HAVE YOU TRIED MY TIMEFORM?

- ✓ Create your own horse to follow list
- ✓ Choose from multiple alert options
- ✓ Make notes on race & result screens
- ✓ Save and sort your horse list
- ✓ Free to registered users

Track any horse, any time. It's a helping hand that's in your hands!

Available at timeform.com and on the mobile App

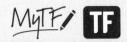

RACEHORSES
OF 2015

Price £79.00

A TIMEFORM PUBLICATION

CONTENTS

The age, weight and distance tables, for use in applying the ratings in races involving horses of different ages, appear at the end of the book

Compiled and produced by

Geoff Greetham (Publishing Editor), John Ingles (Senior Editor & 'Top Horses Abroad' & Editor for pedigrees), Chris Williams (Editor & Handicapper), Andrew Mealor (Managing Editor), Adam Brookes (Essays), Keith Wilkinson (noteforms), David Johnson, Pat Jupp, Mark Milligan, James Thomas, Billy Nash, Simon Baker, Martin Dixon (Handicappers), Sally Wright (pedigree updates), David Holdsworth, Wendy Muncaster, Rachel Todd, Chris Wright, Ivan Gardiner, Michael Williamson (Production)

© **Timeform Limited 2016**   ISBN 978-0-9933900-1-2

TIMEFORM CHAMPIONS IN EUROPE 2015

HORSE OF THE YEAR
BEST THREE-YEAR-OLD COLT
BEST MIDDLE-DISTANCE HORSE RATED AT 134
GOLDEN HORN

BEST TWO-YEAR-OLD FILLY RATED AT 120p
MINDING

BEST TWO-YEAR-OLD MALE RATED AT 128p
AIR FORCE BLUE

BEST THREE-YEAR-OLD FILLY RATED AT 123
FOUND

BEST OLDER HORSE
BEST MILER RATED AT 129
SOLOW

BEST OLDER FEMALES RATED AT 129
MECCA'S ANGEL and TREVE

BEST SPRINTER RATED AT 132
MUHAARAR

BEST STAYER RATED AT 129
ORDER OF ST GEORGE

BEST PERFORMANCE IN A HANDICAP IN BRITAIN
TROPICS
ran to 123 when finishing fifth in Qatar Stewards' Cup at Goodwood

BEST PERFORMANCES ON ALL-WEATHER IN BRITAIN
TRYSTER
ran to 123 when winning totepool Supporting The Sport You Love
Conditions Stakes at Chelmsford
PRETEND
ran to 123 when winning Unibet Hever Sprint Stakes at Lingfield

Racehorses of 2015

Introduction

'I always turn to the sports section first. The sports section records people's accomplishments; the front pages nothing but man's failures.' The words of Earl Warren, the liberal-minded Chief Justice of America's Supreme Court for most of the 'fifties and 'sixties, provide some justification for spending a working life writing about sport. Leaving aside the rather spurious argument about whether competitive sport can be seen as a metaphor for life's struggles, there is no doubting its influence on many people's lives. Take the fortunes of the England cricket team, for example, especially when the Australians arrive on English soil to defend the Ashes. The performance of the team becomes of intense interest and can even cause the mood of the whole nation to swing. 'Australia—bowled Broad 60' was the headline above one account of a scarcely believable opening morning of what proved the decisive Fourth Test at Trent Bridge in August when England fast bowler Stuart Broad put up a performance—eight wickets for fifteen runs—that will enter Ashes folklore as Australia were bowled out in just 18.3 overs before lunch. There was also Andy Murray leading Great Britain over the year to a first Davis Cup crown since 1936, his commitment remarkable to witness, as when fighting back from the brink against French opponent Gilles Simon in a nail-biting quarter final at Queen's. The Rugby World Cup was held in the United Kingdom in 2015, too, and the 'impossible' 34-32 triumph of underdogs Japan over South Africa, with an injury-time try scored after spurning a penalty that would have given them a sensational draw, provided world rugby with the biggest upset in its history.

Those stories not only dominated the back pages but led the wider news agenda on the day. Sport at its most glorious generates a sense of wonder that is equal to any experienced in the field of the arts, and sport provides entertainment and pleasure that is no less 'worthy' than that provided by visiting art galleries, going to the theatre or listening to symphony concerts. The problem, though, is that among 'man's failures' recorded on the front pages in 2015 were an increased number of stories of corruption and cheating in sport, from villains such as football's Blatter and Platini to the exposure of Russia's systematic doping in athletics which, sadly, illustrated one of the depressing realities of modern professional sport. The age of innocence is well and truly over and exceptional deeds in sport will always run the risk of being the subject of cynicism in some quarters from now on. It is an unholy mess that couldn't have been envisaged by Earl Warren when he gave his interview to *Sports Illustrated* nearly half a century ago.

Evidence of corruption in British horse racing is not hard to find—the twelve-year ban imposed on once-promising apprentice Darren Egan (now living in the States) for 'stopping' horses laid by a professional punter isn't the first such case and it won't be the last—and racing cannot afford to be

There haven't been many more exciting racing years in recent times than 'the year of Golden Horn and American Pharoah.' Europe's Horse of the Year Golden Horn ran eight times for owner-breeder Anthony Oppenheimer and champion trainer John Gosden, and his four Group 1 victories lit up the season; his Derby-winning performance (Frankie Dettori pictured doing a flying dismount in the winner's circle) has been bettered only twice in the last quarter of a century. The highest rated horse in this edition is American Pharoah (inset), the first American Triple Crown winner for thirty-seven years and the first winner of what will be known as the 'Grand Slam', incorporating the Breeders' Cup Classic.

complacent. It must prove to the public that the sport is run strictly. Levy Board figures show that British racing spent £16.4m on integrity in 2013/14 (down from a peak of £25m) and more money is needed to ensure the right level of vigilance. The trust of racegoers and punters in the integrity of racing, particularly as a betting medium, is fragile at the best of times, as discussed in the entry on Breeders' Cup Juvenile Turf winner **Hit It A Bomb**. The essay looks mainly at the efforts being made to 'clean up' racing in North America where the widespread use of raceday medication banned in nearly all other countries is holding back the sport's international development.

Racing's declining popularity in the States was temporarily arrested in the latest season by the achievements of **American Pharoah** who was the first Triple Crown winner for thirty-seven years and went on to become the first winner of the 'Grand Slam' when successful in North America's most valuable race the Breeders' Cup Classic, the climax of the Breeders' Cup which itself is dubbed the 'World Championships' by its organisers. Europe's Horse of the Year, the very good Derby winner **Golden Horn** ran in the Breeders' Cup Turf, in which he was surprisingly beaten by **Found**, one of only two horses to get the better of him all year (the other **Arabian Queen**—whose 50/1 win in the Juddmonte International was the biggest shock in that race's history—was also a filly). American Pharoah and Golden Horn had something in common with another of the stars of the European season, the French-trained mare **Treve** whose pursuit of a record-breaking third victory in Europe's richest race, the Prix de l'Arc de Triomphe (one of six races won by Golden Horn), was one of the big stories of the racing year. All three went through the sale-ring as yearlings but failed to reach their reserves and were returned to their breeders, with both American Pharoah and Golden Horn racing throughout their careers for their respective owner-breeders, Ahmed Zayat and Anthony Oppenheimer (one of a diminishing band of English owner-breeders who still maintain a broodmare band of any size), both of whom deserve tremendous credit for campaigning their horses in the true spirit of the sport.

The racing year was certainly not short of star performers and American Pharoah, Golden Horn and Treve were among a number who still had unbeaten records in the year up to the end of July. The top three-year-old miler **Gleneagles** was also among them after completing the Anglo-Irish Guineas/St James's Palace Stakes treble, as was the top older miler, French-trained **Solow**, who was the only champion still remaining unbeaten, winning all six of his races, by the end of the campaign. Solow ran three times in Britain because of the ban on geldings in most Group 1 races in France and his lucrative wins in the Queen Anne, the newly-enriched Sussex Stakes and the Queen Elizabeth II Stakes leave him poised to usurp **Cirrus des Aigles** (who won in pattern company for the seventh year in a row) as Europe's leading money-earner. The essay on Gleneagles examines his absence from the big summer races and also recounts the success enjoyed by Ryan Moore (including his record nine Royal Ascot winners) under the new arrangement to ride as first jockey at Ballydoyle, displacing trainer's son Joseph O'Brien (one of the possible reasons behind the summer rumours of an impending split between Aidan O'Brien and the Coolmore partners which is also examined).

Gleneagles stood out for Ballydoyle in the first part of the season—he was even considered for the Derby (as was Found) because of the yard's weaker than usual batch of middle-distance colts—but, by the end of the season, 'normal service' had been resumed at Ballydoyle. Two three-year-old colts emerged to challenge the number-one status of Gleneagles, the runaway Irish St Leger winner **Order of St George** (whose essay updates Aidan O'Brien's amazing training record in the classics; he also won the Oaks with 50/1-shot **Qualify**) and globe-trotting **Highland Reel** whose story illustrates the increasingly cosmopolitan nature of top-level Flat racing. Both Highland Reel and Order of St George are sons of Galileo (as is Gleneagles) and aspects of the career of Coolmore's phenomenal stallion are covered in the essays on that pair. An interesting change in direction for Coolmore—now showing more interest in the Danzig line which has always been keenly supported by

Ryan Moore's nine winners created a new record at Royal Ascot for the era since the end of World War II but injury put paid to his chance of winning a fourth jockeys' championship in Britain (his season is covered in the essay on the leading three-year-old miler Gleneagles); he is pictured receiving the trophy from the Queen for the leading jockey at the Royal meeting

arch rivals the Maktoums—is one of the topics touched on in the entry on its champion two-year-old colt **Air Force Blue** who looks every inch a Two Thousand Guineas winner in waiting (the essay also outlines further changes to the autumn two-year-old pattern-race programme, this time for the better). Aidan O'Brien also had the highest-rated two-year-old filly **Minding** who, after reversing Debutante Stakes form in the Moyglare Stud Stakes with her ambitiously-named stablemate **Ballydoyle**, put up a fine display in the Fillies' Mile at Newmarket, on the same weekend that Air Force Blue recorded as good a performance in the Dewhurst as any for nearly twenty years.

The battle lines between Ballydoyle/Coolmore and Britain's perennial leading owners Godolphin are not so clearly drawn as they once were. Territories and Lucida carried the royal blue into the runners-up spot behind Gleneagles and the David Wachman-trained and Coolmore-owned **Legatissimo** in the Two Thousand Guineas and One Thousand Guineas respectively, but those two races were not billed beforehand as clashes between racing's superpowers, as they once might have been. There was more of the flavour of a head-to-head when Godolphin's **Emotionless** met Air Force Blue in the Dewhurst, though the anticipated duel failed to materialise and Emotionless was found to have chipped a bone in his knee. The essays on **Emotionless** and **Tryster** cover the plans to 'streamline' the Godolphin operation (the breeding arm Darley is being merged) and turn its two private stables at Newmarket into a more potent force on the big stage once again. The superb start to the year on the all-weather in Britain by Charlie Appleby at Moulton Paddocks, and a string of successes for Saeed bin Suroor's team at the Dubai Carnival (**Prince Bishop** won the World Cup which was back on dirt for the first time since 2009) proved something of a false dawn, but, through weight of numbers, Godolphin still walked away with the owners' championship in Britain. The stables of champion trainer John

The Godolphin royal blue dominated the all-weather scene over the winter (star performer Tryster, second left, pictured winning the Winter Derby); all-weather meetings account for roughly a third of the Flat fixtures in Britain, and Newcastle, which has ripped up its turf course, will be a new venue offering floodlit all-weather racing in 2016 (jumps course Wetherby staged Flat turf meetings for the first time in 2015); Godolphin went on to win its tenth British owners' championship in 2015 with record first-three earnings of £5,217,268.

Gosden, Richard Hannon, Richard Fahey and Roger Varian—and Jim Bolger in Ireland with **Pleascach**—did well with horses they continued to train after being purchased by Godolphin (which has usually transferred such recruits in-house). Mark Johnston also enjoyed a higher profile after receiving more two-year-olds from Darley, **Buratino** (whose essay discusses changes to the two-year-old programme coming into effect in 2016) and **Lumiere** spearheading another excellent year for Kingsley Park. Richard Fahey (whose connection with Godolphin is covered under **Ribchester**) and Mark Johnston are two of the trainers mentioned in the essay on **Odeliz** which discusses the number of thriving northern Flat stables, which also include those of David O'Meara (**Amazing Maria** and **Mondialiste**), Kevin Ryan (**The Grey Gatsby**) and Odeliz's own trainer Karl Burke.

The excellent season enjoyed at home and abroad by John Gosden's Clarehaven Stables (Golden Horn's essay contains details of the stable's spectacular achievements overseas) included the trainer's first Irish Derby winner **Jack Hobbs**, who was purchased by Godolphin before finishing runner-up to stablemate Golden Horn in the Derby at Epsom. The latest running of the Irish Derby—which hadn't been won by a British-trained horse for twenty-two years—was the one hundred and fiftieth, but the essay on Jack Hobbs reflects on the 1962 running which heralded the arrival of the Irish Derby as a truly major race. There have been concerns about the race in recent years—when it has been dominated by Ballydoyle and Aidan O'Brien—and it is still possible that its distance could be cut to a mile and a quarter, following in the footsteps of the decision taken ten years ago to shorten the distance of the Prix du Jockey Club. That move still has its critics, as outlined in the essay on the latest winner **New Bay** who went on to finish third to Golden Horn in the Prix de l'Arc, a place behind his older stablemate **Flintshire** who replicated his performance in the race twelve months earlier. Both are trained by Andre Fabre who was champion trainer in France for the twenty-seventh time; he also had the Poule d'Essai des Poulains winner **Make Believe** (an appropriate name for the holder of Longchamp's seven-furlong record!), as well as the very smart mare **Esoterique** and the Jean-Luc Lagardere winner **Ultra** (whose essay traces the changes made to the Grand Criterium over the years and reflects on its influence on the founding of the Timeform Gold Cup, now the Racing Post Trophy). The Prix Royal-Oak winner **Vazirabad** (whose entry looks at the redevelopment of Longchamp) was the second French classic winner of the year for his owner the Aga Khan who won the Poule d'Essai des Pouliches with the Rouget-trained **Ervedya** who was beaten only once all year. The owner's other leading filly **Dolniya** won the Dubai Sheema Classic for Vazirabad's trainer Alain de Royer Dupre. A third of France's Group 1 races in 2015 were won by British challengers—the Prix Morny winner **Shalaa** and Prix de Diane winner **Star of Seville** (in whose essay there are more details) made it a trio of successes for John Gosden in France—and the essay on **Robin of Navan** mentions the lucrative bonuses that can be earned in French races, on top of the prize money.

Australia is becoming a regular port of call for Europe's globe-trotters but French-trained **Gailo Chop** was the only one to win a race in the latest season, though **Max Dynamite** finished second in the Melbourne Cup, the ill-fated **Red Cadeaux** took second in Australia's most valuable weight-for-age event the Queen Elizabeth Stakes (becoming the first British-trained horse to top £5m in prize-money earnings) and Gold Cup winner **Trip To Paris** finished second in the Caulfield Cup and fourth in the Melbourne Cup. As well as attracting international runners, the Melbourne Cup field nowadays usually features a number of stayers who have been imported from Britain and the essay on Trip To Paris highlights the need to improve the domestic programme for staying-breds who are a vital dimension of British racing. There are only two Group 1s in Britain for three-year-olds and upwards over a mile and three quarters or more, yet there are now no fewer than seven Group 1s for the sprinters, following the upgrading of the programme (outlined in the essay on **Limato**) and the introduction of the Commonwealth Cup for three-year-olds.

The Commonwealth Cup was one of four Group 1s won during an excellent campaign by the champion sprinter **Muhaarar**. His victories also included the British Champions Sprint which was upgraded in the latest season from Group 2 and Muhaarar will make a valuable addition to the Shadwell stallion roster (his outstanding performances came in the same year as the death of his grandsire Green Desert whose influence is touched on in Muhaarar's essay). Muhaarar was the best six-furlong sprinter but mention should also be made of the speedsters **Goldream**, who won both the King's Stand and the Prix de l'Abbaye, **Mecca's Angel**, who won the Nunthorpe, and the veteran **Sole Power** (his essay outlines the upgrades to the sprinting programme in Ireland, though that country still has no Group 1). The victory by **Undrafted** in the Diamond Jubilee Stakes at Royal Ascot was the first by a North American-trained challenger in a Group 1 race in Britain.

Royal Ascot is an international meeting nowadays. As well as saddling Undrafted, American trainer Wesley Ward won the Queen Mary Stakes with **Acapulco**, while the Australian sprinter Brazen Beau was runner-up to Undrafted. Hong Kong's champion miler **Able Friend** was another of the world's top horses attracted to the Royal meeting. Ascot hasn't been so successful, though, in attracting top overseas performers to its mid-summer championship, the King George VI and Queen Elizabeth Stakes, which would have been a purely domestic affair but for the challenge by Italy's top horse Dylan Mouth. The essay on the King George winner **Postponed** returns to the vexed subject of the whip rules in Britain, again arguing that the emphasis should be on *incorrect* use, rather than on the number of times the whip is used (the latest King George was also the fortieth anniversary of the epic clash between the Derby winner Grundy and Bustino, which is recalled in the essay).

If the Ascot stewards drew attention to themselves by dishing out needless and counter-productive whip suspensions after the pulsating finish between Postponed and Eagle Top, the stewards at Doncaster were even more in the public spotlight after demoting the filly **Simple Verse** in the St Leger.

Seeing double ... two jockeys were presented with the St Leger trophy;
Colm O'Donoghue (right) received it on the day after Bondi Beach was awarded the race
by the Doncaster stewards, but the presentation was restaged on Racing Post Trophy day
when Simple Verse, ridden by Andrea Atzeni (left) was reinstated on appeal

The evidence to the stewards' inquiry given by the jockeys on Simple Verse and **Bondi Beach**, who was initially awarded the race, made interesting viewing on Channel 4 (whose shrinking racing audience contributed to its losing the terrestrial contract to cover British racing, which switches to ITV in 2017, as outlined in the essay on Solow). Simple Verse was reinstated on appeal eleven days after the St Leger (her essay recalls a similar case in 1981 in Timeform in which Timeform was caught up in the controversy). Simple Verse is owned by the Qatar Racing team which also found itself at the centre of another controversial disqualification on the other side of the Atlantic. Secret Gesture's demotion in the Beverly D Stakes is discussed in the essay on her stable-companion Simple Verse which points to the limited powers of the International Federation of Horseracing Authorities as one of the major stumbling blocks to bringing about harmonisation of racing's rules around the world (and harmonisation of the rules governing raceday medication).

Racecourse attendances in Britain passed the six-million mark for the first time since 2011 (the aim is to reach seven million by 2020), in part due to favourable weather and the continued successful promotion of themed racedays (with ladies' days and after-racing concerts still proving particularly popular). The trade in racehorses during the year was strong at the upper end, but demand wasn't strong enough at the middle and bottom of the market to match the slightly increased production of foals, which will come as a blow to the powers-that-be at the British Horseracing Authority who have set an optimistic target of having an extra thousand horses in training by 2020 (worryingly for breeders, who are already finding it difficult to sell some of their produce, there are further increases on the way in the size of the foal crops). A significant increase in prize money at the grassroots will probably be needed for the BHA to achieve the expansion in the racehorse population that it feels is necessary. The new tripartite structure at the top of racing—with the BHA (which manages only 13% of the fixture list), the racecourses and the horsemen's group representing owners, trainers and other professionals—finally came into being officially towards the end of 2015 though it had already been warning of a grim future for the sport if the BHA chairman Steve Harman's much trumpeted 'Strategy for Growth' is not delivered.

The grand vision is to attract £120m of new income into the sport by 2018 and 'the racing industry' is looking to 'the betting industry' to provide a good deal of it. Most of the new money—if it materialises—will be channelled through the racecourses which own any of their own fixtures established before 2004, and receive the revenue from them including money from media rights and prize money grants from the levy, two of the largest providers of racing's revenue. The latest levy talks ended without agreement at the end of October (the Department for Culture, Media and Sport quickly announced a roll-over of the existing levy, worth around £60m), with racing turning down an offer from six of the top ten major bookmakers to pay an additional £30m over three years—on top of the statutory levy payments—from their profits on racing that are not subject to the levy. The BHA said that the offer was not sufficient, claiming racing would lose £110m over the next three years in revenue 'leaked' through offshore operators (the BHA, which wanted an escalating percentage agreement over the offshore revenue, was meanwhile warning the government that 12,000 jobs in racing would be lost if the proposed plan for a new horserace betting right—which would capture offshore income—was not in place by 2017).

Timeform's founder Phil Bull was fond of describing the bookmakers as 'the whipping boys of British racing,' saying that too many of those who make their living from racing regard the bookmakers (who provide a valuable shop window for the sport, focussing interest and providing publicity) as 'the source of all racing's ills and problems.' The acquisitive instincts of racing's leaders came to the fore again with the concept of racecourses having 'authorised betting partners', with most tracks deciding not to accept new race sponsorship from bookmakers who did not pay their 'rightful' share of levy. Betfair (which completed a £6bn merger with Paddy Power in early 2016), bet365 and 32Red were each accredited as 'authorised betting partners' as they already paid the full amount of levy, or the equivalent sum through a commercial deal. As negotiations with racing's new tripartite body continued into the early months of 2016 to try to reach a funding deal, the leading betting operators warned racing that it was playing 'Russian roulette'. Betfred, which also owns the Tote and claimed to have put £150m into racing through sponsorship over the previous four years, withdrew its sponsorship of jumping's most prestigious event, the Cheltenham Gold Cup, and the 2016 Sprint Cup at Haydock, among other races, and has said it will 'walk away from racing.' In an interesting development, given that money raised from the betting operators comes, in the end, from punters, the BHA set up the Horseracing Bettors Forum to give those who bet on the sport a voice. The nine forum members are unpaid and will serve for an initial period of three years, deciding the issues to be pursued, as well as providing feedback on proposals submitted to them by the BHA. Simon Rowlands is the first chair. Phil Bull represented punters and racegoers in the 'seventies on a similar committee (RILC) and eventually took up a more prominent position as the first chairman of the Horseracing Advisory Council in 1980. He resigned after six months, describing the HAC as 'no more than a cosmetic charade whose existence suits both the Levy Board and the Jockey Club'! The Horseracing Bettors Forum has no teeth but let's hope this new channel of communication is more successful than its predecessors in making the punter's opinion count.

The year's obituary columns had more of a racing flavour than usual, with plenty of column inches devoted to the passing of eleven-times champion jockey Pat Eddery, from a heart attack at the age of sixty-three, and to those pioneers of racing broadcasting Peter Dimmock and Sir Peter O'Sullevan, both of whom were nonagenarians. Pat Eddery's riding career, summarised in *Racehorses of 2003* when he retired from the saddle, ranked him among the greatest Flat jockeys (only Sir Gordon Richards stands ahead of him on the all-time list in Britain). One of his first big-race successes came while still a 7-lb claiming apprentice on Phil Bull's Philoctetes in the 1969 Vaux Gold Tankard, five years before he became champion jockey for the first time. Grundy was the first superstar with whom Eddery was associated ('Two strides past the line, Grundy had gone, the poor bugger just stopped, he had no more to give … I'm not the most emotional but it brought a lump to my throat,' was how he described the finish of that indelible King George of 1975 in his autobiography; the listed Winkfield Stakes which opens the King George programme has been renamed the Pat Eddery Stakes). Grundy's epic battle with Bustino and Dancing Brave's brilliant victory (under a vintage Eddery waiting ride) in the 1986 Prix de l'Arc de Triomphe were voted first and second among Flat races in a poll of *Racing Post* readers in 2005 to name the '100 Greatest Races'. Eddery himself regarded the second of his three Derby winners, Golden Fleece, as 'maybe just' the best horse he rode (he rode a Derby winner for each of the three main retainers in his career, Grundy's trainer Peter Walwyn, Vincent O'Brien who trained Golden Fleece, and Dancing Brave's owner Khalid Abdullah, for whom he rode Quest For Fame). Eddery briefly enjoyed some success as a trainer, but that career never looked likely to reach the dizzy heights of his years in the saddle as he struggled with alcohol-related problems, one of his daughters explaining after his death that 'a lot of people had tried to help him, among them Kieren Fallon, and John Magnier and Derrick Smith of Coolmore, who arranged for him to attend an addiction centre in 2009, but we always knew he would drink again, it was only a matter of time.'

Peter O'Sullevan was quick to spot Pat Eddery's potential, writing in his *Daily Express* column after the seventeen-year-old's first winner in April 1969 (having had more than fifty rides) that 'Frenchie Nicholson has another bright pupil in Pat Eddery who handled Alvaro with exemplary sang-froid.' Jockeys wore black armbands at the Qatar Goodwood Festival on Goodwood Cup day to mark the passing of O'Sullevan whose voice became inextricably linked with the sport during his fifty years as a BBC TV commentator (there is a flavour of his commentary on Grundy and Bustino in the essay on Postponed). O'Sullevan began his broadcasting career racereading for Peter Dimmock for whom race commentaries were, for a time, part of his role during his rapid rise with Outside Broadcasts at BBC TV in the years when television was first starting to develop into a mass phenomenon. After becoming head of Outside Broadcasts, Dimmock continued his career in front of the camera for a time, presenting *Sportsview* and early editions of *Grandstand*, the first Saturday afternoon rolling sports programme, within which live coverage of racing was a staple (in his management role, he was responsible for securing—after a lengthy pursuit of the reluctant Mirabel Topham—the rights to televise the Grand National for the first time in 1960).

The death was also announced of the prolific bloodstock writer and author Peter Willett, who made an important contribution to the Norfolk Committee's review of British racing in the 'sixties which led to the introduction of the pattern system in 1971; Willett was also, at one time or another, chairman

Racing was saddened by the passing of those pioneers of racing broadcasting Sir Peter O'Sullevan (left) and Peter Dimmock (O'Sullevan began as a racereader for Dimmock who was a racing commentator for the BBC before becoming head of Outside Broadcasts); eleven-times champion jockey Pat Eddery, one of the greatest Flat jockeys in British racing history (4,633 winners in Britain) died from a heart attack at only 63 in November

of the European Breeders' Fund, president of the Thoroughbred Breeders' Association and a director of the National Stud and of Goodwood racecourse. Another blessed with a long life was Ron Pollard who pioneered political and novelty betting for Ladbrokes in the 'sixties when he became a regular on TV, radio and in the newspapers. Pollard once offered odds on Elvis Presley being found alive, which generated such a flurry of bets that Pollard's boss Peter George burst into his office pointing to a clipboard saying 'It must be true, he must be alive, look at all these bets!' Pollard reassured him that he had spoken to the man who cut the singer's hair before he was put into the coffin (which he had!). Ron Muddle, who did much to introduce all-weather racing to Britain, Yorkshire-based trainer Mel Brittain, who held a licence for thirty years and saddled nearly five hundred winners, Colin Tinkler Snr, who opened the door for many to group ownership in the mid-'eighties with the launch of Full Circle Thoroughbreds, and Ray Gilpin, a popular member of the press room in the North, were others who passed away in 2015. Sir Peter O'Sullevan and Peter Willett were both former Racing Journalists of the Year and the death, after heart surgery, of three-times winner of that accolade Alan Lee at sixty-one, no age at all, came as a great shock. Lee, something of a lone hunter in the O'Sullevan mode, was the much respected racing correspondent of *The Times* for the last seventeen years, having spent eleven as the paper's cricket correspondent before that. He also wrote countless books and, coincidentally, worked with Pat Eddery on his autobiography.

Among those who retired in the latest season was the champion jockey for the three previous seasons Richard Hughes who hung up his saddle at the age of forty-two on the final day of the Goodwood Festival to start a new career as a trainer. Hughes, who picked himself up after descending into alcoholism for a time in his late-'twenties, owed his three 'official' jockeys' championships largely to being stable jockey to the huge Hannon training operation. However, Hughes found his prospects of winning a fourth championship weakened by the sales of some of the stable's best horses to owners, such as Godolphin and Al Shaqab, who have their own jockeys. 'Across Herridge and East Everleigh we now have around a hundred horses I can't ride, and I don't feel happy watching these horses win major races without me,' he wrote in his weekly *Racing Post* column on the eve of Royal Ascot. He had told readers in an earlier column that he had found it 'excruciating' watching **Pether's Moon** win the Coronation Cup at Epsom without him being in the saddle (Richard Hannon was himself preparing for Hughes's departure by giving some of his

Richard Hughes, winner of the 'official' jockeys' championship—which was decided over the turf season—for the three previous years, had his last ride on Fox Trotter on the final day of the Goodwood Festival; the revamped 2015 Stobart-sponsored jockeys' championship ran from Two Thousand Guineas day to British Champions' Day, when fellow jockeys formed a guard of honour for the competition's first champion Silvestre de Sousa

other regular jockeys greater opportunities, the stable also employing two of the season's leading apprentices Tom Marquand, who ended up as champion, and Cam Hardie, as well as the long-serving Pat Dobbs who was given the mount on Pether's Moon). The combination of Hannon and Hughes was a most effective one—Richard Hannon senior handed over to his son, also Richard, in 2014—and the intuitive, sometimes exquisite, Hughes riding style paid off time and again, particularly on the stable's good two-year-olds. His thoughtful *Racing Post* column served to enhance his reputation as one of the sport's most clear-thinking and articulate riders. Britain's leading female jockey Hayley Turner, whose career is one of the subjects covered in the essay on **Litigant**, also announced her retirement. Like Hughes, Turner was a fine ambassador for racing but expressed frustration at a lack of opportunities.

Hayley Turner enjoyed a pattern victory on Shaden at Ayr in September for Lady Cecil who ended her short career as a trainer at the end of the season after confirming that the executors of her late husband Sir Henry—from whom she took over in June 2013—had sold the famous Warren Place establishment in Newmarket to Sheikh Mohammed. One of Newmarket's longest-serving trainers, the pioneering Clive Brittain, who did not add to the significant list of achievements outlined in the essay on Rizeena in last year's *Racehorses*, also decided to call it a day because of the deteriorating health of his wife Maureen ('It has always been me and Maureen, we're a team and she spent sixty years looking after me, so I think it's only fair I spend some time looking after her'). A presentation was made to Brittain on Dewhurst day at Newmarket when a compilation of his big-race wins was shown on the track's big screen. Two of his greatest victories were achieved with Pebbles in the Breeders' Cup Turf and Jupiter Island in the Japan Cup, both of them ridden by Pat Eddery.

The training ranks will be further depleted by the decisions not to renew their licences taken by a number of others who have enjoyed success over the years, including Barry Hills (retiring for a second time, leaving son Charlie as the only one of the famous racing family still holding a racing licence), Jonathan Pease (who oddly never had a winner in Britain in over thirty-five years as a trainer, but had plenty of success from his French base, as described in the essay on **Erupt**), Peter Makin (who had nearly 800 winners including dual King's Stand winner Elbio), James Toller (trainer of 2004 Irish Guineas winner Bachelor Duke) and the promising Olly Stevens (who had only three years at Sheikh Fahad's Robins Farm Racing yard in Surrey before deciding to relinquish his licence for family reasons).

This edition of *Racehorses* contains a wealth of facts and informed opinion on the 10,980 horses who are dealt with individually in the A to Z. That number includes all those who ran on the Flat in Britain in 2015. 'Top Horses Abroad' provides extensive editorial coverage and Timeform ratings for the top horses around the world that are not covered in the main body of the book. The attention of regular readers is drawn to the first changes made to Timeform's Flat weight-for-age scale (pages 1213-16) since the early-'nineties. These have the general effect of reducing the allowances younger horses receive. The essays on the year's leading horses—including those highlighted in bold in this Introduction—set out to entertain and enlighten, but *Racehorses* would be nothing if it was not fully comprehensive. The long-standing aim of the series has always been to provide an accurate, authoritative and permanent record of the achievements of *all* Britain's thoroughbreds. As a result, Britain is the only country to possess a complete 'directory' of its racehorses stretching back almost seventy years.

March 2016

TIMEFORM HORSE OF THE YEAR

Timeform's 'Racehorses' series stretches back to 1948 when the first prototype Annual—the 'Timeform Supplement'—was produced covering the 1947 season. The selecting of a 'horse of the year' began in the 'sixties. The title has usually been awarded to the highest rated horse, except in 1969 (when Habitat was rated higher at 134), 1984 (El Gran Senor 136), 1985 (Slip Anchor 136) and 2003 (Hawk Wing 136). Raven's Pass was also rated 133 in 2008.

Year	Horse	Rating	Year	Horse	Rating
1960	Charlottesville	**135**	1987	Reference Point	**139**
	Floribunda	**135**	1988	Warning	**136**
1961	Molvedo	**137**	1989	Zilzal	**137**
1962	Match	**135**	1990	Dayjur	**137**
1963	Exbury	**138**	1991	Generous	**139**
1964	Relko	**136**	1992	St Jovite	**135**
1965	Sea-Bird	**145**	1993	Opera House	**131**
1966	Danseur	**134**	1994	Celtic Swing	**138**
1967	Petingo	**135**	1995	Lammtarra	**134**
1968	Vaguely Noble	**140**	1996	Mark of Esteem	**137**
1969	Levmoss	**133**	1997	Peintre Celebre	**137**
1970	Nijinsky	**138**	1998	Intikhab	**135**
1971	Brigadier Gerard	**141**	1999	Daylami	**138**
	Mill Reef	**141**	2000	Dubai Millennium	**140**
1972	Brigadier Gerard	**144**	2001	Sakhee	**136**
1973	Apalachee	**137**	2002	Rock of Gibraltar	**133**
	Rheingold	**137**	2003	Falbrav	**133**
1974	Allez France	**136**	2004	Doyen	**132**
1975	Grundy	**137**	2005	Hurricane Run	**134**
1976	Youth	**135**	2006	George Washington	**133**
1977	Alleged	**137**	2007	Manduro	**135**
1978	Alleged	**138**	2008	Zarkava	**133**
1979	Troy	**137**	2009	Sea The Stars	**140**
1980	Moorestyle	**137**	2010	Harbinger	**140**
1981	Shergar	**140**	2011	Frankel	**143**
1982	Ardross	**134**	2012	Frankel	**147**
1983	Habibti	**136**	2013	Treve	**134**
1984	Provideo	**112**	2014	Kingman	**134**
1985	Pebbles	**135**	2015	Golden Horn	**134**
1986	Dancing Brave	**140**			

HIGHEST ANNUAL RATINGS (3-y-os+ in Europe)

147	Frankel
145	Sea-Bird
144	Brigadier Gerard, Tudor Minstrel
142	Abernant, Ribot
141	Mill Reef
140	Dancing Brave, Dubai Millennium, Harbinger, Sea The Stars, Shergar, Vaguely Noble
139	Generous, Pappa Fourway, Reference Point
138	Alleged, Alycidon, Daylami, Exbury, Nijinsky

THE TIMEFORM 'TOP HUNDRED'

Here are listed the 'Top 100' two-year-olds, three-year-olds and older horses in the annual. Fillies and mares are denoted by (f).

2 YEAR OLDS

128p	Air Force Blue
125p	Songbird (f)
123p	Shalaa
122p	Emotionless
120p	Minding (f)
119p	Hit It A Bomb
118	Buratino
118	Marcel
117	Ajaya
117	Gutaifan
116p	Ultra
116	Cymric
115p	Lumiere (f)
115	Johannes Vermeer
115	Ribchester
115	Stormy Antarctic
114p	Foundation
114p	Massaat
114	Acapulco (f)
114	Besharah (f)
114	Donjuan Triumphant
114	Gifted Master
114	Ornate
114	Robin of Navan
113p	Ballydoyle (f)
113	Beacon Rock
113	Birchwood
113	Galileo Gold
113	Illuminate (f)
113	Log Out Island
112p	Blue de Vega
112p	La Rioja (f)
112p	Nemoralia (f)
112p	Quiet Reflection (f)
112	Deauville
112	First Selection
112	Shogun
111p	Recorder
111p	Wajeez
111	Attendu
111	Smash Williams
111	Steady Pace
110p	George Patton
110	Alice Springs (f)
110	Biz Heart
110	Cloth of Stars
110	Herald The Dawn
110	Promising Run (f)
110	Sasparella (f)
109p	Very Talented
109	Aim To Please (f)
109	Blue Bayou (f)
109	Ibn Malik
109	Raucous
109	Tashweeq
109	Tourny (f)

108p	Kachy
108p	Sanus Per Aquam
108p	Steel of Madrid
108p	Suits You
108p	Washington DC
108	Easton Angel (f)
108	No Education
108	Turret Rocks (f)
107p	Air Vice Marshal
107p	Bing Bang Dong
107p	Dhahmaan
107p	Hawkbill
107p	Qemah (f)
107p	Round Two
107	Nathra (f)
107	Painted Cliffs
107	Tasleet
106p	Crazy Horse
106p	Mustajeer
106p	Tony Curtis
106p	Trixia (f)
106p	Von Blucher
106	Areen
106	Lawmaking
106	Most Beautiful (f)
106	Mr Lupton
106	Muntazah
106	Waterloo Bridge
105p	First Victory (f)
105p	Marsha (f)
105p	Thetis (f)
105	Antonoe (f)
105	Gracious John
105	King of Rooks
105	Mayfair Lady (f)
105	Race Day
105	Shaden (f)
104p	Abe Lincoln
104p	Eltezam
104p	Ennaadd
104p	Thanksfortellingme
104	Belvoir Bay (f)
104	Fireglow (f)
104	Hawksmoor (f)
104	Katie's Diamond (f)
104	Only Mine (f)
104	Port Douglas
104	Rouleau
104	Sixth Sense
104	Ventura Storm

3 YEAR OLDS

138	American Pharoah
134	Golden Horn
132	Muhaarar
129	Highland Reel
129	Jack Hobbs

129	Order of St George
128	Gleneagles
128	New Bay
127	Make Believe
127	Vazirabad
126	Limato
125p	Intilaaq
125	Erupt
125	Time Test
125	Twilight Son
123	Belardo
123	Dariyan
123	Found (f)
123	Kodi Bear
123	Silverwave
123	Storm The Stars
123	Strath Burn
123	Territories
122	Bondi Beach
122	Dutch Connection
122	Legatissimo (f)
122	Ming Dynasty
121	Consort
121	Endless Drama
121	Estidhkaar
121	Fields of Athenry
121	Impassable (f)
121	Magical Memory
121	Simple Verse (f)
120p	Racing History
120	Candarliya (f)
120	Circus Couture
120	Covert Love (f)
120	Ervedya (f)
120	Jazzi Top (f)
120	Migwar
120	Mubtaahij
120	Nutan
120	The Tin Man
119	Adaay
119	Latharnach
119	Lucida (f)
119	Toscanini
118	Elm Park
118	Home of The Brave
118	Ivawood
118	Journey (f)
118	Karaktar
118	Karpino
118	Lovelyn (f)
118	Mattmu
118	Nightflower (f)
118	Queen's Jewel (f)
118	Sea Calisi (f)
118	Waady
117	Akatea (f)
117	Ampere

17

117 Arabian Queen (f)	126 Gold-Fun	120 Gordon Lord Byron
117 Beautiful Romance (f)	126 Hunter's Light	120 Magic Artist
117 Festive Fare	126 Maurice	120 Mindurownbusiness
117 Full Mast	126 Postponed	120 Spielberg
117 Let's Go	126 Prince Bishop	119 Agent Murphy
117 Lightscameraction	126 Undrafted	119 Air Pilot
117 Maljaa	125 Al Kazeem	119 Arab Spring
117 Pleascach (f)	125 Arod	119 Balty Boys
117 Scottish	125 Eagle Top	119 Cable Bay
117 Sumbal	125 Ito	119 Cannock Chase
117 Taniyar	125 Manatee	119 Catcall
116 Bossy Guest	125 Prince Gibraltar	119 Danzeno
116 Exosphere	124 Max Dynamite	119 Forgotten Rules
116 Hootenanny	124 Second Step	119 Gabrial
116 Irish Rookie (f)	124 Snow Sky	119 Gospel Choir
116 Make It Up	124 Vercingetorix	119 Integral (f)
116 Markaz	123 Cougar Mountain	119 Kingfisher
116 Palace Prince	123 Dolniya (f)	119 Lightning Spear
116 Realtra (f)	123 Esoterique (f)	119 Medicean Man
116 Star of Seville (f)	123 Goldream	119 Mille Et Mille
116 Star Storm	123 Night of Thunder	119 Mount Logan
116 War Envoy	123 Pretend	119 Mustajeeb
116 Western Reserve	123 Safety Check	119 Mutakayyef
116 Zawraq	123 Sole Power	119 Take Cover
115p Fort del Oro (f)	123 Tamarkuz	
115p Mitchum Swagger	123 Telescope	
115 Balios	123 Tropics	
115 Burnt Sugar	123 Tryster	
115 Cotai Glory	123 Wandjina	
115 Curvy (f)	122 African Story	
115 Fadhayyil (f)	122 Custom Cut	
115 Hathal	122 Gailo Chop	
115 Johnny Barnes	122 Mondialiste	
115 Miss Temple City (f)	122 Muthmir	
115 My Dream Boat	122 Rangali	
115 Osaila (f)	122 Spiritjim	
115 Peacock	122 Steps	
115 Ride Like The Wind	122 Tac de Boistron	
115 Sir Isaac Newton	122 The Corsican	
115 Tashaar	122 Toormore	
	122 Trip To Paris	

OLDER HORSES

132 Shared Belief	122 Western Hymn	
131 Beholder (f)	121 Big Orange	
130 Able Friend	121 Bow Creek	
130 Lankan Rupee	121 Brown Panther	
130 Liam's Map	121 Clever Cookie	
129 Mecca's Angel (f)	121 Dylan Mouth	
129 Solow	121 French Navy	
129 Treve (f)	121 GM Hopkins	
128 Cirrus des Aigles	121 Lancelot du Lac	
128 Flintshire	121 Litigant	
128 Free Eagle	121 Pether's Moon	
128 Peniaphobia	121 Red Cadeaux	
128 The Grey Gatsby	121 Siljan's Saga (f)	
127 A Shin Hikari	121 Sky Hunter	
127 Criterion	121 Sloane Avenue	
127 Fascinating Rock	121 Wadi Al Hattawi	
126p Winx (f)	120 Ahtoug	
126 Brazen Beau	120 Ahzeemah	
126 California Chrome	120 Amazing Maria (f)	
126 Designs On Rome	120 Dubday	
	120 Flying Officer	

18

PROMISING HORSES

Selected British- and Irish-trained horses with either a p or P in *Racehorses of 2015* are listed under their trainers for 2016.

CHARLIE APPLEBY
Albernathy 2 ch.c 86p
Archaic (IRE) 2 b.c 84p
Chess Master (IRE) 2 br.c 80p
Disobedience (USA) 2 b.g 82p
Emotionless (IRE) 2 b.c 122p
Folkswood 2 b.c 90p
G K Chesterton (IRE) 2 ch.c 90p
Hawkbill (USA) 2 ch.c 107p
Hornsby 2 b.c 88p
Mandrell (USA) 2 b.f 87p
Mirror City 2 b.f 84p
Roundsman 2 b.c 88p
Spennithorne (IRE) 2 b.f 89p
White Witch (USA) 2 b.f 80p

ANDREW BALDING
Brorocco 2 b.g 80p
Dancing Star 2 b.f 80p
Dream of Summer (IRE) 2 b.c 83p
Husbandry 2 b.g 93p
Sunflower 2 ch.f 93p
Zoffanys Pride (IRE) 2 b.c 80p

DAVID BARRON
Poet's Prize 2 b.c 100p
Wolowitz (IRE) 2 b.g 90p

RALPH BECKETT
Andastra (GER) 2 b.f 85p
Cape Banjo (USA) 2 ch.g 82p
Carntop 2 b.c 100p
Chicadoro 2 b.f 87p
Gold Faith (IRE) 2 gr.g 84p
Hereawi 2 b.f 84p
Mountain Bell 2 b.f 86p
Secret Sense (USA) 2 b.f 86p

MICHAEL BELL
Towerlands Park (IRE) 2 b.c 89p

MARCO BOTTI
Aljazzi 2 b.f 94p
Dhahmaan (IRE) 2 b.c 107p
Knife Edge (IRE) 2 ch.c 94p
Mr Khalid 2 b.c 86p

K. R. BURKE
Bandit Bob (IRE) 2 b.c 82p
Explosive Power (IRE) 2 gr.c 94p
Percy Street 2 br.c 97p
Quiet Reflection 2 b.f 112p
Southern Gailes (IRE) 2 ch.c 90p
Timeless Art (IRE) 2 b.c 80p
Wholesome (USA) 2 b. or br.f 88p

OWEN BURROWS
Ehtiraas 2 b.c 98p
Fawaareq (IRE) 2 b.c 89p
Massaat (IRE) 2 b.c 114p
Mustajeer 2 b.c 106p

HENRY CANDY
Bounce 2 b.f 93p
Jack Nevison 2 b.g 82p
La Rioja 2 b.f 112p
Teresar (IRE) 2 ch.f 85p

MICK CHANNON
Harlequeen 2 b.f 93p
Harrison 2 b.c 87p

PETER CHAPPLE-HYAM
Gunnery (FR) 2 ch.c 82p
Marshal Dan Troop (IRE) 2 b.c 81p
Times Legacy 2 b.c 82p

ROGER CHARLTON
Chester Street 2 b.c 87p
Intermittent 2 b.f 84p
Kummiya 2 b. or br.g 90p
Paling 2 b.c 87p
Quick March 2 b.f 85p
Rock Steady (IRE) 2 ch.g 81p

ROBERT COWELL
King Cole (USA) 2 ch.c 82p

CLIVE COX
Bobby Wheeler (IRE) 2 b.c 90p
Pine Ridge 2 b.f 83p

SIMON CRISFORD
Celebration Day (IRE) 2 b.g 87p
Daqeeq (IRE) 2 b.c 84p
Discreet Hero (IRE) 2 ch.c 80p
Silk Cravat 2 ch.g 84p

LUCA CUMANI
Al Khafji 2 ch.c 87p
Banksea 2 b.c 83p
Beautiful Morning 2 b.f 96p
Farandine 2 ch.f 88p
Four On Eight 2 gr.c 86p
Materialistic 2 b.f 82p
Tiptree (IRE) 2 b.f 91p
Very Dashing 2 br.f 82p
War Story (IRE) 2 gr.c 85p

TOM DASCOMBE
Calder Prince (IRE) 2 gr.c 90p
Dutch Gallery 2 b.c 85p
Happy Tidings 2 b.f 82p
Kachy 2 b.c 108p

MICHAEL DODS
Baltic Raider (IRE) 2 b.g 83p
Kraftwork (IRE) 2 gr.c 83p

ED DUNLOP
Red Verdon (USA) 2 ch.c 85p

HARRY DUNLOP
D'Niro (IRE) 2 br.c 85p

DAVID ELSWORTH
Justice Law (IRE) 2 gr.c 97p

DAVID EVANS
Play Gal 2 b.f 80p

RICHARD FAHEY
Appleton 2 ch.c 91p
Balance 2 ch.f 80p
Curtain Call 2 b.f 85p
Dancing Years (IRE) 2 ch.f 81p
Dark Devil (IRE) 2 gr.g 81p
Gallipoli (IRE) 2 b.g 81p
Garcia 2 b.g 85p
Novinophobia 2 ch.c 81p
Yosemite 2 gr.f 85p

JAMES FANSHAWE
Column 2 b.c 86p
Enreaching 2 b.g 82p
Lord George (IRE) 2 gr.c 85p
Mazzini 2 ch.c 84p
Zest (IRE) 2 b.f 86p

JOHN GOSDEN
Always Welcome (USA) 2 ch.g 90p
Amanaat (IRE) 2 b.c 91p
Auntinet 2 b.f 85p
Chastushka (IRE) 2 b.f 84p
City of Ideas 2 b.c 80p
Crazy Horse 2 b.c 106p
Daily Bulletin (USA) 2 b.c 85p
Eternally 2 b.f 86p
Exist 2 b.f 84p
Foundation (IRE) 2 ch.c 114p
Generalship (IRE) 2 b.c 63P
Khaleesy (IRE) 2 b.f 80p
Linguistic (IRE) 2 b.c 98p
Persuasive (IRE) 2 gr.f 88p
Predilection (USA) 2 b.c 93p
Pursuitofthestars (IRE) 2 b.f 84p
Rex Bell (IRE) 2 b.c 82p
Royal Artillery (USA) 2 b. or br.c 95P
Satish 2 b.c 93p
Shalaa (IRE) 2 b.c 123p
Snow Moon 2 b.f 83p
So Mi Dar 2 b.f 84P
Southern Stars 2 b.f 73P
Swiss Range 2 b.f 86p
Taqdeer (IRE) 2 ch.c 80p
Tathqeef (USA) 2 b.c 84P
The Black Princess (FR) 2 b. or br.f 79P
Vincent's Forever 2 b.c 90p
Von Blucher (IRE) 2 ch.c 106p
Wajeez (IRE) 2 ch.c 111p

WILLIAM HAGGAS
Bedrock 2 b.g 87p
Dal Harraild 2 ch.g 92p
Dutch Destiny 2 b.f 87p
Dwight D 2 b.c 84p
Easy Code 2 b.c 80p
Fastnet Tempest (IRE) 2 b.g 80p
Grey Morning 2 gr. or ro.c 87p
In The City 2 ch.c 88p
Light Music 2 b.f 101p

Muzdawaj 2 b.c 90p
Out And About (IRE) 2 b.g 96p
Recorder 2 ch.c 111p
Victory Bond 2 b.c 85p

RICHARD HANNON
Alkhor 2 b.c 81p
Altarsheed (IRE) 2 b.g 101p
Ancient Trade (USA) 2 ch.c 85p
Chief Whip (USA) 2 ch.c 82P
Eltezam (IRE) 2 b.c 104p
Fashaak (IRE) 2 b.c 80p
George William 2 b.g 81p
Melfit (IRE) 2 b.c 86p
Nisser 2 b.c 90p
Not Touch 2 ch.c 80p
Paris Protocol 2 b.c 98p
See You When (IRE) 2 b.c 82p
Shaan (IRE) 2 b.f 86p
Shwaimsa (IRE) 2 b.f 87p
Steel of Madrid (IRE) 2 b.c 108p
Taqwaa (IRE) 2 ch.c 87p
Tony Curtis 2 b.c 106p
War Glory (IRE) 2 b.c 86p
War Whisper (IRE) 2 b.c 85p

CHARLES HILLS
Dark Crescent (IRE) 2 b.c 86p
Frenchman (FR) 2 b.c 80p
Gunmetal (IRE) 2 gr.c 82p
Moorside 2 b.f 82p
Mootaharer (IRE) 2 b.c 92p
Zaakhir (IRE) 2 b.f 86p

DEAN IVORY
Fighting Temeraire (IRE) 2 b.c 85p

MARK JOHNSTON
Ahdaf 2 ch.c 87p
Deodoro (USA) 2 b.f 86p
Gold Medallion (IRE) 2 b.c 94p
Juste Pour Nous 2 b.c 80p
Lumiere 2 gr.f 115p
Richie McCaw 2 b.c 84p
Samaawy 2 b.c 81p
Twobeelucky 2 b.g 86p

ALAN KING
Jim Dandy 2 ch.g 81p
Primitivo 2 b.g 86p
Rainbow Dreamer 2 b.c 91p

WILLIAM KNIGHT
Ballard Down (IRE) 2 b.g 85p

DAVID LANIGAN
Gershwin 2 b.c 89p
Wapping (USA) 2 b.c 81p

PHILIP MCBRIDE
Quatrieme Ami 2 b.c 101p

MARTYN MEADE
Aclaim (IRE) 2 b.c 83p
C Note (IRE) 2 b.c 98p
De Veer Cliffs (IRE) 2 b.f 83p

BRIAN MEEHAN
Kitaaby (IRE) 2 b.g 81p

Maccus (IRE) 2 b.c 94p
Magnum (IRE) 2 gr.g 82p
Ocean Jive 2 b.c 89p
Qamarain (USA) 2 ch.f 80p
September Stars (IRE) 2 ch.f 87p

HUGHIE MORRISON
Last Tango Inparis 2 ch.f 89p
Maestro Mac (IRE) 2 b.c 83p
Saucy Spirit 2 b.f 83p
Top Beak (IRE) 2 b.c 91p

JEREMY NOSEDA
Abe Lincoln (USA) 2 b.c 104p
Nemoralia (USA) 2 b. or br.f 112p

AIDAN O'BRIEN, IRELAND
Air Vice Marshal (USA) 2 b.c 107p
Ballydoyle (IRE) 2 b.f 113p
Coolmore (IRE) 2 ch.f 101p
Hit It A Bomb (USA) 2 b.c 119p
Landofhopeandglory (IRE) 2 b.c 103p
Minding (IRE) 2 b.f 120p
Washington DC (IRE) 2 b.c 108p

DAVID O'MEARA
Cape Love (USA) 2 ch.c 82p
Flyboy (IRE) 2 b.c 82p

JAMIE OSBORNE
Every Chance (IRE) 2 b.c 92p
Ice Royal (IRE) 2 b.c 80p
Monteverdi (FR) 2 b.c 84p

HUGO PALMER
Architecture (IRE) 2 b.f 87p
Baydar 2 b.c 85p
Harry Champion 2 b.g 87p
Mengli Khan (IRE) 2 b.c 97p
Paris Magic 2 b.c 88p
Sacred Trust 2 b.c 84p
To Be Wild (IRE) 2 br.c 86p

SIR MARK PRESCOTT BT
Marsha (IRE) 2 b.f 105p
Status Quo (IRE) 2 br.g 81p
Time Warp 2 ch.c 101p

JOHN QUINN
Speed Company (IRE) 2 b.c 96p

DAVID SIMCOCK
Algometer 2 gr.c 87p
Chinoiseries 2 b.f 90p
High Hopes 2 b.f 85p
King of Dreams 2 ch.g 81p
Singyoursong (IRE) 2 b.f 86p
Turning The Table (IRE) 2 gr.f 86p
Veena (FR) 2 b.f 82p

BRYAN SMART
Kentuckyconnection (USA) 2 b.c 94p

SIR MICHAEL STOUTE
Abdon 2 b.c 92p
Across The Stars (IRE) 2 b.c 87p
Alyday 2 ch.f 86p
Arab Poet 2 ch.c 88p

Aristocratic 2 b.f 83p
Autocratic 2 b.c 81P
Ballet Concerto 2 b.c 90p
Dollar Reward 2 b.c 87p
Engage (IRE) 2 b.f 83p
Estidraak (IRE) 2 ch.c 96p
Fidaawy 2 ch.g 72P
Honorina 2 ch.f 85p
Mainstream 2 b.c 84p
Midterm 2 b.c 91P
Queen's Trust 2 b.f 90p
Rostova (USA) 2 b.f 88p
Sky Ship 2 ch.c 80p
Stargazer (IRE) 2 b.c 91p
Statuesque 2 b.f 64P
Thetis (IRE) 2 b.f 105p
Thikriyaat (IRE) 2 b.g 81p
Ulysses (IRE) 2 ch.c 81p
Under Attack (IRE) 2 b.g 83p
Vaunting (USA) 2 gr.f 92p

SAEED BIN SUROOR
Brave Hero 2 ch.c 95p
Ebtihaal (IRE) 2 ch.c 97p
First Victory (IRE) 2 b.f 105p
Good Run (FR) 2 ch.c 97p
Great Order (USA) 2 b. or br.c 91p
Impressive Day (IRE) 2 b.f 82p
Jufn 2 b.c 86P
More To Come 2 b.c 83p
Move Up 2 b.c 99p
Next Life 2 b.f 86p
Next Stage 2 ch.c 92p
Nice Future (IRE) 2 b.c 81p
Prize Money 2 b.c 94p
Quality Time (IRE) 2 b.f 87p
Simple Attack 2 b.g 82p
Strong Challenge (IRE) 2 ch.c 98p
Very Talented (IRE) 2 b.c 109p
Yattwee (USA) 2 b. or br.g 102p

ALAN SWINBANK
Zealous (IRE) 2 br.g 83p

MARCUS TREGONING
Storm Ahead (IRE) 2 b.g 85p

ROGER VARIAN
Ennaadd 2 b.c 104p
First Rate 2 b.c 80p
Fourth Way (IRE) 2 b.f 93p
Notary 2 b.f 82p
Shabeeb (USA) 2 b.c 76P
Spanish City 2 ch.c 80p
Sun Lover 2 b.c 86p
Tailwind 2 b.c 80p
Taneen (USA) 2 b. or br.c 92p
Tiercel 2 b.c 82p

ED WALKER
Experto Crede (IRE) 2 b.g 88p
Marylebone 2 b.c 84p

CHRIS WALL
Cambodia (IRE) 2 ch.g 81P
Mix And Mingle (IRE) 2 ch.f 100p

2015 STATISTICS

The following tables cover Jan 1-Dec 31. The prize money statistics, compiled by *Timeform*, relate to first-three prize money and win money. Win money was traditionally used to decide the trainers' championship until, in 1994, the BHB and the National Trainers' Federation established a championship decided by total prize money as determined by *Racing Post*. In 2007, 2008 and 2009 the trainers' and owners' championships were decided over the turf season (March-November) but, in 2010, the championship was changed to run from November to November (ending with the November Handicap meeting). The jockeys' championship has traditionally been decided by the number of winners ridden during the year, though between 1997 and 2014 the Jockeys' Association recognised a championship that ran for the turf season (March-November). The 2015 'title' was decided over a shorter period, starting on Two Thousand Guineas day and ending on British Champions' Day at Ascot in October.

OWNERS (1,2,3 earnings)	Horses	Wnrs	Indiv'l Races Won	Runs	%	Stakes £
1 Godolphin	370	186	287	1194	24.0	5,217,268
2 Mr Hamdan Al Maktoum	215	100	137	738	18.6	3,327,457
3 Mr M. Tabor, D. Smith & Mrs John Magnier	14	4	6	26	23.1	1,832,284
4 Mr A. E. Oppenheimer	13	6	9	43	20.9	1,429,560
5 Wertheimer et Frere	2	1	3	5	60.0	1,396,673
6 Sheikh Hamdan Bin Mohammed Al Maktoum	70	41	80	378	21.2	1,083,297
7 Sheikh Mohammed Obaid Al Maktoum	23	12	12	83	14.5	993,159
8 Al Shaqab Racing	61	33	45	191	23.6	975,425
9 Qatar Racing Limited	81	31	39	277	14.1	927,462
10 Mr D. Smith, Mrs J. Magnier, Mr M. Tabor	12	5	5	18	27.8	896,231
11 Mr K. Abdullah	90	37	48	258	18.6	837,568
12 Dr Marwan Koukash	34	18	35	285	12.3	837,486

OWNERS (win money, £2m+)	Horses	Wnrs	Indiv'l Races Won	Runs	%	Stakes £
1 Godolphin	370	186	287	1194	24.0	3,622,999
2 Mr Hamdan Al Maktoum	215	100	137	738	18.6	2,463,981

TRAINERS (1,2,3 earnings)	Horses	Wnrs	Indiv'l Races Won	Runs	%	Stakes £
1 John Gosden	191	88	133	577	23.1	5,066,018
2 Richard Fahey	296	148	235	1691	13.9	3,644,822
3 Richard Hannon	305	145	194	1382	14.0	3,313,802
4 Aidan O'Brien, Ireland	47	15	16	79	20.3	3,277,310
5 Mark Johnston	199	114	204	1208	16.9	2,556,402
6 William Haggas	144	78	113	533	21.2	2,225,909
7 Charles Hills	145	57	71	580	12.2	2,101,707
8 Charlie Appleby	186	88	151	663	22.8	2,082,341
9 Saeed bin Suroor	131	72	105	392	26.8	1,603,124
10 Luca Cumani	73	43	50	266	18.8	1,562,156
11 Roger Varian	126	66	100	474	21.1	1,548,711
12 Sir Michael Stoute	148	64	80	455	17.6	1,519,495

TRAINERS (win money, £2m+)	Horses	Wnrs	Indiv'l Races Won	Runs	%	Stakes
1 John Gosden	191	88	133	577	23.1	3,092,893
2 Richard Fahey	296	148	235	1691	13.9	2,462,734
3 Richard Hannon	305	145	194	1382	14.0	2,027,872
4 Aidan O'Brien, Ireland	47	15	16	79	20.3	2,015,997

TRAINERS (with 100+ winners)	Horses	Wnrs	Indiv'l Races Won	2nd	3rd	Runs	%
1 Richard Fahey	296	148	235	220	200	1691	13.9
2 Mark Johnston	199	114	204	167	148	1208	16.9
3 Richard Hannon	305	145	194	180	173	1382	14.0
4 Charlie Appleby	186	88	151	113	96	663	22.8
5 John Gosden	191	88	133	101	77	577	23.1
6 David O'Meara	150	79	122	119	105	931	13.1
7 William Haggas	144	78	113	87	50	533	21.2
8 Saeed bin Suroor	131	72	105	67	51	392	26.8
9 Roger Varian	126	66	100	79	66	474	21.1

JOCKEYS (by winners)	1st	2nd	3rd	Unpl	Mts	%
1 Luke Morris	189	208	170	941	1508	12.5
2 Adam Kirby	177	136	135	635	1083	16.3
3 Silvestre de Sousa	155	105	96	475	831	18.7
4 Joe Fanning	132	115	105	586	938	14.1
5 Paul Hanagan	125	93	78	400	696	18.0
6 George Baker	123	98	80	395	696	17.7
7 James Doyle	121	100	77	310	608	19.9
8 Jim Crowley	118	119	110	509	856	13.8
9 William Buick	113	81	75	304	573	19.7
10 Graham Lee	108	103	88	653	952	11.3
11 Pat Cosgrave	104	99	74	436	713	14.6
12 Tony Hamilton	103	97	91	539	830	12.4

Note: Silvestre de Sousa won the Stobart-sponsored jockeys' championship (with 132 wins)

JOCKEYS (1,2,3 earnings)	Races Won	Rides	%	Stakes £
1 Ryan Moore	82	381	21.5	4,807,313
2 Frankie Dettori	75	340	22.1	4,716,935
3 William Buick	113	573	19.7	3,171,111
4 Andrea Atzeni	76	517	14.7	3,142,309
5 Paul Hanagan	125	696	18.0	3,004,861
6 James Doyle	121	608	19.9	2,920,431
7 Jamie Spencer	85	625	13.6	2,245,700
8 Silvestre de Sousa	155	831	18.7	2,095,914
9 Pat Smullen	9	72	12.5	1,829,697
10 Graham Lee	108	952	11.3	1,615,368
11 Adam Kirby	177	1083	16.3	1,600,990
12 Luke Morris	189	1508	12.5	1,478,515

JOCKEYS (win money, £2m+)	Races Won	Rides	%	Stakes £
1 Frankie Dettori	75	340	22.1	3,330,542
2 Ryan Moore	82	381	21.5	3,233,483
3 Andrea Atzeni	76	517	14.7	2,331,750
4 Paul Hanagan	125	696	18.0	2,062,811

APPRENTICES (by winners)	1st	2nd	3rd	Unpl	Mts	%
1 Tom Marquand	67	55	80	400	602	11.1
2 Shane Gray	65	50	45	333	493	13.2
3 Jack Garritty	58	65	67	245	435	13.3

Note: Tom Marquand won the Stobart-sponsored apprentice championship (with 54 wins)

		Races Won	Runs	%	Stakes £
SIRES OF WINNERS (1,2,3 earnings)					
1	Dubawi (by Dubai Millennium)	106	579	18.3	3,474,813
2	Galileo (by Sadler's Wells)	54	473	11.4	3,213,923
3	Cape Cross (by Green Desert)	102	642	15.9	2,691,088
4	Invincible Spirit (by Green Desert)	123	938	13.1	2,198,813
5	Dark Angel (by Acclamation)	104	785	13.2	2,138,037
6	Oasis Dream (by Green Desert)	94	800	11.8	2,131,183
7	Shamardal (by Giant's Causeway)	123	709	17.3	1,968,283
8	Kodiac (by Danehill)	136	1065	12.8	1,899,256
9	Teofilo (by Galileo)	65	461	14.1	1,673,368
10	Exceed And Excel (by Danehill)	131	998	13.1	1,575,212
11	Singspiel (by In The Wings)	12	136	8.8	1,542,016
12	Fastnet Rock (by Danehill)	29	268	10.8	1,429,710

		Horses	Indiv'l Wnrs	Races Won	Stakes £
SIRES OF WINNERS (win money)					
1	Dubawi (by Dubai Millennium)	157	74	106	2,616,226
2	Cape Cross (by Green Desert)	129	68	102	2,045,938
3	Galileo (by Sadler's Wells)	138	46	54	1,844,249
4	Oasis Dream (by Green Desert)	155	60	94	1,783,711
5	Invincible Spirit (by Green Desert)	157	80	123	1,500,533
6	Singspiel (by In The Wings)	22	8	12	1,435,625
7	Shamardal (by Giant's Causeway)	153	73	123	1,418,712
8	Kodiac (by Danehill)	187	80	136	1,403,063
9	Fastnet Rock (by Danehill)	76	25	29	1,303,999
10	Dark Angel (by Acclamation)	146	68	104	1,272,078
11	Duke of Marmalade (by Danehill)	74	24	45	1,241,190
12	Exceed And Excel (by Danehill)	180	89	131	1,107,097

		Races Won	Runs	Stakes £
LEADING HORSES (1,2,3 earnings)				
1	Solow 5 gr.g Singspiel – High Maintenance	3	3	1,396,673
2	Golden Horn 3 b.c Cape Cross – Fleche d'Or	4	5	1,376,725
3	Muhaarar 3 b.c Oasis Dream – Tahrir	4	4	906,124
4	Simple Verse 3 b.f Duke of Marmalade – Guantanamera	5	8	798,233
5	Fascinating Rock 4 b.c Fastnet Rock – Miss Polaris	1	2	770,547
6	Postponed 4 b.c Dubawi – Ever Rigg	1	3	724,522
7	Legatissimo 3 b.f Danehill Dancer – Yummy Mummy	2	3	669,521
8	Arabian Queen 3 b.f Dubawi – Barshiba	2	6	622,799
9	Jack Hobbs 3 br.c Halling – Swain's Gold	2	5	533,410
10	Gleneagles 3 b.c Galileo – You'resothrilling	2	3	512,695
11	Trip To Paris 4 b.g Champs Elysees – La Grande Zoa	4	8	388,657
12	Found 3 b.f Galileo – Red Evie	0	2	379,274

2015 IRISH STATISTICS

The following tables show the leading owners, trainers, jockeys, sires of winners and horses on the Flat in Ireland during 2015 (Jan 1-Dec 31). The prize money statistics, compiled by *Timeform*, relate to winning prize money only, converted to sterling at the prevailing rate at the time.

OWNERS		Horses	Wnrs	Indiv'l Races Won	Runs	%	Stakes £
1	Godolphin & Partners	1	1	1	1	100.0	517,857
2	Michael Tabor/Derrick Smith/ Mrs Magnier	28	17	21	64	32.8	496,478
3	H. H. Aga Khan	53	30	40	143	28.0	468,247
4	Mr A F. Oppenheimer	2	1	1	2	50.0	465,693
5	Mrs J. S. Bolger	107	34	40	455	8.8	459,611
6	Godolphin	54	26	33	160	20.6	404,124
7	Derrick Smith, Mrs J. Magnier & M. Tabor	30	15	20	70	28.6	328,956
8	Sean Jones	26	16	28	127	22.0	289,321
9	Qatar Racing Limited	30	14	19	107	17.8	246,435
10	Mr K. Abdullah	22	9	12	58	20.7	242,861
11	MrsJohnMagnier/MichaelTabor/ DerrickSmith	9	1	2	12	16.7	229,120
12	Newtown Anner Stud Farm Ltd	18	8	11	75	14.7	167,755

TRAINERS (by prize money)		Horses	Wnrs	Indiv'l Races Won	Runs	%	Stakes £
1	Aidan O'Brien, Ireland	157	81	108	505	21.4	1,987,069
2	D. K. Weld, Ireland	142	58	78	424	18.4	1,161,705
3	John Gosden	3	2	2	3	66.7	983,550
4	J. S. Bolger, Ireland	135	52	67	529	12.7	818,694
5	G. M. Lyons, Ireland	80	46	65	359	18.1	787,176
6	David Wachman, Ireland	68	28	37	261	14.2	600,512
7	M. Halford, Ireland	107	41	50	448	11.2	396,010
8	Edward Lynam, Ireland	45	17	24	204	11.8	320,017
9	W. McCreery, Ireland	54	21	29	232	12.5	283,981
10	Mrs J. Harrington, Ireland	54	16	22	215	10.2	263,829
11	Andrew Oliver, Ireland	61	17	22	231	9.5	217,588
12	T. Stack, Ireland	34	13	18	129	14.0	211,312

JOCKEYS (by winners)		1st	2nd	3rd	Unpl	Mts	%
1	Pat Smullen	112	98	79	321	610	18.4
2	C. T. Keane	75	61	67	330	533	14.1
3	Francis-Martin Berry	71	60	56	355	542	13.1
4	Shane Foley	71	74	61	412	618	11.5
5	K. J. Manning	63	61	54	301	479	13.2
6	C. D. Hayes	53	45	66	399	563	9.4
7	W. M. Lordan	54	52	68	390	564	9.4
8	Joseph O'Brien	49	34	23	107	213	23.0
9	William James Lee	48	39	53	277	417	11.5
10	Declan McDonogh	46	43	49	277	415	11.1
11	Connor King	40	37	41	313	431	9.3
12	Seamie Heffernan	36	25	28	265	354	10.2

SIRES OF WINNERS

		Horses	Indiv'l Wnrs	Races Won	Stakes £
1	Galileo (by Sadler's Wells)	112	51	69	1,339,266
2	Cape Cross (by Green Desert)	35	13	15	665,917
3	Halling (by Diesis)	6	2	2	524,463
4	Fastnet Rock (by Danehill)	50	19	27	477,368
5	Teofilo (by Galileo)	46	18	25	382,203
6	Dark Angel (by Acclamation)	53	17	25	376,211
7	Azamour (by Night Shift)	30	15	24	368,923
8	Danehill Dancer (by Danehill)	30	7	10	297,174
9	War Front (by Danzig)	15	5	8	291,343
10	Dubawi (by Dubai Millennium)	15	7	10	208,240
11	Holy Roman Emperor (by Danehill)	48	20	30	206,382
12	Big Bad Bob (by Bob Back)	46	16	21	189,243

LEADING HORSES

		Runs	Races Won	Stakes £
1	Jack Hobbs 3 br.c Halling – Swain's Gold	1	1	517,857
2	Golden Horn 3 b.c Cape Cross – Fleche d'Or	1	1	465,693
3	Air Force Blue 2 b.c War Front – Chatham	3	3	238,120
4	Order of St George 3 b.c Galileo – Another Storm	4	3	184,863
5	Covert Love 3 b.f Azamour – Wing Stealth	1	1	165,714
6	Pleascach 3 b.f Teofilo – Toirneach	5	2	164,043
7	Legatissimo 3 b.f Danehill Dancer – Yummy Mummy	4	2	157,106
8	Minding 2 b.f Galileo – Lillie Langtry	4	2	135,139
9	Gleneagles 3 b.c Galileo – You'resothrilling	1	1	126,087
10	Diamondsandrubies 3 b.f Fastnet Rock – Quarter Moon	3	2	114,458
11	Sovereign Debt 6 gr.g Dark Angel – Kelsey Rose	6	3	113,177
12	Al Kazeem 7 b.c Dubawi – Kazeem	1	1	112,319

TWO-YEAR-OLDS	THREE-YEAR-OLDS	OLDER HORSES
128p Air Force Blue	129 Highland Reel	128 Free Eagle
120p Minding (f)	129 Order of St George	127 Fascinating Rock
119p Hit It A Bomb	128 Gleneagles	124 Max Dynamite
115 Johannes Vermeer	123 Found (f)	123 Cougar Mountain
113p Ballydoyle (f)	122 Bondi Beach	123 Sole Power
113 Beacon Rock	122 Legatissimo (f)	120 Gordon Lord Byron
112p Blue de Vega	121 Endless Drama	119 Forgotten Rules
112 Deauville	121 Fields of Athenry	119 Kingfisher
112 Shogun	119 Lucida (f)	119 Mustajeeb
111 Smash Williams	119 Toscanini	118 Moviesta
110 Alice Springs (f)	117 Pleascach (f)	117 Maarek
110 Herald The Dawn	116 War Envoy	116 Great Minds
	116 Zawraq	116 Simenon

EXPLANATORY NOTES

'Racehorses of 2015' deals individually, in alphabetical sequence, with every horse that ran on the Flat in Britain in 2015, plus a good number of overseas-trained horses. For each of these horses is given (1) its age, colour and sex followed by the name of its sire, its dam and the sire of the dam, with highest Timeform Annual rating where the information is available, (2) its breeding, and for most horses, where this information has not been given in a previous Racehorses Annual, a family outline, (3) a form summary giving its Timeform rating at the end of the previous year, followed by an abbreviated summary of all its performances during the past year and the date of its last run, (4) a Timeform rating, or ratings, of its merit in 2015 (which appears in the margin), (5) a Timeform commentary on its racing or general characteristics as a racehorse, with some suggestions, perhaps, regarding its prospects for 2016, and (6) the name of its trainer when it last ran. For each two-year-old the foaling date is also given.

TIMEFORM RATINGS

The Timeform Rating is a measure of the *best* form a horse displayed, expressed in pounds. Without going into complexities, the scale used for Timeform ratings represents around 4 lb a length at five furlongs, 3.5 lb a length at six furlongs, 3 lb a length at seven furlongs, 2.5 lb a length at a mile, 2 lb a length at a mile and a quarter, over 1.5 lb a length at a mile and a half and over 1 lb a length at two miles, though the precise poundage will depend on circumstances, not least the conversion from times to margins used officially in each instance. When a horse has raced on turf and on an artificial surface and its form on one is significantly different from the other, the two ratings are given, the one for artificial surfaces set out below the turf preceded by 'a'. Some of the ratings may be different from those in the final issue of the 2015 Timeform Black Book series. The 'Racehorses Annual' figure is the definitive Timeform Rating.

The following may be attached to, or appear instead of, a rating:-

p   likely to improve.

P   capable of *much* better form.

+   the horse may be better than we have rated it.

d   the horse appears to have deteriorated, and might no longer be capable of running to the rating given.

§   unreliable (for temperamental or other reasons).

§§   so temperamentally unsatisfactory as not to be worth a rating.

?   the horse's rating is suspect. If used without a rating the symbol implies that the horse can't be assessed with confidence, or, if used in the in-season Timeform publications, that the horse is out of form.

RATINGS AND WEIGHT-FOR-AGE

The ratings in this book embrace all the horses in training it is possible to weigh up, ranging from tip-top performers, with ratings from 130 upwards, through categories such as high-class, very smart, smart, useful, fairly useful, fair and modest, down to the poorest, rated around the 20 mark. All the ratings are at weight-for-age, so that equal ratings mean horses of equal merit: the Timeform handicap is really not a single handicap, but four handicaps side by side: one for two-year-olds, one for three-year-olds, one for four-year-olds and one for older horses. Thus, a three-year-old rated, for argument's sake, at 117 is deemed to be identical in point of 'merit' with a four-year-old also rated at 117: but for them to have equal chances in, say, a mile race in May, the three-year-old would need to be receiving 9 lb from the four-year-old, the weight difference specified by the Age, Weight and Distance Tables at the end of the book.

USING THE RATINGS

A. Horses of the Same Age

If the horses all carry the same weight there are no adjustments to be made, and the horses with the highest ratings have the best chances. If the horses carry different weights, jot down their ratings, and to the rating of each horse add one point for every pound the horse is set to carry less than 10 st, or subtract one point for every pound it has to carry more than 10 st.

B. Horses of Different Ages

Treat each horse separately, and compare the weight it has to carry with the weight for age prescribed for it in the tables, according to the age of the horse, the distance of the race and the time of the year. Then, add one point to the rating for each pound the horse has to carry less than the weight given in the tables: or, subtract one point from the rating for every pound it has to carry more than the weight prescribed by the tables.

For the purposes of rating calculations it should, in general, be assumed that any allowance a rider is able to claim is nullified by his or her inexperience.

WEIGHING UP A RACE

The ratings tell you which horses in a race are most favoured by the weights; but the commentaries should also be studied carefully to see if there is any reason—suitability of going and distance among the most important points to consider—why the horse might be expected not to run up to its rating or indeed, with a lightly raced or inexperienced horse, might improve on it. The quality of jockeyship is also an important factor when deciding between horses with similar chances.

In setting out the various characteristics, requirements and peculiarities of each horse in its commentary, we have expressed ourselves in as critical a manner as possible, endeavouring to say just as much, and no more, than the facts seem to warrant. Where there are clear indications, and conclusions can be drawn with fair certainty, we have drawn them; if it is a matter of probability or possibility we have put it that way; and where real conclusions are not to be drawn, we have been content to state the facts.

THE FORM SUMMARIES

The distance of each race is given in furlongs, fractional distances being expressed in the decimal notation to the nearest tenth of a furlong. The prefix 'a' signifies a race on an artificial surface (except for 'f' for fibresand, 'p' for polytrack and 't' for tapeta).

The going is symbolised as follows: f=firm (turf) or fast (artificial surface); m=good to firm, or standard to fast (artificial surface); g=good (turf) or standard (artificial surface); d=good to soft/dead, or standard to slow (artificial surface); s=soft (turf) or slow, sloppy, muddy or wet (artificial surface); v=heavy.

Placings are indicated, up to sixth place, by the use of superior figures, an asterisk being used to denote a win.

Where sale prices are considered relevant F denotes the price as a foal, Y the price as a yearling, 2-y-o as a two-year-old, and so on. These are given in guineas unless prefixed by $ (American dollars) ¥ (Japanese yen) or € (euros). Other currencies are converted approximately into guineas or pounds sterling at the prevailing exchange rate.

RACEHORSES OF 2015

Horse	Commentary	Rating

AABIR (IRE) 3 b.c. Invincible Spirit (IRE) 121 – Phillippa (IRE) (Galileo (IRE) 134) **83** [2015 81p: 9.9m² 10.3m⁵ p11g⁴ May 27] fairly useful handicapper: second at Beverley in April: stays 10.5f. *Marco Botti*

AAMAN (IRE) 9 gr.g. Dubai Destination (USA) 127 – Amellnaa (IRE) 86 (Sadler's Wells **–** (USA) 132) [2015 16.2sᵖᵘ 14g 18d 13.1d Sep 2] tall gelding: fair at best, no form in 2015. *Bernard Llewellyn*

AARANYOW (IRE) 7 ch.g. Compton Place 125 – Cutpurse Moll 76 (Green Desert (USA) **43** 127) [2015 56, a69: 5m p5g⁶ Jul 22] poor handicapper: stays 7f: acts on polytrack, tapeta, good to firm and good to soft going: tried in headgear/tongue tie. *Clifford Lines*

ABACO RIDGE 2 b.f. (Feb 12) Bahamian Bounty 116 – Echo Ridge (IRE) 78 (Oratorio **74** (IRE) 128) [2015 6d⁵ 6v² Nov 7] first foal: dam, 2-y-o 6f winner, half-sister to useful 6f winner City Girl out of smart 6f/7f winner Lochridge: better effort when second in maiden at Doncaster (length behind Times Legacy) in November. *Ralph Beckett*

ABADOO 2 b.f. (Apr 12) Multiplex 114 – Agooda (Rainbow Quest (USA) 134) [2015 p8f **–** 8.3g 8.3s Nov 4] £2,500Y: third foal: sister to winner up to 1¼m Agadoo (2-y-o 7f winner): dam unraced: no form. *Shaun Harris*

ABAQ 3 b.f. Oasis Dream 129 – Indian Ink (IRE) 122 (Indian Ridge 123) [2015 79p: p7g **–** Aug 19] fair at best, no form in 2015: best effort at 6f. *Richard Hannon*

ABBA ZABBA (IRE) 3 b.g. Bushranger (IRE) 119 – Tipperary Boutique (IRE) 86 (Danehill **–** Dancer (IRE) 117) [2015 –: f8g t9.5f t12.2g Mar 19] maiden: no form in 2015. *David Evans*

ABBERLEY DANCER (IRE) 2 b.f. (Feb 13) Lilbourne Lad (IRE) 111 – Babberina (IRE) **67** 75 (Danehill Dancer (IRE) 117) [2015 5m⁵ p5f* 5m 5f Jun 17] €2,200Y: lengthy filly: fourth foal: half-sister to 3 winners, including 6f winner Barbeque (by Elusive City) and 7f winner Period Piece (by Intikhab): dam maiden (stayed 8.5f): fair performer: won maiden at Chelmsford in April: raced only at 5f. *J. S. Moore*

ABBEY ANGEL (IRE) 3 b.f. Arcano (IRE) 122 – Sanna Bay (IRE) (Refuse To Bend **88** (IRE) 129) [2015 93p: 10.3m³ 10g⁴ 10.4m⁵ 12m 10g⁴ 10.3m 10.4d 10.4s 8.3s⁴ t9.5m⁵ Dec 30] fairly useful handicapper: third in minor event at Doncaster in June: stays 10.5f: acts on tapeta, soft and good to firm going: tried in cheekpieces in 2015. *Richard Fahey*

ABBEYLEIX 2 gr.g. (Apr 30) Sir Percy 129 – Alvarita 104 (Selkirk (USA) 129) [2015 **75 p** t8.6f⁵ p8g³ p8g⁶ Nov 18] €55,000Y: brother to useful winner up to 1¼m Alla Speranza (2-y-o 8.4f winner) and half-brother to several winners, including 1¼m-1¾m winner Alcaeus and 11f winner Altesse (both useful and by Hernando): dam, 1m-10.5f winner, out of dual Champion Stakes winner Alborada: fair form in maidens, best effort when third at Kempton (2¾ lengths behind D'Niro) in November: has been gelded: remains open to improvement, especially over 1¼m+. *Sir Mark Prescott Bt*

ABBOTSFIELD (IRE) 5 ch.m. Sakhee's Secret 128 – May Day Queen (IRE) 79 (Danetime **51 §** (IRE) 121) [2015 72: 7g 8.3d⁵ 7g Jul 22] modest handicapper: stays 1m: acts on soft and good to firm going: tried in cheekpieces: temperamental. *Ben Haslam*

ABDON 2 b.c. (Feb 10) Cacique (IRE) 124 – Kinnaird (IRE) 113 (Dr Devious (IRE) 127) **92 p** [2015 8v* Aug 25] 175,000Y: sixth foal: closely related to 8.3f/9f winner Keene Dancer (by Danehill Dancer) and half-brother to 1¼m-1½m winner Keenes Royale (by Red Ransom), now dam of smart performer up to 1m Ivawood, and very smart winner up to 9f Berkshire (2-y-o 7f/1m winner, by Mount Nelson): dam 6f (at 2 yrs) to 1¼m (Prix de l'Opera) winner: 12/1, looked useful prospect when won maiden at Newbury (by ½ length from Navajo War Dance) in August, readily: will be suited by 1¼m: sure to progress. *Sir Michael Stoute*

ABE LINCOLN (USA) 2 b.c. (Apr 21) Discreet Cat (USA) 127 – Truly Blushed (USA) **104 p** (Yes It's True (USA) 116) [2015 p7g* p7m³ p7m Nov 21] $75,000Y, resold $120,000, $235,000 2-y-o: third foal: half-brother to winners in USA by Hard Spun and Street Sense: dam North American 5f (including at 2 yrs)/6f winner: won maiden at Kempton (by length from Ballet Concerto) in September: better effort when third in minor event at Lingfield (¾ length behind Race Day) in November, left poorly placed: will go on improving. *Jeremy Noseda*

ABERLADY (USA) 2 b.f. (Apr 4) Arch (USA) 127 – Visit 116 (Oasis Dream 129) [2015   **71 p**
6m³ p6g² 6g⁴ p6f⁵ Sep 24] second foal: half-sister to smart 1m winner Western Reserve
(by Indian Charlie): dam, winner up to 7f (2-y-o 6f winner) who stayed 1¼m, half-sister to
Prix de l'Opera winner Promising Lead: fair form: shaped well when fifth on nursery debut
at Chelmsford: will be suited by 7f+: remains with potential. *Sir Michael Stoute*

ABERTILLERY 3 b.g. Shamardal (USA) 129 – Nantyglo 101 (Mark of Esteem (IRE)   **64**
137) [2015 7m 7m⁴ 8g 7s⁴ 7d⁴ Oct 24] 90,000Y: fifth foal: half-brother to 8.6f winner
Valley Tiger (by Tiger Hill): dam, winner up to 1m (2-y-o 6f winner), half-sister to useful
winner up to 1½m Resplendent Light: modest maiden: stays 7f: acts on soft and good to firm
going: often races prominently: sold 18,000 gns, joined Michael Blanshard. *John Gosden*

ABHAJAT (IRE) 3 b.f. Lope de Vega (IRE) 125 – Starry Messenger 82 (Galileo (IRE)   **77**
134) [2015 p8g⁵ 8g³ Sep 4] €125,000F, 400,000Y: fourth foal: half-sister to 3 winners,
including useful 7-y-o 1m winner Starbright (by Duke of Marmalade) and 8.3f (including
at 2 yrs) winner (stayed 1½m) The Giving Tree (by Rock of Gibraltar): dam, 1½m winner,
half-sister to very smart US Grade 1 9f winner Tuscan Evening: better effort when fifth in
maiden in August. *Charles Hills*

ABILITY N DELIVERY 10 gr.g. Kyllachy 129 – Tryptonic (FR) (Baryshnikov (AUS))   **53**
[2015 71: p5g⁴ t5.1f² p5g² t5.1f⁶ p5g⁵ 5d³ 5s p5g 5dᵖᵘ Oct 17] modest handicapper: stays   **a62**
6f, races mainly at 5f: acts on polytrack, tapeta, good to firm and heavy going: often in
headgear prior to 2015. *Michael J. Browne, Ireland*

ABINGDON (USA) 2 b.f. (Feb 11) Street Cry (IRE) 130 – Justlookdontouch (IRE)   **74 p**
(Galileo (IRE) 134) [2015 p8d⁴ Nov 30] first foal: dam unraced close relative/half-sister to
very smart 1¼m-1½m performers Islington and Mountain High out of Yorkshire Oaks
winner/St Leger runner-up Hellenic: 9/1, shaped well when fourth in maiden at Kempton
(3¼ lengths behind Diamonds Pour Moi) in November, caught further back than ideal: sure
to progress. *Sir Michael Stoute*

ABI SCARLET (IRE) 6 b.m. Baltic King 120 – Petarga 87 (Petong 126) [2015 85: f6d*   **82**
f6d⁴ f6g⁴ f6g² f6d² f6g³ f6g Dec 18] small mare: fairly useful performer: won seller at
Southwell in January: stays 6f: acts on fibresand: often in blinkers in 2015: often leads.
Scott Dixon

ABLE DASH 5 ch.g. Dutch Art 126 – Evasive Quality (FR) (Highest Honor (FR) 124) [2015   **80**
80: p12m* p11g² 12g³ 13.3m⁶ p12g⁶ 14.1g Sep 30] workmanlike gelding: fairly useful
handicapper: won at Kempton in April: stays 1½m: acts on polytrack: tried in cheekpieces.
Michael Blake

ABLE FRIEND (AUS) 6 ch.g. Shamardal (USA) 129 – Ponte Piccolo (NZ)   **130**
(Volksraad 109) [2015 130: 8m* 7g* 8m* 8m* 8f⁶ 6m* 8g³ 8g³ Dec 13]
    'The way he won today showed everyone around the world and in Hong
Kong that he's the best miler, but he's got to go overseas to prove himself. I do
think we've seen today that we have another Silent Witness here in Hong Kong.
Silent Witness went to Japan and proved himself, but for what Able Friend's done
so far, I think the world will stand up and take note of this horse and look forward
to seeing him in an overseas campaign.' Able Friend's trainer John Moore, speaking
in January after what proved to be the first of the gelding's Group 1 wins of 2015 at
Sha Tin, the Stewards' Cup, was well aware of the need for Hong Kong's champion
miler to take up the sporting challenge of performing outside his own backyard.
Silent Witness, who ten years earlier had been Hong Kong's champion sprinter, beat
Japan's best sprinters on their home turf—having run up a sequence of seventeen
wins at Sha Tin—but he never raced outside the Far East, the prize money on offer
for Europe's top sprints at the time being insufficient to tempt him further afield.
Whilst his essay in *Racehorses of 2005* acknowledged his status as the world's best
sprinter, it concluded with something of a challenge to the gelding's connections.
'A newly-refurbished Ascot would be an ideal stage on which to perform to a wider
audience, and no overseas runner's visit to Britain would be more keenly anticipated
if Silent Witness were to make the trip.'
    As it happened, Silent Witness was a shadow of his former self in 2006, never
ran at Royal Ascot, and was retired early the following year without winning another
race. Able Friend, on the other hand, arrived at Ascot in the form of his life and
was the biggest international star to line up at the latest Royal meeting, a billing
he would have had to share with the previous season's Kentucky Derby winner
California Chrome until that horse was ruled out of the Prince of Wales's Stakes with

a foot abscess. Performances at Royal Ascot, which nowadays regularly attracts top horses from around the world, have enhanced the standing of a number of overseas performers this century—ever since Australian colt Choisir made history with his double in the King's Stand Stakes and Golden Jubilee Stakes in 2003. Choisir was sent off at 25/1 in the King's Stand, but, inevitably, other stars who have come with far bigger reputations have, for various reasons, not been able to perform to their top-class best at the Royal meeting. Unbeaten Australian mare Black Caviar arrived with the biggest reputation of all, starting at 6/1-on for the Diamond Jubilee Stakes in 2012. She kept her unbeaten record, but only after scrambling home by a head, her performance partly accounted for by her being below par on the day, though it was also compounded by a near-calamitous misjudgement by her jockey who eased off prematurely inside the final furlong. Twelve months later, the Kentucky Derby and Dubai World Cup winner Animal Kingdom topped the Royal Ascot bill but was a bitterly disappointing 5/4 favourite for the Queen Anne Stakes which turned out to be the final start of his career. In 2014, the Prix de l'Arc de Triomphe winner Treve started at 13/8-on on her only start in Britain, in the Prince of Wales's Stakes, but finished only third, looking ill at ease on the good to firm ground, an early manifestation of the physical problems which plagued much of her four-year-old season until she returned to form to repeat her Arc win.

Able Friend—dubbed the 'Sha Tin Express'—didn't have the burden of being a hot favourite for the latest Queen Anne Stakes but he was expected to play his part in a mouth-watering clash with another prolific winner, the French gelding Solow, in the Royal meeting's opening event. The one note of caution, a prophetic one as it turned out, came from Able Friend's regular rider Joao Moreira before the horse's departure from Hong Kong earlier in June. 'The thing is that it's his first trip overseas from Hong Kong and that's the only thing that concerns me.' Able Friend arrived in Britain over a week before Ascot and was stabled with Michael Bell at Newmarket. He was reported to have taken his long journey well and when his trainer later joined him in Britain the weekend before the Royal meeting, he declared him to be 'a picture of health.' So far so good, but in a performance reminiscent of Animal Kingdom's in the same race two years earlier, Able Friend failed to mount any sort of challenge after being held up and struggling with over two furlongs still to run. He finished sixth of the eight runners, nearly nine lengths behind the winner Solow. 'Maybe he ran his race before his race,' reflected John Moore afterwards, a reference to the reportedly normally calm Able Friend being 'on the toe a little bit' beforehand, in the words of his trainer, and needing to have sweat wiped from his neck before he entered the stalls.

The 'real' Able Friend clearly hadn't turned up at Ascot, but there was enough evidence from Sha Tin, both before and after his trip to Britain, that Able Friend was fully deserving of a rating that made him, in Timeform's view at least, superior to all the horses in the Queen Anne line-up, Solow included. By the end of 2014, Able Friend had won seven of his twelve starts at Sha Tin and no Hong Kong-trained horse had got the better of him over a mile. His only defeat at the trip had come in the 2014 Champions Mile when beaten by the top-class South African horse Variety Club. Able Friend ended 2014 with an impressive victory in the Hong Kong Mile, though his winning margin of over four lengths was to some extent due to the runner-up Gold-Fun tiring after contesting an overly-strong pace. Rated 130, Able Friend shared top spot in Timeform's Hong Kong ratings with his stable-companion Designs On Rome who had beaten him twice over longer trips earlier in the year, including in the Hong Kong Derby over a mile and a quarter. Named Horse of the Year at the end of the 2013/14 Hong Kong season, Designs On Rome had himself been successful at the International meeting in December when successful in the Hong Kong Cup, again over ten furlongs. Over a mile, though, it was hard to see any horse preventing Able Friend from continuing to dominate at that distance in Hong Kong in 2015.

Able Friend duly proved in a different league to his Sha Tin rivals, at least in the first half of the year, notching four wins with varying degrees of ease in the run up to Royal Ascot. After the Stewards' Cup in January came the seven-furlong Queen's Silver Jubilee Cup in March, and then, back at a mile, the Chairman's

Trophy in April and the Champions Mile in May. The first two of those races, formerly local Group 1 contests only, enjoyed international recognition for the first time, though the only overseas competitor either race attracted was the Irish gelding Gordon Lord Byron who finished ninth in the Queen's Silver Jubilee Cup. Able Friend was chased home by the same rival, Beauty Flame, in both races, looking in danger of being boxed in on the rail over a furlong out on the second occasion before quickening clear when a gap came. In the end, the two and a quarter lengths Able Friend had to spare at the line was the widest margin of victory he achieved all year. Able Friend's style of racing doesn't lend itself to winning by wide margins—he is always held up and produced late to make best use of his potent turn of foot. Beauty Flame (winner of the Britannia Handicap at Royal Ascot in 2013 when named Roca Tumu) finished runner-up to him for the third start running when Able Friend repeated his 2014 win in the Group 2 Chairman's Trophy, Beauty Flame this time in receipt of weight. Able Friend's final win before Ascot—his sixth in a row—was also his most impressive as he won the Champions Mile on the bridle from just five rivals, three of them his own stable companions, with Rewarding Hero and Dan Excel completing a one, two, three for the stable.

When the 2014/15 Hong Kong season ended in July, there were awards for Able Friend's trainer and jockey, both championship winners, besides Able Friend himself who was named Horse of the Year as well as Champion Miler and Most Popular Horse. Sixty-five-year-old John Moore had cause to be thankful that the Hong Kong Jockey Club had reviewed its policy of compulsory retirement for trainers at that age only two years earlier. As for Joao Moreira, he was living proof that jockeys, as well as horses, sometimes have to go overseas to further their careers. A Brazilian, like Britain's latest champion Silvestre de Sousa, Moreira was champion four times in Singapore before finishing runner-up in his first year in Hong Kong in 2013/14 despite missing the first month of the season. In his first full season in Hong Kong, he smashed the previous record for number of wins (114) with a total of 145, fifty clear of his nearest pursuer. By the end of 2015, approaching halfway through the current season, he was already well on schedule to improve his new mark.

For once, however, Moreira, was not in the saddle for Able Friend's return in the new season in October, having already been booked to ride rival Peniaphobia when the decision was taken to bring Able Friend back in the Group 2 Premier Bowl. Conceding weight all round (the race is a handicap) and up against some of Hong Kong's best sprinters over a trip supposedly short of his best, Able Friend was allowed to go off at 9/1 (he had been long odds-on for his four wins earlier in the year) for a race in which he had suffered his last defeat at Sha Tin twelve months earlier, when finishing a close fourth. Now off a mark 10 lb higher, Able Friend faced the 2014 Premier Bowl winner Aerovelocity who had gone on to beat Peniaphobia in the Hong Kong Sprint and was favourite to win his second Premier Bowl in receipt of 9 lb from Able Friend. Ridden this time by Mauritian-born jockey Karis Teetan, Able Friend ran a remarkable race from the widest draw, travelling strongly at the back of the fourteen-runner field as they turned for home. Denied a run towards the outside of the pack early in the straight, Able Friend was switched wide, going out of camera shot when still having ground to make up over a furlong out, and only reappearing with just over a hundred yards to go as he stormed home to lead in the last strides. Able Friend got up to win by half a length from Gold-Fun, who had finished behind Able Friend again when third in the Queen's Silver Jubilee Cup earlier in the year.

A successful defence of his Hong Kong Mile title now looked very much on the cards for Able Friend. But a shock defeat in the trial for that contest, with Moreira back in board, in the Jockey Club Mile in November, proved to be a portent of another below-par effort at the International meeting. Able Friend lacked his usual finishing kick when finishing only third, conceding weight to old rival Beauty Flame. Sent off at odds-on nonetheless for the Hong Kong Mile, Able Friend was beaten a length into third behind the high-class Japanese miler Maurice, initially quickening past the eventual winner over a furlong out only to falter in the closing stages. Beauty Flame was behind him this time, but Giant Treasure, only fourth in the Jockey Club Mile, got the better of Able Friend for second. Able Friend had only

Dr & Mrs Cornel Li Fook Kwan's "Able Friend"

been given the go-ahead to take part at around midday on the day of the race after needing to pass three separate veterinary checks on a foot problem. After finishing sore in a subsequent workout, Able Friend was sent for scans which revealed a tendon injury that will cause him to miss the rest of the Hong Kong season.

		Giant's Causeway		Storm Cat
	Shamardal (USA)	(ch 1997)		Mariah's Storm
	(b 2002)	Helsinki		Machiavellian
Able Friend (AUS)		(b 1993)		Helen Street
(ch.g. 2009)		Volksraad		Green Desert
	Ponte Piccolo (NZ)	(b 1988)		Celtic Assembly
	(b 2001)	Baronia		Half Iced
		(gr 1985)		Barron Fey

Able Friend is a big, strong gelding, which has apparently earned him the nickname 'Elephant' within his stable, and is typical of his sire's stock. Shamardal's best horses in Europe in the latest season included the all-weather performer Tryster and the two-year-olds Lumiere and Emotionless, but Able Friend, a result of Shamardal shuttling to Australia, is the pick of his progeny to date in either hemisphere. Bought for A$550,000 as a yearling by George Moore, John Moore's son, Able Friend won the second of just two starts in Australia late in 2012 before being exported to Hong Kong where he rose rapidly through the ranks. The dam's side of Able Friend's pedigree will be much less familiar in Europe. His New Zealand-bred dam Ponte Piccolo won three races in Australia for Gai Waterhouse at up to around a mile and a quarter, including a listed event over a mile. She was a half-sister to a Group 1 winner in South Africa, Global News, successful in the South African Nursery Plate. Able Friend's grandam Baronia, by the American-trained Japan Cup winner Half Iced, won five times in Australia at up to a mile,

33

though her brother Big Barron stayed much further, finishing second in the Adelaide Cup over two miles to the subsequent Melbourne Cup winner Subzero. The wider family has become very successful in Australia where it took root following the sale of Able Friend's fourth dam Royal News for 6,200 guineas as a three-year-old at the Newmarket December Sales in 1968. Her entry in *Racehorses* of that year read: 'tried to get her head in front all season, and finally managed it at Newmarket in October'. Royal News was a sister to an Irish Two Thousand Guineas third but she ended up running in blinkers before finally breaking her duck in a weak maiden event. Best at up to a mile, Able Friend acts on good to firm going and wears cheekpieces. *J. Moore, Hong Kong*

ABLE JACK 2 b.g. (Feb 21) Iffraaj 127 – Solva 110 (Singspiel (IRE) 133) [2015 7m 7g⁴ **80**
7.1s² 7m Oct 3] 90,000F, 120,000Y: useful-looking gelding: third foal: half-brother to 1¼m winner Solvanna (by Haafhd): dam 1¼m winner: fairly useful maiden: will stay 1m: tried in cheekpieces. *Andrew Balding*

ABLE SPIRIT 3 b.g. Invincible Spirit (IRE) 121 – Sierra 65 (Dr Fong (USA) 128) [2015 – 73: 5g⁵ May 22] strong gelding: modest maiden: stayed 7f: acted on tapeta and good to firm going: tried in blinkers: temperament was under suspicion: dead. *Brian Meehan*

ABONOS (IRE) 3 b.f. Approve (IRE) 112 – Topiary (IRE) (Selkirk (USA) 129) [2015 t7.1f **61**
f5g² t7.1f f5m f5f⁶ Dec 17] 40,000 2-y-o: sixth foal: half-sister to 3 winners, including useful winner up to 7f Gramercy and winner up to 1m Whipper Snapper (both 2-y-o 6f winners, by Whipper): dam French 9f winner: modest maiden: should be suited by 6f: acts on fibresand: tried in eyeshields. *Simon West*

ABOUT TURN 4 ch.c. Pivotal 124 – Doctor's Glory (USA) 91 (Elmaamul (USA) 125) – [2015 –: p6m t6g 7.6d p6g 6.1m Jun 30] fairly useful at best, no form in 2015: sometimes in cheekpieces in 2015: tends to find little: sent to Sweden. *Ronald Harris*

ABOVE N BEYOND 2 ch.c. (Apr 27) Exceed And Excel (AUS) 126 – Hill Welcome 52 **100**
(Most Welcome 131) [2015 p6g t5.1m³ p6g⁴ 6d² 7g³ Dec 29] £85,000Y: brother to useful 5f (including at 2 yrs) winner Exceedance and half-brother to several winners, including useful winner up to 1m Dubai Hills (2-y-o 6f winner, by Dubai Destination): dam maiden (stayed 7f): useful performer: won maiden at Kempton in September: good second in listed race at Doncaster (1¾ lengths behind Dhahmaan) in October: promises to stay 7f: acts on polytrack and good to soft going. *Tom Dascombe*

ABOVE THE REST (IRE) 4 b.g. Excellent Art 125 – Aspasias Tizzy (USA) 85 (Tiznow **98**
(USA) 133) [2015 95: 8g p8g⁵ 7m² 7g* 7m 7.6m³ 7g 8.5s Oct 9] good-topped gelding: useful handicapper: won at Haydock (by ¾ length from Equally Fast) in July: second at Doncaster (nose behind Free Code) in June and third at Chester (1½ lengths behind Sound Advice) in August: stays 8.5f: acts on soft and good to firm going: often races prominently/travels strongly. *Timothy Jarvis*

A BOY NAMED SUE 2 b.g. (Apr 8) Monsieur Bond (IRE) 120 – Elusive Sue (USA) 83 – (Elusive Quality (USA)) [2015 7m 6m 6d Aug 17] no form. *Peter Niven*

ABSEIL (USA) 5 b.g. First Defence (USA) 119 – Intercontinental 122 (Danehill (USA) **108**
126) [2015 105: 8m³ 8.5g³ 9g Sep 26] useful-looking gelding: useful handicapper: third at York (neck behind Alfred Hutchinson) in May and Epsom (length behind Gratzie) in June: stays 8.5f: acts on good to firm and heavy going: tried in hood prior to 2015: suspect attitude. *Sir Michael Stoute*

ABSENT LADY (USA) 3 b.f. Lemon Drop Kid (USA) 131 – Missing Miss (USA) **47**
(Unaccounted For (USA) 124) [2015 t8.6g p8g⁶ p8f⁶ 11.5g f14s³ p14f⁵ p12g⁴ Oct 20] $62,000F, $115,000Y: medium-sized filly: sixth foal: half-sister to 3 winners in USA: dam US 6f (at 2 yrs) to 8.5f (minor stakes) winner: poor maiden: stays 1¾m: acts on polytrack: tried in blinkers. *Ed Vaughan*

ABSOLUTE CHAMPION (USA) 3 b.g. Henrythenavigator (USA) 131 – Alegendin- **90**
myownmind (Cape Cross (IRE) 129) [2015 85: 6d 6.1d³ 6v⁵ p6g* t6g⁶ 5m* 5m³ 5g⁶ 5m² 6.1g Sep 30] fairly useful handicapper: won at Kempton in June and Bath (by 1¾ lengths from Equally Fast) in July: second at Salisbury in September: stays 6f: acts on polytrack and good to firm going. *Jamie Osborne*

ABSOLUTELY SO (IRE) 5 b.g. Acclamation 118 – Week End (Selkirk (USA) 129) **115**
[2015 117, a103: 7d³ 6m* Jun 14] rather leggy gelding: smart performer: won listed race at Salisbury (by 1¼ lengths from Justineo) in June: third in Timeform Jury Stakes (John of Gaunt) at Haydock (length behind Cable Bay) in May: effective at 6f/7f: acts on polytrack, heavy and good to firm going. *Andrew Balding*

ABSOLUTE ZERO (IRE) 2 b.c. (Feb 3) Cape Cross (IRE) 129 – Emsiyah (USA) 53 **78**
(Bernardini (USA) 132) [2015 7g 8.1g² 8.5m³ Oct 1] fair maiden: best effort when second
in maiden at Sandown (3 lengths behind Valitop) in September. *Roger Varian*

ABSOLUTLYFANTASTIC 8 b.g. Alhaarth (IRE) 126 – Persian Walk (FR) (Persian **63**
Bold 123) [2015 p16d⁵ Sep 4] modest handicapper: stays 17f: acts on polytrack, best turf
form on good to firm going: in tongue tie sole start in 2015. *Martin Hill*

ABUELO (FR) 5 bl.g. Califet (FR) 126 – Quolcevyta (FR) (Ungaro (GER) 119) [2015 **–**
p13g⁶ Feb 11] failed to complete all starts over hurdles/fences: 33/1, sixth in maiden at
Lingfield (16¼ lengths behind Fergall) in February. *Gary Moore*

ABU KHADRA (IRE) 2 b.c. (May 10) Oasis Dream 129 – Flashy Wings 115 (Zafonic **– p**
(USA) 130) [2015 6v Nov 7] fifth foal: half-brother to useful 7f winner Flashy Approach
(by New Approach) and winner up to 8.3f Flashy Memories (2-y-o 7f winner, by Dubawi):
dam 2-y-o 5f/6f (including Queen Mary/Lowther Stakes) winner who stayed 1m: 13/2,
better than result when eighth in maiden at Doncaster (17½ lengths behind Times Legacy)
in November, met some trouble: better to come. *Richard Fahey*

ABUSHAMAH (IRE) 4 b.g. Nayef (USA) 129 – Adaala 108 (Sahm (USA) 112) **89**
[2015 91: 7d 7m 8d³ 8m* 8m 8g⁵ Oct 3] rangy gelding: fairly useful handicapper: won at
Redcar in August: left Kevin Prendergast after second start: stays 11f, effective at shorter:
acts on good to firm going: tried in hood prior to 2015. *Ruth Carr*

ABYAAT (IRE) 4 b.g. Halling (USA) 133 – Why Dubai (USA) 93 (Kris S (USA)) [2015 **75**
10.2s² 10.2m⁵ 12.1v⁶ 10.2s³ Nov 4] fair maiden: first past the post in handicap at Chepstow
in May (demoted to second after causing interference): stays 1¼m: acts on soft going: tried
in tongue tie in 2015. *Victor Dartnall*

ACADEMY HOUSE (IRE) 2 b.c. (Mar 4) Kodiac 112 – Joyfullness (USA) (Dixieland **84**
Band (USA)) [2015 5f³ 6m* 6d⁴ 7g³ 8.3d⁴ Oct 5] €72,000Y: closely related to 1m winner
Song In My Heart (by Spartacus) and half-brother to several winners, including useful
winner up to 1m Chesturo (2-y-o 7f winner, by Manduro): dam unraced: fairly useful
performer: won maiden at Leicester in June: third in maiden at Newmarket in May and
third in nursery at Newmarket in August: stays 7f: acts on firm and good to soft going: in
cheekpieces last 2 starts: sold 26,000 gns, sent to Italy. *Michael Bell*

ACADEMY (IRE) 7 br.g. Montjeu (IRE) 137 – Rock The Casbah (FR) (Lavirco (GER) **–**
125) [2015 13.1g Oct 8] maiden: no form in 2015: best effort at 1¼m: in hood sole start in
2015. *N. W. Alexander*

ACAPULCO (USA) 2 ch.f. (Jan 26) Scat Daddy (USA) 120 – Global Finance (USA) **114**
(End Sweep (USA)) [2015 a4.5f³ 5f* 5g² Aug 21]
　'As I've said before, she is only two but to look at her you would swear
she is four. She is a huge, monstrous, imposing filly and her coat is in amazing
condition. She looks like a leopard, all dappled out and with spots everywhere.'
Wesley Ward could not have been more bullish about Acapulco before she won the
Queen Mary Stakes at Royal Ascot and he was arguably just as ebullient before
she took on her elders on a return visit to Britain for the Nunthorpe Stakes at York,
which is where he described her in the above terms. Acapulco was beaten in the
Nunthorpe after starting at 13/8, in receipt of upwards of 24 lb all around, but she
had any number of smart or better sprinters in trouble over a furlong out and was
only pegged back late on by Mecca's Angel who announced herself a top-notch
performer that day, recording a timefigure of 1.16 fast which was the second fastest
by any horse over any distance all season and owed plenty to Acapulco's controlled
trailblazing performance. Acapulco's physique provides hope that she may turn out
to be more than just a two-year-old. Acapulco's 'catch me if you can' racing style
strongly suggests five furlongs is her trip, though it is worth pointing out that her
trainer had success handling those previous supposed 'speedballs' No Nay Never
and Hootenanny, Royal Ascot winners over five furlongs as two-year-olds who both
trained on and showed their form over further.
　　Wesley Ward is always keen to run two-year-old fillies against colts early in the
season because of the weight allowance they receive, and Acapulco took on colts
on her debut in a four and a half furlong maiden at Churchill Downs in early-May.
Sporting blinkers and starting at odds-on in a field of six, Acapulco was quickly
away and made the running until being headed a furlong out, eventually finishing
seven and three quarter lengths third to Cat Tree. 'It was so disappointing when she

Queen Mary Stakes, Royal Ascot—the first of two wins at the meeting for US trainer Wesley Ward as the well-backed Acapulco (second left) lives up to her reputation; Easton Angel (left) is clear best of the rest, ahead of Besharah (centre)

[Acapulco] had her first run on the dirt,' Ward said later, 'but we brought her home, breezed her on the grass, and that was the making of her.' With reports that her timed workouts against her stablemate Bruised Orange at Keeneland the previous month had suggested she was indeed a different proposition on turf, Acapulco was well backed for the twenty-runner Queen Mary Stakes on firm ground at Royal Ascot. She started 5/2 favourite, ahead of Besharah (6/1), Easton Angel (13/2) and Rah Rah (8/1) who had all won maidens and minor events from their two starts. As has become the norm with juveniles from the Ward yard at the meeting, Acapulco's physical maturity, as well as her size, made her stand out in the paddock, looking so much more developed and forward than her rivals, and she proved in a different league in the race as she bounded along close up under Ryan Moore before leading two furlongs out and storming clear to win by a length and a half from Easton Angel, with the third Besharah, fourth Kurland and fifth Kassia finishing at intervals of around two lengths. The field split into two groups, with the pace possibly more even on the stand side where Acapulco raced (Bruised Orange raced on the far side and led overall until fading into twelfth), but there was little advantage and Acapulco would have won whichever side she had been on. She ran to a very high level for a two-year-old sprinting filly at that stage of the season—her form backed up by a timefigure of 0.68 fast (equivalent to a timerating of 117) which was matched only by Minding among the year's juvenile fillies—and her performance has been bettered in the Queen Mary in the last quarter of a century only by the Wesley Ward-trained Jealous Again (in 2009).

In conjunction with his owners, which had included Acapulco's owners the Coolmore partners No Nay Never in 2013 and Hootenanny in 2014, Ward had resisted the temptation to run any of his Royal Ascot-winning two-year-olds in the Nunthorpe until the latest season, though juveniles receive a significant and overly-generous weight concession. Acapulco lined up in the Nunthorpe as the only two-year-old in the field—she had also been entered in the Lowther at the meeting in which she would have had to carry a penalty—and she was clearly the pick at the weights and the only runner still with a Timeform 'p'. Acapulco was just the tenth two-year-old to run in the Nunthorpe since its last juvenile winner Kingsgate Native in 2007 (Radiohead had come closest when third in 2009). The Nunthorpe came nine weeks after the Queen Mary and the spacing out of Acapulco's races was deliberate according to Ward who wanted to allow her 'back end to catch up with the front.' Ward also reported that Acapulco was 'still doing some sensational breezes, just as she was before Ascot.' Acapulco's low weight—8-0, which was 27 lb less than her older male opponents such as the previous year's first and second Sole Power and Stepper Point—meant that Ryan Moore was unable to ride her, his lowest riding weight nowadays being around 8-7. The next choice Johnny Velazquez was unable to make the trip, so Ward turned to Irad Ortiz Jr who only a few days before had featured as a controversial figure in the British media after his mount was awarded the Beverly D Stakes on the disqualification of British-trained Secret Gesture. Acapulco finished two lengths second of nineteen to Mecca's Angel, but she couldn't have done any more after again blazing the trail and looking to have all bar the winner cooked until being shaken up a furlong out and then headed only

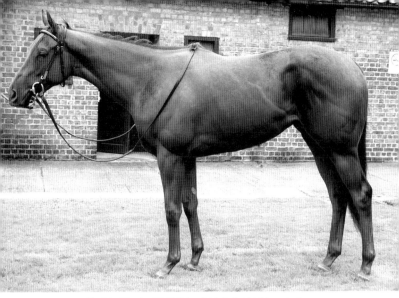

Mrs John Magnier, Mr M. Tabor & Mr D. Smith's "Acapulco"

inside the final fifty yards. She gave the rest a pretty comprehensive beating, Mattmu finishing two lengths away in third, followed by Sole Power, Goldream and Muthmir.

	Scat Daddy (USA) (b or br 2004)	Johannesburg (b 1999)	Hennessy Myth
Acapulco (USA) (ch.f. 2013)		Love Style (ch 1999)	Mr Prospector Likeable Style
	Global Finance (USA) (ch 2000)	End Sweep (b 1991)	Forty Niner Broom Dance
		Friendly Wave (b 1993)	Pentelicus Friendly Gesture

Given Acapulco's physique and stature, it is no surprise that her value rose from the 180,000 dollars paid for her as a yearling to 750,000 dollars at the Ocala Breeze-Up Sale. She is the seventh foal out of Global Finance who raced eight times as a two-year-old in the USA in 2002, winning four races (including minor stakes) between four and a half furlongs and six furlongs. Ironically, given Acapulco's record so far, Global Finance ran solely on dirt. Acapulco is a half-sister to several winners, including six-year-old Spinning Lady (by Hard Spun), also a sprinter, who was sold, believed in foal to To Honor And Serve, for just 25,000 dollars in January. Acapulco's grandam Friendly Wave ran thirty-six times, winning two races on dirt over seven furlongs and a mile, while Acapulco's third dam Friendly Gesture (a granddaughter of the Cheveley Park and One Thousand Guineas winner Night Off) was an unraced half-sister to the very smart miler Montekin. Acapulco's sire Scat Daddy, who raced exclusively on dirt and won Grade 1s over a mile at two (Champagne Stakes) and nine furlongs at three (Florida Derby), is also the sire of No Nay Never and was building a solid reputation. His stud fee was set to almost treble from 35,000 dollars in 2015 to 100,000 dollars in 2016, but he died suddenly at Coolmore's Ashford Stud in Kentucky at the age of eleven in December and will be a big loss to Coolmore's American operation. Acapulco has worn blinkers on all her starts and wore a tongue tie for both her outings in Britain (she might also have worn one on her debut but tongue ties are not included in equipment that has to be declared in North America). *Wesley A. Ward, USA*

37

ACASTER MALBIS (FR) 3 ch.c. Arcano (IRE) 122 – Acatama (USA) (Efisio 120) **88**
[2015 98: 8.3s⁴ 7m³ p7g² p6m* May 19] well-made colt: fairly useful performer: won
maiden at Chelmsford in May: stayed 1m: acted on polytrack, soft and good to firm going:
usually raced close up: dead. *Richard Hannon*

ACCESSION (IRE) 6 b.g. Acclamation 118 – Pivotal's Princess (IRE) 107 (Pivotal 124) **100**
[2015 98: p7g³ 6f⁴ 6g 7m⁴ 7m³ 7g p8g 7g³ 7s Oct 13] strong, sturdy gelding: useful
handicapper: third at Lingfield (1½ lengths behind Valbchek) in April, Newmarket (head
behind Mr Win) in July and Leicester (1¼ lengths behind Kakatosi) in September: stays
1m: acts on polytrack, good to firm and heavy going: sometimes in headgear prior to 2015:
usually races prominently. *Charlie Fellowes*

ACCIPITER 3 ch.f. Showcasing 117 – Mexican Hawk (USA) 98 (Silver Hawk (USA) **97**
123) [2015 92: 6m⁶ 5g 5.7g³ 5m 5g 6g t6f Oct 3] sturdy filly: useful handicapper: third at
Bath (neck behind Rathaath) in July: stays 6f: acts on polytrack and good to firm going:
usually races in rear. *Chris Wall*

ACCLAMATE (IRE) 3 b.c. Acclamation 118 – Rouge Noir (USA) (Saint Ballado **72**
(CAN)) [2015 78: p7f⁵ 6.1d t6g⁴ Jun 22] fair maiden: stays 1m: acts on polytrack: often in
headgear in 2015: wears tongue tie. *Marco Botti*

ACCLIO (IRE) 4 b.f. Acclamation 118 – Hovering (IRE) 100 (In The Wings 128) [2015 **86**
93: p8g² 7.6d 9.9g⁴ 8.3m³ 7d⁴ 7.6v⁶ 7.1g⁵ 6m* 6.1d⁶ 7v Oct 24] lengthy filly: fairly useful
handicapper: won at Yarmouth in September: second at Chelmsford in April and third at
Nottingham in July: stays 8.5f: acts on polytrack, good to firm and heavy going. *Clive Brittain*

ACCRA BEACH (USA) 3 ch.g. Speightstown (USA) 124 – Didina 115 (Nashwan **91 p**
(USA) 135) [2015 84p: 6g² 6m* Jun 1] fairly useful form, lightly raced: blinkered,
won maiden at Windsor in June: raced only at 6f: remains with potential. *Roger Charlton*

ACCRA GIRL 3 b.f. Captain Gerrard (IRE) 113 – Ela d'Argent (IRE) 74 (Ela-Mana-Mou **–**
132) [2015 –: 7g Apr 22] maiden: no form in 2015. *Marjorie Fife*

ACE MASTER 7 ch.g. Ballet Master (USA) 92 – Ace Maite (Komaite (USA)) [2015 90: **83**
f7d⁵ t6g³ f6s* f7d⁵ 7d⁴ 6m³ 6s 5.1m⁶ 6m* 6g Aug 1] plain gelding: fairly useful **a92**
handicapper: won at Southwell (by 7 lengths from Viva Verglas) in February and Thirsk in
June: stays 1m: acts on polytrack, fibresand, good to firm and heavy going: often wears
headgear: front runner/races prominently. *Roy Bowring*

ACE OF MARMALADE (IRE) 3 b.g. Duke of Marmalade (IRE) 132 – Pharapache (USA) **–**
(Lyphard (USA) 132) [2015 –: 9.9m 7.5g May 12] maiden: no form in 2015. *Brian Ellison*

ACES (IRE) 3 b.c. Dark Angel (IRE) 113 – Cute Ass (IRE) 99 (Fath (USA) 116) [2015 104: **94**
8g⁵ 7g 7f Jun 17] lengthy colt: has scope: fairly useful performer: front runner/races prominently to
firm and good to soft going: front runner/races prominently: sold 92,000 gns in October,
joined J. Hammond in France. *Charles Hills*

ACLAIM (IRE) 2 b.c. (Feb 8) Acclamation 118 – Aris (IRE) 94 (Danroad (AUS) 112) **83 p**
[2015 p6g* Dec 9] €130,000Y: first foal: dam, 7f winner, closely related to Irish 1000
Guineas winner Again out of half-sister to Montjeu: 9/4, won maiden at Kempton (by ½
length from Enreaching) in December: will improve. *Martyn Meade*

ACOLYTE (IRE) 3 b.g. Acclamation 118 – Obsara (Observatory (USA) 131) [2015 87: 6m² **93**
6d³ 6g² p6g* t6g* 6m⁵ p6g² t6f⁴ Oct 3] lengthy gelding: useful handicapper: won at Kempton **a104**
and Wolverhampton in July: second at Kempton (head behind Seeking Magic) in September:
stays 6f: acts on polytrack and tapeta: front runner/races prominently: sent to UAE.
Roger Charlton

ACOM 3 ch.g. Compton Place 125 – Pudding Lane (IRE) 64 (College Chapel 122) [2015 **56**
t5.1f⁵ p6f⁵ 6g t6g 5.7g⁵ 5.1g t6m⁴ p6f p7g p8f t7.1f Dec 22] modest maiden: stays 7f: acts
on polytrack and tapeta: tried in blinkers: often races towards rear. *Jeremy Gask*

Betfred Hungerford Stakes, Newbury—Adaay (far side) beats Coulsty (No.4) and
Breton Rock (quartered cap) in a race given a significant boost in prize money for 2015

ACQUAINT (IRE) 4 gr.f. Verglas (IRE) 118 – Azia (IRE) 71 (Desert Story (IRE) 115) – [2015 7.5m⁵ 10d Oct 26] big, good-bodied filly: maiden: no form in 2015: stays 1¼m: best form on good going: tried in headgear prior to 2015: signs of temperament. *Tony Coyle*

ACQUITTAL 3 b.f. Lawman (FR) 121 – Zamid (FR) 47 (Namid 128) [2015 61: p7f⁵ 7d⁶ **74** p6g⁴ p6g² p6g³ Aug 24] neat filly: fair maiden: stays 7f: acts on polytrack: sometimes in hood in 2015: sent to Spain. *James Fanshawe*

ACROSS THE STARS (IRE) 2 b.c. (Mar 28) Sea The Stars (IRE) 140 – Victoria Cross **87 p** (IRE) 101 (Mark of Esteem (IRE) 137) [2015 8.3v² t8.6f² Nov 13] 600,000Y: half-brother to several winners, including very smart winner up to 1½m Bronze Cannon (2-y-o 1m winner) and useful 1m-11f winner Valiant Girl (both by Lemon Drop Kid): dam 7f winner: better effort when second in maiden at Nottingham (3¼ lengths behind Mengli Khan) in October: will stay 1¼m: remains with potential. *Sir Michael Stoute*

ACTIVATION 3 b.g. Stimulation (IRE) 121 – Patteresa Girl 66 (Auction House (USA) **59** 120) [2015 58: t8.6f⁶ f8s⁴ f8g 10d³ p10f⁵ 11s² p12g⁵ p15.8g³ p16g² Dec 16] rather leggy gelding. modest maiden. stays 2m: acts on all-weather, firm and soft going: tried in headgear: often leads. *Hughie Morrison*

ACTONETAKETWO 5 b.m. Act One 124 – Temple Dancer (Magic Ring (IRE) 115) **60 §** [2015 p7g* p8f 8m t9.5f p8g* p8g t8.6f² Dec 21] modest handicapper: won at Kempton in January and November (apprentice): stays 8.5f: acts on polytrack, tapeta and heavy going: tried in headgear: sometimes slowly away, often races in rear: unreliable, and one to treat with caution. *Ron Hodges*

ACT YOUR SHOE SIZE 6 b.m. Librettist (USA) 124 – Howards Heroine (IRE) 70 **64** (Danehill Dancer (IRE) 117) [2015 67: 8s⁵ 9.1s² 10d⁴ 8.3d 10.1m 12.1g Jun 17] modest handicapper: stays 1¼m: acts on tapeta, good to firm and heavy going. *Keith Dalgleish*

ADAAY (IRE) 3 b.c. Kodiac 112 – Lady Lucia (IRE) 51 (Royal Applause 124) [2015 102: **119** 6f³ 6m* 6d* 6f 7d⁶ 6d 6d⁶ Oct 17] sturdy colt: smart performer: won listed race at Newbury (by 1¾ lengths from Jungle Cat) and Sandy Lane Stakes at Haydock (by length from Limato) in May, and Hungerford Stakes at Newbury (by ½ length from Coulsty) in August: respectable 5¼ lengths sixth to Muhaarar in Champions Sprint Stakes at Ascot final start, nearest finish: stays 7f: acts on firm and good to soft going: usually races towards rear. *William Haggas*

Mr Hamdan Al Maktoum's "Adaay"

ADA LOVELACE 5 b.m. Byron 117 – Satin Braid 78 (Diktat 126) [2015 78: p6g⁵ p6f⁶ **80**
t6m⁶ 6m⁵ 5g³ 5.3m* 5g⁶ 5.3g² p5g⁴ 5.3d⁶ p5g⁵ p5f² t5.1m² p5g⁴ t5.1f Dec 21] fairly useful
handicapper: won at Brighton in June: stays 6f: acts on polytrack, tapeta and good to firm
going: tried in hood prior to 2015: often races prominently. *John Gallagher*

ADA MISOBEL (IRE) 2 b.f. (Apr 18) Alfred Nobel (IRE) 110 – Startarette (USA) **55**
(Dixieland Band (USA)) [2015 6m 6m 6m⁶ 7d* 7.2g⁶ 7.2g f6g² f7g⁶ Nov 26] €16,000Y:
seventh foal: half-sister to 3 winners, including useful winner up to 9.5f Star Links (2-y-o
7f winner, by Bernstein) and 2-y-o 6f winner Angels Wings (by Dark Angel): dam lightly-
raced half-sister to dam of Dewhurst Stakes winner Mujahid: modest performer: won seller
at Catterick in August: best effort at 7f: acts on fibresand and good to soft going: usually in
headgear: usually races prominently. *K. R. Burke*

ADAM'S ALE 6 b.g. Ishiguru (USA) 114 – Aqua 51 (Mister Baileys 123) [2015 95: 5g 6d⁴ **98**
6d² 6m 5m² 6m 6m³ 6d³ 6g 5s² 5v² 5d⁶ 7v Nov 7] useful handicapper: runner-up at York
(length behind Union Rose) and Catterick (nose behind Arctic Feeling) in October: stays
6f: acts on good to firm and heavy going: tried in headgear in 2015: front runner/races
prominently. *Mark Walford*

AD DABARAN (GER) 3 b.g. Dubawi (IRE) 129 – Allure (GER) (Konigsstuhl (GER)) **75**
[2015 8d⁵ p8g 9.9v² Aug 24] fair maiden: best effort when seventh in maiden at Kempton
in August. *Charlie Appleby*

ADDICTED TO LUCK 2 b.f. (Feb 3) Myboycharlie (IRE) 118 – Fortunately 95 (Forzando **76**
122) [2015 5m⁴ 5.1s⁴ 6g⁴ 6.1g⁶ f5g⁵ 6v* 6s³ 5d² 5g⁶ 7v Oct 24] fifth foal: half-sister to
2-y-o 6f winner Mitchelton (by High Chaparral) and German 7f winner Firuza (by Oasis
Dream): dam, 2-y-o 5f winner, later 4.5f/5f winner in USA: fair performer: won nursery at
Brighton in August: stays 6f: acts on heavy going: usually races close up. *David Evans*

ADDICTIVE DREAM (IRE) 8 ch.g. Kheleyf (USA) 116 – Nottambula (IRE) **81**
(Thatching 131) [2015 113: 5g 5m 5g 5g² 5m 6m 5g 5.1d 5s Oct 19] robust gelding: fairly
useful handicapper: second in minor event at Hamilton in June: left Fred Watson after sixth
start: stays 6f: acts on polytrack and good to firm going: tried in headgear: tried in tongue
tie in 2015: usually races close up. *Garry Moss*

ADDICTIVE NATURE (IRE) 5 b.g. Acclamation 118 – Movie Queen (Danehill –
(USA) 126) [2015 56: t6g t8.6g 5.7m Jul 8] well-made gelding: maiden: no form in 2015:
tried in headgear. *Dai Burchell*

A DEFINITE DIAMOND 2 ch.f. (Mar 26) Assertive 121 – By Definition (IRE) 54 –
(Definite Article 121) [2015 t7.1g 6.1m 8.1v⁵ 8m p6g 5g Oct 18] fourth foal: half-sister to
1¼m-11.6f winner April Ciel (by Septieme Ciel): dam maiden (stayed 1m): no form: tried
in blinkers/tongue tie. *Milton Bradley*

ADELASIA (IRE) 3 ch.f. Iffraaj 127 – Flaming Song (IRE) (Darshaan 133) [2015 86: **79**
8m⁵ 7g⁶ 8m Jun 6] strong filly: fair handicapper: stays 1m: acts on firm going: sometimes
slowly away, usually races nearer last than first. *Charlie Appleby*

ADELE (GER) 3 b.f. Intikhab (USA) 135 – Adalawa (IRE) (Barathea (IRE) 127) [2015 **88**
72: p10g² 9.3m⁵ 12m² 12.3g⁵ 11.1d* 13.7g* Sep 12] fairly useful handicapper: won at
Hamilton and Musselburgh (by length from Agent Gibbs), both in September: stays 13.5f:
acts on good to soft going: sold 25,000 gns, sent to Saudi Arabia. *Mark Johnston*

ADHAM (IRE) 2 b.c. (Apr 14) Dream Ahead (USA) 133 – Leopard Creek 60 (Weldnaas **90**
(USA) 112) [2015 5.1g⁵ 5m* 5.1m² 5m* 5g 5g Oct 9] €75,000Y: well-made colt: fifth foal:
half-brother to useful 2-y-o 5f winner Ponty Acclaim (by Acclamation) and a winner in
Greece by One Cool Cat: dam, maiden (stayed 6f), sister to smart 5f/6f winner Astonished:
fairly useful performer: won maiden at Lingfield in June and minor event at Bath (by neck
from Sixties Sue) in July: second in minor event at Chepstow in July: raced only at 5f: acts
on good to firm going: front runner/races prominently. *James Tate*

ADHERENCE 2 b.g. (Mar 14) Sir Percy 129 – Straight Laced 68 (Refuse To Bend (IRE) **59**
128) [2015 6g 5v⁶ 6m 8.3d 8d Oct 19] modest maiden: stays 1m: acts on good to soft going.
Tony Coyle

ADIATOR 7 b.m. Needwood Blade 117 – Retaliator 80 (Rudimentary (USA) 118) [2015 **72**
71: 5g² 6g 6m 6s 5m⁶ 5g 6g 5m² 5.1d⁴ 6v⁴ Nov 3] fair handicapper: stays 6f: acts on good
to firm and heavy going: tried in cheekpieces: tried in tongue tie in 2015. *Neville Bycroft*

ADILI (IRE) 6 ch.g. Dubai Destination (USA) 127 – Adirika (IRE) 81 (Miswaki (USA) **62 §**
124) [2015 f16d⁴ p16g⁴ f14d⁵ Jan 27] modest handicapper: stays 2m: acts on polytrack and
fibresand, best turf form on good going or softer (acts on heavy): tried in headgear: lazy
sort, and one to treat with caution. *Michael Appleby*

ADMIRABLE ART (IRE) 5 b.g. Excellent Art 125 – Demi Voix (Halling (USA) 133) **65**
[2015 69: t7.1g* p7f p8m t7.1g³ t8.6g³ 8d⁶ 7g⁵ t7.1g* t8.6g Aug 6] angular gelding: fair
handicapper: won at Wolverhampton in January and June: stays 8.5f: acts on polytrack,
tapeta and heavy going: often wears cheekpieces. *Tony Carroll*

ADMIRAL MILLER 5 b.g. Multiplex 114 – Millers Action (Fearless Action (USA) 116) **70**
[2015 10s⁶ 11.8s p12g⁵ 16s t16.5f Nov 16] fair maiden: half-sister to 3 winners: stays 2m: acts on polytrack, soft
going. *Eve Johnson Houghton*

ADMIRALS CHOICE 2 b.g. (Mar 12) Mount Nelson 125 – Admirable Spirit 92 **–**
(Invincible Spirit (IRE) 121) [2015 p8g p7f Dec 17] no form. *Robert Eddery*

ADMIRAL'S GOLD (IRE) 3 ch.c. Mount Nelson 125 – Lolita's Gold (USA) 66 (Royal **52**
Academy (USA) 130) [2015 –: p8g p8f 11.5g³ Jul 15] leggy colt: modest maiden: should
prove suited by middle distances: acts on polytrack: usually races towards rear: sent to
Italy. *John Best*

ADMIRAL'S SUNSET 2 b.f. (Apr 18) Mount Nelson 125 – Early Evening 84 (Daylami **56 p**
(IRE) 138) [2015 8m⁶ Sep 11] 8,500Y: sixth foal: half-sister to 3 winners, including 1m
winner Early Applause (by Royal Applause): dam 9f/1¼m winner: 9/2, green when sixth
in maiden at Salisbury (6¼ lengths behind In The Red) in September, unable to sustain
effort: will improve. *Hughie Morrison*

ADVANCE (FR) 4 b.g. Aqlaam 125 – Rabeera 62 (Beat Hollow 126) [2015 69: 7g⁵ 8g⁶ **83**
7d* 6.9mᵖᵘ 7m⁴ 8g* 8g³ 9.1g* 8m* 8.3m³ 8d Sep 17] fairly useful handicapper: won at
Newcastle in May, Redcar in June, Ayr in July and again at Newcastle (by length from
Taqneen) in August: stayed 9f: acted on good to firm and good to soft going: often raced
towards rear: dead. *Ruth Carr*

ADVENTUREMAN 3 b.g. Kyllachy 129 – Constitute (USA) 85 (Gone West (USA)) **77**
[2015 72: p8g⁶ p8g³ p8g⁶ 8m 8g³ 8m³ 8g 8.5m 7s Oct 16] fair maiden: left Edward Lynam
after fifth start: stays 1m: acts on polytrack and good to firm going: tried in headgear in
2015: often races prominently. *Ruth Carr*

ADVENTURE SEEKER (IRE) 4 gr.g. Dalakhani (IRE) 133 – Adventure (USA) **97**
(Unbridled's Song (USA) 125) [2015 110: 12d 12f 12m t12.2m⁴ Sep 5] neat gelding: useful
handicapper: not at best in 2015: stays 1¾m: acts on polytrack and good to firm going:
tried in tongue tie in 2015. *Ed Vaughan*

ADVENTURE ZONE (IRE) 2 b.c. (Feb 16) Elnadim (USA) 128 – Eliza Doolittle 67 **65**
(Royal Applause 124) [2015 6mᵖᵘ p7f⁶ p6g⁵ f8f³ Dec 17] angular colt: fair maiden: best
effort at 7f. *Richard Hannon*

ADVENTUROUS (IRE) 2 b.c. (Feb 15) Invincible Spirit (IRE) 121 – Rosia (IRE) (Mr **103**
Prospector (USA)) [2015 6m⁵ 6m* 6m⁴ 7d 6g³ 7g² 7g⁵ Oct 10] lengthy, useful-looking
colt: half-brother to several winners, including useful 1m-1½m winner Crimson And Gold
(by Singspiel) and 2m winner Raslan (by Lomitas): dam unraced daughter of Prix Saint-
Alary winner Rosefinch: useful performer: won maiden at Newbury in July: best efforts
when third in Somerville Tattersall Stakes at Newmarket (½ length behind Sanus Per
Aquam) in September and fifth in Dewhurst Stakes at same course (made running when 7
lengths fifth to Air Force Blue) in October: stays 7f: acts on good to firm going: races
prominently. *Mark Johnston*

AD VITAM (IRE) 7 ch.g. Ad Valorem (USA) 125 – Love Sonnet (Singspiel (IRE) 133) **71**
[2015 69: 7g⁵ 8d 6g³ 7m⁴ 6m² 6g³ 6mᵖ 6g³ 7s 6d t6g* t8.6g⁶ Dec 5] angular gelding:
fair handicapper: won at Wolverhampton in November: has won over 9.5f, races at shorter
nowadays: acts on polytrack, tapeta, good to firm and good to soft going: usually wears
headgear: usually wears tongue tie: often races towards rear. *Suzanne France*

AE FANANAH (IRE) 2 b.f. (Mar 24) Poet's Voice 126 – Miss Marvellous (USA) 78 **58**
(Diesis 133) [2015 p6g⁵ 7m 6s 5d³ 5d² 6g Sep 23] 9,500Y, £26,000 2-y-o: fifth foal: dam,
1¼m winner, closely related to dam of Breeders' Cup Juvenile winner Action This Day:
modest maiden: best form at 5f: acts on good to soft going: front runner/races prominently,
often races freely, tends to find little. *Ismail Mohammed*

AEOLUS 4 b.g. Araafa (IRE) 128 – Bright Moll 88 (Mind Games 121) [2015 112: 7s⁴ 6m* **117**
7g⁶ 6m⁶ 6d 6s Oct 31] small gelding: smart performer: better than ever when winning
Chipchase Stakes at Newcastle (by ½ length from Mattmu) in June: respectable efforts at
best after: best form at 6f: acts on good to firm and heavy going. *Ed Walker*

AETNA 5 b.m. Indesatchel (IRE) 120 – On The Brink 88 (Mind Games 121) [2015 115: 6d⁵ **105**
6g 6g 6m 6s⁵ 6d Oct 23] smart performer in 2014: struggled to make an impact in 2015,
though still showed useful form: stays 7f: goes very well on soft/heavy going: tried in
cheekpieces in 2015. *Michael Easterby*

41

AEVALON 3 b.f. Avonbridge 123 – Blaina 76 (Compton Place 125) [2015 63: p7f 6m –
Apr 6] maiden: no form in 2015: stays 6f: acts on polytrack, soft and good to firm going: in
hood first start in 2015. *Eve Johnson Houghton*

AFFAIRE SOLITAIRE (IRE) 5 b.h. Danehill Dancer (IRE) 117 – Arlesienne (IRE) **116**
108 (Alzao (USA) 117) [2015 113: p9.9g p9.9g² 9.9d* 9.9s² Apr 6] closely related to
French 13f winner Agent de Change (by Westerner) and half-brother to several winners,
including smart French 9.5f-15f winner Aizavoski (by Monsun): dam, French 11.5f-12.5f
winner, sister to smart US Grade 1 9f/9.5f winner Angara: smart performer: won Prix
Exbury at Saint-Cloud (by neck from Meadow Creek) in March: good second in Prix
d'Harcourt at Longchamp (¾ length behind Al Kazeem) in April: missed rest of year: stays
1¼m: acts on viscoride and soft going. *P. Khozian, France*

AFFECTIONATE LADY (IRE) 4 b.f. Dandy Man (IRE) 123 – Agouti (Pennekamp **60**
(USA) 130) [2015 63: 7m 5m⁵ 6g³ 6s* 7.2d⁴ 6g⁵ 6g Sep 21] modest handicapper: won at
Hamilton in July: stays 7f: acts on soft and good to firm going: often wears headgear:
sometimes slowly away, often races towards rear. *Keith Reveley*

AFFILEO 3 b.f. Teofilo (IRE) 126 – Asinara (GER) (Big Shuffle (USA) 122) [2015 t7.1f* **92**
t9.5m* 11.5s⁵ 8.5f 10.5f 11f² Nov 4] 31,000Y: third foal: half-sister to 2-y-o 7f winner
Complexity (by Multiplex): dam, German 2-y-o 7.5f winner, half-sister to useful performer
up to 1¼m Ameer: fairly useful performer: won maiden at Wolverhampton in February and
handicap on same course in April: second in allowance race at Aqueduct in November: left
Daniel Kubler after third start: stays 11f: acts on tapeta and firm going: tried in blinkers.
H. Graham Motion, USA

AFJAAN (IRE) 3 b.g. Henrythenavigator (USA) 131 – Elusive Galaxy (IRE) 98 (Elusive **107 p**
City (USA) 117) [2015 74p: 7.5m* p8g² t7.1f* Nov 16] useful performer: won maiden at
Beverley (by ½ length from Pensax Boy) in October and handicap at Wolverhampton (by
4 lengths from Shootingsta) in November: stays 1m: will go on improving. *William Haggas*

AFKAR (IRE) 7 b.g. Invincible Spirit (IRE) 121 – Indienne (IRE) 69 (Indian Ridge 123) **68**
[2015 78: p8g² 8g p6g³ 7g p7g* f7g⁴ t8.6f⁴ Dec 22] strong gelding: fair handicapper: won
at Kempton in December: left Clive Brittain after fourth start: stays 8.5f: acts on all-weather,
soft and good to firm going: sometimes wears headgear. *Ivan Furtado*

AFNAAN 2 ch.c. (Mar 29) Raven's Pass (USA) 133 – Almansoora (USA) 78 (Bahri (USA) **– p**
125) [2015 p8m Nov 17] seventh foal: half-brother to winner up to 1½m Dahaam (2-y-o
1m winner, by Red Ransom) and useful 7f-9.5f winner Ostaad (by Marju): dam, 2-y-o 7f
winner, half-sister to dam of Breeders' Cup Filly & Mare Turf winner Lahudood: 3/1, badly
needed experience when eighth in maiden at Lingfield (9 lengths behind Kummiya) in
November: capable of better. *Saeed bin Suroor*

AFONSO DE SOUSA (USA) 5 br.g. Henrythenavigator (USA) 131 – Mien (USA) **108**
(Nureyev (USA) 131) [2015 109: p10f⁶ p8f³ p10g p10g² p12g t9.5m⁴ Dec 26] rather
unfurnished gelding: useful performer: second in listed race at Kempton (2½ lengths
behind Romsdal) in March: stays 10.5f: acts on polytrack and good to firm going: often in
headgear in 2015. *David O'Meara*

AFRICAN SHOWGIRL 2 ch.f. (Mar 22) Showcasing 117 – Georgie The Fourth (IRE) **65**
79 (Cadeaux Genereux 131) [2015 6m 6g³ 6m Jun 25] £25,000Y: second foal: dam maiden
(stayed 1½m): fair maiden: best effort when third in maiden at Goodwood (3 lengths
behind Lido Lady) in June. *George Baker*

AFRICAN STORY 8 ch.g. Pivotal 124 – Blixen (USA) 90 (Gone West (USA)) [2015 **122**
128: a9.4f a9.9g* a9.9f⁶ Mar 28] high-class performer at best: successful in Dubai World
Cup at Meydan in 2014: didn't need to reproduce that form when winning Maktoum
Challenge Round 3 there in March, beating Prince Bishop a neck, despite going in snatches:
below-form sixth to same rival in Dubai World Cup next time: stayed 1¼m: acted on dirt/
synthetics and heavy going: usually raced prominently: retired. *Saeed bin Suroor*

AFTER THE SUNSET 4 ch.c. Pivotal 124 – Abandon (USA) 94 (Rahy (USA) 115) **75**
[2015 t7.1g³ t7.1g* 7d 7s⁶ p8g⁴ May 27] fair performer: won maiden at Wolverhampton in
February: stays 1m: acts on polytrack and tapeta: usually races prominently. *Clive Cox*

AGADOO 3 b.f. Multiplex 114 – Agooda (Rainbow Quest (USA) 134) [2015 63: 8.3g **60**
8.3m 7.2d 7.1s⁴ 10s* 7s 10d Oct 26] modest performer: won seller at Leicester in October:
stays 1¼m: acts on good going: often wears headgear: usually leads. *Shaun Harris*

AGAINST THE ODDS 2 b.c. (Mar 20) Champs Elysees 124 – Generous Diana 90 (Generous **73 p**
(IRE) 139) [2015 p8g⁵ Dec 9] 75,000Y: closely related to very smart 9f-13.5f winner (stays
2m) Dandino (by Dansili): dam 9f-10.3f winner: 33/1, shaped well when fifth in maiden at
Kempton (5¾ lengths behind Towerlands Park) in December: will stay 1¼m: will improve.
Paul Cole

AGAPANTHUS (GER) 10 b.g. Tiger Hill (IRE) 127 – Astilbe (GER) (Monsun (GER) **57**
124) [2015 14g² Jul 12] sturdy gelding: modest handicapper: stays 1¼m: acts on good to
firm and good to soft going: tried in headgear. *Neil Mulholland*

AGENT GIBBS 3 ch.g. Bertolini (USA) 125 – Armada Grove 75 (Fleetwood (IRE) 107) **93**
[2015 8.3m 8g⁶ 8.3m⁶ 10.2g* 9.9g* p12f* 13.7g² 11.8s* 14s⁴ Oct 9] workmanlike gelding:
brother to useful 2-y-o 1m winner Henderson Park (later successful in Hong Kong) and
1½m-16.5f winner Ninepointsixthree and half-brother to 9.5f-1½m winner Covert Decree
(by Proclamation): dam 2-y-o 7f winner: fairly useful handicapper: won at Nottingham,
Brighton and Lingfield in August, and Leicester (by 3¼ lengths from More Mischief) in
October: stays 1¾m: acts on polytrack and soft going: usually races close up, often travels
strongly. *Ali Stronge*

AGENT MURPHY 4 b.c. Cape Cross (IRE) 129 – Raskutani (Dansili 127) [2015 106p: **119**
12m* 11.9g³ 13.3d* 14d² 16d Oct 17] good-quartered colt: smart performer: won listed
race at Ascot (by 3 lengths from Red Galileo) in May and Geoffrey Freer Stakes at
Newbury (by 5 lengths from Windshear) in August: third in Grand Prix de Chantilly at
Chantilly (2½ lengths behind Manatee) in May and second in Irish St Leger at the Curragh
(respectable effort when 11 lengths behind Order of St George) in September: should stay
2m: acts on firm and soft going. *Brian Meehan*

AGE OF ELEGANCE (IRE) 3 b.f. Makfi 130 – Elegant Pride (Beat Hollow 126) [2015 **74**
66p: 8.3s p10g* p10g² 12g⁴ 10.2d p12g p10g³ p10g² t9.5f p12g Dec 2] rather leggy filly: **a80**
fairly useful performer: won maiden at Lingfield in May: stays 1¼m: acts on polytrack:
front runner/races prominently. *Olly Stevens*

AGE OF EMPIRE 2 b.c. (Feb 17) Royal Applause 124 – Age of Chivalry (IRE) 110 **101**
(Invincible Spirit (IRE) 121) [2015 5f 6g* 6f⁶ 6g* Jun 29] fourth foal: half-brother to 6f
(including at 2 yrs) winner Oxlip (by Three Valleys): dam, winner up to 6f (2-y-o 5f
winner), half-sister to smart winner up to 9f Sebastian Flyte: useful performer: won maiden
at York in May and minor event at Pontefract in June: stays 6f: sent to Hong Kong.
Richard Hannon

AGE OF INNOCENCE 4 b.g. Invincible Spirit (IRE) 121 – Elusive Legend (USA) **76**
(Elusive Quality (USA)) [2015 t6m p6d p5g⁶ 6g p5g f6d⁴ p8g 5s f7g f6g² f6g* f5g
Dec 29] ex-French gelding: fair handicapper: won at Southwell in December: stays 7f: acts
on polytrack and fibresand: usually in headgear in 2015. *Derek Shaw*

AGERZAM 5 b.g. Holy Roman Emperor (IRE) 125 – Epiphany 81 (Zafonic (USA) 130) **83**
[2015 100: 6m 6m p6g t5.1g² p5g⁴ t6g² 5g* 6g 6g⁶ Aug 7] attractive gelding: fairly useful
handicapper: won at Bath in July: stays 6f: acts on polytrack and tapeta: sometimes wears
headgear. *Ronald Harris*

AGHAANY 2 gr.f. (Apr 26) Dubawi (IRE) 129 – Hathrah (IRE) 113 (Linamix (FR) 127) **57 p**
[2015 7d⁶ Oct 31] half-sister to several winners, including smart 7f-1¼m winner Hadaatha
(by Sea The Stars) and useful 1¼m-16.4f winner Itlaaq (by Alhaarth): dam winner up to
1m (2-y-o 7f winner) and third in 1000 Guineas: 13/2, sixth in maiden at Newmarket
(10¾ lengths behind Aljazzi) in October: should do better in time. *Roger Varian*

*Betfred Geoffrey Freer Stakes, Newbury—a runaway success for up-and-coming stayer
Agent Murphy; Windshear and a below-par Red Cadeaux fill the places in a strung-out field*

AGRAPART (FR) 4 b.g. Martaline 118 – Afragha (IRE) 88 (Darshaan 133) [2015 87: 11.9s Apr 5] has had all 4 races in France: fairly useful form in 2014: well held in handicap at Saint-Cloud on reappearance: stays 1¾m: acts on soft going: slowly away first 2 outings: fairly useful winner over hurdles. *Nick Williams* — —

A GREATER FORCE (FR) 4 gr.c. Montjeu (IRE) 137 – Dibenoise (FR) (Kendor (FR) 122) [2015 86p: 13.3s Aug 14] fairly useful at best, no form in 2015: should stay 1¾m: tried in blinkers prior to 2015: sent to Italy. *Clive Cox* — —

AGREEMENT (IRE) 5 b.g. Galileo (IRE) 134 – Cozzene's Angel (USA) (Cozzene (USA)) [2015 t16.5f⁵ 12g 14.1g 16.2m⁶ 17.2f⁵ 16.2s⁴ 17.2m⁶ 16d* 18d⁴ Aug 20] lengthy gelding: fair handicapper: won at Ffos Las in August: stays 2½m: acts on any turf going: often wears headgear: often races prominently. *Nikki Evans* — **67**

AGUEROOO (IRE) 2 b.g. (Feb 13) Monsieur Bond (IRE) 120 – Vision of Peace (IRE) (Invincible Spirit (IRE) 121) [2015 6d⁴ 6m⁵ 7.6g⁶ f7m⁵ t5.1f² p5m* p6g* Dec 30] 70,000Y: first foal: dam unraced half-sister to useful sprinter Victory Laurel: fairly useful performer: won nurseries at Chelmsford and Lingfield in December: stays 6f: acts on polytrack, tapeta, good to firm and good to soft going: sometimes in headgear. *Richard Hannon* — **84**

AHDAF 2 ch.c. (Apr 23) Pastoral Pursuits 127 – Bayja (IRE) (Giant's Causeway (USA) 132) [2015 5s⁴ 5.3s³ 5g³ 5.9m* Sep 9] £20,000Y, £52,000 2-y-o: second foal: closely related to useful 5f/6f winner (including at 2 yrs) New Providence (by Bahamian Bounty): dam once-raced daughter of useful 1¼m performer Bayberry: fairly useful performer: won nursery at Carlisle (by 5 lengths from Cuppatee) in September: best effort at 6f: likely to progress further. *Mark Johnston* — **87 p**

AHLAN EMARATI (IRE) 3 b.c. Holy Roman Emperor (IRE) 125 – Indaba (IRE) 98 (Indian Ridge 123) [2015 108: 6m⁶ 6f Jun 19] neat colt: fairly useful performer: stays 6f: acts on good to firm going: has joined S. Seemar in UAE. *Peter Chapple-Hyam* — **93**

AHOY THERE (IRE) 4 ch.g. Captain Rio 122 – Festivite (IRE) (Fasliyev (USA) 120) [2015 73: 8.9g 8m* 8g 8d t8.6f Oct 17] fair handicapper: won at Ripon in July: stays 8.5f: acts on good to firm and heavy going. *Tom Tate* — **70**

AHRAAM (IRE) 2 b.g. (Apr 24) Roderic O'Connor (IRE) 119 – Simla Sunset (IRE) 102 (One Cool Cat (USA) 123) [2015 t7.1g 7g p6f Nov 5] €18,000F, 23,000Y: rather unfurnished gelding: first foal: dam, 7f/1m winner, half-sister to useful winner up to 1½m Swift Alhaarth: modest form in maidens: gelded: should do better. *Peter Chapple-Hyam* — **55 p**

AHTOUG 7 b.h. Byron 117 – Cherokee Rose (IRE) 122 (Dancing Brave (USA) 140) [2015 118: 5g⁶ 5g* 5g² 5g Mar 28] well-made horse: very smart performer: won handicap at Meydan (by head from Lancelot du Lac) in January: second in Meydan Sprint (short head behind Sir Maximilian) in March: below form when eighth to Sole Power in Al Quoz Sprint there final outing: best form at 5f: acts on polytrack, good to firm and good to soft going: in cheekpieces last 2 starts: usually travels strongly. *Charlie Appleby* — **120**

AHZEEMAH (IRE) 6 b.g. Dubawi (IRE) 129 – Swiss Roll (IRE) 96 (Entrepreneur 123) [2015 119: 14g² 14g 15.9g³ Mar 28] good-topped gelding: very smart performer: second in handicap at Meydan (¾ length behind Famous Kid) in February and third in Dubai Gold Cup at Meydan (3¼ lengths behind Brown Panther) in March: stays 16.5f: acts on polytrack, firm and good to soft going: wears cheekpieces: usually races prominently. *Saeed bin Suroor* — **120**

AILSA ON MY MIND (IRE) 2 br.f. (Mar 30) Dark Angel (IRE) 113 – Embassy Pearl (IRE) 80 (Invincible Spirit (IRE) 121) [2015 6g³ Jun 8] 20,000Y: second foal: half-sister to 7f winner Mr Christopher (by Bahamian Bounty): dam 7f winner: 7/2, some encouragement when third in maiden at Thirsk (length behind Quick N Quirky) in June, clear of rest: entitled to progress. *Hugo Palmer* — **72 p**

AIM HIGH 2 gr.f. (Apr 11) Intense Focus (USA) 117 – Way To The Stars 75 (Dansili 127) [2015 6m t7.1g Jul 7] third foal: dam maiden half-sister to smart South African winner up to 11f winner Dancer's Daughter: no form. *Jonathan Portman* — —

AIM TO PLEASE (FR) 2 b.f. (Jan 25) Excellent Art 125 – Midnight Flash (IRE) (Anabaa Blue 122) [2015 p6.5g³ 7g* 7d* 7g⁶ Sep 6] first foal: dam, unraced, out of sister to smart German performer up to 1¾m Moonlady, herself dam of very smart Japanese performer up to 2m Eishin Flash: useful form: won maiden at Vichy in July and listed race at Deauville (by 3½ lengths from Mangusto) in August: beaten only 1½ lengths when last of 6 to Attendu in Prix La Rochette at Longchamp final outing: stays 7f. *Francois Doumen, France* — **109**

AINIPPE (IRE) 3 b.f. Captain Rio 122 – Imitation (Darshaan 133) [2015 100: 5s⁵ 5.8d² 6g* 7g* 8g³ Sep 12] smart performer: won Ballyogan Stakes at the Curragh (by ½ length from Newsletter) in June and Brownstown Stakes at Fairyhouse (by 1½ lengths from — **111**

Majestic Queen) in July: creditable third in Matron Stakes at Leopardstown (4½ lengths behind Legatissimo) in September: stays 1m: acts on good to firm and good to soft going. *G. M. Lyons, Ireland*

AINSLIE (IRE) 3 gr.g. Mastercraftsman (IRE) 129 – Capriole (Noverre (USA) 125) **82**
[2015 65: t7.1g 8.3m 8.3d* t9.5g² 9.9v³ 9.2m* Sep 20] fairly useful handicapper: won at Leicester in July and Hamilton in September: stays 9.5f: acts on tapeta, good to firm and good to soft going: often in cheekpieces in 2015: usually races nearer last than first. *David Simcock*

AIR FORCE BLUE (USA) 2 b.c. (May 2) War Front (USA) 119 – Chatham (USA) **128 p**
(Maria's Mon (USA) 121) [2015 6g* 6f² 6g* 7d* 7g* Oct 10]
'In theory, there is no difference between theory and practice, but in practice there is.' One of the many witticisms attributed to Hall of Fame baseball player Yogi Berra, who died in September aged ninety, should be a byword for ante-post punters tempted to take short odds about any winter favourite for the classics. The imposing Air Force Blue, lauded by his trainer as 'something we haven't had before … the best two-year-old we've ever had', is one of the shortest-priced ante-post favourites in years for the Two Thousand Guineas, available at only marginally longer odds than the mighty Frankel when he was odds-on over the winter for the 2011 Guineas. Aidan O'Brien's pronouncements about his best horses aren't always backed up by the form-book (the claim that Gleneagles was the 'best miler we've had' was wide of the mark) but his words are spot-on with regard to Air Force Blue. None of O'Brien's previous champion two-year-olds has been rated so highly as Air Force Blue who is the best champion of his age group in Europe for nearly twenty years, with the exception of Frankel (133p). Air Force Blue's rating is 1 lb ahead of that earned by Johannesburg in 2001 when O'Brien-trained horses won nine of the ten European Group 1s open to two-year-old colts, in a season when the other Group 1-winning Ballydoyle juveniles included Rock of Gibraltar, Hawk Wing and High Chaparral.

There has never been any guarantee that the best two-year-old will go on to be the best three-year-old, with evidence that Frankel was something of a rarity—on that account alone—not hard to find. Nayef, Bago, Oasis Dream, Shamardal, New Approach and Dawn Approach are other champion two-year-olds this century who progressed well and held their own in top company as three-year-olds, but it wasn't so long ago when cynics could safely observe that heading the two-year-old rankings was almost the kiss of death to a colt's prospects in the top races at three. Ballydoyle itself provided some notable examples in an eight-year period from 1973 to 1980 when four champion juveniles handled by Vincent O'Brien, Apalachee, Try My Best, Monteverdi and Storm Bird, all failed to live up to expectations as three-year-olds, Apalachee managing only third when starting the shortest-priced favourite for the Two Thousand Guineas in forty years (9/4-on) and Try My Best trailing in last of nineteen when evens for the race (Monteverdi and Storm Bird didn't even make it to Newmarket). The simple affirmation of the obvious—that there is no such thing as a certainty in racing—should caution against assuming that Air Force Blue merely has to turn up fit and well at Newmarket on the last Saturday in April to give his trainer an outright record eighth Two Thousand Guineas winner. However, barring something untoward happening, it is hard to see anything to beat him. On any rational interpretation of his striking victory in the Dubai Dewhurst Stakes, the most valuable and prestigious race for two-year-old colts in Europe, Air Force Blue is a top-class miler in the making. His physique very much suggests that he will train on, and he should progress again as a three-year-old. Even a reproduction of his bare Dewhurst form would give him a very good chance in an average running of the Two Thousand Guineas.

Air Force Blue was his trainer's fourth Dewhurst winner, following Rock of Gibraltar (who led home a one, two, three for the stable), Beethoven (who had two of his Ballydoyle stablemates also in the frame) and War Command. O'Brien's distinguished predecessor at Ballydoyle won the Dewhurst seven times (one short of the record for the race) and his winners included those notables Nijinsky, The Minstrel and El Gran Senor, as well as the aforementioned Try My Best, Monteverdi and

Keeneland Phoenix Stakes, the Curragh—a remarkable fourteenth success in the race for Aidan O'Brien as Air Force Blue (No.1) gains his revenge on his Coventry conqueror Buratino, the pair split by another Royal Ascot winner Washington DC (left)

Storm Bird. The last Dewhurst winner to go on to win a classic was the 2012 winner Dawn Approach, the only horse to carry the Godolphin colours to Dewhurst success. The latest Dewhurst was billed as a showdown between Ballydoyle and Godolphin, with Air Force Blue (6/4-on) and the Charlie Appleby-trained Champagne Stakes winner Emotionless (7/4) dominating the betting in the seven-runner field. The clash dominated the build-up to the new two-day Dubai Future Champions' Festival, staged at Newmarket over Cesarewitch weekend in October which featured the Dubai Fillies' Mile as the centre-piece of Friday's card and the Dubai Dewhurst Stakes as the main attraction on the Saturday, both those races being more than doubled in value to £500,000 in total prize money to make them the richest Group 1 races for two-year-olds in Europe. The new programme hopefully brings to an end the controversial tinkering with the autumn two-year-old programme, originally prompted in 2011 by a perceived need to create a Future Champions' Day at Newmarket to support the inaugural British Champions' Day at Ascot. The Fillies' Mile had been added to the Future Champions' Day programme only in 2014 (when the card had a short-lived move to the same weekend as British Champions' Day). The Middle Park, the third Group 1 on Future Champions' Day in 2014, sensibly reverted in the latest season to its traditional place in the calendar alongside the Cheveley Park Stakes for fillies, at the earlier Newmarket Cambridgeshire meeting. The Fillies' Mile (along with the Cornwallis for juvenile sprinters, another long-standing pattern race that used to be on Ascot's autumn schedule before being moved to Newmarket) found itself in no less than its fourth different place in the calendar in the space of six years, a far from ideal situation for an event that has been one of the two most important races in Britain (and is now arguably *the* most important) for two-year-old fillies.

The Dubai Fillies' Mile also featured an impressive winner saddled by Ballydoyle, with Minding following up her success in the Moyglare Stud Stakes on Irish Champions' Weekend to establish herself as winter favourite for the One Thousand Guineas. Ryan Moore, who had won both Newmarket classics in May on horses owned by the Coolmore partners, had missed the season's midsummer highlights after damaging vertebrae in his neck in a starting stalls accident at Newmarket's July meeting. He returned to action in timely fashion for the important autumn programme and rode both Minding and Air Force Blue at Newmarket. The normally phlegmatic Moore returned to the unsaddling enclosure much taken with Minding, reportedly telling connections that he had 'never ridden anything like her'. Aidan O'Brien is said to have told him 'Wait until you ride Air Force Blue tomorrow, Minding would probably lead him halfway in his work.' Moore had ridden Air Force Blue twice before, firstly when he made a winning debut in the traditionally strong maiden that opens Irish One Thousand Guineas day at the Curragh, and then when he was beaten two lengths by the much more experienced Buratino in the Coventry Stakes at Royal Ascot on his second start (his trainer later described Air Force Blue, a May foal, as 'only a baby early on, totally unfurnished, but still head and shoulders above everything else at home'). Joseph O'Brien took over in Moore's absence on Air Force Blue's next two starts at the Curragh, in the Keeneland Phoenix Stakes in August and the Goffs Vincent O'Brien National Stakes on Irish Champions' Weekend in September. Both races are Group 1s, and the Phoenix was an above-average renewal for which Buratino started 11/10 favourite to confirm his Coventry superiority over Air Force Blue. In the eight weeks since Royal Ascot, however, Air Force Blue had clearly thrived and he marked himself as one of the best juveniles around, being produced to lead a furlong out and seeing the race out well to win by two lengths and half a length from his stablemate Washington DC (successful at Royal Ascot in the Windsor Castle) and Buratino. The performance put Air Force Blue at the head of the early ante-post betting (at around 8/1) on the Two Thousand Guineas.

Having given his trainer an incredible fourteenth success in the Phoenix, Air Force Blue went on to provide his tenth in the National Stakes (a race won a record fifteen times by Vincent O'Brien). Air Force Blue had been displaced at the head of the Two Thousand Guineas betting by Emotionless, after that horse ran out an impressive winner of the previous day's Champagne Stakes at Doncaster, but an authoritative three-length victory over Dawn Approach's brother Herald The Dawn in the National Stakes saw Air Force Blue on top again (generally priced at around 4/1). Air Force Blue travelled strongly all the way in the five-runner field (the third year in a row the race had attracted just five) and quickened impressively as soon as he was given the office a furlong out. The sole British challenger Birchwood finished a creditable third, a further length and three quarters behind Herald The Dawn, but no-one could call it a vintage National Stakes field and it was left to stronger opponents in the Dewhurst to really put Air Force Blue to the test.

Air Force Blue's six rivals at Newmarket also included two promising colts stepping up in class and carrying the Hamdan Al Maktoum colours, Massaat and Tashweeq, as well as the Somerville Tattersall Stakes winner Sanus Per Aquam

Goffs Vincent O'Brien National Stakes, the Curragh—an easy success for odds-on Air Force Blue, who is chased home by Herald The Dawn and Birchwood

(trained by Jim Bolger whose stable had registered five victories in the last nine Dewhursts). But the Dewhurst betting—20/1 bar the front two—reflected the general expectation that the race would be a match between the heavily-backed Air Force Blue and Emotionless, both of whom had already shown form well up to winning an average renewal. The anticipated battle didn't materialise, with Emotionless later found to have chipped a bone in his knee after dropping away and finishing last. Any feeling of anti-climax, however, was partly tempered by the performance of Air Force Blue who put up a display as good as any seen in the race since Xaar's exceptional seven-length victory in 1997 (Frankel's two-year-old rating came from his performance in the Royal Lodge, rather than his Dewhurst win). Held up as usual, Air Force Blue made eye-catching headway to lead a furlong out, once more producing a good turn of foot and keeping on well under just hands and heels to win with something to spare by three and a quarter lengths and two and three quarters from Massaat and Sanus Per Aquam, with Tashweeq a nose further away in fourth. Air Force Blue's superiority was overwhelming and assured him of champion two-year-old status; some bookmakers installed him afterwards at a shade of odds-on for the Two Thousand Guineas, though Ladbrokes made him a 5/4 chance, which are the longest odds generally available at the time of writing.

Air Force Blue (USA) (b.c. 2013)	War Front (USA) (b 2002)	Danzig (b 1977)	Northern Dancer
			Pas de Nom
		Starry Dreamer (gr or ro 1994)	Rubiano
			Lara's Star
	Chatham (USA) (b 2004)	Maria's Mon (gr or ro 1993)	Wavering Monarch
			Carlotta Maria
		Circle of Gold (b 1999)	Seeking The Gold
			Starlet Storm

The growing impact of American-breds on racing in Europe in the 'seventies and 'eighties eventually resulted in a shift in the balance of power in thoroughbred breeding, as more of the best imports were retired to stud on this side of the Atlantic rather than being sold back to America. The expansion of Coolmore into the empire it has become has been founded principally on the achievements at stud of sons and grandsons of the phenomenal North American stallion Northern Dancer, most notably Northern Dancer's son Sadler's Wells and, in more recent times, Sadler's Wells's son Galileo. Another of the best stallion sons of Northern Dancer, Danzig, who spent his stud career in America, has been more keenly supported over the years by that other racing superpower run by the Maktoum brothers, but it is apparent that the Danzig line, which gave Coolmore the redoubtable Danehill, is again featuring in the thoughts of those hunting for suitable stallions for its host of Sadler's Wells and Galileo mares. Coolmore is looking to North America again, more particularly to the fashionable stallion War Front, a son of Danzig, who burst to prominence in Europe in 2013 when he was represented, among others, by the tough four-year-old Declaration of War, winner of the Queen Anne and the Juddmonte International, and the Dewhurst winner War Command, both of whom were part-owned by their American breeder Joseph Allen but raced for Ballydoyle and are now on the roster at Coolmore. Air Force Blue looks set to become another descendant of Danzig to join the Coolmore stallion ranks. He is among a number of colts by Danzig's son War Front who have been purchased for racing in the last two or three years by the Coolmore partners at the American yearling sales—he cost 490,000 dollars at the Keeneland September Sale—and his achievements as a two-year-old have boosted his sire's burgeoning reputation even further.

Danzig himself barely had a racing career, unbeaten in three starts at up to seven furlongs (none of them in stakes company) before being retired because of a knee injury, and he had only twenty-nine named foals in his first crop, the pick of which were turned down by the selection panel for the prestigious Keeneland July Selected Sale, an event that came to be targeted annually by Europe's richest owners in the 'seventies and 'eighties. Only one of Danzig's second crop made it into the 1984 July Sale catalogue, but the exploits of Danzig's first crop, in particular of his son Chief's Crown and his daughter Contredance, meant that there was plenty of competition at the Keeneland September Sale for the eight Danzig yearlings on offer there, including the first foal out of the unraced mare Foreign Courier. The colt took after his sire in being only neat but was purchased on behalf of Sheikh Mohammed for 650,000 dollars, the top price for a Danzig that year, and was named Green Desert. He raced for Maktoum Al-Maktoum, finishing second in the Two Thousand Guineas and the St James's Palace Stakes before making his name as a sprinter by winning the July Cup and the Sprint Cup at Haydock. Green Desert's significant influence at stud is recounted in the essay on Muhaarar but, as a racehorse, he was fairly typical of the Danzigs who were bought to race in Europe, virtually all of whom were sprinters and milers.

Air Force Blue's sire War Front, who is said to bear a close physical resemblance to Danzig (who was just 15.3 hands), won only four of his thirteen starts, his best victory coming at four in the Grade 2 Alfred G. Vanderbilt Handicap at Saratoga over six furlongs on dirt (he was never tried on turf). He was also second twice in Grade 1 sprinting company. War Front began his career at stud at a fee of 12,500 dollars but, following in the footsteps of his own sire, he had three Grade 1 winners in North America in his first crop and soon had some of the major European operations falling over themselves to purchase his progeny at the yearling sales. War Front was also represented in the latest season by Hit It A Bomb, owned and bred—out of a Sadler's Wells mare (a sign of things to come?)—by the mother of Coolmore supremo John Magnier and successful for Ballydoyle in the Breeders' Cup Juvenile Turf. The in-demand War Front stands at Claiborne Farm in Kentucky (where Danzig stood) and his fee continues its sharp upward trajectory, having been raised by a third for 2016 when he will stand at 200,000 dollars (Air Force Blue and Hit It A Bomb are from War Front's sixth crop and were bred the year his fee leapt from 15,000 dollars to 60,000 dollars, after which it went to 80,000 dollars and then 150,000 dollars in the next two years).

Air Force Blue is the fifth foal out of the Maria's Mon mare Chatham, a winning sprinter who was placed in listed company. In addition to a winner in Japan by Arch, Chatham's other winner is Air Force Blue's year-older sister Bugle who won at up to nine furlongs in the States in the latest season. Chatham's sire Maria's Mon has sired two Kentucky Derby winners (Monarchos and Super Saver), while Seeking The Gold, sire of Air Force Blue's grandam Circle of Gold, finished a close second in the Breeders' Cup Classic over a mile and a quarter. Circle of Gold is a sister to the most distinguished member of Air Force Blue's family in recent times, the champion American two-year-old filly of 1994 Flanders who gamely held off Serena's Song in the Breeders' Cup Juvenile Fillies' despite going lame (Flanders went on to produce the Group 1-winning filly Surfside who was runner-up in the Breeders' Cup Distaff in 2000). Air Force Blue looked half asleep the day he made his debut (his pre-race demeanour in sharp contrast to his performance, it should be said) and his initially rather angular frame filled out as the season went on. He developed into a strong, lengthy individual, and has the potential to grow into a handsome three-year-old. He will stay a mile and acts on good to soft going, and probably on firm. He has a good turn of foot and the best of him is almost certainly still to come, with his expected reappearance in the Two Thousand Guineas eagerly anticipated. *Aidan O'Brien, Ireland*

Irish Thoroughbred Marketing Gimcrack Stakes, York—a valuable success
for the connections of Ajaya, who beats Ribchester (spots on cap) and Raucous (right)

AIR OF ASTANA (IRE) 3 b.g. Equiano (FR) 127 – Fairnilee 67 (Selkirk (USA) 129) **77**
[2015 10m³ 10mᵖᵘ Aug 3] useful-looking gelding: fair form when third in maiden at
Leicester on debut: dismounted after losing action in similar event at Windsor: should
prove as effective at 1m. *Hugo Palmer*

AIR OF GLORY (IRE) 5 ch.g. Shamardal (USA) 129 – Balloura (USA) 80 (Swain **68**
(IRE) 134) [2015 10m 10.2m p12g Aug 15] strong gelding: fairly useful handicapper: best
effort at 1¼m: acts on polytrack: tried in tongue tie. *Martin Bosley*

AIR OF MYSTERY 3 ch.f. Sakhee's Secret 128 – Belle des Airs (IRE) 92 (Dr Fong **85**
(USA) 128) [2015 83p: 7m 6m³ 5.7g⁶ 6m⁴ Aug 9] unfurnished filly: fairly useful performer:
third in minor event at Newmarket in June: should be suited by 7f: acts on firm going.
Marcus Tregoning

AIR OF YORK (IRE) 3 b.g. Vale of York (IRE) 117 – State Secret (Green Desert (USA) **100**
127) [2015 45, a55: f5g³ p5g⁶ f5s* t5.1g t6f t5.1g⁴ 6.1m⁴ 5g 5.1g³ t6g 5d³ 5.7f* 5m 5.1m
6g 5f⁴ 5g³ 6g⁶ p5f* t5.1f³ f6g* t6g* t7.1g* p5g⁶ f7g² p6g Dec 30] smallish gelding: useful
handicapper: won at Southwell in February, Bath in June, Chelmsford in October, Southwell
and Wolverhampton in November and Wolverhampton (apprentice) in December: second
at Southwell (nose behind Ian's Memory) in December: left Ronald Harris after sixteenth
start: stays 7f: acts on all-weather and firm going: often wears headgear. *David Evans*

AIR PILOT 6 b.g. Zamindar (USA) 116 – Countess Sybil (IRE) 73 (Dr Devious (IRE) **119**
127) [2015 118: 10.3s³ 10m* 9.7m³ 10d⁵ Oct 17] compact gelding: smart performer: won
International Stakes at the Curragh (by 1¼ lengths from Parish Hall) in June: also placed
in Huxley Stakes at Chester (¾ length third behind Maverick Wave) in May and Prix Dollar
at Longchamp (¾ length third to Free Port Lux) in October: 33/1, best effort when 3½
lengths fifth to Fascinating Rock in Champion Stakes at Ascot final start: stays 1½m: acts
on soft and good to firm going: wore blinkers sole start at 3 yrs (in France). *Ralph Beckett*

AIR SQUADRON 5 b.g. Rail Link 132 – Countess Sybil (IRE) 73 (Dr Devious (IRE) **86**
127) [2015 77: 12.1m* 14m* 14.1m*? 21g⁶ 14.1s Oct 12] good-topped gelding: fairly
useful handicapper: won at Chepstow and Newmarket in May, and Salisbury in June:
effective at 1½m, barely stays 21f: acts on good to firm going: sometimes in cheekpieces
prior to 2015: often races prominently. *Ralph Beckett*

AIRTON 2 b.g. (Mar 23) Champs Elysees 124 – Fly In Style (Hernando (FR) 127) [2015 **72 p**
7g⁶ 7m⁴ 8d⁴ 8d⁵ Oct 19] 22,000F, 30,000Y: half-brother to several winners, including
winner up to 1m Percy Jackson (2-y-o 5.7f-7f winner, by Sir Percy) and 6f winner Shotgun
Start (by Kyllachy): dam unraced: fair form: promising fifth to Harlequin Rock on nursery
debut at Pontefract: stays 1m: has been gelded: remains with potential. *James Bethell*

AIR VICE MARSHAL (USA) 2 b.c. (Feb 6) War Front (USA) 119 – Gold Vault (USA) **107 p**
(Arch (USA) 127) [2015 6g³ 7m* 7f² Jul 11] $2,200,000Y: fourth foal: brother to useful
US 7f/1m winner Mosler and half-brother to 2 winners, notably very smart US Grade 1
7f/1m winner Contested (by Ghostzapper): dam, US 1m/9f winner, half-sister to very smart
US Grade 1 7f winner Pomeroy: useful form: won maiden at Gowran (by 2½ lengths from

50

Hoppala) in June: marked improvement when second in Superlative Stakes at Newmarket (length behind Birchwood) in July: stays 7f: remains open to improvement. *Aidan O'Brien, Ireland*

AIZU 2 b.g. (Jan 27) Sakhee's Secret 128 – Lemon Rock 78 (Green Desert (USA) 127) **64** [2015 6m⁴ 6m 5.1g⁵ 7.2m⁵ 7d² Aug 24] modest maiden: stays 7f: acts on good to firm and good to soft going: tried in blinkers: sent to Qatar. *Giles Bravery*

AJAADAT 3 b.f. Shamardal (USA) 129 – Taarkod (IRE) (Singspiel (IRE) 133) [2015 88: **100** 8m² 8m* 8m⁵ p8f* 8m⁴ p10g² p9.4g t9.5m Dec 12] useful handicapper: won at Salisbury in July and Chelmsford in September: second at Lingfield (head behind Oakley Girl) in November: stays 1¼m: acts on polytrack and good to firm going: often in hood in 2015. *Roger Varian*

AJAYA 2 b.c. (Feb 26) Invincible Spirit (IRE) 121 – Nessina (USA) (Hennessy (USA) 122) **117** [2015 5.1g² 5f 5.4m* 5.5g² 6g* 6g⁴ Sep 26] first foal: dam unraced half-sister to smart 7f winner Tantina, herself dam of high-class performers Bated Breath (sprinter) and Cityscape (stayed 9f): smart performer: won maiden at York in July and Gimcrack Stakes at same course (by 1¼ lengths from Ribchester) in August: second in Prix Robert Papin at Maisons-Laffitte (head behind Gutaifan) in between: better than bare result (3 lengths fourth to Shalaa) in Middle Park Stakes at Newmarket final start, going with enthusiasm close up until seemingly struggling with the Dip: will prove best kept to 5f/6f: acts on good to firm going (unraced on softer than good). *William Haggas*

A J COOK (IRE) 5 b.g. Mujadil (USA) 119 – Undertone (IRE) 84 (Noverre (USA) 125) **62** [2015 63: 6g³ 6g² 5.9g 6m 5g³ 6s 6d 6d Aug 26] modest handicapper: stays 6f: acts on soft going: often wears headgear: tried in tongue tie prior to 2015. *Ron Barr*

AJIG 4 ch.f. Bahamian Bounty 116 – Atwirl 67 (Pivotal 124) [2015 79: 8m² 8.3s 8m⁶ 10g⁵ **72** 8.1g 8.1g 8g⁶ p10f⁶ p8g² p7g Dec 16] smallish, angular mare: fair handicapper: stays 1¼m: acts on polytrack and good to firm going: often wears headgear: tried in tongue tie in 2015: often races prominently. *Eve Johnson Houghton*

Saleh Al Homaizi & Imad Al Sagar's "Ajaya"

AJJAADD (USA) 9 b.g. Elusive Quality (USA) – Millstream (USA) 107 (Dayjur (USA) **104**
137) [2015 111: 5g 5g 6g 5g 6m Aug 1] tall, useful-looking gelding: useful handicapper:
struggled to make an impact in 2015: stays 6f: acts on polytrack, soft and good to firm
going: tried in headgear. *Ted Powell*

AJMAL IHSAAS 3 b.f. Acclamation 118 – Secret History (USA) 105 (Bahri (USA) 125) **72**
[2015 82p: 8g^{ur} p7f 8.3g^3 p8g^4 10m^4 Jul 17] useful-looking filly: has scope: fair maiden:
best effort at 5f: acts on polytrack, best turf form on good going. *Marco Botti*

AJMAN BRIDGE 5 ch.g. Dubawi (IRE) 129 – Rice Mother (IRE) 69 (Indian Ridge 123) **114**
[2015 103: 10.3m^2 12m^3 12f^2 10.4m^5 14g^4 14g^6 Aug 22] strong gelding: smart handicapper:
best efforts when in frame at Royal Ascot (Duke of Edinburgh Stakes, ½-length second to
Arab Dawn) in June and Goodwood (½-length fourth to Blue Wave) in July: stays 1¾m:
acts on polytrack and any turf going: tried in blinkers prior to 2015: often travels strongly:
joined Roger Varian. *Luca Cumani*

AKATEA (IRE) 3 ch.f. Shamardal (USA) 129 – Altamira 108 (Peintre Celebre (USA) **117**
137) [2015 p9.4g* 8.9s* 9.2s^4 8d^{2d} 8s^2 8m^3 Oct 3] third foal: half-sister to useful 11f winner
Abilene (by Samum) and French 10.5f/11f winner Adam's Peak (by Zamindar): dam
French 9f/11f winner: smart performer: won maiden at Chantilly in March and listed race
at Longchamp (by head from Burma Sea) in April: best efforts on last 2 starts, in Prix du
Moulin at Longchamp (length second to Ervedya) and Prix Daniel Wildenstein on same
course (¾-length third to Impassable): stays 9.5f: acts on polytrack and soft going: sent
to USA. *A. de Royer Dupre, France*

AKAVIT (IRE) 3 b.g. Vale of York (IRE) 117 – Along Came Molly (Dr Fong (USA) 128) **81**
[2015 43: t8.6m^5 t9.5f^6 t9.5f* p11g* 11.7f* 12m^6 11.6g* 14f^2 13.4m^3 11.9m^6 p14f^6 13.7g
Sep 12] compact gelding: fairly useful handicapper: won at Wolverhampton in March,
Kempton and Bath in April and Windsor (by 3 lengths from Al) in June: second at Sandown
in July: stays 1¾m: acts on polytrack, tapeta and firm going: tried in blinkers in 2015:
usually leads. *Ed de Giles*

AKEED CHAMPION 3 b.c. Dubawi (IRE) 129 – Shy Lady (FR) 91 (Kaldoun (FR) 122) **91**
[2015 90p: 7m^6 7m^2 7g^2 7s* 7m* 7m 7m^6 Oct 2] fairly useful performer: won maiden at
Redcar in July and handicap at Newmarket in August: raced only at 7f: acts on soft and
good to firm going: usually travels strongly: sent to UAE. *Richard Fahey*

AKSOUN (IRE) 7 b.g. Red Ransom (USA) – Akdara (IRE) 84 (Sadler's Wells (USA) **57**
132) [2015 t12.2m^6 t9.5f^6 p12f 16.2s^{pu} Jul 24] modest maiden: stays 2m: acts on tapeta and
soft going: in tongue tie in 2015. *Michael Blake*

AKSUM 2 b.f. (Feb 5) Cacique (IRE) 124 – Quiet 91 (Observatory (USA) 131) [2015 p6g **52**
t6f^5 Dec 22] second foal: dam, 2-y-o 8.3f winner, half-sister to useful dam of high-class
1¼m performer Twice Over: better effort when fifth in maiden at Wolverhampton (7½ lengths
behind Go On Go On Go On) in December: trained by Pat Eddery on debut. *Emma Owen*

AKTABANTAY 3 b.c. Oasis Dream 129 – Splashdown 105 (Falbrav (IRE) 133) [2015 **110 ?**
106: 8f^4 8g 8m 7g Aug 21] big, useful-looking colt: useful performer: seemingly good
fourth in St James's Palace Stakes at Royal Ascot (5¾ lengths behind Gleneagles) on
reappearance: well below form after: may prove best short of 1m: acts on firm going: wears
headgear. *Hugo Palmer*

AKULA (IRE) 8 ch.g. Soviet Star (USA) 128 – Danielli (IRE) 79 (Danehill (USA) 126) [2015 **54**
t16.5f^3 t16.5g^5 14.6d^5 Jun 14] workmanlike gelding: modest maiden: left Tim Vaughan
after second start: stays 16.5f: acts on tapeta, soft and good to firm going. *Barry Leavy*

AL 3 b.c. Halling (USA) 133 – Incarnation (IRE) 72 (Samum (GER) 126) [2015 70p: 8.3g **90**
11.6g^2 12g* 14g 14.1s^4 Oct 28] angular colt: fairly useful handicapper: won at Newmarket
(by 7 lengths from Deep Blue Diamond) in July: stays 1¾m: best form on good going:
often races towards rear. *Luca Cumani*

ALABAALY 2 b.g. (Feb 6) Tamayuz 126 – Tatbeeq (IRE) 78 (Invincible Spirit (IRE) 121) **67**
[2015 6g 6.1g^5 7m^5 8.3g^3 7d Oct 11] strong gelding: fair maiden: best effort at 6f: tried in
blinkers: sent to Italy. *Brian Meehan*

ALAKAZAM 2 b.g. (Apr 20) Archipenko (USA) 127 – Alakananda 92 (Hernando (FR) **–**
127) [2015 t7.1g 7m 7g 8.5g^6 7g Sep 8] no form: tried in blinkers. *Sir Mark Prescott Bt*

ALAMODE 2 ch.f. (Mar 27) Sir Percy 129 – Almamia 78 (Hernando (FR) 127) [2015 6m^4 **100**
6g* 7g^2 7v Oct 24] leggy filly: fourth foal: half-sister to 11.5f winner Aloha (by With
Approval): dam lightly-raced half-sister to smart winner up to 1¼m Algonquin out of dual
Champion Stakes winner Alborada: useful performer: won maiden at Goodwood in July:
second in Oh So Sharp Stakes at Newmarket (length behind First Victory) in October: will
be suited by 1m+. *Marcus Tregoning*

ALANS PRIDE (IRE) 3 ch.g. Footstepsinthesand 120 – True Crystal (IRE) 94 (Sadler's 75
Wells (USA) 132) [2015 83: 8s 8.3m 10.4d 8m 8.5f⁶ 8g⁴ 7m⁵ 8d⁴ 8g Sep 18] fair
handicapper: stays 10.5f: acts on good to firm and heavy going: sometimes in headgear in
2015: front runner/races prominently. *Michael Dods*

ALAN TURING (IRE) 3 b.c. Exceed And Excel (AUS) 126 – Maggie Lou (IRE) 83 –
(Red Ransom (USA)) [2015 p8m Jun 3] 20/1, green when ninth in maiden at Chelmsford
(18¾ lengths behind Pick Your Choice) in June. *Ed Dunlop*

ALASAAL (USA) 3 b.g. War Front (USA) 119 – A P Investment (USA) (A P Indy (USA) 82
131) [2015 p7g³ 8m³ 7f³ 7m² Jul 23] $550,000Y: second foal: dam, unraced, out of half-
sister to smart US miler Free Thinking: fairly useful maiden: third in maiden at Kempton
in May: stays 7f: tried in cheekpieces. *William Haggas*

ALASKAN PHANTOM (IRE) 2 b.f. (Mar 2) Kodiac 112 – Alexander Phantom (IRE) 65
(Soviet Star (USA) 128) [2015 5m² 5f⁵ 6m⁵ p6f p8m⁵ t7.1g Dec 1] rather unfurnished filly:
sixth foal: sister to useful 2-y-o 6f winner Alaskan Spirit, later successful in Hong Kong,
and closely related to untrustworthy 7f winner Alkhor (by Invincible Spirit): dam unraced
half-sister to useful performer up to 1¾m Goodwood Mirage: fair maiden: stays 1m: acts
on polytrack and good to firm going: often in headgear: sent to Qatar. *Daniel Kubler*

ALASKAN WING (IRE) 3 br.g. Kodiac 112 – Canary Bird (IRE) 59 (Catrail (USA) 82
123) [2015 69: 5g⁴ 5m⁶ 6d 6d⁴ 5d⁴ 5g³ 6m⁴ 7d⁵ 6s⁴ Oct 27] fairly useful handicapper: won
at Catterick and Hamilton in July, and Catterick (by neck from Tavener) in August: stays
6f: acts on soft and good to firm going: front runner/races prominently: sold 7,500 gns, sent
to Italy. *Keith Dalgleish*

ALAWEER (IRE) 3 ch.c. Makfi 130 – Dolydille (IRE) 108 (Dolphin Street (FR) 125) 85
[2015 8f⁶ 8d³ 10d⁴ 12g⁵ p11g³ 13.4d⁵ Sep 26] 45,000Y: half-brother to several winners,
including smart 1¼m-1½m winner (stayed 2m) Drill Sergeant and useful French 10.5f
winner Nobilis (both by Rock of Gibraltar): dam 9f-1½m winner: fairly useful performer:
won maiden at Pontefract in July: third in handicap at Kempton in September: bred to stay
beyond 11f: acts on polytrack and good to soft going: sold 17,000 gns, sent to Saudi Arabia.
Charlie Fellowes

ALBA DAWN (IRE) 2 ch.f. (Feb 14) Compton Place 125 – Pink Delight (IRE) (Rock of 65
Gibraltar (IRE) 133) [2015 6m⁶ 5g 5m 5m 6s 6g³ Oct 8] £14,000Y: first foal: dam twice-
raced half-sister to Prix Robert Papin winner Irish Field: fair maiden: stays 6f: acts on good
to firm going: tried in cheekpieces. *Keith Dalgleish*

ALBAHAR (FR) 4 gr.g. Dark Angel (IRE) 113 – Downland (USA) 63 (El Prado (IRE) 83
119) [2015 p13.3f⁵ 16g⁵ 16d Oct 11] fairly useful handicapper: stays 2m: acts on polytrack
and soft going. *Chris Gordon*

AL BANDAR (IRE) 3 b.c. Monsieur Bond (IRE) 120 – Midnight Mystique (IRE) 70 98
(Noverre (USA) 125) [2015 85: 8d⁴ 8g³ 7g⁴ Jun 5] useful handicapper: won at Epsom (by
3 lengths from Make It Up) in June: stays 7f: best form on good going: sent to Hong Kong,
where renamed Magnetism. *Simon Crisford*

ALBE BACK 2 gr.c. (Apr 9) Archipenko (USA) 127 – Alba Stella 92 (Nashwan (USA) 80
135) [2015 7m 7.6g² 8m³ p10g³ 8s* Oct 15] 30,000Y: compact colt: closely related to
1¼m-1½m winner (stayed 2m) Aleatricis (by Kingmambo) and half-brother to several
winners, including useful winner up to 1½m Hernandoshideaway (2-y-o 7f winner) and
useful 2m winner Moscato (both by Hernando): dam 1½m/12.4f winner: fairly useful
performer: won maiden at Brighton in October: worth another try at 1¼m: acts on soft and
good to firm going: sold 42,000 gns, sent to Czech Republic. *Richard Hannon*

ALBECQ 3 b.g. Paco Boy (IRE) 129 – Helen Sharp (Pivotal 124) [2015 59: 10.2m 8.3g 54
6.1m⁵ 7m 10s⁵ Aug 31] modest maiden: left David Evans after fourth start: stays 6f: acts
on soft and good to firm going. *Mrs A. Malzard, Jersey*

ALBEN STAR (IRE) 7 b.g. Clodovil (IRE) 116 – Secret Circle (Magic Ring (IRE) 115) 115
[2015 119: p6f t7.1m p5g² p6f² 5g⁴ Aug 29] good-topped gelding: smart performer:
runner-up in listed race at Lingfield (1¼ lengths behind Pretend) in March and valuable
event at Lingfield (beaten 1 length behind Pretend) in April: stays 6.5f: acts on polytrack, good to
firm and good to soft going: usually races nearer last than first. *Richard Fahey*

ALBERNATHY 2 ch.c. (Mar 15) Dubawi (IRE) 129 – La Pelegrina (USA) (Redoute's 86 p
Choice (AUS)) [2015 6g 7.1m* 7m² Jun 26] good-bodied colt: first foal: dam, placed up to
9.5f in France, sister to very smart Australian Group 1 6f-12.5f winner Miss Finland: fairly
useful performer: won maiden at Sandown (by neck from Von Blucher) in June: good
second in minor event at Doncaster (2 lengths behind Champagne City), caught further
back than ideal: stays 7f: open to further improvement. *Charlie Appleby*

ALBERT BOY (IRE) 2 ch.g. (Mar 9) Falco (USA) 122 – Trumbaka (IRE) 115 (In The **62** Wings 128) [2015 6s t7.1g 7g⁵ 8.3d⁶ f8m Dec 8] modest maiden: stays 8.5f: acts on good to soft going. *Scott Dixon*

ALBERT BRIDGE 7 gr.g. Hernando (FR) 127 – Alvarita 104 (Selkirk (USA) 129) [2015 **84** 16.2g 16m 14f 12d* 11.6d⁶ Oct 5] rangy gelding: fairly useful handicapper: won at Newbury (amateur, by 1¼ lengths from Pin Up) in August: stays 17.5f: seems best on ground softer than good (acts on heavy): often races prominently: useful hurdler. *Ralph Beckett*

ALBERT HERRING 3 b.g. Tobougg (IRE) 125 – Balsamita (FR) (Midyan (USA) 124) **57** [2015 –: p10g 11m 14.1g⁶ 16.2s³ 16d⁶ Aug 28] angular gelding: modest maiden: stays 2m: acts on soft going: front runner/races prominently. *Jonathan Portman*

ALBONNY (IRE) 6 b.g. Aussie Rules (USA) 123 – Silk Law (IRE) 80 (Barathea (IRE) **73** 127) [2015 79: 16m 16d⁵ p16g⁴ p16g² p16g⁵ p16g⁴ 16s Oct 23] workmanlike gelding: fair handicapper: stays 2m: acts on polytrack, good to firm and good to soft going: often races towards rear. *Timothy Jarvis*

ALBORETTA 3 b.f. Hernando (FR) 127 – Alvarita 104 (Selkirk (USA) 129) [2015 p10g **69** p10f p10g 12.1g⁴ 16g* 18d⁵ Aug 20] sister to 3 useful winners, including 1¼m-1¾m winner Alcaeus, and half-sister to useful winner up to 1¼m Alla Speranza (2-y-o 8.4f winner, by Sir Percy): dam, 1m-10.5f winner, out of dual Champion Stakes winner Alborada: fair performer: won handicap at Nottingham in July: best effort at 2m. *Ralph Beckett*

ALCAEUS 5 b.h. Hernando (FR) 127 – Alvarita 104 (Selkirk (USA) 129) [2015 108: 12s **–** 16m Oct 2] well-made horse: useful at best, no form in 2015: stays 1¾m: acts on polytrack, good to firm and good to soft going: sold 4,000 gns, sent to Italy. *Sir Mark Prescott Bt*

ALCATRAZ (IRE) 3 b.g. Camacho 118 – Spring Opera (IRE) 82 (Sadler's Wells (USA) **87** 132) [2015 84: 7v⁴ 8.1s* 8.3g³ Jun 22] lengthy gelding: fairly useful performer: won maiden at Chepstow in May: third in handicap at Windsor in June: left J. F. Levins after first start: stays 8.5f: acts on heavy going. *George Baker*

ALDAIR 2 b.c. (Feb 27) Pastoral Pursuits 127 – Tremelo Pointe (IRE) 73 (Trempolino **72** (USA) 135) [2015 6d 8.1g⁴ Aug 2] better effort when fourth in maiden at Chepstow (4½ lengths behind Fleeting Visit) in August. *Richard Hannon*

AL DALLAH (IRE) 2 b.f. (Mar 12) Footstepsinthesand 120 – Fillthegobletagain (IRE) **75** (Byron 117) [2015 6g⁶ 6g³ 6d² 6d³ 6g* 7g* 6g⁶ 6g⁵ Dec 29] €26,000Y: first foal: dam unraced half-sister to smart winner up to 1m Romancero: fair performer: left Charlie Fellowes after third start: later won twice at Doha: stays 7f. *Jassim Al Ghazali, Qatar*

ALDAYHA (IRE) 3 b.f. Acclamation 118 – Galistic (IRE) 104 (Galileo (IRE) 134) [2015 **95** 6d⁵ 7m* 6m³ 8.1g 6g p7m³ p6f⁵ Nov 7] 42,000F, €580,000Y: strong filly: third foal: half-sister to 2-y-o 7f/1m winner Hala Hala (by Invincible Spirit) and useful German 7f/1m winner Guinnevre (by Duke of Marmalade): dam 1¼m-1¾m winner: useful performer: won maiden at Salisbury in July: third in handicaps at Windsor (¾ length behind Stellarta) in August and Kempton (1¼ lengths behind dead-heaters Mr Bossy Boots and Elemraan) in October: stays 7f: acts on polytrack and good to firm going: usually races close up, often travels strongly: sent to France. *Richard Hannon*

ALDEBURGH 6 b.g. Oasis Dream 129 – Orford Ness 107 (Selkirk (USA) 129) [2015 74: **94** p11g* p11m³ t12.2f* t12.2g* p11f² 10.3s⁵ p11g³ 10d t9.5f² t9.5f³ p11g Dec 3] fairly useful handicapper: won at Kempton in January and Wolverhampton (2) in February: stays 1½m: acts on polytrack and tapeta: races towards rear. *Nigel Twiston-Davies*

ALDERAAN (IRE) 3 gr.f. Zebedee 113 – Rublevka Star (USA) 77 (Elusive Quality **?** (USA)) [2015 68: f5g⁶ f6d⁵ Jan 22] fair at 2 yrs: well held both starts in Britain in 2015, but later won at 6.5f at Frankfurt in June: acts on soft and good to firm going: tried in headgear prior to 2015. *Tony Coyle*

AL DESTOOR 5 ch.g. Teofilo (IRE) 126 – In A Silent Way (IRE) 102 (Desert Prince **84** (IRE) 130) [2015 a8g³ a9.9g³ 10.3d² p10g² 12g⁶ Apr 18] fairly useful maiden: second in handicaps at Doncaster in March and Chelmsford in April: stays 1½m: acts on polytrack, good to firm and good to soft going: often wears hood: sometimes wears tongue tie: often races towards rear. *Anthony Middleton*

ALDO 8 b.g. Lucky Owners (NZ) 122 – Chaperone 51 (Shaamit (IRE) 127) [2015 67: **–** p13.3g⁵ Feb 4] close-coupled gelding: fair at best, no form in 2015: best up to 1½m: acts on polytrack, tapeta, raced only on good going on turf: in cheekpieces sole start in 2015: often wears tongue tie. *Sean Curran*

ALDRETH 4 b.g. Champs Elysees 124 – Rowan Flower (IRE) 67 (Ashkalani (IRE) 128) **77** [2015 16.1m* 16m* 16.2m² 16.4m 16.4g 16.2m⁶ 16.4s 15.8s⁶ Oct 27] fair handicapper: won at Newcastle and Musselburgh in June: stays 16.5f: acts on good to firm going: tried in headgear prior to 2015: often races towards rear. *Michael Easterby*

ALEATOR (USA) 3 b.g. Blame (USA) 129 – Alma Mater 102 (Sadler's Wells (USA) **98** 132) [2015 t8.6g⁶ 7.9g* 11m 14d t9.5g* 10.2d² p10f p8m³ p10f² p10g⁴ Dec 7] big, well-made gelding: useful performer: won maiden at Carlisle in July and handicap at Wolverhampton in September: placed on 3 occasions in handicaps after, including when second at Lingfield (1¼ lengths behind Man of Harlech) in November: stays 1¼m: acts on polytrack, tapeta and good to soft going: often in cheekpieces in 2015. *Sir Mark Prescott Bt*

ALEDAID (IRE) 3 b.g. Acclamation 118 – Lanark Belle (Selkirk (USA) 129) [2015 83: **75** p6f* p7m⁶ 6m³ 6g 6.1g Aug 2] good sort: fair performer: won maiden at Kempton in March: stays 6f: acts on polytrack and good to firm going. *Richard Hannon*

ALEEF (IRE) 2 b.c. (Mar 17) Kodiac 112 – Okba (USA) (Diesis 133) [2015 6g May 30] **–** 8/1, eighth in maiden at York (21¼ lengths behind Age of Empire) in May. *Charles Hills*

A LEGACY OF LOVE (IRE) 4 b.f. Sea The Stars (IRE) 140 – Nashmiah (IRE) 114 **76** (Elusive City (USA) 117) [2015 73, a80: p7g⁴ p8f⁴ p6g⁶ Apr 8] fair handicapper: stays 7f: acts on polytrack and good to firm going: often in hood in 2015: front runner/races prominently. *Amanda Perrett*

AL EGDA 2 b.f. (Feb 3) Poet's Voice 126 – Perfect Spirit (IRE) (Invincible Spirit (IRE) **– p** 121) [2015 8.3g Oct 20] 700,000Y: fifth foal: closely related to smart winner up to 7f Perfect Tribute (2-y-o 5f winner, by Dubawi) and 2-y-o 7f winner Tadqeeq (by Makfi) and half-sister to 1¼m winner Perfect Delight (by Dubai Destination): dam unraced close relative to smart performer up to 7m Swift Tango: 7/1, ninth in maiden at Windsor (11¼ lengths behind So Mi Dar) in October, slowly away: will improve. *John Gosden*

ALEJANDRO (IRE) 6 b.g. Dark Angel (IRE) 113 – Carallia (IRE) 101 (Common **97** Grounds 118) [2015 105: 7g⁴ 7.6v⁶ 7g 7g⁶ 7g⁴ 7m 7g⁵ 7d⁵ 7g⁵ 7d Sep 26] compact gelding: useful handicapper: stays 7.5f: acts on polytrack, firm and good to soft going: tried in cheekpieces prior to 2015: often leads. *David O'Meara*

ALEKO 2 b.c. (Apr 13) Cape Cross (IRE) 129 – Monnavanna (IRE) 109 (Machiavellian **80** (USA) 123) [2015 6g* 6m 7f 8m³ 6g Sep 18] 70,000Y: good-quartered, attractive colt: sixth foal: brother to useful winner up to 1m Manassas (2-y-o 6f winner), closely related to winner up to 1m Massenzio (2-y-o 5f winner, by Green Desert) and half-brother to 7f winner Monna Valley (by Exceed And Excel): dam, 6f/7f winner, half-sister to smart 1m-1¼m winner Monturani: fairly useful performer: won maiden at Haydock (by 2¼ lengths from Menai) in May: should stay at least 7f: acts on firm going. *Mark Johnston*

ALEKSANDAR 6 ch.g. Medicean 128 – Alexander Celebre (Peintre Celebre **72** (USA) 137) [2015 80: 12.5m 16m⁶ 16m⁴ 16g⁴ 14.6m² 15.8m² 13.7g* 13.8d 12.1m 15.8g⁴ Oct 13] close-coupled gelding: fair handicapper: won at Musselburgh in August: stays 2m: acts on polytrack, soft and good to firm going: tried in visor prior to 2015: often races prominently. *Jim Goldie*

ALERT 3 b.f. Zamindar (USA) 116 – Tereshkina (IRE) (Sadler's Wells (USA) 132) [2015 **70** –: 10m⁶ 9.9s 11.6g 13.3m 12.1d p12m³ t13.9f⁶ Nov 30] workmanlike filly: fair maiden: stays 1½m: acts on polytrack, soft and good to firm going: tried in headgear in 2015. *Jonathan Portman*

ALEXANDRAKOLLONTAI (IRE) 5 b.m. Amadeus Wolf 122 – Story (Observatory **90** (USA) 131) [2015 94: 6g 7.2g⁶ 7.9g 5.9g* 7d 8m³ 7d 6d⁵ 8g⁵ 6m* 6m⁴ 8g⁵ 7v Nov 7] smallish, strong mare: fairly useful handicapper: won at Carlisle in July and Hamilton (by 2 lengths from Lacing) in September: third at Ripon in August: stays 1m, effective at shorter: acts on polytrack, good to firm and heavy going: usually wears headgear: often races towards rear. *Alistair Whillans*

ALEX MY BOY (IRE) 4 b.c. Dalakhani (IRE) 133 – Alexandrova (IRE) 123 (Sadler's **117** Wells (USA) 132) [2015 114: 15.4s² 15.4s* 14.9d* 15.4d Oct 25] tall colt: smart performer: won Prix de Barbeville at Longchamp (by 3 lengths from Fly With Me) in May and Prix Kergorlay at Deauville (by 2½ lengths from Oriental Fox) in August: creditable 7½ lengths seventh to Vazirabad in Prix Royal-Oak at Saint-Cloud final outing: stays 15.5f: acts on soft and good to firm going. *A. Wohler, Germany*

ALFAHAD (IRE) 2 b.c. (Feb 13) New Approach (IRE) 132 – Al Tamooh (IRE) 84 **68** (Dalakhani (IRE) 133) [2015 p8f⁵ Nov 25] 16/1, some encouragement when fifth in maiden at Lingfield (9¼ lengths behind Brave Hero) in November. *Ed Dunlop*

ALFAJER 3 b.f. Mount Nelson 125 – Sakhee's Song (IRE) 102 (Sakhee (USA) 136) [2015 **102**
78p: 8m³ 7m⁴ p7g² 7m⁴ 7m² 7.6v² 7m³ p8g⁶ t7.1g³ p7.5g⁵ Dec 27] well-made filly: useful
handicapper: third in listed race at Ascot (¾ length behind Pelerin) in October and third in
minor event at Wolverhampton (2½ lengths behind Lamar) in November: stays 1m: acts on
polytrack and good to firm going: consistent. *Marco Botti*

ALFARAABY (IRE) 3 ch.g. Tamayuz 126 – Aphorism 84 (Halling (USA) 133) [2015 **70**
t8.6f p7f⁵ f7d 8.3g³ 10g² 12v 8d⁶ t9.5m² t12.2f⁵ p8f⁴ Oct 15] fair maiden: stays 1½m: acts
on tapeta, best turf form on good going: tried in blinkers. *David Evans*

AL FAREEJ (IRE) 3 b.f. Iffraaj 127 – Shining Hour (USA) 104 (Red Ransom (USA)) **97**
[2015 94: p5m³ Sep 26] lengthy, quite attractive filly: useful handicapper: third at
Chelmsford (1¾ lengths behind Doctor Sardonicus) in September: raced only at 5f: acts on
polytrack, good to firm and good to soft going. *James Tate*

AL FATIH (IRE) 4 b.g. Montjeu (IRE) 137 – Sky High Flyer 102 (Anabaa (USA) 130) **71**
[2015 7.1s⁴ 12d 10.2g³ 8d⁵ t8.6f Nov 20] rather leggy gelding: fair maiden: stays 1½m:
acts on good to soft going: tried in hood in 2015: sometimes slowly away. *Steve Flook*

AL FATTAN 2 b.g. (Apr 7) Dubawi (IRE) 129 – Ocean Silk (USA) 119 (Dynaformer –
(USA)) [2015 t8.6m t8.6g Dec 5] no form: in cheekpieces final start. *Saeed bin Suroor*

ALFIE BOND 3 ch.g. Monsieur Bond (IRE) 120 – Assuage (Wolfhound (USA) 126) –
[2015 –: 7f Jul 3] maiden: no form in 2015. *Tony Coyle*

ALFIE THE PUG 3 b.g. Pastoral Pursuits 127 – Kapsiliat (IRE) 76 (Cape Cross (IRE) **39**
129) [2015 56: p8f p8g p7g⁶ 8d Sep 14] tall gelding: poor maiden: stays 1m: acts on
polytrack: often in tongue tie in 2015. *Pat Phelan*

ALFRED HUTCHINSON 7 ch.g. Monsieur Bond (IRE) 120 – Chez Cherie 108 **110**
(Wolfhound (USA) 126) [2015 102, a109: p8m² p8f 7g⁵ 8m* 7g² 7g⁵ 8m 7m⁴ 8m⁴ 8d² 8d
p8g⁶ Nov 18] good-topped gelding: smart handicapper: won at York (by neck from You're
Fired) in May: second in minor event at Lingfield (1¼ lengths behind Captain Joy) in
January and second at York (head behind Chil The Kite) in August: stays 9.5f: acts on
polytrack, good to firm and heavy going: in headgear in 2015: usually races close up.
Geoffrey Oldroyd

AL FURAT (USA) 7 b.g. El Prado (IRE) 119 – No Frills (IRE) 62 (Darshaan 133) [2015 – §
64§: 12g 10g⁵ 10m⁶ Jul 19] fair at best, no form in 2015: tried in headgear prior to 2015:
untrustworthy. *Ron Barr*

ALGAITH (USA) 3 b.c. Dubawi (IRE) 129 – Atayeb (USA) 81 (Rahy (USA) 115) [2015 **109**
97p: 9m 8m⁵ 8m³ p8g* 8f* 9g Oct 10] strong, attractive colt: useful performer: won minor
event at Chelmsford (by 1¼ lengths from Calling Out) in August and minor event at Bath
(by neck from The Rectifier) in September: stays 1m: acts on polytrack, tapeta and firm
going: often leads. *B. W. Hills*

ALGAR LAD 5 ch.g. Kheleyf (USA) 116 – Winding (USA) (Irish River (FR) 131) [2015 **107**
105: 5m⁵ 6g⁴ 6g* 6f 6m⁶ 6g Sep 19] useful handicapper: won at York (by 1¼ lengths from
Boy In The Bar) in May: effective at 5f/6f: acts on firm and good to soft going: often travels
strongly. *David O'Meara*

ALGHAAZ 3 b.g. Dansili 127 – Thakafaat (IRE) 107 (Unfuwain (USA) 131) [2015 –
11.8m⁵ Jun 18] 6/1, tailed off in maiden at Leicester. *William Haggas*

AL GHAF (IRE) 3 gr.g. Zebedee 113 – Baby Bunting 63 (Wolfhound (USA) 126) [2015 **53**
6g⁶ 7m⁶ Jun 16] modest form in 2 maidens at Thirsk: later sent to Qatar, and won 6f maiden
at Doha in December. *Kevin Ryan*

ALGOMETER 2 gr.c. (Apr 9) Archipenko (USA) 127 – Albanova 119 (Alzao (USA) 117) **87 p**
[2015 9d⁴ 8s* Oct 23] 140,000Y: half-brother to several winners, including smart French
1¼m/11f winner All At Sea (by Sea The Stars) and useful winner up to 19f Alwilda (2-y-o
1m winner, by Hernando): dam winner up to 1½m (2-y-o 7f winner): better effort when
winning maiden at Newbury (by ¾ length from Victory Bond) in October: will be suited by
middle distances: open to further improvement. *David Simcock*

AL GOMRY 3 b.g. Exceed And Excel (AUS) 126 – Welsh Cake 76 (Fantastic Light (USA) **85**
134) [2015 87: p6m⁶ 7g⁶ 6g⁶ 6g² 6g* 5.5d* Oct 16] close-coupled gelding: fairly useful
performer: left Richard Fahey after second start: won claimers at Maisons-Laffitte in
September and October: sent to Qatar after: may prove best at 5f/6f: acts on polytrack,
good to firm and good to soft going: blinkered last 3 starts. *J. Reynier, France*

ALGONQUIN 3 gr.c. Archipenko (USA) 127 – Alborada 122 (Alzao (USA) 117) [2015 **113**
88p: 10g* 8m* 8.5m* 8d Aug 30] smart performer: won handicap at the Curragh (by ½
length from Manny Owens) in June, handicap at Naas (by neck from Shannon Soul) in July

and listed race at Killarney (by neck from Devonshire) in August: worth another try at 1¼m: acts on polytrack and good to firm going: usually responds generously to pressure: sent to Hong Kong. *J. S. Bolger, Ireland*

AL HAMD (IRE) 2 b.g. (Feb 13) Intikhab (USA) 135 – Bakoura 85 (Green Desert (USA) **81** 127) [2015 7m 7v⁵ 8m² Sep 11] good-bodied gelding: first foal: dam, 7f/1m winner, half-sister to useful winner up to 1m Lanansaak out of useful performer up to 1½m Bunood: fairly useful maiden: best effort when second in maiden at Salisbury (neck behind Jim Dandy) in September. *Ed Dunlop*

ALHANIA (USA) 3 b.f. Medaglia d'Oro (USA) 129 – Dessert (USA) 109 (Storm Cat – (USA)) [2015 69p: p10fᵖᵘ Nov 7] lightly-raced maiden: off 12 months, pulled up sole outing in 2015. *Saeed bin Suroor*

ALHELLA 3 b.f. Kyllachy 129 – Maid In The Shade (Forzando 122) [2015 74: 6g* 6.9g⁴ **84** 6d² 6g⁶ 6m⁴ p6g² p7g³ Dec 16] fairly useful performer: won maiden at Redcar in April: left Kevin Ryan after sixth start: stays 7f: acts on polytrack, good to firm and good to soft going. *William Knight*

ALI BIN NAYEF 3 b.g. Nayef (USA) 129 – Maimoona (IRE) 96 (Pivotal 124) [2015 72: – 8m t9.5f Dec 21] maiden: no form in 2015: stays 8.5f: acts on polytrack and tapeta. *Michael Wigham*

ALICE SPRINGS (IRE) 2 ch.f. (May 4) Galileo (IRE) 134 – Aleagueoftheirown (IRE) **110** 107 (Danehill Dancer (IRE) 117) [2015 7g* 7g² 7g⁵ 7d³ 6g⁴ 7m* 8d² Oct 30] 550,000Y: big, attractive filly: fourth foal: sister to 3 winners, including 2-y-o 7f winner (stayed 1¼m) Kingston Jamaica and 1½m winner (stays 14.5f) Criteria, both useful: dam 8.7f winner: smart performer: won maiden at the Curragh in June and £300,000 Tattersalls Millions 2YO Fillies Trophy at Newmarket (by 4 lengths from Clear Skies) in October: third in Moyglare Stud Stakes at the Curragh (1¼ lengths behind Minding) and fourth in Cheveley Park Stakes at Newmarket (beaten 1¼ lengths by Lumiere), both in September, and second in Breeders' Cup Juvenile Fillies Turf at Keeneland (¾ length behind Catch A Glimpse) in October: stays 1m: acts on good to firm and good to soft going: tried in hood. *Aidan O'Brien, Ireland*

ALINSTANTE 2 b.f. (Apr 22) Archipenko (USA) 127 – Algarade 92 (Green Desert **88** (USA) 127) [2015 p6g² 7.1f⁵ 7m* p8f* 8g Sep 8] second foal: half-sister to 13f-16.5f winner Alba Verde (by Verglas): dam, winner up to 10.3f (2-y-o 1m winner), out of half-sister to very smart 1¼m performer Last Second: fairly useful performer: won maiden at Chelmsford in June, and minor events at Haydock and Chelmsford (2 ran) in August: in cheekpieces, last of 7 behind Antonoe in Prix d'Aumale at Chantilly final outing: bred to be suited by at least 1¼m: acts on polytrack and good to firm going. *Sir Mark Prescott Bt*

£300,000 Tattersalls Millions 2YO Fillies Trophy, Newmarket—a distinct lack of depth for such a valuable contest, and odds-on Alice Springs makes the most of a good opportunity; Clear Skies (white cap) and Ninetta fill the places

A LITTLE BIT DUSTY 7 ch.g. Needwood Blade 117 – Dusty Dazzler (IRE) 102 (Titus **68**
Livius (FR) 115) [2015 f12g⁵ f14d p12g⁵ 12d³ 12.4g p10f³ t9.5m⁶ t12.2g³ t12.2f⁶ Oct 17]
leggy gelding: fair handicapper: stays 13f: acts on all-weather, soft and good to firm going:
usually wears headgear. *Conor Dore*

ALIZOOM (IRE) 2 gr.g. (Jan 27) Invincible Spirit (IRE) 121 – Lady Springbank (IRE) **81**
109 (Choisir (AUS) 126) [2015 5f⁶ p6g⁵ 5m² 5d* 5g² p6g⁴ Aug 12] 120,000F, 120,000Y,
75,000 2-y-o: sturdy gelding: first foal: dam 6f/7f winner, including at 2 yrs: fairly useful
performer: won maiden at Windsor in July: second in maiden at Lingfield in June and
second in nursery at Thirsk in August: best form at 5f: acts on good to firm and good to soft
going. *Roger Varian*

ALJAMAAHEER (IRE) 6 ch.h. Dubawi (IRE) 129 – Kelly Nicole (IRE) 84 (Rainbow **114 §**
Quest (USA) 134) [2015 121: 7m² 8m 7d May 30] strong, attractive horse: very smart
performer on his day: won Summer Mile at Ascot in 2013: below best in listed race at
Leicester (though should have won when beaten nose by Coulsty (hampered)), Lockinge
Stakes at Newbury (eighth) and Timeform Jury Stakes (John of Gaunt) at Haydock in 2015:
stayed 1m: acted on firm and good to soft going: tried in headgear prior to 2015: hard to
win with, and was one to treat with plenty of caution: to stand at Tara Stud, Co. Meath,
Ireland, fee €4,000. *Roger Varian*

AL JAMAL 5 b.m. Authorized (IRE) 133 – Kydd Gloves (USA) 99 (Dubai Millennium **61**
140) [2015 –: p8g p10g⁵ p10g⁵ Feb 20] good-topped mare: modest handicapper: stays
1¼m: acts on polytrack and any turf going: tried in hood: often in tongue tie in 2015: front
runner/races prominently, tends to find little. *Jeremy Gask*

ALJAZZI 2 b.f. (Jan 31) Shamardal (USA) 129 – Nouriya 108 (Danehill Dancer (IRE) **94 p**
117) [2015 7d* Oct 31] first foal: dam, 1¼m/10.4f winner, half-sister to smart 1m winner
Yuften: 8/1, won maiden at Newmarket (by 4½ lengths from Alyday) in October, forging
clear: will stay 1m: better to come. *Marco Botti*

ALJULJALAH (USA) 2 b.f. (Feb 14) Exchange Rate (USA) 111 – Ruler's Charm **85**
(USA) (Cape Town (USA) 125) [2015 7g* 7g Oct 9] $45,000Y, 350,000 2-y-o: lengthy filly:
half-sister to several winners in North America: dam unraced: won maiden at Newmarket
(by length from Gale Song) in September: better form when ninth in Oh So Sharp Stakes
at Newmarket (5¾ lengths behind First Victory). *Roger Varian*

ALKAWN 3 ch.g. Dubawi (IRE) 129 – Anna Oleanda (IRE) (Old Vic 136) [2015 8.3s² t8.6g³ **99**
8d² 8g* 8m* 8.1g² Sep 11] 240,000F: strong gelding: brother to smart 2-y-o 6f/7f (Horris
Hill Stakes) winner Piping Rock and half-brother to several winners, including useful
winner up to 9.5f Middle Club (2-y-o 7f/1m winner, by Fantastic Light): dam German
1¼m/10.5f winner: useful performer: won maiden at Newmarket in July and handicap at
Salisbury in August: second in handicap at Sandown (3 lengths behind McCreery) in
September: stays 1m: acts on good to firm going: usually races close up: sent to UAE.
John Gosden

AL KAZEEM 7 b.h. Dubawi (IRE) 129 – Kazeem 73 (Darshaan 133) [2015 128: **125**
9.9s* 10.4s² 10.5g* May 24]

Al Kazeem's second spell as a racehorse lasted, in the end, little more than
ten months from his first start to his last before it was ended by injury, though it
will go down as one of the most successful by a horse returned to training after
disappointing at stud. Al Kazeem did not race in Britain in the latest season, his three
starts being divided between Longchamp and the Curragh. On his reappearance, he
won the Group 2 Prix d'Harcourt at Longchamp by three quarters of a length from
Affaire Solitaire. On his next two starts, both in Group 1 company, Al Kazeem
showed form virtually on a par with that he had achieved at his very best. On the
first occasion, returned to Longchamp, he finished second to another veteran, the
nine-year-old Cirrus des Aigles, in the Prix Ganay before going on, three weeks
later, to the Curragh for the Tattersalls Gold Cup, a race that in 2015 had a little
more significance than usual, as it had been revealed in January that it was one
of seven Group 1 races being considered for demotion by the European Pattern
Committee. The others were the Prix Royal-Oak at Longchamp, the Criterium
de Saint-Cloud and four of Italy's six Group 1s—the Premio Presidente della
Repubblica and Premio Roma at Rome, and the Gran Premio di Milano and Gran
Premio del Jockey Club at Milan (the Presidente della Repubblica and the Gran
Premio di Milano have been downgraded to Group 2 in 2016). The European Pattern
Committee rather arbitrarily uses a three-year rolling average of the end-of-season

ratings of the first four finishers in a race to determine its worthiness for a certain grade. For a Group 1, the average is not expected to drop below 115. Were only the winners of a race considered, it is unlikely that the Tattersalls Gold Cup would have been facing any immediate danger. But the race has struggled to draw runners and the knock-on effect of that has resulted in its status coming into question. In the last ten years, the final field has only once contained more than six runners, nine having contested the 2007 renewal in which Notnowcato beat Dylan Thomas. Pacemakers and middle-ranking performers entered in anticipation of a payday in a weak field, have dragged down the average in many other years.

Ireland's race planners must have been relieved at the field of six that lined up for the 2015 Tattersalls Gold Cup. Among the runners were four horses of either proven or potential Group 1 standard. Besides 3/1-shot Al Kazeem, they were the 2014 Prix du Jockey Club and Irish Champion Stakes winner The Grey Gatsby, who was sent off 11/10 favourite, and the other four-year-olds Postponed (3/1) and Fascinating Rock (15/2), both winners at pattern level as three-year-olds and still relatively unexposed. The field was completed by the six-year-old Parish Hall, himself a Group 1 winner at two in the Dewhurst, and 200/1-shot Highly Toxic. In a race that lacked an obvious front runner, Postponed set a moderate pace followed by The Grey Gatsby, with Al Kazeem tucked on the rail in third ahead of Fascinating Rock. The order remained largely unchanged until Al Kazeem and Fascinating Rock made their moves as the field turned into the straight, with Fascinating Rock having a clear path in front of him out wide and Al Kazeem reliant on finding a gap between the first two. A gap appeared just over a furlong out and Al Kazeem was able to force his way into it to set up a thrilling finish in which he always looked like getting the better of Postponed and The Grey Gatsby, and was eventually able to hold off the final challenge of Fascinating Rock by a neck. Al Kazeem became the second horse to win two renewals of the Tattersalls Gold Cup since it was raised to Group 1 in 1999, following So You Think who won in 2011 and 2012, immediately before Al Kazeem achieved his first win.

The subsequent success of the beaten horses looks to have ensured the Group 1 status of the Tattersalls Gold Cup for the time being. Fascinating Rock went on to win the Champion Stakes, Postponed took the King George, while The Grey Gatsby finished second in both the Prince of Wales's Stakes and the Eclipse. The first four ended the season with an average BHA rating of exactly 122. Unfortunately,

Tattersalls Gold Cup, the Curragh—
a second success in this race for seven-year-old Al Kazeem (No.1) who beats
Fascinating Rock (No.2), Postponed (rail) and The Grey Gatsby in a thrilling finish

Al Kazeem contested no more of the big middle-distance prizes. It was reported soon after the Curragh that he had suffered an injury during the race and would have to miss both the Prince of Wales's Stakes and the Eclipse, races he had won two years earlier. There was still some hope at first that he might be able to return for an autumn campaign, but his retirement was announced in early-August, owing to a suspensory injury to a foreleg. He will stand in 2016 at Oakgrove Stud, which belongs to his owner John Deer, and his fee has been set at £12,000 with a live foal concession. He had originally been retired in 2014 to the Royal Studs at a fee of £18,000, but managed to get only around twenty-five mares in foal which led to his being withdrawn from stallion duties. Al Kazeem, incidentally, isn't the first smart performer owned by Deer to be returned to racing after his first year at stud; the sprinter Averti returned from stallion duties to run three more times (without success) in 1999 before resuming at stud in 2000 (Averti's sire the Prix de l'Abbaye winner Avonbridge also stands at Oakgrove).

Al Kazeem (b.h. 2008)	Dubawi (IRE) (b 2002)	Dubai Millennium (b 1996)	Seeking The Gold
			Colorado Dancer
		Zomaradah (b 1995)	Deploy
			Jawaher
	Kazeem (b 1998)	Darshaan (br 1981)	Shirley Heights
			Delsy
		Kanz (b 1981)	The Minstrel
			Treasure Chest

Al Kazeem's sire Dubawi had an excellent year and is now firmly established as one of Europe's premier sires. His other Group 1 successes included races such as the King George (the aforementioned Postponed), Grand Prix de Paris (Erupt), Prix du Jockey Club (New Bay), International Stakes (Arabian Queen) and Dubai World Cup (Prince Bishop). The distaff side of Al Kazeem's pedigree has been dealt with extensively in previous Annuals. There have been no further runners out of his dam the thrice-raced maiden Kazeem, though she does have a two-year-old close relative to Al Kazeem by Dubawi's son Makfi, while a yearling full brother to Al Kazeem was offered at the Newmarket October Sales but was bought back for 485,000 guineas. The tall, attractive Al Kazeem stayed a mile and a half but showed his very best form at a mile and a quarter, while he acted on soft and firm going. He ran once in cheekpieces but was generally straightforward and was a thoroughly genuine racehorse. *Roger Charlton*

ALKETIOS (GR) 4 b.g. Kavafi (IRE) 111 – Mazea (IRE) (Montjeu (IRE) 137) [2015 90: **77** p8m p8f 10m 7.6d⁴ 7.6g² 8g⁵ p8g* p8g f7g p7g⁴ p7f⁴ Dec 21] good-bodied gelding: fair handicapper: won at Kempton in September: acts on polytrack, best turf form on good going: often races towards rear: temperament under suspicion. *Gary Moore*

AL KHAFJI 2 ch.c. (Mar 1) New Approach (IRE) 132 – Wadaat 102 (Diktat 126) [2015 **87 p** 7m 7m3 7m3 8v³ p7g* Nov 13] 150,000Y: third foal: dam 1m winner (stayed 11f): fairly useful form: won nursery at Lingfield in November: should be suited by 1m+: will go on improving. *Luca Cumani*

AL KHAN (IRE) 6 b.g. Elnadim (USA) 128 – Popolo (IRE) 66 (Fasliyev (USA) 120) **100** [2015 89, a80: 7g* 7.2g* 7g 7g 7.6m² 6m³ 6g 7g 7.2g² 7.2g⁴ p7f p7g⁶ Dec 9] lengthy gelding: useful handicapper: won at Catterick and Ayr in April: third at York (2½ lengths behind Tanzeel) in July and second at Ayr (neck behind Right Touch) in September: left David O'Meara after fifth start: stays 8.5f: acts on polytrack, fibresand, soft and good to firm going: sometimes in cheekpieces prior to 2015: often races towards rear. *Kevin Ryan*

AL KHATEYA 2 b.f. (Feb 13) Acclamation 118 – Grenadia (USA) 104 (Thunder Gulch **56 p** (USA) 121) [2015 6m Aug 3] €80,000F, €350,000Y: attractive filly: has scope: third foal: dam, French 9.5f winner, half-sister to smart French/US 9.5f-12.5f winner Slew The Red: 15/2, seventh in maiden at Windsor (4 lengths behind Stylistik) in August: better to come. *Richard Hannon*

ALKHOR 2 b.c. (Mar 14) Exceed And Excel (AUS) 126 – Ruse 66 (Diktat 126) [2015 5g² **81 p** 5m* Jun 15] 230,000Y: well-grown colt: fourth foal: half-brother to 3 winners, including useful 7f/1m winner Flying Hammer (by Acclamation): dam, maiden (stayed 1½m), half-sister to smart winner up to 7f Ardkinglass: better effort when winning maiden at Windsor (by ¾ length from Raj To Riches) in June, readily: should be suited by at least 6f: remains open to improvement. *Richard Hannon*

AL KIRANA (IRE) 2 b.f. (Mar 2) Exceed And Excel (AUS) 126 – Ripalong (IRE) 68 **61** (Revoque (IRE) 122) [2015 7g⁶ 5.4s⁶ Oct 9] closely related to smart 7f and (including at 2 yrs) 1m winner Imperial Rome (by Holy Roman Emperor) and 1¼m winner Royal Toast (by Duke of Marmalade) and half-sister to 3 winners, including smart winner up to 1m Shamwari Lodge (2-y-o 6f winner, by Hawk Wing): dam, smart maiden, half-sister to Sprint Cup winner Pipalong: better effort when sixth in maiden at Newmarket (9½ lengths behind First Victory) in September: will be suited by return to 6f+. *Richard Hannon*

ALL ABOUT TIME 3 b.f. Azamour (IRE) 130 – Up And About 77 (Barathea (IRE) 127) **93 p** [2015 80p: 7.9m⁵ 10.4m² 9.8g* Aug 15] leggy filly: fairly useful handicapper, lightly raced: won at Ripon in August: will be suited by at least 1½m: acts on soft and good to firm going: front runner/races prominently, usually responds generously to pressure: likely to progress further. *David O'Meara*

ALLA BREVE 3 b.f. Dansili 127 – Allegretto (IRE) 118 (Galileo (IRE) 134) [2015 59p: **80** 12g* 12g⁵ 14.1m³ Sep 15] fairly useful performer: won maiden at Ffos Las in July: third in handicap at Yarmouth in September: should be suited by 2m+: in blinkers in 2015. *Sir Michael Stoute*

ALLEGRA ROYALE 3 b.f. Royal Applause 124 – Rapsgate (IRE) 78 (Mozart (IRE) **–** 131) [2015 8m¹¹ 8.3m¹⁶ 8g⁵ 7v⁶ p8f Sep 17] 13,000Y: lengthy filly: fifth foal: half-sister to 3 winners, including winner up to 13f Hawdyerwheesht (2-y-o 7f winner, by Librettist) and 2-y-o 6f winner Sonsie Lass (by Refuse To Bend): dam 5f winner (including at 2 yrs): no form: often races in rear: sent to Italy. *William Knight*

ALLEGRI (IRE) 6 b.g. Key of Luck (USA) 126 – Bermuxa (FR) 60 (Linamix (FR) 127) **–** [2015 f8d p6g p10g Dec 7] maiden: no form in 2015: tried in headgear prior to 2015. *Alan Coogan*

ALL FOR THE BEST (IRE) 3 b.g. Rip Van Winkle (IRE) 134 – Alleluia 117 (Caerleon **83** (USA) 132) [2015 t8.6g p8m p8g⁴ p11g² 13.1f* 14.4g⁴ 11.7f² p15.8g⁴ p16g⁴ t13.9f² t13.9f* t13.9f³ Nov 20] closely related to 2 winners by Galileo, including smart 1½m-16.4f winner Allegretto, and half-brother to 3 winners, including useful 1½m winner Altaayil (by Sea The Stars): dam 1¼m-2¼m (Doncaster Cup) winner: fairly useful handicapper: won at Bath in July and Wolverhampton in October: left Sir Mark Prescott after eleventh start: stays 1¾m: acts on tapeta and firm going: often in headgear. *Robert Stephens*

ALLFREDANDNOBELL (IRE) 2 b.g. (Mar 15) Alfred Nobel (IRE) 110 – Its In The **65** Air (IRE) (Whipper (USA) 126) [2015 6m⁶ 6g² 6m⁴ 6d Oct 5] fair maiden: raced only at 6f: tried in cheekpieces. *Micky Hammond*

ALL MY LOVE (IRE) 3 b.f. Lord Shanakill (USA) 121 – Afilla (Dansili 127) [2015 70: **79** 9.9m⁴ 8g³ 9.8d⁶ 10.3m³ 9g⁶ 9.9g² 10.4d⁵ 11.6d* 12d⁵ Oct 30] leggy filly: fair handicapper: won at Windsor in October: stays 11.5f: acts on heavy going. *Pam Sly*

ALL OR NOTHIN (IRE) 6 b.g. Majestic Missile (IRE) 118 – Lady Peculiar (CAN) **–** (Sunshine Forever (USA)) [2015 68: p6g t6g⁶ 7m May 3] well-made gelding: useful at best, no form in 2015: often wears headgear: tried in tongue tie prior to 2015. *Paddy Butler*

ALL REDDY 4 ch.g. Compton Place 125 – Raphaela (FR) (Octagonal (NZ) 126) [2015 74: **57** t7.1g t9.5f t7.1g t8.6g 11.5d t8.6g² p8g 10.2d p8g Sep 9] quite attractive gelding: modest maiden: stays 10.5f: acts on polytrack, tapeta and good to soft going: often in headgear in 2015: tried in tongue tie in 2015: often races prominently. *Ian Williams*

ALL ROUNDER (USA) 3 gr.f. Mizzen Mast (USA) 121 – Summer Shower (Sadler's **81** Wells (USA) 132) [2015 69: 9.9s⁶ 14.1v³ f14f⁴ f16g⁶ Dec 29] sturdy filly: fairly useful handicapper: won at Southwell (by 8 lengths from Hall of Beauty) in December: best effort at 1¾m: acts on fibresand: tried in cheekpieces prior to 2015. *Geoffrey Deacon*

ALL SET TO GO (IRE) 4 gr.g. Verglas (IRE) 118 – Firecrest (IRE) 107 (Darshaan 133) **–** [2015 9m May 2] well-made gelding: useful at best, no form in 2015: stays 1¼m: acts on good to firm and heavy going: in tongue tie sole start in 2015. *Paul Nicholls*

ALLSINGINGNDANCING (IRE) 2 b.f. (Feb 18) Vocalised (USA) 114 – Sanan **84** Dancer (IRE) (Danehill Dancer (IRE) 117) [2015 t5.1g⁵ 6g 5.5g* 5g² 5.5g⁴ 5.5g³ p6.5g 6s p7.5g² p8g 7.5g Dec 3] €1,500 2-y-o: first foal: dam ran twice: fairly useful performer: improved to win claimer at Maisons-Laffitte in June (left J. S. Moore after): probably stays 7.5f: acts on polytrack: tried in cheekpieces. *T. Castanheira, France*

ALL TALK N NO DO (IRE) 4 b.g. Kodiac 112 – Woodren (USA) 91 (Woodman (USA) **100** 126) [2015 86: 11.6g* 12g 14.6m* 14f* 14g Jul 28] sturdy gelding: useful handicapper: won at Windsor in April, Doncaster in June and Ascot (by ½ length from Antiquarium) in July: stays 14.5f: acts on polytrack, firm and good to soft going: sometimes wears cheekpieces: sometimes wears tongue tie: usually races close up. *Seamus Durack*

ALL THE ACES (IRE) 10 b.g. Spartacus (IRE) 107 – Lili Cup (FR) (Fabulous Dancer (USA) 124) [2015 t13.9g Jan 23] strong, lengthy gelding: smart at best, no form in 2015: stays 1½m: acts on polytrack, good to firm and good to soft going: tried in blinkers prior to 2015: sometimes slowly away. *Keith Dalgleish* –

ALL THE RAGE 2 b.f. (Apr 1) Dubawi (IRE) 129 – Intrigued 105 (Darshaan 133) [2015 7s 7.5g t7.1m⁶ Sep 25] half-sister to several winners, including smart 1¼m/11f winner Michelangelo and useful 1½m winner (stayed 2m) No Heretic (both by Galileo): dam, 2-y-o 8.5f winner who stayed 1½m, half-sister to very smart miler Aussie Rules: modest form in maidens: will stay at least 1¼m: capable of better. *Sir Mark Prescott Bt* **61 p**

ALL THE WINDS (GER) 10 ch.g. Samum (GER) 126 – All Our Luck (GER) (Spectrum (IRE) 126) [2015 t12.2f⁶ m1.3g* 14.1m* 14f* 14.6m³ Jul 23] fairly useful handicapper: won at Chelmsford in June, and Nottingham and Haydock in July: stays 14.5f: acts on polytrack, tapeta, firm and good to soft going: tried in blinkers prior to 2015: often wears tongue tie: often travels strongly. *Shaun Lycett* **85**

ALLUMAGE 3 b.f. Montjeu (IRE) 137 – Alaia (IRE) 88 (Sinndar (IRE) 134) [2015 9.9d p10f* 12g⁶ p13g Oct 29] 100,000Y: rather leggy filly: first foal: dam, 9f winner, half-sister to smart performer up to 1¼m Alasha: useful performer: won maiden at Chelmsford in September: stays 1½m: usually in hood. *Roger Charlton* **97**

ALL YOU (IRE) 3 b.g. Siyouni (FR) 122 – Diamond Light (USA) 70 (Fantastic Light (USA) 134) [2015 t8.6f* 8g³ 7.1s² 10.4g⁵ 10g Jun 8] fair performer: won maiden at Wolverhampton in March: should prove best at around 1m: acts on tapeta and soft going. *David O'Meara* **79**

ALMANACK 5 b.g. Haatef (USA) 117 – Openness (Grand Lodge (USA) 125) [2015 74, a87; p8g⁴ p7g t7.1g t8.6g Jun 26] fair handicapper: left Ian Williams after second start: stays 8.5f: acts on polytrack, tapeta and good to firm going: tried in cheekpieces: sometimes wears tongue tie. *Ronald Thompson* **71**

ALMARED 3 b.c. Makfi 130 – Starstone (Diktat 126) [2015 8d 8m 8m⁵ 8.3d Jul 29] fair maiden: best effort at 1m: sent to Greece. *James Fanshawe* **69**

AL MEEZAN 5 ch.g. Nayef (USA) 129 – Festivale (IRE) 107 (Invincible Spirit (IRE) 121) [2015 10.2m p12g* p12g⁵ p12g⁶ Aug 1] fair performer: won seller at Lingfield in June: stays 1½m: acts on polytrack: usually in blinkers in 2015. *Peter Hiatt* **73**

ALMODOVAR (IRE) 3 b.g. Sea The Stars (IRE) 140 – Melodramatic (IRE) 101 (Sadler's Wells (USA) 132) [2015 10m⁵ 10g* 10d* 12m² Aug 16] second foal: dam, 8.3f winner, closely related to Sprint Cup winner Tante Rose and half-sister to dam of high-class French 7f/1m winner Make Believe: useful performer: won maiden at Ayr and handicap at Leicester in July: good second in handicap at Pontefract (½ length behind Headline News) in August, hung left after going on over 1f out: stays 1½m: open to further improvement. *David Lanigan* **97 p**

ALMOHTASEB 3 b.g. Oasis Dream 129 – Cuis Ghaire (IRE) 113 (Galileo (IRE) 134) [2015 8g 7m² 7m* 8m⁶ Aug 8] good-bodied gelding: second foal: dam, 2-y-o 6f winner and second in 1000 Guineas, sister to smart miler Gile Na Greine and smart performer up to 1½m Scintillula: useful performer: won maiden at Doncaster in July: will stay 1m: sent to UAE. *Roger Varian* **100**

ALMOQATEL (IRE) 3 b.g. Clodovil (IRE) 116 – Majestic Night (IRE) (Mujadil (USA) 119) [2015 64: p8f 8f 8mᵘʳ 7m⁵ 8f⁵ Sep 12] sturdy gelding: modest handicapper: stays 1m: acts on polytrack, firm and good to soft going: usually in headgear in 2015: often races freely. *Tony Newcombe* **52**

ALMOST GUILTY (USA) 4 ch.f. Distorted Humor (USA) 117 – Rolling Sea (USA) (Sefapiano (USA)) [2015 6m⁵ a8f⁴ a8f² a8f⁴ 8.5f Nov 26] $240,000Y: second foal: half-sister to a winner in USA by Tapit: dam US Grade 2 1m/8.5f winner: fair maiden: left Brian Meehan after first start: stays 1m. *Edward R. Freeman, Canada* **75**

ALMOST NOWHERE (IRE) 3 br.f. Erewhon (USA) – Lianda (USA) (Danzig (USA)) [2015 –: f8s² f8g³ 9.9g Jun 16] poor maiden: left John Butler after second start: probably stays 1¼m: acts on fibresand and soft going: in headgear in 2015: often races lazily: sent to Morocco. *Dr Jon Scargill* **45**

ALMOST SPANISH (IRE) 2 b.f. (Feb 6) Rock of Gibraltar (IRE) 133 – Spanish Quest (Rainbow Quest (USA) 134) [2015 7.5g⁴ 7m 7m p6g Aug 22] 7,000Y: closely related to 3 winners, including 1½m winner Supreme Quest (by Exceed And Excel) and 9.5f/11¼m winner Vaguely Spanish (by Oratorio), and half-sister to 2-y-o 7f winner Hey Up Dad (by Fantastic Light): dam unraced half-sister to smart 1m-1¼m winner Spanish Don: no form. *Scott Dixon* –

ALMUHALAB 4 b.g. Dansili 127 – Ghanaati (USA) 122 (Giant's Causeway (USA) 132) **76**
[2015 77: 10.3d 10.1g 12g 12m⁶ 9.9m 9.3g³ 10m² 11.9d⁴ 9.3g Sep 15] fair maiden: stays
1¼m: acts on good to firm going: usually races prominently. *Ruth Carr*

AL MUHEER (IRE) 10 b.g. Diktat 126 – Dominion Rose (USA) 65 (Spinning World **78**
(USA) 130) [2015 85, a73: t7.1g t7.1g t7.1m² t8.6m² t8.6m⁶ f8g* f7g t8.6f* t8.6m* t8.6g*
f8g⁶ 7.6d t8.6g⁵ t8.6g 8d 7.6g² t8.6g t8.6m t8.6g Dec 4] close-coupled gelding: fair
performer: won handicap at Southwell (apprentice) in February, seller at Wolverhampton
in March, and claimer and seller at Wolverhampton in April: stays 8.5f: acts on all-weather
and any turf going: usually wears headgear: tried in tongue tie prior to 2015: races freely.
Tom Dascombe

ALMUHEET 4 b.g. Dansili 127 – Arwaah (IRE) 106 (Dalakhani (IRE) 133) [2015 98: **92**
p7g³ 7.1m 7m 6m 8m* 8g Oct 3] sturdy gelding: fairly useful handicapper: won at
Redcar (by length from Dual Mac) in September: stays 1m: acts on polytrack, tapeta and
firm going: often wears hood: sent to UAE. *Brian Ellison*

AL MUSHEER (FR) 4 gr.c. Verglas (IRE) 118 – Canzonetta (FR) (Kahyasi 130) [2015 **62 §**
t12.2g t16.5g⁵ 12d Aug 14] modest handicapper: stays 13.5f: acts on good to soft going:
often in blinkers in 2015: temperamental. *Donald McCain*

ALMUTAMARRED (USA) 3 ch.g. Street Cry (IRE) 130 – Sortita (GER) 98 (Monsun **–**
(GER) 124) [2015 10g May 14] 12/1, very green when eighth in maiden at Newmarket
(tailed off behind Resonant) in May. *Roger Varian*

AL NAAMAH (IRE) 3 b.f. Galileo (IRE) 134 – Alluring Park (IRE) 97 (Green Desert **108**
(USA) 127) [2015 10.4g² 12g 11.9m² 12.4d³ 11.9s Sep 13] 5,000,000Y: sister to Oaks
winner Was (2-y-o 1m winner) and half-sister to 3 winners, including useful 2-y-o 6f/7f
winner (stays 1½m) Janood (by Medicean): dam, 2-y-o 6f winner, half-sister to Derby
winner New Approach: useful performer: won minor event at Chantilly at 2 yrs: placed in
2015 in Prix Cleopatre at Saint-Cloud (head second to Little Nightingale), listed race at
Longchamp and Prix Minerve at Deauville (1¼ lengths third to Candarliya): well held in
Oaks at Epsom and Prix Vermeille at Longchamp on other starts: stays 12.5f: acts on good
to firm and good to soft going: often races prominently. *A. Fabre, France*

ALNASHAMA 3 b.g. Dubawi (IRE) 129 – Ghanaati (USA) 122 (Giant's Causeway **83**
(USA) 132) [2015 83p: 8m⁴ 8d⁴ 8m* 8d² 9d⁴ p8g³ 10s⁵ t7.1f⁶ Nov 3] fairly useful
performer: won maiden at Bath (by ¾ length from Important Message) in July: stays 1m:
acts on tapeta, good to firm and good to soft going: races prominently. *Charles Hills*

AL NEHAYY 3 gr.c. Mastercraftsman (IRE) 129 – Yacht Woman (USA) (Mizzen Mast **78**
(USA) 121) [2015 p12f⁴ 9.9m² 12m⁴ 12m⁶ 12g⁵ 9.9v Sep 17] fair maiden: left Kevin Ryan
after fifth start: stays 1½m: acts on polytrack and good to firm going: often in headgear.
G. E. Mikhalides, France

AL NOFOR (IRE) 3 b.f. Shamardal (USA) 129 – First Fleet (USA) 106 (Woodman **79 p**
(USA) 126) [2015 68p: 8.3g² Jun 28] lightly-raced maiden: second in maiden at Windsor
(2¼ lengths behind Rosslare) on sole outing in 2015, needing stronger gallop: sent to
France: sure to progress. *Richard Hannon*

ALOFT (IRE) 3 b.g. Galileo (IRE) 134 – Dietrich (USA) 115 (Storm Cat (USA)) [2015 **109**
109: 16f* 12d Aug 19] strong gelding: useful performer: won Queen's Vase at Royal Ascot
(by ½ length from Tommy Docc) in June: well held in Great Voltigeur Stakes at York
subsequent outing: stays 2m: acts on firm and good to soft going: in headgear/tongue tie in 2015:
sent to Australia. *Aidan O'Brien, Ireland*

ALONSOA (IRE) 3 ch.f. Raven's Pass (USA) 133 – Alasha (IRE) 115 (Barathea (IRE) **–**
127) [2015 96: 10m Jun 11] big, scopey filly: useful at best, no form in 2015: stays 7f: acts
on good to firm going: tends to find little. *Henry Candy*

A LOVABLE ROGUE 3 b.g. Dutch Art 126 – Dance Card 77 (Cape Cross (IRE) 129) **65**
[2015 51: 7.2d³ 8.3g⁵ 7.2d⁴ 6m* 6d² 8g⁶ 7.2g Oct 8] fair handicapper: won at Hamilton in
August: best effort at 6f (probably stays 8.5f): acts on good to firm and good to soft going:
often in cheekpieces in 2015: often races prominently. *R. Mike Smith*

ALOYSIUS 2 b.g. (Mar 1) Oasis Dream 129 – Alaia (IRE) 88 (Sinndar (IRE) 134) [2015 **–**
6m Aug 17] 10/1, very green when tenth in maiden at Windsor (10¾ lengths behind
Dancing Star) in August. *Roger Charlton*

ALPHABETICAL ORDER 7 b.g. Alflora (IRE) 120 – Lady Turk (FR) (Baby Turk 120) **–**
[2015 t12.2g Dec 5] 20/1, eighth in maiden at Wolverhampton (23¾ lengths behind Sign
of A Victory) in December. *Tim Vaughan*

ALPHA DELPHINI 4 b.g. Captain Gerrard (IRE) 113 – Easy To Imagine (USA) **85**
(Cozzene (USA)) [2015 –: 6g² 6d⁵ 5g* 5s⁵ Oct 19] fairly useful performer: won maiden at
Beverley (by 1½ lengths from Grand Beauty) in August: stays 6f: acts on good going.
Bryan Smart

ALPHA DELTA WHISKY 7 ch.g. Intikhab (USA) 135 – Chispa 94 (Imperial Frontier **71**
(USA) 112) [2015 80: t5.1g⁶ p5f³ 5.1d 5m 5.2m* 5m 5.1g 5g t5.1f⁶ Nov 14] strong
gelding: fair handicapper: won at Newbury (apprentice) in July: best form at 5f: acts on
polytrack, tapeta, good to firm and good to soft going: sometimes wears headgear: front
runner/races prominently. *John Gallagher*

ALPHA SPIRIT 3 b.f. Sixties Icon 125 – Queen of Narnia 67 (Hunting Lion (IRE) 115) **56**
[2015 67: t6f p6m p7f Feb 3] rather leggy filly: modest maiden: stays 7f: acts on polytrack,
good to firm and good to soft going: tried in hood prior to 2015. *Mick Channon*

ALPHA TAURI (USA) 9 b.g. Aldebaran (USA) 126 – Seven Moons (JPN) (Sunday **82**
Silence (USA)) [2015 82: f6d⁵ f5g f5d³ f5g f6g² f6s f6g⁴ f6g³ f7g⁴ p5f 7d f7d* 7m f8d
f8s⁶ 6.1m⁶ 6.1m⁶ f5g f6g⁴ f6g⁴ f6g⁵ Dec 18] smallish, sturdy gelding: fairly useful handicapper:
won at Southwell (by 4 lengths from Quadriga) in May: races mainly at 6f nowadays: acts
on fibresand, good to firm and heavy going: tried in headgear prior to 2015: usually in
tongue tie prior to 2015. *Charles Smith*

ALPINE DREAM (IRE) 2 b.f. (Feb 12) Dream Ahead (USA) 133 – Infamous Angel 101 **71**
(Exceed And Excel (AUS) 126) [2015 6d* 6.5m Sep 10] 40,000F: third foal: dam 2-y-o
5f/6f (Lowther Stakes) winner: better effort when winning maiden at Thirsk (by ½ length
from Lady Canford) in August. *William Haggas*

ALQUBBAH (IRE) 2 b.f. (Feb 25) Arcano (IRE) 122 – Musharakaat (IRE) 95 (Iffraaj **89**
127) [2015 6m⁶ 6d³ 6g* 7s² Sep 18] good-topped filly: first foal: dam 2-y-o 7f winner who
stayed 9f: fairly useful performer: won maiden at Yarmouth (by neck from Fourth Way) in
August: stays 7f. *Ed Dunlop*

ALQUFFAAL 2 br.c. (Apr 2) Dansili 127 – Cuis Ghaire (IRE) 113 (Galileo (IRE) 134) **64 p**
[2015 8.3d⁵ Oct 14] third foal: half-brother to useful 7f winner Almohtaseb (by Oasis
Dream): dam, 2-y-o 6f winner and second in 1000 Guineas, sister to smart miler Gile Na
Greine and smart performer up to 1½m Scintillula: 3/1, some encouragement when fifth in
maiden at Nottingham (9½ lengths behind Mr Khalid) in October, not knocked about:
better to come. *Roger Varian*

AL RAYYAN (IRE) 3 ch.c. Danehill Dancer (IRE) 117 – Inca Trail (USA) (Royal **92**
Academy (USA) 130) [2015 79: 8g⁴ 8g 6g³ p8g p6.5g² 7d* Dec 11] fairly useful performer:
won minor event at Toulouse in December: left Kevin Ryan after first start: stays 1m: acts
on polytrack, good to firm and good to soft going. *G. E. Mikhalides, France*

AL RIFAI (IRE) 3 b.c. Galileo (IRE) 134 – Lahaleeb (IRE) 121 (Redback 116) [2015 **90 p**
p12g* Apr 27] first foal: dam 7f (at 2 yrs) to 1¼m (E P Taylor Stakes) winner: 9/2, won
maiden at Kempton (by 3½ lengths from Royal History) in April, storming clear: looked
an exciting prospect, but not seen after. *John Gosden*

ALSAADEN 2 b.f. (Feb 13) Acclamation 118 – Bahia Breeze 109 (Mister Baileys 123) **92**
[2015 6.5m² 6m* 7g² 6g Aug 1] 85,000F: third foal: half-sister to 7f winner Khalaas (by
Iffraaj) and useful Polish 7f-11f winner Brioniya (by Pivotal): dam winner up to 1m (2-y-o
6f winner) who stayed 10.5f: fairly useful performer: won maiden at Doncaster in June:
second in nursery at Chester in July: stays 7f. *Richard Hannon*

ALSACIENNE 2 gr.f. (Mar 1) Dalakhani (IRE) 133 – Alabastrine 56 (Green Desert **59 p**
(USA) 127) [2015 7v⁴ t8.6g t9.5f⁵ Oct 23] €35,000Y: half-sister to 3 winners, including
useful winner up to 1½m Hail Caesar (2-y-o 7.4f winner, by Montjeu) and 2-y-o 7f winner
Albaspina (by Selkirk): dam lightly-raced half-sister to very smart winner up to 1¼m Last
Second: modest form in maidens: will be suited by at least 1¼m: remains with potential.
Sir Mark Prescott Bt

AL SAILIYAH (IRE) 2 b.f. (Mar 30) Acclamation 118 – Raja (IRE) 87 (Pivotal 124) **–**
[2015 7g Sep 26] third foal: half-sister to smart 5f/6f winner Great Minds (by Bahamian
Bounty): dam, 5.5f/6f winner (including at 2 yrs), half-sister to very smart sprinter
Pipalong: 12/1, well held in maiden at Newmarket: bred to prove best at 5f/6f. *Richard
Hannon*

ALSHAAHRAMAN (USA) 3 b.c. Daaher (CAN) 120 – Bashoosha (USA) (Distorted **54**
Humor (USA) 117) [2015 61p: 10.1d⁶ 8g⁵ Jun 20] lengthy, unfurnished colt: modest
maiden: better effort in 2015 when fifth in maiden at Newmarket in June, slowly away.
Brian Meehan

AL SHAHANIYA (IRE) 2 ch.f. (Mar 22) Zoffany (IRE) 121 – Sweet Kristeen (USA) 69   **85**
(Candy Stripes (USA) 115) [2015 6m* p7d* 7g⁵ Sep 26] €29,000F, £36,000Y, €340,000
2-y-o: seventh foal: half-sister to 3 winners, including useful 8.3f winner Cliche (by Diktat)
and 7.4f/1m winner Rule Breaker (by Refuse To Bend): dam 7f winner: fairly useful
performer: won maiden at Hamilton (by 1½ lengths from Doeadeer) in August and minor
event at Kempton (by ½ length from Sun'aq) in September: stays 7f: in hood. *John Quinn*

ALSHALAAL (IRE) 2 ch.g. (Mar 9) Arcano (IRE) 122 – Geesala (IRE) 82 (Barathea   **82**
(IRE) 127) [2015 5d⁶ 6m 6m² 5g⁴ 5d Sep 25] strong, compact gelding: second foal: dam
2-y-o 5f winner: fairly useful maiden: second in maiden at Haydock in July: best effort at
6f: acts on good to firm going: often in blinkers: often races prominently: sent to Italy.
Brian Meehan

ALSHAN FAJER 5 ch.g. Lemon Drop Kid (USA) 131 – Illuminise (IRE) 109 (Grand   **86**
Lodge (USA) 125) [2015 p12m² f12g³ p12m⁶ p10g* p12g* p12g² Dec 30] fairly useful
handicapper: won at Lingfield (twice) in December, awarded race on second occasion:
stays 1½m: acts on polytrack and good to firm going: often races prominently. *J. R. Jenkins*

ALSHAQFF 2 b.c. (Mar 24) Equiano (FR) 127 – Impressible 95 (Oasis Dream 129) [2015   **82**
5.4g 5g⁴ p6g² t5.1m² p5g* Dec 7] £16,000Y, resold 50,000Y: second foal: brother to useful
2-y-o 5f/6f winner Dark Reckoning: dam, 5f and (at 2 yrs) 6f winner, half-sister to high-
class sprinter Reverence: fairly useful performer: won maiden at Chelmsford (by ¾ length
from Krystallite) in December: stays 6f: acts on polytrack and tapeta. *William Haggas*

AL'S MEMORY (IRE) 6 b.g. Red Clubs (IRE) 125 – Consensus (IRE) 91 (Common   **80**
Grounds 118) [2015 86: p7g* t7.1g² p7g⁶ t7.1f³ t7.1g³ t7.1g⁶ 7.6d 7m³ 7m³ 8.1m⁴ p7g²
t8.6g² 7g³ 8g* 7.6g⁴ p8f p8g p8f⁵ t8.6g⁶ t7.1f p8m Dec 31] small, sturdy gelding: fairly
useful handicapper: won at Lingfield in January and Salisbury (amateur) in August: stays
8.5f: acts on polytrack, tapeta and any turf going: tried in visor prior to 2015: often leads.
David Evans

ALTAAYIL (IRE) 4 br.g. Sea The Stars (IRE) 140 – Alleluia 117 (Caerleon (USA) 132)   **84**
[2015 101: t12.2g* Apr 18] fairly useful performer: won maiden at Wolverhampton (by 4
lengths from Smart Motive) in April: stays 1¾m: acts on tapeta. *Sir Michael Stoute*

ALTARSHEED (IRE) 2 b.g. (Feb 23) Lilbourne Lad (IRE) 111 – Lilakiya (IRE) 60 (Dr   **101 p**
Fong (USA) 128) [2015 8m³ 8d³ p8f* Sep 22] €50,000F, 100,000Y: fifth foal: half-brother
to 3 winners, including useful winner up to 13.3f Karam Albaari (2-y-o 6f winner, by
King's Best) and 2-y-o 7f winner Run The Red Light (by Alfred Nobel): dam, 1½m winner,
half-sister to very smart winner up to 1¼m Linngari: best effort when
winning maiden at Lingfield (by 6 lengths from Cabinet Room) in September, staying on
strongly: likely to stay beyond 1m: will go on improving. *Richard Hannon*

AL THAKHIRA 4 b.f. Dubawi (IRE) 129 – Dahama 66 (Green Desert (USA) 127) [2015   **105**
108: t7.1m³ 7s⁶ 6g⁵ May 23] neat filly: useful performer: third in listed race at
Wolverhampton (2 lengths behind Sovereign Debt) in March: stayed 7f: acted on tapeta,
good to firm and good to soft going: often travelled strongly: covered by Toronado, sent to
France. *Marco Botti*

ALTHANIA (USA) 3 ch.f. Street Cry (IRE) 130 – Gabriellina Giof (Ashkalani (IRE) 128)   **83**
[2015 80: 8.3s 7m⁵ 8m² t9.5g* Jul 7] fairly useful performer: won maiden at Wolverhampton
(by 1¼ lengths from Amazing Speed) in July: stays 9.5f: acts on polytrack, tapeta and good
to firm going: front runner/races prominently. *John Gosden*

ALTHAROOS (IRE) 5 b.g. Sakhee (USA) 136 – Thamara (USA) (Street Cry (IRE) 130)   **94**
[2015 –: 8.5g⁴ 8.5g* 8d² 7.9g 10g* 8d* 9.8d 9g 8d Oct 16] good-topped, attractive gelding:
fairly useful handicapper: won at Beverley in May, Wetherby in July and Thirsk (by length
from Amood) in August: stays 1¼m: acts on any turf going. *Sally Hall*

ALWAYS A DREAM 2 b.f. (Jan 19) Oasis Dream 129 – Always Remembered (IRE)   **67**
(Galileo (IRE) 134) [2015 7.6g⁶ p7g p7g⁴ p7g p7m Dec 31] sturdy filly: first foal: dam
unraced close relative to Derby winner Motivator: fair maiden: will stay 1m+: acts on
polytrack. *Chris Wall*

ALWAYS RESOLUTE 4 b.g. Refuse To Bend (IRE) 128 – Mad Annie (USA) (Anabaa   **71**
(USA) 130) [2015 73: p12f⁶ p11g 10.4g 14.6m² 14.1g⁴ 13.3m² 14d* 16.2d⁶ Oct 16]
workmanlike gelding: fair handicapper: won at Haydock in September: stays 2m: acts on
good to firm and good to soft going: sometimes slowly away. *Timothy Jarvis*

ALWAYS SMILE (IRE) 3 b.f. Cape Cross (IRE) 129 – Eastern Joy (Dubai Destination   **112 p**
(USA) 127) [2015 78p: t8.6g* 8g* 8f² Jun 17] smallish, angular filly: smart form: won
handicaps at Wolverhampton in April and Doncaster (by ¾ length from Sahaafy) in May:

should also have won when nose second to Osaila in listed Sandringham Handicap at Royal Ascot, hanging left in front and caught post: stays 8.5f: not entirely straightforward (wanders/hangs in front), but remains with potential all being well. *Saeed bin Suroor*

ALWAYS WELCOME (USA) 2 ch.g. (Apr 23) Elusive Quality (USA) – No Matter **90 p**
What (USA) 110 (Nureyev (USA) 131) [2015 p8m² p8f² f7m² t7.1f* Dec 22] half-brother to several winners, including very smart winner up to 8.5f Rainbow View (2-y-o 7f/1m winner, by Dynaformer) and smart US performer up to 1½m Just As Well (by A P Indy): dam, 1m (in France)/9f (US Grade 1) winner, half-sister to US Grade 1 1¼m winner E Dubai: fairly useful form: won maiden at Wolverhampton by 1¼ lengths from War Glory) in December: stays 7f: tried in hood: open to further improvement. *John Gosden*

ALWAYS WILL 3 b.g. Sleeping Indian 122 – China Beads (Medicean 128) [2015 8.3g **60**
8.3m 10.2m⁵ p10f⁵ t12.2m² Nov 21] tall gelding: modest maiden: stays 1½m: acts on polytrack and tapeta: sometimes in headgear. *William Muir*

ALWILDA 5 gr.m. Hernando (FR) 127 – Albanova 119 (Alzao (USA) 117) [2015 100: **101**
16.4m 15.9g² 14m 13.4m 19.1s* p13g Oct 29] lengthy mare: useful performer: won listed race at Cologne by 1¾ lengths from Wasir) in October: second in listed race at Hamburg (½ length behind Eye In The Sky) in June: stays 19f: acts on polytrack, fibresand, soft and good to firm going: tried in headgear. *Sir Mark Prescott Bt*

ALYAA (IRE) 2 b.f. (Jan 17) Iffraaj 127 – Queenie Keen (IRE) 92 (Refuse To Bend (IRE) **70**
128) [2015 7g⁵ 6d⁶ p5m⁵ Nov 21] €46,000Y, €10,000 2-y-o: angular filly: first foal: dam, 6f winner, half-sister to useful winner up to 1m Diosypros Blue: fair maiden: best effort when fifth in maiden at Newmarket (4½ lengths behind Aljuljalah) in September. *Conrad Allen*

ALYDAY 2 ch.f. (Apr 13) Kyllachy 129 – Dayrose 94 (Daylami (IRE) 138) [2015 7d² **86 p**
Oct 31] sixth foal: half-sister to 3 winners, including very smart 1¼m-1½m winner Dubday (by Dubawi) and useful 1¾m winner Dannyday (by Dansili): dam, 9.7f/10.6f winner, half-sister to dam of high-class 1¼m performer Notnowcato: 14/1, not seen to best effect when second in maiden at Newmarket (4½ lengths behind Aljazzi) in October, not ideally placed: sure to progress. *Sir Michael Stoute*

ALYSSA 2 b.f. (Jan 28) Sir Percy 129 – Almiranta 63 (Galileo (IRE) 134) [2015 8g² 8v³ **77 p**
Oct 24] second foal: half-sister to smart French 2-y-o 1m winner Alea Iacta (by Invincible Spirit): dam, ran once, granddaughter of dual Champion Stakes winner Alborada: better effort when second in maiden at Ascot (2¼ lengths behind Dawn of Hope) in September, finishing well: will be suited by middle distances: remains open to improvement. *Ralph Beckett*

ALZAMMAAR (USA) 4 b.g. Birdstone (USA) 129 – Alma Mater 102 (Sadler's Wells **–**
(USA) 132) [2015 16d Oct 11] maiden: no form in 2015: best effort at 1¾m: acts on soft going: tried in headgear: in tongue tie sole start in 2015. *Warren Greatrex*

ALZEBARH (IRE) 2 ch.f. (Mar 9) Poet's Voice 126 – Dubai Pearl (IRE) (Refuse To **53 p**
Bend (IRE) 128) [2015 p7g 7.5g⁶ Sep 16] first foal: dam unraced half-sister to useful performer up to 1½m Saab Almanal: better effort when sixth in maiden at Beverley (10¼ lengths behind Renfrew Street) in September: should do better. *James Fanshawe*

AL ZUBARAH 2 b.f. (Mar 5) Exceed And Excel (AUS) 126 – Tropical Paradise (IRE) 116 **55 p**
(Verglas (IRE) 118) [2015 5g⁶ t5.1m⁶ Sep 5] 52,000F, £120,000Y: first foal: dam won up to 7f (2-y-o 6f winner): better effort when sixth in maiden at Wolverhampton (4½ lengths behind Fataawy) in September: entitled to do better. *John Quinn*

AMADEITY (IRE) 3 b.g. Amadeus Wolf 122 – Magadar (USA) 78 (Lujain (USA) 119) **68**
[2015 70: t8.6g² p10m⁶ t8.6m⁴ 11.6g 9.9g⁶ 13.1f Sep 13] fair maiden: stays 11.5f: acts on tapeta, best turf form on good going: often in headgear in 2015. *Jo Hughes*

AMADEUS DREAM (IRE) 3 b.g. Amadeus Wolf 122 – Spring Glory 73 (Dr Fong **–**
(USA) 128) [2015 –: 5.7f Apr 17] maiden: no form in 2015: in tongue tie sole start in 2015. *Milton Bradley*

AMANAAT (IRE) 2 b.c. (Feb 21) Exceed And Excel (AUS) 126 – Pietra Dura 96 (Cadeaux **91 p**
Genereux 131) [2015 p7g* Nov 18] 280,000Y: half-brother to 3 winners, including smart 7f-1¼m (US Grade 3) winner Turning Top (by Pivotal) and useful 2-y-o 6f winner Curly Wee (by Excellent Art): dam 2-y-o 7f winner who stayed 9.5f: 10/11, value for extra when won maiden at Kempton (by 1½ lengths from Enreaching) in November, readily: sure to progress. *John Gosden*

AMANTO (GER) 5 b.g. Medicean 128 – Amore (GER) (Lando (GER) 128) [2015 16s **67**
Oct 23] fair handicapper: should stay beyond 1½m: acts on soft going: in cheekpieces sole start in 2015. *Paul Nicholls*

AMAZE ME 3 ch.f. Aqlaam 125 – Princess Miletrian (IRE) 80 (Danehill (USA) 126) **98**
[2015 75: t8.6f² 10f³ 10.4g⁴ 8f 11.9g⁶ 12g 12d p10m Nov 14] lengthy filly: useful maiden:
third in listed race at Newmarket (2¾ lengths behind Jazzi Top) in May: stays 1½m: acts
on firm going: tried in hood in 2015. *Nick Littmoden*

AMAZEMENT (GER) 2 ch.c. (Mar 25) Lope de Vega (IRE) 125 – Aglow 90 (Spinning **– p**
World (USA) 130) [2015 p8f Dec 21] €28,000Y, resold 48,000Y: half-brother to several
winners abroad, including smart German 9.5f-11f winner Altair Star (by Kris Kin): dam
2-y-o 1m winner who stayed 1¼m: 5/1, eighth in maiden at Chelmsford (8¼ lengths
behind Cape Speed) in December: capable of better. *James Tate*

AMAZING BLUE SKY 9 b.g. Barathea (IRE) 127 – Azure Lake (USA) (Lac Ouimet **50**
(USA)) [2015 f12g³ f12d³ f11s* t12.2f³ f12g³ f12g⁵ 10g 9.9m 10.1g⁵ 10d 12d⁵ 12.4g 12d⁴ **a56**
12.1g⁶ t12.2f³ t12.2m f12g* f14g⁶ f12g² f11g Dec 29] workmanlike gelding: modest
handicapper: won at Southwell (amateur) in February and November: stays 12.5f: acts on
all-weather, good to firm and heavy going: tried in headgear. *Ruth Carr*

AMAZING CHARM 3 ch.f. King's Best (USA) 132 – Bint Doyen 83 (Doyen (IRE) 132) **77**
[2015 8.3d² p9.2g⁴ 8s² 7d Sep 27] strong filly: first foal: dam, 2-y-o 7f winner who stayed
1¼m, half-sister to smart winner up to 9f Zoning: fair maiden: stays 9f. *Clive Brittain*

AMAZING MARIA (IRE) 4 gr.f. Mastercraftsman (IRE) 129 – Messias da Silva **120**
(USA) 89 (Tale of The Cat (USA) 113) [2015 88: 8m³ 8g³ 8f* 8m* 8g* 8g Sep 12]
      In August, racecourse rumour had it that Aidan O'Brien might be leaving his
role as trainer at Ballydoyle at the end of the season. The rumours, examined more
closely in the essay on Gleneagles, were never substantiated and eventually died
down altogether, though there was something to be gleaned from an understanding
that the Coolmore partners, John Magnier, Michael Tabor and Derrick Smith, had
considered David O'Meara a likely successor in the event that they might need one.
O'Meara's exceptional rise through the ranks from virtually a standing start to a top
ten trainer in little more than five years has made him a hot prospect among the new,
younger crop of trainers in British Flat racing. O'Meara's stock-in-trade has been
the improvement he has wrought in horses taken from other yards but that model
will take a trainer only so far, regardless of his skill. The patronage of one or more
of the leading owners is vital if a yard is to enjoy sustained top-level success and
O'Meara is already approaching the stage where he will need that sort of support
if he is to continue his rise to the top. In the latest season, O'Meara sent out nine
pattern winners and added three more Group 1s to the two he won in 2014 when
his breakthrough finally came in the biggest races. Two of his Group 1 wins in the

*Qipco Falmouth Stakes, Newmarket—Amazing Maria (centre) comes out on top in a tactical affair,
beating Euro Charline (No.4) and Avenir Certain (spots); Bawina (widest) and Lucida (second left)
are chief amongst those not seen to best effect*

Prix Rothschild, Deauville—
a second Group 1 success for the thriving Amazing Maria (third from right);
Ervedya (right) suffers her only defeat of the season in second, ahead of Bawina (second left)

latest season came from Amazing Maria, a four-year-old filly who very much fits the O'Meara blueprint, having joined him from the Ed Dunlop stable after making little impact in pattern races as a three-year-old.

Amazing Maria had been a highly promising two-year-old, winning a maiden at Glorious Goodwood (by six lengths) and the Prestige Stakes at the same course little more than three weeks later. She had been available at around 14/1 in the days leading up to the One Thousand Guineas the following spring, but wasn't declared after an unsatisfactory scope. Amazing Maria failed to stay in the Oaks on her eventual reappearance and subsequently finished down the field in Group 3 events at Deauville and Doncaster (starting at 25/1 in the Sceptre Stakes). Her owner Sir Robert Ogden, one of the most powerful jumps owners in the country until turning his attentions to the Flat in recent years, sent Amazing Maria to O'Meara over the winter to see if a change of scenery and routine might revive her fortunes. O'Meara started off Amazing Maria in a handicap at Ascot where she shaped quite well to finish third behind Temptress and she ran to a similar level on form when third in the Group 3 Lanwades Stud Stakes at the Curragh a fortnight later.

Stepped up in class, Amazing Maria appeared next in the much stronger Group 2 Duke of Cambridge Stakes at Royal Ascot where she was virtually unconsidered, sent off at 25/1. The 11/8-on shot Integral was a flop which, along with a steady pace in the race, increased Amazing Maria's chances, enabling her to make the best use of her speed. She quickened from behind to beat Rizeena by two lengths, creating one of the shocks of the meeting and, at the same time, putting her trainer's name in lights again after his string of big-race successes the previous autumn, headed by wins in the Sprint Cup at Haydock for G Force and the Prix de l'Abbaye by Move In Time, the first of them having helped to put the stable into the top ten in the end-of-year tables in Britain.

The Falmouth Stakes at Newmarket is traditionally the first opportunity for three-year-old fillies to take on the older fillies and mares over a mile. The field in 2015 contained neither the One Thousand Guineas winner Legatissimo nor Coronation Stakes winner Ervedya, leaving Lucida, second at Newmarket and third at Ascot, beaten less than a length each time, to carry the mantle for the classic generation. She started 2/1 favourite, with the previous year's Poule d'Essai des Pouliches and Prix de Diane winner Avenir Certain next at 7/2. Bawina at 5/1 and Fintry at 6/1, successful in the Group 2 Prix du Muguet and Group 3 Prix Bertrand du Breuil respectively earlier in the season, were also shorter in the betting than Amazing Maria who was sent off at 17/2, just ahead of Arabian Queen, the only three-year-old in the race besides Lucida, and Euro Charline, who had been withdrawn after refusing to load in the Duke of Cambridge. Arabian Queen took the field along at a steady pace from Euro Charline on her outside, with Amazing Maria settled by James Doyle into second-last. Doyle made a move just under three furlongs from the finish, drawing alongside Euro Charline at the two-furlong pole as Arabian Queen began to drop away. Amazing Maria got on top inside the final furlong and won by a length, with little more than a quarter of a length separating the next five runners, Euro Charline finishing a head in front of Avenir Certain for second. Lucida managed only sixth of seven in a race which favoured those, like Amazing Maria, with a turn of foot. Timeform now publishes a finishing speed percentage as a part of its results service and that percentage for the last three furlongs of the Falmouth was 116.0%; a well-run race over a mile on the July Course would normally produce a figure of around 101.5% for the same three-furlong sectional.

After winning two races that had primarily tested speed, Amazing Maria faced a much tougher test when she lined up for the Prix Rothschild at Deauville on her next start, on the first Sunday in August. She had beaten such as Rizeena, Fintry and Bawina, who were among her rivals, but she had not met Ervedya who had remained unbeaten as a three-year-old before the Rothschild, winning the Prix Imprudence, Poule d'Essai des Pouliches and Coronation Stakes. The Rothschild turned into yet another steadily-run race, in which outsider Amulet took them along. Amazing Maria was eventually settled in mid-field, just behind Ervedya who raced in third. The favourite was moved to the rail around three furlongs out, while Olivier Peslier on Amazing Maria kept a straight course four horses wide. The sprint for home started about two furlongs out, with the field fanning out across the track. Amazing Maria and Ervedya had the race between them over the final furlong and, once again, it was Amazing Maria's turn of foot that gave her a decisive edge and she crossed the line a length and a quarter ahead of Ervedya, who finished the same distance ahead of third-placed Bawina. Though the race had again panned out ideally for Amazing Maria, it couldn't have gone much more smoothly for Ervedya, either, so it seemed unfair to say that the winner was flattered. She ended the season as the only horse to beat Ervedya, who won the Prix du Moulin at Longchamp on her only subsequent start. Amazing Maria was also seen only once more, in the Matron Stakes at Leopardstown. The prospect of her completing a four-timer looked bleak from some way out and she eventually finished a tame seventh of nine behind Legatissimo. No specific reason was found for Amazing Maria's performance, which seemed to be taken as an indication that the exertions of her summer campaign had finally caught up with her.

Amazing Maria (IRE) (gr.f. 2011)	Mastercraftsman (IRE) (gr 2006)	Danehill Dancer (b 1993)	Danehill
			Mira Adonde
		Starlight Dreams (gr 1995)	Black Tie Affair
			Reves Celestes
	Messias da Silva (USA) (b or br 2005)	Tale of The Cat (b or br 1994)	Storm Cat
			Yarn
		Indy Power (b or br 1997)	A P Indy
			Clever Power

The tall, lengthy Amazing Maria is the second foal out of the Tale of The Cat mare Messias da Silva, who ran half a dozen times for Jeremy Noseda in Sir Robert Ogden's colours, winning a six-furlong maiden on the all-weather at Lingfield on the second of two starts as a juvenile. Messias da Silva had been bought by Ogden for 700,000 dollars (having gone through the ring for 250,000 dollars as a yearling) at Fasig-Tipton's sale for two-year-olds in training in March 2007. At the end of her racing career, Messias da Silva was entered in the 2008 December Sales, but she was withdrawn and has since produced four foals that have all raced in the mauve and pink check, white sleeves of Ogden. The first, a colt by Tiger Hill named Vulcan, ran just once for David Simcock in 2012 and has since been reported as dead. The two progeny that followed Amazing Maria also made the track in 2015. The three-year-old filly Madame Butterfly (by Rip Van Winkle) showed fair form when runner-up in a couple of maidens for David O'Meara, and the two-year-old colt Constantino, a Danehill Dancer close relative of Amazing Maria (who is by a son of Danehill Dancer, Mastercraftsman), won a maiden at Ayr over seven furlongs for Richard Fahey. Messias da Silva, who also has a yearling sister and a foal brother to Amazing Maria, is one of four winners produced by Indy Power, who ran in the States at three without success. Indy Power comes from a good North American family, her dam Clever Power having won the Morven Stakes at Meadowlands in the last year which that race held graded status. Clever Power in turn is one of eight winners out of Clever Miss, who won four times from twenty-six starts and went on to produce three graded winners, the others being Grade 2 winner Integra and Grade 3 winner Secret Odds. Clever Miss was a half-sister to a good sprinter called Clever Trick, an eighteen-time winner who went on to be a successful sire. For all her North American-centric pedigree, Amazing Maria has raced only on turf and has proved herself on firm ground (raced only once on softer than good). She stays a mile and usually responds generously to pressure, her most potent weapon being her turn of finishing speed. She reportedly stays in training. *David O'Meara*

AMAZING SPEED (IRE) 3 gr.f. Shamardal (USA) 129 – Kind Words (USA) (A P Indy (USA) 131) [2015 79§ p7f² 8f³ 8g² t9.5g² 8m² 8d⁴ Oct 5] second foal: dam twice-raced sister to top-class US 9f/1¼m performer Bernardini out of US Grade 1 2-y-o 8.5f winner Cara Rafaela: fairly useful maiden: probably stays 9.5f: acts on good to firm going: tried in headgear: usually races prominently, often travels strongly: temperamental: sold 42,000 gns, sent to Saudi Arabia. *Saeed bin Suroor* **83 §**

AMAZING STAR (IRE) 10 b.g. Soviet Star (USA) 128 – Sadika (IRE) 55 (Bahhare (USA) 122) [2015 83§, a76§: p10m t9.5f⁴ t12.2g⁴ 11.6m p8f Sep 12] lengthy gelding: fair handicapper: left John Flint after fourth start: stays 1½m: acts on polytrack, tapeta and any turf going: tried in cheekpieces: sometimes wears tongue tie: often races towards rear: one to be wary of. *Alan Berry* **66 §**

AMAZOUR (IRE) 3 b.g. Azamour (IRE) 130 – Choose Me (IRE) 109 (Choisir (AUS) 126) [2015 75: 6s* 7g* 8f⁶ 7m 6g 7g Sep 26] angular gelding: useful handicapper: won at Hamilton and Haydock in May: stays 1m: acts on firm and soft going. *Ismail Mohammed* **102**

AMBELLA (IRE) 5 gr.m. Dark Angel (IRE) 113 – Showmesomething (IRE) 62 (Mujadil (USA) 119) [2015 66: t7.1f Jan 5] modest handicapper: stays 8.5f: acts on polytrack, tapeta and soft going: often wears visor: sometimes slowly away, often races towards rear. *Ian Williams* **54**

AMBER CRYSTAL 3 b.f. Multiplex 114 – Glitz (IRE) 54 (Hawk Wing (USA) 136) [2015 75: f5s⁶ p7g 7m 5g² 6m* 6m⁶ 5.7f⁴ 6g 7d² Jul 29] fair performer: won seller at Leicester in June: stays 6f: acts on firm and soft going: often wears headgear: usually leads. *John Gallagher* **71**

AMBER FLUSH 6 b.m. Sir Harry Lewis (USA) 127 – Sari Rose (FR) (Vertical Speed (FR) 120) [2015 18s² Oct 19] modest hurdler: 50/1, possibly flattered when second in minor event at Pontefract (10 lengths behind Nearly Caught) on Flat debut. *Martin Smith* **73**

AMBER MYSTIQUE 2 ch.f. (Jan 31) Sakhee (USA) 136 – Dame de Noche 102 (Lion Cavern (USA) 117) [2015 6d² t6m⁴ 8g³ Sep 24] fourth foal: sister to winner up to 1¼m Nemushka (2-y-o 7f winner) and half-sister to 11.5f winner Mendelita (by Archipenko): dam 5f-1m winner: fair maiden: best effort when second in maiden at Leicester (2 lengths behind Continental Lady) in July: bred to be suited by 7f+. *Richard Fahey* **75**

AMBITIOUS BOY 6 bl.g. Striking Ambition 122 – Cherished Love (IRE) (Tomba 119) [2015 80, a91: 6d 6g t6f² t7.1f p7d⁶ Nov 30] fairly useful handicapper: second at Wolverhampton in October: stays 6f: acts on polytrack, tapeta and good to firm going: usually races nearer last than first. *Sarah Hollinshead* **82**

AMBITIOUS ICARUS 6 b.g. Striking Ambition 122 – Nesting Box (Grand Lodge (USA) 125) [2015 84: 6d 5d³ 6s⁶ 5.1s* 5s⁴ 6g 6d³ 6m⁶ 5g⁴ 5m⁶ 5g 6g⁵ 5m* 6g 6d 6g 6.1g 5.1d Oct 14] tall, leggy gelding: fairly useful handicapper: won at Nottingham in May and Newcastle (by 1¾ lengths from Chilworth Icon) in August: third at Doncaster in June: stays 6f: acts on polytrack, good to firm and heavy going: usually wears headgear. *Richard Guest* **90**

AMBITIOUS ROSIE 4 b.f. Striking Ambition 122 – Cerulean Rose 78 (Bluegrass Prince (IRE) 110) [2015 p7f 6g⁶ t7.1g p8g p7g p8g p7g⁶ Dec 10] third foal: dam, 5f winner, half-sister to smart sprinter Turn On The Style: modest maiden: best effort at 6f: tried in cheekpieces. *Tony Carroll* **56**

AMBLESIDE 5 b.g. Cape Cross (IRE) 129 – Zarara (USA) (Manila (USA)) [2015 85: **85**
10s⁴ 12.1m³ 12m 12g 12g⁴ 15.9m³ 16.4m 12g 10g² t9.5m* t8.6f Oct 20] fairly useful
handicapper: won at Wolverhampton (by ¾ length from Scurr Mist) in October: stays 2m:
acts on tapeta and good to firm going: tried in headgear: not totally straightforward.
Michael Easterby

AMBONNAY ROUGE (IRE) 3 ch.f. Arakan (USA) 123 – Ambonnay 89 (Ashkalani –
(IRE) 128) [2015 –: t7.1f⁶ p6m⁶ Mar 5] maiden: no form in 2015: in headgear in 2015.
John Butler

AMBRIEL (IRE) 2 gr.f. (Mar 7) Dark Angel (IRE) 113 – Skehana (IRE) 69 (Mukaddamah **77**
(USA) 125) [2015 7.2d⁵ 7g³ 7.2g* Sep 18] 32,000Y: half-sister to several winners,
including useful winner up to 1m Jake's Destiny (2-y-o 6f winner, by Desert Style) and 1m
winner Molten Lava (by Rock of Gibraltar): dam, 2-y-o 7f winner, half-sister to smart
sprinter Fayr Jag: fair performer: best effort when winning maiden at Ayr (by 2¾ lengths
from Prying Pandora) in September: raced only at 7f. *Michael Dods*

AMBUSCADE 2 b.f. (Mar 6) Dick Turpin (IRE) 127 – Tarqua (IRE) (King Charlemagne **57**
(USA) 120) [2015 p8m⁶ t1.1g p6g⁶ Dec 16] second foal: half-sister to useful 2-y-o 5f
winner Field Game (by Pastoral Pursuits): dam, of little account, half-sister to useful
sprinter Cool Creek: modest maiden: best effort when sixth in maiden at Lingfield (8½
lengths behind Natural Beauty) in November. *Hughie Morrison*

AMENABLE (IRE) 8 b.g. Bertolini (USA) 125 – Graceful Air (IRE) 69 (Danzero **78**
(AUS)) [2015 80: f7d² f6d² f6g* f7g* f7g f7d p6f p6g⁶ f7g² t7.1g⁶ f6g⁴ f6g⁴ 6s² 5g f7d⁶ **a68**
7m f7d p6f 5.1g p6f 6d f8g⁵ f7g f6g³ f7m³ f7g³ f8g⁵ Dec 18] fair handicapper: won at
Southwell (twice) in January: stays 7f: acts on polytrack, fibresand, good to firm and heavy
going: often wears headgear. *Conor Dore*

AMERICAN ARTIST (IRE) 3 ch.c. Danehill Dancer (IRE) 117 – American Adventure **97**
(USA) (Miswaki (USA) 124) [2015 87p: 8.5g p8g⁶ 8.1m* 8.3m* 8.3m² 10.3m* 9g³
Sep 25] sturdy colt: useful performer: won handicaps at Sandown in July and Windsor in
August, and minor event at Doncaster (by 1¾ lengths from Super Kid) in September: stays
10.5f: acts on good to firm going: front runner/races prominently. *Roger Varian*

AMERICAN HOPE (USA) 4 b.g. Lemon Drop Kid (USA) 131 – Cedrat (FR) (Enrique **106**
121) [2015 116: p7g² 6g 7m 8f⁶ Jun 17] lengthy gelding: useful performer: second in
minor event at Kempton (head behind Ninjago) in March: stays 1m: acts on polytrack and
firm going: often races freely: sold 210,000 gns in July, has joined Saeed bin Suroor.
Mike Murphy

AMERICAN HUSTLE (IRE) 3 b.f. Jeremy (USA) 122 – Love In May (IRE) 80 (City **75**
On A Hill (USA) 114) [2015 7g⁴ 8g³ 8d² 8g² 8g² 7.2g² Oct 13] fourth foal: sister to smart
7f-8.5f winner (including at 2 yrs) Gabrial's Kaka: dam 2-y-o 5f/6f winner: fair maiden:
best effort at 7f: best form on good going. *Brian Ellison*

AMERICAN PHAROAH (USA) 3 b.c. Pioneerof The Nile (USA) 117 – Little- **138**
princessemma (USA) (Yankee Gentleman (USA)) [2015 126: a8.5s* a9f* a10f*
a9.5s* a12f* a9f* a10f² a10f* Oct 31]

England's triple crown, once regarded as the pinnacle of achievement for a
thoroughbred on the British turf, seemed on the way to being reduced to the status
of a sporting anachronism until Camelot's connections revived interest in it by
aiming the 2012 Two Thousand Guineas and Derby winner Camelot at the St Leger.
Camelot's defeat at 5/2-on at Doncaster—the first of his career—by 25/1-shot Encke
was a big anti-climax at the time, though the winner's reputation was subsequently
tarnished when it was discovered in April 2013 that he had been injected with
banned anabolic steroids. The ill-fated Encke kept the St Leger (he had passed a
routine test after that race) but, along with another twenty-one Godolphin horses
uncovered in the biggest and most shocking doping scandal in the history of British
racing, he was suspended from racing for six months and missed the whole of his
four-year-old season (he failed to repeat the St Leger form in three starts as a five-
year-old before suffering a fatal injury on the gallops). Nijinsky did something that
no colt had done for thirty-five years when he won all three English classics open to
him, back in 1970, and Camelot is the only colt to have lined up in the St Leger since
then with an opportunity to land the triple crown (Oh So Sharp won the so-called
fillies' triple crown in 1985). The American Triple Crown of the Kentucky Derby,
the Preakness Stakes and the Belmont Stakes was won no fewer than three times
in the space of six runnings in the 'seventies. Although nearly four decades passed

Kentucky Derby presented by Yum! Brands, Churchill Downs—
favourite American Pharoah overcomes a wide draw, beating Firing Line (spots on silks)
and stablemate Dortmund (out of picture) in front of a record crowd

until the oddly-spelled American Pharoah became America's twelfth Triple Crown winner, North American racing fans continued to regard winning the series as a realistic target for the country's top three-year-olds.

Like England's triple crown, the American version is decided in races over different distances, though the Kentucky Derby, the Preakness and the Belmont are much closer together in distance than the English triple crown races, and they take place in the space of only five weeks in May and June. The list of Triple Crown challengers who had failed in the final race, since Affirmed triumphed in all three in 1978, was a lengthy one, stretching from Spectacular Bid in 1979 to California Chrome in 2014. There were twelve in all, thirteen if I'll Have Another, scratched the day before the Belmont in 2012 with a tendon injury, is counted. The others in the dozen who kept American racing fans on the edge of their seats during the editions of the Belmont Stakes for which they lined up (two-thirds of them starting odds-on) were: Pleasant Colony (1981), Alysheba (1987), Sunday Silence (1989), Silver Charm (1997), Real Quiet (1998), Charismatic (1999), War Emblem (2002), Funny Cide (2003), Smarty Jones (2004) and Big Brown (2008). All except Alysheba, War Emblem, Big Brown and California Chrome reached a place, with Real Quiet coming closest, beaten a nose by Victory Gallop, while Sunday Silence, Silver Charm and Smarty Jones also finished second in the Belmont. The demands made on an American three-year-old going for the Triple Crown are notoriously tough (most of them arrive there race-hardened sometimes by several preparatory races in the months beforehand) and there have been seasons when very few of the good three-year-olds have been left standing by the autumn, with a knock-on effect on the major late-season championship events such as the Breeders' Cup. Silver Charm, for example, was off the track for six months after the Belmont (though he did come back to win the Dubai World Cup at four) and Real Quiet wasn't seen out at all (although he also returned to the track at four), while Charismatic fractured his near-fore in the Belmont (fortunately saved for stud) and Smarty Jones wasn't raced again due to chronic bruising in all four fetlock joints. Fewer horses run in all three classics nowadays—American Pharoah was the only one to contest all three in the latest season—and that has led to speculation that American horses are not so tough as they used to be 'because the use of drugs has weakened the breed.' Whether that particular statement is true or not, the fact that drugs banned nearly everywhere else are used so liberally in American racing has undoubtedly contributed to the game's fading popularity over the years with the domestic sporting audience, making the aggressive promotion of racing's biggest days, which still manage to attract plenty of media coverage, more important than ever. When a horse like American Pharoah comes along, racing's problems seem to be put into suspended animation as those in the sport put aside their differences to capitalise on the latest star's popularity.

Let's be honest, British racing isn't in the best position to be criticising others—readers need look no further than the opening paragraph of this essay for evidence of drug cheating—but, when interest in American Pharoah has faded, American racing will again have to address its problems with drugs and its alarming equine fatality rates, among other things. The attitude towards drug use on racehorses in North America is far too permissive and a long way out of line with other major racing countries. As well as alienating American sports fans, this has increasingly come to affect the international perception of performances recorded on North American racecourses and has depressed international demand over the years for American bloodstock (though European spending on yearlings has shown some signs of recovery in the last couple of years based on the success in Europe of the progeny of stallions such as War Front and the now-deceased Scat Daddy). The efforts of the Water, Hay, Oats Alliance in trying to lobby Congress to legislate—on horse welfare grounds—against the use of raceday medication have certainly been laudable, but its supporters have come up against very strong opposition from leading trainers, backed up by their vets and others. The majority of horses in North America (up to 95% on some calculations) race on the diuretic drug furosemide (lasix) which has been proven in extensive field trials in South Africa to enhance performance. American Pharoah's trainer Bob Baffert, who is in the sport's Hall of Fame, is just one of many of the leading lights of North American racing wedded to the use of furosemide on racedays. He is on record as saying that a ban on furosemide would mean 'the end of the sport'. This subject has been covered many times over the years in *Racehorses* (and there is more on it in the essay on Hit It A Bomb) but it is not one to dwell on when celebrating a horse whose magnificent achievements have earned him a place among the giants of racing history.

When American Pharoah went on to win America's richest race the Breeders' Cup Classic, after completing the Triple Crown, he became the first winner of what has been dubbed American racing's 'Grand Slam' (the Breeders' Cup began in 1984). In the process, he earned the joint-highest rating (with Cigar) of any North American-trained thoroughbred since Timeform began publishing ratings for that continent's best horses in 1993, the year that the 'Top Horses Abroad' section first appeared in this Annual. His trainer, who has had many top-class performers through his stable, called American Pharoah 'the perfect racehorse' and there is no doubt that the horse's emergence was a welcome tonic for American racing. Coolmore purchased him, with additional increments for further victories, for around a rumoured twenty million dollars (probably half his value by the end of the campaign) just before he won the Belmont. American Pharoah will begin his stallion career at Ashford Stud in Kentucky in 2016 when he will stand at a fee of 200,000 dollars (the most expensive stallion in North America at the current time is champion sire Tapit at 300,000 dollars).

Like Europe's Horse of the Year, the Derby and Prix de l'Arc winner Golden Horn, American Pharoah was offered as a yearling but failed to reach his reserve (bought back at Saratoga for 300,000 dollars). He ran three times as a two-year-old and, after finishing fifth on his debut, he made all in Grade 1 company on his last two starts—in the Del Mar Futurity (one of the final big races at Del Mar on polytrack before its switch back to dirt) and in the FrontRunner Stakes at Santa Anita (on dirt). Those wins, by nearly five lengths and by a comfortable three and a quarter lengths respectively, would have made him favourite for the Breeders' Cup Juvenile but he wasn't seen out after Santa Anita, suffering a foot injury in training. American Pharoah began his three-year-old career towards the head of the market for the Kentucky Derby (sponsored by Yum! Brands) for which he was warmed up in two races at Oaklawn Park, both of which he won by a wide margin. He outclassed six rivals in the Grade 2 Rebel Stakes in March and never looked in the slightest danger when starting at 10/1-on and trouncing a better field in the Arkansas Derby by eight lengths. The Arkansas Derby, which attracted a crowd of 67,500, is a race that American Pharoah's stable has tended to target in recent years with its best three-year-old, but, in the latest season, the string also included the big, powerful Dortmund who lined up for the Kentucky Derby as second favourite to American Pharoah after stretching his unbeaten run to six, his most recent win coming in the Santa Anita Derby (the pair had different owners and their trainer diplomatically dodged questions before the Kentucky Derby about which was the better). Third favourite behind the Baffert-trained pair in a strong field was one of three saddled by Todd Pletcher, Carpe Diem, whose only defeat in five races had come when second in the Breeders' Cup Juvenile on his final two-year-old start. Pletcher had another fancied contender in the unbeaten Materiality, unraced at two but having most recently completed an impressive hat-trick with victory over the Breeders' Cup Juvenile third Upstart in the Florida Derby. Also prominent in the betting was Firing Line, trained by former Newmarket trainer Simon Callaghan, son of Neville Callaghan. Firing Line had been beaten in a protracted battle with Dortmund in the Robert B. Lewis Stakes at Santa Anita in February before completing his preparation with an easy win in the Grade 3 Sunland Derby.

The Godolphin-owned Wood Memorial winner Frosted was also among those Kentucky Derby runners with connections familiar to European racegoers, as was the Mike de Kock-trained UAE Derby winner Mubtaahij, who was the only runner not on lasix. The field was reduced from the maximum permitted twenty to eighteen by two late withdrawals and American Pharoah's wide draw meant that he was always likely to have to cover more ground than his main rivals. He raced wide, shadowing the rail-hugging Dortmund who set the pace from Firing Line in front of a record crowd for the race of 170,513. It became clear from some way out that only these three were going to count. They turned for home with Dortmund still in front and Firing Line edging out towards the middle of the track, with American Pharoah on his outside. Firing Line headed Dortmund over a furlong out but the very strongly-ridden American Pharoah collared him inside the final furlong to win by a length, with Dortmund a further two lengths away third, just ahead of the staying-on Frosted in fourth. Materiality came sixth and Carpe Diem tenth. Veteran jockey Victor Espinoza, riding his third Kentucky Derby winner and his second in succession, was criticised by some European watchers for being too hard on American Pharoah, using his whip no fewer than twenty-six times in the home straight, but he justified his ride—which would have earned him a long suspension and a sizeable fine had it been in Britain—by saying that 'the other horse was tough, he wasn't going away … American Pharoah had never been tested before and I had to ride him hard.'

American Pharoah's winning performance was the best in the race since Big Brown's in 2008 and he gave his trainer a fourth Kentucky Derby winner, putting him joint second in the list behind six-times winning trainer Ben Jones who handled the 1941 and 1948 Triple Crown winners Whirlaway and Citation (although Ben Jones is shown as the trainer of Citation for the Kentucky Derby and his prep race, his son Jimmy had taken over the stable and stepped aside to allow father Ben to be designated as the winning trainer; Jimmy Jones is shown in the official records as

Citation's trainer when he won the Preakness and the Belmont). Baffert's three other Kentucky Derby winners, Silver Charm (1997), Real Quiet (1998) and War Emblem (2002, ridden by Espinoza), each went on to take the second leg of the Triple Crown, the Preakness, to earn their own shot at becoming America's Triple Crown champion. American Pharoah's victory in the Kentucky Derby provided an overdue success in the race for Egyptian-born owner Ahmed Zayat, who first came to the States to study as a teenager and whose large Zayat Stables operation had housed the runner-up three times in the six previous years—with American Pharoah's sire Pioneerof The Nile in 2009 followed by Nehro in 2011 and Bodemeister in 2012—and had also had the hot ante-post favourite Eskendereya (trained by Todd Pletcher) in 2010, only for that horse to suffer a career-ending leg injury just before the race.

The Xpressbet.com Preakness Stakes at Pimlico, two weeks after the Kentucky Derby, featured a rematch (over half a furlong shorter) between the first three at Churchill Downs. Joining the trio in a field of eight, watched by another record crowd of 131,680, were the Kentucky Derby fifth Danzig Moon and the thirteenth Mr Z (sold by Zayat Stables to Calumet Farm between the two races). However, the pair who eventually chased home odds-on American Pharoah in a mudbath, after torrential rain hit the course, had not made the line-up at Churchill Downs. The long shot Tale of Verve had missed the cut by one—Kentucky Derby places are allocated according to points earned in nominated preparatory races—and Kentucky Derby plans for Divining Rod had been shelved after he came a well-beaten third to Carpe Diem in the Tampa Bay Derby. American Pharoah was soon in the lead at Pimlico and comfortably forged clear in the home straight to win by seven lengths and a length from Tale of Verve and Divining Rod, without Espinoza having to resort to his whip at all this time. Dortmund and Firing Line were both well below their best, almost certainly unsuited by the very sloppy conditions on the day (the winning time was the slowest for sixty-five years). American Pharoah was Bob Baffert's sixth winner of the Preakness and he admitted to being 'scared' beforehand when the heavens opened to change the going into a quagmire from the expected fast, dry conditions ('Mind you, the day I don't get nervous you better check my pulse, I'm dead!').

Xpressbet.com Preakness Stakes, Pimlico—a deluge prior to racing turns conditions sloppy but proves no barrier to American Pharoah who runs out an impressive winner; Tale of Verve (only third in the photo) stays on from a long way back to overhaul Divining Rod for second

Following up his trainer's post-race statement after the Preakness that American Pharoah was an 'incredible horse … great horses do great things', American Pharoah's owner added that 'the sign of a good horse is no matter what is thrown in his face he finds a way to win … if he comes out of this race well, we could be talking history.' Andrew Beyer, the *Washington Post*'s long-serving columnist whose speed figures are revered by many in North America, was among the doubters, urging his readers 'not to bet on him … he won't be on any of my exacta or trifecta tickets.' Beyer pointed out that the factors that had foiled previous Triple Crown bids since 1978 applied just as forcefully to American Pharoah as to those before him who had failed. American racehorses were 'less robust and need more time to recuperate between races than when Secretariat, Seattle Slew and Affirmed swept the Triple Crown.' The tradition of the Triple Crown, with its three races in five weeks, was 'out of place in contemporary racing' and 'now formidably difficult.' The difficulty, Beyer wrote, was heightened by the fact that the final leg is over a mile and a half, a distance that 'no U.S. horses are bred to run.' The Belmont Stakes, run over a more galloping track than either Churchill Downs or Pimlico, was the 'only really significant mile-and-a-half race on dirt … it's a crap shoot as to who will get the distance, in fact when you look at the terrible speed figures in recent years, nobody gets the distance.'

Ironically, the expansion and influence of Coolmore, who pulled off something of a coup to secure the breeding rights to American Pharoah, initially probably played a part in creating a shortage of what might be called 'staying' sires in North America. Coolmore's success was founded on the strategy devised by Vincent O'Brien, John Magnier and Robert Sangster in the 'seventies of purchasing the best yearlings, with top pedigrees, from North America, with the aim of turning them into European classic winners and standing the successful ones at stud. Some of the best North American middle-distance bloodlines ended up being concentrated at Coolmore, largely through sons of Northern Dancer who became the height of fashion, with a beneficial knock-on for the whole of Ireland's bloodstock industry whose influence has spread worldwide. The year before Affirmed won his Triple Crown, the O'Brien-trained American-bred import, The Minstrel, bought as a yearling at Keeneland in 1975, became the first big success for the new strategy. Another of the 1977 racing successes was Alleged, purchased at a two-year-old horses-in-training auction. The embryonic Coolmore operation made the best possible start when the syndications of The Minstrel and Alleged—both sold back to the States—returned a combined twenty-five million dollars to swell the coffers for further purchases and provide the financial security to allow Coolmore to begin keeping some of the best trained at Ballydoyle for stud in Ireland. Northern Dancer's

Belmont Stakes Presented by DraftKings, Belmont Park—history is made as American Pharoah becomes the first since Affirmed in 1978 to win the Triple Crown; Frosted (blinkers) is no match for the winner in the straight but hangs on for second ahead of Keen Ice (left of the two horses behind Frosted)

son Sadler's Wells went on to establish himself as the greatest sire in European bloodstock history and his own sons, most notably Galileo, have maintained the pre-eminence of the Northern Dancer line, especially in Europe.

Commercial breeders in North America have, at the same time, tended to concentrate on speed as the racing there has increasingly featured a programme of big races centred around a mile to a mile and a quarter, the latter becoming more and more the theoretical distance limit for horses bred for North America's dirt. Robustness and soundness are also needed for the Triple Crown and it is interesting that modern-day top horses in America tend to be raced less often than their predecessors, the three-year-old campaigns of Triple Crown contenders rarely reaching double figures, as they once used to. Secretariat ran twelve times in his Triple Crown-winning season, while Affirmed had eleven races as a three-year-old; further back, Citation won nineteen (including a walkover) of his twenty starts from six furlongs to two miles at three, his campaign including taking in a race between the Preakness and the Belmont. Gone are the days when it was the norm for a top three-year-old to contest all three Triple Crown races. There has been a growing perception, for example, that running in the Preakness, so soon after the Kentucky Derby, can take the edge off a horse for the Belmont (one of California Chrome's owners found himself in hot water when suggesting that horses who don't run in the Kentucky Derby should not be able to contest the two other legs, accusing the connections of Tonalist and Commissioner—who didn't run in either the Derby or the Preakness—of taking 'the coward's way out' after their horses had finished first and second in the 2014 Belmont).

Tale of Verve was the only runner from the Preakness to take on American Pharoah again at Belmont Park, but five of the six other runners in the latest Belmont Stakes (sponsored by DraftKings) had been rested since the Kentucky Derby, headed by Frosted, Materiality, Keen Ice and Mubtaahij, who had come fourth, sixth, seventh and eighth at Churchill Downs (Firing Line and Dortmund were notable absentees from the Belmont after their below-form efforts in the Preakness). American Pharoah's entry into the history books was achieved with a convincing 'wire-to-wire' victory, his rivals gifting him an uncontested lead which allowed Espinoza to dictate an even pace which resulted in American Pharoah setting one of the fastest times in Belmont history, the fastest since the outstanding Point Given (the only previous winner of the race trained by Bob Baffert) who won the 2001 running by twelve and a quarter lengths. Point Given won the last two legs of the Triple Crown, after being beaten in the Kentucky Derby, but he suffered a career-ending injury to his near-fore when winning the Travers Stakes at Saratoga at the end of August, his retirement shattering the summer dream of a clash between him and dual Derby and King George winner Galileo in the Breeders' Cup Classic (Galileo managed only sixth behind Tiznow in that race on his only start on dirt, reportedly returning with swollen eyes and sore heels). American Pharoah's superiority at Belmont Park was manifest—he saw the trip out really well, travelling as strongly at the finish as at any stage—and, with the crowd of 90,000 in raptures, he won by five and a half lengths and two lengths from Frosted, who was within a couple of lengths rounding the home turn, and Keen Ice, with Mubtaahij a creditable fourth.

Although American Pharoah's owner had sold the breeding rights, he had insisted on controlling the horse's racing programme until the end of his three-year-old career. 'This is for the sport,' Zayat said as he hoisted the trophy after the Belmont Stakes. 'We need to enjoy our stars and race them as long as we possibly can.' Of the three Triple Crown winners in the 'seventies, Secretariat was retired to stud at the end of his three-year-old season, while both Seattle Slew—the only horse to win the Triple Crown while still undefeated—and Affirmed remained in training at four, when they added to their reputations, Seattle Slew being champion older male and Affirmed Horse of the Year. Seattle Slew and Affirmed met twice, the second occasion being in the 1978 Jockey Club Gold Cup, by which time the distance of that iconic dirt race had been reduced to a mile and a half from its traditional two miles (it is now run at a mile and a quarter), but ex-European turf performer Exceller touched off Seattle Slew by a nose with three-year-old Affirmed only fifth after his saddle slipped. Secretariat's Belmont Stakes victory is widely acknowledged as the greatest performance in the history of North America's Triple Crown races—he won by thirty-one lengths—and *The Wall Street Journal* conducted an interesting, split-screen exercise of putting together some mock, grainy, black and white footage of Secretariat's romp alongside the film of American Pharoah's performance. If nothing else, the direct comparison provided an indication of just why Secretariat is still regarded as the outstanding American champion of the modern era (he set track records in all three legs of the Triple Crown which still stand, the essay on I'll Have Another in *Racehorses of 2012* explaining how his 'official' winning time in the Preakness was finally corrected after nearly forty years). Secretariat had six more races after the Belmont, recording four more victories, one of them in a world record time for nine furlongs in the inaugural Marlboro Cup at Belmont Park (the now-discontinued race also featured the first of the two encounters in 1978 between Triple Crown winners Seattle Slew and Affirmed, which Seattle Slew won by three lengths). Secretariat's last two wins, incidentally, came on turf in the Man o' War Stakes (track record) and the Canadian International. Seattle Slew lost his unbeaten record when fourth behind J. O. Tobin in the Swaps Stakes on his only subsequent start as a three-year-old after landing the Triple Crown, while Affirmed lost three of his four remaining races at three (including a disqualification in the Travers Stakes). Like Affirmed, who extended his three-year-old campaign to eight wins in a row in the Jim Dandy Stakes, American Pharoah also followed up his Belmont Stakes win on his next appearance.

American Pharoah's Triple Crown certainly put racing in the spotlight—and on to the front page of the *New York Times* and the cover of *Vogue*, among others. Victor Espinoza, who had paraded American Pharoah down the full length of the grandstand after the Belmont, didn't ride in the week after the race, barely having time to catch his breath as he appeared on TV talk shows and pitched the first ball at various Major League baseball games across the country, among numerous celebrity appearances. The newly-crowned Triple Crown hero recorded his sixth successive victory of the campaign (and his eighth in a winning sequence stretching back to his two-year-old days) in the William Hill Haskell Invitational. His trainer may have been calling him 'a gift from God' but American Pharoah was also proving a gift to the racecourse turnstiles and the Haskell took place before yet another record crowd of 60,983 which was drawn to Monmouth Park. American Pharoah hacked up at 10/1-on, winning eased down and with plenty in hand by two and a quarter lengths and three lengths from Keen Ice and Upstart, after travelling strongly all the way and taking the lead two furlongs out. American Pharoah had been imperious against horses of his own age, and it was hard to envisage his coming unstuck in the Travers Stakes at Saratoga later in August, a race chosen in preference to the Pacific Classic which would have seen him take on his elders for the first time. Saratoga has witnessed its fair share of shock results over the years. The legendary Man o' War suffered his only defeat there (as a two-year-old, beaten by a horse called Upset), and Secretariat was beaten at long odds on by Onion in the Whitney Handicap, two races after his magnificent performance in the Belmont; in the Travers itself, Triple Crown winner Gallant Fox had been beaten in 1930 by 100/1-shot Jim Dandy. Saratoga's nickname of 'the graveyard of champions' was quoted widely before American Pharoah's defeat.

The ten-runner Travers saw odds-on American Pharoah up against some familiar rivals, including Keen Ice and Upstart, as well as Frosted and Tale of Verve. Also in the line-up was the Breeders' Cup Juvenile winner Texas Red who had missed the Triple Crown series but had beaten Frosted in the Jim Dandy at Saratoga earlier in the month. The interest was immense. An estimated 15,000 turned up just to watch American Pharoah work on the course the day before the Travers, but he ran a long way below form in the race itself and connections partly blamed the public workout, which they believed had 'lit up' the horse and caused him to expend more energy than desirable the day before a big race. The normally imperturbable American Pharoah sweated up in the Travers preliminaries and his cause wasn't helped in the race when Frosted was sent up to harry him for the lead from halfway. Although he eventually beat off Frosted's persistent challenge in the home straight, American Pharoah was spent and couldn't find any more to hold off the staying-on

Breeders' Cup Classic, Keeneland—a dominant display from US Horse of the Year American Pharoah, who produces one of the best performances in North America in the past twenty years; rank outsider Effinex (sheepskin noseband) fares best of the rest, with Honor Code staying on from out of the picture to finish third

Keen Ice who collared him in the last sixty yards. American Pharoah, who took twenty-six and a half seconds to cover the final two furlongs, went down by three quarters of a length and, for a time, the possibility of early retirement loomed as connections considered the effects on American Pharoah, not only of his hard race, but of a programme comprising seven races over six months at six different tracks, and involving plenty of travelling. For American Pharoah's jockey, defeat at Saratoga was compounded by a 15,000-dollar fine imposed after the race for 'wearing promotional material without permission … after having been specifically instructed not to do so by the stewards.' Victor Espinoza's boots had carried the logo of Monster energy drinks in the Haskell and he sported the logo again in the Travers; others associated with American Pharoah, including the Zayat family, wore black caps with the same logo.

If American Pharoah simply needed a break, he got one. It was two months to America's richest race the Breeders' Cup Classic and, as the Breeders' Cup meeting approached, American Pharoah was said to be giving his trainer all the right signs at home. For his owner, American Pharoah's appearance at the Breeders' Cup, which provided his only test against older horses, was 'not about the money, the prestige or the honour … it's about greatness, defining greatness.' The Breeders' Cup was staged for the first time at Keeneland racecourse in Lexington, Kentucky, the heartland of the American thoroughbred breeding industry. The course removed its polytrack surface, which had been in place for eight years, and replaced it with traditional dirt in the latest season. The presence of American Pharoah ensured that the Breeders' Cup meeting was higher up North America's sporting agenda in the last weekend of October (the meeting usually has a fight on its hands with the nation's attention firmly on baseball's World Series and college gridiron football at that time of the year). American Pharoah's challengers were whittled down to seven when champion mare Beholder—the likely second favourite—and the Awesome Again Stakes winner Smooth Roller were late scratchings. There were four representatives of the classic generation in the eventual line-up, American Pharoah joined by Keen Ice, Frosted and the only European contender, dual Two Thousand Guineas winner Gleneagles, the last-named representing those perennial challengers Ballydoyle and running for the first and only time on dirt. The previous year's Belmont Stakes winner Tonalist, winner of the Jockey Club Gold Cup on his most recent outing, and the Whitney Stakes winner Honor Code looked the biggest dangers among the older horses, though the in-and-out Effinex had beaten Tonalist narrowly earlier in the season in the Grade 2 Suburban Handicap at Belmont Park. The Breeders' Cup Dirt Mile, introduced in 2007, has, since its inception, had the potential to draw runners away from the Breeders' Cup Classic and there was widely-felt disappointment with

79

the decision to run the progressive Liam's Map in the Dirt Mile rather than the Classic. Honor Code's owners Lanes End Racing had bought an interest in Liam's Map—who had finished a good second to Honor Code in the Whitney and then made all in the Woodward, also at Saratoga—and it was thought the change in ownership might have influenced the choice of race.

Liam's Map won the Dirt Mile impressively and there is no doubt that his absence from the Breeders' Cup Classic removed a potentially dangerous opponent for American Pharoah, as well as altering the shape of that race. With no Liam's Map to contend with, American Pharoah was able to take an easy early lead in the Classic and never looked like relinquishing it. American Pharoah was never in the slightest danger and stretched further and further clear in the home straight, with Espinoza just giving him a couple of slaps entering the final furlong, to crush the opposition by six and a half lengths and four and a half lengths. Effinex, who chased American Pharoah throughout, finished second and the keeping-on Honor Code third, with Keen Ice fourth, Tonalist fifth and Frosted seventh, and Gleneagles trailing in a long way behind the others. The fact that the winner broke the track record was not particularly significant in itself but his 'Beyer' speed figure was the best of his career and was the highest recorded in the Breeders' Cup Classic—indeed in any Breeders' Cup race—since Ghostzapper, who ended his career with a Timeform rating of 137 after running away with the 2004 running. Beyer conceded that American Pharoah had given 'the performance that certified his place in history.' For American Pharoah's trainer, however, it was about much more than one performance. 'I have had some really good horses and, on a given day, some of them were as fast as him, but their window for producing top performances was short … his window has been wide open the whole time and he has sustained his performance, just like the old-time thoroughbreds that you could run every week. The special horses do it effortlessly—I've never had a horse who travels over the ground like he does—and I'm just glad the Pharoah goes out as the champ he is, he's the greatest horse I will ever be involved with and he's going to be a tough act to follow.'

American Pharoah (USA) (b.c. 2012)	Pioneerof The Nile (USA) (b or br 2006)	Empire Maker (b or br 2000)	Unbridled
			Toussaud
		Star of Goshen (b 1994)	Lord At War
			Castle Eight
	Littleprincessemma (USA) (ch 2006)	Yankee Gentleman (b 1999)	Storm Cat
			Key Phrase
		Exclusive Rosette (ch 1993)	Ecliptical
			Zetta Jet

The long-striding American Pharoah is a strong, muscular individual who stands just over 16.1 hands; he was reportedly something of a handful going to post on his racecourse debut when he was equipped with blinkers (which were removed next time when his ears were stuffed with cotton wool), but, except for getting a little on edge before the Travers, he impressed with his equable temperament as a three-year-old. The sprinting influences in his pedigree, which encouraged serious doubts about his ability to get the trip in the Belmont, are plain to see on the distaff side. He is the second foal out of Littleprincessemma, who showed little in two outings in sprint company as a juvenile and is a half-sister to a couple of sprinters by the Storm Cat stallion Stormin Fever. The first of them, Storm Wolf, won the Grade 2 Lazaro Barrera Memorial over seven furlongs, and the second, Misty Rosette, won the Grade 3 Old Hat Stakes over six and a half furlongs. Littleprincessemma is herself a daughter of a Storm Cat stallion, Yankee Gentleman (a minor stakes winner over six furlongs who stands in Louisiana), and her first foal Xixixi (by Maimonides) was successful twice over six furlongs. American Pharoah's grandam Exclusive Rosette was also a sprinter, successful twice at around five furlongs. After American Pharoah's successes as a two-year-old, Littleprincessemma was one of the star lots when sent to Fasig-Tipton's November Sale in 2014 and she made 2,100,000 dollars, carrying a brother to American Pharoah who was foaled in the latest season; Ahmed Zayat retained the yearling sister to American Pharoah.

Ahmed Zayat bred and owned American Pharoah's sire Pioneerof The Nile and he still has a large stake in his stallion career which began at a fee of 20,000 dollars at Vinery Stud in Kentucky in 2010, after Pioneerof The Nile's three-year-

Zayat Stables LLC's "American Pharoah"

old campaign was cut short by injury in mid-season. Pioneerof The Nile, who won the Hollywood Futurity at two and the Santa Anita Derby at three before finishing second in the Kentucky Derby, was transferred to WinStar Farm when Vinery's American stallion division closed down. He stood his first season at his new base in 2013 at 15,000 dollars, a fee that had risen to 60,000 dollars by the latest season. Pioneerof The Nile will stand in 2016 at 125,000 dollars. American Pharoah is from his second crop but there were three Grade 2 winners in his first one and his book of mares in 2015 included nine Grade 1 winners and fifteen who had bred Grade 1 winners. Pioneerof The Nile is much more likely to have been the source of American Pharoah's stamina than his family on the distaff side. He has sired other winners at a mile and a half and is by Juddmonte's Belmont Stakes winner Empire Maker (exported to Japan but now back in Kentucky) who was regarded as an influence for stamina when he was first at stud in North America. Empire Maker is also the sire of the Arkansas Derby winner Bodemeister, another Zayat-owned and Baffert-trained Kentucky Derby runner-up who failed to last a full season as a three-year-old, being retired in the summer because of a shoulder injury, after also finishing second in the Preakness (he too stands at WinStar Farm and his first crop were yearlings in 2015). American Pharoah, who raced prominently, stayed a mile and a half and acted on polytrack and dirt (including wet conditions). He won nine of his eleven races, with eight of his victories coming in Grade 1 company. Not only was American Pharoah the first for thirty-seven years to land the Triple Crown, but by going on to add America's premier open-aged championship event, the Breeders' Cup Classic, he became the inaugural winner of what will be acknowledged from now on as the American Grand Slam. It may be a very long time before American Pharoah's unprecedented feat is achieved again. *Bob Baffert, USA*

AMETRINE (IRE) 4 b.f. Fastnet Rock (AUS) 127 – Amethyst (IRE) 111 (Sadler's Wells – (USA) 132) [2015 66: f8g Jan 13] maiden: blinkered, well held only outing in Britain in 2015: stays 1¼m: acts on soft and good to firm going: sent to New Zealand. *William Jarvis*

AMIRLI (IRE) 4 ch.g. Medicean 128 – Amenapinga (FR) (Spinning World (USA) 130) **68** [2015 9.2d³ 12d⁴ Jul 8] fair ex-French-trained maiden: stays 11f: acts on polytrack and good to soft going: in headgear in 2015: often leads. *Donald McCain*

AMIR PASHA (UAE) 10 br.g. Halling (USA) 133 – Clarinda (IRE) 91 (Lomond (USA) **– §** 128) [2015 14.1m Jun 20] well-made gelding: fair at best, no form in 2015: stays 2m: acts on any turf going: usually wears headgear: temperamental. *Micky Hammond*

AMIS REUNIS 6 b.m. Bahamian Bounty 116 – Spring Clean (FR) 89 (Danehill (USA) **61** 126) [2015 62, a55: t6g⁵ 6s* 6s² 5g³ 6m 5m² 5g 5.9s⁶ 6g 6g 5.9d 6d⁶ 6d 6g⁴ 6m³ t6m Dec 30] sturdy mare: modest handicapper: won at Hamilton in May: has won at 7f, races at 5f/6f nowadays: acts on polytrack, fibresand, soft and good to firm going: often wears cheekpieces. *Alan Berry*

A MOMENTOFMADNESS 2 b.c. (Mar 19) Elnadim (USA) 128 – Royal Blush 68 **79** (Royal Applause 124) [2015 5m² p6g⁶* 6m 6g Aug 20] strong colt: fair performer: won maiden at Lingfield in July: will prove at least as effective at 5f as 6f. *Charles Hills*

AMONG ANGELS 3 b.g. Acclamation 118 – Love Action (IRE) 80 (Motivator 131) **92** [2015 79: 5g⁵ 5m⁶ 6m³ 6d⁶ 6m 5s⁶ Sep 21] good-quartered gelding: fairly useful handicapper: won at Thirsk (by ¾ length from Northgate Lad) in April: third at Ripon in June: stays 6f: acts on soft and good to firm going. *Michael Easterby*

AMOOD (IRE) 4 ch.c. Elnadim (USA) 128 – Amanah (USA) 100 (Mr Prospector (USA)) **85** [2015 90: 8g⁵ 10m* 10.4m 8d³ 8m⁵ 8d² 10.4m 8g 7.9g⁴ p8g 8d Sep 25] fairly useful handicapper: won at Newmarket (by head from Zugzwang) in May: third at Haydock in July and second at Thirsk in August: stays 1¼m: acts on polytrack, tapeta, good to firm and good to soft going: often in headgear in 2015: tried in tongue tie in 2015: front runner/races prominently. *Simon West*

AMORESHARI 3 b.f. Paco Boy (IRE) 129 – Brilliance 74 (Cadeaux Genereux 131) **–** [2015 9.2m⁶ Jun 10] £9,000Y: closely related to a winner up to 1m in Hong Kong by Desert Style and half-sister to several winners, including useful 7f winner Tora Bora (by Grand Lodge) and useful 7f (including at 2 yrs) winner Chorus of Angels (by Rock of Gibraltar): dam 1m winner: 40/1: beaten in maiden at Hamilton. *L. Smyth, Ireland*

AMOR INVICTO (IRE) 2 b.g. (May 10) Holy Roman Emperor (IRE) 125 – Love In **67** The Mist (USA) 69 (Silver Hawk (USA) 123) [2015 7g p8f⁶ 6d⁶ Sep 15] good-topped gelding: fair maiden: third past the post in maiden at Salisbury on debut (disqualified after rider failed to weigh in): below that form after. *Daniel Kubler*

AMOSITE 9 b.m. Central Park (IRE) 123 – Waterline Dancer (IRE) 69 (Danehill Dancer **63** (IRE) 117) [2015 79: t6ft6g⁵ p7f⁶ p6g⁵ t7.1g Apr 28] lightly-made mare: modest handicapper: stays 7f: acts on polytrack and firm going: usually wears headgear: often leads. *J. R. Jenkins*

AMOUR DE NUIT (IRE) 3 b.g. Azamour (IRE) 130 – Umthoulah (IRE) 81 (Unfuwain **109** (USA) 131) [2015 61p: 14.1m⁶ 13m² 14.1g² 16g* 16m* 16.1m² 16.4g* 17.5g* 16d Oct 17] big gelding: useful handicapper: won at Lingfield in July, Ripon in August, and York (by ½ length from Longshadow) and Ayr (by 3¼ lengths from Hidden Justice) in September: stays 17.5f: acts on good to firm and good to soft going: tried in hood: front runner/races prominently. *Sir Mark Prescott Bt*

AMOURITA (IRE) 4 b.f. Azamour (IRE) 130 – Akarita (IRE) 92 (Akarad (FR) 130) **–** [2015 67: p11f Mar 18] maiden: no form in 2015: stays 16.5f, usually over shorter: acts on polytrack and tapeta: tried in headgear. *Jonathan Portman*

AMPERE (FR) 3 b.c. Galileo (IRE) 134 – Amorama (FR) 118 (Sri Pekan (USA) 117) **117** [2015 10.9s* 10.9g* 11.9m² 9.9d³ Aug 15] fifth foal: closely related to French 10.5f/11.5f winner Amorine (by Montjeu) and half-brother to 2 winners in France, including 11f winner Amoa (by Ghostzapper): dam French/US 7f (at 2 yrs) to 9f (Grade 1) winner: smart performer: won minor event at Longchamp in April and Prix Hocquart on same course (by length from Cape Clear Island) in May: second in Grand Prix de Paris at Longchamp (2 lengths behind Erupt) in July and third in Prix Guillaume d'Ornano at Deauville (4 lengths behind New Bay) in August: stays 1½m: acts on good to firm and good to soft going, winner on soft ground. *A. Fabre, France*

AMPLE 2 b.c. (Mar 30) Arakan (USA) 123 – Ambonnay 89 (Ashkalani (IRE) 128) [2015 **89**
p5g* 6g⁵ 5.1v* Oct 7] £8,000Y: seventh foal: dam, 2-y-o 6f winner, half-sister to useful 5f
winner Deep Finesse: fairly useful performer: won maiden at Chelmsford (by 5 lengths
from Lone Angel) in April and nursery at Nottingham (by neck from Celebration) in
October: should stay 6f. *Richard Hannon*

AMTIRED 9 gr.g. Beauchamp King 117 – Rising Talisker (Primitive Rising (USA) 113) **–**
[2015 f11g⁵ Apr 14] good-topped gelding: fair at best, no form in 2015: stays 1½m: acts on
fibresand and good to soft going: often in headgear prior to 2015. *Marjorie Fife*

AMULET 5 gr.m. Ishiguru (USA) 114 – Loveofmylife 59 (Dr Fong (USA) 128) [2015 99: **104**
8v³ 8.5g 8g* 8g Aug 2] rather leggy, close-coupled mare: useful performer: won listed race
at Nantes (by short head from Chika Dream) in June: third in Park Express Stakes at the
Curragh (2½ lengths behind Ramone) in March: stays 8.5f: acts on polytrack, best turf
form on good going or softer (acts on heavy): sometimes wears blinkers. *Eve Johnson
Houghton*

AMY BLAIR 2 b.c. (May 7) Captain Gerrard (IRE) 113 – Shalad'or 97 (Golden Heights **58 p**
82) [2015 6m⁵ 7g 6g⁴ Oct 8] 800F, €4,500Y, €21,000 2-y-o: half-brother to 1¼m winner
Golden Sprite (by Bertolini) and 2-y-o 1m winner Imperial Oak (by Imperial Dancer): dam
winner up to 8.3f (2-y-o 7f winner): best effort (modest form) when fourth in maiden at Ayr
(6½ lengths behind Cheeky Angel) in October: remains with potential. *Keith Dalgleish*

AMY ERIA (IRE) 4 b.f. Shamardal (USA) 129 – Berroscoberro (FR) (Octagonal (NZ) **113**
126) [2015 8m² 6.5s² 7m* 7m⁴ Oct 4] €85,000Y: angular filly: fifth foal: half-sister to 12.5f
winner Anna Rosaires (by Anabaa) and 9f-11.5f winner Passion Eria (by Holy Roman
Emperor): dam French 1½m winner: smart performer: 33/1, won Oak Tree Stakes at
Goodwood (by ½ length from Osaila) in July: creditable 3 lengths fourth to Make Believe
in Prix de la Foret at Longchamp final outing: stays 7.5f: acts on viscoride and good to firm
going: often races prominently. *Francois Rohaut, France*

ANABEL 2 ch.f. (Jan 27) Lord of England (GER) 119 – Adalawa (IRE) (Barathea (IRE) **82**
127) [2015 7m² 7.2d² 8.5g* 8dᶠ Sep 12] fairly useful form: landed the odds in maiden at
Beverley in August: appeared to suffer leg injury after 4f in listed race at Dusseldorf in
September: stayed 8.5f: dead. *Mark Johnston*

ANAGALLIS (IRE) 2 b.f. (Apr 6) Elusive Pimpernel (USA) 117 – Adjtiya (IRE) (Green **60**
Desert (USA) 127) [2015 5.1m² 5m² f5g⁵ Dec 29] £3,500Y: sixth foal: half-sister to 7f/1m
winner Ashton Rose (by Intikhab): dam unraced half-sister to Irish 2000 Guineas runner-
up Adjareli: modest maiden: best effort when second in maiden at Nottingham (¾ length
behind Midnight Malibu) in July: left Alan McCabe after second start: likely to stay at least
6f. *John Balding*

ANAHORISH 2 bl.c. (Feb 9) Showcasing 117 – Zagarock 56 (Rock of Gibraltar (IRE) **–**
133) [2015 5g⁵ May 1] 4/1, last of 5 in maiden at Musselburgh: dead. *David Barron*

ANARCHISTE 3 ch.f. Archipenko (USA) 127 – Hermanita 64 (Hernando (FR) 127) **91**
[2015 p7g⁴ p7f⁴ t8.6f² t8.6m* 10f 10m⁶ 10.9g 10.2d⁶ 10g Oct 9] rather leggy filly: fourth
foal: half-sister to 3 winners, including winner up to 1½m Sbraase (2-y-o 9.5f winner, by
Sir Percy): dam 1½m winner: fairly useful performer: won maiden at Wolverhampton in
March: should be suited by 1½m: acts on tapeta and good to firm going: usually races
nearer last than first. *Philip McBride*

ANA SHABABIYA (IRE) 5 ch.m. Teofilo (IRE) 126 – Call Later (USA) (Gone West **– §**
(USA)) [2015 77§: p11g Jan 7] fair at best, no form in 2015: stays 1¼m: acts on polytrack,
firm and soft going: front runner/races prominently: temperamental. *Ismail Mohammed*

ANASTAZIA 3 br.f. Kyllachy 129 – Meddle (Diktat 126) [2015 74, a80: p5g⁵ t7.1g³ t7.1m⁶ **84**
8m³ 8.3m³ 6m t7.1g 7s³ 7g⁴ p6g⁵ t7.1f³ t9.5g⁵ p7g⁴ p8m⁵ Dec 31] fairly useful handicapper:
stays 1m: acts on polytrack, tapeta, soft and good to firm going: tried in headgear. *Paul
D'Arcy*

ANCIENT ASTRONAUT 2 b.g. (Apr 23) Kodiac 112 – Tatora (Selkirk (USA) 129) **89**
[2015 6s* 7m Oct 3] 70,000F: rather leggy gelding: half-brother to 3 winners, including
very smart winner up to 7f Tariq (2-y-o 6f winner) and smart 6.5f/7f winner Tariq Too (both
by Kyllachy): dam unraced: better effort when winning maiden at Ayr (dead-heated with
Ferryover) in May: should stay 7f. *John Quinn*

ANCIENT CROSS 11 b.g. Machiavellian (USA) 123 – Magna Graecia (IRE) 112 **91**
(Warning 136) [2015 97: 6d 5m⁴ 6m⁴ 5g 6m⁶ 5g⁴ 5m 6m 6g 5d 5m⁵ 6g⁵ f6g⁶ f6m² Dec 8]
good-bodied gelding: fairly useful handicapper: stays 1m: acts on any turf going: tried in
headgear: usually wears tongue tie: somewhat inconsistent nowadays. *Michael Easterby*

ANCIENT GREECE 8 b.g. Pivotal 124 – Classicism (USA) 82 (A P Indy (USA) 131) **76**
[2015 82: 8.3d⁴ p8g 12m² p8g 9g³ Jun 26] well-made gelding: fair handicapper: stays 1½m:
acts on polytrack, snow and heavy going: tried in cheekpieces prior to 2015: often in
tongue tie prior to 2015: sometimes slowly away, often races lazily. *George Baker*

ANCIENT TRADE (USA) 2 ch.c. (May 3) Speightstown (USA) 124 – Nafisah (IRE) **85 p**
109 (Lahib (USA) 129) [2015 6m⁵ 6g⁴ p6f* Sep 10] $485,000Y: good-topped colt: closely
related to 11.3f winner Waaheb (by Elusive Quality) and half-brother to 3 winners, including
very smart 7f/1m winner Snaafy (by Kingmambo): dam winner up to 1¼m (2-y-o 7f winner)
who stayed 1½m: fairly useful form: best effort when winning maiden at Chelmsford
(by length from Cosmopolitan Girl) in September: will stay 7f: should do better still.
Richard Hannon

ANCIENT WORLD (USA) 2 ch.g. (Apr 19) Giant's Causeway (USA) 132 – Satulagi **–**
(USA) 98 (Officer (USA) 120) [2015 7g 8.3s Oct 13] no form. *Charles Hills*

ANDALUSITE 2 br.f. (Mar 18) Equiano (FR) 127 – Kammaan 85 (Diktat 126) [2015 **60**
5.1d³ 6g⁵ May 26] first foal: dam, 7f winner, sister to smart winner up to 1¼m Toolain:
better effort when third in maiden at Nottingham (5 lengths behind Kept Under Wraps) in
May. *Ed McMahon*

ANDAR 2 gr.c. (Apr 12) Hellvelyn 118 – Rioliina (IRE) 84 (Captain Rio 122) [2015 6m **85**
6.1m² 6.1g² p6f⁴ 6d² Oct 11] £13,000Y: second foal: dam winner up to 7f (2-y-o 5.7f
winner): fairly useful maiden: second in maiden at Goodwood in October: raced only at 6f:
acts on good to soft going: tried in cheekpieces. *Clive Cox*

ANDASTRA (GER) 2 b.f. (Feb 2) Kamsin (GER) 124 – Arpista (GER) (Chief Singer **85 p**
131) [2015 8.3g* Sep 30] €190,000Y: sister to useful German 8.5f-11f winner Amazonit,
closely related to smart French 10.5f winner Adelar and useful French 2-y-o 7f/1m winner
(stayed 1¼m) Aquatina (both by Samum) and half-sister to 3 winners abroad: dam
German 7f winner: 5/2, looked useful prospect when won maiden at Nottingham (by 3
lengths from Norse Magic) in September, easily: likely to stay at least 1¼m: open to
improvement. *Ralph Beckett*

ANDAZ 2 b.f. (May 2) Makfi 130 – Waafiah 57 (Anabaa (USA) 130) [2015 p8g² Dec 15] **83 p**
half-sister to several winners, including winner up to 7f Telwaar (2-y-o 6f winner, by
Haafhd) and 1m winner (including at 2 yrs) Jaser (by Alhaarth), both useful: dam, second
at 7f on only start, out of Prix Morny winner First Waltz: 7/1, shaped well when second in
maiden at Kempton (1½ lengths behind Cajoled) in December, not ideally placed: sure to
progress. *Roger Varian*

ANDHAAR 9 b.g. Bahri (USA) 125 – Deraasaat 92 (Nashwan (USA) 135) [2015 16s **59**
17.2d 15.8g Aug 26] quite good-topped gelding: modest handicapper: stays 1½m: acts
on polytrack, soft and good to firm going: fair/ungenuine staying hurdler nowadays.
N. W. Alexander

ANDRETTI 3 b.g. Oasis Dream 129 – Anna Amalia (IRE) (In The Wings 128) [2015 80p: **–**
8.3g⁶ 8.3g Jun 28] strong, compact gelding: fairly useful at best, no form in 2015: stays
8.5f: acts on polytrack and tapeta: tried in headgear. *Roger Varian*

ANDRY BRUSSELLES 5 b.m. Hurricane Run (IRE) 134 – Dont Dili Dali 102 (Dansili **93**
127) [2015 11.9d May 30] 20,000Y, €30,000 2-y-o: second foal: closely related to French
13f winner Surrey Storm (by Montjeu): dam, 7f/1m winner (including at 2 yrs) who stayed
1½m, sister to useful 7f/1m winner Balducci: useful performer in 2014, winning listed race
at Saint-Cloud: ran respectably only outing in 2015: best effort at 1¾m: acts on soft going:
often races towards rear. *David Simcock*

AN DUINE UASAL (IRE) 2 b.c. (Apr 11) Alfred Nobel (IRE) 110 – Dany Song (USA) **77**
(Yankee Victor (USA) 121) [2015 5v 5.8g* 5.1d 5.8m³ 5g p6g³ p7g 7g Oct 20] fair performer:
won maiden at Cork in April: stays 6f: acts on polytrack: often in headgear: often in tongue
tie. *A. P. Keatley, Ireland*

ANEEDH 5 b.g. Lucky Story (USA) 128 – Seed Al Maha (USA) (Seeking The Gold **74**
(USA)) [2015 12g 14.6d³ 12.1m² 12g 12g⁶ 17.1m⁵ 14.1m⁶ 10.4d³ 10.3d² 10.2s⁶ Nov 4]
attractive gelding: fair handicapper: stays 14.5f: acts on good to firm and good to soft
going: often wears headgear. *Clive Mulhall*

ANEESAH 2 b.f. (Jan 31) Canford Cliffs (IRE) 133 – Decorative (IRE) 100 (Danehill **79 p**
Dancer (IRE) 117) [2015 6.5m 7m* 7.1f Jul 23] 23,000F, £180,000Y: first foal: dam,
winner up to 8.3f (2-y-o 6f winner), sister to useful 1m winner Regulation: fair form: won
maiden at Chester in June by head from Tholen: failed to settle when finding little in listed
race at Sandown next time: best effort at 7f: remains open to improvement. *Roger Varian*

ANFIELD 4 b.f. Captain Gerrard (IRE) 113 – Billie Holiday (Fairy King (USA)) [2015 50: f5s p5g⁵ 5g⁶ 5g⁵ p5g² t5.1f p5g⁴ Sep 30] poor maiden: raced only at 5f: acts on polytrack and good to firm going: tried in cheekpieces prior to 2015: tried in tongue tie: front runner/races prominently. *Mick Quinn*   **49**

ANGEL DELIGHT (IRE) 3 b.f. Dark Angel (IRE) 113 – Roof Fiddle (USA) 95 (Cat Thief (USA) 126) [2015 p7g p6g⁶ p7g p8f⁵ 7m⁶ 8m Jun 14] €28,000Y: second foal: half-sister to 1¼m winner Thatchereen (by Mastercraftsman): dam, 2-y-o 5f winner, half-sister to useful 7f winner Sylvestris: no form: suspect temperament. *James Fanshawe*   **–**

ANGELENA BALLERINA (IRE) 8 ch.m. Indian Haven 119 – Nom Francais 39 (First Trump 118) [2015 –: p10m t8.6g p10f⁴ p10f Feb 19] rather leggy mare: poor handicapper: stays 1¼m: acts on polytrack, fibresand, firm and good to soft going: usually wears headgear: tends to find little. *Andy Turnell*   **49**

ANGEL FLORES (IRE) 4 b.f. Art Connoisseur (IRE) 121 – Emmas Princess (IRE) 96 (Bahhare (USA) 122) [2015 83: p6g p6f² 5.7f⁵ t7.1g 6s⁵ p6g 5s Sep 16] close-coupled filly: fair maiden: stays 6f: acts on polytrack and good to firm going: tried in blinkers prior to 2015: sometimes slowly away. *Lee Carter*   **72**

ANGEL GABRIAL (IRE) 6 b.g. Hurricane Run (IRE) 134 – Causeway Song (USA) (Giant's Causeway (USA) 132) [2015 12g² 18.7d 14g³ 16.1m⁴ 16.4m² 16m 14g 14d⁵ 16g² 18g Oct 10] good-topped gelding: smart performer: best efforts when fourth in Northumberland Plate (Handicap) at Newcastle (beaten 1½ lengths by Quest For More) in June, and runner-up in listed races at Sandown (head behind Eye of The Storm) in July and Newmarket (2 lengths behind Flying Officer) in September: stays 2¼m: acts on firm and good to soft going. *Richard Fahey*   **113**

ANGEL GRACE (IRE) 2 gr.f. (Mar 11) Dark Angel (IRE) 113 – Light Sea (IRE) 59 (King's Best (USA) 132) [2015 7s⁴ p8f⁶ Nov 12] €26,000F, 30,000Y: second foal: half-sister to useful 2-y-o 5f/6f winner Squats (by Dandy Man): dam, staying maiden, half-sister to very smart stayer Aaim To Prosper and smart 1m/9f performer Hurricane Alan: better effort when sixth in maiden at Chelmsford (5½ lengths behind Flyweight) in November. *David Menuisier*   **64**

ANGELIC LORD (IRE) 3 b.g. Dark Angel (IRE) 113 – Divine Design (IRE) 77 (Barathea (IRE) 127) [2015 106: p7g² 6g 6m⁶ 6g* Jul 4] rangy, attractive gelding: smart performer: won minor event at Haydock (by length from Intibaah) in July: stays 6f: acts on good to firm and good to soft going: often in headgear in 2015: front runner/races prominently. *Tom Dascombe*   **112**

ANGELIC UPSTART (IRE) 7 b.g. Singspiel (IRE) 133 – Rada (IRE) 52 (Danehill (USA) 126) [2015 95: t8.6g² 9m⁵ p10m² p10g⁶ 9m³ 10.3m⁶ Sep 10] close-coupled gelding: useful handicapper: third at Goodwood (apprentice, length behind Balmoral Castle) in August: stays 1¼m: acts on polytrack, tapeta, good to firm and good to soft going: tried in visor prior to 2015. *Andrew Balding*   **96**

ANGEL IN THE SNOW 2 ch.g. (Mar 14) Haafhd 129 – Chilly Filly (IRE) 99 (Montjeu (IRE) 137) [2015 t8.6m f7f Dec 17] first foal: dam, unreliable 1½m-1¾m winner, closely related to useful stayer Endless Intrigue: down the field in maidens: should do better over 1¼m+. *Brian Ellison*   **– p**

ANGELITO 6 ch.g. Primo Valentino (IRE) 116 – Supreme Angel 85 (Beveled (USA)) [2015 86: p5f³ p6m³ p6g⁴ t5.1g² 5m⁴ 6g³ 5m⁴ 5m⁴ 5.7f³ p6g⁴ 5.7m 6d p7m Oct 28] sturdy gelding: fairly useful handicapper: left Ed McMahon after eleventh start: stays 6f: acts on polytrack, tapeta, firm and good to soft going: often races towards rear. *Natalie Lloyd-Beavis*   **84**

ANGEL OF THE NIGHT (IRE) 2 br.f. (Apr 23) Footstepsinthesand 120 – Princess Sabaah (IRE) 90 (Desert King (IRE) 129) [2015 p5f² 5.1m⁵ 7m⁴ Jul 21] 2,000Y: sixth foal: half-sister to useful 9.5f winner (stayed 14.6f) Prince Sabaah (by Spectrum): dam 2-y-o 6f winner: fair maiden: best effort when second in maiden at Chelmsford (½ length behind Abberley Dancer) in April, not clear run: should stay 7f: sent to Qatar. *K. R. Burke*   **66**

ANGEL ROSA 4 b.f. Multiplex 114 – Rosi Quest (Rainbow Quest (USA) 134) [2015 t7.1f⁴ t8.6f⁶ p10f p8m 6s⁵ 6m⁶ 7.6g Jun 9] modest handicapper: stays 8.5f: acts on tapeta, best turf form on good going: often in headgear in 2015: temperament under suspicion. *Mrs Ilka Gansera-Leveque*   **53**

ANGELS ABOVE (IRE) 3 b.g. Dark Angel (IRE) 113 – Fag End (IRE) 88 (Treasure Kay 114) [2015 58: p7m 7.2g⁵ 8.3d⁵ 10d⁶ t8.6m³ Aug 21] modest maiden: left John Butler after first start: stays 8.5f: acts on polytrack, tapeta and good to soft going: sometimes in headgear in 2015. *John Quinn*   **53**

ANGELS WINGS (IRE) 3 b.f. Dark Angel (IRE) 113 – Startarette (USA) (Dixieland **82**
Band (USA)) [2015 77: t6m³ 7g⁴ 6.1m⁵ 6.1g⁴ t6f² t7.1m Oct 2] tall filly: has scope: fairly
useful handicapper: stays 6f: acts on tapeta and good to firm going. *Charles Hills*

ANGEL VISION (IRE) 3 b.f. Oasis Dream 129 – Islington (IRE) 124 (Sadler's Wells **105**
(USA) 132) [2015 69p: 7g* 8m² 8m* 7m 8.1m⁶ 10.1m⁵ 8f³ 7.5f Dec 27] useful-looking
filly: useful performer: won maiden at Newmarket in May and handicap on same course
(by 2½ lengths from Spirit Raiser) in June: good fifth to Talmada in listed race at Yarmouth
on sixth outing, then left Sir Michael Stoute: stays 1¼m: raced only on good going and
firmer. *Michael Dilger, USA*

ANGEL WAY (IRE) 6 br.m. Trans Island 119 – Zilayah (USA) 79 (Zilzal (USA) 137) **77**
[2015 82: p5f⁴ 5f² May 16] strong mare: fair handicapper: stays 6f: acts on polytrack and
any turf going: usually leads. *Mike Murphy*

ANGIE'S GIRL 2 b.f. (Mar 8) Exceed And Excel (AUS) 126 – Expedience (USA) 74 **74**
(With Approval (CAN)) [2015 6g² 5.7f³ 6m⁵ 6d³ Sep 21] 50,000F, 130,000Y: rather
unfurnished filly: fifth foal: half-sister to winners abroad by Bahamian Bounty and
Azamour: dam, 1m winner, half-sister to smart 2-y-o 7f/1m winner Fantastic View: fair
maiden: stays 6f. *Clive Cox*

ANGINOLA (IRE) 6 b.m. Kodiac 112 – Lady Montekin (Montekin 125) [2015 64: 10.2s **52**
t13.9f p12g⁶ t12.2f⁶ Dec 21] angular mare: modest handicapper: stays 1½m: acts on
polytrack, good to firm and heavy going: sometimes wears headgear. *David Dennis*

ANGLOPHILE 4 ch.g. Dubawi (IRE) 129 – Anna Palariva (IRE) 108 (Caerleon (USA) **109**
132) [2015 109: p12g² p15.8g* p15.8f² p14f² t16.5m² Dec 12] useful performer: won
minor event at Lingfield (by 4½ lengths from Uramazin) in January: runner-up in valuable
event at Lingfield (head behind Mymatechris) in April, handicap at Chelmsford in
November and minor event at Wolverhampton in December: stays 16.5f: acts on polytrack,
tapeta, good to firm and good to soft going: often races prominently, often travels strongly.
Charlie Appleby

ANGROVE FATRASCAL 3 pt.g. Angrove Spottedick – Marshal Plat Club 56 **–**
(Monsieur Bond (IRE) 120) [2015 7d 12gᵖᵘ Sep 26] no form. *Micky Hammond*

ANGUS GLENS 5 gr.g. Dalakhani (IRE) 133 – Clara Bow (IRE) 84 (Sadler's Wells **75**
(USA) 132) [2015 76: t13.9f⁴ p15.8g t12.2f⁴ t13.9f Dec 14] tall gelding: fair handicapper:
stays 2m: acts on polytrack, tapeta, soft and good to firm going: often wears headgear:
usually leads. *David Dennis*

ANGUS OG 5 b.g. Pastoral Pursuits 127 – Winter Moon (Mujadil (USA) 119) [2015 93: **69**
p6g⁴ t6f Jan 29] sturdy gelding: fair performer: stays 6f: acts on good to firm and good to
soft going: tried in eyeshields: sometimes slowly away. *K. R. Burke*

ANIERES BOY 3 b.g. Kheleyf (USA) 116 – Place Morny (IRE) (Cadeaux Genereux 131) **64 p**
[2015 7m⁶ 7d³ 7d⁵ t6m 5m* Oct 1] third foal: dam unraced: modest performer, lightly
raced: won handicap at Beverley in October: best effort at 5f: acts on good to firm going:
front runner/races prominently: still unexposed. *Michael Easterby*

ANJUNA BEACH (USA) 5 b.g. Artie Schiller (USA) 124 – Hidden Temper (USA) **55**
(Miswaki (USA) 124) [2015 74: t9.5f t7.1f p8f p13.3g p7g³ p8f³ Dec 17] tall, useful-
looking gelding: modest handicapper: stays 1½m: acts on all-weather, good to firm and
good to soft going: tried in hood: sometimes slowly away, often races in rear, often races
freely. *Ann Stokell*

ANNA DOLCE (FR) 3 b.f. Areion (GER) 115 – Anna Spectra (IRE) (Spectrum (IRE) **41**
126) [2015 –: 7.1m⁴ 7d⁴ 8.6m t7.1m⁵ Sep 25] poor maiden: best effort at 7f: acts on tapeta.
Harry Dunlop

ANNALUNA (IRE) 6 b.m. Whipper (USA) 126 – Annaletta 89 (Belmez (USA) 131) **77**
[2015 76, a65: p13.3g³ 14m³ 16.2m³ 14g* 16g⁵ 16d² 15.9m 17.2f Sep 13] fair handicapper:
won at Ffos Las in July: stays 17f: acts on polytrack, tapeta and any turf going: often wears
visor. *David Evans*

ANNEANI (IRE) 3 b.f. Bushranger (IRE) 119 – Hazium (IRE) 69 (In The Wings 128) **56**
[2015 –: 7g* 7.1m³ 6.9v⁴ 8.3m³ 8.3m 9.9g⁶ 9m³ 10.4g 7s t9.5f Nov 13] modest handicapper:
won at Catterick in April: stays 9f: acts on good to firm going: often races towards rear.
Paul Green

ANNE'S VALENTINO 5 b.m. Primo Valentino (IRE) 116 – Annie's Gift (IRE) **57**
(Presenting 120) [2015 66: 12d 15.8s 15s⁴ 15.8m² Aug 4] modest handicapper: stays 16.5f:
acts on good to firm and heavy going. *Malcolm Jefferson*

ANNIE SALTS 2 b.f. (Apr 22) Zebedee 113 – Dazzling View (USA) (Distant View (USA) **69**
126) [2015 5m t5.1f⁵ p6f⁶ p5m² Nov 17] 1,700F, 12,000Y: compact filly: fourth foal: half-
sister to German 6f-8.5f winner Mister Mackenzie (by Kodiac) and 2-y-o 6f winner Flashy
Diva (by Showcasing): dam unraced: fair maiden: should stay 6f. *Martyn Meade*

ANNIE T 2 b.f. (Apr 21) Makfi 130 – Hanella (IRE) 91 (Galileo (IRE) 134) [2015 7m 7d   –
Aug 14] fifth foal: half-sister to 3 winners, including 1¼m-2m winner Rutherglen (by Tiger
Hill) and 1m-1½m winner Zambeasy (by Zamindar): dam, 1¼m-11.6f winner, half-sister
to smart performer up to 1½m Chiming: no form. *Paul Midgley*

ANNIVERSARIE 3 ch.f. Major Cadeaux 121 – Razzle (IRE) 68 (Green Desert (USA) **64**
127) [2015 55: t9.5f² t9.5f t8.6m² t9.5f* t9.5g³ 10g⁶ t9.5f t9.5g⁶ f11g Dec 29] modest
handicapper: won at Wolverhampton in March: best effort at 9.5f: acts on tapeta: usually
races nearer last than first. *John Norton*

ANNOUNCEMENT 4 ch.f. Proclamation (IRE) 130 – Anapola (GER) (Polish Precedent   –
(USA) 131) [2015 73: f12g p10g Nov 25] fair at best, no form in 2015: stays 7f: acts on
good to soft going: sometimes wears headgear. *Ronald Thompson*

ANONYMOUS JOHN (IRE) 3 gr.g. Baltic King 120 – Helibel (IRE) 73 (Pivotal 124) **100**
[2015 95: p8g² p5g³ p6g² p7f² t5.1f⁴ 5.1v⁵ 5.1f⁴ 7m⁵ 6.1g² 5.7g⁴ t6g⁵ 6m 5g⁶ 6g⁶ 7m⁵ 6g³
6g* 7v p6m⁶ t6g³ t6m² t6m² Dec 18] useful handicapper: won at Windsor in October:
placed on several other occasions, including when second at Wolverhampton (neck behind
Spring Loaded) final outing: stays 7f: acts on polytrack, tapeta and heavy going: tried in
visor prior to 2015. *David Evans*

ANONYMOUS LADY (IRE) 3 b.f. Le Cadre Noir (IRE) 113 – Dany Song (USA) **84**
(Yankee Victor (USA) 121) [2015 70: 5g³ 5f³ 6g⁴ 5.8m* 6g p5g² 5g³ 5d⁶ 5g⁵ p6g⁶ Nov 6]
fairly useful handicapper: won at Navan in July: stays 6f: acts on polytrack and good to
firm going: often wears headgear: tried in tongue tie prior to 2015: often races towards rear.
A. P. Keatley, Ireland

ANOTHER BOY 2 ch.g. (Apr 7) Paco Boy (IRE) 129 – Kurtanella 86 (Pastoral Pursuits **74**
127) [2015 5.2m⁶ 5.1s* 6.1m⁴ 6f⁵ 5.2m 6v³ 6v³ 6g³ Oct 20] compact gelding: fair performer:
won maiden at Chepstow in May: stays 6f: acts on soft going: tried in cheekpieces.
Ralph Beckett

ANOTHER FOR JOE 7 b.g. Lomitas 129 – Anna Kalinka (GER) (Lion Cavern (USA) **79**
117) [2015 87: 8.3s² 8.3s⁶ 9.2d 7.9g 8g² 8s⁵ 8d 7.9g⁵ 8.3m³ Sep 28] fair handicapper: stays
10.5f: acts on good to firm and heavy going: front runner/races prominently. *Jim Goldie*

ANOTHER PARTY (FR) 4 ch.c. Pomellato (GER) 110 – Jummana (FR) 96 (Cadeaux **112**
Genereux 131) [2015 112: 7g² a7f a6f Feb 12] strong, lengthy colt: smart ex-French-
trained performer: creditable 2¾ lengths second to Safety Check in handicap at Meydan on
reappearance: below form after: stayed 7f: acted on polytrack and soft going, probably
probably on heavy: had worn blinkers: dead. *Jamie Osborne*

ANOTHER ROYAL 4 b.f. Byron 117 – Royal Punch (Royal Applause 124) [2015 74: **83**
6g⁵ 6s³ 5.9g⁴ 5g* 6g⁶ 6m⁶ 5g⁴ 6g² 6s⁶ 5.9s³ Sep 15] fairly useful handicapper: won at
Pontefract in June: second at Newcastle in August: stays 6f: acts on soft and good to firm
going: usually wears headgear. *Tim Easterby*

ANOTHER TOUCH 2 b.g. (Mar 25) Arcano (IRE) 122 – Alsalwa (IRE) 102 (Nayef **92**
(USA) 129) [2015 6m⁴ 6g 5.9g² 7g* 7m² 6.5m 8g* Sep 19] €80,000Y: second foal: half-
brother to 10.4f winner Mufrad (by New Approach): dam, 1m winner, half-sister to smart
performer up to 1m Bossy Guest: fairly useful performer: won nurseries at Newcastle in
August and Ayr (by head from Robinnielly) in September: will probably stay further than
1m: acts on good to firm going. *Richard Fahey*

ANOTHER TRY (IRE) 10 b.g. Spinning World (USA) 130 – Mad Annie (USA)   – §
(Anabaa (USA) 130) [2015 79§: 7d⁶ 7d Jun 23] strong gelding: fairly useful at best, no
form in 2015: stays 7f: acts on polytrack, fibresand, firm and good to soft going: front
runner/races prominently: hard to catch right, and one to treat with plenty of caution.
Timothy Jarvis

ANOTHER WISE KID (IRE) 7 b.g. Whipper (USA) 126 – Romancing 79 (Dr Devious **109**
(IRE) 127) [2015 108: 6g² 6g 5m³ 5g⁴ 6s⁶ 6m 6g 6d² 5.6d³ 6g* 6m⁵ Sep 28] leggy gelding:
useful handicapper: won at Ripon (by ¾ length from Nameitwhatyoulike) in September:
2¾ lengths third to Steps in Portland at Doncaster earlier in September: stays 6f: acts on
good to firm and heavy going. *Paul Midgley*

ANSAAB 7 b.g. Cape Cross (IRE) 129 – Dawn Raid (IRE) 94 (Docksider (USA) 124) **97**
[2015 94: p10m² p10g* p10f t9.5f⁶ 10.3g 9.8d⁶ 10g⁶ 8g² 8d p10m² p10g⁴ p12g⁵ Dec 19]
useful handicapper: won at Lingfield in February: runner-up at same track in January and
November: left Tony Coyle after seventh start: stays 10.5f: acts on polytrack, good to firm
and heavy going: often in tongue tie prior to 2015. *Michael Appleby*

AN SAIGHDIUR (IRE) 8 b.g. Acclamation 118 – Brief Sentiment (IRE) 96 (Brief Truce **105**
(USA) 126) [2015 113: p6g³ 6d³ 6s³ 6g 7d 6m⁵ 6.3m⁶ 7d 5d⁶ p6g 6s* 6d 6g 6d³ p7g Oct 23]
strong gelding: useful handicapper: won at the Curragh (by 1¼ lengths from Have A Nice
Day) in August: has form at 8.5f, races at shorter: acts on polytrack, best turf form on good
going or softer (acts on heavy): tried in headgear: usually leads. *A. Slattery, Ireland*

ANSGAR (IRE) 7 b.g. Celtic Swing 138 – Jemmy's Girl (IRE) (Pennekamp (USA) 130) **102**
[2015 119: 7d 6f 6g 7d 7.5g Oct 4] tall, lengthy gelding: smart at best, just useful in 2015:
has won over 10.5f, best form at shorter: acts on polytrack and good to firm going: tried in
blinkers in 2015: usually wears tongue tie: front runner/races prominently. *Sabrina J. Harty,
Ireland*

ANSWERED 4 b.c. Authorized (IRE) 133 – Dublino (USA) 116 (Lear Fan (USA) 130) **115**
[2015 110: 12.5g* 14d² 10s² 12d⁵ Sep 12] smart performer: won listed race at Limerick
(by 5½ lengths from Waltzing Matilda) in April: second in Vintage Crop Stakes at Navan
(1¼ lengths behind Forgotten Rules) in May: well below form final start (reportedly
finished lame): stayed 1¾m: acted on soft going: dead. *J. S. Bolger, Ireland*

ANTHEM ALEXANDER (IRE) 3 ch.f. Starspangledbanner (AUS) 128 – Lady **112**
Alexander (IRE) 112 (Night Shift (USA)) [2015 116p: 6d* 6f³ 6f⁶ 6g⁴ Aug 9] good-topped
filly: has scope: smart performer: won Lacken Stakes at Naas (by length from The Happy
Prince) in June: third in Commonwealth Cup at Royal Ascot (4½ lengths behind Muhaarar)
next time: stays 6f: acts on good to firm and good to soft going: often travels strongly.
Edward Lynam, Ireland

ANTIOCO (IRE) 2 b.c. (Mar 8) Motivator 131 – Haraplata (GER) (Platini (GER) 126) **73**
[2015 7g⁵ p8g² 8.3v⁵ Oct 7] fair maiden: best effort when second in maiden at Chelmsford
(4 lengths behind Danehill Kodiac) in August, never nearer. *Marco Botti*

ANTIQUARIUM (IRE) 3 b.g. New Approach (IRE) 132 – Antillia 82 (Red Ransom **108**
(USA)) [2015 t9.5f² t9.5f* 9.9m* 12f* 16f 14f² 12m² 14g⁵ 12g Sep 5] rangy gelding:
second foal: dam, 1½m winner, half-sister to very smart 1¼m-1¾m winner Scott's View:
useful performer: won maiden at Wolverhampton in February, and handicaps at Beverley
in April and Newmarket (by 3¾ lengths from Process) in May: second in handicaps at
Ascot (½ length behind All Talk N No Do) in July and Goodwood (2 lengths behind
Dartmouth) in August: stays 1¾m: acts on tapeta and firm going. *Charlie Appleby*

ANTONOE (USA) 2 b.f. (Jan 26) First Defence (USA) 119 – Ixora (USA) (Dynaformer **105**
(USA)) [2015 7.5g* 8g* 8m Oct 4] tall, angular, rather leggy filly: fourth foal: half-sister
to 3 winners, including 1¼m winner Mixora (by Mizzen Mast): dam unraced close relative
to dam of smart French miler Mutual Trust: useful form: won newcomers race at Deauville
(by 6½ lengths from Qemah) in August and Prix d'Aumale at Chantilly (comfortably by
2½ lengths from Pleasemetoo, making all) in September: evens, sustained hairline fracture
to pelvis when 8¼ lengths behind 8 to Ballydoyle in Prix Marcel Boussac at Longchamp
next time: stays 1m. *P. Bary, France*

ANUSHKA NOO NOO 2 b.f. (Apr 15) Makfi 130 – Triple Edition (USA) (Lear Fan **65**
(USA) 130) [2015 6g⁵ 6m* 6d⁴ 8g Sep 26] 10,000Y: fourth foal: half-sister to useful
5f-8.5f winner Ana Emarati (by Forestry): dam lightly-raced half-sister to smart French/US
performer up to 8.5f Etoile Montante: fair performer: won maiden at Ripon in July: likely
to stay 7f. *Ollie Pears*

ANWAR (IRE) 2 gr.f. (Mar 26) Dark Angel (IRE) 113 – Salt Rose (Sleeping Indian 122) **66**
[2015 p5g² p5g² p5g³ 5.3d⁴ Aug 5] 15,000F, 78,000Y: first foal: dam unraced half-sister to
smart French 1m-10.5f winner In Clover, herself dam of Prix de l'Opera winner We Are:
fair maiden: best effort at 5f. *Richard Hannon*

ANYA 6 b.m. Monsieur Bond (IRE) 120 – Dyanita 76 (Singspiel (IRE) 133) [2015 92: p8g⁴ **99**
p8g² p8g* p8g⁵ Sep 5] leggy mare: useful handicapper: won at Kempton (by neck from
Strong Steps) in June: stays 1¼m: acts on polytrack, good to firm and heavy going:
sometimes slowly away, often races towards rear, usually responds generously to pressure.
Henry Candy

ANY GUEST (IRE) 2 b.c. (Mar 12) Zoffany (IRE) 121 – Princess Speedfit (FR) 77 **– p**
(Desert Prince (IRE) 130) [2015 7f 6g 6d Sep 4] 38,000F, 45,000Y: rangy colt: half-brother
to several winners, including smart winner up to 7f Imperial Guest (2-y-o 6f winner, by

Imperial Dancer) and useful winner up to 1m Excellent Guest (2-y-o 6f winner, by Exceed And Excel): dam 8.3f winner: poor form in maidens: well bred, and type to do better in handicaps. *George Margarson*

ANZHELIKA (IRE) 3 ch.f. Galileo (IRE) 134 – Ange Bleu (USA) (Alleged (USA) 138) **77 p** [2015 9.9m* Sep 11] half-sister to several winners, including French/US 9f-1½m winner Angara (by Alzao) and French 9f-10.5f winner Actrice (by Danehill), both smart: dam, French maiden (third at 1¼m), half-sister to Breeders' Cup Classic winner Arcangues: 20/1, very green when won maiden at Salisbury (by ¾ length from Reetaj) in September: sure to progress. *David Lanigan*

APACHE GLORY (USA) 7 b.m. Cherokee Run (USA) 122 – Jumeirah Glory (USA) **77** (Deputy Minister (CAN)) [2015 82: p10g⁴ p10f* p10g² p10f⁶ t9.5f³ t9.5g⁴ p10f 10g⁶ 10m p10f⁵ p10f³ p10g² Dec 9] fair handicapper: won at Lingfield in February: stays 1¼m: acts on polytrack, tapeta and good to firm going: often wears headgear: often races towards rear. *Daniel Loughnane*

APACHE SONG 2 ch.f. (Feb 16) Mount Nelson 125 – Pantita 74 (Polish Precedent **53** (USA) 131) [2015 8.3m⁴ Aug 9] sixth foal: half-sister to 2-y-o 6f winner La Pantera (by Captain Rio) and 6f/7f winner Clara Zetkin (by Elusive City): dam maiden (stayed 1½m): 14/1, fourth in maiden at Windsor (7 lengths behind Lord Kelvin) in August. *Rod Millman*

APACHE STORM 3 ch.f. Pivotal 124 – Best Side (IRE) 100 (King's Best (USA) 132) **95** [2015 82: f6d* p5g² p5f⁵ p5f 6g 5s² 6m 6d² p6m⁴ Nov 19] rather unfurnished filly: useful handicapper: won at Southwell in January: runner-up at Chelmsford (minor event) in February, Leicester in September and Newmarket (minor event, neck behind Mobsta) in October: stays 6f: acts on polytrack, fibresand and soft going: usually leads. *Michael Appleby*

APASIONA (IRE) 2 b.f. (Mar 24) Invincible Spirit (IRE) 121 – Azia (IRE) 71 (Desert **48** Story (IRE) 115) [2015 5f⁵ 5.1d⁵ Aug 5] €40,000F, 45,000Y, 36,000 2-y-o: sixth foal: half-sister to 3 winners, including useful 2-y-o 6f winner Hold Your Colour (by Verglas), later successful in Hong Kong, and 2-y-o 8.3f winner Arcano Gold (by Arcano): dam 2-y-o 7f winner: better effort when fifth in maiden at Sandown (5½ lengths behind Tawwaaq) in July. *Alan McCabe*

APICUS (USA) 2 b.f. (May 1) Speightstown (USA) 124 – Apple of Kent (USA) 118 (Kris **70 p** S (USA)) [2015 5m⁶ May 8] useful-looking filly: half-sister to several winners, including 2-y-o 1m winner Flower of Kent (by Diesis) and useful 1m (in USA)/1½m winner Imperial Pippin (by Empire Maker): dam 1m winner, later US Grade 2 8.5f winner: 14/1, sixth in maiden at Ascot (2¾ lengths behind Besharah) in May: sure to progress. *John Gosden*

APOLLO ELEVEN (IRE) 6 b.g. Manduro (GER) 135 – Arlesienne (IRE) 108 (Alzao **74** (USA) 117) [2015 –: t16.5g² p16d* t16.5g⁵ f14g⁶ t13.9f Nov 20] fair handicapper: won at Chelmsford in March: stays 16.5f: acts on polytrack, tapeta and soft going: front runner. *Michael Appleby*

APOSTLE (IRE) 6 gr.g. Dark Angel (IRE) 113 – Rosy Dudley (IRE) 72 (Grand Lodge **97** (USA) 125) [2015 102: 8g 8m 7.6g 7m 7.6g³ 8m 7.6m⁴ 7g³ p8f* Oct 24] compact gelding: useful handicapper: won at Chelmsford (by ½ length from Mulzamm) in October: stays 1m: acts on polytrack, fibresand and any turf going: tried in headgear. *David Simcock*

APPARATCHIKA 4 b.f. Archipenko (USA) 127 – Kesara (Sadler's Wells (USA) 132) **78** [2015 54p: p10g* t12.2g* t12.2f⁴ Feb 7] fair performer: won maiden at Lingfield and handicap at Wolverhampton in January: stays 1½m. *Rae Guest*

APPLEBERRY (IRE) 3 b.f. Approve (IRE) 112 – Passage To India (IRE) 74 (Indian **88** Ridge 123) [2015 87: 5g 5s* 6.1s⁶ 5g⁴ 6g 5s 5v 5.1d f5g p7d Nov 30] good-topped filly: fairly useful performer: won minor event at Hamilton (by nose from Canny Kool) in May: stays 6f: acts on soft going: tried in cheekpieces in 2015: temperament under suspicion. *Michael Appleby*

APPLEJACK LAD 4 ch.g. Three Valleys (USA) 119 – Fittonia (FR) 66 (Ashkalani (IRE) **65** 128) [2015 71: t7.1f⁴ p8g⁶ p7g⁵ f8g⁶ 12.4d⁵ 12.5m³ 10.1m² 10.1m² 12.2g 9.3m² Aug 11] good-topped gelding: fair handicapper: left John Ryan after fourth start: stays 1¼m: acts on polytrack, tapeta, good to firm and good to soft going: sometimes wears headgear: usually wears tongue tie. *Michael Smith*

APPLETON 2 ch.c. (Apr 8) Showcasing 117 – Valentina Guest (IRE) 102 (Be My Guest **91 p** (USA) 126) [2015 5m* 6.5m Sep 10] 73,000Y: fifth foal: half-brother to 2 winners, including 6f winner Beardwood (by Dutch Art): dam winner up to 1¼m (2-y-o 7f winner) who stayed 1¾m: won maiden at Pontefract (by length from Shaka Zulu) in August: better form when ninth in valuable sales race at Doncaster (5¼ lengths behind Mr Lupton): remains open to improvement. *Richard Fahey*

APPROACHING DAWN 3 ch.c. New Approach (IRE) 132 – Colorado Dawn (Fantastic **60** Light (USA) 134) [2015 p10g⁶ p10f t9.5f Mar 2] modest maiden: best effort when sixth in maiden at Lingfield in January: left John Gosden after second start. *John Butler*

APPROACHING (IRE) 4 ch.c. New Approach (IRE) 132 – Dust Dancer 116 (Suave **70** Dancer (USA) 136) [2015 66: 8m² 10g 9d p10g⁴ 9.9m³ 10.2m⁶ p8f Sep 12] lengthy colt: fair maiden: stays 1¼m: acts on polytrack and good to firm going: often in hood prior to 2015: wears tongue tie. *Amanda Perrett*

APPROACHING SQUALL (IRE) 3 ch.c. New Approach (IRE) 132 – Lady Miletrian **85** (IRE) 103 (Barathea (IRE) 127) [2015 t8.6g² 9.2m* Jun 10] fair form: won maiden at Hamilton in June: dead. *Sir Michael Stoute*

APPROACHING STAR (FR) 4 ch.f. New Approach (IRE) 132 – Madame Arcati (IRE) **–** (Sinndar (IRE) 134) [2015 76: t12.2g⁵ 8m 16g 7m⁵ 8v³ 10s⁶ Sep 13] sturdy filly: maiden: no form in 2015: often in headgear in 2015. *Ann Stokell*

APPROCAILLIS (IRE) 2 ch.c. (Apr 27) New Approach (IRE) 132 – Capercaillie **66** (USA) 101 (Elusive Quality (USA)) [2015 6d⁶ t6g⁴ p7g⁴ p8f Oct 29] good-topped colt: fair maiden: best effort at 6f. *Marco Botti*

APRICOT SKY 5 ch.g. Pastoral Pursuits 127 – Miss Apricot 48 (Indian Ridge 123) [2015 **86** 94: 6g 6m 6m 6m 6g 5g 5s 5m* 5g 5d* 5.1s⁴ 5g 5.1d Oct 14] lengthy gelding: fairly useful handicapper: won at Hamilton in August and Haydock (by length from Thorntoun Lady) in September: stays 6f: acts on good to firm and good to soft going: tried in cheekpieces in 2015: usually races prominently. *David Nicholls*

APROVADO (IRE) 3 b.g. Approve (IRE) 112 – Aldburgh (Bluebird (USA) 125) [2015 **86** 72: 6m² 6d⁵ 6g* 6g* 6.1m* 6m³ 6m⁴ 6g 6g 7d Oct 24] fairly useful handicapper: won at Redcar in May, and Pontefract (by 4 lengths from Danot) and Nottingham in June: stays 6f: acts on good to firm going: often in cheekpieces in 2015: usually races close up. *Michael Dods*

APTERIX (FR) 5 b.g. Day Flight 122 – Ohe Les Aulmes (FR) (Lute Antique (FR)) [2015 **91** t12.2g³ 12m* 14m³ 12g* 11.9g 11.8d Jul 31] fairly useful performer: won maiden at Thirsk in May and handicap at York (amateur, by ½ length from Marmion) in June: stays 1¾m: acts on good to firm going: usually races close up: fairly useful hurdler. *Brian Ellison*

AQLETTE 3 ch.f. Aqlaam 125 – Violette 106 (Observatory (USA) 131) [2015 62: f6s⁵ **48** t8.6f³ Jan 5] poor maiden: stays 8.5f: acts on tapeta and good to firm going: tried in visor. *David Evans*

AQUA ARDENS (GER) 7 b.g. Nayef (USA) 129 – Arduinna (GER) (Winged Love **96** (IRE) 121) [2015 93, a99: 7m 7g 8g 9m 7.1s* p7.5g⁵ t8.6m³ p8g Dec 7] workmanlike gelding: useful handicapper: won at Chepstow in September: third at Wolverhampton (1¼ lengths behind Home Cummins) in November: stays 8.5f: acts on all-weather, firm and soft going: tried in cheekpieces prior to 2015: often wears tongue tie: often races towards rear. *George Baker*

AQUA LIBRE 2 b.f. (Mar 26) Aqlaam 125 – Be Free 60 (Selkirk (USA) 129) [2015 p6g² **83** t7.1g* 8d⁶ 7g² 8d⁶ Oct 31] third foal: half-sister to 9.3f winner Freedom Rock (by Rock of Gibraltar): dam 1m winner: fairly useful performer: won maiden at Wolverhampton (by 1½ lengths from Fool To Cry) in August: second in nursery at Newmarket in September: stays 1m: acts on tapeta and good to soft going: often races freely. *Philip McBride*

ARAB DAWN 4 gr.g. Dalakhani (IRE) 133 – Victoire Celebre (USA) (Stravinsky (USA) **110** 133) [2015 101: 12f³ 12f* 10.4m 14g p12g³ Sep 5] workmanlike gelding: smart handicapper: won Duke of Edinburgh Stakes at Royal Ascot (by ½ length from Ajman Bridge) in June: third in September Stakes at Kempton (4 lengths behind Jack Hobbs) in September: stays 1½m: acts on polytrack, firm and good to soft going: sent to Australia. *Hughie Morrison*

ARABIAN COMET (IRE) 4 b.f. Dubawi (IRE) 129 – Aviacion (BRZ) (Know Heights **105** (IRE) 118) [2015 110: 12m³ 12m⁴ 14m 14g 14.6m 16g⁴ Sep 24] tall, attractive filly: useful performer: third in listed race at Goodwood (1½ lengths behind Miss Marjurie) in May: stays 2m: acts on polytrack and good to firm going: usually races towards rear. *William Haggas*

ARABIAN FLIGHT 6 b.m. Exceed And Excel (AUS) 126 – Emirates First (IRE) 77 (In **66** The Wings 128) [2015 72: t7.1g⁶ t7.1f³ f6g Feb 26] good-topped mare: fair handicapper: stayed 8.5f: acted on all-weather: in headgear latterly: usually made running: covered by Sepoy, sent to France. *Michael Appleby*

ARABIAN ILLUSION (FR) 3 ch.g. Makfi 130 – Arabian Spell (IRE) 100 (Desert   **92 p**
Prince (IRE) 130) [2015 75p: 8m² p8g³ 9.9s* 8.9s³ Oct 10] fairly useful form: won maiden
at Goodwood in September: good third in handicap at York in October: will prove suited
by a return to 1¼m+: acts on soft going: often races prominently: should do better still.
Andrew Balding

ARABIAN OASIS 3 b.g. Oasis Dream 129 – Love Divine 120 (Diesis 133) [2015 83:   **74**
t9.5g* p8g⁵ t8.6g Apr 28] fair performer: won maiden at Wolverhampton in March: stays
9.5f: acts on tapeta and soft going: tried in blinkers in 2015: front runner/races prominently:
temperament under suspicion. *Charlie Appleby*

ARABIAN QUEEN (IRE) 3 b.f. Dubawi (IRE) 129 – Barshiba (IRE) 116 (Barathea   **117**
(IRE) 127) [2015 100: 8.5g* 8f⁵ 8m 9.9m³ 10.4d* 11.9s⁶ 12d⁶ Oct 17]
    The track nicknamed North America's 'graveyard of champions', Saratoga
racecourse in New York, features in the essay on American Triple Crown winner
American Pharoah who suffered his only defeat of the season there at 100/35-on in
August. That reverse came only ten days after Europe's Horse of the Year Golden
Horn suffered his only defeat on European soil at York, a racecourse that itself earned
a reputation for being a 'graveyard of champions' in the 'seventies and 'eighties. The
50/1-shot Arabian Queen did the giant-killing in York's richest race, the Juddmonte
International, an event which was known as the Benson and Hedges Gold Cup for its
first fourteen runnings when Brigadier Gerard (beaten for the only time in his career),
Rheingold, Grundy, Artaius and Oh So Sharp (who completed the English fillies'
triple crown in the same season) were among the race's beaten odds-on favourites.
Upsets in the International have been much less frequent in recent times, with twelve
winning favourites (five of them odds-on, including most recently Australia, Frankel
and Sea The Stars) in the twenty runnings before the latest one, and just three beaten
odds-on shots in that time, Bosra Sham, Dylan Thomas and Await The Dawn.
    The latest edition of the International had something else in common with
the very first running in 1972, in which four-year-old Brigadier Gerard—seeking
a sixteenth straight win—was beaten at 3/1-on by the Derby winner Roberto in a
race that contained more than its share of drama, both before and during the race
(Roberto was forsaken by his Derby-winning jockey Lester Piggott who switched
to Epsom runner-up Rheingold at York, resulting in Panamanian Braulio Baeza
being flown in for Roberto on whom he adopted previously untried forcing tactics).
Although the inaugural Benson and Hedges attracted Brigadier Gerard and the first
two in the Derby, it had been thought, until a week before, that the field would
also include that other great champion of the era Mill Reef. It was being dubbed
as 'the race of the century'. Brigadier Gerard and Mill Reef had finished first and
second in the previous year's Two Thousand Guineas (after which Mill Reef was
never beaten again) and Mill Reef's absence from the Benson and Hedges with a
swollen hock, after a somewhat rushed preparation following a viral infection, was
a big disappointment. Mill Reef's stablemate and erstwhile pacemaker Bright Beam

Juddmonte International Stakes, York—a huge upset as 50/1-shot Arabian Queen
(second left) holds off the unbeaten Derby winner Golden Horn in a muddling renewal;
The Grey Gatsby (cheekpieces) finishes third ahead of Time Test (partly hidden against rail)
but the proximity of 100/1-shot Dick Doughtywylie (right) holds the form down

curiously still took part in the race despite Mill Reef being struck out, but Bright Beam was virtually run to a standstill before the home turn after trying to match strides with Roberto. The latest International also seemed to have all the ingredients to make it a race to savour, if not 'the race of the century' then certainly a candidate for 'the race of the season'. It promised a mouthwatering clash, with the top three-year-old miler Gleneagles, a dual Two Thousand Guineas winner and successful in the St James' Palace Stakes at Royal Ascot, stepping up in distance to take on the very good Derby winner Golden Horn, who had yet to taste defeat and had already beaten top older horses in the Coral-Eclipse (the ante-post betting for York was 11/8-on Golden Horn, 7/2 Gleneagles). An unexpected and prolonged spell of rain the day before the race changed the going to good to soft (from good) and eventually resulted in Gleneagles being pulled out on the day. Had the encounter taken place, it would have been the first time since the 1992 International (Rodrigo de Triano and Dr Devious) that the winners of the same season's Two Thousand Guineas and the Derby had crossed swords on a British racecourse.

With Gleneagles out and the field reduced to seven, Golden Horn started at 9/4-on with the other three-year-old colt in the International line-up, the unexposed Khalid Abdullah-owned Royal Ascot winner Time Test, sent off as second favourite at 4/1, ahead of Eclipse runner-up The Grey Gatsby at 5/1, with 22/1 bar. Only the pacemaker for Golden Horn, his lead horse at home Dick Doughtywylie (supplemented for £75,000), started at longer odds than Arabian Queen, the only filly in the field (none of her sex had won the race since One So Wonderful in 1998). Arabian Queen's trainer, who won the International with another three-year-old filly In The Groove in 1990, took umbrage afterwards at the fact that 'not one journalist phoned me in the build-up to the race … there was all that talk about the two big horses, but our filly has proper Group 1 form.' That Group 1 form before York comprised creditable efforts against her own sex when fifth in the Coronation Stakes at Royal Ascot and third in the Nassau, stepped up to a mile and a quarter, at Goodwood (with a last of seven in the Falmouth at Newmarket in between). Those three most recent efforts before the International had followed a four-length, all-the-way victory against four- and five-year-olds in the Princess Elizabeth Stakes (sponsored by Investec) on Oaks day at Epsom on her first outing for eight months. Arabian Queen's reappearance—she had been aimed at the One Thousand Guineas—had been delayed by the recurrence of a sinus problem which had also affected her at two when she won the Duchess of Cambridge Stakes (former Cherry Hinton) at Newmarket, a pattern race for which she did not incur a penalty under the conditions of the Princess Elizabeth. Even on the pick of her form, however, Arabian Queen had plenty to find to make her mark in the International and even her trainer admitted afterwards that he had thought the Group 3 Prix Minerve at Deauville on the Sunday before York might have been the more rational option, but owner Jeff Smith had been keen to go for the International in which his high-class Norse Dancer had excelled himself when runner-up in 2004.

As predicted by her trainer, there were plenty willing to regard Arabian Queen's neck victory over Golden Horn, with The Grey Gatsby and Time Test beaten into third and fourth, as a 'fluke'. 'If we hadn't run, they'd have looked at the finishing order and been calling Golden Horn the best since Frankel, but, as it is, they'll be saying we fluked it,' said David Elsworth who took no part in the presentation ceremony reportedly because he felt he had been 'patronised'. Arabian Queen's victory, on the face of it, defied logic and was the biggest shock in the International since 1993 when Ezzoud (who, incidentally, went on to win the race again the following year) won at 28/1. The longest-priced winner in the history of the race before Arabian Queen was Relkino at 33/1 in 1977. The latest International, however, turned into a muddling, tactical affair—Golden Horn's pacemaker set up a clear lead but was ignored by the others—and Arabian Queen was always in prime position, taking a keen hold but allowed by her rider to set only a modest gallop at the head of the main pack, with Golden Horn fighting for his head in behind and not settling fully until approaching the home turn. Arabian Queen took over in front from Dick Doughtywylie just inside the last two furlongs and was almost immediately challenged by Golden Horn who threw down the gauntlet over the final

Mr J. C. Smith's "Arabian Queen"

furlong but could not get past a tenacious rival, his usual finishing kick not there in the softest conditions he encountered in his career. The Grey Gatsby was three and a quarter lengths behind Golden Horn at the line, with Time Test a further length and a quarter away in fourth. The bare form, though, had to be treated with caution, with seven-year-old Dick Doughtywylie—an irrelevance in the race itself from a very early stage—finishing only a little over five lengths behind the winner and clearly flattered (he hadn't appeared on a racecourse for fourteen months). The muddling nature of the race was underlined by Arabian Queen's timefigure of 0.04 slow which was distinctly substandard for a Group 1.

Silvestre de Sousa deserved plenty of credit for his canny ride on Arabian Queen which provided him with his biggest success in a season in which he won the inaugural Stobart-sponsored jockeys' championship which ran from Two Thousand Guineas day to British Champions' Day when de Sousa received his trophy and £25,000 prize in a ceremony before racing. Paul Hanagan edged out de Sousa for the Jockeys' Association Championship in 2011, when it was decided by the number of winners ridden during the turf season (from the Lincoln to the November Handicap), and de Sousa's victory in the revamped championship was testament to his work ethic and his resilience as he fought back strongly from being sacked by Godolphin in 2014 (he was 33/1 for the title in May but ended up being the only jockey to ride a hundred winners in the mini-season, stretching clear in the second half of the campaign after being third at the end of Royal Ascot behind Ryan Moore, who was subsequently sidelined by injury, and reigning champion Richard

93

Hughes, who decided to retire from the saddle after Goodwood). One of Arabian Queen's two outings after the International also came on British Champions' Day in a good renewal of the British Champions Fillies' And Mares' Stakes. It was her second appearance at a mile and a half but she fared little better than she had in the Prix Vermeille in September, when she managed only sixth behind Treve, failing to see out the longer trip in testing ground. Starting at 14/1, she was found wanting for stamina at Ascot too after rather surprisingly being sent for home in earnest from a long way out, eventually fading into sixth of twelve behind the St Leger winner Simple Verse, beaten a little under five lengths.

Arabian Queen (IRE) (b.f. 2012)	Dubawi (IRE) (b 2002)	Dubai Millennium (b 1996)	Seeking The Gold
			Colorado Dancer
		Zomaradah (b 1995)	Deploy
			Jawaher
	Barshiba (IRE) (ch 2004)	Barathea (b 1990)	Sadler's Wells
			Brocade
		Dashiba (ch 1996)	Dashing Blade
			Alsiba

Golden Horn's campaign was a reminder that, even though the European Flat programme is dominated by racing superpowers nowadays, there is still room for a member of that endangered species, the traditional English owner-breeder, to break through from time to time with a home-bred champion. It was ironic, in some ways, that Golden Horn's unbeaten run should be ended at York by another British owner-breeder who has enjoyed consistent success against the odds. Jeff Smith's purple, light blue chevron, light blue cap has been carried by some very popular horses over the last thirty years or so, including the top sprinter-miler Chief Singer, the outstanding home-bred sprinting mare Lochsong and the prolific stayer Persian Punch whose achievements in the Cup races are commemorated with a statue at Newmarket where he won three Jockey Club Cups. Arabian Queen's family has been at Smith's Littleton Stud in Hampshire since the mid-'eighties, shortly after the stud came into his possession. Arabian Queen's great grandam Alsiba was a daughter of a half-sister to Irish Two Thousand Guineas winner Northern Treasure and Oaks d'Italia winner Paris Royal; Alsiba's dam Etoile Grise went on to become the grandam of an Irish St Leger winner, Oscar Schindler, while a half-sister to Etoile Grise became the dam of dual Yorkshire Oaks winner Only Royale whose grandson Prince of Penzance was a 100/1 winner of the Melbourne Cup in November. Alsiba's progeny have done their bit to contribute to the reputation of a most successful family, of which another branch descending from the grandam of Etoile Grise, Etoile de France, through another of that broodmare's granddaughters Sunbittern, includes Arabian Queen's sire Dubawi. Alsiba stayed well but wasn't any great shakes on the racecourse and went through the ring at the December Sales as both a three-year-old and a four-year-old, gaining her only win (at 33/1) before being acquired on behalf of Littleton Stud on her second appearance as a racemare in the Newmarket sale-ring. Home-bred Dashing Blade, who won the Dewhurst in the Smith colours, started out as a stallion at Littleton (before ending up in Germany) and sired Arabian Queen's grandam Dashiba who was a useful performer at a mile and a mile and a quarter for her breeder and then bred him five winners. Dashiba was trained by Arabian Queen's trainer, as was the pick of her offspring Arabian Queen's dam Barshiba who had sight in only one eye after being kicked as a foal by her dam. The front-running Barshiba carried her head awkwardly when racing but having one eye didn't prevent her enjoying a splendid career on the track. She ran until she was six, her seven wins including the Lancashire Oaks two years running. Both Dashiba and Barshiba were big mares, but Barshiba's first foal Arabian Queen is only sparely made. Barshiba also has a two-year-old filly by Fastnet Rock, named Australian Queen, who showed promise on her debut at Kempton in November, as well as a filly foal who is a sister to Arabian Queen. Arabian Queen will eventually join her dam among the two dozen or so Jeff Smith-owned broodmares at Littleton, but that won't be for at least another season—and possibly longer if she takes after her dam by improving with age. Arabian Queen stays ten and a half furlongs and acts on good to firm and soft going. She often races freely and, like her dam, makes the running or races prominently. *David Elsworth*

ARAB POET 2 ch.c. (Mar 15) Poet's Voice 126 – Floral Beauty 85 (Shamardal (USA) **88 p**
129) [2015 6g⁵ 7m 7d² p6g* Oct 27] first foal: dam 10.3f winner: fairly useful form: won
maiden at Lingfield (by 2¼ lengths from Alshaqee) in October: likely to prove best at 7f+:
open to further improvement. *Sir Michael Stoute*

ARAB SPRING (IRE) 5 b.h. Monsun (GER) 124 – Spring Symphony (IRE) 94 (Darshaan **119**
133) [2015 121: 12m* 10m² May 28] attractive horse: smart performer: won John Porter
Stakes at Newbury (by length from Pether's Moon) in April: creditable second in Brigadier
Gerard Stakes at Sandown (head behind Western Hymn) in May: stays 1½m: acts on
polytrack, good to firm and good to soft going: front runner/races prominently, often
travels strongly. *Sir Michael Stoute*

ARAGON KNIGHT 2 b.g. (Feb 23) Kheleyf (USA) 116 – Midnight Allure 85 (Aragon **77**
118) [2015 5.2mᵘʳ 5f⁵ 5d² 5f 5d⁶ p5g² Aug 1] workmanlike gelding: fair maiden: raced only
at 5f: acts on polytrack and good to soft going: tried in blinkers: usually leads. *Heather Main*

ARAMIST (IRE) 5 gr.g. Aussie Rules (USA) 123 – Mistic Sun (Dashing Blade 117) **100**
[2015 96: 14s³ 13s* 14f² 16.1m 21g 14d 14d Sep 26] compact gelding: useful handicapper:
won at Hamilton in May: second at Newmarket (2¼ lengths behind Elidor) next time: stays
2m: acts on any turf going: often races towards rear. *Alan Swinbank*

ARANKA 3 ch.f. Iffraaj 127 – Vallota (Polish Precedent (USA) 131) [2015 6g³ 6m* 8m⁴ **91**
7m³ Jul 18] lengthy filly: seventh foal: half-sister to smart 5f-7f winner Ialysos (by So
Factual) and 1m winner Wistar (by Dubawi): dam unraced half-sister to useful performer
up to 1m Epagris: fairly useful performer: won maiden at Windsor in June: third in
handicap at Newmarket in July: stays 1m. *Luca Cumani*

ARANTES 4 b.g. Sixties Icon 125 – Black Opal (Machiavellian (USA) 123) [2015 10.2s³ **80**
12.1m² 11m 10.2m³ 10.1m* 10d 12v 10g Sep 29] rather leggy gelding: fairly useful
handicapper: won at Epsom (apprentice, by ½ length from Lu's Buddy) in July: left Mick
Channon after seventh start: stays 1¾m: acts on polytrack, good to firm and heavy going:
tried in headgear: often races towards rear. *R. Mike Smith*

ARASHI 9 b.g. Fantastic Light (USA) 134 – Arriving 105 (Most Welcome 131) [2015 77: **68**
t13.9g² t12.2f³ t13.9g² p13.3g Feb 1] good-topped gelding: fair handicapper: stays 2m:
acts on polytrack, tapeta, good to firm and good to soft going: usually wears headgear.
Derek Shaw

ARCAMANTE (ITY) 4 b.g. High Chaparral (IRE) 132 – Caractere (IRE) (Indian Ridge **76**
123) [2015 83: 16m⁵ 16v³ 15.8m* 16d⁵ 14m³ p15.8g 13.1g⁴ 14.1s 16s⁵ Oct 23] good-
topped gelding: fair handicapper: won at Catterick in May: stays 2m: acts on soft and good
to firm going: usually in headgear prior to 2015: usually races close up. *K. R. Burke*

ARCAMIST 2 gr.f. (Feb 22) Arcano (IRE) 122 – Good Enough (FR) 109 (Mukaddamah **66 p**
(USA) 125) [2015 p7f⁴ Nov 12] 30,000Y: closely related to smart 6f-1m winner Oasis
Dancer (2-y-o 7f winner, by Oasis Dream) and half-sister to several winners, including
smart 1m-1¼m winner Smart Enough (by Cadeaux Genereux): dam, maiden in France
(fourth in Prix de Diane), later 9f winner in USA: 16/1, shaped well when fourth in maiden
at Chelmsford (2¾ lengths behind Jufn) in November: will improve. *Charles Hills*

ARCANADA (IRE) 2 ch.g. (Mar 5) Arcano (IRE) 122 – Bond Deal (IRE) 104 (Pivotal **84**
124) [2015 6m³ 7g* 7g⁴ Sep 6] 5,000F, £42,000Y: fourth foal: dam, Italian/US winner up
to 9.5f (2-y-o 7.5f winner), half-sister to useful 6f winner Dawn Eclipse: fairly useful
performer: won maiden at Chester (by ¾ length from Dark Devil) in August: best effort
when fourth in nursery at York (1¾ lengths behind Desert Ruler) in September: stays 7f.
Tom Dascombe

ARCANE DANCER (IRE) 2 b.f. (Apr 6) Arcano (IRE) 122 – La Reine Mambo (USA) **69**
(High Yield (USA) 121) [2015 5s⁶ 5m 6m 6g 6s³ 7v⁶ 7s f7g⁴ f8g* f8m⁴ f8g³ Dec 29]
€14,000Y: sixth foal: half-sister to 3 winners, including 2-y-o 6f/7f winner Pearl Arch
(by Arch) and 6f/7f winner Alumina (by Invincible Spirit): dam, useful French 1m winner
(including at 2 yrs), half-sister to smart French/US 1m/9f performer Danzon: fair performer:
won nursery at Southwell in November: stays 1m: acts on fibresand: often in headgear:
front runner/races prominently. *Lawrence Mullaney*

ARCANISTA (IRE) 2 ch.f. (Mar 14) Arcano (IRE) 122 – Cattiva Generosa 109 (Cadeaux **65**
Genereux 131) [2015 5m 6.1s⁴ 7g⁵ 6.1s² Sep 15] €12,000F, €15,000Y: lengthy filly:
seventh foal: closely related to useful French/UAE 6f winner Hattaash (by Oasis Dream)
and half-sister to French 2-y-o 9.5f winner Catmoves (by Medicean): dam French 1m
winner (including at 2 yrs): fair maiden: will be suited by a return to 7f. *Malcolm Saunders*

ARCANMAN (IRE) 3 b.g. Arcano (IRE) 122 – Rose Bourbon (USA) (Woodman (USA) 126) [2015 –: t9.5f⁶ t9.5f 7g Apr 22] maiden: no form in 2015: left Ronald Harris after first start: often in headgear in 2015. *Ollie Pears* —

ARCANO GOLD (IRE) 3 ch.g. Arcano (IRE) 122 – Azia (IRE) 71 (Desert Story (IRE) 115) [2015 84: 8s⁵ 10m 8g² 10.4m³ 10.3m 12m 10.1v Aug 31] smallish gelding: fairly useful handicapper: third at York in July: should stay 1½m: acts on good to firm and good to soft going: often races prominently. *Richard Fahey* — 92

ARC CARA (ITY) 3 b.g. Arcano (IRE) 122 – Folcara (IRE) (Brief Truce (USA) 126) [2015 73: p7f⁴ p7g² 7m⁴ 6m³ 7m² 7.1m* 7.1s⁴ 7g p8f Oct 10] rather leggy gelding: fair performer: won maiden at Chepstow in June: stays 7f: acts on polytrack and good to firm going: often in headgear in 2015: front runner/races prominently: sold 30,000 gns, sent to Singapore. *Ralph Beckett* — 76

ARCHAIC (IRE) 2 b.c. (Apr 20) Acclamation 118 – Classic Legend 96 (Galileo (IRE) 134) [2015 p7g⁵ t6f* p6g³ Dec 30] £120,000Y: second foal: dam, winner up to 10.4f (2-y-o 1m winner), sister to 1½m-1¾m winner I Have A Dream and half-sister to winner up to 7f Jallota (both smart): fairly useful form: best effort when winning maiden at Wolverhampton (by ¾ length from Munira Eyes) in October, sticking to task: will prove suited by a return to 7f+: remains with potential. *Charlie Appleby* — 84 p

ARCHANGE (FR) 3 b.f. Arcano (IRE) 122 – Carinae (USA) 99 (Nureyev (USA) 131) [2015 6s² 7g⁶ 7g⁶ 6g⁵ 5.5g 5.5g⁴ 6s 6g p6.5g⁵ p7.5g⁶ p7g t7.1f² p8m Dec 31] fair handicapper: first past the post at Wolverhampton in December (demoted to second for causing interference): left H-A. Pantall after tenth start: stays 1m: acts on polytrack, tapeta and soft going: tried in hood in 2015. *J. J. Feane, Ireland* — 77

ARCHANGEL RAPHAEL (IRE) 3 b.c. Montjeu (IRE) 137 – La Sylvia (IRE) 102 (Oasis Dream 129) [2015 88p: 12g* 11.9m⁶ 10d Sep 13] useful performer: won minor event at Fairyhouse (by 2 lengths from Outspoken) in July: in rear after in Grand Prix de Paris at Longchamp and handicap at the Curragh: likely to stay at least 1¾m: acts on good to firm going: in headgear/tongue tie in 2015. *Aidan O'Brien, Ireland* — 101

ARCHIBALD THORBURN (IRE) 4 br.g. Duke of Marmalade (IRE) 132 – Winged Harriet (IRE) 85 (Hawk Wing (USA) 136) [2015 74: p6m p6f⁴ 6g³ Jun 7] fair handicapper: left Peter Hedger after second start: stays 7f: acts on polytrack: tried in headgear: often starts slowly, usually races nearer last than first. *Aidan Anthony Howard, Ireland* — 69

ARCHIE (IRE) 3 b.g. Fast Company (IRE) 126 – Winnifred (Green Desert (USA) 127) [2015 88p: 7m 8d⁴ 10d Jul 25] fairly useful handicapper: stays 1m: often in hood in 2015. *Tom Dascombe* — 90

ARCHIE RICE (USA) 9 b.g. Arch (USA) 127 – Gold Bowl (USA) (Seeking The Gold (USA)) [2015 11.6m⁶ Aug 9] lengthy gelding: useful at best, no form in 2015: stays 1½m: acts on polytrack and good to firm going. *Jimmy Frost* —

ARCHIE'S ADVICE 4 b.g. Archipenko (USA) 127 – Flylowflylong (IRE) 74 (Danetime (IRE) 121) [2015 82: p11g⁶ p10m 8.3s* 9.2d⁴ 10m³ 11.5g 9.2d² 10g⁴ 10d 10g⁵ 12s t9.5f f11g⁵ Dec 15] fairly useful handicapper: won at Hamilton (by ½ length from Sakhalin Star) in May: third at Ayr in June and second at Hamilton in July: stays 1¼m: acts on polytrack, soft and good to firm going: tried in cheekpieces in 2015: often races prominently: not straightforward (carries head awkwardly/looks ungainly under pressure). *Keith Dalgleish* — 81 a73

ARCHIE STEVENS 5 b.g. Pastoral Pursuits 127 – Miss Wells (IRE) (Sadler's Wells (USA) 132) [2015 p7g t6m⁶ t5.1m⁵ f6s t5.1m p6f² t6g⁴ 6m² 6f⁵ 5.3s² t5.1g* 5.3m² 5m⁵ 5.2m* 5.1m³ 5g³ 6g⁵ 6.1m t7.1g³ t5.1f* p7m⁶ Dec 31] fairly useful performer: won claimer at Wolverhampton and handicap at Newbury in June, and handicap at Wolverhampton (by 1½ lengths from Eland Ally) in December: left Michael Wigham after second start: effective at 5f to 7f: acts on polytrack, tapeta and good to firm going: tried in cheekpieces prior to 2015. *David Evans* — 75 a86

ARCHILLES (USA) 3 gr.g. Arch (USA) 127 – Niceling (USA) (Maria's Mon (USA) 121) [2015 t8.6g⁵ 10m⁶ 10m⁴ 8.3f⁴ 8g 11.7f² 13.1f⁴ 12g⁴ 11.9g 9.9g Sep 17] lengthy gelding: fair maiden: stays 13f: best form on firm going: tried in headgear: usually leads. *Jo Hughes* — 74

ARCHIMEDES (IRE) 2 b.g. (Mar 27) Invincible Spirit (IRE) 121 – Waveband 102 (Exceed And Excel (AUS) 126) [2015 5g² 5s⁵ 5m* 5f p5f⁶ t6f⁶ Oct 31] €240,000Y: good-topped gelding: second foal: dam, winner up to 7f (2-y-o 5f winner), half-sister to very smart sprinter Muarrab: fairly useful performer: won maiden at Bath in June: best form at 5f: acts on firm going: tried in hood: often in tongue tie. *Paul Cole* — 81

ARCHIMENTO 2 ch.c. (Mar 25) Archipenko (USA) 127 – Caribana 77 (Hernando (FR) **79**
127) [2015 7s³ Oct 13] 16/1, third in maiden at Leicester (2 lengths behind Vincent's
Forever) in October, possibly helped by way race developed. *Ed Dunlop*

ARCHIPELIGO 4 b.g. Archipenko (USA) 127 – Red Slew (Red Ransom (USA)) [2015 **77**
80: t12.2f* t13.9g⁵ 10m³ 10.4f⁶ 10s 9.2g 8m 12.2g⁶ 9.2m* t12.2f² t12.2f t9.5g⁶ Dec 1] **a83**
fairly useful handicapper: won at Wolverhampton in January and Hamilton (apprentice) in
September: stays 1½m: acts on tapeta and good to firm going: tried in hood prior to 2015:
often races towards rear. *Iain Jardine*

ARCHITECTURE (IRE) 2 b.f. (Feb 23) Zoffany (IRE) 121 – Brigayev (ITY) (Fasliyev **87 p**
(USA) 127) [2015 8d³ 8.3d* Oct 14] €4,800F, £26,000Y: second foal: half-sister to Italian
6f-1m winner Norbanus (by Footstepsinthesand): dam Italian maiden: better effort when
winning maiden at Nottingham (by 1½ lengths from De Veer Cliffs) in October: will go on
improving. *Hugo Palmer*

ARCH WALKER (IRE) 8 ch.g. Choisir (AUS) 126 – Clunie 84 (Inchinor 119) [2015 53: **50**
6s³ 5d⁶ 6g 6d⁴ 5.9g 5spu Oct 6] good-bodied gelding: modest handicapper: pulled up at
Catterick: stays 6f: acted on soft and good to firm going: often wore headgear: dead.
John Weymes

ARC LIGHTER (USA) 6 b.g. Street Cry (IRE) 130 – Flamelet (USA) 94 (Theatrical **92**
(IRE) 128) [2015 –: p8f⁶ t9.5f⁵ p11g² 11.6m² 10g² 14f 12g p16g⁶ 10g⁴ 10d Aug 15] big
gelding: fairly useful handicapper: twice runner-up at Windsor in April: stays 11.5f: acts on
polytrack, tapeta and good to firm going: tried in headgear in 2015: often wears tongue tie.
Seamus Durack

ARCTIC FEELING (IRE) 7 ch.g. Camacho 118 – Polar Lady 69 (Polar Falcon (USA) **103**
126) [2015 105: p5g 6g* 6g 5m 6m³ 6s 6m 5m 5g⁵ 5.4g 6g⁶ 6g⁵ 5s⁴ 5v* 5d Oct 24] lengthy
gelding: useful handicapper: won at Newcastle (by neck from Withernsea) in April and
Catterick in October: stays 6f: acts on polytrack, fibresand, good to firm and heavy going:
tried in headgear prior to 2015: often races towards rear. *Richard Fahey*

ARCTIC FLOWER (IRE) 2 gr.f. (Apr 29) Roderic O'Connor (IRE) 119 – Just In Love **55**
(FR) (Highest Honor (FR) 124) [2015 6m 6m 7m⁴ 6g 6m² 7v⁵ 7s p7g p5g⁴ p5f² p7g⁴ p6d³
p6g³ Dec 15] 10,000F: rather leggy filly: half-sister to several winners, including 2-y-o 1m
winner Dauberval (by Noverre) and 1¼m winner (including at 2 yrs) Stiff Upper Lip (by
Sakhee's Secret): dam unraced sister to useful French performer up to 11f Justful: modest
maiden: stays 7f: acts on polytrack, good to firm and heavy going: front runner/races
prominently. *John Bridger*

ARCTIC LYNX (IRE) 8 b.g. One Cool Cat (USA) 123 – Baldemara (FR) (Sanglamore **83**
(USA) 126) [2015 90: f5g* t5.1g³ t5.1f² f5d⁶ t5.1f* t5.1m⁶ p5d* t5.1g² p5g* p5f³ p5g⁴
p5m³ p5m⁶ p5g p5g p5g⁴ p5g Aug 22] sturdy gelding: fairly useful performer: won claimer
at Southwell in January, and handicaps at Wolverhampton in February, and Chelmsford in
March and April: stays 6f: acts on all-weather, firm and good to soft going: sometimes
wears headgear: tried in tongue tie prior to 2015. *Conor Dore*

ARCTIC ROYAL (IRE) 2 ch.f. (Feb 27) Frozen Power (IRE) 108 – Bronze Queen (IRE) **–**
(Invincible Spirit (IRE) 121) [2015 6d Oct 26] €8,000F, €28,000Y: third foal: half-sister to
smart 5f (including at 2 yrs) winner Abstraction (by Majestic Missile) and 5f/6f winner The
Dandy Yank (by Dandy Man): dam well held in maidens: 28/1, well held in maiden at
Redcar. *Ann Duffield*

ARDLUI (IRE) 7 b.g. Galileo (IRE) 134 – Epping 81 (Charnwood Forest (IRE) 125) **96**
[2015 100: 16g³ 16.4m Jul 11] strong, sturdy gelding: useful handicapper: third at Ripon
(5¼ lengths behind Trip To Paris) in April: stays 2m: acts on good to firm and heavy going:
tried in blinkers: front runner/races prominently. *Tim Easterby*

ARDMAY (IRE) 6 b.g. Strategic Prince 114 – Right After Moyne (IRE) (Imperial Ballet **88**
(IRE) 110) [2015 90: 10.3d⁴ 10.1g⁶ 10.3s² 10.3g 10d⁵ 10v Nov 3] good-bodied gelding:
fairly useful handicapper: second at Chester in May: stays 10.5f: acts on good to firm and
heavy going: sometimes wears headgear. *Kevin Ryan*

ARD SAN AER (IRE) 2 b.c. (Apr 8) Acclamation 118 – Allannah Abu 102 (Dubawi **87**
(IRE) 129) [2015 5d² 5d 6v* 5f 7g Dec 29] €75,000Y: useful-looking colt: second foal: half-
brother to 2-y-o 7f winner Plus Ca Change (by Invincible Spirit): dam 11f/1½m winner:
fairly useful performer: won maiden at Leopardstown (by length from Mint Chai) in May:
left J. S. Bolger after third start: should stay 7f: usually in cheekpieces. *M. Hamad Al Attiya,
Qatar*

AREEN (IRE) 2 b.c. (Mar 19) Kodiac 112 – Falcolnry (IRE) 86 (Hawk Wing (USA) 136) **106**
[2015 5g* 5m⁶ 5f² 6m⁶ 5.5g³ 6g⁶ 5m Sep 11] £18,000Y, 85,000 2-y-o: sturdy colt: third
foal: dam 2-y-o 7f winner: useful performer: won minor event at York (by 1½ lengths from
Ravenhoe) in May: second in listed Windsor Castle Stakes at Royal Ascot (head behind
Washington DC) in June and third in Prix Robert Papin at Maisons-Laffitte (2 lengths
behind Gutaifan) in July: should stay 6f: acts on firm going: temperament under suspicion.
Kevin Ryan

AREIOPAGOS (IRE) 3 br.g. Lawman (FR) 121 – Athene (IRE) 83 (Rousillon (USA) –
133) [2015 10m p8g May 28] lengthy gelding: no form: sent to France. *Sir Michael Stoute*

ARETHUSA 3 b.f. Rip Van Winkle (IRE) 134 – Acquifer 75 (Oasis Dream 129) [2015 84p: **89**
9.9g⁶ 8.1m³ 8g⁴ p8g³ p8g p8m³ Nov 21] good-topped filly: fairly useful handicapper: third
at Kempton in September and third at Lingfield in November: stays 1m: acts on polytrack
and good to firm going: usually races nearer last than first. *Ed Dunlop*

ARGAKI (IRE) 5 ch.g. Strategic Prince 114 – Amathusia (Selkirk (USA) 129) [2015 88, **85**
a75: t8.6g⁶ 9s³ t8.6g* 10g⁴ 8g⁶ 8g⁴ 9.9m⁶ 8g* 7.2g⁴ 10s⁴ 8.3s⁶ 7.9m 8.9m² 8d⁵ 7.9g* 8m² **a67**
8g* p8f Oct 1] fairly useful handicapper: won at Wolverhampton in April, Ayr in July,
Carlisle in August and Ayr (by 1½ lengths from Kiwi Bay) in September: stays 1¼m: acts
on tapeta, soft and good to firm going: tried in headgear prior to 2015: front runner/races
prominently. *Keith Dalgleish*

ARGANTE (FR) 6 b.g. Singspiel (IRE) 133 – Abyaan (IRE) 106 (Ela-Mana-Mou 132) **81**
[2015 14m t16.5f³ Sep 19] sturdy gelding: fairly useful handicapper: won at Chantilly and
Saint-Cloud in 2014: creditable third at Wolverhampton in September: stays 16.5f: acts on
polytrack, tapeta and soft going: usually wears blinkers: tried tongue tied. *Henry Spiller*

ARGENT TOUCH 4 gr.g. Elnadim (USA) 128 – The Manx Touch (IRE) 70 (Petardia 113) **52 §**
[2015 68: p5m⁴ f5g t5.1f⁴ t5.1f⁵ p5m⁵ 5.1d 5m 5m 5.1m⁵ 5.1d⁵ t5.1f p5g* p5g³ t5.1f f5g **a58 §**
t5.1m Dec 18] good-topped gelding: modest handicapper: won at Kempton in September:
stays 6f: acts on all-weather, soft and good to firm going: often in headgear in 2015:
untrustworthy. *Derek Shaw*

ARGOT 4 b.g. Three Valleys (USA) 119 – Tarot Card 100 (Fasliyev (USA) 120) [2015 80: **70**
p12f³ Apr 21] fair handicapper: stays 1½m: acts on polytrack, best turf form on good
going: often races towards rear. *Charlie Longsdon*

ARGUS (IRE) 3 b.c. Rip Van Winkle (IRE) 134 – Steel Princess (IRE) 106 (Danehill **98**
(USA) 126) [2015 8g⁵ 9.8d* 10g* 12g⁶ 12d* Oct 24] 400,000Y: good-bodied colt: sixth
foal: half-brother to very smart French 1½m/13f winner Sarah Lynx (by Montjeu) and
smart winner up to 1¼m Sugar Boy (2-y-o 7.5f-9f winner, by Authorized): dam French
winner up to 10.5f (2-y-o 7.5f winner): useful performer: won maiden at Ripon and
handicap at Windsor in June, and handicap at Doncaster in October: stays 1½m: acts on
good to soft going: usually races prominently. *Ralph Beckett*

ARGYLE (IRE) 2 gr.c. (Feb 4) Lawman (FR) 121 – All Hallows (IRE) (Dalakhani (IRE) **73**
133) [2015 8.3g 9s⁶ 10d² Oct 5] fair maiden: best effort when second in maiden at
Pontefract (2¼ lengths behind Heaven Scent) in October: will be suited by 1¼m+.
William Muir

ARISTOCLES (IRE) 2 b.g. (Feb 28) High Chaparral (IRE) 132 – Amathusia (Selkirk **55 p**
(USA) 129) [2015 t8.6g Dec 5] half-brother to several winners, including useful 1¼m
winner (stayed 13f) Troas (by Dalakhani) and 1¼m/11f winner Kinyras (by Peintre
Celebre): dam unraced half-sister to very smart winner up to 1½m Posidonas: 50/1, showed
something when seventh in maiden at Wolverhampton (12 lengths behind Mutawaaly)
in December, having hopeless task from position: bred to stay 1¼m+: better to come.
Sir Michael Stoute

ARISTOCRACY 4 b.g. Royal Applause 124 – Pure Speculation 80 (Salse (USA) 128) –
[2015 78: t12.2g p10f t13.9f Oct 13] rather unfurnished gelding: fair at best, no form in
2015: tried in blinkers in 2015: often races prominently. *Andy Turnell*

ARISTOCRATIC 2 b.f. (Feb 18) Exceed And Excel (AUS) 126 – Peeress 124 (Pivotal **83 p**
124) [2015 7g³ 7g³ Sep 26] good-topped, attractive filly: fourth foal: closely related to
useful 1m winner (stayed 10.5f) Enobled (by Dansili) and half-sister to useful 6f/7f winner
Ladyship (by Oasis Dream): dam 7f/1m (including Sun Chariot Stakes and Lockinge
Stakes) winner: better effort when third in maiden at Newmarket (2 lengths behind First
Victory) in September, not knocked about: remains with potential. *Sir Michael Stoute*

ARISTOCRATIC DUTY 4 b.f. Zamindar (USA) 116 – Duty Paid (IRE) 99 (Barathea **59**
(IRE) 127) [2015 71: 10g⁴ 8g⁵ 10.1m⁴ 9.9m⁶ t12.2g⁵ 12d² 15.8s⁴ 10s Oct 16] modest
maiden: stays 1½m: acts on polytrack, good to firm and good to soft going: tried in
cheekpieces in 2015. *Geoffrey Harker*

ARITHMETIC (IRE) 2 b.c. (Feb 22) Invincible Spirit (IRE) 121 – Multiplication 82 **70**
(Marju (IRE) 127) [2015 7s⁴ 6g Aug 29] better effort when fourth in maiden at Newbury
(6¼ lengths behind Storm Rising) in August. *Charles Hills*

ARIZE (IRE) 2 b.f. (Mar 31) Approve (IRE) 112 – Raise (USA) (Seattle Slew (USA)) **70**
[2015 5v⁴ t7.1f³ t7.1f³ t7.1f⁵ Nov 20] 12,000Y: half-sister to 3 winners, including 2-y-o 6f
winner X Raise (by Aussie Rules): dam, US 1m winner, half-sister to smart 2-y-o 6f
(Railway Stakes) winner Lizard Island: fair maiden: best effort at 7f. *David Brown*

ARIZONA JOHN (IRE) 10 b.g. Rahy (USA) 115 – Preseli (IRE) 115 (Caerleon (USA) **79**
132) [2015 89, a81: 12.1m⁴ 12m² 10g³ 12g* 11.5d³ 12.1mᵖᵘ Aug 12] lengthy gelding: fair
handicapper: won at Thirsk in July: stays 13f: acts on any turf going: tried in blinkers prior
to 2015. *John Mackie*

ARIZONA SNOW 3 b.g. Phoenix Reach (IRE) 124 – Calgary (Pivotal 124) [2015 60· t6f **57**
t5.1g t6m⁶ 6.1m 7s 6g 7.4d⁵ 8.1d 6s² p6f³ f6g* Dec 29] modest performer: won minor
event at Southwell in December: stays 6f: acts on polytrack, fibresand, best turf form on
good going: usually wears headgear. *Ronald Harris*

ARIZONA SUNRISE 2 b.g. (Mar 3) Sakhee's Secret 128 – Phoenix Rising (Dr Fong **69**
(USA) 128) [2015 p6f 6s⁵ p6f⁵ 6d⁴ 7g p6f t5.1g Nov 27] rather leggy gelding: fair maiden: **a60**
left Richard Hannon after fifth start: should be suited by at least 7f: acts on soft going.
David Brown

ARJEED (IRE) 2 b.f. (Apr 29) Arcano (IRE) 122 – Jeed (IRE) 86 (Mujtahid (USA) 118) **56**
[2015 6g 5m 5g⁴ 7.2d 7.2g p6g⁶ Nov 13] half-sister to several winners, including
useful 2-y-o 6f winner Nidhaal (by Observatory) and useful 11.6f-1¾m winner Maslak (by
In The Wings): dam 2-y-o 6f winner: modest maiden: stays 6f: acts on polytrack: tried in
blinkers. *L. Smyth, Ireland*

ARKANSAS SLIM (IRE) 3 b.g. Montjeu (IRE) 137 – Janoubi (Dansili 127) [2015 69: **69**
p8g⁶ 8.3m⁵ 9.9g 10.2m 8.3d 8v² 8m³ 7s t8.6f Oct 23] rather leggy gelding: fair maiden:
stays 8.5f: acts on good to firm going: front runner/races prominently. *Charles Hills*

ARLECCHINO (IRE) 5 b.g. Hernando (FR) 127 – Trullitti (IRE) 91 (Bahri (USA) 125) **57**
[2015 79: p12f⁶ Jan 21] sturdy gelding: fair handicapper: stayed 13f: acted on polytrack,
firm and good to soft going: usually in headgear (not sole outing in 2015): had worn tongue
tie: often raced towards rear: dead. *Gary Moore*

ARLECCHINO'S LEAP 3 br.g. Kheleyf (USA) 116 – Donna Giovanna 74 (Mozart **80**
(IRE) 131) [2015 72: p6f⁴ t6g² p7g³ 7m* 5.7f³ 7g² 7v⁵ t7.1m² t7.1f* p6g⁵ Dec 7] lengthy **a86**
gelding: fairly useful handicapper: won at Brighton in June and Wolverhampton in
October: stays 7f: acts on polytrack, tapeta and good to firm going: usually wears headgear.
Mark Usher

ARLECCHINO'S ROCK 2 ch.g. (Mar 6) Rock of Gibraltar (IRE) 133 – Xtra Special **73**
69 (Xaar 132) [2015 5m³ 5f⁶ 6m² t6g⁵ 7v⁴ 7g 7d³ Sep 27] fair maiden: stays 7f: acts on
good to firm and good to soft going: often races in rear. *Mark Usher*

ARMADILLO (FR) 2 ch.c. (Mar 29) Heliostatic (IRE) 115 – Vivement Dimanche (Royal –
Applause 124) [2015 7d Sep 21] 100/1, very green when tailed off in maiden at Leicester.
Ismail Mohammed

ARMELLE (FR) 4 b.f. Milk It Mick 120 – Park Ave Princess (IRE) 63 (Titus Livius (FR) **70**
115) [2015 70, a58: 6d³ 7g 5g 6.1m⁴ 6m⁴ 6g⁶ 6g 6d² 6v Nov 3] fair handicapper: stays 6f:
acts on polytrack, fibresand, good to firm and good to soft going: sometimes in cheekpieces
prior to 2015: front runner/races prominently. *Scott Dixon*

ARMS AROUND ME (IRE) 3 ch.g. Lope de Vega (IRE) 125 – Mexican Milly (IRE) 60 **75**
(Noverre (USA) 125) [2015 57: 6d² 6m² 7.9g³ 7m³ 6m³ t7.1g Dec 5] fair maiden:
left Bryan Smart after fifth start: stays 1m: acts on good to firm and good to soft going.
James Given

ARMSEY 2 b.g. (Mar 26) Bahamian Bounty 116 – Carina Ari (IRE) (Imperial –
Ballet (IRE) 110) [2015 p5g p6g Nov 25] no form. *Gary Moore*

ARNOLD LANE (IRE) 6 b.h. Footstepsinthesand 120 – Capriole (Noverre (USA) 125) **96**
[2015 103: 6d 6g 7.6v 6g 6d 7s* 7v p7f* p7g² p7f⁶ Dec 21] leggy horse: useful handicapper:
won at Catterick in October and Chelmsford in November: second at Lingfield (½ length
behind Certificate) in December: stays 1m: acts on polytrack, tapeta, good to firm and
heavy going: front runner/races prominently. *Mick Channon*

Qatar Racing Limited's "Arod"

AROD (IRE) 4 b.c. Teofilo (IRE) 126 – My Personal Space (USA) 80 (Rahy (USA) 115) **125**
[2015 115: 9g² 8m³ 8.5g* 8f* 8g² 10.1g 8d Nov 7] tall, useful-looking colt: high-class
performer: won Diomed Stakes at Epsom (by 2 lengths from Custom Cut) in June and
Summer Mile Stakes at Ascot (by 1½ lengths from Lightning Spear) in July: also ran well
when third in Lockinge Stakes at Newbury (length behind Night of Thunder) in May and
second in Sussex Stakes at Goodwood (½ length behind Solow) in July: trip/ground
excuses in Australia last 2 starts when in rear in Cox Plate at Moonee Valley and Emirates
Stakes (Handicap) at Flemington: best around 1m: acts on firm going: front runner/races
prominently, often travels strongly. *Peter Chapple-Hyam*

AROUSAL 3 b.f. Stimulation (IRE) 121 – Midnight Mover (IRE) 73 (Bahamian Bounty —
116) [2015 34: 5g 7g 7m 9m 7m Aug 4] angular filly: maiden: no form in 2015: tried in
headgear. *Ron Barr*

ARRACOURT 3 b.g. Multiplex 114 – Retaliator 80 (Rudimentary (USA) 118) [2015 63: —
8.5m⁵ 12.2m Sep 4] maiden: no form in 2015: should stay beyond 8.5f: often races
prominently. *Tim Easterby*

ARRANMORE BOY 2 b.g. (Feb 11) Archipenko (USA) 127 – Highly Spiced (Cadeaux **55**
Genereux 131) [2015 7g 7.5g⁶ 7.5d⁵ 8.3s⁴ 7s p8g Nov 11] modest maiden: stays 8.5f: acts
on soft going: tried in cheekpieces: sometimes slowly away, often races in rear: temperament under suspicion. *Nigel Tinkler*

ARRANMORE GIRL (IRE) 2 b.f. (Apr 9) Approve (IRE) 112 – Annmary Girl (Zafonic **68**
(USA) 130) [2015 5m⁴ 5m* 5m May 23] €9,000Y: half-sister to 3 winners, including
useful 11.7f/1½m winner Tooreen Legend (by Rakti) and 2-y-o 6f winner Dry Speedfit
(by Desert Style): dam, Italian 6f (at 2 yrs)/6.5f winner, half-sister to smart winner up to 9f
Noll Wallop: fair performer: best effort when winning maiden at Beverley (by 2¼ lengths
from Bond Bombshell) in April, making all: raced only at 5f: sent to USA. *Nigel Tinkler*

ARRAYAN 10 b.g. Catcher In The Rye (IRE) 115 – Ganga (IRE) 94 (Generous (IRE) 139) **66**
[2015 p12g³ f12s³ Feb 3] fair maiden: better effort in 2015 when third in handicap at
Southwell in February: in blinkers final start in 2015. *Alexandra Dunn*

ARRIELLA 3 b.f. Dapper – Bedtime Blues 48 (Cyrano de Bergerac 120) [2015 10g 11.5s[6] **42**
8m[6] f8g[4] Nov 3] fourth foal: dam, maiden (stayed 6f), out of useful 6f/7f performer
Boomerang Blade: poor maiden: stays 1m. *John Davies*

ARROWTOWN 3 b.f. Rail Link 132 – Protectress 110 (Hector Protector (USA) 124) **77**
[2015 57p: p12g[4] p11g p13.3f[4] Oct 22] fair maiden: best effort at 1½m: usually wears hood.
Roger Charlton

ARROWZONE 4 b.g. Iffraaj 127 – Donna Giovanna 74 (Mozart (IRE) 131) [2015 94: **93**
p8g[6] t9.5m[5] 8g* 7.6s[2] 8m 8g 8g 8.5s 10d[2] 10v Nov 3] lengthy gelding: fairly useful
handicapper: won at Pontefract in April: second at Lingfield in May and Pontefract in
October: left Garry Moss after fourth start: stays 1¼m: acts on polytrack and heavy going:
tried in cheekpieces prior to 2015. *David Barron*

ARRUCIAN 2 b.f. (Feb 19) Medicean 128 – Arruhan (IRE) 87 (Mujtahid (USA) 118) **–**
[2015 6d Sep 15] half-sister to several winners, including 1m-1½m winner Sohgol (by
Singspiel) and 8.6f-1¼m winner (stayed 1½m) Kidlat (by Cape Cross): dam winner up to
7f (2-y-o 6f winner): 50/1, shaped as if amiss in maiden at Catterick. *John Weymes*

ARRYZONA 4 b.g. Phoenix Reach (IRE) 124 – Southwarknewsflash 59 (Danetime (IRE) **– §**
121) [2015 –§: p10f p14g p12f 11.5d[5] Jun 4] temperamental maiden, little form: tried in
cheekpieces. *Christine Dunnett*

ARSENALE (GER) 4 b.f. Nicaron (GER) 116 – Alte Rose (GER) (Monsun (GER) 124) **54**
[2015 10g[5] f12g* 10.3d[6] 12.4g f14g f14f[6] Dec 17] modest handicapper: won at Southwell **a63**
in April: best effort at 1½m: acts on fibresand: tried in cheekpieces in 2015. *Michael Appleby*

ARTBEAT (IRE) 3 b.f. Dutch Art 126 – Easy Beat (IRE) (Orpen (USA) 116) [2015 6d 7d **56**
6d[6] f6g[2] Dec 29] neat filly: second foal: half-sister to 5f/6f winner (including at 2 yrs)
Simple Rhythm (by Piccolo): dam unraced: modest maiden: best effort at 6f. *Julia Feilden*

ART BLEU 2 b.c. (Jan 26) Dutch Art 126 – Deep Bleu (Kyllachy 129) [2015 p7g p7g **–**
Oct 7] no form. *Sir Mark Prescott Bt*

ART CHARTER (FR) 3 b.f. Artiste Royal (IRE) 116 – Lady Sylvester (USA) (Elusive **–**
Quality (USA)) [2015 65: t12.2m[6] p12g Dec 19] maiden: no form in 2015: usually wears
headgear. *K. R. Burke*

ART COLLECTION (FR) 2 b.g. (Mar 18) Shakespearean (IRE) 120 – Renascent Rahy **87**
(Rahy (USA) 115) [2015 5.7f[2] 5.3s* 6m 7m 7s[3] 6v[5] 6g* p5f[2] Nov 19] €13,000Y, £40,000
2-y-o: neat gelding: fourth foal: dam unraced: fairly useful performer: won maiden at
Brighton in May and nursery at Windsor in October: second in nursery at Chelmsford in
November: will be suited by a return to 6f: acts on polytrack and soft going: tried in
blinkers. *Gary Moore*

ART DZEKO 6 b.g. Acclamation 118 – Delitme (IRE) (Val Royal (FR) 127) [2015 62: **–**
f7d[5] f6d[5] Mar 11] big, workmanlike gelding: fair at best, no form in 2015: stays 7f: acts on
fibresand and any turf going: tried in cheekpieces: sometimes slowly away, often races
towards rear. *Brian Baugh*

ART ECHO 2 b.g. (Mar 8) Art Connoisseur (IRE) 121 – Madhaaq (IRE) 87 (Medicean **81**
128) [2015 7g[2] 6d[3] 7s 7s* p7m[5] Oct 21] neat unfurnished gelding: second foal: brother to
Italian winner up to 1m Beauty of Art (2-y-o 6f winner): dam, ungenuine 1¼m winner,
half-sister to useful performer up to 1m Mutahayya: fairly useful performer: won maiden
at Brighton in October: stays 7f: acts on polytrack and soft going: front runner/races
prominently. *Jonathan Portman*

ARTEMIS (IRE) 4 b.f. Marju (IRE) 127 – Silver Arrow (USA) 67 (Shadeed (USA) 135) **35**
[2015 64: p5m[6] Jan 9] poor maiden: acts on polytrack, best turf form on good to
firm going: sometimes wears hood: tried in tongue tie prior to 2015. *Conrad Allen*

ARTESANA 3 ch.f. Mastercraftsman (IRE) 129 – Koniya (IRE) (Doyoun 124) [2015 60: **63**
12.1s[3] 11.5d 11.6m[2] 14m[5] 12d 12.1m[6] p11g p12g f8g t9.5m Dec 26] lengthy, rather
sparely-made filly: modest maiden: left William Knight after seventh start: should stay
1¾m: acts on soft and good to firm going: tried in headgear in 2015: usually races nearer
last than first. *David Evans*

ARTFUL MIND 2 b.c. (Feb 25) Cape Cross (IRE) 129 – Tiriana (Common Grounds 118) **67**
[2015 t7.1f[4] t7.1m[4] t8.6f[3] Dec 14] fair maiden: best effort when fourth in maiden at
Wolverhampton (3¾ lengths behind Sky Ship) in November: will stay 1m. *Jamie Osborne*

ARTFUL PRINCE 5 ch.g. Dutch Art 126 – Royal Nashkova (Mujahid (USA) 125) [2015 **92**
85: 8.3d 8.3m[2] 8.3s[2] 8.3m[3] 8.9g 9g* 10m* t9.5g[5] 10.3m 9m 9.8d 9g t8.6f Oct 20] rangy
gelding: fairly useful handicapper: won at Ripon and Newmarket in June: stays 1¼m: acts
on soft and good to firm going: usually wears blinkers. *James Given*

ARTHENUS 3 b.g. Dutch Art 126 – Lady Hen 68 (Efisio 120) [2015 62p: 8d³ 8g³ p8g² **109 p** 8.3d* 8d* 8.9s* Oct 10] useful performer: won maiden at Nottingham (by ½ length from Amazing Charm) in August, minor event at Ascot (by ½ length from Robert The Painter) in September and handicap at York (by head from Librisa Breeze) in October: stays 9f: acts on polytrack and soft going: often races in rear: will go on improving. *James Fanshawe*

ARTHUR'S CHOICE 2 b.g. (Mar 11) Dandy Man (IRE) 123 – Miss Sharapova (IRE) **–** 69 (Almutawakel 126) [2015 6g 6m Jun 15] no form. *Bill Turner*

ARTHURS SECRET 5 ch.g. Sakhee's Secret 128 – Angry Bark (USA) 62 (Woodman **77** (USA) 126) [2015 12.4g⁴ 14g⁵ 16.1d* 16m⁶ 17.1d 14.1s t12.2m Dec 26] close-coupled gelding: fair handicapper: won at Newcastle in May: stays 2m: acts on tapeta and heavy going: sometimes wears headgear: front runner/races prominently. *John Quinn*

ARTIGIANO (USA) 5 ch.g. Distorted Humor (USA) 117 – Angel Craft (USA) (A P Indy **113** (USA) 131) [2015 112: a9.4f³ a9.9f³ Feb 19] good-bodied, attractive gelding: smart handicapper: third at Meydan in January (3¼ lengths behind I'm Back) and February (blinkered, 4½ lengths behind Storm Belt): stays 1¼m: acts on dirt, heavy and good to firm going: carried head awkwardly/hung left in 2015. *Charlie Appleby*

ARTISAN 7 ch.g. Medicean 128 – Artisia (IRE) (Peintre Celebre (USA) 137) [2015 p12g⁶ **52 §** p13.3g⁶ p12f Mar 11] rather leggy gelding: modest handicapper: stays 2m: acts on polytrack, fibresand, best turf form on good to firm going: in cheekpieces in 2015: tried in tongue tie: sometimes slowly away, often races towards rear: ungenuine. *Shaun Lycett*

ARTISANDRA (FR) 2 ch.f. (Jan 27) Mastercraftsman (IRE) 129 – Kezia (FR) (Spectrum **53 p** (IRE) 126) [2015 p7g⁶ 7.4g 7m Jul 30] €60,000Y: fourth foal: half-sister to French 5.5f winner Ammia (by Medicean) and French 7f winner Menandore (by Invincible Spirit): dam useful French winner up to 1m (2-y-o 6f winner): modest form in maidens: open to improvement in handicaps. *William Knight*

ARTIST CRY 3 ch.g. Dutch Art 126 – Twenty Seven (IRE) 75 (Efisio 120) [2015 49: p5g⁵ **52** f5s⁵ t7.1m 7.2g 6g 6sᵖᵘ Oct 15] modest maiden: stays 7f: acts on polytrack and tapeta: tried in cheekpieces in 2015: sent to Spain. *Richard Fahey*

ARTISTICALLY 2 b.f. (Apr 15) Holy Roman Emperor (IRE) 125 – Artistry 69 (Night **–** Shift (USA)) [2015 6m p5g 5.1g Sep 30] seventh foal: half-sister to 3 winners, including 5f/6f winner Greenhead High (by Statue of Liberty): dam, 7f winner, half-sister to useful 7f/1m winner Attune: no form: tried in blinkers. *Robert Eddery*

ARTISTIC FLARE 3 ch.f. Dutch Art 126 – Pantile (Pivotal 124) [2015 –: 9.2s⁶ 7g⁶ 10g **–** Jul 5] maiden: no form in 2015: often in blinkers in 2015. *Michael Dods*

ARTISTIC FLIGHT (IRE) 3 b.g. Art Connoisseur (IRE) 121 – Robin (Slip Anchor **71** 136) [2015 63: p10f³ p12m⁴ p10f⁶ p10g* 10.1v⁵ p10f p12m⁵ p12g* Nov 13] fair handicapper: won at Lingfield in August and November (apprentice): stays 1½m: acts on polytrack: usually in cheekpieces in 2015. *Jim Boyle*

ARTISTS MODEL (IRE) 2 b.f. (Apr 24) Dutch Art 126 – Zarwala (IRE) 92 (Polish **63** Precedent (USA) 131) [2015 t6f³ p6g³ Dec 2] £38,000 2-y-o: sixth foal: dam, 11f winner, half-sister to useful 1½m winner Zarebiya: better effort when third in maiden at Kempton (7½ lengths behind Field of Stars) in December, well positioned. *Henry Candy*

ART LOOKER (IRE) 3 b.g. Excellent Art 125 – Looker 75 (Barathea (IRE) 127) [2015 **–** t8.6f⁵ 10m Apr 13] no form. *Jo Hughes*

ART OBSESSION (IRE) 4 b.g. Excellent Art 125 – Ghana (IRE) (Lahib (USA) 129) **88** [2015 87p: 7.2s² 7d 6g⁴ 6g 6d 7.2g Sep 29] fairly useful handicapper: stays 1m: acts on polytrack, soft and good to firm going. *David Barron*

ART OF WAR (IRE) 4 b.g. Invincible Spirit (IRE) 121 – Chica Roca (USA) 49 **–** (Woodman (USA) 126) [2015 90: 8m May 15] fairly useful at best, no form in 2015: stays 9f: acts on good to firm going. *Ed Walker*

ART SCHOLAR (IRE) 8 b.g. Pyrus (USA) 106 – Marigold (FR) 88 (Marju (IRE) 127) **86** [2015 89: t9.5f p11g⁵ Dec 9] sturdy gelding: fairly useful handicapper: stays 1½m: acts on polytrack, tapeta and any turf going: tried in headgear prior to 2015. *Michael Appleby*

ARTSY 2 b.f. (Jan 30) Dutch Art 126 – Penang Cry (Barathea (IRE) 127) [2015 7g 7.6g 7g **65** p6f* p6m Oct 28] 45,000F, 58,000Y: fourth foal: half-sister to 1½m winners Harbinger Lass (by Thousand Words) and Avenue des Champs (by Champs Elysees): dam unraced half-sister to King George VI and Queen Elizabeth Stakes winner Harbinger: fair performer: won nursery at Chelmsford in October: best effort at 6f: acts on polytrack: often races in rear. *Roger Varian*

ART WORLD (IRE) 3 b.g. Art Connoisseur (IRE) 121 – Human Touch (Oasis Dream 129) [2015 t7.1f t6g³ 5g⁴ 5g* 5m 5g* Sep 12] fair performer: won maiden at Thirsk in July and handicap at Musselburgh in September: best form at 5f: best form on good going. *Brian Ellison* **65**

ARTY CAMPBELL (IRE) 5 b.g. Dylan Thomas (IRE) 132 – Kincob (USA) 63 (Kingmambo (USA) 125) [2015 t16.5g* 16m² 16m³ 18g³ 21g⁴ 16m Oct 2] good-bodied gelding: fairly useful handicapper: won at Wolverhampton (amateur) in April: third at Goodwood and Pontefract in June: stays 21f: acts on polytrack, tapeta, good to firm and heavy going: often races in rear. *Bernard Llewellyn* **87**

ARU CHA CHA 4 b.g. Myboycharlie (IRE) 118 – Royal Arruhan 69 (Royal Applause 124) [2015 77: 7g p6g p8f t6m 7s p7g⁵ p8f⁴ Dec 17] neat gelding: modest maiden: stays 1m: acts on polytrack and good to firm going. *Roger Ingram* **56**

ARUN SANDS (IRE) 2 b.c. (Feb 2) Duke of Marmalade (IRE) 132 – Without Precedent (FR) (Polish Precedent (USA) 131) [2015 8.3s⁶ Oct 28] 25/1, held back by inexperience when sixth in maiden at Nottingham: dead. *David Simcock* **–**

ARYIZAD (IRE) 6 b.m. Hurricane Run (IRE) 134 – Daziyra (IRE) (Doyoun 124) [2015 79: 12.1g⁶ 10m 10g Sep 17] fair handicapper: stays 1½m: acts on good to firm and heavy going. *Alan Swinbank* **67**

AS A DREAM (IRE) 3 b.f. Azamour (IRE) 130 – Wedding Dream 81 (Oasis Dream 129) [2015 65: t8.6f⁴ t9.5f p10g t9.5f t9.5g Jun 26] close-coupled filly: modest handicapper: stays 9.5f: acts on polytrack, tapeta, best turf form on good to soft going: tends to find little. *Nikki Evans* **56**

ASAFOETIDA (IRE) 2 b.f. (May 21) Pivotal 124 – Embraced 103 (Pursuit of Love 124) [2015 p8f⁵ Nov 12] sister to 8.6f winner Abbraccio and half-sister to several winners, including useful 1m winner Fondled (by Selkirk) and useful 7f-9f winner (stayed 1½m) Tartan Gunna (by Anabaa): dam, 1m winner (including at 2 yrs), half-sister to very smart miler Cesare: 10/1, promising fifth in maiden at Chelmsford (5½ lengths behind Flyweight) in November, never nearer: open to plenty of improvement. *Peter Chapple-Hyam* **67 p**

ASBEAU 3 b.g. Captain Gerrard (IRE) 113 – Your Gifted (IRE) 96 (Trans Island 119) [2015 t7.1m⁴ t8.6f Oct 9] better effort when fourth in maiden at Wolverhampton in September, not knocked about. *Michael Appleby* **50**

ASBURY BOSS (IRE) 4 gr.g. Dalakhani (IRE) 133 – Nick's Nikita (IRE) 109 (Pivotal 124) [2015 100: 16g³ 20f 16d⁶ Jul 19] sturdy gelding: useful handicapper: third at the Curragh (2¼ lengths behind Pyromaniac) in May: stays 2m: best form on good going: often in cheekpieces in 2015: usually races close up. *M. Halford, Ireland* **97**

ASCRIPTION (IRE) 6 b.g. Dansili 127 – Lady Elgar (IRE) (Sadler's Wells (USA) 132) [2015 8m 7d² 7g⁵ 7s² 7g Oct 9] sturdy gelding: has reportedly had breathing operation: smart performer: missed 2014: runner-up in Timeform Jury Stakes (John of Gaunt) at Haydock (½ length behind Cable Bay) in May and listed race at Newbury (¾ length behind Hathal) in September: stays 1m: acts on soft going: often wears hood: often wears tongue tie: usually travels strongly. *Hugo Palmer* **115**

ASEELA (IRE) 5 b.m. Teofilo (IRE) 126 – Valse Mystique (IRE) (Grand Lodge (USA) 125) [2015 63: 10.1d 10g 10.3m⁴ Jun 27] poor handicapper: stays 10.5f: acts on soft and good to firm going: often races towards rear: one to treat with caution. *George Moore* **48 §**

AS GOOD AS GOLD (IRE) 3 b.f. Oasis Dream 129 – You'll Be Mine (USA) 107 (Kingmambo (USA) 125) [2015 79: 7g⁵ 6.1g³ 6m* 6g² 5.9g³ 6.1g⁴ 6d Aug 28] fairly useful performer: won maiden at Ripon in June and handicap at Nottingham (by 2½ lengths from Lolita) in August: stays 7f: acts on good to firm going: tried in cheekpieces in 2015: front runner/races prominently. *Richard Fahey* **90**

ASHA 4 ch.f. Dutch Art 126 – Golden Asha 96 (Danehill Dancer (IRE) 117) [2015 67: 6g⁶ 5f 6g³ 6m³ 6d p6m f8g Nov 24] modest maiden: stays 6f: acts on good to firm and good to soft going: tried in visor in 2015. *David C. Griffiths* **62**

ASHADIHAN 2 b.f. (Mar 2) Kyllachy 129 – Miss Delila (USA) (Malibu Moon (USA)) [2015 6g* 6f² 6g Aug 20] 48,000 2-y-o: good-topped filly: half-sister to several winners, including useful 1¼m winner Mythical Madness (by Dubawi) and 2-y-o 6f/7f winner Lady of The House (by Holy Roman Emperor): dam twice-raced half-sister to smart 2-y-o 6f winner Sander Camillo: useful performer: won maiden at Haydock in May: best effort when second in Albany Stakes at Royal Ascot (1½ lengths behind Illuminate) in June, suited by way race developed: bumped at start and never travelling in Lowther Stakes at York: raced only at 6f. *Kevin Ryan* **103**

ASHAPURNA (IRE) 3 ch.f. Tamayuz 126 – Bond Deal (IRE) 104 (Pivotal 124) [2015 –: — 10d Apr 24] workmanlike filly: maiden: no form in 2015: in visor sole start in 2015. *William Knight*

ASHDOWN LASS 3 b.f. Sir Percy 129 – Antibes (IRE) (Grand Lodge (USA) 125) [2015 **66** 10m⁶ 10f p10g 11.5g p10g* Oct 27] rather leggy filly: third foal: sister to 1¼m-1½m winner Ashdown Lad: dam, French 7.5f winner, half-sister to smart winner up to 1½m Forgotten Voice: fair performer: won handicap at Lingfield in October: best effort at 1¼m: acts on polytrack: tried in visor. *Lucy Wadham*

ASHFORD ISLAND 2 b.g. (Feb 20) Munnings (USA) 118 – Falling Angel 86 (Kylian (USA)) [2015 6m t6g⁶ 6d 8.1m⁶ Sep 10] £12,000Y, £31,000 2-y-o: strong gelding: first foal: dam 7f winner: little form in maidens/nursery. *Mike Murphy*

A SHIN HIKARI (JPN) 4 gr.c. Deep Impact (JPN) 134 – Catalina (USA) (Storm Cat **127** (USA)) [2015 8.9g* 8.9f* 8.9f* 9.9f 9.9g* Dec 13] half-brother to several winners in Japan: dam US 5.5f and (including at 2 yrs) 6f winner: high-class performer: has won 9 of his 11 races, including listed race at Kyoto in May, Group 3 Epsom Cup at Tokyo in June, Group 2 Mainichi Okan at Tokyo in October and Hong Kong Cup at Sha Tin (by length from Nuovo Record) in December: only ninth of 18 behind Lovely Day in Tenno Sho (Autumn) at Tokyo on penultimate start: stays 1¼m: acts on firm going: wears a hood. *Masanori Sakaguchi, Japan*

ASHJAN 2 b.c. (Mar 18) Medicean 128 – Violet (IRE) 77 (Mukaddamah (USA) 125) [2015 — 8.3v Oct 7] 100/1, green when well held in maiden at Nottingham. *Mick Channon*

ASHPAN SAM 6 b.g. Firebreak 125 – Sweet Patoopie 72 (Indian Ridge 123) [2015 111: **112** 6g 6m* 5g 6m 5.6d 5s³ Oct 13] leggy gelding: smart handicapper: won at Epsom (by 2½ lengths from Newton's Law) in June: third at Leicester (length behind Demora) in October: stays 6f: acts on good to firm and heavy going: often in cheekpieces in 2015: front runner/ races prominently. *John Spearing*

ASHRIDGE LAD 3 b.g. Invincible Spirit (IRE) 121 – Leavingonajetplane (IRE) 76 **102** (Danehill (USA) 126) [2015 77: 8f² 8m⁴ 8g* 8d³ 8m* 8g Aug 21] strong, lengthy gelding: useful performer: won maiden at Newmarket in June and handicap at Newmarket in August: third in handicap at Ascot (2¼ lengths behind Portage) in July: stays 1m: acts on good to firm and good to soft going: usually races close up. *Brian Meehan*

ASIA MINOR (IRE) 6 ch.m. Pivotal 124 – Anka Britannia (USA) (Irish River (FR) 131) **71** [2015 85: p13.3g⁴ Feb 4] good-topped mare: fair handicapper: stays 1½m: acts on polytrack: sometimes in tongue tie prior to 2015: often races in rear. *Dr Jon Scargill*

ASIAN TRADER 6 b.g. Acclamation 118 – Tiger Waltz (Pivotal 124) [2015 93: 5v Apr — 3] fairly useful at best, no form in 2015: stays 5.5f: acts on firm and good to soft going: often in tongue tie prior to 2015: usually races nearer last than first. *Ruth Carr*

ASIAN WING (IRE) 6 ch.g. Hawk Wing (USA) 136 – Blue Beacon 68 (Fantastic Light **84** (USA) 134) [2015 58: p12g⁵ p12m³ p16g* p12g* p12g 14g⁶ 17g³ 15s* 18d⁵ 16.4s³ Oct 10] **a74** fairly useful handicapper: won at Dundalk in March and April (apprentice), and Ayr in August: stays 2¼m: acts on polytrack and soft going: usually wears headgear: usually wears tongue tie. *J. J. Feane, Ireland*

ASIMA (IRE) 3 ch.f. Halling (USA) 133 – Sospira (Cape Cross (IRE) 129) [2015 69: p8m* **77** p10m⁴ 8.3m³ p10g³ 9.9d⁵ May 14] fair performer: won maiden at Lingfield in January: stays 1¼m: acts on polytrack and good to firm going. *Charles Hills*

ASK DAD 5 b.g. Intikhab (USA) 135 – Don't Tell Mum (IRE) 99 (Dansili 127) [2015 86: **77** p6g 7m² 6m* 6g⁵ 5m⁶ 6g 7d 6s 5s p5g a6g 6dᵘʳ Sep 23] fair handicapper: won at Naas in **a50** June: stays 7f: acts on polytrack, good to firm and good to soft going: often wears headgear/ tongue tie: often starts slowly: usually held up. *Damian Joseph English, Ireland*

ASKER (IRE) 7 b.g. High Chaparral (IRE) 132 – Pay The Bank 81 (High Top 131) [2015 — 12v p15.8g Dec 2] rather leggy gelding: fairly useful at best, no form in 2015: stays 17.5f: best form on heavy going: wears headgear: temperament under suspicion. *Zoe Davison*

ASKNOTWHAT (IRE) 4 ch.g. Dylan Thomas (IRE) 132 – Princess Roseburg (USA) **69** (Johannesburg (USA) 127) [2015 80: p10.7g⁶ 10.2m⁴ 11.9d⁴ Jun 23] fair handicapper: left W. McCreery after first start: stays 1½m: acts on good to firm and heavy going: sometimes wears headgear. *David Bridgwater*

ASK THE GURU 5 b.g. Ishiguru (USA) 114 – Tharwa (IRE) 63 (Last Tycoon 131) [2015 **80** 79: p5g p6f p5f* p5f⁶ p6f p5g* p5g³ 5m² 5.3d³ 5f 5m 5g p5g⁶ Dec 19] lengthy gelding: fairly useful handicapper: won at Lingfield in February (dead-heated) and March: second at Sandown in June: stays 6f: acts on polytrack, good to firm and heavy going: usually wears headgear. *Michael Attwater*

ASPASIUS (GER) 3 b.g. Desert Prince (IRE) 130 – Aspasia Lunata (GER) (Tiger Hill **68 d**
(IRE) 127) [2015 7s² 7.5d⁵ p8m p7g p10g Dec 15] fair performer: won maiden at Baden-
Baden at 2 yrs: left K. Demme, Germany after second start in 2015: stays 7.5f: acts on soft
going. *Gary Moore*

ASPIRANT 4 b.g. Rail Link 132 – Affluent 89 (Oasis Dream 129) [2015 77: 6m 6g 5s Oct **44**
6] rather unfurnished gelding: poor handicapper: stays 7f: acts on polytrack: tried in
headgear: tried in tongue tie prior to 2015. *Marjorie Fife*

ASSAULT ON ROME (IRE) 3 b.f. Holy Roman Emperor (IRE) 125 – Naomh Geileis **91**
(USA) 95 (Grand Slam (USA) 120) [2015 82: 8d 9.8g⁶ 7.9v 7d* 8.5m² 8.3d⁵ 7g* 7.2s⁵ **a85**
7.6m⁴ 7d⁶ 7g 7.6v⁵ 8d* 8g 7g⁶ 8g⁴ 8d⁴ 7.2g 8g t8.6f⁵ p8m⁴ p7g t7.1f* Dec 21] big,
workmanlike filly: fairly useful handicapper: won at Leicester in June and July, Goodwood
in August and Wolverhampton (awarded race) in December: stays 8.5f: acts on tapeta,
good to firm and good to soft going: usually in headgear in 2015: inconsistent, and
temperament under suspicion. *Mark Johnston*

ASSERTIVE AGENT 5 b.m. Assertive 121 – Agent Kensington 65 (Mujahid (USA) **59**
125) [2015 69: p6g⁵ p7g⁴ p6g⁶ p6f³ t6g³ t5.1m⁶ t6m⁵ Dec 30] modest handicapper: stays 6f:
acts on polytrack, tapeta, firm and good to soft going: tried in headgear. *Tony Carroll*

ASSISTED 2 ch.g. (May 7) Motivator 131 – More Sirens (IRE) 91 (Night Shift (USA)) – **–**
[2015 p7g t7.1f Dec 22] well held in maidens: will be suited by at least 1m: in hood.
George Peckham

ASSOCIATION 2 b.c. (Feb 24) Kyllachy 129 – Steal The Curtain (Royal Applause 124) **–**
[2015 5g 5g 8s Oct 16] no form. *John Weymes*

ASTAIRE (IRE) 4 b.c. Intense Focus (USA) 117 – Runway Dancer (Dansili 127) [2015 **118**
117: 6d² 6g* 6g⁶ 6g⁵ 6f³ 6f Jul 11] big, good-topped colt: smart performer: won Abernant
Stakes at Newmarket (by ½ length from Watchable) in April: creditable effort after when
third in Diamond Jubilee Stakes at Royal Ascot (2¼ lengths behind Undrafted) in June:
below form in July Cup at Newmarket final start: suffered fatal bout of colic in August:
stayed 6f: acted on firm and soft going: usually led. *Kevin Ryan*

ASTEROIDEA 4 b.f. Sea The Stars (IRE) 140 – Speciosa (IRE) 115 (Danehill Dancer **80**
(IRE) 117) [2015 90: 12d 12.1m Apr 23] leggy filly: fairly useful handicapper: stays 1½m:
acts on good to firm going: usually leads. *Pam Sly*

ASTLEY HALL 2 ch.g. (Feb 15) Dutch Art 126 – Haigh Hall 84 (Kyllachy 129) [2015 5g* **92**
5.1d 6m⁵ 5m² 5g* 7g² Dec 29] second foal: half-brother to 6f winner Robin Park (by
Invincible Spirit); dam, 2-y-o 5f winner, half-sister to useful 7f-8.3f winner Balducci: fairly
useful performer: won maiden at Redcar in April and nursery at Thirsk in August: left
Richard Fahey £45,000 after fifth start: best form at 5f: best form on good going: has been
slowly away: often races prominently. *Mohammed Jassim Ghazali, Qatar*

ASTRA HALL 6 ch.m. Halling (USA) 133 – Star Precision 103 (Shavian 125) [2015 91: **59**
f12g⁶ p13g⁶ 12s t12.2g 10.2g 10d⁴ f12g Nov 24] angular mare: modest handicapper: left
Simon Hodgson after fourth start: stays 1½m: acts on heavy going: tried in cheekpieces in
2015. *Michael Appleby*

ASTRAL STORM 3 br.g. High Chaparral (IRE) 132 – Highland Shot 91 (Selkirk (USA) **–**
129) [2015 7.1s 10.1d Sep 27] no form: sent to Italy. *Andrew Balding*

ASTRAL WEEKS 4 b.f. Sea The Stars (IRE) 140 – Miss Universe (IRE) 99 (Warning **72**
136) [2015 69p: p12m* p13.3m² 14m May 2] fair performer: won maiden at Lingfield in
January: stays 13.5f. *Michael Bell*

ASTRELLE (IRE) 3 br.f. Makfi 130 – Miss Mariduff (USA) (Hussonet (USA)) [2015 98: **96**
7m⁴ 7s 6.9g Jun 24] close-coupled filly: useful performer: creditable 2 lengths fourth to
Osaila in Nell Gwyn Stakes at Newmarket on reappearance: below form after: stays 7f:
acts on good to firm and good to soft going: front runner/races prominently. *Marco Botti*

ASTROMAJOR 3 b.g. Royal Applause 124 – Astromancer (USA) 62 (Silver Hawk **–**
(USA) 123) [2015 p8m t9.5f⁵ p10g 16g Jul 30] no form. *Mark H. Tompkins*

ASTRONEREUS (IRE) 4 ch.c. Sea The Stars (IRE) 140 – Marie Rheinberg (GER) **117**
(Surako (GER) 114) [2015 101: 10s⁴ 12f* 12f³ 14m* 14g³ 14g Aug 22] rangy colt: smart
handicapper: won at Newmarket (by head from Quest For More) in May and York (by 1¼
lengths from Dashing Star) in July: also ran well when third in Duke of Edinburgh Stakes
at Royal Ascot (beaten 2¼ lengths by Arab Dawn) in June and third at Goodwood (½ length
behind Blue Wave) in July: stays 1¾m: acts on firm and good to soft going: usually races
prominently. *Amanda Perrett*

ASTROPHYSICS 3 ch.g. Paco Boy (IRE) 129 – Jodrell Bank (IRE) 63 (Observatory – (USA) 131) [2015 104: 5g 6g 5s 5v p5g f5g Dec 12] sturdy, close-coupled gelding: useful at best, below form in 2015: tried in blinkers in 2015: tried in tongue tie in 2015. *Ann Duffield*

ASTROVIRTUE 4 b.g. Virtual 122 – Astrolove (IRE) (Bigstone (IRE) 126) [2015 58: – 12.1f 10g Jul 15] workmanlike gelding: maiden: no form in 2015: best effort at 11f: acts on polytrack (has shown nothing on turf). *Mark H. Tompkins*

ASTROWOLF 4 b.g. Halling (USA) 133 – Optimistic 90 (Reprimand 122) [2015 –: p12g **53** f12d⁵ Jan 22] modest maiden: should stay 1½m: acts on polytrack, best turf form on good to soft going. *Mark H. Tompkins*

ASYAD (IRE) 4 b.f. New Approach (IRE) 132 – Elle Danzig (GER) 118 (Roi Danzig **108** (USA)) [2015 99: 10m³ 12f* 12g³ 14.6m³ 12g Sep 25] useful performer: won handicap at Ascot (by ¾ length from Dreamlive) in July: third in Park Hill Stakes at Doncaster (¾ length behind Gretchen) in September: stays 14.5f: acts on any turf going: usually races prominently. *Sir Michael Stoute*

ATAB (IRE) 3 b.f. New Approach (IRE) 132 – Moon's Whisper (USA) (Storm Cat (USA)) **72** [2015 79p: 10.3m⁶ 10m³ Jul 15] fair handicapper: stays 1¼m. *Charles Hills*

ATALAN 3 b.c. Azamour (IRE) 130 – Capriolla 55 (In The Wings 128) [2015 56p: 11.6g **75** p13.3m* 14.1m p16g² p16g* 14.1d Oct 26] workmanlike colt: fair handicapper: won at Chelmsford in May and August: stays 2m: acts on polytrack. *Hughie Morrison*

ATAMAN (IRE) 3 b.g. Sholokhov (IRE) 121 – Diora (Dashing Blade 117) [2015 **81** 10f² t12.2g² 10m³ 12s² Oct 19] €30,000F, 110,000Y: well-made gelding: first foal: dam, German 1m winner, half-sister to useful German 11f winner Dominante: fairly useful maiden: stays 1½m. *Roger Charlton*

ATHAS AN BHEAN 2 b.f. (Apr 18) Royal Applause 124 – Dusty Moon 78 (Dr Fong **90** (USA) 128) [2015 5d* 5m⁴ 5g 5m⁴ 6g⁶ 7s⁶ 7s⁶ Nov 24] 5,500F, 1,500Y: smallish filly: fourth foal: half-sister to 7.4f winner (stays 1½m) Mariners Moon (by Mount Nelson): dam, 2-y-o 7f winner, out of smart winner up to 1½m Dust Dancer: fairly useful performer: won maiden at Cork in April: stays 7f: acts on soft and good to firm going: tried in blinkers: tried in tongue tie. *A. P. Keatley, Ireland*

ATHENIAN GARDEN (USA) 8 b.m. Royal Academy (USA) 130 – Webee (USA) **55 §** (Kingmambo (USA) 125) [2015 t6f t7.1f⁶ f7g p10m 7s⁶ p10g³ 8g⁶ p10g⁶ p10g² p12g⁴ p10f p12g* p12g³ p12g³ p12f⁵ p10g Dec 30] modest handicapper: won at Lingfield (apprentice) in October: left Heather Dalton after third start: stays 1½m: acts on polytrack: tried in hood in 2015: tried in tongue tie prior to 2015: one to treat with caution. *Paddy Butler*

ATHLETIC 6 b.g. Doyen (IRE) 132 – Gentle Irony 65 (Mazilier (USA) 107) [2015 102: **97** p7g 7g 7d⁵ 6m⁴ 7g 7m³ 7m 7m* 7m⁶ 7.6g 7m⁵ 7s 8g² 8m³ 8.3s t9.5m Dec 26] sturdy gelding: useful handicapper: won at Newmarket in July: second at Newmarket (½ length behind Haaf A Sixpence) in September and third in minor event at Ascot (3¼ lengths behind Sir Robert Cheval) in October: stays 1m: acts on polytrack, good to firm and heavy going: usually wears headgear: sometimes slowly away: consistent. *Andrew Reid*

ATHLON (IRE) 2 b.g. (Apr 25) Arakan (USA) 123 – Alexander Divine (Halling (USA) **65** 133) [2015 p8g⁴ t9.5f⁵ p8g Nov 18] fair maiden: hung left second start: has been gelded. *David Lanigan*

ATHOLLBLAIR BOY (IRE) 2 ch.g. (Mar 29) Frozen Power (IRE) 108 – Ellxell (IRE) **76** (Exceed And Excel (AUS) 126) [2015 6m 6m⁵ 6m* 6d⁴ Aug 28] fair performer: won maiden at Ripon in August: raced only at 6f. *Nigel Tinkler*

ATLANTIC AFFAIR (IRE) 4 gr.f. Clodovil (IRE) 116 – Adultress (IRE) (Ela-Mana- **82** Mou 132) [2015 –: p8f⁴ p10f⁴ t9.5f⁴ p8m⁴ 8g² 8.3s 10.2s 8m⁶ 8g³ 8.5g 8.3m² 8.9g* 8d⁴ 8m p8g⁴ 8g² 9.2g² 8m⁵ 8.3d⁴ p8f⁶ Oct 22] fairly useful handicapper: won at Musselburgh and Newmarket in July: stays 9f: acts on polytrack, firm and good to soft going: tried in blinkers in 2015: front runner/races prominently. *Mark Johnston*

ATLANTIC SUN 2 br.c. (Feb 15) Roderic O'Connor (IRE) 119 – Robema 89 (Cadeaux **95** Genereux 131) [2015 7g² 8s* 7g² Oct 21] 48,000G, £52,000Y: tall, useful-looking colt: fourth foal: dam, 7.4f/1m winner, half-sister to smart US performer up to 1¼m Lucky Chappy: useful performer: won maiden at Ffos Las (by 1½ lengths from Ormito) in September: best effort when second in minor event at Newmarket (2½ lengths behind Hayadh) in October: will benefit from return to 1m. *Richard Hannon*

ATLANTIS CROSSING (IRE) 6 b.g. Elusive City (USA) 117 – Back At de Front (IRE) 70 (Cape Cross (IRE) 129) [2015 79§, a98§: p8m p6g 6m⁶ t7.1g⁵ p7g p7g² t7.1g⁵ 7g* 7g⁶ p7g⁶ Sep 5] lengthy gelding: fairly useful handicapper: won at Lingfield in July: second at Kempton in June: stays 1m: acts on polytrack, firm and good to soft going: wears headgear: unreliable: sent to Italy. *Jim Boyle* **71 §**
a85 §

ATLETICO (IRE) 3 b.c. Kodiac 112 – Queenofthefairies (Pivotal 124) [2015 90p: 6m³ t6g* 6g² Aug 1] useful-looking colt: useful performer: won maiden at Wolverhampton in June: second in handicap at Newmarket (2 lengths behind Cartmell Cleave) in August: raced only at 6f: acts on tapeta: often races prominently. *Roger Varian* **98**

ATRAYU (IRE) 2 b.g. (Mar 3) Jeremy (USA) 122 – Feis Ceoil (IRE) 86 (Key of Luck (USA) 126) [2015 6m 6m 6d³ p5f⁵ Sep 22] 50,000Y, 44,000 2-y-o: first foal: dam, 7f winner, half-sister to smart 1½m-15.5f winner Stretarez: modest form in maidens/nursery: should be suited by at least 1m: remains with potential. *Paul D'Arcy* **64 p**

ATREUS 3 b.g. Indesatchel (IRE) 120 – Devassa 60 (Reel Buddy (USA) 118) [2015 64: 6m 5g² 6s⁵ 6d 5g 6.1m⁶ 7m³ 7m³ 8d⁶ 6g t7.1f⁶ t8.6f* Oct 20] fair handicapper: won at Wolverhampton in October: stays 8.5f: acts on tapeta, soft and good to firm going: sometimes in headgear in 2015. *Michael Easterby* **67**

ATTAIN 6 b.g. Dansili 127 – Achieve (Rainbow Quest (USA) 134) [2015 71: p8g p10g* p10g³ 9.9m³ 10.2m* 9g 9.9m⁴ p10g* 10.1g⁶ 9.9v 10.1g³ 9.9d⁵ t8.6f p10f p10g³ Dec 7] good-topped gelding: fair handicapper: won at Lingfield in February, Nottingham (apprentice) in May and Lingfield in July: stays 1¼m: acts on polytrack, good to firm and heavy going: sometimes wears headgear: usually in tongue tie in 2015. *Julia Feilden* **62**
a70

ATTENDU (FR) 2 b.c. (Apr 2) Acclamation 118 – Gwenseb (FR) 113 (Green Tune (USA) 125) [2015 6d² 6g* 7g* 8m 7s³ Nov 1] half-brother to smart French 7f/1m (Prix de Sandringham) winner Impassable and useful French winner up to 1m Foreign Tune (5.5f winner at 2 yrs), both by Invincible Spirit: dam French winner up to 1m (5f winner at 2 yrs): smart performer: won maiden at Deauville in August and Prix La Rochette at Longchamp (by head from Lawmaking) in September: good 1½ lengths third to Johannes Vermeer in Criterium International at Saint-Cloud final outing: will prove best up to 1m: acts on soft and good to firm going. *C. Laffon-Parias, France* **111**

ATTENTION SEAKER 5 b.m. Bollin Eric 125 – Pay Attention 68 (Revoque (IRE) 122) [2015 17.1d³ 15g⁴ Sep 29] fair handicapper: stays 17f: acts on firm and good to soft going. *Tim Easterby* **73**

ATTENZIONE (IRE) 4 b.g. Shamardal (USA) 129 – Fig Tree Drive (USA) 94 (Miswaki (USA) 124) [2015 73: p16g p16g p12g t16.5g⁶ Dec 5] close-coupled gelding: modest maiden: stays 16.5f: acts on polytrack, tapeta and good to firm going: often wears headgear: usually wears tongue tie. *Shane Donohoe, Ireland* **61**

ATWIX 3 br.f. Sakhee (USA) 136 – Atwirl 67 (Pivotal 124) [2015 p10g* p10f³ 11.6f⁶ 8.3m p10g³ p12g 9.9g⁴ 10s⁵ p10g* Oct 20] 3,000Y: lengthy filly: fourth foal: half-sister to winner up to 11.5f Amistress (2-y-o 1m winner, by Kalanisi) and winner up to 1m Ajig (2-y-o 7f winner, by Bahamian Bounty): dam 7f winner: fairly useful performer: won maiden at Lingfield in February and handicap at Lingfield (by 1¼ lengths from Yorkindred Spirit) in October: stays 1¼m: acts on polytrack: tried in cheekpieces. *Lucy Wadham* **83**

AUDACIOUS 7 b.g. Motivator 131 – Flash of Gold 76 (Darshaan 133) [2015 t9.5f Mar 20] lengthy, attractive gelding: fairly useful at best, no form in 2015: stays 1½m: acts on good to firm and good to soft going: tried in hood prior to 2015: tried in tongue tie prior to 2015: often races prominently: not one to trust. *Mandy Rowland* **–**

AUDEN (USA) 7 b.g. Librettist (USA) 124 – Moyesii (USA) (Diesis 133) [2015 74, a66: f8g f8d⁴ p8m⁵ f8g p10f Mar 13] modest handicapper: stays 11f: acts on polytrack, fibresand, soft and good to firm going: often wears headgear: tried in tongue tie prior to 2015. *J. R. Jenkins* **62**

AUGUSTA ADA 4 b.f. Byron 117 – Preference (Efisio 120) [2015 97: 5.5g 7m⁶ 6g Jun 29] fair handicapper: stays 6f: acts on good to firm going: often races towards rear. *Ollie Pears* **65**

AULD FYFFEE (IRE) 3 b.f. Haatef (USA) 117 – Lucky Fountain (IRE) (Lafontaine (USA) 117) [2015 64: t9.5f 10m May 26] modest at best, no form in 2015: stays 9.5f: acts on polytrack, tapeta, good to firm and good to soft going. *Tom Gretton* **–**

AUMERLE 3 b.g. Authorized (IRE) 133 – Succinct 104 (Hector Protector (USA) 124) [2015 10g 11.9d p12g 13.1s⁴ p12g p13.3f* p13.3m* Dec 27] lengthy gelding: sixth foal: half-brother to 3 winners, including 2-y-o 7f winner Starry Sky (by Oasis Dream) and winner up to 6f Itsthursdayalready (2-y-o 5f winner, by Exceed And Excel): dam 1¼m **80**

winner: fairly useful handicapper: won at Chelmsford in October and December (by 1¾ lengths from Kelly's Finest): left James Fanshawe after sixth start: stays 13.5f: acts on polytrack. *Shaun Lycett*

AUMIT HILL 2 b.c. (Apr 2) Authorized (IRE) 133 – Eurolinka (IRE) (Tirol 127) [2015 9d t9.5f f8g Nov 26] no form. *John Quinn* —

AUNTIE BARBER (IRE) 2 b.f. (Apr 10) Elusive City (USA) 117 – Lady Stardust 95 (Spinning World (USA) 130) [2015 7g⁵ 7g 7d⁵ Oct 31] 28,000Y: smallish filly: fourth foal: dam, 7f/1m winner, out of half-sister to Irish 1000 Guineas winner Matiya: modest form in maidens: remains with potential. *Stuart Williams* **64 p**

AUNTIE DIF 3 b.f. Equiano (FR) 127 – Meditation 88 (Inchinor 119) [2015 37: t5.1f p5g⁶ 5d Apr 8] maiden: no form in 2015: often in visor in 2015: sometimes slowly away. *Derek Shaw*

AUNTIE ELSIE 3 b.f. Piccolo 121 – Aunt Hilda 69 (Distant Relative 128) [2015 t7.1g t8.6f t7.1f Feb 16] seventh foal: sister to a winner abroad and half-sister to 2 winners, including 2-y-o 6f winner Cashed Up (by Baryshnikov): dam, maiden (stayed 11.7f), sister to useful 7f/1m winner Aunty Jane: no form. *Michael Easterby*

AUNTIE MAY (IRE) 3 b.f. Steppe Dancer (IRE) 117 – Auntie Mame 73 (Diktat 126) [2015 p7g 8m⁶ 8.3m p10g 11.9g⁶ Sep 7] lengthy filly: first foal: dam 1¼m-11.6f winner: no form. *Denis Coakley* —

AUNTINET 2 b.f. (Mar 7) Invincible Spirit (IRE) 121 – Cozy Maria (USA) 105 (Cozzene (USA)) [2015 p7g⁶ p7m* Dec 16] sister to smart 2-y-o 5f/6f winner Zebedee, closely related to 7f winner Pategonia (by Oasis Dream) and half-sister to a winner abroad by Lemon Drop Kid: dam 1¼m winner: better effort when winning maiden at Lingfield (by 2 lengths from Peaceful Journey) in December, well on top finish: will stay 1m: will go on improving. *John Gosden* **85 p**

AUREOLIN GULF 6 b.g. Proclamation (IRE) 130 – Vermilion Creek 68 (Makbul 104) [2015 57: t7.1g⁶ t8.6g t8.6g 10.2m 7m⁵ 8.3g t8.6g 8.1d Aug 20] poor maiden: left Andrew Hollinshead after first start: best effort at 7f: acts on soft going: tried in headgear. *Sarah Hollinshead* **35**

AURORA GRAY 2 gr.f. (May 11) Rip Van Winkle (IRE) 134 – Summer's Eve 104 (Singspiel (IRE) 133) [2015 p8f Nov 12] third foal: closely related to useful 1m winner Early Morning (by New Approach): dam, 9f winner who stayed 1½m, sister to Gold Cup winner Papineau and half-sister to St Leger winner Silver Patriarch: 8/1, shaped as if needed experience when seventh in maiden at Chelmsford (6¼ lengths behind Khaleesy) in November, not knocked about. *Hughie Morrison* **63**

AUSPICION 3 b.g. Dansili 127 – Superstar Leo (IRE) 114 (College Chapel 122) [2015 82: 8d* 7m³ 8m⁴ 8f 8m p8g 6g⁶ Oct 20] fairly useful performer: won maiden at Ripon (by ¾ length from Count Montecristo) in April: stays 1m: acts on good to firm and good to soft going: often in blinkers in 2015: temperament under suspicion. *William Haggas* **88**

AUSSIE ANDRE 4 b.g. High Chaparral (IRE) 132 – Hana Dee 72 (Cadeaux Genereux 131) [2015 –p: p11g² p12m* 13s p16g p12g* 12s² 11.6d⁴ t12.2f⁴ Oct 17] well-made gelding: useful performer: won maiden at Kempton in April and handicap at Kempton in August: second in handicap at Ascot (¾ length behind Richard of Yorke) in September: stays 1½m: acts on polytrack, tapeta and soft going. *Jeremy Noseda* **95**

AUSSIE BERRY (IRE) 3 gr.g. Aussie Rules (USA) 123 – Berry Baby (IRE) 74 (Rainbow Quest (USA) 134) [2015 8g³ p10m⁴ 7m⁵ 12g⁶ p13f Jul 25] modest maiden: unproven beyond 1m: acts on polytrack: tried in visor. *Michael Bell* **63**

AUSSIE EXPRESS 2 br.g. (Apr 9) Aussie Rules (USA) 123 – Bolshaya 74 (Cadeaux Genereux 131) [2015 6g Jul 20] 12/1, well held in maiden at Ayr: dead. *Keith Dalgleish* —

AUSSIE REIGNS (IRE) 5 b.g. Aussie Rules (USA) 123 – Rohain (IRE) (Singspiel (IRE) 133) [2015 112: 12.1g 14g 9.9g p10g⁴ 12m 13.4v⁶ 16.4m³ 16.4m⁵ 16m p12g 18g Oct 10] angular gelding: useful performer: third in Henry II Stakes at Sandown (2¼ lengths behind Vent de Force) in May: left William Knight after tenth start: stays 16.5f: acts on polytrack, good to firm and good to soft going: often wears headgear. *Gary Moore* **108**

AUSSIE RULER (IRE) 5 br.g. Aussie Rules (USA) 123 – Experiment (IRE) (Whipper (USA) 126) [2015 77: t6g³ 6g⁴ 5m Jun 9] good-quartered gelding: fair maiden: stays 6f: acts on good to firm going: tried in cheekpieces in 2015. *Ronald Harris* **69**

AUSTIN FRIARS 3 b.g. New Approach (IRE) 132 – My Luigia (IRE) (High Estate 127) [2015 72: t9.5g² p10m* t9.5f² 10.2f⁴ Apr 23] good-topped, attractive gelding: fair handicapper: won at Lingfield in February: stays 1¼m: acts on polytrack and tapeta: in blinkers in 2015: one to treat with caution. *Charlie Appleby* **73 §**

AUSTRALIA DAY (IRE) 12 gr.g. Key of Luck (USA) 126 – Atalina (FR) (Linamix **73**
(FR) 127) [2015 14m⁴ Jun 13] good-topped gelding: fair handicapper: stays 1¼m: acts on
soft and good to firm going. *Paul Webber*

AUSTRALIAN QUEEN 2 b.f. (May 7) Fastnet Rock (AUS) 127 – Barshiba (IRE) 116 **73 p**
(Barathea (IRE) 127) [2015 p8d⁵ Nov 30] second foal: half-sister to smart (including
Juddmonte International) winner up to 10.4f Arabian Queen (2-y-o 5f/6f winner, by
Dubawi): dam 1m-1½m (including dual Lancashire Oaks) winner: 3/1, not seen to best
effect when fifth in maiden at Kempton (5 lengths behind Zaakhir) in November, left
poorly placed: sure to progress. *David Elsworth*

AUTHENTICITY 4 b.g. Authorized (IRE) 133 – Jubilee 66 (Selkirk (USA) 129) [2015 **74**
t12.2m⁵ t13.9g² Nov 27] fair maiden: better effort in 2015 when fifth in maiden at
Wolverhampton in October, closing all way to line. *Richard Ford*

AUTHINGER (IRE) 7 b.g. Sadler's Wells (USA) 132 – Ange Bleu (USA) (Alleged (USA) **–**
138) [2015 73: 17.2d Aug 3] maiden: no form in 2015: best effort at 1½m: acts on soft
going: tried in checkpieces prior to 2015: tried in tongue tie prior to 2015. *Barry Murtagh*

AUTHORIZED SPIRIT 3 b.f. Authorized (IRE) 133 – World Spirit 97 (Agnes World **56**
(USA) 123) [2015 –: 10m 10g 10m⁶ p12g p10f⁴ Sep 10] lengthy filly: modest maiden:
stays 1¼m: acts on polytrack: sometimes in visor in 2015. *Stuart Williams*

AUTHOR'S DREAM 2 gr.g. (Mar 16) Authorized (IRE) 133 – Spring Dream (IRE) 93 **62**
(Kalanisi (IRE) 132) [2015 8.3s p8m Nov 17] better effort when seventh in maiden at
Nottingham (9 lengths behind Good Trip) in November, nearest finish: will prove suited by
1¼m+. *William Knight*

AUTOCRATIC 2 b.c. (Jan 22) Dubawi (IRE) 129 – Canda (USA) 100 (Storm Cat (USA)) **81 P**
[2015 7g⁵ Oct 21] good sort: half-brother to 3 winners, including 2-y-o 7f winners Evasive
(smart, by Elusive Quality) and Cantal (by Pivotal): dam, French maiden (raced at 5f/6f),
out of Poule d'Essai des Pouliches and Prix de Diane winner East of The Moon: 14/1,
caught eye when fifth in maiden at Newmarket (5½ lengths behind Colour Me Happy)
in October, nearest finish after running green: should make considerable progress.
Sir Michael Stoute

AUTOMATED 4 b.g. Authorized (IRE) 133 – Red Blooded Woman (USA) 71 (Red **77**
Ransom (USA)) [2015 94: 10m p8g 10m⁵ p10m³ t8.6g⁴ 14g⁶ p12g³ p10.7m³ p10.7g* **a83**
Dec 4] good-topped gelding: fairly useful performer: won maiden at Dundalk in December:
third in handicap at Dundalk in November: left Clive Brittain after fifth start: stays 1¾m:
acts on polytrack, tapeta, good to firm and heavy going: tried in headgear: front runner/
races prominently. *G. M. Lyons, Ireland*

AUTOMOTIVE 7 b.g. Beat Hollow 126 – Bina Ridge 90 (Indian Ridge 123) [2015 73: **69**
t9.5g⁴ p12f² 12g 10m 10m⁵ 8g⁴ 8s³ 9s p10f³ t9.5f* p12m t9.5f Dec 14] attractive gelding:
fair handicapper: won at Wolverhampton in October: stays 10.5f: acts on polytrack, tapeta,
good to firm and good to soft going: tried in blinkers prior to 2015: often races towards rear,
often travels strongly. *Julia Feilden*

AUTRE PRINCESS (IRE) 2 b.f. (May 15) Strategic Prince 114 – Molly Marie (IRE) 75 **–**
(Fasliyev (USA) 120) [2015 t6m Dec 18] seventh foal: half-sister to 5f (including at 2 yrs)
winner Rat Catcher (by One Cool Cat): dam 6f winner: 25/1, very green when well beaten
in maiden at Wolverhampton. *Eric Alston*

AUTUMN BLOSSOM (USA) 2 b.f. (Feb 10) Bernardini (USA) 132 – Late Romance **72 p**
(USA) (Storm Cat (USA)) [2015 f7f* Dec 17] first foal: dam, French 6f and (at 2 yrs) 7f
winner, half-sister to smart winner up to 1m Gamilati: 11/4, won maiden at Southwell by
½ length from Phantom Flipper) in December: better to come. *Mark Johnston*

AUTUMN TONIC (IRE) 3 b.g. Approve (IRE) 112 – Trempjane 71 (Lujain (USA) 119) **69 §**
[2015 –: p7m³ p5g³ p6m* p6g⁵ 7.1m p7g⁶ p7g⁶ p8g⁶ t7.1m⁶ p6f p6m⁵ p6m⁵ p7g Dec 9]
rather leggy gelding: fair performer: won maiden at Chelmsford in March: stays 7f: acts on
polytrack: tried in hood in 2015: not straightforward, and one to treat with plenty of
caution. *Simon Dow*

AUTUN (USA) 5 b.g. Empire Maker (USA) 129 – Sense of Joy 108 (Dansili 127) [2015 **–**
8m 8.5g 10.4m 7.9g Jun 24] well-made gelding: useful at best, no form in 2015: tried in
hood prior to 2015: often races towards rear. *Brian Ellison*

AUXILIARY 2 b.g. (Feb 1) Fast Company (IRE) 126 – Lady Xara (IRE) (Xaar 132) [2015 **82**
5g⁴ 6s⁵ 6g² 7g* 7m* 7.1m 7g⁴ 8g 7d³ Oct 11] 21,000F, £70,000Y: stocky gelding: fourth
foal: half-brother to 6f winner Lady Horatia (by Mount Nelson): dam unraced half-sister to

useful dam of high-class 1¼m-1½m performer Predappio: fairly useful performer: won nurseries at Chester (by length from Alsaaden) and Newbury in July: stays 7f: acts on good to firm going: often in headgear: sometimes slowly away. *William Haggas*

AVAILABLE (IRE) 6 b.m. Moss Vale (IRE) 126 – Divert (IRE) 91 (Averti (IRE) 117) **78** [2015 87: t7.1f⁴ t7.1g² t7.1g² 7m³ 7m³ 7m⁶ t7.1m⁵ t7.1m² t6f* t7.1f t7.1m⁶ t7.1f Nov 30] close-coupled mare: fair handicapper: won at Wolverhampton in October: stays 7f: acts on polytrack, tapeta and firm going: often wears cheekpieces: often wears tongue tie. *John Mackie*

AVAIL (IRE) 3 b.g. Moss Vale (IRE) 126 – Mistress Bailey (IRE) 93 (Mister Baileys 123) **59** [2015 –: t7.1g⁵ 8.3f 8m Jun 25] angular gelding: modest maiden: best effort at 7f: acts on tapeta: in tongue tie in 2015. *Jonathan Portman*

AVALANCHE EXPRESS 3 ch.c. Pivotal 124 – Irresistible 98 (Cadeaux Genereux 131) **81** [2015 7d⁵ 7s² 6.9m⁴ 7d⁶ Aug 28] 60,000Y: brother to several winners, including smart 6f winner Watchable, smart 7f (including at 2 yrs) winner Infallible and useful 7f (including at 2 yrs) winner Thrill: dam 5f/6f winner (including at 2 yrs): fairly useful maiden: second in maiden at Redcar in July: raced only at 7f. *William Muir*

AVENIR CERTAIN (FR) 4 b.f. Le Havre (IRE) 124 – Puggy (IRE) 101 (Mark of **116** Esteem (IRE) 137) [2015 119: 8g 8g² 8m³ 9.9d² Aug 23] strong, well-made filly: smart performer: won 4 times at 3 yrs, including in Poule d'Essai des Pouliches at Longchamp and Prix de Diane at Chantilly: at least respectable efforts last 3 starts in 2015, in Prix Bertrand du Breuil at Chantilly (½-length second to Fintry), Falmouth Stakes at Newmarket (length third to Amazing Maria) and Prix Jean Romanet at Deauville (length third to Odeliz, later promoted to second), on all 3 occasions running on after being poorly placed: stays 10.4f: acts on polytrack, good to firm and good to soft going: sent to Japan. *Jean-Claude Rouget, France*

AVENUE DES CHAMPS 3 b.g. Champs Elysees 124 – Penang Cry (Barathea (IRE) 127) **64** [2015 41: p11g⁵ p11g² 12.1g⁴* 12.1m* p12g⁴ 9.9m³ 12g Jul 31] modest handicapper: won at Beverley in May and June: stays 1½m: acts on polytrack and good to firm going: sometimes wears cheekpieces: races prominently, often travels strongly. *Jane Chapple-Hyam*

AVENUE DU MONDE (FR) 3 ch.f. Champs Elysees 124 – Marla (GER) (Pentire 132) **69** [2015 56: 8f³ 10.2m* 10.2f 12f² 10.2m⁶ Jun 11] fair handicapper: won at Bath in May: stays 1½m: acts on firm going: sent to France. *Richard Hannon*

AVENUE OF DREAMS 3 b.g. New Approach (IRE) 132 – Caro George (USA) 69 **70 p** (Distant View (USA) 126) [2015 10.1m³ Jun 6] 45,000F, 270,000Y: third foal: dam, maiden (raced at 7f/1m), closely related to Irish 2000 Guineas winner Bachelor Duke: 9/2, shaped well when third in maiden at Newcastle (8¾ lengths behind Neymar) in June, unable to sustain effort: better to come. *Charlie Appleby*

AVENUE OF STARS 2 b.c. (Feb 25) Makfi 130 – Clifton Dancer 98 (Fraam 114) [2015 **67** 5s² 6d³ 6g⁵ 5m 6g³ Sep 1] fair maiden: stays 6f: acts on soft going: front runner/races prominently. *Karen McLintock*

AVERTOR 9 b.g. Oasis Dream 129 – Avessia 65 (Averti (IRE) 117) [2015 71: t7.1m³ Mar **66** 10] fair handicapper: stays 7f: acts on tapeta, soft and good to firm going: tried in headgear prior to 2015. *Robert Stephens*

AVIATOR (GER) 7 br.g. Motivator 131 – Amore (GER) (Lando (GER) 128) [2015 17.1d* **82** 16d³ Oct 11] fairly useful handicapper: won at Pontefract in September: third at Goodwood in October: stays 17f: acts on good to soft going: often in headgear prior to 2015: fairly useful hurdler. *James Eustace*

AVIDLY 5 b.m. Beat Hollow 126 – Balmy 89 (Zafonic (USA) 130) [2015 66§, a76§: p10f⁴ **52 §** t12.2g 11.5d May 20] modest maiden: stays 11f: acts on polytrack, tapeta and good to firm going: tried in headgear: temperamental. *Julia Feilden*

AVOCADEAU (IRE) 4 b.g. Lawman (FR) 121 – Christmas Cracker (FR) (Alhaarth (IRE) **77** 126) [2015 77: 10m⁴ 12g³ 10.2m* 12m 10m 10.2f⁵ 9.9g 10.2g p10g Dec 15] good-topped gelding: fair handicapper: won at Chepstow in May: left William Muir after eighth start: stays 1¼m: acts on firm going: often wears headgear: often races towards rear. *Ron Hodges*

AVON BREEZE 6 b.m. Avonbridge 123 – African Breeze 79 (Atraf 116) [2015 93: 6g⁶ 6g **95** 6d⁶ 6m 5g* 6g 6g 5.5m⁴ 5m⁶ 6d⁵ 5g⁵ 5s* Oct 19] useful handicapper: won at Beverley in July and Pontefract (by ½ length from Hoofalong) in October: stays 6f: acts on soft and good to firm going: tried in cheekpieces: usually slowly away, often races in rear. *Richard Whitaker*

AVON PEARL 6 ch.g. Avonbridge 123 – Warden Rose 61 (Compton Place 125) [2015 **105** 113: 8g 8g 9.9g a8f³ a8.6g⁴ 8f 8g⁵ 8m⁶ a8g³ 8g* Oct 18] well-made gelding: useful performer in 2015: won listed race at Taby in October by 1½ lengths from Captain

America: not discredited at Ascot on sixth/eighth starts, in Royal Hunt Cup and Shergar Cup Mile (sixth of 10 to Halation): stays 8.5f: acts on dirt/tapeta, firm and soft going: often wears headgear/tongue tie. *Rune Haugen, Norway*

AVON SCENT 5 b.m. Avonbridge 123 – Ferrybridge (IRE) (Mister Baileys 123) [2015 **47** 54: 8m 6.1m 7.1m⁵ 8.1g 8.1d⁵ 7.1s⁶ 8m⁶ Sep 28] poor maiden: stays 1m: acts on good to firm and good to soft going: usually in headgear in 2015. *Christopher Mason*

AWAKE MY SOUL (IRE) 6 ch.g. Teofilo (IRE) 126 – Field of Hope (IRE) 119 (Selkirk **104** (USA) 129) [2015 107: 10.9m⁶ 8m 9.9f³ 8.9m 9.9f⁶ 10.4s³ 12v Nov 7] rather leggy gelding: useful handicapper: third at York (2¾ lengths behind Chancery) in October: left Gianluca Bietolini, Italy after fifth start and rejoined former trainer: stays 1½m: acts on good to firm and heavy going: tried in hood once. *David O'Meara*

AWAYWITHTHEGREYS (IRE) 8 gr.g. Whipper (USA) 126 – Silver Sash (GER) 83 **91** (Mark of Esteem (IRE) 137) [2015 11.9g⁵ 10.2m⁵ 11.9d* 18g⁵ 12.1d³ 14d Sep 5] fairly useful performer: won maiden at Haydock in May: third in handicap at Chepstow in August: stays 2¼m: acts on good to soft going: often in cheekpieces. *Peter Bowen*

AWESOME POWER 3 b.c. Dubawi (IRE) 129 – Fairy Godmother 113 (Fairy King **93** (USA)) [2015 88p: 9m⁴ 10m 9.9m 8.1g⁶ Sep 11] tall colt: fairly useful handicapper: won at Sandown (by 1¼ lengths from Western Reserve) in June: stays 9f: acts on polytrack and good to firm going: tried in blinkers in 2015: often races prominently. *William Haggas*

AWESOME QUALITY (USA) 2 b.c. (Apr 28) Elusive Quality (USA) – Awesome **63** Maneuver (USA) (Awesome Again (CAN) 133) [2015 6m⁴ 6g⁶ Aug 29] better effort when fourth in maiden at Newmarket (2¼ lengths behind Shadow Game). *James Tate*

AWESOME ROCK (IRE) 6 ch.g. Rock of Gibraltar (IRE) 133 – Dangerous Diva (IRE) **53** 105 (Royal Academy (USA) 130) [2015 53: p12m p12g p12f* p10m³ 11.5d⁶ t12.2g⁵ 11.7g³ 13.1m² p12g⁵ p12g⁵ p12g⁴ 13.1m p12g⁴ p10g Dec 30] modest handicapper: won at Kempton in April: stays 13f: acts on polytrack and good to firm going: usually in headgear in 2015: often races in rear. *Roger Ingram*

AWJAB (IRE) 3 b.g. Bahamian Bounty 116 – Applause (IRE) 102 (Danehill Dancer (IRE) **81** 117) [2015 81: f7g⁵ 8g² 6.1s* 6d³ 6d⁴ 6m⁵ 6g p6f 7v 7v Nov 3] smallish gelding: fairly useful performer: won maiden at Nottingham in May: stays 7f: acts on soft going: tried in cheekpieces in 2015. *Brian Ellison*

AWOHAAM (IRE) 2 b.f. (Apr 25) Iffraaj 127 – Horatia (IRE) 106 (Machiavellian (USA) **79** 123) [2015 5g 6g³ 7.2m⁴ 7m⁴ 7g⁵ 7g* Sep 19] 75,000Y: half-sister to several winners, including smart 1m-1½m winner Moment In Time (by Tiger Hill) and useful winner up to 1m Fontley (2-y-o 7f winner, by Sadler's Wells): dam 1m-1¼m winner: fair performer: won maiden at Musselburgh in July and nursery at Catterick in September: stays 7f: acts on good to firm going. *Richard Fahey*

AYAAR (IRE) 5 b.g. Rock of Gibraltar (IRE) 133 – Teide Lady 75 (Nashwan (USA) 135) **109** [2015 106: 8m* 8f 7f 8m⁵ 8d⁶ 8d Oct 17] useful-looking gelding: useful handicapper: won Spring Cup at Newbury (by 2 lengths from Spark Plug) in April: respectable efforts at best after: stays 1m: acts on firm and good to soft going: tried in visor prior to 2015: slowly away last 2 starts: sent to Australia. *Luca Cumani*

AYAHUASCA (USA) 5 ch.h. Johar (USA) 130 – Eulogize 70 (Pivotal 124) [2015 9.9g **85** 12g 14g p10.7g³ Sep 25] fairly useful performer: third in minor event at Dundalk in September: stays 13f: best form on firm going: tried in headgear. *Takashi Kodama, Ireland*

AYE AYE SKIPPER (IRE) 5 b.g. Captain Marvelous (IRE) 114 – Queenfisher 101 **70** (Scottish Reel 123) [2015 66: p7g t7.1f t6g 7g 6m⁵ 6m 7.5s⁵ 8.5m* 6s* 7.9s⁵ 8s 6d p8g² p8g⁵ 8g⁶ 8d² p8g⁴ Oct 23] fair handicapper: won at Killarney (apprentice) and the Curragh in August: left Dean Ivory after third start: stays 8.5f: acts on polytrack, soft and good to firm going: sometimes wears headgear: tried in tongue tie in 2015: front runner/races prominently. *J. F. Levins, Ireland*

AYLA'S EMPEROR 6 b.m. Holy Roman Emperor (IRE) 125 – Ayla (IRE) 101 (Daylami **66** (IRE) 138) [2015 12d 11.7s* 10.2d³ 10.2s* 10.2m* 10.2g p11g Nov 11] fair handicapper: won at Bath (apprentice) in August, and Chepstow and Bath in September: stays 11.5f: acts on soft and good to firm going: usually in cheekpieces in 2015. *John Flint*

AYRAD (IRE) 4 ch.c. Dalakhani (IRE) 133 – Sweet Firebird (IRE) 103 (Sadler's Wells **115** (USA) 132) [2015 113: 10d⁵ 12g² 12m⁴ 13.3d⁵ Aug 15] sturdy gelding: smart performer: won listed race at Goodwood (by ½ length from Rawaki) in May: best effort when fourth in Princess of Wales's Stakes at Newmarket (2½ lengths behind Big Orange) in July: below form in Geoffrey Freer Stakes at Newbury final start: stays 1½m: acts on good to firm and good to soft going. *Roger Varian*

AYRESOME ANGEL 2 ch.f. (Mar 19) Captain Gerrard (IRE) 113 – Almunia (IRE) **84** (Mujadil (USA) 119) [2015 5v³ 5m³ 5m² 5.1g* 5m⁴ 5g 5m² Sep 20] 7,000F, 10,000Y: fifth foal: half-sister to 6f winner Lewisham (by Sleeping Indian): dam unraced: fairly useful performer: won maiden at Chester in July: raced only at 5f: acts on good to firm going: front runner. *Bryan Smart*

AYR OF ELEGANCE 3 b.f. Motivator 131 – Gaelic Swan (IRE) 80 (Nashwan (USA) **72** 135) [2015 9.9g 10m 9.9m² 12g⁴ 9.9v⁴ Aug 25] workmanlike filly: seventh foal: half-sister to 11f winner Straight Laced (by Refuse To Bend): dam, maiden (placed at 1½m), sister to smart 1¼m-1½m winner Mary Stuart and half-sister to smart winner up to 1½m Bonny Scot: fair maiden: stays 1½m: acts on good to firm going: usually races in rear. *Philip Hide*

AZAGAL (IRE) 4 b.f. Azamour (IRE) 130 – Brave Madam (IRE) (Invincible Spirit (IRE) **90** 121) [2015 102: 8.3m⁴ 8m⁵ 7m⁵ 7g 8m³ 7m 8m⁴ 8g 7d 7.2m⁵ 7s Oct 27] long-backed filly: fairly useful handicapper: won at Nottingham (by ½ length from Stosur) in April: stays 8.5f: acts on good to firm and heavy going: sometimes slowly away. *Tim Easterby*

AZAMAARA (IRE) 3 b.f. Azamour (IRE) 130 – Causeway Queen (IRE) (Giant's **47** Causeway (USA) 132) [2015 57: t7.1g 8g 12m p10m⁶ 9.9g⁵ 8d⁶ 16.2m⁵ f14s p12g⁵ Sep 2] poor maiden: left James Tate after first start: stays 1¼m: acts on polytrack and good to firm going: tried in headgear in 2015: tried in tongue tie in 2015: usually slowly away. *Conrad Allen*

AZAMESSE (IRE) 3 b.f. Azamour (IRE) 130 – Jeunesse Doree (IRE) 68 (Rock of **77** Gibraltar (IRE) 133) [2015 p10.7g² p10.7g² 12.5d⁵ 10.5g⁵ 10m³ 11.8g 12.1m³ 13.1g² 14.1d* p16g Nov 20] first foal: dam, lightly raced (best effort at 1¼m), out of sister to high-class stayer Yeats: fair performer: won handicap at Redcar in October: best effort at 1¾m: acts on polytrack, good to firm and good to soft going: tried in cheekpieces: tried in tongue tie: front runner/races prominently. *J. J. Feane, Ireland*

AZERELLE (IRE) 3 ch.f. Arcano (IRE) 122 – Simply Topping (IRE) 64 (Exceed And **57** Excel (AUS) 126) [2015 63: 5g t5.1g³ t6m 5s f5g³ t5.1m⁴ t6m Dec 30] modest maiden: should stay 6f: acts on fibresand, tapeta and soft going: sometimes in cheekpieces in 2015: often races prominently. *Tim Easterby*

AZHAR 2 b.f. (Jan 23) Exceed And Excel (AUS) 126 – Nitya (FR) (Indian Ridge 123) **79** [2015 5d⁶ p6g* 6f Jun 19] 210,000F: useful-looking filly: third foal: closely related to 1m winner Pleasure Bent and 1¼m winner Heho (both by Dansili): dam unraced sister to Breeders' Cup Mile winner Domedriver: fair performer: best effort when winning maiden at Kempton (by 2½ lengths from Gwendolyn) in June: will stay 7f. *Saeed bin Suroor*

AZILIAN 3 b.c. Azamour (IRE) 130 – Zietory 107 (Zieten (USA) 118) [2015 74: 10m³ 8m⁶ **82** 10.1m² p12g³ p12g* 12g² p16g p12g p12g Dec 20] well-made colt: fairly useful handicapper: won at Lingfield in August: stays 1½m: acts on polytrack and good to firm going: tried in blinkers in 2015: usually wears tongue tie: front runner/races prominently. *Paul Cole*

AZMAAM (IRE) 3 gr.c. Dark Angel (IRE) 113 – Miss Indigo 62 (Indian Ridge 123) **105** [2015 99: 10g⁵ 10m⁵ 10m² 10m³ 10s³ 10m⁶ 10g Sep 19] good-topped, attractive colt: useful handicapper: second at Newmarket (1¼ lengths behind Master The World) in June, and third at Newmarket (7 lengths behind Resonant) and Ascot (1¾ lengths behind Great Park) in July: stays 1¼m: acts on soft and good to firm going: sent to UAE. *Richard Hannon*

AZRAFF (IRE) 3 b.g. Paco Boy (IRE) 129 – Gee Kel (IRE) 91 (Danehill Dancer (IRE) **103** 117) [2015 99: p8g² 10f² 10m⁴ 8m² 8d 8d⁴ 8.9s⁶ p10f⁴ Oct 28] sturdy gelding: useful handicapper: second at Newmarket (2 lengths behind Marma's Boy) in May and Doncaster (2½ lengths behind Oracolo) in June: stays 1¼m: acts on polytrack, firm and good to soft going: often in headgear in 2015. *Marco Botti*

AZRUR (IRE) 5 b.g. Sir Percy 129 – Tiger Spice 68 (Royal Applause 124) [2015 90: **72** 10.1g 8g 6s 7m⁶ 8g 7.2g 7.2g* 7.2g 7s Oct 16] good-topped gelding: fair handicapper: won at Musselburgh in September: left Kenny Johnson after sixth start: stays 1m: acts on firm and good to soft going: sometimes wears hood: tried in tongue tie prior to 2015. *Keith Dalgleish*

AZURE AMOUR (IRE) 3 b.f. Azamour (IRE) 130 – Al Euro (FR) 57 (Mujtahid (USA) **70** 118) [2015 p10f⁵ p12m 8.3m 8m⁴ 9.9m² 12.1d⁵ 10.2s³ 10.2m⁶ p10g⁵ p12g² Nov 4] sturdy, quite attractive filly: fair handicapper: won at Bath in July: left Ralph Beckett after second start: stays 1½m: acts on polytrack, soft and good to firm going: tried in visor in 2015. *Rod Millman*

AZURITE (IRE) 4 b.g. Azamour (IRE) 130 – High Lite 54 (Observatory (USA) 131) **89**
[2015 103: 9.7g 11.9s⁶ 12f Jun 19] useful performer at 3 yrs: new trainer, below best in
2015: well held in Duke of Edinburgh Stakes at Royal Ascot final outing: stays 1½m: acts
on polytrack and good to firm going: sent to Australia. *J. E. Hammond, France*

AZYAAN (IRE) 3 gr.f. Mastercraftsman (IRE) 129 – Hidden Heart (USA) 62 (Kingmambo **67**
(USA) 125) [2015 12.1g³ 11.8m 11.9f⁵ 12g Jun 29] €12,500Y, 20,000 2-y-o: fourth foal:
half-sister to 6f winner Red Valerian (by Royal Applause): dam Canadian 6.5f winner: fair
maiden: raced only at 1½m: tried in cheekpieces: sold £4,000, sent to Germany. *Kevin Ryan*

AZZIR (IRE) 3 gr.g. Echo of Light 125 – Lady Georgina 88 (Linamix (FR) 127) [2015 63: **82**
10.4f² 8m³ 10.1g⁴ 14.1s³ Oct 28] fairly useful handicapper: won at Epsom in September:
should stay 1½m (stamina stretched final start): acts on firm going. *Timothy Jarvis*

B

BAADI 3 b.g. Dansili 127 – Dashing (IRE) (Sadler's Wells (USA) 132) [2015 10m 10.2d² **87 p**
9.8d² Jun 3] third foal: closely related to 7f winner Azenzar (by Danehill Dancer): dam
unraced half-sister to high-class winner up to 1¼m Alexander Goldrun: fairly useful form:
best effort when second in maiden at Ripon (1¾ lengths behind Argus) in June, not clear
run: should do better. *Roger Varian*

BAARS CAUSEWAY (IRE) 4 ch.f. Intense Focus (USA) 117 – Barbera (GER) (Night **–**
Shift (USA)) [2015 65, a56: p8g t6g Apr 27] leggy filly: maiden: no form in 2015: stays 7f:
acts on polytrack, firm and good to soft going: tried in visor. *Timothy Jarvis*

BABY BALLERINA 2 b.f. (Feb 4) Kheleyf (USA) 116 – Markova's Dance 64 (Mark of **74**
Esteem (IRE) 137) [2015 5v² 5g⁶ 5m 6m³ 5g² 6g² 5d* 6.5m 7s³ Oct 6] 5,000F, £7,000Y:
half-sister to several winners, including useful 2-y-o 7f winner Evening Attire (by Pastoral
Pursuits) and useful winner up to 7f Perfect Act (by Act One): dam lightly-raced half-sister
to smart 1¼m-15f winner Khamaseen: fair performer: won maiden at Catterick in August:
stays 6f: acts on good to firm and good to soft going: tried in cheekpieces. *Brian Ellison*

BABYFACT 4 b.f. Piccolo 121 – Pennyspider (IRE) 74 (Redback 116) [2015 t8.6m⁴ f6⁶ **74**
6.1m⁴ 7.6g² 6g⁴ 5.7m* 5.7m⁶ 6g⁵ 5.7d³ 5.7f* 5.7m⁵ 5.7g³ Oct 18] useful filly: fair
handicapper: won at Bath in July and September (apprentice): stays 5.5f: acts on firm
going: usually races close up. *Malcolm Saunders*

BACALL 3 b.f. Paco Boy (IRE) 129 – Xtrasensory 96 (Royal Applause 124) [2015 –: f6g* **71**
6m³ 6g⁶ t7.1g f6d Jul 27] strong filly: fair performer: won maiden at Southwell in January:
stays 6f: acts on fibresand and good to firm going: often starts slowly, often races towards
rear. *Kevin Ryan*

BACK AT THE RANCH (USA) 2 b.f. (Feb 3) Artie Schiller (USA) 124 – Major Allie **78**
(USA) (Officer (USA) 120) [2015 a4.5f² a5f* 6f Jun 19] $110,000Y: well-made filly: third
foal: half-sister to useful 2-y-o 6f/7f winner Lieutenant Kaffee and 6f winner Ballerina
Belle (both by First Defence): dam lightly-raced half-sister to useful/untrustworthy 2-y-o
6f winner Rudik: fair performer: won maiden at Belmont in May by 2¼ lengths from
Assoulin: well held in Albany Stakes at Royal Ascot only subsequent outing, hanging right
and finding nothing: stays 5f: wears blinkers. *Wesley A. Ward, USA*

BACK BURNER (IRE) 7 br.g. Big Bad Bob (IRE) 118 – Marl 94 (Lycius (USA) 124) **61**
[2015 85: f12g f11g² f12g⁴ Mar 10] good-topped gelding: modest handicapper: left Dai
Burchell after first start: stays 1¾m: acts on all-weather, good to firm and heavy going:
tried in headgear: tried in tongue tie prior to 2015. *David Evans*

BACK TO BOND 2 ch.g. (Feb 16) Monsieur Bond (IRE) 120 – Nicola's Dream 76 **76**
(Alhaarth (IRE) 126) [2015 6g⁵ 5m⁶ 6m³ 5.2m 6m³ 7g³ 8s Oct 9] sturdy gelding: fair
maiden: stays 7f: acts on good to firm going. *Richard Fahey*

BADALONA BREEZE (IRE) 2 br.f. (Apr 18) Big Bad Bob (IRE) 118 – Rose Mandarin **–**
(IRE) (Tiger Hill (IRE) 127) [2015 p8g p8m f7g⁴ p7g Dec 16] €8,500Y, £12,000 2-y-o:
second foal: dam unraced half-sister to useful 5 7f-7f winner Redvers: no form. *Michael
Appleby*

BADDILINI 5 b.g. Bertolini (USA) 125 – Baddi Heights (FR) (Shirley Heights 130) [2015 **91**
99: p5g⁵ p6f² p6g* p7f* t7.1m p7g³ 6f 7.6g 7m 7d 6g 7v p7f⁵ p6g Nov 25] strong gelding: **a105**
useful handicapper: won at Lingfield (twice) (stays 6f from Grey Mirage latter occasion)
in February: third in minor event at Kempton (¾ length behind Ninjago) in March: stays
7f: acts on polytrack, tapeta, firm and soft going: often wears headgear: often races towards
rear. *Alan Bailey*

BAD GIRL CAOIMHE (IRE) 2 br.f. (Mar 30) Big Bad Bob (IRE) 118 – Sumostars **49**
(IRE) (Refuse To Bend (IRE) 128) [2015 6d Oct 26] €3,000Y: first foal: dam once-raced
half-sister to smart 5f/6f winner Tiger Royal: 25/1, very green when eighth in maiden at
Redcar (4¾ lengths behind Gowanless) in October, never nearer. *Brian Ellison*

BAD PENNY (IRE) 2 b.f. (Apr 3) Kodiac 112 – Double Fantasy (GER) (Indian Ridge **68**
123) [2015 7.2d⁴ 6d⁵ Sep 4] €45,000Y, 105,000 2-y-o: fifth foal: closely related to winner
up to 7f George Rooke and 1¼m winner Legal Trip (both by Rock of Gibraltar) and half-
sister to 5f/6f winner Pantella (by Fasliyev): dam, 1m winner, half-sister to smart 1m
winner Zafeen Speed: better effort when fourth in maiden at Ayr (4½ lengths behind
Forever A Lady) in August: should be suited by a return to 7f. *John Quinn*

BAG OF DIAMONDS 2 b.c. (Mar 8) Lilbourne Lad (IRE) 111 – Milnagavie 95 **81**
(Tobougg (IRE) 125) [2015 8.1g⁴ 7g⁴ 7.1g p8f⁴ 8.3d p8m⁵ p8g* p8g² Dec 15] 30,000Y:
rangy colt: first foal: dam, 11f/1½m winner (stayed 21.5f) Elyaadi out of useful 1¼m winner (stayed 12.5f) Abyaan: fairly useful performer:
won nursery at Lingfield in December: second in similar event at Kempton next time: stays
1m: acts on polytrack: usually responds generously to pressure. *Richard Hannon*

BAHAARAH (IRE) 2 b.f. (Jan 27) Iffraaj 127 – Love Intrigue (IRE) 107 (Marju (IRE) **97**
127) [2015 6m³ 7f* 7m* 6s⁵ Sep 3] 55,000Y: sturdy filly: second foal: half-sister to 10.7f
winner Eloge (by Elnadim): dam 5f/6f winner (including at 2 yrs): useful performer: won
maiden at Doncaster in July and nursery at Newmarket in August: stays 7f. *Richard Hannon*

BAHAMA DANCER 4 ch.f. Bahamian Bounty 116 – Arlene Phillips 54 (Groom Dancer **–**
(USA) 128) [2015 –: t12.2f Jan 5] maiden: no form in 2015: in blinkers sole start in 2015.
Jason Ward

BAHAMA MOON (IRE) 3 b.g. Lope de Vega (IRE) 125 – Bahama Bay (GER) (Dansili **86**
127) [2015 10.4g³ 11.9g⁴ 8.5g⁶ Aug 30] fairly useful performer: won newcomers race at
Maisons-Laffitte at 2 yrs: in frame in minor events at Saint-Cloud and Longchamp in 2015:
left A. Fabre, well held in handicap at Beverley final outing: stays 1½m. *David Barron*

BAHAMIAN BIRD 2 b.f. (Feb 27) Bahamian Bounty 116 – Ride The Wind 72 (Cozzene **68**
(USA)) [2015 5m² 5d⁴ 6m Oct 3] strong filly: first foal: dam maiden (stayed 1¼m) out of
1m/8.5f (minor Canadian stakes) winner Wind Surf: fair maiden: best effort when second
in maiden at Redcar (½ length behind Twentysvnthlancers) in September, caught further
back than ideal. *Richard Fahey*

BAHAMIAN BOY 2 ch.g. (Apr 18) Paco Boy (IRE) 129 – Bahamian Babe 94 (Bahamian **70**
Bounty 116) [2015 5f⁶ 5.1d³ t5.1m⁴ 6.1s 5d p6f t7.1f² p7g* Dec 10] fair performer: won
nursery at Chelmsford in December: likely to stay 1m: acts on polytrack and tapeta: starts
slowly, often races in rear. *Hughie Morrison*

BAHAMIAN C 4 b.g. Bahamian Bounty 116 – Amandian (IRE) 84 (Indian Ridge 123) **81**
[2015 88: 9s 10.4m 8m³ 7.9g⁴ 8m⁵ 8.3m⁶ 8g 10.3d⁵ 10v³ t9.5f³ t9.5g⁴ Dec 1] fairly useful
handicapper: stays 10.5f: acts on good to firm and heavy going: tried in cheekpieces: tried
in tongue tie in 2015: usually responds generously to pressure. *Richard Fahey*

BAHAMIAN DESERT 3 b.g. Bahamian Bounty 116 – Noble Desert (FR) (Green **95**
Desert (USA) 127) [2015 –: 5g 8m² 8m² 9m* 10.1m² 8.9m* 10s² 8g* 9.8g² Aug 31] useful
handicapper: won at Redcar and Musselburgh in July, and on latter course in August:
second at Ripon (nose behind The Wee Bairn) later in August: stays 1¼m: acts on good to
firm going: strong traveller: sold 20,000 gns, sent to Bahrain. *David O'Meara*

BAHAMIAN HEIGHTS 4 b.g. Bahamian Bounty 116 – Tahirah 99 (Green Desert **91**
(USA) 127) [2015 95: 6f 6m 6g 6m* 5g p6m 16m Dec 12] fairly useful handicapper: won
at Doncaster (by head from The Hooded Claw) in June: left Clive Brittain after fourth start:
stays 6f: acts on good to firm going: often wears headgear: sometimes slowly away, usually
races nearer last than first. *Robert Cowell*

BAHAMIAN SUNRISE 3 ch.g. Bahamian Bounty 116 – Tagula Sunrise (IRE) 101 **82**
(Tagula (IRE) 116) [2015 77: 6g⁴ 6.5m 6s 5g* 5.6m² 5g 6g t5.1f⁵ p5f⁵ Oct 29] fairly useful
handicapper: won at Redcar (by 2½ lengths from Choppy Water) in June: left Richard
Fahey after sixth start: stays 5.5f: acts on tapeta and good to firm going: often in blinkers
in 2015: front runner/races prominently. *John Gallagher*

BAHAMIAN SUNSHINE 2 ch.c. (Mar 27) Bahamian Bounty 116 – Tagula Sunrise **54**
(IRE) 101 (Tagula (IRE) 116) [2015 6m 5m 5g³ 6.1g⁶ 6d⁶ 6g³ 8d t6f* f6g* t6g Dec 1] **a69**
close-coupled colt: fair performer: won seller at Wolverhampton in October and claimer at
Southwell in November: stays 6f: acts on fibresand, tapeta and good to firm going: tried in
cheekpieces: usually leads. *Richard Fahey*

BAHANGO (IRE) 3 b.g. Bahamian Bounty 116 – Last Tango (IRE) 94 (Lion Cavern (USA) 117) [2015 72: 5.1m⁵ 5d⁵ 5g³ 5g 5g* Aug 3] modest handicapper: won at Ripon in August: best form at 5f: acts on tapeta and soft going: often wears headgear: front runner/ races prominently. *Patrick Morris* **62**

BAHRIKATE 2 b.f. (Mar 22) Bahri (USA) 125 – Dispol Katie 90 (Komaite (USA)) [2015 6g 6m Jun 16] sixth foal: half-sister to 5f winner Made In The Shade (by Ishiguru) and 1m winner Riponian (by Trade Fair): dam winner up to 7f (2-y-o 5f winner): no form. *Michael Herrington* **–**

BAILEYS CONCERTO (IRE) 9 b.g. Bach (IRE) 121 – None The Wiser (IRE) (Dr Massini (IRE) 117) [2015 11.5s⁵ 9.3d² 8d⁶ 12.1g⁵ 15g Sep 29] fair maiden: should prove suited by at least 1½m: acts on good to soft going: sometimes slowly away, often races in rear. *Dianne Sayer* **66**

BAILEYS EN PREMIER (FR) 4 b.g. Exceed And Excel (AUS) 126 – Numberonedance (USA) (Trempolino (USA) 135) [2015 65: t12.2f p8g⁴ p8m⁴ p8f p10f 8m* 8d p8m* p8g* 8m⁴ 7.6d 8.1g⁵ p8f* p8t³ p8f³ p8f p7.5g p8f Nov 17] ex-French gelding: fair performer: won minor event at Brighton in April, and handicaps at Chelmsford in May, June and August: stays 1½m: acts on polytrack and good to firm going: usually in headgear in 2015: front runner/races prominently. *Chris Dwyer* **63 a76**

BAILEYS GALAXY (FR) 2 b.c. (Apr 27) Elusive City (USA) 117 – Kosmic View (USA) (Distant View (USA) 126) [2015 t9.5f t8.6f p7f Nov 12] modest maiden: best effort when eighth in maiden at Chelmsford (5¼ lengths behind Jufn) in November. *Mark Johnston* **61**

BAILEYS PURSUIT 3 ch.f. Pastoral Pursuits 127 – Royal Mistress (Fasliyev (USA) 120) [2015 62: p6g t6g³ p6m⁶ 6d³ t6g² t7.1g³ t6g* 6g* p6f p6g p6g Dec 7] good-topped filly: fair handicapper: won at Wolverhampton in June and Lingfield in July: stays 6f: acts on tapeta and firm going: sometimes wears headgear: sometimes slowly away. *Christine Dunnett* **74**

BAILIWICK 4 b.g. Oratorio (IRE) 128 – Imperial Bailiwick (IRE) 104 (Imperial Frontier (USA) 112) [2015 74p: p8g t7.1f p7f⁴ p8g³ Nov 26] fair handicapper: may prove best at short of 1m: acts on polytrack and tapeta: front runner/races prominently. *Daniel Kubler* **70**

BAINNE (IRE) 5 b.m. Strategic Prince 114 – Laemeen (IRE) (Danehill Dancer (IRE) 117) [2015 70, a77; f8g⁶ 5g⁴ 6g* 6.3m 6g³ 6d³ 6v⁴ Sep 24] sturdy mare: fairly useful handicapper: won at the Curragh in June: left James Eustace after first start: stays 7f: acts on fibresand and heavy going: tried in headgear: tried in tongue tie prior to 2015. *M. D. O'Callaghan, Ireland* **82**

BAINO HOPE (FR) 4 b.f. Jeremy (USA) 122 – Baino Ridge (FR) (Highest Honor (FR) 124) [2015 10.4g* 11.9g² 12.4d⁴ 11.9s³ Sep 13] smart performer: won minor event at Saint-Cloud in May and Prix de Pomone at Deauville (readily by 1¾ lengths from Cocktail Queen, despite wandering) in August: good 2 lengths third to Postponed in Prix Foy at Longchamp final outing: stays 15f: acts on soft and good to firm going. *Jean-Claude Rouget, France* **117**

BAITHA ALGA (IRE) 3 b.c. Fast Company (IRE) 126 – Tawaafur 89 (Fantastic Light (USA) 134) [2015 106: 6m 6d 6mᵘʳ Aug 8] useful-looking colt: useful handicapper: left Richard Hannon after first start: stays 6f: acts on good to firm and heavy going: in headgear last 2 starts. *Jassim Al Ghazali, Qatar* **100**

BAJAN REBEL 4 ch.f. Bahamian Bounty 116 – Silca Key 94 (Inchinor 119) [2015 64: 8.5m⁴ 8d 10.2g⁵ 8.3m³ 8m⁶ 8.5m³ 7dᵘʳ 8.5g⁵ 8.5d Sep 22] modest handicapper: stays 1¼m: acts on good to firm and heavy going: tried in headgear. *Michael Easterby* **57**

BAJAN STORY 6 b.g. Lucky Story (USA) 128 – Bajan Rose 89 (Dashing Blade 117) [2015 7g p7m 6g⁴ 5.3g⁶ 7g Aug 6] poor handicapper: stays 7f: acts on soft going: tried in headgear: sometimes slowly away, usually races nearer last than first, often races lazily. *Paul Fitzsimons* **47**

BAJAN (USA) 4 b.f. Speightstown (USA) 124 – Critikal Reason (USA) (Aptitude (USA) 128) [2015 8.9g⁶ Feb 22] useful performer: won listed race at Hollywood at 2 yrs: left Simon Callaghan in USA, respectable 9 lengths sixth to Parranda in Singapore Cup at Kranji only outing in 2015: stays at least 8.5f: acts on dirt and synthetics. *Roger Varian* **92 +**

BAKER 3 b.g. Teofilo (IRE) 126 – Meydan Princess (IRE) 109 (Choisir (AUS) 126) [2015 p8m⁵ t7.1g 7m 10.3m⁴ p8f 10.2v p10f² p11g³ Nov 11] fair maiden: stays 11f: acts on polytrack, tapeta and good to firm going: tried in tongue tie. *Nick Littmoden* **75**

*King Edward VII Stakes, Royal Ascot—Balios (blaze) wins from Mr Singh,
with Father Christmas (striped cap) edging out stablemate Ol' Man River for third*

BAKHT A RAWAN (IRE) 3 b.g. Rip Van Winkle (IRE) 134 – Foolish Ambition (GER) **76**
95 (Danehill Dancer (IRE) 117) [2015 58: 10.2m2 10.2m4 8.3m* 8.5g* 8.3m5 8m5 8.5v3
8.5g3 8.3g Oct 19] stocky gelding: fair handicapper: won at Nottingham in June and Epsom
in July: stays 8.5f: acts on good to firm and heavy going. *Mark Usher*

BALANCE 2 ch.f. (Apr 11) Pivotal 124 – Danella (FR) 109 (Highest Honor (FR) 124) **80 p**
[2015 6g* Oct 16] sister to useful 1m winner Azabara and half-sister to 3 winners,
including winner up to 9f Kentish Dream (2-y-o 7f winner, by Oasis Dream) and 1¼m
winner (stays 1½m) Ella's Honour (by Makfi): dam winner up to 1m (2-y-o 6f winner): 4/1,
knew job when won maiden at Haydock (by 1¾ lengths from Tanaasub) in October,
responding well: will stay 7f+: has scope for plenty of improvement. *Richard Fahey*

BALAYAGE (IRE) 3 b.f. Invincible Spirit (IRE) 121 – Shamwari Lodge (IRE) 114 **73**
(Hawk Wing (USA) 136) [2015 74p: p7g p6g5 p6g2 p6d Sep 4] sturdy filly: fair maiden:
stays 6f: acts on polytrack: often in blinkers in 2015: sometimes slowly away. *Marco Botti*

BALDUCCI 8 b.g. Dansili 127 – Miss Meltemi (IRE) 100 (Miswaki Tern (USA) 120) **92**
[2015 106: 8m 8m 7.6m* 8g 8m4 8m3 8d 8g Aug 31] strong, close-coupled gelding: fairly
useful performer: won claimer at Chester (by neck from Al Khan) in June: third in handicap
at Haydock in August: stays 8.5f: acts on good to firm and good to soft going: sometimes
wears headgear: tried in tongue tie prior to 2015: usually leads. *David O'Meara*

BALER BOY 3 b.g. Sakhee (USA) 136 – Olindera (GER) (Lomitas 129) [2015 8g 7f6 7m **–**
10.3g 10.2sur Oct 28] no form. *Des Donovan*

BALINUS (GER) 7 ch.g. Tertullian (USA) 115 – Brighella (GER) (Lomitas 129) [2015 **–**
t6g 7m 8m Jul 7] handicapper: won at Magdeburg and Dresden in 2014: no form in 2015:
stays 1m: acts on good to soft going: usually wears cheekpieces. *David Bridgwater*

BALIOS (IRE) 3 ch.c. Shamardal (USA) 129 – Elle Galante (GER) (Galileo (IRE) 134) **115**
[2015 93p: 10m2 12f* 11.9m5 12d6 Aug 19] lengthy colt: smart performer: won King
Edward VII Stakes at Royal Ascot (by 1¼ lengths from Mr Singh) in June: race not run to
suit when fifth to Erupt in Grand Prix de Paris at Longchamp next outing: softer ground,
well held in Great Voltigeur Stakes at York final start: stays 1½m: acts on polytrack and
firm going: held up. *David Simcock*

BALLAD OF MULAN (IRE) 2 b.f. (Feb 24) Bahamian Bounty 116 – Salonga (IRE) 77 **42**
(Shinko Forest (IRE)) [2015 5.9m 6m6 6g5 7g 7s Oct 16] £10,000Y: third foal: half-sister
to 2-y-o 6f winner Hardy Red (by Mujadil): dam 8.6f winner: poor maiden: best effort at
6f. *K. R. Burke*

BALLAD SINGER 2 ch.c. (Mar 15) Kyllachy 129 – Clear Voice (USA) (Cryptoclearance **– p**
(USA)) [2015 7g Aug 28] 70,000Y: compact colt: fourth foal: half-brother to useful winner
up to 1m Mutasayyid (2-y-o 7f winner, by Bahamian Bounty): dam unraced half-sister to
very smart US Grade 1 9f/1¼m winner Tinners Way: 50/1, green when well held in maiden
at Newmarket (12¾ lengths behind Tashweeq) in August: sent to UAE: should do better.
Richard Hannon

BALLARD DOWN (IRE) 2 b.g. (Apr 6) Canford Cliffs (IRE) 133 – Mackenzie's **85 p**
Friend (Selkirk (USA) 129) [2015 p8g5 p8g* Dec 16] €30,000Y: half-brother to several
winners, including useful 2-y-o 9f/1¼m winner Sallen (by Oratorio) and 1½m winner

116

Know The Law (by Danehill Dancer): dam unraced: better effort when winning maiden at Kempton (by nose from Bandit Bob) in December, always holding on: will be suited by further than 1m: still unexposed. *William Knight*

BALLESTEROS 6 ch.g. Tomba 119 – Flamenco Dancer (Mark of Esteem (IRE) 137) **91** [2015 105: 5.1s⁵ 5m 6.1f 5.1m⁵ 5m 6g² 5.5m* 5g⁴ 5d 6d 5v Oct 17] close-coupled gelding: fairly useful handicapper: won at Chester (by short head from Deauville Prince) in August: stays 6f: acts on good to firm and heavy going: tried in hood prior to 2015: often leads. *Richard Fahey*

BALLET CONCERTO 2 b.c. (Apr 13) Dansili 127 – Ballet Ballon (USA) 81 (Rahy **90 p** (USA) 115) [2015 7g⁵ p7g² Sep 23] 300,000Y: sixth foal: half-brother to 3 winners, including smart winner up to 7.5f Havane Smoker (by Dubawi) and 9.5f-1½m winner (stays 1¾m) Maxie T (by Dalakhani): dam 1¼m winner who stayed 1½m: better effort when fifth in maiden at Ascot (2¾ lengths behind Culturati) in September, met some trouble: remains with potential. *Sir Michael Stoute*

BALLIOL 3 b.g. Exceed And Excel (AUS) 126 – Cinerama (IRE) 68 (Machiavellian **77** (USA) 123) [2015 5g⁴ 6m* 5m³ p7f Dec 17] fair performer: won maiden at Windsor in June: left Charlie Appleby after third start: stays 7f: in tongue tie. *Ronald Harris*

BALLISTA (IRE) 7 b.g. Majestic Missile (IRE) 118 – Ancient Secret (Warrshan (USA) **96** 117) [2015 107: p6f p6g³ p6g³ t6m⁴ t6m⁶ Dec 18] useful-looking gelding: useful handicapper: third at Lingfield (½ length behind Baddilini) in February: has won at 7f, races at sprint trips nowadays: acts on polytrack, tapeta, good to firm and heavy going: tried in headgear prior to 2015: usually leads. *Tom Dascombe*

BALLROOM ANGEL 3 gr.f. Dark Angel (IRE) 113 – Ballroom Dancer (IRE) 91 **–** (Danehill Dancer (IRE) 117) [2015 –: p8f p10g⁶ f7g³ 6m p6g 6d⁶ Aug 5] maiden: no form in 2015: tried in blinkers in 2015: tried in tongue tie in 2015: often races prominently. *Philip Hide*

BALLYBACKA QUEEN (IRE) 4 b.f. Hurricane Run (IRE) 134 – Zankara (FR) **106** (Linamix (FR) 127) [2015 99: 12v⁵ 12v* 12g 12m* 11.9g 12d⁴ 12.4m 12g Oct 18] rather leggy filly: useful performer: won handicaps at Leopardstown (by 2 lengths from Theophilus) in May and Cork (by head from Shadagann) in June: stays 12.5f: acts on good to firm and heavy going: usually in hood in 2015. *P. A. Fahy, Ireland*

BALLYCOYLE GIRL (IRE) 2 b.f. (Apr 5) Manduro (GER) 135 – Gwyllion (USA) 71 **–** (Red Ransom (USA)) [2015 7g Oct 3] 5,000Y: fourth foal: half-sister to 3 winners, including 1½m-13.4f winner Bayan Kasirga (by Aussie Rules) and 7.4f winner Montefalcon (by Footstepsinthesand): dam maiden half-sister to smart winner up to 10.4f Barefoot Lady: 100/1, very green when well held in maiden at Redcar, hanging badly left. *Tony Coyle*

BALLYDOYLE (IRE) 2 b.f. (Jan 27) Galileo (IRE) 134 – Butterfly Cove (USA) **113 p** (Storm Cat (USA)) [2015 6g⁴ 7f² 7f* 7g* 7d² 8m* Oct 4]

The clues that there might be a particularly strong bunch of two-year-old fillies at Ballydoyle were there from early in the year, as soon as the names of some of the new draft were published. Ballydoyle, Coolmore and Best In The World stood out for obvious reasons, their names very likely to have been reserved for some time, and all three fillies went on to win 'black type' races and all have the potential to add further to their reputations as three-year-olds. The pick of the Ballydoyle classic prospects among the fillies is Minding, whose name reflects a relatively recent penchant for single-word names following such as Was and Found. For all that Minding won both the Moyglare and the Fillies' Mile it still might prove significant that Ballydoyle started a short-priced favourite both times the pair met on the track. Ballydoyle beat Minding in the Debutante Stakes before being caught late on by her in the Moyglare Stud Stakes, and Ballydoyle didn't need to improve on her form in Ireland to win the Prix Marcel Boussac on her final start. A good-topped filly with plenty of scope, Ballydoyle is deservedly among the favourites for the One Thousand Guineas, for which her stablemate Minding is the clear market leader.

Ballydoyle was beaten on her first two starts, never going the pace in a six-furlong maiden at the Curragh (odds-on) in May and just failing in the Chesham Stakes, short-headed by Suits You, at Royal Ascot. Ballydoyle made no mistake back in maiden company at Newmarket in July, winning by two and three quarter lengths from Nemoralia in a race that worked out well (six of the nine that finished behind Ballydoyle won their next start, including the runner-up who went on to be placed in two Grade 1s in America). There was a field of eight for the Group 2 Breast Cancer Research Debutante Stakes at the Curragh in August, when Ballydoyle started at 11/8 for a race Aidan O'Brien had already won a record nine times. O'Brien also saddled Alice Springs (9/2) and Minding (8/1), while the David Wachman-trained Group 3 winner Most Beautiful started at 7/2. Ballydoyle showed smart form as she made all to win by two lengths from Minding, with Most Beautiful and 14/1-shot Turret Rocks close behind in third and fourth and Alice Springs in fifth. Ballydoyle quickened well to score with something up her sleeve and she was sent off a well-backed favourite for the Moyglare Stud Stakes over the same course and distance three weeks later. The race was run on rain-softened ground—the good to soft was the softest encountered by Ballydoyle so far—and conditions were believed by connections at the time to have played a part in Ballydoyle's defeat. Minding beat her by three quarters of a length, with Alice Springs completing a one, two, three for the stable.

Ballydoyle wore a first-time tongue tie in her next race, the Total Prix Marcel Boussac at Longchamp in October, in which she was back on firmer ground and also stepped up in trip. Starting second favourite at 15/10, Ballydoyle was driven out to win by a length and a quarter from Turret Rocks, who had won the May Hill Stakes at Doncaster since contesting the Debutante. Five of the six other runners, including third-placed Qemah, were from France, while the only runner from Britain, Katie's Diamond, finished fifth after making the running. The even-money favourite, the previously unbeaten Group 3 winner Antonoe, beat only one home and was found to have sustained a pelvic injury. While the form could not be rated so highly as that of the 2014 renewal, in which the Aidan O'Brien-trained Found beat Ervedya, there were some promising types on show and Ballydoyle recorded a faster time than Ultra when he won the following Prix Jean-Luc Lagardere over the same course and distance. Ballydoyle did take time to master the leaders—which included Turret Rocks—after joining them, and her rider Ryan Moore (who had ridden Ballydoyle on her first two starts, with Joseph O'Brien deputising in between) had to get fairly serious before she finally asserted in the closing stages. Interestingly, Ballydoyle's odds for the One Thousand Guineas at various stages were 8/1 after the Moyglare (Minding was cut to 12/1 from 25/1), as low as 6/1 after the Boussac (Minding 10/1) and then 5/1 after the Fillies' Mile won by Minding (who was shortened to 4/1 for the Guineas after that race and is 7/2 at the time of writing). The programme mapped

Breast Cancer Research Debutante Stakes, the Curragh—Ballydoyle beats stablemate Minding (No.4) and Most Beautiful (No.6) in a strong renewal of this Group 2

Total Prix Marcel Boussac - Criterium des Pouliches, Longchamp—Ballydoyle emulates her sister Misty For Me, who won this race for the same connections in 2010; Turret Rocks (checked cap) completes a 1, 2 for Ireland, with Qemah (No.2) faring best of the home contingent

out for Ballydoyle of the Debutante, Moyglare and Boussac was the one followed by her small, workmanlike sister Misty For Me who ran in those races for the same connections in 2010, finishing runner-up in the Debutante before winning both the Moyglare (reversing the form with the Debutante winner) and the Boussac. Misty For Me went on to win the Irish One Thousand Guineas and the Pretty Polly Stakes at three.

Coolmore and Best In The World are worth mentioning in a little more detail. Coolmore is the third foal out of You'resothrilling, following the classic winners Marvellous and Gleneagles, and she got off the mark at the third time of asking in the Group 3 C. L. Weld Park Stakes at the Curragh and then finished a good fourth in the Fillies' Mile. She will stay a mile and a quarter. Found's full sister Best In The World progressed from her debut when taking the listed Staffordstown Stud Stakes at the Curragh, a race the same connections won with the subsequent Group 1 winners Homecoming Queen in 2011 and Together Forever in 2014. Best In The World only did the bare minimum in front as she turned around Gowran form with Rayisa and will do better once she races over longer distances as a three-year-old. Another two-year-old filly from Ballydoyle to keep an eye on is Even Song who improved from her debut when winning a Leopardstown maiden over a mile eight days later in October. She is a half-sister to the St Leger winner Simple Verse and will be suited by at least a mile and a quarter.

Ballydoyle (IRE) (b.f. 2013)	Galileo (IRE) (b 1998)	Sadler's Wells (b 1981)	Northern Dancer / Fairy Bridge
		Urban Sea (ch 1989)	Miswaki / Allegretta
	Butterfly Cove (USA) (b or br 2001)	Storm Cat (b or br 1983)	Storm Bird / Terlingua
		Mr P's Princess (ch 1993)	Mr Prospector / Anne Campbell

As well as being a sister to the aforementioned Misty For Me, who was a very smart winner at up to a mile and a quarter, Ballydoyle is also a full sister to Twirl, a useful winner at up to an extended nine furlongs. Twirl won two of her eight starts for Aidan O'Brien, including a listed race as a three-year-old, before running seven times without success in the States. Ballydoyle is also a half-sister to the Italian seven-furlong/mile winner Alexanor (by Pivotal) and to the unraced Come Touch The Sun (by Fusaichi Pegasus), whose second foal Sun Lover showed promise in two starts in 2015. Ballydoyle's dam Butterfly Cove is an unraced half-sister to the very smart sprinting two-year-old Fasliyev (who did not race at three due to injury) and to the useful seven-furlong winner Kamarinskaya who got off the mark in a One Thousand Guineas trial and was eventually sold for 3,200,000 dollars as a four-year-old, believed in foal to Kingmambo. Fasliyev and Kamarinskaya were trained by Aidan O'Brien. Butterfly Cove's half-brother by Kris S, incidentally, made 3,900,000 dollars as a yearling in 1999 when bought by Sheikh Mohammed's bloodstock adviser John Ferguson. Ballydoyle's grandam Anne Campbell was a useful stakes winner and numbered the Grade 1 winners Menifee and Desert Wine among her seven successful progeny. Ballydoyle will stay a mile and a quarter but she isn't sure to stay a mile and a half (Misty For Me didn't stay when fifth in the Oaks and Twirl was well beaten in the same race). Ballydoyle showed she isn't inconvenienced by good to soft ground when second in the Moyglare, though it remains to be seen whether it suits her ideally and she certainly acts well on firm (Aidan O'Brien said after the Boussac that Ballydoyle is 'a beautiful mover and loves fast ground'; Misty For Me won the Boussac on soft but encountered good ground or firmer on her ten other starts). *Aidan O'Brien, Ireland*

BALLYER RALLYER (IRE) 2 ch.c. (Apr 2) Dylan Thomas (IRE) 132 – Ridiforza **50** (FR) (Starborough 126) [2015 t7.1f[6] Oct 30] 50/1, showed something when sixth in maiden at Wolverhampton (8¾ lengths behind Ice Royal) in October, slowly away. *Ronald Thompson*

BALLYFARSOON (IRE) 4 ch.g. Medicean 128 – Amzara (IRE) (Montjeu (IRE) 137) **61 §** [2015 58: t16.5f* t16.5g[5] t13.9f[3] p15.8f[2] 14.1m t13.9g 14.1g 14.1m[3] p15.8f[6] t16.5f[5] t13.9f t12.2m[3] t12.2m Dec 18] modest handicapper: won at Wolverhampton (apprentice) in January: stays 16.5f: acts on polytrack, tapeta and good to firm going: often wears headgear: tried in tongue tie in 2015: often races in rear: lazy sort, and one to treat with caution. *Ian Williams*

BALLYGLASHEEN (IRE) 5 ch.g. Galileo (IRE) 134 – Luas Line (IRE) 115 (Danehill **77** (USA) 126) [2015 10.2m[2] 14g[2] Jul 21] fair maiden: likely to stay 2m: acts on firm and soft going: in cheekpieces final start in 2015. *Evan Williams*

BALLYHEIGUE (IRE) 6 b.g. High Chaparral (IRE) 132 – Lypharden (IRE) (Lyphard's **56** Special (USA) 122) [2015 66: f14s[3] 12m[ur] p13.3m[3] 11.9d 10m 13.3m 11.6m[6] 11.6m[5] p12g Aug 26] modest handicapper: left Brian Barr after fourth start: stays 1¾m: acts on polytrack, fibresand, soft and good to firm going: often wears headgear: often races prominently. *Ron Hodges*

BALLYLARE 2 b.g. (Feb 16) Mullionmileanhour (IRE) 116 – Retainage (USA) (Polish **73** Numbers (USA)) [2015 p6.5g[6] 6g[3] 5d[2] Jul 25] fair maiden: best effort when second in maiden at Lingfield (4 lengths behind Jakaby Jade) in July: will be suited by a return to 6f+. *John Best*

BALLYMORE CASTLE (IRE) 3 br.g. Invincible Spirit (IRE) 121 – Ballymore Lady **103** (USA) (War Chant (USA) 126) [2015 97: 6m[2] 7g 7m[5] 7.6m 6m[3] 7s[4] Oct 13] rather unfurnished gelding: useful performer: second in £150,000 Tattersalls Millions 3-Y-O Sprint at Newmarket (1¼ lengths behind Bossy Guest) in April: stays 7f: acts on soft and good to firm going: temperament under suspicion. *Richard Fahey*

BALLYNANTY (IRE) 3 gr.c. Yeats (IRE) 128 – Reina Blanca 102 (Darshaan 133) [2015 **98** 12.1m[3] 11.8s[5] p11g[2] p12g* t13.9g[2] Dec 5] €62,000Y: sixth foal: closely related to 2 winners by Sadler's Wells, including 1½m/12.5f winner Notion and half-brother to useful 7f (including at 2 yrs) winner Bellomi (by Lemon Drop Kid): dam, 1m/9f winner, closely related to winner up to 11f Silver Sign and 2-y-o 6f winner Miss Universe (both useful): useful performer: won maiden at Lingfield in November: stays 1¾m: acts on polytrack and tapeta: usually travels strongly. *Andrew Balding*

BALMONT MAST (IRE) 7 b.g. Balmont (USA) 117 – Corn Futures 78 (Nomination **106** 125) [2015 111: p6g[2] 6s[5] 6g 5g[4] 7d[6] 5.8m* 6m[2] 6.3m p6g* 6g[6] 6d p6g Oct 2] smart **a112** handicapper: won at Navan (by 2 lengths from Oor Jock) in June and Dundalk (by neck from Have A Nice Day) in August: stays 7f: acts on polytrack, tapeta, soft and good to firm going: tried in headgear prior to 2015: tried in tongue tie: often races prominently. *Edward Lynam, Ireland*

BALMORAL CASTLE 6 b.g. Royal Applause 124 – Mimiteh (USA) 77 (Maria's Mon **91** (USA) 121) [2015 89: 10m[4] 10m[3] 9m* 9s 10g[5] Oct 19] angular gelding: fairly useful handicapper: won at Goodwood (apprentice) in August: third at Windsor in May: stays 1¼m: acts on polytrack, good to firm and good to soft going. *Jonathan Portman*

BALMUSETTE 6 b.m. Halling (USA) 133 – Tcherina (IRE) 90 (Danehill Dancer (IRE) **54 p** 117) [2015 8m 12m[2] 12m May 16] useful bumper/hurdles winner: best effort in maidens (modest form) when second at Doncaster in April: will be suited by 1¾m+: should do better. *Keith Reveley*

BALQEES (IRE) 2 b.f. (Mar 25) Bushranger (IRE) 119 – Alexander Confranc (IRE) 73 – (Magical Wonder (USA) 125) [2015 t5.1g 6g 5.7f p10f Oct 22] €15,500Y: sister to 2-y-o 6f winner Pleasant Bay and half-sister to several winners, including useful/moody winner up to 12.4f (stayed 2m) Capable Guest (2-y-o 7f winner, by Cape Cross) and winner up to 6f Petardias Magic (by Petardia): dam 2-y-o 7f winner: no form. *David Evans*

BALTIC BRAVE (IRE) 4 b.g. Baltic King 120 – Negria (IRE) (Al Hareb (USA) 123) 92 [2015 97: t7.1g 7s² 7m⁶ 7m² 7m⁶ 7g² 7g⁵ 7g⁴ p7g Oct 29] workmanlike gelding: fairly useful handicapper: runner-up at Newmarket in June and July: stays 7f: acts on soft and good to firm going: usually wears tongue tie: inconsistent. *Hughie Morrison*

BALTIC HISTOIRE (IRE) 2 b.f. (Apr 7) Baltic King 120 – Petite Histoire (IRE) 96 – (Desert Story (IRE) 115) [2015 t5.1g p5g 5.1g p5f Oct 24] £33,000 2-y-o: fourth foal: half-sister to 5f winner Storyline (by Kodiac): dam, 2-y-o 5f winner, half-sister to useful winner up to 7f Whitbarrow: no form. *Jamie Osborne*

BALTIC KNIGHT (IRE) 5 b.g. Baltic King 120 – Night of Joy (IRE) 87 (King's Best 109 (USA) 132) [2015 116: p8f² 8d⁵ 8.1d⁵ 7d⁴ 8g⁴ 8m p8g⁵ Aug 17] sturdy gelding: useful performer: best effort in 2015 when 2½ lengths fourth to Cable Bay in Timeform Jury Stakes (John of Gaunt) at Haydock: stays 1¼m: acts on polytrack, soft and good to firm going: often in blinkers in 2015: sold 20,000 gns, sent to Bahrain. *Richard Hannon*

BALTIC PRINCE (IRE) 5 b.g. Baltic King 120 – Brunswick (Warning 136) [2015 52, 76 a79: p7g⁴ p7m⁴ t7.1f t7.1m p6f* p6m* 7g* 8f 6g 8m² 8.5m 7.6g* 8.3g⁴ Oct 19] fair handicapper: won at Kempton in March (apprentice) and April, Les Landes later in April and Chester (amateur) in September: stays 8.5f: acts on all-weather and good to firm going: tried in blinkers prior to 2015: usually leads: none too consistent. *Tony Carroll*

BALTIC RAIDER (IRE) 2 b.g. (Apr 10) Baltic King 120 – Frippet (IRE) 87 (Ela-Mana- 83 p Mou 132) [2015 5g 6g* 6d⁴ Sep 5] €6,500F, €27,000Y: sixth foal: half-brother to 3 winners, including useful 9f winner Carefree Smile (by Invincible Spirit) and 1½m winner Pagano (by Night Shift): dam, 11f winner, sister to useful 2-y-o 1¼m winner Trigger Happy: fairly useful performer: won maiden at Newcastle (by neck from Extortion) in August: good fourth in nursery at Haydock (2¾ lengths behind Receding Waves) in September, inadequate test: will be suited by 7f+: remains open to improvement. *Michael Dods*

BALTY BOYS (IRE) 6 b.g. Cape Cross (IRE) 129 – Chatham Islands (USA) 77 (Elusive 119 Quality (USA)) [2015 109: 7g² 9m* 12m⁵ 8f⁴ 10.4m 7d² 8d* p9.2m⁶ 8d 8d Oct 31] useful-looking gelding: smart performer: won handicap at Newmarket (by 2¼ lengths from Halation) in May and Superior Mile at Haydock (by 1½ lengths from Sovereign Debt) in September: second in valuable handicap at Ascot (head behind Heaven's Guest) in July: stays 9f: acts on any turf going: often wears headgear. *Brian Ellison*

BAMAKO DU CHATELET (FR) 4 gr.g. Voix du Nord (FR) 119 – Royale du Chatelet 71 (FR) (Sleeping Car (FR) 116) [2015 p12g⁵ p10.7g⁴ p8g⁴ Dec 28] fair maiden: best effort when fourth in maiden at Dundalk in April, nearest finish: left Charlie Swan after second start. *Ian Williams*

betfred.com Superior Mile, Haydock—a first pattern success for Balty Boys, who is chased home by Sovereign Debt (No.6); the other horse in shot is the eventual fifth Master Carpenter

BAMBINO 2 b.f. (Apr 20) Lilbourne Lad (IRE) 111 – Venus Rising (Observatory (USA) **58**
131) [2015 7m 7.6v 6s p6g p7g Oct 27] €25,000 2-y-o: lengthy, rather unfurnished filly:
sixth foal: closely related to 2-y-o 6f winner Businessman and useful winner up to 7f
Guiding Light (2-y-o 6f winner) (both by Acclamation) and half-sister to 7f-2m winner
Songsmith (by Librettist): dam unraced half-sister to smart winner up to 1½m Kandidate:
modest maiden: best effort at 6f: acts on soft going: sometimes slowly away, often races
towards rear. *Amanda Perrett*

BANANA SPLIT 3 b.f. Kyllachy 129 – Chicita Banana 69 (Danehill Dancer (IRE) 117) **91**
[2015 6g⁵ 6g 6g³ 5d⁵ 6g³ 7g 6g Oct 10] fairly useful performer: good third in listed race at
Hoppegarten (2¼ lengths behind Penmaen) on fifth start: well held in similar event at
Newmarket final outing: stays 6f: acts on soft going: tried in cheekpieces/tongue tie. *Paul
Harley, Germany*

BANCNUANAHEIREANN (IRE) 8 b.g. Chevalier (IRE) 115 – Alamanta (IRE) (Ali- **114**
Royal (IRE) 127) [2015 108: 8.3m⁵ 8f 8m³ 8m³ 10.4d² p10f* p10f* Nov 5] big, workmanlike
gelding: smart handicapper: won at Chelmsford (by ½ length from Croquembouche) in
October and Chelmsford (by nose from Spanish Squeeze) in November: stays 11f, effective
at shorter: acts on polytrack, good to firm and heavy going. *Michael Appleby*

BANDIT BOB (IRE) 2 b.c. (Apr 10) Manduro (GER) 123 – Neat Shilling (IRE) (Bob **82 p**
Back (USA) 124) [2015 8d p8g³ p8g² Dec 16] 12,000Y: half-brother to several winners,
including very smart 6f/7f winner Kalahari Gold (by Trans Island) and useful winner up to
1¼m (stayed 1½m) Mr Jack Daniells (2-y-o 7f winner, by Mujadil): dam unraced: fairly
useful maiden: best effort when second in maiden at Kempton (nose behind Ballard Down)
in December: will stay at least 1¼m: capable of better. *K. R. Burke*

BANDITRY (IRE) 3 b.g. Iffraaj 127 – Badalona 90 (Cape Cross (IRE) 129) [2015 77: **89**
8.3s³ 10m² 9.9g² 10.1m* 10.3g² 9.9m 9.8d 10.1d Sep 27] fairly useful handicapper: won at
Epsom (by 2¼ lengths from Triple Dip) in July: stays 10.5f: acts on soft and good to firm
going: wears headgear: sometimes slowly away, often races in rear. *Michael Bell*

BANE (IRE) 4 ch.g. Tamayuz 126 – Hidden Heart (USA) 62 (Kingmambo (USA) 125) –
[2015 58: p10g Aug 26] maiden: no form in 2015: stays 8.5f: acts on good to firm going:
in blinkers sole start in 2015. *Mike Murphy*

BANGERS (IRE) 3 b.g. Alfred Nobel (IRE) 110 – Sandbox Two (IRE) (Foxhound –
(USA) 103) [2015 –: t7.1g Jan 19] maiden: no form in 2015. *Tom Dascombe*

BANHAM (USA) 2 gr.c. (May 4) Exchange Rate (USA) 111 – Palisade (USA) 87 (Gone **73 p**
West (USA)) [2015 7s p8f⁶ Oct 22] half-brother to several winners, including smart US
5.5f-8.5f winner Jibboom (by Mizzen Mast) and useful winner up to 1m Self Evident
(by Known Fact): dam 2-y-o 7f winner: better effort when sixth in maiden at Chelmsford
(3 lengths behind Thikriyaat) in October, never nearer: open to further improvement.
Roger Charlton

BANK OF GIBRALTAR 3 ch.g. Rock of Gibraltar (IRE) 133 – Banksia (Marju (IRE) **85**
127) [2015 52p: 10m² 11.5d³ 10.1m² p8g² 9.9m p10f² Dec 21] tall, angular gelding: fairly
useful maiden: second in maiden at Newcastle in June and handicap at Lingfield in July:
left Peter Chapple-Hyam after fourth start: stays 1¼m: acts on polytrack and good to firm
going. *Richard Hughes*

BANKSEA 2 b.c. (Mar 12) Lawman (FR) 121 – Stars In Your Eyes 75 (Galileo (IRE) 134) **83 p**
[2015 7m* 9d³ Oct 31] 14,000Y: first foal: dam, 1½m winner, closely related to smart
winner up to 1¼m Coordinated Cut: won maiden at Yarmouth (by head from Tears In My
Eyes) in September: better effort when third in nursery at Newmarket (3¾ lengths behind
Good Run) in October: remains open to improvement. *Luca Cumani*

BANNISTER BELL (IRE) 3 b.c. Holy Roman Emperor (IRE) 125 – Bells of Ireland **59**
(UAE) (Machiavellian (USA) 123) [2015 62: f6s² f7g* t7.1g⁴ f6d⁴ Feb 8] modest
handicapper: won at Southwell in January: stays 7f: acts on all-weather: tried in headgear
prior to 2015: often leads. *David Evans*

BANNOCK TOWN 4 b.g. Denounce 89 – Miss Pigalle 55 (Good Times (ITY)) [2015 –: –
6s 6g 6g 7.2d 6s⁶ 7.2d 7.2g 6g 5m Sep 28] maiden: no form in 2015: sometimes wears
headgear. *Linda Perratt*

BANREENAHREENKAH (IRE) 5 b.m. Steppe Dancer (IRE) 117 – Carmencita –
(Rock of Gibraltar (IRE) 133) [2015 63: f16g Jan 6] fair at best, no form in 2015: stays
1½m: acts on polytrack, fibresand and any turf going: tried in headgear: tried in tongue tie.
Paul Fitzsimons

BAN SHOOF 2 b.c. (Feb 11) Shirocco (GER) 129 – Pasithea (IRE) 101 (Celtic Swing **53 p**
138) [2015 7g 7v Nov 3] 32,000F: half-brother to 3 winners, including smart 1m-10.4f
winner Educate (by Echo of Light) and 1¼m winner Hippolytus (by Observatory): dam,
winner up to 1½m (2-y-o 7.4f winner), half-sister to high-class winner up to 7f Somnus:
better effort when tenth in maiden at Salisbury (6¼ lengths behind Royal Reserve) in
September: remains capable of better. *Ismail Mohammed*

BANTRY BAY (IRE) 3 ch.g. Galileo (IRE) 134 – Play Misty For Me (IRE) 74 (Danehill **92**
Dancer (IRE) 117) [2015 12v² 10g* 16f⁶ 12g Jul 6] lengthy, good sort: fifth foal: brother
to 3 winners, including very smart 1¼m-1¾m winner Quest For Peace and useful 1¼m
winner The Vatican: dam 2-y-o 6f winner: fairly useful performer: won maiden at the
Curragh in May: sixth in Queen's Vase at Royal Ascot next time: stays 2m: sent to Australia.
Aidan O'Brien, Ireland

BANZARI 3 b.f. Motivator 131 – Bantu 80 (Cape Cross (IRE) 129) [2015 88p: 11.4d⁴ **85**
13 4m 10.4d⁶ Sep 26] fairly useful handicapper: should stay 1½m: acts on good to firm and
heavy going: usually races prominently. *Michael Bell*

BAPAK ASMARA (IRE) 3 ro.g. Zebedee 113 – Sheba Five (USA) 73 (Five Star Day **96**
(USA) 120) [2015 80: 5.1d⁵ 5d⁵ 5m* 5g* Jul 4] useful performer: won maiden at Thirsk
in May and handicap at Haydock (by 3¾ lengths from Snow Cloud) in July: stays 6f,
best form at 5f: acts on good to firm and heavy going: front runner/races prominently.
Kevin Ryan

BAPAK BANGSAWAN 5 b.g. Pastoral Pursuits 127 – Nsx 74 (Roi Danzig (USA)) [2015 **80**
81: f5g⁶ f5d* p5g p5f⁵ t5.1f f5g² 5v⁶ 5.1d 5g⁶ 5.1d 5m 5d⁶ 5.2m⁶ 5.3m⁵ 5m 5g⁴ t5.1g⁵ 5d⁴
5v* 5s³ f5g* f5g⁵ Dec 29] fairly useful handicapper: won at Southwell in January, Ffos Las
in August and Southwell (by ½ length from Powerful Wind) in December: acts on
polytrack, fibresand and any turf going: tried in headgear: tried in tongue tie prior to 2015:
usually leads, often travels strongly. *Ann Stokell*

BAQQA (IRE) 3 b.f. Shamardal (USA) 129 – Love Excelling (FR) (Polish Precedent **73**
(USA) 131) [2015 8.3d⁵ 8g⁵ p8g⁴ p10f⁵ Aug 11] 400,000Y: useful-looking filly: sister to
smart winner up to 1¼m (stays 1½m) Dunboyne Express (2-y-o 6.3f/7f winner) and half-
sister to 3 winners, including useful 2-y-o 7f winner Race And Status (by Raven's Pass)
and useful 1¼m/10.4f winner Angels Story (by Galileo): dam once-raced half-sister to
Oaks winner Love Divine and smart 1m-1¼m winner Dark Promise (by Shamardal): fair
maiden: stays 1¼m: possibly not straightforward. *John Gosden*

BARABAU (USA) 2 b.c. (Apr 2) Bernardini (USA) 132 – Balanchine (USA) 131 (Storm **53**
Bird (CAN) 134) [2015 7.1g 7m 8.3m³ 7g 8.3s Oct 13] modest maiden: best effort at 8.5f:
acts on good to firm going: often races towards rear: sent to Hungary. *Mark Johnston*

BARABOY (IRE) 5 b.g. Barathea (IRE) 127 – Irina (IRE) 91 (Polar Falcon (USA) 126) **69**
[2015 9.2d⁶ 10d* Jun 8] fair handicapper: won at Ayr in June: stays 1¼m: acts on heavy
going: tried in cheekpieces prior to 2015. *Barry Murtagh*

BARAWEEZ (IRE) 5 b.g. Cape Cross (IRE) 129 – Aquarelle Bleue (Sadler's Wells **111**
(USA) 124) [2015 109: 8d 7m 7.6g⁴ 8f 7m⁵ 8.3d² 7d* 7g Sep 12] smart handicapper: won
at Galway (by neck from Pintura) in August: good second at same course (½ length behind
Hint of A Tint) on previous start: stays 9f: acts on good to firm and good to soft going: tried
in cheekpieces in 2015. *Brian Ellison*

BARBAROUS RELIC (USA) 2 b.c. (May 3) Scat Daddy (USA) 120 – Electric Gold **85**
(USA) (Seeking The Gold (USA)) [2015 5m⁴ 6m* 5f⁴ 6m 6g⁵ 6g⁵ 7g Dec 29] $77,000Y:
second foal: dam, 6f-1m winner, half-sister to smart 6f-1m winner Elusive Warning: fairly
useful performer: won maiden at Ayr (by ½ length from Kraftwork) in June: left K. R. Burke
after fifth start: stays 6f: acts on firm going. *Jassim Al Ghazali, Qatar*

BARBARY (IRE) 4 b.g. Rock of Gibraltar (IRE) 133 – Silver Cache (USA) 59 (Silver **50**
Hawk (USA) 123) [2015 68: p8g Apr 8] modest handicapper: stays 1m: acts on polytrack:
tried in hood prior to 2015. *Charlie Fellowes*

BARBICAN 7 b.g. Hurricane Run (IRE) 134 – The Faraway Tree 113 (Suave Dancer **79**
(USA) 136) [2015 14f 12g Jun 13] big, useful-looking gelding: fair handicapper: stays 2m:
acts on polytrack and good to firm going. *Don Cantillon*

BARBS PRINCESS 5 ch.m. Bahamian Bounty 116 – Halland Park Girl (IRE) 106 **82**
(Primo Dominie 121) [2015 80: t6g* f6d* f6s f6d³ 6g⁴ 5f³ 6g 6m⁵ 6s p5g³ Oct 20] sturdy
mare: fairly useful handicapper: won at Wolverhampton and Southwell (by 5 lengths from
Musical Molly) in January: stays 6f: acts on all-weather and any turf going: tried in
cheekpieces: usually races close up. *Charles Hills*

BARCHAN (USA) 3 b.g. War Front (USA) 119 – Malamado (USA) (Broken Vow (USA) **81** 117) [2015 82: t7.1f* p6g³ Feb 14] rangy gelding: fairly useful handicapper: won at Wolverhampton by 2¼ lengths from Biting Bullets) in January: stays 7f: acts on polytrack and tapeta: tried in cheekpieces prior to 2015: often wears tongue tie: usually races freely: sometimes looks hard ride. *Charlie Appleby*

BAREFOOT DANCER 3 b.g. Dansili 127 – Charlotte O Fraise (IRE) 106 (Beat Hollow **88** 126) [2015 11.9g² 11.5d p12g⁴ 11.8m³ 14f⁶ p12g³ p12g² p13.3f* Oct 8] sturdy gelding: fifth foal: closely related to 1m winner (stayed 1¼m) Empress Charlotte (by Holy Roman Emperor) and half-brother to useful 1¼m-16.4f winner Big Thunder and 1½m winner Charlotte's Day (both by Dalakhani): dam, 2-y-o 6f/7f winner, half-sister to smart winner up to 1m Luck Money: fairly useful performer: won maiden at Chelmsford in October: second in handicap at Kempton in September: stays 13.5f: acts on polytrack: tried in cheekpieces: usually races close up: sold 65,000 gns, sent to Saudi Arabia. *Michael Bell*

BARI (IRE) 4 b.f. Cape Cross (IRE) 129 – Genoa 96 (Zafonic (USA) 130) [2015 p12g⁴ **79** p11g⁶ t12.2g² 12g* 13.3m⁵ 12g² 14d 14.1g 11.6g Oct 20] 6,000Y: half-sister to several **a71** winners, including useful 1m winner (stayed 1¼m) Brindisi (by Dr Fong) and useful 1¼m winner (stays 1½m) Torphichen (by Alhaarth): dam temperamental 11.5f winner: fair handicapper: won at Newbury (apprentice) in May: stays 1½m: best form on good going: tried in cheekpieces: often races prominently: temperament under suspicion. *Lucy Wadham*

BARISTA (IRE) 7 b.g. Titus Livius (FR) 115 – Cappuccino (IRE) (Mujadil (USA) 119) **72** [2015 8.3d⁵ 7.1s³ 7.1s* 7s⁶ 8.3g Oct 20] compact gelding: fair handicapper: won at Chepstow in August: stays 8.5f: acts on polytrack, good to firm and heavy going: tried in visor prior to 2015. *Brian Forsey*

BARIZAN (IRE) 9 b.g. Kalanisi (IRE) 132 – Behra (IRE) 101 (Grand Lodge (USA) 125) **–** [2015 11.6m Apr 20] useful hurdler/chaser: first outing on Flat since 2008, well held in handicap at Windsor: tried in visor/blinkers. *Brendan Powell*

BARKSTON ASH 7 b.g. Kyllachy 129 – Ae Kae Ae (USA) (King of Kings (IRE) 125) **97** [2015 105: 6d 6g 6g² 6g 6m⁴ 6g 6d² 6m 6d 6g 6d 6d 6d 6d 6g 6d Sep 26] compact gelding: useful handicapper: runner-up at Pontefract (2 lengths behind Out Do) in April and Ripon (neck behind Mississippi) in June: stays 6f: acts on good to firm and heavy going: often wears headgear: often races prominently. *Eric Alston*

BARLEYSUGAR (IRE) 2 b.f. (Feb 28) Kyllachy 129 – Caster Sugar (USA) 87 (Cozzene **88** (USA)) [2015 p7g² p7g* 7g Oct 10] lengthy filly: second foal: half-sister to useful 2-y-o 7f/1m winner Mukhayyam (by Dark Angel): dam, 1m-11f winner, half-sister to dam of Melbourne Cup winner Prince of Penzance: fairly useful performer: best effort when winning maiden at Kempton (by 2¼ lengths from Dutch Destiny) in September: raced at 7f. *Sir Michael Stoute*

BARNET FAIR 7 br.g. Iceman 117 – Pavement Gates 81 (Bishop of Cashel 122) [2015 **100** 103: 5mᵘʳ 5m⁶ 5m 5m⁴ 6m 5f⁶ 5d⁶ 6m² 5.4g 5.6d 6g⁴ 6g⁶ 5m⁵ Oct 3] lengthy gelding: useful handicapper: second at Goodwood (1½ lengths behind Golden Steps) in August: stays 6f: acts on polytrack, firm and good to soft going: tried in cheekpieces in 2015: usually races nearer last than first. *David Nicholls*

BARNEY MCGREW (IRE) 12 b.g. Mark of Esteem (IRE) 137 – Success Story 60 **81** (Sharrood (USA) 124) [2015 83: 6d⁵ 6s* 6d² 6m³ 6g 6g⁴ Jul 20] rather leggy gelding: fairly useful performer: won seller at Thirsk in May: stays 7f: acts on polytrack, firm and soft going: tried in headgear prior to 2015: often races towards rear. *Michael Dods*

BARNSDALE 2 b.g. (Mar 18) Stimulation (IRE) 121 – Seren Teg 80 (Timeless Times **–** (USA) 99) [2015 7m 7d 6g⁴ 6g f6g f7g Nov 26] no form: often races towards rear. *John Holt*

BARON BOLT 2 br.g. (Mar 6) Kheleyf (USA) 116 – Scarlet Royal 43 (Red Ransom **55** (USA)) [2015 t7.1m t7.1g⁶ p6g⁵ Dec 16] modest maiden: best effort when sixth in maiden at Wolverhampton (9¼ lengths behind Harry Champion) in December, doing too much too soon. *Paul Cole*

BARON RUN 5 ch.g. Bertolini (USA) 125 – Bhima (Polar Falcon (USA) 126) [2015 88: **80** 7d 6s 6g 6d⁴ Jun 25] well-made gelding: fairly useful handicapper: stays 6f: acts on firm and good to soft going: tried in hood prior to 2015: usually leads. *K. R. Burke*

BARON SPIKEY (IRE) 3 ch.g. Lord Shanakill (USA) 121 – Sharp Diversion (USA) 42 **57 §** (Diesis 133) [2015 68: 7dᵘʳ 7g 8m⁶ 7.5f² 7.5m 7g³ t7.1g 8m 8g Aug 31] modest maiden: stays 1m: acts on firm going: often in cheekpieces in 2015: temperamental: sold £2,000, sent to Germany. *Ann Duffield*

BAROOT 3 ch.g. Dubawi (IRE) 129 – Time Honoured 83 (Sadler's Wells (USA) 132) **75**
[2015 –: 6m³ 7m² a6f⁵ Dec 3] fair maiden: stays 7f: acts on good to firm going. *M. F. de Kock, South Africa*

BARRACUDA BOY (IRE) 5 b.g. Bahamian Bounty 116 – Madame Boulangere 100 **105**
(Royal Applause 124) [2015 107: 6g 6m² 6f 5m² 6m 5.1m² 5g³ 6m* Sep 15] robust gelding: useful performer: won minor event at Yarmouth (by neck from Basil Berry) in September: stays 6f: acts on polytrack, good to firm and good to soft going: tried in headgear prior to 2015: inconsistent. *Tom Dascombe*

BARREESH (IRE) 3 ch.g. Giant's Causeway (USA) 132 – Astrologie (FR) 110 (Polish **90**
Precedent (USA) 131) [2015 8g⁴ 10.2d⁴ 8g⁴ 10.2m* 10.4m* 12m 12g Oct 9] €300,000Y: good-topped gelding: second foal: half-brother to 10.5f winner San Sicario (by Smart Strike): dam, 10.5f-1½m winner, half-sister to useful winner up to 1¼m Quest For Honor: fairly useful performer: won maiden at Nottingham in June and handicap at York (by ¾ length from Primogeniture) in July: stays 1½m: acts on good to firm going: often races towards rear: sold 18,000 gns, sent to Bahrain. *Richard Hannon*

BARREN BROOK 8 b.g. Beat Hollow 126 – Carinthia (IRE) 82 (Tirol 127) [2015 89: **82**
8m⁶ 10.4g 8m⁴ 8.9g⁶ 8m³ t8.6g³ 6.9d⁶ 10.3g⁵ 10.4g³ 8.5d Sep 22] strong, sturdy gelding: fairly useful handicapper: third at Wolverhampton in July and third at York in September: stays 10.5f: acts on tapeta, soft and good to firm going: sometimes wears headgear: usually races close up. *Michael Easterby*

BARSANTI (IRE) 3 b.g. Champs Elysees 124 – Silver Star 105 (Zafonic (USA) 130) **75**
[2015 8g⁵ 8g³ p10g² 10v³ Aug 19] fair maiden: stays 1¼m. *Luca Cumani*

BARTEL (IRE) 3 b.c. Aussie Rules (USA) 123 – Kirunavaara (IRE) (Galileo (IRE) 134) **104**
[2015 97p: p7g* 8f 8m² Jul 9] useful handicapper: won at Kempton in June: second in listed race at Newmarket (2¾ lengths behind Tupi) in July: stays 1m: acts on polytrack and good to firm going: usually responds generously to pressure: sent to Hong Kong. *Ed Vaughan*

BARTHOLOMEW FAIR 3 b.g. Dansili 127 – Rebecca Sharp 122 (Machiavellian **–**
(USA) 123) [2015 95p: 11.5s⁵ 8f 8.1g⁶ Aug 21] useful at best, no form in 2015: tried in blinkers: often travels strongly: sold 20,000 gns, sent to Saudi Arabia. *Luca Cumani*

BARWAH (USA) 4 b.f. Discreet Cat (USA) 127 – Enfiraaj (Kingmambo (USA) **62**
125) [2015 65p: p7g* p7m³ t1.1m⁶ p8m⁴ 7m⁴ 7.5s⁵ 7d 6m⁵ t8.6m⁵ 8.5d Sep 22] modest handicapper: won at Kempton in January: left Anthony Carson after fifth start: stays 1m: acts on polytrack, tapeta and good to firm going: often wears tongue tie. *Peter Niven*

BARWICK 7 b.g. Beat Hollow 126 – Tenpence 60 (Bob Back (USA) 124) [2015 93: 12g³ **93**
12m p12g⁶ 12m³ 14.1d 12v Nov 7] fairly useful handicapper: third at Epsom in April and third at Ascot in August: left Graham Mays after third start: stays 1½m: acts on polytrack and any turf going. *Ian Williams*

BARYE 4 b.g. Archipenko (USA) 127 – Oblige 101 (Robellino (USA) 127) [2015 83: **105**
t9.5g² p10g* p10g* p10g² p10g³ 8.1m 10g p11g² p12g* Dec 19] useful handicapper: won at Chelmsford in February (by 3 lengths from Topamichi) and March (by 5 lengths from Mr Red Clubs), and Lingfield (by 2 lengths from Paddys Motorbike) in December: left David Simcock after seventh start: stays 1½m: acts on polytrack and good to firm going: often races in rear. *Richard Hughes*

BASATEEN (IRE) 3 ch.g. Teofilo (IRE) 126 – Tasha's Dream (USA) 74 (Woodman **106**
(USA) 126) [2015 103p: 8m 10.4m⁵ 10m Aug 22] tall, lengthy, good-topped gelding: useful handicapper: fifth in handicap at Haydock (3¾ lengths behind Rembrandt Van Rijn) in August: stays 10.5f: acts on good to firm going: tried in blinkers in 2015: sent to UAE. *Richard Hannon*

BASEM 4 b.c. Pivotal 124 – Gonbarda (GER) 117 (Lando (GER) 128) [2015 106: 8.1m* **116**
8.1m* 8m³ 8.9g³ 9.9s⁴ Sep 23] useful-looking colt: smart handicapper: won at Sandown in June (by neck from Jacob Black) and July (by ½ length from Munaaser): third (promoted from fourth) in Betfred Mile (Handicap) at Goodwood in July and Strensall Stakes at York (best effort, 1½ lengths behind Mondialiste) in August: stays 9f: acts on good to firm and good to soft going: tried in cheekpieces in 2015. *Saeed bin Suroor*

BASHIBA (IRE) 4 ch.g. Iffraaj 127 – Nightswimmer (IRE) 75 (Noverre (USA) 125) **87**
[2015 82: 6g³ 5.1m³ 5g 5g² 5m* 6m⁴ 5m⁴ 5d⁶ 5m* 5g³ Sep 26] fairly useful handicapper: won at Doncaster in July and September: best form at 5f: acts on good to firm going: tried in visor prior to 2015: often wears tongue tie: often races prominently. *Nigel Tinkler*

125

BASIL BERRY 4 b.g. Tobougg (IRE) 125 – Dolly Coughdrop (IRE) 72 (Titus Livius (FR) **106**
115) [2015 97: p6g² t5.1f² t6m⁵ 6d p6f t7.1g* 6m* 6f 7g⁵ 6m 6m² 6s p7f t6g* t6m⁵ Dec 18]
workmanlike gelding: useful handicapper: won at Wolverhampton (by neck from Realize)
in April, Ascot (by head from Major Jack) in May and Wolverhampton (by 1¼ lengths
from It Must Be Faith) in December: stays 1m: acts on polytrack, tapeta, good to firm and
good to soft going: tried in headgear: sometimes slowly away, often races towards rear.
Chris Dwyer

BASINGSTOKE (IRE) 6 b.g. Elusive City (USA) 117 – Ryninch (IRE) 79 (Dr Devious **58**
(IRE) 127) [2015 84: f8g⁴ f7m⁴ Dec 8] lengthy gelding: modest handicapper: stays 8.5f:
acts on fibresand and soft going. *Simon Hodgson*

BASLE 8 b.m. Trade Fair 124 – Gibaltarik (IRE) 68 (Jareer (USA) 115) [2015 –: t7.1g f6g⁶
Mar 5] fairly useful at best, no form in 2015: stays 7f: acts on polytrack, fibresand, best turf
form on good going or softer (acts on heavy): tried in headgear: often wears tongue tie.
Roy Brotherton

BASMA 2 b.f. (Mar 9) Exceed And Excel (AUS) 126 – Miss Chicane 77 (Refuse To Bend **70**
(IRE) 128) [2015 6g⁵ 6f² 6m t5.1f Oct 13] 58,000F, €325,000Y: rather unfurnished filly:
first foal: dam, temperamental 9f winner, half-sister to smart 2-y-o 5f/6f winner Best Terms
(by Exceed And Excel): fair maiden: best effort at 6f. *B. W. Hills*

BASSETT BLEU 2 b.c. (Mar 14) Wootton Bassett 119 – Lafontaine Bleu 66 (Piccolo **–**
121) [2015 6g 7m 5.9g 6g 8g Oct 13] no form. *Iain Jardine*

BASTILLE DAY 3 ch.g. Champs Elysees 124 – Vivianna (Indian Ridge 123) [2015 10m⁴ **88**
10.3g⁶ p8g⁴ 8.3d⁴ 8g⁴ p8g* 8d² Oct 30] 15,500F, €32,000Y: strong gelding: closely related
to smart winner up to 1m Diamond Diva (2-y-o 7f winner, by Dansili) and half-brother to
several winners, 2 useful, including 1¼m winner (stayed 1½m) Kaylianni (by Kalanisi):
dam 11f winner: fairly useful performer: won maiden at Kempton in September: stays
1¼m: acts on polytrack, good to firm and good to soft going: often travels strongly.
David Elsworth

BATEEL (IRE) 3 b.f. Dubawi (IRE) 129 – Attractive Crown (USA) 105 (Chief's Crown **104 p**
(USA)) [2015 9.9d* 12s* 12g* Sep 19] half-sister to 3 winners, including winner up to
10.5f Basemah (2-y-o 1m winner, by Lemon Drop Kid) and 1¼m winner (stayed 1½m)
Feathered Crown (by Indian Ridge): dam winner up to 1m (2-y-o 6f winner) who stayed
11.4f: useful performer: won maiden at Salisbury in May, and handicaps at Goodwood in
August and Newmarket (by 2¾ lengths from Twitch) in September: stays 1½m: open to
further improvement. *David Simcock*

BATHOS (IRE) 2 b.c. (Apr 7) Poet's Voice 126 – Santolina (USA) 101 (Boundary (USA) **90**
117) [2015 5g 5g⁴ 6g 7g⁵ 8.3g² 7.5m* 8g* 8s* 8g* 9v⁵ Oct 7] 62,000F: tall colt: half-
brother to 3 winners, including 2-y-o 1m winner (stays 1¼m) Leitrim Pass (by Raven's
Pass) and 1½m winner Flower Fairy (by Dynaformer): dam, 2-y-o 6f winner, half-sister to
smart winner up to 1m (stayed 1½m) Etizaaz: fairly useful performer: won nurseries at
Beverley and Newmarket in August, and Thirsk and Newmarket in September: stays 1m:
acts on soft and good to firm going: usually races close up, usually responds generously to
pressure. *Mark Johnston*

BATHWICK STREET 6 ch.g. Compton Place 125 – Bahawir Pour (USA) (Green **67**
Dancer (USA) 132) [2015 72: t13.9g³ Jan 19] fair handicapper: stays 15f: acts on polytrack,
tapeta, soft and good to firm going: tried in headgear prior to 2015: front runner/races
prominently, tends to find little. *David Evans*

BATHYRHON (GER) 5 b.h. Monsun (GER) 124 – Be My Lady (GER) (Be My Guest **118**
(USA) 126) [2015 116: 15.9g 15.4m* 20f⁵ 13.9m² 11.9s 19.9m⁵ Oct 4] smart performer:
won Prix Vicomtesse Vigier at Longchamp (by 2½ lengths from dead-heaters Mille Et
Mille and Glaring) in May: creditable efforts next 2 starts, 2 lengths fifth behind Trip To
Paris in Gold Cup at Royal Ascot then short-head second to Walzertakt in Prix Maurice de
Nieuil at Longchamp: just fair fifth to Mille Et Mille in Prix du Cadran at Longchamp final
outing: stays 2½m (finds 1½m too sharp nowadays): acts on viscoride, firm and good to
soft going. *Mme Pia Brandt, France*

BATTALION (IRE) 5 b.g. Authorized (IRE) 133 – Zigarra (Halling (USA) 133) [2015 **115 §**
115§: p10g⁶ 10.4m 10d³ 9.9s* p10m⁵ p10g* p10g⁶ Dec 19] tall, attractive gelding: smart **a108 §**
performer: won listed race at Goodwood (by ¾ length from Wannabe Yours) in September
and minor event at Lingfield (by 1½ lengths from Energia Davos) in December: third in
Winter Hill Stakes at Windsor (1¼ lengths behind Racing History) in August: stays 1½m:
acts on polytrack and soft going: tried in cheekpieces: sometimes slowly away: not
straightforward. *William Haggas*

BATTERSEA 4 b.c. Galileo (IRE) 134 – Gino's Spirits 98 (Perugino (USA) 84) [2015 **107**
110p: 11.9g 14g 14.6m² Sep 11] attractive colt: useful handicapper: light campaign in 2015,
and shaped well when 1¼ lengths second to Curbyourenthusiasm in Mallard Stakes at
Doncaster final start, shuffled back 3f out: stays 14.5f: acts on firm and good to soft going.
Roger Varian

BATTLE OF BOSWORTH (IRE) 2 b.g. (May 16) Duke of Marmalade (IRE) 132 – **65 p**
Muskoka Dawn (USA) (Miswaki (USA) 124) [2015 t6g 6.5m p7g 8.1m² Sep 10] 45,000Y:
brother to 2-y-o 1m winner Chinotto and half-brother to several winners, including useful
2-y-o 6f-1m winner Mousse Au Chocolat (by Hennessy): dam lightly raced: fair maiden:
good second in nursery at Chepstow: should be suited by further than 1m: open to further
improvement. *Paul Cole*

BATTLE OF MARATHON (USA) 3 b.g. War Front (USA) 119 – Sayedah (IRE) 105 **100**
(Darshaan 133) [2015 98: 9d⁶ 8.5m⁴ Aug 19] useful performer: stays 8.5f: acts on good to
firm going: often wears headgear: sold 23,000 gns, joined John Ryan. *Aidan O'Brien, Ireland*

BATTLE PRIDE (IRE) 2 b.c. (May 15) Acclamation 118 – Heavens Peak 64 (Pivotal **90**
124) [2015 6m 7d⁴ 7g* 7.1m⁵ 8d⁴ 8d p8m⁴ f7g² Nov 24] 40,000Y: third foal: dam maiden
half-sister to smart winner up to 1½m Centennial out of smart 7f winner Lurina: fairly
useful performer: won maiden at Salisbury in August: stays 1m: acts on good to firm and
good to soft going: tried in cheekpieces. *Richard Hannon*

BATTLE SUCCESS (USA) 2 b.g. (Jan 11) Kitten's Joy (USA) 128 – Elusive **72**
Champagne (USA) (Elusive Quality (USA)) [2015 p8g f7f⁴ Dec 17] better effort when
fourth in maiden at Southwell (length behind Autumn Blossom) in December: in cheekpieces final start. *Saeed bin Suroor*

BATTS ROCK (IRE) 2 b.c. (Mar 16) Fastnet Rock (AUS) 127 – Be My Queen (IRE) **74 p**
104 (Sadler's Wells (USA) 132) [2015 8.3s³ Nov 4] fifth foal: half-brother to 7f winner
Vibe Queen (by Invincible Spirit) and winner up to 1½m Relco Nordic (2-y-o 7f-9f winner,
by Raven's Pass): dam, 1m winner who stayed 1½m, closely related to smart winner up to
6f Imperial Beauty: 8/1, some encouragement when third in maiden at Nottingham
(11½ lengths behind Wajeez) in November, not knocked about: better to come. *Michael Bell*

BAWINA (IRE) 4 b.f. Dubawi (IRE) 129 – Esneh (IRE) (Sadler's Wells (USA) 132) [2015 **117**
115: 8g* 8m⁴ 8g³ 9.9d²ᵈ 8m⁶ Oct 3] good-topped filly: smart performer: won Prix du
Muguet at Saint-Cloud (by 1¼ lengths from Spoil The Fun) in May: placed at Deauville
after, in Prix Rothschild (2½ lengths third behind Amazing Maria) and Prix Jean Romanet
(neck second to Odeliz, but later disqualified after failing drugs test): below form when
sixth to Esoterique in Sun Chariot Stakes at Newmarket final outing: stays 10.4f: acts on
soft and good to firm going: often races towards rear. *C. Laffon-Parias, France*

BAYAN (IRE) 6 b.g. Danehill Dancer (IRE) 117 – Kindling 105 (Dr Fong (USA) 128) **88**
[2015 96: 14s⁵ 18g Oct 10] sturdy, close-coupled gelding: fairly useful handicapper: stays
2¼m: acts on polytrack, good to firm and heavy going: often wears headgear: often wears
tongue tie. *Gordon Elliott, Ireland*

BAYAN KASIRGA (IRE) 5 b.m. Aussie Rules (USA) 123 – Gwyllion (USA) 71 (Red **71**
Ransom (USA)) [2015 78: 12g⁵ 12.3m⁶ 12.3g 12.4g⁴ 13.1g 10s 14.1v t12.2m* p12g⁴ **a77**
t12.2m* Dec 26] rather leggy mare: fair handicapper: won at Wolverhampton in November
and December: stays 1¾m: acts on polytrack, tapeta, firm and good to soft going: tried in
headgear. *Richard Fahey*

BAYDAR 2 b.c. (Mar 21) Rock of Gibraltar (IRE) 133 – Splashdown 105 (Falbrav (IRE) **85 p**
133) [2015 8d² p8m* Nov 17] 85,000Y: third foal: closely related to 7f winner Synergise
(by Danehill Dancer) and half-brother to useful 2-y-o 6f-7f winner Aktabantay (by Oasis
Dream): dam winner up to 1¼m (2-y-o 7f winner): won maiden at Lingfield (by 3¾ lengths
from Gabster) in November: remains with potential. *Hugo Palmer*

BAY KNIGHT (IRE) 9 b.g. Johannesburg (USA) 127 – Sabeline (IRE) (Caerleon (USA) **–**
132) [2015 64: f8d Mar 11] rather leggy gelding: useful at best, no form in 2015: stays 8.5f:
acts on polytrack, best turf form on good going or softer (acts on heavy): tried in headgear
prior to 2015: tried in tongue tie prior to 2015: often races in rear. *Heather Dalton*

BAYLAY (USA) 3 b.g. Blame (USA) 129 – Rock Candy (USA) (Mineshaft (USA) 132) **88**
[2015 p10f² 10m⁶ 10.3s 10g* 10.4g³ 10.2m* 10.2m p11g⁴ Sep 23] $180,000F, $300,000Y:
second foal: half-brother to 5.5f winner Rock Shaft (by Dixie Union): dam, 7f-1m winner
(2-y-o 6.5f winner), also third in US Grade 3 8.5f event: fairly useful performer: won
maiden at Redcar in June and handicap at Bath in July: stays 11f: acts on polytrack and
good to firm going: sold 20,000 gns, sent to Saudi Arabia. *B. W. Hills*

BAY MIRAGE (IRE) 2 b.g. (Mar 30) Kheleyf (USA) 116 – Choosey Girl (IRE) (Choisir 77
(AUS) 126) [2015 7.5m⁵ 7.2g³ 7.2g² 8s⁵ Sep 5] smallish gelding: fair maiden: stays 7f.
Kevin Ryan

BAY OF ST MALO (IRE) 2 b.f. (Jan 9) Canford Cliffs (IRE) 133 – Distant Skies (Tiger 76
Hill (IRE) 127) [2015 6d p7g³ 8g³ p7g⁴ 8v Oct 24] €24,000F, 45,000Y: sturdy filly: first
foal: dam unraced half-sister to smart 6f winner Primo Valentino and winner 2-y-o 6f
winner Dora Carrington: fair maiden: stays 1m: acts on polytrack: often races prominently.
Richard Hannon

BAY STREET BELLE 4 ch.f. Bahamian Bounty 116 – Donna Anna (Be My Chief –
(USA) 122) [2015 60: f11g⁶ p8f Jan 21] maiden: no form in 2015: in visor final start in
2015: front runner/races prominently, tends to find little. *Alison Hutchinson*

BAYTOWN KESTREL 4 b.f. Captain Gerrard (IRE) 113 – Litewska (IRE) 86 (Mujadil –
(USA) 91) [2015 91: f5s⁶ Jan 20] fairly useful at best, no form in 2015: best form at 5f:
acts on polytrack, fibresand and good to firm going: sometimes wears headgear: usually
races close up, usually finds little. *Jamie Osborne*

BAZOOKA (IRE) 4 b.g. Camacho 118 – Janadam (IRE) 55 (Mukaddamah (USA) 125) 79
[2015 p6g⁶ t7.1g³ t7.1g³ p8g² 9.2g* 10d² 12v⁵ p14f t12.2f Dec 11] fair performer:
won seller at Hamilton in September: left Ed de Giles after sixth start: stays 1½m: acts on
polytrack, tapeta and heavy going. *David Flood*

BAZ'S BOY 2 b.g. (Jan 29) Compton Place 125 – Spunger 73 (Fraam 114) [2015 6s⁵ –
10.2m 8.3d Oct 5] no form. *John Flint*

BAZULA (IRE) 2 b.g. (Apr 18) Tagula (IRE) 116 – Lilly Be (IRE) 81 (Titus Livius (FR) –
115) [2015 5.4g Sep 6] 33/1, green when well held in maiden at York. *Tim Easterby*

BAZZAT (IRE) 2 ch.g. (Jan 24) Roderic O'Connor (IRE) 119 – Compradore 82 (Mujtahid –
(USA) 118) [2015 7m p6g p5f 8g Sep 24] no form. *Alan Bailey*

BEACH ACTION (FR) 3 b.g. Footstepsinthesand 120 – Shagadellic (USA) (Devil's 70
Bag (USA)) [2015 –: t6f³ p7f⁶ 7.1s² 7.5m 7.1m 6d⁶ Jun 4] fair maiden: best effort at 7f:
acts on soft going: often in hood in 2015: won 10,000 gns, sent to France. *David O'Meara*

BEACH BAR (IRE) 4 b.g. Azamour (IRE) 130 – Toasted Special (USA) 89 (Johannesburg 103
(USA) 127) [2015 99: p8f⁶ p10g² p10f p8g 6d 8f 7s* 7g p8g 7g⁵ 7.4g* 7g⁵ 7d⁴ 6v⁵ 8.3s* **a92**
8.3s⁴ Nov 4] sturdy gelding: useful handicapper: won at Lingfield in May, Ffos Las in July
and Leicester (by 5 lengths from Starboard) in October: left William Knight after fifteenth
start: stays 8.5f: acts on polytrack and soft going: sometimes wears hood: usually leads.
Brendan Powell

BEACH PLAZA (IRE) 3 b.f. Moss Vale (IRE) 126 – Uhud (IRE) (Mujtahid (USA) 118) 53
[2015 –: p7g⁶ p6g² p6f 6g p6f Sep 17] modest maiden: stays 7f: acts on polytrack: tried in
cheekpieces: sold £600, sent to Germany. *Robert Mills*

BEACH WALKER 3 b.f. Footstepsinthesand 120 – Danemere (IRE) 90 (Danehill (USA) 36
126) [2015 70: p8f⁶ 11.6m 10m p12g⁶ Jun 6] lengthy filly: poor maiden: best effort at 1m:
acts on polytrack and good to soft going: tried in hood in 2015: sometimes slowly away.
Robert Eddery

BEACON 3 b.g. Paco Boy (IRE) 129 – Key Light (IRE) 81 (Acclamation 118) [2015 104: 101
6f 6d 5m⁶ Jul 4] lengthy gelding: useful performer: best effort in 2015 when 3¼ lengths
sixth to Waady in Sprint Stakes at Sandown: best form at 5f: acts on soft and good to firm
going. *Richard Hannon*

BEACON ROCK (IRE) 2 ch.c. (Feb 18) Galileo (IRE) 134 – Remember When (IRE) 113
111 (Danehill Dancer (IRE) 117) [2015 8g⁶ 8d* 8d³ 8g² Oct 10] neat colt: second foal:
brother to smart 9f winner Wedding Vow: dam, maiden (promoted second in Oaks), closely
related to top-class winner up to 1½m Dylan Thomas: smart performer: won maiden at the
Curragh (by short head from Precious Gold) in August: marked progress when third in
Beresford Stakes at the Curragh (beaten ¼ lenght by Port Douglas) in September and
second in Autumn Stakes at Newmarket (½ length behind Gifted Master) in October: will
stay at least 1¼m: often in cheekpieces. *Aidan O'Brien, Ireland*

BEAR CHEEK (IRE) 2 b.f. (Jan 16) Kodiac 112 – See Nuala (IRE) 73 (Kyllachy 129) 101
[2015 5m* 5g* 5m⁴ 6g⁵ Sep 26] €125,000 2-y-o: fourth foal: dam, 6f winner, half-sister to
smart winner up to 1m Aspectoflove: useful performer: won maiden at Naas in July and
Curragh Stakes (by 1½ lengths from Independence Day) in August: may prove best at 5f.
G. M. Lyons, Ireland

BEARDWOOD 3 ch.g. Dutch Art 126 – Valentina Guest (IRE) 102 (Be My Guest (USA) **92**
126) [2015 82p: 6g* 6d³ 6m⁶ 7g⁵ 6g 7s⁴ 7v⁵ Nov 7] big, strong gelding: fairly useful
performer: won maiden at Pontefract in April: third in handicap at Pontefract in July: likely
to stay 1m: acts on good to soft going. *Richard Fahey*

BEAR FACED 2 b.g. (Jan 16) Intikhab (USA) 135 – Hulcote Rose (IRE) 100 (Rock of **79 p**
Gibraltar (IRE) 133) [2015 6g 6.1m² Jun 30] 40,000Y: good-quartered gelding: first foal:
dam winner up to 8.6f (2-y-o 6f winner): better effort when second in maiden at Chepstow
(3 lengths behind Tasleet) in June, no match for winner: will go on improving. *Sir Mark
Prescott Bt*

BEARING KISSES (IRE) 4 gr.f. Clodovil (IRE) 116 – Masakira (IRE) 58 (Royal **–**
Academy (USA) 130) [2015 –: 7g May 29] lengthy, rather unfurnished filly: maiden: no
form in 2015: sometimes wears headgear: tried in tongue tie prior to 2015. *Shaun Harris*

BEARSKIN (IRE) 4 br.g. Kodiac 112 – Dark Arts (USA) 64 (Royal Anthem (USA) 135) **54**
[2015 72: 7g 6g* 6s 6g 6g⁵ 6s Jul 11] modest handicapper: stays 6f: acts on soft and good
to firm going: usually wears headgear. *Ann Duffield*

BEAST MODE (IRE) 2 b.c. (Apr 7) Cape Cross (IRE) 129 – Faithful One (IRE) 93 **102**
(Dubawi (IRE) 129) [2015 7m 7g* 8g⁵ 8s² Oct 19] €130,000Y: compact colt: first foal:
dam 6.5f-1m winner: useful performer: won maiden at Newcastle in August: second in
listed race at Pontefract (¾ length behind Thanksfortellingme) in October: stays 1m. *Peter
Chapple-Hyam*

BEATABOUT THE BUSH (IRE) 4 b.g. Bushranger (IRE) 119 – Queen of Fibres **61**
(IRE) 65 (Scenic 128) [2015 57: t12.2g* Sep 29] sturdy gelding: modest handicapper: won
at Wolverhampton in September: stays 1½m: acts on tapeta and firm going: tried in hood
prior to 2015. *Henry Oliver*

BEATBYBEATBYBEAT 2 ch.f. (Mar 13) Poet's Voice 126 – Beat As One (Medicean **73**
128) [2015 7g 7.1m⁴ 7g* 7s⁶ Oct 6] sturdy filly: second foal: dam unraced half-sister to 6f
winner So Will I and 5f/6f winner Sand Vixen (both smart): fair performer: won maiden at
Redcar in September: raced only at 7f. *Ismail Mohammed*

BEAT GOES ON 3 gr.g. Piccolo 121 – Cherrycombe-Row 77 (Classic Cliche (IRE) 128) **92**
[2015 t1.1g⁶ t7.1m* 8g 7.1m⁵ 8.3g⁶ t8.6g* p9f⁴ Sep 20] 30,000F, €70,000Y: workmanlike
gelding: sixth foal: brother to smart 7f-9.5f winner St Trinians: dam 2-y-o 7f winner who
stayed 1¼m: fairly useful performer: won maiden at Wolverhampton in February and
handicap at Wolverhampton in July: stays 8.5f: acts on tapeta and good to firm going: often
races towards rear. *Charles Hills*

BEAT THE BLUES 3 b.f. Aqlaam 125 – Beat As One (Medicean 128) [2015 p10f⁴ 10.3g **65**
10.3d p8g⁵ p7g Dec 9] first foal: dam unraced half-sister to 6f winner So Will I and 5f/6f
winner Sand Vixen (both smart): fair maiden: left Clive Brittain after third start: stays 1¼m:
acts on polytrack. *Miss Joey Ellis*

BEAT THE SHOWER 9 b.g. Beat Hollow 126 – Crimson Shower 61 (Dowsing (USA) **55**
124) [2015 67: 15.8s 16d Jun 3] big, workmanlike gelding: modest handicapper: stays
2¼m: acts on good to firm and heavy going: tried in hood prior to 2015: often races
towards rear. *Peter Niven*

BEAU AMADEUS (IRE) 6 b.g. Amadeus Wolf 122 – Degree of Honor (FR) 49 (Highest **66**
Honor (FR) 124) [2015 p5g³ p6g* p6g⁶ p6f 7s Oct 26] fair handicapper: won at Lingfield
in July: stays 1m: acts on polytrack and heavy going: sometimes wears headgear.
Phil McEntee

BEAUCHAMP ACE 3 b.g. Compton Admiral 121 – Aquarelle (Kenmare (FR) 125) **–**
[2015 66?: p6f t9.5f 7d⁴ Apr 8] maiden: no form in 2015: tried in blinkers in 2015: front
runner/races prominently. *Paul Fitzsimons*

BEAUCHAMP AMIGO 2 b.g. (Mar 29) Cockney Rebel (IRE) 127 – Beauchamp Xiara **–**
79 (Compton Admiral 121) [2015 6m 6m⁶ 7g Jun 20] no form. *Paul Fitzsimons*

BEAUCHAMP DAME 2 ch.f. (May 1) Archipenko (USA) 127 – Beauchamp Utopia 75 **37**
(Compton Admiral 121) [2015 p7g⁶ Sep 22] fifth foal: dam once-raced sister to smart
winner up to 9f Beauchamp Viceroy: 50/1, sixth in claimer at Kempton (5½ lengths behind
Poldark) in September. *Paul Fitzsimons*

BEAUCHAMP MELBA 4 b.f. Compton Admiral 121 – Ashford Castle (USA) (Bates **–**
Motel (USA)) [2015 t12.2f Feb 16] maiden: no form in 2015: stays 1½m: acts on polytrack:
often wears headgear: in tongue tie sole start in 2015: front runner/races prominently, tends
to find little. *Paul Fitzsimons*

BEAUCHAMP MONARK 2 b.g. (Apr 16) Pastoral Pursuits 127 – Orange Sunset (IRE) **61** 99 (Roanoke (USA)) [2015 t7.1g p7g³ t7.1g³ 7s⁶ t7.1f Oct 30] workmanlike gelding: modest maiden: raced only at 7f: acts on tapeta: usually in headgear. *Paul Fitzsimons*

BEAU EILE (IRE) 3 b.f. Arcano (IRE) 122 – Mona Em (IRE) (Catrail (USA) 123) [2015 **82** 84: 5g⁴ 5m³ 5.1f³ 5.6m 5m 5s Sep 5] fairly useful handicapper: best effort at 5f: acts on firm going: tried in blinkers in 2015: sometimes slowly away. *David Barron*

BEAUFORT TWELVE 6 b.g. Hurricane Run (IRE) 134 – Violette 106 (Observatory **76** (USA) 131) [2015 p12g Dec 9] attractive gelding: fair handicapper: stays 1½m: acts on polytrack and good to firm going: tried in headgear prior to 2015. *Graham Mays*

BEAU KNIGHT 3 b.g. Sir Percy 129 – Nicola Bella (IRE) 98 (Sadler's Wells (USA) 132) **79** [2015 72p: p10f* 12.1m 12.3g³ 13m⁵ 12.3g 11.9m² 12s t9.5m Sep 25] sturdy gelding: fair performer: won maiden at Lingfield in January: stays 12.5f: acts on polytrack and good to firm going: front runner/races prominently. *William Jarvis*

BEAU MISTRAL (IRE) 6 ch.m. Windsor Knot (IRE) 118 – Carpet Lover (IRE) 46 **70** (Fayruz 116) [2015 80: 5.1m⁵ 5.1s 5.3s³ 5d* p6g⁶ 6d 5m⁴ 5s⁶ 5g 5.1d Oct 14] fair handicapper: won at Leicester in June: stays 6f, all wins at 5f: acts on polytrack, good to firm and heavy going: tried in visor prior to 2015. *Tony Carroll*

BEAUMONT'S PARTY 8 b.g. High Chaparral (IRE) 132 – Miss Champagne **78 §** (FR) (Bering 136) [2015 10.1g 12m⁶ 10.1d 12v Oct 17] well-made, attractive gelding: fair handicapper: stays 1½m: acts on good to firm and heavy going: tried in cheekpieces prior to 2015: often races prominently: moody, and one to treat with caution. *Chris Grant*

BEAUSANT 3 ch.g. Orientor 118 – Hanella (IRE) 91 (Galileo (IRE) 134) [2015 –p: 9.9m **72** p12g 12.1g⁵ t12.2g² p13.3f⁴ Oct 10] fair maiden: stays 13.5f: acts on polytrack and tapeta: sometimes in cheekpieces in 2015. *George Baker*

BEAU SPARKLE (IRE) 3 b.f. Baltic King 120 – Cabopino (IRE) 58 (Captain Rio 122) **44** [2015 47: t7.1g 8f 7d³ p7m⁵ 7d t6m 7s⁵ Oct 26] poor maiden: stays 8.5f: acts on polytrack, tapeta and good to soft going: usually in headgear in 2015: often in tongue tie in 2015. *Steph Hollinshead*

BEAUTIFUL ENDING 3 ch.f. Exceed And Excel (AUS) 126 – Pearl Kite (USA) 106 **74** (Silver Hawk (USA) 123) [2015 78p: p8g⁵ 8.3m⁴ 7d Aug 5] fair handicapper: stays 8.5f: acts on polytrack, tapeta and good to firm going: often in headgear in 2015: sometimes slowly away, often races freely: temperament under suspicion. *Saeed bin Suroor*

BEAUTIFUL FIRTH 2 b.f. (Mar 15) Poet's Voice 126 – Roslea Lady (IRE) 63 (Alhaarth **–** (IRE) 126) [2015 6.5m 7.5g Jul 4] 17,000Y: sixth foal: half-sister to 3 winners, including 2-y-o 6f winner Hoot (by Invincible Spirit) and 1¼m winner Royal Roslea (by Royal Applause): dam maiden half-sister to smart/unreliable 5f/6f winner Conquest: no form. *Tim Easterby*

BEAUTIFUL MORNING 2 b.f. (Mar 15) Galileo (IRE) 134 – Date With Destiny (IRE) **96 p** 93 (George Washington (IRE) 133) [2015 7m⁴ 7g* 8g⁵ Oct 10] 650,000Y: rangy, rather unfurnished filly: first foal: dam, 2-y-o 7f winner who stayed 11.5f, half-sister to useful 10.5f winner Ombre Legere: useful performer: won maiden at York (by length from Very Talented) in August: best effort when fifth in Fillies' Mile at Newmarket (8¼ lengths behind Minding) in October: will stay beyond 1m: remains open to improvement. *Luca Cumani*

BEAUTIFUL ROMANCE 3 b.f. New Approach (IRE) 132 – Mazuna (IRE) 110 (Cape **117** Cross (IRE) 129) [2015 97p: 7m³ 9.9g⁶ 11.6d* 11.9s⁵ 12d³ Oct 17] sturdy filly: smart performer: won listed race at Windsor (by 4½ lengths from Gospel Choir) in August: third in Fillies' And Mares' Stakes at Ascot (2¾ lengths behind Simple Verse) in October: should stay beyond 1½m: acts on soft going. *Saeed bin Suroor*

BEAUTIFUL STRANGER (IRE) 4 b.g. Iffraaj 127 – Monarchy (IRE) (Common **80 §** Grounds 118) [2015 82§: f7d⁴ t8.6f⁵ p7g p8g⁶ 7d² 7.2g³ 8m* 8.5m³ Jun 10] leggy gelding: fairly useful handicapper: won at Pontefract in May: third at Beverley in June: stays 8.5f: acts on fibresand, tapeta, good to firm and good to soft going: usually wears headgear: quirky sort, and one to treat with caution. *Keith Dalgleish*

BEAUTY INDEX (IRE) 3 b.g. Dylan Thomas (IRE) 132 – Tencarola (IRE) (Night Shift **67** (USA)) [2015 t8.6g⁶ 8.3g⁶ 8.6m³ p8f⁶ Sep 12] 56,000Y: half-brother to 2 winners, including 6f/7f winner Impel (by Excellent Art): dam, 1m winner, half-sister to useful 1¼m winner (stayed 1½m) Torcello: fair form: stayed 8.5f: dead. *Chris Wall*

BEAUTY NIGHT 2 b.g. (Mar 22) Showcasing 117 – Night Symphonie (Cloudings (IRE) **71** 112) [2015 8s p7g³ p8f⁶ Nov 25] fair maiden: best effort when sixth in maiden at Lingfield (5¼ lengths behind Next Stage) in November. *Clive Cox*

BEAUTY PRINCE 3 b.g. Arcano (IRE) 122 – Singed (Zamindar (USA) 116) [2015 66p: **86**
p7g* Mar 28] fairly useful performer: still green when winning maiden at Kempton (by 1¼
lengths from Fire And Passion) in March: will stay at least 1m: sent to Hong Kong.
Clive Cox

BEAUTY'S FORTE (IRE) 4 b.g. Kyllachy 129 – Viking Fair (Zamindar (USA) 116) **51**
[2015 –: 7d 5g 7s 6g 5g 6m⁶ 5m⁵ t7.1g⁴ 5m⁶ 6g⁶ f6d t6g² 7d⁶ t6m 6d⁵ 5m 6g 5m t6f t7.1m* **a65**
t7.1f Dec 22] fair handicapper: won at Wolverhampton in November: stays 7f: acts on
tapeta: sometimes in headgear in 2015. *Declan Carroll*

BEAVERBROOK 2 b.c. (Mar 21) Cape Cross (IRE) 129 – Bint Almatar (USA) 75 **99**
(Kingmambo 125) [2015 5m⁴ 5m² 6m² 6.1g* 6f⁴ 7f⁵ 7g⁶ 7.1m 7d⁵ Sep 12] well-
grown colt: first foal: dam, 1m winner (including at 2 yrs), half-sister to smart 2-y-o 7f
winner Latharnach and useful winner up to 9.5f Falls of Lora: useful performer: won
maiden at Chester in May: best effort when 4¾ lengths fourth to Buratino in Coventry
Stakes at Royal Ascot: better form at 6f than 7f: acts on firm going. *Mark Johnston*

BEAVER CREEK 4 ch.g. Three Valleys (USA) 119 – Delta (Zafonic (USA) 130) [2015 **–**
–: 10m 16g Jul 8] maiden: no form in 2015. *Ralph Smith*

BE BOLD 3 ch.g. Assertive 121 – Marysienka 78 (Primo Dominie 121) [2015 85: 6m⁴ 7m⁵ **88**
6m 6d⁵ 8.3g⁴ p8g 7g 6v* 6d³ 7s 6d² Oct 12] sturdy gelding: fairly useful handicapper: won
at Newbury in August: stays 6f: acts on heavy going: tried in headgear. *Richard Hannon*

BE BOP TANGO (FR) 2 b.g. (Apr 29) Soul City (IRE) 114 – Divine Poesie (FR) **78**
(Enrique 121) [2015 5g⁴ 5d* 6m⁶ 5g 6g Sep 18] good-quartered gelding: fair performer:
won maiden at Catterick in May: best effort at 5f: acts on good to soft going: front runner/
races prominently. *K. R. Burke*

BECCABUDDYBLUES (GR) 3 ch.f. Reel Buddy (USA) 118 – Second of May 72 **–**
(Lion Cavern (USA) 117) [2015 –: 9g 11.7f⁵ 16.2m Jul 20] maiden: no form in 2015: often
in hood prior to 2015. *Amanda Perrett*

BECCA CAMPBELL (IRE) 2 b.f. (Apr 10) Roderic O'Connor (IRE) 119 – Scottendale **58**
58 (Zilzal (USA) 137) [2015 5m⁴ 6g⁴ 6.1m³ p7f⁶ 8.3g 6.3d Sep 13] €15,000Y: fifth foal:
half-sister to 6f-7f winner Bush Beauty (by Bushranger): dam highly-raced half-sister to
smart 1½m-13.3f winner (stayed 2½m) Compton Ace: modest maiden: stays 6f: acts on
good to firm going: often races towards rear. *Eve Johnson Houghton*

BECKY THE THATCHER 2 b.f. (Feb 25) Mastercraftsman (IRE) 129 – Fairmont **67**
(IRE) 53 (Kingmambo (USA) 125) [2015 8d 7s² 7.5m⁶ 7v Oct 17] 12,000F, £12,000 2-y-o:
fourth foal: half-sister to winner up to 1m Emperatriz (2-y-o 7f winner, by Holy Roman
Emperor) and winner up to 7f (stays 1¼m) Fair Ranger (by Bushranger): dam ran once: fair
maiden: should stay 1m. *Micky Hammond*

BECOME AWARE 3 b.g. Sakhee (USA) 136 – Sainte Gig (FR) (Saint Cyrien (FR) 128) **–**
[2015 –: 12d 10g⁶ 14.1g 14.1v t9.5m t12.2f⁵ Dec 14] maiden: no form in 2015: tried in
headgear in 2015. *Tim Etherington*

BEDAZZLING LADY (IRE) 2 gr.f. (Feb 17) Zebedee 113 – Malta (USA) (Gone West **–**
(USA)) [2015 5g p6g⁶ p6g Dec 16] €15,500Y, €16,000 2-y-o: lengthy filly: third foal: half-
sister to useful winner up to 7f Comino (by Tagula): dam once-raced half-sister to smart 7f
winner Tombelaine: no form. *Robert Eddery*

BEDLOE'S ISLAND (IRE) 10 b.g. Statue of Liberty (USA) 115 – Scenaria (IRE) **67**
(Scenic 128) [2015 86: f5s³ f6g⁵ 5g⁴ Apr 13] big gelding: fair performer: stays 6f: acts on
all-weather, good to firm and heavy going: tried in headgear prior to 2015. *John Balding*

BEDROCK 2 b.g. (Feb 1) Fastnet Rock (AUS) 127 – Gemstone (IRE) 108 (Galileo (IRE) **87 p**
134) [2015 6s⁴ 7m 6.5s* Oct 23] 150,000Y: compact gelding: first foal: dam, 2-y-o 7f/1m
winner who stayed 1½m, half-sister to 7f winner Karamela: fairly useful form: best effort
when winning maiden at Newbury (by neck from Make Music) in October, driven out:
should be suited by at least 7f: remains with potential. *William Haggas*

BEEDEE 5 b.g. Beat Hollow 126 – Dawnus (IRE) 103 (Night Shift (USA)) [2015 –: p8g **67**
p10g⁶ 10.2m May 30] smallish gelding: fair handicapper: left Richard Hannon after second
start: stayed 1¼m: acted on polytrack, good to firm and good to soft going: was sometimes
slowly away: dead. *Tim Vaughan*

BEEP 5 b.m. Beat Hollow 126 – Dialing Tone (USA) 100 (Distant View (USA) 126) [2015 **62**
66: 11m² Jun 7] tall mare: modest maiden: stayed 11f: acted on polytrack, soft and good to
firm going: had worn headgear: front runner/raced prominently: dead. *Lydia Richards*

BEGGERS LUCK 5 b.m. Lucky Story (USA) 128 – Dropitlikeit's Hot (IRE) (Tagula **65** (IRE) 116) [2015 60: p10g⁴ p8f² p7g* p7g 8.3m 7m⁴ t7.1g² t7.1g² 7g p8f p7g p7m⁴ f7g² p7g² Dec 30] fair handicapper: won at Lingfield in February: stays 7f: acts on all-weather: races prominently. *Eric Wheeler*

BEHOLDER (USA) 5 b.m. Henny Hughes (USA) 125 – Leslie's Lady (USA) (Tricky **131** Creek (USA)) [2015 123: a8.5f* a8.5f* a8.5f* a10f* a8.5f* Sep 26] top-class performer, Grade 1 winner in each season to race: successful in Breeders' Cup Juvenile Fillies at Santa Anita in 2012 and Breeders' Cup Distaff on same course in 2013: won all 5 of her races in 2015, namely non-graded stakes at Santa Anita in April, Grade 3 Adoration Stakes on same course in June, Clement L. Hirsch Stakes and Pacific Classic (by 8¼ lengths from Catch A Flight, travelling powerfully and storming clear over 1f out), both at Del Mar in August, and Zenyatta Stakes at Santa Anita (for third year running, landed odds very easily by 3¼ lengths from My Sweet Addiction) in September: stays 1¼m: acts on polytrack and dirt: often races prominently: missed Breeders' Cup Classic at Keeneland in October after being found to have bled in gallop 2 days before (the second year in succession she had been forced to miss the meeting). *Richard E. Mandella, USA*

BEIJING STAR 3 ch.g. Dylan Thomas (IRE) 132 – Signella 66 (Selkirk (USA) 129) **66** [2015 –: 8m 10m* 9.9m⁵ 8.9m³ 7.9g⁴ 8g⁶ 12.2m⁴ 12.2g⁵ 9.2m 8g 7.2g 7.2g Oct 13] sturdy gelding: fair performer: won claimer at Windsor in July: left David Pipe after second start: stays 1½m: acts on good to firm going. *Linda Perratt*

BE KOOL (IRE) 2 b.g. (Apr 26) Approve (IRE) 112 – Accounting (Sillery (USA) 122) **67** [2015 6m 7m⁵ 6g t7.1f² Oct 27] fair maiden: will stay 1m. *Brian Ellison*

BELAHODOOD 4 b.c. New Approach (IRE) 132 – Broken Peace (USA) (Devil's Bag **74** (USA)) [2015 67: f8g⁶ t9.5f⁴ 8s May 9] fair maiden: left William Haggas after second start: best effort at 9.5f: often in cheekpieces in 2015. *Ismail Mohammed*

BELARDO (IRE) 3 b.c. Lope de Vega (IRE) 125 – Danaskaya (IRE) 106 (Danehill **123** (USA) 126) [2015 119: 7m 8g⁴ 8g 8d 6d 7g³ 8d² Oct 17] smallish, compact colt: very smart performer: in the frame in Irish 2000 Guineas at the Curragh (1¾ lengths fourth to Gleneagles), Challenge Stakes at Newmarket (¾-length third to Cable Bay) and Queen Elizabeth II Stakes at Ascot (best effort, ¾-length second to Solow, again finished well from off pace): stays 1m: acts on good to firm and good to soft going: often wears headgear. *Roger Varian*

BELEAVE 2 gr.f. (Mar 21) Avonbridge 123 – Grezie 63 (Mark of Esteem (IRE) 137) [2015 **68 p** p7m⁴ Dec 16] fourth foal: dam 7f winner (including at 2 yrs): 100/1, some encouragement when fourth in maiden at Lingfield (5¾ lengths behind Auntinet) in December, not knocked about: capable of better. *Luke Dace*

BELGIAN BILL 7 b.h. Exceed And Excel (AUS) 126 – Gay Romance 71 (Singspiel **112** (IRE) 133) [2015 113: 8g* 9.9g³ 9.9g⁴ 8d 8m* 10d 8d 8d Oct 17] lengthy, well-made horse: smart handicapper: won at Meydan (by neck from Dark Emerald) in January and Goodwood (Betfred Mile, finished second but later awarded race after So Beloved failed drugs test) in July: stays 1¼m: acts on polytrack, firm and soft going: sometimes wears headgear: usually wears tongue tie. *George Baker*

BELGRADE 3 b.c. Rock of Gibraltar (IRE) 133 – Powder Blue 64 (Daylami (IRE) 138) **91** [2015 84: 10d² 10.3m³ 11.7m* 12f Jun 18] fairly useful handicapper: won at Bath (by 5 lengths from Master Zephyr) in May: stayed 11.5f: acted on polytrack, tapeta, good to firm and good to soft going: often raced towards rear: dead. *Richard Hannon*

BELIEVE IT (IRE) 3 b.c. Rip Van Winkle (IRE) 134 – Have Faith (IRE) 87 (Machiavellian **71 p** (USA) 123) [2015 6m⁶ 8g t6f⁴ t7.1f* Dec 22] 170,000Y: sixth foal: half-brother to 3 winners, including 6.5f-1m winner Faithful One (by Dubawi) and 7f winner Nur Jahan (by Selkirk): dam, 2-y-o 7f winner, half-sister to very smart 7f-1¼m winner Favourable Terms: fair performer: won handicap at Wolverhampton in December: left Richard Hannon after second start: should be suited by 1m: open to further improvement. *Richard Hughes*

BELLA ALAMOTO 3 b.f. Almaty (IRE) 113 – Mtoto Girl 46 (Mtoto 134) [2015 –: p12g **–** 6d p7m Oct 21] maiden: no form in 2015: sometimes slowly away. *John Bridger*

BELLA BLUR 3 ch.f. Showcasing 117 – Ellablue 63 (Bahamian Bounty 116) [2015 p8f⁶ **59** t7.1m² p8g p10g Dec 9] 6,500Y, 15,000 2-y-o: fourth foal: half-sister to 3 winners, including 2-y-o 9.5f winner Amoralist (by Tobougg) and 6f/7f winner Dumbarton Rock (by Kyllachy): dam, maiden (stayed 6f), half-sister to useful winner up to 1m Espartero: modest maiden: best effort at 7f. *Michael Bell*

BELLA IMPERATRIX 2 b.f. (Feb 7) Holy Roman Emperor (IRE) 125 – Be Amazing **53** (IRE) 71 (Refuse To Bend (IRE) 128) [2015 5m 6g 6m⁵ Jul 20] 52,000Y: sturdy filly: first foal: dam, maiden (stayed 7f), half-sister to very smart/unreliable winner up to 1m Asset: modest maiden: best effort when fifth in maiden at Windsor (8¼ lengths behind Justice Lass) in July. *Ed de Giles*

BELLAJEU 3 b.f. Montjeu (IRE) 137 – Arbella 106 (Primo Dominie 121) [2015 86p: **96** 11.5s² 12g 12.3m² 12v² 11.8s³ p13.3f³ p13.3f* Oct 22] rather unfurnished filly: useful performer: won maiden at Chelmsford in October: second in listed Oaks Trial at Lingfield (1¼ lengths behind Toujours L'Amour) in May: stays 13.5f: acts on polytrack and heavy going: tried in hood: front runner/races prominently. *Ralph Beckett*

BELLA LULU 3 b.f. Iffraaj 127 – Loulwa (IRE) 103 (Montjeu (IRE) 137) [2015 65p: 8m² **85** 7f* 8.3m⁶ p8g Sep 22] rangy, good sort: fairly useful performer: won maiden at Doncaster (by 2 lengths from Saguna) in July: stays 1m: acts on firm going: usually races prominently. *Roger Varian*

BELLAMOI 3 b.f. Arabian Gleam 122 – Wenden Belle (Brave Act 119) [2015 8m **56** 9.8m⁶ p12g 8s⁶ p8g⁶ f8g Nov 3] third foal: half-sister to 6f/7f winner My Own Way Home (by Danbird): dam unraced half-sister to useful 5f winner Calm Bay: modest maiden: best effort at 1m: acts on soft going: tried in cheekpieces. *Michael Appleby*

BELLA NOSTALGIA (IRE) 3 ch.f. Raven's Pass (USA) 133 – Fafinta (IRE) (Indian **100** Ridge 123) [2015 60p: 7m² 7m* 8.1m¹ 8s⁵ 8m⁶ 7m 7m Oct 3] well-made filly: useful performer: won maiden at Thirsk in June: third in listed race at Sandown (2¼ lengths behind Blond Me) in July: stays 1m: acts on good to firm going: usually races close up, tends to find little. *Hugo Palmer*

BELLA NOUF 3 b.f. Dansili 127 – Majestic Sakeena (IRE) (King's Best (USA) 132) **91** [2015 74p: 8.3g² 9g* 10g³ 10g 10s* 10.3v Nov 7] close-coupled filly: fairly useful performer: won maiden at Goodwood in June and handicap at Newbury (by 3¼ lengths from Eager Beaver) in October: stays 1¼m: acts on soft going: tried in cheekpieces in 2015. *William Haggas*

BELLA'S BOY (IRE) 2 b.g. (Apr 17) Lovelace 117 – Cosa Deasa (IRE) 48 (Barathea **50** (IRE) 127) [2015 6d 5g⁴ Oct 19] better effort when seventh in maiden at Goodwood (9¾ lengths behind Yosemite) in October: will be suited by 7f+. *John Ryan*

BELLEDESERT 2 b.f. (Apr 1) Pastoral Pursuits 127 – Ocean Blaze 91 (Polar Prince **73** (IRE) 117) [2015 5m 5m⁴ 5s² 5.4g⁵ 5.7m* Sep 28] second foal: dam, 5f winner, half-sister to useful winner up to 6f Phantom Whisper: fair performer: won nursery at Bath in September: best effort at 5.5f: acts on good to firm going. *Steph Hollinshead*

BELLE DORMANT (IRE) 3 b.f. Rip Van Winkle (IRE) 134 – Lady Rockfield (IRE) 71 **75** (Rock of Gibraltar (IRE) 133) [2015 65: p7m⁵ t9.5f⁶ 8.3s 7m³ 6g* 5.7f¹⁴ 6m⁴ 7v p7g Nov 9] fair handicapper: won at Brighton in June: stays 7f: acts on firm going: often starts slowly. *Joseph Tuite*

BELLE D'OR (USA) 4 b.f. Medaglia d'Oro (USA) 129 – Glatisant 104 (Rainbow Quest **107** (USA) 134) [2015 110p: 9f³ 10.4m May 14] big, rather unfurnished filly: useful performer: third in Dahlia Stakes at Newmarket (2¼ lengths behind Bragging) in May: should stay 1¼m: acts on firm going. *John Gosden*

BELLE FILLE 3 ch.f. Makfi 130 – Belle Allemande (CAN) (Royal Academy (USA) 130) **61** [2015 74: p7g 7.1m⁴ Jun 22] good-topped filly: modest maiden: best effort at 5f: acts on good to firm going: often races prominently. *David Brown*

BELLE MARE PLAGE 2 b.f. (Apr 5) Canford Cliffs (IRE) 133 – Flora Trevelyan 106 **67** (Cape Cross (IRE) 129) [2015 5f 6m⁵ 6g f5g p5m² p5g⁶ Dec 7] 60,000Y: second foal: dam, 1m winner who stayed 1¼m, half-sister to smart 7f-10.6f winner Leporello: fair maiden: stays 6f: acts on polytrack and good to firm going. *Stuart Williams*

BELLE NELLIE (IRE) 3 b.f. Kodiac 112 – Mildmay (USA) (Elusive Quality (USA)) **63** [2015 56p: 5d⁶ 5g² 5.1g 5g⁴ 5g⁴ 5m 5g⁴ 5d³ t5.11f* t5.1m Oct 2] modest handicapper: won at Wolverhampton in September: raced only at 5f: acts on tapeta, best turf form on good going: tried in visor in 2015: usually races prominently. *Nigel Tinkler*

BELLE PARK 8 b.m. Hamairi (IRE) 112 – Cape Siren (Warning 136) [2015 76: 8.1s² **75** May 19] fair handicapper: stays 1¼m: acts on polytrack and any turf going: often starts slowly, often races in rear, usually travels strongly. *Victor Dartnall*

BELLE PEINTURE (FR) 4 ch.f. Peintre Celebre (USA) 137 – Grosgrain (USA) (Diesis **46** 133) [2015 55: f12g⁵ 14.1m 12.4g 9.9m 12.1m⁵ 16.1g⁶ 14.1v⁶ Nov 3] poor maiden: stays 2m: acts on polytrack, good to firm and heavy going, well held both fibresand starts: often in cheekpieces in 2015: often races towards rear. *Alan Lockwood*

133

BELLE TRAVERS 3 ch.f. Bahamian Bounty 116 – Forthefirstime 99 (Dr Fong (USA) **86**
128) [2015 73p: 10g⁴ 10.3m⁵ 10.3g³ 10.3m⁴ 8m² 8g² 8.1v² 10g⁶ Oct 8] fairly useful
handicapper: second at Musselburgh in August and second at Sandown in September:
worth another try at around 1m: acts on good to firm and heavy going: often races
prominently, often travels strongly: consistent. *Richard Fahey*

BELLE VALE (IRE) 2 b.f. (Mar 1) Cape Cross (IRE) 129 – Belle Josephine 80 (Dubawi **70**
(IRE) 129) [2015 p7g⁶ 7.4v² 6.9m⁵ t8.6g⁶ p8f⁵ Oct 10] first foal: dam, 1½m-2m winner,
half-sister to smart 11.7f winner Yankee Doodle: fair maiden: stays 1m: acts on polytrack
and good to firm going: front runner/races prominently. *Mark Johnston*

BELL HEATHER (IRE) 2 b.f. (Mar 30) Iffraaj 127 – Burren Rose (USA) (Storm Cat **85**
(USA)) [2015 7.6v* 8s³ Sep 3] €100,000Y: fifth foal: half-sister to useful 1½m winner
Burren Quality (by Elusive Quality) and 2-y-o 8.4f winner Bleu Ciel Et Rouge (by
Manduro): dam 1m-1½m winner: better effort when winning maiden at Lingfield (by 4
lengths from Giveaway Glance) in August. *Charles Hills*

BELL WEIR 7 gr.g. Tobougg (IRE) 125 – Belly Dancer (IRE) 88 (Danehill Dancer (IRE) **68**
117) [2015 80: 13.8m⁶ 14.1g⁴ 14.1s² 16.4s Oct 10] fair handicapper: stays 16.5f: acts on
soft and good to firm going: tried in cheekpieces prior to 2015: sometimes slowly away,
often races in rear. *Dianne Sayer*

BELROG 4 ch.g. New Approach (IRE) 132 – Millennium Dash 94 (Nashwan (USA) 135) **54**
[2015 81: p12m³ p12m³ p12g p11g 12g 11.5d⁵ 10.2m³ p8g⁵ 11.8m f8d p10f p16f² p14f* **a78**
t16.5f* p13.3g* p13.3m³ Dec 27] fair handicapper: won at Chelmsford in September,
Wolverhampton in October and Chelmsford in December: left Ralph Beckett after second
start: stays 16.5f: acts on polytrack, tapeta and heavy going: sometimes in visor in 2015:
often races in rear, often travels strongly: formerly temperamental but did little wrong in
latter part of 2015. *J. R. Jenkins*

BE LUCKY 5 ch.m. Kyllachy 129 – Spritzeria 81 (Bigstone (IRE) 126) [2015 80: 5d⁶ f6g² **87**
f7d³ 6g* 6m⁵ 6m* 7.2m f6s³ 6m* 6s Sep 5] fairly useful handicapper: won at Pontefract in **a74**
June, July and August (by head from Gold Club): stays 6f: acts on good to firm going: often
wears tongue tie: front runner/races prominently. *Michael Easterby*

BELVOIR BAY 2 ch.f. (Apr 19) Equiano (FR) 127 – Path of Peace 86 (Rock of Gibraltar **104**
(IRE) 133) [2015 5m² 5m* 5.2m⁶ 6m* 7s⁴ 8g 8f* Dec 27] 20,000Y: rather unfurnished
filly: second foal: dam, 1m winner, half-sister to smart winner up to 1¼m Mountain Song
and useful 2-y-o 5f/6f winner (stayed 1m) Please Sing: useful performer: won maiden at
Windsor in June, nursery at Goodwood in July and listed race at Santa Anita (by 7¼ lengths
from Family Meeting) in December: left Richard Hannon after fifth start, William I. Mott
after sixth: stays 1m: acts on firm and soft going. *Peter Miller, USA*

BELVOIR DIVA 3 br.f. Exceed And Excel (AUS) 126 – Merry Diva 81 (Bahamian **82**
Bounty 116) [2015 76p: t6f⁶ 6m⁴ p6g⁴ p5f⁴ Oct 29] fairly useful handicapper: stays 6f: acts
on polytrack and good to firm going: often races prominently. *Chris Wall*

BENANDONNER (USA) 12 ch.g. Giant's Causeway (USA) 132 – Cape Verdi (IRE) **65**
126 (Caerleon (USA) 132) [2015 64: t8.6g* p8f² Mar 20] good-topped gelding: fair
handicapper: won at Wolverhampton in January: stays 1¼m: acts on all-weather, soft and
good to firm going: tried in headgear prior to 2015: tried in tongue tie prior to 2015.
Mike Murphy

BENBECULA 6 b.g. Motivator 131 – Isle of Flame (Shirley Heights 130) [2015 80: **75**
14.1m² 14.1g⁵ 14.1g⁴ Aug 21] rangy gelding: fair handicapper: stays 1¾m: acts on
polytrack and any turf going: tried in headgear prior to 2015: often leads. *Richard Mitchell*

BEN HALL (IRE) 4 b.g. Bushranger (IRE) 119 – Sassy Gal (IRE) 93 (King's Best (USA) **62**
132) [2015 99: f6g⁶ t5.1g 6s 6g 5g⁴ 5.5m⁶ 5d 6m⁵ t6g² p6f* p6f³ p6g⁶ p6f Oct 28] sturdy **a71**
gelding: fair handicapper: won at Chelmsford in September: stays 7f, mostly races over
sprint trips: acts on polytrack, tapeta and firm going: often wears headgear: front runner/
races prominently. *Ruth Carr*

BENIDORM 7 b.g. Bahamian Bounty 116 – Famcred 89 (Inchinor 119) [2015 55: f7g⁶ **41**
t7.1g p7m t7.1m³ t7.1g⁵ f7g Mar 3] poor maiden: stays 9f: acts on all-weather, good to firm
and good to soft going: usually wears headgear. *Richard Guest*

BENJAMIN DISRAELI (IRE) 3 b.c. Champs Elysees 124 – Strike Lightly (Rainbow **– p**
Quest (USA) 134) [2015 –: p8f p7g Apr 8] hinted at ability in maidens: should do better in
handicaps. *John Best*

BEN MUIR 3 b.g. Observatory (USA) 131 – Chapel Corner (IRE) (Alhaarth (IRE) 126) **53**
[2015 –: 7d 11.5g 10.2f⁵ 9.9g⁵ t8.6m⁶ p15.8f³ p16f⁴ t12.2m Nov 21] close-coupled
gelding: modest maiden: best effort at 2m: acts on polytrack: usually leads. *Stuart Williams*

BENNELONG 9 b.g. Bahamian Bounty 116 – Bundle Up (USA) (Miner's Mark (USA) **60** 120) [2015 68, a74: p10g³ p8g p12f⁵ p12f² p8f² p13g⁴ p8f 9.9g³ 9.9d³ p11g⁵ p11g² p8g³ **a71** p8g³ p10g⁵ 10.1g p8f⁶ p10m* p12g p10d² p11g² p8g² p12g³ Dec 30] rangy gelding: fair handicapper: won at Kempton in October: stays 13f: acts on polytrack, fibresand, firm and soft going: often wears headgear: tried in tongue tie prior to 2015. *Lee Carter*

BENOORDENHOUT (IRE) 4 br.g. Footstepsinthesand 120 – Tara Too (IRE) 97 **57** (Danetime (IRE) 121) [2015 69: p10g 7g⁶ 8.5m⁶ 14g² May 24] modest handicapper: left Jonathan Portman after first start: stays 1¾m: acts on polytrack: wears headgear. *T. Le Brocq, Jersey*

BE PERFECT (USA) 6 b.g. Street Cry (IRE) 130 – Binya (GER) 106 (Royal Solo (IRE) **99** 113) [2015 101: p12g³ 16s 13g² 14.6m⁴ 16.1g⁵ 16m 12.3m* 12.3g 13.8m* 14.1d t12.2m⁵ 15.9g² 17.5g Sep 18] useful handicapper: won at Chester in June and Catterick in August: second at Chester (½ length behind Steve Rogers) in September: stays 2¼m: acts on polytrack, viscoride, soft and good to firm going: tried in cheekpieces: tried in tongue tie prior to 2015: front runner. *Ruth Carr*

BERBICE (IRE) 10 gr.g. Acclamation 118 – Pearl Bright (FR) 80 (Kaldoun (FR) 122) **44 §** [2015 54§: 5g 6g 56m⁶ 7.2g Sep 29] tall, close-coupled gelding: poor handicapper: probably best at 6f/7f: acts on polytrack, good to firm and heavy going: tried in headgear prior to 2015: tried in tongue tie prior to 2015: sometimes slowly away: ungenuine. *Linda Perratt*

BERET (FR) 2 b.g. (May 11) Sageburg (IRE) 123 – Moonavvara (IRE) (Sadler's Wells **65** (USA) 132) [2015 8g 8.3s⁶ p8g t9.5f⁵ Dec 11] fair maiden: best effort at 8.5f. *Harry Dunlop*

BERGHOLT (IRE) 2 b.c. (Apr 5) Sir Percy 129 – Sularina (IRE) 74 (Alhaarth (IRE) 126) **76 p** [2015 7.1f⁴ 7.6g⁴ 7v⁴ Aug 25] €36,000F, 55,000Y, 100,000 2-y-o: fourth foal: half-brother to useful 8.3f-1½m winner Khione (by Dalakhani): dam once-raced half-sister to smart 1¼m-14.6f winner Discreet Brief: fair maiden: best effort when fourth in maiden at Lingfield (1¼ lengths behind Machine Learner) in August: should do better. *Philip Hide*

BERKELEY VALE 4 b.g. Three Valleys (USA) 119 – Intriguing Glimpse 100 (Piccolo **83** 121) [2015 70: p8f² p8g* 8m⁴ p7g⁴ 8g² 9s⁴ 8.1g Sep 11] fairly useful handicapper: won at Lingfield in May: second at Salisbury (amateur) in July: stays 1m: acts on polytrack, best turf form on good going: usually in visor in 2015. *Roger Teal*

BERKSHIRE BEAUTY 3 b.f. Aqlaam 125 – Salim Toto 107 (Mtoto 134) [2015 61: **66** p11g 12f 11.6m t8.6g³ f8g² Dec 22] leggy filly: fair maiden: stays 11f: acts on all-weather and good to firm going: sometimes in hood in 2015. *Andrew Balding*

BERLAND (IRE) 3 b.g. Cape Cross (IRE) 129 – Ballantrae (IRE) 96 (Diktat 126) [2015 **92** 83p: 8s 8.3g³ 10m⁴ 10s⁴ 10d² 10d Oct 30] lengthy gelding: fairly useful handicapper: won at Leicester in June: second at Windsor in October: stays 1¼m: acts on good to firm and good to soft going: front runner/races prominently. *Michael Bell*

BERLUSCA (IRE) 6 b.g. Holy Roman Emperor (IRE) 125 – Shemanikha (FR) (Sendawar **91** (IRE) 129) [2015 92: t9.5g* 8d 8m² 10.4m⁶ t8.6g² 7.9g t9.5g³ t9.5f⁵ t8.6f t9.5f⁵ t9.5m* Dec 30] strong gelding: fairly useful handicapper: won at Wolverhampton in January (dead-heated) and December: stays 10.5f: acts on polytrack, tapeta, good to firm and heavy going. *David O'Meara*

BERMONDSEY 3 b.g. Galileo (IRE) 134 – Barter 62 (Daylami (IRE) 138) [2015 8g 8f* **84 p** 10.4m³ 10v³ Sep 16] second foal: closely related to 1¼m winner Petticoat Lane (by High Chaparral): dam lightly-raced half-sister to very smart 1½m-2m winner (stayed 2½m) Golden Quest: fairly useful performer, lightly raced: won maiden at Haydock in June: third in handicaps at Haydock in July and Sandown in September: should prove suited by 1½m: better to come. *Luca Cumani*

BERNHARD (IRE) 3 b.c. Bernardini (USA) 132 – Nasheej (USA) 112 (Swain (IRE) **58** 134) [2015 –: 8.3s p8f 9.9f May 23] modest maiden: best effort at 1m. *Sir Michael Stoute*

BERNIE'S BOY 2 b.c. (Feb 16) Lilbourne Lad (IRE) 111 – Stoney Cove (IRE) **84** (Needwood Blade 117) [2015 6m³ 7f² 7m² 7m² p7g² Dec 28] 18,000Y: rather leggy colt: tthird foal: half-brother to ungenuine 5f/6f winner Gentlemen (by Ad Valorem): dam unraced half-sister to smart winner up to 1m Golden Nepi: fairly useful maiden: second in maidens at Goodwood and Newmarket in August: stays 7f: acts on good to firm going: front runner/races prominently. *Andrew Balding*

BERNISDALE 7 ch.m. Bertolini (USA) 125 – Carradale 73 (Pursuit of Love 124) [2015 **61** 67: t13.9g⁵ 10m 12.1m⁵ 12.1s² 12.1g⁶ 13.1d* Sep 2] close-coupled mare: modest handicapper: won at Bath in September: stays 13f: acts on polytrack and any turf going: front runner/races prominently. *John Flint*

Pinsent Masons Lowther Stakes, York—
Besharah shows no signs of a busy campaign as she runs out a clear-cut winner;
the grey Lumiere still looks green in second, followed home by Easton Angel (noseband)

BERN ME BABY (USA) 5 b.m. Bernstein (USA) 115 – Clever Maid (USA) (Confide **81**
(USA)) [2015 a5.5g* a6g 5g p6f Sep 24] fairly useful performer: won minor event at Doha
in January: stays 6f: acts on dirt and good to firm going: has worn blinkers, including last
2 starts: tried in tongue tie. *Zuhair Mohsen*

BE ROYALE 5 b.m. Byron 117 – Sofia Royale 61 (Royal Applause 124) [2015 78: f7g **80**
p7m* p7f 7d³ 7m³ 7.6d⁴ f7d p7g f7g p7f² f7g⁵ p7g² Dec 16] fairly useful handicapper:
won at Kempton in January: second at Chelmsford in November and Kempton in
December: stays 8.5f: acts on polytrack, fibresand and good to firm going: often races
prominently. *Michael Appleby*

BERRAHRI (IRE) 4 b.g. Bahri (USA) 125 – Band of Colour (IRE) (Spectrum (IRE) **85**
126) [2015 77d: p8f³ p8g⁵ a8g² a8g* a8g² p8f* t8.6g³ p8f* p8g⁴ p8g* 8g⁵ 7f 9d³ 8m⁵ 10m⁴
10.3g* 10d² p10g² 10.3s² 10.4s⁵ Oct 10] rather leggy gelding: fairly useful performer: won
minor event at Saint Moritz in February, and handicaps at Kempton and Chelmsford in
March, Kempton in April and Chester in August: stays 10.5f: acts on polytrack, snow and
heavy going: tried in headgear: usually races close up: consistent. *John Best*

BERTHA BURNETT (IRE) 4 gr.f. Verglas (IRE) 118 – Starsazi (Observatory (USA) **44**
131) [2015 62: 8.5m 10.3d⁴ 8d May 19] poor maiden: stays 1m: acts on good to firm and
good to soft going: tried in cheekpieces in 2015. *Brian Rothwell*

BERTIE BLU BOY 7 b.g. Central Park (IRE) 123 – Shaymee's Girl 59 (Wizard King **90**
122) [2015 70: p7g* p7f² p7g p8m³ p8f⁵ p6g* p6g* p6g* p5g* p5g² p5g⁵ p6f 6g
Sep 26] workmanlike gelding: fairly useful handicapper: won at Lingfield (apprentice) in
January, Chelmsford in March and April, Lingfield in May and Chelmsford in June: stays
9.5f, effective at shorter (5f winner): acts on polytrack and good to firm going: often wears
headgear: usually leads. *Lisa Williamson*

BERTIE BUOY 2 b.g. (Apr 24) Bertolini (USA) 125 – Tide of Love (Pursuit of Love 124) **–**
[2015 5m 5s⁴ 5m 7m⁴ 6g 5d Oct 26] no form: often in visor. *Richard Guest*

BERTIE MOON 5 b.g. Bertolini (USA) 125 – Fleeting Moon 70 (Fleetwood (IRE) 107) **78**
[2015 87: 10m⁴ 10.3g 8.1m 10g Oct 19] fair handicapper: stays 1¼m: acts on polytrack,
fibresand, firm and good to soft going. *Polly Gundry*

BERTIEWHITTLE 7 ch.g. Bahamian Bounty 116 – Minette 55 (Bishop of Cashel 122) **101**
[2015 111: 8d 7m 7g⁶ 7.6g 7g 7m 7d 7.6g 7g² 7g⁶ 6g 7g 7s* 8d 7v t6m⁴ Dec 12] smallish
gelding: useful handicapper: won at York (apprentice) in October: stays 1m: acts on
polytrack, tapeta, good to firm and heavy going: tried in headgear: often races towards rear.
David Barron

BERWIN (IRE) 6 b.m. Lawman (FR) 121 – Topiary (IRE) (Selkirk (USA) 129) [2015 61: **–**
p8m p8f Mar 4] rather leggy mare: maiden: no form in 2015: stays 11f: acts on polytrack
and good to firm going: tried in cheekpieces prior to 2015: often starts slowly, often races
in rear. *Sylvester Kirk*

136

Sheikh Rashid Dalmook Al Maktoum's "Besharah"

BESHARAH (IRE) 2 b.f. (Feb 18) Kodiac 112 – Dixieland Kiss (USA) (Dixie Union **114**
(USA) 121) [2015 5m* 5m* 5f³ 6m² 6d* 6g* 6g³ Sep 26] 30,000F, 85,000Y: useful-
looking filly: first foal: dam unraced half-sister to useful US Grade 3 8.5f winner Kiss
Moon: smart performer: won maiden at Ascot in May, minor event at Windsor in June,
Princess Margaret Stakes at Ascot (by 3 lengths from Great Page) in July and Lowther
Stakes at York (by 2¼ lengths from Lumiere) in August: also placed in Queen Mary Stakes
at Royal Ascot (4 lengths third to Acapulco) in June, Duchess of Cambridge Stakes at
Newmarket (nose second to Illuminate) in July and Cheveley Park Stakes at Newmarket
(½-length third to Lumiere) in September: likely to stay 1m: acts on good to firm and good
to soft going: tough and reliable. *William Haggas*

BESS OF HARDWICK 3 b.f. Dansili 127 – Request 87 (Rainbow Quest (USA) 134) **92 P**
[2015 12m³ t12.2m* Oct 2] half-sister to several winners, including high-class 1¼m-15.5f
winner Ask (by Sadler's Wells) and useful 1½m winner Require (by Montjeu): dam ran
twice: promising third to Gretchen in maiden at Newmarket on debut: off 5 months, easily
won maiden at Wolverhampton in October by 2¾ lengths from Red Cardinal: will stay
beyond 1½m: sort to improve markedly. *Luca Cumani*

BEST BOY 3 b.c. Myboycharlie (IRE) 118 – Best Dancer (King's Best (USA) 132) [2015 **75**
–: 8d 7g 9.9m 10.2g⁵ 9.9m* 9.9g³ p10m³ 10s Oct 13] fair handicapper: won at Beverley in
August: stays 1¼m: acts on polytrack and good to firm going: usually in tongue tie in 2015.
David C. Griffiths

BEST ENDEAVOUR 3 b.c. Medicean 128 – Striving (IRE) 66 (Danehill Dancer (IRE) **85**
117) [2015 84: p7f 7d⁴ 8f p8g⁵ 7.1m³ 7g⁵ 7.4d⁴ 7s³ t7.1m* p8f⁴ Oct 10] angular colt: fairly
useful handicapper: won at Wolverhampton (by length from Lone Star Boy) in October:
stays 7f: acts on polytrack and tapeta: often in headgear in 2015. *William Muir*

BEST EXAMPLE (USA) 3 ch.g. King's Best (USA) 132 – Born Something (IRE) 105 **93**
(Caerleon (USA) 132) [2015 77: p6f⁴ p8f* t8.6f² t9.5f p8g⁴ Dec 16] fairly useful
handicapper: won at Chelmsford in October: second at Wolverhampton in November:
stays 9.5f: acts on polytrack and tapeta: sometimes in cheekpieces in 2015: often races
prominently. *Saeed bin Suroor*

BEST KEPT 4 ch.g. Sakhee's Secret 128 – Ashlinn (IRE) 86 (Ashkalani (IRE) 128) [2015 **77**
88: 8.3m* 7m³ Jun 27] workmanlike gelding: fair handicapper: won at Nottingham in
April: stays 1¼m: acts on polytrack, soft and good to firm going: tried in headgear prior to
2015: tried in tongue tie prior to 2015. *Roger Varian*

BEST NEW SHOW (IRE) 2 gr.f. (Mar 29) Clodovil (IRE) 116 – Serious Delight **68**
(Lomond (USA) 128) [2015 6m² 6s⁵ t6f³ p7m⁵ Dec 31] €5,000Y, €45,000 2-y-o: good-
topped filly: sister to useful 6f-7f winner Maid In Heaven and half-sister to several winners,
including useful winner up to 7f Delphie Queen (2-y-o 6f winner) and 5f-9f winner
Everygrainofsand (both by Desert Sun): dam unraced: fair maiden: left Robert Cowell after
second start: stays 7f. *David Evans*

BEST OF OREGON (USA) 2 ch.c. (Apr 26) Cape Blanco (IRE) 130 – Wicked Sting **74**
(USA) (Devil His Due (USA) 126) [2015 7m 8.3g² Sep 7] better effort when second in
maiden at Windsor (2 lengths behind Four On Eight) in September: will stay beyond 1m:
in tongue tie final start. *Ed Walker*

BEST OF TIMES 3 b.c. Dubawi (IRE) 129 – Nabati (USA) (Rahy (USA) 115) [2015 **111**
102p: 10m* 11g² May 22] strong colt: smart performer: won listed race at Newmarket (by
½ length from Balios) in May: second in similar event at Goodwood (1½ lengths behind
Storm The Stars): may prove best short of 11f: acts on good to firm going: usually races
prominently. *Saeed bin Suroor*

BEST TAMAYUZ 4 ch.g. Tamayuz 126 – Pink Ivory 81 (Sakhee (USA) 136) [2015 52, **73**
a82: f7g² 7.2g f8d p8g⁵ 8m 7d⁶ 9g⁴ 10.3d p8f f7g² f8m⁴ f7f⁶ Dec 17] fair handicapper: **a79**
stays 9f: acts on polytrack and fibresand: usually wears headgear: sometimes slowly away,
usually races towards rear. *Scott Dixon*

BEST TRIP (IRE) 8 b.g. Whipper (USA) 126 – Tereed Elhawa 75 (Cadeaux Genereux **88**
131) [2015 94: f6d³ 7s* 6g² 6g³ 6g⁶ 5d 5g⁴ 7v⁵ 6s² f5g Dec 15] fairly useful handicapper:
won at Catterick in May: second at York in June and Catterick in October: left Brian
Ellison after first start: stays 7.5f, effective at shorter: acts on polytrack, soft and good to
firm going: tried in tongue tie prior to 2015: front runner/races prominently. *Marjorie Fife*

BETA TAURI (USA) 3 b.f. Oasis Dream 129 – Beta 101 (Selkirk (USA) 129) [2015 66: **–**
t6f Jan 12] maiden: no form in 2015: best effort at 6f: acts on polytrack. *Charlie Appleby*

BETHAN 6 b.m. Nayef (USA) 129 – Elizabethan Age (FR) 78 (King's Best (USA) 132) **64**
[2015 65: t12.2g² 11.8m* 11.5d² t12.2g² Jun 26] workmanlike mare: modest handicapper:
won at Leicester (apprentice) in May: stays 1½m: acts on fibresand, tapeta, good to firm
and good to soft going: often wears cheekpieces: usually races prominently, usually travels
strongly. *Julia Feilden*

BETHNAL GREEN 3 ch.f. Cockney Rebel (IRE) 127 – Exodia 63 (Dr Fong (USA) 128) **51**
[2015 p7m⁶ Jan 14] fourth foal: half-sister to 2-y-o 7f winner Bousfield (by Duke of
Marmalade): dam lightly-raced half-sister to useful 1½m winner (stayed 2m) Drifting Mist:
20/1, sixth in maiden at Lingfield (4¼ lengths behind Dat Il Do) in January: will stay at
least 1m. *Nick Littmoden*

BETSY COED (IRE) 2 b.f. (Apr 21) Raven's Pass (USA) 133 – Lucky Norwegian (IRE) **–**
(Almutawakel 126) [2015 6m⁵ 7m⁶ 8g⁶ Sep 19] €95,000Y: strong filly: sixth foal: closely
related to 6f/7f winner Charter (by Elusive City) and half-sister to 2-y-o 7f winner
Astonishment (by Desert Style): dam 5f winner: little form: sent to Germany. *Mick Channon*

BETTY BLUE 2 b.f. (Mar 27) Sir Percy 129 – Artistic Blue (USA) 109 (Diesis 133) [2015 **70**
6g⁴ 6s⁴ p6g Sep 30] 52,000Y: half-sister to several winners, including useful 2-y-o 6f
winner Heartbreak Hero (by Exceed And Excel) and useful winner up to 1¼m Indigo Way
(by Encosta de Lago): dam 2-y-o 7f winner: fair maiden: best effort when fourth in maiden
at Lingfield (1½ lengths behind Lolla Fincess) on debut: sent to Sweden. *David Simcock*

BETTY BOO (IRE) 5 ch.m. Thousand Words 113 – Poker Dice (Primo Dominie 121) **51**
[2015 73: 7.2d⁶ 6m 6g² 7g Jul 22] modest handicapper: stays 6f: best form on soft/heavy
going: tried in headgear prior to 2015: often races prominently. *Shaun Harris*

BETTY THE THIEF (IRE) 4 b.f. Teofilo (IRE) 126 – Siphon Melody (USA) (Siphon **83 p**
(BRZ) 130) [2015 59: 8.3m⁴ 10.3m* Jun 27] fairly useful performer, very lightly raced:
won handicap at Doncaster in June: stays 10.5f: will go on improving. *Ed Walker*

BETTY TURPIN 2 b.f. (Feb 7) Dick Turpin (IRE) 127 – Protectress 110 (Hector Protector (USA) 124) [2015 6.9m 8s Oct 16] 8,000F: half-sister to 3 winners, including useful 8.6f-1¾m winner (stays 2m) Stand Guard (by Danehill) and 2-y-o 1m winner Wafeira (by Dansili): dam, 2-y-o 7f winner who stayed 1¼m, half-sister to useful 1½m-15f winner Market Forces: no form. *Jedd O'Keeffe* —

BEVERLEY BULLET 2 b.g. (Apr 16) Makfi 130 – Don't Tell Mary (IRE) 94 (Starcraft (NZ) 128) [2015 6g 6d⁵ 7s⁶ 7.2g⁵ 8d⁴ Oct 19] leggy gelding: fair maiden: probably stays 1m: acts on soft going. *Les Eyre* 67

BEWDLEY 10 b.m. Best of The Bests (IRE) 122 – Garota de Ipanema (FR) (Al Nasr (FR) 126) [2015 t8.6f Nov 3] maiden: no form in 2015: stays 8.5f: acts on firm going: tried in visor prior to 2015. *Ray Peacock* —

BEYOND ARGUMENT (IRE) 3 b.g. Galileo (IRE) 134 – Thought Is Free 88 (Cadeaux Genereux 131) [2015 12g6 p10f p10f Sep 24] no form. *David Simcock* —

BEYOND THE EDGE 3 ch.f. Compton Place 125 – Edge of Gold 81 (Choisir (AUS) 126) [2015 7.4g⁵ Jul 21] first foal: dam, 2-y-o 5f/6f winner, closely related to useful 6f winner Bright Edge: 66/1, shaped as if needed experience when fifth in maiden at Ffos Las (23¼ lengths behind War Strike) in July, very slowly away. *Christopher Mason* —

B FIFTY TWO (IRE) 6 br.g. Dark Angel (IRE) 113 – Petite Maxine 70 (Sharpo 132) [2015 107: p5g 5.1s 5f 5g 5d² 5.6d 7d* Oct 24] smallish, leggy gelding: useful performer: won minor event at Doncaster (by 1½ lengths from Justice Well) in October: stays 7f: acts on soft and good to firm going: sometimes wears blinkers: sometimes wears tongue tie. *Charles Hills* 105

BICKERSHAW 3 b.g. Equiano (FR) 127 – Ring of Love 77 (Magic Ring (IRE) 115) [2015 –: p8g 8.3g 6g³ p6g⁶ p6f p8g Oct 14] sturdy gelding: poor maiden: best effort at 6f: often in blinkers in 2015. *Roger Ingram* 46

BIFF JOHNSON (IRE) 3 b.g. Dansili 127 – Sagacious (IRE) 92 (Dalakhani (IRE) 133) [2015 p8m⁶ 10g² 9.3d⁴ 10v⁵ 8.1g 9.9s Oct 12] close-coupled gelding: fair maiden: stays 1¼m: acts on soft going: often races prominently. *Ed Dunlop* 67

BIG AMIGO (IRE) 2 b.c. (Mar 4) Bahamian Bounty 116 – Goldamour (IRE) (Fasliyev (USA) 120) [2015 t7.1f Dec 22] €65,000Y: first foal: dam, maiden, out of half-sister to Goldikova: 7/2, held back by inexperience in maiden at Wolverhampton, not knocked about: capable of better. *Tom Dascombe* – p

BIGBADBOY (IRE) 2 b.g. (Apr 24) Big Bad Bob (IRE) 118 – Elegantly (IRE) (Rock of Gibraltar (IRE) 133) [2015 p8f p8g p8m³ f7m Dec 8] modest maiden: left Marco Botti after third start: best effort at 1m. *Clive Mulhall* 52

BIG BAZ (IRE) 5 b.g. Pivotal 124 – Gracefully (IRE) 102 (Orpen (USA) 116) [2015 105: p8m⁵ p8g² p8f 8m³ 7m 8.3m* 8f 10m⁵ 8m 8d* p8g* Nov 18] strong, quite attractive gelding: smart performer: won handicap at Nottingham (by 1¾ lengths from Homage) in June, listed race at Newmarket (by head from Mitchum Swagger) in October and listed race at Kempton (by 1¼ lengths from Very Special) in November: stays 8.5f: acts on polytrack, good to firm and good to soft going: often races prominently. *William Muir* 116

BIG BEAR (FR) 3 b.g. Thewayyouare (USA) 117 – Alivera (FR) (Danehill (USA) 126) [2015 53p: 8d⁶ p7m⁵ t7.1g* 7m⁵ p8g 7g 8.3g Sep 30] fairly useful handicapper: won at Wolverhampton in June: likely to stay 1m: acts on tapeta and good to firm going: tried in visor in 2015: often races towards rear: sent to France. *George Peckham* 86

BIG CHILL (IRE) 3 b.g. Acclamation 118 – Royal Consort (IRE) (Green Desert (USA) 127) [2015 80: p7f 8.3m³ 8g² 8.3g² 7.1m² 7g² 6d 7s Sep 19] close-coupled gelding: fairly useful maiden: stays 8.5f: acts on good to firm going: tried in headgear. *Patrick Chamings* 83

BIG CITY BOY (IRE) 7 b.g. Tamarisk (IRE) 127 – Cuddles (IRE) 89 (Taufan (USA) 119) [2015 54: p5f⁴ p6g⁴ p5g² 7g⁵ t6g² p5g t6g⁶ p7g p6g⁴ p6g* 6v⁵ t6f⁵ p5g Dec 2] modest handicapper: won at Chelmsford in August: stays 7f: acts on all-weather and good to firm going: tried in headgear: sometimes wears tongue tie. *Phil McEntee* 57

BIG EASY (GER) 8 b.g. Ransom O'War (USA) 117 – Basilea Gold (GER) 105 (Monsun (GER) 124) [2015 18g Sep 19] good-topped gelding: useful handicapper: won Cesarewitch at Newmarket in 2014: well held at same course on return to Flat (useful hurdler): stays 2½m: acts on good to firm going: in cheekpieces last 2 starts. *Philip Hobbs* —

BIGGER AND BETTER 2 b.c. (Mar 10) Fastnet Rock (AUS) 127 – Interlace 78 (Pivotal 124) [2015 7g 7m Oct 13] lengthy colt: well held in maiden/valuable sales race. *Richard Hannon* —

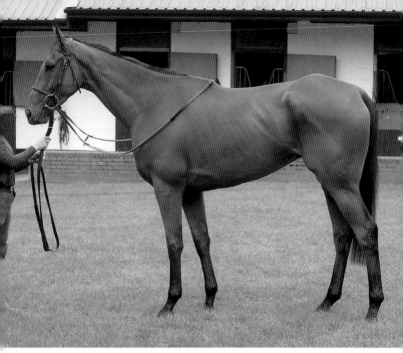

W. J. and T. C. O. Gredley's "Big Orange"

BIG LARRY (IRE) 2 b.g. (Apr 7) Windsor Knot (IRE) 118 – Telltime (IRE) 83 (Danetime **53** (IRE) 121) [2015 5.9g⁴ 5g 6g Sep 26] modest maiden: best effort when fourth in maiden at Carlisle (8 lengths behind First To Post) in August. *Nigel Tinkler*

BIG MCINTOSH (IRE) 3 b.g. Bushranger (IRE) 119 – Three Decades (IRE) 83 **69** (Invincible Spirit (IRE) 121) [2015 62: 6m p6f f6d⁴ 5m 7g⁴ p8g p12g 9g* 10g 8.3d⁶ 9.9g³ p8g* 8s² t9.5m⁶ Sep 25] lengthy gelding: fair handicapper: won at Lingfield in July and Kempton in August: stays 9f: acts on polytrack, fibresand, soft and good to firm going: often in headgear in 2015: in tongue tie prior to 2015: front runner/races prominently. *John Ryan*

BIGMOUTH STRIKES (IRE) 2 ch.g. (Feb 14) Raven's Pass (USA) 133 – Chiosina **–** (IRE) (Danehill Dancer (IRE) 117) [2015 6m 6fᵇᵘ Jul 10] sturdy gelding: no form. *David Menuisier*

BIG ORANGE 4 b.g. Duke of Marmalade (IRE) 132 – Miss Brown To You (IRE) 84 **121** (Fasliyev (USA) 120) [2015 117: 13.4v⁴ 14g 12m* 16m* 16.4d 15.9g⁵ Nov 3] big gelding: very smart performer: further progress in 2015, successful in Princess of Wales's Stakes at Newmarket (by ½ length from Second Step) and Goodwood Cup (dug deep to beat Quest For More by neck), both in July: good 2½ lengths fifth to Prince of Penzance in Melbourne Cup (Handicap) at Flemington final outing, headed 2f out and keeping on gamely: stays 2m: acts on polytrack, soft and good to firm going: in cheekpieces last 4 starts: usually leads. *Michael Bell*

BIG RED 3 ch.f. Sakhee's Secret 128 – Hickleton Lady (IRE) 64 (Kala Shikari 125) [2015 **45** 49: 8m 7g 7g⁴ 7.9d⁴ Sep 15] poor maiden: probably stays 1m: seems to act on good to firm and good to soft going: often in hood in 2015: usually races towards rear. *Rebecca Bastiman*

BIG SHOES (IRE) 2 br.c. (Apr 15) Big Bad Bob (IRE) 118 – Caro Mio (IRE) (Danehill **–** Dancer (IRE) 117) [2015 7m 7.1g 7g Sep 8] sturdy colt: no form. *Charles Hills*

BIG SKY 2 b.f. (Apr 19) Fastnet Rock (AUS) 127 – Sheppard's Watch 108 (Night Shift (USA)) [2015 6g³ 6g 6g p7f* p8f⁴ p7g⁵ Oct 27] well-grown filly: seventh foal: half-sister to 1m winner Satwa Star (by King's Best): dam winner up to 8.5f (2-y-o 6f winner): fair performer: won nursery at Lingfield in August: should stay 1m: acts on polytrack: front runner/races prominently. *Michael Bell* **60 a70**

BIG STORM COMING 5 b.g. Indesatchel (IRE) 120 – Amber Valley 88 (Foxhound (USA) 103) [2015 89: 7m 7f⁶ 7m 7m 10g⁵ 10s³ 9.9m⁵ 8g 8m³ f8m f11g⁵ Dec 22] fair handicapper: left Ruth Carr after ninth start: stays 1¼m: acts on polytrack, fibresand, soft and good to firm going: often races towards rear. *David C. Griffiths* **75**

BIG THUNDER 5 gr.g. Dalakhani (IRE) 133 – Charlotte O Fraise (IRE) 106 (Beat Hollow 126) [2015 103: 10m⁶ 12m 20f 16.4m* 16.4d 18g Oct 10] big, strong gelding: useful handicapper: won at York (by length from Saved By The Bell) in July: left Sir Mark Prescott Bt after third start: stays 2¼m: acts on any turf going: tried in headgear in 2015: sometimes slowly away: temperament under suspicion. *David O'Meara* **95**

BIG TIME (IRE) 4 br.g. Kheleyf (USA) 116 – Beguine (USA) 77 (Green Dancer (USA) 132) [2015 93: 6d 7d 8.5d 7d⁶ 6g⁵ 8,3s² 7v p8f³ p7d³ p8g² Dec 9] strong gelding: useful handicapper: second at Lingfield (2½ lengths behind Forceful Appeal) in December: left John Joseph Murphy after third start: stays 8.5f: acts on polytrack, soft and good to firm going: tried in headgear: usually leads. *David Nicholls* **93 a99**

BIG WHISKEY (IRE) 5 ch.g. Ad Valorem (USA) 125 – El Opera (IRE) 100 (Sadler's Wells (USA) 132) [2015 85: 7.1f² 7.1g² 8s⁵ p7g* 7m³ p7g⁵ p8g³ p8f* p8f² p8g³ p8g Dec 28] sturdy gelding: useful handicapper: won at Kempton in September and Chelmsford (by 1¾ lengths from Volunteer Point) in November: stays 1m, worth a try at 6f: acts on polytrack, soft and firm going: tried in tongue tie prior to 2015: often travels strongly: consistent. *John Best* **94 a103**

BILASH 8 gr.g. Choisir (AUS) 126 – Goldeva 104 (Makbul 104) [2015 72: t5.1f t5.1g⁵ t6g t6gᵘʳ t5.1g t5.1g⁶ t6m Sep 14] small gelding: poor handicapper: stays 6f: acts on polytrack, tapeta, firm and good to soft going: tried in cheekpieces prior to 2015: tried in tongue tie in 2015. *Sarah Hollinshead* **49**

BILIDN 7 b.m. Tiger Hill (IRE) 127 – Brightest Star 77 (Unfuwain (USA) 131) [2015 p16g⁶ Feb 26] good-topped mare: useful at best, no form in 2015: stays 2m: acts on polytrack, good to firm and heavy going: tried in tongue tie. *Laura Young* **–**

BILLET DOUX (IRE) 2 br.f. (Mar 31) Dark Angel (IRE) 113 – Tullawadgeen (IRE) (Sinndar (IRE) 134) [2015 p7g⁶ 8g⁵ Sep 19] workmanlike filly: fifth foal: closely related to 6f/7f winner Eager To Bow (by Acclamation) and half-sister to useful winner up to 1¼m Weapon of Choice (2-y-o 9f winner, by Iffraaj) and winner up to 1m Percythepinto (by Tiger Hill): dam twice-raced half-sister to smart winner up to 1m Tie Black: better effort when fifth in maiden at Newmarket (5½ lengths behind Haggle) in September, unable to sustain effort. *David Elsworth* **71**

BILLINGSGATE (IRE) 4 b.g. Exceed And Excel (USA) 126 – Island Babe (USA) (Kingmambo (USA) 125) [2015 107: 8g t8.6m Mar 7] good sort: useful handicapper: stays 1m: acts on polytrack and good to firm going: often races prominently: quirky sort. *Charlie Appleby* **99**

BILL'S PAID (IRE) 2 b.g. (Feb 13) Bushranger (IRE) 119 – Auspicious 103 (Shirley Heights 130) [2015 4.5d p5g³ t6f t7.1f Oct 3] modest maiden: best effort at 4.5f: often in visor. *Bill Turner* **53**

BILLY BOND 3 b.g. Monsieur Bond (IRE) 120 – Princess Cocoa (IRE) 86 (Desert Sun 120) [2015 53p: 7.1s³ 7.5m 7.5g³ 8d³ 7m 7.5m 7.9g t7.1f² t9.5f⁴ 18.6f⁵ f8g² f8g² p8m² Dec 31] fair maiden: stays 1m: acts on fibresand, tapeta and soft going: tried in visor in 2015. *Richard Fahey* **74**

BILLYOAKES (IRE) 3 b.g. Kodiac 112 – Reality Check (IRE) 73 (Sri Pekan (USA) 117) [2015 86: 6d⁴ 6g⁵ 7m⁴ 7m⁶ 6d⁶ 6g t6g Dec 4] fairly useful handicapper: stays 7f: acts on tapeta, good to firm and heavy going: often races towards rear. *David Barron* **89**

BILLY RANGER (IRE) 3 b.g. Bushranger (IRE) 119 – Prealpina (IRE) (Indian Ridge 123) [2015 6m 9.2m³ 8.3g³ 8.3d² 9.3m⁴ 9.3s³ 12.2m³ 14.1s* 12d Oct 5] fair handicapper: won at Carlisle in September: stays 1¾m: acts on soft and good to firm going: often races towards rear. *Alan Swinbank* **68**

BILLY RED 11 ch.g. Dr Fong (USA) 128 – Liberty Bound 85 (Primo Dominie 121) [2015 74: p6f p5m* p5d t5.1m p6g⁵ p5g* p5f p6f p5g Dec 19] lengthy gelding: fair handicapper: won at Lingfield in February and July: stays 6f: acts on polytrack, soft and good to firm going: usually wears headgear: tried in tongue tie. *J. R. Jenkins* **72**

BILLY ROBERTS (IRE) 2 b.g. (Feb 21) Multiplex 114 – Mi Amor (IRE) 47 (Alzao **73** (USA) 117) [2015 6d⁵ 7.2g⁴ 7.2m⁴ 8d⁵ 7.5g* 8d³ 9d⁴ Oct 31] compact gelding: fair performer: won maiden at Beverley in September: stays 1m: acts on good to soft going: often races towards rear. *Richard Guest*

BILLY SLATER 3 br.c. Pastoral Pursuits 127 – Procession 72 (Zafonic (USA) 130) [2015 **81** 75: 7.6s² 8g May 23] fairly useful maiden: second in handicap at Chester in May: best effort at 7.5f: acts on soft going: sometimes slowly away. *Richard Fahey*

BIMBO 3 b.f. Iffraaj 127 – Birthday Suit (IRE) 94 (Daylami (IRE) 138) [2015 80: 6m² 6g **94** 6g 6m* 7m⁶ 7d⁵ 5.9s* Aug 24] smallish, close-coupled filly: fairly useful handicapper: won at Newmarket in June and Carlisle (by 1¼ lengths from Cadeaux Power) in August: stays 6f: acts on soft and good to firm going: usually wears hood. *Richard Fahey*

BING BANG BONG (IRE) 2 b.g. (Feb 2) Big Bad Bob (IRE) 118 – Dreamaway (IRE) **107 p** (Oasis Dream 129) [2015 6m³ 6d* 7d² Aug 19] €15,000Y: second foal: dam, unraced, closely related to useful 6f-7f winner Foss Way: useful performer: won maiden at Newmarket (by 3 lengths from Guanabara Bay) in July: best effort when second in Acomb Stakes at York (1¼ lengths behind Recorder) in August, sticking to task: stays 7f: sent to Hong Kong: remains with potential. *David Barron*

BINGO GEORGE (IRE) 2 b.g. (Feb 9) Holy Roman Emperor (IRE) 125 – Kalleidoscope **75** 78 (Pivotal 124) [2015 6m 6m 6m⁴ 7m Jul 30] good-topped gelding: fair maiden: best effort at 6f. *Andrew Balding*

BINKY BLUE (IRE) 3 b.f. Approve (IRE) 112 – Sabander Bay (USA) 51 (Lear Fan **69** (USA) 130) [2015 70: 16g⁴ t7.1g⁶ 16g 16g 6g⁶ 6g⁶ t7.1g 6m 7.1m⁴ 8.1g⁵ 8.1d⁴ 11.9g 8.5d t9.5f⁵ t8.6f t7.1m² Dec 30] fair handicapper: stays 7f: acts on tapeta, good to firm and heavy going: tried in headgear. *Daniel Loughnane*

BINT ALDAR 2 b.f. (May 6) Zoffany (IRE) 121 – Maggie Lou (IRE) 83 (Red Ransom **79** (USA)) [2015 6g⁵ 6g* 6m⁴ 5m* 6.5m Sep 10] 22,000Y: third foal: half-sister to useful 2-y-o 7f/1m winner (probably stays 1¼m) Bremner (by Manduro): dam, 2-y-o 5f winner, half-sister to smart winner up to 6f One Putra: fair performer: won maiden at Hamilton in June and nursery at York in July: stays 6f: acts on good to firm going: often leads. *Kevin Ryan*

BINT AL REEM (IRE) 2 b.f. (Apr 20) Elusive Quality (USA) – Causeway Lass (AUS) **89** (Giant's Causeway (USA) 132) [2015 7m* 7m 6g⁴ Sep 30] tall filly: fifth foal: half-sister to winner up to 1¼m Press Room (2-y-o 9.5f winner) and 2-y-o 7f/1m winner Good Place (both useful and by Street Cry): dam, 5f/5.5f winner (including at 2 yrs), out of Australian Group 1 winner up to 1m Canny Lass: fairly useful performer: won maiden at Newmarket by ¾ length from Heroic Heart) in July: not beaten far when best of seven to Blue Bayou in Sweet Solera Stakes at same track next time: stays 7f. *Charlie Appleby*

BINT DANDY (IRE) 4 b.f. Dandy Man (IRE) 123 – Ceol Loch Aoidh (IRE) 74 (Medecis **96** 119) [2015 88: p7m⁴ p8f⁶ p8f* p8f³ p8g* p8g³ 8.3m² 7m³ p8m⁵ p8g² 8m⁶ p10g³ 7g³ p8f² p10m² p10f³ p10f p10f⁶ p8g⁴ Dec 7] smallish, sparely-made filly: useful handicapper: won at Chelmsford in February and March: stays 1¼m: acts on polytrack, tapeta and good to firm going: tried in cheekpieces in 2015: usually races close up. *Chris Dwyer*

BINT KODIAC (IRE) 2 b.f. (Mar 12) Kodiac 112 – Magnificent Bell (IRE) (Octagonal **61** (NZ) 126) [2015 6s⁶ 5f⁵ 15.1m⁵ 6g⁴ Sep 21] €70,000Y: closely related to 6f winner Crystalized (by Rock of Gibraltar) and half-sister to 3 winners, including useful winner up to 1½m Inventor (2-y-o 1¼m winner, by Alzao) and useful winner up to 10.3f Las Verglas Star (2-y-o 5f winner, by Verglas): dam unraced: modest maiden: should be suited by 6f+: sold 3,000 gns, sent to Italy. *Richard Fahey*

BINZART (IRE) 2 ch.c. (Apr 20) Dandy Man (IRE) 123 – Silca Conegliano (IRE) 69 **92** (Alhaarth (IRE) 126) [2015 t6g³ p6g* 6g⁶ p7g⁶ 6g² 7g⁶ Dec 29] first foal: dam 6f winner: fairly useful performer: won maiden at Chelmsford (by ½ length from Rasheeq) in July: left Marco Botti after fourth start: best effort at 6f: acts on polytrack: tried in cheekpieces/tongue tie. *Majed Seifeddine, Qatar*

BIODYNAMIC (IRE) 2 b.c. (Feb 25) New Approach (IRE) 132 – Doctrine 97 (Barathea **68 p** (IRE) 127) [2015 8.3s⁵ Nov 4] 80,000Y: brother to 2-y-o 1m winner (stays 1¼m) Gay Marriage and half-brother to several winners, including useful 6f (including at 2 yrs) winner Sunraider (by Namid) and useful 7f winner (stayed 9f) Always Be True (by Danehill Dancer): dam 2-y-o 7f-1m winner who stayed 1¼m: 4/1, some encouragement when fifth in maiden at Nottingham (6½ lengths behind Good Trip) in November: better to come. *K. R. Burke*

BIOGRAPHER 6 b.g. Montjeu (IRE) 137 – Reflective (USA) (Seeking The Gold (USA)) –
[2015 116: 14d May 17] useful-looking gelding: smart performer: below form when
seventh to Forgotten Rules in Vintage Crop Stakes at Navan sole outing in 2015: stayed
2¼m: acted on firm and soft going: wore headgear: often raced towards rear: dead.
David Lanigan

BIONIC INDIAN 3 b.g. Acclamation 118 – Strawberry Moon (IRE) 80 (Alhaarth (IRE) 57
126) [2015 –: 8.5m⁵ 7d⁴ 5g 6v t7.1m³ 16m⁴ t7.1m Dec 30] sturdy, quite good-topped
gelding: modest maiden: stays 7f: acts on tapeta and good to soft going: tried in cheekpieces
in 2015. *Michael Easterby*

BIOTIC 4 b.g. Aqlaam 125 – Bramaputra (IRE) 88 (Choisir (AUS) 126) [2015 81: p7f⁴ 90
p8f³ p8g 10m⁴ 10m³ 10m* 10g² p11g* 10.2g p11g⁵ p11g Nov 9] tall, good-topped gelding:
fairly useful handicapper: won at Windsor in July and Kempton (by 4 lengths from Ninety
Minutes) in September: stays 11f: acts on polytrack and good to firm going. *Rod Millman*

BIPARTISAN (IRE) 3 b.f. Bahamian Bounty 116 – Bijou A Moi (Rainbow Quest (USA) 76
134) [2015 68: p7g³ 8g⁵ 8.3m 8.1d² 8s* 8g⁵ 8g* Oct 18] fair performer: won maiden at
Thirsk in September and handicap at Bath in October: stays 1m: acts on soft going: often
in hood in 2015. *Michael Bell*

BIRCHWOOD (IRE) 2 b.c. (Jan 21) Dark Angel (IRE) 113 – Layla Jamil (IRE) 85 113
(Exceed And Excel (AUS) 126) [2015 5m* 6m* 6d³ 7f* 7g⁵ 7d³ 8d³ Oct 30] 77,000Y:
good-topped colt: first foal: dam 7f winner: smart performer: won maiden at Doncaster and
minor event at Newbury (by 1½ lengths from Beaverbrook) in May, and Superlative Stakes
at Newmarket (by length from Air Vice Marshal) in July: third in National Stakes at the
Curragh (ran just respectably when 4¼ lengths behind Air Force Blue) in September and
Breeders' Cup Juvenile Turf at Keeneland (best effort, ½ length behind Hit It A Bomb) in
October: stays 1m: acts on firm and good to soft going: front runner/races prominently.
Richard Fahey

BIRDIE QUEEN 5 b.m. Pastoral Pursuits 127 – Silver Miss (FR) (Numerous (USA)) 76
[2015 79, a85: p6f 6g⁶ 7s⁴ 7d 6m³ 7m⁴ p6g* 6g⁵ 5d⁵ 6g p6g³ p6f⁵ Nov 25] fairly a83
useful handicapper: won at Lingfield (by 1½ lengths from Acquittal) in July: stays 6f:
acts on polytrack, soft and good to firm going: often wears hood: usually races close up.
Gary Moore

BIRDMAN (IRE) 5 b.g. Danehill Dancer (IRE) 117 – Gilded Vanity (IRE) 83 (Indian 115
Ridge 123) [2015 99§: 7g* 7m* 7m* 8d³ 8f² 8d* 8m* 8d³ 8d 8d⁵ 8d³ 9g 7s Oct 13] rather
leggy gelding: smart handicapper: won at Thirsk and Doncaster in April, Thirsk in May,
and Haydock (by 2½ lengths from Simply Shining) and York (by 1¼ lengths from
Musaddas) in July: third at Doncaster (1½ lengths behind Bronze Angel) in September:
stays 1m: acts on polytrack, good to firm and heavy going: sometimes in headgear prior to
2015. *David O'Meara*

BIRKDALE BOY (IRE) 3 br.g. Alfred Nobel (IRE) 110 – Yaky Romani (IRE) (Victory 76
Note (USA) 120) [2015 53: t6f² p8f p7m* p7m* 7d 7v⁶ t7.1f t7.1f² p7f⁴ p7g⁴ Dec 9] fair
handicapper: won at Lingfield (twice) in February: stays 7f: acts on polytrack and tapeta:
usually races prominently in 2015: often races prominently. *Richard Fahey*

BIRKDALE (IRE) 2 b.g. (Feb 15) Elnadim (USA) 128 – Duquesa (IRE) 82 (Intikhab 79
(USA) 135) [2015 6s³ 6d² Jun 8] better effort when third in maiden at Ayr (2¼ lengths
behind dead-heaters Ancient Astronaut and Ferryoven) in May: will stay 7f. *Richard Fahey*

BIRTHDAY BOND 2 ch.g. (Mar 29) Monsieur Bond (IRE) 120 – Birthday Belle 70 –
(Lycius (USA) 124) [2015 6m May 26] 80/1, very green when well beaten in maiden at
Leicester. *George Baker*

BIRTHDAY GUEST (GER) 6 ch.g. Areion (GER) 115 – Birthday Spectrum (GER) –
(Spectrum (IRE) 126) [2015 12g Jul 22] fair at best, no form in 2015: stays 10.5f: acts on
sand and good to soft going. *Philip Kirby*

BISCUITEER 4 ch.f. Byron 117 – Ginger Cookie 47 (Bold Edge 123) [2015 63: 5mᵘʳ Jun – §
16] modest at best: unseated rider at start sole outing in 2015: stays 6f: acts on polytrack
and good to firm going: usually wears headgear: one to treat with caution. *Scott Dixon*

BISHARA (USA) 3 ch.f. Dubawi (IRE) 129 – Kaseema (USA) 95 (Storm Cat (USA)) 58
[2015 64p: p10g³ Apr 9] third in maiden at Chelmsford (5¾ lengths behind Martlet) on sole
outing in April. *Sir Michael Stoute*

BISHOP'S LEAP 3 ch.g. Major Cadeaux 121 – Ocean Grove (IRE) 84 (Fairy King 97 p
(USA)) [2015 10m³ p10g* 10m* 10m* Aug 10] 13,000Y: angular gelding: half-brother to
several winners, including 5f-7f winner Silaah (by Mind Games), winner up to 7f Sea
Hunter (2-y-o 5f winner, by Lend A Hand), both smart, and useful 2-y-o 5f winner Eastern

Romance (by Oasis Dream): dam 2-y-o 6f winner who stayed 1m: useful form: won maiden at Lingfield in June, and handicaps at Newbury in July and Windsor in August: raced only at 1¼m: sent to Hong Kong: open to further improvement. *Andrew Balding*

BISON GRASS 5 b.g. Halling (USA) 133 – Secret Blend (Pivotal 124) [2015 54: p7g³ **54** p10m⁶ p10f p8f f7g⁵ t8.6g⁵ 8d 7.6g⁶ t8.6g p10g Aug 15] modest maiden: stays 1¼m: acts on polytrack and tapeta: sometimes wears headgear: sometimes slowly away. *Giles Bravery*

BITING BULLETS (USA) 3 b.c. Bluegrass Cat (USA) 120 – Mary Ellise (USA) (In **86** Excess) [2015 89: t7.1f² p8mᵖᵘ Feb 18] fairly useful handicapper: second at Wolverhampton in January: stayed 1m: acted on polytrack, tapeta and good to firm going: often raced towards rear: dead. *Jo Hughes*

BIT OF A LAD (IRE) 2 b.g. (Jan 5) Lilbourne Lad (IRE) 111 – Sacred Love (IRE) 69 **63** (Barathea (IRE) 127) [2015 f5g p5g⁴ t5.1m Nov 28] modest maiden: best effort when fourth in maiden at Kempton (2¼ lengths behind Fruit Salad) in November: often in headgear. *David Brown*

BITTER LAKE (USA) 3 b.f. Halling (USA) 133 – Suez 109 (Green Desert (USA) 127) **87** [2015 84p: p8g⁶ 10m⁴ p10g Aug 4] well-made filly: fairly useful handicapper: stays 1¼m: acts on soft and good to firm going. *Charlie Appleby*

BITTERN (IRE) 3 ch.f. New Approach (IRE) 132 – Oiseau Rare (FR) 118 (King's Best **87** (USA) 132) [2015 75: t8.6f⁵ t8.6g³ 10m* 10.2m 9s p12g² p12g* Nov 27] fairly useful handicapper: won at Pontefract in May and Dundalk in November: left Charlie Appleby after fourth start: stays 1½m: acts on polytrack, tapeta and good to firm going: tried in hood prior to 2015: often races prominently. *Emmet Mullins, Ireland*

BITTER ORANGE (IRE) 2 ch.f. (Feb 9) Dutch Art 126 – Pearl Mountain (IRE) 64 **58** (Pearl of Love (IRE) 112) [2015 6m 7g 6g 7g* p8m p8g⁵ Nov 11] £27,000Y: sturdy filly: first foal: dam, lightly raced, including in bumpers, half-sister to smart 5f-1m winner Social Harmony: modest performer: won seller at Leicester in September: stays 1m: acts on polytrack: often in headgear: often races towards rear, often races lazily. *Roger Charlton*

BITUSA (USA) 5 b.g. Roman Ruler (USA) 122 – Richen (USA) (Well Decorated (USA)) **51** [2015 –: p8g⁵ t7.1f³ 6.7s Apr 16] workmanlike gelding: modest maiden: stays 1m: acts on tapeta and heavy going: tried in headgear: often starts slowly. *Muredach Kelly, Ireland*

BIX (IRE) 5 b.g. Holy Roman Emperor (IRE) 125 – Belle Rebelle (IRE) (In The Wings **–** 128) [2015 55: 7f⁴ 7g⁶ 6g 7d⁶ 5d⁶ 6m Sep 28] stocky gelding: fair at best, no form in 2015: tried in blinkers prior to 2015: often races towards rear. *Alan Berry*

BIZ HEART (IRE) 2 ch.c. (Apr 24) Roderic O'Connor (IRE) 119 – Biz Bar (Tobougg **110** (IRE) 125) [2015 7g* 7.5m⁴ 7.5m* 8s* Oct 18] fourth foal: half-brother to 3 winners in Italy, including very smart winner up to 1½m Biz The Nurse (2-y-o 8.5f winner, by Oratorio): dam useful Italian 2-y-o 7f/7.5f winner (stayed 11f): smart form: won maiden at Milan in June, minor event at Rome in September and Gran Criterium on former course (by 2¼ lengths from Basileus, making 1f out) in October: left A. Marcialis after second start: stays 1m: acts on soft and good to firm going. *Stefano Botti, Italy*

BIZZARIO 3 b.g. Raven's Pass (USA) 133 – All's Forgotten (USA) 81 (Darshaan 133) **72** [2015 80: 12.3g⁴ 12g⁶ 13m⁴ 12g⁴ 12d³ 16d³ 14.1m Sep 8] tall gelding: fair handicapper: stays 12.5f: acts on good to firm going: sometimes in headgear in 2015: front runner/races prominently. *Mark Johnston*

BLACKADDER 3 b.g. Myboycharlie (IRE) 118 – Famcred 89 (Inchinor 119) [2015 54: **52** p8f⁶ 7s² 6g⁶ 8g Aug 6] modest maiden: stays 1m: acts on polytrack and soft going: usually wears hood. *Pat Phelan*

BLACKASYOURHAT (IRE) 3 b.g. Le Cadre Noir (IRE) 113 – Mattrah (USA) **65** (Machiavellian (USA) 123) [2015 55: p7f p5g⁵ 5g² p5g⁴ p5g² 5m p6g 5f⁶ p5f Sep 22] good-topped gelding: fair maiden: best form at 5f: acts on polytrack, best turf form on good going: sometimes in headgear in 2015: usually wears tongue tie. *Michael Attwater*

BLACK BEACH 2 b.c. (Feb 10) Footstepsinthesand 120 – Eraadaat (IRE) 59 (Intikhab **96** (USA) 135) [2015 5d² 5g³ 6f Jun 16] 42,000Y: good-topped colt: first foal: dam once-raced half-sister to smart 7f/1m winner Fajr out of smart 7f/1m winner Ta Rib: best effort (useful form) when third in listed race at the Curragh (2½ lengths behind Round Two) in May: tenth in Coventry Stakes at Royal Ascot next time: should be suited by 6f: sold £220,000, sent to Qatar. *J. F. Levins, Ireland*

BLACK BESS 2 br.f. (Jan 21) Dick Turpin (IRE) 127 – Spring Clean (FR) 89 (Danehill **69** (USA) 126) [2015 6d⁶ 6g³ p6g³ 6s Oct 26] half-sister to several winners, including useful 6f-7f winner Duster (by Pastoral Pursuits) and 5f/6f winner Clearing (by Sleeping Indian): dam 2-y-o 6f winner: fair maiden: raced only at 6f. *Jim Boyle*

BLACK CAESAR (IRE) 4 b.g. Bushranger (IRE) 119 – Evictress (IRE) 70 (Sharp **71**
Victor (USA) 114) [2015 84: 7v² 8s² 6d* p6g⁴ 7g 6s⁵ 7s p7g Dec 9] good-topped gelding:
fair handicapper: won at Brighton in June: stays 1m: acts on polytrack and heavy going:
tried in blinkers prior to 2015: often races prominently. *Philip Hide*

BLACK CHERRY 3 b.f. Mount Nelson 125 – Arctic Char 102 (Polar Falcon (USA) 126) **107**
[2015 82: 7g 7g* 8.1m* 8.1m³ 8g² Sep 25] useful-looking filly: useful performer:
won maiden at Goodwood (by 3¼ lengths from Privileged) in May and handicap at
Sandown (by 5 lengths from Merritt Island) in June: third in Atalanta Stakes at Sandown
(¾ length behind Nakuti) in August and second in listed race at Newmarket (½ length
behind Solar Magic) in September: stays 1m: acts on good to firm going: often travels
strongly. *Richard Hannon*

BLACK DAVE (IRE) 5 b.g. Excellent Art 125 – Miss Latina (IRE) 74 (Mozart (IRE) **80**
131) [2015 76: f5d² t6g⁴ p6m⁵ t5.1f⁴ p6g³ p6f³ t5.1g* f6s² p7f* 7f 7.6g⁵ 7.4g³ t7.1g* 7.4d²
7.4v⁵ 5g 7.6gᵘʳ 6d p8f⁴ t7.1g f7f⁴ t7.1f Dec 21] tall gelding: fairly useful handicapper: won
at Wolverhampton in March, Kempton in April and Wolverhampton (by ¾ length from
Crack Shot) in July: stays 8.5f: acts on all-weather, good to firm and heavy going: tried in
visor in 2015. *David Evans*

BLACK DIAMOND GIRL 2 b.f. (Feb 27) Kheleyf (USA) 116 – Tripti (IRE) 72 (Sesaro **52**
(USA) 81) [2015 5g 5m⁵ 5m 5g⁶ 5m Sep 27] 3,500Y: sixth foal: half-sister to 3 winners,
including winner up to 6.5f Captain Dimitrios (by Dubai Destination) and 8.6f/9.5f winner
Tangramm (by Sakhee's Secret): dam 5.3f winner: modest maiden: raced only at 5f: acts on
good to firm going: often leads. *Noel Wilson*

BLACKDOWN WARRIOR 2 b.g. (Apr 16) Showcasing 117 – Showery 76 (Rainbow **–**
Quest (USA) 134) [2015 5m⁵ 6m f5g⁶ Jul 27] no form. *Rod Millman*

BLACKFOOT BRAVE (IRE) 3 ch.g. Iffraaj 127 – Beatrix Potter (IRE) 75 (Cadeaux **65**
Genereux 131) [2015 60: 8g⁵ 10g⁶ 8g 8g² 8g² 7.9g⁶ 8g 9.9g 7m 8g Sep 29] fair maiden:
stays 1m: best form on good going: usually in headgear in 2015. *Michael Dods*

BLACK GRASS 2 b.g. (Apr 2) Monsieur Bond (IRE) 120 – Alustar 71 (Emarati (USA) **61**
74) [2015 5.4m⁵ 5g 5g⁵ 5g⁴ 5d⁴ 5d³ Oct 26] modest maiden: stays 5.5f: acts on good to firm
going: often races prominently. *Michael Easterby*

BLACK HAMBLETON 2 b.g. (Feb 23) Dick Turpin (IRE) 127 – Duena (Grand Lodge **66**
(USA) 125) [2015 6s³ 7.2m⁶ 7g⁶ 8d Oct 19] fair maiden: best effort at 6f. *Bryan Smart*

BLACK HOLE SUN 3 ch.f. Black Sam Bellamy (IRE) 121 – Black Annie (IRE) **–**
(Anshan 93) [2015 t8.6f⁵ Dec 14] £900 2-y-o: first foal: dam bumper winner/winning
hurdler: 40/1, probably flattered when fifth in maiden at Wolverhampton (6½ lengths
behind St Patrick's Day) in December. *Tony Carroll*

BLACK ICEMAN 7 gr.g. Iceman 117 – Slite 55 (Mind Games 121) [2015 60: t13.9g³ **54**
t13.9m² p13.3g² t13.9f³ p13.3g³ t13.9f⁴ p14g³ t13.9g³ p15.8f p13.3g² p16g⁴ p14f Sep 17]
modest handicapper: stays 16.5f: acts on polytrack and tapeta: tried in headgear. *Lydia
Pearce*

BLACK KEY 3 b.g. Authorized (IRE) 133 – Pentatonic 100 (Giant's Causeway (USA) **91 p**
132) [2015 10m⁴ p12.3g³ 11.9d³ 12d* 14g 14d² Sep 25] 40,000Y: third foal: dam 1¼m-1½m
winner who stayed 1¾m: fairly useful performer, lightly raced: won maiden at Catterick in
July: second in handicap at Haydock in September: stays 1¾m: acts on good to soft going:
often races towards rear: type to do better again at 4 yrs. *Hughie Morrison*

BLACKLISTER 2 br.g. (Apr 1) Lawman (FR) 121 – Lebenstanz 66 (Singspiel (IRE) **80**
133) [2015 6m² 6m⁴ 6d⁴ 7d p8f² 8.3d³ t7.1f⁴ p8f⁴ p8m p8g² t8.6m⁴ Dec 26] 22,000Y:
sixth foal: half-brother to winner up to 1m Sapperton (by Key of Luck) and 1¼m winner
(stays 1½m) My Renaissance (by Medicean): dam, 11.5f winner, closely related to smart
1¼m-2¼m winner Boreas: fairly useful maiden: second in nursery at Kempton in
December: stays 8.5f: acts on polytrack, tapeta, good to firm and good to soft going:
sometimes slowly away. *Mick Channon*

BLACK MAGIC (IRE) 2 gr.g. (Mar 9) Poet's Voice 126 – Centifolia (FR) 112 (Kendor **73**
(FR) 122) [2015 5g* 5g⁴ May 13] better effort when winning maiden at Pontefract (by 3
lengths from Tawakkol) in April: will be suited by 6f. *Richard Fahey*

BLACK MINSTREL (IRE) 6 b.g. Dylan Thomas (IRE) 132 – Overlook 60 (Generous **–**
(IRE) 139) [2015 73: p12g⁶ Dec 20] strong, workmanlike gelding: fair at best, no form in
2015: stays 1½m: acts on polytrack. *John O'Shea*

BLACK NIGHT (IRE) 3 b.c. Excellent Art 125 – Starfish (IRE) (Galileo (IRE) 134) **73**
[2015 67p: 9.8m⁴ p12g* 11.8s⁶ Oct 6] fair performer: won maiden at Lingfield in
September: best effort at 1½m. *Stuart Williams*

BLACKOUT (FR) 2 b.c. (Jan 17) Dream Ahead (USA) 133 – Belle Masquee (IRE) **80** (Oratorio (IRE) 128) [2015 7.1m 6.1d* 8s Sep 18] €85,000Y: well-made colt: first foal: dam, 9.5f/10.5f winner, closely related to useful 7f-8.4f winner Rock On Ciara: fairly useful performer: best effort when winning maiden at Nottingham (by short head from Cautious Optimism) in August: best effort at 6f. *Richard Hannon*

BLACK PUDDING (IRE) 3 b.g. Baltic King 120 – Top of The Ridge (IRE) (Celtic **51** Swing 138) [2015 62: 6m 5g⁴ 6m May 27] modest handicapper: stays 6f: acts on good to firm going: often wears headgear: often races prominently. *Ollie Pears*

BLACK SHADOW 4 b.g. New Approach (IRE) 132 – Shadow Dancing 110 (Unfuwain **90** (USA) 131) [2015 102: 11.6g⁴ 12mᵖᵘ 11.6m⁶ 10g p11d p12g² p11g² t12.2f Oct 23] attractive gelding: fairly useful handicapper: second twice at Kempton in September: stays 1½m: acts on polytrack, soft and good to firm going: often in headgear in 2015: sold 16,000 gns, sent to Saudi Arabia. *Amanda Perrett*

BLACK SHEBA 3 b.f. Aqlaam 125 – Duty Paid (IRE) 99 (Barathea (IRE) 127) [2015 7d – Apr 10] seventh foal: half-sister to 7f/1m winner Duty Doctor (by Dr Fong): dam, 2-y-o 5f/6f winner who stayed 1m, sister to useful 1m winner Lady Miletrian: 25/1, badly needed experience in maiden at Leicester. *James Eustace*

BLACKTHORN STICK (IRE) 6 b.g. Elusive City (USA) 117 – Hi Lyla (IRE) (Lahib **64** (USA) 129) [2015 70: p7g² p6g³ p6m* p7g⁴ Dec 2] modest handicapper: won at Lingfield in February: left John Butler after third start: stays 1m: acts on polytrack and soft going: tried in headgear prior to 2015: tried in tongue tie prior to 2015: often races towards rear, often travels strongly. *Paul Burgoyne*

BLACK TRUFFLE (FR) 5 b.g. Kyllachy 129 – Some Diva 75 (Dr Fong (USA) 128) **71** [2015 63: p6g⁶ p6m p6g⁴ p7g² p6f⁴ p7g³ t6g³ t6g³ t7.1m* p7m³ t7.1g² t7.1g* p7g t7.1g* p6d t6f⁵ 7s t7.1f⁶ t7.1g² t7.1f p7g Dec 28] sturdy gelding: fair handicapper: won at Wolverhampton in April, July and August (apprentice): stays 1m, races mostly over shorter: acts on polytrack, tapeta and good to firm going: often wears headgear: often races freely. *Mark Usher*

BLACK VALE (IRE) 4 b.g. Moss Vale (IRE) 126 – Limit (IRE) 69 (Barathea (IRE) 127) **50 §** [2015 77§: p6m³ p6m p5f⁵ 6m 6f 8g 5g p6g p6m p8m⁶ Dec 31] lengthy gelding: modest **a64 §** handicapper: stays 1m: acts on polytrack and fibresand: sometimes wears headgear: often wears tongue tie: unreliable. *Ralph Smith*

BLACK WIDOW 4 b.f. Bertolini (USA) 125 – Malvadilla (IRE) 77 (Doyoun 124) [2015 – 46: f11d Jan 2] maiden: no form in 2015: should stay 1m: in hood sole start in 2015. *Pat Eddery*

BLADES LAD 6 ch.g. Haafhd 129 – Blades Girl 100 (Bertolini (USA) 125) [2015 80: **72** 12g⁶ 12.4g f12g² Nov 12] fair handicapper: stays 1½m: acts on fibresand and soft going: tried in cheekpieces in 2015. *Peter Niven*

BLAGGER 2 ch.g. (Mar 16) Major Cadeaux 121 – Brogue Lanterns (IRE) 88 (Dr Devious – (IRE) 127) [2015 7.5g 6g 6v⁴ Oct 17] no form: often in visor. *Richard Guest*

BLAINE 5 ch.g. Avonbridge 123 – Lauren Louise 55 (Tagula (IRE) 116) [2015 114: 5v⁴ 6f **106 §** 6g 7g 6f 6m 6g 6s 6d Oct 23] strong, good-topped gelding: smart handicapper at his best: on the downgrade in 2015, in both form and attitude: stays 6f: acts on soft and good to firm going: often wears blinkers: lazy, and one to treat with caution. *Kevin Ryan*

BLAKENEY POINT 2 b.g. (Jan 22) Sir Percy 129 – Cartoon 81 (Danehill Dancer (IRE) **64 p** 117) [2015 7g 8.3d p8g⁶ Nov 11] 5,000Y, €58,000 2-y-o: third foal: brother to smart 8.3f-1½m winner Lady Tiana: dam, 8.3f winner, half-sister to 7f/1m winner Smirk and winner up to 7.5f Stetchworth Prince (both smart): modest form: best effort when sixth in maiden at Kempton (7¼ lengths behind Prince of Arran) in November, not knocked about: should do better still. *Roger Charlton*

BLAME LOVE (USA) 3 b.c. Blame (USA) 129 – Twisted Tale (USA) (Tale of The Cat **76** (USA) 113) [2015 65p: p10f⁵ p8f³ t9.5m p8f p10g Oct 20] fair maiden: best effort at 1m: acts on polytrack: sometimes in blinkers in 2015: sold 800 gns, sent to Greece. *Mark Johnston*

BLAZEOFENCHANTMENT (USA) 5 b.g. Officer (USA) 120 – Willow Rush (USA) **80** (Wild Rush (USA) 123) [2015 83: p8g p8g f8d² f8s f8g² 7s p8g 9m f8s³ Aug 6] fairly useful handicapper: second at Southwell in March and April: stays 1m: acts on polytrack and fibresand: sometimes wears headgear: tried in tongue tie prior to 2015: often races in rear. *John Wainwright*

BLAZE OF HEARTS (IRE) 2 b.c. (Apr 8) Canford Cliffs (IRE) 133 – Shesthebiscuit – 76 (Diktat 126) [2015 7d Oct 23] 25/1, shaped as if needed experience when tenth in maiden at Doncaster (23½ lengths behind Royal Artillery) in October: should do better in time. *Dean Ivory*

BLENHEIM WARRIOR 3 br.c. Galileo (IRE) 134 – Crystal Swan (IRE) 88 (Dalakhani **62 p** (IRE) 133) [2015 10.3g Aug 1] second foal: dam, 1¼m winner who stayed 1½m, half-sister to useful 1m-1¼m winner Grande Melody: 14/1, better than result when seventh in maiden at Doncaster (16¼ lengths behind Koora) in August, left poorly placed: open to plenty of improvement. *William Haggas*

BLETCHLEY PARK 3 ch.c. Mastercraftsman (IRE) 129 – Puzzling (Peintre Celebre **70** (USA) 137) [2015 57p: p8g3 9.8g5 10.4g4 14.1m Jun 3] fair maiden: bred to stay beyond 10.5f: acts on polytrack: often races towards rear: sold 10,000 gns, sent to Italy. *Richard Fahey*

BLEU ASTRAL (FR) 3 b.g. Astronomer Royal (USA) 121 – Passion Bleue (In The Wings **83** 128) [2015 75: 7.1m5 7g3 t7.1g6 8v* 8v* p9.4g p6.5g Dec 21] fairly useful performer: won handicaps at Ffos Las (twice) in August. left Alexandra Dunn after fifth start: stays 1m: acts on heavy going: in cheekpieces final outing. *Mme G. Rarick, France*

BLHADAWA (IRE) 4 b.f. Iffraaj 127 – Trois Heures Apres (Soviet Star (USA) 128) **109** [2015 t6g2 p6m* p6f* 6m 6g* 6g6 Jun 7] lengthy, useful-looking filly: useful performer: won maiden at Lingfield (by 6 lengths from Lady In White) in February, handicap at Lingfield (by 3¼ lengths from Major Crispies) in March and listed race at Haydock (by ¾ length from Interception) in May: stays 6f: acts on polytrack and good to firm going: tried in cheekpieces in 2015: races prominently. *James Tate*

BLING KING 6 b.g. Haafhd 129 – Bling Bling (IRE) 70 (Indian Ridge 123) [2015 82: **78** 9.9m2 9.9g5 12g6 8g 10m5 8m6 8d6 8.5d6 8g Oct 3] sturdy, compact gelding: fair handicapper: stays 1½m: acts on any turf going: sometimes wears headgear. *Geoffrey Harker*

BLING RING (USA) 3 b.f. Arch (USA) 127 – Youcan'ttakeme (USA) (He's Tops – (USA)) [2015 68: 7.5g 8.1s6 Jul 24] maiden: no form in 2015: left Charles Hills after first start: stays 7f: acts on soft and good to firm going: sometimes wears hood: often races in rear. *Stuart Kittow*

BLISTERING DANCER (IRE) 5 b.g. Moss Vale (IRE) 126 – Datura 74 (Darshaan **44** 133) [2015 60, a53: 6m 8d 6m 5g3 6s4 5g 6s p6g Dec 3] poor handicapper: stays 8.5f: acts on polytrack, sand, soft and good to firm going: tried in headgear: usually races close up. *Ralph Smith*

BLITHE SPIRIT 4 b.f. Byron 117 – Damalis (IRE) 106 (Mukaddamah (USA) 125) [2015 **100** 100: 5.1d2 5.1s 5.1g 5m 5.1m* 5m6 5.5m 5d3 5d 5s Oct 9] rather leggy filly: useful handicapper: won at Chester (by length from Vimy Ridge) in June: third at Haydock (¾ length behind Maljaa) in September: stays 5.5f: acts on good to firm and heavy going: often races prominently. *Eric Alston*

BLOND ME (IRE) 3 ch.f. Tamayuz 126 – Holda (IRE) 81 (Docksider (USA) 124) [2015 **109** 7m 8.3g2 8m* 8.1m* 8.1m2 9g2 9f6 Oct 10] 65,000Y: good-bodied filly: fourth foal: half-sister to 10.4f winner Antarctic (by Alhaarth) and 6f (including at 2 yrs) winner Red Larkspur (by Red Clubs): dam, 2-y-o 7f winner, half-sister to winner up to 11f Glass Harmonium and 1¼m-1½m winner Arab Spring, both very smart: useful performer: won maiden at Salisbury in June and listed race at Sandown (by neck from Montalcino) in July: second on next 2 starts, in Atalanta Stakes at Sandown (beaten a neck by Nakuti) and Grade 2 Sands Point Stakes at Belmont (3¾ lengths behind Sentiero Italia): bumped start when sixth to Her Emmynency in QEII Challenge Cup at Keeneland final outing: will stay 1¼m: acts on good to firm going: has been slowly away. *Andrew Balding*

BLOODSWEATANDTEARS 7 b.g. Barathea (IRE) 127 – Celestial Princess 84 **73** (Observatory (USA) 131) [2015 74: 8d4 8s3 8.1g 9s5 8d* 8v6 8d Oct 30] tall gelding: fair handicapper: won at Brighton in September: stays 1¼m: acts on polytrack, good to firm and heavy going: tried in headgear prior to 2015: sometimes slowly away: carries head awkwardly. *William Knight*

BLOSSOM MILLS 3 ch.f. Bahamian Bounty 116 – Countess Sybil (IRE) 73 (Dr **57** Devious (IRE) 127) [2015 6g6 8.5d 7g t7.1m f7g Dec 12] half-sister to several winners, including smart 1¼m-1½m winner Air Pilot (by Zamindar) and 1¼m-1¾m winner Air Squadron (by Rail Link): dam 1¾m winner who stayed 2m: modest maiden: left Joseph G. Murphy after third start: stays 8.5f: acts on good to soft going: tried in hood. *Ralph Beckett*

BLOSSOMTIME 2 b.f. (Apr 17) Shamardal (USA) 129 – Bal de La Rose (IRE) 110 **95**
(Cadeaux Genereux 131) [2015 6m² 6m* 6f* 6g 7m⁶ 6s⁵ Sep 1] €150,000Y: sturdy filly:
fifth foal: half-sister to 9f winner Askania Nova (by New Approach): dam, winner up to
1¼m (2-y-o 7.5f/1m winner), half-sister to high-class (Poule d'Essai/Prix du Jockey Club)
winner up to 10.5f Lope de Vega (by Shamardal): useful performer: won maiden at
Newmarket in May and nursery at Doncaster (by 2¼ lengths from Saturn Lace) in July:
stays 6f: acts on firm going: front runner/races prominently. *Charlie Appleby*

BLUE AEGEAN 3 b.f. Invincible Spirit (IRE) 121 – Blue Azure (USA) 67 (American **103**
Chance (USA) 117) [2015 88: p5g* p6f³ p5m³ p5f* p5f² 5m⁶ May 14] leggy filly: useful
handicapper: won at Chelmsford in January and Lingfield (by 2¾ lengths from Mignolino)
in March: second in valuable event at Lingfield (neck behind Lightscameraction) in April:
best at 5f: acts on polytrack and soft going: often in hood in 2015: usually leads. *Charlie
Appleby*

BLUE AMAZON (IRE) 3 b.f. Acclamation 118 – Amazon Beauty (IRE) 105 (Wolfhound **66**
(USA) 126) [2015 –: p6g³ p6f³ t7.1g⁴ p5g³ 5s⁴ p7g⁶ p6g Dec 3] fair maiden: stays 7f: acts
on polytrack: tried in cheekpieces in 2015: often races prominently. *Lee Carter*

BLUE BAYOU 2 ch.f. (Jan 26) Bahamian Bounty 116 – Oshiponga 72 (Barathea (IRE) **109**
127) [2015 6f* 6m³ 7m* 7d⁵ Sep 13] strong filly: half-sister to several winners, including
smart winner up to 7f Hatta Fort (by Cape Cross) and 6f-7f winner Caramack (by Danehill
Dancer): dam 9f winner: useful performer: won maiden at Haydock in June and Sweet
Solera Stakes at Newmarket (by ½ length from Fireglow) in August: good third in Duchess
of Cambridge Stakes at Newmarket (head behind Illuminate) in between: not seen to best
effect when fifth to Minding in Moyglare Stud Stakes at the Curragh final start, shuffled
back over 2f out: stays 7f. *Brian Meehan*

BLUEBEARD 2 b.g. (Feb 28) Dansili 127 – Arabesque 100 (Zafonic (USA) 130) [2015 **83 §**
6g⁶ 7m⁴ 7g² 8m³ p8m* Oct 21] good-bodied gelding: closely related to smart 6f (including
at 2 yrs) winner Camacho (by Danehill) and half-brother to several winners, including
smart 2-y-o 6f winners Showcasing and Tendu (both by Oasis Dream): dam 6f winner who
stayed 1m: fairly useful performer: won maiden at Kempton in October: stays 1m: acts on
polytrack: front runner/races prominently: one to treat with caution (has awkward head
carriage). *John Gosden*

BLUE BLAZE 2 ch.c. (Mar 31) Sleeping Indian 122 – Lilly Blue (IRE) 65 (Hawk Wing **–**
(USA) 136) [2015 5m 6.1d 5.1d 6.1v Oct 7] no form. *Roy Brotherton*

BLUE BOUNTY 4 ch.g. Bahamian Bounty 116 – Laheen (IRE) 60 (Bluebird (USA) 125) **55**
[2015 76: p8g 6d⁶ 6g 6d⁴ 7s⁶ p7g⁵ Dec 2] workmanlike gelding: modest maiden: stays 7.5f:
acts on polytrack: tried in headgear. *Mark H. Tompkins*

BLUE BULLET (IRE) 5 b.g. Red Clubs (IRE) 125 – Blue Holly (IRE) 83 (Blues **76**
Traveller (IRE) 119) [2015 67, a78: 5.9g* 7d 7d³ 6d 8.3d 7.3d 6g p7g Nov 11] fair
handicapper: won at Carlisle in June: left Brian Ellison after third start: stays 1m: acts on
polytrack, soft and good to firm going. *Conor O'Dwyer, Ireland*

BLUE BURMESE (IRE) 3 ch.f. Camacho 118 – Love City (IRE) 74 (Spectrum (IRE) **40**
126) [2015 66: t9.5f f8s⁵ t8.6m Feb 17] plain filly: poor maiden: stays 1m: acts on fibresand,
tapeta, best turf form on good to soft/soft going: sometimes wears headgear: often races in
rear: sold £1,100, sent to Morocco. *Mark Usher*

BLUE CANNON (IRE) 7 b.g. High Chaparral (IRE) 132 – Blushing Barada (USA) 53 **46**
(Blushing Groom (FR) 131) [2015 13.1g⁴ 12d Aug 17] poor handicapper: stays 2¼m: acts
on polytrack, good to firm and good to soft going: tried in cheekpieces prior to 2015. *Stuart
Crawford, Ireland*

BLUE CHIP 3 gr.f. Galileo (IRE) 134 – Intrigued 105 (Darshaan 133) [2015 p13.3g³ 11.8m⁴ **83**
12.3m³ 14.1m* Sep 15] fifth foal: sister to useful 1½m winner (stays 2m) No Heretic and
smart 1¼m/11f winner Michelangelo and half-sister to 1m winner Curious Mind (by
Dansili): dam, 2-y-o 8.5f winner who stayed 1½m, half-sister to very smart winner up to
1m (stayed 1¼m) Aussie Rules: fairly useful performer: won handicap at Yarmouth in
September: stays 1¾m. *John Gosden*

BLUE CLUMBER 5 b.m. Sleeping Indian 122 – Blue Nile (IRE) 70 (Bluebird (USA) **42 §**
125) [2015 t7.1f p8m t9.5m t8.6g p7g 7.1m 6g Jul 31] leggy mare: poor handicapper: stays
8.5f: acts on polytrack, tapeta, good to firm and good to soft going: tried in headgear: tried
in tongue tie prior to 2015: front runner/races prominently: has flashed tail, and one to treat
with caution. *Shaun Harris*

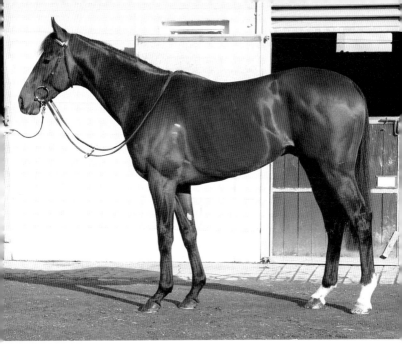

BLUE DE VEGA (GER) 2 b.c. (Mar 28) Lope de Vega (IRE) 125 – Burning Heights **112 p**
(GER) (Montjeu (IRE) 137) [2015 p7g3 7d* 7d* Oct 24] €32,000Y, €75,000 2-y-o: third
foal: dam maiden half-sister to smart 1¼m-1¾m winner Burma Gold: smart performer:
won maiden at Naas (by 4¾ lengths from Tribal Beat) in September: further progress when
winning Killavullan Stakes at Leopardstown (by 3½ lengths from Tribal Beat) in October,
impressively: bred to stay at least 1¼m: likely to progress further. *M. D. O'Callaghan,
Ireland*

BLUE EYED BOY 3 b.g. Stimulation (IRE) 121 – Lilly Blue (IRE) 65 (Hawk Wing **–**
(USA) 136) [2015 –: t5.1f t6g 7.1m6 Jun 30] maiden: no form in 2015: left Eric Wheeler
after second start: tried in blinkers. *Nikki Evans*

BLUE GERANIUM (IRE) 2 b.f. (Mar 8) Dansili 127 – Super Sleuth (IRE) 113 (Selkirk **72 p**
(USA) 129) [2015 8v5 Oct 24] second foal: dam maiden, third in 1000 Guineas: 11/2,
promise when fifth in maiden at Newbury (4½ lengths behind Chastushka) in October, not
knocked about: will improve. *John Gosden*

BLUEGRASS BLUES (IRE) 5 gr.g. Dark Angel (IRE) 113 – Dear Catch (IRE) 69 **69**
(Bluebird (USA) 125) [2015 98: p8g Feb 13] strong gelding: fair performer: stays 7f: acts
on polytrack, good to firm and heavy going: tried in blinkers prior to 2015: tried in tongue
tie prior to 2015. *Paul Cole*

BLUE HUMOR (USA) 2 b.g. (Mar 18) Distorted Humor (USA) 117 – Wile Cat (USA) **82**
(Storm Cat (USA)) [2015 6m6 6g2 6m4 7m6 p7g2 Oct 7] $260,000Y: good-topped gelding:
has scope: fourth foal: brother to useful 5f/6f (including at 2 yrs) winner Shumoos: dam
unraced sister to US Grade 2 9f winner Cat Fighter and half-sister to smart winner up to 6f
Ishiguru: fairly useful maiden: first past the post at Kempton in October, but demoted to
second after hanging left final 1f: stays 7f: acts on polytrack: usually leads: sold 42,000 gns,
sent to USA. *Kevin Ryan*

BLUE HUSSAR (IRE) 4 b.g. Montjeu (IRE) 137 – Metaphor (USA) (Woodman (USA) **95**
126) [2015 110: 12g 12m 12f 12m 12g6 12g* 12d 12v Nov 7] good-topped gelding: useful
handicapper: won at Ripon in September: stays 15f: acts on firm and soft going: sometimes
in cheekpieces in 2015. *Micky Hammond*

BLUE JACKET (USA) 4 ro.f. Mizzen Mast (USA) 121 – Complex (USA) (Unbridled's **65**
Song (USA) 125) [2015 7.1s4 7.1s2 7d4 7.2d* 5m2 6g2 7g* 5.9d4 7g Sep 4] fair handicapper:
won at Ayr in June and Thirsk in July: stays 7f: acts on good to firm and good to soft going.
Dianne Sayer

BLUE JAY (FR) 2 b.g. (Apr 30) Anabaa Blue 122 – Romantic Notion (IRE) 92 (Mujadil **–**
(USA) 119) [2015 5g 6d t7.1g Dec 4] no form. *Ronald Thompson*

BLUE MAISEY 7 b.m. Monsieur Bond (IRE) 120 – Blue Nile (IRE) 70 (Bluebird (USA) **64**
125) [2015 76: 8s 7g 8m 8.5m 8.5g 8.5m 8g6 7g2 7.5m 7s Oct 16] angular mare: modest
handicapper: stays 1¼m: acts on any turf going: tried in cheekpieces in 2015. *Edwin Tuer*

BLUE MELODY GIRL (IRE) 3 b.f. Captain Rio 122 – Salingers Star (IRE) 78 **–**
(Catcher In The Rye (IRE) 115) [2015 6s 6m 8s 7m t8.6g4 f8d Jul 27] first foal: dam 2-y-o
6f winner: no form. *James Given*

BLUE MOON RISING (IRE) 2 ch.f. (Feb 2) Dream Ahead (USA) 133 – Wedding **72 p**
Gown (Dubai Destination (USA) 127) [2015 7g5 7s5 Oct 12] rather unfurnished filly: third
foal: half-sister to useful 7f winner Ijmaaly (by Makfi): dam, third at 9f, half-sister to high-
class winner up to 1m Poet's Voice: better effort when fifth in maiden at Salisbury (4¾
lengths behind Rostova) in October, left with lot to do: should still improve. *Michael Bell*

BLUE RAMBLER 5 b.g. Monsun (GER) 124 – La Nuit Rose (FR) 109 (Rainbow Quest **–**
(USA) 134) [2015 101: 14.1s Apr 8] useful at best, no form in 2015: stays 1½m: acts on
good to soft going: in cheekpieces sole start in 2015. *Charlie Appleby*

BLUES DANCER 3 b.g. Norse Dancer (IRE) 127 – Indiana Blues 90 (Indian Ridge 123) **54**
[2015 60: t8.6g6 8f 9.9g 9g Jul 8] modest maiden: stays 8.5f: acts on tapeta: temperament
under suspicion. *Sylvester Kirk*

BLUE SEA OF IBROX (IRE) 7 gr.m. Subtle Power (IRE) 115 – Jerpoint Rose (IRE) **76**
(Roselier (FR)) [2015 10.3g 10d2 t12.2m6 12s* 16d Oct 30] lengthy mare: fair performer:
won maiden at Pontefract in October: best effort at 1½m: acts on soft going. *John Berry*

BLUE SMOKE 2 gr.f. (Feb 1) Hellvelyn 118 – Easy Mover (IRE) 77 (Bluebird (USA) **–**
125) [2015 p5g5 5d Apr 16] seventh foal: half-sister to 2-y-o 5f winner Dispol Keasha (by
Kheleyf): dam 2-y-o 7f winner who stayed 1¼m: no form. *Bill Turner*

BLUE SONIC 5 gr.m. Proclamation (IRE) 130 – Big Mystery (IRE) 53 (Grand Lodge **75**
(USA) 125) [2015 65: 6g3 6s 6d 5g* 6d* 5d* 6d 6g 5g Oct 13] fair handicapper: completed
hat-trick at Ayr in July and August (2): has form at 7f, best efforts at shorter: acts on good
to firm and good to soft going: sometimes slowly away, often races towards rear.
Linda Perratt

BLUE SURF 6 ch.g. Excellent Art 125 – Wavy Up (IRE) (Brustolon 117) [2015 107: 12m* **108**
16.1m 9.9g 14s4 Aug 29] useful-looking gelding: useful handicapper: won at Epsom (by
length from Gothic) in June: stays 1¾m: acts on good to firm and heavy going: tried in
cheekpieces prior to 2015: usually races prominently. *Amanda Perrett*

BLUE TALISMAN (IRE) 4 ch.g. Alhaarth (IRE) 126 – Amaniy (USA) 96 (Dayjur **–**
(USA) 137) [2015 16.2s6 May 19] fair at best, no form in 2015: stays 1¾m: acts on
fibresand and heavy going: often wears headgear: front runner/races prominently, usually
finds little. *Peter Bowen*

BLUE TOP 6 b.g. Millkom 124 – Pompey Blue 71 (Abou Zouz (USA) 109) [2015 t9.5g **60**
16.2m3 16.2s3 10.2g4 Oct 18] plain gelding: modest handicapper: stays 14.5f: acts on soft
and good to firm going: often in headgear prior to 2015: tried in tongue tie prior to 2015:
often starts slowly. *Dai Burchell*

BLUE WALTZ 4 b.f. Pivotal 124 – Blue Symphony 73 (Darshaan 133) [2015 103p: 9.9m3 **105**
10m 10.3m* 10g 10.3v Nov 7] sturdy, quite attractive filly: useful handicapper: won at
Doncaster (by 2¾ lengths from Forgotten Hero) in September: stays 10.5f: acts on good to
firm and good to soft going. *Luca Cumani*

BLUE WAVE (IRE) 5 b.g. Raven's Pass (USA) 133 – Million Waves (IRE) 92 (Mull of **107**
Kintyre (USA) 114) [2015 105, a111: 14g* 12m 13.4m3 14d 12d Sep 12] strong gelding:
useful handicapper: won at Goodwood (by neck from Forgotten Voice) in July: third at
Chester (length behind Gabrial's King) in August: stays 1¾m: acts on polytrack, fibresand
and firm going: tried in headgear prior to 2015. *Mark Johnston*

BLUFF CRAG 2 b.g. (Feb 11) Canford Cliffs (IRE) 133 – Camp Riverside (USA) (Forest **74**
Camp (USA) 114) [2015 6g⁶ 8f⁴ 8s⁶ Oct 9] fair maiden: best effort when sixth in maiden
at York (5 lengths behind Dolphin Vista) in October. *Andrew Balding*

BLUSHED (IRE) 2 b.f. (May 1) Invincible Spirit (IRE) 121 – Subtle Charm (Machiavellian **54 p**
(USA) 123) [2015 6g⁴ Jul 30] 75,000 2-y-o: sister to useful 5f (including at 2 yrs) winner
Indescribable and half-sister to 1m-1½m winner Cipher (by Reset) and winner up to 7f
Spinning Yarn (2-y-o 6f winner, by Pivotal): dam lightly-raced half-sister to Oaks winner
Snow Bride, herself dam of Lammtarra: 20/1 and tongue tied, considerable introduction
when fourth in maiden at Ffos Las (5½ lengths behind Lilbourne Prince) in July, not
knocked about: better to come. *Alan McCabe*

BLUSHES (FR) 2 b.f. (May 5) Siyouni (FR) 122 – Pink And Red (USA) (Red Ransom **57 p**
(USA)) [2015 p7g⁵ 7.1m p6f Sep 24] €25,000Y: half-sister to several winners, including
10.5f winner Parisham (by Cadeaux Genereux) and 1½m winner Parandeh (by Kahyasi):
dam 7f/7.5f winner (including at 2 yrs): modest maiden: best effort when seventh in
maiden at Chepstow (7 lengths behind Puzzled Look) in September: will stay 1m: capable
of better. *Ed Dunlop*

BLYTHE PRINCE 3 b.c. Dutch Art 126 – Arculinge 64 (Paris House 123) [2015 –: 6m **–**
6s Oct 16] maiden: no form in 2015. *Danielle McCormick*

BLYTHE STAR (IRE) 3 b.g. Thewayyouare (USA) 117 – Run To Jane (IRE) (Doyoun **48**
124) [2015 46: t12.2g⁸ 8g 12.1g t9.5f t8.6f t13.9f Nov 10] poor maiden: stays 1¾m: acts on
tapeta, good to firm and good to soft going: often wears headgear: sometimes slowly away.
Danielle McCormick

BNEDEL (IRE) 3 b.c. Teofilo (IRE) 126 – Dance Club (IRE) 71 (Fasliyev (USA) 120) **90**
[2015 85p: 10m⁴ 10.4m⁴ 10.4g² 9.9m⁶ 12g³ 10s Sep 18] fairly useful handicapper: won at
Haydock in June: second at Haydock in July and third at Salisbury in August: stays 1½m:
acts on polytrack and good to firm going: usually races prominently: sent to Qatar.
Richard Hannon

BOARDING PARTY (USA) 3 ch.g. More Than Ready (USA) 120 – Oceans Apart 90 **77**
(Desert Prince (IRE) 130) [2015 64p: 7g 7m 5.7f⁵ p7g⁴ p8g⁵ p8f² p8m⁵ Oct 28] workmanlike
gelding: fair maiden: stays 1m: acts on polytrack: tried in visor in 2015: sold 16,000 gns,
sent to UAE. *Charlie Fellowes*

BOBBY BENTON (IRE) 4 b.g. Invincible Spirit (IRE) 121 – Remarkable Story (Mark **77**
of Esteem (IRE) 137) [2015 79: p10m² p10g⁵ p10f³ p8g² 10m 8g⁴ Apr 28] fair handicapper:
stays 1¼m: acts on polytrack, fibresand and good to firm going: tried in hood prior to 2015.
Luke Dace

BOBBY JEAN (IRE) 4 b.f. Jeremy (USA) 122 – Madam's View (IRE) (Entrepreneur **79**
123) [2015 59: 7.5s* 6.7s² 8v* 7v³ 7d⁶ 9s³ 7.3d 8d⁶ Oct 30] fair handicapper: won at
Tipperary in April and the Curragh in May: stays 9f: best form on soft/heavy going:
sometimes in tongue tie in 2015. *Miss Tara Lee Cogan, Ireland*

BOBBY'S BABE 2 b.f. (Mar 16) Big Bad Bob (IRE) 118 – Express Logic (Air Express **75**
(IRE) 125) [2015 7s⁴ 6d² 6g* Sep 26] 12,000Y: fifth foal: half-sister to smart winner up to
1m Pure Poetry (2-y-o 6f winner, by Tagula) and 7f winner Eljowzah (by Acclamation):
dam ran once: fair performer: best effort when winning maiden at Ripon (by ½ length from
Kyllukey) in September, driven out: best effort at 6f. *Tim Easterby*

BOBBY WHEELER (IRE) 2 b.c. (Apr 23) Pivotal 124 – Regal Rose 110 (Danehill **90 p**
(USA) 126) [2015 6g⁵ 7g²* 7s³ Sep 1] €16,000Y: well-grown colt: half-brother to several
winners, including useful/ungenuine winner up to 6f Regal Royale and 7f (including at
2 yrs) winner (stays 1m) Royal Banker (both by Medicean): dam, 2-y-o 6f (Cheveley Park
Stakes) winner, half-sister to smart winner up to 1¾m (stayed 2m) Regal Flush: fairly
useful performer: best effort when finishing second at Salisbury (by 3¼ lengths from Art
Echo) in August, well on top finish: best effort at 7f: should do better. *Clive Cox*

BOBOLI GARDENS 5 b.g. Medicean 128 – Park Crystal (IRE) (Danehill (USA) 126) **72**
[2015 70: p7g* t7.1g* p6m⁵ p8f* t7.1f 8.3d t8.6g 7m t7.1g⁵ t7.1g t9.5m Sep 25] fair
handicapper: won at Kempton and Wolverhampton in January, and Kempton in February:
left Noel Quinlan after fifth start, Giles Bravery after tenth: stays 1m: acts on polytrack and
tapeta: sometimes in hood prior to 2015: tried in tongue tie: often starts slowly. *Alan Berry*

BO BRIDGET (IRE) 2 gr.f. (Feb 24) Mastercraftsman (IRE) 129 – Greta d'Argent (IRE) **73**
103 (Great Commotion (USA) 123) [2015 8d² 8.3g p10g⁵ 8d Oct 19] €37,000Y: leggy,
unfurnished filly: half-sister to several winners, including winner up to 7f Coolminx (2-y-o

5f/5.4f winner) and 2-y-o 5f winner Baycat (both useful and by One Cool Cat): dam, winner up to 1½m (2-y-o 8.4f winner), half-sister to smart/ungenuine 1¼m-2m winner (stayed 2½m) Winged d'Argent: fair maiden: best effort at 1m. *Mark Johnston*

BOB'S BOY 2 b.g. (Apr 2) Showcasing 117 – Tech Zinne (Zinaad 114) [2015 8v 8.3d⁵ 8s Oct 23] modest maiden: best effort when fifth in maiden at Windsor (5½ lengths behind Gawdawpalin) in October, unable to sustain effort: tried in cheekpieces. *Jose Santos* **56**

BOB'S WORLD 6 b.g. Multiplex 114 – Vocation (IRE) 74 (Royal Academy (USA) 130) **–**
[2015 t16.5fᵇᵘ Sep 19] fairly useful at best, no form in 2015: stays 16.5f: acts on polytrack and soft going: sometimes in cheekpieces prior to 2015: sometimes wears tongue tie. *Jennie Candlish*

BOCA SHAM 2 b.f. (Jan 14) Shami 105 – Reluctant Heroine (USA) 52 (Medaglia d'Oro **–**
(USA) 129) [2015 7d 7v Oct 17] first foal: dam lightly raced: no form. *John Davies*

BOCCA BACIATA (IRE) 3 b.f. Big Bad Bob (IRE) 118 – Sovana (IRE) 103 (Desert **112**
King (IRE) 129) [2015 88p: 10d* 8g⁵ 10f 9d³ 9d* 10d³ 12d⁵ Oct 17] tall, leggy filly: tends to sweat/get on edge: smart performer: won listed race at Navan (by 1½ lengths from Pleascach) in April and Dance Design Stakes at the Curragh (by 4 lengths from Easter) in August: third in Blandford Stakes at the Curragh (1¾ lengths behind Ribbons) in September and fifth in Fillies' And Mares' Stakes at Ascot (beaten 3½ lengths by Simple Verse) in October: stays 1½m: acts on good to firm and good to soft going. *Mrs J. Harrington, Ireland*

BOCHART 2 ch.g. (Apr 2) Dubawi (IRE) 129 – Camlet 94 (Green Desert (USA) 127) **80**
[2015 6g 7m³ p6g² 6.1m⁵ 5m² 5.3d² 6v³ t5.1f³ p7g³ Nov 13] brother to ungenuine 7f winner Hollie Point and half-brother to 3 winners, including smart winner up to 7.5f Cheviot (2-y-o 6f winner, by Rahy): dam, 6f winner (including at 2 yrs), half-sister to high-class winner up to 1m Barathea: fairly useful maiden: third in maiden at Leicester in June and nursery at Wolverhampton in October: stays 7f: acts on tapeta, polytrack, good to firm and good to soft going: often in blinkers. *Charlie Appleby*

BOCKING END (IRE) 2 b.f. (Mar 1) Paco Boy (IRE) 129 – Miss Wells (IRE) (Sadler's **75**
Wells (USA) 132) [2015 7f 7g 8.3g⁴ 9d⁵ Oct 31] 30,000F: third foal: sister to 7f winner Cisco Boy and half-sister to winner up to 6f Archie Stevens (by Pastoral Pursuits): dam unraced sister to useful winner up to 10.3f Temple Place: fair maiden: best effort at 8.5f. *Michael Bell*

BOETHIUS 2 b.c. (Mar 19) Manduro (GER) 135 – Perfect Note 80 (Shamardal (USA) **70 p**
129) [2015 t8.6g⁴ p8f Dec 21] second foal: half-brother to useful winner up to 1m Romance Story (2-y-o 7f winner, by New Approach): dam, 1m winner, half-sister to smart/ungenuine 11f-1¾m winner Claremont out of smart winner up to 1½m (2-y-o 1m winner) Mezzo Soprano: better effort when fourth in maiden at Wolverhampton (6¼ lengths behind Mutawaaly) on debut: badly hampered at Chelmsford: remains open to improvement. *Charlie Appleby*

BOGARDUS (IRE) 4 b.g. Dalakhani (IRE) 133 – Sugar Mint (IRE) 100 (High Chaparral **74**
(IRE) 132) [2015 85: 12g 9.2d 10.1m⁵ 12g⁵ 12g³ 12.1g 12.1g 11.1g⁵ 12.2g t12.2m⁴ p10g* Dec 15] fair handicapper: won at Kempton in December: stays 1½m: acts on polytrack, tapeta, soft and good to firm going: tried in headgear. *Patrick Holmes*

BOGART 6 ch.g. Bahamian Bounty 116 – Lauren Louise 55 (Tagula (IRE) 116) [2015 105: **101**
5m³ 6g⁶ 5g 5m³ 6m 5.4g 5.6d Sep 12] sturdy, good-quartered gelding: useful handicapper: third at Beverley (1½ lengths behind Pipers Note) in April and third at York (¾ length behind Kimberella) in July: stays 6f: acts on soft and good to firm going: tried in cheekpieces. *Kevin Ryan*

BOGEY HOLE (IRE) 6 gr.m. Aussie Rules (USA) 123 – Sticky Green 75 (Lion Cavern **–**
(USA) 117) [2015 t13.9g Jan 19] maiden: no form in 2015: stays 8.6f: tried in headgear: in tongue tie sole start in 2015. *Nikki Evans*

BOGNOR (USA) 4 b.g. Hard Spun (USA) 124 – Ms Blue Blood (USA) (A P Indy (USA) **72**
131) [2015 66, a89: f8d⁴ f7d³ p8m⁴ f8g³ p8f f7g² 8.3m⁵ 8.3s⁴ 11.1d⁶ May 27] fairly useful **a86**
handicapper: best up to 1m: acts on polytrack, fibresand and good to firm going: tried in cheekpieces in 2015. *Michael Appleby*

BOGSNOG (IRE) 5 b.g. Moss Vale (IRE) 126 – Lovers Kiss 52 (Night Shift (USA)) **74**
[2015 71, a77: t6g* t7.1g t6f⁶ t5.1g⁵ t5.1m² t6g 5g² 6m 5d⁵ 6m* 6m 5m³ 6m⁶ t6g⁴ t7.1f t6f³ **a68**
p6f⁶ t6g³ t6m⁴ Dec 12] fair handicapper: won at Wolverhampton in January and Thirsk in July: stays 7f: acts on polytrack, tapeta, good to firm and good to soft going: often in cheekpieces prior to 2015: often races prominently. *Kristin Stubbs*

BOHEMIAN DIAMOND 2 b.f. (Feb 20) Bahamian Bounty 116 – Parsonagehotelyork – p
(IRE) 62 (Danehill (USA) 126) [2015 5.9g Jun 15] £2,000Y: fourth foal: dam, ran once,
closely related to useful 6f-1m winner Picture Perfect: 11/2, eighth in maiden at Carlisle
(10 lengths behind Kelly's Dino) in June: entitled to do better. *Richard Fahey*

BOHEMIAN ORIGIN (IRE) 2 ch.g. (Mar 31) Zoffany (IRE) 121 – Rainbow Lyrics –
(IRE) (Rainbow Quest (USA) 134) [2015 t7.1g 8f⁵ 6d p7g Dec 10] no form. *J. S. Moore*

BOHEMIAN RHAPSODY (IRE) 6 b.g. Galileo (IRE) 134 – Quiet Mouse (USA) 80
(Quiet American (USA)) [2015 p16g 14.1f⁵ 16m⁶ 21g 14.4g³ 17.1d⁵ 16s² 12v³ Oct 24]
rather leggy gelding: fairly useful handicapper: third at Newcastle in August and second at
Newbury (apprentice) in October: stays 2m: acts on soft and good to firm going: tried in
cheekpieces: fairly useful hurdler. *Joseph Tuite*

BOHEMIAN SYMPHONY 2 b.f. (Feb 19) Paco Boy (IRE) 129 – Wish You Luck 47
(Dubai Destination (USA) 127) [2015 t7.1g⁵ 7m p7g⁶ t7.1m Sep 14] £11,000Y: second
foal: dam once-raced half-sister to smart winner up to 10.6f Simeon: little form in Britain,
but won 7.5f seller at Pisa in November. *Marco Botti*

BOITE (IRE) 5 b.g. Authorized (IRE) 133 – Albiatra (USA) (Dixieland Band (USA)) 96
[2015 14g² 20f 21g Jul 29] quite good-topped gelding: useful handicapper: third at
Goodwood (3½ lengths behind Quest For More) in May: stays 2m: acts on any turf going:
tried in tongue tie in 2015: usually races close up: fairly useful hurdler. *Warren Greatrex*

BOLD 3 b.c. Oasis Dream 129 – Minority 106 (Generous (IRE) 139) [2015 74p: p7f* 7m 88
7.1m⁵ Jun 13] sturdy colt: fairly useful performer: won maiden at Kempton in April: best
effort at 7f: acts on polytrack. *Roger Charlton*

BOLD ADVENTURE 11 ch.g. Arkadian Hero (USA) 123 – Impatiente (USA) (Vaguely 53
Noble 140) [2015 p16g⁵ p16g p16g⁴ p16g⁵ p15.8f⁴ p16g⁴ Aug 17] good-bodied gelding:
modest handicapper: stays 16.5f: acts on polytrack, soft and good to firm going: tried in
cheekpieces prior to 2015: usually races towards rear. *Willie Musson*

BOLD APPEAL 3 b.g. Nayef (USA) 129 – Shy Appeal (IRE) 71 (Barathea (IRE) 127) 84
[2015 70: 9.9m⁴ p12g³ 11.6g³ 12m³ 12.1g* 12.1m² 13.1f p12g³ Oct 6] sturdy gelding:
fairly useful handicapper: won at Chepstow in August: third at Kempton in October: stays
1½m: acts on polytrack and tapeta: usually in blinkers in 2015: races prominently: sold
45,000 gns, sent to UAE. *Ralph Beckett*

BOLDBOB (IRE) 3 gr.g. Verglas (IRE) 118 – Special Park (USA) (Trempolino (USA) –
135) [2015 55: 8g 8g 12.1g 12g 16.2m Jul 20] maiden: no form in 2015. *Micky Hammond*

BOLD CAPTAIN (IRE) 4 ch.g. Captain Rio 122 – Indianaca (IRE) 67 (Indian Danehill –
(IRE) 124) [2015 8s 8g⁶ 9g 8g 8d Aug 18] fairly useful at best, no form in 2015: tried in
blinkers in 2015. *John Quinn*

BOLD CROSS (IRE) 12 b.g. Cape Cross (IRE) 129 – Machikane Akaiito (IRE) (Persian 56
Bold 123) [2015 57: 10.2m 10.2m² 12.1m⁵ 9.9d 10m Aug 18] leggy gelding: modest
handicapper: stays 1½m: acts on polytrack, firm and soft going: sometimes slowly away,
usually races nearer last than first. *Edward Bevan*

BOLD DUKE 7 b.g. Sulamani (IRE) 130 – Dominant Duchess 97 (Old Vic 136) [2015 61
p16g 14.6m⁵ f12g Nov 12] modest handicapper: stays 1½m: acts on good to firm and
heavy going: tried in headgear: often races towards rear. *Edward Bevan*

BOLD GROVE 3 b.g. Proclamation (IRE) 130 – Trysting Grove (IRE) 64 (Cape Cross 54
(IRE) 129) [2015 –: t6f³ t7.1m⁵ t6g⁴ t7.1g t8.6g 8.1d⁵ 7.1s⁵ Aug 31] modest maiden: stays
6f: acts on tapeta: tried in hood in 2015. *Edward Bevan*

BOLD HENMIE (IRE) 4 b.g. Henrythenavigator (USA) 131 – Seminole Lass (USA) 63
(Indian Charlie (USA) 126) [2015 63: t8.6g t8.6g² 9m⁵ 9.9m⁵ p10f² t12.2m* 10.9g³
t12.2m² Sep 14] modest handicapper: won at Wolverhampton in August: left Paul John
Gilligan after fourth start: stays 1½m: acts on polytrack and tapeta: tried in headgear.
Philip Kirby

BOLD LASS (IRE) 4 b.f. Sea The Stars (IRE) 140 – My Branch 111 (Distant Relative 103
128) [2015 98p: 8.3m* 8.5g⁴ 8m⁴ 8.1m 7m Sep 10] lengthy filly: useful performer: won
handicap at Windsor in May: good fourth in Princess Elizabeth Stakes at Epsom (4¾
lengths behind Arabian Queen) in June: stays 8.5f: acts on firm going: tried in cheekpieces
in 2015: strong traveller, tends not to find much: sent to USA. *David Lanigan*

BOLD MAX 4 b.g. Assertive 121 – Jane's Payoff (IRE) 72 (Danetime (IRE) 121) [2015 60
45, a55: f7g³ t7.1g⁴ t7.1f⁵ t6f² t6g t6g* t5.1m³ t6g t6g t6f⁴ t6f t7.1m² t6m³ Dec 30]
lengthy gelding: modest handicapper: won at Wolverhampton in April: stays 7f: acts on
tapeta and fibresand: often wears headgear: often races towards rear. *Zoe Davison*

BOLD PREDICTION (IRE) 5 b.g. Kodiac 112 – Alexander Eliott (IRE) 73 (Night **90**
Shift (USA)) [2015 101: p8g p8g 8g p8f p7g p8m* Dec 31] useful-looking gelding: fairly
useful handicapper: won at Lingfield (by 3 lengths from Billy Bond) in December: stays
8.5f: acts on polytrack, good to firm and good to soft going: tried in hood prior to 2015:
usually races prominently. *Ed Walker*

BOLD RUNNER 4 ch.g. Mount Nelson 125 – Music In Exile (USA) 58 (Diesis 133) **81**
[2015 85: p12f³ p12f⁵ p12f* p12f³ 14d* 14.1g⁵ p12g³ 14.1g² 14.1g³ 12v³ p12g⁶ 14.1g²
16d* 12v⁵ Oct 24] tall gelding: fairly useful handicapper: won at Kempton in April,
Lingfield in May and Goodwood (by 1½ lengths from Mr Fickle) in October: stays 2m:
acts on polytrack and heavy going: often wears cheekpieces: front runner/races prominently.
Jose Santos

BOLD SPIRIT 4 b.g. Invincible Spirit (IRE) 121 – Far Shores (USA) (Distant View **71**
(USA) 126) [2015 80: 6g 5.1d 5.9v 6g³ 7m³ 7m 6m 5d 6g 5d 7g 6d³ 6m⁶ 5m 7.2g* 6g
Oct 20] compact gelding: fair handicapper: won at Musselburgh in October: stays 7f: acts
on polytrack, firm and soft going: often wears headgear: often in tongue tie in 2015: front
runner/races prominently: inconsistent. *Declan Carroll*

BOLLIHOPE 3 ch.g. Medicean 128 – Hazy Dancer 81 (Oasis Dream 129) [2015 78p: **78**
10.2d 10m⁵ 11.9f* 12.4g⁴ 12g⁴ 13.1g 12d⁶ 11.6g⁵ p12g Nov 13] fair performer: won
maiden at Haydock in June: left John Gosden after fourth start: stays 12.5f: acts on firm
and good to soft going. *Richard Guest*

BOLLYWOOD DREAM 3 b.f. Sleeping Indian 122 – Act Three 76 (Beat Hollow 126) **47**
[2015 –: t9.5g⁵ t12.2g⁴ p11g 10.2m May 4] poor maiden: stays 1½m: acts on polytrack and
tapeta. *Jonathan Portman*

BOMBALURINA (IRE) 3 ch.f. Rip Van Winkle (IRE) 134 – Real Cat (USA) (Storm Cat **–**
(USA)) [2015 –: p10m⁵ t8.6g 9.9m Jun 23] maiden: no form in 2015: tried in visor in 2015.
George Peckham

BOMBILATE (USA) 2 b.f. (Mar 23) Kitten's Joy (USA) 128 – Wild Chant (USA) (War **70 p**
Chant (USA) 126) [2015 t8.6g p8g² Nov 4] $350,000Y: third foal: dam, 2-y-o 7f winner,
half-sister to Breeders' Cup Distaff winner Untapable: better effort when second in maiden
at Kempton (2 lengths behind The Black Princess) in November, barely adequate test:
should be suited by further than 1m: remains with potential. *Charlie Appleby*

BON CHANCE 4 b.g. Byron 117 – Stolen Melody 74 (Robellino (USA) 127) [2015 –: **–**
f7m t6f Dec 21] maiden: no form in 2015: tried in blinkers. *Peter Niven*

BOND ARTIST (IRE) 6 b.m. Excellent Art 125 – Pitrizza (IRE) (Machiavellian (USA) **51**
123) [2015 67: t8.6g⁵ p8f t8.6f t8.6f Mar 26] modest handicapper: stays 8.5f: acts on
polytrack, tapeta and good to soft going: often races towards rear. *Geoffrey Oldroyd*

BOND BLADE 7 ch.g. Needwood Blade 117 – Bond Cat (IRE) 51 (Raise A Grand (IRE) **46**
114) [2015 36: t5.1g⁴ t5.1f³ Mar 26] poor handicapper: stays 6f: acts on fibresand and
tapeta: tried in headgear prior to 2015. *Suzzanne France*

BOND BOMBSHELL 2 ch.f. (Apr 20) Monsieur Bond (IRE) 120 – Fashion Icon (USA) **66**
76 (Van Nistelrooy (USA) 108) [2015 t5.1g⁶ 5m² 5d³ 5m² 5g 5s³ 5m* 5m⁴ 5m⁵ 5g⁵ 5m³
Sep 27] first foal: dam 5f winner: fair performer: won maiden at Beverley in July: raced
only at 5f: acts on good to firm going: tried in cheekpieces. *David O'Meara*

BOND EMPIRE 5 b.g. Misu Bond (IRE) 114 – At Amal (IRE) (Astronef 116) [2015 62: **–**
t7.1f Mar 23] modest maiden: best effort at 7f: acted on good to firm going: sometimes
slowly away, often raced towards rear: dead. *Geoffrey Oldroyd*

BOND FASTRAC 5 b.g. Monsieur Bond (IRE) 120 – Kanisfluh 89 (Pivotal 124) [2015 **73**
79: f5s² f6s t6m* t7.1f p6f f6g 7.2m 5.9g p6f p7g 6v Nov 3] tall, close-coupled gelding:
fair performer: won seller at Wolverhampton (dead-heated) in February: left Geoffrey
Oldroyd after third start: stays 6f: acts on tapeta, good to firm and heavy going: tried in
headgear: often races in rear. *Shaun Harris*

BONDI BEACH BABE 5 b.m. Misu Bond (IRE) 114 – Nice One (Almaty (IRE) 113) **73**
[2015 61: f5g⁵ 6g² 5g* 6m² 5m² 6m² 5m⁴ 5.9g 6g³ 6d* 6g Sep 26] fair handicapper:
won at Catterick (apprentice) in May, Beverley (apprentice) in June and Catterick in
September: stays 6f: acts on tapeta, good to firm and good to soft going: usually in
cheekpieces in 2015. *James Turner*

BONDI BEACH BOY 6 b.g. Misu Bond (IRE) 114 – Nice One (Almaty (IRE) 113) **85**
[2015 94: 5m 5m 5g⁵ 5f⁶ 5.5m³ 5g 5m* 5m⁵ 5m 5g⁶ Sep 26] lengthy gelding: fairly useful
handicapper: won at Haydock (by 1¼ lengths from Nocturn) in July: third at Wetherby in
June: stays 5.5f: has won on soft going, probably best under less testing conditions (acts on
firm). *James Turner*

BONDI BEACH (IRE) 3 b.c. Galileo (IRE) 134 – One Moment In Time (IRE) **122**
(Danehill (USA) 126) [2015 12v* 12g² 14m* 12d² 14.6d² 15.9g Nov 3]

Bondi Beach held the status of 'classic winner' for just eleven days—until
the first past the post in the St Leger, Simple Verse, was reinstated on appeal by a
British Horseracing Authority disciplinary panel, after three hours of evidence and
legal argument at High Holborn. Bondi Beach had been the first promoted 'winner'
of the St Leger since the favourite Pewett was awarded the race in 1789 when an
objection for jostling was sustained against the first-past-the-post Zanga. Pewett was
the eighth filly to win the oldest classic and Simple Verse became the forty-second,
and the first for almost a quarter of a century. On balance, the correct decision
was arrived at in the end and Bondi Beach's connections accepted the disciplinary
panel's verdict with good grace. However, on the day, the stewards at Doncaster
decided that the cumulative effect of two bumps in the closing stages by Simple
Verse 'improved her placing' and therefore effectively cost Bondi Beach victory.
Disqualifications are few and far between nowadays in British racing, with the first
past the post enjoying a sometimes seemingly-weighty benefit of the doubt under
the rules, which made the Doncaster stewards' decision at the time more than a little
surprising. With the disciplining of riding offences judged separately under British
rules, the stewards had to adjudicate only on whether the interference caused by
Simple Verse had 'improved her placing'.

The process did not specifically involve looking at whether Bondi Beach
would have won had he not suffered interference, a subtle but important point
which emphasises that, under the rules, the stewards are concerned with the effect
of any interference on the winner's chance, rather than on that of the runner-up. The
evidence considered by the Doncaster stewards included the testimony of the two
jockeys involved—both of whom incurred punishments for separate riding offences
in the race—and there was no doubt that, in Colm O'Donoghue, Bondi Beach and
his connections had an impressive advocate. The stewards' inquiry was televised
live by Channel 4 and, after outlining the interference ('my horse was taken off his
line and bumped quite severely for the second time'), the composed O'Donoghue
asked the stewards in his closing statement—'Has an incident occurred? Yes. Has
it taken me off a straight course? Yes. For the second time in the race my horse has
received a severe bump which has obviously taken his breath and knocked him
off his stride and his rhythm, and he's doing his best and trying his heart out to
get back at a filly that obviously has a weight allowance against him. Well, he's
suffered interference and he's been beaten a head on the line.' How much influence
O'Donoghue's persuasive testimony had on the Doncaster stewards can only be
guessed at, but, as Simple Verse's jockey pointed out, the interference wasn't all one
way, with Bondi Beach also leaning on Simple Verse for some of the closing stages
of a protracted battle. The way Timeform looked at the race, Bondi Beach wasn't
gaining on a most responsive Simple Verse inside the last half furlong, or as the line
was reached, which made it hard to justify changing the result under the rules as they
stand (it is worth repeating that whether the jockeys had kept strictly to the rules
was not relevant in this case, with O'Donoghue's being a whip offence and Atzeni
on Simple Verse found guilty of nothing more serious than careless riding when
pushing his way out from the rails two furlongs out).

Colm O'Donoghue would not have ridden Bondi Beach in the St Leger but
for a late decision taken unilaterally in Ireland (after a forecast of significant rain)
to bring forward the start of the Irish Champion Stakes by sixty-five minutes, which
reduced the time between the St Leger and the Irish Champion to two hours. The
flight from Doncaster to Leopardstown takes an hour and a half in a high-speed
helicopter and Sheikh Fahad, the face of Irish Champions' Weekend sponsors Qipco,
made it from Doncaster in time for the big-race presentation in Ireland, though the
change unfortunately meant that jockeys couldn't ride in both races because of the
declaration deadline. Frankie Dettori was originally booked for Bondi Beach but
he was committed to Golden Horn in the Irish Champion, and William Buick was
booked to replace him until O'Donoghue's intended mount Order of St George was
an eleventh-hour switch from Doncaster to the next day's Irish St Leger (which he

N. C. Williams & Mr and Mrs L. J. Williams' "Bondi Beach"

won), leaving O'Donoghue free to ride Bondi Beach (with Ryan Moore still on the sidelines, Joseph O'Brien was earmarked to ride Gleneagles, eventually declared a non-runner, in the Irish Champion).

Bondi Beach (IRE) (b.c. 2012)	Galileo (IRE) (b 1998)	Sadler's Wells (b 1981)	Northern Dancer / Fairy Bridge
		Urban Sea (ch 1989)	Miswaki / Allegretta
	One Moment In Time (IRE) (b 2003)	Danehill (b 1986)	Danzig / Razyana
		Hotelgenie Dot Com (gr 1998)	Selkirk / Birch Creek

The St Leger was the second race in succession in which Bondi Beach failed to get a clear run in a tight finish. Reportedly too big and backward to be raced as a two-year-old, he wasted no time in working his way up the ladder, winning a maiden at Leopardstown in May on his debut and then beating Order of St George by a short head in the Curragh Cup in June on his third start, despite his rider that day Seamus Heffernan dropping his whip. Bondi Beach had his St Leger credentials put to the test in the Great Voltigeur Stakes at York in August (his stable had nine in the race at the six-day stage, with Giovanni Canaletto and Aloft joining Bondi Beach in the eventual seven-runner line-up). Bondi Beach moved upsides the leader Storm The Stars a furlong out but was carried across the course by him in the last half furlong, receiving a bump in the process as he pressed Storm The Stars strongly all the way to the line. Bondi Beach went down by half a length and it was hard to argue that the result would have been different had the winner not taken Bondi Beach off a true line. It came as no surprise when Storm The Stars survived the inevitable stewards' inquiry. After his good effort in the St Leger, Bondi Beach was purchased by Australian interests, among them leading owner Lloyd Williams, and put into quarantine for a tilt at the Melbourne Cup in November. He faced a stiffish task as the only northern hemisphere three-year-old in the line-up and was far from discredited, finishing sixteenth of twenty-four but beaten only just over half a dozen lengths.

Bondi Beach is by Galileo out of One Moment In Time, an unraced sister (who cost 520,000 guineas as a yearling) to the smart miler Simply Perfect who won the May Hill and the Fillies' Mile, as well as the Falmouth Stakes, for the Coolmore partners when trained by Jeremy Noseda. One Moment In Time has had two previous winners, a Fusaichi Pegasus filly who won in Malaysia, and the useful mile and a quarter winner for Aidan O'Brien, Bazaar, a brother to Bondi Beach. The immediate influences on the distaff side of the pedigree are more for speed than stamina. Bondi Beach's grandam Hotelgenie Dot Com, who was at her best at two when placed in the Moyglare Stud Stakes and Fillies' Mile, is a half-sister to the Lowther and Moyglare Stud Stakes winner Bianca Nera. Further back, however, Bondi Beach's fifth dam Aurorabella was a sister to the Goodwood Cup winner Double Bore while Bianca Nera is now grandam of the latest King George and Queen Elizabeth Stakes winner Postponed. Bondi Beach stays two miles and he acts on good to firm and heavy going. He often wears a tongue tie. *Aidan O'Brien, Ireland*

BONDI MIST (IRE) 6 gr.m. Aussie Rules (USA) 123 – Akoya (IRE) (Anabaa (USA) – 130) [2015 57: 12m⁴ 11m Jun 25] leggy mare: fair at best, no form in 2015: stays 1½m: acts on good to firm and heavy going: sometimes wears visor: temperament under suspicion. *Jonathan Geake*

BOND MYSTERY 3 b.g. Monsieur Bond (IRE) 120 – Scooby Dooby Do 62 (Atraf 116) **47** [2015 –: 7g 8g 12.1m⁶ 9.9m 8.5g Sep 16] poor maiden: best effort at 1½m: acts on good to firm going: tried in cheekpieces in 2015: tried in tongue tie in 2015: sometimes slowly away, often races lazily. *Richard Whitaker*

BONDS CHOICE 3 ch.f. Monsieur Bond (IRE) 120 – Collette's Choice 72 (Royal – Applause 124) [2015 71: 6s⁶ 7d Oct 24] maiden: no form in 2015: stays 6f: acts on soft and good to firm going: usually races prominently. *Richard Fahey*

BOND'S GIFT 5 ch.m. Monsieur Bond (IRE) 120 – Bond Shakira 54 (Daggers Drawn **73** (USA) 114) [2015 65: t7.1g² t7.1m² t7.1g⁴ Aug 27] fair maiden: stays 7f: acts on tapeta: often wears headgear: often races towards rear. *Geoffrey Oldroyd*

BOND'S GIRL 3 ch.f. Monsieur Bond (IRE) 120 – Blades Girl 100 (Bertolini (USA) 125) **96** [2015 96: 7m⁵ 7m 6g 7m 6m 7s⁴ 6g Sep 24] sturdy, close-coupled filly: second at Newmarket (1½ lengths behind Teruntum Star) in July: stays 6.5f: acts on soft and good to firm going: often races towards rear. *Richard Fahey*

BOND'S PEARL 2 ch.f. (Apr 29) Monsieur Bond (IRE) 120 – Janet's Pearl (IRE) 72 – (Refuse To Bend (IRE) 128) [2015 6m 6g Jul 31] first foal: dam, winner up to 1¼m (2-y-o 7f winner), also won over hurdles: no form. *Michael Easterby*

BOND STARPRINCESS 3 ch.f. Monsieur Bond (IRE) 120 – Presidium Star (Presidium **43** 124) [2015 –: 7g 10g 16.2m⁶ Jul 20] poor maiden: best effort at 2m: acts on good to firm going: sometimes slowly away, usually races in rear. *George Moore*

BOND'S TRICKS 2 ch.g. (Apr 1) Monsieur Bond (IRE) 120 – Triple Tricks (IRE) 70 **51** (Royal Academy (USA) 130) [2015 6m⁶ 5m 6g³ 7d² 6d² f7g⁶ Dec 18] modest maiden: left Michael Easterby after fifth start: stays 7f: acts on fibresand and good to soft going. *Ronald Thompson*

BONFIRE HEART 3 b.f. Exceed And Excel (AUS) 126 – Marisa (GER) (Desert Sun **61** 120) [2015 71: 6mᵘʳ 6.1g⁴ 7m Aug 18] modest handicapper: stays 6f: acts on polytrack and tapeta: tried in blinkers in 2015: often races prominently. *Daniel Loughnane*

BONHOMIE 2 b.f. (Apr 23) Shamardal (USA) 129 – Bonnie Doon (IRE) (Grand Lodge **71 p** (USA) 125) [2015 p7g³ p7g⁴ Nov 26] rather unfurnished filly: fifth foal: half-sister to 1m-11.6f winner Banks And Braes (by Red Ransom) and useful 8.3f-1¼m winner Border Legend (by Selkirk): dam unraced half-sister to useful winner up to 9f Calista: better effort when third in maiden at Lingfield (5¼ lengths behind Our Joy) in October: will be suited by at least 1m: should still improve. *Michael Bell*

BONJOUR BABY 2 ch.f. (Mar 14) Duke of Marmalade (IRE) 132 – Briery (IRE) 66 **69** (Salse (USA) 128) [2015 7m 8d⁴ t7.1g⁴ Sep 29] 22,000Y: sister to 1¼m winner (stays 1½m) Rosaceous, closely related to 7f/1m winner Deduction (by Holy Roman Emperor) and half-sister to several winners, including useful 6f/7f winner Great Charm (by Orpen): dam 7f winner: fair maiden: best effort when fourth in maiden at Haydock (5 lengths behind Peru) in September. *K. R. Burke*

BONJOUR STEVE 4 b.g. Bahamian Bounty 116 – Anthea 66 (Tobougg (IRE) 125) [2015 **76** 65: 7d* 6.1s* 7m 6.1m² 6.1m⁴ 5.1s* 5.1d² 6m 5.1v² 6.1s⁴ 6s Oct 6] tall, unfurnished gelding: fair handicapper: won at Newcastle and Chepstow in May, and Chepstow in July: stays 7f: acts on firm and soft going: often wears headgear: often races towards rear. *Richard Price*

BONNIE GREY 3 gr.f. Hellvelyn 118 – Crofters Ceilidh 101 (Scottish Reel 123) [2015 **88** 95: 7m⁶ 6f⁵ May 16] rather leggy filly: fairly useful performer: stays 7f: acts on soft and good to firm going: front runner/races prominently. *Rod Millman*

BOOGANGOO (IRE) 4 b.f. Acclamation 118 – Spice World (IRE) (Spinning World **80** (USA) 130) [2015 81: p8m³ p8f² t7.1f p8g⁶ 8m* 7m² 7g⁵ t7.1g⁴ 14.1g⁴ Sep 30] fairly useful handicapper: won at Bath in May: stays 1¾m: acts on polytrack, tapeta, soft and good to firm going: sometimes in hood in 2015. *Grace Harris*

BOOKMAKER 5 b.g. Byron 117 – Cankara (IRE) 62 (Daggers Drawn (USA) 114) [2015 **68 §** 66: p7g p6m* p7m³ p7f⁴ p6g⁵ p7g⁵ p8g⁵ 7g 7m² p8g 7g p7g⁴ 6s* 6d p7g⁴ 8.3g⁵ p7g³ p7m p8d p7g³ p10m⁴ Dec 16] lengthy gelding: fair handicapper: won apprentice events at Lingfield in January and August: stays 1¼m: acts on polytrack, soft and good to firm going: often wears blinkers: sometimes slows away: one to treat with caution. *John Bridger*

BOOLASS (IRE) 3 b.f. Bushranger (IRE) 119 – Silent Secret (IRE) 81 (Dubai Destination **69** (USA) 127) [2015 f6g⁵ f8g² 7g⁵ 8g⁴ f7g⁵ f8g⁵ f6g⁵ f6g* Dec 15] €16,000Y: second foal: half-sister to 2-y-o 5f winner Gwen Lady Byron (by Dandy Man): dam, 2-y-o 7.4f winner, half-sister to smart winner up to 1m Cheyenne Star out of useful performer up to 1¼m Charita: fair performer: won maiden at Southwell in December: stays 7f: acts on fibresand: tried in blinkers. *Brian Ellison*

BOOM AND BUST (IRE) 8 b.g. Footstepsinthesand 120 – Forest Call 67 (Wolfhound **85** (USA) 126) [2015 103: 8d 8m 8m⁴ 8.1mᵖᵘ May 28] sturdy gelding: useful handicapper: stayed 9f: acted on firm and good to soft going: tried in cheekpieces: often raced prominently, tended to find little: dead. *Marcus Tregoning*

BOOMERANG BOB (IRE) 6 b.h. Aussie Rules (USA) 123 – Cozzene's Pride (USA) **104** (Cozzene (USA)) [2015 105: t6m² p6g⁵ 6f 6m² 6m 6g 6g⁵ t6f 6d⁴ p6g f6g* p6g* Dec 30] sturdy horse: useful performer: won claimer at Southwell and handicap at Lingfield (by neck from Mythmaker) in December: second in handicap at Wolverhampton (1¼ lengths behind Pretend) in March: left Charles Hills after tenth start: races mostly at 6f: acts on all-weather, soft and good to firm going: often races towards rear. *Jamie Osborne*

BOOM JUNIOR 2 b.c. (Mar 28) Compton Place 125 – Khyber Knight (IRE) 56 (Night **–** Shift (USA)) [2015 t7.1g 5g p6g p6g Dec 7] no form. *Tony Carroll*

BOOMSHACKERLACKER (IRE) 5 gr.g. Dark Angel (IRE) 113 – Allegrina (IRE) **111** 70 (Barathea (IRE) 127) [2015 113: a8f a7f⁴ a6f⁴ a7f⁶ 8v 8f 8g* 7s Aug 29] leggy gelding: smart performer: won listed race at Vichy (by 1¼ lengths from Stillman) in July: ran creditably at Maydan second/third outings, 2¾ lengths third to Reynaldothewizard in Al Shindagha Sprint on first occasion: stays 8.5f: acts on dirt, best turf form on good going or softer (acts on heavy): sometimes wears headgear. *George Baker*

BOOM THE GROOM (IRE) 4 b.g. Kodiac 112 – Ecco Mi (IRE) (Priolo (USA) 127) **108** [2015 86, a106: p6g* p6m⁴ p6g⁵ t5.1f p5m* p5g³ p6f⁶ 5.2m⁵ 5m³ 5m⁵ 5m 5g⁴ 5m 5v³ 6g Sep 19] lengthy gelding: useful handicapper: won at Lingfield in January (by neck from Firmdecisions) and February (by ¾ length from Dynamo Walt): third in listed race at Lingfield (2¼ lengths behind Pretend) in March and in 'Dash' at Epsom (1¼ lengths behind Desert Law) in June: stays 6f: acts on polytrack, tapeta, good to firm and heavy going: sometimes in tongue tie in 2015. *Tony Carroll*

BOONGA ROOGETA 6 b.m. Tobougg (IRE) 125 – Aberlady Bay (IRE) 62 (Selkirk **89** (USA) 129) [2015 95: t9.5f⁵ p10g* 9.9d³ p10m³ p8m* 7.9g 8m⁴ p10g⁶ 7g⁴ 8g p8f⁴ p10g⁴ p8f Dec 21] small mare: fairly useful handicapper: won at Chelmsford in April and June (by 1¾ lengths from Taaqah): stays 10.5f: acts on polytrack, good to firm and heavy going: tried in visor: front runner/races prominently. *Peter Charalambous*

BOOTS AND SPURS 6 b.g. Oasis Dream 129 – Arctic Char 102 (Polar Falcon (USA) **79** 126) [2015 95: 8d 8f⁴ 8g⁴ 7s⁶ 7s p7f⁵ p8g⁵ f8g* Dec 22] lengthy gelding: fairly useful **a85** handicapper: won at Southwell in December (by 1½ lengths from Clockmaker): left Stuart Williams after third start: stays 1m: acts on polytrack, fibresand and heavy going: often wears headgear: tried in tongue tie. *Scott Dixon*

BOP IT 6 b.g. Misu Bond (IRE) 114 – Forever Bond (Danetime (IRE) 121) [2015 90: 6d 6m 6g 6g 6g 6m³ 6g* 6m⁴ 6m⁵ Sep 20] good-topped gelding: fairly useful handicapper: won at Haydock (by ½ length from See The Storm) in August: third at York in July: stays 6f: acts on firm and soft going: tried in headgear: tried in tongue tie prior to 2015: usually races close up. *Geoffrey Oldroyd* **80**

BORAK (IRE) 3 b.g. Kodiac 112 – Right After Moyne (IRE) (Imperial Ballet (IRE) 110) [2015 75: p10g² 10.4g 10.3d* 10.2m⁴ 10g⁶ 12.1d² 12.1s* 13.4d³ Sep 26] compact gelding: fairly useful performer: won minor event at Doncaster in June and handicap at Chepstow (by 1¼ lengths from Late Shipment) in September: left Marco Botti after fourth start: stays 1½m: acts on polytrack, good to firm and soft going: often in cheekpieces in 2015. *Bernard Llewellyn* **82**

BORDER BANDIT (USA) 7 b.g. Selkirk (USA) 129 – Coretta (IRE) 118 (Caerleon (USA) 132) [2015 91: 8g⁶ 8g 8.5g² 8.5g³ 8d 7.9g⁵ 8g 8.5s 8g² Sep 23] fairly useful handicapper: stays 1¼m: acts on soft and good to firm going: often wears cheekpieces: has shown signs of temperament. *Tracy Waggott* **84**

BORDERLESCOTT 13 b.g. Compton Place 125 – Jeewan 82 (Touching Wood (USA) 127) [2015 103: 5v² 5m⁴ 5.1g³ 5m⁵ Jun 20] smallish, strong, close-coupled gelding: useful handicapper: second in minor event at Musselburgh (1¼ lengths behind Tangerine Trees) in April and third at Nottingham (1½ lengths behind Double Up) in May: best at 5f/6f: acts on polytrack and any turf going: usually races close up. *Rebecca Bastiman* **98**

BORIS GRIGORIEV (IRE) 6 b.g. Excellent Art 125 – Strategy 92 (Machiavellian (USA) 123) [2015 74§: 5s³ 5d⁴ 6d t6g 5g³ Sep 23] leggy gelding: fair handicapper: stays 6f: acts on soft and good to firm going: usually wears headgear: temperamental: sold 3,500 gns, won 6f seller at Rome in December. *Michael Easterby* **73 §**

BORN TO BE BAD (IRE) 3 b.g. Arcano (IRE) 122 – Lady of Kildare (IRE) 100 (Mujadil (USA) 119) [2015 66p: t7.1f p6f⁶ t6g p8g⁴ t8.6g* p8g² 10.3m* 10g⁴ t12.2g³ 10.1g t9.5m⁴ p10f² Oct 24] fairly useful handicapper: won at Wolverhampton in June and Doncaster in July: stays 10.5f: acts on polytrack, tapeta and good to firm going: front runner/races prominently. *Jamie Osborne* **80**

BORN TO FINISH (IRE) 2 b.g. (Mar 16) Dark Angel (IRE) 113 – Music Pearl (IRE) 77 (Oratorio (IRE) 128) [2015 p6d t7.1m⁴ 7g⁶ p7g p7g Nov 13] fair maiden: best effort at 7f. *Jeremy Gask* **75**

BORN TO FLY (IRE) 4 b.f. Kodiac 112 – Cayambe (IRE) (Selkirk (USA) 129) [2015 68: 7m p7g 7v⁴ 7g⁶ t7.1g⁶ t7.1g t7.1g 6m⁶ 7.6d³ 7.6s 7g t7.1f Oct 23] modest handicapper: stays 8.5f: acts on polytrack, tapeta and any turf going: sometimes wears headgear: inconsistent. *Christine Dunnett* **62 a56**

BORN TO REIGN 4 b.g. Sir Percy 129 – Oat Cuisine 92 (Mujahid (USA) 125) [2015 57: t12.2f³ p13.3g* p14g⁶ t12.2g 11.5d 13.1m⁴ 13.1m³ p16g³ p14g⁵ 13.1m Sep 28] modest handicapper: won at Chelmsford in February: stays 2m: acts on polytrack, tapeta and good to firm going: often wears headgear: front runner/races prominently: temperamental. *Michael Bell* **51 §**

BOROUGH BOY (IRE) 5 b.g. Jeremy (USA) 122 – Ostrusa (AUT) (Rustan (HUN)) [2015 71: p6g² 6.1m⁵ 6.1m⁵ p6g p5g* t5.1g* p5g* 5s³ 5.1g 5.1d⁵ 5.1d f5g⁴ f5g² Dec 29] sturdy gelding: fairly useful handicapper: won at Chelmsford (apprentice) and Wolverhampton in July, and Chelmsford (dead-heated) in August: stays 6f: acts on all-weather and soft going: often wears visor. *Derek Shaw* **81**

BORROCO 3 ch.g. Dutch Art 126 – Straitjacket 73 (Refuse To Bend (IRE) 128) [2015 7g 6d May 13] no form. *Michael Dods* **–**

BORSAKOV (IRE) 3 b.g. Dylan Thomas (IRE) 132 – Million Wishes (Darshaan 133) [2015 8g³ 8g 8g⁵ p6.5g* p7f Dec 21] useful performer: won minor event at Deauville in December: stiff task in similar race at Chelmsford next time: stays 1m: acts on polytrack, raced only on good going on turf: often races towards rear. *Mme Pia Brandt, France* **95**

BOSHAM 5 b.g. Shamardal (USA) 129 – Awwal Malika (USA) 73 (Kingmambo (USA) 125) [2015 73: 5g⁶ 5m 5m⁴ 5m⁴ 5g 5d⁶ t6m* 5s⁴ t6f* t5.1g³ Nov 27] fairly useful handicapper: won at Wolverhampton in August and September: stays 6f: acts on polytrack, tapeta and firm going: often wears headgear: usually leads. *Michael Easterby* **64 a86**

BOSSA NOVA 2 b.f. (Jan 21) High Chaparral (IRE) 132 – Marcellinas Angel (Anabaa (USA) 130) [2015 7g Oct 9] 8,000Y: workmanlike filly: second foal: dam unraced half-sister to smart winner up to 12.5f Maroussies Wings out of smart 1¼m/10.5f winner Maroussie: 66/1, well held in maiden at Newmarket. *Nick Littmoden* **–**

BOSSIPOP 2 ch.g. (Apr 23) Assertive 121 – Opopmil (IRE) 68 (Pips Pride 117) [2015 5m⁴ 5g⁴ 5g² 6d³ Jun 25] fair maiden: may prove best at bare 5f. *Tim Easterby* **68**

BOSSTIME (IRE) 5 b.g. Clodovil (IRE) 116 – Smoken Rosa (USA) (Smoke Glacken **70** (USA) 120) [2015 77: p8g⁶ 8s Sep 3] fair handicapper: stays 1m: acts on polytrack: usually wears headgear: often travels strongly. *John Holt*

BOSSY GUEST (IRE) 3 b.c. Medicean 128 – Ros The Boss (IRE) 80 (Danehill (USA) **116** 126) [2015 101: 6m* 8m⁴ 7f³ 8m³ 8g 7g Aug 21] good-topped colt: smart performer: won £150,000 Tattersalls Millions 3-Y-O Sprint at Newmarket by 1¼ lengths from Ballymore Castle) in April: in the frame in 2000 Guineas at Newmarket (3½ lengths fourth to Gleneagles) and Jersey Stakes at Royal Ascot (1¼ lengths third to Dutch Connection) next 2 starts: below form after: stays 1m: acts on firm and soft going: usually races towards rear: temperament under suspicion. *Mick Channon*

BOSTON BLUE 8 b.g. Halling (USA) 133 – City of Gold (IRE) 91 (Sadler's Wells (USA) **– §** 132) [2015 61§: 12d Mar 29] workmanlike gelding: fairly useful at best, no form in 2015: stays 2¼m: acts on polytrack, good to firm and heavy going: tried in headgear prior to 2015: untrustworthy. *Tony Carroll*

BOSTON TWO STEP 3 b.g. Pivotal 124 – Danse Arabe (IRE) (Seeking The Gold **45** (USA)) [2015 –: t8 6g t8.6g t8.6g t6g f7s⁷ p8g³ t8.6m 11.9d⁵ 8s³ Oct 15] poor maiden: left Mark Johnston after second start: stays 1m: acts on polytrack and soft going: usually in blinkers in 2015. *Chris Dwyer*

BOTANIST 8 b.g. Selkirk (USA) 129 – Red Camellia 116 (Polar Falcon (USA) 126) [2015 **60** 67: t9.5f p8f 11.8m 8.3m⁶ 8m 7g* 10g⁵ 8.1d⁶ 10.9g Aug 31] good-topped gelding: modest handicapper: won at Leicester (amateur) in July: stayed 1¼m: acted on good to firm and heavy going: had worn headgear: had worn tongue tie: dead. *Shaun Harris*

BOTANY BAY (IRE) 3 b.g. Galileo (IRE) 134 – Honour Bright (IRE) (Danehill (USA) **96** 126) [2015 –: 10g⁴ 10.5g³ 12m* 12g³ p10.7g 14g⁴ 16d Sep 27] useful performer: won handicap at Down Royal in June: should stay 2m: acts on good to firm going: sometimes slowly away, often races in rear. *Charles O'Brien, Ireland*

BOTH SIDES 2 b.g. (Feb 10) Lawman (FR) 121 – Pearl Dance (USA) 102 (Nureyev **70** (USA) 131) [2015 7.1m⁵ 7g⁶ Aug 2] good-topped gelding: better effort when fifth in maiden at Sandown (5 lengths behind Albernathy) in June. *Andrew Balding*

BOUCLIER (IRE) 5 ch.h. Zamindar (USA) 116 – Bastet (IRE) 110 (Giant's Causeway **77** (USA) 132) [2015 87: 6m 5m⁵ 5g p6g t7.1f p8g Dec 16] fair handicapper: stays 1m: acts on polytrack and good to firm going. *Tony Carroll*

BOUNCE 2 b.f. (Apr 2) Bahamian Bounty 116 – Black Belt Shopper (IRE) 82 (Desert **93 p** Prince (IRE) 130) [2015 6d⁵ p6g* Sep 30] 32,000Y: closely related to 6f winner Exit Strategy (by Cadeaux Genereux) and half-sister to several winners, including useful 7f winner Star Asset (by Dutch Art) and 1½m winner Black Label (by Medicean): dam 2-y-o 6f winner who stayed 1m: better effort when winning maiden at Kempton (by 4½ lengths from Porta Rosa) in September, quickening clear: will go on improving. *Henry Candy*

BOUNCING CZECH 3 b.g. Dandy Man (IRE) 123 – Correlandie (USA) (El Corredor **57** (USA) 123) [2015 –: p6f² t6f⁵ p6f 5g p7m⁴ 7m Jun 13] lengthy gelding: modest maiden: stays 7f: acts on polytrack and tapeta: tried in headgear in 2015: sometimes slowly away, often races towards rear. *Amanda Perrett*

BOUNTY BAH 3 ch.g. Bahamian Bounty 116 – Eternity Ring (Alzao (USA) 117) [2015 **47** –: p8f p7g p6m⁴ 5.1g t6g⁶ 7m 6.1m Jun 30] poor maiden: stays 7f: acts on polytrack: often in cheekpieces in 2015: sometimes slowly away, often races towards rear. *Mark Usher*

BOUNTYBEAMADAM 5 b.m. Bahamian Bounty 116 – Madamoiselle Jones 76 **64** (Emperor Jones (USA) 119) [2015 85: p7f 7m⁵ 7d⁶ 8m 8.1m⁴ 8.1m⁶ 7.1g 8.1v² 7.1s² 8s Sep 3] modest handicapper: stays 8.5f: acts on heavy going: often wears headgear: usually races close up. *George Baker*

BOUNTY TIME 3 b.g. Bahamian Bounty 116 – Pressed For Time (IRE) 64 (Traditionally **62** (USA) 117) [2015 f7g³ t7.1g³ p8g Dec 9] modest maiden: best effort when third in maiden at Wolverhampton in December, not ideally placed. *Michael Appleby*

BOURBONDI 4 b.g. Sakhee (USA) 136 – Lake Diva 70 (Docksider (USA) 124) [2015 **–** p13.3g⁴ Apr 7] sturdy gelding: maiden: no form in 2015: tried in blinkers prior to 2015. *Conrad Allen*

BOURNEMOUTH BELLE 2 b.f. (Mar 14) Canford Cliffs (IRE) 133 – Ellbeedee (IRE) **80** 84 (Dalakhani (IRE) 133) [2015 5f³ 6g* 6m³ Jun 27] €22,000Y, resold 30,000Y: close-coupled filly: first foal: dam, 1¼m winner, half-sister to US Grade 2 1m/9f winner Uncharted Haven: fairly useful performer: won maiden at Goodwood (by 1¾ lengths from Angie's Girl) in May: third in listed race at Newmarket (length behind Katie's Diamond) in June: stays 6f. *Richard Hannon*

BOURNE SYMPHONY (IRE) 2 b.f. (Mar 31) Lilbourne Lad (IRE) 111 – Song To The **46**
Moon (IRE) 88 (Oratorio (IRE) 128) [2015 5g p6g 5g p6g p8f p8f² p10f p8g p8m⁵ Nov 21]
€10,000Y: sturdy filly: first foal: dam, 8.3f-1¼m winner, closely related to very smart
winner up to 6f Charles The Great: poor maiden: stays 1m: acts on polytrack: often in
cheekpieces. *Jim Boyle*

BOUTAN 2 gr.f. (Feb 11) Tobougg (IRE) 125 – High Tan (High Chaparral (IRE) 132) **72**
[2015 7m 7f 7v* 8.3g² 8g Sep 24] first foal: dam unraced half-sister to useful winner up to
7f My Sharona: fair performer: won maiden at Brighton in August: stays 8.5f: acts on
heavy going: often travels strongly. *George Baker*

BOW AND ARROW 3 b.g. Iffraaj 127 – Isobel Archer (Oasis Dream 129) [2015 87p: **102**
p8g² p7m* 7.5m* 7g* 8f 8f 7m³ Aug 1] well-made gelding: useful handicapper: won at
Lingfield, Beverley and Redcar in April: third at Goodwood (1¼ lengths behind Enlace) in
August: stays 1m: acts on polytrack and good to firm going. *Charlie Appleby*

BOWBERRY 4 b.f. Cockney Rebel (IRE) 127 – Blaeberry 69 (Kirkwall 118) [2015 60, **77**
a67: p12f⁵ t12.2f* p13.3m⁴ t12.2g t12.2g* t12.2g³ 11.6m³ 16.2m Jun 30] fair handicapper:
won at Wolverhampton in February and April: stays 1½m: acts on tapeta: usually in
headgear in 2015. *Clive Cox*

BOW CREEK 4 b.c. Shamardal (USA) 129 – Benevota 110 (Most Welcome 131) **121**
[2015 119: 8.1d⁶ 8f⁶ 7.9g² 8d Nov 7] good-topped colt: very smart performer: below form
in Britain first 2 starts in 2015, then left Charlie Appleby: good ½-length second to Turn
Me Loose in Group 2 Crystal Mile at Moonee Valley in October: finished lame on near-
final outing: stays 1m: acts on polytrack, good to firm and good to soft going: tried in
cheekpieces. *John O'Shea, Australia*

BOWDICCA 2 b.f. (Mar 13) Monsieur Bond (IRE) 120 – Bow Bridge 95 (Bertolini (USA) **– p**
125) [2015 5m 5g 5m Jul 20] sixth foal: sister to 2-y-o 5f winner Bowson Fred and half-
sister to winner up to 6f Black Annis Bower (by Proclamation) and 5f/6f winner Towbee
(by Doyen): dam, 2-y-o 5f winner, third in Queen Mary Stakes: well held in maidens: type
to do better in sprint handicaps. *Michael Easterby*

BOWDLER'S MAGIC 8 b.g. Hernando (FR) 127 – Slew The Moon (ARG) (Kitwood **71 §**
(USA) 119) [2015 82: 12.4g³ t16.5g² 16.1d⁵ 14.1m² 14.1m³ 16.5m² 14.1m⁵ 14.4g³ 15.8m⁴
14.4g⁵ 14.1m² 12.8m⁵ Sep 27] big, rather leggy gelding: fair handicapper: effective around
1½m-2m: acts on polytrack, firm and soft going: tried in headgear: tried in tongue tie: hard
to win with, and one to treat with caution. *David Thompson*

BOWSERS BOLD 4 gr.g. Firebreak 125 – Cristal Clear (IRE) 92 (Clodovil (IRE) 116) **64 §**
[2015 68: p12f⁵ p12f² p12f⁴ 11.5d p11g³ Jun 4] sturdy gelding: modest maiden: stays
1½m: acts on polytrack, tapeta and firm going: tried in headgear: races towards rear, tends
to find little: not straightforward (often flatters to deceive), and one to treat with plenty of
caution. *Marcus Tregoning*

BOWSON FRED 3 b.g. Monsieur Bond (IRE) 120 – Bow Bridge 95 (Bertolini (USA) **87**
125) [2015 85: 5g³ 5m² 5m² 5.1f⁵ 5.4m 5g⁴ 5m² 5g⁵ 5s² Oct 19] fairly useful
handicapper: runner-up at Musselburgh in May and Pontefract in October: best form at 5f:
acts on soft and good to firm going: tried in visor in 2015: front runner/races prominently.
Michael Easterby

BOXING SHADOWS 5 b.g. Camacho 118 – Prima Ballerina 73 (Pivotal 124) [2015 79: **65**
p6f p5g² t5.1g³ t5.1g³ 5m 5g 5g⁵ 6g 5g³ 5.5m Jul 21] fair handicapper: best form at 5f: acts **a71**
on polytrack, tapeta, soft and good to firm going: tried in headgear: front runner/races
prominently. *Les Eyre*

BOYCHICK (IRE) 2 b.g. (Apr 26) Holy Roman Emperor (IRE) 125 – Al Saqiya (USA) **–**
68 (Woodman (USA) 126) [2015 7v t8.6g p8f Dec 21] no form. *Ed Walker*

BOYCIE 2 b.c. (Mar 16) Paco Boy (IRE) 129 – Eve 81 (Rainbow Quest (USA) 134) [2015 **77**
5.3g³ p6g⁴ t7.1g² 8.3m⁵ 7d⁵ p6f 6m 7g⁴ p6f² p8g⁵ p7g⁴ Dec 9] compact colt: fair performer:
won maiden at Wolverhampton in July: stays 8.5f: acts on polytrack, tapeta and good to
firm going. *Richard Hannon*

BOY IN THE BAR 4 ch.g. Dutch Art 126 – Lipsia (IRE) (Dubai Destination (USA) 127) **99**
[2015 97: 6m⁵ 6g² 6d⁶ 6s⁴ 7s 6g 7.2g⁶ p8f p6g t6m Dec 12] lengthy, angular gelding: useful
handicapper: second at York (1¼ lengths behind Algar Lad) in May: left Richard Fahey
after fourth start, Ed de Giles after eighth: stays 7f: acts on soft and good to firm going:
sometimes wears blinkers. *Ian Williams*

BRACKA LEGEND (IRE) 3 ch.g. Approve (IRE) 112 – Glyndebourne (USA) (Rahy **–**
(USA) 115) [2015 64: t6f Jan 12] modest maiden: best effort at 6f: dead. *David Barron*

BRACKEN BRAE 3 b.f. Champs Elysees 124 – Azure Mist 79 (Bahamian Bounty 116) **65**
[2015 –: 10m⁴ p10g⁶ p12g⁵ 14.1g⁶ 11.9g⁵ p13.3m² p13.3f² t16.5f⁴ Oct 27] big, unfurnished
filly: fair maiden: may prove best short of 2m: acts on polytrack and tapeta. *Mark H.
Tompkins*

BRADBURY (IRE) 7 ch.g. Redback 116 – Simonaventura (IRE) (Dr Devious (IRE) 127) –
[2015 73: t13.9f⁶ Oct 31] plain gelding: fair at best, no form in 2015: stays 2¼m: acts on
polytrack, soft and good to firm going: usually wears headgear. *Julia Brooke*

BRADLEYSINTOWN (IRE) 2 ch.g. (Feb 16) Thousand Words 113 – Anazah (USA) **58 p**
(Diesis 133) [2015 7m⁶ Jul 19] €21,000Y: half-brother to several winners, including useful
2-y-o 7f/7.5f winner Sorella Bella (by Clodovil) and winner up to 8.4f Thrust Control
(2-y-o 7f winner, by Fath): dam of little account: 12/1, some encouragement when sixth
in maiden at Redcar (8¾ lengths behind Kentuckyconnection) in July: capable of better.
Michael Dods

BRAES OF LOCHALSH 4 b.g. Tiger Hill (IRE) 127 – Gargoyle Girl 75 (Be My Chief **81**
(USA) 122) [2015 74p: 16s 14.6m 16.1d⁴ 14.6m⁶ 16.1m⁵ 13.1g* 13 1d* 17.5g³ 15g³ 16.2d
Oct 16] fairly useful handicapper: won at Ayr (twice) in July: stays 17.5f: acts on good to
firm and good to soft going: often in cheekpieces in 2015: usually races close up. *Jim Goldie*

BRAGGING (USA) 4 b.f. Exchange Rate (USA) 111 – Boasting (USA) (Kris S (USA)) **110**
[2015 113: 9f* 10.4m⁶ 8f⁴ 10.4m Jul 25] well-made, attractive filly: smart performer: won
Dahlia Stakes at Newmarket (by ¾ length from Kleo) in May: failed to progress after:
should stay 1¼m: acts on firm going: front runner/races prominently: sent to USA.
Sir Michael Stoute

BRANDBERG (IRE) 2 b.c. (Feb 15) Cape Cross (IRE) 129 – Eaton Street (Discreet Cat –
(USA) 127) [2015 7.6g⁶ Sep 11] 9/1, tailed off in maiden at Chester. *Mark Johnston*

BRANDO 3 ch.g. Pivotal 124 – Argent du Bois (USA) (Silver Hawk (USA) 123) [2015 88: **97 p**
6m* 5s⁵ 6d* Sep 26] strong gelding: useful performer: won maiden at Hamilton in August
and handicap at Haydock in September: stays 6f: acts on soft and good to firm going: front
runner/races prominently, often travels strongly: should do better. *Kevin Ryan*

BRANDON CASTLE 3 b.g. Dylan Thomas (IRE) 132 – Chelsey Jayne (IRE) 57 **93**
(Galileo (IRE) 134) [2015 76: t9.5g⁴ 11.6g⁵ p11g⁴ 14.4g² p13f⁵ 12.1v³ 12s* 13.4d² 14s²
t16.5f⁴ t12.2m² t12.2f⁶ Dec 11] sturdy gelding: fairly useful handicapper: won at Ffos Las
in September: runner-up 3 of next 4 starts: likely to stay beyond 1¾m: acts on polytrack,
tapeta and heavy going: usually in hood in 2015: usually travels strongly. *Andrew Balding*

BRANDYBEND (IRE) 3 b.f. Galileo (IRE) 134 – Elusive Wave (IRE) 120 (Elusive City **103**
(USA) 117) [2015 p10g² 10d* 10m⁵ 12f 10g³ 10.3v⁴ Nov 7] good-topped filly: first foal:
dam, won Poule d'Essai des Pouliches, also 2-y-o 6f/7f winner: useful performer: won
maiden at Sandown in April: third in listed race at Newmarket (1½ lengths behind Chain
of Daisies) in October: stays 1¼m: acts on good to soft going: tried in hood. *Marco Botti*

BRASSBOUND (USA) 7 b.g. Redoute's Choice (AUS) – In A Bound (AUS) (Ashkalani **93**
(IRE) 128) [2015 75: f12g* t16.5g⁵ p16g* f16g* 16m f16g² t16.5f⁴ f11g² Dec 15] rather
leggy gelding: fairly useful handicapper: won at Southwell in January, Chelmsford in
February and Southwell in April: stays 2m: acts on polytrack and fibresand: front runner/
races prominently. *Michael Appleby*

BRASTED (IRE) 3 ch.g. Footstepsinthesand 120 – Ellen (IRE) (Machiavellian (USA) **75**
123) [2015 10m⁶ 8f⁴ 7m³ 8d p8f³ p8f* p8m² p8f* Dec 17] fair performer: won claimers at
Chelmsford in October and December: stays 1m: acts on polytrack: often in tongue tie:
often races prominently. *Ian Williams*

BRAVE ARCHIBALD (IRE) 2 b.g. (Apr 21) Arch (USA) 127 – Muneefa (USA) 82 **77**
(Storm Cat (USA)) [2015 7m⁵ 7g⁶ 6m p7g* p7g² p8m t7.1f² p8f* Oct 29] useful-looking
gelding: fair performer: won nurseries at Lingfield in August and Chelmsford in October:
stays 1m: acts on polytrack and tapeta. *Paul Cole*

BRAVE DECISION 8 gr.g. With Approval (CAN) – Brave Vanessa (USA) 62 (Private **68**
Account (USA)) [2015 70: p10g* p10g² p10g² p10m p10f p10m⁵ Dec 16] fair performer:
won claimer at Lingfield in January: left Suzy Smith after fourth start: stays 1¼m: acts on
polytrack: tried in headgear prior to 2015: front runner/races prominently. *Brett Johnson*

BRAVE HERO 2 ch.c. (Mar 29) Poet's Voice 126 – Classical Dancer 98 (Dr Fong (USA) **95 p**
128) [2015 p8f* Nov 25] 70,000F, 75,000Y: seventh foal: half-brother to winner up to
1½m Zaaqya (2-y-o 7f-1m winner) and 9.5f winner Topanga Canyon (both by Nayef):
dam, 8.3f winner, half-sister to very smart winner up to 1½m Imperial Dancer: 5/2, won
maiden at Lingfield (by 4½ lengths from Severini) in November, forging clear: open to
improvement. *Saeed bin Suroor*

BRAVE LEADER 3 ch.g. Pivotal 124 – Assabiyya (IRE) 91 (Cape Cross (IRE) 129) **107 p**
[2015 t6g* Jun 4] second foal: half-brother to smart winner up to 11.6f Solidarity (2-y-o
8.5f winner, by Dubawi): dam 1¼m winner out of smart 1¼m winner (stayed 1½m)
Coretta: 6/4, looked good prospect on debut when won maiden at Wolverhampton
(impressively by 7 lengths from Tough Call): one to note if all is well. *Saeed bin Suroor*

BRAVE RICHARD (IRE) 4 b.g. Jeremy (USA) 122 – Certainly Brave 77 (Indian Ridge **53**
123) [2015 f12g⁴ Dec 22] 5/2, fourth in maiden at Southwell (17¾ lengths behind Busy
Street) in December. *J. R. Jenkins*

BRAVE SPARTACUS (IRE) 9 b.g. Spartacus (IRE) 107 – Peaches Polly 76 (Slip **55**
Anchor 136) [2015 12g⁴ Sep 26] 17/2, showed a bit when fourth in maiden at Ripon (24
lengths behind Pecking Order) in September. *Keith Reveley*

BRAVO ECHO 9 b.g. Oasis Dream 129 – Bold Empress (USA) (Diesis 133) [2015 88, **86**
a97: p8m⁴ p7f³ p7g³ p7f p7f² p7g⁴ p7g 7g³ 7m⁵ 7g⁴ 6m² 7g 6m Aug 14] big, strong gelding: **a97**
useful handicapper: stays 1m: acts on polytrack, viscoride, firm and good to soft going:
tried in tongue tie prior to 2015. *Michael Attwater*

BRAVO ZOLO (IRE) 3 b.g. Rip Van Winkle (IRE) 134 – Set Fire (IRE) 90 (Bertolini **107**
(USA) 125) [2015 88p: t7.1g* 7f⁴ 7m⁶ p8g² Dec 28] useful handicapper: won at
Wolverhampton (by 2 lengths from Mulzamm) in April: second at Lingfield (3¼ lengths
behind Mulzamm) in December: left Marco Botti after third start: stays 1m: acts on
polytrack and tapeta. *Jeremy Noseda*

BRAZEN BEAU (AUS) 4 br.c. I Am Invincible (AUS) – Sansadee (AUS) (Snaadee **126**
(USA) 114) [2015 121: 5g² 6g* 6f² 6f Jul 11] strong colt: fifth foal: half-brother to
Australian 6f/1¼m winner Epic Faith (by Dash For Cash): dam Australian 5f/6f winner,
including at 2 yrs: high-class performer: won Newmarket Handicap at Flemington (by 2¼
lengths from Chautauqua) in March: second in Lightning Stakes at Flemington (2¾ lengths
behind Lankan Rupee) in February and Diamond Jubilee Stakes at Royal Ascot (½ length
behind Undrafted) in June: only seventh behind Muhaarar in July Cup at Newmarket final
outing: stayed 6f: acted on firm going: standing at Northwood Park, Victoria, Australia, fee
A$44,000 and to stand at Dalham Hall Stud, Newmarket, fee £10,000. *Chris Waller, Australia*

Godolphin's "Brazen Beau"

BRAZEN SPIRIT 3 gr.g. Zebedee 113 – Never Say Deya 55 (Dansili 127) [2015 82: 6m⁴ **81** 5.7f* 5m⁴ 5f⁴ 5.7g⁵ p6g⁴ Nov 13] close-coupled gelding: fairly useful handicapper: won at Bath (by neck from You're My Cracker) in July: stays 6f: acts on polytrack and firm going: tried in headgear prior to 2015. *Clive Cox*

BRAZOS (IRE) 4 gr.c. Clodovil (IRE) 116 – Shambodia (IRE) (Petardia 113) [2015 114: **107** p7g⁵ 8m 7.6v³ 7d 7g 7d Sep 12] rather leggy colt: useful handicapper: third at Chester (2½ lengths behind Newstead Abbey) in May: stays 7.5f: acts on polytrack, good to firm and heavy going: tried in blinkers in 2015: usually races prominently. *Clive Brittain*

BREAD 3 b.g. Alfred Nobel (IRE) 110 – Sweet Power (Pivotal 124) [2015 58: 8.3m 6.1m **75** t6g* t7.1g⁵ p6g² Oct 20] fair handicapper: won at Wolverhampton in August: stays 6f: acts on polytrack and tapeta: often in cheekpieces in 2015: usually races close up. *Ivan Furtado*

BREAKABLE 4 ch.f. Firebreak 125 – Magic Myth (IRE) 81 (Revoque (IRE) 122) [2015 **90** 83: 7m 8g 7m* 7g³ 7m* 7.6f* 7g 8m² 7s³ 7v² 7v Nov 7] fairly useful handicapper: won at Catterick in May and June, and Chester later in June: second at Musselburgh in September and Newbury in October: stays 1m: acts on any turf going: often wears cheekpieces: usually races prominently. *Tim Easterby*

BREAK FREE 2 b.f. (Jan 22) Oasis Dream 129 – Penny's Gift 108 (Tobougg (IRE) 125) **57** [2015 5.7f⁵ 6g 5.1d⁶ 5.3v⁶ 7g² t5.1f⁶ t6f² p6d⁴ p6g⁴ Dec 7] lengthy, rather unfurnished filly: second foal: half-sister to 2-y-o 5f winner Dittander (by Exceed And Excel): dam winner up to 1m (2-y-o 5f-6.5f winner): modest maiden: left Richard Hannon after fifth start: stays 7f: acts on polytrack, tapeta and firm going. *David O'Meara*

BREAKHEART (IRE) 8 b.g. Sakhee (USA) 136 – Exorcet (FR) 78 (Selkirk (USA) 129) **78** [2015 79: p8g² p10g³ p8f p8f* p10g⁴ 8g⁶ 8m⁴ 8.1s³ p8g³ p8f⁶ p8d p8m³ Dec 31] strong gelding: fair handicapper: won at Kempton in March: stays 10.5f: acts on polytrack, tapeta, soft and good to firm going: often wears headgear: tried in tongue tie prior to 2015: often races towards rear. *Andrew Balding*

BREAN GOLF BIRDIE 3 br.f. Striking Ambition 122 – Straight As A Die 47 (Pyramus **46** (USA) 78) [2015 –: p5g 8m 7s⁶ t6f p10f⁵ Dec 21] poor maiden: stays 1¼m: acts on polytrack: tried in hood in 2015: sometimes slowly away. *Bill Turner*

BREAN SPLASH SUSIE 4 b.f. Tobougg (IRE) 125 – Straight As A Die 47 (Pyramus **59** (USA) 78) [2015 56, a45: 5.1m 6g* 6d 5s* 6s³ 6v⁵ Oct 6] compact filly: modest performer: won sellers at Lingfield in June and August: stays 6f: acts on soft going: tried in headgear prior to 2015: front runner/races prominently. *Bill Turner*

BREATHLESS 3 b.g. Royal Applause 124 – Ada River 102 (Dansili 127) [2015 p7m⁵ **76** p8m⁶ f8g³ Nov 24] fair maiden: best effort when fifth in maiden at Kempton in October: tongue tied. *Andrew Balding*

BRECCBENNACH 5 b.g. Oasis Dream 129 – Next (In The Wings 128) [2015 89: 5g⁵ 5g – Sep 11] good-topped gelding: fairly useful at best, no form in 2015: has won over 7f, best form at shorter: acts on polytrack, best turf form on good to firm going: often wears cheekpieces: often wears tongue tie: front runner/races prominently. *Seamus Durack*

BREDEN (IRE) 5 b.g. Shamardal (USA) 129 – Perfect Touch (USA) 107 (Miswaki **102 p** (USA) 124) [2015 10m² Aug 10] lengthy gelding: useful handicapper at 3 yrs: off 22 months, second at Windsor (½ length behind Bishop's Leap) sole outing in 2015 (hooded): stays 1¼m: acts on polytrack, good to firm and good to soft going: probably open to further improvement if all is well. *John Gosden*

BREEZOLINI 7 b.m. Bertolini (USA) 125 – African Breeze 79 (Atraf 116) [2015 64, a71: **60** 6v² p6m⁵ Nov 25] small mare: modest handicapper: best at 5f/6f: acts on polytrack, good to firm and heavy going: tried in headgear: often races prominently. *Muredach Kelly, Ireland*

BRENDAN BRACKAN (IRE) 6 b.g. Big Bad Bob (IRE) 118 – Abeyr 106 (Unfuwain **110** (USA) 131) [2015 117: 7d 8g³ 9d³ 8.3d⁵ 8d⁵ 9gᵘʳ 8.5g* Oct 17] big, rather leggy gelding: smart performer: won listed race at Cork (by 1¼ lengths from Akira) in October: third in Meld Stakes at Leopardstown (2 lengths behind Carla Bianca) in July: stays 10.5f: acts on polytrack, tapeta, soft and good to firm going. *G. M. Lyons, Ireland*

BRESLIN 2 ch.g. (Mar 9) Atlantic Sport (USA) 115 – Aries (GER) 79 (Big Shuffle (USA) **69** 122) [2015 7f⁶ t7.1g⁶ 7m⁶ 8.3g⁶ 8g t8.6g* t8.6f⁴ 9g Oct 21] close-coupled gelding: fair performer: won nursery at Wolverhampton in September: best effort at 8.5f: acts on tapeta: tried in visor. *Mick Channon*

BRETON BLUES 5 b.g. Street Cry (IRE) 130 – Many Colours 112 (Green Desert (USA) **50** 127) [2015 10g⁴ 10g⁶ Jul 5] better effort when fourth in maiden at Redcar in June. *Fred Watson*

BRETONCELLES (FR) 2 b.f. (Feb 22) Le Havre (IRE) 124 – Carolles (FR) (Medicean **71**
128) [2015 p8g⁴ p8m² Nov 19] €5,000Y, resold 15,000Y: first foal: dam unraced out of
useful 10.5f winner Anna Mona: better effort when second in maiden at Lingfield (short
head behind Danilovna) in November. *Harry Dunlop*

BRETON ROCK (IRE) 5 b.g. Bahamian Bounty 116 – Anna's Rock (IRE) 106 (Rock **118**
of Gibraltar (IRE) 133) [2015 120: 8m 7d 7d³ 8s³ 7d³ 7g² Oct 9] good-topped gelding:
shows plenty of knee action: smart performer: third in Hungerford Stakes at Newbury
(½ length behind Adaay) and Celebration Mile at Goodwood (4 lengths behind Kodi Bear),
both in August, and Park Stakes at Doncaster (5 lengths behind Limato) in September, and
second in Challenge Stakes at Newmarket (neck behind Cable Bay) in October: stays 1m,
best efforts at 7f: races mostly on ground softer than good. *David Simcock*

BREUGHEL (GER) 4 b.g. Dutch Art 126 – Bezzaaf 97 (Machiavellian (USA) 123) –
[2015 7g Apr 26] 25/1, very green when well held in maiden at Wetherby. *Ollie Pears*

BRIAN NOBLE 4 b.g. Royal Applause 124 – Little Greenbird 39 (Ardkinglass 114) –
[2015 –: t8.6g t8.6f Feb 7] smallish gelding: fairly useful at best, no form in 2015: best
effort at 6f. *Richard Fahey*

BRIAN THE LION 4 b.g. Byron 117 – Molly Pitcher (IRE) 59 (Halling (USA) 133) –
[2015 –: p10g f11s Feb 3] maiden: no form in 2015: often races towards rear. *Shaun Harris*

BRIARDALE (IRE) 3 b.g. Arcano (IRE) 122 – Marine City (JPN) 77 (Carnegie (IRE) **79**
129) [2015 9.9m* 10d 10.4s 10v Nov 3] fair performer: won maiden at Beverley in April:
raced only around 1¼m. *James Bethell*

BRIDALGOWN 3 b.f. Arabian Gleam 122 – Bridal White 66 (Robellino (USA) 127) [2015 –
p8g May 28] fifth foal: dam maiden: 50/1, well beaten in maiden at Lingfield. *Lydia Pearce*

BRIDEY'S LETTUCE (IRE) 3 b.g. Iffraaj 127 – Its On The Air (IRE) (King's Theatre **74**
(IRE) 128) [2015 p8g⁵ p7g⁶ p12g⁵ 12g p12g⁴ p12g Sep 22] fair maiden: stays 1½m: acts
on polytrack: tried in hood. *Dean Ivory*

BRIDGE BUILDER 5 b.g. Avonbridge 123 – Amazing Dream (IRE) 98 (Thatching 131) **56**
[2015 –: p7f⁵ Nov 25] modest maiden: stays 7f: acts on polytrack and good to firm going:
usually wears headgear. *Peter Hedger*

BRIDGE OF SIGHS 3 b.g. Avonbridge 123 – Ashantiana 64 (Ashkalani (IRE) 128) **74**
[2015 10m 10m⁶ p8g 7d⁴ 7s⁴ p8f* p8f² p8m* Dec 27] sturdy gelding: fair performer: won
handicaps at Chelmsford in November and December: stays 1m: acts on polytrack and soft
going: often races towards rear. *Martin Smith*

BRIDGE THAT GAP 7 b.h. Avonbridge 123 – Figura 87 (Rudimentary (USA) 118) **55**
[2015 70: p12m⁵ 11.6m Jun 15] good-topped horse: modest handicapper: stays 11f: acts on
polytrack and tapeta: often wears cheekpieces. *Roger Ingram*

BRIDIE FFRENCH 4 b.f. Bahamian Bounty 116 – Wansdyke Lass 59 (Josr Algarhoud **76**
(IRE) 118) [2015 83: p8g⁶ p8m 8m² 8.3m⁴ 8d⁵ 7s³ 7.6f⁵ 8.3m⁶ 8m³ Jul 23] workmanlike
filly: fair handicapper: stays 1m: acts on polytrack and any turf going. *Mick Channon*

BRIGADOON 8 b.g. Compton Place 125 – Briggsmaid 70 (Elegant Air 119) [2015 94: **88**
11.9f⁵ 11.5g Jun 24] leggy gelding: fairly useful handicapper: stays 14.5f: acts on polytrack
and any turf going: often leads. *Michael Appleby*

BRIGAND CHIEF 3 ch.g. Aqlaam 125 – Soundwave (Prince Sabo 123) [2015 –: p7f **64**
p7m p10m⁶ 11.5d² 11.7f³ 12g³ p15.8g 13.1f Sep 13] modest maiden: stays 1½m: acts on
good to soft going. *Luke Dace*

BRIGANTIAN (IRE) 3 b.f. Makfi 130 – Cartimandua 115 (Medicean 128) [2015 p8m –
7m p8g p10f Dec 21] 42,000Y: third foal: dam 6f winner: no form: tried in cheekpieces.
David Simcock

BRIGHT ABBEY 7 ch.g. Halling (USA) 133 – Bright Hope (IRE) 84 (Danehill (USA) –
126) [2015 84: 16s Apr 5] well-made gelding: fairly useful gelding, no form in 2015: stays
16.5f: acts on polytrack, good to firm and good to soft going: tried in visor prior to 2015.
Dianne Sayer

BRIGHT APPLAUSE 7 b.g. Royal Applause 124 – Sadaka (USA) 77 (Kingmambo **67**
(USA) 125) [2015 78: 10s 12g² Apr 22] fair handicapper: stays 12.5f: acts on good to firm
and heavy going: tried in headgear prior to 2015. *Tracy Waggott*

BRIGHT APPROACH (IRE) 4 ch.f. New Approach (IRE) 132 – Zam Zoom (IRE) –
(Dalakhani (IRE) 133) [2015 96p: 9.9m 12d Aug 20] rangy filly: useful at best, no form in
2015: stays 11.5f: acts on good to firm and good to soft going. *John Gosden*

BRIGHT FLASH 3 ch.f. Dutch Art 126 – Quadri (Polish Precedent (USA) 131) [2015 **85**
78p: 8m⁴ 6.9g 8g³ 10.1g⁴ 10g* Oct 8] unfurnished filly: fairly useful handicapper: won at
Ayr (by short head from Clear Spell) in October: stays 1¼m: acts on good to firm going.
David Brown

BRIGHTSIDE 3 b.g. Indesatchel (IRE) 120 – Romantic Destiny 90 (Dubai Destination **53**
(USA) 127) [2015 –: 9.8v⁵ 7g 9m 10s⁶ 8m⁵ 9.8d⁵ 7.5g⁵ 8g⁴ 8.5d f8g Nov 3] modest maiden:
probably stays 1¼m: acts on good to soft going: often races prominently. *Tracy Waggott*

BRIGLIADORO (IRE) 4 ch.g. Excellent Art 125 – Milady's Pride 82 (Machiavellian **92**
(USA) 123) [2015 98: p7g* p7f⁴ p8f⁴ p7f⁴ p7g 7m³ 6m 7m 6m Aug 7] angular gelding:
fairly useful handicapper: won at Kempton (by ½ length from History Book) in January:
third at Newmarket in May: needs further than 6f, and stays 1m: acts on polytrack and
good to firm going: sometimes in visor in 2015: usually races nearer last than first.
Philip McBride

BRILLIANT TOY 3 b.f. Champs Elysees 124 – Beautiful Lady (IRE) 77 (Peintre **68**
Celebre (USA) 137) [2015 10g 8m² 8m⁵ 7d t12.2f t9.5f t9.5f³ Nov 20] 5,000F: second foal:
half-sister to 1m winner Practising (by Rail Link): dam, 1½m winner, half-sister to useful
winner up to 8.6f (stayed 1½m) Putra Sas: fair maiden: left John M. Oxx after second start,
Geoffrey Harker after fifth: stays 9.5f: acts on tapeta and good to firm going: tried in
cheekpieces. *David O'Meara*

BRILLIANT VANGUARD (IRE) 2 b.g. (May 4) Fast Company (IRE) 126 – Alyska **– p**
(IRE) 80 (Owington 123) [2015 6m⁶ Jul 25] €18,000F, 50,000 2-y-o: half-brother to 2
winners, including useful 1½m-1¾m winner Asiya (by Dilshaan): dam, 1m winner, half-
sister to useful 2-y-o 7f/1m winner Athlumney Lady: 5/1, some encouragement when sixth
in maiden at York (7 lengths behind Reputation) in July: will improve. *Kevin Ryan*

BRING ON A SPINNER 2 b.g. (Mar 4) Kheleyf (USA) 116 – Posy Fossil (USA) 70 **50 p**
(Malibu Moon (USA)) [2015 5.3s³ Aug 23] second foal: brother to 2-y-o 7f winner
Danseur Noble: dam 6f winner: 8/1 and blinkered, showed a bit when third in maiden at
Brighton (7¾ lengths behind Florencio) in August: entitled to progress. *Stuart Williams*

BRISE COEUR (FR) 4 b.g. Daramsar (FR) 116 – Rose Bombon (FR) (Cadoudal (FR) **59**
124) [2015 13.9s 15.9g⁶ Apr 12] better effort when seventh in minor event at Compiegne
in March. *Nick Williams*

BRITANNIA BOY 2 b.g. (May 5) Royal Applause 124 – Caledonia Princess 86 (Kyllachy **–**
129) [2015 6m 6g 5g p6g p6f Oct 1] no form: tried in cheekpieces. *Mark Usher*

BRITISH ART 3 b.g. Iffraaj 127 – Bush Cat (USA) 93 (Kingmambo (USA) 125) [2015 **72**
79: p7g⁵ 8.3m p10.7g Oct 23] strong gelding: fair maiden: left Paul Cole after second start:
stays 7f: acts on polytrack and good to firm going. *R. K. Watson, Ireland*

BRITISH EMBASSY (IRE) 3 b.g. Clodovil (IRE) 116 – Embassy Belle (IRE) 82 **73**
(Marju (IRE) 127) [2015 74: 5.7f³ t6m⁶ 7m⁵ t7.1g⁵ t7.1g⁴ p8g⁴ 8s* 8.5g⁵ p8m⁶ Oct 28]
rather unfurnished gelding: fair handicapper: won at Bath in August: stays 1m: acts on
polytrack, tapeta, firm and soft going: tried in hood in 2015: front runner/races prominently.
Eve Johnson Houghton

BRITTLETON 3 b.g. Aqlaam 125 – Fairy Dance (IRE) (Zafonic (USA) 130) [2015 56: **89**
p12f² 12f⁴ p11g⁵ p12g* p13f² 14.1g* 16d* 15.9s³ 16d Oct 30] strong gelding: fairly useful
handicapper: won at Lingfield in July, and Salisbury and Goodwood (by 5 lengths from
Mistamel) in August: stays 2m: acts on polytrack and good to soft going: often in headgear
in 2015. *Harry Dunlop*

BRIYOUNI (FR) 2 b.g. (Mar 15) Siyouni (FR) 122 – Brianza (USA) 61 (Thunder Gulch **72**
(USA) 129) [2015 8g⁴ 7g⁴ 7d⁴ Oct 23] fair maiden: best effort when fourth in maiden at
Doncaster (7¾ lengths behind Royal Artillery) in October, doing too much too soon.
Kevin Ryan

BROADWAY ICON 2 b.c. (Jan 29) Sixties Icon 125 – Funny Girl (IRE) 78 (Darshaan **79**
133) [2015 6m⁵ p7g³ t7.1g³ p7m⁴ Dec 31] fair maiden: will stay at least 1m. *Jeremy Noseda*

BROADWAY MELODY 2 b.f. (Feb 22) Arcano (IRE) 122 – Oriental Melody (IRE) 72 **71**
(Sakhee (USA) 136) [2015 6m 7m³ 8.3g⁵ Sep 8] fourth foal: dam, 2-y-o 7f winner, half-
sister to smart 7f winner Green Coast out of smart winner up to 1m (including at 2 yrs)
Oriental Fashion: fair maiden: best effort when fifth in maiden at Leicester (3¼ lengths
behind Sepal) in September, well positioned. *B. W. Hills*

BROCKFIELD 9 ch.g. Falbrav (IRE) 133 – Irish Light (USA) 91 (Irish River (FR) 131) **64**
[2015 70: 9.9g⁵ 9.9d Sep 22] lengthy, good-topped gelding: modest handicapper: stays
12.5f: acts on polytrack, fibresand, good to firm and heavy going: tried in visor prior to
2015: usually races close up. *Antony Brittain*

BROCKLEBANK (IRE) 6 b.g. Diamond Green (FR) 121 – La Stellina (IRE) 100 **96**
(Marju (IRE) 127) [2015 80, a102: p10m³ p10f⁶ p8f p8m p10g² t9.5m Dec 26] lengthy
gelding: useful handicapper: third at Lingfield (2 lengths behind Maverick Wave) in
January and second at Lingfield (2¾ lengths behind Super Kid) in December: stays 1¼m:
acts on polytrack, tapeta, soft and good to firm going: tried in headgear prior to 2015: tried
in tongue tie to 2015: usually races in rear. *Simon Dow*

BROCKWELL 6 b.g. Singspiel (IRE) 133 – Noble Plum (IRE) 87 (King's Best (USA) **84**
132) [2015 96: p16g⁴ t16.5f⁵ p16g Dec 9] fairly useful handicapper: stays 21f: acts on firm
and soft going: tried in headgear prior to 2015: usually races prominently. *Gary Moore*

BROCTUNE PAPA GIO 8 b.g. Tobougg (IRE) 125 – Fairlie 70 (Halling (USA) 133) **69**
[2015 79: 7m 9g 10.1d⁶ 8g² 8m³ 8g Jun 19] good-topped gelding: fair handicapper: stays
1m: acts on soft and good to firm going: inconsistent. *Keith Reveley*

BROMYARD (IRE) 3 b.g. Dark Angel (IRE) 113 – Zoudie 79 (Ezzoud (IRE) 126) [2015 **93**
8.3g² t8.6f² t8.6f* p10g² Dec 10] €22,000F, 34,000Y: half-brother to several winners,
including smart/unreliable winner up to 6f Croisultan (2-y-o 5f winner) and 1m winner
Diesel Ten (both by Refuse To Bend): dam 1¼m winner who stayed 1½m: fairly useful
performer: won maiden at Wolverhampton in November: stays 1¼m. *David Simcock*

BRON FAIR 6 b.m. Multiplex 114 – Spectacular Hope 55 (Marju (IRE) 127) [2015 t7.1f⁶ **59**
t8.6g t8.6f⁶ t7.1m 9.5f Mar 2] modest maiden: best effort at 7f: acts on tapeta: often races
towards rear. *Edward Bevan*

BRONTE FLYER 2 ch.f. (Jan 21) Nayef (USA) 129 – Shohrah (IRE) 103 (Giant's **78 p**
Causeway (USA) 132) [2015 7.9m* Sep 9] sixth foal: half-sister to 2-y-o 8.5f winner
Shaayeq (by Dubawi): dam, 2-y-o 6f winner, half-sister to 7f winner (stayed 1¼m) Ma-Arif
and 1¼m winner (stayed 1½m) Haadef (both useful): 14/1, won maiden at Carlisle (by ¾
length from Good Run) in September, driven out: will stay 1¼m: will improve. *Ann Duffield*

BRONZE ANGEL (IRE) 6 b.g. Dark Angel (IRE) 113 – Rihana (IRE) 68 (Priolo (USA) **116**
127) [2015 119: 8d 8m 9m 7m⁶ 8f 7f 8m 8d 8d* 9g 8d Oct 17] good attractive gelding:
smart handicapper (dual winner of Cambridgeshire): won at Doncaster (by 1½ lengths
from Man of Harlech) in September: stays 9f: acts on polytrack, soft and good to firm
going: usually wears headgear. *Marcus Tregoning*

BRONZE BEAU 8 ch.g. Compton Place 125 – Bella Cantata (Singspiel (IRE) 133) [2015 **81**
88: 5v⁵ 5d⁵ 5s* 5g 5m² 5g⁵ 5m² 5s² 5m⁶ 5s* 5m⁵ 5d 5g 5s 5g Oct 3] lengthy gelding: fairly
useful handicapper: won at Hamilton in May and August (by 2 lengths from Economic
Crisis): best form at 5f: acts on firm and soft going: tried in cheekpieces: usually wears
tongue tie: usually leads. *Kristin Stubbs*

BRONZE MAQUETTE (IRE) 3 b.f. Dark Angel (IRE) 113 – Precious Citizen (USA) **91**
57 (Proud Citizen (USA) 122) [2015 98: 8g⁵ 8g* 6gᵘʳ 10m 8f 7m 7g² 8g⁵ 9.2g* 9.9g*
Dec 29] smallish, workmanlike filly: fairly useful performer: successful at Doha in minor
event in February, Oaks Trial in November and Qatar Oaks (beat Akeed Misk 2½ lengths)
in December: little impact in 3 races in Britain in the summer: trained by Jassim Al Ghazali
for fifth/sixth starts, then returned to former trainer: stays 1¼m: acts on firm and good to
soft going. *Mohammed Hussain, Qatar*

BROOCH (USA) 4 b.f. Empire Maker (USA) 129 – Daring Diva (Dansili 127) [2015 **112**
113p: 8g* 10m 9d² 9d³ 8g Sep 12] smart performer: won Lanwades Stud Stakes at the
Curragh (by 2¼ lengths from Ramone) in May: second in Kilboy Estate Stakes at the
Curragh (2 lengths behind Wedding Vow) in July and third in Dance Design Stakes at the
Curragh (4¼ lengths behind Bocca Baciata) in August: should stay 1¼m: acts on good to
firm going: blinkered last 2 starts: races prominently: sent to USA. *D. K. Weld, Ireland*

BROOKE'S BOUNTY 5 ch.g. Bahamian Bounty 116 – Choysia 92 (Pivotal 124) [2015 **59**
73: p7g 8e² 8m 8.3d 8.3g 8.3s⁶ 8.9g² 8.9m 12.4g 10d Oct 26] modest handicapper: left
Richard Fahey after first start: stays 9f: acts on good to firm and heavy going: tried in
cheekpieces in 2015: usually races close up: inconsistent. *Ian Semple*

BROROCCO 2 b.g. (Mar 31) Shirocco (GER) 129 – Lady Brora 83 (Dashing Blade 117) **80 p**
[2015 8.1g⁶ 7.1m 8.3v⁴ Oct 7] good-bodied gelding: third foal: half-brother to smart
winner up to 1m Elm Park (2-y-o 7f/1m winner, by Phoenix Reach): dam 1m winner who
stayed 1¼m: fairly useful form: best effort when ninth in Solario Stakes at Sandown
(7¾ lengths behind First Selection) in August, not knocked about: has been gelded:
remains with potential. *Andrew Balding*

BROSNAN (IRE) 3 ch.f. Champs Elysees 124 – Clytha 57 (Mark of Esteem (IRE) 137) **79**
[2015 61: 10.2s 7.5g⁶ 8g² 8g 8g p8g³ p10.7g* p10.7g² p12g⁶ p10.7g² Dec 18] fair
handicapper: won at Dundalk in November: left Noel Quinlan after first start, Giles
Bravery after fourth: stays 10.5f: acts on polytrack: often wears headgear: often races
towards rear. *J. F. Levins, Ireland*

BROTHERLY COMPANY (IRE) 3 b.g. Fast Company (IRE) 126 – Good Lady (IRE) **85**
(Barathea (IRE) 127) [2015 78p: p8g³ 10g* 10f⁴ 11.9g³ 12.5m⁶ 10.9g⁴ Oct 18] fairly useful
performer: won maiden at Redcar in April: third in handicap at Haydock in May: left
Richard Fahey after fifth start: stays 12.5f: acts on firm going: usually leads: joined
Harry Fry. *A. Wohler, Germany*

BROTHER TIGER 6 b.g. Singspiel (IRE) 133 – Three Secrets (IRE) 92 (Danehill (USA) **95**
126) [2015 86: p5g⁴ p5f* p5g* p6f 6m 5m p5m⁴ p5f² p5g² Dec 2] big, strong gelding:
useful handicapper: won at Lingfield in February and March: second at Chelmsford (length
behind Medicean Man) in November and second at Lingfield (1¼ lengths behind Lightscameraction) in December: stays 6f: acts on polytrack, soft and good to firm going. *David
C. Griffiths*

BROUGHTONS BANDIT 8 b.g. Kyllachy 129 – Broughton Bounty 68 (Bahamian **64**
Bounty 116) [2015 p15.8f² 15g Sep 29] angular gelding: modest handicapper: stays 16.5f:
acts on polytrack: in cheekpieces in 2015. *Gordon Elliott, Ireland*

BROUGHTONS BERRY (IRE) 4 b.f. Bushranger (IRE) 119 – Larrocha (IRE) 116 **61**
(Sadler's Wells (USA) 132) [2015 f11d² p10g⁵ t12.2m p12f t12.2g f12d 10m 11.6d⁶
t12.2f³ t12.2f³ t12.2m⁴ p12g t12.2f³ Dec 21] €23,000Y, 20,000 2-y-o: half-sister to several
winners, including very smart 8.4f-1½m winner Razkalla (by Caerleon) and useful 1m-11f
winner Western Adventure (by Gone West): dam 1¼m-1½m winner: modest maiden: stays
1½m: acts on all-weather: sometimes in headgear. *Willie Musson*

BROUGHTONS FANCY 2 b.f. (Feb 12) Pastoral Pursuits 127 – Lifetime Romance **75**
(IRE) 92 (Mozart (IRE) 131) [2015 7m² 7.4v³ 7s³ 7.1m³ 7d² 6g² t6f⁵ t7.1g² t7.1m⁴ t7.1f⁴
Dec 22] fifth foal: half-sister to winner up to 7f Amoure Medici (by Medicean) and 9f-13f
winner Madjani (by Nayef): dam, 2-y-o 7f winner, half-sister to useful 7f-1½m winner
Hanoverian Baron out of useful 1½m winner Josh's Pearl: fair maiden: left Willie Musson
after first start: stays 7f: acts on tapeta, soft and good to firm going: often races prominently.
David Evans

BROUGHTONS HARMONY 3 ch.f. Nayef (USA) 129 – Park Melody (IRE) 64 **70**
(Refuse To Bend (IRE) 128) [2015 p10f² p10g² p10g⁵ Dec 30] 32,000Y: second foal: half-
sister to 6f winner Lyra (by Myboycharlie): dam, maiden (stayed 1¼m), half-sister to
useful winner up to 7f Rum Charger out of useful 1m-1¼m winner Park Charger: fair
maiden: best effort when second in maiden at Chelmsford in October, not ideally placed.
Willie Musson

BROUGHTONS MYSTERY 2 b.f. (Mar 3) Sakhee's Secret 128 – Enchanted Princess **57**
82 (Royal Applause 124) [2015 6m 6.1g p6f 6m p7f Nov 12] sturdy filly: half-sister to
several winners, including smart winner up to 7f Morache Music (2-y-o 6f winner, by
Sleeping Indian) and useful 6f/7f winner Never Lose (by Diktat): dam 1m/8.3f winner:
modest maiden: best effort at 6f: acts on polytrack. *Willie Musson*

BROUGHTONS VISION 2 b.g. (Apr 30) Kheleyf (USA) 116 – Read Federica 90 **72 p**
(Fusaichi Pegasus (USA) 130) [2015 p6g³ Sep 22] fifth foal: half-brother to 3 winners,
including useful 2-y-o 1m winner (stays 1½m) Won Diamond (by Mount Nelson) and
winner up to 11f Jazri (2-y-o 1m winner, by Myboycharlie): dam, 2-y-o 7f winner, half-
sister to 1m/9f winner Grafitti and 7.5f winner Reine Magique, both useful: 66/1, some
encouragement when third in maiden at Kempton (1½ lengths behind Nassuvian Pearl) in
September: entitled to progress. *Willie Musson*

BROWN PANTHER 7 b.h. Shirocco (GER) 129 – Treble Heights (IRE) 107 **121**
(Unfuwain (USA) 131) [2015 123: 15.9g* 14m² 14dᵖᵘ Sep 13]

The very smart stayer Brown Panther was probably best known among
casual racegoers for his connection with former England footballer Michael Owen,
who owned him with Betfair co-founder Andrew Black. Owen bred Brown Panther
whose performances on the track in a lengthy career made him very popular with the
racing public in his own right. He won eleven of his twenty-eight starts and earned
over £1m, including £405,405, the biggest single prize that winning for his owners
have won, for justifying favouritism in the Group 2 Dubai Gold Cup at Meydan in
March. Brown Panther's biggest success in Europe came in the Irish St Leger in

Dubai Gold Cup Sponsored by Al Tayer Motors, Meydan—
a final career success for Brown Panther who is clear from early in the straight;
Star Empire (noseband) gets the better of Ahzeemah for second

2014—he also won the Ormonde and Henry II Stakes that year—but he was fatally injured trying to repeat his Irish St Leger success in the latest renewal, suffering a compound fracture of a hind leg which meant he could not be saved.

Brown Panther's 2014 campaign ended rather ignominiously when he bolted to post before being withdrawn from the Canadian International and then beat just one home in the Breeders' Cup Turf, albeit over a trip short of his best. However, he was back on song after five months off in the fifteen-runner Dubai Gold Cup Sponsored by Al Tayer Motors over two miles. Although overshadowed by bigger events on the card—primarily the Dubai World Cup—the Dubai Gold Cup would have been considered a competitive staying contest by Group 2 standards in Europe, and Brown Panther did well to have things sewn up soon after going clear turning for home. Brown Panther had three and a quarter lengths to spare over Star Empire, the only one of the principals to come from off the pace, and Ahzeemah. Credit was also due to trainer Tom Dascombe who had Brown Panther spot on for his return against rivals who'd had preparatory runs—and indeed had kept Brown Panther at the top of his game for five seasons—and to Brown Panther's jockey Richard Kingscote who had not long returned from multiple injuries sustained in a fall the previous November. Kingscote rode Brown Panther on all but four of his career outings and was very instrumental in his Irish St Leger success, when, after riding Brown Panther close to the pacemaker (well clear of the rest), he won the race with a decisive move turning into the straight. Brown Panther went on to repeat his Dubai Gold Cup form when half a length second of six to Snow Sky in the Yorkshire Cup at York in May, conceding at least 4 lb all round (and 5 lb to Snow Sky). Brown Panther was keen to begin with and was ridden with restraint and he was just unable to peg back Snow Sky. Brown Panther was ruled out of a second crack at the Gold Cup in June after injuring a leg in the days before the race and had only one more run in the Irish St Leger in September when he was suddenly pulled up at around halfway.

	Shirocco (GER) (b 2001)	Monsun (br 1990)	Konigsstuhl
Brown Panther (b.h. 2008)			Mosella
		So Sedulous (b 1991)	The Minstrel
			Sedulous
	Treble Heights (IRE) (b 1999)	Unfuwain (b 1985)	Northern Dancer
			Height of Fashion
		Height of Passion (b 1982)	Shirley Heights
			Maladie d'Amour

Brown Panther's demise came fourteen months after his dam Treble Heights had to be put down. Michael Owen bought Treble Heights for 135,000 guineas as a yearling and she carried his dark blue and grey colours (as did Brown Panther at two and three, including when winning the King George V Stakes Handicap at Royal Ascot) to success twice from seven starts, including in listed company over twelve furlongs. Brown Panther's full brother Cocker, Treble Heights' final foal, showed modest form at up to fourteen furlongs in the latest season before being sold for £6,500. The good-topped Brown Panther was a very smart performer who was best at thirteen furlongs to an extended two miles (he won the Goodwood Cup in 2013 but seemed stretched by the trip when third in the 2014 Gold Cup). He usually raced prominently and acted on fibresand, heavy and good to firm going. *Tom Dascombe*

BROWN PETE (IRE) 7 b.g. Aussie Rules (USA) 123 – Banba (IRE) 87 (Docksider **55** (USA) 124) [2015 55: p11f6 p10g4 t12.2g2 t12.2g t12.2g3 12.1m2 11.5d4 p16g4 Jun 18] rangy gelding: modest handicapper: stays 1½m: acts on polytrack, tapeta, soft and good to firm going: sometimes wears headgear: tried in tongue tie: sometimes slowly away. *Heather Dalton*

BROWNSEA BRINK 5 b.g. Cadeaux Genereux 131 – Valiantly 103 (Anabaa (USA) 130) **95** [2015 105: 8m 7m4 May 2] workmanlike gelding: useful handicapper: fourth at Goodwood in May: stays 1m: acts on polytrack and soft going: sold £5,000. *Richard Hannon*

BROXBOURNE (IRE) 6 b.m. Refuse To Bend (IRE) 128 – Rafting (IRE) 87 (Darshaan **96** 133) [2015 20f6 Jun 16] strong, workmanlike mare: useful handicapper: sixth in Ascot Stakes at Royal Ascot sole start on Flat in 2015: stays 21f: acts on polytrack and firm going: useful hurdler. *Nicky Henderson*

BRUISED ORANGE (USA) 2 ch.f. (Mar 23) City Zip (USA) 112 – Ain't She Awesome **90** (USA) (Awesome Again (CAN) 133) [2015 a4.5m* 5f 5.5g2 a6f5 Nov 1] $33,000Y, resold $80,000Y: good-topped filly: half-sister to several winners, including 1m/8.5f winner Literary Lady (by Birdstone) and 5.5f/6f winner Balotelli (by Roman Ruler): dam once-raced half-sister to very smart 6f-9f winner Whiskey Wisdom: fairly useful performer: won maiden at Keeneland in April: good neck second of 4 behind Too Discreet in non-graded stakes at Saratoga in August: well held in Queen Mary Stakes at Royal Ascot on second outing: stays 5.5f: blinkered first 3 starts. *Wesley A. Ward, USA*

BRUNELLO 7 b.g. Leporello (IRE) 118 – Lydia Maria 70 (Dancing Brave (USA) 140) **–** [2015 15.8s Oct 27] fair at best, no form in 2015: stays 1¾m: acts on all-weather and good to firm going: often wears headgear. *Michael Smith*

BRUNTINGTHORPE (IRE) 2 b.g. (Feb 28) Thousand Words 113 – Cooke's Bar (IRE) **–** (Invincible Spirit (IRE) 121) [2015 p6g 6.1v5 Oct 7] no form: in hood. *Dean Ivory*

BRUTUS (FR) 3 b.g. Desert Style (IRE) 121 – Belle Alicia (FR) 111 (Smadoun (FR)) **82 §** [2015 89: 8.1m6 8.1f3 10v2 10.2g5 8.3d3 t9.5f4 Oct 20] useful-looking gelding: fairly useful maiden: second in handicap at Sandown in September: stays 1¼m: acts on polytrack and heavy going: tried in blinkers in 2015: temperamental: sold 28,000 gns, sent to Saudi Arabia. *Richard Hannon*

BRYANT PARK (USA) 6 ch.g. Street Cry (IRE) 130 – Cala (FR) 98 (Desert Prince **–** (IRE) 130) [2015 50: t12.2f Mar 13] maiden: no form in 2015: stays 8.5f: acts on polytrack and tapeta: tried in tongue tie. *Noel Quinlan*

BRYCEWISE 4 b.g. Firebreak 125 – Jan Mayen 60 (Halling (USA) 133) [2015 –p: 8s **–** p11g t8.6g Jun 26] maiden: no form in 2015: in hood in 2015: sometimes slowly away. *Michael Wigham*

BRYGHT BOY 2 b.g. (Mar 21) Paco Boy (IRE) 129 – Bright Moll 88 (Mind Games 121) **– p** [2015 6d p8g Dec 7] half-brother to several winners, including smart 6f (including at 2 yrs) winner Aeolus (by Araafa) and useful 6f/7f winner Hezmah (by Oasis Dream): dam 2-y-o 5f/6f winner: green in maidens: should do better. *Ed Walker*

BUBBLY BAILEY 5 b.g. Byron 117 – Night Gypsy 74 (Mind Games 121) [2015 60, a68: **70** p5m5 p5f4 p5f4 p5g6 6m p5g4 p5g* p5g2 p6f5 p6f4 p5f* p5f6 p6m Nov 17] smallish gelding: fair handicapper: won at Lingfield in July and September: stays 6f: acts on polytrack, firm and soft going: usually wears headgear: usually races prominently. *J. R. Jenkins*

BUBBLY BELLINI (IRE) 8 b.g. Mull of Kintyre (USA) 114 – Gwapa (IRE) 84 **110** (Imperial Frontier (USA) 112) [2015 105: p6g6 p7m p5g3 6v* 7g2 6s* 5d3 5g* 5m 7.5m* **a90 +** 6.3m 5.8m5 6d 7s2 5d5 7.5g2 6s 6d Oct 17] smart performer: won handicaps at the Curragh in March and Naas (by 2¾ lengths from In Salutem) in April, and minor events at Cork (by ½ length from Russian Soul) in May and Tipperary (by 1½ lengths from Intensical) in July: effective from 5f to 7.5f: acts on polytrack, fibresand, good to firm and heavy going: usually wears headgear. *Adrian McGuinness, Ireland*

BUCCANEERS VAULT (IRE) 3 gr.g. Aussie Rules (USA) 123 – Heaven's Vault (IRE) **89** 103 (Hernando (FR) 127) [2015 84: 6s 7g5 7m4 6m5 6.1g3 6g4 6m* Sep 8] fairly useful handicapper: won at Redcar (by neck from Edgar Balthazar) in September: stays 7f: acts on firm and soft going: often in blinkers in 2015. *Michael Dods*

BUCKENHILL 5 gr.g. Intikhab (USA) 135 – Trauquebise (FR) (Kaldounevees (FR) 118) **78**
[2015 p11f* 15.4g 13.4d³ Jun 16] won maiden at Kempton in January: left David Simcock
after: stays 13.4f. *Mlle Louisa Carberry, France*

BUCKLAND BEAU 4 b.g. Rock of Gibraltar (IRE) 133 – Heavenly Whisper (IRE) 105 **83**
(Halling (USA) 133) [2015 67, a77: p7f² 6m⁶ p7g³ 7m² 6g 7.5m³ 7g³ t7.1g p8g⁵ p10g⁵
p10g² t9.5g⁰ t9.5f* Dec 21] useful-looking gelding: fairly useful handicapper: won at
Wolverhampton (by ¾ length from Hickster) in December: stays 1¼m: acts on polytrack,
tapeta and good to firm going: sometimes in visor in 2015: tried in tongue tie in 2015: often
races towards rear. *Charlie Fellowes*

BUCKLAND (IRE) 7 b.g. Oratorio (IRE) 128 – Dollar Bird (IRE) 103 (Kris 135) [2015 **91**
95: p16f² 16m⁴ 20f 14f⁴ 16m² 16m Oct 2] good-topped gelding: fairly useful handicapper:
runner-up at Kempton in April and Ascot in August: stayed 2m: acted on polytrack and firm
going: tried in headgear prior to 2015: tried in tongue tie: front runner/raced prominently:
retired. *Charlie Fellowes*

BUCKLEBERRY 3 ch.g. Sakhee's Secret 128 – Smart Hostess 101 (Most Welcome 131) **75**
[2015 73: p8m* 8.1m¹ 9.9g¹ 8g⁴ 8.3g⁴ Jul 27] fair handicapper: won at Kempton in April:
stays 1¼m: acts on polytrack and good to firm going: usually races prominently. *Jonathan
Portman*

BUCKSTAY (IRE) 5 b.g. Lawman (FR) 121 – Stella Del Mattino (USA) (Golden Gear **115**
(USA) 116) [2015 103: 8d² 8m 7m⁴ 7m³ 7m² 7m* 6g⁵ 7m* 8d Oct 17] lengthy gelding:
smart handicapper: won at Newmarket (by neck from Flash Fire) in August and Ascot
(Challenge Cup, by short head from Gabriel's Lad) in October: staying-on fifth in Ayr Gold
Cup (beaten length by Don't Touch) in between: stays 1¼m, best form at shorter: acts on
polytrack, soft and good to firm going: sometimes in cheekpieces in 2015: usually responds
generously to pressure: consistent. *Peter Chapple-Hyam*

BUDDING ROSE (USA) 3 ch.f. New Approach (IRE) 132 – White Rose (GER) 105 **– p**
(Platini (GER) 126) [2015 p7f Jan 21] closely related to useful 1¼m winner Promesse de
L'Aube (by Galileo) and half-sister to 3 winners, including smart winner up to 1¼m (stays
1½m) Elite Army (by Authorized) and useful 2-y-o 7f winner (stays 11.4f) Champagne-
lifestyle (by Montjeu): dam 2-y-o 7f winner who stayed 11f: 4/1, some encouragement
when seventh in maiden at Kempton (9½ lengths behind Waldnah) in January: bred to be
suited by 1m+: open to improvement. *Charlie Appleby*

BUFFALO SOLDIER (IRE) 2 b.c. (Mar 4) Big Bad Bob (IRE) 118 – Fusili (IRE) 100 **73**
(Silvano (GER) 126) [2015 5.1g⁶ t7.1g² p8g⁴ 7v⁶ t7.1f² Oct 20] fair maiden: should stay
1m: acts on tapeta. *Dave Morris*

BUKLE (IRE) 2 b.c. (Feb 26) Approve (IRE) 112 – Rumline 55 (Royal Applause 124) [2015 **70**
5f⁵ 5m⁴ 5.1s³ 6d⁵ 7m⁴ 7s* 8s⁴ Sep 13] close-coupled colt: fair performer: won nursery
at Salisbury in September: should stay 1m: acts on soft going: often races prominently.
Rod Millman

BULAS BELLE 5 b.m. Rob Roy (USA) 122 – Bula Rose (IRE) 57 (Alphabatim (USA) **80**
126) [2015 12.4g 13.8d² 12g⁶ 14.1s² 15.8s* Oct 27] fairly useful handicapper: won at
Catterick (by head from Sinakar) in October: stays 2m: acts on soft going. *Edwin Tuer*

BULGE BRACKET 2 b.g. (Feb 17) Great Journey (JPN) – Baldovina 73 (Tale of The **61**
Cat (USA) 113) [2015 6m 7f³ 7.1g p8g⁴ Aug 17] strong gelding: modest maiden: best
effort at 7f. *Tom Dascombe*

BUMPTIOUS 2 b.f. (Mar 16) Acclamation 118 – Cast In Gold (USA) 92 (Elusive Quality **78**
(USA)) [2015 8.3g⁵ 7d³ Oct 31] 62,000Y: fourth foal: half-sister to 3 winners, including
useful winner up to 7f Wedding Ring (by Oasis Dream) and 1m winner Mustaqqil
(by Invincible Spirit): dam, 2-y-o 7f winner, half-sister to St Leger winner Rule of Law:
better effort when fifth in maiden at Windsor (2½ lengths behind So Mi Dar) in October,
not knocked about: will be suited by a return to 1m. *Ismail Mohammed*

BUNCE (IRE) 7 b.g. Good Reward (USA) 120 – Bold Desire 58 (Cadeaux Genereux 131) **77**
[2015 80: 5v 5g² 5g* 5s² 5m 5m 5g⁴ 5g⁵ 5m 5d⁵ 5g 5m³ 5g 6g Sep 29] compact gelding:
fair handicapper: won at Musselburgh in May: has form at 7f, races over shorter nowadays:
acts on good to firm and heavy going: tried in headgear prior to 2015: tried in tongue tie
prior to 2015. *Linda Perratt*

BUNKER HILL LASS 3 ch.f. Kheleyf (USA) 116 – Incony 54 (Daggers Drawn (USA) **63**
114) [2015 8.3m 10.3m t12.2g⁴ 8.3m 10.2g t8.6m 8.5g³ 8s* p10f f7m⁵ f8g⁵ Dec 22] second **a56**
foal: dam maiden (stayed 7f): modest handicapper: won at Brighton in October: stays 1m:
acts on soft and good to firm going: sometimes in cheekpieces. *Michael Appleby*

BUONAROTTI BOY (IRE) 3 b.g. Galileo (IRE) 134 – Funsie (FR) (Saumarez 132)   **62**
[2015 10m t12.2m Oct 2] better effort when seventh in maiden at Wolverhampton in
October. *Jeremy Noseda*

BUONARROTI (IRE) 4 b.g. Galileo (IRE) 134 – Beauty Is Truth (IRE) 114 (Pivotal   **93**
124) [2015 101: 12m 16.2g t9.5g⁶ 10.3g⁴ 12d 11.9d² 10g 10.2d⁶ 12d⁵ 12v² Nov 7] strong,
well-made gelding: fairly useful handicapper: second at Haydock in September and
Doncaster (November Handicap, beaten 4½ lengths by Litigant) in November: stays 1½m:
acts on tapeta and heavy going. *Declan Carroll*

BURANO (IRE) 6 ch.g. Dalakhani (IRE) 133 – Kalimanta (IRE) 89 (Lake Coniston (IRE)   **93 §**
131) [2015 108§: p8m 8d p10g 10s* 10.1g⁵ 10f⁴ 9.9g 9s⁴ 10s 10.1d⁶ 10g Oct 19] smallish,
sturdy gelding: fairly useful handicapper: won at Lingfield (by ½ length from Nancy From
Nairobi) in May: seemingly stays 1½m: acts on polytrack and any turf going: tried in
headgear prior to 2015: usually races prominently: ungenuine. *Amanda Perrett*

BURATINO (IRE) 2 ch.c. (Mar 1) Exceed And Excel (AUS) 126 – Bergamask (USA)   **118**
(Kingmambo (USA) 125) [2015 p5g* 5f³ 6m* 5m² 6m* 6f* 6g³ 6g² Sep 26]
    Mark Johnston had three two-year-old runners on Saturday March 28th, the
day the first juvenile races were staged in Britain. All three won, Rah Rah landing
a maiden at Kempton, Ravenhoe winning the Brocklesby Stakes at Doncaster and
Buratino a maiden at Chelmsford. Johnston trained significantly more juveniles than
usual—a change in the make-up of the stable discussed in the essay on Lumiere—
and many of the better ones were out early, including Buratino and the subsequent
listed winners Sixth Sense, Delizia and Riflescope. Buratino had had five races—and
won three of them—by the time he lined up for the Coventry Stakes at Royal Ascot,
that fact alone particularly interesting in the light of the changes to the programme
of two-year-old races which comes into effect in 2016. In order to 'address a long-
held concern that two-year-olds who win in the early part of the season, prior to the
introduction of nursery handicaps, have very few opportunities to assist them along
the path of development after an initial early season success,' the BHA announced in
October that around ninety per cent of maidens (roughly one hundred and seventy-
five races) from March to July will be converted into novice events. The changes
will be on a trial basis, and the penalty structure for the races is still to be finalised at
the time of writing, with trainers being consulted for their views. Any impact on the
development of two-year-olds will have to be monitored over time, but the change
has the support of a number of well-respected trainers—William Haggas thinks
'they should include three-year-old races in the system as well'. One of the other
aims is to increase field sizes which may help to boost betting turnover on races that
haven't always been among the most attractive to punters. Buratino would certainly
have been able to defy a penalty in one of the new races given that he proved himself
smart and consistent in an eight-race campaign, winning four of his races and being
placed in the remainder, picking up over £100,000 in prize money along the way.

*Coventry Stakes, Royal Ascot—Buratino is already having his sixth outing of the season
as he lands this prestigious event from Air Force Blue and Eltezam (third left)*

His two defeats before the Coventry came behind the Richard Hannon-trained pair Log Out Island in a minor conditions event at Ascot and King of Rooks in the National Stakes at Sandown.

Buratino gained his second win in a four-runner Newmarket minor event (from Gifted Master) over six furlongs, and his two placed efforts on his first four outings were over five, but he showed himself something out of the ordinary when returned to six furlongs in the nine-runner Investec Woodcote Stakes at Epsom on Derby Day. Buratino carried the second colours of his owner Sheikh Hamdan bin Mohammed Al Maktoum (stablemate Aleko carried the first), but was sent off the 2/1 favourite and justified the market support easily, despite being slowly into his stride (as he had been for his two defeats). Buratino travelled well held up, was produced to lead after two furlongs out and stayed on strongly inside the final furlong to win by six lengths from Nelspruit, showing himself to be one of the best early-season two-year-olds seen in Britain.

Mark Johnston ran twelve two-year-olds at Royal Ascot, and Buratino—transferred to Godolphin ownership in the meantime—was joined by 33/1-shots Beaverbrook and Ode To Evening in the seventeen-runner Coventry Stakes, which came just ten days after the Woodcote. The 9/4 favourite Round Two, winner of the Marble Hill Stakes at the Curragh, wore the Godolphin first colours (with Buratino in a distinguishing white cap). Another Irish-trained challenger, the Curragh maiden winner Air Force Blue, representing Ballydoyle, was 7/2 second favourite ahead of Buratino at 6/1, with the Leicester maiden winner War Department at 7/1 and the rest available at 12/1 or longer. Buratino ran out a decisive winner, beating Air Force Blue by two lengths, his performance at least up to the recent standards for the Coventry which nearly always produces very smart horses (subsequent classic winners Canford Cliffs, Power and Dawn Approach are recent winners). Buratino raced in touch and travelled strongly, tracking Beaverbrook (who finished fourth) and then Ode To Evening (fifth) before being produced to lead entering the final furlong and quickening clear. Buratino's performance was backed up by a timefigure of 0.57 fast, equivalent to a timerating of 114 and bettered at the Royal meeting only by the American filly Acapulco in the Queen Mary. Buratino was clearly thriving, his busy schedule in contrast to that of most Coventry winners, only four of whom in the previous thirty years had raced more than twice before Royal Ascot, those being Mac's Imp (1990) who ran four times before Royal Ascot and Sri Pekan (1994), Red Clubs (2005) and Dawn Approach (2012) who all ran three times.

Buratino's two subsequent starts—both in Group 1s—were noticeably more spaced out. He finished two and a half lengths third to Air Force Blue in the Phoenix Stakes at the Curragh in early-August and then a length second to Shalaa in the Middle Park Stakes at Newmarket in late-September. Buratino ran respectably in the Phoenix, but he didn't produce the finishing burst that had been a feature of his Coventry success. He was back in tip-top form in the Middle Park when he turned in his best effort of the season, chasing Shalaa gamely and finishing clear of the rest, in the process suggesting he will stay at least seven furlongs and may well get a mile.

		Danehill (b 1986)	Danzig
	Exceed And Excel (AUS)		Razyana
	(b 2000)	Patrona (ch 1994)	Lomond
Buratino (IRE)			Gladiolus
(ch.c. 2013)		Kingmambo (b 1990)	Mr Prospector
	Bergamask (USA)		Miesque
	(ch 2005)	Adonesque (b 1998)	Sadler's Wells
			Mira Adonde

A Darley home bred, Buratino is by the top Australian sprinter Exceed And Excel and is the fourth foal out of Bergamask who won three races in France over a mile from ten starts and was third in a listed race at Deauville over an extended nine furlongs for Sheikh Mohammed. Bergamask is a half-sister to the fairly useful two-year-old six-furlong winner Alderney, who showed enough during a brief campaign at three, before being retired to stud, to suggest that she trained on, and to the useful seven- to ten-furlong winner Busker for whom the latest season was his sixth on the track (he has been trained in Dubai since 2011). Bergamask is a daughter of the useful Irish nine/ten-furlong (listed) winner Adonesque, who is herself a half-

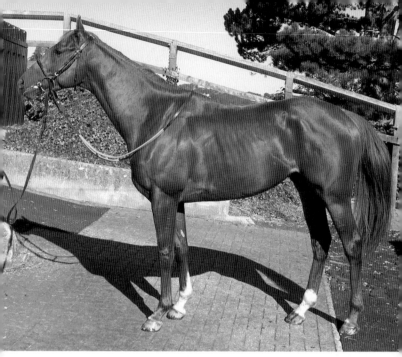

Godolphin's "Buratino"

sister to the smart six/seven-furlong performer and successful sire Danehill Dancer, the smart sprinting two-year-old (a listed winner for Aidan O'Brien) Colossus and the useful sprinting two-year-old (a Group 3 winner) Unilateral. Adonesque is also the dam of Split Rock, a fairly useful two-year-old in 2013 for Buratino's original connections, though he failed to win again after his debut in a busy season. Split Rock finished well beaten on a belated return in Dubai in November for a new yard. Another daughter of Adonesque, China Creek, also represented Buratino's original connections, racing only at three and winning a mile handicap on her fifth and final start. Buratino's great grandam Mira Adonde ran once at three. The good-quartered Buratino acts on polytrack and firm going (yet to race on ground softer than good on turf). He is a 25/1-shot in ante-post lists for the Two Thousand Guineas but has achieved enough at least to deserve a place in the line-up. *Mark Johnston*

BURAUQ 3 b.g. Kyllachy 129 – Riccoche (IRE) 63 (Oasis Dream 129) [2015 63: 5.1d 6m t6f p6m* p6g* t6m Dec 12] fair handicapper: won at Lingfield in November and Kempton in December: stays 6f: acts on polytrack: often wears headgear: often races prominently. *Milton Bradley* **71**

BURMA BRIDGE 3 ro.g. Avonbridge 123 – Mandalay Lady (Environment Friend 128) [2015 74: 8.3m 8v 8.3g Oct 20] maiden: no form in 2015. *Richard Hannon* **–**

BURMA ROAD 2 b.f. (Jan 11) Poet's Voice 126 – Strawberry Moon (IRE) 80 (Alhaarth (IRE) 126) [2015 6m Jul 2] lengthy filly: has scope: third foal: dam, 6f/7f winner, half-sister to useful winner up to 6f Jewel In The Sand out of useful 2-y-o 6f winner (stayed 1m) Dancing Drop: 66/1, green when eighth in maiden at Newbury (9 lengths behind La Rioja) in July: capable of better. *Charles Hills* **58 p**

BURMESE 3 b.g. Sir Percy 129 – Swan Queen 101 (In The Wings 128) [2015 8.3g² 10m² **103 p**
10m² 13.1m* p16g* 16m* Oct 2] leggy, angular gelding: second foal: dam, 1½m-1¾m
winner who stayed 2m, half-sister to smart winner up to 1m Snow Goose: useful performer:
won maiden at Bath in August, and handicaps at Kempton in September and Ascot (by 2¼
lengths from Deauville Dancer) in October: will stay beyond 2m: acts on polytrack and
good to firm going: often races prominently, usually responds generously to pressure:
likely to progress further. *Marcus Tregoning*

BURMESE WHISPER 2 b.c. (Apr 1) Approve (IRE) 112 – Annellis (UAE) (Diesis **70**
133) [2015 6.1m 7d³ 7v 7d⁶ p6f⁴ t7.1g⁴ p6g² p6g³ f5g² Dec 29] fair maiden: stays 6f: acts
on polytrack and fibresand: often leads. *Andrew Balding*

BURNER (IRE) 3 b.g. High Chaparral (IRE) 132 – Breathe (FR) (Ocean of Wisdom **72**
(USA) 106) [2015 8d⁴ 8.3m⁶ 8.3g⁴ 10.1d³ p8m f12g⁴ Nov 24] fair maiden: attractive gelding:
fair maiden: left Lady Cecil after fifth start: best effort at 1¼m: acts on good to soft going:
tried in visor: often in tongue tie. *Olly Williams*

BURNESTON 3 br.g. Rock of Gibraltar (IRE) 133 – Grain of Gold 74 (Mr Prospector **71**
(USA)) [2015 50p: 10s⁴ 9.8g⁶ 12g 9.8m⁵ Aug 4] fair maiden: best effort at 1¼m: acts on
soft going: tried in blinkers in 2015. *James Bethell*

BURNHOPE 6 b.g. Choisir (AUS) 126 – Isengard (USA) 76 (Cobra King (USA) 122) **70**
[2015 60, a80: f7g⁴ f8g³ p7m⁵ f7g⁵ Apr 14] workmanlike gelding: fair handicapper:
stays 1m: acts on polytrack, fibresand and good to firm going: usually wears headgear.
Scott Dixon

BURNING BLAZE 5 b.g. Danroad (AUS) 112 – Demeter (USA) 79 (Diesis 133) [2015 **84**
88: p6g a6.5g* a6.5g³ 6.1d⁵ t7.1f f6g⁵ Dec 15] good-bodied gelding: fairly useful
performer: won minor event at Saint Moritz (by 8 lengths from Sheikh The Reins) in
February: left Olly Stevens after fourth start: stays 1m: acts on polytrack, fibresand, snow,
firm and good to soft going: tried in blinkers prior to 2015: often starts slowly, usually races
towards rear. *Brian Ellison*

BURNING DESIRE (IRE) 4 b.g. Galileo (IRE) 134 – Flames (Blushing Flame (USA) **78**
109) [2015 –p: 12m³ 11.5g⁵ 14.1g 17.2g⁴ p15.8m f16g⁵ Dec 29] rangy gelding: fair maiden:
left M. F. de Kock after second start: stays 17f: acts on polytrack and good to firm going:
tried in cheekpieces in 2015: sometimes slowly away. *Richard Hughes*

BURNINGFIVERS (IRE) 2 b.g. (Apr 4) Paco Boy (IRE) 129 – All Embracing (IRE) 82 **75**
(Night Shift (USA)) [2015 7.1m 7g 6d⁶ 6.1d* 8g⁵ 8.3g 7d² Oct 16] compact gelding: fair
performer: won nursery at Chepstow in August: should stay 1m: acts on good to soft going.
Richard Hannon

BURNING LOVE (IRE) 2 b.f. (Apr 28) Kodiac 112 – Think (FR) 99 (Marchand de **54**
Sable (USA) 117) [2015 6m p6g⁴ 7d⁶ Jun 14] 10,000Y, £41,000 2-y-o: sixth foal: half-
sister to 3 winners, including 9f-12.4f winner Card High (by Red Clubs) and 1m winner
(stays 1¼m) Filosofo (by Teofilo): dam 2-y-o 6f winner: modest maiden: best effort when
fourth in maiden at Lingfield (8 lengths behind Tutu Nguru) in May. *Dave Morris*

BURNING SHADOW (IRE) 2 br.f. (Feb 26) Elusive Pimpernel (USA) 117 – Child **–**
Bride 73 (Invincible Spirit (IRE) 121) [2015 5g 5m 6m Jun 6] €3,500F, £4,800Y: first foal:
dam 2-y-o 5f winner: no form. *Alan Brown*

BURNING THREAD (IRE) 8 b.g. Captain Rio 122 – Desert Rose (Green Desert **86**
(USA) 127) [2015 99§: 5m 5.1g 5m 6g⁶ 5m 5d⁶ 5m⁶ 6m 5m⁶ 5.1g² 5.3s 5.7g* p5m⁴ p5g* **a95**
p5g⁴ Dec 15] sturdy gelding: useful handicapper: won at Bath in October and Kempton (by
¾ length from Pensax Lad) in December: stays 6f: acts on polytrack and any turf going:
often wears headgear: inconsistent. *David Elsworth*

BURNT CREAM 8 b.m. Exceed And Excel (AUS) 126 – Basbousate Nadia 92 **65**
(Wolfhound (USA) 126) [2015 70: p5m* p5f³ p6m p5g⁵ 5.3g⁵ 5.2m 5m⁵ 5f* 5m⁶ p5f⁶
p5m⁵ Dec 31] good-bodied mare: fair handicapper: won at Lingfield in January and Bath
in August: best form at 5f: acts on polytrack and firm going: usually wears hood: usually
wears tongue tie: often starts slowly, often races towards rear. *Martin Bosley*

BURN THE BOATS (IRE) 6 br.g. Big Bad Bob (IRE) 118 – Forever Phoenix 106 **99**
(Shareef Dancer (USA) 135) [2015 108: p7g⁴ 7d 8m Jun 27] lengthy gelding: useful
handicapper: stays 1m: acts on polytrack and good to firm going: tried in cheekpieces prior
to 2015. *G. M. Lyons, Ireland*

BURNT PAVLOVA (USA) 2 b.f. (Apr 12) Big Brown (USA) 132 – Pavlova (USA) **62**
(Stravinsky (USA) 133) [2015 6v 7.5g⁶ 7s⁵ Oct 6] $20,000F, $18,000 2-y-o, resold €26,000
2-y-o: half-sister to several winners, including 1m (including at 2 yrs) winner Palang

(by Hat Trick) and minor US winner by Purim: dam ran once: modest maiden: best effort when sixth in maiden at Beverley (2¼ lengths behind Billy Roberts) in September, not knocked about. *Ismail Mohammed*

BURNT SUGAR (IRE) 3 b.c. Lope de Vega (IRE) 125 – Lady Livius (IRE) 102 (Titus **115**
Livius (FR) 115) [2015 110: 7g a8f⁵ p7g⁵ 6f⁵ 6d 6g 6m⁵ 7d⁴ 6m² 7g Sep 5] well-made colt: smart performer: career-best effort when second in handicap at Newmarket (neck behind Mubtaghaa) in August: stays 6f: acts on polytrack and good to firm going: often in blinkers in 2015: often races towards rear. *Richard Hannon*

BURREN VIEW LADY (IRE) 5 br.m. Dansili 127 – Westerly Gale (USA) (Gone West **76**
(USA)) [2015 83, a93: p7g p6g p7g* 7g⁶ 6m* 7d 7g 8.5m⁵ 7s 6d² 6d⁶ t6f² t5.1f* p5g³ **a83**
p6g Dec 11] fairly useful handicapper: won at Dundalk in March, Naas in July and Wolverhampton (by head from You're Cool) in November: stays 7f: acts on polytrack, tapeta, good to firm and good to soft going: often wears headgear: usually in tongue tie in 2015: front runner/races prominently. *Denis Hogan, Ireland*

BURTONWOOD 3 b.g. Acclamation 118 – Green Poppy 68 (Green Desert (USA) 127) **73**
[2015 81: t7.1g 8g⁶ 8g 7m 5.9g⁵ 6g* 5.9s 6g* t6f⁷ Oct 16] strong, close-coupled gelding: fair handicapper: won at Newcastle (apprentice) in August and Ripon (apprentice) in September: stays 6f: acts on tapeta, good to firm and good to soft going: tried in headgear prior to 2015. *Julie Camacho*

BUSH BABE 2 b.f. (Apr 15) Bushranger (IRE) 119 – Cliche (IRE) 108 (Diktat 126) [2015 **39**
6m 6d⁶ 7.5g 8g t8.6f⁶ Oct 3] 4,200F: fifth foal: half-sister to 3 winners, including 6f/7f winner Bretherton (by Exceed And Excel) and winner up to 1m Only Joking (2-y-o 5f winner, by Aussie Rules): dam 8.3f winner: poor maiden: stays 1m: acts on good to soft going: usually in headgear. *Tim Easterby*

BUSH BEAUTY (IRE) 4 b.f. Bushranger (IRE) 119 – Scottendale 58 (Zilzal (USA) 137) **73**
[2015 74: t7.1f² t7.1f² t7.1g* t7.1g 7m 6m t6m t7.1m t6g² t6f* t6g⁶ t7.1f³ t6m⁵ t8.6f⁶ Dec 22] fair performer: won handicap in January, claimer in July and apprentice handicap in October, all at Wolverhampton: left Philip McBride after third start, William Jarvis after eighth: stays 8.5f: acts on polytrack and tapeta: tried in blinkers in 2015. *Eric Alston*

BUSHCRAFT (IRE) 4 b.g. Bushranger (IRE) 119 – Lady Lucia (IRE) 51 (Royal **103**
Applause 124) [2015 6m* 6m* 6m* 7d Jul 25] good-quartered gelding: useful handicapper: won at Windsor in May, and Windsor and Newcastle (by 1¼ lengths from See The Sun) in June: stays 6f: acts on fibresand and good to firm going. *Ed Walker*

BUSHEL (USA) 5 b.g. Street Cry (IRE) 130 – Melhor Ainda (USA) 120 (Pulpit (USA) **86 §**
117) [2015 f12d² t13.9g f11g* f12s² f11g³ Dec 15] fairly useful handicapper: won at Southwell in January: third in claimer at Southwell in December: stays 1½m: acts on fibresand and good to firm going: sometimes wears headgear: often races lazily: untrustworthy. *James Given*

BUSHEPHALUS (IRE) 3 gr.g. Dark Angel (IRE) 113 – White Daffodil (IRE) 76 (Foot- **76**
stepsinthesand 120) [2015 p5f³ p6g² 6m² 7m³ Jun 7] £48,000Y: first foal: dam, winner up to 6f (2-y-o 5f winner), half-sister to useful 6f winner Lady Links: fair form in maidens/ handicap: still looked green when third on handicap debut at Goodwood: sold £14,000. *Ed Walker*

BUSHRANGER BAY (IRE) 3 b.g. Bushranger (IRE) 119 – Zafaraya (IRE) 68 **50**
(Ashkalani (IRE) 128) [2015 54: 8g 8g 7.5g⁵ f6d 6m May 27] modest maiden: likely to prove best up to 7f: acts on good to firm going: sometimes in blinkers in 2015: sometimes in tongue tie in 2015. *Tim Easterby*

BUSHTIGER (IRE) 3 b.g. Bushranger (IRE) 119 – Emma's Surprise 69 (Tobougg (IRE) **48**
125) [2015 –: f7g t5.1g⁴ f6d² t6m³ 6m⁶ 7g⁶ 7.1m May 22] poor maiden: stays 6f: acts on fibresand, tapeta and good to firm going: usually in blinkers in 2015. *David Barron*

BUSH WARRIOR (IRE) 4 b.g. Bushranger (IRE) 119 – Lady Corduff (IRE) 78 (Titus **80**
Livius (FR) 115) [2015 75: f5d p6f⁴ 6m³ 6m⁵ 6.1m³ p6g* 6m⁴ p6g² 6m³ 6s p6g t6m 6g Oct 19] tall gelding: fairly useful handicapper: won at Lingfield (by 4 lengths from Toast of Newbury) in June: second at Kempton (apprentice) in July: stays 6f: acts on polytrack and good to firm going: sometimes wears headgear: often races prominently. *Robert Eddery*

BUSHWISE (IRE) 2 b.f. (Apr 6) Bushranger (IRE) 119 – Validate (Alhaarth (IRE) 126) **46**
[2015 6.1m 7g 6.1m f5g 6.1d⁵ 6.1s⁶ p6f p6f⁶ t6f Nov 10] 3,000F, £3,500Y: half-sister to several winners, including 7f winner Carnival King (by Arcano) and winner up to 7f Personal Touch (2-y-o 7f winner, by Pivotal): dam unraced half-sister to 6f winner Enact and 6f-7f winner Enrol, both useful: poor maiden: stays 6f: acts on good to firm and good to soft going. *Milton Bradley*

BUSHY GLADE (IRE) 4 b.f. Bushranger (IRE) 119 – Cladantom (IRE) 70 (High Estate **51**
127) [2015 56: f12g⁶ p12g t12.2f² t12.2g 9.9d t12.2gᵖᵘ Jun 2] rather leggy filly: modest
maiden: stays 1½m: acts on tapeta and good to soft going: tried in cheekpieces in 2015:
tends to find little. *Julia Feilden*

BUSSA 7 b.g. Iceman 117 – Maid To Dance 62 (Pyramus (USA) 78) [2015 56: t7.1m⁵ t6g **60**
8m* 9.2s⁵ 9.3d a7g* p8g Nov 11] tall gelding: modest performer: won handicap at Bath in
July and claimer at Laytown in September: left Emmet Michael Butterly after sixth start:
stays 1¼m: acts on polytrack, sand, soft and good to firm going: tried in headgear: often
wears tongue tie. *S. J. Mahon, Ireland*

BUSTA NELLIE 2 ch.f. (May 1) Pastoral Pursuits 127 – Vezere (USA) 67 (Point Given **37**
(USA) 134) [2015 p6g 6g p7g p8m p7f⁵ p7g Nov 18] angular filly: second foal: dam,
maiden (stayed 1¼m), half-sister to smart 5f winner Stern Opinion: poor maiden: stays 7f:
acts on polytrack: sometimes slowly away, often races towards rear. *Simon Dow*

BUSTER BROWN (IRE) 6 ch.g. Singspiel (IRE) 133 – Gold Dodger (USA) (Slew O' **62**
Gold (USA)) [2015 p10g⁶ Jan 16] leggy gelding: modest handicapper: stays 1¼m: acts on
polytrack, good to firm and good to soft going. *Gary Moore*

BUSY BIMBO (IRE) 6 b.m. Red Clubs (IRE) 125 – Unfortunate 55 (Komaite (USA)) **69**
[2015 61§, a44§: 5g 5m 5g³ 5m 5m³ 5g⁵ 5d³ 5f³ 5g² 5g² 5m* 5m³ 5m⁴ 5m³ 5d* 5m⁴ 5d⁶
5m³ 5m⁵ 5g⁶ 5s Oct 27] fair handicapper: won at Musselburgh in July and Catterick in
August: stays 6f: acts on firm and soft going: often wears headgear. *Alan Berry*

BUSY STREET 3 b.g. Champs Elysees 124 – Allegro Viva (USA) (Distant View (USA) **80 p**
126) [2015 f12g* Dec 22] 18,000 3-y-o: fifth foal: closely related to smart 1½m-15f winner
Canticum (by Cacique) and half-brother to useful 1m-1½m winner Uphold (by Oasis
Dream) and 1¼m winner Allegrezza (by Sir Percy): dam unraced sister to high-class
winner up to 9f Distant Music: 5/1, won maiden at Southwell by 3¾ lengths from Kay
Sera) in December: entitled to progress. *Alan Swinbank*

BUTE HALL 6 ch.g. Halling (USA) 133 – Les Hurlants (IRE) (Barathea (IRE) 127) [2015 **79**
92: t12.2f⁴ t12.2m⁶ t13.9g⁶ Mar 24] rather leggy gelding: fair handicapper: stays 14.5f:
acts on polytrack, tapeta, soft and good to firm going: tried in headgear. *David Thompson*

BUTEO BAI (IRE) 2 b.f. (Mar 1) Big Bad Bob (IRE) 118 – Spring Will Come (IRE) **–**
(Desert Prince (IRE) 130) [2015 7.6v⁶ 7.5g⁶ 7.6g⁵ f7g Nov 3] 4,000F: third foal: half-sister
to 2-y-o 5f winner Pinodeipalazzi (by Kheleyf): dam unraced: no form. *Martin Smith*

BUTHELEZI (USA) 7 b.g. Dynaformer (USA) – Ntombi (USA) (Quiet American **101**
(USA)) [2015 14s* 18.7d 12m⁵ 16.1m Jun 27] big, well-made gelding: useful handicapper:
won at Musselburgh in April: effective at 13f, barely stays 2¼m: acts on soft and good to
firm going: sometimes in headgear prior to 2015: tried in tongue tie prior to 2015: front
runner/races prominently. *Brian Ellison*

BUY NOW PAY LATER 3 b.g. Sir Percy 129 – Great Quest (IRE) 78 (Montjeu (IRE) **57**
137) [2015 8.3m p8g⁵ 10m Jun 15] little impact in maidens: should have stayed 1½m+:
dead. *Rod Millman*

BUY OUT BOY 4 gr.g. Medicean 128 – Tiger's Gene (GER) (Perugino (USA) 84) [2015 **–**
59: t9.5f t9.5g Jan 23] rather leggy gelding: maiden: no form in 2015: stays 1¼m: acts on
polytrack, fibresand and good to firm going: tried in headgear. *Brian Baugh*

BUZZ LIGHTYERE 2 b.c. (Feb 8) Royal Applause 124 – Lady Gloria 114 (Diktat 126) **63**
[2015 p8g p8g Dec 7] modest form in maidens: better effort when seventh in maiden at
Kempton (7¼ lengths behind D'Niro) in November, not ideally placed. *Michael Attwater*

BY FAR (FR) 2 b.g. (May 1) Shamardal (USA) 129 – Perfidie (IRE) (Monsun (GER) 124) **– p**
[2015 6m Aug 4] half-brother to several winners, including 1m-1¼m winner Don Bosco
(by Barathea), 9f-10.5f winner Vodkato (both smart) and useful winner up to 8.5f Orcus
(2-y-o 6f/7f winner) (both by Russian Blue): dam unraced: 5/2, eleventh in maiden at
Ripon (24¼ lengths behind Athollblair Boy) in August: should do better. *Saeed bin Suroor*

BYGONES FOR COINS (IRE) 7 ch.m. Danroad (AUS) 112 – Reservation (IRE) 78 **–**
(Common Grounds 118) [2015 7m 12.4d 10.1d⁵ 12.4g 16.1m Jun 6] fair at best, no form in
2015: tried in headgear prior to 2015: front runner/races prominently. *Kenny Johnson*

BYRD IN HAND (IRE) 8 b.g. Fasliyev (USA) 120 – Military Tune (IRE) (Nashwan **60**
(USA) 135) [2015 72, a65: 7m 7d⁴ 9g 8d³ 8m⁵ 8g 8v² 8g³ 8d⁵ 8s² p10m² p10m p10m
Nov 14] good-topped gelding: modest handicapper: stays 1¼m: acts on polytrack, good to
firm and heavy going: sometimes wears headgear: front runner. *John Bridger*

BY RIGHTS 4 b.f. Byron 117 – Legend House (FR) 70 (Grand Lodge (USA) 125) [2015 **77** 82: 6.1m 5m² 5g⁶ 5.1g⁶ 5.1v⁶ 5g 5s² 5.1d 5.1d² f6g³ t6m² t5.1m² Dec 30] fair handicapper: stays 6f: acts on fibresand, tapeta, good to firm and heavy going: often wears hood. *Tony Carroll*

BYRON BLUE (IRE) 6 br.g. Dylan Thomas (IRE) 132 – High Society (IRE) 97 (Key of **–** Luck (USA) 126) [2015 p12g Jan 14] compact gelding: fair at best, no form in 2015: best effort at 1¾m: acts on soft going: tried in hood prior to 2015. *Mark Gillard*

BYRONEGETONEFREE 4 b.g. Byron 117 – Lefty's Dollbaby (USA) (Brocco (USA) **49** 124) [2015 57: 9.1s 13.1d⁵ 14.1v⁴ f14g Dec 12] poor maiden: may prove best at shorter than 13f: acts on polytrack and heavy going: tried in hood in 2015: front runner/races prominently. *Stuart Coltherd*

BYRON'S GOLD 4 ch.f. Byron 117 – Dance To The Blues (IRE) 73 (Danehill Dancer **–** (IRE) 117) [2015 79: p6g Feb 14] fair at best, no form in 2015: stays 6f: acts on soft and good to firm going. *Zoe Davison*

BY THE RULES 2 b.f. (May 20) Aussie Rules (USA) 123 – Bay Tree (IRE) 100 (Daylami **–** (IRE) 138) [2015 7.6g p8g Aug 18] smallish filly: half-sister to several winners, including useful 2-y-o 6f winner (stays 8.5f) Mezmaar (by Teofilo) and useful 1½m winner The Bells O Peover (by Selkirk): dam, 2-y-o 6f/7f winner who stayed 10.4f, half-sister to high-class winner up to 7f Tante Rose: no form. *Paul Cole*

C

CABAL 8 br.m. Kyllachy 129 – Secret Flame 78 (Machiavellian (USA) 123) [2015 55: **83** f8g³ t9.5f* t8.6m³ t9.5m⁴ 8.5m² 8g³ t9.5g² 9.9m⁵ 10.1m⁶ t9.5g³ 10.1m 8m⁴ t9.5m 8.5d³ **a76** t9.5m* 7.5m* 7s* t8.6f⁶ t9.5f⁶ Nov 13] lengthy mare: fairly useful handicapper: won at Wolverhampton in January (apprentice) and September, and Beverley and Redcar (by 2¾ lengths from Cliff) in October: stays 12.5f: acts on polytrack, tapeta, firm and soft going: usually wears headgear: often travels strongly. *Geoffrey Harker*

CABBIES LOU 3 b.f. Sakhee's Secret 128 – Regal Run (USA) (Deputy Minister (CAN)) **–** [2015 69: 8g 7.1s May 11] fair at best, no form in 2015: best effort at 5f: acts on good to soft going: tried in headgear: often starts slowly, often races in rear. *Noel Wilson*

CABELO (IRE) 3 b.f. Azamour (IRE) 130 – Fringe 93 (In The Wings 128) [2015 78: 7d **91** 7g* 8g 7m⁶ 6.9g² 6.9g⁵ 8.9m 7d* 7d⁴ 7v² Oct 17] fairly useful performer: won maiden at Catterick in April and handicap at Catterick in August: stays 1m: acts on good to firm and heavy going: sometimes in cheekpieces in 2015. *Brian Ellison*

CABINET ROOM (USA) 2 ch.c. (May 18) Exchange Rate (USA) 111 – Private Line **87** (USA) 105 (Private Account (USA)) [2015 t7.1g⁴ p8f² p7g² Oct 7] brother to 1¼m winner Convocate, closely related to useful 1m winner Discuss (by Danzig) and half-brother to several winners, including smart French 7f-10.5f winner Dance Dress (by Nureyev): dam winner up to 1m (2-y-o 7f winner): fairly useful maiden: best effort when second in maiden at Kempton (nose behind Chester Street) in October, having run of race. *Lady Cecil*

CABLE BAY (IRE) 4 b.c. Invincible Spirit (IRE) 121 – Rose de France (IRE) (Diktat **119** 126) [2015 114: 7d³ 8m⁵ 7d* 8f³ 7d⁴ 8s⁴ 7d⁶ 6m⁴ 7g* Oct 9] compact colt: smart performer: won Timeform Jury Stakes (John of Gaunt) at Haydock (by ½ length from Ascription) in May and Challenge Stakes at Newmarket (by neck from Breton Rock) in October: also ran

Dubai Challenge Stakes, Newmarket—Cable Bay (No.4) wins from Breton Rock (No.3), Belardo (No.9), So Beloved (far side) and Markaz (striped cap)

Julie Martin & David R. Martin & Partner's "Cable Bay"

well when fifth in Lockinge Stakes at Newbury (beaten 1¾ lengths by Night of Thunder) in May: stayed 1m: acted on firm and soft going: to stand at Highclere Stud, Burghclere, Berkshire, fee £6,500. *Charles Hills*

CABUCHON (GER) 8 b.g. Fantastic Light (USA) 134 – Catella (GER) 119 (Generous (IRE) 139) [2015 70: t12.2f⁴ p13g⁴ t12.2m⁶ t12.2m 11.7f⁶ 12m² p10g² 11.9m⁵ 10.2m⁴ 10m⁴ p10gᵘʳ p10g⁶ 10m³ 10.9g⁶ p10m⁶ t12.2f² p12g* 10.2s⁵ Oct 28] workmanlike gelding: modest handicapper: won at Lingfield in October: stays easy 2m, effective at much shorter: acts on polytrack, tapeta and firm going: sometimes wears headgear: usually wears tongue tie: often races towards rear. *David Evans* **61**

CACHAO 2 br.c. (Mar 14) New Approach (IRE) 132 – Mambo Halo (USA) (Southern Halo (USA)) [2015 p7g⁵ t8.6g⁶ Dec 5] better effort when fifth in maiden at Kempton (1¾ lengths behind Marylebone) in November, unsuited by emphasis on speed: will stay 1¼m. *John Gosden* **79**

CACICA 2 b.f. (May 3) Cacique (IRE) 124 – Moonlight Mystery 77 (Pivotal 124) [2015 7g⁶ 8.3g⁶ f7m⁶ Dec 8] 35,000F, 160,000Y: compact filly: first foal: dam 7f winner out of useful winner up to 1m Mauri Moon: fair maiden: best effort when sixth in maiden at Newmarket (6¼ lengths behind Promising Run) in August: should stay 1m. *Richard Hannon* **69**

CACTUS VALLEY (IRE) 6 b.g. Lawman (FR) 121 – Beech Gardens 66 (Sadler's Wells (USA) 132) [2015 98: 8m 10.4g 9.8d² 10.4m 10.4m 10.3g 9.8d Aug 18] useful-looking gelding: fairly useful handicapper: second at Ripon in June: stays 1½m: acts on good to firm and good to soft going: tried in headgear: often in tongue tie in 2015. *Michael Easterby* **91**

CADEAU MAGNIFIQUE 3 b.g. Dutch Art 126 – Cadeau Speciale 54 (Cadeaux Genereux 131) [2015 68p: 8.3s* 12.5m 10.4m⁵ 8d⁴ 9.8g³ Aug 3] rather leggy gelding: fairly useful handicapper: won at Nottingham in May: third at Ripon in August: stays 10.5f: acts on soft and good to firm going. *Richard Fahey* **85**

CADEAUX 3 b.g. Major Cadeaux 121 – Bikini 80 (Trans Island 119) [2015 7g⁴ 6g³ 7g⁴ **70** 7m⁵ 8g 7d⁵ 7g² 8g 7s Oct 16] fair maiden: stays 7f: acts on good to firm going: tried in cheekpieces: front runner/races prominently: sold 4,000 gns, sent to USA. *Michael Dods*

CADEAUX PEARL 7 b.g. Acclamation 118 – Anneliina 80 (Cadeaux Genereux 131) **67** [2015 68: f6d⁵ f7g⁶ f6s⁴ f6g⁴ p6f f6s⁵ 5d³ 6m 6.1m³ 5m⁴ 6g 6m⁵ 6s 6d² 6g⁴ 7s² f7g p6m f7m* f7g Dec 15] sturdy gelding: fair handicapper: won at Southwell in January and December: stays 7f: acts on polytrack, fibresand, soft and good to firm going: usually wears headgear. *Scott Dixon*

CADEAUX POWER 4 b.f. Major Cadeaux 121 – Right Answer 95 (Lujain (USA) 119) **87** [2015 82: t6f* p6g 6.1d³ 5.9s² 6d² 6d⁶ 6.1d³ 6.1g 7v* 7s Oct 27] good-topped filly: fairly useful performer: won maiden at Wolverhampton in March and handicap at Catterick (by neck from Red Tycoon) in October: has form over 1¼m, races over shorter: acts on tapeta, best turf form on soft/heavy going. *Tim Easterby*

CADLAND LAD (IRE) 2 b.g. (Feb 8) Lilbourne Lad (IRE) 111 – Hari's Gift (IRE) (Ivan **56** Denisovich (IRE) 115) [2015 7m p8f 7m p6f³ p6f³ p7f² Nov 12] lengthy, rather unfurnished gelding: modest maiden: stays 7f: acts on polytrack and good to firm going: often in tongue tie: front runner/races prominently. *John Ryan*

CADMIUM 4 b.f. Major Cadeaux 121 – Miss Mirasol 92 (Sheikh Albadou 128) [2015 56, **75** a70: p8g⁵ p8g 8d⁶ 8d* 7.9v² 8.3m* 8.3m 8.3s⁵ 8.3s* 8m Aug 5] fair handicapper: won at Newcastle in May, and Hamilton in June and July (apprentice): left Harry Dunlop after second start: stays 8.5f: acts on polytrack, soft and good to firm going: tried in cheekpieces. *Micky Hammond*

CAERLEON KATE 3 ch.f. Medicean 128 – Towaahi (IRE) (Caerleon (USA) 132) [2015 **–** p8g⁴ p8f t8.6g 11.5d⁶ Jun 4] closely related to winner up to 1¼m (in Hong Kong) Towering Storm (2-y-o 1m winner, by Storming Home) and half-sister to 1m winner Mezoglam (by Kris): dam unraced daughter of Yorkshire Oaks winner Untold: no form. *Rod Millman*

CAESER THE GAESER (IRE) 3 b.g. Captain Rio 122 – Alchimie (IRE) (Sri Pekan **65** (USA) 117) [2015 –: 7g⁵ 7m 5.9g* 5.9s 7.2g Oct 13] fair handicapper: won at Carlisle in August: left Richard Guest after second start: best effort at 6f: usually races in rear. *Nigel Tinkler*

CAFE CAPRICE 3 ch.f. Duke of Marmalade (IRE) 132 – Midpoint (USA) (Point Given **52** (USA) 134) [2015 p7g t9.5g⁵ p10g⁵ 10g p12g p12g p13.3m* p16f⁵ Oct 15] 12,000Y: sturdy filly: fourth foal: half-sister to 5f/6f winner Invigilator (by Motivator) and 1m winner Mezogiorno (by Zamindar): dam unraced half-sister to US Grade 3 9f winner Ocean Queen: modest handicapper: won at Chelmsford in September: best effort at 13.5f: acts on polytrack: often in headgear: usually races prominently. *Ed Vaughan*

CAGED LIGHTNING (IRE) 5 b.g. Haatef (USA) 117 – Rainbow Melody (IRE) 83 **85** (Rainbows For Life (CAN)) [2015 –: t9.5f f12g⁶ f12g³ f14s* f14g* f16g³ 14.1s² Oct 28] fairly useful handicapper: won twice at Southwell in March (amateur event on first occasion): left Ronald O'Leary after first start: stays 1¾m: acts on polytrack, fibresand and soft going: tried in headgear. *Steve Gollings*

CAHALA DANCER (IRE) 7 ch.m. Elnadim (USA) 128 – Ranma (In The Wings 128) **76** [2015 –: 8.1d* 8v* 10.1v² Sep 1] fair handicapper: won at Chepstow and Brighton in August: stays 1m: acts on polytrack and heavy going: in tongue tie in 2015. *Robert Mills*

CAHAL (IRE) 4 b.g. Bushranger (IRE) 119 – Cabopino (IRE) 58 (Captain Rio 122) [2015 **–** 68: f6d⁶ Jan 4] fair at best, no form in 2015: stays 7f: acts on soft going. *David Nicholls*

CAHAR FAD (IRE) 3 b.g. Bushranger (IRE) 119 – Tarbiyah 89 (Singspiel (IRE) 133) **42** [2015 52: t12.2g t12.2m⁴ 11.7f⁴ p10m³ 11.7f 12.1f⁶ 11.5g⁴ 16g p12g³ t12.2m t9.5m³ **a61** t9.5f* t9.5f³ t9.5f³ t9.5f⁶ t9.5g³ Dec 4] angular gelding: modest handicapper: won at Wolverhampton in October: stays 1¼m: acts on polytrack and tapeta: often wears headgear: usually in tongue tie in 2015: races prominently. *Steph Hollinshead*

CAHILL (IRE) 3 b.g. Lawman (FR) 121 – Malaspina (IRE) (Whipper (USA) 126) [2015 **72** 75: 11.8g⁴ 12m⁴ 14m p12g⁶ t13.9f* t13.9g² Dec 1] useful-looking gelding: fairly useful **a89** handicapper: won at Wolverhampton (apprentice, by 19 lengths from Goodby Inheritence) in October: stays 1¾m: acts on tapeta: tried in cheekpieces in 2015. *Alan King*

CAIGEMDAR (IRE) 3 b.f. Tagula (IRE) 116 – Honey Feather (IRE) 51 (Intikhab (USA) **87** 135) [2015 81: 6.1s⁴ 6g 7m² 7.6g² 7.2m⁵ 7d Aug 20] fairly useful handicapper: second at Newcastle in June and Chester (apprentice) in July: will probably stay 1m: acts on soft and good to firm going: sent to Germany. *David Barron*

CAITIE (IRE) 2 b.f. (Mar 3) Canford Cliffs (IRE) 133 – The Shrew 108 (Dansili 127) **75** [2015 5.1m⁵ 5f t6g² 6.5m Sep 10] 40,000Y: lengthy filly: first foal: dam winner up to 1m (2-y-o 7.4f winner): fair maiden: best effort at 6f. *Paul Cole*

CAIUS COLLEGE GIRL (IRE) 3 b.f. Royal Applause 124 – Galeaza (Galileo (IRE) **78**
134) [2015 83p: 6g 7m⁵ f6d p7g⁵ 6g⁴ 6g³ 6s* t7.1f⁵ p7g Dec 16] sturdy filly: fair
handicapper: won at Leicester in October: left David Menuisier after seventh start: stays 7f:
acts on polytrack, tapeta and soft going: tried in blinkers in 2015: front runner/races
prominently. *Heather Main*

CAJOLED (FR) 2 b.f. (Feb 15) High Chaparral (IRE) 132 – Dolphina (USA) 83 (King- **87 p**
mambo (USA) 125) [2015 p8g* Dec 15] second foal: dam, 1¼m winner, out of US Grade 3
8.5f winner Sea of Showers, herself half-sister to high-class US performers Aldebaran
(best at 7f/1m) and Good Journey (miler): 16/1, value for extra when won maiden at
Kempton (by 1½ lengths from Andaz) in December, overcoming pace bias: likely to stay
1¼m: will improve. *George Scott*

CALCULATED RISK 6 ch.g. Motivator 131 – Glen Rosie (IRE) 102 (Mujtahid (USA) **75**
118) [2015 13.8m⁵ 15.9m 13.8d Sep 15] tall gelding: fair handicapper: stays 2¼m: acts on
good to firm and heavy going: tried in cheekpieces in 2015. *John Quinn*

CALDER PRINCE (IRE) 2 gr.c. (May 22) Dark Angel (IRE) 113 – Flame of Ireland **90 p**
(IRE) 85 (Fasliyev (USA) 120) [2015 6d* p6f* Nov 7] €30,000Y: leggy colt: third foal:
half-brother to a winner abroad by Marju: dam, 2-y-o 6f winner, half-sister to useful
1m-10.3f winner Prince Kalamoun: won maiden at Pontefract in October and minor event
at Chelmsford (by 1¾ lengths from Harvard Man) in November: will stay 7f: likely to
progress further. *Tom Dascombe*

CALEDONIA DUCHESS 2 b.f. (Apr 14) Dutch Art 126 – Granuaile O'Malley (IRE) 55 **72**
(Mark of Esteem (IRE) 137) [2015 6m 6g t6m³ Sep 14] half-sister to several winners,
including useful 5f (including at 2 yrs)/6f winner Caledonia Lady (by Firebreak) and 1m
winner Caledonia Prince (by Needwood Prince): dam maiden (should have stayed 7f):
fair maiden: best effort when third in maiden at Wolverhampton (1¾ lengths behind
Symposium) in September. *Jo Hughes*

CALEDONIA LAIRD 4 b.g. Firebreak 125 – Granuaile O'Malley (IRE) 55 (Mark of **73**
Esteem (IRE) 137) [2015 66: p7g⁴ p8f* p8f⁴ p8f⁵ 8m⁵ p8f⁵ t7.1f t7.1f² Dec 22] good-topped
gelding: fair handicapper: won at Chelmsford in February: stays 1m: acts on polytrack,
tapeta, firm and soft going: tried in cheekpieces: tried in tongue tie in 2015. *Jo Hughes*

CALEDONIAN GOLD 2 b.f. (Jan 1) Acclamation 118 – Moonlight Rhapsody (IRE) 73 **65**
(Danehill Dancer (IRE) 117) [2015 p6g 5f 7g⁴ 6s³ t7.1f⁵ 7s Oct 26] 43,000F, 40,000Y,
48,000 2-y-o: first foal: dam, 1¼m winner who stayed 1½m, half-sister to smart performer
up to 12.5f Fantastic Love: fair maiden: stays 7f: acts on tapeta and soft going. *Paul D'Arcy*

CALIFORNIA CHROME (USA) 4 ch.c. Lucky Pulpit (USA) – Love The Chase **126**
(USA) (Not For Love (USA)) [2015 127: a9f² a9.9f² Mar 28] high-class performer:
successful 6 times in 2014 (when voted US Horse of The Year), including Kentucky Derby
at Churchill Downs, Preakness Stakes at Pimlico and Hollywood Derby at Del Mar:
runner-up both outings in 2015, in Grade 2 San Antonio Invitational at Santa Anita (beaten
1½ lengths by Shared Belief) and Dubai World Cup at Meydan (2¾ lengths behind Prince
Bishop, chasing strong pace out wide): stabled in Britain during spring/summer and had
been due to race but missed several engagements, including because of an abscess on off-
fore: sent back to USA but reported in July to have bruised a cannon bone: stays 1¼m: acts
on synthetics/dirt and firm going (successful only start on turf): wears blinkers: usually
tracks pace: genuine: stays in training. *Art Sherman, USA*

CALIFORNIA (IRE) 3 b.f. Azamour (IRE) 130 – Maskaya (IRE) 92 (Machiavellian **102**
(USA) 123) [2015 10m* 10.3m* 9.9g p13g² Oct 29] 75,000Y: good-topped filly: seventh
foal: half-sister to 3 winners, including useful performer up to 1¼m Drumbeat (2-y-o 7f
winner, by Montjeu) and 7.6f winner Red Blooded Woman (by Red Ransom): dam, 2-y-o
5f winner, half-sister to dam of Dewhurst Stakes winner Belardo: useful performer: won
maiden at Wetherby in July and handicap at Doncaster in September: second in listed race
at Lingfield (length behind Urban Castle) in October: stays 13f. *John Gosden*

CALIFORNIA LAD 2 b.g. (Jan 29) Aussie Rules (USA) 123 – Medaille d'Or 80 (With **76**
Approval (CAN)) [2015 7.1m 7m² 7f Jul 11] sturdy gelding: fair maiden: best effort when
second in maiden at Salisbury (¾ length behind Montsarrat) in June, sticking to task.
Harry Dunlop

CALIMA BREEZE 3 b.f. Oasis Dream 129 – Paris Winds (IRE) 110 (Galileo (IRE) 134) **85**
[2015 55p: 7m³ 8m* 8m³ 7g p7g⁵ Oct 14] fairly useful performer: won maiden at Thirsk in
July: stays 1m: acts on polytrack and good to firm going: front runner/races prominently.
Charles Hills

CALITXO (SPA) 6 b.g. Diamond Green (FR) 121 – Citadelle (CHI) (Hussonet (USA)) **56** [2015 t7.1g² p8m 8g t8.6m 8s⁶ p10m Oct 21] modest maiden: stays 7f: acts on tapeta and dirt: tried in cheekpieces in 2015. *Ralph Smith*

CALLAC 3 b.g. Aqlaam 125 – Fifty (IRE) 86 (Fasliyev (USA) 120) [2015 p7g⁴ p7f³ p7g⁴ **70** 7g⁴ 7d² Jul 25] fair maiden: raced only at 7f: acts on polytrack: sent to Sweden. *David Simcock*

CALLAGHAN (GER) 2 b.c. (May 3) Cacique (IRE) 124 – Cent Cheveux Blanc (GER) **69** (Pentire 132) [2015 6.1m 7g p7g² p8f 7g⁶ Sep 19] fair maiden: best effort at 7f: acts on polytrack: sometimes slowly away, often races towards rear. *James Given*

CALLENDULA 3 ch.f. Halling (USA) 133 – Oatey 68 (Master Willie 129) [2015 60: **82** t12.2g³ 11.6g³ 10.2f⁴ t12.2g² 13.1f² 14m 11.9g* 11s 11.7g* p12g t12.2f⁵ Dec 11] lengthy filly: fairly useful handicapper: won at Brighton in August and Bath in October: stays 1½m: best form on good going: usually in cheekpieces in 2015. *Clive Cox*

CALLING OUT (FR) 4 b.g. Martaline 118 – Exit The Straight (IRE) (Exit To Nowhere **108** (USA) 122) [2015 110: 9.9g 8.9g 8.5g⁵ 10m⁴ p8g² p8g* Dec 19] tall gelding: useful ex-French-trained performer: won minor event at Lingfield (by ½ length from dead-heaters Our Channel and Spiritual Star) in December: stays 1¼m: acts on polytrack, good to firm and good to soft going: often races towards rear. *David Simcock*

CALLIOPE 2 b.f. (Mar 26) Poet's Voice 126 – Costa Brava (IRE) (Sadler's Wells (USA) **68** 132) [2015 7g p7g 7s⁶ Oct 12] €85,000Y: useful-looking filly: fifth foal: half-sister to French 8.5f winner Soho Theatre (by Indian Ridge) and French 1¼m winner Mr Chance (by Dalakhani): dam unraced sister to Arc fourth Acropolis and closely related to Falmouth Stakes winner Tashawak and smart performer up to 12.5f Fairy Queen: fair form: best effort when sixth in maiden at Salisbury (6¼ lengths behind Rostova) in October: should be suited by 1m+. *Andrew Balding*

CALL IT ON (IRE) 9 ch.g. Raise A Grand (IRE) 114 – Birthday Present (Cadeaux **86** Genereux 131) [2015 f14d t13.9g⁵ p16g² 16g³ t16.5g 17.2d* 18d* 17.1d* 16.4s Oct 10] **a63** sturdy gelding: fairly useful handicapper: won at Carlisle (amateur) and Chepstow in August, and Pontefract (by 8 lengths from Ivanhoe) in September: stays 2½m: acts on good to firm and good to soft going: usually in cheekpieces in 2015: usually in tongue tie in 2015. *Philip Kirby*

CALL ME CROCKETT (IRE) 3 ch.g. Intense Focus (USA) 117 – Forest Storm **72** (USA) (Woodman (USA) 126) [2015 60: 7g f7g² 8g² 7g⁶ 10.1m 8m² 9.8d² 7.2g³ 8f³ 7.2g 7.2g* 7.2g⁶ 8v³ t8.6f² t9.5f² t9.5m Dec 18] fair handicapper: won at Ayr in October: left Richard Guest after second start: stays 9.5f: acts on tapeta: often wears headgear. *Iain Jardine*

CALL OF DUTY (IRE) 10 br.g. Storming Home 128 – Blushing Barada (USA) 53 **64** (Blushing Groom (FR) 131) [2015 t8.6m⁴ 10.3d 8d³ 10.4d⁴ 10m* 10.1m 9.3s⁴ 8.9g⁶ 9.3d⁴ 9.3g Aug 19] close-coupled gelding: modest handicapper: won at Wetherby in June: stays 1½m: acts on polytrack, soft and good to firm going: tried in headgear: tried in tongue tie in 2015: sometimes slowly away, races well off pace. *Dianne Sayer*

CALL OUT LOUD 3 b.c. Aqlaam 125 – Winner's Call (Indian Ridge 123) [2015 –p: **74** 7.6g⁴ 8.3m⁵ 10m⁵ 8g 7.4v* 8v³ 10.3d f8g⁵ Nov 12] fair handicapper: won at Ffos Las in August: left Sir Michael Stoute after second start, Heather Dalton after sixth: stays 8.5f: acts on good to firm and heavy going: usually in tongue tie in 2015. *Michael Appleby*

CALM ATTITUDE (IRE) 5 ch.m. Dutch Art 126 – Turban Heights (IRE) 88 (Golan **87** (IRE) 129) [2015 90: 9.9d 10.2g⁴ 10d* 10d⁵ 10s² 10s⁶ Oct 23] fairly useful handicapper: won at Newmarket in July: second at Newbury in September: stays 1¼m: best form on good going or softer (acts on heavy): usually races towards rear. *Rae Guest*

CALPURNIA 2 b.f. (Mar 21) Sleeping Indian 122 – Africa's Star (IRE) 63 (Johannesburg **–** (USA) 127) [2015 5g³ 6g 6d 5m⁶ 7.2g 7.2g Sep 29] second foal: half-sister to 1m winner Thanks Harry (by Lucky Story): dam maiden (stayed 7f): no form: sometimes slowly away. *Sharon Watt*

CALRISSIAN (IRE) 4 ch.g. Lando (GER) 128 – Dallaah 94 (Green Desert (USA) 127) **60** [2015 70: p8f 8.3s² 10.2m⁵ 9g⁶ Jul 13] lengthy gelding: modest maiden: stays 8.5f: acts on tapeta, soft and good to firm going: tried in visor prior to 2015: inconsistent. *Timothy Jarvis*

CALTRA COLLEEN 3 b.f. Sixties Icon 125 – Mistic Magic (IRE) 95 (Orpen (USA) **75** 116) [2015 75: p7f⁵ 9.9m⁴ 8.3s³ 8.3d³ 8.1d⁴ 7d 7s² 6s 7s* 7v t7g t8.6g³ f8g⁴ Dec 15] fair performer: won claimer at Leicester in October: left Mick Channon after ninth start: barely stays 1¼m: acts on tapeta, soft and good to firm going: tried in blinkers in 2015. *Gay Kelleway*

CALVADOS SPIRIT 2 b.c. (Feb 5) Invincible Spirit (IRE) 121 – Putois Peace (Pivotal **71 p**
124) [2015 7g 7d⁶ Oct 30] €220,000Y: sturdy colt: first living foal: dam unraced half-sister
to smart winner up to 1¾m Lion Sands and Lancashire Oaks winner Pongee: fair form:
better effort when sixth in maiden at Newmarket (2¼ lengths behind Chelsea Lad) in
October: should do better still. *William Muir*

CALVINIST 2 b.g. (Feb 20) Holy Roman Emperor (IRE) 125 – Sharp Relief (IRE) 78 **91**
(Galileo (IRE) 134) [2015 8m⁴ 10.2m* 10g Oct 10] 55,000Y: neat gelding: first foal:
dam 11.5f-1¾m winner: fairly useful performer: won maiden at Bath by 5 lengths from
Southfields) in September: best effort when seventh in listed race at Newmarket (6½ lengths
behind Glamorous Approach) in October: stays 1¼m. *Brian Meehan*

CALYPSO BEAT (USA) 3 b.f. Speightstown (USA) 124 – African Skies 99 **102**
(Johannesburg (USA) 127) [2015 99: 7v 6.9g² 7m 7.5s³ a8.5f a8f³ Nov 22] rather leggy
filly: useful performer: best efforts in 2015 in listed race at Carlisle (good 1¼ lengths
second to Excilly) and Fairy Bridge Stakes at Tipperary (2 lengths third to Tested): left
Kevin Ryan, below form final outing: stays 7.5f: acts on soft and good to firm going: often
in headgear: front runner/races prominently. *Brendan P. Walsh, USA*

CALYPSO CHOIR 2 ch.f. (Feb 22) Bahamian Bounty 116 – Heavenly Song (IRE) 61 **84**
(Oratorio (IRE) 128) [2015 5.7f* 5.2s 5g Oct 9] angular filly: first foal: dam twice-raced
daughter of smart sprinter Lochangel: fairly useful performer: best effort when winning
maiden at Bath (by 6 lengths from David's Beauty) in June: best effort at 5.5f. *Sylvester Kirk*

CALYPSO DELEGATOR (IRE) 2 b.g. (Apr 14) Lilbourne Lad (IRE) 111 – Amber **58**
Nectar (IRE) (Barathea (IRE) 127) [2015 5.9s 8g⁶ Sep 24] better effort when sixth in
maiden at Pontefract (17 lengths behind Percy Street) in September. *Micky Hammond*

CALYPSO MUSIC 4 ch.f. Bahamian Bounty 116 – Songsheet 74 (Dominion 123) [2015 **53**
6d 7g⁵ 6m 5g⁴ 5m⁴ 5d³ 6d 5m 5g⁴ 5m⁶ 5m Sep 27] £24,000Y: sister to smart winner up to
1m Fareer (2-y-o 6f winner) and half-sister to 3 winners, including winner up to 1m
Monsieur Boulanger (2-y-o 5f/6f winner) and 1m-1¼m winner Ferryview Place (both by
Compton Place): dam 5f winner: modest maiden: best form at 5f: acts on good to soft
going: often races in rear. *Jim Goldie*

CAMAGUEYANA 3 b.f. Archipenko (USA) 127 – Caribana 77 (Hernando (FR) 127) **86**
[2015 85p: 10m 10g⁴ 9d² 10.4s Oct 10] sturdy filly: fairly useful handicapper: second at
Ffos Las in August: stays 9f: acts on polytrack and good to soft going. *Ralph Beckett*

CAMAKASI (IRE) 4 b.g. Camacho 118 – Innocence 73 (Unfuwain (USA) 131) [2015 **87**
82: p8g² 10g³ p10.7g⁴ 8g⁵ 8g³ Aug 27] fairly useful handicapper: second at Dundalk in
March and third at Musselburgh in August: stays 1¼m: acts on polytrack and soft going:
tried in cheekpieces prior to 2015: often starts slowly, often races in rear. *J. J. Feane,
Ireland*

CAMANCHE GREY (IRE) 4 gr.g. Camacho 118 – Sense of Greeting (IRE) 46 (Key of **66**
Luck (USA) 126) [2015 75: f6g⁵ f5g 5d 5g⁵ 5g* 5m Aug 4] fair performer: won seller at
Thirsk in July: best form at 5f: acts on good to firm going: tried in cheekpieces in 2015:
often races towards rear. *Ben Haslam*

CAMBODIA (IRE) 2 ch.g. (Apr 25) Fast Company (IRE) 126 – Remarkable Story **81 P**
(Mark of Esteem (IRE) 137) [2015 p7g² p7m² Dec 31] 45,000Y: sixth foal: half-brother to
3 winners, including smart 1¼m-1½m winner Grendisar (by Invincible Spirit) and 5f/6f
winner Alnoomaas (by Oasis Dream): dam once-raced close relative to Moyglare Stud
Stakes winner Necklace (by Desert King): better effort when second in maiden at Lingfield (neck behind
Shypen) in December, not having run of race: will stay 1m: certain to progress further and
is one to note. *Chris Wall*

CAMELEY DAWN 4 b.f. Alhaarth (IRE) 126 – Apply Dapply 89 (Pursuit of Love 124) **58**
[2015 67: 13.1m 9.9s 11.7g³ 16.2m⁶ 13.1g² 16.2s 11.9g² 17.2f⁴ 13.1d² 17.2g Oct 18]
workmanlike filly: modest handicapper: stays 17f: acts on firm and soft going: sometimes
wears headgear: front runner/races prominently, often races freely. *Malcolm Saunders*

CAMERAMAN 2 b.g. (Feb 17) Rail Link 132 – Photographic 99 (Oasis Dream 129) **84**
[2015 9s² 9d² Oct 11] first foal: dam, 1m winner, half-sister to very smart Australian winner
up to 1¼m Foreteller out of Cheveley Park Stakes winner Prophecy: better effort when
second in maiden at Goodwood (1½ lengths behind Harrison) in October: likely to stay
1¼m. *Amanda Perrett*

CAMEROONEY 12 b.g. Sugarfoot 118 – Enkindle 39 (Relkino 131) [2015 82: 7g 8m 7m **–**
8m⁵ Aug 7] workmanlike gelding: useful at best, no form in 2015: tried in headgear:
usually leads. *Marjorie Fife*

CAMINEL (IRE) 4 b.f. Kyllachy 129 – Jalissa 83 (Mister Baileys 123) [2015 71: p6g* **71** p6m⁶ p7f 6.1m* 6g⁵ 6s⁶ p6d p6g² p6g p6m⁶ p6g⁶ p6m⁵ Dec 16] fair handicapper: won at Lingfield in January and Nottingham in June: worth another try at 7f: acts on polytrack and good to firm going: often wears headgear: usually races in rear. *Jeremy Gask*

CAMINO 2 b.f. (Mar 4) Equiano (FR) 127 – Juncea 76 (Elnadim (USA) 128) [2015 t6g3 **64** 5m³ 5d 6m p6f Nov 12] 12,500Y: lengthy filly: fourth foal: half-sister to useful 2-y-o 5f/6f winner Juncart (by Dutch Art): dam 2-y-o 6f winner: modest maiden: stays 6f: acts on tapeta and good to firm going. *Willie Musson*

CANADIAN DIAMOND (IRE) 8 ch.g. Halling (USA) 133 – Six Nations (USA) **67** (Danzig (USA)) [2015 f12g f12d² 11.6g Oct 19] fair handicapper: left Brendan Powell after second start: stays 1¾m: acts on fibresand: sometimes wears headgear. *Jo Hughes*

CANCAN KATY 2 b.f. (Mar 1) Canford Cliffs (IRE) 133 – Katy Nowaitee 112 (Komaite **79** (USA)) [2015 p7g 6d² Sep 4] 50,000Y: half-sister to 3 useful winners, including winner up to 2m (in Australia) Mister Impatience (2-y-o 8.3f winner) and 1¼m-11f winner Harry Tricker (both by Hernando): dam 1m-1¼m winner: better effort when second in maiden at Haydock (1¼ lengths behind Shwaimsa) in September. *Tom Dascombe*

CANCELLARA 3 b.c. Kheleyf (USA) 116 – Royal Ivy 71 (Mujtahid (USA) 118) [2015 **–** p8g p8g Aug 24] rather leggy colt: no form: in headgear. *Michael Attwater*

CANDARLIYA (FR) 3 gr.f. Dalakhani (IRE) 133 – Candara (FR) (Barathea (IRE) 127) **120** [2015 10.9g² 11.9g* 13.9g* 11.9m* 12.4d* 11.9s² 12.4m* 12d Oct 17] rather leggy filly: first foal: dam twice second at 1½m from 3 starts in France: very smart performer: won minor events at Chantilly in May and Longchamp in June, listed race at Longchamp in July, Prix Minerve at Deauville in August and Prix de Royallieu at Longchamp (by 1½ lengths from Lady of Kyushu) in October: best effort when second in Prix Vermeille at Longchamp (6 lengths behind Treve) in September: disappointing when well held in Fillies' And Mares' Stakes at Ascot final outing: stays 1¾m: acts on soft and good to firm going. *A. de Royer Dupre, France*

CANDELISA (IRE) 2 br.c. (Feb 20) Dream Ahead (USA) 133 – Vasilia (Dansili 127) **95** [2015 6g⁵ 6g² 6g* 6g² 6.5m⁵ Sep 10] 31,000F: fourth foal: half-brother to 3 winners, including winner up to 1m Silverheels (2-y-o 5f winner) and winner up to 1¼m Fiftyshadesfreed (2-y-o 7f winner) (both by Verglas): dam unraced half-sister to very smart sprinter (also 1m winner) Airwave: useful performer: won maiden at Ayr in July: improved when 4 lengths fifth to Mr Lupton in valuable event at Doncaster final start: stays 6.5f: raced only on good going. *Jedd O'Keeffe*

CANDELITA 8 b.m. Trade Fair 124 – Gramada (IRE) 78 (Cape Cross (IRE) 129) [2015 **–** 11.5d 12.1m f12g Nov 26] rather leggy mare: fair at best, no form in 2015: left Alan Berry after second start: tried in headgear. *Clare Ellam*

CANDELLA 3 b.f. Stimulation (IRE) 121 – Wolumla (IRE) (Royal Applause 124) [2015 **76** 58: p10g* 10.4d⁴ 11.6d² p10g⁶ Oct 29] leggy, sparely-made filly: fair handicapper: won at Lingfield in August: stays 11.5f: acts on polytrack and good to soft going. *Roger Varian*

CANDESTA (USA) 5 b.g. First Defence (USA) 119 – Wandesta 121 (Nashwan (USA) **65** 135) [2015 70: f11g² t9.5g⁵ p8g² p10f p8f⁴ f8g² p8f⁵ p10m⁵ p8f³ p8g* p10m Nov 17] fair performer: won minor event at Kempton in October: stays 13f: acts on all-weather: often wears headgear: in tongue tie in 2015: often races towards rear. *Julia Feilden*

CANDLELIGHT (IRE) 3 b.f. Zebedee 113 – Masai Queen (IRE) (Mujadil (USA) 119) **71** [2015 65: 5.1m p6m 5g* 5.1g² 5.7g⁶ 5g⁵ Jul 4] fair handicapper: won at Redcar in May: best form at 5f: best form on good going: usually races prominently. *Charles Hills*

CANDY BANTER (USA) 2 b.f. (Jan 30) Distorted Humor (USA) 117 – Sweet Hope **58** (USA) 106 (Lemon Drop Kid (USA) 131) [2015 5g³ 6m t6f Dec 22] second foal: dam, 2-y-o 7f winner, later Grade 3 6f winner in USA: modest maiden: best effort when third in maiden at Pontefract (12 lengths behind Mayfair Lady) in July, slowly away: should be suited by further than 5f. *Kevin Ryan*

CANDY HILL (IRE) 2 b.f. (Feb 10) Jeremy (USA) 122 – Luggala (IRE) 90 (Kahyasi **71** 130) [2015 6d⁶ 5d² 6g² 7.2m³ 6g⁶ 5.9m³ 6g t7.1f⁵ Oct 3] €15,000 2-y-o: sister to useful 6f/7f winner Fairway To Heaven and half-sister to 3 winners, including 6f winner Vale of Clara (by Iffraaj): dam 1m-1¼m winner: fair maiden: stays 7f: acts on good to firm and good to soft going: sent to Italy. *Keith Dalgleish*

CANDYMAN CAN (IRE) 5 b.g. Holy Roman Emperor (IRE) 125 – Palwina (FR) **82** (Unfuwain (USA) 131) [2015 78: p10d⁵ p11g* p12g* Dec 3] fairly useful handicapper: won at Kempton in November and December: stays 1½m: acts on polytrack, fibresand and heavy going: often in hood in 2015: front runner/races prominently. *Willie Musson*

CANDY VAL (IRE) 3 b.f. Captain Rio 122 – Candy Rock (IRE) (Rock of Gibraltar (IRE) **60** 133) [2015 p8m p6m³ 7m⁵ 6g⁴ 5m³ 6m⁶ 7s Oct 6] €10,000 2-y-o: lengthy filly: second foal: dam, unraced, out of sister to 2000 Guineas winner King of Kings: modest maiden: best effort at 6f: acts on polytrack: usually in hood/tongue tie: sold 800 gns, sent to Belgium. *Jose Santos*

CANFORD BELLE 2 b.f. (Feb 12) Canford Cliffs (IRE) 133 – Ballyea (IRE) 70 **70** (Acclamation 118) [2015 5m 6g 5f 5.3v⁴ 5.1m² p6g* p6f² p6f⁶ Oct 10] 20,000Y: sturdy filly: first foal: dam, 2-y-o 6f winner, half-sister to useful winner up to 1¼m Rakaan: fair performer: won nursery at Kempton in September: stays 6f: acts on polytrack: often races prominently. *Amanda Perrett*

CANFORD CROSSING (IRE) 2 b.c. (Jan 10) Canford Cliffs (IRE) 133 – Smartest **74** (IRE) 76 (Exceed And Excel (AUS) 126) [2015 7f² p8g³ p8d⁴ p7f² t8.6g² t8.6m Dec 26] fair maiden: stays 8.5f: acts on polytrack, tapeta and firm going. *Richard Hannon*

CANFORD KILBEY (IRE) 2 b.f. (Mar 22) Canford Cliffs (IRE) 133 – Sweet Namibia **53** (IRE) 67 (Namid 128) [2015 5g⁶ 6g⁵ 5m⁴ 6g⁵ 6s 6m³ 6d⁴ 7g⁵ 7s² Oct 16] £24,000Y: fifth foal: half-sister to 3 winners, including useful 7f (including at 2 yrs) winner Whimsical (by Strategic Prince) and 2-y-o 5.5f winner Doomah (by Holy Roman Emperor): dam 5f winner: modest performer: won maiden claimer at Thirsk in August: stays 7f: acts on soft going: often races towards rear. *Richard Fahey*

CANFORD LILLI (IRE) 2 b.f. (Feb 20) Canford Cliffs (IRE) 133 – Aine (IRE) 105 **75 p** (Danehill Dancer (IRE) 117) [2015 6s² 7m³ 6d⁵ Oct 11] €22,000Y: lengthy, useful-looking filly: second foal: dam 5f/6f winner: fair maiden: best effort when second in maiden at Goodwood (neck behind Forgotten Wish) in August: remains open to improvement. *Eve Johnson Houghton*

CANFORD STAR (IRE) 2 b.f. (Feb 24) Canford Cliffs (IRE) 133 – Alexander Alliance **–** (IRE) 106 (Danetime (IRE) 121) [2015 6g 6m 5d⁵ 5.1m p6g t6f Nov 10] €26,000Y: angular filly: third foal: half-sister to 6f (including at 2 yrs) winner Dream Ally (by Oasis Dream): dam, 2-y-o 6f winner, half-sister to smart 6f winner Ruby Rocket: no form: tried in cheekpieces. *Ronald Harris*

CANFORD THOMPSON 2 b.c. (Apr 12) Canford Cliffs (IRE) 133 – Sadie Thompson **71** (IRE) 79 (King's Best (USA) 132) [2015 t7.1g³ p7g p8g Dec 16] fair maiden: best effort when third in maiden at Wolverhampton (2¼ lengths behind Status Quo) in September: should prove suited by further than 1m. *Marco Botti*

CANNOCK CHASE (USA) 4 b.c. Lemon Drop Kid (USA) 131 – Lynnwood Chase **119** (USA) (Horse Chestnut (SAF) 119) [2015 115p: 10d³ 10.3s² 10f 10d² 12g* 12g* 11.9g Dec 13] rather leggy, attractive colt: smart performer: won listed race at Newmarket (by 3¾ lengths from Tashaar) in September and Canadian International at Woodbine (by 1½ lengths from Up With The Birds) in October: runner-up in Huxley Stakes at Chester (½ length behind Maverick Wave) in May and Winter Hill Stakes at Windsor (beaten length by Racing History) in August: stays 1½m: acts on firm and soft going. *Sir Michael Stoute*

Pattison Canadian International Stakes, Woodbine—Cannock Chase (No.2) gives Sir Michael Stoute and Ryan Moore a second successive win in this Grade 1 following Hillstar in 2014

CANNY KOOL 3 b.g. Kheleyf (USA) 116 – Kool Acclaim 75 (Royal Applause 124) **106** [2015 85: 5g* 5s² 5d⁴ 5m⁶ 6.1g² 5g 5m³ Sep 27] useful performer: won handicap at Ripon (by 3¼ lengths from Rita's Boy) in April: second in listed race at Chester (¾ length behind Eastern Impact) in August: stays 6f: acts on good to firm and good to soft going: front runner/races prominently. *Brian Ellison*

CANNY STYLE 2 b.f. (Jan 21) Canford Cliffs (IRE) 133 – Stylish One (IRE) 101 **73** (Invincible Spirit (IRE) 121) [2015 6.5m³ 7m³ 7f³ 7g⁵ 6d³ 6.5m Sep 10] £22,000Y: first foal: dam, 2-y-o 7f winner, half-sister to useful performer up to 1¼m Reckoning: fair maiden: stays 7f: acts on firm and good to soft going. *Kevin Ryan*

CANONBURY (IRE) 2 b.f. (Jan 30) Oasis Dream 129 – Islington (IRE) 124 (Sadler's **64 p** Wells (USA) 132) [2015 p7g⁵ 7d⁴ Sep 26] rather unfurnished filly: sister to useful 7f/1m winner Angel Vision and half-sister to 3 winners, including useful 8.5f-1½m winner Bohemian Dance and 1¼m winner Upper Street (both by Dansili): dam 1¼m-1½m winner (including Yorkshire Oaks twice and Breeders' Cup Filly & Mare Turf): better effort when fourth in maiden at Chester (5¼ lengths behind Invermere) in September, slowly away: will be suited by 1m+: sure to progress. *Sir Michael Stoute*

CANON LAW (IRE) 5 b.g. Holy Roman Emperor (IRE) 125 – Delisha (Salse (USA) **76** 128) [2015 76: p12g² p12g⁶ t9.5f* t9.5g⁶ p11g p8g⁴ p8m⁶ p10.7g Dec 4] fair handicapper: won at Wolverhampton in March: left Albert Moriarty after second start, Muredach Kelly after fifth: stays 9.5f: acts on polytrack and tapeta: tried in headgear. *Adrian Brendan Joyce, Ireland*

CANTANKEROUS 4 b.g. Myboycharlie (IRE) 118 – Akhira 90 (Emperor Jones (USA) **49** 119) [2015 t7.1f t7.1g p7g t8.6g t9.5g t8.6g⁵ 10.2m⁵ 8.5d t9.5m⁵ Sep 25] poor maiden: stays 1¼m: acts on polytrack, tapeta and good to firm going: tried in cheekpieces. *Daniel Loughnane*

CAN'T CHANGE IT (IRE) 4 gr.g. Verglas (IRE) 118 – All Tied Up (IRE) 76 (Desert **96** Prince (IRE) 130) [2015 88: 7v⁴ 7g 7g⁵ 6m 7s 7g* Sep 12] lengthy gelding: useful handicapper: won at Lingfield (by 3¾ lengths from Ejbaar) in September: stays 1m: acts on polytrack and soft going: often in cheekpieces in 2015: sometimes slowly away. *David Simcock*

CANYARI (IRE) 4 b.g. Dandy Man (IRE) 123 – Morna's Fan (FR) (Lear Fan (USA) 130) **95** [2015 89: p6f t7d⁴ 7d 6d⁴ 6m* 6g⁴ 6d* 6m 6m 6d³ Oct 23] compact gelding: useful handicapper: won at Leicester in April and Doncaster (by short head from Adam's Ale) in June: third at Doncaster (2½ lengths behind Nameitwhatyoulike) in October: stays 6f: acts on good to firm and good to soft going: often wears headgear: front runner/races prominently. *Richard Fahey*

CAN YOU CONGA 5 b.g. Piccolo 121 – Takes Two To Tango 69 (Groom Dancer (USA) **91** 128) [2015 92: 6d⁶ 5.9m⁴ 5.9v⁴ 5f a7f³ a6f* Dec 3] fairly useful handicapper: won at Meydan (by 1¾ lengths from Padlock) in December: left Michael Easterby after fourth start: has form at 7f, better at shorter: acts on dirt and good to firm going: tried in headgear/ tongue tie. *M. Ramadan, UAE*

CAN YOU REVERSE 3 b.g. Piccolo 121 – Give Her A Whirl 63 (Pursuit of Love 124) **58** [2015 7m⁶ 6g⁴ 6g⁴ 7.5m 7m⁶ 7.2g 8.5d⁶ t8.6f⁵ Oct 20] modest maiden: stays 7.5f: acts on good to firm going: tried in blinkers. *Kevin Ryan*

CAPATOSTA (USA) 3 ch.g. Flashy Bull (USA) 118 – Da River Hoss (USA) (River **56** Special (USA)) [2015 f8g⁵ p10d² t12.2g Mar 24] modest maiden: best effort when second in maiden at Chelmsford in March. *David O'Meara*

CAP CANAILLE (USA) 2 br.c. (Apr 12) Giant's Causeway (USA) 132 – Cassis (USA) **76 p** 106 (Red Ransom (USA)) [2015 p8m³ Nov 17] half-brother to 7f winner Cassini Flight and a winner in USA (both by Bernardini): dam 5f (at 2 yrs) and 10.4f (Musidora Stakes) winner: 7/2, showed plenty when third in maiden at Lingfield (2¼ lengths behind Kummiya) in November: should do better. *Jeremy Noseda*

CAPE BANJO (USA) 2 ch.g. (Mar 26) Cape Blanco (IRE) 130 – Magic of Love 99 **82 p** (Magic Ring (IRE) 115) [2015 p7g² p8g² Dec 9] $140,000Y, 52,000 2-y-o: half-brother to several winners, including useful 1m winner Nordic Sky (by Arch): dam 5f/6f winner: runner-up in maidens at Kempton, did too much too soon when beaten 2½ lengths by Towerlands Park on second occasion: remains with potential. *Ralph Beckett*

CAPE CASTLE (IRE) 4 b.f. Cape Cross (IRE) 129 – Kaabari (USA) 89 (Seeking The **85**
Gold (USA)) [2015 –: p13.3g² 10m t13.9g* p12g* 12m* 14m p13.3f* 16m Oct 2] angular
filly: fairly useful handicapper: won at Wolverhampton, Lingfield and Doncaster (dead-
heated) in June, and Chelmsford in August: stays 1¾m: acts on polytrack, tapeta and good
to firm going. *Clive Brittain*

CAPE CAY 3 gr.f. Cape Cross (IRE) 129 – White Cay (Dalakhani (IRE) 133) [2015 74: **70**
t8.6f³ p8g⁵ 7.1m* 7m⁴ 10.2f⁴ p8f⁵ p8g³ Oct 27] fair performer: won maiden at Chepstow
in May: stays 1m: acts on polytrack, tapeta and good to firm going: tried in cheekpieces in
2015. *Ralph Beckett*

CAPE CLEAR ISLAND (IRE) 3 b.c. Fastnet Rock (AUS) 127 – Kushnarenkovo 101 **109**
(Sadler's Wells (USA) 132) [2015 89: 10g* 10d² 10.9g² 10.4g 10f Jun 18] well-made colt:
useful performer: won £200,000 Tattersalls Millions 3-Y-O Trophy at Newmarket (by neck
from Greatest Journey) in April: second in Classic Trial at Sandown (½ length behind
Master Apprentice) in April and Prix Hocquart at Longchamp (length behind Ampere) in
May: will stay 1½m: acts on good to firm going: blinkered last 2 starts (creditable seventh
in Prix du Jockey Club at Chantilly on first occasion, looked less than straightforward on
second one): usually races towards rear: sent to Hong Kong. *Aidan O'Brien, Ireland*

CAPE CRUSADER (IRE) 2 br.g. (Apr 2) Kheleyf (USA) 116 – Naddwah 85 (Pivotal **56**
124) [2015 5m⁴ 5m Sep 8] better effort when fourth in maiden at Beverley (5¼ lengths
behind Copacobana) in August. *Michael Dods*

CAPE CRYSTAL (IRE) 2 b.f. (Apr 24) Cape Cross (IRE) 129 – Lady Rockfield (IRE) **58 p**
71 (Rock of Gibraltar (IRE) 133) [2015 7v⁶ 7.1m⁶ p7g Sep 21] 30,000Y: third foal: half-
sister to 6f winner Belle Dormant (by Rip Van Winkle): dam, maiden (stayed 1m), half-
sister to smart winner up to 7f Ugo Fire: modest form: best effort when sixth in maiden at
Chepstow (6¾ lengths behind Puzzled Look) in September: should do better. *Sir Mark
Prescott Bt*

CAPE FACTOR (IRE) 4 b.f. Oratorio (IRE) 128 – Crossanza (IRE) (Cape Cross (IRE) **85**
129) [2015 104: 7s³ 6g⁵ 7s⁵ 7s Sep 18] fairly useful performer: stays 7f: acts on polytrack,
best turf form on soft/heavy going. *Rae Guest*

CAPE HIDEAWAY 3 b.g. Mount Nelson 125 – Amiata 89 (Pennekamp (USA) 130) **63**
[2015 74: 10d⁶ 10.3d 7v Nov 3] modest handicapper: best effort at 7f: acts on soft going:
often races prominently. *Mark Walford*

CAPELENA 4 br.f. Cape Cross (IRE) 129 – Roslea Lady (IRE) 63 (Alhaarth (IRE) 126) **58**
[2015 p10f p8g³ Dec 9] modest maiden: better effort in 2015 when third in maiden at
Kempton in December. *Miss Joey Ellis*

CAPE LION (IRE) 3 b.c. Kodiac 112 – Cheal Rose (IRE) 83 (Dr Devious (IRE) 127) **77**
[2015 t7.1f³ 8.1s⁶ 7.1m³ 7d⁵ 7g* 7.2m p7g⁴ 7.5g 8s⁶ p8g² p8g p8g Nov 24] fair performer:
won handicap at Leicester in July: won then Mark Johnston after eighth start, P. & F. Montfort
after eleventh: stays 1m: acts on polytrack: tried in cheekpieces. *Alain Lyon, France*

CAPELITA 4 b.f. Cape Cross (IRE) 129 – Zamhrear 73 (Singspiel (IRE) 133) [2015 83: **76**
p8g p8m⁶ 6.1g⁴ t6g³ 5g⁶ 7m⁵ 6m² 6g² p7g* f8g* f8g⁵ Dec 22] good-topped filly: fairly **a93**
useful performer: won maiden at Kempton in August and handicap at Southwell in
December: left Clive Brittain after ninth start: stays 1m: acts on all-weather, good to firm
and good to soft going: usually races close up. *Michael Appleby*

CAPELLANUS (IRE) 9 b.g. Montjeu (IRE) 137 – Secret Dream (IRE) (Zafonic (USA) **63**
130) [2015 t16.5g⁴ Mar 27] modest handicapper: stays 2m: acts on good to firm and good
to soft going: tried in headgear prior to 2015. *Brian Ellison*

CAPE LOVE (USA) 2 ch.c. (Feb 4) Cape Blanco (IRE) 130 – Matroshka (IRE) (Red **82 p**
Ransom (USA)) [2015 8d² 8d* 8d⁵ Sep 5] $110,000Y: fourth foal: half-brother to 2-y-o 5f
winner Stand of Glory (by Oasis Dream) and a winner in USA by Tale of The Cat: dam,
unraced, out of half-sister to Prix de Diane winner Rafha: fairly useful form: best effort
when winning maiden at Thirsk (by head from Bo Bridget) in August: raced only at 1m:
should do better. *David O'Meara*

CAPEL PATH (USA) 3 b.c. Street Cry (IRE) 130 – Miss Lucifer (FR) 119 (Noverre **100**
(USA) 125) [2015 86p: 7m³ 7m² 8f^pu Jun 18] well-made colt: useful performer: second in
handicap at Ascot (2 lengths behind Mister Universe) in May: injured when pulled up in
Britannia Stakes (Handicap) at Royal Ascot: would have stayed 1m: acted on good to firm
going: dead. *Sir Michael Stoute*

CAPE OF GLORY (IRE) 2 br.c. (Apr 20) Cape Cross (IRE) 129 – Stairway To Glory **75**
(IRE) 86 (Kalanisi (IRE) 132) [2015 t8.6m⁴ p8f³ p8f³ p8g³ Nov 26] fair maiden: will stay
beyond 1m. *James Tate*

CAPE ROSIE 3 b.f. Cape Cross (IRE) 129 – Rosika 112 (Sakhee (USA) 136) [2015 **72**
p12m⁴ 12m 9.9g⁶ 10g 9g p10f⁴ 13.1s³ 13.1f⁴ Sep 13] first foal: dam, 1¼m-1½m winner,
half-sister to smart dam of high-class 1¼m performer Notnowcato: fair maiden: stays 13f:
acts on polytrack and firm going: front runner/races prominently. *Eve Johnson Houghton*

CAPERS ROYAL STAR (FR) 4 b.g. What A Caper (IRE) – Arundhati (IRE) (Royal –
Academy (USA) 130) [2015 69: p10g p12f Mar 11] plain, rather leggy gelding: maiden: no
form in 2015: stays 1¼m: acts on polytrack, soft and good to firm going: tried in headgear:
front runner/races prominently. *Ralph Smith*

CAPE SPEED (FR) 2 b.c. (Jan 15) Cape Cross (IRE) 129 – At A Great Rate (USA) 82 **85 p**
(Arch (USA) 127) [2015 6m⁵ p8f* Dec 21] 47,000Y: first foal: dam, 1¼m winner, half-
sister to dam of very smart US Grade 1 8.5f-1¼m winner Emollient out of half-sister to
dam of Prix de l'Arc de Triomphe winner Bago: better effort when winning maiden at
Chelmsford (by neck from Dwight D) in December: will stay 1¼m: open to further
improvement. *Mark Johnston*

CAPE SPIRIT (IRE) 3 b.f. Cape Cross (IRE) 129 – Fearless Spirit (USA) 74 (Spinning **63**
World (USA) 130) [2015 67p: 7v⁵ 8g 9.9g⁶ 8.1m² 10.4g⁵ 11.6d³ 10v Sep 16] rather
unfurnished filly: modest maiden: stays 11.5f: acts on good to firm going, probably on
heavy: tried in cheekpieces in 2015. *Andrew Balding*

CAPE VICTORIA 4 b.f. Mount Nelson 125 – Victoria Montoya 104 (High Chaparral **86**
(IRE) 132) [2015 64p: t12.2g* 11.6m³ p12g⁵ 11.9m* 12g* 11.9g⁶ 12v⁵ p12g Sep 23] fairly **a79**
useful performer: won maiden at Wolverhampton in April, and handicaps at Brighton and
Ffos Las in July: will stay beyond 1½m: acts on tapeta and good to firm going: often in
cheekpieces in 2015. *Andrew Balding*

CAPE WRATH 4 gr.g. Verglas (IRE) 118 – Capades Dancer (USA) (Gate Dancer (USA)) **67**
[2015 75: 8g 8g⁵ 9.9m 8g 8g 9.8d⁶ 7g 7g 8.5m t8.6f Oct 17] fair handicapper: best effort at
6f: acts on good to soft going: often in headgear in 2015: often races towards rear: sent to
Greece. *Micky Hammond*

CAPE XENIA 3 b.f. Cape Cross (IRE) 129 – Xaphania (Sakhee (USA) 136) [2015 67: **83**
p8g³ 8m³ 8g³ 7m³ 6g* 6m* 6d⁶ Sep 4] sturdy filly: fairly useful handicapper: won at
Leicester in July and Windsor in August: stayed 1m, best efforts at 6f: acted on polytrack,
good to firm and good to soft going: dead. *Henry Candy*

CAPITAL GEARING 2 b.g. (Feb 10) Makfi 130 – Dicara (GER) (Royal Applause 124) **67**
[2015 6.1d³ p6g 7m 8s³ 8.9g⁵ 8s³ Oct 29] sturdy gelding: fair maiden: stays 9f: acts on soft
going: tried in headgear. *Henry Spiller*

CAPONOVA (IRE) 2 b.g. (Apr 11) Bushranger (IRE) 119 – Satin Cape (IRE) 62 (Cape **64**
Cross (IRE) 129) [2015 6m t6g⁴ 7m⁵ t7.1f Oct 20] modest maiden: best effort at 6f.
Tom Dascombe

CAPO ROSSO (IRE) 5 b.g. Red Clubs (IRE) 125 – Satin Cape (IRE) 62 (Cape Cross **106**
(IRE) 129) [2015 108: t7.1m p8g p8f⁵ 8g² 8m 7f² 8f⁵ Sep 13] compact gelding: useful
performer: runner-up in handicap (1¼ lengths behind Wilde Inspiration) in April and minor
event (nose behind Hawkesbury) in July, both at Haydock: stays 8.5f: acts on polytrack,
tapeta and firm going: tried in headgear: tried in tongue tie prior to 2015: usually front
runner/races prominently. *Tom Dascombe*

CAPPELLA SANSEVERO 3 b.c. Showcasing 117 – Madam President 76 (Royal **104**
Applause 124) [2015 109: 8m 8g 7g⁶ Jun 18] smallish, sturdy, good-bodied colt: useful
performer: won Round Tower Stakes at the Curragh at 2 yrs: may have proven best at sprint
trips: acted on polytrack, soft and good to firm going: tried in cheekpieces in 2015: usually
raced towards rear: to stand at Bridge House Stud, Co. Westmeath, Ireland, fee €4,500. *G.
M. Lyons, Ireland*

CAPPIELOW PARK 6 b.g. Exceed And Excel (AUS) 126 – Barakat 93 (Bustino 136) **53**
[2015 p12g⁵ Dec 2] well-made gelding: modest maiden: stays 1½m: acts on polytrack, soft
and good to firm going: sometimes wears cheekpieces: often starts slowly, often travels
strongly. *Ali Stronge*

CAPPY BROWN 2 b.g. (May 2) Showcasing 117 – Corndavon (USA) 95 (Sheikh Albadou **58**
128) [2015 5m⁶ p6g⁵ 5.1m⁵ p7g p6f⁵ Nov 5] modest maiden: stays 7f: acts on polytrack:
tried in cheekpieces. *Alan Bailey*

CAPRIOR BERE (FR) 3 b.g. Peer Gynt (JPN) – Hush Hush (USA) (Horse Chestnut **93**
(SAF) 119) [2015 92: p8m² p7g⁶ 7.6s⁵ 6m 7m² 6g 7.2g 7v Nov 7] fairly useful handicapper:
second at Kempton in February and Doncaster in September: stays 1m: acts on polytrack
and good to firm going: often races prominently. *K. R. Burke*

CAPSIZE 3 b.g. Showcasing 117 – Change Course 67 (Sadler's Wells (USA) 132) [2015 – 67: 8.3f 12f⁶ t9.5g Jul 28] close-coupled gelding: maiden: no form in 2015: tried in visor prior to 2015: often races prominently. *Alex Hales*

CAPTAIN BOB (IRE) 4 b.g. Dark Angel (IRE) 113 – Birthday Present (Cadeaux 92 Genereux 131) [2015 94: 7.6s⁶ 7m 7f² 7m² 7d⁵ 7d⁴ 7g Sep 26] good-topped gelding: fairly useful handicapper: runner-up at Ascot and York in July: stays 7.5f: acts on firm and soft going: tried in headgear. *Charles Hills*

CAPTAIN CAT (IRE) 6 b.g. Dylan Thomas (IRE) 132 – Mother of Pearl (IRE) 113 117 (Sadler's Wells (USA) 132) [2015 122: p10g⁵ 8m 7d 8g⁶ 8s⁵ 8d⁵ p9.2m⁴ Sep 26] big gelding: smart performer: creditable efforts in 2015 when fifth in Winter Derby at Lingfield (beaten 1¼ lengths by Tryster) and fourth in minor event at Chelmsford (1¾ lengths behind same rival) first/final starts: stays 1¼m: acts on polytrack, soft and good to firm going: tried in headgear (blinkered final start): usually races in rear. *Roger Charlton*

CAPTAIN COLBY (USA) 3 b.g. Bernstein (USA) 115 – Escape To Victory (Salse 101 (USA) 128) [2015 92: 6f* May 16] useful handicapper: won at Newmarket (by 1½ lengths from Steve Prescott) in May: stays 6f: acts on firm and good to soft going: often wears headgear: usually leads. *Kevin Ryan*

CAPTAIN DION 2 gr.c. (Mar 25) Equiano (FR) 127 – Bandanna 98 (Bandmaster (USA) 74 p 97) [2015 6s⁴ 6d⁴ Oct 26] £35,000Y: half-brother to several winners, including useful winner up to 1m Markazzi (2-y-o 7f winner, by Dansili) and 5f winner Mandy's Hero (by Compton Place): dam 5f/6f winner (including at 2 yrs): better effort when winning maiden at Redcar (by short head from Never In Doubt) in October, holding on gamely: open to further improvement. *Kevin Ryan*

CAPTAIN DUNNE (IRE) 10 b.g. Captain Rio 122 – Queen Bodicea (IRE) (Revoque 93 (IRE) 122) [2015 87: 5m* 5m* 5g 5m³ 5.1m³ 5g* 5g 5v⁴ 5d 5s 5v Oct 17] lengthy, workmanlike gelding: fairly useful handicapper: won at Thirsk (twice) (by 1½ lengths from Master Bond latter occasion) in May and Catterick (by 1½ lengths from Irish Girls Spirit) in July: stays 5.5f: acts on fibresand, good to firm and heavy going: tried in headgear prior to 2015: usually leads. *Tim Easterby*

CAPTAIN FELIX 3 b.g. Captain Gerrard (IRE) 113 – Sweet Applause (IRE) 84 85 (Acclamation 118) [2015 –: 8g⁶ 9.9g* 10v 8d p8m* p8d⁶ t9.5f² Dec 14] good-topped gelding: fairly useful handicapper: won handicap at Beverley in August and claimer at Lingfield in November: second in handicap at Wolverhampton (amateur) in December: stays 1¼m: acts on polytrack and tapeta. *Gay Kelleway*

CAPTAIN FUTURE 3 b.g. Captain Gerrard (IRE) 113 – Saorocain (IRE) (Kheleyf 56 (USA) 116) [2015 –p: t5.1f² f6d² t5.1f* t6g⁵ 5.1m⁶ 5m⁶ t5.1g⁴ 5d⁵ 5m⁵ t6m Aug 21] fair a65 handicapper: won at Wolverhampton in February: best form at 5f: acts on tapeta: in headgear in 2015: tried in tongue tie in 2015. *Bryan Smart*

CAPTAIN GEORGE (IRE) 4 b.g. Bushranger (IRE) 119 – High Society Girl (IRE) 53 (Key of Luck (USA) 126) [2015 78: 8.3m p11g 12.1m p12g 13.1d 11.9d⁵ t12.2f* Oct 16] a62 modest handicapper: won at Wolverhampton in October: stays 1½m: acts on polytrack, tapeta and good to firm going: sometimes wears headgear: often races prominently. *Michael Blake*

CAPTAIN GERALD 2 b.g. (Apr 29) Captain Gerrard (IRE) 113 – My Heart's On Fire 61 (IRE) 81 (Beat Hollow 126) [2015 5g⁶ 5.1g 7g⁶ 7m⁴ p8g² p8g p8f² 10.2f⁴ p8m p8f³ p10f³ Oct 22] compact gelding: modest maiden: stays 1¼m: acts on polytrack and firm going: often in cheekpieces: often leads. *John Ryan*

CAPTAIN JOEY (IRE) 2 b.g. (Mar 1) Kodiac 112 – Archetypal (IRE) (Cape Cross – (IRE) 129) [2015 6g 7g Sep 25] useful-looking gelding: no form. *Charles Hills*

CAPTAIN JOY (IRE) 6 gr.g. Dark Angel (IRE) 113 – Ardea Brave (IRE) 83 (Chester 106 House (USA) 123) [2015 107, a115: p8m* p8g² p8f³ 8g² 8m Jun 27] smart performer: won a114 minor event at Lingfield (by 1¼ lengths from Alfred Hutchinson) in January: second in listed race at Leopardstown (beaten ¾ length by Tennessee Wildcat) in June: stays 1m: acts on polytrack, tapeta and good to firm going: usually races close up. *Tracey Collins, Ireland*

CAPTAIN KENDALL (IRE) 6 b.g. Clodovil (IRE) 116 – Queen's Lace (IRE) (King's 60 Best (USA) 132) [2015 63: 7.6d 7.1s⁵ p8m p7m⁵ p7g* Dec 30] lengthy gelding: modest handicapper: won at Lingfield in December: stays 7f: acts on polytrack and good to firm going: tried in headgear. *Harry Chisman*

CAPTAIN KOKO 3 b.g. Selkirk (USA) 129 – Lady Artemisia (IRE) 103 (Montjeu (IRE) 56 137) [2015 66: p8f⁵ 12d p12g⁵ May 26] modest maiden: stays 1m: acts on polytrack and fibresand: often races freely. *Marco Botti*

CAPTAIN LARS (SAF) 6 b.g. Captain Al (SAF) – Polar Charge 106 (Polar Falcon **97**
(USA) 126) [2015 8g 8g p8g 7g p6g⁵ 6d p7g² p8m* Dec 31] useful performer: won seller
at Lingfield in December: left M. F. de Kock after second start, Ken Cunningham-Brown
after sixth: stays 9f: acts on polytrack and good to soft going: often in headgear in 2015.
Michael Bell

CAPTAIN MARMALADE (IRE) 3 gr.g. Duke of Marmalade (IRE) 132 – Elisium **78**
(Proclamation (IRE) 130) [2015 75: p6f 6s³ 6.1m* 6m⁴ Jul 11] good-bodied gelding: fair
handicapper: won at Chepstow in June: best effort at 6f: acts on polytrack, good to firm
going and soft going: often in hood in 2015. *Roger Charlton*

CAPTAIN MIDNIGHT (IRE) 4 b.g. Bushranger (IRE) 119 – Beverley Macca 73 **70**
(Piccolo 121) [2015 88: 7v 6g 6g 7.2m⁴ 7m 7.2d⁶ a7g⁶ p7g* p7g* Nov 13] workmanlike
gelding: fair handicapper: won at Dundalk (twice) in November: left J. J. Feane after
seventh start: stays 1m: acts on polytrack and good to firm going: often in headgear in
2015: tried in tongue tie in 2015. *Joseph Anthony Murray, Ireland*

CAPTAIN MORLEY 4 b.g. Hernando (FR) 127 – Oval Office 99 (Pursuit of Love 124) **106**
[2015 100: 11.6g² 10m⁵ 10.3g⁶ 12d* Sep 12] big gelding: useful handicapper: won at
Doncaster (by 4 lengths from Kinema) in September: likely to stay 1¾m: acts on polytrack,
good to firm and heavy going: held up. *David Simcock*

CAPTAIN NAVARRE 3 b.g. Excellent Art 125 – Quantum (IRE) 89 (Alhaarth (IRE) **86**
126) [2015 85: 10.3d 10g p10g³ 11.9g⁵ p12g³ t12.2g³ 11.6d⁴ 13d² 11.9m² p14f³ 11.5m²
12g⁶ 10d⁴ Oct 30] smallish, close-coupled gelding: fairly useful maiden: second in
handicaps at Newmarket in July and Yarmouth in September: stays 1¾m: acts on polytrack,
tapeta, good to firm and good to soft going: front runner/races prominently: consistent.
Lydia Pearce

CAPTAIN OATS (IRE) 12 b.g. Bahhare (USA) 122 – Adarika (Kings Lake (USA) 133) **58 §**
[2015 68§: 12.1m⁶ 12.1s⁵ 14.1g³ 10.2d² 10.2d⁶ Sep 2] angular gelding: modest handicapper:
stays 2¼m: acts on any turf going: tried in cheekpieces prior to 2015: sometimes slowly
away, often races towards rear: irresolute. *Pam Ford*

CAPTAIN PEACOCK 2 b.c. (Feb 4) Champs Elysees 124 – Blast Furnace (IRE) 74 **– p**
(Sadler's Wells (USA) 132) [2015 8.3g 8.1s 8.3d Oct 14] second foal: dam, maiden (stayed
1m), closely related to very smart winner up to 7f King Charlemagne and smart winner up
to 7f Meshaheer: little impact in maidens: should do better in handicaps. *William Knight*

CAPTAIN REVELATION 3 ch.g. Captain Rio 122 – Agony Aunt 81 (Formidable **81**
(USA) 125) [2015 83: t6g² p8g³ 6.1s t7.1g² 7f 7g* 7g t7.1g 7.6g⁵ p8g Sep 21] fairly useful
handicapper: won at Chester (by short head from Gatepost) in July: stays 7.5f: acts on
fibresand, tapeta and good to firm going: sometimes in headgear in 2015. *Tom Dascombe*

CAPTAIN RHYRIC 6 ch.g. Dylan Thomas (IRE) 132 – Nuts In May (USA) 63 (A P Indy **–**
(USA) 131) [2015 16.1d 13.1d Jun 8] maiden: no form in 2015: stays 11f: acts on soft and
good to firm going: front runner/races prominently. *James Moffatt*

CAPTAIN ROYALE (IRE) 10 ch.g. Captain Rio 122 – Paix Royale (Royal Academy **66**
(USA) 130) [2015 88: 6g 5d 6s 5g⁵ 5g 5g Oct 13] strong, good-topped gelding: fair
handicapper: stays 7f: acts on any turf going: usually wears headgear: often races
prominently. *Tracy Waggott*

CAPTAIN RYAN 4 b.g. Captain Gerrard (IRE) 113 – Ryan's Quest (IRE) 67 (Mukad- **69**
damah (USA) 125) [2015 73: 6m⁶ 6g³ 5.7m⁶ 6g⁴ 5m* 5.7m 5m² 5s² 5.3d 5.7m⁶ 6g Oct 20]
sturdy gelding: fair handicapper: won at Bath in July: stays 5.5f: acts on firm and good to
soft going: tried in headgear prior to 2015. *Peter Makin*

CAPTAIN SCOOBY 9 b.g. Captain Rio 122 – Scooby Dooby Do 62 (Atraf 116) [2015 **68**
64: t5.1f f6d² t6g⁵ 5m⁵ 5s² 6.1d 5.1d⁴ 5m³ 6g³ 6m⁵ 5g 6m³ 6g⁴ 6s⁵ 5g⁵ 5g 5.1d* 5s³ 6d⁵ 6g⁶ **a56**
6g³ 5.1d 6g* 5.1d t6f Nov 13] good-topped gelding: fair handicapper: won at Nottingham
in August and Windsor in October: stays 6f: acts on polytrack, good to firm and heavy
going: sometimes wears headgear: usually races towards rear. *Richard Guest*

CAPTAIN SHARPE 7 ch.g. Tobougg (IRE) 125 – Helen Sharp (Pivotal 124) [2015 16m **–**
Apr 6] workmanlike gelding: fair at best, no form in 2015: stays 17f: acts on good to firm
and heavy going: often wears headgear: tried in tongue tie prior to 2015. *Robert Johnson*

CAPTAIN STARLIGHT (IRE) 5 b.g. Captain Marvelous (IRE) 114 – Jewell In The **–**
Sky (IRE) (Sinndar (IRE) 134) [2015 p7m p7f t8.6g t8.6mᵖᵘ t8.6gᵖᵘ Dec 1] fairly useful at
best, no form in 2015: left Jo Crowley after second start: often in headgear in 2015.
Aytach Sadik

CAPTAIN SWIFT (IRE) 4 br.g. Captain Rio 122 – Grannys Reluctance (IRE) 63 **78**
(Anita's Prince 126) [2015 78: t13.9f⁴ t12.2g 11.8d² 11.9d* 12s Oct 27] compact gelding:
fair handicapper: won at Haydock in September: best effort at 1½m: acts on tapeta and
good to soft going: tried in blinkers prior to 2015. *John Mackie*

CAPTAINTHUNDERBOLT (IRE) 2 b.g. (Mar 4) Bushranger (IRE) 119 – Dream **60**
Date (IRE) 78 (Oasis Dream 129) [2015 5m⁴ 6g 6m 6.1d p8g³ p8g Aug 24] compact
gelding: modest maiden: stays 1m: acts on polytrack and good to firm going: often in
headgear. *Brian Meehan*

CAPTAIN WHOOSH (IRE) 4 gr.g. Dandy Man (IRE) 123 – Caerella (IRE) (Alzao **66**
(USA) 117) [2015 79: t5.1f⁵ p5m⁴ 5m⁴ 5g⁵ 5m⁶ 7.2d Jul 27] fair handicapper: best form at
5f: acts on tapeta and firm going: tried in headgear. *John Quinn*

CARAMBA (IRE) 3 b.f. Lord Shanakill (USA) 121 – Known Class (USA) (Known Fact **–**
(USA) 135) [2015 –: p6g 8g⁶ p12g Aug 19] maiden: no form in 2015. *Brendan Powell*

CARA'S MUSE (IRE) 2 b.f. (Feb 3) Zoffany (IRE) 121 – Shenkara (IRE) 79 (Night **71**
Shift (USA)) [2015 5.1d p6g 6g² 6.1m p7g* Sep 9] €26,000Y: rather leggy filly: half-sister
to several winners, including useful 5f-7f winner You Da One (by Footstepsinthesand) and
useful/untrustworthy winner up to 8.4f Crocodile Bay (2-y-o 5f winner, by Spectrum): dam
maiden (stayed 1m): fair performer: in hood, won nursery at Kempton in September: best
effort at 7f: acts on polytrack: often races towards rear: sent to Spain. *Eve Johnson Houghton*

CARA'S REQUEST (AUS) 10 gr.g. Urgent Request (IRE) 120 – Carahill (AUS) **70**
(Danehill (USA) 126) [2015 83: f7g³ 7d² 7.1m 7d f7g Nov 3] compact gelding: fair
handicapper: left Michael Dods after third start: stays 8.5f: acts on fibresand and any turf
going: usually leads. *David C. Griffiths*

CARBON DATING (IRE) 3 b.c. The Carbon Unit (USA) 106 – Advertising Space **86**
(IRE) (Galileo (IRE) 134) [2015 10.2v⁵ 10.1g⁵ 10v³ 8g 12m 12m 11.1s⁵ 12g³ a8f⁵ a9.9f³
Dec 17] good-topped colt: third foal: half-brother to smart 1¼m-1¾m winner Ralston
Road (by Dylan Thomas): dam unraced: fairly useful maiden: third in Derrinstown Stud
Derby Trial at Leopardstown (15½ lengths behind Success Days) in May: highly tried next
4 outings: left John Patrick Shanahan after eighth start: stays 1½m: acts on dirt and good to
firm going: tried in blinkers. *S. Seemar, UAE*

CARBUTT'S RIDGE (IRE) 2 br.g. (Apr 24) Alfred Nobel (IRE) 110 – Tallassee 60 **59 §**
(Indian Ridge 123) [2015 6g 6d⁴ 5m 7.1m 6g 8d f8g³ t9.5f Dec 11] workmanlike gelding:
modest maiden: stays 1m: acts on good to soft going: often in headgear: temperamental. *K.
R. Burke*

CARCHARIAS (IRE) 2 b.c. (May 12) Kodiac 112 – Princess Atoosa (USA) (Gone West **58**
(USA)) [2015 7.4d 7g 7s p6f⁵ p7g⁵ Oct 6] modest maiden: stays 7f: acts on polytrack and
good to soft going. *Ed de Giles*

CARD HIGH (IRE) 5 b.g. Red Clubs (IRE) 125 – Think (FR) 99 (Marchand de Sable **83**
(USA) 117) [2015 63: 12.5s⁶ 10d⁴ 12.4g* 11.1m² 11.5d² 11.5m³ 12.1g⁴ 13.1g 12g* 12v²
12s* 10.2s Nov 14] fairly useful handicapper: won at Newcastle in May, Pontefract
(apprentice) in September and Catterick (by 1½ lengths from Multellie) in October: stays
12.5f: acts on soft going: often wears tongue tie. *Wilf Storey*

CARDINAL 10 ch.h. Pivotal 124 – Fictitious 100 (Machiavellian (USA) 123) [2015 76, **57**
a66: p5m 5.1s⁴ 5.1d³ 5.3s Jun 2] plain horse: modest handicapper: stays 6f: acts on
polytrack, good to firm and heavy going: tried in cheekpieces: tried in tongue tie prior to
2015. *Robert Cowell*

CARDINAL PALACE (IRE) 5 b.g. Papal Bull 128 – Heat (King's Best (USA) 132) **85**
[2015 107: p12g¹¹ 14v² 16.4d Aug 19] fairly useful handicapper: second in minor event at
Listowel in May: likely to prove best at short of 2m: acts on polytrack, good to firm and
heavy going: tried in headgear: tried in tongue tie in 2015: useful hurdler. *James A. Nash,
Ireland*

CARDINAL SIN 3 b.g. Major Cadeaux 121 – Golden Nun 108 (Bishop of Cashel 122) **42**
[2015 5m⁵ 6g⁵ 5g⁴ 5s⁶ 5m⁵ 5s p7m f7m Dec 8] poor maiden: best effort at 7f: acts on
polytrack: often in cheekpieces. *Les Eyre*

CARELESS RAPTURE 2 ch.f. (Feb 1) Champs Elysees 124 – Cushat Law (IRE) 75 **–**
(Montjeu (IRE) 137) [2015 7s⁶ p8g p8f Nov 12] third foal: dam 1½m winner: no form.
Mark H. Tompkins

CARENOT (IRE) 2 b.f. (Mar 11) Iffraaj 127 – Sahara Sky (IRE) (Danehill (USA) 126) **76 p**
[2015 7s² 8s² Oct 9] €35,000Y: fifth foal: half-sister to 3 winners, including useful 2-y-o 6f
(including Phoenix Stakes) winner Dick Whittingtson (by Rip Van Winkle) and useful 2-y-o

5f winner Sign From Heaven (by Raven's Pass): dam, unraced, closely related to July Cup winner Owington: fair form in maidens: better effort when second in maiden at Salisbury (3 lengths behind Robanne) in September: remains with potential. *William Haggas*

CARLA BIANCA (IRE) 4 gr.f. Dansili 127 – Majestic Silver (IRE) (Linamix (FR) 127) **111** [2015 113p: 9.5g⁴ 12m² 9d* 9.5d⁶ 10d p10.7g² Oct 2] close-coupled, attractive filly: smart performer: won Meld Stakes at Leopardstown (by ¾ length from Elleval) in July: second in Munster Oaks at Cork (¾ length behind Words) in June and Diamond Stakes at Dundalk (3 ran, beaten length by Panama Hat) in October: stays 1½m: acts on good to firm and good to soft going: tried in visor in 2015: usually races close up. *D. K. Weld, Ireland*

CARLANDA (FR) 5 ch.m. Lando (GER) 128 – Carousel Girl (USA) (Gulch (USA)) **74 §** [2015 74: f12g⁵ f12d* f12d* f14gᵗᵗ f12g⁵ Mar 10] fair handicapper: won at Southwell in January and February: stays 1¾m: acts on fibresand and good to firm going: sometimes wears headgear: one to treat with caution. *Michael Appleby*

CARLOVIAN 2 b.g. (Apr 30) Acclamation 118 – Mimisel 92 (Selkirk (USA) 129) [2015 **71** 7f⁶ 6g⁴ 6.1m⁴ 6g⁴ 5m⁴ 5g 6g⁴ 6d Oct 19] strong gelding: fair maiden: best effort at 6f: acts on good to firm going: front runner/races prominently. *Danielle McCormick*

CARNACHY (IRE) 3 gr.f. Mastercraftsman (IRE) 129 – Market Day 105 (Tobougg **99 p** (IRE) 125) [2015 9.3m² 8.1m² 10s* 12d* Oct 11] £68,000Y: third foal: half-sister to 7f/1m winners Coach Montana (by Proud Citizen) and Saucy Minx (by Dylan Thomas), latter useful but irresolute: dam, 2-y-o 6f/7f winner, later 1m winner in USA: useful performer: won maiden at Newbury in August and handicap at Goodwood by 4 lengths from Revision) in October: stays 1½m: open to further improvement. *David Simcock*

CARNAGEO (FR) 2 b.g. (Mar 11) Pivotal 124 – Sudarynya (IRE) (Sadler's Wells (USA) **64 p** 132) [2015 7.5m 6d⁴ t7.1f Nov 13] €55,000 2-y-o: fifth foal: half-brother to winners abroad by Dalakhani and Kentucky Dynamite: dam, second at 5f at 2 yrs in France on only start, half-sister to US Grade 1 2-y-o 8.5f winner Consolidator: modest maiden: best effort when fourth in maiden at Redcar (2 lengths behind Gowanless) in October, nearest finish: will stay 7f+: should do better. *Richard Fahey*

CARNIVAL KING (IRE) 3 b.c. Arcano (IRE) 122 – Validate (Alhaarth (IRE) 126) **92** [2015 74: 7m⁴ 7m⁶ 7g⁴ Jul 29] tall, angular colt: fairly useful performer: won maiden at Newmarket (by length from Hakam) in April: may prove best up to 7f: acts on good to firm going. *Brian Meehan*

CARNTOP 2 b.c. (Feb 10) Dansili 127 – Milford Sound (Barathea (IRE) 127) [2015 8m³ **100 p** 8m* Oct 3] good-topped colt: third foal: brother to French 10.5f winner Quebec: dam, French 1m winner, half-sister to Prix de l'Arc de Triomphe winner Rail Link (by Dansili): better effort when winning maiden at Newmarket (by 2¾ lengths from Schubert) in October, staying on strongly: will be suited by 1¼m+: will go on improving. *Ralph Beckett*

CAROLINAE 3 ch.f. Makfi 130 – You Too 74 (Monsun (GER) 124) [2015 t9.5g⁴ f12g⁶ **–** Dec 22] 10,000Y: fifth foal: half-sister to 3 winners, including useful 1¼m-1¾m winner (stays 16.5f) Totalize (by Authorized) and 11f winner Sharareh (by Sir Percy): dam 1¾m winner: no form. *Charlie Fellowes*

CAROLINE NORTON (USA) 3 b.f. Henrythenavigator (USA) 131 – Fifth Avenue **65** Doll (USA) (Marquetry (USA) 121) [2015 –p: 10g p10g⁶ p12g⁶ 16.2m p15.8g⁶ Aug 13] sturdy filly: fair maiden: seems to stay 2m: acts on polytrack: in headgear last 3 starts. *John Gosden*

CARPE DIEM LADY (IRE) 2 b.f. (May 2) Acclamation 118 – Greenisland (IRE) 100 **68** (Fasliyev (USA) 120) [2015 p7g⁵ 7.6g³ 7s⁵ Oct 12] 85,000Y: lengthy filly: third foal: half-sister to useful 5f (including at 2 yrs) winner Shamshon (by Invincible Spirit): dam 7f and (at 2 yrs) 1m winner: fair maiden: best effort when third in maiden at Lingfield (5½ lengths behind Mix And Mingle) in September. *Clive Cox*

CARPE VITA (IRE) 3 b.f. Montjeu (IRE) 137 – Dance Parade (USA) 107 (Gone West **83 p** (USA)) [2015 10m 11.5d⁶ p12g 14.1m* 13.1g² Sep 17] sister to 3 winners, notably St Leger/Gold Cup winner Leading Light (2-y-o 9f winner), and half-sister to several winners, including smart 6f/7f winner Castles In The Air (by Oasis Dream): dam 5f (Queen Mary Stakes) to 1m (US Grade 2) winner: fairly useful performer: won handicap at Redcar in August: good second in similar event at Ayr: left Charles Hills after third start: stays 1¾m: acts on good to firm going: sometimes in hood: usually races nearer last than first: will go on improving. *David O'Meara*

CARRABAMABABE 4 b.f. Beat All (USA) 120 – Carranita (IRE) 111 (Anita's Prince **–** 126) [2015 f5g⁴ f5d³ p5g³ f5g Nov 3] half-sister to useful 5f/6f winner Go Far (by Dutch Art): dam winner up to 7f (2-y-o 5f/6f winner): no form. *J. R. Jenkins*

CARRAGOLD 9 b.g. Diktat 126 – Shadow Roll (IRE) 79 (Mark of Esteem (IRE) 137) **77**
[2015 75: f11g² f11g* f12g⁵ t12.2f³ t9.5f⁵ Dec 21] workmanlike gelding: fair handicapper:
won at Southwell in February: stays 1½m: acts on all-weather, good to firm and heavy
going: tried in headgear. *Antony Brittain*

CARRINGTON (FR) 2 b.g. (May 25) New Approach (IRE) 132 – Winning Family **90 §**
(IRE) (Fasliyev (USA) 120) [2015 5f⁵ p5m* 6m² 7d² 7.1m³ 7d* 7m³ p7g⁴ Sep 30] rather
unfurnished gelding: fifth foal: closely related to French 9f winner Winografa (by Teofilo)
and half-brother to 2 winners in France, including smart 1¼m-12.5f winner La Conquerante
(by Hurricane Run): dam French 2-y-o 6f/7.5f winner: fairly useful performer: won maiden
at Chelmsford in May and nursery at Goodwood in August: stays 7f: acts on polytrack,
good to firm and good to soft going: pulls hard and is not an easy ride, often starts slowly:
best treated with caution. *Charlie Appleby*

CARR LANE 2 b.f. (Apr 6) Piccolo 121 – Leominda 67 (Lion Cavern (USA) 117) [2015 **–**
f7m f8f Dec 17] £4,500Y: seventh foal: half-sister to 3 winners, including winner up to 11f
Hidden Glory (2-y-o 1m winner, by Mujahid): dam maiden (stayed 6f): no form. *Michael
Easterby*

CARRON VALLEY 3 b.g. Royal Applause 124 – Clear Impression (IRE) 103 (Danehill **–**
(USA) 126) [2015 52: f7d t6m Feb 27] maiden: no form in 2015: stays 1m: acts on
polytrack and fibresand: in blinkers final start in 2015: sometimes slowly away, usually
races nearer last than first. *Keith Dalgleish*

CARROWBEG (IRE) 7 b.g. Cape Cross (IRE) 129 – Love And Affection (USA) **42**
(Exclusive Era (USA)) [2015 55: p11g Jun 4] lengthy, angular gelding: poor maiden: best
efforts at 1m: acts on good to firm going: often wears headgear/tongue tie: often races
prominently: sold £1,800, sent to Germany. *Lawney Hill*

CARRY ME HOME 2 b.g. (Apr 14) Dark Angel (IRE) 113 – Toffee Vodka (IRE) 86 **74 p**
(Danehill Dancer (IRE) 117) [2015 p7g⁴ p7g⁵ Oct 20] £20,000Y: half-brother to several
winners, including 2-y-o 6f winners Toffee Tart (by Dutch Art) and No One Knows (by
Pastoral Pursuits): dam winner up to 1m (2-y-o 6f winner): better effort when fourth in
maiden at Kempton (2¾ lengths behind Blue Humor) in October: remains open to
improvement. *Charles Hills*

CARRY ON DERYCK 3 b.g. Halling (USA) 133 – Mullein 110 (Oasis Dream 129) **107**
[2015 95: p7f⁵ p7g 7.6s* 8g³ 8f⁴ Jun 18] useful handicapper: won at Chester (by ¾ length
from Billy Slater) in May: third at Haydock (length behind Mutarakez) next time: stays 1m:
acts on firm and soft going: sometimes slowly away: has joined Saeed bin Suroor. *David
Evans*

CARTAGO 2 b.c. (Mar 7) Dansili 127 – Kilo Alpha 104 (King's Best (USA) 132) [2015 **96**
7g³ 7.1f³ 7.1g² p7f³ 8.3g* 8m* 10g⁵ Oct 10] sturdy colt: second foal: half-brother to useful
French 2-y-o 1m winner Alpha Bravo (by Oasis Dream): dam, French 7.5f (at 2 yrs)/1m
winner, sister to smart performer up to 1½m Runaway out of close relative to Dancing
Brave: useful performer: won nurseries at Windsor and Yarmouth in September: stays
1¼m: acts on good to firm going. *John Gosden*

CARTER PACE (IRE) 2 b.f. (Mar 6) Lawman (FR) 121 – Kyniska (IRE) 108 (Choisir **– p**
(AUS) 126) [2015 7g p8m Nov 19] €110,000Y: sturdy filly: second foal: dam, 2-y-o 7f
winner, later successful up to 9f in USA: well held in maidens: in hood: should do better.
Michael Bell

CARTHAGE (IRE) 4 b.g. Mastercraftsman (IRE) 129 – Pitrizzia (Lando (GER) 128) **86**
[2015 85: 10.3d 11.6m* 12g⁴ 13.4g³ 11.5g 10g 14.1s t12.2m Nov 28] attractive gelding:
fairly useful handicapper: won at Windsor in April: stays 13.5f: acts on good to firm and
heavy going: tried in headgear: often starts slowly, often races towards rear. *Brian Ellison*

CARTIER (IRE) 3 b.f. Montjeu (IRE) 137 – Rosamixa (FR) (Linamix (FR) 127) [2015 **79**
83p: 10.4g⁵ 8g³ 8m⁶ t8.6g⁴ Aug 6] angular filly: fair handicapper: stays 1m: acts on
polytrack: usually races nearer last than first, often travels strongly. *David Simcock*

CARTMELL CLEAVE 3 br.g. Pastoral Pursuits 127 – There's Two (IRE) 85 (Ashkalani **99**
(IRE) 128) [2015 76: 5.7f* 6.1s⁶ 5m² 6m² 6g* 6g⁶ Sep 5] angular gelding: useful
handicapper: won at Bath in April and Newmarket (by 2 lengths from Atletico) in August:
stays 6f: acts on tapeta and firm going: usually travels strongly. *Stuart Kittow*

CARTWRIGHT 2 b.g. (Apr 4) High Chaparral (IRE) 132 – One So Marvellous 86 (Nash- **60 p**
wan (USA) 135) [2015 7v⁵ t7.1f f8g⁵ Nov 26] 160,000Y: seventh foal: half-brother to 3
useful winners, including winner up to 1¼m (stayed 1½m) Coquet (2-y-o 1m/8.6f winner,
by Sir Percy) and 1m-9.5f winner Genius Boy (by New Approach): dam, 1¼m winner,

sister to Juddmonte International winner One So Wonderful: modest form: best effort when fifth in maiden at Redcar (10¾ lengths behind Roundsman) in November, staying on strongly: should be suited by 1m+: remains open to improvement. *Sir Mark Prescott Bt*

CASCADIA (IRE) 4 br.f. Mujadil (USA) 119 – Tucum (IRE) (Diktat 126) [2015 63: **63** t12.2f⁵ f12g⁴ f12d f12d² t12.2f⁴ f12g* f12g⁶ f14g³ t12.2g f12g² f12g t8.6g f11g⁵ Dec 29] modest handicapper: won at Southwell in March: left Alison Hutchinson after tenth start: stays 1¾m: acts on fibresand, tapeta and good to firm going: tried in headgear: tried in tongue tie in 2015: often races prominently. *Ivan Furtado*

CASCADING STARS (IRE) 3 b.f. Tagula (IRE) 116 – Subtle Affair (IRE) 96 (Barathea **74** (IRE) 127) [2015 80: 8g 8g⁶ 7m 7m⁴ 7d² p7g³ p8g² p7g³ p8g⁶ p7g Dec 16] fairly useful **a81** handicapper: second at Kempton in August and third at Kempton in October: stays 1m: acts on polytrack and good to firm going: often races prominently. *J. S. Moore*

CASE KEY 2 gr.c. (Apr 29) Showcasing 117 – Fluttering Rose 71 (Compton Place 125) **80** [2015 5g* 5m 5g 5m² 5.5s 6d⁴ Oct 5] £35,000Y, 55,000 2-y-o: strong colt: fourth foal: dam, 2-y-o 5f winner, half-sister to very smart sprinter Masamah: fairly useful performer: won maiden at Leicester (by 2¼ lengths from Miniaturist) in May: second in nursery at Leicester in August: best form at 5f: acts on good to firm and good to soft going: front runner/races prominently. *Charles Hills*

CASH IS KING 5 b.g. Bahamian Bounty 116 – Age of Chivalry (IRE) 110 (Invincible **–** Spirit (IRE) 121) [2015 66: 7g 8d 7d May 13] lengthy, unfurnished gelding: maiden: no form in 2015: tried in headgear prior to 2015: often races prominently. *Kenny Johnson*

CASH OR CASUALTY (IRE) 7 b.g. Footstepsinthesand 120 – La Quinta (IRE) 67 **73** (Indian Ridge 123) [2015 78, a84: 7v* 6d³ p7g⁴ 7v⁴ 7g⁴ 7g⁵ 7m⁴ 8m⁴ 7.2g³ 7.5s² 6.9s² 7.9s* a7g Sep 10] fair handicapper: won at Cork in April and Bellewstown in August: has won at 10.5f, but mostly races over shorter nowadays: acts on polytrack, good to firm and heavy going: tried in headgear prior to 2015: usually wears tongue tie: usually leads. *Damian Joseph English, Ireland*

CASHPOINT 10 b.g. Fantastic Light (USA) 134 – Cashew 80 (Sharrood (USA) 124) **88** [2015 95: f11g² 8.9s⁶ 8.9g³ 8m* 10g* Jul 8] smallish gelding: fairly useful performer: won sellers at Goodwood in June and Lingfield in July: stays 1½m: acts on polytrack, fibresand and any turf going: sometimes in headgear in 2015: usually races prominently. *Ian Williams*

CASILA (IRE) 3 b.f. High Chaparral (IRE) 132 – Miletrian (IRE) 113 (Marju (IRE) 127) **69** [2015 59p: 8m³ t12.2g² 10.2m⁴ 11.9v⁴ 10.4g³ 9.9g³ 12g³ 12g⁵ 12g⁵ Aug 15] fair maiden: stays 1½m: acts on tapeta and good to firm going: tried in blinkers in 2015: usually races prominently: temperament under suspicion. *Mark Johnston*

CASIUS 3 b.c. Teofilo (IRE) 126 – Mary Pekan (IRE) 97 (Sri Pekan (USA) 117) [2015 –: **–** t9.5f Jan 29] maiden: no form in 2015: tried in blinkers prior to 2015. *Harry Dunlop*

CASO DO LAGO (IRE) 4 b.g. Balmont (USA) 117 – Dasha 69 (Kyllachy 129) [2015 **–** 66: 5.3m⁴ Jun 30] fair at best, no form in 2015: stays 7f: acts on polytrack and good to firm going: often in visor prior to 2015. *Sheena West*

CASPAR NETSCHER 6 b.h. Dutch Art 126 – Bella Cantata (Singspiel (IRE) 133) [2015 **118** 115: 5g³ 5g 6g⁴ 6f Jun 20] rather leggy, medium-sized horse: smart performer: third in Meydan Sprint at Meydan (head behind Sir Maximilian) in March and fourth in Duke of York Stakes at York (½ length behind Glass Office) in May: effective at 1m, campaigned as sprinter nowadays: acts on soft and good to firm going. *David Simcock*

CASPIAN PRINCE (IRE) 6 ch.g. Dylan Thomas (IRE) 132 – Crystal Gaze (IRE) **116** (Rainbow Quest (USA) 134) [2015 111: 5g³ a6f 5g* 5g 5g 5m 5m 5m⁵ 5m 5.4g⁶ 5.2s⁶ 5m Oct 4] strong, workmanlike gelding: smart performer: won handicaps at Meydan (by length from Hototo) in February and York (by ½ length from Highland Acclaim) in August: left Tony Carroll after eighth start: best form at 5f: acts on polytrack, good to firm and good to soft going: often wears headgear: sometimes wears tongue tie: usually leads. *Dean Ivory*

CASSANDANE (IRE) 3 br.f. Jeremy (USA) 122 – Princess Atoosa (USA) (Gone West **63** (USA)) [2015 –: 8f⁴ t8.6g⁵ 8.3d⁶ 8.3g 8m 11.1s 10g⁵ 12.1m* 12d p13.3f Oct 24] modest handicapper: won at Bath in April and Beverley in August: left Mark Johnston after eighth start: stays 1½m: acts on firm going: often leads. *Shaun Harris*

CASSELLS ROCK (IRE) 5 br.g. Rock of Gibraltar (IRE) 133 – Se La Vie (FR) **–** (Highest Honor (FR) 124) [2015 18g 18g 15s Oct 25] sturdy gelding: useful at best, no form in 2015: tried in headgear prior to 2015: sometimes wears tongue tie: often races towards rear. *A. J. Martin, Ireland*

CASSIE 5 b.m. Refuse To Bend (IRE) 128 – Strictly Cool (USA) (Bering 136) [2015 12s **–** Oct 19] 33/1, shaped as if amiss when well held in maiden at Pontefract. *Ben Pauling*

CASTANEA 3 ch.g. Pivotal 124 – Invitee 74 (Medicean 128) [2015 t8.6g⁶ 7d 7.1m⁴ 7m⁶ **56** 8.1g 8.1d 12.1s 10.2s⁶ 9.9s p11g³ t12.2f Dec 21] modest maiden: stays 11f: acts on polytrack and good to firm going: tried in hood: often races towards rear. *Ronald Harris*

CASTERBRIDGE 3 b.g. Pastoral Pursuits 127 – Damalis (IRE) 106 (Mukaddamah **99** (USA) 125) [2015 81: 5.1d⁶ 5g⁵ 6s 5g* 5.4m 5.5m⁶ 5g⁵ 5.1d* Oct 28] useful handicapper: won at Haydock in July and Nottingham (by 3¾ lengths from Indian Tinker) in October: best form at 5f: acts on soft going: usually in hood in 2015: front runner/races prominently. *Eric Alston*

CASTILO DEL DIABLO (IRE) 6 br.g. Teofilo (IRE) 126 – Hundred Year Flood **95** (USA) (Giant's Causeway (USA) 132) [2015 108: p12g⁶ p15.8g³ p11g p16g² 14f³ 12f³ **a102** 16m t12.2m³ t12.2f⁵ Oct 17] tall, useful-looking gelding: useful handicapper: third in minor event at Lingfield (7½ lengths behind Anglophile) in January, second at Kempton (2 lengths behind Ridgeway Storm) in April and third at Wolverhampton (5¾ lengths behind Newmarch) in September: stays 2m: acts on polytrack, tapeta, firm and good to soft going: often wears headgear: often races in rear. *David Simcock*

CASTLE COMBE (IRE) 4 b.g. Dylan Thomas (IRE) 132 – Mundus Novus (USA) **93** (Unbridled's Song (USA) 125) [2015 83: p11g* 11.6m⁴ 12m⁴ 13.3m* 16m¹ 14g p16g² p14f* 12s⁵ p14f⁵ Nov 6] fairly useful handicapper: won at Kempton in April, Newbury in July and Chelmsford (by ¾ length from Devon Drum) in September: stayed easy 2m: acted on polytrack and good to firm going: had worn headgear: dead. *Marcus Tregoning*

CASTLE GUEST (IRE) 6 b.g. Rock of Gibraltar (IRE) 133 – Castelletto 105 (Komaite **99** (USA) [2015 105: a9.9f 9.9g 10m 10g* 10d Sep 13] useful performer: won minor event at Leopardstown (by ½ length from Xebec) in July: stays 1¼m: acts on soft and good to firm going: often wears tongue tie. *M. Halford, Ireland*

CASTLELYONS (IRE) 3 br.g. Papal Bull 128 – Summercove (IRE) 72 (Cape Cross **93** (IRE) 129) [2015 8.5g* 10.4m⁶ p8g⁴ 8.1g⁵ Sep 11] second foal: dam maiden (may have proven best up to 1½m): fairly useful performer: won maiden at Cork in April: left John Joseph Murphy after first start: stays 8.5f: often in hood. *Robert Stephens*

CASTLEREA TESS 2 ch.f. (Mar 21) Pastoral Pursuits 127 – Zartwyda (IRE) (Mozart **47** (IRE) 131) [2015 5s⁶ 7s 6.1s⁵ t5.1f⁴ t5.1g⁴ t5.1f⁵ Dec 11] first foal: dam Italian winner up to 1½m (2-y-o 9.5f winner): poor maiden: best form at 5f: acts on tapeta and soft going. *Sarah Hollinshead*

CASTLE TALBOT (IRE) 3 b.g. Rock of Gibraltar (IRE) 133 – Louve Sacree (USA) **69** (Seeking The Gold (USA)) [2015 70: 7.6g³ 8.5g⁵ 8.5g⁴ p10g p10g p12g⁵ f11g³ Dec 29] fair **a62** maiden: left Charles Hills after second start: stays 8.5f: raced only on good going on turf: sometimes wears headgear: sometimes slowly away. *Richard Hughes*

CASTORIENTA 4 ch.f. Orientor 118 – The Lady Caster 61 (City On A Hill (USA) 114) **66** [2015 82: p6g⁵ p6f 5.7f 6g³ p6g² 6m³ p7.5g⁶ 5.5s⁵ p7.5g p6.5g p7.5g Dec 28] close- **a77** coupled filly: fair performer: left George Baker after sixth start: probably stays 7.5f: acts on polytrack, good to firm and heavy going: tried in cheekpieces in 2015. *S. Cerulis, France*

CATAKANTA 3 b.g. Notnowcato 128 – Akanta (GER) (Wolfhound (USA) 126) [2015 –p: **–** p10m 11.9d Sep 14] maiden: no form in 2015. *Denis Coakley*

CATALINAS DIAMOND (IRE) 7 b.m. One Cool Cat (USA) 123 – Diamondiferous **72** (USA) (Danzig (USA)) [2015 67: p6m⁶ p6m⁶ p6m² p6f p6f³ 5m⁵ 6.1s⁶ 5m* 5.2m 5m⁴ **a58** 5.7m³ 5s² 5.7f⁵ 5m* 5g p6m Nov 17] leggy, angular mare: fair handicapper: won at Bath in June and September: stays 7f: acts on polytrack, firm and soft going: sometimes wears hood: usually wears tongue tie: often races in rear. *Pat Murphy*

CATARIA GIRL (USA) 6 b.m. Discreet Cat (USA) 127 – Elaflaak (USA) 104 (Gulch **–** (USA)) [2015 75: p10g Jan 28] fair at best, no form in 2015: stays 11.5f: acts on polytrack, best turf form on good going or firmer (acts on firm): often wears hood: usually wears tongue tie. *Marcus Tregoning*

CATASTROPHE 2 b.g. (Jan 26) Intikhab (USA) 135 – Mrs Snaffles (IRE) 99 (Indian **75** Danehill (IRE) 124) [2015 7m⁵ 7.2m⁴ 7.5g³ 8d² t9.5f⁴ Nov 10] small gelding: fair maiden: should stay 1¼m: acts on good to soft going. *John Quinn*

CATCALL (FR) 6 b.g. One Cool Cat (USA) 123 – Jurata (IRE) (Polish Precedent (USA) **119** 131) [2015 120: 5.5d* 5g⁵ 5g² 6g 5s 5.5g⁴ 6s Oct 31] tall, lengthy gelding: smart performer: won listed race at Fontainebleau (by ¾ length from Azagba) in March: good second in Prix du Gros-Chene at Chantilly (beaten short head by Muthmir, losing out on the nod) in May: fair efforts at best after: winner at 10.5f, but best at up to 5.5f nowadays: acts on soft and good to firm going: has worn headgear, including last 2 starts: none too consistent nowadays. *P. Sogorb, France*

CATCHMENT 2 b.f. (Feb 14) Oasis Dream 129 – Mirror Lake 112 (Dubai Destination (USA) 127) [2015 6m 6d⁶ p6g² Oct 14] well-made filly: first foal: dam 1¼m winner: fair form: best effort when second in maiden at Kempton (¾ length behind Veena) in October: should stay 7f: remains with potential. *Amanda Perrett* **77 p**

CATEGORICAL 12 b.g. Diktat 126 – Zibet 90 (Kris 135) [2015 82: 18s⁶ Apr 7] leggy gelding: modest handicapper: stays 2m: acts on fibresand and any turf going: usually races nearer last than first. *Keith Reveley* **59**

CATHEDRAL 6 b.g. Invincible Spirit (IRE) 121 – Capades Dancer (USA) (Gate Dancer (USA)) [2015 84: t16.5f f14g⁵ f14g⁴ 11.1s³ p13.3m⁵ p13.3m³ p13.3g⁵ Jun 17] compact, attractive gelding: fair handicapper: stayed 13.5f: acted on polytrack and heavy going: wore headgear: dead. *Philip Kirby* **71**

CAT ROYALE (IRE) 2 b.c. (Apr 2) Lilbourne Lad (IRE) 111 – Call This Cat (IRE) 66 (One Cool Cat (USA) 123) [2015 6g² 6m⁶ p6g p8m p7g t8.6m⁶ Dec 30] fair maiden: stays 8.5f: acts on tapeta: front runner/races prominently. *Jane Chapple-Hyam* **74**

CATSBURY (IRE) 3 b.f. Teofilo (IRE) 126 – Chatham Islands (USA) 77 (Elusive Quality (USA)) [2015 p10f⁵ p10f* Oct 28] 50,000Y: fourth foal: half-sister to smart winner up to 9f Balty Boys (2-y-o 6f winner, by Cape Cross) and useful 5.7f/6f winner Shore Step (by Footstepsinthesand): dam, 2-y-o 6f winner, sister to smart French/UAE winner up to 1m Time Prisoner: better effort when winning maiden at Chelmsford (by ¾ length from Broughtons Harmony) in October, driven out: open to further improvement. *Roger Varian* **75 p**

CAT SILVER 2 b.c. (Feb 21) Dansili 127 – Catopuma (USA) (Elusive Quality (USA)) [2015 8.1g⁵ p8m² Oct 21] second foal: dam unraced half-sister to Breeders' Cup Juvenile Turf winner Pounced: better effort when second in maiden at Kempton (½ length behind Bluebeard) in October: will go on improving. *Sir Michael Stoute* **76 p**

CATWILLDO (IRE) 5 b.m. One Cool Cat (USA) 123 – Hypocrisy 85 (Bertolini (USA) 125) [2015 77: p5g p5g⁵ p5g⁴ p6g 6.9g⁶ 6m³ 5m* 5m* 5m² 5d⁴ 5.8m 6g 5d⁶ p5g³ p6m p5g⁴ Dec 4] modest handicapper: won at Bellewstown and Navan (apprentice) in July: stays 7f: acts on polytrack, good to firm and good to soft going: usually wears blinkers. *Garvan Donnelly, Ireland* **64** **a58**

CAUSE AND EFFECT (IRE) 2 b.g. (May 4) Big Bad Bob (IRE) 118 – Special Cause (IRE) (Fasliyev (USA) 120) [2015 7sᵖᵘ p8m³ Oct 21] 35,000€, 34,000Y: seventh foal: half-brother to useful Italian 6f winner (including at 2 yrs) Victory Laurel (by Holy Roman Emperor) and 7f winner Fashion Forward (by Manduro): dam French 6.5f winner: better effort when third in maiden at Kempton (3½ lengths behind Southern Gailes) in October: remains with potential. *Ralph Beckett* **74 p**

CAUSEY ARCH (IRE) 2 b.g. (Feb 16) Jeremy (USA) 122 – Coill Cri (IRE) 51 (Shinko Forest (IRE)) [2015 6d⁵ Jul 8] €26,000Y: third foal: dam maiden half-sister to very smart 1½m winner Phoenix Reach: 16/1, very green when fifth in maiden at Ayr (3¾ lengths behind Dark Defender) in June, nearest finish: capable of better. *Michael Dods* **70 p**

CAUTIONARY NOTE 2 b.f. (Mar 30) Roderic O'Connor (IRE) 119 – Precautionary 73 (Green Desert (USA) 127) [2015 6s 5m⁵ 6m² 5.9m⁶ 5d⁵ Sep 22] €10,000F, €5,500Y, €20,000 2-y-o: sixth foal: half-sister to 5f (including at 2 yrs) winner Best Be Careful (by Exceed And Excel) and 2-y-o 7f winner Summer Stroll (by Hurricane Run): dam, maiden (stayed 7f), closely related to very smart sprinter Prohibit: modest maiden: best effort at 6f: acts on good to firm going. *Nigel Tinkler* **62**

CAUTIOUS OPTIMISM 2 ch.g. (Mar 29) Showcasing 117 – Queen of Havana (USA) (King of Kings (IRE) 125) [2015 6g³ 6.1d² 6v² 6s² p7g t6f³ Oct 31] 40,000Y: sixth foal: half-brother to 1¼m winner Havanavich (by Xaar) and 1m winner Valley Queen (by Three Valleys): dam unraced half-sister to Prix Robert Papin winner Ozone Friendly: fairly useful maiden: second in maidens at Nottingham in August and Ffos Las in September: should stay 7f: acts on tapeta and heavy going: tried in blinkers: front runner/races prominently: not straightforward (has high head carriage). *William Muir* **80**

CAVALIERI (IRE) 5 b.g. Oratorio (IRE) 128 – Always Attractive (IRE) (King's Best (USA) 132) [2015 82: 12g 11.9m 14.1m⁵ 14.1m⁶ 12g 16d 14.1s t13.9m² t16.5f³ t16.5f* t16.5g⁴ p16f³ Dec 21] fair handicapper: won at Wolverhampton in November: stays 16.5f: acts on polytrack, tapeta, good to firm and good to soft going: tried in headgear. *Philip Kirby* **62** **a71**

CAVALRYMAN 9 b.h. Halling (USA) 133 – Silversword (FR) 102 (Highest Honor (FR) 124) [2015 121: 14gᵖᵘ Feb 28] strong, well-made horse: often impressed in appearance: very smart performer: winner of 10 races during career, including Grand Prix de Paris in 2009 and Nad Al Sheba Trophy at Meydan, Princess of Wales's Stakes at Newmarket and **–**

Goodwood Cup in 2014: put down after breaking a hind leg in Nad Al Sheba Trophy in 2015: stayed 16.5f: acted on good to firm and good to soft going: tried in visor: usually responded generously to pressure. *Saeed bin Suroor*

CAYJO 4 b.g. Josr Algarhoud (IRE) 118 – Caysue (Cayman Kai (IRE) 114) [2015 –: f12g⁶ f8g Mar 31] maiden: no form in 2015. *Tracy Waggott* — **–**

CAY LOCATION (IRE) 2 b.g. (Mar 2) Bahamian Bounty 116 – Desert Location 66 (Dubai Destination (USA) 127) [2015 p7g 8.1g 8s⁴ Sep 13] no form. *Ed de Giles* — **–**

CAYMUS 2 b.f. (Mar 9) Compton Place 125 – Midnight Sky 52 (Desert Prince (IRE) 130) [2015 6m 6d 5g* 5s⁵ Oct 27] 8,000F, £25,000Y: fifth foal: half-sister to 3 winners, including German 5f (including at 2 yrs) winner Matchday (by Acclamation) and 6f winner Deepest Blue (by Sakhee's Secret): dam, 5f winner, half-sister to smart/ungenuine sprinter Out After Dark: fair performer: won claimer at Beverley in September: left William Haggas after third start: best effort at 5f: often in hood. *Tracy Waggott* — **69**

CAYUGA 6 b.g. Montjeu (IRE) 137 – Ithaca (USA) 100 (Distant View (USA) 126) [2015 92: p10g³ t9.5f⁵ t9.5f p8m⁶ 8f 10p² 10m³ 8.5g⁶ 10m² 10g p8f⁶ p10f Nov 6] good-toppcd gelding: fairly useful handicapper: third at Lingfield in January: stays 8f: acts on polytrack, tapeta and good to firm going: tried in cheekpieces: tried in tongue tie in 2015. *Brett Johnson* — **85** **a91**

CEASELESS (IRE) 3 b.f. Iffraaj 127 – Sheer Bliss (IRE) 86 (Sadler's Wells (USA) 132) [2015 79p: 7g* 8m 8.9g² 9.9d⁴ Jul 12] fairly useful performer: won maiden at Newmarket in April: creditable efforts in listed races last 3 starts, at Baden-Baden (6 lengths second to Val d'Hiver) and Hanover (5½ lengths fourth to Holy Moly) last 2 occasions: stays 1¼m: acts on good to soft going. *James Tate* — **93**

CEECUBED (IRE) 2 b.f. (Mar 21) Canford Cliffs (IRE) 133 – Chincoteague (IRE) 75 (Daylami (IRE) 138) [2015 8.3d Oct 14] second foal: half-sister to 1m and (at 2 yrs) 9f winner Maftoon (by Dark Angel): dam, maiden (stayed 13f), half-sister to smart performer up to 1½m Indian Creek and to dam of Irish Derby winner Treasure Beach: 50/1, shaped as if amiss (later reported to have lost action) in maiden at Nottingham: should do better. *Ed Walker* — **– p**

CEE JAY 2 ch.c. (Feb 18) Kyllachy 129 – Intermission (IRE) (Royal Applause 124) [2015 p6g⁵ 6d² 6v³ p7g Dec 9] fair maiden: best effort at 6f. *Jeremy Noseda* — **75**

CELEBRATION 2 b.c. (Mar 20) Equiano (FR) 127 – Bold Bidder 92 (Indesatchel (IRE) 120) [2015 6g³ 5.1g⁵ 6g⁵ 5m* 5d* 6d⁶ 5d⁴ 5.1v² Oct 7] 75,000Y: strong colt: first foal: dam, 2-y-o 5f winner, out of half-sister to very smart sprinter Mind Games: fairly useful performer: won nurseries at Carlisle and Sandown in August: second in nursery at Nottingham in October: best form at 5f: acts on good to firm and heavy going. *Richard Fahey* — **83**

CELEBRATION DAY (IRE) 2 b.g. (Feb 20) Raven's Pass (USA) 133 – Bunting 102 (Shaadi (USA) 126) [2015 p7g p8g² p8d² 10.2g* 9d² Oct 31] half-brother to several winners, including winner up to 10.3f Parasol (2-y-o 6f winner, by Halling) and winner up to 1¼m (stayed 1½m) Mot Juste (2-y-o 1m winner, by Mtoto), both smart: dam winner up to 1¼m (2-y-o 1m winner): fairly useful performer: won nursery at Nottingham in September: second in nursery at Newmarket in October: best effort at 1¼m: acts on good to soft going: remains open to improvement. *Simon Crisford* — **87 p**

CELESTIAL BAY 6 b.m. Septieme Ciel (USA) 123 – Snowy Mantle 54 (Siberian Express (USA) 125) [2015 71, a80: p12g³ t13.9g⁴ t12.2g² p13.3g⁴ p13.3m* p13g⁵ 12g t13.9m p11g p14f⁶ t12.2f* t12.2m³ p15.8m⁶ t12.2m³ Dec 26] fairly useful handicapper: won at Chelmsford (apprentice) in March and Wolverhampton in November: stays 13.5f: acts on polytrack, tapeta and good to firm going: tried in hood prior to 2015: often races towards rear. *Sylvester Kirk* — **83**

CELESTIAL DANCER (FR) 3 b.f. Dr Fong (USA) 128 – Rabeera 62 (Beat Hollow 126) [2015 –: t9.5f f8s⁶ f8s f11g Dec 29] maiden: no form in 2015: front runner/races prominently. *Michael Appleby* — **–**

CELESTIAL DAWN 6 b.m. Echo of Light 125 – Celestial Welcome 96 (Most Welcome 131) [2015 41, a59: t7.1f Jan 2] poor handicapper: stays 7f: acts on polytrack, best turf form on good going or softer: tried in headgear prior to 2015: tried in tongue tie prior to 2015: often races in rear. *John Weymes* — **36**

CELESTIAL FIRE 3 b.f. Medicean 128 – Celeste (Green Desert (USA) 127) [2015 8.3g 8m⁵ 8.3g⁵ 8d 10.4d t8.6f^bu Oct 23] third foal: half-sister to 7f winner Endless Light (by Pivotal): dam unraced half-sister to smart US Grade 1 9f/1¼m winner Megahertz and — **70**

smart 1m/1¼m performer Heaven Sent: fair maiden: left James Fanshawe after third start: best effort at 1m: acts on good to firm going: often starts slowly, often races towards rear. *David O'Meara*

CELESTIAL KNIGHT 4 b.g. Compton Place 125 – Garter Star 56 (Mark of Esteem **80** (IRE) 137) [2015 77: p8f⁶ 7f p8g⁵ p7g 8g³ p8f³ p8g* Oct 6] workmanlike gelding: fairly useful handicapper: won at Kempton in October: stays 1m: acts on polytrack: usually wears visor: not straightforward. *James Fanshawe*

CELESTIAL LAD (FR) 2 b.c. (Feb 2) Lilbourne Lad (IRE) 111 – Heavenly Quest (IRE) **67** (Dubawi (IRE) 129) [2015 6d 6.1g³ Aug 3] €90,000Y: first foal: dam unraced half-sister to smart winner up to 1m Tell: better effort when third in maiden at Nottingham (3¼ lengths behind In Ken's Memory) in August: sold 9,000 gns, sent to Spain. *Richard Hannon*

CELESTIAL PATH (IRE) 3 br.c. Footstepsinthesand 120 – Miss Kittyhawk (IRE) 66 **110** (Hawk Wing (USA) 136) [2015 108p: 8m⁵ 7g p8g³ Nov 18] tall, lengthy colt: smart performer: good fifth in 2000 Guineas at Newmarket (5½ lengths behind Gleneagles) in May: in first-time cheekpieces, shaped well when 2½ lengths third to Big Baz in listed race at Kempton final start, doing best of those patiently ridden: stays 1m: acts on polytrack, soft and good to firm going: usually races nearer last than first. *Sir Mark Prescott Bt*

CELESTIAL VISION (USA) 3 b.g. Henrythenavigator (USA) 131 – Damini (USA) 76 **–** (Seeking The Gold (USA)) [2015 70: p8f p8f Dec 17] maiden: no form in 2015: tried in tongue tie prior to 2015. *Miss Joey Ellis*

CELESTINE ABBEY 3 b.f. Authorized (IRE) 133 – Billie Jean 65 (Bertolini (USA) **59** 125) [2015 58: t7.1g³ p8f t7.1m* p7m t7.1m⁵ t7.1f⁴ t7.1g⁶ p8f 8g⁵ Apr 26] compact filly: modest handicapper: won at Wolverhampton in February: stays 7f: acts on tapeta. *John Ryan*

CELTIC ARTISAN (IRE) 4 ch.g. Dylan Thomas (IRE) 132 – Perfectly Clear (USA) **58** (Woodman (USA) 126) [2015 t12.2g² t9.5g² 10.1d p10m⁴ t8.6f Dec 21] modest maiden: stays 1½m: acts on polytrack, tapeta and soft going: usually wears headgear: tried in tongue tie prior to 2015. *Rebecca Menzies*

CELTIC AVA (IRE) 3 b.f. Peintre Celebre (USA) 137 – Denices Desert 53 (Green Desert **59** (USA) 127) [2015 51: p10m p12g⁴ p11g⁶ p8g p7g⁵ Dec 30] rather sparely-made filly: modest maiden: may prove best short of 1½m: acts on polytrack. *Pat Phelan*

CELTIC POWER 3 b.g. Rail Link 132 – Biloxi (Caerleon (USA) 132) [2015 9.2d⁴ 10g **74** 9.3d³ 10.1d 12.2m⁶ 11.1g* Sep 21] fair performer: won handicap at Hamilton in September: stays 11f: acts on good to firm going: often races towards rear. *Jim Goldie*

CELTIC SIXPENCE (IRE) 7 b.m. Celtic Swing 138 – Penny Ha'penny 84 (Bishop of **80** Cashel 122) [2015 81: 7m² 8.3m 7g⁶ 6.1g* 6.1g⁵ 7s⁶ 6s 7v 7s³ t8.6f Nov 20] angular mare: fairly useful handicapper: won at Nottingham (by 1¼ lengths from Imtiyaaz) in June: stays 8.5f: acts on good to firm and good to soft going: tried in cheekpieces prior to 2015: front runner/races prominently. *Nick Kent*

CENSORIUS 4 b.g. Notnowcato 128 – Meredith (Medicean 128) [2015 74, a82: p12m³ **74** 16m⁶ p15.8g⁴ 12m⁴ p12g p15.8g⁶ p12g⁵ Sep 22] good-topped gelding: fair handicapper: may prove best at short of 2m: acts on polytrack, tapeta and good to firm going: often wears headgear: often races in rear. *Lee Carter*

CENTRALIZED 4 ch.g. Central Park (IRE) 123 – Millie The Filly (Erhaab (USA) 127) **–** [2015 –: p12m Jan 9] maiden: no form in 2015: often wears blinkers. *Eric Wheeler*

CENTRAL SQUARE (IRE) 3 b.g. Azamour (IRE) 130 – Lucky Clio (IRE) 59 (Key of **87 p** Luck (USA) 126) [2015 10.3g² 10.3d⁴ Sep 26] €50,000Y: fourth foal: half-brother to 3 winners, including smart winner up to 6f Lucky Beggar (2-y-o 5f winner, by Verglas) and useful winner up to 10.3f Kingsdesire (2-y-o 1m winner, by King's Best): dam maiden (stayed 7f): promising second in maiden at Doncaster (length behind Koora) on debut: disappointed on softer ground at Chester: remains open to improvement. *Roger Varian*

CENTRE HAAFHD 4 b.g. Haafhd 129 – Deira Dubai 75 (Green Desert (USA) 127) **56 §** [2015 79§: 6s³ 7m 6d 5.9g Jun 15] unfurnished gelding: modest handicapper: stays 7f: acts on soft and good to firm going: tried in blinkers: tried in tongue tie in 2015: often races prominently: temperamental. *Dianne Sayer*

CENTURO (USA) 2 ch.g. (Apr 17) Cape Blanco (IRE) 130 – Cats Copy (USA) (Cat's **59** Career (USA)) [2015 8m 8s t8.6f⁶ Oct 31] modest maiden: best effort when sixth in maiden at Wolverhampton (6¼ lengths behind Loading) in October. *Jonjo O'Neill*

CENTURY FIGHTER 3 b.g. Shamardal (USA) 129 – Bergamask (USA) (Kingmambo **–** (USA) 125) [2015 9.9m 12m³ 12m 10g May 18] no form: tried in blinkers. *Tony Coyle*

CERISE FIRTH 3 b.f. Pastoral Pursuits 127 – Vermilion Creek 68 (Makbul 104) [2015 **42**
54: 8.3g⁴ 7d⁵ t8.6m 7d⁵ t6m Oct 2] poor maiden: stays 8.5f: acts on heavy going: often
wears headgear. *Steph Hollinshead*

CERSEI 2 b.f. (Mar 20) Invincible Spirit (IRE) 121 – Elle Galante (GER) (Galileo (IRE) **84**
134) [2015 7g 7g² 7d⁵ Oct 31] sturdy filly: fifth foal: half-sister to French 1½m winner
Shutterfly (by Dalakhani) and smart winner up to 1½m Balios (2-y-o 1m winner, by
Shamardal): dam, German 10.5f-15f winner, half-sister to smart German performer up to
11f Elle Shadow: fairly useful maiden: best effort when second in maiden at Newmarket
(2½ lengths behind Promising Run) in August: will stay at 1m. *David Simcock*

CERTERACH (IRE) 7 b.g. Halling (USA) 133 – Chartres (IRE) 105 (Danehill (USA) **107**
126) [2015 119: 14d⁴ 12g⁵ 14d 16d⁴ Sep 27] tall, lengthy, angular gelding: just useful
performer nowadays: best effort of 2015 when 2¼ lengths fourth to Silwana in listed race
at the Curragh final start: stays 2m: acts on polytrack, good to firm and good to soft going:
tried in cheekpieces in 2015: often starts slowly, usually races nearer last than first.
M. Halford, Ireland

CERTIFICATE 4 ch.g. Pivotal 124 – Graduation 102 (Lomitas 129) [2015 95p: 8d 8d⁶ **103**
p8g² 8.1s p7g* Dec 9] well-made gelding: useful handicapper: won at Lingfield in
December: stays 8.5f: acts on polytrack and good to firm going: tried in visor in 2015: often
races prominently. *Roger Varian*

CERTIFICATION (IRE) 5 b.g. Authorized (IRE) 133 – Most Charming (FR) (Darshaan **78**
133) [2015 t12.2m* t13.9m⁵ t13.9f³ 12.4g² 12m⁵ 12g Sep 24] fair performer: won maiden **a67**
at Wolverhampton in February: stays 1¾m: acts on tapeta. *Andrew Crook*

CERTIFIED (IRE) 2 ch.f. (Mar 10) Raven's Pass (USA) 133 – Guarantia 92 (Selkirk **76 p**
(USA) 129) [2015 p6f* Nov 5] fifth foal: half-sister to 6f winners Daraa (at 2 yrs) and
Surety (both by Cape Cross): dam, 7f winner, half-sister to very smart 1¼m-1½m winner
Laaheb: 6/4, won maiden at Chelmsford (by ½ length from Turn On The Tears) in
November: will stay 7f: better to come. *James Tate*

CERULEAN SILK 5 b.m. Striking Ambition 122 – Cerulean Rose 78 (Bluegrass Prince **–**
(IRE) 110) [2015 6.1v⁵ 7.1sᵖᵘ 7s t5.1f⁵ p5g p6g Nov 26] no form: often races in rear.
Tony Carroll

CERUTTY (IRE) 4 b.c. Shamardal (USA) 129 – Mouriyana (IRE) (Akarad (FR) 130) **88**
[2015 92: p11g² p13.3m² p13.3g Jun 18] fairly useful handicapper: third at Kempton in
March and second at Chelmsford in May: stays 13.5f: acts on polytrack and tapeta: often
races prominently. *Marco Botti*

CESCA (IRE) 3 b.f. Fastnet Rock (AUS) 127 – Mark of An Angel (IRE) 86 (Mark of **70**
Esteem (IRE) 137) [2015 p7f 8.3g p12g⁵ p10f 11.6d p10fᵖᵘ Nov 25] 52,000Y: lengthy filly:
second foal: closely related to a winner in Spain by Duke of Marmalade: dam placed at 7f:
fair maiden: left Olly Stevens after fifth start: stays 1½m: acts on polytrack: sometimes
slowly away, often races in rear. *William Knight*

CHADIC 3 b.g. Echo of Light 125 – Hawsa (USA) (Rahy (USA) 115) [2015 86: 8s 8.1m **86**
10g² 12.4g* 14.4g³ 13.4m* 13.1d 15.9m 9.9g 13.7g⁵ Sep 12] workmanlike gelding: fairly
useful performer: won minor event at Newcastle in June and handicap at Chester (by 3¼
lengths from Distain) in July: stays 14.5f: acts on good to firm going: in blinkers in 2015:
usually races prominently. *Mark Johnston*

CHAIN OF DAISIES 3 b.f. Rail Link 132 – Puya 88 (Kris 135) [2015 72: p8f⁴ 9.9g* **106**
10m* 10.4m* 9.9m⁴ 10g* Oct 9] tall, useful-looking filly: useful performer: won handicaps
at Goodwood (apprentice) (by 1¾ lengths from Banditry) in June, and Sandown (by 3¼
lengths from Pacify) and York (by neck from All About Time) in July, and listed race at
Newmarket (by neck from Crystal Zvezda) in October: stays 10.5f: acts on good to firm
going: front runner, often travels strongly. *Henry Candy*

CHAIN OF EVENTS 8 ch.g. Nayef (USA) 129 – Ermine (IRE) 86 (Cadeaux Genereux **80**
131) [2015 90, a80: 10g 10m⁶ 10m⁵ 10m⁶ 10m* 10g⁵ 9g 10m 10d Oct 30] rather leggy
gelding: fairly useful handicapper: won at Sandown (by 2½ lengths from Zambeasy) in
August: stays 11f: acts on polytrack, soft and good to firm going: tried in tongue tie prior to
2015. *Michael Wigham*

CHAMBERLAIN 4 b.g. Indesatchel (IRE) 120 – Citron (Reel Buddy (USA) 118) [2015 **–**
–: 7m 7.1s May 11] maiden: no form in 2015: stays 7.5f: acts on good to firm and good to
soft going: usually in headgear prior to 2015: tends to find little. *Fred Watson*

CHAMPAGNE BOB 3 gr.g. Big Bad Bob (IRE) 118 – Exclusive Approval (USA) (With 78
Approval (CAN)) [2015 83: 8.3s⁶ 10.3s⁶ 7.6m 7m⁶ 7.1s⁶ 9.2m⁵ 7s* t9.5f⁵ 7s* 7v Nov 3]
workmanlike gelding: fair handicapper: won at Salisbury and Leicester (amateur) in
October: left Tom Dascombe after fourth start: stays 8.5f: acts on tapeta and soft going:
tried in headgear in 2015. *Richard Price*

CHAMPAGNE CERI 3 b.f. Montjeu (IRE) 137 – Freni (GER) (Sternkoenig (IRE) 122) 80
[2015 10m 11.8s² p12g³ t13.9g³ Nov 27] sister to smart 1¼m-1½m winner Clowance,
closely related to useful 2m winner Keys (by Doyen) and half-sister to 2-y-o 6.5f winner
(stayed 9f) Club Tahiti (by Hernando): dam German 10.5f/11f (including Group 2) winner:
fairly useful maiden: second in maiden at Leicester in September: best effort at 1½m.
Roger Charlton

CHAMPAGNE CHAMP 3 b.g. Champs Elysees 124 – Maramba 97 (Rainbow Quest 84
(USA) 134) [2015 11m 10m p12g⁶ 11.6g 12d* 12v* 12s⁴ 14.1s Oct 12] 11,000Y: tall,
rather unfurnished gelding: closely related to 1½m winner Warneford (by Dansili) and
half-brother to 2-y-o 5f-6.5f winner Nyramba (by Night Shift) and winner up to 1¼m Cape
Amber (2-y-o 7f winner, by Cape Cross), both useful: dam 1m winner: fairly useful
handicapper: won at Ffos Las (twice) (by 5 lengths from Duc de Seville latter occasion) in
August: should stay further than 1½m: acts on heavy going. *Rod Millman*

CHAMPAGNE CHARLEY 4 b.f. Myboycharlie (IRE) 118 – Crossed Wire 77 (Lycius 54
(USA) 124) [2015 66: 7m 5.1s⁶ 6g 6g Jul 4] modest maiden: stays 6f: acts on polytrack,
soft and good to firm going: tried in cheekpieces in 2015: tried in tongue tie prior to 2015:
often races in rear: temperament under suspicion. *Des Donovan*

CHAMPAGNE CITY 2 ch.g. (Feb 26) Tobougg (IRE) 125 – City of Angels (Woodman 96
(USA) 126) [2015 6g⁴ 7.5m* 7m* 7f 8d* 8d² 8g Sep 19] half-brother to numerous winners,
including useful winner up to 11f I'm So Lucky (2-y-o 7f winner, by Zilzal) and useful
1m-1¼m winner Del Mar Sunset (by Unfuwain): dam unraced: useful performer: won
maiden at Beverley and minor event at Doncaster in June, and minor event at Ripon (by
length from Fleeting Visit) in August: second in listed race at Haydock (3 lengths behind
Foundation) in September: will stay beyond 1m: acts on good to firm and good to soft
going: usually races close up. *Mark Johnston*

CHAMPAGNE DUCHESS (IRE) 2 ch.f. (Mar 17) Zebedee 113 – Zafaraya (IRE) 68 –
(Ashkalani (IRE) 128) [2015 f7g⁶ p5g⁶ t7.1g f6g⁵ Dec 15] €12,000Y: half-sister to useful
6.7f-8.4f winner If Per Chance (by Danetime) and 1m winner The Educator (by Chineur):
dam, maiden (stayed 1¼m), half-sister to useful performer up to 1½m Zafaraniya: no form.
Richard Fahey

CHAMPAGNE RANSOM (FR) 3 gr.f. Mastercraftsman (IRE) 129 – Linorova (USA) 59
(Trempolino (USA) 135) [2015 t9.5g³ p10f⁶ t9.5f t12.2g⁶ t12.2m³ 12.1g⁶ 14.1g³ p13.3m²
12.1m⁵ p12g p14f⁶ Sep 17] €30,000Y: seventh foal: half-sister to 3 winners in France,
including useful 2-y-o 5f-7f winner Lixirova (by Slickly) and 11f winner Pythagoras (by
Oratorio): dam unraced half-sister to smart/ungenuine French 1½m winner (stayed 15.5f)
Mashoor: modest maiden: left Mark Johnston after tenth start: stays 1¾m: acts on polytrack
and tapeta: tried in blinkers. *Nicky Henderson*

CHANCERY (USA) 7 b.g. Street Cry (IRE) 130 – Follow That Dream 90 (Darshaan 133) 109
[2015 108: 9.8d* 10.4g 10m³ 11.9f 10m⁵ 12m⁶ 12m⁴ 9.8d* 12d⁴ 11.9d⁵ 10g 10.4s* 10d⁶
Oct 31] well-made gelding: useful handicapper: won at Ripon (by 2¼ lengths from Puzzle
Time) in April, Ripon (by 5 lengths from Puzzle Time) in August and York (by 2¼ lengths
from Off Art) in October: stays 1½m: acts on soft and good to firm going: tried in
cheekpieces: often races towards rear. *David O'Meara*

CHANCES ARE (IRE) 3 ch.f. Dandy Man (IRE) 123 – Incendio (Siberian Express 76
(USA) 125) [2015 78: 5d⁶ 5d⁵ 6g⁵ 6.9g⁶ 6.9g³ 7.5m 7.2m t7.1g³ 7.9g* t8.6f⁵ Oct 30] fair
handicapper: won at Carlisle in August: stays 7.5f, effective at shorter: acts on tapeta, good
to firm and good to soft going. *Keith Dalgleish*

CHANCEUSE 4 b.f. Lucky Story (USA) 128 – Miss Madame (IRE) 74 (Cape Cross (IRE) 59
129) [2015 68, a60: p8g⁶ p8g³ t7.1g⁶ Feb 9] modest handicapper: stays 1¼m: acts on
polytrack, fibresand and good to firm going: tried in headgear prior to 2015: sent to France,
where won minor event at Montier-En-Der in August. *Gary Moore*

CHANDRAYAAN 8 ch.g. Bertolini (USA) 125 – Muffled (USA) 67 (Mizaaya 104) [2015 45
54: p8g p6g p8f p8m³ 7g⁴ 7v 7.6g 8g f7d p7g² p7g p7g Dec 30] lengthy gelding: modest a53
handicapper: stays 1m: acts on polytrack, good to firm and good to soft going: usually
wears visor. *John E. Long*

CHANDRESH 2 b.f. (Feb 10) Holy Roman Emperor (IRE) 125 – Cloud's End 87 **59** (Dubawi (IRE) 129) [2015 5.1g 5s³ 6d⁴ 5.7m Sep 28] first foal: dam, winner up to 7f (2-y-o 6f winner), half-sister to very smart winner up to 1m Airwave and smart 5f winner Jwala: modest maiden: stays 6f. *Robert Cowell*

CHANGE THE GAME (USA) 2 ch.g. (Feb 23) Distorted Humor (USA) 117 – Joanie's **81** Catch (USA) (First Tour (USA)) [2015 t8.6f² 10d⁴ p8m Oct 21] $550,000Y: first foal: dam useful US 5f-8.5f winner: fairly useful maiden: best effort when second in maiden at Wolverhampton (¾ length behind Maestro Mac) in September, slowly away: tried in cheekpieces. *Saeed bin Suroor*

CHANSON DE MARINS (FR) 3 b.f. Le Havre (IRE) 124 – Easy To Sing (Johannesburg **–** (USA) 127) [2015 –: p8m 8.3m⁵ p10m Jun 1] maiden: no form in 2015: in tongue tie in 2015. *Dean Ivory*

CHANTECLER 4 b.g. Authorized (IRE) 133 – Snow Goose 111 (Polar Falcon (USA) **78** 126) [2015 65, a75: p11g⁶ t12.2g² p10g⁵ Jun 17] has scope: fair handicapper: left Hughie Morrison after second start: stays 1½m: acts on polytrack and tapeta: tried in hood prior to 2015: often races freely. *Robert Stephens*

CHANT (IRE) 5 b.g. Oratorio (IRE) 128 – Akarita (IRE) 92 (Akarad (FR) 130) [2015 83: **79** 12.4g⁴ 14g² 12m⁴ 11.5m* 12.5m³ Jun 6] fair handicapper: won at Carlisle in May: stays 16.5f, effective at much shorter: acts on good to firm and good to soft going: tried in cheekpieces. *Ann Duffield*

CHAPEAU BLEU (IRE) 3 b.f. Haatef (USA) 117 – La Petite Bleue (GER) 74 (Fantastic **65** Light (USA) 134) [2015 t6g³ p6f* p7g p6g 7.1s⁶ p6g² p8g p6f⁵ t7.1f⁵ Oct 23] €6,000F, €3,500Y, £11,000 2-y-o: first foal: dam 1¼m/10.4f winner out of smart German 1m-1¼m performer La Blue: fair performer: won maiden at Kempton in March: should stay at least 7f: acts on polytrack: tried in tongue tie: usually races towards rear. *Seamus Durack*

CHAPEL CHOIR 3 gr.f. Dalakhani (IRE) 133 – Chorist 120 (Pivotal 124) [2015 70p: **73 p** p12g⁵ 11.8m² p14f⁴ Sep 3] fair maiden, lightly raced: stays 1¾m: acts on polytrack and good to firm going: often races prominently: remains open to improvement. *Sir Michael Stoute*

CHAPELLERIE (IRE) 6 b.m. Acclamation 118 – Castellane (FR) (Danehill (USA) **66** 126) [2015 76: p6m⁴ Jan 10] angular mare: fair handicapper: stays 6f: acts on polytrack, tapeta and good to soft going: often wears headgear: usually slowly away, races towards rear. *Brendan Powell*

CHAPTER AND VERSE (IRE) 9 gr.g. One Cool Cat (USA) 123 – Beautiful Hill **75** (IRE) 74 (Danehill (USA) 126) [2015 75, a93: t9.5g⁵ t9.5f p8m 10m* 10m² 10m⁶ 10m³ Aug 7] compact gelding: fair handicapper: won at Leicester in April: stays 11f: acts on polytrack, tapeta and good to firm going: usually races close up, often travels strongly. *Mike Murphy*

CHAPTER SEVEN 6 ch.g. Excellent Art 125 – My First Romance 61 (Danehill (USA) **99** 126) [2015 109: 8v 12.9m² 13.8d³ 12s* 16d⁶ Sep 27] rather leggy gelding: useful performer: won minor event at Bellewstown in August: stays 13f: acts on good to firm and heavy going: tried in headgear prior to 2015. *G. M. Lyons, Ireland*

CHARACTER ONESIE (IRE) 3 b.g. Dark Angel 128 – Flame Keeper (IRE) 113 – **85** (Pivotal 124) [2015 68p: 6g⁶ 7d 7g² 8.3g* 10.3m⁴ 7.6g* 7.6m³ 7.6g 7.9g⁶ 7.6g t8.6f Oct 13] fairly useful handicapper: won at Hamilton in June and Chester (apprentice) in July: stays 8.5f: acts on good to firm going: often races towards rear. *Richard Fahey*

CHARAVA (IRE) 3 br.g. Captain Marvelous (IRE) 114 – Sweet Compliance 71 (Safawan **69** 118) [2015 66: 8g⁴ 7m 8m 8m 7.2d⁵ 7.2d* 7.2g² 7g³ 7.2g³ Oct 13] fair handicapper: won at Ayr in August: stays 7f: acts on good to soft going: tried in cheekpieces in 2015. *Patrick Holmes*

CHARLEMAGNE DIVA 5 b.m. Holy Roman Emperor (IRE) 125 – Opera Ridge (FR) **–** (Indian Ridge 123) [2015 –: t6g 6m Apr 24] fair at best, no form in 2015: stays 7f: acts on polytrack and good to soft going: tried in headgear: sometimes wears tongue tie: front runner/races prominently, tends to find little. *Richard Guest*

CHARLES CAMOIN (IRE) 7 b.g. Peintre Celebre (USA) 137 – Birthday (IRE) **105** (Singspiel (IRE) 133) [2015 97: p11g* p11g³ p12g⁴ t9.5m² Dec 12] lengthy gelding: useful handicapper: won at Kempton (by ¾ length from Black Shadow) in September: third at Kempton (1¼ lengths behind The Steward) in November and second at Wolverhampton (1¾ lengths behind Festive Fare) in December: stays 1½m: acts on polytrack, tapeta, firm and soft going. *Sylvester Kirk*

CHARLES DE MILLE 7 b.g. Tiger Hill (IRE) 127 – Apple Town 91 (Warning 136) **64 §** [2015 68§: 8m³ 8g 8g⁵ 8m⁶ 8m 9.9m 8.5g Sep 16] strong gelding: modest handicapper: stays 1½m: acts on good to firm and heavy going: unreliable. *George Moore*

CHARLES MESSIER 3 b.g. Acclamation 118 – Praesepe 71 (Pivotal 124) [2015 58: f5s **–** t6m 5d⁵ 6m 5m 5m 5g Aug 27] maiden: no form in 2015: tried in blinkers in 2015: front runner/races prominently. *Bryan Smart*

CHARLES MOLSON 4 b.g. Monsieur Bond (IRE) 120 – Arculinge 64 (Paris House **107** 123) [2015 94: 7s 6m³ 6m* 6m² 6m 6g² p6g⁵ 6d Oct 23] useful handicapper: won at Lingfield (by 1½ lengths from Royal Brave) in June: second at Windsor (neck behind Huntsmans Close) in June and second at Ascot (½ length behind Right Touch) in September: stays 6f: acts on soft and good to firm going: tried in blinkers prior to 2015: usually races towards rear. *Patrick Chamings*

CHARLIE CROKER (IRE) 3 b.c. Fast Company (IRE) 126 – Officious Madam (USA) **92** 69 (Officer (USA) 120) [2015 85: 6m* 6m 5g a6f⁴ Dec 18] fairly useful handicapper: won at Doncaster (by head from Bimbo) in April: left Kevin Ryan after third start: likely to stay 7f: acts on good to firm going: often races towards rear. *D. Watson, UAE*

CHARLIE LAD 3 b.g. Myboycharlie (IRE) 118 – Night Owl 73 (Night Shift (USA)) **65** [2015 75: 5.1m⁴ 5g 6d 6g 6d⁵ t6f 6d t6f t5.1f⁴ f5m³ t5.1m² t6m Dec 30] fair handicapper: left Ollie Pears after fifth start: stays 6f: acts on fibresand, tapeta and soft going: tried in blinkers in 2015: often races prominently. *Daniel Loughnane*

CHARLIE PARKER (IRE) 2 b.g. (Apr 27) Myboycharlie (IRE) 118 – Solaria (IRE) 53 **–** (Desert Prince (IRE) 130) [2015 10.2m⁶ 7s p8m Nov 17] lengthy, rather unfurnished gelding: no form. *Dominic Ffrench Davis*

CHARLIE'S APPROVAL (IRE) 3 b.f. Approve (IRE) 112 – Authenticate 69 (Dansili **–** 127) [2015 –: 6v 8.3d⁴ Jul 16] maiden: no form in 2015. *Ben Haslam*

CHARLIES MATE 4 br.g. Myboycharlie (IRE) 118 – Retainage (USA) (Polish Numbers **56** (USA)) [2015 48: p10f* p11f³ p8m* p10m² p10g⁴ p11g² 10m² 9.9m⁴ 10d³ p12g* p12g² **a82** p8f⁵ p10f⁴ p8f* p8m* p8f³ p12g p8f Dec 21] leggy gelding: fairly useful handicapper: won at Kempton in March, Lingfield in April, Kempton in August, Chelmsford in October and Kempton in October: stays 1½m, effective at shorter: acts on polytrack, good to firm and good to soft going: sometimes in headgear prior to 2015. *John Best*

CHARLIE'S STAR 3 b.f. Hellvelyn 118 – Sweet Sorrow (IRE) 105 (Lahib (USA) 129) **61** [2015 80d: p7m p7m⁶ 7.6m⁶ 7v⁴ 8g² p10f² 9.9v⁵ p10m p10m⁵ p10d⁶ p11g⁶ p10m⁶ p10g⁴ Dec 30] close-coupled filly: modest handicapper: stays 1¼m: acts on polytrack, good to firm and good to soft going: tried in headgear: often races prominently. *Laura Mongan*

CHARLOTTE'S SECRET 3 ch.g. Sakhee's Secret 128 – Charlotte Point (USA) 97 **69** (Distorted Humor (USA) 117) [2015 64: 8m² 8.3g 8g⁴ 8.3m⁶ 7d Jul 8] fair maiden: stays 8.5f: acts on good to firm going: sometimes in headgear in 2015. *Richard Fahey*

CHARLTON HEIGHTS (IRE) 3 b.g. Strategic Prince 114 – Personal Design (IRE) **–** (Traditionally (USA) 117) [2015 70: t7.1g 8.1m p7g 7sᵖᵘ Oct 13] fair at best, no form in 2015: often wears cheekpieces. *J. S. Moore*

CHARMY 2 b.f. (Mar 22) Yeats (IRE) 128 – Saturday Girl (Peintre Celebre (USA) 137) **75** [2015 7m⁵ p8g³ p8g⁵ p7m³ Dec 31] useful-looking filly: second foal: half-sister to useful 2-y-o 6f winner (stays 1¼m) Room Key (by Mount Nelson): dam unraced half-sister to useful performers up to/around 1¼m Boogie Shoes, Cosmodrome and Splashdown: fair maiden: bred to stay beyond 1m, though pulled hard third start. *Andrew Balding*

CHARPENTIERE 4 b.f. Shirocco (GER) 129 – Lumiere d'Espoir (FR) 81 (Saumarez **55** 132) [2015 p10g⁶ 11.9d⁵ 12s Oct 19] seventh foal: half-sister to 1¼m/11f winner Sahf London (by Vettori) and useful 1¼m-1½m winner Plaisterer (by Best of The Bests): dam 1¼m-14.6f winner: modest maiden: best effort when fifth in maiden at Haydock in September, slowly away: should prove suited by 1½m: often in headgear. *Lucy Wadham*

CHASING RUBIES (IRE) 3 b.f. Tamayuz 126 – Laureldean Lady (IRE) (Statue of **57** Liberty (USA) 115) [2015 60p: f6g⁴ p6g⁵ p6m⁴ p7f p7g t7.1g May 11] modest maiden: stays 6f: acts on all-weather: tried in headgear in 2015. *Michael Bell*

CHASTUSHKA (IRE) 2 b.f. (Apr 20) Poet's Voice 126 – Sesmen 106 (Inchinor 119) **84 p** [2015 8v* Oct 24] €100,000Y: fifth foal: half-sister to 1m winner Batrana (by Cape Cross) and Italian 1m-1¼m winner Fifun (by Pivotal): dam 7f/1m winner (including at 2 yrs): 10/3, won maiden at Newbury (by 2 lengths from Norse Magic) in October: better to come. *John Gosden*

CHATEZ (IRE) 4 b.g. Dandy Man (IRE) 123 – Glory Days (GER) 59 (Tiger Hill (IRE) **115** 127) [2015 107: 8d* Mar 28] rather leggy gelding: smart handicapper: won Spring Mile at Doncaster (by 3 lengths from Buckstay) in March: not seen out again: stays 8.5f: acts on heavy going: usually races towards rear. *Alan King*

CHATTY MAN (IRE) 3 b.g. Approve (IRE) 112 – Grenouillere (USA) (Alysheba **–** (USA)) [2015 –: 10m 12.1m Jun 10] small, close-coupled gelding: maiden: no form in 2015: tried in blinkers prior to 2015. *Deborah Sanderson*

CHAUVELIN 4 b.g. Sir Percy 129 – Enforce (USA) 109 (Kalanisi (IRE) 132) [2015 77: **75** p12m* 11.6m p12g⁴ 12m² 12g⁵ 15.8g⁵ t16.5f t13.9f⁵ f14f⁵ Dec 17] fair handicapper: won at Lingfield (apprentice) in January: left Roger Charlton after fourth start: best effort at 1½m: acts on polytrack and good to firm going: often in headgear in 2015: tried in tongue tie in 2015: often races towards rear. *Richard Guest*

CHEBSEY BEAU 5 b.g. Multiplex 114 – Chebsey Belle (IRE) (Karinga Bay 116) [2015 **85** 12d* 17.5g Sep 18] fairly useful performer: better effort in 2015 when winning maiden at Catterick (by 2½ lengths from Our Thomas) in August, suited by emphasis on stamina: best effort at 1½m: fairly useful hurdler. *John Quinn*

CHECKPOINT 6 ch.g. Zamindar (USA) 116 – Kalima (Kahyasi 130) [2015 72: 8m 8.5d **–** Sep 22] fairly useful at best, no form in 2015: best effort at 11f: acts on polytrack, best turf form on good going: tried in cheekpieces: often races towards rear. *Tony Coyle*

CHEECO 3 ch.g. Shami 105 – Mandarin Lady 60 (Timeless Times (USA) 99) [2015 –: **–** f7d³ f8s⁶ f8g t9.5f t9.5f Oct 16] maiden: no form in 2015. *Ruth Carr*

CHEEKY ANGEL (IRE) 2 gr.f. (Feb 25) Dark Angel (IRE) 113 – Cheeky Weeky **75 p** (Cadeaux Genereux 131) [2015 5.9s² 6g 6g* Oct 8] 18,000F: half-sister to several winners, including useful/untrustworthy 6f and (at 2 yrs) 7f winner Golden Shaheen and 2-y-o 6f winner Pretty Majestic (both by Invincible Spirit): dam French maiden (stayed 1½m): fair performer: best effort when winning maiden at Ayr (by ½ length from Lydiate) in October, responding well: likely to stay 7f: likely to progress further. *Michael Dods*

CHEEKY CHAPMAN 3 ch.g. Stimulation (IRE) 121 – Athboy Auction 66 (Auction **–** House (USA) 120) [2015 56: 5g⁶ 7d 7d⁶ Aug 26] maiden: no form in 2015: often in cheekpieces in 2015: sent to Italy. *Clive Mulhall*

CHEENI 3 ch.f. Orientor 118 – Class Wan 74 (Safawan 118) [2015 6g 6g 5g⁵ 5g 6d⁶ Aug 8] **–** sister to 5f winner Classy Anne and half-sister to 5f winner Killer Class (by Kyllachy) and 6f winner Sleeper Class (by Sleeping Indian): dam 2-y-o 5f/6f winner: no form: usually races in rear. *Jim Goldie*

CHEERIO SWEETIE (IRE) 3 b.f. Captain Rio 122 – Curve (IRE) (Desert Style (IRE) **57** 121) [2015 80: p6g⁶ t5.1m⁴ t7.1m Mar 7] modest handicapper: best effort at 5f: acts on polytrack. *David Evans*

CHEERS BUDDY (IRE) 7 b.g. Acclamation 118 – Victorian Dancer (IRE) 60 (Groom **71** Dancer (USA) 128) [2015 66, a75: p8g⁶ p8g p8g p8g p8g* p8g 7m* 8.3g 8m* 8.3s 7m p8g **a64** a7g² p8g p8g p8g p8g p8g Dec 11] fair handicapper: won at Dundalk in April, Down Royal in June and Bellewstown in July: best form at 1m: acts on polytrack, sand, firm and soft going: tried in headgear prior to 2015. *L. Smyth, Ireland*

CHEFCHAOUEN (IRE) 3 b.f. Dylan Thomas (IRE) 132 – Love Thirty 93 (Mister **67** Baileys 123) [2015 62: t9.5f⁶ p7m⁴ p8f⁴ p7m t8.6f⁴ p8f⁴ p10f² p11g³ p10g⁴ t9.5m⁴ p10g* Dec 30] fair handicapper: won at Lingfield in December: stays 11f: acts on polytrack and tapeta: tried in cheekpieces: often races towards rear. *J. S. Moore*

CHELABELLA 2 b.f. (Feb 22) Medicean 128 – Agrippina 99 (Timeless Times (USA) 99) **73 p** [2015 7m p8g p8m² Nov 19] 70,000Y: lengthy filly: sister to smart 6f winner Cartimandua and half-sister to 3 winners, including useful 5f (including at 2 yrs) winner Terentia (by Diktat) and 2-y-o 8.6f winner Sejanus (by Dubai Destination): dam 2-y-o 7f winner: fair maiden: best effort when second in maiden at Lingfield (2½ lengths behind Natural Beauty) in November, unsuited by emphasis on speed: open to further improvement. *Michael Bell*

CHELLA THRILLER (SPA) 6 b.m. Chevalier (IRE) 115 – Arundhati (IRE) (Royal **72** Academy (USA) 130) [2015 63: p12g² 10g⁶ 14.1g⁵ p10f² t9.5m⁵ p8g² Dec 9] good-topped mare: fair handicapper: stays 1½m: acts on polytrack: often in headgear prior to 2015: tried in tongue tie prior to 2015. *Ralph Smith*

CHELSEA LAD (IRE) 2 b.c. (Feb 21) Clodovil (IRE) 116 – Yali (IRE) 95 (Orpen (USA) **84**
116) [2015 7d* Oct 30] 20,000F, 10,000Y: lengthy colt: has scope: second foal: closely
related to Italian winner up to 9f Dubai Palace (2-y-o 7f winner, by Oratorio): dam 2-y-o
7f winner who stayed 9.5f: 33/1, knew job when won maiden at Newmarket (by short head
from Clear Cut) in October. *Martyn Meade*

CHELSEA'S BOY (IRE) 2 gr.c. (Apr 30) Rip Van Winkle (IRE) 134 – St Roch (IRE) **– p**
(Danehill (USA) 126) [2015 8g Oct 21] 110,000Y: good-topped colt: sixth foal: closely
related to 2-y-o 1m winner (stayed 1½m) Last Crusade and 10.7f-13f winner (stays 15f)
Venezia (both by Galileo), both useful: dam unraced sister to smart US Grade 1 9f winner
Luas Line and closely related to smart performer up to 2m Lost In The Moment: 20/1,
eighth in maiden at Newmarket (16¼ lengths behind Prize Money) in October: will
improve. *Clive Cox*

CHELWOOD GATE (IRE) 5 b.g. Aussie Rules (USA) 123 – Jusoor (USA) (El Prado **82**
(IRE) 119) [2015 77: p7g² p7m² p8g* p8g³ p8g⁴ p8g* p8f p7m p8g p7f³ p8m³ Dec 31]
smallish gelding: fairly useful handicapper: won at Lingfield in February and Lingfield (by
½ length from Bobby Benton) in March: stays 1m: acts on polytrack and good to soft going:
often wears headgear. *Patrick Chamings*

CHEMISTRY MASTER 7 b.g. Doyen (IRE) 132 – Elemental 82 (Rudimentary (USA) **–**
118) [2015 p10g Jun 6] maiden: no form in 2015: effective at 8.5f to 1½m. *Alexandra Dunn*

CHEMPEDAK BAY (IRE) 2 ch.g. (Apr 1) Exceed And Excel (AUS) 126 – Snowdrops **64**
(Gulch (USA)) [2015 6g p6f⁴ 6s² p6f Nov 12] modest maiden: raced only at 6f: often in
blinkers. *Paul Cole*

CHENONCEAU (IRE) 7 b.m. Fasliyev (USA) 120 – Isengard (USA) 76 (Cobra King **–**
(USA) 122) [2015 12.1m p12g 10s Aug 14] maiden: no form in 2015. *Sophie Leech*

CHEROKEE PRINCESS (IRE) 5 ch.m. Iffraaj 127 – Radiancy (IRE) 77 (Mujtahid **–**
(USA) 118) [2015 8.9g 10.2m 10m 10.1g Aug 30] maiden: no form in 2015: usually wears
hood: temperament under suspicion. *Michael Appleby*

CHERRY KOOL 2 b.f. (Feb 27) Kheleyf (USA) 116 – Pretty Kool 68 (Inchinor 119) **80**
[2015 5d⁶ p5g* 5d⁵ p5f² 6m Oct 3] neat filly: fifth foal: half-sister to 3 winners, including
5f/6f winner The Strig (by Mujahid) and 5f winner Oh So Kool (by Bertolini): dam 5f/6f
winner: fairly useful performer: won maiden at Lingfield in August: second in nursery at
Lingfield in September: best form at 5f: acts on polytrack. *Stuart Williams*

CHERRY PRINCESS 5 gr.m. Act One 124 – Francia 59 (Legend of France (USA) 124) **53**
[2015 64: t9.5f 12d Aug 17] good-topped mare: modest handicapper: left Stuart Williams
after first start: stays 2m, often races over shorter: acts on polytrack and good to firm going:
often races prominently. *Dianne Sayer*

CHERRY STREET 6 b.g. Alhaarth (IRE) 126 – Weqaar (USA) 83 (Red Ransom (USA)) **63**
[2015 75: p10m³ p10g³ 10m p10g⁴ p10g 12m⁵ 10g⁶ t8.6f⁴ p10f⁴ Nov 7] lengthy gelding: **a70**
fair handicapper: stays 1½m: acts on polytrack, tapeta and good to firm going: sometimes
wears headgear. *Denis Quinn*

CHERRY TIGER 5 b.g. Tiger Hill (IRE) 127 – Lolla's Spirit (IRE) 68 (Montjeu (IRE) **52**
137) [2015 65: t8.6f f11s t12.2f⁴ t8.6gᵖᵘ Aug 26] modest handicapper: stayed 1½m: acted
on polytrack, tapeta, best turf form on good going or softer: tried in headgear: tried in
tongue tie in 2015: front runner/raced prominently: fatally injured at Wolverhampton.
Graeme McPherson

CHESHAM ROSE (IRE) 2 gr.f. (Apr 24) Mastercraftsman (IRE) 129 – Rose's **52**
Destination (IRE) (Dubai Destination (USA) 127) [2015 7s³ f8g⁴ Dec 18] €22,000Y:
fourth foal: closely related to Italian winner up to 1m Choisir Roses (2-y-o 7f winner, by
Choisir): dam unraced half-sister to smart winner up to 8.4f Golden Arrow: better effort
when third in maiden at Leicester (16¾ lengths behind Light Music) in October: left Tom
Dascombe after first start. *Dave Roberts*

CHESIL BEACH 4 b.f. Phoenix Reach (IRE) 124 – Seaflower Reef (IRE) 68 (Robellino **98**
(USA) 127) [2015 95, a67: 13.1f² 14g⁵ 12f⁴ 12m⁵ 14m 13.4m 12.3s⁵ 14d Sep 26] rather
leggy filly: useful handicapper: stays 2m: acts on polytrack, firm and soft going: tried in
cheekpieces in 2015: usually races nearer last than first. *Andrew Balding*

CHESS MASTER (IRE) 2 br.c. (May 7) Shamardal (USA) 129 – Cassandra Go (IRE) **80 p**
119 (Indian Ridge 123) [2015 7g³ Sep 8] 1,700,000Y: half-brother to several winners,
including winner up to 1¼m (Nassau Stakes) Halfway To Heaven (2-y-o 7f winner, by
Pivotal), 5f/6f winner Tickled Pink (by Invincible Spirit) and 6f (including at 2 yrs) winner

Theann (by Rock of Gibraltar), all smart: dam 5f-7f winner, including King's Stand Stakes: 5/1, promise when third in maiden at Leicester (4¼ lengths behind Muntazah) in September, nearest finish: will improve. *Charlie Appleby*

CHESTER BOUND 3 gr.f. Equiano (FR) 127 – Varanasi (High Chaparral (IRE) 132) – [2015 –: p7f Jan 21] no form: sent to Germany. *Jo Hughes*

CHESTER DEELYTE (IRE) 7 b.m. Desert Style (IRE) 121 – Bakewell Tart (IRE) 92 **53** (Tagula (IRE) 116) [2015 43, a53: 5.1m² 5m⁵ p5g⁶ 5.1g⁴ 6g⁶ p6f t5.1f p6g p8g t6m Dec 30] **a38** lengthy mare: modest handicapper: stays 6f: acts on polytrack, tapeta and firm going: usually wears headgear: often races prominently. *Lisa Williamson*

CHESTER STREET 2 b.c. (Apr 22) Invincible Spirit (IRE) 121 – Expressive 81 **87 p** (Falbrav (IRE) 133) [2015 7g p7g* Oct 7] 70,000Y: third foal: brother to 2-y-o 6f winner Expect and half-brother to smart 6f winner Don't Touch (by Dutch Art): dam, 9.5f winner, half-sister to 7f/1m winner Chic and winner up to 9f Echelon (both very smart) out of Coronation Stakes winner Exclusive, herself half-sister to 2000 Guineas winner Entrepreneur: better effort when winning maiden at Kempton (by nose from Cabinet Room) in October: open to further improvement. *Roger Charlton*

CHESTNUT STORM (IRE) 2 ch.f. (Feb 6) Rip Van Winkle (IRE) 134 – Always Attractive (IRE) (King's Best (USA) 132) [2015 8.3g Oct 20] 28,000Y: third foal: half-sister to 1½m-16.5f winner Cavalieri (by Oratorio): dam ran twice: 50/1, badly needed experience when tenth in maiden at Windsor (11¼ lengths behind So Mi Dar) in October. *Ed Dunlop*

CHETAN 3 b.g. Alfred Nobel (IRE) 110 – Island Music (IRE) 74 (Mujahid (USA) 125) **61** [2015 58, a67: p6f⁶ 6s 7m⁶ 6g³ 7m 6.1m⁶ p7g p7m p6g³ Dec 3] fair handicapper: left **a68** Milton Bradley after sixth start: stays 7f: acts on polytrack and good to firm going: sometimes in headgear: tried in tongue tie in 2015. *Charlie Wallis*

CHEVALGRIS 5 gr.g. Verglas (IRE) 118 – Danzelline 83 (Danzero (AUS)) [2015 78: **74** f12s⁴ 13.8d⁵ 21.6g 11.1s⁴ 17.2d³ 17.1m* 17.1d 16.2d Oct 16] fair handicapper: won at Pontefract in August: stays 17f: acts on good to firm and heavy going: tried in blinkers in 2015. *Alan Swinbank*

CHEVALLIER 3 b.g. Invincible Spirit (IRE) 121 – Magical Romance (IRE) 110 **87** (Barathea (IRE) 127) [2015 77: p6g³ p6f² 6d* 7g 7m* 7.1m* 8.1g* 7g⁴ 8.1g³ Sep 11] neat gelding: fairly useful performer: won handicap at Brighton and claimer at Leicester in May, and handicaps at Sandown in July and August: third in handicap at Sandown in September: left Richard Hannon after fifth start: stays 1m: acts on good to firm and good to soft going: usually races prominently. *K. R. Burke*

CHEVISE (IRE) 7 b.m. Holy Roman Emperor (IRE) 125 – Lipica (IRE) 99 (Night Shift **71** (USA)) [2015 70: p6m² p6m⁴ p6f p6g⁴ p6f⁴ 6g 6m² p6g p6m p6m p7g Dec 28] fair handicapper: stays 7f: acts on polytrack and good to firm going: often wears headgear: tried in tongue tie prior to 2015: often races lazily. *Steve Woodman*

CHEWY ROUND TOWN (IRE) 2 b.c. (Mar 15) Roderic O'Connor (IRE) 119 – **64** Happy Land (IRE) (Refuse To Bend (IRE) 128) [2015 t7.1g⁵ Dec 14] 40/1, showed a bit when fifth in maiden at Wolverhampton (5¾ lengths behind Take The Helm) in December. *Shane Donohoe, Ireland*

CHEZ VRONY 9 b.g. Lujain (USA) 119 – Polish Abbey (Polish Precedent (USA) 131) – [2015 57: p8f p8f Feb 19] maiden: no form in 2015: stays 1m: acts on polytrack, fibresand, best turf form on ground softer than good (acts on heavy): tried in headgear: tried in tongue tie prior to 2015. *Dave Morris*

CHIBERTA KING 9 b.g. King's Best (USA) 132 – Glam Rock 102 (Nashwan (USA) **87** 135) [2015 –: 14f⁶ 16m⁶ Jun 7] big, strong gelding: fairly useful handicapper: stays 21.5f, effective over shorter: acts on soft and good to firm going: sometimes wears cheekpieces: usually races close up. *Andrew Balding*

CHICADORO 2 b.f. (Apr 8) Paco Boy (IRE) 129 – Going For Gold 84 (Barathea (IRE) **87 p** 127) [2015 7g⁵ 8.1s² 8d* Sep 26] second foal: dam, 1½m winner, half-sister to useful winner up to 1½m Mustard: fairly useful form: won maiden at Haydock (by short head from Zest) in September: stays 1m: should do better. *Ralph Beckett*

CHICAGO BERE (FR) 3 b.c. Peer Gynt (JPN) – Fitness Queen (USA) (Gilded Time **68** (USA)) [2015 77: p8m⁴ Jan 10] fair handicapper: stays 8.5f: acts on polytrack and tapeta: sent to Belgium. *Richard Hannon*

CHICAGO SCHOOL (IRE) 2 ch.g. (Mar 22) Approve (IRE) 112 – Ms Sasha Malia **75** (IRE) (Verglas (IRE) 118) [2015 5m² 5v 5m 5.1g³ 5m³ p5f⁴ 6g t7.1f² Oct 30] fair maiden: stays 7f: acts on tapeta and good to firm going: tried in blinkers. *Mark Johnston*

CHICA RAPIDA 3 ch.f. Paco Boy (IRE) 129 – Tora Bora 101 (Grand Lodge (USA) 125) **67**
[2015 7.1m⁴ 7.1f 8.3d p7g p8f Nov 19] 22,000Y: seventh foal: dam 7f winner: fair maiden:
stays 7f: acts on polytrack and tapeta: sometimes in blinkers. *Daniel Kubler*

CHICLET (IRE) 4 b.f. Dandy Man (IRE) 123 – Springfort (IRE) 79 (Captain Rio 122) **85**
[2015 84: p5g* p5g* 5m 5m 5g p5g p5g* Nov 27] strong filly: useful handicapper: won at **a98**
Dundalk in April (2) and November: best form at 5f: acts on polytrack and good to soft
going: often travels strongly. *Tracey Collins, Ireland*

CHIEF ENTERTAINER (IRE) 2 ch.c. (Mar 19) Captain Rio 122 – Grand Minstrel **66**
(IRE) 63 (Ashkalani (IRE) 128) [2015 5g⁵ 7g⁴ 5v³ 5d³ p6g⁶ 5d Oct 12] fair maiden: best
effort at 5f: acts on good to soft going: tried in hood: sent to Greece. *Stuart Williams*

CHIEF EXECUTIVE (IRE) 5 gr.g. Dalakhani (IRE) 133 – Lucky (IRE) 95 (Sadler's **60**
Wells (USA) 132) [2015 –: p10f 12d⁶ 8s⁶ 10.1d⁴ 9.1s* 9.2d⁴ May 27] well-made gelding:
modest handicapper: won at Ayr (apprentice) in May: stays 11f: acts on soft going: tried in
headgear: tried in tongue tie prior to 2015: front runner/races prominently. *Shaun Harris*

CHIEF SPIRIT 3 b.g. Norse Dancer (IRE) 127 – Indian Angel (Indian Ridge 123) [2015 **86**
76: 8m³ 8.1m 10g³ 10.4g p11g Dec 9] lengthy gelding: fairly useful maiden: stays 1¼m:
acts on good to firm going: often races prominently. *James Eustace*

CHIEF WHIP (USA) 2 ch.c. (Mar 9) Giant's Causeway (USA) 132 – Canterbury Lace **82 P**
(USA) (Danehill (USA) 126) [2015 7.1g* Jul 29] $250,000F: closely related to winner up
to 1m Chachamaidee (2-y-o 6f winner) and winner up to 7f J Wonder (2-y-o 6f winner)
(both smart and by Footstepsinthesand) and half-brother to 2 winners: dam unraced sister
to Irish Derby runner-up Alexander of Hales and half-sister to 1000 Guineas winner
Virginia Waters: 15/2, looked good prospect when won maiden at Sandown (by ¾ length
from Cartago) in July, readily: sure to progress. *Richard Hannon*

CHILDESPLAY 4 ch.f. Byron 117 – Parting Gift (Cadeaux Genereux 131) [2015 79, a71: **94**
p8f² p7f* p7f* p7f⁵ 17.1g² 6m* 6g 6m² 7s⁵ p6g Sep 21] smallish, plain filly: fairly useful **a79**
handicapper: won at Kempton in February, Kempton in March and Ascot (by 3½ lengths
from Stellarta) in May: second in minor event at Newmarket in June: stays 7f: acts on
polytrack and good to firm going. *Heather Main*

CHILLI JAM 2 b.c. (Jan 21) Mastercraftsman (IRE) 129 – Wosaita 70 (Generous (IRE) **62**
139) [2015 8v 8.3d p8m⁶ p8m⁶ Nov 19] modest maiden: probably stays 1m. *Ed de Giles*

CHILL (IRE) 7 b.g. Diamond Green (FR) 121 – Time To Relax 68 (Orpen (USA) **–**
116) [2015 14m May 2] well-made gelding: fairly useful at best, no form in 2015: stays 2m:
acts on heavy going: tried in headgear: in tongue tie sole start in 2015. *Paul Henderson*

CHILLY MISS 6 b.m. Iceman 117 – Fairlie 70 (Halling (USA) 133) [2015 66: 10.3d **53**
13.8d Apr 8] modest maiden: should be suited by 1½m+: acts on good to soft going:
sometimes slowly away. *Malcolm Jefferson*

CHIL THE KITE 6 b.g. Notnowcato 128 – Copy-Cat 60 (Lion Cavern (USA) 117) [2015 **118**
119: 7m 8f³ 7f 8m 8d* 10g⁴ 8d 8d⁶ Oct 31] workmanlike gelding: smart handicapper: won
at York (by head from Alfred Hutchinson) in August: third in Hunt Cup at Royal Ascot (1¾
lengths behind GM Hopkins) in June: effective from 7f to 1¼m: acts on firm and soft
going: tried in headgear prior to 2015: usually races in rear. *Hughie Morrison*

CHILWORTH BELLS 3 ch.g. Sixties Icon 125 – Five Bells (IRE) (Rock of Gibraltar **69**
(IRE) 133) [2015 59: f8s* 8g² 10g* 12m⁴ 11.9m⁵ 10.4f⁴ Jun 11] fair handicapper: won at
Southwell in January and Ayr in April: will probably stay 1¾m: acts on fibresand and good
to firm going: often races prominently. *David Barron*

CHILWORTH ICON 5 b.g. Sixties Icon 125 – Tamara Moon (IRE) 75 (Acclamation **101**
118) [2015 102: p6g 5m 6m 6g 5g 6d³ 6.1f³ 6m⁴ 5.1m⁵ 5g⁴ 5m² 5g² 5g* Aug 22] rather
leggy gelding: useful handicapper: won at Sandown (by 2¼ lengths from Noble Storm) in
August: effective from 5f to 7f: acts on polytrack, tapeta, firm and soft going: sold £36,000,
sent to Qatar, and won 6f handicap at Doha in December. *Mick Channon*

CHINA CLUB (IRE) 3 b.c. Shamardal (USA) 129 – Twyla Tharp (IRE) 107 (Sadler's **70 §**
Wells (USA) 132) [2015 75: p7m³ p6g³ Jan 21] rather unfurnished colt: fair maiden: stays
1m: acts on polytrack: sometimes wears headgear: front runner/races prominently:
temperamental: sent to Qatar. *John Gosden*

CHINA EXCELS 8 b.g. Exceed And Excel (AUS) 126 – China Beauty 64 (Slip Anchor **72**
136) [2015 59: t5.1f⁵ p5m t6f 5m* t6m* t5.1f⁶ t5.1f⁴ t6g⁶ t6m⁶ Dec 12] fair handicapper:
won at Leicester in August and Wolverhampton in September: stays 7f: acts on tapeta, soft
and good to firm going: tried in headgear: front runner/races prominently. *Mandy Rowland*

CHINA GIRL (IND) 3 b.f. Dancing Forever (USA) 119 – Oriental Lady (IRE) (King's **70**
Best (USA) 132) [2015 8.3d² p10f³ p10m⁴ Nov 19] fifth foal: half-sister to 3 winners,
including useful 1m-1½m winner Beacon Lady (by Haafhd): dam, French 1½m winner,
half-sister to smart French 11f-1¾m winner Ostankino: fair maiden: best effort when
second in maiden at Windsor in October: bred to stay 1½m+: tried in cheekpieces.
William Knight

CHINAWOOD 2 b.f. (May 18) Ferrule (IRE) – Wedgewood Star 74 (Bishop of Cashel **–**
122) [2015 5m 7g⁶ 7d Aug 14] well held in 3 maidens: dead. *John Davies*

CHINOISERIES 2 b.f. (Feb 4) Archipenko (USA) 127 – Robe Chinoise 103 (Robellino **90 p**
(USA) 127) [2015 8.1s⁴ 8s⁵ Oct 19] leggy filly: sixth foal: sister to smart winner up to 1½m
(Fillies' And Mares' Stakes) Madame Chiang (2-y-o 1m winner) and half-sister to winner
up to 1½m Mannlichen (2-y-o 1m winner) and useful 1m winner Oriental Scot (both by
Selkirk): dam 1¼m-11.6f winner who stayed 1¾m: won maiden at Chepstow (by length
from Chicadoro) in August: similar level when fifth in listed race at Pontefract: will be
suited by 1¼m+: remains open to improvement. *David Simcock*

CHIP OR PELLET 2 b.g. (Feb 18) Hellvelyn 118 – Concentration (IRE) (Mind Games **–**
121) [2015 6g⁶ 5.4s 6d Oct 26] no form. *Nigel Tinkler*

CHIRINGUITA (USA) 2 gr.f. (Apr 6) Hard Spun (USA) 124 – Silver Games (IRE) 95 **94**
(Verglas (IRE) 118) [2015 6g⁸ 7.1f⁶ 6g² 6g 7v⁴ Oct 24] second foal: dam, winner up to 1m
(2-y-o 7f winner), half-sister to Lowther/Falmouth Stakes winner Nahoodh: fairly useful
performer: won maiden at Pontefract in June: second in listed race at Ripon (head behind
Whitman) in August: should stay 7f: acts on heavy going. *James Bethell*

CHISWICK BEY (IRE) 7 b.g. Elusive City (USA) 117 – Victoria Lodge (IRE) (Grand **80**
Lodge (USA) 125) [2015 76: 7m 6s 6.9m* 7.1m* 7.9g⁵ 7d² 8g²² 7.5g 6.9s³ 7.2g 7v p7g*
Oct 29] compact gelding: fairly useful handicapper: won at Carlisle in May, Musselburgh
in June and Lingfield (apprentice) in October: second at Ascot (amateur) in July: stays 1m:
acts on polytrack, soft and good to firm going: tried in headgear prior to 2015: tried in
tongue tie: often races towards rear. *Richard Fahey*

CHIVERS (IRE) 4 b.g. Duke of Marmalade (IRE) 132 – Thara (USA) (Hennessy (USA) **83**
122) [2015 79: 12s² 14m⁴ 14.1v* 14m 15.8d p10m⁶ Dec 16] fairly useful handicapper: won
at Carlisle (by 9 lengths from Jan Smuts) in June: left Tim Easterby after fifth start: stays
1¾m: acts on good to firm and heavy going: sometimes wears cheekpieces: front runner/
races prominently. *Sheena West*

CHLOE'S IMAGE 5 b.m. Lucky Story (USA) 128 – Iwunder (IRE) 73 (King's Best (USA) **63**
132) [2015 t12.2f t12.2g⁴ t13.9g* Apr 25] modest handicapper: won at Wolverhampton in
April: stays 1½m: acts on tapeta and polytrack. *Philip Kirby*

CHOC'A'MOCA (IRE) 8 b.g. Camacho 118 – Dear Catch (IRE) 69 (Bluebird (USA) **60**
125) [2015 73: 5g⁶ 5m 5g⁵ 6g 5m⁶ Jun 10] workmanlike gelding: modest handicapper:
effective at 5f-7f: acts on any turf going: usually wears headgear. *Paul Midgley*

CHOCOLATE DIAMOND (IRE) 4 ch.g. Intense Focus (USA) 117 – Sagemacca **46**
(IRE) (Danehill Dancer (IRE) 117) [2015 74: 9g 10g⁵ 16m 12d 10.9g 7g⁶ t8.6f Oct 17]
poor handicapper: best effort at 1¼m: acts on good to firm going: usually wears headgear.
Micky Hammond

CHOICE OF DESTINY 4 ch.f. Haafhd 129 – Lumpini Park (Halling (USA) 133) [2015 **58**
73: t8.6f⁵ Jan 29] modest handicapper: stays 8.5f: acts on tapeta and soft going: tried in
visor prior to 2015: sold 2,000 gns, sent to Germany. *Philip McBride*

CHOOKIE ROYALE 7 ch.g. Monsieur Bond (IRE) 120 – Lady of Windsor (IRE) 73 **95**
(Woods of Windsor (USA)) [2015 112: p7f⁵ t8.6m³ p6g* t7.1m² p6f³ 6g 8m 7.6g 6.5m⁵ 6g **a118**
p6g⁴ p7g* t6m⁴ t6m* Dec 26] smart performer: won handicap at Chelmsford (by 2 lengths
from Golden Amber) in February, minor event at Kempton (by head from Justice Well) in
November and minor event at Wolverhampton (by 2¼ lengths from Sir Maximilian) in
December: stays 9.5f, effective over shorter: acts on polytrack, tapeta, soft and good to firm
going: usually wears headgear: front runner/races prominently. *Keith Dalgleish*

CHOOKIE'S LASS 4 ch.f. Compton Place 125 – Lady of Windsor (IRE) 73 (Woods of **71**
Windsor (USA)) [2015 75: t6f⁶ p7f p6g² t6f⁴ 6g 5d⁵ 5d² 5.9g³ 6d⁵ 5.9g⁵ 5d² 5g⁴ 5s⁵ 5m⁶
5g⁵ 5g Sep 17] fair handicapper: has form at 7f, races mainly over shorter: acts on polytrack,
tapeta and soft going: usually in cheekpieces in 2015. *Keith Dalgleish*

CHOOKIE VALENTINE 2 b.g. (Mar 5) Approve (IRE) 112 – Lady of Windsor (IRE) **–**
73 (Woods of Windsor (USA)) [2015 6d Oct 26] 25/1, twelfth in maiden at Redcar
(19¾ lengths from Captain Dion) in October. *Keith Dalgleish*

CHOPIN (GER) 5 b.g. Santiago (GER) 117 – Caucasienne (FR) 79 (Galileo (IRE) 134) **93** [2015 118: 8s⁶ 10g⁶ 8.3d 8d Aug 30] good-topped ex-German-trained gelding: formerly smart, just fairly useful nowadays: stays 1½m: acts on soft going: often in headgear in 2015. *G. M. Lyons, Ireland*

CHOPPY WATER (IRE) 3 b.g. Zebedee 113 – Brewing Storm (IRE) (King **65** Charlemagne (USA) 120) [2015 49: 6g⁵ 6g 5g² t5.1g³ 6d⁶ 6s 5g⁴ Aug 27] fair maiden: best form at 5f: acts on tapeta, best form on good going: often in blinkers in 2015: often races prominently. *Tim Easterby*

CHORAL CLAN (IRE) 4 b.g. Oratorio (IRE) 128 – Campbellite (Desert Prince (IRE) **72** 130) [2015 65: 8.3m 7m² 9g 10m 7g⁶ p8f p7m* p8f² p8d³ Nov 30] close-coupled gelding: fair performer: won minor event at Kempton in October: stays 1m: acts on polytrack and firm going: tried in headgear. *Philip Mitchell*

CHORAL FESTIVAL 9 b.m. Pivotal 124 – Choirgirl 106 (Unfuwain (USA) 131) [2015 **73** 77: 11.6g 10g 9m 10g² 10d* 10g³ 10m³ 10m³ 10.1v* 8.3d 11.6g⁵ p10g p10g p11g Dec 9] sturdy mare: fair handicapper: won at Windsor in July and Epsom in September: stays 1½m: acts on polytrack, fibresand, good to firm and heavy going: tried in headgear prior to 2015. *John Bridger*

CHORLTON HOUSE 3 ch.g. Compton Place 125 – Really Ransom 85 (Red Ransom **70** (USA)) [2015 62: p10f² 10g⁶ 10.3m⁶ 10.2m⁴ 10.2m 8d p7g t9.5f³ t9.5f² Oct 20] fair maiden: left Johnny Farrelly after first start: stays 1¼m: acts on polytrack, tapeta and good to firm going: sometimes in headgear in 2015: tried in tongue tie in 2015. *Ian Williams*

CHORUS OF LIES 3 b.g. Teofilo (IRE) 126 – Cherry Orchard (IRE) (King's Best (USA) **75** 132) [2015 71: p12f³ p12m⁴ 11.9g⁴ 14.1s 14.1d⁶ Oct 26] well-made gelding: fair maiden: left Charlie Appleby after third start: stays 1¾m: acts on polytrack and good to soft going: tried in tongue tie in 2015: often races prominently. *Tracy Waggott*

CHOSEN CHARACTER (IRE) 7 b.g. Choisir (AUS) 126 – Out of Thanks (IRE) 89 **91** (Sadler's Wells (USA) 132) [2015 100: 8.3s⁵ 7v² 8f 7g 7.6g⁶ 8g⁶ 7d 18.6m 8d Oct 16] workmanlike gelding: fairly useful handicapper: second at Chester in May: stays 8.5f: acts on any turf going: usually wears headgear: usually wears tongue tie: front runner/races prominently. *Tom Dascombe*

CHRISTCHURCH (USA) 2 b.g. (Mar 20) Henrythenavigator (USA) 131 – Saintlike **90** (USA) (Saint Ballado (CAN)) [2015 7s³ 7g³ 6s* Sep 18] €36,000Y: half-brother to several winners in North America: dam, US 6f-8.5f winner, half-sister to smart performer up to 2m Pompeyano: fairly useful form: won maiden at Newbury (by 1¾ lengths from Operative) in September: stays 7f. *Brian Meehan*

CHRISTMAS HAMPER (IRE) 3 b.g. Dubawi (IRE) 129 – Gift Range (IRE) 106 **70** (Spectrum (IRE) 126) [2015 –p: 10m 10g 12f* 12mᵖᵘ t12.2g⁶ p14g⁴ Aug 22] tall gelding: fair handicapper: won at Salisbury in May: stays 1¾m: acts on polytrack and firm going: often in headgear in 2015. *Sir Michael Stoute*

CHRISTMAS LIGHT 8 b.m. Zafeen (FR) 123 – Arabian Dancer 86 (Dansili 127) [2015 **61** 71: 10.3d 12g 12g⁶ 10m 10.2m⁶ 12g³ 12d⁶ 14.1m 9.9d 12s Oct 6] medium-sized mare: modest handicapper: stays 1½m: acts on soft and good to firm going: tried in headgear: often races towards rear. *Alan Lockwood*

CHRISTMAS SPIRIT (IRE) 2 b.f. (Jan 23) Tamayuz 126 – Invincibile Stella (IRE) **–** (Invincible Spirit (IRE) 121) [2015 6m 6m⁶ p6g Sep 22] €3,500Y: second foal: half-sister to Italian 5f/6f winner (including at 2 yrs) Disappointing (by Excellent Art): dam second in Italy at 5.5f at 2 yrs: no form: often in hood. *Seamus Durack*

CHRISTOPHERMARLOWE (USA) 3 b.c. Tapit (USA) 118 – Dress Rehearsal (IRE) **108** 102 (Galileo (IRE) 134) [2015 107p: 10.1g* 11.5s³ May 9] useful performer: won Derby Trial at Epsom (by 4 lengths from Future Empire) in April: stays 1¼m: sent to Hong Kong, where renamed Cloud Nine. *John Gosden*

CHUFFT 4 b.f. Sleeping Indian 122 – Relkida 76 (Bertolini (USA) 125) [2015 –: t5.1g⁵ **–** p6m Jun 1] maiden: no form in 2015. *Seamus Durack*

CIAO CIELO (GER) 3 br.g. Lord of England (GER) 119 – Celebration Night (IRE) **86** (Hawk Wing (USA) 136) [2015 82p: f8d⁴ 8s⁶ 7m 8g* 8.3g t8.6f Oct 20] tall gelding: fairly useful handicapper: won at Southwell in January and Haydock (by ¾ length from Dutch Law) in May: stays 1m: acts on fibresand and tapeta: often in hood in 2015: sometimes slowly away, often races freely. *David Barron*

CIARA'S BEAUTY 2 b.f. (Feb 14) Aqlaam 125 – Tanasie (Cadeaux Genereux 131) **64**
[2015 6m p5g² 5m 5.7m p6g² t6f Oct 16] £10,000Y: half-sister to several winners,
including 5f/6f winner Doric Lady (by Kyllachy) and 1m-1½m winner Jamhoori (by Tiger
Hill): dam French 1m winner: modest maiden: best effort at 5f: acts on polytrack: tried in
cheekpieces: sent to Italy. *Richard Hannon*

CIARAS COOKIE (IRE) 3 b.f. Approve (IRE) 112 – Preach (IRE) (Danehill Dancer **54**
(IRE) 117) [2015 65: t7.1g 6d 6m⁵ 6d³ p5g 5.1d⁶ f5g⁶ Dec 12] lengthy filly: modest
handicapper: left Jo Crowley after fourth start: stays 7f: acts on soft and good to firm going.
Heather Dalton

CILENTO (IRE) 3 b.g. Raven's Pass (USA) 133 – Kapria (FR) 103 (Simon du Desert **92**
(FR) 116) [2015 80p: 8m* 8m⁴ Jun 25] good-topped gelding: fairly useful handicapper:
won at Ascot (by ½ length from Weld Al Emarat) in May: stays 1m. *John Gosden*

CINCUENTA PASOS (IRE) 4 ch.g. Footstepsinthesand 120 – Sweet Nicole 54 **96**
(Okawango (USA) 115) [2015 77: p8f p7g 7s* 7g 6m* 6g 7.1m⁶ 7g* p8g 7m 7d⁵ 7v³ Nov **a68**
7] tall gelding: useful handicapper: won at Salisbury in May and June (both apprentice
events) and Newmarket in July: stays 7f: acts on polytrack, good to firm and heavy going:
often in headgear in 2015: usually races towards rear. *Joseph Tuite*

CINDERS AND ASHES 8 b.g. Beat Hollow 126 – Moon Search 110 (Rainbow Quest **78**
(USA) 134) [2015 12m⁶ 11.9d May 29] useful hudler: better effort on Flat (fair form) when
sixth in maiden at Thirsk in May. *Donald McCain*

CINDERS (IRE) 2 b.f. (Jan 28) Lilbourne Lad (IRE) 111 – The Fairies Did It (USA) **73**
(Elusive Quality (USA)) [2015 5g² 5.1m³ t6g⁶ Aug 10] 70,000F, €62,000Y: workmanlike
filly: second foal: half-sister to 6.5f winner Tohfa (by Dutch Art): dam unraced: fair
maiden: best effort when third in maiden at Nottingham (length behind Shaden) in June:
will stay 6f. *Hughie Morrison*

CINNILLA 4 b.f. Authorized (IRE) 133 – Caesarea (GER) (Generous (IRE) 139) [2015 **96**
99: 14.1s⁴ 12g⁶ 16.4m 16s⁶ 14.1d 14.1s³ 18g Oct 10] tall filly: useful performer: stays 1¼m:
acts on good to soft going: tried in headgear prior to 2015. *Ralph Beckett*

CIRCUITOUS 7 b.g. Fasliyev (USA) 120 – Seren Devious (Dr Devious (IRE) 127) [2015 **77**
86: 5.9s 7.2m⁴ 5.9m⁴ 7.2g⁴ 6d 7.2g³ 6g² 6g⁴ p7g³ 7.2g⁴ Oct 13] fair handicapper: stays 7f:
acts on polytrack, firm and soft going: usually wears headgear: tried in tongue tie prior to
2015: front runner/races prominently. *Keith Dalgleish*

CIRCUS COUTURE (IRE) 3 ch.c. Intikhab (USA) 135 – Bois Joli (IRE) 84 (Orpen **120**
(USA) 116) [2015 9.9d* 8.9d* 9.9m² 8m* 8m² 8.9m* 7.5g* 8g³ 8g² 9.9g² Nov 8] third
foal: half-brother to useful Italian winner up to 1¼m Celticus (2-y-o 6f/1m winner, by
Stroll) and Italian 2-y-o 1m winner Muad'dib (by Manduro): dam, won up to 1½m (9f
winner at 2 yrs), half-sister to smart Italian performer up to 1½m Kidnapping (by Intikhab),
Derby Italiano winners Awelmarduk and Crackerjack King and high-class performer up to
2m Jakkalberry: very smart performer: unraced at 2 yrs: won newcomers race at Pisa in
February, minor event at Milan in March, listed race at Rome in May, Premio del Giubileo
at Milan in June and minor event at Rome (by 5 lengths) in September: best effort when
short-head second to Dylan Mouth (pair clear) in Premio Roma at Rome final outing: stays
1¼m: acts on good to firm and good to soft going: often races prominently. *Stefano Botti,
Italy*

CIRRUS DES AIGLES (FR) 9 b.g. Even Top (IRE) 127 – Taille de Guepe (FR) **128 d**
(Septieme Ciel (USA) 123) [2015 129: 10.4s* 9.2m⁴ 10g 9.7m⁵ 15.4d⁴ 11.9g
Dec 13]

At the age of nine, Cirrus des Aigles, older than the winners of both the
latest Cheltenham Gold Cup and Grand National, was back again in the spring to
begin another campaign in some of Europe's top Flat races. At his age, it might
have been expected that there would be little scope to tick off many more 'firsts',
but the career of this exceptional veteran produced a few novelties in the latest
season. He had never before won first time out, for example, but that was something
he accomplished when returned to action at Longchamp in the Prix Ganay at the
beginning of May. He had won the race twice before, in 2012 and 2014, but both
times with the benefit of races beforehand in Dubai. Cirrus des Aigles may not have
had Treve to beat in the latest Ganay (he had ended her unbeaten record after a
stirring duel between the pair twelve months earlier), but his rivals included a race-
fit and high-class rival in Al Kazeem who had had Cirrus des Aigles back in fifth
when going down narrowly to Noble Mission in another of the previous season's

Prix Ganay, Longchamp—
Cirrus des Aigles wins Europe's first Group 1 for older horses for the third time,
chased home by Al Kazeem; it was also the first time he'd won first time out in his lengthy career

most thrilling finishes in the Champion Stakes at Ascot. Al Kazeem had won the Prix d'Harcourt at Longchamp a month before the Ganay, a race also contested by Fate (third) and Fractional (ninth of ten) who also went on to the Ganay. Fractional had been awarded the Prix Dollar at Longchamp the previous autumn when Cirrus des Aigles was demoted from first for causing interference. Conditions for Cirrus des Aigles were the same as for his two previous wins in the Ganay, the ground being soft, conditions which he relishes. Cirrus des Aigles won the latest edition in the same manner as he had gained his first win three years earlier, making all and having his rivals in trouble some way out. He didn't have eight lengths to spare this time—Al Kazeem almost got on terms a furlong out—but he kept on well to beat the favourite by a length and three quarters, Al Kazeem finishing three lengths ahead of Fate in third. It was Cirrus des Aigles' thirteenth win at Longchamp (out of a total of twenty-two career victories) and will almost certainly prove to be his final win at the track which was closed after the Arc meeting and won't see racing again until 2017. An important figure missing from the traditional group photo after the Ganay, though, was his breeder, Yvon Lelimouzin, who died in January.

While Al Kazeem went on to win the Tattersalls Gold Cup at the Curragh three weeks later, Cirrus des Aigles was returned to Longchamp on the same day for the Prix d'Ispahan in a potentially mouth-watering clash with Solow. A high-class gelding himself, Solow might well have beaten an in-form Cirrus des Aigles on merit anyway, but the d'Ispahan turned into a one-sided contest when Cirrus des Aigles, having loomed up early in the straight, produced an uncharacteristically tame finish and trailed in last of the four runners, as it turned out having lost half of one of his stick-on shoes. No harm was done on that occasion, but a bruised fetlock later prevented Cirrus des Aigles from renewing rivalry with Treve in his next intended target, the Grand Prix de Saint-Cloud at the end of June, and it was to be nearly four months before he was back on a racecourse, though this time, in another career first, in Ireland. For the second start running, though, Cirrus des Aigles failed to beat a single rival, finishing last of seven behind Golden Horn in the Irish Champion Stakes at Leopardstown after never threatening. Back on home turf, Cirrus des Aigles started favourite to win the Prix Dollar once again at Longchamp. It was a contest he had won three times in addition to his demotion in 2014, but he still wasn't at his best on the day, finishing only fifth of the eight runners behind Free Port Lux. The Dollar followed by the Champion Stakes (which he won in 2011 before twice finishing second) has been Cirrus des Aigles' autumn routine for several seasons, but he missed Ascot in the latest season in favour of another new challenge at Saint-Cloud a week later. Cirrus des Aigles had never previously been raced beyond twelve and a half furlongs but had gained one of the most comprehensive wins of his career at the trip when routing his field by upwards of eight lengths in the 2011 Grand Prix de Deauville. As well as racing over an extra three furlongs in the Prix Royal-Oak, Cirrus des Aigles also had a new jockey, with Frankie Dettori taking over from his regular partner of late, Christophe Soumillon, who was contracted to ride the eventual winner Vazirabad for the Aga Khan. Cirrus des Aigles threatened only briefly in the straight before finishing seven lengths behind the winner in fourth, giving the impression the trip wasn't the only reason behind another below-par performance. In truth, he simply didn't look the same horse who had begun the year so well.

The Royal-Oak had been won at its usual home, Longchamp, in 2005 by the ten-year-old gelding Alcazar who became only the second horse of that age to win a Group 1 in Europe. The first was Yavana's Pace, winner of the Credit Suisse Private Banking Pokal at Cologne three years earlier. Alcazar, who also won the Sagaro Stakes and the Prix Kergorlay at the age of ten, was rated 118 that season, while Yavana's Pace had a rating of 120 at the same age. The oldest winner of a Group 1 race in Britain is Bahamian Pirate who was nine when winning the Nunthorpe Stakes in 2004 when he was rated 118. In his prime, Cirrus des Aigles was in a different league to those record holders in terms of ability, earning Annual ratings of 133 in 2011, when he won five pattern races in all, and 135 (the highest Timeform rating earned by a gelding) in 2012, when successful in another three pattern events before getting to within a couple of lengths of Frankel at Ascot. Alcazar was plagued by injury, resulting in lengthy absences at various times during his career, and, although Cirrus des Aigles has had the odd setback himself, his remarkable durability is something else that has set him apart. When he won the Ganay again in April, it was the seventh consecutive season in which he had won a pattern race (four-times Gold Cup winner Yeats was retired as an eight-year-old after six seasons of winning pattern races). If there's a secret behind Cirrus des Aigles' longevity in the top flight, it certainly isn't down to being wrapped in cotton wool in his early years. He had seventeen races as a three-year-old, for example, the first of them in a maiden at Cagnes-sur-Mer in January of that year and the last of them when fifth in the Hong Kong Vase in December, earning him the tailpiece for his efforts of 'remarkably tough and consistent' in *Racehorses* at the end of a season which included six wins, among them his first couple of pattern-race victories in the Prix du Prince d'Orange and Prix du Conseil de Paris.

Cirrus des Aigles (FR) (b.g. 2006)	Even Top (IRE) (br 1993)	Topanoora (b 1987)	Ahonoora
			Topping Girl
		Skevena (b 1983)	Niniski
			Skhiza
	Taille de Guepe (FR) (ch 1999)	Septieme Ciel (b 1987)	Seattle Slew
			Maximova
		Roots (ch 1992)	Funambule
			Ruma

As previously detailed in *Racehorses*, the well-made Cirrus des Aigles is far from being fashionably bred, so that even at the end of 2011, the year in which he first showed top-class form, his then six-year-old half-sister Vie des Aigles (by Alamo Bay), who had failed to make the frame from ten attempts, fetched just €12,000 when going through the ring at Deauville's December Sale. There was much more interest, however, in her first foal who was by the Prix du Jockey Club winner Vision d'Etat. Originally sold for €110,000 as a yearling, he was then bought privately for €130,000 as a two-year-old after appearing at the Saint-Cloud breeze-up sale in May 2014. Named Vision des Aigles, he made a winning debut in the Al Shaqab colours for Henri-Francis Graffard in the Prix Juigne for newcomers at Longchamp a few weeks before Cirrus des Aigles returned in the Ganay. While Vision des Aigles was seen out only twice more, finishing third in minor events at Longchamp and Vichy, the Juigne runner-up Dariyan made into a very smart colt, winning the Prix Eugene Adam. Coincidentally, Dariyan is the first foal of Daryakana who won that

2009 Hong Kong Vase in which Cirrus des Aigles finished fifth. Dariyan was among Cirrus des Aigles' rivals in the latest renewal of that race which marked the sixth time in the last seven years that Cirrus des Aigles has rounded off the year with a run at Sha Tin; a strained ligament had caused him to miss the Hong Kong Cup in 2012. In the frame twice from four attempts in the Cup over two furlongs shorter, Cirrus des Aigles finished only tenth in the latest Vase in which Dariyan ran a good race to come third. Vision des Aigles will be joined in training by his two-year-old half-sister Vision Intense (by Siyouni) in 2016 who was also bought to race for Al Shaqab for €250,000 at Deauville in October. Probably best at up to twelve and a half furlongs, Cirrus des Aigles acts on good to firm ground but goes particularly well on soft ground. He wasn't at his best in the second half of 2014 (having pulled up lame after winning the Coronation Cup) but he bounced back in the latest season to win the Ganay, though that victory now looks like proving the final highlight of what has been an extraordinary career in which he has set a prize-money earnings record for a horse based in Europe (calculated at prevailing exchange rates, he has won £6,089,233 to the end of 2015). It would surely be Cirrus des Aigles' most remarkable feat yet if he could stage another comeback at the age of ten and add to his seven career Group 1 wins. *Mme C. Barande-Barbe, France*

CISCO BOY 3 b.g. Paco Boy (IRE) 129 – Miss Wells (IRE) (Sadler's Wells (USA) 132) **70** [2015 62: t7.1g* 7.1m² 7.9v² 8.3g 8.5f⁴ 7g⁴ 8g t7.1g⁴ 7.9g⁶ 8g Sep 18] fair handicapper: won at Wolverhampton in May: stays 8.5f: acts on tapeta and any turf going: often in headgear in 2015: often races prominently: sent to Greece. *Tim Easterby*

CITADEL 2 ch.g. (Apr 11) Haafhd 129 – Preference (Efisio 120) [2015 5g 6g 6m⁶ 7.2g **–** Aug 27] no form: tried in visor. *Ollie Pears*

CITISONSMITH (IRE) 3 b.g. Amadeus Wolf 122 – Ink Pot (USA) 73 (Green Dancer **35** (USA) 132) [2015 –: t6g t8.6m p8f p11g 14.1m⁵ 12.1s⁶ p10m Jun 1] poor maiden: stays 11f: acts on polytrack and tapeta: sometimes wears headgear. *Tony Carroll*

CITY BY THE BAY 2 b.c. (Apr 2) Myboycharlie (IRE) 118 – October Winds (USA) **– p** (Irish River (FR) 131) [2015 7d Sep 21] €27,000Y: fifth foal: dam US 8.5f/9f winner: 50/1, tenth in maiden at Leicester (16¾ lengths behind Massaat) in September, not knocked about: entitled to progress. *Richard Hannon*

CITY CHIC (USA) 2 b.f. (Mar 8) Street Cry (IRE) 130 – Divine Dixie (USA) (Dixieland **74 p** Band (USA)) [2015 7f p7g* Aug 24] strong filly: sister to smart 2-y-o 6f/7f (Sweet Solera Stakes) winner Discourse and useful 8.6f/10.3f winner Serene Beauty, and half-sister to several winners, including very smart US Grade 1 9f winner Bandini (by Fusaichi Pegasus): dam US 6f-8.5f winner: better effort when winning maiden at Kempton (by 1½ lengths from Pure Happiness) in August: likely to progress further. *Charlie Appleby*

CITY DREAMS (IRE) 5 b.m. Rakti 130 – Attymon Lill (IRE) (Marju (IRE) 127) [2015 **59** t12.2g⁴ t9.5f⁴ t12.2f⁵ t9.5f t8.6g Dec 1] fifth foal: half-sister to 3 winners, including winner up to 1¼m If I Were A Boy (2-y-o 8.6f winner, by Invincible Spirit) and winner up to 2m Ninfea (2-y-o 1m winner, by Le Vie dei Colori): dam of little account: modest maiden: left Michael Blake after first start: stays 1½m: acts on tapeta: usually races nearer last than first. *Philip Kirby*

CITY GROUND (USA) 8 b.g. Orientate (USA) 127 – Magnet (USA) (Seeking The Gold **68** (USA)) [2015 78: 10.3d⁵ 12.4g 9g 9g⁶ 9.9m³ 8.5m⁶ 8.5m Oct 1] angular gelding: fair handicapper: stays 1¼m: acts on polytrack, firm and good to soft going: tried in visor prior to 2015. *Michael Easterby*

CITY OF ANGKOR WAT (IRE) 5 b.g. Elusive City (USA) 117 – Kathleen Rafferty **82** (IRE) (Marju (IRE) 127) [2015 73: t9.5g² p11m⁴ f8d² t9.5f³ p8f* t8.6m⁵ p8g* f8g² p8f* p8f⁴ p7f* p8m⁶ p7g t7.1g p7g p7g t8.6g⁶ t8.6g² f8d t8.6g p8f t8.6f p8m Oct 21] fairly useful handicapper: won at Kempton and Lingfield in February, and Kempton (2) in March: left Jo Hughes after fourth start: stays 9.5f: acts on polytrack and tapeta: usually in cheekpieces in 2015: tried in tongue tie: front runner/races prominently. *Conor Dore*

CITY OF IDEAS 2 b.c. (Mar 4) Dansili 127 – Gertrude Bell 112 (Sinndar (IRE) 134) **80 p** [2015 7m 8s t9.5f* Nov 14] first foal: dam, 1¼m-1½m (Lancashire Oaks) winner, half-sister to smart 1¼m winner Dick Doughtywylie: fairly useful performer: best effort when winning maiden at Wolverhampton (by 1½ lengths from Plenary) in November: will prove suited by at least 1¼m: open to further improvement. *John Gosden*

CITY OF NIGHT (IRE) 3 b.g. Elusive City (USA) 117 – Testama (FR) 106 (Testa **68 p** Rossa (AUS) 128) [2015 6d p6m⁴ p7m⁶ Oct 28] €47,000Y: second foal: dam French winner up to 1m (2-y-o 6.5f winner): fair form: best effort when sixth in maiden at Kempton in October: remains with potential. *Martyn Meade*

CITY OF STARS (IRE) 2 b.g. (Mar 8) Lilbourne Lad (IRE) 111 – City Vaults Girl (IRE) **72** 78 (Oratorio (IRE) 128) [2015 5m² 5.1d 6.1d⁴ p6g³ 6d⁴ 7s* 7.5g² 7.5g Dec 13] fair performer: won nursery at Brighton in October: left Michael Appleby after fifth start, Charlie Fellowes after sixth: should stay 1m: acts on polytrack and soft going: often leads. *Marco Gasparini, Italy*

CIVIL WAR (IRE) 6 b.g. Scorpion (IRE) 126 – Silvestre (ITY) (Unfuwain (USA) 131) **81** [2015 89: 11.6g² 16g May 21] tall gelding: fairly useful handicapper: second at Windsor in April: stays 1¾m: acts on polytrack and good to soft going: in visor latest start in 2015: usually races nearer last than first: quirky sort. *Gary Moore*

CLABARE 4 b.g. Proclamation (IRE) 130 – Choral Singer (Daylami (IRE) 138) [2015 60: **58** 7.1m 6g⁴ 5m² 5m 5g 6g⁶ t5.1f⁴ Oct 31] modest maiden: stays 6f: acts on tapeta and good to firm going: sometimes slowly away, often races towards rear: inconsistent. *Ian Semple*

CLADOCERA (GER) 4 b.f. Oasis Dream 129 – Caesarine (FR) 106 (Pivotal 124) [2015 **116** 110: 8g* 8.9g* 8.9g⁶ 8f³ 9.9m⁴ 8g² 9.9m⁵ Oct 4] sturdy filly: smart performer: successful in Group 2 events at Meydan early in year, namely Cape Verdi (by 2 lengths from Zurigha) in January and Balanchine (by 1¾ lengths from Anahita) in February: at least creditable efforts last 2 starts, in Matron Stakes at Leopardstown (2¼ lengths second to Legatissimo) and Prix de l'Opera at Longchamp (2¼ lengths fifth to Covert Love): stays 1¼m: acts on polytrack, firm and good to soft going. *A. de Royer Dupre, France*

CLAIM THE ROSES (USA) 4 b.g. Speightstown (USA) 124 – Reboot (USA) (Rubiano **97** (USA)) [2015 89: p8f t7.1m* t8.6g⁶ 6g* 6f t6g³ p6f⁵ Oct 28] rather leggy gelding: useful handicapper: won at Wolverhampton in March and Haydock in May: third at Wolverhampton (½ length behind Don't Touch) in July: stays 7f: acts on polytrack and tapeta: often wears headgear. *Ed Vaughan*

CLAMPDOWN 3 ch.g. Kheleyf (USA) 116 – Miss McGuire 72 (Averti (IRE) 117) [2015 **70** 66: t9.5f³ p8f* p8g² 8g⁵ 8g Jun 19] fair handicapper: won at Kempton in March: stays 1m: acts on polytrack: tried in cheekpieces prior to 2015. *James Tate*

CLAP IN TIME 2 b.f. (Apr 15) Royal Applause 124 – Nahab 92 (Selkirk (USA) 129) – [2015 p7g Aug 26] first foal: dam, 1m/8.6f winner, half-sister to useful 5f-7f winner Air of York: 9/2, well held in maiden at Lingfield. *Hugo Palmer*

CLARA SCHUMANN 3 b.f. Medicean 128 – Zarzuela (IRE) (Rock of Gibraltar (IRE) – 133) [2015 7g⁶ 8m⁵ 8.3d⁴ t9.5m Sep 25] 17,000F: first foal: dam unraced half-sister to winner up to 11f Glass Harmonium and 1¼m-1½m winner Arab Spring (both very smart): no form: usually in hood. *David O'Meara*

CLARATY 5 b.m. Firebreak 125 – Claradotnet 82 (Sri Pekan (USA) 117) [2015 –: t12.2m³ **63** t12.2f³ t12.2g³ 12d⁵ t13.9g Apr 25] modest maiden: stays 1½m: acts on tapeta and good to soft going: tried in cheekpieces in 2015: usually races towards rear. *James Unett*

CLARENTINE 3 b.f. Dalakhani (IRE) 133 – Clarietta 100 (Shamardal (USA) 129) [2015 **98** p8m⁵ p10g² t12.2g³ p10g⁶ p12g³ 9.8g⁵ p8f* p8f* p8g³ Oct 29] angular filly: first foal: dam, 2-y-o 7f winner who stayed 1¼m, half-sister to smart winner up to 11.5f Cassydora: useful handicapper: won at Lingfield in September and Chelmsford in October: third in listed race at Lingfield (1¼ lengths behind Lamar) later in October: stays 1m: acts on polytrack. *Ed Dunlop*

CLA ROCK (IRE) 2 b.f. (Apr 7) Iffraaj 127 – Blessed Biata (USA) 95 (Mr Greeley **61** (USA) 122) [2015 8v p8g p7g Nov 26] dam, 8.3f winner, closely related to milers Dupont and Pacino and 1m/9f winner Moon Dazzle (all smart): modest maiden: best effort when seventh in maiden at Kempton (8¾ lengths behind Persuasive) in November. *William Haggas*

CLARY (IRE) 5 b.m. Clodovil (IRE) 116 – Kibarague (Barathea (IRE) 127) [2015 51: **60** 7.4d* 8v³ t8.6m* p8f* p8f* t7.1f³ 7s⁵ t7.1g² t8.6f² Dec 22] fair handicapper: won at Ffos **a78** Las in August, and Wolverhampton (apprentice) and Chelmsford (2) in September: stays 8.5f: acts on polytrack, tapeta and good to soft going: tried in cheekpieces prior to 2015: tried in tongue tie prior to 2015: usually races towards rear. *James Unett*

CLASS HONOURS (IRE) 2 b.c. (Mar 17) Alfred Nobel (IRE) 110 – Margaret's Dream **67** (IRE) 61 (Muhtarram (USA) 125) [2015 6g 7s⁶ 7s 8.3d Oct 14] useful-looking colt: fair maiden: best effort at 7f. *Richard Hannon*

CLASSICAL DIVA 4 b.f. Amadeus Wolf 122 – America Lontana (FR) (King's Theatre **42 §**
(IRE) 128) [2015 52§: f8g p6m⁵ Feb 12] poor handicapper: stays 7f: acts on polytrack,
fibresand and good to firm going: often wears headgear: sometimes slowly away: unreliable.
Michael Appleby

CLASSICAL ROSE 3 b.f. Amadeus Wolf 122 – Monaazalah (IRE) 81 (Green Desert **77**
(USA) 127) [2015 57: p7g p7g³ 6m p7g p7g* p7g* 7g³ Sep 19] lengthy filly: fair handicapper: won at Kempton (twice) in August: stays 7f: acts on polytrack. *Charlie Fellowes*

CLASSIC COLLECTION 3 b.g. Cape Cross (IRE) 129 – Local Spirit (USA) 101 (Lion **105 p**
Cavern (USA) 117) [2015 95: 11.6d² 10.3d* Oct 23] useful handicapper: won at Doncaster
(by 2¾ lengths from Pacify) in October: stays 10.5f: acts on polytrack and good to soft
going: often races freely: should do better still. *Saeed bin Suroor*

CLASSIC COLORI (IRE) 8 b.g. Le Vie dei Colori 126 – Beryl 77 (Bering 136) [2015 **46**
82: p10g p12f⁵ Jan 17] good-topped gelding: poor performer: stays 1¼m: acts on polytrack,
firm and soft going: sometimes wears headgear: tried in tongue tie prior to 2015: often
races in rear, often races lazily. *Martin Keighley*

CLASSIC FLYER 3 b.g. Stimulation (IRE) 121 – Tranquil Flight (Oasis Dream 129) **76**
[2015 76: 5g* 5m* 5g⁶ 6d⁵ 5m 5g⁴ 6g 6tg² t6f³ t7.1g p6g Dec 16] fair handicapper: won at
Newcastle in May and June: will probably stay 7f: acts on tapeta and good to firm going:
often in headgear in 2015. *David O'Meara*

CLASSIC IMAGE 3 b.f. Exceed And Excel (AUS) 126 – Reflected Image (IRE) 71 **66 p**
(Refuse To Bend (IRE) 128) [2015 –: 6d 5.3g³ 5.1m⁶ t5.1g⁴ 5.3g t5.1g* Aug 27] fair
handicapper: won at Wolverhampton in August: best effort at 5f: acts on tapeta: front
runner/races prominently: still unexposed. *Rae Guest*

CLASSIC MISSION 4 ch.g. Bahamian Bounty 116 – Triple Cee (IRE) 73 (Cape Cross **70**
(IRE) 129) [2015 60, a76: p11m⁵ 10.2m⁵ 10m² p12g 10d p12m p12g² Dec 20] good-topped **a81**
gelding: fairly useful maiden: first past the post in handicap at Lingfield (demoted to
second after causing interference) in December: stays 1½m: acts on polytrack: often wears
headgear. *Jonathan Portman*

CLASSIC PURSUIT 4 b.g. Pastoral Pursuits 127 – Snake's Head 81 (Golden Snake **78**
(USA) 127) [2015 77: t6g³ p6f⁶ p6f 5.7m 6m³ 6g² 5.7m² 5g* 6m 5d³ 5g⁵ 5.7m t6f⁶ 6g p6d⁶ **a69**
Nov 30] good-topped colt: fair handicapper: won at Salisbury in July: stays 6f: acts on
polytrack, tapeta, firm and good to soft going: often wears headgear: often starts slowly,
often races towards rear. *Ronald Harris*

CLASSIC ROSES 3 b.f. Youmzain (IRE) 131 – Masque Rose (Oasis Dream 129) [2015 **–**
7m 7v Sep 2] first foal: dam, French 1m winner, closely related to useful French 7f-9f
winner Nid d'Abeilles: no form: in cheekpieces final start. *Robert Cowell*

CLASSIC SENIORITY 3 b.g. Kyllachy 129 – Dramatic Solo 76 (Nayef (USA) 129) **86**
[2015 69, a78: t6g* 6m³ 6.9s⁶ 6m 6m⁵ 5.5m⁵ 6g* 6g 7v Oct 17] angular gelding: fairly
useful performer: won claimer at Wolverhampton in January and handicap at Ripon (by ½
length from Only Just) in August: third in handicap at Thirsk in June: left Richard Hannon
after first start: stays 6f: acts on polytrack, tapeta and good to firm going. *Marjorie Fife*

CLASSIC VILLAGER 3 b.g. Authorized (IRE) 133 – Sablonne (USA) 100 (Silver **94**
Hawk (USA) 123) [2015 75: p10g* 12d* 12d* 12d³ Oct 11] lengthy gelding: fairly useful
handicapper: won at Lingfield in July, and Thirsk and Catterick in August: third at
Goodwood in October: stays 1½m: acts on polytrack and good to soft going: often races
prominently. *Chris Wall*

CLASSIC WIN (IRE) 3 b.c. Invincible Spirit (IRE) 121 – Birthstone 109 (Machiavellian **98 p**
(USA) 123) [2015 6g* 7.1m⁶ 6m² Jul 6] compact colt: fifth foal: half-brother to useful
French 1m winner Charm Bracelet (by Tiger Hill): dam, French 2-y-o 1m (including Prix
d'Aumale) winner, half-sister to smart winner up to 1¾m winner Songcraft: useful
performer: won maiden at Leicester (by neck from Accra Beach) in May: best effort when
second in handicap at Ripon (neck behind Showstoppa) in July, clear of rest: will be suited
by a return to 7f+: likely to progress further. *Saeed bin Suroor*

CLASSY ANNE 5 ch.m. Orientor 118 – Class Wan 74 (Safawan 118) [2015 93: 5v 6s 5s* **87**
5m 5m⁶ 5d⁶ 6d 5g Sep 18] fairly useful handicapper: won at Ayr (by 1¾ lengths from
Bunce) in May: best form at 5f: acts on soft going: usually races prominently. *Jim Goldie*

CLAUDE GREENWOOD 5 b.g. Lucky Story (USA) 128 – Greenmeadow 70 (Sure **52**
Blade (USA) 130) [2015 56: p8m⁶ p8f⁴ p8f² p8g² 7g p8m⁶ 8s⁶ p8f p8f⁶ p8g p8f⁵
p10f⁴ Dec 21] smallish, rather sparely-made gelding: modest handicapper: stays 1¼m: acts
on polytrack, soft and good to firm going: often wears headgear: front runner/races
prominently. *Linda Jewell*

CLAYMORE (IRE) 2 gr.c. (Feb 28) Kodiac 112 – Krasotka (IRE) (Soviet Star (USA) **78**
128) [2015 7g 7g 7g³ Oct 21] neat colt: first maiden: best effort when third in maiden at
Newmarket (4½ lengths behind Mootaharer) in October. *David Lanigan*

CLEAR CUT 2 b.c. (Mar 1) Acclamation 118 – Claiomh Solais (IRE) 111 (Galileo (IRE) **85**
134) [2015 6d² 8g⁶ 7d² Oct 30] 57,000F, €300,000Y: sturdy colt: first foal: dam, 1m winner,
sister to Cuis Ghaire and Gile Na Greine (both placed in 1000 Guineas) and 1m/9f winner
(stayed 1½m) Scintillula (all smart): fairly useful maiden: best effort when second in
maiden at Fairyhouse (short head behind Golden Pearl) in September. *J. S. Bolger, Ireland*

CLEAR EVIDENCE 2 b.c. (Apr 5) Cape Cross (IRE) 129 – Rainbow's Edge 85 **66 p**
(Rainbow Quest (USA) 134) [2015 8.1g p8f Oct 22] fifth foal: half-brother to 3 winners,
including smart winner up to 1¼m Peacock (2-y-o 6f winner, by Paco Boy) and useful
1¼m-16.5f winner Purple Spectrum (by Verglas): dam 1½m winner: better effort when
eighth in maiden at Chelmsford (5½ lengths behind Thikriyaat) in October: better to come.
Sir Michael Stoute

CLEARING 5 br.m. Sleeping Indian 122 – Spring Clean (FR) 89 (Danehill (USA) 126) **82**
[2015 87: p5g⁶ p5f* p5g Mar 27] fairly useful handicapper: won at Lingfield (by neck from
Dishy Guru) in February: stays 6f: acts on polytrack and tapeta. *Jim Boyle*

CLEAR PRAISE (USA) 8 b.g. Songandaprayer (USA) 118 – Pretty Clear (USA) 89 (Mr **74**
Prospector (USA)) [2015 81, a87: p5m⁶ p6g³ 6g May 6] workmanlike gelding: fair
handicapper: stays 6f: acts on polytrack, firm and soft going: tried in hood prior to 2015:
often starts slowly. *Simon Dow*

CLEAR SKIES 2 b.f. (May 1) Sea The Stars (IRE) 140 – Out West (USA) 103 (Gone **89 p**
West (USA)) [2015 7m⁴ 8d⁵ 7m² Oct 3] 500,000Y: good-topped filly: half-sister to several
winners, notably Derby winner Motivator (2-y-o 1m winner, including Racing Post
Trophy) and high-class winner up to 13.4f Macarthur (2-y-o 1m winner) (both by Montjeu):
dam winner up to 1m (2-y-o 7.5f winner): fairly useful form: best effort when second in
valuable sales event at Newmarket (4 lengths behind Alice Springs) in October: will benefit
from return to 1m+: should do better in time. *David Wachman, Ireland*

CLEAR SPELL (IRE) 4 b.g. Tamayuz 126 – Beat The Rain 76 (Bahri 126) [2015 **77**
85, a75: 13s 10d⁵ 12.1g⁶ 11.5d 10s⁵ 12.4g⁶ 10g² 12v Oct 17] fair handicapper: stays 13f:
acts on polytrack and good to soft going: tried in cheekpieces in 2015: starts slowly, often
races towards rear: quirky sort. *Alistair Whillans*

CLEAR SPRING (IRE) 7 b.h. Chineur (FR) 123 – Holly Springs 81 (Efisio 120) [2015 **110**
103: 6g⁵ 6s* 6g* 6m 6m 6g⁵ 6mᵘʳ 6g 6m⁶ 6g 6d² 6d Oct 23] leggy horse: smart performer:
won minor event at Haydock (by 2¼ lengths from Intibaah) and handicap at Newbury (by
short head from Golden Steps), both in May: stays 7f: acts on fibresand, soft and good to
firm going. *John Spearing*

CLEMENT (IRE) 5 b.g. Clodovil (IRE) 116 – Winnifred (Green Desert (USA) 127) **64 §**
[2015 76: t7.1f⁴ p7g⁵ p7m⁶ p8g⁵ p8f⁶ p6m⁶ t8.6g⁶ 6.1s 7m⁵ p8g⁴ p7g p7g³ 7.4d⁶ p7g⁴ 7s **a72 §**
p7g³ p7g⁶ Dec 30] fair handicapper: stays 8.5f: acts on polytrack, tapeta, soft and good to
firm going: often in headgear in 2015: tried in tongue tie prior to 2015: sometimes slowly
away: best treated with caution. *John O'Shea*

CLEO FAN (ITY) 4 b.c. Mujahid (USA) 125 – Cuprea (IRE) (Best of The Bests (IRE) **114**
122) [2015 114: 9.9g² 9.9m* 11.9m⁵ 10.9m³ 11.9s Oct 18] second foal: half-brother to
Italian 1m winner (including at 2 yrs) Catnip Fan (by Johnny Red Kerr): dam Italian
7.5f/1m winner (including at 2 yrs): smart performer: won Premio Presidente della
Repubblica at Rome (by neck from Magic Artist, making all and clear for much of straight)
in May: had earlier finished short-head second to same rival in Premio Ambrosiano at
Milan: below form last 3 starts, including when third in Premio Federico Tesio at Milan
(7 lengths behind Dylan Mouth): stays 11f: acts on good to firm going: tried in tongue tie
prior to 2015: often leads. *Stefano Botti, Italy*

CLEVEDON COURT 2 b.f. (Mar 11) Royal Applause 124 – Bow River Arch (USA) 77 **55**
(Arch (USA) 127) [2015 6.5s p8m p7m⁵ Dec 16] 15,000Y: first foal: dam maiden (stayed
1¾m), sister to useful 1m-1¼m winner Ehtedaam: modest maiden: best effort when sixth
in maiden at Lingfield (9¼ lengths behind Auntinet) in December. *Gary Moore*

CLEVER BOB (IRE) 2 br.c. (Mar 29) Big Bad Bob (IRE) 118 – Clever Millie (USA) 81 **80**
(Cape Canaveral (USA) 115) [2015 6g² 6m 7v⁴ 7d Sep 27] €12,500F, €20,000Y, €60,000
2-y-o: sturdy colt: fourth foal: half-brother to 3 winners, including useful 9.5f-11f winner
Majeed and 2-y-o 7f winner Clever Miss (both by Mount Nelson): dam, 7f winner, half-
sister to smart 7f/1m winner Fatefully, herself dam of Nassau Stakes winner Favourable
Terms: fairly useful maiden: second in maiden at Windsor in June: best effort at 6f.
Joseph Tuite

Boodles Diamond Ormonde Stakes, Chester—the mud is flying as Clever Cookie takes advantage of the 7 lb he receives from the grey Tac de Boistron

CLEVERCONVERSATION (IRE) 2 ro.f. (Apr 18) Thewayyouare (USA) 117 – Monet's Lady (IRE) 51 (Daylami (IRE) 138) [2015 p5g 8g³ 10g 9g Oct 21] €10,000Y: lengthy filly: fourth foal: half-sister to 2-y-o 1m winner Running Wolf (by Amadeus Wolf): dam maiden (stayed 1¾m): fairly useful maiden: third in maiden at Newmarket in September: stays 1¼m: usually in eyeshields: has flashed tail. *Jane Chapple-Hyam* **80**

CLEVER COOKIE 7 b.g. Primo Valentino (IRE) 116 – Mystic Memory 74 (Ela-Mana- Mou 132) [2015 116p: 13.4v* 14g* 12d⁵ 16.4d⁴ 16d² Oct 17] big, strong gelding: very smart performer: won Ormonde Stakes at Chester (by 1¼ lengths from Tac de Boistron) and listed race at York (by 2¾ lengths from Nabatean), both in May: below best in King George VI and Queen Elizabeth Stakes at Ascot (fifth to Postponed) and Lonsdale Cup at York (fourth to Max Dynamite), but back to form when second in Long Distance Cup at Ascot (length behind Flying Officer, stayed on strongly from poor position) final outing: stays 2¼m: best form on good going or softer (acts on heavy): usually races in rear. *Peter Niven* **121**

CLEVER DIVYA 2 b.f. (Apr 14) Archipenko (USA) 127 – Clever Omneya (USA) 73 (Toccet (USA) 118) [2015 5g May 18] good-topped filly: second foal: dam, 7f winner, half-sister to smart UAE sprinter Terrific Challenge: 66/1, tenth in maiden at Windsor (17¼ lengths behind Dream Dreamer) in May. *J. R. Jenkins* **–**

CLEVER LOVE (FR) 3 gr.g. Silver Frost (IRE) 122 – Sharp's Love (IRE) (Fasliyev (USA) 120) [2015 71: t6f* p7f t6g⁶ 8g 5g 7.1s⁶ 6d⁶ 9.2d⁵ 7.2d 5d⁶ 5d 6d 10g⁵ 10v⁵ Nov 3] modest performer: won maiden at Wolverhampton in February: left David O'Meara after fourth start, R. Mike Smith after eleventh, Linda Perratt after twelfth: best effort at 6f: acts on polytrack, tapeta, soft and good to firm going: tried in cheekpieces in 2015: tried in tongue tie in 2015: often races towards rear. *Kenny Johnson* **63**

CLICK AND ROLL (USA) 2 b.f. (Mar 21) Smart Strike (CAN) 121 – More Hennessy (USA) (Hennessy (USA) 122) [2015 7g p8g Oct 6] $350,000Y: third foal: closely related to a winner in USA by Not For Love and half-sister to smart 4.5f-1m (Breeders' Cup Juvenile Turf) winner Hootenanny (by Quality Road): dam once-raced close relative to smart US Grade 1 6f winner Cat Moves: no form. *David Brown* **–**

CLIFF (IRE) 5 b.g. Bachelor Duke (USA) 122 – Silesian (IRE) (Singspiel (IRE) 133) **77**
[2015 79: 8d⁴ 8m³ 7m³ 7.5s² 7d² 8m 6g 7s² Oct 16] fair maiden: stays 1m: acts on soft and good to firm going: sometimes wears headgear. *Nigel Tinkler*

CLIFFMEENA (IRE) 2 b.f. (Mar 30) Canford Cliffs (IRE) 133 – Yasmeena (USA) 80 **59**
(Mr Greeley (USA) 122) [2015 p7g⁵ t7.1f Nov 20] €25,000Y: rather unfurnished filly: first foal: dam 2-y-o 5f winner out of smart sprinter La Cucaracha: better effort when fifth in maiden at Lingfield (6½ lengths behind Vaunting) in October, nearest finish. *Alex Hales*

CLIFFS OF DOVER 2 b.g. (Mar 13) Canford Cliffs (IRE) 133 – Basanti (USA) 80 **71**
(Galileo (IRE) 134) [2015 7g⁵ 7g 8m⁶ Sep 11] fair maiden: best effort when fifth in maiden at Salisbury (6½ lengths behind Battle Pride) in August, never nearer: will stay at least 1m. *Charles Hills*

CLIFTON MISS (IRE) 6 b.m. Whipper (USA) 126 – Clifton Lass (IRE) (Up And At **68**
'Em 109) [2015 62: 8g 8v 10g⁴ 8.7m³ 10m 10g* 8.3d 15s⁵ Aug 8] fair maiden: won at Ayr in July: best effort at 1¼m: acts on polytrack and good going: often wears headgear: sometimes slowly away, usually races nearer last than first. *A. P. Keatley, Ireland*

CLINE 2 ch.f. (Apr 5) Pivotal 124 – Graduation 102 (Lomitas 129) [2015 t6m t6f p7g³ p7m **72**
Dec 16] fifth foal: sister to useful 7f/1m winner Certificate and half-sister to 2 winners, including useful 9.5f/1¼m winner (stays 1½m) Marma's Boy (by Duke of Marmalade): dam 1m winner: fair maiden: will stay at least 1m. *Sir Mark Prescott Bt*

CLIODHNA (IRE) 2 b.f. (Feb 6) Bahamian Bounty 116 – Clodilla (IRE) (Clodovil (IRE) **46**
116) [2015 5m⁵ 6m 6m 7m³ p7g³ 8.3g⁶ p7g⁶ 6v⁶ Aug 19] first foal: dam, Italian 5f winner, half-sister to smart 7f/1m performer One Word More: poor maiden: stays 7f: acts on polytrack and good to firm going: sometimes slowly away. *Mick Channon*

CLIVE CLIFTON (IRE) 2 b.g. (Mar 5) Wootton Bassett 119 – Dearest Daisy 84 **65**
(Forzando 122) [2015 5m⁵ 6g 6m³ 7g⁴ 7m² 7d⁴ 8.3g p8m³ p8g⁶ p8g Dec 15] fair maiden: stays 8.5f: acts on polytrack, good to firm and good to soft going. *David Evans*

CLOAK AND DEGAS (IRE) 3 b.g. Sakhee's Secret 128 – Coup de Torchon (FR) 61 **74**
(Namid 128) [2015 65: 16g³ t6g⁴ 6d² 6g f6d⁵ t6m⁴ 6s² 6d 6g t7.1f p6f* p6g Dec 7] fair handicapper: won at Chelmsford in October: stays 6f: acts on polytrack and soft going: often wears headgear: usually races close up. *Scott Dixon*

CLOCKMAKER (IRE) 9 b.g. Danetime (IRE) 121 – Lady Ingabelle (IRE) 71 (Catrail **92**
(USA) 123) [2015 99: p6f⁴ f7g* f7d³ f8f² f8g² f8s⁴ p6g 7m* p7g 7.6g⁴ 7.6m 7.6s⁴ 7d⁶ t7.1f **a81**
t7.1f⁴ t7.1m³ t7.1g⁴ t7.1f⁵ f8g² Dec 22] well-made gelding: fairly useful handicapper: won at Southwell (apprentice) in January and Chester (by 2¼ lengths from Gatepost) in June: stays 1¼m: acts on all-weather, good to firm and heavy going: tried in headgear: often leads. *Conor Dore*

CLOCK ON TOM 5 b.g. Trade Fair 124 – Night Owl 73 (Night Shift (USA)) [2015 –: **48**
p10m p12m t7.1f⁶ p8m p10f⁵ t9.5f Oct 16] poor handicapper: stays 1¼m: acts on polytrack and good to firm going: often in hood in 2015. *Denis Quinn*

CLOCK OPERA (IRE) 5 b.m. Excellent Art 125 – Moving Diamonds 70 (Lomitas 129) **–**
[2015 74: p6g t5.1f Feb 20] smallish, angular mare: fair at best, no form in 2015: stays 6f: acts on polytrack, best turf form on good to firm going: races prominently, usually finds little. *William Stone*

CLOCK WATCHER 2 b.c. (Jan 24) Shamardal (USA) 129 – Hypnology (USA) (Gone **78 p**
West (USA)) [2015 6g 7d⁴ Sep 21] 380,000Y: third foal: half-brother to 1m winner Trust The Wind (by Dansili): dam unraced half-sister to smart winner up to 1¼m Gentleman's Deal out of 1000 Guineas winner Sleepytime: better effort when fourth in maiden at Leicester (6½ lengths behind Massaat) in September, not knocked about: better to come. *Charlie Appleby*

CLODIANNA (IRE) 2 gr.f. (Apr 24) Clodovil (IRE) 116 – Indiannie Moon (Fraam 114) **76**
[2015 6m 6g² 6g⁵ p7g² p7m³ Dec 31] 25,000Y: fifth foal: sister to a winner abroad and half-sister to useful 1m-1¼m winner Audacia (by Sixties Icon) and 2-y-o 7f winner Fingal's Cave (by Fast Company): dam once-raced half-sister to useful sprinters Kickboxer (by Clodovil) and Ajigolo: fair maiden: will stay 1m: acts on polytrack: sometimes in hood. *Roger Charlton*

CLONARD STREET 3 b.g. Archipenko (USA) 127 – Moi Aussi (USA) 88 (Mt **99**
Livermore (USA)) [2015 100: 10g⁶ 9.5m² 9.5g⁴ Oct 20] useful performer: second in minor event at Gowran (¾ length behind Lat Hawill) in June: stays 9.5f: acts on soft and good to firm going: often in hood in 2015. *A. J. Martin, Ireland*

CLON BRULEE (IRE) 6 ch.g. Modigliani (USA) 106 – Cloneden (IRE) 79 (Definite – Article 121) [2015 116, a103: 7d May 30] smart handicapper: probably needed run when well held in John of Gaunt Stakes at Haydock sole outing in 2015: stayed 10.5f: acted on tapeta, soft and good to firm going: dead. *Saeed bin Suroor*

CLONDAW WARRIOR (IRE) 8 br.g. Overbury (IRE) 116 – Thespian (IRE) (Tiraaz **114** (USA) 115) [2015 20f* 11.8d* 14g 18m² 19.9m 16d Oct 17] good-topped gelding: smart performer: won Ascot Stakes (Handicap) at Royal Ascot (by ½ length from Fun Mac) in June and handicap at Galway (by 1½ lengths from Golden Spear) in July: good second in Doncaster Cup (¾ length behind Pallasator) in September: acts on firm and good to soft going: tried in headgear: often races towards rear. *W. P. Mullins, Ireland*

CLOSING 3 ch.f. Compton Place 125 – Rosewood Belle (USA) 70 (Woodman (USA) – 126) [2015 61: p7m t7.1m p5f Mar 20] maiden: no form in 2015: usually races prominently. *Nick Littmoden*

CLOTH OF STARS (IRE) 2 b.c. (Apr 6) Sea The Stars (IRE) 140 – Strawberry Fledge **110** (USA) (Kingmambo (USA) 125) [2015 8g* 8g* 8.9g³ 9.9s² Nov 1] 400,000Y: third foal: half-brother to useful winner up to 1½m Warrior of Light (2-y-o 1m winner, by High Chaparral): dam, third at 1m in France at 2 yrs on only start, sister to Oaks winner Light Shift and half-sister to high-class 8.5f-10.5f winner Shiva: smart performer: won newcomers race at Deauville in August and Prix des Chenes at Longchamp (by 1¾ lengths from Vedevani) in September: good second in Criterium de Saint-Cloud (2½ lengths behind Robin of Navan) in November: wore cheekpieces on debut. *A. Fabre, France*

CLOTILDE 3 br.f. Dubawi (IRE) 129 – Mary Boleyn (IRE) 108 (King's Best (USA) 132) **75** [2015 10m⁵ 9.9g⁵ 12d t8.6g⁶ Jul 8] strong filly: first foal: dam, French 9f/1¼m winner, sister to smart 6f winner Kaldoun Kingdom: fair maiden: may prove best at around 1m. *William Knight*

CLOUDBERRY 2 b.g. (Feb 26) Pivotal 124 – Clouded Leopard (USA) 81 (Danehill – **P** (USA) 126) [2015 8s Oct 23] fourth foal: half-brother to 6f and (at 2 yrs) 1m winner Tiger Cub (by Dr Fong) and a winner in Qatar by Dubawi: dam, maiden (stayed 7f), half-sister to Breeders' Cup Juvenile Turf winner Pounced: 18/1, promising debut when eleventh in maiden at Newbury (9¼ lengths behind Midterm) in October, not knocked about: sort to improve markedly. *Roger Charlton*

CLOUDED GOLD 3 ch.g. Resplendent Glory (IRE) 115 – Segretezza (IRE) 48 (Perugino – (USA) 84) [2015 7d f7g t7.1g⁴ Dec 1] little solid form in maidens. *Michael Appleby*

CLOUD MONKEY (IRE) 5 b.g. Marju (IRE) 127 – Sweet Clover 67 (Rainbow Quest **82** (USA) 134) [2015 79: 12g⁴ 12g* 12m* 14.6m⁴ 12m⁶ 12g 12s² 12s Oct 27] fairly useful handicapper: won at Catterick in May and Doncaster (dead-heated with Cape Castle) in June: second at Catterick in October: stays 12.5f: acts on polytrack, soft and good to firm going: often in headgear prior to 2015: often races in rear, tends to find little. *Martin Todhunter*

CLOUD NINE (FR) 2 b.f. (Mar 1) Sakhee (USA) 136 – Heaven 84 (Reel Buddy (USA) – 118) [2015 p6g⁶ Dec 16] second foal: half-sister to 6f winner Wedgewood Estates (by Assertive): dam 5f winner (including at 2 yrs): 25/1, sixth in maiden at Kempton (8¼ lengths behind Desirable) in December, very slowly away. *Tony Carroll*

CLOUDSCAPE (IRE) 4 b.c. Dansili 127 – Set The Scene (IRE) 79 (Sadler's Wells **107** (USA) 132) [2015 113: p10f³ p10g 12d⁴ Mar 29] big, rangy colt: useful performer: third in listed race at Lingfield (length behind Grendisar) in February: may prove best at short of 1½m: acts on polytrack, soft and good to firm going: often in blinkers in 2015: wears tongue tie: sent to Australia. *John Gosden*

CLOUD SEVEN 3 br.g. New Approach (IRE) 132 – Regrette Rien (USA) (Unbridled's **89** Song (USA) 125) [2015 72p: p8g* 8.3m⁵ p11g* p11g⁴ Aug 26] fairly useful handicapper: won at Kempton in April and August: stays 11f: acts on polytrack: often travels strongly. *Chris Wall*

CLOUDS REST 3 b.f. Showcasing 117 – Ahwahnee (Compton Place 125) [2015 89: 5f **80** 5m 6m⁵ 5.5g⁵ 5m⁴ 5g⁶ 5f 5g⁴ Oct 13] smallish filly: fairly useful handicapper: stays 6f: acts on good to firm going: front runner/races prominently. *Richard Fahey*

CLOUDY GIRL (IRE) 2 gr.f. (Feb 11) Lawman (FR) 121 – Vespetta (FR) (Vespone – (IRE) 125) [2015 6g 5s⁵ Aug 26] €58,000F, £40,000Y: sturdy filly: first foal: dam unraced half-sister to dam of smart performers Spin Cycle (sprinter) and Same World (up to 1¼m in Hong Kong): no form. *Charles Hills*

CLOVELLY BAY (IRE) 4 b.g. Bushranger (IRE) 119 – Crystalline Stream (FR) (Polish **83** Precedent (USA) 131) [2015 62p: p7m⁴ p8m⁴ 9s² 8.3d⁴ 10.3d³ p10f* p11g p12g² Dec 20] fairly useful handicapper: won at Chelmsford in November: second at Goodwood (amateur) in August and Lingfield in December: stays 1½m: acts on polytrack: often races prominently, often travels strongly. *Marcus Tregoning*

CLOWANCE KEYS 6 b.g. High Chaparral (IRE) 132 – Seasons Parks 64 (Desert Prince **42** (IRE) 130) [2015 p7g⁵ p8f Jan 21] poor maiden: should be suited by at least 1m: acts on polytrack and soft going: tried in headgear. *Peter Hedger*

CLOWANCE ONE 3 b.g. Oasis Dream 129 – Clowance 117 (Montjeu (IRE) 137) [2015 **91** 10g³ 12v³ p12g* 10d⁵ p12g⁴ Nov 18] sturdy gelding: first foal: dam 1¼m-1½m (St Simon Stakes) winner and second in Irish St Leger: fairly useful performer: won maiden at Kempton in October: third in maiden at Newbury in May: stays 1½m: acts on polytrack: usually travels strongly. *Roger Charlton*

CLUB HOUSE (IRE) 5 b.g. Marju (IRE) 127 – Idesia (IRE) 78 (Green Desert (USA) **68** 127) [2015 82: p8g³ p8g⁶ p8g⁶ p8f p8g⁴ p8g² p7f⁶ t8.6g³ 8m t7.1g t9.5m Sep 25] workmanlike gelding: fair handicapper: left Robert Mills after third start, John O'Shea after eighth: stays 1m: acts on polytrack and good to firm going: sometimes wears headgear. *Kevin Frost*

CLUBLAND (IRE) 6 b.g. Red Clubs (IRE) 125 – Racjilanemm 77 (Kyllachy 129) [2015 **89** 85: t6g⁶ f5d⁴ t6g³ 6g* 6m⁴ 6v³ 6.1m 6m 7m f6d* 6m⁵ 6s 7d 6.1d* 5.1d p6g f7f⁵ Dec 17] **a81** compact gelding: fairly useful handicapper: won at Thirsk in April, Southwell in July and Chester (by 2¼ lengths from Funding Deficit) in September: stays 6f: acts on all-weather, soft and firm going: tried in cheekpieces in 2015. *Roy Bowring*

CLUMBER PLACE 9 ch.m. Compton Place 125 – Inquirendo (USA) 81 (Roberto – (USA) 131) [2015 74: 7m 7m 7.2g Jul 6] fairly useful at best, no form in 2015. *Shaun Harris*

CLUMBER STREET 4 ch.g. Compton Place 125 – Tinnarinka 84 (Observatory (USA) **88** 131) [2015 p5f* p5g³ Apr 7] fairly useful performer: won maiden at Chelmsford in March: raced only at 5f: acts on polytrack and firm going. *David Brown*

C NOTE (IRE) 2 b.c. (Apr 18) Iffraaj 127 – Alexander Queen (IRE) 96 (King's Best **98 p** (USA) 132) [2015 7g³ Sep 25] 55,000Y: half-brother to several winners, including smart 6f/7f winner Alkasser (by Shamardal) and useful 6f (including at 2 yrs) winner Dragon King (by Dylan Thomas): dam, 2-y-o 5f winner, half-sister to very smart sprinter Dandy Man: 14/1, showed plenty when third in maiden at Newmarket (head behind Crazy Horse) in September: open to improvement. *Martyn Meade*

COACH BOMBAY (IRE) 7 b.g. Ad Valorem (USA) 125 – Molly-O (IRE) 101 (Dolphin **68** Street (FR) 125) [2015 63: p10.7g³ p10.7g³ p8g² p8g p8g p12g* 14g 12g³ p8g* p8g* p10.7g t8.6f³ p12g⁶ p8g⁶ Dec 11] fair handicapper: won at Dundalk in May and September (2): stays 1½m, effective at shorter: acts on polytrack, tapeta and good to firm going: often wears headgear: sometimes wears tongue tie: front runner/races prominently. *Adrian Brendan Joyce, Ireland*

COARSE CUT (IRE) 2 b.g. (Mar 2) Duke of Marmalade (IRE) 132 – Keladora (USA) **69** (Crafty Prospector (USA)) [2015 7d 8.3g 8.3d Oct 5] fair maiden: best effort when seventh in maiden at Windsor (4¼ lengths behind Four On Eight) in September. *Eve Johnson Houghton*

COBANA SAND (IRE) 2 br.f. (Apr 16) Captain Rio 122 – Five Sisters (Mujahid (USA) **89 ?** 125) [2015 6g⁵ 5m* 6m 5.1m⁴ 5g³ p5g⁵ 5.2v³ 5d⁵ Oct 9] €7,200Y: leggy filly: third foal: half-sister to 2-y-o 6f winner Mr Matthews (by Diamond Green): dam unraced: fairly useful performer: won maiden at Leicester (by ¾ length from Belvoir Bay) in May: beaten in nurseries sixth/seventh starts: blinkered, seemed to show improved form when 1¼ lengths fifth to Fine Blend in listed race at Chantilly final outing: best form at 5f: acts on good to firm and good to soft going: often races prominently. *Giles Bravery*

COBHAM'S CIRCUS (IRE) 4 ch.g. Hernando (FR) 127 – Protectorate 91 (Hector **71** Protector (USA) 124) [2015 54: 10g⁴ p12g⁶ Sep 22] lengthy gelding: fair maiden: stays 1½m: acts on polytrack and good to firm going. *Marcus Tregoning*

COCKER 3 b.g. Shirocco (GER) 129 – Treble Heights (IRE) 107 (Unfuwain (USA) 131) **60** [2015 61: f8g⁶ t12.2m⁵ 14.1g 11.7g² 16g⁶ 12v⁴ Aug 19] modest maiden: stays 1¾m: acts on tapeta: often in cheekpieces in 2015. *Tom Dascombe*

COCKLE TOWN BOY 3 ch.g. Cockney Rebel (IRE) 127 – Rare Cross (IRE) 90 (Cape **49** Cross (IRE) 129) [2015 p7f⁶ t6f⁶ p6f² p6f 7s p7g⁵ p6f t6m 7s 8sᵘʳ p7g⁶ p8g⁶ p8g Dec 3] **a58** modest maiden: left David Bridgwater after fifth start: best effort at 7f: acts on polytrack: often in hood. *Brendan Powell*

COCKNEY BOY 2 ch.g. (Mar 24) Cockney Rebel (IRE) 127 – Menha 70 (Dubawi (IRE) –
129) [2015 7g Sep 30] 66/1, eleventh in maiden at Salisbury (7¾ lengths behind Royal
Reserve) in September. *John Gallagher*

COCKNEY ISLAND 3 b.f. Cockney Rebel (IRE) 127 – Island Rhapsody 78 (Bahamian   59
Bounty 116) [2015 86: p6f³ Nov 6] small, rather sparely-made filly: modest maiden: stays
6.5f: acts on good to firm going: sometimes wears cheekpieces. *Philip McBride*

COCONELL 5 b.m. Rock of Gibraltar (IRE) 133 – Marula (IRE) (Sadler's Wells (USA) –
132) [2015 53: 14.1g 14.6d 17.1m⁴ p15.8fᵖᵘ Sep 22] fair at best, no form in 2015.
Peter Hiatt

CODE RED 3 ch.c. Bahamian Bounty 116 – Just Devine (IRE) 69 (Montjeu (IRE) 137)   111
[2015 105p: 7m⁶ 8m 7g* 7m⁴ 7g⁴ 7d Sep 12] tall, good-topped colt: smart performer: won
listed race at Epsom (by 1¼ lengths from Mister Universe) in June: creditable effort after
when 1½ lengths fourth to Toormore in Lennox Stakes at Goodwood penultimate outing:
stays 7f: acts on soft going: front runner/races prominently. *William Muir*

CODGER'S GIFT (IRE) 3 b.f. Footstepsinthesand 120 – Moonbi Ridge (IRE) 102 –
(Definite Article 121) [2015 54p: 7.2g 10.2s t9.5f Nov 20] maiden: no form in 2015.
Richard Fahey

COGENT 2 b.g. (Apr 4) Paco Boy (IRE) 129 – Logic 94 (Slip Anchor 136) [2015 6.1d 6m   69
t6g⁴ p8f⁴ t7.1f Oct 20] sturdy gelding: fair maiden: stays 1m: acts on polytrack and tapeta:
usually races nearer last than first: sent to Spain. *Ed Dunlop*

COHERENT (IRE) 2 b.c. (Apr 30) Rip Van Winkle (IRE) 134 – Hold Off (IRE) (Bering   79
136) [2015 7g p7g² t8.6m* Nov 21] 80,000 2-y-o: rather unfurnished colt: half-brother
to several winners in Germany, including useful 11f winner High Heat (by Boreal) and
12.5f winner High Chance (by Kandahar Run): dam lightly-raced half-sister to top-class
winner up to 1½m Hurricane Run: fair performer: best effort when winning maiden at
Wolverhampton (by nose from Red Verdon) in November, having run of race: best effort at
8.5f. *William Haggas*

COILLTE CAILIN (IRE) 5 b.m. Oratorio (IRE) 128 – Forest Walk (IRE) (Shinko   88
Forest (IRE)) [2015 75: t9.5g* t9.5g³ p10.7g⁵ t9.5m* t9.5f³ t9.5m⁴ 10.3g³ 8.3g⁶ 9d⁶ 10.3s
t9.5m⁶ t12.2f t9.5f² t9.5m³ Dec 30] fairly useful handicapper: won at Wolverhampton in
January and February: stays 10.5f: acts on tapeta: tried in blinkers prior to 2015: sometimes
slowly away, often races towards rear. *Daniel Loughnane*

COIN A PHRASE 3 b.f. Dubawi (IRE) 129 – French Bid (AUS) (Anabaa (USA) 130)   –
[2015 t7.1f Feb 16] sixth foal: half-sister to several winners, including useful French 2-y-o
5.5f winner Forum Magnum (by Elusive Quality) and 2-y-o 1m winner Kind Invitation (by
New Approach): dam Australian 6f (including at 2 yrs) winner, including Group 2: 9/2,
well beaten in maiden at Wolverhampton in February. *Charlie Appleby*

COINCIDENTLY 5 b.m. Acclamation 118 – Miss Chaussini (IRE) 76 (Rossini (USA)   –
118) [2015 90: p10m Jan 10] unfurnished mare: fairly useful at best, no form in 2015: stays
10.5f: acts on polytrack and any turf going: usually wears headgear: often leads. *Alan Bailey*

COISTE BODHAR (IRE) 4 b.g. Camacho 118 – Nortolixa (FR) (Linamix (FR) 127)   71
[2015 71: p6g p6g⁴ f6g* f6g⁵ 6m³ 6g³ 5m 6m 5d* 6s 5d t6m 6d t6f⁶ f6g* f6m f6g Dec 15]
fair performer: won handicap at Southwell in March, seller at Thirsk in August and
handicap at Southwell in November: stays 6f: acts on polytrack, fibresand and heavy going:
usually wears headgear: front runner/races prominently. *Scott Dixon*

COLD AS ICE (SAF) 4 b.f. Western Winter (USA) 116 – Viva (SAF) (National Assembly 114
(CAN)) [2015 6g* 8g² t7.1g⁴ p7f* Dec 21] second foal: half-sister to a winner in South
Africa by Var: dam South African Group 3 6f winner: smart performer: won Grade 2
Sceptre Stakes at Kenilworth (by 2¼ lengths from Double Whammy) in January and minor
event at Chelmsford (by ¾ length from Realize) in December: second in Majorca Stakes at
Kenilworth (short head behind Inara) in January: left Joey Ramsden, South Africa after
second start: stays 7f, effective at shorter: acts on polytrack. *William Haggas*

COLLABORATION 4 b.g. Halling (USA) 133 – Red Shareef (Marju (IRE) 127) [2015   107
90: 10m* 10.1g* 10.3s* 10f 9.9g 10.4m⁵ 10.1v³ p9.2m Sep 26] rather leggy gelding: useful
handicapper: won at Windsor and Epsom (by 4½ lengths from Hold The Line) in April, and
Chester (by 2¼ lengths from Tres Coronas) in May: stays 10.5f: acts on polytrack and any
turf going: wore hood final outing: wears tongue tie: usually races freely: sent to Australia.
Andrew Balding

COLLEGE DOLL 6 ch.m. Piccolo 121 – Southwarknewsflash 59 (Danetime (IRE) 121) **53**
[2015 65: f5d⁵ f5g f5.1f⁶ f5g⁶ f5s⁵ f5g⁴ p5g⁴ 5m⁵ 5.1d Aug 14] lengthy, angular mare:
modest handicapper: stays 6f: acts on all-weather, firm and soft going: often wears tongue
tie: often races prominently. *Christine Dunnett*

COLLODI (GER) 6 b.g. Konigstiger (GER) 112 – Codera (GER) (Zilzal (USA) 137) **76**
[2015 83: 8.3m³ p7g 8.3s 8.3v p8m² p10g⁶ p8d² t9.5f Dec 14] fair handicapper: stays 10.5f:
acts on polytrack, good to firm and heavy going: tried in cheekpieces in 2015: often starts
slowly, usually races nearer last than first. *David Bridgwater*

COLLOSIUM (IRE) 3 ch.g. Showcasing 117 – Ragsta (IRE) 68 (Key of Luck (USA) **72**
126) [2015 81p: 6g* 6g 6.9s Jul 4] fairly useful form: won maiden at Newcastle in April:
stayed 6f: dead. *Michael Dods*

COLOMBE BLEU 2 b.f. (Mar 12) Manduro (GER) 135 – Blue Dream (IRE) 100 **61**
(Cadeaux Genereux 131) [2015 7g* 7f Jul 11] sixth foal: half-sister to Italian winner up
to 10.5f Dream Hall (2-y-o 1m winner, by Halling) and 2-y-o 7f winner Medicoe (by
Medicean): dam, French 6f winner, half-sister to useful winner up to 9f Equity Princess:
better effort when winning seller at Redcar (by 7 lengths from Workaday) in June: left Sir
Mark Prescott after: will stay 1m+. *Tony Coyle*

COLOMBIA (IRE) 3 b.f. Art Connoisseur (IRE) 121 – Credibility 65 (Komaite (USA)) **52**
[2015 48: t5.1f⁴ t5.1g* t5.1g Feb 13] modest handicapper: won at Wolverhampton in
January: raced only at 5f: acts on tapeta: in hood in 2015: usually races prominently.
Ann Duffield

COLONEL BOSSINGTON (IRE) 2 b.c. (Mar 27) Azamour (IRE) 130 – Ros The **– p**
Boss (IRE) 80 (Danehill (USA) 126) [2015 6g Aug 29] €20,000F, 50,000Y: half-brother to
several winners, including smart 6f (including at 2 yrs) winner Bossy Guest (by Medicean)
and useful 1m winner Alsalwa (by Nayef): dam 7f/1m winner: 33/1, better than result
when eighth in maiden at Newmarket (8 lengths behind Taneen) in August, unable to
sustain effort: should do better. *William Knight*

COLONEL MAK 8 br.g. Makbul 104 – Colonel's Daughter 61 (Colonel Collins (USA) **–**
122) [2015 101: f7d⁶ 6d 6s 6d 6g Aug 1] small, sturdy gelding: smart at best, no form in
2015: tried in tongue tie in 2015: usually races prominently. *David Barron*

COLONIAL CLASSIC (FR) 2 br.f. (Apr 9) Dansili 127 – Flame of Hestia (IRE) 79 **81**
(Giant's Causeway (USA) 132) [2015 8g⁴ 7g² Oct 9] good-topped, attractive filly: first foal:
dam, maiden (stayed 11.5f), half-sister to dam of useful winner up to 1¼m Don't Be: better
effort when second in maiden at Newmarket (½ length behind Materialistic) in October.
John Gosden

COLONIAL STYLE (IRE) 5 b.g. Gamut (IRE) 124 – The Dukes Pert (IRE) (Revoque **–**
(IRE) 122) [2015 8m Jul 6] 66/1, eighth in maiden at Ripon (well beaten behind Pyjama
Party) in July. *George Moore*

COLORADA 3 ch.f. Lope de Vega (IRE) 125 – Isabella Glyn (IRE) 75 (Sadler's Wells **72**
(USA) 132) [2015 75p: t7.1m p7g p6f⁵ p6m⁶ Dec 16] tall filly: has scope: fair maiden:
stays 7f: acts on tapeta and good to firm going: tried in hood in 2015: tried in tongue tie in
2015: sometimes slowly away, usually races towards rear. *William Knight*

COLOR FORCE (IRE) 2 gr.f. (Apr 3) Dark Angel (IRE) 113 – Amistad (GER) (Winged **–**
Love (IRE) 121) [2015 7d Oct 31] €26,000Y: closely related to 2 winners by Acclamation,
including winner up to 7f Amary (2-y-o 6f winner), and half-sister to 2 winners, including
useful 6f/7f winner Amazing Amoray (by Tagula): dam, German 2-y-o 7f winner, sister to
smart German 1½m performer Acamani: 20/1, eighth in maiden at Newmarket (17 lengths
behind Tiptree) in October. *Gay Kelleway*

COLOR MODEL (IRE) 2 b.f. (Mar 3) Zoffany (IRE) 121 – Green Green Grass 56 **67**
(Green Desert (USA) 127) [2015 5v⁵ 6g⁵ 5.9m⁵ 5m⁴ 6m⁵ 7.2g⁵ 6g p5g p8g Dec 18]
£20,000Y: half-sister to several winners, including 2-y-o 6f/1m winner Mr Spiggott (by
Intikhab) and 5f winner (including at 2 yrs) Liberty Green (by Statue of Liberty): dam
maiden (stayed 6f): fair maiden: left John Patrick Murtagh after second start, Michael
Dods after seventh: stays 6f: acts on good to firm and heavy going: tried in eyeshields.
J. J. Feane, Ireland

COLOURBEARER (IRE) 8 ch.g. Pivotal 124 – Centifolia (FR) 112 (Kendor (FR) 122) **80**
[2015 77: p6g f6g* f6s* p6f* p6g⁶ 6d f6g f6d p6f⁴ p6g Sep 22] fairly useful handicapper:
won at Southwell in February and March, and Chelmsford (by neck from Oscars Journey)
later in March: stays 6f: acts on polytrack, fibresand and soft going: tried in headgear prior
to 2015: usually wears tongue tie. *Charlie Wallis*

COLOUR BLUE (IRE) 4 b.f. Holy Roman Emperor (IRE) 125 – Catch The Blues (IRE) **98** 115 (Bluebird (USA) 125) [2015 100: 8v 7.5s* 7.6v⁴ 8g⁶ 7m* 6m⁵ 7g 7g⁴ 8v³ 7.5g Oct 4] smallish filly: useful performer: won minor event at Tipperary in April and handicap at the Curragh (by short head from Military Angel) in June: third in minor event at Cork (5½ lengths behind Akira) in September: stays 8.5f: acts on soft and good to firm going: tried in tongue tie prior to 2015. *W. McCreery, Ireland*

COLOURFILLY 3 ch.f. Compton Place 125 – Where's Broughton 77 (Cadeaux Genereux **65** 131) [2015 63: 8.3m⁴ p10g Aug 7] fair maiden: stays 8.5f: acts on polytrack, tapeta and good to firm going: often races prominently. *Ed Walker*

COLOUR ME HAPPY 2 ch.c. (May 8) Poet's Voice 126 – Za Za Zoom (IRE) 99 (Le **95** Vie dei Colori 126) [2015 8m² 8.3d² 7g² 7g* Oct 21] 20,000Y: workmanlike colt: second foal: dam, 2-y-o 6f winner, sister to very smart 5f-1m winner Highland Colori and half-sister to smart 6f winners Genki and Highland Acclaim: useful performer: won maiden at Newmarket (by short head from Wave Reviews) in October: should prove as effective at 1m: sent to USA. *K. R. Burke*

COLOUR MY WORLD 5 gr.g. With Approval (CAN) – Nadeszhda 91 (Nashwan – (USA) 135) [2015 73: 7g Apr 18] fair at best, no form in 2015: stays 9.5f: acts on polytrack and soft going: sometimes wears blinkers: front runner/races prominently, often travels strongly. *Ed McMahon*

COLOUR PLAY (USA) 2 b.f. (Mar 10) Medaglia d'Oro (USA) 129 – Blue Duster **52 p** (USA) 118 (Danzig (USA)) [2015 7d⁴ Aug 5] half-sister to 3 winners, including 1½m winner Federal Blue (by Elusive Quality) and 1¼m winner Blue Leader (by Cadeaux Genereux): dam 5f (at 2 yrs) to 7f winner, including Cheveley Park Stakes: 7/4, very green when fourth in maiden at Brighton (8¾ lengths behind Mansfield) in August: entitled to do better. *Mark Johnston*

COLUMBANUS (IRE) 4 b.g. Jeremy (USA) 122 – Shamah 96 (Unfuwain (USA) 131) – [2015 75: 10.1m Jun 6] maiden: no form in 2015: best effort at 8.5f: tried in blinkers prior to 2015. *S. Wilson, Ireland*

COLUMBINA 3 b.f. Proclamation (IRE) 130 – La Columbina 84 (Carnival Dancer 123) – [2015 t7.1f t8.6f Mar 14] first foal: dam 1m and (including at 2 yrs) 1¼m winner: no form. *John Spearing*

COLUMN 2 b.c. (Apr 25) Mount Nelson 125 – Tottie 96 (Fantastic Light (USA) 134) **86 p** [2015 7g⁶ 7.5m* Oct 1] second foal: dam, 2-y-o 1m winner (later winner up to 11f in USA, including Grade 3 9f event), half-sister to useful performer up to 2m Mister Impatience: better effort when winning maiden at Beverley (by 8 lengths from Red Tea) in October: will stay at least 1m: open to further improvement. *James Fanshawe*

COMADOIR (IRE) 9 ch.g. Medecis 119 – Hymn of The Dawn (USA) 73 (Phone Trick **51** (USA)) [2015 6m⁶ t7.1m⁴ Nov 28] rather leggy, workmanlike gelding: modest handicapper: stays 7.5f: acts on polytrack, tapeta and any turf going: sometimes wears headgear: tried in tongue tie prior to 2015. *Jo Crowley*

COMANCHE CHIEFTAIN (CAN) 3 b.g. Broken Vow (USA) 117 – Platinum **73** Preferred (CAN) (Vindication (USA) 122) [2015 66p: 10.4g 10m³ 10.3m⁵ 10.1g⁵ 8.3s⁶ 10.2g t9.5f* p10f² t9.5g Nov 27] fair handicapper: won at Wolverhampton in October: stays 1¼m: acts on polytrack, tapeta and good to firm going: tried in cheekpieces in 2015: usually leads. *Michael Appleby*

COMBE HAY (FR) 2 b.f. (Feb 20) Elusive City (USA) 117 – Coiffure (King's Best **80** (USA) 132) [2015 8g³ 8d² 8.9g² Oct 1] second foal: closely related to French 10.5f winner Win Coiff (by Raven's Pass): dam unraced daughter of Yorkshire Oaks winner/St Leger runner-up Quiff: fairly useful maiden: runner-up in maidens at Haydock and Compiegne. *Henry Spiller*

COMEDY HOUSE 7 b.g. Auction House (USA) 120 – Kyle Akin (Vettori (IRE) 119) **59** [2015 74: p12g p12f² 11.9d⁵ 14.1g² 11.9s p12f³ p12g⁵ Dec 20] fair handicapper: stays 2m: **a68** acts on polytrack and good to firm going: sometimes wears headgear: often races towards rear. *Michael Madgwick*

COMEDY KING (IRE) 4 b.g. Dansili 127 – Comic (IRE) 87 (Be My Chief (USA) 122) **88** [2015 87: 12m² 12g⁵ 11.5g 12m Aug 15] fairly useful handicapper: second at Doncaster (apprentice) in May: stays 1½m: acts on good to firm going. *Luca Cumani*

COMEDY NIGHT 2 b.c. (Apr 28) Royal Applause 124 – Acicula (IRE) 96 (Night Shift (USA)) [2015 5.3g² 5g⁵ 5m² 5m⁴ 5g² 5f³ 5s⁶ 5.1g* 6m t5.1f 7g⁴ Dec 30] sturdy colt: fair performer: won maiden at Nottingham in September: left Robert Cowell 14,000 gns after tenth start: stays 6f: acts on good to firm going: often in headgear: front runner/races prominently. *A. Al Qathiri, Qatar* **78**

COMEDY QUEEN (USA) 3 b.f. Distorted Humor (USA) 117 – Miss Caerleona (FR) 106 (Caerleon (USA) 132) [2015 86p: a7f⁶ Jan 15] fairly useful winner at 2 yrs: well held in minor event at Meydan, sole outing in 2015: stays 7f: wears hood. *Charlie Appleby* **–**

COME ON DAVE (IRE) 6 b.g. Red Clubs (IRE) 125 – Desert Sprite (IRE) 62 (Tagula (IRE) 116) [2015 91: p5g* p5g² p5g* 5.1s⁴ 5m³ 5m p6f t6f p5f⁴ f5g⁴ Dec 12] useful handicapper: won at Chelmsford (by 5 lengths from Dynamo Walt) in February and March: left John Butler after third start: best form at 5f: acts on polytrack, fibresand, soft and good to firm going: tried in headgear: usually leads. *Phil McEntee* **85 a95**

COME ON LULU 4 ch.f. Calcutta 112 – Flashing Floozie 54 (Muhtarram (USA) 125) [2015 –: f8g 6d 9.3m 8m 7g Jun 20] maiden: no form in 2015: left Shaun Harris after first start. *Kenny Johnson* **–**

COME ON SUNSHINE 4 b.g. Authorized (IRE) 133 – Tagula Sunrise (IRE) 101 (Tagula (IRE) 116) [2015 71: 14.1m Jul 19] good-topped gelding: maiden: no form in 2015: stays 2m: acts on soft going: tried in headgear. *Brian Ellison* **–**

COME UPPENCE 3 b.g. Captain Gerrard (IRE) 113 – Waterline Twenty (IRE) 89 (Indian Danehill (IRE) 124) [2015 72: f5g² f5d* f5g² f5s⁴ Mar 17] angular gelding: fairly useful performer: won maiden at Southwell in January: second in handicap at Southwell in February: best form at 5f: acts on fibresand: tried in visor: usually leads. *David Evans* **82**

COMICAS (USA) 2 ch.c. (Mar 20) Distorted Humor (USA) 117 – Abby's Angel (USA) (Touch Gold (USA) 127) [2015 7g⁵ 7m² 7m* Jul 23] good-bodied colt: third foal: brother to 2 winners in USA: dam, US 7f-8.5f (minor stakes) winner, half-sister to Irish Oaks runner-up Miss Jean Brodie: useful form: won maiden at Doncaster (by ½ length from Dragon Mall) in July: raced only at 7f: open to further improvement. *Charlie Appleby* **96 p**

COMINO (IRE) 4 b.g. Tagula (IRE) 116 – Malta (USA) (Gone West (USA)) [2015 95: 7g 8m 8g 7.1m 7d⁴ 7d 7v 6s* Oct 27] strong gelding: fairly useful handicapper: won at Thirsk in August and Catterick (by 1¼ lengths from Best Trip) in October: stays 7f: acts on soft going: tried in cheekpieces in 2015: front runner/races prominently. *Kevin Ryan* **90**

COMMANCHE 6 ch.g. Sleeping Indian 122 – Happy Memories (IRE) (Thatching 131) [2015 85: p6g³ 6m p5m⁵ p6g³ t6g⁵ 6d* 6m 6g⁶ p6f⁶ 6s⁴ 6g⁶ Oct 19] compact gelding: fair handicapper: won at Leicester in July: stays 7f: acts on polytrack, good to firm and heavy going: tried in headgear. *Chris Dwyer* **77**

COMMANDER PATTEN (IRE) 3 ro.g. Clodovil (IRE) 116 – Idle Rich (USA) 104 (Sky Classic (CAN)) [2015 84: p5g t6g⁶ p5mʳʳ Feb 4] modest handicapper: stays 6f: acts on polytrack and good to firm going: tried in headgear: refused to race final start, and one to treat with plenty of caution: sold €5,500, sent to Germany. *Alan Bailey* **57 §**

COMMANDING ROLE 2 ch.f. (Apr 30) Major Cadeaux 121 – Cultural Role 95 (Night Shift (USA)) [2015 p6g 6g 6d⁵ 5.3v³ 7s⁵ 6g Oct 20] good-quartered filly: half-sister to numerous winners, including useful 1m-16.5f winner Dont Call Me Derek (by Sri Pekan) and 2-y-o 7f/7.5f winner Mister Benedictine (by Mister Baileys): dam 2-y-o 7f winner: modest maiden: stays 6f: acts on heavy going. *Michael Blanshard* **50**

COMMEMORATE 3 ch.c. Zamindar (USA) 116 – Revered 94 (Oasis Dream 129) [2015 109p: 10d⁴ Apr 24] strong, good-topped colt: useful at best, no form in 2015: should stay at least 1¼m: acts on good to firm going. *Charles Hills* **–**

COMMISSAR 6 b.g. Soviet Star (USA) 128 – Sari 83 (Faustus (USA) 118) [2015 81, a90: p10g⁴ 10m 8m⁶ 9g* 9g² 10g³ 10.3g⁶ 10m² 8m 10.2g⁶ f11g² f12g⁶ f11g⁴ Dec 15] tall, unfurnished gelding: fairly useful handicapper: won at Goodwood (amateur) in June: left Ian Williams after tenth start: stays 1½m: acts on polytrack, fibresand, firm and soft going: usually in headgear in 2015: often wears tongue tie. *Heather Dalton* **73 a81**

COMMODORE (IRE) 3 b.g. Kodiac 112 – Deportment 90 (Barathea (IRE) 127) [2015 76p: p7g³ 6.5m³ 7g 7.1m² 7m⁶ p7g² p7g² p8g² p7m⁴ Oct 21] compact gelding: useful handicapper: stays 1m: acts on polytrack and soft going: often races towards rear, usually responds generously to pressure. *George Baker* **84 a96**

COMMUNICATOR 7 b.g. Motivator 131 – Goodie Twosues 91 (Fraam 114) [2015 103: 16m 15.9g⁴ 18g p16g p15.8g Dec 28] leggy gelding: useful handicapper: stays 2¼m: acts on polytrack, soft and good to firm going: tried in hood prior to 2015. *Andrew Balding* **95**

COMPANY ASSET (IRE) 2 ch.f. (Apr 15) Fast Company (IRE) 126 – Changari (USA) **82** 90 (Gulch (USA)) [2015 t5.1g³ 5m⁶ 6m⁵ t6g² 5.9m* 6.5m³ Sep 10] £22,000Y: seventh foal: half-sister to 6f/7f winner Stir Trader (by Titus Livius) and 6f (including at 2 yrs) winner The Hooded Claw (by Dandy Man): dam 2-y-o 5f winner: fairly useful performer: won maiden at Carlisle in August: third in nursery at Doncaster in September: stays 6.5f: acts on good to firm going: has twice been slowly away. *Kevin Ryan*

COMPANY SECRETARY (USA) 4 gr.g. Awesome Again (CAN) 133 – Maria Elena **68** (USA) (El Prado (IRE) 119) [2015 69: t9.5f² Jan 30] good-topped gelding: fair maiden: may prove best at short of 11f: acts on all-weather: usually wears headgear. *Jo Hughes*

COMPARATIVE 3 b.g. Oasis Dream 129 – Indication 76 (Sadler's Wells (USA) 132) **70** [2015 6m³ t5.1f³ p6f⁵ p7g⁴ Dec 9] fair maiden: stays 7f: acts on polytrack: in headgear in 2015. *Lydia Pearce*

COMPARINKA 2 ch.f. (Apr 26) Compton Place 125 – Tinnarinka 84 (Observatory **61** (USA) 131) [2015 5d² 5.1g³ f5g³ 6g 5g Sep 19] 5,500Y: fourth foal: sister to 5f winner Clumber Street and half-sister to 2-y-o 7f winner Mystical Moment (by Dutch Art): dam 1m winner: modest maiden: best form at 5f: acts on good to soft going. *Scott Dixon*

COMPASS HILL (USA) 3 ch.g. Mizzen Mast (USA) 121 – Zamindarling (USA) **91** (Zamindar (USA) 116) [2015 82p: 6g 6d² p7g⁶ 7d⁶ 6v* Sep 24] fairly useful performer: won maiden at Cork (by 3¾ lengths from Falcao) in September: stays 6f: acts on heavy going: often in headgear in 2015. *John Joseph Murphy, Ireland*

COMPEL (FR) 2 ch.f. (Mar 31) Exceed And Excel (AUS) 126 – Good Hope (GER) 95 **74** (Seattle Dancer (USA) 119) [2015 5m 5m 5g* 6g 5.9m² p6f t7.1f* Oct 20] €37,000F, €45,000Y: second foal: half-sister to French 1½m winner Gwalchaved (by Silver Frost): dam German 2-y-o 6f winner (stayed 1¼m): fair performer: won maiden at Beverley in July and nursery at Wolverhampton in October: stays 7f: acts on tapeta and good to firm going: often races prominently: sent to USA. *Roger Varian*

COMPETENT 3 b.g. Compton Place 125 – Pantita 74 (Polish Precedent (USA) 131) **76** [2015 –p: 8g⁴ p11g⁶ t12.2m⁶ Dec 26] fair maiden: stays 1½m. *Kristin Stubbs*

COMPLICIT (IRE) 4 b.g. Captain Rio 122 – Molomo 104 (Barathea (IRE) 127) [2015 **114** 106, a112: p10g⁴ p10f² 8.3f² 8.5g³ 8.3m⁵ p9.4g⁴ 8.9g⁶ Aug 19] good-topped gelding: smart performer: fourth in Winter Derby at Lingfield (length behind Tryster) in March, second in valuable Easter Classic at Lingfield (¾ lengths behind Tryster) in April, second in listed race at Windsor (1¾ lengths behind Shifting Power) in May and third in Diomed Stakes at Epsom (3¼ lengths behind Arod) in June: stays 1¼m: acts on all-weather and any turf going: tried in blinkers prior to 2015. *Paul Cole*

COMPTON BIRD 6 b.m. Motivator 131 – Noble Peregrine (Lomond (USA) 128) [2015 **89** 86: p8g⁵ 10m⁶ p11g 10g* 10.1g³ 10.3g 12d³ p11g⁴ 10g² 10d³ p8g⁵ t9.5f Nov 20] sturdy mare: fairly useful handicapper: won at Newbury in May: third at Newmarket in October: stays 1½m: acts on polytrack, good to firm and good to soft going: usually wears hood: tried in tongue tie prior to 2015: often starts slowly, often races in rear. *Paul Fitzsimons*

COMPTON HEIGHTS 6 ch.g. Compton Place 125 – Harrken Heights (IRE) (Belmez **96** (USA) 131) [2015 5d* 5m* 5g² 5g* p5g³ Nov 11] useful handicapper: won at Ayr in July, Haydock in August and Ayr (by length from El Viento) in September: stays 6f: acts on good to firm and good to soft going: often in hood prior to 2015: usually races close up, usually travels strongly: formerly quirky sort, but doing nothing wrong for current connections. *Keith Dalgleish*

COMPTON LADY (IRE) 2 b.f. (Mar 27) Compton Place 125 – Treble Seven (USA) 58 **66** (Fusaichi Pegasus (USA) 130) [2015 7m 5.1d⁴ 5m⁵ 7s⁴ 10.2g Sep 30] 18,000 2-y-o: seventh foal: half-sister to 3 winners, including useful UAE 7f winner Hazaz (by Dubawi) and 11f winner Stadium of Light (by Fantastic Light): dam, maiden (stayed 1¼m), half-sister to Falmouth Stakes winner Lovers Knot: fair maiden: stays 7f: acts on soft going. *Ismail Mohammed*

COMPTON MAGIC 4 b.g. Compton Place 125 – Phantasmagoria 75 (Fraam 114) [2015 **–** 6m⁶ 5g Aug 29] no form: in blinkers/tongue tie final start. *Martin Bosley*

COMPTON MEWS 2 ch.f. (Mar 29) Compton Place 125 – Dhuyoof (IRE) (Sinndar (IRE) **–** 134) [2015 5g 5d 7v Oct 17] 10,000Y, 20,000 2-y-o: fourth foal: half-sister to winner up to 12.4f Gioia Di Vita (2-y-o 9.5f winner, by Sakhee) and smart winner up to 1m Salford Secret (2-y-o 7f winner, by Sakhee's Secret): dam unraced: no form: often in hood. *Les Eyre*

COMPTON MILL 3 b.g. Compton Place 125 – Classic Millennium 72 (Midyan (USA) **82**
124) [2015 79p: f7g² p8f* 10m⁵ 8.3g⁴ 8v⁴ 8.3s² p10g Oct 27] rather leggy gelding: fairly
useful handicapper: won at Chelmsford in April: second at Leicester in September: stays
1¼m: acts on polytrack and soft going: in tongue tie in 2015: front runner/races prominently.
Hughie Morrison

COMPTON PARK 8 ch.h. Compton Place 125 – Corps de Ballet (IRE) 92 (Fasliyev **82**
(USA) 120) [2015 109: 7f⁵ 6d 6d⁵ Sep 4] tall horse: fairly useful handicapper: stays 7f: acts
on polytrack, tapeta, good to firm and heavy going: often wears tongue tie: usually races
towards rear. *Les Eyre*

COMPTON PRINCE 6 ch.g. Compton Place 125 – Malelane (IRE) 48 (Prince Sabo **57**
123) [2015 74: p6m⁴ p6g² p6f p6g⁴ t6g⁴ 6m⁵ 6m 6m³ p6g 6s t6m³ t6m t6f p6g² t6m* p6f² **a66**
t6m² Dec 30] lengthy gelding: fair handicapper: won at Wolverhampton in December:
stays 1m: acts on polytrack, tapeta and good to firm going: usually wears headgear: usually
races prominently. *Milton Bradley*

COMPTON RIVER 3 b.g. Compton Place 125 – Inagh River 71 (Fasliyev (USA) 120) **69**
[2015 67: 5.1m⁵ 5m³ 5m⁶ 5g³ 5d² 5m⁴ 5d² 5g 5g f7g Nov 26] fair maiden: best form at 5f:
acts on good to firm and good to soft going: usually in headgear in 2015: front runner/races
prominently: temperament under suspicion. *Bryan Smart*

COMPTON SKY (USA) 2 b.g. (Feb 20) Sky Mesa (USA) 116 – See How She Runs **59**
(USA) (Maria's Mon (USA) 121) [2015 7m⁵ 7m⁵ p8g⁶ p7g t8.6f⁶ 7s Oct 26] lengthy
gelding: has scope: modest maiden: stays 7f: acts on good to firm going: tried in headgear.
Paul Fitzsimons

COMPTONSSECRET 3 ch.f. Compton Place 125 – Ashfield 67 (Zilzal (USA) 137) **–**
[2015 t6f⁶ 6s t5.1g⁶ 6m 5d Jun 13] fourth foal: half-sister to 7f winner Piccolo Express (by
Piccolo): dam ran twice (second at 7f): no form: tried in hood: sometimes slowly away,
often races in rear. *Brian Baugh*

COMPTON VIKING (IRE) 3 ch.g. Equiano (FR) 127 – Feather Boa (IRE) 81 (Sri **–**
Pekan (USA) 117) [2015 –: 7.1m t6g Jun 22] maiden: no form in 2015: in hood final start:
tried tongue tied. *Paul Fitzsimons*

COMRADE BOND 7 ch.g. Monsieur Bond (IRE) 120 – Eurolink Cafe (Grand Lodge **68**
(USA) 125) [2015 77: p8g t8.6m³ p8g 7.6d⁴ 7m 7.6d 7g⁶ 7s⁶ Oct 26] close-coupled gelding:
fair handicapper: stays 8.5f: acts on polytrack, tapeta, good to firm and heavy going: tried
in headgear: inconsistent. *Mark H. Tompkins*

CONCORD (IRE) 3 b.g. Mawatheeq (USA) 126 – Amhooj 77 (Green Desert (USA) 127) **70**
[2015 p10g⁵ 10m⁶ 10m p15.8g³ Aug 26] sturdy gelding: fair maiden: stays 2m. *Marcus
Tregoning*

CONCUR (IRE) 2 ch.g. (Apr 20) Approve (IRE) 112 – Tradmagic (IRE) (Traditionally **–**
(USA) 117) [2015 5m 6m Jun 9] no form. *Rod Millman*

CONDUCTING 7 b.g. Oratorio (IRE) 128 – Aiming 76 (Highest Honor (FR) 124) [2015 **–**
76: f11g⁵ Mar 5] workmanlike gelding: fairly useful at best, no form in 2015: stays 11.5f:
acts on polytrack and soft going: tried in headgear. *David Bridgwater*

CONFESSIONAL 8 b.g. Dubawi (IRE) 129 – Golden Nun 108 (Bishop of Cashel 122) **99**
[2015 102: 6g 5.1s² 5m 5m 5m³ 5g³ 6s 5g 5.5m 5g 5m² 5d² 5v⁵ 5d Oct 24] lengthy, good-
topped gelding: useful handicapper: runner-up at Chester (1¼ lengths behind Lexi's Hero)
in May, and Doncaster (neck behind Bashiba) and Haydock (neck behind Maljaa) in
September: stays 6f: acts on fibresand, tapeta, good to firm and heavy going: usually wears
headgear. *Tim Easterby*

CONFIDENT KID 2 b.c. (Apr 2) Dubawi (IRE) 129 – Longing To Dance 98 (Danehill **– p**
Dancer (IRE) 117) [2015 6g⁶ Jul 31] 500,000Y: fourth foal: half-brother to smart 1m-1¼m
winner Be My Gal (by Galileo) and useful 6f/7f winner Foreign Diplomat (by Oasis
Dream): dam, maiden (stayed 7f), half-sister to dam of high-class performer up to 1m
Dutch Art: 8/11, well below expectations when sixth in maiden at Newmarket (13 lengths
behind Dutch Gallery) in July, slowly away: almost certainly capable of better. *Saeed bin
Suroor*

CONFLICTING ADVICE (USA) 3 b.c. Iffraaj 127 – Assertive Lass (AUS) (Zeditave **59**
(AUS)) [2015 81p: p7g³ 8.3f May 11] lengthy colt: disappointing since debut (on heavy
ground). *Sir Michael Stoute*

CONGAREE WARRIOR 5 ch.g. Congaree (USA) 127 – Peace And Love (IRE) 75 **–**
(Fantastic Light (USA) 134) [2015 52: t9.5f⁶ Jan 12] maiden: no form in 2015. *John Butler*

CONJURING (IRE) 3 b.f. Showcasing 117 – Trick (IRE) 76 (Shirley Heights 130) [2015 **68**
69: 8.3s 7m 7.1m 8s* 8g 7v³ Aug 25] workmanlike filly: fair handicapper: won at
Newmarket in July: stays 1m: acts on soft going. *Mike Murphy*

CONJUROR'S BLUFF 7 b.g. Tiger Hill (IRE) 127 – Portmeirion 96 (Polish Precedent –
(USA) 131) [2015 –: 8g Sep 23] leggy gelding: maiden: no form in 2015: stays 8.5f: acts
on good to firm going: tried in cheekpieces prior to 2015: tends to find little. *Fred Watson*

CONNECTICUT 4 b.c. New Approach (IRE) 132 – Craigmill 85 (Slip Anchor 136) **116**
[2015 113: 12g⁷ 12m⁵ 11.9g* Sep 6] attractive colt: smart performer: won listed race at
Pontefract (by 16 lengths from Nancy From Nairobi) in June and Bosphorus Cup at
Veliefendi (beat Maftool ½ length) in September: possibly not at ease on track when fifth
to Dubday in Glorious Stakes at Goodwood in between: stays 1¾m: acts on good to firm
going: often races prominently. *Luca Cumani*

CONO ZUR (FR) 8 b.g. Anabaa (USA) 130 – Alaskan Idol (USA) (Carson City (USA)) **68**
[2015 71: f8g t9.5f 8s 8g* 8s³ 8.5m⁵ 7.5m⁴ Jun 10] big gelding: fair handicapper: won at
Ayr in April: stayed 9f: acted on polytrack, firm and good to soft going: had worn headgear:
dead. *Ruth Carr*

CONRY (IRE) 9 ch.g. Captain Rio 122 – Altizaf 66 (Zafonic (USA) 130) [2015 92, a80: **74**
t7.1f p8f³ 7s³ f7d⁴ 7m³ 8m³ 7.6m⁶ 10s³ 7.5m⁵ Aug 12] close-coupled gelding: fair handicapper: stays 8.5f: acts on all-weather, good to firm and heavy going: tried in headgear:
often races in rear. *Ian Williams*

CONSERVE (IRE) 5 b.m. Duke of Marmalade (IRE) 132 – Minor Point (Selkirk (USA) **74**
129) [2015 78: t12.2g³ t16.5g* f14g t16.5g⁶ Apr 21] fair handicapper: won at Wolverhampton
in March: stays 16.5f: acts on polytrack, tapeta and heavy going: often wears blinkers.
Neil King

CONSISTANT 7 b.g. Reel Buddy (USA) 118 – Compact Disc (IRE) 48 (Royal Academy **65**
(USA) 130) [2015 68: t6g 6.1d 6.1s³ 5.9g 6.1m⁵ 6.1m 6m³ 6d⁵ 6s* 5.7f⁶ Sep 12] leggy
gelding: fair handicapper: won at Leicester in August: stays 7f, races over shorter trips
nowadays: acts on polytrack, soft and good to firm going. *Brian Baugh*

CONSORT (IRE) 3 gr.c. Lope de Vega (IRE) 125 – Mundus Novus (USA) (Unbridled's **121**
Song (USA) 125) [2015 95p: 8.1m* 8f³ 10m² Jul 18] good-topped colt: has scope: very
smart performer: won listed race at Sandown (by 2½ lengths from Secret Brief) in May:
good efforts both outings after, third in St James's Palace Stakes at Royal Ascot (3 lengths
behind Gleneagles) in June and second in listed race at Newbury (2½ lengths behind
Intilaaq) in July: stays 1¼m: sent to Hong Kong. *Sir Michael Stoute*

CONSORTIUM (IRE) 3 b.g. Teofilo (IRE) 126 – Wish List (IRE) 98 (Mujadil (USA) **73**
119) [2015 60p: p12m² p12g³ 11.6m³ 11.8g³ p12g³ p13.3f⁴ Sep 24] stocky gelding: fair
maiden: left David Simcock after fifth start: will stay beyond 13.5f: acts on polytrack and
good to firm going: tried in headgear in 2015. *Neil King*

CONSTABLE BUCKLEY 3 b.g. Naaqoos 117 – Naadrah (Muhtathir 126) [2015 86: **72**
12m 12.3g May 30] fair maiden: stays 1½m. *Mick Channon*

CONSTABLE CLOUDS (USA) 2 b.c. (Apr 23) Blame (USA) 129 – For Spacious –
Skies (USA) (Golden Missile (USA) 123) [2015 6f⁵ 7.1g 7.1g Aug 21] strong, attractive
colt: no form: tried in cheekpieces. *Gary Moore*

CONSTANTINO (IRE) 2 b.c. (Mar 29) Danehill Dancer (IRE) 117 – Messias da Silva **79 p**
(USA) 89 (Tale of The Cat (USA) 113) [2015 7g 7.2g* Sep 18] fourth foal: closely related
to very smart winner up to 1m Amazing Maria (2-y-o 7f winner, by Mastercraftsman): dam
2-y-o 6f winner: better effort when winning maiden at Ayr (by neck from Weekend
Offender) in September, having run of race: remains with potential. *Richard Fahey*

CONSULTING 2 ch.c. (Mar 16) Kyllachy 129 – Doctor's Note (Pursuit of Love 124) **79**
[2015 6d⁵ 5.4s³ p6g* Nov 11] fair performer: best effort when winning maiden at Kempton
(by nose from Mutarajjil) in November: best effort at 6f. *Martyn Meade*

CONTENDIT 2 b.g. (Apr 5) Indesatchel (IRE) 120 – Hope Chest 70 (Kris 135) [2015 6v⁶ –
t7.1m t5.1m Dec 12] no form. *Michael Easterby*

CONTINENTAL LADY 2 ch.f. (Apr 16) Medicean 128 – Paquerettza (FR) 96 (Dr Fong **87 p**
(USA) 128) [2015 6d* 6g⁶ 7m⁴ Aug 29] second foal: closely related to 6f winner Lady
Atlas (by Dutch Art): dam, 1m-10.3f winner, half-sister to smart stayer Shipmaster: fairly
useful maiden: won maiden at Leicester (by 2 lengths from Amber Mystique) in July: best
effort when sixth in Lowther Stakes at York (7 lengths behind Besharah) in August: found
race coming too soon final outing: bred to stay at least 7f: remains with potential.
David Brown

CONTINUUM 6 b.g. Dansili 127 – Clepsydra 78 (Sadler's Wells (USA) 132) [2015 106: **94** 14g⁶ 12f Jun 19] tall, good-topped gelding: fairly useful handicapper: stays 1¾m: acts on good to firm and good to soft going: usually wears headgear: often races towards rear: not straightforward. *Peter Hedger*

CONVERGENCE (IRE) 3 b.c. Cape Cross (IRE) 129 – Zahoo (IRE) 105 (Nayef (USA) **111** 129) [2015 102: p7g* 8g 7g* 8g³ 8g⁵ 9.2g⁵ 9.2g⁵ 9.9g Dec 30] compact colt: smart performer: won listed race at Dundalk (by length from War Envoy) in April and Ballycorus Stakes at Leopardstown (by neck from Tested) in June: third in Desmond Stakes at Leopardstown (¾ length behind Cougar Mountain) in August: left G. M. Lyons after fifth start: stays 1m: acts on polytrack, good to firm and good to soft going: front runner/races prominently. *Debbie Mountain, Qatar*

CONVEY 3 b.r. Dansili 127 – Insinuate (USA) 99 (Mr Prospector (USA)) [2015 100P: 8m⁴ **109** 8.9g Aug 22] well-made, attractive rig: useful performer, very lightly raced: promising fourth in Thoroughbred Stakes at Goodwood (3¾ lengths behind Malabar) on reappearance: amiss in Strensall Stakes at York (reportedly suffered from a breathing problem): stays 1m. *Sir Michael Stoute*

CONVICTED (FR) 3 b.g. Lawman (FR) 121 – Passiflore (FR) (Sillery (USA) 122) [2015 **70** 64: p10f t9.5f⁵ t12.2g⁴ p11g* p11g⁴ 11.9s 11.9g³ 14.9g 11g⁵ 10.5g⁴ 9.9d⁶ 9.5g³ a10.7g⁵ 10g p9.4g Oct 23] fair handicapper: won at Kempton in April and La Teste in August: left Ian Williams after sixth start: stays 1½m: acts on polytrack, tapeta and good to soft going: often in headgear in 2015: often leads. *P. Monfort, France*

COOKIE RING (IRE) 4 b.g. Moss Vale (IRE) 126 – Talah 87 (Danehill (USA) 126) **56** [2015 53: t6f³ t7.1f³ t9.5m* 10g⁵ 9.2d 8.3m 10.1m 7.5f 7.9s 7g t9.5f t8.6f t9.5m⁵ Dec 26] modest handicapper: won at Wolverhampton in February: stays 9.5f: acts on tapeta, firm and soft going: blinkered once in 2014: sometimes tongue tied in 2015. *Patrick Holmes*

COOL BAHAMIAN (IRE) 4 b.g. Bahamian Bounty 116 – Keritana (IRE) (One Cool Cat **92** (USA) 123) [2015 92: p7g 7s⁵ 7.1m⁴ 6.1m² 6.1m² t6g⁵ 6g* 6.1g³ 6d p6m⁴ p7g Dec 9] sparely-made gelding: fairly useful handicapper: won at Newmarket in August: second at Chepstow in July and third at Nottingham in September: stays 8.5f: acts on polytrack, good to firm and good to soft going: often wears headgear: races towards rear. *Eve Johnson Houghton*

COOL BARANCA (GER) 9 b.m. Beat Hollow 126 – Cool Storm (IRE) 58 (Rainbow **58** Quest (USA) 134) [2015 61: 15s⁶ 13d⁵ 14g² 17.2d 12.4g 13.8v Oct 17] modest handicapper: stays 2m: acts on good to firm and heavy going: often races in rear. *Dianne Sayer*

COOL BEANS 3 b.g. Kyllachy 129 – Stellar Brilliant (USA) 85 (Kris S (USA)) [2015 59: **60** f8s 10.2s 8s 10m t12.2g⁶ 8.3m⁴ f11g² Dec 29] modest maiden: stays 11f: acts on fibresand, good to firm and good to soft going: tried in headgear in 2015: tried in tongue tie in 2015. *Roy Bowring*

COOLCALMCOLLECTED (IRE) 3 b.f. Acclamation 118 – Jalissa 83 (Mister **76** Baileys 123) [2015 67p: 6.5m 7m³ 7.1m* p8g³ p8f t7.1m f7g f8g⁵ Dec 15] fair handicapper: won at Sandown in July: left Chris Wall after sixth start: stays 1m: acts on polytrack, tapeta and good to firm going: sometimes slowly away. *Andrew Crook*

COOL CRESCENDO 2 b.f. (Apr 2) Royal Applause 124 – Cool Catena (One Cool Cat **60** (USA) 123) [2015 6m 6g⁶ 7.2d 7.2g² 7.2g 7d p6f⁴ t7.1f⁵ t6f⁵ Dec 22] 11,000E, €14,000, €15,000 2-y-o: second foal: dam unraced half-sister to useful winner up to 8.3f Cochabamba: modest maiden: stays 7f: acts on polytrack, tapeta and good to soft going: front runner/races prominently. *Rebecca Menzies*

COOL IMAGE 2 b.f. (Apr 1) Elnadim (USA) 128 – Key Light (IRE) 81 (Acclamation **–** 118) [2015 5.1g 5.1m p5f⁶ t5.1f Oct 31] £20,000Y: second foal: half-sister to useful 2-y-o 5f winner (including Flying Childers Stakes) Beacon (by Paco Boy): dam 6f winner (including at 2 yrs): no form: tried in hood. *Derek Shaw*

COOL IT 2 ch.f. (May 2) Medicean 128 – Pantile (Pivotal 124) [2015 f7g t8.6g Dec 5] **–** £5,000Y: second foal: dam unraced half-sister to useful performer up to 1½m Little Rocky: no form. *James Given*

COOLMORE (IRE) 2 ch.f. (Jan 16) Galileo (IRE) 134 – You'resothrilling (USA) 117 **101 p** (Storm Cat (USA)) [2015 8g³ 7d² 7d* 8g⁴ Oct 9] lengthy filly: third foal: sister to Irish 1000 Guineas winner Marvellous (also 1m winner at 2 yrs) and dual Guineas and St James's Palace winner Gleneagles (2-y-o 7f winner): dam, 2-y-o 6f winner (including Cherry Hinton Stakes) who probably stayed 1¼m, stays top-class winner up to 10.4f Giant's Causeway and half-sister to dam of very smart 1½m performer Storm The Stars: useful performer: won C. L. Weld Park Stakes at the Curragh (by ½ length from Anamba) in

September: similar form when 6¾ lengths fourth to Minding in Fillies' Mile at Newmarket final start: will stay at least 1¼m: in cheekpieces last 2 starts: should do better again at 3 yrs. *Aidan O'Brien, Ireland*

COOL MUSIC (IRE) 5 b.m. One Cool Cat (USA) 123 – Musicology (USA) (Singspiel (IRE) 133) [2015 75: 6s 7g 6g 8.5d⁴ t8.6f t9.5f Nov 20] modest handicapper: stays 8.5f: acts on good to soft going. *Antony Brittain* — **64**

COOL SILK BOY (IRE) 2 b.c. (Mar 18) Big Bad Bob (IRE) 118 – Kheleyf's Silver (IRE) 86 (Kheleyf (USA) 116) [2015 5.1m⁶ 5m 5.1g⁴ f5g* 5m³ p5f⁶ f5g⁴ Dec 18] fair performer: won nursery at Southwell in July: raced only at 5f: acts on fibresand: tried in blinkers: keen sort, makes running. *James Given* — **68 a77**

COOL SILK GIRL 2 br.f. (May 12) Motivator 131 – Captain's Paradise (IRE) (Rock of Gibraltar (IRE) 133) [2015 7m Oct 3] 38,000F, 160,000Y: second foal: dam twice-raced half-sister to very smart winner up to 1½m Kutub: 66/1, well held in valuable sales race at Newmarket. *James Given* — **–**

COOL SKY 6 b.g. Millkom 124 – Intersky High (USA) (Royal Anthem (USA) 135) [2015 87: 13g⁵ 14.1s* 15.9m 14.1m² 14d³ Sep 26] good-topped gelding: fairly useful handicapper: won at Nottingham in May: stays 1¾m: acts on polytrack, tapeta, good to firm and heavy going. *Ian Williams* — **93**

COOL STRUTTER (IRE) 3 b.g. Kodiac 112 – Cassava (IRE) (Vettori (IRE) 119) [2015 92: 5g 6g 5.1m 5.7g 6.1g³ 6m 6v³ 6.1m Sep 10] fairly useful handicapper: third at Chepstow in August: left David O'Meara after first start: stays 6f: acts on soft and good to firm going: often races towards rear. *Andrew Balding* — **84**

COOPER 3 b.g. Sir Percy 129 – Blossom (Warning 136) [2015 –p: p6g⁵ t7.1g⁴ t8.6g² 8m³ 8.3s⁴ t8.6g 8m³ 7.9g² 8f³ 9.8g² 8d* Aug 18] fair performer: won handicap at Ripon in August: stays 1¼m: acts on tapeta, soft and good to firm going: sometimes in cheekpieces in 2015: temperamental. *Kevin Ryan* — **79 § a72 §**

COOPERESS 2 b.f. (Mar 27) Sixties Icon 125 – Vilnius 67 (Imperial Dancer 123) [2015 7s p7g 6g⁴ 6d t7.1f³ Oct 3] second foal: half-sister to 2-y-o 5f/6f winner Honest Bob's (by Winker Watson): dam 5f (including at 2 yrs)/6f winner: fair maiden: best effort at 6f. *Mick Channon* — **65**

COORG (IRE) 3 ch.g. Teofilo (IRE) 126 – Creese 88 (Halling (USA) 133) [2015 63p: 10.2d 8g p8f⁵ p10m p13.3f 11.6g p10m t12.2g⁶ f14g* p15.8g³ Dec 20] modest handicapper: won at Southwell in December: left Sir Michael Stoute after first start: stays 2m: acts on polytrack, fibresand and soft going: tried in blinkers in 2015. *Chris Dwyer* — **63**

COPACOBANA 2 b.f. (Feb 17) Monsieur Bond (IRE) 120 – Cocabana 69 (Captain Rio 122) [2015 5g³ t5.1g⁴ 5g⁴ 6d 5g² 5m 5m* Aug 12] fair performer: won maiden at Beverley in August: best form at 5f: acted on good to firm going: sometimes in visor: front runner/raced prominently: dead. *Tim Easterby* — **71**

COPIOUS KATIE 3 ch.f. Notnowcato 128 – Abundant 96 (Zafonic (USA) 130) [2015 p10g⁴ 10v 9.9m p10f Sep 24] sixth foal: half-sister to 1m winners Merrqaad (by Haafhd) and Pendo (by Denounce): dam 2-y-o 7f winner: no form. *John Holt* — **–**

COPPER CAVALIER 4 ch.g. Haafhd 129 – Elle Crystal (Mozart (IRE) 131) [2015 62: p6g⁶ t6m² t6m² Sep 25] modest handicapper: left Robert Cowell after first start: stays 7f: acts on polytrack and tapeta: usually wears headgear: usually leads. *James Toller* — **59**

COPPER TO GOLD 6 ch.m. Avonbridge 123 – Faithful Beauty (IRE) (Last Tycoon 131) [2015 52: 6g Jul 22] modest maiden: stayed 7f: best form on good going or firmer: was sometimes slowly away: dead. *John Weymes* — **–**

COPPULL MOOR 3 ch.f. Pivotal 124 – Dea Caelestis (FR) 70 (Dream Well (FR) 127) [2015 8m 9.5s 12d p12g Oct 28] third foal: dam, French 11f winner, closely related to 2000 Guineas runner-up Enrique: no form: left Richard Fahey after first start. *Anthony Mullins, Ireland* — **–**

COPRAH 7 b.g. Bertolini (USA) 125 – Oatcake 68 (Selkirk (USA) 129) [2015 9.7s⁵ 9.7g³ 8f 8g⁴ 9g³ 8.9g⁵ a8g⁵ 8g³ a9.9g⁶ Nov 12] useful performer: third in Stockholms Stora Pris at Taby (3 lengths behind Hurricane Red), listed race at Klampenborg (beaten ¾ length by Falconet) and listed race at Taby (2 lengths behind Avon Pearl): in rear in Hunt Cup at Royal Ascot on third start: stays 9.7f: acts on soft and good to firm going: has worn tongue tie. *Ms C. Erichsen, Norway* — **104**

CORAL CLUSTER (IRE) 3 b.f. Intense Focus (USA) 117 – Balloura (USA) 80 (Swain (IRE) 134) [2015 57: p8g⁶ p7g 8d 7.2g⁵ p8g Oct 9] modest maiden: left Shane Donohoe after second start: stays 7f: acts on polytrack: often in blinkers in 2015. *Adrian McGuinness, Ireland* — **51**

CORAL GARDEN 3 b.f. Halling (USA) 133 – Coraline (Sadler's Wells (USA) 132) **– p**
[2015 11.9g⁶ Apr 25] sister to 2 winners, including very smart 1½m-15.5f winner (stayed
2½m) Coastal Path, and half-sister to several winners, including winner up to 1¾m
Martaline (2-y-o 1m winner) and 1½m-2½m (Prix du Cadran) winner Reefscape (both
smart, by Linamix): dam French 12.5f winner: 9/2, green when sixth in maiden at Haydock
(16 lengths behind The Lampo Genie) in April: entitled to do better. *Lady Cecil*

CORAL ISLAND 2 ch.f. (Apr 10) Equiano (FR) 127 – Windermere Island 81 (Cadeaux **49**
Genereux 131) [2015 p6g 6d t6f t7.1f⁶ p7g⁶ f7g Dec 18] 16,000Y, 22,000 2-y-o: half-sister
to several winners, including 6f/7f winner Flexible Flyer (by Exceed And Excel): dam, 7f
winner, half-sister to smart 2-y-o 5f/6f winner Nevisian Lad: poor maiden: left Olly
Stevens after second start: stays 7f: acts on polytrack. *David O'Meara*

CORAL QUEEN 4 b.f. Desideratum 118 – Queen's Lodge (IRE) 93 (Grand Lodge (USA) **54**
125) [2015 10s² 9.8d⁴ 7g⁴ 8.5m Oct 1] third foal: dam 6f winner (including at 2 yrs):
modest maiden: left Peter Niven after second start: stays 1¼m: in hood. *Ray Craggs*

CORDIAL 4 b.f. Oasis Dream 129 – Mirabilis (USA) 114 (Lear Fan (USA) 130) [2015 95: **93**
6.1g⁵ 5m 6m 6.1g 5d⁴ 5g 6g 5d 6v Nov 7] sturdy filly: fairly useful performer: stays 6f: acts
on good to firm and good to soft going: often races towards rear. *Stuart Williams*

CORDITE (IRE) 4 ch.g. Footstepsinthesand 120 – Marion Haste (IRE) 69 (Ali-Royal **97**
(IRE) 127) [2015 111: 7g 8m p8g⁶ 7g 7s³ 7d⁶ 8d p7f⁴ f7g⁴ f7g Dec 22] angular gelding:
useful handicapper: third at Leicester (4 lengths behind Dinkum Diamond) in October:
stays 8.5f: acts on polytrack, fibresand, good to firm and heavy going: often in headgear in
2015: front runner/races prominently: quirky sort. *Michael Appleby*

CORECZKA (IRE) 4 b.f. Intense Focus (USA) 117 – Szewinska 87 (Green Desert **60**
(USA) 127) [2015 64: p12g p12g 7.2d³ 7.2d² 8.3g⁵ 7.2g⁶ p7g³ p7g* p7g⁴ Dec 11] fair **a68**
handicapper: won at Dundalk (apprentice) in October: stays 7f: acts on polytrack and good
to soft going: tried in blinkers in 2015. *Miss Clare Louise Cannon, Ireland*

CORKED (IRE) 2 b.f. (Feb 20) Mastercraftsman (IRE) 129 – Dama'a (IRE) 85 (Green **65 p**
Desert (USA) 127) [2015 p8d⁶ Nov 30] €40,000F: sixth foal: half-sister to 2-y-o 7f winner
Darkening (by Shamardal) and 2-y-o 6f/7f winner Art Official (by Excellent Art), both
useful: dam, 6f winner, half-sister to smart 6f/7f winner Himalya: 7/1, some encouragement when sixth in maiden at Kempton (8 lengths behind Zaakhir) in November: capable
of better. *Hugo Palmer*

CORLOUGH MOUNTAIN 11 ch.g. Inchinor 119 – Two Step 60 (Mujtahid (USA) 118) **–**
[2015 –: p12m t12.2f Feb 16] workmanlike gelding: fair at best, no form in 2015: stays
1½m: acts on polytrack and good to soft going: tried in headgear: tried in tongue tie prior
to 2015. *Paddy Butler*

CORNBOROUGH 4 ch.g. Sir Percy 129 – Emirates First (IRE) 77 (In The Wings 128) **80**
[2015 82: 8s⁵ 7g 9.3g⁴ 10g³ 8d² 8d³ 8d⁵ 10.2v³ Oct 7] leggy gelding: fairly useful
handicapper: stays 1¼m: acts on heavy going: sometimes in cheekpieces in 2015: often
races prominently: fairly useful hurdler. *Mark Walford*

CORNELIOUS (IRE) 3 b.g. Cape Cross (IRE) 129 – Fantastic Spring (USA) (Fantastic **82**
Light (USA) 134) [2015 p10g² p8g³ 10m* 11.7m³ 10.1m 10d⁵ 9.9g² 10d⁶ p10f* t12.2f Nov
16] €16,000 2-y-o: rather leggy gelding: fourth foal: half-brother to useful 1m-10.4f winner
Queensberry Rules (by Teofilo) and a winner in USA by Mr Greeley: dam, US 5f/6f winner,
half-sister to smart 1½m Kid Mambo: fairly useful performer: won maiden
at Windsor in April and seller at Chelmsford in October: third in handicap at Bath in May:
stays 11.5f: acts on polytrack and good to firm going: tried in headgear: front runner/races
prominently. *Robert Eddery*

CORNISH PATH 4 b.f. Champs Elysees 124 – Quintrell 92 (Royal Applause 124) [2015 **85**
86: 8m⁵ 8m² 8.9g 10.3m* 9.9g⁶ 10.2m² 10.3m Sep 10] sparely-made filly: fairly useful
handicapper: won at Doncaster (by 1¾ lengths from Merchant of Dubai) in July: second at
Bath in August: stays 10.5f: acts on polytrack, good to firm and good to soft going: sold
18,000 gns, sent to USA. *Henry Candy*

CORN MAIDEN 6 b.m. Refuse To Bend (IRE) 128 – Namat (IRE) 93 (Daylami (IRE) **48**
138) [2015 70: p13.3m⁶ p13.3m⁵ p10f⁶ p12g Dec 15] good-topped mare: poor handicapper:
stays 1¾m: acts on fibresand, firm and soft going: tried in blinkers prior to 2015: tried in
tongue tie prior to 2015: often races towards rear. *Phil McEntee*

CORNTON ROAD 3 b.g. Bertolini (USA) 125 – Sister Rose (FR) (One Cool Cat (USA) **–**
123) [2015 p6m⁵ f6g⁶ Dec 15] no form. *Phil McEntee*

CORONA BOREALIS 4 b.g. Galileo (IRE) 134 – Incheni (IRE) 100 (Nashwan (USA) **94**
135) [2015 89: 13g* 16.4m⁵ 14.1g² 16.4g³ 13.1g² Sep 19] fairly useful handicapper: won
at Wetherby in April: stays 16.5f: acts on soft and good to firm going: tried in cheekpieces
prior to 2015. *Michael Dods*

CORPORAL MADDOX 8 b.g. Royal Applause 124 – Noble View (USA) 68 (Distant **89**
View (USA) 126) [2015 96§: p7g⁴ p7g 7.1v⁶ 6.1m⁵ p6g p7m p6g³ t7.1f* t7.1f* p7m²
Dec 31] good-topped gelding: fairly useful performer: won seller at Wolverhampton in
November and handicap at Wolverhampton in December: races mainly at 6f/7f: acts on
polytrack, tapeta, firm and soft going: often wears headgear: tried in tongue tie prior to
2015: formerly unreliable. *Ronald Harris*

CORPUS CHORISTER (FR) 2 b.f. (Apr 22) Soldier of Fortune (IRE) 131 – Bridge of –
Peace (Anabaa (USA) 130) [2015 8.3d Oct 14] second foal: dam, placed up to 1½m in
France, out of useful French 2-y-o 1m/8.5f winner Hope Town: 100/1, eleventh in maiden
at Nottingham (10 lengths behind Architecture) in October. *David Menuisier*

CORREGGIO 5 ch.g. Bertolini (USA) 125 – Arian Da 81 (Superlative 118) [2015 8m³ **88**
10m⁵ 8.9g* 10.4m⁴ 10g* 10g⁶ 10d⁴ 10.4s Oct 10] rangy gelding: fairly useful handicapper:
won at York in June and Pontefract in July: stays 1¼m: acts on firm and good to soft going:
tried in cheekpieces prior to 2015. *Micky Hammond*

CORRIDOR KID (IRE) 2 b.g. (Apr 24) Kodiac 112 – All In Clover (IRE) 74 (Bahri **67**
(USA) 125) [2015 5.1m⁵ 5d⁴ p6g Jun 10] fair maiden: best effort when fourth in maiden at
Haydock (4½ lengths behind Jazz Legend) in May: will be suited by 6f. *Derek Shaw*

CORTON LAD 5 b.g. Refuse To Bend (IRE) 128 – Kelucia (IRE) 101 (Grand Lodge **93**
(USA) 125) [2015 91: p10g⁶ 16s 10.1d⁵ 10.3g⁴ 12.5m 10.4f² 10g* 10g⁴ 11.5d² 9.8g⁴ 14.1g³
12.1d t12.2f* Dec 11] fairly useful handicapper: won at Ayr in July and Wolverhampton
(by ¾ length from Gabrial The Hero) in December: stays 1¾m: acts on polytrack, tapeta,
good to firm and good to soft going: usually wears headgear: often wears tongue tie.
Keith Dalgleish

CORZETTI (FR) 3 ch.g. Linngari (IRE) 124 – Green Maid (USA) (Green Dancer (USA) **52**
132) [2015 p8f³ 8.9g f8g⁴ p8f⁴ 7s 8m⁶ 7d⁶ 7g⁵ t7.1g 8.3g 8v Nov 3] modest maiden: left **a59**
Charles Hills after fifth start: stays 1m: acts on polytrack and fibresand: often starts slowly.
Alan Berry

COSETTE (IRE) 4 b.f. Champs Elysees 124 – Luanas Pearl (IRE) (Bahri (USA) 125) [2015 **79**
88: 11.6m⁴ 13.1f⁵ 11.6m³ 14m³ 16.2m⁵ 14.1g p12g⁶ 11.7g⁶ Oct 18] rather leggy filly: fair
handicapper: stays 2m: acts on any turf going: tried in cheekpieces in 2015. *Henry Candy*

COSMEAPOLITAN 2 b.g. (Apr 3) Mawatheeq (USA) 126 – Cosmea 87 (Compton **85**
Place 125) [2015 7m⁵ 7.1g⁴ 7.1s* 8g Oct 10] strong gelding: second foal: dam, 1¼m-11.6f
winner (also won over hurdles), half-sister to useful 5f winner Master of Disguise: fairly
useful performer: won maiden at Chepstow (by 4 lengths from Able Jack) in September:
should be suited by 1m+. *Alan King*

COSMIC CHATTER 5 b.g. Paris House 123 – Paradise Eve 81 (Bahamian Bounty 116) **90**
[2015 97: 6d 6g 6d³ 6.1m³ 6d 6g 7.1m⁶ 6d⁶ 5s² 5g⁵ 5g* 5m² 5g 5.1d Oct 14] fairly useful
handicapper: won at Beverley (by 2¾ lengths from El Viento) in August: third at
Nottingham in May and second at Musselburgh in September: stays 6f: acts on good to
firm and heavy going: often in headgear in 2015: often races in rear. *Ruth Carr*

COSMIC DUST 2 b.f. (Apr 5) Equiano (FR) 127 – Cosmic Song 58 (Cosmonaut) [2015 **47**
6g 5g 5g 5s⁵ 5d 6s Oct 16] seventh foal: half-sister to 3 winners, including useful 7f winner
Marmoom (by Dutch Art) and winner up to 7f Cosmic Art (2-y-o 6f winner, by Bertolini):
dam 9f/1¼m winner: poor maiden: should be suited by 6f: acts on soft going. *Richard
Whitaker*

COSMIC HALO 6 ch.m. Halling (USA) 133 – Cosmic Case 66 (Casteddu 111) [2015 87: **76**
10.4g 10g p10g⁵ t12.2f⁵ p10f⁵ Dec 17] small mare: fair handicapper: stays 11f: acts on
polytrack, firm and good to soft going. *Richard Fahey*

COSMIC RAY 3 b.g. Phoenix Reach (IRE) 124 – Beat Seven 102 (Beat Hollow 126) **82**
[2015 83: 8.5g⁶ 8.1m⁴ 10.1m⁶ p8g* 10m⁵ 8.5g³ 8g⁴ 8.5v⁵ 8.5d² t8.6f Dec 14] sturdy
gelding: fairly useful handicapper: won at Lingfield in July: left Andrew Balding after
ninth start: should stay 1¼m: acts on polytrack, good to firm and heavy going: often in
hood in 2015: front runner/races prominently, often races freely. *Daniel Loughnane*

COSMIC STATESMAN 3 ch.g. Halling (USA) 133 – Cosmic Case 66 (Casteddu 111) **71**
[2015 60p: 14.1m² 12m⁴ 14.1g² 14f² 13m³ 14.1g³ 16.2m 12g³ 14.1m 13.1g 13.1g⁴ t13.9m³
Dec 30] rather leggy gelding: fair maiden: stays 1¾m: acts on tapeta and firm going: tried
in cheekpieces in 2015. *Richard Fahey*

COSMIC STORM 2 br.f. (Mar 18) Sea The Stars (IRE) 140 – Riotous Applause 104 **68 p**
(Royal Applause 124) [2015 7g Oct 9] 200,000F: useful-looking filly: fifth foal: half-sister
to 3 winners, including 6f (including at 2 yrs) winner Invincible Warrior (by Invincible
Spirit) and 7f winner Riot of Colour (by Excellent Art), both useful: dam, 6f winner
(including at 2 yrs), half-sister to Racing Post Trophy winner/smart performer up to 1¼m
Crowded House: 20/1, shaped as if needed experience when eighth in maiden at Newmarket
(4¾ lengths behind Materialistic) in October: will stay 1m: will improve. *David Simcock*

COSMOPOLITAN GIRL (IRE) 2 b.f. (Apr 4) Dream Ahead (USA) 133 – Absolute **74**
Music (USA) 98 (Consolidator (USA) 121) [2015 p6g 6m² 5g² p6f² p6f³ 6d³ p7g Dec 9]
90,000 2-y-o: lengthy filly: second foal: half-sister to 2-y-o 5f winner (stayed 7f) Tecumseh
(by Danehill Dancer): dam 2-y-o 5f winner: fair maiden: stays 6f: acts on polytrack and
good to firm going: tried in cheekpieces. *Ed Walker*

COSTA FILEY 4 b.g. Pastoral Pursuits 127 – Cosmic Destiny (IRE) 79 (Soviet Star **76**
(USA) 128) [2015 75: p6m p6f f5g 6m* 5.2m³ 6g³ 6g⁴ 6s* 5g² 5s⁶ p6m² Nov 17] leggy
gelding: fair handicapper: won at Lingfield in June and August: stays 6f: acts on polytrack,
soft and good to firm going: sometimes wears headgear: usually races prominently.
Ed Vaughan

COTAI GLORY 3 ch.c. Exceed And Excel (AUS) 126 – Continua (USA) (Elusive **115**
Quality (USA)) [2015 109: 5m³ 5m⁵ 5g 5m* Sep 9] tall, rather unfurnished colt: smart
performer: won listed Scarbrough Stakes at Doncaster (by length from Kingsgate Native)
in September: third in listed race at York (neck behind Out Do) in July: best form at 5f: acts
on good to firm going: front runner/races prominently. *Charles Hills*

COTE D'AZUR 2 ch.c. (Feb 25) Champs Elysees 124 – Florentia 75 (Medicean 128) **72 p**
[2015 p6g⁶ 6.1g 7.5m p8g³ p7g* p8f⁵ Oct 1] strong, compact colt: second foal: half-brother
to 2-y-o 6f-7.4f winner Flora Medici (by Sir Percy): dam, 1m-9.7f winner, half-sister to
useful winner up to 7f Flying Officer: fair performer: won nursery at Kempton in
September: best effort at 7f: acts on polytrack: has looked hard ride, but remains with
potential. *Sir Mark Prescott Bt*

COTILLION 9 b.g. Sadler's Wells (USA) 132 – Riberac 110 (Efisio 120) [2015 15.9m **79**
10.3g 13.8d 11.9d³ p16g⁴ p15.8m* Dec 16] close-coupled gelding: fair handicapper: won
at Lingfield in December: stays 2m: acts on polytrack and soft going: often in cheekpieces
in 2015: often starts slowly/races in rear. *Ian Williams*

COTO (IRE) 3 b.f. Fast Company (IRE) 126 – Let Me Shine (USA) 79 (Dixie Union **83**
(USA) 121) [2015 78: 5s⁶ 5m⁶ 5m² p5d⁴ 5d p5g p5g 5g p5g⁵ f5g⁵ f5f* Dec 17] small,
close-coupled filly: fairly useful handicapper: won at Southwell in December: second at
Bellewstown in July: raced only at 5f: acts on polytrack, fibresand, soft and good to firm
going: tried in hood prior to 2015: tried in tongue tie in 2015: usually races prominently.
M. J. Tynan, Ireland

COTTESLOE (IRE) 6 b.g. Teofilo (IRE) 126 – Vignelaure (IRE) 74 (Royal Academy **84**
(USA) 130) [2015 82: p16g⁴ p10g* 12f² 10g⁴ p12g* 12v² t13.9m³ 10m⁴ t12.2f⁴ p12g⁴
p12g³ Dec 20] tall gelding: fairly useful handicapper: won at Lingfield in June and August:
left Charles O'Brien after first start: stays 1¾m: acts on polytrack, tapeta, good to firm and
heavy going: sometimes wears headgear: tried in tongue tie prior to 2015: often races
towards rear. *John Berry*

COTTON CAMERA (IRE) 2 b.f. (Feb 13) Lilbourne Lad (IRE) 111 – Dffra (IRE) 64 **66**
(Refuse To Bend (IRE) 128) [2015 5m⁵ 5g⁵ 5d⁴ 7g² 6s⁴ 7.2m³ 8s² 8g Sep 24] €6,000Y: first
foal: dam lightly-raced half-sister to useful 2-y-o 6f/7f winner Albabilia: fair maiden: best
effort at 1m: acts on soft and good to firm going. *Richard Fahey*

COTTON CLUB (IRE) 4 b.g. Amadeus Wolf 122 – Slow Jazz (USA) 106 (Chief's **82**
Crown (USA)) [2015 87, a75: p12m⁵ 11.6m⁵ 10.2s 10m⁶ 14.1m 12m⁵ 13.3m² 17.2m* 16d⁵ **a92**
p16d³ 18g⁵ p16f* t16.5f³ p16f³ p16g⁵ p15.8g² Dec 28] quite good-topped gelding: fairly
useful handicapper: won at Bath in July and Chelmsford in October: stays 2¼m: acts on
polytrack, tapeta, good to firm and good to soft going: often races towards rear. *Rod Millman*

COTTRELL 5 b.g. Acclamation 118 – Asheyana (IRE) (Soviet Star (USA) 128) [2015 64: **56**
p6g³ p5g⁶ p6g⁶ t6g⁵ t5.1m⁵ t6g 6g⁵ Jun 9] modest handicapper: left Colin Thomas Kidd
after second start: stays 1m: acts on polytrack and heavy going: often wears headgear:
often wears tongue tie. *Daniel Loughnane*

COUGAR MOUNTAIN (IRE) 4 b.c. Fastnet Rock (AUS) 127 – Descant (USA) **123**
(Nureyev (USA) 131) [2015 118: 8s⁴ 8m 8f³ 10m⁴ 8g⁵ 8g* 10.4d Aug 19] strong, attractive
colt: very smart performer: won Desmond Stakes at Leopardstown (by ¾ length from

Raydara) in August: best effort when third in Queen Anne Stakes at Royal Ascot (1¼ lengths behind Solow) in June: probably better at 1m than 1¼m: acts on firm and good to soft going: often in headgear, and also tried in tongue tie, in 2015. *Aidan O'Brien, Ireland*

COULSTY (IRE) 4 b.c. Kodiac 112 – Hazium (IRE) 69 (In The Wings 128) [2015 113: **116** 7m* 6.5g 7d² 7d⁵ 7g 6d Oct 17] useful-looking colt: smart performer: won listed race at Leicester (by nose from Aljamaaheer) in August: second in Hungerford Stakes at Newbury (½ length behind Adaay) in August: stays 7.5f: acts on firm and soft going. *Richard Hannon*

COUNTERMAND 3 b.g. Authorized (IRE) 133 – Answered Prayer (Green Desert (USA) **78** 127) [2015 66p: 10m² 10.2m² 12g p11m⁵ f12g* f12f³ Dec 17] fairly useful **a87** performer: won maiden at Southwell (by 11 lengths from Rebel Collins) in November: third in handicap at Southwell in December: stays 1½m: acts on polytrack and fibresand: front runner/races prominently, races freely. *Andrew Balding*

COUNTERPROOF (IRE) 3 br.c. Authorized (IRE) 133 – Ellasha (Shamardal (USA) – 129) [2015 76p: 10m 10m Jun 12] well-made colt: fair at 2 yrs, no form in 2015: should stay 1¼m: acts on tapeta: sold £9,000, sent to Italy. *John Gosden*

COUNTER RIDGE (SAF) 6 b.m. Tiger Ridge (USA) – Counterpoise (SAF) (Counter **86** Action (SAF)) [2015 95: 6m⁶ 6.1g 5g p6g⁵ p6g Nov 20] fairly useful performer: left Marco Botti after second start: stays 6f: acts on polytrack and good to firm going: tried in headgear. *Thomas J. Farrell, Ireland*

COUNT MONTECRISTO (FR) 3 b.g. Siyouni (FR) 122 – Blackberry Pie (USA) 74 **97** (Gulch (USA)) [2015 75: 8d² 9g² 8m² 7d² 8.3g* Sep 21] useful performer: won maiden at Hamilton (by 6 lengths from Bromyard) in September: stays 9f: tall form on good going: front runner/races prominently. *Kevin Ryan*

COUNTY WEXFORD (IRE) 4 b.g. Teofilo (IRE) 126 – Tiffed (USA) (Seattle Slew **71** (USA)) [2015 61: p8g* p8g³ 10m⁵ p10g² Aug 17] sturdy gelding: fair handicapper: won at Dundalk (apprentice) in March: left J. S. Bolger after second start: stays 1¼m: acts on polytrack and good to firm going: tried in hood prior to 2015: usually in tongue tie prior to 2015: usually leads. *Miss Joey Ellis*

COUP DE GRACE (IRE) 6 b.g. Elusive City (USA) 117 – No Way (IRE) (Rainbows **71** For Life (CAN)) [2015 p15.8f* p15.8g 16s Oct 23] good-topped gelding: fair handicapper: won at Lingfield in February: stays 2m: acts on polytrack and soft going: tried in cheekpieces prior to 2015. *Pat Phelan*

COUP DE VENT 4 b.f. Tobougg (IRE) 125 – Pigment (Zamindar (USA) 116) [2015 **63** 10.2f⁴ 10.2m⁶ p12g p10f⁶ t8.6g⁴ p10g* Dec 30] £15,000 3-y-o: third foal: half-sister to 6f winner Jordanstown (by Piccolo): dam unraced: modest performer: won handicap at Lingfield in December: stays 1½m: acts on polytrack: tried in hood. *John O'Shea*

COURIER 3 b.f. Equiano (FR) 127 – Pivotal Drive (IRE) (Pivotal 124) [2015 58: p8f² **74** p7f² p10g⁴ p8m³ p8f² 9m² p11g 9g² 8.3m² p8g p8f⁵ p8m⁴ Nov 14] rather leggy filly: fair maiden: stays 9f: acts on polytrack and good to firm going: usually in cheekpieces in 2015: races prominently. *Lee Carter*

COURSING 3 b.f. Kyllachy 129 – Granuaile O'Malley (IRE) 55 (Mark of Esteem (IRE) **79** 137) [2015 55: t6f* p5f* p6m² Feb 18] fair handicapper: won at Wolverhampton and Lingfield in January: stays 6f: acts on polytrack and tapeta: in blinkers in 2015. *Sir Mark Prescott Bt*

COURTSIDER 3 b.f. Kyllachy 129 – Elhareer (IRE) 71 (Selkirk (USA) 129) [2015 t7.1f³ **72 p** Nov 16] 10,000Y: fourth foal: half-sister to useful 1¼m winner (stays 16.5f) Kashmir Peak (by Tiger Hill): dam 2-y-o 5f winner: 11/4, third in maiden at Wolverhampton (1¾ lengths behind Never Change) in November, not ideally placed: will stay at least 1m: sure to progress. *Lucy Wadham*

COUSIN KHEE 8 b.g. Sakhee (USA) 136 – Cugina 99 (Distant Relative 128) [2015 98: **94** t16.5f⁶ p12g² p15.8f⁶ 16.4m 15.8d⁴ 14.1s* 12v Nov 7] well-made gelding: fairly useful handicapper: won at Nottingham (by 7 lengths from Caged Lightning) in October: stays 2m: acts on polytrack, fibresand and soft going: fairly useful hurdler. *Hughie Morrison*

COVENANT 3 b.g. Raven's Pass (USA) 133 – Love Everlasting 112 (Pursuit of Love **91** 124) [2015 8m 10g⁴ 9.9m² 13d⁴ 10.1d* 10g⁴ 11s² Sep 23] strong gelding: half-brother to 3 winners, including useful 1½m winner Acquainted (by Shamardal) and 2-y-o 7f winner (stayed 1¼m) Penny Rose (by Danehill Dancer): dam, winner up to 1½m (2-y-o 7.4f winner), half-sister to smart 1¼m winner Baron Ferdinand: fairly useful performer: won maiden at Newcastle in August: second in handicap at Goodwood in September: stays 11f: acts on soft going: in hood: front runner/races prominently. *Daniel Kubler*

COVER CHARGE 2 ch.c. (Mar 17) Kheleyf (USA) 116 – Perfect Cover (IRE) 48 (Royal –
Applause 124) [2015 6m 6m 6g 5.1m Sep 10] sturdy colt: no form: tried in cheekpieces:
sent to Greece. *Clive Cox*

COVERT LOVE (IRE) 3 b.f. Azamour (IRE) 130 – Wing Stealth (IRE) 76 (Hawk **120**
Wing (USA) 136) [2015 62p: p10g* 10.4g* 10.1g* 12m* 12d² 9.9m* 12d⁴ Oct 17]

Having a privileged background can be a hindrance, as well as an obvious
help, to a young racehorse trainer. (The Honourable) Hugo Palmer, master of
Kremlin Cottage Stables in Newmarket, is from the family that owned the biscuit
manufacturers Huntley & Palmers, and he is the eldest son of the 4th Baron Palmer
whose ancestral seat is in Berwickshire. Thirty-five-year-old Palmer, who worked
for a stockbroker, a law firm and a property developer, among others, before
becoming a trainer, admits he is 'enormously lucky' to have had the support of
his father ('I wouldn't have come anywhere near to getting the mortgage I needed
without his help'). Palmer is well aware of his 'posh boy' image—'When you talk
like I do and have been at the school I have [Eton], some people think you are
not prepared to work as hard as everyone else … they think you have been given
things on a plate and they may want you to fail because of it.' Any misconceptions
about Palmer must finally have been laid to rest by his stable's profile in the latest
season—which included a first classic victory thanks to Covert Love, a filly that
nobody wanted—and by the obvious conclusion to be drawn from his interviews in
the media and his co-operation during TV broadcasts that he is very much a young
trainer for the modern age. 'Horses can't talk, so the humans have a responsibility to
make racing come alive … the sport is not any more a private club and, if we drag
our feet, it's going to get harder. We have to make the sport more appealing and, if
my generation can't embrace that concept, we're all in trouble.'

Hugo Palmer is an up-and-coming trainer more concerned about where he
wants to go—his ultimate ambition is to be champion trainer—than with where he
has come from, and he certainly has a bright future. Importantly, he knows how to
promote himself, as well as doing his bit to promote the sport itself. He was only six
months into his first season in 2011, with a dozen horses in his care, when he paid
£20,000 at Doncaster Sales for the filly Born To Run whose every step was being
followed and featured by the *Racing Post*. 'I'm afraid she turned out to be absolutely
useless, but to have my business promoted in the trade newspaper as her career
unfolded seemed like a golden opportunity, and she did me an enormous amount of
good. I'd have thought someone with greater resources would have bought her for
the publicity alone.' In the latest season, Palmer's quietly developing stable strength
suddenly doubled to around eighty and it looks set to keep on growing (the yard has
been added to the roster of Khalid Abdullah's trainers from 2016) after his string of
successes, which included passing the £1m mark in prize-money in Britain for the
first time, as well as chalking up two pattern victories from two runners in Ireland,
Covert Love's in the Irish Oaks and that of Home of The Brave in the following
day's Minstrel Stakes, though the latter was later disqualified after testing positive
for a prohibited substance (New Providence and Galileo Gold also won in pattern
company on home soil in July to make it a notable month for the yard).

Covert Love is syndicate-owned, not unusual for horses trained by Palmer
('I originally bought all my horses on tick and formed syndicates … looking back,
foolhardy doesn't come close to describing it, my father would have gone crazy if
he'd known!'). Covert Love was led out unsold at Goffs as a yearling when the
bidding reached only €26,000. Her co-breeders sent her into training with Palmer
who helped to form the seven-member FOMO [Fear Of Missing Out] Syndicate
to spread the cost. Once-raced at the back end as a two-year-old, Covert Love
made rapid strides at three, well backed when getting off the mark in a maiden
at Chelmsford in early-May and following up, switched to turf and making her
handicap debut, at York later that month. The hat-trick was completed in an all-aged
listed event at Newcastle at the end of June when she improved again to beat the
promising four-year-old Talmada by a length, battling on well after being prominent
all the way. Covert Love completed her meteoric rise, making it four wins from
four appearances as a three-year-old, in the Darley Irish Oaks at the Curragh in

Darley Irish Oaks, the Curragh—
the supplemented Covert Love is given a masterful ride by Pat Smullen as she wins from
Jack Naylor (right), Curvy (No.2) and the only previous Group 1 winner Together Forever

mid-July for which she was supplemented at €40,000 (the syndicate members having agreed to pool the winnings from her three earlier races to pay for the entry). Bearing in mind that it cost more to supplement Covert Love for the Irish Oaks than it would have cost to buy her outright as a yearling, her triumph provided an unlikely story, but one that will undoubtedly encourage owners who have to operate with a restricted budget.

Up against four contenders owned by the Coolmore partners, including the first and second favourites Curvy (bidding for a five-timer) and the unbeaten Words, Covert Love started at 7/1 in the field of nine for the Irish Oaks (the Oaks winner Qualify was a late withdrawal on account of the good to firm going). The Coolmore-owned Fillies' Mile winner Together Forever was the only Group 1 winner in the line-up, in which Newbury listed winner Speedy Boarding and Gretchen (fifth behind Curvy in the Ribblesdale at Royal Ascot) made up a three-strong challenge from British stables which had won four of the six previous renewals. The forcing tactics employed on Together Forever saw her in a clear lead for a long way, but she was kept in range by Covert Love on whom Pat Smullen was seen to very good effect. Covert Love was the first to chase after Together Forever in earnest and she collared her a furlong out, getting first run on the pair that eventually filled the places, Jack Naylor (who had finished in the frame in the Irish One Thousand Guineas) and Curvy, with Together Forever dropping back to finish fourth. Covert Love held on well to win by a length and three quarters from Jack Naylor, whose own story—a €10,500-yearling, she was in utero when her dam was sold by Juddmonte for just 10,000 guineas—provided more food for the optimist. Curvy was run out of second place close home, finishing a head behind Jack Naylor, while Speedy Boarding and Gretchen managed only fifth and seventh, and Words beat only one home. As well as being her trainer's first classic winner, Covert Love was also the first Irish Oaks winner for her jockey who went on to be champion in Ireland for the eighth time and needs an Irish Two Thousand Guineas win to complete his collection of Irish classic victories.

Covert Love had three more races after winning the Irish Oaks and continued to give plenty of enjoyment to her enthusiastic connections who had been there in force for her success at the Curragh. Her trainer had earmarked her as an intended Yorkshire Oaks entry before that race closed, but had then crossed her name from his list at the last minute ('She was just a 92-rated handicapper and I'm conscious of not spending my owners' money needlessly on entry fees'). Covert Love's owners didn't have to think twice about supplementing her for York (although it cost £35,000) and her bid for a five-timer was only narrowly denied by the Irish One Thousand Guineas winner Pleascach. The classic generation accounted for nine of

Prix de l'Opera Longines, Longchamp—Covert Love battles for another Group 1 success as she beats Jazzi Top (spots) and strong-finishing We Are (right)

the eleven runners in the Yorkshire Oaks (with the two older runners starting at 25/1 and 50/1) and front-running Covert Love, on whom Smullen again controlled the race tempo well, confirmed her Irish Oaks superiority over Curvy (fourth) and Jack Naylor (sixth) but was just unable to repel the late challenge of the winner, keeping on gamely but going down by a neck, as little over a length separated the first five home. Covert Love just came out on the right side of a similarly close encounter in the Prix de l'Opera Longines at Longchamp on Arc de Triomphe weekend, again giving everything after leading most of the way and being tackled by fellow British-trained challenger Jazzi Top with whom she had a sustained duel over the final two furlongs. Covert Love had a head to spare over Jazzi Top with the strong-finishing We Are (successful in the race twelve months earlier) two and a half lengths away third. There were four other Group 1 winners further down the field, headed by Jazzi Top's Prix de Diane-winning stablemate Star of Seville (Dettori opted to ride Jazzi Top) and the Prix Saint-Alary winner Queen's Jewel in eighth and ninth in the thirteen-runner field. Covert Love's campaign was completed with a creditable fourth of twelve to the St Leger winner Simple Verse in the British Champions Fillies' And Mares' Stakes at Ascot in October. Covert Love started favourite ahead of French challenger Candarliya and Simple Verse but, taking a keen hold and racing in touch behind the free-running Arabian Queen in the home straight and finished a little under three lengths adrift of Simple Verse, with Journey and Beautiful Romance also ahead of her.

		Night Shift		Northern Dancer
	Azamour (IRE)	(b 1980)		Ciboulette
	(b 2001)	Asmara		Lear Fan
Covert Love (IRE)		(b 1993)		Anaza
(b.f. 2012)		Hawk Wing		Woodman
	Wing Stealth (IRE)	(b 1999)		La Lorgnette
	(br 2005)	Starlight Smile		Green Dancer
		(b or br 1997)		Bubinka

The big, lengthy Covert Love looks just the type to train on as a four-year-old and, provided she does so, she will add further to her laurels in what is already a remarkable racing career. Covert Love became the third Group 1 winner for her ill-fated sire Azamour who died after injuring himself in an accident in his box at Gilltown Stud in 2014. Azamour won the King George VI and Queen

FOMO Syndicate's "Covert Love"

Elizabeth Stakes for the Aga Khan but never became a fashionable stallion—his two other Group 1 winners, Valyra and Dolniya, were Aga Khan home breds—and his fee when he died had dropped to just €8,000. Covert Love's dam Wing Stealth—a maiden who stayed a mile and a half—was by Hawk Wing who was a top-class racehorse at his best who failed to make the grade as a stallion at Coolmore and was quickly on his way, last heard of in South Korea where he reportedly covered just nine mares in 2014. The distaff side of Wing Stealth's family contains some distinguished names, however, her grandam Bubinka also being the grandam of Irish Derby winner Grey Swallow and the great grandam of Hong Kong Horse of the Year Designs On Rome. Bubinka, successful in pattern company at a mile in Italy, is out of Stolen Date, a half-sister to another notable broodmare Best In Show, the grandam of the brothers El Gran Senor and Try My Best. Wing Stealth, who went through the sale-ring unsold at €19,000 at Deauville while Covert Love was still a two-year-old, will be worth plenty now and looks set for an upgrade in the stallions she visits, after being covered by Style Vendome and Rio de La Plata in 2014 and 2015. She produced a filly foal to Style Vendome, her fifth filly from five foals, of which Covert Love's year-older half-sister Stealth Missile (by Invincible Spirit) was the only other to be successful on the racecourse, developing into a useful handicapper, twice successful at seven furlongs. Wing Stealth's first foal Montjess (by Montjeu) was a fair maiden, runner-up four times at a mile and three quarters to an extended two miles (Montjess was led out unsold after bidding reached only £2,500 at the Doncaster January 2015 Sales—before her pedigree enjoyed the reflected glory of Covert Love's classic 'black type' which resulted in her being sold at the Newmarket December Sales for 50,000 guineas). The game and

236

genuine Covert Love stays a mile and a half and acts on polytrack and good to firm and good to soft going. She is a keen-going sort, usually equipped with a crossed noseband, who makes the running or races handily, as do so many from her stable, to which she is a credit. *Hugo Palmer*

COWSLIP 6 b.m. Tobougg (IRE) 125 – Forsythia 63 (Most Welcome 131) [2015 16m – 17.1d Sep 17] rangy mare: modest at best, no form in 2015: stays 2¼m: acts on heavy going: tried in blinkers prior to 2015: often races lazily. *George Moore*

CRACK SHOT (IRE) 3 ch.c. Lope de Vega (IRE) 125 – Slap Shot (IRE) 115 (Lycius   **85** (USA) 124) [2015 73: p6g² 7.5m⁴ 7g 7m⁷ 6g⁴ 7.1m⁴ t7.1g² p7m Dec 31] rather unfurnished colt: fairly useful handicapper: won at Newbury in June: second at Wolverhampton in July: left Clive Brittain after seventh start: stays 7f: acts on polytrack, tapeta and good to firm going. *James Tate*

CRAFTSMANSHIP (FR) 4 ch.c. Mastercraftsman (IRE) 129 – Jennie Jerome (IRE) 87   **90** (Pivotal 124) [2015 85: p8f⁵ 8.3s⁴ 8.3m⁶ 10m⁴ 10m 10s 10.2g³ 10m⁵ 10s² 10.4s 10g⁴ Oct 19] workmanlike colt: fairly useful handicapper: won at Windsor in May: third at Nottingham in July and second at Newbury in September: stays 1¼m: acts on firm and soft going: often wears cheekpieces: often races in rear. *Robert Eddery*

CRAGGAKNOCK 4 b.g. Authorized (IRE) 133 – Goodie Twosues 91 (Fraam 114)   **90** [2015 81: 12s* 11.9d⁴ 14.1d⁴ 16.4g⁶ 14d⁴ 16.4s⁴ 14.6d² Oct 23] fairly useful handicapper: won at Thirsk and Haydock in May: second at Doncaster in October: stays 16.5f: acts on soft going. *Mark Walford*

CRAKEHALL LAD (IRE) 4 ch.g. Manduro (GER) 135 – My Uptown Girl (Dubai   **55** Destination (USA) 127) [2015 76: f12d* p12f² f14d⁶ f14g⁵ 18s 15.8s 15.8m³ 16.1m⁵ **a68** 14.1m 15.8s³ 13.8v⁴ 14.1v Nov 3] smallish, leggy gelding: fair handicapper: won at Southwell in January: left Keith Dalgleish after second start: stays 2m: acts on fibresand, firm and good to soft going: often in headgear in 2015: often races in rear. *Andrew Crook*

CRANACH 6 b.g. Rail Link 132 – Hachita (USA) 99 (Gone West (USA)) [2015 12v⁶ p11g   **71** p12g⁴ t13.9fᵖᵘ Oct 13] fair handicapper: stays 11f: acts on polytrack: usually in cheekpieces in 2015. *David Bridgwater*

CRANBERRY PARK (IRE) 2 b.f. (Apr 13) Acclamation 118 – Queen Padme (IRE)   **53** (Halling (USA) 133) [2015 5g⁶ 5.9g 5m⁴ 5m³ 7.2g⁴ Sep 12] £26,000Y, £9,000 2-y-o: fifth foal: half-sister to 2-y-o 7f winners Gregoria (by Holy Roman Emperor) and Graser (by Motivator), latter also 1m winner in USA: dam unraced sister to smart 11f/1½m winner Counterpunch: modest maiden: stays 7f: acts on good to firm going. *Brian Ellison*

CRANWELL 3 b.f. Nayef (USA) 129 – First Bloom (USA) 71 (Fusaichi Pegasus (USA)   – 130) [2015 p10f⁶ p8g p7g⁴ Nov 25] fourth foal: half-sister to 6f winner At A Clip (by Green Desert): dam lightly-raced half-sister to very smart winner up to 7f Diffident: no form. *Marcus Tregoning*

CRASHING THEW LIFE 5 b.g. Tobougg (IRE) 125 – Kalmina (USA) (Rahy (USA)   **59** 115) [2015 p12f⁵ p11g p12m 13.1m⁶ p12m⁵ Jun 1] modest maiden: stays 13f: acts on polytrack and good to firm going: sometimes slowly away. *Sheena West*

CRAZY CHIC (IRE) 4 gr.g. Exceed And Excel (AUS) 126 – Martines (FR) (Linamix   **85** (FR) 127) [2015 86: t7.1g* p6g⁴ 7.6f 7g⁴ 6m⁴ p7g* p7g* p7f p7g⁵ p8g⁵ Dec 28] lengthy **a101** gelding: useful handicapper: won at Wolverhampton in April, Kempton in September and Lingfield (by ½ length from Hold Tight) in October: stays 7f: acts on polytrack and tapeta. *Marco Botti*

CRAZY HORSE 2 b.c. (Mar 15) Sleeping Indian 122 – Mainstay 86 (Elmaamul (USA)   **106 p** 125) [2015 7g⁴ 7v* Oct 24] second foal: half-brother to smart 7f (including at 2 yrs) winner Richard Pankhurst (by Raven's Pass): dam, 1m winner, sister to smart winner up to 10.4f Lateen Sails: won maiden at Newmarket (by short head from Ehtiraas) in September: better form when winning Horris Hill Stakes at Newbury (by nose from Start Time) in October, overcoming slow start: will stay 1m: open to further improvement. *John Gosden*

CREATIVE DREAM 2 br.g. (Feb 1) Rock of Gibraltar (IRE) 133 – Emonoja (IRE)   – (Sadler's Wells (USA) 132) [2015 t7.1g 8d 7.5g t8.6f t9.5f f8g Nov 26] no form: often in visor. *Derek Shaw*

CREDIT SWAP 10 b.g. Diktat 126 – Locharia 91 (Wolfhound (USA) 126) [2015 10s 9g   **77** Sep 25] lengthy gelding: fair handicapper: stays 9f: acts on any turf going. *Michael Wigham*

CRESCENT (IRE) 3 ch.c. Galileo (IRE) 134 – Coralita (IRE) 98 (Night Shift (USA)) **100**
[2015 78: 8g⁶ 8g* 8.9g* 8.9m⁴ 10m 8f 8m 8g* 9.2g 9.9g Dec 30] angular colt: useful
performer: won 2 minor events at Doha in February and Thoroughbred Guineas there (beat
The Blue Eye ¾ length) in November: little impact in 3 races in Britain in the summer:
stays 1¼m: acts on firm going. *Ahmed Kobeissi, Qatar*

CRESCENT QUEEN 2 ch.f. (Feb 19) Nayef (USA) 129 – Lilac Moon (GER) 75 (Dr **–**
Fong (USA) 128) [2015 5.1g p6g⁴ Aug 7] first foal: dam 1m-1½m winner: no form. *Tom
Dascombe*

CREW CUT (IRE) 7 gr.g. Acclamation 118 – Carabine (USA) (Dehere (USA) 121) **90**
[2015 83: 6m* 6m 6g⁴ 6m⁶ 6f² 6m* 6m² 6.1g 6d⁵ 7d 7v Nov 7] workmanlike gelding:
fairly useful handicapper: won at Leicester in April and Newmarket in July: runner-up at
Ascot in July and Newmarket in August: stays 6f: acts on polytrack, firm and soft going:
sometimes in headgear prior to 2015: tried in tongue tie prior to 2015. *Stuart Williams*

CRICKLEWOOD GREEN (USA) 4 ch.g. Bob And John (USA) 117 – B Berry **86**
Brandy (USA) (Event of The Year (USA) 125) [2015 91: p8g p8g 7g⁴ 8g⁵ 7m* 8g² 7g² 7m*
10v⁴ p8g p7f Nov 19] workmanlike gelding: fairly useful handicapper: won at Salisbury
(apprentice) in August and Ascot (by nose from Shady McCoy) in October: second at
Epsom in September: left Richard Hannon after first start: stays 1¼m: acts on polytrack
and good to firm going: sometimes slowly away. *Sylvester Kirk*

CRIMINALISTIC 2 b.c. (Mar 30) Dubawi (IRE) 129 – Forensics (AUS) 121 (Flying **69**
Spur (AUS)) [2015 t6g³ p6g² t7.1g p7g p8m² p8f⁶ Oct 1] fair maiden: best effort at 1m:
acts on polytrack: tried in cheekpieces: front runner/races prominently. *Charlie Appleby*

CRISSCROSSED 3 b.c. Oasis Dream 129 – Double Crossed 102 (Caerleon (USA) 132) **84**
[2015 72p: p10g² 11.5d 9.9m² Jun 10] fairly useful maiden: second in handicap at Brighton
in June: best effort at 1¼m: tried in blinkers in 2015: sold 55,000 gns, sent to Qatar.
Amanda Perrett

CRITERIA (IRE) 4 b.f. Galileo (IRE) 134 – Aleagueoftheirown (IRE) 107 (Danehill **104**
Dancer (IRE) 117) [2015 106: 12m 11.9d⁵ 11.9g 14m Jul 30] tall, lengthy filly: useful
performer: stays 14.5f: acts on polytrack, soft and good to firm going: usually in headgear
in 2015: front runner/races prominently. *John Gosden*

CRITERION (NZ) 5 ch.h. Sebring (AUS) 123 – Mica's Pride (AUS) (Bite The Bullet **127**
(USA)) [2015 124: 6.5g³ 7.5g² 9.9s* 9.9m³ 10f⁵ 10.4d⁶ 9.9g* 10.1g² 15.9g³ 9.9g Dec 13]
strong horse: half-brother to 3 winners in Australia, including Group 2 6.5f winner Varenna
Miss (by Redoute's Choice): dam Australian 5f/6f (Group 3) winner: high-class performer:
won Queen Elizabeth Stakes at Randwick (by 2½ lengths from Red Cadeaux) in April and
Caulfield Stakes (by ½ length from Happy Trails) in October: placed next 2 starts, in Cox
Plate at Moonee Valley (4¾ lengths second to Winx) and Melbourne Cup (Handicap) at
Flemington (good 1¼ lengths third to Prince of Penzance): not at best either start in Britain
in the summer, in Prince of Wales's Stakes at Royal Ascot and International Stakes at York,
or in Hong Kong Cup at Sha Tin (ninth behind A Shin Hikari) final outing: effective at
1¼m to 2m: acts on good to firm and heavy going: wears headgear. *David Hayes & Tom
Dabernig, Australia*

CRITICAL RISK (IRE) 3 ch.g. Pivotal 124 – High Reserve 95 (Dr Fong (USA) 128) **94**
[2015 74: 8d* 8.1m* 8.3d² 10.1m³ 10m⁶ Oct 3] unfurnished gelding: fairly useful
handicapper: won at Doncaster and Sandown (dead-heated) in May: second at Windsor in
August and third at Yarmouth in September: left Brian Meehan after second start: stays
8.5f: acts on good to firm and good to soft going: sometimes slowly away, often races in
rear: sold £190,000, sent to Australia. *Luca Cumani*

CROARA (IRE) 2 b.f. (May 11) Exceed And Excel (AUS) 126 – Alleviate (IRE) 91 **72**
(Indian Ridge 123) [2015 p6g⁶ p7g⁴ 7v² 7g⁶ Oct 21] €40,000Y, 35,000 2-y-o: fourth foal:
dam, 1¾m/15f winner, half-sister to Allegretto out of Alleluia, both smart stayers: fair
maiden: will stay 1m+. *Marco Botti*

CROCKETT 4 b.g. Rail Link 132 – Tarocchi (USA) (Affirmed (USA)) [2015 12m 9.2s⁴ **62**
11.9d 13.1d 15.8s⁵ f12g Nov 24] modest maiden: should stay 2m: acts on soft and good to
firm going. *Noel Wilson*

CROFT RANGER (IRE) 2 b.g. (Apr 24) Bushranger (IRE) 119 – Alexander Duchess **63**
(IRE) 103 (Desert Prince (IRE) 130) [2015 6g⁴ 6s Oct 16] modest maiden: best effort
when fourth in maiden at Newcastle (4¾ lengths behind Mont Kiara) in September, nearest
finish: will prove suited by 7f. *Michael Dods*

CROMBAY (IRE) 2 b.f. (Mar 26) Approve (IRE) 112 – Ms Cromby (IRE) (Arakan **75** (USA) 123) [2015 5m² 5.1f⁴ 5g⁴ 5m 5m² 5s² 5g* 5g⁵ 5g 6g Oct 3] €11,000Y: first foal: dam unraced half-sister to smart French/US 1m-1¼m winner Lord Cromby: fair performer: won maiden at Thirsk in August: best form at 5f: acts on soft and good to firm going: often in hood: front runner/races prominently. *Tim Easterby*

CROPLEY (IRE) 6 gr.g. Galileo (IRE) 134 – Niyla (IRE) (Darshaan 133) [2015 77d: – f16g Jan 6] maiden: no form in 2015: stays 2m: acts on heavy going: often wears headgear: often races towards rear. *Ann Stokell*

CROQUEMBOUCHE (IRE) 6 b.g. Acclamation 118 – Wedding Cake (IRE) 71 (Groom **96** Dancer (USA) 128) [2015 92: 10g* 12m² 13.7m 12d 12d⁶ 10.1d p10f² p10f⁵ Nov 5] good-topped gelding: useful handicapper: won at Windsor in April: second at York (1¼ lengths behind Notarised) in May and second at Chelmsford (½ length behind Bancnuanaheireann) in October: stays 1½m: acts on polytrack, firm and soft going: front runner. *Ed de Giles*

CROSSED ARROW 2 b.f. (Feb 27) Cape Cross (IRE) 129 – Snoqualmie Star 98 **64** (Galileo (IRE) 134) [2015 p8g⁶ Nov 4] 9/2, better for run when sixth in maiden at Kempton: dead. *Ralph Beckett*

CROSSE FIRE 3 b.g. Monsieur Bond (IRE) 120 – Watersilk (IRE) (Fasliyev (USA) 120) **71** [2015 70: f5s* t5.1g⁴ 5g⁵ 5g³ 5.1g³ f5g⁵ t5.1m f5g³ f5g* Dec 29] fairly useful handicapper: **a80** won at Southwell in March and Southwell (by neck from Borough Boy) in December: best form at 5f: acts on fibresand and good to soft going: usually wears headgear: sometimes slowly away. *Scott Dixon*

CROSS EXAMINE (IRE) 2 b.g. (Mar 12) Roderic O'Connor (IRE) 119 – Red Vale – (IRE) (Halling (USA) 133) [2015 6s⁶ 6.5m p6g 6m Aug 8] no form. *David Simcock*

CROSSLEY 6 ch.g. Monsieur Bond (IRE) 120 – Dispol Diamond 72 (Sharpo 132) [2015 **47** 55: t8.6g⁵ 7d t8.6g 8s Jul 29] poor maiden: stays 8.5f: acts on tapeta and heavy going: sometimes wears headgear: often races prominently. *Geoffrey Oldroyd*

CROUCHING HARRY (IRE) 6 b.g. Tiger Hill (IRE) 127 – Catwalk Dreamer (IRE) **54** (Acatenango (GER) 127) [2015 64: t13.9g⁵ 11.5d Aug 3] modest handicapper: stays 2m: acts on polytrack, tapeta and soft going: often wears headgear: often races towards rear. *Anabel K. Murphy*

CROWLEY'S LAW 4 b.f. Dubawi (IRE) 129 – Logic 94 (Slip Anchor 136) [2015 104: **106** 8m² 8.5g² 8g² 8m³ 8f³ 8s² 8g* 8f Nov 29] good-topped filly: useful performer: landed the odds in non-graded stakes at Woodbine in October by 1¾ lengths from Notte d'Oro: notable placed efforts earlier in year in Princess Elizabeth Stakes at Epsom, listed race at Cologne, Grade 3 Noble Damsel Stakes at Belmont (length third to Recepta) and First Lady Stakes at Keeneland (7 lengths second to Tepin): left Tom Dascombe before final outing: stays 8.5f: acts on firm and soft going: usually front runner/races prominently. *Peter Miller, USA*

CROWN COMMAND (IRE) 3 ch.c. Lope de Vega (IRE) 125 – Pivotal Role 66 – (Pivotal 124) [2015 75p: p8mᵖᵘ Nov 14] useful-looking colt: maiden: no form in 2015. *William Muir*

CROWNED WITH STARS (IRE) 3 b.g. Sea The Stars (IRE) 140 – Drifting (IRE) 85 **82** (Sadler's Wells (USA) 132) [2015 12m⁵ 11.9d⁴ p12gᵖᵘ Jul 1] fairly useful form: pulled up at Kempton: would have proved suited by further than 1½m: dead. *David Simcock*

CROWN GREEN 3 b.f. Royal Applause 124 – Grasshoppergreen (IRE) (Barathea (IRE) – 127) [2015 –: 8m f8g⁵ 10.1d May 13] maiden: no form in 2015. *Karen Tutty*

CROWNING GLORY (FR) 2 b.f. (Feb 13) Speightstown (USA) 124 – Forest Crown **73 p** 105 (Royal Applause 124) [2015 6g p7g⁶ p7g* Nov 26] rather unfurnished filly: first foal: dam, winner up to 8.3f (2-y-o 6f winner), half-sister to Racing Post Trophy winner Crowded House: fair form: best effort when winning maiden at Chelmsford (by neck from Star of Lombardy) in November, driven out: will stay at least 1m: open to further improvement. *Ralph Beckett*

CROWNING STAR (IRE) 6 b.g. Royal Applause 124 – Dossier 103 (Octagonal (NZ) **55** 126) [2015 58: p8f⁴ p8f* p8g³ p8g p10g 8g⁵ 8v p8m⁵ Dec 31] modest handicapper: won at Kempton in March: stays 8.5f: acts on polytrack, best turf form on good going: tried in blinkers prior to 2015: often in tongue tie prior to 2015: often races prominently. *Steve Woodman*

CROWN PLEASURE (IRE) 4 b.f. Royal Applause 124 – Tarbiyah 89 (Singspiel (IRE) **75** 133) [2015 70: t9.5f⁵ p12f² p10.7g⁴ p12g 11.3m⁵ 11d² 11g* 12d⁵ 10s⁵ Oct 25] smallish filly: fair handicapper: won at Wexford in August: left Willie Musson after second start: stays 1½m: acts on polytrack, tapeta and good to firm going: tried in cheekpieces in 2015. *T. G. McCourt, Ireland*

CRUCIBLE 4 b.g. Danehill Dancer (IRE) 117 – Baize 95 (Efisio 120) [2015 –: t6f f7d⁵ **53** f8g⁶ Mar 31] modest maiden: best effort at 7f: often in blinkers in 2015. *Daniel Kubler*

CRUISE TOTHELIMIT (IRE) 7 b.g. Le Vie dei Colori 126 – Kiva (Indian Ridge 123) **83** [2015 94: t5.1g⁵ 5.1s³ p5m⁴ 6m 5g 5g⁶ 5v⁴ 6s 5g t6f⁶ 5g⁴ 5.1d Oct 28] lengthy gelding: **a76** fairly useful handicapper: third at Chester in May: stays 6f: acts on polytrack, soft and good to firm going: tried in cheekpieces in 2015: usually races close up. *Patrick Morris*

CRUISING ALONG 5 ch.g. Byron 117 – Rosapenna (IRE) 84 (Spectrum (IRE) 126) **–** [2015 t12.2g⁶ Mar 6] maiden: no form in 2015. *Kevin Frost*

CRUSADING (USA) 3 b.g. Street Cry (IRE) 130 – Danelagh (AUS) (Danehill (USA) **61** 126) [2015 62: p8m⁶ Jan 24] modest maiden: sixth in maiden at Lingfield (6 lengths behind Festive Fare) on sole outing in 2015 in January: sent to Greece. *Mark Johnston*

CRY FURY 7 b.g. Beat Hollow 126 – Cantanta 74 (Top Ville 129) [2015 85: 12g 8.3g³ **70** 10m⁵ 13.3m⁶ Jul 23] fair handicapper: left Gary Moore after second start: barely stays 13.5f: acts on polytrack and good to firm going: tried in cheekpieces in 2015: often starts slowly, usually races in rear: temperament under suspicion. *Sophie Leech*

CRY ME A RIVER (IRE) 2 b.f. (Apr 8) Danehill Dancer (IRE) 117 – River Flow (USA) **82** (Affirmed (USA)) [2015 5g⁴ 5f Jun 17] £50,000Y: sturdy filly: sister to 2-y-o 5f winner Danehill Brook and half-sister to 2 winners abroad by Generous: dam unraced: better effort when fourth in listed race at the Curragh (4½ lengths behind Round Two) in May. *T. Stack, Ireland*

CRYPTIC (IRE) 2 br.g. (Apr 28) Lord Shanakill (USA) 121 – Privet (IRE) 79 (Cape **79 p** Cross (IRE) 129) [2015 p6f⁵ t7.1f t8.6f³ p7g* Dec 19] 37,000F, 65,000Y: half-brother to French winner up to 1m Bilge Kagan (2-y-o 6f winner, by Whipper) and UAE 6f winner Just A Penny (by Kodiac): dam, maiden (stayed 1m), sister to useful 2-y-o 6f winner Mokabra: fair form: won nursery at Kempton in December: will stay 1m: will go on improving. *Luca Cumani*

CRYPTONYM 3 b.f. Dansili 127 – Codename (Sadler's Wells (USA) 132) [2015 9.9s **93 p** p12g² p12g² p9.2g* p10f³ Sep 3] fourth foal: half-sister to 7f-11f winner Never Forever (by Sir Percy): dam unraced half-sister to 6f/7f winner Main Aim and 1¼m performer Weightless, both very smart: fairly useful performer: won maiden at Chelmsford in August: third in handicap at Chelmsford in September: stays 1¼m: acts on polytrack: often races prominently, usually travels strongly: sold 27,000 gns, sent to Saudi Arabia: capable of better. *Sir Michael Stoute*

CRYSTALIN (IRE) 3 b.f. Arcano (IRE) 122 – Loose Julie (IRE) (Cape Cross (IRE) 129) **58** [2015 62: p7m* Jan 14] modest performer: won claimer at Lingfield in January: stays 7f: sold 11,000 gns, sent to Kazakhstan. *Marco Botti*

CRYSTALISE (IRE) 3 b.f. Nayef (USA) 129 – Crystal Power (USA) (Pleasant Colony **62** (USA)) [2015 p12g⁴ p13.3f Oct 22] half-sister to several winners, including useful 2-y-o 7f winner Misdaqeya (by Red Ransom) and 7f (including at 2 yrs) winner Intimidate (by Royal Applause): dam, 1m winner, closely related to US Grade 1 1¼m winner Chelsey Flower: better effort when fourth in maiden at Lingfield in July. *Robert Stephens*

CRYSTALIZED (IRE) 4 ch.f. Rock of Gibraltar (IRE) 133 – Magnificent Bell (IRE) **–** (Octagonal (NZ) 126) [2015 60: p6m p6g p6g Feb 20] neat filly: modest at best, no form in 2015: tried in cheekpieces prior to 2015: often races towards rear. *Dean Ivory*

CRYSTAL MALT (IRE) 3 b.f. Intikhab (USA) 135 – Elegantly (IRE) (Rock of Gibraltar **79** (IRE) 133) [2015 76: 6d² 6g* 7m² 8m⁴ 7f 7.1v³ 8.3v² 8.3d³ t9.5f³ p8m* p7g⁶ Dec 7] lengthy filly: fair performer: won maiden at Doncaster in May and handicap at Lingfield in November: stays 9.5f: acts on polytrack, tapeta, good to firm and heavy going: usually races towards rear. *Richard Hannon*

CRYSTAL QUARTZ (IRE) 4 ch.f. Rock of Gibraltar (IRE) 133 – Crystal Gaze (IRE) **67** (Rainbow Quest (USA) 134) [2015 p5g* Feb 5] fair ex-French performer: won maiden at Chelmsford in February: stays 6.5f. *David Evans*

CRYSTAL ROSE (IRE) 2 b.f. (May 2) Holy Roman Emperor (IRE) 125 – True Crystal (IRE) 94 (Sadler's Wells (USA) 132) [2015 7s p8g p8g Nov 26] 14,000Y: smallish, light-framed filly: half-sister to several winners, including smart 7f-1½m winner Libran (by Lawman) and 2-y-o 7f/7.4f winner (stays 10.5f) Alans Pride (by Footstepsinthesand): dam 1¼m winner: modest maiden: best effort when seventh in maiden at Salisbury (5½ lengths behind Hermarna) in October. *Eve Johnson Houghton* **51**

CRYSTAL WISH 3 b.f. Exceed And Excel (AUS) 126 – Crystal Mountain (USA) (Monashee Mountain (USA) 115) [2015 61: f5g p7f Jan 23] lengthy filly: maiden: no form in 2015: best effort at 5f: tried in tongue tie: often races prominently. *Kevin Ryan* **–**

CRYSTAL ZVEZDA 3 ch.f. Dubawi (IRE) 129 – Crystal Star 100 (Mark of Esteem (IRE) 137) [2015 86p: 10m* 12g 10.4m^2 12d 10g^2 Oct 9] rather unfurnished filly: smart performer: won listed race at Newbury (by 3½ lengths from Montalcino) in May: runner-up in similar events at York (2¾ lengths behind French Dressing) in July and Newmarket (neck behind Chain of Daisies) in October: stays 1½m: acts on polytrack, good to firm and good to soft going: tried in hood in 2015. *Sir Michael Stoute* **110**

CRY WOLF 2 ch.g. (Feb 17) Street Cry (IRE) 130 – Love Charm (Singspiel (IRE) 133) [2015 t8.6m t8.6g^4 Dec 5] better effort when fourth in maiden at Wolverhampton (1¾ lengths behind Red Verdon) in December, well positioned: in cheekpieces. *Charlie Appleby* **74**

CUBAN QUEEN (USA) 2 ro.f. (Apr 1) Elusive Quality (USA) – One Smokin' Lady (USA) (Smoke Glacken (USA) 120) [2015 6g 6m 6g Sep 7] $75,000Y, 80,000 2-y-o: second foal: dam US 5.5f/6f winner, including minor stakes: well held in maidens: type to do better in handicaps. *Jeremy Gask* **– p**

CUDDLE 2 b.f. (Apr 14) Intikhab (USA) 135 – Karlovy 78 (Halling (USA) 133) [2015 p8f^6 p8m Nov 19] 1,000Y, 6,500 2-y-o: third foal: half-sister to 9f winner Al Karlovyyh (by Authorized): dam twice-raced half-sister to Prix de l'Arc de Triomphe winner Marienbard: better effort when sixth in maiden at Chelmsford (4 lengths behind Purple Magic) in November, not knocked about: likely to stay 1¼m. *Eve Johnson Houghton* **59**

CULLENTRY ROYAL 7 b.g. Royal Applause 124 – Fleur A Lay (USA) 53 (Mr Greeley (USA) 122) [2015 100: p12g^4 p10.7g^3 t12.2m^5 8v p12g^4 12v^5 12.5m 12g 10m^4 14d^5 8g^2 10g^2 p10.7g^3 8d p12g Nov 6] fairly useful handicapper: third at Dundalk in February and second at Leopardstown (apprentice) in August: left J. F. Levins after fourteenth start: winner at 1¾m, effective at much shorter: acts on polytrack, soft and good to firm going: often wears headgear: usually races nearer last than first. *E. Sheehy, Ireland* **91**

CULLODEN 3 b.c. Kyllachy 129 – Mamounia (IRE) 101 (Green Desert (USA) 127) [2015 p6g^4 p6g^4 t8.6m^3 p6g^6 6m^3 p7g 6v^6 t7.1f f5g^3 p6m^2 f6g^5 f5m f6g Dec 29] lengthy colt: modest maiden: left Richard Hannon after seventh start: stays 6f: acts on polytrack, fibresand and good to firm going: tried in blinkers: usually leads. *Shaun Harris* **62**

CULTURATI 2 b.c. (Feb 23) Dubawi (IRE) 129 – Whazzis 109 (Desert Prince (IRE) 130) [2015 7d^2 8g^2 7g* 6s* Oct 9] lengthy, good sort: fifth foal: half-brother to 3 winners, including French performer up to 1½m Whim (2-y-o 1m winner, by Nayef) and 1¼m/10.4f winner Valiant (by Galileo), both useful: dam winner up to 1m (2-y-o 7f winner): useful performer: won maiden at Ascot in September and nursery at York (by neck from Hyland Heather) in October: stays 1m. *Charlie Appleby* **95**

CULTURED KNIGHT 2 ch.c. (Mar 17) Compton Place 125 – Cultured Pride (IRE) 81 (King's Best (USA) 132) [2015 p6g^5 Dec 16] second foal: half-brother to 6f winner The Big Lad (by Kheleyf): dam 2-y-o 6f winner who stayed 8.3f: 7/1, fifth in maiden at Kempton (9½ lengths behind Soofiah) in December, not knocked about: should do better. *Richard Hughes* **– p**

CUMBRIANNA 3 b.f. Hellvelyn 118 – Positivity 79 (Monsieur Bond (IRE) 120) [2015 65: 6.1d^4 6g^5 t6g^F Jul 7] modest handicapper: stayed 6f: acted on tapeta and heavy going: front runner/raced prominently: fell and fatally injured at Wolverhampton. *Bryan Smart* **63**

CUPPATEE (IRE) 2 b.f. (Mar 21) Canford Cliffs (IRE) 133 – Fanditha (IRE) 101 (Danehill Dancer (IRE) 117) [2015 5f 6s^2 6f^6 7m 7g* 6d^3 6g* 5.9m^2 6g^5 6d^5 t6f 6v^2 Nov 7] angular filly: first foal: dam winner up to 11f (2-y-o 7f winner): fair performer: won sellers at Catterick in July and Ripon in August: left Mick Channon after fifth start: stays 7f: acts on any turf going. *Ann Duffield* **74**

CURBYOURENTHUSIASM (IRE) 4 gr.g. Mastercraftsman (IRE) 129 – Mohican Princess (Shirley Heights 130) [2015 83: 11.6m* 11.6m* 12m^2 12d 14.6m* Sep 11] big gelding: useful handicapper: won at Windsor in May and June, and Mallard Stakes at Doncaster (by 1¼ lengths from Battersea) in September: stays 14.5f: acts on good to firm going: usually races nearer last than first, often travels strongly. *David Simcock* **107**

CURIOUS FOX 2 b.f. (Feb 26) Bertolini (USA) 125 – Doric Lady 91 (Kyllachy 129)   –
[2015 p6f Oct 29] second foal: dam 5f/6f winner: 50/1, eighth in maiden at Chelmsford (14¼ lengths behind Saucy Spirit) in October. *Anthony Carson*

CURLYLOCKS (IRE) 3 ch.f. Galileo (IRE) 134 – Meow (IRE) 108 (Storm Cat (USA))   **65**
[2015 86p: 7g⁴ 6d Aug 3] fair maiden: best effort at 7f. *David Wachman, Ireland*

CURRICULUM 2 b.g. (Mar 19) New Approach (IRE) 132 – Superstar Leo (IRE) 114   **73 p**
(College Chapel 122) [2015 7d⁴ Oct 30] rather unfurnished gelding: half-brother to several winners, including 5f (including at 2 yrs) winner Enticing (by Pivotal) and 7f/1m winner Sentaril (by Danehill Dancer), both smart: dam 2-y-o 5f (including Flying Childers Stakes) winner: 12/1, green when fourth in maiden at Newmarket (1½ lengths behind Chelsea Lad) in October: sure to progress. *William Haggas*

CURTAIN CALL 2 b.f. (Mar 8) Acclamation 118 – Apace (IRE) 94 (Oasis Dream 129)   **85 p**
[2015 5.1g* 6s⁶ 6d 5g* Oct 16] first foal: dam, 5f and (at 2 yrs) 7f winner, half-sister to smart winner up to 1¼m High Twelve out of Prix Robert Papin winner Much Faster: fairly useful form: won maiden at Nottingham in July and nursery at Haydock in October: best form at 5f: open to further improvement. *Richard Fahey*

CURVY 3 b.f. Galileo (IRE) 134 – Frappe (IRE) 93 (Inchinor 119) [2015 79: 10d*   **115**
10d* 10g* 12f* 12m³ 12d⁴ 10s⁵ 10g* Oct 18]

When the Coolmore partners paid 775,000 guineas at Newmarket's principal yearling sale, the October Sales Book 1, for a Galileo half-sister to their Irish Two Thousand Guineas winner Power, they could hardly have imagined she would be trying to resurrect her career, after three unplaced efforts in maidens, in a handicap at Navan off an Irish Turf Club mark of just 72. By the same token, anyone outside the circle of her connections picking up Curvy's story at that point—in mid-April—would have found it equally difficult to visualise her emulating Power, and another illustrious relative, her half-sister Thakafaat, by winning a pattern event at Royal Ascot, then finishing in the frame in the Irish Oaks and the Yorkshire Oaks and finally rounding off an eight-race three-year-old campaign with an all-important Grade 1 win in the E. P. Taylor Stakes at Woodbine in October. Rapidly improving fillies turn up regularly in end-of-season reviews—on form there was the best part of three stone between Curvy's first win at Navan and her last at Woodbine—but Curvy's story is most unusual for a top filly with her background. Only the Andre Fabre-trained 5,000,000-guinea filly Al Naamah, the most expensive yearling ever sold at auction in Europe, who has failed to add to her two-year-old debut success in a fillies conditions event, cost more than Curvy among the yearling fillies offered at Newmarket in 2013.

Curvy's two-year-old career began with a respectable fourth behind Pleascach in a fillies maiden at Leopardstown at the start of July (sixth of seven in the same race, incidentally, was Curvy's stablemate Legatissimo, ridden by the stable's number-

Ribblesdale Stakes, Royal Ascot—
Curvy, successful in handicaps on her first two starts in the latest season, follows up her Gallinule Stakes win by a length from the Irish One Thousand Guineas winner Pleascach

E. P. Taylor Stakes Presented by HPIBet, Woodbine—
Curvy (No.9) beats fellow European raider Talmada (light cap) and Rosalind (rail)

one Wayne Lordan). Curvy took on colts on her second start and finished over ten lengths seventh to Vert de Grece, who went on to finish second to Gleneagles in the Futurity Stakes before winning the Criterium International at Saint-Cloud. Curvy's third and final run—which opened up the possibility of her running in handicaps—was back in another fillies maiden, stepped up to a mile, at Navan where, starting at 25/1, she managed only eighth of eighteen, beaten fourteen lengths by the winner Bocca Baciata. Curvy was fitted with cheekpieces for the first time when she reappeared as a three-year-old at Navan, stepped up further in trip to a mile and a quarter. There was money for her—she started third favourite at 5/1 in a field of nine—and she ran out a ready winner from the favourite Ringside Humour. Raised 12 lb by the handicapper, Curvy won again over the course and distance a month later, sent off favourite this time, in a handicap restricted to fillies. Seven days after that, Curvy was out for the third time in five weeks, taking on the colts, including Derby-bound Giovanni Canaletto, in the Group 3 Airlie Stud Gallinule Stakes at the Curragh. Showing the first real signs that she might be capable of living up to her choice pedigree, Curvy beat Giovanni Canaletto—who went on to finish fourth at Epsom—by a neck. She made it four wins in a row when stepped up again in class and distance in the Ribblesdale Stakes at Royal Ascot where, ridden by Ryan Moore for the first time (and one of his nine winners at the meeting), her transformation into one of the best of her generation was completed by her victory over the Irish One Thousand Guineas winner Pleascach in a good renewal. Curvy had to barge her way out in a fairly rough race as the field approached the final furlong, but she readily caught Pleascach to win by a length, with Pamona, knocked sideways in Curvy's manoeuvre, finishing four lengths further back in third. None of the Oaks field came on to Royal Ascot for the Ribblesdale but the form of the first two was certainly on a par with that shown by the Epsom winner Qualify.

Like Qualify, Curvy earned herself free entry to the Irish Derby (for winning the Gallinule) but she was supplemented instead for the Irish Oaks, at a cost of €40,000 (Qualify was a late withdrawal from that race on account of the good to firm ground). Curvy started favourite at the Curragh but she couldn't complete her five-timer. She ran well, though, virtually repeating her Ribblesdale form to finish third, just run out of second close home and beaten a length and three quarters and a head behind Covert Love and Jack Naylor, despite the winner getting first run on her. Covert Love finished ahead of Curvy again when they were second and fourth behind Pleascach in the Yorkshire Oaks, in which a little over a length covered the first five. There was a change of headgear for Curvy at York, where a visor replaced the cheekpieces she had worn in all her earlier races, and, although the official returns for her two appearances in North America in October show that she wore blinkers there, she may have been visored there also (no distinction is made in North America). Curvy was a little below her best when fifth on soft going behind Stephanie's Kitten in the Flower Bowl at Belmont, in which she was the only

Mrs John Magnier, Mr M. Tabor & Mr D. Smith's "Curvy"

three-year-old, but returned to her best in the E. P. Taylor on a sounder surface. She stayed on well, after leading a furlong out, to win by a length and a half from the British-trained four-year-old Talmada. It was another red letter day for her jockey Ryan Moore who also won the Canadian International on Cannock Chase on the same card.

Curvy (b.f. 2012)	Galileo (IRE) (b 1998)	Sadler's Wells (b 1981)	Northern Dancer
			Fairy Bridge
		Urban Sea (ch 1989)	Miswaki
			Allegretta
	Frappe (IRE) (b 1996)	Inchinor (ch 1990)	Ahonoora
			Inchmurrin
		Glatisant (b 1991)	Rainbow Quest
			Dancing Rocks

Curvy will be a valuable addition to Coolmore's broodmare band when she starts her stud career in 2016. As well as being the third Royal Ascot winner bred by her dam—Power (by Oasis Dream) won the Coventry and Thakafaat (by Unfuwain) also won the Ribblesdale—Curvy descends from a family cultivated by the Oppenheimer family at the Hascombe and Valiant studs, the breeders of Horse of the Year Golden Horn. By coincidence, the dams of Golden Horn and Curvy are both now at Norelands Stud in County Kilkenny which bred Curvy. Curvy's dam Frappe (completely Oppenheimer bred, being by the miler Inchinor out of Glatisant, both of whom carried the Oppenheimer black and white halved colours to success in pattern company) was sold privately after her racing career in which she showed fairly useful form at up to seven furlongs for Geoff Wragg, who also trained Curvy's grandam the Prestige Stakes winner Glatisant, while his father Harry trained her great grandam Dancing Rocks who won the Nassau Stakes for Sir Philip

Oppenheimer, the father of Golden Horn's owner. Dancing Rocks bred nine winners and most of her daughters went on to breed winners, though Glatisant has been the star turn, responsible for Two Thousand Guineas winner Footstepsinthesand and Phoenix Stakes winner Pedro The Great, both of whom were purchased as yearlings on behalf of various Coolmore partners and trained by Aidan O'Brien. Another of Glatisant's winners, the smart filly Belle d'Or, was retained by her breeder, winning in listed company at a mile as a three-year-old and finishing a good third in the Dahlia Stakes at Newmarket in the latest season. Curvy's dam Frappe had a dead Frankel foal in 2014, then failed to get in foal to Oasis Dream before slipping a foal to Kingman in the autumn of the latest season. Norelands Stud also has one of Frappe's daughters, the fairly useful seven-furlong winner Applauded (by Royal Applause), who has bred a stakes winner in the States called Amnesia and has a yearling filly by Lawman and a colt foal by Oasis Dream. Curvy stayed a mile and a half and acted on firm and good to soft going. She wore headgear as a three-year-old. *David Wachman, Ireland*

CURZON LINE 6 b.g. Dubawi (IRE) 129 – Polska (USA) 103 (Danzig (USA)) [2015 8g⁶ **82** 7m⁵ 6m⁵ 7.6g 6.1d 7v f7f Dec 17] lengthy gelding: fairly useful handicapper: stays 1m: acts on polytrack and good to firm going: sometimes in eyeshields in 2015: tried in tongue tie: often races towards rear. *Michael Easterby*

CUSTARD THE DRAGON 2 b.g. (Apr 12) Kyllachy 129 – Autumn Pearl 102 (Orpen **66 p** (USA) 116) [2015 6s⁶ p6g⁴ p6g⁴ Dec 9] brother to 6f (including at 2 yrs) winner (stays 1m) Fillionaire and half-brother to 3 winners, including smart winner up to 6f Pabusar (by Oasis Dream) and 5f (including at 2 yrs) winner Montaigne (by Exceed And Excel): dam winner up to 6f (2-y-o 5f winner): fair form: best effort when fourth in maiden at Kempton (2¾ lengths behind Mywayistheonlyway) in November: should do better. *Ralph Beckett*

CUSTODIAL (IRE) 2 b.f. (Mar 16) Lawman (FR) 121 – Chervil 80 (Dansili 127) [2015 **53** 6m⁶ 6m⁵ 6.1s 6m³ 8.1m³ p7g³ t8.6f³ Oct 3] 6,000Y: sixth foal: half-sister to 3 winners, including 1m winner Zeyran (by Galileo) and 2-y-o 7f winner (stays 1¼m) Laurelita (by High Chaparral): dam, 2-y-o 6f winner, closely related to very smart 1m-1¼m winner (stayed 1½m) Light Jig: modest maiden: stays 8.5f: acts on polytrack, tapeta and good to firm going: tried in tongue tie: sent to Greece. *Eve Johnson Houghton*

CUSTOM CUT (IRE) 6 b.g. Notnowcato 128 – Polished Gem (IRE) 89 (Danehill (USA) **122** 126) [2015 124: 8.1d* 8m 8.5g² 10.4m⁴ 8g³ 8g* 8g² 7m Oct 4] smallish, workmanlike gelding: very smart performer: won Mile at Sandown (by 1½ lengths from Here Comes When) in April and Boomerang Stakes at Leopardstown (by 1¾ lengths from Top Notch Tonto) in September: good second in Diomed Stakes at Epsom (beaten 2 lengths by Arod) in June and Joel Stakes at Newmarket (length behind Time Test) in September: well below form in Prix de la Foret at Longchamp final outing: best up to 9f: acts on good to firm and heavy going: has worn headgear: front runner/races prominently. *David O'Meara*

Clipper Logistics Boomerang Stakes, Leopardstown—the admirable Custom Cut lands his sixth pattern-race success from Top Notch Tonto and Lightning Spear

CUSTOM (IRE) 2 b.f. (Feb 20) Lilbourne Lad (IRE) 111 – Margaux Magique (IRE)   **55**
(Xaar 132) [2015 8.3g 7s⁵ t6f 8.3s Oct 28] 13,000Y: narrow filly: second foal: dam, 6f
winner, sister to useful winner up to 1m Royal Power: modest maiden: best effort at 7f.
Mick Channon

CUTHBERT (IRE) 8 ch.g. Bertolini (USA) 125 – Tequise (IRE) 97 (Victory Note (USA)   **–**
120) [2015 40: p7g⁵ p8m Feb 18] fair at best, no form in 2015: stays 1m: acts on polytrack
and good to firm going: often wears headgear. *Michael Attwater*

CYCLOGENISIS (USA) 3 gr.c. Stormy Atlantic (USA) – Mighty Renee (USA)   **109**
(Maria's Mon (USA) 121) [2015 t6f* 6f 5.5f⁴ 6g Oct 18] $185,000Y: strong-quartered colt:
fourth foal: brother to useful US 2-y-o 5f-6.5f (Grade 3) winner Mighty Caroline and
closely related to useful US 2-y-o 1m winner Renee's Queen (by After Market): dam
unraced granddaughter of US 2-y-o Grade 1 winner Over All: useful performer: won both
starts at 2 yrs and listed race at Presque Isle Downs (by 2¾ lengths from Fast Flying
Rumor) in May: respectable fourth to Ready For Rye in listed race at Saratoga in August:
well held on other starts, in Commonwealth Cup at Royal Ascot and Grade 2 Nearctic
Stakes at Woodbine: stays 6f: acts on tapeta: wears headgear: has worn tongue tie. *George
Weaver, USA*

CYFLYMDER (IRE) 9 b.g. Mujadil (USA) 119 – Nashwan Star (IRE) 68 (Nashwan   **63**
(USA) 135) [2015 58, a64: f7d 7.1s³ 8m* p7m³ 7.1m³ 7.6g* 7.1m⁴ 7m 7.2g⁶ Oct 13]
smallish gelding: modest handicapper: won at Musselburgh in May and Lingfield in June:
stays 1m: acts on polytrack and any turf going: tried in headgear: tried in tongue tie prior
to 2015. *David C. Griffiths*

CYMRAEG BOUNTY 3 ch.g. Bahamian Bounty 116 – Croeso Cusan 75 (Diktat 126)   **68**
[2015 10.2d 10.1d 8f³ 7g³ 10.3g 12d 8d Sep 17] fair maiden: stays 10.5f: acts on firm
going: usually races freely. *Michael Appleby*

CYMRIC (USA) 2 b.c. (Feb 25) Kitten's Joy (USA) 128 – Fastbridled (USA) (Unbridled's   **116**
Song (USA) 125) [2015 7f 7.1m* 7d³ 7.1s* 8m² 8d Oct 30] $300,000Y: tall, attractive colt:
fourth foal: half-brother to 2-y-o 4.5f winner Tiecat (by Bluegrass Cat): dam, unraced,
closely related to smart US Grade 2 9f winner Interactivf: smart performer: won maiden at
Sandown in July and minor event on same course (by 1¼ lengths from Risk Adjusted) in
September: much improved when short-neck second to Ultra in Prix Jean-Luc Lagardere
at Longchamp next time, staying on strongly: only eighth behind Hit It A Bomb in Breeders'
Cup Juvenile Turf at Keeneland final outing, hanging left and weakening: stays 1m: acts on
soft and good to firm going. *John Gosden*

CYMRO (IRE) 3 gr.g. Dark Angel (IRE) 113 – Dictatrice (FR) (Anabaa (USA) 130) [2015   **107**
79: 8d³ 10.3s* 10.1m 10.4g* 9.9m 10.4d³ 10s³ Sep 19] lengthy gelding: useful performer:
won maiden at Chester in May, and handicaps at Haydock in July and September (by
2¼ lengths from Bancnuanaheireann): stays 10.5f: acts on heavy going: often races
prominently. *Tom Dascombe*

CYRIL 3 b.g. Rail Link 132 – Nurse Gladys (Dr Fong (USA) 128) [2015 79p: t7.1g³ 7m³   **90**
8.3g⁴ 10g* 10.3g* 10.4m² 11.9m⁴ 12d 10.3g⁶ 10.3d Oct 23] fairly useful handicapper: won
at Pontefract in June and Chester in July: stays 1½m: acts on good to firm going: usually
leads. *Kevin Ryan*

CZABO 2 b.f. (Feb 18) Sixties Icon 125 – Fiumicino 87 (Danehill Dancer (IRE) 117) [2015   **89**
7m 6d* Aug 15] unfurnished filly: second foal: dam 2-y-o 1m winner who stayed easy
1½m: better effort when winning maiden at Newbury (by neck from Jadaayil) in August.
Mick Channon

CZECH IT OUT (IRE) 5 b.g. Oratorio (IRE) 128 – Naval Affair (IRE) 101 (Last Tycoon   **99**
131) [2015 92: 7g* 8g 7d² 7s⁶ 8g⁶ 7v Nov 7] good-topped gelding: useful handicapper:
won at Goodwood in May: second at Newbury (neck behind Mullionheir) in August: stays
7f: acts on firm and soft going. *Amanda Perrett*

D

DABADIYAN (IRE) 5 b.g. Zamindar (USA) 116 – Dabista (IRE) 70 (Highest Honor   **89**
(FR) 124) [2015 113: 12g 12f 14f 16m p11g f11g⁵ p12g⁵ t13.9g Dec 1] compact gelding:
fairly useful handicapper: stays 2m: acts on polytrack, good to firm and good to soft going:
usually in headgear in 2015: often races towards rear. *Gary Moore*

DACOITY 2 b.g. (May 4) Dick Turpin (IRE) 127 – Todber 80 (Cape Cross (IRE) 129) **77 p**
[2015 5d³ 6.1v³ 6v² Oct 17] third foal: half-brother to 2-y-o 6f winner Bandolier (by
Bahamian Bounty): dam 5f/6f winner out of smart 5f (including at 2 yrs) winner Dominica:
fair maiden: best effort when second in maiden at Catterick (neck behind Indian Pursuit) in
October, clear of rest: likely to progress further. *Richard Fahey*

DAD'S GIRL 3 ch.f. Sakhee's Secret 128 – China Cherub 94 (Inchinor 119) [2015 68: **66**
5.1m⁶ 5m 5g⁶ 7.5m³ 7m² 17.1g⁶ 7.2g 5m Oct 1] fair handicapper: stays 7.5f: acts on good
to firm going: tried in cheekpieces in 2015: front runner/races prominently. *Ollie Pears*

DAGHASH 6 b.g. Tiger Hill (IRE) 127 – Zibet 90 (Kris 135) [2015 83: p14g⁴ 14.1m* 14f³ **87**
16g⁵ 16g* 15.9m⁴ 17.2f² 16m⁴ Oct 2] sturdy gelding: fairly useful handicapper: won at
Nottingham in June and Ffos Las in July: second at Bath in September: stays 17f: acts on
firm and good to soft going: tried in headgear prior to 2015. *Stuart Kittow*

DAGHER 3 b.c. New Approach (IRE) 132 – Sakhya (IRE) (Barathea (IRE) 127) [2015 **94**
81p: 8g⁴ 7.1m³ 8m² 8g⁵ 7d* Aug 28] smallish colt: fairly useful handicapper: won at Thirsk
(by length from Fullon Clarets) in August: stays 1m: acts on good to firm and good to soft
going: sold 13,000 gns, sent to Bahrain. *Peter Chapple-Hyam*

DAILY BULLETIN (USA) 2 b.c. (Jan 29) Medaglia d'Oro (USA) 129 – Life At Ten **85 p**
(USA) 121 (Malibu Moon (USA)) [2015 7g⁴ t8.6f* Nov 13] $140,000Y: first foal: dam
US Grade 1 8.5f/9f winner: better effort when winning maiden at Wolverhampton (by 3½
lengths from Across The Stars) in November, having run of race: likely to progress further.
John Gosden

DAINTY DAISEY (IRE) 3 b.f. Pastoral Pursuits 127 – Nursling (IRE) 57 (Kahyasi 130) **–**
[2015 p10g⁶ 12s⁵ p12f⁵ p12g Aug 26] €2,500F, 2,500Y: seventh foal: half-sister to 11f-17f
winner Callisto Moon (by Mujahid) and 11f winner Sunday's Fantasy (by Carnival
Dancer): dam lightly-raced half-sister to useful dam of Oaks winner Qualify: no form: tried
in cheekpieces. *Clive Drew*

DAIONI 2 b.f. (Apr 20) Green Horizon – Calon Lan (Nayef (USA) 129) [2015 p8g p6f⁵ **51**
p7g Dec 3] first foal: dam unraced: modest maiden: best effort when fifth in maiden at
Chelmsford (8¾ lengths behind Saucy Spirit) in October. *Simon Dow*

DAISY BOY (IRE) 4 b.g. Cape Cross (IRE) 129 – Muluk (IRE) 83 (Rainbow Quest (USA) **81**
134) [2015 79: 10.4g⁴ 10m* 12g³ 10.1v⁶ 12d⁵ 10.2g³ p12g² Dec 2] big gelding: fairly
useful handicapper: won at Sandown (apprentice, by ½ length from Jack of Diamonds)
in July: stays 1¼m: acts on good to firm going: front runner/races prominently. *Stuart
Williams*

DAISY CHAINSAW (IRE) 2 b.f. (Apr 2) Frozen Power (IRE) 108 – Dark Albatross **–**
(USA) 89 (Sheikh Albadou 128) [2015 5g Sep 16] fifth foal: half-sister to 1m-1¼m winner
Night Knight (by Bachelor Duke) and 5f (including at 2 yrs) winner Dark Opal (by
Camacho): dam, winner up to 1½m (2-y-o 6f winner), half-sister to useful winner up to 9f
Unusual Heat: 80/1, well held in maiden at Beverley. *Kristin Stubbs*

DAISY DIP 3 b.f. Sixties Icon 125 – Silk Daisy 74 (Barathea (IRE) 127) [2015 10m p10g⁶ **–**
Jun 20] seventh foal: half-sister to 3 winners, including useful 9.5f-2m winner William's
Way (by Fraam) and 2-y-o 8.6f winner Golan Way (by Golan): dam 7f-8.2f winner: no
form. *Mick Channon*

DAISY'S SECRET 4 ch.f. Sakhee's Secret 128 – Darling Daisy (Komaite (USA)) [2015 **40**
62: 7.6d 8g 6s p8f Oct 29] angular filly: poor maiden: best effort at 8.5f: acts on polytrack
and soft going: often in tongue tie in 2015. *George Baker*

DAKOTA CITY 4 b.g. Three Valleys (USA) 119 – West Dakota (USA) (Gone West **61**
(USA)) [2015 p10g⁴ 10g⁴ 10g 10g² 10.2g 10m⁴ p10f* p12g² 12v 10.2f p12g p10g⁴ **a78**
Nov 18] fair handicapper: won at Lingfield in July: stays 1½m: acts on polytrack, good to
firm and good to soft going: often in headgear in 2015. *Julia Feilden*

DALAKI (IRE) 4 b.g. Dalakhani (IRE) 133 – Lunda (IRE) 60 (Soviet Star (USA) 128) **80**
[2015 76, a66: p11m* p10m⁵ p12m² p13.3m⁶ p12g p12g p10g p13.3f⁶ Nov 19] good-
topped gelding: fairly useful handicapper: won at Kempton in January: second at Kempton
in April: left Jim Boyle after third start: stays 1½m: acts on polytrack and firm going: often
wears headgear: often races towards rear. *Des Donovan*

DALALAH 2 b.f. (Feb 16) Exceed And Excel (AUS) 126 – Bashasha (USA) 69 **59**
(Kingmambo (USA) 125) [2015 6f p6g 6s⁵ p7g⁶ t6f Dec 22] first foal: dam twice-raced out
of useful 9f winner Dessert: modest maiden: left Roger Varian after fourth start: stays 7f:
acts on polytrack and tapeta. *Richard Guest*

DALAMAR 3 b.f. Montjeu (IRE) 137 – Dalasyla (IRE) (Marju (IRE) 127) [2015 7m 10.3g **57** p10f p13f 9.9s Oct 15] fourth foal: closely related to useful 7f/1m winner Dalkova (by Galileo) and half-sister to 1½m winner Diavola (by Duke of Marmalade): dam, 15f winner, half-sister to very smart winner up to 1¾m Daliapour out of smart 1½m/12.5f winner Dalara: modest maiden: sometimes in hood: often starts slowly/held up: sold 45,000 gns. *Rae Guest*

DALBY SPOOK (IRE) 5 b.m. Jeremy (USA) 122 – Lamassu (IRE) (Entrepreneur 123) **59** [2015 7g 7s⁶ 8s 9.2d 12.1g³ 12.2g⁵ 9.3d² 12d 11.5s* 16.1g 12.1g Sep 21] modest handicapper: won at Carlisle (apprentice) in August: stays 1½m: acts on soft going: often races towards rear. *Dianne Sayer*

DALEELAK (IRE) 2 b.c. (May 29) Arcano (IRE) 122 – Alshamatry (USA) (Seeking The **79** Gold (USA)) [2015 6g⁴ 7m² 6.1m² 6g⁵ 7.2m** 7d⁶ Oct 24] fair performer: won maiden at Musselburgh in September: stays 7f: acts on good to firm going: front runner. *Mark Johnston*

DALGIG 5 b.g. New Approach (IRE) 132 – Bright Halo (IRE) (Bigstone (IRE) 126) [2015 **61 §** 86§, a78§: 11.9d 10m⁵ p12g⁴ Jun 27] compact gelding: modest performer: stays 1½m: acts on polytrack, tapeta, good to firm and good to soft going: tried in hood: refused to race penultimate start in 2014: temperamental. *Peter Bowen*

DAL HARRAILD (IRE) 3 ch.g. (Mar 24) Champs Elysees 124 – Dalvina 113 (Grand Lodge **92 p** (USA) 125) [2015 7m⁴ 7g² 8d* 9v² Oct 7] first foal: dam, winner up to 1½m (including US Grade 3 event), also 2-y-o 7f winner, half-sister to smart 1¼m winner French Dressing: fairly useful performer: won maiden at Haydock in September: second in nursery at Nottingham in October: stays 9f: will go on improving. *William Haggas*

DALIAKOVA (IRE) 2 b.f. (Mar 21) Big Bad Bob (IRE) 118 – Daliyra (IRE) 92 (Refuse – To Bend (IRE) 128) [2015 7g 6d p7g p8f Sep 3] €8,000Y: second foal: dam 2-y-o 1m winner who stayed 1¼m: no form. *Ed Walker*

DALMARELLA DANCER (IRE) 4 gr.f. Mastercraftsman (IRE) 129 – Ting A Greeley **72** (Mr Greeley (USA) 122) [2015 78: f8d 13.8d f11g⁴ 10.1d⁴ 10m³ 10d² 10g* 10d² 10m³ 10m* 9.3g 10.2g Sep 30] workmanlike filly: fair handicapper: won at Windsor in June and August: stays 1¼m: acts on all-weather, good to firm and good to soft going: sometimes in headgear prior to 2015: often races prominently. *K. R. Burke*

DAMBUSTER (IRE) 5 b.g. Dalakhani (IRE) 133 – Threefold (USA) 99 (Gulch (USA)) **87** [2015 p11g² 12s⁶ 16.1m 16.2g p11g⁰ Oct 7] good-bodied gelding: fairly useful handicapper: second at Kempton (head behind Fresh Kingdom) in June: stayed 11.5f: acted on polytrack and good to firm going: usually raced prominently: dead. *Martyn Meade*

DAME LIBERTY (IRE) 3 ch.f. Tamayuz 126 – Elizabeth Swann 95 (Bahamian Bounty – 116) [2015 83p: 6d May 8] fairly useful winner at 2 yrs, well held sole outing in 2015: sold 2,500 gns, sent to Bahrain. *Richard Hannon*

DAME LUCY (IRE) 5 b.m. Refuse To Bend (IRE) 128 – Sheer Glamour (IRE) 57 **84** (Peintre Celebre (USA) 137) [2015 91: t12.2f² t9.5f³ 12m May 2] sturdy mare: fairly useful handicapper: stays 16.5f: acts on tapeta, best turf form on good going or softer (acts on heavy): tried in hood prior to 2015. *Michael Appleby*

DAME ROSSIE 3 b.f. Virtual 122 – Resal (IRE) (Montjeu (IRE) 137) [2015 p8g 7v⁵ p8f – 8s Oct 15] first foal: dam unraced: no form. *Phil McEntee*

DAMES AND DIAMONDS (IRE) 2 b.f. (Apr 11) Bushranger (IRE) 119 – Storm Lady – (IRE) (Alhaarth (IRE) 126) [2015 5v 6m⁶ 5g 5m t7.1f Dec 22] fifth foal: half-sister to winner up to 7f Paker (2-y-o 6f winner, by Kodiac) and 7f winner (stays 1¼m) Dylan's Storm (by Zebedee): dam unraced half-sister to smart 11f-1¾m winner Bay Willow: no form: left Mrs A. M. O'Shea after fourth start: tried in blinkers. *Shaun Harris*

DANA'S PRESENT 6 ch.g. Osorio (GER) 114 – Euro Empire (USA) 111 (Bartok (IRE) **86** 94) [2015 76: t9.5g* t9.5g* t9.5g⁵ p8f p8f⁶ 7.6d⁶ 9.9s² 8.3m* 7m⁶ 8.1m⁴ 8g² 8g⁵ 10.3s⁵ p8g **a76** Dec 2] lengthy, useful-looking gelding: fairly useful performer: won handicaps at Wolverhampton (2) in January and claimer at Leicester in June: second in handicap at Goodwood in July: left George Baker after first start: stays 9.5f: acts on polytrack, tapeta, firm and good to soft going: tried in hood in 2015: tricky ride (often races freely/carries head high). *Tom Dascombe*

DANCE 6 b.m. Erhaab (USA) 127 – Shi Shi (Alnasr Alwasheek 117) [2015 54: p11g⁶ Jun **44** 4] poor maiden: stays 1½m: acts on polytrack: tried in tongue tie prior to 2015: front runner/races prominently. *Rod Millman*

DANCE ALONE 2 gr.g. (Feb 4) Bahamian Bounty 116 – Palais Glide 85 (Proclamation **74** (IRE) 130) [2015 6s³ 6m² 6s⁶ Oct 16] fair maiden: best effort when second in maiden at Hamilton (neck behind Extortion) in September, conceding first run. *Kevin Ryan*

DANCE AND DANCE (IRE) 9 b.g. Royal Applause 124 – Caldy Dancer (IRE) 97 **87**
(Soviet Star (USA) 128) [2015 103: 8d 10.1g 8m⁵ 8m Oct 2] sturdy gelding: fairly useful
handicapper: stays 9f: acts on polytrack, firm and good to soft going: tried in headgear:
sometimes slowly away, usually races nearer last than first. *Ed Vaughan*

DANCE FOR LIVVY (IRE) 7 br.m. Kodiac 112 – Dancing Steps (Zafonic (USA) 130) **50**
[2015 p12g t16.5g t16.5m⁵ Mar 10] top-topped mare: modest handicapper: stays 16.5f:
acts on polytrack, tapeta, good to firm going: tried in hood in 2015. *Robin Dickin*

DANCEINTOTHELIGHT 8 gr.g. Dansili 127 – Kali 83 (Linamix (FR) 127) [2015 63: **50**
15.8m⁵ 16m 17.2d Aug 3] modest handicapper: stays 17f: acts on soft and good to firm
going: tried in cheekpieces in 2015: tried in tongue tie in 2015. *Micky Hammond*

DANCE KING 5 ch.g. Danehill Dancer (IRE) 117 – One So Wonderful 121 (Nashwan **91**
(USA) 135) [2015 92: 9.8d 10.1d³ 12g² 10g⁶ 11.5d⁶ 9.8d³ 8g⁴ 10g⁵ 10.4s² 10d* p10f
Oct 28] rather leggy gelding: fairly useful handicapper: won at Pontefract (by ¾ length
from Arrowzone) in October: effective at 1¼m/1½m: acts on soft and good to firm going:
sometimes in cheekpieces in 2015: sometimes in tongue tie in 2015: often travels strongly.
Tim Easterby

DANCE OF FIRE 3 b.g. Norse Dancer (IRE) 127 – Strictly Dancing (IRE) 95 (Danehill **86**
Dancer (IRE) 117) [2015 84: 10.3d² 10.1g⁴ 10m 8m⁴ 8f⁵ Jul 10] good-topped gelding:
fairly useful handicapper: second at Doncaster in March: stays 10.5f: acts on good to firm
and heavy going: sometimes in headgear in 2015: usually leads. *Andrew Balding*

DANCETRACK (USA) 3 b.c. First Defence (USA) 119 – Jazz Drummer (USA) **111**
(Dixieland Band (USA)) [2015 87p: p8g³ 8.1m⁶ 8d* 8d Oct 31] lengthy colt: smart
performer: won handicap at Haydock (by 1½ lengths from McCreery, easily best effort) in
September: stays 1m: acts on polytrack and good to soft going: sent to USA. *Charles Hills*

DANCIN ALPHA 4 ch.g. Bahamian Bounty 116 – Phoebe Woodstock (IRE) 76 (Grand **62**
Lodge (USA) 125) [2015 76: 9g³ 8.3s⁵ 10s⁴ 13.1d 10.1m Jun 25] modest maiden: stays
9.5f: acts on good to firm going: often races prominently. *Alan Swinbank*

DANCING ACES 3 ch.c. Shamardal (USA) 129 – Rainbow Dancing 108 (Rainbow **60**
Quest (USA) 134) [2015 10m p8g⁵ 9.9s⁵ p8g Dec 30] modest maiden: best effort at 1m:
tried in tongue tie. *Paul Cole*

DANCING ADMIRAL 4 b.g. Kyllachy 129 – Dream Dance 62 (Diesis 133) [2015 8.3d **–**
Oct 12] 50/1 and blinkered, green when well held in maiden at Windsor. *Mrs Ilka Gansera-
Leveque*

DANCING DUDE (IRE) 8 ch.g. Danehill Dancer (IRE) 117 – Wadud 59 (Nashwan **–**
(USA) 135) [2015 18s Apr 7] lengthy, angular gelding: fair performer in 2010: first start on
Flat since (fair hurdler), well held in handicap at Pontefract: stayed 12.5f: acted on
polytrack, soft and good to firm going: dead. *Barry Leavy*

DANCING MAITE 10 ch.g. Ballet Master (USA) 92 – Ace Maite (Komaite (USA)) **60**
[2015 65, a51: f7d⁶ f6d³ 5.1m* 6.1d 6g 6.1m 6.1m⁵ Aug 11] compact gelding: modest
handicapper: won at Nottingham in April: stays 7f: acts on polytrack, fibresand, firm and
soft going: sometimes wears headgear: usually races towards rear. *Roy Bowring*

DANCING PRIMO 9 b.m. Primo Valentino (IRE) 116 – Tycoon's Last 64 (Nalchik **66**
(USA)) [2015 67: t12.2g t13.9g⁶ t13.9m⁴ 11.7f 11.9m⁴ 11.9f² 11.9d 11.5g⁶ 11.7g⁵ **a58**
11.9m⁶ 11.7s⁴ 11.9d⁶ 11.9d Sep 25] leggy mare: fair handicapper: won at Lingfield in June:
stays 1¾m: acts on tapeta, firm and good to soft going. *Mark Brisbourne*

DANCING SAL (IRE) 4 b.f. Azamour (IRE) 130 – Miss Tango Hotel 77 (Green Desert **54**
(USA) 127) [2015 56, a63: p7g⁵ p8f p6g Feb 5] lengthy, angular filly: modest maiden:
stays 1m: acts on polytrack, best turf form on good going: tried in blinkers: tried in tongue
tie in 2015. *Gary Moore*

DANCING SPRINGS (IRE) 3 b.f. Bushranger (IRE) 119 – Deep Springs (USA) **–**
(Storm Cat (USA)) [2015 –: 7m 5.7m⁴ t6g Jun 22] maiden: no form in 2015. *Bill Turner*

DANCING STAR 2 b.f. (Apr 17) Aqlaam 125 – Strictly Dancing (IRE) 95 (Danehill **80 p**
Dancer (IRE) 117) [2015 5m⁴ 6m* 6.1m Aug 22] sturdy filly: second foal: half-sister to
2-y-o 1m/8.5f winner (stays 10.5f) Dance of Fire (by Norse Dancer): dam 6f winner out of
smart winner up to 6f (including at 2 yrs) Lochangel: fairly useful form: best effort when
winning maiden at Windsor in August: excuses in minor event at Chester: remains with
potential. *Andrew Balding*

DANCING YEARS (IRE) 2 ch.f. (Mar 29) Iffraaj 127 – Daganya (IRE) 104 (Danehill **81 p**
Dancer (IRE) 117) [2015 5g⁴ t6g 6g³ 6d* Sep 21] €175,000Y: half-sister to several winners,
including 5f/6f winner Kernoff (by Excellent Art) and 7f-10.7f winner Akasaka (by King's

Best), both smart: dam 6f winner (including at 2 yrs): fairly useful performer: won nursery at Leicester (by neck from Novantae) in September: best effort at 6f: likely to progress further. *Richard Fahey*

DANCRUISE (IRE) 3 b.g. Dandy Man (IRE) 123 – Crua Mna (Bahamian Bounty 116) **58** [2015 –: 6g³ 6d 5m⁴ May 23] modest maiden: best effort at 6f. *Kristin Stubbs*

DANDARRELL 8 b.g. Makbul 104 – Dress Design (IRE) 84 (Brief Truce (USA) 126) **65** [2015 72: f8g p8m³ p10m² p10f³ f8g 8d May 13] fair handicapper: stays 1½m: acts on polytrack, fibresand, soft and good to firm going: tried in headgear. *Julie Camacho*

DANDY (GER) 6 b.g. Nayef (USA) 129 – Diacada (GER) 108 (Cadeaux Genereux 131) **76** [2015 86: p10g p10f 10.2f⁴ 10m 10.2m* 10.1m 10.2d Aug 5] good-topped gelding: fair handicapper: won at Chepstow in June: stays 1½m: acts on polytrack and any turf going: often wears headgear: front runner/races prominently. *Andrew Balding*

DANDYS PERIER (IRE) 4 br.g. Dandy Man (IRE) 123 – Casual Remark (IRE) 67 **69** (Trans Island 119) [2015 56, a64: p6m f6g⁵ t6g t7.1g 7.6d⁶ t6g 7.1m* 7g² 8.1g² 7.4d² 7.1s³ 7d⁶ 8.3g p8d² f8g t7.1f* Dec 22] good-topped gelding: fair handicapper: won at Chepstow in July and Wolverhampton in December: stays 1m: acts on polytrack, fibresand, good to firm and heavy going: tried in cheekpieces in 2015. *Ronald Harris*

DANECASE 2 ch.g. (Apr 10) Showcasing 117 – Yding (IRE) (Danehill (USA) 126) [2015 **87 p** 6m 6.1m³ 6.1m* Jul 17] 22,000Y, 55,000 2-y-o: neat, good-quartered gelding: seventh foal: dam unraced: fairly useful performer: best effort when winning maiden at Nottingham (by 1¾ lengths from Daleelak) in July, slowly away: raced only at 6f: will go on improving. *David Dennis*

DANEGELD 3 b.g. Danehill Dancer (IRE) 117 – Kirkinola (Selkirk (USA) 129) [2015 –: **69** p8f⁴ 10d⁴ 8m p8g 7.2s 8g Oct 20] fair performer: won maiden at Kempton in February: left Paul Cole after fourth start: best effort at 1m: acts on polytrack: tried in tongue tie in 2015: sometimes slowly away. *J. Morrison, Ireland*

DANEGLOW (IRE) 5 ch.m. Thousand Words 113 – Valluga (IRE) (Ashkalani (IRE) **–** 128) [2015 54: p6g Feb 1] useful-looking mare: modest at best, no form in 2015: best effort at 5f: acts on polytrack: often wears eyeshields: often races in rear. *Mike Murphy*

DANEHILL KODIAC (IRE) 2 b.c. (Apr 6) Kodiac 112 – Meadow 72 (Green Desert **88** (USA) 127) [2015 7g⁴ p8g² p8g* 8d* Sep 12] £30,000Y: workmanlike colt: seventh foal: half-brother to 3 winners, including 2-y-o 6f winner Reliant Robin (by Moss Vale) and winner up to 6f (stayed 1m) Scantily Clad (2-y-o 5f winner, by Acclamation): dam, 7f winner, sister to smart 7f/1m winner Green Line: fairly useful performer: won maiden at Chelmsford in August and nursery at Doncaster (by short head from Prince of Arran) in September: stays 1m. *Richard Hannon*

DAN EMMETT (USA) 5 ch.g. Flower Alley (USA) 127 – Singing Dixie (USA) (Dixie- **68** land Band (USA)) [2015 81: 16s Oct 23] fair handicapper: stays 2¼m: acts on fibresand and heavy going: sometimes in cheekpieces prior to 2015: usually races towards rear. *Michael Scudamore*

DANGEROUS AGE 5 br.m. Sleeping Indian 122 – Rye (IRE) 75 (Charnwood Forest **79** (IRE) 125) [2015 86, a93: p5g p5f³ 5g p5g⁵ t5.1g⁴ p5g² 5m² 5.7g* 6g⁴ 6g p6g⁵ Aug 26] lengthy mare: fair handicapper: won at Bath in July: stays 6f: acts on polytrack and firm going: tried in cheekpieces in 2015. *J. S. Moore*

DANGEROUS MOONLITE (IRE) 3 b.f. Acclamation 118 – Light It Up (IRE) 79 **81** (Elusive City (USA) 117) [2015 90: p5f⁶ 5d⁶ 5m⁴ 5m 5f⁶ Jun 24] lengthy filly: fairly useful performer: best form at 5f: acts on good to firm going. *Jim Boyle*

DANGEROUS THOUGHT (USA) 2 ch.c. (Mar 15) Super Saver (USA) 121 – **67 p** Trepidation (USA) (Seeking The Gold (USA)) [2015 p8m³ Dec 16] $250,000Y: half-brother to several winners, including smart 7f/1m winner Tiz Now Tiz Then (by Tiznow) and useful winner up to 7f Maoineach (2-y-o 6f winner, by Congaree): dam unraced: evens, only a fair third in maiden at Lingfield (6½ lengths behind Hombre Rojo) in December: should do better. *John Gosden*

DANGLYDONTASK 4 b.g. Lucky Story (USA) 128 – Strat's Quest 65 (Nicholas (USA) **66** 111) [2015 61: p15.8g t12.2g 11.5d⁴ 14.1g* 16g⁵ 13.1m² 17.2g* Oct 18] fair handicapper: won at Nottingham in June and Bath in October: stays 17f: best form on good going: usually in headgear prior to 2015. *David Arbuthnot*

DANIEL THOMAS (IRE) 13 b.g. Dansili 127 – Last Look (Rainbow Quest (USA) 134) **51** [2015 59: 10.2m t12.2g⁶ t9.5f p10m p10f² p8g³ p10f Dec 21] good-topped gelding: modest handicapper: stays 1½m: acts on polytrack, soft and good to firm going: often wears headgear: often wears tongue tie: sometimes slowly away. *Heather Dalton*

DANILOVNA (IRE) 2 br.f. (May 10) Dansili 127 – Hoity Toity (Darshaan 133) [2015 **77 p**
p8m* Nov 19] closely related to very smart winner up to 1m Lillie Langtry (2-y-o 6f/7f
winner, by Danehill Dancer), now dam of Moyglare Stud Stakes and Fillies' Mile winner
Minding, and smart winner up to 1¼m Count of Limonade (2-y-o 7f-8.4f winner, by Duke
of Marmalade): dam unraced: 8/1, won maiden at Lingfield (by short head from
Bretoncelles) in November, overcoming positional bias: sure to progress. *David Lanigan*

DANISA 6 b.m. Shamardal (USA) 129 – Divisa (GER) 107 (Lomitas 129) [2015 –: f16d⁵ **55**
f14s Mar 25] sturdy mare: modest handicapper: stays 2m: acts on good to firm and good to
soft going: tried in headgear: sometimes wears tongue tie. *David Bridgwater*

DANISH DUKE (IRE) 4 ch.g. Duke of Marmalade (IRE) 132 – Bridge Note (USA) 49 **68**
(Stravinsky (USA) 133) [2015 84: 7m 6m 7.5d t7.1f⁶ f7g² f7g* f7g Dec 15] fair
handicapper: won at Southwell in November: acts on fibresand and good to firm
going: often in headgear prior to 2015. *Ruth Carr*

DANNYDAY 3 b.c. Dansili 127 – Dayrose 94 (Daylami (IRE) 138) [2015 77p: 10s⁵ p11g³ **94**
14f* 14d² 14g Aug 22] plain, rather leggy colt. fairly useful handicapper: won at Haydock
in June: second at Haydock in July: will stay 2m: acts on firm and good to soft going: often
races towards rear. *Sir Michael Stoute*

DANNY O'RUAIRC (IRE) 3 b.c. Fast Company (IRE) 126 – Tawoos (FR) 104 (Rainbow **57**
Quest (USA) 134) [2015 69: 10.1d 10d 8.3g 7.9g⁴ 11.5m⁴ 11.5s⁴ 14.1v Nov 3] modest
maiden: may prove best at around 1¼m: acts on soft and good to firm going: tried in
cheekpieces prior to 2015: often races towards rear. *James Moffatt*

DANNY THE DANCER 5 ch.g. Indian Haven 119 – Invincible 76 (Slip Anchor 136) **–**
[2015 10m Jul 21] 100/1, well held in maiden at Wetherby. *Micky Hammond*

DANOT (IRE) 3 ch.g. Zebedee 113 – Hapipi (Bertolini (USA) 125) [2015 71: 6s⁵ 6m 7g **76**
6d⁶ 6g² 6g⁴ 6.9d³ 7d³ 7g³ 7.2g Sep 17] fair handicapper: stays 7f: acts on soft and good
to firm going: usually races close up. *Jedd O'Keeffe*

DANSEUR NOBLE 3 b.g. Kheleyf (USA) 116 – Posy Fossil (USA) 70 (Malibu Moon **79**
(USA)) [2015 83p: f8d³ t7.1m³ t7.1g t7.1m⁶ t7.1f⁵ Oct 13] fair handicapper: stays 7f: acts
on fibresand and tapeta: sometimes slowly away, often races in rear. *James Tate*

DANSILI DASH 3 b.g. Dansili 127 – Dashiba 102 (Dashing Blade 117) [2015 p8f p10f⁵ **61 §**
p8f t12.2g 10.2m Apr 28] modest maiden: best effort at 1¼m: acted on polytrack: often
raced towards rear: was temperamental: dead. *David Elsworth*

DANZEB (IRE) 2 gr.g. (Apr 14) Zebedee 113 – Daneville (IRE) (Danetime (IRE) 121) **72**
[2015 5.9g² 5g⁶ 6g 5m* Sep 20] fair performer: won nursery at Hamilton in September:
stays 6f. *Ann Duffield*

DANZELLA 3 b.f. Desideratum 118 – Danzatrice 76 (Tamure (IRE) 125) [2015 –: 12s **–**
t12.2f Oct 31] maiden: no form in 2015. *Chris Fairhurst*

DANZENO 4 b.g. Denounce 89 – Danzanora (Groom Dancer (USA) 128) [2015 124p: 5g⁴ **119**
6m³ 6f⁵ 6d⁶ 5m* 6d³ Oct 17] strong gelding: smart performer: won minor event at Musselburgh (by 2½ lengths from Red Baron) in September: third in Chipchase Stakes at Newcastle
(½ length behind Aeolus) in June, fifth in July Cup at Newmarket (beaten 2 lengths by
Muhaarar), sixth in Sprint Cup at Haydock (5 lengths behind Twilight Son) in September
and third in Champions Sprint Stakes at Ascot (3½ lengths behind Muhaarar) in October:
stays 6.5f: acts on soft and good to firm going. *Michael Appleby*

DANZKI (IRE) 4 b.g. Bushranger 119 – Miniver (IRE) (Mujtahid (USA) 118) **37**
[2015 64: p8f Mar 18] poor maiden: stays 7f: acts on good to soft going: sometimes wears
headgear: sold 1,500 gns, sent to Italy. *Ed Walker*

DANZOE (IRE) 8 br.g. Kheleyf (USA) 116 – Fiaba 66 (Precocious 126) [2015 66§: p6g **62 §**
t5.1f p5g⁴ p6f⁵ p6m⁴ t6g* p5f⁶ p6g⁶ t6g⁵ t6g⁵ 6.1m p6g 6g t6m Sep 25] lengthy gelding:
modest handicapper: won at Wolverhampton in April: stays 6f: acts on all-weather, good to
firm and heavy going: sometimes wears headgear: often races towards rear, often races
lazily: untrustworthy. *Christine Dunnett*

DANZ STAR (IRE) 4 ch.g. Ad Valorem (USA) 125 – Await (IRE) (Peintre Celebre **50**
(USA) 137) [2015 67: t7.1g⁵ t8.6g Apr 25] modest maiden: stays 1m: acts on soft going.
Malcolm Saunders

DAPHNE 2 b.f. (Feb 12) Duke of Marmalade (IRE) 132 – Daring Aim 89 (Daylami (IRE) **67 p**
138) [2015 8v⁶ Oct 24] closely related to 2-y-o 7f winner Queen's Prize (by Dansili) and
half-sister to several winners, including smart 1¼m-1½m winner Bold Sniper (by New
Approach) and useful/ungenuine 1¼m-1½m winner Highland Glen (by Montjeu): dam

1½m winner who stayed 1¾m: 10/1, showed promise when sixth in maiden at Newbury (6½ lengths behind Chastushka) in October: bred to be suited by 1¼m+: should do better in time. *William Haggas*

DAQEEQ (IRE) 2 b.c. (Apr 21) New Approach (IRE) 132 – Asawer (IRE) 110 (Darshaan 133) [2015 8.3v³ t8.6f² Oct 31] sixth foal: closely related to useful 2-y-o 1m winner Ghaawy (by Teofilo) and half-brother to 11f-15f winner Ashwaat (by Authorized) and useful 1¼m winner Monasada (by Nayef): dam, 1¼m winner, third in Ribblesdale Stakes: better effort when third in maiden at Nottingham (4¼ lengths behind Mengli Khan) in October: likely to stay 1¼m: should still improve. *Simon Crisford* **84 p**

DAREBIN (GER) 3 ch.g. It's Gino (GER) 128 – Delightful Sofie (GER) (Grand Lodge (USA) 125) [2015 11.5d⁵ 10m⁴ p10g² 11m Jul 31] workmanlike gelding: fair maiden: best effort at 1¼m. *Gary Moore* **75**

DARING DAY 2 b.f. (Mar 21) Acclamation 118 – Silver Kestrel (USA) (Silver Hawk (USA) 123) [2015 6m³ Sep 15] 60,000Y: sixth foal: closely related to useful 2-y-o 5f/6f winner Habaayib and 5f (including at 2 yrs) winner Golden Flower (both by Royal Applause): dam 7f winner: 16/1, shaped well when third in maiden at Yarmouth (1¼ lengths behind Fourth Way) in September: will improve. *George Peckham* **81 p**

DARING DRAGON 5 gr.g. Intikhab (USA) 135 – The Manx Touch (IRE) 70 (Petardia 113) [2015 58, a81: p6g⁶ t7.1f p6f p5d⁵ t5.1g² t5.1m⁴ 5g 5m³ 5.1g³ 6m p6g* p6f³ 5g p5f 5.1d³ Nov 4] fair handicapper: won at Chelmsford in August: stays 7f: acts on polytrack, tapeta, good to firm and good to soft going: usually wears headgear: tried in tongue tie: sometimes slowly away. *Derek Shaw* **57 a66**

DARING INDIAN 7 ch.g. Zamindar (USA) 116 – Anasazi (IRE) (Sadler's Wells (USA) 132) [2015 t13.9f⁵ p15.8g t12.2g 12g 14.1g 14.1g⁵ t12.2g² 12.1s p13f p11g p12g² p12g p12f⁶ Nov 25] fair handicapper: left Graeme McPherson after eighth start: stays 16.5f: acts on polytrack, tapeta, soft and good to firm going: sometimes wears cheekpieces: usually in tongue tie in 2015: usually races prominently. *Roger Teal* **56 a68**

DARING KNIGHT 2 b.g. (Feb 25) Dick Turpin (IRE) 127 – Fairy Slipper (Singspiel (IRE) 133) [2015 7.1m Jul 22] sturdy gelding: 100/1, showed something when seventh in maiden at Sandown (7¼ lengths behind Cymric) in July. *Martin Smith* **–**

DARIYAN (FR) 3 b.c. Shamardal (USA) 129 – Daryakana (FR) 120 (Selkirk (USA) 129) [2015 9.9g² 9.9s* 11.9g* 11.9g⁴ 9.9g* 9.9d² 11.9g³ Dec 13] first foal: dam, won Hong Kong Vase, half-sister to smart French middle-distance performer Daramsar, and daughter of Prix de Diane and Prix Vermeille winner Daryaba: very smart performer: won maiden and minor event, both at Saint-Cloud in May, and Prix Eugene Adam at Maisons-Laffitte (by 1½ lengths from War Dispatch) in July: good efforts when placed last 2 starts, in Prix Guillaume d'Ornano (1½ lengths second to New Bay) and Hong Kong Vase at Sha Tin (3 lengths third to Highland Reel): effective at 1¼m/1½m: acts on good going. *A. de Royer Dupre, France* **123**

DARK AMBER 5 b.m. Sakhee (USA) 136 – Donna Vita 85 (Vettori (IRE) 119) [2015 10m⁶ 11.7g* 11m³ 10m* 13.3m⁴ 10.2m⁴ 9s* 10s³ 10g 12v⁴ Oct 24] rather leggy mare: fair handicapper: won at Bath in June, Newbury and Goodwood (amateur) in July and at Goodwood (amateur) in August: stays 1½m: acts on soft and good to firm going: often in cheekpieces in 2015: tried in tongue tie prior to 2015: often races in rear. *Brendan Powell* **77**

DARK AND DANGEROUS (IRE) 7 b.g. Cacique (IRE) 124 – Gilah (IRE) (Saddlers' Hall (IRE) 126) [2015 p12f p15.8g⁶ Feb 11] rather leggy gelding: modest handicapper: stays 2m: acts on polytrack, good to firm and heavy going: tried in headgear: tried in tongue tie prior to 2015. *Brendan Powell* **50**

DARKAN (IRE) 3 b.f. Dark Angel (IRE) 113 – Divine Quest 81 (Kris 135) [2015 63: 11.8m⁵ 11.3m 10m⁶ 8m Jul 22] maiden: no form in 2015: tried in headgear in 2015. *M. J. Tynan, Ireland* **–**

DARK AVENGER (USA) 3 b.g. Scat Daddy (USA) 120 – Luxaholic (USA) (Macho Uno (USA) 124) [2015 p10f⁴ t8.6f³ p8f² 9.9f² 10.3d³ t9.5g⁴ p12g⁴ 9.9m⁵ 10.2m² 8m⁵ p8f² p10f⁶ p10f³ Oct 24] sturdy gelding: fair maiden: stays 1¼m: acts on polytrack and good to firm going: tried in headgear: front runner/races prominently. *Jamie Osborne* **79**

DARK AVENUE 2 b.f. (Mar 10) Champs Elysees 124 – Dark Quest 75 (Rainbow Quest (USA) 134) [2015 8s 8.3g p8g⁶ Nov 4] first foal: dam, maiden (stayed 1½m), half-sister to smart winner up to 10.6f Goncharova out of very smart winner up to 1½m (2-y-o 7f winner) Pure Grain: fair form: best effort when sixth in maiden at Kempton (4¾ lengths behind Persuasive) in November, not ideally placed: better to come. *William Knight* **75 p**

DARK CASTLE 6 b.g. Dark Angel (IRE) 113 – True Magic 80 (Magic Ring (IRE) 115) [2015 93: 6d 6m 6m 6m 6m Jul 23] useful at best, no form in 2015. *Micky Hammond* **–**

DARK COMMAND 2 b.g. (Feb 25) Kheleyf (USA) 116 – Desert Liaison 68 (Dansili 127) [2015 6g⁴ 5.9m 6m⁶ 6g³ Sep 23] modest maiden: raced only at 6f. *Michael Dods* **60**

DARK CONFIDANT (IRE) 2 b.g. (Apr 2) Royal Applause 124 – Sleek Gold 81 (Dansili 127) [2015 7m⁴ 6g³ 7m² 7m² 7d⁶ 5.5s 6d⁶ Oct 5] fair maiden: stays 7f: acts on good to firm going: tried in visor. *Richard Guest* **71**

DARK CRESCENT (IRE) 2 b.c. (Feb 6) Elnadim (USA) 128 – Zenella 95 (Kyllachy 129) [2015 6m⁶ p6f³ p6g⁴ 7d* Oct 16] 35,000Y: first foal: dam 2-y-o 6f-1m winner: fairly useful performer: won nursery at Haydock (by 2¼ lengths from Master Mirasol) in October: best effort at 7f: likely to progress further. *Charles Hills* **86 p**

DARK CRUSADER (IRE) 5 b.m. Cape Cross (IRE) 129 – Monty's Girl (IRE) (High Chaparral (IRE) 132) [2015 103: 14d³ 12.5g⁶ 14d⁶ 11.9g⁵ 13.8d* 12d³ 12d Sep 7] rather leggy mare: useful performer: won minor event at Galway in July: third in listed race at York (4¼ lengths behind Martlet) in August: stays 1¾m: acts on soft and good to firm going: tried in hood. *A. J. Martin, Ireland* **104**

DARK CRYSTAL 4 b.f. Multiplex 114 – Glitz (IRE) 54 (Hawk Wing (USA) 136) [2015 70: 8g⁶ 8s⁶ 8d⁶ 7.2d⁴ 8g 7.2g 7.2m* 7.2m³ 8d* 7.2g³ 8m 8g⁴ 7.2g² 8.3g Sep 21] fair handicapper: won at Musselburgh in July and Ayr in August: stays 1m: acts on soft and good to firm going. *Linda Perratt* **71**

DARK DEED 3 b.c. Dansili 127 – High Heeled (IRE) 122 (High Chaparral (IRE) 132) [2015 78p: 10m² 10m³ May 21] good-topped colt: fairly useful form in maidens: tried in hood: dead. *Sir Michael Stoute* **86**

DARK DEFENDER 2 b.c. (Jan 26) Pastoral Pursuits 127 – Oh So Saucy 90 (Imperial Ballet (IRE) 110) [2015 6g⁶ 6d* 6m* 6g⁵ 6g 7g⁶ 5m⁴ 6g Oct 3] £15,000Y: first foal: dam, 7f-1m winner, half-sister to useful 5f/6f winner Oh So Sassy (by Pastoral Pursuits): fairly useful performer: won maiden at Ayr in June and nursery at York (by neck from Shawaahid) in July: stays 6f: acts on good to firm and good to soft going: often races prominently. *Keith Dalgleish* **85**

DARK DEVIL (IRE) 2 gr.g. (Feb 15) Dark Angel (IRE) 113 – Ride For Roses (IRE) (Barathea (IRE) 127) [2015 7g² 7g² 7g* Sep 23] 70,000 2-y-o: first foal: dam, 1m winner, half-sister to smart winner up to 6f Mister Manannan out of winner up to 1m (2-y-o 6f/7f winner) Cover Girl: fairly useful performer: best effort when winning maiden at Redcar (by neck from Heir To A Throne) in September: raced only at 7f: remains with potential. *Richard Fahey* **81 p**

DARK DIAMOND (IRE) 5 b.g. Dark Angel (IRE) 113 – Moon Diamond (Unfuwain (USA) 131) [2015 f8d² f8g³ p10m⁵ f8g⁵ 10m⁵ 12m³ 11.9d³ 10g² t12.2g⁴ 9.9g⁶ 8.3g² 10.2s f8g³ f12g* Dec 22] fair handicapper: won at Southwell in December: left Robert Cowell after fourth start: stays 1½m: acts on fibresand, best turf form on good going: often in visor in 2015. *Julia Feilden* **70 a76**

DARK ELEGANCE 3 b.f. Observatory (USA) 131 – Fairy Slipper (Singspiel (IRE) 133) [2015 10m 11.8m t9.5g t8.6m⁴ p10f⁵ p10f⁴ t12.2g⁵ Sep 29] plain filly: first foal: dam of little account: modest maiden: stays 1½m: acts on polytrack and tapeta: often in headgear. *Philip McBride* **57**

DARK EMERALD (IRE) 5 gr.g. Dark Angel (IRE) 113 – Xema (Danehill (USA) 126) [2015 108: 8g² 6g* 7g* 8g² a8f 8f 7d³ 8g² 7d² 7s³ 6m* Sep 28] lengthy gelding: smart performer: won handicaps at Meydan (twice, by 2½ lengths from Fils Anges latter occasion) in February and minor event at Hamilton (by 6 lengths from Straightothepoint) in September: second in Zabeel Mile at Meydan (length behind Safety Check) in February: effective at 6f to 8.5f: acts on polytrack, soft and good to firm going: tried in visor: tried in tongue tie prior to 2015: often races prominently. *Brendan Powell* **118**

DARKENING NIGHT 3 b.g. Cape Cross (IRE) 129 – Garanciere (FR) (Anabaa (USA) 130) [2015 –p: 8m 8.3m⁶ t9.5g Jun 26] maiden: no form in 2015: tried in blinkers in 2015. *James Tate* **–**

DARK FOREST 2 b.g. (Feb 2) Iffraaj 127 – Through The Forest (USA) 62 (Forestry (USA) 121) [2015 6m⁶ 6m² 7g² 8g Sep 24] 42,000F, 120,000Y: second foal: half-brother to 2-y-o 5f winner Bountiful Forest (by Bahamian Bounty): dam, 11f winner, half-sister to 8.5f (minor US stakes) winner Dattts Our Girl: fairly useful maiden: second in maiden at Leicester in September: best effort at 7f. *Richard Hannon* **81**

DARK ILLUSTRATOR 2 b.f. (Mar 19) Dutch Art 126 – Xtrasensory 96 (Royal Applause 124) [2015 t5.1m⁶ t6f Dec 22] £40,000Y: sister to 2-y-o 5.7f winner Responsive and half-sister to several winners, including winner up to 7f Tassel (2-y-o 5f/6f winner) and **54**

2-y-o 5f/6f winner Tishtar (both by Kyllachy): dam, 2-y-o 6f winner, later 5.5f winner in USA: modest form: better effort when sixth in maiden at Wolverhampton (4¼ lengths behind Lydiate) in November, not knocked about: may do better. *David O'Meara*

DARK INTENTION (IRE) 2 b.f. (Feb 25) High Chaparral (IRE) 132 – Ajiaal 72 (Cape Cross (IRE) 129) [2015 6m 7d⁴ 7.9d² 8s³ Oct 9] €10,000Y: first foal: dam, maiden (stayed 1½m), half-sister to high-class 1½m dual Hardwicke winner Maraahel: fair form in maidens: will be suited by 1¼m+: open to further improvement. *Lawrence Mullaney*   **73 p**

DARK JUSTICE (IRE) 5 b.m. Lawman (FR) 121 – Dark Raider (IRE) 77 (Definite Article 121) [2015 p11g Aug 24] sturdy mare: maiden: no form in 2015: stays 1¾m: acts on firm going: in blinkers sole start in 2015. *Michael Madgwick*   **–**

DARK LIGHT (IRE) 3 b.g. Dark Angel (IRE) 113 – Spring View (Fantastic Light (USA) 134) [2015 p7g⁶ t8.6g⁶ t7.1g³ 8.3m² Jul 4] fair form in Britain: stays 8.3f: tried in hood: temperament under suspicion (hung left first 3 starts): sent to Qatar, and won 1m maiden at Doha in November. *Charles Hills*   **76**

DARK OCEAN (IRE) 5 b.g. Dylan Thomas (IRE) 132 – Neutral (Beat Hollow 126) [2015 80. 8s* 8.5g³ 8.5g⁵ 8d³ 8d* 7.9s⁴ 8g⁵ t8.6g³ 8d* 8d⁶ 8d Oct 31] leggy gelding: fairly useful handicapper: won at Pontefract in April, Doncaster in June and Pontefract (by ¾ length from Red Charmer) in September: stays 1¼m: acts on tapeta, best turf form on good going or softer (acts on heavy): often races prominently. *Jedd O'Keeffe*   **87**

DARK PHANTOM (IRE) 4 b.g. Dark Angel (IRE) 113 – Stoneware (Bigstone (IRE) 126) [2015 46: p8f⁵ 8g⁴ 8.1d⁴ p8g t8.6g² t8.6f⁶ t7.1m Dec 30] good-topped gelding: poor maiden: left Peter Makin after first start: stays easy 1¼m: acts on polytrack, tapeta and good to firm going: tried in blinkers: sometimes in tongue tie prior to 2015: usually races close up. *Geoffrey Deacon*   **48**

DARK PROFIT (IRE) 3 gr.g. Dark Angel (IRE) 113 – Goldthroat (IRE) 79 (Zafonic (USA) 130) [2015 82: t7.1m² 6g⁵ t6g³ 5g⁴ p5g* p5g⁴ Oct 20] good-topped gelding: fair performer: won maiden at Chelmsford in August: left Charles Hills after fourth start: stays 7f: acts on polytrack, tapeta and good to firm going: tried in cheekpieces in 2015. *Robert Cowell*   **77**

DARK REDEEMER 2 b.g. (Apr 13) Dark Angel (IRE) 113 – Lush (IRE) 78 (Fasliyev (USA) 120) [2015 6g t6g⁵ 7g p7.5g* p7.5g* a9g⁴ p7.5g p8.9g² p8.9g⁶ p7.5g Dec 17] good-quartered gelding: fair performer: won 2 claimers at Deauville in August, leaving J. S. Moore after first one: stays 9f: acts on polytrack: blinkered last 3 starts, wore cheekpieces on third outing. *N. Caullery, France*   **79**

DARK RED (IRE) 3 gr.g. Dark Angel (IRE) 113 – Essexford (IRE) 92 (Spinning World (USA) 130) [2015 7d⁴ 8d⁴ 7g² 7.5g² 9g³ 8.5m³ Jun 16] €34,000F, 82,000Y: third foal: dam, 2-y-o 7f winner, best at 1m: fairly useful maiden: second in maiden at Wetherby in April and third in handicap at Beverley in June: stays 9f: acts on good to firm going. *Ed Dunlop*   **82**

DARK RULER (IRE) 6 b.g. Dark Angel (IRE) 113 – Gino Lady (IRE) 79 (Perugino (USA) 84) [2015 96: p10g⁵ 12g 10.3s³ 12.1s² 12m 12m 12.1d⁶ 14d 13.1g 10g⁶ Sep 29] fairly useful handicapper: stays 1¾m: acts on good to firm and heavy going: often races towards rear. *Alan Swinbank*   **93**

DARK SHOT 2 b.c. (Feb 21) Acclamation 118 – Dark Missile 114 (Night Shift (USA)) [2015 6d⁵ 6m² p6d³ 6.1s² p6m⁵ Nov 19] sturdy colt: fair maiden: raced at 6f, will prove at least as effective at 5f: acts on polytrack, soft and good to firm going. *Andrew Balding*   **79**

DARK SIDE DREAM 3 b.g. Equiano (FR) 127 – Dream Day 98 (Oasis Dream 129) [2015 78: p6g⁴ t6f² p5f³ p5f³ t5.1g* 5d⁴ 5m p5g p6g⁶ f5g Dec 12] tall gelding: fairly useful handicapper: won at Wolverhampton (by 1½ lengths from Showstoppa) in April: stays 6f: acts on polytrack and tapeta. *Chris Dwyer*   **89**

DARK SIDE PRINCESS 2 b.f. (Jan 12) Strategic Prince 114 – Brazilian Breeze (IRE) 87 (Invincible Spirit (IRE) 121) [2015 p5m² t6f p5g⁴ Dec 7] £32,000Y, 46,000 2-y-o: first foal: dam, 5f winner who stayed 7f, sister to smart 6f winner Rivellino out of useful 2-y-o 5f/6f winner Brazilian Bride: fair maiden: best effort when second in maiden at Chelmsford (length behind Wedge) in June, nearest finish. *Chris Dwyer*   **66**

DARKSITEOFTHEMOON (IRE) 2 b.g. (Mar 28) Dark Angel (IRE) 113 – Moon Club (IRE) (Red Clubs (IRE) 125) [2015 7d p8g³ t7.1g² Aug 27] fair maiden: best effort when fourth in maiden at Wolverhampton (4½ lengths behind Aqua Libre) in August. *Marco Botti*   **74**

DARK TSARINA (IRE) 4 b.f. Soviet Star (USA) 128 – Dark Raider (IRE) 77 (Definite Article 121) [2015 61: p12g p15.8f⁶ Jan 30] angular filly: maiden: no form in 2015: likely to prove best up to 13f: acts on polytrack: sometimes wears headgear. *Michael Madgwick*   **–**

DARK WAR (IRE) 3 b.g. Dark Angel (IRE) 113 – Waroonga (IRE) (Brief Truce (USA) **55** 126) [2015 71: t7.1f p7m* p8f² t7.1m² p7f* p8g⁶ 8.3m 7d 8g t7.1g 6mᵘʳ Jun 26] fair **a73** handicapper: won at Kempton in February and March: stayed 1m: acted on polytrack and tapeta: tried in headgear: front runner/raced prominently: fatally injured at Doncaster. *James Given*

DARK WAVE 3 ch.g. Zebedee 113 – Rule Britannia 89 (Night Shift (USA)) [2015 87: **91** 10.3d* 11.8m⁴ 10g p11g⁴ 8.3d⁴ 10.2v 8s p9.4g⁶ p12.4g⁴ Dec 27] useful-looking gelding: fairly useful performer: won handicap at Doncaster in March: left Ed Walker, creditable efforts last 2 starts: stays 12.4f: acts on polytrack and heavy going: has worn tongue tie. *S. Cerulis, France*

DARK WONDER (IRE) 3 b.g. Dark Angel (IRE) 113 – Wondrous Story (USA) 91 **71** (Royal Academy (USA) 130) [2015 64: p7f⁵ t8.6g³ t8s⁵ 8m* 8.3g⁴ 7m⁶ 7.5g⁶ 8g p8f 8d t7.1f* t7.1m p7f t8.6g⁵ p8m⁴ Dec 31] attractive gelding: fair handicapper: won at Thirsk in May and Wolverhampton in September: stays 8.5f: acts on tapeta and good to firm going: often wears headgear: usually races prominently. *James Given*

DARMA (IRE) 3 b.f. Acclamation 118 – Dark Dancer (FR) (Danehill (USA) 126) [2015 **75** 76: 5.1d³ 5d⁵ 5m³ 6v⁶ p6g³ t5.1g⁶ Jun 22] fair handicapper: stays 6f: acts on polytrack, tapeta, good to soft and good to firm going. *Martyn Meade*

DARRELL RIVERS 3 b.f. Hellvelyn 118 – First Term 64 (Acclamation 118) [2015 49: **70** p6g⁴ p6m⁵ p6f 6d 6g³ 6m⁶ 6.1m⁴ 7m² 7m³ 8.3d³ 8.3d Oct 12] fair maiden: stays 8.5f: acts on good to firm and good to soft going: tried in hood. *Giles Bravery*

DARRINGTON 3 b.g. Archipenko (USA) 127 – Rosablanca (IRE) (Sinndar (IRE) 134) **90** [2015 78: 10.3d⁵ 8m² 7g 8m⁵ 8f⁴ p8g 8d* 8m³ 8g 10.3m⁴ 10.3d³ 10.4s⁶ Oct 10] lengthy gelding: fairly useful handicapper: won at Newmarket in July: third at Newmarket in August and third at Chester in September: stays 10.5f: acts on firm and soft going. *Richard Fahey*

DARSHINI 3 b.c. Sir Percy 129 – Fairy Flight (USA) 80 (Fusaichi Pegasus (USA) 130) **95** [2015 88: 8m* 9g² 12m⁵ 10.2d Oct 14] useful-looking colt: useful handicapper: won at Doncaster in April: second at Goodwood (1¼ lengths behind Resonant) in May: stays 9f: acts on good to firm going: tried in cheekpieces in 2015. *Sir Michael Stoute*

DARTMOUTH 3 b.c. Dubawi (IRE) 129 – Galatee (FR) 115 (Galileo (IRE) 134) [2015 **107** 76p: 10d⁴ 10m* 12f⁶ 12f* 12m* 12g⁵ p12g³ Nov 4] strong colt: useful handicapper: won at Sandown (by nose from Putting Green) in May, Ascot (by 4 lengths from Space Age) in July and Goodwood (by 2 lengths from Antiquarium) in August: third in listed race at Kempton (¾ length behind Missed Call) in November: stays 1½m: acts on polytrack and firm going. *Sir Michael Stoute*

DASAATEER (IRE) 3 b.g. Mount Nelson 125 – Trishuli (Indian Ridge 123) [2015 –: **78** 10m³ 12d² 10.3m 10g² p11g Oct 7] useful-looking gelding: fair maiden: stays 1¼m: acts on good to firm going: tried in blinkers in 2015: temperament under suspicion. *Roger Varian*

DASHING APPROACH 2 ch.f. (Feb 15) New Approach (IRE) 132 – Dashiba 102 **67 p** (Dashing Blade 117) [2015 7s³ 7s Sep 19] closely related to smart winner up to 12.4f Dashing Star (2-y-o 8.3f winner, by Teofilo) and half-sister to several winners, including smart 1m-1½m winner Barshiba (by Barathea), now dam of Juddmonte International winner Arabian Queen, and useful 2-y-o 1m winner Doctor Dash (by Dr Fong): dam 9f-1¼m winner: better effort when third in maiden at Salisbury (8¾ lengths behind Nathra) in September: remains open to improvement. *David Elsworth*

DASHING DYNAMO (IRE) 4 b.g. Alhaarth (IRE) 126 – Dashing Diva (IRE) (Sri **49** Pekan (USA) 117) [2015 72: 10.5g 17g p10.7g⁶ f12g⁵ Nov 26] poor maiden: bred to stay at least 1¼m: acts on soft going. *Andrew Oliver, Ireland*

DASHING STAR 5 b.g. Teofilo (IRE) 126 – Dashiba 102 (Dashing Blade 117) [2015 110: **107** p15.8g⁵ 12m² 12f 14m² Jul 11] lengthy gelding: useful handicapper: runner-up at Newmarket (1¾ lengths behind Watersmeet) in May and York (1¼ lengths behind Astronereus) in July: stays 1¾m: acts on good to firm and heavy going: usually in hood prior to 2015: usually leads, usually races freely. *David Elsworth*

DASTARHON (IRE) 5 b.h. Dansili 127 – Top Toss (IRE) 107 (Linamix (FR) 127) [2015 **102** 112: p8m³ p8g³ p9.4g³ 8d⁵ p6.5g⁶ Sep 30] just useful performer nowadays: won minor event at Maisons-Laffitte in 2014: best efforts in 2015 when third in similar races at Lingfield (beaten 4¼ lengths by Captain Joy) and Deauville (3 lengths behind Al Waab) on first/third outings: stays 1¼m: acts on polytrack and good to firm going: wears cheekpieces: has worn tongue tie. *Mme Pia Brandt, France*

DAT IL DO 3 b.f. Bahamian Bounty 116 – Broughtons Revival 88 (Pivotal 124) [2015 76p: **74**
p7m* p7m² 8.3s⁴ 7m t7.1g⁴ Aug 10] fair performer: won maiden at Lingfield in January:
left Noel Quinlan after first start: stays 7f: acts on polytrack: often races prominently.
Giles Bravery

DAVEY BOY 2 ch.g. (Mar 27) Paco Boy (IRE) 129 – She's So Pretty (IRE) 76 (Grand **79**
Lodge (USA) 125) [2015 p7g f7g* Nov 12] better effort when winning maiden at
Southwell (by neck from Underdressed) in November. *Michael Bell*

DAVID LIVINGSTON (IRE) 6 b.h. Galileo (IRE) 134 – Mora Bai (IRE) (Indian Ridge **96**
123) [2015 9.9s³ 10.4s 10v³ Oct 24] useful-looking horse: smart performer in 2013: seemed
amiss only outing in 2014 (at Meydan): just useful form in 2015: third in listed race at
Goodwood (8¾ lengths behind Battalion) in September and handicap at Newbury (9¼
lengths behind Passover) in October: best form around 1¼m: acts on good to firm and
heavy going. *Roger Charlton*

DAVID'S BEAUTY (IRE) 2 b.f. (Apr 24) Kodiac 112 – Thaisy (USA) (Tabasco Cat **63**
(USA) 126) [2015 6g 6.5m 5g³ 5.7f² 5f² 6g³ p6g* 6.1g 6s⁵ 6.3d t6f³ 6s⁴ Oct 6] €8,500F,
€26,000Y: fifth foal: half-sister to 8.3f winner Ice Box (by Pivotal): dam maiden half-sister
to high-class winner up to 1½m Fruits of Love: modest performer: won claimer at Lingfield
in July: left David Evans after eleventh start: stays 6f: acts on polytrack, firm and soft
going: front runner/races prominently. *Brian Baugh*

DAVID'S DUCHESS (IRE) 2 b.f. (Feb 16) Zebedee 113 – Blue Daze 75 (Danzero **79**
(AUS)) [2015 6g⁴ 5m² 5.2m⁴ Jul 18] €28,000Y: compact filly: half-sister to several
winners, including 2-y-o 5f/6f winner Strange Magic (by Diamond Green) and 2-y-o 6f
winner Fight The Chance (by Elusive City): dam 2-y-o 6f winner who barely stayed 9f: fair
maiden: best effort when fourth in Super Sprint at Newbury (2 lengths behind Lathom) in
July, suited by way race developed. *Richard Fahey*

DAVIDS PARK 4 b.g. Lucky Story (USA) 128 – Dijital Power (Pivotal 124) [2015 98: **90**
10.2v 14v⁵ 7.1s² 7m Oct 2] fairly useful handicapper: second at Chepstow in September:
left John Joseph Murphy after second start: stays 8.5f: best form on soft/heavy going: tried
in headgear: races prominently: sold 17,000 gns, sent to UAE. *Clive Cox*

DAVID'S SECRET 5 ch.g. Sakhee's Secret 128 – Mozie Cat (IRE) 72 (Mozart (IRE) **–**
131) [2015 53: 6m 10.2m 8m Jul 22] good-topped gelding: maiden: no form in 2015:
sometimes wears headgear: tried in tongue tie in 2015: usually races nearer last than first.
Roy Brotherton

DAWAA 2 ch.f. (Apr 24) Tamayuz 126 – Athreyaa (Singspiel (IRE) 133) [2015 5m⁴ 6m² **97**
6g³ 6.1m* 6s* 7g Oct 10] sturdy filly: third foal: half-sister to useful 1m winner Inaad (by
New Approach): dam unraced half-sister to very smart 11.3f-21.7f winner Honolulu out of
smart performer up to 1½m Cerulean Sky: useful performer: won nurseries at Nottingham
in August and Goodwood (by 1¼ lengths from Sixties Sue) in September: should stay 7f:
acts on soft and good to firm going: front runner/races prominently. *Mark Johnston*

DAWN CATCHER 5 ch.m. Bertolini (USA) 125 – First Dawn 68 (Dr Fong (USA) 128) **80**
[2015 86: 6.1m 5v³ 5g 6g 6d 5.1d p6m⁴ p6g³ p6m⁶ Dec 31] fairly useful handicapper: third **a70**
at Ffos Las in August: best at 5f: acts on any turf going. *Geoffrey Deacon*

DAWN MISSILE 3 b.g. Nayef (USA) 129 – Ommadawn (IRE) 75 (Montjeu (IRE) 137) **102**
[2015 p10g* 12m² 12g* 11.9m* 14d² 12g Oct 9] 12,500Y: useful-looking gelding: third
foal: half-brother to 1¼m winner Dawn Rock (by Rock of Gibraltar): dam, 1½m winner,
half-sister to smart 7f/1m winner Carribean Sunset: useful performer: won maiden at
Chelmsford in April, handicap at Goodwood in June and handicap at Haydock in August:
second in handicap at Haydock (nose behind Pin Up) in September: will stay 2m: acts on
polytrack, good to firm and good to soft going: often races towards rear, usually responds
generously to pressure. *William Haggas*

DAWN OF HOPE (IRE) 2 ch.f. (Feb 10) Mastercraftsman (IRE) 129 – Sweet Firebird **88**
(IRE) 103 (Sadler's Wells (USA) 132) [2015 7g³ 8g* 8g⁶ Oct 9] €220,000Y: compact filly:
half-sister to several winners, including smart 8.3f-1½m winner Ayrad (by Dalakhani) and
6f winner (stayed 1m) Alsium (by Invincible Spirit): dam, 1¼m winner who stayed 1½m,
closely related to top-class winner up to 6f Stravinsky: fairly useful performer: best effort
when winning maiden at Ascot (by 2¼ lengths from Alyssa) in September: well-held sixth
in Fillies' Mile at Newmarket: best effort at 1m. *Roger Varian*

DAWN'S EARLY LIGHT (IRE) 3 gr.g. Starspangledbanner (AUS) 128 – Sky Red 75 **106**
(Night Shift (USA)) [2015 t5.1f² 6g² 6v³ 6g* 6f* 6m³ 6g⁵ 6m² Oct 2] €32,000F, £60,000Y:
good-quartered gelding: half-brother to several winners, including smart 2-y-o 5f/6f
winner Orpen Grey (by Orpen) and 2-y-o 5f winner Rose of Battle (by Averti): dam 5f
winner: useful handicapper: won at Pontefract (by 2¼ lengths from Normandy Barriere) in

June and Ascot (by 3 lengths from Crew Cut) in July: third at Newmarket (length behind Mubtaghaa) in August and second at Ascot (4½ lengths behind The Tin Man) in October: stays 6f: acts on firm going: races prominently, usually travels strongly. *Tom Dascombe*

DAYBREAK LADY 2 ch.f. (Apr 17) Firebreak 125 – Musical Day 80 (Singspiel (IRE) **65**
133) [2015 t7.1f⁶ t7.1m³ Dec 18] 1,500Y: sixth foal: half-sister to 2-y-o 1m winner
Mindblowing (by Mind Games): dam, 2-y-o 1m winner, half-sister to useful 2-y-o 7f/1m
winner Day of Conquest: better effort when sixth in maiden at Wolverhampton (2½ lengths
behind Turn On The Tears) in November. *Jo Hughes*

DAYDREAM BELIEVER 3 b.f. Acclamation 118 – Idonea (CAN) (Swain (IRE) 134) **43**
[2015 6m⁵ 6g⁵ p8g⁶ 6m 6s p8m Nov 14] 50,000Y: rather leggy filly: second foal: dam 2-y-o
7f/1m winner: poor maiden: stays 1m: acts on polytrack and good to firm going. *Richard
Hannon*

DAYDREAMER 4 b.g. Duke of Marmalade (IRE) 132 – Storyland (USA) 103 (Menifee **78**
(USA) 124) [2015 72, a83: p12g⁴ t16.5g⁶ p15.8g⁵ Jun 9] well-made gelding: fair
handicapper: stays 16.5f: acts on polytrack, firm and good to soft going. *Alan King*

DAYDREAM (IRE) 2 b.f. (Apr 7) Dream Ahead (USA) 133 – Intricate Dance (USA) **64**
(Aptitude (USA) 128) [2015 p6f⁶ Sep 24] €19,000 2-y-o: fourth foal: half-sister to 6f
winner Garfunkel (by Excellent Art) and 2-y-o 6f winner Youcanseeme (by Le Vie Dei
Colori): dam twice-raced half-sister to winner up to 1m Short Dance and ungenuine 7f
winner (stayed 1¼m) Yankadi, both useful: 33/1, sixth in maiden at Chelmsford (3½
lengths behind Hide Your Fires) in September. *Jamie Osborne*

DAYLIGHT 5 ch.g. Firebreak 125 – Dayville (USA) 86 (Dayjur (USA) 137) [2015 90: **74**
f6g f6g⁵ 6d 7s 6g⁵ 5.9s³ 7.2g 7.5d 6d* f6g⁶ f7g⁶ Dec 15] fair handicapper: won at Redcar **a66**
(apprentice) in October: stays 6f: acts on polytrack, firm and soft going: sometimes wears
eyeshields prior to 2015: often wears tongue tie. *Michael Easterby*

DAYLIGHT ROBBERY 2 br.g. (Feb 2) Dick Turpin (IRE) 127 – Imperialistic (IRE) 99 **– p**
(Imperial Ballet (IRE) 110) [2015 p7g Nov 4] 70,000F: half-brother to several winners,
including winner up to 1m Electrelane (2-y-o 7f winner, by Dubawi) and winner up to 9f
Imperialistic Diva (2-y-o 5f winner, by Haafhd), both useful: dam winner up to 8.3f (2-y-o
6f winner): 25/1, well held in maiden at Kempton: has been gelded: should do better in
time. *David Elsworth*

DAY OF THE EAGLE (IRE) 9 b.g. Danehill Dancer (IRE) 117 – Puck's Castle 92 **77**
(Shirley Heights 130) [2015 74: t9.5g⁴ t8.6g* 8.3d* 8m⁴ 8m³ 7.9d² 8d 8g* 7.5d Sep 22]
lengthy gelding: fair performer: won handicap at Wolverhampton in April, handicap at
Hamilton in June and claimer at Newcastle in August: stays 8.5f: acts on tapeta, good to
firm and heavy going: often wears headgear prior to 2015. *Michael Easterby*

DAY STAR LAD 4 b.g. Footstepsinthesand 120 – Eurolink Mayfly 55 (Night Shift **50**
(USA)) [2015 71: t7.1g p8f t7.1m 7g p8f⁶ p8f 8.5d p8f Oct 15] modest handicapper: stays
1m: acts on fibresand: often wears visor: usually races nearer last than first, often races
freely. *Derek Shaw*

DAZEEKHA 2 b.f. (May 5) Captain Gerrard (IRE) 113 – Dazakhee 74 (Sakhee (USA) **50**
136) [2015 5m 6g t7.1m Dec 18] £2,000Y: first foal: dam 1m winner: modest maiden: best
effort when seventh in maiden at Wolverhampton (6½ lengths behind Outback Blue) in
December. *Michael Herrington*

DAZEEN 8 b.g. Zafeen (FR) 123 – Bond Finesse (IRE) 61 (Danehill Dancer (IRE) 117) **52**
[2015 73: t7.1f Feb 16] tall gelding: modest handicapper: stays 1m: acts on tapeta, firm and
soft going: tried in headgear prior to 2015: usually races towards rear. *Michael Herrington*

DAZZA 4 ch.f. Bertolini (USA) 125 – Another Secret 87 (Efisio 120) [2015 73: 5g 5g 6g **57**
p7g Dec 2] modest handicapper: stays 6f: acts on polytrack, good to firm and heavy going:
often in headgear in 2015. *Gary Moore*

DAZZLE THE DUEL (IRE) 4 b.g. Oasis Dream 129 – Roo 97 (Rudimentary (USA) **82**
118) [2015 –: 8g⁴ 5.8g 8s* 8d Sep 27] fairly useful performer: won handicap at Newbury
(by ¾ length from Hard To Handel) in August: stays 1m: acts on soft going. *Darren Bunyan,
Ireland*

DEACON'S LADY 3 b.f. Compton Place 125 – Mistress Cooper 71 (Kyllachy 129) **–**
[2015 t6g⁶ 5m⁴ p5g⁵ p6f p7g Dec 30] lengthy, angular filly: third foal: dam 2-y-o 5f winner:
no form: tried in cheekpieces. *Willie Musson*

DE AGUILAR (USA) 2 b.c. (Feb 28) Cape Blanco (IRE) 130 – Golden Aster (USA) 68 **70**
(Seeking The Gold (USA)) [2015 p7g⁶ 8s t8.6f³ p8g Dec 9] fair maiden: stays 8.5f.
Roger Charlton

DEANSGATE (IRE) 2 b.g. (Mar 24) Dandy Man (IRE) 123 – Romarca (IRE) 61 (Raise **73**
A Grand (IRE) 114) [2015 6g 6d 7.5m⁴ 8.5g⁴ 8.5m⁴ Oct 1] fair maiden: left Richard Fahey
after third start: likely to prove best up to 1m: acts on good to firm going. *Julie Camacho*

DEAR BEN 6 b.g. Echo of Light 125 – Miss Up N Go (Gorytus (USA) 132) [2015 54: t6g **–**
Jan 8] maiden: no form in 2015: best form at 5f: acts on polytrack: tried in hood prior to
2015: tried in tongue tie prior to 2015. *Brian Baugh*

DEAR BRUIN (IRE) 3 b.f. Kodiac 112 – Namu 76 (Mujahid (USA) 125) [2015 66: 7d⁶ **78**
7d³ 7.5m³ 7m² 7d* 7g³ 6g 7g⁴ Sep 7] close-coupled filly: fair handicapper: won at Lingfield
in July: stays 7f: acts on good to soft going: usually in cheekpieces in 2015: front runner.
John Spearing

DEAUVILLE DANCER (IRE) 4 b.g. Tamayuz 126 – Mathool (IRE) (Alhaarth (IRE) **95**
126) [2015 91p: 17.2m² 16.1g 16m t16.5f⁵ 16m² 18g 15s⁶ Oct 25] rather unfurnished
gelding: fairly useful handicapper: runner-up at Bath in May and Ascot in October: stays
17f: acts on tapeta, good to firm and heavy going: tried in hood in 2015: often races
prominently/races freely: sold 40,000 gns, joined David Dennis. *Sir Mark Prescott Bt*

DEAUVILLE (IRE) 2 b.c. (Mar 2) Galileo (IRE) 134 – Walklikeanegyptian (IRE) 77 **112**
(Danehill (USA) 126) [2015 7v* 7g* 8g² 8d⁵ Oct 24] fourth foal: brother to very smart
1¼m-1½m winner The Corsican and 2-y-o 1m winner Heatstroke and closely related to
2-y-o 6f winner Absolute Soul (by Perfect Soul): dam winner up to 9f (2-y-o 5f winner):
smart performer: won maiden at Listowel in May and Tyros Stakes at Leopardstown (by ½
length from Sanus Per Aquam) in July: second in Royal Lodge Stakes at Newmarket
(¾ length behind Foundation) in September: below form when fifth to Marcel in Racing
Post Trophy at Doncaster final start: sure to stay beyond 1m: tried in cheekpieces final start.
Aidan O'Brien, Ireland

DEAUVILLE PRINCE (FR) 5 b.g. Holy Roman Emperor (IRE) 125 – Queen of **96 §**
Deauville (FR) (Diableneyev (USA) 112) [2015 102: 7g⁴ 7d 8d 6.1f* 6d³ 6d 5.5m² 7gᵘʳ 7d³
6g Oct 16] quite good-topped gelding: useful handicapper: won at Chester in June: third at
Pontefract (2¾ lengths behind Nameitwhatyoulike) in July, second at Chester (short head
behind Ballesteros) in August and third at Chester (2½ lengths behind Maggie Pink) in
September: effective from 5.5f to 1m: acts on tapeta, firm and soft going: tried in headgear:
tried in tongue tie prior to 2015: unreliable. *Tom Dascombe*

DEBEN 2 b.g. (May 24) Lilbourne Lad (IRE) 111 – Mocca (IRE) 99 (Sri Pekan (USA) 117) **– p**
[2015 6g 7g Oct 21] leggy gelding: seventh foal: half-brother to smart winner up to 7f
Kiyoshi (2-y-o 6f winner, by Dubawi): dam winner up to 1¼m (2-y-o 8.3f winner) who
stayed 1½m: green in maidens: should do better. *Kevin Ryan*

DEBIT 4 b.g. Pivotal 124 – Silver Kestrel (USA) (Silver Hawk (USA) 123) [2015 81: 7m **71**
8g 6d³ 7g⁶ 5g 6s³ 7s f6m Dec 8] rather leggy gelding: fair maiden: left Brian Ellison after
seventh start: stays 7f: acts on soft and good to firm going: often wears cheekpieces. *Simon Hodgson*

DEBT FREE DAME 3 ch.f. Arcano (IRE) 122 – Runkerry Point (USA) (Giant's **76**
Causeway (USA) 132) [2015 –: 8g⁴ f7g³ 7d 6m² t6g* 5m² 5m⁶ 7d⁴ f6d⁶ 5.9g t7.1m² 6d⁶
t7.1m³ t7.1f² t6f⁶ Oct 17] fair handicapper: won at Wolverhampton in June: stays 7f: acts
on tapeta and firm going: usually in headgear in 2015: front runner/races
prominently. *Michael Easterby*

DECENT FELLA (IRE) 9 b.g. Marju (IRE) 127 – Mac Melody (IRE) 91 (Entrepreneur **62**
123) [2015 77: t5.1m⁴ t6g p6f Sep 10] sturdy gelding: modest handicapper: stays 1m: acts
on polytrack, tapeta, good to firm and good to soft going: often wears headgear: usually
wears tongue tie. *Heather Dalton*

DECIMUS MAXIMUS 4 b.g. Elnadim (USA) 128 – Sempre Sorriso 52 (Fleetwood **–**
(IRE) 107) [2015 p5g⁴ p6f p5f⁴ Oct 28] poor maiden: left Chris Gordon after first start:
dead. *Andi Brown*

DECISIVE (IRE) 3 ch.f. Iffraaj 127 – Guarantia 92 (Selkirk (USA) 129) [2015 t6g⁶ 6.1s³ **61**
5m⁴ 5g⁵ 6m² p8f⁶ p8f⁵ 8s⁴ Oct 15] 80,000Y: fourth foal: half-sister to 2-y-o 6f winner
Daraa and 6f winner (stays 8.5f) Surety (both by Cape Cross): dam, 7f winner, half-sister
to very smart 1¼m-1½m winner Laaheb: modest maiden: left Robert Cowell after fifth
start: stays 1m: acts on polytrack and good to firm going: tried in hood. *Anthony Carson*

DECLAMATION (IRE) 5 ch.g. Shamardal (USA) 129 – Dignify (IRE) 105 (Rainbow **67**
Quest (USA) 134) [2015 52: t7.1f* 7.2d⁶ t7.1m² Nov 28] fair handicapper: won at
Wolverhampton in February: stays 8.5f: acts on polytrack, tapeta, best turf form on firm
going. *Alistair Whillans*

DECLAN 3 ch.g. Dylan Thomas (IRE) 132 – Fleurissimo 79 (Dr Fong (USA) 128) [2015 **72 p** 8.3m t8.6g² p13.3g³ Dec 10] first foal: dam, maiden (stayed 1¼m), half-sister to smart 1m winner Dolores: fair form: best effort when third in maiden at Chelmsford in December, unsuited by way race developed: capable of better. *Jamie Osborne*

DECORATED KNIGHT 3 ch.c. Galileo (IRE) 134 – Pearling (USA) (Storm Cat **110** (USA)) [2015 90p: 9.8g² 8g* 8.1g* 8g³ 9g⁴ Oct 10] useful-looking colt: smart performer: won maiden at Haydock and handicap at Sandown (by ¾ length from Pyjama Party), both in July: good third in Joel Stakes at Newmarket (5½ lengths behind Time Test) in September: not disgraced when 3¼ lengths fourth to Energia Davos in Darley Stakes at Newmarket final start: stays 9f: best form on good going. *Roger Varian*

DEEBAJ (IRE) 3 br.g. Authorized (IRE) 133 – Athreyaa (Singspiel (IRE) 133) [2015 73p: **75 p** 12g⁵ Jul 30] fair maiden: fifth in maiden at Ffos Las (3½ lengths behind Alla Breve) on sole outing in 2015: will be suited by 1¼m+: should still improve. *Mark Johnston*

DEEDS NOT WORDS (IRE) 4 b.g. Royal Applause 124 – Wars (IRE) 60 (Green **86** Desert (USA) 127) [2015 103§: 5m 6m 6m 6m 6g⁵ 5.7s⁶ 6g⁵ 6.1m* 5.7m² 6d* p6g p8g Dec 18] smallish gelding: fairly useful handicapper: won at Chepstow in September and Windsor (by ¾ length from Be Bold) in October: left Mick Channon after tenth start: stays 6f: acts on soft and good to firm going: tried in visor in 2015: usually races prominently. *J. F. Levins, Ireland*

DEEMAH (IRE) 3 b.f. Iffraaj 127 – Princess Iris (IRE) 99 (Desert Prince (IRE) 130) **77** [2015 62p: p7g⁴ p7g³ p8g³ p7g 8g⁴ 8.1d* 10.1d⁴ 8.3d 8.3s Sep 21] fair handicapper: won at Chepstow in August: left David Marnane after fifth start: stays 8.5f: acts on polytrack and soft going. *Ismail Mohammed*

DEEP BLUE DIAMOND 3 b.f. Sir Percy 129 – Apple Blossom (IRE) 81 (Danehill **75** Dancer (IRE) 117) [2015 –: 7g 10m 12m⁴ 12.1f* 12g² 12g² 12.1g² 12.1g² Sep 16] fair handicapper: won at Beverley in July: stays 1½m: acts on firm going: in hood in 2015: often races prominently. *Denis Quinn*

DEEP BLUE SEA 3 b.f. Rip Van Winkle (IRE) 134 – Semaphore (Zamindar (USA) 116) **79** [2015 77: 8g² 8.3m² 8.1m⁴ 10g⁶ 8d³ 7s 8.5g⁶ Sep 10] useful-looking filly: has scope: fair handicapper: stays 8.5f: acts on good to firm and good to soft going: sometimes in cheekpieces in 2015. *Anthony Carson*

DEEP RESOLVE (IRE) 4 b.g. Intense Focus (USA) 117 – I'll Be Waiting (Vettori (IRE) **75** 119) [2015 f12g⁵ 12.1g 11.9d* 11.9d⁴ 12v⁴ 12s⁶ f12g⁴ Nov 24] fair handicapper: won at Haydock (amateur) in September: stays 1½m: acts on fibresand and heavy going: tried in cheekpieces in 2015. *Alan Swinbank*

DEEPSAND (IRE) 6 br.g. Footstepsinthesand 120 – Sinamay (USA) (Saint Ballado **66** (CAN)) [2015 87: p15.8g 12.1s⁴ 16d 15.8s⁴ Oct 27] fair handicapper: barely stays 2¼m: acts on good to firm and heavy going: often wears headgear: often races towards rear. *Ali Stronge*

DEERFIELD 3 b.g. New Approach (IRE) 132 – Sandtime (IRE) 92 (Green Desert (USA) **85** 127) [2015 80: 8.5g³ 8.9m⁴ p10g Sep 2] fairly useful handicapper: third at Epsom in April: should stay 1¼m+: in cheekpieces in 2015. *Charlie Appleby*

DEER SONG 2 b.g. (Feb 18) Piccolo 121 – Turkish Delight 67 (Prince Sabo 123) [2015 **59** 5g 5.3g⁴ 5f⁴ 5g⁵ 5m 5d 5.3v⁵ p6g⁵ p6g p6m⁴ p7g p6d² p6g³ Dec 16] compact gelding: modest maiden: stays 6f: acts on polytrack: sometimes in headgear. *John Bridger*

DEFIANT CHOICE 2 b.c. (Feb 27) Teofilo (IRE) 126 – Endorsement 107 (Warning – 136) [2015 p8g p8g 8d 8.3d Oct 14] no form. *Derek Shaw*

DEFICIT (IRE) 5 gr.g. Dalakhani (IRE) 133 – Venturi 103 (Danehill Dancer (IRE) 117) **79** [2015 p16f⁵ Apr 15] angular gelding: fair handicapper: stays 2m: acts on polytrack, good to firm and heavy going: sent to USA. *Steve Gollings*

DEFROCKED (IRE) 2 b.c. (Feb 28) Lope de Vega (IRE) 125 – Portelet 91 (Night Shift **66 p** (USA)) [2015 f7m³ Dec 8] €90,000Y: brother to useful 7f-1m winner Back On Top and half-brother to several winners, including very smart 6f and (including at 2 yrs) 7f winner Etlaala and smart 7f-1m winner Selective (both by Selkirk): dam 5f winner: 10/1, some encouragement when third in maiden at Southwell (13½ lengths behind Yattwee) in December: capable of better. *Jamie Osborne*

DEFTERA FANTUTTE (IRE) 4 b.f. Amadeus Wolf 122 – Carranza (IRE) (Lead On **53** Time (USA) 123) [2015 67: f6s⁴ p6f t5.1m Apr 2] modest maiden: stays 7f: acts on all-weather: tried in cheekpieces in 2015: usually races close up. *Natalie Lloyd-Beavis*

DEFTERA LAD (IRE) 3 b.g. Fast Company (IRE) 126 – Speedbird (USA) 76 (Sky **57** Classic (CAN)) [2015 55: p8m p6g⁶ p7m p8f 7s⁴ 6d⁴ p6g² p7g⁶ p7g² 6g⁴ Sep 7] modest maiden: stays 1m: acts on polytrack and soft going: tried in hood in 2015. *Pat Phelan*

DEINONYCHUS 4 b.g. Authorized (IRE) 133 – Sharp Dresser (USA) 80 (Diesis 133) **91** [2015 70: p10g² p12g* 11.8d* 13g² 12m 12s⁶ p12g Nov 18] fairly useful performer: won maiden at Lingfield in January and handicap at Leicester in June: stays 13f: acts on polytrack and good to soft going: often wears hood: usually races close up. *William Knight*

DEIRA MIRACLE (IRE) 3 b.f. Duke of Marmalade (IRE) 132 – Naval Affair (IRE) 101 – (Last Tycoon 131) [2015 t8.6m⁴ Mar 7] €30,000Y: closely related to useful 7f winner Czech It Out (by Oratorio) and half-sister to 3 winners, including useful winner up to 1m (stayed 1¼m) Field Day (2-y-o 7f winner, by Cape Cross) and 1m-1½m winner (stayed 2m) War At Sea (by Bering): dam, 2-y-o 7f winner, half-sister to smart winner up to 10.3f King Adam: 8/1, held back by inexperience when fourth in maiden at Wolverhampton (12¼ lengths behind Anarchiste) in March: sold 7,500 gns, sent to Italy. *Marco Botti*

DELAGOA BAY (IRE) 7 b.m. Encosta de Lago (AUS) – Amory (GER) (Goofalik **49** (USA) 118) [2015 57: p16g⁵ t16.5g p16g⁵ t13.9m Dec 30] compact mare: poor handicapper: stays 16.5f: acts on polytrack, tapeta, soft and good to firm going: tried in blinkers prior to 2015. *Sylvester Kirk*

DELAIRE 3 b.g. Sakhee's Secret 128 – Moody Margaret (Bahamian Bounty 116) [2015 **69** 79p: p10g³ 9.9m⁵ 8.3m⁵ 7.1m³ 8g³ p10f Nov 25] leggy gelding: fair maiden: left Roger Varian after fifth start: stays 8.5f: acts on good to firm going: tried in cheekpieces in 2015. *Martin Bosley*

DE LESSEPS (USA) 7 ch.g. Selkirk (USA) 129 – Suez 109 (Green Desert (USA) 127) – [2015 58: f6g Dec 29] lengthy gelding: modest at best, no form in 2015: best effort at 7f: acts on fibresand. *John David Riches*

DELIZIA (IRE) 2 b.f. (Feb 14) Dark Angel (IRE) 113 – Jo Bo Bo (IRE) (Whipper (USA) **97** 126) [2015 t5.1g* 5m* 5f 6g⁴ 6g 6g³ 6s Oct 10] 34,000F, £48,000Y: close-coupled filly: first foal: dam unraced half-sister to smart 5f winner Dominica out of useful 2-y-o 5f winner Dominio: useful performer: won maiden at Wolverhampton in April and listed race at York (by 1½ lengths from Silk Bow) in May: third in listed Two-Year-Old Trophy at Redcar (3¾ lengths behind Log Out Island) in October: stays 6f: acts on tapeta and good to firm going: usually races prominently. *Mark Johnston*

DELLBUOY 6 b.g. Acclamation 118 – Ruthie 72 (Pursuit of Love 124) [2015 71: p12g Jul – 14] workmanlike gelding: fairly useful at best, no form in 2015: stays 1½m: acts on polytrack and soft going: tried in cheekpieces prior to 2015. *Pat Phelan*

DELUXE 3 b.g. Acclamation 118 – Ainia 83 (Alhaarth (IRE) 126) [2015 81: p7g⁵ 8m 7g³ **77** 7g⁵ 7g⁶ p8g⁴ 8s³ 7s⁵ p8m p7g p10f⁴ p7g⁵ Dec 9] useful-looking gelding: fair maiden: left **a71** Richard Hannon after fifth start: stays 1m: acts on polytrack, soft and good to firm going. *Pat Phelan*

DELVE (IRE) 2 b.f. (Mar 18) Dansili 127 – Cool And Composed (USA) (Buddha (USA) **65 p** 122) [2015 7s Oct 12] useful-looking filly: third foal: dam, 1m-9.5f winner, half-sister to 6f winner (stayed 1m) Shadowland: 8/1, considerate introduction when eighth in maiden at Salisbury (5¼ lengths behind Dutch Destiny) in October, not knocked about: capable of better. *Sir Michael Stoute*

DELYSDREAM 3 br.c. Dutch Art 126 – Goodbye Cash (IRE) 82 (Danetime (IRE) 121) **44** [2015 –: t6g 5g⁴ 6d 5m Aug 9] poor maiden: best form at 5f: acts on good to firm going: usually in tongue tie in 2015. *Christine Dunnett*

DEMAND RESPECT 2 ch.g. (Mar 25) Paco Boy (IRE) 129 – Brilliance 74 (Cadeaux – Genereux 131) [2015 7d Aug 24] 33/1, eighth in maiden at Leicester (15¼ lengths behind Le Roi du Temps) in August, merely closing up late. *Henry Spiller*

DEMBABA (IRE) 3 b.g. Moss Vale (IRE) 126 – Wildsplash (USA) (Deputy Minister **60** (CAN)) [2015 p7m⁵ t7.1f⁶ p8m⁶ 8g f7g⁶ Apr 23] modest maiden: best effort at 7f: acts on polytrack: often in blinkers: tried in tongue tie. *Michael Wigham*

DEMOCRETES 6 ch.g. Cadeaux Genereux 131 – Petite Epaulette 80 (Night Shift **91** (USA)) [2015 105: p7g 6m⁴ Apr 20] strong gelding: fairly useful handicapper: stays 1m: acts on firm and soft going: tried in headgear: often in tongue tie in 2015: temperament under suspicion. *Seamus Durack*

DEMONSTRATION (IRE) 3 b.g. Cape Cross (IRE) 129 – Quiet Protest (USA) **94** (Kingmambo (USA) 125) [2015 10g 10m² 10m² 10.3g 8g t9.5f* t9.5f* t9.5m³ Dec 12] 48,000Y: good-topped gelding: second foal: half-brother to 6f winner Reaffirmed (by Pivotal): dam 1m winner out of useful 10.5f winner Rosa Parks: fairly useful performer:

won maiden at Wolverhampton in October and handicap at Wolverhampton (by head from Ready) in November: left James Toller after sixth start: stays 9.5f: acts on tapeta: sometimes in cheekpieces: front runner. *William Jarvis*

DEMORA 6 b.m. Deportivo 116 – Danzanora (Groom Dancer (USA) 128) [2015 112: 5f⁵ 5m 5m 6m 5s* 5d³ Oct 24] close-coupled mare: useful handicapper: won at Leicester (by length from Maljaa) in October: best form at 5f: acts on any turf going: usually leads. *Michael Appleby* **109**

DEMPSEY ROLL 2 b.g. (Mar 11) Bushranger (IRE) 119 – Suzie Quw 83 (Bahamian Bounty 116) [2015 7m 6g 7.2g Aug 26] no form. *Ann Duffield* **–**

DENHAM SOUND 2 ch.f. (Feb 7) Champs Elysees 124 – Presbyterian Nun (IRE) 100 (Daylami (IRE) 138) [2015 8.1g³ 8s³ Sep 1] sturdy, lengthy filly: first foal: dam, ungenuine 2-y-o 7f winner who stayed 1¾m, half-sister to smart 7f winner Jedburgh: better effort when third in maiden at Goodwood (5¾ lengths behind Harlequeen) in September. *Henry Candy* **72**

DENISON FLYER 8 b.g. Tobougg (IRE) 125 – Bollin Victoria 51 (Jalmood (USA) 126) [2015 –: 9.9m⁶ 16m⁴ Aug 10] smallish, sturdy gelding: poor handicapper: stays 1¾m: acts on good to firm and heavy going: often wears headgear. *Lawrence Mullaney* **47**

DEN MASCHINE 10 b.g. Sakhee (USA) 136 – Flamingo Flower (USA) (Diesis 133) [2015 p13f⁴ t12.2g² t12.2f⁶ t13.9f⁵ Mar 20] workmanlike gelding: fair handicapper: stays 1½m: acts on polytrack, tapeta, good to firm and good to soft going: tried in cheekpieces prior to 2015: tried in tongue tie prior to 2015. *Paul Morgan* **78**

DENMEAD 2 b.g. (Apr 7) Champs Elysees 124 – Glorious Dreams (USA) 76 (Honour And Glory (USA) 122) [2015 7.1g 8m 7s⁶ Sep 23] workmanlike gelding: modest form in maidens. *Michael Madgwick* **63**

DENTON DAWN (IRE) 3 b.f. Fast Company (IRE) 126 – Rectify (IRE) (Mujadil (USA) 119) [2015 77: 6g⁵ 5d⁵ 6g⁶ 7m 7g Sep 19] modest maiden: best form at 5f: acts on soft going: sent to Greece. *Michael Dods* **60**

DENWOOD LAD 5 ch.g. Resplendent Glory (IRE) 115 – Heather Valley 47 (Clantime 101) [2015 p8g Aug 5] 100/1 and in cheekpieces, well held in maiden at Kempton. *Linda Jewell* **–**

DENZILLE LANE (IRE) 3 ch.g. Iffraaj 127 – Alexander Youth (IRE) 98 (Exceed And Excel (AUS) 126) [2015 88: p5g⁵ 7.1m⁴ 7.1m 7m* 7.5f* 7.1m² 7g* 6d 7m⁵ 7g Aug 15] lengthy gelding: fairly useful handicapper: won at Newmarket in June, and Beverley and Epsom (by neck from Swiss Cross) in July: stays 7.5f: acts on fibresand and firm going: tried in blinkers prior to 2015: front runner/races prominently: sent to UAE. *Mark Johnston* **92**

DEODORO (USA) 2 b.f. (Mar 1) Medaglia d'Oro (USA) 129 – Anna Wi'yaak (JPN) (Dubai Millennium 140) [2015 7.5d⁴ 8.5m* 8.3g² Oct 19] fifth foal: half-sister to 2-y-o 6f winner Appointee (by Exceed And Excel): dam, unraced, closely related to smart 1m winner Anna Salai and half-sister to smart but unreliable winner up to 1m Iguazu Falls: fairly useful performer: won maiden at Beverley (by 2½ lengths from Wapping) in October: further progress when second in nursery at Windsor (2 lengths behind Primitivo): stays 8.5f: open to further improvement. *Mark Johnston* **86 p**

DEPTH CHARGE (IRE) 3 b.g. Fastnet Rock (AUS) 127 – Myrtle 96 (Batshoof 122) [2015 7m 8d 7f⁴ p7g⁴ p7g t8.6g³ t8.6f² t8.6f³ Dec 14] useful-looking gelding: fair maiden: left Jeremy Noseda after seventh start: stays 8.5f: acts on tapeta: often in headgear: often in tongue tie. *Kristin Stubbs* **74**

DE REPENTE (IRE) 4 b.f. Captain Rio 122 – Suddenly 86 (Puissance 110) [2015 65: f5d⁶ t5.1f 5.1m 6.1d May 8] leggy filly: poor handicapper: stays 5.5f: acts on fibresand, tapeta, soft and good to firm going. *Michael Appleby* **45**

DERULO (IRE) 4 ch.g. Arakan (USA) 123 – Bratislava 54 (Dr Fong (USA) 128) [2015 85: p8f 8.3m³ 8.3s³ 10m² 8d 8.1g 9.9g* 10g² p10m Nov 17] fairly useful performer: won claimer at Salisbury in September: second in handicap at Windsor in October: stays 1¼m: acts on good to firm going: tried in cheekpieces in 2015: front runner/races prominently. *David Elsworth* **89**

DESCARO (USA) 9 gr.g. Dr Fong (USA) 128 – Miarixa (FR) (Linamix (FR) 127) [2015 t9.5g 12.1m Jul 10] quite good-topped gelding: fairly useful at best, no form in 2015: stays 21.5f: acts on good to firm and heavy going: sometimes wears headgear: front runner/races prominently. *John O'Shea* **–**

DESDICHADO 3 ch.g. Pivotal 124 – Murrieta 57 (Docksider (USA) 124) [2015 10m 10v* 12.1s⁶ 12d⁶ Oct 11] €150,000Y: fifth foal: closely related to useful 1½m-1¾m winner Wildomar (by Kyllachy) and half-brother to useful 1m (including at 2 yrs) winner **87**

Maywood (2-y-o 1m winner, by Cape Cross): dam, maiden (stayed 1½m), half-sister to very smart winner up to 9f Charlie Farnsbarns: fairly useful performer: won maiden at Ffos Las in August: likely to stay at least 1½m. *Ralph Beckett*

DESERT ACE (IRE) 4 ch.g. Kheleyf (USA) 116 – Champion Place 109 (Compton Place 125) [2015 104: 5m 5m² 5g⁶ 5g⁴ 5g 5d 6g 5s 5d Oct 24] good-topped gelding: useful handicapper: second at Thirsk (1½ lengths behind Red Baron) in May: best form at 5f: acts on firm and soft going: often wears cheekpieces: often wears tongue tie: sometimes slowly away. *Michael Dods* — **99**

DESERT APOSTLE (IRE) 3 b.f. Tagula (IRE) 116 – Cambara 97 (Dancing Brave (USA) 140) [2015 44: t7.1g p6g t5.1g⁴ 6d 5.1g t6g⁶ 6.1m 5m p6g⁵ Aug 22] poor maiden: stays 6f: acts on polytrack and tapeta: usually in visor in 2015: usually races nearer last than first. *Derek Shaw* — **32 a39**

DESERT CHIEF 3 b.g. Kheleyf (USA) 116 – African Breeze 79 (Atraf 116) [2015 –: 6m 6g 7g⁴ 7g 8v⁵ Nov 3] maiden: no form in 2015: sometimes in cheekpieces in 2015: usually slowly away, often races towards rear, often races lazily. *Richard Whitaker* — **–**

DESERT COMMAND 5 b.g. Oasis Dream 129 – Speed Cop 104 (Cadeaux Genereux 131) [2015 93: p6f⁵ p6m⁴ p6g 5m⁻ 6m² 5v⁶ 5.2m⁵ p5g² p5g Dec 15] strong gelding: fairly useful handicapper: won at Salisbury in June: second at Epsom in July and second at Kempton in November: left Andrew Balding after fifth start: stays 6f: acts on polytrack, soft and good to firm going: often in headgear in 2015: front runner/races prominently. *Robert Cowell* — **92**

DESERT CROSS 2 b.g. (Apr 30) Arcano (IRE) 122 – Secret Happiness (Cape Cross (IRE) 129) [2015 6s 6d 6.1v Oct 7] no form. *Jonjo O'Neill* — **–**

DESERT ENCOUNTER (IRE) 3 b.g. Halling (USA) 133 – La Chicana (IRE) (Invincible Spirit (IRE) 121) [2015 80p: 10.1d³ 12.2g* Oct 13] fairly useful form, lightly raced: won maiden at Musselburgh (by 6 lengths from Spring Dixie) in October: stays 1½m: remains with potential. *David Simcock* — **88 p**

DESERT FORCE 3 b.c. Equiano (FR) 127 – Mail The Desert (IRE) 110 (Desert Prince (IRE) 130) [2015 89p: 7m⁴ 6m² 6m 6d 6m³ 6g 6g Sep 19] well-made colt: useful handicapper: won at Newbury in April: second at Newmarket (2 lengths behind Twilight Son) in May and third at Ascot (3 lengths behind Moonraker) in August: stays 7f: acts on soft and good to firm going. *Richard Hannon* — **101**

DESERT HAZE 2 br.f. (Apr 8) New Approach (IRE) 132 – Ensemble (FR) (Iron Mask (USA) 117) [2015 7g 8v³ Oct 24] 420,000Y: first foal: dam, 9f winner, half-sister to very smart winner up to 1m Occupandiste, herself dam of very smart miler Mondialiste and grandam of high-class performer up to 1½m Intello: better effort when third in maiden at Newbury (3¼ lengths behind Chastushka) in October: open to further improvement. *Ralph Beckett* — **75 p**

DESERT LAW (IRE) 7 b.g. Oasis Dream 129 – Speed Cop 104 (Cadeaux Genereux 131) [2015 103: 6d 5m 5m³ 5g⁴ 5m* 5m³ 5f³ 5.1m⁷ 5.4g⁴ 5m Sep 9] strong gelding: smart performer: won 'Dash' (Handicap) at Epsom (by length from Monsieur Joe) in June and minor event at Nottingham (by 1½ lengths from Barracuda Boy) in August: third in handicap at Ascot (length behind Double Up) in July: stays 6f: acts on firm and good to soft going: tried in hood prior to 2015: front runner/races prominently. *Paul Midgley* — **112**

DESERT MORNING (IRE) 2 b.f. Pivotal 124 – Arabian Mirage 103 (Oasis Dream 129) [2015 68p: p10g p6g³ t7.1f⁵ p6m* Dec 27] fair performer: won maiden at Chelmsford in December: left David Simcock after first start: will prove suited by a return to 7f: acts on polytrack. *Anthony Carson* — **72**

DESERT RECLUSE (IRE) 8 ch.g. Redback 116 – Desert Design (Desert King (IRE) 129) [2015 79: t12.2f Dec 22] close-coupled gelding: useful at best, no form in 2015: best at 2m+: acts on polytrack, soft and good to firm going: tried in headgear prior to 2015. *Henry Oliver* — **–**

DESERT RIVER (IRE) 2 b.c. (May 3) Showcasing 117 – Kathy's Rocket (USA) (Gold Legend (USA)) [2015 5.1m 5m t7.1g⁵ 6s⁶ p7g⁵ p6f² Oct 10] 55,000Y: sixth foal: half-brother to 3 winners, including 6f/7f winner Cailin Coillteach (by Woodman) and 7f winner Beaupreau (by Mr Sidney): dam 5.5f/6f (including at 2 yrs) winner: fair form: tongue tied, shaped well in nurseries last 2 starts: best effort at 6f: acts on polytrack and tapeta: often leads: open to further improvement. *Ismail Mohammed* — **69 p**

DESERT RULER 2 b.g. (Mar 20) Kheleyf (USA) 116 – Desert Royalty (IRE) 96 (Alhaarth (IRE) 126) [2015 6d⁶ 6g* 7g* 7d⁵ Oct 24] 15,000Y: seventh foal: half-brother to 3 winners, including 1½m-2m winner Kian's Delight (by Whipper) and 11.6f/1½m winner — **86**

(stays 2m) Lady of Yue (by Manduro): dam 8.3f-1½m winner: fairly useful performer: won maiden at Ayr in July and nursery at York (by ½ length from Reputation) in September: stays 7f. *Jedd O'Keeffe*

DESERT SNOW 4 gr.f. Teofilo (IRE) 126 – Requesting (Rainbow Quest (USA) 134) **102** [2015 95, a108: 12m³ 12d 12g² p13g Oct 29] rangy filly: useful performer: third in listed race at Newmarket (1½ lengths behind Jordan Princess) in July and second in listed race at Newmarket (8 lengths behind Journey) in September: stays 2m: acts on polytrack, tapeta and good to firm going: often in hood prior to 2015. *Saeed bin Suroor*

DESERT STRIKE 9 b.g. Bertolini (USA) 125 – Mary Jane 77 (Tina's Pet 121) [2015 88: **93** p5g f6s⁵ p6f⁴ p6f* p5g⁵ p6g* p5f⁴ p5m² p5m⁴ p5g⁶ p5g⁴ p5g* p6f p6g p6g³ p5g p5m p5g f5g⁶ Dec 29] rangy gelding: fairly useful handicapper: won at Kempton in March, Lingfield in April and Chelmsford in August: stays 6f: acts on polytrack, tapeta, firm and good to soft going: usually wears headgear: tried in tongue tie prior to 2015. *Conor Dore*

DESERT TANGO 2 ch.f. (Apr 13) Paco Boy (IRE) 129 – Photographie (USA) (Trempolino **54** (USA) 135) [2015 7.1m 8.1s⁵ 7s t9.5f⁴ Nov 3] smallish filly: half-sister to several winners, including useful 1½m-1¾m winner Duty Free (by Rock of Gibraltar) and winner up to 1½m Little Dutch Girl (2-y-o 1m winner, by Dutch Art): dam maiden: modest maiden: best effort at 9.5f. *Jonathan Portman*

DESIDERADA (IRE) 2 b.f. (May 9) Acclamation 118 – Turning Light (GER) 108 **76 p** (Fantastic Light (USA) 134) [2015 p6g⁵ p7g* Oct 14] 35,000Y: fourth foal: brother to useful winner up to 9f Sikeeb (2-y-o 6f winner) and half-brother to 2-y-o 7f winner (stayed 1¾m) Gypsie Queen (by Xaar): dam 1½m winner: better effort when winning maiden at Kempton (by length from Pirouette) in October, well positioned: likely to stay 1m: will go on improving. *Hugo Palmer*

DESIGNS ON ROME (IRE) 5 b.g. Holy Roman Emperor (IRE) 125 – Summer Trysting **126** (USA) 83 (Alleged (USA) 138) [2015 130: 8.9m* 9.9m* 12g⁴ 9.9m⁴ 8g⁶ 9.9g⁴ Dec 13] lengthy, leggy gelding: high-class performer: won Group 3 Centenary Vase (Handicap) in February and Hong Kong Gold Cup (readily by 1¼ lengths from Helene Super Star) in March, both at Sha Tin: fourth on 3 of next 4 starts, in Dubai Sheema Classic at Meydan (4¾ lengths behind Dolniya, left with too much to do), Queen Elizabeth II Cup at Sha Tin (beaten 2 lengths by Blazing Speed) and Hong Kong Cup on latter course (3¾ lengths behind A Shin Hikari): stays at least 1¼m: acts on good to firm and good to soft going: has worn tongue tie: had bone chips removed and off 7 months after fourth outing: patiently ridden. *J. Moore, Hong Kong*

DESIRABLE 2 b.f. (Mar 18) Stimulation (IRE) 121 – Hot Pursuits 89 (Pastoral Pursuits **58 p** 127) [2015 p6g p6g* Dec 16] first foal: dam winner up to 5.7f (2-y-o 5f winner): better effort when winning maiden at Kempton (by neck from Don't Blame Me) in December: likely to progress further. *Hughie Morrison*

Investec Corporate Banking 'Dash' (Heritage Handicap), Epsom—
Desert Law and Monsieur Joe (both jockeys wearing striped sleeves) give trainer Paul Midgley a
1, 2 in this valuable event; Boom The Groom (checked cap) finishes third and the blinkered Steps
takes fourth for the second year running

DESIRE 3 ch.f. Kyllachy 129 – Colonel's Daughter 61 (Colonel Collins (USA) 122) [2015 **70**
–: 5m⁴ 6m⁴ 5g⁶ 7g 7.2d 7m* 7.2g 7g* 7.2g 7s Oct 16] fair handicapper: won at Leicester
and Newcastle in August: stays 7f: acts on good to firm going: often in cheekpieces in 2015.
Richard Fahey

DESKTOP 3 b.g. Desideratum 118 – First Harmony (First Trump 118) [2015 8s⁶ 10.1d² **63**
8m⁶ 12g³ 14.1m⁶ 15.8s⁵ t13.9f Oct 13] modest maiden: stays 1¾m: acts on good to firm
and good to soft going. *Antony Brittain*

DESPERADO DANCER 4 b.g. Iffraaj 127 – Madam Ninette (Mark of Esteem (IRE) –
137) [2015 –: t8.6f Jan 30] maiden: no form in 2015. *Peter Hiatt*

DESSERTOFLIFE (IRE) 2 gr.f. (Feb 24) Mastercraftsman (IRE) 129 – Cranky Spanky **100**
(IRE) (Spectrum (IRE) 126) [2015 6.5m⁴ 7d* 7f⁶ 7.1f² 7d² 7g* 8g Oct 9] €18,000F, 42,000Y:
rather unfurnished filly: fourth foal: half-sister to 1m (including at 2 yrs) winner Hotkiss (by
Footstepsinthesand): dam, 7f/1m winner, half-sister to useful 1m winner Pepper Popper:
useful performer: won maiden at Doncaster in June and Zukunfts-Rennen at Baden-Baden
(by 1¼ lengths from Shy Witch) in September: second in listed race at Sandown (2¼
lengths behind Fireglow) in July: should stay 1m: acts on good to soft going. *Mark Johnston*

DESTALINK 3 b.f. Rail Link 132 – Modesta (IRE) 105 (Sadler's Wells (USA) 132) [2015 **83**
10m⁴ 12m⁴ 12m³ Jun 5] sturdy filly: closely related to useful winner up to 1m Intense
(2-y-o 7f winner) and 1½m winner Archive (both by Dansili) and half-sister to 3 winners,
including smart 1¼m-1½m winner (stays 2½m) Model Pupil (by Sinndar): dam, 11.5f-1¾m
winner, half-sister to high-class 1½m-1¾m winner Manifest: fairly useful maiden: best
effort when fourth in maiden at Newmarket (3¾ lengths behind Gretchen) in May: in hood/
tongue tie. *Lady Cecil*

DESTINATION AIM 8 b.g. Dubai Destination (USA) 127 – Tessa Reef (IRE) (Mark **82**
of Esteem (IRE) 137) [2015 68: 9.3g⁵ 7.9m 7.9m⁴ 7g* 7.5d² 7s Oct 16] fairly useful
handicapper: won at Newcastle (by 3¼ lengths from Oak Bluffs) in September: stays 7f:
acts on good to soft going: usually races close up: inconsistent. *Fred Watson*

DESTINY BAY (IRE) 2 b.g. (Mar 24) Dubai Destination (USA) 127 – Banutan (IRE) 73 –
(Charnwood Forest (IRE) 125) [2015 p7g 8m 7s Oct 12] no form: tried in visor. *Mark Usher*

DESTINY BLUE (IRE) 8 b.g. Danehill Dancer (IRE) 117 – Arpege (IRE) (Sadler's **42**
Wells (USA) 132) [2015 64: t9.5f t9.5m⁶ t9.5f⁵ Mar 23] big, strong gelding: poor
handicapper: stays 1¼m: acts on soft and good to firm going: tried in cheekpieces prior to
2015: tried in tongue tie prior to 2015: often races in rear. *Suzzanne France*

DESTINY'S SHADOW (IRE) 3 gr.g. Dark Angel (IRE) 113 – Lunar Love (IRE) (In –
The Wings 128) [2015 –: p10g t12.2g⁴ p10g 8.5g Apr 6] no form: in headgear last 3 starts.
George Baker

DESTROYER 2 b.g. (Feb 10) Royal Applause 124 – Good Girl (IRE) 100 (College **76**
Chapel 122) [2015 6g 6g³ 6f 6d² 7.6g⁵ p6f Sep 24] strong gelding: fair maiden: stays 6f:
acts on good to soft going. *William Muir*

DESTRUCT 5 b.g. Rail Link 132 – Daring Miss 113 (Sadler's Wells (USA) 132) [2015 –
18.7dᵖᵘ May 6] useful performer in France in 2013 (for Andre Fabre), winning 3 times,
including listed race at Deauville: off 21 months, pulled up in Chester Cup only subsequent
outing: stays 15f: acts on polytrack and soft going. *Ian Williams*

DEUCE AGAIN 4 b.f. Dubawi (IRE) 129 – Match Point (Unfuwain (USA) 131) [2015 **105**
85p: f11d* f12s⁶ p14f* 14.1s* 14.3v³ 12.4d Aug 14] useful performer: won maiden at
Southwell in January, handicap at Chelmsford in February and listed race at Nottingham
(by 1½ lengths from Island Remede) in April: creditable 7¼ lengths third to Clever Cookie
in Ormonde Stakes at Chester next time: off over 3 months, last of 10 in Prix de Pomone at
Deauville final outing: stays 1¾m: acts on polytrack/fibresand, best turf form on soft/heavy
going: usually travels strongly. *John Gosden*

DE VEER CLIFFS (IRE) 2 b.f. (May 8) Canford Cliffs (IRE) 133 – Mill Guineas **83 p**
(USA) (Salse (USA) 128) [2015 8.3d² Oct 14] half-sister to several winners, including
winner up to 9f Mill Marin (2-y-o 5f winner, by Pivotal) and 7f/7.5f (including at 2 yrs)
winner Olvia (by Giant's Causeway), both useful: dam useful (stayed 1¼m): 100/1,
showed plenty when second in maiden at Nottingham (1½ lengths behind Architecture) in
October: entitled to progress. *Martyn Meade*

DEVILS IN MY HEAD 5 b.m. Kheleyf (USA) 116 – Alexandra S (IRE) (Sadler's Wells –
(USA) 132) [2015 –: p10g Jan 11] maiden: no form in 2015. *Keiran Burke*

DEVILUTION (IRE) 3 b.g. Bluegrass Cat (USA) 120 – Meniatarra (USA) 68 (Zilzal **47**
(USA) 137) [2015 –: t5.1f t5.1g⁶ f5s² t5.1g² t5.1f³ p6g p6g f6g⁴ Dec 15] poor maiden:
stays 6f: acts on all-weather: usually races nearer last than first. *Derek Shaw*

DEVIOUS SPIRIT (IRE) 3 br.g. Intikhab (USA) 135 – Unintentional 60 (Dr Devious **79** (IRE) 127) [2015 65: 7m 7.9g³ 6.9d⁴ 8.3m² 9.3s 8g* 8.3g 8d⁴ Oct 30] workmanlike gelding: fair handicapper: won at Ayr in September: best effort at 1m: acts on good to firm going: usually races towards rear. *Richard Fahey*

DEVON DRUM 7 b.g. Beat Hollow 126 – West Devon (USA) (Gone West (USA)) [2015 **84** 83: 11.6g⁶ 14.4gʳʳ p13.3f² p14f² t13.9f* t12.2f t12.2f Dec 11] fairly useful handicapper: won at Wolverhampton (by neck from All For The Best) in October: second at Chelmsford in September: left Paul Webber after first start: stays 1¾m: acts on polytrack and tapeta. *David Brown*

DEVONIAN 3 b.g. Hellvelyn 118 – Overcome (Belmez (USA) 131) [2015 t7.1f t6g t8.6f⁴ **59** f8d³ t8.6f⁶ p6f Apr 15] modest maiden: best effort at 8.6f: acts on tapeta: sold 4,500 gns, sent to Italy. *Rod Millman*

DEVONSHIRE (IRE) 3 b.f. Fast Company (IRE) 126 – Nova Tor (IRE) 86 (Trans Island **109** 119) [2015 87: 7v³ 8v² 8g³ 7f8.5m² 9d⁴ 9s* 10g Oct 18] workmanlike filly: useful performer: won listed race at Listowel (by 4½ lengths from Alive Alive Oh) in September: good third in Irish 1000 Guineas at the Curragh (2 lengths behind Pleascach) in May: respectable seventh behind Curvy in E. P. Taylor Stakes at Woodbine final outing: should stay 1¼m: acts on soft and good to firm going: often races prominently. *W. McCreery, Ireland*

DEVONSHIRE PLACE (IRE) 3 b.f. Rip Van Winkle (IRE) 134 – Councilofconstance **82** (IRE) 78 (Footstepsinthesand 120) [2015 61: p8m⁵ 10.3m² 10m⁴ 10.2d* p12g 10d* Oct 12] fairly useful handicapper: won at Bath in September and Windsor (by ½ length from Berland) in October: stays 1¼m: acts on good to soft going. *Roger Charlton*

DEWALA 6 b.m. Deportivo 116 – Fuwala (Unfuwain (USA) 131) [2015 f11s³ Jan 1] big **68** mare: fair handicapper: stays 1½m: acts on fibresand and good to soft going. *Michael Appleby*

DEW POND 3 b.g. Motivator 131 – Rutland Water (IRE) (Hawk Wing (USA) 136) [2015 **72** 52: 14.1gᵘʳ 12.1m² 12g² 14.1g⁴ 16.2m² 14.1m* 14.1m² 17.1d³ 14.1d² 14.1v⁴ Nov 3] fair handicapper: won at Redcar in August: stays 17f: acts on good to firm and good to soft going. *Tim Easterby*

DEXTEROUS 3 b.f. Mastercraftsman (IRE) 129 – Daring Aim 89 (Daylami (IRE) 138) **66** [2015 56: p12g p14f⁴ Sep 17] fair maiden: stays 1¾m. *Roger Charlton*

DHA CHARA (IRE) 5 b.g. Ramonti (FR) 126 – Campiglia (IRE) (Fairy King (USA)) **78** [2015 –: f8g³ f8g 8s² 8d 8.3v⁵ Oct 7] fair maiden: left Andrew Hollinshead after second start: stays 1m: acts on synthetics, soft and good to firm going: front runner/races prominently. *Sarah Hollinshead*

DHAHMAAN (IRE) 2 b.c. (Apr 13) Kodiac 112 – Heroine Chic (IRE) 69 (Big Bad Bob **107 p** (IRE) 118) [2015 5.1g* p5g* 6s² 6d* Oct 24] €35,000F, 58,000 2-y-o: first foal: dam, maiden (stayed 8.5f), sister to winner up to 13f Banksters Bonus and winner up to 11f Backbench Blues, both smart: useful performer: won maiden at Nottingham in May, minor event at Chelmsford in June and listed race at Doncaster (by 1¾ lengths from Above N Beyond) in October: second in listed race at York (1¼ lengths behind Donjuan Triumphant) earlier in October: should prove best at 5f/6f: likely to progress further. *Marco Botti*

DHAULAR DHAR (IRE) 13 b.g. Indian Ridge 123 – Pescara (IRE) 108 (Common **86** Grounds 118) [2015 69: t12.2g* 14g 12g* 12.5m² 12g* 13.8m² 11.1d⁴ 13.7m* 12.8m² Sep 27] leggy gelding: fairly useful handicapper: won at Wolverhampton in January, Thirsk in June, Catterick (amateur) in July and Musselburgh (by 3 lengths from Trafalgar Rock) in September: stays 1¾m: acts on tapeta, firm and soft going: tried in headgear prior to 2015: often waited with. *Jim Goldie*

DHEBAN (IRE) 2 gr.g. (Feb 7) Exceed And Excel (AUS) 126 – Comeback Queen 91 **88** (Nayef (USA) 129) [2015 5f² 5g³ 6m 5d⁵ p6f* Oct 10] 240,000Y: half-brother to useful 8.5f winner (stays 1½m) Nonchalant (by Oasis Dream): dam, 2-y-o 1m winner, half-sister to smart winner up to 1m Donativum: fairly useful performer: won maiden at Chelmsford (by 2½ lengths from Munira Eyes) in October: stays 6f: acts on polytrack and firm going: front runner/races prominently. *Richard Hannon*

DHEYAA (IRE) 2 b.f. (Mar 11) Dream Ahead (USA) 133 – Lady Livius (IRE) 102 (Titus **51** Livius (FR) 115) [2015 7s⁵ 7g Oct 9] 210,000Y: rather unfurnished filly: half-sister to several winners, including smart 2-y-o 5f/6f winner Burnt Sugar (by Lope de Vega) and useful 2-y-o 5f/6f winner Brown Sugar (by Tamayuz): dam, winner up to 6f (2-y-o 5f winner), half-sister to smart winner up to 7f Galeota: better effort when eleventh in maiden at Newmarket (7½ lengths behind Materialistic) in October. *B. W. Hills*

DIAKTOROS (IRE) 5 b.g. Red Clubs (IRE) 125 – Rinneen (IRE) 67 (Bien Bien (USA) **80** 125) [2015 t12.2g* 11.6m* 14.1m⁶ Apr 28] fairly useful performer: won maiden at Wolverhampton in March and handicap at Windsor in April: should stay 1¼m. *Ian Williams*

DIALOGUE 9 b.g. Singspiel (IRE) 133 – Zonda 100 (Fabulous Dancer (USA) 124) [2015 **77** 68, a77: t9.5g⁵ t9.5f t8.6m² t8.6f² t8.6m² t8.6g⁴ p8g² t8.6g⁵ 8m⁶ t8.6g p8f³ f8g* Nov 12] close-coupled, useful-looking gelding: fair handicapper: won at Southwell in November: stays 1½m: acts on all-weather and good to firm going: tried in cheekpieces prior to 2015: tried in tongue tie prior to 2015: often races prominently. *Andrew Reid*

DIAMOND BLAISE 3 b.f. Iffraaj 127 – See You Later 98 (Emarati (USA) 74) [2015 7m³ **77** 7g p6m² 7.5m⁴ Jun 16] 95,000Y: good-topped filly: half-sister to several winners, including smart winner up to 6f Aahayson (2-y-o 5f winner, by Noverre) and useful 5f/6f (including at 2 yrs) winner Take Ten (by Bahamian Bounty): dam 5f winner (including at 2 yrs): fair maiden: bred to prove best at around 7f. *Marcus Tregoning*

DIAMOND CHARLIE 7 br.g. Diamond Green (FR) 121 – Rosy Lydgate 53 **94** (Last Tycoon 131) [2015 79, a92: p6g³ p6f p5m p5g⁶ 5m 5g⁵ p6g p5f² p5m p5g Dec 2] compact gelding: fairly useful handicapper: third at Lingfield in January: stays 6f: acts on polytrack, soft and good to firm going: tried in cheekpieces. *Simon Dow*

DIAMOND JOEL 3 b.g. Youmzain (IRE) 131 – Miss Lacroix 32 (Picea 99) [2015 62: **82** t12.2g² p12f² 11.6m 12d³ 14.1m⁵ 14.4g* 14g³ 14.1g² 15.9m⁴ Sep 12] plain gelding: fairly useful handicapper: won at Chester in July: stays 14.5f: best form on good going: usually leads. *Mick Channon*

DIAMOND LADY 4 b.f. Multiplex 114 – Ellen Mooney 83 (Efisio 120) [2015 93: p6g² **89** 6m² 5f⁴ 6m⁶ 6m 6m³ f6s⁴ 6d p6f⁵ p6g* p6g³ Dec 7] rather leggy filly: fairly useful handicapper: won at Lingfield in November: second at Leicester in April: stays 6f: acts on polytrack, firm and good to soft going: usually races prominently. *William Stone*

DIAMOND MAN 3 b.g. Exceed And Excel (AUS) 126 – Inaminute (IRE) 86 (Spectrum – (IRE) 126) [2015 p5g⁶ t6g p5m p5g Jun 18] no form: in hood. *Derek Shaw*

DIAMOND REFLECTION (IRE) 3 b.g. Oasis Dream 129 – Briolette (IRE) 112 **70** (Sadler's Wells (USA) 132) [2015 10.1m⁴ 10g² Jun 19] better effort when second in maiden at Redcar in June: worth a try in handicaps: joined Tom Watson. *Charlie Appleby*

DIAMOND RIDGE (IRE) 3 gr.c. Zebedee 113 – Porky Pie (IRE) (Grand Lodge (USA) **80** 125) [2015 p8m⁴ p10g³ t8.6g² 11m p10f Aug 18] €8,500F, £30,000Y: half-brother to several winners, including 9f winner Rey de Trebol (by Shinko Forest) and winner up to 1¼m Red Surprise (2-y-o 1m winner, by Great Exhibition): dam unraced: fairly useful maiden: best effort at 1¼m: acts on polytrack. *Richard Hannon*

DIAMOND RUNNER (IRE) 3 b.g. Amadeus Wolf 122 – Hawk Eyed Lady (IRE) 75 **55** (Hawk Wing (USA) 136) [2015 56: 10g 9.9m 8.3d² 8m* t8.6m² t8.6m³ 8.5g 7s³ t9.5f³ 7s⁴ Oct 26] modest handicapper: won at Thirsk in August: stays 1¼m: acts on tapeta, firm and soft going: wears headgear: front runner/races prominently. *Deborah Sanderson*

DIAMONDS A DANCING 5 ch.g. Delta Dancer – Zing (Zilzal (USA) 137) [2015 76: **70** p7g p7g⁴ 8.3g p7g Oct 29] sturdy gelding: fair handicapper: best form at 7f: acts on polytrack and tapeta: usually wears headgear. *Brian Gubby*

DIAMOND SAM 3 ch.g. Compton Place 125 – Kurtanella 86 (Pastoral Pursuits 127) [2015 **53** –: 7.1m² 8m 7m p6f⁶ᵘ 6s⁶ p8f⁴ t7.1m⁴ Nov 28] good-quartered gelding: modest maiden: stays 1m: acts on polytrack and tapeta: usually wears tongue tie: often races prominently. *Sylvester Kirk*

DIAMONDSANDRUBIES (IRE) 3 b.f. Fastnet Rock (AUS) 127 – Quarter Moon **114** (IRE) 120 (Sadler's Wells (USA) 132) [2015 60p: 9s* 10d³ 11.4d* 12g⁴ 10m* 9.9m 11.9s 9.9m Oct 4]

    The Aga Khan's studs arguably house the finest collection of broodmares in Europe, a collection that has periodically been enhanced by the addition of blue-chip mares in lock-stock-and-barrel purchases of the studs of those noted French owner-breeders Marcel Boussac, Mme Francois Dupre and Jean-Luc Lagardere. The Aga Khan whittles down his broodmare band annually to keep the numbers at around two hundred and there is always keen interest in the studs' castoffs. Watership Down, for example, paid 470,000 guineas at the December Sales for the Prix Vermeille winner Darara as an eleven-year-old and she went on to great success, becoming the dam of major Group 1 winners Dar Re Mi and Rewilding among others. Darara and her illustrious half-brother Darshaan are descended on

the dam's side from the celebrated Boussac mare Tourzima whom the Aga Khan describes as his 'rock, just as Mumtaz Mahal was for my grandfather.' Mumtaz Mahal, 'the fastest filly in the annals of the turf', was one of the foundation mares of the stud when it was started by the Aga Khan's grandfather in the 'twenties. The 'old' families have continued to serve the Aga Khan well, his brilliant, unbeaten Arc-winning filly Zarkava (a distant descendant of Mumtaz Mahal) the most recent outstanding example. One of the fillies from this long-established line who wasn't given a chance to join the Aga Khan's broodmare band was Alruccaba, a tall, leggy, rather lightly-built individual who gained her only success for the Aga Khan in a six-furlong maiden at Brighton and made her final racecourse appearance when fifth in a nursery at Catterick. The Aga Khan didn't keep her and she was weeded out of Michael Stoute's string at the end of her two-year-old days, fetching 19,000 guineas (only just reaching her reserve) at the 1985 December Sales.

Purchased by Kirsten Rausing, owner of Lanwades Stud, and Sonia Rogers, owner of Airlie Stud in Ireland, Alruccaba has gone on to found a dynasty of her own. Three of Mumtaz Mahal's daughters also became famous broodmares (including Mumtaz Begum the sixth dam of Shergar, the best horse bred by the Aga Khan); Alruccaba is from the branch descended from Mah Mahal (dam of Derby winner Mahmoud), through Mah Iran (dam of Migoli who beat Tudor Minstrel in the 1947 Eclipse and won the 1948 Prix de l'Arc), Mah Behar (a sister to the dam of the brilliant Petite Etoile, the fifth dam of Zarkava), Nucciolina (grandam of a French Two Thousand Guineas winner in Nishapour) and Alruccaba's dam Allara (a half-sister to the dam of the Aga Khan's disqualified 1989 Oaks winner Aliysa, as well as to the dam of Nishapour). The female line then continues as illustrated in the tabulated pedigree which accompanies this essay. Kirsten Rausing and Sonia Rogers were richly rewarded for their decision to purchase Alruccaba, who bred eight winners, including the Nassau Stakes and Sun Chariot winner Last Second (whose own progeny include Poule d'Essai des Poulains winner Aussie Rules), and two other fillies who have gone on to breed Group 1 winners for Mrs Rogers and Ms Rausing after carrying their respective colours with distinction on the racecourse, namely Alleluia who won the Doncaster Cup and Alouette who finished third in the Moyglare. Alleluia is the dam of Prix Royal-Oak and Goodwood Cup winner Allegretto, and Alouette is the dam of dual Champion Stakes winner Alborada and of Albanova, who won three Group 1s in Germany and was nearly as good as her sister.

One of Alruccaba's daughters, Jude, by the Aga Khan's stallion Darshaan and a sister to Alouette and the Irish Oaks third Arrikala, didn't manage to win, making the frame only once in four starts for Paul Cole as a three-year-old, her only season to race. Jude carried the colours of Prince Fahd Salman who sent her to the December Sales at the end of her three-year-old season when she changed hands for 92,000 guineas. She may have been a modest performer on the racecourse but she hailed from a family which was to become one of the most sought after in the stud book. Purchased on behalf of Richard Henry and his wife Roisin, Jude became the foundation mare of Premier Bloodstock, the breeding arm of Primus Advertising, the marketing and advertising agency (Richard Henry is the CEO) which has

267

promoted Coolmore Stud internationally since the mid-'eighties. Jude has produced numerous winners for them, notably Irish One Thousand Guineas winner Yesterday (also runner-up in the Oaks) and her year-older sister the Moyglare Stud Stakes winner Quarter Moon, who went on to finish runner-up in the Irish One Thousand Guineas, Oaks and Irish Oaks. That pair raced in the ownership of Mrs Henry and Mrs John (Sue) Magnier, Yesterday carrying the Magnier dark blue and Quarter Moon the dark blue and emerald green check, white sleeves and cap, of Mrs Henry.

Mrs Henry's colours were also carried in the latest season by Quarter Moon's three-year-old daughter Diamondsandrubies, who also raced in the ownership of Mrs Henry and Mrs Magnier and lived up to her name by becoming yet another gem among the descendants of Alruccaba. Diamondsandrubies saw a racecourse only once as a two-year-old, finishing sixth of thirteen in a back-end fillies maiden at Leopardstown, but she was out early in the latest season, getting off the mark in a fillies maiden at Tipperary in early-April and then finishing a good third to Bocca Baciata and Pleascach in listed company at Navan nine days later. With an eye to finding out whether she was good enough to follow in the footsteps of her dam and other distinguished relatives by taking up an Oaks challenge, Diamondsandrubies ran next in the Arkle Finance Cheshire Oaks at the beginning of May. Starting favourite in a field of ten at Chester, she stormed clear to win by six lengths from Entertainment. Diamondsandrubies was clearly progressing well, but more was going to be needed at Epsom where she started at 14/1, one of five Irish-trained challengers including her stablemates Together Forever and 50/1-shot Qualify, and the One Thousand Guineas winner Legatissimo who was the 5/2 favourite. It was a fairly strong Oaks field, also featuring the winners of most of the other key trials, and Diamondsandrubies enhanced her reputation by finishing fourth, despite being badly hampered and losing several lengths—and all momentum—when badly baulked by Together Forever approaching the final furlong while still holding every chance. It

Sea The Stars Pretty Polly Stakes, the Curragh—
Diamondsandrubies, who met trouble when fourth to Qualify in the Oaks on her previous start,
gains consolation as she holds off Oaks runner-up Legatissimo (far side) and Ribbons

was wretched luck but Diamondsandrubies recovered and rallied well, finishing with plenty of running left in her, to be beaten just under six lengths by the shock winner Qualify who caught Legatissimo on the post. Exactly how close Diamondsandrubies would have finished with a clear run is speculation, but she deserved plenty of credit for her effort.

The Irish Oaks looked an obvious target for Diamondsandrubies after her performance at Epsom, but both her and Legatissimo were instead dropped back to a mile and a quarter for their next start. The pair met again in the Sea The Stars Pretty Polly Stakes at the Curragh at the end of June and Diamondsandrubies narrowly turned the tables, showing that she might well have finished there or thereabouts in the Oaks but for the serious trouble she encountered. The Pretty Polly provides the first opportunity of the season in Britain and Ireland for the classic fillies to test themselves against the best of their elders who have remained in training. Five older horses and four three-year-olds, who also included Irish One Thousand Guineas winner Pleascach, made for a high quality renewal with the line-up also including a third Group 1 scorer in five-year-old Ribbons who had won the 2014 Prix Jean Romanet. Diamondsandrubies made all under a well-judged ride from Seamus Heffernan, who had partnered her at Epsom and felt she had been most unlucky. Responding gamely when really asked to stretch out, Diamondsandrubies held off Legatissimo and Ribbons at the Curragh by a short head and a neck, with another five-year-old Secret Gesture, who had won the Middleton Stakes at York with Ribbons third, filling fourth place and Pleascach fifth. Three-year-olds haven't had a great record in the Pretty Polly since it was elevated to Group 1 in 2004 with only Peeping Fawn and Misty For Me, both also trained by Aidan O'Brien, being successful before Diamondsandrubies. Peeping Fawn completed the Pretty Polly/Irish Oaks double when there was only a fortnight between the races, and, with a three-week gap nowadays, it seemed as if the Irish Oaks was the plan for both Diamondsandrubies and Pleascach after the Pretty Polly. In the event, none of the three-year-olds that took part in the Pretty Polly went on to the Irish Oaks. Diamondsandrubies was given an extra week and ran next in the newly-enriched Nassau Stakes at Goodwood which was worth over twice as much as the Irish Oaks in the latest season. Starting second favourite to Legatissimo (who won readily), Diamondsandrubies was disappointing, pushed along over three furlongs out before finishing last of nine. She fared little better on her two other subsequent outings, never involved and beating only one home in the Prix Vermeille and the Prix de l'Opera, both at Longchamp.

Diamondsandrubies (IRE) (b.f. 2012)	Fastnet Rock (AUS) (b 2001)	Danehill (b 1986)	Danzig
			Razyana
		Piccadilly Circus (b 1995)	Royal Academy
			Gatana
	Quarter Moon (IRE) (b 1999)	Sadler's Wells (b 1981)	Northern Dancer
			Fairy Bridge
		Jude (b 1994)	Darshaan
			Alruccaba

The medium-sized, attractive Diamondsandrubies will be joining her dam in the paddocks in the next season, alongside other members of the Jude 'tribe' still owned by Premier Bloodstock—Yesterday, You'll Be Mine and Jude's four-year-old daughter Ruby Tuesday (Premier Bloodstock also has the Nunthorpe winner Margot Did among its half dozen broodmares). A sister to the winning Irish two-year-old How High The Moon, who was placed in listed company at the Curragh in August, Diamondsandrubies is now one of eight winners bred by Quarter Moon. She is closely related to two of the others, Moonless Night, who won four races on the Flat (and two over jumps) in Japan, successful at up to twelve and a half furlongs on the Flat (including on dirt), and the two-year-old mile winner Dance With Another, who were by Danehill and Danehill Dancer respectively, Danehill being the sire of Diamondsandrubies' and How High The Moon's champion Australian sire Fastnet Rock (about whom there is more in the essays on Fascinating Rock and Qualify). Being covered by a son of Danehill also brought success to two of Quarter Moon's sisters, All My Loving (who was placed in the Oaks and Irish Oaks) and Hold Me Love Me, who both produced 'black type' winners to Dansili (Hardwicke winner

Thomas Chippendale and Godolphin Stakes winner Renew respectively, the latter subsequently a listed winner in Australia). Quarter Moon's other winners include Born To Be King (by Storm Cat), a useful miler, and King of Westphalia (by Kingmambo), useful at up to a mile and a quarter, both of whom acted on occasions as pacemaker for some of their better Ballydoyle contemporaries. The aforementioned You'll Be Mine, a sister to King of Westphalia, looked to have plenty of potential when coming third in the Fillies' Mile as a two-year-old after just two starts in maidens, but she didn't go on at three, running her best race when sixth in the Pride Stakes over a mile and a half at Newmarket. You'll Be Mine's first foal is the fairly useful three-year-old sprinter As Good As Gold and she is set to be represented by a Frankel colt in the next season who made 150,000 guineas as a yearling at Newmarket in October. Premier Bloodstock were also in action at Newmarket, paying 2,100,000 guineas for a Dubawi yearling filly out of Loveisallyouneed, an unraced sister to Quarter Moon and Yesterday whom the operation had sold just before Jude died. Another of Quarter Moon's daughters, the Duke of Marmalade filly Half Moon who showed only modest form in maidens, was sold for 675,000 guineas, in foal to Frankel, at the 2014 December Sales. Diamondsandrubies stayed a mile and a half and acted on soft and good to firm going. She flashed her tail under pressure at Navan and was mulish at the stalls before the Prix de l'Opera on her final outing, but that shouldn't be held against her, given how gamely she responded after suffering interference in the Oaks (she was also hit in the face by a rival's whip just as she was beginning her winning effort in the Cheshire Oaks). *Aidan O'Brien, Ireland*

DIAMONDSARETRUMPS (IRE) 2 b.f. (Feb 5) Dick Turpin (IRE) 127 – Serial **53**
Sinner (IRE) 65 (High Chaparral (IRE) 132) [2015 p7g p8f p7g⁶ Dec 20] €8,000F,
£25,000Y: sturdy filly: first foal: dam, maiden (stayed 8.3f), half-sister to useful 2-y-o 5f/6f
winner Palanca: modest maiden: best effort when sixth in maiden at Lingfield (5¾ lengths
behind Foxinthehenhouse) in December. *Charles Hills*

DIAMONDSINTHESKY (IRE) 4 b.f. Dandy Man (IRE) 123 – Colourpoint (USA) 81 **57**
(Forest Wildcat (USA) 120) [2015 58: f5s² f5d⁴ t6f⁵ t5.1f³ p5m⁴ 5m p5g⁶ 5.1d t5.1g
Aug 27] modest maiden: stays 6f: acts on all-weather and good to firm going: often wears
visor. *Derek Shaw*

DIAMONDS POUR MOI 2 b.f. (Apr 2) Pour Moi (IRE) 125 – Diamond Light (USA) **79 p**
70 (Fantastic Light (USA) 134) [2015 p8d* Nov 30] half-sister to several winners, including
useful 2-y-o 1m winner Double Diamond (by Muhtathir) and 7f winner Mac's Superstar
(by Elusive City): dam 1¼m winner: 12/1, won maiden at Kempton (by length from
Mytimehascome) in November, well positioned all the way: will improve. *Ralph Beckett*

DIAMOND VINE (IRE) 7 b.g. Diamond Green (FR) 121 – Glasnas Giant 60 (Giant's **57 §**
Causeway (USA) 132) [2015 55: t6g t6f* t6f⁶ p6f⁴ t6g⁴ t6g² 6m⁵ 5.1m³ 5.1m t6g 6d 5.1m
5.1g⁵ 5.7f t6m⁴ 6s⁴ p6g⁴ p6f Dec 17] good-topped gelding: modest handicapper: won at
Wolverhampton (apprentice) in February: stays 6f: acts on polytrack, tapeta, soft and good
to firm going: usually wears headgear: often races towards rear: one to treat with caution.
Ronald Harris

DIATOMIC (IRE) 3 b.g. Bushranger (IRE) 119 – Glidled Truffle (IRE) 69 (Peintre **63**
Celebre (USA) 137) [2015 64: 10.2s 9.9g⁴ 9.2d³ 7.2d 6m⁵ 5.7m² 6m² 6g² 5s² 5m 5.9s* 6g⁶
6g Oct 20] modest handicapper: won at Carlisle in September: stays 6f: acts on soft and
good to firm going: often in headgear in 2015. *Tom Dascombe*

DICK DOUGHTYWYLIE 7 b.g. Oasis Dream 129 – Sugar Mill (FR) 104 (Polar Falcon **109**
(USA) 126) [2015 112: 10.4d⁵ Aug 19] good-topped gelding: one-time smart performer:
first outing for 14 months, acted as pacemaker—virtually ignored by rest of field—when
5¼ lengths fifth to Arabian Queen in Juddmonte International at York sole outing in 2015:
stays 10.5f: acts on polytrack, good to firm and good to soft going: tried in tongue tie.
John Gosden

DICK WHITTINGTON (IRE) 3 b.c. Rip Van Winkle (IRE) 134 – Sahara Sky (IRE) **96 +**
(Danehill (USA) 126) [2015 109: 7m⁴ Apr 18] well-made colt: useful performer: better
than result when 8 lengths fourth to Muhaarar in Greenham Stakes at Newbury sole outing
in 2015, having plenty to do (dropped out): should stay 7f: acts on good to firm and good
to soft going: tried in hood prior to 2015. *Aidan O'Brien, Ireland*

DIDDY ERIC 5 b.g. Oratorio (IRE) 128 – Amber Queen (IRE) 92 (Cadeaux Genereux **59**
131) [2015 10.1d 10d 11.1s² 9.2s³ 10s² 9.2g 11.5s 12d 10s Oct 16] modest handicapper:
stays 1½m: acts on soft and good to firm going: often wears blinkers: usually races nearer
last than first. *Micky Hammond*

DIESCENTRIC (USA) 8 b.g. Diesis 133 – Hawzah (Green Desert (USA) 127) [2015 –: **105**
t8.6m² 7s⁶ 7g May 30] big, strong gelding: useful performer: second in minor event at
Wolverhampton (length behind Graphic) in February: stays 1¼m: acts on polytrack, tapeta,
good to firm and good to soft going. *Julie Camacho*

DIFFERENT SCENARIO 4 b.f. Araafa (IRE) 128 – Racina 103 (Bluebird (USA) 125) **63**
[2015 54: t12.2f² f12g* f12d² f12g⁴ 12.1f⁵ 14g 12.1m² 12.4g t13.9f⁴ f14g⁴ Dec 12]
modest handicapper: won at Southwell in January: stays 1¾m: acts on fibresand, tapeta and
firm going: front runner/races prominently. *Antony Brittain*

DIGEANTA (IRE) 8 b.g. Helissio (FR) 136 – Scolboa Gold (IRE) (Accordion) [2015 **102**
15g⁴ 20f 16d* 14d 16g⁴ 15s Oct 25] rather leggy gelding: useful handicapper: won at the
Curragh in July and October (by ¾ length from Guard of Honour): stays 17f: acts on good
to firm and good to soft going: tried in cheekpieces prior to 2015: usually wears tongue tie.
W. P. Mullins, Ireland

DIGI (IRE) 2 b.f. (Mar 6) Baltic King 120 – Lorena (IRE) (Bishop of Cashel 122) [2015 **51**
6.1m⁴ 5g⁴ 7m 7.1f 8.3s Oct 13] €5,500Y: second foal: dam unraced half-sister to useful
winner up to 7f Queenfisher: modest maiden: stays 6f: acts on good to firm going. *David
Evans*

DIKTA DEL MAR (SPA) 3 b.f. Diktat 126 – Marmaria (SPA) (Limpid 119) [2015 5s⁴ **97**
5m³ 5m⁶ 5m⁵ 5m 5d³ 5g⁵ 5d Sep 13] useful performer: third in listed race at Ayr (2 lengths
behind Katawi) in June: should stay 6f: acts on soft and good to firm going: often in tongue
tie in 2015. *T. Hogan, Ireland*

DILETTATOMMASA (IRE) 5 ch.m. Dylan Thomas (IRE) 132 – Chronicle (Observatory **72**
(USA) 131) [2015 78: t9.5g 10m p10m³ p10g 10m⁵ t9.5g⁶ p10f³ t9.5m³ p10f⁵ t9.5f² p10f⁵
p8g⁶ p8g² Dec 30] fair handicapper: stays 1¼m: acts on polytrack, tapeta and good to firm
going: often wears cheekpieces: tried in tongue tie prior to 2015: often races towards rear.
Daniel Loughnane

DILGURA 5 b.m. Ishiguru (USA) 114 – Dilys 84 (Efisio 120) [2015 f6d⁵ p5g p6g³ Dec 28] **82**
fairly useful handicapper: third at Lingfield in December: stays 6f: acts on polytrack,
fibresand, best turf form on good going. *Stuart Kittow*

DIMINUTIVE (IRE) 3 ch.f. Fast Company (IRE) 126 – Take It Easee (IRE) 89 (Noverre **56**
(USA) 125) [2015 60: t6f⁶ p7f p6f⁶ p5m² 5.1m 6d³ t6g 5d³ 5.1d² 5v² 5s³ p6g⁴ Oct 20] neat
filly: modest handicapper: stays 6f: acts on polytrack, fibresand, good to firm and good to
soft going: often wears headgear: sometimes slowly away. *Grace Harris*

DIMITAR (USA) 6 b.g. Mizzen Mast (USA) 121 – Peace And Love (IRE) 75 (Fantastic **50**
Light (USA) 134) [2015 75: t9.5f t7.1g t7.1g f8d⁴ p8g p7m Jun 1] modest handicapper:
stayed 8.5f: acted on polytrack, tapeta and good to firm going: tried in headgear: dead.
Johnny Farrelly

DINARIA (IRE) 3 b.f. Holy Roman Emperor (IRE) 125 – Logica (IRE) 81 (Priolo (USA) **82**
127) [2015 8.3g³ 8m² 8.3d² 8d² p10g³ Oct 29] compact filly: fairly useful maiden: third in
handicap at Lingfield in October: best effort at 1¼m: acts on polytrack: usually wears
headgear: sometimes slowly away (refused to race only outing in France at 2 yrs).
K. R. Burke

DING DING 4 ch.f. Winker Watson 118 – Five Bells (IRE) (Rock of Gibraltar (IRE) 133) **–**
[2015 p8g Jan 7] small, angular filly: modest at best, no form in 2015: stays 11f: acts on
soft and good to firm going. *Mick Channon*

DINKUM DIAMOND (IRE) 7 b.h. Aussie Rules (USA) 123 – Moving Diamonds 70 **113**
(Lomitas 129) [2015 113: 6d⁵ 6f⁵ 6m³ 6f 6m⁴ 6g⁶ 6g 7s* 7d⁵ Oct 24] leggy horse: smart
handicapper: won at Leicester (by 1¾ lengths from Hillbilly Boy) in October: stays 7f: acts
on soft and good to firm going. *Henry Candy*

DINNERATMIDNIGHT 4 b.g. Kyllachy 129 – The Terrier 76 (Foxhound (USA) 103) **80**
[2015 93: p6m p6g⁴ May 27] fairly useful handicapper: stays 6f: acts on polytrack: in
blinkers latest start in 2015: often races towards rear. *Ralph Beckett*

DIPLOMA 2 b.f. (Apr 26) Dubawi (IRE) 129 – Enticement 102 (Montjeu (IRE) 137) **90**
[2015 7g 7g* 7g Oct 9] well-made filly: third foal: half-sister to useful 1m winner Pick
Your Choice (by Elusive Quality): dam, winner up to 1¼m (2-y-o 1m/8.3f winner), half-

sister to smart winner up to 7f Surfrider: fairly useful performer: best effort when winning maiden at Newmarket (by neck from Doubly Motivated) in August, always holding on: will stay 1m. *Sir Michael Stoute*

DIPLOMATIC (IRE) 10 b.g. Cape Cross (IRE) 129 – Embassy 114 (Cadeaux Genereux 131) [2015 85: p8g Apr 27] fairly useful at best, no form in 2015: stays 1m: acts on polytrack: often wears headgear: usually races in rear. *Michael Squance* –

DIPPINGANDDIVING (IRE) 3 ch.f. Captain Rio 122 – Arabis 88 (Arazi (USA) 135) [2015 44: p5g⁵ t6g 8f 6d⁵ 6m⁶ 7m³ 7d* 7.4d⁶ 8v³ 8g 7d³ 8m³ 7s³ Oct 12] small filly: modest performer: won seller at Leicester in July: stays 1m: acts on soft and good to firm going: tried in headgear in 2015: front runner/races prominently: sold 1,800 gns, sent to Greece. *Jose Santos* **62**

DIRECT APPROACH (IRE) 11 b.g. Tel Quel (FR) 125 – Miss Telimar (IRE) (Montelimar (USA) 122) [2015 t16.5f⁶ t16.5g Mar 24] maiden: no form in 2015: seemingly stays 1½m. *Lynn Siddall* –

DIRECTOR (IRE) 3 b.g. Danehill Dancer (IRE) 117 – Toolentidhaar (USA) 78 (Swain (IRE) 134) [2015 –p: p7g⁶ 7.5g⁶ p10g⁶ 10.2m Jul 4] fair maiden: stays 1¼m: acts on polytrack: in cheekpieces final outing: sold 11,000 gns, sent to USA. *William Haggas* **65**

DIRECTORSHIP 9 br.g. Diktat 126 – Away To Me (Exit To Nowhere (USA) 122) [2015 95: 8f* 8.1m⁵ 8.3g² 8m* 8m 8g Sep 19] well-made gelding: useful handicapper: won at Ascot (apprentice) in April and Newmarket (by length from Ifwecan) in July: second at Windsor (¾ length behind Secret Art) in June: stays 8.5f: acts on polytrack, firm and soft going. *Patrick Chamings* **100**

DIRECT TIMES (IRE) 4 b.g. Acclamation 118 – Elegant Times (IRE) 68 (Dansili 127) [2015 66p: 6m* 6g² 6g⁴ 6m⁵ Aug 1] useful handicapper: won at Newmarket in May (apprentice) and June (by 1¼ lengths from Syrian Pearl): raced only at 6f: acts on good to firm and heavy going: usually races prominently, strong traveller. *Peter Chapple-Hyam* **105**

DISAVOW 3 b.f. Shamardal (USA) 129 – Dunnes River (USA) 84 (Danzig (USA)) [2015 79: p7g p8f Dec 21] fair at best, no form in 2015: stays 7f: acts on good to firm and good to soft going: usually races close up. *Mark Johnston* –

DISCLOSURE 4 b.g. Indesatchel (IRE) 120 – Gemini Gold (IRE) 97 (King's Best (USA) 132) [2015 80: t9.5g⁴ t8.6m t9.5m⁴ t8.6g* 8s⁴ 7g⁶ 7.5m 8m 5g⁶ 6m* 6m 6m 5g t6f Oct 9] fair handicapper: won at Wolverhampton in March and Doncaster in July: stays 9.5f: acts on tapeta and good to firm going: usually wears headgear: often starts slowly/races in rear. *Les Eyre* **75**

DISCO DALE (IRE) 4 gr.g. Verglas (IRE) 118 – Artisia (IRE) (Peintre Celebre (USA) 137) [2015 –: t12.2f⁶ Jan 5] maiden: no form in 2015. *Richard Fahey* –

DISCO DAVE (IRE) 7 ch.g. Dalakhani (IRE) 133 – Amoureux (USA) (Deputy Minister (CAN)) [2015 69: t8.6g⁶ Jun 4] modest handicapper: will prove best up to 1½m: acts on polytrack: tried in tongue tie prior to 2015: often travels strongly. *Daniel Loughnane* **50**

DISC PLAY 3 b.f. Showcasing 117 – Gitane (FR) (Grand Lodge (USA) 125) [2015 8.3m May 4] 2,000F: half-sister to 3 winners, including winner up to 1¼m Mega Back (by Zamindar) and 6f/7f winner Pool House (by Sakhee's Secret), both useful: dam 11f winner: 50/1 and blinkered, very green when well held in maiden at Windsor. *John Bridger* –

DISCREET HERO (IRE) 2 ch.c. (Apr 12) Siyouni (FR) 122 – Alfaguara (USA) (Red Ransom (USA)) [2015 5.1m⁴ 6.1m⁵ 7m⁶ 6v⁵ p5f* Sep 22] €20,000Y, £90,000 2-y-o: closely related to winner up to 1¼m Rouing (2-y-o 9f winner, by Pivotal) and half-brother to several winners, including useful winner up to 11.3f Ard Na Greine (2-y-o 1m winner, by Galileo): dam 1m winner: fairly useful performer: won nursery at Lingfield in September: left Alan McCabe after third start: stays 6f: acts on polytrack: often in tongue tie: often races prominently: likely to progress further. *Simon Crisford* **90 p**

DISCUSSIONTOFOLLOW (IRE) 5 b.g. Elusive City (USA) 117 – Tranquil Sky 91 (Intikhab (USA) 135) [2015 107: 6m⁶ 5m² 5f⁵ 6m Aug 1] lengthy gelding: useful handicapper: second at the Curragh (2¼ lengths behind Foxy Forever) in June: stays 6.5f: acts on polytrack and firm going. *Mike Murphy* **105**

DISEGNO (IRE) 3 b.g. Fastnet Rock (AUS) 127 – Seven Magicians (USA) 106 (Silver Hawk (USA) 123) [2015 100: 9m³ 10.3v² 10f⁴ 12g³ Jul 29] good-topped gelding: smart performer: in frame in listed race at Newmarket (2 lengths third to Golden Horn) in April, Dee Stakes at Chester (short-head second to Not So Sleepy) in May, Tercentenary Stakes at Royal Ascot (7½ lengths fourth to Time Test) in June and Gordon Stakes at Goodwood (6½ lengths third to Highland Reel) in July: barely stays 1¼m: acts on polytrack and any turf going: often in visor in 2015. *Sir Michael Stoute* **111**

DI'S GIFT 6 b.g. Generous (IRE) 139 – Di's Dilemma (Teenoso (USA) 135) [2015 10.4g^6 **77**
12g^6 17.2d^2 17.1m^2 15.8d* 13.8d^4 17.1d^5 12s^3 14.1s Oct 16] fair handicapper: won at
Catterick in August: stays 17f: acts on soft and good to firm going: wears hood: sometimes
slowly away, usually races nearer last than first. *Richard Guest*

DISHY GURU 6 ch.g. Ishiguru (USA) 114 – Pick A Nice Name 85 (Polar Falcon (USA) **79 §**
126) [2015 79: p5f^2 p5g p6g p5f^5 5m* 5m 5m^4 6g 5.7f 5g p6f^6 Nov 25] plain,
sturdy gelding: fair handicapper: won at Leicester in May: stays 7f: acts on polytrack, good
to firm and heavy going: often wears headgear: starts slowly, races well off pace: best
treated with caution (often loses all chance at start). *Michael Blanshard*

DISMANTLE (IRE) 2 b.f. (Mar 19) Invincible Spirit (IRE) 121 – Dismay (Dubawi **74**
(IRE) 129) [2015 5m 7v^3 t6m^2 p6g^3 5d^5 p5g Dec 7] good-topped filly: first foal: dam
maiden half-sister to very smart 1¼m-12.5f winner Poet Laureate: fair maiden: stays 7f:
acts on polytrack, tapeta and heavy going: tried in blinkers. *Charlie Appleby*

DISOBEDIENCE (USA) 2 b.g. (Jan 28) Street Cry (IRE) 130 – Rosa Parks 103 (Sadler's **82 p**
Wells (USA) 132) [2015 p8g t8.6m* Dec 30] seventh foal: half-brother to 3 winners,
including useful 6f/7f winner Swooning (by Raven's Pass) and 12.5f winner Emancipation
(by Kingmambo): dam, 10.6f winner, sister to very smart winner up to 1¼m Mikado: better
effort when winning maiden at Wolverhampton (by ½ length from King of Dreams) in
December, suited by emphasis on stamina: likely to stay 9f+: will go on improving. *Charlie
Appleby*

DISSENT (IRE) 6 b.g. Dansili 127 – Centifolia (FR) 112 (Kendor (FR) 122) [2015 87: **74**
t6f^5 p6f^5 p6f Nov 19] fair performer: stays 7f: acts on polytrack, tapeta and good to firm
going: often wears headgear: front runner. *James Given*

DISSERTATION 3 b.f. Champs Elysees 124 – Reel Style (Rainbow Quest (USA) 134) **61**
[2015 p9.4g 11.9g p12g^6 p13.3f^6 11.6g p11g t12.2g^5 p15.8g^4 Dec 20] fifth foal: closely
related to 1m winner Official Style (by Dansili) and half-sister to winners in Greece by Rail
Link and Oasis Dream: dam 9f winner: modest maiden: left Mme C. Head-Maarek after
second start: stays 2m: acts on polytrack: tried in headgear. *Julia Feilden*

DISSOLUTION 3 b.c. New Approach (IRE) 132 – Portodora (USA) 92 (Kingmambo **99**
(USA) 125) [2015 84: 10g* 10m^2 12f 10m^6 12g Sep 5] unfurnished colt: useful handicapper:
won at Newmarket in April: second at Newbury (1¼ lengths behind Time Test) in May:
stays 1½m: acts on firm going: sometimes wears visor: sold 60,000 gns, sent to Saudi
Arabia. *Sir Michael Stoute*

DISTAIN 3 b.f. Champs Elysees 124 – Market Forces 107 (Lomitas 129) [2015 10s^2 10g* **92**
13.4m^2 10.4g^2 12g^3 10s^5 Oct 23] good-topped filly: fourth foal: half-sister to 1¼m winner
Fast Pace (by Observatory) and 1½m winner Limousine (by Beat Hollow): dam, 1½m-15f
winner, half-sister to smart 2-y-o 7f winner (stayed 1¼m) Protectress: fairly useful
performer: won maiden at Redcar in May: second in handicap at York in September:
effective at 1¼m to 13.5f: acts on soft and good to firm going: tried in cheekpieces: sold
68,000 gns, sent to Germany. *Lady Cecil*

DISTANT HIGH 4 b.f. High Chaparral (IRE) 132 – Distant Dreamer (USA) (Rahy (USA) **69**
115) [2015 68: 10.2m 11d 12.2g 11.6m 12.1m^2 10.2m* 12.1g^2 12d 10.2v* 10g 10.2s^3 9.9v
11.7g Oct 18] fair handicapper: won at Chepstow in July and August: stays 1¼m: acts on
good to firm and heavy going: often wears headgear. *Richard Price*

DISTANT PAST 4 b.g. Pastoral Pursuits 127 – Faraway Lass 94 (Distant Relative 128) **99**
[2015 81: 5v* 5m* 6g^5 5m* 5m^4 5d^2 5.4g 5d^6 5.6d 5d^6 Sep 26] compact gelding: useful
handicapper: won at Musselburgh and Doncaster in April, and Musselburgh (apprentice, by
1¾ lengths from Master Bond) in June: second at Ascot (¾ length behind Midlander) in
July: stays 6f, all wins at 5f: acts on polytrack, good to firm and heavy going: tried in
cheekpieces in 2015. *Kevin Ryan*

DISTANT SHADOW 4 gr.f. Rock of Gibraltar (IRE) 133 – Daheeya 76 (Daylami (IRE) **50**
138) [2015 –: t7.1f^4 p8f^6 t7.1f^6 6g 7g Jun 16] rather leggy filly: modest maiden: stays 1m:
acts on polytrack and tapeta: usually travels strongly: weak finisher: sent to Belgium.
Michael Wigham

DISTRICT ATTORNEY (IRE) 6 b.g. Lawman (FR) 121 – Mood Indigo (IRE) 91 **50**
(Indian Ridge 123) [2015 60: 16.1d 14.1m 14.4g^5 Aug 6] strong gelding: modest maiden:
stays 14.5f: acts on good to firm going: tried in headgear prior to 2015. *Chris Fairhurst*

DISTRICT TWELVE (FR) 3 b.f. Aqlaam 125 – Zanna (FR) (Soviet Star (USA) 128) **–**
[2015 6.1v^4 7.1m 7.1f t5.1m Dec 18] €17,000 2-y-o: fifth foal: half-sister to 1m winner
Catch The Cider (by Medicean): dam, maiden (placed up to 7f), half-sister to dam of Poule
d'Essai des Pouliches winner Zalaiyka: no form: tried in tongue tie. *Tony Carroll*

DISUSHE STAR 3 ch.g. Kheleyf (USA) 116 – Canis Star (Wolfhound (USA) 126) [2015 –
–: 6g 5g 6d Jun 4] maiden: no form in 2015: tried in blinkers in 2015. *Keith Dalgleish*

DIVASESQUE (IRE) 2 ch.f. (Mar 29) Poet's Voice 126 – Lily Again 95 (American Post –
121) [2015 p6g 6g p5g⁵ p5f p7f Nov 12] 50,000Y: first foal: dam 2-y-o 6f-7f winner: no
form. *Derek Shaw*

DIVERTIDO (USA) 2 ch.c. (Mar 11) Eskendereya (USA) 126 – La Capella (USA) –
(Smart Strike (CAN) 121) [2015 7m Aug 14] well-made colt: 20/1 and in hood, very green
when well held in maiden at Newmarket. *John Gosden*

DIVERTIMENTI (IRE) 11 b.g. Green Desert (USA) 127 – Ballet Shoes (IRE) 75 (Ela- **56**
Mana-Mou 132) [2015 60: f5d⁴ f5d³ 6g⁴ 5g⁵ 6.1m 6m 6m⁴ 6.1m* t6m 5.1d³ f5m f6g⁵
Dec 22] sturdy gelding: modest handicapper: won at Nottingham in August: stays 7f: acts
on polytrack, fibresand, firm and soft going: usually wears headgear: tried in tongue tie.
Roy Bowring

DIVINE CALL 8 b.g. Pivotal 124 – Pious 74 (Bishop of Cashel 122) [2015 74: t6g p6m⁵ **77**
t6f t7.1m² t6g² p7f 6.1s⁴ 6g* 5.7m 6.1m 6.1m 6m 6m t6g⁶ 6.1m 6s* 5.7g⁶ 6g⁵ Oct 20] **a65**
well-made gelding: fair handicapper: won at Goodwood in May and September: stays 7f:
acts on all-weather, good to firm and heavy going: sometimes wears headgear: tried in
tongue tie prior to 2015: usually races nearer last than first. *Milton Bradley*

DIVINE (IRE) 4 b.f. Dark Angel (IRE) 113 – Carallia (IRE) 101 (Common Grounds 118) **108**
[2015 97: 6m* 6m⁴ 6f 6m⁶ 6m³ 6m* 6g⁴ 5m 6g³ Oct 10] good-topped filly: useful
performer: won handicap at Windsor (by 3¾ lengths from Panther Patrol) in April and
listed race at Pontefract (by neck from Online Alexander) in August: third in Hackwood
Stakes at Newbury (1¼ lengths behind Strath Burn) in July: stays 6f: acts on polytrack,
good to firm and good to soft going. *Mick Channon*

DIVINE JOY 2 b.f. (Mar 3) Rip Van Winkle (IRE) 134 – Joyeaux 78 (Mark of Esteem –
(IRE) 137) [2015 p8d Nov 30] 28,000Y: first foal: dam, 5f/6f winner, half-sister to smart
7.5f-1¼m winner Aoife Alainn: 40/1, shaped as if needed experience when eighth in
maiden at Kempton (8 lengths behind Diamonds Pour Moi) in November, left poorly
placed. *Marco Botti*

DIVINE LAW 3 ch.c. Major Cadeaux 121 – Yanomami (USA) 71 (Slew O' Gold (USA)) **87**
[2015 76: 8.3s⁴ 9.9m 8.3f* 8.3m* 8.3m* 8.3g² 8.3m⁵ 8.1g 8.3d Oct 5] sturdy colt: fairly
useful handicapper: won at Windsor in May (2) and June: stays 8.5f: acts on firm going:
front runner/races prominently: sold 15,000 gns, sent to Bahrain. *Richard Hannon*

DIVINE RULE (IRE) 7 br.g. Cacique (IRE) 124 – Island Destiny 79 (Kris 135) [2015 **56**
66: p7g⁶ p7f⁴ p7g⁶ p10m⁴ Mar 5] workmanlike gelding: modest handicapper: stays 1¼m:
acts on polytrack, tapeta and good to soft going: usually wears headgear: tried in tongue tie
prior to 2015. *Laura Mongan*

DIVINE TOUCH 2 b.f. (Feb 26) Kheleyf (USA) 116 – Easy To Love (USA) 86 (Diesis – p
133) [2015 6m 7m p7g Sep 21] 5,000F, 10,000Y: closely related to 2-y-o 7f winner Pezula
Bay (by Oasis Dream) and half-sister to 3 winners, including 7f-1m (including at 2 yrs)
winner Easy Lover (by Pivotal) and 1½m-13f winner Right of Appeal (by Dubawi): dam
11.5f winner: little impact in maidens: should do better in handicaps. *Robert Eddery*

DIVISIONIST 2 b.c. (Jan 23) Oasis Dream 129 – Exemplify (Dansili 127) [2015 7s Aug –
14] 20/1, very green when well held in maiden at Newbury. *Sir Michael Stoute*

DIZOARD 5 b.m. Desideratum 118 – Riviere (Meadowbrook 83) [2015 12m 10g 10d³ **57**
10.1m 14.1m⁵ Aug 8] modest maiden: best effort at 1¼m: acts on good to soft going: often
in hood: often races towards rear. *Ollie Pears*

DIZZEY HEIGHTS (IRE) 3 b.f. Halling (USA) 133 – Extreme Pleasure (IRE) 72 **80**
(High Chaparral (IRE) 132) [2015 54: 9.9s² 12m⁴ 14g 10.2d⁴ 10v² Sep 16] fairly useful
maiden: will prove best at 1½m+: acts on heavy going. *Stuart Kittow*

DNANEER (IRE) 2 b.f. (Feb 14) Invincible Spirit (IRE) 121 – Lulua (USA) (Bahri (USA) **52**
125) [2015 6d⁶ 6d⁶ Sep 25] 50,000F, 28,000Y, 75,000 2-y-o: sister to 1m winner Estifzaaz
and 5f winner My Inspiration and half-sister to 6.7f-1m winner Samba School (by Sahm):
dam, 5.5f winner, half-sister to useful 2-y-o 6f winner (stayed 1m) Shuhrah: better effort
when sixth in maiden at Haydock (7¾ lengths behind Silken Skies) in September. *Kevin
Ryan*

D'NIRO (IRE) 2 br.c. (Mar 5) Big Bad Bob (IRE) 118 – Causeway Charm (USA) 60 **85 p**
(Giant's Causeway (USA) 132) [2015 7d⁵ p8g* Nov 12] €75,000Y: fourth foal: half-
brother to useful 2-y-o 6f/7f winner (stays 1½m) Lily Rules (by Aussie Rules): dam,
maiden (stayed 1m), half-sister to useful winner up to 1m Chan Chan: better effort when
winning maiden at Kempton (by 2¾ lengths from Imperial Aviator) in November, finding
extra: will go on improving. *Harry Dunlop*

DOCALI (IRE) 3 b.g. Dark Angel (IRE) 113 – Housekeeping (Dansili 127) [2015 8d⁶ 8d **70** 8g⁵ 10g 7g⁶ 8g 8g⁶ Sep 4] fair maiden: left G. M. Lyons after fourth start: stays 1m: acts on good to soft going: tried in cheekpieces: tried in tongue tie. *Ian Semple*

DOC CHARM 3 b.g. Hellvelyn 118 – Songsheet 74 (Dominion 123) [2015 81: t6m 6s⁴ **92** 7m 6g² 6d² 6g⁴ 5.1v* 5d 5s⁶ Oct 19] fairly useful handicapper: won at Chepstow (by 6 lengths from Bonjour Steve) in August: stays 6f: best form on heavy going: usually in headgear in 2015: front runner/races prominently: sold 9,000 gns, sent to Italy. *K. R. Burke*

DOC HAY (USA) 8 b.g. Elusive Quality (USA) – Coherent (USA) (Danzig (USA)) [2015 **65 §** a98§: p6m 6m 6g⁵ May 18] strong gelding: fair handicapper: stays 7.5f: acts on polytrack, good to firm and heavy going: tried in headgear: tried in tongue tie prior to 2015: often starts slowly: has hung right: best treated with caution. *Lee Carter*

DOCS LEGACY (IRE) 6 b.g. Ad Valorem (USA) 125 – Lunamixa (GER) (Linamix **95** (FR) 127) [2015 98: p10g³ 8g⁴ 8.5f³ 8f a8f⁵ 8.5f⁶ t8.5f* 8.5f* t8.5f* 8.5f* t8.5f⁵ Dec 26] close-coupled gelding: useful performer: left Richard Fahey 14,000 gns after first start: won claimers at Golden Gate Fields in September, October and November (2): stays 10.5f: acts on polytrack/tapeta, and any turf going. *Manuel Badilla, USA*

DOCTOR BONG 3 b.g. Sleeping Indian 122 – Vax Rapide 80 (Sharpo 132) [2015 7.1m² **78** 7.6m* 7.1m⁴ 7.1v² 7s⁶ p7g⁵ p8g Nov 9] tall, angular gelding: fair performer: won maiden at Chester in June: stays 7.5f: acts on good to firm going: tried in cheekpieces. *Andrew Balding*

DOCTOR HILARY 13 b.g. Mujahid (USA) 125 – Agony Aunt 81 (Formidable (USA) **46** 125) [2015 58: p6f p6m f6g³ f6g⁵ Apr 9] strong gelding: poor handicapper: stays 7f: acts on polytrack, fibresand, dirt, soft and good to firm going: usually wears headgear: tried in tongue tie prior to 2015. *Mark Hoad*

DOCTOR KEHOE 3 b.g. Cockney Rebel (IRE) 127 – Ogre (USA) 84 (Tale of The Cat **69** (USA) 113) [2015 68: t6g p6d 7s 9.9g⁶ 10.2m⁴ 11.7g* 12.1d⁴ 12d⁵ t12.2m² 13.1f³ 13.9m* t13.9f⁴ p13.3f⁵ Oct 24] fair handicapper: won at Bath in July and Wolverhampton in October: stays 1¾m: acts on tapeta, firm and good to soft going: often in headgear in 2015: tried in tongue tie in 2015. *David Evans*

DOCTOR PARKES 9 b.g. Diktat 126 – Lucky Parkes 108 (Full Extent (USA) 113) **82** [2015 93: p5g⁴ p5g³ p5g* p5m p5g² p5g⁵ 5g⁵ 5m 5m p6g 6m p6f 5.2m⁴ t5.1f² p5m⁶ p5g⁴ **a92** p5g² t5.1f⁴ Dec 22] strong gelding: fairly useful handicapper: won at Lingfield (by ¾ length from Come On Dave) in February: second at Chelmsford in March and December: stays 6f: acts on polytrack, tapeta and good to firm going: tried in eyeshields prior to 2015: often races towards rear. *Stuart Williams*

DOCTOR SARDONICUS 4 ch.g. Medicean 128 – Never A Doubt 107 (Night Shift **98** (USA)) [2015 88: p6g* p6g³ p6f³ p5m* Sep 26] useful handicapper: won at Chelmsford in May and September (by 1¼ lengths from Secret Missile): stays 7f: acts on polytrack: usually leads. *David Simcock*

DOCTOR SERENA (USA) 2 ch.f. (Mar 28) Cape Blanco (IRE) 130 – Seek Easy (USA) **68 p** (Seeking The Gold (USA)) [2015 p8m⁶ p8d Nov 30] $150,000: half-sister to several winners, including useful 2-y-o 1m winner Dancing David (by Danehill Dancer) and useful 6f-1½m winner Ordination (by Fantastic Light): dam unraced: better effort when sixth in maiden at Lingfield (3 lengths behind Danilovna) in November, unsuited by emphasis on speed: should do better. *John Gosden*

DOCTORS PAPERS 3 ch.g. Stimulation (IRE) 121 – Inya Lake 101 (Whittingham **–** (IRE) 104) [2015 –: 7m Jun 16] maiden: no form in 2015: in visor sole start in 2015. *David Brown*

DOCTOR WATSON 3 ch.g. Winker Watson 118 – Cibenze 74 (Owington 123) [2015 –: **–** 6d 10d Sep 17] maiden: no form in 2015. *Tom Tate*

DODGY BOB 2 b.g. (Apr 21) Royal Applause 124 – Rustam (Dansili 127) [2015 5m³ 6g* **87** 6.1m² 6g⁵ 6g⁴ 6g Sep 18] 21,000Y: second foal: half-brother to 5f winner Foxtrot Knight (by Kyllachy): dam, 1m winner, half-sister to smart winner up to 9f Cornelius: fairly useful performer: won maiden at Ripon (by 1½ lengths from Sahreej) in May: second in minor event at Chepstow in June: should prove as effective at 5f as 6f: acts on good to firm going: tried in cheekpieces: usually leads. *Kevin Ryan*

DOEADEER (IRE) 2 b.f. (Apr 26) Dandy Man (IRE) 123 – Bloomsday Babe (USA) **72 p** (Cherokee Run (USA) 122) [2015 6m² Aug 20] €30,000 2-y-o: first foal: dam, of little account, half-sister to useful 2-y-o 6f winner Steaming Home: 7/1, shaped with promise when second in maiden at Hamilton (1½ lengths behind Al Shahaniya) in August: will prove as effective at 5f: better to come. *Keith Dalgleish*

DOLLAR REWARD 2 b.c. (Apr 11) Shamardal (USA) 129 – Cape Dollar (IRE) 107 **87 p**
(Cape Cross (IRE) 129) [2015 7d⁶ 7g⁴ t7.1m* Sep 25] first foal: dam 2-y-o 7f winner: fairly
useful form: best effort when winning maiden at Wolverhampton (by 1¼ lengths from
Nokhada) in September: raced only at 7f: will go on improving. *Sir Michael Stoute*

DOLNIYA (FR) 4 b.f. Azamour (IRE) 130 – Daltama (IRE) (Indian Ridge 123) **123**
[2015 121: p9.4g* 12g* 12m² 11.9m³ 11.9s⁴ 11.9m Oct 4]
Dubai World Cup night provided its usual colourful celebration of
international competition. The big prizes were spread around, with the winners
coming from six different countries, the United States, South Africa, Britain, Ireland,
France and the home nation the United Arab Emirates (which pulled off the night's
biggest surprise when Prince Bishop beat the Kentucky Derby winner California
Chrome in the World Cup itself). France had the winners of both major turf races,
Dolniya in the Dubai Sheema Classic and Solow in the Dubai Turf (formerly the
Dubai Duty Free), and both represented long-standing owner-breeders whose
bloodstock empires have been synonymous with French racing for generations.
Solow carried the famous Wertheimer colours, which were first registered in 1911
by Pierre Wertheimer, the grandfather of Gerard and Alain who race the Wertheimer
horses under the banner of Wertheimer et Frere nowadays, while Dolniya carried
the green, red epaulets of the Aga Khan who still retains his family's original 'green,
chocolate hoops', which were worn, for example, by Kahyasi in the 1988 Derby
(with Two Thousand Guineas winner Doyoun in the first colours), by Alamshar
when he beat the same owner's Dalakhani in the 2003 Irish Derby and by Enzeli
in the 1999 Gold Cup. The hooped colours belonged to the Aga Khan's grandfather
who founded the famous stud in the 'twenties.
More of the Aga Khan's pattern-winning fillies race on beyond their three-
year-old days than used to do so, now that there is a lucrative programme for older
fillies and mares. Dolniya was probably too big and backward to be raced as a two-
year-old and the classics had been run by the time she was ready to take on the cream
of the fillies as a three-year-old. She won the Prix de Malleret at Saint-Cloud but her
two best performances came in the autumn when third in the Prix Vermeille and fifth
in the Prix de l'Arc. Clearly progressive and relatively lightly raced, she was always
a prime contender to be kept in training at four. The Dubai Sheema Classic at the
end of March was also the target for the Prix de l'Arc runner-up Flintshire who had
gone on to finish second in the Breeders' Cup Turf before winning the Hong Kong
Vase. Dolniya, who had been put away after the Arc, narrowly beat Flintshire in a
preparatory race over nine furlongs on the polytrack at Chantilly at the beginning
of March, but Flintshire was widely expected to reverse the form over a mile and
a half at Meydan where the high-class Japanese-trained filly Harp Star, sixth in the
Arc after coming from a long way back, started 11/4 favourite, ahead of Flintshire
at 3/1, the Breeders' Cup Turf winner Main Sequence at 9/2, the top-class Hong
Kong performer Designs On Rome at 5/1 and Dolniya at 7/1 in a field which also
included the previous year's Japanese Derby winner One And Only (16/1) and two
British-trained challengers, the Irish One Thousand Guineas and the E. P. Taylor
Stakes winner Just The Judge (28/1) and the well-travelled Sheikhzayedroad (33/1
outsider of the nine). Dolniya ran out a worthy winner, well placed throughout and
just kept up to her work, after taking over a furlong out, to beat Flintshire by two and
a quarter lengths, with One And Only two lengths further back in third and Designs
On Rome fourth, ahead of the two British challengers and Main Sequence. It had not
been clear beforehand where the pace in the race was likely to come from and, with
Just The Judge (running at the trip for the first time) allowed to dictate, the Sheema
Classic turned into more of a test of speed than stamina and Dolniya seemed to get
first run on some of her patiently-ridden rivals (Designs On Rome, in particular, was
left with plenty to do).
Dolniya couldn't add to her richly-endowed success in the Sheema Classic
in four remaining outings as a four-year-old. She was headed late on when beaten a
neck by Pether's Moon (with Flintshire third) in a muddling four-runner race for the
Coronation Cup at Epsom, possibly being sent for home a shade too early given the
fairish rise towards the finish, after the race turned into a tactical affair. Dolniya then

Dubai Sheema Classic Presented by Longines, Meydan—
Dolniya reverses placings from the previous season's Arc with her compatriot Flintshire

finished a place behind Flintshire when the pair filled second and third behind Treve in the Grand Prix de Saint-Cloud, Dolniya being held up on this occasion. Given a break in preparation for a second tilt at the Prix de l'Arc de Triomphe, Dolniya was warmed up against the colts in the Prix Foy on Longchamp's 'day of trials', avoiding having to take on Treve again in the Prix Vermeille. Dolniya finished fourth to Postponed but probably needed the outing (it had been two and a half months since the Grand Prix de Saint-Cloud) and she also had to cope with the softest ground she encountered in her career. Unfortunately, Dolniya's racing career was ended by an injury sustained in the Prix de l'Arc three weeks later. She was kept in touch with the leaders from the start and had every chance entering the final two furlongs, but she was squeezed and badly hampered just inside the final furlong as Treve hung right. Dolniya looked held at the time, and set to run just a little below the form of her good fifth the previous year, but her eventual finishing position of thirteenth gives no idea of how creditably she ran. Her jockey eased her considerably after she suffered interference and she returned to the unsaddling enclosure with a badly swollen foreleg, which turned out to be caused by a hairline fracture of her cannon bone. She had been invited to the Japan Cup in November before she ran in the Arc.

			Night Shift	Northern Dancer
Dolniya (FR)	Azamour (IRE)	(b 1980)	Ciboulette
(b.f. 2011)	(b 2001)	Asmara	Lear Fan
		(b 1993)	Anaza
	Daltama (IRE)	Indian Ridge	Ahonoora
	(gr 2005)	(ch 1985)	Hillbrow
		Daltawa	Miswaki
		(gr 1989)	Damana

The big, rangy Dolniya is an Aga Khan home bred through and through. Her sire Azamour, who won the King George VI and Queen Elizabeth Stakes, among other races, for his owner-breeder sadly had to be put down at Gilltown Stud after sustaining a serious injury in his box in April 2014. Dolniya had given her sire his second Group 1 winner after that of another home bred, the ill-fated Prix de Diane winner Valyra, and Dolniya's Sheema Classic was followed later in the latest season by a third Group 1 winner for Azamour when Covert Love won the Irish Oaks. On the distaff side, Dolniya is descended from one of the families acquired by the Aga Khan when he bought the bloodstock of French textile tycoon Marcel Boussac in the late-'seventies. Marcel Boussac was France's dominant owner-breeder for decades, leading owner nineteen times and leading breeder seventeen, his record including six Prix de l'Arcs and twelve Prix du Jockey Clubs. Dolniya comes from the Boussac family founded on Astana whose daughters included the last of five Prix de Diane winners for Boussac, Crepellana, as well as Dolniya's fifth dam Rose Ness. Dolniya's grandam Daltawa died in July at the age of twenty-six after making a name for herself as the dam of the Aga Khan's Poule d'Essai des Poulains winner Daylami (who added considerably to his record when racing for Godolphin at four and five) and his Prix du Jockey Club and Prix de l'Arc winner Dalakhani. Dolniya's dam

Daltama ran only once and Dolniya is her second foal, her first being the French ten and a half furlong winner Daldena (by Anabaa). The 2013 Prix de l'Opera winner Dalkala is a great granddaughter of Daltawa and, together with Dolniya, should help to keep the family name in lights for years to come. Dolniya stayed twelve and a half furlongs and acted on polytrack, good to firm and good to soft going. *A. de Royer Dupre, France*

DOLPHIN ROCK 8 b.g. Mark of Esteem (IRE) 137 – Lark In The Park (IRE) 57 (Grand Lodge (USA) 125) [2015 76: 9.1s 8.3m³ 9.2g⁶ 8d* 8.1v* 8d* Sep 2] stocky gelding: fair handicapper: won at Ayr (apprentice) in July, Chepstow (apprentice) in August and Bath in September: stays 10.5f: acts on polytrack, fibresand, good to firm and heavy going: tried in headgear: front runner/races prominently, often travels strongly. *Richard Ford* **74**

DOLPHIN VILLAGE (IRE) 5 b.g. Cape Cross (IRE) 129 – Reform Act (USA) 112 (Lemon Drop Kid (USA) 131) [2015 95: p12g⁵ p12f⁶ p11f⁶ p11f³ 11.6m 10m 10f⁵ p12g² p11g⁶ p12g p11g 11.6g⁶ t9.5g³ p12g* p12g* Dec 20] smallish gelding: fairly useful handicapper: won at Lingfield (2) in December: left Roger Ingram after twelfth start: stays 1½m: acts on polytrack, good to firm and heavy going: tried in hood in 2015: often in tongue tie in 2015. *Jane Chapple-Hyam* **73 a86**

DOLPHIN VISTA (IRE) 2 b.c. (Apr 6) Zoffany (IRE) 121 – Fiordiligi (Mozart (IRE) 131) [2015 6s⁴ 6m⁶ 7s² 8g³ 8s* 8d² Oct 23] €16,000Y, £32,000 2-y-o: sturdy colt: fifth foal: half-brother to winner up to 1m Celtic Filly (by Footstepsinthesand) and 2-y-o 5f-7f winner Magdalen Love (by King's Best): dam unraced half-sister to 1¼m-15f winner Bayreuth: fairly useful performer: won maiden at York (by 3 lengths from Carenot) in October: stays 1m: acts on soft going: front runner/races prominently. *Richard Fahey* **89**

DOMINADA (IRE) 3 b.g. Mastercraftsman (IRE) 129 – Red Blossom (USA) (Silver Hawk (USA) 123) [2015 84p: 10.3d⁵ 8s 10.1d⁴ 8d⁴ 12g* 12.3g³ 12d⁵ 16.4g 12g* Sep 19] compact gelding: fairly useful handicapper: won at Catterick in July and September (by length from Poetic Verse): stays 1½m: acts on good to firm going: front runner/races prominently. *Brian Ellison* **85**

DOMINAE (IRE) 3 b.f. Motivator 131 – White Turf (GER) (Tiger Hill (IRE) 127) [2015 p10g Jun 18] 8,000Y: fourth foal: half-sister to winner up to 7f Winter Hill (2-y-o 5f winner, by Three Valleys): dam 1m winner out of 5f winner Wonderful Dreams: 50/1, well held in maiden at Chelmsford, very slowly away. *Conor Dore* **–**

DOMINANCE 2 b.f. (Mar 22) Lilbourne Lad (IRE) 111 – Christmas Tart (IRE) 74 (Danetime (IRE) 121) [2015 t5.1m² Dec 12] ffifth foal: closely related to 5f/6f winner Tarando (by Equiano) and half-sister to 2-y-o 6f winner Make Up (by Kyllachy) and useful 2-y-o 5f winner Hoyam (by Royal Applause): dam 2-y-o 5f winner: 33/1, not seen to best effect when second in maiden at Wolverhampton (6 lengths behind Gwendolyn), sticking to task. *Rae Guest* **71**

coral.co.uk Rockingham Stakes, York—
Donjuan Triumphant shows smart form as he follows up his nursery win in this listed event from Dhahmaan and Gracious John, both successful in similar races next time

DOMINANDROS (FR) 4 b.g. Teofilo (IRE) 126 – Afya (Oasis Dream 129) [2015 90, **89** a100: p12g⁴ 10m 10m 10.1m p12g⁶ t16.5f⁶ p11g Dec 9] lengthy, angular gelding: fairly useful handicapper: stays 1½m: acts on polytrack: tried in tongue tie in 2015: often races prominently: temperament under suspicion. *Gay Kelleway*

DOMINANNIE (IRE) 2 b.f. (Apr 23) Paco Boy (IRE) 129 – English Rose (USA) (Kafwain **52** (USA) 118) [2015 5m⁵ 6v⁵ Nov 7] €3,500F, €8,200Y, £14,000 2-y-o: fourth foal: half-sister to 1m winner Jhon Grass (by Refuse To Bend): dam, 1m winner, half-sister to 1m/9f winner Snowdrops out of useful 1m winner Roses In The Snow: better effort when fifth in maiden at Doncaster (7¾ lengths behind Times Legacy) in November. *Alan Swinbank*

DOMINATE 5 b.g. Assertive 121 – Blue Goddess (IRE) 94 (Blues Traveller (IRE) 119) **89 §** [2015 90§: 6m³ 7g⁵ 6m⁶ 6f 6m 6.1s⁶ 5g⁶ Sep 7] tall gelding: fairly useful handicapper: third at Ascot in May: stays 6f: acts on any turf going: tried in blinkers: one to treat with caution. *Richard Hannon*

DOMINEENO 2 b.g. (May 5) Stimulation (IRE) 121 – Shining Oasis (IRE) 73 (Mujtahid **48** (USA) 118) [2015 6g 6g 6m 6d 8.3s 7s 8.3s⁵ Oct 28] poor maiden: stays 8.5f: acts on soft going. *Richard Guest*

DOMINIUM (USA) 8 b.g. E Dubai (USA) 124 – Sudenlylastsummer (USA) (Rinka Das **86** (USA) 107) [2015 78, a84: p6m² p6g⁴ 6g³ 6g 5.7g² 6f p6f* p6g⁵ p7m⁶ p6f p6g p6g⁴ Dec 28] leggy gelding: fairly useful handicapper: won at Chelmsford (by neck from Milady) in September: third at Doncaster in May and second at Bath in June: stays 7f, usually races over shorter: acts on polytrack, tapeta and good to firm going: often wears headgear: sometimes slowly away, often races in rear. *Jeremy Gask*

DOMMERSEN (IRE) 2 ch.c. (Feb 26) Dutch Art 126 – Kelowna (IRE) 93 (Pivotal 124) **– P** [2015 7g Oct 21] 340,000Y: strong colt: second foal: half-brother to useful winner up to 11f Nebulla (2-y-o 8.3f winner, by Iffraaj): dam 1m winner out of useful winner up to 8.5f (2-y-o 7f/7.5f winner) Kootenay: 11/2, shaped well when seventh in maiden at Newmarket (13¼ lengths behind Colour Me Happy) in October, not knocked about: has scope for plenty of improvement. *John Gosden*

DON CAMILLO (USA) 3 b.c. Ghostzapper (USA) 137 – Potra Clasica (ARG) (Potrillon **103** (ARG)) [2015 71p: p10.7g* p12g² 10f 12g p10.7d³ Jul 12] useful performer: won maiden at Dundalk in March: second in handicap on same course (neck behind Hardstone) in May: stays 1½m: acts on polytrack and firm going: tried in visor in 2015: sent to USA. *D. K. Weld, Ireland*

DONE DREAMING (IRE) 5 b.g. Diamond Green (FR) 121 – Wishing Chair (USA) **54** (Giant's Causeway (USA) 132) [2015 58: p6m³ f6g⁵ Jan 29] modest handicapper: stays 6f: acts on polytrack, tapeta, good to firm and good to soft going: races prominently. *Richard Fahey*

DONETSK 3 b.g. Medicean 128 – Seasonal Blossom (IRE) (Fairy King (USA)) [2015 **57** p7f⁴ p8f⁴ 7d 10m 8g Jul 13] modest maiden: stays 1m: acts on polytrack: sometimes in hood: often races towards rear. *William Jarvis*

DONJUAN TRIUMPHANT (IRE) 2 b.c. (Mar 24) Dream Ahead (USA) 133 – **114** Mathuna (IRE) (Tagula (IRE) 116) [2015 6m² 6g³ 5.9m² 6d² 6g* 6s* 6d* 7s⁴ Nov 1] €58,000F, 30,000 2-y-o: fourth foal: half-brother to useful winner up to 1m Caledonian Spring (by Amadeus Wolf) and 7f winner Eusepio (by One Cool Cat): dam, 2-y-o 7.5f winner, half-sister to useful 1m/9f winner Wilside: smart performer: won nursery at Ayr in September, and listed race at York (by 1¼ lengths from Dhahmaan) and Criterium de Maisons-Laffitte (by 5½ lengths from Dressed In Fur) in October: unsuited by step up in trip when 2½ lengths fourth to Johannes Vermeer in Criterium International at Saint-Cloud final outing: stays 6f: acts on soft going. *Richard Fahey*

DON KEYHOE TAY (IRE) 3 b.c. Danehill Dancer (IRE) 117 – Arosa (IRE) 97 **79** (Sadler's Wells (USA) 132) [2015 10.5g⁶ 8d² 8g² 8.3g⁴ Sep 21] fair maiden: left John Patrick Murtagh after first start: should be suited by 1¼m+. *Richard Fahey*

DONNA GRACIOSA (GER) 3 b.f. Samum (GER) 126 – Donna Alicia (GER) 105 **84** (Highland Chieftain 121) [2015 61: p12m⁵ 9.9m⁵ 9.9g* 10d 11.6m⁵ 10m² 12g² 12.1g* 12.2g* 12.8m* 12d Oct 30] close-coupled filly: fairly useful handicapper: won at Beverley in May and August, and Musselburgh (2) in September: stays 13f: acts on good to firm going: usually races prominently/responds generously to pressure. *Mark Johnston*

DONNCHA (IRE) 4 br.c. Captain Marvelous (IRE) 114 – Seasonal Style (IRE) 93 **106** (Generous (IRE) 139) [2015 97: 8.3s⁶ 7.6s* 8.1m 7m* 7m* 7d³ 8m⁶ 9g 8d⁴ Oct 17] tall colt: useful handicapper: won at Lingfield in May, and Goodwood (by ¾ length from

Excilly) and Redcar (by ½ length from Major Crispies) in June: third at Ascot (length behind Heaven's Guest) in July: stays 8.5f: acts on polytrack, good to firm and heavy going: often races towards rear. *Robert Eddery*

DONNY ROVER (IRE) 4 b.g. Excellent Art 125 – My Lass 91 (Elmaamul (USA) 125) **99** [2015 103: 8d 12g⁵ 12f 10m 10.4m* 10m⁶ 12m 10.3g 10g Aug 29] leggy gelding: useful handicapper: won at York (by 1½ lengths from Mistiroc) in June: stays 10.5f: acts on good to firm and heavy going: often wears headgear: often races prominently: sold £40,000, sent to Bahrain. *Michael Appleby*

DON PADEJA 5 br.g. Dansili 127 – La Leuze (IRE) (Caerleon (USA) 132) [2015 –: **60** 11.8d⁵ 12f⁶ t8.6f Dec 22] modest handicapper: left Jonjo O'Neill after second start: stays 1¾m: acts on good to firm going. *Ronald Harris*

DON'T BE 5 b.m. Cape Cross (IRE) 129 – Faslen (USA) 92 (Fasliyev (USA) 120) [2015 **96 +** 94: p7m* t7.1m* t7.1m⁶ p7f³ 8m* 8.5g⁵ 8f 7m 8g p8g* p10m p9.4g p10g* Dec 19] useful **a108** performer: won handicaps at Lingfield in January and Wolverhampton in February, and listed races at Goodwood (by short head from Crowley's Law) in May, Dundalk (by 3 lengths from Façade) in October and Lingfield (by neck from Grendisar) in December: stays 1¼m: acts on polytrack, tapeta and good to firm going: tried in blinkers prior to 2015. *Sir Mark Prescott Bt*

DON'T BLAME ME 2 b.g. (May 10) Captain Gerrard (IRE) 113 – Dragon Flyer (IRE) **62 p** 105 (Tagula (IRE) 116) [2015 p6g⁶ p6g² Dec 16] £20,000Y: fourth foal: dam 5f winner (including at 2 yrs): better effort when sixth in maiden at Kempton (4 lengths behind Mywayistheonlyway) in November: remains open to improvement. *Clive Cox*

DONT BOTHER ME (IRE) 5 br.h. Dark Angel (IRE) 113 – Faleh (USA) 85 (Silver **88** Hawk (USA) 123) [2015 107: 6g 7d Aug 2] rangy, useful-looking horse: fairly useful handicapper: effective at 6f-1m: acts on soft and good to firm going: tried in cheekpieces prior to 2015: often races prominently. *Niall Moran, Ireland*

DON'T CALL ME (IRE) 8 ch.g. Haafhd 129 – Just Call Me (NZ) (Blues Traveller **93** (IRE) 119) [2015 107: t9.5g³ p8g⁶ t8.6m 8d p8f 8m 7.6m³ 8f² 7d 7.5g² 8g⁴ Sep 19] compact **a102** gelding: useful handicapper: third at Wolverhampton (1¾ lengths behind Tryster) in February: stays 1¼m: acts on all-weather, firm and soft going: tried in cheekpieces in 2015: usually wears tongue tie: often races prominently. *David Nicholls*

DONT HAVE IT THEN 4 b.g. Myboycharlie (IRE) 118 – Mondovi 97 (Kyllachy 129) **80** [2015 89: p6g³ 6m 6f 6m⁴ 6g 6m 6g⁴ 6s³ t7.1m Nov 21] smallish gelding: fairly useful handicapper: third at Lingfield in April: stays 6f: acts on polytrack, soft and good to firm going: usually races nearer last than first. *Willie Musson*

William Hill Great St Wilfrid Stakes (Handicap), Ripon—the only three-year-old in the line-up Don't Touch narrowly justifies favouritism in this valuable event from Kimberella (No.14), with the winner's stablemate Tatlisu in third

DON'T STARE 5 b.g. Zamindar (USA) 116 – Joshua's Princess 92 (Danehill (USA) 126) **98**
[2015 104: 12m 12g⁵ 10f 10.3m Sep 10] good-topped gelding: useful performer: stays
1½m: acts on polytrack, good to firm and good to soft going: often in hood prior to 2015:
often wears tongue tie. *James Fanshawe*

DON'T TELL ANNIE 3 b.f. Royal Applause 124 – Oasis Breeze 88 (Oasis Dream 129) **–**
[2015 87: 5gᵖᵘ May 22] fairly useful performer: fatally injured at Haydock: raced only at
5f: raced only on good going: often raced prominently. *Tim Easterby*

DONT TELL CHRIS (FR) 3 b.g. Lawman (FR) 121 – Enigma (GER) 107 (Sharp Victor **66 p**
(USA) 114) [2015 –: 8m⁴ 8m⁵ 8.9g⁵ 8.5d Sep 22] fair form, lightly raced: shaped well in
handicap at Musselburgh penultimate start: badly hampered in similar event at Beverley
final outing: best effort at 9f: front runner/races prominently: type to do better at 4 yrs.
David O'Meara

DON'T TELL HER (IRE) 2 b.f. (Mar 17) Tagula (IRE) 116 – Annouska (IRE) (Ad **58**
Valorem (USA) 125) [2015 6.1m 6g³ p7.5g⁶ 7d³ p6f 5g⁵ Oct 19] €2,000Y, £2,000 2-y-o:
first foal: dam unraced half-sister to winner up to 11f Prince Nureyev and winner up to 15f
Anousa, both useful: modest maiden: probably stays 7.5f: acts on polytrack and good to
soft going: tried in blinkers: often in tongue tie: sent to Greece. *Jo Hughes*

DON'T TELL JO JO 2 b.g. (Apr 28) Hellvelyn 118 – Shake Baby Shake (Reel Buddy **–**
(USA) 118) [2015 t6f p8m p6g⁶ Dec 19] no form. *Bill Turner*

DON'T TELL LOUISE 3 b.f. Medicean 128 – Lyra's Daemon 82 (Singspiel (IRE) 133) **62**
[2015 –: 9g 10m p10f p12g² 10.2s⁴ 10s⁵ Oct 6] lengthy filly: modest maiden: stays 1½m:
acts on polytrack and soft going: sometimes slowly away. *William Muir*

DONT TELL NAN 4 b.f. Major Cadeaux 121 – Charlie Girl 70 (Puissance 110) [2015 53: **–**
f5g Jan 29] maiden: no form in 2015: best form at 5f: acts on polytrack and fibresand: in
visor sole start in 2015: usually races prominently: has shown signs of temperament.
Derek Shaw

DON'T TELL NIK (IRE) 2 b.f. (Mar 24) Lawman (FR) 121 – Karliysha (IRE) (Kalanisi **–**
(IRE) 132) [2015 8s Oct 16] £5,000 2-y-o: fourth foal: half-sister to 7f-1¼m winner Maude
Adams (by Rock of Gibraltar): dam, 9.5f winner who stayed 12.5f, half-sister to 1¼m-2¼m
winner Kasthari and 7f-8.4f winner Kargali, both smart: 150/1 and in hood, well held in
maiden at Redcar. *Geoffrey Harker*

DON'T TOUCH 3 b.g. Dutch Art 126 – Expressive 81 (Falbrav (IRE) 133) [2015 6d* 6d* **114 p**
t6g* 6g* 6g* Sep 19] 60,000Y: second foal: half-brother to 2-y-o 6f winner Expect (by
Invincible Spirit): dam, 9.5f winner, half-sister to 7f/1m winner Chic and winner up to 9f
Echelon, both very smart: smart performer: unbeaten in 5 starts, namely maiden at
Newcastle in May, and handicaps at Haydock later in May, Wolverhampton in July, Ripon
(Great St Wilfrid Stakes, beat Kimberella by head) in August and Ayr (Ayr Gold Cup, beat
Poyle Vinnie by ½ length) in September: will stay 7f: acts on tapeta and good to soft going:
responds generously to pressure: open to further improvement at 4 yrs. *Richard Fahey*

DONTTOUCHTHECHIPS (IRE) 2 b.g. (Apr 8) Lilbourne Lad (IRE) 111 – Trim **64**
(IRE) (Ela-Mana-Mou 132) [2015 5.1d⁶ 5.7d⁶ 7.1s³ 8s⁴ 6s³ t7.1f Oct 27] modest maiden:
stays 1m: acts on soft going: usually leads, often races freely. *Nikki Evans*

*William Hill Ayr Gold Cup (Heritage Handicap), Ayr—Don't Touch completes his five-timer in a
cracking renewal of one of the season's top sprint handicaps, beating Poyle Vinnie (star on cap),
Ninjago (diamonds) and Toofi (right) in a blanket finish*

DOPPLER EFFECT 3 ch.g. Monsieur Bond (IRE) 120 – Scarlet Oak 77 (Zamindar (USA) 116) [2015 71: f6d⁴ t6g⁴ t7.1m⁵ p7g² p7g 7m 7m p7d⁵ 6s 7g⁴ p6g⁵ Oct 23] modest maiden: left Ann Duffield after third start: stays 7f: acts on polytrack, tapeta, good to firm and good to soft going: tried in headgear: often races towards rear: sent to Greece. *John Joseph Murphy, Ireland* **62**

DORA'S FIELD (IRE) 2 b.f. (Mar 4) Rip Van Winkle (IRE) 134 – Rydal Mount (IRE) 96 (Cape Cross (IRE) 129) [2015 7g p7g Oct 14] third foal: half-sister to 6f/7f winner Ptolemy (by Royal Applause): dam, 7f winner, half-sister to smart winner up to 1m Chagall: better effort when tenth in maiden at Kempton (5½ lengths behind Desiderada) in October, not knocked about: should do better in time. *Ed Dunlop* **60 p**

DORNOCH (USA) 4 b.g. Mizzen Mast (USA) 121 – Gainful (USA) (Gone West (USA)) [2015 7m⁶ 7d⁵ 8f⁵ Jun 10] useful handicapper: stays 9f: acts on soft and good to firm going: tried in cheekpieces in 2015: temperament under suspicion: sent to UAE. *Robert Cowell* **96**

DOSE 2 b.f. (Apr 15) Teofilo (IRE) 126 – Prescription 103 (Pivotal 124) [2015 7g³ t7.1f³ t8.6m⁵ p7g p7m⁴ Dec 31] second foal: dam, 6f winner, half-sister to smart winner up to 1¼m Cupid's Glory and useful winner up to 8.5f Clinical: fair maiden: likely to stay 1m: acts on polytrack and tapeta. *Richard Fahey* **68**

DOSTOYEVSKY (IRE) 2 b.c. (Mar 6) Galileo (IRE) 134 – My Branch 111 (Distant Relative 128) [2015 t8.6m Dec 30] closely related to high-class winner up to 7f Tante Rose (2-y-o 6f winner, by Barathea), 8.3f winner Melodramatic (by Sadler's Wells) and winner up to 8.3f Bold Lass (2-y-o 7f winner, by Sea The Stars), both useful, and half-brother to winners: dam winner up to 7f (2-y-o 5f/6f winner): 8/1, very green when seventh in maiden at Wolverhampton (6½ lengths behind Disobedience) in December, left poorly placed: sure to progress. *David Lanigan* **66 p**

DOT DASH DOT 3 b.f. Rainbow High 121 – Never Lost (Golden Snake (USA) 127) [2015 p10f t12.2f⁶ Dec 14] second foal: dam maiden hurdler: no form in hood final start. *Christopher Kellett* **—**

DOT GREEN (IRE) 2 b.f. (Feb 1) Lawman (FR) 121 – Katajan (Halling (USA) 133) [2015 8g² 8s Oct 19] 29,000F: second foal: dam unraced out of very smart 1¼m winner Kartajana: better effort when seventh in listed race at Pontefract (4½ lengths behind Thanksfortellingme) in October. *Mark H. Tompkins* **85**

DOUBLE CZECH (IRE) 4 b.g. Bushranger (IRE) 119 – Night of Joy (IRE) 87 (King's Best (USA) 132) [2015 77: 8.3m² p8f² 8.1s* 9.9s³ 8.3m 8.1m⁴ 8.1g 8s² Aug 23] good-quartered gelding: fair handicapper: won at Chepstow in May: stays 8.5f: acts on polytrack, good to firm and heavy going: often in headgear prior to 2015: usually leads: has hinted at temperament. *Patrick Chamings* **76**

DOUBLE DISCOUNT (IRE) 5 b.g. Invincible Spirit (IRE) 121 – Bryanstown Girl (IRE) (Kalanisi (IRE) 132) [2015 103: t12.2g² t12.2m 12g p11g p12g p10g⁶ t12.2m Sep 5] useful handicapper: second at Wolverhampton (¾ length behind Dream Child) in January: stays 11f: acts on polytrack and firm going: sometimes wears headgear: sometimes slowly away. *Tom Dascombe* **95**

DOUBLE HAPPINESS 5 ch.m. Sakhee (USA) 136 – Fu Wa (USA) 53 (Distant View (USA) 126) [2015 8d 10d⁶ 12d 10m Jul 21] maiden: no form in 2015. *Brian Rothwell* **—**

DOUBLE HEAVEN 3 b.g. Dutch Art 126 – Popocatepetl (FR) 66 (Nashwan (USA) 135) [2015 68p: p7m² 8d⁵ 8.1g* 8.3d² Oct 5] fairly useful performer: won handicap at Sandown in September: second in similar event at Windsor in October well worth a try at 1¼m: acts on good to soft going: usually responds generously to pressure: likely to progress further. *Ed Walker* **88 p**

DOUBLE UP 4 b.g. Exceed And Excel (AUS) 126 – My Love Thomas (IRE) 84 (Cadeaux Genereux 131) [2015 89: 5f* 5.1g* 5m³ 5f* 5g² 5m⁵ Aug 8] workmanlike gelding: smart handicapper: won at Newmarket and Nottingham (by 1½ lengths from Top Boy) in May, and Ascot (by ½ length from Taajub) in July: second at Goodwood (1½ lengths behind Ridge Ranger) later in July: stays 6f: acts on polytrack and firm going: sometimes wears tongue tie: often travels strongly. *Roger Varian* **115**

DOUBLY CLEVER (IRE) 3 ch.g. Iffraaj 127 – Smartest (IRE) 76 (Exceed And Excel (AUS) 126) [2015 73: t7.1g p7m⁴ 10.2m² Jun 5] modest maiden: left Charles Hills after second start: stays 7f: acts on tapeta and good to firm going: signs of temperament. *Michael Blake* **63**

DOUBLY MOTIVATED (IRE) 2 ch.f. (Feb 3) Iffraaj 127 – Chicane 76 (Motivator 131) [2015 7g² 7.6g* 7g⁶ Sep 25] 65,000Y: well-made filly: second foal: dam, 11.6f winner, half-sister to useful winner up to 1m Whazzis: fairly useful performer: best effort **89**

when winning maiden at Lingfield (by 8 lengths from Percy's Romance) in September: stays 7.5f. *Charles Hills*

DOUGAL MAGIC (IRE) 2 b.c. (May 10) Zebedee 113 – Kissing The Sky (IRE) **38** (King's Best (USA) 132) [2015 6m 5m 6g 7.2g 6g 6s 7d f7g Nov 3] poor maiden: stays 7f: acts on soft and good to firm going: often in hood: often races in rear: temperament under suspicion (has carried head awkwardly/refused to settle). *Micky Hammond*

DOUGAN 3 b.g. Dutch Art 126 – Vive Les Rouges 91 (Acclamation 118) [2015 8.3d⁴ p7m* **89 p** p6g* t7.1m² p7m* Dec 31] 130,000Y, £3,500 3-y-o: second foal: half-brother to useful 6f winner Speedfiend (by Bahamian Bounty): dam, 2-y-o 6f winner, half-sister to smart 6f winner Bounty Box: fairly useful performer: won maiden at Kempton in October, and handicaps at Lingfield in November and December: effective at 6f/7f: acts on polytrack and tapeta: will go on improving. *David Evans*

DOUNEEDAHAND 4 b.f. Royal Applause 124 – Our Sheila 82 (Bahamian Bounty 116) **61** [2015 70: p6g t7.1g p6f* 5m 16g⁵ 6m p6g t6f p6m p6g³ Dec 3] modest handicapper: won at Kempton in March: stays 6f: acts on polytrack, tapeta and firm going: sometimes wears headgear: often races in rear. *Seamus Mullins*

DOVE MOUNTAIN (IRE) 4 b.g. Danehill Dancer (IRE) 117 – Virginia Waters (USA) **61** 116 (Kingmambo (USA) 125) [2015 62: 7g 7.2m⁵ 10m 7.2g* p8g p7g⁵ t8.6f* p8m⁵ p12g⁴ **a75** p8g Dec 11] fair handicapper: won at Ayr in September and Wolverhampton in November: stays 8.5f: acts on polytrack, tapeta and good to firm going: sometimes wears headgear: often in tongue tie in 2015: often starts slowly, usually races towards rear. *Gordon Elliott, Ireland*

DOVILS DATE 6 gr.g. Clodovil (IRE) 116 – Lucky Date (IRE) 91 (Halling (USA) 133) **70** [2015 84: 14.1f May 23] sturdy gelding: fair handicapper: stays 1¾m: acts on soft and good to firm going. *Tim Vaughan*

DOVIL'S DUEL (IRE) 4 b.g. Clodovil (IRE) 116 – Duelling 80 (Diesis 133) [2015 73: **73** 7d 7m⁵ 6m 5.2m³ 6m⁵ 6m 6s p10f⁶ p11g³ 10d* p10g t9.5f Dec 11] leggy, dipped-backed gelding: fair performer: won claimer at Windsor in October: left Rod Millman after tenth start: stays 11f, though effective at much shorter: acts on polytrack, good to firm and good to soft going: tried in headgear: sometimes slowly away, usually races in rear. *Tony Newcombe*

DOWN TO EARTH 3 gr.c. Aussie Rules (USA) 123 – May Fox (Zilzal (USA) 137) **83** [2015 62p: 8.3m* p8g³ May 28] fairly useful form: won maiden at Nottingham in April: stayed 8.5f: acted on good to firm ground: dead. *Michael Bell*

DOWNTOWN BOY (IRE) 7 b.rg. Kheleyf (USA) 116 – Uptown (IRE) 72 (Be My **61** Guest (USA) 126) [2015 –: 16m⁴ 12.4d² 15.8s³ May 5] good-topped gelding: modest handicapper: stays 2m: acts on polytrack, soft and good to firm going: sometimes wears headgear. *Ray Craggs*

DOZY JOE 7 b.g. Sleeping Indian 122 – Surrey Down (USA) (Forest Wildcat (USA) 120) **56** [2015 74: t9.5f t9.5f² Feb 7] plain gelding: modest handicapper: stays 1½m: acts on all-weather, best turf form on good to firm going: often wears headgear: tried in tongue tie: starts slowly, often races towards rear. *Joseph Tuite*

DRACO'S CODE 4 b.g. Galileo (IRE) 134 – Lady Karr 76 (Mark of Esteem (IRE) 137) **79** [2015 p12m² p13g² 11.8s⁴ p12g⁴ p13.3f⁵ Oct 22] fair maiden: stays 1½m: acts on polytrack and soft going. *Gary Moore*

DRAGO (IRE) 3 b.c. Cape Cross (IRE) 129 – Eden (USA) (Holy Bull (USA) 134) [2015 **71** 12v p10f⁴ p10f t9.5f² Oct 27] fair maiden: stays 1¼m. *David Simcock*

DRAGON FALLS (IRE) 6 b.g. Distorted Humor (USA) 117 – Tizdubai (USA) 114 **108** (Cee's Tizzy (USA)) [2015 102: a9.4f⁵ a9.9f a8f Feb 19] useful handicapper: ran only at Meydan in 2015, creditable 4¼ lengths fifth to I'm Back on reappearance: well held after: probably best around 1m: acts on dirt/synthetics and soft going: often in headgear: often travels strongly. *Charlie Appleby*

DRAGON FEI (IRE) 5 b.m. Jeremy (USA) 122 – Wallonia (IRE) 70 (Barathea (IRE) **97** 127) [2015 87: 10v* 10d² 11.9d 9d 9g 9g Sep 26] useful handicapper: won at the Curragh in May: second at Navan (½ length behind Curvy) later in May: stays 1½m: acts on good to firm and heavy going: tried in hood prior to 2015: fairly useful hurdler. *Dermot Anthony McLoughlin, Ireland*

DRAGON KING (IRE) 3 ch.g. Dylan Thomas (IRE) 132 – Alexander Queen (IRE) 96 **100** (King's Best (USA) 132) [2015 72p: 6d* 6s 6g³ 6m³ 6g* 6g⁵ 6d Oct 23] useful handicapper: won at Ripon in April and Newmarket (by 3¾ lengths from My Dad Syd) in August: stays 6f: acts on soft going: usually races close up. *Michael Dods*

DRAGON MALL (USA) 2 b.c. (Feb 19) Blame (USA) 129 – Petition The Lady (USA) **97**
(Petionville (USA)) [2015 p7g⁵ 7m² p8m* 8g⁵ Oct 10] $105,000Y: good-topped colt: first
foal: dam, 6.5f/7.5f (minor US stakes) winner, half-sister to useful 7f-8.5f (minor US
stakes, including at 2 yrs) winner Saucey Evening: useful performer: won minor event at
Chelmsford (by ¾ length from Lazzam) in September: stays 1m. *David Simcock*

DRAGON TREE 3 ch.g. Halling (USA) 133 – Doggerbank (IRE) 106 (Oasis Dream 129) **–**
[2015 t7.1f p8m Feb 12] no form. *Lady Cecil*

DRAGOON GUARD (IRE) 4 b.g. Jeremy (USA) 122 – Elouges (IRE) (Dalakhani **78**
(IRE) 133) [2015 85: p10d⁶ 10.1g 11.6g³ p11g f11g Dec 22] fair handicapper: left Marco
Botti after fourth start: stays 11.5f: acts on polytrack and good to soft going: sometimes in
cheekpieces in 2015: tried in tongue tie in 2015. *Anthony Honeyball*

DRAMATIC VOICE 2 ch.f. (Apr 18) Poet's Voice 126 – Darwinia (GER) (Acatenango **–**
(GER) 127) [2015 p7g 7s p8g Oct 27] rather unfurnished filly: half-sister to several
winners, including smart 9f-11f winner Daveron (by Black Sam Bellamy) and 7f winner
Don Libre (by Librettist): dam 1¼m winner: no form. *Paul Cole*

DRASTIC ART 3 ch.f. Dutch Art 126 – Drastic Measure 73 (Pivotal 124) [2015 –: 7s **–**
p10g Jun 20] maiden: no form in 2015. *Henry Spiller*

DRAWNFROMTHEPAST (IRE) 10 ch.g. Tagula (IRE) 116 – Ball Cat (FR) (Cricket **–**
Ball (USA) 124) [2015 77: p5m⁵ Feb 18] sturdy gelding: useful at best, no form in 2015:
stays 6f: acts on polytrack, fibresand, best turf form on good going or firmer (acts on firm):
tried in cheekpieces: tried in tongue tie prior to 2015. *Ed Walker*

DRAWN TO BE A LADY 2 b.f. (Mar 13) Avonbridge 123 – Lady Killer (IRE) 76 **–**
(Daggers Drawn (USA) 114) [2015 t6f p5g Nov 13] fifth foal: dam 2-y-o 5f winner: no
form. *Bill Turner*

DR DORO (IRE) 2 b.f. (Mar 31) Holy Roman Emperor (IRE) 125 – Stellarina (IRE) 71 **89**
(Night Shift (USA)) [2015 5f 5m² 5m² 5g* 5g5 5g p5g⁴ Oct 9] second foal: dam, 6f winner,
half-sister to smart 1m-1¼m winner Fanjura: fairly useful performer: won nursery at the
Curragh (by 3½ lengths from Know) in August: raced only at 5f: in headgear: tried in
tongue tie: usually leads. *T. Stack, Ireland*

DR DREY (IRE) 2 ch.c. (Mar 28) Bahamian Bounty 116 – Mount Lavinia (IRE) 92 **71**
(Montjeu (IRE) 137) [2015 p7g p8g³ Oct 20] better effort when third in maiden at Lingfield
(½ length behind Sahalin) in October. *Jamie Osborne*

DREAM ALLY (IRE) 5 b.g. Oasis Dream 129 – Alexander Alliance (IRE) 106 **63**
(Danetime (IRE) 121) [2015 70: t6f² t6g³ 5g t6g t6g³ p6g⁵ t6m³ t6f t6g⁴ Nov 27] modest
handicapper: stays 6f: acts on polytrack, tapeta and good to firm going: tried in headgear:
tried in tongue tie prior to 2015: usually races prominently. *John Weymes*

DREAM AND HOPE 4 b.f. Royal Applause 124 – Senta's Dream (Danehill (USA) 126) **49**
[2015 62: t7.1g⁶ p7g Jan 21] angular, quite attractive filly: poor handicapper: stays 7f: acts
on polytrack: tried in hood prior to 2015: other starts slowly: sent to Italy. *Philip McBride*

DREAM APPROACH (IRE) 3 b.f. New Approach (IRE) 132 – Witch of Fife (USA) 91 **–**
(Lear Fan (USA) 130) [2015 10.2g⁶ 10.3g Sep 11] 60,000Y: closely related to useful 2-y-o
7f winner Cabaret and 11f winner Galaya (both by Galileo) and half-sister to several
winners, including smart winner up to 1m Ho Choi (2-y-o 6f winner, by Pivotal): dam
2-y-o 6f/7f winner: no form. *Alan McCabe*

DREAM BOUNTY 3 b.f. Bahamian Bounty 116 – Dream In Waiting 88 (Oasis Dream **65 p**
129) [2015 6d² 6s* Oct 16] 26,000Y, 800 3-y-o; first foal: dam 2 y-o 6ff winner who
stayed 1¼m out of smart winner up to 10.4f (2-y-o 5f/6f winner) Lady In Waiting: better
effort when winning maiden at Redcar (by ½ length from Havre de Paix) in October, driven
out: likely to stay at least 1m: should do better still. *John Holt*

DREAM CHILD (IRE) 4 ch.f. Pivotal 124 – Poseidon's Bride (USA) 103 (Seeking The **109**
Gold (USA)) [2015 98p: t12.2g* t9.5f² t12.2m* 12m² 10.2m² p9.4g* 12m² Jul 18] smart
performer: won handicaps at Wolverhampton in January and February (by 1½ lengths from
Kings Bayonet), and listed event at Deauville (by 2 lengths from Persona Grata) in June:
runner-up all other outings in 2015, including in listed races at Goodwood (neck behind
Miss Marjurie), Nottingham and Newmarket (1½ lengths behind Jordan Princess): stays
1½m: acts on polytrack, tapeta and good to firm going: often races prominently. *Charlie
Appleby*

DREAM DANA (IRE) 2 b.f. (Feb 2) Dream Ahead (USA) 133 – Lidanna 113 (Nicholas **– p**
(USA) 111) [2015 t7.1m Sep 25] 100,000Y: half-sister to several winners, including smart
winner up to 7.6f (stays 1¼m) Yaa Wayl (2-y-o 5f winner), useful winner up to 8.4f Robert
The Painter (2-y-o 6f winner) (both by Whipper) and useful 6.7f winner Lidanski (by

Soviet Star): dam winner up to 6f (2-y-o 5f winner): 20/1, badly needed experience when tenth in maiden at Wolverhampton (8 lengths behind Dollar Reward) in September: should do better. *Jamie Osborne*

DREAM DESTINATION (IRE) 2 b.c. (Jan 25) Showcasing 117 – Never Let You **99**
Down (IRE) (Barathea (IRE) 127) [2015 5g² 5g* 7.1m p6g² 5g⁴ 6d Oct 24] 15,000F, 100,000Y: strong colt: first foal: dam, third at 10.5f, closely related to smart winner up to 1½m Glencadam Gold: useful performer: won maiden at Sandown in August: second in Sirenia Stakes at Kempton (½ length behind Rouleau) in September: stays 6f: acts on polytrack. *Sylvester Kirk*

DREAM DREAMER 2 b.f. (Jan 14) Dream Ahead (USA) 133 – Moonlit Garden (IRE) **82**
95 (Exceed And Excel (AUS) 126) [2015 5g² 5m⁴ 5g* 5m⁶ 5f p5g³ 5s² t5.1f⁵ t5.1f⁵ t5.1f **a73**
Nov 13] 26,000F, £35,000Y: lengthy, rather unfurnished filly: first foal: dam 2-y-o 6f winner: fair to useful performer: won maiden at Windsor (by 4½ lengths from Cinders) in May: raced only at 5f: acts on polytrack, tapeta, soft and good to firm going. *Jamie Osborne*

DREAM FARR (IRE) 2 b.g. (Feb 16) Dream Ahead (USA) 133 – French Lady (NZ) **–**
(Entrepreneur 123) [2015 t7.1f Nov 20] 16/1, tenth in maiden at Wolverhampton (17¼ lengths behind Turn On The Tears) in November, finding little. *Ed Walker*

DREAMFULLY (USA) 3 b.f. Oasis Dream 129 – Tizaqueena (USA) 117 (Tiznow **–**
(USA) 133) [2015 p10g 8s Sep 5] quite attractive filly: first foal: dam US Grade 2 1m winner: no form. *Charlie Appleby*

DREAM IMPOSSIBLE (IRE) 4 b.f. Iffraaj 127 – Romea (Muhtarram (USA) 125) **–**
[2015 69: 8m 8.1m 8.3g Oct 20] fair at best, no form in 2015: tried in tongue tie in 2015: often races prominently, tends to find little. *Peter Makin*

DREAMING AGAIN 5 b.g. Young Ern 120 – Maedance 83 (Groom Dancer (USA) 128) **56**
[2015 58: p10g p8g* 8.1g p8g³ 7s⁶ p8f⁵ t8.6f⁵ t8.6f³ Dec 21] modest handicapper: won at Kempton (apprentice) in June: stays 1¼m: acts on polytrack and tapeta: sometimes slowly away. *Jimmy Fox*

DREAMING OF RIO (IRE) 2 b.g. (Mar 3) Captain Rio 122 – Inourthoughts (IRE) 106 **54**
(Desert Style (IRE) 121) [2015 6g 6m⁵ 7g Sep 8] modest maiden: best effort when fifth in maiden at Ripon (6¼ lengths behind Atholl blair Boy) in August. *Tom Dascombe*

DREAMING VOICE (IRE) 2 ch.c. (Mar 5) Poet's Voice 126 – North East Bay (USA) **63 p**
(Prospect Bay (CAN) 117) [2015 7.2m 8d⁶ Sep 3] 35,000F, 60,000Y: closely related to high-class 9f-1½m winner Prince Bishop (by Dubawi) and half-brother to several winners, including useful winner up to 1¼m Strategic Mission (2-y-o 1m winner, by Red Ransom) and 2-y-o 6f winner Acquiesced (by Refuse To Bend): dam ran once: better effort when sixth in maiden at Haydock (9 lengths behind Dal Harraild) in September, slowly away: open to further improvement. *Kevin Ryan*

DREAM ISLAND (IRE) 2 b.f. (Feb 18) Kheleyf (USA) 116 – Takawiri (IRE) (Danehill **73**
(USA) 126) [2015 p6g* p6g⁵ 6f p6g⁵ 6m Oct 3] 12,000Y: lengthy filly: half-sister to several winners, including useful 6f (including at 2 yrs) winner Midnight Flower (by Haafhd) and 6f-9f winner Strident Force (by Refuse To Bend): dam unraced: fair performer: won maiden at Lingfield in May and minor event at Kempton in June: raced only at 6f: acts on polytrack. *James Tate*

DREAM JOB 3 b.f. Dubawi (IRE) 129 – Coretta (IRE) 118 (Caerleon (USA) 132) [2015 **86**
–p: 10.3g* p11g⁵ 10s Oct 23] fairly useful performer: won maiden at Chester in September: stays 11f: tried in cheekpieces in 2015. *Saeed bin Suroor*

DREAM JOURNEY (IRE) 2 ch.f. (Mar 26) Dream Ahead (USA) 133 – Khibraat 57 **–**
(Alhaarth (IRE) 126) [2015 t7.1f Nov 10] 55,000Y: fifth foal: half-sister to 3 winners, including useful 2-y-o 1m winner (stays 1¾m) Cavaleiro (by Sir Percy) and 10.7f winner Westpieser (by Azamour): dam, lightly raced, closely related to smart 1¼m-14.6f winner Ranin: 10/1, eighth in maiden at Wolverhampton (22¾ lengths behind Eternally) in November. *Charles Hills*

DREAMLIKE 3 b.f. Oasis Dream 129 – So Silk (Rainbow Quest (USA) 134) [2015 91p: **90**
10.4g 10m² 12f² Jul 10] unfurnished filly: fairly useful handicapper: runner-up at Newbury in June and Ascot in July: stays 1½m: acts on polytrack and firm going: often races prominently. *Luca Cumani*

DREAM MOVER (IRE) 2 ch.c. (Apr 3) Dream Ahead (USA) 133 – Maramba (USA) **81**
97 (Hussonet (USA) 125) [2015 6m⁴ 6.1g* 7d Aug 19] €52,000F, €58,000Y, 160,000 2-y-o: fourth foal: half-brother to 7f/1m winner (stays 1¼m) Wakeup Little Suzy (by Peintre Celebre) and 2-y-o 7f-8.3f winner (stays 10.5f) Taper Tantrum (by Azamour): dam 2-y-o 6f winner: fairly useful performer: best effort when winning maiden at Nottingham (by 2 lengths from Waslawi) in July, easily: should stay 7f. *Marco Botti*

DREAM OF SUMMER (IRE) 2 b.c. (May 6) Canford Cliffs (IRE) 133 – Danehill's **83 p**
Dream (IRE) (Danehill (USA) 126) [2015 6g 7s⁵ 8m² 8.3d⁶ p8m* Nov 19] €80,000Y: sixth
foal: half-brother to smart 1½m-1¾m winner Viking Storm (by Hurricane Run) and useful
10.7f winner Moldowney (by Dalakhani): dam unraced: fairly useful performer: won
nursery at Lingfield (by 2¼ lengths from Lady Canford) in November: stays 1m: acts on
polytrack: open to further improvement. *Andrew Balding*

DREAM REVIVAL 2 br.f. (Apr 16) Captain Gerrard (IRE) 113 – Passkey 83 (Medicean **–**
128) [2015 t7.1g t8.6m Dec 30] second foal: dam maiden, likely to have stayed 1¼m: no
form. *James Unett*

DREAM RULER 4 b.g. Holy Roman Emperor (IRE) 125 – Whatcameoverme (USA) **70**
(Aldebaran (USA) 126) [2015 80: p10f 10g 11.6m³ 11.7g Oct 18] fair handicapper: stays
11.5f: acts on polytrack and good to firm going: often races prominently. *Jo Crowley*

DREAM SCENARIO 5 b.m. Araafa (IRE) 128 – Notjustaprettyface (USA) 98 (Red **69**
Ransom (USA)) [2015 62, a83: t6g t7.1g t6f⁵ 7s⁴ 7g* 7s f7g f8m Dec 8] tall, quite good-
topped mare: fair handicapper: won at Newcastle in August: stays 7f: acts on polytrack,
tapeta, soft and good to firm going: often wears visor. *Antony Brittain*

DREAM SERENADE 2 b.f. (Apr 11) Dream Eater (IRE) 119 – Lady Santana (IRE) 61 **–**
(Doyoun 124) [2015 7g 8g 8.3g Sep 30] sixth foal: half-sister to 1m winner First Glance
(by Passing Glance): dam maiden: no form. *Michael Appleby*

DREAM SIKA (IRE) 4 b.g. Elnadim (USA) 128 – Enchantment 108 (Compton Place **58**
125) [2015 61: t5.1m³ 5.1m⁶ t5.1m² 5d⁴ 5g 5m⁵ 5m⁶ Jun 29] sturdy gelding: modest
handicapper: best form at 5f: acts on tapeta and good to soft going: tried in eyeshields prior
to 2015: usually races close up. *Ruth Carr*

DREAMS OF GLORY 7 ch.g. Resplendent Glory (IRE) 115 – Pip's Dream 52 (Glint of **77**
Gold 128) [2015 86: p5m² p5g⁶ p5f⁴ 5.3d⁴ 5.7m³ 5.7g⁴ 5.2m⁵ 5.7f⁵ 5.1v⁵ 5g⁴ t6m 5g* 5g*
t5.1f⁵ t5.1g Nov 27] rather leggy gelding: fair handicapper: won twice at Windsor in
October (amateur event on first occasion): stays 5.5f: acts on polytrack and any turf going:
tried in blinkers. *Ron Hodges*

DREAM SPIRIT (IRE) 4 b.g. Invincible Spirit (IRE) 121 – Dream Valley (IRE) 61 **94**
(Sadler's Wells (USA) 132) [2015 106: 7m 8m 7g 10m 10.2m³ 10.4d 10.2d⁵ t9.5f p8g*
p10g⁶ Dec 20] tall, leggy gelding: fairly useful handicapper: won at Lingfield in December:
left William Haggas after seventh start: stays 1¼m: acts on polytrack, soft and good to firm
going: tried in cheekpieces in 2015: sometimes slowly away. *Jamie Osborne*

DREAM TUNE 6 b.g. Oasis Dream 129 – Play Bouzouki 70 (Halling (USA) 133) [2015 **79 §**
7g a7f 7m³ 8d² 7g 8gʳʳ 8s⁵ Aug 23] tall, good-topped gelding: fair handicapper: left Salem
Al Ketbi, UAE after second start: stays 1m: acts on sand, firm and soft going: tried in
headgear: refused/virtually refused to race last 2 starts, and one to treat with plenty of
caution: sent to France. *Gay Kelleway*

DREAM WALKER (FR) 6 gr.g. Gold Away (IRE) 125 – Minnie's Mystery (FR) **88**
(Highest Honor (FR) 124) [2015 100: 8m 8m 8d 8m⁶ 8.9g 7.9m⁵ 7.6s 8d 7s⁴ 8d⁵ 8d⁶
Oct 30] strong gelding: fairly useful handicapper: stays 1m: acts on good to firm and heavy
going: tried in headgear in 2015: tried in tongue tie. *Brian Ellison*

DREESE (IRE) 4 b.g. Dandy Man (IRE) 123 – Lucky Flirt (USA) (Gulch (USA)) [2015 **80**
87: 6v⁴ 7.2s 6g* 6m 5d 5d 6m Sep 8] fairly useful performer: won seller at Catterick in
May: left Richard Fahey after third start: stays 6f: acts on polytrack and good to firm going:
usually in headgear in 2015: often in tongue tie in 2015: sometimes slowly away, often
races in rear. *Marjorie Fife*

DRESSED IN FUR (IRE) 2 b.f. (Feb 19) Excellent Art 125 – Little Empress (IRE) **99**
(Holy Roman Emperor (IRE) 125) [2015 t5.1gᵘʳ 5m⁵ 5s* 6m⁴ 5.5g* 5d⁴ 6.5d³ 6d² 7s²
Oct 31] €19,000Y: rather unfurnished filly. second foal: dam unraced half-sister to high-
class winner up to 1m Araafa: useful performer: won maiden at Hamilton in May and
claimer at Dieppe in July (left K. R. Burke after): continued progress after, placed at
Maisons-Laffitte last 3 starts, in listed race, Criterium de Maisons-Laffitte (5½ lengths
second to Donjuan Triumphant) and Prix Miesque (head second of 4 to Aboulie): stays 7f:
acts on soft going: has worn hood: has looked hard ride. *Mme Pia Brandt, France*

DRESSED TO THRILL 2 b.f. (Mar 19) Dick Turpin (IRE) 127 – Birthday Suit (IRE) 94 **60**
(Daylami (IRE) 138) [2015 5.9g⁴ Jul 9] 25/1, showed some promise when fourth in maiden
at Carlisle: dead. *Richard Fahey*

DR FINLEY (IRE) 8 ch.g. Dr Fong (USA) 128 – Farrfesheena (USA) 89 (Rahy (USA) **53**
115) [2015 63: p16g³ p16f⁴ p15.8f⁵ Sep 22] angular gelding: modest handicapper: stays
17f: acts on polytrack, good to firm and heavy going: sometimes in headgear prior to 2015.
Lydia Pearce

DRIFTING SPIRIT (IRE) 2 b.f. (Mar 20) Clodovil (IRE) 116 – Laureldean Spirit (IRE) **90**
71 (Whipper (USA) 126) [2015 6.5m⁵ 6m⁴ 7f⁵ 7.5m* 7g* 7g* 7g Oct 9] 38,000F, 52,000Y:
lengthy filly: second foal: dam, maiden (stayed 7f), half-sister to smart winner up to 1m
Nahoodh: fairly useful performer: won maiden at Beverley and nursery at Newmarket in
August, and nursery at Newmarket in September: stays 7.5f: acts on good to firm going:
often races prominently. *Richard Fahey*

DRINKS FOR LOSERS (IRE) 4 b.g. Mastercraftsman (IRE) 129 – Heart's Desire **48**
(IRE) 79 (Royal Applause 124) [2015 –: 9.1g⁵ 7.2g 12.1g 7.2g⁴ Sep 29] poor maiden: left
R. Mike Smith after second start: best effort at 7f: acts on soft going: usually races
prominently. *Linda Perratt*

DR IRV 6 ch.g. Dr Fong (USA) 128 – Grateful 69 (Generous (IRE) 139) [2015 84: 13g⁴ **77 §**
16.4m 16.1g⁶ 14m⁶ 16m² 16m² 14.6m⁵ 16m³ 16.1g⁵ Sep 6] smallish gelding: fair
handicapper: stays 2¼m: acts on good to firm and good to soft going: tried in cheekpieces:
irresolute, and one to treat with caution. *Micky Hammond*

DRIVE ON (IRE) 4 b.g. Tagula (IRE) 116 – Thelma Louise (IRE) (Desert Style (IRE) **81**
121) [2015 84: p7g* p7g³ p8f³ p7f 8m⁵ 6.1g⁶ p6g p6f p8g⁴ p8m Oct 21] rangy gelding:
fairly useful handicapper: won at Kempton (by neck from Picks Pinta) in January: barely
stays 1m: acts on polytrack and firm going: usually wears headgear: tried in tongue tie:
usually races towards rear. *Eve Johnson Houghton*

DROMCUS 3 b.c. Teofilo (IRE) 126 – Storming Sioux 79 (Storming Home 128) [2015 **82 p**
8.3s 10g⁵ 12d p11g⁵ Jul 8] sturdy colt: second foal: dam, maiden, closely related to very
smart winner up to 1¼m Best of The Bests out of useful performer up to 1½m Sueboog:
fairly useful form: promising fifth on handicap debut at Kempton: likely to prove best up
to 1¼m: capable of better. *James Fanshawe*

DR RED EYE 7 ch.g. Dr Fong (USA) 128 – Camp Fire (IRE) 81 (Lahib (USA) 129) [2015 **82**
94: f7g 7m² 7g³ 7s f7d⁵ 7m² 7g 6.1f⁴ 6m⁵ 7g⁶ 8g 7s 7g⁶ Sep 10] strong gelding: fairly
useful handicapper: stays 8.5f, usually races over shorter: acts on polytrack, fibresand and
any turf going: often wears headgear: front runner/races prominently. *Scott Dixon*

DRUID'S DIAMOND 2 b.g. (Mar 16) Piccolo 121 – Faithful Beauty (IRE) (Last Tycoon **–**
131) [2015 6m⁵ Jun 20] 33/1, very green when fifth in maiden at Redcar (14½ lengths
behind Receding Waves) in June. *Mark Walford*

DRUIDS RIDGE 3 b.c. Paco Boy (IRE) 129 – Miss Queen (USA) (Miswaki (USA) 124) **90 p**
[2015 8m² 8d⁴ 7m² 8g² 7f* Jul 3] useful-looking colt: half-brother to several winners,
including winner up to 1m (stayed 10.5f) Prince of Light (2-y-o 6f winner, by Fantastic
Light) and winner up to 1m Mandobi (2-y-o 7f winner, by Mark of Esteem), both smart:
dam 6f winner: fairly useful performer: won maiden at Doncaster by 2½ lengths from
Headquarters) in July: stays 1m: acts on good to firm going: still unexposed. *John Gosden*

DRUMLIN 2 gr.g. (Apr 21) Hellvelyn 118 – Live To Tell 68 (Primo Dominie 121) [2015 **–**
7g p7m Dec 31] no form. *Geoffrey Deacon*

DRUMMOND 6 b.g. Zamindar (USA) 116 – Alrisha (IRE) 90 (Persian Bold 123) [2015 **46**
–: 12d⁶ 10.2d⁵ Aug 20] sturdy gelding: poor maiden: stays 1½m: acts on good to firm and
heavy going: tried in headgear: tried in tongue tie. *Bernard Llewellyn*

DRUOT 3 b.g. Champs Elysees 124 – Trick of Ace (USA) (Clever Trick (USA)) [2015 68p: **–**
7g 10m Jul 20] sturdy gelding: maiden: no form in 2015: bred to be suited by at least 1¼m.
Peter Makin

DRY YOUR EYES (IRE) 4 b.f. Shamardal (USA) 129 – Kindling 105 (Dr Fong (USA) **72**
128) [2015 77: 12g⁴ Jun 8] big, workmanlike filly: fair handicapper: stays 1½m: acts on
good to firm and heavy going. *David O'Meara*

DUAL MAC 8 br.g. Paris House 123 – Carol Again 48 (Kind of Hush 118) [2015 79: 8g⁵ **86**
8.5s³ 7.5g² 8m² 6.9s² 8.5d* 8g 8.3s Oct 28] fairly useful handicapper: won at Beverley in
September: stays 8.5f: acts on soft and good to firm going: often wears headgear. *Neville
Bycroft*

DUBAI BREEZE (IRE) 3 b.f. Lope de Vega (IRE) 125 – Expectation (IRE) 59 (Night **62**
Shift (USA)) [2015 75: p8g p7g 7d 6g² 5.1m 7.5g 7.6m³ p8f⁵ p6f⁵ Sep 10] modest maiden:
stays 7.5f: acts on good to firm going. *Clive Brittain*

287

DUBAI CELEBRATION 7 b.g. Dubai Destination (USA) 127 – Pretty Poppy 67 (Song **70**
132) [2015 80: 8m⁴ t9.5g⁵ Apr 25] big, strong gelding: fair handicapper: stays 9.5f: acts on
polytrack, soft and good to firm going: often wears headgear: tried in tongue tie prior to
2015. *Julie Camacho*

DUBAI CELEBRITY 3 b.g. Sakhee (USA) 136 – Aljana (IRE) (Exceed And Excel **73**
(AUS) 126) [2015 8s 10.1d 12m⁴ 12.4g⁵ 14.1g 12g⁴ 14.4g⁶ Aug 6] fair maiden: stays 12.5f:
acts on good to firm going: tried in visor: sometimes slowly away, often races towards rear.
Chris Grant

DUBAI DYNAMO 10 b.g. Kyllachy 129 – Miss Mercy (IRE) 62 (Law Society (USA) **97**
130) [2015 97: 7d⁵ 8g⁵ 8g² 8g* 8d⁶ 8d⁵ 8m 7m 8g⁴ 8m* 8g 7.6g 7g 8g* 7.6s 8g⁵ 7.2g Oct 8]
stocky gelding: useful handicapper: won at Ripon in May, July (by 3¼ lengths from Johnny
Cavagin) and August: stays 8.5f: acts on polytrack and any turf going: tried in headgear
prior to 2015: inconsistent nowadays. *Ruth Carr*

DUBAI EMPRESS (IRE) 2 b.f. (Apr 21) Dubawi (IRE) 129 – The World (Dubai **–**
Destination (USA) 127) [2015 7s Oct 12] useful-looking filly: fourth foal: sister to 7f
winner (stays 9.5f) Conquerant and 1¼m winner Wild Storm, both useful, and half-sister
to 11f-12.5f winner Cosmic Flame (by Doyen): dam, 1¼m winner, half-sister to high-class
winner up to 1m Poet's Voice: 16/1, badly needed experience when well held in maiden at
Salisbury. *William Haggas*

DUBAI FASHION (IRE) 2 b.f. (Mar 3) Dubawi (IRE) 129 – Oriental Fashion (IRE) 110 **85 p**
(Marju (IRE) 127) [2015 t8.6g⁸ 8d⁵ Oct 31] half-sister to several winners, including smart
7f winner Green Coast (by Green Desert), winner up to 1¼m Famous Warrior (2-y-o
6f-8.4f winner, by Alhaarth) and 1m-1½m winner St Jean (by Teofilo), latter 2 useful: dam
1m winner, including at 2 yrs: easily won maiden at Wolverhampton (by 2¾ lengths from
Sagely) in October: not seen to best effect when fifth in listed race at Newmarket: remains
with potential. *Saeed bin Suroor*

DUBAI HILLS 9 b.g. Dubai Destination (USA) 127 – Hill Welcome 52 (Most Welcome **95**
131) [2015 96: f7s 8g² 8g 7.2d 7.9g 8d 8g³ 8d⁴ t8.6m f7g f7g³ Dec 22] strong gelding:
useful handicapper: second at Redcar (head behind Taghreeb) in April and third at
Southwell (2½ lengths behind Ian's Memory) in December: stays 1m: acts on fibresand,
soft and good to firm going: tried in visor in 2015. *David O'Meara*

DUBAI IN BLOOM (IRE) 2 b.f. (Mar 17) Kheleyf (USA) 116 – Weood (IRE) (Dubawi **–**
(IRE) 129) [2015 7v⁵ Aug 25] first foal: dam, of little account, half-sister to useful winner
up to 1m (stayed 1¼m) Desert Realm: 5/1, last of 5 in maiden at Brighton. *Simon Crisford*

DUBAI SKYLINE (USA) 4 b.f. Medaglia d'Oro (USA) 129 – Love of Dubai (USA) 106 **–**
(More Than Ready (USA) 120) [2015 –: p12g Jun 4] maiden: no form in 2015. *Clive Brittain*

DUBAI'S SECRET 2 ch.c. (Mar 29) Paco Boy (IRE) 129 – Lilli Marlane 82 (Sri Pekan **83**
(USA) 117) [2015 6m 6.1m* 7m 8.3m* 8g⁴ 8.3g³ Oct 19] 65,000Y: angular colt: seventh
foal: half-brother to 3 winners, including 6f winner Treadstone (by Myboycharlie) and
winner up to 7f Pearl Rebel (2-y-o 6f winner, by Cockney Rebel): dam, 1m-9.7f winner,
half-sister to smart 1m/9f winner Medici Code: fairly useful performer: won maiden at
Chepstow in July and nursery at Windsor in August: stays 8.5f: acts on good to firm going:
often starts slowly. *Richard Hannon*

DUBAWI DIAMOND 3 b.c. Dubawi (IRE) 129 – Darrfonah (IRE) 106 (Singspiel (IRE) **63**
133) [2015 71: f8g³ f8s⁴ t8.6gᵖᵘ Feb 9] modest maiden: stayed 8.5f: acted on all-weather:
often in headgear in 2015: fatally injured at Wolverhampton. *James Tate*

Betfred Glorious Stakes, Goodwood—
the first success for a Qatari-trained horse in Britain as Dubday beats The Corsican

DUBAWI LIGHT 4 b.g. Dubawi (IRE) 129 – Shesadelight 67 (Shirley Heights 130)   **86**
[2015 77: 8.3g p10g* p10g³ Nov 25] fairly useful handicapper: won at Kempton in
November: stays 1¼m: acts on polytrack: often travels strongly. *Gary Moore*

DUBDAY 5 ch.h. Dubawi (IRE) 129 – Dayrose 94 (Daylami (IRE) 138) [2015 10.9g* 11.9g*   **120**
15.9g⁵ 12m² 12m² 12m* 11.9s³ Sep 27] rangy horse: third foal: dam, 9.7f/10.5f winner,
half-sister to dam of high-class 1¼m performer Notnowcato: very smart performer: won
twice at Doha in February, namely Qatar Gold Trophy and H. H. Emir's Trophy (by neck
from Ponfeigh), both for second successive year, and Glorious Stakes at Goodwood (by ¾
length from The Corsican) in July: creditable efforts all other starts, placed in listed races
at Newbury and Newmarket (beaten short head by Gospel Choir) and Preis von Europa at
Cologne (2 lengths third to Nightflower): stayed 2m: acted on good to firm going:
to stand at Qatar Racing and Equestrian Club, fee private. *Jassim Al Ghazali, Qatar*

DUC DE SEVILLE (IRE) 3 b.g. Duke of Marmalade (IRE) 132 – Splendid (IRE)   **62**
(Mujtahid (USA) 118) [2015 62: p11g p12g⁴ 14.1g 12v² 12.1s³ 13.1m³ Sep 28] modest
handicapper: stays 13f: acts on tapeta, good to firm and heavy going: usually in cheekpieces
in 2015: front runner/races prominently: temperament under suspicion. *Clive Cox*

DUCHESSOFMARMALADE 3 b.f. Duke of Marmalade (IRE) 132 – Helena Molony   **–**
(IRE) 105 (Sadler's Wells (USA) 132) [2015 7m 8m Jul 17] 62,000Y: angular filly: fifth
foal: closely related to 1m-1¼m winner Dance of Heroes (by Danehill Dancer) and half-
sister to 1¼m winner Red Hand (by Mr Greeley) and 9.5f winner Heavenly Sound (by
Street Cry): dam, 1¼m winner who stayed 1¾m, sister to top-class winner up to 1½m High
Chaparral: no form. *Ralph Smith*

DUCHESS OF MARMITE (IRE) 3 b.f. Duke of Marmalade (IRE) 132 – Reprise 66   **92**
(Darshaan 133) [2015 p10g² p10g³ 11m 12d⁵ 11.6g p10g⁵ p12m³ p16g* t13.9f² p16f*
p16g* Dec 9] €65,000Y: lengthy filly: sixth foal: half-sister to 3 winners, including smart
winner up to 1½m (stayed 14.5f) Hazel Lavery (2-y-o 7f winner, by Excellent Art) and
useful 1¼m-13f winner Leo Gali (by Galileo): dam ran twice: fairly useful handicapper:
won at Kempton and Chelmsford in November, and Kempton in December: left Charles
Hills after sixth start: stays 2m: acts on polytrack, tapeta and good to soft going: often in
headgear: usually races in rear, strong traveller: quirky. *Richard Hughes*

DUCHY 2 b.f. (Feb 25) Kyllachy 129 – Albavilla 82 (Spectrum (IRE) 126) [2015 7g⁶ 8.3g⁴   **79 p**
Oct 20] 105,000Y: fifth foal: half-sister to 9f-11f winner Antinori (by Fasliyev) and 2-y-o
5f-1m winner Pure Excellence (by Exceed And Excel), both useful: dam, 1¾m winner,
half-sister to very smart 1¼m-1¾m winner Barolo and useful/ungenuine 2-y-o 7f winner
Propinquity: better effort when fourth in maiden at Windsor (2¼ lengths behind So Mi Dar)
in October, unsuited by emphasis on speed: will prove best at 1m+: remains with potential.
Michael Bell

DUCK A L'ORANGE (IRE) 2 ch.g. (Mar 15) Duke of Marmalade (IRE) 132 – Incheni   **74**
(IRE) 100 (Nashwan (USA) 135) [2015 8g 8.3g³ 8s⁵ Oct 15] sturdy gelding: fair maiden:
best effort when third in maiden at Windsor (2¼ lengths behind Four On Eight) in
September, met some trouble: will be suited by 1¼m. *Michael Bell*

DUDE ALERT (IRE) 5 b.g. Windsor Knot (IRE) 118 – Policy (Nashwan (USA) 135)   **29**
[2015 p13.3m⁴ Feb 12] poor maiden: best effort at 1m: acts on polytrack: in visor sole start
in 2015. *Anna Newton-Smith*

DUE DILIGENCE (USA) 4 b.c. War Front (USA) 119 – Bema (USA) (Pulpit (USA)   **106**
117) [2015 120: 7d 6f 6f 6d⁵ Sep 5] good-topped colt: smart performer at 3 yrs, injured
pelvis when runner-up in Diamond Jubilee Stakes at Royal Ascot final outing (off 10
months after): failed to recapture that form in 2015, best effort (just useful form) when 4½
lengths fifth to Twilight Son in Sprint Cup at Haydock final start: best form at 6f: acted on
firm and good to soft going: sometimes wore tongue tie: to stand at Whitsbury Manor Stud,
Fordingbridge, Hampshire, fee £6,500. *Aidan O'Brien, Ireland*

DUELLING DRAGON (USA) 4 b.g. Henrythenavigator (USA) 131 – Ometsz (IRE)   **86**
111 (Singspiel (IRE) 133) [2015 80: 7d* 8d p8g 8.5m³ Jul 9] lengthy gelding: fairly
useful handicapper: won at Leicester in April: stayed 8.5f: acted on firm and good to soft
going: dead. *Stuart Kittow*

DUET 3 ch.f. Pivotal 124 – Miswaki Belle (USA) 73 (Miswaki (USA) 124) [2015 8g p10f⁴   **61 p**
p12g Sep 9] sister to 3 winners, including smart 1¼m winner (stayed 1½m) Mighty and
smart 1m-11f winner Humouresque and half-sister to several winners, including smart
winner up to 6f Danehurst (2-y-o 5f winner, by Danehill): dam ran once: modest form in
maidens: remains with potential. *Jeremy Noseda*

DUFAY (IRE) 2 b.f. (Feb 16) Dubawi (IRE) 129 – White Moonstone (USA) 115 **78 p**
(Dynaformer (USA)) [2015 p7m³ Dec 16] first foal: dam, 2-y-o 6f-1m (Fillies' Mile)
winner, half-sister to smart 1¼m/10.3f winner Albasharah: 11/4, shaped well when third in
maiden at Lingfield (3 lengths behind Auntinet) in December, caught further back than
ideal: sure to progress. *Charlie Appleby*

DUFFEL 3 ch.c. Shamardal (USA) 129 – Paisley 80 (Pivotal 124) [2015 8f 7m⁶ 7m⁶ t6g* **75**
6v³ p6d⁵ t6g 7d Oct 24] fair handicapper: won at Wolverhampton in August: best effort at
6f: acts on tapeta: often travels strongly. *Luca Cumani*

DUFOOF (IRE) 3 b.f. Shamardal (USA) 129 – Evensong (GER) (Waky Nao 122) [2015 **61**
7f³ p8g Jul 21] 90,000Y: fourth foal: half-sister to 8.6f-1¼m winner Night And Dance (by
Danehill Dancer) and 5f/6f winner Diamond Klitoui (by Holy Roman Emperor): dam,
1m-1¼m winner, half-sister to 1m winner Eagle Rise and 9f-2m winner Eye of The Tiger,
both smart: better effort when third in maiden at Doncaster in July: will prove suited to
1m+. *William Haggas*

DUKE COSIMO 5 ch.g. Pivotal 124 – Nannina 121 (Medicean 128) [2015 95: 6g⁵ 6g 6m **90**
6.1f 6m 6g Sep 19] fairly useful handicapper: stays 6f: acts on polytrack, good to firm and
good to soft going: sometimes wears blinkers. *David Barron*

DUKE OF CLARENCE (IRE) 6 gr.g. Verglas (IRE) 118 – Special Lady (FR) (Kaldoun **102**
(FR) 122) [2015 110: 18.7d 12m⁵ May 15] well-made gelding: useful handicapper: stays
1¾m: acts on polytrack, good to firm and heavy going: tried in headgear: often races
prominently. *Richard Fahey*

DUKE OF DIAMONDS 3 gr.g. Duke of Marmalade (IRE) 132 – Diamond Line (FR) **57**
(Linamix (FR) 127) [2015 12s⁴ p12g⁵ p13.3f⁵ Oct 8] modest maiden: best effort when
fourth in maiden at Newmarket in July. *Julia Feilden*

DUKE OF DUNTON (IRE) 4 b.g. Duke of Marmalade (IRE) 132 – Southern Migration **53**
(USA) (Kingmambo (USA) 125) [2015 49: p8g p10m p8f p7m 7.6g⁶ p12g³ p11g⁴ p10g³
p10f⁶ t9.5f² t8.6f⁴ t8.6f p8g⁵ t8.6g Dec 1] lengthy gelding: modest maiden: left Tony
Carroll after fifth start: stays 1¼m: acts on polytrack and tapeta: often in cheekpieces in
2015: tried in tongue tie in 2015: sold £800, sent to Germany. *Dean Ivory*

DUKE OF FIRENZE 6 ch.g. Pivotal 124 – Nannina 121 (Medicean 128) [2015 109: 5.1s **–**
5g 5m 5v Aug 31] good-topped gelding: useful at best, no form in 2015: sometimes wears
cheekpieces: often races prominently, tends to find little. *Robert Cowell*

DUKE OF HANOVER 4 b.g. Duke of Marmalade (IRE) 132 – Caro George (USA) 69 **–**
(Distant View (USA) 126) [2015 t12.2m f7g f12g⁵ Nov 24] no form. *Clare Ellam*

DUKE OF NORTH (IRE) 3 b.g. Danehill Dancer (IRE) 117 – Althea Rose (IRE) (Green **75**
Desert (USA) 127) [2015 69p: p7g⁵ p7g p7g* p6g* p6g p6m⁵ Dec 31] fair handicapper:
won at Lingfield in October: left James Fanshawe after fourth start: best effort at 6f: acts
on polytrack: tried in cheekpieces in 2015. *Jim Boyle*

DUKE OF ROMANCE 3 ch.g. Duke of Marmalade (IRE) 132 – Chance For Romance **–**
81 (Entrepreneur 123) [2015 –: 10m 8g 12.1g p10m 13.1fᵇᵘ p13.3f 10d Oct 5] maiden: no
form in 2015: tried in visor in 2015. *John Ryan*

DUKE OF SONNING 3 ch.g. Duke of Marmalade (IRE) 132 – Moonshadow 75 (Diesis **79**
133) [2015 70p: 14m⁵ 14.1m 12.1m* 11s⁶ Sep 23] big, strong gelding: fair handicapper:
won at Chepstow in September: best effort at 1½m: acts on good to firm going. *Alan King*

DUKE OF YORKSHIRE 5 b.g. Duke of Marmalade (IRE) 132 – Dame Edith (FR) (Top **66**
Ville 129) [2015 78: 9.9g 10m 9.9m³ 9.9m² 12.1m³ 10.2m 12g 10m² 10.4g 10m 9.9d 10.3d
10.7s³ Oct 20] full handicapper: stays 14.5f: acts on good to firm and heavy going: tried in
headgear in 2015: often in tongue tie in 2015. *Tim Easterby*

DUKES DEN 4 b.g. Duke of Marmalade (IRE) 132 – Green Room (FR) 108 (In The **60**
Wings 128) [2015 71: p15.8g⁶ t16.5m³ p16d⁴ p15.8g⁵ 17.2f⁵ t16.5g³ 16.2s 13.1m² 16.2m⁴ **a67**
p16g³ 16g Jul 8] useful-looking gelding: fair handicapper: stays 17f: acts on polytrack,
tapeta and firm going: tried in blinkers in 2015. *Sylvester Kirk*

DUKES MEADOW 4 b.g. Pastoral Pursuits 127 – Figura 87 (Rudimentary (USA) 118) **77**
[2015 75p: p8f⁵ p8g p8f* p8d Nov 30] fair handicapper: won at Chelmsford in November:
likely to stay 1¼m: raced only on polytrack. *Roger Ingram*

DUKE STREET (IRE) 3 b.g. Duke of Marmalade (IRE) 132 – Act of The Pace (IRE) 86 **93**
(King's Theatre (IRE) 128) [2015 p10g⁵ p10g³ p10g³ f12g³ 12.1s t12.2g* 11.9m⁴
t13.9g* p16g* 16.2s* 16m² 16.2m* 14g Aug 22] €20,000Y: fifth foal: half-brother to 3
winners, including 1½m-2¼m winner Act of Kalanisi (by Kalanisi) and 1½m winner
Cluain Dara (by Hawk Wing): dam, 12.3f winner who stayed 15f, closely related to very
smart 7f-15.5f winner Yavana's Pace and smart winner up to 1¼m Littlepacepaddocks:

fairly useful handicapper: won at Wolverhampton in June and July, Chelmsford and Chepstow later in July and Beverley (by 1¼ lengths from Sea of Heaven) in August: stays 2m: acts on polytrack, tapeta, soft and good to firm going: front runner/races prominently: joined Dr Richard Newland, successful over hurdles. *Mark Johnston*

DULJANAH (IRE) 2 ch.f. (Feb 17) Dream Ahead (USA) 133 – Centreofattention (AUS) (Danehill (USA) 126) [2015 p7g Jul 14] 45,000Y: dam lightly-raced sister to high-class 2-y-o 6f/7f winner Holy Roman Emperor: 66/1, green when well held in maiden at Lingfield (23 lengths behind Hawkbill). *Ed Walker* —

DUMBFOUNDED (FR) 7 b.g. Vettori (IRE) 119 – Take The Light (FR) (Take Risks (FR) 116) [2015 77: p13g⁴ 16m p15.8g Aug 7] sturdy gelding: fair handicapper: won at Lingfield (apprentice) in March: stays 1¾m: acts on polytrack and good to firm going. *Graham Mays* **79**

DU MOTO (IRE) 2 b.c. (May 5) Galileo (IRE) 134 – Mauralakana (FR) 116 (Muhtathir 126) [2015 7.1g⁶ p8g⁴ Aug 18] 510,000Y: good sort: fourth foal: brother to useful 7f winner Hail The Hero and half-brother to 1m winner Calissa (by Danehill Dancer): dam winner up to 11f (including US Grade 1 9.5f winner, and 2-y-o 5f/6f winner): fair form in maidens: better effort when fourth in maiden at Kempton (10¼ lengths behind Pure Diamond) in August: open to further improvement. *Sir Michael Stoute* **72 p**

DUNCAN OF SCOTLAND (IRE) 2 ch.c. (Apr 28) Roderic O'Connor (IRE) 119 – Cantando (IRE) (Hamas (IRE) 125) [2015 6d³ 7m 7.2g p7g p6g p7g⁶ p6g³ Nov 13] fair maiden: stays 6f: acts on polytrack and good to soft going: sometimes in blinkers. *L. Smyth, Ireland* **70 a61**

DUNE DANCER (IRE) 2 b.c. (Apr 6) Footstepsinthesand 120 – Leonica 92 (Lion Cavern (USA) 117) [2015 p8m⁵ Oct 21] 65,000Y: half-brother to 3 winners, including useful winner up to 8.3f Rodrigo de Torres (2-y-o 6f winner, by Bahamian Bounty) and 2-y-o 5f winner Old Master Expert (by Royal Applause): dam, 1m winner, half-sister to smart winner up to 1½m Greek Envoy: 10/1, showed plenty when fifth in maiden at Kempton (2¼ lengths behind Bluebeard) in October: will improve. *David Lanigan* **71 p**

DUNGANNON 8 b.g. Monsieur Bond (IRE) 120 – May Light 62 (Midyan (USA) 124) [2015 115: f5s² p5g p5g 5m⁴ 5m 5d 5s 5d f5g³ Dec 12] good-topped gelding: useful handicapper: second in minor event at Southwell (head behind Woolfall Sovereign) in January and third at Southwell (2¼ lengths behind Meadway) in December: stays 7f: acts on polytrack, fibresand, good to firm and heavy going: sometimes wears headgear: often races towards rear. *Andrew Balding* **86 a100**

DUNNSCOTIA 3 b.g. Showcasing 117 – Black And Amber 45 (Weldnaas (USA) 112) [2015 68: 6.1d 5.7g² 6g² 6g² 6m² Aug 9] sturdy gelding: fair maiden: stays 6f: acts on good to firm going: usually wears tongue tie. *Paul Webber* **74**

DUNQUIN (IRE) 3 b.g. Cape Cross (IRE) 129 – Last Resort 116 (Lahib (USA) 129) [2015 84: 7v 8s⁵ t9.5m⁶ Dec 30] good-bodied gelding: fairly useful maiden: left J. S. Bolger after second start: likely to stay at least 1¼m: acts on tapeta and good to soft going: usually races prominently. *John Mackie* **81**

DURETTO 3 ch.g. Manduro (GER) 135 – Landinium (ITY) 109 (Lando (GER) 128) [2015 85p: 10m p11g⁴ 12d* 12g* 12g⁴ Oct 9] tall gelding: useful handicapper: won at Ascot in July and September (dead-heated with Wonder Laish): fourth to Mustard in valuable event at Newmarket final start: stays 1½m: acts on polytrack and good to soft going: usually in hood in 2015: races towards rear. *Andrew Balding* **96**

DURHAM EXPRESS (IRE) 8 b.g. Acclamation 118 – Edwina (IRE) 63 (Caerleon (USA) 132) [2015 50: 6s 6g 5g May 29] tall gelding: fairly useful at best, no form in 2015: often wears headgear. *Colin Teague* —

DUSKY QUEEN (IRE) 5 b.m. Shamardal (USA) 129 – Sanna Bay (IRE) (Refuse To Bend (IRE) 128) [2015 100: 7s² 7m* 7g³ 7g* 7m⁶ 7d² 7m⁵ 7g⁵ p8g Oct 29] rangy mare: useful performer: won handicap at York (by 1¼ lengths from Royal Seal) in May and listed race at Chester (by head from Intransigent) in July: second in listed race at Haydock (1¼ lengths behind That Is The Spirit) in May and handicap at York (neck behind Mistrusting) in August: stays 7f: acts on firm and good to soft going. *Richard Fahey* **108**

DUSKY RAIDER (IRE) 2 gr.g. (Apr 30) Clodovil (IRE) 116 – Rahila (IRE) (Kalanisi (IRE) 132) [2015 5.9g 7m 7s Sep 5] modest maiden: best effort when seventh in maiden at Thirsk (5 lengths behind Midnight Macchiato) in August. *Michael Dods* **55**

DUSTY BLUE 3 ch.f. Medicean 128 – Jazz Jam 100 (Pivotal 124) [2015 67: p5g* p5m⁵ p6f³ p6.5g 5g⁶ 5.1s⁵ 5.7m* 5.7d⁵ 5f⁶ 5g² t5.1f t5.1g Nov 27] fair performer: won maiden at Lingfield in January and handicap at Bath in August: stays 6f: acts on polytrack and good to firm going: often wears tongue tie: sometimes slowly away, often races in rear. *Tony Carroll* **75 a67**

DUSTY RAVEN 2 ch.g. (Apr 30) Raven's Pass (USA) 133 – Dust Dancer 116 (Suave – **p** Dancer (USA) 136) [2015 p7g t7.1f f7m Dec 8] half-brother to several winners, including smart winner up to 9f Spotlight (2-y-o 7f/1m winner, by Dr Fong) and useful 7f winner Tyranny (by Machiavellian): dam 7f-1½m winner: little impact in maidens: will do better in handicaps over 1m+. *Sir Mark Prescott Bt*

DUTCHARTCOLLECTOR 4 b.g. Dutch Art 126 – Censored 79 (Pivotal 124) [2015 67: p8d Nov 30] tall, angular gelding: fair at best, no form in 2015: stays 1¼m: acts on polytrack: tried in headgear prior to 2015: sometimes slowly away. *Tim McCarthy*

DUTCH ART DEALER 4 b.g. Dutch Art 126 – Lawyers Choice 86 (Namid 128) [2015 **97** 100: p8g⁶ p8g Dec 7] lengthy, useful-looking gelding: useful handicapper: stays 1m: acts on polytrack, tapeta and firm going: tried in cheekpieces. *Paul Cole*

DUTCH BREEZE 4 ch.g. Dutch Art 126 – Oasis Breeze 88 (Oasis Dream 129) [2015 86: **85** 6d 6v 5.9m³ 6g 7v* Oct 17] fairly useful handicapper: won at Catterick (by short head from Cabelo) in October: stays 7f: acts on good to firm and heavy going: sometimes wears cheekpieces: front runner/races prominently. *Tim Easterby*

DUTCH CONNECTION 3 ch.c. Dutch Art 126 – Endless Love (IRE) (Dubai **122** Destination (USA) 127) [2015 106: 8m 7f* 8g² 7g² 8d⁵ Oct 3] rangy, good sort: very smart performer: won Jersey Stakes at Royal Ascot (by ½ length from Fadhayyil) in June: second after in Prix Jean Prat at Chantilly (best effort, beaten ½ length from Territories) and Lennox Stakes at Goodwood (respectable ¾ length behind Toormore): possibly unsuited by softer ground when fifth (beaten 3½ lengths by Grand Arch) in Shadwell Turf Mile at Keeneland final outing: likely to prove best up to 1m: acts on firm going: often races prominently, usually travels strongly. *Charles Hills*

DUTCH DESCENT (IRE) 4 b.g. Royal Applause 124 – Wagtail 101 (Cape Cross (IRE) **80** 129) [2015 61: 7m⁵ 8.3s³ 8d* 8g⁴ 7.5f⁶ 8g 8d³ 8.3v p8f f8m Dec 8] fairly useful handicapper: won at Ayr (by 1¼ lengths from Funding Deficit) in May: stays 8.5f: acts on soft going. *David Barron*

DUTCH DESTINY 2 b.f. (Mar 8) Dutch Art 126 – Danehill Destiny 104 (Danehill **87 p** Dancer (IRE) 117) [2015 p7g² 7s* Oct 12] compact filly: third foal: half-sister to useful 6f winner Danehill Revival (by Pivotal): dam winner up to 6f (2-y-o 5f winner): better effort when winning maiden at Salisbury (by length from Girling) in October: open to further improvement. *William Haggas*

DUTCH DIVA 3 b.f. Dutch Art 126 – Hiddendale (IRE) 97 (Indian Ridge 123) [2015 5m – May 27] sixth foal: dam, 2-y-o 6f winner, half-sister to winner up to 7f That's The Way: 10/1, green when seventh in maiden at Thirsk (8½ lengths behind Bapak Asmara) in May. *Scott Dixon*

DUTCH DREAM 2 ch.f. (Mar 18) Dutch Art 126 – Starry Sky 81 (Oasis Dream 129) **56** [2015 7.2g 6m 6g Oct 8] 45,000Y: fourth foal: half-sister to 2-y-o 6f winners Tarn (by Royal Applause) and Blackbriar (by Kyllachy): dam 2-y-o 7f winner out of useful 1¼m winner Succinct: modest maiden: best effort when seventh in maiden at Hamilton (3¾ lengths behind Extortion) in September. *Linda Perratt*

DUTCHESS OF ART 3 br.f. Dutch Art 126 – Kind of Light 83 (Primo Dominie 121) **68**
[2015 –: p6g² p6g⁵ p7f⁴ 6d t6g³ Apr 27] fair maiden: stays 7f: acts on polytrack and tapeta:
usually in blinkers in 2015: sometimes slowly away, often races towards rear. *Olly Stevens*

DUTCH FALCON 3 ch.g. Pivotal 124 – Luminance (IRE) (Danehill Dancer (IRE) 117) **57**
[2015 –: t8.6g³ 8g 8.3m t8.6g⁴ p8g⁶ 7.4d⁵ 7d Sep 21] fair maiden: stays 8.5f: acts on tapeta: **a70**
tried in cheekpieces in 2015: often races prominently. *William Muir*

DUTCH FREDIE G 3 ch.f. Dutch Art 126 – Flawless Diamond (IRE) 54 (Indian Haven **39**
119) [2015 –: p7f p6g p8g 7s⁶ Jun 2] poor maiden: best effort at 7f: acts on polytrack: races
prominently. *Gary Moore*

DUTCH GALLERY 2 b.c. (Feb 28) Dutch Art 126 – Luluti (IRE) 55 (Kheleyf (USA) **85 p**
116) [2015 6g* Jul 31] 65,000Y: second foal: dam once-raced half-sister to useful 2-y-o 5f
winner Excellerator: 12/1, won maiden at Newmarket (by neck from Wimpole Hall) in July,
responding well: should progress if all is well. *Tom Dascombe*

DUTCH GARDEN 3 b.g. Fastnet Rock (AUS) 127 – Swan Wings 89 (Bahamian Bounty **57**
116) [2015 70p: t9.5g⁵ f7g⁴ Dec 29] modest maiden: better effort in 2015 when fourth in
maiden at Southwell in December. *David Brown*

DUTCH GOLDEN AGE (IRE) 3 b.g. Kodiac 112 – Magic Melody 62 (Petong 126) **79**
[2015 80p: p6f² p6f³ p6g* Dec 2] fair performer: won maiden at Kempton in December:
likely to stay 7f: tried in tongue tie in 2015. *Gary Moore*

DUTCH HEIRESS 2 b.f. (Feb 7) Dutch Art 126 – Regal Heiress 76 (Pivotal 124) [2015 **82**
6d⁴ 5.7f p7g² 7.2s* 7.2m* 7.5m² 7s⁵ p8g³ Sep 9] strong filly: first foal: dam, maiden (stayed
8.3f), out of Cheveley Park Stakes winner Regal Rose: fairly useful performer: won maiden
at Ayr in July and nursery at Musselburgh in August: stays 7.5f: acts on soft and good to
firm going: tried in cheekpieces: front runner/races prominently. *Sir Mark Prescott Bt*

DUTCH LADY ROSEANE 4 b.f. Dutch Art 126 – Lady Rose Anne (IRE) 67 (Red **–**
Ransom (USA)) [2015 53: t12.2g 13.1m 7g 10.2d Aug 14] maiden: no form in 2015:
sometimes in headgear prior to 2015: sometimes slowly away. *James Unett*

DUTCH LAW 3 b.g. Dutch Art 126 – Lawyers Choice 86 (Namid 128) [2015 72p: p7m⁴ **91**
8g² 8m* 8f² p8g⁵ 8.3g⁵ 8.9s Oct 10] close-coupled gelding: fairly useful handicapper: won
at Newmarket in June: second at Ascot in July: stays 1m: acts on firm going: tried in
blinkers in 2015: often races in rear. *Hughie Morrison*

DUTCH MASTERPIECE 5 b.g. Dutch Art 126 – The Terrier 76 (Foxhound (USA) **113**
103) [2015 –: 5.1d⁵ 5.1s⁶ 5m³ 5m² 5.4g 5g² 5.2s⁵ 5m* p6g² Oct 7] strong gelding: smart
performer: won listed race at Ascot (by neck from Speed Hawk) in October: best form at
5f: acts on fibresand, good to firm and heavy going: sometimes wears headgear: often starts
slowly, often races towards rear: has hung right. *Gary Moore*

DUTCH MIST 2 ch.f. (Mar 18) Dutch Art 126 – Solstice 84 (Dubawi (IRE) 129) [2015 **94**
5.1m⁵ 6m* 6d* 6g* 6g 7s⁶ 6g⁵ 6s⁶ 7v⁵ Oct 24] 38,000F: neat filly: second foal: half-sister
to 11f winner (stays 1¾m) Solstalla (by Halling): dam 6f winner: fairly useful performer:
won maiden at Thirsk in June, and nurseries at Catterick and Thirsk (by length from Baby
Ballerina) in July: stays 6f: acts on good to firm and good to soft going: usually races nearer
last than first. *Kevin Ryan*

DUTCH MISTRESS 6 b.m. Dutch Art 126 – Royal Mistress (Fasliyev (USA) 120) [2015 **55**
–: 7g⁶ 7g⁴ 8g⁵ Aug 13] strong mare: modest handicapper: stays 1m: acts on polytrack and
good to firm going: tried in cheekpieces in 2015: often races prominently. *David Bridgwater*

DUTCH RIFLE 4 b.f. Dutch Art 126 – Vodka Shot (USA) 53 (Holy Bull (USA) 134) **75**
[2015 77, a87: t8.6g t9.5m Feb 27] fair handicapper: stays 11.5f, effective at shorter: acts
on polytrack, tapeta and good to firm going: in hood in 2015. *James Tate*

DUTCH ROBIN (IRE) 3 b.f. Fast Company (IRE) 126 – Autumn Star (IRE) (Mujadil **–**
(USA) 119) [2015 63: 7.5m⁵ 8d 10m Jun 15] maiden: no form in 2015. *Mick Channon*

DUTCH S 4 ch.f. Dutch Art 126 – Park Law (IRE) 94 (Fasliyev (USA) 120) [2015 83: p7g⁴ **74**
p7f 7m⁶ 8m⁴ 10g Jun 22] tall filly: fair handicapper: stays 7f: acts on polytrack, good to
firm and heavy going: sometimes wears headgear. *Clive Cox*

DUTCH UNCLE 3 b.g. Dutch Art 126 – Evasive Quality (FR) (Highest Honor (FR) 124) **91**
[2015 84p: t9.5f* 10.3m² 10m³ 10m 10.1m⁴ 12f 10g³ Jul 17] compact gelding: fairly useful
performer: won maiden at Wolverhampton in January: second in handicap at Doncaster in
April: stays 10.5f: acts on tapeta and good to firm going. *Ed Dunlop*

DUTIFUL SON (IRE) 5 b.g. Invincible Spirit (IRE) 121 – Grecian Dancer 114 (Dansili **97**
127) [2015 101: p6g p5g p7g⁶ p6g* p6g⁶ p8g³ p8g³ p7g⁴ p8g³ p8g³ p7g⁴ p7g* p8f p8g⁴
p8g⁴ Dec 28] sturdy gelding: useful handicapper: won at Chelmsford in April and Kempton

in November: third at Kempton (½ length behind Librisa Breeze) in September: left David C. Griffiths after third start: stays 1m: acts on polytrack: tried in cheekpieces in 2015. *Simon Dow*

DWIGHT D 2 b.c. (Feb 1) Duke of Marmalade (IRE) 132 – Almatinka (IRE) (Indian Ridge 123) [2015 p8g⁶ p8f² Dec 21] 75,000Y: fourth foal: half-brother to 1m winner Easter Chorus (by Oasis Dream): dam, 7f winner, half-sister to smart winner up to 1m Alanza out of smart performer up to 1¼m Alasha: better effort when second in maiden at Chelmsford (neck behind Cape Speed) in December, sticking to task: will go on improving. *William Haggas*   **84 p**

DYLAN ALEXANDER (IRE) 2 b.f. (Apr 30) Dylan Thomas (IRE) 132 – Kindest 92 (Cadeaux Genereux 131) [2015 6m 6d⁵ 7m⁴ 7m² p7g* 8g 6.1s⁴ t7.1f p7g⁶ Nov 13] second foal: dam, 1m/9f winner, half-sister to 11f/1½m winner (stayed 15f) Without A Trace and 2-y-o 5f winner Patience Alexander, both useful: fair performer: won nursery at Lingfield in July: stays 7f: acts on polytrack and tapeta: usually leads. *David Evans*   **60 a68**

DYLAN EXPRESS (IRE) 4 ch.g. Dylan Thomas (IRE) 132 – Miss Gorica (IRE) 110 (Mull of Kintyre (USA) 114) [2015 55: 5d p5g* 5d 5m 5m² Jul 2] modest handicapper: won at Dundalk in April: best form at 5f: acts on polytrack and good to firm going: often wears headgear: in tongue tie in 2015: front runner/races prominently. *Damian Joseph English, Ireland*   **55**

DYLAN MOUTH (IRE) 4 b.c. Dylan Thomas (IRE) 132 – Cottonmouth (IRE) 109 (Noverre (USA) 125) [2015 117: 11.9m* 11.9m* 12d 10.9m* 11.9s² 9.9g* Nov 8] strong, compact colt: very smart performer: won Premio Carlo d'Alessio at Rome in May, Gran Premio di Milano at Milan (beat Billabong 5 lengths) in June, Premio Federico Tesio at Milan (by 5 lengths from Bertinoro) in September and Premio Roma at Rome (by short head from Circus Couture) in November: only defeat in 12 starts in Italy when 3 lengths second to Lovelyn in Gran Premio del Jockey Club at Milan on penultimate start: sweated up, last of 7 behind Postponed in King George VI and Queen Elizabeth Stakes at Ascot in July: stays 1½m: acts on firm and good to soft going, possibly not at best on very soft: races prominently: has joined Marco Botti. *Stefano Botti, Italy*   **121**

DYLAN'S CENTENARY 4 b.g. Kyllachy 129 – Sheka 68 (Ishiguru (USA) 114) [2015 58: t7.1g 8.1d p7g⁵ p6gʳʳ Nov 26] sturdy gelding: modest maiden: stays 1m: acts on polytrack and good to firm going: often in headgear in 2015: usually slowly away, usually races in rear: refused to race final start, and one to treat with plenty of caution. *David Simcock*   **50 §**

DYLAN'S STORM (IRE) 3 b.g. Zebedee 113 – Storm Lady (IRE) (Alhaarth (IRE) 126) [2015 67: t6g 7g⁵ 7m² 7d* 6.1m⁴ 8.1m³ 8f² 9.9g⁴ 11.7f³ Aug 12] fair handicapper: won at Brighton in June: stays 1¼m: acts on firm and good to soft going. *David Dennis*   **73**

DYLANTELLE 2 b.f. (Feb 18) Dylan Thomas (IRE) 132 – Bay Swallow (IRE) 77 (Daylami (IRE) 138) [2015 t7.1m t7.1f⁴ p8g⁵ p7g t6f Dec 22] first foal: dam 1½m winner who stayed 1¾m: modest maiden: stays 1m: acts on polytrack and tapeta: often races towards rear. *Harry Dunlop*   **54**

DYLLAN (IRE) 2 b.g. (Apr 2) Zebedee 113 – Luvmedo (IRE) 57 (One Cool Cat (USA) 123) [2015 6m⁴ 6m⁴ 6g⁵ p7g⁵ 7d⁶ Oct 11] compact gelding: fair maiden: stays 7f: acts on polytrack and good to firm going: often races towards rear. *Richard Hannon*   **75**

DYNAMIC IDOL (USA) 8 b.g. Dynaformer (USA) – El Nafis (USA) 73 (Kingmambo (USA) 125) [2015 t16.5g⁴ f14d² May 18] fair maiden: stayed 1¾m: acted on fibresand and good to soft going: had worn headgear: dead. *Johnny Farrelly*   **64**

DYNAMIC RANGER (USA) 4 b.g. U S Ranger (USA) 124 – Dynamous (USA) (Dynaformer (USA)) [2015 68: p10g p8f p10g 7.6g p10g 11.9d⁶ Aug 5] poor maiden: stays 1¼m: acts on polytrack: often in blinkers in 2015: often in tongue tie in 2015. *Gary Moore*   **46**

DYNAMITE DIXIE (IRE) 6 b.g. Dylan Thomas (IRE) 132 – Lavender Blue (Galileo (IRE) 134) [2015 88: 8.3d p10g t8.6g t8.6g 8d t8.6m p8f t8.6m p8fᵇᵘ Oct 15] modest handicapper: stays 1¼m: acts on heavy going: tried in headgear: sometimes wears tongue tie. *Phil McEntee*   **60**

DYNAMITE SAMMY 2 ch.f. (Feb 26) Black Sam Bellamy (IRE) 121 – Darcique (Cacique (IRE) 124) [2015 7.6g Sep 12] first foal: dam unraced half-sister to smart 9f-11f winner Daveron (by Black Sam Bellamy): 25/1, very green when well held in maiden at Lingfield. *Paul Cole*   **–**

DYNAMO (IRE) 4 b.g. Galileo (IRE) 134 – Trading Places (Dansili 127) [2015 p8g Dec 9] maiden: no form in 2015. *Richard Hughes*   **–**

DYNAMO WALT (IRE) 4 b.g. Acclamation 118 – Cambara 97 (Dancing Brave (USA) **98**
140) [2015 70, a82: p5g* p5g² t5.1f⁴ p5m² p5g⁴ p5g³ p5g⁴ t5.1g² p5m* p5m* p5m⁶ p5g⁵
p5f³ Nov 23] useful handicapper: won at Chelmsford in January, May and June: third at
Chelmsford (1½ lengths behind Medicean Man) in November: best form at 5f: acts on
polytrack and tapeta: usually wears visor. *Derek Shaw*

E

EAGER BEAVER 3 b.f. Duke of Marmalade (IRE) 132 – Kahlua Kiss 103 (Mister **80**
Baileys 123) [2015 –: t9.5g⁴ p10g³ 10g⁶ 10s² p11g⁵ 10s² p12g² Nov 13] angular filly: fairly
useful maiden: second in handicaps at Ffos Las in September and Newbury in October:
stays 1¼m: acts on polytrack and soft going. *William Muir*

EAGLE EMPIRE (IRE) 3 b.g. Jeremy (USA) 122 – Red Eagle (IRE) 62 (Eagle Eyed **66**
(USA) 111) [2015 65: 10g³ 7d⁴ 7.2g³ 7d⁴ Oct 26] fair maiden: left Richard Hannon after
second start: will prove suited by a return to 1m: acts on polytrack: often races prominently.
Garry Moss

EAGLE FALLS 2 b.g. (Jan 26) Paco Boy (IRE) 129 – Miss Excel 60 (Exceed And Excel **63 p**
(AUS) 126) [2015 p7g p6f⁴ Oct 1] 18,000Y: first foal: dam maiden (stayed 1¼m) out
of smart 1¼m/15f winner Shaiybara: better effort when fourth in maiden at Chelmsford
(1¾ lengths behind Staintondale Lass) in October: sold 7,500 gns, sent to Austria: should
do better in time. *Chris Wall*

EAGLE TOP 4 ch.c. Pivotal 124 – Gull Wing (IRE) 108 (In The Wings 128) [2015 123: **125**
10m⁴ 12f² 12d² 11s³ 11.9m Oct 4] smallish colt: high-class performer: second in Hardwicke
Stakes at Royal Ascot (beaten 3¾ lengths by Snow Sky) in June and King George VI and
Queen Elizabeth Stakes at Ascot (best effort, nose behind Postponed) in July: below form

Lady Bamford's "Eagle Top"

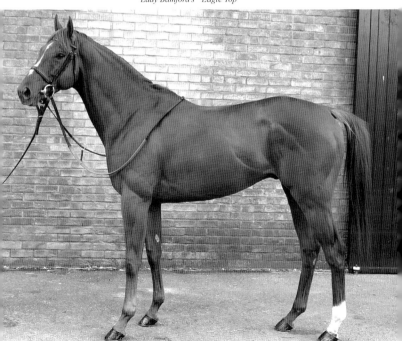

both subsequent starts, 12½ lengths fifteenth of 17 to Golden Horn in Prix de l'Arc de Triomphe at Longchamp final outing: stays 1½m: acts on good to firm and good to soft going. *John Gosden*

EARLS QUARTER (IRE) 9 b.g. Shantou (USA) 125 – Par Street (IRE) (Dolphin Street 72 (FR) 125) [2015 14.6m³ May 2] unfurnished gelding: fairly useful maiden: stayed 2m: acted on good to soft going: had worn tongue tie: dead. *Ian Williams*

EARLY BIRD (IRE) 2 ch.f. (Feb 10) Exceed And Excel (AUS) 126 – Crossmolina (IRE) 76 (Halling (USA) 133) [2015 6m⁴ 6g³ 5.9s⁴ 5g² 5s* Oct 6] 85,000F: fifth foal: half-sister to smart winner up to 1m Neebras (2-y-o 6f winner, by Oasis Dream) and 7f winner Jolyne (by Makfi): dam French 1½m winner: fair performer: won maiden at Catterick in October: stays 6f: acts on soft going. *Richard Fahey*

EARLY MORNING (IRE) 4 gr.g. New Approach (IRE) 132 – Summer's Eve 104 104 (Singspiel (IRE) 133) [2015 83: p8g* p8g² 8.1m³ 8m* p8g 9g Sep 26] useful handicapper: a98 won at Kempton in April and Haydock (by 2¼ lengths from Manchestar) in August: well held last 2 starts, in Cambridgeshire final one: stays 10.5f: acts on polytrack and good to firm going. *Harry Dunlop*

EARNESTINE (GER) 3 b.f. New Approach (IRE) 132 – Earthly Paradise (GER) (Dashing 75 Blade 117) [2015 p9.9g⁵ p9.9g 7.1m⁶ 7.1s³ 10.2g² p10m t12.2fᵇᵘ Nov 16] half-sister to a69 several winners abroad, including smart German winner up to 1½m (stays 2m) Earl of Tinsdal (2-y-o 1m winner, by Black Sam Bellamy) and useful German 1m-1¼m winner Emily of Tinsdal (by Librettist): dam German 7f winner: fair maiden: left H-A. Pantall after second start: best effort at 1¼m: acts on polytrack. *David Evans*

EARTH DRUMMER (IRE) 5 b.g. Dylan Thomas (IRE) 132 – In Dubai (USA) 91 108 (Giant's Causeway (USA) 132) [2015 106: 12.1g³ 8m² 10.4g⁶ 9g 10.4s⁶ Oct 10] useful handicapper: third at Meydan in January and second at Ascot (½ length behind Halation) in August: has form at 1½m, probably best at shorter (effective at 1m): acts on tapeta and good to firm going: tried in hood: often travels strongly. *David O'Meara*

EARTH GODDESS 3 b.f. Invincible Spirit (IRE) 121 – Clara Bow (IRE) 84 (Sadler's – Wells (USA) 132) [2015 p7g 7.1s p8f³ Nov 5] fourth foal: half-sister to 11.5f/1½m winner Angus Glens (by Dalakhani): dam, 7f winner, sister to Fillies' Mile winner Listen and Moyglare Stud Stakes winner Sequoyah, latter dam of top-class 1m/1¼m performer Henrythenavigator: no form. *Charles Hills*

EAST COAST LADY (IRE) 3 b.f. Kodiac 112 – Alexander Anapolis (IRE) 94 (Spectrum 86 (IRE) 126) [2015 91: p8g⁴ 8m 7m 7d 10m 9.9s³ 8g 10s² 11.6g Oct 20] useful-looking filly: fairly useful handicapper: second at Leicester in October: best up to 1¼m: acts on polytrack, soft and good to firm going: tried in headgear in 2015: often races prominently. *Robert Eddery*

EASTER (IRE) 3 b.f. Galileo (IRE) 134 – Missvinski (USA) 116 (Stravinsky (USA) 133) 107 [2015 95P: 8v⁵ 10m³ 8.5g³ 12g² 9.5g* 12d 9d² 10d⁵ 9.5s² 8s Oct 3] useful performer: won listed race at Gowran (by 2 lengths from Stellar Glow) in August: second after in Dance Design Stakes at the Curragh (4 lengths behind Bocca Baciata) and Denny Cordell Lavarack & Lanwades Stud Fillies Stakes at Gowran (1¾ lengths behind Jack Naylor): below form in First Lady Stakes at Keeneland final outing: stays 1½m: acts on soft going: wears blinkers/tongue tie: sometimes slowly away. *Aidan O'Brien, Ireland*

EASTER MATE (IRE) 2 b.g. (Apr 5) Acclamation 118 – Greek Easter (IRE) 85 (Namid 81 128) [2015 6m³ 6.1m⁴ 6m⁴ 7m⁵ 8d⁴ 8d⁵ Oct 23] 70,000Y: third dam, 7f 1½m winner who stayed 1½m, half-sister to useful winner up to 1m Doc Holiday: fairly useful maiden: may prove best at short of 1m: acts on good to firm and good to soft going: tried in cheekpieces. *Ralph Beckett*

EASTERN DRAGON (IRE) 5 b.g. Elnadim (USA) 128 – Shulammite Woman (IRE) 73 (Desert Sun 120) [2015 89, a72: p7g p7g⁶ p8m⁶ 7d⁶ 6m 7.9v 7.6g⁵ 7.1m³ 7g 7.4d⁵ p6d³ p6f a67 p10m p7g t6f⁶ p8d Nov 30] sturdy gelding: fair handicapper: left Michael Scudamore after tenth start: has form at 8.5f, best efforts at shorter: acts on polytrack, good to firm and heavy going: tried in visor. *Sally Randell*

EASTERN DYNASTY 4 b.g. Exceed And Excel (AUS) 126 – Agooda (Rainbow Quest – (USA) 134) [2015 6g May 29] no form. *Ben Haslam*

EASTERN IMPACT (IRE) 4 b.g. Bahamian Bounty 116 – Kate The Great 79 (Xaar 117 132) [2015 111: 6f* 6m 6m⁴ 6f³ 6.1g* 6d 6m* 6d Oct 17] good-topped gelding: smart performer: won handicap at Newmarket (by short head from Huntsmans Close) in May, listed race at Chester (by ¾ length from Canny Kool) in August and Bengough Stakes at

Exors of the late Mr D. W. Barker's "Eastern Impact"

Ascot (by neck from Naadirr) in October: good third in July Cup at Newmarket (1½ lengths behind Muhaarar): stays 6f: acts on firm and good to soft going: usually races close up. *Richard Fahey*

EASTERN MAGIC 8 b.g. Observatory (USA) 131 – Inchtina 85 (Inchinor 119) [2015 65: 13.1m² 17.2f 16.2s⁵ 14.1g 18d Aug 20] smallish gelding: modest handicapper: stays 17f: acts on soft and good to firm going: has worn cheekpieces. *Ben Case* **59**

EASTERN RACER (IRE) 3 b.g. Bushranger (IRE) 119 – Queen Cobra (IRE) 80 (Indian Rocket 115) [2015 80: 7.1s³ 6g² 6v² 6.1g* 6m* 6m⁴ 6g⁵ 6.1g Sep 30] good-topped gelding: fairly useful performer: won maiden at Chester in May and handicap at Redcar (by ½ length from Grissom) in July: stays 6f: acts on good to firm and heavy going: often wears cheekpieces: front runner/races prominently. *Brian Ellison* **87**

EASTERN RULES (IRE) 7 b.g. Golden Snake (USA) 127 – Eastern Ember 85 (Indian King (USA) 128) [2015 115: 7g² 7g⁶ 6g⁴ 7d⁶ 7g⁴ 7d 7g⁵ Sep 12] smart performer: best efforts when in frame at Meydan in Al Fahidi Fort (4 lengths second to Safety Check) in January and handicap (fourth to Ertijaal) in February: respectable fifth to Kelinni in handicap at Leopardstown final outing: stays 1m: acts on synthetics, good to firm and good to soft going: tried in cheekpieces once. *M. Halford, Ireland* **112**

EAST INDIES 2 b.g. (Mar 9) Authorized (IRE) 133 – Elan (Dansili 127) [2015 8.1g⁴ p10g* 7m Oct 3] 48,000F, 100,000Y: good-topped gelding: second foal: half-brother to a winner abroad by Azamour: dam unraced daughter of very smart 7f/1m winner Chic: fairly useful form: won 10-runner maiden at Kempton in September by 7 lengths from Press Gang: 6/1, well held in valuable sales race at Newmarket final start: best effort at 1¼m: has been gelded. *John Gosden* **86**

EASTON ANGEL (IRE) 2 gr.f. (Mar 24) Dark Angel (IRE) 113 – Staceymac (IRE) 59 (Elnadim (USA) 128) [2015 5s* 5m* 5f² 6m⁴ 6g³ 5g⁵ Sep 18] 18,000F, £30,000Y: good-topped filly: sixth foal: dam, 5f winner, half-sister to very smart 6.5f/7f winner Kalahari **108**

Gold: useful performer: won maiden at Musselburgh (by 3¼ lengths from Fishergate) in May and minor event at Beverley (by length from Opal Tiara) in May: second in Queen Mary Stakes at Royal Ascot (1½ lengths behind Acapulco) in June and third in Lowther Stakes at York (4½ lengths behind Besharah) in August: may prove best at 5f: acts on firm and soft going: usually travels strongly. *Michael Dods*

EAST RIVER (IRE) 3 ch.c. Captain Rio 122 – Eastern Blue (IRE) 68 (Be My Guest (USA) 126) [2015 f6s⁴ f5g² Feb 26] modest form in maidens at Southwell: dead. *John Wainwright* **59**

EAST STREET REVUE 2 ch.g. (Apr 17) Pastoral Pursuits 127 – Revue Princess (IRE) 80 (Mull of Kintyre (USA) 114) [2015 6g⁶ 6d 5.9g⁶ Jun 15] modest maiden: best effort when sixth at Carlisle (5¾ lengths behind Kelly's Dino) in June. *Tim Easterby* **55**

EASTWARD HO 7 ch.g. Resplendent Glory (IRE) 115 – Mofeyda (IRE) 70 (Mtoto 134) [2015 62: p8g³ p8f p8g Feb 1] modest handicapper: stayed 9.5f: acted on polytrack, tapeta, good to firm and heavy going: had worn headgear: usually raced prominently: dead. *Sarah Humphrey* **51**

EASY CODE 2 b.c. (Feb 14) Bahamian Bounty 116 – Skirrid (Halling (USA) 133) [2015 7m 6d⁵ 6g* Sep 24] 35,000F, 80,000Y: sturdy colt: first foal: dam unraced half-sister to smart winner up to 1½m Spice Route out of Oaks d'Italia winner Zanzibar: fairly useful performer: won maiden at Pontefract (by 1¼ lengths from Happy Call) in September, having run of race: best effort at 6f: open to further improvement. *William Haggas* **80 p**

EASYDOESIT (IRE) 7 b.g. Iffraaj 127 – Fawaayid (USA) 92 (Vaguely Noble 140) [2015 t16.5g⁶ p12f 12.1m⁵ t12.2g³ 11.9d* 18d 13.1d⁴ t12.2g⁶ t13.9f⁶ t12.2m⁵ p16g⁴ t13.9m⁵ Dec 30] modest handicapper: won at Brighton in August: stays 16.5f: acts on polytrack, tapeta and good to soft going: sometimes wears headgear. *Tony Carroll* **63**

EASY EASY 2 ch.g. (Mar 20) Rip Van Winkle (IRE) 134 – Nizza (GER) (Acatenango (GER) 127) [2015 9s⁴ 9d Oct 11] better effort in maidens at Goodwood when fourth of 7 to Good Run in September: has been gelded. *Alan King* **68**

EASY GOLD 2 ch.c. (Mar 21) Mastercraftsman (IRE) 129 – Aiming Upwards (Blushing Flame (USA) 109) [2015 7v Nov 3] 50/1, thirteenth in maiden at Redcar (well beaten behind Roundsman) in November. *Ed Walker* **–**

EASY ROAD 5 b.h. Compton Place 125 – Broughtons Revival 88 (Pivotal 124) [2015 6.8s² 5.7g² 5.8g² 6.8g* 4.5g* 5.7d* 5d* Oct 24] smart performer: won Polar Cup at Ovrevoll (by head from Silver Ocean) in July, minor event on same course (by ½ length from Weisse Socken) in August, listed race at Taby (by ½ length from Mr David) in September and handicap at Doncaster (by ½ length from El Viento) in October: effective from 5f to 1m: acts on soft going: often wears blinkers: has worn tongue tie. *Ms C. Erichsen, Norway* **116**

EASY TERMS 8 b.m. Trade Fair 124 – Effie (Royal Academy (USA) 130) [2015 –: 10s⁵ 10m² 12m May 15] useful-looking mare: fairly useful handicapper: stays 1½m: acts on good to firm and heavy going: tried in headgear prior to 2015. *Edwin Tuer* **82**

betdaq.com 2% Commission Handicap, Doncaster—Easy Road, a prolific and reliable performer in Scandinavia (successful in a Group 3 earlier in the year), wins on his first start in Britain from El Viento (checked sleeves), Demora (noseband) and Perfect Pasture (near side)

EASY TIGER 3 b.g. Refuse To Bend (IRE) 128 – Extremely Rare (IRE) 82 (Mark of Esteem **85**
(IRE) 137) [2015 77p: 8m⁵ 7m* 7.1m⁶ 7.4g² 7m² 7g² 7g⁵ 6m⁶ 6g⁴ Oct 20] rangy gelding:
fairly useful handicapper: won at Goodwood in June: runner-up twice at Newmarket in
August: stays 7f: acts on polytrack and good to firm going: sometimes in cheekpieces in
2015: usually races close up. *William Muir*

EATSLEEPRACEREPEAT 3 b.g. Myboycharlie (IRE) 118 – Highland Jewel (IRE) 58 **66**
(Azamour (IRE) 130) [2015 70: t7.1g t8.6g⁶ 10m⁴ 9.9m⁴ 8m t8.6g⁴ 7g⁴ p10g⁴ t9.5g³ p10g⁵
Aug 1] fair maiden: left Lady Cecil after first start: stays 1¼m: acts on polytrack, tapeta and
good to firm going: tried in hood prior to 2015: sometimes slowly away. *John Ryan*

EBBISHAM (IRE) 2 b.g. (Mar 9) Holy Roman Emperor (IRE) 125 – Balting Lass (IRE) **–**
(Orpen (USA) 116) [2015 p6d 6d p6g Oct 27] no form. *Jim Boyle*

EBEN DUBAI (IRE) 3 b.g. New Approach (IRE) 132 – Eldalil 106 (Singspiel (IRE) 133) **69 p**
[2015 –: 10g⁵ May 14] rather unfurnished gelding: fair maiden, lightly raced: visored,
some encouragement when fifth at Newmarket (14¾ lengths behind Resonant) on sole
outing in 2015, slowly away: should be suited by 1½m: remains open to improvement. *Sir
Michael Stoute*

EBREEZ 3 b.g. Dutch Art 126 – Half Sister (IRE) 63 (Oratorio (IRE) 128) [2015 10m **–**
p13.3f Oct 22] no form: left Clive Brittain after first start. *David Evans*

EBTIHAAL (IRE) 2 ch.c. (Feb 4) Teofilo (IRE) 126 – Dance Troupe 85 (Rainbow Quest **97 p**
(USA) 134) [2015 7m⁴ 8s* 8d⁴ Oct 23] brother to 1½m winner Aquilla and 1¼m winner
Improvisation, both useful, and half-brother to 2 winners, including useful winner up to
10.7f Puncher Clynch (2-y-o 1m/8.4f winner, by Azamour): dam, maiden (stayed 12.5f),
half-sister to smart winner up to 13.5f Self Defense: useful performer: won maiden at
Brighton (by 1¾ lengths from Prince of Arran) and nursery at Doncaster (best effort, by 5
lengths from Dolphin Vista) in October, slowly away both times: will be suited by middle
distances: will go on improving. *Saeed bin Suroor*

ECCLESTON 4 b.g. Acclamation 118 – Miss Meggy 97 (Pivotal 124) [2015 103: 5m 6g* **105**
6d 6m 6s⁵ 6g⁵ 6g⁴ 6d* 6g⁶ 6g 6s Oct 10] sparely-made gelding: useful handicapper: won at
Haydock (by ½ length from My Name Is Rio) in May and Thirsk (by ¾ length from
Another Wise Kid) in August: stays 6f: acts on any turf going: wears headgear nowadays
(visored last 6 starts): sometimes slowly away. *David O'Meara*

ECHO BRAVA 5 gr.g. Proclamation (IRE) 130 – Snake Skin 68 (Golden Snake (USA) **91**
127) [2015 89: p12g⁵ p12g⁶ t13.9g⁴ p16f 12g* 14g⁴ 12m* 13.3s⁵ 12v² Aug 31] lengthy **a80**
gelding: fairly useful handicapper: won at Goodwood in June and Epsom in July: good 6
lengths second to English Summer in amateur event at Epsom final start: stays 1¼m: acts
on polytrack, tapeta, good to firm and heavy going: has worn hood: joined Jim Best 20,000
gns in October. *Luke Dace*

ECHOES OF WAR 6 b.g. Echo of Light 125 – Waraqa (USA) 76 (Red Ransom (USA)) **–**
[2015 –: p5g⁵ Feb 7] workmanlike gelding: no form. *John Bridger*

ECHO OF LIGHTNING 5 b.g. Echo of Light 125 – Classic Lass 68 (Dr Fong (USA) **82**
128) [2015 71: 7g 7.5g* 7.1m² 8.3s⁴ 8d² 7.2d³ 7.2g* 8d Oct 30] quite good-topped gelding:
fairly useful handicapper: won at Beverley in May and Ayr (by 1¼ lengths from Dark
Crystal) in September: stays 1m: acts on soft and good to firm going: often wears headgear.
Brian Ellison

ECLIPTIC SUNRISE 4 b.f. Compton Place 125 – Winter Moon (Mujadil (USA) 119) **73**
[2015 62: p5m³ p6g⁵ p6m p6g⁶ 5.1m⁴ t5.1m⁴ 6.1d p5g² 5.3s* 6m² 5.3g* 5.3m³ t5.1g⁶ 6s⁴ **a60**
5s⁵ 5.3d² Sep 14] fair handicapper: won at Brighton (twice) in June: stays 5.5f: acts on soft
going: often wears headgear: sometimes wears tongue tie: often races freely. *Des Donovan*

ECLOGUE 2 b.f. (May 19) Pastoral Pursuits 127 – Ecstasy 81 (Pursuit of Love 124) [2015 **–**
p8g p8g Dec 7] half-sister to several winners, including useful 7f (including at 2 yrs and
Fred Darling Stakes) winner Redstart (by Cockney Rebel) and 1½m winner Oneiric (by
Act One): dam winner up to 1¼m (2-y-o 7f winner): no form. *Ralph Beckett*

ECONOMIC CRISIS (IRE) 6 ch.m. Excellent Art 125 – Try The Air (IRE) (Foxhound **80**
(USA) 103) [2015 81: 5s³ 5s* 5m⁴ 6d* 5m⁶ 5m⁶ 5.1m⁶ 5g 5s² 5d³ 5.9s⁶ 6d⁴ 6m⁶ 5g² 6s
Oct 27] leggy mare: fairly useful handicapper: won twice at Hamilton in May: stays 6f:
acts on good to firm and heavy going: tried in cheekpieces prior to 2015. *Alan Berry*

ECTOT 4 b.c. Hurricane Run (IRE) 134 – Tonnara (IRE) (Linamix (FR) 127) [2015 123: **110**
10f 9.9s³ 11.9d Oct 18] strong, long-backed colt: very smart performer at 3 yrs: not in same
form in 2015, last of 9 in Prince of Wales's Stakes at Royal Ascot, 7½ lengths third to Gailo

Chop in La Coupe de Maisons-Laffitte and 7¾ lengths seventh to Ming Dynasty in Prix du Conseil de Paris at Chantilly: free-going sort, should prove best at shorter than 1½m: acts on soft and good to firm going: in cheekpieces last 2 starts. *E. Lellouche, France*

EDAS 13 b.g. Celtic Swing 138 – Eden (IRE) 88 (Polish Precedent (USA) 131) [2015 58: 8d 11.9m⁵ 9.3g⁶ 9.3g 9.9s² 9.3d⁵ 8d² 9.3s⁴ 10m Aug 29] good-topped gelding: modest handicapper: stays 12.5f: acts on fibresand and any turf going: tried in headgear prior to 2015. *Thomas Cuthbert* — **53**

EDE'S THE BUSINESS 4 ch.f. Halling (USA) 133 – My Amalie (IRE) 92 (Galileo (IRE) 134) [2015 p11f p10g t12.2g 7g 8.1g⁶ Aug 2] modest maiden: left Pat Phelan after second start: stays 1¼m: acts on polytrack: has worn headgear, including usually of late: tends to find little. *Ken Wingrove* — **54**

EDE'S THE MOVER 2 b.f. (Feb 23) Bahamian Bounty 116 – Run For Ede's 89 (Peintre Celebre (USA) 137) [2015 8s³ 7s² Oct 6] first foal: dam 8.3f-1½m winner: better effort when second in maiden at Brighton (3 lengths behind Art Echo) in October: will be suited by a return to 1m. *Pat Phelan* — **64**

EDGAR BALTHAZAR 3 b.g. Pastoral Pursuits 127 – Assistacat (IRE) (Lend A Hand 124) [2015 81p: 6s⁶ 6m⁶ 6.1s 6g³ 6g 5m² 5g³ 5g² 6d³ 6g* 6m² 7d² 7.2g*⁷ 7.2g² Oct 8] useful handicapper: won at Newcastle in August and Ayr (by 1½ lengths from Zacynthus) in September: good second at Ayr (1¾ lengths behind Majestic Myles) in October: will probably stay 1m: acts on good to firm and good to soft going: often in headgear in 2015: quirky sort, but usually responds generously to pressure. *Keith Dalgleish* — **95**

EDGAR (GER) 5 b.g. Big Shuffle (USA) 122 – Estella (GER) (Acatenango (GER) 127) [2015 t12.2g² Jun 22] fair maiden: blinkered, second in seller at Wolverhampton on sole outing in 2015. *David Bridgwater* — **67**

EDGED OUT 5 b.m. Piccolo 121 – Edge of Light 94 (Xaar 132) [2015 78: 5.7f³ 5.7m* 5m³ 5g² 6.1g⁵ 5.7f² 5f⁵ 5.7m⁴ 5.7g⁶ Oct 18] plain mare: fairly useful handicapper: raced mainly at Bath in 2015 and successful there in June: stays 6f: acts on firm and soft going: front runner/races prominently. *Christopher Mason* — **81**

EDGE (IRE) 4 b.g. Acclamation 118 – Chanter (Lomitas 129) [2015 8.3s 10.2m³ 10.2m³ 10g⁴ 8.1g² 8.1d⁶ 8.1v⁵ 10.2s⁴ 10.2m⁴ Sep 28] modest handicapper: stays 11f: acts on soft and good to firm going: often wears headgear: temperamental. *Bernard Llewellyn* — **60 §**

EDGE OF HEAVEN 3 b.f. Pastoral Pursuits 127 – Halfwaytoparadise 69 (Observatory (USA) 131) [2015 66: t8.6g* 8.3m* 8.3d* 9g 8d² t8.6f⁶ Oct 3] compact filly: fairly useful handicapper: won at Wolverhampton in May, Leicester in June and Windsor in July: good second at Goodwood in August: stays 8.5f: acts on polytrack, tapeta, good to firm and good to soft going: often races prominently. *Jonathan Portman* — **89**

EDGE OF LOVE 3 b.f. Kyllachy 129 – Upskittled (Diktat 126) [2015 61p: 6m⁶ 7d* 7g⁴ p8f⁶ t7.1f Oct 30] fair performer: won maiden at Thirsk in August: stays 1m: acts on polytrack and good to soft going: usually races prominently. *Ed Walker* — **73**

EDGE OF SANITY (IRE) 6 b.g. Invincible Spirit (IRE) 121 – Saor Sinn (IRE) 60 (Galileo (IRE) 134) [2015 108: 12d⁶ 18.7d May 6] leggy gelding: useful handicapper at best: well beaten both starts in 2015: gelded after: stays 2m: acts on polytrack, soft and good to firm going: has worn tongue tie. *Brian Ellison* — **–**

EDGEOFTHEFOREST (IRE) 2 b.f. (Jan 22) Bushranger (IRE) 119 – Beguilor (Refuse To Bend (IRE) 120) [2015 5m* 7m³ t8.6f⁶ Nov 14] €9,500F, €3,000Y: neat filly: second foal: half-sister to a winner in Italy by Amadeus Wolf: dam, lightly raced, closely related to smart winner up to 1m Tian Shan: modest performer: won seller at Thirsk in July: stays 7f: acts on good to firm going. *David Evans* — **£0**

EDGWARE ROAD 7 ch.g. Selkirk (USA) 129 – Bayswater 76 (Caerleon (USA) 132) [2015 71: t9.5f t9.5f t8.6g p10g t9.5g⁴ 10.2d⁵ Aug 14] modest handicapper: stays 1¼m: acts on polytrack, tapeta, soft and good to firm going: sometimes wears headgear. *Andy Turnell* — **56**

EDIFICATION 2 b.g. (Apr 1) Dream Ahead (USA) 133 – Elegant Pride (Beat Hollow 126) [2015 6g⁴ 6m² 6m 6m⁵ 7m 8g* Sep 15] good-topped gelding: fifth foal: half-brother to 3 winners, including 1¼m winner Age of Elegance (by Makfi) and French 11f winner Kierena (by Choisir): dam, unraced, out of half-sister to Dewhurst Stakes winner Xaar: fairly useful performer: won nursery at Salisbury in August: further improvement when second in nursery at Yarmouth in September: stays 1m: acts on good to firm going: tried in blinkers. *Martyn Meade* — **85**

EDITH WESTON 2 b.f. (Mar 22) Showcasing 117 – Twitch Hill 67 (Piccolo 121) [2015 **44** 5.1g 5m p6f⁶ p6m t6f⁵ t7.1f p7g Dec 10] 1,000Y: fifth foal: half-sister to temperamental winner up to 1m Tableforten (2-y-o 6f winner, by Pastoral Pursuits) and 2-y-o 5f winner The Wispe (by Kyllachy): dam 6f winner: poor maiden: stays 6f: acts on polytrack and tapeta: often in headgear. *Robert Cowell*

EDIYE (IRE) 2 b.f. (Mar 30) Fast Company (IRE) 126 – Sweet Home Alabama (IRE) 56 **72** (Desert Prince (IRE) 130) [2015 6m⁵ 6g* 6g 5.9m⁵ 6d⁴ 7d⁴ Oct 16] €32,000F, £29,000Y: good-topped filly: half-sister to several winners, including smart winner up to 16.4f Havana Beat (2-y-o 1m winner, by Teofilo) and 5f winner (stays 1m) Rahmah (by Vale of York): dam, maiden (stayed 8.5f), half-sister to top-class miler Proclamation: fair performer: won maiden at Lingfield in July: stays 7f: acts on good to soft going: sold 13,000 gns, sent to Qatar. *Hugo Palmer*

EDMAAJ (IRE) 7 ch.g. Intikhab (USA) 135 – Lady Angola (USA) 83 (Lord At War **–** (ARG)) [2015 10.4g 10.4m 10d Aug 15] sturdy gelding: useful handicapper in 2012: well beaten back on Flat in 2015: stays 1½m: acts on good to firm and heavy going. *Jonjo O'Neill*

EDUCATE 6 b.g. Echo of Light 125 – Pasithea (IRE) 101 (Celtic Swing 138) [2015 119: **109** p10g 9g⁶ 9m³ 9.9g² 10f 10.4m 10.3m 9g 8.3s⁶ Oct 26] rather leggy gelding: useful performer: best efforts in 2015 when third in handicap at Newmarket (3¾ lengths behind Balty Boys) and second in listed race at Goodwood (2 lengths behind The Corsican), both in May: stays 10.5f: acts on tapeta, good to firm and heavy going: tried in visor prior to 2015. *Ismail Mohammed*

EDU QUERIDO (BRZ) 6 ch.h. Holzmeister (USA) – Kournikova (BRZ) (Irish Fighter **103** (USA)) [2015 112: a8f a8f⁵ Feb 19] smart performer at best: better effort (useful form) at Meydan in 2015 when 7 lengths fifth to Layl in handicap: best form at 1m/9f: acts on polytrack, probably on any turf going: usually in headgear nowadays (not last time): sold 26,000 gns in July, sent to Saudi Arabia. *Marco Botti*

EDWARD ELGAR 4 ch.g. Avonbridge 123 – Scooby Dooby Do 62 (Atraf 116) [2015 **55 §** 60§: 8.5g² 9.9m⁴ 11.9g² 11.5d² 10g² 14.1g 12.1m³ 12.1m t12.2f Nov 3] modest handicapper: stays 1½m: acts on good to firm and good to soft going: has worn headgear, including lately: unreliable: won twice over hurdles in November. *Natalie Lloyd-Beavis*

EDW GOLD (IRE) 3 ch.g. Fast Company (IRE) 126 – Hams (USA) 67 (Dixie Union **44** (USA) 121) [2015 41: t8.6f⁵ t7.1m⁵ Feb 5] poor maiden: best effort at 7f: acts on tapeta: tried in visor: sometimes slowly away, usually races towards rear. *David Evans*

EENY MAC (IRE) 8 ch.g. Redback 116 – Sally Green (IRE) 79 (Common Grounds 118) **55** [2015 83: 7.5g 8.5m 7.5m 7.5f 9m 8s⁵ 9.3d⁵ 10.2m 8.9g 8.5d Sep 22] modest handicapper: stays 1¼m: acts on good to firm and heavy going: tried in headgear: front runner/races prominently. *John Wainwright*

EFFECTUAL 3 b.f. Exceed And Excel (AUS) 126 – Our Faye 106 (College Chapel 122) **82 p** [2015 72p: 6d⁴ 6g Oct 10] rather leggy filly: fairly useful performer: won maiden at Lingfield (by nose from Swiss Affair) in May: better form when eleventh in listed race at Newmarket (7¼ lengths behind Mistrusting) in October: stays 6f: in hood in 2015: remains open to improvement. *Roger Varian*

EFFUSIVE 3 ch.f. Starspangledbanner (AUS) 128 – Thrill 97 (Pivotal 124) [2015 83: **81** 5.1g⁴ 6.1d⁵ 5f 6m³ t7.1m⁵ t6f t7.1f p6g⁴ Dec 16] fairly useful handicapper: third at Yarmouth in September: stays 7f: acts on tapeta and good to firm going: sometimes in headgear in 2015. *William Haggas*

E FOURTEEN 2 b.f. (Apr 29) Nayef (USA) 129 – Pale Blue Eyes (IRE) (Peintre Celebre **35** (USA) 137) [2015 5f p6g 6m p7f⁶ Nov 12] fifth foal: half-sister to 3 winners in Italy, including 10.5f winner Tropical Music (by Distant Music): dam Italian maiden (second at 1½m): poor maiden: stays 7f. *Nick Littmoden*

EFRON (IRE) 2 b.c. (Jan 29) Frozen Power (IRE) 108 – Ribald 69 (Alhaarth (IRE) 126) **48** [2015 6g 7.1m 5.7m p7g⁵ 6v p7g² 10.2f⁶ Sep 13] poor maiden: best effort at 7f: acts on polytrack and good to firm going. *Richard Hannon*

F.GLANTYNE DREAM (FR) 2 b.f. (Apr 14) Oasis Dream 129 – Bright Morning (USA) **52** (Storm Cat (USA)) [2015 5m³ 5g 6m 6g¹ 6m⁴ p6g p5g⁵ p5f⁵ Oct 24] rather unfurnished filly: third foal: dam unraced half-sister to top-class winner up to 9f Observatory: modest maiden handicapper: stays 6f: acts on polytrack and good to firm going: blinkered last 3 starts: sold 5,500 gns, sent to France. *Roger Charlton*

EGMONT 3 b.g. Notnowcato 128 – Salutare (IRE) (Sadler's Wells (USA) 132) [2015 –: **–** 14.1m³ 14.1g May 26] little form: often starts slowly: winning hurdler. *George Moore*

EHTIRAAS 2 b.c. (Mar 24) Oasis Dream 129 – Kareemah (IRE) (Peintre Celebre (USA) **98 p**
137) [2015 7g² Sep 25] fourth foal: half-brother to 1½m winner Saraha (by Dansili): dam,
useful French 1¼m/11f winner, half-sister to Breeders' Cup Filly & Mare Turf winner
Lahudood: 33/1, promise when second in maiden at Newmarket (always prominent, beaten
short head by Crazy Horse) in September: open to improvement. *B. W. Hills*

EILEAN MOR 7 ch.g. Ishiguru (USA) 114 – Cheviot Heights 72 (Intikhab (USA) 135) **63**
[2015 61: 8g³ 12.5s⁴ 9.1s⁵ 13d³ 12.1g 16m* 13.1g² 13.1s⁴ 13.1g⁵ Jul 20] fair handicapper:
won at Musselburgh (apprentice) in June: stayed 2m: acted on fibresand, soft and good to
firm going: usually raced close up: dead. *R. Mike Smith*

EIUM MAC 6 b.g. Presidium 124 – Efipetite 54 (Efisio 120) [2015 53: f8s* f8g² f8g² f7d⁴ **60**
f8g⁵ 8d⁴ 8g f8g² Dec 18] modest handicapper: won at Southwell in January: stays 1¼m:
acts on fibresand, good to firm and good to soft going: often wears headgear: often leads.
Neville Bycroft

EJAAZAH (IRE) 2 b.f. (May 14) Acclamation 118 – English Ballet (IRE) 104 (Danehill **87**
Dancer (IRE) 117) [2015 5m 5.1f* 5f² 5.2s⁵ 5.5s⁶ Sep 12] €115,000Y: quite attractive filly:
fourth foal: dam, 2-y-o 6f/7f winner, closely related to Prix de Diane winner Star of Seville:
fairly useful performer: won maiden at Chester in June: good second in listed race at
Sandown (length behind Riflescope) in July: likely to prove best at 5f: acts on firm going.
Richard Hannon

EJAYTEEKAY 2 b.f. (Mar 15) Big Bad Bob (IRE) 118 – Lovely Dream (IRE) 69 **80**
(Elnadim (USA) 128) [2015 8m⁴ 7s³ 7g² t7.1f³ t7.1g Dec 4] rather leggy filly: fourth foal:
half-sister to 2-y-o 5f winner Mosstang (by Moss Vale): dam, maiden (best form at 7f),
closely related to very smart US Grade 1 9f/1¼m winner Janet: fairly useful maiden:
placed at Salisbury and Newmarket in October and at Wolverhampton in November:
should stay 1m: acts on tapeta and soft going. *Jo Crowley*

EJBAAR 3 b.g. Oasis Dream 129 – Habaayib 108 (Royal Applause 124) [2015 t8.6g⁴ 7.5g³ **81**
p8g³ 8m 8d* 8s⁴ 7g² p6g Oct 6] first foal: dam 2-y-o 5f/6f (Albany Stakes) winner: fairly **a67**
useful performer: won maiden at Pontefract in July: second in handicap at Lingfield in
September: stays 1m: acts on good to soft going: usually races close up. *Ed Dunlop*

ELA GOOG LA MOU 6 b.m. Tobougg (IRE) 125 – Real Flame (Cyrano de Bergerac **65**
120) [2015 73: 10.3d³ 10m⁶ p10g³ 10.1g³ p10f p12g⁵ 10g² p10f 8.3g p10f* p10f⁵ p10g⁶
Dec 7] fair handicapper: won at Chelmsford in October: stays 1¼m: acts on polytrack, soft
and good to firm going: tried in headgear. *Peter Charalambous*

ELAGWEN 2 b.f. (Apr 6) Equiano (FR) 127 – Perfect Night 79 (Danzig Connection **–**
(USA)) [2015 t5.1m t6m 6g Sep 26] 9,000F: half-sister to smart 5f to (at 2 yrs) 7f winner
Definightly (by Diktat) and 1m winner Why Not Now (by Notnowcato): dam 6f/7f winner:
no form: tried in tongue tie. *Nikki Evans*

ELAND ALLY 7 b.g. Striking Ambition 122 – Dream Rose (IRE) 80 (Anabaa (USA) 130) **69**
[2015 78: 6g 5g 5s³ 6s 5d³ 5m⁵ 6d⁶ 6g³ 6s 5d* 5d 5d 5m⁴ 5s⁶ t5.1f² Dec 21] big gelding:
fair handicapper: won at Catterick in August: left Karen Tutty prior to final start: has form
at 7f, best at sprint trips: acts on tapeta, good to firm and good to soft going: tried in
headgear: sometimes slowly away, often races prominently. *Anabel K. Murphy*

EL ASTRONAUTE (IRE) 2 ch.c. (Apr 30) Approve (IRE) 112 – Drumcliffe Dancer **89**
(IRE) 66 (Footstepsinthesand 120) [2015 5m⁵ 5v³ 5m⁵ 5 1m² f8* 6⊑¹ 5m¹¹ 5.5d¹ Sep 26]
€19,000Y, £38,000 2-y-o: second foal: dam maiden (seemed to stay 1m): fairly useful
performer: won maiden at Thirsk in July, nursery at Leicester in August and nursery at
Chester (by ½ length from Sixties Sue) in September: likely to stay 6f: acts on good to firm
and good to soft going: usually races close up, often travels strongly. *John Quinn*

EL BEAU (IRE) 4 ch.g. Camacho 118 – River Beau (IRE) 47 (Galileo (IRE) 134) [2015 **91**
84: 9.2g⁵ 10.4g* 10g³ 10g⁴ 10.4s³ 10v⁵ Nov 3] fairly useful handicapper: won at York in
September: third at Ayr in September and York in October: stays 10.5f: acts on soft and
good to firm going: usually travels strongly. *John Quinn*

ELBERETH 4 b.f. Mount Nelson 125 – Masandra (IRE) (Desert Prince (IRE) 130) [2015 **102**
89: t9.5g⁴ 9.9d² 10.1g* 11.9g⁵ 12m² 10.1m³ Sep 16] useful performer: won handicap at
Epsom in June: further improvement when second in handicap at Ascot (short head behind
Missed Call) in August and third in listed race at Yarmouth (2½ lengths behind Talmada) in
September: will benefit from return to 1½m: acts on polytrack, tapeta and good to firm
going: responds generously to pressure. *Andrew Balding*

EL BRAVO 9 ch.g. Falbrav (IRE) 133 – Alessandra 101 (Generous (IRE) 139) [2015 78: p12f t12.2m t12.2g 12g⁵ 12.1m⁶ 13.7g³ 13.8v t13.9f p12g t12.2f⁴ Dec 21] good-topped gelding: modest handicapper: stays 1¾m: acts on polytrack, tapeta, soft and good to firm going: tried in headgear: front runner/races prominently. *Shaun Harris* **59 a53**

EL CAMPEON 3 b.g. Multiplex 114 – Villabella (FR) (Hernando (FR) 127) [2015 54: p11g⁵ p10m* t9.5g* p12g³ p13f³ p12g* 12v* p12g⁵ 12d² t13.9f* t13.9g Dec 1] fairly useful handicapper: won at Lingfield and Wolverhampton in June, Lingfield in August, Epsom in September and Wolverhampton in November: stays 1¾m: acts on polytrack, tapeta and heavy going: often races prominently. *Simon Dow* **83**

EL CHE 3 gr.f. Winker Watson 118 – Rose Cheval (USA) 74 (Johannesburg (USA) 127) [2015 77: t6f² p5g³ p5g⁴ p5g² p5f² 5g⁵ 5gᵘʳ p5m² Jun 1] angular filly: modest maiden: best form at 5f: acts on polytrack and soft going. *Mick Channon* **59**

EL DUQUE 4 b.g. Byron 117 – Royal Tavira Girl (IRE) 62 (Orpen (USA) 116) [2015 50, a67: f6d⁴ p6g⁵ p8f⁶ t7.1f⁴ p8g² p10m 8m² 8d² 7.1m³ 8m⁵ 8v⁵ 8g⁴ t8.6m⁴ 8m² t9.5f⁴ f8g⁴ p8f* t8.6g³ p7g Dec 9] modest handicapper: won at Chelmsford in November: stays 8.5f: acts on all-weather, soft and good to firm going. usually wears headgear: tried in tongue tie prior to 2015: often races prominently. *Bill Turner* **63**

ELECTRA VOICE 2 b.f. (Feb 1) Poet's Voice 126 – Electra Star 99 (Shamardal (USA) 129) [2015 6d 6m³ 6m² 7m 6s⁴ 6d² p7g* p7f* t7.1m⁶ p7g⁵ Dec 28] lengthy, rather unfurnished filly: first foal: dam 1m winner: fairly useful performer: won nurseries at Lingfield in October and Chelmsford in November: stays 7f: acts on polytrack, good to soft and good to firm going. *William Haggas* **81**

ELECTRIC QATAR 6 b.g. Pastoral Pursuits 127 – Valandraud (IRE) (College Chapel 122) [2015 76: f5s⁵ f5g³ f5d⁶ f5g f6s⁶ f6g³ p5f⁵ 5d⁴ 5g 5g² 5m⁴ 5.7m t5.1g³ 5d 5s⁵ t6g Sep 29] tall, useful-looking gelding: fair performer: won claimer at Southwell in February: left Michael Appleby after seventh start: best form at 5f: acts on all-weather and good to soft going: sometimes wears headgear: sent to the Netherlands. *Alan Berry* **71**

ELECTROSTATIC (IRE) 2 b.f. (Apr 26) Invincible Spirit (IRE) 121 – Laywaan (USA) 104 (Fantastic Light (USA) 134) [2015 t6g 6s⁶ 6g⁶ p7.5g Dec 27] 67,000Y: rather unfurnished filly: fifth foal: sister to 7f (including at 2 yrs) winner (stays 10.5f) Madhmoonah and half-sister to 10.7f winner Nabat Ali (by Haatef): dam 8.4f-1¼m winner: fair form in maidens/minor event: left Charles Hills 8,500 gns after third start. *N. Caullery, France* **67**

ELEGANT ANNIE 2 b.f. (Mar 6) Lawman (FR) 121 – An Ghalanta (IRE) 97 (Holy Roman Emperor (IRE) 125) [2015 6m 7m⁵ 7m⁴ p7f⁵ Aug 11] 22,000Y: first foal: dam, 2-y-o 5f winner, closely related to smart 1m-11f winner Bancnuanaheireann: fair maiden: best effort at 7f. *Jonathan Portman* **66**

ELEGANT SUPERMODEL (GER) 2 b.f. (Mar 5) Lope de Vega (IRE) 125 – Elegant As Well (IRE) (Sadler's Wells (USA) 132) [2015 5.5d* 5g* 6f³ Jun 19] €13,000Y: sturdy filly: seventh foal: sister to 1m winner Treasury Notes and half-sister to 3 winners, including 1½m winner Ebony Boom (by Boreal): dam unraced: useful performer: won maiden at Chateaubriant and minor event at Lyon Parilly (by 2½ lengths from Princess Emma), both in May: best effort when third in Albany Stakes at Royal Ascot (1½ lengths behind Illuminate) in June: not seen out again (sent to USA): stays 6f. *J-P. Perruchot, France* **103**

ELEMRAAN 4 b.g. Shamardal (USA) 129 – Tadris (USA) 106 (Red Ransom (USA)) [2015 8m 7.6s⁵ 8.1m 8.1m p7g p8d³ p8g⁶ p7m* Oct 21] compact ex-French-trained gelding: fairly useful handicapper: won at Kempton (dead-heated with Mr Bossy Boots) in October: stays 1m: acts on polytrack, soft and good to firm going: in headgear first 4 starts in 2015: sold 29,000 gns, sent to Saudi Arabia. *Roger Charlton* **89**

ELEUSIS 4 b.f. Elnadim (USA) 128 – Demeter (USA) 79 (Diesis 133) [2015 84: 6m⁶ 5m⁴ 5.5m² 5m³ 6m 5g⁴ Sep 7] sturdy filly: fairly useful handicapper: second at Wetherby in June and third at Sandown in July: stays 6f: acts on good to firm going: tried in hood prior to 2015: usually races prominently: sold 34,000 gns, sent to USA. *Chris Wall* **84**

ELEUTHERA 3 ch.g. Bahamian Bounty 116 – Cha Cha Cha 90 (Efisio 120) [2015 6d⁴ Jun 4] second foal: dam 6f/7f winner: 11/1, badly needed experience when fourth in maiden at Hamilton (5¾ lengths behind Under Siege) in June: should do better. *Kevin Ryan* **53 p**

EL FENIX (IRE) 3 b.c. Lope de Vega (IRE) 125 – Woodmaven (USA) (Woodman (USA) 126) [2015 65p: 8.3m 6g* t7.1g³ 7g p8f t7.1f* Oct 31] fair handicapper: won at Goodwood in June and Wolverhampton in October: stays 7f: acts on tapeta: in cheekpieces last 3 starts: often travels strongly. *Gary Moore* **79**

ELHAAME (IRE) 5 b.g. Acclamation 118 – Gold Hush (USA) 96 (Seeking The Gold **114** (USA)) [2015 105: 12m⁴ 11.6m* 9.9g² 10.4g* 10.3m* 12.4d⁴ Oct 31] strong, sturdy gelding: smart performer: won handicaps at Windsor in June and York (by neck from Roseburg) in August, and minor event at Doncaster (3 ran, by short head from Red Galileo) in September: respectable 2½ lengths fourth to Excess Knowledge in Group 3 Lexus Stakes (Handicap) at Flemington final outing: stays 1½m: acts on good to firm and good to soft going: usually travels strongly. *Saeed bin Suroor*

ELHAAM (IRE) 4 b.f. Shamardal (USA) 129 – Loulwa (IRE) 103 (Montjeu (IRE) 137) **70** [2015 70: t6f³ t6g³ Jan 15] sturdy filly: fair handicapper: stays 7f: acts on polytrack and tapeta: front runner/races prominently. *George Margarson*

ELIDOR 5 br.g. Cape Cross (IRE) 129 – Honorine (IRE) 89 (Mark of Esteem (IRE) 137) **115** [2015 112: 12.1g 14g 12g³ 14f* 14g⁶ 14g⁵ Jul 28] strong, rangy gelding: smart handicapper: won at Newmarket (by 2¼ lengths from Aramist) in May: good ½-length fifth to Blue Wave at Goodwood final start: worth another try at 2m: acts on firm and soft going: tried in visor: often races freely: consistent. *Mick Channon*

ELIS ELIZ (IRE) 3 b.f. Lord Shanakill (USA) 121 – Suailce (IRE) 103 (Singspiel (IRE) **95** 133) [2015 78p: t6m² 7m p6m³ p7g³ p6g³ p5g³ p6g* p6f² p6g t6m³ Dec 12] useful handicapper: won at Kempton (by head from Salvatore Fury) in October: second at Chelmsford (2¼ lengths behind Secret Missile) in October and third at Wolverhampton (2 lengths behind My Call) in December: stays 6f: acts on polytrack and tapeta: races prominently. *Michael Wigham*

ELISHPOUR (IRE) 5 b.g. Oasis Dream 129 – Elbasana (IRE) (Indian Ridge 123) [2015 **105** 20f³ Jun 16] tall gelding: useful handicapper: third in Ascot Stakes at Royal Ascot (2 lengths behind Clondaw Warrior) in June: stays 2½m: acts on any turf going: in tongue tie sole start in 2015. *A. J. Martin, Ireland*

ELITE ARMY 4 b.g. Authorized (IRE) 133 – White Rose (GER) 105 (Platini (GER) 126) **–** [2015 115p: 12m May 16] lengthy, attractive gelding: smart handicapper in 2014: well held in listed race at Newbury only outing in 2015: gelded after: stays 1½m: acts on polytrack, soft and good to firm going. *Saeed bin Suroor*

ELITE FORCE (IRE) 4 ch.g. Medicean 128 – Amber Queen (IRE) 92 (Cadeaux Genereux **75 §** 131) [2015 75§: t9.5g² t9.5g² 10.2f² 12g 11.9d⁵ 14.1g Sep 30] well-made gelding: fair maiden: stays 1½m: acts on tapeta and firm going: often wears headgear: sometimes in tongue tie prior to 2015: often races prominently: ungenuine and best treated with caution. *Roger Charlton*

ELITE FREEDOM (IRE) 4 b.f. Acclamation 118 – Jebel Musa (IRE) 73 (Rock of **37** Gibraltar (IRE) 133) [2015 59: t7.1f p7g t7.1m⁴ t7.1g⁶ f7g Mar 10] angular filly: poor maiden: stays 7f: acts on polytrack, tapeta, best turf form on ground firmer than good (acts on firm): sometimes wears cheekpieces. *Brian Baugh*

ELIZA 3 ch.f. Cockney Rebel (IRE) 127 – Royal Arruhan 69 (Royal Applause 124) [2015 **–** f8s⁴ 10.3m 12d³ 13.3m f14s Aug 6] second foal: dam maiden (stayed 1½m): no form. *Scott Dixon*

ELIZABETH COFFEE (IRE) 7 b.m. Byron 117 – Queens Wharf (IRE) 104 (Ela- **–** Mana-Mou 132) [2015 10g⁶ 10.3m⁵ Jun 27] fairly useful at best, no form in 2015: stays 12.5f: acts on polytrack, soft and good to firm going: sometimes wears headgear: tried in tongue tie prior to 2015: often races prominently, often races freely. *John Weymes*

ELIZABETH ERNEST 3 b.f. Exceed And Excel (AUS) 126 – Elusive Sue (USA) 83 **–** (Elusive Quality (USA)) [2015 52: 6m 5g Apr 22] maiden: no form in 2015: stays 6f: acts on good to soft going. *Richard Fahey*

ELIZONA 4 b.f. Pastoral Pursuits 127 – Morning After 84 (Emperor Jones (USA) 119) **86** [2015 89: p7f⁴ 6m⁴ 6m⁴ 7m⁴ p7g³ p7g⁵ Sep 5] lengthy filly: fairly useful handicapper: third at Kempton in August: stays 7f: acts on polytrack and good to firm going: in cheekpieces final start: sold 14,000 gns, sent to Saudi Arabia. *James Fanshawe*

ELJADDAAF (IRE) 4 b.g. Shamardal (USA) 129 – Almansoora (USA) 78 (Bahri (USA) **–** 125) [2015 t8.6f Nov 14] 16/1 and wearing hood, last of 7 in maiden at Wolverhampton (15½ lengths behind Bromyard) in November. *Dean Ivory*

ELJEEMI (IRE) 2 b.c. (Feb 9) Shamardal (USA) 129 – Arthur's Girl 103 (Hernando **– p** (FR) 127) [2015 7v Nov 3] 140,000Y: third foal: dam, 1¼m winner who stayed 1½m, half-sister to useful winner up to 1¼m Apple Charlotte: 4/1, seventh in maiden at Redcar (13¼ lengths behind Roundsman) in November, unable to sustain effort: better to come. *William Haggas*

ELKAAYED (USA) 5 ch.g. Distorted Humor (USA) 117 – Habibti (USA) 121 (Tabasco **99**
Cat (USA) 126) [2015 111: 12d 10.1g 10.3s 10.3f 10g² 10.3g* 10m 10.3m Sep 10] strong,
well-made gelding: useful handicapper: won at Doncaster (by short head from Roseburg)
in August: second at Newbury (2½ lengths behind Jakey) previous start: stays 13.5f: acts
on firm going. *B. W. Hills*

ELLAAL 6 b.g. Oasis Dream 129 – Capistrano Day (USA) 110 (Diesis 133) [2015 83: f8s **79**
8m² 8g⁵ 7.1g⁵ 8d 8g⁵ 8g⁴ 8.3s⁵ 7.9m³ 8.9m⁶ 8m 7.9m 8.5d⁴ 18.6f t8.6f Nov 3] big, strong, **a56**
close-coupled gelding: fair handicapper: stays 1¼m: acts on polytrack, soft and good to
firm going: tried in cheekpieces prior to 2015: front runner/races prominently. *Ruth Carr*

ELLA'S DELIGHT (IRE) 5 b.m. Camacho 118 – Swift Alchemist 78 (Fleetwood (IRE) **72**
107) [2015 79: 5s⁴ 5d 6d 6m³ 6g² 6g² 6m 6g 7s Oct 16] fair handicapper: stays 6f: acts on
good to firm and good to soft going: sometimes slowly away. *Martin Todhunter*

ELLA'S HONOUR 3 b.f. Makfi 130 – Danella (FR) 109 (Highest Honor (FR) 124) [2015 **81**
8.3d⁴ 8g² 8g² 8g² 10.1d⁴ 12s³ 10.4d⁵ 10d Oct 19] good-topped filly: half-sister to several
winners, including useful French 1m winner Azabara (by Pivotal): dam French winner up
to 1m (2-y-o 6f winner). fairly useful performer: won handicap at Newcastle (by 4½ lengths
from Field of Light) in August: stays 1½m: acts on soft going: often races prominently:
sold 30,000 gns, sent to France. *Rae Guest*

ELLE DORADO 3 ch.f. Paco Boy (IRE) 129 – Clever Millie (USA) 81 (Cape Canaveral **68**
(USA) 115) [2015 74: t9.5f 10g² 12.3s 10mᵖᵘ 10.3m 9.3d⁶ 10.4d 8g Oct 18] fair
handicapper: best effort at 8.5f: acts on tapeta, best turf form on good going: in cheekpieces
last 3 starts: often races lazily. *Tom Dascombe*

ELLE REBELLE 5 b.m. Cockney Rebel (IRE) 127 – Lille Ida 73 (Hawk Wing (USA) **63**
136) [2015 66: t8.6g t9.5g 8g² 8d² t8.6g t8.6g 8m³ 8g⁴ 8.5m 9.9g³ 10.2d⁵ 9.9d³ t9.5f³ t9.5f*
p10f³ t9.5m² t8.6f⁶ p10f* Dec 21] modest handicapper: won at Wolverhampton in October
and Chelmsford in December: stays 1¼m: acts on polytrack, tapeta, good to firm and good
to soft going: tried in cheekpieces prior to 2015. *Mark Brisbourne*

ELLERINA 3 b.f. Stimulation (IRE) 121 – Dream Quest 102 (Rainbow Quest (USA) 134) **57**
[2015 –: 8m⁵ 8g 10g² 12.1m 10.2m⁶ f8d⁶ t12.2f⁴ t13.9f⁵ t16.5m² t12.2m Dec 18] modest
maiden: best effort at 16.5f: acts on tapeta. *Chris Fairhurst*

ELLE SHADE 3 ch.f. Shamardal (USA) 129 – Elle Danzig (GER) 118 (Roi Danzig **76**
(USA)) [2015 t8.6f* p10m⁵ 10.2d³ 8.3m⁶ 8.1m² Jun 22] €150,000Y: sister to smart German
winner up to 1¼m Elle Shadow (2-y-o 7f winner) and half-sister to numerous winners,
including useful winner up to 1½m Asyad (2-y-o 1m winner, by New Approach): dam
1m-11f winner, including Premio Roma twice: fair performer: won maiden at Wolverhampton in February: stays 1¼m: acts on tapeta, good to firm and good to soft going: races
prominently, usually travels strongly. *John Gosden*

ELLEVAL (IRE) 5 b.g. Kodiac 112 – Penny Rouge (IRE) 59 (Pennekamp (USA) 130) **112**
[2015 112, a118: 9.9g⁴ 9.9g² 8.9g³ 9.9g³ 8.9g 8g 8m 10m⁴ 9d² 10d⁵ 12d⁴ Sep 12] strong
gelding: smart performer: second in handicap at Meydan (1¼ lengths behind Hunter's
Light) in January and Meld Stakes at Leopardstown (¾ length behind Carla Bianca) in
July: stays 1¼m: acts on polytrack, tapeta, good to firm and good to soft going: tried in
headgear. *David Marnane, Ireland*

EL LIBERTADOR (USA) 9 b.g. Giant's Causeway (USA) 132 – Istikbal (USA) (King- **40**
mambo (USA) 125) [2015 –: p10m⁶ p12g Feb 7] good-topped gelding: poor handicapper:
stays 13f: acts on polytrack and good to firm going: often wears headgear: tried in tongue
tie prior to 2015. *Eric Wheeler*

ELLIES IMAGE 8 b.m. Lucky Story (USA) 128 – Crown City (USA) 56 (Coronado's **–**
Quest (USA) 130) [2015 56, a47: 7.2d t7.1g Jun 22] fair at best, no form in 2015: stays 7f:
acts on good to firm and heavy going: tried in cheekpieces prior to 2015. *Richard Ford*

ELLINGHAM (IRE) 4 b.f. Bushranger (IRE) 119 – No Way (IRE) (Rainbows For Life **–**
(CAN)) [2015 –: p8f 11.5d t8.6g p5g⁵ Jul 14] compact filly: maiden: no form in 2015: tried
in headgear. *Christine Dunnett*

ELLTAAF (IRE) 2 b.f. (Mar 27) Invincible Spirit (IRE) 121 – Qasirah (IRE) 97 **66 p**
(Machiavellian (USA) 123) [2015 p6f³ Oct 15] sister to useful winner up to 7f Tantshi
(2-y-o 6f winner) and half-sister to several winners, including smart winner up to 1¼m
Toolain (2-y-o 7f winner, by Diktat) and 1¾m/2m winner Harry Hunt (by Bertolini): dam
2-y-o 7f winner: 13/8, seemed in need of experience and not unduly knocked about when
third in maiden at Chelmsford (3¾ lengths behind Wimpole Hall) in October: capable of
better. *Saeed bin Suroor*

ELLUSIVANCE (IRE) 5 b.g. Elusive Quality (USA) – Germance (USA) 113 (Silver — Hawk (USA) 123) [2015 8d f11d May 18] maiden: no form in 2015: stays 1m: tried in cheekpieces prior to 2015. *Nick Kent*

EL MASSIVO (IRE) 5 b.g. Authorized (IRE) 133 – Umthoulah (IRE) 81 (Unfuwain **70** (USA) 131) [2015 15.8s⁵ 14.1g² 13.1d* 15s⁶ Aug 8] good-topped gelding: fair handicapper: won at Ayr (amateur) in June: stays 1¾m: acts on polytrack, good to firm and good to soft going: tried in hood: sometimes slowly away, usually races nearer last than first. *Brian Ellison*

ELM PARK 3 b.c. Phoenix Reach (IRE) 124 – Lady Brora 83 (Dashing Blade 117) [2015 **118** 117b: 10.4m³ 12m 8.1d* 8d⁵ Oct 17] tall, good-topped colt: smart performer: won listed race at Sandown (by 2 lengths from Gabrial) in September: 16/1, good 2½ lengths fifth of 9 to Solow in Queen Elizabeth II Stakes at Ascot final start, having run of race from front: bred to be suited by 1¼m+, but best form at 1m: acts on good to firm and heavy going: front runner/races prominently, often races freely. *Andrew Balding*

ELOCUTION 2 b.f. (Mar 24) Paco Boy (IRE) 129 – Speech (Red Ransom (USA)) [2015 — 6m 7g 7s Sep 3] 15,000Y: rather unfurnished filly: third foal: half-sister to winner up to 11f Zamoyski (2-y-o 7f winner, by Dutch Art) and 1½m winner Hatch Hall (by Sleeping Indian): dam unraced half-sister to useful winner up to 1¼m Spoken out of Lancashire Oaks winner Spout: no form. *Denis Coakley*

ELOQUENCE 4 b.f. Oratorio (IRE) 128 – Noble Plum (IRE) 87 (King's Best (USA) 132) **57** [2015 55: 11.7f t9.5m² t12.2g f11d May 18] modest maiden: best effort at 9.5f: acts on tapeta: in headgear last 2 starts. *Tom Dascombe*

EL PRINCIPE 2 b.g. (Apr 7) Strategic Prince 114 – Shamrock Lady (IRE) 88 (Orpen **63** (USA) 116) [2015 5g⁴ 5m 8.5g⁵ 6s⁵ p6m² Oct 28] modest maiden: best effort at 6f: acts on polytrack: tried in eyeshields: front runner/races prominently. *Les Eyre*

ELRONAQ 2 b.g. (Apr 3) Invincible Spirit (IRE) 121 – Cartimandua 115 (Medicean 128) **100** [2015 6g² 6m* 6m³ 6m⁵ 6m⁴ 6g Sep 30] 90,000F: fourth foal: dam 6f winner: useful performer: won maiden at Newmarket in June: best effort next start when third in July Stakes at Newmarket (3 lengths behind Shalaa): raced only at 6f: acts on good to firm going. *Charles Hills*

EL TEL 3 ch.g. Sixties Icon 125 – Chelsea (USA) (Miswaki (USA) 124) [2015 8m t8.6g² **70 p** t8.6g⁴ Jun 2] 12,000Y: rather leggy gelding: half-brother to 3 winners, including unreliable winner up to 1m Cedar Rangers (2-y-o 6f winner, by Anabaa) and 7f winner Donna Giovanna (by Mozart): dam French 9f winner: fair maiden: best effort when second at Wolverhampton in May, sticking to task: gelded after final start: open to improvement. *Roger Varian*

ELTEZAM (IRE) 2 b.c. (Jan 18) Kodiac 112 – Tymora (USA) 63 (Giant's Causeway **104 p** (USA) 132) [2015 6m³ 6g* 6f³ 6m⁴ Jul 9] 60,000F, 280,000Y: lengthy colt: first foal: dam, disappointing maiden, out of high-class 8.5f-10.5f winner Shiva, herself half-sister to Oaks winner Light Shift: useful form: won maiden at Haydock (by 1¼ lengths from Elronaq) in May: third in Coventry Stakes at Royal Ascot (4 lengths behind Buratino) and fourth in July Stakes at Newmarket (3¼ lengths behind Shalaa) subsequently: will be suited by 7f: remains open to improvement. *Richard Hannon*

ELTHAM 2 ch.f. (Mar 8) Kheleyf (USA) 116 – Baddi Heights (FR) (Shirley Heights 130) **48** [2015 p6g Jul 2] 5,000Y: half-sister to several winners, including winner up to 7f Baddilini (2-y-o 5f/6f winner) and 2-y-o 1m winner Uvinza (both useful and by Bertolini): dam French 9f-10.5f winner: 50/1, last of 7 in maiden at Lingfield (6 lengths behind A Momentofmadness) in July. *Nick Littmoden*

ELTHEEB 8 gr.g. Red Ransom (USA) – Snowdrops (Gulch (USA)) [2015 86: 12.4g* 12g **85** 11.5g⁵ 10g⁴ 10.2g⁴ 9.8d⁵ 10g³ Sep 29] tall, close-coupled gelding: fairly useful handicapper: won at Newcastle in April and Nottingham in July: third at Ayr in September: stays 12.5f: acts on good to firm and heavy going: sometimes wears headgear: consistent: sold 6,500 gns, sent to Saudi Arabia. *Michael Dods*

ELUSIVE ELLEN (IRE) 5 b.m. Elusive City (USA) 117 – Ellen's Girl (IRE) 82 (Desert **73** Prince (IRE) 130) [2015 73: p10g p7f* p7f⁴ p7f* p7f* p8f⁵ 7s³ 7m 8g⁵ p7g⁵ 7d³ 7v² 7g p8f³ Oct 22] fair performer: won claimer at Lingfield in January and handicap at Kempton in March: stays 8.5f: acts on polytrack and heavy going: tried in hood prior to 2015: usually wears tongue tie. *Brendan Powell*

ELUSIVE EPONA (USA) 3 b.f. Elusive Quality (USA) – Genuine Charm (USA) (Dixie Union (USA) 121) [2015 72p: 5g 5m⁶ 7m Jun 25] fair form when successful only start in 2014: well held in handicaps in 2015. *Richard Fahey* —

ELUSIVE GENT (IRE) 8 b.g. Elusive City (USA) 117 – Satin Cape (IRE) 62 (Cape Cross (IRE) 129) [2015 54, a61: 9.5d² 11.3g⁴ 10d⁵ 9.5g³ 10.5g² 9.1g* 8m⁵ 8d³ 10d⁵ Aug 10] tall, good-topped gelding: modest handicapper: won at Ayr in July: stays 10.5f: acts on polytrack, soft and good to firm going: often wears headgear: front runner/races prominently. *A. P. Keatley, Ireland* **63**

ELUSIVE GUEST (FR) 4 b.g. Elusive City (USA) 117 – Mansoura (IRE) (Kalanisi (IRE) 132) [2015 86: 10g 8.3m⁶ 8.3m³ 10g 8g² 8.1g 7m p8f⁶ p8g* p8m* Dec 27] well-made gelding: fairly useful handicapper: won at Kempton in November and December and Chelmsford (by neck from Kalon Brama) in December: stays 8.5f: acts on polytrack and good to firm going: tried in hood in 2015. *George Margarson* **85 a93**

ELUSIVITY (IRE) 7 b.g. Elusive City (USA) 117 – Tough Chic (IRE) 82 (Indian Ridge 123) [2015 98: p6g⁶ 5m² 5m 6g 5m⁵ p6g 5.2s² 5v² 5m 5.1d 5.1d⁴ f5g⁵ p6m p5g f5g⁶ f6g⁴ p6g² Dec 28] well-made gelding: fairly useful handicapper: best efforts in 2015 when second at Windsor in April and Newbury and Epsom in August: left Peter Crate after tenth start: effective at 5f/6f: acts on polytrack, good to firm and heavy going: tried in headgear prior to 2015: usually races prominently: not one to trust. *Conor Dore* **88 § a80 §**

EL VALLE (FR) 3 b.c. Dobby Road (FR) 106 – Dohibane (FR) (Danehill (USA) 126) [2015 p6.5g⁴ 5.5s* 5.5s 6g* 6f 7g⁵ 6s⁶ 6s Nov 19] sturdy colt: fifth foal: brother to 5f (in Belgium) and 7f (at 2 yrs in France) winner Dobby Girl and half-brother to French winners around 1¼m Finnigan and Mont Calpe (both by Bachir): dam French maiden: useful performer: won minor event at Fontainebleau in March and Prix Sigy at Chantilly (by head from Finsbury Square) in April: creditable efforts in Prix du Pin at Longchamp (3¾ lengths fifth to Taniyar) and Prix de Seine-et-Oise at Maisons-Laffitte (3¼ lengths sixth to Gammarth) sixth/seventh starts: well held in Commonwealth Cup at Royal Ascot on fifth outing: stays 7f: acts on heavy going: blinkered last 5 starts. *Mlle V. Dissaux, France* **107**

EL VIENTO (FR) 7 ch.g. Compton Place 125 – Blue Sirocco (Bluebird (USA) 125) [2015 95: 6g 6m 5m² 5s³ 6m⁶ 5d* 5g² 5g² 5.1d² 5d² p5g⁴ p6m* t6g⁴ t6m Dec 18] lengthy gelding: useful handicapper: won at Sandown in August and Lingfield (by ¾ length from Mythmaker) in November: best other effort of 2015 when second at Doncaster (½ length behind Easy Road) tenth start: best at 5f/6f: acts on polytrack, soft and good to firm going: usually wears headgear. *Richard Fahey* **98**

ELYSIAN FIELDS (GR) 4 ch.f. Champs Elysees 124 – Second of May 72 (Lion Cavern (USA) 117) [2015 73p: 11.7f* 11.7m* 13.1f* 12m* 12f³ 14m Jul 30] good-topped filly: useful performer: thrived in 2015 and won at Bath in April and May (twice) and at Salisbury (by 4 lengths from Sunny Future) in June: 33/1, stiff task when good 8 lengths ninth of 14 to Simple Verse in Lillie Langtry Stakes at Goodwood final start: stays 1¾m: acts on polytrack and firm going: front runner/races prominently. *Amanda Perrett* **98**

ELYSIAN FLYER (IRE) 3 b.g. Majestic Missile (IRE) 118 – Starisa (IRE) (College Chapel 122) [2015 100p: 6m 5m³ 5.2s t6m t6m Dec 26] good-quartered gelding: useful performer: third in listed race at Sandown (2¼ lengths behind Waady) in June: left Richard Hannon, well held last 3 starts: stays 6f: acts on good to firm and good to soft going: tried in cheekpieces in 2015: front runner/races prominently, tends to find little. *Richard Hughes* **99**

EMARATIYA ANA (IRE) 4 b.f. Excellent Art 125 – Tina Heights 79 (Shirley Heights 130) [2015 94: 10.3g May 16] rangy, unfurnished filly: fairly useful at best: in cheekpieces, well held sole start in 2015: stays 1½m: acts on polytrack, soft and good to firm going. *Marco Botti*

EMBALLER (IRE) 2 ch.f. (Feb 18) Fast Company (IRE) 126 – French Doll (IRE) 66 (Titus Livius (FR) 115) [2015 5m⁵ 5g 6d⁵ p6f Oct 1] €7,000F, £24,000 2-y-o: first foal: dam maiden half-sister to smart winner up to 1¼m Road To Love: poor maiden: will be suited by at least 6f. *John Quinn* **46**

EMBANKMENT 6 b.g. Zamindar (USA) 116 – Esplanade 77 (Danehill (USA) 126) [2015 77§: p8g⁵ p8m² p8g⁶ p8f² p7f³ p8m p8f p8g⁵ 7s p8g* p8g 8.1g 8g⁴ 8v³ 7d² 7m 8d 8d Oct 30] sturdy, attractive gelding: fair handicapper: won at Kempton in May: stays 8.5f: acts on polytrack and soft going: tried in cheekpieces prior to 2015: usually slowly away, often races in rear: untrustworthy (usually blows chance at start). *Michael Attwater* **78 §**

EMBLAZE 3 b.f. Showcasing 117 – Chushka 81 (Pivotal 124) [2015 64: 6g 6g 6g t5.1m⁵ **61**
t6f Nov 13] modest maiden: stays 6f: acts on tapeta: tried in visor in 2015: usually races
close up. *Bryan Smart*

EMELL 5 ch.h. Medicean 128 – Londonnetdotcom (IRE) 101 (Night Shift (USA)) [2015 **113**
108: 8d 7g* 7m⁵ 7m⁵ 7d⁵ 8g⁵ 7m⁶ 7m³ 7g⁵ 7s³ 8f⁴ 7s⁴ Oct 12] strong horse: useful performer:
won handicap at Haydock (by 3¼ lengths from Professor) in April: mainly creditable
efforts subsequently, including when 2¼ lengths third of 5 to So Beloved in Supreme
Stakes at Goodwood tenth start: stays 8.5f: acts on soft and good to firm going: wears
headgear. *Richard Hannon*

EMERAHLDZ (IRE) 4 b.f. Excellent Art 125 – Sancia (IRE) 76 (Docksider (USA) 124) **93**
[2015 94: 12g⁶ 12m* 12m 12d 12d³ 14d⁶ 12d Oct 30] lengthy filly: fairly useful handicapper:
won at Thirsk in June: third at Doncaster in September: stays 1¾m: acts on polytrack, good
to firm and heavy going: sold 20,000 gns, sent to Saudi Arabia. *Richard Fahey*

EMERALD ASSET (IRE) 2 b.g. (Apr 30) Frozen Power (IRE) 108 – Balance The **60**
Books 75 (Elmaamul (USA) 125) [2015 5g 6g 6m 5d² 6g Sep 23] modest maiden: best
effort at 5f on good to soft going. *Paul Midgley*

EMERALD BAY 2 b.f. (Feb 5) Kyllachy 129 – Bahia Emerald (IRE) 80 (Bahamian **65**
Bounty 116) [2015 5d⁴ 5g⁴ t5.1m* 5g⁶ p6f t5.1f² t5.1g t5.1f⁴ Dec 11] neat filly: first foal:
dam, 6f winner, half-sister to useful 6f/7f performer Vital Statistics out of useful 5f
performer Emerald Peace: fair performer: won seller at Wolverhampton in August: left
William Haggas after: best form at 5f: acts on tapeta. *Ivan Furtado*

EMERALD (ITY) 3 b.g. High Chaparral (IRE) 132 – Ekta 101 (Danehill Dancer (IRE) **96 p**
117) [2015 8g p9.2g³ 8g* 8.9s⁵ 8d* Oct 31] first foal: dam Italian 6f-1m winner: useful
performer: won maiden at Ripon in August and handicap at Newmarket (had bit in hand
when beating Jack's Revenge by 1¼ lengths, again displaying high head carriage) in
October: stays 9f: acts on good to soft going: will go on improving. *Marco Botti*

EMILIE BRONTE 2 b.f. (Mar 9) Mullionmileanhour (IRE) 116 – Yorke's Folly (USA) **57**
54 (Stravinsky (USA) 133) [2015 5d⁶ 5g⁴ 6g Oct 16] second foal: dam maiden (stayed 6f):
modest maiden: best effort when fourth at Beverley (6¾ lengths behind Poet's Prize) in
September: may prove best at 5f. *Chris Fairhurst*

EMILIO LARGO 7 b.g. Cadeaux Genereux 131 – Gloved Hand 105 (Royal Applause **62**
124) [2015 7g p8g 12.1s⁵ 12v Oct 24] good-topped gelding: modest handicapper: left
Joseph Tuite after second start: stays 1m: acts on firm and soft going: tried in tongue tie
prior to 2015. *Mark Pitman*

EMILY DAVISON (IRE) 4 gr.f. Moss Vale (IRE) 126 – Carabine (USA) (Dehere (USA) **62**
121) [2015 67: p5m³ p5g* t5.1g³ 5.3g² 5m⁶ p5g 5d² p5g³ p5g 5m Aug 4] modest
handicapper: won at Chelmsford in March: stays 6f: acts on polytrack, tapeta, good to firm
and good to soft going: often wears headgear: often races prominently. *Heather Dalton*

EMILY GOLDFINCH 2 ch.f. (Mar 14) Prime Defender 118 – Lakelands Lady (IRE) 85 **–**
(Woodborough (USA) 112) [2015 7d Oct 31] fifth foal: dam 2-y-o 6f-1m winner: 100/1,
last of 9 in maiden at Newmarket (20¾ lengths behind Tiptree) in October. *Phil McEntee*

EMILYROSIE (IRE) 2 br.f. (Feb 14) Captain Rio 122 – Delira (IRE) 75 (Namid 128) **41**
[2015 5m⁵ f5d⁶ 5.1m 5m⁴ 5d 5d Sep 15] £6,000Y: first foal: dam, 5.5f winner, half-sister
to smart winner in Scandinavia up to 1½m Barrier Reef: poor maiden: raced only at 5f: acts
on good to firm going: usually races close up. *Tim Easterby*

EMILY YEATS 4 b.f. Yeats (IRE) 128 – Lasso 58 (Indian Ridge 123) [2015 65: 10.2m⁵ **–**
11.6m⁴ t12.2g Sep 29] maiden: showed little in 2015: best effort at 1¼m: dead. *Paul Webber*

EMINENTT 3 b.g. Exceed And Excel (AUS) 126 – Antediluvian 106 (Air Express (IRE) **52 ?**
125) [2015 7m 7.9g⁴ 8d⁴ 9.3m Aug 11] seemingly modest form on third outing. *John Davies*

EMIRATES AIRLINE 3 b.g. Dubawi (IRE) 129 – Moonlife (IRE) 114 (Invincible Spirit **98 p**
(IRE) 121) [2015 60p: p8g* 10g⁶ 8f 8d⁴ Oct 31] good sort: useful performer: won maiden
at Chelmsford (by 7 lengths from Regards) in March: off 4 months, 11/1, improved despite
not seen to best effect when 1½ lengths fourth of 11 to Emerald in handicap at Newmarket
final start, short of room over 1f out: likely to prove best up to 1¼m: acts on polytrack and
good to soft going: in hood last 2 starts: often races towards rear: open to further
improvement. *Saeed bin Suroor*

EMIRATES COMFORT (IRE) 3 ch.f. Dubawi (IRE) 129 – Royal Highness (GER) **78**
119 (Monsun (GER) 124) [2015 p12g3 p13.3f² p12g⁴ Nov 13] €500,000Y: fourth foal: half-
sister to 3 winners abroad, including smart French winner up to 11f Free Port Lux (2-y-o

9f winner, by Oasis Dream): dam French/US 9.5f-1½m winner: fair maiden: best effort when second at Chelmsford in October: in cheekpieces, signs of temperament final start. *Saeed bin Suroor*

EMIRATES HOLIDAYS (USA) 3 b.f. Dubawi (IRE) 129 – New Morning (IRE) 115 —
(Sadler's Wells (USA) 132) [2015 –p: t8.6f Feb 7] twice-raced maiden: no form. *Charlie Appleby*

EMIRATES SKYCARGO (IRE) 3 b.g. Iffraaj 127 – Catchline (USA) (Bertolini (USA) **108**
125) [2015 –p: t7.1f² p8f* p8m* p8f⁵ 8m² 8.1m 8m Jul 18] good-topped, attractive geld- **a98**
ing: useful performer: won maiden at Lingfield (by 2½ lengths from Goathland) in January
and handicap at Chelmsford (by 6 lengths from International Name) in March: unlucky
second to Mutasayyid in handicap at Newmarket (promoted from third) in May: stays 1m:
acts on polytrack and good to firm going: tried in tongue tie in 2015. *Charlie Appleby*

EMIRATES SKYWARDS (IRE) 3 b.g. Dubawi (IRE) 129 – Mont Etoile (IRE) 112 **81**
(Montjeu (IRE) 137) [2015 81: p13.3g* 14.1g⁶ p11g Aug 26] sturdy gelding: fairly useful
performer: won maiden at Chelmsford in April: probably stays 1¾m: acts on polytrack and
good to firm going: in visor in 2015: temperament under suspicion. *Charlie Appleby*

EMJAYEM 5 ch.g. Needwood Blade 117 – Distant Stars (IRE) 69 (Distant Music (USA) **88**
126) [2015 89: 5m 5g² 5.2m* t5.1f Oct 9] strong gelding: fairly useful handicapper: won at
Yarmouth (by 1½ lengths from Flexible Flyer) in September: best form at 5f: acts on tapeta,
firm and good to soft going. *Ed McMahon*

EMMESSESS (IRE) 4 b.g. Desert Millennium (IRE) – Azira 45 (Arazi (USA) 135) —
[2015 –: t7.1f t7.1g f6g Mar 3] no form: dead. *Christine Dunnett*

EMOTIONLESS (IRE) 2 b.c. (Mar 12) Shamardal (USA) 129 – Unbridled Elaine **122 p**
(USA) 124 (Unbridled's Song (USA) 125) [2015 7m* 7d* 7g Oct 10]
   Old battle lines were redrawn between Ballydoyle and Godolphin in the
latest season when Air Force Blue and Emotionless faced each other in the Dewhurst
Stakes. Tensions between the operations do appear, however, to have eased in recent
years since the days when each boycotted the other's stallions. At the Newmarket
October Sales, in the week leading up to the Dewhurst, M. V. Magnier, bidding
for Premier Bloodstock, paid 2,100,000 guineas for a daughter of Dubawi, with
Godolphin the underbidders. Coolmore connections have also bought colts by
Exceed And Excel (The Warrior, for 600,000 guineas as a yearling in 2013) and
by Bernardini (for 900,000 dollars—in partnership with Stonestreet Stables—at the
breeze-ups in March). There was also an old-fashioned tug of war in 2014 for a
colt whose lineage represented both parties, with Godolphin having the final say at
1,700,000 guineas (the colt, later named Chess Master, came third on his only start in
the latest season). Perhaps the apparent armistice between Ballydoyle/Coolmore and
Godolphin/Darley has something to do with the fact that they are no longer the only
superpowers in European racing, with operations based in Qatar, South Africa and
the Far East becoming increasingly influential, some of them teaming up together
(as Coolmore has done with Al Shaqab Racing and The China Horse Club).
   Godolphin has taken a new direction with a number of things in recent
years and it was announced in late-December that, in another adjustment, John
Ferguson, Sheikh Mohammed's long-standing adviser, will no longer be training
jumpers (which he has been doing successfully for five years) and will become
chief executive and racing manager to what was described as a new 'streamlined'
Godolphin operation. The move will see Godolphin and Darley merge into one
with the aim of sparking a revival in fortunes. The appointment of two new jockeys,
William Buick and James Doyle, did not coincide with the expected resurgence
at Godolphin. Saeed bin Suroor, a stalwart in the training ranks, saddled Group 1
winners at Meydan in March, including the winner of the Dubai World Cup (the
eight-year-old gelding Prince Bishop), but neither he nor Charlie Appleby, who
has charge of the other large yard belonging to Godolphin in Newmarket, saddled
a Group 1 winner in Europe in the latest season. The Godolphin colours were carried
to success in the Irish Derby, and to second place in the Two Thousand Guineas,
the One Thousand Guineas and the Derby in Britain, as well as to success in the
Lockinge, the Prix Jean Prat and the Yorkshire Oaks, but they were for other trainers.
Whether the riding or the training of the in-house Godolphin horses is more of an

At The Races Champagne Stakes, Doncaster—the highly-touted Emotionless wins very comfortably from the Vintage Stakes runner-up Ibn Malik, who is well clear of the rest

issue than the quality of many of the home breds they have had to deal with in recent years is a moot point. Either way, Sheikh Mohammed will be expecting John Ferguson to engineer a much needed reinvigoration of the operation.

While the anticipated duel between the National Stakes winner Air Force Blue and the Champagne Stakes winner Emotionless, the two highest-rated runners going into a Dewhurst together since Frankel and Dream Ahead in 2010, failed to materialise (as in 2010), there was a genuine excuse for Emotionless as he was found to have chipped a bone in a knee. Emotionless has undergone surgery which does leave a question mark of sorts over his career, as it did over Godolphin's much vaunted 2010 Champagne Stakes winner Saamidd who finished last in Frankel's Dewhurst before being well beaten in the Two Thousand Guineas, after which he was found to be lame. That Saamidd never won again gives food for thought, but horses do return to their best after surgery, as Kingman did in 2014 (he had ankle surgery at the end of his two-year-old campaign). Emotionless is a good sort physically and looked a top-class prospect when winning at Doncaster, so he has to be given the chance to confirm that form if and when he returns to action in the spring. He will stay a mile.

Emotionless started a well-backed 6/4-shot on his debut in an eleven-runner newcomers event at Newmarket in August and, after overcoming a slow start and being taken to the far side after a furlong, he won by three and a half lengths under a hands-and-heels ride; the runner-up Perkunas went on to show useful form himself soon afterwards, as did Emotionless' stablemate Venturous who finished fifth (he won his next two starts before running in the Middle Park Stakes). Emotionless held a number of big-race entries and he already looked ready for the step up to pattern races. The At The Races Champagne Stakes at Doncaster in September was a somewhat disappointing renewal in many ways, only three of the six runners having run to 100 or more on Timeform ratings, though Ibn Malik (7/2) had pattern-placed form having finished second to Galileo Gold in the Vintage Stakes after making a winning debut at Newmarket. Emotionless started at 13/8-on and looked something very special, winning as his rider William Buick liked, after racing keenly enough in the early stages with the pace set by Ibn Malik hardly fast enough for him. He cruised past Ibn Malik approaching the final furlong to win by three and a half lengths, barely appearing to hit top gear. Ibn Malik finished clear of the rest and the form put Emotionless in the same bracket at the time as Group 1 winners Shalaa and Air Force Blue. Emotionless was joined in the Dewhurst by two other Maktoum-owned horses in Massaat and Tashweeq, but strong support for Air Force Blue saw him go off at 6/4-on, with one-time ante-post favourite Emotionless drifting to 7/4 by start time. Emotionless made an effort over two furlongs out but soon wandered off a true line and dropped away inside the final furlong.

310

Emotionless (IRE) (b.c. 2013)	Shamardal (USA) (b 2002)	Giant's Causeway (ch 1997)	Storm Cat / Mariah's Storm
		Helsinki (b 1993)	Machiavellian / Helen Street
	Unbridled Elaine (USA) (gr 1998)	Unbridled's Song (gr 1993)	Unbridled / Trolley Song
		Carols Folly (b or br 1987)	Taylor's Falls / No Trespassing

Darley paid 4,400,000 dollars in 2005 for a mare carrying a Forestry foal. The foal was Etched who showed very smart form at up to nine furlongs in North America, his seven wins including two Grade 2s. The mare herself, Unbridled Elaine, who had cost her original owner 230,000 dollars, had won six of her eleven races including the 2001 Breeders' Cup Distaff over nine furlongs (she would have stayed a mile and a quarter) before having to be retired at the start of her four-year-old year (without running) because of ankle problems. Her first foal sold for 260,000 dollars two months before Darley purchased her; that foal was initially named Rogers Girl but had been renamed Seresa's Spirit by the time she herself was sold, believed in foal to Curlin, for 23,000 dollars in 2014. Unbridled Elaine's only other winner prior to Emotionless was the 2009 colt Out of Bounds (by Discreet Cat) who showed useful form at up to an extended ten furlongs on dirt, synthetics and turf, winning two of his first three starts in the States before being switched to the Saeed bin Suroor yard; Etched had had his final outing (in Dubai) for Mahmood Al Zarooni. Like Emotionless, Etched and Out of Bounds were both two-year-old winners. Unbridled Elaine's dam Carols Folly won five of her twelve races (all but one of them at two), including a minor stakes race, and has also produced another Grade 1 winner, the Ashland Stakes winner Glitter Woman, herself the dam of the Suburban Handicap winner Political Force. Unbridled Elaine's half-brother Your Eminence made 700,000 dollars as a yearling in 2002 and her close relative Unbridled's Folly fetched 675,000 dollars as a yearling in 2003. Emotionless has won on good to firm and good to soft ground. Should he bounce back, he could prove just the home-bred superstar Godolphin have been looking for after a couple of quiet seasons since being hit by the shocking doping scandal uncovered in 2013 at the Moulton Paddocks stable then run by Mahmood Al Zarooni. *Charlie Appleby*

EMPEROR FERDINAND (IRE) 4 b.g. Holy Roman Emperor (IRE) 125 – Moon Flower (IRE) 95 (Sadler's Wells (USA) 132) [2015 59: p10g⁵ p13g Jan 21] poor maiden: stays 1½m: acts on polytrack. *Marcus Tregoning* — **48**

EMPEROR MAX (AUS) 6 b.g. Holy Roman Emperor (IRE) 125 – Maxerelle (AUS) (Strategic (AUS)) [2015 6g³ 6g² 6g* 6d Oct 17] strong gelding: smart performer: won Group 3 Garden City Trophy at Kranji (by ½ length from Super Winner) in September: placed earlier on same course in Lion City Cup (very close third to War Affair) and KrisFlyer International Sprint (1½ lengths second to Aerovelocity): respectable 5¼ lengths seventh to Muhaarar in Champions Sprint Stakes at Ascot final outing: raced only at 6f/7f: raced mainly on good going: wears headgear. *S. Gray, Singapore* — **118**

EMPEROR NAPOLEON 2 b.c. (Mar 3) Champs Elysees 124 – Amarullah (FR) (Daylami (IRE) 138) [2015 p8f Nov 25] 39,000F: third foal: half-brother to 7f winner Song of Norway (by Halling): dam unraced sister to Champion stayer Amerigo: 33/1, green and never a threat when eighth in maiden at Lingfield (18½ lengths behind Brave Hero) in November: should do better. *Andrew Balding* — **– p**

EMPERORS WARRIOR (IRE) 3 ch.g. Thewayyouare (USA) 117 – World Sprint (GER) (Waky Nao 122) [2015 67: p8f 6.1m⁶ 7m 8.3m⁴ 6m 8gᵖᵘ p6m* p7m⁶ p6g² Dec 3] smallish gelding: fair performer: left Richard Hannon after fifth start: won maiden at Kempton in October: best form at 6f: acts on polytrack: usually in blinkers in 2015: often leads. *Gary Moore* — **59 a69**

EMPIRE STORM (GER) 8 b.h. Storming Home 128 – Emy Coasting (USA) 78 (El Gran Senor (USA) 136) [2015 116: a8f a8f³ a8f³ 8g⁶ 9.9s⁵ 7m³ 8d Oct 17] smart performer: third in handicap at Meydan (5¼ lengths behind Tamarkuz) in January, Firebreak Stakes at Meydan (7¾ lengths behind Tamarkuz) in February and handicap at Ascot (2½ lengths behind Buckstay) in October: stays 1¼m: acts on tapeta, dirt, soft and good to firm going: tried in hood prior to 2015: wears tongue tie: usually races close up. *Michael Attwater* — **115**

EMPRESS ALI (IRE) 4 b.f. Holy Roman Emperor (IRE) 125 – Almansa (IRE) (Dr **93**
Devious (IRE) 127) [2015 92: 10.3s 10.3g 10g⁴ 12.1d 10.3s* 10.4d³ 10.4s* 10v² 10.3v
Nov 7] smallish, sturdy filly: fairly useful handicapper: won at Chester in September and
York (by 1¼ lengths from Dance King) in October: stays 10.5f: acts on good to firm and
heavy going: in cheekpieces sixth to eighth starts in 2015: front runner/races prominently.
Tom Tate

EMPRESS TOORAH (IRE) 4 b.f. Holy Roman Emperor (IRE) 125 – Toorah Laura La **90**
(USA) (Black Minnaloushe (USA) 123) [2015 87: 8d 7g⁴ 7g* 7d* 8g Aug 22] fairly useful
handicapper: won at Cork and Roscommon in August: effective at 7f to 1¼m: acts on good
to soft going: usually races prominently. *Sabrina J. Harty, Ireland*

ENCANTAR 2 b.f. (Apr 6) Equiano (FR) 127 – Enrapture (USA) 85 (Lear Fan (USA) **77**
130) [2015 6d⁴ 5m² t5.1g* 5m* 6g 5g t5.1f⁶ Oct 16] 14,000F: seventh foal: half-sister to 3
winners, including smart 7f/1m winner Red Gulch (by Kyllachy) and 1¼m winner
Entrance (by Iceman): dam 7f winner: fair performer: won maiden at Wolverhampton in
July and nursery at Carlisle in July: stays 6f: acts on tapeta and good to firm going.
Ann Duffield

ENCAPSULATED 5 b.g. Zamindar (USA) 116 – Star Cluster 106 (Observatory (USA) **54**
131) [2015 66, a57: p6m² p6f² p6f² p6g 6m⁴ 6m 8m⁴ 7g p6g* p6g² p6f* p6g⁴ p6f⁵ p6m **a71**
p6m³ p6m⁶ p6m* Dec 31] good-topped gelding: fair handicapper: won at Lingfield in
August, Chelmsford in September and Lingfield in December: stays 7f: acts on polytrack,
good to firm and good to soft going: sometimes wears cheekpieces. *Roger Ingram*

ENCHANTED GARDEN 7 ch.g. Sulamani (IRE) 130 – Calachuchi 74 (Martinmas 128) **68**
[2015 16.1m² Aug 5] fair handicapper: stays 2m: acts on soft going: useful hurdler/fairly
useful chaser. *Malcolm Jefferson*

ENCHANTED MOMENT 3 b.f. Lawman (FR) 121 – Gentle Thoughts 73 (Darshaan **67**
133) [2015 p8g 10.3g⁵ 10.1d⁵ 11.6d Oct 12] 34,000Y: lengthy filly: half-sister to several
winners, including smart winner up to 16.4f Blue Bajan (2-y-o 9.5f winner, by Montjeu)
and 2m/16.5f winner Black Or Red (by Cape Cross): dam lightly raced: fair maiden: best
effort at 10.5f. *Chris Wall*

ENCODED (IRE) 2 ch.f. (Apr 13) Sakhee's Secret 128 – Confidentiality (IRE) 93 **– p**
(Desert Style (IRE) 121) [2015 5d Sep 22] €8,000 2-y-o: third foal: half-sister to 7f
(including at 2 yrs) winner Madame Mirasol (by Sleeping Indian): dam 1m-1¼m winner:
5/1, seventh in maiden at Beverley (9¼ lengths behind Fashionata) in September, not
knocked about: sure to progress. *Ann Duffield*

ENCORE D'OR 3 b.c. Oasis Dream 129 – Entente Cordiale (IRE) 72 (Ela-Mana-Mou **94**
132) [2015 93p: 6m⁴ 6m 6m⁶ 6m Jul 25] strong colt: useful performer: creditable sixth of
17 to Magical Memory in handicap at Newmarket in July: likely to stay 7f: acts on tapeta
and good to firm going. *Ralph Beckett*

ENCORE L'AMOUR 3 b.f. Azamour (IRE) 130 – Centime 75 (Royal Applause 124) **100**
[2015 76+: 9.9g² 10m 12.4d 10g⁴ Oct 9] compact filly: useful performer: creditable 3¼
lengths second of 8 to Lady of Dubai in listed race at Goodwood: not disgraced last 2 starts:
stays 1¼m: acts on heavy going. *David Simcock*

ENCRYPTED MESSAGE (IRE) 6 b.g. Dansili 127 – Where We Left Off (Dr Devious **87**
(IRE) 127) [2015 –: 14m³ 16d 15g⁴ 18d³ 18g² 16g⁶ Oct 11] fairly useful handicapper: best
efforts of season last 2 starts, when second of 13 to Lein Itcy at Newmarket and sixth of 20
to Digeanta at the Curragh: stays 2¼m: acts on soft and good to firm going: has worn
headgear: wears tongue tie. *A. J. Martin, Ireland*

ENDEAVOR 10 ch.g. Selkirk (USA) 129 – Midnight Mambo (USA) 53 (Kingmambo **–**
(USA) 125) [2015 8.9g Aug 27] close-coupled gelding: winning hurdler/chaser: maiden on
Flat: should stay beyond 12.5f: acts on heavy going: in cheekpieces sole start in 2015.
Dianne Sayer

ENDERBY SPIRIT (GR) 9 gr.g. Invincible Spirit (IRE) 121 – Arctic Ice (IRE) 82 **51**
(Zafonic (USA) 130) [2015 78: 6g 6d 6s⁶ Jul 17] tall gelding: modest handicapper: stays
6f: acts on firm and soft going: tried in headgear prior to 2015: tried in tongue tie prior to
2015: usually races prominently. *Bryan Smart*

ENDLESS CREDIT (IRE) 5 b.g. High Chaparral (IRE) 132 – Pay The Bank 81 (High **84**
Top 131) [2015 12g 12f² 12m² 12g⁴ 12g Sep 6] fairly useful handicapper: second at
Newmarket in July and Ripon in July: stays 1½m: acts on firm going: front runner/races
prominently: fairly useful hurdler. *Micky Hammond*

ENDLESS DRAMA (IRE) 3 b.c. Lope de Vega (IRE) 125 – Desert Drama (IRE) 106 **121**
(Green Desert (USA) 127) [2015 97p: 8v² 7v² 8g² May 23] big colt: very smart form: 9/1,
much improved when ¾-length second of 11 to Gleneagles in Irish 2000 Guineas at the
Curragh, doing better under change of tactics (held up): runner-up previously in listed
races at Leopardstown (to Zawraq) and the Curragh (to Tombelaine): stays 1m. *G. M. Lyons,
Ireland*

ENDLESS SEAS 4 ch.f. Refuse To Bend (IRE) 128 – Ocean Ballad (Bering 136) [2015 **44**
–: t8.6f f11d⁶ p13.3g⁴ 11.8m⁴ Jul 16] poor maiden: likely to prove best at short of 13f: acts
on polytrack, tapeta and good to firm going. *Michael Appleby*

ENDLESS TIME (IRE) 3 b.f. Sea The Stars (IRE) 140 – Mamonta 65 (Fantastic Light **110**
(USA) 134) [2015 84p: 9.9d* 12g* 12g 12m* 12g* Oct 18] leggy filly: smart performer:
progressed well in 2015 and won handicaps at Salisbury (by 8 lengths from Justice Belle)
and Goodwood (by ¾ length from Simple Verse) in May and Newmarket (by 1¾ lengths
from Twitch) in October, and listed race at Naas (by 4½ lengths from Almela) in October:
stays 1½m: acts on polytrack, good to firm and good to soft going: often travels strongly.
Charlie Appleby

ENERGIA DAVOS (BRZ) 7 gr.g. Torrential (USA) 117 – Star Brisingamen (USA) **113**
(Maria's Mon (USA) 121) [2015 113: a9.9f³ a9.9f 8d* 9g 9g* 9.9g p10g² p10g⁴ Dec 19]
sturdy gelding: smart performer: won handicap at Ascot (by ½ length from Puissant) in
September and Darley Stakes at Newmarket (by ¾ length from Sovereign Debt) in
October: third in handicap at Meydan (6½ lengths behind Le Bernardin) in January, left
Marco Botti after next start: stays 1½m: acts on polytrack, tapeta, soft and good to firm
going: tried in headgear: tricky customer. *Jane Chapple-Hyam*

ENERGIA FLAVIO (BRZ) 5 gr.h. Agnes Gold (JPN) 115 – Lira da Guanabara (BRZ) **89**
(Pitu da Guanabara (BRZ)) [2015 100: t8.6f² p8f³ p8g 8m 7m⁶ 7.6m 10.3m 8.3m³ Aug 9] **a96**
angular horse: useful handicapper: second at Wolverhampton (short head behind Pearl
Nation) and third at Lingfield (2¼ lengths behind Spiritual Star), both in January: stays
9.5f: acts on polytrack, tapeta, soft and good to firm going: tried in cheekpieces. *Marco Botti*

ENERGIA FOX (BRZ) 5 ch.m. Agnes Gold (JPN) 115 – Super Eletric (BRZ) (Choctaw **96**
Ridge (USA)) [2015 103: p12g² a9.9f 8.9g 10.3s 10.3g⁴ 10m⁶ 12.3f³ 11.6m⁵ 12.3g² 10m⁴
10.3m Sep 10] lengthy mare: useful handicapper: second at Lingfield (1¼ lengths behind
John Reel) in January and Chester (nose behind Leaderene) in July: stays 12.5f: acts on
polytrack and any turf going. *Marco Botti*

ENERGIA FRIBBY (BRZ) 5 b.m. Agnes Gold (JPN) 115 – Karla Dora (BRZ) (Nugget **101**
Point) [2015 105: 8g⁵ 8.9g 8f³ 8.5f 11f Nov 21] smallish, sparely-made mare: useful
performer: mostly inadequate trips in 2015, leaving Marco Botti 80,000 gns after second
outing: third in non-graded event at Santa Anita (1¼ lengths behind Alexis Tangier) in
October: stays 12.3f: acts on heavy going. *Neil Drysdale, USA*

ENGAGE (IRE) 2 b.f. (Apr 28) Pour Moi (IRE) 125 – Brooklyn's Storm (USA) (Storm **83 p**
Cat (USA)) [2015 8g* 7m⁵ Oct 3] 160,000Y: neat filly: half-sister to 3 winners abroad,
including useful French/US 1m/8.5f winner Stormina (by Gulch), herself dam of smart
French performer up to 1¼m Silasol: dam, 6f (at 2 yrs in France)/8.5f (in USA) winner,
half-sister to Prix de l'Arc de Triomphe winner Solemia: won maiden at Doncaster (by
short head from Langlauf) in August: better effort when fifth in valuable event at
Newmarket (6¼ lengths behind Alice Springs) in October: will be suited by a return to
1m+: remains with potential. *Sir Michael Stoute*

ENGAGING SMILE 3 b.f. Exceed And Excel (AUS) 126 – Bronze Star 76 (Mark of **73**
Esteem (IRE) 137) [2015 74p: p7m³ 8.1m 8g t7.1m Sep 25] good-topped filly: fair
handicapper: stays 7f: acts on polytrack: tried in blinkers in 2015: often races prominently.
Ralph Beckett

ENGAI (GER) 9 b.g. Noroit (GER) 116 – Enigma (GER) 107 (Sharp Victor (USA) 114) **69**
[2015 10m³ 9.9m* 9.9s f8g f8g p10g Dec 30] fair handicapper: won at Beverley (amateur) **a57**
in July: stays 1¼m: acts on polytrack and good to soft going: sometimes slowly away,
usually races nearer last than first. *David Bridgwater*

ENGELBERG (IRE) 3 gr.f. Zebedee 113 – Chingford (IRE) 64 (Redback 116) [2015 **68**
t7.1f⁶ 8.3d Oct 12] third foal: half-sister to 2-y-o 5f winner Courtland Avenue (by Kodiac)
and 5.7f winner Connaught Water (by Aussie Rules): dam maiden (stayed 7f): better effort
when sixth in maiden at Wolverhampton in October, never nearer. *Jonathan Portman*

ENGLISH HERO 2 b.g. (Feb 14) Royal Applause 124 – Merton Matriarch 64 (Cadeaux **76** Genereux 131) [2015 p6g 5.1g 5.4s* 6d Oct 24] first foal: dam, second at 6f at 2 yrs on only start, half-sister to useful 6f/7f performer Englishman: fair form: won maiden at York (by neck from Shine Likeadiamond) in October: 20/1, 8½ lengths seventh of 9 to Dhahmaan in listed race at Doncaster final start: stays 6f: acts on soft going: has been gelded. *Olly Stevens*

ENGLISHMAN 5 b.g. Royal Applause 124 – Tesary 98 (Danehill (USA) 126) [2015 100: **86** 6g⁴ 6m 6d Aug 28] big, good-topped gelding: fairly useful handicapper: stays 7f: acts on good to firm and heavy going: tried in cheekpieces prior to 2015. *Milton Bradley*

ENGLISH STYLE (IRE) 4 b.g. Bushranger (IRE) 119 – Fuerta Ventura (IRE) 102 **87** (Desert Sun 120) [2015 8g⁶ 7m⁴ 7.4g² Jul 21] 90,000Y: second foal: half-brother to useful winner up to 7f The Gold Cheongsam (2-y-o 6f/6.5f winner, by Red Clubs): dam, 1m-9.4f winner who stayed 1¾m, half-sister to useful 5.7f-7f winner Redvers: fairly useful maiden: best effort when second in maiden at Ffos Las (neck behind War Strike) in July, clear of rest: will benefit from return to 1m: sold 30,000 gns, sent to Macau. *David Lanigan*

ENGLISH SUMMER 8 b.g. Montjeu (IRE) 137 – Hunt The Sun (Rainbow Quest (USA) **97** 134) [2015 92: 12.3v⁴ 13.4g 11.9f³ 12.3m³ 13.2g⁶ 11.8g² 12g* 12m³ 12v* 11.8g* 14d 12v* Oct 17] sturdy, close-coupled gelding: useful performer: won amateur handicaps at Epsom in July and August (by 6 lengths from Echo Brava), handicap at Leicester (by 2¼ lengths from Eton Rambler) in September and claimer at Catterick in October: stays 16.5f: acts on polytrack and any turf going: tried in headgear prior to 2015: often wears tongue tie: often travels strongly. *Richard Fahey*

ENGLISHWOMAN 2 b.f. (Feb 27) Acclamation 118 – Tesary 98 (Danehill (USA) 126) **60** [2015 6d p6g t7.1f⁵ Dec 22] £20,000Y: fifth foal: closely related to useful winner up to 6f Englishman (2-y-o 5f winner, by Royal Applause) and half-sister to 1m winner (stayed 1½m) Merton Lady (by Beat Hollow) and winner up to 9f in Hong Kong Verbeeck (2-y-o 5f winner, by Dutch Art): dam winner up to 7f (2-y-o 5f winner): modest maiden: best effort when eighth at Kempton (4½ lengths behind Nassuvian Pearl) in September on second start: left Charles Hills after. *David Evans*

ENIGMATIC ANGEL (IRE) 3 b.g. Arcano (IRE) 122 – Seraphina (IRE) 99 (Pips Pride **–** 117) [2015 p8g 8.3d⁵ 8g Aug 28] little form. *Sir Michael Stoute*

ENLACE 3 b.f. Shamardal (USA) 129 – Crossover 105 (Cape Cross (IRE) 129) [2015 95: **105** p7f² t6f³ 7.5m⁵ p8g³ 7g* p8m⁴ 8.1m⁴ 7g* 7m* 7g 7m 7.6m 7d 7m* 7d 7s 6g 7g⁶ Oct 3] **a85 +** lengthy filly: useful handicapper: won at Goodwood in May/June, Chester in June and again at Goodwood (by ¾ length from Mambo Paradise) in August: below form last 4 starts: stays 7f: acts on good to firm going: usually races close up. *Mark Johnston*

ENNAADD 2 b.c. (Mar 2) King's Best (USA) 132 – Zayn Zen 107 (Singspiel (IRE) 133) **104 p** [2015 8.3d⁴ p8g² p8g* Dec 7] fifth foal: half-brother to 3 winners, including 5f winner Foolaad (by Exceed And Excel) and 1¼m winner Mezyaad (by Tiger Hill): dam 1m-1¼m winner: useful form: 5/4, impressive when winning 12-runner maiden at Lingfield in December by 6 lengths from Imperial Aviator: likely to stay beyond 1m: will go on improving. *Roger Varian*

ENREACHING 2 b.g. (Feb 13) Dutch Art 126 – Czarna Roza (Polish Precedent (USA) **82 p** 131) [2015 p7g³ p7g² p6g² Dec 9] 135,000F, 130,000Y: good-topped gelding: half-brother to several winners, including smart winner up to 8.3f Mabait (2-y-o 6f winner) and 6f/7f winner Jay Bee Blue (both by Kyllachy): dam unraced: fairly useful maiden: second at Kempton in November (1½ lengths behind Amanaat) and December (½ length behind Aclaim): likely to stay 1m: tried in tongue tie: remains with potential. *James Fanshawe*

ENRICHING (USA) 7 ch.g. Lemon Drop Kid (USA) 131 – Popozinha (Rahy **74** (USA) 115) [2015 76: t9.5f² t8.6f* 8f⁴ 8m p8f³ p10f² p8g⁶ p10f* Nov 7] close-coupled gelding: fair handicapper: won at Wolverhampton in January and Chelmsford in November: stays 1½m: acts on polytrack, tapeta, best turf form on good going or firmer (acts on firm): tried in blinkers prior to 2015: tried in tongue tie prior to 2015. *Nick Littmoden*

ENTENTE 3 b.g. Mawatheeq (USA) 126 – Amarullah (FR) (Daylami (IRE) 138) [2015 **62** 67: 7m 7g 10g p10f 8s⁵ t9.5f Oct 23] modest maiden: stays 1¼m: acts on polytrack, tapeta and good to firm going: in cheekpieces final start: often races freely: sold 3,500 gns, sent to Italy. *Peter Makin*

ENTERTAINING BEN 2 b.g. (Apr 14) Equiano (FR) 127 – Fatal Attraction 65 (Oasis **75** Dream 129) [2015 p5g 5.1g p5g² t5.1m³ Dec 12] fair maiden: raced only at 5f: usually in cheekpieces. *William Muir*

ENTERTAINMENT 3 ch.f. Halling (USA) 133 – Opera Comique (FR) 100 (Singspiel (IRE) 133) [2015 84p: p8g* 11.4d² 10m 12f⁴ 12.4d Aug 16] lengthy, good-topped filly: useful performer: won maiden at Chelmsford in March: ran well when 5¾ lengths fourth to Curvy in Ribblesdale Stakes at Royal Ascot on fourth outing: in cheekpieces, last of 10 in Prix Minerve at Deauville final start: stays 1½m: acts on polytrack, firm and good to soft going: front runner/races prominently. *John Gosden* — **102**

ENTIHAA 7 b.g. Tiger Hill (IRE) 127 – Magic Tree (UAE) 52 (Timber Country (USA) 124) [2015 91, a101: t16.5m⁴ t12.2g⁴ 13.1g 16.4s 14.6d⁶ p16g⁵ t16.5f* t16.5m Dec 12] sturdy gelding: useful handicapper: won at Wolverhampton in November: stays 2¼m: acts on tapeta, sand and good to firm going: often races prominently. *Alan Swinbank* — **78 + a99**

ENTITY 3 ch.f. Shamardal (USA) 129 – Echelon 120 (Danehill (USA) 126) [2015 –p: 10s p10g² p12g⁵ 10m* 12g⁶ 10d* 10.2v⁶ Oct 7] sturdy filly: fairly useful handicapper: won at Pontefract in July and September: stays 1¼m: acts on good to firm and good to soft going: usually wears hood: front runner/races prominently. *Sir Michael Stoute* — **90**

ENVISIONING (IRE) 3 b.g. Dylan Thomas (IRE) 132 – Lady Taufan (IRE) (Taufan (USA) 119) [2015 60: p7m³ p7f 11.3g 9.5g 11d Jul 14] smallish gelding: modest maiden: left Richard Hannon after second start: stays 8.5f: acts on polytrack, firm and good to soft going: tried in blinkers in 2015: usually races prominently: hinted at temperament. *Eric McNamara, Ireland* — **57**

ENZAAL (USA) 5 b.g. Invasor (ARG) 133 – Ekleel (IRE) (Danehill (USA) 126) [2015 64: f16g 12g 16.5m Jul 9] fairly useful at best, no form in 2015: tried in headgear: tried in tongue tie prior to 2015: often races prominently. *Philip Kirby* — **–**

EPEIUS (IRE) 2 b.c. (Apr 28) Arakan (USA) 123 – Gilda Lilly (USA) 80 (War Chant (USA) 126) [2015 7g⁵ 7.5g⁴ 8s Oct 9] fair maiden: best effort when fifth at Newcastle (6¾ lengths behind Marcel) in August. *Ben Haslam* — **70**

EPIC EMIRATES 2 b.f. (May 7) Dubawi (IRE) 129 – Nabati (USA) (Rahy (USA) 115) [2015 p7g⁵ Dec 20] fourth foal: sister to smart winner up to 1¼m Best of Times (2-y-o 7f/1m winner) and half-sister to French 10.5f winner Louisa M Alcott (by King's Best) and French 1¼m winner Rosewater (by Pivotal): dam, French 1¼m-1½m winner, closely related to St Leger winner Nedawi: 3/1, showed something when fifth in maiden at Lingfield (4¼ lengths behind Foxinthehenhouse) in December, left poorly placed: will improve. *Charlie Appleby* — **58 p**

EPICURIS 3 b.g. Rail Link 132 – Argumentative 101 (Observatory (USA) 131) [2015 111p: 9.9s² 12m⁵ 9.9g⁴ Jul 19] rangy gelding: smart performer: won Criterium de Saint-Cloud at 2 yrs: just respectable efforts in 2015, in Prix La Force at Longchamp (4 lengths second to Silverwave), Derby at Epsom (11¾ lengths fifth to Golden Horn) and Prix Eugene Adam at Maisons-Laffitte (3¼ lengths fourth to Dariyan): stays 1½m: acts on soft and good to firm going: has worn tongue tie: often leads: nervy sort, refused to enter stalls intended second outing: has been gelded. *Mme C. Head-Maarek, France* — **111**

EPIPHANEIA (JPN) 5 b.h. Symboli Kris S (USA) 132 – Cesario (JPN) 124 (Special Week (JPN) 125) [2015 132: a9.9f Mar 28] top-class performer at best: won Japan Cup at Tokyo (by 4 lengths) in 2014: ran only once in 2015, finishing last of 9 behind Prince Bishop in Dubai World Cup at Meydan (dirt debut, folded tamely over 4f out): retired in July after injuring suspensory ligament: stayed 15f: acted on firm and soft going: had worn tongue tie: to stand at Shadai Stallion Station, Japan. *Katsuhiko Sumii, Japan* — **–**

EPPING FOREST (IRE) 3 b.f. Bushranger (IRE) 119 – Ringmoor Down 113 (Pivotal 124) [2015 p6m 6m⁴ 7m⁶ 7.6m⁴ 6v⁵ 5.7f 8m⁴ Sep 28] fifth foal: half-sister to unreliable 9f-1½m winner Cuckoo Rock (by Refuse To Bend) and 6f winner Tregereth (by Footstepsinthesand): dam 5f and (at 2 yrs) 6f winner: modest maiden: stays 1m: acts on good to firm going: in headgear. *Jonathan Portman* — **60**

EPSOM DAY (IRE) 2 b.c. (Mar 21) Teofilo (IRE) 126 – Dubai Flower (Manduro (GER) 135) [2015 7g p8f⁶ p7g⁵ t9.5f² p10g³ Nov 26] good-topped colt: fair maiden: best effort at 9.5f: acts on tapeta: often starts slowly, usually races towards rear. *John Gosden* — **75**

EPSOM FLYER 5 ch.g. Haafhd 129 – River Cara (USA) 86 (Irish River (FR) 131) [2015 –: p15.8g⁵ p11g³ p10g Jun 20] sturdy gelding: modest maiden: stays 11f: acts on polytrack and soft going: tried in visor prior to 2015. *Pat Phelan* — **50**

EPSOM ICON 2 b.f. (Mar 22) Sixties Icon 125 – Hairspray 92 (Bahamian Bounty 116) [2015 6m 7g* 7d* 7s Aug 29] compact filly: second foal: dam 6f winner (including at 2 yrs): useful performer: won maiden at Epsom in July and listed race at Newbury (by length from Dessertodlife) in August: well held in Prestige Stakes at Goodwood final start: stays 7f: acts on good to soft going. *Mick Channon* — **95**

EPSOM POEMS 3 b.g. Pastoral Pursuits 127 – My Amalie (IRE) 92 (Galileo (IRE) 134) – [2015 53: p8f⁶ 9d Jun 4] maiden: no form in 2015: stays 1m: acts on polytrack: tried in tongue tie. *Pat Phelan*

EQLEEM 2 b.g. (Mar 25) Acclamation 118 – Blessing (Dubai Millennium 140) [2015 6g* **98** 6d³ 6g³ Aug 15] 75,000F: sixth foal: half-brother to useful 2-y-o 6f winner Sweetie Time (by Invincible Spirit): dam unraced half-sister to smart Japanese performer up to 11f Shinko Calido out of smart French miler Hydro Calido, herself half-sister to Machiavellian and Exit To Nowhere: useful performer: won maiden at Haydock (by ¾ length from Phantom Flipper) in July: best effort when third in minor event at Newmarket (length behind Raucous, hampered close home) later in month: likely to stay 7f. *Mark Johnston*

EQUALLY FAST 3 b.g. Equiano (FR) 127 – Fabulously Fast (USA) 120 (Deputy Minister **89** (CAN)) [2015 89p: 5d 5.1g² 5.6m⁵ 5m³ 5m² 5m² 5m 5g* 5m⁴ Oct 3] good-quartered gelding: fairly useful handicapper: won at Windsor (by head from Emjayem) in September: best form at 5f: acts on tapeta and good to firm going: blinkered last 6 starts: usually leads, usually travels strongly. *William Muir*

EQUAL POINT 2 b.g. (Feb 11) Equiano (FR) 127 – Point Perfect (Dansili 127) [2015 p8f – p Oct 15] fourth foal: half-brother to 2-y-o 7.6f winner Timothy T (by Pastoral Pursuits) and 6f winner Suitsus (by Virtual): dam ran twice: 25/1, very green when last of 7 in maiden at Chelmsford: should do better. *William Knight*

EQUILICIOUS 3 b.f. Equiano 127 – Fabine 70 (Danehill Dancer (IRE) 117) [2015 **48** –: p6g⁴ p7f⁵ 6m f7m Dec 8] poor maiden: left Charles Hills after second start: stays 6f: acts on polytrack and good to firm going: often races towards rear. *Ollie Pears*

EQUILLINSKY 3 ch.f. Equiano (FR) 127 – Millinsky (USA) 85 (Stravinsky (USA) 133) – [2015 p5m⁶ 6g⁴ 5g⁶ Jul 22] 8,500F, £10,500 2-y-o: fourth foal: half-sister to 5f/6f winner Moiety (by Myboycharlie): dam, 5f winner, half-sister to smart sprinter Mirza: no form. *Anthony Carson*

EQUINETTE (IRE) 2 b.f. (Mar 31) Equiano (FR) 127 – Rougette 86 (Red Ransom **75** (USA)) [2015 6g⁵ p5g² p6g Sep 30] first foal: dam, 1m winner, half-sister to useful winner up to 7f Royal Confidence out of Prix Robert Papin winner Never A Doubt: fair maiden: best effort when second at Kempton (1½ lengths behind Teresar) in September, conceding first run: will be suited by a return to 5f. *Amanda Perrett*

EQUISTAR 2 ch.g. (Mar 31) Equiano (FR) 127 – Halfwaytoparadise 69 (Observatory **82** (USA) 131) [2015 6m⁴ 7g² 7m 6g² p7g 6s³ Oct 26] rather leggy gelding: fourth foal: half-brother to 1m/8.6f winner Edge of Heaven (by Pastoral Pursuits): dam 7f winner: fairly useful maiden: second at Newbury in July and Newmarket in August: stays 7f: acts on polytrack, best form on good going. *Jonathan Portman*

EQUITA 3 b.f. Equiano (FR) 127 – Oasis Jade 65 (Oasis Dream 129) [2015 42: t5.1f³ t5.1f **46** Jan 12] poor maiden: raced only at 5f: acts on tapeta: hung right last 2 starts: sent to Greece. *Robert Stephens*

EQUITANUS (IRE) 3 b.c. Shamardal (USA) 129 – Wedding Gift (FR) 108 (Always Fair **52** (USA) 121) [2015 83p: 9g⁴ p8g⁴ p12g Sep 9] modest maiden: stays 1½m: acts on polytrack, raced only on good going on turf: tried in hood. *Jo Davis*

EQUITY RISK (USA) 5 b.g. Henrythenavigator (USA) 131 – Moon's Tune (USA) **84** (Dixieland Band (USA)) [2015 85: 6m 6d t8.6g t8.6m³ 9.9g* Sep 7] good-topped gelding: fairly useful handicapper: won at Brighton (by ½ length from Sixties Love) in September: stays 1¼m: acts on polytrack, tapeta, firm and good to soft going: sometimes slowly away, usually races nearer last than first: sold 9,000 gns, sent to Saudi Arabia. *Roger Charlton*

EQUIVOCAL 2 b.f. (Mar 27) Street Cry (IRE) 130 – Innuendo (IRE) 110 (Caerleon – (USA) 132) [2015 7m Aug 8] sturdy filly: sister to 1m-1¼m winner Hikma, closely related to smart French/US 9f-1½m winner Criticism (by Machiavellian) and half-sister to 3 winners, including smart 1¼m/10.4f winner Libel Law (by Kingmambo): dam 1¼m-1½m winner, including in USA: 4/1, last of 11 in maiden at Newmarket in August, possibly amiss. *Charlie Appleby*

EQULEUS 3 b.g. Equiano (FR) 127 – Merle (Selkirk (USA) 129) [2015 63p: 6g⁶ 6s⁴ t7.1f **73** p10m⁶ p8d⁴ t9.5m² Dec 18] fair handicapper: won at Kempton in November: should stay 1½m: acts on polytrack and tapeta: tried in cheekpieces in 2015. *Jeremy Gask*

ERELIGHT (IRE) 7 b.m. Erewhon (USA) – Caradene (IRE) 64 (Ballad Rock 122) [2015 **52 §** 54§: t7.1g² t7.1f f8f6] modest maiden: best effort at 7f: acts on polytrack, tapeta, best turf form on good to soft going: sometimes wears headgear: sometimes in tongue tie prior to 2015: often races prominently: has suspect attitude: one to avoid. *Shane Donohoe, Ireland*

ERETARA (IRE) 6 b.m. Erewhon (USA) – Hi Fasliyev (IRE) (Fasliyev (USA) 120) **55**
[2015 55: t7.1f⁶ t7.1m p8g 8m 10.1g p8g³ p8g Oct 9] modest maiden: barely stays 1¼m:
acts on polytrack, good to firm and heavy going: often wears headgear: tried in tongue tie
prior to 2015. *Shane Donohoe, Ireland*

ERICA STARPRINCESS 5 b.m. Bollin Eric 125 – Presidium Star (Presidium 124) **–**
[2015 13.8d 16v⁶ May 8] maiden: no form in 2015. *George Moore*

ERIC THE VIKING 3 b.g. Monsieur Bond (IRE) 120 – Whatdo You Want (IRE) **–**
(Spectrum (IRE) 126) [2015 –: 10.2d Aug 14] no form. *Richard Guest*

ERIK THE RED (FR) 3 b.g. Kendargent (FR) 112 – Norwegian Princess (IRE) (Fairy **99**
King (USA)) [2015 82p: 8g² 7.5m² 8m³ 8d* 8.5g* 10.3d* Sep 26] good-topped gelding:
useful performer: won maiden at Thirsk and handicap at Beverley in August and handicap
at Chester (by 1¼ lengths from Hakka, hampered before halfway) in September: stays
10.5f: acts on good to firm and good to soft going: tried in hood in 2015: formerly front
runner, ridden more patiently last 2 starts. *Kevin Ryan*

ERMYN LODGE 9 br.g. Singspiel (IRE) 133 – Rosewood Belle (USA) 70 (Woodman **–**
(USA) 126) [2015 73: p15.8g Jan 16] tall gelding: useful at best, well held sole start in
2015: stays 2m: acts on polytrack, good to firm and good to soft going: often wears
headgear: tried in tongue tie. *Pat Phelan*

ERNEST 3 b.g. Showcasing 117 – Excello 94 (Exceed And Excel (AUS) 126) [2015 p6g **64**
p5g⁶ f5g* f5d⁶ Mar 11] modest performer: won maiden at Southwell in February: best
effort at 5f: acts on fibresand: sent to Belgium. *Robert Cowell*

ERSHAADAAT (IRE) 3 b.f. Cape Cross (IRE) 129 – Almansoora (USA) 78 (Bahri **75**
(USA) 125) [2015 75: p7g⁴ 7.5m 6m⁶ p8g³ p8f Oct 22] fair maiden: stays 1m: acts on
polytrack and good to firm going: sometimes in cheekpieces in 2015. *Saeed bin Suroor*

ERSHAAD (IRE) 3 b.g. Acclamation 118 – Emerald Peace (IRE) 103 (Green Desert **75**
(USA) 127) [2015 77: p6g* t7.1f Dec 21] fair form: won maiden at Lingfield in January:
left Roger Varian £4,500/off 11 months, well held in handicap at Wolverhampton: stays 6f.
Shaun Harris

ERTIDAAD (IRE) 3 b.c. Kodiac 112 – Little Scotland 92 (Acclamation 118) [2015 72: **69**
p6f⁵ 6g³ 6.1m³ 5.7f⁵ p6f p6m⁶ Oct 21] fair maiden: stays 7f: acts on polytrack and good to **a62**
firm going: races prominently. *Pat Eddery*

ERTIKAAN 8 b.g. Oasis Dream 129 – Aunty Mary 82 (Common Grounds 118) [2015 86: **–**
7g Sep 19] good-topped gelding: fairly useful at best, well held sole start in 2015: stays 1m:
acts on polytrack, soft and good to firm going: sometimes in headgear prior to 2015: tried
in tongue tie prior to 2015: races towards rear. *Miss Joey Ellis*

ERUPT (IRE) 3 b.c. Dubawi (IRE) 129 – Mare Nostrum 117 (Caerleon (USA) 132) **125**
[2015 10.9g* 11.9d* 11.9g* 11.9m* 11.9s⁴ 11.9m⁵ 11.9f⁶ Nov 29]
     Fifth place in the Prix de l'Arc de Triomphe and then sixth in the Japan Cup
were good efforts from the three-year-old colt Erupt in the most competitive races
he contested. Although he came up short in the best company in the autumn, he
proved himself a high-class performer, confirming the promise he had shown earlier
in the year when unbeaten on his first four starts. Erupt booked his ticket to the big
end-of-season races with much his biggest win in the Juddmonte Grand Prix de
Paris at Longchamp in July. Reportedly having shown little at home to warrant any
big-race entries, Erupt had had to be supplemented for the Grand Prix de Paris after
progressing rapidly in the first half of the year, winning a maiden at Lyon Parilly
on his debut in April, a listed race at the same course (by three quarters of a length
from the Andre Fabre-trained favourite Big Blue) just a fortnight later, and then the
Prix du Lys Longines at Chantilly in June. Erupt beat another Fabre colt at Chantilly,
holding on by a neck from the listed winner Sarrasin who stayed on strongly from
further back than the winner.
     Sarrasin would have been a worthy contender for the Grand Prix de Paris
himself (he wasn't seen out again) but Erupt faced yet another colt from the same
stable at Longchamp, Ampere, who had won both his starts at the track, including
the Prix Hocquart. Ampere started at even money to give Fabre a fourteenth win in
the Grand Prix de Paris after Gallante had given him his fourth winner in the last six
runnings in 2014. Judged on classic form, however, the pick of the six-runner field
was 3/1 second favourite Storm The Stars (another supplementary entry) who had
finished third to Golden Horn in the Derby and then second to Epsom runner-up Jack

Hobbs in the Irish Derby. Storm The Stars was joined from Britain by the lightly-raced King Edward VII Stakes winner Balios at 7/2, while Erupt was fourth in the betting at 73/10. The field was completed by outsiders Silverwave, who had lost his unbeaten record when only ninth in the Prix du Jockey Club, and the Aidan O'Brien representative Archangel Raphael who faced a stiff task, having made a winning reappearance in a three-runner minor event at Fairyhouse just nine days earlier. Archangel Raphael made the running, with Storm The Stars the first to challenge starting the turn for home. However, Erupt was on the heels of the two leaders and soon joined issue once into the straight before going ahead under two furlongs out. Keeping on well, Erupt had two lengths to spare over Ampere who stayed on best of the remainder, but it was tight for third just over a length behind him, with Storm The Stars narrowly depriving Silverwave and Balios of that position, that trio clear of the eased-down Archangel Raphael.

Erupt's first Group 1 success was also a first for his thirty-eight-year-old trainer Henri-Francis Graffard who started training, with backing from Erupt's owners the Niarchos Family, in 2011 after three years as assistant to Alain de Royer Dupre. The latest season was therefore a pivotal year for the Niarchos operation as it also said goodbye to one of its established trainers Jonathan Pease who retired at the end of the season. Pease had trained the 2004 Niarchos-owned Grand Prix de Paris winner Bago who had just three rivals to beat that year (the latest renewal drew the smallest field since then) which was the final running of the race over a mile and a quarter. Coincidentally, Pease had also trained the winner of the final edition of the Grand Prix de Paris over its old distance of fifteen furlongs as well when Swink was successful in 1986 for Nelson Bunker Hunt. Another important American owner to support the yard, right up to the present day in his case, was George Strawbridge whose Tikkanen won the 1994 Breeders' Cup Turf three years after that horse's close relative Turgeon won the Irish St Leger and Prix Royal-Oak. Spinning World provided Pease with another Breeders' Cup winner when winning the Mile in the Niarchos colours in 1997, while the same race was won by Karakontie for the same connections in 2014. Karakontie was unsuccessful at Keeneland in October in his bid to win a second Breeders' Cup Mile but Pease's training career still ended on a high the following month. The trainer's final runner Siyoushake won a listed race at Fontainebleau (for another of the trainer's long-standing owners, Larry Roy), while earlier in November George Strawbridge's mare Sparkling Beam won a similar contest at Chantilly. Pease's last runner for the Niarchos Family was also a winner when, three days later, the two-year-old colt Bolting (who has since joined Graffard) won a minor event at the same track.

Juddmonte Grand Prix de Paris, Longchamp—the unbeaten Erupt completes his four-timer from Ampere (chevron) with Storm The Stars (left) third

After his Grand Prix de Paris win, Bago was a beaten favourite in the Juddmonte International and the Prix Niel (third in both) before bouncing back to win the Prix de l'Arc de Triomphe. Erupt was firmly on course for the Arc himself now, after the almost obligatory preparatory outing in the Prix Niel. This promised to be an exciting clash with another son of Dubawi, New Bay, the pair of them dominating the betting in a field of seven. However, after moving easily into the lead off the home turn, Erupt was readily brushed aside in the straight before weakening to finish a well-beaten fourth behind the Prix du Jockey Club winner, with Silverwave turning around the Grand Prix de Paris form by finishing second. Erupt must have disappointed connections all the more because they had stressed, after both the Prix du Lys and the Grand Prix de Paris, that he would be seen to better effect under softer conditions than he encountered in those two races. However, Erupt's performances on his two subsequent starts appeared to confirm that he is better suited by firmer conditions. He got much closer to New Bay when putting up a career-best effort to finish fifth in the Arc, always in touch and keeping on at one pace to be beaten less than four lengths behind Golden Horn. Erupt then went closer still in a blanket finish to the Japan Cup at Tokyo where he fared best of the four European runners, running in similar fashion to the Arc to finish sixth to the Japanese four-year-old filly Shonan Pandora, beaten less than two lengths. For the record, the Gold Cup winner Trip To Paris came fourteenth, while the German Group 1 winners Nightflower and Ito were eleventh and a tailed-off last respectively.

Erupt (IRE) (b.c. 2012)	Dubawi (IRE) (b 2002)	Dubai Millennium (b 1996)	Seeking The Gold Colorado Dancer
		Zomaradah (b 1995)	Deploy Jawaher
	Mare Nostrum (b 1998)	Caerleon (b 1980)	Nijinsky Foreseer
		Salvora (ch 1982)	Spectacular Bid Grand Luxe

Erupt is his dam's ninth foal in what has been something of a mixed record at stud for a mare who was a smart filly on the track. Mare Nostrum's only other winner in the Niarchos colours was her very first foal Hurricane Mist (a filly by Spinning World), successful in a minor event at two over a mile at Chantilly. Mare Nostrum's two other winners were useful performers in Britain for Mark Johnston, the handicapper Roman Republic (by Cape Cross), a winner up to a mile and a quarter, and Marie de Medici (by Medicean) whose wins included the listed Pretty Polly Stakes at Newmarket. Marie de Medici is now the dam of the useful Godolphin filly Local Time whose wins in the latest season included the UAE 1000 Guineas and Oaks and a Group 3 contest in Turkey. Another daughter of Mare Nostrum, the twice-raced Danehill filly Hespera, produced the French listed winner Lady Penko and a good jumper in France called Nando. Mare Nostrum was one of the best middle-distance three-year-old fillies of her year in France for Pascal Bary, winning the Prix Vanteaux before being beaten a neck in the Prix Saint-Alary, finishing fifth in the Prix de Diane and then running her best race when third in the Prix Vermeille. Mare Nostrum's half-sister Aube Indienne had fared less well in the Prix de Diane but went on to Grade 1 success in the States when winning the Yellow Ribbon Invitational Handicap at Santa Anita. Grandam Salvora was a mile and a quarter winner at Maisons-Laffitte for Stavros Niarchos and trainer Francois Boutin, while she was out of Grand Luxe, a winner of ten races in North America and a daughter of the Canadian Horse of the Year and very influential broodmare Fanfreluche. As well as other Canadian champions, Fanfreluche's descendants include grandson Holy Roman Emperor who was a high-class two-year-old for Aidan O'Brien in 2006. Fanfreluche lived to be thirty-two but she had an eventful as well as a long and productive life. In foal to Secretariat in 1977, she was kidnapped or stolen (there was no ransom demand) and then found wandering beside a road a hundred and fifty miles away from her home at Claiborne Farm. Unaware of her identity or value, the couple who found her named her Brandy and kept her in a woodshed until, after being 'missing' for over five months, she was eventually tracked down by the FBI and, with her true identity revealed, returned to Claiborne. The foal she was carrying was later named Sain Et Sauf—safe and sound. *Francis-Henri Graffard, France*

ERVEDYA (FR) 3 b.f. Siyouni (FR) 122 – Elva (IRE) 107 (King's Best (USA) 132) **120**
[2015 110: 7s* 8g* 8f* 8g² 8s* Sep 13]

Over the last thirty years, Royal Ascot's Coronation Stakes has been won by fillies representing some of the most successful and well-known owner-breeders. Hamdan Al Maktoum, Sheikh Mohammed, Stavros Niarchos, Jacques Wertheimer, Cheveley Park Stud, Khalid Abdullah and the Coolmore partners have each won the race at least once, as has Golden Horn's owner-breeder Anthony Oppenheimer, including with Rebecca Sharp, a half-sister to the dam of his Derby and Arc winner. Surprisingly, perhaps, the present Aga Khan was missing from the list of winning owners of more recent times until the latest season when the Coronation Stakes went to his Poule d'Essai des Pouliches winner Ervedya. Few of Europe's top fillies' races have not been won by a product of the Aga Khan's studs at one time or another in the long and illustrious history of the family's breeding operation, and Ervedya was not, in fact, the first filly to carry the silks of the Aga Khan to victory. The famous 'green, chocolate hoops' of the Aga Khan's grandfather were carried by the 1950 Coronation Stakes winner Tambara who had dead-heated for second in the One Thousand Guineas.

Ervedya's win was also significant because it had been ten years since the present Aga Khan's familiar 'green, red epaulets' had last been successful in a Group 1 at the Royal meeting. The four-year-old colts Valixir and Azamour won the Queen Anne Stakes and Prince of Wales's Stakes respectively in 2005 when the meeting was held at York during Ascot's redevelopment. It was also on the Knavesmire that the Aga Khan had last had a Group 1 winner in Britain before the latest season when Shareta won the 2012 Yorkshire Oaks. Azamour, sire of the Aga Khan's Sheema Classic winner Dolniya, also won the King George VI and Queen Elizabeth Stakes in 2005, another race transferred from Ascot (to Newbury), though the previous season he had won the St James's Palace Stakes at the Royal meeting's traditional home. The Aga Khan's other 2005 Royal meeting winner Valixir had been in his ownership only a matter of months, having been among the wholesale acquisition of the late Jean-Luc Lagardere's bloodstock earlier that year. Besides new bloodlines, that transfer also brought two new trainers into the Aga Khan fold, with the ex-Lagardere horses retaining their respective trainers Andre Fabre and Jean-Claude Rouget. Valixir was trained by Fabre whose association with the Aga Khan didn't last, but Rouget remains on the roster of trainers. Following Behkhabad in the 2010 Grand Prix de Paris and the ill-fated Valyra in the Prix de Diane two years later, Ervedya became the most successful horse to date trained by Rouget for the Aga Khan when landing a third Group 1 of the year in the Prix du Moulin back at Longchamp in September.

Poule d'Essai des Pouliches, Longchamp—the favourite Ervedya gets the better of British-trained outsider Irish Rookie (nearest to rail) and Mexican Gold

Coronation Stakes, Royal Ascot—Ervedya gets up late to beat Found and Lucida to give her owner the Aga Khan his first win in this race

Ervedya had won her first three starts as a two-year-old, graduating from a newcomers race at Tarbes, via a minor event at Maisons-Laffitte, to a ready Group 3 success in the Prix de Cabourg at Deauville. She improved again when third behind the colts The Wow Signal and Hootenanny in the Prix Morny back at Deauville three weeks later and then started favourite for the Prix Marcel Boussac, stepping up from sprint trips to a mile for the first time. Ervedya ran well at Longchamp considering she had the worst of the draw but proved no match for Found in the last half furlong and went down by two and a half lengths. Ervedya and Found renewed rivalry in the Coronation Stakes in which they were two of the leading contenders, along with the One Thousand Guineas runner-up Lucida. Found was sent off the 13/8 favourite after being beaten by Lucida's stable-companion Pleascach in the Irish One Thousand Guineas, while Ervedya and Lucida were next in the betting at 3/1, the remaining six fillies at 12/1 or longer.

While her two chief rivals were still seeking a first success of the year, Ervedya had won both her starts in France in the spring, prefacing her Poule d'Essai des Pouliches win with a comfortable victory on soft ground in the Prix Imprudence at Maisons-Laffitte in early-April. That made Ervedya the short-priced favourite for the fourteen-runner Poule d'Essai des Pouliches at Longchamp in May. The placed horses from the Imprudence, Ameenah and Queen Bee, were among those who took her on again, but a bigger danger looked to be the Andre Fabre-trained Mexican Gold who had taken her record to two wins from two starts when winning the Prix de la Grotte over the same course and distance three weeks earlier. Still with only one behind her two furlongs from home, Ervedya impressed with the way she finished down the outside to lead well inside the final furlong. Ervedya's winning margin was three quarters of a length but, given the ground she had made up from the rear, that didn't really reflect her superiority over the British-trained runner-up Irish Rookie, a 63/1 outsider who had finished sixth in the One Thousand Guineas just seven days earlier, while Mexican Gold was a neck behind the runner-up in third. Ervedya was Jean-Claude Rouget's second consecutive winner of the Poule d'Essai des Pouliches after Avenir Certain and the Aga Khan's first winner since the brilliant Zarkava in 2008.

Irish Rookie was among the longer-priced runners again in the Coronation Stakes but it was the three market leaders who fought out a close finish at Ascot, Christophe Soumillon producing Ervedya later still this time for a victory which again didn't fully reflect her superiority over Found and Lucida who were just a neck and half a length behind her at the line. It was Found who got first run, taking over in front from the pace-setting Arabian Queen a furlong out with Ervedya tracking her through before finding plenty for Soumillon's urgings to get up in the dying strides. Lucida finished strongly too, coming from even further back and wider out but not quite able to match Ervedya's acceleration. The American filly Miss Temple

Qatar Prix du Moulin de Longchamp, Longchamp—Ervedya justifies short-priced favouritism in a race weakened significantly by withdrawals while outsider Akatea stays on wide from the rear to take second from Karakontie (white cap)

City outran her odds of 50/1 to complete the frame, just ahead of Arabian Queen. Both Found and Arabian Queen went on to better things over longer trips later in the season, earning notoriety as the only two horses to lower the colours of Golden Horn, but Ervedya, whose strong-finishing efforts suggested she would stay further herself, was kept to a mile for her remaining starts.

Ervedya looked like being more than a match for a field of mainly older fillies in the Prix Rothschild at Deauville next time but, ridden more prominently than she had been at either Longchamp or Ascot, she lacked the same finishing kick, hitting the front over a furlong out when a gap opened on the rail but having no answer to the much improved four-year-old Amazing Maria who beat her a length and a quarter. Having skipped the Prix Jacques le Marois at the same course a fortnight later, Ervedya was one of ten originally declared for the Qatar-sponsored Prix du Moulin de Longchamp the following month. However, with the ground turning soft over the following forty-eight hours, the complexion of the race altered dramatically with the defection of the two British-trained entries, Arod and Dutch Connection, along with the Fabre pair Esoterique and Territories, who had been the first two home in the Jacques le Marois. That made Ervedya's task considerably easier, leaving Karakontie as the most noteworthy of her rivals to stand their ground, though he had finished a never-dangerous sixth in the Jacques le Marois after a lengthy absence since winning the Breeders' Cup Mile the previous autumn. The Moulin field was completed by the German-trained four-year-olds Wild Chief (third in the Jacques le Marois) and Guiliani and two other three-year-old fillies, Maimara and Akatea. The latter pair had been the first two past the post in the Group 3 Prix de Lieurey at Deauville but looked to have plenty on against Ervedya who had had Maimara back in eighth in the Pouliches.

With no obvious candidate to make the running, it was Karakontie who dictated just a steady pace, and at the line only around four lengths covered the entire field. Ervedya emerged comfortably the best, though, travelling smoothly behind Karakontie and quickening to lead well inside the final furlong after having to wait for a gap on his outer. Akatea finished best of the rest to be beaten a length in second, the same distance ahead of Karakontie in third, with the hard-pulling Maimara, Wild Chief and Guiliani close behind. Ervedya was put away for the season afterwards, thus ending her three-year-old campaign on a much more satisfactory note in the Moulin than the same stable's Elusive Wave six years earlier. Elusive Wave had been Rouget's first winner of the Pouliches (also his first classic winner all told), after also finishing runner-up in the previous season's Marcel Boussac. At three she contested the same five races as Ervedya in the latest season, also winning the Imprudence but finishing only fourth in the Coronation Stakes. Like Ervedya, Elusive Wave found an older filly too good in the Prix Rothschild (coming up against Goldikova) but then disgraced herself when favourite for the Moulin by refusing to race.

Ervedya comes from the first crop of the Aga Khan's own stallion Siyouni whose best effort in a three-year-old season in which he failed to win came when beaten two heads into third in the Prix du Moulin. By Pivotal, Siyouni was a speedier and more precocious colt than most of those associated with his owner, gaining his first three wins at two over five furlongs before winning the Prix Jean-Luc Lagardere over seven later in the season. That was an appropriate success because Siyouni's dam Sichilla was among the horses involved in the transfer of the Lagardere bloodstock to the Aga Khan. Sichilla's high-class half-brother Slickly won the Prix du Moulin, though by then he had been sold to Godolphin after earlier successes in the Lagardere colours, notably in the Grand Prix de Paris. Due largely to Ervedya's success, Siyouni will be standing at a fee of €30,000 at the Aga Khan's Haras de Bonneval in 2016, up from €20,000 in 2015.

		Pivotal	Polar Falcon
	Siyouni (FR)	(ch 1993)	Fearless Revival
	(b 2007)	Sichilla	Danehill
Ervedya (FR)		(b 2002)	Slipstream Queen
(b.f. 2012)		King's Best	Kingmambo
	Elva (IRE)	(b 1997)	Allegretta
	(b 2004)	Evora	Marju
		(b 1999)	Eviyrna

It is something of a surprise that Ervedya's family has been persevered with, as the Aga Khan's broodmare band is subject to regular culling of surplus, less successful stock. You have to go back four generations to find any other pattern winners, though further back this is a family that did well for Marcel Boussac (whose bloodstock empire was absorbed into the Aga Khan's studs in the late-'eighties); Ervedya's great great grandam Euliya won the Prix de Royallieu for the Aga Khan at Longchamp when it was a Group 3 contest. She was a half-sister to Erdelistan who finished third in the Prix du Jockey Club in the Aga Khan colours but was sold to Italian connections days before his Group 1 win in the Gran Premio del Jockey Club at Milan. Euliya produced eight winners but only one of them was so much as placed at listed level. Ervedya's great grandam was not one of those winners—she failed to reach the frame in three starts in France—while grandam Evora also ran only three times, winning a nine-furlong maiden at Fairyhouse as a two-year-old for John Oxx. Evora produced two foals, but one of those was Ervedya's useful dam Elva, also trained by Rouget. Like her dam, she won over a long distance for a two-year-old (an extended nine furlongs at Bordeaux) but was also successful over a mile at three at Saint-Cloud and finished second in the Prix Vanteaux at Longchamp. Elva's three foals before Ervedya are all winners, but none remotely so good as Ervedya herself. Ennaya (by Nayef) won at up to a mile and a quarter in the Provinces for Rouget, while Elmal (by Dalakhani), also a winner on the Flat in France, became a successful jumper in the Czech Republic. Elva is also dam of the five-year-old mare Elayouna (by Dr Fong) who was offered at the December Sales where the catalogue described her rather coyly as having 'won one race abroad'. That turned out to be in Morocco, after she had been sold for just €6,000 as an unraced two-year-old. Ervedya's two-year-old half-sister Elennga (by Exceed And Excel) has had three runs to date, including finishing third over a mile at Deauville.

Ervedya is a rangy filly who, despite coming to hand quickly at two, still looked to have plenty of scope ahead of her three-year-old season. She stays in training at four, as more of her owner's good fillies do nowadays, and she will presumably be aimed at some of the top mile contests again, her connections always having the option of races confined to her own sex if need be. Judging from her wins on very firm ground at Ascot and then on soft at Longchamp, the state of the going shouldn't be too much of a factor in how she is campaigned. She tends to travel strongly held up and has a good turn of foot. *Jean-Claude Rouget, France*

ESCALATE (IRE) 2 b.f. (Apr 12) Fast Company (IRE) 126 – Nova Tor (IRE) 86 (Trans – Island 119) [2015 p6g t6f Dec 22] €48,000Y: fourth foal: sister to useful winner up to 9f Devonshire (2-y-o 7f winner) and half-sister to useful 2-y-o 5f winner Hurryupharriet (by Camacho): dam 5f winner (including at 2 yrs): well held in 2 maidens. *Jeremy Noseda*

ESCALATING 3 ch.c. Three Valleys (USA) 119 – Pure Joy (Zamindar (USA) 116) [2015 **79**
89: 5f³ 5m⁴ 5m⁶ Aug 17] strong, attractive colt: fair handicapper: best form at 5f: acts on
polytrack, firm and soft going. *Pat Eddery*

ESCRICK (IRE) 3 b.f. Vale of York (IRE) 117 – Dubai Power 89 (Cadeaux Genereux **84**
131) [2015 73: 6d² 6g⁶ 6m⁶ 6g* 6g² 6m³ 7v⁶ Oct 24] neat filly: fairly useful handicapper:
won at Newcastle in August: good second at Brighton in September: stays 6f: acts on soft
going: sold 4,500 gns, sent to Italy. *David Simcock*

ESEEJ (USA) 10 ch.g. Aljabr (USA) 125 – Jinaan (USA) 72 (Mr Prospector (USA)) [2015 **–**
–: 7m⁵ 11.6m p15.8g⁶ Dec 2] big gelding: fairly useful at best, no form in 2015: tends to
find little. *Geoffrey Deacon*

ESHTIAAL (USA) 5 b.g. Dynaformer (USA) – Enfiraaj (USA) (Kingmambo (USA) 125) **91**
[2015 89: 12.3v³ 12g⁵ 16.4m* 16d Jul 27] tall gelding: fairly useful handicapper: won at
York (by ¾ length from William of Orange) in July: stays 16.5f: acts on soft and good to
firm going: often wears headgear: often wears tongue tie: front runner/races prominently:
fairly useful hurdler. *Gordon Elliott, Ireland*

ESHTYAAQ 8 b.g. Mark of Esteem (IRE) 137 – Fleet Hill (IRE) 99 (Warrshan (USA) **72**
117) [2015 75: 16m p13.3m⁴ 14.1g 16.2m² Jun 12] fair handicapper: stays 17f: acts on
polytrack, soft and good to firm going. *David Evans*

ESKANDARI (IRE) 2 b.c. (Feb 27) Kodiac 112 – Alexander Icequeen (IRE) 106 (Soviet **51 p**
Star (USA) 128) [2015 f7m Dec 8] 60,000Y: fourth foal: half-brother to useful 2-y-o 1m
winner Musaafer (by Marju) and 7f winner The Eyes Have It (by Arcano): dam, 2-y-o 7f
winner, half-sister to useful 9.4f-1½m winner Gavroche: 10/1, not seen to best effect when
seventh in maiden at Southwell (19¼ lengths behind Yattwee) in December, not knocked
about: better to come. *Simon Crisford*

ESOTERIQUE (IRE) 5 b.m. Danehill Dancer (IRE) 117 – Dievotchka (Dancing **123**
Brave (USA) 140) [2015 120: 8g³ 8f² 6.5g² 8d* 8m* 8g 8g⁴ Dec 13]

Bred at the Haras de Meautry which is just a stone's throw from the course,
a return to Deauville's sea air in August clearly suited Esoterique again. Having
won the Prix Rothschild there in 2014, for her owner Baron Edouard de Rothschild,
Esoterique was set a far stiffer task in the latest season when asked to attempt a
double in two of the other Group 1 contests at the Normandy track, the Prix Maurice
de Gheest and the Prix Jacques le Marois which are run just a week apart. Foiled only
by the season's champion sprinter Muhaarar in the first of those races, Esoterique
went one better seven days later when beating her stable-companion, the Two
Thousand Guineas runner-up Territories, in the top French mile race of the summer,
a much more valuable contest than the Rothschild which is restricted to fillies and
mares. Another five-year-old mare, Moonlight Cloud, had become the first to win
both races in the same season just two years earlier when she was successful in the
Maurice de Gheest for the third year running. Moonlight Cloud had also attempted
the double as a four-year-old but finished fourth in the Jacques le Marois on that
occasion. The Robert Collet-trained Whipper won the Maurice de Gheest and
Jacques le Marois in consecutive years, 2004 and 2005, and went close to winning
both races in each of those two seasons; in 2004 he was beaten a neck by Somnus
in the Maurice de Gheest, while in 2005 he was denied in the Jacques le Marois by
the three-year-old colt Dubawi. The only other horse to contest the two races in the
period between Whipper and Moonlight Cloud was Whipper's stable-companion
New Girlfriend who finished down the field in both contests in 2006.

Until the latest season, Esoterique had done all her winning against her own
sex and had never run at distances short of a mile, but she was better than ever at
the age of five and showed more speed than she had previously been given credit
for. On pedigree, she could have been expected to stay a mile and a quarter, but
she had pulled hard when finishing only seventh to Treve in the Prix de Diane on
her final three-year-old start. However, she had won a very muddling Rothschild
the year before from her stable companion, the One Thousand Guineas winner
Miss France, starting the outsider of four in a rather bizarre contest in which the
runners had started on one side of Deauville's straight mile and ended up on the
opposite rail. It might have been dubious form but the Rothschild at least showed
that Esoterique was well equipped for a test of speed, at least against other milers.
She also went to Deauville in the latest season after a much better showing at Royal

Ascot than the year before, belying odds of 16/1 when getting to within a length of Solow in the Queen Anne Stakes, a big improvement on her poor performance in the Duke of Cambridge Stakes against other fillies and mares twelve months earlier. Esoterique was beaten just half a length by Muhaarar in the Maurice de Gheest after challenging him briefly in the final furlong once a gap came. With Solow ineligible for the Jacques le Marois as a gelding and Gleneagles ruled out because of the ground (which had softened a little since the Maurice de Gheest), Esoterique's biggest danger the following week looked to be her own stable's three-year-old colt Territories who had won the Prix Jean Prat since chasing home Gleneagles at Newmarket. Territories started at 13/10 and Esoterique at 33/10 in a race which also saw the belated reappearance of the previous season's Breeders' Cup Mile winner Karakontie who was next in the betting at 53/10. The remainder in a field of nine for the Jacques le Marois, sponsored as usual by the Haras de Fresnay-le-Buffard, included a quartet of colts from Britain. Toormore had won the Lennox Stakes at Goodwood after finishing behind Esoterique when fourth in the Queen Anne, while his three-year-old stable-companion Estidkhaar had run Muhaarar to a neck in the Greenham at Newbury earlier in the season. Belardo was still trying to recapture the form which had won him the previous season's Dewhurst Stakes, while lightly-raced four-year-old Lightning Spear was contesting his first Group 1.

It was Toormore and Estidkhaar who set a sound pace down the centre of the track in the Jacques le Marois, with the patiently-ridden Esoterique having only Karakontie behind her as she bided her time travelling strongly under Pierre-Charles Boudot who had become her regular rider since partnering her for the first time in the previous season's Rothschild. With the race beginning in earnest two furlongs out, most of the field were hard at work as they fanned out from behind the two leaders to attempt to make their challenges, but Esoterique was still cruising as she made ground on to the heels of the leaders. A gap opened over a furlong out and Esoterique burst to the front through the middle of the pack before keeping on well. Running on softer ground than previously, Territories didn't have the same finishing kick after making his ground towards the outside and finished a length and a half back in second, with the same distance to the German colt Wild Chief who stayed on well to deprive Lightning Spear of third by a nose on the line. Toormore faded into fifth ahead of a never-nearer Karakontie, while Belardo and Estidkhaar ended up beating only the outsider Spoil The Fun who brought up the rear. Francois Boutin, who won the Jacques le Marois seven times, five of those wins for Stavros Niarchos (including with Karakontie's great grandam Miesque who won it twice in the 'eighties), still holds the record as the race's most successful trainer and nowadays has a listed race

Prix du Haras de Fresnay-le-Buffard - Jacques le Marois, Deauville—only seven days after pushing Muhaarar close in the Prix Maurice de Gheest, Esoterique grabs the limelight herself as she beats her stablemate Territories while Wild Chief (right) stays on for third

Kingdom of Bahrain Sun Chariot Stakes, Newmarket—Esoterique continues her excellent season, beating her old rival Integral (rail) and the Pouliches runner-up Irish Rookie (star on cap)

named after him earlier on the Jacques le Marois card. But Andre Fabre has now won the race six times himself and had twice been successful previously with fillies, the three-year-old Miss Satamixa in 1995 and the four-year-old Banks Hill in 2002.

Khalid Abdullah's Banks Hill went on to finish second in the Breeders' Cup Filly & Mare Turf that year (she had won the same race the year before), and the Breeders' Cup meeting was also the autumn target for Esoterique. First, though, came the Prix du Moulin at Longchamp and then the Sun Chariot Stakes at Newmarket for which she had to be supplemented, races in which she had ended her previous campaign by finishing fourth in both. Although Esoterique had looked very much at home on the good to soft ground at Deauville, the first time she had encountered such conditions since winning on her debut, she was taken out of the Moulin, along with Territories, when the ground softened appreciably after the pair had been declared to run. At Newmarket, Esoterique took on a field of mostly younger fillies in the Kingdom of Bahrain Sun Chariot Stakes, though her chief rival was another five-year-old mare, Integral, the 2014 winner whom Esoterique had met four times in all the previous season. Honours between the two were even from those encounters. There had been just a head between them in the Dahlia Stakes, when Esoterique had the advantage of being race-fit and better positioned in a steadily-run race, while in the Rothschild Integral had finished a disappointing third, returning with a bruised foot. In the 2014 Sun Chariot, it was Esoterique who had underperformed when unsuited by the way the race developed. There were no excuses needed for either mare in the latest Sun Chariot, though Esoterique came into the race in the better form of the two and was sent off at 11/8 with Integral next in the betting at 4/1. There were two other French fillies in the field of nine, the three-year-old Maimara who had finished fourth in the Moulin and the four-year-old Bawina who had been getting weight from Esoterique when having her back in third when both made their reappearance in the Prix du Muguet at Saint-Cloud at the beginning of May. Integral dictated a modest pace before kicking on two furlongs out, but Esoterique was always stalking her, and picked her off in the last fifty yards despite her rider dropping his whip. Esoterique won with a little in hand by half a length with the Poule d'Essai des Pouliches runner-up Irish Rookie faring best of the three-year-olds another length and a half back in third, while third favourite Bawina managed only sixth, already beaten when hampered over a furlong out. Esoterique therefore went to Keeneland for the Breeders' Cup Mile at the top of her form, along with stable-companion Make Believe who had won the Prix de la Foret the same weekend, but neither gave their running, with Esoterique never able to get into the race and finishing seventh, two places behind Make Believe. Esoterique was closer to her best when a respectable fourth to Japan's high-class miler Maurice in the Hong Kong Mile at Sha Tin in December.

Esoterique (IRE) (b.m. 2010)	Danehill Dancer (IRE) (b 1993)	Danehill (b 1986)	Danzig
			Razyana
		Mira Adonde (b or br 1986)	Sharpen Up
			Lettre d'Amour
	Dievotchka (b 1989)	Dancing Brave (b 1983)	Lyphard
			Navajo Princess
		High And Dry (b 1983)	High Line
			Photo Flash

The pedigree of the workmanlike Esoterique was covered in her essay in *Racehorses of 2014*. To recap, her dam Dievotchka, a 250,000-dollar yearling, never ran but made up for that by becoming a hugely successful broodmare at the Rothschilds' Haras de Meautry. Esoterique, her penultimate foal in a long innings at stud, was her tenth winner and fourth to be successful in pattern company. They include the Prix Eugene Adam winner Archange d'Or (by Danehill, Esoterique's grandsire), while local success at Deauville has been a feature of the records of Dievotchka's other pattern winners, with Russian Cross (by Cape Cross) winning the Prix Guillaume d'Ornano there and Russian Hope (by Rock Hopper) the Grand Prix de Deauville. Grandam High And Dry ran twice at Goodwood as a two-year-old, winning a maiden there before finishing third in the Candelabra Stakes for Jim Joel and Henry Cecil. A daughter of the One Thousand Guineas runner-up Photo Flash and rated 95p at two, High And Dry never raced again and was among her ninety-two-year-old owner's breeding stock from his Childwick Bury Stud that was dispersed the following year at the 1986 Newmarket December Sales where High And Dry was sold for 155,000 guineas. Another very smart miler to descend from High And Dry in the latest season was her great grandson Kodi Bear whose wins included the Celebration Mile at Goodwood.

Finally, a note on Esoterique's jockey. Having made his breakthrough at Group 1 level just a year earlier, Boudot finished up sharing the French jockeys' title with Christophe Soumillon in a dramatic conclusion to the championship. He actually ended the year one in front when beating Soumillon into third in the final Flat race of the year at Pau on New Year's Eve but the scores were levelled again when Soumillon's mount Walzertakt was awarded the Prix Gladiateur from earlier in the season after the winner of that race had tested positive. Ideally suited by a mile, Esoterique acts on firm and good to soft ground and usually travels strongly held up. *A. Fabre, France*

ESPECIAL 3 b.g. Misu Bond (IRE) 114 – Lady In The Bath (Forzando 122) [2015 78: 6v* **87** 6d 6m³ 6s² 7d⁶ 6g⁶ Oct 16] fairly useful performer: won maiden at Ripon in May: better form when placed in handicaps at Doncaster in July and Hamilton in August: left Bryan Smart after fifth start: worth another try at 7f: acts on good to firm and heavy going. *Michael Dods*

ESPOIR 2 b.f. (Mar 20) Cockney Rebel (IRE) 127 – Quiquillo (USA) 73 (Cape Canaveral **50 p** (USA) 115) [2015 p6g t7.1g t6m⁴ Dec 18] second foal: sister to 2-y-o 5f winner Perardua: dam 6f winner who stayed 1m: modest maiden: best effort when fourth at Wolverhampton (6 lengths behind Tesoro) in December, not knocked about: likely to stay 7f: capable of better. *Richard Fahey*

ESSAKA (IRE) 3 b.g. Equiano (FR) 127 – Dream Vision (USA) (Distant View (USA) **69** 126) [2015 66: t6g³ t7.1f 5d⁴ 7s⁵ 7s³ 6d⁴ 6.1m⁴ 6s² 6v² 6g 6d³ t6g p6g² t5.1f⁵ Nov 10] fair handicapper: left Mick Channon, won at Brighton in August: best at 6f: acts on tapeta, good to firm and heavy going: usually races towards rear. *Tony Carroll*

ESSENAITCH (IRE) 2 b.c. (Apr 14) Zoffany (IRE) 121 – Karlisse (IRE) 90 (Celtic **94** Swing 138) [2015 6m 6d* 7d⁴ 7s* 7s² p8m⁶ Sep 26] 13,000Y, 36,000 2-y-o: sturdy colt: second foal: dam, French 7f/1m winner who stayed 10.5f, half-sister to useful winner up to 1½m Filios: fairly useful performer: won maiden at Windsor in July and minor event at Lingfield (by 3 lengths from Sakada) in August: second in minor event at Goodwood in September: stays 7f: acts on soft going: usually leads. *David Evans*

ESSPEEGEE 2 b.g. (Apr 18) Paco Boy (IRE) 129 – Goldrenched (IRE) 78 (Montjeu — (IRE) 137) [2015 6v f8g Nov 26] well held in 2 maidens. *Alan Bailey*

ESTEAMING 5 b.g. Sir Percy 129 – Night Over Day 57 (Most Welcome 131) [2015 102: **99** 14s² 13s⁴ 12m 12m³ 10.3g 12m⁴ 12.1d⁵ 10.2d³ 12d 12v³ Nov 7] compact gelding: useful handicapper: second at Musselburgh (1¼ lengths behind Buthelezi) in April and third at York (5¼ lengths behind Wadi Al Hattawi) in July and Nottingham (3½ lengths behind Lahayeb) in October: stays 2m: acts on good to firm and heavy going. *David Barron*

ESTEEMABLE 3 ch.f. Nayef (USA) 129 – Ring of Esteem (Mark of Esteem (IRE) 137) **74 p** [2015 p8g⁶ p8g² Aug 24] 44,000F: rather leggy filly: half-sister to several winners, including smart 6f-9f winner Montpellier (by Montjeu) and useful 9.5f/1¼m winner Tinshu (by Fantastic Light): dam unraced half-sister to smart German winner up to 1½m Catella: better effort when 4 lengths second to Power Game in maiden at Kempton in August: open to further improvement. *James Fanshawe*

ESTIBDAAD (IRE) 5 b.g. Haatef (USA) 117 – Star of Siligo (USA) (Saratoga Six **74** (USA)) [2015 66: p12g⁶ p10g* p12f* t8.6f² p12f² t12.2f⁴ p12g t9.5g⁴ p11g⁴ p11g⁴ p11g* p10g* 10g p10g 8g⁴ t12.2g p10g* t9.5f Dec 14] lengthy gelding: fair handicapper: won at Lingfield in January (2, latter amateur event), Kempton and Chelmsford in June and Lingfield in October: stays 1½m: acts on polytrack, tapeta and soft going: wears tongue tie: front runner/races prominently. *Paddy Butler*

ESTIDHKAAR (IRE) 3 b.c. Dark Angel 113 – Danetime Out (IRE) (Danetime **121** (IRE) 121) [2015 114: 7m² 8m 8d Aug 16] rangy, good-looking colt: very smart performer: best effort when neck second to Muhaarar in Greenham Stakes at Newbury in April: well beaten in 2000 Guineas next time: off 4 months, better than result (6 lengths eighth of 9 to Esoterique) in Prix Jacques le Marois at Deauville, leading over 1f out: may prove best at short of 1m: acts on good to firm and good to soft going: usually races close up. *Richard Hannon*

ESTIDRAAK (IRE) 2 ch.c. (Mar 5) Iffraaj 127 – Gold Hush (USA) 96 (Seeking The Gold **96 p** (USA)) [2015 t7.1f² p7g* Nov 4] 130,000Y: fourth foal: half-brother to smart 1¼m-11.6f winner Elhaame (by Acclamation) and a winner in Italy by Tiger Hill: dam, 1m-1¼m winner, out of half-sister to Lammtarra: 8/13, created highly favourable impression when winning 13-runner maiden at Kempton in November by 7 lengths from Coherent, shaken up under 2f out then storming clear: will be suited by 1m+: smart prospect. *Sir Michael Stoute*

ESTIKHRAAJ 3 b.c. Dansili 127 – Shimah (USA) 107 (Storm Cat (USA)) [2015 73: 8g* **88** 8g² 8g³ 8g³ p8f³ Oct 1] fairly useful performer: won maiden at Thirsk in July: creditable efforts when placed in handicaps subsequently: stays 1m: acts on polytrack, raced only on good going on turf: sold 30,000 gns, sent to Australia. *Roger Varian*

ESTOURNEL 3 b.f. Danehill Dancer (IRE) 117 – Estephe (IRE) 91 (Sadler's Wells **58** (USA) 132) [2015 –: 9.9s⁶ 7m⁶ 8d⁶ p10f p10f p16f⁶ Oct 15] compact filly: modest maiden: stays 1¼m: acts on polytrack and soft going. *Harry Dunlop*

ESTRELLA ERIA (FR) 2 gr.f. (Feb 1) Mastercraftsman (IRE) 129 – Madrid Beauty — (FR) (Sendawar (IRE) 129) [2015 8.3d Oct 14] €50,000Y: fourth foal: dam, French 10.5f winner, half-sister to useful French 9.5f winner Northern Blue: 100/1 and in hood, held in maiden at Nottingham: sent to UAE. *George Peckham*

ETAAD (USA) 4 b.g. Intidab (USA) 115 – Red's Lucky Lady (USA) (Lucky Lionel **75** (USA) 112) [2015 57: p12g t7.1m* t7.1f² p8g p7g³ p8f³ p8g* t6f³ p7m* p7f⁵ Dec 21] fair performer: won handicap (apprentice) at Wolverhampton in February, minor event at Kempton in October and handicap at Lingfield in November: left Shane Donohoe after fifth start: stays 1m: acts on polytrack and tapeta: often wears headgear. *Gary Moore*

ETERNALLY 2 b.f. (Mar 22) Dutch Art 126 – Ardent 92 (Pivotal 124) [2015 t7.1f* **86 p** Nov 10] second foal: dam, 6f winner, half-sister to useful winner up to 6f Irresistible, herself dam of smart performers Watchable (6f winner) and Infallible (7f/1m performer): 9/2, overcame difficulties (slowly away, forced wide home turn) when winning maiden at Wolverhampton (by ½ length from Make Music) in November: sure to progress. *John Gosden*

ETERNITYS GATE 4 b.g. Dutch Art 126 – Regency Rose (Danehill (USA) 126) [2015 **86** 88: t5.1g⁴ 6g⁶ 5m⁶ 5.1m⁶ 6g² 5d⁵ Aug 17] sturdy gelding: fairly useful handicapper: second at Pontefract in August: left Peter Chapple-Hyam after fourth start: stays 6f: acts on tapeta and firm going: front runner/races prominently. *David O'Meara*

ETIBAAR (USA) 3 b.g. Kitten's Joy (USA) 128 – Oh Deanne O (USA) (Dynaformer **76** (USA)) [2015 54p: 10g⁶ 11.9d⁵ 14f⁶ p13g² p16g Sep 5] strong gelding: fair maiden: stays 13f: acts on polytrack and good to soft going: sometimes in blinkers in 2015. *Brian Meehan*

ETIENNE GERARD 3 b.g. Captain Gerrard (IRE) 113 – Alucica 64 (Celtic Swing 138) **74**
[2015 70: 6d 6.5m 6g⁴ 6g 6mᵘʳ 6m⁴ 6m* 6g⁵ 6m* 6m² 6g² t7.1f³ t7.1m Oct 2] fair
handicapper: won at Ripon in July and Leicester in August: stays 7f: acts on tapeta and
good to firm going: in cheekpieces last 5 starts. *Nigel Tinkler*

ETON NESS 3 b.g. Mullionmileanhour (IRE) 116 – Neissa (USA) (Three Wonders –
(USA)) [2015 10f p13.3f⁵ Nov 5] lengthy gelding: well held in 2 maidens. *John Best*

ETON RAMBLER (USA) 5 b.g. Hard Spun (USA) 124 – Brightbraveandgood (USA) **92**
(Smart Strike (CAN) 121) [2015 83: 11.6m⁶ 12.1m³ 11m* 12m² 12g² 11.8g² p12g* 11.9g⁵
12v Nov 7] sturdy gelding: fairly useful handicapper: won at Goodwood in June and
Kempton in September: stays 1½m: acts on polytrack, soft and good to firm going: often in
headgear prior to 2015. *George Baker*

ETTIE HART (IRE) 2 b.f. (Feb 11) Bushranger (IRE) 119 – Miss Megs (IRE) 81 (Croco **63 p**
Rouge (IRE) 126) [2015 p6g² Aug 26] €8,000Y: seventh foal: closely related to a winner
in Norway by Danetime and half-sister to 2-y-o 6f winner Chips O'Toole (by Fasliyev),
later successful in Scandinavia, and 6f-1m winner Presumido (by Iffraaj): dam 9f-11f
winner: 9/2, some encouragement when second in maiden at Lingfield (2 lengths behind
Harmony Bay) in August, left poorly placed: will improve. *Mick Channon*

ET TOI (IRE) 2 b.c. (Apr 3) Pour Moi (IRE) 125 – O' Bella Ballerina (USA) 80 (Fusaichi **83**
Pegasus (USA) 130) [2015 7m⁶ 7.1m³ 8v⁵ 8f² 7m⁶ Oct 3] 100,000Y: rather unfurnished
colt: second foal: dam, 1½m winner, half-sister to St Leger winner Millenary: fairly useful
maiden: bred to be suited by 1m+: acts on good to firm going: blinkered final start (stiff
task, ran creditably): has joined Doug O'Neill in USA. *Brian Meehan*

EUCHEN GLEN 2 b.g. (Mar 23) Authorized (IRE) 133 – Jabbara (IRE) 65 (Kingmambo **82 p**
(USA) 150) [2015 8g² Sep 17] fifth foal: brother to 9.5f-1½m winner Naru and 13f winner
Sir Chauvelin: dam 5f/6f winner out of smart French/US winner up to 12.5f Isle de France:
66/1, green when second in minor event at Ayr (1¾ lengths behind Speed Company) in
September, nearest finish: likely to stay 1¼m: sure to progress. *Jim Goldie*

EURATO (FR) 5 ch.g. Medicean 128 – Double Green (IRE) 104 (Green Tune (USA) 125) **62**
[2015 69: f12d⁶ p12f⁶ p10g⁵ t12.2g p12g⁵ Oct 20] good-topped gelding: modest handicapper:
stays 1½m: acts on polytrack and soft going: tried in cheekpieces. *John Spearing*

EURO CHARLINE 4 b.f. Myboycharlie (IRE) 118 – Eurolink Artemis 75 (Common **116**
Grounds 118) [2015 119: 8.9g⁴ 8m² 9.5d⁴ 8g⁵ Sep 12] good-topped filly: smart performer:
length second to Amazing Maria in Falmouth Stakes at Newmarket in July: better effort
after when 2¼ lengths fourth to Secret Gesture in Beverly D Stakes (won race in 2014) at
Arlington: stays 9.5f: acts on polytrack and firm going: front runner/races prominently:
refused to enter stall intended second outing. *Marco Botti*

EURO MAC 3 ch.f. Sir Percy 129 – Oomph 83 (Shareef Dancer (USA) 135) [2015 –: 7m⁵ –
9.9m Jul 14] no form. *Neville Bycroft*

EUROPA (GER) 3 b.f. Arcano (IRE) 122 – Easy Sunshine (IRE) 96 (Sadler's Wells **75**
(USA) 132) [2015 p10g 12g* 13d⁵ Jul 25] €10,000Y: seventh foal: half-sister to 3 winners,
including 8.6f-1½m winner Muwalla (by Bahri) and 1¼m winner (stayed 1¾m) Second
Glance (by Lemon Drop Kid): dam 7f winner: fair performer: best effort when winning
maiden at Pontefract (by 1¾ lengths from Spring Dixie) in June, suited by step up to 1½m.
Ed Dunlop

EUROQUIP BOY (IRE) 8 b.g. Antonius Pius (USA) 123 – La Shalak (IRE) 79 (Shalford **67**
(IRE) 124) [2015 70: 8.3d² 10m² 8.1s⁵ 10.2m⁶ 10.2m 6d 7s Sep 21] compact gelding: fair
handicapper: stays 1¼m: acts on any turf going: tried in visor prior to 2015: often races
freely: inconsistent. *Michael Scudamore*

EUROQUIP SUSIE 7 b.m. Monsieur Bond (IRE) 120 – Fizzy Lady 70 (Efisio 120) [2015 –
–: 16.2s 8.1m⁶ Jun 12] no form. *Michael Scudamore*

EURYSTHEUS (IRE) 6 b.g. Acclamation 118 – Dust Flicker 63 (Suave Dancer (USA) **89**
136) [2015 97: 8d 8g 8m 10m⁴ 7.9g 10.4m 9m 10.4g⁵ 8m⁶ 7d 7v Nov 7] well-made gelding:
fairly useful handicapper: stays 10.5f: acts on polytrack, soft and good to firm going:
sometimes wears cheekpieces: tried in tongue tie. *Michael Appleby*

EUTHENIA 3 b.f. Winker Watson 118 – Funny Girl (IRE) 78 (Darshaan 133) [2015 68: **67**
p10g⁵ p8m 7g² p6m* 6s⁶ 5m 5.7g Jun 13] fair handicapper: won at Lingfield in April: stays
1¼m: acts on polytrack, firm and good to soft going: often races prominently. *Mick Channon*

EUTROPIUS (IRE) 6 b.g. Ad Valorem (USA) 125 – Peps (IRE) (Val Royal (FR) 127) **94**
[2015 90: 8m⁴ 10m* 9.2d⁶ 10m⁴ 8m* 8g 8m 8g Aug 27] lengthy, angular gelding: fairly
useful handicapper: won at Redcar in May and Newcastle (dead-heated with Red Avenger)
in June: stays 1¼m: acts on fibresand, good to firm and heavy going: often races
prominently. *Alan Swinbank*

EUXTON 3 ch.f. Equiano (FR) 127 – Mystic Love (Pivotal 124) [2015 6v⁴ 5d² 6d³ 6m⁵ 7d⁴ **66**
6g t7.1f⁶ Oct 23] second foal: dam unraced half-sister to high-class 1m-1¼m winner
Medicean: fair maiden: left Richard Fahey after first start: stays 7f: acts on good to firm
and heavy going: tried in headgear. *Ronald Thompson*

EVA CLARE (IRE) 4 b.f. Majestic Missile (IRE) 118 – College of Arms (Lujain (USA) **63**
119) [2015 70: f5g⁵ f5g⁴ f5g⁴ p5f² Apr 26] modest handicapper: raced only at 5f: acts on
polytrack and fibresand. *K. R. Burke*

EVACUSAFE LADY 4 ch.f. Avonbridge 123 – Snow Shoes 84 (Sri Pekan (USA) 117) **68**
[2015 80: t9.5g p11m p10f p13.3m³ f12g⁶ p10f⁵ p10g t12.2g⁵ 10.1g 10.2d p10f² t8.6m³
t9.5m⁴ p10f* t9.5f⁶ p10f p10m³ t9.5g⁶ p10d Nov 30] angular filly: fair handicapper: won
at Chelmsford in October: stays easy 13f: acts on polytrack, tapeta and good to soft going:
often in cheekpieces prior to 2015: often wears tongue tie. *John Ryan*

EVANESCENT (IRE) 6 b.g. Elusive City (USA) 117 – Itsanothergirl 77 (Reprimand 122) **90**
[2015 93: 7m² 7.2d⁶ 7d³ 7.2g⁶ 7d⁶ 7s 7s p6f⁵ Nov 19] fairly useful handicapper: placed at
Thirsk in May and August: stays 7f: acts on soft and good to firm going. *John Quinn*

EVANGELICAL 2 b.f. (Apr 11) Dutch Art 126 – Pious 74 (Bishop of Cashel 122) [2015 **74**
6g⁴ 6d² 6d⁴ 6g⁴ Oct 20] sister to 2-y-o 5f winner My Boy Bill and half-sister to numerous
winners, including very smart 7f/1m winner Penitent and useful 2-y-o 5f/6f (including Mill
Reef Stakes) winner Supplicant (both by Kyllachy): dam 6f winner (including at 2 yrs): fair
maiden: raced only at 6f. *Richard Fahey*

EVELITH HALL (FR) 4 b.c. Teofilo (IRE) 126 – Dream For Life (FR) (Oasis Dream –
129) [2015 12m⁴ 11.5g p13g⁵ Aug 7] sturdy colt: no form. *Ian Williams*

EVENING ATTIRE 4 b.g. Pastoral Pursuits 127 – Markova's Dance 64 (Mark of Esteem **90**
(IRE) 137) [2015 96: p7g² 7d⁵ 8m 7g⁴ 7m⁶ 7g 6g³ 6g² p6m Nov 17] good-topped gelding:
fairly useful handicapper: second at Lingfield in January, best effort of 2015: stays 7f: acts
on polytrack and good to soft going: races prominently. *William Stone*

EVENING STARLIGHT 2 gr.f. (Mar 7) Kyllachy 129 – Night Haven 99 (Night Shift –
(USA)) [2015 p7m Dec 16] 15,000Y, £30,000 2-y-o: half-sister to several winners,
including useful winner up to 1¼m Rosa Grace (2-y-o 7f winner, by Lomitas) and useful
winner up to 7f Secret Night (2-y-o 5f/6f winner, by Dansili): dam winner up to 6f (2-y-o
5f winner): 100/1, well held in maiden at Lingfield in December. *Ron Hodges*

EVEN STEVENS 7 br.g. Ishiguru (USA) 114 – Promised (IRE) 90 (Petardia 113) [2015 **72**
80, a110: f5s⁶ 5g 5.2s⁵ 5d 5s f5g² p5f f5g Dec 12] close-coupled gelding: fairly useful **a90**
handicapper: second at Southwell in November: stays 6f: acts on all-weather and heavy
going: often wears headgear: front runner/races prominently. *Scott Dixon*

EVERGREEN FOREST (IRE) 7 ch.g. Haafhd 129 – Inaaq 109 (Lammtarra (USA) **47**
134) [2015 64: 11.9g⁵ t12.2g 16.5m 12g⁶ 13.1m⁶ 11.5d 12.1m p10f t11.7s³ 11.9d Sep 14]
smallish gelding: poor handicapper: left Jim Best after first start: stays 13f: acts on
polytrack, soft and good to firm going: often wears headgear: tried in tongue tie prior to
2015. *Alan Berry*

EVER PHEASANT (IRE) 3 b.g. Alfred Nobel (IRE) 110 – Indian Bounty 68 (Indian –
Ridge 123) [2015 –: 8.1s 8m May 28] no form. *J. S. Moore*

EVERVESCENT (IRE) 6 b.g. Elnadim (USA) 128 – Purepleasureseeker (IRE) (Grand **75**
Lodge (USA) 125) [2015 80: 10.2m² 10m⁵ 10g⁵ 9s 9.3g⁵ 10.2v Oct 7] good-topped
gelding: fair handicapper: stays 1½m: acts on good to firm and good to soft going: tried in
headgear prior to 2015: often races prominently. *Graeme McPherson*

EVERY CHANCE (IRE) 2 b.c. (Apr 23) Frozen Power (IRE) 108 – Runway Dancer **92 p**
(Dansili 127) [2015 t7.1f⁵ p8g⁴ t9.5f* Dec 14] 75,000Y, 100,000 2-y-o: fifth foal: half-
brother to 2 winners, including smart 6f (including Middle Park Stakes at 2 yrs) winner
Astaire (by Intense Focus): dam unraced: useful performer: improved to win maiden at
Wolverhampton (by 7 lengths from Van Dyke) in December: best effort at 9.5f: should
continue to progress. *Jamie Osborne*

EVERY INSTINCT (IRE) 3 b.g. Danehill Dancer (IRE) 117 – Phrase 72 (Royal Anthem **77**
(USA) 135) [2015 10g⁴ 12g² p12g² p10f³ p10f⁶ Dec 21] fair maiden: stays 1½m: acts on
polytrack. *David Simcock*

EVER YOURS (IRE) 4 br.f. Tagula (IRE) 116 – Quiet Please (IRE) 38 (Rock of Gibraltar 57
(IRE) 133) [2015 60: p6g p8f* p10f t8.6f⁴ t8.6f p8m⁶ Apr 8] modest handicapper: won at
Kempton in February: stays 8.5f: acts on polytrack, tapeta and good to soft going: often
wears headgear. *Noel Quinlan*

EVERYTHING GONE (IRE) 5 b.m. Erewhon (USA) – Atuf (USA) 88 (Danzig –
(USA)) [2015 –: 7d Oct 26] in headgear, well held both starts in maidens. *Kevin Ryan*

EVERYWISH 4 b.f. Quatre Saisons 69 – Reine de Violette 68 (Olden Times 121) [2015 –
p12g⁶ 10m⁶ 10m⁵ 12.1m p12g Aug 26] rather leggy filly: second foal: dam maiden (third
at 1m): no form: tried in blinkers: often starts slowly. *Jonathan Portman*

EVIDENCE (FR) 2 b.f. (Mar 31) Excellent Art 125 – Peachmelba (USA) (Theatrical) 57 p
[2015 7g³ Aug 13] €26,000Y, €25,000 2-y-o: lengthy filly: third foal: half-sister to useful
French 2-y-o 6f winner City Money (by Elusive City): dam French 9f-10.5f winner: 33/1,
shaped as if needed experience when third (promoted) in maiden at Salisbury (9½ lengths
behind Bobby Wheeler) in August: should do better. *Harry Dunlop*

EVIDENT (IRE) 5 b.g. Excellent Art 125 – Vestavia (IRE) (Alhaarth (IRE) 126) [2015 79, 63
a66: p6g* p6m p6f p7m⁴ 8.3m t6g³ 7.6d⁶ t7.1g⁶ 6s² 7v³ p6f p7g f6g⁶ Dec 18] strong, a73
lengthy gelding: fair handicapper: won at Kempton in January: effective at 6f to 8.5f: acts
on all-weather, soft and good to firm going: tried in headgear: often races prominently.
Tony Carroll

EVITA PERON 4 ch.f. Pivotal 124 – Entente Cordiale (IRE) 72 (Ela-Mana-Mou 132) 108
[2015 109: 7s³ 8g² 8s* 8.1m Aug 22] tall, angular filly: useful performer: won listed race
at Ascot (by neck from Solar Magic) in July: third in Chartwell Stakes at Lingfield (2¾
lengths behind Majestic Queen) and second in Group 3 at Hamburg (neck behind Odeliz)
previously: well below best final start: stays 1m: acts on soft going. *Ralph Beckett*

EXALTED (IRE) 4 b.g. Acclamation 118 – Eman's Joy 68 (Lion Cavern (USA) 117) [2015 68
7m 7m 8.3m⁵ p8d⁵ p8g* Dec 15] fair performer: won handicap at Kempton (apprentice) in
December: best effort at 1m: acts on polytrack: in tongue tie: sometimes slowly away.
William Knight

EXAMINER (IRE) 4 ch.g. Excellent Art 125 – Therry Girl (IRE) (Lahib (USA) 129) 99
[2015 98: 8m 10.4g 10s⁵ 9g³ 10v⁶ Oct 24] sturdy gelding: useful handicapper: best effort
when third in Cambridgeshire Handicap at Newmarket (length behind Third Time Lucky)
in September, only one to make frame who didn't race in far-side group: stays 1¼m: acts
on polytrack and good to firm going. *Stuart Williams*

EXCEEDINGLY 3 b.f. Exceed And Excel (AUS) 126 – Miss Rochester (IRE) 84 71
(Montjeu (IRE) 137) [2015 80: p5g⁴ p5m⁴ p6m⁶ Feb 18] fair handicapper: stays 6f: acts on
polytrack, tapeta, best turf form on good going: tried in cheekpieces in 2015. *Robert Cowell*

EXCEEDING POWER 4 b.g. Exceed And Excel (AUS) 126 – Extreme Beauty (USA) 75
89 (Rahy (USA) 115) [2015 79: p7g⁵ p7g⁶ 7s⁵ p7g² 7g² 7g² p7f³ p7g* p8f² Dec 21] a87
sturdy gelding: fairly useful handicapper: won at Lingfield in December: stays 1m: acts on
polytrack, fibresand and heavy going: tried in cheekpieces in 2015: tried in tongue tie:
often travels strongly. *Martin Bosley*

EXCEEDWELL 3 b.f. Exceed And Excel (AUS) 126 – Muja Farewell 94 (Mujtahid –
(USA) 118) [2015 59: t8.6g 8d 9g 11.5g p13f 6d⁵ Aug 5] angular filly: maiden: no form in
2015: often in headgear in 2015: front runner/races prominently, tends to find little.
John Ryan

EXCELLENT AIM 8 b.g. Exceed And Excel (AUS) 126 – Snugfit Annie 49 (Midyan 77
(USA) 124) [2015 62: t6g² p5g² 5.3g⁴ p5f³ p5g² f5m* p6m Dec 31] tall, lengthy gelding:
fair handicapper: won at Southwell in December: effective at 5f to 7f: acts on polytrack,
fibresand and good to firm going: tried in tongue tie prior to 2015. *George Margarson*

EXCELLENT ALIBI 2 ch.c. (Feb 7) Exceed And Excel (AUS) 126 – Indian Love Bird –
(Efisio 120) [2015 6g Aug 29] 33/1, well held in maiden at Newmarket in August.
Andrew Balding

EXCELLENT GEORGE 3 b.g. Exceed And Excel (AUS) 126 – Princess Georgina 78 86
(Royal Applause 124) [2015 74: p5f² t5.1f* 6m⁶ 5m 5g⁵ p5g³ p6f⁴ 5f³ Sep 13]
fairly useful performer: won maiden at Wolverhampton in March: third in handicaps at
Chelmsford in July and Bath in September: stays 6f: acts on polytrack, tapeta and firm
going. *Stuart Williams*

EXCELLENT GUEST 8 b.g. Exceed And Excel (AUS) 126 – Princess Speedfit (FR) 77 **87**
(Desert Prince (IRE) 130) [2015 97: 8m 8m 7m 7f 7d 8.3m⁴ 7g³ 7m p8f⁵ p8g⁴ p8g³
p8f³ Dec 21] strong gelding: fairly useful handicapper: third at Windsor and Yarmouth in
August: stays 8.5f: acts on polytrack, firm and good to soft going: tried in cheekpieces in
2015: tried in tongue tie in 2015. *George Margarson*

EXCELLENT JEM 6 b.g. Exceed And Excel (AUS) 126 – Polar Jem 109 (Polar Falcon –
(USA) 126) [2015 f8d p6g⁵ p6g May 20] fair at best, no form in 2015: often wears
headgear. *David C. Griffiths*

EXCELLENT PUCK (IRE) 5 b.g. Excellent Art 125 – Puck's Castle 92 (Shirley **84**
Heights 130) [2015 91: 12g* 11.5g 12m⁶ 12v⁵ p11g t9.5f* t9.5m Dec 12] sturdy gelding:
fairly useful handicapper: won at Newmarket (awarded race) in May and Wolverhampton
in October: stays 12.5f: acts on polytrack, tapeta, soft and good to firm going: tried in
blinkers prior to 2015: has edged/hung left under pressure. *Shaun Lycett*

EXCELLENT RESULT (IRE) 5 b.g. Shamardal (USA) 129 – Line Ahead (IRE) **111**
(Sadler's Wells (USA) 132) [2015 116: 12.1g⁵ 11.9g³ 14g 11.9g⁶ 14g 14g 14d 14d⁵ Sep 26]
lengthy gelding: smart handicapper: creditable efforts at Meydan first 2 starts, including
3¾ lengths third to Songcraft in February: respectable fifth of 17 to Nakeeta at Haydock
final outing: stays 1¾m: acts on firm going, probably on good to soft: tried in headgear in
2015. *Saeed bin Suroor*

EXCELLENT TEAM 3 b.g. Teofilo (IRE) 126 – Seradim 95 (Elnadim (USA) 128) **75**
[2015 59p: 12m³ May 29] useful-looking gelding: improved from debut when third in
maiden at Newmarket (10¾ lengths behind Horseshoe Bay) on sole outing in 2015: will
stay beyond 1½m. *Saeed bin Suroor*

EXCELLING OSCAR (IRE) 3 b.g. Excellent Art 125 – Three Pennies 72 (Pennekamp **70**
(USA) 130) [2015 64: f7g f6d³ f6d* f7d⁴ f5d³ t6f³ p6g² t6g⁴ p6g t7.1g 7m f7g⁶ f7m²
f7g² f8g* Dec 18] fair handicapper: won at Southwell in February and December: stays
1m: acts on all-weather: usually wears headgear. *Conor Dore*

EXCESSABLE 2 ch.c. (Jan 26) Sakhee's Secret 128 – Kummel Excess (IRE) 81 (Exceed **96**
And Excel (AUS) 126) [2015 5g* 5f² 5.2m⁵ 6g 5g Sep 18] 8,000F, £6,000Y: workmanlike
colt: first foal: dam winner up to 6f (2-y-o 5f winner): useful performer: won maiden at
Ripon (by 3½ lengths from Risk Adjusted) in April: second in minor event at Beverley
(neck behind Lydia's Place) in July: well below form last 2 starts: may prove best at 5f: acts
on firm going: often races prominently, often travels strongly. *Tim Easterby*

EXCHEQUER (IRE) 4 ch.g. Exceed And Excel (AUS) 126 – Tara's Force (IRE) 56 **99**
(Acclamation 118) [2015 94: 8f⁶ p7g* 6d⁴ 7f³ p7g⁶ 7d² 6d² Sep 26] lengthy gelding: useful
handicapper: won at Kempton (by 1¼ lengths from Great Fun) in May: twice second at
Haydock in September, ½ length behind Peril then ¾ length behind Brando: stays 1m:
unexposed on all-weather (successful 2 of 4 starts on surface), also acts on firm and good
to soft going: usually races prominently. *Richard Hannon*

EXCILLY 3 br.f. Excellent Art 125 – Afra Tsitsi (FR) (Belong To Me (USA)) [2015 84: 6g* **101**
7m* 7m² 6.9g* 8d³ 7m Sep 10] useful performer: won maiden in March in April, handicap
at Leicester in May and listed race at Carlisle (by 1¼ lengths from Calypso Beat) in June:
good fourth (later promoted to third) behind Maimara in Prix de Lieurey at Deauville in
August: stays 1m: acts on good to firm and good to soft going. *Tom Dascombe*

EXCLUSIVE CONTRACT (IRE) 4 br.f. High Chaparral (IRE) 132 – Birthday (IRE) **66**
(Dingsplat (IRE) 133) [2015 70: 112d⁴ 14.1m³ 12g* 12g³ 16g* 16.1m⁴ 14.4g⁴ 17.1d 16.2m
Oct 1] lengthy filly: fair handicapper: won at Thirsk in June and July: stays 17f: acts on
firm and good to soft going: tried in cheekpieces prior to 2015. *Ollie Pears*

EXCLUSIVE DIAMOND 3 b.f. Iffraaj 127 – Poppets Sweetlove 73 (Foxhound (USA) **55**
103) [2015 –p: f8d5 t9.5f³ Feb 23] modest maiden: left Bryan Smart, best effort when third
of 6 at Wolverhampton in February. *Geoffrey Oldroyd*

EXCLUSIVE WATERS (IRE) 5 b.g. Elusive City (USA) 117 – Pelican Waters (IRE) **72**
97 (Key of Luck (USA) 126) [2015 73, a80: 10s 12.4g⁵ 12g 10.1d 8g⁵ 10.1m* 9.3g⁴ 10.1m²
10.4m 10m⁴ 8m 9.3g 8g Aug 31] good-topped gelding: fair handicapper: won at Newcastle
in June: stays 1¼m: acts on polytrack, fibresand, good to firm and good to soft going: often
in headgear prior to 2015. *Tracy Waggott*

EXECUTIVE BAY 2 b.c. (Mar 11) Bushranger (IRE) 119 – Munaawashat (IRE) 87 **62**
(Marju (IRE) 127) [2015 6m⁵ 7m⁴ Aug 22] better effort when fourth of 5 in maiden at
Chester (6 lengths behind Kingston Kurrajong) in August. *Tom Dascombe*

EXECUTOR 2 b.c. (Mar 1) Cacique (IRE) 124 – Star Cluster 106 (Observatory (USA) **81**
131) [2015 7s 8f* 8g Sep 24] sixth foal: half-brother to 1½m winner Asterism (by
Motivator) and 5.7f/6f winner Encapsulated (by Zamindar): dam, winner up to 1m (2-y-o
7f winner), half-sister to US Grade 2 8.5f winner Didina: fairly useful form: won 5-runner
maiden at Bath in September by 2¼ lengths from Et Toi: below expectations in nursery at
Newmarket next time: best effort at 1m. *Roger Charlton*

EXENTRICITY 3 b.f. Paco Boy (IRE) 129 – Wansdyke Lass 59 (Josr Algarhoud (IRE) **81**
118) [2015 79: p7f³ p6g³ t7.1f⁵ t6f⁵ 7s² 5g⁴ t7.1f⁵ 5.7g p6f* p6m t6m* Dec 12] quite
attractive filly: fairly useful performer: won maiden at Chelmsford in November and
handicap at Wolverhampton in December: stays 7f: acts on polytrack, tapeta and soft going.
Mick Channon

EXIST 2 b.f. (Feb 5) Exceed And Excel (AUS) 126 – Harryana 79 (Efisio 120) [2015 7s³ **84 p**
6g* Oct 20] 180,000Y: half-sister to several winners, including smart 2-y-o 5f/6f (Mill
Reef Stakes) winner Temple Meads (by Avonbridge) and useful 2-y-o 6f winner Sneak
Preview (by Monsieur Bond): dam 2-y-o 5f winner: better effort when winning maiden at
Windsor (by length from Welsh Rose) in October, rallying: may prove best at 5f/6f: will go
on improving. *John Gosden*

EXIT EUROPE 3 ch.g. Bahamian Bounty 116 – Depressed 80 (Most Welcome 131) **77**
[2015 –: t8.6g 7v⁶ 7s² t7.1f* t8.6f³ p7g* p7m³ Nov 21] sturdy gelding: fair handicapper:
won at Wolverhampton in October and Kempton in November: stays 7f: acts on polytrack
and tapeta: races prominently. *Andrew Reid*

EXKALIBER 6 b.g. Exceed And Excel (AUS) 126 – Kalindi 102 (Efisio 120) [2015 50§: **– §**
t6f p5m⁶ Feb 28] maiden: no form in 2015: best effort at 5f: acts on all-weather: often
wears headgear: often wears tongue tie: usually races nearer last than first: untrustworthy.
Richard Ford

EXOPLANET BLUE 3 b.f. Exceed And Excel (AUS) 126 – Tut (IRE) 84 (Intikhab **82**
(USA) 135) [2015 66p: 5.7f³ 6m² 6g p7g* 7m⁴ 6s 7s 6d t7.1f⁴ t7.1f⁴ p7g⁶ Dec 16] fairly
useful handicapper: won at Lingfield in July: stays 7f: acts on polytrack and good to firm
going: usually races close up. *Henry Candy*

EXOSPHERE 3 b.c. Beat Hollow 126 – Bright And Clear 106 (Danehill (USA) 126) **116**
[2015 8g⁶ p10m* 10.3m* 10s⁴ 10m* 10g³ Sep 19] angular colt: sixth foal: half-brother to
useful 11f/1½m winner Blog (by Peintre Celebre) and 11.7f winner Tuscan Light (by
Medicean): dam, 2-y-o 7f winner (stayed 1¾m), half-sister to Grand Criterium/Dante
Stakes winner Tenby: smart performer: won maiden at Lingfield in April, minor event at
Doncaster in June and handicap at Sandown (by 2¼ lengths from Mount Logan) in August:
good third in listed race at Ayr (2¼ lengths behind Scottish) in September: stays 10.5f: acts
on polytrack, soft and good to firm going. *Sir Michael Stoute*

EXOTERIC 2 b.c. (Feb 22) Champs Elysees 124 – Short Dance (USA) 105 (Hennessy **77 p**
(USA) 122) [2015 t8.6m⁴ Dec 30] sixth foal: brother to winner up to 1m Fray (2-y-o 7f
winner) and half-brother to 2 winners, including 7f winner (stays 1¼m) Plover (by Oasis
Dream): dam winner up to 1m (2-y-o 6f/7f winner): 10/1, shaped well when fourth in
maiden at Wolverhampton (1¾ lengths behind Disobedience) in December, nearest finish:
sure to progress. *Charles Hills*

EXOTIC GUEST 5 ch.g. Bahamian Bounty 116 – Mamoura (IRE) 97 (Lomond (USA) **80**
128) [2015 74: f6g⁶ 6g⁵ 6s⁶ 6m⁵ 6g 6g* 6g² 6g² 6m* 6g⁵ 5.9s⁴ 6g Sep 29] fairly useful
handicapper: won at Ayr in July and Newcastle (by 1¼ lengths from Off The Scale) in
August: stays 7f: acts on good to firm going: sometimes wears cheekpieces. *Ruth Carr*

EXPENSIVE DATE 3 ch.f. Monsieur Bond (IRE) 120 – Cheap Thrills 79 (Bertolini **96**
(USA) 125) [2015 87: 6m* 6m⁴ 6m⁵ 6m Oct 2] lengthy filly: useful handicapper: won at
Epsom (by 1¼ lengths from Cartmell Cleave) in July: stays 6f: acts on polytrack, good to
firm and good to soft going: tried in cheekpieces in 2015: often races prominently.
Paul Cole

EXPENSIVE TASTE (IRE) 4 b.g. Moss Vale (IRE) 126 – Priceoflove (IRE) 72 **–**
(Inchinor 119) [2015 84d: p8f⁶ p10m 7m 8g 6m p6g⁶ 7g p8f p10f Sep 24] fairly useful
at best, no form in 2015: tried in headgear: usually wears tongue tie. *Phil McEntee*

EXPERTO CREDE (IRE) 2 b.g. (Mar 9) Exceed And Excel (AUS) 126 – Shepherdia **88 p**
(IRE) (Pivotal 124) [2015 6m* 6m Jul 9] 80,000Y, 290,000 2-y-o: first foal: dam, French
maiden (third at 9f at 2 yrs), half-sister to US Grade 3 1m winner Chattahoochee War out
of US Grade 3 8.5f winner Buffalo Berry: won 11-runner maiden at Newmarket in June by
1¼ lengths from Show Legend: 9/1, well held in July Stakes there last time: gelded after:
should still improve. *Ed Walker*

EXPIRY DATE 3 ch.c. Makfi 130 – Midnight Shift (IRE) 73 (Night Shift (USA)) [2015 **67** p7f 8.3s⁶ 8d⁶ May 11] fair maiden: best effort when sixth at Nottingham in April. *Charlie Fellowes*

EXPLAIN 3 ch.g. Kyllachy 129 – Descriptive (IRE) 83 (Desert King (IRE) 129) [2015 85: **83** 5.7f² 6d⁴ 6m* 6d³ 6m⁶ 6m 5.5m Aug 22] good-topped gelding: fairly useful performer: won minor event at Windsor (by 4½ lengths from You're My Cracker) in June: placed in handicaps at Bath in April and Leicester in June: stays 7f: acts on good to firm and good to soft going: often in blinkers in 2015. *Martyn Meade*

EXPLOSIVE LADY (IRE) 3 gr.f. Alfred Nobel (IRE) 110 – My Girl Lisa (USA) (With **94** Approval (CAN)) [2015 94: 6g³ 6g 6m 6g 7.2g⁵ 7m⁶ p7g⁶ Nov 11] fairly useful performer: third in listed race at Haydock (3½ lengths behind Blhadawa) in May: respectable efforts in handicaps fifth/sixth starts: stays 7f: acts on good to firm going: tried in cheekpieces in 2015. *K. R. Burke*

EXPLOSIVE POWER (IRE) 2 gr.c. (Mar 20) Alfred Nobel (IRE) 110 – My Girl Lisa **94 p** (USA) (With Approval (CAN)) [2015 5.4g 6g³ 6s* 6d⁵ Oct 24] €47,000Y: brother to 2-y-o 5f winner Explosive Lady and half-brother to several winners, including 10.3f winner Darling Lexi (by Dylan Thomas): dam US 5f/5.5f winner, including at 2 yrs: fairly useful form: won maiden at Redcar (by 2½ lengths from Regal Response) in October: 8/1, improved when 3½ lengths fifth of 9 to Dhahmaan in listed race at Doncaster next time: will stay 7f: likely to progress further. *K. R. Burke*

EXPRESS HIMSELF (IRE) 4 b.g. Dylan Thomas (IRE) 132 – Lightwood Lady (IRE) **108** 84 (Anabaa (USA) 130) [2015 93: 8g³ 8m³ 8f* 8m² 10.3g³ 9g 8d* Oct 16] good-topped gelding: useful handicapper: won at Haydock in June (by ¾ length from Birdman) and October (by neck from Mitchum Swagger): has form at 10.5f, may prove best at 1m/9f: acts on any turf going: tried in cheekpieces prior to 2015: held up (has started slowly), often travels strongly. *Ed McMahon*

EXPRESS METRO (IRE) 2 b.c. (Apr 15) Poet's Voice 126 – Star Express 80 (Sadler's **–** Wells (USA) 132) [2015 7f p8g p6f Sep 10] compact colt: no form. *Ed Walker*

EXTORTION 2 b.g. (Mar 14) Kheleyf (USA) 116 – Virtuality (USA) 60 (Elusive Quality **79** (USA)) [2015 6s² 6g² 5g² 6m* Sep 28] fair form: won maiden at Hamilton in September by neck from Dance Alone: stays 6f: signs of temperament: has been gelded. *Bryan Smart*

EXTORTIONIST (IRE) 4 b.c. Dandy Man (IRE) 123 – Dream Date (IRE) 78 (Oasis **–** Dream 129) [2015 121: 5g Mar 7] strong, close-coupled colt: smart performer in 2014: reportedly lost a front shoe when tailed-off last in Meydan Sprint sole outing in 2015: was best at 5f: acted on firm and good to soft going: dead. *Olly Stevens*

EXTRASOLAR 5 b.g. Exceed And Excel (AUS) 126 – Amicable Terms 88 (Royal **91** Applause 124) [2015 97: p6g⁶ p6g⁵ 5m 5d⁶ 6m 5m³ 6g⁵ 5.3d⁶ 5m* 6m⁵ 5m 5m* 6g⁵ 6g Sep 30] sturdy gelding: fairly useful handicapper: won at Bath in July and Salisbury (by ½ length from Absolute Champion) in September: stays 7f, races at shorter: acts on polytrack, firm and good to soft going: tried in blinkers in 2015: usually wears tongue tie: often races towards rear. *Amanda Perrett*

EXTRATERRESTRIAL 11 b.g. Mind Games 121 – Expectation (IRE) 59 (Night Shift **73 §** (USA)) [2015 86§: p8g Jan 14] lengthy gelding: fairly useful handicapper at best: below form sole start in 2015: stays 9.5f: acts on tapeta and any turf going: has worn headgear: ungenuine. *Richard Fahey*

EXTREME SUPREME 4 b.g. Piccolo 121 – Kitty Kitty Cancan 73 (Warrshan (USA) **77** 117) [2015 84: f5g² t5.1g p5g³ 5g p5g p5g² 5g p5f⁶ Sep 10] small gelding: fair handicapper: raced only at 5f: acts on all-weather: often wears visor: usually races nearer last than first: temperament under suspicion. *Derek Shaw*

EXTREMITY (IRE) 4 ch.g. Exceed And Excel (AUS) 126 – Chanterelle (IRE) 88 **95** (Indian Ridge 123) [2015 105: 8g 8m 8.3m⁴ 8d 7.9m t6f Oct 3] good-topped gelding: useful handicapper: largely well below form in 2015: stays 8.5f: acts on polytrack, soft and good to firm going: wears headgear. *Hugo Palmer*

EYE GLASS (IRE) 3 b.f. Intense Focus (USA) 117 – Petite Arvine (USA) (Gulch **58** (USA)) [2015 68p: 5g³ 6m⁵ 7s f5g⁴ p6g³ p7g Dec 11] modest maiden: left Tim Easterby after fourth start: stays 6f: acts on polytrack, soft and good to firm going. *T. G. McCourt, Ireland*

EYE OF THE STORM (IRE) 5 ch.h. Galileo (IRE) 134 – Mohican Princess (Shirley **112** Heights 130) [2015 114: 12g³ 16.4m* 16m 16g⁶ Sep 24] angular horse: reportedly has only one eye: smart performer: won listed race at Sandown (by head from Angel Gabrial) in

July: third in listed race at Goodwood (length behind Ayrad) on reappearance, below form last 2 starts: stays 16.5f: acts on good to firm and heavy going: tried in hood prior to 2015. *Amanda Perrett*

F

FABLE OF ARACHNE 2 b.f. (Feb 4) Dick Turpin (IRE) 127 – Las Hilanderas (USA) **58** (El Prado (IRE) 119) [2015 5m 6g³ 7m⁵ p6g* 6d p6g² p6f⁴ p7f* p7g⁴ Dec 10] small filly: first foal: dam, ran 3 times, out of smart winner up to 1½m Lilium, herself half-sister to Middle Park Stakes winner Lujain: modest performer: won nurseries at Chelmsford in August and November: stays 7f: acts on polytrack: often in tongue tie. *Stuart Williams*

FAB LOLLY (IRE) 5 b.m. Rock of Gibraltar (IRE) 133 – Violet Ballerina (IRE) 85 **72** (Namid 128) [2015 86: t1.3m³ p7g⁶ t7.1m⁴ t6f² p7f 5.5g⁶ 7m 7m⁴ t7.1f p7f Dec 21] fairly **a80** useful handicapper: third at Wolverhampton in February and second at Wolverhampton in March: stays 7f: acts on polytrack, tapeta and good to firm going: often wears headgear. *James Bethell*

FABRICATE 3 b.g. Makfi 130 – Flight of Fancy 114 (Sadler's Wells (USA) 132) [2015 **106** 11m³ 12m* 11.9g* 11.8s³ Oct 26] well-made gelding: seventh foal: half-brother to 1¼m winner Fleeting Memory (by Danehill) and useful 1½m-1¾m winner Aladdins Cave (by Rainbow Quest): dam 2-y-o 7f winner and second in Oaks: useful performer: won maiden at Salisbury (by 2½ lengths from Yarrow) and handicap at Haydock (by 1¾ lengths from Hernandoshideaway), both in May: off 5 months/in cheekpieces, below form final start: likely to stay 1¾m: tried in cheekpieces. *Michael Bell*

FABULOUS DARLING 2 ch.f. (May 3) Dutch Art 126 – Fabuleux Cherie 71 (Noverre **62** (USA) 125) [2015 6m³ 6g 6d t7.1m⁵ p6f⁶ Oct 1] €16,000F, €37,000Y: compact filly: third foal: dam 2-y-o 5f/6f winner: modest maiden: best effort at 6f: acts on good to firm going: tried in cheekpieces: sent to Greece. *Eve Johnson Houghton*

FABULOUS FLYER 2 b.f. (Feb 10) Equiano (FR) 127 – Lucky Flyer 79 (Lucky Story **–** (USA) 128) [2015 p5g⁶ 5.1g 5d Aug 18] first foal: dam 5f winner: no form. *Bill Turner*

FACE OF GLORY (IRE) 2 b.c. (Apr 8) Big Bad Bob (IRE) 118 – Interchange (IRE) 92 **– p** (Montjeu (IRE) 137) [2015 6g 8d Oct 16] 42,000Y: third foal: half-brother to useful 7f/7.5f winner Bronte (by Oasis Dream): dam, 1½m winner, out of Yorkshire Oaks winner Key Change: well held in maidens, but still in need of experience final start: will do better at some stage. *Ismail Mohammed*

FACE YOUR DEMONS 2 b.f. (Mar 29) Stimulation (IRE) 121 – Psychic's Dream 87 (Oasis Dream 129) [2015 6m Jun 25] 3,000Y: first foal: dam 6f winner: 25/1, ninth of 15 in maiden at Newbury (13 lengths behind Poster Girl) in June. *Jimmy Fox*

FADDWA (IRE) 3 b.f. Arcano (IRE) 122 – Heart's Desire (IRE) 79 (Royal Applause 124) **75** [2015 t8.6g* t8.6g⁵ t9.5g⁶ Sep 29] €30,000Y: half-sister to several winners, including winner up to 1¼m Unsinkable (2-y-o 6f winner, by Verglas) and winner up to 1¾m (stayed 2m) Knight Eagle (2-y-o 1m winner, by Night Shift) both useful: dam maiden (best effort at 7f): fair form: won maiden at Wolverhampton in July: sixth of 13 to Aleator in handicap there final start: stays 8.5f. *Roger Varian*

FADHAYYIL (IRE) 3 b.f. Tamayuz 126 – Ziria (IRE) 109 (Danehill Dancer (IRE) 117) **115** [2015 109p: 8f⁵ 7f² 7m 7g* 7m⁴ 8m⁴ Oct 3] big, unfurnished filly: smart performer: won listed race at York (by ½ length from Speculative Bid, leading final 1f) in August: also ran well when ½-length second of 16 to Dutch Connection in Jersey Stakes at Royal Ascot in June and 2¼ lengths fourth of 9 to Esoterique in Sun Chariot Stakes at Newmarket in October: stays 1m: acts on firm going: strong traveller. *B. W. Hills*

FAERY SONG (IRE) 3 b.f. Lawman (FR) 121 – Chervil 80 (Dansili 127) [2015 70: 7g **79** 8m⁴ 10g³ 9.9m* 10.2m³ 10.2f⁵ Sep 13] smallish filly: fair handicapper: won at Salisbury in August: stays 1¼m: acts on good to firm going: tried in cheekpieces in 2015. *David Lanigan*

FAINTLY (USA) 4 b.g. Kitten's Joy (USA) 128 – Tinge (USA) (Kingmambo (USA) 125) **84** [2015 82: p8g⁶ t7.1g t7.1m² t7.1f p8m² Nov 19] fairly useful handicapper: second at Wolverhampton in September and Lingfield in November: stays 1m: acts on polytrack, tapeta and firm going: in hood in 2015. *Simon Crisford*

FAIR COMMENT 5 b.m. Tamayuz 126 – Cliche (IRE) 108 (Diktat 126) [2015 72: p10f⁶ **65** p12g⁵ p10g⁵ 10m⁶ 10g⁴ p10f² p10g⁴ p11g* 12.1m² p12g Sep 22] rather leggy mare: fair handicapper: won at Kempton in August: stays 1½m: acts on polytrack, firm and soft going. *Michael Blanshard*

FAIR LOCH 7 gr.g. Fair Mix (IRE) 123 – Ardentinny (Ardross 134) [2015 t12.2m 8g **66** 10.4m 14.6m 14.4g Aug 6] fair maiden: left K. R. Burke after first start: best effort at 1½m: best form on soft/heavy going: sometimes in cheekpieces in 2015: tried in tongue tie in 2015: usually races nearer last than first: fairly useful hurdler. *Brian Ellison*

FAIR RANGER 4 b.g. Bushranger (IRE) 119 – Fairmont (IRE) 53 (Kingmambo (USA) **54** 125) [2015 p10f p12f Mar 11] quite attractive gelding: modest handicapper: best at short of 1¼m: acts on polytrack, best turf form on good going or firmer: in cheekpieces in 2015: sent to Belgium, and won over 7.5f at Mons in April. *Chris Gordon*

FAIR'S FAIR (IRE) 3 b.f. Lawman (FR) 121 – Winning Sequence (FR) (Zafonic (USA) **75 p** 130) [2015 t9.5f⁵ p10f² Nov 7] €30,000Y: fourth foal: half-sister to French 9f winner Calitor (by Marju) and 7f winner (stayed 9f) Circle (by Galileo): dam, French 2-y-o 7.5f winner, closely related to Prix Saint-Alary winner Coquerelle: better effort when second in maiden at Chelmsford in November, no match for winner: in hood: better to come. *Ralph Beckett*

FAIR TRADE 8 ch.g. Trade Fair 124 – Ballet 61 (Sharrood (USA) 124) [2015 –: 11.1s⁵ **69** 12g³ 14.1m⁶ Jun 20] tall gelding: fair handicapper: stays 1½m: acts on good to firm and good to soft going: in tongue tie in 2015. *Wilf Storey*

FAIR VALUE (IRE) 7 b.m. Compton Place 125 – Intriguing Glimpse 100 (Piccolo 121) **75** [2015 89: p5f p5g 5g Apr 22] sturdy mare: fair handicapper: stays 6f: acts on polytrack, good to firm and good to soft going: tried in hood prior to 2015: sometimes slowly away. *Simon Dow*

FAIRWAY TO HEAVEN (IRE) 6 b.g. Jeremy (USA) 122 – Luggala (IRE) 90 (Kahyasi **90** 130) [2015 100: p6f⁴ p6g p6d⁵ 5m⁵ 5g 5m² 5m 5g⁵ 6d⁴ 6g² p6m⁶ f7g Dec 22] rather leggy gelding: fairly useful handicapper: second at Goodwood in June and Windsor in October: stays 7f: acts on polytrack, soft and good to firm going: tried in headgear in 2015: often starts slowly. *Michael Wigham*

FAIRY DUCHESS (IRE) 3 b.f. Duke of Marmalade (IRE) 132 – Fairybook (USA) (El **59** Prado (IRE) 119) [2015 7m³ p8g⁴ 8s Sep 5] 21,000Y: sturdy filly: third foal: dam, French 1¼m winner, half-sister to very smart French winner up to 12.5f Penglai Pavilion: modest maiden: best effort when third at Newmarket in July: bred to be suited by further than 1m. *Martin Bosley*

FAIRY FOXGLOVE (IRE) 5 b.m. Albano (IRE) 105 – Aegean Magic 76 (Wolfhound **54** (USA) 126) [2015 54, a63: p7g³ p8g³ p7g³ p7g² p7m⁵ p6g p7g 6g² 6m² 7g p5g⁵ p6g⁴ t7.1m* **a66** Dec 30] fair handicapper: won at Wolverhampton in December: stays 1m: acts on polytrack, tapeta, soft and good to firm going: sometimes wears headgear: front runner/races prominently. *P. J. F. Murphy, Ireland*

FAIRY GLADE 2 b.f. (Apr 9) Monsieur Bond (IRE) 120 – Fairy Shoes 77 (Kyllachy 129) **–** [2015 5m 5.9g 6g t5.1m Aug 21] second foal: half-sister to useful 5f/6f winner (including at 2 yrs) Vimy Ridge (by American Post): dam, 5f winner, sister to Corrybrough and half-sister to dam of Amour Propre, both smart sprinters: no form. *Richard Fahey*

FAIRYINTHEWIND (IRE) 6 ch.m. Indian Haven 119 – Blue Daze 75 (Danzero **80** (AUS)) [2015 –: 10m⁶ 10.2g* Oct 18] sturdy mare: fairly useful handicapper: in tongue tie, won at Bath (by neck from Earnestine) in October: stays 1¼m: acts on polytrack and good to firm going: tried in headgear prior to 2015: fairly useful chaser. *Brendan Powell*

FAIRY MIST (IRE) 8 b.g. Oratorio (IRE) 128 – Prealpina (IRE) (Indian Ridge 123) **61** [2015 65, a46: 7v 7.6g³ 7d² 6m³ 7.6g⁴ 7.6s⁵ 7v² 7d⁴ 6v⁴ p5g p7g³ Dec 30] modest handicapper: stays 1¼m: acts on polytrack and any turf going: often wears headgear: tried in tongue tie prior to 2015: sometimes slowly away, usually races nearer last than first. *John Bridger*

FAIRY POOLS 4 ch.f. Halling (USA) 133 – Maritima (Darshaan 133) [2015 f8g f12g **–** Dec 22] 10,000 3 y or fifth foal: half-sister to 1m winner Port Hollow (by Beat Hollow): dam once-raced half-sister to Racing Post Trophy winner/St Leger second Armiger: no form, including in bumpers: usually in hood. *Les Eyre*

FAIRY WING (IRE) 8 b.g. Hawk Wing (USA) 136 – Mintaka (IRE) (Fairy King (USA)) **49** [2015 61: f6g⁴ Mar 5] poor handicapper: stays 1m, usually over shorter: acts on polytrack, fibresand and soft going: often wears headgear: tried in tongue tie prior to 2015. *Heather Dalton*

FAISEUR DE MIRACLE 3 b.g. Makfi 130 – Flawly 106 (Old Vic 136) [2015 9.2s May **–** 15] 4/1, shaped as if amiss when tailed off in maiden at Hamilton. *Mark Johnston*

FAITHFUL CREEK (IRE) 3 b.g. Bushranger (IRE) 119 – Open Verse (USA) 69 (Black **107** Minnaloushe (USA) 123) [2015 108: a9.4f 10m⁵ 10f⁵ 9.9d⁵ 10s 9.9g 10v Oct 24] compact gelding: useful performer: best effort of 2015 when seventh of 17 to What About Carlo in handicap at Newbury in September on fifth outing: stays 1¼m: acts on firm and soft going: has worn blinkers, including last 5 starts: in tongue tie last 2 starts: has been gelded. *Brian Meehan*

FAITHFUL MOUNT 6 b.g. Shirocco (GER) 129 – Lady Lindsay (IRE) 105 (Danehill **90** Dancer (IRE) 117) [2015 p10m p14g³ 14.1g* 13.3s² 12s⁵ 14.1s* Oct 12] fairly useful handicapper: won at Salisbury in July and October (by neck from Mark Hopkins): stays 15f: acts on soft going. *Ian Williams*

FAITH JICARO (IRE) 8 b.m. One Cool Cat (USA) 123 – Wings To Soar (USA) 67 **48** (Woodman (USA) 126) [2015 17.2f Aug 12] angular mare: poor maiden: stays 17f: acts on firm and good to soft going: tried in headgear: in tongue tie sole start in 2015. *David Bridgwater*

FAITH MATTERS (IRE) 3 ch.f. Arcano (IRE) 122 – Luanas Pearl (IRE) (Bahri (USA) **72** 125) [2015 7p: p10g⁴ 12g³ p10g p12g⁴ 11.6g Oct 20] sturdy filly. fair maiden: stays 1½m: acts on polytrack: sometimes in headgear in 2015: often races prominently. *Marco Botti*

FAKEITTILYAMAKEIT (IRE) 2 gr.f. (Apr 29) Dark Angel (IRE) 113 – Halliwell House 59 (Selkirk (USA) 129) [2015 p5m⁵ 6m 6m p7f Nov 12] 28,000Y: angular filly: fourth foal: sister to 1m winner What Could She Be and half-sister to 5f winner (including at 2 yrs) Dusty Storm (by Kyllachy) and 6f winner Inciting Incident (by Camacho): dam once-raced half-sister to useful performers up to 1¼m/11f Flag Officer and Counterclaim: no form. *David Evans*

FALCON ANNIE (IRE) 2 b.f. (Mar 16) Kodiac 112 – Frosted 65 (Dr Fong (USA) 128) **66** [2015 5.1s⁵ 6m⁵ Jul 9] better effort in maidens when fifth of 9 to Salvo at Newmarket final start: dead. *Tom Dascombe*

FALCONIZE (IRE) 3 b.f. Henrythenavigator (USA) 131 – Crystal Crossing (IRE) 99 **70** (Royal Academy (USA) 130) [2015 64p: p7m² p8f⁶ 7g⁵ 7.1m⁵ t7.1g⁶ Jul 7] fair maiden: stays 7f: acts on polytrack and good to firm going. *Charles Hills*

FALCON'S FIRE (IRE) 2 ch.g. (Feb 3) Thewayyouare (USA) 117 – Matadora (IRE) 69 **–** (Kris 135) [2015 f5g⁴ Dec 29] 9/2, well-held fourth of 5 in maiden at Southwell in December. *Keith Dalgleish*

FALCON'S REIGN (FR) 6 ch.g. Haafhd 129 – Al Badeya (IRE) 68 (Pivotal 124) [2015 **62** 65: f8s² f8g⁶ 8s 10.2s f7g f7g⁵ Dec 12] rather leggy gelding: modest handicapper: stays 1¼m: acts on fibresand, best turf form on good going or softer (acts on heavy): sometimes wears headgear: front runner/races prominently: temperament under suspicion. *Michael Appleby*

FALCON'S SONG (USA) 3 b.f. U S Ranger (USA) 124 – Saudia (USA) 84 (Gone West **73 p** (USA)) [2015 p8f² p10g* Apr 28] $80,000F, 85,000Y: closely related to smart winner up to 1m Red Duke (2-y-o 7f winner, by Hard Spun) and half-sister to several winners, including useful French 1½m winner The West's Awake (by Theatrical): dam, 2-y-o 6f winner, out of Yorkshire Oaks/Prix Vermeille winner Bint Pasha: better effort when winning maiden at Chelmsford (by short head from Regal Ways) in April, sticking to task: likely to stay beyond 1m: open to further improvement. *David Simcock*

FALLEN ANGEL (FR) 2 ch.f. (Feb 28) Dalghar (FR) 122 – Angel Voices (IRE) 81 **58** (Tagula (IRE) 116) [2015 5.9g³ Jun 24] 7/2, green when 6 lengths third of 10 to Hawatif in maiden at Carlisle on only start: dead. *K. R. Burke*

FALLEN FOR A STAR 3 b.g. Sea The Stars (IRE) 140 – Fallen Star 112 (Brief Truce **92** (USA) 126) [2015 8g³ 10m² 10g² p10m² t9.5g* Dec 4] closely related to useful performer up to 1½m Fallen In Love (2-y-o 1m winner, by Galileo) and half-brother to several winners, including very smart winner up to 1m (Coronation Stakes) Fallen For You (2-y-o 7f winner, by Dansili): dam 7f/1m winner: fairly useful performer: 2/5, won maiden at Wolverhampton in December: stays 1¼m: acts on polytrack and tapeta: front runner/races prominently. *John Gosden*

FALLING PETALS (IRE) 3 ch.f. Raven's Pass (USA) 133 – Infinite Spirit (USA) 108 **85 p** (Maria's Mon (USA) 121) [2015 81p: p8g² May 6] well-made filly: fairly useful handicapper: in hood, second at Chelmsford (length behind Gentlemusic) on sole outing in 2015 in May, sticking to task: stays 1m: may do better still. *John Gosden*

FALMOUTH HARBOUR 3 b.g. Champs Elysees 124 – Divina Mia 66 (Dowsing (USA) –
124) [2015 –: p12g p10g⁵ Jun 20] no form: tried in cheekpieces/tongue tie. *Paul Cole*

FALSE ID 2 b.c. (Feb 7) Aqlaam 125 – Miss Dutee 68 (Dubawi (IRE) 129) [2015 7g⁴ Sep **54 p**
10] €15,000Y, £25,000 2-y-o: first foal: dam, winner up to 7f (2-y-o 6f winner), half-sister
to useful 2-y-o 6f winner Yajbill: 10/1, fourth in maiden at Epsom (11¼ lengths behind
Lytham St Annes) in September, weakening final 1f: should do better. *Robert Eddery*

FALSIFY 3 ch.f. Compton Place 125 – Swindling (Bahamian Bounty 116) [2015 t6g⁴ p6m³ **78**
p6m⁴ t6g⁴ p5g* p5f² p5f² p5f³ t5.1g² p5g⁵ Dec 10] 35,000Y: fourth foal: half-sister to
winner up to 6f Above The Stars (2-y-o 5f winner, by Piccolo): dam unraced: fair
handicapper: won at Chelmsford in August: best form at 5f: acts on polytrack and tapeta:
often in visor: front runner/races prominently. *Robert Cowell*

FAMOUS KID (USA) 4 ch.c. Street Cry (IRE) 130 – Moyesii (USA) (Diesis 133) [2015 **117**
108: a9.9f² 14g* 18.7d 12f⁶ 14m p14f* t16.5m³ Dec 12] well-made colt: smart performer:
won handicaps at Meydan (by ¾ length from Ahzeemah) in February and Chelmsford (by
6 lengths from Anglophile) in November: raced freely when disappointing in minor event
at Wolverhampton final start: stays 1¾m: acts on polytrack, good to firm and heavy going.
Saeed bin Suroor

FANCIFUL ANGEL (IRE) 3 gr.g. Dark Angel (IRE) 113 – Fanciful Dancer (Groom **110**
Dancer (USA) 128) [2015 98: p7g³ p8g* 8g² 7f 8d⁴ 8g⁶ Sep 27] good-topped gelding:
smart performer: won listed race at Lingfield (by neck from Lexington Times) in April:
second in Mehl-Mulhens-Rennen (German 2000 Guineas) at Cologne (4½ lengths behind
Karpino) in May: at least respectable efforts abroad, including seventh to Dutch Connection
in Jersey Stakes at Royal Ascot fourth start: stays 1m: acts on polytrack, firm and good to
soft going: gelded after final start. *Marco Botti*

FANCIFY 2 b.f. (Feb 15) Exceed And Excel (AUS) 126 – Shane (GER) 106 (Kornado 120) – **p**
[2015 p7g p6f 7v Oct 17] fifth foal: half-sister to French 1m winner Malicho (by Manduro)
and 1¼m winner Zaeemah (by Shamardal): dam, German 2-y-o 6f-1m winner, sister to
smart German miler Shapira: well held in 3 maidens, not persevered once held final one:
should do better. *Mark Johnston*

FANCI THAT (IRE) 2 b.f. (Mar 9) Elnadim (USA) 128 – Featherlight 78 (Fantastic Light **56 p**
(USA) 134) [2015 5g⁵ Oct 18] third foal: dam 11f-2m winner: 14/1, some encouragement
when fifth in maiden at Bath (6¾ lengths behind Pine Ridge) in October, slowly away: will
be suited by 6f+: better to come. *Rae Guest*

FANDANGO (GER) 2 b.c. (Feb 8) Lord of England (GER) 119 – Fitness (IRE) (Monsun **66**
(GER) 124) [2015 p8g⁶ p8g⁴ Nov 11] better effort when fourth in maiden at Kempton (6¼
lengths behind Prince of Arran) in November: likely to stay 1¼m. *Jeremy Gask*

FANG 2 b.g. (Feb 22) Lawman (FR) 121 – Desert Tigress (USA) 83 (Storm Cat (USA)) **82**
[2015 6g⁴ 6m² 7g 7s³ 7g³ Oct 3] sturdy gelding: sixth foal: half-brother to 2-y-o 6f winner
Growl (by Oasis Dream) and a winner in USA by A P Indy: dam, 2-y-o 5f winner, sister to
Horris Hill Stakes winner Hurricane Cat out of high-class US Grade 1 winner up to 1¼m
Sky Beauty: fairly useful maiden: second at Newmarket in May and third at Newbury
in September: stays 7f: acts on soft and good to firm going: in tongue tie: usually leads.
Brian Meehan

FANNAAN (USA) 3 ch.g. Speightstown (USA) 124 – Titian Time (USA) 107 (Red –
Ransom (USA)) [2015 103p: 7m Apr 18] useful form at 2 yrs: never dangerous in
Greenham Stakes at Newbury only start in 2015: stays 7f: has been gelded. *John Gosden*

FANNY AGAIN 3 b.f. Nayef (USA) 129 – Sweet Wilhelmina 87 (Indian Ridge 123) **62 p**
[2015 56p: 10m p10g p12g⁵ t12.2g⁴ Sep 29] modest maiden: will prove suited by further
than 1½m: acts on tapeta and polytrack: remains open to improvement. *Denis Coakley*

FANTASY GLADIATOR 9 b.g. Ishiguru (USA) 114 – Fancier Bit (Lion Cavern (USA) **87**
117) [2015 81: p8f⁵ t9.5f³ t9.5g³ 8.3g* 8.3m² 8.3s² 8.3g* p8g⁶ 8m* 7m 8.3s⁶ p8f² p8g p8f
Dec 21] fairly useful handicapper: won at Nottingham in June and July and Musselburgh
in September: good second at Chelmsford in November: stays 8.5f: acts on polytrack,
fibresand, soft and good to firm going: usually wears headgear: sometimes slowly away:
quirky sort. *Michael Appleby*

FANTASY JUSTIFIER (IRE) 4 b.g. Arakan (USA) 123 – Grandel (Owington 123) **76**
[2015 77: 6m⁵ 6g⁵ 6.1m* 5.7s⁵ 6d Sep 4] lengthy gelding: fair handicapper: won at
Nottingham in June: stays 6f: acts on good to firm and good to soft going: sometimes
slowly away. *Ronald Harris*

FANTASY KING 9 b.g. Acclamation 118 – Fantasy Ridge 92 (Indian Ridge 123) [2015 **81** 84: 14g⁴ Aug 6] fairly useful handicapper: stays 2m: acts on polytrack, good to firm and good to soft going: often in tongue tie prior to 2015: fairly useful chaser. *James Moffatt*

FANTASY QUEEN 2 b.f. (Mar 8) Aqlaam 125 – Regal Curtsy 67 (Royal Applause 124) – [2015 7s 8m Sep 11] fourth foal: half-sister to a winner in Spain by Halling: dam, maiden (stayed 1¼m), sister to smart 7f-1¼m winner Take A Bow: well held in maidens. *Eve Johnson Houghton*

FARANDINE 2 ch.f. (Mar 26) Rock of Gibraltar (IRE) 133 – Rivara (Red Ransom (USA)) **88 p** [2015 7m² p7g³ 7g* Oct 21] angular filly: second foal: dam unraced half-sister to smart winners Gravitas (up to 1½m) and Armure (up to 15.5f): fairly useful performer: best effort when winning maiden at Newmarket (by 2¾ lengths from Ejayteekay) in October, readily: will be suited by 1m+: remains open to improvement. *Luca Cumani*

FARANG JAI DEE (IRE) 3 b.g. Approve (IRE) 112 – Fruit O'The Forest (IRE) (Shinko **42** Forest (IRE)) [2015 –: 6g 6m 6g 7m 5.9s Sep 15] poor maiden: best effort at 6f: acts on soft going: sometimes in blinkers in 2015: often races prominently. *Declan Carroll*

FARENDOLE (USA) 3 b.f. First Defence (USA) 119 – Quick To Please (USA) 101 **59** (Danzig (USA)) [2015 57p: p7f² Jan 23] modest maiden: will be suited by return to 1m: sold 25,000 gns, sent to Qatar. *Roger Charlton*

FARHAM (USA) 3 b.g. Smart Strike (CAN) 121 – Diamondrella 120 (Rock of Gibraltar **79** (IRE) 133) [2015 77p: t8.6f⁴ p8m⁵ p10g³ p12g⁶ Dec 20] useful-looking gelding: fair maiden: best effort at 1¼m: acts on polytrack. *Richard Fahey*

FARKLE MINKUS 2 b.g. (Jan 18) Kheleyf (USA) 116 – Majestic Diva (IRE) (Royal **89** Applause 124) [2015 5g² 6g* 6g⁴ 6.5m 6g Oct 3] fourth foal: brother to useful winner up to 7f Stonefield Flyer (2-y-o 5f/6f winner): dam unraced: fairly useful performer: won maiden at Ayr (by 5 lengths from Strummer) in July: below form after, not seen to best effect when well held in listed Two-Year-Old Trophy at Redcar final start: best effort at 6f. *Keith Dalgleish*

FARLETTI 3 b.f. Royal Applause 124 – Le Badie (IRE) (Spectrum (IRE) 126) [2015 71: **80** p7m 8.3m⁴ 8.1m* 8m⁵ 8d p8m⁵ p7g Dec 16] lengthy filly: fairly useful performer: won **a74** minor event at Chepstow (by 2¾ lengths from Elle Shade) in June: stays 1m: acts on polytrack and good to firm going. *Andrew Balding*

FARLOW (IRE) 7 ch.g. Exceed And Excel (AUS) 126 – Emly Express (IRE) (High Estate **112** 127) [2015 97: 6d² 6g⁴ 7d 7g³ 7d 7g² 7g* 7s⁴ 7m 8d 7v³ Nov 7] good-topped gelding: smart handicapper: won 16-runner event at Doncaster (by length from Bertiewhittle) in August: better than ever when 1¼ lengths third of 21 to Withernsea there in November: stays 8.5f: acts on any turf going: tried in headgear prior to 2015. *Richard Fahey*

FARMSHOP BOY 4 b.g. Sagamix (FR) 129 – Littleton Zephir (USA) 74 (Sandpit (BRZ) – 129) [2015 –: 10m⁴ 9.9m Jun 10] no form: left Natalie Lloyd-Beavis after first start. *Barry Brennan*

FARMTRUCK (IRE) 2 b.c. (Feb 20) Bushranger (IRE) 119 – Nice One Clare (IRE) 117 **57** (Mukaddamah (USA) 125) [2015 6g 7g p6f⁵ p6m⁶ p7f Nov 12] modest maiden: stayed 6f: acted on polytrack: dead. *Ronald Thompson*

FARQUHAR (IRE) 4 ch.g. Archipenko (USA) 127 – Pointed Arch (IRE) 68 (Rock of **107** Gibraltar (IRE) 133) [2015 105: 12m⁶ 11.9g³ 14g 12m² 13g⁴ Aug 29] sturdy gelding: useful handicapper: best efforts when third in Old Newton Cup at Haydock (2½ lengths behind Notarised) in July and second at Newmarket (length behind Gold Trail) in August: stays 1½m: acts on soft and good to firm going: sometimes slowly away, often races in rear. *Peter Chapple-Hyam*

FARRAH'S CHOICE 3 b.f. Equiano (FR) 127 – Esplanade 77 (Danehill (USA) 126) **62** [2015 5d⁴ 6m³ 6m³ 5g⁶ 6m³ 6s 6d⁶ 6m t8.6f⁶ t9.5f Nov 13] sixth foal: half-sister to useful 2-y-o 6f winner Seasider and untrustworthy 1m winner Embankment (both by Zamindar): dam, 1¼m winner, half-sister to smart French 1¼m-1½m winner Tenuous: modest maiden: left Tim Easterby after eighth start: stays 6f: acts on good to firm going: sometimes in headgear. *James Grassick*

FAR RANGING (USA) 4 b.f. U S Ranger (USA) 124 – Hutchinson (USA) (Gregorian – (USA) 124) [2015 63: t12.2f Mar 26] modest maiden: well held in handicap at Wolverhampton only start in 2015: stays 8.5f: best form on good going: sometimes slowly away, usually races towards rear. *Julie Camacho*

FARSAKH (USA) 3 b.f. Smart Strike (CAN) 121 – Ethaara 106 (Green Desert (USA) **85**
127) [2015 6m* 7m Oct 3] third foal: half-sister to useful 1m winner Estiqaama (by Nayef)
and smart 7f/1m winner Etaab (by Street Cry): dam, 6f/7f winner, closely related to smart
7f /1m performer Muwaary: won 6-runner maiden at Yarmouth in September by 6 lengths
from Jaarih: well below that form in listed race at Ascot: should stay 7f. *William Haggas*

FASCINATING ROCK (IRE) 4 b.c. Fastnet Rock (AUS) 127 – Miss Polaris 93 **127**
(Polar Falcon (USA) 126) [2015 114: 8s* 10v* 10.5g² 10d⁵ 12d* 10d* Oct 17]
British Champions' Day is the country's richest raceday, with over £4m in
prize money, but it is still in its infancy and has a long way to go to match the
cosmopolitan appeal of the much more richly-endowed Prix de l'Arc and Breeders'
Cup meetings, between which it is rather uncomfortably sandwiched. The long-term
backing of Qatar-based Qipco, a privately-owned commercial entity which has
committed its hefty sponsorship until 2024, will help British Champions' Day to
establish itself in the calendar but there is still plenty of work to do. 'This Is The
One That Matters' was the promotional line for Ascot's big day in the latest season,
when 'racing's explosive finale' found itself having to begin at 12.45 to squeeze in
its five pattern races before the start of a Rugby World Cup quarter final later in the
afternoon (there was a lower average Channel 4 audience than for the racing on the
two October Saturdays that preceded it).

British Champions' Day might not be 'the one that matters' for everyone—
the challenge from outside the British Isles comprised just half a dozen from France
and one each from Germany and Singapore—but Irish trainer Dermot Weld is one
who has certainly embraced the lucrative opportunities provided. It is a quarter of
a century since Weld won the Belmont Stakes with Go And Go (he is still the only
European trainer to win a leg of the American Triple Crown), and he was also the
first European trainer to saddle a Melbourne Cup winner (he has won that race
twice). Weld has always kept his sights on the horizon—he has had big winners
on four continents—but he was never going to miss the rich pickings on offer just
across the Irish Sea at Ascot's new championship meeting. Rosewell House has
had four winners on British Champions' Day in the five years since its inception,
Rite of Passage (Long Distance Cup) and Sapphire (Fillies' And Mares') in 2012,
Forgotten Rules (Long Distance Cup) in 2014 and Fascinating Rock in the latest
season in the main feature, the Qipco Champion Stakes which had a first prize of
£770,547, putting it behind only the Derby among Britain's most valuable races.
Forgotten Rules suffered interference when attempting a repeat in the Long Distance
Cup, for which he started joint favourite, but Fascinating Rock proved a more than
able deputy for the stable's top horse Free Eagle who was aimed instead at the Prix
de l'Arc in which he came a creditable sixth behind Golden Horn, the most notable
British-trained absentee from British Champions' Day.

The Champion Stakes wasn't the first time that Fascinating Rock had stood
in for Free Eagle, the one-time ante-post favourite for the 2014 Derby. Free Eagle
didn't reappear as a three-year-old until September, after suffering a stress fracture
of the tibia in the spring, and Fascinating Rock took his place in the main Irish
trial for the Derby, the Derrinstown Stud Derby Trial at Leopardstown. Fascinating
Rock had won a maiden at the same course and followed up in the Ballysax Stakes
at Navan, and he made it a hat-trick in the Derby Trial, being awarded the race
after being bumped by the narrow winner Ebanoran late on. Fascinating Rock went
on to contest both the Derby (eighth to Australia) and the Irish Derby (last of five
behind the same horse). However, he wasn't seen out after finishing eight and a half
lengths behind Australia at the Curragh, while Free Eagle came a good third in the
Champion Stakes at Ascot after an impressive victory in the Group 3 Enterprise
Stakes on his return to action on Irish Champions' Weekend. Fascinating Rock's
performances on firmish going in the Derby and Irish Derby convinced his trainer
that he was a better horse on a softer surface ('He loves soft ground and is very
effective on it and under more testing conditions').

Once Fascinating Rock got his career back on track by winning on his first
two starts at four—landing the odds in the listed Heritage Stakes at Leopardstown
in April and in the Mooresbridge Stakes at the Curragh in May—his trainer began

to turn his thoughts to an autumn campaign, with the Champion Stakes the main target, given the likelihood of suitable underfoot conditions at Ascot in October. After splitting British challengers Al Kazeem and Postponed in a close finish to the Tattersalls Gold Cup at the Curragh on good going, Fascinating Rock was given a break over the summer. He reappeared at the very end of August at Windsor, reportedly his stable's first runner there, and, conceding weight to seven rivals in the Winter Hill Stakes, managed only fifth, shaping as if needing the race (though he was a strong market order, sent off 6/5 favourite). Fascinating Rock completed his preparation for the Champion Stakes by following successfully in the footsteps of Free Eagle with a wide-margin win in the KPMG Enterprise Stakes at Leopardstown, forging clear to win by six lengths from Panama Hat. The Enterprise was run over a mile and a half for the first time, having previously been staged over ten furlongs.

The Champion Stakes would have been strengthened by the presence of the likes of Golden Horn and Free Eagle (who had won the Prince of Wales's Stakes at Royal Ascot before an unlucky third to Golden Horn in the Irish Champion). However, the high-class line-up still meant that Fascinating Rock would have to produce a career best to play anything other than a supporting role and, on the morning of the race, he was available in places at 20/1 in a betting market dominated by Golden Horn's stablemate Jack Hobbs (evens), winner of the Irish Derby, and the Ballydoyle-trained filly Found (9/2), who had been runner-up to Golden Horn in the Irish Champion before meeting trouble in running when ninth in the Arc. Fascinating Rock was eventually sent off fourth favourite at 10/1, the smart but unexposed French challenger Vadamos being third in the betting at 8/1. Six of the thirteen runners started at odds ranging from 33/1 to 80/1, including Maverick Wave in the race as pacemaker for Jack Hobbs. The softish conditions were in Fascinating Rock's favour, as was the flat-out gallop back at a mile and a quarter, and he stayed on to lead inside the final furlong, after being held up, to win by a length and a quarter from the stable's patiently-ridden Found, with Jack Hobbs a further half a length away in third after taking over from his pacemaker over two furlongs out. Fourth place went to 16/1-shot Racing History (a brother to the 2013 winner Farhh), who had won the Winter Hill Stakes, while Vadamos folded tamely and trailed in last. Fascinating Rock reportedly stays in training and, on his Champion Stakes form, will have to be respected in any top middle-distance race staged under similar

Qipco Champion Stakes, Ascot—
Fascinating Rock beats Found and the even-money favourite Jack Hobbs in a strongly-run renewal

Newtown Anner Stud Farm's "Fascinating Rock"

conditions. Since his debut as a two-year-old, he has been beaten only once when encountering going softer than good (when presumably not fully fit in the Winter Hill Stakes).

Fascinating Rock (IRE) (b.c. 2011)	Fastnet Rock (AUS) (b 2001)	Danehill (b 1986)	Danzig
			Razyana
		Piccadilly Circus (b 1995)	Royal Academy
			Gatana
	Miss Polaris (b 2001)	Polar Falcon (b or br 1987)	Nureyev
			Marie d'Argonne
		Sarabah (b 1988)	Ela-Mana-Mou
			Be Discreet

    Fascinating Rock is a strong, lengthy colt with plenty of size and substance about him. His sire Fastnet Rock, also sire of the Oaks winner Qualify and another of the season's good fillies Diamondsandrubies, was a sprinter, but he has sired Group 1 winners in Australia—where he has twice been champion sire—at a mile and a quarter plus, and has not made his name as a sire of sprinters so far in Europe. Fascinating Rock is from Fastnet Rock's first European crop, which was around eighty strong, and is out of Miss Polaris, a daughter of the Haydock Sprint Cup winner Polar Falcon. Miss Polaris was a fairly useful racemare who won twice at a mile and stayed a mile and a quarter, while Fascinating Rock's grandam Sarabah, a half-sister to the smart miler Gothenberg, won at a mile and a quarter and went on to breed nine winners including three useful brothers to Miss Polaris, one of whom was successful at a mile and a half (in Germany and Slovakia). Fascinating Rock's great grandam Be Discreet, who was out of a half-sister to July Cup and Sussex Stakes winner Chief Singer, won at up to seven furlongs and was herself a half-sister to Kirov Premiere, the dam of Japanese Oaks winner Cesario who made history by becoming the first Japanese horse to win a Grade 1 in North America when successful in the 2005 American Oaks on turf at Hollywood Park, having crossed continents after landing the Japanese version earlier that year. Miss Polaris bred two winners before Fascinating Rock, the mile and a quarter maiden winner Secretsubstitute (by High Chaparral) and the smart and versatile Quick Jack (by Footstepsinthesand), winner of the 2015 Galway Hurdle and placed in both the Chester Cup and the Cesarewitch (the last-named for the second time) in the latest season. The genuine Fascinating Rock has shown himself to be versatile too, though in terms of distance, having been successful at a mile, a mile and a quarter and a mile and a half in the latest season. He has shown his best form on good going or softer and acts on heavy. *D. K. Weld, Ireland*

FASHAAK (IRE) 2 b.c. (Jan 31) Starspangledbanner (AUS) 128 – Szabo (IRE) 88 (Anabaa **80 p** (USA) 130) [2015 8m⁵ 6g⁵ 7m Oct 3] 260,000Y: strong, compact colt: half-brother to several winners, including useful 1½m-21f winner Teak (by Barathea) and 1½m winner Artful Rogue (by Excellent Art): dam, maiden (stayed 1½m), half-sister to smart performer up to 1m Edinburgh Knight: fairly useful form: fifth of 8 to Very Talented in maiden at Doncaster in September: 25/1, stiff task when well held in valuable sales race at Newmarket final start: will be suited by further than 6f: remains open to improvement. *Richard Hannon*

FASHIONABLE SPIRIT (IRE) 2 b.f. (Mar 4) Invincible Spirit (IRE) 121 – White And **77** Red (IRE) 93 (Orpen (USA) 116) [2015 p5g² 5.1d³ 5m⁵ 5g* 5g³ 5m² 6m⁴ 5.2v² 6.5m 6g⁶ **a66** 5d t5.1f p5f³ Nov 19] 85,000Y: lengthy filly: second foal: dam, 6.5f winner, half-sister to useful German performer up to 1¾m Wild Passion: fair performer: won maiden at Ripon in June: stays 6f: acts on good to firm going. *Mark Johnston*

FASHIONATA (IRE) 2 ch.f. (Mar 25) Fast Company (IRE) 126 – Red Red Rose (Piccolo **77** 121) [2015 5m⁶ p6f⁶ 5d* 6g⁶ Oct 20] €26,000Y: second foal: half-sister to 2-y-o 5f winner Pillar Box (by Sakhee's Secret): dam unraced half-sister to smart 2-y-o 5f/6f winner Temple Meads: fair form: won maiden at Beverley in September: just respectable effort in nursery final start: stays 6f. *William Haggas*

FASHION FIT (IRE) 2 ch.f. (Apr 25) Raven's Pass (USA) 133 – Mike's Wildcat (USA) **–** (Forest Wildcat (USA) 120) [2015 6g 6d p6f Oct 8] 80,000Y: sister to useful 7f winner Future Reference and half-sister to several winners, including smart 2-y-o 6f winner Jungle Cat (by Iffraaj): dam US 2-y-o 5f/5.5f (minor stakes) winner: no form. *Brian Meehan*

FASHION LINE (IRE) 5 b.m. Cape Cross (IRE) 129 – Shadow Roll (IRE) 79 (Mark of **95** Esteem (IRE) 137) [2015 98: p7m² p7f t7.1m⁴ Feb 2] useful handicapper: second at Lingfield (¾ length behind Don't Be) in January, best effort of 2015: stays 8.5f: acts on polytrack, good to firm and good to soft going. *Michael Bell*

FAST ACT (IRE) 3 ch.g. Fast Company (IRE) 126 – Nullarbor (Green Desert (USA) 127) **–** [2015 101: t5.1f 5m May 14] useful at best, no form in 2015: best at 5f: acts on good to firm going: races prominently. *Kevin Ryan*

FAST AND FURIOUS (IRE) 2 b.g. (Jan 30) Rock of Gibraltar (IRE) 133 – Ocean **90** Talent (USA) (Aptitude (USA) 128) [2015 6g⁴ 6g² 6g* 7m 6g* 6g p7f⁴ Nov 23] 25,000Y: second foal: dam unraced daughter of Prix du Moulin winner/Oaks runner-up All At Sea: fairly useful performer: successful twice at Hamilton, in maiden in June and nursery (by 2 lengths from Candelisa) in September: stays 6f: best form on good going. *James Bethell*

FAST AND HOT (IRE) 2 gr.c. (Apr 2) Fastnet Rock (AUS) 127 – Hotelgenie Dot Com **65** 107 (Selkirk (USA) 129) [2015 6g³ 7s 8g⁶ p7g⁶ p8g Dec 2] fair maiden: should stay 1m: acts on polytrack, best turf form on good going. *Richard Hannon*

FAST APPROACH (IRE) 3 ch.f. New Approach (IRE) 132 – Exorcet (FR) 78 (Selkirk **51** (USA) 129) [2015 p8g p10f p8g³ Dec 20] half-sister to several winners, including smart 6f (including at 2 yrs) winner Dark Missile (by Night Shift) and useful 1m-1¼m winner Breakheart (by Sakhee): dam 6f winner: modest maiden: best effort when third at Lingfield in December. *Andrew Balding*

FAST CAT (IRE) 2 ch.f. (Apr 13) Rock of Gibraltar (IRE) 133 – Real Cat (USA) (Storm **36** Cat (USA)) [2015 6m 5g t7.1g 7m⁶ 7d⁴ 7g⁶ t8.6g Sep 29] €10,000Y: sister to a winner in USA and half-sister to winners in USA by Unbridled's Song and Corinthian: dam unraced half-sister to US Grade 3 6f/7f winner Ifyoucouldseemenow: poor maiden: stays 7f: acts on tapeta, good to firm and good to soft going: sold 1,500 gns, sent to Portugal. *Mark Johnston*

FAST CHARLIE (IRE) 3 b.g. Fast Company (IRE) 126 – Where's Charlotte 53 (Sure **73** Blade (USA) 130) [2015 76: 8g² 7.9v 7f 7m 7d⁴ 7g* 8.3s⁶ 7d⁴ 8v⁴ p8g⁶ p8.9g a12g² a12g⁶ Dec 9] fair handicapper: won at Thirsk in July: left Ann Duffield after eighth start: stays 1½m: acts on fibresand, tapeta and soft going. *P. & F. Montfort, France*

FAST DANCER (IRE) 3 b.g. Fast Company (IRE) 126 – Tereed Elhawa 75 (Cadeaux **90** Genereux 131) [2015 82: t5.1g² 5m* 5f⁵ 6.1g* 5.4m 5.5m² 7g² p7m⁵ Oct 21] fairly useful performer: won maiden at Windsor in May and handicap at Chester in July: second in handicaps at Chester in August and September: stays 7f: acts on polytrack and good to firm going: often in cheekpieces in 2015. *Joseph Tuite*

FAST ENOUGH (IRE) 2 b.g. (Apr 21) Kodiac 112 – La Chicana (IRE) (Invincible Spirit **82** (IRE) 121) [2015 p6g⁴ 6m³ 5g² 6g* 5m⁵ Aug 18] 50,000Y, 160,000 2-y-o: compact gelding: second foal: half-brother to 1½m winner Desert Encounter (by Halling): dam lightly-raced sister to smart 1¼m-12.3f winner Allied Powers: fairly useful performer: won maiden at Brighton (by 3¼ lengths from Rosy Morning) in August: will benefit from return to 6f: best form on good going: tried in cheekpieces: often races prominently. *Saeed bin Suroor*

FASTER COMPANY (IRE) 2 b.g. (Apr 29) Fast Company (IRE) 126 – Lily Rio (IRE) **65 d** 63 (Marju (IRE) 127) [2015 6m³ p7g 7s 8.3d p8m p7m Dec 31] fair maiden: best effort at 6f on good to firm going. *J. S. Moore*

FAST FINIAN (IRE) 6 gr.g. Clodovil (IRE) 116 Delphie Queen (IRE) 104 (Desert Sun **–** 120) [2015 81: 6g Jun 30] fairly useful winner in 2014, well held only start in 2015: subsequently sold £1,000: stays 7f: acts on polytrack, good to firm and good to soft going: has worn headgear, including usually of late: often leads. *Heather Dalton*

FAST GOLD (IRE) 2 b.g. (Mar 20) Fast Company (IRE) 126 – Gold Tobougg 72 (Tobougg **85** (IRE) 125) [2015 5f⁴ 5.3g² 5.3g* 6f³ 7m 7.1m⁴ 8g⁴ 8d 8.3g⁴ Oct 19] €33,000F, £20,000Y: close-coupled gelding: first foal: dam, 6f winner, sister/half-sister to useful winners up to 10.4f Sweet Lilly and Ofaraby: fairly useful performer: won maiden at Brighton in May: respectable efforts after when in frame in nurseries: stays 1m: acts on firm going: tried in headgear: often races prominently: sold 10,000 gns, sent to Qatar. *Marcus Tregoning*

FAST LAYNE 2 gr.g. (May 8) Sakhee's Secret 128 – Tiger's Gene (GER) (Perugino **–** (USA) 84) [2015 p7g t7.1f Oct 30] no form: left Alan Bailey after first start. *Joseph Tuite*

FASTNET PRINCE 2 b.c. (Mar 20) Fastnet Rock (AUS) 127 – Lucky Spin 116 **58** (Pivotal 124) [2015 7m⁵ 7g 6g⁴ Jul 27] modest maiden: best effort when fourth at Windsor (3¼ lengths behind Shakerattlenroll) in July, suited by drop in trip. *David Evans*

FASTNET RED 4 b.g. Fastnet Rock (AUS) 127 – Gyroscope 97 (Spinning World (USA) **–** 130) [2015 82: p11g 12g 18d 12s t8.6f Oct 30] good-bodied gelding: maiden: no form in 2015: usually in headgear in 2015. *Simon West*

FASTNET TEMPEST (IRE) 2 b.g. (Jan 26) Fastnet Rock (AUS) 127 – Dame Blanche **80 p** (IRE) 67 (Be My Guest (USA) 126) [2015 7g⁵ Oct 21] lengthy gelding: closely related to 3 winners, including useful/ungenuine French 1¼m winner Excellent Girl and 5f and (at 2 yrs) 6f winner Moon River (both by Exceed And Excel), and half-brother to a winner abroad by Xaar: dam lightly-raced half-sister to US Grade 1 9f winner Luas Line and smart performer up to 2m Lost In The Moment: 50/1, caught eye when fifth in maiden at Newmarket (5¼ lengths behind Mootaharer) in October, not clear run: sure to progress. *William Haggas*

FAST OPERATOR (IRE) 2 b.f. (Apr 21) Fast Company (IRE) 126 – Dialing Tone **–** (USA) 100 (Distant View (USA) 126) [2015 7s 7g Sep 23] €2,500F, €10,000Y: half-sister to 3 winners, including 2-y-o 7f winner Avenue Montaigne (by Showcasing) and German 7f-1¼m winner Intercom (by Dansili). dam 2-y-o 7f winner: no form. *Nigel Tinkler*

FAST PICK (IRE) 3 b.f. Fastnet Rock (AUS) 127 – Dream Time 75 (Rainbow Quest **69** (USA) 134) [2015 7m 7g⁵ 12s³ 13.1s² p12f⁵ p13.3f Oct 10] €59,000Y: lengthy filly: half-sister to winners abroad by Spinning World and Verglas: dam third at 1½m from 3 starts: fair maiden: stays 13f: acts on polytrack and soft going: often in cheekpieces. *Charles Hills*

FAST PLAY (IRE) 3 b.f. Fast Company (IRE) 126 – Akariyda (IRE) (Salse (USA) 128) **–** [2015 8.3g May 18] 23,000Y: sturdy filly: seventh foal: half-sister to 5f winner Captain Coke (by Fath), later 1¼m winner in Qatar, and 1m winner Purple Affair (by Clodovil): dam unraced half-sister to smart winner up to 2m Akbar: 33/1, well held in maiden at Windsor in May. *Peter Makin*

FAST SCAT (USA) 3 ch.f. Scat Daddy (USA) 120 – Furusato (USA) (Sendawar (IRE) **56** 129) [2015 53, a59: t7.1g 7.6d⁴ t8.6g p10g² 10.2m³ p10g p12g t7.1f Nov 16] modest maiden: left David Evans after seventh start: stays 1¼m: acts on polytrack: tried in visor: often races in rear, often races freely. *Steve Flook*

FAST SHOT 7 b.g. Fasliyev (USA) 120 – Final Pursuit 92 (Pursuit of Love 124) [2015 **102** 104: 6g³ 6g 6g 6d 7g 6s 6g 6g 6d Sep 26] useful handicapper: third at Newcastle (¼ length behind Arctic Feeling) in April: below form after: stays 7f, races mostly at 6f: acts on good to firm and heavy going: sometimes in headgear in 2015: tried in tongue tie prior to 2015. *Tim Easterby*

FAST SPRITE (IRE) 3 b.g. Fast Company (IRE) 126 – Salty Air (IRE) (Singspiel (IRE) **76 p** 133) [2015 8.3d⁵ p7m⁴ p6m² p7g³ p7f³ Dec 21] €9,000F: seventh foal: half-brother to 6f winner Mr Skipiton (by Statue of Liberty) and 1¼m-11.5f winner Giantstepsahead (by Footstepsinthesand): dam unraced half-sister to useful US Grade 3 8.5f winner Eye of Taurus: fair maiden: stays 7f: acts on polytrack: remains with potential. *John Best*

FAST TRACK 4 b.g. Rail Link 132 – Silca Boo 99 (Efisio 120) [2015 99: 6g⁵ 5m² 6m⁶ 5d **103** 5.6d 6g Sep 19] strong gelding: useful handicapper: easily best efforts of 2015 when 1½ lengths second of 17 to Red Baron at Musselburgh in June and sixth of 27 to Golden Steps at Goodwood in August: effective at 5f/6f: acts on good to firm and good to soft going. *David Barron*

FATAAWY (IRE) 2 b.f. (Feb 7) Invincible Spirit (IRE) 121 – Jamaayel 99 (Shamardal **74** (USA) 129) [2015 5m⁴ 6g² 5.1g² t5.1m* p5f³ Sep 22] compact filly: second foal: closely related to useful 5f and (including at 2 yrs) 5.7f winner Rathaath (by Oasis Dream): dam 2-y-o 6f/7f winner out of useful sister to smart 6f/7f winner Haatef: fair performer: won maiden at Wolverhampton in September: stays 6f: acts on tapeta, best turf form on good going: usually races close up. *Brian Meehan*

FATEH (IRE) 2 b.g. (Feb 18) Big Bad Bob (IRE) 118 – Passarelle (USA) 78 (In The **–** Wings 128) [2015 p8g t8.6g Dec 5] no form. *David Dennis*

FATHER BERTIE 3 b.g. Firebreak 125 – Magical Music 96 (Fraam 114) [2015 77: 7m³ **97** 7.5g 8d² 7m* 7d⁴ 8m⁴ 8s* 8g 8s² 8g* 10.3d⁶ Oct 23] useful performer: won maiden at Wetherby in June and handicaps at Catterick and Redcar in July and Redcar (by nose from Mystic Miraaj) in October: stays 1m: acts on soft and good to firm going: often in cheekpieces in 2015: front runner/races prominently. *Tim Easterby*

FATHER CHRISTMAS (IRE) 3 b.c. Bernardini (USA) 132 – Christmas Kid (USA) **110** 114 (Lemon Drop Kid (USA) 131) [2015 53p: 8s² 10.4d* 12f³ Jun 19] good-topped colt: smart form: won maiden at Roscommon (by length from Alertness) in June: in first-time cheekpieces, 16/1, much improved when 2 lengths third of 7 to Balios in King Edward VII Stakes at Royal Ascot, sticking to task very well: will probably stay further than 1½m. *Aidan O'Brien, Ireland*

FATHER FRED 5 br.g. Pastoral Pursuits 127 – Gramada (IRE) 78 (Cape Cross (IRE) **81** 129) [2015 p6f* p6f* Nov 19] fairly useful performer: won 2 claimers at Chelmsford in November, latter by length from Yeeoow: stays 6f: acts on polytrack: tried in cheekpieces prior to 2015. *Chris Dwyer*

FATHER FROST (IRE) 3 b.c. Rip Van Winkle (IRE) 134 – Yaria (IRE) 98 (Danehill **105** (USA) 126) [2015 7g* 5.8d⁴ 7d 7f 7.5m³ p6g Aug 16] 85,000F, 300,000Y: rather leggy colt: fourth foal: half-brother to 1m winner Hurricane Lady (by Hurricane Run) and 6f winner Hard Walnut (by Cape Cross): dam, winner up to 7f (2-y-o 6f winner), half-sister to smart winner up to 1m Emirates Gold: useful performer: won maiden at Cork (by neck from Frozen Lake) in April: 50/1, best effort when ninth of 16 to Dutch Connection in Jersey Stakes at Royal Ascot on fourth start: stays 7f: acts on firm going: often in hood: in tongue tie last 3 starts. *Aidan O'Brien, Ireland*

FATHERLY FRIEND (USA) 2 b.c. (Jan 31) Scat Daddy (USA) 120 – Grimace (USA) **76** (Vindication (USA) 122) [2015 6g⁴ 6g⁵ 7.2g³ Sep 18] fair maiden: best effort when third in maiden at Ayr (2¾ lengths behind Ambriel) in September, racing freely. *K. R. Burke*

FATHOM FIVE (IRE) 11 b.g. Fath (USA) 116 – Ambria (ITY) (Final Straw 127) [2015 **58** 67, a49: 5d 5g⁵ 5m⁶ 5s⁵ 6s² 6s 5g 5d 6m⁶ 6g f7d 5.1d Aug 14] strong, compact gelding: modest handicapper: stays 6f: acts on fibresand, good to firm and heavy going: tried in headgear prior to 2015: usually races prominently. *Shaun Harris*

FATTSOTA 7 b.g. Oasis Dream 129 – Gift of The Night (USA) (Slewpy (USA)) [2015 **114** 108: a9.9f⁶ a9.9f p16g⁵ 12d³ 12g* 13.4v 10.1g⁶ 10f⁶ 10f⁴ 10.4m⁴ 12m 10.1v² 10g³ Sep 24] **a98** lengthy gelding: smart handicapper: won at Ripon (by 8 lengths from Angel Gabrial) in April: good sixth of 13 at Epsom (behind Elbereth) and Royal Ascot (listed event won by Mahsoob) in June: stays 1½m: acts on dirt, firm and soft going: front runner/races prominently. *David O'Meara*

FAVORITE GIRL (GER) 7 b.m. Shirocco (GER) 129 – Favorite (GER) (Montjeu (IRE) **71**
137) [2015 74: 10s³ Oct 13] fair handicapper: will prove suited by a return to 1½m: acts on
fibresand, tapeta, soft and good to firm going. *Michael Appleby*

FAVOURITE TREAT (USA) 5 b.g. Hard Spun (USA) 124 – Truart (USA) (Yes It's **79**
True (USA) 116) [2015 86: 8m 7s 7g⁶ 8g* 8g⁵ 7.9s⁵ 7.5m⁴ 7.2m⁵ 7m⁶ 8d Aug 17] fair
handicapper: won at Thirsk in June: stays 1m: acts on polytrack, good to firm and heavy
going: in eyeshields last 5 starts: front runner/races prominently: no battler in general.
Ruth Carr

FAWAAREQ (IRE) 2 b.c. (Feb 24) Invincible Spirit (IRE) 121 – Ghandoorah (USA) **89 p**
(Forestry (USA) 121) [2015 6d⁴ 7g 7g² Sep 8] useful-looking colt: first foal: dam unraced
close relative to 1000 Guineas winner Ghanaati and half-sister to high-class 1m-1½m
winner Mawatheeq: fairly useful maiden: best effort when second at Leicester (neck
behind Move Up) in September: will stay 1m: still unexposed. *B. W. Hills*

FAYDHAN (USA) 3 b.c. War Front (USA) 119 – Agreeable Miss (USA) (Speightstown **103 p**
(USA) 124) [2015 107p: 7m³ Apr 15] strong, attractive colt: below expectations when third
in listed Free Handicap at Newmarket (3¼ lengths behind Home of The Brave) on sole
outing in 2015 in April, not ideally placed: reportedly suffered leg problem after: sure to
stay 1m: remains with potential. *John Gosden*

FAZENDA'S GIRL 3 b.f. Stimulation (IRE) 121 – Goes A Treat (IRE) 82 (Common **48**
Grounds 118) [2015 50: 8g⁶ 8.3m t12.2g⁶ 7.5f p10g p12g⁴ Aug 12] poor maiden: left
Michael Easterby after fourth start: probably stays 8.5f: acts on good to firm and good to
soft going: sometimes wears headgear: sold £3,000, sent to Germany. *Ian Williams*

FAZZA 8 ch.g. Sulamani (IRE) 130 – Markievicz (IRE) 73 (Doyoun 124) [2015 85: 10s² **75**
9.9m⁵ 9.8d⁵ 10g⁵ 9.3s⁶ 8.3s³ 8g⁶ 9.3g⁶ 7.9m 8.5d² 8.5m⁵ 10.3d Oct 23] close-coupled
gelding: fair handicapper: stays 1¼m: acts on polytrack, good to firm and heavy going: in
cheekpieces last 5 starts. *Edwin Tuer*

FEARLESS LAD (IRE) 5 b.g. Excellent Art 125 – Souffle 105 (Zafonic (USA) 130) **70**
[2015 72: p10f³ p10g p10f p12m⁴ p11g Nov 11] fair handicapper: stays 1½m: acts on
polytrack: usually in tongue tie prior to 2015. *John Best*

FEAR OR FAVOUR (IRE) 4 b.g. Haatef (USA) 117 – Insaaf 100 (Averti (IRE) 117) **76**
[2015 92: p6g⁶ t6m 6m 6m 5.7g⁵ p6g⁶ p7m Oct 21] compact gelding: fairly useful handi- **a85**
capper: stays 6f: acts on polytrack and firm going: tried in cheekpieces in 2015. *Clive Cox*

FEB THIRTYFIRST 6 ch.g. Shirocco (GER) 129 – My Mariam 79 (Salse (USA) 128) **64**
[2015 p15.8f* p15.8g* p16m³ p16d³ p15.8g² p15.8f³ p15.8g⁵ p16g⁶ Dec 16]
modest handicapper: won at Lingfield in January and February: stays 2m: acts on polytrack:
in blinkers in 2015: sometimes slowly away. *Sheena West*

FEED THE GOATER (FR) 2 b.g. (Jan 30) Fastnet Rock (AUS) 127 – Lumiere Astrale **71 p**
(FR) (Trempolino (USA) 135) [2015 7g² Jul 18] €80,000Y: third foal: half-brother to
German 1¼m-1½m winner Anaximenes (by Anabaa) and useful French 13.5f winner
Theme Astral (by Cape Cross): dam, French 12.5f winner, half-sister to smart French/US
winner up to 1¼m Desert Blanc: 3/1, showed plenty when second in maiden at Lingfield
(neck behind Nucky Thompson) in July, sticking to task: will stay at least 1m: sure to
progress. *Richard Hannon*

FEELIN DICKY 2 b.g. (Apr 23) Dick Turpin (IRE) 127 – Feelin Foxy 91 (Foxhound **76 p**
(USA) 103) [2015 f5g* Nov 3] second foal: dam, winner up to 6f (7½f?) 5f winner),
half-sister to useful 7½f/m 6f winner Josh. 14/1, won 13-runner maiden at Southwell (by
1¼ lengths from Specialv) in November, sticking to task: will stay 6f: capable of better.
James Given

FEELING EASY (IRE) 3 b.f. Bushranger (IRE) 119 – Easy Feeling (IRE) 84 (Night **83**
Shift (USA)) [2015 87: 6m⁵ 6m³ 6g 6m³ 6m³ 7g 6g 6g Oct 20] leggy filly: fairly useful
handicapper: third at Newmarket in May and June and Leicester in August: stays 6.5f: acts
on good to firm going. *Robert Eddery*

FEEL THE HEAT 8 ch.g. Firebreak 125 – Spindara (IRE) 64 (Spinning World (USA) **66 §**
130) [2015 78§: 6g⁴ 6d 6m 5.9m 6m³ 6g Oct 8] plain gelding: tubed: fair handicapper: stays
7f: acts on good to firm and good to soft going: usually wears headgear: front runner/races
prominently: best treated with caution. *Bryan Smart*

FEELTHERHYTHM (IRE) 4 b.f. Yeats (IRE) 128 – Queen Althea (IRE) 89 (Bach **54**
(IRE) 121) [2015 12g³ t12.2f p10g⁴ Dec 30] modest maiden: left John Patrick Murtagh
after first start: will benefit from return to 1½m+: acts on polytrack, raced only on good
going on turf: tried in cheekpieces in 2015. *Des Donovan*

FEI KUAI 3 b.f. Paco Boy (IRE) 129 – Goldrenched (IRE) 78 (Montjeu (IRE) 137) [2015 **81**
8.3g⁴ p8g 8g⁵ 7.1m* t7.1f⁵ Oct 13] lengthy filly: third foal: half-sister to 2 winners abroad,
including German winner up to 1m Goldbraid (2-y-o 7f winner, by Exceed And Excel):
dam, 2m winner, sister to useful 1¼m-1½m winner Sunny Game: fairly useful performer:
won maiden at Chepstow (by 3½ lengths from Star of Spring) in September: best effort at
7f: acts on good to firm going. *Luca Cumani*

FELICE (IRE) 5 b.m. Papal Bull 128 – Tarabaya (IRE) 90 (Warning 136) [2015 –: f12g³ **56**
f11d* 11.1m⁵ 12.1g f12d⁶ p13.3m⁵ t16.5m f14g Dec 12] modest handicapper: won at
Southwell in May: stays 13.5f: acts on polytrack, fibresand and good to firm going: often
wears cheekpieces: often leads. *Scott Dixon*

FELIX DE VEGA (IRE) 3 b.g. Lope de Vega (IRE) 125 – Lafite 100 (Robellino (USA) **90**
127) [2015 81: 9.8g⁵ 10.4d 10g³ 10.3m³ 12m³ 11.9m 10m* 10.4g⁴ 10.4s Oct 10] fairly
useful handicapper: won at Redcar (amateur) in August: good fourth of 19 to El Beau at
York in September: stays 1½m: acts on good to firm and heavy going: usually races
prominently. *Michael Easterby*

FELIX FABULLA 5 b.g. Lucky Story (USA) 128 – Laser Crystal (IRE) 67 (King's **90**
Theatre (IRE) 128) [2015 f11g² 11.6g⁵ 12g⁶ p12g² 12m* p12g⁵ 11.9m⁴ 12d* p15.8g⁴ 12s **a79**
14.1s Oct 12] good-topped gelding: fairly useful handicapper: won at Salisbury in June and
Ffos Las in August: third at Ffos Las in September: stays 1¾m: acts on polytrack, good to
firm and soft going: often in cheekpieces in 2015: usually races close up. *Hughie Morrison*

FELIX LEITER 3 ch.g. Monsieur Bond (IRE) 120 – Spiralling (Pivotal 124) [2015 89: **99**
6m 7g 6m⁴ 6m⁴ 6g² 6g⁴ 6m³ 7d³ 7v² Nov 7] workmanlike gelding: useful handicapper:
good efforts when placed in apprentice events at Doncaster last 2 starts, ¾ length third to
Sea Wolf in May: head second of 22 to Westwood Hoe: stays 7f: acts on good to firm and
heavy going: front runner/races prominently, usually responds generously to pressure.
K. R. Burke

FELIX MENDELSSOHN (IRE) 4 b.g. Galileo (IRE) 134 – Ice Queen (IRE) 118 **110**
(Danehill Dancer (IRE) 117) [2015 90p: 12m³ 12g⁴ 11.6d⁵ Aug 29] rangy gelding: second
foal: brother to 1½m winner Exotic: dam, 1¼m-1½m winner, second in Irish Oaks: smart
performer: raced only in listed races in 2015, best effort when third at Ascot (3 lengths
behind Agent Murphy) in May: not seen to best effect (left poorly placed) at Windsor final
outing: stays 1½m: acts on good to firm and good to soft going. *David Simcock*

FENCING (USA) 6 ch.g. Street Cry (IRE) 130 – Latice (IRE) 121 (Inchinor 119) [2015 **– §**
115§] strong, lengthy gelding: smart at best: well held in Firebreak Stakes at
Meydan sole outing in 2015: stays 9f: acts on soft and good to firm going: tried in hood:
tried in tongue tie prior to 2015: no battler, and one to treat with caution. *Charlie Appleby*

FENDALE 3 b.g. Exceed And Excel (AUS) 126 – Adorn 105 (Kyllachy 129) [2015 99: 5m **101**
6m⁴ 6g³ 6g Sep 19] strong, good-topped gelding: useful handicapper: left Bryan Smart
after reappearance: creditable efforts next 2 starts, including third of 19 at York (3¾ lengths
behind George Dryden) in September: stays 6f: acts on good to firm going. *Michael Dods*

FEN FLYER 6 ch.g. Piccolo 121 – Maraffi (IRE) (Halling (USA) 133) [2015 51: p12m⁵ **49**
t16.5g⁴ t16.5m Mar 10] leggy gelding: poor maiden: stays 16.5f: acts on tapeta: tried in
headgear prior to 2015. *John Berry*

FENG SHUI 3 b.g. Iffraaj 127 – Whazzis 109 (Desert Prince (IRE) 130) [2015 81p: p8g³ **81**
p8f² 7d* p7f t7.1f Dec 11] rangy, useful-looking gelding: fairly useful performer: won
maiden at Redcar (by 1¾ lengths from Playboy Bay) in October: best effort when second
in similar event at Chelmsford in September: may prove best at around 1m: usually races
prominently. *Jamie Osborne*

FEN LADY 3 b.f. Champs Elysees 124 – Query (USA) (Distant View (USA) 126) [2015 **–**
8.3m t7.1m⁶ t8.6f t8.6f⁴ f8g⁴ Dec 22] 2,000Y: sturdy filly: fourth foal: half-sister to 2-y-o
7f winner Sensei (by Dr Fong), later successful abroad, and ungenuine 9.5f/1¼m winner
Saturation Point (by Beat Hollow): dam unraced daughter of useful performer up to 1¼m
Questonia: no form. *John Berry*

FENNER HILL NEASA (IRE) 2 b.f. (Apr 13) Alfred Nobel (IRE) 110 – A Woman In **–**
Love 87 (Muhtarram (USA) 125) [2015 8.5d⁵ 6s⁶ p6g Dec 16] fourth foal: half-sister to
useful 1¼m-1½m winner Leah Freya (by Aussie Rules): dam 7f/1m winner: no form: in
hood. *Pat Phelan*

FERAL (IRE) 2 b.f. (Mar 18) Kodiac 112 – Zaynaba (IRE) (Traditionally (USA) 117) **62**
[2015 5g 6g⁵ 5g³ Aug 27] €20,000Y: second foal: dam unraced half-sister to smart
1¼m-1½m winner Zanughan: modest maiden: tongue tied, best effort when third at
Musselburgh (1½ lengths behind Searanger) in August, needing stiffer test: should stay at
least 6f: sold 1,500 gns, sent to France. *Michael Dods*

FERDY (IRE) 6 b.h. Antonius Pius (USA) 123 – Trinity Fair (Polish Precedent (USA) **62**
131) [2015 66, a60: t9.5f⁴ 8g² 10.4g³ 12.3m⁴ 10.4g 8m⁴ 9.3g 7.9d Sep 15] small horse:
modest handicapper: stays 12.5f: acts on polytrack, fibresand, good to firm and good to soft
going: tried in headgear: usually slowly away/races in rear. *Paul Green*

FERENTINA 2 b.f. (Apr 8) Sixties Icon 125 – The Screamer (IRE) 53 (Insan (USA) 119) **–**
[2015 8.3v 8s⁶ t6f Oct 23] sixth foal: sister to winner up to 7f Juventas (2-y-o 6f winner)
and half-sister to a winner in Sweden by Imperial Dancer: dam, 1½m winner, also winning
jumper: no form. *Mick Channon*

FERGALL (IRE) 8 br.g. Norwich 118 – Gaybrook Girl (IRE) (Alderbrook 120) [2015 **77**
p13g* p13.3g Apr 1] fairly useful form: won 6-runner maiden at Lingfield in February by
9 lengths from Draco's Code, better effort: useful hurdler/chaser. *Seamus Mullins*

FERNGROVE (USA) 4 gr.g. Rockport Harbor (USA) 114 – Lucky Pipit 102 (Key of **57**
Luck (USA) 126) [2015 51: 12g² 13.1d⁶ t12.2m Sep 14] tall gelding: modest maiden: best
effort at 1½m: acts on tapeta and heavy going: tried in hood in 2015: often wears tongue
tie: often races freely. *Warren Greatrex*

FERN OWL 3 ch.g. Nayef (USA) 129 – Snow Goose 111 (Polar Falcon (USA) 126) [2015 **78**
10f³ 12.1m⁴ p12g⁵ 11.6g t8.6f⁴ p10g⁴ t9.5f⁵ Dec 11] rangy gelding: fair maiden: stays
1¼m: acts on polytrack, tapeta and firm going: tried in cheekpieces: often starts slowly.
Hughie Morrison

FERRYOVER 2 ch.c. (Mar 29) Pastoral Pursuits 127 – Charlotte Vale 84 (Pivotal 124) **95**
[2015 5g² 6s* 6g² 7m⁵ Sep 9] 6,500F, £15,000Y: fourth foal: half-brother to 11.5f-1¾m
winner Spats Colombo (by Notnowcato): dam, 1½m-13f winner, also won over hurdles:
useful form: won maiden at Ayr (dead-heated with Ancient Astronaut) in May: second in
valuable sales race at York (½ length behind Tasleet) in August: not seen to best effect in
nursery at Doncaster final outing, left poorly placed: should stay 7f: sent to Hong Kong,
where renamed Favouritism. *Kevin Ryan*

FERRYVIEW PLACE 6 b.g. Compton Place 125 – Songsheet 74 (Dominion 123) [2015 **56**
59: t8.6f t8.6g t9.5f* t9.5m* t8.6f³ p11f⁶ p10g⁵ 10m 8.3g⁴ 10m⁴ t9.5g Jul 23] tall gelding:
modest handicapper: won at Wolverhampton (twice) in February: stays 11.5f: acts on
polytrack, tapeta and good to firm going: usually wears headgear: tried in tongue tie: often
races prominently. *Ian Williams*

FESTIVE FARE 3 b.g. Teofilo (IRE) 126 – Al Joza 73 (Dubawi (IRE) 129) [2015 p8m* **117**
p8m* 9m⁴ 12f⁵ 11.1s⁶ 10.4m⁴ t9.5m* Dec 12] 150,000Y: strong, attractive gelding: first
foal: dam, 8.3f winner, half-sister to Racing Post Trophy/Dante Stakes winner Dilshaan:
smart performer: won maiden at Lingfield in January, handicap at Kempton (by 4½ lengths
from Caprior Bere) in February and handicap at Wolverhampton (by 1¾ lengths from
Charles Camoin) in December: stays 9.5f: acts on polytrack and tapeta: often races
prominently, usually races freely. *Charlie Appleby*

FEVER FEW 6 b.m. Pastoral Pursuits 127 – Prairie Oyster 68 (Emperor Jones (USA) 119) **85**
[2015 81: 6m² 6m⁶ 7g* 6m p7g⁶ p6f⁴ Dec 17] tall, lengthy mare: fairly useful handicapper:
won at Lingfield (by neck from Unseeding Power) in August: stays 7f: acts on polytrack
and good to firm going: tried in cheekpieces prior to 2015. *Chris Wall*

FEY 3 b.f. New Approach (IRE) 132 – Persinette (USA) (Kingmambo (USA) 125) [2015 **67**
80p: t9.5m⁵ Apr 2] below winning debut form when fifth in handicap at Wolverhampton on
sole outing in 2015 in April. *Charlie Appleby*

FIBRE OPTIC 3 b.g. Rip Van Winkle (IRE) 134 – Wind Surf (USA) (Lil's Lad (USA) **80**
121) [2015 77p: 10m² 13d³ 10.3g Aug 15] attractive gelding: fairly useful maiden: second
in handicap at Newmarket in June: stays 1¼m: acts on good to firm and heavy going: tried
in blinkers in 2015: often races towards rear. *Luca Cumani*

FIDAAWY 2 ch.g. (Feb 9) New Approach (IRE) 132 – Haymana (IRE) (Pivotal 124) [2015 **72 P**
7g Sep 25] first foal: dam unraced out of smart 1¼m-1½m winner Briolette, herself half-
sister to top-class 1¼m-1½m performer Pilsudski: 11/4, shaped well (looked in need of
experience) when 6½ lengths eighth of 16 to Crazy Horse in maiden at Newmarket on
debut, late headway not knocked about: has been gelded: should make considerable
progress. *Sir Michael Stoute*

FIDELITY 3 b.g. Halling (USA) 133 – Sir Kyffin's Folly 73 (Dansili 127) [2015 –: 10.2m   –
May 22] well held both starts in maidens. *Jonathan Geake*

FIDELMA MOON (IRE) 3 b.f. Dylan Thomas (IRE) 132 – Ridiforza (FR) (Starborough   **73**
126) [2015 81: t7.1g⁵ 10.3m⁶ 9.8d 10.3d⁶ 7.9g* 9.3d⁴ 8g³ 8m Sep 9] leggy filly: fair
handicapper: won at Carlisle in July: probably stays 9.5f: acts on tapeta and good to soft
going: tried in hood: front runner/races prominently, usually races freely. *K. R. Burke*

FIDRA BAY (IRE) 2 b.f. (Mar 27) Roderic O'Connor (IRE) 119 – Halicardia 104   **68**
(Halling (USA) 133) [2015 5m⁶ 6.9m⁶ 7g⁶ Sep 23] €23,000F, €23,000Y: half-sister to
8.6f-1¼m winner Hector Spectre (by Verglas): dam winner up to 1¼m (2-y-o 7f winner):
fair maiden: best effort when sixth at Carlisle in September on second start. *Alan Swinbank*

FIELD FORCE 4 b.g. Champs Elysees 124 – Fairy Steps (Rainbow Quest (USA) 134)   –
[2015 67: t8.6f Feb 7] lightly-raced maiden: best effort at 7f: acted on polytrack: often in
headgear: tried in tongue tie: looked temperamental: dead. *Kevin Bishop*

FIELD GAME 3 b.g. Pastoral Pursuits 127 – Tarqua (IRE) (King Charlemagne (USA)   **94**
120) [2015 97p· p6g³ p5m⁴ 6f³ 6g 7g² 8d⁶ 7g³ 6m Oct 2] rather leggy gelding: fairly useful
handicapper: third at Newmarket in May and second at Leicester in July: barely stays 1m:
acts on polytrack, firm and soft going: usually wears tongue tie. *Hughie Morrison*

FIELDGUNNER KIRKUP (GER) 7 b.g. Acclamation 118 – Fire Finch 83 (Halling   **89**
(USA) 133) [2015 89: 8m* 7m* 8d 7.5g 8m 8g 7v⁴ 7s 7v Nov 7] good-topped gelding:
fairly useful handicapper: won at Redcar in April and Catterick (by neck from Khelman) in
May: stays 1m: acts on good to firm and heavy going: tried in blinkers prior to 2015.
David Barron

FIELDMOUSE 3 b.f. Champs Elysees 124 – Intervene (Zafonic (USA) 130) [2015 55:   **62**
7m 10m 10.2m⁵ p10g⁵ p12g² Dec 15] rather unfurnished filly: modest maiden: best effort
at 1½m: acts on polytrack. *Eve Johnson Houghton*

FIELD OF DREAM 8 b.g. Oasis Dream 129 – Field of Hope (IRE) 119 (Selkirk (USA)   **104**
129) [2015 114: 8f 7f 7g⁴ 7g⁴ 7g 7g 7g p7g p8g t8.6m* p7f* p8g Dec 7] big, attractive gelding: **a93**
useful performer: won claimers at Wolverhampton in November and Lingfield in
November: stays 8.5f: acts on polytrack, tapeta, firm and good to soft going: often wears
headgear: usually races in rear. *Jamie Osborne*

FIELD OF FAME 4 b.g. Champs Elysees 124 – Aswaaq (IRE) 74 (Peintre Celebre (USA)   **98**
137) [2015 10m³ 10.4g⁵ 10m⁴ 11.6m² 10s⁶ 10g* 10s 10.4s⁵ Oct 10] useful-looking gelding:
useful handicapper: won at Newmarket (by 1½ lengths from Uele River) in August: good
4½ lengths fifth of 8 to Chancery at York final start: stays 11.5f: acts on good to firm and
heavy going. *Andrew Balding*

FIELD OF LIGHT 3 b.g. Pastoral Pursuits 127 – Luminda (IRE) (Danehill (USA) 126)   **77**
[2015 8.3g t8.6g⁵ 8.3d² 8d³ p12g² t12.2g³ 10.1d² p12g² 10g⁵ t13.9f⁵ Oct 9] lengthy gelding:
fair maiden: stays 1¾m: acts on polytrack, tapeta and good to soft going: often in headgear:
consistent. *Ed Dunlop*

FIELD OF STARS 2 b.f. (Jan 19) Acclamation 118 – Map of Heaven 82 (Pivotal 124)   **90**
[2015 5.1g⁵ 6m² p6g² p6g* Dec 2] first foal: dam, 7f winner, sister to 5f winner Enticing
and 7f/1m winner Sentaril (both smart) out of smart 2-y-o 5f winner Superstar Leo: fairly
useful performer: improved and value for extra when winning maiden at Kempton in
December by 6 lengths from The Lillster: best effort at 6f. *William Haggas*

FIELD OF VISION (IRE) 2 b.c. (Mar 2) Pastoral Pursuits 127 – Grand Design 64   **103**
(Danzero (AUS)) [2015 5.1s² 5.3s² 5.1f³ 5.1g² 5.2m³ 5g p5f* 5m⁵ 5g² 5g² Oct 9] lengthy,
dipped-backed colt: fifth foal: brother to useful 2-y-o 5f/6f winner Drawing Board: dam,
maiden (stayed 1¼m), half-sister to useful 10.4f-1½m winner Jalousie: useful performer:
won maiden at Chelmsford (by 6 lengths from Men United) in August: good 2½ lengths
second of 11 to Quiet Reflection in Cornwallis Stakes at Newmarket final start: speedy,
best kept to 5f: acts on polytrack and good to firm going: front runner/races prominently.
Joseph Tuite

FIELDSMAN (USA) 3 b.g. Hard Spun (USA) 124 – R Charlie's Angel (USA) (Indian   **95**
Charlie (USA) 126) [2015 93: 8m⁶ 7g 7g² 7.2g 7m Oct 2] useful handicapper: second at
Yarmouth (2 lengths behind Mujassam) in August: stays 7f: best form on good going: often
races prominently. *Ed Dunlop*

FIELDS OF ATHENRY (IRE) 3 b.c. Galileo (IRE) 134 – Last Love (IRE) 87 (Danehill   **121**
(USA) 126) [2015 54p: p10.7g* 12m² 14d* 12g* 14g⁵ 14.6d³ Sep 12] sixth foal: brother to
useful 1¼m winner League of Nations and half-brother to a winner in USA by Fusaichi
Pegasus: dam, 7f winner, sister to smart performer up to 1½m Summerland: very smart
performer: won maiden at Dundalk (by 5½ lengths from Game Set Dash) in May, listed

race at Leopardstown (by 10 lengths from Silwana) in July and Ballyroan Stakes at Leopardstown (by 1¾ lengths from Edelpour) in August: creditable third in St Leger at Doncaster (1¾ lengths behind Simple Verse) final start: will stay 2m: acts on polytrack and good to soft going: in hood in 2015: front runner/races prominently: sent to Denmark. *Aidan O'Brien, Ireland*

FIESOLE 3 b.c. Montjeu (IRE) 137 – Forgotten Dreams (IRE) 44 (Olden Times 121) **80 p** [2015 78: 9.9m³ 12m³ 9.9g* Aug 7] fairly useful handicapper: won at Brighton (by 1¼ lengths from Pensionnat) in August: stays 1½m: acts on polytrack and good to firm going: should do better still. *Luca Cumani*

FIFTYSHADESFREED (IRE) 4 gr.g. Verglas (IRE) 118 – Vasilia (Dansili 127) [2015 **92** 100: p11g 12g⁶ p11g⁵ 10.4m t9.5g² 9m 10g* 10m p11g Nov 9] rather leggy gelding: fairly useful handicapper: won at Sandown (by head from Symphony of Kings) in September: second at Wolverhampton in July: stays 11f: acts on polytrack and tapeta: often wears cheekpieces. *George Baker*

FIFTYSHADESOFGREY (IRE) 4 gr.g. Dark Angel (IRE) 113 – Wohaida (IRE) 71 **102** (Kheleyf (USA) 116) [2015 87, a95: 7d⁷ 7m* 7g* 7m⁶ 7g 7g⁵ p6.5g⁵ Oct 22] good-topped gelding: useful performer: won 2 handicaps at Goodwood (latter by ½ length from Mr Win), both in May: creditable 1¼ lengths fifth to Phu Hai in minor event at Deauville final start: stays 1m: acts on polytrack, firm and good to soft going: tried in headgear: has worn tongue tie: often travels strongly. *George Baker*

FIFTYSHADESOFPINK (IRE) 2 b.f. (Mar 18) Pour Moi (IRE) 125 – Maakrah – (Dubai Destination (USA) 127) [2015 p8d Nov 30] 42,000F: second foal: dam unraced sister to high-class winner up to 7f/1m winner Matravers (by Oasis Dream): dam unraced sister to high-class winner up to 10.4f Farraaj and half-sister to high-class 6f/7f performer Iffraaj: 16/1, shaped as if needed experience when tenth in maiden at Kempton (13¼ lengths behind Diamonds Pour Moi) in November. *Hugo Palmer*

FIFTYTINTSOFSILVER (IRE) 2 gr.f. (Apr 18) Clodovil (IRE) 116 – Marju Guest **51** (IRE) 67 (Marju (IRE) 127) [2015 p5g⁵ p6g f5g³ Dec 29] €2,000F, €12,000 2-y-o: half-sister to several winners, including 2-y-o 7f winner Sapphire Stone (by Intikhab), later successful abroad, and 5f winner Roring Samson (by Art Connoisseur): dam maiden (placed up to 9.4f): modest maiden: best effort when fifth at Kempton (3½ lengths behind Fruit Salad) in November, unable to sustain effort. *Gay Kelleway*

FIGHTING TEMERAIRE (IRE) 2 b.c. (Jan 13) Invincible Spirit (IRE) 121 – Hot **85 p** Ticket (IRE) (Selkirk (USA) 129) [2015 6g² 6s³ 6d* p7f² Nov 23] €75,000Y, 140,000 2-y-o: first foal: dam unraced sister/half-sister to smart performers up to 1½m Scottish Stage and Eleanora Duse: fairly useful form: won maiden at Windsor (by 2¾ lengths from Cee Jay) in October: shaped well when ¾-length second of 4 to Electra Voice in nursery at Chelmsford final start: stays 7f: remains with potential. *Dean Ivory*

FIGHT KNIGHT 3 ch.g. Sir Percy 129 – Great White Hope (IRE) (Noverre (USA) 125) **55** [2015 p8f⁶ f8s³ p7g f8g⁴ p10g² p11g Aug 24] rather leggy gelding: modest maiden: stays 1¼m: acts on polytrack: usually races towards rear: sold 1,000 gns, sent to Germany. *Dr Jon Scargill*

FIGMENT 3 b.f. Acclamation 118 – First Exhibit (Machiavellian (USA) 123) [2015 78p: **92** 7g⁴ 8.3g³ 8m² 7m* 7.1g⁶ Sep 11] useful-looking filly: fairly useful performer: won maiden at Newmarket (by 7 lengths from Fine View) in August: best effort at 7f: acts on good to firm going: usually leads, strong traveller: sold 30,000 gns in December. *John Gosden*

FIGURANTE (IRE) 2 ch.f. (May 13) Excellent Art 125 – Savignano (Polish Precedent **69 p** (USA) 131) [2015 6m² Aug 17] half-sister to several winners, including smart Italian 1m (including at 2 yrs) winner Saint Bernard (by Three Valleys) and 1½m-1¾m winner Who Dares Wins (by Jeremy): dam, French 7f winner, half-sister to Prix de la Foret winner Field of Hope: 33/1, shaped well when second in maiden at Windsor (2¼ lengths behind Dancing Star) in August: will stay 7f: will improve. *Jamie Osborne*

FIGURE OF SPEECH (IRE) 4 b.g. Invincible Spirit (IRE) 121 – Epic Similie (Lomitas – 129) [2015 a7f a6f⁶ Jan 22] strong, well-made gelding: useful performer at 2 yrs: below form in 4 races at Meydan since, well held in handicaps in 2015: best at 6f: acts on polytrack and good to firm going: often in headgear prior to 2015. *Charlie Appleby*

FILAMENT OF GOLD (USA) 4 b.g. Street Cry (IRE) 130 – Raw Silk (USA) (Malibu **73** Moon (USA)) [2015 82: p12g 10.2f t8.6f t8.6g Dec 4] good-topped gelding: fair handicapper: stays 1½m: acts on polytrack: usually in cheekpieces in 2015. *Roy Brotherton*

FILE OF FACTS (IRE) 2 b.g. (Apr 18) Iffraaj 127 – Clever Day (USA) (Action This **61** Day (USA) 121) [2015 7m 7m⁶ 8d Sep 3] lengthy gelding: modest maiden: best effort when seventh at Haydock (9¾ lengths behind Dal Harraild) in September. *Tom Dascombe*

FILLYDELPHIA (IRE) 4 b.f. Strategic Prince 114 – Lady Fonic 77 (Zafonic (USA) **59**
130) [2015 58: t12.2g⁴ 12.4d⁴ 12.5m 11.1m 12m⁴ 14.1m³ 14g 11.5s⁵ 12d* 12.1m Sep 28]
modest handicapper: won at Catterick in September: best effort at 1½m: acts on good to
firm and good to soft going: often wears hood. *Patrick Holmes*

FILOSOFO (IRE) 4 b.c. Teofilo (IRE) 126 – Think (FR) 99 (Marchand de Sable (USA) **72**
117) [2015 78: p10m p8g⁴ p10f³ 8.3m⁵ 10g 10m⁵ 8.1g² 8g* 8s⁶ 8.3g Oct 19] rather leggy
colt: fair handicapper: won at Salisbury in August: stays 1¼m: acts on polytrack and good
to firm going: often races prominently. *Richard Hannon*

FINAL 3 b.g. Arabian Gleam 122 – Caysue (Cayman Kai (IRE) 114) [2015 t7.1g³ t7.1m* **71 p**
Feb 27] sixth foal: half-brother to 1½m/12.4f winner Discay (by Distant Music) and a
winner in Denmark by Garrison Savannah: dam unraced: better effort when winning
maiden at Wolverhampton (by 4½ lengths from Starlight Genie) in February, staying on
strongly: will stay 1m+: will go on improving. *Mark Johnston*

FINAL CHOICE 2 b.c. (May 1) Makfi 130 – Anasazi (IRE) (Sadler's Wells (USA) 132) **– p**
[2015 p8m t8.6g p8m Dec 16] half-brother to several winners, including smart French/
Scandinavian 7f-1¼m winner Runaway (by King's Best) and useful 1m winner Zonergem
(by Zafonic): dam lightly-raced half-sister to Dancing Brave: no form in maidens but looks
type to do better in time. *Roger Charlton*

FINAL COUNTDOWN 4 ch.g. Selkirk (USA) 129 – Culture Queen 91 (King's Best **92**
(USA) 132) [2015 82: t12.2f 10s* 10.4g* 10.1d² 10.4m 10d⁵ 9.8d 10d² Sep 17] fairly
useful handicapper: won at Pontefract in April and Haydock in April: second at Newcastle
in May and at Pontefract in September: stays 10.5f: acts on polytrack, tapeta, soft and good
to firm going: usually in cheekpieces in 2015. *John Quinn*

FINAL DRIVE (IRE) 9 b.g. Viking Ruler (AUS) – Forest Delight (IRE) 58 (Shinko **51**
Forest (IRE)) [2015 p10g p10f p8f Feb 19] good-topped gelding: modest handicapper:
stays 9.5f: acts on polytrack, tapeta, good to firm and good to soft going: tried in headgear:
sometimes wears tongue tie. *John Butler*

FINAL SPRING (IRE) 2 b.f. (Apr 7) Zebedee 113 – Baileys Cream 79 (Mister Baileys **–**
123) [2015 7v 6d Sep 25] €47,000F, 82,000Y: closely related to useful 2-y-o 5f/6f winner
Baileys Cacao (by Invincible Spirit) and half-sister to several winners, including French
10.5f winner Morny's Place (by Clodovil): dam 2-y-o 7f winner: well held in 2 maidens.
John Gosden

FINAL VENTURE 3 b.g. Equiano (FR) 127 – Sharplaw Venture 95 (Polar Falcon (USA) **76**
126) [2015 5d* 6s⁶ 6d³ 5g³ Jun 26] fair form: won maiden at Newcastle (by neck from
Soie d'Leau) in April: creditable third in handicaps at Ripon and Newcastle: stays 6f.
Alan Swinbank

FINAL WARNING 2 b.f. (Mar 31) Piccolo 121 – Karminskey Park 71 (Sabrehill (USA) **–**
120) [2015 5g⁵ 5m 6m Jun 15] £1,000Y: sixth foal: dam 5f/6f winner: no form: often in
tongue tie. *Bill Turner*

FINCH FLYER (IRE) 8 ch.g. Indian Ridge 123 – Imelda (USA) (Manila (USA)) [2015 **41**
t13.9f t8.6g t12.2m Dec 18] stocky gelding: poor handicapper: stays 13f: acts on any turf
going: often wears headgear. *Aytach Sadik*

FINDHORN MAGIC 4 b.f. Kyllachy 129 – Enchanted Princess 82 (Royal Applause **52**
124) [2015 72: 5.1m 5g⁴ 5d⁵ p6g t6f Oct 16] modest handicapper: best effort at 6f: acts on
polytrack: tried in cheekpieces in 2015: usually races close up. *Peter Makin*

FINDOG 5 b.g. Pastoral Pursuits 127 – Night Home (ITY) (Night Shift (USA)) [2015 63§: **58**
5v⁶ 7.1g² 7.1s 5.9d 7.2d 8.3g 7.2g Oct 13] modest handicapper: won at Musselburgh in
May: stays 7f: acts on good to firm going: tried in hood: inconsistent. *Linda Perratt*

FINE BLEND (IRE) 2 br.f. (Feb 15) Sakhee's Secret 128 – Coffee Time (IRE) 88 (Efisio **96**
120) [2015 5m* 5g² 6g⁶ 5d* 6d Oct 30] €10,000 2-y-o: rather unfurnished filly: sister to
useful 6f winner Caffeine and half-sister to 3 winners, including 5f (including at 2 yrs)
winner Cuppacocoa (by Bertolini): dam, ungenuine maiden (stayed 1m), half-sister to
useful winner up to 9f Fine Silver: useful performer: won maiden at Lingfield in June and
listed race at Chantilly (by neck from Lil's Joy) in October: may prove best at 5f: acts
on good to firm and good to soft going. *William Muir*

FINE EXAMPLE 2 b.g. (May 12) Showcasing 117 – Belle Reine (King of Kings (IRE) **56 p**
125) [2015 7m 7s⁵ 6g³ Sep 24] 47,000Y, £35,000 2-y-o: half-brother to several winners,
including useful winner up to 16.5f Layline (2-y-o 1m winner, by King's Best) and useful
2-y-o 5f/6f winner Ishbelle (by Invincible Spirit): dam unraced half-sister to 1m/9f winner

Smart Enough and winner up to 1m Oasis Dancer (both smart): modest maiden: best effort when third at Pontefract (7¾ lengths behind Yorkee Mo Sabee) in September, running on late: open to further improvement. *Kevin Ryan*

FINE JUDGMENT 3 b.f. Compton Place 125 – Blue Lyric 81 (Refuse To Bend (IRE) 128) [2015 54: t5.1g p5g* 5g⁵ p5g⁶ p5f Sep 22] modest handicapper: won at Lingfield in July: best effort at 5f: acts on polytrack: front runner/races prominently. *William Muir* **63**

FINELCITY (GER) 2 b.g. (Mar 19) Elusive City (USA) 117 – Finity (USA) 94 (Diesis 133) [2015 7s³ Oct 12] rather leggy gelding: 25/1 and blinkered, third in maiden at Salisbury (1½ lengths behind Kismet Hardy) in October, edging right approaching final 1f but keeping on. *Harry Dunlop* **72**

FINE 'N DANDY (IRE) 4 ch.g. Dandy Man (IRE) 123 – Pearly Brooks 77 (Efisio 120) [2015 –: p5f 5d 6g⁶ 7m 7m 5g⁵ 5g² 5m* f5f⁴ Dec 17] strong, close-coupled gelding: fair handicapper: won at Musselburgh in September: best form at 5f: acts on good to firm and heavy going: tried in visor in 2015: tried in tongue tie prior to 2015: usually leads. *J. R. Jenkins* **72**

FINE SHARE (IRE) 2 b.g. (Apr 7) Art Connoisseur (IRE) 121 – Novel Fun (IRE) 42 (Noverre (USA) 125) [2015 7g 6d p7g p7g⁶ 7s p7g p8g p8m⁶ Dec 16] lengthy gelding: poor maiden: stays 1m: acts on polytrack and good to soft going: often in headgear: usually in tongue tie: temperament under suspicion. *John Bridger*

FINE TUNE (IRE) 4 b.g. Medicean 128 – Phillippa (IRE) (Galileo (IRE) 134) [2015 –: – p10g p12g p10f Sep 24] rather leggy gelding: maiden: no form in 2015: tried in cheekpieces in 2015: sometimes slowly away. *Linda Jewell*

FINE VIEW (USA) 3 b.f. Arch (USA) 127 – Nesselrode (USA) (Lemon Drop Kid (USA) 84 131) [2015 74p: p8m⁴ 7.5m² 7g² 7m² 7m² t7.1f* p8f³ Oct 10] angular filly: fairly useful performer: won maiden at Wolverhampton (by length from Real Smart) in October: stays 7.5f: acts on tapeta and good to firm going: in cheekpieces last 2 starts: tried in tongue tie in 2015: sold 32,000 gns, sent to Saudi Arabia. *Saeed bin Suroor*

FINFLASH (IRE) 4 b.g. Jeremy (USA) 122 – Sinegronto (IRE) (Kheleyf (USA) 116) 57 [2015 67: 5.3g⁴ 6d⁵ 6m 5v⁴ Aug 28] angular gelding: modest handicapper: stays 6f: acts on good to firm and good to soft going: tried in headgear. *John Spearing*

FINGAL'S CAVE (IRE) 3 ch.g. Fast Company (IRE) 126 – Indiannie Moon (Fraam 66 114) [2015 84: p7g⁵ 7g⁵ 6m⁵ Jun 8] leggy, angular gelding: fair performer: stays 7f: acts on firm and soft going: sometimes slowly away. *Mick Channon*

FINN CLASS (IRE) 4 b.g. Exceed And Excel (AUS) 126 – Finnmark (Halling (USA) 94 133) [2015 88: 8g⁴ 7.2g² 7m 7g⁵ 7.2d² 8m* 8g* 8d 8g 7.2g⁵ 8d³ Oct 16] useful-looking gelding: fairly useful handicapper: won at Haydock in June and Ayr (by neck from Sound Advice) in July: good third of 16 to Express Himself at Haydock final start: stays 1m: acts on polytrack, good to firm and good to soft going: often races prominently. *Michael Dods*

FINNEGAN (IRE) 2 ch.c. (Feb 9) Unbridled's Song (USA) 125 – Untouched Talent 97 (USA) 110 (Storm Cat (USA)) [2015 a4.5f² 5f* 6g Aug 22] fifth foal: closely related to high-class US Grade 1 9f winner and Kentucky Derby/Preakness Stakes runner-up Bodemeister (by Empire Maker) and half-brother to 2 winners in USA, including smart 1m winner Fascinating (by Smart Strike): dam US 2-y-o 5f/6.5f (Grade 2) winner who stayed 8.5f: useful performer: won maiden at Pimlico in May by 5 lengths from La Nina: off 3 months, below that form when 7¾ lengths seventh of 10 to Ajaya in Gimcrack Stakes at York next time, weakening: best effort at 5f: blinkered first outing: has worn tongue tie. *Wesley A. Ward, USA*

FINTON FRIEND (IRE) 3 b.c. Fast Company (IRE) 126 – Right Ted (IRE) 78 (Mujadil – § (USA) 119) [2015 60, a67: p10m Jan 14] maiden: well held only start in 2015, subsequently sold 2,500 gns: stays 7f: acts on polytrack: in blinkers last 3 starts: best treated with caution. *Charles Hills*

FINTRY (IRE) 4 b.f. Shamardal (USA) 129 – Campsie Fells (UAE) 111 (Indian Ridge 117 123) [2015 119: 9f⁵ 8g* 8m⁵ 8g⁵ 8s⁶ Nov 1] smart performer: won Prix Bertrand du Breuil at Chantilly (by ½ length from Avenir Certain) in June: respectable fifth to Amazing Maria next 2 starts, in Falmouth Stakes at Newmarket and Prix Rothschild at Deauville: below form in Prix Perth at Saint-Cloud final outing: stays 1m: acts on soft and good to firm going. *A. Fabre, France*

FIRE AND PASSION 3 b.g. Dutch Art 126 – Mary Goodnight 86 (King's Best (USA) 81 132) [2015 p7g² p7g³ 7g⁵ 7f p7m⁶ t7.1m² Dec 12] 48,000Y, £190,000 2-y-o: compact gelding: second foal: half-brother to 7f winner Marydale (by Aqlaam): dam, 1¼m winner, half-sister to smart winner up to 2m Namibian: fairly useful maiden: best effort when second at Kempton in March: raced only at 7f: acts on polytrack: tried in blinkers. *Jeremy Gask*

FIREDANSER 2 b.c. (Jan 29) Firebreak 125 – Citron (Reel Buddy (USA) 118) [2015 6g⁶ **89** 5.9m³ 6g* 6.5m 7d Sep 27] fifth foal: half-brother to 5f winner Bitter Lemon (by Indesatchel): dam unraced half-sister to useful winner up to 6.5f Golden Nun, herself dam of smart sprinter Confessional: fairly useful performer: won maiden at Haydock in August: should stay 7f (run free excused next try at trip): acts on good to firm going. *Richard Fahey*

FIRE DIAMOND 2 b.c. (Mar 4) Firebreak 125 – Diapason (IRE) 80 (Mull of Kintyre **51** (USA) 114) [2015 6m 5.9m Jul 26] better effort when seventh in maiden at Haydock (10 lengths behind Wayward Hoof) on debut. *Tom Dascombe*

FIRE EMPRESS 2 b.f. (Feb 9) Firebreak 125 – Tedsmore Dame 81 (Indesatchel (IRE) **–** 120) [2015 6d Jul 29] 1,000F: first foal: dam, a 2-y-o 6f winner, half-sister to useful 2-y-o 7f/1m winner Day of Conquest and to dam of smart performer up to 9f Hearts of Fire: 100/1, well held in maiden at Leicester. *James Unett*

FIRE FIGHTING (IRE) 4 b.g. Soldier of Fortune (IRE) 131 – Savoie (FR) (Anabaa **118** (USA) 130) [2015 115: 12.1g² 11.9g⁶ 14g p16g³ p11g² 14s p12g² 10.1g³ 12f 10m* 10.1g² 10f³ 10.4m⁶ 10m³ 9.9g³ 10.4m³ 9.9d p12g⁵ 10g⁵ 9g p10f* p10.7g* p12g⁴ p10m p12g* Nov 25] medium-sized gelding: smart performer: thrived during very busy 2015 and won handicap at Redcar (by 3¾ lengths from Yeager) in May, minor event at Chelmsford (by 2 lengths from Merritt Island) and listed race at Dundalk (by 5 lengths from Hot Sauce) in October and listed race at Kempton (by 2¼ lengths from Hamelin) in November: several other good efforts, including when third to Mahsoob in Wolferton Handicap at Royal Ascot and to Mount Logan in another good-quality handicap at Goodwood twelfth/fifteenth starts: stays 1½m: acts on polytrack, firm and good to soft going: often wears headgear: usually responds generously to pressure: very tough. *Mark Johnston*

FIREGLOW 2 b.f. (Mar 26) Teofilo (IRE) 126 – Fading Light 103 (King's Best (USA) **104** 132) [2015 5g* 6f⁴ 7.1f* 7m² 7s² 8s⁴ 8d* Oct 31] strong, compact filly: fourth foal: half-sister to UAE 7f-1¼m winner Paschendale (by Refuse To Bend) and winner up to 2m Moon Trip (2-y-o 8.3f winner, by Cape Cross), both useful: dam, French 2-y-o 1m winner, half-sister to grandam of 2000 Guineas/Derby winner Camelot: useful performer: won maiden at Catterick in May, listed race at Sandown (by 2¼ lengths from Dessertoflife) in July and listed race at Newmarket (by 4 lengths from Rioca) in October: second in Sweet Solera Stakes at Newmarket (½ length behind Blue Bayou) and Prestige Stakes at Goodwood (nose behind Hawksmoor) in August: stays 1m: acts on firm and soft going: front runner/races prominently. *Mark Johnston*

FIRE IN BABYLON (IRE) 7 b.g. Montjeu (IRE) 137 – Three Owls (IRE) 79 (Warning **59** 136) [2015 71: t12.2f⁶ f12g t12.2f² p12f⁶ t12.2g t12.2g p13.3m p13.3m⁴ t12.2g* t13.9g⁴ f12d p16g² p16g⁶ p13.3m Sep 26] modest handicapper: left Noel Quinlan after third start: won at Wolverhampton in June: stays 2m: acts on all-weather and good to firm going: often wears headgear: tried in tongue tie prior to 2015: races well off pace: none too consistent. *Giles Bravery*

FIRE KING 9 b.g. Falbrav (IRE) 133 – Dancing Fire (USA) (Dayjur (USA) 137) [2015 **54** 57: p7g² p7g⁵ p8f Mar 4] workmanlike gelding: modest handicapper: stays 1¼m: acts on polytrack, firm and good to soft going: often wears headgear. *Paul Burgoyne*

FIRE SHIP 6 b.g. Firebreak 125 – Mays Dream (Josr Algarhoud (IRE) 118) [2015 114: 8d **107** 8v³ 8g³ 8d⁵ 8s⁶ 8d 8.1v³ 10d⁵ 8.3s⁵ Nov 4] well-made gelding: useful performer: third in Amethyst Stakes at Leopardstown (neck behind Onenightidreamed) in May and in listed races at York (3 lengths behind Top Notch Tonto) in June and Sandown (2 lengths behind Elm Park) in September: stays 8.5f: acts on good to firm and heavy going: front runner/races prominently. *William Knight*

FIRESNAKE (IRE) 2 b.g. (Apr 3) Dandy Man (IRE) 123 – La Bataille (USA) (Out of **75** Place (USA)) [2015 5f⁶ t5.1g³ t7.1g² 6.1d⁶ p7g³ t7.1f² t8.6f Oct 27] good-topped gelding: fair maiden: stays 7f: acts on polytrack and tapeta. *Tom Dascombe*

FIRESTORM (GER) 4 b.g. Dylan Thomas (IRE) 132 – Fitness (IRE) (Monsun (GER) **108 d** 124) [2015 10.4s³ 9.9g⁶ 9.4g³ 12m⁴ 12m 11.9g 10.1d⁵ 9.9g 10v Oct 24] sturdy gelding: useful performer at best: third in listed races at Cologne (good effort, ½ length behind Vif Monsieur) in April and Bordeaux in May: left P. Schiergen after, subsequently below form: stays 12.3f: acts on soft going: has been gelded. *Michael Attwater*

FIRGROVE BRIDGE (IRE) 3 ch.g. Dandy Man (IRE) 123 – Over Rating 74 (Desert **79**
King (IRE) 129) [2015 80: p6f p8g⁴ p7f p8m 8g 7m⁵ 6d⁴ 6m* 6m⁶ 6.1g⁵ 7d⁶ 5.7m 6g **a67**
Oct 19] stocky, close-coupled gelding: fair handicapper: won at Doncaster in June: left
Kevin Ryan after eleventh start: stays 6f: acts on good to firm going: often wears headgear:
sometimes slowly away. *Grace Harris*

FIRMAMENT 3 b.g. Cape Cross (IRE) 129 – Heaven Sent 116 (Pivotal 124) [2015 86: **98**
8s² 9g⁶ 8.1g⁵ 8v p8g⁴ t8.6f⁴ p8g³ p8g² Dec 16] good-topped gelding: useful handicapper:
left Jeremy Noseda, third at Chelmsford (neck behind Volunteer Point) and second at
Kempton (½ length behind Elusive Guest) in December: worth a try at 1¼m: acts on
polytrack, tapeta, best turf form on soft/heavy going. *David O'Meara*

FIRMDECISIONS (IRE) 5 b.g. Captain Rio 122 – Luna Crescente (IRE) (Danehill **102**
(USA) 126) [2015 88, a98: p6g² p7f p7f p7g⁶ 6m⁴ 7f* 7m* 7f 6m 7g Sep 8] big, workmanlike
gelding: useful handicapper: won at Newmarket (twice, by ½ length from Russian Realm
latter occasion) in May: best other effort when second at Lingfield in January: stays 7f: acts
on polytrack and firm going: has worn headgear: usually races close up. *Dean Ivory*

FIRNAS 2 b.c. (Apr 1) Dubawi (IRE) 129 – Crystal Music (USA) 114 (Nureyev (USA) **73 p**
131) [2015 7g⁵ Aug 28] 1,600,000Y: rangy colt: half-brother to 3 winners, including 2-y-o
7f winner Treasury Devil (by Bernardini) and 2-y-o 6f winner Crystany (by Green Desert),
both useful: dam, 2-y-o 7f/1m (Fillies' Mile) winner and second in 1000 Guineas, closely
related to smart performer up to 1¾m Dubai Success: 4/1, shaped as if in need of race when
fifth in maiden at Newmarket (6¼ lengths behind Tashweeq) in August: will improve.
Charlie Appleby

FIRST BOMBARDMENT 2 br.g. (Apr 26) Pastoral Pursuits 127 – Magic Myth (IRE) **84**
81 (Revoque (IRE) 122) [2015 5d² 5v² 5g³ 5m⁴ 5d⁵ 5g⁴ 5m³ 5.4s⁴ t6f⁴ 5.1d² Nov 4]
£18,000Y: seventh foal: half-brother to 7f/7.5f winner Breakable (by Firebreak) and a
winner abroad by Monsieur Bond: dam, unreliable 2-y-o 5f/6f winner, half-sister to smart
5f winner Flanders (dam of very smart sprinter G Force) and to dam of high-class performer
up to 7f Lethal Force: fairly useful maiden: best effort when second in minor event at
Doncaster in March on debut: best form at 5f: acts on good to firm and heavy going: tried
in hood. *David O'Meara*

FIRST COMMANDMENT 4 b.g. Major Cadeaux 121 – Golden Nun 108 (Bishop of **–**
Cashel 122) [2015 –: f6d t8.6f Feb 23] no form: often wears headgear. *Les Eyre*

FIRST DREAM (IRE) 3 b.g. Oasis Dream 129 – First 103 (Highest Honor (FR) 124) **93**
[2015 –: p6m⁵ f7d³ p8g* p8g* p10g 10.3m² 8.5g* 8m⁴ 9s 8.3g* Sep 30] good-topped
gelding: fairly useful handicapper: won at Chelmsford in February and April, Epsom in
July and Nottingham (by 1½ lengths from La Superba) in September: stays 10.5f: acts on
polytrack, best turf form on good going: often in headgear in 2015: often travels strongly:
sold 35,000 gns, sent to Saudi Arabia. *Roger Varian*

FIRST EXCEL 3 ch.g. First Trump 118 – Exceedingly Good (IRE) 71 (Exceed And Excel **56**
(AUS) 126) [2015 5m⁵ 6m⁶ 6m⁶ Jul 9] modest maiden: best effort when fifth in maiden at
Thirsk in May on debut, very slowly away. *Roy Bowring*

FIRST EXPERIENCE 4 b.f. Tamayuz 126 – Lolla's Spirit (IRE) 68 (Montjeu (IRE) **81**
137) [2015 84: p7m⁵ p7m⁴ p8g² p8g³ 8.3m⁵ 7d² p7g³ p8g⁴ p7g⁴ p6m p8g Dec 16] fairly
useful handicapper: second at Brighton and third at Kempton in August: left Rae Guest
after eighth start: stays 1m: acts on polytrack, tapeta, good to firm and good to soft going:
tried in headgear prior to 2015. *Lee Carter*

FIRST FLIGHT (IRE) 4 b.g. Invincible Spirit (IRE) 121 – First of Many 83 (Darshaan **111**
133) [2015 109: 10.4g³ 10f 10.4m Jul 11] attractive gelding: smart handicapper: best effort
when third at York (¾ length behind Mahsoob) in May: in cheekpieces, well held latter start:
stays 10.5f: acts on firm and soft going: usually races towards rear. *Saeed bin Suroor*

FIRST MOHICAN 7 ch.g. Tobougg (IRE) 125 – Mohican Girl 112 (Dancing Brave (USA) **111**
140) [2015 114: p12f² 12d⁵ 12s² 12g 12v t13.9g* Dec 5] smallish, well-made gelding:
smart handicapper: won at Wolverhampton (by neck from Ballynanty) in December: best
other efforts of 2015 when second at Lingfield and Goodwood: stays 1¾m: acts on
polytrack, tapeta, good to firm and heavy going: wears headgear: often races towards rear.
Alan King

FIRST PARTY 2 gr.f. (Apr 17) Royal Applause 124 – Third Party 63 (Terimon 124) [2015 **73**
5.1m* 6f 5g³ 6g⁶ 5.1v⁶ t6m⁵ t8.6f Nov 30] 20,000F, 37,000 2-y-o: neat filly: sister to 2-y-o
6f winner Nardin and half-sister to several winners, including smart winner up to 8.6f
Party Boss (2-y-o 7f winner, by Silver Patriarch) and useful winner up to 2m/high-class

hurdler Countrywide Flame (2-y-o 1m winner, by Haafhd): dam 6f winner: fair performer: won maiden at Nottingham in May: best effort at 5f: acts on good to firm going: often starts slowly, often races towards rear. *Mark Johnston*

FIRST RATE 2 b.c. (Apr 13) Kyllachy 129 – Hooray 121 (Invincible Spirit (IRE) 121) **80 p** [2015 6d 5g^3 Oct 18] first foal: dam 6f (at 2 yrs, including Lowther and Cheveley Park Stakes) and 7f winner: much better effort when third in maiden at Bath (2 lengths behind Pine Ridge, fading late on) in October: open to further improvement. *Roger Varian*

FIRST REBELLION 6 ch.g. Cockney Rebel (IRE) 127 – First Dawn 68 (Dr Fong (USA) **53** 128) [2015 63: p5f t5.1m* t5.1m^3 t5.1f^5 t5.1g 5.1m 5.1m 5.1m 7.1m^6 7g^4 t6m t6m^3 p5g^2 t6f **a60** t7.1m^3 t6m^4 Dec 30] lengthy gelding: modest handicapper: won at Wolverhampton in February: stays 7f: acts on polytrack, tapeta, good to firm and heavy going: sometimes wears headgear: usually races close up. *Tony Carroll*

FIRST SARGEANT 5 gr.g. Dutch Art 126 – Princess Raya 58 (Act One 124) [2015 67§: **77** 10.3d^2 9.1s 10m* 10s* 10.3g^3 9.2g* 12g^6 10g^6 10.4s 10d Oct 19] close-coupled gelding: fair handicapper: won at Wetherby (apprentice) and Redcar in July and Hamilton in August: stays 1½m: acts on any turf going: often wears headgear: often starts slowly: quirky. *Lawrence Mullaney*

FIRST SELECTION (SPA) 2 b.c. (Feb 11) Diktat 126 – Villa Sonata 77 (Mozart (IRE) **112** 131) [2015 f5g* 5m* 6f 7f* 7.1m* 8m^5 Oct 4] €23,000Y, £42,000 2-y-o: close-coupled colt: sixth foal: half-brother to 3 winners abroad, including French/Spanish winner up to 9.5f Tout A Coeur (2-y-o 5f winner, by Silent Times): dam, 1¼m winner, half-sister to useful performer up to 1½m Ceilidh House: smart performer: won maiden at Southwell (by 2½ lengths from Mistymoistymorning) in April, minor event at Beverley (by 1¼ lengths from Lathom) in May, nursery at Newmarket (by short head from Spongy) in July and Solario Stakes at Sandown (by ½ length from Manaafidh) in August: improved again when 1½ lengths fifth of 11 to Ultra in Jean-Luc Lagardere at Longchamp final start: stays 1m: acts on fibresand and firm going: often leads. *Simon Crisford*

FIRST SITTING 4 b.g. Dansili 127 – Aspiring Diva (USA) (Distant View (USA) 126) **106** [2015 84: 8s^2 9.2d* 8.9g^2 12m 10d^6 12.1d 10g* 10.2v^3 Oct 7] useful handicapper: won at Hamilton (by 2¼ lengths from Sakhalin Star) in June and Ayr (by 6 lengths from Gworn) in September: third at Nottingham (¾ length behind Ready) in October: stays 1¼m: acts on heavy going. *David O'Meara*

FIRST SUMMER 3 b.g. Cockney Rebel (IRE) 127 – Silken Dalliance 91 (Rambo Dancer **53** (CAN) 107) [2015 61: p8g Sep 9] modest maiden: may prove best at 1m: acts on polytrack and tapeta: tried in cheekpieces prior to 2015. *Shaun Harris*

FIRST TO POST (IRE) 2 b.g. (Feb 22) Acclamation 118 – Aoife Alainn (IRE) 117 (Dr **78** Fong (USA) 128) [2015 5m^2 5s^5 5.9g* 6g 6g t5.1f Oct 16] fair performer: won maiden at Carlisle in August: stays 6f: acts on good to firm going: sold 5,000 gns, sent to Qatar. *Richard Fahey*

FIRST VICTORY (IRE) 2 b.f. (Mar 7) Teofilo (IRE) 126 – Eastern Joy (Dubai Destination **105 p** (USA) 127) [2015 7g* 7g* Oct 9] angular filly: third foal: half-sister to winner up to 9.5f Ihtimal (2-y-o 7f/1m winner, by Shamardal) and winner up to 8.6f Always Smile (2-y-o 6f winner, by Cape Cross), both smart: dam, French 9f winner, half-sister to Prix de Diane winner West Wind: won 11-runner maiden at Newmarket in September by ½ length from Wholesome: 9/2, useful form when following up in 12-runner Oh So Sharp Stakes at Newmarket in October by length from Alamode, keeping on well: will stay at least 1m: open to further progress. *Saeed bin Suroor*

FIRST WHEAT 2 b.g. (Apr 10) Monsieur Bond (IRE) 120 – Ballet Fame (USA) 79 **70 p** (Quest For Fame 127) [2015 6s^3 6d^4 Oct 26] seventh foal: half-brother to 6f winner Slingsby (by Dutch Art) and 8.6f winner Fame Again (by Gentleman's Deal): dam 2-y-o 7f winner: better effort when third in maiden at Redcar (3½ lengths behind Explosive Power) in October, nearest finish: remains with potential. *Michael Easterby*

FISHER 6 br.g. Jeremy (USA) 122 – Elfin Laughter 76 (Alzao (USA) 117) [2015 69: p12g **63** 16m^5 Apr 6] modest handicapper: stays 12.5f: acts on soft and good to firm going: in cheekpieces first start in 2015: tried in tongue tie. *John Quinn*

FISHERGATE 2 b.g. (May 4) Pastoral Pursuits 127 – Miss Meggy 97 (Pivotal 124) [2015 **79** 5s^2 5v^2 6g* 6g t7.1m Dec 18] fair performer: won maiden at Ripon in June: left Richard Fahey after fourth start: stays 6f: acts on heavy going. *Richard Rowe*

FIT (IRE) 2 b.f. (Jan 20) Kodiac 112 – Greenflash 80 (Green Desert (USA) 127) [2015 5m^6 **47** 5g^6 5.7f Jun 24] €12,000F: first foal: dam 7f winner: poor maiden: best effort when sixth in maiden at Bath (4¾ lengths behind Princess Kodia) in June on second start. *Richard Hannon*

FIT THE BILL (IRE) 3 b.c. Iffraaj 127 – Najam 75 (Singspiel (IRE) 133) [2015 53: **90**
p11g² t9.5g* p12f* 11.6f² p11g² 10g* t9.5g 10m⁵ p10g⁶ 10g⁶ p12g³ p10m* Dec 16]
lengthy colt: fairly useful handicapper: won at Wolverhampton and Lingfield in April,
Redcar in June and Lingfield (by 1¼ lengths from Sheila's Buddy) in December: stays
1½m: acts on polytrack, tapeta and firm going: temperament under suspicion. *James Tate*

FITZWILLIAM 3 ch.g. Sixties Icon 125 – Canadian Capers 70 (Ballacashtal (CAN)) **66**
[2015 –: p8m p8g⁴ t12.2g⁵ 11.6m⁶ 9.9m p11g⁵ 9.9s³ t16.5f p10m Nov 14] fair maiden:
probably stays 11f: acts on polytrack and soft going. *Mick Channon*

FITZWILLY 5 b.g. Sixties Icon 125 – Canadian Capers 70 (Ballacashtal (CAN)) [2015 **83**
80: 14m⁴ 16g* 16m 14.1m⁴ 16g⁴ 16.1m⁴ 16s⁴ 17.2f³ 14.1g* 16d⁵ Oct 11] workmanlike
gelding: fairly useful handicapper: won at Goodwood in May and Salisbury (by 2¼ lengths
from Bold Runner) in September: stays 17f: acts on any turf going. *Mick Channon*

FIX UP LOOK SHARP 4 b.c. Sakhee (USA) 136 – Featherlight 78 (Fantastic Light **62**
(USA) 134) [2015 12v⁵ p10f Sep 24] better effort when fifth in maiden at Newbury in
August. *Jamie Poulton*

FLAG OF GLORY 8 b.g. Trade Fair 124 – Rainbow Sky 79 (Rainbow Quest (USA) 134) **69**
[2015 70: 12g 11.9d 9.9s⁶ 9.9g⁵ 10.2d² 10.2d* 9.9v* 10.9g 10.2s⁴ 10.4d 10.2v⁶ 12v Oct 24]
compact gelding: fair handicapper: won amateur events at Chepstow and Brighton in
August: stays 1¼m: acts on polytrack, good to firm and heavy going: tried in headgear.
Peter Hiatt

FLAG WAR (GER) 4 ch.g. Dubawi (IRE) 129 – Fantastic Flame (IRE) 79 (Generous **103**
(IRE) 139) [2015 99: t8.6g* 10s⁴ p10g* 10m Aug 22] lengthy gelding: useful handicapper:
successful at Wolverhampton in April and Chelmsford in June: stays 1½m: acts on polytrack/tapeta, best turf form on soft/heavy going: in cheekpieces last
2 starts. *Saeed bin Suroor*

FLAMBEUSE 4 b.f. Cape Cross (IRE) 129 – Flamenba (USA) (Kingmambo (USA) 125) **82**
[2015 p13.4g⁵ p13.4g² 12.9g⁶ 11.9g* 12g p12.4g² p9.4g⁵ Dec 12] fourth foal: half-sister to
3 winners in France, including 1¼m/11f winner Falcolina (by Falco) and 1½m winner
Flamenko (by Green Tune): dam French 1½m winner: fairly useful handicapper: won at
Chantilly in July: second at Deauville in October: stays 1½m: acts on polytrack and good
to soft going. *Harry Dunlop*

FLAMBOROUGH BREEZE 6 ro.m. Ad Valorem (USA) 125 – Lothian Lass (IRE) 67 **64 §**
(Daylami (IRE) 138) [2015 68, a77: p8g² p8f p7f³ p8g⁶ p8g Jun 24] workmanlike mare:
modest handicapper: stays 1m: acts on polytrack and good to firm going: usually in
headgear/tongue tie: often races freely: one to treat with caution. *Ed Vaughan*

FLAMING FYNN 2 ch.g. (Jan 29) Paco Boy (IRE) 129 – La Polka 69 (Carnival Dancer –
123) [2015 5f 7g 8.1s² p8g t9.5f Dec 11] no form: tried in tongue tie. *Mark Gillard*

FLAMING SPEAR (IRE) 3 ch.g. Lope de Vega (IRE) 125 – Elshamms 107 (Zafonic **100**
(USA) 130) [2015 99P: 7m 8g p10f⁵ Oct 8] useful form: eleventh in Poule d'Essai des
Poulains at Longchamp (7½ lengths behind Make Believe) on second outing: off 5 months,
6¾ lengths fifth to Fire Fighting in minor event at Chelmsford final start: stays 1¼m: has
been gelded. *Kevin Ryan*

FLAMME FANTASTIQUE (GER) 3 b.f. Nayef (USA) 129 – Flames To Dust (GER) **63**
(Oasis Dream 120) [2015 . p10g³ 11.8g³ May 18] fair maiden: best effort at 1¼m: in
blinkers last start in 2015. *William Haggas*

FLANDERS FLAME 2 ch.g. (Mar 17) Dutch Art 126 – Pink Flames (IRE) (Redback **56**
116) [2015 6.1g 6g⁶ 7g 7.1m⁴ 7.2g⁴ Sep 29] modest maiden: stays 7f: acts on tapeta, raced
only on good going on turf: visored last 2 starts: sometimes slowly away, often races
towards rear: sold 2,000 gns, sent to Portugal. *Richard Fahey*

FLASH CITY (ITY) 7 b.g. Elusive City (USA) 117 – Furnish 87 (Green Desert (USA) **83**
127) [2015 86, a66: 5v⁵ 5m 5m⁵ 5m⁶ 5g⁴ 5g² 5d* 5g 5m 5m² 5d⁴ 5d 5g³ 5.1g³ t5.1f³ 5g⁵
Oct 13] strong gelding: fairly useful handicapper: won at Hamilton (by 1¼ lengths from
Rothesay Chancer) in June: best form at 5f: acts on fibresand, firm and soft going: often
wears headgear: tried in tongue tie prior to 2015. *Ruth Carr*

FLASH CRASH 6 b.g. Val Royal (FR) 127 – Tessara (GER) 103 (Big Shuffle (USA) 122) –
[2015 84: f14d⁴ May 18] fairly useful at best, well held sole start in 2015: stays 16.5f: acts
on polytrack, fibresand, best turf form on good going: tried in cheekpieces: sometimes in
tongue tie prior to 2015. *Jim Best*

FLASH FIRE (IRE) 3 b.c. Shamardal (USA) 129 – Flamelet (USA) 94 (Theatrical (IRE) **108**
128) [2015 93: 7.1m 7.1m* 7m 7m² 7.6m Aug 22] useful-looking colt: useful handicapper:
won at Sandown (by 6 lengths from Harbour Patrol) in July: second at Newmarket (neck
behind Buckstay) in August: stays 7f: acts on good to firm going: front runner/races
prominently. *Charlie Appleby*

FLASHMAN 6 ch.g. Doyen (IRE) 132 – Si Si Si (Lomitas 129) [2015 84: p13.3g* p16m* **95**
p16g⁴ p16f² Nov 23] good-topped gelding: useful handicapper: won at Chelmsford in
January and February: better form when second at Chelmsford (short head behind Duchess
of Marmite) in November: stays 16.5f: acts on polytrack, best turf form on good going or
firmer (acts on firm): tried in headgear: front runner/races prominently, often travels
strongly. *Gary Moore*

FLASH N SMART 2 b.f. (Mar 15) Sakhee's Secret 128 – Lady Trish (Red Ransom **45**
(USA)) [2015 5m⁶ 6.1m 7.4g 8.1s⁶ 8.1m⁵ t8.6f⁵ Nov 16] second foal: dam of little account:
poor maiden: stays 1m: acts on tapeta and good to firm going. *Nikki Evans*

FLASHY DIVA 3 ch.f. Showcasing 117 – Dazzling View (USA) (Distant View (USA) **69**
126) [2015 80: 6m 5g⁵ 6g p6g⁶ p6g 6m⁴ p7g² 6g⁶ t7.1f t6f Oct 16] smallish, close-coupled
filly: fair handicapper: stays 7f: acts on polytrack, tapeta and good to firm going: often
races towards rear. *Henry Candy*

FLASHY MEMORIES 3 ch.g. Dubawi (IRE) 129 – Flashy Wings 115 (Zafonic (USA) **93**
130) [2015 82p: p8g² 8m⁴ 8g⁴ 9m⁶ 10.2g⁴ 8.3m* 9g Sep 25] leggy, narrow gelding: fairly
useful handicapper: won at Leicester in August: stays 1¼m: acts on polytrack, good to firm
and good to soft going: in cheekpieces last 2 starts: sold 38,000 gns, sent to Saudi Arabia.
Richard Fahey

FLASHY QUEEN (IRE) 4 ch.f. Bahamian Bounty 116 – Somersault 69 (Pivotal 124) **85**
[2015 83: p6g⁴ 5m p5g 5g 6s³ 5.1g* 5s 5.1d Nov 4] sturdy, close-coupled filly: fairly
useful handicapper: won at Nottingham (by neck from Burning Thread) in September:
stays 6f: acts on polytrack and soft going: tried in cheekpieces in 2015: front runner/races
prominently. *Joseph Tuite*

FLASHY STAR 6 ch.m. Mr Greeley (USA) 122 – Galileo's Star (IRE) 101 (Galileo (IRE) **47**
134) [2015 49: p12f p16m⁵ t16.5m Mar 10] leggy mare: poor maiden: stays 2m: acts on
polytrack, firm and good to soft going: often wears headgear. *Paul Henderson*

FLAWLESS FILLY (IRE) 5 gr.m. Clodovil (IRE) 116 – Min Asl Wafi (IRE) 75 (Octagonal **–**
(NZ) 126) [2015 10s 9g Jul 13] fairly useful at best, no form in 2015: stays 1¼m: acts on
good to firm and good to soft going: usually in headgear prior to 2015: in tongue tie in 2015.
Rose Dobbin

FLECKERL (IRE) 5 b.g. Danehill Dancer (IRE) 117 – Spinola (FR) 103 (Spinning World **85**
(USA) 130) [2015 85: 7d⁴ 7m⁴ 7.6d 7m⁶ p7g 8.3m⁴ 7.6g* 8.3m* 8.1m* p8d⁴ p8g⁶ 8.3d⁵
t8.6f⁵ t8.6m² p8g⁵ p10g Dec 20] lengthy gelding: fairly useful handicapper: won at Lingfield
(apprentice), Windsor and Sandown in August: second in claimer at Wolverhampton in
November, then left William Muir: stays 8.5f: acts on polytrack, tapeta, good to firm and
good to soft going: tried in headgear in 2015. *Conor Dore*

FLEDERMAUS (IRE) 5 br.g. Jeremy (USA) 122 – Khayrat (IRE) (Polar Falcon (USA) **–**
126) [2015 8g⁴ 9.2d 10.2m 10.3d Oct 23] no form: in tongue tie. *Tina Jackson*

FLEETING DREAM (IRE) 2 b.f. (Apr 16) Dream Ahead (USA) 133 – Flanders (IRE) **– p**
110 (Common Grounds 118) [2015 6g Oct 20] 400,000Y: half-sister to numerous winners,
including high-class 5f/6f (Sprint Cup) winner G Force (by Tamayuz) and smart 1m-1¼m
winner Laajooj (by Azamour): dam 5f winner (including at 2 yrs): 5/1, eleventh in maiden
at Windsor (8¾ lengths behind Exist) in October, not knocked about: better to come.
William Haggas

FLEETING INDIAN (IRE) 6 b.g. Sleeping Indian 122 – Glebe Garden 86 (Soviet Star **49**
(USA) 128) [2015 54: p7m p6f p6f⁴ p5m⁵ p5g³ t5.1f 7g⁶ 6g³ p5g⁵ 8d⁶ Jun 23] poor maiden:
stays 7f: acts on polytrack and good to firm going: often wears headgear: tried in tongue tie
prior to 2015: usually races nearer last than first. *Linda Jewell*

FLEETING STRIKE 3 b.c. Acclamation 118 – Cursory (Hurricane Run (IRE) 134) **82**
[2015 p7g⁴ 7d² 6.1g⁴ 7m² 6m⁵ Jun 27] 92,000F: first foal: dam unraced daughter of May
Hill Stakes winner Half Glance: fairly useful maiden: second in handicap at Newbury in
June: best effort at 7f: acts on good to firm going. *Richard Hannon*

FLEETING VISIT 2 b.g. (Mar 19) Manduro (GER) 135 – Short Affair 99 (Singspiel **90**
(IRE) 133) [2015 7.1m³ 8.1g* 8d² 8s⁵ Sep 18] 12,000Y: second foal: half-brother to Italian
9f winner Romp (by Pivotal): dam, winner up to 10.3f (2-y-o 7.5f winner in Italy), half-

sister to useful/ungenuine 1½m-1¾m winner Great Hall: fairly useful performer: won maiden at Chepstow in August: good second in minor event at Ripon later in month: will be suited by 1¼m+. *Eve Johnson Houghton*

FLEETWOOD BELLA 4 ch.f. Byron 117 – Royal Ivy 71 (Mujtahid (USA) 118) [2015 –: p8g p8g⁶ Dec 28] no form. *Michael Attwater* —

FLEETWOOD NIX 5 b.m. Acclamation 118 – Antediluvian 106 (Air Express (IRE) 125) [2015 –: p15.8f Jan 30] no form. *Pat Phelan* —

FLEETWOOD POPPY 3 br.f. Kheleyf (USA) 116 – Steppin Out 63 (First Trump 118) [2015 55: p7f⁴ p8f p7m p8f p8g p12g⁵ p11g p12g² p12g⁶ p12f p12g⁶ Dec 19] smallish filly: modest maiden: stays 1½m: acts on polytrack. *Michael Attwater* **54**

FLEMISH SCHOOL 5 ch.m. Dutch Art 126 – Rosewood Belle (USA) 70 (Woodman (USA) 126) [2015 99: p11g 16g p13.3m⁵ May 19] leggy mare: fair handicapper: stays 16.5f: acts on polytrack, good to firm and good to soft going: usually wears headgear. *K. R. Burke* **77**

FLEUR DES MERS 4 ch.f. Mount Nelson 125 – Fidelio's Miracle (USA) 108 (Mountain Cat (USA)) [2015 t7.1f³ p8g f8d⁶ Jan 22] seventh foal: sister to smart 6f (including at 2 yrs)/7f winner Ninjago and half-sister to 6f winner Florestans Match (by Medicean): dam French 7.5f-1¼m winner (2-y-o 9f winner): fair maiden: trained in France at 3 yrs: stays 7.5f: acts on synthetics, best turf form on good going: often wears headgear. *Richard Fahey* **67**

FLEURTILLE 6 b.m. Tillerman 123 – Miss Fleurie 50 (Alzao (USA) 117) [2015 81: 5m² 5.5g 6s 6m 7d Sep 15] fair handicapper: left Kenny Johnson after fourth start: stays 7f: acts on good to firm and heavy going: often races towards rear. *Ray Craggs* **79**

FLEXIBLE FLYER 6 b.g. Exceed And Excel (AUS) 126 – Windermere Island 81 (Cadeaux Genereux 131) [2015 83: p6f² p6m t7.1g⁴ 6m² 6g* 6v² 6g* p6g 6d 5.2m² 6.1g Sep 30] lengthy gelding: fairly useful handicapper: won at Brighton in May and Haydock (by 1½ lengths from Mukaynis) in July: second at Yarmouth in September: stays 7f: acts on soft and good to firm going: often wears headgear: tried in tongue tie prior to 2015. *Chris Dwyer* **90** **a80**

FLICKA'S BOY 3 b.g. Paco Boy (IRE) 129 – Selkirk Sky 65 (Selkirk (USA) 129) [2015 75: 5.1m* 5g³ 5m⁴ 5m² 5g³ 5.4m 5m⁵ 5g⁴ 5s Sep 5] strong gelding: fairly useful handicapper: won at Nottingham (by ½ length from Foxtrot Knight) in April: second at Musselburgh and third at Redcar in June: best form at 5f: acts on good to firm going: tried in cheekpieces in 2015. *Tony Coyle* **83**

FLIGHT FIGHT 4 b.g. Raven's Pass (USA) 133 – Sunspear (IRE) (Montjeu (IRE) 137) [2015 65: p10g 9.9d Aug 5] good-topped gelding: maiden: no form in 2015: raced only at 1¼m: sometimes slowly away. *Chris Wall* —

FLIGHTY CLARETS (IRE) 5 ch.m. Bahamian Bounty 116 – Flying Clarets (IRE) 115 (Titus Livius (FR) 115) [2015 73, a67: t6g² p6g p6f² Jan 31] fair handicapper: stays 6f: acts on polytrack, tapeta, best turf form on good going: often in headgear in 2015: often races freely. *Richard Fahey* **71**

FLIGHTY FILIA (IRE) 3 gr.f. Raven's Pass (USA) 133 – Coventina (IRE) 108 (Daylami (IRE) 138) [2015 71p: 12s⁴ p12f p13.3f³ p16g² p15.8g² Dec 20] good-topped filly: fair maiden: stays 2m: acts on polytrack. *Amanda Perrett* **76**

FLINTSHIRE 5 b.h. Dansili 127 – Dance Routine 116 (Sadler's Wells (USA) 132) [2015 128. p9.4g² 12g² 12m³ 11.9m² 12f* 11.9m² 11.9g² Dec 13] **178**

'First is first, second is nowhere.' What would Bill Shankly, the highly successful Liverpool football manager of the 'sixties and early-'seventies, have made of Flintshire? The three largest purses won by this most consistent five-year-old have come from being runner-up in the Dubai Sheema Classic (£810,811) and in successive editions of the Prix de l'Arc de Triomphe (£892,969 and £840,441). Those three prizes alone account for just over half of all the prize money won by Flintshire, whose total earnings (converted at exchange rates prevailing at the time of each race) now stand at £4,887,562, taking him past Workforce, Frankel and Cityscape to make him the highest-earning horse ever to carry the green, pink sash and cap, white sleeves of one of the world's leading owner-breeders Khalid Abdullah. Flintshire's huge prize-money earnings may have been built on efforts in races that he lost but, as Khalid Abdullah's racing manager said, after Flintshire picked up another £309,992 for second in the Hong Kong Vase on his final outing in the latest season, 'We're disappointed to be beaten but can't complain.'

Sword Dancer Invitational Stakes, Saratoga—
Flintshire gains a deserved third success at the top level in this US Grade 1 turf contest

It is perhaps understandable that Flintshire's 'seconditis'—he has been runner-up in nine of his thirteen races over the past two seasons—should have become such a talking point. However, all except two of the races he has contested in that time have been Grade 1s and his string of good efforts includes two successes at the highest level, one in each of those campaigns—the Hong Kong Vase (£762,769) in 2014 and the Sword Dancer Invitational at Saratoga (£340,764) in the latest season. Flintshire won three of his six races as a three-year-old, his only other season to race, including the Grand Prix de Paris (£295,552). The latest season was Flintshire's most lucrative so far and the first of his four six-figure paydays came in the Dubai Sheema Classic at Meydan in March. Fellow French challenger Dolniya (fifth in the 2014 Arc) had pipped odds-on Flintshire in a warm-up in a minor event on the all-weather at Chantilly earlier in the month and Flintshire again found her a thorn in his side on the big day, going down by two and a quarter lengths after Dolniya stole a march on her opponents when sent for home in earnest over a furlong out. Flintshire wasn't quite at his peak in the first part of the season and he also finished a place behind Dolniya at Epsom in a muddling Coronation Cup, in which both were surprisingly beaten by Pether's Moon. Flintshire finally got the better of Dolniya when they met for a fourth time in the latest season, Flintshire returning to his very best in the Grand Prix de Saint-Cloud in which he found only the dual Prix de l'Arc winner Treve too good for him on the day, running her to a length and a quarter and finishing a little closer than he had at Longchamp the previous October. Sent across the Atlantic for the Sword Dancer Invitational at the end of August, Flintshire continued in good form. He was the only horse in the line-up running without the permitted raceday medication furosemide when justifying short-priced favouritism with a convincing victory from the home-trained pair Red Rifle and the consistent Twilight Eclipse, neither of whom could make any impression on Flintshire after he quickened into the lead over two furlongs out.

Flintshire was sent to Saratoga after missing Britain's midsummer middle-distance championship, the King George VI and Queen Elizabeth Stakes at Ascot in July, for the second year running, a late absentee when the going turned soft after a torrential downpour the day before (he had been an eleventh-hour withdrawal from the 2014 King George with a high temperature). Fortune has smiled more kindly on Flintshire in France's counterpart the Prix de l'Arc de Triomphe, Europe's richest race, in which, for the second time, he encountered his optimum conditions (it had been clear since his three-year-old days—when he came eighth in a soft-ground Arc—that Flintshire needed good going or firmer to show his best). Flintshire was no match at Longchamp for the Derby winner Golden Horn, who beat him by two lengths (the same margin by which he had lost to Treve twelve months earlier), but Flintshire ran right up to form, keeping on well to hold on to second from his better-backed stablemate the Prix du Jockey Club winner New Bay and the odds-on favourite Treve. There was no Breeders' Cup challenge for Flintshire this time—he had earned £335,404 for finishing second in the 2014 Breeders' Cup Turf—and he was prepared especially for an attempt to repeat the previous year's victory in the Hong Kong Vase. He had been considered for the Japan Cup beforehand which had been the reason for his missing the Breeders' Cup as the Japanese quarantine rules precluded him from contesting both races. Flintshire was sent off 6/4 favourite in a strong field at Sha Tin but, as so often, found one just too good for him in the Irish-trained Prix du Jockey Club runner-up Highland Reel who beat him by a length and a half, Flintshire leading over a furlong out and keeping on well. It was announced afterwards that Flintshire remains in training as a six-year-old. British racegoers haven't quite seen the best of him on either of his appearances so far, both of them in the Coronation Cup. It must be hoped that he finally gets a chance to show his paces in 'Britain's Arc', the King George VI and Queen Elizabeth Stakes. A top-form Flintshire would be an asset in the field for that race, as for any race. He must be a pleasure to own.

The pedigree of the close-coupled, good-topped Flintshire has been covered fully in previous editions of this Annual. He is a Juddmonte home bred through and through, both his excellent sire Dansili and his dam Dance Routine running in the Abdullah colours for Flintshire's trainer. Dansili has been one of the stallion success stories of recent times, starting his stud career in 2001 at a fee of just £8,000 and standing at £85,000 for 2016, along with Galileo and Pivotal, he is one of only three active stallions who have sired the winners of more than a hundred European pattern races. Dance Routine, who was runner-up in the Prix de Diane, has bred four winners so far, the best of the others being Flintshire's year-older brother Dance Moves, a smart stayer who finished a close third in the Prix Kergorlay. Flintshire stays a mile and a half and needs good going or firmer to be fully effective. He has a good turn of foot and is a high-class performer under his favoured conditions. *A. Fabre, France*

FLIPPING 8 br.g. Kheleyf (USA) 116 – Felona 92 (Caerleon (USA) 132) [2015 68: 8.3m⁶ **66** 8d⁵ 8m 9s⁶ 7.1s⁶ Aug 31] angular gelding: fair handicapper: stays 9f: acts on tapeta, good to firm and heavy going: tried in headgear. *Stuart Kittow*

FLORENCIO 2 b.c. (May 6) Equiano (FR) 127 – Mary Pekan (IRE) 97 (Sri Pekan (USA) **89** 117) [2015 5d⁴ 5f² 5.3s* 5.5s⁵ p6f* Oct 15] 10,000Y: sixth foal: half-brother to 3 winners in Italy, including 2-y-o 6f-1m winner Mantissa (by Oratorio) and winner up to 11f Mandadrera (2-y-o 9f/1¼m winner, by Duke of Marmalade): dam, Italian winner up to 9f

(7.5f winner at 2 yrs), half-sister to smart Italian 1¼m-1½m winner Wild Wolf: fairly useful performer: won maiden at Brighton in August and nursery at Chelmsford (by nose from Hope Cove) in October: stays 6f: acts on polytrack and soft going. *William Muir*

FLORENZA 2 b.f. (Apr 25) Haafhd 129 – Danzatrice 76 (Tamure (IRE) 125) [2015 6d⁴ 6m³ Jun 26] second foal: dam 13f-2m winner: better effort when third in maiden at Doncaster (2½ lengths behind Alsaaden) in June: will be suited by 7f+. *Chris Fairhurst* **67**

FLORIANE (IRE) 3 b.f. Arcano (IRE) 122 – Kay Es Jay (FR) 99 (Xaar 132) [2015 p10f⁵ Sep 3] €34,000Y: second foal: half-sister to 2-y-o 1m/8.6f winner Act of Charity (by Royal Applause): dam, 2-y-o 7f winner, later 6f winner in USA: 14/1, promise when fifth in maiden at Chelmsford (5½ lengths behind Allumage) in September, still going well when denied a run over 1f out: sure to progress. *Marco Botti* **62 p**

FLORISS 3 b.f. Medicean 128 – Joshua's Princess 92 (Danehill (USA) 126) [2015 p7g⁵ 7m³ 8m⁵ 8m⁵ 7.1g* 7m Oct 3] fourth foal: half-sister to 3 winners, including useful 1m-10.3f winner Don't Stare (by Zamindar) and 1m winner Walk of Shame (by Muhtathir): dam 1m winner: useful performer: won maiden at Newmarket (by 2 lengths from Figment) in July and handicap at Sandown (by 5 lengths from Privileged) in September: stays 1m: acts on good to firm going. *James Fanshawe* **105**

FLOWER CUP 2 b.f. (Apr 14) Acclamation 118 – Amber Queen (IRE) 92 (Cadeaux Genereux 131) [2015 p7g³ Aug 24] 50,000Y: good-topped filly: fourth foal: half-sister to 9.3f/1¼m winner Diddy Eric (by Oratorio) and 2-y-o 5f winner (1½m) Mountain Rescue (by High Chaparral): dam, 7f winner, half-sister to Sun Chariot Stakes winner Spinning Queen: 12/1, tongue tied, green when third in maiden at Kempton (2 lengths behind City Chic) in August: will stay 1m: should do better. *Simon Crisford* **68 p**

FLOWERS ON VENUS (IRE) 3 ch.g. Raven's Pass (USA) 133 – Chelsea Rose (IRE) 121 (Desert King (IRE) 129) [2015 t6f* Dec 21] €220,000F, £12,500 3-y-o: fifth foal: half-brother to useful 6f/6f winner Pale Orchid (by Invincible Spirit) and smart French 6f-1m winner Thawaany (by Tamayuz): dam winner up to 1½m (2-y-o 7f winner, including Moyglare Stud Stakes): 6/4, looked useful prospect when winning maiden at Wolverhampton (by 3¼ lengths from Inshaa) in December, soon in front and quickening over 1f out: will stay 7f: sure to progress. *David Evans* **86 p**

FLOWING CLARETS 2 ch.f. (Feb 9) Pastoral Pursuits 127 – Flying Clarets (IRE) 115 (Titus Livius (FR) 115) [2015 6s* t6f⁶ Nov 14] £2,000Y: second foal: closely related to 6f (including at 2 yrs) winner Flighty Clarets (by Bahamian Bounty): dam 1m-11f winner: won 12-runner maiden at Leicester in October by 2½ lengths from Zippy: run best excused when sixth of 10 to Parkour in nursery at Wolverhampton, stumbling home turn. *Richard Fahey* **74**

FLOW (USA) 5 b.h. Medaglia d'Oro (USA) 129 – Enthused (USA) 109 (Seeking The Gold (USA)) [2015 101: p8m² 8d⁶ 9.8d⁶ 8m⁶ Jul 18] useful handicapper: best efforts of 2015 on first 2 starts (both in March), second to Ruban at Chelmsford and sixth to Chatez at Doncaster: stays 10.5f: acts on polytrack, tapeta, good to firm and good to soft going: usually wears tongue tie: sent to Saudi Arabia. *David Brown* **98**

FLUMMOXED 2 ch.g. (Feb 1) Monsieur Bond (IRE) 120 – Slightly Foxed (Royal Applause 124) [2015 6v t8.6f Oct 27] no form. *David O'Meara* **–**

FLUTTERBEE 3 b.f. Equiano (FR) 127 – Dunya (Unfuwain (USA) 131) [2015 7m p7g 9.9d p7m⁶ 7m* 8g³ 11.9d* 9.9v⁴ Oct 6] 25,000F, 50,000Y: rather leggy filly: fourth foal: half-sister to 2-y-o 5f winner Glas Burn (by Avonbridge), later successful in Greece, and useful winner up to 9f in Qatar Beach Club (2-y-o 6f winner, by Footstepsinthesand): dam unraced half-sister to smart Y winner up to 7f An Tadh: fair handicapper: won at Brighton in July and September: stays 1½m: acts on good to firm and good to soft going: often in cheekpieces. *George Baker* **68**

FLY 3 ch.f. Pastoral Pursuits 127 – Hannda (IRE) 74 (Dr Devious (IRE) 127) [2015 7v* p8g* p8m* Oct 21] half-sister to several winners, including smart 11f/1½m winner Seal of Approval (by Authorized) and useful 15.5f/2m winner Gale Force (by Shirocco): dam 1¼m winner: fairly useful performer: won maiden at Lingfield and handicap at Kempton in September and handicap at Kempton (best effort, readily by ¾ length from Lu's Buddy) in October: will stay 1¼m: will go on improving. *James Fanshawe* **88 p**

FLY ALONE 4 ch.f. Volochine (IRE) 121 – Solicitude 75 (Bertolini (USA) 125) [2015 t8.6g 10v⁶ 8v⁵ 6d p7m Oct 21] first foal: dam 7f winner (including at 2 yrs): no form: tried in cheekpieces. *John Flint* **–**

FLY

FLYBALL 3 gr.g. Proclamation (IRE) 130 – Bella Bertolini 67 (Bertolini (USA) 125) [2015 77: 5m 6d 6g 8g 8m⁴ Aug 8] well-made gelding: fair at best, no form in 2015: tried in cheekpieces in 2015. *Tony Coyle* — **–**

FLYBOY (IRE) 2 b.c. (May 2) Zoffany (IRE) 121 – In Dubai (USA) 91 (Giant's Causeway (USA) 132) [2015 8g³ Oct 13] €29,000Y, £52,000 2-y-o: fifth foal: half-brother to 1m winner (stayed 1½m) Hurricane In Dubai (by Hurricane Run) and useful 7f-9.5f winner Earth Drummer (by Dylan Thomas); dam, 2-y-o 1m winner, closely related/half-sister to smart performers up to 1¼m Sarrsar, Nahrain and Baharah: 10/1, badly in need of experience and shaped well when 3¼ lengths third of 9 to Nokhado in maiden at Musselburgh on debut, keeping on: will improve. *David O'Meara* — **82 p**

FLYING AUTHOR (IRE) 4 b.g. Authorized (IRE) 133 – Fly Free 97 (Halling (USA) 133) [2015 54: p10g² p10f³ p10f p10f p10g⁶ Apr 1] tall gelding: modest maiden: stays 1½m: acts on polytrack and fibresand: often wears headgear: often wears tongue tie: sometimes slowly away. *Phil McEntee* — **51**

FLYING BEAR (IRE) 4 b.g. Kodiac 112 – Marinebird (IRE) 66 (Bad As I Wanna Be (IRE) 115) [2015 87: p5f⁵ p5f* 5d⁴ 5g³ 5g⁵ 5.3d⁴ 5m p6g 5s p6f f5g p5g Dec 2] rather leggy gelding: fairly useful handicapper: won at Chelmsford in March and Lingfield (by nose from Waseem Faris) in May: stays 6f, races mostly at 5f: acts on polytrack and good to firm going: tried in headgear. *Jeremy Gask* — **76 a87**

FLYING BOND GIRL 2 b.f. (Mar 9) Monsieur Bond (IRE) 120 – Flying Visitor (Magic Ring (IRE) 115) [2015 6m 6s⁶ 6g p6m Oct 28] third foal: dam of little account: no form. *Ali Stronge* — **–**

FLYING EMPRESS 2 b.f. (Apr 22) Holy Roman Emperor (IRE) 125 – Fly Free 97 (Halling (USA) 133) [2015 6g* 7.1f⁴ 8g⁵ 7m* 7g⁴ 7v Oct 24] 9,000Y, £60,000 2-y-o: unfurnished filly: fourth foal: dam, 2-y-o 7f winner who stayed 10.7f, half-sister to winner up to 2m Illustrious Blue and 6f winner Mullein (both smart): fairly useful performer: won maiden at Windsor in June and 3-runner minor event at Salisbury (by ½ length from Shwaimsa) in September: creditable fourth of 7 to Promising Run in Rockfel Stakes at Newmarket later in September: stays 7f: acts on good to firm going: blinkered fourth/fifth starts, below form in visor final outing: often leads, often races freely: sent to Qatar. *Ralph Beckett* — **93**

FLYING FANTASY 3 b.g. Oasis Dream 129 – Disco Volante 105 (Sadler's Wells (USA) 132) [2015 75p: p8f³ 8m* 10m⁶ 8m⁴ 6g 7v 7d p8d p7f⁵ Dec 17] lengthy gelding: fair handicapper: won at Newmarket in May: left William Haggas after fourth start: stays 1m: acts on polytrack, good to firm and heavy going: sometimes in hood in 2015: often races towards rear. *Stuart Williams* — **78**

FLYING HAMMER 3 b.c. Acclamation 118 – Ruse 66 (Diktat 126) [2015 71p: 7.1d* p8g* 7m* Oct 22] useful form: won maiden at Chepstow, and handicaps at Kempton in August and Ascot (by head from Them And Us, value bit extra) in October: stays 1m: sent to Hong Kong: will go on improving. *William Haggas* — **102 p**

FLYING OFFICER (USA) 5 b.g. Dynaformer (USA) – Vignette (USA) 93 (Diesis 133) [2015 116: 14.1s* 16g* 16d* Oct 17] tall, lengthy gelding: very smart performer, winner of 6 of just 9 starts in 4 seasons: unbeaten in 3 races in 2015, namely minor event at Salisbury (by 4½ lengths from Melodious) and listed race at Newmarket (by 2 lengths from Angel Gabrial) in September and 13-runner Long Distance Cup at Ascot (better than ever when beating Clever Cookie a length, leading 2f out) in October: stays 2m: acts on soft and good to firm going: wears hood: usually travels strongly. *John Gosden* — **120**

Qipco British Champions Long Distance Cup, Ascot—Flying Officer makes it three from three in 2015 as he beats Clever Cookie (noseband) and Wicklow Brave

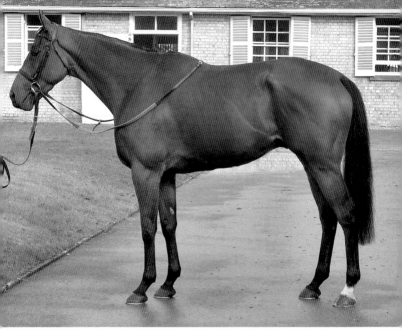

FLYING PHOENIX 7 b.m. Phoenix Reach (IRE) 124 – Rasmalai 71 (Sadler's Wells (USA) 132) [2015 t8.6m Apr 29] workmanlike mare: fair at best, well held sole start in 2015: stays 1¼m: acts on polytrack, soft and good to firm going: sometimes in headgear prior to 2015: temperamental. *Michael Blake* –

FLYING POWER 7 b.g. Dubai Destination (USA) 127 – Rah Wa (USA) (Rahy (USA) 115) [2015 87: t12.2f³ t12.2f³ t12.2g⁴ t13.9f² 12.4g² t12.2g² 11.8g 11.9m⁵ 12.1g⁶ t13.9m⁶ 12s⁵ t12.2f⁶ t12.2m⁵ t12.2m³ t12.2f³ Dec 22] stocky gelding: fairly useful handicapper: second at Wolverhampton in March and July: stays 2m: acts on polytrack, tapeta, good to firm and good to soft going: tried in headgear prior to 2015: usually leads. *John Norton* **80**

FLYING PURSUIT 2 ch.g. (Apr 6) Pastoral Pursuits 127 – Choisette 75 (Choisir (AUS) 126) [2015 5g 6d² 6g⁶ 6d² 6m⁴ 6g* 7g 6g² 6g⁶ 6v* Nov 7] £21,000Y: fourth foal: half-brother to 6f (including at 2 yrs) winner Straighttothepoint (by Kyllachy): dam, 5f winner (including at 2 yrs), half-sister to useful 6f winner Fast Shot: fairly useful performer: won maiden at Ripon in August and nursery at Doncaster (by neck from Cuppatee) in November: stays 6f: acts on heavy going: front runner/races prominently. *Tim Easterby* **88**

FLYMAN 5 b.g. Pastoral Pursuits 127 – Satin Bell 99 (Midyan (USA) 124) [2015 110: 6g 7d 6d⁶ 7f³ 6g* 6g 8g 6g⁴ 6d⁵ 6g Oct 16] leggy, quite attractive gelding: useful handicapper: won at Ripon (by ½ length from Snap Shots) in August: fourth at Ayr (2½ lengths behind Go Far) in September: stays 7f: acts on good to firm and good to soft going: usually wears headgear: front runner/races prominently. *David O'Meara* **97**

FLYWEIGHT (IRE) 2 b.f. (Mar 18) Teofilo (IRE) 126 – Morinqua (IRE) 99 (Cadeaux Genereux 131) [2015 7m p8f* Nov 12] €80,000F, 200,000Y: second foal: half-sister to useful French winner up to 1m Cornwallville (2-y-o 6f-1m winner, by Makfi): dam 5f winner (including at 2 yrs): off 5 months and in first-time tongue strap, progressed from debut when winning 10-runner maiden at Chelmsford in November by 1¾ lengths from Pirouette, edging ahead 2f out and asserting final ½f: will go on improving. *John Gosden* **79 p**

FLY

FLY WITH EMIRATES (IRE) 3 b.g. Lawman (FR) 121 – Keriyka (IRE) 70 (Indian **70**
Ridge 123) [2015 7g² 7g⁵ 7mʳʳ Jun 6] fair form: second of 11 to Mount Tahan in maiden at
Wetherby in April: refused to race final outing: sold £4,500. *Saeed bin Suroor*

FLY WITH ME (FR) 5 gr.h. Beat Hollow 126 – Bird of Paradise (FR) (Highest Honor **115**
(FR) 124) [2015 115: 15.4s* 15.4s² 14.9d* 15.4g⁵ 15.4sᴰ 15.4d Oct 25] smart performer:
first past post in 2015 in listed races at Saint-Cloud in April and Chantilly in June, and
Prix Gladiateur at Longchamp (beat Walzertakt a length, later disqualified for failing drugs
test) in September: second in Prix de Barbeville at Longchamp (3 lengths behind Alex
My Boy) on second outing: not discredited when tenth of 13 behind Vazirabad in Prix
Royal Oak at Longchamp final start: stays 15.4f: acts on polytrack and heavy going: wears
headgear. *E. Libaud, France*

FOCAIL MEAR 4 b.f. Oratorio (IRE) 128 – Glittering Image (IRE) (Sadler's Wells **53**
(USA) 132) [2015 53: p8g² p10f t8.6g* t8.6f t8.6mᵖᵘ Apr 29] modest handicapper: won at
Wolverhampton in March: stays 8.5f: acts on polytrack and tapeta. *John Ryan*

FOIE GRAS 5 b.g. Kyllachy 129 – Bint Zamayem (IRE) 95 (Rainbow Quest (USA) 134) **72**
[2015 73: p6g² t7.1g* t7.1f t6f² p6f³ f6g² p6g² p6d p6f p6g⁴ p6f Oct 28] good-topped
gelding: fair handicapper: won at Wolverhampton in January: stays 7f: acts on all-weather,
good to firm and good to soft going: tried in headgear prior to 2015: sometimes slowly
away, usually races nearer last than first. *Chris Dwyer*

FOLKSWOOD 2 b.c. (Mar 14) Exceed And Excel (AUS) 126 – Magic Nymph (IRE) **90 p**
(Galileo (IRE) 134) [2015 7m³ 7m* Aug 1] 160,000Y: rangy colt: first foal: dam unraced
sister to very smart 1¼m-1½m winner Galactic Star and smart stayer El Salvador out of
Coronation Stakes winner Balisada: fairly useful form both starts in maidens, winning at
Goodwood (by 1½ lengths from Bernie's Boy) in August: will stay 1m: remains open to
improvement. *Charlie Appleby*

FOLLOW THE FAITH 3 b.f. Piccolo 121 – Keeping The Faith (IRE) 88 (Ajraas (USA) **44**
88) [2015 69: 8.3m 9.9g p10g 8v⁶ Aug 24] poor handicapper: left Mick Channon after
second start: best effort at 1m: acts on polytrack, good to firm and heavy going: often in
tongue tie in 2015. *Simon Hodgson*

FOLLOW THE RULES 2 b.c. (Mar 14) Kheleyf (USA) 116 – It's The War (USA) **–**
(Consolidator (USA) 121) [2015 5.3s⁶ 6m Jun 25] no form in maidens: sent to UAE.
Giles Bravery

FOLLY BERGERE (IRE) 2 ch.f. (Feb 17) Champs Elysees 124 – Rainbow Queen (FR) **59 p**
88 (Spectrum (IRE) 126) [2015 7d³ Oct 31] seventh foal: half-sister to 7f winner Sir Isaac
(by Key of Luck) and useful 1¼m-1½m winner (stayed 2m) Quixote (by Singspiel): dam,
French/Belgian 6.5f-1m winner, half-sister to useful French/Canadian winner up to 8.5f
Stella Blue: 40/1, considerate introduction when third in maiden at Newmarket (9½ lengths
behind Tiptree) in October, running on late: better to come. *James Eustace*

FOL O'YASMINE 2 b.f. (Mar 5) Dubawi (IRE) 129 – Sewards Folly 70 (Rudimentary **– p**
(USA) 118) [2015 7g Oct 9] good-topped filly: half-sister to useful 2-y-o 5f/6f winner
Hunter Street (by Compton Place), later 7f winner in Italy, and very smart 6f winner Sayif
(by Kheleyf), later 1m winner in USA: dam disappointing maiden: 14/1, in need of
experience when twelfth in maiden at Newmarket (8½ lengths behind Materialistic) in
October: should do better in time. *William Haggas*

FONDIE (IRE) 2 b.f. (Feb 8) Oasis Dream 129 – Prima Luce (IRE) 111 (Galileo (IRE) **58 p**
134) [2015 7s⁵ 7v Oct 17] €40,000Y: third foal: sister to 1m winner Dawn Mirage: dam 7f
winner (including at 2 yrs): better effort when eighth in maiden at Catterick (5½ lengths
behind Sunnua) in October: remains with potential. *Mark Johnston*

FONDLY (IRE) 3 b.f. Dansili 127 – Mrs Marsh (Marju (IRE) 127) [2015 p8m t7.1f* **80**
t7.1g⁴ 8g 7d² 10.2m⁵ 8s⁶ Jul 24] angular filly: sixth foal: closely related to 6f-8.3f winner **a70**
Mayo Lad (by Holy Roman Emperor) and half-sister to 2 winners, notably top-class miler
Canford Cliffs (2-y-o 6f winner, by Tagula): dam unraced: fairly useful performer: won
maiden at Wolverhampton in March: second in handicap at Lingfield in June: stays 1m:
acts on tapeta and good to soft going. *Richard Hannon*

FOOLAAD 4 ch.g. Exceed And Excel (AUS) 126 – Zayn Zen 107 (Singspiel (IRE) 133) **83**
[2015 6m² 6.1s² 5m* 6.1m³ 7d f5g f7f Dec 17] £2,500 3-y-o: third foal: closely related to
1¼m winner Mezyaad (by Tiger Hill) and half-brother to 6f winner Maakirr (by Street
Cry): dam 1m-1¼m winner: fairly useful performer: won maiden at Doncaster in June:
third in handicap at Nottingham later in month: stays 6f: acts on soft and good to firm
going: in tongue tie. *Roy Bowring*

FOOL'S DREAM 2 ch.f. (Apr 6) Showcasing 117 – Folly Lodge 93 (Grand Lodge (USA) – 125) [2015 8d Oct 23] 42,000Y: fourth foal: half-sister to 10.4f-1½m winner Azzuri (by Azamour): dam, winner up to 1m (2-y-o 7f winner), half-sister to smart French sprinter Sabratah: 50/1, well held in maiden at Doncaster in October. *Bryan Smart*

FOOL TO CRY (IRE) 2 ch.f. (Mar 25) Fast Company (IRE) 126 – Islandagore (IRE) 97 **82** (Indian Ridge 123) [2015 6d³ t7.1g² 7.5g* 8g⁵ Sep 26] 17,000Y: half-sister to several winners, including 2-y-o 6f winner Iron Range and winner up to 7f Alice's Dancer (2-y-o 6f winner) (both useful and by Clodovil): dam 7f winner: fair form: won maiden at Beverley (by neck from Gold Trade) in September: ¾ lengths fifth of 13 to Move Up in nursery at Ripon final start: stays 1m. *Roger Varian*

FOOTLIGHT 2 br.f. (May 20) Showcasing 117 – Wood Fairy 74 (Haafhd 129) [2015 p6g – p6g t6f⁶ Dec 22] first foal: dam, 7f-9f winner, half-sister to winner up to 1m Polar Ben and winner up to 1¾m Franklins Gardens (both smart): no form. *Richard Fahey*

FOOTSTEPSINTHERAIN (IRE) 5 b.g. Footstepsinthesand 120 – Champagne Toni **73** (IRE) (Second Empire (IRE) 124) [2015 80, a88: p8g p8f³ p10g⁴ 8.3g p8f Sep 24] sturdy gelding: fair handicapper: stays 8.5f: acts on polytrack, tapeta and good to firm going: tried in tongue tie. *David Dennis*

FOR AYMAN 4 b.g. Bertolini (USA) 125 – Saharan Song (IRE) 64 (Singspiel (IRE) 133) **77** [2015 76: p6m³ p6g² p6f³ p6f² t6g* 6m² 6g t7.1m p6f² t7.1f⁶ p6f³ p6d Nov 30] fair handicapper: won at Wolverhampton (apprentice) in April: stays 7f: acts on polytrack, tapeta, good to firm and good to soft going: often wears tongue tie: often races in rear. *Joseph Tuite*

FORBIDDEN CITY (IRE) 9 b.g. Elusive City (USA) 117 – Blueberry (USA) **65** (Bertrando (USA) 127) [2015 t7.1g* p8g p8g Mar 20] fair handicapper: won at Wolverhampton in February: left Des Donovan after: stays 7f: acts on polytrack, tapeta, best turf form on good to firm going: tried in blinkers prior to 2015: often wears tongue tie. *Peter Fahey, Ireland*

FORBIDDEN LOVE 3 b.f. Dubawi (IRE) 129 – Indian Love Bird (Efisio 120) [2015 –: **68** f8g² p8m May 12] fair maiden: best effort at 1m. *Simon Crisford*

FORCE AWAKENS (IRE) 2 b.f. (Apr 12) Raven's Pass (USA) 133 – Natural Skill **67** (USA) (Aptitude (USA) 128) [2015 6m⁴ 6d² 5.2m 6g Aug 3] €11,000Y: rather leggy filly: fourth foal: dam unraced half-sister to smart US Grade 1 9f winner Monzante: fair maiden: will be suited by 7f: sold 4,000 gns, sent to Spain. *Richard Fahey*

FORCED FAMILY FUN 5 b.g. Refuse To Bend (IRE) 128 – Juniper Girl (IRE) 108 **87** (Revoque (IRE) 122) [2015 f12g⁶ 12g² 13.1g⁴ 16.2d Oct 16] lengthy gelding: fairly useful handicapper: second at York (apprentice) in September: stays 13f: best form on ground softer than good: tried in hood prior to 2015. *John Quinn*

FORCEFUL APPEAL (USA) 7 b.g. Successful Appeal (USA) 118 – Kinetic Force **98** (USA) (Holy Bull (USA) 134) [2015 83, a96: p7g³ p8g* p8g* p8m⁴ p8g p8g 8.5g 10.1m p8g p8f p8g³ p8g* Dec 9] workmanlike gelding: useful handicapper: won at Chelmsford in January and February: better than ever when also winning 8-runner event at Lingfield in December by 2½ lengths from Big Time: stays 8.5f: acts on polytrack, firm and soft going: often races towards rear. *Simon Dow*

FORCEFUL BEACON 5 ch.g. Assertive 121 – Shore Light (USA) (Gulch (USA)) **49** [2015 50: t7.1g p6f t5.1g² p6g⁴ t5.1f⁶ Mar 26] poor maiden: stays 6f: acts on polytrack and tapeta: tried in headgear prior to 2015: often in tongue tie in 2015. *Tony Carroll*

FORCE (IRE) 2 ch.g. (Jan 30) Raven's Pass (USA) 133 – Holly's Kid (USA) (Pulpit **87** (USA) 117) [2015 6g³ 7f⁵ 6m⁶ 6d* p6f³ Oct 15] €30,000F, £160,000 2-y-o: compact gelding: fourth foal: half-brother to 2-y-o 1m winner Posh Cracker (by Johannesburg) and 9f winner (stays 12.5f) Rawaafed (by Invasor): dam, US winner up to 9f winner (2-y-o 1m winner), sister to smart US Grade 1 9f winner Rutherienne: fairly useful performer: won maiden at Haydock in September: should stay 7f: in hood last 2 starts. *John Gosden*

FORECASTER 2 b.f. (Jan 31) Fastnet Rock (AUS) 127 – Aurore (IRE) (Fasliyev (USA) **68 p** 120) [2015 7.1m⁵ 8d⁶ p7g Oct 29] lengthy filly: third foal: closely related to 7f winner Enliven (by Dansili) and a winner in Sweden by Holy Roman Emperor: dam, French maiden (stayed 7f), half-sister to very smart French 1¼m-1½m performer Aquarelliste: fair maiden: best effort when fifth at Chepstow (3½ lengths behind Puzzled Look) in September: never dangerous but not knocked about final start: will benefit from return to 1m+: remains open to improvement. *Michael Bell*

FOREIGN DIPLOMAT 3 b.g. Oasis Dream 129 – Longing To Dance 98 (Danehill **92**
Dancer (IRE) 117) [2015 87: 7m* 7g 6d⁴ 5m 5g 7.2m⁵ p7m⁴ t7.1f² p7d p6f* t7.1m⁵
Dec 26] useful-looking gelding: fairly useful performer: won maiden at Thirsk in May and
handicap at Chelmsford (by neck from Hoofalong) in December: left William Haggas after
fifth start: worth another try at sprint distances: acts on polytrack, tapeta, soft and good to
firm going: sometimes in headgear in 2015. *David O'Meara*

FOREIGN RHYTHM (IRE) 10 ch.m. Distant Music (USA) 126 – Happy Talk (IRE) **56**
74 (Hamas (IRE) 125) [2015 68: 6m⁶ 5g 6d² 6m Aug 29] rather leggy, close-coupled mare:
modest handicapper: stays 6f: acts on fibresand, good to firm and heavy going: tried in
headgear prior to 2015: tried in tongue tie prior to 2015. *Ron Barr*

FORESIGHT (FR) 2 b.c. (Apr 19) Dream Ahead (USA) 133 – Madhya (USA) 103 **78 p**
(Gone West (USA)) [2015 6v³ Nov 7] €65,000Y, €100,000 2-y-o: half-brother to 3 winners
abroad, including German 8.5f-1¼m winner Madhyana (by Monsun) and German
1¼m/11f winner Medinella (by Pivotal): dam French 1m winner: 7/2, caught eye when
third in maiden at Doncaster (length behind Times Legacy) in November, not knocked
about: sure to progress. *David Simcock*

FOREST LAKES (IRE) 2 b.f. (Feb 2) Iffraaj 127 – Cala (FR) 98 (Desert Prince (IRE) **78**
130) [2015 7v² p8g⁴ p8g³ Dec 15] seventh foal: half-sister to 7f winner Top Draw (by
Elusive Quality) and useful winner up to 12.3f Shrewd (2-y-o 7f-9f winner, by Street
Sense): dam, 6f/7f winner, half-sister to useful winner up to 7f Badminton: fair maiden:
best effort when third at Kempton (3½ lengths behind Mandrell) in December: tried in
cheekpieces. *Saeed bin Suroor*

FOREST MAIDEN (IRE) 3 b.f. Invincible Spirit (IRE) 121 – Lady Marian (GER) 125 **99**
(Nayef (USA) 129) [2015 83p: t7.1m* p8g⁴ 7m⁴ 8m* 8m³ 8m* 9g³ 8g⁶ Sep 5] sturdy filly:
useful handicapper: won at Wolverhampton in March, Thirsk in June and Newbury (by
short head from Rekdhat) in July: third at Newmarket (2½ lengths behind Angel Vision) in
June and Goodwood (4¼ lengths behind Tazffin) in July: effective at 9f, may prove ideally
suited by shorter: acts on polytrack, tapeta and good to firm going: front runner, often
travels strongly. *Charlie Appleby*

FOREST MISSILE (IRE) 3 b.g. Majestic Missile (IRE) 118 – Garnock Academy
(USA) (Royal Academy (USA) 130) [2015 –: 5g 6g 8.5m⁵ 7.5g 5g⁵ 6.9m⁵ 5g⁶ Aug 29]
maiden: no form in 2015: in cheekpieces final start. *John Wainwright*

FOREVER A LADY (IRE) 2 b.f. (Feb 23) Dark Angel (IRE) 113 – Unicamp 84 (Royal **85**
Academy (USA) 130) [2015 6g⁴ 7.2d* 6.1m² 6g 7s⁵ Oct 6] €10,000F, £27,000Y: half-sister
to several winners, including smart 7f and (including at 2 yrs) 1m winner Smarty Socks (by
Elnadim) and useful winner up to 13f Kempes (2-y-o 7f/1m winner, by Intikhab): dam
2-y-o 6f winner: fairly useful performer: won maiden at Ayr in August: second in minor
event at Chester later in month: stays 7f: acts on good to firm and good to soft going.
Keith Dalgleish

FOREVER NOW 4 b.c. Galileo (IRE) 134 – All's Forgotten (USA) 81 (Darshaan 133) **116**
[2015 116: 14.1s³ 16f³ 16.4m⁴ 20f 16g⁵ Sep 24] good-looking colt: smart performer: best
efforts of 2015 when third in Sagaro Stakes at Ascot (3¼ lengths behind Mizzou) in April
and eighth in Gold Cup at Royal Ascot (4 lengths behind Trip To Paris) in June: left John
Gosden/off 3 months, only fifth of 8 to Flying Officer in listed race at Newmarket final
start: stays 2½m: acts on firm going: front runner/races prominently. *Martyn Meade*

FOREVER POPULAR (USA) 3 b.f. Dynaformer (USA) – Pussycat Doll (USA) 120 **88 p**
(Real Quiet (USA) 131) [2015 10m² 12m² 12.1m* 12f⁵ Jul 10] useful-looking filly: first
foal: dam, US Grade 1 7f winner, half-sister to very smart US Grade 1 7f winner Jimmy
Creed: fairly useful performer: won maiden at Chepstow in June: excuses in handicap final
start: stays 1½m: remains open to improvement. *William Haggas*

FOREVER SCOTLAND (IRE) 3 b.c. The Carbon Unit (USA) 106 – Green Glen (IRE) **–**
(Hawk Wing (USA) 136) [2015 –: 8g 7g 9.5g 8.3g⁶ Aug 20] maiden: no form in 2015: left
John Patrick Shanahan after first start, P. J. Prendergast after third: tried in visor in 2015.
John Patrick Shanahan, Ireland

FOREVER YOURS (IRE) 2 b.g. (Apr 6) Canford Cliffs (IRE) 133 – Gilded (IRE) 101 **–**
(Redback 116) [2015 p7g⁶ Dec 10] 11/1, very green when sixth in maiden at Chelmsford
(16½ lengths behind Sweet Temptation) in December. *Dean Ivory*

FORGE 2 b.c. (Feb 18) Dubawi (IRE) 129 – Heat Haze 120 (Green Desert (USA) 127) [2015 **69 p**
7g Aug 28] good sort: brother to useful winner up to 1m Radiator (2-y-o 7f winner): dam,
French/US 6.5f-9.5f winner, out of outstanding broodmare Hasili: 7/2, seventh in maiden
at Newmarket (7½ lengths behind Tashweeq) in August: sure to progress. *Sir Michael Stoute*

FORGIVING FLOWER 2 ch.f. (Apr 3) New Approach (IRE) 132 – Dance Lively **69 p**
(USA) (Kingmambo (USA) 125) [2015 7.9d³ 8.3d p8g³ Nov 4] 70,000Y: sister to German
6f winner Emirati Spirit and half-sister to several winners, including smart Japanese miler
Live Concert (by Singspiel) and useful winner up to 13f Charleston Lady (2-y-o 1m winner,
by Hurricane Run): dam unraced: fair maiden: best effort when third at Kempton (2 lengths
behind The Black Princess) in November, needing stiffer test: will be suited by at least
1¼m: still unexposed. *K. R. Burke*

FORGIVING GLANCE 3 gr.f. Passing Glance 119 – Giving 98 (Generous (IRE) 139) **65**
[2015 51: 9g³ 10.2m² 10.2g⁴ t12.2m³ 13.1f² p16f² t16.5f⁴ Oct 30] fair maiden: stays 2m:
acts on polytrack, tapeta and firm going: often races towards rear. *Alan King*

FORGOTTEN HERO (IRE) 6 b.g. High Chaparral (IRE) 132 – Sundown 71 (Polish **103**
Precedent (USA) 131) [2015 101: 10.1g⁴ 12m 10m* 12f 10.4m⁴ 9.9g 10.3m² 9g 12v
Oct 24] strong, sturdy gelding: useful handicapper: won at Newmarket (by 1¾ lengths
from Squire) in May: second at Doncaster (2¾ lengths behind Blue Waltz) in September:
stays 1½m: acts on polytrack, good to firm and good to soft going: usually wears hood:
usually races nearer last than first. *Charles Hills*

FORGOTTEN RULES (IRE) 5 b.g. Nayef (USA) 129 – Utterly Heaven (IRE) 107 **119**
(Danehill (USA) 126) [2015 14d* 20f³ 14m⁴ 14d⁵ 16d Oct 17] smart performer: won
Vintage Crop Stakes at Navan (by 1¼ lengths from Answered) in May: 5/2 favourite, 1½
lengths third of 12 to Trip To Paris in Gold Cup at Royal Ascot next time: disappointing
subsequently, 7 lengths eighth of 13 to Flying Officer in Long Distance Cup at Ascot final
start (looked held when hampered 2f out): stays 2½m: best form on going softer than good:
strong traveller. *D. K. Weld, Ireland*

FORGOTTEN VOICE (IRE) 10 b.g. Danehill Dancer (IRE) 117 – Asnieres (USA) **115**
(Spend A Buck (USA)) [2015 16.4m⁶ 16.4m³ 14g² 14.6m⁵ 12m⁶ Oct 3] big, strong gelding:
smart performer: third in listed race at Sandown (½ length behind Eye of The Storm) and
second in handicap at Goodwood (neck behind Blue Wave), both in July: well below form
final start: stays 16.5f: acted on polytrack and firm going: tried in visor prior to 2015:
usually raced in rear: retired. *Nicky Henderson*

FORGOTTEN WISH (IRE) 2 b.f. (Mar 24) Lilbourne Lad (IRE) 111 – Khatela (IRE) **83**
91 (Shernazar 131) [2015 6g⁶ 6s* 7s³ 7g t6f⁴ p7g Nov 13] €50,000F, €75,000Y: sturdy
filly: half-sister to several winners, including useful winner up to 1m Massive (2-y-o 7f
winner, by Marju) and useful French 12.5f winner Irish Kind (by Cape Cross): dam 1m/9f
winner: fairly useful performer: won maiden at Goodwood in August: third in nursery at
Newbury in September: stays 7f: acts on soft going. *Richard Hannon*

FOR SHIA AND LULA (IRE) 6 b.g. Majestic Missile (IRE) 118 – Jack-N-Jilly (IRE) **79**
43 (Anita's Prince 126) [2015 72, a82: p8g² p8g⁴ t1.7g⁶ t7.1g³ t7.1g* 8m³ t7.1g 8g⁵ 7g³
7.4d³ t7.1g t7.1m⁴ t7.1f t7.1f Oct 31] fair handicapper: won at Wolverhampton in April:
stays 8.5f: acts on polytrack, tapeta and firm going: sometimes in headgear prior to 2015:
often races prominently. *Daniel Loughnane*

FORT BASTION (IRE) 6 b.g. Lawman (FR) 121 – French Fern (IRE) 81 (Royal **106**
Applause 124) [2015 105: 8m 8m⁵ 8d* 8f 8.3m⁶ 8m 7d⁶ 8d 8g⁵ 8d⁶ 7v Nov 7] well-made
gelding: useful handicapper: won at Ayr (by 3¾ lengths from Pintura) in May: respectable
efforts at best subsequently: best form up to 1m: acts on firm and soft going: has worn
headgear, including last 5 starts. *David O'Meara*

FORT BELVEDERE 7 ch.g. King's Best (USA) 132 – Sweet Folly (IRE) 109 (Singspiel **52**
(IRE) 133) [2015 –: 8g 8g 8m 8m 8g Aug 5] modest handicapper: stays 1¼m: acts on firm
and soft going: tried in hood prior to 2015: often races towards rear. *Micky Hammond*

FORT DEL ORO (IRE) 3 b.f. Lope de Vega (IRE) 125 – Gilded (IRE) 101 (Redback **115 p**
116) [2015 6v² 6g* 6g³ 6g² 6g* Oct 11] 50,000Y: fourth foal: half-sister to a winner in
Denmark by Nayef: dam 2-y-o 5f winner (including Queen Mary Stakes): smart performer:
won maiden at the Curragh (by 4¼ lengths from Creggs Pipes) in June and listed race at the
Curragh (by 1½ lengths from The Happy Prince) in October: raced only at 6f: best form on
good going: often races towards rear, often travels strongly: will go on improving. *Edward
Lynam, Ireland*

FORTE 3 ch.f. New Approach (IRE) 132 – Prowess (IRE) 103 (Peintre Celebre (USA) **101 ?**
137) [2015 92: 10f⁶ 12f⁶ 11.1s 9.9m Aug 12] unfurnished filly: useful form: best effort
when 6 lengths sixth to Curvy in Ribblesdale Stakes at Royal Ascot on second start:
probably stays 1½m: acts on polytrack, firm and good to soft going: in hood in 2015:
sometimes slowly away, usually races freely. *Ralph Beckett*

FORTINBRASS (IRE) 5 b.g. Baltic King 120 – Greta d'Argent (IRE) 103 (Great **64**
Commotion (USA) 123) [2015 76: f5d⁵ f5g f6s 5m⁶ 6m⁶ 5m t5.1f³ t6f t6g⁵ f7m³ f6g²
Dec 22] smallish gelding: modest handicapper: stays 7f: acts on all-weather and good to
firm going: tried in cheekpieces prior to 2015: tried in tongue tie. *John Balding*

FORT JEFFERSON 2 br.g. (Apr 8) Passing Glance 119 – Florida Heart 78 (First Trump **70**
118) [2015 7s p7g 7g⁶ Oct 21] lengthy gelding: fair maiden: best effort when sixth at
Newmarket (7¾ lengths behind Colour Me Happy) in October: will be suited by 1m.
Andrew Balding

FORZA BLACKY 3 br.g. Manduro (GER) 135 – Rightside 78 (High Chaparral (IRE) **67**
132) [2015 74: 11.6m⁵ 9.9g 11.5g t8.6g⁴ 8.3g t8.6m Sep 5] lengthy gelding: fair maiden:
best effort at 8.5f: acts on polytrack, tapeta and good to firm going: tried in visor in 2015.
Philip McBride

FORZARZI (IRE) 11 b.g. Forzando 122 – Zarzi (IRE) (Suave Dancer (USA) 136) [2015 **–**
48: t7.1g Jan 15] modest at best, well held sole start in 2015: stays 8.5f: acts on polytrack,
tapeta and good to firm going: tried in cheekpieces prior to 2015: usually races nearer last
than first. *John David Riches*

FOSSA 5 b.g. Dubai Destination (USA) 127 – Gayanula (USA) 67 (Yonaguska (USA) 112) **67**
[2015 77: p7g p6m p6m² p7f p6g⁵ p6f⁶ p6f³ 5m t6f⁶ p6f t7.1g Dec 4] good-topped gelding:
fair handicapper: stays 1m: acts on polytrack, fibresand and good to firm going: sometimes
in cheekpieces in 2015: front runner/races prominently. *Dean Ivory*

FOSTER'S ROAD 6 b.g. Imperial Dancer 123 – Search Party 78 (Rainbow Quest (USA) **70**
134) [2015 16m³ 14m p16g⁶ 17.1g 16m⁵ Jul 1] close-coupled gelding: fair handicapper:
stays 16.5f: acts on polytrack, good to firm and good to soft going: tried in visor: usually
races towards rear. *Mick Channon*

FOUDROYER DEUX 2 ch.f. (Apr 8) Sakhee's Secret 128 – Lighted Way 66 (Kris 135) **–**
[2015 6s f7f Dec 17] half-sister to several winners, including 2-y-o 6f winner Lightning
Charlie (by Myboycharlie) and 2-y-o 7f winner Beam of Light (by Bertolini): dam, sprint
maiden, half-sister to useful sprinter Connect: no form: in hood. *Bryan Smart*

FOULRICE FLYER 2 b.g. (Apr 9) Winker Watson 118 – Big Old Unit (Byron 117) **–**
[2015 5m 6g 7.5g Sep 16] no form. *Patrick Holmes*

FOUNDATION (IRE) 2 ch.c. (Feb 24) Zoffany (IRE) 121 – Roystonea (Polish **114 p**
Precedent (USA) 131) [2015 8m³ 8g⁴ 8g* 8d³ Oct 24]
Shalaa was hailed as 'the fastest juvenile I've trained' by John Gosden, and
Clarehaven also seemed to house several once-raced two-year-olds that 'could be
anything', but there is absolutely no doubting the classic hopes entertained for
Foundation by those closest to him. It is not often you see a trainer so unruffled after
one of his horses has lost a big race in such unfortunate circumstances as Foundation
encountered in the Racing Post Trophy at Doncaster. The Racing Post Trophy had
been won by the favourite six years in a row, but the prospects of odds-on Foundation
extending that sequence had virtually evaporated by the time he found himself in
the clear. The seven-runner field had converged on the stand rail and, with Frankie
Dettori riding a waiting race, Foundation found himself pocketed, with no room to
manoeuvre, as the race began in earnest. His chance wasn't helped by the fact that he
stalked the second favourite Deauville, with whom he was closely matched on earlier
form, before that horse unexpectedly folded in front of him, leaving Foundation
with no way out, at the same time as the eventual winner Marcel and runner-up
Johannes Vermeer were enjoying an uninterrupted run down the outside. Foundation
quickened effortlessly once Dettori got him extricated in the last furlong, but the
gap didn't come until it was far too late and the considerably-handled Foundation,
who didn't have anything like a hard race, finished full of running in third, beaten
a diminishing length and a half and two and a half behind Marcel and Johannes
Vermeer (who went on to frank the form by winning the Criterium International at
Saint-Cloud). 'I would have loved to have seen him get free at the two-furlong pole,
but that's racing,' said John Gosden after the Racing Post Trophy, 'but the horse
has had a lovely experience, he has just done a nice piece of work. He's a gorgeous
horse.' Foundation certainly made a big impression and should more than make up
for his Doncaster misfortune as a three-year-old. To all intents and purposes, he is
already a Group 1 horse and has the physical scope to make up into an even better
performer with a winter on his back. At the time of writing, he is a 16/1-shot for the

Two Thousand Guineas, in a market dominated by the exceptional Air Force Blue, but most bookmakers have Foundation at the head of their ante-post list for the Derby at around 14/1. Those odds might look to have been generous if he bypasses Newmarket and follows the Derby trial route to Epsom. He looks a natural for the Dante in which the stable had the first two in the latest season, Golden Horn and Jack Hobbs. That pair went on to win the Derby and the Irish Derby respectively.

Foundation was unbeaten until the Racing Post Trophy. He made his racecourse debut in August in a maiden over a mile at Haydock, holding all the big autumn entries and starting a short-priced favourite. Foundation overcame a slow start (giving away several lengths) to win in taking style from fellow newcomers Colour Me Happy and Altarsheed, both of whom went on to show fairly useful form. Looking every inch a pattern performer in the making, Foundation was returned to Haydock a month later for the Ascendant Stakes, a listed contest, again over a mile. He proved a cut above his four rivals, beating the three-times winner Champagne City and the Solario Stakes runner-up Manaafidh with plenty in hand despite once more missing the break. The Juddmonte Royal Lodge Stakes at Newmarket provided a sterner test of Foundation's credentials, up against another unbeaten colt in the Aidan O'Brien-trained Deauville who had followed up a debut success in a Listowel maiden by winning the Tyros Stakes at Leopardstown from the useful Sanus Per Aquam (subsequently third in the Dewhurst to Air Force Blue). The betting market had the Group 2 Royal Lodge as a virtual match between Foundation (5/4 favourite) and Deauville (11/8), and that is the way the race turned out, with Foundation the winner by three quarters of a length in a race run at a sound gallop. Foundation had to work harder than for his two Haydock wins, but he was away on terms this time, settled in mid-division, and kept on well after taking the lead under two furlongs out. Third-placed Muntazah and the others were no match for Foundation and Deauville who both recorded smart efforts that were in line with the standards of recent editions of the race (with the notable exception of Frankel's year). John Gosden's first Derby winner Benny The Dip won the Royal Lodge as a two-year-old. He also finished third in the Racing Post Trophy when a well-backed favourite (though with no obvious explanation for his defeat) and went on to win the Dante before triumphing by the skin of his teeth at Epsom from Silver Patriarch.

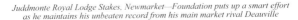

Juddmonte Royal Lodge Stakes, Newmarket—Foundation puts up a smart effort
as he maintains his unbeaten record from his main market rival Deauville

Highclere T'Bred Racing (Wellington)'s "Foundation"

Foundation (IRE) (ch.c. 2013)	Zoffany (IRE) (b 2008)	Dansili (b 1996)	Danehill
			Hasili
		Tyranny (b 2000)	Machiavellian
			Dust Dancer
	Roystonea (b 2000)	Polish Precedent (b 1986)	Danzig
			Past Example
		Alleluia Tree (gr 1992)	Royal Academy
			Thistlewood

Just as with Benny The Dip, there are pedigree doubts about Foundation's ability to get a mile and a half, but unlike Benny The Dip, who had an abundance of speed on the distaff side, they stem from Foundation's sire. Zoffany won five of his seven races at two, including the Phoenix Stakes, and trained on into a smart miler at three (his most notable performance coming when a strong-finishing, very good second to Frankel in the St James's Palace Stakes). Zoffany's first two-year-olds, bred on a fee of just €6,000, gave him a flying start in the latest season when Illuminate, Washington DC and Waterloo Bridge landed an eye-catching Royal Ascot treble. Already one of the busiest Flat stallions, with two hundred and twenty mares in 2015, Zoffany's fee will rise from €12,500 in 2015 to €45,000 for 2016 when it will be interesting to see how his first crop turn out as three-year-olds. Zoffany's sire Dansili was a miler himself, but he has had some notable middle-distance performers and, until there is evidence to the contrary, it would be precipitate to label Zoffany as purely a sire of two-year-olds, sprinters and milers. Foundation's dam Roystonea won at seven furlongs and a mile in France and her five winners so far include the fairly useful two-year-old seven furlong winner Take

A Chance (by Hawk Wing) who later won abroad, including over a mile and three quarters in Belgium; the pick of her winners before Foundation, who changed hands as a foal for €55,000 and as a yearling for €190,000, were the useful pair Vastonea (by Verglas) and the three-year-old Misterioso (by Iffraaj), the former showing that he stayed ten and a half furlongs but the latter not so far raced beyond a mile. There is plenty of stamina a little further back on the distaff side, Foundation's unraced great grandam Thistlewood, a half-sister to dual Gold Cup winner Ardross (also runner-up in an Arc), being the grandam of St Leger winner Scorpion. The fact that the long-striding Foundation stayed a mile so well as a two-year-old adds to the case for the Derby trip proving within his compass. He has won on good to firm and good to soft going. *John Gosden*

FOUND (IRE) 3 b.f. Galileo (IRE) 134 – Red Evie (IRE) 117 (Intikhab (USA) 135) **123**
[2015 115p· 7v² 8g² 8f² 10s* 10g² 11.9m 10d² 12g* Oct 31]

The European challengers again proved too good for the best of North America's middle-distance grass performers in the Breeders' Cup Turf. Europe's two runners—both three-year-olds—filled the first two places in the twelve-strong field at Keeneland, though they didn't finish in the order generally expected, with the Irish-trained filly Found just mastering odds-on Golden Horn inside the final furlong. Found had finished behind Europe's Horse of the Year on two of her last three starts, when runner-up to him in the Irish Champion Stakes and when ninth after a nightmare passage in the Prix de l'Arc de Triomphe (which Golden Horn also won), after which she had gone on to contest the Champion Stakes on British Champions' Day when second to Fascinating Rock. Golden Horn's connections campaigned their Derby winner with a boldness which is rarely seen with a classic winner nowadays (he was making his eighth appearance of the year at Keeneland) and there was an inevitable sense of anticlimax when he failed to end a splendid three-year-old campaign on a winning note. However, Found was also running for the eighth time and the Breeders' Cup Turf was her fourth championship race in four different countries in quick succession. She had finished second four times in all in Group 1 company during the year, the two earlier occasions coming against her own age and sex in the Irish One Thousand Guineas and the Coronation Stakes, and she had looked like ending the campaign as 'bridesmaid of the year', as one Irish journalist dubbed her. Found's triumph in the Breeders' Cup Turf was worth £1,078,431 and was handsome reward for a string of good efforts, her victory made all the more meritorious by the fact that, in the space of seven weeks, she had appeared consecutively at the major end-of-season championship meetings in Ireland, France, Britain and North America. 'As tough as old boots' scarcely does justice to Found's constitution.

Found began the latest season looking sure to make her mark in the fillies' classics. She was ante-post favourite for both the One Thousand Guineas and the Oaks over the winter after winning the Prix Marcel Boussac by two and a half lengths from the best of the French-trained fillies Ervedya who looked a natural contender for the 'French Guineas', the Poule d'Essai des Pouliches. Ervedya duly won the Pouliches (and suffered only one defeat all season) but Found's preparation for the One Thousand Guineas was interrupted by a temperature and she missed her first major target. The Group 3 Athasi Stakes over seven furlongs at the Curragh, the day after the Guineas, was chosen for her reappearance but she was beaten by one of the four-year-olds, 25/1-shot Iveagh Gardens, though Found travelled much the best through the race before running out of steam in the closing stages. Returned to a mile, Found was back in top company on her next two starts, though she found one too good for her in both the Irish One Thousand Guineas at the Curragh (in which Pleascach beat her by half a length) and the Coronation Stakes at Royal Ascot (in which Ervedya headed her close home to win by a neck). With the Ballydoyle classic colts not looking so strong as in recent years, there was some discussion among the Coolmore partners about supplementing Found for the Derby but, in the end, it came to nothing. Nor did Found contest the Oaks, her trainer having expressed some concerns earlier in the season about whether such a heavy-topped filly might be at risk of jarring herself coming down Tattenham Hill on firmish going.

Longines Breeders' Cup Turf, Keeneland—
Found gains her reward for a string of good efforts as she beats Golden Horn in what is her fourth
top-level race in just seven weeks; Big Blue Kitten (armlets) pips Slumber for third

It was ten weeks before Found reappeared and she was warmed up for her late-season tour of the grand theatres in the Group 3 Royal Whip Stakes at the Curragh where she got her head in front for the first time since the Prix Marcel Boussac. Ryan Moore had apparently told the Coolmore partners and trainer Aidan O'Brien after that race—'This filly will win an Arc.' That race was announced as her target after the Royal Whip Stakes, with either the Prix Vermeille or the Irish Champion Stakes to act as a stepping stone. With dual Arc winner Treve being targeted at the Vermeille, Found joined the Prix du Jockey Club runner-up Highland Reel in a two-pronged challenge by Ballydoyle for the Irish Champion, from which the stable's principal hope, dual Two Thousand Guineas winner Gleneagles, was a late absentee after overnight rain. Found started 6/1 third favourite and turned in a career-best effort at up to that time, staying on to go down by a length to Golden Horn, though she would probably have come third if Free Eagle had not been almost stopped in his tracks, and then carried right, when the winner veered off a straight line a furlong out. The Irish Champion was the first race in the latest season for which Found did not start favourite, and she started at 28/1 in the Arc on her next start when very little went right for her. Having her first outing beyond a mile and a quarter and dropped out from her wide draw, Found had plenty to do turning for home and twice met trouble when trying to make her run. She was never able to challenge but finished well with running left in her, beaten five lengths by Golden Horn. Found started second favourite to Golden Horn's Irish Derby-winning stablemate Jack Hobbs in the Champion Stakes at Ascot but there was one too good for her on the day as she went down by a length and a quarter to fellow Irish raider Fascinating Rock, after again being dropped out and finishing well.

The Breeders' Cup Turf over a mile and a half has been the strongest of the Breeders' Cup races (of which there are thirteen nowadays) for the European visitors. They now lead their North American rivals, as a group, in the Turf by eighteen and a half victories to thirteen and a half (the 'half' was the dead-heat between High Chaparral and Johar in 2003). The latest Breeders' Cup was the first hosted by Keeneland where the circuit on the turf course is inside the dirt track and just seven and a half furlongs round. The Breeders' Cup Turf was the last of the six turf races at the self-proclaimed 'Breeders' Cup World Championships' and, to that point, Hit It A Bomb's victory in the Juvenile Turf on the first day had been the only one for the Europeans. Heavy rain in the days before the meeting resulted in the going on the turf course being on the soft side for the first day. It continued to dry out overnight, however, and Timeform returned the ground as 'good' on the second day, though jockeys described the surface as 'loose'. Dettori said afterwards that Golden Horn was 'spinning his wheels all the time and just couldn't pick up on the ground.' On the day and under the prevailing conditions, though, Found ran out a worthy winner after she and Golden Horn fought a protracted battle most of the way up the short home straight before Found finally got on top inside the final furlong and was driven

372

right out to prevail by half a length. The smart seven-year-olds Big Blue Kitten and his stablemate Slumber (once trained in Britain by Charlie Hills) fared best of the home defence, beaten a further three quarters of a length and half a length, with the Arlington Million winner The Pizza Man fifth. Big Blue Kitten, a close second in the Arlington Million, had won Grade 1s on either side of that performance, but his form and that of the other leading home-trained contenders left them with plenty to find to beat a top-form Golden Horn and a few pounds to find on Found at the weights. One way of putting Found's performance into context is to say that Golden Horn was undoubtedly some way below his peak at Keeneland, but, even so, Found still had to put up the best effort of her career to beat him.

Found's triumph gave the Coolmore partners, trainer Aidan O'Brien and jockey Ryan Moore a double at the meeting, following the success of Hit It A Bomb. Moore also came second on Alice Springs in the Juvenile Fillies' Turf and on Legatissimo in the Filly & Mare Turf, his combined efforts enough to earn him the Bill Shoemaker Award as top jockey at the meeting (Moore stopped off in France—on the way to ride in the Melbourne Cup—and won the Criterium International for O'Brien on Johannes Vermeer just sixteen hours after winning on Found). Ballydoyle has usually taken a 'When in Rome' stance to using permitted raceday medication on its North American runners, and both Hit It A Bomb and Found raced on furosemide—which has been shown in field studies to enhance performance—while most of the rival European visitors raced 'clean' (Golden Horn among them). Hit It A Bomb and Found took Aidan O'Brien, already the most successful European-based trainer at the Breeders' Cup, to ten Breeders' Cup winners, half of those coming in the Breeders' Cup Turf which he had previously won with High Chaparral (twice), St Nicholas Abbey and Magician. Hit It A Bomb was O'Brien's third winner of the Juvenile Turf in the last five years, following Wrote and George Vancouver.

Found (IRE) (b.f. 2012)			
Galileo (IRE) (b 1998)	Sadler's Wells (b 1981)	Northern Dancer	
		Fairy Bridge	
	Urban Sea (ch 1989)	Miswaki	
		Allegretta	
Red Evie (IRE) (b 2003)	Intikhab (b 1994)	Red Ransom	
		Crafty Example	
	Malafemmena (b 1992)	Nordico	
		Martinova	

The big, strong, workmanlike Found was the third Breeders' Cup Turf winner for her sire Galileo, who was also responsible for Red Rocks and Magician. Found's dam Red Evie has been a perennial visitor to Galileo since she was retired and has now produced four winners by him for the Coolmore partners, her fifth foal, the promising two-year-old Best In The World, becoming the latest of them when successful in the listed Staffordstown Stud Stakes at the Curragh on the second of her two starts. Red Evie's second foal, Magical Dream, also earned 'black type', winning the C. L. Weld Park Stakes as a two-year-old before being placed in Group 2 and Group 3 company at three (she got a mile and a half as a three-year-old). Red Evie herself won at the highest level at a mile, taking the Matron Stakes at three and the Lockinge as a four-year-old; a big, lengthy filly (Found takes after her in physique), she was bought privately by the Coolmore partners after being led out unsold for 1,000,000 guineas at the December Sales at the end of her four-year-old season. Found's grandam Malafemmena raced only as a two-year-old, winning in listed company over six furlongs in Italy, and is a half-sister to the smart French sprinter Export Price. Found's great grandam Martinova won the Athasi Stakes over seven furlongs and finished a good third in the Irish One Thousand Guineas (Martinova's eight winners also included, in complete contrast to Export Price, the top American steeplechaser Ninepins who won the Colonial Cup). Although speed has been the predominant characteristic in recent generations of Found's family on the distaff side, there is stamina further back, Martinova being out of a half-sister (who won at a mile and a half) to the very smart stayer Random Shot who was awarded the 1971 Gold Cup after the first-past-the-post Rock Roi failed a drugs test. Found stays a mile and a half and acts on soft and good to firm going. She remains in training. *Aidan O'Brien, Ireland*

FOUR NATIONS (USA) 7 ch.g. Langfuhr (CAN) 124 – Kiswahili 105 (Selkirk (USA) **75 §**
129) [2015 67: p15.8g⁵ p12f⁵ t16.5g* 16.2m t13.9g* t12.2g⁵ p16g⁴ p16d⁶ t13.9f⁶ 16s
t16.5f⁵ Nov 16] strong gelding: fair handicapper: won at Wolverhampton in April and May:
stays 16.5f: acts on polytrack, tapeta, soft and good to firm going: tried in headgear in 2015:
often starts slowly. *George Baker*

FOUR ON EIGHT 2 gr.c. (Apr 3) Lawman (FR) 121 – Pocket Watch (Pivotal 124) [2015 **86 p**
7g 7m³ 8.3g* 9g³ Oct 21] good-topped colt: first foal: dam unraced half-sister to smart
performer up to 2m Bauer: fairly useful performer: won maiden at Windsor in September:
creditable third in nursery at Newmarket final start: will be suited by at least 1¼m: remains
with potential. *Luca Cumani*

FOUR POETS 2 ch.g. (Feb 14) Poet's Voice 126 – O Fourlunda 71 (Halling (USA) 133) **66**
[2015 p10g t8.6m⁵ 8.3s Oct 28] fair maiden: best effort when fifth at Wolverhampton (7
lengths behind Lord George) in October, left poorly placed. *David Simcock*

FOUR'S COMPANY (IRE) 2 b.f. (Jan 24) Fast Company (IRE) 126 – Mrs Beeton **84**
(IRE) 80 (Dansili 127) [2015 5g⁴ 5.1s 5m³ 6f³ t7.1g* 6.1g² 7m 6.1m* 7g³ 5.5d⁶ Sep 26]
€5,000Y, resold €13,000Y: angular filly: second foal: dam, 1m winner, half-sister to very
smart 1¼m winner Stotsfold: fairly useful performer: won maiden at Wolverhampton in
July and minor event at Chester in August: good third in nursery at Chester in September:
stays 7f: acts on tapeta and good to firm going: sold 10,000 gns, sent to Italy. *Tom Dascombe*

FOUR SEASONS (IRE) 3 b.c. Dubawi (IRE) 129 – Please Sing 103 (Royal Applause **105**
124) [2015 103: p7f* p7g⁴ p8f* 7m May 8] lengthy colt: useful performer: won handicap
at Lingfield (by 1¾ lengths from Anonymous John) in March and AW 3YO Mile
Championships Stakes at Lingfield (by 1¼ lengths from Tempus Temporis) in April: stays
1m: acts on polytrack and heavy going. *Charlie Appleby*

FOURSQUARE FUNTIME 6 b.g. Common World (USA) 116 – Farina (IRE) 73 **–**
(Golan (IRE) 129) [2015 t8.6g t9.5f Oct 16] fair at best, no form in 2015: stays 8.5f: acts
on polytrack, soft and good to firm going: often in tongue tie in 2015. *Trevor Wall*

FOURTH WAY (IRE) 2 b.f. (May 6) Iffraaj 127 – Spiritual Air 93 (Royal Applause 124) **93 p**
[2015 6g² 6m* 7v³ Oct 24] £78,000Y: sister to useful 7f winner Perfect Step and half-sister
to 3 winners, including 7f/1m winner Emeralds Spirit (by Rock of Gibraltar): dam, 6f (at
2 yrs) and 9f (in USA) winner, half-sister to dam of smart winner up to 1m Forjatt: fairly
useful performer: won maiden at Yarmouth (by ¾ length from Field of Stars) in September:
best effort when third in listed race at Newbury (1½ lengths behind Light Music) in
October: will stay 1m: should do better still. *Roger Varian*

FOXCOVER (IRE) 4 ch.g. Raven's Pass (USA) 133 – Cover Girl (IRE) 78 (Common **68**
Grounds 118) [2015 78: t7.1f p8g⁶ t8.6g² t7.1g⁶ p8g³ p10g² p10g p12g t8.6g t8.6f Nov 14]
fair maiden: left Philip McBride after third start: stays 1¼m: acts on polytrack, tapeta and
good to soft going: usually in headgear in 2015. *Conor Dore*

FOXFORD 4 b.f. Clodovil (IRE) 116 – Pulau Pinang (IRE) 101 (Dolphin Street (FR) 125) **68 §**
[2015 73, a62: p8g 6m p6g³ p6g* p6f⁴ p6g 6gᵘʳ Oct 20] lengthy filly: fair handicapper: won
at Kempton in August: stays 7f: acts on polytrack and good to soft going: often races
prominently: has high head carriage. *Patrick Chamings*

FOXHAVEN 13 ch.g. Unfuwain (USA) 131 – Dancing Mirage (IRE) 83 (Machiavellian **59**
(USA) 123) [2015 74: p12m⁴ p12f p11g⁵ 12v p12m Nov 19] smallish, sturdy gelding:
modest handicapper: stays 12.5f: acts on polytrack and any turf going: often wears visor.
Patrick Chamings

FOXINTHEHENHOUSE 2 ch.f. (Apr 9) Bahamian Bounty 116 – Pants 78 (Pivotal **71**
124) [2015 p7g p7g⁵ p7g* Dec 20] fifth foal: half-sister to winners up to 7f Little Knickers
(2-y-o 5f winner, by Prince Sabo) and Chambles (2-y-o 6f winner, by Shamardal): dam 7f
winner: fair performer: best effort when winning maiden at Lingfield (by ½ length from
Rahyah) in December, having run of race: raced only at 7f. *J. R. Jenkins*

FOXTROT JUBILEE (IRE) 5 b.g. Captain Marvelous (IRE) 114 – Cool Cousin (IRE) **65**
102 (Distant Relative 128) [2015 74: p6g f5d⁶ f6s 6m 7s 7.1s Aug 31] fair handicapper:
stays 6f: acts on polytrack and soft going: tried in cheekpieces in 2015. *Ralph Beckett*

FOXTROT KNIGHT 3 b.g. Kyllachy 129 – Rustam (Dansili 127) [2015 63: f5d⁵ 5d* **88**
5.1m² p5g* 5m* p5g⁴ 5g 5m³ 6g³ 5s⁴ 5g 5s Oct 19] smallish, robust gelding: fairly
useful handicapper: won at Catterick and Chelmsford in April and Windsor (by 1¼ lengths
from Cartmell Cleave) in June: third at Windsor and Newmarket in August: stays 6f: acts
on polytrack, soft and good to firm going: tried in blinkers prior to 2015. *Ruth Carr*

FOXTROT ROMEO (IRE) 6 b.g. Danehill Dancer (IRE) 117 – Hawala (IRE) 97 **99**
(Warning 136) [2015 111: p6f⁴ p8g p6f⁵ 6f 7g 7m³ 7m 6.5m 6g Sep 19] lengthy, well-made **a107**
gelding: useful performer: best effort in 2015 when fifth to Pretend in AW Sprint
Championships Stakes at Lingfield on third start: below form after, leaving Marco Botti
after seventh outing: stays 1m, effective at shorter: acts on polytrack, tapeta, good to firm
and good to soft going: wears headgear: sometimes wears tongue tie: sold 7,000 gns, sent
to USA. *David O'Meara*

FOX TROTTER (IRE) 3 br.g. Bushranger (IRE) 119 – Miss Brief (IRE) 72 (Brief Truce **110**
(USA) 126) [2015 99: 7m⁴ 7s 7g⁶ Sep 5] rangy gelding: smart performer: fourth in
handicap at Goodwood (2 lengths behind Enlace) in August: creditable sixth of 16 to
Majestic Moon in handicap at Ascot final start, left with too much to do: stays 7f: acts on
good to firm going: tried in hood. *Brian Meehan*

FOXY FOREVER (IRE) 5 b.g. Kodiac 112 – Northern Tara (IRE) 84 (Fayruz 116) **108**
[2015 94: p6g p5g* p5m² 5m* 6d Sep 13] lengthy gelding: useful handicapper: won at
Chelmsford (by 1¼ lengths from Sir Billy Wright) in May and the Curragh (by 2¼ lengths
from Discussiontofollow) in June: stays 5.5f: acts on polytrack and good to firm going:
sometimes wears headgear: front runner/races prominently. *Michael Wigham*

FOYLESIDEVIEW (IRE) 3 b.g. Dark Angel (IRE) 113 – Showerproof (Peintre Celebre **56**
(USA) 137) [2015 62: p7m 7.1s³ 7.6m 6g p6f⁵ p5g p7m t7.1m⁶ 18.6f* Dec 21] sturdy
gelding: modest handicapper: won at Wolverhampton in December: left Luke Dace after
first start: stays 8.5f: acts on polytrack, tapeta and good to firm going: tried in headgear
prior to 2015: often races in rear. *Harry Chisman*

FRACTAL 4 b.g. High Chaparral (IRE) 132 – Clincher Club 77 (Polish Patriot (USA) 128) **105**
[2015 100p: 12m 14m 12m⁴ 11.9d³ 12s* Sep 18] good-topped gelding: useful handicapper:
value for extra when winning 4-runner event at Newbury in September by 1¼ lengths from
Memorial Day, quickly settling matters final 1f despite carrying head bit awkwardly: stays
1½m: acts on polytrack, soft and good to firm going: sometimes slowly away: often races
in rear/travels strongly: sent to Saudi Arabia. *David Simcock*

FRAGILE EARTH (IRE) 3 b.f. The Carbon Unit (USA) 106 – Mad Madam Mym 75 **69**
(Hernando (FR) 127) [2015 72: 7g⁴ 8m 8.5g 8.3s³ 9.2d² 9.5v⁵ p10.7g f8g⁴ Nov 26] fair
maiden: stays 9f: acts on soft going. *John Patrick Shanahan, Ireland*

FRAMLEY GARTH (IRE) 3 b.g. Clodovil (IRE) 116 – Two Marks (USA) 73 **75**
(Woodman (USA) 126) [2015 76§, a68§: 12m 10d 10g 11.1s⁶ 8s⁴ 7.9g⁵ 8d* 8m 8g Oct 3]
rather leggy gelding: fair handicapper: won at Thirsk (apprentice) in August: stays 10.5f:
acts on good to soft going: tried in visor prior to 2015: tried in tongue tie in 2015: one to
treat with some caution (carries head awkwardly). *Patrick Holmes*

FRANCISCO 3 b.g. Paco Boy (IRE) 129 – Blue Goddess (IRE) 94 (Blues Traveller (IRE) **92 p**
119) [2015 67p: p7m* 5m² 6g* Jun 12] fairly useful performer: won maiden at Lingfield in
April and handicap at Goodwood (by neck from Subversive) in June: stays 7f: should do
better still. *Richard Hannon*

FRANCO'S SECRET 4 b.g. Sakhee's Secret 128 – Veronica Franco 90 (Darshaan 133) **89**
[2015 83: p8g² p8f⁵ p8f⁵ p8g⁵ p8m 10m⁵ 10m⁴ 8.1m⁵ 8g 8.3m* 8.1g³ t9.5g⁵ p8g⁴ p10g³
Dec 20] fairly useful handicapper: won at Lingfield in January and Windsor in August:
stays 1¼m: acts on polytrack and good to firm going: usually wears headgear: usually
races towards rear. *Peter Hedger*

FRANGARRY (IRE) 3 b.g. Lawman (FR) 121 – Divert (IRE) 91 (Averti (IRE) 117) **69 p**
[2015 6m⁵ 6g 7.5m³ p6f³ Nov 6] 55,000Y, £62,000 2-y-o: fourth foal: half-brother to 3
winners, including useful 2-y-o 5f winner Reroute (by Acclamation) and 5f-7f winner
Available (by Moss Vale): dam, 5f winner, half-sister to useful 5f-7f winner Zero Money:
fair maiden: off 5 months/well backed, creditable effort in handicap final start: stays 7.5f:
should do better still. *Alan Bailey*

FRANK BRIDGE 2 b.c. (Mar 26) Avonbridge 123 – First Among Equals 59 (Primo **44**
Valentino (IRE) 116) [2015 p5g⁵ 5g³ 5.3s⁵ 5m⁶ t5.1g Aug 10] poor maiden: stays 5.5f: tried
in cheekpieces. *Bill Turner*

FRANK COOL 2 b.c. (Mar 8) Royal Applause 124 – Queen of Heaven (USA) 54 **–**
(Mr Greeley (USA) 122) [2015 7g 7d p7g Sep 23] compact colt: no form. *David Lanigan*

FRANKLIN D (USA) 3 b.c. Medaglia d'Oro (USA) 129 – Kissed By A Star (USA) **101 p**
(Kingmambo (USA) 125) [2015 81p: p8f⁴ 8.1f* 8m² 8d⁴ 9g p10m* Nov 17] well-made
colt: useful performer: won maiden at Sandown in July and handicap at Lingfield (by ¾
length from Ansaab) in November: stays 1¼m: acts on polytrack and firm going: open to
further improvement. *Michael Bell*

FRANK SANDATRA 2 b.g. (Apr 14) Equiano (FR) 127 – Alhufoof (USA) 100 (Dayjur (USA) 137) [2015 p6g 6d 5g⁶ Oct 19] no form. *Peter Crate* —

FRANKSTER (FR) 2 b.g. (May 8) Equiano (FR) 127 – Milwaukee (FR) (Desert King (IRE) 129) [2015 6g⁶ 7s 6d² Oct 19] fair maiden: best effort when second at Pontefract (½ length behind Calder Prince) in October. *Micky Hammond* **76**

FRANK THE BARBER (IRE) 3 gr.g. Zebedee 113 – Red Rosanna 82 (Bertolini (USA) 125) [2015 62: p5g² t5.1g² t5.1m⁶ 5m³ 5.1g⁵ 5d 5f⁴ 5m⁴ t5.1g² t5.1f³ 5m t5.1m* t5.1f⁶ t5.1f³ t5.1m⁴ Dec 18] modest handicapper: won at Wolverhampton in October: raced only at 5f: acts on polytrack, tapeta and good to firm going: often wears headgear: in tongue tie in 2015: often races prominently. *Steph Hollinshead* **52 a61**

FRANKTHETANK (IRE) 4 ch.g. Captain Gerrard (IRE) 113 – Mi Amor (IRE) 47 (Alzao (USA) 117) [2015 71, a79: f8g Jan 8] fair at best, well held sole start in 2015: stays 9f: acts on fibresand and good to soft going: often wears cheekpieces: sent to Denmark. *Keith Dalgleish* —

FRANTICAL 3 b.g. Observatory (USA) 131 – Quest For Freedom (Falbrav (IRE) 133) [2015 65: 8m p12g⁶ 8.1g⁴ p10f 9.9g f8g p8g f7g p8m² Dec 27] fair handicapper: left Luke Dace after fifth start: stays 8.5f: acts on polytrack and good to firm going. *Tony Carroll* **70**

FRAP 2 b.g. (May 15) Makfi 130 – Frizzante 121 (Efisio 120) [2015 7s 6d 8f³ 10.2g 8.3s* Oct 13] seventh foal: half-brother to 3 winners, including useful winner up to 7f Greensward (2-y-o 6f winner, by Green Desert) and 6f/7f winner Frangipanni (by Dansili): dam 5f/6f winner, including July Cup: modest performer: won nursery at Leicester in October: stays 8.5f: acts on firm and soft going: open to further improvement. *Richard Hannon* **63 p**

FRAY 4 b.f. Champs Elysees 124 – Short Dance (USA) 105 (Hennessy (USA) 122) [2015 94: 8d³ 7m⁴ 8g 8g⁵ 8g⁶ Sep 17] strong, attractive filly: fairly useful handicapper: stays 1m: acts on good to firm and heavy going: often races in rear. *Jim Goldie* **81**

FREDDIE BOLT 9 b.g. Diktat 126 – Birjand 99 (Green Desert (USA) 127) [2015 –: 7.5f⁵ 7.2g⁶ 5.9d 7g⁶ 8g Sep 23] poor maiden: stays 1¼m: acts on firm going: tried in cheekpieces prior to 2015: tried in tongue tie prior to 2015: often races prominently. *Fred Watson* **44**

FREDDIE FREELOADER (IRE) 2 b.c. (Mar 2) Zoffany (IRE) 121 – Spinning Wings (IRE) 102 (Spinning World (USA) 130) [2015 5g⁵ 7.5m p6g³ Jul 2] sturdy colt: modest maiden: best effort when seventh at Beverley (9¾ lengths behind Champagne City) on second start: sold 15,000 gns, sent to Qatar. *Peter Chapple-Hyam* **58**

FREDDY WITH A Y (IRE) 5 b.g. Amadeus Wolf 122 – Mataji (IRE) (Desert Prince (IRE) 130) [2015 81: 7d* 7d* 7g p8g 7g² 8d⁴ 8.1m⁵ 8.5v p7g p8g Dec 9] tall gelding: fairly useful handicapper: won at Brighton in May and Lingfield (amateur, by head from Jonnie Skull) in May: second in claimer at Epsom in July: stays 1m: acts on polytrack, good to firm and good to soft going: often wears headgear: sometimes in tongue tie in 2015. *Gary Moore* **85**

FREDERIC CHOPIN 4 ch.g. Tamayuz 126 – Eliza Gilbert 80 (Noverre (USA) 125) [2015 74, a66: 14m³ p16g* 14.1m³ p15.8g³ p15.8g³ p16g³ Aug 26] fairly useful handicapper: won at Kempton in May: third at Lingfield and Kempton in August: stays 2m: acts on polytrack and good to firm going: often wears tongue tie: sold £16,000 in September and joined James Moffatt. *Michael Appleby* **80**

FREDRICKA 4 ch.f. Assertive 121 – Vintage Steps (IRE) 76 (Bahamian Bounty 116) [2015 82, a66: 5m* 5p² 5m⁵ 5 5m 5f² 6d¹ 5d³ 5m³ 3g⁶ 5.1d⁴ 5v⁴ Oct 17] workmanlike filly: fairly useful handicapper: won at Redcar in April: second at Thirsk in August and third at Doncaster in September: left Garry Moss after second start: best form at 5f: acts on good to firm and good to soft going: tried in cheekpieces prior to 2015. *Ivan Furtado* **94**

FRED'S FILLY 2 ch.f. (Mar 29) Avonbridge 123 – Regal Quest (IRE) 91 (Marju (IRE) 127) [2015 5m 6m⁵ 6m p6g 5.3v² 5.1m⁶ p6g⁶ p5g³ Oct 14] third foal: dam 2-y-o 7f winner: modest maiden: stays 6f: acts on polytrack, good to firm and heavy going: often in headgear: usually races close up. *Bill Turner* **51**

FREE BOUNTY 2 b.c. (Mar 4) Dick Turpin (IRE) 127 – Native Ring (FR) (Bering 136) [2015 p8d⁵ 8m⁵ t9.5f³ Nov 10] angular colt: half-brother to several winners, including useful 1¼m-1½m winners Old Town Boy (by Myboycharlie) and John Louis (by Bertolini): dam French 10.5f winner: fair maiden: best effort when third in maiden at Wolverhampton (6¾ lengths behind Soldier In Action) in November: remains with potential. *Philip McBride* **70 p**

FREE CODE (IRE) 4 b.g. Kodiac 112 – Gerobies Girl (USA) 86 (Deposit Ticket (USA)) [2015 98: 6g 6f 7d* 7m* 7g 7g 7.2g Sep 19] lengthy gelding: useful handicapper: won at Newcastle in May and Doncaster (by nose from Above The Rest) in June: stays 1m: acts on good to firm and good to soft going: tried in headgear prior to 2015. *David Barron* **99**

FREEDOM FLYING 12 b.m. Kalanisi (IRE) 132 – Free Spirit (IRE) (Caerleon (USA) –
132) [2015 –: 15.8s Oct 27] maiden: no form in 2015: often in cheekpieces prior to 2015:
sometimes wears tongue tie. *Lee James*

FREEDOM MARCH 2 b.f. (Mar 17) Oasis Dream 129 – Liberally (IRE) 87 (Statue of **54 p**
Liberty (USA) 115) [2015 6m 6g Jul 15] well-made filly: second foal: dam, 1m-1¼m
winner, half-sister to 1000 Guineas winner Speciosa: better effort when seventh in maiden
at Lingfield (5¼ lengths behind Ediye) in July: will be suited by 7f: in hood: sent to USA:
remains with potential. *Brian Meehan*

FREEDOM ROCK 3 b.f. Rock of Gibraltar (IRE) 133 – Be Free 60 (Selkirk (USA) 129) **73**
[2015 7m 8.3g 9.3g* 10.1m p11m⁶ p10g Nov 25] 12,000Y: good-topped filly: second foal:
dam 1m winner: fair performer: won maiden at Carlisle in June: stays 11f: acts on polytrack.
Philip McBride

FREEDOM ROSE (IRE) 3 br.f. Alfred Nobel (IRE) 110 – Colourpoint (USA) 81 –
(Forest Wildcat (USA) 120) [2015 –: p6f Feb 3] maiden: well held sole start in 2015: best
effort at 6f: acts on polytrack: in visor sole start in 2015: often races towards rear.
Derek Shaw

FREE EAGLE (IRE) 4 b.c. High Chaparral (IRE) 132 – Polished Gem (IRE) 89 **128**
(Danehill (USA) 126) [2015 128p: 10f* 10g³ 11.9m⁶ 9.9g Dec 13]

It would be neither fair nor accurate to describe 2015 as a breakthrough year
for Pat Smullen, who has been riding big-race winners for Dermot Weld for nearly
twenty years, though the latest season showed in the clearest terms just how much
of an asset he has been to the Weld operation in that time. It is increasingly not just
Weld nowadays either, as in 2015 Smullen rode six pattern winners for other yards,
the most he has ever achieved. His association with Covert Love in particular drew
him plaudits, with his ride on that filly in the Irish Oaks justifiably viewed as one
of the rides of the season. Smullen also had two strong candidates for that notional
accolade at Royal Ascot, in the two major middle-distance contests. His expertly-
judged ride on Snow Sky in the Hardwicke Stakes was the sort of front-running ride
seen only rarely, subsequently shown to be near-perfect judged on analysis of the
sectional times. A slightly different but no less deft piece of judgement had shown
Smullen in a good light when landing the Prince of Wales's Stakes on Free Eagle
three days earlier.

One-time ante-post favourite for the Derby before injury intervened, Free
Eagle started the 2015 season as one of the top middle-distance prospects around,
having shown high-class form in a total of just four starts at two and three. The last
of those starts had been a third-placed finish in the Champion Stakes at Ascot and,
following an interrupted preparation with a head cold (he had reportedly always been
hard to train), he reappeared for his four-year-old season over the same course and
distance in the Prince of Wales's Stakes on the second day of Royal Ascot. It wasn't
a particularly strong renewal of the Prince of Wales's Stakes, with only Free Eagle
(129p), The Grey Gatsby (127) and the Australian-trained Criterion (127) having
Timeform ratings that put them in the high-class bracket. Despite being the least
experienced in the line-up and not having had a preparatory race, there was plenty of
stable confidence behind Free Eagle and he was sent off the 5/2 favourite. The Grey
Gatsby was next at 9/2, following a couple of merely respectable showings in the
Dubai Turf and the Tattersalls Gold Cup in the latest season. French-trained Ectot
and Japanese raider Spielberg were 7/1, ahead of the Gordon Richards Stakes and
Brigadier Gerard Stakes winner Western Hymn at 8/1 with Cannock Chase. Gailo
Chop (10/1) and The Corsican (14/1) also started at shorter odds than Criterion, who
was sent off the outsider of the field at a surprising 20/1. California Chrome, the
Kentucky Derby and Preakness winner of 2014, had been declared for the race and
was available at 8/1 before he was withdrawn because of a foot abscess.

Gailo Chop, drawn widest of all in stall ten, took the Prince of Wales's field
along in the early stages at a steady pace, with Criterion second and Pat Smullen on
Free Eagle in third. The Grey Gatsby and Western Hymn sat just behind in fourth and
fifth. Around halfway, Smullen took the chance to move Free Eagle up on Criterion's
outside to take second. Jamie Spencer and Frankie Dettori, on The Grey Gatsby
and Western Hymn respectively, followed, keen not to allow the favourite too much
rope. Smullen moved Free Eagle alongside the leader as they turned into the straight,

Prince of Wales's Stakes, Royal Ascot—
Free Eagle is well ridden by Pat Smullen to prevail from the slightly unfortunate The Grey Gatsby
who meets trouble and only just fails; Western Hymn leads home the rest

best placed as the race was about to begin in earnest. With The Grey Gatsby held in by Western Hymn on his outside, Smullen asked Free Eagle for maximum effort fully two furlongs out and managed to break away to lead by a couple of lengths just inside the final furlong. It was here that The Grey Gatsby finally had the room to attack and he finished strongly, closing on Free Eagle all the way to the line and failing only by a short head with a photo required to separate the pair. That none of the rest, with the exception of fourth-placed The Corsican, who had been set too much to do, were closing on the first two in the later stages showed how well-judged Smullen's ride had been. He certainly hadn't gone too soon, as some might have suspected at the time.

For once in his career, it seemed that Free Eagle's connections might be able to set about the rest of his campaign as planned, with a summer break followed by the Irish Champion Stakes, then the Arc, as the nominated course after Ascot. Free Eagle finished third at Leopardstown, and would have been second but for receiving a broadside from the veering winner Golden Horn, and he came sixth at Longchamp behind the same horse, both creditable efforts, though he was done no favours in the Arc by the eventual fourth Treve who leaned on him in the straight, causing Pat Smullen to stop riding momentarily. However, when Free Eagle was then sent to Hong Kong, where he started favourite for the Hong Kong Cup at Sha Tin's International meeting in December, he shaped as though amiss and finished last of the thirteen runners.

	High Chaparral (IRE) (b 1999)	Sadler's Wells (b 1981)	Northern Dancer / Fairy Bridge
Free Eagle (IRE) (b.c. 2011)		Kasora (b 1993)	Darshaan / Kozana
	Polished Gem (IRE) (b 2003)	Danehill (b 1986)	Danzig / Razyana
		Trusted Partner (ch 1985)	Affirmed / Talking Picture

Free Eagle's pedigree was dealt with at length in *Racehorses of 2014* and there is only a little to add. His dam Polished Gem's latest foal to race, Valac (by Dark Angel), eventually made the track as a three-year-old in 2015, running eight times for Weld without success despite showing fairly useful form. Polished Gem also has a yearling colt by Dubawi and a colt foal by Galileo following on and is in foal to Galileo again. Custom Cut, Polished Gem's most successful offspring after Free Eagle, won the Sandown Mile in April and the Boomerang Stakes at Leopardstown on the same day that Free Eagle finished third in the Irish Champion Stakes. Polished Gem's first foal Sapphire, who won the British Champions Fillies' And Mares' Stakes, delivered her own first foal, a colt by Invincible Spirit, in the latest season. Free Eagle will be at stud himself in 2016 when he will stand at the Irish National Stud for an initial fee of €20,000. He stayed a mile and a half on his only try at the trip in the Arc, but did most of his racing over ten furlongs, and was effective on firm and soft going (unraced on heavy). Victory in the Prince of Wales's Stakes gave Free Eagle the Group 1 win that his career deserved and represented a notable triumph not only for the skill of his jockey but for the skill and patience of

his master trainer, something reinforced by the trainer himself who is not one to be self-effacing at such times. 'Running him here was a calculated risk and a personal triumph for me,' he said afterwards. *D. K. Weld, Ireland*

FREE ENTRY (IRE) 3 b.f. Approve (IRE) 112 – Dear Catch (IRE) 69 (Bluebird (USA) 125) [2015 80: 6m $6v^2$ May 29] good-topped filly: fair handicapper: stays 6f: acts on good to firm and heavy going: in cheekpieces final start. *James Tate*   **77**

FREEMASON 4 b.g. Cape Cross (IRE) 129 – Candy Mountain 86 (Selkirk (USA) 129) [2015 85: p7m 10m p10g* Jun 9] fair handicapper: won at Lingfield in June: stays 1¼m: acts on polytrack and tapeta. *Gary Moore*   **73**

FREE ONE (IRE) 3 b.g. Fast Company (IRE) 126 – Tatamagouche (IRE) 70 (Sadler's Wells (USA) 132) [2015 72: 8.3m³ 8g t7.1m* p8f p8m Dec 31] sturdy gelding: fair performer: won maiden at Wolverhampton in September: stays 8.5f: acts on tapeta and good to firm going: often in hood in 2015. *Jeremy Noseda*   **78**

FREE PASSAGE 2 ch.g. (Mar 1) Medicean 128 – Free Offer 94 (Generous (IRE) 139) [2015 7m 7g 7d Oct 30] rather unfurnished gelding: fourth foal: half-brother to 3 winners at 1m, including smart Cape Peron (by Beat Hollow): dam winner up to 1¼m (2-y-o 7f winner): modest maiden: best effort when eleventh in maiden at Newmarket (4½ lengths behind Chelsea Lad) in October on final start, not knocked about: will stay at least 1m: capable of better. *Henry Candy*   **64 p**

FREE RUNNING (IRE) 3 b.f. Iffraaj 127 – Street Star (USA) 91 (Street Cry (IRE) 130) [2015 7m 8m³ 8g⁶ Aug 28] 60,000Y: rather leggy filly: second foal: dam, 2-y-o 6f winner, half-sister to smart winners up to 1¼m Shrewd Idea and Alva Glen: fair maiden: best effort when third at Thirsk in August: likely to stay further than 1m. *Clive Brittain*   **72**

FREE STATE 3 ch.g. New Approach (IRE) 132 – Firenze 109 (Efisio 120) [2015 9.9m⁵ p10f p8g Dec 11] 160,000F: third foal: half-brother to ungenuine 6f winner Isola Verde (by Oasis Dream) and 5f/6f winner Green Monkey (by Green Desert): dam, 6f winner, sister to July Cup winner Frizzante: fair form: left Charlie Appleby 10,000 gns/off 11 weeks and dropped in trip, 66/1, very much caught eye when 8¾ lengths tenth of 14 to Eagle Valley in maiden at Dundalk final start, racing well off the pace, pushed along early in straight and keeping on: remains with potential. *Denis Hogan, Ireland*   **68 p**

FREE TO LOVE 3 br.f. Equiano (FR) 127 – All Quiet 87 (Piccolo 121) [2015 77: 6m³ **85** 5g³ 5.7f* 5.7g⁴ 5f* 6d⁶ Oct 12] rather leggy filly: fairly useful performer: won minor event at Bath in June and handicap at Bath (by ½ length from Stocking) in September: stays 5.5f: best form on firm going: front runner/races prominently. *Charles Hills*

FREE TO ROAM (IRE) 2 gr.f. (Mar 10) Bushranger (IRE) 119 – Operissimo (Singspiel **– p** (IRE) 133) [2015 7g p6f⁶ f7g f8g Nov 26] 7,000Y: good-topped filly: fifth foal: sister to 1¼m winner The Character and half-sister to useful winner up to 1¼m Silver Grey (2-y-o 6f winner, by Chineur) and French 2-y-o 1m winner Allegrissimo (by Redback): dam unraced sister to smart performer up to 2m Songlark: modest form in maidens: possibly unsuited by conditions when well held on nursery debut at Southwell: may still do better. *Philip McBride*

FREE WHEELING (AUS) 7 b.g. Ad Valorem (USA) 125 – Miss Carefree (AUS) (Last **117** Tycoon 131) [2015 112: 8g³ a7f⁶ 7g³ a8f³ Mar 28] sturdy gelding: smart performer: better than ever when third in Godolphin Mile at Meydan (1½ lengths behind Tamarkuz) on final start: stays 1m: acts on tapeta, best turf form on good going or firmer: sometimes in headgear prior to 2015: wears tongue tie. *Saeed bin Suroor*

FREEWHEEL (IRE) 5 br.g. Galileo (IRE) 134 – La Chunga (USA) 109 (More Than **79** Ready (USA) 120) [2015 89: t12.2g⁵ 13s⁶ 10.1d May 19] fair handicapper: stays 1½m: acts on tapeta, best turf form on soft/heavy going: tried in cheekpieces in 2015: often races prominently. *Fred Watson*

FREEZE A CROWD (IRE) 2 b.f. (Mar 28) Frozen Power (IRE) 108 – Skies Are Blue **–** 70 (Unfuwain (USA) 131) [2015 6g 5.9g 5g 6g Sep 23] €5,000Y, £15,000 2-y-o: seventh foal: half-sister to 3 winners, including 9f/1¼m winner (stayed 13.5f) Lyric Ballad (by Byron) and 1m/9f winner Ledgerwood (by Royal Applause): dam placed at 7f/1m at 2 yrs: no form: tried in hood. *Ben Haslam*

FREEZE STYLE (IRE) 2 ch.g. (Apr 23) Frozen Power (IRE) 108 – Seasonal Style **58** (IRE) 93 (Generous (IRE) 139) [2015 5m³ 6.1m 5s⁴ 6g p7f f7g⁶ f7g⁴ f8f Dec 17] modest **a48** maiden: best form at 5f: acts on soft and good to firm going: in cheekpieces last 3 starts. *Kevin Ryan*

FREEZE THE SECRET (IRE) 3 b.f. Kodiac 112 – Campiglia (IRE) (Fairy King **47** (USA)) [2015 55: f5g⁵ 5m 5.1m 5g⁴ p6f⁴ p6f Oct 28] poor maiden: stays 6f: acts on polytrack and good to firm going: tried in headgear. *David C. Griffiths*

FREE ZONE 6 b.g. Kyllachy 129 – Aldora 109 (Magic Ring (IRE) 115) [2015 98: 5m **89** 5.1g 5m p5g⁵ 5m⁵ 5m 5d⁴ 5v² 5.1d 5s⁴ Oct 19] smallish, good-topped gelding: fairly useful handicapper: second at Ffos Las in August: stays 5.5f: acts on good to firm and heavy going: tried in headgear. *Robert Cowell*

FREIGHT TRAIN (IRE) 3 b.g. Manduro (GER) 135 – Sigonella (IRE) (Priolo (USA) **81** 127) [2015 74p: 10g⁶ 10.4g 12g⁵ 10g* 10d Oct 12] fairly useful handicapper: won at Redcar (by ¾ length from High Baroque) in October: stays 1¼m: acts on good to firm going: front runner/races prominently. *Mark Johnston*

FRENCH 2 ch.f. (Mar 25) Monsieur Bond (IRE) 120 – Guadaloup 70 (Loup Sauvage **77** (USA) 125) [2015 5d* 5m 6f 6m 6g Oct 3] £800Y: workmanlike filly: third foal: dam 6f/7f winner: fair performer: won maiden at Ripon in April: best effort at 5f: acts on good to soft going. *Antony Brittain*

FRENCH DRESSING 2 b.f. Oea The Stars (IRE) 140 – Foodbroker Fancy (IRE) 113 **113 p** (Halling (USA) 133) [2015 10s* 10.4m* Jul 24] rangy filly: half-sister to 3 winners, including winner up to 1m Pretzel (2-y-o 7f winner, by New Approach) and winner up to 1½m Dalvina (2-y-o 7f winner, by Grand Lodge), both smart: dam winner up to 1¼m (2-y-o 6f winner): won 9-runner maiden at Ascot in May by 1½ lengths from Distain: off 11 weeks, looked excellent prospect when following up in 8-runner listed race at York by 2¾ lengths from Crystal Zvezda, leading over 1f out and finding plenty: likely to stay 1½m. *John Gosden*

FRENCH ENCORE 2 b.g. (Feb 27) Showcasing 117 – French Connexion (IRE) 54 **92** (Chineur (FR) 123) [2015 4.5g* 5g³ 5m* 5f⁶ 6g* 7g Dec 29] good-topped colt: dam maiden (stayed 6f): fairly useful performer: successful in newcomers race at Saint-Cloud in March and minor event at Bath in May: 2¾ lengths sixth to Waterloo Bridge in Norfolk Stakes at Royal Ascot next time: left J. S. Moore, also won minor event at Doha in November: stays 6f: acts on firm going. *Debbie Mountain, Qatar*

FRENCH LEGEND 2 b.f. (Apr 22) Pour Moi (IRE) 125 – Fast Flow (IRE) (Fasliyev **–** (USA) 120) [2015 8.1s p8g p7g Nov 9] second foal: dam unraced half-sister to smart winner up to 12.5f Cocktail Queen: no form. *Andrew Balding*

FRENCHMAN (FR) 2 b.c. (Apr 27) Le Havre (IRE) 124 – Como (USA) 95 (Cozzene **80 p** (USA)) [2015 p7g⁴ Oct 7] €6,500Y, resold 45,000Y: half-brother to several winners, including useful 5f/6f (including at 2 yrs) winner Pencil Hill (by Acclamation) and 2-y-o 7f winner Hot Diggity (by Librettist): dam 6f winner: 16/1, encouragement when 2½ lengths fourth of 10 to Chester Street in maiden at Kempton on debut, slowly away but good headway under 2f out: sure to progress. *Charles Hills*

FRENCH NAVY 7 b.h. Shamardal (USA) 129 – First Fleet (USA) 106 (Woodman (USA) **121** 126) [2015 121: 9g* 9.7m⁶ Oct 3] rather leggy horse: very smart performer: looked as good as ever when winning Earl of Sefton Stakes at Newmarket in April by ¾ length from Arod, sweeping through and asserting quickly: off 5½ months, below form when sixth of 8 to Free Port Lux in Prix Dollar at Longchamp: stayed 1¼m: acted on soft and good to firm going: held up: to stand at Kildangan Stud, Co. Kildare, Ireland, fee €4,000. *Charlie Appleby*

FRENCH PRESS (IRE) 5 ch.g. Kheleyf (USA) 116 – Coffee Cream 87 (Common **86** Grounds 118) [2015 –: p6g p6g t9.5m² 7v* 6g* p6f* 6g* 7s² 6s Oct 27] fairly useful **a80** handicapper: left Shane Donohoe after second start: won at Brighton in May and Hamilton (amateur), Chelmsford and Redcar in September: second at Brighton in October: stays 7f: acts on polytrack and heavy going: tried in headgear: tried in tongue tie prior to 2015: front runner/races prominently. *Michael Appleby*

FRENZIFIED 3 b.f. Yeats (IRE) 128 – Librettista (AUS) 81 (Elusive Quality (USA)) **93** [2015 76p: p10g⁴ 9.9f* 10.2m³ 12f* 12g* 12s⁵ 12g⁶ t12.2f* p12g⁶ Nov 4] fairly useful performer: won minor event at Salisbury in May and handicaps at Doncaster in July, Salisbury in August and Wolverhampton (by length from Scurr Mist) in October: stays 1½m: acts on polytrack, tapeta and firm going. *Luca Cumani*

FRESH ARUGULA (IRE) 2 b.c. (Feb 4) Fast Company (IRE) 126 – Temecula (IRE) 86 **—** (High Chaparral (IRE) 132) [2015 5.1m Apr 18] 6/1, better than result when last of 7 in maiden at Nottingham: dead. *Tom Dascombe*

FRESH KINGDOM (IRE) 4 ch.g. Dubawi (IRE) 129 – Polyquest (IRE) 73 (Poliglote **91** 121) [2015 87p: 11.9d p11g* 12s 13.3s p16g⁵ Aug 26] rather leggy gelding: fairly useful handicapper: won at Kempton in June: should be suited by a return to 1½m: acts on polytrack, tapeta and good to soft going: often wears cheekpieces: sold 15,500 gns, sent to Saudi Arabia. *James Fanshawe*

FRESLES (IRE) 4 b.f. Royal Applause 124 – Luna Celtica (IRE) (Celtic Swing 138) **101** [2015 107: p6.5g⁴ p7f* 7s⁴ 8g Sep 6] useful performer: won AW Fillies and Mares Championship Stakes at Lingfield (by neck from Lamar) in April: respectable 4 lengths fourth to Majestic Queen in Chartwell Stakes at same course next time: last of 9 behind Sonnerie in listed race at Longchamp final outing: stays 7.5f: acts on polytrack, best turf form on good going: tried in hood: usually leads. *Mme Pia Brandt, France*

FREUD (FR) 5 b.g. Dalakhani (IRE) 133 – Ailette (Second Set (IRE) 127) [2015 p8g f7s **71** t8.6g t7.1g⁶ 8m t9.5f⁵ Dec 14] fair handicapper: best effort at 1m: acts on soft going: sometimes slowly away, often races towards rear. *Ian Williams*

FRIDGE KID 3 b.f. Kheleyf (USA) 116 – Snow Shoes 84 (Sri Pekan (USA) 117) [2015 **57** 61: 8.3m⁵ 8.3g² p10f p8f p8f⁶ Dec 17] modest maiden: stays 8.5f: acts on good to firm going: tried in cheekpieces in 2015. *Dr Jon Scargill*

FRIGHTENED RABBIT (USA) 3 b.g. Hard Spun (USA) 124 – Champagne Ending **67** (USA) (Precise End (USA)) [2015 8.3s⁵ 9.2m⁴ 6g⁶ 8.3d³ 10.5m⁵ 9.2s* 12.1g Aug 20] fair performer: won handicap at Hamilton in August: best effort at 9f: acts on soft going: tried in blinkers: front runner/races prominently. *L. Smyth, Ireland*

FRIVOLOUS LADY (IRE) 2 b.f. (Mar 14) Bushranger (IRE) 119 – Ufallya (IRE) 74 **71** (Statue of Liberty (USA) 115) [2015 5m 5d* f7g t7.1g³ f8f Dec 17] €1,000F, €4,000Y: leggy filly: second foal: dam, 8.4f winner, half-sister to useful sprinter Bear Behind: fair performer: won maiden at Salisbury in May: will stay 6f: acts on good to soft going: visored last 2 starts. *David Evans*

FRIVOLOUS PRINCE (IRE) 2 b.g. (Apr 5) Baltic King 120 – Sweet Reflection (IRE) **50** (Victory Note (USA) 120) [2015 7m 7g⁶ 6g 8.1m t9.5f⁴ Dec 11] modest maiden: will probably stay 1¼m: acts on tapeta. *David Evans*

FROCK COAT (IRE) 2 ch.g. (Mar 6) Street Cry (IRE) 130 – Peacoat 104 (Doyen (IRE) **65** 132) [2015 7m⁵ 7s⁵ 7g⁴ Sep 7] fair form first 2 starts in maidens: will stay 1m+: has been gelded. *Charlie Appleby*

FROGNAL (IRE) 9 b.g. Kheleyf (USA) 116 – Shannon Dore (IRE) 81 (Turtle Island – (IRE) 123) [2015 –: f6d² f6s Mar 25] lengthy, angular gelding: fairly useful at best, no form in 2015: stays 7f: acts on polytrack, good to firm and good to soft going: often wears headgear: sometimes wears tongue tie. *Heather Dalton*

FRONT FIVE (IRE) 3 b.g. Teofilo (IRE) 126 – Samdaniya 79 (Machiavellian (USA) 82 123) [2015 10g 9.9m 10m⁴ 12m⁴ p13f⁴ p12g³ p16f³ 17.2g⁶ Oct 18] 50,000Y: good-topped gelding: fourth foal: brother to 1¾m/14.6f winner Samtu: dam, 9.7f winner, half-sister to smart performers up to 1½m winner Reverie Solitaire and Queen's Best: fairly useful maiden: third in handicap at Kempton in September: stays 2m: acts on polytrack and good to firm going: front runner/races prominently. *Amanda Perrett*

FRONTIER FIGHTER 7 b.g. Invincible Spirit (IRE) 121 – Rawabi (Sadler's Wells 86 (USA) 132) [2015 110: a7f a9.4f f7s 7g t9.5m* 7g Jun 20] strong gelding: one-time smart performer: just fairly useful in 2015, winning claimer at Wolverhampton in April: stays 11f: acts on all-weather, soft and good to firm going: tried in visor third start: front runner/ races prominently, tends to find little. *David O'Meara*

FRONTLINE PHANTOM (IRE) 8 b.g. Noverre (USA) 125 – Daisy Hill (Indian 67 Ridge 78) [2015 80: 10.3d 10m⁵ 9g⁵ 11.9m 9g 10.2m 9.9s 10s t8.6f Oct 30] strong, close-coupled gelding: fair handicapper: left K. R. Burke after third start: stays 10.5f: acts on firm and good to soft going: tried in headgear: tried in tongue tie prior to 2015. *Tom Dascombe*

FRONT RUN (IRE) 4 b.c. Amadeus Wolf 122 – Prima Volta 80 (Primo Dominie 121) 74 [2015 77: 12g 10.2g² p10g² Jun 17] fair maiden: stays 1½m: acts on polytrack, tapeta and good to soft going: usually races towards rear: sent to Qatar. *Marco Botti*

FROSTMAN (FR) 3 gr.g. Silver Frost (IRE) 122 – Santa Marina (FR) (Kendor (FR) 122) 80 [2015 69: 6d³ 5.7f* p6m² 6g 7m p6g⁵ 6g⁴ 7g p6.5g p6f⁵ Oct 15] fairly useful performer: a88 won maiden at Bath in April: second in handicap at Chelmsford in June: best effort final start: stays 6f: acts on polytrack and firm going: tried in blinkers in 2015: sold 25,000 gns, sent to Sweden. *Jo Hughes*

FROSTY BERRY 6 gr.m. Proclamation (IRE) 130 – Star Entry 67 (In The Wings 128) 78 [2015 73: 12d 9g 12g 14.1v* f12g* f14m* f16g* Dec 18] workmanlike mare: useful a95 handicapper on all-weather, fairly useful on turf: successful last 4 starts, at Redcar and Southwell in November and twice at Southwell in December, latest by neck from Handiwork: stays 2m: acts on polytrack, fibresand and heavy going: in hood nowadays. *Ed de Giles*

FROSTY FLYER (FR) 3 gr.g. Silver Frost (IRE) 122 – Perruche Grise (FR) (Mark of 55 Esteem (IRE) 137) [2015 56: f8g⁵ 10g⁵ 8g³ 6.9v⁵ 7.5m⁵ Jun 23] modest maiden: stays 1m: acts on good to firm going: in headgear last 3 starts. *Richard Fahey*

FROSTY THE SNOWMAN (IRE) 4 gr.g. Mastercraftsman (IRE) 129 – Sleeveless 61 (USA) 76 (Fusaichi Pegasus (USA) 130) [2015 71: f12g 10.3d⁶ f11g² 12.4d⁶ f11d² 12.4g³ 11.9f⁴ 12g⁶ 16m⁴ 14g 16.1m⁶ f12s³ 15.8g⁴ 16.1g Sep 4] modest maiden: stays 2m: acts on fibresand, firm and good to soft going: often in headgear in 2015: front runner/races prominently. *Ruth Carr*

FROZEN FORCE (IRE) 2 ch.c. (Mar 3) Frozen Power (IRE) 108 – La Mere Germaine 72 (IRE) 88 (Indian Ridge 123) [2015 7g 8s⁴ 6.5s⁵ p7g⁶ p8g³ p8g* Dec 15] fair performer: won nursery at Kempton in December: best effort at 1m: acts on polytrack. tried in blinkers. *Amanda Perrett*

FROZEN PRINCESS 3 b.f. Showcasing 117 – Super Midge 50 (Royal Applause 124) – [2015 64: p5g Dec 2] good-quartered filly: modest at best, well held sole start in 2015: stays 6f: acts on tapeta and good to firm going: often races prominently. *Jamie Osborne*

FROZEN VENTURE (IRE) 2 b.c. (Apr 9) Frozen Power (IRE) 108 – Taqarub (IRE) 54 p (Marju (IRE) 127) [2015 7m⁵ Jun 22] £48,000Y: third foal: dam, French 7f winner, half-sister to 5f/6f winner Khasayl and 2-y-o 7f winner Muklah (both useful): 11/1, fifth in maiden at Wetherby (11¾ lengths behind King's Pavilion) in June: may do better. *John Quinn*

FROZON 2 b.g. (Apr 20) Kheleyf (USA) 116 – Crozon 68 (Peintre Celebre (USA) 137) – [2015 6.1v⁶ Oct 7] 25/1, showed something amidst greenness when 13 lengths sixth of 9 to Kadrizzi in maiden at Nottingham on debut, very slowly away but making late headway. *Brian Ellison*

FRUGAL (IRE) 2 b.f. (May 8) Bahamian Bounty 116 – Naayla (IRE) 85 (Invincible – Spirit (IRE) 121) [2015 6g⁴ 7g⁴ Jul 22] 11,000Y: fifth foal: half-sister to 5f (including at 2 yrs) winner La Sylphe (by Refuse To Bend): dam 2-y-o 6f winner: no form in sellers. *Nick Littmoden*

FRUIT PASTILLE 4 b.f. Pastoral Pursuits 127 – Classic Millennium 72 (Midyan (USA) **98** 124) [2015 94: 8m 8m⁶ p8m 10f⁶ 8v² 8d 8g² 8d⁵ Nov 3] rather leggy filly: useful performer: second in handicaps at Newbury and Newmarket (beaten 1¼ lengths by Volunteer Point): good 3¼ lengths fifth to Sparkling Beam in listed race at Chantilly final start, leading till over 1f out: stays 8.5f: acts on polytrack, tapeta and heavy going: usually wears headgear: often starts slowly. *Hughie Morrison*

FRUIT SALAD 2 ch.f. (May 7) Monsieur Bond (IRE) 120 – Miss Apricot 48 (Indian **68** Ridge 123) [2015 5.4s⁵ t6f² p5g* Nov 25] £3,000Y: fourth foal: sister to 8.6f winner Charlcot and half-sister to 5f/6f winner Apricot Sky (by Pastoral Pursuits) and 1m winner Princess Peaches (by Notnowcato): dam ran twice: fair performer: won maiden at Kempton (by short head from Shine Likeadiamond) in November: stays 6f. *James Bethell*

FRUITY (IRE) 3 b.f. Camacho 118 – Belle of The Blues (IRE) (Blues Traveller (IRE) **89** 119) [2015 84: 7m⁴ 8.1m 7m* 7.1g³ p7g³ t8.6f⁵ p8g⁴ Nov 9] rather leggy filly: fairly useful handicapper: won at Leicester (by 1¼ lengths from Fine View) in July: third at Kempton in September: should prove suited by a return to 7f: acts on polytrack and good to firm going: front runner/races prominently: sold 40,000 gns, sent to USA. *Clive Cox*

FUEL INJECTION 4 gr.g. Pastoral Pursuits 127 – Smart Hostess 101 (Most Welcome **71** 131) [2015 67, a73: 5g f5m f5f² Dec 17] rather leggy gelding: fair handicapper: best form at 5f: acts on fibresand, soft and good to firm going: often wears headgear: often races prominently. *Paul Midgley*

FUJIANO 3 b.f. Equiano (FR) 127 – The Fugitive 94 (Nicholas (USA) 111) [2015 70: 6d* **67** 6g 6s⁶ Aug 23] good-topped filly: fair performer: won maiden at Brighton (by 3¼ lengths from General Potempkin) in May: stayed 6f: acted on soft going: tried in hood: dead. *Mike Murphy*

FUJIN 4 b.g. Oasis Dream 129 – Phantom Wind (USA) 111 (Storm Cat (USA)) [2015 62: **61** 6g⁶ 5m⁴ p5g² 5g⁴ 5m* 5s 6v p6g f6g* 16m³ Dec 30] fair handicapper: won at Beverley in **a71** October and Southwell in December: stays 6f: acts on fibresand, tapeta and good to firm going: often wears headgear. *Shaun Harris*

FULL COVERAGE (IRE) 3 b.g. Bushranger (IRE) 119 – Incense 73 (Unfuwain (USA) **–** 131) [2015 7g 7g⁶ Apr 30] no form. *Nigel Tinkler*

FULL DAY 4 ch.f. Champs Elysees 124 – Capistrano Day (USA) 110 (Diesis 133) [2015 **87** 82: 12.1m² 11.7m⁴ 12g 16m⁴ 16.4m⁵ 16.4m⁴ 15.9g⁶ 18g³ 16.4s⁵ Oct 10] sturdy, attractive filly: fairly useful handicapper: third at Newmarket in September: stays 2¼m: acts on good to firm and heavy going: usually in cheekpieces in 2015. *Brian Ellison*

FULL MAST (USA) 3 b.c. Mizzen Mast (USA) 121 – Yashmak (USA) 118 (Danzig **117** (USA)) [2015 111p: 8g² 8g Jul 12] big, strong, attractive colt: smart performer: won all 3 starts at 2 yrs, including when awarded Prix Jean-Luc Lagardere at Longchamp: even better form when short-neck second to Almanaar in Prix Paul de Moussac at Chantilly on reappearance: disappointing seventh behind Territories in Prix Jean Prat at Chantilly only subsequent outing: stays 1m: acts on polytrack and good to firm going: sent to USA. *Mme C. Head-Maarek, France*

FULL OF PROMISE 2 b.f. (Apr 14) Kyllachy 129 – Arculinge 64 (Paris House 123) **53** [2015 6s⁴ 6s⁵ Nov 7] sixth foal: half-sister to 3 winning sprinters, including useful winner up to 6f Charles Molson (2-y-o 5f winner, by Monsieur Bond): dam, maiden (stayed 6f), half-sister to smart sprinter Corrybrough (by Kyllachy): modest form in maidens at Brighton and Doncaster, testing conditions both times. *Richard Fahey*

FULL OF SPEED (USA) 3 ch.g. Raven's Pass (USA) 133 – Knock Twice (USA) (Two **68** Punch (USA)) [2015 66: p8g p10g 11.6m³ p12g² t12.2g² t12.2m⁴ 9.9d t9.5f⁴ Oct 23] fair maiden: stays 1½m: acts on polytrack and tapeta. *James Fanshawe*

FULLON CLARETS 3 ch.g. Equiano (FR) 127 – Palinisa (FR) 106 (Night Shift (USA)) **94** [2015 81: 7d⁵ p6g* 6m⁴ 6f⁴ 7d³ 7m⁴ 7m⁵ 7d² 7.2m² 7s Oct 9] good-topped gelding: fairly useful performer: won maiden at Lingfield in April: second in handicaps at Thirsk in August and Musselburgh in September: stays 7f: acts on polytrack, good to firm and good to soft going: tried in cheekpieces in 2015: front runner/races prominently: temperament under suspicion (has hung left/carried head awkwardly). *Richard Fahey*

FULL SPEED (GER) 10 b.g. Sholokhov (IRE) 121 – Flagny (FR) (Kaldoun (FR) 122) **–** [2015 t12.2m⁵ t12.2m t12.2m Sep 14] strong gelding: fairly useful at best, no form in 2015: tried in cheekpieces in 2015. *Philip Kirby*

FUMATA BIANCA (IRE) 2 b.f. (Apr 22) Acclamation 118 – Divine Authority (IRE) **68**
(Holy Roman Emperor (IRE) 125) [2015 6d 6s 6g⁶ 6s 6g p7g³ Oct 27] €70,000Y: useful-
looking filly: second foal: dam unraced half-sister to Richmond Stakes winner Carrizo
Creek: fair maiden: likely to stay 1m: acts on polytrack and soft going: often starts slowly:
sold 7,500 gns, sent to France. *Hughie Morrison*

FUMBO JUMBO (IRE) 2 b.f. (Feb 25) Zebedee 113 – Baraloti (IRE) 71 (Barathea **67**
(IRE) 127) [2015 5d 6g² 7g⁵ 6m⁴ 5d⁴ Oct 26] €7,000 2-y-o: half-sister to several winners,
including smart UAE 6f/7f winner Garbah and 7f/1m winner Kodiac's Back (both by
Kodiac): dam maiden (raced at 1m): fair maiden: left David Nicholls after second start:
stays 6f: acts on good to firm going. *Garry Moss*

FUNDING DEFICIT (IRE) 5 ch.g. Rakti 130 – Bukat Timah (Inchinor 119) [2015 75: **87**
7.1g⁴ 8d² 7.2d* 7m⁴ 7m 7d⁵ 6m* 5g 6.1d² Sep 26] fairly useful handicapper: won at Ayr in
June and Redcar in August: second at Chester in September: stays 8.5f, at least as effective
over shorter: acts on firm and good to soft going: sometimes wears hood: often races
towards rear. *Jim Goldie*

FUNKY MUNKY 10 b.g. Talaash (IRE) 110 – Chilibang Bang 68 (Chilibang 120) [2015 **58**
60: t16.5g⁵ 8d 12.4g 15.8s* 13.8v³ Oct 17] modest handicapper: won at Catterick in
October: stays 2m: acts on polytrack and heavy going: sometimes wears headgear: tried in
tongue tie prior to 2015. *Alistair Whillans*

FUN MAC (GER) 4 ch.g. Shirocco (GER) 129 – Favorite (GER) (Montjeu (IRE) 137) **115**
[2015 91: 14.1m* 20f² 14s² 18m⁴ 19.9m³ 15.4d Oct 25] good-topped gelding: smart
performer: won handicap at Salisbury (by 11 lengths from William of Orange) in May:
even better form after, including when second in Ascot Stakes (Handicap) at Royal Ascot
(½ length behind Clondaw Warrior) in June, fourth in Doncaster Cup (2¾ lengths behind
Pallasator) in September and third in Prix du Cadran at Longchamp (4 lengths behind Mille
Et Mille) in October: stays 2½m: acts on any turf going: tried in blinkers prior to 2015:
sometimes wears tongue tie: usually races towards rear. *Hughie Morrison*

FUNNY OYSTER (IRE) 2 gr.f. (Apr 12) Dark Angel (IRE) 113 – Carpet Lover (IRE) **59**
46 (Fayruz 116) [2015 6g⁵ p7g 8s⁵ p6g 6d⁴ 7s³ Oct 26] £32,000Y: sturdy filly: seventh foal:
half-sister to 5f (including at 2 yrs) winner Beau Mistral (by Windsor Knot): dam once-
raced half-sister to smart 2-y-o 5f winner Misty Eyed: modest maiden: stays 1m: acts on
soft going: tried in cheekpieces. *George Baker*

FURAS (IRE) 4 br.g. Shamardal (USA) 129 – Albaraari 79 (Green Desert (USA) 127) –
[2015 80: 5.9m May 25] well-made gelding: fairly useful at best, no form in 2015: stays 6f:
acts on polytrack: tried in blinkers prior to 2015. *Ruth Carr*

FURIANT 2 b.g. (Mar 10) Invincible Spirit (IRE) 121 – Save Me The Waltz (FR) (Halling **86**
(USA) 133) [2015 5g* 5m⁶ 5m⁵ p6g² 5f³ 6f⁴ 6m² 6.5m 5.5d³ 6s 5s* Oct 27] €105,000F,
€140,000Y: sturdy gelding: seventh foal: half-brother to 3 winners, including smart French/
US winner up to 10.5f Dealbata (2-y-o 1m winner, by Dubawi) and useful/ungenuine 10.5f
winner King's Warrior (by King's Best): dam French 11f winner: fairly useful performer:
won maiden at Musselburgh in May and minor event at Catterick in October: stays 6f: acts
on soft and good to firm going: front runner/races prominently. *Mark Johnston*

FURIOUSLY FAST (IRE) 3 b.g. Fast Company (IRE) 126 – Agouti (Pennekamp (USA) **72**
130) [2015 58p: 8g 7.6m⁴ 8.5g⁵ 12.1m⁵ 11.6d³ f12g⁴ t12.2m Nov 28] fair maiden: left
Clive Brittain after second start: stays 1½m: acts on fibresand, good to firm and good to soft
going: often races prominently. *Richard Fahey*

FUTOON (IRE) 2 b.f. (Jan 8) Kodiac 112 – Vermilliann (IRE) 98 (Mujadil (USA) 119) **75**
[2015 6g² 6g³ Oct 16] 12,000F, €40,000Y: fifth foal: half-sister to 5.5f winner Marjong (by
Mount Nelson) and a winner abroad by One Cool Cat: dam, 2-y-o 5f winner, sister to smart
winner up to 7f Galeota: second of 10 to Ring of Truth in maiden at Haydock in May: left
Clive Cox/off 5 months, below that form in maiden at Haydock: sold 3,000 gns in
December. *Kevin Ryan*

FUTURE EMPIRE 3 ch.g. New Approach (IRE) 132 – Fann (USA) 96 (Diesis 133) **107**
[2015 102: 10.1g² 12.3s⁶ 16f³ 13m² 13.7m² 14.6m Sep 11] good-topped gelding: useful
performer: second in Bahrain Trophy at Newmarket (2½ lengths behind Mr Singh) in July
and in handicap at Musselburgh (neck behind Pressure Point) in August: stays 2m: acts on
firm going: tried in cheekpieces in 2015: has hung/carried head awkwardly. *Saeed
bin Suroor*

FUTURE SECURITY (IRE) 6 ch.g. Dalakhani (IRE) 133 – Schust Madame (IRE) 46 –
(Second Set (IRE) 127) [2015 a9g a9.9g Feb 22] fairly useful at best, no form in 2015:
stays 1½m: acts on snow, best turf form on good going: in cheekpieces latest start in 2015.
Anthony Middleton

FUWAIRT (IRE) 3 b.g. Arcano (IRE) 122 – Safiya Song (IRE) (Intikhab (USA) 135) – [2015 90: 6m⁶ 9.9s 11.9d Oct 18] stocky, close-coupled gelding: fairly useful at best, little form in 2015: left John Quinn after first start: stays 6f (acted as pacemaker over much longer trips last 2 starts): acts on soft and good to firm going: front runner/races prominently: sold €5,000 in November. *E. Lellouche, France*

FUZZY LOGIC (IRE) 6 b.g. Dylan Thomas (IRE) 132 – Gates of Eden (USA) 71 **55** (Kingmambo (USA) 125) [2015 16.2m⁶ 16.2s⁴ 18d³ Aug 20] sturdy gelding: modest maiden: stays 2¼m: acts on good to firm and heavy going: tried in headgear: often races prominently: temperament under suspicion. *Bernard Llewellyn*

FYRECRACKER (IRE) 4 ch.g. Kheleyf (USA) 116 – Spirit of Hope (IRE) (Danehill **85** Dancer (IRE) 117) [2015 90: 6m³ 6m⁶ 7f 7g 6.1m³ p6g Oct 6] angular gelding: fairly useful handicapper: third at Ascot in May and Chepstow in September: stays 6f: acts on good to firm going: tried in hood in 2015. *Marcus Tregoning*

G

GABBIANO 6 b.g. Zafeen (FR) 123 – Hollybell 87 (Beveled (USA)) [2015 96: t5.1f⁵ 6m **78** p7g p6g Oct 6] compact gelding: fair handicapper: best at 6f: acts on polytrack, firm and good to soft going: tried in headgear prior to 2015: held up (often starts slowly). *Jeremy Gask*

GABBYS LAD (IRE) 2 b.f. (Jan 31) Lilbourne Lad (IRE) 111 – Phantom Waters 79 – (Pharly (FR) 130) [2015 6m p7g Aug 24] 5,000Y: angular filly: half-sister to several winners, including useful winner up to 1¼m (stays 1¾m) Goodwood Mirage (2-y-o 7f winner, by Jeremy) and 5f/6f winner Diman Waters (by Namid): dam 1½m winner who stayed 1¾m: no form. *Brendan Powell*

GABRIAL (IRE) 6 b.g. Dark Angel (IRE) 113 – Guajira (FR) (Mtoto 134) [2015 114: 8d* **119** 8m 10.3s⁴ 8m⁴ 8g² 8f 8.3m³ 7g³ 8g³ 8.9g⁶ 8s² 8.1v² 8d³ Oct 17] big, strong gelding: smart performer: won 22-runner Lincoln (Handicap) at Doncaster (by neck from Mondialiste) in March, leading near finish: showed himself better than ever when third in Sussex Stakes at Goodwood (2¾ lengths behind Solow) in July, second in Celebration Mile at Goodwood (3¼ lengths behind Kodi Bear) in August and third in Queen Elizabeth II Stakes at Ascot (2¼ lengths behind Solow) in October, ninth/eleventh/final starts: stays 10.5f, all wins at shorter: acts on any turf going: tried in headgear prior to 2015: usually races nearer last than first: formerly quirky, more reliable nowadays. *Richard Fahey*

GABRIAL'S HOPE (FR) 6 b.g. Teofilo (IRE) 126 – Wedding Night (FR) (Valanour **66** (IRE) 125) [2015 74, a67: 12.4g 10.1d 12g⁶ 10.1m 10m 10.1m⁴ 9g⁵ 9m² 12.4g⁵ 12.4g⁴ 12.4g² Sep 4] fair handicapper: stays 12.5f: acts on polytrack and good to firm going: tried in headgear: sometimes in tongue tie prior to 2015: often races towards rear. *Tracy Waggott*

Betway Lincoln (Heritage Handicap), Doncaster—
Gabrial (noseband) gives owner Marwan Koukash his second triumph in the race in three years
as he wins from the future Grade 1 winner Mondialiste, with Moohaarib (left) third

GABRIAL'S KAKA (IRE) 5 b.g. Jeremy (USA) 122 – Love In May (IRE) 80 (City On 98
A Hill (USA) 114) [2015 114: 8d 8g⁶ 10.3s⁵ 7.6g⁶ 10.3f 8.1m 8m⁶ 7.6m 7.6s³ 8g 9g 8.5s⁶
Oct 9] lengthy gelding: smart handicapper in 2014 but just useful form at best in 2015:
stays 10.5f: acts on soft and good to firm going: tried in visor in 2015. *Richard Fahey*

GABRIAL'S KING (IRE) 6 b.g. Hurricane Run (IRE) 134 – Danella (IRE) (Platini 101
(GER) 126) [2015 100: 16g² 18.7d⁴ 16.2g 16.1m 12m 12m⁶ 13.4m* 14d 18g Oct 10]
sturdy gelding: useful handicapper: won at Chester in August: not at best subsequently:
stays 2¼m: acts on polytrack, good to firm and heavy going: has worn headgear:
inconsistent. *Richard Fahey*

GABRIAL'S STAR 6 b.g. Hernando (FR) 127 – Grain Only (Machiavellian (USA) 123) 104
[2015 97: t12.2g³ f12s² t16.5m² 18.7d⁵ 16.1m 11.9g 21g 13.4m² 14d 17.5g^pu Sep 18] leggy a95
gelding: useful handicapper: second at Chester (neck behind Gabrial's King) in August:
shaped as if amiss when pulled up final start: stays 2¼m: acts on all-weather and any turf
going: usually in headgear, *Richard Fahey*

GABRIAL'S WAWA 5 b.g. Dubai Destination (USA) 127 – Celestial Welcome 96 (Most 77
Welcome 131) [2015 71: p6m* p6f* p6g² t6f⁴ 6m⁵ 6g² t7.1g Jun 29] fair handicapper: won
at Lingfield (twice) in January: left Michael Squance after fourth start: stays 9.5f, but has
taken well to sprinting: acts on polytrack, best turf form on good to soft/soft going: tried in
blinkers prior to 2015: often races prominently. *Phil McEntee*

GABRIAL THE BOSS (USA) 5 ch.g. Street Boss (USA) 124 – Bacinella (USA) (El –
Gran Senor (USA) 136) [2015 76: 9.9s 10.2d 8.6m 9.5m 10g⁶ Oct 3] good-topped
gelding: fairly useful at best, no form in 2015: tried in cheekpieces: often wears tongue tie.
Michael Mullineaux

GABRIAL THE DUKE (IRE) 5 ch.g. Duke of Marmalade (IRE) 132 – Literacy (USA) 89
74 (Diesis 133) [2015 81§: t9.5g p11m² f12s* f12d³ f12g⁵ t13.9f* 12.5s* 12g⁵ 14m*
13.4g² 16m² 15.9m⁵ 16.4m⁶ 15.9m Aug 22] fairly useful handicapper: won at Southwell in
February, Wolverhampton in March and Musselburgh in April and May: second at Chester
in May and Musselburgh in June: stays 16.5f: acts on all-weather, soft and good to firm
going: sometimes wears headgear: formerly untrustworthy. *Richard Fahey*

GABRIAL THE HERO (USA) 6 b.g. War Front (USA) 119 – Ball Gown (USA) (Silver 101
Hawk (USA) 123) [2015 95: 14.6d t12.2m⁴ t12.2f² f12f* p15.8g* Dec 28] strong gelding:
useful handicapper: in cheekpieces, won at Southwell and Lingfield (by neck from Cotton
Club) in December: stays 2m: acts on all-weather, firm and good to soft going: sometimes
slowly away, often travels strongly. *Richard Fahey*

GABRIAL THE TERROR (IRE) 5 b.g. Kheleyf (USA) 116 – Simla Bibi 69 (Indian 86
Ridge 123) [2015 77: t8.6g t9.5g t12.2f* t12.2f³ t16.5g* t13.9g* 14s 14m 16.4m Jul 11]
fairly useful handicapper: won at Wolverhampton in February (twice) and March (twice):
stays 16.5f: acts on tapeta and good to firm going: sometimes wears cheekpieces: usually
races towards rear. *Richard Fahey*

GABRIAL THE THUG (FR) 5 b.g. Azamour (IRE) 130 – Baliyna (USA) (Woodman 65
(USA) 126) [2015 68§, a61§: t9.5g⁵ t8.6g* t8.6f* t8.6f* 8g 8m⁵ 8.5m⁶ t8.6g³ t8.6g⁶ a73
7.5m t8.6m* 10 3s t8.6g⁵ t8.6f p8g⁴ t8.6g 8.6f Dec 22] fair handicapper: won at
Wolverhampton in January, February (twice) and September (apprentice): stays 10.5f: acts
on polytrack, tapeta, good to firm and good to soft going: usually wears tongue tie: quirky.
Richard Fahey

GABRIAL THE TIGER (IRE) 3 b.g. Kodiac 112 – Invincible 76 (Slip Anchor 136) 84
[2015 72: t7.1g p6m⁶ f5g t6g⁴ 7.1s* 7m⁴ 7g³ 6.9v² 7.1m* 7.6m⁶ 6.1g² 5.5m Aug 22] fairly
useful handicapper: won at Musselburgh in April and June: second at Chester in July: stays
7f: acts on soft and good to firm going: tried in hood in 2015: front runner/races prominently.
Richard Fahey

GABRIAL THE VIKING (IRE) 3 b.g. Approve (IRE) 112 – Xarzee (IRE) (Xaar 132) 69 §
[2015 78: p10f⁴ 8g 8g 8g May 27] fair handicapper: stays 1m: acts on soft and good to firm
going: usually races prominently, tends to find little. *Richard Fahey*

GABRIEL'S LAD (IRE) 6 b.g. Dark Angel (IRE) 113 – Catherine Wheel 83 (Primo 118
Dominie 121) [2015 118: 7g 7s⁶ 7m² 8d Oct 17] tall, rather leggy gelding: smart performer:
easily best effort of season when short-head second of 17 to Buckstay in handicap at Ascot
in October: stays 7f: acts on polytrack, firm and soft going: often starts slowly, usually
races nearer last than first. *Denis Coakley*

GABSTER (IRE) 2 ch.f. (Feb 12) Iffraaj 127 – Mozie Cat (IRE) 72 (Mozart (IRE) 131) **67**
[2015 6g p7g[6] p8m[2] Nov 17] €12,000 2-y-o: angular filly: third foal: dam, 8.6f winner,
half-sister to smart 7f/1m winner Pounced out of useful 1m winner (stayed 1¼m) Golden
Cat: fair maiden: best effort when second at Lingfield (3¾ lengths behind Baydar) in
November, well positioned. *Amanda Perrett*

GAELIC ANGEL (IRE) 2 b.f. (Feb 15) Pour Moi (IRE) 125 – Missionary Hymn (USA) **64**
(Giant's Causeway (USA) 132) [2015 6.1s p7g Oct 14] £27,000 2-y-o: second foal: half-
sister to 1¼m winner (stays 1½m) High And Flighty (by High Chaparral): dam unraced:
better effort when eighth in maiden at Kempton (4 lengths behind Desiderada) in October,
needing stiffer test. *Michael Scudamore*

GAELIC ICE 6 b.m. Iceman 117 – Gaelic Lime (Lomitas 129) [2015 p12f t13.9m[5] p13f[5] **59**
Mar 4] modest handicapper: stays easy 1¾m: acts on polytrack, tapeta, good to firm and
heavy going: often in headgear prior to 2015. *Martin Hill*

GAELIC O'REAGAN 4 b.g. Refuse To Bend (IRE) 128 – Gaelic Roulette (IRE) 78 **–**
(Turtle Island (IRE) 123) [2015 54: p8f p8f Dec 17] maiden: no form in 2015: often in
tongue tie in 2015. *Robert Eddery*

GAELIC SILVER (FR) 9 b.g. Lando (GER) 128 – Galatza (FR) (Johann Quatz (FR) **79**
120) [2015 83, a98: p10g[2] p10m[5] p10f[3] p10f 10.1g 10.1d 10g p10m p11g[3] p10g[4] Dec 20] **a97**
fairly useful handicapper on turf, useful on all-weather: stays 11f: acts on polytrack and
good to soft going: tried in cheekpieces: usually races towards rear. *Gary Moore*

GAELIC WIZARD (IRE) 7 b.g. Fasliyev (USA) 120 – Fife (IRE) 95 (Lomond (USA) **66**
128) [2015 70: f8s f6g[6] t7.1g f7g 7.1g[6] 7d 7.1m[6] 6g[2] 6m[2] 5m[2] 5d[2] 6d[4] 6m[4] 5m* 5m[2] 6d
Oct 26] fair handicapper: won at Hamilton in September: stays 7.5f, effective at shorter:
acts on polytrack, fibresand, soft and good to firm going: sometimes wears headgear: often
races prominently. *Karen Tutty*

GAILO CHOP (FR) 4 ch.g. Deportivo 116 – Grenoble (FR) (Marignan (USA) 117) **122**
[2015 119: 9.2m[2] 10f 9.9s* 10.1g 9.9d* Oct 31]

    While there was disappointment for his compatriots at the Breeders' Cup,
French-trained Gailo Chop had more luck the same weekend in Australia where he
ran out a game winner of the Mackinnon Stakes at Flemington. Gailo Chop struck
a wider blow for Europe, in fact, as the now annual raid by northern hemisphere
challengers on Australia's most prestigious autumn races, the Melbourne Cup,
Caulfield Cup and Cox Plate, drew a blank. Like the Andrew Balding-trained
Side Glance, before his victory in the Mackinnon in 2013, Gailo Chop had been
unsuccessful just seven days earlier in the Cox Plate, Australia's most prestigious
weight-for-age contest. Gailo Chop finished only eighth behind
the Australian-trained filly Winx who was an impressive winner in record time over
the idiosyncratic, turning track. Ridden more patiently than usual, Gailo Chop made
ground rapidly approaching the home turn but was forced to come wide before
his effort petered out in the very short home straight. The Aidan O'Brien-trained
Highland Reel, representing the connections who had been successful in the Cox
Plate with Adelaide twelve months earlier, finished third, but the British-trained
colt Arod was another who failed to give his running back in eleventh. Gailo Chop
reportedly took very little out of himself in the Cox Plate and was supplemented
with the aim of trying to gain quick consolation in the Mackinnon. Back on a more
conventional track, he was duly seen to much better effect, his rivals including
two others who had contested the Cox Plate, fourth-placed Pornichet and the
2014 Mackinnon winner Happy Trails who had been only tenth at Moonee Valley.
Gailo Chop had often been a front runner in Europe, and he got to the front in the
Mackinnon after a couple of furlongs. He looked in trouble when asked to quicken in
the straight and was headed entering the final furlong by the mare Rising Romance
before rallying well to beat the previous season's Caulfield Cup runner-up by half a
length. The same distance back in third, representing Godolphin's Australian stable,
was Contributor who had won the Wolferton Stakes at Royal Ascot in 2014 when
trained by Ed Dunlop. With little covering the first half dozen, the other European
runner, German-trained Magic Artist, stayed on well for a close fourth, right on the
heels of the winner and tight up against the rail, all in all probably unlucky not to
finish closer still. There is a photo of the finish in 'Top Horses Abroad'.

Besides being a career-best effort, Gailo Chop's Mackinnon win represented a marked improvement on his previous unsuccessful forays outside France, a record which contrasted with his excellent record on home turf. Starting out in the Provinces, Gailo Chop won a maiden at La Teste and a listed race at Nantes from four starts as a two-year-old. The following spring, he made a perfect transition to the bigger tracks, completing a hat-trick in a listed race at Saint-Cloud and the Prix La Force and Prix Noailles at Longchamp. Had he been a colt, those wins would have put him firmly on course for the Prix du Jockey Club but, with the French Derby closed to geldings, Gailo Chop was sent abroad for the first time, contesting the inaugural running of the Belmont Derby Invitational Stakes instead. In a field which included Adelaide from Ireland, the future Breeders' Cup Classic runner-up Toast of New York and the ex-French Pornichet having his first start for Gai Waterhouse, Gailo Chop wasn't entirely discredited in finishing just over four lengths fourth to Mr Speaker, who beat Adelaide by a neck. Gailo Chop had changed hands after the Prix La Force, having raced in the colours of his breeder until then, but his new Australian owners had to wait until the latest season for him to make his debut Down Under. In what turned out to be his final start at three, Gailo Chop was returned to France and took his record to six wins from nine starts with another improved effort, making all in the Prix Guillaume d'Ornano to win by three and a half lengths from Free Port Lux who had finished much closer to him when also runner-up in the Prix La Force in the spring.

The performances of the likes of Cirrus des Aigles and, in the latest season, Solow too, have exposed the absurdity of the French Group 1 programme which results in geldings who graduate to the top flight being barred from many of the best races. It was no coincidence that Gailo Chop met that illustrious pair in a four-runner field for the Prix d'Ispahan at Longchamp in May, one of the few Group 1 contests of the season open to them on home soil. Gailo Chop was the only one of the quartet who lacked the benefit of a recent run, having had his reappearance delayed by a setback earlier in the spring, but he made an encouraging return without proving any match in the closing stages for Solow who beat him very comfortably by a length and a half. Gailo Chop actually lasted longer in the lead than had looked likely after Cirrus des Aigles loomed up to him early in the straight, that particular challenge coming to nothing with Cirrus des Aigles having, it turned out, broken one of his racing plates. Gailo Chop again made much of the running in the Prince of Wales's Stakes at Royal Ascot the following month but was not up to the task in a high-class contest and beat only fellow French runner Ectot home in a field of nine. However, taking a drop in class and after a three-month break, Gailo Chop successfully warmed up for his Australian campaign when having Ectot over seven lengths behind in third when winning La Coupe de Maisons-Laffitte in September by four lengths from outsider Al Waab. After his two races in Australia, Gailo Chop was due to end the year in the Hong Kong Cup in December but failed a veterinary examination after returning lame from a workout the day before the race.

Gailo Chop (FR) (ch.g. 2011)	Deportivo (b 2000)	Night Shift (b 1980)	Northern Dancer
			Ciboulette
		Valencia (b 1994)	Kenmare
			De Stael
	Grenoble (FR) (ch 2000)	Marignan (ch 1989)	Blushing Groom
			Madelia
		Blue Wings (ch 1992)	In The Wings
			Blue Rider

Anyone who remembers Gailo Chop's sire Deportivo, a smart performer for Khalid Abdullah and Roger Charlton who was best at five furlongs, will be surprised that much his best horse to date is suited by twice that distance. Deportivo's only other runner of real note, the smart sprinting mare Demora, takes much more after her sire. Interestingly, both Gailo Chop and Demora are out of mares by sons of Blushing Groom, and in Gailo Chop's case it is his dam's sire who is one of the stamina influences in his pedigree, as Marignan finished second in the Prix du Jockey Club when it was still run over a mile and a half. Gailo Chop's dam Grenoble gained her only win (from thirty starts) over the same trip in a maiden at La Teste. Grenoble has bred three other winners from her four foals before Gailo Chop, all of whom, like their dam, have had busy careers at a modest level. City Chope (by Sagacity) won over five furlongs at two, Noble Rocket has won twice at around seven furlongs and Captain Rocket has won up to nine and a half furlongs, the latter pair both being by Indian Rocket. Gailo Chop's breeder Alain Chopard (whose horses all contain 'chop' in their names) is one of France's most successful breeders, specialising mainly in early-season two-year-olds bred from mares with modest backgrounds. Chopard's broodmare band reportedly numbers nearly a hundred, though they no longer include Grenoble who was among a batch of mares sent to Libya in the year Gailo Chop was foaled (she was in foal to Deportivo again at the time). Grenoble's dam Blue Wings won three races in France at up to ten and a half furlongs and was out of an unraced daughter of Thoroly Blue, winner of the Del Mar Oaks. Thoroly Blue was the dam of the very smart Cresta Rider, winner of the Criterium de Maisons-Laffitte and Prix Jean Prat and third in the Poule d'Essai des Poulains. She was also the grandam of the useful out-and-out stayer Zero Watt and his brother the Stewards' Cup and Ayr Gold Cup winner Green Ruby, and great grandam of the Poule d'Essai des Pouliches winner Ta Rib. Cresta Rider was by Northern Dancer and Ta Rib by Mr Prospector, in a different league from the sires close up in Gailo Chop's own pedigree. Gailo Chop's success in Australia evidently did little to boost the career of his fifteen-year-old sire. Deportivo was one of a number of active stallions who went through the ring at the December Breeding Stock Sale at Deauville where he was sold for just €15,000. Gailo Chop, a very smart and genuine gelding, is suited by around a mile and a quarter and effective on soft and good to firm going. He has worn a tongue tie, and was fitted with cheekpieces for his last three starts at two. *A. de Watrigant, France*

GALA CASINO STAR (IRE) 10 ch.g. Dr Fong (USA) 128 – Abir 73 (Soviet Star **70** (USA) 128) [2015 75: 9g⁴ 10.1d² 10s³ 9g Jul 13] tall gelding: fair handicapper: stays 10.5f: acts on any turf going: usually wears headgear: others races prominently, usually travels strongly. *Lawrence Mullaney*

GALACTIC HALO 4 b.f. Rail Link 132 – Star Cluster 106 (Observatory (USA) 131) **62** [2015 65: t9.5g⁶ 14.1g 12.1s Aug 31] modest maiden: stays 1½m: acts on polytrack and tapeta: usually races prominently. *Michael Blanshard*

GALAGO (IRE) 3 b.g. Bushranger (IRE) 119 – She's A Softie (IRE) (Invincible Spirit **68** (IRE) 121) [2015 69: t6f³ p6f⁶ p6g* Jan 28] fair performer: won maiden at Kempton in January: stays 6f: acts on polytrack and tapeta, best turf effort on good to soft going: tried in cheekpieces prior to 2015: usually races prominently: sold 7,000 gns, sent to Qatar. *Sylvester Kirk*

GALE FORCE 4 b.f. Shirocco (GER) 129 – Hannda (IRE) 74 (Dr Devious (IRE) 127) **107** [2015 71: 12g² p16g* 14.1d³ 16s* 16g³ 16d 15.4v* Nov 20] compact filly: useful performer: won handicaps at Kempton (by 8 lengths) in July and Goodwood (by 2½ lengths from Shades of Silver) in September, and listed race at Saint-Cloud (by ¾ length from Soriano) in November: third in listed race at Newmarket (4½ lengths behind Flying Officer) fifth start: will stay beyond 2m: acts on polytrack and heavy going: often travels strongly: sold 270,000 gns. *James Fanshawe*

GALEOTTI 3 ch.g. Paco Boy (IRE) 129 – Bella Lambada 87 (Lammtarra (USA) 134) **71** [2015 p8m p8g² Mar 14] much better effort when 3 lengths second of 4 to Newmarch in maiden at Lingfield: dead. *Andrew Balding*

GALESBURG (IRE) 2 b.g. (Mar 4) Shamardal (USA) 129 – Calista 108 (Caerleon (USA) **84** 132) [2015 6g³ 6g 6d* 6g 7v* 7s⁵ Sep 19] half-brother to 2-y-o 6f winner Calligrapher (by Rahy) and 1½m winner (stays 2m) Za'lan (by Street Sense): dam winner up to 9f (2-y-o 1m winner): fairly useful performer: won maiden at Leicester (by neck from Musical Taste) in July and nursery at Epsom in September: stays 7f: acts on heavy going. *Mark Johnston*

GALE SONG 2 b.f. (Feb 10) Invincible Spirit (IRE) 121 – Please Sing 103 (Royal **80** Applause 124) [2015 7m⁴ 7g² 7s⁴ p6f² Oct 29] 120,000F: lengthy filly: second foal: half-sister to useful winner up to 1m Four Seasons (2-y-o 6f-7f winner, by Dubawi): dam, 2-y-o 5f/6f winner who stayed 1m, half-sister to smart winner up to 1¼m Mountain Song: fairly useful maiden: second at Newmarket in September and Chelmsford in October: stays 7f. *Ed Walker*

GALILEANO (IRE) 3 ch.f. Galileo (IRE) 134 – Flamingo Sea (USA) (Woodman (USA) 72
126) [2015 56: p12m³ t12.2g² t12.2m² 14.1m* 11.8g² 14.1m t13.9f⁴ p13.3f⁵ Nov 19] fair
handicapper: won at Nottingham in April: stays 1¼m: acts on tapeta and good to firm
going: tried in cheekpieces prior to 2015. *Marco Botti*

GALILEE CHAPEL (IRE) 6 b.g. Baltic King 120 – Triple Zero (IRE) 70 (Raise A 66
Grand (IRE) 114) [2015 57: t7.1f t8.6g t8.6f⁴ 8s⁵ t8.6g⁴ 8d* 7.1g 8d³ 9.2d³ 10.1m⁵ a53
9.1g 5.9g⁶ t8.6m⁶ 7.2g 7s Oct 26] compact gelding: fair handicapper: won at Newcastle in
April: stays 1¼m: acts on polytrack, good to firm and good to soft going: usually wears
headgear. *Alistair Whillans*

GALILEO GOLD 2 ch.c. (Jan 31) Paco Boy (IRE) 129 – Galicuix (Galileo (IRE) 134) 113
[2015 6g² 6m* 7d² 7g* 8m³ Oct 4] €33,000Y: useful-looking colt: first foal: dam
twice-raced half-sister to King's Stand/Abbaye winner Goldream: smart performer: won
maiden at Salisbury (by 2¾ lengths from Zeeoneandonly) in June, minor event at Haydock
(by 1¼ lengths from Hayadh) in July and Vintage Stakes at Goodwood (by ¾ length from
Ibn Malik) in July: further improvement when third in Prix Jean-Luc Lagardere at
Longchamp (1¼ lengths behind Ultra, keeping on well) in October: stays 1m: acts on good
to firm and good to soft going: often travels strongly, usually responds generously under
pressure. *Hugo Palmer*

GALLEY PROOF 3 b.c. Galileo (IRE) 134 – Fictitious 100 (Machiavellian (USA) 123) 73
[2015 p10f⁵ t12.2g⁵ Dec 5] better effort when fifth in maiden at Wolverhampton latter start
(wore hood). *William Haggas*

GALLIPOLI (IRE) 2 b.g. (May 9) Compton Place 125 – Altadena Lady (IRE) (Imperial 81 p
Ballet (IRE) 110) [2015 5m* 5m⁴ May 23] €48,000F, 30,000Y: second foal: dam unraced
half-sister to useful 5f winner Our Little Secret: won maiden at Doncaster in April: still
looked green and never nearer when 3¼ lengths fourth of 7 to First Selection in minor
event at Beverley in May: gelded after: should still improve. *Richard Fahey*

GALLOPING ANGER 3 b.f. Makfi 130 – Whispering Blues (IRE) (Sadler's Wells –
(USA) 132) [2015 p12g⁶ 10s Aug 14] 24,000F, 22,000Y: fifth foal: dam unraced half-sister
to smart winner up to 9f Petroselli: no form. *James Fanshawe*

GALUPPI 4 b.g. Galileo (IRE) 134 – La Leuze (IRE) (Caerleon (USA) 132) [2015 83: 72
p11g p10g⁵ 14m 10g p13.3g³ 8.1s³ p10g⁴ 11s³ f12g⁵ Dec 22] tall, rather unfurnished
gelding: fair maiden: stays 13.5f: acts on polytrack and heavy going: sometimes in
headgear in 2015: often races towards rear. *J. R. Jenkins*

GALVANIZE 4 b.g. Bahamian Bounty 116 – Xtrasensory 96 (Royal Applause 124) [2015 65
88: 5d 7.2g 8m 5d⁵ 6m 5g f6g t7.1f⁵ Dec 22] workmanlike gelding: fair handicapper: stays
1m: acts on tapeta, firm and good to soft going: tried in cheekpieces/tongue tie in 2015.
Noel Wilson

GALVANIZE (USA) 2 b.c. (Mar 26) Medaglia d'Oro (USA) 129 – Enthused (USA) 109 79
(Seeking The Gold (USA)) [2015 7g 7g² p8f³ Oct 22] angular colt: fair form when placed
in maidens, second of 12 to Tafteesh at Salisbury and third of 10 to Thikriyaat at
Chelmsford: wore tongue tie first start. *Sir Michael Stoute*

GAMBINO (IRE) 5 b.g. Red Clubs (IRE) 125 – Temptation Island (IRE) 67 (Spectrum 85
(IRE) 126) [2015 79: 9s⁵ 8g³ 8d⁴ 8d* 7.6f³ 7.9g² 7.9s⁶ 7.9d⁵ 9.2g³ 8d 6m⁶ Sep 28] fairly
useful handicapper: won at Haydock in May: good second at Carlisle in June: stays 8.5f:
acts on tapeta, good to firm and good to soft going: tried in cheekpieces prior to 2015:
sometimes slowly away. *John David Riches*

GAMBIT 2 b.c. (Jan 22) New Approach (IRE) 132 – Sospel (Kendor (FR) 122) [2015 8m⁵ – p
Aug 7] 75,000Y: half-brother to numerous winners, including smart 6f winner Charming
Woman (by Invincible Spirit) and 7f/1m (including at 2 yrs) winner Men's Magazine (by
Dr Devious): dam 2-y-o 6f winner: 5/4, much better than result when fifth in maiden at
Haydock (10¾ lengths behind Foundation) in August, still going well when stumbling
(nearly unseated) 3f out: has scope for plenty of improvement. *Tom Dascombe*

GAMBOL (FR) 5 ch.g. New Approach (IRE) 132 – Guardia (GER) 109 (Monsun (GER) 74
124) [2015 90: 14m 14.6m⁵ 10f Jul 11] workmanlike gelding: fair handicapper: probably
stays 2m: acts on good to firm going: sometimes wears hood. *Ian Williams*

GAME MASCOT 5 ch.g. Kheleyf (USA) 116 – Tolzey (USA) 94 (Rahy (USA) 115) 55
[2015 78d: f7g⁶ t8.6g⁶ f7g⁴ 8.3s 8.3m³ 8.3m⁵ 9.9m p8f⁵ t9.5f 10.3d f8g⁵ Nov 3] modest
handicapper: left Peter Hiatt after sixth start: stays 10.5f: acts on all-weather, good to firm
and good to soft going: sometimes wears blinkers: tried in tongue tie: often races in rear.
Shaun Harris

GAMEPLAY 2 b.g. (Apr 30) Lawman (FR) 121 – Top Toss (IRE) 107 (Linamix (FR) 127) **66**
[2015 7m p8g⁵ p8g t8.6g³ p10f Oct 22] sturdy gelding: fair maiden: best effort at 8.5f: acts
on tapeta: in cheekpieces last 2 starts. *Charlie Appleby*

GAME SET DASH (USA) 3 b.g. Arch (USA) 127 – Proudeyes (GER) (Dashing Blade **84**
117) [2015 74p: 10s⁴ p10.7g² 12g* 16f Jun 19] fairly useful performer: won maiden at the
Curragh (by ½ length from Here For The Craic) in June: 33/1, stiff task when 7¼ lengths
eleventh of 13 to Aloft in Queen's Vase at Royal Ascot final start: probably stays 2m: acts
on polytrack and firm going: usually races prominently: has been gelded. *G. M. Lyons,
Ireland*

GAME SHOW 3 b.g. Dubawi (IRE) 129 – Dream Play (IRE) 112 (In The Wings 128) **81**
[2015 88p: 11.8m² 14m⁶ 12g⁵ 10m 10.2m² p10g Jul 21] lengthy, good sort: fairly useful
handicapper: second at Leicester in April and Nottingham in July: stays 1½m: acts on
polytrack and good to firm going: in cheekpieces last 3 starts: often races prominently.
Charlie Appleby

GAMESOME (FR) 4 b.g. Rock of Gibraltar (IRE) 133 – Hot Coal (USA) (Red Ransom **107**
(USA)) [2015 105: 6g⁶ 6f⁵ 6f⁶ 6m³ 5f 6m Aug 1] compact gelding: useful handicapper:
third at Windsor (length behind Huntsmans Close) in June: stays 6f: acts on good to firm
going: tried in blinkers in 2015. *Olly Stevens*

GAMESTERS LAD 3 b.g. Firebreak 125 – Gamesters Lady 84 (Almushtarak (IRE) 122) **60**
[2015 55: t12.2g 9.9g³ 9g 10g 9.9g² 10.2f² 9.9g³ 11.9g³ 13.1f Sep 13] modest maiden: best
effort at 1¼m: acts on firm going: sometimes wears headgear. *Mark Brisbourne*

GAMMARTH (FR) 7 ch.h. Layman (USA) 121 – Emouna Queen (IRE) (Indian Ridge **115**
123) [2015 115: 5.5d³ 6g 5g⁵ 6g³ 6.5g 6d⁵ 6s* Oct 31] smart performer: won Prix de Seine-
et-Oise at Maisons-Laffitte (for second successive year, beat Porthilly 1½ lengths) in
October: third earlier in year in listed race at Fontainebleau and Prix de Ris-Orangis at
Maisons-Laffitte (2 lengths behind Son Cesio): ideally suited by 6f: acts on polytrack,
viscoride and soft going: wears headgear. *H.-A. Pantall, France*

GANDVIK (IRE) 2 b.g. (Mar 30) Baltic King 120 – Regal Lustre 50 (Averti (IRE) 117) **68**
[2015 5.7f 7.1g⁵ 6m⁴ 7d³ Aug 24] fair maiden: stays 7f. *Mick Channon*

GANG WARFARE 4 b.g. Medicean 128 – Lunar Impact (IRE) (Fantastic Light (USA) **92**
134) [2015 79: 10m⁶ 12.1m* 12f⁴ 14.1g³ p15.8g* t16.5f* Sep 19] sturdy gelding: fairly
useful handicapper: won at Beverley in June, Lingfield in August and Wolverhampton (by
1¾ lengths from Longshadow) in September: stays 2m+: acts on polytrack, tapeta
and good to firm going: in hood in 2015: usually travels strongly. *Simon Crisford*

GANNICUS 4 b.g. Phoenix Reach (IRE) 124 – Rasmani 40 (Medicean 128) [2015 79: **80**
p8g³ 8m* 8v² 8m⁴ 7.1f⁵ 8s* 8m* 8d³ 8d⁵ Oct 30] strong, close-coupled gelding: fairly
useful performer: won handicaps at Brighton in April and August (apprentice) and minor
event at Doncaster (by 2 lengths from Next Stop) in September: stays 1m: acts on polytrack,
good to firm and heavy going: often wears headgear: tried in tongue tie: front runner/races
prominently. *Brendan Powell*

GANYMEDE 4 b.g. Oasis Dream 129 – Gaze 74 (Galileo (IRE) 134) [2015 84: 7m³ 7g* **85**
7m 7g⁶ 7g p7g⁵ 6d 7d p7m Oct 28] leggy gelding: fairly useful handicapper: won at
Brighton (twice) in April: stays 7f: acts on polytrack and good to firm going: often wears
headgear: sometimes slowly away, often races towards rear. *Eve Johnson Houghton*

GARCIA 2 b.g. (Feb 17) Paco Boy (IRE) 129 – Birdie 99 (Alhaarth (IRE) 126) [2015 6m³ **85 p**
7s* Oct 10] 50,000Y: seventh foal: half-brother to 1½m-13f winner Salvation (by Montjeu)
and useful 7f (including at 2 yrs) winner Il Paparazzi (by Royal Applause): dam, 1m-11.5f
winner, half-sister to grandam of 2000 Guineas/Derby winner Camelot: better effort when
winning maiden at York (by length from Prying Pandora, staying on well to lead near
finish) in October: will prove suited by 1¼m+: open to further improvement. *Richard Fahey*

GARCON DE SOLEIL 2 b.c. (Feb 11) Danehill Dancer (IRE) 117 – Darinza (FR) **57**
(Dalakhani (IRE) 133) [2015 7.1g 7s 8.3d p8g² f8m Dec 8] modest maiden: stays 8.5f: acts
on polytrack and good to soft going. *Michael Blanshard*

GARDEN WORLD (IRE) 2 b.f. (Feb 26) Canford Cliffs (IRE) 133 – Elizabeth Swann **78**
95 (Bahamian Bounty 116) [2015 5m⁶ 5s* 6s Aug 24] €22,000Y: fourth foal: half-sister to
2-y-o 5f winner Dame Liberty (by Tamayuz): dam 7f winner: fair performer: best effort
when winning maiden at Beverley (by ½ length from Crombay) in July: raced too freely
upped to 6f next start. *Nigel Tinkler*

GASPIRALI 2 b.g. (Mar 5) Oasis Dream 129 – Lion Forest (USA) (Forestry (USA) 121) **77** [2015 6d 6m³ 6g p8f² p8f³ 7g* Oct 21] neat gelding: fair performer: won nursery at Newmarket in October: stays 1m: acts on polytrack and good to firm going: blinkered first 2 starts: usually races close up: temperament under suspicion: sold 25,000 gns, sent to Qatar. *Hugo Palmer*

GATEPOST (IRE) 6 br.g. Footstepsinthesand 120 – Mandama (IRE) 95 (Warning 136) **88** [2015 92: 7m⁶ 7m² 7g² Jul 10] tall, leggy gelding: fairly useful handicapper: second at Chester in June and July: stays 7f: acts on soft and good to firm going: tried in hood prior to 2015: usually races prominently. *Richard Fahey*

GATEWOOD 7 b.h. Galileo (IRE) 134 – Felicity (IRE) 108 (Selkirk (USA) 129) [2015 **101** 115: 12m⁶ 12m³ Jun 27] leggy, attractive horse: smart performer at best: better effort in listed races in 2015 (useful form) when third at Newmarket (9 lengths behind Gospel Choir) in June: stayed 12.5f: acted on soft and good to firm going: to stand at Windmill View Stud, Co. Galway, Ireland, fee €1,500. *John Gosden*

GATHERING POWER (IRE) 5 b.m. Kyllachy 129 – Nutkin 91 (Act One 124) [2015 **108** 105+: 6d³ 6g 6g 5d 6g³ 6d Oct 17] good-topped mare: useful performer: stays 6f: acts on polytrack, good to firm and heavy going: races towards rear. *Edward Lynam, Ireland*

GATHURST 3 b.g. Royal Applause 124 – Rivalry (Medicean 128) [2015 7.1m³ 6g² 6s² **72** 6m² Aug 20] fair maiden: left David O'Meara after second start: stays 6f: sold £16,000 in September, sent to Qatar. *Richard Fahey*

GAVARNIE ENCORE 3 b.c. Intikhab (USA) 135 – Greeley Bright (USA) 64 (Mr **57** Greeley (USA) 122) [2015 63: p8f p8g⁶ 8.3g⁵ 9g 10.2m 8g⁶ p7g* p8g³ f7m⁶ Dec 8] modest handicapper: won at Kempton in August: stays 8.5f: acts on polytrack and fibresand: often races towards rear. *Michael Blanshard*

GAVLAR 4 b.g. Gentlewave (IRE) 120 – Shawhill 93 (Dr Fong (USA) 128) [2015 80: **98** 11.6m⁴ 14m² 16g³ 16m* p16g³ 21g p16g* p16g* 18g⁴ 18g Oct 10] sturdy gelding: useful handicapper: won at Goodwood in June and at Kempton (twice) in August: stays 2¼m: acts on polytrack, soft and good to firm going: often in headgear prior to 2015: held up. *William Knight*

GAWDAWPALIN (IRE) 2 b.c. (Apr 17) Holy Roman Emperor (IRE) 125 – Dirtybirdie **78** 63 (Diktat 126) [2015 7s⁶ 8.3g 8.3d* p8f³ Oct 29] fair form: won maiden at Windsor (by 1¼ lengths from Jazzy) in October: further improvement when 1¾ lengths third to Brave Archibald in nursery at Chelmsford: stays 1m. *Sylvester Kirk*

GAWN SID 4 b.g. Exceed And Excel (AUS) 126 – Only In Dreams 78 (Polar Falcon **50** (USA) 126) [2015 f5g t6f⁶ Nov 20] better effort when sixth in maiden at Wolverhampton in November, slowly away. *Stuart Coltherd*

GAYATH (GER) 3 b.g. High Chaparral (IRE) 132 – Gallivant 93 (Danehill (USA) 126) **–** [2015 p8g⁵ 8.5g⁶ Apr 22] no form. *Richard Hannon*

G'DAY AUSSIE 2 b.g. (May 1) Aussie Rules (USA) 123 – Moi Aussi (USA) 88 (Mt **67** Livermore (USA)) [2015 6m 7m 6d⁵ 7.2m³ p8f Oct 10] fair maiden: stays 1m: acts on polytrack, good to firm and good to soft going. *Brian Ellison*

GEANIE MAC (IRE) 6 ch.m. Needwood Blade 117 – Dixie Evans 96 (Efisio 120) [2015 **56** 65: 11.1d 12.5m³ 12.1g⁴ 16m 13.1g 12.8m 15.8m⁶ 12.1g 13.7g Aug 26] modest handicapper: stays 2m: acts on polytrack, good to firm and good to soft going: usually wears headgear: temperament under suspicion. *Linda Perratt*

GECKO (IRE) 2 b.c. (Mar 29) Zoffany (IRE) 121 – Chameleon 79 (Green Desert (USA) **63** 127) [2015 8d p7g t7.1f Oct 20] modest maiden: best effort when eighth at Haydock on debut, very slowly away: sold 2,000 gns, sent to Sweden. *Richard Hannon*

GEEAITCH 6 ch.g. Cockney Rebel (IRE) 127 – Grand Rebecca (IRE) (Namid 128) [2015 **53** 72: f12s 10g 13.1m⁶ 11.6g⁴ f11g⁴ t12.2m⁵ f12g³ Dec 22] big, workmanlike gelding: **a59** modest handicapper: stays 13f: acts on polytrack, fibresand and any turf going: tried in headgear prior to 2015. *Peter Hiatt*

GENAX (IRE) 4 b.f. Green Desert (USA) 127 – Steam Cuisine 104 (Mark of Esteem **46** (IRE) 137) [2015 54: t7.1f⁵ t7.1g⁴ t8.6f t7.1g⁵ Feb 9] poor maiden handicapper in Britain: acts on tapeta and good to firm going: wears headgear nowadays: sent to Germany, running 11 times and winning 9.2f amateur handicap at Bad Harzburg in July. *Ian Williams*

GENERAL ALEXANDER (IRE) 2 gr.g. (Feb 12) Zebedee 113 – Alexander Express **81** (IRE) 102 (Sri Pekan (USA) 117) [2015 5d³ 5g² 6.1g⁴ 6g 6g 7d² Oct 24] €10,000F, £30,000Y: half-brother to several winners, including useful 6f-10.7f winner Political

Policy (by Bushranger) and 2-y-o 7f winner Andalacia (by Choisir): dam 1m winner: fairly useful maiden: good second in nursery at Doncaster on final start: stays 7f: acts on good to soft going. *Brian Ellison*

GENERAL BROOK (IRE) 5 b.g. Westerner 130 – Danse Grecque (IRE) (Sadler's Wells (USA) 132) [2015 97: 8d 10m 10m 10.2v⁵ 8.1m Sep 10] lengthy gelding: useful at best, no form in 2015: tried in hood in 2015. *John O'Shea* —

GENERAL POTEMPKIN (IRE) 3 b.g. Rip Van Winkle (IRE) 134 – Muskoka Dawn (USA) (Miswaki (USA) 124) [2015 6d² 8.1g³ Aug 2] second of 6 to Fujiano in maiden at Brighton in May: 10/11, well-beaten last of 3 in apprentice seller at Chepstow only other start: sent to Belgium. *Paul Cole* — 66

GENERALSHIP (IRE) 2 b.c. (Mar 8) New Approach 132 – Ahla Wasahl 111 (Dubai Destination (USA) 127) [2015 8g⁵ Oct 21] 600,000Y: well-made, attractive colt: second foal: dam winner up to 1m (2-y-o 6f winner, also third in Cherry Hinton Stakes): 9/2, much better than result when 11½ lengths fifth of 12 to Prize Money in maiden at Newmarket on debut, leading briefly 1f out but carried left/hampered soon after: will prove a very different proposition in time. *John Gosden* — 63 P

GENERAL TUFTO 10 b.g. Fantastic Light 134 – Miss Pinkerton 104 (Danehill (USA) 126) [2015 63§: f8s² f8g* f8g* f8s⁶ f8g* f8g⁵ f8g⁶ f8d⁴ f12s 10.3d f11g⁶ p8f 8.3s⁴ f8d⁶ 8.5m 9.9m f12d 10g 8.5m 9.9g 8.5d f8g⁶ f8g f8g⁶ f8g³ Dec 18] sturdy gelding: modest handicapper: won 3 times at Southwell in January (has won 14 times there during career): stays 2m, races mainly around 1m: acts on all-weather, firm and soft going: wears headgear: usually races in rear, often races lazily: one to treat with caution. *Charles Smith* — 48 § a68 §

GENERALYSE 6 b.g. Cadeaux Genereux 131 – Dance To The Blues (IRE) 73 (Danehill Dancer (IRE) 117) [2015 82§: 6.1m 6.1g p6d² f6f p6g p6d³ p6g Dec 16] lengthy gelding: fair handicapper: stays 6f: acts on polytrack, fibresand, firm and good to soft going: usually wears headgear: tried in tongue tie prior to 2015: unreliable. *Anabel K. Murphy* — 76 §

GENEROUS DREAM 7 ch.m. Generous (IRE) 139 – First Harmony (First Trump 118) [2015 63: f16g 12.1s² 16d³ 15.8d t13.9f t13.9f Nov 30] modest handicapper: stays 2m: acts on fibresand, tapeta and heavy going: often in cheekpieces in 2015. *Antony Brittain* — 60

GEN I AM 3 ch.f. Aqlaam 125 – Gennie Bond 73 (Pivotal 124) [2015 64: p6f³ 6.1m⁵ 8.3f³ 7d* 7m³ 8m² 7m² 9s³ 8.3d⁵ 8g⁴ Oct 18] smallish filly: fair handicapper: won at Lingfield in June: stays 9f: acts on soft and good to firm going: sold 10.000 gns, sent to Bahrain. *Sylvester Kirk* — 73

GENO (IRE) 2 b.g. (May 16) Holy Roman Emperor (IRE) 125 – Abama Lady (CAN) (Mr Greeley (USA) 122) [2015 5m² 5m⁴ 6d² 6d² 6g Oct 3] fair maiden: stays 6f: acts on good to firm and good to soft going. *Kevin Ryan* — 76

GENRES 3 b.g. Champs Elysees 124 – Musical Horizon (USA) (Distant View (USA) 126) [2015 p10m² 10f* 10m⁵ 10m Jun 19] big gelding: fourth foal: half-brother to winner up to 6f Musical Valley (2-y-o 5f winner, by Three Valleys) and useful 7f/1m winner Country Western (by Oasis Dream): dam thrice-raced sister to high-class winner up to 9f Distant Music: fairly useful form: won maiden at Windsor (by 1½ lengths from Ataman) in May: raced only at 1¼m: has been gelded. *John Gosden* — 88

GENTLEMEN 4 ch.g. Ad Valorem (USA) 125 – Stoney Cove (IRE) (Needwood Blade 117) [2015 –§: t6g* t7.1g³ 6m t6g² t6g² 5.3g* p5g⁶ p7f² Dec 17] fairly useful performer: won maiden at Wolverhampton in March and handicap at Brighton in August: stays 7f: acts on polytrack and tapeta: usually wears headgear: tried in tongue tie prior to 2015: often races in rear: has been reluctant (refused to race once) and best treated with caution. *Phil McEntee* — 85 §

GENTLEMUSIC (FR) 3 b.f. Gentlewave (IRE) 120 – Makhalina (IRE) (Red Ransom (USA)) [2015 72: p8f* t9.5m⁴ p8g* p8m 8g⁴ 8g p10g⁴ Nov 13] fairly useful handicapper: won at Chelmsford in February and May (by length from Falling Petals): barely stays 1¼m: acts on polytrack and tapeta. *Marco Botti* — 88

GENTLE PERSUASION 3 b.f. Rock of Gibraltar (IRE) 133 – Play Bouzouki 70 (Halling (USA) 133) [2015 –: p7f 5m Jun 6] maiden: no form in 2015. *Amanda Perrett* —

GENUINE APPROVAL (IRE) 2 ch.f. (Mar 26) Approve (IRE) 112 – Genuinely (IRE) 43 (Entrepreneur 123) [2015 t9.5f Dec 14] €16,500Y, 32,000 2-y-o, resold 2,500 2-y-o: half-sister to several winners, including winner up to 1m Get Knotted (2-y-o 6f winner, by Windsor Knot) and winner up to 9f Right Rave (2-y-o 5f winner, by Soviet Star): dam maiden (stayed 1½m): 66/1, well-held eighth of 11 in maiden at Wolverhampton on debut. *Jonathan Portman* —

GEOFF POTTS (IRE) 2 ch.g. (Mar 31) Zebedee 113 – Our Sheila 82 (Bahamian Bounty **76 p**
116) [2015 5g⁴ 6d Sep 25] €21,000F, £55,000Y, £95,000 2-y-o: fifth foal: half-brother to
6f/7f winner Captain McCaw (by Exceed And Excel) and winner up to 6f Douneedahand
(2-y-o 5.7f winner, by Royal Applause): dam, 5f/6f winner, half-sister to useful winner up
to 6f Shifting Place: better effort when fourth in maiden at Sandown (5¼ lengths behind
Southern Belle) in September, considerately handled: refused to settle next time: has been
gelded: remains with potential. *Jeremy Gask*

GEOLOGICAL (IRE) 3 b.g. Rock of Gibraltar (IRE) 133 – Bean Uasal (IRE) 94 (Oasis **90**
Dream 129) [2015 89: 7g 6m³ p6g⁴ Dec 11] compact gelding: fairly useful handicapper:
third at Epsom in July: left Richard Hannon after: stays 7f: acts on polytrack, tapeta and
good to firm going. *Damian Joseph English, Ireland*

GEOLOGY 3 b.g. Rock of Gibraltar (IRE) 133 – Baralinka (IRE) 93 (Barathea (IRE) 127) **69**
[2015 –: 6g 7m⁴ 8m⁶ 8.3g⁵ 8g⁶ Sep 18] fair maiden: may prove best at sprint trips: acts on
good to firm going: front runner/races prominently. *Kevin Ryan*

GEORDAN MURPHY 4 b.g. Firebreak 125 – Sukuma (IRE) 55 (Highest Honor (FR) **77**
124) [2015 92: t8.6g⁶ Jan 8] fair handicapper: stays 8.5f: acts on polytrack, raced only on
ground softer than good on turf: often travels strongly. *Philip Kirby*

GEORDIE GEORGE (IRE) 3 b.g. Kodiac 112 – Trika (First Trump 118) [2015 93: 6s² **93**
7.6s³ 7g⁶ 6m 7.6m 7g 6.1d Sep 26] quite attractive gelding: fairly useful handicapper:
second at Pontefract in April and third at Chester in May: stays 7.5f: acts on good to firm
and heavy going: tried in cheekpieces in 2015: usually races prominently. *John Quinn*

GEORDIE MAN 5 b.g. Manduro (GER) 135 – Opening Ceremony (USA) 89 (Quest For **–**
Fame 127) [2015 10d p12g Oct 6] won maiden at Haydock in 2012: off 3 years, tailed off
in handicaps at Kempton. *Pat Eddery*

GEORGE BAILEY (IRE) 3 b.g. Zebedee 113 – Zuzu (IRE) 94 (Acclamation 118) **59**
[2015 62: 7d⁵ 6m 5d⁵ 5f 5m* 5d 6m⁵ 5d⁶ 5m³ t6g f5g² Dec 12] modest handicapper: won
at Beverley in July: left Bryan Smart after eighth start: best form at 5f: acts on fibresand
and good to firm going: often in headgear in 2015. *Suzzane France*

GEORGE BAKER (IRE) 8 b.g. Camacho 118 – Petite Maxine 70 (Sharpo 132) [2015 **72**
80: t7.1f t7.1g² p8g⁵ p7g* 8.5m* 8g³ p7g⁴ 8.3d 8m Sep 9] fair performer: won handicap at
Kempton in April and minor event at Les Landes in May: stays 8.5f: acts on polytrack,
tapeta and good to firm going: tried in cheekpieces/tongue tie prior to 2015. *George Baker*

GEORGE BOWEN (IRE) 3 gr.g. Dark Angel (IRE) 113 – Midnight Oasis 49 (Oasis **109**
Dream 129) [2015 91: t6f* 7g 7g⁴ 7.1m* 7m⁴ 7m 6m* 6d* 6g² 6s⁶ Oct 10] sturdy gelding:
useful handicapper: won at Wolverhampton (by head from Wanting) in March, Newmarket
(by length from Crew Cut) in August and the Curragh (by 1¾ lengths from In Salutem) in
September: good second at Ayr (head behind Tatlisu) later in September: stays 6f: acts on
tapeta, good to firm and good to soft going: tried in headgear in 2015. *Richard Fahey*

GEORGE CINQ 5 b.g. Pastoral Pursuits 127 – Fairnilee 67 (Selkirk (USA) 129) [2015 **97 §**
98: p8g² 7d² 7d 7m⁵ 7g⁵ 7f* 7d 7g 7d³ 8d⁴ 8m⁴ Oct 2] good-bodied gelding: useful
performer: won minor event at Doncaster (by neck from King Torus) in July: creditable
efforts other in both handicaps and a minor event: stays 1m: acts on polytrack,
tapeta, firm and soft going: has worn headgear: often races in rear: not straightforward and
one to be wary of. *Michael Bell*

GEORGE DRYDEN (IRE) 3 gr.g. Zebedee 113 – Key To Fortune (GER) 86 (Big **108**
Shuffle (USA) 122) [2015 94: 6m 5m 6m² 6m 6d⁶ 6g* 5.6d⁴ Sep 12] useful handicapper:
won at York (by 3¾ lengths from Felix Leiter) in September: respectable 2¼ lengths fourth
of 20 to Steps in Portland at Doncaster only subsequent start: stays 6f: acts on good to firm
going: has been gelded. *Ann Duffield*

GEORGE FENTON 6 ch.g. Piccolo 121 – Mashmoum 85 (Lycius (USA) 124) [2015 78: **64**
f6d⁴ t7.1g f6g⁶ Apr 14] sturdy, close-coupled gelding: modest handicapper: stays 7f: acts
on polytrack, fibresand, good to firm and heavy going: usually wears headgear: tried in
tongue tie prior to 2015: tends to find little. *Ann Stokell*

GEORGE GURU 8 b.g. Ishiguru (USA) 114 – Waraqa (USA) 76 (Red Ransom (USA)) **87**
[2015 105: p10f⁵ p11g⁵ p8g p8f p10g Aug 17] fairly useful handicapper: stays 11f: acts on
polytrack and soft going: tried in headgear. *John Bridger*

GEORGE PATTON (USA) 2 gr.c. (Feb 21) War Front (USA) 119 – Photograph (USA) **110 p**
(Unbridled's Song (USA) 125) [2015 p6.5g* 7.5g* Aug 9] second foal: brother to smart
winner up to 1¼m (2-y-o 9f winner) War Dispatch: dam unraced half-sister to UAE Derby
winner Lines of Battle, later very smart performer up to 1½m in Hong Kong as Helene
Super Star (by War Front): smart form: successful on both his starts, namely maiden at
Deauville in June and minor event on same course (pushed out by 1½ lengths from
subsequent pattern-race winner Robin of Navan) in August: will stay 1¼m: likely to make
his mark at 3 yrs. *Jean-Claude Rouget, France*

GEORGE WILLIAM 2 b.g. (Apr 19) Paco Boy (IRE) 129 – Basque Beauty 96 (Nayef **81 p**
(USA) 129) [2015 6g⁴ 7f³ 6m⁵ 7.1m⁶ Aug 22] good-topped gelding: third foal: dam 1m
winner who probably stayed 1¼m: fair form: 8/1, caught eye when 3 lengths sixth of 11 to
Time Warp in nursery at Sandown final start, left with a lot to do but keeping on well under
considerate handling, finishing with running left: will stay 1m: has been gelded: capable of
better. *Richard Hannon*

GEORGIAN BAY (IRE) 5 b.g. Oratorio (IRE) 128 – Jazzie (FR) (Zilzal (USA) 137) **89**
[2015 106: p7g⁵ p8g⁵ 8g 7m⁴ 7g³ 7m 7g p8g⁴ p8g* 8m⁵ p8m⁵ p7f² p7f⁴ Dec 21] **a106**
lengthy gelding: useful handicapper: won at Kempton (by 1½ lengths from Spirit Raiser)
in September: second at Chelmsford (head behind Arnold Lane) in November: will prove
suited by a return to 1m: acts on polytrack and any turf going: often wears headgear: tried
in tongue tie in 2015: often races prominently. *K. R. Burke*

GEORGIA'S GAMBLE (IRE) 3 b.g. Strategic Prince 114 – My Sweet Georgia (IRE) **–**
79 (Royal Applause 124) [2015 –: p10f p12f Feb 21] maiden: no form in 2015: in
cheekpieces last start. *Lee Carter*

GERRARD'S QUEST 2 b.c. (Apr 23) Captain Gerrard (IRE) 113 – Ryan's Quest (IRE) **92**
67 (Mukaddamah (USA) 125) [2015 6m⁵ 6d² p6g* 6f² 7m² 6.5m⁶ p8g³ 8s³ 7g Dec 29]
7,000Y, resold 13,000Y: sturdy colt: sixth foal: brother to winner up to 5.7f Captain Ryan
(2-y-o 5f winner) and half-brother to 2-y-o 5f winner Multi Quest (by Multiplex): dam,
ungenuine maiden (best at 5f), half-sister to smart winner up to 6f Guinea Hunter: fairly
useful performer: won maiden at Chelmsford in June: good third on seventh/eighth starts,
in minor event at Kempton and Gran Criterium at Milan (7¼ lengths behind Biz Heart): left
Marco Botti before final outing (blinkered): stays 1m: acts on polytrack, firm and soft
going. *Mohammed Hussain, Qatar*

GERRARD'S SLIP 3 b.g. Captain Gerrard (IRE) 113 – Park's Girl 71 (Averti (IRE) 117) **74**
[2015 –: f6s* f5g³ t6g³ Jun 22] fair form: won maiden at Southwell in February: stays 6f.
Bryan Smart

GERRY THE GLOVER (IRE) 3 b.g. Approve (IRE) 112 – Umlani (IRE) (Great **96**
Commotion (USA) 123) [2015 84: 7m 7.5m² 5m³ 8g⁶ 8m* 7.6m 8g 7m⁴ 8g³ Sep 19]
workmanlike gelding: useful handicapper: won at Haydock in May and Newcastle (by 2
lengths from Volunteer Point) in June: third at Ayr (1¼ lengths behind Mutasayyid) in
September: stays 1m: acts on soft and good to firm going: often races in rear. *Brian Ellison*

GERSHWIN 2 b.c. (Apr 2) Shamardal (USA) 129 – Gradara 108 (Montjeu (IRE) 137) **89 p**
[2015 7m 7g⁶ 8d* Oct 16] €100,000Y: first foal: dam, 9.5f-12.5f winner, half-sister to
1m-1¼m winner Giofra and 1m/8.6f winner Big Baz, both smart: fairly useful performer:
best effort when winning maiden at Haydock (by ½ length from Baydar) in October: will
stay 1¼m: likely to progress further. *David Lanigan*

GET KNOTTED(IRE) 3 ch.g. WindsorKnot(IRE)118 – Genuinely(IRE)43(Entrepreneur **94 §**
123) [2015 82p: 8d³ 8gᵘʳ 7.9v* 8m³ 8g* 8g³ 8s³ 8g 8d⁶ Oct 5] tall, quite good-topped
gelding: fairly useful handicapper: won at Carlisle in June and Ayr (by nose from Instant
Attraction) in July: good third at York (3¼ lengths behind My Dream Boat) next start: stays
1m: acts on good to firm and heavy going: wears cheekpieces: not straightforward and can't
be relied on. *Michael Dods*

GET PRANCER 3 ch.g. Archipenko (USA) 127 – Clever Omneya (USA) 73 (Toccet **–**
(USA) 118) [2015 7m⁶ 8.3g 7.1d Aug 5] no form. *J. R. Jenkins*

GETTIN' LUCKY 2 ch.g. (Apr 3) Bertolini (USA) 125 – Loose Caboose (IRE) 82 **–**
(Tagula (IRE) 116) [2015 7.1s 5.1g Sep 30] no form: left Alan McCabe after first start.
John Balding

G FORCE (IRE) 4 b.c. Tamayuz 126 – Flanders (IRE) 110 (Common Grounds 118) [2015 **110**
126: 5g 5f 6d⁴ 7m Oct 4] good-topped colt: very smart performer at best, won 2014
Sprint Cup at Haydock: well below that form in 2015, easily best effort when 3½ lengths
fourth of 15 to Twilight Son in latest renewal of Sprint Cup in September, not ideally
placed near side: stayed 6.5f: acted on good to firm and heavy going: usually raced towards
rear: to stand at Tally-Ho Stud, Co. Westmeath, Ireland, fee €8,000. *David O'Meara*

GHALIB (IRE) 3 ch.c. Lope de Vega (IRE) 125 – Gorband (USA) 59 (Woodman (USA) **105**
126) [2015 70: p6f* 6s* 6g t6g² 6m 6v* 6v Nov 7] quite attractive colt: useful handicapper:
won at Kempton in April, Salisbury in May and Ffos Las (by 2 lengths from Personal
Touch, best effort) in August: stays 6f: acts on polytrack and tapeta, best turf form on soft/
heavy going: tried in hood/tongue tie. *Ed Walker*

GHINIA (IRE) 4 b.f. Mastercraftsman (IRE) 129 – Jorghinia (FR) (Seattle Slew (USA)) **93**
[2015 82: 10g 8d³ 8m² 8.3m* 8.3m⁶ 8g 8d² 8.3d* 8d³ Oct 31] lengthy filly: fairly useful
handicapper: won at Leicester in July and Windsor (by length from Miss Van Gogh) in
October: stays 8.5f: acts on good to firm and good to soft going: often races prominently.
Pam Sly

GHOSTING (IRE) 4 ro.g. Invincible Spirit (IRE) 121 – Exclusive Approval (USA) **66**
(With Approval (CAN)) [2015 79: t9.5f⁶ Jan 30] fair maiden: stays 1¼m: acts on polytrack,
tapeta, good to firm and good to soft going: sometimes wears headgear: usually wears
tongue tie: sometimes slowly away, often races freely. *Tom Dascombe*

GHOSTLY ARC (IRE) 3 b.g. Arcano (IRE) 122 – Cheyenne's Spirit (IRE) 56 (Sadler's **63**
Wells (USA) 132) [2015 –: 10.3d 12.1g² 9.8d⁴ 10g⁶ 12d² 12.2g⁵ Oct 13] modest maiden:
stays 1½m: acts on good to soft going: usually leads. *Noel Wilson*

GHOST TRAIN (IRE) 6 b.g. Holy Roman Emperor (IRE) 125 – Adrastea (IRE) **73**
(Monsun (GER) 124) [2015 72: p6f³ p6m² p6g² p6g⁶ p6f² p6g p6f⁴ p6m⁶ p6g p6m* p6m³
Dec 31] fair handicapper: won at Lingfield in December: stays 7f: acts on polytrack and
firm going: usually wears headgear: quirky. *Tim McCarthy*

GHOSTWRITER (IRE) 2 b.g. (Mar 20) High Chaparral (IRE) 132 – Diara Angel (IRE) **74 p**
(Hawk Wing (USA) 136) [2015 p8m⁵ p8g³ Dec 9] 35,000Y: first foal: dam, 9f/1¼m winner,
half-sister to Breeders' Cup Juvenile Turf winner Wrote (by High Chaparral): better effort
when third in maiden at Kempton (5½ lengths behind Towerlands Park) in December: open
to further improvement. *Hugo Palmer*

GIANTOUCH (USA) 3 b.g. Giant's Causeway (USA) 132 – Beauty O' Gwaun (IRE) **89**
107 (Rainbow Quest (USA) 134) [2015 83p: p10g* 10g⁵ 10m⁴ 10g⁵ p10g² p11g³ Aug 5]
useful-looking gelding: fairly useful performer: won maiden at Chelmsford in April:
placed in handicaps on same course in July and Kempton in August: stays 11f: acts on
polytrack, tapeta and good to firm going: tried in tongue tie prior to 2015: sent to Saudi
Arabia. *Marco Botti*

GIANT SEQUOIA (USA) 11 ch.g. Giant's Causeway (USA) 132 – Beware of The Cat **61**
(USA) (Caveat (USA)) [2015 p10m p13.3g* p10f⁵ p12f* Apr 15] modest handicapper:
won at Chelmsford in February and Kempton in April: stays 13.5f: acts on polytrack,
good to firm and heavy going: tried in cheekpieces in 2015: usually wears tongue tie.
Des Donovan

GIANT SHADOW (IRE) 2 b.g. (Apr 10) Clodovil (IRE) 116 – Aldburgh (Bluebird **37**
(USA) 125) [2015 5m⁶ 6g 6m 5.1d⁵ p7f⁴ f8g Nov 26] tall gelding: poor maiden: bred to be
suited by at least 1m: acts on polytrack: tried in visor. *Michael Bell*

GIANT SPARK 3 b.g. Orientor 118 – Annie Gee (Primo Valentino (IRE) 116) [2015 6m **70 p**
8.3g 6s⁴ 6v³ Nov 3] third foal: dam unraced: fair form: 33/1, improved though still green
when neck third of 19 to Posh Bounty in handicap at Redcar last time, hanging left under
pressure but nearest finish: best effort at 6f: will go on improving. *Paul Midgley*

GIANTSTEPSAHEAD (IRE) 6 br.g. Footstepsinthesand 120 – Salty Air (IRE) **89**
(Singspiel (IRE) 133) [2015 90: 10m⁵ p10m* 12v p10f⁶ p10g² Dec 20] fairly useful
handicapper: won at Chelmsford in June: second at Lingfield in December: stays 11.5f:
acts on polytrack and soft going: often in hood prior to 2015: usually leads. *Brian McMath*

GIBEON (IRE) 3 b.c. Cape Cross (IRE) 129 – Gravitation 112 (Galileo (IRE) 134) [2015 **114**
89: 10m⁵ 8m³ 10m⁶ 10.1m² 9.9g⁶ 10m² 9.9m* 11.6d³ Aug 29] lengthy colt: smart
performer: won handicap at Goodwood (by neck from Keble) in July: respectable 6 lengths
third of 8 to Beautiful Romance in listed race at Windsor final start: stays 1¼m: acts on
good to firm and good to soft going: usually races close up. *Richard Hannon*

GIDDY 2 b.f. (Mar 21) Kyllachy 129 – Light Hearted 90 (Green Desert (USA) 127) [2015 **84**
5m* 6g Sep 18] fourth foal: half-sister to 2-y-o 6f winner Merletta (by Raven's Pass): dam,
6f winner, sister to smart winner up to 7f Byron out of smart 2-y-o 5f/6f winner (stayed 1m)
Gay Gallanta: won 8-runner maiden at Beverley in August by 2¾ lengths from Harmonic
Wave: disappointing in nursery only other start. *Richard Fahey*

£500,000 Tattersalls Millions 2YO Trophy, Newmarket—
Gifted Master returns from three months off to draw clear in the final running of this most valuable
of sales races; he follows up in the Autumn Stakes seven days later

GIFTED MASTER (IRE) 2 b.g. (Apr 3) Kodiac 112 – Shobobb (Shamardal (USA) **114**
129) [2015 5m* 5f⁴ 6m² 6m* 7m* 8g* Oct 10] 75,000Y: rather leggy gelding: second foal:
half-brother to 6f winner Mary Ann Bugg (by Bushranger): dam unraced half-sister to
useful 2-y-o 5f/6f winner Alzerra out of smart 1m winner (stayed 10.5f) Belle Argentine:
smart performer: successful in minor events at Newmarket in April and Newcastle in June:
off 3 months, much improved to win valuable sales race (beat Waterloo Bridge 4½ lengths)
and 8-runner Autumn Stakes (by ½ length from Beacon Rock) at Newmarket in October,
making all both times: stays 1m: acts on good to firm going: front runner. *Hugo Palmer*

GIGAWATT 5 b.g. Piccolo 121 – Concubine (IRE) 76 (Danehill (USA) 126) [2015 82: **77**
p6f⁵ t7.1f* p7g⁴ p6g³ t7.1g⁵ Apr 27] fair handicapper: won at Wolverhampton in February:
stays 7f: acts on polytrack, tapeta and heavy going: tried in headgear: usually in tongue tie
in 2015: often travels strongly. *Jim Boyle*

GILDED LILI (IRE) 3 b.f. Big Bad Bob (IRE) 118 – City Vaults Girl (IRE) 78 (Oratorio **–**
(IRE) 128) [2015 77p: 8.3g p11g Jun 10] lengthy, rather unfurnished filly: maiden: no form
in 2015: sent to Bahrain. *Charles Hills*

GILD MASTER 3 b.g. Excellent Art 125 – Nirvana 82 (Marju (IRE) 127) [2015 75: 11g **81**
11.6g t13.9f³ t12.2f³ p13.3f³ p12g⁵ Dec 3] good-topped gelding: fairly useful maiden:
third in handicap at Chelmsford in November: stays 13.5f: acts on polytrack and tapeta:
tried in hood in 2015: often races in rear. *Alan King*

GILMER (IRE) 4 b.g. Exceed And Excel (AUS) 126 – Cherokee Rose (IRE) 122 **63**
(Dancing Brave (USA) 140) [2015 74: t9.5g 6m t8.6g² 8d t8.6g³ p10g t8.6g⁵ t8.6g⁴ t9.5g²
8.1g³ t6m t7.1f Dec 22] modest maiden: stays 9.5f: acts on tapeta: often wears hood:
usually in tongue tie in 2015. *Laura Young*

GILT EDGED (IRE) 2 br.f. (Mar 24) Big Bad Bob (IRE) 118 – Caona (USA) 69 **–**
(Miswaki (USA) 124) [2015 7g Oct 3] €3,000Y, €15,000 2-y-o: fifth foal: dam, 2-y-o 7f
winner, half-sister to smart 7f/1m winner (stays 1¼m) Diescentric: 100/1, well held in
maiden at Redcar on debut. *Julie Camacho*

GIMLET 2 b.g. (Mar 31) Poet's Voice 126 – Poppo's Song (CAN) (Polish Navy (USA)) **65**
[2015 p10g p8m⁶ t8.6g Dec 5] fair maiden: best effort when sixth in maiden at Lingfield
(4¼ lengths behind Kummiya) in November: in tongue tie. *Hugo Palmer*

GIMME FIVE 4 b.g. Champs Elysees 124 – Waitingonacloud (In The Wings 128) [2015 **69**
p15.8f² 12d³ 16m 12g May 15] sturdy gelding: fair handicapper: stays 16.5f: acts on
polytrack, tapeta and soft going: wears cheekpieces: sent to USA. *Alan King*

GINGER FIZZ 8 ch.m. Haafhd 129 – Valagalore 91 (Generous (IRE) 139) [2015 p15.8g² **67**
t16.5m² t16.5g³ 18s Apr 7] lengthy, angular mare: fair maiden: stays 16.5f: acts on
polytrack and tapeta: sometimes wears hood: often wears tongue tie. *Ben Case*

GINGER JACK 8 ch.g. Refuse To Bend (IRE) 128 – Coretta (IRE) 118 (Caerleon (USA) **96**
132) [2015 10.3d 8m 10.3s⁶ 8m* 7.9g⁶ 7.9s* 9.9g 8d⁶ 10.4m 8g 9g p8f t8.6m p8g Dec 7] **a90**
workmanlike gelding: useful handicapper: won at Thirsk in May and Carlisle (by 1¾
lengths from Imshivalla) in July: left Keith Dalgleish after eleventh start: stays 10.5f: acts
on polytrack, soft and good to firm going: tried in cheekpieces. *Garry Moss*

GINGER JOE 2 ch.g. (Mar 21) Medicean 128 – Susi Wong (IRE) (Selkirk (USA) 129) **66**
[2015 5.2m 7g⁵ 8.3d p6f⁶ f7g* Nov 26] fair performer: left Peter Chapple-Hyam after
debut: won seller at Southwell on final outing, making all: subsequently sold 9,500 gns:
possibly stays 8.5f: acts on fibresand and good to soft going. *Richard Hannon*

GIN IN THE INN (IRE) 2 b.g. (Mar 28) Alfred Nobel (IRE) 110 – Nose One's Way **89**
(IRE) 57 (Revoque (IRE) 122) [2015 5d* 6m³ 6.5m 6g Oct 3] €35,000Y: fifth foal:
closely related to 1m winner Kavaco (by Choisir) and half-brother to 1m/9f winner Bobolit
(by Oratorio) and useful winner up to 6f Grandad's World (2-y-o 5f winner, by Kodiac):
dam, Flat maiden/winning hurdler, half-sister to smart winner up to 6f Guinea Hunter:
fairly useful performer: won maiden at Leicester in April: third in minor event at Pontefract
in May: stays 6f: acts on good to firm and good to soft going: often races prominently/
travels strongly. *Richard Fahey*

GINZAN 7 b.m. Desert Style (IRE) 121 – Zyzania 96 (Zafonic (USA) 130) [2015 82: p5f* **85**
5.3d* 5m 5.1m t6g³ 6g³ 5v 6.1s 6d² 6d Oct 12] good-topped mare: fairly useful handicapper:
won at Kempton in April and Brighton in May: stays 6f: acts on polytrack, tapeta, firm and
soft going: tried in cheekpieces prior to 2015. *Malcolm Saunders*

GIOIA DI VITA 5 b.g. Sakhee (USA) 136 – Dhuyoof (IRE) (Sinndar (IRE) 134) [2015 **78**
11.6m² 12d² Aug 11] good-topped gelding: fair handicapper: stays 1¾m: acts on polytrack,
firm and soft going: tried in headgear prior to 2015. *Dr Richard Newland*

GIOS LAST (GER) 5 gr.g. Paolini (GER) 121 – Giovanella (IRE) (Common Grounds **68**
118) [2015 60: t12.2f* t12.2m* p13f³ p14g⁵ Apr 9] fair handicapper: won amateur event
and apprentice event at Wolverhampton in February: stays 1½m: acts on polytrack, tapeta
and dirt: tried in cheekpieces: sold £15,000 and joined Sarah-Jane Davies. *James Eustace*

GIOVANNI CANALETTO (IRE) 3 ch.c. Galileo (IRE) 134 – Love Me True (USA) **113**
99 (Kingmambo (USA) 125) [2015 100P: 10g² 12m⁴ 12m³ 12d³ Aug 19] tall, lengthy,
rather unfurnished colt: smart performer: second in Gallinule Stakes at the Curragh (neck
behind Curvy) in May, fourth in Derby (10 lengths behind Golden Horn), third in Irish
Derby at the Curragh (10½ lengths behind Jack Hobbs) in June and third in Great Voltigeur
Stakes at York (5 lengths behind Storm The Stars) in August: stays 1½m: acts on good to
firm and good to soft going: in cheekpieces last 3 starts: has an awkward head carriage: sent
to Hong Kong. *Aidan O'Brien, Ireland*

GIOVANNI DI BICCI 3 b.g. Medicean 128 – Marula (IRE) (Sadler's Wells (USA) 132) **–**
[2015 –: p10g p8g 9d Jun 4] sturdy gelding: maiden: no form in 2015: left Lady Cecil after
first start: tried in tongue tie in 2015. *Jim Boyle*

GIRLING (IRE) 2 b.f. (Feb 23) Rock of Gibraltar (IRE) 133 – Gravitation 112 (Galileo **78 p**
(IRE) 134) [2015 7s² Oct 12] rather unfurnished filly: third foal: closely related to 9f
winner (stays 1¾m) Galaxy (by Oratorio) and half-sister to smart winner up to 1¼m
Citron (2-y-o 7f winner, by Cape Cross): dam 1½m-1¾m winner: 8/1, shaped well when
second in maiden at Salisbury (length behind Dutch Destiny) in October, sticking to task:
will be suited by 1m+: sure to progress. *Ralph Beckett*

GIRLS IN A BENTLEY 2 b.f. (Feb 9) Acclamation 118 – Laurelei (IRE) (Oratorio **–**
(IRE) 128) [2015 5g⁶ 5m⁴ 5g 6m p6g⁶ Aug 22] £60,000Y: first foal: dam, 1¼m winner,
half-sister to top-class winner up to 1½m Cape Blanco out of useful 5f (including at 2 yrs)
winner Laurel Delight: no form. *James Given*

GIRL WITH A PEARL (IRE) 2 ch.f. (Mar 31) Dutch Art 126 – Pointed Arch (IRE) 68 **62**
(Rock of Gibraltar (IRE) 133) [2015 6m 6d⁶ p7g Jul 1] 110,000F, 120,000Y: fourth foal:
half-sister to 2-y-o 5.7f/6f winner Dream Maker (by Bahamian Bounty) and useful winner
up to 1½m Farquhar (2-y-o 8.3f winner, by Archipenko): dam, 1½m winner, half-sister to
very smart 1¼m-1¾m winner Pugin: modest form in maidens: will be suited by at least 7f.
Ed Dunlop

GITTAN 2 b.c. (Mar 19) Kodiac 112 – Apple Dumpling 50 (Haafhd 129) [2015 5.1m⁶ p7g **68**
p8g⁵ Oct 27] fair form in maidens at Kempton and Lingfield last 2 starts: left Richard
Hannon after debut. *Ed Walker*

GIVEAGIRLACHANCE (IRE) 6 b.m. Iffraaj 127 – Farewell To Love (IRE) (Darshaan – 133) [2015 p10g⁶ t13.9g Nov 27] no form. *Seamus Mullins*

GIVEAWAY GLANCE 2 br.f. (Mar 20) Passing Glance 119 – Giving 98 (Generous **76** (IRE) 139) [2015 7.6v² 7v* 7g Sep 26] fourth foal: dam, 2-y-o 7f winner who stayed 1¼m, half-sister to smart 1¼m/10.5f winner (stayed 12.5f) Burn The Breeze: fair performer: best effort when winning maiden at Lingfield (by 1½ lengths from Croara) in September: will stay at least 1m: acts on heavy ground. *Alan King*

GIVE US A BELLE (IRE) 6 b.g. Kheleyf (USA) 116 – Bajan Belle (IRE) 72 (Efisio **63** 120) [2015 53, a70: p5m t5.1g² t5.1f² t5.1f³ t5.1g⁴ t5.1g⁶ t5.1m* t6g³ 5.1d² p5m 5m² **a73** p5g⁴ t5.1g² p5f³ 5.3d 5g⁴ p5f⁴ t5.1f t5.1f⁶ f5f t5.1m³ Dec 30] fair handicapper: won at Wolverhampton in April: stays 6f: acts on polytrack, tapeta, good to firm and heavy going: usually wears headgear: usually wears tongue tie. *Christine Dunnett*

G K CHESTERTON (IRE) 2 ch.c. (Feb 20) Poet's Voice 126 – Neptune's Bride (USA) **90 p** 110 (Bering 136) [2015 8.3d³ 8s* Oct 16] half brother to several winners, including smart 1¼m-1½m winner Submariner (by Singspiel) and useful 6f-7.5f winner Poseidon's Bride (by Seeking The Gold): dam 1m-10.5f winner: better effort when winning maiden at Redcar (by 4½ lengths from Muzdawaj) in October, leading on bridle 2f out and storming clear: potentially useful. *Charlie Appleby*

GLADIATRIX 6 b.m. Compton Place 125 – Lady Dominatrix (IRE) 112 (Danehill Dancer – (IRE) 117) [2015 97: 5.5d Mar 27] workmanlike mare: useful performer: stiff task when last in listed race at Fontainebleau sole start in 2015: stays 5.5f: acts on fibresand, good to firm and heavy going: has worn blinkers: often races prominently. *Rod Millman*

GLADSOME 7 b.m. Resplendent Glory (IRE) 115 – Christening (IRE) (Lahib (USA) **52** 129) [2015 60: p7m p6g⁶ p6g² p6f p7g f7g Dec 12] modest maiden: left Sarah Humphrey after first start: stays 7f: acts on polytrack, good to firm and heavy going: tried in headgear prior to 2015. *Charlie Wallis*

GLADSTONE (FR) 4 b.g. Mizzen Mast (USA) 121 – Bahia Gold (USA) (Woodman – (USA) 126) [2015 16d Oct 11] one-time fairly useful performer in France: well held only start in 2015: stays 15f: acts on polytrack and soft going: tried in blinkers/hood. *Warren Greatrex*

GLAD TIDINGS 3 b.g. Shamardal (USA) 129 – Time Away (IRE) 114 (Darshaan 133) **90 p** [2015 7m⁵ 8m² 8.3d* 8g² Aug 6] 180,000Y, 16,000 3-y-o: half-brother to 3 winners, including smart 9.7f-1½m winner Time On and temperamental 10.3f winner Time Control (both by Sadler's Wells): dam winner up to 10.4f (2-y-o 1m winner): fairly useful form: won maiden at Hamilton (by 8 lengths from Billy Ranger) in July: further progress when neck second of 5 to Pyjama Party in handicap at Haydock: stays 8.5f: wears hood: capable of better still. *David O'Meara*

GLADYS COOPER (IRE) 2 b.f. (Apr 20) Arcano (IRE) 122 – Anthyllis (GER) (Lycius **62** (USA) 124) [2015 7g p7g⁶ p7g Nov 26] half-sister to several winners, including useful winner up to 2m Andorn (2-y-o 1m winner, by Monsun) and winner up to 11f Galilivia (2-y-o 1m winner, by Teofilo): dam 2-y-o 6f winner: modest maiden: best effort when sixth at Lingfield (2 lengths behind Little Kipling) in October: should prove suited by 1m+. *Ed Walker*

GLADYS' GAL 7 b.m. Tobougg (IRE) 125 – Charming Lotte 80 (Nicolotte 118) [2015 8g – 8m May 2] useful at best, no form in 2015: stays 7f: acts on polytrack and good to firm going. *Ruth Carr*

GLAMOROUS APPROACH (IRE) 2 ch.f. (Feb 7) New Approach (IRE) 132 – Maria **99 p** Lee (IRE) (Rock of Gibraltar (IRE) 133) [2015 7.5m* 7.5s³ 8d³ 10g* Oct 10] tall filly: has scope: first foal: dam ran once: useful form: successful debut in maiden at Tipperary in July: 15/2, further improvement when winning 10-runner listed race at Newmarket in October by 1¼ lengths from Landofhopeandglory, leading from over 2f out: stays 1¼m: should continue to progress. *J. S. Bolger, Ireland*

GLANCE MY WAY (IRE) 2 ch.c. (Mar 10) Rock of Gibraltar (IRE) 133 – Glympse **81** (IRE) 59 (Spectrum (IRE) 126) [2015 8.1s 10.2m⁴ 8s⁴ 9.5f Nov 14] 38,000F: sixth foal: half-brother to 3 winners, including useful 2-y-o 7f winner (stays 10.5f) Whipper's Boy (by Whipper) and 5f winner Supercharged (by Iffraaj): dam maiden: fairly useful maiden: best effort at 1m. *Richard Hannon*

GLAN Y GORS (IRE) 3 b.g. High Chaparral (IRE) 132 – Trading Places (Dansili 127) **85** [2015 10m* 11g⁶ 10.3m⁴ p11g t9.5m⁶ Dec 26] 12,000Y: leggy gelding: fifth foal: dam unraced half-sister to smart winner up to 9f Wharf: fairly useful performer: won maiden at Pontefract in April: left Gay Kelleway after third start: stays 11f: acts on good to firm going: tried in hood. *David Simcock*

GLASGON 5 gr.g. Verglas (IRE) 118 – Miss St Tropez (Danehill Dancer (IRE) 117) [2015 **72**
–: t8.6m⁴ 7d³ 8.3m⁴ 10.1m⁶ 8d² 9.3d* 9.3s⁵ 10.1g⁵ t9.5f* Oct 16] fair handicapper: won at
Carlisle (amateur) in August and Wolverhampton in October: left Declan Carroll after
second start: stays 9.5f: acts on tapeta and good to soft going. *David Barron*

GLASGOW CENTRAL 4 b.g. Rail Link 132 – Musical Key 71 (Key of Luck (USA) **76**
126) [2015 t12.2f³ p10f⁵ 11.6m² 10.2f² 12.1m⁵ 10.2m⁶ t8.6g t9.5f p8m Dec 27] rather
unfurnished gelding: fair maiden: left Nigel Twiston-Davies after sixth start: stays 1½m:
acts on tapeta and firm going: tried in visor in 2015. *Phil McEntee*

GLASS OFFICE 5 gr.h. Verglas (IRE) 118 – Oval Office 99 (Pursuit of Love 124) [2015 **116**
–: 5m 6g* 6f Jun 20] tall, good-topped horse: smart performer: won Duke of York Stakes at
York in May by head from Mattmu, finding plenty to lead close home: below-form ninth of
15 to Undrafted in Diamond Jubilee Stakes at Royal Ascot only subsequent start: stays 6f:
acts on polytrack and firm going. *David Simcock*

GLASTONBERRY 7 gr.m. Piccolo 121 – Elderberry (Bin Ajwaad (IRE) 119) [2015 85: **81**
p6f* p6m p6f² p6g² 6m* 6m* 5.7f² 6.1d⁴ 6d⁴ p6g Oct 6] sturdy mare: fairly useful **a88**
handicapper: won at Lingfield in January and Windsor in April and May (apprentice):
winner at 7f, races mainly over shorter nowadays: acts on polytrack, good to firm and good
to soft going. *Geoffrey Deacon*

GLEAMING GIRL 3 b.f. Arabian Gleam 122 – Desert Liaison 68 (Dansili 127) [2015 **78**
77: p8g² p8m⁵ 7d⁴ 8m⁶ 8.3d³ 7d⁶ Oct 24] fair handicapper: stays 8.5f: acts on polytrack,
good to firm and good to soft going: often races towards rear. *David Simcock*

GLEESE THE DEVIL (IRE) 4 br.g. Manduro (GER) 135 – Causeway Song (USA) **91**
(Giant's Causeway (USA) 132) [2015 86p: 9.9m⁴ 12m³ 12d⁶ 15.9m² 15.9g 16.4s* Oct 10]
fairly useful handicapper: improved when winning 16-runner event at York in October by
neck from Hidden Justice, leading around 2f out then idling: stays 16.5f: acts on good to
firm and heavy going: front runner/races prominently. *Richard Fahey*

GLENALMOND (IRE) 3 b.g. Iffraaj 127 – Balladonia 103 (Primo Dominie 121) [2015 **105**
106: 7m⁴ 8m 6d 6m 6m 7.6m⁵ 7v Nov 7] attractive gelding: fairly useful performer: fourth
in listed Free Handicap at Newmarket (4 lengths behind Home of The Brave) in April: well
below form subsequently: stays 7f: acts on good to firm going: often in headgear: often
races towards rear. *K. R. Burke*

GLENBUCK LASS (IRE) 3 gr.f. Dandy Man (IRE) 123 – Certainlei (IRE) 81 (Definite **52**
Article 121) [2015 55: t5.1f t6g³ 7m 7m⁵ p5g⁵ f5g⁴ Dec 12] fairly useful maiden: stays 6f: acts
on fibresand and tapeta: sometimes slowly away. *Alan Bailey*

GLENEAGLES (IRE) 3 b.c. Galileo (IRE) 134 – You'resothrilling (USA) 117 **128**
(Storm Cat (USA)) [2015 113: 8m* 8g* 8f* 8d⁶ a10f Oct 31]
        Socrates, Aristotle and Einstein are among those accredited with variations
on the dictum 'The more we know, the more there is to know.' A visit to Ballydoyle,
the racing arm of the Coolmore empire, serves only to confirm the increasing
complexity of racehorse evaluation and training nowadays. In addition to the
modern veterinary checks and blood tests, all the horses are linked to a heart monitor
during exercise, for example, and every gallop is videoed and every work rider
quizzed personally about the well-being of their horses by trainer Aidan O'Brien.
O'Brien is in constant touch with the riders by walkie-talkie during exercise, as well
as being linked by mobile at all times to key stable and office staff. Six statisticians
are employed to keep a wealth of data on the horses up to date, so that the Coolmore
partners and their various advisers can log in to check every horse's well-being,
progress and training plan—O'Brien does all the work plans himself—and watch
videos of the gallops. Listening to Aidan O'Brien discussing his methods can, at
times, be like being at a masterclass with Sir Dave Brailsford (though Ballydoyle
hasn't yet got round to following British Cycling by appointing a 'head of marginal
gains'). O'Brien's renowned sharp-eyed attention to detail and innate understanding
of the thoroughbred remains his greatest asset but that apparently isn't enough on
its own to succeed in the modern era. The data crunchers have certainly increased
the depth of preparation involved in racehorse training and planning, though, of
course, it is one thing accumulating all the information and another being able to
make the best use of it. The decision-making process around running plans for
Ballydoyle's top horses can be tortuous, with the involvement of the different
Coolmore partners and their advisers, and it would come as no surprise to learn

that interpreting the detailed dossier kept on each horse can sometimes make that an extremely complicated process. No running plans are issued from Ballydoyle until they have been agreed by all three major partners— 'the lads'—which often leaves Aidan O'Brien hedging his bets about future plans in post-race interviews (a process he describes as 'trying to say something without saying anything').

The three-year-old career of Gleneagles, whose victory in the Two Thousand Guineas gave Aidan O'Brien a seventh success in the race and made him jointly the most successful trainer in the long history of the event, provided a number of apparent examples of the trainer and the owners not always being in unison. The poor attendance record of Gleneagles in the major open-aged championship mile races in the second half of the season, usually after 'will-he-won't-he' dilemmas about whether the going was suitable for him, became a sore point with some racegoers who perhaps felt that not all of those connected with Gleneagles valued entertainment and excitement as much as they did. After he had completed a fine Group 1 hat-trick against horses of his own age in the Irish Two Thousand Guineas and the St James's Palace Stakes at Royal Ascot in the first part of the season, Gleneagles wasn't seen in racing action until British Champions' Day in mid-October.

It is sometimes said that the Two Thousand Guineas is the last important target of the two-year-old season and Gleneagles, a mature-looking individual as a juvenile, had passed the post in front on the last five of his six appearances in that first season. There were other classic hopes at Ballydoyle who seemed clearly open to more improvement at three and the Two Thousand Guineas always looked the natural number-one target for Gleneagles. As with his trainer's previous winners, Gleneagles lined up at Newmarket without a preparatory outing. The trainer's son Joseph had ridden Gleneagles on all his starts after his debut as a two-year-old but there was a new jockey for the Two Thousand Guineas, with Ryan Moore taking over. Weight issues seemed at first to be behind the decision to replace O'Brien who, by his father's admission, had increasingly found 'doing nine stone a problem, last year it was a big problem and this year he's heavier than he was at this time last year.' Joseph O'Brien, who had a number of early-season rides over hurdles, was unable to give an assurance in the spring that he could ride Gleneagles at the nine stone allotted in the Two Thousand Guineas, with his father saying 'Joseph will go gently and we'll see what will happen.' The Coolmore partners reacted to the uncertainty over their jockey by putting their relationship with Ryan Moore on a more formal basis (he had been used a little more regularly the previous year on some of the stable's leading horses).

The replacement of his son as Ballydoyle's number-one must have been uncomfortable at the very least for Aidan O'Brien who seemed even more conscious in his public pronouncements over the latest season of emphasising that it is 'the lads' who take the key decisions. At one point over the summer, the rumour mill was feverish with speculation of an impending split. O'Brien, it was said, was planning, after twenty years at Ballydoyle, to return to his jumping roots at the Piltown yard in County Kilkenny where he and his wife started, and from which Joseph O'Brien –who retained a central role at Ballydoyle—sent out point-to-point runners

Qipco 2000 Guineas Stakes, Newmarket—the favourite Gleneagles runs out an impressive winner from Territories, Ivawood (left, star on cap) and outsider Bossy Guest, giving trainer Aidan O'Brien a record-equalling seventh win in this classic

Tattersalls Irish 2000 Guineas, the Curragh—Gleneagles joins an elite group, including former Ballydoyle inmates Henrythenavigator and Rock of Gibraltar, by completing an Anglo/Irish Two Thousand Guineas double; Endless Drama (checks) takes second, Ivawood (rail) third and the hooded Belardo fourth

later in the season. The up-and-coming David O'Meara found his name linked to Ballydoyle during all the speculation, though he himself dismissed the story and none of the rumours was ever validated. For his part, Ryan Moore wasted no time in demonstrating his value to the Coolmore partners by riding the winners for them of both the Two Thousand Guineas and the One Thousand Guineas (in which he partnered the David Wachman-trained Legatissimo).

Gleneagles needed to step up on his two-year-old form to win an average Guineas but there had been a shortage of tip-top performances in the leading two-year-old championship events and the Qipco Two Thousand Guineas field potentially looked far from vintage. Gleneagles was sent off 4/1 favourite in a field of eighteen on the day (he had been 2/1 and shorter in places earlier in the week), with the supplemented, Andre Fabre-trained Territories next in the betting at 5/1. Territories had finished three quarters of a length behind the subsequently-demoted Gleneagles when third (promoted to second) in a bunched finish to the Prix Jean-Luc Lagardere at Longchamp; Gleneagles edged right that day after taking the lead—as he had when winning the National Stakes at the Curragh—and he fell foul of the stricter French rules on interference, being put back to third. In an open betting market at Newmarket, the Champagne Stakes winner Estidhkaar, who had shaped well when a close second in the Greenham at Newbury on his reappearance, shared third favouritism at 6/1 with the second Ballydoyle runner Ol' Man River (ridden by Joseph O'Brien at 9-0) who had looked an exciting prospect at two and was among what had seemed, over the winter, to be an embarrassment of riches for his stable in the Derby, a race it had won three years in succession. Estidhkaar's owner had stumped up the £30,000 supplementary fee for twice-raced Intilaaq after he ran away with a Newbury maiden in April, and he came next in the betting at 8/1, ahead of the Middle Park runner-up Ivawood, who had come third in the Greenham. The only other runner to start at shorter than 20/1 was Celestial Path, the Racing Post Trophy third (the winner of that race Elm Park was an eleventh-hour withdrawal from the Guineas on account of the firmish ground).

There had been comment after the 2014 Two Thousand Guineas that, because the field split into two groups which raced on opposite sides, the race had been an unsatisfactory spectacle. The 40/1-shot Night of Thunder won that edition from 6/4 favourite Kingman and Ballydoyle's top three-year-old Australia, and that outcome also prompted speculation about whether the result would have been different had the race been run more conventionally. In a bid to avoid a repeat, Newmarket positioned the stalls for the latest edition against the stand rail (they were in the middle in 2014 where they had usually been in recent times) and the track also installed a false running rail on the stand side to narrow the course by three or four metres in the first five furlongs or so; the course returned to its full width when the false rail cut back to the original rail about two and a half furlongs from the finish, providing more room in the later stages for runners that had been tucked in the main pack. Gleneagles was drawn in stall sixteen, close to the stand rail, and he was settled in the middle of the field before making good progress over two furlongs out and then producing a sharp turn of acceleration to quicken into a clear lead approaching the final furlong. Ridden out to maintain his advantage, Gleneagles won by two and a quarter lengths and three quarters of a length from Territories, who chased him throughout the final furlong, and Ivawood, who fared best of a cluster that still raced further apart, towards the centre of the course. The 50/1-shot Bossy Guest excelled himself in fourth, close behind the placed horses, despite meeting trouble around two furlongs out when making ground in the stand-side group, while fifth-placed Celestial Path was second home in the centre group which seemed slightly disadvantaged the way the race developed (the stand-side group was ahead throughout). Estidhkaar folded tamely after seeming to lose his action in the Dip and Ol' Man River found nothing when shaken up and was eased markedly in the closing stages.

Gleneagles looked the finished article at Newmarket, showing none of the tendency to wander off a true line that had been apparent in his two-year-old performances at the Curragh and Longchamp and he responded well under pressure to keep going all the way to the line (he had idled in front more than once in his two-year-old races). He did again sweat in the preliminaries, being described by his trainer afterwards as 'a free sweater, he sweats quick but dries off quick.' Victory for Gleneagles enabled Aidan O'Brien to equal the number of wins in the Two Thousand Guineas set by John Scott, the 'Wizard of the North', who trained a record forty English classic winners at Malton in the nineteenth century. Gleneagles gave Ryan Moore his first winning ride in the race. The middle one of John Scott's seven Two Thousand Guineas winners was West Australian, the first horse to win the Two Thousand Guineas, the Derby and the St Leger, which he did in 1853 at around the time the terms 'classics' and 'triple crown' came into use. The last winner of the Two Thousand Guineas sent out from Ballydoyle, Camelot in 2012, had gone on to win the Derby before being beaten by Encke in the St Leger, a defeat that also denied his trainer the unique feat of saddling all five winners of the British classics in a single season. There was never any question of Gleneagles following in Camelot's hoofprints, his trainer describing him after the Two Thousand Guineas as being 'as exciting a miler as we've had … it's all pace with him.'

Two of the earlier O'Brien-trained Two Thousand Guineas winners, Rock of Gibraltar and Henrythenavigator, both went on to complete the Anglo-Irish Guineas double but another, George Washington, was beaten at 7/4-on at the Curragh on heavy ground (O'Brien's first Two Thousand Guineas winner King of Kings had his only subsequent race in the Derby while Footstepsinthesand wasn't seen out at all after his Guineas win). Gleneagles duly joined Rock of Gibraltar and Henrythenavigator on the list of eight horses who have now completed the double at Newmarket and the Curragh, but his trainer said afterwards that it had been a borderline decision to run and that the prevailing going at the Curragh (Timeform returned it as good after drying weather) was 'as slow as he'd want it'. Gleneagles was sent off at 5/2-on but didn't match his Newmarket form in the Tattersalls Irish Two Thousand Guineas. He had to battle after finding himself briefly stuck in a pocket two furlongs out, and he kept on gamely, once Moore extricated him, to take the lead well inside the final furlong. Gleneagles confirmed his position at the head of the list of the three-year-old milers by beating Endless Drama (the least exposed horse in the field) and Ivawood by three quarters of a length and half a length, with the Dewhurst winner Belardo a further half a length back in fourth, returning to form after missing the Newmarket classic following a poor run in the Greenham. Gleneagles was the tenth winner of the Irish Two Thousand Guineas saddled by Aidan O'Brien who hailed him afterwards as 'the best miler we've had', drawing comparisons with Giant's Causeway (Gleneagles is out of a sister to that very tough top-class mile- to mile-and-a-quarter performer). 'He was always exceptional … I always thought he was Giant's Causeway with more speed and today he showed he has that pure Giant's Causeway courage,' O'Brien told the assembled media (no doubt fully conscious, a cynic might say, that Gleneagles was ultimately destined for a leading place on the Coolmore stallion roster).

With Gleneagles a notable exception, the form of some of the Ballydoyle three-year-olds had given cause for concern in the opening part of the season. Ol' Man River's poor effort in the Two Thousand Guineas and the eclipse of the winter favourite John F Kennedy on his seasonal debut at Leopardstown had focussed attention on some of the supposed lesser lights among the Ballydoyle Derby entries and on their performances in the various trials in Britain and Ireland. Gleneagles himself was left in the Derby until fairly late, though Aidan O'Brien said after the Irish Two Thousand Guineas that he had 'always viewed him as a miler and he works like a miler.' O'Brien, it seems, was overruled when it came to the decision to keep Gleneagles in the Derby after he had been entered (at a cost of £8,000) at the second entry stage in April. 'I was going through the Derby forfeits and I had a line through Gleneagles until the lads told me to leave him in—so obviously they're clearly thinking about it.' In the end, Gleneagles wasn't sent to Epsom where Giovanni Canaletto fared best of Ballydoyle's three Derby runners when just making the frame (ten lengths behind the winning favourite Golden Horn).

Gleneagles went on to emulate Rock of Gibraltar and Henrythenavigator by completing the Anglo-Irish Guineas/St James's Palace Stakes treble, something only Right Tack, in 1969, had achieved before the twenty-first-century Ballydoyle trio. O'Brien's six previous winners of the St James's Palace, which also included Giant's Causeway (who had finished second in both Guineas), had put him level with that great nineteenth-century figure Mat Dawson as the most successful trainer in the history of the race. O'Brien is now out on his own after Gleneagles joined exalted company when landing the odds in a small field which contained none of those who had taken him on at Newmarket (runner-up Territories missed Royal Ascot with a foot problem) or the Curragh, but did include the Poule d'Essai des Poulains winner Make Believe. The prevailing very firm ground may have been the cause of Make Believe's poor effort (well-beaten last of five) but Gleneagles revelled in the conditions, quickening well and running out a ready winner, under just hands and heels, from the progressive pair Latharnach and Consort. As well as the expected comparisons between Gleneagles and Giant's Causeway, Aidan O'Brien's post-race media briefing included an unexpectedly fulsome tribute to Gleneagles' deposed jockey. 'Joseph rides Gleneagles every day and does absolutely everything with him, I am very happy to be sitting in the back seat, believe me, and I'm looking forward to staying the odd night away in future. We go back to Ireland every day, we never stay anywhere and I have never seen any of the cities we go to. I come racing and go home.' He added that Joseph had told him that 'this was the best he's had Gleneagles for a race and I was happy to hear that.' Whether all the Coolmore partners were just as happy to hear their forty-five-year-old trainer implying that he might be looking to slow down'—something that few who knew him could quite believe—was a matter for conjecture. It would have been very hard, however, to find fault with the performance of the Ballydoyle horses at Royal Ascot. Irish-trained horses won eight races at the meeting and five of them hailed from Ballydoyle (O'Brien was leading trainer at the meeting for the sixth time).

All five of the Ballydoyle winners were ridden by Ryan Moore who had nine winners in all over the five days (thirty races), three short of the all-time Royal Ascot record of twelve set by Fred Archer at the four-day meeting (twenty-nine races) in 1878. Moore's nine winners were a record for the era since the end of World War II, one more than Lester Piggott's total in 1965 and 1975 and Pat Eddery's in 1989. Ryan Moore is just thirty-two and he has a long way to go to match some of the other achievements of Piggott and Eddery—both of whom were champion jockey eleven times—but he could be painted as a present-day version of either in his taciturnity. Like Piggott and Eddery, Moore is undemonstrative and he spurns the limelight and can seem uncooperative at times. Ascot presented him with a number-nine saddle cloth after he won the Queen's Vase, the last race on Friday, to surpass the mark set by Piggott and Eddery; but he did not pause to celebrate, dashing off straight away to catch a helicopter to the evening fixture at Newmarket. 'I'm not thinking about records, I'm thinking about tomorrow, then we will worry about this,' he said. Even when eventually allowing a little more time for the media, his low-key manner was typical for someone who is undoubtedly his own man in an age when jockeys are encouraged to be more 'media friendly'. Asked how highly the achievement ranked in his career so far, Moore replied: 'Well, not everything went right … I didn't win the Gold Cup, I was on the best horse [Kingfisher], we were unfortunate, he should have won … and I was disappointed with the Saturday [no winners].' It is not Moore's style to seek to boost his celebrity by proclaiming his own achievements, or through showmanship (though he is unstinting in his admiration for Frankie Dettori—'We can't all be like him').

Moore also explained that it is in his nature to stay 'level' in victory and defeat. 'We don't talk about records, things can go wrong quickly,' Moore said, prophetically as it turned out. A mishap when his mount reared and crushed him against the back of the stalls, before the final race on the opening day of the Newmarket July meeting, resulted in Moore suffering a neck injury which kept him out of the saddle until a surprise return in October. The injury put paid to Moore's chance of winning a fourth jockeys' championship in Britain—he had a narrow lead over Silvestre de Sousa at the time of his accident—and, until his unheralded late return, it seemed he might miss the rest of the season. The impressive victories of Minding in the Fillies' Mile and Air Force Blue in the Dewhurst gave Moore and the Coolmore partners plenty to look forward to in 2016, and Moore was also the leading jockey (winning on Found and Hit It A Bomb for Ballydoyle) at the Breeders' Cup before enjoying a successful spell in Japan and then riding two winners (including Highland Reel for Ballydoyle) and a second on Hong Kong's International raceday in December.

With Moore sidelined, Joseph O'Brien was pencilled in to ride Gleneagles in the newly-enriched Sussex Stakes at Goodwood which looked set to be his first outing against older horses, headed by the French-trained five-year-old Solow who, like Gleneagles, brought an unbeaten seasonal record to the race (most recently winning the Queen Anne at Royal Ascot) and had actually won his last seven races. Gleneagles would have completed an eight-race winning run but for his disqualification in the Prix Jean-Luc Lagardere. The scratching of Gleneagles at the forty-eight-hour declaration stage denied Goodwood its most marketable duel of the week. It came after more rain fell on the Friday and Sunday before the meeting than had been forecast, leaving the ground on the soft side. After the ground dried out on the run up to the race, the decision not to declare Gleneagles was widely criticised as having been premature. However, when a horse is left among the possible runners, with doubts over its participation until the last moment, it puts some racegoers in a quandary about whether to travel, and it also has a dampening effect on betting turnover until a call is finally made one way or the other. The withdrawal of

St James's Palace Stakes, Royal Ascot—Gleneagles finishes first past the post for the eighth successive start as he readily beats Latharnach (white cap), Consort (rail) Aktabantay and the disappointing Poule d'Essai des Poulains winner Make Believe

M. Tabor, Mrs J. Magnier & D. Smith's "Gleneagles"

Gleneagles at Goodwood (which O'Brien still thought had been the right decision when he walked the course on Sussex Stakes morning) may have been deflating for the sport, but its timing was infinitely preferable to the 'will-he-won't-he' sagas that ensued before the International at York and the Irish Champion at Leopardstown.

The Prix Jacques le Marois at Deauville had seemed the next viable option for Gleneagles at a mile after the Sussex, though Aiden O'Brien had let it be known that a step up to a mile and a quarter—something he described pointedly as 'a very sporting gesture by the owners'—was now figuring in future plans. Gleneagles didn't get his preferred 'good, fast ground' at Deauville—where he would have renewed rivalry with Two Thousand Guineas runner-up Territories among others—and, for a time, it seemed that York would host a headline clash in the Juddmonte International between Gleneagles and Golden Horn, the first time the same season's Two Thousand Guineas and Derby winners had taken each other on in Britain since the 1992 International (when Rodrigo de Triano had Derby winner Dr Devious back in fourth). Unexpectedly persistent rain the day before the race in the end scuppered 'the race of the season', but not before Gleneagles had been brought from Ireland on the morning of the International to allow connections to assess conditions, before finally announcing at a very late stage that they were pulling him out (he was led around the pre-parade ring so racegoers could see him, but the York stewards refused permission for him to work on the course after racing). The next attempt to get Gleneagles back on the racecourse came in the Irish Champion Stakes in September (the Prix du Moulin over a mile was the next day in France, but Gleneagles wasn't entered as, under French rules, he couldn't have run if he had been withdrawn from the Irish Champion after being declared for that race). He was withdrawn again on the day of racing at Leopardstown, with Aidan O'Brien saying connections were 'sorry about not running, but we had to do what was the right thing by the horse, it wouldn't be fair to ask him to go a mile and a quarter for the first time with the ground like this.' The Leopardstown executive had controversially brought forward the time of the Irish Champion by sixty-five minutes, after Friday night's rain was forecast, in the hope that running it on virgin ground might secure the participation of Gleneagles against Golden Horn and company. When Gleneagles was scratched, the stewards gave permission for him to be cantered on the course after racing.

There was serious talk for the first time between York and Leopardstown of a tilt at the Breeders' Cup Classic, the race in which Gleneagles' sire Galileo (unplaced) and Giant's Causeway (an excellent second) also ended their careers, and it was probably the 'need to get a race into him before that' which tilted the balance to run Gleneagles on good to soft in the Queen Elizabeth II Stakes on British Champions' Day at Ascot. It was another decision that went down to the wire and one that, in hindsight, Aidan O'Brien said he regretted. Had he and connections been consistent, Gleneagles would have been withdrawn. On going that was softer than any he had encountered since his racecourse debut (fourth in a Leopardstown maiden), Gleneagles managed only sixth behind Solow, after being waited with and then edging right when brought to challenge. Gleneagles was probably a shade ring-rusty after his four-month absence but was still beaten only about two and a half lengths by the winner, possibly prompting thoughts among some of his connections that he might have done better had Moore sat closer to the pace. That said, Gleneagles ran some way below his best form and finished behind four horses who were manifestly his inferiors (the Irish Two Thousand Guineas fourth Belardo came second to Solow). The Breeders' Cup Classic at Keeneland provided an ignominious end to Gleneagles' career. The least said about his performance the better. On his only start beyond a mile, and his only start on dirt, he clearly didn't handle the surface, finding nothing when ridden two furlongs out and clearly beaten before stamina became an issue, eventually trailing in a long way behind the others. Galileo himself cut no ice in the Classic and, as a sire, his three winners at the Breeders' Cup have all come in the Breeders' Cup Turf.

Gleneagles (IRE) (b.c. 2012)	Galileo (IRE) (b 1998)	Sadler's Wells (b 1981)	Northern Dancer
			Fairy Bridge
		Urban Sea (ch 1989)	Miswaki
			Allegretta
	You'resothrilling (USA) (b or br 2005)	Storm Cat (b or br 1983)	Storm Bird
			Terlingua
		Mariah's Storm (b 1991)	Rahy
			Immense

The heavy-topped Gleneagles is only around medium-sized. Galileo himself was a neat, attractive individual, bearing a closer resemblance in that respect to his grandsire Northern Dancer than to his sire Sadler's Wells. Gleneagles has similar markings to Galileo, something which has actually been used to promote Gleneagles as a potential sire, though the most important similarity between father and son (who both had a tendency to sweat) is that they were fluent movers. Galileo was one of the finest movers anyone could wish to see, with a tremendous stride. Galileo has been responsible for some very good milers at stud—headed by that paragon Frankel (like Gleneagles, a son of Galileo with four white feet)—but Galileo has become more widely regarded as a source of stamina and has had three Derby winners and four Irish Derby winners. The dam of Gleneagles, the useful You'resothrilling, who probably stayed a mile and a quarter, has been a perennial visitor to Galileo since being retired to the paddocks. Gleneagles is her second foal and her second classic winner, following the Irish One Thousand Guineas winner Marvellous who should have got further than a mile, though she failed to reproduce her Curragh form on her two subsequent appearances, when down the field in the Oaks (for which she started favourite) and the Irish Oaks (in which she was equipped with blinkers). You'resothrilling's third foal is the useful two-year-old filly Coolmore, winner of the C. L. Weld Park Stakes at the Curragh and fourth behind stablemate Minding in the Fillies' Mile at Newmarket. There is a yearling brother and a foal sister to Gleneagles following on. As has already been stated, You'resothrilling is a sister to Giant's Causeway, the horse to whom Gleneagles was most frequently likened, in racing character at least, by his trainer. Giant's Causeway has been champion sire in North America three times and his progeny in Europe include winners of the Two Thousand Guineas and the One Thousand Guineas. Giant's Causeway was the foal that Gleneagles' grandam, the very smart miler Mariah's Storm, was carrying when the Coolmore partners secured her for 2,600,000 dollars at the Keeneland November Sale in 1996. Other offspring of Mariah's Storm—who has yearling, two-year-old and three-year-old fillies by Galileo—were in the news in the latest season, including an unraced Sadler's Wells half-sister to You'resothrilling and Giant's Causeway, Love Me Only, who was represented on the racecourse by Storm The Stars who was placed in the Derby at both Epsom and the Curragh. A twice-raced sister to You'resothrilling and Giant's Causeway, Pearling, added her name to the list of successful broodmares in the immediate family when Decorated Knight (also by Galileo) developed into a smart miler, winning twice before finishing third in the Joel Stakes and fourth in the Darley Stakes, both at Newmarket. The useful five-year-old Galileo half-sister to You'resothrilling and Giant's Causeway, Hanky Panky who won at a mile, made headlines when fetching a sale-topping 2,700,000 guineas, in foal to Dubawi, at the December Sales. The great grandam of Gleneagles, Immense, was a graded winner on turf in North America over eight and a half furlongs and also enjoyed success as a broodmare. Gleneagles, who was usually held up travelling strongly in mid-division, stayed a mile and acted on firm going. He begins his career as a stallion at a fee of €60,000, the highest-priced sire at Coolmore among those with an advertised fee, €10,000 more than the Derby winner Australia who was advertised as 'the heir apparent to Galileo' when he was retired at the end of 2014. It would seem that Australia now has a serious rival for that title. The fact that Gleneagles was a Group 1-winning two-year-old who went on to classic success, and could hardly have a more fashionable stallion pedigree, makes him a highly attractive commercial proposition and he is also assured of the best support, given the strength of the Coolmore broodmare band. *Aidan O'Brien, Ireland*

GLENEELY GIRL (IRE) 3 b.f. Intense Focus (USA) 117 – Timber Tops (UAE) **75** (Timber Country (USA) 124) [2015 73: p8m⁵ 7.5m⁶ 8g⁴ 8.3m² 8.5f² 8.3m⁶ 9.9g³ 9.9g Sep 30] fair handicapper: stays 8.5f: acts on firm going: usually races towards rear: sold 1,800 gns, sent to Hungary. *Rae Guest*

GLENEVE (IRE) 2 b.g. (May 3) Intikhab (USA) 135 – Dalannda (IRE) (Hernando (FR) **59** 127) [2015 7v⁴ t7.1m f7m⁴ Dec 8] modest maiden: best effort when fourth at Southwell (16 lengths behind Yattwee) final start: will stay 1m. *Richard Fahey*

GLEN LEA (IRE) 6 b.g. Indian Danehill (IRE) 124 – Masquerade Ball (IRE) (Presenting **59** 120) [2015 9.3d⁵ 8m⁵ 5.9s⁵ 14.1m 7.9d⁵ Sep 15] modest maiden: stays 1m: acts on good to firm and good to soft going: front runner/races prominently. *Susan Corbett*

GLEN MOSS (IRE) 6 b.h. Moss Vale (IRE) 126 – Sail With The Wind 74 (Saddlers' Hall **108** (IRE) 126) [2015 115: p6g⁵ p6f² t7.1m⁴ p6f 7m 7m Jun 27] attractive horse: useful performer: in frame in listed races at Lingfield (head behind Rivellino) in February and Wolverhampton (2½ lengths fourth to Sovereign Debt) in March: well below form after: stays 7f: acts on polytrack, tapeta, firm and good to soft going. *Martyn Meade*

GLENNTEN 6 b.g. Ishiguru (USA) 111 – Uplifting 77 (Magic Ring (IRE) 115) [2015 69, **75** a79: 18d⁴ t8.6t⁶ t8.6f⁵ p10f⁵ 11.7f⁴ 9.9g* 9.9d* 10g⁴ 9g⁴ 10m³ 10m 8g⁵ 11.6m⁴ p10g² 10g³ p10f³ 10.2m² 10.2g³ Oct 18] angular gelding: fair handicapper: won at Brighton in April and May (apprentice): stays 11f: acts on polytrack, tapeta, good to firm and heavy going: tried in headgear: often races prominently. *Jose Santos*

GLENROWAN ROSE (IRE) 2 b.f. (Feb 2) Bushranger (IRE) 119 – Choice House **92** (USA) (Chester House (USA) 123) [2015 5g² 5m* 6f⁵ 6m⁶ 6g 5m² 6g 6g Sep 19] £6,000Y: fifth foal: half-sister to 3 winners, including 2m winner Jan Smuts (by Johannesburg) and 1¼m winner Chez Marina (by Duke of Marmalade): dam unraced: fairly useful performer: won maiden at Catterick (by neck from Comedy Night) in June: second in minor event at Musselburgh (short head behind Lil's Joy) in August: out of depth last 2 starts: stays 6f: acts on firm going. *Keith Dalgleish*

GLENS WOBBLY 7 ch.g. Kier Park (IRE) 114 – Wobbly (Atraf 116) [2015 t13.9g **79** p15.8g 11.7f² 13.1m* 13.1m* 11.7g² 14.1m 13.3m 10.2d³ 14.1g 13.1f⁵ 11.7g⁵ 12v² **a64** p12g⁵ Dec 9] fair handicapper: won at Bath in May and June: stays 13f: acts on polytrack and any turf going: tried in cheekpieces prior to 2015: front runner/races prominently. *Jonathan Geake*

GLIMMER OF HOPE 4 b.g. Tiger Hill (IRE) 127 – Fontaine House (Pyramus (USA) – 78) [2015 p10g Dec 9] 100/1, tailed off in maiden at Lingfield. *Mark Hoad*

GLOBAL AVENGER (IRE) 2 b.c. (Feb 2) Kodiac 112 – Silent Serenade (Bertolini 60 (USA) 125) [2015 7g t6g⁶ p8g t7.1f² p7g Dec 10] modest maiden: best effort at 7f: acts on tapeta: tried in blinkers. *Ed Dunlop*

GLOBAL FORCE (IRE) 3 b.g. Shamardal (USA) 129 – Pioneer Bride (USA) (Gone 97 West (USA)) [2015 85p: 10m* 10f⁶ 10d⁴ 10g Aug 29] tall gelding: useful performer: won maiden at Newmarket (by 2 lengths from Great Glen) in April: below that form in handicaps after: best effort at 1¼m: acts on good to firm going: usually races close up. *Saeed bin Suroor*

GLORIOUS ASSET 3 b.g. Aqlaam 125 – Regal Asset (USA) (Regal Classic (CAN)) 65 [2015 73p: t7.1g² Dec 1] fair maiden: second at Wolverhampton (2¼ lengths behind Lady Pinnacle) on sole outing in 2015 in December: will stay at least 1m. *Ivan Furtado*

GLORIOUS DANCER 3 br.g. Royal Applause 124 – Provence 83 (Averti (IRE) 117) 69 [2015 68: t7.1g³ p8g* 9g⁵ 10.4g p8g⁵ p7g p11g Aug 24] workmanlike gelding: fair handicapper: won at Chelmsford in February: left Ed Walker after fifth start: stays 9f: acts on polytrack: often in headgear in 2015. *Lee Carter*

GLORIOUS DAYS (AUS) 8 b.g. Hussonet (USA) – San Century (NZ) (Centaine 113 (AUS)) [2015 117: 8m 8m⁶ p7gᵘʳ Nov 11] high-class performer at best, winner of Hong Kong Mile at Sha Tin in 2013: just smart nowadays: left J. Size/off 7 months, unseated rider as stall opened in minor event at Kempton on final outing in 2015: stays 1m: acts on soft and good to firm going: wears headgear. *Ed Walker*

GLORY AWAITS (IRE) 5 ch.g. Choisir (AUS) 126 – Sandbox Two (IRE) (Foxhound 112 § (USA) 103) [2015 113§: 8d² 9g 8f 7g 6g 7g Oct 9] rather leggy, close-coupled gelding: smart performer: second in listed race at Doncaster (½ length behind Tullius) in March: subsequently disappointing: stays 1m: acts on soft and good to firm going: often wears headgear: front runner/races prominently: one to treat with caution: has joined David Simcock. *Kevin Ryan*

GM HOPKINS 4 b.g. Dubawi (IRE) 129 – Varsity 109 (Lomitas 129) [2015 113p: 8d 8m² 121 8f* 8m 8.9g 9g⁶ 8d² 8d⁴ Oct 31] attractive, good-quartered gelding: very smart handicapper: won Royal Hunt Cup at Royal Ascot (by neck from Temptress, edging ahead close home) in June: creditable sixth of 34 to Third Time Lucky in Cambridgeshire at Newmarket in September, and better than ever when 1½ lengths second of 20 to Musaddas in Balmoral Handicap at Ascot in October: stays 9f: acts on firm and good to soft going: tried in hood: usually races nearer last than first. *John Gosden*

Royal Hunt Cup (Heritage Handicap), Royal Ascot—
GM Hopkins (chevrons) catches the similarly progressive four-year-old Temptress to land this valuable handicap, with Chil The Kite and Balty Boys (far side) completing the frame

GOADBY 4 gr.f. Kodiac 112 – Gone Sailing (Mizzen Mast (USA) 121) [2015 66, a60: 6m⁴ **67**
6.1d* 6f² 6m 6g 6m 6.1m³ 6s³ 6d⁴ 6d² 6g⁵ 6d⁵ 6v⁵ Nov 3] fair handicapper: won at
Nottingham (apprentice) in May: stays 6f: acts on any turf going: often races prominently.
John Holt

GOAL (IRE) 7 b.g. Mujadil (USA) 119 – Classic Lin (FR) (Linamix (FR) 127) [2015 p10f **60**
9g p10g⁶ 10m 11.6m f8g Nov 24] rather leggy gelding: modest handicapper: stays 14.5f:
acts on polytrack, fibresand, good to firm and heavy going: tried in headgear: often wears
tongue tie. *Sally Randell*

GO AMBER GO 3 ch.f. Compton Place 125 – Lady Chef 75 (Double Trigger (IRE) 123) **50**
[2015 p8f p7f p7f⁶ p5g p7m p6g⁴ Nov 26] third foal: half-sister to 7f-11f winner (stays
2m) Yes Chef (by Best of The Bests) and 1m winner My Boy Ginger (by Byron): dam
2-y-o 7f winner: modest maiden: best effort at 6f: acts on polytrack: tried in cheekpieces.
Rod Millman

GOATHLAND (IRE) 3 b.g. Teofilo (IRE) 126 – Royals Special (IRE) 72 (Caerleon **98**
(USA) 132) [2015 66p: p8f² t9.5f³ 11.9d² 13.1f* 13.8g² 12g² Oct 9] good-topped gelding:
useful performer: won handicap at Bath (by 3 lengths from Vanishing) in September: 16/1,
resumed progress/shaped well when length second of 14 to Mustard in handicap at
Newmarket final start: stays 13f: acts on firm and good to soft going: often races towards
rear. *Peter Chapple-Hyam*

GO CHARLIE 4 b.g. Myboycharlie (IRE) 118 – Branston Gem 59 (So Factual (USA) **52**
120) [2015 53: 5m 5m 5m³ 5m³ 5m³ 5m⁵ t5.1f³ p5g² p6m t5.1f² t6f³ t6g f5g t5.1m* **a58**
t5.1m⁶ Dec 30] modest handicapper: won at Wolverhampton in December: stays 6f: acts
on polytrack, tapeta and firm going: usually wears hood: often starts slowly, usually races
nearer last than first. *Lisa Williamson*

GO DAN GO (IRE) 3 b.g. Dandy Man (IRE) 123 – Without Words 71 (Lion Cavern **102**
(USA) 117) [2015 60: 7.1s² 8g² 7.5m* 7.1s* 8g 8m³ 7.1m³ 7.9g* 6.9s* 9.2g 7g* 9.2g 9.9g⁴
Dec 30] tall gelding: useful performer: won handicaps at Beverley in April, Musselburgh
in May and Carlisle in June and July (by ½ length from Special Venture, left Keith
Dalgleish after) and minor event at Doha in December: stays 1¼m: acts on soft and good
to firm going. *Jassim Al Ghazali, Qatar*

GODDESS EPONA 3 b.f. Dylan Thomas (IRE) 132 – Cloudchaser (IRE) (Red Ransom **57**
(USA)) [2015 p10g p12f⁴ p12m 8.1d⁶ Aug 20] second foal: half-sister to 7f-1½m winner
Marengo (by Verglas): dam unraced: modest maiden: stays 1½m: often in hood. *Ed de Giles*

GOD WILLING 4 b.g. Arch (USA) 127 – Bourbon Ball (USA) (Peintre Celebre (USA) **101**
137) [2015 105: p8g² 7g⁴ 8.5g 8m p8g⁵ 8d 8d⁵ Sep 26] lengthy, quite attractive gelding:
useful handicapper: in frame at Chelmsford and Goodwood first 2 starts, below form after:
stays 9f: acts on polytrack and soft going: has been gelded. *Ed Dunlop*

GODWIT 7 b.m. Noverre (USA) 125 – Hen Harrier 94 (Polar Falcon (USA) 126) [2015 **–**
t12.2f Jan 5] maiden, modest at best: effective at 8.5f to 1½m: acts on fibresand and
polytrack. *Eugene Stanford*

GO FAR 5 b.g. Dutch Art 126 – Carranita (IRE) 111 (Anita's Prince 126) [2015 108: p6g⁴ **107**
p6f t6m 6g 6f 7m 7m 5g 6m³ p7g 6g* 6s² p5g⁵ t6m Dec 18] good-topped gelding: useful **a100**
handicapper: won at Ayr (by 1¾ lengths from Tiger Jim) in September: creditable second
at York (3 lengths behind Shared Equity) in October: best at 5f/6f: acts on all weather, soft
and good to firm going: usually wears headgear: often races towards rear. *Alan Bailey*

GO GLAMOROUS (IRE) 4 b.f. Elnadim (USA) 128 – Glamorous Air (IRE) (Air **–**
Express (IRE) 125) [2015 68: 5m⁵ 6m Jun 18] lengthy filly: fairly useful at best, no form
in 2015: best form at 5f: acts on good to firm going: tried in cheekpieces prior to 2015.
Ronald Harris

GO GO GREEN (IRE) 9 b.g. Acclamation 118 – Preponderance (IRE) 85 (Cyrano de **80**
Bergerac 120) [2015 78: 5v³ 6d⁵ 5g³ 5g 6s⁴ 5s⁴ 5m⁴ 5m⁵ 6m⁴ 5m² 5g 5m 5d⁴ 5m* 5g
Oct 13] angular gelding: fairly useful handicapper: won at Musselburgh in September:
stays 6f: acts on good to firm and heavy going: tried in tongue tie prior to 2015: sometimes
slowly away, often races in rear. *Jim Goldie*

GO GRAZEON 3 ch.f. Monsieur Bond (IRE) 120 – Graze On And On (Elmaamul (USA) **49**
125) [2015 55: 6g⁵ 8g 7m⁵ 8.5m⁶ Aug 13] poor maiden: stays 1m: acts on fibresand, good
to firm and heavy going. *John Quinn*

GOKEN (FR) 3 b.c. Kendargent (FR) 112 – Gooseley Chope (FR) (Indian Rocket 115) **113**
[2015 110: 6g³ 5.5g* 6f 5m p6m* Nov 14] close-coupled, quite attractive colt: smart
performer: won Prix Texanita at Maisons-Laffitte (by head from Finsbury Square) in May

and listed race at Lingfield (by 1½ lengths from Jamesie) in November: third in Prix Sigy at Chantilly (¾ length behind El Valle) in April: left H-A. Pantall after fourth start: raced only at 5f/6f: acts on polytrack, soft and good to firm going. *Kevin Ryan*

GOLDAN JESS (IRE) 11 b.g. Golan (IRE) 129 – Bendis (GER) (Danehill (USA) 126) **68** [2015 p16g p16g² t16.5f Nov 16] neat gelding: fair handicapper: stays 16.5f: acts on polytrack, good to firm and heavy going: tried in headgear prior to 2015: usually leads, usually finds little. *Philip Kirby*

GOLD BEAU (FR) 5 b.g. Gold Away (IRE) 125 – Theorie (FR) (Anabaa (USA) 130) **76** [2015 84: p7f² 6m 6g 7g 6g 6g 5.9m⁵ 7g³ p6f⁵ 6g* p6f³ p6f⁶ p6d Nov 30] workmanlike gelding: fair handicapper: won at Hamilton in September: stays 7f: acts on polytrack and good to firm going: usually wears headgear. *Kristin Stubbs*

GOLD CHAIN (IRE) 5 b.m. Authorized (IRE) 133 – Mountain Chain (USA) (Royal **61 §** Academy (USA) 130) [2015 t16.5g 12.5m 16m⁶ 15s Aug 8] medium-sized mare: modest handicapper: stays 2m: acts on soft and good to firm going: usually in headgear in 2015: often races towards rear: temperamental. *Dianne Sayer*

GOLD CHIEF (IRE) 3 b.c. Acclamation 118 – Easter Heroine (IRE) 72 (Exactly Sharp (USA) 121) [2015 7m Jun 16] 25/1, well held in maiden at Thirsk in June. *Ismail Mohammed*

GOLD CLUB 4 b.g. Multiplex 114 – Oceana Blue 89 (Reel Buddy (USA) 118) [2015 74: **86** p6f⁵ p6f* t7.1f* t7.1g⁵ 7m⁴ 6.1m⁴ 6.1m* 6m² 6m² 6.1m 6.1d⁴ Sep 26] big gelding: fairly **a76** useful handicapper: won at Kempton and Wolverhampton in March and Chepstow in June: good second at Pontefract in August: stays 7f: acts on polytrack, tapeta, good to firm and good to soft going: tried in cheekpieces prior to 2015: consistent. *Ed McMahon*

GOLDCREST 3 ch.f. Assertive 121 – Level Pegging (IRE) 48 (Common Grounds 118) **89** [2015 92: 5f³ 5m Jun 20] workmanlike filly: fairly useful performer: stays 6f: acts on firm and good to soft going: tried in hood prior to 2015: front runner/races prominently. *Henry Candy*

GOLD ELIZA (IRE) 2 ch.f. (Jan 22) Pivotal 124 – Srda (USA) 93 (Kingmambo (USA) **–** 125) [2015 p7g 7s 8g Sep 19] 50,000Y: good-topped filly: first foal: dam 6f-9.5f winner: no form. *Richard Hannon*

GOLDEN AMBER (IRE) 4 b.f. Holy Roman Emperor (IRE) 125 – Time of Gold (USA) **106** (Banker's Gold (USA) 116) [2015 95: p7m t1.1m² p6g² 6d p6m* 6g³ p6g² p6f* 6g⁴ 6g* 6g⁵ 6v Nov 7] workmanlike filly: useful handicapper: won at Chelmsford in May (by ¾ length from Picture Dealer) and August (by 2 lengths from Mukhmal) and Newmarket (by nose from Iseemist) in September: stays 6f: acts on polytrack and soft going: often wears hood. *Dean Ivory*

GOLDEN BIRD (IRE) 4 b.g. Sinndar (IRE) 134 – Khamsin (USA) (Mr Prospector **71** (USA)) [2015 73: p15.8g⁴ 17.2f⁴ 14d p16g t12.2g² 13.1m⁵ p16f⁶ Sep 10] fair maiden: left Dean Ivory after fifth start: stays 17f: acts on polytrack, tapeta and firm going: sometimes wears headgear: races prominently. *Brendan Powell*

GOLDEN BULLET 3 ch.c. New Approach (IRE) 132 – Gleam of Light (IRE) 81 **74** (Danehill (USA) 126) [2015 8.3m 11.5g⁴ Jul 15] tall colt: better effort when fourth in maiden at Lingfield in July: will be suited by 1¾m. *Saeed bin Suroor*

GOLDEN CAPE 2 ch.f. (Mar 14) Native Ruler 119 – Lake Sabina 77 (Diktat 126) [2015 **–** 6s⁶ Oct 26] first foal: dam maiden (stayed 6f): 150/1, sixth in maiden at Leicester (8 lengths behind Flowing Clarets) in October, unable to sustain effort. *Michael Mullineaux*

GOLDEN CHAPTER 2 b.f. (Jan 26) Danehill Dancer (IRE) 117 – Farfala (FR) 106 **77 p** (Linamix (FR) 127) [2015 p8g⁵ Dec 15] 200,000Y: closely related to 11f winner Strawberry Jam (by Duke of Marmalade) and half-sister to several winners, including useful 1½m winner Starfala (by Galileo) and useful 2-y-o 8.3f-1¼m winner (stayed easy 2¼m) Under The Rainbow (by Fantastic Light): dam 1¼m-1½m winner: 5/2, some encouragement when fifth in maiden at Kempton (3¾ lengths behind Mandrell) in December, taking good hold up with pace and not knocked about once held: better to come. *Ralph Beckett*

GOLDEN DOYEN (GER) 4 b.g. Doyen (IRE) 132 – Goldsamt (GER) (Rienzi (EG)) **84** [2015 14d Sep 26] fairly useful handicapper: ninth at Haydock (5¼ lengths behind Nakeeta) on sole outing in 2015, needing stiffer test: likely to stay 2m: useful hurdler. *Philip Hobbs*

GOLDEN EMERALD 4 b.g. Peintre Celebre (USA) 137 – Flying Finish (FR) (Priolo **79** (USA) 127) [2015 83: p8g⁶ 10g* 11.6g 10s⁶ 10s Oct 13] fair handicapper: won at Newmarket in August: stays 1¼m: acts on polytrack and good to soft going: tried in hood: usually leads. *Mike Murphy*

GOLDENFIELD (IRE) 2 b.g. (Jan 24) Footstepsinthesand 120 – Society Gal (IRE) **71** (Galileo (IRE) 134) [2015 6.5m 7.4g⁶ 7g⁴ 8.3d t9.5f² p10g² Nov 26] fair maiden: left Olly Stevens after third start: stays 1¼m: acts on polytrack and tapeta: often in cheekpieces: often races prominently. *Gary Moore*

GOLDEN HELLO (IRE) 2 b.g. (Apr 28) Zebedee 113 – Your Opinion (IRE) (Xaar 132) **64** [2015 6g⁵ 6m p6g³ 6f 7d⁶ t7.1m³ Sep 14] attractive gelding: modest maiden: stays 7f: acts on polytrack and tapeta: tried in headgear: sold 5,000 gns, sent to Italy. *Michael Bell*

GOLDEN HERITAGE 4 b.g. Halling (USA) 133 – Summertime Legacy 109 (Darshaan **90** 133) [2015 p8g* Dec 16] fairly useful handicapper: third at Lingfield in December: stays 8.5f: acts on polytrack, viscoride, raced only on good going on turf: often in blinkers in 2015. *Charlie Appleby*

GOLDEN HIGHWAY (USA) 3 ch.g. Elusive Quality (USA) – Awesome Chic (USA) **71** (Awesome Again (CAN) 133) [2015 p8g* p8g⁴ 8d 8.3m p10g Jul 21] fair performer: won maiden at Chelmsford in January: subsequently disappointing: best effort at 1m: acts on polytrack: tried in cheekpieces: tried in tongue tie: often races lazily. *Michael Appleby*

GOLDEN HORN 3 b.c. Cape Cross (IRE) 129 – Fleche d'Or (Dubai Destination **134** (USA) 127) [2015 107p: 9m* 10.4m* 12m* 10m* 10.4d² 10g* 11.9m* 12g² Oct 31]
When the great Sea The Stars recorded six Group 1 wins from six starts in 2009, he successfully completed just about the toughest programme that could be set for a European classic three-year-old in the modern era. Two Thousand Guineas, Derby, Eclipse, International, Irish Champion and Prix de l'Arc de Triomphe—Sea The Stars displayed sustained excellence in six genuine championship races over a variety of distances at the rate of one every month from May to October. Just six years later, another three-year-old son of Cape Cross dominated the European programme for a horse of his type in similar fashion and was thoroughly deserving of the title of Europe's Horse of the Year. In the end, Golden Horn's winning Group 1 tally of the Derby, Eclipse, Irish Champion and Arc didn't match that of Sea The Stars, and he suffered two defeats in the course of a splendidly bold eight-race campaign. It could also be said that Golden Horn's best performances fell a little way short of the best that Sea The Stars recorded but that, in itself, is no disgrace. Only Frankel, Sea-Bird, Brigadier Gerard, Tudor Minstrel, Abernant, Ribot and Mill Reef have achieved a higher rating (among three-year-olds and upwards in Europe) than Sea The Stars in the sixty-nine years of the *Racehorses* series, which stretches back to the first prototype Annual produced in 1948, covering the 1947 season.

History will ultimately decide Golden Horn's place in the racing pantheon, but very few of the top middle-distance performers in Timeform's experience have equalled his achievement of winning at least four of Europe's greatest championship events in a classic-winning season. Among the other Derby winners in the now-extensive period covered by *Racehorses*, Nijinsky (138 in 1970) won the Irish Derby, the King George and the St Leger after completing the Two Thousand

Betfred Dante Stakes, York—
Golden Horn continues his exceptionally promising start to his career as he comes clear of his stablemate Jack Hobbs and the previous year's Racing Post Trophy winner Elm Park

Guineas/Derby double; Tulyar (134 in 1952) went on to success in the Eclipse, the King George and the St Leger; Sea-Bird (145 in 1965) had won the Prix Lupin before the Derby and then added the Grand Prix de Saint-Cloud and the Arc; Sir Ivor (135 in 1968) won the Champion Stakes and the Washington DC International after completing the Guineas/Derby double; Mill Reef (141 in 1971) won the Eclipse, the King George and the Arc; and Nashwan (135 in 1989) won the Eclipse and the King George after completing the Guineas/Derby double. Frankel's last nine victories in his fourteen-race unbeaten career were achieved in Group 1 races but, before him, Mill Reef and the miler Rock of Gibraltar were the only other European-trained horses, apart from Sea The Stars, to have won as many as six Group 1 races in succession since the official pattern began in 1971 (Mill Reef added the Ganay and the Coronation Cup to his record in a truncated campaign as a four-year-old, while Rock of Gibraltar had won the Grand Criterium and the Dewhurst at two before stretching his winning streak in Group 1s with five more as a three-year-old).

The latest season was noteworthy for divisional champions who ran up a sequence in their particular series of races. Kingman had been the only horse to win four Group 1s the previous year, but champion sprinter Muhaarar won four Group 1s in 2015 like Golden Horn, while Europe's top miler, the French-trained five-year-old gelding Solow, won all six of his races, the last five of them Group 1s. The year's top two-year-old Air Force Blue won three Group 1s in a row to clinch his title, while those admirable classic fillies Legatissimo and Ervedya also won three Group 1s, as did the leading three-year-old colt at a mile, Gleneagles. None of the season's champions ran more often than Golden Horn, though, and, of the iconic Derby winners mentioned in the preceding paragraph, only Sir Ivor had a busier campaign, running nine times between early-April (when he won the Ascot Two Thousand Guineas Trial) and mid-November (when he won the Washington International); he had a few setbacks along the way—losing four races in a row after winning the Derby—but he captured the hearts of racing fans and, unusually for a top horse at that time, won top-class races in four countries, in Ireland, England, France (the Grand Criterium as a two-year-old) and North America. In terms of races won, Golden Horn's admirable record as a three-year-old made him one of the most talked-about Derby winners in recent memory and he proved a great credit to his connections who deserved plenty of praise for campaigning him in the true spirit of the sport.

Golden Horn's seventy-eight-year-old owner Anthony Oppenheimer, whose wealth is founded on the success of De Beers, which controls around a third of global diamond production, is one of a diminishing number of English owner-breeders who still maintain a broodmare band of any size. Oppenheimer keeps about thirty mares at his Hascombe and Valiant studs in Newmarket, which he took over on the death of his father Sir Philip Oppenheimer in 1995. Golden Horn's victory in the Derby was the crowning achievement of the Oppenheimer family's lengthy involvement in racing. 'It's what my father wanted and it's what I've wanted all my life, it's the biggest race in the world and it's why I breed racehorses,' said Anthony Oppenheimer afterwards. That was only the start, though, as Golden Horn set out to follow in the footsteps of the likes of Sir Ivor and Sea The Stars, his owner clearly relishing the challenge. 'We really want people to know how good this horse is,' he declared. The last owner-bred Derby winner with strong British connections before Golden Horn was the 2004 winner North Light who carried the colours of the Weinstock family's Ballymacoll Stud. Lord Arnold Weinstock, who died when North Light was a yearling, acquired Ballymacoll in Ireland with his father-in-law Sir Michael Sobell in 1960 and Sir Michael won the 200th Derby in 1979 with home bred Troy. English owner-breeders won the Derby three times in the 'eighties, with Teenoso in 1983, Slip Anchor in 1985 and Reference Point in 1987, but the traditional indigenous owner-breeder was already an endangered species in the face of the influx of enormous, corporate-style operations supported by Middle Eastern wealth.

In the year that Teenoso, a product of the Moller brothers' White Lodge Stud, carried the colours of Eric Moller to Derby success, Moller and Sir Michael Sobell finished second and third in the owners' table in Britain behind pools

Investec Derby, Epsom—as Hans Holbein leads Elm Park (noseband), Epicuris and Storm The Stars around Tattenham Corner, the favourite Golden Horn (black and white halves) tracks his main market rival Jack Hobbs in mid-field ...

magnate Robert Sangster. Two years later, when Lord Howard de Walden's home bred (Plantation Stud) Slip Anchor was successful, his owner finished third in the table behind Sheikh Mohammed and Khalid Abdullah, and just ahead of Hamdan Al Maktoum and the Aga Khan. Reference Point, a product of Louis Freedman's Cliveden Stud, helped his owner into second behind Sheikh Mohammed, but Robert Sangster, Helena Springfield Ltd and Charles St George were the only other British owners in a Middle East-dominated top twelve. The year before Teenoso's Derby victory, the Oppenheimer silks of black and white (halved), sleeves reversed, red cap were carried to classic victory in the One Thousand Guineas by stable-companion On The House, a home bred out of Lora, a poor racemare by Lorenzaccio who was best known for overturning odds-on Nijinsky in the Charles St George colours in the Champion Stakes on the triple crown winner's eighth start as a three-year-old. Over thirty years and several generations later, the racing world is a different place, but Lora's appearance in Golden Horn's extended pedigree as his fourth dam at least serves as a reminder of an era when the old-school English owner-breeders with twenty or thirty mares were the backbone of the game.

Golden Horn had something else in common with On The House, as both went through the sale-ring as yearlings and were returned to their breeder after failing to meet their reserve (as also, incidentally, did Pelerin whose fourth in the 1980 Derby was the best performance in that race by an Oppenheimer home bred before Golden Horn). On The House failed to reach only a modest reserve and Golden Horn was led out unsold at 190,000 guineas in 2013 at Newmarket's principal yearling sale, the October Sales Book 1. Sent into training with John Gosden, Golden Horn ran only once as a two-year-old, winning a maiden over a mile at Nottingham at the end of October in the style of a colt who had a very bright future. Golden Horn showed a sparkling turn of foot to come from last to first to get the better of Storm The Stars, both recording impressive closing sectionals and finishing well clear of the rest (Golden Horn's owner said at the Cartier Awards, when receiving Golden Horn's Horse of the Year award for 2015, that he 'knew we had a good horse' when he earned a Timeform rating of 107p for that first run).

With Clarehaven's stable jockey William Buick signing a lucrative retainer for Godolphin, John Gosden turned at the start of the latest season to Frankie Dettori, who had had a retainer with the trainer back in the mid-'nineties. Dettori had found it difficult in recent seasons to maintain his profile after losing his job as first jockey to Godolphin in 2012 and lapsing into drug-taking which earned him a six-month ban from the sport when he failed a test on Longchamp's 'day of trials' shortly after his eighteen-year association with Sheikh Mohammed had been terminated. Dettori got the job as first jockey to Qatari owner Sheikh Joaan in July 2013, shortly after his return to riding, but he found that few trainers in Britain wanted him for rides outside those for Sheikh Joaan. Dettori struggled to reach just over two hundred rides in Britain in 2013 and rode only sixteen winners, his campaign ending when he broke a bone in his foot in a fall on the way to post for a class 5 handicap at Nottingham just four days before he was due to take the mount on Treve in the Prix de l'Arc de Triomphe. Sheikh Joaan's horses ran in the name of Al Shaqab Racing in 2014 when Dettori again missed the winning ride in the Arc on Treve, though this time he lost the mount when Arc-winning jockey Thierry Jarnet was recalled after Treve was beaten on her first two starts as a four-year-old. Thirty-seven winners was Dettori's final score by the end of the calendar year in Britain, hardly a sign of the imminent renaissance which was to be one of the stories of the Flat racing year in 2015.

Dettori's prospects in the latest season seemed to suffer a setback when Sheikh Joaan—whose string increased in size—signed up Gregory Benoist at the start of April to ride the Al Shaqab horses trained in France (except for Treve for whom Jarnet was retained). The appointment of Benoist at least meant that Dettori did not have to keep criss-crossing the Channel—though he continued to ride the British-trained Al Shaqab challengers in France—and he was able to spend more time on the link with Clarehaven. John Gosden later recounted that Golden Horn was the horse he put Dettori on when he first rode work 'in the sleet and rain of March'. Dettori reported that Golden Horn was 'a lovely horse but he's not clued up yet and wouldn't be mentally sharp enough for a Guineas [in which he held an entry].' Dettori was on Golden Horn when he made a winning reappearance in the listed Feilden Stakes at Newmarket's Craven meeting, again coming from last to first to win impressively from the more experienced pair Peacock and Disegno, both of whom had been placed in similar company before. Golden Horn was the only winning favourite in twelve races for three-year-olds at the two-day meeting, one of his stable's more high profile classic hopes at the time, Faydhan, effectively

... Golden Horn reaches the line with three and a half lengths to spare over Jack Hobbs, who is himself clear of Storm The Stars (rail) and the chief Ballydoyle hope Giovanni Canaletto (stripes)

ruling himself out of the Two Thousand Guineas when beaten favourite in the Free Handicap. Another of Golden Horn's stablemates Richard Pankhurst would have started favourite for the Craven but didn't make the line-up after a weekend setback.

Dettori also partnered another of the stable's once-raced promising types, Jack Hobbs, to a wide-margin victory in a handicap at Sandown (one of four winners on the card for Dettori) the week after the Craven meeting, and he chose to ride him rather than Golden Horn when the pair lined up for the Betfred Dante Stakes at York, which was eagerly anticipated after a largely uninformative set of Derby trials in the preceding weeks. After his Sandown win, Jack Hobbs had been installed as ante-post favourite for the Derby, on which the winter market—dominated by colts trained at Ballydoyle which had won the last three editions—had undergone major changes. Ballydoyle ran its two principal winter Derby hopes, John F Kennedy and Ol' Man River, in the Dante after both had finished last on their reappearance, the former in the three-runner Ballysax Stakes at Leopardstown and the latter in the Two Thousand Guineas. The Racing Post Trophy winner Elm Park, a late withdrawal from the Two Thousand Guineas on account of the firmish going, made his reappearance instead in the Dante, starting second favourite behind Jack Hobbs. The Gosden-trained pair dominated the finish after Elm Park was headed entering the final furlong, with Golden Horn again quickening impressively to beat Jack Hobbs by two and three quarter lengths, with Elm Park a further three and a quarter behind, the first three well clear of the rest (Ol' Man River and John F Kennedy filled the last two places in the field of seven). Golden Horn held an entry in the Prix du Jockey Club but had been left out of the Derby because his owner-breeder had considered he would lack the necessary stamina (the best members of the family on the distaff side had been milers and Golden Horn's sire, both his grandsires and his four great grandsires had all been either sprinters or milers). In the immediate aftermath of the Dante, Golden Horn was as short as 6/4 'with a run' for a race in which he was not even entered.

In the light of the evidence provided by Golden Horn's victory in the Dante, in which he finished strongly at the end of a well-run race, it was soon confirmed that his owner-breeder would be stumping up the £75,000 supplementary entry fee for Epsom. William Buick, who rode Golden Horn at York, had jokingly offered to pay the fee himself 'if I can keep the ride'. By the time the Investec Derby came round, Buick was on Jack Hobbs in whom a significant interest was purchased in the run up to Epsom by Godolphin (with original owners, Gosden's wife Rachel Hood and two of her friends from university, retaining shares). Golden Horn and Jack Hobbs, who were both given a sight of Epsom at the now well-established Breakfast With The Stars event, started 13/8 favourite and 4/1 second favourite respectively at Epsom, with Giovanni Canaletto (6/1) and Elm Park (9/1) the only others at shorter than 12/1 in a field of twelve (the ante-post second favourite Zawraq, trained by Dermot Weld, was a late absentee after a training setback). Giovanni Canaletto, a brother to the 2013 Derby winner Ruler of The World, had emerged as Ballydoyle's number-one, ahead of the Chester Vase winner Hans Holbein and the Lingfield Derby Trial winner Kilimanjaro, both of whom incidentally were Coolmore yearling purchases. There had been speculation that the Two Thousand Guineas winner Gleneagles might be drafted in at Epsom to bolster the weaker than usual team of middle-distance colts trained at Ballydoyle (all three of its Derby runners wore headgear), or even that the Irish One Thousand Guineas runner-up Found, or the Coolmore-owned but David Wachman-trained One Thousand Guineas winner Legatissimo could be supplemented.

Among the other Derby runners was a rare French-trained challenger the Criterium de Saint-Cloud winner Epicuris, rerouted to Epsom after French officials refused a request for a horse behaviour expert to help with his loading in the Prix du Jockey Club. The Irish challenge was bolstered by Success Days, supplemented after completing the Ballysax/Derrinstown Derby Trial double, and there was a challenge from Germany in the shape of 50/1-shot Rogue Runner, giving Elm Park's owners Qatar Racing a second runner. Al Shaqab Racing was represented by 25/1-shot Moheet, from whom Frankie Dettori was released to ride Golden Horn. Moheet was the only Derby runner who had contested the Two Thousand Guineas in which he had finished eighth, seven and three quarter lengths behind Gleneagles. Golden

Horn also renewed rivalry with Storm The Stars, a first Derby runner for his sire Sea The Stars, who had developed into a smart performer since their encounter at Nottingham and had already run four times as a three-year-old, being successful on his latest start in the Goodwood trial known nowadays as the Cocked Hat Stakes (Troy had been the last winner to go on to Derby success, back in the days when the race was run as the Predominate Stakes). One point of difference between the latest Derby field and most of its recent predecessors was that the twelve runners were by eleven different sires, High Chaparral being the only one doubly represented (Kilimanjaro and Moheet); those other Sadler's Wells stallions who had had such an influence on the race, Galileo (three winners) and Montjeu (four winners), had just Giovanni Canaletto and Hans Holbein to represent them respectively this time.

Golden Horn was Frankie Dettori's first Derby ride since his split with Godolphin but he repaid the faith shown in him by John Gosden with a confident ride. Golden Horn was too keen in the early part of the race, as was Elm Park, but while the latter burned himself out up front, Dettori successfully settled Golden Horn towards the rear of the field in a race run at a sound pace from the start. Hans Holbein disputed the lead with Elm Park initially before pressing on in front after the first four furlongs. Elm Park, Epicuris, Storm The Stars, Jack Hobbs and Giovanni Canaletto made up the first six rounding Tattenham Corner where Golden Horn had only three behind him, and was some way adrift of the leaders. If Golden Horn's supporters were beginning to feel concern, Dettori apparently couldn't have been happier ('I can't believe how smoothly it went,' he said afterwards, 'It took me three furlongs to put him to sleep but then the job was done, I was happy to take him back because he wanted to race too much'). Jack Hobbs quickened to lead halfway up the straight, chased by Storm The Stars, in what looked initially as if it might be a race-winning move, but Golden Horn produced a storming finish once he was fully opened out and sent after the leaders, and he overhauled Jack Hobbs with a furlong still left to run. Keeping on well, as Jack Hobbs began to hang left with the camber towards the rail, Golden Horn was comfortably on top at the finish. He won by three and a half lengths and four and a half from Jack Hobbs and Storm The Stars, with a further two lengths back to Giovanni Canaletto in fourth, Epicuris in fifth, and the two other Ballydoyle runners, Kilimanjaro and Hans Holbein, sixth and seventh.

Golden Horn's performance was right out of the top drawer. His winning time of 2m 33.32sec was the fourth fastest that has been recorded at Epsom in the race's history (at least back to 1900), bettered only by Workforce in 2010, Lammtarra in 1995 and Galileo in 2001. All those winning performances were recorded under conditions that were conducive to fast times—on going that was firm or good to firm—and the *time value* of Golden Horn's performance was confirmed by a Timeform timefigure of 1.08 fast (equivalent to a timerating of 127), one bettered in the latest season only by the 1.17 fast and 1.16 fast recorded by the sprinters Muhaarar (British Champions Sprint) and Mecca's Angel (Nunthorpe). The Derby field was strung out at the finish—the eight lengths that separated Golden Horn from Storm The Stars was the biggest margin between winner and third since Motivator's year—and the form looked even stronger than the time value of the performance. Golden Horn's Derby-winning display earned him a Timeform rating on the day of 132 which has been bettered in the race in the last quarter of a century only by Generous (ran to 135 in 1991) and Workforce (133 in 2010). The post-race celebrations focussed on Frankie Dettori as he produced his trademark flying dismount before cavorting round the winner's enclosure, all of which provided entertainment for Channel 4's audience of 1.46m (slightly below that of the previous year, despite a half-an-hour later Derby start at 4.30). The Derby, though, also represented a notable triumph for Golden Horn's trainer who became only the sixth in the last hundred years to saddle first and second in the Derby, following Alec Taylor (Gainsborough and Blink in 1918), Frank Butters (Mahmoud and Taj Akbar in 1936), Fred Darling (Owen Tudor and Morogoro in 1941), Dick Carver (My Love and Royal Drake in 1948) and Aidan O'Brien (High Chaparral and Hawk Wing in 2002). Because it was war-time, the 1918 and 1941 editions were run as the New Derby at Newmarket. Golden Horn was the second Derby winner for forty-four-year-old Dettori (the oldest jockey in the race), following Authorized on his fifteenth Derby ride in 2007, and the second for Gosden who won the 1997 edition with Benny The Dip. Golden Horn and Jack Hobbs were the biggest earners for Clarehaven in another excellent season for the Newmarket stable. John Gosden was champion trainer in Britain for the second time, with record first three earnings for a calendar year of £5,066,018, beating the mark set by Richard Hannon in 2014. Gosden also won the two most valuable races in Ireland with Jack Hobbs and Golden Horn, and three further Group 1s in France.

Timeform's assessment of the Derby form provoked quite a reaction at the time on social media where the general consensus seemed to be that Golden Horn's rating was 'much too high', but the subsequent performances of the principals showed that it was not at all too high. Golden Horn went on to do plenty to advertise the form himself, while Jack Hobbs, Storm The Stars, Giovanni Canaletto and Kilimanjaro proceeded to fill the first four places next time in the Irish Derby, ahead of the Prix du Jockey Club runner-up Highland Reel and the Oaks winner Qualify. Golden Horn hadn't been entered in the Irish Derby but the first four at Epsom were among those who qualified for a place in the field under a free entry incentive introduced to celebrate the Irish Derby's hundred and fiftieth running. Golden Horn's connections opted instead to wait a week and test the Derby winner against older horses for the first time in the Coral-Eclipse (it was the fortieth anniversary of Coral's sponsorship which began in 1976 when Frankie Dettori's father was the winning jockey on Wollow who was awarded the race when the French-trained Trepan failed a drugs test).

The late absence from the 2015 Eclipse of French challenger New Bay, winner of the Prix du Jockey Club, left Golden Horn facing four rivals on a sweltering day at Sandown, the most dangerous of which looked to be the seasoned mile and a quarter performer The Grey Gatsby who had won the previous year's Prix du Jockey Club and gone on to beat the Derby winner Australia in the Irish Champion Stakes. The Grey Gatsby was bang in form, having looked a shade unlucky when hemmed in before being short-headed by Free Eagle in the Prince of Wales's Stakes at Royal Ascot on his most recent appearance. Golden Horn started at 9/4-on, though the Eclipse represented a very different test from a strongly-run Derby. The Grey Gatsby pushed Golden Horn close until the final furlong, with the pair upsides for much of the straight as The Grey Gatsby kept up a determined challenge to his front-running rival, on whom the change of tactics had been adopted to avoid the race turning into a tactical contest. Although the outcome looked uncertain for a furlong or so, after The Grey Gatsby loomed up, Golden Horn stayed on very strongly and, as in the Derby, was well on top at the line. The winning distance was the same as at Epsom—three and a half lengths—and was a fair reflection of the merits of the first two. Golden Horn's very smart four-year-old stablemate Western Hymn, third in the Prince of Wales's, finished a further four and a half lengths back in a creditable third, giving the form a solid look, with Golden Horn even improving a little on his Derby performance. The Eclipse is by no means straightforward for a Derby winner taking on older horses for the first time and also stepping back to a shorter trip. Although Golden Horn successfully followed in the historic footsteps of the four most recent Derby winners to achieve the double, Tulyar, Mill Reef, Nashwan and Sea The Stars, it is worth pointing out that five Derby winners were beaten in the Eclipse in the twenty-one years between 1987 and 2007. By coincidence, all five of them—Reference Point, Erhaab, Benny The Dip, Motivator and Authorized—had also won the Dante on the way to Epsom. Sir Ivor, by the way, also suffered one of his four defeats after the Derby in the Eclipse.

One interesting postscript to the Eclipse came when Frankie Dettori was approached, as he returned along the Sandown horse-walk on Golden Horn, by Channel 4's interviewer (with extendable microphone in hand) for the now seemingly-obligatory instant reaction to victory. The most recognisable jockey in British racing, a national celebrity since those 'Magnificent Seven' winners at Ascot in 1996, whose career was now enjoying something of a rebirth after it had seemed in decline—here surely was another public relations godsend for the sport, just like the Derby had provided. To general surprise, though, the normally ebullient Dettori, who is seldom lost for words when things are going his way, unexpectedly cut short the interview, saying 'Let me enjoy the moment, I'll talk to you later.' The snatched

*Coral-Eclipse, Sandown—Golden Horn stretches his unbeaten record to five
with another performance right out of the top drawer, beating his elders headed by
The Grey Gatsby by three and a half lengths and more*

post-race interview has become a staple of Channel 4's coverage, but it is so often completely predictable in its triteness as the victors draw on familiar banalities and platitudes to satisfy the broadcaster's desire to be 'first'. For Dettori, it seemed important, on this occasion at least, not only to 'enjoy the moment' but to gather his thoughts before debriefing Golden Horn's owner and trainer, who surely had the right in any case to be the first to hear their jockey's views on the performance. Most jockeys have scarcely got their breath back, let alone had time to think, when the Channel 4 microphone is pushed under their nose. Even a natural communicator like Frankie Dettori—who has worked as part of the Channel 4 team—cannot be expected to be at his most fluent in those first few moments after a victory. Dettori's temporary stand against Channel 4 provided a much needed reminder that the best interviews are nearly always those conducted after both interviewer and interviewee have been given sufficient time for consideration. Dettori's relaxed interview with Channel 4 later on Eclipse afternoon was both reflective and informative, and well worth waiting for—'Golden Horn is up there with the very best I have ridden, and I would say he is probably the best three-year-old [Dettori rode the Derby winner Lammtarra when he followed up in the King George and the Arc in 1995] … I hope you all saw it today, he never finishes tired and he hits the line running every time, he must have some constitution … Jamie [Spencer] was very good, he took me on three out and if my horse was weak he had every chance to give in … The Grey Gatsby came to within a head and I thought "when I show my horse the whip he will give me a length", but he gave me that and more.'

Dubai Millennium (Timeform 140 as a 4-y-o) and Daylami (138 as a 5-y-o) are the two best horses Frankie Dettori has ridden, and any discussion about the best three-year-old with which he has been associated would have to include the first of his Two Thousand Guineas winners Mark of Esteem (137) who was also one of the 'Magnificent Seven' on that epic day at Ascot in 1996 when he recorded a performance in the Queen Elizabeth II Stakes that hadn't been bettered in the race since its elevation to Group 1 status (Frankel is the only horse to have put up a better performance in the Queen Elizabeth II Stakes since). For Dettori to be talking about Golden Horn in such glowing terms after the Eclipse spoke volumes and served only to heighten anticipation when it was announced that the horse would be aimed next at the King George VI and Queen Elizabeth Stakes at Ascot three weeks later (the Prix de l'Arc, for which Golden Horn would have to be supplemented, was also announced as his major end-of-season objective—'It could easily be his last race, I'm a breeder and I'm not enthusiastic about racing him next year,' said his owner).

Golden Horn's owner was actively involved at De Beers in the days when the company backed the King George, which his father won as part of the syndicate which owned 1978 winner Ile de Bourbon, while trainer John Gosden had won the

Qipco Irish Champion Stakes, Leopardstown—Gleneagles is pulled out at the eleventh hour after overnight rain from a race that has a dramatic and unsatisfactory conclusion with front-running Golden Horn hanging right a furlong out and badly hampering Free Eagle (star on cap), who loses second to Found (rail); the stewards very quickly decide that Golden Horn had not improved his position and allow the result to stand

race with three-year-olds Nathaniel and Taghrooda in 2011 and 2014 (the only three-year-old winners in the eleven previous runnings). Golden Horn would have been seeking to extend his unbeaten run to six in the King George, in which he would have started odds-on to emulate Tulyar, Mill Reef and Nashwan by completing the Derby/Eclipse/King George treble (Sea The Stars would probably have been aimed at the King George had he run in the Irish Derby—pulled out two days before following heavy rain—instead of the Eclipse). In the end, Golden Horn's participation in the King George was thwarted by significant rain which arrived the day before the race, John Gosden explaining his late withdrawal, after walking the course on the day of racing, by saying that 'It was a close decision, but holding ground over a mile and a half is not fair to him, my stick went in twelve inches in Swinley Bottom, though we'd probably still have run if it had been a mile and a quarter.' Ascot's loss was York's and Leopardstown's gain as Golden Horn's post-Derby campaign continued to mirror that of Sea The Stars by taking in first the Juddmonte International in August and then the Qipco Irish Champion Stakes in September before his tilt at the Prix de l'Arc. Golden Horn was reported by his trainer to be thriving. 'I've been asked if we're going to the well too often but he has a great attitude and takes his races well so I'm certainly not frightened that we might be overfacing him.' Even after Golden Horn lost his unbeaten record in the International—beaten a neck by 50/1-shot Arabian Queen—there was no thought of curtailing his campaign.

The International at York looked all set to feature a rare clash between the same season's Two Thousand Guineas and Derby winners until Gleneagles was pulled out after overnight rain eased the ground to good to soft. The three most recent three-year-old winners of the International, a race dominated historically by older horses, had all been Derby winners and, in the absence of Gleneagles, Golden Horn was sent off at 9/4-on to emulate Authorized, Sea The Stars and Australia. The fact that he was beaten by a three-year-old filly racing in prime position throughout, who became the first of her age and sex to win the race for a quarter of a century, probably owed a good deal to the muddling nature of the race. It was run at a modest tempo after Golden Horn's seven-year-old stablemate Dick Doughtywylie, put in as a pacemaker to avoid him having to make his own running, was virtually ignored in a clear lead. Golden Horn had been sent to the front in the Eclipse specifically to avoid the race turning into a muddling affair and there's not much doubt that, if those tactics had been repeated at York, he would have won. Unfortunately, as soon as the runners left the stalls with Dick Doughtywylie having to be rushed past Golden Horn after missing the kick, Golden Horn could be seen fighting for his head. He had seemed excitable on the way to the start and Dettori had taken him to post very quietly behind the others, but he proved impossible to settle in the race itself, travelling much too freely under restraint until around halfway. He eventually threw down a strong challenge to Arabian Queen but never got his head in front and ran some way below his top form.

Gleneagles was also pulled out of another much heralded clash with Golden Horn in the Irish Champion Stakes, the centre-piece of Irish Champions' Weekend, a festival in its second year staged over successive days at Leopardstown and the Curragh. The Irish Champion attracted a field of seven, four three-year-olds up against the first two in the Prince of Wales's Stakes, Free Eagle and The Grey Gatsby (the last-named seeking to become only the second, after Dylan Thomas, to win the race in successive seasons), and nine-year-old Cirrus des Aigles, who was having his first start in Ireland. Golden Horn headed the market at 5/4, ahead of Free Eagle at 100/30, in which the classic generation was also represented by the Prix du Jockey Club runner-up Highland Reel, fresh from victory in the Secretariat Stakes at Arlington, and the first two in the Irish One Thousand Guineas, Pleascach and Found. In a race controversially brought forward in the programme by an hour from its original advertised time, after the forecast of heavy rain, Golden Horn picked up the winning thread. However, he had to survive a stewards' inquiry before being confirmed the winner, after shying away sharply to the right in the closing stages and knocking the challenging Free Eagle sideways.

After the defeat at York, and with the pacemaker dispensed with, John Gosden said he would 'leave it to the jockey' at Leopardstown. Gosden isn't one for tying down his jockeys with too many instructions—'You have to let them feel and read a race'—and he tells a story about his days as assistant to Vincent O'Brien which influenced him. 'I remember in the paddock before the 1977 Arc [the first of two won by the O'Brien-trained Alleged], Vincent giving the most extraordinarily detailed instructions to Lester Piggott. You could see Lester's eyes beginning to glaze over and he half-turned to me and murmured out of the corner of his mouth "Have you got a notebook?" He then proceeded to ignore everything Vincent had told him!' Piggott rode a brilliant race that day, audaciously taking Alleged to the front after only three furlongs and setting a steady pace until pressing on turning into the straight and opening up a four-length lead. None of Alleged's pursuers ever looked like getting to him and he ran out a comfortable winner. Dettori adopted similar tactics on Golden Horn in the Irish Champion, allowing him to stride on, as he had in the Eclipse, before quickening the pace sharply early in the home straight. Golden Horn, however, very nearly threw the race away when suddenly jinking right about a furlong out—possibly at the shadow cast by the grandstand. Free Eagle hadn't helped his own cause by first hanging right and then left (away from his rider's whip) but he was stopped in his tracks when carried right by Golden Horn, with the outcome still in the balance, and wasn't able to recover. Golden Horn was driven out, after being straightened, and won by a length from Found, who avoided trouble and kept on to take second well inside the final furlong, half a length ahead of Free Eagle. Pleascach produced another creditable effort in fourth, ahead of Highland Reel, The Grey Gatsby and Cirrus des Aigles. The interference suffered by Free Eagle almost certainly cost him second place but the Leopardstown stewards quickly reached the conclusion—probably the correct one—that Golden Horn himself had not 'improved his position' in the process and they let the result stand (they might have found the adjudication harder if Free Eagle had finished second instead of third, while in France, for example, where horses are placed behind rivals with whom they have interfered, Golden Horn would have been demoted to third).

France was the next port of call for Golden Horn after he was one of three supplemented at a cost of €120,000 each for the Qatar Prix de l'Arc de Triomphe three days before the race. Connections were satisfied that the going would be no softer than good to soft with the weather looking set fair for Arc weekend. The Longchamp turf dried out to good to firm on the day, a prospect which had ruled out Jack Hobbs who was instead aimed at British Champions' Day at Ascot. Treve was attempting an historic third win in the Arc—her pacemaker Shahah and the Prix Foy runner-up Spiritjim were the two other supplementary entries—and she had shown herself to be in top form with a scintillating, wide-margin victory in the Prix Vermeille on Longchamp's 'day of trials'. The Prix du Jockey Club winner New Bay had won the Prix Niel on the same card and headed the Arc challenge of the Andre Fabre stable, along with the previous year's runner-up Flintshire. Fabre, incidentally, who has won the Arc seven times, did not adopt the traditional French approach with New Bay of giving a classic-winning three-year-old a summer break before building up to the Arc. In the same way that Golden Horn was kept going over the summer, New Bay won the Prix Guillaume d'Ornano at Deauville in August and the Arc was his sixth race of the campaign, his only defeat having come when a strong-finishing second in the Poule d'Essai des Poulains. Treve always looked likely to start at odds-on (New Bay and Golden Horn were the only others sent off at single-figure odds) and her chance seemed to be emphasised when the Prix Vermeille runner-up Candarliya broke the course record when winning the Prix de Royallieu the day before the Arc. Ground conditions might have been regarded positively by Golden Horn's connections, but they were similar to those which had obtained on Arc day the previous year and there was no reason to think that Treve would be inconvenienced by them, while Flintshire would be in his element. Found and Free Eagle (both tackling a mile and a half for the first time) renewed rivalry with Golden Horn from the Irish Champion, heading a five-strong Anglo-Irish challenge in the field of seventeen. Among the other home-trained Group 1 winners were the Grand Prix de Paris winner Erupt (only fourth to New Bay in the Niel), and the Dubai Sheema Classic winner Dolniya and Grosser Preis von Baden winner Prince Gibraltar who had come fifth and seventh respectively in the 2014 Arc.

If the drying ground encouraged Golden Horn's supporters, some among them seemed concerned about his wide draw—fourteen—though Treve had won the 2013 Prix de l'Arc from stall fifteen after her jockey steered a wide course, instead of easing her back and crossing to the inside. Dalakhani and Sakhee were others who had won the Arc from a wide draw in recent times, Sakhee scoring by six lengths in 2001 for Frankie Dettori who had no difficulty settling him close to the pace before moving readily to the front soon after entering the home straight. It seemed unlikely that Golden Horn would be asked to make all the running at Longchamp, but it was a near-certainty that connections would want him at least to be ridden handily. Dettori adopted the very unorthodox course of staying noticeably wide of the main pack in the early stages of the race (owner Anthony Oppenheimer wasn't privy to the plan and said afterwards that he thought at the time that Golden Horn's reins must have broken!). After half a mile or so, when the initial pace had slackened a little, Dettori moved Golden Horn across to slot in behind Treve's pacemaker Shahah who was

Qatar Prix de l'Arc de Triomphe, Longchamp—Golden Horn, kept very wide in first from his outside draw, turns in another top-class effort to cap a tremendous campaign in Europe by beating the previous year's runner-up Flintshire, Prix du Jockey club winner New Bay (rail) and Treve (dark cap), who fails in her bid to record an historic third Arc win

taking the field along. Golden Horn was ideally positioned from that point, travelling strongly in a race in which the pace was a little slower than usual, which made it an advantage to lay handy. Taking over in front two furlongs out, Golden Horn was two lengths clear entering the final furlong and kept on well to win by that margin from Flintshire, with New Bay a neck away third, just ahead of Treve in fourth. Like the winner, Flintshire and New Bay both raced prominently. The patiently-ridden Treve, who took a keen hold before making headway rounding the home turn to have every chance out wide, edged right over a furlong out and, in the dash to the finish, failed to produce the turn of foot, relative to her opponents, that had characterised her very best performances. Erupt and Free Eagle, who suffered some interference from Treve, completed the first six in a finish in which less than five lengths covered the first ten home (who included rank outsiders Siljan's Saga and Silverware). The compressed field at the finish suggested it was an average Prix de l'Arc, at best. Ninth-placed Found, switched behind the field to the rail from stall fifteen, met plenty of trouble as she tried to get through in the home straight and never reached a challenging position, while the luckless Dolniya, who held every chance two furlongs out before being badly hampered when Treve edged right, was found afterwards to have suffered a career-ending injury.

Golden Horn's victory may not have been what Treve's legion of fans were expecting, but cries of 'Come on, come on' from an ecstatic Dettori helped to muster for the winner the type of reception that his performance deserved (Dettori's flying dismount was something many felt he might not produce because of his retainer with Treve's owner). A significant number of Derby winners have tried over the years to add the Arc to their record but Golden Horn is only the seventh to have achieved the double, following Sea-Bird, Mill Reef, Lammtarra, Sinndar, Sea The Stars and Workforce. Victory on Golden Horn gave Frankie Dettori a record-equalling fourth Arc, following his wins on Lammtarra, Sakhee and Marienbard for Saeed bin Suroor. Jacko Doyasbere, Freddie Head, Yves Saint-Martin, Pat Eddery, Olivier Peslier and Thierry Jarnet are the other jockeys with four Arc wins to their name. Golden Horn was the first Prix de l'Arc winner for trainer John Gosden (Taghrooda's third place in 2014 had been the stable's previous best in the race). Gosden could have been forgiven for thinking, as Golden Horn lined up, that it perhaps wasn't going to be his day; the stable's Cymric and Jazzi Top had both been touched off earlier on the card in the Prix Jean-Luc Lagardere and Prix de l'Opera respectively. Golden Horn's triumph in Europe's richest race was, however, the third Group 1 victory for Clarehaven in France in 2015, following Star of Seville's win in the Prix de Diane and Shalaa's in the Prix Morny. Added to the lucrative victories of Golden Horn and Jack Hobbs in Ireland, the Clarehaven overseas winners ensured that John Gosden headed the trainers' table for earnings on foreign soil by a very wide margin. According to figures compiled by the International Racing Bureau, Clarehaven horses picked up £4,452,892 on their travels, contributing to a total haul of £16,403,214 (a little below the 2014 total) won by British-trained horses on foreign soil. In a stellar year for Gosden, in particular, he finished fifth in the trainers' table in Ireland and third in France, to add to his British trainers' championship.

The Prix de l'Arc de Triomphe is the most valuable race in Europe by some margin and it has long been the event that counts most in the European racing year. The field is usually the strongest and most representative assembled for any of the year's middle-distance races, and the race tends to take a lot out of a horse. With generally four weeks between the two fixtures, a number of Arc runners have gone on to run well at the Breeders' Cup meeting, but the story with Arc *winners* has proved very different. The emergence of the Arc as a race of truly international importance can be traced back to 1949, when its value was raised five-fold, but since then only three winners of the race who have run again—anywhere—in the same season have managed to win. Those Italian superstars Ribot (who won the Arc twice in the 'fifties) and Ribot's son Molvedo, the 1961 winner, both had one more race as three-year-olds on returning to Italy, winning the Gran Premio del Jockey Club at Milan impressively (Molvedo broke the course record). Both owners turned down an invitation to run in the richly-endowed Washington International at Laurel Park, but, twenty-two years after Molvedo's Arc win, the connections of the

French-trained four-year-old filly All Along jumped at an invitation after she won the Arc. In fact, All Along ran three times in North America after her triumph at Longchamp, winning the Rothmans International at Woodbine (a fortnight after the Arc), the Turf Classic at Aqueduct and the Washington International, in the process landing a million-dollar bonus offered by the three racecourse executives for any horse that could complete the treble, which was given the name of the International Classic Series. Unfortunately for Woodbine, Aqueduct and Laurel, the Breeders' Cup was inaugurated the following year and quickly became the focus for Europe's transatlantic challengers.

The decision to send Golden Horn for the Breeders' Cup Turf came as a surprise to some, but it was in keeping with the way he had been campaigned over the season. History did appear to be against him, though, as none of the five Arc winners who had tried the same season to win the Washington International, before All Along, had succeeded (Ballymoss and Ivanjica managed a place) and five Arc winners had since been defeated in the Turf after going on to the Breeders' Cup. The 1987 Arc winner Trempolino finished a creditable second in the Turf but the four others failed to make the first three. Dancing Brave's fourth at 2/1-on behind Manila at Santa Anita in 1986 was the biggest disappointment; he was a great champion as a three-year-old (Timeform 140), winner of the Two Thousand Guineas, the Eclipse (after an unlucky second in the Derby), the King George and the Arc (which he won in scintillating style), and the Breeders' Cup Turf was his eighth race of the campaign. Saumarez (1990), Subotica (1992) and Dylan Thomas (2007) all finished fifth in the Turf. Sakhee had also been sent to the Breeders' Cup after winning his Arc and, after some contemplation, his connections spurned the chance to follow up in the Turf (which they won with Fantastic Light) in order to take on the top domestic dirt performers in the Classic, the richest race at the meeting. It was a very bold decision that nearly came off as he was beaten a nose by Tiznow, who was winning the race for the second successive time, having just got the better of another European challenger, Irish-trained Giant's Causeway, the previous year.

Golden Horn faced eleven opponents in the Breeders' Cup Turf and started at odds-on to end his racing career on a winning note. He beat the best turf performers that North America could field against him, including the first three in both the Turf Classic at Belmont and the Arlington Million, but he couldn't hold off Found, the only one to renew rivalry from Longchamp. Found beat Golden Horn by half a length, the pair having the race between them in the home straight after Dettori sent Golden Horn for home almost immediately on turning in. Setting aside any marginal advantage Found may have enjoyed by racing on the permitted raceday medication furosemide (Golden Horn's connections opted to race 'clean'), it was clear that Golden Horn, who didn't settle as well as he might have done early on, was some way from his best on the day. There had been three inches of rain at Keeneland in the week preceding the Breeders' Cup and, although the going dried out to good, Golden Horn's trainer had feared that the racing surface might prove his undoing. 'If it wasn't for the rain, I'd be as confident as you can be running first time in America around tight turns,' Gosden said before the race. 'It is not ideal for a horse with a beautiful action who flies off the ground, but we are not going to run and hide.' Dettori reported afterwards that the surface was too loose to enable Golden Horn to show his best—'He was laboured and couldn't pick up, he was spinning his wheels all the time'—and defeat in North America should not detract from the legacy that Golden Horn leaves behind. His performances illuminated the European season and his virtually uninterrupted progress from one championship race to the next was a joy to see, among other things providing ample evidence, if any were needed, that the modern thoroughbred is a tougher and more resilient animal than it is sometimes given credit for. Golden Horn lost two of his eight races, but he came out the best horse at the weights on all his starts as he was conceding the statutory 3 lb allowance to the pair of three-year-old fillies that beat him. Perhaps the last word should be left to his trainer who said after the Breeders' Cup, 'He has done everything and we could not have asked for more ... horses as good as him don't come along very often.'

Mr A. E. Oppenheimer's "Golden Horn"

Golden Horn (b.c. 2012)	Cape Cross (IRE) (b 1994)	Green Desert (b 1983)	Danzig
			Foreign Courier
		Park Appeal (br 1982)	Ahonoora
			Balidaress
	Fleche d'Or (b 2006)	Dubai Destination (b 1999)	Kingmambo
			Mysterial
		Nuryana (b 1984)	Nureyev
			Loralane

Golden Horn is a lengthy, good-topped, attractive individual, and a good mover. He has been retired to Dalham Hall Stud in Newmarket at a fee of £60,000 and joins eleven other winners of the Derby who are currently available at widely varied fees to European breeders, five of them standing at Coolmore in Ireland (Workforce, the only one of the last eleven Derby winners to have 'got away', made a good start with his first crop of two-year-olds in Japan in the latest season). Top-class mile and a half horses don't always enjoy the wholehearted support of commercial breeders, who can get a better return in the sale-ring by using sprinting and miling stallions, but Galileo has shown that a Derby winner can sire good two-year-olds (he has had three champion juveniles and has been the leading sire of two-year-olds in Europe on a number of occasions, including in each of the last two seasons). Golden Horn's pedigree contains plenty of speed elements, his long-serving sire Cape Cross (also sire of an Oaks winner in Ouija Board, the dam of Australia) being a high-class miler who also stands under the Darley banner, at Kildangan Stud in County Kildare (at a fee of €20,000). Golden Horn's dam Fleche d'Or was an unraced daughter of

425

another miler in Dubai Destination (also the sire of the dam of King George winner Postponed but a commercial failure at stud who was sold to Saudi Arabia during the year). Fleche d'Or was sold by Golden Horn's owner-breeder, in foal to Champs Elysees, for 62,000 guineas at the December Sales in 2012, before the first of the two foals she left for Hascombe and Valiant had reached the racecourse. That first foal, Eastern Belle (by Champs Elysees), carried the Oppenheimer colours to success in the listed Ballymacoll Stakes over a mile and a quarter at Newbury before being sent to continue her racing career for the Oppenheimers in the States as a four-year-old (when she was placed three times in graded company at up to a mile and a half, including the Grade 2 New York Stakes over a mile and a quarter at Belmont the day before Golden Horn won the Derby).

Golden Horn's dam may never have run but she is a half-sister to another of the top performers produced by the family, the Coronation Stakes winner Rebecca Sharp who met trouble in running when narrowly beaten in the Queen Elizabeth II Stakes later the same season. Rebecca Sharp and Golden Horn's grandam, the useful miler Nuryana, were both trained by Geoff Wragg who, like his father Harry before him, had most of the Oppenheimer home breds of that era (Harry trained On The House—half-sister to Golden Horn's great grandam Loralane, a seven-furlong winner—and Pelerin, who have both been mentioned earlier). Nuryana bred ten winners for the Oppenheimers, also producing a smart mile and a half performer in Mystic Knight who won the Lingfield Derby Trial and finished sixth in Shaamit's Derby in which he carried the family colours prominently for a long way. Another of Nuryana's offspring Hidden Hope won the Cheshire Oaks and is the dam of the 2013 Galtres Stakes winner Our Obsession who was trained for Anthony Oppenheimer by William Haggas, another of the half-dozen trainers used by the owner-breeder nowadays. Golden Horn's fourth dam Lora was a granddaughter of the One Thousand Guineas runner-up Tessa Gillian who was acquired in 1965 when Sir Philip Oppenheimer bought Hascombe Stud and all its stock, which he amalgamated with his own at Valiant Stud (the name an amalgamation of the Christian names of his two children).

Tessa Gillian, who stemmed from an Aga Khan family (Mumtaz Mahal was her great grandam), was already fifteen and she had bred a Gimcrack winner in Test Case and a Richmond Stakes winner in Gentle Art. Tessa Gillian had also produced a sister to Test Case named Courtessa, a twin who didn't race. Several years further on, Courtessa herself had been represented on the racecourse by the high-class sprinter D'Urberville, winner of the King's Stand Stakes, when Sir Philip Oppenheimer purchased a closely-related younger sibling for 28,000 guineas at the 1973 Newmarket yearling sales. That filly was Lora (by Lorenzaccio, a son of D'Urberville's sire Klairon) who went on to play such a huge role in the Hascombe and Valiant story. Hascombe and Valiant has bred other classic winners—the Coolmore partners purchased the 2001 Poule d'Essai des Pouliches winner Rose Gypsy and the 2005 Two Thousand Guineas winner Footstepsinthesand from them—but both classic winners to carry the Oppenheimer colours, On The House and Golden Horn, descended from Lora. The tough and genuine Golden Horn was equally effective at a mile and a quarter and a mile and a half, and acted on good to firm going. He usually raced prominently and always found plenty under pressure. *John Gosden*

GOLDEN ISLES (IRE) 2 ch.f. (Feb 6) Mastercraftsman (IRE) 129 – Aphorism 84 **65** (Halling (USA) 133) [2015 p8m³ p8d⁶ Nov 30] 55,000F, 31,000Y: fifth foal: half-sister to winner up to 1m Danz Choice (2-y-o 5f/5.3f winner, by Kheleyf): dam, 1½m-2¼m winner, half-sister to very smart winner up to 14.6f Craigsteel: modest form in maidens at Lingfield and Kempton. *J. S. Moore*

GOLDEN JUBILEE (USA) 6 b.g. Zavata (USA) 111 – Love Play (USA) (Friendly **83** Lover (USA) 117) [2015 p10m⁶ p12m⁴ 10m⁵ 10.2s⁶ 10m³ t12.2g* 12d⁵ 12g² 10g* 10d **a74** Oct 30] good-topped gelding: fairly useful handicapper: won at Wolverhampton in July and Newmarket (by 4½ lengths from Compton Bird) in September: stays 1½m: acts on all-weather, soft and good to firm going: often wears headgear: front runner/races prominently. *Nigel Twiston-Davies*

GOLDEN KINGDOM (IRE) 2 b.g. (Mar 2) Elusive City (USA) 117 – Sea Paint (IRE) **63** (Peintre Celebre (USA) 137) [2015 p6g 6m p6m⁶ Nov 19] workmanlike gelding: modest maiden: best effort when sixth at Lingfield (5¾ lengths behind Happy Call) in November: should stay at least 7f: sent to Singapore. *William Jarvis*

GOLDEN LAUGHTER (USA) 3 b.f. Bernardini (USA) 132 – Glatisant 104 (Rainbow **60** Quest (USA) 134) [2015 7g p10g⁵ 10.3m Jun 26] half-sister to several winners, including 2000 Guineas winner Footstepsinthesand (2-y-o 6f/7f winner, by Giant's Causeway), smart 1m winner Belle d'Or (by Medaglia d'Oro) and smart 2-y-o 6f winner (including Phoenix Stakes) Pedro The Great (by Henrythenavigator): dam 2-y-o 6f/7f winner: modest maiden: blinkered, best effort when ninth at Doncaster final start. *John Gosden*

GOLDEN ROSANNA 2 b.f. (Apr 10) Equiano (FR) 127 – Goldeva 104 (Makbul 104) **39** [2015 5f 6s⁵ 6v t7.1f t5.1f Dec 11] fourth foal: half-sister to 5f/5.7f winner Bilash (by Choisir) and 5f/6f winner Gold Pursuit (by Pastoral Pursuits): dam, winner up to 6f (2-y-o 5f winner), half-sister to useful 9.4f-1½m winner (stayed 1¾m) Royal Cavalier: poor maiden: stays 6f: acts on tapeta, firm and soft going: usually in headgear. *Steph Hollinshead*

GOLDEN SPUN (USA) 3 b.g. Hard Spun (USA) 124 – Scarlet's Tara (USA) (Goodbye **62** Doeny (USA)) [2015 81: 6m 7g 6g 6g 6g Jul 5] modest handicapper: stays 6f: acts on soft going: tried in hood in 2015. *David O'Meara*

GOLDEN STEPS (FR) 4 b.g. Footstepsinthesand 120 – Kocooning (IRE) (King's Best **112** (USA) 132) [2015 112: 6g⁵ 6g² 6m 6m* 6g 6s 6v Nov 7] smart handicapper: won at Goodwood (by 1½ lengths from Barnet Fair) in August: stays 6f: acts on polytrack, soft and good to firm going: tried in hood prior to 2015: often races towards rear. *Marco Botti*

GOLDEN STUNNER (IRE) 2 ch.f. (Feb 26) Dream Ahead (USA) 133 – Pina Colada **84** 77 (Sabrehill (USA) 120) [2015 6m⁶ 6.9m² 8.3g² p8d³ Nov 30] €43,000F, €115,000Y: rather unfurnished filly: half-sister to 1m-1¼m winner Colonel Carter and useful winner up to 1m Mr Mojito (2-y-o 5f winner) (both by Danehill Dancer): dam, winner up to 7f (2-y-o 5.3f winner), half-sister to smart winner up to 1¼m (stays 1½m) Triple Threat: fairly useful maiden: second at Windsor in October and third at Kempton in November: stays 8.5f. *Ralph Beckett*

GOLDEN THREAD 5 ch.g. Singspiel (IRE) 133 – Alpenrot (IRE) (Barathea (IRE) 127) **69** [2015 t9.5f t9.5f³ t8.6f⁶ t12.2m Nov 28] fair maiden: stays 9.5f. *Neil King*

GOLDEN WEDDING (IRE) 3 b.g. Archipenko (USA) 127 – Peace Lily 69 (Dansili **74** 127) [2015 68: 7.5m⁴ 8m⁶ 10m⁶ 7.1m 7.1m⁶ 8s* p7g p10g Dec 15] fair handicapper: won at Brighton in October: stays 1m: acts on soft going: often in cheekpieces in 2015. *Eve Johnson Houghton*

GOLD FAITH (IRE) 2 gr.g. (Feb 26) Dark Angel (IRE) 113 – Livadream (IRE) **84 p** (Dalakhani (IRE) 133) [2015 7m⁴ p7g* Sep 23] 33,000F, 200,000Y: first foal: dam unraced half-sister to useful 1¼m-13f winner Ukrainian out of smart 1m-1¼m winner Livadiya: better effort when winning maiden at Kempton (by 1¼ lengths from Rock Warbler) in September, driven clear: will stay at least 1m: open to further improvement. *Ralph Beckett*

GOLD FLASH 3 b.g. Kheleyf (USA) 116 – My Golly (Mozart (IRE) 131) [2015 76p: 6m³ **83** 6m 5m 6m p7g Aug 12] lengthy gelding: fairly useful handicapper: third at Doncaster in April: below form after: best effort at 6f: acts on polytrack: sometimes in blinkers in 2015: sometimes slowly away. *Ralph Beckett*

GOLD-FUN (IRE) 6 ch.g. Le Vie dei Colori 126 – Goodwood March 66 (Foxhound **126** (USA) 103) [2015 127: 8m⁶ 6g⁴ 7g³ 6m² 6m² 6g* 6g² Dec 13] high-class performer: won Chairman's Sprint Prize at Sha Tin (by short head from Aerovelocity) in February and Group 2 Jockey Club Sprint on same course (by 1¼ lengths from Peniaphobia) in November: creditable ½-length second to same rival in Hong Kong Sprint there final outing: effective at 6f to 1m: acts on good to firm and good to soft going: wears headgear. *R. Gibson, Hong Kong*

GOLD HUNTER (IRE) 5 b.g. Invincible Spirit (IRE) 121 – Goldthroat (IRE) 79 **89** (Zafonic (USA) 130) [2015 t8.6g³ 8g⁵ 7d 7m t8.6g 7.1s 7d² t9.5g 7d Oct 31] sturdy gelding: fairly useful handicapper: stays 8.5f: acts on tapeta, firm and good to soft going: usually races close up, tends to find little. *Steve Flook*

GOLD LEAF 3 ch.f. Kheleyf (USA) 116 – Lefty's Dollbaby (USA) (Brocco (USA) 124) **–** [2015 –: p6g⁶ p5g p6g f6d 6g 6s Aug 15] little form: tried in blinkers in 2015. *John E. Long*

GOLDMADCHEN (GER) 7 b.m. Ivan Denisovich (IRE) 115 – Goldkatze (GER) **66**
(Czaravich (USA)) [2015 66: t12.2f* p13.3g⁴ f12g² p10f* f11g⁵ f12g t12.2m f12g⁶ Dec
22] fair handicapper: won at Wolverhampton (amateur) in February and Chelmsford in
March: stays 1½m: acts on all-weather, best turf form on heavy going: tried in cheekpieces
prior to 2015: front runner/races prominently. *James Given*

GOLD MEDAL (IRE) 5 b.g. Dylan Thomas (IRE) 132 – Sogno Verde (IRE) 82 (Green **60**
Desert (USA) 127) [2015 12d⁴ t16.5g⁵ Apr 21] well-made gelding: modest maiden: best
effort at 1½m: acts on good to soft going. *Jonjo O'Neill*

GOLD MEDALLION (IRE) 2 b.c. (Mar 9) Acclamation 118 – Gold Bubbles (USA) **94 p**
105 (Street Cry (IRE) 130) [2015 6m* 6g² Jun 29] €70,000Y: second foal: half-brother to
useful 8.3f winner Spiriting (by Invincible Spirit): dam 2-y-o 6f winner who stayed 10.4f:
won maiden at Leicester (by ¾ length from Shahbar) in May: better effort when second in
minor event at Pontefract (1¾ lengths behind Age of Empire) in June, sticking to task: will
be suited by 7f: sent to Hong Kong: will go on improving. *Mark Johnston*

GOLDMEMBER 2 ch.c. (Jan 25) New Approach (IRE) 132 – Sister Act 85 (Marju (IRE) **73 p**
127) [2015 8s Oct 23] 300,000Y: third foal: half-brother to smart winner up to 1¼m
Ribbons (2-y-o 1m winner, by Manduro): dam, 1m winner, sister to high-class winner up
to 1m Soviet Song: 12/1, better for run when eighth in maiden at Newbury (4¼ lengths
behind Midterm) in October, not knocked about: better to come. *David Simcock*

GOLD MERLION (IRE) 2 b.f. (Mar 29) Alhaarth (IRE) 126 – Sea of Time (USA) **76**
(Gilded Time (USA)) [2015 7g* 7d³ 6.3d Sep 13] €1,800F, €15,000Y: half-sister to useful
1½m-2¼m winner Desert Sea (by Desert Sun): dam unraced: fair form: won maiden at
Thirsk in July by neck from Ribbing: easily better effort after when third of 5 to Carrington
in nursery at Goodwood in August: will be suited by 1m+. *Mark Johnston*

GOLD NOT SILVER (IRE) 6 b.g. Celtic Swing 138 – Molly-O (IRE) 101 (Dolphin **62**
Street (FR) 125) [2015 59: p10.7g t12.2f² p12g² p10.7g* Dec 18] modest handicapper:
won at Dundalk (apprentice) in December: stays 1¾m: acts on polytrack, tapeta and heavy
going: sometimes wears headgear: often races prominently. *Adrian Brendan Joyce, Ireland*

GOLD PRINCE (IRE) 3 b.g. Nayef (USA) 129 – Premier Prize 106 (Selkirk (USA) **92**
129) [2015 85: 8.1g⁶ 8m² 8v* 12g 8.5d 10v Oct 24] lengthy gelding: fairly useful
handicapper: won at Newbury (by neck from Fruit Pastille) in August: stays 1m: acts on
good to firm and heavy going. *Sylvester Kirk*

GOLDREAM 6 br.g. Oasis Dream 129 – Clizia (IRE) (Machiavellian (USA) 123) **123**
[2015 114: 5m* 5g 5f* 5g⁵ 5m* Oct 4]
    Perhaps one of the more surprising success stories at the top level in 2015
was Goldream, who landed both the King's Stand and Prix de l'Abbaye—as well
as Newmarket's Palace House Stakes—during a very fruitful campaign in the
top five-furlong events. Goldream hadn't even contested a pattern race in his four
previous seasons, though he had shown decidedly smart form in good-quality sprint
handicaps as a five-year-old in 2014, winning on One Thousand Guineas day at
Newmarket and on the Shergar Cup card at Ascot, as well as finishing fourth to
Muthmir in the Portland. Goldream's success in the latest season—which he ended
ranked behind only Nunthorpe winner Mecca's Angel among the top five-furlong
performers in Europe—is a further feather in the cap of his Newmarket-based
trainer Robert Cowell who, as mentioned in these pages before, has a well-earned
reputation as a dab hand with sprinters. Cowell's nine wins at pattern level have
all been achieved in races over five furlongs. In addition to his two other Group 1
winners, Prohibit (2011 King's Stand) and Jwala (2013 Nunthorpe), Cowell has
won pattern races with Monsieur Joe, Spirit Quartz and Kingsgate Native, while
his biggest success outside pattern races came with Intrinsic in the 2014 Stewards'
Cup. Cowell recorded twenty-five wins in 2015, his second highest total following
a career-high thirty-seven in 2014, and Goldream's wins at Newmarket and Ascot
helped the yard accrue just short of half a million pounds in prize money.

    Cowell also has a knack for improving horses recruited from other yards. Of
the big-race winners mentioned above, only Jwala started her career with Cowell.
Prohibit and Intrinsic came from John Gosden and Sir Michael Stoute respectively,
and Goldream was sourced from another of the leading stables in Newmarket,
having raced twelve times at two and three for Luca Cumani. Goldream started out

over seven furlongs and a mile but was soon dropped back to sprint trips as a three-year-old, winning twice over six furlongs and showing useful form before making the short move across Newmarket to Cowell's yard at Bottisham Heath Stud at the end of the 2012 season. Although he failed to win in his first campaign for Cowell in 2013, Goldream has made rapid progress in the two seasons since. Such was the level of Goldream's handicap form in 2014 that he started 5/1 third favourite for the Pearl Bloodstock Palace House Stakes on Two Thousand Guineas day at Newmarket on his reappearance. Sole Power, the winner of the two previous renewals, was a notable absentee from the final field of nine but Goldream had to produce a very smart effort nonetheless to prevail by a length and a quarter and the same from Justice Day and his own veteran stablemate Kingsgate Native, the latter still going strongly as a ten-year-old and reaching a place in the Palace House for the third consecutive season (he landed a listed race at Haydock two outings later).

Sole Power had been clearly the best horse in Europe over five furlongs the previous season and was seeking a hat-trick of wins in the latest King's Stand Stakes, though he was challenged in the betting by the up-and-coming Muthmir, who had gained his first pattern-race win in the Group 2 Prix du Gros-Chene at Chantilly the previous month. Aussie raider Shamal Wind—the only runner trained outside Europe—and the 2014 Sprint Cup winner G Force were the only others to start at shorter than 14/1 in the eighteen-runner field which contained no three-year-olds, almost certainly due to the rival attraction of the inaugural Commonwealth Cup for three-year-olds over six furlongs later at the meeting (three-year-olds can no longer run in the Diamond Jubilee). Goldream was a 20/1-shot in the King's Stand having disappointed since the Palace House in the Temple Stakes at Haydock (won by another King's Stand runner, Pearl Secret). With outsider Take Cover making the running on the flank towards the far side, those drawn high struggled to get involved, as did those held up in a race in which the overall gallop was far from strong. The first three were all drawn in single figures and raced in touch, including Goldream who found plenty over the final two furlongs to edge out nine-year-old Medicean Man and Muthmir in a tight finish, the margins between the trio being a short head and a neck. Pearl Secret did best of those held up in finishing fourth, a place ahead of Sole Power, who didn't have the race run to suit but failed to show his trademark turn of foot nonetheless. Goldream sidestepped Goodwood's King George Stakes, with connections concerned about his having to shoulder a Group 1 penalty as well as harbouring reservations about the suitability of the track, and he appeared next in the Nunthorpe Stakes at York. Despite his Royal Ascot win, Goldream started at 20/1 again in a market dominated this time by the short-priced Queen Mary winner Acapulco. Although he didn't fully repeat his Newmarket and Ascot form in finishing four and a half lengths fifth behind Mecca's Angel, Goldream was far from discredited in a stronger race than the King's Stand, especially as the ground (officially good to soft, but good by Timeform's reckoning) wasn't quite so firm as suits him.

King's Stand Stakes, Royal Ascot—Goldream makes his breakthrough at the top level as he beats a better-than-ever Medicean Man (cheekpieces) and Muthmir (striped cap) in a tight finish; Pearl Secret is fourth and Sole Power (No.12) fifth in his bid to win for the third year running

Qatar Prix de l'Abbaye de Longchamp, Longchamp—Goldream edges out the previous year's runner-up Rangali, with Muthmir and Pearl Secret completing the frame

Having been withdrawn, due to soft ground, from the Prix du Petit Couvert on Longchamp's 'day of trials' (the race was won by 2014 Abbaye winner Move In Time), Goldream had much firmer conditions for his final outing when he was part of a typically large British-trained contingent contesting the Qatar Prix de l'Abbaye on Arc day itself. The poor record of home-trained runners in the Abbaye has been alluded to in these pages before, and, in the latest renewal, just two of the eighteen runners (which included fourteen from Britain) were trained in France, both of them by Alex Pantall. In the absence of Nunthorpe winner Mecca's Angel, who was among the final declarations before being withdrawn the day before due to the drying ground, the favourite for the Abbaye was the King George Stakes winner Muthmir (who had finished a place behind Goldream in the Nunthorpe), with Sole Power—representing Ireland alongside 2013 winner Maarek—and the juvenile Gutaifan next in the market, ahead of Move In Time and Goldream who were the only others at single-figure odds. Goldream was ridden a little more conservatively than usual which served him well in a race in which the leaders went off hard. The previous year's runner-up Rangali looked like becoming only the fourth home-trained winner since 1996 as he scythed through the pack over a furlong out, quickening past Goldream among others, but in hindsight his move was arguably made too soon and he was overhauled by the rallying Goldream close home. Goldream got home by a short neck, with Muthmir in third, followed by Pearl Secret (who came from a long way back as in the King's Stand) and then Move In Time. Goldream was the eleventh British-trained winner of the Abbaye this century, and he completed a treble for British-trained horses in the seven Group 1 races on Arc day, following the wins of Covert Love in the Prix de l'Opera and Golden Horn in the Arc (the Abbaye was moved down the card from its recent place as the day's curtain raiser, a change that enabled an earlier start for the Arc).

		Oasis Dream (b 2000)	Green Desert (b 1983)	Danzig
Goldream (br.g. 2009)				Foreign Courier
			Hope (b 1991)	Dancing Brave
				Bahamian
		Clizia (IRE) (gr 2002)	Machiavellian (b 1987)	Mr Prospector
				Coup de Folie
			Cuixmala (gr 1991)	Highest Honor
				Floripedes

Although by Oasis Dream, it was far from certain, based on pedigree, that Goldream would develop into a sprinter. Indeed, given the stamina on the distaff side of his pedigree it is not surprising that he was started off at seven furlongs and a mile as a juvenile. His dam, the unraced Machiavellian mare Clizia, is a half-sister to the smart mile and a half winner Mont Rocher and their dam Cuixmala (also unraced) is a half-sister to none other than Montjeu out of the French mare Floripedes, who finished second in the Prix Royal-Oak. Goldream has proved much the best of Clizia's three foals who have reached the track, though his year-older half-sister Galicuix (by Galileo), who shaped as though amiss on both of her outings in maidens as a three-year-old (for Luca Cumani), has not taken long to

Mr J Sargeant & Mrs J Morley's "Goldream"

make an impression in her short time at stud. She has produced two foals by Paco Boy, the first being the smart juvenile Galileo Gold who won the Vintage Stakes at Goodwood in the latest season, and the second going through the ring as a yearling for £280,000 at the Doncaster Sales and set to join Galileo Gold with Hugo Palmer. Oasis Dream isn't simply a sire of good sprinters—triple Nassau Stakes-winner Midday is testament to that—but champion sprinter Muhaarar and Goldream were his two star performers in the latest season. Goldream has been raced only at five and six furlongs since his reappearance at three. Although he has winning form over six, five furlongs and firm ground (conditions were described as firm by Timeform when he won the King's Stand) are the ideal combination for him. He has also won on polytrack, scoring in a maiden as a three-year-old. Goldream may well encounter ideal conditions for his first big target of 2016, the Al Quoz Sprint on Dubai World Cup night at Meydan, a race won in the latest season by Sole Power. A close-coupled gelding who usually races prominently, Goldream has worn cheekpieces for all of his runs since mid-2013 but he is most reliable for a sprinter. *Robert Cowell*

GOLD SANDS (IRE) 3 b.f. Cape Cross (IRE) 129 – Lil's Jessy (IRE) 101 (Kris 135) **91**
[2015 86p: 8g² 10m⁴ 10m² p12g* 11.1s 10.3m Sep 10] tall filly: fairly useful performer: won maiden at Kempton in July: stays 1½m: acts on polytrack and good to firm going: front runner/races prominently. *James Tate*

GOLDSLINGER (FR) 3 b.g. Gold Away (IRE) 125 – Singaporette (FR) (Sagacity (FR) **89**
125) [2015 –: p7g p10m⁵ 11.7m* 12.1s* 12g⁶ 13.1s* 13.4d* Sep 26] sturdy gelding: fairly useful handicapper: won at Bath and Chepstow in July, Bath in August and Chester (by ¾ length from Brandon Castle, showing further marked improvement) in September: stays 13.5f: acts on soft and good to firm going: tried in hood in 2015: front runner, often travels strongly. *Dean Ivory*

GOLD TRADE (IRE) 2 b.c. (Apr 9) Raven's Pass (USA) 133 – Trading Places (Dansili 127) [2015 7d³ p7g² 7.5g² p8f² Oct 15] 20,000Y: sixth foal: half-brother to 1¼m winner Glan Y Gors (by High Chaparral): dam unraced half-sister to smart winner up to 9f Wharf: fairly useful maiden: best effort when second at Beverley in September on third start: stays 1m. *Hugo Palmer*   **86**

GOLD TRAIL (IRE) 4 ch.c. Teofilo (IRE) 126 – Goldthroat (IRE) 79 (Zafonic (USA) 130) [2015 100: p10m* p12f* t12.2g* p15.8m² p12g² 12f 9.9g⁶ 12m* 13.4m⁴ Aug 22] rangy colt: useful handicapper: won at Lingfield (twice, by ½ length from Masterpaver latter occasion) in January, Wolverhampton (by neck from Luv U Whatever) in February and at Newmarket (by length from Farquhar) in August: stays 13.5f: acts on polytrack, tapeta and good to firm going: often races prominently. *Charlie Appleby*   **108**

GOLD WALTZ 3 b.f. Acclamation 118 – Corps de Ballet (IRE) 92 (Fasliyev (USA) 120) [2015 63, a76: 5m⁵ 6v³ p6g⁶ p6g³ 6.1m* 6.1g⁴ t6f* Oct 9] leggy, close-coupled filly: fairly useful handicapper: won at Chepstow in July and Wolverhampton (by neck from Ambitious Boy) in October: stays 6f: acts on polytrack, tapeta, good to firm and heavy going: sometimes wears headgear. *Ralph Beckett*   **80**

GOLD WILL (IRE) 3 b.g. Invincible Spirit (IRE) 121 – Ermine And Velvet 87 (Nayef (USA) 129) [2015 76: p7g³ p7g³ 7g⁴ p8g Sep 21] fairly useful maiden: third at Kempton on second start, best effort: stays 7f: acts on polytrack: usually races close up: sold 6,000 gns, sent to Saudi Arabia. *Ralph Beckett*   **82**

GOLLY MISS MOLLY 4 b.f. Exceed And Excel (AUS) 126 – Amicable Terms 88 (Royal Applause 124) [2015 72: p13g² p12g² p10g⁵ 10m⁶ p11g t12.2m⁵ p11g⁵ p16g* Dec 16] sturdy filly: fair handicapper: won at Kempton in December: stays 2m: acts on polytrack and good to firm going: often wears headgear: races towards rear. *Jeremy Gask*   **68**

GO MARNIE 2 b.g. (May 2) Multiplex 114 – Sopran Cross (ITY) (Cape Cross (IRE) 129) [2015 f5g⁵ 6g 5.1m⁶ 8g⁵ 10.2f Sep 13] rather leggy gelding: fair maiden: best effort at 1m: sometimes in blinkers: usually races nearer last than first. *Jo Hughes*   **68**

GO NANI GO 9 b.g. Kyllachy 129 – Go Between 91 (Daggers Drawn (USA) 114) [2015 94: t5.1f p5g³ 5m⁴ p5f* 5f⁶ 5m⁶ 5m⁵ 5m⁴ 5m p5f² Oct 28] smallish, stocky gelding: fairly useful handicapper: won at Lingfield (from Sandfrankskipsgo) in May: stays 6f: acts on polytrack, firm and good to soft going. *Ed de Giles*   **80 a89**

GONEINAMINUTE 3 b.f. Bushranger (IRE) 119 – Nevada Princess (IRE) (Desert Prince (IRE) 130) [2015 63: f8g⁶ Apr 27] thrice-raced maiden, form only on debut. *Tony Coyle*   **–**

GONE VIRAL (IRE) 4 ch.g. Virtual 122 – Dorinda Gray (IRE) (Docksider (USA) 124) [2015 89: 10.3d⁶ 10m p10m⁴ p11g 9.9g³ 10.3d⁴ 10.2s² Nov 4] workmanlike gelding: fairly useful handicapper: third at Brighton in September and second at Nottingham (amateur) in November: stays 10.5f: acts on soft going: tried in hood in 2015: sometimes in tongue tie in 2015: often races in rear, often travels strongly. *George Baker*   **85**

GONE WITH THE WIND (GER) 4 b.g. Dutch Art 126 – Gallivant 93 (Danehill (USA) 126) [2015 81: 8g 7m 8.1m 7.2g⁵ 7g⁵ 8d⁵ 8.9g² 7.9d⁴ 10.2v⁵ Oct 7] useful-looking gelding: fair handicapper: won at Carlisle in September: stays 9f: acts on polytrack and good to soft going: tried in cheekpieces: sometimes in tongue tie in 2015: usually races nearer last than first. *Rebecca Bastiman*   **72**

GONINODAETHAT 7 b.g. Proclamation (IRE) 130 – Big Mystery (IRE) 53 (Grand Lodge (USA) 125) [2015 73§: 6g 6s 7.2d³ 5.9g 6g* 6d⁴ 6g³ 5g⁶ 6d² 7.2d⁶ 5d⁴ 5g 6g Oct 8] fair handicapper: won at Ayr in July: stays 1m: acts on good to firm and heavy going: tried in hood: quirky sort who can't be relied on. *Jim Goldie*   **69 §**

GOOD AUTHORITY (IRE) 8 b.g. Chineur (FR) 123 – Lady Alexander (IRE) 112 (Night Shift (USA)) [2015 91: 6m⁴ p7g Sep 5] sturdy gelding: fairly useful handicapper: stays 1m: acts on polytrack, tapeta, good to firm and good to soft going: in cheekpieces latest start in 2015: tried in tongue tie. *Victor Dartnall*   **84**

GOOD BOY ALEX 3 gr.c. Arabian Gleam 122 – Animal Cracker 73 (Primo Dominie 121) [2015 –: 7m 6g 7g⁶ 6s 6.9m⁶ Aug 11] no form. *Alan Berry*   **–**

GOODBY INHERITANCE 3 b.c. Medicean 128 – Chili Dip (Alhaarth (IRE) 126) [2015 58: t8.6f³ 9.9m⁴ 10m⁵ 10.4g² 10.1m⁶ 10m p12g 11.7g⁴ t13.9f² p13.3f^pu Nov 19] close-coupled colt: fair maiden: stays 1½m: acts on polytrack and good to firm going: usually in headgear in 2015: usually wears tongue tie: usually races close up, often races freely. *Seamus Durack*   **76**

GOOD CONTACT (USA) 3 b.g. Teofilo (IRE) 126 – Mayoress (Machiavellian (USA) **109** 123) [2015 102: 7g⁵ 10.3f 8f⁶ 10.3g* 10.3d⁵ Sep 26] strong, close-coupled gelding: useful handicapper: won at Chester (by 2 lengths from Taraz) in September: creditable 3 lengths fifth of 9 to Erik The Red on same course final start: stays 10.3f: acts on good to soft going: tried in hood. *Saeed bin Suroor*

GOOD INTENT (USA) 2 b.g. (Feb 4) Scat Daddy (USA) 120 – Liza Lu (USA) (Menifee **86** (USA) 124) [2015 7m* 7f³ 8.5f⁴ Oct 23] $37,000Y: third foal: dam 5.5f-7f winner out of US Grade 2 9f winner Chamrousse: fairly useful performer: won maiden at Newcastle (by short head from Street Duel) in July: left Kevin Ryan, good efforts when in frame after in non-graded event at Kentucky Downs and allowance race at Keeneland: stays 8.5f. *Brendan P. Walsh, USA*

GOOD JUDGE (USA) 3 gr.g. Cape Cross (IRE) 129 – Summer Fete (IRE) 104 (Pivotal **81 p** 124) [2015 –: t12.2f* Oct 31] in cheekpieces on only second start, won maiden at Wolverhampton in October by ½ length from Red Cardinal, having run of race from the front: stays 1½m: entitled to progress. *Saeed bin Suroor*

GOODKNIGHT PERCY (IRE) 2 ch.g. (Feb 8) Sir Percy 129 – Ekhraaj (USA) (El **69** Prado (IRE) 119) [2015 6.1d⁶ 7f⁴ 7.1m⁵ 8.3g⁴ 8d⁴ 10.2f⁵ Sep 13] fair maiden: best effort at 7f, should prove effective over further: acts on firm going: tried in cheekpieces. *Kevin Ryan*

GOOD LUCK CHARM 6 b.g. Doyen (IRE) 132 – Lucky Dice (Perugino (USA) 84) **81** [2015 90, a83: 7.6d 5.7m 7m⁵ 7.1f⁴ 7g⁴ 7v⁵ 7d* 7s 7s p7m³ p7f Nov 23] rather leggy gelding: fairly useful handicapper: won at Brighton (by 7 lengths from Mendacious Harpy) in September: stays 8.5f: acts on polytrack, firm and soft going: sometimes wears headgear: sometimes in tongue tie in 2015: usually races nearer last than first. *Gary Moore*

GOOD MOVE (IRE) 3 b.f. Aussie Rules (USA) 123 – Lady Lafitte (USA) 73 (Stravinsky **–** (USA) 133) [2015 –: 7g 7.5g 10g 8g 7.5m 8.5m⁴ 7.5m⁶ Oct 1] no form: sometimes in headgear in 2015. *Brian Rothwell*

GOODNIGHTSUZY (IRE) 3 b.f. Azamour (IRE) 130 – Suzy Bliss 105 (Spinning **81** World (USA) 130) [2015 80p: 7m³ 8g³ 10m⁶ t8.6g⁶ 10.3g⁴ 10v³ 10.4d² p10f² t12.2f p11g Dec 9] leggy filly: fairly useful handicapper: second at Haydock (apprentice) in September and Chelmsford in October: stays 10.5f: acts on polytrack and good to soft going. *Ed Walker*

GOOD PLACE (USA) 3 ch.f. Street Cry (IRE) 130 – Causeway Lass (AUS) (Giant's **99** Causeway (USA) 132) [2015 97: a7f⁴ a8f² a9.4f⁴ Feb 26] lengthy filly, has scope: useful performer: good second in listed UAE 1000 Guineas at Meydan (3¼ lengths behind Local Time) in February: below-form fourth of 5 behind same rival in UAE Oaks on same course next time: should stay 1¼m: acts on dirt and firm going, below form on good to soft. *Saeed bin Suroor*

GOOD RUN (FR) 2 ch.c. (Feb 20) Iffraaj 127 – Tadawul (USA) 73 (Diesis 133) [2015 **97 p** 7.9m² 9s* 9d* Oct 31] €35,000F, €120,000Y: half-brother to 3 winners, including 1m (including at 2 yrs) winner Absolutly Me (by Anabaa Blue) and 9f-10.5f winner Mrs Nobody (by Footstepsinthesand), both useful: dam 8.5f winner: useful performer: won maiden at Goodwood (by 1¾ lengths from Cameraman) in September and nursery at Newmarket (by 1¼ lengths from Celebration Day) in October: stays 9f: open to further improvement. *Saeed bin Suroor*

GOOD TRIP (IRE) 2 b.c. (Apr 7) Dansili 127 – Counterclaim 98 (Pivotal 124) [2015 **101** 8.3s* f7g²* p8g² Dec 19] fourth foal: closely related to 6f winner Mukhabarat (by Exceed And Excel) and half-brother to useful 1m winner Power Game (by Shamardal): dam, 10.5f winner, half-sister to useful 7f-8.3f winner Grand Inquisitor (by Dansili): useful form: won maiden at Nottingham and minor event at Southwell (by 11 lengths from Battle Pride), both in November: 4/6, 2½ lengths second of 3 to Special Season in minor event at Lingfield final start: stays 8.5f. *Saeed bin Suroor*

GOODWOOD MIRAGE (IRE) 5 b.g. Jeremy (USA) 122 – Phantom Waters 79 **85** (Pharly (FR) 130) [2015 10s 11.6g 10g Jul 17] well-made gelding: fairly useful handicapper: stays 1¾m: acts on soft and good to firm going: temperament under suspicion. *Jonjo O'Neill*

GOODWOOD MOONLIGHT 3 gr.g. Azamour (IRE) 130 – Corrine (IRE) 99 (Spectrum **60** (IRE) 126) [2015 65: 8m 9.9m 9d⁶ p8g 8.1s⁵ 8g² 8v⁴ p8f⁴ p8f⁶ 7s p8g p10f³ Dec 21] good-topped gelding: modest maiden: left William Knight after tenth start: stays 1¼m: acts on polytrack and good to soft going: often in headgear in 2015: sometimes slowly away. *Ian Williams*

GOODWOOD ZODIAC (IRE) 2 b.g. (Jan 28) Kodiac 112 – Insieme (IRE) 68 (Barathea **91** (IRE) 127) [2015 6m 6m² 6g 7s* 7d* 7d Oct 11] 40,000Y: compact gelding: first foal: dam, 1m winner, half-sister to useful 1m winner Aldovrandi: fairly useful performer: won maiden at Brighton in August and nursery at Epsom (by 1¾ lengths from Hope Cove) in September: likely to stay 1m: acts on soft going. *William Knight*

GOODYEARFORROSES (IRE) 3 b.f. Azamour (IRE) 130 – Guilia 106 (Galileo **91** (IRE) 134) [2015 83p: 10.1g⁶ 12g Sep 25] fairly useful form, raced only 3 times: better effort in listed races in 2015 when sixth at 1¼m at Newcastle (8½ lengths behind Covert Love) in June: sent to USA. *Rae Guest*

GOOLAGONG GIRL (IRE) 3 b.f. Avonbridge 123 – Lady Berta 65 (Bertolini (USA) **67** 125) [2015 56: p10g⁴ p10g⁴ t9.5g² 8f* p8g* p8m Dec 27] fair handicapper: won at Bath in May and Lingfield in June: stays 1m: acts on polytrack and firm going: tried in cheekpieces. *Jane Chapple-Hyam*

GO ON GAL (IRE) 2 b.f. (Apr 13) Approve (IRE) 112 – Jeritza (Rainbow Quest (USA) **–** 134) [2015 t5.1g 6m 5g⁶ Jun 28] workmanlike filly: sixth foal: half-sister to 1¼m winner Joker Hill (by Tiger Hill): dam, 11f/1½m winner, sister to useful 9f-13f winner Jade Quest: no form. *Julia Feilden*

GO ON GO ON GO ON 2 b.f. (Mar 24) Medicean 128 – Piranha (IRE) 82 (Exceed And **79 p** Excel (AUS) 126) [2015 p6g² t6f* Dec 22] £23,000Y: first foal: dam 2-y-o 5f winner: better effort when winning maiden at Wolverhampton (by 1¾ lengths from Mondial) in December: in tongue tie first start: open to further improvement. *Clive Cox*

GO PACKING GO 3 br.g. Equiano 127 – Khubza 86 (Green Desert (USA) 127) **67** [2015 t7.1f p8m³ p7f² t7.1g⁵ 7m p7g Aug 24] sturdy gelding: fair maiden in Britain: stays 1m: acts on polytrack and tapeta: usually in headgear: front runner/races prominently: sold 800 gns, sent to Italy, winning 7f claimer at Varese in December. *Marco Botti*

GORDON LORD BYRON (IRE) 7 b.g. Byron 117 – Boa Estrela (IRE) (Intikhab **120** (USA) 135) [2015 124: 7g 6g 6f 6m* 7d* 6.5g³ 6g³ 6d 7m⁶ 6d p5g⁴ p8g⁵ Nov 18] tall, good-topped gelding: very smart performer: won listed race at the Curragh (by 3 lengths from Balmont Mast) in June: 3½ lengths second in Minstrel Stakes there in July, but awarded race following disqualification of Home of The Brave on technical grounds: best subsequent effort on next start, when length third to Muhaarar in Prix Maurice de Gheest at Deauville: stays 8.5f: acts on polytrack and any turf going: genuine. *T. Hogan, Ireland*

GORGEOUS GEEZER 2 b.c. (Apr 22) Kheleyf (USA) 116 – Arctic High 62 (Polar **75** Falcon (USA) 126) [2015 p7g p6m³ p6g³ Dec 16] workmanlike colt: fair form when third in maidens at Lingfield in November and Kempton (slowly away) in December: in hood. *Martin Smith*

GORGEOUS GEORGIE (IRE) 4 b.g. Nayef (USA) 129 – Sterope (FR) 76 (Hernando **–** (FR) 127) [2015 12d p12g p13g⁴ Aug 7] no form: tried in blinkers: sold £4,000, sent to Italy. *Tony Carroll*

GORING (GER) 3 b.g. Areion (GER) 115 – Globuli (GER) (Surako (GER) 114) [2015 **94** 81: 8.5m⁵ 8g² 7g 8m³ 8d 8s³ 7s* 7m⁴ 8s⁴ Oct 23] compact gelding: fairly useful performer: won maiden at Beverley in April and handicap at Newbury (by length from Harlequin Striker) in September: stays 8.5f: acts on soft and good to firm going: has been gelded. *Eve Johnson Houghton*

GORUKAI (IRE) 2 b.g. (Jan 18) Kodiac 112 – Damask (IRE) 66 (Red Clubs (IRE) 125) **74 p** [2015 5m⁵ 6.1s³ 6g t5.1m² Dec 26] 65,000Y: first foal: dam maiden half-sister to very smart winner up to 1¼m Zafisio and useful winner up to 1½m Gold Trail: fair maiden: left Alan McCabe after first start: gelded after third, and best effort on return over 3 months later: still unexposed. *David Simcock*

GO SAKHEE 4 br.g. Sakhee's Secret 128 – Bling Bling (IRE) 70 (Indian Ridge 123) **94** [2015 91: 10g³ 10m⁴ 9.8m³ 10.2m* Jul 4] good-topped gelding: fairly useful handicapper: improved to win at Nottingham in July by 7 lengths from Game Show, making all: stays 1¼m: acts on good to firm and good to soft going: blinkered penultimate start: front runner/races prominently: sold 88,000 gns, sent to Qatar. *Roger Varian*

GOSPEL CHOIR 6 ch.g. Galileo (IRE) 134 – Chorist 120 (Pivotal 124) [2015 121: 12m* **119** 12m³ 11.6d² 14d⁶ Sep 13] well-made gelding: smart performer: won listed race at Newmarket (by short head from Dubday) in June: third in Princess of Wales's Stakes at Newmarket (½ length behind Big Orange) in July and second in listed race at Windsor (4½ lengths behind Beautiful Romance) in August: below form in Irish St Leger at the Curragh final start: stays 1¾m: acts on firm and good to soft going. *Sir Michael Stoute*

GOSSIPING 3 b.g. Dubawi (IRE) 129 – Gossamer 118 (Sadler's Wells (USA) 132) [2015 **85** 7m⁴ 8.3g* 8g⁶ p8g⁵ 8.3g⁵ Jun 22] sturdy gelding: half-brother to several winners, including smart 2-y-o 7f/1m winner Ibn Khaldun (by Dubai Destination), 7f-10.4f winner Memory Cloth (by Cape Cross) and 1½m winner (stayed 1¾m) Calico Cat (by Tiger Hill), both useful: dam, 1m winner (including at 2 yrs) who stayed 1¼m, sister to high-class winner up to 1m Barathea: fairly useful performer: won maiden at Windsor (by length from Mister Brightside) in April: best effort at 8.5f: has been gelded. *Charlie Appleby*

GOTASINGGOTADANCE 3 b.f. Royal Applause 124 – Water Gipsy 81 (Piccolo 121) – [2015 6m 7s⁴ p6f⁴ p5g Sep 30] angular filly: first foal: dam 7f winner: no form: tried in hood. *Philip Hide*

GOTCHA 4 gr.f. Fair Mix (IRE) 123 – Shazana 62 (Key of Luck (USA) 126) [2015 70p: **57** 9s⁶ Apr 5] modest maiden: best effort at 7f: in hood sole start in 2015. *James Bethell*

GOTHIC 4 b.g. Danehill Dancer (IRE) 117 – Riberac 110 (Efisio 120) [2015 99: 10s³ 12f **100** 12m² 11.6m³ Jun 27] rangy gelding: useful handicapper: second at Epsom (length behind Blue Surf) and third at Windsor (½ length behind Elhaame), both in June: stays 1½m: acts on any turf going: tried in headgear. *Sir Michael Stoute*

GOTHIC EMPIRE (IRE) 3 b.g. Dark Angel (IRE) 113 – Box of Frogs (IRE) 50 (One **84** Cool Cat (USA) 123) [2015 7d⁴ t7.1g* 7m⁵ 7m³ 7.1g⁶ t7.1g⁴ Aug 27] €25,000F, 80,000Y: lengthy gelding: first foal: dam ran a few times: fairly useful performer: won maiden at Wolverhampton (by 4½ lengths from Virile) in April: raced only at 7f: acts on tapeta: in hood last 3 starts. *Marco Botti*

GOWANHARRY (IRE) 6 ch.m. Choisir (AUS) 126 – Aahgowangowan (IRE) 88 **94** (Tagula (IRE) 116) [2015 85: 5.5g 5.1m⁴ 5g² 5g² 5m⁴ 5d* 5d* 5g⁴ 5.1d Oct 14] fairly useful handicapper: won at Ayr and Thirsk (by short head from Fredricka) in August: stays 6f: acts on good to firm and heavy going: sometimes wears cheekpieces: often wears tongue tie: front runner/races prominently: consistent. *Michael Dods*

GOWANLESS 2 b.g. (May 1) Monsieur Bond (IRE) 120 – Aahgowangowan (IRE) 88 **78 p** (Tagula (IRE) 116) [2015 6d* Oct 26] sixth foal: closely related to 5f winner Gowanharry (by Choisir): dam 5f-6f winner (including at 2 yrs): 11/1, overcame inexperience when winning 13-runner maiden at Redcar by ¾ length from Wernotfamusanymore, staying on to lead final ½f: will improve. *Michael Dods*

GOWER PRINCESS 4 ch.f. Footstepsinthesand 120 – Hollow Quaill (IRE) 82 **65** (Entrepreneur 123) [2015 64: 5m 5.1m* 6g² 5.7g 5g⁵ 5s³ 5m t6m p5m⁶ Dec 31] fair handicapper: won at Chepstow in June: stays 6f: acts on polytrack and good to firm going. *Ronald Harris*

GRACCHUS (USA) 9 b.g. Black Minnaloushe (USA) 123 – Montessa (USA) (Montbrook – (USA)) [2015 t12.2m Feb 27] fair at best, well held sole start in 2015: stays 1m: acts on good to firm and heavy going: tried in headgear: sometimes in tongue tie prior to 2015. *Richard Price*

GRACE AND FAVOUR 4 b.f. Montjeu (IRE) 137 – Gryada 93 (Shirley Heights 130) **91** [2015 79: 10.2m* 13.4g 14.1m⁵ Jun 24] sturdy, lengthy filly: fairly useful handicapper: won at Chepstow in May: stays 1¾m: acts on good to firm and heavy going. *Andrew Balding*

GRACEFILLY 4 b.f. Invincible Spirit (IRE) 121 – Marula (IRE) (Sadler's Wells (USA) **74** 132) [2015 69: p8g* t8.6f⁶ Jan 29] fair handicapper: won at Chelmsford in January: stays 9.5f: acts on polytrack and tapeta: usually races prominently. *Ed Walker*

GRACEFUL ACT 7 b.m. Royal Applause 124 – Minnina (IRE) (In The Wings 128) **56** [2015 63: 10g³ 10.1d 12d⁴ 9.3g⁵ 10g² 8m⁵ 8.9m 10m⁶ 6v Nov 3] modest handicapper: has form at 1½m, better over shorter: acts on good to firm and heavy going: tried in headgear prior to 2015: often starts slowly. *Ron Barr*

GRACEFUL JAMES (IRE) 2 ch.c. (Apr 14) Rock of Gibraltar (IRE) 133 – Little Miss **78 p** Gracie 105 (Efisio 120) [2015 p7g³ p8g* Dec 9] fourth foal: closely related to winner up to 1m Gracious George (2-y-o 7f winner) and 1m winner Henry Grace (both by Oratorio): dam 1m winner (including at 2 yrs): better effort when winning maiden at Kempton (by 2 lengths from High Shields) in December, kept up to work: open to further improvement. *Jimmy Fox*

GRACEFUL LADY 2 b.f. (Feb 15) Sixties Icon 125 – Leitzu (IRE) 74 (Barathea (IRE) **64** 127) [2015 8d Oct 23] 4,000F, £4,800 2-y-o: first foal: dam, 1m winner (including at 2 yrs) who stayed 1¾m, closely related to useful 1¼m-1½m winner (stayed 1¾m) Sgt Schultz: 66/1, seventh in maiden at Doncaster (8¼ lengths behind Zest) in October, slowly away. *Robert Eddery*

GRACEFUL WILLOW 5 b.m. Phoenix Reach (IRE) 124 – Opera Belle 77 (Dr Fong (USA) 128) [2015 –: p10m f7g Mar 3] no form. *John E. Long* —

GRACELAND (FR) 3 b.f. Mastercraftsman (IRE) 129 – Jeunesse Lulu (IRE) (Montjeu (IRE) 137) [2015 73: t12.2g* 12.3s³ 10.2d² 12.1m* 12m⁴ 12g² 14g⁶ 12g Sep 19] fairly useful performer: won maiden at Wolverhampton in April and handicap at Beverley in June: stays 1¾m: acts on tapeta, soft and good to firm going: often races towards rear. *Michael Bell* **91**

GRACESOME (IRE) 4 b.f. Shirocco (GER) 129 – Simonda 95 (Singspiel (IRE) 133) [2015 8.3m⁴ 8g 10d⁵ 10.2m p10m Oct 21] lengthy filly: modest maiden: stays 1¼m: acts on polytrack, good to firm and good to soft going. *Michael Blanshard* **57**

GRACIOUS GEORGE (IRE) 5 b.g. Oratorio (IRE) 128 – Little Miss Gracie 105 (Efisio 120) [2015 82: p8g* p8m³ p8f⁶ p8f 8m⁵ 10g⁶ t8.6m p8m p8g³ Dec 3] sturdy gelding: fairly useful handicapper: won at Kempton in January: stays 1¼m: acts on polytrack, soft and good to firm going: sometimes in headgear prior to 2015: usually races nearer last than first. *Jimmy Fox* **80**

GRACIOUS JOHN (IRE) 2 b.c. (Mar 6) Baltic King 120 – Dorn Hill 55 (Lujain (USA) 119) [2015 7.6g³ 7.4d 5.4g* 5d* 6s³ 6s* Oct 31] €10,000 2-y-o: fourth foal: brother to 1½m winner Helmsley Flyer and half-brother to 5f/6f winner Nonmeloricordo (by Chineur): dam, 6f winner, half-sister to useful 1m-1¼m winner Brocheta: useful performer: won maiden at York (by 2½ lengths from Poet's Prize) and nursery at Haydock (by 3 lengths from Point of Woods), both in September, and listed race at Maisons-Laffitte (by 1¾ lengths from Jimmy Two Times) in October: stays 5.5f: acts on good to soft going: front runner/races prominently. *David Evans* **105**

GRACIOUS LADY 4 b.f. Royal Applause 124 – Succinct 104 (Hector Protector (USA) 124) [2015 8v⁴ p10f⁵ Sep 22] maiden: no form in 2015. *Jo Davis* —

GRADIENT 2 b.c. (Jan 15) Oasis Dream 129 – Very Good News (USA) (Empire Maker (USA) 129) [2015 p8f⁵ p8m⁶ Oct 21] fair form in maidens at Lingfield and Kempton, some late headway when sixth of 10 to Southern Gailes in latter. *John Gosden* **70**

GRAFFITI ART 6 b.m. Kayf Tara 130 – Art Affair (GER) (Germany (USA) 124) [2015 68: p8f³ p12m² 11.6m⁶ p16g³ Jul 8] lengthy mare: fair maiden: stays 2m: acts on polytrack and good to firm going: sent to France. *Brendan Powell* **69**

GRAMERCY (IRE) 8 b.g. Whipper (USA) 126 – Topiary (IRE) (Selkirk (USA) 129) [2015 96§: 7v⁶ 6m³ 6g 6.1f² 7.6m⁴ 6.1g⁵ 6g 5.5m³ 6d* 7g* 6g Sep 18] well-made gelding: useful handicapper: won at Haydock and Chester (by 1¼ lengths from Fast Dancer), both in September: effective at 6f to 1m: acts on polytrack, firm and soft going: has worn headgear: none too resolute. *Richard Fahey* **101**

GRAMMAR 6 b.g. Rail Link 132 – Comma (USA) 88 (Kingmambo (USA) 125) [2015 12.1f 12.1m 11.5s⁶ 12.4g Aug 31] poor handicapper: stays 1½m: acts on firm and soft going: usually wears headgear. *David Thompson* **43**

GRAMS AND OUNCES 8 b.g. Royal Applause 124 – Ashdown Princess (IRE) (King's Theatre (IRE) 128) [2015 11.8d⁶ 8.1m 8.3m⁵ p16f⁵ 13.1m* 17.2g² 15.8s p10g⁵ p13.3g² p12g Dec 20] strong gelding: fair handicapper: won at Bath in September: left Adrian Wintle after fourth start: stays 17f: acts on polytrack, soft and good to firm going: tried in cheekpieces in 2015: sometimes wears tongue tie: often starts slowly. *Grace Harris* **70**

GRAN CANARIA QUEEN 6 b.m. Compton Place 125 – Ex Mill Lady 60 (Bishop of Cashel 122) [2015 89: 5d 5.5g⁴ 6g* 6.1g² 6m* 6g* 6m 6g⁵ 5.6d 6g 6d Oct 23] fairly useful handicapper: won at Ripon, York and Pontefract in May/June: well below form last 3 starts: stays 6f: acts on polytrack, soft and good to firm going: has worn headgear. *Tim Easterby* **98**

GRANDAD CHUNK (IRE) 4 gr.c. Acclamation 118 – Silverdreammachine (IRE) 51 (Marju (IRE) 127) [2015 f7g⁵ Dec 29] twice-raced maiden: off 31 months, fifth of 6 to Karmadal at Southwell. *Tracy Waggott* —

GRANDAD'S WORLD (IRE) 3 b.g. Kodiac 112 – Nose One's Way (IRE) 57 (Revoque (IRE) 122) [2015 88p: 6s* 5s⁵ 6f 6g² 6m 6m 6m⁶ Aug 8] lengthy gelding: useful handicapper: won at Pontefract (by ¾ length from Geordie George) in April: best effort when second at York (1½ lengths behind Twilight Son) in June: stays 6f: acts on soft going: tried in hood. *Richard Fahey* **106**

GRAND BEAUTY (IRE) 3 ch.f. Kheleyf (USA) 116 – Grand Zafeen 86 (Zafeen (FR) 123) [2015 82p: 5g³ 5g² 5g* 5f* 5m Oct 3] fairly useful performer: won maiden at Newcastle and handicap at Bath (by 2¼ lengths from Red Stripes) in September: best form at 5f: acts on firm going: front runner/races prominently, often travels strongly. *Robert Cowell* **92**

436

GRAND CANYON (IRE) 3 b.g. High Chaparral (IRE) 132 – Cleide da Silva (USA) 84 **71 p**
(Monarchos (USA) 129) [2015 73p: 10g⁵ 9.9m⁴ Jun 7] lengthy gelding: fair form in
maidens: fourth of 9 to Keble at Goodwood last start, not unduly punished: capable of
better. *Ralph Beckett*

GRAND DEPART 3 b.f. Royal Applause 124 – Path of Peace 86 (Rock of Gibraltar (IRE) **55**
133) [2015 –: 7m 7.1m⁴ 8g 9.9m Jun 23] modest maiden: best effort at 7f, probably stays
1¼m: acts on good to firm going: usually in headgear in 2015. *James Bethell*

GRAND DIAMOND (IRE) 11 b.g. Grand Lodge (USA) 125 – Winona (IRE) 120 **–**
(Alzao (USA) 117) [2015 62: 14g 15s 13.1d 13.1g⁶ Jul 20] good-bodied gelding: fair at
best, no form in 2015: often in cheekpieces prior to 2015: sometimes slowly away, usually
races in rear. *Jim Goldie*

GRANDEST 4 b.g. Dansili 127 – Angara 119 (Alzao (USA) 117) [2015 87: p8g⁶ 8m 8g **80**
7.5g 8d 7d t8.6f⁵ Nov 20] fairly useful handicapper: left Roger Charlton after first start:
best effort at 7f: acts on fibresand and good to firm going: tried in cheekpieces prior to
2015: often starts slowly, usually races in rear. *Brian Ellison*

GRANDEUR (IRE) 6 gr.g. Verglas (IRE) 118 – Misskinta (IRE) 81 (Desert Sun 120) **113**
[2015 120: p10f⁴ p10g³ 9g⁵ 9.9g⁴ 10d⁶ 10.3m⁴ Sep 10] rather unfurnished gelding: smart
performer: won 10 times during career: third in Winter Derby at Lingfield (¾ length
behind Tryster) in March: 3½ lengths fourth of 10 to Blue Waltz in handicap at Doncaster
final start: stayed 1½m: acted on polytrack and firm going: wore cheekpieces: retired.
Jeremy Noseda

GRAND FACILE 3 b.g. Henrythenavigator (USA) 131 – Santolina (USA) 101 (Boundary **61**
(USA) 117) [2015 8g 8.3g 8.3m p10m p12g⁴ p15.8g⁴ p15.8g* Dec 20] strong gelding:
modest handicapper: won at Lingfield in December: stays 2m: acts on polytrack: often in
headgear. *Gary Moore*

GRAND INQUISITOR 3 b.c. Dansili 127 – Dusty Answer 97 (Zafonic (USA) 130) **102**
[2015 8m 8.3d* 7.1m* 8d⁵ 8g⁵ 7g³ Sep 26] 250,000Y: good-topped colt: half-brother to
several winners, including 2-y-o 7f/1m winner (stays 10.4f) Flag Officer (by Dubai
Destination) and 10.5f winner Counterclaim (by Pivotal), both useful: dam 2-y-o 7f
winner: useful performer: won maiden at Nottingham in May and handicap at Sandown in
June: good third in handicap at Newmarket (¾ length behind Mr Win) in September: stays
8.5f: acts on good to firm and good to soft going. *Sir Michael Stoute*

GRAND LIAISON 6 b.m. Sir Percy 129 – Dancinginthedark (IRE) 60 (Fasliyev (USA) **76**
120) [2015 65: t12.2m* 10.3d* 10.4g⁵ p12g 12g³ 9.8g⁵ 14d Sep 4] medium-sized mare: fair
handicapper: won at Wolverhampton in April and Doncaster in May: stays 1½m: acts on
polytrack, tapeta and heavy going: often races towards rear. *John Berry*

GRAND MEISTER 4 gr.g. Mastercraftsman (IRE) 129 – Wait It Out (USA) (Swain **87**
(IRE) 134) [2015 86: 9.9m³ 10.4s t12.2f² t13.9g* p15.8g⁴ Dec 28] big gelding: fairly
useful handicapper: won at Wolverhampton (by ½ length from Cahill) in December: stays
2m: acts on polytrack, tapeta, good to firm and good to soft going. *John Quinn*

GRAND PROPOSAL 3 gr.g. Exceed And Excel (AUS) 126 – Si Belle (IRE) 95 **53**
(Dalakhani (IRE) 133) [2015 71, a63: 8f 7m p7g⁶ p7g Dec 30] modest maiden: left Jim
Boyle after second start: stays 7.5f: acts on polytrack, good to firm and good to soft going:
tried in cheekpieces prior to 2015: often starts slowly, often races in rear. *Mike Murphy*

GRAND SPIRIT (IRE) 3 b.g. Lord Shanakill (USA) 121 – Spirit Watch (IRE) 70 **84**
(Invincible Spirit (IRE) 121) [2015 85p: p7m⁴ 8m 8.1m 8.3m⁵ 6g 6m t7.1m* p7g Oct 7]
fairly useful handicapper: won at Wolverhampton (by neck from Faintly) in September:
stays 7f: acts on polytrack, tapeta and good to soft going: blinkered last 4 starts: sold
22,000 gns, sent to Macau. *Luca Cumani*

GRANITA (USA) 2 b.f. (Jan 15) Blame (USA) 129 – Youre So Sweet (USA) (Storm Cat **63**
(USA)) [2015 6g⁴ 7g p7g Oct 29] good-topped filly: third foal: half-sister to winner abroad
by Dixie Union: dam unraced half-sister to Derby winner Kris Kin: modest form when
fourth to Sunflower in maiden at Windsor: well held both subsequent starts. *Lady Cecil*

GRANITE CITY DOC 2 b.g. (Apr 3) Arabian Gleam 122 – Hansomis (IRE) 73 (Titus **–**
Livius (FR) 115) [2015 7.2s 6g 7g⁶ Aug 31] no form. *Lucy Normile*

GRAN MAESTRO (USA) 6 ch.g. Medicean 128 – Red Slippers (USA) 111 (Nureyev **79**
(USA) 131) [2015 81: 12.1m³ 11.8d² 16m³ 14d³ Sep 4] fair handicapper: should prove best
at short of 2m: acts on any turf going: usually wears headgear: usually in tongue tie in
2015: usually races prominently. *Dr Richard Newland*

GRANOLA 3 b.f. Makfi 130 – Common Knowledge (Rainbow Quest (USA) 134) [2015 **62**
55: f6d 8g* 8v⁵ 7.2g t8.6f⁴ t9.5m Nov 28] modest handicapper: won at Wetherby in July:
stays 8.5f: acts on tapeta. *David Brown*

GRAPEVINE (IRE) 2 b.c. (Mar 20) Lilbourne Lad (IRE) 111 – High Vintage (IRE) 97 **72 p**
(High Chaparral (IRE) 132) [2015 7s⁵ 7g 7d Oct 30] €28,000F, 40,000Y: lengthy colt:
second foal: half-brother to 1¼m winner Nice Vintage (by Big Bad Bob): dam, 1¼m
winner who stayed 1½m, closely related to useful 5f/5.5f winner Lisselan Diva: fair form
in maidens at Newbury and Newmarket first/final starts: type to do better at 3 yrs.
Charles Hills

GRAPHIC (IRE) 6 ch.g. Excellent Art 125 – Follow My Lead 72 (Night Shift (USA)) **116**
[2015 116: t8.6m* a8f Mar 28] rangy gelding: smart performer: at least as good as ever
when winning 5-runner minor event at Wolverhampton in February by length from
Diescentric, driven out: switched to dirt, well-held last of 15 behind Tamarkuz in
Godolphin Mile at Meydan: stays 8.6f: acts on polytrack, tapeta, good to firm and heavy
going: wears cheekpieces/blinkers: front runner/races prominently. *William Haggas*

GRASS ROOTS 3 gr.g. Pastoral Pursuits 127 – Southern Psychic (USA) (Alwasmi (USA) **–**
115) [2015 –p: 7m 7m 8d⁶ 7m Jun 27] little form: sold 6,000 gns, sent to Italy. *Charles Hills*

GRATZIE 4 b.f. Three Valleys (USA) 119 – La Gazzetta (IRE) 59 (Rossini (USA) 118) **100**
[2015 90: 8m⁴ 8.5g* 8.3m⁴ 8d⁵ 7m 8.1m 8d Sep 4] good-topped filly: useful handicapper:
won at Epsom (by neck from Merry Me) in June: best effort when fourth in listed race
at Windsor (2½ lengths behind Kodi Bear) in June: stays 8.5f: acts on firm going.
Mick Channon

GRAVITY FLOW (IRE) 2 ch.f. (Apr 22) Exceed And Excel (AUS) 126 – Landela 64 **77 p**
(Alhaarth (IRE) 126) [2015 6g² p7g² Sep 21] £165,000Y: seventh foal: closely related to
winner up to 1m Impendor (by Holy Roman Emperor) and half-sister to winner up to 9f
Get A Grip (2-y-o 1m winner, by Royal Applause) and 1m/8.6f winner Trumpington Street
(by Noverre), both useful: dam twice-raced half-sister to very smart 1¼m-1½m winner
Zambezi Sun: fair form when second in maidens at Windsor and Kempton in September,
beaten 3¼ lengths by Queen's Trust in latter: open to further improvement. *William Haggas*

GREAT AND SMALL 2 b.f. (Jun 1) Galileo (IRE) 134 – Gryada 93 (Shirley Heights **– p**
130) [2015 p8g Dec 15] sister to 1¼m winner (stayed easy 1¾m) Gaze and closely related
to several winners, including Irish Derby/Gold Cup winner Fame And Glory (2-y-o
1m-1¼m winner, by Montjeu) and useful 1¼m-1½m winner Rain Forest (by Sadler's Wells):
dam 2-y-o 7f/1m winner: 14/1, green when eighth in maiden at Kempton (8 lengths behind
Cajoled) in December: should do better given time and longer distances. *Andrew Balding*

GREAT COLACI 2 b.g. (Mar 5) Sulamani (IRE) 130 – Fairlie 70 (Halling (USA) 133) **–**
[2015 7g 7g 8s Oct 16] no form. *Keith Reveley*

GREAT DEMEANOR (USA) 5 b.g. Bernstein (USA) 115 – Hangin Withmy Buds **–**
(USA) (Roar (USA) 116) [2015 70: f7g t7.1m t8.6g 7.2d 9.1g Jul 6] fairly useful at best,
no form in 2015: tried in headgear. *Dianne Sayer*

GREATEST HITS (USA) 3 b.c. Cape Cross (IRE) 129 – Northern Melody (IRE) **–**
(Singspiel (IRE) 133) [2015 87p: 8s Oct 23] strong, attractive colt: fairly useful winner in
2014: well held only outing in 2015: sent to UAE. *John Gosden*

GREATEST JOURNEY 3 ch.g. Raven's Pass (USA) 133 – Sensationally 77 (Montjeu **98**
(IRE) 137) [2015 93p: p8g* p7f³ 10g² 8m⁵ May 2] useful handicapper: won at Kempton
(by 2¼ lengths from Gleaming Girl) in January: third at Lingfield (3¼ lengths behind Four
Seasons) in March and second in valuable sales race at Newmarket (neck behind Cape
Clear Island) in April: stays 1¼m: acts on polytrack and tapeta: tried in headgear: often
travels strongly. *Saeed bin Suroor*

GREATEST PLACE (IRE) 3 ch.f. Shamardal (USA) 129 – Texas Tammy (USA) **–**
(Seeking The Gold (USA)) [2015 p10f^pu Oct 28] closely related to very smart US Grade 2
1m/9f winner (stays 1¼m) Cowboy Cal (by Giant's Causeway) and half-sister to 3 winners:
dam once-raced half-sister to top-class US Grade 1 9f/1¼m winner Behrens: 6/4, pulled up
(reportedly suffered breathing problem) in maiden at Chelmsford on debut: clearly thought
capable of better. *Saeed bin Suroor*

GREAT EXPECTATIONS 7 b.g. Storming Home 128 – Fresh Fruit Daily 92 (Reprimand **79**
122) [2015 82: p8g⁴ p10g³ p10g⁵ p8m⁶ p8f⁶ p8g³ 8.3d³ 7m³ 7d⁵ 7m 6.1m 6.1m² 6g⁵ 6d³ 6m* **a70**
6s⁵ 6d* 5.7g⁴ p6f⁶ p6g⁴ p6m p7g⁶ Dec 28] compact gelding: fair handicapper: won at
Lingfield in August and Brighton in September: stays 1¼m: acts on polytrack, fibresand,
good to firm and heavy going: usually in headgear in 2015: sometimes wears tongue tie:
often races towards rear. *J. R. Jenkins*

GREAT FUN 4 b.g. Kyllachy 129 – Have Fun (Indian Ridge 123) [2015 7g* p7g² p6g³ **88**
7m² p7g⁴ Sep 5] 24,000F, £40,000Y: seventh foal: half-brother to 7f winner Nice Dream
(by Oasis Dream) and 6f winner Enjoyment (by Dansili): dam, 7.5f-11f winner, half-sister
to winner up to 1½m Day Or Night and winner up to 9f Pipette, both useful: fairly useful
performer: won maiden at Wetherby (by ½ length from Dark Red) in April: second in
handicaps at Kempton in May and Wetherby in July: likely to stay 1m: acts on polytrack.
Brian Meehan

GREAT GLEN 3 b.g. High Chaparral (IRE) 132 – Grand Opening (IRE) 108 (Desert **101**
King (IRE) 129) [2015 86p: 10m² 11g⁴ 16f Jun 19] attractive gelding: useful form: fourth
in listed race at Goodwood (2¾ lengths behind Storm The Stars) in May: tenth of 13 to
Aloft in Queen's Vase at Royal Ascot final start, probably would have benefited from
stronger gallop: gelded after: bred to be suited by at least 1½m. *Ralph Beckett*

GREAT HALL 5 b.g. Halling (USA) 133 – L'Affaire Monique 101 (Machiavellian (USA) **105 §**
123) [2015 107: 12m⁴ 11.9g 14m³ 14g 13.4m 14d Sep 5] rather leggy gelding: useful
handicapper: third at York (1¼ lengths behind Astronercus) in July: left John Quinn after
fifth start: stays 14.5f: acts on good to firm and good to soft going: sometimes wears
headgear: often races towards rear: ungenuine: fairly useful hurdler. *Kevin Frost*

GREAT MINDS (IRE) 5 ch.g. Bahamian Bounty 116 – Raja (IRE) 87 (Pivotal 124) **116**
[2015 109p: 6v⁴ 6d* 5s* 5g 5d⁵ 6d Oct 17] tall gelding: smart performer: won listed races
at Cork (by 2½ lengths from Bold Thady Quill) and Naas (by ¾ length from Musical
Comedy), both in April: below form after, though won disgraced when fifth of 12 to Sole
Power in Flying Five Stakes at the Curragh: effective at 5f/6f: raced only on good going or
softer. *T. Stack, Ireland*

GREAT ORDER (USA) 2 b.c. (Feb 16) Distorted Humor (USA) 117 – Michita (USA) **91 p**
113 (Dynaformer (USA)) [2015 7g⁴ Sep 25] third foal: half-brother to 1m-9.5f winner
Thatchmaster (by Street Cry): dam, winner up to 1½m (2-y-o 1m winner), sister to very
smart 10.3f-1¾m winner Willing Foe and smart winner up to 11f Cat O'Mountain: 2/1,
shaped well when 2½ lengths fourth of 16 to Crazy Horse in maiden at Newmarket on
debut, running on without being knocked about: sure to progress. *Saeed bin Suroor*

GREAT PAGE (IRE) 2 b.f. (Jan 16) Roderic O'Connor (IRE) 119 – Areeda (IRE) 77 **102**
(Refuse To Bend (IRE) 128) [2015 5m* 5m² 6d* 6m⁴ 5.2m 6d² 7g* 7d 7g⁵ Sep 25]
€35,000Y: quite attractive filly: second foal: dam 7f winner out of 2-y-o 6f winner (stayed
1m) Raindancing: useful performer: won maiden at Windsor in April, listed race at Naas
(by 3 lengths from Special Focus) in June and Prix du Calvados at Deauville (by neck from
Marenko) in August: second in Princess Margaret Stakes at Ascot (3 lengths behind
Besharah) in July: well held last 2 starts: stays 7f: acts on good to firm and good to soft
going. *Richard Hannon*

GREAT PARK (IRE) 3 br.c. Vale of York (IRE) 117 – Telesina (ITY) (Marju (IRE) 127) **106**
[2015 86: 8f³ 8m* 8f² 10s* Jul 24] close-coupled colt: useful handicapper: won at
Newmarket (by neck from Dagher) in June and Ascot (by length from Master of Finance)
in July: stays 1¼m: acts on firm and soft going: responds generously to pressure: sent to
Hong Kong, where renamed Packing Genius. *Martyn Meade*

GREAT THOUGHTS (IRE) 2 ch.f. (Apr 1) Iffraaj 127 – Fascination (IRE) 76 (Galileo **–**
(IRE) 134) [2015 8.3d 8v Oct 24] 40,000Y: first foal: dam, maiden (stayed 1½m), half-
sister to smart 1¼m-1½m winner (stayed 2m) Drill Sergeant out of useful 9f-1½m winner
Dolydille: behind in maidens at Nottingham and Newbury. *David Simcock*

GREEB 4 b.g. Oasis Dream 129 – Shamtari (IRE) (Alhaarth (IRE) 126) [2015 91: 6.1m² **103**
6m 6.1m* 6m Aug 1] useful handicapper: won at Nottingham (by short head from
Lexington Abbey) in July: raced only at 6f: acts on good to firm going: sent to UAE.
Charles Hills

GREEK ISLANDS (IRE) 7 b.g. Oasis Dream 129 – Serisia (FR) 107 (Exit To Nowhere **58**
(USA) 122) [2015 64: p8f⁶ 7g p8m³ p8g p8g 10.2m* 8g² 11.7s⁶ 8m f8g t8.6f⁶ t8.6g* **a70**
p8f* Dec 17] good-topped gelding: fair performer: won handicaps at Bath in July and
Wolverhampton and Chelmsford in December: stays 1¼m: acts on polytrack, tapeta, good
to firm and good to soft going: has worn headgear: often travels strongly. *Neil Mulholland*

GREELEYS LOVE (USA) 5 ch.g. Mr Greeley (USA) 122 – Aunt Winnie (IRE) **77**
(Deputy Minister (CAN)) [2015 64, a70: t9.5f² t12.2f⁵ Feb 23] fair performer: stays 1½m:
acts on polytrack, tapeta, firm and good to soft going: sometimes wears headgear: tried
in tongue tie prior to 2015: often starts slowly: sent to Belgium, where won 4 times.
Luke Dace

DFS Park Hill Stakes, Doncaster—
a trio of progressive fillies fight out the finish as Gretchen (left) beats Melodious (stripes) and Asyad

GREEN DOOR (IRE) 4 b.g. Camacho 118 – Inourhearts (IRE) 111 (Pips Pride 117) **116**
[2015 107: p5g⁶ 5.2m³ 5g 6f 5m 5d* Sep 22] attractive gelding: smart performer: better
than ever when winning 6-runner minor event at Beverley in September by 6 lengths from
Pipers Note, unchallenged: left Olly Stevens after fourth start: best form at 5f: acts on
polytrack, firm and good to soft going: often in headgear (visored first time at Beverley).
Robert Cowell

GREEN DU CIEL (FR) 10 gr.g. Smadoun (FR) 111 – Sucre Blanc (FR) (Green Tune –
(USA) 125) [2015 63: 12m Jun 9] well beaten only start on Flat in 2015: has worn
cheekpieces/tongue tie: poor hurdler/modest chaser. *Brian Barr*

GREENFYRE (IRE) 2 b.f. (Mar 15) Kodiac 112 – Miss Chaumiere 60 (Selkirk (USA) **73**
129) [2015 6m² 6m 7m⁴ 6.5m 6d Sep 21] €13,000F, 72,000Y: good-topped filly: first foal:
dam, maiden (stayed 8.3f), sister to smart 1m-1¾m winner (stayed 2m) Moyenne
Corniche: fair maiden: second at Newbury on debut but failed to progress: should stay 7f:
acts on good to firm going. *Richard Hannon*

GREENGAGE SUMMER 4 b.f. Sixties Icon 125 – Linda Green 82 (Victory Note –
(USA) 120) [2015 68: p8f 11.7f Apr 17] angular filly: maiden: no form in 2015: stays 7f:
sometimes slowly away, usually races in rear. *Seamus Mullins*

GREENHEAD HIGH 7 b.g. Statue of Liberty (USA) 115 – Artistry 69 (Night Shift (USA)) **49**
[2015 63, a70: f6d⁵ f5g⁴ f6s Jan 20] leggy gelding: poor performer: stays 6f: acts on polytrack, fibresand, good to firm and heavy going: sometimes wears headgear. *David Nicholls*

GREEN HOWARD 7 ch.g. Bahamian Bounty 116 – Dash of Lime 67 (Bold Edge 123) **94**
[2015 100: 7m⁴ 7m 7f 7d 8g² 8g⁵ 7.6s Sep 12] fairly useful handicapper: second at Ripon
in August: stays 1m: acts on soft and good to firm going: tried in cheekpieces. *Rebecca
Bastiman*

GREEN LIGHT 4 b.g. Authorized (IRE) 133 – May Light 62 (Midyan (USA) 124) [2015 **95**
90: 10.2s* 10.3f⁴ 10.4m 10m⁴ 10d 10.2v¹ 12d³ 12v Nov 7] lengthy gelding: useful
handicapper: won at Nottingham (by ½ length from Kinema) in May: shaped well several
times subsequently, including when close third to Argus at Doncaster: stays 1½m: acts on
firm and soft going: visored last 2 starts: held up. *Ralph Beckett*

GREEN NOMAD 3 b.c. Green Horizon – Fontaine Way (Nomadic Way (USA) 104) –
[2015 10.2m 12s⁶ Jul 24] no form. *Michael Appleby*

GREEN PASTURES (IRE) 7 b.g. Diamond Green (FR) 121 – Continuous (IRE) 89 –
(Darshaan 133) [2015 f11g Feb 26] little form in maidens/handicaps. *John Wade*

GREENSIDE 4 b.c. Dubawi (IRE) 129 – Katrina (IRE) (Ela-Mana-Mou 132) [2015 81p: **97**
8d* p8f Nov 19] useful form: won handicap at Newmarket (by 5 lengths from Tatting) in
October: possibly found pace coming too soon when always behind in similar event at
Chelmsford: will prove suited by 1¼m+. *Henry Candy*

GREEN TORNADO (IRE) 3 b.g. Equiano (FR) 127 – Loch Verdi 108 (Green Desert **69**
(USA) 127) [2015: p6m⁵ Jan 24] fair maiden: improved form though seen to full
advantage when ¾-length fifth to Justice First in handicap at Lingfield, only outing in 2015:
gelded after: best effort at 6f. *Ralph Beckett*

440

GREEN ZONE (IRE) 4 b.g. Bushranger (IRE) 119 – Incense 73 (Unfuwain (USA) 131) **68**
[2015 81: 8s 8.3s⁴ 8m 9.2d 10.1m 9g 8.9g⁴ 10.1g² 10.2m 9.9g⁴ 10g 10d Oct 26] good-
topped gelding: fair handicapper: stays 1¼m: acts on soft and good to firm going: usually
wears cheekpieces: tried in tongue tie in 2015. *Nigel Tinkler*

GREGARIOUS (IRE) 2 gr.g. (Mar 5) Big Bad Bob (IRE) 118 – Sense of Greeting (IRE) **76**
46 (Key of Luck (USA) 126) [2015 7d³ p8g⁴ Nov 18] €40,000 2-y-o: workmanlike gelding:
second foal: half-brother to 5f winner Camanche Grey (by Camacho): dam, maiden (stayed
8.5f), half-sister to smart 5f/6f winner Tiger Royal: fair form when in frame in maidens at
Newmarket in October and Kempton in November: has been gelded. *Lucy Wadham*

GREGORI (IRE) 5 b.g. Invincible Spirit (IRE) 121 – Three Wrens (IRE) 99 (Second **–**
Empire (IRE) 124) [2015 90: p5g p5g Mar 27] compact gelding: fairly useful at best, no
form in 2015: stays 7f: acts on polytrack and good to firm going: sometimes wears
cheekpieces: usually wears tongue tie. *Brian Meehan*

GRENADE 3 b.g. Paco Boy (IRE) 129 – Amira 70 (Efisio 120) [2015 70: 6d⁴ 5g⁶ 6m 5m⁵ **57**
5g 5f⁵ 5m⁶ 5d⁴ 5g 5m 7d Oct 26] modest maiden: stays 7f: acts on good to firm and good
to soft going: tried in headgear in 2015: often races towards rear. *Patrick Holmes*

GRENDISAR (IRE) 5 b.h. Invincible Spirit (IRE) 121 – Remarkable Story (Mark of **115**
Esteem (IRE) 137) [2015 116: p10f* p10g² p10f³ a9.9g⁵ p10f⁴ p12g⁵ p10m² p10g² Dec 19]
strong horse: smart performer: won listed race at Lingfield (by short head from Lamar) in
February: runner-up 3 times there, in Winter Derby in March (¾ length behind Tryster) and
in listed races in November (¾ length behind Let's Go) and December (neck behind Don't
Be): stays 1½m: acts on polytrack: usually wears cheekpieces: often races towards rear,
usually travels strongly. *Marco Botti*

GRETCHEN 3 ch.f. Galileo (IRE) 134 – Dolores 111 (Danehill (USA) 126) [2015 12m* **109 p**
12f⁵ 12m 12g* 14.6m* Sep 10] half-sister to several winners, including very smart
1¼m-1¾m winner (stayed 2m) Duncan (by Dalakhani), smart 1¾m-2¼m winner Samuel
(by Sakhee) and useful 2-y-o 1m winner Deirdre (by Dubawi): dam 1m winner: useful
performer: won maiden at Newmarket (by 1¾ lengths from Forever Popular) in May, listed
race at Newmarket (by nose from Sahrawi) in August and Park Hill Stakes at Doncaster (by
neck from Melodious, showing good attitude) in September: will stay 2m: acts on firm
going: open to further improvement. *John Gosden*

GREY DESTINY 5 gr.g. Desideratum 118 – Mother Corrigan (IRE) 64 (Paris House 123) **62**
[2015 60: f8s⁶ 8d⁵ 6g² 6m³ 7m 6g* 6s 6g⁴ 7d t7.1f⁴ f7g³ t6f² t7.1m⁵ f7m² f7g* Dec 12] **a75**
fair performer: won seller at Catterick in July and handicap at Southwell in December:
stays 7f: acts on fibresand, best turf form on good going: usually in cheekpieces in 2015:
often starts slowly, usually races nearer last than first, often races freely. *Antony Brittain*

GREYEMKAY 7 gr.g. Fair Mix (IRE) 123 – Magic Orb 81 (Primo Dominie 121) [2015 **49**
70: t9.5f t9.5f⁵ t9.5f⁵ p11f 11.7f 10.2g 8f 8.3m 8.1s Jul 24] poor handicapper: stays 1¼m:
acts on polytrack, good to firm and heavy going: tried in headgear. *Richard Price*

GREYFRIARSCHORISTA 8 ch.g. King's Best (USA) 132 – Misty Heights 105 **79**
(Fasliyev (USA) 120) [2015 94: p6f p6f⁶ p6m* 8d] tall, angular gelding: fair performer:
won claimer at Southwell in December: stays 9.5f: acts on fibresand and firm going: tried
in headgear: often in tongue tie in 2015: often races prominently. *Giles Bravery*

GREY GEM (IRE) 4 gr.g. Danehill Dancer (IRE) 117 – Tiffany Diamond (IRE) 101 **63**
(Sadler's Wells (USA) 132) [2015 t12.2g⁴ 7d 11.5d³ p12m² 12m⁵ 11m⁶ p12g⁴ p12g⁵ p12g **a70**
9s t12.2g⁵ t16.5f Oct 27] fair maiden: stays 1½m: acts on polytrack and tapeta: front
runner/races prominently. *Sylvester Kirk*

GREY MIRAGE 6 b.g. Oasis Dream 129 – Grey Way (USA) 109 (Cozzene (USA)) **109**
[2015 109: p7f² p7f² t7.1m⁵ p8f* p7g* p8f f7g Dec 12] lengthy, good-topped gelding:
useful performer: won AW Mile Championships Stakes at Lingfield (by neck from
Sovereign Debt) in April: also ran well when second in handicap there (head behind
Baddilini) on second outing: stays 8.5f: acts on all-weather, good to firm and heavy going:
often wears headgear. *Marco Botti*

GREY MORNING 2 gr.c. (Feb 18) Zebedee 113 – Break of Dawn (USA) (Mt Livermore **87 p**
(USA)) [2015 6g 6g² 7.2m* p7m³ Oct 21] 11,000F, £48,000Y: seventh foal: half-brother to
3 winners, including winner up to 9f Maremmasanta (2-y-o 5f-7.5f winner, by Kodiac) and
7f winner Whitstable Native (by Bertolini): dam unraced: fairly useful performer: won
maiden at Musselburgh in September: good third in nursery at Kempton in October: stays
7f: sent to Hong Kong: will go on improving. *William Haggas*

GREY ODYSSEY 4 gr.g. Verglas (IRE) 118 – Reading Habit (USA) (Half A Year (USA) –
130) [2015 –: p12g p8g Jan 22] lengthy gelding: maiden: no form in 2015: best effort at
1¼m: best form on good to firm going: in tongue tie in 2015, also in cheekpieces final start.
Dean Ivory

GREY'S ANGEL 3 gr.f. Notnowcato 128 – Kryena 72 (Kris 135) [2015 t8.6g³ t9.5g² **71**
t8.6f² t12.2m² t12.2g² 12.1m² p10m² 12.1m⁵ 11.9d p10f p16g³ Nov 4] 4,000Y: sixth foal:
half-sister to 5f/6f winner Luckyreno (by Kyllachy) and winner up to 1m Haafkry (2-y-o
6f winner, by Haafhd): dam maiden: fair maiden: stays 1½m: acts on polytrack and good
to firm going. *Philip McBride*

GRIFFIN STREET 2 gr.g. (Apr 8) Zebedee 113 – Twilight Belle (IRE) 53 (Fasliyev **35**
(USA) 120) [2015 5m⁴ 5g 5d⁴ 6m⁶ 5m⁶ 5d 5d⁵ f6g⁶ Nov 12] poor maiden: best effort at 5f:
acts on good to firm and good to soft going: tried in hood. *Iain Jardine*

GRIGOLO 3 b.c. Shamardal (USA) 129 – Dubai Opera (USA) (Dubai Millennium 140) –
[2015 85: 10.3dᵖᵘ Sep 26] fairly useful handicapper: fatally injured at Chester: stayed 1m:
acted on good to firm going: front runner/raced prominently. *Mark Johnston*

GRISSOM (IRE) 9 b.g. Desert Prince (IRE) 130 – Misty Peak (IRE) 83 (Sri Pekan (USA) **94**
117) [2015 92: 6g 7v 7d² 6g⁴ 7.2d⁴ 6d 6m² 6d⁵ 6g⁴ 6g⁶ 6d 6s* 6g 6g³ Sep 26] small gelding:
fairly useful handicapper: won at Thirsk (by 4 lengths from Orion's Bow) in September:
stays 7.5f: acts on good to firm and heavy going: tried in tongue tie prior to 2015.
Tim Easterby

GRIZZLY BEAR 2 b.g. (Jan 24) Kodiac 112 – Pearl Magic (USA) (Speightstown (USA) **69**
124) [2015 5g³ 6m 6d 7m 7g³ Oct 21] small gelding: fair maiden: stays 7f: acts on good to
firm going: tried in cheekpieces: withdrawn before intended debut after giving trouble in
stalls: sent to Greece. *Jeremy Noseda*

GROOR 3 b.c. Archipenko (USA) 127 – Alta Moda (Sadler's Wells (USA) 132) [2015 90: **93**
10g 9.9g⁶ p11g⁶ Sep 23] fairly useful handicapper: stays 1¼m: acts on good to firm going:
blinkered final start: sold 20,000 gns, sent to Qatar. *James Tate*

GROOVEJET 4 b.f. Cockney Rebel (IRE) 127 – Vino Veritas (USA) 72 (Chief's Crown **102**
(USA)) [2015 105: 10.2m 14m⁶ 14m 16.4d 14.6m⁵ 16g p13g Oct 29] sturdy mare: useful
performer: stays 14.5f: acts on polytrack, fibresand, good to firm and heavy going: often
races prominently. *Dave Morris*

GROSMONT 3 br.g. Hellvelyn 118 – Aimee's Delight 85 (Robellino (USA) 127) [2015 **67 §**
73: f5s³ t6g* p5f⁶ p6f² p6m⁵ p7f⁶ t6g² 7.5m⁵ 6.5m⁵ 7m t6g f6m Dec 8] fair performer:
won maiden at Wolverhampton in January: stays 7.5f: acts on all-weather and good to firm
going: in headgear in 2015: usually races towards rear: not straightforward and best treated
with caution. *James Given*

GROUNDBREAKING 5 b.g. New Approach (IRE) 132 – Ladeena (IRE) 80 (Dubai **100**
Millennium 140) [2015 107: a9.4f 10f Jun 20] good-topped gelding: useful handicapper:
looked reluctant when 5 lengths twelfth of 13 to Mahsoob in Wolferton Handicap at Royal
Ascot final outing: stays 1½m: acts on firm going: in hood last 2 starts: often starts slowly,
usually races nearer last than first: joined John Ferguson. *Charlie Appleby*

Betfred Cesarewitch (Heritage Handicap), Newmarket—
Grumeti causes a 50/1 shock in a typically open renewal of this historic marathon, narrowly
beating the gambled-on Oriental Fox (spots on cap) and Irish raiders Quick Jack (white cap) and
Renneti (right); winning jockey Adam Beschizza had also won the first leg of the 'autumn double',
the Cambridgeshire, on Third Time Lucky two weeks earlier

GROUND CONTROL (IRE) 2 b.c. (Feb 21) Air Chief Marshal (IRE) 115 – Maya de **94**
La Luz (Selkirk (USA) 129) [2015 5d⁵ 6m⁴ 5m² 7f⁵ 7m 6g* 6.5m 6s² Oct 23] €8,500F,
£12,000Y: fourth foal: dam, 7f-9.5f winner, half-sister to smart 9f-1¼m winner Minakshi:
fairly useful performer: won maiden at Salisbury (by 4 lengths from Clodianna) in August:
best effort when neck second of 8 to Tawdheef in nursery at Newbury final start: should
prove as effective back at 7f: acts on firm and soft going: often races prominently.
Richard Hannon

GROUND DEPENDENT (IRE) 2 ch.c. (Apr 27) Art Connoisseur (IRE) 121 – Ipanema **–**
Beach 67 (Lion Cavern (USA) 117) [2015 7g Oct 3] 100/1, well held in maiden at Redcar:
sent to Greece. *David C. Griffiths*

GROUND DOVE 2 b.f. (Mar 4) Showcasing 117 – Tenable (Polish Precedent (USA) 131) **59**
[2015 6v⁴ p7g Nov 18] 5,000F, £20,000Y, 42,000 2-y-o: half-sister to 3 winners, including
1m-9.5f winner Milla's Rocket (by Galileo) and 6f (including at 2 yrs) winner Armour
(by Azamour): dam unraced half-sister to very smart 1¼m-13.4f winner Day Flight: better
effort when fourth in maiden at Doncaster (6¼ lengths behind Sainted) in November,
considerably handled: sold 7,000 gns, sent to Saudi Arabia. *Olly Stevens*

GROUNDWORKER (IRE) 4 b.g. Tagula (IRE) 116 – Notepad 63 (King's Best (USA) **82**
132) [2015 84: 5m⁶ 5m⁵ 5m⁴ 5.1m 6g* 6m⁴ 6m² 5.2s 5g 5g 5s⁴ 5.7g⁴ Oct 18] compact
gelding: fairly useful handicapper: won at Newbury (apprentice) in July: stays 6f: acts on
soft and good to firm going: usually in tongue tie in 2015: inconsistent. *Sylvester Kirk*

GROWING GLORY (FR) 3 b.f. Orpen (USA) 116 – Trois Rivieres (IRE) (Dr Fong **103**
(USA) 128) [2015 p8g² p8g* 8g⁶ p8f⁶ 7g² 8g³ 8dᵖᵘ 8.7g³ Nov 21] useful performer: won
listed race at Cagnes-sur-Mer (by neck from Djoko) in February: second in listed race at
Maisons-Laffitte (length behind Lady Sybil) in July: stays 1m: acts on polytrack. *Francois
Rohaut, France*

GROWL 3 b.c. Oasis Dream 129 – Desert Tigress (USA) 83 (Storm Cat (USA)) [2015 88: **94**
6d² 6f 6m⁵ 6g 6m⁵ t6f Oct 3] attractive colt: fairly useful performer: fifth in listed race at
Newbury (5¾ lengths behind Adaay) in May: stays 6f: acts on firm and good to soft going:
blinkered final start: usually in tongue tie. *Brian Meehan*

GRUMETI 7 b.g. Sakhee (USA) 136 – Tetravella (IRE) (Groom Dancer (USA) 128) [2015 **97**
12m⁵ 14g 16.4m⁶ 18g* Oct 10] tall, good-topped gelding: useful handicapper (at least
that good as hurdler/chaser): off 3 months, 50/1, back to best when winning 34-runner
Cesarewitch Handicap at Newmarket in October by short head from Oriental Fox, leading
narrowly over 1f out and battling well: stays 2¼m: acts on soft and good to firm going.
Alan King

GRUMPY ANGEL 3 b.f. Exceed And Excel (AUS) 126 – Eye To Eye (Exit To Nowhere **53**
(USA) 122) [2015 –p: 6s³ 6m 6g⁶ Aug 1] modest maiden: best effort at 6f: acts on soft
going: often wears headgear. *Richard Fahey*

GUANABARA BAY (IRE) 2 b.c. (Apr 2) Clodovil (IRE) 116 – Sakaka (Tobougg (IRE) **76**
125) [2015 7m⁵ 6d² 6d² 7d⁶ 6g Oct 8] fair maiden: should stay 7f: acts on good to soft
going. *Martyn Meade*

GUANTOSHOL (IRE) 4 ch.g. Sholokhov (IRE) 121 – Glicine (GER) (Tiger Hill (IRE) **–**
127) [2015 11.6m⁶ 10d Oct 30] leggy gelding: won maiden at Durtal and minor event at
Le Lion-d'Angers in 2014: left A. Couetil, well held both starts in Britain in 2015: stays
1½m: acts on viscoride and soft going. *Venetia Williams*

GUAPO BAY 2 b.f. (Feb 1) Showcasing 117 – Cumana Bay 90 (Dansili 127) [2015 6m 6s³ **61**
6v⁵ p6g⁵ 7s⁵ p6g⁴ p6g⁵ Dec 15] neat filly: second foal: half-sister to 2-y-o 5f/6f winner La
Tinta Bay (by Compton Place): dam winner up to 1m (2-y-o 5f winner) out of useful winner
up to 1m (2-y-o 6f winner) Mayaro Bay: modest maiden: stays 6f: best form on soft/heavy
going: often races towards rear. *Richard Hannon*

GUARACHA 4 ch.g. Halling (USA) 133 – Pachanga (Inchinor 119) [2015 76: p8g 7m 7m **77**
8.5g² 7.5m t8.6g³ 8gᵖ* t8.6m⁴ 8g⁶ 7.9m t9.5g Sep 29] fair handicapper: won at Pontefract
in August: stays 8.5f: acts on tapeta and good to firm going: often wears headgear: often
races prominently. *Clive Brittain*

GUARD OF HONOUR (IRE) 4 b.g. Galileo (IRE) 134 – Queen of France (USA) 95 **96**
(Danehill (USA) 126) [2015 16g³ p15.8g² p16d² 13.1f* 16g² 15s² Oct 25] angular gelding:
useful handicapper: won at Bath in September: second at the Curragh (¾ length behind
Digenta) in October and at Leopardstown (neck behind Silver Concorde) in October:
stays 2m: acts on firm and soft going: in headgear in 2015: usually races towards rear.
George Baker

GUARDS CHAPEL 7 b.g. Motivator 131 – Intaaj (IRE) (Machiavellian (USA) 123) **71**
[2015 69: p15.8g* p13g³ p15.8g* p15.8f³ p15.8g 16d Oct 11] attractive gelding: fair
handicapper: won at Lingfield in January and February: stays 2m: acts on polytrack and
good to firm going: usually wears headgear: usually races in rear. *Gary Moore*

GUIDING LIGHT (IRE) 3 b.g. Acclamation 118 – Venus Rising (Observatory (USA) **96**
131) [2015 74: p7g⁴ 8.1m⁶ 7m⁶ 7.1m* 7.6g⁴ 7.1s* 7g² Jul 30] useful handicapper: won at
Chepstow in June and again (by 11 lengths from Prefect) in July: stays 7f: acts on soft and
good to firm going. *Andrew Balding*

GUILDED ROCK 2 gr.g. (Apr 30) Hellvelyn 118 – Once Removed 65 (Distant Relative –
128) [2015 6m Jun 9] 66/1, very green when well held in maiden at Salisbury. *Stuart Kittow*

GUILIANI (IRE) 4 br.c. Tertullian (USA) 115 – Guadalupe (GER) 113 (Monsun (GER) **116**
124) [2015 8d² 8g* 8g² 8.7g² 9.9g* 8s⁶ 9.9d² 9.9g⁴ Nov 8] seventh foal: half-brother to 3
winners, including smart 11f winner Guantana (by Dynaformer) and useful 1¼m winner
Glee (by Dansili): dam, winner up to 11f (2-y-o 1m winner), sister to high-class 1½m-15f
winner Getaway: smart performer: won listed race at Cologne in May and Grosser
Dallmayr-Preis Bayerisches Zuchtrennen at Munich (by ½ length from Erveda) in July: far
from discredited when last of 6 in Prix du Moulin de Longchamp (3 lengths behind
Ervedya) in September: not at best last 2 starts: stays 1¼m: acts on soft going: races nearer
last than first. *J-P. Carvalho, Germany*

GUILTLESS (USA) 2 b.f. (May 5) Bernardini (USA) 132 – Getaway Girl (USA) (Silver **50**
Deputy (CAN)) [2015 5m 5g⁴ 5m⁶ p6f 7v⁶ p7f Nov 12] $100,000Y: good-topped filly:
sister to a winner in USA, closely related to 2 winners by Malibu Moon and half-sister to
2 winners, including Canadian Grade 3 9f winner Northern Causeway (by Giant's
Causeway): dam, US 4f/5.5f winner, closely related to Breeders' Cup Classic winner
Ghostzapper: modest maiden: will be suited by a return to 5f/6f: acts on good to firm going:
tried in visor: sold 32,000 gns, sent to USA. *David Brown*

GUILTY TWELVE (USA) 3 b.f. Giant's Causeway (USA) 132 – Arkadina (IRE) 102 **78 p**
(Danehill (USA) 126) [2015 t9.5g² p10g⁴ 10.3g⁴ Sep 11] third foal: half-sister to useful
1½m/12.5f winner Iltemas (by Galileo): dam, 9.4f winner who stayed 1½m, closely related
to Irish 1000 Guineas winner Again: fair form in maidens, second at Wolverhampton in
July: should be suited by 1½m: wore hood final start: sent to USA: remains with potential.
Roger Varian

GUISHAN 5 b.m. Ishiguru (USA) 114 – Fareham (Komaite (USA)) [2015 90: f5g³ p6g* **92**
p6g 6g⁶ 6.1m⁴ 6m⁴ 6m⁵ 6m 6d* 6d³ 6d 6g p6m³ p6g³ p6f⁶ Dec 17] fairly useful handicapper:
won at Chelmsford in January and Hamilton (by nose from Cadeaux Power) in August:
best at 6f nowadays: acts on polytrack, fibresand, good to firm and good to soft going: tried
in cheekpieces prior to 2015: front runner/races prominently. *Michael Appleby*

GUISING 6 ch.g. Manduro (GER) 135 – Trick Or Treat 108 (Lomitas 129) [2015 76: 12d **61**
p13.3g⁴ 14.1g p16g³ p16g⁴ Jul 21] rather leggy gelding: modest handicapper: stays 2m:
acts on polytrack, soft and good to firm going: tried in headgear: usually races close up.
Julia Feilden

GULLAND ROCK 4 b.g. Exceed And Excel (AUS) 126 – Sacre Coeur 90 (Compton **64**
Place 125) [2015 73: 5.3g⁵ 5.1d⁶ 5m⁵ 7m 6s 6v² 7d³ 5g 8s p6m⁴ t7 1m f7g⁴ f6g⁷ Dec 22] **a56**
attractive gelding: modest handicapper left William Muir after fourth start: stays 6f: acts
on polytrack, fibresand and any turf going: tried in headgear in 2015: front runner/races
prominently: inconsistent. *Anthony Carson*

GUMHREAR (IRE) 3 b.f. Kodiac 112 – Tip The Scale (USA) (Valiant Nature (USA) **50**
118) [2015 56: f8s⁵ Jan 20] modest maiden: stays 1m: acts on polytrack, fibresand and firm
going: often wears hood. *James Tate*

GUN CASE 3 b.c. Showcasing 117 – Bassinet (USA) 84 (Stravinsky (USA) 133) [2015 81: **81**
6d⁶ 6.1m 7.1m* 7m² 8s² 8.1m⁶ p8g Sep 21] good-bodied colt: fairly useful handicapper:
won at Sandown in June: stays 1m: acts on soft and good to firm going. *Ed Walker*

GUNG HO JACK 6 b.g. Moss Vale (IRE) 126 – Bijan (IRE) 75 (Mukaddamah (USA) **78**
125) [2015 64: p6g⁴ p6g* p6m* p6g* p6f p6g⁴ p6g² p6f* 6mᵘʳ 6g p7g⁴ 6m⁴ 6g³ 6m⁶ 6m⁵
Aug 8] good-topped gelding: fair handicapper: won at Chelmsford and Lingfield (twice) in
February and at Kempton in April: stays 7f: acts on polytrack and good to firm going.
John Best

GUNMAN 2 ch.c. (Feb 23) Monsieur Bond (IRE) 120 – Honesty Pays (Dr Fong (USA) **66**
128) [2015 6g 7g⁶ 7d p8m Sep 26] sturdy colt: fair maiden: best effort at 6f. *Richard Hannon*

GUNMETAL (IRE) 2 gr.c. (Mar 3) Clodovil (IRE) 116 – March Star (IRE) 109 (Mac's Imp (USA) 116) [2015 7g³ Oct 21] €45,000F, 33,000Y: rangy colt: closely related to 6f-7f winner Scuba (by Indian Danehill) and half-brother to 5f-7f winner Kensington (by Cape Cross) and 2-y-o 5f winner Spiders of Spring (by Redback): dam 6f winner (including at 2 yrs): 33/1, third in maiden at Newmarket (4 lengths behind Colour Me Happy) in October, not knocked about once held: will improve. *Charles Hills* **82 p**

GUNNER LINDLEY (IRE) 8 ch.g. Medicean 128 – Lasso 58 (Indian Ridge 123) [2015 87: 8g 9.8v⁵ 9.2d 9.2d⁶ 12.8m⁶ Jul 31] useful-looking gelding: useful at best, no form in 2015: tried in blinkers once in 2015: often races in rear. *Stuart Coltherd* **–**

GUNNER MOYNE 3 b.c. Excellent Art 125 – Maramkova (IRE) (Danehill Dancer (IRE) 117) [2015 p8g⁵ p8f p7g t7.1g³ t8.6g Jun 2] modest maiden: stays 1m: acts on polytrack and tapeta: in tongue tie: usually races nearer last than first. *Gary Moore* **50**

GUNNERY (FR) 2 ch.c. (Mar 29) Le Havre (IRE) 124 – Loup The Loup (FR) (Loup Solitaire (USA) 117) [2015 8s⁴ Oct 23] €17,000F, €75,000Y. half-brother to several winners, including useful 5f (including at 2 yrs) winner Louve Rouge (by Gold Away) and 2-y-o 7f winner Nulera (by Poliglote): dam, 9f-12.5f winner, half-sister to useful 7f/1m winner Caointiorn: 25/1 and green, shaped well when fourth in maiden at Newbury (2¼ lengths behind Algometer) in October: sure to progress. *Peter Chapple-Hyam* **82 p**

GUNS OF LEROS (USA) 2 b.c. (Mar 5) Cape Blanco (IRE) 130 – Zappeuse (USA) (Kingmambo (USA) 125) [2015 8d⁴ Oct 22] better effort when fourth in maiden at Goodwood (4¼ lengths behind Ocean Jive) in August, not knocked about. *Gary Moore* **71**

GURKHA FRIEND 3 b.c. Showcasing 117 – Parabola 72 (Galileo (IRE) 134) [2015 82: 6d* 6g 5s 6g Oct 16] fairly useful performer: won minor event at Leicester (by ½ length from Growl) in April: should prove suited by at least 6f: acts on good to soft going. *Karen McLintock* **89**

GURU MAC 5 b.m. Ishiguru (USA) 114 – Zacinta (USA) (Hawkster (USA)) [2015 8m f8g⁴ Apr 27] no form. *Neville Bycroft* **–**

GUTAIFAN (IRE) 2 gr.c. (Apr 7) Dark Angel (IRE) 113 – Alikhlas 81 (Lahib (USA) 129) [2015 6g² 6m* 5.1g* 5.5g* 6d² 5m* 5m Oct 4] **117**
The influential American post-war sires Hail To Reason and Raise A Native were both retired to stud after their two-year-old seasons because of injury, as was the unbeaten Irish juvenile Fasliyev who topped the International Classification for two-year-olds in 1999. The 2006 Group 1-winning two-year-old Holy Roman Emperor, who represented the same connections as Fasliyev, did not run beyond his two-year-old year season after being plucked out of training as a three-year-old—completely sound and being prepared for the Two Thousand Guineas—to replace the subfertile George Washington at Coolmore. Retiring sound racehorses at the end of their two-year-old year is no longer such a rare occurrence, since the notable example set in Britain with the Barry Hills-trained Dark Angel in 2007. Dark Angel had plenty of racing as a two-year-old, winning four of his nine starts, including the Mill Reef Stakes and the Middle Park Stakes, though he was not obviously one to be pigeon-holed as just a two-year-old on either looks or pedigree. Dark Angel's own sire the sprinter Acclamation had enjoyed a stunning season with his first crop, but the reason for Dark Angel's retirement, according to one of his owners, was that the better quality two-year-old sprinters faced an uphill battle at three, usually forced into tackling their elders too quickly, especially so with a Group 1 winner like Dark Angel. This was probably still a factor when the two-year-old retirements of Approve and Zebedee came along in 2010, followed by Lilbourne Lad (whose first crop were two-year-olds in the latest season) and Requinto in 2011 and Sir Prancealot in 2012, albeit none of those had won Group 1s. The addition of the Group 1 Commonwealth Cup at Royal Ascot, as well as the upgrading of other races before the Commonwealth Cup, such as the Sandy Lane Stakes at Haydock (now a Group 2), has gone a long way to addressing the issue, but it was still not enough to persuade connections to keep the Prix Robert Papin and Flying Childers winner Gutaifan in training (his owners Al Shaqab Racing have a very strong candidate for the 2016 Commonwealth Cup in Shalaa). Gutaifan was trained, like Zebedee, Lilbourne Lad

Fly Aer Lingus From Doncaster Sheffield Flying Childers Stakes, Doncaster—
the smart Gutaifan doesn't need to be at his best to resume winning ways, value for more than the
narrow margins over Ornate (left) and Log Out Island

and Sir Prancealot, by the Hannons and he will stand in 2016 for €12,500, alongside Dark Angel and Camacho at Morristown Lattin, the sister stud to Yeomanstown Stud in County Kildare which bred Dark Angel. Gutaifan looks set to attract a three-figure book of mares, based on the largely unexpected success and popularity of his sire. Dark Angel's fee has more than doubled to €60,000 for 2016 after he was available for as little as €7,000 as recently as 2011. He had seven individual pattern winners in the latest season, headed by Nunthorpe winner Mecca's Angel, and was again among the leading sires of two-year-olds, which generated demand for his yearlings which averaged over 90,000 guineas (the first crop foals of Dark Angel's first Group 1 winner Lethal Force averaged 37,500 guineas).

Gutaifan improved on his debut second to Strong Challenge at Goodwood when winning a Salisbury maiden later in June by a short head from Husbandry, and he followed up by the same margin in a four-runner minor event at Chester in July, having no trouble with the drop to five furlongs, even on such a sharp track. Later the same month, Gutaifan led home a British one, two, three in the Group 2 Prix Robert Papin over five and a half furlongs at Maisons-Laffitte, winning by a head from Ajaya (who won the Gimcrack Stakes on his next start), with two lengths further back to Areen. Gutaifan worked his way across from the highest stall and was in front throughout with Ajaya, his much improved performance providing Richard Hannon with successive victories in the race, following Kool Kompany. Gutaifan ran well on his next outing when a length and three quarters second of five to the odds-on Shalaa in the Prix Morny at Deauville in August, and, starting at 7/4, he didn't need to improve on that to get back to winning ways in the nine-runner Flying Childers Stakes at Doncaster the following month. The quality of the Flying Childers, a race won by Zebedee, Requinto and Sir Prancealot (Lilbourne Lad was a close fourth, while Dark Angel finished down the field), can vary quite a bit from year to year, but the latest edition appealed as one of the better recent renewals. The field initially raced in two groups before coming together after two furlongs or so, with Gutaifan chasing the leaders before edging ahead a furlong out and just being kept up to his work by Frankie Dettori (who'd ridden Gutaifan in the Papin but had chosen Shalaa instead in the Morny) to get home by a head from Ornate. Gutaifan was ridden by Al Shaqab Racing's number-one jockey in France, Gregory Benoist, when starting at 58/10 to become the first two-year-old to win the Prix de l'Abbaye since Sigy in 1978, but he faced a stiff task from his wide draw and finished well held after weakening over a furlong out.

				Royal Applause
Gutaifan (IRE) (gr.c. 2013)	Dark Angel (IRE) (gr 2005)		Acclamation (b 1999)	Princess Athena
		Midnight Angel (gr 1994)	Machiavellian
			Night At Sea
	Alikhlas (b or br 1994)		Lahib (b 1988)	Riverman
			Lady Cutlass
		Mathaayl (br 1989)	Shadeed
			Manal

The sturdy Gutaifan cost €75,000 as a foal and is a half-brother to several winners, including the useful trio of Silk Fan (by Unfuwain), who won over seven furlongs (including at two) and stayed a mile and a quarter, Blasket Spirit (by King's Best), who won over a mile on the last of his three starts in Ireland before further success in Hong Kong, and Cest Notre Gris (by Verglas), who was a two-year-old seven-furlong/mile winner and later stayed a mile and a half (he also raced over hurdles). Gutaifan is the eleventh foal out of Alikhlas, who was bred and owned by Hamdan Al Maktoum and won a mile maiden at Brighton as a three-year-old from ten starts before being sold for 18,000 guineas. Alikhlas was the first foal out of Mathaayl and is a half-sister to the useful pair Nasanice (stayed ten furlongs) and Sahool (stayed twelve furlongs and runner-up in the Ribblesdale and Lancashire Oaks). Nasanice is the dam of the very smart middle-distance performer Maraahel, who twice won the Hardwicke at Royal Ascot, and the smart performer at around a mile Mostashaar who won the Britannia Stakes a couple of days before Maraahel won his first Hardwicke. Mathaayl was successful at six furlongs to a mile and a quarter and is a half-sister to the 1988 Princess Margaret winner Muhbubh. Gutaifan, who usually raced close up, stayed six furlongs, and both the dam's side of his pedigree and his own relaxed demeanour provided some hope that he might have stayed seven. Though genuine enough, he had a tendency just to do enough in his races and all four of his wins were narrow ones, gained by no more than a head. Gutaifan acted on good to firm and good to soft going. *Richard Hannon*

GUY FAWKES 2 b.g. (Mar 4) Big Bad Bob (IRE) 118 – Flight of Fancy 114 (Sadler's **71 p** Wells (USA) 132) [2015 p8f⁶ t9.5f³ Dec 14] half-brother to 3 winners, including useful 1½m winner Fabricate (by Makfi) and useful 1½m-1¾m winner Aladdins Cave (by Rainbow Quest): dam, 2-y-o 7f winner (runner-up in Oaks), sister to smart 7f winner Golden Stream: better effort when third in maiden at Wolverhampton (9 lengths behind Every Chance) in December: will stay 1½m: open to further improvement. *William Haggas*

GWENDOLYN (GER) 2 b.f. (Jan 10) Invincible Spirit (IRE) 121 – Golden Whip (GER) **89** 105 (Seattle Dancer (USA) 119) [2015 5g⁴ p6g² 6m⁵ 6f⁴ t5.1m* Dec 12] 60,000Y: sturdy filly: first foal: dam 6f/7f winner: fairly useful performer: left Roger Varian, improved to win maiden at Wolverhampton in December by 6 lengths from Dominance: best effort at 5f: acts on tapeta. *Robert Cowell*

GWORN 5 b.g. Aussie Rules (USA) 123 – Crochet (IRE) (Mark of Esteem (IRE) 137) **91** [2015 93: p10g p8m 8d* 10d* 12.1d 10g⁵ 10g² 10.4s Oct 10] good-topped gelding: fairly useful handicapper: won at Ayr in July and August (by nose from Mica Mika): stays 10.5f: acts on polytrack, soft and good to firm going: tried in blinkers. *R. Mike Smith*

GYPSY EYES (IRE) 2 b.f. (Apr 22) High Chaparral (IRE) 132 – Brown Eyes 86 **89** (Danehill (USA) 126) [2015 7m⁵ 8m⁵ 7g Oct 9] 25,000Y: good-topped filly: closely related to 2m-17.5f winner Nashville (by Galileo) and half-sister to several winners, including ungenuine 8.5f winner Giant Step (by Giant's Causeway): dam 2-y-o 7f winner: fairly useful performer: won maiden at Newmarket (by 1¾ lengths from Farandine) in August: best effort when fifth in May Hill Stakes at Doncaster (5¾ lengths behind Turret Rocks) in September: stays 1m: not disgraced when ninth in final final start. *Charles Hills*

GYPSY MAJOR 3 ch.g. Major Cadeaux 121 – Romany Gypsy (Indesatchel (IRE) 120) **58** [2015 –: t9.5g⁶ 7g⁶ 7g 8m f7s³ 7m* 7m 7.2g t8.6f t7.1m t8.6g⁶ Dec 1] modest performer: left Fred Watson after third start: won maiden at Redcar in August: best effort at 7f: acts on good to firm going: often in headgear in 2015. *Garry Moss*

GYPSY RIDER 6 b.g. Ishiguro (USA) 114 – Spaniola (IRE) (Desert King (IRE) 129) **57** [2015 60: t6g p5g³ 6m³ 6m⁵ 6m* 7.1m 6m⁵ p6g⁴ p8f⁴ p8f⁶ Sep 17] close-coupled gelding: modest handicapper: won at Brighton in July: stays 1m: acts on polytrack, tapeta and good to firm going: tried in headgear prior to 2015. *Henry Tett*

H

HAADEETH 8 b.g. Oasis Dream 129 – Musical Key 71 (Key of Luck (USA) 126) [2015 **64** 75: t6f² f5g⁵ p6f 5.1m² 5m² t5.1g⁵ 6m⁴ 5.5m Jul 21] well-made gelding: modest performer: stays 7f: acts on polytrack, tapeta, best turf form on good going or firmer (acts on firm): tried in headgear: sometimes wears tongue tie. *David Evans*

HAAFAGUINEA 5 ch.g. Haafhd 129 – Ha'penny Beacon 74 (Erhaab (USA) 127) [2015 **115** 114: 9.9g* 9.9g 9.9g* Feb 28] good-bodied gelding: smart handicapper: won at Meydan in January (by short head from Mr Pommeroy) and February (by ¾ length from Silent Bullet): stays 11f: acts on polytrack, tapeta and good to soft going. *Saeed bin Suroor*

HAAF A SIXPENCE 6 b.g. Haafhd 129 – Melody Maker 62 (Diktat 126) [2015 –: t8.6f⁴ **95** f8d* 8v 8m 8d 8.1s⁵ 8g* 8d⁵ Oct 31] rather leggy gelding: useful handicapper: won at Southwell (by 1¼ lengths from Patriotic) in February and Newmarket (by ½ length from Athletic) in September: stays 8.5f: acts on polytrack, fibresand and soft going: front runner/races prominently. *Ralph Beckett*

HAAJES 11 ch.g. Indian Ridge 123 – Imelda (USA) (Manila (USA)) [2015 81: 5g⁵ 6g⁴ 5s⁵ **72** 5m May 25] compact gelding: fair performer: won seller at Redcar in April: stays 6f: acts on polytrack, good to firm and heavy going: tried in headgear: tried in tongue tie prior to 2015. *Paul Midgley*

HAALAN 3 b.f. Sir Percy 129 – Fin (Groom Dancer (USA) 128) [2015 73: 8f⁴ 7v⁶ 12m⁴ **92** 9.9m² 10.2m⁴ 9.9g⁵ 8.3m⁵ 10.1g* 10.3m³ 10.3d Sep 26] rather leggy filly: fairly useful handicapper: won at Yarmouth (by length from Mezajy) in August: third at Doncaster in September: stays 10.5f: acts on firm going: front runner/races prominently. *Clive Brittain*

HAALICK (IRE) 2 ch.c. (Apr 14) Roderic O'Connor (IRE) 119 – Lucky Pipit 102 (Key **102** of Luck (USA) 126) [2015 7g* 7m² 7g⁶ Sep 24] €50,000F, 170,000Y: half-brother to several winners in North America: dam, 7f winner (including at 2 yrs), out of smart winner up to 1¼m Meadow Pipit: useful performer: won maiden at Haydock (by ½ length from Jayjinski) in July: best effort when second in listed race at Doncaster (1½ lengths behind Tashweeq) in October: raced only at 7f. *Roger Varian*

HAAMES (IRE) 8 b.g. Kheleyf (USA) 116 – Jumilla (USA) 100 (El Gran Senor (USA) **56** 136) [2015 56: p8g p8g⁴ p11g p8g p8g Dec 15] modest maiden: stays 1m: acts on polytrack, best turf form on good going: tried in cheekpieces in 2015. *Kevin Morgan*

HAATEFINA 5 b.m. Haatef (USA) 117 – Felona 92 (Caerleon (USA) 132) [2015 t8.6g **–** Dec 1] angular mare: well held only start in 2015: stays 8.5f: acts on soft and good to firm going: tried in visor prior to 2015. *Mark Usher*

HABESHIA 5 ch.g. Muhtathir 126 – Lumiere Rouge (FR) (Indian Ridge 123) [2015 60: **68** f8g⁵ p8f² p8f⁴ 9.2d* 7.5f* 7.5m* 8g⁴d 9m⁸ 8g⁴ p9.4g* Jul 1] fair performer: left Michael Bell after third start: won claimer at Hyeres in March, 2 minor events at Carpentras in April, and minor event at Deauville in July: stays 1m: acts on polytrack, firm and good to soft going: sometimes wears headgear: tried in tongue tie prior to 2015: usually races prominently. *J. Reynier, France*

HABESH (IRE) 6 b.g. Rock of Gibraltar (IRE) 133 – Haratila (IRE) 81 (Marju (IRE) 127) **65** [2015 74: p16g³ p12g t12.2m⁵ p10.7g Feb 27] fair handicapper: stayed 2m, effective over shorter: acted on polytrack, tapeta, best turf form on good going: tried in headgear: sometimes wore tongue tie: dead. *Eugene M. O'Sullivan, Ireland*

HAD REEH 7 gr.g. Diktat 126 – Asian Love (Petong 126) [2015 67, a54: f6g² f6d³ Mar **60** 11] big, good-topped gelding: modest handicapper: stays 6f: acts on polytrack, fibresand, soft and good to firm going: sometimes in headgear/often in tongue tie prior to 2015: races towards rear. *Ruth Carr*

HADLEY 2 b.g. (Apr 29) Royal Applause 124 – Brush Strokes (Cadeaux Genereux 131) **54** [2015 6m 7g⁵ Sep 23] better effort when fifth in maiden at Redcar (7½ lengths behind Beatbybeatbybeat) in September. *Tracy Waggott*

HAFINA 3 b.f. Multiplex 114 – Danifah (IRE) 77 (Perugino (USA) 84) [2015 –: t8.6f t7.1f **–** 7m Apr 6] no form. *Michael Easterby*

HAGGLE 2 ch.f. (Mar 29) Pivotal 124 – Barter 62 (Daylami (IRE) 138) [2015 7f³ 8g* 8d³ **92** Oct 31] third foal: half-sister to 1m winner Bermondsey (by Galileo) and 1¼m winner (stays 1½m) Petticoat Lane (by High Chaparral): dam lightly-raced half-sister to very smart stayer Golden Quest and to dam of Oaks winner Alexandrova and Cheveley Park Stakes winner Magical Romance: fairly useful performer: won maiden at Newmarket (by 2½ lengths from Hereawi) in September: best effort when third in listed race at Newmarket (4 lengths behind Fireglow) in October: stays 1m. *Luca Cumani*

HAGREE (IRE) 4 b.g. Haatef (USA) 117 – Zuniga's Date (USA) (Diesis 133) [2015 89: **56** f7g f7d f6g⁶ 7g t7.1m 7m⁴ t8.6g⁵ t8.6g f12d f7s⁵ Aug 6] well-made gelding: modest handicapper: stays 8.5f: acts on all-weather, good to firm and good to soft going: tried in headgear: sometimes wears tongue tie: sometimes slowly away. *Declan Carroll*

HAIDEES REFLECTION 5 b.m. Byron 117 – Exchanging Glances (Diktat 126) [2015 **69** 6g⁴ 7.2g⁵ 7.2d⁴ 7.2d² 8g⁴ 7g⁴ 8.3g Sep 21] fair handicapper: won at Ayr in July and Newcastle in August: stays 1m: acts on good to soft going. *Jim Goldie*

HAIL BOLD CHIEF (USA) 8 b.g. Dynaformer (USA) – Yanaseeni (USA) (Trempolino **56** (USA) 135) [2015 65: 12.1g 10.1m 10g⁴ 9.1g⁴ 9.2s⁶ 8.9g Aug 27] sturdy, close-coupled gelding: modest handicapper: stays 11f: acts on good to firm and good to soft going. *Alan Swinbank*

HAIL THE HERO (IRE) 3 b.g. Galileo (IRE) 134 – Mauralakana (FR) 116 (Muhtathir **102** 126) [2015 92: 7d⁸ 8g⁶ 8m 7g⁴ 8f 8m⁴ 8d⁴ Jul 26] useful performer: won maiden at Doncaster (by 3 lengths from Mockingbird Hill) in March: stiff tasks subsequently, including when fourth of 6 in listed races at Newmarket and Pontefract last 2 starts: stays 1m: acts on good to firm and good to soft going: sold £290,000, gelded and sent to Hong Kong, where renamed See Me Now. *David O'Meara*

HAINES 4 ch.g. Shirocco (GER) 129 – Spring Dream (IRE) 93 (Kalanisi (IRE) 132) [2015 **81** 73p: p13.3f* f14g* t16.5g² p16g² 14m⁵ 14g t12.2m⁴ Dec 26] lengthy gelding: fairly useful handicapper: won at Chelmsford in March and Southwell (apprentice) in April: will benefit from return to at least 1¾m: acts on all-weather and good to soft going. *Andrew Balding*

HAIRDRYER 2 b.c. (May 9) Motivator 131 – Londonnetdotcom (IRE) 101 (Night Shift **72** (USA)) [2015 7m⁴ 7m⁶ 8d⁵ 7d³ Oct 16] well-made colt: fair maiden: stays 7f. *Richard Hannon*

HAJEER (IRE) 2 b.f. (Jan 22) Cape Cross (IRE) 129 – Mejala (IRE) 74 (Red Ransom **51** (USA)) [2015 p6g⁵ 6m 6m p7g³ p7g⁴ 8.1m⁴ Sep 10] sturdy filly: second foal: dam, 1¼m **a59** winner, half-sister to smart 7f/1m performer Muwaary: modest maiden: stays 7f: acts on polytrack: tried in cheekpieces: sometimes slowly away: sent to Hungary. *Ed Dunlop*

HAKAM (USA) 3 b.g. War Front (USA) 119 – Lauren Byrd (USA) (Arch (USA) 127) **93 p** [2015 p7f² 7m² Apr 15] $450,000Y: first foal: dam, US 2-y-o 6f/1m winner, half-sister to smart US Grade 2 9f winner Hudson Steele: runner-up in maidens at Lingfield and Newmarket: looked unlucky when beaten length by Carnival King in latter, hampered over 1f out, forced to switch and finishing with running left: has been gelded: open to further improvement. *Charles Hills*

HAKKA 3 b.c. Dansili 127 – African Rose 119 (Observatory (USA) 131) [2015 t8.6g² **103 p** t8.6g* 8m³ p8g* t8.6m² 10.3d² Sep 26] second foal: dam 6f (Sprint Cup) and (including at 2 yrs) 7f winner: useful performer: won maiden at Wolverhampton in June and handicap at Chelmsford in August: second in handicaps at Wolverhampton (head behind Intrude) and Chester (1¼ lengths behind Erik The Red) on last 2 starts: may prove best at shorter than 1¼m: acts on polytrack, tapeta and good to soft going: often races prominently, strong traveller: sold 85,000 gns, sent to Saudi Arabia: capable of better still. *Sir Michael Stoute*

HALA MADRID 3 ch.f. Nayef (USA) 129 – Ermine (IRE) 86 (Cadeaux Genereux 131) **79** [2015 –p: 8.3m² 8.1s³ 7m³ 8.3m² 8g* 9g⁶ 8.1g³ Aug 21] rather leggy filly: fair performer: won maiden at Wetherby in July: stays 8.5f: acts on good to firm going: front runner/races prominently. *Andrew Balding*

HALATION (IRE) 4 b.g. Azamour (IRE) 130 – Ghenwah (FR) (Selkirk (USA) 129) **104** [2015 99: p8g p8m* 18.6m⁵ 8d⁴ 9m² 8.1m⁴ 8m* 10.3m 9g 8d Oct 17] useful handicapper: **a97** won at Lingfield in February and Ascot (by ½ length from Earth Drummer) in August: also ran well when in frame in between: stays 9f: acts on polytrack, tapeta, good to firm and good to soft going: sometimes wears a hood: usually races in rear: sold 70,000 gns, sent to UAE. *David Simcock*

HALEY BOP (IRE) 2 ch.f. (May 4) Dream Ahead (USA) 133 – Hallie's Comet (IRE) **93** 108 (One Cool Cat (USA) 123) [2015 6g³ 7f 6s* 6d* 6g Oct 3] €30,000Y: second foal: dam, unreliable winner up to 1m (2-y-o 6f winner), half-sister to smart 1m-9.4f winner Along Came Casey: fairly useful performer: won maiden at Redcar in July and nursery at Hamilton (by 5 lengths from Young Windsor) in August: should stay 7f: acts on soft going. *Mark Johnston*

HALF A BILLION (IRE) 6 b.g. Acclamation 118 – Amankila (IRE) 62 (Revoque (IRE) **80** 122) [2015 86: 6d⁵ 5.9v 5.5m⁴ 6m 5g 5m 6s⁵ 6m 6d Sep 17] rather unfurnished gelding: fairly useful handicapper: stays 7f: acts on fibresand and heavy going: often in headgear in 2015. *Michael Dods*

HAL

HALFSIN (IRE) 7 b.g. Haafhd 129 – Firesteed (IRE) 91 (Common Grounds 118) [2015 –
94: t9.5g Jan 15] big, good-topped gelding: useful at best, well held only start in 2015:
stays 11f: acts on polytrack and any turf going: tried in headgear prior to 2015: sometimes
wears tongue tie: edgy sort, has run well when sweating. *Alexandra Dunn*

HALF WAY 4 b.g. Haafhd 129 – Amhooj 77 (Green Desert (USA) 127) [2015 79: p7g p6m   70
p8g p6f p7m⁶ 7m* Jun 1] angular gelding: fair handicapper: successful at Leicester in June:
stays 7f: acts on polytrack and good to firm going: tried in blinkers/tongue tie in 2015:
sometimes finds little: sold 7,000 gns, sent to Italy, and won 6f seller at Rome in November.
Lee Carter

HALJAFERIA (UAE) 9 ch.g. Halling (USA) 133 – Melisendra (FR) (Highest Honor   –
(FR) 124) [2015 12.4g 11.1s 10.1d 12.4g 10.1m 10.1m Jun 25] lengthy, angular gelding:
fairly useful at best, no form in 2015: tried in cheekpieces in 2015: usually slowly away,
usually races nearer last than first. *Kenny Johnson*

HALLELUJAH 7 b.m. Avonbridge 123 – My Golly (Mozart (IRE) 131) [2015 109: p6m*   102
p6f³ p6g p6g⁶ Nov 25] strong mare: useful performer: won minor event at Kempton (by
length from Happy Valentine) in January: third in listed race at Lingfield (1½ lengths
behind Rivellino) in February: raced only at 6f: acts on polytrack, good to firm and heavy
going: sometimes in tongue tie prior to 2015. *James Fanshawe*

HALLINGHAM 5 b.g. Halling (USA) 133 – In Luck 72 (In The Wings 128) [2015 77:   73
10g³ 10m 10m² 11m⁴ 10m² 10m⁴ 10g 12.1m Sep 28] workmanlike gelding: fair
handicapper: left Jonathan Portman after seventh start: stays 1½m: acts on polytrack, good
to firm and heavy going: often wears headgear. *Chris Gordon*

HALLINGS COMET 6 ch.g. Halling (USA) 133 – Landinium (ITY) 109 (Lando (GER)   72
128) [2015 10.2m⁵ 13.3m⁴ 11.6g³ 10.2d⁵ 12.1m² 11.9d⁶ Sep 25] fair handicapper: stays 1½m:
acts on good to firm and heavy going: usually leads: none too consistent. *Adrian Wintle*

HALLING'S WISH 5 br.g. Halling (USA) 133 – Fair View (GER) (Dashing Blade 117)   72
[2015 16g² 14.1g* 17.2f² Aug 12] fair handicapper: won at Salisbury in August: stays 17f:
acts on any turf going: in blinkers in 2015: tried in tongue tie: often travels strongly.
Gary Moore

HALL OF BEAUTY 3 ch.f. Halling (USA) 133 – Victorian Era (Cape Cross (IRE) 129)   59
[2015 7f⁵ p8g 10.2g⁵ t9.5f p13.3f² p16g⁴ f12g³ f14f² Dec 17] 3,500 2-y-o: first foal: dam,
French maiden (stayed 10.5f), out of sister to Dubai Millennium: modest maiden: best
effort at 13.5f: acts on polytrack and fibresand. *Michael Appleby*

HALLO SEXY 3 br.f. Halling (USA) 133 – Maziona 89 (Dansili 127) [2015 p12g Aug 5]   –
3,000Y: second foal: dam, 2-y-o 7f winner who stayed 10.5f, half-sister to St Leger runner-
up The Geezer (by Halling): 150/1, well held in maiden at Kempton. *Clive Drew*

HALLSTATT (IRE) 9 ch.g. Halling (USA) 133 – Last Resort 116 (Lahib (USA) 129)   75
[2015 80: 14.1g⁶ 16m* 15.8d⁵ 14.6m⁶ 14.1m⁴ 17.1d² 16.2m⁴ 18d² 16.2d Oct 16] fair
handicapper: won at Wetherby in June: stays 2¼m: acts on polytrack, good to firm and
good to soft going: tried in cheekpieces prior to 2015: often wears tongue tie: often races
towards rear. *John Mackie*

HALSALL 2 b.c. (Apr 4) Kodiac 112 – Albeed 80 (Tiger Hill (IRE) 127) [2015 5m² 5g⁴   76
5m* 5f 5f⁵ Jul 3] neat colt: fair performer: won maiden at Redcar in May: will stay 6f+:
acts on good to firm going: front runner/races prominently: sold 30,000 gns, sent to Qatar.
David O'Meara

HAMELIN (IRE) 5 b.g. Cape Cross (IRE) 129 – Love Divine 120 (Diesis 133) [2015   107
106: t12.2m² 14d t12.2f* p12g² p12g² Nov 25] useful performer: won handicap at
Wolverhampton (by ½ length from The Steward) in October: second in 2 listed races at
Kempton in November, beaten neck by Missed Call then (after leaving Lady Cecil) 2¼
lengths by Fire Fighting: stays 1½m: acts on polytrack, tapeta, good to firm and good to
soft going: often leads. *George Scott*

HAMILTON TERRACE 2 b.f. (Mar 21) Mount Nelson 125 – Striking Pose (IRE) 77   –
(Darshaan 133) [2015 8d p8g Nov 18] sixth foal: dam, maiden (stayed 1½m), half-sister to
useful winner up to 1m Beautiful Fire: no form. *Henry Candy*

HAMIS AL BIN (IRE) 6 b.g. Acclamation 118 – Paimpolaise (IRE) (Priolo (USA) 127)   67
[2015 67: p6m t6f³ t7.1f t6g⁴ t6g⁶ t6g⁶ 5.1m⁶ 6m t6g p6g t6g p6m⁴ p6m* t5.1m³ t6m*
Dec 30] fair handicapper: won at Lingfield and Wolverhampton in December: stays 8.5f,
races at shorter these days: acts on polytrack, tapeta and firm going: tried in blinkers in
2015: often wears tongue tie. *Milton Bradley*

HAMISH MCGONAGAIN 2 b.c. (Apr 21) Kyllachy 129 – Inya Lake 101 (Whittingham   61
(IRE) 104) [2015 p5g 5g p5g⁴ t6f Dec 22] modest maiden: best effort at 5f. *Jeremy Gask*

HAMMER GUN (USA) 2 b.c. (Feb 6) Smart Strike (CAN) 121 – Caraboss 98 (Cape Cross (IRE) 129) [2015 7g 8.3d² Oct 14] first foal: dam, 1¼m winner, half-sister to smart performers Four Winds (stayed 1¼m) and Kingdom of Fife (stayed 1½m): better effort when second in maiden at Nottingham (7 lengths behind Mr Khalid) in October, needing stiffer test: will prove suited to middle distances: still unexposed. *Sir Michael Stoute*   **69 p**

HAMOODY (USA) 11 ch.g. Johannesburg (USA) 127 – Northern Gulch (USA) (Gulch (USA)) [2015 85: f5s⁴ p5f⁶ t6m⁴ p5m⁴ Feb 27] strong, lengthy gelding: fair performer: left Joseph Tuite after third start: stays 7f: acts on all-weather, firm and good to soft going: often races prominently. *Jo Davis*   **71**

HANALEI BAY (IRE) 5 b.g. Tamayuz 126 – Genial Jenny (IRE) 70 (Danehill (USA) 126) [2015 86: t9.5g⁶ t9.5f⁴ Jan 30] fairly useful handicapper at best: stayed 9.5f: acted on polytrack, tapeta and good to firm going: had worn headgear: was a front runner/raced prominently: dead. *Keith Dalgleish*   **73**

HANDAZAN (IRE) 6 b.g. Nayef (USA) 129 – Handaza (IRE) 93 (Be My Guest (USA) 126) [2015 20f Jun 16] workmanlike gelding: useful performer at best: first-time tongue strap and fit from hurdling when well held in Ascot Stakes at Royal Ascot: stays 2m: acts on good to firm and heavy going: in cheekpieces last 3 starts. *Ben Case*   **–**

HANDBELL (IRE) 3 b.f. Acclamation 118 – Dulcian (IRE) (Shamardal (USA) 129) [2015 7m t6g* t7.1g³ 6m⁵ Sep 16] £175,000Y: first foal: dam unraced half-sister to smart 7f/1m performer Army of Angels and to dam of Cheveley Park Stakes winner Serious Attitude: fair performer: won maiden at Wolverhampton in July: stays 7f. *Luca Cumani*   **72**

HANDHELD 8 ch.g. Observatory (USA) 131 – Kid Gloves (In The Wings 128) [2015 87: 10.2s⁶ May 9] fairly useful handicapper at best: below form only start in 2015: stays 10.5f: acts on viscoride and good to soft going: wears cheekpieces: inconsistent. *Julia Feilden*   **66**

HANDIWORK 5 ch.g. Motivator 131 – Spinning Top 105 (Alzao (USA) 117) [2015 16s² 17.1g² 16.2d² 16d³ f16g² p15.8g Dec 28] workmanlike gelding: fairly useful handicapper: good second at Southwell (neck behind Frosty Berry) in December on penultimate start: stays 2m: acts on fibresand, good to firm and heavy going: usually wears cheekpieces: visored final outing: usually travels strongly. *Steve Gollings*   **93**

HANDSOME DAN (IRE) 9 b.g. Busy Flight 122 – Beautiful City (IRE) (Jurado (USA)) [2015 t13.9g⁵ Nov 27] fairly useful over hurdles and fences: only outing on Flat when fifth in maiden at Wolverhampton in November, very slowly away. *Sarah Hollinshead*   **64**

HANDSOME DUDE 3 b.g. Showcasing 117 – Dee Dee Girl (IRE) 60 (Primo Dominie 121) [2015 93p: 5m 5g³ 5.5g* 6d³ 6m⁴ 5g³ 6g Sep 6] useful handicapper: won at Wetherby (by neck from Straightothepoint) in July: worth a try at 7f: acts on good to firm and good to soft going: in blinkers last 3 starts: often races prominently. *David Barron*   **96**

HANDYTALK (IRE) 2 b.c. (Apr 14) Lilbourne Lad (IRE) 111 – Dancing With Stars (IRE) (Where Or When (IRE) 124) [2015 5m* 5f² 6m⁴ 5m⁴ 6m⁶ 6g Oct 3] €16,500F, £32,000Y: rather leggy colt: third foal: half-brother to 8.5f winner Jackie Ellis (by Excellent Art): dam unraced half-sister to smart Spanish miler Cielo Canarias: fairly useful performer: won maiden at Windsor in April: best efforts when in frame in minor events at Ascot and Newbury next 2 starts: stays 6f: acts on firm going: often races towards rear. *Rod Millman*   **94**

HANGON HARRIET 3 b.f. Sir Percy 129 – Black Salix (USA) 54 (More Than Ready (USA) 120) [2015 52: p10f³ p10f³ p10m⁵ Sep 26] fair maiden: stayed 1¼m: acted on polytrack: often raced prominently: dead. *Pam Sly*   **69**

HANK WILLIAMS 3 b.g. Schiaparelli (GER) 120 – Jezadil (IRE) 66 (Mujadil (USA) 119) [2015 p13.3g⁴ Dec 10] well beaten in bumper: 66/1, green when fourth in maiden at Chelmsford (14¼ lengths behind Kelly's Finest) in December. *Kristin Stubbs*   **–**

HANNAHS LAD 2 b.g. (Apr 13) Assertive 121 – Beyond The Rainbow (Mind Games 121) [2015 5g f7m t5.1m Dec 26] no form. *Ronald Thompson*   **–**

HANNAHS TURN 5 b.m. Dubai Destination (USA) 127 – Fontaine House (Pyramus (USA) 78) [2015 85§, a94§: p5g⁶ p5g Feb 5] good-topped mare: fair handicapper: stays 7f: acts on fibresand, best turf form on good going: usually races close up, tends to find little. *Chris Dwyer*   **73**

HANNINGTON 4 ch.g. Firebreak 125 – Manderina (Mind Games 121) [2015 84p: 7.6d* 8g⁴ 8.3m⁴ 8f* 8g 8.1g 8.3d p8g* t8.6m⁴ p8g⁶ p10g Dec 20] fairly useful handicapper: won at Lingfield in May, Ascot (apprentice) in July and Lingfield (by 1¼ lengths from Tuco) in November: stays 8.5f: acts on polytrack, firm and good to soft going: sometimes in cheekpieces in 2015: often wears tongue tie. *Andrew Balding*   **88**

HANNO (USA) 4 b.g. Henrythenavigator (USA) 131 – Archstone (USA) (Arch (USA) **76 §**
127) [2015 84: p10g⁶ 8.3d 7.6d³ 8v* 10.2g³ 10g 8g 8.1m⁴ Sep 10] strong gelding: fair
handicapper: won at Brighton in May: stays 1¼m: acts on good to firm and heavy going:
tried in cheekpieces prior to 2015: tried in tongue tie in 2015: clear signs of temperament
and one to treat with caution: sent to USA. *Ed Dunlop*

HANSEATIC 6 b.g. Galileo (IRE) 134 – Insinuate (USA) 99 (Mr Prospector (USA)) **80**
[2015 8m 8m⁵ 10.4g 10.3m 13.1g Sep 19] rangy gelding: fairly useful handicapper: stays
10.5f: acts on polytrack and good to soft going: often in tongue tie in 2015: often races
prominently. *Michael Easterby*

HANS HOLBEIN 3 b.c. Montjeu (IRE) 137 – Llia 94 (Shirley Heights 130) [2015 80p: **111**
10.2v² 10s* 12.3s* 12m Jun 6] 50,000Y: tall, good-topped colt: closely related to 2 winners,
including high-class winner up to 1¾m (Irish St Leger) Sans Frontieres (2-y-o 7f winner,
by Galileo) and half-brother to several winners, including useful winner up to 8.5f
Kootenay (2-y-o 7f/7.5f winner, by Selkirk): dam 2-y-o 7f winner who stayed 1½m: smart
performer: won maiden at Leopardstown in April and Chester Vase (by 1¼ lengths from
Storm The Stars) in May: 14/1, not seen to best effect when 14½ lengths seventh of 12 to
Golden Horn in Derby at Epsom final start, ridden too aggressively: will stay beyond 12.3f:
acts on soft going: in cheekpieces last 3 starts: front runner/races prominently: sent to
Australia. *Aidan O'Brien, Ireland*

HAPPY CALL 2 b.g. (Mar 3) Kodiac 112 – Munaa's Dream (Oasis Dream 129) [2015 **85**
5.4m⁴ 6g² 6d² 6g² p6m* Nov 19] 12,500F, £28,000Y, £110,000 2-y-o: first foal: dam, little
form, out of half-sister to useful performers Anna Karenina (stayed 9.5f) and Windsor
Palace (stayed 10.5f): fairly useful handicapper: visored, made all when winning maiden at
Lingfield final start by 2 lengths from Sir Roger Moore: stays 6f: acts on polytrack: tried in
cheekpieces. *Simon Crisford*

HAPPY DEAL (IRE) 3 b.g. Tagula (IRE) 116 – Jeu Set Et Match (IRE) (Shantou (USA) **–**
125) [2015 t7.1f f8d Jan 27] no form. *Scott Dixon*

HAPPYDOINGNOTHING 4 b.g. Avonbridge 123 – Neferura 51 (Mister Baileys 123) **61**
[2015 63: p7g 7.1g² t8.6f⁶ t8.6f* t8.6g³ t8.6g p8f p8g t9.5g 11.6m Aug 3] modest
handicapper: won at Wolverhampton in March: best effort at 8.5f: acts on tapeta: often
wears headgear: tried in tongue tie in 2015. *Christine Dunnett*

HAPPY DREAMS (IRE) 3 b.c. Fastnet Rock (AUS) 127 – Timeless Dream 79 (Oasis **63**
Dream 129) [2015 p8f p8f³ p8f⁴ Feb 25] modest maiden: dead. *David Simcock*

HAPPY JACK (IRE) 4 b.g. Elusive City (USA) 117 – Miss Pelling (IRE) 75 (Danehill **51**
Dancer (IRE) 117) [2015 –: p10m t8.6g⁴ t9.5f³ p10m 12.1m p10g³ 9.9d⁵ p12g³ t12.2f⁵
Dec 21] modest maiden: stays 1½m: acts on polytrack, tapeta and good to soft going:
usually in headgear in 2015. *Michael Wigham*

HAPPY PURSUIT 3 b.f. Pastoral Pursuits 127 – Carollan (IRE) 68 (Marju (IRE) 127) **42**
[2015 –: t7.1g⁵ p7f⁶ Feb 3] poor handicapper: sold €7,000 in November. *Stuart Williams*

HAPPY TIDINGS 2 b.f. (Apr 12) Exceed And Excel (AUS) 126 – Helena Molony (IRE) **82 p**
105 (Sadler's Wells (USA) 132) [2015 7g p7g⁵ Sep 21] €105,000Y: tall filly: sixth foal:
closely related to 7f-1¼m winner Dance of Heroes (by Danehill Dancer) and half-sister to
1¼m winner Red Hand (by Mr Greeley) and 9.5f winner Heavenly Sound (by Street Cry):
dam, 1¼m winner who stayed 1¾m, sister to top-class winner up to 1½m High Chaparral:
better effort when fifth in maiden at Kempton (4 lengths behind Barleysugar) in September,
considerately handled: remains open to improvement. *Tom Dascombe*

HAPPY VALENTINE (SAF) 5 ch.m. Silvano (GER) 126 – Happy Ever After (SAF) **94**
(National Assembly (CAN)) [2015 p6m² 5s* 6g 5g May 10] third foal: half-sister to a
winner in South Africa by Var: dam unraced: useful performer in 2013, winning Grade 1 at
Scottsville: missed 2014: length second to Hallelujah in minor event at Kempton on first
outing in 2015: didn't need to reproduce best when winning minor event at Moulins in
March: stays 6f: acts on polytrack, winner on soft going. *A. de Royer Dupre, France*

HARBOUR PATROL (IRE) 3 b.c. Acclamation 118 – Traou Mad (IRE) 107 (Barathea **81**
(IRE) 127) [2015 81: 6m* 8m⁶ 7g⁵ 7.1m² 7.2m 7d 7v Nov 3] workmanlike colt: fairly
useful performer: won maiden at Salisbury (by 3¾ lengths from Bushephalus) in May: left
Richard Hannon after fourth start, below form subsequently: stays 7f: acts on good to firm
going: front runner/races prominently. *Rebecca Bastiman*

HARDINGTON 3 b.c. (Mar 28) Fastnet Rock (AUS) 127 – La Cucina (IRE) (Last Tycoon **71**
131) [2015 7s t7.1f* p8g Dec 16] fair maiden: best effort when fourth at Wolverhampton
(2 lengths behind Turn On The Tears) in November. *Alan King*

HARDSTONE (USA) 4 b.c. Birdstone (USA) 129 – Songerie 115 (Hernando (FR) 127) **100**
[2015 91: p12g* 15g⁵ 20f 13.7mᵖᵘ 13.1g* 14.6d⁵ Oct 23] lengthy colt: useful handicapper:
won at Dundalk in May and Ayr (by length from Corona Borealis) in September: left John
Patrick Murtagh after third start: stays 15f: acts on polytrack, soft and good to firm going:
sometimes in tongue tie prior to 2015. *Michael Dods*

HARD TO HANDEL 3 b.g. Stimulation (IRE) 121 – Melody Maker 62 (Diktat 126) **89**
[2015 84: 7m⁶ 8.1m⁶ 8m 8.3g* 8m⁵ 8s² 8s⁵ Oct 23] rather leggy gelding: fairly useful
handicapper: won at Windsor in June: stays 8.5f: acts on tapeta and soft going: often in
cheekpieces in 2015: front runner/races prominently. *Ralph Beckett*

HARDY BLACK (IRE) 4 b.g. Pastoral Pursuits 127 – Wondrous Story (USA) 91 (Royal **73**
Academy (USA) 130) [2015 81: p7g⁶ p7m t7.1m³ t7.1f⁵ t7.1g p7g t8.6g 6m³ 6m⁴ 5.5m*
5.1m⁶ t6f⁴ 6g Sep 26] fair handicapper: won at Wetherby in July: left Jamie Osborne after
third start: stays 1m, but effective at shorter: acts on polytrack, tapeta and good to firm
going: often wears headgear: tried in tongue tie in 2015: sometimes slowly away, often
races towards rear. *Kevin Frost*

HARLEQUEEN 2 b.f. (Mar 26) Canford Cliffs (IRE) 133 – Aurelia 80 (Rainbow Quest **93 p**
(USA) 134) [2015 8s* Sep 11] 32,000Y: seventh foal: half-sister to 3 winners, including
winner up to 1½m (stayed 2m) Aurorian (2-y-o 7f winner, by Fantastic Light) and 7f/1m
winner Wardell (by Rip Van Winkle): dam 2-y-o 1¼m winner: 11/2, promising debut when
winning maiden at Goodwood (by 4½ lengths from Renfrew Street) in September, waited
with after dwelling, quickening to lead over 1f out and storming clear: sure to progress.
Mick Channon

HARLEQUIN ROCK 2 bl.g. (Feb 25) Rock of Gibraltar (IRE) 133 – Berry Baby (IRE) **69**
74 (Rainbow Quest (USA) 134) [2015 6.5m 7m⁶ 7m⁶ 8.3g* 6m⁵ 8.3m³ 8g⁶ 8g p8f⁷³ 8d*
p10g f8m* Dec 8] leggy gelding: fair performer: won nurseries at Nottingham in August,
Pontefract in October (left Mick Channon after) and Southwell in December: should be
suited by further than 1m: acts on fibresand, polytrack and good to soft going. *Mick Quinn*

HARLEQUIN STRIKER (IRE) 3 b.g. Bahamian Bounty 116 – Air Maze 80 (Dansili **91**
127) [2015 82: 7d 7.1m 7g⁴ 7g 7.4d* 7v* 7s² 7m Oct 2] fairly useful handicapper: won at
Ffos Las in August and Epsom (by neck from Live Dangerously) in September: stays 7.5f:
acts on heavy going: front runner/races prominently. *Mick Channon*

HARLESTONE HOPES 3 b.g. Olden Times 121 – Harlestone Lady (Shaamit (IRE) **71**
127) [2015 t8.6f⁴ p8g³ 7g³ 9.9m t12.2f p13.3g² Dec 10] fair maiden: stays 13.5f: acts on
polytrack and tapeta. *Ed Dunlop*

HARLEY REBEL 3 br.g. Cockney Rebel (IRE) 127 – Al Kahina (Mark of Esteem (IRE) **65**
137) [2015 –: p11g² p11g* 10.2m³ May 4] fair handicapper: won at Kempton in April:
likely to stay 1½m: acts on polytrack and good to firm going: sometimes slowly away,
often races towards rear. *Neil Mulholland*

HARLY FOREST 2 b.g. (Mar 21) Holy Roman Emperor (IRE) 125 – Goslar 92 (In The **–**
Wings 128) [2015 7.5m 7m⁶ 7s Sep 5] no form. *Brian Ellison*

HARMONICAL 4 ch.f. Desideratum 118 – First Harmony (First Trump 118) [2015 55: **57**
16.1d⁶ 14.1g Jun 15] modest maiden: best effort at 2m: acts on good to soft going.
Antony Brittain

HARMONIC LADY 5 ch.m. Trade Fair 124 – First Harmony (First Trump 118) [2015 **51**
68: 10.3d 9.5g 12.1s 15.8d Aug 26] modest handicapper: best effort at 1¼m: acts on heavy
going: tried in hood in 2015: often leads. *Antony Brittain*

HARMONIC WAVE (IRE) 2 b.f. (May 13) Zebedee 113 – Pure Folly (IRE) 58 **82**
(Machiavellian (USA) 123) [2015 5g⁵ 5g⁴ 5m² 5d⁴ 5g* 5g² Oct 16] €6,500F, €30,000Y,
40,000 2-y-o: fifth foal: half-sister to 3 winners, including 2-y-o 1m winner Koko Loca (by
Kodiac), later 6.5f/8.5f winner in USA, and useful 5f/6f winner (including at 2 yrs) Lucky
Numbers (by Key of Luck): dam sprint maiden: fairly useful performer: won nursery at
Musselburgh in September: raced only at 5f: best form on good going. *Ann Duffield*

HARMONY BAY (IRE) 2 b.f. (Apr 12) Fast Company (IRE) 126 – Consensus (IRE) 91 **67**
(Common Grounds 118) [2015 5m p6g* 6.5m 6d⁶ p7g Nov 13] £16,000Y: sixth foal: half-
sister to 3 winners, including 2-y-o 5f winner (stayed 8.5f) Cloneylass (by Verglas) and
winner up to 1m Al's Memory (2-y-o 6f winner, by Red Clubs), both useful: dam 5f and (at
2 yrs) 6f winner: fair performer: won maiden at Lingfield in August: best effort at 6f: acts
on polytrack. *Sylvester Kirk*

HAROLD LLOYD (IRE) 3 b.g. Cape Cross (IRE) 129 – Silent Act (USA) 86 (Theatrical (IRE) **86**
128) [2015 –: 8.3d³ 10m³ 10m* Jul 15] sturdy gelding: fairly useful performer: won
handicap at Sandown (by ½ length from Zamperini) in July: will stay 1½m. *Henry Candy*

HARPERS RUBY 5 b.m. Byron 117 – La Belle Katherine (USA) (Lyphard (USA) 132) **52**
[2015 –: 7g 8.5m t5.1f f5g f6m⁴ Dec 30] modest maiden: best effort at 6f: acts on tapeta:
tried in hood in 2015. *Lynn Siddall*

HARPS OF BRETAGNE 3 b.f. Monsieur Bond (IRE) 120 – Lavernock Lady (Don't **–**
Forget Me 127) [2015 –: t12.2g⁴ p10m t13.9m Dec 30] no form. *Lisa Williamson*

HARP STAR (JPN) 4 b.f. Deep Impact (JPN) 134 – Historic Star (JPN) (Falbrav (IRE) **112**
133) [2015 125: 10.9f⁵ 12g Mar 28] good-topped filly: high-class performer at best:
successful 3 times in 2014, including Oka Sho (Japanese 1000 Guineas) at Hanshin and
sixth in Prix de l'Arc de Triomphe at Longchamp: disappointing in 2015, including when
eighth of 9 behind Dolniya in Dubai Sheema Classic at Meydan on second outing: stayed
1½m: raced only on good going or firmer: usually ridden well off pace: reported in May to
have been retired due to off-hind leg injury. *Hiroyoshi Matsuda, Japan*

HARRISON 2 b.c. (Feb 23) Sixties Icon 125 – Excellent Day (IRE) 78 (Invincible Spirit **87 p**
(IRE) 121) [2015 8g⁵ 9d* Oct 11] second foal: dam winner up to 7f (?-y-o 5f winner): won
maiden at Goodwood in October by 1½ lengths from Cameraman, leading over 1f out and
keeping on well: will stay 1¼m: open to further progress. *Mick Channon*

HARRISON'S CAVE 7 b.g. Galileo (IRE) – Sitara 74 (Salse (USA) 128) [2015 68: **56**
t12.2g 12.4d³ 11.8m⁶ 13d 13.1d⁶ 12.5m³ 14g 12.2g⁴ 12.1s⁵ Jul 28] tall gelding: modest
handicapper: stays 2m: acts on polytrack, tapeta and any turf going: tried in headgear: tried
in tongue tie: usually races close up. *Sharon Watt*

HARRISON STICKLE 3 gr.g. Hellvelyn 118 – Hollybell 87 (Beveled (USA)) [2015 **75**
5m³ 6m³ 5g² 6s 5.7m* Sep 28] fair performer: won handicap at Bath (apprentice) in
September: stays 6f: acts on good to firm going. *John Gallagher*

HARROGATE FAIR 5 b.g. Trade Fair 124 – Starbeck (IRE) 94 (Spectrum (IRE) 126) **79**
[2015 79: p6m³ 5.1d* 5.1gᵖᵘ p5g Oct 20] close-coupled gelding: fair handicapper: won at
Nottingham in May: left Michael Squance after third start: stays 6f: acts on polytrack and
heavy going: tried in headgear: sometimes slowly away. *Kevin Morgan*

HARRYANA'S SECRET 2 ch.f. (Feb 12) Sakhee's Secret 128 – Harryana To 57 **48**
(Compton Place 125) [2015 5g 5m⁶ 6g 6m⁵ 5d⁵ 5d Sep 15] 10,000Y: first foal: dam, maiden
(stayed 7f), half-sister to smart 2-y-o 5f/6f (Mill Reef Stakes) winner Temple Meads: poor
maiden: may prove best at 5f: acts on good to firm going: often in blinkers. *Tim Easterby*

HARRY BOSCH 5 b.g. Kyllachy 129 – Fen Guest 73 (Woodborough (USA) 112) [2015 **59**
87d: t6g t7.1g t7.1f 8.3m 8d³ 8m* 8s⁵ 8m⁵ 8m³ 8m⁵ 8g 8m Sep 28] useful-looking
gelding: modest handicapper: won at Bath in May: left James Unett after third start: stays
8.5f: acts on polytrack, good to firm and good to soft going: sometimes wears headgear.
Julia Feilden

HARRY CHAMPION 2 b.c. (Apr 25) Cockney Rebel (IRE) 127 – Nine Red 63 (Royal **87 p**
Applause 124) [2015 6g⁵ 6g⁴ t7.1g* t7.1m² Dec 18] sturdy colt: fifth foal: half-brother to
1¼m winner Nonagon (by Pastoral Pursuits): dam, maiden (stayed 7f), half-sister to smart
6f/7f winner Snow Kid: fairly useful form: won maiden at Wolverhampton (by 2 lengths
from Broughtons Fancy) in December: head second to Take The Helm in nursery there next
time: stays 7f: sometimes in hood: likely to progress further. *Hugo Palmer*

HARRY HURRICANE 3 b.g. Kodiac 112 – Eolith 99 (Pastoral Pursuits 127) [2015 77: **102**
t7.1f* p6f² t7.1g* t5.1f² p5f⁵ 7f 6m 5m 5d 5.6d² Sep 12] useful handicapper: won at
Wolverhampton in January (maiden) and February: 25/1, best effort when 1¼ lengths
second of 20 to Steps in Portland at Doncaster final outing: effective at 5f to 7f: acts on
tapeta, good to firm and good to soft going: has worn cheekpieces: has been gelded.
George Baker

HARRY'S ENDEAVOUR 2 b.g. (Apr 24) Paco Boy (IRE) 129 – Crabapple (Alhaarth **–**
(IRE) 126) [2015 p8g Dec 9] 100/1, well held in maiden at Kempton. *Seamus Mullins*

HARRY SPEED (IRE) 2 b.c. (Mar 7) Dark Angel (IRE) 113 – Starfly (IRE) 79 **78**
(Invincible Spirit (IRE) 121) [2015 5.9m 6d⁴ 6g⁶ 6s 7d³ Oct 24] fair performer: won
maiden at Thirsk in August: likely to prove best at 5f/6f: acts on good to soft going: has
joined Garvan Donnelly. *Jedd O'Keeffe*

HARTFORD STARTS (IRE) 5 b.g. Chineur (FR) 123 – Desert Design (Desert King **56**
(IRE) 129) [2015 f8g f8s 12m 8.5g 7g⁵ 8g 10.2s² t9.5f⁴ t12.2m² Nov 21] modest maiden:
stays 1½m: acts on tapeta, soft and good to firm going: often races towards rear.
Brian Ellison

HARVARD MAN 2 b.g. (Feb 22) Equiano (FR) 127 – Fabulously Fast (USA) 120 **88**
(Deputy Minister (CAN)) [2015 5.2m* 6m⁶ 5f 5.5s⁴ p6f² Nov 7] 50,000F, 120,000Y: good-
quartered gelding: brother to 5f (including as 2 yrs) winner Equally Fast and half-brother

to several winners, including 1m winner Fabulouslyspirited (by Selkirk): dam US Grade 1 7f winner: fairly useful performer: won maiden at Newbury (by short head from Ring of Truth) in April: stays 6f: acts on polytrack, soft and good to firm going: sent to USA. *Brian Meehan*

HARVEY'S HOPE 9 b.g. Sinndar (IRE) 134 – Ancara 109 (Dancing Brave (USA) 140) **64** [2015 18s 12.4d 16.1d² 16.1m 14.1m* 14.1v³ Nov 3] modest handicapper: won at Redcar in September: stays 2m: acts on good to firm and heavy going: tried in blinkers in 2015: tried in tongue tie: sometimes slowly away, often travels strongly. *Keith Reveley*

HARWOODS STAR (IRE) 5 b.g. Danehill Dancer (IRE) 117 – Showbiz (IRE) 89 **71** (Sadler's Wells (USA) 132) [2015 69, a61: f5d* t5.1f t7.1f³ f5g* f5s² p6g⁵ 6m⁴ 6m 6s 6g⁴ 6g* 6s f6m⁵ Dec 8] fair handicapper: won at Southwell (apprentice) in January and March and Epsom in September: stays 1m: acts on fibresand, soft and good to firm going: tried in headgear: sometimes wears tongue tie: inconsistent. *Stuart Williams*

HARWOODS VOLANTF (IRE) 4 ch.g. Kheleyf (USA) 116 – Semiquaver (IRE) **98** (Mark of Esteem (IRE) 137) [2015 96: 6g⁶ 8m² 7m³ 6g* 7ııı* 7.2g³ 7d⁴ 6m⁴ 6d 6d² 7.2g 6d Sep 26] useful handicapper: won at York and Wetherby (by ½ length from Twin Point) in June: good second at Haydock (head behind Gramercy) in September: stays 7f: acts on polytrack, good to firm and good to soft going: tried in headgear: often races prominently. *David O'Meara*

HASHTAG FRENZY 2 ch.g. (Feb 18) Compton Place 125 – One Night In May (IRE) 50 **–** (Choisir (AUS) 126) [2015 6d 6d 5d 7s Oct 16] no form: tried in blinkers. *Rebecca Menzies*

HASOPOP (IRE) 5 b.g. Haatef (USA) 117 – Convenience (IRE) (Ela-Mana-Mou 132) **–** [2015 107: p7f Jan 23] leggy gelding: smart at best, well held only outing in 2015: stays 7f: acts on polytrack, good to firm and heavy going: tried in headgear: sold 11,000 gns, sent to Saudi Arabia. *Marco Botti*

HASSAH 3 b.f. Halling (USA) 133 – Regent's Park 83 (Green Desert (USA) 127) [2015 **89** 88p: 8f⁵ 10m 9.5f 8f³ Nov 9] rather unfurnished filly: fairly useful performer: fifth in minor event at Ascot in April: left Marco Botti after next start: good third in allowance race at Aqueduct final outing: stays 1m: acts on firm going: often wears cheekpieces. *Kelly Rubley, USA*

HASSLE (IRE) 6 b.g. Montjeu (IRE) 137 – Canterbury Lace (USA) (Danehill (USA) **107** 126) [2015 103: 16s³ 16m⁴ 14d³ 14d² Sep 26] sturdy gelding: useful handicapper: placed at Ascot and Haydock (twice), career-best effort when ½-length second of 17 to Nakeeta on latter course final start (forced to switch soon after 2f out): stays 2m: acts on soft and good to firm going: wears cheekpieces: quirky. *Clive Cox*

HATHAL (USA) 3 ch.c. Speightstown (USA) 124 – Sleepytime (IRE) 121 (Royal **115** Academy (USA) 130) [2015 91P: 7m* 7f 8m 8g² 7s* Sep 18] attractive colt: smart performer: won maiden at Lingfield (by 2¼ lengths from Druids Ridge) in June: first-time cheekpieces, further improvement when winning 9-runner listed race at Newbury in September by ¾ length from Ascription, well on top at line: will be suited by a return to 1m: acts on soft and good to firm going. *William Haggas*

HATSAWAY (IRE) 4 b.g. Dubawi (IRE) 129 – Scotch Bonnet (IRE) 95 (Montjeu (IRE) **75** 137) [2015 86: 8g 8m⁶ p7g 8.5m⁶ p8f 9.3m² p10m Sep 26] fair maiden: seemingly effective at 1m to 2m: acts on good to firm and good to soft going: wears headgear. *Clive Brittain*

HATTA STREAM (IRE) 9 b.g. Oasis Dream 129 – Rubies From Burma (USA) 104 **–** (Forty Niner (USA)) [2015 61: p6m p6g t6g 6m p6g 6s Aug 24] workmanlike gelding: one-time fairly useful handicapper, no form in 2015: stayed 7f: acted on polytrack, firm and soft going: dead. *Lydia Pearce*

HATTON SPRINGS (IRE) 4 b.f. Jeremy (USA) 122 – Oopsadaisy (IRE) (High **55** Chaparral (IRE) 132) [2015 –: 15s² 13.1d² 12.1g⁵ Jun 17] modest maiden: stays 15f: acts on soft going. *Stuart Coltherd*

HAUGHMOND 2 b.g. (Jan 25) Kheleyf (USA) 116 – Orapids (Oratorio (IRE) 128) [2015 **68** 5m³ 6g⁶ 5g⁵ p6g⁶ 6d⁵ 5g² 5s² 5g⁵ Oct 13] fair maiden: best form at 5f: acts on soft going: usually in headgear: sold 12,000 gns, sent to Italy. *K. R. Burke*

HAVANA BEAT (IRE) 5 b.g. Teofilo (IRE) 126 – Sweet Home Alabama (IRE) 56 **115** (Desert Prince (IRE) 130) [2015 111: 14g⁴ 15.9g⁴ 14m³ 20f 16.4m⁶ 14g 18m 12g³ Sep 25] leggy gelding: useful performer: career-best efforts when 4½ lengths fourth to Brown Panther in Dubai Gold Cup at Meydan in March and 2 lengths third to Snow Sky in Yorkshire Cup at York in May: in first-time visor, 25/1, respectable third of 7 to Cannock Chase in listed race at Newmarket final start, though did have run of race: stays 2½m: acts on firm and good to soft going. *Andrew Balding*

HAVISHAM 3 b.g. Mount Nelson 125 – Ile Deserte (Green Desert (USA) 127) [2015 **91** p12f³ p13.3g² 12m⁴ 14m³ 16f⁵ 12f³ 16s⁵ 12m 14g Aug 22] €320,000Y: well-made gelding: fourth foal: half-brother to useful 2-y-o 6f winner St Barths (by Cadeaux Genereux): dam unraced half-sister to St Leger winner Kingston Hill: fairly useful maiden: 2¼ lengths fifth to Aloft in Queen's Vase at Royal Ascot on fifth start: stays 2m: acts on firm and soft going: in cheekpieces final start (raced too freely): front runner/races prominently: has been gelded. *Andrew Balding*

HAVRE DE PAIX (FR) 3 b.f. Le Havre (IRE) 124 – Bridge of Peace (Anabaa (USA) **96** 130) [2015 7g² 8s⁶ 8s² 6s² Oct 16] first foal: dam, placed up to 1½m in France, out of useful French 2-y-o 1m/8.5f winner Hope Town: useful maiden: best effort when 2 lengths sixth of 9 to Night of Light in listed race at Chantilly in May: stays 1m. *David Menuisier*

HAWATIF (IRE) 2 b.f. (Apr 9) Royal Applause 124 – Excellerator (IRE) 101 (Exceed **77** And Excel (AUS) 126) [2015 6f⁴ 5.9g* 5.2m 6g Aug 1] £32,000Y: lengthy filly: first foal: dam 2-y-o 5f winner: fair performer: won maiden at Carlisle in June: stays 6f. *Mark Johnston*

HAWEEYA (IRE) 2 b.f. (Jan 21) Iffraaj 127 – Yin 58 (Dansili 127) [2015 t7.1f² t7.1f p8g **68** Dec 16] £40,000Y, 14,000Y, £14,000 2-y-o: second foal: dam lightly-raced half-sister to smart winner up to 1m Emirates Gold: fair maiden: easily best effort when second at Wolverhampton on debut: tried in tongue tie. *Marco Botti*

HAWKBILL (USA) 2 ch.c. (Mar 6) Kitten's Joy (USA) 128 – Trensa (USA) (Giant's **107 p** Causeway (USA) 132) [2015 5.2m p7g³ p7g* p7g* p8g* Sep 9] $350,000Y: compact colt: second foal: dam, US 8.5f winner (second in Grade 3 11f event), closely related to US Grade 3 8.5f/9f winner Batique: useful performer: won maiden at Lingfield (by neck from Lazzam) in July, nursery at Kempton (by 3¼ lengths from Powderhorn) in August and minor event at Kempton (by head from Steel of Madrid) in September: stays 1m: acts on polytrack: tried in hood: front runner/races prominently: will go on improving. *Charlie Appleby*

HAWKE (IRE) 3 b.g. Oratorio (IRE) 128 – Australie (IRE) 114 (Sadler's Wells (USA) **102** 132) [2015 8d⁴ 7g* 8g 8g³ 8g.8g⁵ p7.5g⁴ p8g⁴ p9.4g⁵ p10g Dec 15] half-brother to useful French 7f/1m winner Mireille (by Dalakhani): dam, French 1m (at 2 yrs) to 10.5f winner, half-sister to smart performer up to 2m Forgotten Voice: useful performer: won maiden at Longchamp in April: best effort when fifth in listed race at Deauville (1½ lengths behind Vodkato) on penultimate start: last of 12 in similar race at Lingfield final outing: stays 9.5f: acts on polytrack, raced mainly on good going on turf: often blinkered. *Mme Pia Brandt, France*

HAWKERLAND (IRE) 2 b.c. (Apr 17) Sea The Stars (IRE) 140 – Zarara (USA) **– p** (Manila (USA)) [2015 7m Aug 1] 140,000F: tall colt: closely related to 9.5f-1½m winner Ambleside (by Cape Cross) and half-brother to 3 winners, including very smart winner up to 1¾m All The Good (2-y-o 1¼m winner, by Diesis): dam unraced half-sister to Oaks winner Ramruma: 50/1, well held in maiden at Goodwood on debut: should do better in time. *Marcus Tregoning*

HAWKESBURY 3 gr.g. Shamardal (USA) 129 – Nahoodh (IRE) 119 (Clodovil (IRE) **114 §** 116) [2015 97: p6g* 6f⁶ 7m³ 7f* 7g² 7g t6m³ Dec 26] useful-looking gelding: smart performer: won minor events at Kempton (by 2½ lengths from Merdon Castle) in January and Haydock (by nose from Capo Rosso) in July: best other effort when third in handicap at Ascot in between: stays 7f: acts on polytrack and firm going: usually races prominently, often travels strongly: has a most awkward head carriage, one to treat with caution. *Charlie Appleby*

HAWKEYETHENOO (IRE) 9 b.g. Hawk Wing (USA) 136 – Stardance (USA) (Rahy **100 §** (USA) 115) [2015 110§: 5v⁵ 7g 7m³ 5m 7d 5m⁴ 7g 6g 6d Oct 23] good-topped gelding: useful handicapper: third in Victoria Cup at Ascot (2¾ lengths behind Speculative Bid) in May: has won at 8.5f, usually races over shorter: acts on polytrack and any turf going: tried in headgear prior to 2015: often races in rear: quirky and hard to win with. *Jim Goldie*

HAWK GOLD (IRE) 11 ch.g. Tendulkar (USA) 114 – Heiress of Meath (IRE) 34 **–** (Imperial Frontier (USA) 112) [2015 p15.8g Dec 2] good-topped gelding: maiden: best effort at 1½m: acts on good to firm going: tried in headgear. *Paddy Butler*

HAWKIN (IRE) 3 b.f. Big Bad Bob (IRE) 118 – Margaux Magique (IRE) (Xaar 132) **74** [2015 82: 7d⁴ 7m 8.3m⁶ 8g⁵ 7m³ 8.1d² 8s⁵ t7.1f⁴ 8g² p10g p8f³ Dec 17] close-coupled filly: fair maiden: stays 1m: acts on good to firm going: in headgear nowadays: often races prominently. *Ralph Beckett*

HAWKMEISTER (IRE) 3 gr.g. Mastercraftsman (IRE) 129 – Lake Ladoga (Green **62**
Desert (USA) 127) [2015 73: 9.9m⁶ 11.6f 10.2m³ 9.9m 10g⁶ Jul 21] modest maiden: stays
1¼m: acts on polytrack and good to firm going: often wears headgear: tends to find little.
Michael Blanshard

HAWK MOTH (IRE) 7 b.g. Hawk Wing (USA) 136 – Sasimoto (USA) (Saratoga Six **69**
(USA)) [2015 70: 8g⁵ 7s 8g t7.1g 7m⁶ 8m* 7g⁴ 7g⁶ t7.1g 8g² 8d² t8.6f³ p7g⁴ p8d p8g p8g³
Dec 9] rather leggy gelding: fair handicapper: won at Brighton in July: stays 8.5f: acts on
polytrack, tapeta, firm and good to firm going: often wears headgear: sometimes slowly
away, often races in rear. *John Spearing*

HAWKSMOOR (IRE) 2 b.f. (Mar 14) Azamour (IRE) 130 – Bridal Dance (IRE) 62 **104**
(Danehill Dancer (IRE) 117) [2015 p7g* 7m⁶ 7s* 7g³ 8g³ Oct 9] €80,000Y: well-made
filly: third foal: dam maiden half-sister to smart winner up to 1m Millennium Dragon:
useful performer: won maiden at Kempton in July and Prestige Stakes at Goodwood (by
nose from Fireglow) in August: third in Rockfel Stakes at Newmarket (4½ lengths behind
Promising Run) in September and in Fillies' Mile at Newmarket (6¾ lengths behind
Minding) in October: likely to stay 1¼m: acts on polytrack and soft going: sometimes
slowly away. *Hugo Palmer*

HAWRIDGE DANCER 3 b.g. Danehill Dancer (IRE) 117 – Thermopylae 81 (Tenby **71**
125) [2015 8m 8d⁵ 8m 10.3d⁵ 10.2m⁴ Jul 4] rangy gelding: fair maiden: likely to have
stayed at least 1½m: acted on good to firm going: was sometimes slowly away: dead.
Rod Millman

HAYADH 2 gr.g. (Feb 4) Oasis Dream 129 – Warling (IRE) 101 (Montjeu (IRE) 137) [2015 **103**
7f* 7d² 7f⁶ 8g⁴ 7g* Oct 21] 195,000F, 550,000Y: well-made gelding: first foal: dam, 11f
winner who stayed 14.6f, closely related to smart French performer up to 1½m War Is War:
useful performer: won maiden at Haydock in June: off 9 weeks/gelded, improved to win
minor event at Newmarket in October by 2½ lengths from Atlantic Sun: should stay 1m:
acts on firm going: usually leads. *John Gosden*

HAYBA 3 b.f. Invincible Spirit (IRE) 121 – Loch Jipp (USA) 95 (Belong To Me (USA)) **64**
[2015 –: 8g⁴ Apr 25] twice-raced maiden: still green when fourth at Haydock on sole
outing in 2015. *Marco Botti*

HAYMARKET 6 b.g. Singspiel (IRE) 133 – Quickstyx 72 (Night Shift (USA)) [2015 67: **79**
9.2d² 10d² 10g² 10s* 9.2g³ 13m⁴ 10g 10g⁵ Oct 8] fair handicapper: won at Ayr in August:
stays 1¼m: acts on soft and good to firm going: often races prominently. *R. Mike Smith*

HAZEL BLUE 4 b.f. Kodiac 112 – Pure Folly (IRE) 58 (Machiavellian (USA) **62**
123) [2015 53, a59: t8.6f⁶ t6f⁵ t9.5m* t8.6f Dec 21] modest handicapper: won at
Wolverhampton in November: left Geoffrey Harker after first start: stays 9.5f: acts on
polytrack and tapeta: tried in cheekpieces in 2015. *David O'Meara*

HAZEL'S SONG 3 b.f. Orpen (USA) 116 – Songbook (Singspiel (IRE) 133) [2015 8.3s **–**
May 8] sixth foal: dam unraced half-sister to smart 7f-1¼m performer Two-Twenty-Two:
100/1 and in hood, well held in maiden at Nottingham. *Steph Hollinshead*

HAZELY 2 b.f. (May 1) Cape Cross (IRE) 129 – Sentimental Value (USA) 107 (Diesis **–**
133) [2015 7.5g⁶ t8.6f p8g Dec 15] 15,000Y: half-sister to several winners, including useful
winner up to 1½m Personal Opinion (2-y-o 9.5f winner, by New Approach) and useful
9f/1¼m winner Oriental Cat (by Tiger Hill): dam 1m/9f winner: no form. *James Bethell*

HAZZA THE JAZZA 5 b.g. Jeremy (USA) 122 – Zagaleta 81 (Sri Pekan (USA) 117) **–**
[2015 58: t9.5f Oct 16] fair at best, well held sole start in 2015: stays 7f: acts on polytrack
and good to firm going: usually wears headgear: sometimes slowly away. *Nigel Tinkler*

HEAD COACH 3 ch.g. Medicean 128 – Lilli Marlane 82 (Sri Pekan (USA) 117) [2015 **62**
10m p8g⁴ p12g 9g⁴ 7.6m Aug 8] modest maiden: best effort at 1m: acts on polytrack: tried
in blinkers: in tongue tie: sometimes slowly away. *Luke Dace*

HEAD EAST (IRE) 2 ch.c. (Mar 15) Showcasing 117 – Seeking Dubai 93 (Dubawi (IRE) **85 p**
129) [2015 5m³ 5m³ Jun 20] €22,000Y, 52,000 2-y-o: second foal: dam, 2-y-o 6f winner,
half-sister to useful winner up to 7f Presto Vento: better effort when third in maiden at
Haydock (½ length behind Mr Lupton) in June, nearest finish: will stay 6f: will go on
improving. *Ivan Furtado*

HEAD HIGH (IRE) 2 gr.c. (Mar 24) Mastercraftsman (IRE) 129 – Elisium (Proclamation **70**
(IRE) 130) [2015 8.3m² t8.6f⁴ Oct 31] fair maiden: better effort when 1½ lengths fourth to
Loading at Wolverhampton, having run of race. *Kevin Ryan*

HEADING HOME (FR) 3 b.g. Dutch Art 126 – Nelly Dean (Pivotal 124) [2015 58: 10g **53 §**
12.1m⁴ 13.8v Oct 17] modest maiden: stays 1½m: acts on soft and good to firm going: in
headgear in 2015: unreliable. *John Quinn*

HEADING TO FIRST 8 b.g. Sulamani (IRE) 130 – Bahirah 71 (Ashkalani (IRE) 128) **?**
[2015 9.9m t12.2g Jun 26] lengthy gelding: fair at best, little form in Britain in 2015: stays
1½m: acts on any turf going: usually wears headgear: tried in tongue tie prior to 2015: sent
to Belgium, and won there in November. *Jim Best*

HEADLINE NEWS (IRE) 6 ch.m. Peintre Celebre (USA) 137 – Donnelly's Hollow **102**
(IRE) 71 (Docksider (USA) 124) [2015 96: 9.9m⁴ 12s³ 12m* 11.6d⁴ 12.3s⁴ 12g⁵ p13g³
p12g³ Nov 25] workmanlike mare: useful handicapper: won at Pontefract (by ½ length
from Almodovar) in August: even better form when in frame in listed races subsequently,
2½ lengths third to Fire Fighting at Kempton final start: stays 13f: acts on polytrack, good
to firm and heavy going: sometimes slowly away, races towards rear: sold 38,000 gns, sent
to Qatar. *Rae Guest*

HEADQUARTERS (IRE) 3 b.c. Oasis Dream 129 – Front House (IRE) 114 (Sadler's **83**
Wells (USA) 132) [2015 68p: 7f² 8g⁴ 7g Sep 19] second foal: brother to a winner in South
Africa: dam 1m-1½m winner in South Africa/UAE: fairly useful maiden: best effort at 7f:
blinkered first 2 starts in 2015. *M. F. de Kock, South Africa*

HEAD SPACE (IRE) 7 b.g. Invincible Spirit (IRE) 121 – Danzelline 83 (Danzero **80**
(AUS)) [2015 92: p7g p5m³ p5f⁴ p6f 6g⁵ 6v⁴ 5.7g 5.2m² 6m* 6m p6g⁶ p6g 6g p6f⁵ p6d
p6g² Dec 16] rangy gelding: fairly useful handicapper: won at Newbury (by 1¼ lengths
from Gold Club) in July: left Michael Attwater prior to final start: stays 7.5f: acts on
polytrack and any turf going: often wears headgear: often races towards rear. *Brian Barr*

HEADS YOU WIN 2 ch.f. (Mar 4) Compton Place 125 – Miss Rimex (IRE) 84 (Ezzoud **53**
(IRE) 126) [2015 t6m Dec 30] 8,000F: sister to 3 winners, including useful 6f-9f winner
(including in Hong Kong) Warden Complex, and half-sister to 3 winners, including
1m-1½m winner Baileys Best (by Mister Baileys): dam winner up to 1m (2-y-o 6f winner):
33/1, green when eighth of 10 in maiden at Wolverhampton in December. *Jamie Osborne*

HEARMENOW (IRE) 2 b.g. (Mar 9) Kodiac 112 – Crystalline Stream (FR) (Polish **77**
Precedent (USA) 131) [2015 p6f³ 6d⁶ p5f⁶ t5.1f t7.1g² p6g* p6g² p6g² Dec 30] fair
performer: won seller at Lingfield in December: likely to stay 1m: acts on polytrack: often
in cheekpieces: often in tongue tie: usually races close up. *J. S. Moore*

HEARTBREAK CITY (FR) 5 b.g. Lando (GER) 128 – Moscow Nights (FR) (Peintre **92**
Celebre (USA) 137) [2015 16g³ 16.4d* 18g 15s Oct 25] good-topped gelding: fairly useful
handicapper: won at York (by 2½ lengths from Saved By The Bell) in August: stays 2m:
acts on viscoride, raced only on good going or softer on turf: usually in tongue tie in 2015.
A. J. Martin, Ireland

HEARTBREAK HERO 3 b.g. Exceed And Excel (AUS) 126 – Artistic Blue (USA) 109 **97**
(Diesis 133) [2015 104: 6m 6f 8f 7m² 7m⁶ 7m 6m Oct 2] good-bodied gelding: useful
handicapper: second at York (apprentice, ¾ length behind Sakhee's Return) in July: stays
7f: acts on firm going: sometimes slowly away, often races towards rear: sold 42,000 gns,
sent to Macau. *William Haggas*

HEARTLESS 3 ch.f. New Approach (IRE) 132 – Honorine (IRE) 89 (Mark of Esteem **85 p**
(IRE) 137) [2015 10m⁶ 10.3m 10m* 10d³ Aug 15] useful-looking filly: sixth foal: closely
related to very smart winner up to 1½m (including Irish Derby) Treasure Beach (2-y-o 7f
winner, by Galileo) and half-sister to smart 1½m-1¾m winner Elidor (by Cape Cross) and
useful 1¼m-11.5f winner Honor Bound (by Authorized): dam 1m-1¼m winner: fairly
useful performer: won maiden at Newbury in July: better form when third in handicap
there: will stay at least 1½m. open to further improvement. *Andrew Balding*

HEART LOCKET 3 b.f. Champs Elysees 124 – Zante 108 (Zafonic (USA) 130) [2015 –: **75**
12.1m⁴ 11.7f* 11.6m 13.8m³ 14d² 16.2d t13.9f⁵ Nov 20] fair performer: won maiden at
Bath in June: left Roger Charlton after: worth another try at 2m: acts on tapeta, firm and
good to soft going. *Michael Easterby*

HEART OF AN ANGEL 2 ro.f. (Mar 8) Dark Angel (IRE) 113 – How High The Sky **–**
(IRE) (Danehill Dancer (IRE) 117) [2015 p7g Aug 24] smallish filly: third foal: half-sister
to French winners around 1¼m Across The Sky (by Cape Cross) and Rat Pack (by Verglas):
dam, unraced, closely related to smart French winner up to 1¼m High Rock and half-sister
to dam of very smart French performers Silver Frost (best at 1m) and Spiritjim (stays
12.5f): 7/1, well held in maiden at Kempton. *Philip McBride*

HEARTSONG (IRE) 6 b.m. Kheleyf (USA) 116 – Semiquaver (IRE) (Mark of Esteem **91**
(IRE) 137) [2015 80, a65: 6m 6g² 6.1m 7g³ 6g² 6g⁴ 6s⁴ 6.1s* 6g* 6d 6g Oct 20] lengthy
mare: fairly useful handicapper: won at Chepstow in August and Brighton (by ½ length
from Escrick) in September: stays 6f: acts on good to firm and heavy going: wears
headgear: often races prominently. *John Gallagher*

HEARTSTONE (IRE) 2 b.f. (Mar 20) Fastnet Rock (AUS) 127 – Eva's Request (IRE) **75**
115 (Soviet Star (USA) 128) [2015 7.6g² 7g Oct 9] third foal: dam 6f (at 2 yrs) to 1¼m
(Premio Lydia Tesio) winner: better effort when second in maiden at Lingfield (3¾ lengths
behind Mix And Mingle) in September, slowly away. *Charles Hills*

HEARTY (IRE) 2 b.g. (Mar 15) Big Bad Bob (IRE) 118 – Ulanova (IRE) (Noverre (USA) **–**
125) [2015 8g p8g p8g⁶ Dec 9] lengthy, rather unfurnished gelding: no form. *Jeremy Noseda*

HEATHFIELD PARK (IRE) 2 b.f. (Apr 28) Bushranger (IRE) 119 – Alexander **–**
Anapolis (IRE) 94 (Spectrum (IRE) 126) [2015 t6f Dec 22] 10,000Y: closely related to
useful 6f winner Film Maker (later successful at 1m in Italy) and winner up to 7f Cut The
Cackle (2-y-o 5f winner) (both by Danetime) and half-sister to several winners, including
2-y-o 6f winner East Coast Lady (by Kodiac): dam 1½m winner: 80/1, well held in maiden
at Wolverhampton. *William Stone*

HEAT STORM (IRE) 4 b.g. Lawman (FR) 121 – Coconut Show (Linamix (FR) 127) **58**
[2015 t8.6m⁵ t9.5g⁴ 8.3d Oct 12] modest maiden: best effort when fourth at Wolverhampton
in March. *James Unett*

HEAVENLYFRIENDSHIP 3 b.f. Multiplex 114 – Nut (IRE) 65 (Fasliyev (USA) 120) **–**
[2015 51: p7m Jun 1] maiden, modest form at best: best effort at 7f: acts on polytrack.
Brendan Powell

HEAVENLY RIVER (FR) 4 b.f. Stormy River (FR) 123 – Aaliyah (GER) (Anabaa **61**
(USA) 130) [2015 60: 10.3d³ 10.3d 10.1m³ 10g 11.9m Aug 7] modest maiden: stays 10.5f:
acts on good to firm and good to soft going: tried in visor: often races in rear. *K. R. Burke*

HEAVENS ABOVE (IRE) 3 b.f. Montjeu (IRE) 137 – Sharplaw Star 97 (Xaar 132) **51**
[2015 55: p10f⁴ p10g Feb 24] modest maiden: stays 1¼m: acts on polytrack: in blinkers in
2015: often races towards rear. *Ed Dunlop*

HEAVEN SCENT 2 ch.f. (Jan 30) Phoenix Reach (IRE) 124 – Hel's Angel (IRE) 86 **72**
(Pyrus (USA) 106) [2015 8.3m⁴ 8.5m⁶ 10d* Oct 5] first foal: dam 1m-1½m winner: fair
performer: best effort when winning maiden at Pontefract (by 2¼ lengths from Argyle) in
October: will be suited by further than 1¼m. *Ann Duffield*

HEAVENS EYES (IRE) 4 b.f. Oasis Dream 129 – Snowtime (IRE) (Galileo (IRE) 134) **86**
[2015 77: f11d³ p11f⁴ f8d³ t9.5g⁴ t9.5g* 8.9g 10g t9.5f* Nov 10] fairly useful
handicapper: won at Southwell and Wolverhampton in July, and Wolverhampton (by neck
from Miss Minuty) in November: stays 9.5f: acts on all-weather: front runner/races
prominently: sold 26,000 gns, sent to Saudi Arabia. *Jo Hughes*

HEAVEN'S GUEST (IRE) 5 b.g. Dark Angel (IRE) 113 – Bakewell Tart (IRE) 92 **112**
(Tagula (IRE) 116) [2015 115: 6d 7g* 7m 7d* 7g 7f³ 7d* 7d⁵ 7g⁴ 6g 7m 6d Oct 17] good-
topped gelding: smart performer: won minor event at Thirsk (by 1¼ lengths from Balty
Boys) in April, listed race at Naas (by ½ length from Lat Hawill) in June and International
Stakes (Handicap) at Ascot (by head from Balty Boys) in July: third in Bunbury Cup
(Handicap) at Newmarket (length behind Rene Mathis) in July: stays 7f: acts on any turf
going: often races prominently. *Richard Fahey*

*Gigaset International Stakes (Heritage Handicap), Ascot—over a quarter of the original field is
withdrawn on the day due to the softened ground, but Heaven's Guest (No.8) still has to get the better
of twenty rivals to win from Balty Boys (No.2), Donncha (whip in air) and Burnt Sugar (star on cap);
there is plenty of controversy in the aftermath with favourite Speculative Bid, who didn't come out
of the stalls because his head was over the side and jockey Jamie Spencer was out of the saddle,
officially declared a non-runner after the 'weighed-in' signal had been given, only for that decision
to be later reversed (there is a court case in progress, with bookmaker Geoff Banks challenging the
BHA and seeking compensation for losses sustained in the confusion over whether or not there was
a Rule 4 deduction on winnings)*

HECTOR'S CHANCE 6 ch.g. Byron 117 – Fleur A Lay (USA) 53 (Mr Greeley (USA) **74**
122) [2015 75: p10f² p10m² p10f² 10m 10g⁶ t8.6g³ 8m² 8m⁶ p10g⁶ 8.1g⁶ 10.2s⁵ p8g p8g **a82**
Oct 6] well-made gelding: fairly useful handicapper: stays 1½m: acts on polytrack, tapeta,
soft and good to firm going: tried in headgear: tried in tongue tie in 2015: front runner/races
prominently. *Heather Main*

HEDGE END (IRE) 4 gr.f. Verglas (IRE) 118 – Trilemma 84 (Slip Anchor 136) [2015 89: **78**
t9.5f⁴ 11.6m 10m 9.9m p8g p8g 8.1g⁵ t9.5f p10g⁴ t9.5f Dec 11] strong filly: fair
handicapper: left Richard Hannon after first start: stays 11.5f: acts on polytrack, tapeta,
firm and soft going. *Jimmy Fox*

HEEZARARITY 7 b.g. Librettist (USA) 124 – Extremely Rare (IRE) 82 (Mark of Esteem **77**
(IRE) 137) [2015 77: p10g² 10.2s⁵ t8.6g p10g⁶ Dec 10] tall gelding: fair handicapper: stays
1¼m: acts on polytrack, firm and soft going: tried in tongue tie prior to 2015. *Jonathan Geake*

HEHO 4 b.f. Dansili 127 – Nitya (FR) (Indian Ridge 123) [2015 82: p8g⁴ t9.5g³ p8m⁵ Feb **75**
12] fair handicapper: stays 1¼m: acts on polytrack, best turf form on good to soft going:
tried in headgear. *William Knight*

HEIR TO A THRONE (FR) 2 ch.g. (Mar 10) Siyouni (FR) 122 – Boaka (FR) (Kahyasi **80**
130) [2015 7.5s⁵ 7g² 7g² Sep 23] €13,000Y, €60,000 2-y-o: fourth foal: half-brother to
French 1m winner Alexandra Blue (by High Yield) and French 10.5f winner Xellent (by
Naaqoos): dam French 2-y-o 1m winner: fairly useful form: improved again when neck
second to Dark Devil in maiden at Redcar final start. *Kevin Ryan*

HEISMAN (IRE) 4 b.g. Teofilo (IRE) 126 – Luminata (IRE) 103 (Indian Ridge 123) **97**
[2015 100p: 8.1m 10f⁴ t8.6m⁴ 8.5s⁴ Oct 9] tall gelding: useful handicapper: stays 1¼m:
acts on polytrack, tapeta and firm going: usually wears tongue tie: often races towards rear.
Olly Stevens

HELAMIS 5 b.m. Shirocco (GER) 129 – Alnoor (USA) (Danzig (USA)) [2015 –: t12.2f⁶ **39**
Oct 16] poor handicapper: stays 11.5f: acts on good to firm going: tried in headgear prior
to 2015. *Barry Leavy*

HELEN'S ARMADA (IRE) 4 b.f. Oratorio (IRE) 128 – The Real Thing (IRE) 84 **63**
(Traditionally (USA) 117) [2015 70: 7s 7d 8s* 8g⁴ 7g Oct 20] modest handicapper: won at
Gowran in September: stays 8.5f: acts on polytrack, good to firm and heavy going: often
wears tongue tie. *Adrian McGuinness, Ireland*

HELFIRE 2 b.f. (Feb 12) Archipenko (USA) 127 – Relkida 76 (Bertolini (USA) 125) **57 p**
[2015 6m Aug 17] third foal: half-sister to useful 6f-1m winner Realize (by Zafeen): dam,
2-y-o 5f winner, half-sister to smart winner up to 8.6f Nazreef: 50/1 and very green, some
encouragement when seventh in maiden at Windsor (5¾ lengths behind Dancing Star) in
August: will improve. *Hughie Morrison*

HELIUM (FR) 10 b.g. Dream Well (FR) 127 – Sure Harbour (SWI) (Surumu (GER)) **56**
[2015 f16d² f14s⁵ t12.2g May 11] modest maiden, very lightly raced on Flat: best effort at
2m: acts on fibresand: blinkered final start: fair hurdler/modest chaser. *Alexandra Dunn*

HELLBENDER (IRE) 9 ch.g. Exceed And Excel (AUS) 126 – Desert Rose (Green **58**
Desert (USA) 127) [2015 59, a77: t7.1g⁵ p7f p7g³ f7g⁵ 7.1s³ 7d⁶ 7.2d² t7.1g 7.2d³ p7g² **a64**
t7.1f 7s p7g Dec 2] strong gelding: modest handicapper: stays 7f: acts on all-weather, good
to firm and heavy going: tried in headgear: tried in tongue tie prior to 2015. *Shaun Harris*

HELLO BEAUTIFUL (IRE) 4 ch.f. Captain Rio 122 – Tekhania (IRE) (Dalakhani **54**
(IRE) 133) [2015 68: t5.1g 5m⁵ 6m³ 5d 6g 5m⁴ 5d² 5d³ Jun 25] modest handicapper: best
form at 5f: acts on good to firm and good to soft going: tried in headgear. *Brian Ellison*

HELL OF A LORD 3 br.g. Hellvelyn 118 – Miss Brookie 70 (The West (USA) 107) **–**
[2015 81: f5g³ t6g 7d 6d p8g⁴ 10.2s⁶ Aug 31] sturdy gelding: maiden: no form in 2015:
tried in headgear in 2015: tried in tongue tie in 2015. *Bill Turner*

HELLOLINI 5 b.m. Bertolini (USA) 125 – Smiddy Hill 85 (Factual (USA) 108) [2015 48: **–**
t5.1f f6s t5.1g Feb 9] maiden: no form in 2015: sometimes wears headgear. *Rebecca
Bastiman*

HELLS BABE 2 gr.f. (Apr 23) Hellvelyn 118 – Blues In Cee (IRE) 91 (Sinndar (IRE) 134) **83**
[2015 p6g 6m⁴ 7s* 8d⁴ Oct 31] good-topped filly: second foal: dam, 1½m winner, half-
sister to 2-y-o 7f winner History Note and 1m winner Stepwise (both useful): fairly useful
form: won maiden at Leicester (by ½ length from Intermittent) in October: 20/1, 8 lengths
fourth of 9 to Fireglow in listed race at Newmarket final start: should stay beyond 7f.
Seamus Durack

HELLVELYN WINDS 2 gr.f. (Mar 19) Hellvelyn 118 – Mix It Up (Linamix (FR) 127) **54**
[2015 6d⁴ 6.1d⁶ Aug 14] 1,200F: fifth foal: dam twice-raced half-sister to useful 7f/1m
winner Bishr: better effort in maidens when fourth at Newmarket (7½ lengths behind Bing
Bang Bong) in July. *Dr Jon Scargill*

HELL YEAH 4 b.g. Raven's Pass (USA) 133 – Go Between 91 (Daggers Drawn (USA) **82 p**
114) [2015 p12g* Aug 17] 70,000Y, £800 3-y-o: fifth foal: half-brother to 3 winning
sprinters, including 5f (including at 2 yrs) winner Go Nani Go (by Kyllachy): dam, winner
up to 7f (2-y-o 6f winner), half-sister to smart 5f-1m winner Grecian Dancer: 25/1, won
maiden at Kempton (by 1½ lengths from Every Instinct, patiently ridden and leading well
inside final 1f) in August: capable of better. *Brendan Powell*

HELMSLEY FLYER (IRE) 5 b.g. Baltic King 120 – Dorn Hill 55 (Lujain (USA) 119) **–**
[2015 75: t12.2f Jan 16] fair handicapper: well held only start in 2015: likely to prove best
up to 1¾m: acts on polytrack, good to firm and good to soft going: wears headgear.
Trevor Wall

HELMSMAN (IRE) 3 b.g. Alhaarth (IRE) 126 – La Cuvee 48 (Mark of Esteem (IRE) **65**
137) [2015 75: p10m⁵ p8f⁵ 10.2m⁵ 10d⁴ 10m³ p12g⁴ 11.9g⁴ 14.4g² Aug 10] tall gelding: fair
maiden: stays 14.4f: acts on polytrack, good to firm and good to soft going: often wears
headgear. *J. S. Moore*

HELVETIA (USA) 3 b.f. Blame (USA) 129 – Helstra (USA) (Nureyev (USA) 131) [2015 **74**
6g 6g⁴ 6m⁵ t5.1f* p5f Oct 24] closely related to a winner in Canada by Arch and half-sister
to several winners, including smart French 5f winner (including at 2 yrs) Stern Opinion (by
Mizzen Mast): dam, US 6f winner, out of US Grade 1 8.5f winner Hail Atlantis: fair
performer: won maiden at Wolverhampton in October: left P. Bary after second start: best
effort at 5f: acts on tapeta: in hood last 2 starts. *Rae Guest*

HELVIS 3 gr.g. Hellvelyn 118 – Easy Mover (IRE) 77 (Bluebird (USA) 125) [2015 6g² 6s⁴ **48**
6m⁴ Sep 8] poor maiden: best effort when second at Hamilton in July. *Bryan Smart*

HENLEY 3 b.g. Royal Applause 124 – Making Waves (IRE) 70 (Danehill (USA) 126) **61**
[2015 81: 5m² 6m⁶ 5.5g Jul 13] angular gelding: modest maiden: stays 6f: acts on good to
firm going: temperament under suspicion. *William Jarvis*

HENPECKED 5 b.m. Footstepsinthesand 120 – Poule de Luxe (IRE) 75 (Cadeaux **66**
Generous 131) [2015 69: 13d⁴ 13d³ 10g² 11.1s² 9.2s² 10d* 10d⁶ 10g 10.4d 10s² Oct 16] fair
handicapper: first past the post at Hamilton (demoted to second after causing interference)
in July and Ayr in August: stays 11f: acts on soft going: tried in cheekpieces in 2015.
Alistair Whillans

HENRI DE BOISTRON (FR) 5 b.g. Enrique 121 – Highness Royale (FR) (Garde **–**
Royale 120) [2015 t12.2g Jun 3] 33/1, well held in claimer at Wolverhampton: winning
chaser. *Tom George*

HENRIETTA DANCER 3 ch.f. Sakhee's Secret 128 – Craic Sa Ceili (IRE) 83 (Danehill **–**
Dancer (IRE) 117) [2015 –: t6g⁵ t6g Aug 6] no form: in hood in 2015. *Malcolm Saunders*

HENRY GRACE (IRE) 4 b.c. Oratorio (IRE) 128 – Little Miss Gracie 105 (Efisio 120) **62**
[2015 61: p8g* p8f² p8g⁴ p8g⁶ p8g Sep 9] modest handicapper: won at Kempton in
January: stays 1m: acts on polytrack: sometimes wears blinkers: often races towards rear.
Jimmy Fox

HENRYHUDSONBRIDGE (USA) 3 b.g. Henrythenavigator (USA) 131 – Harlan Ash **59**
(USA) (Harlan (USA) 118) [2015 63: 8.1s⁴ 7m 16g³ 5.7d t7.1f Sep 19] modest maiden: left
Brian Meehan after third start: stays 8.5f: acts on good going: sometimes wears headgear.
Edward Bevan

HENRY MORGAN 8 ch.g. Bahamian Bounty 116 – Hill Welcome 52 (Most Welcome **62**
131) [2015 45: 7g 5m² 5g² 5g* 5m⁴ 5d² 5m 5m Sep 28] modest handicapper: won at
Hamilton in July: stays 6f: acts on firm and soft going: tried in cheekpieces prior to 2015:
usually races close up. *David Brown*

HENRY SMITH 3 b.g. Firebreak 125 – So Discreet (Tragic Role (USA)) [2015 7g⁵ 6m⁶ **59**
8m t8.6f⁶ t9.5f⁵ p10f³ Oct 29] modest maiden: left Fred Watson after second start: stays
9.5f: acts on tapeta: in headgear: sometimes acts slowly away, often races prominently.
Garry Moss

HENRY THE EXPLORER (CAN) 2 b.c. (Apr 11) Henrythenavigator (USA) 131 – **71**
Game (FR) (Montjeu (IRE) 137) [2015 7m⁶ 7.1m² 7g² 7d⁵ 8s⁴ p7g⁵ Sep 23] quite good-
topped colt: fair maiden: should stay 1m: acts on good to soft going: usually races
prominently. *Jo Hughes*

HEPPLEWHITE 2 b.c. (Mar 29) Rail Link 132 – Millistar 88 (Galileo (IRE) 134) [2015 **82**
8.3g t8.6m² 8g² Oct 21] £18,000Y: good-topped colt: fifth foal: half-brother to 3 winners,
including 1¼m-1½m winner Syncopate (by Oratorio) and 9.5f winner (stays 1½m) Le
Notre (by Champs Elysees): dam 1¼m winner: fairly useful form: 14/1, improved again/
seen to advantage when 4½ lengths second of 12 to Prize Money in maiden at Newmarket
final start, racing stand side. *Robert Eddery*

HEPWORTH MARBLE (IRE) 2 b.f. (Mar 15) Lilbourne Lad (IRE) 111 – Angel **69**
Nights (IRE) (Night Shift (USA)) [2015 6g⁵ 5d³ Jul 25] £20,000Y: strong filly: fourth foal:
half-sister to 2-y-o 5f winner Monkey Bar Flies (by Elusive City), later 6f winner in
Scandinavia: dam unraced half-sister to smart Hong Kong performer up to 1m Sunny Sing:
better effort when third in maiden at Lingfield (4½ lengths behind Jakaby Jade) in July.
Gary Moore

HERALDIC (USA) 2 b.c. (Apr 9) Discreet Cat (USA) 127 – Chilukki's Song (USA) **85**
(Elusive Quality (USA)) [2015 5s³ p6g* 7d⁵ p6g³ p6f⁶ Sep 24] £20,000Y: first foal: dam US 6f winner
(on sole start) out of smart US Grade 1 2-y-o 7f/1m winner Chilukki: fairly useful
performer: won maiden at Lingfield (by 6 lengths from Criminalistic) in June: stays 6f: acts
on polytrack. *Mark Johnston*

HERALD THE DAWN (IRE) 2 b.c. (May 20) New Approach (IRE) 132 – Hymn of **110**
The Dawn (USA) 73 (Phone Trick (USA)) [2015 6m² 7g* 7s* 7d² 8m Oct 4] strong, close-
coupled colt: brother to 2000 Guineas winner Dawn Approach (2-y-o 5f-7f winner) and
half-brother to 5f-7f winner Comadoir (by Medecis): dam disappointing maiden: smart
performer: won maiden at Naas in August and Futurity Stakes at the Curragh (by 1¼
lengths from Now Or Never) in August: creditable efforts both subsequent starts, 3 lengths
second of 5 to Air Force Blue in National Stakes at the Curragh and 3 lengths seventh of 11
to Ultra in Prix Jean-Luc Lagardere at Longchamp: should stay 1m: acts on soft going: not
settle fully last 2 starts. *J. S. Bolger, Ireland*

Godolphin & Mrs J S Bolger's "Herald The Dawn"

HERCULLIAN PRINCE 3 b.g. Royal Applause 124 – Thara'a (IRE) 69 (Desert Prince **83**
(IRE) 130) [2015 p7g⁴ p7f³ 7g³ t8.6g* 8.5g⁴ p8g³ 8.1g p12g p8m³ t8.6g² t8.6f³
t9.5f⁶ Dec 21] 50,000F: fifth foal: half-brother to temperamental 7f winner Straitjacket (by
Refuse To Bend): dam, maiden (stayed 1m), half-sister to smart French sprinter Tycoon's
Hill: fairly useful handicapper: won at Wolverhampton in July: left Olly Stevens after
eighth start: stays 8.5f: acts on polytrack and tapeta: often in headgear: often travels
strongly: has hinted at temperament. *Conor Dore*

HEREAWI 2 b.f. (Mar 1) Dubawi (IRE) 129 – Look Here 123 (Hernando (FR) 127) **84 p**
[2015 8g² 8.3d⁵ Oct 14] second foal: dam winner up to 1½m (2-y-o 1m winner), including
Oaks: better effort when second in maiden at Newmarket (2½ lengths behind Haggle) in
September: will be suited by 1¼m+: remains open to improvement. *Ralph Beckett*

HERECOMESTHEBAND 3 b.g. Bertolini (USA) 125 – Green Supreme (Primo **61**
Dominie 121) [2015 63: 6d² p7g p6fᵇᵘ t7.1g⁶ p6m Dec 16] modest maiden: stays 7f: acts
on good to soft going: sometimes in blinkers in 2015. *George Baker*

HERE COMES WHEN (IRE) 5 b.g. Danehill Dancer (IRE) 117 – Quad's Melody **116**
(IRE) 107 (Spinning World (USA) 130) [2015 122: 8.1d² 8m⁶ 8f 8g⁴ 7d 7s² 7g⁶ Oct 9] tall,
lengthy gelding: smart performer: second in Mile at Sandown (1½ lengths behind Custom
Cut) in April and in Supreme Stakes at Goodwood (head behind So Beloved) in August:
also ran creditably when fourth to Night of Thunder in Lockinge Stakes at Newbury and
fourth to Solow in Sussex Stakes at Goodwood: stays 1m: acts on good to firm ground,
ideally suited by good or softer (winner on heavy): usually wears hood: sometimes slowly
away: tends to sweat. *Andrew Balding*

HERE FOR GOOD (IRE) 4 b.g. Aqlaam 125 – North East Bay (USA) (Prospect Bay **–**
(CAN) 117) [2015 69: f12s⁶ Feb 3] fair handicapper: well held only start in 2015: should
have stayed beyond 1½m: acted on all-weather: usually raced prominently: dead. *Brian
Ellison*

HERE'S TWO 2 b.f. (Apr 29) Hellvelyn 118 – There's Two (IRE) 85 (Ashkalani (IRE) **64**
128) [2015 8.3m⁶ p7g⁴ 7.6g⁴ t7.1f Oct 13] closely related to 5f-1¼m winner Ken's Girl (by
Ishiguru) and half-sister to several winners, including useful 6f winner (including at 2 yrs)
Cartmell Cleave (by Pastoral Pursuits) and 1¼m-17f winner Sula Two (by Sulamani): dam
2-y-o 6f winner: modest maiden: stays 7f. *Ron Hodges*

HEREWARD THE WAKE 2 gr.c. (Feb 14) Fastnet Rock (AUS) 127 – Miss Universe **– p**
(IRE) 99 (Warning 136) [2015 p8g Dec 9] half-brother to numerous winners, including
smart winner up to 1m (including Breeders' Cup Juvenile Turf) Donativum (by Cadeaux
Genereux) and useful German winner up to 1m Nice Danon (2-y-o 7f winner, by Sakhee):
dam 2-y-o 6f winner: 66/1, green when tailed off in maiden at Kempton: will be better for
experience. *Sylvester Kirk*

HERMARNA 2 br.f. (Feb 11) Heliostatic (IRE) 115 – Louverissa (IRE) (Verglas **73 p**
(IRE) 118) [2015 8g 7s* Oct 12] €16,500 2-y-o: good-topped filly: third foal: half-sister to
2-y-o 1m winner Lulani (by Royal Applause) and a winner abroad by Medicean: dam
unraced half-sister to 2000 Guineas winner Cockney Rebel: better effort when winning
maiden at Salisbury (by 2¾ lengths from The Juggler) in October, forging clear: should
stay 1m: likely to progress further. *Harry Dunlop*

HERMITAGE BAY (USA) 2 b.c. (Feb 2) War Front (USA) 119 – City Sister (USA) **70 p**
(Carson City (USA)) [2015 p8g³ Dec 9] $750,000F: half-brother to 3 winners in USA by
Dixie Union, including smart Grade 2 2-y-o 9f winner Dixie City: dam, US 6f/7f winner,
half-sister to US Grade 3 1m winner Fast Decision: 11/10, encouragement when 3 lengths
third of 12 to Graceful James in maiden at Kempton on debut, not knocked about: has
scope for plenty of improvement. *John Gosden*

HERMOSA VAQUERA (IRE) 5 b.m. High Chaparral (IRE) 132 – Sundown 71 (Polish **66**
Precedent (USA) 131) [2015 –: p12f p10m p13.3g⁵ 9.9d² p12g 11.9d* 11.9s² 9.9s Oct 15]
good-topped mare: fair handicapper: won at Brighton in September: left Anna Newton-
Smith after third start: stays 1½m: acts on heavy going: often wears cheekpieces:
sometimes in tongue tie in 2015: usually races close up. *Gary Moore*

HERNANDOSHIDEAWAY 3 b.g. Hernando (FR) 127 – Alba Stella 92 (Nashwan **102**
(USA) 135) [2015 89P: 12.3s² 11.9g² 12g* 14g 12g Sep 24] useful handicapper: won at
Pontefract (by 1½ lengths from Penhill) in August: good second at Haydock (1¾ lengths
behind Fabricate) in May: should stay further than 1½m: acts on good to soft going: often
travels strongly. *Michael Dods*

HERNANDO TORRES 7 b.g. Iffraaj 127 – Espana 69 (Hernando (FR) 127) [2015 t9.5f* **82**
7g* 7.1g³ 8.9g³ 7d 8d t9.5g 10.3d⁵ t8.6g⁴ t9.5g² t8.6f* Dec 14] workmanlike gelding: fairly
useful handicapper: won at Wolverhampton in January, Newcastle (apprentice) in April
and Wolverhampton in December: stays 1½m, effective over shorter: acts on tapeta and
any turf going: sometimes wears cheekpieces: tried in tongue tie. *Michael Easterby*

HEROIC HEART (FR) 2 b.f. (Mar 27) Invincible Spirit (IRE) 121 – Because (IRE) 87 **80**
(Sadler's Wells (USA) 132) [2015 6.5m 7m² 7m² p7g⁵ 6g² p6g⁴ t5.1f Oct 13] half-sister to **a68**
useful winner up to 1½m Anhar (2-y-o 8.3f winner, by Kingmambo) and 1½m winner
Buchanan (by Dansili): dam, maiden (stayed 1½m), sister to Moyglare Stud Stakes winner
Quarter Moon (dam of Pretty Polly Stakes winner Diamondsandrubies) and Irish 1000
Guineas winner Yesterday, both second in Oaks: fairly useful maiden: best efforts when
second at Newbury and Newmarket : will stay at least 1m: acts on good to firm going: tried
in hood. *John Gosden*

HEROIQUE (IRE) 4 b.f. Acclamation 118 – Gay Heroine 105 (Caerleon (USA) 132) **68**
[2015 78: 5m³ 5g⁶ 5d⁴ 7m⁵ 6g⁴ 5.9s⁴ 5.9g² 6g⁵ 6m 6g Sep 23] leggy filly: fair handicapper:
stays 7.5f: acts on good to firm and heavy going: often wears headgear: front runner/races
prominently. *Tim Easterby*

HERO'S STORY 5 b.g. Mount Nelson 125 – Red Roses Story (FR) 118 (Pink (FR) 123) **61**
[2015 –: 10d³ 10d⁴ 10g³ 13.1s³ 15s³ 15.8g³ 16.1g 12.1g* 13.1g³ t13.9f Nov 20] well-made
gelding: modest handicapper: won at Hamilton in September: stays 2m: acts on soft going:
sometimes wears headgear. *Jim Goldie*

HER RED DEVIL (IRE) 4 b.f. Jeremy (USA) 122 – All Began (IRE) 63 (Fasliyev **42**
(USA) 120) [2015 68: f8d t8.6m⁵ t12.2f t9.5m t7.1f t8.6m 11.8m Jun 23] poor handicapper:
left Christopher Kellett after sixth start: best effort at 8.5f: acts on good to firm going: often
in tongue tie in 2015. *Jennie Candlish*

HERRIDGE (IRE) 2 ch.f. (Apr 29) Bahamian Bounty 116 – Quickstyx 72 (Night Shift **66**
(USA)) [2015 5f p6g³ 6g p7g p7g* t9.5f⁵ t8.6f⁶ f8m Dec 8] 11,000F, 30,000Y: good-topped
filly: sister to 6f (including at 2 yrs) winner Hairspray and 7f winner Collingbourneducis
and half-sister to several winners, including winner up to 1m Watneya (2-y-o 6f winner, by
Dubawi): dam 1m winner who stayed 1¼m: fair performer: won nursery at Kempton in
October: probably stays 9.5f: acts on polytrack and tapeta. *Richard Hannon*

HE'S A DREAMER (IRE) 2 ch.g. (May 20) Dream Ahead (USA) 133 – Illuminise **86**
(IRE) 109 (Grand Lodge (USA) 125) [2015 t7.1m³ p7g² t7.1f⁶ Nov 13] 34,000Y: lengthy
gelding: fifth foal: half-brother to 3 winners, including 1½m winner Break My Mind (by
Nayef) and useful winner up to 1m Oracolo (2-y-o 7f winner, by Cape Cross): dam 7f/1m
winner: fairly useful maiden: best effort when second at Lingfield (length behind Race
Day) in October: has been gelded. *David Simcock*

HESKA (IRE) 4 b.g. Rock of Gibraltar (IRE) 133 – Sweet Sioux 59 (Halling (USA) 133) **66 §**
[2015 78: t12.2f⁶ p13.3g³ 11.8d⁵ 13.7m 11.6g⁴ 15.8s⁵ f11g t9.5f t12.2m Dec 26] angular **a72 §**
gelding: fair handicapper: stays 13.5f: acts on polytrack, tapeta, firm and good to soft
going: usually wears headgear: often wears tongue tie: usually slowly away, often races
towards rear: not one to rely on. *Michael Appleby*

HESKETH BANK 4 b.g. Aqlaam 125 – Wendylina (IRE) (In The Wings 128) [2015 88: **57**
10s 13s May 3] modest handicapper: stays 12.5f: acts on good to soft going: blinkered last
start in 2015. *Richard Fahey*

HE'S MY BOY (IRE) 4 gr.g. Dark Angel (IRE) 113 – Rose of Battle 80 (Averti (IRE) **69**
117) [2015 77: p6g⁴ 6m p7g⁶ 7.5m 8m⁵ 7m 7g⁶ 6m Sep 19] lengthy, rather leggy
gelding: fair handicapper: first past the post at Newmarket in July but disqualified due to
prohibited substance: stays 7f: acts on polytrack and good to firm going: often wears
headgear. *James Fanshawe*

HE'S MY CRACKER 2 ch.g. (Feb 4) Captain Gerrard (IRE) 113 – Dalmunzie (IRE) **64 p**
(Choisir (AUS) 126) [2015 7d⁶ Oct 23] third foal: brother to 2 winners, including 2-y-o 5f
winner (stays 7f) You're My Cracker: dam twice-raced half-sister to useful performer up
to 1m Berenica: 50/1, sixth in maiden at Doncaster (10½ lengths behind Royal Artillery) in
October: should prove as effective at 6f: should do better. *Clive Cox*

HE'S NO SAINT 4 b.g. Dutch Art 126 – Stellar Brilliant (USA) 85 (Kris S (USA)) [2015 **100**
98: 8g 7m⁵ 7m³ 7.9g⁴ 8m* 8d 8d p8f Oct 24] sturdy gelding: useful handicapper: won at
York (by 3¾ lengths from Woody Bay) in July: stays 1m: acts on polytrack and good to firm
going: sometimes wears headgear: front runner/races prominently. *David O'Meara*

HEURTEVENT (FR) 6 b.g. Hold That Tiger (USA) 117 – Sybilia (GER) 99 (Spectrum   –
(IRE) 126) [2015 t13.9g⁵ p12m⁵ p16g Dec 16] winner in France at 2 yrs: well held in
handicaps on Flat in 2015, but won over fences: tried in blinkers. *Tony Carroll*

HEY BEN 2 ch.g. (Apr 9) Sakhee's Secret 128 – Gib (IRE) 81 (Rock of Gibraltar (IRE)   –
133) [2015 f8g t7.1g⁶ Dec 4] no form. *Ronald Thompson*

HEY BOB (IRE) 3 br.g. Big Bad Bob (IRE) 118 – Bounty Star (IRE) (Fasliyev (USA)   –
120) [2015 –: 8s 7g 9m 10s 8m Aug 8] no form: sometimes in headgear/tongue tie in 2015.
Chris Grant

HIBOU 2 ch.g. (Feb 15) Street Cry (IRE) 130 – Arlette (IRE) (King of Kings (IRE) 125)   **85**
[2015 6g⁶ 7f² p7g p8g* 8d³ Aug 18] brother to useful 2-y-o 6f/7f winner Autumn Lily and
half-brother to several winners, including very smart winner up to 9f Alexandros (2-y-o
6f/7f winner, by Kingmambo): dam, French winner up to 9.5f (8.5f/9f winner at 2 yrs),
closely related to high-class 1½m winner In The Wings: fairly useful performer: won
maiden at Lingfield (by 4 lengths from Celebration Day) in August: stays 1m: acts on
polytrack: sometimes in blinkers. *Charlie Appleby*

HICKSTER (IRE) 4 br.g. Intense Focus (USA) 117 – Surrender To Me (USA) (Royal   **77**
Anthem (USA) 135) [2015 55, a65: t9.5g² f5g t9.5f* t8.6g³ t8.6g* 10m* 8.3g⁶ 9.9m³ 12s⁴   **a85**
11.8g³ 13.8d⁵ 10s t9.5f⁴ t9.5f* t9.5f² Dec 21] small gelding: fairly useful handicapper: won
at Wolverhampton in March and June, Leicester in June and Wolverhampton again in
December: best short of 1½m: acts on polytrack, tapeta, soft and good to firm going: tried
in visor: often wears tongue tie: usually leads. *Roy Bowring*

HI DANCER 12 b.g. Medicean 128 – Sea Music (Inchinor 119) [2015 13d Jun 4] useful-
looking gelding: fair at best, well held only start in 2015: stays 2m: acts on fibresand, firm
and soft going. *Ben Haslam*

HIDDEN ASSET 5 ch.g. Sakhee's Secret 128 – Petite Epaulette 80 (Night Shift (USA))   **51**
[2015 68: p8f² p10f f7s t8.6m 10g⁵ 7s t9.5f t7.1f Oct 23] modest handicapper: stays 9.5f:
acts on polytrack and tapeta: tried in cheekpieces: sometimes slowly away. *Michael Appleby*

HIDDEN GOLD (IRE) 4 b.f. Shamardal (USA) 129 – Melikah (IRE) 116 (Lammtarra   **109**
(USA) 134) [2015 110p: p15.8f³ 16f⁵ 14m² 16.4d³ 14.6m 16d⁵ Oct 17] useful performer:
second in Lillie Langtry Stakes at Goodwood (1½ lengths behind Simple Verse) in July and
third in Lonsdale Cup at York (5½ lengths behind Max Dynamite) in August: creditable
fifth of 15 to Flying Officer in Long Distance Cup at Ascot final start: will stay beyond
16.5f: acts on polytrack, tapeta, firm and soft going: sometimes in hood prior to 2015: often
races towards rear. *Saeed bin Suroor*

HIDDEN JUSTICE (IRE) 6 b.g. Lawman (FR) 121 – Uncharted Haven (Turtle Island   **91**
(IRE) 123) [2015 90: 16.4m 15.8d³ 15.8g 16.4g⁴ 17.5g² 16.4s² 16d Oct 30] sturdy gelding:
fairly useful handicapper: second at York (neck behind Gleese The Devil) in October: stays
2¼m: acts on polytrack, good to firm and heavy going: has worn headgear. *John Quinn*

HIDDEN REBEL 3 b.f. Cockney Rebel (IRE) 127 – Medicea Sidera 101 (Medicean 128)   **87**
[2015 60: 8g² 10g² 10d⁵ 8m* 8m* 8m² 7.9g² 8g* 8m Sep 27] fairly useful handicapper:
won at Musselburgh in June, Redcar in July and Musselburgh (by 1½ lengths from Atlantic
Affair) in September: stays 1m: acts on good to firm going: tried in hood in 2015: tail
flasher. *Alistair Whillans*

HIDDEN TREASURES 2 ch.f. (Feb 8) Zoffany (IRE) 121 – Swynford Pleasure 72   **79**
(Reprimand 122) [2015 t6f⁶ p7g² f8g³ Dec 18] £56,000Y: sixth foal: closely related to
2-y-o 7f winner Bee Brave (by Rail Link), later useful 1m/8.5f winner (stayed 1¼m) in
USA, and half-sister to 1m/9f winner Petsas Pleasure (by Observatory) and 6f/7f winner
Saskia's Dream (by Oasis Dream): dam 1m-12.3f winner: fair maiden: best effort when
second at Chelmsford (2 lengths behind Quality Time) in November. *Richard Fahey*

HIDE YOUR FIRES (IRE) 2 b.f. (May 5) Frozen Power (IRE) 108 – Omanah (USA)   **77**
(Kayrawan (USA) 91) [2015 t5.1g⁵ 5m p6f* t7.1f³ t7.1m³ Dec 18] €4,500 2-y-o: half-sister
to several winners, including 8.5f/9.5f winner Cul A Dun (by Soviet Star) and 7f-8.5f
winner Chevie (by Chevalier), both useful: dam ran twice in USA: fair performer: won
maiden at Chelmsford in September: stays 7f: acts on polytrack and tapeta. *Marco Botti*

HI EMPRESS (IRE) 5 b.m. Antonius Pius (USA) 123 – Musthav (IRE) 85 (Fasliyev   **61 §**
(USA) 120) [2015 67: p5g 5g² p6g 6m³ 6m t6g Jul 23] modest handicapper: left Sean P.   **a45 §**
Hennessy, won at Brighton in June: stays 6f: acts on polytrack and good to firm going:
often wears headgear: tried in tongue tie: usually slowly away, often races towards rear:
untrustworthy. *Des Donovan*

465

HIERARCH (IRE) 8 b.g. Dansili 127 – Danse Classique (IRE) 94 (Night Shift (USA)) **68** [2015 77: p8g³ p8f³ p8g p7g⁵ p7g p7f⁵ Dec 21] rangy gelding: fair handicapper: stays 1m: acts on polytrack, soft and good to firm going: sometimes wears headgear: tried in tongue tie prior to 2015. *David Simcock*

HIGH ADMIRAL 3 ch.g. New Approach (IRE) 132 – Wosaita 70 (Generous (IRE) 139) **87** [2015 67P: 10m* 12d⁴ 12.1d⁵ p11g⁵ Sep 23] fairly useful performer: won maiden at Newbury (by length from Mark Hopkins) in July: similar form in handicaps: stays 1½m: acts on polytrack, good to firm and good to soft going: in hood last 4 starts: has been gelded. *Andrew Balding*

HIGH AND FLIGHTY (IRE) 3 b.f. High Chaparral (IRE) 132 – Missionary Hymn **81** (USA) (Giant's Causeway (USA) 132) [2015 9.8m* 11.8g⁶ 12g⁴ 11.8s t12.2f² p12g Dec 9] first foal: dam, unraced, out of half-sister to champion Canadian/US older mare Glorious Song, herself dam of top-class 1¼m-1½m performer Singspiel: fairly useful performer: won maiden at Ripon in August: second in handicap at Wolverhampton in November: stays 1½m: acts on tapeta and good to firm going. tried in cheekpieces: often races prominently. *David O'Meara*

HIGH BAROQUE (USA) 3 b.c. Lookin At Lucky (USA) 127 – Yesterday (IRE) 119 **93 p** (Sadler's Wells (USA) 132) [2015 f7d⁴ t9.5g² 10d* 10g² Oct 3] $500,000F: fourth foal: dam, Irish 1000 Guineas winner (also 7f/9f winner at 2 yrs) and second in Oaks, sister to Moyglare Stud Stakes winner and Oaks runner-up Quarter Moon, herself dam of Pretty Polly Stakes winner Diamondsandrubies: fairly useful performer: won maiden at Pontefract in September: second in handicap at Redcar in October: stays 1¼m: open to further improvement. *Richard Fahey*

HIGHBURGH ROAD (IRE) 2 b.f. (Mar 20) Pour Moi (IRE) 125 – Alta Lena (FR) 103 **–** (Alzao (USA) 117) [2015 8.3s f8g⁵ Dec 18] €30,000Y: sixth foal: half-sister to French winner up to 8.5f Year of The Cat (2-y-o 1m winner, by Footstepsinthesand) and French 1m winner Costanza (by Zamindar): dam, French 9.5f winner, half-sister to several smart French middle-distance performers: well held in 2 maidens. *Mark Johnston*

HIGHER POWER 3 b.g. Rip Van Winkle (IRE) 134 – Lady Stardust 95 (Spinning World **85 p** (USA) 130) [2015 65p: 8m⁶ 10.2m² Jun 25] angular gelding: fairly useful maiden: much better effort in 2015 when second at Nottingham (¾ length behind Barreesh), benefiting from step up to 1¼m: remains open to improvement. *James Fanshawe*

HIGHEST LEVEL (IRE) 3 b.g. Invincible Spirit (IRE) 121 – Halle Bop 92 (Dubai **92** Millennium 140) [2015 74p: p7g* p7g² 8m⁵ 7d Aug 1] fairly useful performer: won maiden at Kempton in April: good second in handicap there in June: stays 7f: acts on polytrack. *Saeed bin Suroor*

HIGHEST QUALITY (IRE) 3 b.f. Invincible Spirit (IRE) 121 – Princess Taise (USA) **70** 100 (Cozzene (USA)) [2015 6m⁴ 7g² t6f⁵ p6m⁶ Dec 27] third foal: half-sister to useful winner up to 9f (in Qatar) Elkhart (2-y-o 7.4f winner, by Refuse To Bend): dam 2-y-o 7f winner: fair maiden: left Saeed bin Suroor after second start: will stay 7f: in hood last 2 starts. *Stuart Williams*

HIGHFIELD LASS 4 b.f. Cayman Kai (IRE) 114 – Jendorcet 57 (Grey Ghost 98) [2015 **50** 46: 8g 10.1m 10.1g⁶ 11.5s 12g⁵ 10d⁵ Oct 26] modest maiden: stays 1½m: best form on good going. *Chris Fairhurst*

HIGH HOPES 2 b.f. (Mar 12) Zamindar (USA) 116 – Dixielake (IRE) 84 (Lake Coniston **85 p** (IRE) 131) [2015 8v² Oct 24] half-sister to several winners, including 1¼m winner Dixie Music (by Montjeu) and 5f/6f winner Chief Crazy Horse (by Dansili), both useful: dam 1m winner: 25/1, showed plenty of ability when 1¾ lengths second of 12 to Last Tango Inparis in maiden at Newbury, finishing well under hands-and-heels: sure to progress. *David Simcock*

HIGH INTENSITY 3 b.g. Sir Percy 129 – Woodbeck 90 (Terimon 124) [2015 68: t9.5g³ **72** f12g³ 14.1d f16g⁴ Nov 3] fair maiden: stays 1¾m: acts on tapeta and good to soft going. *Scott Dixon*

HIGH JINX (IRE) 7 b.g. High Chaparral (IRE) 132 – Leonara (GER) (Surumu (GER)) **110** [2015 120: 15.4s⁴ May 3] good-topped gelding: very smart performer at best, winner of Prix du Cadran at Longchamp in 2014: not discredited when 8½ lengths fourth to Alex My Boy in Prix de Barbeville at Longchamp, only outing in 2015: thorough stayer: acts on good to firm and heavy going: tried in tongue tie: front runner. *James Fanshawe*

HIGH KESTREL 2 b.g. (Feb 19) Poet's Voice 126 – Miss Lacey (IRE) (Diktat 126) **–** [2015 8s Oct 23] 16/1, very green when well held in maiden at Newbury on debut. *John Gosden*

HIGHLAND ACCLAIM (IRE) 4 b.g. Acclamation 118 – Emma's Star (ITY) **106** (Darshaan 133) [2015 115: 7m 6m 6f 7f 6m 6m³ 5.4g² 6g 5.6d⁵ 6g 6s 6d Oct 23] useful handicapper: third at Newmarket (2¼ lengths behind Steve Prescott) and second at York (½ length behind Caspian Prince), both in August: fifth of 20 to Steps in Portland at Doncaster following month: stays 7f: acts on firm and good to soft going: usually wears hood: quirky, needs things to drop right. *David O'Meara*

HIGHLAND BLAIZE 3 ch.g. Dutch Art 126 – Off Stage (IRE) 58 (Danehill Dancer **56** (IRE) 117) [2015 p7g p8f⁵ p8f⁵ 10.2f³ 12.1s 11.5d⁵ 11.7f⁶ Jun 24] modest maiden: stays 11.5f: acts on polytrack and good to soft going: tried in hood: temperament under suspicion: sold 2,500 gns, sent to Italy. *Andrew Balding*

HIGHLAND CASTLE 7 b.g. Halling (USA) 133 – Reciprocal (IRE) 88 (Night Shift **103** (USA)) [2015 95: 12f 14.1f* 12m 16s⁴ 12m⁵ 16.4d Aug 19] strong gelding: useful handicapper: won by length from Lil Rockerfeller at Salisbury in May: stays 2m: acts on any turf going: held up: has shown signs of temperament. *David Elsworth*

HIGHLAND COLORI (IRE) 7 b.g. Le Vie dei Colori 126 – Emma's Star (ITY) **109** (Darshaan 133) [2015 108: 8m 7m³ 7g 7g⁴ 6g 6g⁶ 7s⁵ 7d 7v⁶ f7g² Dec 12] good-bodied gelding: useful performer: creditable efforts when in frame in handicaps at Goodwood, York and Southwell (½-length second to Westwood Hoe), and when sixth of 25 to Don't Touch in Ayr Gold Cup (Handicap) at Ayr on sixth start: effective from 6f to 1m: acts on fibresand, good to firm and heavy going. *Andrew Balding*

HIGHLAND DUKE (IRE) 6 b.g. Dansili 127 – House In Wood (FR) (Woodman (USA) **85** 126) [2015 90: p8m 10m 10m⁵ 8.3m² 8.3m³ 9m Aug 1] leggy gelding: fairly useful handicapper: stays 10.5f: acts on good to firm and good to soft going: sold 4,000 gns, sent to Italy. *Clive Cox*

HIGHLAND GAMES 3 b.g. Cape Cross (IRE) 129 – High Barn 72 (Shirley Heights **71 p** 130) [2015 p10f t12.2m* Feb 17] 7,000Y: half-brother to 3 winners, including 1½m winner Coyote Creek (by Zilzal): dam maiden half-sister to smart 1½m/13f winner and Gold Cup third Compton Ace: still green, better effort when winning maiden at Wolverhampton (by length from Grey's Angel) in February, suited by increase in trip: subsequently gelded: will go on improving. *David Simcock*

HIGHLAND REEL (IRE) 3 b.c. Galileo (IRE) 134 – Hveger (AUS) (Danehill **129** (USA) 126) [2015 111p: 8g⁶ 10.4g² 12m⁵ 12g* 10f* 10g⁵ 10.1g³ 11.9g* Dec 13]

Highland Reel is a good example of the increasingly cosmopolitan nature of Flat racing nowadays. He may be Irish-bred but he is a product of a sire and dam who made their names in different hemispheres, and his racing career so far has also reflected the fact that the world is getting smaller. After a traditional campaign for a classic three-year-old in Europe, which included a creditable second in the Prix du Jockey Club and a decisive victory in the Gordon Stakes at Goodwood in July, Highland Reel set off on an international campaign, his last four races of the season coming on four different continents and yielding lucrative victories in the Secretariat Stakes at Arlington and the Longines Hong Kong Vase at Sha Tin. Highland Reel was always held in high regard at Ballydoyle as a two-year-old—Joseph O'Brien apparently labelled him 'an absolute machine'—and the Coolmore partners paid 750,000 guineas for his yearling full brother at the October Sales after Highland Reel had won two of his three juvenile starts.

Highland Reel wasn't seen out again as a two-year-old after his victory in the Vintage Stakes at Goodwood in July. He displayed an impressive turn of foot that day and looked very much a Group 1 performer in the making, featuring at around 10/1 in winter ante-post betting on the Two Thousand Guineas. In the end, Highland Reel didn't make the Guineas line-up—the race was won by his stablemate Gleneagles— and he made his reappearance the following week in the French version, the Poule d'Essai des Poulains, for which he started favourite, but he could only keep on at one pace for sixth behind Make Believe. After nine months off the course, that effort was still respectable and Highland Reel stepped up noticeably on the form when runner-up to the Poulains second New Bay in the Prix du Jockey Club, keeping on well after travelling smoothly for a long way to finish a length and a half behind the winner. On the strength of that, Highland Reel started second favourite, behind Epsom runner-up Jack Hobbs, in the Irish Derby but failed by some way to repeat his Chantilly form, managing only fifth, beaten not only by Jack Hobbs but by the

Derby third Storm The Stars and by two of his own stablemates, Giovanni Canaletto and Kilimanjaro, who had finished fourth and sixth at Epsom. Reunited with Joseph O'Brien (who had ridden him at Chantilly when Ryan Moore preferred Cape Clear Island), Highland Reel got his head in front for the first time as a three-year-old when justifying favouritism in the Neptune Investment Management Gordon Stakes at Goodwood, O'Brien having to extricate him from a pocket before he stayed on well to win by a length and a half from the smart Scottish, with Disegno five lengths further back in third. The Gordon Stakes is often a trial for the St Leger but Highland Reel was no St Leger candidate. He was a far from certain stayer and, in any case, his stable had numerous other options for the final classic.

Highland Reel embarked instead on an international campaign, following closely in the footsteps of another Ballydoyle three-year-old Adelaide who the previous year had won the Secretariat Stakes and Australia's most prestigious weight-for-age contest, the Cox Plate. Highland Reel gave his stable its fourth victory in the Secretariat Stakes, with Seamus Heffernan in the saddle this time as Highland Reel made all and won readily by five and a quarter lengths from close-finishers Closing Bell and the slow-starting favourite Force The Pass. After a creditable fifth of seven back on home turf in the Irish Champion Stakes (starting the 16/1 rank outsider in the field), Highland Reel was on his travels again. Like Adelaide, he was classed as a four-year-old in the southern hemisphere and carried a stone more than any local three-year-olds would have done, had there been any in the latest Cox Plate line-up. Highland Reel would have had to better Adelaide's ground-breaking performance by some way to beat the very impressive Winx who recorded her fifth victory in a row, winning by a wide margin and in record time. Highland Reel came third, beaten three quarters of a length by the Queen Elizabeth Stakes winner Criterion who had returned to form when winning the Caulfield Stakes a fortnight earlier, after not being seen at his best in the Prince of Wales's Stakes at Royal Ascot or the International at York on a summer visit to Britain (he followed up his Cox Plate second with a good third in the Melbourne Cup). The performances of Adelaide and

Secretariat Stakes, Arlington—
a second successive win in the race (and fourth all told) for Aidan O'Brien courtesy of
Highland Reel, who quickens clear in the straight; Closing Bell (star on silks) stays on for second

Longines Hong Kong Vase, Sha Tin—
a clean sweep for the Europeans as Ireland's Highland Reel leads home the French-trained trio
Flintshire (the 2014 winner), Dariyan (noseband) and Ming Dynasty

Highland Reel should ensure regular challenges from the northern hemisphere for the Cox Plate which is one of the world's richest races (the Sussex Stakes runner-up Arod and French-trained Gailo Chop, who went on to win the Mackinnon at Flemington, were other European runners in the latest edition).

Unlike the Cox Plate, Hong Kong's International race day at Sha Tin in December has long been on the calendar for the top European stables, though Aidan O'Brien had never had a winner at the meeting. Highland Reel became only the third three-year-old to win the Hong Kong Vase in its twenty-two-year history, his two predecessors, Vallee Enchantee in 2003 and Daryakana in 2009, both being French-trained fillies. The Hong Kong-trained contingent usually face their stiffest task in the Vase and the first four places in the latest edition were taken by the Europeans, Highland Reel producing a career-best effort, after being prominent all the way, to win by a length and a half and the same from the previous year's winner Flintshire and Dariyan (Daryakana's first foal), with another French-trained challenger Ming Dynasty in fourth. Highland Reel, Dariyan and Ming Dynasty were the only three-year-olds in the thirteen-runner line-up. Britain's only representative, the Canadian International winner Cannock Chase, was below form on the day and beat only two home. Ryan Moore, who had been in the saddle at Woodbine when Cannock Chase won, enjoyed another fine day at Sha Tin, winning on Highland Reel and on Japanese-trained Maurice in the Hong Kong Mile before finishing second in the Hong Kong Cup on another Japanese visitor, Nuovo Record, who had won the previous year's Yushun Himba (Japanese Oaks) from Harp Star who had gone on to finish sixth in the Prix de l'Arc de Triomphe.

Highland Reel (IRE) (b.c. 2012)	Galileo (IRE) (b 1998)	Sadler's Wells (b 1981)	Northern Dancer
			Fairy Bridge
		Urban Sea (ch 1989)	Miswaki
			Allegretta
	Hveger (AUS) (b 2001)	Danehill (b 1986)	Danzig
			Razyana
		Circles of Gold (ch 1991)	Marscay
			Olympic Aim

Highland Reel, a good-topped individual who tends to spoil his appearance by sweating, contributed only one of the twenty-nine European pattern victories (in the Gordon Stakes) recorded by the progeny of Galileo in 2015. However, taken overall, he showed himself to be at least as good at his very best as any of his sire's big winners in the latest season. Gleneagles won three Group 1s and his Anglo/Irish Guineas double, together with Order of St George's Irish St Leger, took the number of major European classics won by Galileo's offspring to twenty-one from his first ten crops of three-year-olds. They helped Galileo to top the general sires' table in Britain and Ireland for the seventh time in the last eight years. As anticipated, Galileo overtook Danehill to reach second place behind his own sire Sadler's Wells in the tally of European pattern wins by a stallion's progeny. According to the records kept by bloodstock historian Tony Morris since the start of the official pattern in 1971, Sadler's Wells (327 wins) and Galileo (223) are the only stallions to have passed the two-hundred mark, and they are among only thirteen who have reached a century, Pivotal being the latest to join that select band—following Dansili the year before—when Queen's Jewel won the Prix Saint-Alary in May. One point that needs to be made, however, is that the number of races which are included in the pattern nowadays is considerably higher than when the scheme was originally introduced. In its inaugural year, the pattern comprised a total of two hundred and forty-three races in Britain, France, Ireland and Italy. There are five other countries involved nowadays (with Germany contributing the most significant number) and there were four hundred and eleven races in the scheme in 2015, eighty-seven of them Group 1s (the original pattern had fifty Group 1s). The fastest expansion has taken place since the turn of the century, some of the 'inflation' accounted for by the radical overhaul of pattern races for fillies and mares which occurred in 2004, but the general lack of 'quality control' has resulted in there now being more opportunities than ever at the top level for good horses to avoid one another.

To return to Highland Reel's pedigree, his dam Hveger won at a mile in Australia and was placed in the Group 1 Australasian Oaks at Morphettville. She is a sister to Elvstroem, a tough and versatile Australian champion who boosted his reputation with a win in the Dubai Duty Free as a five-year-old which was followed by several other creditable efforts in top company that season in Europe. Hveger's half-brother Haradasun was another notable sibling who had a successful European campaign—winning the Queen Anne Stakes at Royal Ascot having joined Ballydoyle—after establishing himself as a top performer in Australia (champion three-year-old colt in the 2007/8 season). This is the family of another notable Aussie the top sprinter Starspangledbanner, who was also successful at Royal Ascot, in the Golden Jubilee, before following up in the July Cup, both after his permanent transfer to Aidan O'Brien. The dam of Hveger, the Group 1 AJC Oaks (at Randwick) winner Circles of Gold, is a half-sister to Starspangledbanner's grandam National Song. Hveger produced a winner in Australia, the seven-furlong and mile winner Valdemoro (by Encosta de Lago) who was placed in the Victoria Oaks (at Flemington). Hveger was imported into Europe in 2009 and Highland Reel is her fourth foal, her fifth being Highland Reel's year-younger brother Idaho who finished fourth in the Criterium de Saint-Cloud after winning a maiden at the Curragh on his debut in October. Highland Reel stays a mile and a half and acts on firm going. He races prominently and sometimes makes the running. He stays in training. *Aidan O'Brien, Ireland*

HIGHLIFE DANCER 7 br.g. Imperial Dancer 123 – Wrong Bride (Reprimand 122) **70** [2015 72: 10.2m⁵ 9.9s* 10.2m³ 10m⁵ 11.8m⁵ 10.2m² 10.2d* 10.2d³ 11.7s² 9.9g 9.9v² 10.2g 10.2s Nov 4] good-topped gelding: fair handicapper: won at Brighton in June and Nottingham (amateur) in August: stays 13f: acts on any turf going: sometimes in visor prior to 2015: front runner/races prominently. *Mick Channon*

HIGHLY LIKELY (IRE) 6 b.g. Elnadim (USA) 128 – Height of Fantasy (IRE) 101 **53** (Shirley Heights 130) [2015 63: p10f⁵ p11f⁵ p10g p11g Jun 10] quite attractive gelding: modest handicapper: stays 13f: acts on polytrack and good to firm going: tried in blinkers/tongue tie prior to 2015. *Steve Woodman*

HIGHLY PRIZED 2 b.c. (Apr 1) Manduro (GER) 135 – Razzle (USA) (Danzig (USA)) **75** [2015 7m f7s² 8.3g⁴ 8f* Dec 31] good-topped colt: fair form: left Lady Cecil, won maiden at Gulfstream in December: will stay 1¼m: acts on firm sand and firm going. *Niall Saville, USA*

HIGHLY SPRUNG (IRE) 2 b.g. (Mar 31) Zebedee 113 – Miss Donovan 100 (Royal **84** Applause 124) [2015 5m⁶ 6m³ 6g² 5.9g³ 6g* 6m 6g 6g⁵ Sep 1] €15,000Y, 38,000 2-y-o: rather leggy gelding: fourth foal: half-brother to 2-y-o 5f winner Youcouldntmakeitup (by Captain Rio): dam, 6f winner, half-sister to smart sprinter Hellvelyn: fairly useful performer: won maiden at Catterick (by 3½ lengths from Valko) in July: raced mainly at 6f: usually races prominently. *Mark Johnston*

HIGH OFFICE 9 b.g. High Chaparral (IRE) 132 – White House 84 (Pursuit of Love 124) **58** [2015 p12f³ t13.9g p12f Feb 3] rather leggy gelding: modest performer: stays 2¼m, effective over much shorter: acts on polytrack, good to firm and heavy going: in blinkers in 2015. *Conor Dore*

HIGH ON THE HOG (IRE) 7 b.g. Clodovil (IRE) 116 – Maraami 83 (Selkirk (USA) **– §** 129) [2015 52: t7.1f Mar 23] modest handicapper: well held only start in 2015: stays 1m: acts on polytrack, soft and good to firm going: has worn headgear. *Mark Brisbourne*

HIGH RANKING 2 b.c. (Feb 9) Paco Boy (IRE) 129 – Crown (IRE) 91 (Royal Applause **–** 124) [2015 7m 8d Oct 16] well held in 2 maidens. *David Brown*

HIGHSALVIA COSMOS 4 b.g. High Chaparral (IRE) 132 – Salvia (Pivotal 124) [2015 **63** 74: p12f³ p12f* p12f⁶ 11.6m 14d⁶ p13.3g⁶ p12m⁶ Oct 28] modest handicapper: won at Kempton in February: stays 1¾m: acts on polytrack and good to soft going: usually wears blinkers: often wears tongue tie. *Mark Hoad*

HIGH SECRET (IRE) 4 b.g. High Chaparral (IRE) 132 – Secret Question (USA) (Rahy **102** (USA) 115) [2015 89p: p13.3m² p13.3m* p16g p16g² 15.8d* 16s² 17g* 14d⁴ 18g 18s⁵ Oct **a91** 19] rangy gelding: useful performer: won handicaps at Chelmsford in May and Catterick in July and minor event at Killarney in August: also ran well when second in handicap at Ascot (short head behind Seamour) and fourth of 16 to Nakeeta in Old Borough Cup (Handicap) at Haydock sixth/eighth starts: stays 17f: acts on polytrack, tapeta, firm and soft going: usually races prominently. *Sir Mark Prescott Bt*

HIGH SHIELDS (IRE) 2 b.c. (May 11) Shamardal (USA) 129 – Marine City (JPN) 77 **77 p** (Carnegie (IRE) 129) [2015 7g p8g² Dec 9] 100,000Y: brother to 1m winner Falcon In Flight and half-brother to several winners, including 1¼m winner Briardale (by Arcano): dam, 1½m winner (stayed 2m), half-sister to Prix de l'Arc de Triomphe winner Marienbard: better effort when second in maiden at Kempton (2 lengths behind Graceful James) in December, caught further back than ideal: will stay further than 1m: will go on improving. *Roger Charlton*

HIGH SPEED (IRE) 2 b.f. (Apr 17) Kodiac 112 – Scarlet Empress 79 (Second Empire **62** (IRE) 124) [2015 5g⁶ 5.1s³ 6d⁵ 6d⁶ 5d² f5g⁴ 5.7m⁴ p6f p5f³ Oct 24] 65,000Y: sturdy filly: sixth foal: closely related to winner up to 6f Titus Andronicus (2-y-o 5f winner, by Danetime) and half-sister to 2-y-o 5.7f winner Mary Fildes (by Chineur): dam 2-y-o 6f winner: modest maiden: stays 6f: acts on polytrack, soft and good to firm going: often races prominently. *Charles Hills*

HIGHTIME HERO 3 b.g. Pivotal 124 – Hightime Heroine (IRE) 89 (Danetime (IRE) **55** 121) [2015 7.1m⁵ 8d⁵ Jun 2] better effort in maidens when fifth at Ripon final start, never a threat. *David O'Meara*

HIGH VALLEY 3 ch.g. New Approach (IRE) 132 – Bathilde (IRE) 102 (Generous (IRE) **73** 139) [2015 52p: t9.5f⁵ p12f² 13m Jun 26] rather leggy gelding: fair maiden: stays 1½m: tried in cheekpieces in 2015. *Charlie Appleby*

HIGHWAY CODE (USA) 9 b.g. Street Cry (IRE) 130 – Fairy Heights (IRE) 110 (Fairy **75** King (USA)) [2015 81: t12.2g⁶ 12d* t16.5g 12.1m⁶ 12m⁴ Jun 27] fair handicapper: won at Doncaster (amateur) in March: stays 1½m: acts on good to firm and good to soft going: often wears tongue tie: usually races towards rear: fairly useful hurdler/chaser. *Richard Lee*

HIGHWAY DREAM 2 b.f. (Feb 19) Dick Turpin (IRE) 127 – Just Dreams 85 (Salse **62** (USA) 128) [2015 p5f⁴ t5.1g p6g² 6d 6.1m p6g Aug 7] modest maiden: stayed 6f: usually raced close up, tended to find little: blinkered final start: dead. *William Jarvis*

HIGHWAY LASS 2 br.f. (Mar 15) Dick Turpin (IRE) 127 – Light Dreams 70 (Fantastic **56** Light (USA) 134) [2015 6d 8.3g⁵ 6g Oct 16] 10,500F: third foal: dam, maiden (best at 1m), half-sister to smart sprinters Vision of Night and Struggler and smart German performer up to 1½m Baroon: modest maiden: best effort when fifth at Nottingham (11¼ lengths behind Andastra) in September. *Richard Hannon*

HIGHWAYMAN 2 b.g. (Feb 9) Dick Turpin (IRE) 127 – Right Rave (IRE) 84 (Soviet **61** Star (USA) 128) [2015 7g p6f 7d Oct 30] sturdy gelding: modest form in maidens. *William Jarvis*

HIGHWAY PURSUIT 4 b.g. Pastoral Pursuits 127 – Extreme Pleasure (IRE) 72 (High **–** Chaparral (IRE) 132) [2015 –: 12g 13.8m⁵ Jun 5] maiden: no form in 2015: stays 1½m: acts on soft going: tried in cheekpieces: often races in rear. *George Moore*

HIGHWAY ROBBER 2 b.g. (Apr 6) Dick Turpin (IRE) 127 – Lawyers Choice 86 **– p** (Namid 128) [2015 6g May 14] fifth foal: half-brother to useful winner up to 7f Dutch Art Dealer (2-y-o 6f winner) and 1m winner Dutch Dutch (both by Dutch Art): dam 7f/1m winner: 11/4, shaped as if needed experience when last of 9 at Newmarket: subsequently gelded: clearly thought capable of better. *Simon Crisford*

HIJRAN (IRE) 2 ch.f. (Apr 11) Mastercraftsman (IRE) 129 – Sunny Slope 77 (Mujtahid **69** (USA) 118) [2015 8g⁶ 8v⁶ p8f⁵ Nov 12] 60,000Y: half-sister to several winners, including 2-y-o 7f winner Indigo River (by Kodiac), later 6.5f winner in USA, and winner up to 10.7f Lake Pontchartrain (2-y-o 7f/1m winner, by Invincible Spirit), both useful: dam 1m/9f winner: fair maiden: best effort when fifth at Chelmsford (4 lengths behind Khaleesy) final start. *William Haggas*

HILLBILLY BOY (IRE) 5 b.g. Haafhd 129 – Erreur (IRE) 84 (Desert King (IRE) 129) [2015 110: p8g^3 8d 7d^3 6g^3 7s^2 7v p8m^6 p7g^4 Dec 9] useful performer: third in minor event at Haydock (1¾ lengths behind Richard Pankhurst) and handicap at Ayr (2½ lengths behind Tatlisu) in September and second in handicap at Leicester (1¾ lengths behind Dinkum Diamond) in October: left Martin Smith after second start: stays 1m: acts on polytrack and heavy going: tried in cheekpieces: front runner/races prominently. *Tom Dascombe* **105 a96**

HILL FORT 5 ch.g. Pivotal 124 – Cairns (UAE) 107 (Cadeaux Genereux 131) [2015 78: t9.5g^3 p10g p12g Jan 28] fair handicapper: stays 1¼m: acts on polytrack, tapeta and good to soft going: sometimes wears headgear: sometimes slowly away. *Ronald Harris* **66**

HILLGROVE ANGEL (IRE) 3 gr.g. Dark Angel (IRE) 113 – Theben (GER) (Monsun (GER) 124) [2015 70: p10g^4 p10m^3 8.1s^5 9.9m^3 10d* 10g^2 8d^5 8g 10.2s* 10g^4 10.2s* Sep 15] fair performer: won sellers at Windsor in July and at Chepstow in August and September: stays 1¼m: acts on polytrack, soft and good to firm going: tried in blinkers: front runner/races prominently. *David Evans* **76**

HILL OF DREAMS (IRE) 6 b.m. Indian Danehill (IRE) 124 – Shaunas Vision (IRE) 88 (Dolphin Street (FR) 125) [2015 79: p7g^3 p8m Feb 4] angular mare: fair handicapper: stays 1m: acts on polytrack, best turf form on good to soft going: usually wears headgear: sold 5,000 gns, sent to Saudi Arabia. *Dean Ivory* **73**

HILLS AND DALES (IRE) 3 b.g. Acclamation 118 – Soul Mountain (IRE) 88 (Rock of Gibraltar (IRE) 133) [2015 79: t7.1m^2 p6g* p6g^3 p6g* 6g p7g Oct 7] rather leggy gelding: fair performer: won maiden at Lingfield in February and handicap on same course in April: left Charlie Appleby after: stays 7f: acts on polytrack, probably acts on tapeta: usually in blinkers in 2015: sold 12,000 gns, sent to Sweden. *George Peckham* **77**

HILLSIDE DREAM (IRE) 2 b.f. (Mar 12) Dream Ahead (USA) 133 – Knapton Hill 88 (Zamindar (USA) 116) [2015 5g^6 6m^4 6.5m 7m^2 7.5m^3 6.9m 6g^2 7m 6s^2 Oct 26] 82,000Y: fourth foal: half-sister to 3 winning sprinters, including 6f winners Vallado (at 2 yrs, by Clodovil) and Pitlochry (including at 2 yrs, by Chineur): dam 7f winner: fair maiden: stays 7f: acts on good to firm going: tried in cheekpieces. *James Tate* **78**

HILLSTAR 5 b.h. Danehill Dancer (IRE) 117 – Crystal Star 100 (Mark of Esteem (IRE) 137) [2015 121: 12f^5 12m^5 12m^6 11s^4 12m^3 Oct 3] sturdy, close-coupled horse: very smart performer at best: won King Edward VII Stakes at Royal Ascot in 2013 and Arc Trial at Newbury and Canadian International at Woodbine in 2014: best effort of 2015 when fifth in Princess of Wales's Stakes at Newmarket (3¼ lengths behind Big Orange) in July on second start: 4¾ lengths third of 8 to Star Storm in Cumberland Lodge Stakes at Ascot final outing: stayed 13.5f: acted on any turf going: to stand at Garryrichard Stud, Co. Wexford, Ireland, fee on application. *Sir Michael Stoute* **114**

HIMALAYAN PEAK 5 b.g. Tiger Hill (IRE) 127 – Rosy Outlook (USA) 79 (Trempolino (USA) 135) [2015 p12g p16m Feb 18] maiden: no form in 2015: stays 11f: acts on heavy going: sometimes wears headgear/tongue tie. *Sophie Leech* **–**

HIMALAYAN QUEEN 2 b.f. (Mar 30) Poet's Voice 126 – Annapurna (IRE) 101 (Brief Truce (USA) 126) [2015 p7g^6 p8g^5 p8f^4 Nov 12] 32,000F, 70,000Y: half-sister to several winners, including smart 1¼m winner Solva (by Singspiel): dam 2-y-o 7f winner: fair maiden: late headway not knocked about when fourth at Chelmsford final start: remains open to improvement. *William Haggas* **66 p**

HI NOTE 7 b.m. Acclamation 118 – Top Tune (Victory Note (USA) 120) [2015 67: p13.8f^6 p15.8g 17.2f^3 16g^6 Jul 15] light-framed mare: modest handicapper: stays 17f: acts on polytrack, firm and soft going: usually races close up. *Sheena West* **64**

HINT OF GREY (IRE) 2 gr.f. (Apr 26) Mastercraftsman (IRE) 129 – Anamarka 57 (Mark of Esteem (IRE) 137) [2015 7.6g 7g 8g Oct 21] €52,000Y: workmanlike filly: first foal: dam 1½m winner in Czech Republic: no form. *Don Cantillon* **–**

HINTON ADMIRAL 11 b.g. Spectrum (IRE) 126 – Shawanni 105 (Shareef Dancer (USA) 135) [2015 61: p8f Jan 21] good-topped gelding: modest handicapper nowadays: stays 7f: acts on polytrack, good to firm and good to soft going: has worn headgear: has worn tongue tie. *Pat Eddery* **–**

HIORNE TOWER (FR) 4 b.g. Poliglote 121 – Hierarchie (FR) (Sillery (USA) 122) [2015 60: p12g^6 p15.8f^2 p15.8g^2 p16d p15.8f p12m p10m Nov 14] fair maiden: stays 2m: acts on polytrack and good to firm going. *John Best* **65**

HIPZ (IRE) 4 br.f. Intense Focus (USA) 117 – Radha (Bishop of Cashel 122) [2015 71: p6f p7f^4 p6m 6m^5 6m 7v^3 6m* 7d^4 6m* 6g^2 7g^5 6g* 6d 6g^3 6s Oct 6] angular filly: fair handicapper: won at Brighton and Windsor (apprentice) in June and Salisbury in August: stays 6f: acts on polytrack, soft and good to firm going: tried in headgear. *Laura Mongan* **75 a60**

HISTORY BOOK (IRE) 5 b.m. Raven's Pass (USA) 133 – Pure Illusion (IRE) 95 **95**
(Danehill (USA) 126) [2015 92§: p7g² p6f* p6f p7f⁴ Apr 3] lengthy mare: useful
performer: won handicap at Lingfield in January: subsequently left Charlie Appleby, then
left John Butler after third start: has form at up to 8.5f, may prove best around 6f: acts on
polytrack: often in headgear in 2015. *Phil McEntee*

HIT IT A BOMB (USA) 2 b.c. (Feb 20) War Front (USA) 119 – Liscanna (IRE) 105 **119 p**
(Sadler's Wells (USA) 132) [2015 7d* p7g* 8d* Oct 30]
The FIFA football scandals—its president Sepp Blatter and UEFA supremo
Michel Platini have both been banned for eight years—dominated the sporting
headlines for much of the year. Those stories for the most part were about murky
financial dealings and the fixing of bids and votes, not about skewing results on
the field. Of much more worrying significance for the average sports fan was the
continuing evidence emerging on a much wider scale of the use of drugs to enhance
performance in sport. Public trust has gradually been eroded over the years and
there can't be many spectators who still imagine that every memorable sporting
feat they watch is a fair trial of strength and skill. A brilliant documentary about the
systemic use of performance-enhancing drugs in Russian athletics, made by German
broadcaster ARD, brought out into the open the fact that not only have Russian
officials been supplying banned substances to athletes on a massive scale, in return
for a percentage of earnings, but they have also covered up positive drug tests.

When an independent commission, led by its former chief Dick Pound, was
appointed by the World Anti-Doping Agency (WADA) to investigate claims, the
commission discovered the 'intentional and malicious destruction' of more than
1,400 samples by Moscow laboratory officials to prevent closer investigation, in
defiance of notification from WADA to preserve target samples taken from athletes.
Russian secret police, the commission said, have imposed for years an 'atmosphere
of intimidation on laboratory process and staff' and Russia's anti-doping agency has
given athletes advance notice of tests, as well as routinely bullying doping control
officers and their families, and taking bribes to cover up missed tests. Athletes who
said they did not want to be involved in 'the programme' were told they would not
be picked for their country. The commission concluded that 'the Olympic Games
in London were sabotaged by athletes who should not have been competing and
could have been prevented from doing so [Russia was second in the athletics table at
London 2012 with eighteen medals].' A separate investigation by French authorities
found that some of those who held high rank in the International Association of
Athletics Federations (IAAF), right up to former 'spiritual president' Lamine Diack,
accepted huge bribes to cover up positive drugs tests on some top Russian athletes.
Later investigations revealed that the IAAF's former anti-doping chief Gabriel Dolle
turned a blind eye to the corruption and cheating. Athletics is one of those sports that
hasn't smelt right for a long time, while cycling, swimming, biathlon, weightlifting
and skiing were others implicated by the German documentary makers in doping
scandals. WADA has warned that the revelations 'could be the tip of the iceberg'
with widespread doping stretching beyond Russia and the sport of athletics.

The standard parochial view of British athletes as 'whiter than white'—it is
always other nations who have drug problems—is now being challenged. Double
Olympic champion Mo Farah found himself under suspicion by association when
allegations were made, in a BBC *Panorama* programme, about his American coach
Alberto Salazar and his stable of athletes including Galen Rupp (Farah's training
partner), allegedly involving 'microdosing', using small doses of naturally occurring
substances that do not raise levels high enough to attract suspicion on an athlete's
biological passport. The biological passport, a blood-profiling system introduced
in 2009, is said to reveal the hormonal changes that usually result from drug use
though, on their own, unusual readings are not regarded as proof of doping. If
Farah had his reputation affected, he was not alone. The retired marathon champion
Paula Radcliffe found herself having to explain 'fluctuations' in her blood test data
which were published by *Sky News*. Her world record set in 2003 in London, which
obliterated the previous fastest time by more than three minutes and hasn't been
threatened by any other runner since, was suddenly no longer a universal source of

wonder, but the subject of cynicism in some quarters. The world's sporting cheats, it seems, have gradually made a disillusioned sporting public think differently about everything and everyone. A report by WADA into wider claims of blood doping in athletics did clear Radcliffe's name, while another modern British sporting legend, cyclist Chris Froome, put himself through a series of physiological tests, after winning the Tour de France for a second time, to try to convince sceptics that his remarkable performances are possible without doping (hostility in the French media towards Froome and Team Sky seemed at times to spill over to the spectators, one of whom threw urine in Froome's face towards the end of the Tour). Lance Armstrong left cycling with a toxic legacy, so much so that Froome's explosive surge, which left his closest rivals trailing on the key climb to La Pierre-Saint-Martin on stage ten and was up there with some of the greatest exploits in the Tour's history, was considered by some to be too reminiscent of Armstrong's displays for comfort. The journalist who exposed Armstrong as a fraud, David Walsh of *The Sunday Times*, has come out in defence of Froome saying that, in many years of following his career, he has found no evidence that he is doping and is 'inclined to believe' his denials.

The problem for all professional sport nowadays is that suspicion is contagious. It is all too easy to doubt. Athletics—the premier Olympic sport—and cycling may well survive their scandals if they put their houses in order, as baseball has largely done in North America, but horse racing is among the sports that cannot afford to be complacent. The trust of racegoers and punters in the integrity of racing, particularly as a betting medium, is fragile at the best of times and the damaging consequences of a serious breach—such as the Godolphin doping scandal uncovered in Britain in 2013—can take years to repair. If misgivings continue to nag away about just how 'clean' British racing is, they are nothing like so serious as those about the sport in North America. The drug-fuelled veterinary treatment of American thoroughbreds, and the permissive attitude within the sport to different kinds of raceday medication, is so far out of line with the stringent rules in most of the rest of the world that it affects the international perception of performances there. As a result, the demand in the world market for North American bloodstock—once so highly sought after—is nothing like it used to be. Except for the really big days, racing's popularity with its domestic sporting audience is in a parlous state, resulting in general media coverage being virtually restricted to the Triple Crown races and the Breeders' Cup meeting (even the latest Breeders' Cup, which had American Pharoah, came some way after news of baseball's World Series and all the college football on the television sports bulletins). Styled as the 'World Championships', the Breeders' Cup is the richest fixture on the globe and continues to attract strong European representation, concentrated on the Grade 1 turf races over the two days. Attempts by the Breeders' Cup organisers to phase out the raceday use of drugs such as the diuretic furosemide (lasix), beginning with a ban on its use in the four major two-year-old races in 2012 and 2013, met such strong opposition from horsemen's groups that the status quo was reinstated in 2014. Furosemide is widely used on racedays throughout North America to reduce the severity of any exercise-induced bleeding in the lung tissue.

Evidence that furosemide—which is also an effective masking agent—improves performance is difficult to extract from any study of North American racing because an estimated ninety-five per cent of the horses are on it, though it is not hard to find anecdotal evidence (the owner-breeder of Effinex, runner-up to American Pharoah in the Breeders' Cup Classic, campaigned the horse, on principle, without lasix in his early races but eventually 'put him on lasix because I had to in order to compete, it is a stone-cold performance enhancer and, for all the wrong reasons, you have to use it'). American horsemen can be coy about the effects of furosemide—defending it as 'therapeutic'—but a large field study conducted in South Africa several years ago showed that horses on furosemide have an advantage over those who run without it. It is little wonder then that most of the leading European-based trainers—given the choice—have adopted a 'When in Rome' approach to using permitted medication at the Breeders' Cup, prominent among them Aidan O'Brien who says 'It is going to be a hard thing to change because it is part of the culture here.' O'Brien would, however, support a ban as 'it is the right thing to do because it would clear up the muddy picture about ability.' Andre Fabre has always refused to race

Breeders' Cup Juvenile Turf, Keeneland—a sixth win for Europe (and third for Aidan O'Brien) in a race inaugurated only in 2007 as Hit It A Bomb (No.14) beats Airoforce (next to winner) and Birchwood (No.6)

his Breeders' Cup challengers on raceday drugs such as furosemide, and more Europeans are now doing so, in support of the Water, Hay, Oats Alliance (WHOA), launched in May 2012 by prominent figures in the sport in North America, including George Strawbridge ('It's not who has the best horse but the best chemist'), Roy and Gretchen Jackson and Arthur and Staci Hancock. WHOA is lobbying Congress to prohibit the use of raceday medication on welfare grounds. Racing in North America is run state-by-state and not by a central body, something which is a huge barrier to reform, though a bill was introduced in the House of Representatives in the latest season to try to set up a specific anti-doping authority for racing under the United States Anti-Doping Agency whose chief executive Travis Tygart (closely involved in exposing Lance Armstrong) supported the legislation as 'a national solution to the problem of doping in horse racing … and the protection of the integrity of competition and the health and safety of the jockeys and horses.' There is no specific mention of ending the use of raceday drugs such as furosemide, which would be a big step towards creating the level playing field that should be essential in the world's major international races. The International Federation of Horseracing Authorities has limited influence but it does have the power to remove international pattern status from drug-associated races, and it would be a good time to use it in support of those trying to 'clean up' the Breeders' Cup, in particular.

The only British-trained starters at the latest Breeders' Cup to run on furosemide were Nemoralia and Mondialiste (Talmada was declared on lasix but was not allowed to run because it was not administered by an official racecourse vet). Golden Horn, Time Test, Secret Gesture, the two Godolphin-owned runners Cymric and Birchwood, and Illuminate joined the Fabre-trained trio Make Believe, Miss France and Esoterique, and Argentinian challenger Ordak Dan, by racing 'clean'. Only three of the home-trained runners were not declared to run on lasix but two of them—Runhappy in the Breeders' Cup Sprint and Mongolian Saturday in the Turf Sprint—were successful. The only European-trained winners in the thirteen Breeders' Cup races were saddled by Aidan O'Brien, the most successful European-based trainer in the history of the event, now with ten winners. O'Brien supplied seven of the twenty-two-strong European contingent and returned home with two winners, Hit It A Bomb in the Juvenile Turf (a race he also won in 2011 with Wrote and 2012 with George Vancouver) and Found in the Breeders' Cup Turf (which he had previously won with High Chaparral in 2002 and 2003 [dead heat], St Nicholas Abbey in 2011 and Magician in 2013). The stable's representative in the Breeders' Cup Juvenile Fillies' Turf, Alice Springs, was a good second.

Hit It A Bomb didn't reach the racecourse until the end of September when he beat twenty-one rivals—after being strongly supported down to 2/1 favourite—in a fairly useful seven-furlong maiden at the Curragh contested by plenty of other promising types. Ballydoyle newcomers invariably improve a good deal on their second appearance nowadays and Hit It A Bomb hacked up twelve days later, at

5/2-on this time, in the listed Star Appeal Stakes over the same trip on the all-weather at Dundalk. He was most impressive, showing a smart turn of foot to beat Siamsaiocht by four and a half lengths and looking sure to be of interest if taking up his engagement in the Breeders' Cup Juvenile Turf. Hit It A Bomb was part of a strong European challenge for the Breeders' Cup Juvenile Turf over a mile which also included the Godolphin-owned pair Cymric, who had been beaten a short neck in the Prix Jean-Luc Lagardere at Longchamp, and Birchwood, third in the National Stakes at the Curragh behind Hit It A Bomb's stablemate Air Force Blue. Cymric and Hit It A Bomb started second and third favourite respectively behind Airoforce who had maintained his own unbeaten record with a course win in the Grade 3 Dixiana Bourbon Stakes earlier in the month. Hit It A Bomb was dropped out from his outside draw and was last of the fourteen runners in the back straight. Helped by the punishing pace, Hit It A Bomb put in a very strong finishing run, after still having only one behind him turning for home, and just got up to win by a neck and the same from Airoforce and Birchwood; Cymric came eighth, two places in front of Hit It A Bomb's stablemate Shogun (who had finished four places behind Cymric in the Jean-Luc Lagadere). The Juvenile Turf hasn't unearthed a top-notcher since it was inaugurated in 2007—neither Wrote nor George Vancouver made much impact for Ballydoyle as three-year-olds—but Hit It A Bomb made a great impression and should improve further at three. He looks a good prospect.

Hit It A Bomb (USA) (b.c. 2013)	War Front (USA) (b 2002)	Danzig (b 1977)	Northern Dancer
			Pas de Nom
		Starry Dreamer (gr or ro 1994)	Rubiano
			Lara's Star
	Liscanna (IRE) (b 2004)	Sadler's Wells (b 1981)	Northern Dancer
			Fairy Bridge
		Lahinch (b 1999)	Danehill Dancer
			Dublah

Hit It A Bomb is by the same sire as Air Force Blue, the American sprinter-miler War Front, and he became his first Breeders' Cup winner after Declaration of War had gone close for Ballydoyle in the 2013 Breeders' Cup Classic. Hit It A Bomb is the fourth foal and second winner (following a minor winner abroad by Kingmambo) bred from the Ballyogan Stakes winner Liscanna who raced in the colours of Mrs Evie Stockwell, the mother of Coolmore supremo John Magnier. Liscanna is a rarity in being one of the very few foals by Sadler's Wells who won over a trip as short as six furlongs, the distance of the Ballyogan, after the age of two. Hit It A Bomb's grandam Lahinch, an early 'black type' winner for Danehill Dancer, also raced for Aidan O'Brien and, after winning in listed company over five furlongs and finishing fourth in the Cheveley Park and second in the Rockfel, she trained on from two to three to win again in listed company at Leopardstown over seven furlongs and finish a creditable seventh in the One Thousand Guineas before reverting unsuccessfully to sprinting. Not all the family have been sprinters and milers, Liscanna being closely related to Lahinch Classics, a smart performer for David Wachman, who won at up to ten and a half furlongs, and also a half-sister to The Bogberry, who won at up to ten furlongs for Aidan O'Brien and went on to show he stayed a mile and a half. Hit It A Bomb is clearly suited by a mile and may well get a mile and a quarter. He has won on polytrack and good to soft, but has yet to encounter good going or firmer on turf, conditions which tend to favour horses like him whose most potent weapon is a good turn of foot. *Aidan O'Brien, Ireland*

HIT LIST (IRE) 3 ch.g. Makfi 130 – Kassiopeia (IRE) 103 (Galileo (IRE) 134) [2015 **86 p** p8m p8g⁵ 10m⁴ p10m² 9.9s* Oct 12] good-topped gelding: fourth foal: half-brother to winner up to 1¼m Arabian Star (2-y-o 7f winner, by Green Desert) and 6f winner Illustrate (by Oasis Dream), both useful: dam 1½m winner: fairly useful performer: won handicap at Salisbury in October, suited by emphasis on stamina: will stay 1½m: acts on polytrack and soft going: likely to progress further. *Andrew Balding*

HITMAN 2 b.c. (Feb 23) Canford Cliffs (IRE) 133 – Ballymore Celebre (IRE) (Peintre **80** Celebre (USA) 137) [2015 7g 7d 6.5s³ Oct 23] half-brother to several winners, including smart performer up to 7f Anjaal (2-y-o 5f/6f winner, by Bahamian Bounty) and 1¼m-1½m winner Pintrada (by Tiger Hill): dam, French 11.5f-13f winner, half-sister to smart 1¼m performer Nysaean: fairly useful maiden: easily best effort when third at Newbury (1½ lengths behind Bedrock) final start, no extra and hampered close home. *William Muir*

HIT THE JACKPOT (IRE) 6 ch.g. Pivotal 124 – Token Gesture (IRE) 113 (Alzao **105** (USA) 117) [2015 103: 9.8d⁵ 8m 10m⁵ 10m* 12m³ 12d⁶ 12d⁵ Sep 12] leggy gelding: useful handicapper: won at Ayr (by short head from Mica Mika) in June: good third at Ripon (½ length behind Pressure Point) in July: stays 1½m: acts on good to firm and good to soft going: tried in headgear prior to 2015. *David O'Meara*

HIT THE LIGHTS (IRE) 5 b.g. Lawman (FR) 121 – Dawn Chorus (IRE) (Mukaddamah **63** (USA) 125) [2015 61, a51: p5m 5.1m 5m⁴ 6d³ 5m² 5.1m* 5.1g* 5s³ Aug 26] modest handicapper: won at Chepstow in July and August: stays 6f: acts on good to firm and good to soft going: sometimes wears headgear: front runner/races prominently. *Patrick Chamings*

HOBNOB 2 b.f. (Feb 26) Paco Boy (IRE) 129 – Phantasmagoria 75 (Fraam 114) [2015 **52** t5.1m³ t5.1f t6f⁶ Oct 23] 5,000Y: fourth foal: half-sister to useful 5f/6f winner La Fortunata (by Lucky Story): dam ran twice: modest form in sellers and a maiden. *Nick Littmoden*

HOLD FIRM 3 b.c. Refuse To Bend (IRE) 128 – Four Miracles 96 (Vettori (IRE) 119) **62** [2015 45: p10f t8.6m* p8d² p8f² p8f³ t7.1g⁴ t8.6g² t8.6g² p8g⁴ 8.3d⁴ 8.5g* t9.5m² p10m⁵ t9.5f⁵ t8.6g⁴ p8f² Dec 17] modest performer: won handicap at Wolverhampton in February and minor event at Beverley in September: stays 1¼m: acts on polytrack and tapeta: often races prominently: consistent. *Mark H. Tompkins*

HOLD ON MAGNOLIA 2 ch.c. (Apr 2) Monsieur Bond (IRE) 120 – Mawjoodah 80 **72** (Cadeaux Genereux 131) [2015 5d³ 6d⁴ f5g p6f⁵ t6f* Dec 22] fair performer: won nursery at Wolverhampton in December: will stay 7f: acts on tapeta and good to soft going: often places towards rear. *Richard Fahey*

HOLD THE LINE (IRE) 5 b.g. Ivan Denisovich (IRE) 115 – Janna's Jewel (IRE) **95** (Traditionally (USA) 117) [2015 97: p10.7g⁴ 8v 10.1g² 8g 12m Jun 6] useful handicapper: second at Epsom (4½ lengths behind Collaboration) in April: stays 1½m: acts on polytrack, good to firm and heavy going: tried in headgear prior to 2015: often wears tongue tie: usually races prominently. *John Patrick Shanahan, Ireland*

HOLD THE STAR 9 b.m. Red Ransom (USA) – Sydney Star 91 (Machiavellian (USA) **–** 123) [2015 44: t7.1f f7g⁶ Apr 23] rangy mare: fair at best, no form in 2015: stays 7f: acts on polytrack and soft going: tried in headgear. *Ann Stokell*

HOLD TIGHT 3 ch.g. Exceed And Excel (AUS) 126 – Kangra Valley 56 (Indian Ridge **98 p** 123) [2015 7s* p7g² Oct 29] 105,000Y: sturdy gelding: half-brother to several winners, including very smart winner up to 1m Airwave (2-y-o 6f winner, including Cheveley Park Stakes, by Air Express) and smart 5f (including at 2 yrs) winner Jwala (by Oasis Dream): dam 2-y-o 5f winner: won maiden at Leicester (by 2¾ lengths from Merhoob) in October on debut: better effort when second in handicap at Lingfield (½ length behind Crazy Chic), always prominent: already useful, and open to further improvement. *Saeed bin Suroor*

HOLIDAY HENRY (USA) 2 b.g. (Mar 19) Lookin At Lucky (USA) 127 – Lady Ilsley **66** (USA) (Trempolino (USA) 135) [2015 t8.6m t7.1f⁵ t9.5f⁶ p8m* f8m³ t8.6m⁵ Dec 26] fair performer: won seller at Lingfield in November: stays 8.5f: acts on all-weather: visored last 3 starts. *Richard Fahey*

HOLIDAY MAGIC (IRE) 4 gr.g. Dark Angel (IRE) 113 – Win Cash (IRE) (Alhaarth **103** (IRE) 126) [2015 101: p7g² p7f⁵ p8m² p8g p8g³ p8g Aug 19] useful handicapper: second at Lingfield (head behind Halation) in February and third at Chelmsford (2½ lengths behind Hakka) in August: stays 1m: acts on polytrack: tried in blinkers in 2015: often races prominently: has plaited tail/looked ungainly. *Charlie Appleby*

HOLLAND PARK 3 b.c. More Than Ready (USA) 120 – B Berry Brandy (USA) (Event **81** of The Year (USA) 125) [2015 77p: 7m³ 7m² 7m⁵ 6g³ 6g³ p6g p6g p8f 6g Oct 19] well-grown colt: fairly useful maiden: third in handicap at Salisbury in August: left Richard Hannon after sixth start: will be suited by a return to 7f: acts on polytrack and firm going: tried in headgear in 2015: often races towards rear: temperament under suspicion. *Conor Dore*

HOLLEY SHIFTWELL 5 ch.m. Bahamian Bounty 116 – Persario 96 (Bishop of Cashel **96** 122) [2015 91: 5f² 5m² 6m 5g 5m 5m 6g Oct 10] sturdy mare: useful performer: raced solely in listed events in 2015, second at Bath (length behind Zhoor Baynoona) in April and Ayr (2 lengths behind Katawi) in June: also ran creditably fifth/final starts: effective at 5f/6f: acts on polytrack, firm and good to soft going. *Stuart Williams*

HOLLIE POINT 3 b.f. Dubawi (IRE) 129 – Camlet 94 (Green Desert (USA) 127) [2015 **75**
79§: p7g² p7f² p7m* p7f⁴ p7g t7.1m Dec 26] fair performer: won maiden at Kempton in
February: left Charlie Appleby after fifth start: stays 7.5f: acts on polytrack and good to
firm going: often in blinkers in 2015. *Sylvester Kirk*

HOLLYWOOD KEN (IRE) 2 b.g. (Mar 20) Arcano (IRE) 122 – Third Dimension (FR) **73 p**
(Suave Dancer (USA) 136) [2015 7.1m⁴ 5.9g⁵ 7m² Aug 4] €52,000Y, resold €92,000Y:
half-brother to several winners, including useful 1¾m winner Orgilgo Bay (by Lawman)
and 2m-2¼m winner Theola (by Kalanisi): dam French 10.5f winner: fair maiden: best
effort when second at Catterick (8 lengths behind Mohab) in August, clear of rest: remains
with potential. *Keith Dalgleish*

HOLLYWOOD ROAD (IRE) 2 b.c. (Mar 7) Kodiac 112 – Rinneen (IRE) 67 (Bien **75**
Bien (USA) 125) [2015 6s⁵ 7v⁴ 7g² 7g⁵ 8.5g³ 8v⁵ t5.1m⁵ t5.1m⁴ Dec 12] fair maiden: left
Conor O'Dwyer after sixth start: will be suited by a return to 6f+: acts on heavy going:
tried in visor. *Don Cantillon*

HOLY GRAIL (IRE) 2 b.f. (Apr 30) Canford Cliffs (IRE) 133 – Dashing Beauty (IRE) **91**
77 (Daggers Drawn (USA) 114) [2015 5v* 5m⁴ 6d² 6g* 7m³ 6g⁴ 6.5m Sep 10] €25,000Y,
resold £25,000: third foal: half-sister to 1¾m winner Get Out of Jail (by Authorized):
dam, 6f winner, half-sister to useful performer up to 1m Dashing Colours: fairly useful
performer: won maiden at Ripon in May and nursery at Newmarket in August: good third
in nursery at Newmarket next start: stays 7f: acts on good to firm and heavy going. *Richard
Fahey*

HOMAGE (IRE) 5 b.g. Acclamation 118 – Night Sphere (IRE) 74 (Night Shift (USA)) **100**
[2015 109: 8m 8.3m² 8g⁶ 10m 10s 8.3s³ Oct 6] rather leggy gelding: useful handicapper:
second at Nottingham (1¾ lengths behind Big Baz) in June: stays 8.5f: acts on polytrack,
firm and good to soft going: often in cheekpieces in 2015: often races prominently:
temperament under suspicion. *William Haggas*

HOMBRE ROJO (IRE) 2 b.c. (Apr 27) Intikhab (USA) 135 – Sidney Girl (Azamour **86**
(IRE) 130) [2015 p7g⁴ p7f² 7g⁶ p8g³ p8m* Dec 16] €43,000F, 45,000Y: compact colt: first
foal: dam French 1m-10.5f winner: fairly useful performer: confirmed earlier promise
when winning maiden at Lingfield in December by ½ length from Sacred Trust, close up
throughout: stays 1m: acts on polytrack. *Simon Dow*

HOME AGAIN 2 b.g. (Mar 25) Bahamian Bounty 116 – Celestial Welcome 96 (Most **69**
Welcome 131) [2015 5f⁴ 5g 6g² 5m⁵ 6g³ 7.2g² Sep 29] fair maiden: left David Brown after
third start: stays 7f: acts on good to firm going. *Brian Ellison*

HOME CUMMINS (IRE) 3 b.f. Rip Van Winkle (IRE) 134 – Alava (IRE) (Anabaa **96**
(USA) 130) [2015 93: 8g⁶ p10g⁵ t8.6m* p8g⁶ Dec 28] lengthy filly: useful handicapper: won at Wolverhampton (by ½ length from Mont Ras) in November: stays 8.5f: acts
on polytrack, tapeta and good to firm going. *Richard Fahey*

HOME FLYER (IRE) 4 b.g. Tagula (IRE) 116 – Lady Flyer (IRE) (Eagle Eyed (USA) **65**
111) [2015 75?: 8m 7s³ 8g 8m⁵ 10.2m 8d 7g 7.9d³ 8g t8.6f³ t8.6f Oct 23] fair maiden: stays
1¼m: acts on tapeta and soft going: often in cheekpieces in 2015: usually wears tongue tie:
front runner/races prominently. *Mark Walford*

HOMELAND (IRE) 3 b.g. Galileo (IRE) 134 – Withorwithoutyou (IRE) 91 (Danehill **–**
(USA) 126) [2015 79P: 5m 6g⁶ Jul 4] fairly useful winner only start at 2 yrs: left Aidan
O'Brien, well held both starts in 2015 (in face of stiff tasks), subsequently gelded: stays 7f:
in tongue tie in 2015. *Brian Rothwell*

HOME OF THE BRAVE (IRE) 3 ch.c. Starspangledbanner (AUS) 128 – Blissful Beat **118**
(Beat Hollow 126) [2015 104: 7m* 8m⁶ 6f⁶ 7d*dis 7d Sep 12] lengthy colt: smart performer:
won 5-runner listed Free Handicap at Newmarket in April by 1¾ lengths from Tupi: also
first past post in Minstrel Stakes at the Curragh (3½ lengths ahead of Gordon Lord Byron)
in July but disqualified due to prohibited substance: off 7 weeks, well held in Park Stakes
at Doncaster final outing, ridden too aggressively: best at 7f: acts on good to firm and good
to soft going: tongue tied: usually leads. *Hugo Palmer*

HONCHO (IRE) 3 gr.g. Dark Angel (IRE) 113 – Disco Lights 76 (Spectrum (IRE) 126) **83**
[2015 77: 8.3m 7m 7.1m⁶ 6g⁶ 5m³ 5m⁶ 6m⁶ 6m 6m⁶ 6m 5.7s⁴ 6g* 6m 5.7s⁴ 5d² 6m* p6f 5.7g⁵ 6d⁴
Oct 30] close-coupled, sparely-made gelding: fairly useful handicapper: won at Newmarket
in July, Yarmouth in August and Salisbury in September: stays 6f: acts on soft and good to
firm going: tried in headgear. *John Ryan*

HONEST STRIKE (USA) 8 b.g. Smart Strike (CAN) 121 – Honest Lady (USA) 119 **– §**
(Seattle Slew (USA)) [2015 71: f16g⁵ p15.8m⁴ Jan 14] fairly useful at best, no form in

2015: stays 16.5f: acts on all-weather: often wears headgear: tried in tongue tie: often races towards rear: unreliable. *Daniel Loughnane*

HONEY BADGER 4 b.g. Pastoral Pursuits 127 – Taminoula (IRE) 82 (Tagula (IRE) 116) **63** [2015 –: p8f 7.6d 9.9m² 9.9m⁵ p10f p11g² p12m p10d Nov 30] modest maiden: left Denis Quinn after fourth start: stays 11f: acts on polytrack and good to firm going: usually in cheekpieces in 2015: sometimes slowly away. *Eugene Stanford*

HONEYMOON COCKTAIL (FR) 4 gr.g. Martaline 118 – Caipirinia (FR) (Hawk **89** Wing (USA) 136) [2015 8g³ 8g⁵ 10.4g⁴ 8v⁵ 10s t8.6f p8d p12m* Dec 16] fairly useful **a80** handicapper: won at Lingfield (apprentice) in December: left S. Brogi, France, after third start: stays 1½m: acts on polytrack, viscoride and soft going: in hood last 3 starts. *David Pipe*

HONEYMOON EXPRESS (IRE) 5 br.m. Mujadil (USA) 119 – Royal Jelly 82 (King's **43** Best (USA) 132) [2015 87: 5.7f 5m 5m⁶ 6d⁶ p6f⁶ t5.1f⁶ p6f Oct 1] sturdy mare: poor handicapper: stays 6f: acts on good to firm going: often wears headgear. *Julia Feilden*

HONEY REQUIRED 3 b.f. Makfi 130 – Tiger Mist (IRE) (Galileo (IRE) 134) [2015 62, **–** a55: t8.6f 10.2s Oct 28] modest at best, no form in 2015: stays 8.5f: acts on polytrack, good to firm and good to soft going: tried in hood: front runner/races prominently. *Alan Bailey*

HONEYSUCKLE LIL (IRE) 3 b.f. Alfred Nobel (IRE) 110 – Twinberry (IRE) (Tagula **84** (IRE) 116) [2015 78: 6d⁵ 6m 6g⁵ 6d* 6m* 5g³ 6m² 6.1g⁶ 5.9s⁵ 5g Sep 18] fairly useful handicapper: won at Ripon and Leicester in June: good second at Newcastle in July: stays 6f: acts on good to firm and good to soft going: tried in cheekpieces in 2015. *Tim Easterby*

HONG KONG JOE 5 b.g. Oasis Dream 129 – Singed (Zamindar (USA) 116) [2015 65: **61** p7m p8g⁵ p8g 9.9d⁴ 9.9s³ 9.9d³ 8g⁵ p10f³ 9.9v p12g² p11g 9.9s⁵ Oct 15] modest maiden: stays 1½m: acts on polytrack and soft going: often wears headgear. *Lydia Richards*

Flemington Bloodstock Partnership's "Home of The Brave"

HONIARA 2 b.c. (Apr 19) Rock of Gibraltar (IRE) 133 – Indian Maiden (IRE) 115 (Indian **80** Ridge 123) [2015 6g 6m² 7m⁴ 6g⁴ 7s p7.5g² p8g² Nov 6] €34,000F, €60,000Y: good-topped colt: fifth foal: half-brother to 3 winners in France, including 6f-1m winner Love Spirit (by Elusive City) and 7f/1m winner Inner Beauty (by Pivotal): dam 5f/6f winner: fairly useful maiden: second at Windsor, Deauville and Chantilly: stays 1m: acts on polytrack and good to firm going, below form on soft. *Paul Cole*

HONITON LACE 4 ch.f. Tobougg (IRE) 125 – Mellifluous (IRE) 44 (Noverre (USA) **45** 125) [2015 63: p8m p8f 8d t8.6g³ t8.6g 7.6s 8v² p8f p8f⁶ p7g* Dec 10] workmanlike filly: **a58** modest handicapper: won at Wolverhampton in June and Chelmsford in December: stays 1¼m: acts on polytrack, tapeta and soft going: often wears headgear: often wears tongue tie. *Phil McEntee*

HONORINA 2 ch.f. (Apr 8) Sea The Stars (IRE) 140 – Honorine (IRE) 89 (Mark of **85 p** Esteem (IRE) 137) [2015 7f² p7g² Aug 5] seventh foal: closely related to smart 1½m-1¾m winner Elidor (by Cape Cross) and very smart winner up to 1½m (including Irish Derby) Treasure Beach (2-y-o 7f winner, by Galileo) and half-sister to 2 winners, including useful 1¼m-1.5f winner Honor Bound (by Authorized): dam 1m-1¼m winner: promising second in maidens at Doncaster and Kempton, unsuited by emphasis on speed when beaten 2¼ lengths by Nemoralia in latter: will be well suited by 1m+: remains open to improvement. *Sir Michael Stoute*

HONOURABLE ACTION (IRE) 3 b.g. Shamardal (USA) 129 – Saoirse Abu (USA) **71 §** 112 (Mr Greeley (USA) 122) [2015 t9.5f² p10f³ p10g⁴ p11g⁵ 11.7f³ Apr 23] fair maiden: stays 11f: acts on polytrack and tapeta: often in blinkers: tried in tongue tie: sold £21,000, sent to the Netherlands. *Charlie Appleby*

HONOUR PROMISE (IRE) 3 b.f. Jeremy (USA) 122 – Karenaragon (Aragon 118) **63** [2015 –: 10.2m⁶ 12.1s* 11.9m² 14m⁶ 16g 12.1s⁶ p13.3f⁵ t16.5fOct27] modest handicapper: won at Chepstow in May: stays 1¾m: acts on soft and good to firm going: often races prominently. *William Muir*

HOOFALONG 5 b.g. Pastoral Pursuits 127 – Baymist 68 (Mind Games 121) [2015 82: **86** 6m 6.1m 6g⁵ 5.5mᵘʳ 5m⁵ 6m 5g* 5m⁴ 6d 5.1s⁶ t5.1f 5s² p6f² p6g* p6f² Dec 17] useful- **a95** looking gelding: useful handicapper: won at Pontefract in August and Chelmsford (by length from Luis Vaz de Torres) in November: good neck second to Foreign Diplomat at Chelmsford final start: stays 6.5f: acts on polytrack, soft and good to firm going: wears headgear: front runner/races prominently. *Michael Easterby*

HOOF IT 8 b.g. Monsieur Bond (IRE) 120 – Forever Bond (Danetime (IRE) 121) [2015 **105** 111: 6g 6m 6m 6m 6d⁵ 6.5m* 6g 6d⁵ 7v Nov 7] big, strong gelding: useful handicapper: won at Doncaster (by 1½ lengths from Toofi) in September: creditable eighth of 25 to Don't Touch in Ayr Gold Cup next start: stays 6.5f: acts on polytrack, soft and good to firm going: tried in headgear. *Michael Easterby*

HOOFITHULLY 3 ch.g. Stimulation (IRE) 121 – Splicing 82 (Sharpo 132) [2015 41: **41** f7m f6g Dec 29] close-coupled gelding: poor maiden: stays 7f: acts on fibresand and good to soft going. *Michael Easterby*

HOOKERGATE GRAMMAR 3 b.g. Yeats (IRE) 128 – Oulianovsk (IRE) (Peintre **71** Celebre (USA) 137) [2015 –: 8m⁴ 9g 11.9m⁶ 16.2m³ 14.1m³ 14.1m³ 17.1d 14.14d Oct 26] fair maiden: should stay at least 2m: acts on good to firm going. *Keith Reveley*

HOONOSE 6 ch.g. Cadeaux Genereux 131 – Roodeye 100 (Inchinor 119) [2015 p16g⁶ **?** 12.1s 11.9d 8g? 14] compact gelding: modest at best, no form in 2015: often wears headgear: tried in tongue tie prior to 2015. *Pat Eddery*

HOORAYFORHOLLYWOOD 3 b.f. Oasis Dream 129 – Dalisay (IRE) 76 (Sadler's **81** Wells (USA) 132) [2015 78p: 9.9d⁴ 8.1m⁵ 10.2m* 9.9g³ t8.6f⁴ p10f⁴ Nov 5] sturdy filly: fairly useful handicapper: won at Bath by 3¼ lengths from Saumur) in July: stays 1¼m: acts on firm going: tried in cheekpieces once in 2015: sold 16,000 gns, sent to Qatar. *Sir Michael Stoute*

HOOTENANNY (USA) 3 b.c. Quality Road (USA) 131 – More Hennessy (USA) **116** (Hennessy (USA) 122) [2015 116: 5.5g* 6f Jun 19] strong colt: smart performer: successful in Breeders' Cup Juvenile Turf at Santa Anita in 2014: easy winner of allowance race at Keeneland (by 6¼ lengths from Bottle Rocket) in April: below form when 11½ lengths eleventh to Muhaarar in Commonwealth Cup at Royal Ascot, only subsequent outing: stays 1m: acts on polytrack, firm and soft going: wears blinkers: has worn tongue tie: races prominently. *Wesley A. Ward, USA*

HOPE AND FAITH (IRE) 3 gr.f. Zebedee 113 – Fuerta Ventura (IRE) 102 (Desert Sun **79** 120) [2015 6m* 6g⁶ 6m⁵ 6g⁴ p6f t6f⁴ p6f³ Oct 22] 120,000Y: workmanlike filly: third foal: half-sister to useful winner up to 7f The Gold Cheongsam (2-y-o 6f/6.5f winner, by Red

Clubs): dam, 1m-9.4f winner who stayed 1¾m, half-sister to useful 5.7f-7f winner Redvers: fair performer: won maiden at Doncaster in April: raced only at 6f: acts on polytrack, tapeta and good to firm going: in cheekpieces final start. *Jeremy Noseda*

HOPE COVE 2 b.c. (Apr 28) Shamardal (USA) 129 – Deveron (USA) 105 (Cozzene **89** (USA)) [2015 6m⁶ 6m³ 6s² 7.1m 7m* 7d² p6f² t6f* Oct 31] 100,000Y: compact colt: sixth foal: brother to 2-y-o 7f winner Dffar and half-brother to ungenuine 2-y-o 1m winner (stayed 12.5f) Open Letter (by New Approach) and useful winner up to 9.5f Lamar (2-y-o 6f winner, by Cape Cross): dam 2-y-o 7f winner: fairly useful performer: won nurseries at Redcar in September and Wolverhampton in October: stays 7f: acts on polytrack, tapeta and good to firm going. *Ed Walker*

HOPE IS HIGH 2 b.f. (Apr 20) Sir Percy 129 – Altitude 88 (Green Desert (USA) 127) – [2015 8.3d p8g t9.5f Dec 14] 28,000Y: third foal: half-sister to 1m winner (stayed 11.5f) Alegra (by Galileo): dam, 1½m winner, half-sister to dual Champion Stakes winner Alborada: no form: tried in cheekpieces *David Simcock*

HOPES N DREAMS (IRE) 7 b.m. Elusive City (USA) 117 – Hope of Pekan (IRE) (Sri **91** Pekan (USA) 117) [2015 93: p6g⁴ p6f p5f⁶ p6f⁶ t5.1g⁶ 5.5g⁶ 6s* 6g⁴ 6.1g 6m 6m Jul 2] fairly useful handicapper: won at Hamilton (by 2¼ lengths from Norville) in May: stays 6f: acts on polytrack, good to firm and heavy going: tried in headgear: tried in tongue tie prior to 2015. *Kevin Ryan*

HOPE YOU DANCE (FR) 3 ch.f. Mastercraftsman (IRE) 129 – Anna of Dubai (GER) **69** (Dubai Destination (USA) 127) [2015 58: 9.9s⁵ May 14] better effort in maidens when fifth of 9 to Loving Things at Salisbury in May. *David Simcock*

HORATIA THE FLEET 2 ch.f. (Jan 20) Bahamian Bounty 116 – Countermarch 81 – (Selkirk (USA) 129) [2015 p6g p7m Dec 31] £7,000Y: first foal: dam 8.6f winner: well held in seller and a maiden. *Willie Musson*

HORNSBY 2 b.c. (Feb 16) Dubawi (IRE) 129 – Moonlife (IRE) 114 (Invincible Spirit **88 p** (IRE) 121) [2015 7.1m⁶ 7g* 7d³ Jul 2] strong colt: second foal: brother to useful 1m winner Emirates Airline: dam winner up to 1m (2-y-o 7f winner): fairly useful performer: won maiden at Newmarket (by ½ length from Zebadiah) in June: further improvement when third in minor event at Haydock (3½ lengths behind Galileo Gold) in July, never nearer: raced only at 7f: remains with potential. *Charlie Appleby*

HORS DE COMBAT 4 ch.g. Mount Nelson 125 – Maid For Winning (USA) (Gone West **113** (USA)) [2015 114: 8f² 8m 7m² 8f⁴ 8d³ 9g⁶ Oct 10] strong gelding: smart performer: second in listed race at Ascot (1¼ lengths behind Moohaarib) in April and Criterion Stakes at Newmarket (1¼ lengths behind Markaz) in June, and third in Superior Mile at Haydock (3 lengths behind Balty Boys, having met trouble) in September: stays 1m: acts on firm and good to soft going: waited with. *James Fanshawe*

HORSEGUARDSPARADE 4 b.g. Montjeu (IRE) 137 – Honorlina (FR) (Linamix (FR) **78 p** 127) [2015 f12g* t12.2f⁵ Dec 22] 450,000Y: second foal: dam, French 2-y-o 1m winner, sister to very smart French 1m/9f winner Vahorimix: behind in 2 bumpers: won maiden at Southwell (by length from Starving Faithful) in December: fifth in handicap at Wolverhampton final start: will be suited by further than 1½m: should continue to progress. *Nigel Twiston-Davies*

HORSESHOE BAY (IRE) 3 b.g. Arch (USA) 127 – Sweepstake (IRE) 98 (Acclamation **101** 118) [2015 78p: 10m⁴ 12m* 13m⁴ Jul 9] tall gelding: useful form: won maiden at Newmarket (by 7 lengths from Libbard) in May: 9/4, much stiffer task when 4¼ lengths fourth of 5 to Mr Singh in Bahrain Trophy at Newmarket only subsequent start: stays 13f: has been gelded. *Sir Michael Stoute*

HORSFORTH 3 b.f. Kyllachy 129 – Lady McBeth (IRE) (Avonbridge 123) [2015 76: 5g⁶ **73** 5g⁴ 5m 5m³ 5g 5g³ 5.1g⁵ 5d⁶ 5m⁵ 5m Aug 13] rather unfurnished filly: fair handicapper: stays 5.5f: acts on good to firm and good to soft going: tried in headgear in 2015. *Tony Coyle*

HORSTED KEYNES (FR) 5 ch.g. Giant's Causeway (USA) 132 – Viking's Cove **104** (USA) (Miswaki (USA) 124) [2015 112: 8g 8.9g 7f 6.5m⁴ p6g² t6m Dec 26] useful handicapper: second in minor event at Kempton (1¼ lengths behind Lancelot du Lac) in October: should stay 1m: acts on polytrack, best turf form on good to firm going: tried in headgear. *David Simcock*

HOT MUSTARD 5 b.g. Pastoral Pursuits 127 – Lihou Island 89 (Beveled (USA)) [2015 **83** 70: 8.3m⁶ p8m² 9d² 8f* 9g² 8.3m² 8.1g* 8.1g² p8f⁵ 8.3s Oct 28] fairly useful handicapper: won at Bath in June and Sandown in August: stays 8.5f: acts on polytrack and any turf going: races prominently. *William Muir*

HOT RIGHT NOW 5 ch.m. Sleeping Indian 122 – American Rouge (IRE) (Grand Lodge –
(USA) 125) [2015 77: f8d⁵ p8g Feb 1] fair at best, no form in 2015: stays 1m: acts on
fibresand: tried in visor: usually races close up. *K. R. Burke*

HOT SAUCE (IRE) 3 ch.f. Peintre Celebre (USA) 137 – Heat (King's Best (USA) 132)   **102**
[2015 –p: 8.5v⁴ 9.5g* 10g³ 10m² 9d⁶ 12g⁵ 12d p10.7g² Oct 16] fourth foal: half-sister to
useful 10.7f-1½m winner Cardinal Palace (by Papal Bull): dam unraced half-sister to very
smart sprinter Prohibit: useful performer: won maiden at Gowran (by 1¼ lengths from
Variable) in April: better form after including when fifth in Give Thanks Stakes at Cork (3¼
lengths behind Zananda) in August and 5 lengths second to Fire Fighting in listed race at
Dundalk final start: stays 1½m: acts on polytrack and good to firm going: consistent. *John
Joseph Murphy, Ireland*

HOT SPICE 7 b.g. Kodiac 112 – Harlestone Lady (Shaamit (IRE) 127) [2015 83: 13.8d   **84**
13g 16d 16m* 16.5m* 17.5g 16.4s 14.6d Oct 23] good-topped gelding: fairly useful
handicapper: won at Thirsk in July and Doncaster (amateur, by 5 lengths from Bowdler's
Magic) in July: stays 16.5f: acts on good to firm and good to soft going: front runner/races
prominently. *Michael Easterby*

HOT STREAK (IRE) 4 ch.c. Iffraaj 127 – Ashirah (USA) (Housebuster (USA)) [2015   **109**
119: 5g³ 5g⁶ 5f 6g⁵ 5d Sep 13] strong colt: very smart sprinter at his best but just a useful
performer in 2015, best effort when third in Prix de Saint-Georges at Longchamp (2¾
lengths behind Mecca's Angel) in May: left Kevin Ryan after fourth start: won at 6f, but
best at 5f: acted on soft and good to firm going: tried in cheekpieces in 2015: to stand at
Tweenhills Stud, Hartpury, Gloucestershire, fee £7,000. *Robert Cowell*

HOT STUFF 2 b.g. (Mar 3) Assertive 121 – Even Hotter 63 (Desert Style (IRE) 121)   **66**
[2015 5m⁴ 5f t5.1g⁴ t5.1f² Dec 11] useful-looking gelding: fair maiden: left George Baker
after third start: raced only at 5f. *Tony Carroll*

HOUDINI 3 b.c. Pivotal 124 – Regina 97 (Green Desert (USA) 127) [2015 59p: t7.1f p8m   **72**
p6f⁵ t6g⁴ p7g 5m⁴ 5m⁴ 5.7f³ t6g Jul 7] fair handicapper: won at Wolverhampton in May:
stays 6f: acts on tapeta and firm going. *Jamie Osborne*

HOUND MUSIC 3 ch.f. Ashkalani (IRE) 128 – Saffron Fox 89 (Safawan 118) [2015 75:   **73**
8g p11g 11.6m* 11.6m 10g⁴ 10v⁵ 11.6d Oct 12] tall, lengthy, unfurnished filly: fair
handicapper: won at Windsor in June: stays 11.5f: acts on good to firm going: front runner/
races prominently. *Jonathan Portman*

HOUSE OF COMMONS (IRE) 2 b.c. (Mar 23) Sea The Stars (IRE) 140 – Reality   **87**
(FR) (Slickly (FR) 128) [2015 6.5m³ 7m⁴ p8d Sep 4] €45,000F, 100,000Y: first foal: dam
useful French winner up to 1m (2-y-o 6.5f winner): fairly useful maiden: third at Newbury
(2 lengths behind Twin Sails) and fourth at Newmarket (1¾ lengths behind Manaafidh) in
July: should stay 1m. *Paul Cole*

HOUSEWIVES CHOICE 4 ch.f. Black Sam Bellamy (IRE) 121 – Maid of Perth (Mark   –
of Esteem (IRE) 137) [2015 56: 12d Sep 15] lightly-raced maiden: tried in hood prior to
2015. *James Bethell*

HOUSTON DYNIMO (IRE) 10 b.g. Rock of Gibraltar (IRE) 133 – Quiet Mouse   **52**
(USA) (Quiet American (USA)) [2015 12d Mar 29] tall gelding: modest handicapper: stays
1¾m: acts on polytrack, soft and good to firm going: in blinkers/tongue tie sole start in
2015: fairly useful chaser. *David Pipe*

HOWARDIAN HILLS 2 b.c. (Apr 21) Vale of York (IRE) 117 – Handsome Anna   –
(IRE) 67 (Bigstone (IRE) 126) [2015 p6g⁶ Dec 9] 40/1, shaped as if needed experience
when sixth in maiden at Kempton (7 lengths behind Aclaim) in December. *Richard Hannon*

HOWYADOINGNOTSOBAD (IRE) 7 b.g. Kodiac 112 – Beau Petite (Kyllachy 129)   **66**
[2015 67: p5f⁴ 5m⁵ p5f Oct 24] lengthy gelding: fair handicapper: stays 5.5f: acts on
polytrack and firm going: tried in cheekpieces prior to 2015: tried in tongue tie prior to
2015: front runner/races prominently. *John Gallagher*

HOWZ THE FAMILY (IRE) 4 b.g. Myboycharlie (IRE) 118 – Lady Raj (USA) (El   **51**
Prado (IRE) 119) [2015 68: f6d p8f p10f f8g Mar 31] smallish gelding: modest handicapper: stays 1m: acts on polytrack and good to firm going: tried in headgear: tried in
tongue tie prior to 2015: usually races nearer last than first: temperament under suspicion.
John Spearing

HOY HOY (IRE) 4 b.g. Iffraaj 127 – Luxie (IRE) 77 (Acclamation 118) [2015 75: t7.1f⁵   **55**
p7m³ 7d 8.1m⁵ 7g⁴ 6g 7t.1g⁵ p6m t7.1f Dec 22] good-topped gelding: fair handicapper: **a65**
stays 1m: acts on polytrack, tapeta and good to soft going: often in headgear/tongue tie in
2015. *Alexandra Dunn*

HUBERTAS 3 b.g. Lord of England (GER) 119 – Western Eyes (IRE) 57 (Rock of **87 §** Gibraltar (IRE) 133) [2015 50: f8d⁵ t8.6f⁶ 10.2m* 11.8g* 11.9m³ 12m⁶ 12d² 14d⁴ 12g 14.6d⁴ Oct 23] fairly useful handicapper: won at Nottingham in April and Leicester in May: second at Catterick (amateur) in August: stays 14.5f: acts on soft and good to firm going: sometimes in blinkers in 2015: sometimes slowly away. *John Quinn*

HUGIE BOY (IRE) 3 ch.g. Art Connoisseur (IRE) 121 – Piece Unique (Barathea (IRE) **71** 127) [2015 –: 7d 6g⁴ 6m* 6m 6m Jun 26] fair handicapper: won at Thirsk in May: should stay 7f: acts on good to firm going: in cheekpieces last 3 starts. *Scott Dixon*

HULCOLT (IRE) 4 b.g. Acclamation 118 – Fusili (IRE) 100 (Silvano (GER) 126) [2015 **84** 80: 7.5f² 7.5m* 8d 7.5g⁵ 7g Sep 19] fairly useful handicapper: won at Beverley in July: stays 7.5f: acts on polytrack, firm and good to soft going. *Ivan Furtado*

HUMAN NATURE (IRE) 2 b.c. (Apr 29) Kodiac 114 – Sundown 71 (Polish Precedent **95** (USA) 131) [2015 6m³ 6m* 6f² 5m⁴ 5s* Aug 20] 115,000 2-y-o: compact colt: half-brother to several winners, including useful/unreliable 5f-7f winner Copper Dock (by Docksider) and useful 1m-1½m winner Forgotten Hero (by High Chaparral): dam maiden (best up to 1m): useful performer: won maiden at Windsor in June and minor event at Lingfield in August: stays 6f: acts on firm and soft going: tried in cheekpieces: front runner/races prominently. *Saeed bin Suroor*

HUMAN (USA) 3 b.f. Blame (USA) 129 – Angel In My Heart (FR) 119 (Rainbow Quest **64 p** (USA) 134) [2015 8.3g⁶ p10f Sep 3] angular filly: half-sister to several winners, including Derby winner Kris Kin (2-y-o 7f winner, by Kris S) and smart French 1¼m/10.5f winner Bravodino (by Dynaformer): dam French/US 1m-1¼m winner: better effort when sixth in maiden at Windsor in May: remains open to improvement. *David Lanigan*

HUME LOUGH 4 b.g. Teofilo (IRE) 126 – Pink Cristal 13 (Dilum (USA) 115) [2015 **53** 70p: p12g p12g 13g 15.8s Oct 6] modest maiden: left Andrew Oliver after third start: stays 10.5f: acts on polytrack: tried in tongue tie in 2015. *Mark McNiff, Ireland*

HUMIDOR (IRE) 8 b.g. Camacho 118 – Miss Indigo 123 (Indian Ridge 123) [2015 108: **112** 5.1d³ 5m* 6m 5m* 5f 5gᵘʳ 5v* 5m Oct 4] well-made gelding: smart handicapper: won at Goodwood (by ½ length from Long Awaited) in May, Newmarket (by head from Kingsgate Choice) in June and Epsom (by 1¼ lengths from Elusivity) in August: stays 6f: acts on good to firm and heavy going: tried in cheekpieces prior to 2015: sometimes in tongue tie prior to 2015. *George Baker*

HUMOUR (IRE) 4 b.g. Invincible Spirit (IRE) 121 – Hucking Hot 102 (Desert Prince **70** (IRE) 130) [2015 68: t7.1g² p6m p6f³ t5.1g* 5.1s 5.1d² p5m 5.1g 5.1d p5f⁴ p6f* p6f² p6d⁵ **a77** p7f⁴ p7g⁴ p6m Dec 31] fair handicapper: won at Wolverhampton in March and Chelmsford in October: has form at 8.5f, best efforts at sprint distances: acts on polytrack, tapeta and good to soft going: tried in hood: usually races close up. *Christine Dunnett*

HUMPHREY BOGART (IRE) 2 b.c. (Apr 4) Tagula (IRE) 116 – Hazarama (IRE) 91 **103** (Kahyasi 130) [2015 p6g³ 7g* 7d⁴ 6.5m² 8g⁴ Sep 26] €29,000F, £33,000Y: brother to winner up to 1¼m Domino Dancer (2-y-o 6f winner) and half-brother to 3 winners, including 1¼m winner Devote Myself (by Kodiac): dam 13f winner: useful performer: won maiden at Doncaster in August: progressed well and finished second in valuable event at Doncaster (head behind Mr Lupton, carried left late on) and fourth in Royal Lodge Stakes at Newmarket (4¼ lengths behind Foundation) last 2 starts: stays 1m: acts on good to firm and good to soft going. *Richard Hannon*

HUMPHRY REPTON 3 b.g. Virtual 122 – Qilin (IRE) 94 (Second Set (IRE) 127) [2015 **52** –: 6m 7m⁵ 6g⁶ p8f Oct 1] modest maiden: best effort at 6f: acts on good to firm going: often starts slowly. *Mark H. Tompkins*

HUNDI (IRE) 3 b.f. Fastnet Rock (AUS) 127 – Hawala (IRE) 97 (Warning 136) [2015 88: **93** p8m² 7g⁴ 7g² 6f* 8f⁶ 8.1m 10.4m⁵ 8g Oct 17] rather leggy filly: fairly useful performer: won maiden at Salisbury (by short head from Paint The Star) in May: good efforts in listed races next 2 starts: creditable seventh to Belle Hill in Grade 3 Autumn Miss Stakes at Santa Anita final outing: stays 1m: acts on firm going: often wears a hood nowadays. *Charles Hills*

HUNGERFORD 3 b.g. Pastoral Pursuits 127 – Truly Pink (Mr Greeley (USA) 122) [2015 **81** 64p: p8m* 8m³ 7.6m² p8g Jul 8] fairly useful performer: won maiden at Lingfield in January: placed in handicaps at Doncaster in June and Chester (apprentice) in June: stays 1m: acts on polytrack and good to firm going. *Olly Stevens*

HUNTER JACK 2 b.g. (Mar 7) Monsieur Bond (IRE) 120 – Maysarah (IRE) 77 (Green **68** Desert (USA) 127) [2015 6m³ 6d⁴ 6g 7g Sep 23] fair maiden: best effort at 6f (second start): sold 7,000 gns, sent to Sweden. *George Peckham*

HUNTERS BELT (IRE) 11 b.g. Intikhab (USA) 135 – Three Stars 93 (Star Appeal 133) **63**
[2015 69: 16s⁴ May 11] modest handicapper: stays 2m: acts on fibresand, best turf form on
good going or softer: tried in headgear: tried in tongue tie. *George Bewley*

HUNTER'S LIGHT (IRE) 7 ch.h. Dubawi (IRE) 129 – Portmanteau 96 (Barathea **126**
(IRE) 127) [2015 108: 9.9g* 9.9g* 8.9g* Mar 7] strong horse: high-class performer: won
12 of his 27 races: raced only at Meydan after 2013 and unbeaten in 3 outings there when
better than ever in 2015, namely handicap (by 1¼ lengths from Elleval) in January, listed
race (by 1¾ lengths from Umgiyo) in February and Jebel Hatta (by 6½ lengths from Trade
Storm) in March: stayed 11f: acted on synthetics and any turf going: was tried in headgear:
often travelled strongly: reported in March to have been retired after suffering a tendon
injury: to stand at Haras du Logis, France, fee €4,000. *Saeed bin Suroor*

HUNTLAW 2 b.g. (May 6) Oasis Dream 129 – Attraction 125 (Efisio 120) [2015 6g⁶ Oct **– p**
8] brother to smart 5f (including at 2 yrs) winner Fountain of Youth, closely related to 2-y-o
7f winner Elation (by Cape Cross) and half-brother to 3 winners, including useful 9f/1¼m
winner (stays 1½m) Cushion (by Galileo): dam high-class miler (also 2-y-o 5f/6f winner):
3/1, held back by inexperience when sixth in maiden at Ayr (7¾ lengths behind Cheeky
Angel) in October: entitled to do better. *Mark Johnston*

HUNTSMANS CLOSE 5 b.g. Elusive Quality (USA) – Badminton 106 (Zieten (USA) **110**
118) [2015 103: 6f² 6m* 6m⁶ 5.4g Aug 19] lengthy gelding: smart handicapper: won at
Windsor (by neck from Charles Molson) in June: creditable efforts when short-head second
of 22 to Eastern Impact at Newmarket and sixth of 27 to Magical Memory in Stewards'
Cup at Goodwood: stays 6f: acts on any turf going: sometimes wore hood in 2014.
Roger Charlton

HURRICANE ALERT 3 b.g. Showcasing 117 – Raggle Taggle (IRE) 95 (Tagula (IRE) **59**
116) [2015 76: p6g p6f⁴ 6d³ p5m³ 5g⁴ Jul 14] modest maiden: left Ralph Beckett after first
start: stays 6f: acts on polytrack and good to soft going: sometimes in visor in 2015: front
runner/races prominently. *Gary Moore*

HURRICANE HICKS (USA) 2 ch.g. (Mar 16) Speightstown (USA) 124 – Specific **–**
Dream (Danehill Dancer (IRE) 117) [2015 8d 8.3m⁶ Sep 20] well held in 2 maidens. *David
O'Meara*

HURRICANE HIGGINS (IRE) 7 br.g. Hurricane Run (IRE) 134 – Mare Aux Fees **103**
(Kenmare (FR) 125) [2015 p15.8m* p15.8f⁵ 20f Jun 16] tall, attractive gelding: useful
performer: won minor event at Lingfield in February: stays 21f: acts on polytrack, firm and
good to soft going: tried in blinkers prior to 2015: has failed to impress with attitude in past:
fairly useful hurdler. *Nicky Henderson*

HURRICANE VOLTA (IRE) 4 ch.c. Hurricane Run (IRE) 134 – Haute Volta (FR) **–**
(Grape Tree Road 122) [2015 81: 12m 17.2m 11.6d f11g Dec 29] fairly useful at best, no
form in 2015: often wears headgear: tends to find little. *Ralph Smith*

HURRY HOME POPPA (IRE) 5 b.g. Holy Roman Emperor (IRE) 125 – My Renee **74**
(USA) 109 (Kris S (USA)) [2015 72: 13.8d³ 14.1m² 16d² 14.1g³ 16.4g 13.8d* 18d 14.1s⁴
15.8s⁴ 13.9f⁴ t13.9f⁶ Dec 14] fair handicapper: won at Catterick in September: stays 2m:
acts on tapeta and soft going. *John Mackie*

HUSBANDRY 2 b.g. (Feb 7) Paco Boy (IRE) 129 – Humdrum 101 (Dr Fong (USA) 128) **93 p**
[2015 5.1m³ 6m² 6m* Jul 11] first foal: dam, 7f/1m winner (including at 2 yrs), half-sister
to smart 6f winner Musical Comedy: fairly useful performer: won maiden at York (by 1¾
lengths from Mont Kiara) in July: second in maiden at Salisbury (short head behind
Gutaifan) previous start: will stay 7f: will go on improving. *Andrew Balding*

HUSSAR BALLAD 2 b.g. Hard Spun (USA) 124 – Country Melody (USA) **76**
(Gone West (USA)) [2015 75: f12g⁴ f11g⁴ 10g³ 10.1m³ t12.2g³ 9.9m⁵ t12.2m⁶ t9.5f* Dec
14] strong gelding: fair handicapper: won at Wolverhampton (amateur) in December: stays
1½m: acts on fibresand, tapeta, best turf form on good going. *Antony Brittain*

HUTTON (IRE) 2 b.g. (Jan 18) Lawman (FR) 121 – Moynsha Lady (IRE) (Namid 128) **67**
[2015 t7.1m² p7f³ Dec 17] better effort when second in maiden at Wolverhampton (3½
lengths behind Sky Ship) in November. *Richard Fahey*

HYALINE (USA) 2 b.c. (Mar 4) Shamardal (USA) 129 – Looking Glass (USA) (Seeking **65**
The Gold (USA)) [2015 6.1d 6s⁵ 7g³ 7d Oct 16] fair maiden: stays 7f. *Mark Johnston*

HYDRANT 9 b.g. Haafhd 129 – Spring 112 (Sadler's Wells (USA) 132) [2015 83: 10.3d⁵ **79**
10s⁵ 10g* 8s* 10s* 10.4d² 9.8d 8.5s⁵ 10.3g 9.8d 10.3s Sep 12] strong, good-bodied
gelding: fair handicapper: won at Ayr in April and Thirsk and Ayr in May: stays 12.5f: acts
on fibresand, good to firm and heavy going: front runner/races prominently. *Richard Guest*

HYDROGEN 4 b.c. Galileo (IRE) 134 – Funsie (FR) (Saumarez 132) [2015 76p: p10g⁵ **70** Mar 12] twice-raced maiden, fifth at Chelmsford (4½ lengths behind Mister Rockandroll) in March, only outing in 2015. *Peter Chapple-Hyam*

HYGROVE PERCY 2 ch.c. (Jan 29) Sir Percy 129 – Hygrove Welshlady (IRE) 78 **76** (Langfuhr (CAN) 124) [2015 8s⁴ 9s³ 10.2g³ Oct 18] fair maiden: best effort when third at Bath (1¾ lengths behind Wapping) in October: will be suited by 1½m+. *Marcus Tregoning*

HYLAND HEATHER (IRE) 2 b.f. (Mar 6) Lilbourne Lad (IRE) 111 – Maidservant **79 p** (USA) (Seeking The Gold (USA)) [2015 5d² 6g⁶ 7m⁴ 5.9m⁴ 6s² Oct 9] €20,000F, €85,000Y: first foal: dam unraced half-sister to useful French 1m winner Woven Lace out of very smart French sprinter Do The Honours: fair maiden: neck second to Culturati in nursery at York final start: will prove suited by a return to 7f: acts on soft going: open to further improvement. *Richard Fahey*

HYMN FOR THE DUDES 2 br.g. (Apr 5) Sakhee's Secret 128 – Hermione's Dream – (Oasis Dream 129) [2015 6m 6d 6.1g⁶ Aug 3] compact gelding: no form. *John Berry*

HYPERLINK (IRE) 6 b.g. Cape Cross (IRE) 129 – Surf The Web (IRE) (Ela-Mana-Mou – 132) [2015 81: t12.2f 17.2g Oct 18] big, strong gelding: fairly useful at best, no form in 2015: stays 1½m: acts on good to firm and heavy going: tried in headgear: often in tongue tie in 2015: front runner/races prominently. *Heather Dalton*

HYPHAEMA (IRE) 3 b.f. Rock of Gibraltar (IRE) 133 – Kotdiji (Mtoto 134) [2015 67p: **54** 10.2m⁵ 10g Jul 22] modest maiden: should prove suited by middle distances: acts on polytrack and soft going: sometimes wears tongue tie. *Clive Cox*

HYPNOTISM 5 ch.g. Pivotal 124 – Hypnotize 103 (Machiavellian (USA) 123) [2015 –: – 8.1v Aug 25] maiden: best effort at 8.5f: acts on polytrack: sometimes wears headgear. *Michael Scudamore*

I

I AM NOT HERE (IRE) 4 b.g. Amadeus Wolf 122 – Newgate Lodge (IRE) 101 (Namid **73** 128) [2015 62: p12f³ 11.5d 11m* Jun 25] workmanlike gelding: fair handicapper: won at Newbury (apprentice) in June: stays 1½m: acts on polytrack, tapeta and good to firm going. *Timothy Jarvis*

IAN FLEMING 2 b.c. (Apr 29) Makfi 130 – High Cross (IRE) 78 (Cape Cross (IRE) 129) **73** [2015 7m⁵ 7.1g² 7.6g² 7s⁶ Oct 10] compact colt: fair maiden: will be suited by at least 1m. *Andrew Balding*

IAN'S MEMORY (USA) 4 b.c. Smart Strike (CAN) 121 – Rite Moment (USA) (Vicar **105** (USA) 120) [2015 70: p8g³ f8d* p8m³ p7g* f8s* p7g f7g* Dec 2] sturdy colt: useful performer: progressed very well after winning maiden at Southwell in January and was successful in handicaps at Kempton (by ½ length from Atlantis Crossing) in June and Southwell in August (by ½ length from Showboating) and December (by nose from Air of York): should be suited by a return to 1m: acts on polytrack and fibresand: in headgear in 2015: often travels strongly. *Jeremy Noseda*

IBALLISTICVIN 2 b.g. (Feb 22) Rail Link 132 – Guntakal (IRE) (Night Shift (USA)) – [2015 p7g Jul 14] 66/1, last of 12 in maiden at Lingfield. *Sean Curran*

IBN MALIK (IRE) 2 ch.g. (Feb 23) Raven's Pass (USA) 133 – Moon's Whisper (USA) **109** (Storm Cat (USA)) [2015 7m* 7g² 7d² 8g³ Oct 10] strong gelding: half-brother to several winners, including 2-y-o 1m winner Yazamaan (by Galileo) and 5f/6f winner Mutafaakir (by Oasis Dream), both useful: dam unraced daughter of Poule d'Essai des Pouliches/Prix de Diane winner East of The Moon: useful performer: won maiden at Newmarket (by ¼ length from Comicas) in June: second in Vintage Stakes at Goodwood (¾ length behind Galileo Gold) in July and Champagne Stakes at Doncaster (3½ lengths behind Emotionless) in September and third in Autumn Stakes at Newmarket (2 lengths behind Gifted Master) in October: stays 1m. *Charles Hills*

IBROX (FR) 3 b.g. Hamairi (IRE) 112 – Aalsmeer 91 (Invincible Spirit (IRE) 121) [2015 – p7.5g 10.2s⁵ Aug 31] maiden: no form in 2015: left E. J. O'Neill after reappearance (wore cheekpieces). *Victor Dartnall*

ICANBOOGIE 5 b.g. Tobougg (IRE) 125 – Dubai Marina (Polish Precedent (USA) 131) **54** [2015 –: 8g* 8m 8s⁴ p8f⁵ Nov 7] modest handicapper: won at Brighton (apprentice) in September: stays 1m: acts on soft going: tried in cheekpieces prior to 2015. *John Gallagher*

ICANDI 3 b.f. Indesatchel (IRE) 120 – Some Diva 75 (Dr Fong (USA) 128) [2015 52: 6m⁴ – 5d Jun 25] maiden: no form in 2015. *Alan Berry*

ICE AGE (IRE) 2 b.g. (May 22) Frozen Power (IRE) 108 – Incendio (Siberian Express **61**
(USA) 125) [2015 6m p7g² Jul 22] better effort when second in maiden at Lingfield (8
lengths behind Sakada) in July. *Eve Johnson Houghton*

ICE ALERT (IRE) 2 b.c. (Mar 30) Frozen Power (IRE) 108 – Karenka (IRE) (Arakan **54 p**
(USA) 123) [2015 t7.1f t7.1m Dec 18] €13,000Y, 14,000 2-y-o: second foal: dam once-
raced half-sister to smart winner up to 7f Capt Chaos: showed a little ability in 2 maidens
at Wolverhampton: remains with potential. *Marco Botti*

ICEAXE 2 b.f. (Mar 16) Stimulation (IRE) 121 – Laser Crystal (IRE) 67 (King's Theatre **60**
(IRE) 128) [2015 6m 6d³ p6g Sep 30] sixth foal: half-sister to 3 winners, including winner
up to 1½m Felix Fabulla (2-y-o 1¼m winner, by Lucky Story) and 1m-1¼m winner
D'Urberville (by Auction House): dam maiden (stayed 1¼m): modest maiden: will be
suited by 7f+. *John Holt*

ICE BOND 2 b.g. (Mar 3) Monsieur Bond (IRE) 120 – Icing 74 (Polar Falcon (USA) 126) **58**
[2015 7g 6m 5s⁴ p7g p8m⁵ 8.3s² p10f⁶ t8.6f⁶ Nov 16] compact gelding: modest maiden:
best effort at 8.5f: acts on soft going. *Richard Hannon*

ICE CRISTAL (IRE) 2 ch.f. (May 5) Frozen Power (IRE) 108 – Cristalita (IRE) 77 **–**
(Entrepreneur 123) [2015 p8d Nov 30] €5,500Y: sixth foal: half-sister to winner up to 8.5f
Cristal Island (2-y-o 7f winner, by Trans Island) and a winner in Italy by Clodovil: dam,
maiden (stayed 9f), half-sister to smart performer up to 1½m Chiming: 66/1, last of 10 in
maiden at Kempton. *Sylvester Kirk*

ICE DREAM (IRE) 2 b.f. (Mar 30) Frozen Power (IRE) 108 – Mikes Baby (IRE) 72 **81 §**
(Key of Luck (USA) 126) [2015 6g t6g³ t7.1g³ 6d² 7dʳʳ t7.1fʳ Oct 27] €28,000Y: sixth foal:
half-sister to useful US 1m winner (including at 2 yrs) Ace of Aces (by Antonius Pius) and
a winner in Italy by Indian Haven: dam, 6f winner, half-sister to useful winner up to 1½m
winner Palace Royale: fairly useful maiden: will stay 1m: acts on tapeta and good to soft
going: tried in cheekpieces: refused to race last 2 starts, and very much one to avoid.
Tom Dascombe

ICEFALL (IRE) 2 b.g. (Mar 8) Frozen Power (IRE) 108 – Silvertine (IRE) 84 (Alzao **76 p**
(USA) 117) [2015 7s 7.2g³ 8s Oct 9] €20,000Y: fifth foal: half-brother to 2-y-o 6f winner
She's Ok (by Xaar): dam, maiden (stayed 7f), half-sister to Prix de l'Opera winner Kinnaird
and Chester Vase winner Mickdaam: fair maiden: best effort when third in maiden at Ayr
(length behind Constantino) in September: remains open to improvement. *Tim Easterby*

ICE GALLEY (IRE) 2 b.c. (Jan 29) Galileo (IRE) 134 – Ice Queen (IRE) 118 (Danehill **59 p**
Dancer (IRE) 117) [2015 8.3s⁵ Oct 28] 105,000Y: fourth foal: brother to 1½m winner
Exotic and smart 1¼m winner (stays 1½m) Felix Mendelssohn: dam, 1¼m-1½m winner,
second in Irish Oaks: 7/2, fifth in maiden at Nottingham (8 lengths behind Zoffanys Pride)
in October: better to come, particularly over 1¼m+. *Kevin Ryan*

ICE KONIG (FR) 6 gr.g. Epalo (GER) 122 – Isarwelle (GER) (Sternkoenig (IRE) 122) **48**
[2015 10.2d⁴ 10.9g⁵ Aug 31] poor handicapper: stays 14.5f: acts on polytrack and heavy
going: tried in cheekpieces prior to 2015. *Jimmy Frost*

ICE LORD (IRE) 3 gr.g. Verglas (IRE) 118 – Special Lady (FR) (Kaldoun (FR) 122) **94**
[2015 87p: 8m⁵ 6g* 6m 7g⁵ Sep 8] lengthy gelding: fairly useful performer: won maiden
at Salisbury (by 8 lengths from Oat Couture) in July: stays 6f: acts on good to firm going:
front runner/races prominently. *Clive Cox*

ICE ROYAL (IRE) 2 b.c. (Apr 26) Frozen Power (IRE) 108 – Salford Princess (IRE) **80 p**
(Titus Livius (FR) 115) [2015 t7.1f* p7g³ Dec 9] €10,500Y, £62,000 2-y-o: fourth foal:
dam unraced half-sister to very smart performer up to 1½m Definite Article: won maiden
at Wolverhampton (by neck from Chicago School) in October: better effort when third in
nursery at Kempton (¾ length behind Cryptic) in December, needing stronger gallop:
likely to progress further. *Jamie Osborne*

ICE SLICE (IRE) 4 b.g. Dark Angel (IRE) 113 – Ice Rock (IRE) (Rock of Gibraltar **86**
(IRE) 133) [2015 92, a81: 8.3s⁵ 8d p8g⁴ p7g⁶ 8d⁶ 8.3s Oct 28] angular gelding: fairly useful
handicapper: second at Nottingham in April: stays 8.5f: acts on good to firm and heavy
going. *James Eustace*

ICKYMASHO 3 b.f. Multiplex 114 – Icky Woo (Mark of Esteem (IRE) 137) [2015 70: **72**
11.6g² 9.9f⁶ 12m 9.9s p12m* t12.2m* p10f² Dec 17] tall filly: fairly useful handicapper: **a82**
won at Kempton in October and Wolverhampton in November: stays 1½m: acts on
polytrack and tapeta: usually races prominently. *Jonathan Portman*

ICON DREAM (IRE) 8 b.g. Sadler's Wells (USA) 132 – Silver Skates (IRE) 89 (Slip **86 §**
Anchor 136) [2015 14s 16.4m⁶ 14m 16.4m⁴ 13.7m⁵ Aug 7] rather leggy gelding: fairly
useful handicapper: missed 2013 and 2014: stays 16.5f: acts on good to firm and heavy
going: tried in headgear/tongue tie prior to 2015: front runner/races prominently:
ungenuine. *Jim Goldie*

ICONIC FIGURE (IRE) 2 b.g. (Apr 10) Approve (IRE) 112 – Tough Chic (IRE) 82 **74**
(Indian Ridge 123) [2015 5g⁶ f5g³ t5.1m³ p5g Dec 7] fair maiden: likely to stay 6f. *David
O'Meara*

ICONIC (IRE) 3 b.f. Kodiac 112 – Christa Maria (Alhaarth (IRE) 126) [2015 7g³ 8m* **90**
8.1m 8m⁴ 8g² 8d Oct 5] 30,000Y: workmanlike filly: third foal: half-sister to French 1¼m
winner Maria Crista (by Red Clubs) and a winner in Scandinavia by Bushranger: dam
unraced half-sister to smart performer up to 9f Tamweel: fairly useful performer: won
maiden at Salisbury in June: second in handicap at Ascot in September: stays 1m: acts on
good to firm going. *Henry Candy*

ICY BLUE 7 b.g. Iceman 117 – Bridal Path 75 (Groom Dancer (USA) 128) [2015 /0: **63**
7.5m³ 8g² 8.3g 7.5m 7.5s 8m 7.9m 8g Sep 23] sturdy gelding: modest handicapper: stays
8.5f: acts on polytrack, good to firm and heavy going: often wears headgear: often starts
slowly, usually races towards rear. *Richard Whitaker*

IDDER (IRE) 4 br.g. Authorized (IRE) 133 – Epiphany 81 (Zafonic (USA) 130) [2015 89: —
10m May 15] fairly useful at best, well held sole start in 2015: stays 10.5f: acts on soft and
good to firm going: tried in headgear prior to 2015: sometimes slowly away. *Roger Varian*

IDEAL RECRUIT (IRE) 2 br.g. (Mar 16) Lord Shanakill (USA) 121 – Gemma's Pearl —
(IRE) (Marju (IRE) 127) [2015 5m 7g t1.1g 6v t7.1m t7.1f Oct 3] no form: tried in
cheekpieces: signs of temperament. *Tom Dascombe*

IDLE TALKER (IRE) 3 b.g. Dandy Man (IRE) 123 – Special Pearl (IRE) 75 (Alhaarth **71**
(IRE) 126) [2015 54: 10.2m 12.1s⁴ p10m³ 9.9g⁴ p10g* t13.9g² 12.1d* 11.9s* 12v⁴ p13.3f⁵
p13.3f 11.6g² Oct 19] fair performer: won seller at Lingfield in June and handicaps at
Chepstow (apprentice) and Brighton in August: stays 1¾m: acts on polytrack, tapeta and
soft going: usually in cheekpieces in 2015: sometimes in tongue tie prior to 2015: often
races prominently. *Jose Santos*

IDOL DEPUTY (FR) 9 gr.g. Silver Deputy (CAN) – Runaway Venus (USA) (Runaway **86**
Groom (CAN)) [2015 73: p10g t8.6g² t9.5g⁵ p8g⁴ t8.6g² t8.6g t9.5g⁶ t8.6g* t8.6m* p10f⁵
t9.5m t8.6f⁶ t8.6f⁴ t8.6f* t8.6f* t8.6g⁵ Nov 27] fairly useful handicapper: won at
Wolverhampton in August (twice) and November (twice, by neck from Know Your Name
latter occasion): stays 1¼m: acts on polytrack and tapeta: often wears headgear: tried in
tongue tie prior to 2015: usually travels strongly. *James Bennett*

IFAN (IRE) 7 b.g. Ivan Denisovich (IRE) 115 – Montana Miss (IRE) 80 (Earl of Barking **71**
(IRE) 119) [2015 84: 10.2f 12.1m¹ 11.9g⁴ 10.2v² Aug 25] fair handicapper: stays 1½m:
acts on polytrack, good to firm and heavy going: tried in visor prior to 2015: front runner/
races prominently. *Tim Vaughan*

IFFRANESIA (FR) 5 ch.m. Iffraaj 127 – Farnesina (FR) 91 (Anabaa (USA) 130) [2015 **109**
96: 5d* 5g² 5m 5d² 5d 5.5g* Oct 5] useful performer: won handicap at Lingfield (by ½
length from It Must Be Faith) in May and listed race at Chantilly (by head from Finsbury
Square) in October: second in listed races at Chantilly (½ length behind Son Cesio) and
Tipperary (1½ lengths behind Monsieur Joe) in between: best form at up to 5.5f: acts on
polytrack, good to firm and good to soft going: often wears headgear: front runner/races
prominently. *Robert Cowell*

IFITTAKESFOREVER (IRE) 3 b.g. Kodiac 112 – Bobby Jane 72 (Diktat 126) [2015 **89**
67: f5g* p6f* p6f* Feb 11] fairly useful handicapper: won at Southwell in January and
twice at Kempton (by 5 lengths from Grosmont latter occasion) in February: stays 6f: acts
on polytrack and fibresand: often wears headgear: often travels strongly. *John Butler*

IF I WERE A BOY (IRE) 8 b.m. Invincible Spirit (IRE) 121 – Attymon Lill (IRE) **75**
(Marju (IRE) 127) [2015 76: p10m 10.2m⁵ p10g⁵ 10m* 10m 10.1m³ 10.2f² 10m⁵ 10.2f⁶
p10f² p10f³ p10g³ p10g p12g Dec 30] rather leggy mare: fair handicapper: won at
Lingfield in June: stays 1½m: acts on polytrack, firm and good to soft going: usually wears
headgear. *Dominic Ffrench Davis*

IFTIKAAR (IRE) 5 b.g. Cape Cross (IRE) 129 – Anbella (FR) (Common Grounds 118) **73**
[2015 72: 10g⁴ 9.1g⁴ 9.3d* 8d* 10d 10.4g 10s 10.2s t8.6f⁶ Nov 20] fair handicapper: won
at Carlisle (amateur) and Ayr (amateur) in August: stays 1¼m: acts on good to soft going:
tried in cheekpieces prior to 2015: tried in tongue tie in 2015. *Philip Kirby*

Duchess of Cambridge Stakes (sponsored by Qipco), Newmarket—in a three-way photo, joint favourite Illuminate gets the better of Besharah (black seams) and Blue Bayou (far side) in the race that used to be known as the Cherry Hinton; the other joint favourite Easton Angel (left in noseband) looks unlucky after meeting trouble and is promoted to fourth

IFTIRAAQ (IRE) 4 b.g. Muhtathir 126 – Alzaroof (USA) 72 (Kingmambo (USA) 125) **82** [2015 10.3d p11g⁵ 14f⁶ 10g² 12d⁴ Aug 15] fairly useful ex-French-trained maiden: second in handicap at Sandown in July: seems barely to stay 1¾m: acts on polytrack, viscoride and good to soft going: usually in headgear in 2015: fairly useful hurdler. *Seamus Durack*

IFWECAN 4 b.g. Exceed And Excel (AUS) 126 – Kirk 79 (Selkirk (USA) 129) [2015 103: **96** p8m³ p8g⁵ f7s⁴ p7g 7g 8g⁶ 7.9g* 8.1m 8.1m² 8m² 8g 9m⁴ 7.6m 8g⁶ 7.9m 9g 8d* Oct 11] big gelding: useful handicapper: won at Carlisle in June and Goodwood (by ½ length from Mezel) in October: stays 1m: acts on all-weather, good to firm and good to soft going: tried in blinkers in 2015: front runner/races prominently. *Mark Johnston*

IF WINTER COMES 2 br.f. (Feb 16) Dick Turpin (IRE) 127 – Misty Eyed (IRE) 112 **74** (Paris House 123) [2015 p7g² p6f² t6f Oct 16] 32,000Y: fifth foal: half-sister to winner up to 1m Mister Musicmaster (2-y-o 5f/6f winner, by Amadeus Wolf) and 7f winner Sirikoi (by Myboycharlie): dam 2-y-o 5f winner, including Molecomb Stakes: fair maiden: best effort when second at Chelmsford (1¾ lengths behind Hide Your Fires) in September. *James Tate*

IGGY 5 ch.g. Lucarno (USA) 121 – Fujakka (IRE) (Vettori (IRE) 119) [2015 75: 5m* 6.1d⁶ **65** 6g⁵ 7m 7.5m 5m³ 5g 5f² 6g² 5d⁶ 6g 5g p6f⁶ 6d 6v Nov 3] neat gelding: fair handicapper: won at Pontefract (apprentice) in April: stays 6f: acts on polytrack, firm and good to soft going: tried in headgear: usually wears tongue tie. *Michael Easterby*

IGIDER (IRE) 4 b.c. Teofilo (IRE) 126 – Changeable (Dansili 127) [2015 90p: 12.1s 12m* **103** 12f 12d⁴ Sep 12] sturdy colt: useful handicapper: won at Doncaster (by 5 lengths from Arizona John) in June: disappointing both subsequent starts: stays 1½m: acts on good to firm going: sold 70,000 gns, sent to Saudi Arabia. *Roger Varian*

IGUACU 11 b.g. Desert Prince (IRE) 130 – Gay Gallanta (USA) 112 (Woodman (USA) **46** 126) [2015 –: t12.2f² t12.2f³ t12.2g⁶ 14.1g⁴ 13.1d⁵ Sep 2] compact, quite attractive gelding: poor handicapper: stays 12.5f: acts on polytrack, tapeta, good to firm and good to soft going: often in headgear prior to 2015. *Richard Price*

IJMAALY (IRE) 3 ch.g. Makfi 130 – Wedding Gown (Dubai Destination (USA) 127) **98 p** [2015 7d* 8.1m May 28] 300,000Y: rangy gelding: second foal: dam, ran twice in France (third at 9f), half-sister to high-class winner up to 1m Poet's Voice: better effort when winning maiden at Lingfield (by 12 lengths from Fleeting Strike) in May, storming clear: still green when well held in listed race at Sandown next time: subsequently gelded: will stay 1m: remains with potential. *Saeed bin Suroor*

IKERRIN ROAD (IRE) 2 b.c. (Apr 27) Iffraaj 127 – Fantastic Spring (USA) (Fantastic **79** Light (USA) 134) [2015 7d² 6d⁴ Sep 3] better effort when second in maiden at Newcastle (neck behind Simple Attack) in August: found less than looked likely next time. *John Quinn*

ILE DE RE (FR) 9 gr.g. Linamix (FR) 127 – Ile Mamou (IRE) (Ela-Mana-Mou 132) [2015 **–** –: 14.1s⁶ 16.2g 14d Sep 26] lengthy gelding: smart at best, no form since 2013. *Kevin Frost*

I'LL BE GOOD 6 b.g. Red Clubs (IRE) 125 – Willisa 67 (Polar Falcon (USA) 126) [2015 **87** 65§, a75§: 5d* 5d⁴ 5m* 5.1m 5s* 5m³ 5m⁴ 5m³ 5g⁴ 5m⁴ 5.1s* 5g 5d⁵ Sep 26] fairly useful handicapper: won at Hamilton in May, Musselburgh in June, Carlisle in July and Chester (by 2½ lengths from Keep It Dark) in September: stays 6f: acts on polytrack, good to firm and heavy going: tried in cheekpieces/tongue tie prior to 2015: front runner. *Alan Berry*

ILLEGALE (IRE) 9 b.m. Poliglote 121 – Pinkai (IRE) (Caerleon (USA) 132) [2015 46, **43** a56: t12.2f 12.1m 14.1g p16g 16g t16.5g⁴ Jul 28] poor handicapper: stays 1¾m: acts on polytrack, tapeta and good to soft going: often wears headgear: usually wears tongue tie: often starts slowly, usually races in rear. *Nikki Evans*

ILLEGALLY BLONDE (IRE) 2 b.f. (Mar 19) Lawman (FR) 121 – Kayak (Singspiel **98** (IRE) 133) [2015 6m* 6.5m 6d⁵ 5d³ 5.1d* t6f³ t6m* t6g* p6g³ p7g² Dec 28] 14,000Y: half-sister to several winners, including 2-y-o 5f/6.3f winner Midterm Break (by Intense Focus) and 2-y-o 7f winner (stayed 1½m) Goodwood Atlantis (by Elusive City): dam Italian 9f winner (including at 2 yrs): useful performer: won maiden at Leicester in June and nurseries at Nottingham and Wolverhampton in November and Wolverhampton in December: creditable efforts in nurseries at Lingfield last 2 starts: stays 7f: acts on polytrack, tapeta, good to firm and good to soft going: usually travels strongly. *Jamie Osborne*

ILLUMINATE (IRE) 2 b.f. (Feb 13) Zoffany (IRE) 121 – Queen of Stars (USA) (Green **113** Desert (USA) 127) [2015 5m* 6f* 6m* 6g² 8d⁶ Oct 30] £95,000Y: compact filly: sixth foal: half-sister to 5f/6f winner Rhal (by Rahy) and a winner in Japan by Singspiel: dam unraced half-sister to useful performer up to 11f Lady Catherine: smart form: successful on first 3 starts, in minor event at Salisbury in May, Albany Stakes at Royal Ascot (beat Ashadihan

Denford Stud's "Illuminate"

by 1½ lengths) in June and Duchess of Cambridge Stakes at Newmarket (by nose from Besharah) in July: improved again when ½-length second to Lumiere in Cheveley Park Stakes at Newmarket: respectable 2½ lengths sixth of 14 to Catch A Glimpse in Breeders' Cup Juvenile Fillies Turf at Keeneland final outing: best form at 6f: acts on firm going. *Richard Hannon*

ILLUSIVE FORCE (IRE) 3 ch.g. Iffraaj 127 – Geesala (IRE) 82 (Barathea (IRE) 127)   **71**
[2015 73: t9.5f³ p10f Jan 23] fair maiden: stays 9.5f: has been gelded. *Charles Hills*

ILLUSIVE (IRE) 4 b.g. Galileo (IRE) 134 – Looking Back (IRE) (Stravinsky (USA)   **97**
133) [2015 83: p8f p8g⁴ 8.3m² 8d³ 9m² 10d 10.1m* 10.1d³ Sep 27] useful handicapper: won at Yarmouth (by 3½ lengths from Qanan) in September: stays 1¼m: acts on good to firm and good to soft going: has worn blinkers, including last 4 starts: often travels strongly. *Lady Cecil*

ILLUSTRATION (IRE) 7 b.g. Pivotal 124 – In Anticipation (IRE) 93 (Sadler's Wells   **58**
(USA) 132) [2015 11.9s t12.2f t13.9f* t16.5m³ Nov 21] modest handicapper: won at Wolverhampton (apprentice) in November: stays 16.5f: acts on tapeta and heavy going: tried in blinkers prior to 2015. *George Margarson*

ILLUSTRIOUS PRINCE (IRE) 8 b.g. Acclamation 118 – Sacred Love (IRE) 69   **73**
(Barathea (IRE) 127) [2015 87, a72: f7g³ t8.6m f7g 7m 8s 7m⁴ 7m 7d³ 8m³ 7.5s* 8g 7s⁶ 7s² Oct 26] fair handicapper: won at Beverley in July: stays 1m: acts on polytrack, fibresand, soft and good to firm going: tried in headgear: tried in tongue tie prior to 2015: often races prominently. *Julie Camacho*

ILLYA KURYAKIN 3 b.g. Cockney Rebel (IRE) 127 – Vino Veritas (USA) 72 (Chief's   **67**
Crown (USA)) [2015 –: 9d 11.7f³ t13.9g² f14s* p16g⁵ t13.9m⁵ t16.5f* Oct 17] compact, good-bodied gelding: fair handicapper: won at Southwell in August and Wolverhampton in October: stays 16.5f: acts on fibresand and tapeta: in cheekpieces in 2015: temperament under suspicion. *Dave Morris*

IL PICCOLO GRANDE (IRE) 2 ch.c. (Feb 6) Iffraaj 127 – Soxy Doxy (IRE) 51   **84**
(Hawk Wing (USA) 136) [2015 6m 7g p6g⁴ 7m⁴ p7g⁴ 5.9m* p8m⁴ Sep 26] €68,000F, 25,000Y: big, strong colt: third foal: half-brother to 8.3f-1¼m winner Mister Mayday (by Kheleyf) and a winner in Singapore by Verglas: dam, maiden (stayed 1½m), half-sister to smart winner up to 1m Millennium Dragon: fairly useful performer: won nursery at Carlisle in September: stays 1m: acts on polytrack and good to firm going. *Clive Brittain*

ILZAM (IRE) 2 b.g. (Feb 6) Holy Roman Emperor (IRE) 125 – Let's Pretend 69 (Rainbow   **79**
Quest (USA) 134) [2015 7m t6f t6f³ p7m² Dec 31] €20,000Y, £40,000 2-y-o: third foal: closely related to Spanish 1m-11f winner Gang of Ten (by Duke of Marmalade): dam once-raced sister to very smart stayer Rainbow High: fair maiden: will be suited by 1m+: in tongue tie final start. *Marco Botti*

I'M A BUTTERFLY (IRE) 3 b.f. Teofilo (IRE) 126 – Am I (USA) (Thunder Gulch   **–**
(USA) 129) [2015 70: 8g Aug 28] lightly-raced maiden, fair form at best: would have proved suited by at least 1m: dead. *Eve Johnson Houghton*

IMAGERY 6 ch.g. Pivotal 124 – Fantasize 99 (Groom Dancer (USA) 128) [2015 t12.2g   **–**
Sep 29] big, workmanlike gelding: no form. *Ronald Harris*

IMAGINARY DIVA 9 b.m. Lend A Hand 124 – Distant Diva 86 (Distant Relative 128)   **31**
[2015 57: f5d p5m⁶ Feb 4] compact mare: poor handicapper: stays 5.5f: acts on polytrack, fibresand, soft and good to firm going: tried in visor prior to 2015. *George Margarson*

IMAGINARY WORLD (IRE) 7 b.m. Exceed And Excel (AUS) 126 – Plutonia   **65 §**
(Sadler's Wells (USA) 132) [2015 81: f8d f8g³ t7.1g⁵ 8m 7g f7d⁶ 7m³ 7g t7.1f Oct 16] fair handicapper: stays 9.5f: acts on all-weather, soft and good to firm going: usually wears headgear: often races towards rear: unreliable. *John Balding*

IMAN (GER) 5 b.g. Dansili 127 – Ioannina 111 (Rainbow Quest (USA) 134) [2015 9g Apr   **–**
16] useful form: left W. Figge/off 12 months, 100/1, well held in Earl of Sefton Stakes at Newmarket: subsequently joined Sophie Leech: best effort at 1¼m: tried in blinkers. *Mrs Ilka Gansera-Leveque*

IMARI KID (IRE) 2 b.g. (Apr 21) Pour Moi (IRE) 125 – Breathe (FR) (Ocean of   **–**
Wisdom (USA) 106) [2015 8s Oct 23] 66/1, badly needed experience when well held in maiden at Newbury. *Gary Moore*

I'M BACK (IRE) 5 b.h. Exceed And Excel (AUS) 126 – Paracel (USA) (Gone West   **116**
(USA)) [2015 102: a9.4f* a9.4f* a9.9f Feb 19] well-made horse: smart handicapper: much improved when winning twice at Meydan in January, latter by 2¾ lengths from Tiz Now

Tiz Then: reportedly finished lame when last of 15 there final outing: stays 9.5f: acts on dirt/polytrack/tapeta, heavy and good to firm going: sometimes tongue tied prior to 2015: usually races prominently. *Saeed bin Suroor*

IM DAPPER TOO 4 b.g. Dapper – Lonely One (Perryston View 114) [2015 60: f8g 8d⁴ 8d* 9.2d⁵ 8g 9m² 8g² 8g⁴ 8.5d² Sep 22] fair handicapper: won at Newcastle in May: stays 9f: acts on fibresand, good to firm and good to soft going. *John Davies* **67**

I'M FRAAM GOVAN 7 ch.g. Fraam 114 – Urban Dancer (IRE) 89 (Generous (IRE) 139) [2015 103: 12m⁶ 10m 10f³ 9m Aug 1] rather leggy gelding: useful handicapper: third at Sandown (head behind Karraar) in July: stays 11f: acts on polytrack, tapeta and firm going: tried in cheekpieces in 2015: usually in tongue tie prior to 2015. *George Baker* **95**

I'M HARRY 6 b.g. Haafhd 129 – First Approval 78 (Royal Applause 124) [2015 79: 10g³ 11.5d* 12m⁴ 12g⁶ 12g 12d⁶ p10g p12g⁴ p10g⁵ Dec 15] sturdy gelding: fair handicapper: won at Lingfield in May: stays 1½m: acts on polytrack, good to firm and heavy going: often wears headgear: often wears tongue tie: often starts slowly. *George Baker* **79**

IMJIN RIVER (IRE) 8 b.g. Namid 128 – Lady Nasrana (FR) (Al Nasr (FR) 126) [2015 64: p5f t5.1m⁶ t5.1f f5g⁴ f5s⁶ f6g⁴ f5g* p5m p5g 6m⁶ 5.1d t5.1f⁴ p5g⁶ Sep 30] good-topped gelding: modest handicapper: won at Southwell in April: stays 6f: acts on all-weather and good to firm going: tried in headgear: sometimes wears tongue tie. *William Stone* **52**

I'M JUST SAYING 2 ch.f. (Feb 6) Sakhee's Secret 128 – Ice Haven (IRE) (Verglas (IRE) 118) [2015 6g⁴ p7g⁴ p7g p7g Oct 6] first foal: dam unraced: modest maiden: races freely. *Clive Cox* **54**

IMPASSABLE (IRE) 3 b.f. Invincible Spirit (IRE) 121 – Gwenseb (FR) 113 (Green Tune (USA) 125) [2015 p7g* 8s² 8g* 8g* 8m* 8g⁶ Oct 31] third foal: sister to useful French winner up to 1m Foreign Tune (5.5f winner at 2 yrs): dam French winner up to 1m (5f winner at 2 yrs): very smart performer: progressed well, winning maiden in March, and minor event and Prix de Sandringham, both in May, all at Chantilly, and Prix Daniel Wildenstein at Longchamp (by ½ length from Miss France) in October: below form when 5¾ lengths sixth of 12 to Tepin in Breeders' Cup Mile at Keeneland final start: stays 1m: acts on polytrack and good to firm going. *C. Laffon-Parias, France* **121**

IMPECCABILITY 5 b.m. Lucky Story (USA) 128 – Impeccable Guest (IRE) 60 (Orpen (USA) 116) [2015 55: t13.9g Jan 9] poor maiden: stays 16.5f: acts on tapeta and good to firm going: sometimes wears cheekpieces: usually races prominently. *John Mackie* **39**

IMPEDIMENT 2 ch.g. (Apr 15) Pivotal 124 – Pediment 91 (Desert Prince (IRE) 130) [2015 8g 8.3s⁵ t7.1f⁵ Nov 13] 90,000Y: fourth foal: half-brother to Italian 9f winner Ginseng Coffee (by High Chaparral): dam, 11f winner, half-sister to useful winner up to 1m White Lake (by Pivotal) and to useful dam of smart miler Spacious: fair maiden: best effort when fifth at Nottingham (6½ lengths behind Rainbow Dreamer) in October: should be suited by 1¼m+: remains capable of better. *Sir Michael Stoute* **67 p**

IMPERATOR AUGUSTUS (IRE) 7 b.g. Holy Roman Emperor (IRE) 125 – Coralita (IRE) 98 (Night Shift (USA)) [2015 76: t7.1f t7.1f² t7.1f⁶ 5g 7.1g 6.9m⁵ 7m 7d 7d* 7g 8.5m Oct 1] lightly-made gelding: fair handicapper: won at Catterick in August: best around 7f: acts on polytrack, tapeta, soft and good to firm going: tried in headgear. *Patrick Holmes* **66**

IMPERIAL AVIATOR 2 b.c. (Mar 7) Paco Boy (IRE) 129 – Telescopic (Galileo (IRE) 134) [2015 p8g² p8g² p8f³ Dec 21] first foal: dam, of little account, closely related to useful performer up to 1¾m Hovering: fairly useful maiden: second at Lingfield (6 lengths behind Ennaadd) and third at Chelmsford (½ length behind Cape Speed), both in December. *Roger Charlton* **84**

IMPERIALISTA 3 ch.f. Halling (USA) 133 – Empress Maud (USA) (Kingmambo (USA) 125) [2015 8.4d 6.7g 7.5g 8m⁶ 9.8d 14.1m Aug 29] first foal: dam unraced daughter of useful Canadian Grade 2 9f winner Calista: little form: left H-A. Pantall after third start. *Tracy Waggott* **–**

IMPERIAL LEGEND (IRE) 6 b.g. Mujadil (USA) 119 – Titian Saga (IRE) 74 (Titus Livius (FR) 115) [2015 93: 5v 5d 5m² 5m⁵ 5g² 5m³ 5m 5g 5g⁴ 5g 5d³ 5m⁶ 5g² 5g³ 5.1d⁵ Oct 28] fairly useful handicapper: second at Redcar in May and Pontefract in September: best form at 5f: acts on soft and good to firm going: usually wears headgear: often races prominently: inconsistent. *David Nicholls* **84**

IMPERIAL LINK 3 b.f. Rail Link 132 – Imperia (GER) (Tertullian (USA) 115) [2015 70: 10.2m⁵ p8f³ 7s* t7.1g³ 7m⁶ t7.1g⁵ 7.4d³ 8v⁴ t7.1f⁶ 7s³ 10d⁶ t9.5f⁶ f8g Nov 24] modest performer: won claimer at Salisbury in May: left Paul Cole after: stays 8.5f: acts on tapeta and soft going: tried in headgear: sometimes slowly away. *David Evans* **62**

IMPERIAL MARCH (IRE) 3 b.g. Arch (USA) 127 – Sneak Preview 104 (Monsieur   –
Bond (IRE) 120) [2015 58p: 8.3s 8d May 11] lightly-raced maiden, well held in 2015.
Clive Cox

IMPERIOUS ONE (IRE) 2 b.c. (Apr 20) Royal Applause 124 – Never A Doubt 107   **90**
(Night Shift (USA)) [2015 6m* 6.1m³ 7d² 6.5m 8f 8f² Dec 31] tall colt: brother to useful
winner up to 7f Royal Confidence (2-y-o 5f-6.5f winner) and half-brother to 1m winner
Rougette (by Red Ransom) and useful 5f-7f winner Doctor Sardonicus (by Medicean):
dam, 2-y-o 5f/5.5f (Prix Robert Papin) winner, half-sister to smart sprinter Jonny Mudball:
fairly useful performer: won maiden at Windsor in July: second after in nursery at
Goodwood and, having left Charles Hills after fourth start, listed race at Santa Anita
(blinkered, length second to Path of David): stays 1m: acts on firm and good to soft going.
Doug F. O'Neill, USA

IMPORTANT MESSAGE 3 b.c. New Approach (IRE) 132 – Plaza (USA) (Chester   **103**
House (USA) 123) [2015 t8.6g² 8m² p12g* 12m³ Aug 15] second foal: half-brother to a
winner in USA by Dixie Union: dam, French 1¼m winner, out of very smart 10.5f-1½m
winner Jolypha, herself sister to Dancing Brave: useful performer: 8/11, won maiden at
Lingfield in July: further improvement when third in handicap at Newmarket (1½ lengths
behind Gold Trail) in August: stays 1½m. *Saeed bin Suroor*

IMPORTANT POINT (USA) 3 b.g. Street Cry (IRE) 130 – Zofzig (USA) (Danzig   **84 p**
(USA)) [2015 t9.5f* Oct 27] fourth foal: half-brother to smart 2-y-o 7f winner Zip Top
(by Smart Strike) and 1m/9f winner Corn Snow (by Raven's Pass): dam, US 2-y-o 6f/1m
winner, half-sister to smart US Grade 1 1m winner Zaftig: 3/10, overcame inexperience
when winning 6-runner maiden at Wolverhampton on debut easily by 2½ lengths from
Drago, drawing clear from 2f out: sure to progress. *Saeed bin Suroor*

IMPRESSIVE DAY (IRE) 2 b.f. (Apr 18) Cape Cross (IRE) 129 – Shieldmaiden (USA)   **82 p**
85 (Smart Strike (CAN) 121) [2015 p7g⁵ p7g² Oct 29] well-made filly: first foal: dam 1½m
winner: better effort when second in maiden at Lingfield (½ length behind Vaunting) in
October: will be suited by 1m+: open to further improvement. *Saeed bin Suroor*

IMPRESSIVE VICTORY (USA) 3 b.f. Street Cry (IRE) 130 – Long Lashes (USA)   **70**
110 (Rock Hard Ten (USA) 126) [2015 86p: 8.3m³ 8.3g⁶ 9.9m⁶ Jul 20] fair maiden: best
effort at 7f: acts on polytrack and good to firm going: tried in visor in 2015. *Saeed
bin Suroor*

IMPROVIZED 4 b.f. Authorized (IRE) 133 – Rhapsodize (Halling (USA) 133) [2015   **– §**
68§: 11.5d t8.6g 8.3m 8.1g 8v³ 8v⁵ Aug 28] lengthy filly: fair at best, no form in 2015:
sometimes wears headgear: tried in tongue tie prior to 2015: often races towards rear: not
one to trust. *William Muir*

IMPULSIVE AMERICAN 3 b.g. American Post 121 – Impulsive Decision (IRE) 71   **72**
(Nomination 125) [2015 p9.9g 9.9g 10.7s⁵ 9.9s⁶ 11.9d² 11.9g² 11.5s 12.1m* Sep 10] fair
handicapper: won at Chepstow in September: left Mme G. Rarick after sixth start: stays
1½m: acts on good to firm and good to soft going: blinkered fourth outing. *David Pipe*

I'M READY (IRE) 2 ch.f. (Feb 19) Iffraaj 127 – Ready When You Are (IRE) 76 (Royal   **56 p**
Applause 124) [2015 7v p7g f7f⁵ Dec 17] first foal: dam lightly-raced sister to smart US
1m/9f performer Whatsthescript: modest form in maidens: remains with potential. *Richard
Fahey*

IMSHI'S LITTLE BRO (IRE) 2 b.g. (Mar 19) Lilbourne Lad (IRE) 111 – Subtle Affair   **55**
(IRE) 96 (Barathea (IRE) 127) [2015 5g⁶ 6g² 6m Jul 1] modest maiden: second in seller at
Ripon in May, then left Richard Fahey: will stay at least 7f. *Ivan Furtado*

IMSHIVALLA (IRE) 4 b.f. Acclamation 118 – Subtle Affair (IRE) 96 (Barathea (IRE)   **92**
127) [2015 94: 10.1g⁵ 8m 8.5g 9.8m⁴ 7.9s² 7.6m² 9g 9m 9s* 10g 8m³ 8.5s 8g³ 10.3v³ p8f
Nov 19] fairly useful performer: won handicap at Goodwood (by 1¾ lengths from
Kapstadt) in August: third in handicaps at Musselburgh and Newmarket in October and
listed event at Doncaster in November: stays 1¼m: acts on good to firm and heavy going:
wears hood. *Richard Fahey*

I'M SUPER TOO (IRE) 8 b.g. Fasliyev (USA) 120 – Congress (IRE) 86 (Dancing   **69**
Brave (USA) 140) [2015 81, a73: f8d* f8g⁶ f11g f8g⁴ 8s 8g³ 8m⁵ 8.3d 9.2g 7.5f* 7.9m⁶
8m⁵ 8.5m* 7.9s⁵ 8g³ 7.9m⁴ 9.2m⁶ 8.5m Oct 1] workmanlike gelding: fair performer: won
claimer at Southwell in January, seller at Beverley in July and handicap at Beverley
(amateur) in August: left Alan Swinbank after third start: probably stays 11.5f, usually
races over shorter: acts on fibresand and any turf going: tried in blinkers prior to 2015:
usually races nearer last than first. *Karen Tutty*

IMTIYAAZ (IRE) 3 b.f. Starspangledbanner (AUS) 128 – Endure (IRE) (Green Desert **101** (USA) 127) [2015 65p: 7g³ 7pm³ 5.7m* 6.1g² 6m² 5g* 5g² Aug 22] useful performer: won maiden at Bath in June and handicap at Ripon (by ¾ length from Olivia Fallow) in August: respectable second to Thesme in apprentice handicap at York final start: best form at 5f: acts on good to firm going: often travels strongly. *Roger Varian*

IMVULA 3 gr.f. Aqlaam 125 – Reason To Dance 96 (Damister (USA) 123) [2015 8.3s⁵ 8g* **77 p** Jun 5] 30,000Y: half-sister to several winners, including smart South African performer up to 11f Dancer's Daughter (by Act One) and useful winner up to 1m Diktatorial (2-y-o 7f winner, by Diktat): dam, 5f (at 2 yrs) and 6.5f (in USA) winner, stayed 1¼m: better effort when winning maiden at Goodwood (by ¾ length from Ella's Honour) in June, well positioned: likely to progress further. *Ed Dunlop*

INAAM (IRE) 2 b.c. (Apr 28) Camacho 118 – Duckmore Bay (IRE) (Titus Livius (FR) **61** 115) [2015 5s 5.9m⁶ 6m 5g 6s² 7g t6f p6d⁵ f7g³ Dec 18] lengthy colt: modest maiden: stays 7f: acts on polytrack, fibresand, soft and good to firm going: often in headgear: suspect temperament. *Richard Fahey*

INAUGURATION (IRE) 3 b.f. Acclamation 118 – Carraigoona (IRE) 76 (Rock of **51** Gibraltar (IRE) 133) [2015 62: f6g p7m³ p7m p8g⁴ p6g³ 6d⁴ 6d 7m 8m⁶ Jul 7] modest **a58** maiden: left Charles Hills after second start: stays 7f: acts on polytrack and good to firm going: tried in eyeshields in 2015: tried in tongue tie in 2015. *Julia Feilden*

INCANTARE 5 gr.m. Proclamation (IRE) 130 – Mythical Charm 69 (Charnwood Forest **57** (IRE) 125) [2015 63: p8m⁵ p7g t6f⁴ t6g p5g⁶ 6g⁶ p10g³ p10g⁵ p10g⁴ p10f² p12g Oct 20] modest maiden: stays 1¼m: acts on polytrack: tried in headgear in 2015: sometimes slowly away. *Jim Allen*

INCENDO 9 ch.g. King's Best (USA) 132 – Kindle (Selkirk (USA) 129) [2015 83§: 10m – Jul 19] fairly useful at best, well held only start in 2015: stays 13f: acts on polytrack, firm and soft going: often wears headgear: sometimes in tongue tie prior to 2015: usually races in rear: temperamental and best treated with caution. *Ann Stokell*

INCLUDED 3 b.f. Champs Elysees 124 – Cordoba 77 (Oasis Dream 129) [2015 52p: **82 p** 9.9m² 10m⁵ p12g* Sep 22] fairly useful form: won 4-runner maiden at Kempton final start by ¾ length from Persian Breeze, staying on to lead well inside final 1f: stays 1½m: open to further improvement. *Amanda Perrett*

INCOMPARABLE 10 ch.g. Compton Place 125 – Indian Silk (IRE) 74 (Dolphin Street **63** (FR) 125) [2015 62, a68: f5d* f5d f5g⁴ 5d 5s 5d 5m* 5m⁵ 5f 5m⁴ 5m⁶ 5g f6g f5m Dec 8] big, strong gelding: modest handicapper: won at Southwell in January and Beverley in June: stays 6f: acts on polytrack, fibresand, soft and good to firm going: usually wears headgear: tried in tongue tie prior to 2015. *Scott Dixon*

INCREDIBLE THUNDER 2 b.c. (Mar 8) Kheleyf (USA) 116 – Glitz (IRE) 54 (Hawk – Wing (USA) 136) [2015 p6g 7g 7m⁶ 6m p8g p8g 7s t7.1f⁶ Oct 3] tried in tongue tie: in blinkers: hasn't looked straightforward: sold £1,700, sent to Germany. *Harry Dunlop*

INCURS FOUR FAULTS 4 b.g. Halling (USA) 133 – Rapsgate (IRE) 78 (Mozart (IRE) **63** 131) [2015 71: 11.1d 12.5m 9.2g 9.3g 9.3m⁵ 9.3g 13.7m⁵ 9.3m³ 7.9d² 9.2m⁴ p8f² 18.6f⁵ f8g* f8g⁵ Dec 12] modest handicapper: won at Southwell in November: stays 13.5f: acts on polytrack, fibresand and good to firm going: often in hood in 2015. *Keith Dalgleish*

INCUS 2 b.c. (Apr 30) Bertolini (USA) 125 – Cloudchaser (IRE) (Red Ransom (USA)) – [2015 p8m 8.3s t8.6f Nov 13] no form. *Ed de Giles*

INDASTAR 5 b.g. Indesatchel (IRE) 120 – Charcoal (Primo Valentino (IRE) 116) [2015 **64** 68: f6g t6g⁵ 6g* 5m³ 5f 5g p6f³ 6v⁶ p6m⁶ t5.1m³ t5.1m Dec 30] modest handicapper: won at Thirsk in May: stays 6f: acts on tapeta, good to firm and heavy going: tried in cheekpieces in 2015: tried in tongue tie prior to 2015: front runner/races prominently, often travels strongly. *Michael Herrington*

INDEGO BLUES 6 b.g. Indesatchel (IRE) 120 – Yanomami (USA) 71 (Slew O' Gold **70** (USA)) [2015 60: 6g² 6g 6s 6d³ 6m⁴ 5.9s* 6d³ 6s³ 6g⁵ 7g⁶ 6s⁴ 7.2g 6g⁶ 7s⁵ 6d Oct 26] fair handicapper: won at Carlisle (apprentice) in July: stays 6f: acts on soft and good to firm going: sometimes in headgear in 2015. *David Nicholls*

INDELIBLE INK (IRE) 3 b.g. Invincible Spirit (IRE) 121 – Serres (IRE) (Daylami **84** (IRE) 138) [2015 82: 10m⁵ 12.5m 10f* 10g⁵ 10.1g³ Aug 30] good-topped gelding: fairly useful handicapper: won at Sandown in July: should stay 1½m: acts on firm going: tried in visor in 2015: often races prominently. *Sir Michael Stoute*

INDEPENDENCE DAY (IRE) 2 b.c. (Apr 10) Dansili 127 – Damson (IRE) 113 **99** (Entrepreneur 123) [2015 6g⁴ 5m* 5g² 5g² 5m⁶ Sep 11] seventh foal: brother to smart 2-y-o 5f winner (including Flying Childers Stakes) Requinto and half-brother to useful 9.4f-10.7f winner Barbadine (by Giant's Causeway) and 7f winner Compelling (by Kingmambo): dam 2-y-o 5f/6f (including Queen Mary and Phoenix Stakes) winner: useful performer: won maiden at Down Royal (by 5 lengths from Reckless Endeavour) in June: second in listed race at Tipperary (½ length behind Promised Money) in July and in Curragh Stakes at the Curragh (1½ lengths behind Bear Cheek) in August: should stay 6f: acts on good to firm going. *David Wachman, Ireland*

INDESCRIBABLE (IRE) 3 b.g. Invincible Spirit (IRE) 121 – Subtle Charm **97** (Machiavellian (USA) 123) [2015 86: p6f⁴ 5g 5m* 6g 5m² 5.1m 5f 5m* 6m 5.1m³ 5.4g 5d 5.6d Sep 12] good-quartered gelding: useful performer: won handicaps at York in May and Goodwood (by head from Maljaa) in July: second in handicap at Ayr (nose behind Lexington Place) in June and third in minor event at Nottingham (3¼ lengths behind Desert Law) in August: best at 5f/easy 6f: acts on firm going: sent to UAE. *Mark Johnston*

INDIAN AFFAIR 5 h h. Sleeping Indian 122 – Rare Fling (USA) (Kris S (USA)) [2015 **77** 65, a74: p6m⁴ t7.1f² t7.1g³ t7.1m t7.1f³ p6f² t7.1f* t7.1m³ 6.1d⁵ t6g² 6.1m² 6g⁶ t6g* 7.1g⁴ 6m* t6m 6.1m² t6f³ 6s² t7.1f³ 5.7g³ t7.1f Oct 31] stocky horse: fair handicapper: won at Wolverhampton in March and July and Windsor (apprentice) in August: stays 7f: acts on polytrack, tapeta, good to firm and heavy going: usually in headgear in 2015: tried in tongue tie: front runner/races prominently. *Milton Bradley*

INDIAN CHIEF (IRE) 5 b.g. Montjeu (IRE) 137 – Buck Aspen (USA) (Seeking The **88 §** Gold (USA)) [2015 –: 8d 12g⁴ 10.3s 12g 12m⁴ 10.1m⁵ 9.2d⁵ 12m 10.3d³ 10.2s⁴ f12g Nov 24] tall, lengthy, attractive gelding: fairly useful handicapper: left David Nicholls after tenth start: stays 1½m: acts on good to firm and heavy going: tried in headgear: often travels strongly: not one to rely on. *Rebecca Bastiman*

INDIAN GIVER 7 b.m. Indesatchel (IRE) 120 – Bint Baddi (FR) (Shareef Dancer (USA) **66** 135) [2015 62: t7.1f t7.1f² 8s² t7.1g 10d* 8.3d⁵ 9.2g* 9.3s³ 11.1s³ 11.5d⁴ 12.1g 11.9d Sep **a57** 3] small, leggy mare: fair handicapper: won at Ayr in May and Hamilton in June: stays 11.5f: acts on good to firm and heavy going: tried in headgear. *John David Riches*

INDIAN GOLD 2 b.g. (Apr 27) Sleeping Indian 122 – Hiraeth 76 (Petong 126) [2015 5d⁶ **–** 5f 5m p6f p6f Nov 5] no form: tried in blinkers/tongue tie. *Milton Bradley*

INDIAN MONSOON (IRE) 3 b.g. Monsun (GER) 124 – Madhya (USA) 103 (Gone **80** West (USA)) [2015 11m⁶ 10s⁴ 11.8s p10f⁶ Oct 8] €85,000Y: good sort: seventh foal: brother to 2 winners, including German 8.5f-1¼m winner Madhyana, and half-brother to German 1¼m/11f winner Medinella (by Pivotal): dam French 1m winner: fairly useful maiden: will stay 1½m: tried in visor. *Sir Michael Stoute*

INDIAN PURSUIT (IRE) 2 b.g. (Apr 12) Compton Place 125 – Church Melody (Oasis **78** Dream 129) [2015 5.9m 5.9g³ 6d³ 6g³ 6v* 6v⁴ Nov 7] fair performer: won maiden at Catterick in October: will stay 7f: acts on heavy going. *John Quinn*

INDIAN SCOUT 7 b.g. Indesatchel (IRE) 120 – Manderina (Mind Games 121) [2015 55: **54** f16d t16.5g 12.1m⁶ 11.9d* 13.1m⁶ 13.1m⁵ p12g⁵ 11.9d t12.2f Dec 21] modest handicapper: won at Brighton (amateur) in June: stays 1¾m: acts on polytrack, tapeta, good to firm and good to soft going: often wears headgear. *Anabel K. Murphy*

INDIAN TIM 3 b.g. Sleeping Indian 122 – River City Moon (USA) (Riverman (USA) **44** 131) [2015 –: 7.1m t6g⁵ 6g⁶ 5.1d⁴ Sep 13] poor maiden: stays 6f: acts on good to soft going. *Milton Bradley*

INDIAN TINKER 6 b.g. Sleeping Indian 122 – Breakfast Creek 63 (Hallgate 127) [2015 **82** 83: f5g 5.3d² 5m³ 5d³ 5.2s⁴ 5.2m³ 5.1g⁴ 5.3s² 5.1d² 5.1d Nov 4] fairly useful handicapper: second at Brighton in June and Nottingham in October: stays 5.5f: acts on fibresand, good to firm and heavy going: tried in headgear. *Robert Cowell*

INDIA'S SONG 5 b.m. Zamindar (USA) 116 – Sea Chorus 82 (Singspiel (IRE) 133) **76** [2015 75: p10g* p10g³ p10d² p8g⁴ 9.2g³ p8f⁴ p10f⁴ Dec 17] fair handicapper: won at Chelmsford in February: stays 1¼m: acts on polytrack: often wears tongue tie: often races towards rear. *David Simcock*

INDIE MUSIC 2 ch.f. (Mar 8) Sakhee's Secret 128 – Indiana Blues 90 (Indian Ridge 123) **69** [2015 6m p7g⁴ 8.1v³ 8.3g³ 7g Oct 10] rather unfurnished filly: sister to 7f winner Secret Rebel, later successful abroad, and half-sister to 3 winners, including useful winner up to 1m Norse Blues (2-y-o 7f winner) and 8.5f-1¼m winner Inspector Norse (both by Norse Dancer): dam 6f winner: fair maiden: stays 8.5f: acts on polytrack and heavy going. *Sylvester Kirk*

INDIGO 2 gr.f. (Feb 9) Medicean 128 – Jessica Ennis (USA) (English Channel (USA) 126) **74** [2015 5g p6g⁴ p7g 7m³ p7g* p7g p8m* p8f⁵ Oct 29) angular filly: first foal: dam, unraced, out of sister to smart US Grade 1 2-y-o 8.5f winner Tactical Cat: fair performer: won nurseries at Kempton in August and Chelmsford in September: stays 1m: acts on polytrack and good to firm going. *Mark Usher*

INDIRA 4 ch.f. Sleeping Indian 122 – Forever Loved 86 (Deploy 131) [2015 88: 10.1g **80** 12g⁶ 12s⁴ 12s p12g² t12.2f⁷ Dec 22] smallish, close-coupled filly: fairly useful handicapper: second at Kempton and Wolverhampton in December: should stay further than 1½m: acts on polytrack, tapeta, good to firm and good to soft going. *John Berry*

INDOMITABLE SPIRIT 3 b.g. Zebedee 113 – Gayala (IRE) (Iron Mask (USA) 117) **70** [2015 58: t7.1m 10.2m p10g⁶ p8g* p7g* p8f⁵ p7g p6m f7m* Dec 8] fair handicapper: won at Lingfield in July and August and Southwell in December: stays 1m: acts on polytrack and fibresand: front runner/races prominently. *Martin Smith*

INDRAPURA (IRE) 2 ch.c. (Mar 30) Cape Blanco (IRE) 130 – A Mind of Her Own **79** (IRE) 91 (Danehill Dancer (IRE) 117) [2015 6.5m 7f³ p7f⁵ 7g⁵ Sep 11] sturdy colt: fair performer: won maiden at Brighton in July: will stay 1m. *Paul Cole*

IN DUE TIME (IRE) 3 br.g. Big Bad Bob (IRE) 118 – Bravada (GER) (Dai Jin 123) **61** [2015 8g⁶ 9.2s⁵ 6m 11.5g Jun 15] modest maiden: best effort at 1m. *Alan Swinbank*

INDULGENT 2 b.c. (Jan 23) Makfi 130 – Santa Agata (FR) (Anabaa (USA) 130) [2015 **65** 8m⁴ 8d⁴ 8d³ 8d f7g⁵ f8m f8f⁵ f8g Dec 29] compact colt: fair maiden: stays 1m: acts on **a56** good to firm and good to soft going: tried in cheekpieces. *Tony Coyle*

INDUS VALLEY (IRE) 8 ch.g. Indian Ridge 123 – Gloriously Bright (USA) 69 **68** (Nureyev (USA) 131) [2015 64, a70: p6m³ p7f p8f⁴ p7g² p8g⁵ p7g² p7g p8g 6m² 6d⁴ 6g⁴ 7g* p6f p7m p7g p6m⁴ Dec 16] well-made gelding: fair handicapper: won at Brighton in August: left Des Donovan after first start: stays 9f, effective at shorter: acts on polytrack, firm and soft going: tried in headgear: tried in tongue tie prior to 2015: temperament under suspicion. *Lee Carter*

INDY (IRE) 4 b.g. Indian Haven 119 – Maddie's Pearl (IRE) 62 (Clodovil (IRE) 116) **102** [2015 101: 8d 8d² Jun 2] useful handicapper, lightly raced: second at Ripon (length behind Instant Attraction) in June: stays 10.5f: acts on heavy going: front runner/races prominently. *David Barron*

INEXES 3 gr.g. Exceed And Excel (AUS) 126 – Likeable (Dalakhani (IRE) 133) [2015 77: **79** 8.3g⁵ t7.1m⁵ Nov 21] fair maiden: best effort at 7f. *Marjorie Fife*

INEXORABLE TIDE (IRE) 3 gr.g. Verglas (IRE) 118 – Atlas Silk (Dansili 127) [2015 **89** p8m³ p8f⁶ p8f² 8.3m t8.6m* p8g* p8gᵖᵘ t8.6m Sep 14] angular gelding: fairly useful performer: won maiden at Wolverhampton in April and handicap at Chelmsford (by 2 lengths from Mount Tahan) in June: stays 8.5f: acts on polytrack and tapeta: often in blinkers: usually leads: sold only 5,000 gns in October, sent to Italy. *Ralph Beckett*

INFANTRY 4 b.g. Rail Link 132 – Zorleni (Zafonic (USA) 130) [2015 8f⁴ 8.3m Jun 27] **86** fairly useful performer: won newcomers race at Saint-Cloud in 2014 (left Mme C. Head-Maarek for 42,000gns after next start): pulled too hard when well held in listed events in 2015, subsequently gelded: stays 10.5f: sent to Australia. *Andrew Balding*

INFLEXIBALL 3 b.f. Refuse To Bend (IRE) 128 – Sphere (IRE) 77 (Daylami (IRE) 138) **65** [2015 54: t8.6f³ 8m⁵ t9.5g⁴ 10g⁴ t12.2m⁶ t9.5m⁵ Sep 25] fair maiden: stays 1½m: acts on tapeta and good to firm going: often races prominently. *John Mackie*

IN FOCUS (IRE) 4 ch.g. Intense Focus (USA) 117 – Reine de Neige 96 (Kris 135) [2015 **83** 81: 8g* 8m 7m 7m⁵ 7.9g 7m⁶ 6.9d 6m 7m⁵ 6.9s* 7.5d Sep 22] fairly useful handicapper: won at Wetherby in April and Carlisle in September: stays 1m: acts on soft and good to firm going: none too consistent. *Alan Swinbank*

INGEN BRAVE 2 gr.f. (Apr 17) Mastercraftsman (IRE) 129 – Antrim Rose 68 (Giant's **–** Causeway (USA) 132) [2015 t8.6m Dec 30] 35,000Y: third foal: half-sister to a winner abroad by Selkirk: dam maiden (stayed 1¼m) out of useful performer up to 8.5f Aunty Rose: 50/1, green when well held in maiden at Wolverhampton. *David Evans*

INGLEBY ANGEL (IRE) 6 br.g. Dark Angel (IRE) 113 – Mistress Twister 83 (Pivotal **105** 124) [2015 103: 7g 8m 8g* 8g 10.4m⁶ 10.4g 7.9m* Sep 9] leggy gelding: useful handicapper: won at Redcar (by 1¼ lengths from Tizlove Regardless) in June and Carlisle (by 2 lengths from Silver Rime) in September: stays 9f: acts on fibresand, good to firm and heavy going. *David O'Meara*

INGLEBY ERIN 2 b.f. (May 6) Medicean 128 – Mistress Twister 83 (Pivotal 124) [2015 – 6g 6m 7.5g⁵ t8.6f Oct 9] £15,000Y: half-sister to several winners, including useful 6f-9f winner Ingleby Angel (by Dark Angel) and winner up to 1m Ingleby Exceed (2-y-o 6f winner, by Exceed And Excel): dam 1m-1¼m winner: no form. *Michael Easterby*

INGLEBY HOLLOW 3 ch.g. Beat Hollow 126 – Mistress Twister 83 (Pivotal 124) **72** [2015 55p: f8g⁶ 10g⁴ 14.1g⁴ 12.1m 12g* 12g² 16g² 12d² 11.5s² 12d Oct 5] fair handicapper: won at Pontefract in June: stays 1½m: acts on soft going: usually races prominently. *David O'Meara*

INGLEBY SPRING (IRE) 3 br.f. Zebedee 113 – Jouel (FR) (Machiavellian (USA) 123) **65** [2015 65: 7.1m⁴ 8.3m⁶ 7.2g³ 7.2g 7d⁶ 7m* 7.9s² 8g⁵ 8s³ Oct 15] fair handicapper: won at Thirsk in August: stays 1m: acts on soft and good to firm going. *Richard Fahey*

INGLEBY VALLEY 2 ch.c. (Apr 15) Sakhee's Secret 128 – Ingleby Lady 104 (Captain **70** Rio 122) [2015 5g² 6g⁶ 5d⁵ Aug 26] fair maiden: best effort when second at Carlisle in June. *Richard Fahey*

IN HASTE (IRE) 2 gr.g. (May 12) Clodovil (IRE) 116 – Hasty Katie (IRE) 77 (Whipper **78** (USA) 126) [2015 5f² 5.1d⁴ 6g* 5m³ p6g⁴ Jun 24] fair performer: won maiden at Goodwood in May: stays 6f: acts on good to firm going. *Eve Johnson Houghton*

INHERENT VICE 2 b.g. (Apr 27) Kodiac 112 – Ting A Greeley (Mr Greeley **70** (USA) 122) [2015 6g³ 7.1m 6g Jul 27] useful-looking gelding: fair maiden: best effort when third at Newbury in May. *Jamie Osborne*

INIESTA (IRE) 4 b.c. Galileo (IRE) 134 – Red Evie (IRE) 117 (Intikhab (USA) 135) **–** [2015 10.1d Sep 27] fairly useful at best: stays 1¼m: acts on soft going: often in visor prior to 2015. *Gary Moore*

INITIALLY 2 b.f. (Mar 28) Dansili 127 – Emplane (USA) 101 (Irish River (FR) 131) **70 p** [2015 p7g⁵ t7.1f² Nov 10] sister to 3 winners, including French 2-y-o 7f winner Early March and winner up to 10.4f Aviate (2-y-o 1m winner), both smart, and half-sister to 3 winners: dam 1m winner: better effort when second in maiden at Wolverhampton (1¾ lengths behind Izmir) in November: open to further improvement. *Charles Hills*

INJAM (IRE) 2 b.g. (Mar 29) Pour Moi (IRE) 125 – Sniffle (IRE) 60 (Shernazar 131) **53** [2015 8.3d⁴ 8g Sep 24] showed a little ability in maidens at Hamilton and Pontefract. *Jedd O'Keeffe*

INJUN SANDS 4 b.g. Halling (USA) 133 – Serriera (FR) 51 (Highest Honor (FR) 124) **88** [2015 79: p12g* p13.3g* 13.1d⁵ 14g² p13.3f⁴ 14.1m⁴ Sep 15] attractive gelding: fairly useful handicapper: won at Lingfield in May and Chelmsford in June: second at Haydock in August: stays 1¾m: acts on polytrack and good to firm going. *Jane Chapple-Hyam*

INKA SURPRISE (IRE) 5 b.g. Intikhab (USA) 135 – Sweet Surprise (IRE) 69 **74** (Danetime (IRE) 121) [2015 t6f⁶ p6f⁵ Feb 25] good-topped gelding: fair handicapper: stays 6f: acts on polytrack, tapeta, best turf form on good going. *Ralph Beckett*

INKE (IRE) 3 br.f. Intikhab (USA) 135 – Chifney Rush (IRE) (Grand Lodge (USA) 125) **79** [2015 67: 10m⁵ 9.9m⁶ 8.3m 7.1m⁵ 9g³ p8g* 8.1g* 8.5g² Sep 10] lengthy filly: fair handicapper: won at Kempton and Sandown in August: stays 8.5f: acts on polytrack, best turf form on good going: often in cheekpieces in 2015: often travels strongly. *Jim Boyle*

IN KEN'S MEMORY 2 b.f. (Apr 28) Sakhee (USA) 136 – Suzi Spends (IRE) 94 (Royal **73** Applause 124) [2015 6.1g* 7m 6d⁴ 6g⁶ Oct 0] third foal: half-sister to useful winner up to 7f Suzi's Connoisseur (2-y-o 5f/6f winner, by Art Connoisseur): dam winner up to 1¼m (2-y-o 8.3f winner): fair performer: won maiden at Nottingham in August: should be suited by 7f+. *Mark Johnston*

INLAND SEA (USA) 2 b.c. (Feb 23) Scat Daddy (USA) 120 – Cat's Eye Witness (USA) **82** (Elusive Quality (USA)) [2015 6d⁴ 6g* 7d⁶ Aug 16] angular colt: third foal: brother to smart 4.5f-6f winner (including Norfolk Stakes and Prix Morny at 2 yrs) No Nay Never and half-brother to a winner in USA by Flashy Bull: dam US 2-y-o 5.5f winner: fairly useful performer: best effort when winning maiden at Goodwood (by ½ length from Papa Luigi) in July: upped in trip, stiff task and took strong hold when well held in listed race at Deauville next time: best effort at 6f. *Richard Hannon*

IN MY PLACE 2 b.c. (Apr 12) Compton Place 125 – Luxuria (IRE) 59 (Kheleyf (USA) **70** 116) [2015 6g 6.1d⁴ 6d 6g⁴ 6v Nov 7] compact gelding: fair maiden: raced only at 6f. *Richard Fahey*

INNISCASTLE LAD 3 b.g. Kyllachy 129 – Glencal 74 (Compton Place 125) [2015 86: **79** 6m⁵ 7g 6m 6d 6d t7.1m⁶ p8f⁵ 7d Oct 24] fair handicapper: stays 7f: acts on tapeta, good to firm and heavy going: often in headgear in 2015. *William Muir*

INNISH MAN (IRE) 3 b.g. Fastnet Rock (AUS) 127 – Super Gift (IRE) 96 (Darshaan **76**
133) [2015 60: 12m⁶ t12.2g* t12.2f⁴ Dec 22] fair handicapper: won at Wolverhampton in
December: left D. K. Weld after first start: stays 1½m: acts on tapeta: tried in visor in 2015:
often races prominently. *John Mackie*

INNOCENTLY (IRE) 4 ch.g. Kheleyf (USA) 116 – Innocency (USA) (Diesis 133) **83**
[2015 93: 5g⁵ 6d 5g 5g⁶ 5g 5m 5g t5.1f p5f³ t5.1m³ t5.1g⁵ t5.1f⁴ f5g Dec 29] stocky, close-
coupled gelding: fairly useful handicapper: third at Wolverhampton in November: stays
5.5f: acts on tapeta and good to firm going: often in headgear in 2015. *David O'Meara*

INNOCENT TOUCH (IRE) 4 bl.g. Intense Focus (USA) 117 – Guajira (FR) (Mtoto **93**
134) [2015 89: 9.8d 12f⁶ 12g³ 12g⁴ 12g³ 11.5g² 12.3g³ 12m 12.1d³ 13.1g Sep 19] rather
leggy gelding: fairly useful handicapper: creditable efforts most starts in 2015: stays 13f:
acts on good to firm and heavy going: visored twice in 2015. *Richard Fahey*

INNOKO (FR) 5 gr.g. Carlotamix (FR) 113 – Chalana (Ashkalani (IRE) 128) [2015 66, **75**
a79: p11g³ t12.2f⁵ t12.2f⁴ 12.5s 10.4d⁵ 11.7g⁴ t8.6f t9.5f Dec 11] sturdy gelding: fair
handicapper: stays 1¾m: acts on polytrack, tapeta and soft going: sometimes wears hood:
sometimes in tongue tie prior to 2015. *Tony Carroll*

INN THE BULL (GER) 2 ch.g. (Mar 14) Lope de Vega (IRE) 125 – Ile Rousse (Danehill **83**
(USA) 126) [2015 7g⁵ 7s* 7d Oct 11] 65,000 2-y-o: seventh foal: closely related to a
winner in Qatar by Shamardal and half-brother to French/Belgian winner up to 11f Marc
Aurele (2-y-o 9f winner, by Trempolino): dam useful French 1m/9f winner: fairly useful
performer: best effort when winning maiden at Goodwood (by 1¾ lengths from Tadaawol)
in September: will stay 1m. *Alan King*

IN PURSUIT 3 b.f. Makfi 130 – Entre Nous (IRE) (Sadler's Wells (USA) 132) [2015 9.9g **74**
10m⁴ 12g³ p10f³ p10f⁵ t12.2m Nov 28] 27,000Y: third foal: half-sister to 1m winner **a66**
Royal Memory (by Invincible Spirit): dam once-raced sister/half-sister to smart/very
smart performers up to 1¾m Scriptwriter and Courteous: fair maiden: stays 1½m: acts on
polytrack and good to firm going. *Rae Guest*

IN SEINE 4 b.g. Champs Elysees 124 – Fancy Rose (USA) (Joyeux Danseur (USA) 123) **– §**
[2015 52§: p14gᵘʳ Apr 9] maiden: stays 13f: acts on polytrack: one to treat with caution.
John Best

INSHAA 3 b.c. Dansili 127 – Hidden Brief 100 (Barathea (IRE) 127) [2015 –p: 9.8g 10m⁵ **74**
10.2m t6f² f7g³ Dec 29] lengthy colt: fair maiden: left Sir Michael Stoute after third start:
best effort at 6f, though will prove suited by further: acts on fibresand, tapeta and good to
firm going: often in tongue tie in 2015. *Michael Herrington*

INSIGHT (IRE) 4 b.f. Bushranger (IRE) 119 – Ribbon Glade (UAE) (Zafonic (USA) **–**
130) [2015 62: 6m Aug 10] compact filly: maiden: modest form at best: tried in cheekpieces
prior to 2015. *John Spearing*

INSOLENCEOFOFFICE (IRE) 7 b.g. Kodiac 112 – Sharp Diversion (USA) 42 (Diesis **69**
133) [2015 74: t6g f5g* t6f 5d* 5g⁵ t5.1f t5.1m t5.1f f5f Dec 17] fair handicapper: won at
Southwell in January and Hamilton (apprentice) in June: stays 6f: acts on all-weather, good
to firm and good to soft going: usually wears headgear: often races in rear: none too
consistent. *Richard Ford*

INSPECTOR NORSE 4 b.g. Norse Dancer (IRE) 127 – Indiana Blues 90 (Indian Ridge **71**
123) [2015 89: 12g 10m 10m Jun 29] lengthy, rather unfurnished gelding: fair handicapper:
stays 1¼m: acts on good to firm going: front runner/races prominently, tends to find little.
Sylvester Kirk

INSTAGRAM (FR) 3 b.g. Falco (USA) 122 – Trumbaka (IRE) 115 (In The Wings 128) **–**
[2015 11.9d 11.8s Sep 21] fair winning hurdler for F. Nicolle in France: well held in
maidens in Britain. *David Pipe*

INSTANT ATTRACTION (IRE) 4 b.g. Tagula (IRE) 116 – Coup de Coeur (IRE) **104**
(Kahyasi 130) [2015 92: 7d³ t7.1g⁴ 7v* 8d* 7g 8m⁴ 8g² 7g 8g² 8g 7v Nov 7] small, close-
coupled gelding: useful handicapper: won at Chester in May and Ripon in June: better
form when second at Ayr (nose behind Get Knotted) in July and Ripon (neck behind Dubai
Dynamo) in August: stays 1m: acts on polytrack, tapeta and heavy going: front runner/
races prominently. *Jedd O'Keeffe*

INSTANT KARMA (IRE) 4 b.g. Peintre Celebre (USA) 137 – Kotdiji (Mtoto 134) [2015 **84**
86p: 12g 12.1s⁶ 12d 12m p16d⁴ 13.1g³ 11.9d⁵ 11.6g* Oct 20] fairly useful handicapper:
won at Windsor in October: stays 13f: acts on polytrack, good to firm and heavy going:
often in visor in 2015: often travels strongly. *Michael Bell*

INSTILL 3 ch.g. Pivotal 124 – Insijaam (USA) 112 (Secretariat (USA)) [2015 8.3m⁶ 9.9m⁴ 10m⁶ 10.4g* 11.6d* 10g³ Sep 23] £4,500 3-y-o: half-brother to several winners, including smart Maputo (by Cape Cross) and smart performer up to 1½m (third in Oaks) Pictavia (2-y-o 7f winner, by Sinndar): dam, French winner up to 1¼m (2-y-o 9f winner), half-sister to very smart 1m-1½m performer Hatoof: fairly useful performer: won handicaps at Haydock and Windsor in August: stays 11.5f: acts on good to soft going: usually races close up: remains with potential. *Ivan Furtado* **83 p**

INSTINCTUAL 5 ch.g. Observatory (USA) 131 – Be Glad 105 (Selkirk (USA) 129) [2015 t12.2f Oct 16] modest handicapper at best: stays 1½m: acts on good to firm going: sometimes in headgear prior to 2015. *Charlie Longsdon* **–**

INSWING (IRE) 2 b.f. (Apr 11) Intikhab (USA) 135 – Vampire Blues (IRE) 63 (Azamour (IRE) 130) [2015 p7g⁴ t7.1m² Dec 18] £5,500Y: second foal: dam 10.4f winner: showed ability in maidens at Kempton (wore hood) and Wolverhampton: remains with potential. *Ralph Beckett* **66 p**

INTALZA (IRE) 2 b.f. (Mar 29) Intikhab (USA) 135 – Talzaqueen (SWI) (Zilzal Zamaan (USA) 113) [2015 6f 7g 7d³ 8g² t8.6g⁶ 8.3s⁶ f7g⁶ Nov 3] first foal: dam German 9.5f winner: poor maiden: stays 8.5f: acts on soft going: often in cheekpieces. *Michael Herrington* **48**

INTEGRAL 5 b.m. Dalakhani (IRE) 133 – Echelon 120 (Danehill (USA) 126) [2015 121: 8m⁴ 8f⁵ 8m² 8d⁴ Oct 17] smallish, leggy mare: smart performer: fourth in Lockinge Stakes at Newbury (1¼ lengths behind Night of Thunder) in May, second in Sun Chariot Stakes at Newmarket (½ length behind Esoterique) in October and fourth in Queen Elizabeth II Stakes at Ascot (2¼ lengths behind Solow) final start: best form at 1m: acts on firm and good to soft going. *Sir Michael Stoute* **119**

INTENSE STYLE (IRE) 3 ch.g. Galileo (IRE) 134 – Intense Focus (USA) 117 – Style Queen (IRE) 82 (Galileo (IRE) 134) [2015 96: p7g⁴ 8d² 7v⁵ 6d⁴ 7m 8g 6.5m Sep 11] leggy gelding: useful handicapper: second at Naas (short head behind Bold Thady Quill) in April: left J. S. Bolger after fourth start, well held subsequently: stays 1m: acts on polytrack and soft going: tried in cheekpieces in 2015. *Les Eyre* **105**

INTENSE TANGO 4 b.f. Mastercraftsman (IRE) 129 – Cover Look (SAF) (Fort Wood (USA) 117) [2015 12d⁴ 12m³ 13g² 13.1g⁵ Sep 19] rangy filly: fairly useful handicapper: second at Newmarket in August: stays 13f: acts on good to firm and heavy going: useful hurdler. *K. R. Burke* **94**

INTENSIFIED (IRE) 4 b.g. Intense Focus (USA) 117 – Sway Me Now (USA) (Speightstown (USA) 124) [2015 77: 6.9v⁵ 8.5sᵘʳ 7g 7.2d 10m⁵ 10.9g⁴ 10g 9.9d t9.5f⁴ Oct 16] useful-looking gelding: modest maiden: left J. S. Bolger after third start: stays 11f: acts on good to firm going: tried in cheekpieces prior to 2015: tried in tongue tie prior to 2015. *Ruth Carr* **61**

INTERCEPTION (IRE) 5 ch.m. Raven's Pass (USA) 133 – Badee'a (IRE) (Marju (IRE) 127) [2015 103p: 6g² 6f* 6m 6m³ 6m⁵ 6d Oct 17] sturdy mare: smart performer: improved to win 25-runner Wokingham Stakes (Handicap) at Royal Ascot in June by 1¼ lengths from Robert Le Diable, travelling well held up and finding plenty to lead well inside final 1f: 50/1, excuses when 5¾ lengths tenth of 20 to Muhaarar in Champions Sprint Stakes at Ascot final start, having hopeless task from position: stays 7f: acts on polytrack, firm and good to soft going. *David Lanigan* **114**

INTERCHOICE STAR 10 b.g. Josr Algarhoud (IRE) 118 – Blakeshall Girl 64 (Piccolo 121) [2015 70: f7g² t6g 6.1m⁶ t6g t6m Dec 12] fair handicapper: stays 7f: acts on polytrack, fibresand, good to firm and good to soft going: usually wears headgear. *Ray Peacock* **66**

Wokingham Stakes (Heritage Handicap), Royal Ascot—lightly-raced five-year-old Interception improves again to land this valuable prize, beating French raider Robert Le Diable (hidden by winner), Lancelot du Lac (fourth left) and Related (blinkers, partly hidden by third)

INTERCONNECTION 4 ch.g. Mount Nelson 125 – Lacework 91 (Pivotal 124) [2015 **94** 76§: 10m* 12m² 10.1m⁴ 10.1m⁵ 10.3g⁵ 10s* Oct 13] sturdy gelding: fairly useful handicapper: won at Sandown in May: career-best effort when also won at Leicester in October by 3¾ lengths from East Coast Lady, staying on strongly: stays 12.5f: acts on soft and good to firm going: wears headgear: usually races prominently: temperamental in 2014, but did little wrong in 2015. *Ed Vaughan*

INTERIOR MINISTER 5 b.g. Nayef (USA) 129 – Sister Maria (USA) 89 (Kingmambo **82** (USA) 125) [2015 12m³ p16g Jul 1] fairly useful handicapper: third at Salisbury in June: acts on polytrack and good to firm going: in headgear/tongue tie in 2015: sold £5,000, sent to Germany, where won 5 races from 9.7f to 1½m in second half of year. *Warren Greatrex*

INTERMITTENT 2 b.f. (May 2) Cacique (IRE) 124 – Innocent Air 110 (Galileo (IRE) **84 p** 134) [2015 7s² p7g² Oct 29] attractive filly: fifth foal: closely related to useful 1½m-1¾m winner Fledged (by Dansili) and half-sister to 7f winner Angelic Air (by Oasis Dream): dam, winner up to 1¼m (2-y-o 7f winner), half-sister to smart French/US 1¼m-1½m winner Skipping: second in maidens at Leicester (½ length behind Hells Babe) and Lingfield (2¼ lengths behind Our Joy) in October: will be suited by 1m: remains open to improvement. *Roger Charlton*

INTERNATIONAL NAME 3 ch.g. Iffraaj 127 – Dove (IRE) 83 (Sadler's Wells (USA) **72 §** 132) [2015 82p: f8d³ p8m² p8g² 10f³ 9.9m⁴ 12m Jun 25] good-topped gelding: fairly useful **a84 §** maiden: best effort at 1m: acts on polytrack, tapeta and firm going: often in headgear in 2015: often in tongue tie in 2015: often starts slowly, usually races nearer last than first: ungenuine: sold £13,000. *Saeed bin Suroor*

IN THE CITY 2 ch.c. (Apr 3) Exceed And Excel (AUS) 126 – Soft Morning 108 (Pivotal **88 p** 124) [2015 7m⁴ Aug 7] 100,000Y: fourth foal: half-brother to 2-y-o 7f winner (stays 1½m) Savanna La Mar (by Curlin) and French 2-y-o 6f winner (stayed 1m) So In Love (by Smart Strike), both useful: dam, 7f-1¼m winner, half-sister to smart performers at 1½m+ Songerie and Souvenance: 14/1, shaped encouragingly when fourth in maiden at Newmarket (4¾ lengths behind Emotionless) in August: will improve. *William Haggas*

IN THE FAST LANE (SAF) 5 b.m. Jet Master (SAF) – First Arrival (SAF) (Northern **110** Guest (USA)) [2015 p9.2m⁵ 10g p12g Nov 4] good-topped mare: half-sister to several winners in South Africa, including Group 1 6f winner Let's Rock'n Roll (by Muhtafal): dam champion 3-y-o filly in Zimbabwe: smart performer: champion 3-y-o filly in South Africa, winning Cape Fillies Guineas at Kenilworth in 2013 and Woolavington 2000 at Greyville in 2014, both Group 1 events: left S. J. Snaith, fifth in minor event at Chelmsford (2½ lengths behind Tryster) in September: well held in listed events subsequently, in first-time cheekpieces latter occasion: stays 11f: acts on polytrack, has won on soft ground: sold 150,000 gns in December. *William Haggas*

IN THE HOUSE (IRE) 3 b.f. Montjeu (IRE) 137 – O' Bella Ballerina (USA) 80 **71** (Fusaichi Pegasus (USA) 130) [2015 10m⁵ p12g⁶ Aug 5] 105,000Y: compact filly: first foal: dam, 1½m winner, half-sister to St Leger winner Millenary: better effort when fifth in maiden at Newbury in July: should stay 1½m. *Luca Cumani*

IN THE RED (IRE) 2 b.c. (Mar 1) Elusive Pimpernel (USA) 117 – Roses From Ridey **91** (IRE) 78 (Petorius 117) [2015 7g 7s² 8v⁴ 8m* 7d⁴ Oct 11] €13,000F, £36,000Y: good-topped colt: half-brother to 3 winners, including French 1m-1½m winner Armigerent (by In The Wings) and 2-y-o 7f winner Sultans Way (by Indian Ridge): dam ran twice: fairly useful performer: won maiden at Salisbury in September and nursery at Goodwood (by 5 lengths from Many Dreams) in October: stays 1m: acts on good to firm and good to soft going: usually races close up. *Richard Hannon*

INTIBAAH 5 b.g. Elnadim (USA) 128 – Mawaared 61 (Machiavellian (USA) 123) [2015 **111** 119: 6s² 5d 6g² 6.3m 6s* 5.5g 6s Oct 31] good-quartered gelding: smart performer: won minor event at Fontainebleau (by 1½ lengths from Vedeux) in September: second in minor event at Haydock (2¼ lengths behind Clear Spring) in May: stays 6f: acts on polytrack, best turf form on good to soft/soft going: blinkered fourth outing. *George Baker*

INTILAAQ (USA) 3 b.c. Dynaformer (USA) – Torrestrella (IRE) 117 (Orpen (USA) **125 p** 116) [2015 85p: 8m* 8m 10m* 10.4m* Aug 8]
The Sheikh Hamdan-owned three-year-old Nayef—who, for some reason, never enjoyed the popularity he deserved as a racehorse (or now as a sire)—won the 2001 Rose of Lancaster Stakes by five lengths before going on to win four Group 1s. The same owner's Intilaaq won the latest Rose of Lancaster by the same margin and looks a Group 1 performer in the making. Like Nayef, Intilaaq is also a physically imposing colt. He finished well held in the Two Thousand Guineas before he

bounced back after being given time off and stepped up in trip, just like Nayef, and he was being considered for the Champion Stakes (won by Nayef at three) until being scratched earlier in the week after failing to sparkle in a racecourse gallop under Paul Hanagan at Newmarket. In a year when two of Roger Varian's three Group 1-winning two-year-olds from 2014, Cursory Glance (who has been retired and will visit War Front in 2016) and Vert de Grece, did not reappear and the other one, Belardo, failed to win in seven starts, Intilaaq's emergence as a top member of the classic generation will have been satisfying for his excellent trainer. There's more to come from Intilaaq too, just five starts behind him after all, and he'll merit his place in some of the top middle-distance races in 2016, with the Dubai World Cup his first intended target.

Intilaaq had shown promise when third in an Ascot maiden on his only start at two, and he was much improved on his reappearance when stepped up to a mile in a similar race at Newbury in April, making the running and storming eight lengths clear of Keble. Intilaaq's performance was one of rare merit for a maiden event and he was supplemented for the Two Thousand Guineas two weeks later at a cost of £30,000, although his owner already had a live contender for the race in Estidhkaar (Sheikh Hamdan's leading winter Two Thousand Guineas fancy Faydhan had managed only third in the Free Handicap on his return and did not run in the Guineas). Intilaaq was backed from 12/1 to 8/1 on the day—with Paul Hanagan's choice Estidhkaar at 6/1—but it was probably a case of asking too much of him too soon as he managed only fifteenth of the eighteen runners. Intilaaq had shaped as if he'd stay further at Newbury, and he was stepped up to a mile and a quarter after eleven weeks off in the six-runner listed JLT Stakes (Steventon) back at the same course in July, also taking on his elders for the first time. In a slightly unusual race, in that Sheikh Hamdan's second runner Mustadeem set a suicidal pace (though not apparently acting as a pacemaker for the better-fancied Intilaaq), Intilaaq won by two and a half lengths from fellow three-year-old Consort. With the field strung out behind him, Intilaaq looked something out of the ordinary, and the form assessment of his performance was backed up by a good time. Intilaaq stood out on both form and profile for the five-runner Group 3 Betfred Rose of Lancaster at Haydock in August and he started at 3/1-on against his elders, which included the smart in-form pair Master Carpenter and Fire Fighting (Fattsota and Collaboration completed the field). Intilaaq tracked Fattsota early on but was sent to the front after two furlongs, thus avoiding a muddling, tactical race that would not have seen him to best effect, and he stormed clear before being eased approaching the finish to win by five lengths from Master Carpenter. Intilaaq bettered any performance from a winner of the Rose of Lancaster Stakes in recent years, including that of Nayef and the other subsequent Group 1 winners Jukebox Jury (2009) and Hunter's Light (2012). Intilaaq was due to contest the Arc Trial at Newbury in mid-September but he missed that race after knocking a joint (though the soft ground might have ruled him out anyway), and he was also absent from the Champion Stakes.

		Dynaformer (USA) (br 1985)	Roberto (b 1969)	Hail To Reason
Intilaaq (USA) (b.c. 2012)				Bramalea
			Andover Way (b or br 1978)	His Majesty
				On The Trail
		Torrestrella (IRE) (b 2001)	Orpen (b 1996)	Lure
				Bonita Francita
			Sea Ring (b 1990)	Bering
				Blue River

The big, well-made Intilaaq is bred in the purple. His dam Torrestrella was runner-up on both her starts at two and showed smart form when winning her first three outings at up to nine furlongs as a three-year-old in 2004, including the Poule d'Essai des Pouliches. Torrestrella's next run, when well held in the Prix de Diane, was her last for Francois Rohaut in France and she continued her career with Christophe Clement in the States. Torrestrella finished down the field in three starts there, including on her return as a four-year-old. Torrestrella was purchased by Sheikh Hamdan for 1,300,000 dollars, in foal to Dynaformer, at Keeneland in November 2006, though she gave birth to twins which did not survive. Intilaaq is Torrestrella's third live foal and follows the ten-furlong winner Moosir (by Daaher) and the smart winner Farmah (by Speightstown) who made a winning debut as a three-year-old over a mile and a quarter but is best known as a sprinter (Group 3 winner). Farmah was trained by Rohaut, as was Moosir until he was transferred to Dubai at the end of his four-year-old year. Farmah is now part of the Shadwell broodmare band and is in foal to Oasis Dream; she will visit Muhaarar in 2016.

Mr Hamdan Al Maktoum's "Intilaaq"

Torrestrella's two-year-old colt by Smart Strike is named Takatul and is in training with Charlie Hills. Torrestrella did not have a foal in 2014 and she died after giving birth to a full brother to Farmah in 2015. Torrestrella's pedigree was covered in *Racehorses of 2004*, though it bears repeating that she is from a family with plenty of stamina and is a half-sister to the useful French performer at up to fifteen and a half furlongs Torrealta and the winning hurdlers Comandante and the ill-fated Lingo (a Grade 1 winner in that sphere before his career was cut short). Intilaaq is also by a sire who was an influence for stamina—unlike most North American stallions—in Dynaformer who died in 2012. Dynaformer's best progeny are the North American-trained pair Barbaro and Point of Entry and the French-trained Melbourne Cup winner Americain (also trained in the States for a short time), while he is perhaps best known on British shores as the sire of Blue Bunting and the smart or better brothers Lucarno, Thought Worthy and Flying Officer. Intilaaq stays an extended mile and a quarter and shapes like he will stay further. He has raced only on ground firmer than good. *Roger Varian*

INTIMATELY 2 b.g. (Mar 20) Intense Focus (USA) 117 – Midnight Fling 66 (Groom Dancer (USA) 128) [2015 5g 5.1g t5.1g⁴ p7g³ t7.1m⁶ p6g³ p7g⁴ 6g f6g³ Dec 15] compact gelding: modest maiden: stays on polytrack: often races towards rear. *Jonathan Portman* **59**

INTIMATION 3 b.f. Dubawi (IRE) 129 – Infallible 114 (Pivotal 124) [2015 –p: 8.3g* 10g* Jul 4] useful performer: won maiden at Nottingham (by ½ length from Bella Nouf) in May: further improvement when winning handicap at Leicester (by 4½ lengths from Mikandy) in July, forging clear: stays 1¼m: will continue to progress. *Sir Michael Stoute* **96 p**

INTISAAB 4 b.g. Elnadim (USA) 128 – Katoom (IRE) 75 (Soviet Star (USA) 128) [2015 88: 7d 6d* 7m* 7v 7m⁵ 7m⁶ Jun 20] fairly useful handicapper: won at Ripon (by neck from Royal Connoisseur) and Doncaster (amateur, by ½ length from Celtic Sixpence) in April: stays 7f: acts on good to firm and good to soft going: tried in visor prior to 2015. *David O'Meara* **85**

INTIWIN (IRE) 3 b.g. Intikhab (USA) 135 – Muluk (IRE) 83 (Rainbow Quest (USA) 134) [2015 87: 8d* 7g 8m* 8m⁴ 8g 7.6s⁶ 8.5d⁶ 8.9s Oct 10] fairly useful handicapper: won at Ripon (by nose from Tadqeeq) in April and Ayr (awarded race) in June: stays 1m: acts on firm and soft going. *Richard Fahey* **94**

INTO THE WIND 8 ch.m. Piccolo 121 – In The Stocks 59 (Reprimand 122) [2015 p12f May 1] stocky mare: fair at best, no form in 2015: stays 15f: acts on good to firm and heavy going. *Jim Best*

INTRANSIGENT 6 b.g. Trans Island 119 – Mara River 86 (Efisio 120) [2015 119: p6f⁶ t7.1m p6f⁴ 7m³ 8.3f³ 6f 7g² 6.1g⁵ 7g 7m p7g³ p6g² p7f⁵ Dec 21] tall gelding: smart performer: third in listed races at Leicester in April, at Windsor (2¼ lengths behind Shifting Power) in May, and second in listed race at Chester (head behind Dusky Queen) in July and handicap at Kempton (1¼ lengths behind Lancelot du Lac) in November: effective from 6f to 8.5f: acts on polytrack, firm and soft going: in hood last 3 starts. *Andrew Balding* **115**

INTREPID GLORY (IRE) 4 ch.g. Danehill Dancer (IRE) 117 – Ballymore Lady (USA) (War Chant (USA) 126) [2015 p16g p10.7g⁴ p12g p10.7g 10m⁻ Jun 13] modest maiden: left fl005 O'Sullivan after fourth start: stays 2m: acts on polytrack: sometimes in headgear: tried in tongue tie: one to avoid (refused to race final start). *Henry Spiller* **55 §**

INTREPID (IRE) 5 b.g. Invincible Spirit (IRE) 121 – Imiloa (USA) (Kingmambo (USA) 125) [2015 88: 7m* 7.6f⁶ 7m⁵ 7g⁵ 7m 6s p6f Oct 10] compact gelding: fairly useful handicapper: won at Leicester (by 1¼ lengths from Boogangoo) in June: stays 8.5f: acts on polytrack, fibresand and firm going: sometimes wears headgear. *Robert Mills* **80**

INTRIGUE 3 b.f. Fastnet Rock (AUS) 127 – Riberac 100 (Efisio 120) [2015 8m⁵ 8g 8m³ p10f² p10f³ Sep 24] closely related to 1m/8.6f winner Epernay (by Tiger Hill) and useful winner up to 1¼m (stays 1½m) Gothic (2-y-o 8.3f winner, by Danehill Dancer) and half-sister to several winners, including useful winner up to 11.5f Dordogne (2-y-o 9f winner, by Singspiel): dam winner up to 1¼m (2-y-o 5f winner): fair maiden: likely to stay 1½m: acts on polytrack: often in headgear: remains with potential. *William Haggas* **71 p**

INTRINSIC 5 b.h. Oasis Dream 129 – Infallible 114 (Pivotal 124) [2015 114: 6f Jun 20] well-made horse: smart handicapper: won Stewards' Cup at Goodwood in 2014: 10/1, possibly amiss when well held in Wokingham Stakes at Royal Ascot only outing in 2015: stayed 6f: acted on soft and good to firm going: tried in cheekpieces: to stand at Hedgeholme Stud, Winston, County Durham, fee £1,750. *Robert Cowell* **–**

INTRUDE 3 b.g. Intikhab (USA) 135 – Don't Tell Mum (IRE) 99 (Dansili 127) [2015 57: **94** p8g* 8f⁴ 8.3m⁵ t8.6m* Sep 14] good-topped gelding: fairly useful performer: won maiden at Lingfield in May and handicap at Wolverhampton (by head from Hakka) in September: stays 8.5f: acts on polytrack and tapeta. *David Simcock*

INVADE (IRE) 3 ch.f. Intense Focus (USA) 117 – Spinning Well (IRE) 83 (Pivotal 124) **65** [2015 p7m p8m⁶ p7g⁴ 6d⁴ 6m³ 7d⁶ 6m⁴ Aug 9] 70,000Y: second foal: sister to 2-y-o 1m winner Tanqeya: dam, 1½m winner, half-sister to very smart 1¼m-1¾m winner Fox Hunt: fair maiden: stays 1m: acts on polytrack, good to firm and good to soft going: tried in tongue tie: often races towards rear. *Stuart Williams*

INVECTUS HERO 3 b.g. Paco Boy (IRE) 129 – Blur 62 (Oasis Dream 129) [2015 –: **63** t5.1g³ t6f⁵ p6g⁴ f7g Dec 12] modest maiden: best effort at 6f: acts on polytrack. *Derek Shaw*

INVERMERE 2 b.f. (Feb 5) Kyllachy 129 – Kootenay (IRE) 109 (Selkirk (USA) 129) **82** [2015 7m² 7m³ 6.9m³ 7d* 7g⁶ Oct 10] £25,000Y: good-topped filly: seventh foal: closely related to 1m winner Kelowna (by Pivotal), later 6f/1m winner in USA: dam, winner up to 8.5f (2-y-o 7f/7.5f winner), half-sister to Irish St Leger winner Sans Frontieres: fairly useful performer: won maiden at Chester in September: raced only at 7f: acts on good to soft going: front runner/races prominently, often travels strongly. *Richard Fahey*

INVESTISSEMENT 9 b.g. Singspiel (IRE) 133 – Underwater (USA) 109 (Theatrical) **73** [2015 p15.8m² p13f² p15.8f⁵ p10f⁴ p13g* p15.8g³ f14d⁵ p12g⁶ 9g t12.2g⁴ p12g p12m p15.8g² p12g⁴ p12g⁵ Dec 30] lengthy gelding: fair performer: left Lee Carter, won claimer at Lingfield in March: stays 2½m: acts on polytrack, tapeta, good to firm and good to soft going: often wears cheekpieces: tried in tongue tie. *Paddy Butler*

INVESTITURE 2 b.f. (Jan 28) Invincible Spirit (IRE) 121 – Highest 99 (Dynaformer **68 p** (USA)) [2015 t7.1f³ p7g⁶ p7m Dec 16] first foal: dam, 12.4f winner, half-sister to smart performers Wasan (up to 1¼m) and Olaya (US Grade 2 1½m winner): fair maiden: will be suited by at least 1m: should do better. *John Gosden*

INVIGILATOR 7 b.g. Motivator 131 – Midpoint (USA) (Point Given (USA) 134) [2015 **69** 69: p6g* p6f p6f⁴ f6g⁵ p6f⁴ p6f³ p6g³ p6g⁴ Apr 7] useful-looking gelding: fair handicapper: won at Chelmsford in January: stays 6f: acts on polytrack and heavy going: often wears tongue tie: often races towards rear. *Derek Shaw*

INVIGORATE 2 b.c. (Feb 9) Stimulation (IRE) 121 – Pesse (IRE) (Eagle Eyed (USA) **72** 111) [2015 6m 7.1m⁵ t6g² t7.1g³ 7v³ 6d³ t8.6f⁴ Oct 27] fair maiden: stays 8.5f: acts on tapeta and heavy going: front runner/races prominently. *Harry Dunlop*

INVINCIBLE BOND 2 b.c. (Mar 24) Monsieur Bond (IRE) 120 – Royal Pardon 61 **–** (Royal Applause 124) [2015 5m⁶ 6g 7.1m⁶ Jun 29] no form. *Simon Waugh*

INVINCIBLE DIAMOND (IRE) 3 ch.g. Arakan (USA) 123 – Invincible Woman **71** (IRE) 87 (Invincible Spirit (IRE) 121) [2015 84: 6d⁴ Apr 10] fairly useful form in 2014: left Mrs A. M. O'Shea 12,000 gns and gelded, fourth of 5 in minor event at Leicester only outing in 2015: best effort at 7f. *J. S. Moore*

INVINCIBLE LAD (IRE) 11 b.g. Invincible Spirit (IRE) 121 – Lady Ellen 67 (Horage **60** 124) [2015 72: 5.1m 5m 5m⁶ 5m 5m⁴ t5.1f⁴ Oct 31] strong gelding: modest handicapper: left Ed McMahon after fifth start: stays 6f: acts on all-weather, firm and good to soft going (below form all recent starts on soft/heavy): tried in headgear. *David Dennis*

INVINCIBLE RIDGE (IRE) 7 b.g. Invincible Spirit (IRE) 121 – Dani Ridge (IRE) 92 **89** (Indian Ridge 123) [2015 85, a92: t6g² f5s⁵ t6f³ t5.1f⁶ t6m t5.1f⁶ 6d 6s³ 5g* May 18] quite good-topped gelding: fairly useful handicapper: won at Redcar (by length from Mappin Time) in May: effective at 5f-7f: acts on tapeta, soft and good to firm going: tried in blinkers prior to 2015: often wears tongue tie: often races towards rear. *Eric Alston*

INVINCIBLE WISH (IRE) 3 b.g. Vale of York (IRE) 117 – Moonlight Wish (IRE) **69** (Peintre Celebre (USA) 137) [2015 70: p8f⁵ f8d* f8s⁴ 7m⁵ 7.5g 7m⁵ t6g⁶ 10m 10.2s² t9.5f⁵ p10m⁶ Oct 28] fair performer: won seller at Southwell in March: left Brian Ellison after seventh start: stays 1¼m: acts on all-weather and soft going: sometimes wears headgear. *Trevor Wall*

INVINCIBLE ZEB (IRE) 3 gr.g. Zebedee 113 – Cruise Line (Rainbow Quest (USA) **–** 134) [2015 62, a55: t6f Jan 12] maiden: stays 6f: acts on tapeta and soft going: in cheekpieces sole start in 2015. *Ronald Harris*

IN VINO VERITAS (IRE) 4 b.g. Art Connoisseur (IRE) 121 – Robin (Slip Anchor 136) **66** [2015 12g 12g⁴ 12d⁵ 12m³ 11.9d⁶ t13.9f³ t13.9f t16.5g⁵ Dec 5] lengthy gelding: fair maiden: left Ann Duffield after fourth start: stays 15f: acts on tapeta, soft and good to firm going: often wears headgear: front runner/races prominently. *Lynn Siddall*

INVOCATION (FR) 2 b.c. (Apr 12) Intense Focus (USA) 117 – Fabiola (GER) **76**
(Medicean 128) [2015 p8f² t8.6m³ Oct 2] fair form when placed in maidens at Chelmsford
and Wolverhampton: likely to stay 1¼m. *Alan King*

INVOKE (IRE) 4 b.f. Kodiac 112 – Tides 47 (Bahamian Bounty 116) [2015 79: 8d³ 8g³ **96**
7.6f⁴ 6.9g* 8.3d² 7g* 7.2s² 7.6m³ 7.2m* p8g t7.1g⁶ f7g f7g⁶ Dec 22] angular filly:
useful handicapper: much improved in 2015 and won at Carlisle in June, Haydock in July
and Musselburgh in August and September: stays 8.5f: acts on polytrack, fibresand, good
to firm and good to soft going: tried in headgear in 2014: often races prominently.
Keith Dalgleish

INWITHACHANCE (IRE) 2 b.g. (Apr 7) Thousand Words 113 – Sombreffe 71 (Polish **–**
Precedent (USA) 131) [2015 t8.6f t7.1f t9.5f Nov 10] no form. *Daniel Loughnane*

INXILE (IRE) 10 b.g. Fayruz 116 – Grandel (Owington 123) [2015 89: 6g 5m⁶ 5m 6m⁴ **88**
6g* 5.1m⁴ 5g⁴ 5m 5d 5g Sep 16] strong, compact gelding: fairly useful handicapper: won
claimer at Ripon in June: stays 6f: acts on firm and soft going: often wears cheekpieces.
David Nicholls

IOANNOU 6 b.g. Excellent Art 125 – Sandtime (IRE) 92 (Green Desert (USA) 127) [2015 **44**
–: p7g Jan 14] poor handicapper: best effort at 7f: acts on polytrack: in cheekpieces sole
start in 2015. *Ian Williams*

IONA ISLAND 2 b.f. (Mar 9) Dutch Art 126 – Still Small Voice (Polish Precedent (USA) **58 p**
131) [2015 7d⁴ Oct 31] 100,000Y: fourth foal: dam unraced sister to Irish/Yorkshire Oaks
winner Pure Grain: 5/1, not seen to best effect when fourth in maiden at Newmarket
(9½ lengths behind Tiptree) in October, caught further back than ideal: better to come.
Charles Hills

IONIAN LIBRETTA (AUT) 3 b.f. Librettist (USA) 124 – Ionia (IRE) (Montjeu (IRE) **–**
137) [2015 8.3s 12m May 29] compact filly: fourth foal: dam, placed up to 1m in Italy,
half-sister to smart 7f/1m winner Serre Chevalier: in hood, tailed off in 2 maidens: sent to
Austria. *Mrs Ilka Gansera-Leveque*

IRENE HULL (IRE) 4 b.f. Excellent Art 125 – Wing Diva (IRE) 65 (Hawk Wing (USA) **–**
136) [2015 66: f8s Jan 1] maiden: well held only start in 2015: best effort at 1m: acts on
fibresand and good to firm going: usually races close up. *Garry Moss*

IRISH BELLE (IRE) 3 ch.f. Duke of Marmalade (IRE) 132 – Flower of Kent (USA) 78 **–**
(Diesis 133) [2015 –: 6g 8m 11.7f 10m 8.3g⁶ t7.1g Aug 6] leggy filly: no form: tried in
blinkers/tongue tie. *Tony Carroll*

IRISH CAILIN (IRE) 2 b.f. (Apr 6) Desert Millennium (IRE) – Shone Island (IRE) **58**
(Desert Sun 120) [2015 5g⁶ 5d³ 5.1m³ 5m⁵ 5g⁴ 5m⁶ Sep 27] £1,200Y: fifth foal: sister to 5f
winners Irish Boy (temperamental) and Irish Girls Spirit: dam unraced: modest maiden:
raced only at 5f: acts on good to firm and good to soft going: front runner/races prominently.
Paul Midgley

IRISH ECLARE (IRE) 2 br.c. (Mar 23) Equiano (FR) 127 – Delitme (IRE) (Val Royal **73**
(FR) 127) [2015 6d⁶ 6g t6f² p6f* Nov 12] lengthy colt: fair performer: won nursery at
Chelmsford in November: raced only at 6f. *Charles Hills*

IRISH GIRLS SPIRIT (IRE) 6 b.m. Desert Millennium (IRE) – Shone Island (IRE) **73**
(Desert Sun 120) [2015 81: 5d⁶ 5m⁶ 5f⁵ 5f³ 5f² 5g² 5m⁴ 5m⁵ 5m* 5m⁴ 5m Sep 28] fair
handicapper: won at Hamilton in September: best form at 5f: acts on good to firm going:
tried in headgear prior to 2015: front runner/races prominently. *Paul Midgley*

IRISH HAWKE (IRE) 3 b.g. Montjeu (IRE) 137 – Ahdaab (USA) 73 (Rahy (USA) 115) **79**
[2015 9.9m⁴ 11.5g* 14.1g 11.8g Sep 8] good-topped gelding: fair performer: won maiden
at Lingfield in July: best effort at 11.5f. *Luca Cumani*

IRISH ROOKIE (IRE) 3 b.f. Azamour (IRE) 130 – Bold Assumption (Observatory **116**
(USA) 131) [2015 96p: 8f⁶ 8g² 8f 8m³ Oct 3] lengthy filly: smart performer: best efforts
when second in Poule d'Essai des Pouliches at Longchamp (¾ length behind Ervedya,
leading from 2f out until well inside final 1f) in May and third in Sun Chariot Stakes at
Newmarket (2 lengths behind Esoterique) in October: should stay beyond 1m: acts on good
to firm going. *Martyn Meade*

IRON BUTTERFLY 6 b.m. Shirocco (GER) 129 – Coh Sho No 59 (Old Vic 136) [2015 **–**
16.2s⁵ 14.1g Jun 15] good-topped mare: fair at best, no form in 2015: stays 2¼m: acts on
good to firm and heavy going: sometimes wears headgear: fairly useful hurdler. *James
Eustace*

IRONDALE EXPRESS 4 b.f. Myboycharlie (IRE) 118 – Olindera (GER) (Lomitas 129)   **63**
[2015 75§: 7m 8.3s* 8d May 13] modest handicapper: won at Nottingham (apprentice) in
May: stays 8.5f: acts on good to firm and heavy going: tried in headgear: sometimes slowly
away, usually races nearer last than first: best treated with caution. *Des Donovan*

IRVINE LADY (IRE) 2 ch.f. (Mar 28) Footstepsinthesand 120 – Ascot Lady (IRE) 85   **–**
(Spinning World (USA) 130) [2015 6g⁶ 8s Aug 29] €17,000F, €20,000Y: fourth foal: half-
sister to French 2-y-o 7.5f winner Lady Ascot (by Excellent Art) and 7f winner Lady On
Top (by Oratorio): dam, French 2-y-o 5.5f winner, half-sister to smart winner up to 9f Tiger
Shark: well held in 2 maidens at Deauville. *Gay Kelleway*

ISABELLA BEETON 4 b.f. Archipenko (USA) 127 – Famcred 89 (Inchinor 119) [2015   **48**
62: p12g⁶ p7m⁴ Oct 21] tall filly: poor performer: will prove suited by a return to 1m+: acts
on polytrack: usually races nearer last than first. *Pat Phelan*

ISABELLA BIRD 4 b.f. Invincible Spirit (IRE) 121 – Meetyouthere (IRE) (Sadler's   **83**
Wells (USA) 132) [2015 80: 8.3m³ 10.3g 8.5m² 8.3m⁴ 8.3d 8.3s Oct 28] tall filly: fairly
useful handicapper: stays 8.5f: acts on any turf going: front runner/races prominently.
Mick Channon

ISABELLA LIBERTY (FR) 4 b.f. Soldier of Fortune (IRE) 131 – Samsa (FR) (Zafonic   **–**
(USA) 130) [2015 p13.3g⁶ p10f 11.6m⁵ May 25] tall, unfurnished filly: fairly useful at best,
no form in 2015. *Robert Eddery*

ISAMOL 3 b.c. Intikhab (USA) 135 – Uvinza 100 (Bertolini (USA) 125) [2015 p10g² 10m*   **84**
11g 11m⁶ 14.1g⁴ p12g 11s⁵ Sep 23] 41,000F, 170,000Y: strong, compact colt: first foal:
dam, 2-y-o 1m winner who stayed 1½m, sister to useful performer up to 7f Baddilini: fairly
useful performer: won maiden at Windsor in April: stays 1¾m: acts on polytrack and good
to firm going: tried in blinkers: often races prominently: sold 35,000 gns, sent to UAE.
Amanda Perrett

ISDAAL 8 ch.m. Dubawi (IRE) 129 – Faydah (USA) 72 (Bahri (USA) 125) [2015 p11g*   **64**
p12m Oct 28] modest handicapper: won at Kempton in September: stays 1½m: acts on
polytrack, soft and good to firm going: sometimes wears headgear. *Kevin Morgan*

ISEEMIST (IRE) 4 gr.f. Verglas (IRE) 118 – Krasivaya (IRE) (Soviet Star (USA) 128)   **96**
[2015 95: p6m⁵ 6d 6m³ 5.3d² 6m 6m* 6m⁵ 6m⁶ 6g² 6d* Oct 11] workmanlike filly: useful
handicapper: won at Epsom in July and Goodwood (by ½ length from Clear Spring) in
October: stays 6f: acts on good to firm and heavy going: tried in hood prior to 2015: front
runner/races prominently. *John Gallagher*

ISHIAMBER 5 ch.m. Ishiguru (USA) 114 – Black And Amber 45 (Weldnaas (USA) 112)   **100**
[2015 94: p7g² 7m² 7m⁴ 6m⁵ 6m* 7g p6g⁴ 7m⁵ p6m Nov 14] tall mare: useful performer:
won minor event at Newmarket in June: second in handicaps at Lingfield in April and
Salisbury in May, and good fourth in similar event at Kempton in September: stays 7f: acts
on polytrack, good to firm and good to soft going: tried in cheekpieces in 2015.
George Baker

ISHIANICON 2 b.f. (May 2) Sixties Icon 125 – Ishibee (IRE) 64 (Ishiguru (USA) 114)   **–**
[2015 p6g t7.1f Oct 9] 1,500Y: second foal: dam 6f winner (including at 2 yrs): tailed off
in 2 maidens. *Natalie Lloyd-Beavis*

ISHIKAWA (IRE) 7 b.g. Chineur (FR) 123 – Nautical Light (Slip Anchor 136) [2015 90:   **–**
t9.5f 8g 8d 7.9g⁶ 8.1m Aug 22] sturdy, lengthy gelding: fairly useful at best, no form in
2015: left K. R. Burke after fourth start: tried in cheekpieces prior to 2015: front runner/
races prominently. *Ali Stronge*

ISHISOBA 5 ch.m. Ishiguru (USA) 114 – Bundle Up (USA) (Miner's Mark (USA) 120)   **–**
[2015 58: f5g Apr 27] angular mare: poor maiden nowadays: best effort at 7f: acts on good
to firm going: tried in cheekpieces prior to 2015. *Mark Hoad*

ISIS BLUE 5 b.g. Cockney Rebel (IRE) 127 – Bramaputra (IRE) 88 (Choisir (AUS) 126)   **74**
[2015 p10g² p12g⁶ Dec 3] fair handicapper: stays 11f: acts on polytrack: tried in
cheekpieces prior to 2015. *Rod Millman*

ISLAND AUTHORITY 3 b.f. Authorized (IRE) 133 – Island Odyssey 93 (Dansili 127)   **59**
[2015 10m 10.2m⁵ p10g 12.1v⁵ Aug 25] third foal: half-sister to useful performer up to
1¾m Island Remede (2-y-o 9f winner, by Medicean): dam 1¼m-1½m winner: modest
maiden: best effort at 1¼m: in hood. *Ed Dunlop*

ISLAND EXPRESS (IRE) 8 b.g. Chineur (FR) 123 – Cayman Expresso (IRE) 79   **53**
(Fayruz 116) [2015 55: f5g⁶ p6f⁴ p6f⁶ p6g³ t6f p6f⁶ 5d Apr 28] sturdy gelding: modest
maiden: stays 6f: acts on polytrack and firm going: usually wears headgear: usually wears
tongue tie: sometimes slowly away. *Ann Stokell*

ISLAND FLAME (IRE) 2 b.f. (Feb 7) Kodiac 112 – Noble Flame (IRE) 58 (Doyoun **67**
124) [2015 5d³ 6g⁴ 6d⁵ 6.3d 7d⁵ Oct 16] €1,000F, €6,000Y: seventh foal: dam maiden half-
sister to useful 1½m winner Noble Galileo: fair maiden: stays 7f: acts on good to soft going.
Richard Fahey

ISLAND REMEDE 4 b.f. Medicean 128 – Island Odyssey 93 (Dansili 127) [2015 103: **103**
12d² 14.1s² 12m⁶ 14m⁶ 14m 13.4m⁶ 14.6m 12g 12v⁶ Oct 24] good-topped filly: useful
performer: second in minor event at Doncaster (¾ length behind Windshear) in March and
in listed race at Nottingham (1½ lengths behind Deuce Again) in April: stays 1¾m: acts on
good to firm and heavy going: tried in cheekpieces in 2015. *Ed Dunlop*

ISLA ROSE 2 b.f. (May 10) Royal Applause 124 – Impetious 97 (Inchinor 119) [2015 6m **52**
6g 7m⁶ 7.2g t7.1m Sep 14] £14,000Y: fifth foal: half-sister to a winner in Spain by Cockney
Rebel: dam 1m winner (including at 2 yrs): modest maiden: best effort at 7f: acts on good
to firm going: sometimes in headgear. *Tim Easterby*

ISNTSHESOMETHING 3 br.f. Assertive 121 – Princess Almora 88 (Pivotal 124) [2015 **67**
–: 7m² 7g 7g 7.2g⁴ 7.2g³ 7d³ p7g Dec 2] fair maiden: stays 7f: acts on good to firm going:
front runner/races prominently. *Richard Guest*

ISRAFEL 2 b.f. (Apr 27) Dark Angel (IRE) 113 – Border Minstral (IRE) 69 (Sri Pekan **– p**
(USA) 117) [2015 t7.1f p6g⁶ t5.1m Dec 12] half-sister to several winners, including
smart 5f (including at 2 yrs) winner Oldjoesaid and 6f/7f winner Royal Normandy (both by
Royal Applause): dam 2-y-o 6f winner: no form in maidens: type to do better at 3 yrs.
Jamie Osborne

ISTIMRAAR (IRE) 4 b.g. Dansili 127 – Manayer (IRE) (Sadler's Wells (USA) 132) **–**
[2015 13g Apr 26] angular gelding: fairly useful at best: stays 1¾m: acts on polytrack and
good to firm going: often wears cheekpieces: often races prominently. *Philip Kirby*

ISTINFAAR (USA) 3 b.g. Street Cry (IRE) 130 – Yaqeen 107 (Green Desert (USA) 127) **85**
[2015 71p: t8.6g* 10m⁶ 10m t9.5g⁴ a9.9f a9.9f Dec 3] good sort: fairly useful performer:
won maiden at Wolverhampton in April: left Roger Varian after fourth start: stays 1¼m:
acts on tapeta and good to firm going. *A. bin Harmash, UAE*

ITALIAN BEAUTY (IRE) 3 b.f. Thewayyouare (USA) 117 – Edelfa (IRE) (Fasliyev **75**
(USA) 120) [2015 56: p8f 8m* 8.3m* 9g⁵ 7v* 8.5g* 8.3g 10s Oct 23] fair handicapper:
won at Salisbury (apprentice) and Windsor in June, Newbury in August and Epsom in
September: stays 8.5f: acts on good to firm and heavy going: often races prominently.
Timothy Jarvis

ITALIAN TOM (IRE) 8 b.g. Le Vie dei Colori 126 – Brave Cat (IRE) (Catrail (USA) **54**
123) [2015 69, a77: t6f p6f p6g May 20] smallish gelding: modest handicapper: stays 6f:
acts on all-weather, good to firm and heavy going: tried in cheekpieces. *Ronald Harris*

I T GURU 2 b.c. (Feb 19) Bahamian Bounty 116 – Never Say Deya 55 (Dansili 127) [2015 **59**
t5.1g⁴ 6m⁴ p6g² 6m³ 6m⁴ t6f Dec 22] modest maiden: left Richard Hannon after third start:
stays 6f: acts on polytrack and good to firm going: tried in tongue tie: temperament under
suspicion. *Noel Wilson*

ITLAAQ 9 b.g. Alhaarth (IRE) 126 – Hathrah (IRE) 113 (Linamix (FR) 127) [2015 93: **78**
12d⁵ 12.1m⁶ 12g May 13] attractive gelding: fair handicapper: stays 16.5f: acts on firm and
soft going: tried in cheekpieces prior to 2015: often wears tongue tie. *Michael Easterby*

IT MUST BE FAITH 5 b.g. Mount Nelson 125 – Purple Rain (IRE) 46 (Celtic Swing **95**
139) [2015 86: p6f* p6g⁵ f6g⁷ 6g 5d³ 5f* 5.1g* 6m⁴ 7v p5f t6g⁶ p5m⁶ Dec 27] useful
handicapper: second at Lingfield (½ length behind Iffranesia) in May, Thirsk (neck behind
Rex Imperator) in July and second at Wolverhampton (1¼ lengths behind Basil Berry) in
December: stays 6f: acts on polytrack, tapeta, good to firm and good to soft going: tried in
cheekpieces prior to 2015. *Michael Appleby*

ITO (GER) 4 b.c. Adlerflug (GER) 123 – Iota (GER) 115 (Tiger Hill (IRE) 127) **125**
[2015 10.2s* 9.9g* 10.9g* 11.9g² 11.9s⁴ 11.9s* 11.9f Nov 29]
    It took a high-class performer from Britain to lower the colours of Germany's
best horse Ito, but his defeat by Second Step, and another suffered when his rivals
caught him on an off-day, were his only defeats on home soil in 2015. On the other
occasions, the vastly improved four-year-old, a confirmed front runner, proved
impossible to catch and he has now won six of his eleven races, with none of his
victories gained with less than four lengths to spare. Unraced at two, Ito had just
four races as a three-year-old, winning a maiden at Cologne by five lengths and
then a minor event at Mulheim by six. On his final start in 2014 he was beaten
in a handicap at Baden-Baden, finishing only eighth of the eleven runners. A son

Pastorius - Grosser Preis von Bayern, Munich—
the best performance by a German-trained horse in 2015 as Ito slams his rivals;
odds-on Prince Gibraltar (second right among pursuers) stays on for second

of two German classic winners, Ito was clearly bred to be something more than a handicapper, though, and in the latest season he started living up to his pedigree in no uncertain terms. He made a spectacular reappearance in a minor event at Krefeld in March when he had the race won turning for home and hacked up by sixteen lengths. His opponents obviously didn't amount to much on that occasion, but it was equally clear that Ito had returned an improved performer and was ready for stepping up to better company. Two more wide-margin wins duly followed—not by so far as at Krefeld, but his rivals in a listed race at Hoppegarten in April and then in the Grosser Preis der Badischen Unternehmer at Baden-Baden in June were at least useful. At Hoppegarten he easily beat his smart stable-companion Kerosin by five lengths, in receipt of weight, while in the Group 2 contest at Baden-Baden he forged clear impressively in the final furlong for a four-length victory.

Given a break of two months, Ito then faced his biggest test so far in the Grosser Preis von Berlin back at Hoppegarten in August. As well as the Jockey Club Stakes winner Second Step, Ito's rivals included the Deutsches Derby winner Nutan who started favourite. Ito established a clear lead in the back straight and looked to have Second Step in trouble once in line for home, but while he was able to hold off Nutan's challenge, Ito could not repel the staying-on Second Step in the final furlong and went down by three quarters of a length. Ito's connections had won Germany's most important all-aged contest, the Grosser Preis von Baden, the year before when Ivanhowe who inflicted a shock defeat on the previously unbeaten Sea The Moon, the eleven-length winner of that year's Deutsches Derby. Baden-Baden was the next target for Ito (he had also been given a Prix de l'Arc de Triomphe entry) but he ended up missing the race with a temperature and, in his absence, it went to French-trained Prince Gibraltar. Ito was next seen in the Preis von Europa at Cologne at the end of September when his rivals included Nightflower and Sirius who had finished second and third behind Prince Gibraltar at Baden-Baden. Favourite here, however, was the Frankie Dettori-ridden Dubday, successful in the Glorious Stakes at Goodwood last time out, who had begun his career in Germany but had since become the top performer in Qatar. Ito made the running as usual but, evidently not at his best, was headed in the final furlong by Nightflower and then run out of the places close home by both Sirius and Dubday.

The Preis von Europa used to be Germany's final Group 1 of the year, but Munich now hosts the Pastorius Grosser Preis von Bayern at the beginning of November. Ivanhowe won the first running of the race in its new slot in 2014, that renewal attracting a bigger and more competitive field than the race had managed in its former position in the calendar in August, when squeezed between the other big races at Berlin and Baden-Baden. Having been beaten by the placed horses from the Grosser Preis von Baden, Ito started at 46/10 in an interesting clash with the Baden-Baden winner Prince Gibraltar who started odds on. Sirius was also in the field of seven, along with the Irish colt Success Days who was having his first start since sustaining an injury when last in the Derby on good to firm ground after relishing the mud in Ireland before Epsom. Prince Gibraltar had shown high-class form when seventh, for the second year running, in the Prix de l'Arc de Triomphe after Baden-Baden but Ito gave him a sound beating in customary style. Going clear early in the straight, Ito ran out a comfortable four-length winner from Prince Gibraltar who could only keep on without landing a blow, though he himself pulled four and a half lengths clear of the Deutsches Derby third Fair Mountain. Sirius was only fourth and Success Days tailed-off last. Ito might have a Japanese name but it did him little good in Tokyo where, four weeks later, he trailed in a remote last in the Japan Cup. He had the form to figure much more highly in what was a substandard renewal, but conditions were much firmer than he had faced previously and he couldn't pull off his usual front-running tactics from an unfavourable draw in the eighteen-runner field. Twenty years after Lando's success for Germany in the Japan Cup, Nightflower also failed to figure, finishing eleventh from the widest stall of all and not getting a clear run in the straight.

Ito (GER) (b.c. 2011)	Adlerflug (GER) (ch 2004)	In The Wings (b 1986)	Sadler's Wells / High Hawk
		Aiyana (b 1993)	Last Tycoon / Alya
	Iota (GER) (b 2002)	Tiger Hill (b 1995)	Danehill / The Filly
		Iora (br 1996)	Konigsstuhl / Incitation

As has been said, Ito is the product of classic German breeding. His sire Adlerflug won the Deutsches Derby (by seven lengths in soft ground) in 2007—he was also twice runner-up in the Grosser Preis von Baden—while, also in the Schlenderhan colours, Ito's dam Iota won the German Oaks, the Preis der Diana (by four lengths, also in soft ground) two years earlier. Iota was herself by a German Derby winner Tiger Hill, as was her own dam Iora, a daughter of the only horse to complete Germany's version of the triple crown Konigsstuhl. Iota was also a front runner, but gave a headstrong display when sent over to Britain for the Yorkshire Oaks in which she finished fifth behind Punctilious. Ito is Iota's fourth foal and third winner from as many foals to race. The filly Ituila (by Tertullian) showed fairly useful form, winning twice at around nine furlongs, while Iniciar (by Galileo), now hurdling with David Pipe, showed smart form at his best, winning at a mile and a half and contesting the Grosser Preis von Berlin and Grosser Preis von Baden in the role of Ivanhowe's pacemaker. Iota's first foal, the Giant's Causeway filly Iojo, was unraced but Iojo's own first foal Isidor (also by Adlerflug) showed useful form in the latest season, winning his first two starts and finishing eighth in the Deutsches Derby. Adlerflug is also the sire of Iota's three-year-old colt Ilkin who is unraced, as is her two-year-old filly by Galileo, Igraine. Grandam Iora was a useful winner at seven furlongs and a mile who was placed in listed company and finished fourth in the Henkel-Rennen, the German One Thousand Guineas. The dam of numerous winners, Iora has produced two other smart performers besides Iota. The listed-winning filly Ionnina was third in the Preis von Europa, while Illo, a Group 3 winner at Cologne over ten and a half furlongs (also winner of the same listed race at Hoppegarten which Ito won in the latest season), was exported to Australia where he contested the Melbourne Cup for Dart Cummings. This family has been with Gestut Schlenderhan, Germany's oldest private stud, for generations and Ito and Ivanhowe are distantly related, while Ivanhowe's dam Indigo Girl finished third to Iota in the Preis der Diana. Ito stays a mile and a half and acts on soft ground. He should again be a major force in Germany's top mile and a half contests in 2016. *J-P. Carvalho, Germany*

ITORIO (IRE) 3 b.c. Oratorio (IRE) 128 – Image Of (IRE) (Close Conflict (USA) 115)   **104**
[2015 97: 7g² 8g* 8.9g² 8g² 8.9m³ 10m 7g³ 7m³ 9.9g Dec 30] lengthy colt: useful performer: trained in Ireland for most of 2014: won minor event at Doha (by 2 lengths from Izzthatright) in February: ran 3 times in Britain, good third in handicaps at Epsom (3¼ lengths behind Al Bandar) and Chester (½ length behind Enlace) in June: off 6 months before final outing: stays 1m: acts on good to firm going: usually in blinkers in 2015. *Jassim Al Ghazali, Qatar*

IT'S ALL A GAME 4 ch.g. Sleeping Indian 122 – St Edith (IRE) 58 (Desert King (IRE)   **56**
129) [2015 7d 7m 8.3d⁶ 8.3g⁴ f8g⁵ f7m⁶ f8g Dec 18] modest handicapper: left Richard Guest after fourth start: stays 8.5f: acts on polytrack, fibresand and heavy going: usually wears headgear. *Nigel Tinkler*

ITS A SHEILA THING 2 ch.f. (Apr 24) Sir Percy 129 – Sefemm (Alhaarth (IRE) 126) **49**
[2015 5.1d⁶ 7g p8g p6g⁴ p7g² p8f⁴ p8g⁶ t9.5f³ t9.5f Dec 11] fourth foal: half-sister to 1¼m
winner Pennfield Pirate (by Bahamian Bounty): dam unraced: poor maiden: left Julia
Feilden after fifth start: stays 9.5f: acts on polytrack and tapeta: tried in hood. *Linda Jewell*

IT'S A STITCH UP 2 b.f. (Feb 13) Kheleyf (USA) 116 – Colourflash (IRE) (College **–**
Chapel 122) [2015 p7g t7.1m p7m Dec 31] half-sister to 3 winning sprinters, including
5f/6f winner Extremely Rare (by Mark of Esteem): dam unraced half-sister to dam of smart
sprinter Eastern Purple: no form: in blinkers last 2 starts. *Brian Meehan*

ITS IN THE RAIN (FR) 2 b.c. (Apr 7) Slickly (FR) 128 – Try The Air (IRE) (Foxhound **83**
(USA) 103) [2015 5g² 5g² 5.5g² 5.5g* 5f 5g Jun 29] €4,500Y: tall colt: seventh foal: half-
brother to 3 winners, including winner 7f-1¼m winner Hot Rod Mamma (by Traditionally)
and 5f/6f winner Economic Crisis (by Excellent Art): dam, of little account, half-sister to
high-class winner up to 1½m Storming Home: fairly useful performer: won maiden at
Marseilles Borely (by 4 lengths from Lespalem) in June: well-held last both subsequent
starts, in listed Windsor Castle Stakes at Royal Ascot and Prix du Bois at Chantilly: stays
5.5f: blinkered last 3 starts. *M. Palussiere, France*

ITSINTHESTARS 2 b.f. (Mar 5) Zoffany (IRE) 121 – Gemini Gold (IRE) 97 (King's **62**
Best (USA) 132) [2015 5m³ 6g 5m³ 5m Sep 27] £32,000Y: fifth foal: half-sister to 5.7f
winner Lady Gemini (by Myboycharlie) and winner up to 8.6f Disclosure (2-y-o 6f winner,
by Indesatchel): dam, 2-y-o 7f winner, half-sister to smart 1m winner Caughnawaga:
modest maiden: best form at 5f. *James Given*

IT'S ONLY BUSINESS 5 ch.g. Haafhd 129 – Noble Plum (IRE) 87 (King's Best (USA) **66**
132) [2015 72: 8d³ 8d³ t8.6g⁴ 10.4gᵖᵘ Jul 2] workmanlike gelding: fair handicapper: stays
1¼m: acts on polytrack and good to soft going: often wears headgear. *Clive Mulhall*

IT'S THE ICE 2 b.g. (Apr 17) Sakhee's Secret 128 – Vodka Shot (USA) 53 (Holy Bull **79**
(USA) 134) [2015 7m² 7d² 7.6g* Sep 11] fair performer: best effort when winning maiden
at Chester (by 2¾ lengths from Ian Fleming) in September: will stay 1m: sold 55,000 gns,
sent to USA. *Kevin Ryan*

IT'S TIME FOR BED 3 gr.f. Zebedee 113 – Mystical Ayr (IRE) 76 (Namid 128) [2015 **57**
–: 6g⁶ 6m⁴ 5g⁶ 5m 5m⁶ Sep 27] compact filly: modest maiden: best effort at 5f: usually in
hood in 2015. *Linda Perratt*

IVANHOE 5 b.g. Haafhd 129 – Marysienka 78 (Primo Dominie 121) [2015 77: 14.1g⁴ **75**
16m 16g⁴ 15.9m⁶ 17.1d² 16d 16s⁶ Oct 23] workmanlike gelding: fair handicapper: stays
17f: acts on good to firm and heavy going: tried in headgear prior to 2015. *Michael Blanshard*

IVANOVICH GORBATOV (IRE) 3 b.g. Montjeu (IRE) 137 – Northern Gulch (USA) **114 p**
(Gulch (USA)) [2015 79p: 13d* 15g* Aug 6] smart performer: won maiden at Navan (by
1½ lengths from Torcedor) in May: blinkered, better effort when winning handicap at
Leopardstown (by 2 lengths from Venezia) in August, slowly away: stays 15f: open to
further improvement: useful hurdler. *Aidan O'Brien, Ireland*

IVAWOOD (IRE) 3 b.c. Zebedee 113 – Keenes Royale 79 (Red Ransom (USA)) [2015 **118**
118p: 7m³ 8m³ 8g³ 7f 6.5g 7d Sep 12] strong, attractive colt: smart performer: third to
Gleneagles in both 2000 Guineas at Newmarket (beaten 3 lengths) and Irish 2000 Guineas
at the Curragh (beaten 1¼ lengths) in May, second/third starts: only creditable effort after
when seventh to Muhaarar in Prix Maurice de Gheest at Deauville fifth start (met some
trouble): stayed 1m: acted on good to firm and good to soft going: raced prominently: to
stand at Coolmore Stud, Co. Tipperary, Ireland, fee €9,000. *Richard Hannon*

IVEAGH GARDENS (IRE) 4 b.f. Mastercraftsman (IRE) 129 – Woodland Chant (USA) **110**
(War Chant (USA) 126) [2015 103: 8v 7v* 7s² 6v⁴ Nov 7] smart performer: won Athasi
Stakes at the Curragh (by 2 lengths from Found) in May: second in listed race at Leopardstown (½ length behind Sovereign Debt) in October: worth another try at 1m: raced only on
soft/heavy going: usually races nearer last than first. *Charles O'Brien, Ireland*

IVORS INVOLVEMENT (IRE) 3 b.g. Amadeus Wolf 122 – Summer Spice (IRE) 88 **78**
(Key of Luck (USA) 126) [2015 p7m p8f⁴ p8m⁵ t12.2g t12.2g⁴ 10.2s 8.5m³ p8f³ 10.2m²
8.3g* 10.2m⁴ 8m 8d 8s* 8d p8m⁴ Oct 21] fair performer: won handicaps at Nottingham in
May and Salisbury (apprentice) in September: stays 8.5f: acts on polytrack and soft going:
sometimes slowly away, often races in rear. *David Elsworth*

IVORS REBEL 3 b.c. Cockney Rebel (IRE) 127 – Sopran Cross (ITY) (Cape Cross (IRE) **93**
129) [2015 84: p5m* p5m³ t5.1f⁶ Mar 14] good-topped colt: fairly useful performer:
improved in 2015: won handicap at Lingfield (by 4½ lengths from Red Stripes) in January,
then left David Elsworth: creditable third in minor event there following month: best form
at 5f: acted on polytrack: front runner/raced prominently: dead. *Ruth Carr*

IVY MATILDA 2 b.f. (Mar 29) Monsieur Bond (IRE) 120 – Ingleby Princess 78 (Bold Edge 123) [2015 6m 5g 6s 7s Oct 16] second foal: half-sister to 6f winner Thornaby Princess (by Camacho): dam 5f-7f winner (including at 2 yrs): no form: tried in cheekpieces. *Michael Easterby*

IVY TRUMP 4 b.f. First Trump 118 – Ivy Bridge (IRE) (Namid 128) [2015 t7.1g Apr 6] lightly-raced maiden: form only on debut (in 2013): best effort at 6f. *Shaun Harris*

IXCHELL 2 b.f. (Mar 16) Equiano (FR) 127 – Amanda Carter 92 (Tobougg (IRE) 125) – [2015 7d p7g Nov 26] second foal: half-sister to smart 7f (including at 2 yrs) winner Salateen (by Dutch Art): dam, 9.3f-13f winner, also won over hurdles: well held in 2 maidens. *Mark H. Tompkins*

IXELLES DIAMOND (IRE) 4 br.f. Diamond Green (FR) 121 – Silk Point (IRE) 77 (Barathea (IRE) 127) [2015 84: 7f⁵ 7g 7.2s³ 7g² 7.2m² 8.1g⁶ 7v³ 7d⁵ p8m² Dec 31] leggy filly. fair handicapper: stays 7f: acts on good to firm and heavy going: tried in hood in 2015. *Richard Fahey*

IZBUSHKA (IRE) 4 b.g. Bushranger (IRE) 119 – Zaynaba (IRE) (Traditionally (USA) – 117) [2015 66: 14g Jul 13] maiden: fair at best: stays 1¾m: acts on polytrack, good to firm and good to soft going: often wears headgear: tried in tongue tie prior to 2015. *David Thompson*

I ZINGARI 3 b.c. Dansili 127 – Hi Calypso (IRE) 114 (In The Wings 128) [2015 70p: 76 10m³ 10d⁶ p12g⁶ Oct 6] fair maiden: should be suited by 1½m: acts on good to firm going: tried in hood in 2015: tends to race freely. *Sir Michael Stoute*

IZMIR (IRE) 2 b.f. (Feb 15) Sir Percy 129 – Limit (IRE) 69 (Barathea (IRE) 127) [2015 75 p 7g³ t7.1f* Nov 10] angular filly: half-sister to several winners, including 5f/6f winner Kellys Eye (by Noverre) and 2-y-o 6f winner El Manati (by Iffraaj), both useful: dam temperamental 2-y-o 7f winner: better effort when winning maiden at Wolverhampton (by 1¼ lengths from Initially) in November: will be suited by 1m: will go on improving. *William Haggas*

IZZTHATRIGHT (IRE) 3 b.g. Moss Vale (IRE) 126 – Miss Adelaide (IRE) 85 (Alzao 109 (USA) 117) [2015 101: 8g² 6g² 6g* 6g* 6m 6m Jun 27] smallish gelding: useful performer: won minor events at Doha in March and April: good second in Group 3 Qatar 2022 Invitation Cup on same course (short head behind Roi de Vitesse) on second outing: not at best in Britain on last 2 starts: stays 7f: acts on good to firm going. *Jassim Al Ghazali, Qatar*

IZZY TOO 5 b.m. Oratorio (IRE) 128 – Quiet Counsel (IRE) 81 (Law Society (USA) 130) – [2015 p12f 10m p10g p10g p10f Sep 17] close-coupled mare: no form: tried in cheekpieces: often in tongue tie. *Dr Jon Scargill*

J

JAADU (FR) 2 b.c. (May 9) Holy Roman Emperor (IRE) 125 – Reine Violette (FR) (Fly 85 To The Stars 124) [2015 5f⁶ 5m 6g⁵ 7m* 7d Aug 19] €16,000F, €90,000Y: compact colt: third foal: dam unraced: fairly useful performer: won nursery at Goodwood (by 1¼ lengths from Montsarrat) in July: stays 7f: acts on good to firm going. *Mick Channon*

JAAMEH (IRE) 2 b.c. (Feb 16) Iffraaj 127 – Miss Gibraltar (Rock of Gibraltar (IRE) 133) 71 p [2015 p6f⁴ 7d⁵ Oct 30] 75,000Y: useful-looking colt: fourth foal: brother to 2-y-o 6f winner Vigor and half-brother to useful winner Ajay (up to 1m Ewell Place (2-y-o 6f winner, by Namid): dam once-raced half-sister to useful 7f winner Johnny Castle: better effort when fifth in maiden at Newmarket (2 lengths behind Chelsea Lad) in October, hampered: open to further improvement. *Mark Johnston*

JAARIH (IRE) 3 ch.g. Starspangledbanner (AUS) 128 – Bridge Note (USA) 49 75 (Stravinsky (USA) 133) [2015 6m² 6d⁵ t5.1f² Dec 11] fair maiden: left George Peckham/ tongue tied, best effort when second at Wolverhampton final start. *George Scott*

JACBEQUICK 4 b.g. Calcutta 112 – Toking N' Joken (IRE) (Mukaddamah (USA) 125) 79 [2015 87: 7g³ 8.5g⁶ 7m³ 8d 7d⁴ 7.5f⁵ 7.5m 6.9d⁵ Jul 26] fair handicapper: stays 8.5f: acts on any turf going: usually in headgear nowadays. *Ollie Pears*

JACK BEAR 4 b.g. Joe Bear (IRE) 109 – Colins Lady (FR) (Colonel Collins (USA) 122) 74 [2015 53: 12.1s⁴ p13f* 14.1g³ p12m⁵ t16.5f³ Nov 16] fair handicapper: won at Lingfield in September: best effort at 13f: acts on polytrack and tapeta. *Jonathan Portman*

JACK BOND 3 ch.g. Monsieur Bond (IRE) 120 – Floods of Tears 62 (Lucky Story (USA) –
128) [2015 p7f t8.6f⁵ t8.6g t9.5g 8f p10m Jun 1] no form: tried in cheekpieces: often races
lazily. *Daniel Loughnane*

JACK CARTER 2 ch.g. (Jan 31) Medicean 128 – Astrodonna 83 (Carnival Dancer 123) **62**
[2015 6m³ 6m⁶ 6v⁶ p8m 6m Oct 3] workmanlike gelding: modest maiden: stays 1m: acts
on polytrack and good to firm going: tried in blinkers: often races prominently. *Mark H.
Tompkins*

JACK DEXTER 6 b.g. Orientor 118 – Glenhurich (IRE) 59 (Sri Pekan (USA) 117) [2015 **115**
121: 6d⁴ 6g⁴ 6g³ 5g² 5f 6f 6m 6g 6d 6v* Nov 7] lengthy gelding: smart performer: won
listed race at Doncaster (by head from Lightning Moon) in November: also ran well when
third in Duke of York Stakes at York (neck behind Glass Office) and second in Temple
Stakes at Haydock (neck behind Pearl Secret), both in May: has won at 7f, races at 5f/6f
nowadays: acts on any turf going: often races towards rear. *Jim Goldie*

JACK HOBBS 3 br.c. Halling (USA) 133 – Swain's Gold (USA) (Swain (IRE) 134) **129**
[2015 92p: 10d* 10.4m² 12m² 12m* p12g* 10d³ Oct 17]

After leading the Mercedes Formula One team to its second successive
constructors' and drivers' championships, Toto Wolff made an interesting point
about one of the unintended consequences of sustained success. 'It happened with
Michael Schumacher at Ferrari and even to Red Bull who had a superb brand but,
after winning the world title four times in a row, developed into an unsympathetic
brand. Dominance is bad for Formula One, it makes the racing boring, it becomes
predictable … the sport needs multiple winners, the odd freak result … it needs
the underdog to win. The moment you become a dominant force, you suffer and
your brand suffers. Nobody wants the establishment.' Mercedes and its two drivers
Lewis Hamilton and Nico Rosberg crushed the opposition in the latest season, when
the only meaningful rivalry—between the two fiercely ambitious Mercedes drivers
themselves—was kept in check by 'team orders'. The dominance of the Irish Derby,
in particular, by Ireland's Flat racing superpower Ballydoyle is also an illustration
of one of the great contradictions of sport—that winning too much can sometimes
be 'bad for the brand'. Before the latest season, eleven times winning trainer Aidan
O'Brien had saddled the Irish Derby winner in eight of the last nine years (including
seven years in a row between 2006 and 2012, a record for the number of consecutive
victories by a trainer in any of the ten traditional classics in England and Ireland).
The Ballydoyle near-monopoly, interrupted only by the Jim Bolger-trained Trading
Leather in 2013, undoubtedly contributed to a falling off in the competitiveness of
the race and started to cause some unrest (there wasn't a single overseas challenger
in 2009, 2012 and 2014).

The celebrations in the latest season for the one hundred and fiftieth running
of the Irish Derby were accompanied by reminders of earlier renewals won by some
of the sport's household names. No running was more significant, though, than that
in 1962 which heralded the arrival of Ireland's premier classic as a truly major race
and ended nearly a century of the Irish Derby being regarded as the poor relation of
its much mightier Epsom cousin. Sponsorship by the Irish Hospitals' Sweepstake
helped to generate one of the biggest prizes in European racing history up to that
time—the winning horse earned £49,777, nearly half as much again as the first prize
at Epsom that year and second only to the Arc—and Ireland at last had its very own
spectacular on the international stage. Larkspur, the first Epsom Derby winner to
take part in the Irish Derby since Orby won both races in 1907, started favourite
in a strong field of twenty-four but managed only fourth behind French-trained
Tambourine II. Interestingly, BBC TV's Saturday afternoon *Grandstand* programme
broadcast the Irish Derby live for the first time, but only after considerable discussion
among the powers-that-be about whether the race would be appealing enough for
British viewers; it was feared that those watching Wimbledon might turn over to ITV
when *Grandstand* switched from the tennis to the Curragh, but, in the event, five
and a quarter million remained tuned in to the BBC's coverage. Two years after that,
Santa Claus became the first of sixteen horses who have since gone on to complete
the Anglo-Irish Derby double as, for most of its modern history, the Irish Derby has
enjoyed an allure that has made it one of the key races in the European calendar.

Understandable concerns in recent years have produced suggestions for change—one of them being to follow the example of the Prix du Jockey Club and shorten the distance of the race—but innovative free entry incentives for the latest running helped to produce the type of Irish Derby field that was much more in keeping with its 'glory days'. The winners of the Irish Two Thousand Guineas, the Derby and the Prix du Jockey Club, along with the second, third and fourth in those races, qualified for free supplementary entry (worth €100,000) or a refund of original entry costs, if applicable. The offer also applied to the winners only of the Gallinule Stakes, the Nijinsky Stakes (Leopardstown), the Epsom Oaks, the Silver Stakes (Curragh), the Prix de Diane and two races at Royal Ascot, the Tercentenary Stakes and the King Edward VII Stakes at Royal Ascot. The latest Irish Derby— the eighth to be sponsored by Dubai Duty Free—may not have attracted either the winner of the Epsom Derby (Golden Horn ran instead in the Eclipse) or the Prix du Jockey Club (New Bay) but it did at least feature a lesser version of several defining clashes in the race between the winners of the two races. Sinndar and Holding Court had been the last of five such meetings between 1983 and 2000, but there had been none since. The runner-up in the Derby, Jack Hobbs, a stablemate of Golden Horn, lined up against the runner-up at Chantilly, Highland Reel, who led a Ballydoyle team which provided half the field and also included Giovanni Canaletto and Kilimanjaro, who had come fourth and sixth at Epsom and the Oaks winner Qualify. Qualify's presence—courtesy of the entry initiative in which the Curragh paid the €100,000 supplementary entry—evoked memories of the successes in the race of Oaks winners Salsabil and Balanchine in the early-'nineties (Qualify was the first filly to contest the Irish Derby since 1997). Also in the line-up was a second British-trained challenger, the Derby third Storm The Stars who, together with Jack Hobbs, was trying to become the first British-trained winner of the Irish Derby since Commander In Chief beat the Prix du Jockey Club winner Hernando in a rousing finish in 1993, the third time in six years that the Derby winner had beaten the Prix du Jockey Club winner at the Curragh.

The Derby form is usually reliable and Jack Hobbs had come out clear second best behind Golden Horn at Epsom, as in the Dante Stakes at York just over three weeks earlier (when Ballydoyle's leading winter fancies for the Derby, John F Kennedy and Ol' Man River, had both been well beaten). While Ballydoyle had seven of the top eight in the ante-post Derby betting before the spring trials, Clarehaven inmates Jack Hobbs, named after the legendary England cricketer, and Golden Horn had run only once as a two-year-old, both winning back-end maidens off the beaten track in the Midlands. Under the floodlights at Wolverhampton in December—the day after Boxing Day—is an unlikely place to see a potential classic winner but the well-backed Jack Hobbs won his maiden in the style of a good prospect, drawing clear of his strung-out rivals after being slowly into his stride and being forced to race wide early on. He earned his place in the Dante field when making a mockery of a BHA mark of 85 (he was put up 24 lb afterwards) in a handicap at Sandown in April on his reappearance, storming clear to win, eased down in the final fifty yards, by twelve lengths from some useful opposition. Although no match for Golden Horn at York or Epsom, Jack Hobbs acquitted himself really well and came out of the Derby, in which he led two furlongs out and kept on well, with his reputation enhanced (he was four and a half lengths ahead of Storm The Stars at the line and six and a half ahead of Giovanni Canaletto). Although his trainer John Gosden warned that Jack Hobbs 'still has a lot to learn', he started a shade of odds on at the Curragh, with Highland Reel a strong second favourite and expected to give him most to do. They bet 8/1 bar the two. Highland Reel failed by some way to reproduce his Chantilly form, and Qualify proved no match for the colts, neither landing a blow. Storm The Stars made the running and stuck to his task to repeat Epsom form with Giovanni Canaletto and Kilimanjaro, but the progressive Jack Hobbs proved to be in a league of his own, settling the issue in a matter of strides after leading on the bridle over a furlong out and forging clear (despite edging left as he had at Epsom) to win by five lengths and five and a half lengths from Storm The Stars and Giovanni Canaletto, with Kilimanjaro fourth, Highland Reel fifth, Qualify sixth, the Derby eighth Carbon Dating in seventh and Radanpour last of the eight.

Jack Hobbs gave his trainer John Gosden and jockey William Buick (who became the horse's regular rider when Godolphin bought a major share in him before the Derby) their first Irish Derby successes; Gosden completed the notable feat of winning the Derby and the Irish Derby in the same season with different horses (while Aidan O'Brien suffered the rare occurrence for him nowadays of winning neither the Derby at Epsom nor the Curragh, the first time that had happened since 2005). The first British-trained success in the Irish Derby for twenty-two years may help to reinvigorate Anglo-Irish rivalry in the race and should at least dispel any idea that the race might be in danger of turning into a purely domestic affair. Work still needs to be done, perhaps the most urgent task being to try to entice challengers from France to make the Irish Derby the international showpiece that it once was (Darsi was the last winner of the Prix du Jockey Club to contest the race, back in 2006, and there hasn't been a French challenge at all in the last eight years, a situation possibly linked to the reduction of the distance of the Jockey Club in 2005 from a mile and a half to ten and a half furlongs, France's major race for three-year-olds over the traditional Derby distance now being the Grand Prix de Paris which is run just over a fortnight after the Irish Derby (though Storm The Stars contested both).

It was announced after the Irish Derby that Jack Hobbs would miss the King George VI and Queen Elizabeth Stakes at Ascot and be rested for a tilt at the Prix de l'Arc de Triomphe, probably with a preparatory race in the Prix Niel. In the end, he stretched his legs in the totescoop6 September Stakes on the polytrack at Kempton, rather than risk what his trainer called a 'dawdle-and-sprint Arc trial in Paris'. He landed odds of 5/1-on easily from the handicappers Sweeping Up and Arab Dawn, still looking a leading contender for the Arc on the progressive form he had shown at Epsom and the Curragh. However, when it became clear that Golden Horn was also in line for an Arc challenge, Jack Hobbs was rerouted to British Champions' Day at Ascot later in October. 'I don't want his nose bloodied by Golden Horn for a third time,' his trainer said, 'he is an improving horse and he will get better at four and five.' Jack Hobbs was sent off at evens in a high-class field for the Champion Stakes but he didn't run up to his best in finishing only third, beaten a length and a quarter and half a length by Fascinating Rock and Found in a strongly-run affair in which Jack Hobbs had a pacemaker, whom he chased from the outset until going on over two furlongs out and being headed inside the final furlong, still seeing the race out well considering how hard he had worked racing close to the strong gallop. The Champion was just Jack Hobbs's seventh start and, given his physical scope, he should achieve even more as a four-year-old, especially back at a mile and a half. 'He's just a big, overgrown kid and needs to fill out, I couldn't be more thrilled with him, he'll be bigger and stronger next year,' his trainer said afterwards.

Dubai Duty Free Irish Derby, the Curragh—the Derby form is upheld as Jack Hobbs steps out of the shadow of his stablemate Golden Horn with a comprehensive success in Ireland's richest race; Storm The Stars is in turn well clear of the rest, headed by Giovanni Canaletto (striped cap), who does best of the four Ballydoyle runners

Godolphin's "Jack Hobbs"

Jack Hobbs (br.c. 2012)	Halling (USA) (ch 1991)	Diesis (ch 1980)	Sharpen Up
			Doubly Sure
		Dance Machine (b 1982)	Green Dancer
			Never A Lady
	Swain's Gold (USA) (b or br 2001)	Swain (b 1992)	Nashwan
			Love Smitten
		Golden Pond (b 1993)	Don't Forget Me
			Golden Bloom

Jack Hobbs, a strong, good sort in appearance with plenty of scope, is by the now-deceased Darley stallion Halling and was foaled when his sire was twenty-one. Halling won the Eclipse twice and the International at York twice for Godolphin in his racing days (having won the Cambridgeshire as a three-year-old for Gosden) and the sire of Jack Hobbs's dam, Swain, was another top-notch Godolphin performer on the track, twice winning the King George VI and Queen Elizabeth Stakes. Swain wasn't a success as a stallion, possibly because he was based in the States (where he had come very close to winning the Breeders' Cup Classic) rather than in Europe. Jack Hobbs's dam Swain's Gold won three races in the States as a three-year-old, all of them at around six furlongs, but she was brought back to Europe by Minster Stud, whose owner Willie Carson is the only man to have ridden an English classic winner whom he bred himself (1988 St Leger winner Minster Son). Minster Stud now has another classic winner to its name, Jack Hobbs having been sold for 60,000 guineas as a yearling, by which time the first two foals Swain's Gold had produced for the Carsons had both been successful—the fairly useful six/seven-furlong winner Mrs Greeley (by Mr Greeley) and the useful winner at up to eleven furlongs Niceofyoutotellme (by Hernando), the last-named still in training with Ralph Beckett in the latest season when he showed smart form. Golden Pond, the grandam of Jack Hobbs, won the Grade 2 Orchid Handicap over a mile and a half in the States but most of the family's bloodlines are European on the distaff side, Golden Pond herself winning as a three-year-old in listed company at a mile

514

before being exported to the States. Golden Pond's dam Golden Bloom was unraced but was bred by Jim Joel and was a half-sister to his Derby runner-up Connaught. Jack Hobbs stays a mile and a half, and acts on polytrack, tapeta and good to firm and good to soft on turf. He usually travels strongly in his races and often races prominently. *John Gosden*

JACK LUEY 8 b.g. Danbird (AUS) – Icenaslice (IRE) 78 (Fayruz 116) [2015 93: 5m 6g⁴ **88** 5d³ 5.1m 5m³ 5s* 5d³ 5g 5s⁴ 6s³ 5.1d⁵ Nov 4] rather leggy gelding: fairly useful handicapper: won at Beverley (by length from Cosmic Chatter) in July: stays 6f: acts on fibresand, good to firm and heavy going: tried in headgear. *Lawrence Mullaney*

JACK NAYLOR 3 b.f. Champs Elysees 124 – Fashionable 102 (Nashwan (USA) 135) **113** [2015 104: 8g⁴ 12g⁶ 12m² 12d⁶ 9.5s* Sep 20] smallish, workmanlike filly: smart performer: won Denny Cordell Lavarack & Lanwades Stud Fillies Stakes at Gowran (by 1¼ lengths from Easter) in September: in frame in Irish 1000 Guineas (2 lengths fourth to Pleascach) and Irish Oaks (very good 1¾ lengths second to Covert Love), both at the Curragh: stays 1½m: acts on soft and good to firm going. *Mrs J. Harrington, Ireland*

JACK NEVISON 2 b.g. (Apr 27) Dick Turpin (IRE) 79 – Creative Mind (IRE) 95 **82 p** (Danehill Dancer (IRE) 117) [2015 6m³ 5g³ 6.1v⁵ Oct 7] £10,000Y: fourth foal: half-brother to French 2-y-o 1m winner Imagine This (by Excellent Art) and French 2-y-o 6f winner Hidden Talent (by Kyllachy): dam 7f winner (including at 2 yrs): fairly useful maiden: third at Newbury (2½ lengths behind Adventurous) in July and Sandown (4¼ lengths behind Southern Belle) in September: will be suited by a return to 6f+: remains with potential. *Henry Candy*

JACK OF DIAMONDS (IRE) 6 b.g. Red Clubs (IRE) 125 – Sakkara Star (IRE) 94 **83** (Mozart (IRE) 131) [2015 82, a94: p8g³ p8g³ p10g³ t8.6m⁶ p10f 10m 10g⁴ p8g⁴ 10m⁵ 10m² **a92** 8.1g⁴ 8.1m² p8g p11g t8.6f* Nov 3] compact gelding: fairly useful handicapper: won at Sandown (apprentice) in July and Wolverhampton (by ¾ length from Best Example) in November: stays 1¼m: acts on all-weather and good to firm going: tried in headgear prior to 2015. *Roger Teal*

JACKPOT 5 b.m. Avonbridge 123 – Strat's Quest 65 (Nicholas (USA) 111) [2015 39, a51: **52** p8f* p8f p8f t8.6g 8.3m⁴ 7.6g 8s⁶ p8f p7f⁶ Nov 25] sturdy mare: modest handicapper: won at Kempton in January: stays 8.5f: acts on polytrack, tapeta and good to firm going: tried in cheekpieces: often races prominently. *Brendan Powell*

JACKSONFIRE 3 ch.g. Firebreak 125 – Fitolini 72 (Bertolini (USA) 125) [2015 –: f5g **54** t7.1m⁶ 5g 6m⁴ 6.1m² 6m Aug 9] modest maiden: stays 6f: acts on good to firm going: often in blinkers in 2015: often starts slowly, often races in rear. *Michael Mullineaux*

JACK'S REVENGE (IRE) 7 br.g. Footstepsinthesand 120 – Spirit of Age (IRE) 83 **98** (Indian Ridge 123) [2015 108: 8d 8m 8f 8.3d⁶ 7d 7s 7.6s² 8.3s⁴ 8d² 7v Nov 7] leggy gelding: useful handicapper: second at Chester (2¼ lengths behind Marcret) in September and Newmarket (1¼ lengths behind Emerald) in October: stays 1¼m: acts on polytrack, fibresand, soft and good to firm going: usually wears headgear: usually wears tongue tie: often races towards rear. *George Baker*

JACK THE LAIRD (IRE) 2 b.g. (Apr 1) Acclamation 118 – Pretty Demanding (IRE) — 84 (Night Shift (USA)) [2015 7g 6d p6g Oct 27] well held in maidens. *Dean Ivory*

JACOB BLACK 4 b.g. Amadeus Wolf 122 – First Eclipse (IRE) 66 (Fayruz 116) [2015 **105** 93: 8m² 8.1m* 8.1m² 8.1m⁵ 7m 7.9m⁶ Sep 9] lengthy gelding: useful handicapper: won at Sandown (by neck from Secret Art) in May: good second at Newmarket (2 lengths behind Musaddas) in May and Sandown (neck behind Basem) in June: stays 8.5f: acts on good to firm and good to soft going: usually leads. *Keith Dalgleish*

JACOB CATS 6 b.g. Dutch Art 126 – Ballet 61 (Sharrood (USA) 124) [2015 90: p11g* **88** p12g⁶ 14g 14m³ 14g 11.8g⁴ 12d³ p11d p12g p11g⁴ p12g Nov 4] angular gelding: fairly useful handicapper: won at Kempton (by 2½ lengths from Arc Lighter) in March: stays 1¾m: acts on polytrack and good to firm going: often wears headgear: tried in tongue tie prior to 2015: sometimes slowly away, usually races in rear. *William Knight*

JACOBEAN (IRE) 3 b.c. High Chaparral (IRE) 132 – Civility Cat (USA) (Tale of The **91 §** Cat (USA) 113) [2015 94p: 8v⁴ 9s³ 12v² 8m* Jun 19] rangy colt: fairly useful performer: won maiden at Limerick (by 2 lengths from Chenega Bay) in June: stays 1m: acts on good to firm and heavy going: often in hood in 2015: tried in tongue tie in 2015: front runner/races prominently, often travels strongly: has suspect attitude, and one to treat with caution. *Aidan O'Brien, Ireland*

JACOB'S PILLOW 4 b.g. Oasis Dream 129 – Enticing (IRE) 116 (Pivotal 124) [2015 **80** 92: 5m 6m 5g 6m² 6g⁴ 7m 6s⁶ 6m 6m* 5.3s⁵ p6f⁵ f6m³ f6g² f6g³ Dec 18] fairly useful performer: won claimer at Hamilton in September: left Jedd O'Keeffe after eighth start, Rebecca Bastiman after ninth: stays 6f: acts on fibresand, firm and good to soft going: tried in headgear. *Michael Appleby*

JACOBS SON 7 ch.g. Refuse To Bend (IRE) 128 – Woodwin (IRE) 97 (Woodman (USA) **82** 126) [2015 87: f12g² t12.2f⁴ 12s² 10m* 12d 12m⁵ f11g Dec 22] tall, rather unfurnished gelding: fairly useful handicapper: won at Leicester in May: left Michael Appleby after sixth start: stays 1¾m: acts on polytrack, fibresand, soft and good to firm going: tried in headgear. *John Balding*

JACQUOTTE DELAHAYE 4 ch.f. Kyllachy 129 – Mary Read 100 (Bahamian Bounty **91 §** 116) [2015 89: 7g² 7m 8g⁶ 7m p7g* p7g 7.2g Sep 29] fairly useful handicapper: won at Kempton in August: stays 7f: acts on polytrack, tapeta and good to firm going: often wears headgear: tried in tongue tie in 2015: unreliable. *David Brown*

JADAAYIL 2 b.f. (Feb 17) Oasis Dream 129 – Muthabara (IRE) 111 (Red Ransom (USA)) **88** [2015 6d² 6d⁴ Sep 4] well-made filly: second foal: dam, 7f winner (including at 2 yrs, and Fred Darling Stakes), half-sister to smart performers Maraheb (1m winner) and Mustadeem (stays 1¼m): fairly useful form when second of 13 to Czabo in maiden at Newbury in August: 8/11, well below that in similar event at Haydock, carrying head shade awkwardly and faltering final 1f. *Charles Hills*

JAGANORY (IRE) 3 b.g. Dylan Thomas (IRE) 132 – Jacquelin Jag (IRE) (Fayruz 116) **70** [2015 78: p7m⁶ p7f³ p7g⁶ 10.2f⁵ 7s³ 7.6d² 7m⁵ 6.1m³ 6.1m⁶ 6.1s⁵ 6g⁵ 5.1d⁴ 5.1d* 5.7d² 5f² 5.7m 5.7g Oct 18] fair handicapper: won at Chepstow in August: left David Evans after sixth start: stays 7.5f, but effective at shorter: acts on polytrack, firm and good to soft going: tried in headgear: front runner/races prominently. *Christopher Mason*

J'AIME LE FRANCAIS (IRE) 2 b.g. (Apr 1) Arakan (USA) 123 – Bayasiya (IRE) 93 **–** (Pennekamp (USA) 130) [2015 5f⁶ 5.7f⁶ 7.1g Jul 7] no form: in tongue tie last 2 starts. *David Evans*

JAIYANA 3 b.f. Dansili 127 – Jira 95 (Medicean 128) [2015 –p: t7.1f⁴ f6g t7.1g² t7.1f² **78** t7.1f⁴ p6m² t6f³ t6m Dec 12] fair performer: won maiden at Wolverhampton in November: stays 7f: acts on polytrack and tapeta: tried in cheekpieces in 2015: often races prominently. *James Tate*

JAKABY JADE 2 b.f. (Mar 27) Royal Applause 124 – Zia (GER) (Grand Lodge (USA) **93** 125) [2015 5m 5d* 8f* 8f⁶ Oct 10] rather leggy filly: fifth foal: half-sister to 3 winners, including 13f-16.5f winner Face Value (by Tobougg) and 5f winner (including at 2 yrs) Middle East Pearl (by Equiano): dam, Swedish 2-y-o 6f winner (placed up to 1½m), half-sister to smart stayer Zuider Zee: fairly useful performer: won maiden at Lingfield in July and listed event at Del Mar (by 1½ lengths from One Last Shot) in September: below form in listed race at Santa Anita final outing: stays 1m: acts on firm and good to soft going. *Doug F. O'Neill, USA*

JAKEY (IRE) 5 b.g. Cape Cross (IRE) 129 – Off Message (IRE) 84 (In The Wings 128) **100** [2015 89: 12g² 12m 10g* Jul 17] big gelding: useful handicapper: resumed progress when making most to win at Newbury in July by 2½ lengths from Elkaayed, well ridden: stays 1½m: acts on polytrack, good to firm and good to soft going: sometimes slowly away. *Pat Phelan*

JAKODIMA (IRE) 3 b.c. Kodiac 112 – Jasmina (GER) (Monsun (GER) 124) [2015 65: **74** 7m⁴ 8m⁵ 7g* 7.4d³ 9.9g⁴ 10g² Oct 3] fair performer: won claimer at Salisbury in July: stays 1¼m: acts on good to soft going: often races prominently: sold 11,000 gns, sent to Bahrain. *Richard Hannon*

JALLOTA 4 b.g. Rock of Gibraltar (IRE) 133 – Lady Lahar 106 (Fraam 114) [2015 111: **111** 7g⁵ 6g 7m 7.6g² 7g* 7f⁵ 7g⁶ 7s² 7s⁴ 7m Oct 3] tall, good-topped gelding: smart performer: won handicap at York (by head from One Word More) in June: good efforts after when fifth of 17 to Rene Mathis in Bunbury Cup (Handicap) at Newmarket and second of 19 to same horse in handicap at Goodwood, and when 1½ lengths fourth to Hathal in listed race at Newbury: stays 7.5f: acts on firm and soft going: often travels strongly. *Charles Hills*

JAMAICA GRANDE 7 ch.g. Doyen (IRE) 132 – Mary Sea (FR) 67 (Selkirk (USA) 129) **72** [2015 71: p8m* 10.2g⁴ May 31] workmanlike gelding: fair handicapper: won at Chelmsford in May: stays 1½m: acts on polytrack and good to firm going: tried in cheekpieces prior to 2015. *Charlie Wallis*

JAMAICA INN (IRE) 2 b.f. (Apr 11) Fastnet Rock (AUS) 127 – Vintage Tipple (IRE) — 117 (Entrepreneur 123) [2015 p8g Dec 15] 50,000F: sister to unreliable 1m winner (stays 1½m) Athassal Abbey and half-sister to several winners, including 11f winner (stayed 2m) King's Vintage (by King's Best): dam won Irish Oaks (also 2-y-o 7f/1m winner): 25/1, shaped as if needed experience when behind in maiden at Kempton, not knocked about. *John Gosden*

JAMAICAN BOLT (IRE) 7 b.g. Pivotal 124 – Chiming (IRE) 110 (Danehill (USA) **98** 126) [2015 105: 6d6 6g6 7d 6.5m 6g 6d 7v2 Nov 7] rather leggy, close-coupled gelding: useful handicapper: best effort of 2015 when second at Doncaster (length behind Withernsea) in November: stays 7f: acts on fibresand and heavy going: tried in headgear prior to 2015. *Geoffrey Oldroyd*

JAMEERAH 2 b.f. (May 7) Dansili 127 – Jira 95 (Medicean 128) [2015 6g5 p5g3 p6g2 **78** p6f* Oct 22] 65,000F: good-topped filly: second foal: sister to 6f winner Jaiyana: dam, 2-y-o 6f winner who stayed 8.5f, closely related to King Edward VII Stakes winner Plea Bargain and half-sister to smart performer up to 11f Lay Time: fair performer: won maiden at Chelmsford in October: stays 6f. *James Tate*

JAMES BOND GIRL (USA) 3 b.f. Giant's Causeway (USA) 132 – Swan Nebula **81** (USA) 92 (Seeking The Gold (USA)) [2015 8g 6g2 6g2 p6.5g4 7m3 7s3 t6f4 p6m3 Dec 27] $150,000Y: fourth foal: sister to useful 2-y-o 5f winner Vinson Massif and 1½m winner Elpida: dam, 2-y-o 6f/6.5f winner, half-sister to high-class winner up to 1m Poet's Voice: fairly useful maiden: second at Maisons-Laffitte in July and Deauville in August: left A. Fabre after sixth start, well below best last 2 outings (in hood final one): stays 6.5f: acts on polytrack, best turf form on good going. *Robert Cowell*

JAMESBO'S GIRL 5 ch.m. Refuse To Bend (IRE) 128 – Donna Anna (Be My Chief **86** (USA) 122) [2015 88: 5.5g3 6g3 6m3 6m 6m3 6g4 6g5 5.9s4 6d6 6d Sep 17] lengthy, workmanlike mare: fairly useful handicapper: stays 6.5f: acts on good to firm and heavy going: tried in cheekpieces/tongue tie prior to 2015. *David Barron*

JAMESIE (IRE) 7 b.g. Kodiac 112 – Pretty Woman (IRE) 45 (Night Shift (USA)) [2015 **110** 113: 5g 5g4 6g6 5s 6g 5d6 6g 5.8m* 6d6 p6g* p5g5 p6g2 p6m2 p6g2 Dec 11] deep-girthed gelding: smart performer: won minor events at Navan (by length from Alkasser) in September and Dundalk (by ¾ length from Eisenhower) in October: second in handicap at Dundalk (¾ length behind Grey Danube) in December: has won at 1m, best at 5f/6f nowadays: acts on polytrack, tapeta, good to firm and good to soft going: tried in blinkers: often in tongue tie in 2015. *David Marnane, Ireland*

JAMHOORI 7 b.h. Tiger Hill (IRE) 127 – Tanasie (Cadeaux Genereux 131) [2015 96: **90** p10f 10.4g3 10.2s6 10.4m5 t12.2f* Dec 14] well-made horse: fairly useful performer: won seller at Wolverhampton in December: stays 1½m: acts on polytrack, tapeta, good to firm and good to soft going: tried in headgear prior to 2015: sometimes in tongue tie prior to 2015. *Jeremy Gask*

JAM JAR 3 b.f. Duke of Marmalade (IRE) 132 – Rosinka (IRE) 116 (Soviet Star (USA) **83 p** 128) [2015 p8g5 8g3 p7g3 9.3m* p8f* p10f* Oct 28] third foal: closely related to 1½m winner Moshe (by Dansili): dam, 6f (at 2 yrs) to 11f (US Grade 3) winner, half-sister to smart French/US performer up to 1½m King's Drama: fairly useful performer: won handicaps at Chelmsford last 2 starts, both in October: stays 1¼m: acts on polytrack: often races prominently: quirky sort, but should do better still. *Hughie Morrison*

JAMMY GUEST (IRE) 5 b.g. Duke of Marmalade (IRE) 132 – Ardbrae Lady 104 **82** (Overbury (IRE) 116) [2015 92: 7d 6m p7g 6.1m 7g5 6g2 5.1g 6g5 p6f2 p6f3 p6g p6g Dec 7] fairly useful handicapper: best at 6f/7f nowadays: acts on polytrack and firm going: tried in blinkers in 2015: usually races towards rear. *George Margarson*

JAMMY MOMENT 4 ch.f. Duke of Marmalade (IRE) 132 – Special Moment (IRE) 72 **79** (Sadler's Wells (USA) 132) [2015 74: 12.5s 14g* 14m5 12.5m5 16m3 16.2m3 10g 15.8g6 12s Oct 27] fair handicapper: won at Musselburgh in May: stays 2m: acts on good to firm going. *Linda Perratt*

JANAAB (IRE) 5 ch.g. Nayef (USA) 129 – Mood Indigo (IRE) 91 (Indian Ridge 123) **80** [2015 79: 7m2 8s4 6.9m6 8d2 8.5m5 8g* 7.9g6 8m* 7.9d3 8d 8m 8d 8g6 8.3s5 Oct 28] fairly useful handicapper: won at Ripon in June and Haydock (apprentice) in July: stays 8.5f: acts on soft and good to firm going: usually wears headgear: usually wears tongue tie. *Tim Easterby*

JAN DE HEEM 5 ch.g. Dutch Art 126 – Shasta 81 (Shareef Dancer (USA) 135) [2015 56: **66**
12d⁶ 10m 9m⁴ 10.1m* 10.1g* 10.3g 9.9g⁵ 12.4g⁵ 9.9d* 10s⁶ Oct 16] sturdy gelding: fair
handicapper: won apprentice events at Newcastle in July and August and amateur event at
Beverley in September: stays 1½m: acts on good to firm and good to soft going: usually
wears headgear: often races towards rear. *Tina Jackson*

JAN SMUTS (IRE) 7 b.g. Johannesburg (USA) 127 – Choice House (USA) (Chester **75**
House (USA) 123) [2015 74: f14d³ 16m³ 15.8s 16.1d 14.1v² 16.1m² 14.6d² 16m² 16g²
15.8g⁴ 17.2d⁵ 15.8m⁴ 16d⁵ 13.7g² 14.4g² 13.8d⁶ 15.8g² 15.8s² Oct 27] lengthy, useful-
looking gelding: fair handicapper: stays 17f: acts on soft and good to firm going: usually
wears cheekpieces: usually wears tongue tie: races towards rear: consistent. *Wilf Storey*

JAN STEEN (IRE) 2 b.g. (Apr 2) Footstepsinthesand 120 – Mi Rubina (IRE) (Rock of **75**
Gibraltar (IRE) 133) [2015 6g⁵ 6m⁴ p6d⁵ 6s* p7g³ Nov 4] useful-looking gelding: fair
performer: won maiden at Brighton in October: stays 6f: acts on polytrack and soft going.
Denis Coakley

JAN VAN EYCK (USA) 5 ch.g. Raven's Pass (USA) 133 – Layounne (USA) (Mt **80**
Livermore (USA)) [2015 12.5s 12g⁵ 12d 12d 12g⁴ 12d⁴ p12g* p12g⁵ t12.2f* Dec 22] fairly
useful handicapper: won at Dundalk in November and Wolverhampton in December: stays
1½m: acts on polytrack, tapeta, soft and good to firm going: often wears headgear: often in
tongue tie in 2015: usually responds generously to pressure. *G. O'Leary, Ireland*

JAN VAN HOOF (IRE) 4 b.g. Dutch Art 126 – Cosenza 71 (Bahri (USA) 125) [2015 81: **95**
5g* 5m* 6m 6g⁶ 6d³ 6g² 6.1g 7d² t7.1f⁴ Nov 16] useful handicapper: won at Pontefract in
June and Newmarket in July: good second at Pontefract (nose behind Johnny Cavagin) in
September and Newmarket (½ length behind Popeswood) in October: stays 7f: acts on
tapeta, good to firm and good to soft going: tried in cheekpieces in 2015. *Richard Fahey*

JARGON (FR) 3 b.g. Naaqoos 117 – Cobblestone Road (USA) (Grindstone (USA) 124) **–**
[2015 91: 8m 8f 10m⁶ p8g p7.5g Dec 28] rather unfurnished gelding: fairly useful at best,
well held in 2015: left Michael Bell after fourth start: tends to race little. *S. Cerulis, France*

JARIR 2 b.g. (Mar 27) Oasis Dream 129 – Generous Lady 98 (Generous (IRE) 139) [2015 **– p**
7m 7m 8d Sep 3] 185,000Y: sturdy gelding: brother to useful winner up to 13f (stayed 2m)
Oasis Knight (2-y-o 9f winner) and half-brother to several winners, including very smart
winner up to 1½m/St Leger runner-up High Accolade (2-y-o 7f winner, by Mark of
Esteem): dam 1½m-1¾m winner: signs of ability in maidens: should be suited by at least
1m: remains open to improvement. *Richard Hannon*

JARLATH 4 b.g. Norse Dancer (IRE) 127 – Blue Lullaby (IRE) 82 (Fasliyev (USA) 120) **79**
[2015 p13.3g⁵ p11f⁴ p12g² p12m⁶ 12m Jul 11] workmanlike gelding: fair handicapper:
stays 1½m: acts on polytrack, good to firm and good to soft going: sometimes wears
blinkers: often races towards rear, often races freely. *Seamus Mullins*

JASIM JUNIOR 2 b.c. (Mar 21) Oasis Dream 129 – Junior Council (IRE) (Sadler's Wells **62**
(USA) 132) [2015 6m⁵ 6m⁶ 6d⁶ 7d⁵ Aug 24] rather dipped-backed colt: modest maiden:
best effort at 6f: tried in blinkers. *George Margarson*

JASMINE BLUE (IRE) 3 b.f. Galileo (IRE) 134 – Impressionist Art (USA) 70 (Giant's **95**
Causeway (USA) 132) [2015 70p: p8m³ 10m* 10m⁶ 10m³ 11.9m 9.9m Aug 12] well-made
filly: useful performer: won maiden at Newbury in April: best effort when third in listed
race at Newbury (1½ lengths behind Speedy Boarding) in June: stays 1¼m: acts on good
to firm going: usually races close up. *Paul Cole*

J'ASPIRE 3 b.f. Zamindar (USA) 116 – Ipsa Loquitur 69 (Unfuwain (USA) 131) [2015 –: **59**
7g 8.3m³ p8g⁵ Dec 2] modest maiden: stays 8.5f. *Stuart Williams*

JASSUR 2 b.c. (Feb 6) Canford Cliffs (IRE) 133 – Child Bride (USA) (Coronado's Quest **68**
(USA) 130) [2015 7g 7g⁵ 7m t8.6f⁵ p10f* t9.5f p10g⁴ Nov 26] fair performer: won nursery
at Chelmsford in October: best effort at 1¼m: acts on polytrack: often in headgear:
sometimes slowly away, often leads. *Marco Botti*

JAWAAYIZ 2 b.f. (Mar 26) Kodiac 112 – Silkenveil (IRE) 55 (Indian Ridge 123) [2015 **69 p**
p7g⁴ Nov 26] 11,000F, £68,000Y: second foal: sister to 2-y-o 5.7f winner Brown Velvet:
dam lightly-raced half-sister to smart winner up to 1¾m Excellent Result: 4/1, best of
newcomers when staying-on fourth in maiden at Chelmsford (1¼ lengths behind Crowning
Glory) in November: will improve. *Simon Crisford*

JAY BEE BLUE 6 b.g. Kyllachy 129 – Czarna Roza (Polish Precedent (USA) 131) [2015 **67**
87: p6g⁶ t7.1f t7.1f p6m⁵ 6m p6g 7v 6m³ 6m p6g⁶ Jul 14] close-coupled gelding: fair
handicapper: stays 8.5f, usually over shorter: acts on polytrack, firm and soft going: often
wears headgear: usually wears tongue tie: often races towards rear. *Sean Curran*

JAYEFF HERRING (IRE) 4 b.g. Excellent Art 125 – Biasca (Erhaab (USA) 127) [2015 **51** 57: p10f p13.3g^{ur} t12.2f^4 p12g^2 p12f p10m 11.8m May 25] modest maiden: stays 1½m: acts on polytrack and tapeta: in headgear in 2015: tends to find little. *Michael Bell*

JAY EM GEE (IRE) 2 gr.g. (Apr 7) Mastercraftsman (IRE) 129 – Pallas Athena (IRE) — (Sadler's Wells (USA) 132) [2015 6d Oct 26] 12/1, very green when well held in maiden at Redcar. *Bryan Smart*

JAYJINSKI (IRE) 2 gr.c. (Apr 10) Zebedee 113 – Prime Time Girl 73 (Primo Dominie **86** 121) [2015 p7g^2 7g^2 6g^4 Jul 25] 80,000Y: half-brother to several winners, including 5f-7.4f winner Doorock (by Redback) and 7f winner Cannon Bolt (by Chineur): dam ran twice: fairly useful maiden: best effort when second at Kempton (¾ length behind They Seek Him Here) in June. *Richard Hannon*

JAY KAY 6 b.g. Librettist (USA) 124 – Turn Back 73 (Pivotal 124) [2015 71: 7.2g^3 8s* **86** 8.3d* 7.2d* 7.2g^2 7v Oct 17] fairly useful handicapper: won at Ayr (twice, apprentice event first time) and Hamilton in July, and at Ayr again (by ½ length from Lady Ranger) in August: stays 8.5f: acts on fibresand, soft and good to firm going: wears hood: front runner/races prominently. *K. R. Burke*

JAZRI 4 b.g. Myboycharlie (IRE) 118 – Read Federica 90 (Fusaichi Pegasus (USA) 130) **70** [2015 69: p8g t8.6g^4 p10f^6 p10f^2 p10f^2 p10f^3 t8.6f p11f^3 p12f^4 11.9g^3 9.9d^2 p10g^3 t9.5g* 9.9m* p10g^3 10.2m^6 10.2m 10.2g p10d p10m* Dec 27] big, robust gelding: fair handicapper: won at Wolverhampton and Brighton in June and Chelmsford in December: stays 11f: acts on polytrack, tapeta, good to firm and heavy going: often wears headgear: tried in tongue tie in 2015. *Milton Bradley*

JAZZI TOP 3 b.f. Danehill Dancer (IRE) 117 – Zee Zee Top 116 (Zafonic (USA) 130) **120** [2015 79p: p8m* 10f* 12g^5 9.9m* 9.9g* 9.9m^2 Oct 4] tall, attractive filly: very smart performer: won maiden at Kempton (by length from Hundi) in April, listed Pretty Polly Stakes at Newmarket (by 1½ lengths from Zannda) in May and Prix de la Nonette at Deauville (by 1¼ lengths from Holy Moly) in August: further improvement when head second to Covert Love in Prix de l'Opera at Longchamp final start, challenging strongly from over 2f out: best form at 1¼m: acts on polytrack and firm going: often travels strongly. *John Gosden*

JAZZ LEGEND (USA) 2 b.c. (Apr 24) Scat Daddy (USA) 120 – Champion Ride (USA) **85** (Candy Ride (ARG) 133) [2015 5d* 5f 6.1m^4 p6g p5f Sep 17] $37,000Y, £170,000 2-y-o: third foal: half-brother to a winner in USA by Seeking The Dia: dam, US 6f winner, half-sister to dam of very smart US performer up to 1¼m Twirling Candy: fairly useful performer: best effort when winning maiden at Haydock (by 2¼ lengths from Miniaturist) in May: best effort at 5f: acts on good to soft going: often leads. *James Given*

JAZZY (IRE) 2 b.c. (Apr 18) Roderic O'Connor (IRE) 119 – Lucayan Beauty (IRE) 80 **66** (Marju (IRE) 127) [2015 5.9s 8.3d^2 8.3d^3 f8g^6 Dec 29] fair maiden: stays 8.5f. *Martin Keighley*

JEANIE'S PLACE 2 ch.f. (Mar 28) Compton Place 125 – Good Again 104 (Dubai **74** Destination (USA) 127) [2015 5m^5 6m^5 t5.1f^5 t6g^3 p6g^4 Dec 20] 6,000F, 24,000Y: lengthy filly: first foal: dam winner up to 1m (2-y-o 6f winner): fair performer: won maiden at Thirsk in May: creditable efforts in nurseries thid/fourth starts: stays 6f: acts on tapeta and good to firm going. *Richard Fahey*

JEBEDIAH SHINE 3 ch.f. Kyllachy 129 – Ardessie (Bahamian Bounty 116) [2015 65: **95** f5g p5f^2 p5m^2 5m* 5m^4 5.1g^2 5g^5 5m* 5m* 5g* 5g p5m^2 p5g* Dec 15] useful handicapper: won at Thirsk in June, Haydock and Beverley (twice) in August and at Kempton (by ¾ length from Royal Birth, showing further improvement) in December: raced only at 5f: acts on polytrack and good to firm going: tried in cheekpieces in 2015: usually leads. *David O'Meara*

JEBEL TARA 10 b.g. Diktat 126 – Chantilly (FR) (Sanglamore (USA) 126) [2015 53: **73** 7.1s 7g^3 7.1g^3 7.1s^6 8m^4 7.1m^5 7g^4 7.5f^4 7g^2 8s^2 8.5m^4 5.9g* 6m* 6g* 7.2g^5 6d* 6m^6 7s Oct 16] lengthy, good-topped gelding: fair handicapper: won at Carlisle (amateur) and Redcar in August and at Newcastle and Pontefract (apprentice) in September: stays 8.5f, effective at shorter: acts on fibresand, firm and soft going: often wears headgear: usually wears tongue tie: front runner/races prominently. *Alan Brown*

JEBULANI 5 b.g. Jelani (IRE) 115 – Susan's Dowry 74 (Efisio 120) [2015 –: 15.8m^6 **48** 12.1g^3 Sep 21] poor handicapper: stays 2m: best form on good going or softer (acts on heavy): tried in cheekpieces/tongue tie prior to 2015. *Barry Murtagh*

JEFFERSON CITY (IRE) 4 b.g. Montjeu (IRE) 137 – Reina Blanca 102 (Darshaan **85** 133) [2015 12m³ 12m⁶ p13.3g Jun 18] good-topped gelding: fairly useful maiden: reportedly lame final start: will stay beyond 1½m: acts on good to firm and heavy going. *Michael Appleby*

JELLICLE BALL (IRE) 3 b.f. Invincible Spirit (IRE) 121 – Dance Troupe 85 (Rainbow **106** Quest (USA) 134) [2015 104p: 7m² 8f 9.9g³ 8f⁴ 8.1m⁴ 8.5f⁶ 9f Sep 5] well-made filly: useful performer: second in Fred Darling Stakes at Newbury (¾ length behind Redstart) in April: left John Gosden after fifth start: stays 8.5f: acts on polytrack and firm going: often races towards rear. *H. Graham Motion, USA*

JELLY MONGER (IRE) 3 b.f. Strategic Prince 114 – Royal Jelly 82 (King's Best **90** (USA) 132) [2015 88: 7m⁴ 8m 8s⁶ 6m 10g⁶ p10m p10g⁶ Dec 7] tall filly: fairly useful performer: stays 1¼m: acts on polytrack and good to firm going: often in headgear in 2015: has looked ungainly. *Dominic Ffrench Davis*

JERSEY BREEZE (IRE) 2 gr.f. (Jan 20) Dark Angel (IRE) 113 – Sixfields Flyer (IRE) **84** 66 (Desert Style (IRE) 121) [2015 5d³ 5m* 6f 6s Oct 23] €105,000Y: fourth foal: sister to 2-y-o 6f/7f winner Malachim Mist and half-sister to 2 winners by Camacho, including winner up to 1¼m (in Germany) Rich Forever (2-y-o 6f winner): dam maiden (stayed 1m): fairly useful performer: won maiden at Leicester in May, easily best effort: should stay 6f. *Mick Channon*

JERSEY BROWN (IRE) 4 br.f. Marju (IRE) 127 – Daniysha (IRE) 76 (Doyoun 124) **74** [2015 75: 8.3m 8m³ 8v⁴ 8g* 8f² 8m⁴ 8.1g⁵ 8.3m⁵ 8m³ 8d³ 8.3s Sep 21] unfurnished filly: fair handicapper: won at Bath in June: stays 8.5f: acts on firm and soft going: usually travels strongly in rear. *Mick Channon*

JERSEY BULL (IRE) 3 b.g. Clodovil (IRE) 116 – Chaguaramas (IRE) 93 (Mujadil **71** (USA) 119) [2015 71, a62: p7f³ p8f³ p7m p8f⁴ 8f⁴ 10.2f p8g 8d p8g³ 8g³ 7d³ p8m p16g⁵ p12g* Dec 15] good-quartered gelding: fair handicapper: won at Kempton in December: stays 1½m: acts on polytrack, firm and good to soft going: often wears headgear: usually races nearer last than first. *Michael Madgwick*

JERSEY CREAM (IRE) 4 ch.f. Iffraaj 127 – Unicamp 84 (Royal Academy (USA) 130) **67** [2015 55, a68: p10f⁴ p12f* p12m³ 10m⁴ p12f p10f² p10f⁶ Oct 8] sturdy filly: fair handicapper: won at Lingfield in May: stays 1½m: acts on polytrack and tapeta: sometimes slowly away, usually races nearer last than first. *Andi Brown*

JERSEY JEWEL (FR) 3 b.f. Naaqoos 117 – Nikolenka (IRE) (Indian Ridge 123) [2015 **78** 73: 10m⁶ 10.2m² 9.9d³ 12m⁴ 13m 11.6m⁶ 12g⁶ 11.6d² Aug 29] workmanlike filly: fair handicapper: won at Newbury in June: stays 1½m: acts on polytrack, good to firm and good to soft going: sometimes slowly away, usually races nearer last than first. *Richard Hannon*

JERSEY ROY 2 b.g. (Mar 11) Major Cadeaux 121 – Charlie Girl 70 (Puissance 110) **63 p** [2015 6s t7.1f t7.1f⁶ Nov 20] £10,500Y: half-brother to several winners, including useful 2-y-o 6f winners Josh (by Josr Algarhoud) and Valley of Fire (by Firebreak): dam 2-y-o 5f winner: modest maiden: best effort when sixth at Wolverhampton (3 lengths behind Rebel Lightning) final start: open to further improvement. *Richard Fahey*

JESS 2 b.f. (Mar 15) Equiano (FR) 127 – Poyle Meg 91 (Dansili 127) [2015 6f 6m⁵ 7m³ 6g⁵ **66** 5m⁶ Aug 16] £22,000Y: third foal: dam, 8.3f-1¼m winner, closely related to useful performer up to 2m Poyle Thomas: fair maiden: best effort at 6f: acts on good to firm going: sometimes slowly away, front runner/races prominently, often travels strongly. *Kevin Ryan*

JESSIE ALLAN (IRE) 4 b.f. Bushranger (IRE) 119 – Ishimagic 52 (Ishiguru (USA) **–** 114) [2015 6d 6g⁵ 6s⁵ Aug 1] second foal: dam, maiden (stayed 1m), closely related to smart US Grade 2 8.5f/1¼m winner Foxysox: no form. *Jim Goldie*

JESSIE B GOODE (IRE) 2 b.f. (Mar 27) Approve (IRE) 112 – Musica E Magia (IRE) **67** (King's Theatre (IRE) 128) [2015 6g 5g³ 5.2m 6g* 6m* 5.9m p7g⁴ Sep 22] €10,000Y: rather leggy filly: fourth foal: sister to 2-y-o 5f/6f winner Johnny B Goode and half-sister to 7f winner Aanna Heneeih (by Desert Style): dam Italian 1¼m winner: fair performer: won sellers at Thirsk in July and Redcar in August: stays 6f: acts on good to firm going: sold 4.500 gns, sent to Bahrain. *Richard Fahey*

JESSIE K 4 ch.f. Compton Place 125 – Fairnilee 67 (Selkirk (USA) 129) [2015 –: 7.2d Jun **–** 8] poor maiden: left Patrick J. Flynn/off 12 months, well held in handicap at Ayr: tried in visor. *David O'Meara*

JESSY MAE 4 b.f. Oratorio (IRE) 128 – Welsh Valley (USA) 64 (Irish River (FR) 131) **38**
[2015 60: t7.1g f7d⁵ t9.5f⁶ p8m p12f Apr 15] poor maiden: left Derek Haydn Jones after
second start: stays 1m: acts on all-weather: tried in headgear: often races prominently.
Alan Bailey

JE T'AIME ENCORE 3 b.g. Acclamation 118 – Mimisel 92 (Selkirk (USA) 129) [2015 **67**
59: p9.9g 7.5d* 7.5s 7.5s⁴ p8g⁴ 8m t7.1g 8.3g⁴ 8.1g* p8f 8g⁶ 9.9s³ 7s² 8v⁴ f8g p10m Dec
16] fair performer: won claimer at Cagnes-sur-Mer in January and seller at Chepstow in
August: stays 1m: acts on polytrack and soft going. *Gay Kelleway*

JETHOU ISLAND 4 ch.f. Virtual 122 – Lihou Island 89 (Beveled (USA)) [2015 73: **63**
10.2g⁶ p10f⁶ t8.6f⁵ t12.2m t12.2m⁶ Dec 18] modest maiden: left Henry Candy after third
start: stays 1½m: acts on polytrack, tapeta and good to soft going: tried in tongue tie in
2015: front runner/races prominently. *David Menuisier*

JET MATE (IRE) 3 ch.g. Fast Company (IRE) 126 – Anazah (USA) (Diesis 133) [2015 **–**
63: p8g⁵ Apr 1] modest handicapper: stayed 8.5f: acted on polytrack and tapeta: wore
headgear: often raced prominently: dead. *William Muir*

JET SETTING (IRE) 2 b.f. (Feb 16) Fast Company (IRE) 126 – Mean Lae (IRE) 96 **94**
(Johannesburg (USA) 127) [2015 5d⁴ 5.3m² 6m² 6.5m 7s³ Nov 24] €7,000F: close-coupled
filly: second foal: dam 7f winner: fairly useful maiden: left Richard Hannon, first-time
cheekpieces and improved form when third in listed race at Chantilly (2½ lengths behind
La Cressonniere) in November: will stay 1m: acts on soft going. *A. P. Keatley, Ireland*

JEWELLED PRINCESS 2 ch.f. (Feb 25) Zamindar (USA) 116 – Diamond Lass (IRE) **–**
72 (Rock of Gibraltar (IRE) 133) [2015 6d Sep 4] third foal: half-sister to 2-y-o 6f winner
Mr Carbonfootprint (by Footstepsinthesand): dam maiden (stayed 1¼m): 10/1, tailed off in
maiden at Haydock. *Richard Fahey*

JEWELLERY QUARTER (IRE) 2 b.f. (Mar 27) Lilbourne Lad (IRE) 111 – Mary **–**
Spring Rice (IRE) 62 (Saffron Walden (FR) 123) [2015 5m t6g 6.1s⁵ p8g p6g Sep 22]
€8,000Y: rather unfurnished filly: second foal: dam maiden (third at 1½m), half-sister to
smart German performers up to 1¼m Fight Club and Flambo: no form: tried in hood.
Jamie Osborne

JEZZA 9 br.g. Pentire 132 – Lara (GER) 103 (Sharpo 132) [2015 76: p16g f14m Dec 8] **61**
workmanlike gelding: modest handicapper: stays 16.5f: acts on polytrack, fibresand, best
turf form on good going or softer (acts on heavy): wears headgear/tongue tie: sometimes
slowly away, usually races nearer last than first. *Victor Dartnall*

JILLANAR (IRE) 3 b.f. Lawman (FR) 121 – Lunduv (IRE) 103 (Pivotal 124) [2015 71: **77**
p7m⁴ t7.1g² t6f³ 6g³ 5g³ t6g2 6.9m* 5.9g³ Aug 19] fair performer: won maiden at Carlisle
in August: stays 7f: acts on polytrack, tapeta, firm and good to soft going: sometimes in
hood in 2015: front runner/races prominently. *David O'Meara*

JIM DANDY 2 ch.g. (Apr 14) Dandy Man (IRE) 123 – Noctilucent (JPN) (Lammtarra **81 p**
(USA) 134) [2015 7.1g⁶ 8m* Sep 11] 40,000 2-y-o: sturdy gelding: half-brother to 1m
winner Nadema Rose (by Elnadim): dam, useful French winner up to 1½m (2-y-o 1m
winner), sister to smart 1¼m-1½m performer Simeon and closely related to Park Hill
Stakes winner Noble Rose: better effort when winning maiden at Salisbury (by neck from
Al Hamd) in September, shaping as though may stay bit beyond 1m: should do better still.
Alan King

JIMENEZ (IRE) 2 b.c. (Apr 10) Acclamation 118 – Fritta Mista (IRE) (Linamix (FR) **75**
127) [2015 6m⁴ 7m³ Jun 27] fair form when in frame in maidens at Newmarket in May and
Doncaster (1¾ lengths third to Platitude) in June. *Brian Meehan*

JIMMY CRACKLE (IRE) 4 b.g. Intense Focus (USA) 117 – Slieve (Selkirk (USA) **52**
129) [2015 63: t7.1g 8d 10.1m Jun 6] modest maiden: stays 1¼m: acts on soft going:
sometimes wears cheekpieces. *Brian Ellison*

JIMMY'S HALL 3 b.g. Kyllachy 129 – Up At Dawn 51 (Inchinor 119) [2015 73: p5g⁶ **81**
t6g⁶ p7g⁶ p7g⁶ 6v* 6d⁵ 5.7f⁶ 6m* t6g⁶ 6g⁴ 8g p6.5g 6g 6g⁴ p7d t7.1f³ p6g Dec 28] fairly
useful handicapper: won at Brighton in May and July: stays 7f: acts on polytrack, tapeta,
good to firm and heavy going: often wears headgear: usually races nearer last than first:
none too consistent. *J. S. Moore*

JIMMY STYLES 11 ch.g. Inchinor 119 – Inya Lake 101 (Whittingham (IRE) 104) [2015 **88**
108: 6g 6m Jun 27] strong gelding: one-time smart performer, just fairly useful in 2015:
stayed 6.5f: acted on firm and good to soft going: often wore headgear: retired. *Clive Cox*

JINKO'S APPROVAL (IRE) 2 ch.c. (Mar 28) Approve (IRE) 112 – Felin Gruvy (IRE) **67**
69 (Tagula (IRE) 116) [2015 6m 6m⁵ 6g⁵ 6.1m³ 6g Jul 30] workmanlike colt: fair maiden:
raced only at 6f: acted on good to firm going: dead. *Ed de Giles*

JINKY 7 b.g. Noverre (USA) 125 – Aries (GER) 79 (Big Shuffle (USA) 122) [2015 79: 6g* **79**
5s⁵ 6d⁴ 7.2d 6m⁵ 6g 5g 6g⁶ 6d* 5g 5g⁴ 6m² 6g 5g Oct 13] lengthy gelding: fair handicapper:
won at Ayr in April and August: stays 7f: acts on polytrack, good to firm and heavy going.
Linda Perratt

JINSHA LAKE (IRE) 3 b.c. Galileo (IRE) 134 – Al Ihsas (IRE) 99 (Danehill (USA) 126) **94**
[2015 82p: 8d* 11m⁵ 8.5g³ 9.5v⁵ Sep 20] fairly useful performer: won maiden at Navan in
May: stays 11f: acts on good to firm and good to soft going: usually in tongue tie in 2015:
often races prominently: has joined Evan Williams. *Aidan O'Brien, Ireland*

JINTSHI 2 b.c. (May 8) Poet's Voice 126 – Ivory Gala (FR) 101 (Galileo (IRE) 134) [2015 **69 p**
6m⁵ Jun 25] 72,500Y: fifth foal: closely related to smart 2-y-o 1m winner (stays 1½m) Red
Galileo (by Dubawi) and half-brother to useful UAE 6f/7f winner Okimono (by Invincible
Spirit) and 1½m winner Okavango (by Nayef): dam 1½m winner: 9/1, some encouragement
when fifth in maiden at Newmarket (4 lengths behind Experto Crede) in June: bred to stay
1m+: entitled to progress. *Mark Johnston*

JIVE TIME 2 b.c. (Apr 12) Motivator 131 – Lindy Hop (IRE) 68 (Danehill Dancer (IRE) **67 p**
117) [2015 p8g⁶ Dec 16] 15,000Y: second foal: half-brother to 2-y-o 6f winner Jive (by
Major Cadeaux): dam, maiden (stayed 7f), half-sister to Derby runner-up At First Sight:
33/1, showed some promise when sixth in maiden at Kempton (5 lengths behind Ballard
Down) in December: will be better for experience. *James Tate*

JOALDO 3 b.g. Monsieur Bond (IRE) 120 – Labba (Tiger Hill (IRE) 127) [2015 7g⁵ 7s⁶ **–**
Jul 29] well held in 2 maidens. *Antony Brittain*

JO BIBIDIA 3 ch.f. Joe Bear (IRE) 109 – Veni Bidi Vici 55 (Horse Chestnut (SAF) 119) **–**
[2015 58: p11g t9.5g Jul 8] maiden: no form in 2015: left Jonathan Portman after first start:
stays 8.5f: acts on polytrack and tapeta: often starts slowly. *Zoe Davison*

JODIES JEM 5 br.g. Kheleyf (USA) 116 – First Approval 78 (Royal Applause 124) [2015 **92**
98: p8f⁴ t8.6f* p8g⁵ Dec 9] sturdy gelding: fairly useful handicapper: won at Wolverhampton (dead-heated with King Torus) in October: stays 1¼m: acts on polytrack, tapeta,
soft and good to firm going: tried in cheekpieces prior to 2015. *William Jarvis*

JODY 2 ch.f. (May 8) Kheleyf (USA) 116 – Canis Star (Wolfhound (USA) 126) [2015 6g **–**
Jun 30] £2,000Y: half-sister to 1m-17f winner Jawaab (by King's Best) and useful 6f/7f
winner Cansili Star (by Dansili): dam unraced: 100/1, well held in maiden at Hamilton.
Susan Corbett

JOE PACKET 8 ch.g. Joe Bear (IRE) 109 – Costa Packet (IRE) (Hussonet (USA)) [2015 **80 §**
89§: 6g 6m⁵ 6m* 6g⁶ Jul 17] quite good-topped gelding: fairly useful handicapper: won at
Salisbury (by length from Monarch Maid) in July: stays 7f: acts on firm and soft going:
tried in headgear prior to 2015: one to treat with caution. *Jonathan Portman*

JOEY BLACK 3 b.g. Kheleyf (USA) 116 – Black Moma (IRE) 80 (Averti (IRE) 117) **62**
[2015 –: 6d 10.1d³ 10.1m⁵ 8m 12g⁶ 6s⁴ 5m⁴ 6d⁵ 6m³ Aug 20] modest maiden: has form
from 6f to 1¼m: acts on soft and good to firm going: tried in blinkers: sent to Greece.
Susan Corbett

JOEY'S DESTINY (IRE) 5 ch.g. Kheleyf (USA) 116 – Maid of Ailsa (USA) 65 (Pivotal **101**
124) [2015 102: 6m 6d³ 6d 7v⁵ Nov 7] leggy gelding: useful handicapper: best effort of
2015 when third at Goodwood (½ length behind Iseemist) in October: stays 7f: acts on soft
and good to firm going: tried in cheekpieces prior to 2015: often races towards rear.
George Baker

JOFRANKA 5 b.m. Paris House 123 – Gypsy Fair 69 (Compton Place 125) [2015 85: p5g⁵ **67**
5g⁶ Jun 18] fair handicapper: best form at 5f: acts on polytrack, soft and good to firm going:
tried in blinkers prior to 2015: usually leads. *David Barron*

JOHANNES VERMEER (IRE) 2 b.c. (Apr 20) Galileo (IRE) 134 – Inca Princess **115**
(IRE) 82 (Holy Roman Emperor (IRE) 125) [2015 7.5g³ 8.5m* 8d* 8m⁴ 8d² 7s*
Nov 1]
       There can't have been many races that have been won by different horses
named after the same person but, when Johannes Vermeer continued his steady
progress to give Aidan O'Brien his fourth win in the Criterium International at Saint-
Cloud in early-November, he followed the same stable's Mount Nelson (2006), Jan
Vermeer (2009)—another alias of the Dutch painter—and Roderic O'Connor (2010).
Johannes Vermeer was ridden in two of his three Group 1 starts—including in the
Criterium International—by Ryan Moore who took over from Joseph O'Brien as
number-one jockey to the Coolmore partners in April. Moore's dedication to the
task was in evidence from the start, when he rode three horses in Group 1s (including

Cox Plate winner Adelaide who was having his first start for Chris Waller) at Randwick and, with the help of the time difference, three horses (including ante-post Derby favourite John F Kennedy) at Leopardstown the following day. In late-October/early-November, Moore rode at Keeneland, Saint-Cloud and Flemington in the space of four days. Moore's win aboard Johannes Vermeer in the Criterium International came just sixteen hours after he had ridden Found to success in the Breeders' Cup Turf. The Criterium International was run over seven furlongs for the first time, having swapped distances with what is now the one-mile (which it always was before 2001) Prix Jean-Luc Lagardere (Grand Criterium) in which Johannes Vermeer had finished fourth, just eight days after he had fared best of the three runners from Ballydoyle in the Racing Post Trophy when runner-up to Marcel. Both on his breeding and his running style, Johannes Vermeer may have more to offer as he gets a stiffer test of stamina—he's likely to need testing conditions if he goes for a Guineas—though the fact that he is freely available at 20/1 for the Derby at the time of writing suggests that Ballydoyle probably have stronger contenders for the Epsom classic among Johannes Vermeer's less exposed stablemates.

Johannes Vermeer was beaten five and a half lengths at odds-on on his debut in a Tipperary maiden in July, but he clearly learned plenty from that experience and made no mistake in a similar race at Killarney the following month, winning by four and a quarter lengths from Dawenkour. Johannes Vermeer made all over the extended mile, and also finished strongly when following up in the Group 3 Willis Champions Juvenile Stakes over a mile at Leopardstown in September, having a length and a half to spare over True Solitaire, with the favourite Sanus Per Aquam in third. Johannes Vermeer gave Ballydoyle its fourth straight success in the race following John F Kennedy, Australia (who was owned, like Johannes Vermeer, by the Coolmore partners and China Horse Club chairman Teo Ah Khing) and Battle of Marengo (back in 2012 when it was a listed event). Shogun, who looked like the first string for Ballydoyle at Leopardstown before being withdrawn, was in the field when Johannes Vermeer ran next in the Prix Jean-Luc Lagardere, in which

Criterium International, Saint-Cloud—a reduction in trip from a mile to seven furlongs for this Group 1 in which only two of the runners are trained in France; Ballydoyle's Johannes Vermeer (far side) finds extra to repel British-trained Stormy Antarctic

Ryan Moore chose to ride Johannes Vermeer who started the 22/10 favourite. Back on firmer ground, Johannes Vermeer appeared to find the test on the sharp side (as did sixth-placed Shogun, a €400,000 brother to Oaks winner Qualify) and managed only fourth of eleven to Ultra, challenging over a furlong out and keeping on when a bit short of room late on. Johannes Vermeer improved by two places in the Racing Post Trophy at Doncaster twenty days later, with stablemates Port Douglas and Deauville fourth and fifth, first-time cheekpieces not having the desired effect on the latter. Like the winner Marcel, Johannes Vermeer skirted trouble in running—third-placed Foundation had a nightmare passage—but he was unable to quicken as well as Marcel, albeit staying on to finish clear second. Johannes Vermeer's appearance in the shorter Criterium International came as something of a surprise as he might have been expected to prove better suited by the ten-furlong Criterium de Saint-Cloud later on the card (in which the same connections' Idaho started favourite and finished only fourth). As it unfolded, a well-run race on soft ground placed the emphasis on stamina and Johannes Vermeer stuck to his task to win by a head from Stormy Antarctic and six others (the runner-up came out best of the five runners from Britain). The first three home, completed by home-trained Attendu, had all run at a mile on their previous start. The whole field came wide in the straight, as is usual at Saint-Cloud when the going is on the soft side, and Johannes Vermeer came to challenge under two furlongs out and led soon afterwards before finding extra to repel the persistent runner-up in the final furlong.

Johannes Vermeer (IRE) (b.c. 2013)	Galileo (IRE) (b 1998)	Sadler's Wells (b 1981)	Northern Dancer / Fairy Bridge
		Urban Sea (ch 1989)	Miswaki / Allegretta
	Inca Princess (IRE) (b 2008)	Holy Roman Emperor (b 2004)	Danehill / L'On Vite
		Miletrian (b 1997)	Marju / Warg

Johannes Vermeer cost €300,000 as a yearling and he is the first foal out of Inca Princess who was originally bought by the Coolmore partners for €140,000 as a yearling and raced three times as a two-year-old for Aidan O'Brien, winning a six-furlong maiden at Fairyhouse, before presumably being sold on in a private deal. Inca Princess is from the first crop of Holy Roman Emperor and is closely related to the ten-furlong winner Millie's Rock, whose yearling colt by Footstepsinthesand sold for only €15,000 in October. Inca Princess is also a half-sister to the smart winner at up to thirteen furlongs (and Ebor runner-up) Changingoftheguard who was also trained by Aidan O'Brien. Johannes Vermeer's grandam Miletrian was a smart winner at up to an extended fourteen furlongs (after winning over nine furlongs as a two-year-old) for Mick Channon, with her three wins including the Ribblesdale and Park Hill Stakes in 2000. Miletrian raced on at four before being sold later that year for 700,000 guineas. She is a half-sister to the very smart performer at up to an extended fourteen furlongs (third in the 2001 St Leger, also fourth in the Derby) Mr Combustible. Their unraced dam Warg is out of Um Lardaff, a sister to Derby winner Shirley Heights, who won two middle-distance races in the French Provinces. Johannes Vermeer looks a genuine colt and he acts on soft and good to firm going. *Aidan O'Brien, Ireland*

JOHARA (IRE) 4 b.f. Iffraaj 127 – Hurricane Irene (IRE) (Green Desert (USA) 127) **101**
[2015 99: 6d⁴ 6g 6g⁴ Oct 10] lengthy filly: useful performer: lightly raced again in 2015 but further progress, 2½ lengths fourth of 16 to Mistrusting in listed race at Newmarket final start: stays 6f: acts on polytrack, soft and good to firm going. *Chris Wall*

JOHN CAESAR (IRE) 4 b.g. Bushranger (IRE) 119 – Polish Belle (Polish Precedent **70** (USA) 131) [2015 79: 7.5m 8m 8m 6m⁴ 6d 7g⁵ 7.2g 8d⁴ t8.6f⁴ t9.5f³ Oct 27] fair maiden: stays 9.5f: acts on polytrack, tapeta, good to firm and good to soft going: tried in cheekpieces: usually wears tongue tie. *Rebecca Bastiman*

JOHN COFFEY (IRE) 6 b.g. Acclamation 118 – Appleblossom Pearl (IRE) 79 (Peintre **61** Celebre (USA) 137) [2015 61: t7.1f⁴ p6g 7g 7.2g² 7g³ 6d 7.2g t6f t6g² t7.1f³ Dec 22] fair **a71** handicapper: stays 7f: acts on polytrack, tapeta and good to firm going: tried in headgear/ tongue tie prior to 2015: often starts slowly. *Michael Appleby*

JOHN F KENNEDY (IRE) 3 b.c. Galileo (IRE) 134 – Rumplestiltskin (IRE) 116 **105**
(Danehill (USA) 126) [2015 116p: 10v³ 10.4m 12d³ Sep 12] smart at 2 yrs: disappointing
in 2015, best effort when 10¾ lengths third of 5 behind Fascinating Rock in Enterprise
Stakes at Leopardstown final start (blinkered/tongue tied): should stay beyond 1m: acts on
good to firm and good to soft going: sent to USA. *Aidan O'Brien, Ireland*

JOHN JOINER 3 b.g. Captain Gerrard (IRE) 113 – Nigella 92 (Band On The Run 102) **61**
[2015 53: 5m 5m⁴ 5.7f⁵ t5.1f² p5g⁶ Oct 14] modest maiden: stays 5.5f: acts on tapeta and
good to firm going: in headgear prior to 2015. *Peter Makin*

JOHN LOUIS 7 ch.g. Bertolini (USA) 125 – Native Ring (FR) (Bering 136) [2015 11.9d⁴ **81**
14g p16g Jul 1] workmanlike gelding: fairly useful handicapper: stays 1½m: acts on
polytrack, good to firm and heavy going: fairly useful jumper. *Venetia Williams*

JOHNNO 6 br.g. Excellent Art 125 – Vert Val (USA) 103 (Septieme Ciel (USA) 123) [2015 **–**
101: 8m 8d 7.6s Sep 12] strong, good-topped gelding: useful at best, no form in 2015: left
Marjorie Fife after second start: tried in headgear: tried in tongue tie prior to 2015.
David Nicholls

JOHNNY BARNES (IRE) 3 b.c. Acclamation 118 – Mahalia (IRE) 107 (Danehill **115**
(USA) 126) [2015 107: 8.1m⁵ 8m 8d* 8m⁵ 8s Nov 1] good-topped colt: smart performer:
improved to win Prix Quincey at Deauville (by 3 lengths from dead-heaters Spoil The Fun
and Stillman) in August: below that form form both subsequent starts: stays 1m: acts on
heavy going: sometimes slowly away, usually races nearer last than first. *John Gosden*

JOHNNY B GOODE (IRE) 3 b.g. Approve (IRE) 112 – Musica E Magia (IRE) (King's **78**
Theatre (IRE) 128) [2015 80: 6s⁴ 5g⁵ 6.1s 7f² 6.9s³ 7g² 7m² Aug 9] fair handicapper: stays
7f: acts on firm and soft going: front runner/races prominently. *Richard Fahey*

JOHNNY CAVAGIN 6 b.g. Superior Premium 122 – Beyond The Rainbow (Mind **90**
Games 121) [2015 94: 7d* 8m 8d⁶ 7m⁵ 7f⁶ 8m² 7d 7.9g 5m 6g* p6g⁶ Oct 6] fairly useful
handicapper: won at Doncaster in March and Pontefract (by nose from Jan Van Hoof) in
September: left Richard Guest after second start: best at 6f/7f: acts on polytrack, soft and
good to firm going: usually wears tongue tie. *Ronald Thompson*

JOHNNYS LEGACY (IRE) 8 b.g. Ecton Park (USA) 124 – Lexy May (USA) (Lear **–**
Fan (USA) 130) [2015 t13.9f Nov 30] fairly useful at best: stays 2m: acts on polytrack,
good to firm and good to soft going: sometimes wears cheekpieces. *Ken Wingrove*

JOHNNY SORRENTO 3 b.g. Zamindar (USA) 116 – Glorious Dreams (USA) 76 **–**
(Honour And Glory (USA) 122) [2015 48: f5g⁵ 5d 6g 5g May 12] neat gelding: maiden: no
form in 2015: often in headgear/tongue tie prior to 2015. *Karen Tutty*

JOHNNY SPLASH (IRE) 6 b.g. Dark Angel (IRE) 113 – Ja Ganhou (Midyan (USA) **71**
124) [2015 66, a79: p5g⁵ p6g Feb 7] close-coupled gelding: fair handicapper: stays 6f: acts
on polytrack, good to firm and good to soft going: usually wears headgear. *Roger Teal*

JOHN PALMER 2 b.c. (May 4) Dick Turpin (IRE) 127 – Allmost Inti (Intikhab (USA) **–**
135) [2015 p7g Oct 20] 33/1, very slowly away when tenth of 12 in maiden at Lingfield:
sent to Italy. *Chris Wall*

JOHN POTTS 10 b.g. Josr Algarhoud (IRE) 118 – Crown City (USA) 56 (Coronado's **57**
Quest (USA) 130) [2015 69: t9.5g t8.6f⁵ t8.6f⁵ t8.6g t8.6m⁵ t9.5g³ t8.6g⁵ 8g⁶ Aug 6] big,
good-topped gelding: modest handicapper: stays 9.5f: acts on polytrack and tapeta: tried in
cheekpieces. *Brian Baugh*

JOHN REEL (FR) 6 b.g. Country Reel (USA) 113 – John Quatz (FR) (Johann Quatz (FR) **107**
120) [2015 93p: p12g* t16.5m* t12.2g³ p15.8m³ p16g² p15.8f⁴ 18.7d⁶ 16.2g⁶ 11.9g 14g
14g Aug 22] big gelding: useful handicapper: won at Lingfield (by 1¾ lengths from
Energia Fox) in January and Wolverhampton (by ¾ length from Gabrial's Star) in February:
better form after, including when sixth of 17 to Trip To Paris in Chester Cup at Chester on
seventh start: stays 2¼m: acts on polytrack, tapeta and good to soft going: front runner/
races prominently. *David Evans*

JOHN SPLENDID (IRE) 2 b.g. (Apr 9) Acclamation 118 – Affirmative (Pivotal 124) **93**
[2015 6.5m² 7m³ 7f* Jul 18] 70,000Y: useful-looking gelding: second foal: dam unraced
daughter of Nassau Stakes winner Favourable Terms: fairly useful maiden: 2/7, didn't need
to improve to win 4-runner maiden at Haydock in July by 3½ lengths from Canford
Crossing, unchallenged: stays 7f: gelded, and sent to Hong Kong, where renamed Super
Clan. *Brian Meehan*

JOLIE BLONDE 4 ch.f. Sir Percy 129 – Affaire d'Amour 100 (Hernando (FR) 127) **91** [2015 84p: p15.8g* 17.2f⁵ Sep 13] fairly useful handicapper: won at Lingfield in August: stays 17f: acts on polytrack, firm and good to soft going: in cheekpieces in 2015: races prominently. *Sir Mark Prescott Bt*

JOLIEVITESSE (FR) 3 b.g. Elusive City (USA) 117 – Volvoreta 121 (Suave Dancer **82** (USA) 136) [2015 98p: p8g⁴ 11.8m³ 10g 8.9s 10d p8g⁵ p11g⁴ Dec 9] angular gelding: fairly useful handicapper: stays 1½m: acts on polytrack and good to firm going: tried in hood in 2015. *K. R. Burke*

JOLLY GOOD KITTEN (USA) 3 b.c. Kitten's Joy (USA) 128 – Ballade's Girl (USA) **98** (Saint Ballado (CAN)) [2015 8g² 8g 7s³ 8.9g⁵ 8f 8g 8g⁴ p9.4g⁴ p7.5g⁶ Dec 11] fifth foal: brother to smart US Grade 3 9f winner Coalport and half-brother to minor North American winner by Langfuhr: dam unraced: useful performer: in frame in listed races at Saint-Cloud and Longchamp, Premio Ribot at Rome (6¾ lengths fourth to Kaspersky) and minor event at Deauville: well held in Britannia Stakes (Handicap) at Royal Ascot on fifth outing: stays at least 1m: acts on soft going: has worn tongue tie. *Gianluca Bietolini, Italy*

JOLLY RED JEANZ (IRE) 4 ch.f. Intense Focus (USA) 117 – Sovienne (IRE) (Soviet **68** Star (USA) 128) [2015 69, a76: t6f⁵ p6m* p6f² p6f p6f6m⁶ 5.7m³ t6m p6g⁵ p6g⁵ p6f p6f³ t5.1f² t5.1f⁴ t5.1f⁵ t5.1m⁴ Dec 30] sturdy filly: fair handicapper: won at Kempton in January: left Tom Dascombe after sixth start: stays 7f: acts on polytrack and tapeta: often wears headgear. *Daniel Loughnane*

JOLLY ROGER (IRE) 8 b.g. Oratorio (IRE) 128 – Chalice Wells (Sadler's Wells (USA) **67** 132) [2015 16.2m³ 16.2m² 18d⁶ Aug 20] smallish gelding: fair handicapper: stays 2m: acts on good to firm and heavy going. *Bernard Llewellyn*

JON H THE LAWMAN (IRE) 2 b.g. (Mar 22) Lawman (FR) 121 – Lan Pham Ti (IRE) **38** (Librettist (USA) 124) [2015 5m 5g 5m 8g p7g Oct 6] poor maiden: stays 7f: acts on polytrack. *Ronald Thompson*

JONNIE SKULL (IRE) 9 b.g. Pyrus (USA) 106 – Sovereign Touch (IRE) (Pennine Walk **69** 120) [2015 f8s f7d⁴ p6g p8g³ p8f⁵ p8f p8f² p8m⁵ t7.1g* p8f⁴ 7g² p8f* 7m 8d⁵ 8g³ t7.1g⁴ p8f t7.1g 8g p8f p8f p8m⁶ Dec 27] compact gelding: fair handicapper: won at Wolverhampton in April and Lingfield in May: stays 1¼m: acts on all-weather, firm and good to soft going: usually wears headgear/tongue tie: front runner/races prominently: very tough. *Phil McEntee*

JONNY DELTA 8 ch.g. Sulamani (IRE) 130 – Send Me An Angel (IRE) 75 (Lycius **76** (USA) 124) [2015 92: 16.2g 16m⁵ 15.8g⁵ 14g 14d Sep 4] fair handicapper: stays 2¼m: acts on good to firm and heavy going. *Jim Goldie*

JORDAN JAMES (IRE) 2 b.g. (Feb 22) Equiano (FR) 127 – Deira (USA) 79 (Green **–** Desert (USA) 127) [2015 7g 7g⁶ Aug 31] better effort in maidens when 7¼ lengths sixth of 8 to Marcel at Newcastle latter start. *Brian Ellison*

JORDAN PRINCESS 4 b.f. Cape Cross (IRE) 129 – Princess Nada 108 (Barathea (IRE) **105** 127) [2015 105p: 12m⁴ 11.9g⁴ 12m* 14m³ 12d Aug 20] good-topped filly: useful performer: won listed race at Newmarket (by 1½ lengths from Dream Child) in July: creditable third in Lillie Langtry Stakes at Goodwood (4 lengths behind Simple Verse) later in month: stays 1¾m: acts on good to firm and heavy going. *Luca Cumani*

JORDAN SPORT 2 b.c. (Feb 26) Dubawi (IRE) 129 – Wonder Why (GER) (Tiger Hill **78** (IRE) 127) [2015 7.5s³ 7.1g⁶ 7.5d² Sep 22] well-made colt: fair maiden: best effort when second at Beverley (1½ lengths behind Rio's Cliffs) in September. *Richard Fahey*

JORDAURA 9 br.g. Primo Valentino 116 – Christina's Dream 74 (Spectrum (IRE) **58** 126) [2015 50: 10.4d³ 8.3d 11.1s 11.1s⁵ 10.9g* 11.9d 9.9d⁵ 10s⁵ 10.2s Nov 4] sturdy gelding: modest handicapper: won at Ripon (amateur) in August: stays 1½m: acts on polytrack, good to firm and heavy going: tried in eyeshields/tongue tie prior to 2015: often races towards rear. *Alan Berry*

JOSEPHINE K 2 b.f. (Feb 16) Bahri (USA) 125 – Montrachet Belle (Kadeed (IRE)) **–** [2015 7.9d⁵ Sep 15] first foal: dam of little account: 100/1, tailed off in maiden at Carlisle. *Susan Corbett*

JOSEPH JEFFERSON (IRE) 3 b.c. Rip Van Winkle (IRE) 134 – Vas Y Carla (USA) **86** 80 (Gone West (USA)) [2015 10m 12d⁵ p12g³ 14m² 14g t13.9m⁵ Sep 25] fairly useful maiden: second in handicap at Haydock (3 lengths behind Senrima) in July: stayed 1¾m: acted on polytrack, tapeta and good to firm going: dead. *Roger Varian*

JOSH PERRY 2 b.g. (Mar 9) Hellvelyn 118 – Emma Peel 113 (Emarati (USA) 74) [2015 7s **–** Oct 12] lengthy gelding: 16/1, very green when last of 9 in maiden at Salisbury. *Rod Millman*

JOSHUA POTMAN (IRE) 3 gr.g. Zebedee 113 – Road To Reality (IRE) (Indian **74**
Danehill (IRE) 124) [2015 67: 10.2m² 9.9m⁵ 12.3s⁶ 9.8d t9.5g⁵ t12.2g² 11.9m⁴ 12.2m
t12.2f⁴ t13.9m³ Oct 2] good-bodied gelding: fair maiden: stays 1¾m: acts on tapeta and
good to firm going: in headgear in 2015. *Tom Dascombe*

JOSIE JOE 3 ch.f. Stimulation (IRE) 121 – Minette 55 (Bishop of Cashel 122) [2015 53: **–**
f11g³ t9.5f Jan 29] maiden: no form in 2015: stays 7f: acts on fibresand. *David Evans*

JOSIE'S DREAM (IRE) 7 b.g. Tau Ceti 117 – Gallery Breeze 80 (Zamindar (USA) 116) **55**
[2015 f11s t12.2g 17.2f² 13.1m⁵ 13.1g⁵ 17.2f 13.4g 13.1d p13f Sep 12] modest
handicapper: stays 17f: acts on polytrack, fibresand, firm and soft going: tried in headgear.
Jo Hughes

JOULES 2 b.c. (Mar 28) Oasis Dream 129 – Frappe (IRE) 93 (Inchinor 119) [2015 6m⁵ **71**
p6g² p5g⁵ Sep 21] fair maiden: best effort when second in maiden at Kempton (1¼ lengths
behind Valko) in August: will be suited by a return to 6f+. *Charles Hills*

JOURNEY 3 b.f. Dubawi (IRE) 129 – Montare (IRE) 116 (Montjeu (IRE) 137) [2015 66P: **118**
7d² p7f⁴ 9.9g² 10m* 10.1g 9.9m* 12g* 12d² Oct 17] sturdy filly: smart performer: won
maiden at Newbury (by 3¼ lengths from Gold Sands) in June and listed races at Salisbury
(by 2¼ lengths from Suffused) in August and Newmarket (by 8 lengths from Desert Snow)
in September: further improvement when second of 12 in Fillies' And Mares' Stakes at
Ascot (¾ length behind Simple Verse) in October, headed final 50 yds: stays 1½m: acts on
good to firm and good to soft going: in hood last 7 starts: front runner/races prominently,
often travels strongly, usually responds generously to pressure. *John Gosden*

JOYFUL DAY (IRE) 2 b.c. (Mar 16) Lilbourne Lad (IRE) 111 – Blondie's Esteem (IRE) **72**
50 (Mark of Esteem (IRE) 137) [2015 t7.1m f7f³ Dec 17] better effort when third in
maiden at Southwell (length behind Autumn Blossom) in December. *Robert Cowell*

Mr George Strawbridge's "Journey"

JOYFUL RISK (IRE) 5 ch.m. Kheleyf (USA) 116 – Joyfullness (USA) (Dixieland Band (USA)) [2015 64: p8m p8f Mar 4] poor maiden: raced only at 1m on polytrack: acts on polytrack. *Martin Bosley* **46**

JOYFUL STAR 5 b.g. Teofilo (IRE) 126 – Extreme Beauty (USA) 89 (Rahy (USA) 115) [2015 –: 12m 10.1d³ 12.4g 12.4g 9.9d 7d⁶ f8g⁶ f6g Nov 24] modest maiden: stays 12.5f: acts on good to soft going: sometimes in visor in 2015: often races prominently. *Fred Watson* **58**

JUBILEE BRIG 5 b.g. Kheleyf (USA) 116 – Voile (IRE) 102 (Barathea (IRE) 127) [2015 83, a94: p7f³ p7g³ p6f p6f p6m* t6g* 7m⁴ p6m⁵ 6g² p7g⁵ p7g⁶ 6g⁵ 5g 6m⁴ 7.2m² 5.9d* p6f 8m 7s Oct 9] useful-looking gelding: fairly useful performer: won claimer at Lingfield in April, handicap at Wolverhampton (amateur) in April and handicap at Carlisle (amateur) in August: left Sean Curran after eleventh start: stays 7.5f: acts on all-weather, good to firm and good to soft going: used to wear headgear (not on last 9 starts) *Alan Swinbank* **88**

JUBILEE SONG 3 b.f. Royal Applause 124 – Cosmic Song 58 (Cosmonaut) [2015 6m⁵ 7m 6m⁴ 6g 5.9g Aug 19] sixth foal: half-sister to 3 winners, including useful 7f winner Marmoom (by Dutch Art) and winner up to 7f Cosmic Art (2-y-o 6f winner, by Bertolini): dam 9f/1¼m winner: modest maiden: best effort at 6f: acts on good to firm going: tried in cheekpieces. *Richard Whitaker* **53**

JUBILEE SPIRIT 3 b.g. Misu Bond (IRE) 114 – Bond Babe 59 (Forzando 122) [2015 62: t6f⁵ t6f 6m 6m⁶ t7.1g 7m⁵ Aug 9] modest maiden: stays 7f: acts on tapeta and good to firm going: usually wears headgear: sometimes slowly away, usually races towards rear. *Geoffrey Oldroyd* **52**

JUDGE 'N JURY 11 ch.g. Pivotal 124 – Cyclone Connie 98 (Dr Devious (IRE) 127) [2015 99: 5d³ 5.1g⁶ 5.2s³ 5m 5s Oct 9] strong gelding: fairly useful handicapper: third at Lingfield in May and Newbury in August: best form at 5f: acts on polytrack, good to firm and heavy going: usually wears tongue tie: front runner/races prominently: none too consistent. *Ronald Harris* **89**

JUDICIAL ENQUIRY 2 b.g. (Mar 26) Lawman (FR) 121 – Koniya (IRE) (Doyoun 124) [2015 6d 7m 7v 8g 10.2g p8g⁴ f8g⁶ t9.5f* Dec 11] compact gelding: fair performer: won nursery at Wolverhampton in December: best effort at 9.5f: acts on polytrack, tapeta and heavy going: tried in cheekpieces. *Ed Walker* **67**

JUDICIAL (IRE) 3 b.g. Iffraaj 127 – Marlinka 95 (Marju (IRE) 127) [2015 92p: 5m p5g* Nov 11] useful handicapper: left Roger Charlton, won at Kempton (by 2½ lengths from Desert Command) in November: raced only at 5f: acts on polytrack, tapeta and good to firm going: wears headgear. *Julie Camacho* **105**

JUDICIOUS 8 ch.g. Pivotal 124 – Virtuoso 92 (Exit To Nowhere (USA) 122) [2015 51: – 10.4g May 22] sturdy, attractive gelding: fairly useful at best: stays 1½m: acts on good to firm and good to soft going. *Geoffrey Harker* **–**

JUDITH GARDENIER 3 b.f. Rip Van Winkle (IRE) 134 – Millagros (IRE) 86 (Pennekamp (USA) 130) [2015 10.1d 11.9d 8.3g⁶ Sep 21] second foal: half-sister to useful 7f-1½m winner Spes Nostra (by Ad Valorem): dam, 1m-1½m winner, also won over hurdles: no form. *Ian Semple*

JUEN 2 b.c. (Feb 2) Nayef (USA) 120 – Doyuur (USA) (Storm Cat (USA)) [2015 p/t* Nov 12] second foal: half-brother to 2-y-o 6f winner Khobaraa (by Invincible Spirit): dam, unraced, out of very smart US Grade 1 9f/1¼m winner Golden Apples: 5/4, did well under circumstances when winning 9-runner maiden at Chelmsford by 1½ lengths from Canford Crossing, very slowly away but quickening to lead final ½f: will stay at least 1m: open to significant improvement. *Saeed bin Suroor* **86 p**

JULIA DREAM 2 b.f. (Feb 13) Montjeu (IRE) 137 – Winds of Time (IRE) 91 (Danehill (USA) 126) [2015 7g Sep 26] fifth foal: half-sister to useful 2-y-o 6f winner The Paddyman (by Giant's Causeway): dam 6f (at 2 yrs) to 9f (in Canada) winner: 25/1, showed a bit when seventh in maiden at Newmarket (6 lengths behind Aljuljalah) in September, not ideally placed: will be suited by 1m+: better to come. *William Haggas* **69 p**

JULIETA (IRE) 3 ch.f. Teofilo (IRE) 126 – Home You Stroll (IRE) 84 (Selkirk (USA) 129) [2015 10s⁶ 11.8m³ 10m⁶ 10g⁵ p12g⁴ p15.8g* p16g Sep 5] good-topped filly: fourth foal: half-sister to useful 1m winner Romantic Stroll (by Oratorio) and French 1½m-1¾m winner Sango (by Dalakhani): dam, 1¼m winner, half-sister to smart performer up to 1m Prima Luce: fair handicapper: won at Lingfield in August: stays 2m: acts on polytrack, soft and good to firm going. *Roger Charlton* **75**

JUMBO PRADO (USA) 6 gr.g. El Prado (IRE) 119 – Sant Elena 88 (Efisio 120) [2015 **73** t7.1f⁵ p8g² 8g⁴ t9.5g t8.6m t8.6f t8.6f* t8.6f² t8.6f³ Dec 22] rather leggy gelding: fair handicapper: won at Wolverhampton in October: stays 9f: acts on polytrack, tapeta and soft going: sometimes wears headgear: tried in tongue tie prior to 2015. *Daniel Loughnane*

JUMBO STEPS (IRE) 8 b.g. Footstepsinthesand 120 – Night Delight (IRE) 86 (Night **55** Shift (USA)) [2015 77: 5g 5m⁶ 5m 6g 5g 7.2g 5d 7d 6g 5g³ 5m⁵ 5s³ 5s⁶ Oct 27] modest handicapper: will prove suited by a return to 6f: acts on polytrack, good to firm and heavy going: tried in visor in 2015. *Jim Goldie*

JUMEIRAH GLORY (IRE) 3 b.g. Fast Company (IRE) 126 – Lady Dettoria (FR) **96** (Vettori (IRE) 119) [2015 84: 10g 12.3s⁵ 10.4d* 10.4g⁴ 11.9m 10.1g⁴ 10v* 12d Oct 11] useful handicapper: won at Haydock in May and Sandown (by 3¼ lengths from Brutus) in September: stays 10.5f: has form on good to firm ground but seems particularly effective on heavy going: sold 29,000 gns, sent to Bahrain. *Richard Fahey*

JUMEIRAH STAR (USA) 2 b.f. (Mar 18) Street Boss (USA) 124   Cosmic Wing **56** (USA) (Halo (USA)) [2015 p5m⁵ 5g⁵ 5.1m⁶ p7g p6g³ p6f Oct 10] $32,000F, $30,000Y: half-sister to several winners, including smart 5f/6f winner (including at 2 yrs) Speed Hawk (by Henny Hughes): dam US 1m and (at 2 yrs) 8.5f winner: modest maiden: stays 6f: acts on polytrack: tried in cheekpieces: sometimes slowly away. *Robert Cowell*

JUNCART 3 b.g. Dutch Art 126 – Juncea 76 (Elnadim (USA) 128) [2015 94: 5m p6g⁵ t6g **82** 8v⁶ Aug 25] fairly useful handicapper: stays 6f: acts on good to firm and good to soft going. *William Haggas*

JUNE (IRE) 3 b.f. High Chaparral (IRE) 132 – Aguilas Perla (IRE) (Indian Ridge 123) **68** [2015 p8m⁴ 10m⁵ 10d⁵ 11.6f 10.2m Jun 11] €60,000F: rather unfurnished filly: half-sister to several winners, including 2-y-o 5f-6.5f winner Spirit of Pearl (by Invincible Spirit) and 1¼m-1½m winner Saint Thomas (by Alhaarth): dam unraced: fair maiden: stays 11.5f: acts on polytrack, firm and good to soft going: tried in cheekpieces: usually races prominently. *Richard Hannon*

JUNGLE BAY 8 b.g. Oasis Dream 129 – Dominica 115 (Alhaarth (IRE) 126) [2015 82, **82** a90: p7g⁵ p7g² p6m p6d² p6g³ 6m p7g p6g p6g* 6g 6.1g p7g⁶ p6g Dec 7] strong gelding: fairly useful handicapper: won at Salisbury (by neck from Noverre To Go) in August: stays 1m: acts on polytrack, good to firm and heavy going: often wears headgear: untrustworthy. *Jane Chapple-Hyam*

JUNGLE CAT (IRE) 3 b.c. Iffraaj 127 – Mike's Wildcat (USA) (Forest Wildcat (USA) **108** 120) [2015 110: 7m⁵ 6m² 6f Jun 19] good-topped colt: useful performer: second in listed race at Newbury (1¾ lengths behind Adaay) in May, easily best effort of 2015: stays 6f: acts on good to firm going: front runner/races prominently. *Charlie Appleby*

JUNIOR BEN 3 b.g. Equiano (FR) 127 – Pretty Girl (IRE) 103 (Polish Precedent (USA) **–** 131) [2015 49: t5.1f f5g⁵ f6d⁶ Jan 22] lengthy, rather unfurnished gelding: poor maiden: best form at 5f: acted on tapeta: tried in visor/cheekpieces: dead. *Derek Shaw*

JUPITER CUSTOS (FR) 3 b.g. Le Havre (IRE) 124 – Angel Rose (IRE) (Definite **82** Article 121) [2015 7m⁵ 10m² 9.9m² 10.4g⁵ 8m⁴ 7g* 8.5d⁴ p8f⁵ t8.6f⁴ p11g Dec 9] €18,000Y: half-brother to several winners, including useful 2-y-o 7f winner Kay Es Jay (by Xaar), later 6f winner in USA, and 2-y-o 8.6f winner Encore Encore (by Royal Applause): dam, Swedish 2-y-o 1m winner, half-sister to useful 6f winner Wildwood Flower: fairly useful performer: won claimer at Epsom in July: subsequently left Richard Hannon: stays 1¼m: acts on polytrack, tapeta, good to firm and good to soft going: often races prominently. *Michael Scudamore*

JUPITER STORM 6 ch.g. Galileo (IRE) 134 – Exciting Times (FR) (Jeune Homme **78** (USA) 120) [2015 11.6m 14.1f p15.8g⁶ 12m⁶ p15.8f* p15.8g⁵ Aug 7] close-coupled gelding: fair handicapper: won at Lingfield in July: stays 2m: acts on polytrack, good to firm and good to soft going: sometimes wears headgear. *Gary Moore*

JUST A GROOVE (IRE) 2 b.g. (Mar 18) Kodiac 112 – Callanish (Inchinor 119) [2015 **74** 5g⁴ 5m⁶ 5s² t6f Nov 14] fair maiden: best effort at 5f. *Ann Duffield*

JUST BECAUSE 3 b.g. Mawatheeq (USA) 126 – Muwakaba (USA) 97 (Elusive Quality **70** (USA)) [2015 47: p6f⁶ p10d* 11.6g 10m⁶ 10m² 10g p11g p10m⁴ p10f⁴ p10g⁶ Oct 27] lengthy gelding: fair performer: won maiden at Chelmsford in March: should stay beyond 1¼m: acts on polytrack and good to firm going: usually in hood in 2015: often races towards rear. *John Best*

JUST BE LUCKY (IRE) 3 ch.g. Intense Focus (USA) 117 – Anda (Selkirk (USA) 129) **79**
[2015 77: 7d² 8d³ 10d³ 8.3v 7v⁶ Nov 3] fair maiden: left J. S. Bolger after third start: will
prove suited by a return to 1m+: acts on good to soft going: sometimes in headgear in 2015.
Ivan Furtado

JUST CHING (IRE) 3 b.f. Fastnet Rock (AUS) 127 – Adjalisa (IRE) 65 (Darshaan 133) **57**
[2015 7d 10.2m⁵ 10.3s⁴ 12f 14.1m 11.5g Jul 8] sister to 7f winner Brown Diamond and
closely related/half-sister to several winners, including smart South African/UAE 1m-1½m
winner Front House (by Sadler's Wells) and useful 1¾m winner Royal Irish Hussar (by
Galileo): dam maiden (stayed 1m): modest maiden: best effort at 10.5f: acts on soft going.
Charles Hills

JUST DUCHESS 5 b.m. Avonbridge 123 – Red Countess 78 (Pivotal 124) [2015 p12f⁵ **47**
11.9g⁴ 13.1m⁵ May 22] poor maiden: stays 16.5f, effective at shorter: acts on tapeta, firm
and soft going. *Michael Blanshard*

JUST EMMA 2 b.f. (Mar 19) Bertolini (USA) 125 – Royal Obsession (IRE) (Val Royal **77**
(FR) 127) [2015 5.3m³ 5.3g* 6m³ 5f 6f 7g⁶ 7d Sep 27] £1,100Y: angular filly: second foal:
half-sister to 2-y-o 5f winner Harleys Rocket (by Proclamation): dam ran twice: fair
performer: won maiden at Brighton in April: will benefit from return to 6f: acts on good to
firm going. *Joseph Tuite*

JUSTE POUR NOUS 2 b.c. (Mar 5) Pour Moi (IRE) 125 – Steam Cuisine 104 (Mark of **80 p**
Esteem (IRE) 137) [2015 p8g⁴ 8.3d* Sep 1] 27,000Y: fourth foal: half-brother to German
9f winner Genax (by Green Desert): dam 7f/1m winner (including at 2 yrs): better effort
when winning maiden at Hamilton (by ½ length from Colour Me Happy, dictating) in
September: open to further improvement. *Mark Johnston*

JUST FAB (IRE) 2 b.f. (Mar 7) Canford Cliffs (IRE) 133 – Unlock (IRE) 78 (Key of Luck **73**
(USA) 126) [2015 t6m⁵ p6f³ 7v² p8m³ Nov 19] €17,000Y, €54,000 2-y-o: fourth foal: half-
sister to Swiss 10.5f/1½m winner Painted Blue (by Peintre Celebre): dam, 2-y-o 7f winner,
sister to useful winner up to 1m Lock And Key: fair maiden: stays 1m. *Marco Botti*

JUST FABULOUS 6 b.m. Sakhee (USA) 136 – Tipsy Me 70 (Selkirk (USA) 129) [2015 **–**
9.3m⁵ Sep 9] rather leggy mare: fairly useful at best: stays 1¼m: best form on good to soft/
soft going. *Keith Dalgleish*

JUST FIVE (IRE) 9 b.g. Olmodavor (USA) 117 – Wildsplash (USA) (Deputy Minister **52**
(CAN)) [2015 56: t8.6g⁵ t8.6g p8f⁵ p8m⁴ t8.6m* p8m⁵ t9.5g t8.6m Aug 21] workmanlike
gelding: modest handicapper: won at Wolverhampton (apprentice) in April: stays 1¼m:
acts on all-weather, good to firm and heavy going: often wears headgear: tried in tongue tie
prior to 2015. *John Weymes*

JUST FRED (IRE) 2 br.g. (Apr 26) Excellent Art 125 – Consignia (IRE) 67 (Definite **55**
Article 121) [2015 p7g p7g p7g Dec 16] modest form at best in maidens at Kempton.
Denis Coakley

JUST GLAMOROUS (IRE) 2 ch.g. (Feb 27) Arcano (IRE) 122 – Glamorous Air (IRE) **73**
(Air Express (IRE) 125) [2015 5.1m² 5f 5m⁵ 6.1d² 5.1d² 5.4g³ p5f⁴ Sep 22] tall gelding:
fair maiden: stays 6f: acts on good to firm and good to soft going: usually races close up.
Ronald Harris

JUSTICE ANGEL (IRE) 2 gr.f. (Apr 22) Dark Angel (IRE) 113 – Malaica (FR) 103 **82**
(Roi Gironde (IRE) 104) [2015 5m⁶ p6g³ p6g* 7d³ 7m* 7g 8d Oct 31] lengthy filly: fourth
foal: half-sister to smart winner up to 1¼m Success Days (2-y-o 7f winner, by Jeremy):
dam French winner up to 6f (2-y-o 5f/5.5f winner): fairly useful performer: won maiden at
Kempton in July and nursery at Salisbury (by 1¾ lengths from Stylistik) in September:
stays 7f: acts on polytrack and good to firm going. *David Elsworth*

JUSTICE BELLE (IRE) 3 b.f. Montjeu (IRE) 137 – Metaphor (USA) (Woodman **102**
(USA) 126) [2015 72p: 11.6m² 9.9d² 11.5d* p11g* 12s⁴ 12g³ p11g⁴ Nov 9] tall, rather
unfurnished filly: useful performer: won maiden at Lingfield in June and handicap at
Kempton (by 6 lengths from Rosenbaum) in July: good 3¼ lengths fourth to The Steward
in handicap at Kempton final start, though did have run of race: stays 1½m: acts on
polytrack and soft going. *Ed Walker*

JUSTICE DAY (IRE) 4 b.c. Acclamation 118 – Rock Exhibition 86 (Rock of Gibraltar **116**
(IRE) 133) [2015 115: 6d 5m² 6g 5g⁵ 5f 5m 5m 5m³ 5g 5g* 5.2s³ 5m Oct 4] neat colt: smart
performer: won minor event at Leicester (by 2¼ lengths from Dutch Masterpiece) in
September: second in Palace House Stakes at Newmarket (1¼ lengths behind Goldream) in
May, third in handicap at Ascot (¾ length behind Secretinthepark) in August and third in
World Trophy at Newbury (neck behind Steps) later in September: stays 6f: acts on good to
firm and heavy going: tried in blinkers in 2015: sent to Singapore. *David Elsworth*

JUSTICE EARS (IRE) 2 b.c. (Mar 25) Dylan Thomas (IRE) 132 – Shanghai Visit (IRE) **– p** (Peintre Celebre (USA) 137) [2015 8g 7g Oct 21] strong, lengthy colt: sixth foal: half-brother to 5f winner Shanghai Beauty (by Jeremy) and a winner abroad by Red Clubs: dam once-raced half-sister to Prix Morny/Middle Park Stakes winner Bahamian Bounty: behind in 2 maidens at Newmarket: wore hood in latter (didn't settle fully and not knocked about): capable of better. *David Elsworth*

JUSTICE FIRST 3 b.g. Zebedee 113 – Nelly's Glen 71 (Efisio 120) [2015 68p: f8g⁵ p6m* **86** p6f⁵ p7g p6g⁴ p6g 6g² 7d 6d p6g⁶ p7g² p7f* p8m⁶ Dec 31] fairly useful handicapper: won at Lingfield in January and Chelmsford in December: stays 7f: acts on polytrack: often in headgear in 2015. *Ed Dunlop*

JUSTICE FOCUSED (IRE) 2 b.g. (Apr 28) Intense Focus (USA) 117 – Moon Shine **67 p** (FR) (Groom Dancer (USA) 128) [2015 p7g Sep 23] eighth foal: dam unraced half-sister to smart 1m-1¼m winner Mocham Glen: 33/1, seventh in maiden at Kempton (6¾ lengths behind Abe Lincoln) in September: capable of better. *David Elsworth*

JUSTICE GOOD (IRE) 3 b.c. Acclamation 118 – Qui Moi (CAN) 88 (Swain (IRE) 134) **104** [2015 104: 6d⁵ 5.2s 6m 6d⁵ Oct 30] sturdy colt: useful performer: seventh in Bengough Stakes at Ascot (3¾ lengths behind Eastern Impact) in October: well below form only subsequent start: stays 6f: acts on soft and good to firm going: front runner/races prominently. *David Elsworth*

JUSTICE (IRE) 2 b.f. (Feb 23) Lawman (FR) 121 – Sheboygan (IRE) 95 (Grand Lodge **–** (USA) 125) [2015 5m p6g 5m Jun 27] €17,000Y, resold 21,000Y: good-topped filly: fifth foal: half-sister to 7f/1m winner Master Mylo (by Bertolini): dam winner up to 7.6f (2-y-o 7f winner): no form. *Dean Ivory*

JUSTICE LASS (IRE) 2 b.f. (Feb 11) Canford Cliffs (IRE) 133 – Dibiya (IRE) 102 **82** (Caerleon (USA) 132) [2015 5m⁵ 7f⁴ 6m* 6g 6.5m p7m⁴ Oct 21] sturdy filly: half-sister to several winners, including very smart performer up to 1½m in Hong Kong Dibayani (2-y-o 7f winner, by Shamardal) and smart winner up to 1¾m Dirar (2-y-o 1m winner, by King's Best): dam 1½m-1¾m winner: fairly useful performer: won maiden at Windsor in July: stays 7f: acts on polytrack and firm going. *David Elsworth*

JUSTICE LAW (IRE) 2 gr.c. (Apr 4) Acclamation 118 – Inishtearaght (IRE) 71 (Verglas **97 p** (IRE) 118) [2015 6d² 7s* 8s² Sep 3] £25,000Y, £100,000 2-y-o: rather leggy colt: second foal: dam, 1m/8.4f winner, half-sister to Doncaster Cup winner Kasthari: useful performer: won maiden at Newbury (by 1¼ lengths from Tashweeq) in August: best effort when second in minor event at Salisbury (2¼ lengths behind Ventura Storm) in September: stays 1m: should do better still. *David Elsworth*

JUSTICE ROCK 2 b.g. (Apr 14) Acclamation 118 – Fashion Rocks (IRE) 97 (Rock of **72** Gibraltar (IRE) 133) [2015 5.1m 6m 5d³ 6d³ 6g³ 5m⁵ 5.1d⁵ p5g³ p5m⁶ p6g⁶ Dec 3] close- **a64** coupled gelding: fair maiden: stays 6f: acts on polytrack and good to soft going: sometimes in checkpieces: often races towards rear. *David Elsworth*

JUSTICE WELL 3 b.g. Halling (USA) 133 – Porthcawl 93 (Singspiel (IRE) 133) [2015 **108** 86: 6m 7g 7s³ 7d² p7g² f7g Dec 12] rather leggy gelding: useful performer: good second in minor event at Kempton (head behind Chookie Royale) in November on penultimate start: stays 7f: acts on polytrack. *David Elsworth*

JUSTINEO 6 b.h. Oasis Dream 129 – Loulwa (IRE) 103 (Montjeu (IRE) 137) [2015 112: **112** 5.1d⁶ 5d⁵ 6m² 5m* 5m⁶ 5g Aug 21] well-made horse: smart performer: won minor event at Newmarket (by ¾ length from Barracuda Boy) in July: second in listed race at Salisbury (1¼ lengths behind Absolutely So) previous start: effective at 5f/6f: acts on good to firm and good to soft going: sometimes wears headgear: usually leads, often travels strongly. *Roger Varian*

JUST ISLA 5 ch.m. Halling (USA) 133 – Island Rapture 87 (Royal Applause 124) [2015 **63** 69: 7m 7m⁶ 7.6d* 8.1g⁴ 8g⁴ p8g* 8g p8f p8d Nov 30] workmanlike mare: modest handicapper: won at Lingfield in July and Kempton in September: stays 1m: acts on polytrack, firm and good to soft going: usually wears headgear. *Michael Blanshard*

JUST MARION (IRE) 3 b.f. Bushranger (IRE) 119 – Dolphin Stamp (IRE) (Dolphin **70** Street (FR) 125) [2015 61, a68: f6d³ t7.1g⁶ 6g 7m⁴ 7m t6g² t7.1g³ 7m⁵ 7g² t7.1g* t7.1g⁵ p7g³ t7.1m⁵ t7.1m p11g p8g p10g t8.6f Dec 21] small, leggy filly: fair handicapper: won at Wolverhampton in August: left David Evans after thirteenth start: stays 7f: acts on all-weather, good to firm and good to soft going: tried in headgear: often races towards rear. *James Grassick*

JUST PAUL (IRE) 5 b.g. Clodovil (IRE) 116 – Tatamagouche (IRE) 70 (Sadler's Wells **75**
(USA) 132) [2015 91: 7g⁶ 8m 8g⁴ 7m⁵ 7.1m² 7.6g 7m 8d⁴ 7.2g⁶ 6.9s⁴ 8.5m 7s Oct 16] fair
handicapper: stays 1m: acts on firm and soft going: often races prominently: temperament
under suspicion. *Micky Hammond*

JUST RUBIE 4 b.f. Refuse To Bend (IRE) 128 – Island Rapture 87 (Royal Applause 124) **52**
[2015 –: p6g p7g⁶ p7g t7.1g³ 8m 7.6g⁴ 6.1m p6g Jul 14] modest handicapper: stays 7.5f:
acts on polytrack and tapeta: tried in blinkers in 2015: races towards rear. *Michael Blanshard*

JUST SILCA 3 ch.f. Teofilo (IRE) 126 – Silca Chiave 106 (Pivotal 124) [2015 66p: 7f⁴ Jul **52**
3] below debut form when fourth in maiden at Doncaster on sole outing in 2015 (wore
hood). *Mick Channon*

JUST THAT LORD 2 ch.c. (Apr 7) Avonbridge 123 – Lady Filly 92 (Atraf 116) [2015 **67**
5d⁴ p5g³ p5g⁶ Sep 21] fair form when in frame in maidens Doncaster and Kempton, off
almost off 6 months after latter start. *Bill Turner*

JUST THE JUDGE (IRE) 5 b.m. Lawman (FR) 121 – Faraday Light (IRE) (Rainbow **111**
Quest (USA) 134) [2015 115: 12g⁶ Mar 28] lengthy, good-quartered mare: smart performer:
successful in Irish 1000 Guineas at the Curragh in 2013 and E. P. Taylor Stakes at
Woodbine in 2014: just respectable 6¾ lengths sixth to Dolniya in Dubai Sheema Classic
at Meydan sole outing in 2015: stayed 1¼m: acted on firm and good to soft going: retired
in July after suffering minor tendon injury. *Charles Hills*

JUST THE TONIC 8 ch.m. Medicean 128 – Goodwood Blizzard 97 (Inchinor 119) [2015 **60**
56§: 7g 7s⁶ 7.2d⁴ 7d 5.9d⁵ 6d 7g Sep 4] sparely-made mare: modest handicapper: stays 1m:
acts on good to firm and heavy going: tried in hood/tongue tie prior to 2015: none too
genuine. *Marjorie Fife*

JUST US TWO (IRE) 3 b.c. Royal Applause 124 – Sarah's First 68 (Cadeaux Genereux **89**
131) [2015 83: 5m* 5g⁶ Jun 20] fairly useful handicapper: won at Windsor (by length from
Francisco) in May: raced only at 5f: acts on good to firm going. *Robert Cowell*

JUST WHEN 6 b.g. Dalakhani (IRE) 133 – Cape Grace (IRE) 105 (Priolo (USA) 127) **–**
[2015 p12m Oct 28] useful-looking gelding: fairly useful at best, well held only start on
Flat since 2012: stays 11.5f: acts on heavy going: often wears visor. *Patrick Chamings*

JUVENTAS 3 ch.f. Sixties Icon 125 – The Screamer (IRE) 53 (Insan (USA) 119) [2015 79: **83**
p8g³ 9.9g 8.3m 8g⁶ 7m* 7m⁴ 7m⁶ 7g³ 7.5g³ 7g 9.9g³ Dec 29] close-coupled filly: fairly
useful performer: won handicaps at Brighton in June and July: left Mick Channon after
ninth start: third in Qatar Oaks at Doha final outing: stays 1¼m: acts on good to firm going:
front runner/races prominently. *I. Al Malki, Qatar*

K

KAABER (USA) 4 b.g. Daaher (CAN) 120 – Taseel (USA) (Danzig (USA)) [2015 –: **53**
t12.2g t7.1g⁵ 6m 7m 7m t7.1g t6g⁴ t6g³ p6g⁵ t6g 6d³ f7g⁶ t6m Dec 30] modest maiden: best
effort at 6f: acts on tapeta, good to firm and good to soft going: often in headgear in 2015.
Roy Brotherton

KAATSKILL NAP (FR) 2 ch.g. (Apr 8) Rip Van Winkle (IRE) 134 – Last Cast (FR) **–**
(Marju (IRE) 127) [2015 8v Aug 25] 50/1, green when seventh in maiden at Newbury (9¾
lengths behind Abdon) in August, slowly away. *David Menuisier*

KACHOU 3 b.f. Excellent Art 125 – Milwaukee (FR) (Desert King (IRE) 129) [2015 **70**
t8.6g⁶ t8.6f⁶ f8g⁴ p12g³ p10f* p12g⁶ p10f⁴ p10g Dec 9] 24,000Y: fourth foal: half-sister to
3 winners, including 7f-8.6f winner Two No Bids (by Footstepsinthesand) and 2-y-o 7f
winner Choral Society (by Acclamation): dam 10.5f-1½m winner who stayed 15f: fair
performer: left Sir Mark Prescott Bt, won handicap at Chelmsford (apprentice) in August:
stays 1¼m: acts on polytrack: often in headgear: front runner/races prominently. *Ivan
Furtado*

KACHY 2 b.c. (Mar 5) Kyllachy 129 – Dubai Bounty 89 (Dubai Destination (USA) 127) **108 p**
[2015 5.1m* 5g* Jul 29] £52,000Y: useful-looking colt: fourth foal: dam winner up to 12.3f
(2-y-o 8.6f winner) out of useful 2-y-o 5f winner Mary Read: useful form: successful both
starts, namely minor event at Chester (by 2¼ lengths from Muhadathat) in June and
10-runner Molecomb Stakes at Goodwood in July: beat King of Rooks by ¾ length in latter,
travelling well and leading inside final 1f: should stay 6f: smart prospect. *Tom Dascombe*

KADOOMENT DAY (IRE) 2 ch.g. (Feb 12) Lord Shanakill (USA) 121 – Four Poorer 77
(IRE) (Oasis Dream 129) [2015 5.9g 6m 7g² Sep 23] fair maiden: easily best effort when
second at Redcar (neck behind Beatbybeatbybeat) in September, clear of rest: stays 7f.
K. R. Burke

KADRIZZI (FR) 2 ch.g. (Mar 29) Hurricane Cat (USA) 111 – Kadiania (FR) (Indian 101
Rocket 115) [2015 p7g⁴ p6g⁵ 6.1v* 6v t6g² p6g² Dec 20] €16,000Y, £25,000 2-y-o: first
foal: dam unraced: useful performer: won maiden at Nottingham in October: second in
nurseries at Wolverhampton (neck behind Illegally Blonde) and second at Lingfield (head
behind Kingsley Klarion) in December: stays 6f: acts on polytrack, tapeta and heavy going:
front runner/races prominently. *Dean Ivory*

KAFEEL (USA) 4 b.g. First Samurai (USA) 119 – Ishraak (USA) (Sahm (USA) 112) 73
[2015 9.9g⁵ p10g p10.1m^pu Jul 2] sturdy gelding: fair handicapper: stays 1m: acts
on polytrack and good to firm going: tried in cheekpieces in 2015: tried in tongue tie in
2015: often races prominently. *Linda Jewell*

KAFOO 2 b.g. (Apr 18) Dansili 127 – Nidhaal (IRE) 107 (Observatory (USA) 131) [2015 53 p
6m⁵ 6.1m p8g⁶ Aug 4] sixth foal: closely related to useful 2-y-o 5f winner Burwaaz (by
Exceed And Excel) and half-brother to 2-y-o 5f/6f winner Sadafiya and useful winner up to
6f Sharaarah (both by Oasis Dream): dam 2-y-o 6f winner: modest form in maidens:
should do better in time. *Ed Dunlop*

KAGAMI 4 ch.g. Teofilo (IRE) 126 – Sky Wonder (Observatory (USA) 131) [2015 73, 50
a57: p8m p11f⁵ p12f Apr 15] modest maiden: stays 1½m: acts on polytrack, raced only on
good going on turf: sometimes wears hood. *Simon Dow*

KAINE KEIRA 3 ch.g. Archipenko (USA) 127 – Mme de Stael 71 (Selkirk (USA) 129) 58
[2015 –: 8g⁴ 8m May 16] modest maiden: stays 1m. *Paul Midgley*

KAISAN 2 b.g. (May 18) Rip Van Winkle (IRE) 134 – Orinoco (IRE) 53 (Darshaan 133) 69 p
[2015 8.3s⁶ Oct 13] closely related to 1½m winner Intiquilla (by Galileo) and half-brother
to several winners, including smart winner up to 12.5f Kelinni (2-y-o 7f winner, by Refuse
To Bend) and useful 1¼m-1½m winner Bandama (by Green Desert): dam ran once: 33/1,
shaped as if needed experience when sixth in maiden at Leicester (4 lengths behind Little
Avon) in October: will be suited by 1¼m+: capable of better. *Michael Bell*

KAJAKI (IRE) 2 gr.g. (May 8) Mastercraftsman (IRE) 129 – No Quest (IRE) (Rainbow 74
Quest (USA) 134) [2015 8.5m 8d t9.5f⁴ Nov 14] fair maiden: best effort when fourth at
Wolverhampton (2¾ lengths behind City of Ideas) in November. *Kevin Ryan*

KAKAPUKA 8 br.g. Shinko Forest (IRE) – No Rehearsal (FR) (Baillamont (USA) 124) 59
[2015 76: t7.1f⁵ p7f p7g² 7m³ 7g⁵ 7.6g⁵ 7d Sep 14] good-topped gelding: modest
handicapper: stays 7.5f: acts on polytrack and firm going: tried in headgear: front runner/
races prominently. *Anabel K. Murphy*

KAKASHAN (IRE) 2 b.f. (Apr 22) Kodiac 112 – Barracade (IRE) 71 (Barathea (IRE) 81
127) [2015 6d³ 7s³ 7d⁴ p7g* Dec 3] 65,000€, 250,000Y: close-coupled filly: fourth foal:
half-sister to 7f winner Black Rider (by Elnadim) and useful 2-y-o 5f/6f winner Blockade
(by Kheleyf): dam maiden (stayed 1¼m): fairly useful performer: won maiden at Kempton
in December: stays 7f. *John Gosden*

KAKATOSI 8 br.g. Pastoral Pursuits 127 – Ladywell Blaise (IRE) 63 (Turtle Island (IRE) 94
123) [2015 93: 7d 8f⁵ 7f² t7.1g* 7f⁵ 7d 7g* Sep 8] strong gelding: fairly useful handicapper:
won at Wolverhampton in June and Leicester (by ½ length from Provident Spirit) in
September: stays 1m: acts on polytrack, tapeta, firm and soft going: tried in headgear:
usually races towards rear, often travels strongly. *Mike Murphy*

KALAMATA 2 b.f. (Jan 27) Sir Percy 129 – Kalamkas (USA) 59 (Kingmambo (USA) –
125) [2015 7g p7g p8d Nov 30] rather leggy filly: first foal: dam, ran twice, out of useful
2-y-o 6f winner Reach For The Moon: down the field in maidens: will be suited by 1¼m+.
Roger Varian

KALANI'S DIAMOND 5 ch.m. Kalani Bay (IRE) – Cryptonite Diamond (USA) 66 –
(Hennessy (USA) 122) [2015 –: 5m 6m Jul 18] no form: tried in headgear: tried in tongue
tie prior to 2015. *Alan Brown*

KALANN (IRE) 8 b.g. Barathea (IRE) 127 – Karkiyla (IRE) (Darshaan 133) [2015 112?: 100
14g 18m 12g⁵ Oct 11] smart in 2014, third in Doncaster Cup: best effort in 2015 when 12
lengths ninth of 11 to Pallasator in same race: stays 2¼m: acts on polytrack, good to firm
and good to soft going. *Sabrina J. Harty, Ireland*

KALDERA (GER) 4 ch.f. Sinndar (IRE) 134 – Konigstochter (GER) 110 (Dai Jin 123) 109
[2015 109: 15.9g 11.9g³ 14m⁶ Jul 30] useful performer: won 5 times in 2014, including
Deutsches St Leger at Dortmund: creditable third in Grosser Hansa-Preis at Hamburg

(beaten narrowly by Lovelyn) in June: respectable 4½ lengths sixth to Simple Verse in Lillie Langtry Stakes at Goodwood final outing: stays 1¾m: acts on soft going: tried in blinkers (in 2013). *Paul Harley, Germany*

KALIFI (USA) 4 b.f. First Defence (USA) 119 – Out of Reach 109 (Warning 136) [2015 –: p12f t12.2m Feb 17] maiden: no form in 2015: in cheekpieces/tongue last start. *Stuart Kittow*

KALIMANTAN (IRE) 5 b.g. Azamour (IRE) 130 – Kalamba (IRE) (Green Dancer (USA) 132) [2015 t12.2g³ 10.2m 10m 14g⁴ t13.9m⁶ Oct 2] good-topped gelding: fair maiden: stays 1¾m: acts on tapeta: tried in headgear: sometimes slowly away. *Tim Vaughan* **70**

KALK BAY (IRE) 8 b.g. Hawk Wing (USA) 136 – Politesse (USA) (Barathea (IRE) 127) [2015 92: 8g 7g² 7.6f* 7f* 7.5g 8m⁴ 7s 7s p7f⁶ Nov 23] fairly useful handicapper: won at Chester in June and Doncaster (by neck from Victoire de Lyphar) in July: stays 10.5f: acts on fibresand and any turf going: tried in headgear prior to 2015: often wears tongue tie. *Michael Easterby* **88**

KALKRAND (IRE) 2 b.c. (Apr 15) Dubawi (IRE) 129 – Kiltubber (IRE) 104 (Sadler's Wells (USA) 132) [2015 7d p8m⁴ t8.6g⁵ p8g Dec 15] fair maiden: likely to stay 1¼m. *John Gosden* **70**

KALLISHA 4 b.f. Whipper (USA) 126 – Shallika (IRE) (Alhaarth (IRE) 126) [2015 95: 10m 12f 12v* 12g⁵ 10.4s Nov 1] angular filly: useful performer: won handicap at Newbury (by 7 lengths from Cottesloe) in August: creditable fifth to Cannock Chase in listed race at Newmarket next time: stays 1½m: best form on good going or softer (acts on heavy): tried in cheekpieces in 2014: often races towards rear. *Brendan Powell* **98**

KALON BRAMA (IRE) 4 b.f. Kodiac 112 – Gilded Truffle (IRE) 69 (Peintre Celebre (USA) 137) [2015 73: 8m 6m 10m⁶ 8m⁴ 7m⁶ 10m⁵ 10m² p8f⁴ p8f* p10m* p8f* p8f² p8f² p10f³ p8f⁶ p8g p10f³ p8m² Dec 27] lengthy mare: fairly useful handicapper: improved and won at Chelmsford in September (twice) and October: runner-up 3 times there subsequently: stays 1¼m: acts on polytrack and good to firm going: often wears hood. *Peter Charalambous* **60 + a83**

KANO'S GHIRL (IRE) 4 b.f. Kodiac 112 – Southern Barfly (USA) (Southern Halo (USA)) [2015 58: p5g p7g p6g p5g 5m 5g 7.2d Aug 10] poor handicapper: stays 6f: acts on good to firm going: often wears headgear: tends to find little. *L. Smyth, Ireland* **35**

KANTARA CASTLE (IRE) 4 b.g. Baltic King 120 – Arbitration (IRE) (Bigstone (IRE) 126) [2015 75: t9.5f t9.5g⁶ 10.2m³ 10.4d⁶ 8m⁵ 9m⁵ 10.2m³ t12.2f t9.5f⁵ t9.5f³ t9.5f t9.5m Nov 28] modest handicapper: stays 1½m: acts on polytrack, tapeta, soft and good to firm going: usually in cheekpieces in 2015: often wears tongue tie. *John Mackie* **62**

KAPSTADT (FR) 5 b.g. Country Reel (USA) 113 – King's Parody (IRE) (King's Best (USA) 132) [2015 7d 8.3m⁵ 9s² Aug 29] fairly useful handicapper: second at Goodwood in August: should stay 1¼m: acts on good and good to firm going: sometimes in headgear prior to 2015: useful hurdler. *Ian Williams* **88**

KARAKA JACK 8 ch.g. Pivotal 124 – Mauri Moon 104 (Green Desert (USA) 127) [2015 89: 7.2g 7.2s⁶ 8.3g³ 8g³ 7.9g 7m 7m⁴ 8m⁴ 8m² 9g* 8gᵖᵘ Oct 3] strong gelding: fairly useful handicapper: won at Newmarket (by 1¼ lengths from Squire) in September: stays 10.5f: acts on fibresand, soft and good to firm going: tried in blinkers prior to 2015: front runner/races prominently. *Jim Goldie* **83**

KARAKONTIE (JPN) 4 b.c. Bernstein (USA) 115 – Sun Is Up (JPN) (Sunday Silence (USA)) [2015 125: 8d⁶ 8s³ 8g Oct 31] lengthy colt: high-class performer in 2014, winning Poule d'Essai des Poulains at Longchamp and Breeders' Cup Mile at Santa Anita: not the same force in just 3 races in 2015 (reportedly suffered foot problem in May): just smart form in Prix Jacques le Marois at Deauville (sixth to Esoterique) and Prix du Moulin de Longchamp (2 lengths third to Ervedya) on first 2 starts: well held in Breeders' Cup Mile at Keeneland final outing: stayed 1m: acted on firm and soft going: to stand at Gainesway Farm, Kentucky, fee $15,000. *J. E. Pease, France* **110**

KARAKTAR (IRE) 3 b.c. High Chaparral (IRE) 132 – Karawana (IRE) 99 (King's Best (USA) 132) [2015 10.4s* 10.4g* 10.4g 9.9s* Sep 19] fifth foal: half-brother to 2-y-o 6f winner Karamaya (by Invincible Spirit) and 1¼m winner Karatash (by Halling), both useful: dam, 1m/1¼m winner (stayed 1½m), out of half-sister to smart stayer Kasthari: smart performer: improved in 2015, winning listed race at Saint-Cloud (easily, by 7 lengths) in March, Prix Noailles at Longchamp in April and Prix du Prince d'Orange on latter course (off 3½ months, beat Sumbal by a neck, part 7 lengths clear, edging ahead near finish) in September: favourite, only eighth of 14 behind New Bay in Prix du Jockey Club at Chantilly on third outing, finding little (slipped on turn and reported to have displaced pelvis): will stay 1½m: acts on soft going. *A. de Royer Dupre, France* **118**

KARAM ALBAARI (IRE) 7 b.h. King's Best (USA) 132 – Lilakiya (IRE) 60 (Dr Fong **80** (USA) 128) [2015 86: f12g³ p16g² p13.3g* 16m⁶ p13.3m³ May 19] fairly useful handicapper: won at Chelmsford (by 8 lengths from Taaresh) in February: stays easy 2m, may be best over shorter on turf: acts on polytrack, good to firm and good to soft going: tried in cheekpieces prior to 2015: races well off pace, often travels strongly. *J. R. Jenkins*

KARATE QUEEN 10 b.m. King's Best (USA) 132 – Black Belt Shopper (IRE) 82 **–** (Desert Prince (IRE) 130) [2015 36: 6g 7g⁵ Jun 20] close-coupled mare: maiden: no form in 2015: stays 6f: acts on polytrack, soft and good to firm going: tried in headgear prior to 2015: tried in tongue tie prior to 2015. *Ron Barr*

KARCH 2 b.f. (Apr 23) Sulamani (IRE) 130 – Let It Be 83 (Entrepreneur 123) [2015 7g 6d **–** 7g Sep 23] fourth foal: dam 1½m-17f winner: no form. *Keith Reveley*

KARENS STAR 2 b.f. (Feb 23) Piccolo 121 – Maarees (Groom Dancer (USA) 128) [2015 **65** 7d t8.6f⁶ t8.6m⁶ t8.6f t9.5f⁵ Dec 14] fourth foal: dam, maiden, including over hurdles: fair maiden: best effort at 8.5f: acts on tapeta *Steph Hollinshead*

KARISMA (IRE) 2 gr.f. (May 8) Lawman (FR) 121 – Lucky Clio (IRE) 59 (Key of Luck **– p** (USA) 126) [2015 7g Jul 24] good-topped filly: fifth foal: half-sister to 3 winners, including smart winner up to 6f Lucky Beggar (2-y-o 5f winner, by Verglas) and useful winner up to 10.3f Kingsdesire (2-y-o 1m winner, by King's Best): dam, maiden (stayed 7f), half-sister to very smart winner up to 1¼m Special Kaldoun: 25/1, badly needed experience when eighth in maiden at Ascot (10½ lengths behind Marenko) in July: likely to do better. *Roger Varian*

KARMADAL (IRE) 3 b.f. Shamardal (USA) 129 – Karmifira (FR) 111 (Always Fair **81** (USA) 121) [2015 7s³ p7m² p8g² p8g⁶ f7g* Dec 29] 95,000F: half-sister to several winners, including useful 2-y-o 7.5f winner (stayed 9.5f) On Verra (by Smart Strike) and 2-y-o 1m winner Kaminari (by Sea The Stars): dam winner up to 9f (2-y-o 7f winner): fairly useful performer: won maiden at Southwell (by 4½ lengths from Mitre Peak) in December: best effort at 7f: acts on fibresand: usually in hood: front runner/races prominently. *William Haggas*

KARNAGE (IRE) 3 b.g. Lawman (FR) 121 – Kazinoki (UAE) (Timber Country (USA) **79** 124) [2015 7d 8m⁵ 7g 10.3d⁶ t9.5g² p10g³ Dec 15] strong gelding: fair maiden: stays 1¼m: acts on polytrack and tapeta. *Daniel Kubler*

KARPINO (GER) 3 b.c. Cape Cross (IRE) 129 – Kahara 100 (Sadler's Wells (USA) 132) **118** [2015 8.4d* 8g* May 25] third foal: half-brother to 2 winners in Germany, including useful 7f winner Karpina (by Pivotal): dam, 1¼m to 1¾m winner, sister to St Leger winner Milan and daughter of smart 11f/1½m (at St Simon Stakes) winner Kithanga: smart form: has won all 3 of his starts, namely minor event at Hoppegarten (by 4 lengths) at 2 yrs, Dr Busch-Memorial at Krefeld (by 2½ lengths from Ajalo) in April and Mehl-Mulhens-Rennen - German 2000 Guineas at Cologne (beat Fanciful Angel by 4½ lengths) in May: bred to stay 1½m: reported in early-July to have suffered setback and wasn't seen out again: stays in training. *A. Wohler, Germany*

KARRAAR 4 b.g. Dubawi (IRE) 129 – Maghya (IRE) 96 (Mujahid (USA) 125) [2015 90: **96** 10f* 14.1d⁵ 13g⁶ 12s* Sep 13] strong gelding: useful performer: won handicaps at Sandown (by nose from Tom Hark) in July and Ffos Las (by 4 lengths from Royal Warranty, suited by drop in trip) in September: likely to prove best at around 1½m: acts on firm and soft going: sometimes in cheekpieces. *William Haggas*

KASBAH (IRE) 3 b.g. Acclamation 118 – Dance Hall Girl (IRE) 81 (Dansili 127) [2015 **100** 93: 5d 6s p5g² 6d⁴ t6f* Oct 3] useful handicapper: career-best effort when winning at Wolverhampton (by ¾ length from Seeking Magic) in October: stays 6f: acts on tapeta, polytrack and good to firm going: tried in headgear. *John Patrick Murtagh, Ireland*

KASB (IRE) 3 ch.g. Arcano (IRE) 122 – Cape Columbine 106 (Diktat 126) [2015 97p: 7m **–** Jun 27] attractive, good-topped gelding: useful performer at best: stiff task, well held only start in 2015: stays 7f: acts on good to firm and good to soft going: tried in blinkers: sent to UAE. *John Gosden*

KASHGAR 6 b.g. Hernando (FR) 127 – Miss Katmandu (IRE) (Rainbow Quest (USA) **91** 134) [2015 97: 14.1s⁵ 16m 13.4g⁵ 16m⁵ 15.9m⁶ 16d⁶ 16s⁵ 15.9g 16m Oct 2] sturdy gelding: fairly useful handicapper: stays 2m: acts on good and good to firm going: tried in headgear prior to 2015: tried in tongue tie in 2015. *Bernard Llewellyn*

KASHMIR PEAK (IRE) 6 b.g. Tiger Hill (IRE) 127 – Elhareer (IRE) 71 (Selkirk (USA) **88** 129) [2015 89, a99: 12s³ 13.1g⁶ Sep 19] stocky gelding: useful handicapper at best: just respectable efforts in 2 starts in 2015: stays 16.5f: acts on polytrack, best turf form on good going or softer: has worn headgear: often races towards rear. *John Quinn*

KASHSTAREE 4 b.f. Sakhee (USA) 136 – Celestial Welcome 96 (Most Welcome 131) – [2015 54: 16m 16.1g Sep 4] maiden: no form in 2015: stays 1¾m: acts on heavy going: in blinkers last start in 2015: often races in rear. *John Quinn*

KASHTAN 2 ch.f. (Apr 1) Sakhee's Secret 128 – Gitane (FR) (Grand Lodge (USA) 125) **75** [2015 p6g³ 5m² 5m² p6f⁴ t5.1f* t5.1f³ p5g Dec 11] 3,000F, €15,000Y: sister to useful 6f/7f winner Pool House and half-sister to useful winner up to 1¼m Mega Back (by Zamindar) and 9f winner Golshan (by Shirocco): dam 11f winner: fair performer: won maiden at Wolverhampton in October: best form at 5f: acts on tapeta and good to firm going. *Harry Dunlop*

KASPERSKY (IRE) 4 b.c. Footstepsinthesand 120 – Croanda (IRE) (Grand Lodge **118** (USA) 125) [2015 8m* 8m* 8m* 8m* 8g⁴ 8g* Oct 25] smart performer: improved in 2015, winning minor event at Rome in March, listed race on same course in April, Premio Carlo Vittadini at Milan (by 1¾ lengths from Circus Couture) in May, minor event in September and Premio Ribot (by 1½ lengths from Circus Couture, leading 3f out) in October, last 2 also at Rome: raced mainly at 1m: acts on good to firm going: usually tongue tied. *E. Botti, Italy*

KASSBAAN 3 b.g. Kodiac 112 – Town And Gown 72 (Oasis Dream 129) [2015 70: 5g* **85** 5.1g³ 6m² 5m* 6g Aug 29] sturdy, compact gelding: fairly useful handicapper: won at Windsor in June and August: stayed 6f: acted on good to firm going: dead. *Marco Botti*

KASSEOPIA 2 ch.c. (Apr 15) Showcasing 117 – Dream Again 65 (Medicean 128) [2015 **102** 7m⁶ p8g² p8d* p8.5f² Oct 4] 12,500F, 40,000 2-y-o: good-quartered colt: fifth foal: half-brother to 6f/7f winner Debejki (by Where Or When) and 1m winner Dream Melody (by Selkirk): dam, twice-raced daughter of Oaks runner-up Dance A Dream, herself sister to 2000 Guineas winner Entrepreneur: useful performer: much improved when winning maiden at Kempton (by 9 lengths from Celebration Day) in September: creditable second in Grade 3 Grey Stakes at Woodbine (1½ lengths behind Riker) in October: stays 8.5f: acts on polytrack. *Charlie Fellowes*

KASSIA (IRE) 2 b.f. (Apr 27) Acclamation 118 – Speedy Sonata (USA) (Stravinsky **92** (USA) 133) [2015 5m² 5m* 5f⁵ 6d⁶ 6g 6d* Oct 5] €180,000Y: rather unfurnished filly: fifth foal: half-sister to 2-y-o 6f winner Yesnabay (by Grand Slam) and 6f (including at 2 yrs) winner Rufford (by Invincible Spirit), both useful: dam US 5f/5.5f (including at 2 yrs) winner: fairly useful performer: won maiden at Sandown in May and nursery at Pontefract (by neck from Noble Peace) in October: stays 6f: acts on good to firm and good to soft going: often travels strongly. *Mick Channon*

KASTELA STARI 8 b.m. Beat Hollow 126 – Campaspe 79 (Dominion 123) [2015 59: **56** 15.8s t16.5f² t16.5m f14g Dec 12] modest maiden: stays 16.5f: acts on polytrack, tapeta and good to firm going: tried in eyeshields in 2015: often in tongue tie prior to 2015: usually races towards rear. *Tim Fitzgerald*

KASTINI 5 b.g. Halling (USA) 133 – Toucantini 65 (Inchinor 119) [2015 87§: 10m² 10m³ **92** 10m⁶ 10f⁵ 10g 10d* 10.1v³ 10s* 10v⁵ Oct 24] close-coupled gelding: fairly useful handicapper: won at Newbury in August and September, latter by 2 lengths from Craftsmanship: stays 11.5f: acts on good to firm and heavy going: usually visored in 2014: often races towards rear/travels strongly: has sometimes looked temperamental: sold 20,000 gns, sent to Italy. *Denis Coakley*

KATABATIK KATIE 2 b.f. (May 2) Sir Percy 129 – New Choice (IRE) (Barathea (IRE) – 127) [2015 t7.1f Nov 10] fourth foal: half-sister to 6f-7.5f winner Dasho (by Dubawi): dam unraced half-sister to smart 1½m winner (stays 15f) Glaring: 33/1, last of 9 in maiden at Wolverhampton. *Mrs Ilka Gansera-Leveque*

KATANIYA (IRE) 3 b.f. Raven's Pass (USA) 133 – Katiykha (IRE) 117 (Darshaan 133) **113** [2015 p9.4g² 11.9g* 10.9g* 11.9g* 11.9m² 9.9g⁶ 10d Sep 13] big, rangy, attractive filly: half-sister to several winners, including smart winner up to 1¼m Katiyra (2-y-o 7f winner, by Peintre Celebre) and useful 1½m winner Katiola (by Oratorio): dam 1½m-1¾m winner: smart performer: won maiden at Maisons-Laffitte in April, listed race at Longchamp in May and Prix de Royaumont at Chantilly (by neck from Sea Calisi) in May: good second in Prix de Malleret at Saint-Cloud (1½ lengths behind Sea Calisi) in June: below form in Prix de la Nonette at Deauville and Blandford Stakes at the Curragh last 2 starts: stays 1½m: acts on good to firm going. *A. de Royer Dupre, France*

KATAWI 4 b.f. Dubawi (IRE) 129 – Purring (USA) 79 (Mountain Cat (USA)) [2015 101: **105** 6.1s 6g 5m* 5m 5m 5g 5s⁶ 5m⁵ Oct 3] well-made filly: useful performer: won listed race at Ayr (by 2 lengths from Holley Shiftwell) in June: 28/1, one of better other efforts when

3 lengths fifth of 13 to Dutch Masterpiece in listed race at Ascot final start: stays 6f: acts on good to firm and good to soft going: usually wears hood: usually races towards rear. *Chris Wall*

KATHLATINO 8 b.m. Danbird (AUS) – Silver Rhythm 53 (Silver Patriarch (IRE) 125) **57** [2015 66: 12.4d 13.8m² 12g 13d⁴ 14g³ 16d 15.8s Oct 6] modest handicapper: stays 14.5f: acts on good to firm and heavy going: tried in headgear. *Micky Hammond*

KATH'S LEGACY 2 ch.f. (Mar 19) Cockney Rebel (IRE) 127 – It's Dubai Dolly 82 **69** (Dubai Destination (USA) 127) [2015 7s 6g⁶ 6s³ p7g³ p7m⁵ Dec 31] first foal: dam 1¼m-1½m winner: fair maiden: best effort at 7f: acts on polytrack. *Ben De Haan*

KATIE CANFORD 2 b.f. (Feb 17) Canford Cliffs (IRE) 133 – Serafina's Flight 82 **67** (Fantastic Light (USA) 134) [2015 5s³ 5m³ 6g⁵ 5g⁵ 5f⁶ Jul 23] lengthy filly: second foal: half-sister to useful 11f winner Durlindana (by Mastercraftsman): dam 8.6f winner who stayed 1½m: fair maiden: stays 6f: acts on good to firm going: front runner/races prominently. *John Bridger*

KATIE ELDER (FR) 4 b.f. High Chaparral (IRE) 132 – Cool And Composed (USA) **59** (Buddha (USA) 122) [2015 p12m² p12m⁶ p13.3g³ 16d May 19] 4,500 3-y-o: first foal: dam, 1m-9.5f winner, half-sister to 6f winner (stayed 1m) Shadowland: modest maiden: best effort at 1½m. *David Brown*

KATIE GALE 5 b.m. Shirocco (GER) 129 – Karla June (Unfuwain (USA) 131) [2015 74: **84** f12s⁵ f16d⁴ f14d⁴ p15.8f⁵ 16.5m² 16m p16g 14.6m⁴ 15.8g* p16g Aug 19] angular mare: fairly useful handicapper: won at Southwell in February and March and Musselburgh in July: stays 16.5f: acts on polytrack, fibresand and good to firm going: tried in blinkers: front runner/races prominently, sometimes finds little. *Michael Appleby*

KATIE'S DIAMOND (FR) 2 b.f. (Feb 21) Turtle Bowl (IRE) 121 – Aaliyah (GER) **104** (Anabaa (USA) 130) [2015 6g* 6m* 7g³ 8m⁵ Oct 4] €18,000Y: strong, workmanlike filly, type to carry plenty of condition: seventh foal: half-sister to 1¼m/11f winner Perennite (by Vespone) and 9f-10.5f winner Music Hall (by Stormy River): dam, 8.5f winner, half-sister to smart 11f winner Adelar and useful 2-y-o 7f/1m winner (stayed 1¼m) Aquatinta: useful form: won maiden at Redcar in May and listed race at Newmarket (by neck from White Bullet) in June: third to Great Page in Prix du Calvados at Deauville, then improved again when 2½ lengths fifth of 8 to Ballydoyle in Prix Marcel Boussac at Longchamp, having run of race: stays 1m: wears hood. *K. R. Burke*

KATMAI RIVER (IRE) 8 b.g. Choisir (AUS) 126 – Katavi (USA) 56 (Stravinsky **52** (USA) 133) [2015 47, a63: t8.6f⁶ p8f⁵ p7g² p8f⁴ p8m² p8f p8f³ p8g t8.6g t8.6m Apr 29] workmanlike gelding: modest handicapper: stays 9.5f: acts on polytrack, tapeta and heavy going: often wears headgear. *Mark Usher*

KATNISS (IRE) 3 ch.f. Champs Elysees 124 – Nicene (USA) (Pulpit (USA) 117) [2015 **59** –p: 9.9d⁶ p15.8g⁵ p12g* 13.1f⁶ 11.9d p13.3f p12g³ Oct 20] modest handicapper: won at Lingfield in August: stays 13f: acts on polytrack and firm going: usually in tongue tie in 2015. *Stuart Williams*

KAUFMANN 3 b.g. Showcasing 117 – Mini Mosa 73 (Indian Ridge 123) [2015 86: t7.1f⁶ **71** p5g p6g⁴ p8m⁵ t7.1g⁵ t7.1g 7m Apr 25] compact gelding: fair handicapper: left John Gosden after second start: stays 7f: acts on polytrack and tapeta: usually in headgear in 2015: often races lazily. *Chris Dwyer*

KAVACO (IRE) 6 b.g. Choisir (AUS) 126 – Nose One's Way (IRE) 57 (Revoque (IRE) **–** 122) [2015 72: 8m⁴ 5.7m Jul 22] fair at best, no form in 2015: likely to prove best at short of 1m: acts on polytrack and good to soft going: tried in blinkers/tongue tie: front runner/races prominently. *Mark Gillard*

KAWAII 3 b.f. Myboycharlie (IRE) 118 – Aliena (IRE) (Grand Lodge (USA) 125) [2015 –: **71** t8.6g³ 7.5g⁴ 8.3g⁵ 7g t7.1f⁵ p8g p7g Dec 9] fair maiden: stays 8.5f: acts on tapeta: tried in visor in 2015. *Philip McBride*

KAWARTHA 3 b.f. Royal Applause 124 – Zarkavean (Medicean 128) [2015 p10m Nov **–** 19] second foal: half-sister to 7f-1¼m winner Zakayla (by Aqlaam): dam, unraced, closely related to useful 2-y-o 1m winner Emily Bronte: 50/1, tailed off in maiden at Lingfield. *Robert Stephens*

KAY GEE BE (IRE) 11 b.g. Fasliyev (USA) 120 – Pursuit of Truth (USA) 69 (Irish River **–** (FR) 131) [2015 66: 7.2d 8.3g t9.5f Oct 16] tall, good-topped gelding: fairly useful handicapper in 2012, has deteriorated markedly: sometimes in cheekpieces. *Alan Berry*

KAYLAN'S ROSE 5 b.m. Kayf Tara 130 – Ostfanni (IRE) 74 (Spectrum (IRE) 126) **–** [2015 –: 9.2g⁵ 12g Sep 26] maiden: no form in 2015. *Dianne Sayer*

KAYO KOKO (IRE) 3 b.f. Zebedee 113 – Negria (IRE) (Al Hareb (USA) 123) [2015 71: —
7.5m 9.8v³ 7m May 25] fair at best, no form in 2015: tried in headgear in 2015. *Ann Duffield*

KAY SERA 7 b.g. Kayf Tara 130 – Inflation 68 (Primo Dominie 121) [2015 t12.2g f12g² **74**
Dec 22] fair form: best effort in maidens when second of 8 to Busy Street at Southwell in
December: placed in bumpers. *Tony Newcombe*

KAYTOM 4 b.f. Misu Bond (IRE) 114 – Morristown Music (IRE) 71 (Distant Music —
(USA) 126) [2015 –: p7m Jan 18] no form: sometimes wears blinkers. *John Wainwright*

KAZOEY 2 b.f. (Feb 7) Stimulation (IRE) 121 – Dubawi's Spirit (IRE) (Dubawi (IRE) —
129) [2015 6g 7m 6g Aug 15] 2,000Y: first foal: dam unraced half-sister to smart 6f/6.5f
winner Prince Aaron: no form. *Chris Fairhurst*

KAZZIANA 3 b.f. Shamardal (USA) 129 – Kazzia (GER) 121 (Zinaad 114) [2015 10.2g³ **88 p**
p8g* 10.2d⁵ Sep 2] well-made filly: sixth foal: half-sister to 3 winners, including very
smart winner up to 1½m (stayed 1¾m) Eastern Anthem (2-y-o 8.2f winner) and smart
2-y-o 1m/9f winner Zeitoper (both by Singspiel): dam won 1000 Guineas and Oaks (2-y-o
7f/1m winner): fairly useful performer: best effort when winning maiden at Kempton (by
3½ lengths from Saraha) in August, well positioned: should stay at least 1¼m: acts on
polytrack: still unexposed. *Charlie Appleby*

KEBLE (IRE) 3 b.c. Teofilo (IRE) 126 – Vadazing (FR) (Spinning World (USA) 130) **108**
[2015 82p: 8m² 10g² 9.9m* 10g² 9.9m² Jul 30] tall, useful-looking colt: useful performer:
won maiden at Goodwood (by 2 lengths from Covenant) in June: in cheekpieces, best
effort when neck second to Gibeon in handicap there on final start: stays 1¼m: acts on
good to firm going: strong traveller, usually responds generously to pressure: sent to UAE.
John Gosden

KEENE'S POINTE 5 br.g. Avonbridge 123 – Belle's Edge (Danehill Dancer (IRE) 117) **72**
[2015 70: t7.1f⁶ t7.1g p8f⁵ t8.6f⁴ t8.6f 8s³ 7.1g⁵ 7d⁴ 7.2d⁵ 6m³ t7.1g 7g³ 6g* 5.9g³ 6g² 6g³ **a61**
6g² 7s⁴ Oct 26] fair handicapper: won at Newcastle in August: should be suited by a return
to 6f: acts on polytrack, tapeta, soft and good to firm going: sometimes wears headgear.
Kristin Stubbs

KEEN MOVE 3 b.g. Aussie Rules (USA) 123 – Kekova (Montjeu (IRE) 137) [2015 60: **74 §**
10.2m² 10.2m³ p10g 11.9m³ 11.7m² Jul 8] fair maiden: stays 11.5f: acts on good to firm
going: often wears headgear: often races towards rear: not straightforward and isn't one to
trust: sent to Italy, where won over hurdles in November. *Ismail Mohammed*

KEEPER'S RING (USA) 4 b.f. Street Cry (IRE) 130 – Liffey Dancer (IRE) (Sadler's **50**
Wells (USA) 132) [2015 65: p8f⁶ Jan 21] modest maiden: best effort at 8.5f: acts on
polytrack and good to soft going: tried in blinkers prior to 2015. *Roger Varian*

KEEP IN LINE (GER) 3 b.c. Soldier Hollow 121 – Kastila (GER) (Sternkoenig (IRE) **112**
122) [2015 55p: t8.6g⁵ 9g* 12f 11.6d* 12m⁵ 12s³ 12s* 12g Oct 9] useful-looking colt:
smart performer: progressed very well in 2015 and won maiden at Ripon (by neck from
Count Montecristo) in May and handicaps at Windsor (by 1¼ lengths from Royal Altitude)
in July and Newbury (by neck from Satellite) in September: stays 1½m: acts on soft and
good to firm going: in cheekpieces final start (well held). *Saeed bin Suroor*

KEEP IT DARK 6 b.g. Invincible Spirit (IRE) 121 – Tarneem (USA) 87 (Zilzal (USA) **86**
137) [2015 92, a75: 5v² 5m⁶ 5g⁶ 7g p5g⁶ 5m⁶ 5d 5d 5g 5.1s² 5g* 5g² 5g* 5s 5.1d² f5g* f5g
Dec 12] fairly useful handicapper: won at Beverley in September, Ripon (by neck from
Singeur) in September and Southwell (by ¾ length from Even Stevens) in November: stays
1m: acts on fibresand and heavy going: tried in headgear: often races prominently/travels
strongly: quirky sort, carries head high. *Tony Coyle*

KEEP KICKING (IRE) 8 b.g. Tiger Hill (IRE) 127 – Dalannda (IRE) (Hernando (FR) **72**
127) [2015 78: p12m p16g* p15.8g³ p16d⁶ Mar 16] well-made gelding: fair handicapper:
won at Chelmsford in January: stays 2m: acts on polytrack and good to firm going: tried in
cheekpieces prior to 2015: often races in rear. *Simon Dow*

KEEP ON DANCING 2 b.f. (Mar 16) Sakhee's Secret 128 – Dancing Nelly 52 (Shareef —
Dancer (USA) 135) [2015 6m 5g 6d Oct 26] 800F, £8,000Y: sister to winner up to 7.6f
Mystical Man (2-y-o 6f winner) and half-sister to several winners, including 5f/6f
(including at 2 yrs) winner Valhillen (by Bertolini) and temperamental 1¼m winner Ice
Nelly (by Iceman): dam maiden (should have stayed 1m): down the field in maidens.
Michael Easterby

KEEP 'R LIT 3 b.f. Multiplex 114 – Cashel Dancer 47 (Bishop of Cashel 122) [2015 39: —
8v p6f t6f t5.1m Dec 30] small filly: no form: tried in headgear/tongue tie. *Miss
Imogen Pickard*

Irish Stallion Farms European Breeders Fund 'Sovereign Path' Handicap, Leopardstown—a 1, 2 for British stables in this concluding event to the first day of Irish Champions' Weekend, Kelinni producing a smart effort under 9-12 to beat Withernsea (checked cap) who catches Seanie (diamond on cap) who finishes third ahead of Colour Blue (left)

KEEP TO THE BEAT 4 b.f. Beat Hollow 126 – Cadeau Speciale 54 (Cadeaux Genereux 131) [2015 69, a61: f11g⁴ t9.5f t9.5f³ t8.6f³ 8.5m t12.2g⁴ 14.1m Aug 8] modest maiden: stays 1½m: acts on polytrack, tapeta and good to firm going: sometimes wears cheekpieces: tried in tongue tie in 2015: fair hurdler. *Kevin Ryan* **59**

KEEP UP (GER) 3 b.g. Monsun (GER) 124 – Katy Carr 70 (Machiavellian (USA) 123) [2015 57: 10m f14s⁵ 11.9d t12.2f⁵ t16.5f⁵ Oct 27] modest maiden: left Saeed bin Suroor after second start: worth another try at 1¾m: acts on tapeta and good to firm going: tried in cheekpieces in 2015: often races towards rear. *Philip Kirby* **55**

KEIBA (IRE) 2 gr.c. (Apr 24) Dark Angel (IRE) 113 – True Magic 80 (Magic Ring (IRE) 115) [2015 p6d⁶ 5.1g⁶ p6g Oct 27] fair maiden: best effort when sixth at Kempton in September on debut. *Gary Moore* **70**

KELINNI (IRE) 7 b.g. Refuse To Bend (IRE) 128 – Orinoco (IRE) 53 (Darshaan 133) [2015 106: p12f⁴ 14s⁴ 12g* 12f⁵ 12f 10.4m² 10.4m⁵ 8d³ 7g* 8d Oct 3] smart handicapper: won at Thirsk (by ¾ length from Manhattan Swing) in April and Leopardstown (16-runner event, by 1¾ lengths from Withernsea) in September: creditable placed efforts at York in between, including neck second to Master Carpenter in John Smith's Cup: below form in Shadwell Turf Mile at Keeneland final outing: effective at 7f to 1½m: acts on polytrack, good to firm and heavy going: often in headgear prior to 2015: tried in tongue tie prior to 2015: front runner, often travels strongly. *Kevin Ryan* **118**

KELLY'S DINO (FR) 2 b.g. (Mar 1) Doctor Dino (FR) 123 – Sabolienne (FR) (Marchand de Sable (USA) 117) [2015 5.9g* 7d⁶ 8g⁶ Sep 19] fair form: won maiden at Carlisle in June despite starting very slowly: should stay 1m. *K. R. Burke* **73**

KELLY'S FINEST (IRE) 3 ch.f. Intense Focus (USA) 117 – Priory Rock (IRE) 79 (Rock of Gibraltar (IRE) 133) [2015 78: 9.9m⁵ 9.8g⁴ 12g³ 12g³ 12m² 12d⁴ 12.2m⁵ 14.1d⁵ f12g p13.3g³ p13.3g* p13.3m² Dec 27] fair performer: won maiden at Chelmsford in December: left James Bethell after eighth start: stays 1¾m: acts on polytrack, good to firm and good to soft going: often in headgear in 2015: often leads. *Michael Appleby* **73**

KELVIN HALL 2 ch.f. (Mar 21) Halling (USA) 133 – Barawin (IRE) 87 (Hawk Wing (USA) 136) [2015 8d³ 8s t7.1f³ p8f³ Nov 12] 16,000F, 6,000Y: second foal: half-sister to useful winner up to 1½m Sir Jack Layden (2-y-o 7f winner, by Sir Percy): dam 2-y-o 1m winner who stayed 1¾m: fair maiden: should do better when stepped up to 1¼m and more. *Mark Johnston* **72 p**

KEMSING (IRE) 2 ch.g. (Apr 12) Footstepsinthesand 120 – St Edith (IRE) 58 (Desert King (IRE) 129) [2015 7g 6m 6g t8.6g⁵ f7g⁶ Dec 18] rather unfurnished gelding: modest performer: left Olly Stevens, improved form on fibresand debut when winning nursery at Southwell in December: should stay 1m. *Julia Feilden* **58**

KENNY THE CAPTAIN (IRE) 4 ch.g. Captain Rio 122 – Kelso Magic (USA) 98 (Distant View (USA) 126) [2015 78: 6d 6d* 6s⁵ 6g 6m⁵ 5.9d² 6g 5.9s² 6s f6g f6g Dec 15] useful-looking, athletic gelding: fairly useful handicapper: won at Newcastle (by length from Kommander Kirkup) in April: stays 6f: acts on good to firm and heavy going: often in headgear in 2015. *Tim Easterby* **83**

KENOBE STAR (IRE) 3 b.g. Clodovil (IRE) 116 – Maimana (IRE) 105 (Desert King –
(IRE) 129) [2015 8.3m p10m May 19] well held in 2 maidens: has joined Jamie Snowden.
Chris Wall

KENSTONE (FR) 2 gr.g. (Mar 17) Kendargent (FR) 112 – Little Stone (FR) (One Cool **68**
Cat (USA) 123) [2015 6g 6m p6d p6g² p6f² p7g² 7s⁵ p6f Nov 5] angular gelding: fair
maiden: likely to prove best up to 7f: acts on polytrack: tried in cheekpieces. *David Dennis*

KENT RAGSTONE (USA) 6 ch.g. Stonesider (USA) – Sweet Charity (USA) (A P Indy –
(USA) 131) [2015 –: f14g Dec 12] fairly useful at best in 2013, no form since. *Sheena West*

KENTUCKYCONNECTION (USA) 2 b.c. (Feb 14) Include (USA) 121 – Youcanring- **94 p**
mybell (USA) (Street Cry (IRE) 130) [2015 7m* 7d⁶ 7d⁴ 10g⁶ Oct 10] $22,000F, 60,000
2-y-o: lengthy, rather unfurnished colt: first foal: dam unraced half-sister to smart
US Grade 3 8.5f winner Eh Cumpari: useful from: well backed, won maiden at Redcar in
July on debut: well held in pattern company next 2 starts, but progress when 4¾ lengths
sixth of 10 to Glamorous Approach in listed race at Newmarket final outing: stays 1¼m:
remains with potential. *Bryan Smart*

KEPT UNDER WRAPS (IRE) 2 gr.f. (Apr 13) Clodovil (IRE) 116 – Chatifa (IRE) 83 **82**
(Titus Livius (FR) 115) [2015 5.1d* 5m May 23] 40,000Y: half-sister to 9f/1¼m winner
Akaaleel (by Teofilo): dam, 1m winner, half-sister to top-class winner up to 1½m Dylan
Thomas, 1000 Guineas winner Homecoming Queen and Cheveley Park Stakes winner
Queen's Logic: fairly useful form when winning maiden at Nottingham in May on debut,
making all: well held in minor event at Beverley next time, possibly amiss (not seen out
again). *Richard Fahey*

KERBAAJ (USA) 5 b.g. Dixie Union (USA) 121 – Mabaahej (USA) 69 (Belong To Me **70**
(USA)) [2015 –: t6m³ f6s⁶ 7m t6g 7.1g May 1] rangy gelding: fair handicapper: stays 7.5f:
acts on fibresand, tapeta and good to firm going: tried in cheekpieces/tongue tie: often
races towards rear. *Ruth Carr*

KERRY ICON 2 b.f. (Mar 4) Sixties Icon 125 – La Gifted 79 (Fraam 114) [2015 p6m p6g⁵ –
t5.1m⁶ t6f Dec 22] third foal: dam, 7f winner, half-sister to smart winner up to 9f Samitar:
no form. *Mick Channon*

KERRYMERRY (IRE) 3 b.c. Vale of York (IRE) 117 – Reasonably Devout (CAN) (St **78**
Jovite (USA) 135) [2015 58: 12.1g³ p10m* 11.5d* 12m² 12.1g² 10.3m⁶ 12g² Aug 15] fair
handicapper: won at Lingfield (twice) in June: better form when second at Hamilton and
Ripon fifth/final starts: stays 1½m: acts on polytrack, good to firm and good to soft going:
front runner/races prominently. *Ismail Mohammed*

KESTREL CALL (IRE) 2 b.c. (Mar 10) Acclamation 118 – Winged Harriet (IRE) 85 **53**
(Hawk Wing (USA) 136) [2015 6.1m t7.1f⁶ Dec 22] better effort when sixth of 12 in
maiden at Wolverhampton (12 lengths behind Always Welcome) in December. *Simon
Crisford*

KEY ON KODIAC (IRE) 2 b.c. (Apr 8) Kodiac 112 – Kilakey (IRE) (Key of Luck **75**
(USA) 126) [2015 5.1m³ 6d⁵ 6m⁶ p7g⁴ t8.6f² t7.1f⁵ Oct 20] good-topped colt: fair maiden:
likely to prove suited by return to 1m: acts on tapeta: sold 22,000 gns, sent to Singapore.
Charles Hills

KEYS (IRE) 8 b.g. Doyen (IRE) 132 – Freni (GER) (Sternkoenig (IRE) 122) [2015 14s⁶ **79**
16.4m 12g⁵ 12v⁶ Aug 31] compact gelding: fair handicapper: stays 2m: best form on good
going: usually wears blinkers. *Tony Carroll*

KEYSTROKE 3 b.c. Pivotal 124 – Fondled 101 (Selkirk (USA) 129) [2015 8d* 8.3d* 8g **97 p**
Sep 19] 120,000Y: third foal: brother to useful 1m-10.3f winner Cosseted: dam 1m winner:
useful form: won first 2 starts, namely maiden at Doncaster in May and handicap at
Windsor (by length from Critical Risk) in August: better than result when ninth of 10 in
handicap at Newmarket final start: stays 8.5f: should still do better. *Jeremy Noseda*

KEY TO YOUR HEART 4 b.f. Sakhee (USA) 136 – You Too 74 (Monsun (GER) 124) **?**
[2015 59: 18.6f p10m Feb 4] rather leggy filly: maiden in Britain: well held there in 2015:
stays 1½m: acts on polytrack and tapeta: tried in cheekpieces prior to 2015: often wears
tongue tie: sent to Italy, where won 1m handicap at Rome in December. *Michael Bell*

K'GARI SPIRIT 2 b.f. (Feb 14) Major Cadeaux 121 – Ivory Silk 94 (Diktat 126) [2015 **66 p**
t5.1f³ Dec 21] first foal: dam 5f-7f winner out of useful winner up to 6f (2-y-o 5f/6f
winner) Ivory's Joy: third of 7 to Krystallite in maiden at Wolverhampton on debut,
keeping on not knocked about: better to come. *Jeremy Gask*

KHAJAALY (IRE) 8 b.g. Kheleyf (USA) 116 – Joyfullness (USA) (Dixieland Band **60**
(USA)) [2015 80: t7.1g⁵ f7g² 7d⁷ t7.1g f7g³ t7.1g⁶ t7.1g⁶ 7.1m 7d³ 8v² 7g* 7s⁶ 8.3g⁴ **a80**
t7.1f⁴ Nov 16] angular gelding: modest handicapper on turf, fairly useful on all-weather:

won at Southwell in February and Catterick in September: stays 8.5f: acts on polytrack, fibresand, good to firm and heavy going: has worn headgear: wears tongue tie. *Daniel Loughnane*

KHALAAS 3 b.g. Iffraaj 127 – Bahia Breeze 109 (Mister Baileys 123) [2015 82: 7g* 7g⁴ **92** 8m⁶ p8g Sep 21] well-made gelding: fairly useful performer: won maiden at Newcastle (by ¾ length from Akeed Champion) in May: best effort at 7f. *William Haggas*

KHALEESY (IRE) 2 b.f. (Feb 22) Galileo (IRE) 134 – Fleeting Spirit (IRE) 124 **80 p** (Invincible Spirit (IRE) 121) [2015 7g⁶ 8v⁵ p8f* Nov 12] €300,000F: sturdy filly: second foal: dam winner up to 6f (including July Cup), also won at 5f (Flying Childers Stakes) at 2 yrs: fairly useful performer: won maiden at Chelmsford (by 2½ lengths from Shall We) in November: stays 1m: will go on improving. *John Gosden*

KHAMEELA 2 b.f. (Jan 31) Equiano (FR) 127 – Mina 73 (Selkirk (USA) 129) [2015 **74 p** t7.1f³ Oct 20] 75,000Y: fifth foal: closely related to 2-y-o 5f winner Miss Diva (by Acclamation) and half-sister to useful 5f/6f winner Peace Seeker and smart 6f winner Minalisa (both by Oasis Dream): dam 6f winner: 9/1, better for run when third in maiden at Wolverhampton (length behind Swilly Sunset) in October, caught further back than ideal: sure to progress. *B. W. Hills*

KHAREER (IRE) 3 b.g. Acclamation 118 – Fantastic Account (Fantastic Light (USA) **84** 134) [2015 7m⁴ 7s³ 7g* 8g⁵ 7m Oct 2] 150,000Y: useful-looking gelding: half-brother to several winners, including smart winner up to 1¼m Coupe de Ville (2-y-o 7f/1m winner, by Clodovil) and useful winner up to 9f Fantastico Roberto (2-y-o 5f/6f winner, by Refuse To Bend): dam unraced: fairly useful performer: won maiden at Salisbury in August: stays 1m: acts on good to firm going: sold £13,000, sent to Belgium. *Charles Hills*

KHATIBA (IRE) 4 b.f. Kheleyf (USA) 116 – Tempete (Dubai Millennium 140) [2015 88, **87** a101: p7f⁶ 8.3m⁵ p8m p7g Aug 18] workmanlike filly: fairly useful handicapper: stays 7f: acts on polytrack and tapeta: sometimes wears headgear. *Roger Varian*

KHEE SOCIETY 4 b.g. Sakhee (USA) 136 – Society Rose 88 (Saddlers' Hall (IRE) 126) **69** [2015 76, a65: 11.6g⁴ 11.6g² 10.2v⁴ 11.6d⁴ Aug 29] lengthy gelding: fair handicapper: stays 11.5f: acts on good to firm and heavy going: sometimes wears hood: often races towards rear: sent to Greece. *David Evans*

KHELFAN 4 b.f. Kheleyf (USA) 116 – Fanny's Fancy 99 (Groom Dancer (USA) 128) **46** [2015 54: p6f t7.1g 6d p5g³ Jul 21] poor maiden: stays 6f: acts on polytrack: sometimes slowly away, often races towards rear. *Martin Smith*

KHELMAN (IRE) 5 b.g. Kheleyf (USA) 116 – Mandolin (IRE) 69 (Sabrehill (USA) **93** 120) [2015 93: 6d 7m² 7m³ 7g 7m 7d 6v* 6d 6d 6d 7v Nov 7] smallish gelding: fairly useful handicapper: won at Epsom (by 3 lengths from Kinglami) in September: stays 7f: acts on good to firm and heavy going: tried in cheekpieces prior to 2015: temperament under suspicion. *Richard Fahey*

KHESKIANTO (IRE) 9 b.m. Kheleyf (USA) 116 – Gently (IRE) (Darshaan 133) [2015 **– §** 54: 10.2m 11.8m⁴ 9.9m 10m Aug 18] leggy mare: fair at best, no form in 2015: tried in headgear prior to 2015: sometimes wears tongue tie: one to treat with caution. *Michael Chapman*

KHISMET 2 b.f. (Feb 24) Kheleyf (USA) 116 – Bisaat (USA) (Bahri (USA) 125) [2015 **77** 6m t7.1f* 8d t8.6f* p8g⁵ Dec 2] 3,500F: fifth foal: half-sister to 3 winners, including 2m winner Frederick William (by Tobougg) and 1¼m winner Ventura Castle (by Paco Boy): dam, ran once, out of sister to 1000 Guineas winner Lahan: fair performer: won at Wolverhampton in October (maiden) and November (claimer): stays 8.5f: acts on tapeta: in cheekpieces. *Rae Guest*

KHOR AL UDAID 2 b.g. (Feb 26) Invincible Spirit (IRE) 121 – Brusca (USA) **– p** (Grindstone (USA) 124) [2015 p8g Dec 9] 215,000F, 680,000Y: closely related to 7.5f-1¼m winner Brynica (by Desert Style) and half-brother to several winners, including smart 9.5f/10.5f winner Baraan (by Dalakhani) and useful winner up to 10.5f (stayed 15f) Brampour (2-y-o 1¼m winner, by Daylami), also very smart hurdler: dam 1m/8.5f winner: 12/1, tenth of 12 in maiden at Kempton, very slowly away: entitled to do better. *John Gosden*

KHUSOOSY (USA) 3 b.g. Hard Spun (USA) 124 – Elmaleeha 97 (Galileo (IRE) 134) **105** [2015 92: p10g* p11d⁵ p11g* p10f⁶ Oct 28] useful handicapper: won at Kempton in August (by 1½ lengths from Berrahri) and September (by ¾ length from Osipova): will stay 1½m: acts on polytrack and firm going: often wears headgear: often races prominently. *Saeed bin Suroor*

KIBAAR 3 b.g. Pastoral Pursuits 127 – Ashes (IRE) 77 (General Monash (USA) 107) – [2015 97: 6m 6f 6.5m Sep 11] well-made gelding: useful at best, no form in 2015: often in hood in 2015: usually races nearer last than first. *B. W. Hills*

KICKBOXER (IRE) 4 gr.g. Clodovil (IRE) 116 – Ajig Dancer 86 (Niniski (USA) 125) **105** [2015 109: 6g 6m³ 6f Jun 20] close-coupled gelding: useful handicapper: creditable third to Mukhmal at Newmarket in May: possibly unsuited by conditions well below form in Wokingham Stakes at Royal Ascot final start: stays 6f: acts on soft and good to firm going: often races towards rear. *Saeed bin Suroor*

KICKER ROCK 3 b.f. Fastnet Rock (AUS) 127 – Speak Softly To Me (USA) (Ogygian **53** (USA)) [2015 7m 7m⁵ Jul 21] £50,000Y: closely related to 3 winners, including 1m winner High Maintenance (by Danehill) and 7f winner Charlotte Bronte (by Danehill Dancer) and half-sister to 11f/1½m winner Contra Mundum (by Giant's Causeway): dam unraced: better effort when ninth of 12 in maiden at Newmarket on debut. *Charlie Fellowes*

KICKING THE CAN (IRE) 4 gr.g. Aussie Rules (USA) 123 – Silk Meadow (IRE) **70** (Barathea (IRE) 127) [2015 80: p8g p8g 10g p10g³ 9.9d p10g p10g⁵ p10g 11.9d p12m Oct 28] fair maiden: stays 1¼m: acts on polytrack and tapeta: often in headgear in 2015: tried in tongue tie in 2015. *Michael Attwater*

KIDMENEVER (IRE) 2 b.c. (Apr 27) Baltic King 120 – Pepys Tillergirl (IRE) **91** (Tillerman 123) [2015 6m⁵ 6g² 6.5g⁶ 6.5g⁴ p6.5g* 6.5d⁶ p7.5g² p7.5g Dec 27] €10,000 2-y-o: second foal: dam unraced half-sister to useful winner up to 7f Gouray Girl: fairly useful performer: won claimer at Deauville in August: good second in nursery on same course in October: left J. S. Moore after fifth start: stays 7.5f: acts on polytrack and good to soft going: in cheekpieces last 4 outings. *X. Nakkachdji, France*

KIE (IRE) 7 b.g. Old Vic 136 – Asura (GER) (Surumu (GER)) [2015 14.1g⁴ Aug 4] modest **55** maiden: stays 2m: tried in hood: in tongue tie last 3 starts: fairly useful hurdler/useful chaser at best. *David Pipe*

KI KI 3 ch.f. Kheleyf (USA) 116 – Peryllys 67 (Warning 136) [2015 5.9s* 6m Sep 20] half- **70** sister to numerous winners, including useful 6f/7f winner Penelewey (by Groom Dancer) and 7f winner Quintrell (by Royal Applause): dam maiden who stayed 1m: much better effort when winning maiden at Carlisle (by 2½ lengths from Pomme de Terre) in August. *Bryan Smart*

KILIM 2 b.f. (May 5) Dansili 127 – Kibara 88 (Sadler's Wells (USA) 132) [2015 p6f p8f⁶ **69 p** p7g⁵ Nov 26] sixth foal: closely related to useful winner up to 1½m Kikonga (2-y-o 8.3f winner, by Danehill Dancer) and half-sister to 11.4f/1½m winner (stays 16.5f) Kiwayu (by Medicean) and 1m-1½m winner Kinshasa (by Pivotal), both useful: dam, 11.5f winner, sister to St Leger winner Milan: fair form in maidens at Chelmsford, not knocked about when fifth of 11 final start: bred to be suited by 1¼m+: capable of better. *Luca Cumani*

KILIMANJARO (IRE) 3 gr.g. High Chaparral (IRE) 132 – Middle Persia 76 (Dalakhani **107** (IRE) 133) [2015 75: p10.7g* 11.5s* 12m⁶ 12m⁴ Jun 27] lengthy gelding: useful performer: won maiden at Dundalk in April and Derby Trial at Lingfield (by 1¼ lengths from Magic Dancer) in May: sixth in Derby at Epsom (13 lengths behind Golden Horn) and fourth in Irish Derby at the Curragh (11 lengths behind Jack Hobbs): subsequently gelded: worth a try at 1¾m: acts on polytrack, soft and good to firm going: in hood last 4 starts: sent to Australia. *Aidan O'Brien, Ireland*

KILLASSER BOY 2 b.g. (Apr 3) Authorized (IRE) 133 – Tidal 94 (Bin Ajwaad (IRE) – 119) [2015 p10g 8.3d p8g Oct 27] no form. *Lee Carter*

KILL OR CURE (IRE) 3 b.g. Acclamation 118 – Welsh Mist 102 (Damister (USA) 123) **69** [2015 68p: 6s⁵ 7.1m p8f² Aug 11] fair maiden: likely to prove best at shorter than 1m: acts on polytrack. *Charles Hills*

KILTARA (IRE) 3 b.f. Lawman (FR) 121 – Kiltubber (IRE) 104 (Sadler's Wells (USA) **93** 132) [2015 p8g³ p10g* 9.9s⁴ 12.1g* 12g Oct 9] leggy filly: closely related to smart winner up to 7.4f Anam Allta (2-y-o 6f winner, by Invincible Spirit) and half-sister to 3 winners, including very smart 1¼m-1¾m winner Fox Hunt (by Dubawi) and smart 9f-1½m winner Opinion (by Oasis Dream): dam 1½m winner: fairly useful performer: won maiden at Chelmsford in August and handicap at Beverley (by 2¼ lengths from Deep Blue Diamond) in September: stays 1½m: acts on polytrack: front runner/races prominently. *Mark Johnston*

KIMBELLE 2 b.f. (Jan 29) Compton Place 125 – Engaging 62 (Oasis Dream 129) [2015 – p7m Dec 31] first foal: dam lightly raced out of useful 2-y-o 7f winner Dialing Tone: 33/1, well held in maiden at Lingfield. *Mark Usher*

KIMBERELLA 5 b.g. Kyllachy 129 – Gleam of Light (IRE) 81 (Danehill (USA) 126) **104**
[2015 106: 6g 6g 5m 5g⁴ 5m³ 6m 5m* 6m 6m 6g² 5.5m⁵ 5.6d 6g 6g 5m 5s⁶ 5v⁶ 5d Oct 24]
close-coupled, attractive gelding: useful handicapper: won at York (by ¾ length from
Adam's Ale) in July: third at Ayr (neck behind Lexington Place) in June and second in
Great St Wilfrid Stakes at Ripon (head behind Don't Touch) in August: stays 7f: acts on any
turf going: tried in cheekpieces in 2015. *David Nicholls*

KIND INVITATION 4 b.f. New Approach (IRE) 132 – French Bid (AUS) (Anabaa –
(USA) 130) [2015 84: p8f Feb 2] sturdy filly: fairly useful handicapper at best, well held
sole start in 2015: stays 1¼m: acts on polytrack and good to firm going: covered by Farhh,
then sold 20,000 gns in July. *Charlie Appleby*

KINDLELIGHT STORM (USA) 5 b.g. Stormy Atlantic (USA) – Rose of Zollern **68**
(IRE) 111 (Seattle Dancer (USA) 119) [2015 77: p10g⁴ t9.5g⁶ p10g p8m⁶ p10f² t9.5f² Mar
23] fair handicapper: left Nick Littmoden after third start, John Butler after fourth: stays
1½m: acts on polytrack and tapeta: often wears headgear. *Phil McEntee*

KIND OF HUSH (IRE) 3 b.f. Marju (IRE) 127 – Affinity 76 (Sadler's Wells (USA) 132) –
[2015 p10g 8m⁵ p8g 10.2s Sep 15] first foal: dam, 1½m winner, half-sister to high-class
winner up to 1m Soviet Song (by Marju): no form: tried in visor. *Andrew Balding*

KINEMA (IRE) 4 b.g. Galileo (IRE) 134 – Bon Nuit (IRE) 112 (Night Shift (USA)) [2015 **102**
83: 10.1g³ 10.4g⁴ 10.2s² 10.1d* 10.3g⁶ 10.4m⁴ 11.5g* 11.9g 12m² 14.1d² 13g³ 12d² 11.8s²
Oct 26] useful-looking gelding: useful handicapper: won at Newcastle in May and Carlisle
in June: continued his improvement and finished second at Ripon (neck behind Pressure
Point), Nottingham (head behind Rhombus), Doncaster (4 lengths behind Captain Morley)
and Leicester (2¼ lengths behind Noble Gift): stays 1¾m: acts on polytrack, soft and good
to firm going: tried in headgear prior to 2015: usually races towards rear, strong traveller.
Alan Swinbank

KINEMATIC 3 b.f. Kyllachy 129 – Spinning Top 105 (Alzao (USA) 117) [2015 89: 5m⁴ **82**
5.2s 6.1d p5g Oct 20] rather unfurnished filly: fairly useful handicapper: stays 6f: acts on
good to firm going. *Andrew Balding*

KING BOLETE (IRE) 3 b.c. Cape Cross (IRE) 129 – Chanterelle (FR) (Trempolino **101**
(USA) 135) [2015 82p: 10.3m⁴ 11g* 12f⁴ 12f⁴ 11.9m⁴ 14g Aug 22] good-topped colt:
useful handicapper: won at Newbury (by ¾ length from Murgan) in May: good fourth of
17 in King George V Stakes at Royal Ascot (2½ lengths behind Space Age) on next start:
stays 1½m: acts on any turf going. *Luca Cumani*

KING CALYPSO 4 ch.g. Sir Percy 129 – Rosa de Mi Corazon (USA) 86 (Cozzene **90**
(USA)) [2015 78, a85: 11.6m³ 12m p16g² 14g 14f⁵ p16g³ 14.1m⁶ p16g⁴ Nov 18] lengthy
gelding: fairly useful handicapper: second at Kempton in June and third there in August:
stays 2m: acts on polytrack and firm going: tried in headgear. *Denis Coakley*

KING COLE (USA) 2 ch.c. (Feb 28) Scat Daddy (USA) 120 – Volver (IRE) (Danehill **82 p**
Dancer (IRE) 117) [2015 p5f* Oct 24] $115,000Y: second foal: dam French 1m-10.5f
winner: 4/5, won 7-runner maiden at Chelmsford on debut by 1½ lengths from Murdanova,
slowly away, shaken up to lead inside final 1f then drawing clear under hands-and-heels
ride: sure to progress. *Robert Cowell*

KING CRIMSON 3 ch.g. Captain Gerrard (IRE) 113 – Elegant Lady 89 (Selkirk (USA) **83**
129) [2015 87: t5.1m 5g 6m⁶ 5m 5m⁵ 5m 5.1f⁶ 5.1m⁵ 5m² 5d* 5m⁵ 5d⁴ 5.1g 5.3s* 5.1d Oct
28] smallish gelding: fairly useful handicapper: won at Newcastle in August and Brighton
in October: stays 5.5f: acts on firm and soft going: usually leads. *Mick Channon*

KINGDOM (IRE) 5 b.g. Montjeu (IRE) 137 – Shadow Song (IRE) (Pennekamp (USA) **84**
130) [2015 –: 11.6g⁶ 12f⁴ 11.9g 12d Aug 15] fairly useful handicapper: acts on good to firm
and heavy going: usually wears blinkers: in tongue tie in 2015: sold £3,500, sent to
Germany: won at 1¾m at Mons in December. *Gary Moore*

KINGDOM OF ALBA (IRE) 3 ch.g. The Carbon Unit (USA) 106 – Crackling Rosie **64**
(IRE) 55 (Dr Fong (USA) 128) [2015 60: 8.5g⁵ 10d 10g 6m⁶ 8.9g⁴ Aug 27] modest maiden:
stayed 9f: best form on good going: tried in blinkers/cheekpieces: front runner/raced
prominently: dead. *John Patrick Shanahan, Ireland*

KINGFISHER GIRL 2 gr.f. (Apr 9) Hellvelyn 118 – Caribbean Star 81 (Soviet Star –
(USA) 128) [2015 6d 5.9g 5g⁵ Jul 26] 2,000F: half-sister to several winners, including
useful 5f and (including at 2 yrs) 6f winner Caribbean Coral (by Brief Truce) and 6f-1¼m
winner Trip Switch (by Reset): dam 7f winner: well held in maidens. *Michael Appleby*

KINGFISHER (IRE) 4 b.c. Galileo (IRE) 134 – Mystical Lady (IRE) 106 (Halling **119** (USA) 133) [2015 116: 14d⁴ 14g* 20f² 14s³ 14d 15.9g Nov 3] leggy colt: smart performer: won listed race at Leopardstown (by ½ length from Panama Hat) in June: good second in Gold Cup at Royal Ascot (not clear run when 1¼ lengths behind Trip To Paris) next time: not beaten far when nineteenth of 24 in Melbourne Cup (Handicap) at Flemington final start, trying to come from last place and hampered under 2f out: stays 2½m: acts on any turf going: often wears a hood nowadays. *Aidan O'Brien, Ireland*

KING IN WAITING (IRE) 12 b.g. Sadler's Wells (USA) 132 – Ballerina (IRE) 88 – (Dancing Brave (USA) 140) [2015 t12.2g f14d May 18] well-made gelding: useful at best, no form in 2015: stays 21.5f: acts on good to firm and heavy going: sometimes in headgear/ tried in tongue tie prior to 2015. *David Thompson*

KINGLAMI 6 b.g. Kingsalsa (USA) 118 – Red Japonica (Daylami (IRE) 138) [2015 87: **92** 6m² 6m* 6m⁵ 7g³ 6v² 6g p6m p7d Nov 30] sturdy gelding: fairly useful handicapper: won at Windsor in May: has form at 1m, most effective at 6f/7f: acts on polytrack, good to firm and heavy going: often wears headgear: tried in tongue tie prior to 2015: often races prominently. *Brian Gubby*

KING OF CORNWALL (IRE) 2 b.g. (Mar 5) Duke of Marmalade (IRE) 132 – Course – **p** de Diamante (IRE) 78 (Galileo (IRE) 134) [2015 7g 7g⁵ p8f Sep 22] good-topped gelding: second foal: half-brother to 1½m winner Artistic Muse (by Excellent Art): dam lightly-raced half-sister to useful winner up to 9f (stayed 1½m) Distant Mirage: no form in maidens: looks type to do better in time. *David Lanigan*

KING OF COUNTRY 3 b.g. Dubawi (IRE) 129 – Country Star (USA) 116 (Empire **79** Maker (USA) 129) [2015 10m p12g³ 10m⁴ 9.3g² Jun 15] useful-looking gelding: fair maiden: stays 1½m. *Charlie Appleby*

KING OF DREAMS 2 ch.c. (Feb 9) Dream Ahead (USA) 133 – Complexion 92 **81 p** (Hurricane Run (IRE) 134) [2015 8.3m² 8d³ t8.6m² Dec 30] 240,000Y: first foal: dam, 1m winner who stayed 1¼m, half-sister to high-class winner up to 1m Zacinto: fairly useful maiden: best effort when second at Wolverhampton (½ length behind Disobedience) in December: likely to progress further. *David Simcock*

KING OF EDEN (IRE) 9 b.g. Royal Applause 124 – Moonlight Paradise (USA) 111 **72 §** (Irish River (FR) 131) [2015 82§: 7m 7m 8d³ 8m 7.9g⁵ Jun 15] tall, lengthy gelding: fair handicapper: stays 1m: acts on polytrack, good to firm and heavy going: often in headgear: tried in tongue tie prior to 2015: usually races prominently: unreliable. *Eric Alston*

KING OF NAPLES 2 b.g. (Feb 4) Excellent Art 125 – Avon Lady 96 (Avonbridge 123) – **p** [2015 t6g⁶ Jul 13] 16,000Y: first foal: dam winner up to 8.3f (including at 2 yrs): 7/1, sixth in maiden at Wolverhampton (11½ lengths behind Squash) in July, having hopeless task from position: will improve. *James Fanshawe*

KING OF NORMANDY (FR) 3 ch.g. Soldier of Fortune (IRE) 131 – Innocent Affair **74** (IRE) (Night Shift (USA)) [2015 95: 10.3d³ 8.3m* 10m May 16] workmanlike gelding: fairly useful performer at best: fair form in 2015, winning maiden at Windsor in May: stayed 8.5f: acted on good to firm and heavy going: usually led: dead. *Richard Hannon*

KING OF PARADISE (IRE) 6 b.g. Hurricane Run (IRE) 134 – Silly Game (IRE) **75** (Bigstone (IRE) 126) [2015 80: 10d 11.1d* 13d⁶ 10.1m⁶ 10.4g⁵ 10.4f⁴ 12g 11.1s* 11.9m⁵ 12d³ 11.1d⁶ 13m⁵ 10s Oct 13] fair handicapper: won at Hamilton in May and August and Haydock (apprentice) later in August: stays 13f: acts on good to firm and heavy going: tried in headgear: usually leads. *Eric Alston*

KING OF ROOKS 2 b.c. (Mar 14) Acclamation 118 – Slap Shot (IRE) 115 (Lycius **105** (USA) 124) [2015 5m³ 6g* 5m* 5f³ 5g² 6g⁴ p6g⁶ Sep 5] 67,000Y: good-topped colt: half-brother to several winners, including smart 5f/6f winner Sandslash (by Holy Roman Emperor) and useful winner up to 7f Samara Valley (by Dalakhani): dam, 5f/6f winner (including at 2 yrs), runner-up in Prix de l'Abbaye: useful performer: won maiden at Newbury (by 6 lengths from Predilection) and listed race at Sandown (by 5 lengths from Buratino), both in May: third in Norfolk Stakes at Royal Ascot (length behind Waterloo Bridge) in June and second in Molecomb Stakes at Goodwood (¾ length behind Kachy) in July: disappointing last 2 starts: stays 6f: acts on good to firm going. *Richard Hannon*

KING OF SPIN 2 b.c. (Apr 1) Pivotal 124 – Regina 97 (Green Desert (USA) 127) [2015 **64 p** p5g t5.1m³ Dec 26] 30,000Y: sixth foal: brother to 6f winner Houdini and closely related to 2-y-o 5f winner Survived (by Kyllachy) and half-brother to 5f (including at 2 yrs) winner Six Wives (by Kingsalsa): dam 2-y-o 5f winner: better effort when third in maiden at Wolverhampton (2¾ lengths behind Sir Roger Moore) in December: remains with potential. *William Muir*

KING OF SWING 2 b.c. (Apr 5) Dutch Art 126 – Mystic Spirit (IRE) (Invincible Spirit **79**
(IRE) 121) [2015 6d* 5.1d⁵ t6f⁴ Nov 14] fair performer: best effort when winning maiden
at Haydock (by ¾ length from The Perfect Show) in September, very slowly away: stays
6f. *James Given*

KING OF THE CELTS (IRE) 7 b.g. Celtic Swing 138 – Flamands (IRE) 92 (Sadler's **75**
Wells (USA) 132) [2015 77: 9.9m* 9.9m* 10d⁵ 9.9m* 9.9m⁶ 12.1g 10.3d Oct 23] lengthy
gelding: fair handicapper: won at Beverley in May, June and July: stays 1½m: acts on soft
and good to firm going: races prominently. *Tim Easterby*

KING OF THE PICTS (IRE) 6 ch.g. Rock of Gibraltar (IRE) 133 – Belle Rebelle **86**
(IRE) (In The Wings 128) [2015 80: 16.1g² 16.1m² 13d² 16g³ Jul 30] fairly useful
handicapper: stays 2m: acts on soft and good to firm going: front runner/races prominently:
fairly useful chaser. *John Patrick Shanahan, Ireland*

KING OLAV (UAE) 10 ch.g. Halling (USA) 133 – Karamzin (USA) (Nureyev (USA) **74**
131) [2015 79: p11g t16.5f² p15.8g⁶ p12m p12f² p16g p12g³ p12g p14f³ p11g p12g² p16f*
Dec 21] tall, angular gelding: fair handicapper: won at Chelmsford in December: stays
16.5f: acts on polytrack, tapeta, good to firm and good to soft going: front runner/races
prominently. *Tony Carroll*

KING OSWALD (USA) 2 b.c. (Mar 31) Street Cry (USA) 130 – Northern Melody (IRE) **72**
(Singspiel (IRE) 133) [2015 p7g⁶ p7g⁶ Dec 28] better effort when sixth in maiden at
Kempton (4 lengths behind Marylebone) in November on debut. *Charlie Appleby*

KING ROBERT 2 b.g. (Mar 17) Royal Applause 124 – Generously Gifted (Sakhee **100**
(USA) 136) [2015 5v* 6.1g* 6s⁴ 6s⁴ Oct 10] 16,000Y, £26,000 2-y-o: second foal: half-
brother to useful winner up to 6f Son of Africa (by Equiano): dam unraced: useful form:
won first 2 starts, namely maiden at Carlisle in June and 5-runner minor event at Chester
(by 1¼ lengths from Madrinho) in August: 4 lengths fourth to Donjuan Triumphant in
listed race at York final outing: stays 6f: has been gelded. *Bryan Smart*

KINGS BAYONET 8 ch.g. Needwood Blade 117 – Retaliator 80 (Rudimentary (USA) **94**
118) [2015 95: p10m⁴ p12f⁴ t12.2m² t12.2g² p15.8f 12m 12d Aug 21] lengthy gelding:
fairly useful handicapper: second at Wolverhampton in February and March: stays 1¾m:
acts on polytrack, tapeta and any turf going: usually races in rear. *Alan King*

KINGS CHAPEL (USA) 4 b.g. Elusive Quality (USA) – Ladyecho (USA) (Alphabet **54**
Soup (USA) 126) [2015 61: p7m p7f⁶ p8m Apr 8] rather leggy gelding: modest maiden:
stays 7f: acts on polytrack, firm and good to soft going: in headgear in 2015. *Jeremy Gask*

KING'S CHORISTER 9 ch.g. King's Best (USA) 132 – Chorist 120 (Pivotal 124) [2015 **49**
16m Aug 10] workmanlike gelding: poor handicapper: stays 1¼m: acts on good to soft
going: tried in headgear prior to 2015: often wears tongue tie. *Barry Murtagh*

KINGSCOMBE (USA) 6 g.g. Mizzen Mast (USA) 121 – Gombeen (USA) (Private **56**
Account (USA)) [2015 59, a85: f12s p13.3g⁶ f16d³ Feb 10] modest handicapper nowadays:
stays 2m: acts on fibresand, best turf form on good to firm going: tried in cheekpieces.
Linda Jewell

KING'S CONCERTO (IRE) 3 ch.g. Thewayyouare (USA) 117 – Major Minor (IRE) **64**
(Desert Prince (IRE) 130) [2015 –: p8f⁶ 8.3f 7m t9.5g⁶ p12g⁶ 11.9g² 11.9d² 9.9v p10g Oct
27] lengthy gelding: modest maiden: stays 1½m: acts on good to soft going: sometimes in
headgear in 2015: often races prominently. *Dean Ivory*

KINGSCROFT (IRE) 7 b.g. Antonius Pius (USA) 123 – Handsome Anna (IRE) 67 **73**
(Bigstone (IRE) 126) [2015 89: t7.1m t7.1g* 7m 8m t7.1m³ t6m* p6f⁶ 7v t7.1f p6g* p6f⁵ **a92**
p7m⁵ Dec 31] big, strong gelding: fairly useful performer: won at Wolverhampton in April
(handicap) and October (claimer, left Michael Herrington), and at Chelmsford (handicap)
in December: stays 10.5f, races mainly at 6f/7f nowadays: acts on polytrack, tapeta and any
turf going: tried in blinkers: often races towards rear. *Tom Dascombe*

KING'S CURRENCY 2 b.g. (Apr 24) Kheleyf (USA) 116 – Mint Royale (IRE) 44 **57 p**
(Cadeaux Genereux 131) [2015 6.1v⁶ 6d⁶ Oct 19] 6,000Y: half-brother to several winners,
including useful/ungenuine winner up to 9f La Neige (2-y-o 5f winner, by Royal Applause)
and winner up to 7.4f Spying (by Observatory): dam maiden (stayed 6f): better effort
when sixth in maiden at Pontefract (7 lengths behind Calder Prince) in October, slowly
away: should do better. *Jedd O'Keeffe*

KINGSGATE CHOICE (IRE) 8 b.g. Choisir (AUS) 126 – Kenema (IRE) 88 (Petardia **108**
113) [2015 109: 5g 5m 5m² 5f Jul 11] good-bodied gelding: useful handicapper: second at
Newmarket (head behind Humidor) in June: stays 6f: acts on polytrack and any turf going:
tried in blinkers prior to 2015. *Ed de Giles*

KINGSGATE NATIVE (IRE) 10 b.g. Mujadil (USA) 119 – Native Force (IRE) 82 **114**
(Indian Ridge 123) [2015 117: 5m³ 5g 5d* 5m⁵ 5m 5m 5m² 5.2s 5m Oct 3] strong, lengthy
gelding: smart performer: won listed race at Haydock (by 1¼ lengths from Out Do) in May:
third in Palace House Stakes at Newmarket (2½ lengths behind Goldream) earlier that
month and second in listed race at Doncaster (length behind Cotai Glory) in September:
stays 6f: acts on firm and good to soft going: sometimes wears headgear: usually races
nearer last than first. *Robert Cowell*

KINGS HENCHMAN (IRE) 2 b.g. (Mar 31) Lawman (FR) 121 – Millay (Polish **– p**
Precedent (USA) 131) [2015 7g Sep 25] €72,000F, €140,000Y: half-brother to several
winners, including 1m (including at 2 yrs) winner Chief Barker (by Azamour) and winner
up to 11f (stayed 1¾m) Salford Art (2-y-o 6f winner, by Sir Percy), both useful: dam, 1m
winner, sister to smart 1¼m-1½m winner Millstreet: 50/1, better for run when eleventh in
maiden at Newmarket (13 lengths behind Crazy Horse) in September, slowly away: will
improve. *Peter Chapple-Hyam*

KINGSLEY KLARION (IRE) 2 b.c. (Apr 28) Arcano (IRE) 122 – May Day Queen **87 p**
(IRE) 79 (Danetime (IRE) 121) [2015 5s⁶ 6v³ 6s⁵ p6f* t5.1g* p6g* Dec 20] €42,000Y:
third foal: half-brother to 7f winner Abbotsfield (by Sakhee's Secret) and useful winner up
to 6f Mukhmal (2-y-o 5f winner, by Bahamian Bounty): dam 2-y-o 6f winner: fairly useful
performer: won nurseries at Chelmsford and Wolverhampton in November and Lingfield
(by head from Kadrizzi) in December: likely to stay 7f: acts on polytrack and tapeta:
usually races close up: open to further improvement. *Mark Johnston*

KING'S MASQUE 9 b.g. Noverre (USA) 125 – Top Flight Queen 82 (Mark of Esteem **64**
(IRE) 137) [2015 10g 10m⁴ p12g³ 10.2m⁶ Jul 16] good-topped gelding: modest performer:
stays 1½m: acts on polytrack, firm and soft going, seemingly not on heavy: tried in
cheekpieces in 2015. *Bernard Llewellyn*

KING'S MIMIC (IRE) 2 b.g. (Apr 13) Bushranger (IRE) 119 – Annus Iucundus (IRE) **79**
67 (Desert King (IRE) 129) [2015 5m³ 5g* 5m³ May 23] fairly useful form: won maiden
at Beverley in May by 2¾ lengths from Ferryover: would have been suited to 6f: dead.
Ann Duffield

KING'S PAVILION (IRE) 2 b.c. (Feb 20) King's Best (USA) 132 – Embassy 114 **92**
(Cadeaux Genereux 131) [2015 6m² 6d³ 7m* 7g³ 8d* 8g² 7m² 8.5d³ 8d³ Oct 23] brother to
6f/7f winner Felicitous and half-brother to several winners, including useful winner up to
1m Grosvenor Square (2-y-o 7f winner, by Dubai Millennium) and useful 9f-11f winner
Diwaan (by Echo of Light): dam 2-y-o 6f winner who would have stayed 1m: fairly useful
performer: won maiden at Wetherby in June and nursery at Ripon in August: stays 1m: acts
on good to firm and good to soft going: front runner/races prominently. *Mark Johnston*

KING'S PROCESSION (IRE) 4 ch.g. Teofilo (IRE) 126 – Sateen 87 (Barathea (IRE) **–**
127) [2015 p7f⁵ Jan 30] 33/1, tailed off in claimer at Lingfield. *Neil Mulholland*

KING'S REALM (IRE) 8 ch.g. King's Best (USA) 132 – Sweet Home Alabama (IRE) **–**
56 (Desert Prince (IRE) 130) [2015 15.8s May 5] workmanlike gelding: fair handicapper
in 2010, well held both starts on Flat since: stays 2m: acts on polytrack, soft and good to
firm going: tried in eyeshields. *Tina Jackson*

KING'S REQUEST (IRE) 5 ch.g. New Approach (IRE) 132 – Palace Weekend (USA) **68**
(Seattle Dancer (USA) 119) [2015 p15.8f Feb 2] useful-looking gelding: fairly useful
handicapper at best: stayed 2m: acted on polytrack, soft and good to firm going: often raced
prominently: dead. *Laura Mongan*

KING'S ROAD 10 ch.g. King's Best (USA) 132 – Saphire 93 (College Chapel 122) [2015 **–**
11.9d⁶ 9.9s 11.9d⁶ Sep 14] quite good-topped gelding: fair at best, no form in 2015: tried in
cheekpieces prior to 2015: often wears tongue tie. *Anabel K. Murphy*

KINGSTON KURRAJONG 2 b.c. (Mar 27) Authorized (IRE) 133 – Kingston Acacia **95**
87 (King of Roses (AUS)) [2015 7.4g 7g⁶ 7m* 7g² 8.5d² Sep 27] second foal: dam 7f
winner: useful performer: won maiden at Chester in August: better form when second in
nursery at Chester (head behind Powderhorn) and minor event at Epsom (3 lengths behind
Thanksfortellingme): stays 8.5f: acts on good to firm and good to soft going. *Andrew Balding*

KINGSTON MIMOSA 3 b.g. Kheleyf (USA) 116 – Derartu (AUS) (Last Tycoon 131) **58**
[2015 p7g 8.3m 8.3g⁶ 9.9m 10m⁴ 10v² 12.1m⁴ Sep 10] angular gelding: modest maiden:
stays 1¼m: acts on good to firm and heavy going: often in headgear. *Andrew Balding*

KINGSTON SASSAFRAS 3 b.g. Halling (USA) 133 – Kingston Acacia 87 (King of **53**
Roses (AUS)) [2015 61: p10m⁴ p10f 8g 8.1d p8f³ p8f t8.6g⁵ p8f⁴ f8g⁶ Dec 22] modest
maiden: left Andrew Balding after fourth start: probably stays 1¼m: acts on polytrack and
good to soft going: often in headgear/tongue tie in 2015. *Phil McEntee*

KINGSTREET LADY 2 b.f. (Feb 23) Royal Applause 124 – Intellibet One 74 (Compton Place 125) [2015 5.7f 6g 6d⁴ 6.1s⁵ t7.1f⁴ 7s Oct 26] seventh foal: half-sister to 3 winners, including winner up to 6f Decision By One (2-y-o 6f winner, by Bahamian Bounty) and 5f-6f winner Taurus Twins (by Deportivo): dam winner up to 6f (2-y-o 5f winner): modest maiden: best effort at 7f: acts on tapeta and good to soft going. *Richard Price* **60**

KINGSWAY LAD (IRE) 4 b.g. New Approach (IRE) 132 – Obsessive (USA) 102 (Seeking The Gold (USA)) [2015 53: f6d Jan 4] useful-looking gelding: little form: tried in visor: often in tongue tie prior to 2015: sometimes slowly away. *Derek Shaw* **–**

KING'S WHARF (IRE) 6 gr.g. Clodovil (IRE) 116 – Global Tour (USA) (Tour d'Or (USA) 108) [2015 9.2d May 27] modest maiden: stays 1½m: acts on polytrack and soft going: tried in cheekpieces/tongue tie: fair hurdler/poor chaser. *L. Smyth, Ireland* **–**

KINGSWINFORD (IRE) 9 b.g. Noverre (USA) 125 – Berenica (IRE) 101 (College Chapel 122) [2015 59: 18.6g⁵ t8.6m⁶ t12.2g 10.2m 7g Jul 22] leggy gelding: modest handicapper: stays 1½m: acts on polytrack, tapeta, good to firm and heavy going: tried in headgear. *John Norton* **52**

KINGTHISTLE 2 ch.g. (Mar 30) Monsieur Bond (IRE) 120 – Chez Cherie 108 (Wolfhound (USA) 126) [2015 5m⁵ 6s 6g⁵ Aug 6] £30,000Y: seventh foal: brother to smart 7f-9.5f winner Alfred Hutchinson and half-brother to 8.5f winner Chez La Sammana (by Proud Citizen): dam winner up to 11f (2-y-o 7f winner): fair maiden: likely to do better in time. *Michael Easterby* **66 p**

KING TO BE (IRE) 3 b.g. Myboycharlie (IRE) 118 – Becuille (IRE) 79 (Redback 116) [2015 84: 7m* 7g⁵ 7g² 8f 8g Aug 21] lengthy gelding: useful performer: won maiden at Goodwood by 2 lengths from Quite Smart) in May: good second in handicap there (nose behind Enlace) later in month: stays 7f: acts on good to firm going: often races towards rear: has been gelded. *Richard Hannon* **98**

KING TORUS (IRE) 7 b.g. Oratorio (IRE) 128 – Dipterous (IRE) 89 (Mujadil (USA) 119) [2015 99: 8d 8g⁶ 7d⁴ 8g⁶ 7.1m³ 7m 8f* 7f² 8d t7.1m² 7.6s 8g⁵ t8.6f* p10f⁶ Nov 6] strong, sturdy gelding: fairly useful performer: won claimer at Doncaster in July and handicap at Wolverhampton (dead-heated with Jodies Jem, left David O'Meara after) in October: stays 8.5f: acts on polytrack, tapeta and any turf going: tried in headgear: usually races prominently. *Lee Carter* **92**

KINLOCH PRIDE 3 ch.f. Kyllachy 129 – Pride of Kinloch 80 (Dr Devious (IRE) 127) [2015 –: 5d 5g 6m⁵ 5g 5m⁶ 5g³ 6g⁴ 5m 5s² t5.1f³ f5g Dec 12] modest maiden: best effort at 5f: acts on tapeta and soft going: often in cheekpieces in 2015. *Noel Wilson* **61**

KINNARA 3 b.f. Kyllachy 129 – Tinnarinka 84 (Observatory (USA) 131) [2015 63: 7.1m 5d 5.7f⁴ p8g 7.1m 6g t7.1g⁴ p6g t6m p5g³ 6s Oct 15] modest maiden: stays 7f: acts on tapeta and firm going: sometimes in tongue tie in 2015. *Sylvester Kirk* **58 a49**

KIP 3 b.f. Rip Van Winkle (IRE) 134 – Catopuma (USA) (Elusive Quality (USA)) [2015 6p: 9.9s⁴ 12d 10.2m² 10.2m⁴ p12g⁵ p10f Oct 1] tall, rather unfurnished filly: fair maiden: stays 1¼m: acts on good to firm going: tried in visor in 2015: front runner/races prominently. *Sir Michael Stoute* **74**

KIPUKA 3 b.f. Authorized (IRE) 133 – Rakata (USA) 83 (Quiet American (USA)) [2015 65: p8m 10.2m Apr 18] maiden: no form in 2015: best effort at 6f: in hood last start in 2015. *Paul Cole* **–**

KIRINGA 2 ch.f. (May 16) Kyllachy 129 – Good Health 78 (Magic Ring (IRE) 115) [2015 p7m p7g Dec 28] 28,000Y: closely related to 2-y-o 5f/6f winner The Magic of Rio (by Captain Rio) and 6f winner Amoureuse (by Needwood Blade) and half-sister to winner up to 6f Your Pal Tal (by Dark Angel): dam 2-y-o 5f winner: well held in 2 maidens: worth a try at 5f/6f. *William Knight* **–**

KIRI SUNRISE (IRE) 2 b.f. (Mar 15) Iffraaj 127 – Lucky Flirt (USA) (Gulch (USA)) [2015 6g⁴ 7g⁵ Jul 24] €8,000F, €110,000Y: fifth foal: half-sister to 3 winners, including 5f/6f winner Dreese (by Dandy Man) and winner up to 9f Lucked Out (2-y-o 1m winner, by Ramonti): dam lightly raced: better effort when fifth in maiden at Thirsk in July: sold 3,000 gns, sent to Spain. *Richard Fahey* **62**

KIRKHAM 2 b.g. (Apr 18) Pastoral Pursuits 127 – Royal Grace 66 (Royal Applause 124) [2015 5g⁵ 6.1m⁶ 6s⁴ Oct 26] modest maiden: left Richard Fahey after second start. *Julie Camacho* **63**

KIRKMAN (IRE) 4 ch.g. Virtual 122 – Validate (Alhaarth (IRE) 126) [2015 76: 16.5m⁵ 16.1d 16m³ 17.1d⁶ 15.8s Oct 6] fair handicapper: stays 2m: acts on good to firm going. *James Bethell* **69**

KIRTLING 4 gr.g. Araafa (IRE) 128 – Cape Maya 67 (Cape Cross (IRE) 129) [2015 **74** 11.8m* 12g⁶ 14.1g Sep 30] fair handicapper: won at Leicester in June: best effort at 1½m: acts on good to firm going: in tongue tie in 2015: sometimes slowly away, often races towards rear. *Andi Brown*

KISMET HARDY 2 ch.c. (Mar 23) Mount Nelson 125 – Quinzey's Best (IRE) 63 (King's **79** Best (USA) 132) [2015 8s⁵ 9s⁵ 7s* p8f⁵ Nov 23] good-topped colt: fair form: won maiden at Salisbury (by ¾ length from White Shaheen) in October: best effort at 7f. *Richard Hannon*

KISSY SUZUKI 3 b.f. Sakhee's Secret 128 – Yonder 71 (And Beyond (IRE) 113) [2015 **74** –: p7g⁴ t8.6f* t9.5f⁶ Nov 10] fair performer: won maiden at Wolverhampton in October: stays 9.5f. *Hughie Morrison*

KISUMU 3 b.g. High Chaparral (IRE) 132 – Arum Lily (USA) (Woodman (USA) 126) **70 §** [2015 78: 9.9m³ 10.2s p11g Jul 8] fair maiden: stays 1¼m: acts on good to firm going: tried in visor in 2015: ungenuine (carries head awkwardly). *Sir Michael Stoute*

KITAABY (IRE) 2 b.g. (Apr 1) Acclamation 118 – Flower of Kent (USA) 78 (Diesis 133) **81 p** [2015 6m² 6m 6g² 6g⁴ Aug 29] 35,000F: useful-looking gelding: fifth foal: half-brother to 6f/7f winner Gravitational (by Invincible Spirit) and 1¼m winner Crystal Nymph (by Rock of Gibraltar): dam, 2-y-o 1m winner, half-sister to useful 1¼m winner Imperial Pippin out of smart 1m winner Apple of Kent: fairly useful maiden: second at Newbury and Haydock: raced only at 6f: in hood last 2 starts: has been gelded: should do better. *Brian Meehan*

KITTEN'S RED (USA) 3 ch.c. Kitten's Joy (USA) 128 – Arbor (USA) (Forestry (USA) **75** 121) [2015 71p: 11.6g 10.2m* p11g 11.9m² 10.2m 9.9g² p11g 8.5d Sep 22] tall, good-topped colt: has scope: fair performer: won minor event at Bath in May: stays 1½m: acts on good to firm going: in headgear last 2 starts: usually races prominently: sold 10,000 gns, sent to Switzerland. *Ed Dunlop*

KITTY BEQUICK 4 ch.f. Piccolo 121 – Cat Patrol 77 (One Cool Cat (USA) 123) [2015 **–** –: p6g p8m Feb 18] no form: in headgear in 2015: sometimes slowly away. *Peter Hedger*

KIWAYU 6 b.g. Medicean 128 – Kibara 88 (Sadler's Wells (USA) 132) [2015 10.4m **86** 11.5d⁴ 13.7m⁶ 12g⁵ 12g 12v t12.2f t13.9g⁴ Dec 1] good-topped gelding: fairly useful handicapper: left Kevin Ryan after seventh start: stays 16.5f: acts on polytrack, tapeta, soft and good to firm going: sometimes wears headgear: tried in tongue tie prior to 2015: often races towards rear. *Philip Kirby*

KIWI BAY 10 b.g. Mujahid (USA) 125 – Bay of Plenty (FR) (Octagonal (NZ) 126) [2015 **89** 95: 8g 8m⁴ 8d 8g² 7.9s³ 8m² 8d 7.9g⁵ 8g² 7v Nov 7] tall gelding: fairly useful handicapper: stays 10.5f: acts on good to firm and heavy going: tried in cheekpieces prior to 2015: often races prominently. *Michael Dods*

KIYOSHI 4 b.f. Dubawi (IRE) 129 – Mocca (IRE) 99 (Sri Pekan (USA) 117) [2015 112: **107** 7s⁵ 6m³ 7m⁵ 7m Sep 10] strong filly: useful performer: third in Summer Stakes at York (¾ length behind New Providence) in July: stays 1m: acts on firm and soft going: tried in cheekpieces. *Charles Hills*

KIZINGO (IRE) 3 b.f. Oasis Dream 129 – Enora (GER) 111 (Noverre (USA) 125) [2015 **74** 69p: 7m⁴ 8d³ 7m² 7d⁵ Aug 5] fair maiden: should prove fully effective at 1m: acts on good to firm and good to soft going: front runner/races prominently: sold 35,000 gns, sent to Germany. *Charles Hills*

KLEITOMACHOS (IRE) 7 b.g. Barathea (IRE) 127 – Theben (GER) (Monsun (GER) **74** 124) [2015 14.1s⁴ 14.1g⁶ 16d Oct 30] good-topped gelding: fair handicapper: stays 2m: acts on good to firm and heavy going: in tongue tie in 2015. *Stuart Kittow*

KLEO (GR) 4 b.f. Kavafi (IRE) 111 – Selfish 111 (Bluebird (USA) 125) [2015 106: 9f² **108** 11.9d⁶ 10.1g³ Jun 26] tall filly: useful performer: second in Dahlia Stakes at Newmarket (¾ length behind Bragging) in May: stays 10.5f: acts on polytrack and any turf going: usually races prominently. *Luca Cumani*

KNAVERY (USA) 4 b.c. Candy Ride (ARG) 133 – Tight Spin (USA) (Favorite Trick **–** (USA) 121) [2015 97: a9.4f a8f 7g Dec 13] useful at best, well held in 2015: left Simon Crisford after second start: tongue tied final outing. *M. Ramadan, UAE*

KNIFE EDGE (IRE) 2 ch.c. (Feb 15) Zoffany (IRE) 121 – Attalea (IRE) (Monsun **94 p** (GER) 124) [2015 7g* 7g⁴ Oct 21] €43,000Y: strong, attractive colt: first foal: dam unraced sister to useful winner up to 2m Andorn: fairly useful form: won maiden at Ascot in September by ¾ length from Paris Protocol: 4 lengths fourth of 5 to Hayadh in minor event at Newmarket following month, ill at ease on track and not knocked about: remains open to improvement. *Marco Botti*

KNIGHT COMMANDER 2 br.c. (Mar 24) Sir Percy 129 – Jardin (Sinndar (IRE) 134) [2015 7m³ 7f 8.1g³ 8g² 8s³ 8s³ Oct 6] 22,000Y: compact colt: sixth foal: half-brother to 9f winner Jeb Master (by Manduro): dam unraced half-sister to very smart 7f-8.3f winner Sleeping Indian: fairly useful maiden: second in nursery at Salisbury in August: will prove suited by 1¼m: best form on good going: often races prominently. *William Knight* **82**

KNIGHTLY ESCAPADE 7 ch.g. Sakhee (USA) 136 – Queen of Iceni 81 (Erhaab (USA) 127) [2015 87: 16m² 16.4m 16.1g³ 16.1m* 16.4m 13.1g 18g Oct 10] sturdy gelding: fairly useful handicapper: won at Newcastle in June: 100/1, back to form when 3¾ lengths tenth of 34 to Grumeti in Cesarewitch at Newmarket final start: stays 2¼m: acts on good to firm and good to soft going: tried in cheekpieces: held up. *Brian Ellison* **91**

KNIGHT MUSIC 3 b.g. Sir Percy 129 – Lyric Art (USA) 65 (Red Ransom (USA)) [2015 63: p11g p12g* p11g³ p12g 12g² p12g* 11.9v* p12g Sep 9] fairly useful handicapper: won at Lingfield in May and Kempton (by 11 lengths from Full of Speed) and Brighton in August: stays 1½m: acts on polytrack and heavy going: front runner/races prominently. *Michael Attwater* **86**

KNIGHT OF THE AIR 3 b.g. Bushranger (IRE) 119 – Picolette 56 (Piccolo 121) [2015 8m 7.1m⁵ 8.3m 8d³ 8m² p8g⁵ 7.1m³ 8.3d³ 7.6m² 8s⁴ 8d 8m* 8s² Oct 15] angular gelding: fair handicapper: won at Bath in September: stays 1m: acts on soft and good to firm going. *Mick Channon* **67**

KNIGHT OF WANDS 3 b.g. Azamour (IRE) 130 – Maid To Treasure (IRE) 77 (Rainbow Quest (USA) 134) [2015 11.9f² 12v* 12g Sep 24] fifth foal: half-brother to smart 1½m-16.4f winner King of Wands (by Galileo) and 8.5f winner Queen of Wands (by Sakhee): dam maiden: fairly useful performer: best effort when winning maiden at Newbury (by 2¼ lengths from Bellajeu) in August, suited by emphasis on stamina: likely to stay at least 1¾m. *Luca Cumani* **86**

KNIGHT OWL 5 b.g. Rock of Gibraltar (IRE) 133 – Miss Ivanhoe (IRE) 107 (Selkirk (USA) 129) [2015 98: p8f 9m⁴ 8.1m⁶ 8f² 9m⁶ 8g³ p8g* Nov 9] rather leggy gelding: useful handicapper: won at Kempton (by length from Mont Ras) in November: stays 10.5f: acts on polytrack, firm and good to soft going: tried in hood in 2015: often races prominently. *James Fanshawe* **98**

KNOCKAMANY BENDS (IRE) 5 b.g. Majestic Missile (IRE) 118 – Sweet Compliance 71 (Safawan 118) [2015 59§: t6f⁵ 6g⁴ 5m⁵ 5g⁶ 6g⁴ t6g³ 5d* 5.1d⁶ 5g 5g t6f⁶ Oct 23] modest handicapper: won at Pontefract in July: stays 6f: acts on good to firm and good to soft going: usually in cheekpieces in 2015: usually leads: unreliable. *John Wainwright* **62 §** **a52 §**

KNOTTY JACK (IRE) 3 b.g. Zebedee 113 – Half-Hitch (USA) 88 (Diesis 133) [2015 t5.1f⁴ t6f Nov 20] well held in 2 maidens. *Ian Semple* **–**

KNOW YOUR NAME 4 ch.g. Halling (USA) 133 – Lady Agnes 53 (Singspiel (IRE) 133) [2015 82: p7g⁶ 7m 8.1s 7m 7g³ 8f⁴ 7g 7g³ 7.6g³ 7.9m² 8.3g² t8.6f* t8.6f² t8.6f² Nov 20] close-coupled gelding: fairly useful handicapper: won at Wolverhampton in October: left David Evans after ninth start: stays 8.5f: acts on tapeta, good to firm and good to soft going: often wears headgear: races prominently, often travels strongly. *Eric Alston* **76** **a88**

KODACHROME (IRE) 2 b.f. (Feb 21) Kodiac 112 – Sheila Blige 83 (Zamindar (USA) 116) [2015 6m p6g⁴ 6g⁵ p5f⁵ Oct 24] €23,000F, £62,000Y: compact filly: closely related to 8.7f winner (stayed 10.7f) Apt (by Danetime) and half-sister to useful winner up to 6f Lady Lily (2-y-o 5f/6f winner, by Desert Sun) and 2-y-o 5f/6f winner World All Fruit (by Refuse To Bend): dam, 2-y-o 5f winner, half-sister to smart winner up to 1½m Naked Welcome: modest maiden: stays 6f: tried in tongue tie in 2015: sold 6,500 gns, sent to Denmark. *James Tate* **61**

KODAFINE (IRE) 4 br.f. Kodiac 112 – Zafine (USA) 130 (Zafonic 130) [2015 69: p6g⁴ p5f* t6g² p6g⁴ p5m⁴ f5g f6g 6m Apr 24] small, close-coupled filly: fair handicapper: won at Lingfield in January: left David Evans after fifth start: stays 6f: acts on polytrack and good to soft going: tried in visor prior to 2015. *John Wainwright* **67**

KODIAC LADY (IRE) 3 b.f. Kodiac 112 – Weeping Willow (IRE) 57 (Kheleyf (USA) 116) [2015 63: t6f⁴ p6m⁴ t6g² t6g⁵ 6m 7.5m t6g 5d 6.9v⁶ t7.1g⁶ t7.1g³ t6g⁵ t7.1g⁵ t7.1g f8d³ t8.6g³ t7.1g* t9.5m⁴ t8.6m² t7.1f⁴ t8.6g⁶ Sep 29] fair handicapper: won at Wolverhampton (apprentice) in August: left James Tate after second start: stays 8.5f: acts on tapeta: often in headgear in 2015: tried in tongue tie in 2015. *Simon West* **71**

KOD

KODI BEAR (IRE) 3 br.c. Kodiac 112 – Hawattef (IRE) (Mujtahid (USA) 118) [2015 **123**
112: 8.3m* 8g⁴ 8g* 8s* 8d Oct 17] tall colt: developed into a very smart performer in 2015:
won listed race at Windsor (by ¾ length from Short Squeeze) in June and Sovereign Stakes
at Salisbury (by 4½ lengths from Dark Emerald) and Celebration Mile at Goodwood (by
3¼ lengths from Gabrial) in August: below-form eighth of 9 to Solow in Queen Elizabeth
II Stakes at Ascot final start, racing freely and hanging left when beaten: stays 8.5f: acts on
soft and good to firm going: front runner/races prominently. *Clive Cox*

KODICIL (IRE) 7 b.g. Kodiac 112 – Miss Caoimhe (IRE) (Barathea (IRE) 127) [2015 **75**
16v⁴ 16m 14.1m* 15.8d⁴ 16d Oct 11] sturdy, quite good-topped gelding: fair handicapper:
won at Nottingham in August: stays 2m: acts on good to firm and good to soft going: tried
in cheekpieces: usually races close up. *Mark Walford*

KODIMOOR (IRE) 2 b.c. (Apr 29) Kodiac 112 – Victoria Lodge (IRE) (Grand Lodge **73**
(USA) 125) [2015 5m⁵ 5m³ 5,1m⁴ 5.1g⁶ 6.1g⁴ 6d³ 5g Sep 12] fair maiden: stays 6f: acts on
good to firm and good to soft going. *Danielle McCormick*

KODIVA (IRE) 3 b.f. Kodiac 112 – Operissimo (Singspiel (IRE) 133) [2015 9⁄2: 8f 8.5f⁷ **78**
8.5f³ 8f 8.5d Dec 4] good-topped filly: fairly useful maiden: second at Parx in September:
left Charles Hills after first start: best effort at 1m: acts on firm going. *Jonathan E. Sheppard,
USA*

KOHUMA 5 ch.m. Halling (USA) 133 – Kohiba (IRE) (Rock of Gibraltar (IRE) 133) **–**
[2015 p8m Jan 14] 66/1, tailed off in maiden at Lingfield. *Joseph Tuite*

KOKONI (IRE) 2 b.g. (Mar 27) Acclamation 118 – Belgique (IRE) 87 (Compton Place **63 p**
125) [2015 7g 7d⁶ p7g⁴ Oct 29] 75,000Y: neat gelding: second foal: half-brother to 7f
winner Zylan (by Kyllachy): dam, 7f-8.3f winner, half-sister to useful 2-y-o 6f/7f winner
Bruges: modest form: fourth of 8 to Race Day at Lingfield final start, nearest finish and not
knocked about: has been gelded: remains with potential. *Sir Michael Stoute*

KOKOVOKO (IRE) 4 br.g. Trans Island 119 – Khazaria (FR) (Sinndar (IRE) 134) [2015 **–**
73p: t8.6g p8g 8d Sep 2] maiden: no form in 2015: often starts slowly: temperament under
suspicion. *Andrew Balding*

KOLONEL KIRKUP 5 b.g. Dr Fong (USA) 128 – Strawberry Lolly 89 (Lomitas 129) **56 §**
[2015 67: t12.2f t12.2f³ p10f³ p11f² p12g 9.9v⁶ p11g⁶ t12.2g⁴ Jul 13] modest handicapper:
acts on polytrack, tapeta, soft and good to firm going: often wears headgear: tried in tongue
tie prior to 2015: often races towards rear: no battler: sold £7,000, sent to Germany, where
won 3 handicaps at up to 14.7f. *Ali Stronge*

KOMEDY (IRE) 2 b.f. (Mar 16) Kodiac 112 – Dancing Jest (IRE) 71 (Averti (IRE) 117) **68**
[2015 5m⁵ 5m 6g 5d² 6v³ 6.1s³ t7.1f⁵ Oct 20] €70,000Y: neat filly: second foal: half-sister
to useful 5f (including at 2 yrs) winner Jane's Memory (by Captain Rio): dam, 1m-1¼m
winner, half-sister to smart winner up to 7.6f The Kiddykid: fair maiden: stays 7f: acts on
tapeta, good to firm and heavy going: often races prominently: sold 9,000 gns, sent to
Spain. *Charles Hills*

Doom Bar Celebration Mile, Goodwood—
a third win in four starts for the progressive Kodi Bear, who beats Gabrial (left of winner),
Breton Rock (quartered cap) and Cable Bay (between second and third)

Mrs Olive Shaw's "Kodi Bear"

KOMMANDER KIRKUP 4 ch.g. Assertive 121 – Bikini 80 (Trans Island 119) [2015 **88**
88§: 6d² 6v 6g³ 6m 7.2g 6g 6d Sep 4] fairly useful handicapper: left Michael Dods after
sixth start: stays 6f: acts on good to firm and good to soft going: often wears headgear:
often races in rear: none too genuine. *John Davies*

KONNOS BAY 3 b.g. Phoenix Reach (IRE) 124 – Rasmalai 71 (Sadler's Wells (USA) **–**
132) [2015 –: p10g⁵ p12g⁶ Jun 27] well held in maiden/sellers: in headgear last 2 starts.
Shaun Harris

KONSTANTIN (IRE) 7 br.g. Balmont (USA) 117 – Manuka Magic (IRE) (Key of Luck **–**
(USA) 126) [2015 7m 8m Jul 10] good-topped gelding: useful performer: won minor event
and Group 3 in Bahrain in 2014: off 15 months, well held in handicaps at Newmarket in
2015: stays 7f: acts on polytrack and good to firm going. *Martin Smith*

KOOL KOMPANY (IRE) 3 br.c. Jeremy (USA) 122 – Absolutely Cool (IRE) 74 **111**
(Indian Ridge 123) [2015 108: 8g* 8m 6f 7g⁴ 8m² 7s⁵ Oct 31] good-topped colt: smart
performer: won Craven Stakes at Newmarket (by 1¼ lengths from Nafaqa) in April:
creditable second in Thoroughbred Stakes at Goodwood (3 lengths behind Malabar) in
July: left Richard Hannon before final start: stays 1m: acts on good to firm and good to soft
going: front runner/races prominently. *Chris Waller, Australia*

KOORA 3 b.f. Pivotal 124 – Kithanga (IRE) 117 (Darshaan 133) [2015 10.3m³ 10.3g* 12d² **109 p**
14.6m⁶ 12v* Oct 24] sister to 1½m winner Omar Khayyam and 11f winner Kindu and half-
sister to several winners, including St Leger winner Milan (2-y-o 7f winner, by Sadler's
Wells): dam 11f/1½m winner: useful performer: won maiden at Doncaster (by length from
Central Square) in August and St Simon Stakes at Newbury (by 1½ lengths from

Melodious) in October: second in listed race at York (2¼ lengths behind Martlet) in August: stays 1½m (no extra late on when sixth of 11 in Park Hill Stakes at Doncaster over 14.5f): acts on good to firm and heavy going: usually travels strongly: remains with potential. *Luca Cumani*

KOOS (GER) 7 b.m. Konigstiger (GER) 112 – Kiss Me (GER) (Alwasmi (USA) 115) **53** [2015 p15.8g³ p13.3g² t16.6m⁶ p12f Apr 15] modest maiden: stays 2m: acts on polytrack: in tongue tie in 2015. *Suzy Smith*

KOOTHRAPPALI 2 b.g. (Apr 22) Sakhee's Secret 128 – Grandmas Dream 86 (Kyllachy **62** 129) [2015 5g⁵ 5m² 5g⁵ 5m⁵ t5.1g⁵ Aug 10] modest maiden: raced only at 5f: acts on good to firm going: tried in blinkers. *David Barron*

KOPASSUS (IRE) 3 b.g. Holy Roman Emperor (IRE) 125 – Couverture (USA) 82 (Lear **66** Fan (USA) 130) [2015 57: 8d⁴ 8.3m² 8g⁴ 9m³ 7m² 7g 8.5d⁵ Sep 22] fair maiden: stays 9f: acts on good to firm going: often in headgear in 2015. *Lawrence Mullaney*

KOPENHAGEN (IRE) 4 ch.c. Captain Rio 122 – Quizzical Lady 62 (Mind Games 121) **–** [2015 –: p8g Jan 14] lightly-raced maiden: often wears headgear. *Ed de Giles*

KOPTOON 3 b.g. Rip Van Winkle (IRE) 134 – Mania (IRE) (Danehill (USA) 126) [2015 **91** 86: 6m 6.1s 6g t6g* t6g* 7g 6m⁴ 5.5m⁴ Aug 22] fairly useful performer: won claimer and seller at Wolverhampton in June, then left Tom Dascombe: stays 6f: acts on polytrack, tapeta and good to firm going: sometimes wears cheekpieces: usually wears tongue tie: races prominently: temperament under suspicion. *Michael Appleby*

KOREEN (IRE) 4 b.g. Samum (GER) 126 – Pony Girl (IRE) (Darshaan 133) [2015 **66** 10.9m 11.9s 8.9d⁶ 10.2m³ p12g p10g p13.3f⁴ p10g³ p12g³ Dec 20] fairly useful maiden at **a74** best: trained by A. Fabre in France at 2 and 3 yrs (placed 5 times) and by Francesco Santella in Italy first 4 starts in 2015: stays 1¾m: acts on polytrack, viscoride, soft and good to firm going: tongue tied last 3 outings. *John Berry*

KORNGOLD 7 b.g. Dansili 127 – Eve 81 (Rainbow Quest (USA) 134) [2015 f16g t12.2f⁶ **42 §** t9.5f f11g⁶ Apr 14] poor handicapper: stays 1¾m: acts on fibresand, tapeta and heavy going: tried in blinkers: temperamental. *Barry Leavy*

KOVOLINI 5 ch.m. Bertolini (USA) 125 – Petrikov (IRE) (In The Wings 128) [2015 57: **49** p8m p10m 8.3m May 21] poor maiden: stays 1¼m: acts on polytrack. *Geoffrey Deacon*

KRAFTWORK (IRE) 2 gr.c. (Apr 20) Mastercraftsman (IRE) 129 – Paraphernalia **83 p** (IRE) 104 (Dalakhani (IRE) 133) [2015 6m² 6g² Aug 5] €50,000Y: first foal: dam, 7f winner, half-sister to smart winner up to 1m Prince d'Alienor: runner-up in maidens won by Barbarous Relic at Ayr (better effort) and Still On Top at Pontefract (outpaced, finished well): will be suited by 7f: remains open to improvement. *Michael Dods*

KRAFTY ONE 3 ch.f. Mastercraftsman (IRE) 129 – Wonderful Desert 57 (Green Desert **64** (USA) 127) [2015 56p: 7g 7m⁶ 8.3m⁵ 9.9g² 8v³ 10.2mᵖᵘ p10f t8.6f⁶ t12.2g⁴ Dec 4] modest maiden: left John Gosden after fourth start: stays 1½m: acts on polytrack, tapeta and good to firm going. *Michael Scudamore*

KRAZY PAVING 3 b.g. Kyllachy 129 – Critical Path (IRE) 87 (Noverre (USA) 125) **–** [2015 77: 6s 5.7f 6.1m 6s 7.1s Aug 31] fair at best, no form in 2015: tried in cheekpieces in 2015: tends to find little. *Anabel K. Murphy*

KRISSY'S KISSES (IRE) 3 b.f. The Carbon Unit (USA) 106 – Eliza Berry (IRE) **84** (Montjeu (IRE) 137) [2015 –: 10d² 10.4d³ 12.4g⁶ 11.1s² 9.2g 12d² Sep 29] fairly useful maiden: second in handicap at Hamilton in August: left John Patrick Shanahan after first start, P. J. Prendergast after third: stays 1½m: acts on soft going: usually races prominently. *John Patrick Shanahan, Ireland*

KRISTAL HART 6 b.m. Lucky Story (USA) 128 – Moly (FR) (Anabaa (USA) 130) **61** [2015 65, a53: p10f⁴ p12f p10g* p10g⁴ p10m⁴ p10f* p11g⁵ Dec 3] modest handicapper: won at Lingfield in May and Chelmsford in November: stays 11f: acts on polytrack, firm and soft going: often wears cheekpieces: front runner/races prominently. *Neil Mulholland*

KRISTJANO (GER) 3 b.g. Nayef (USA) 129 – Kalahari Dancer (Dalakhani (IRE) 133) **80 p** [2015 10g 10m 10m⁴ t12.2f³ t13.9f⁶ p13.3f² Nov 19] 1,000F, €30,000Y, resold 8,000Y: well-made gelding: third foal: dam unraced half-sister to useful 1¼m winner (stayed 1½m) Design Perfection: fairly useful form: second in handicap at Chelmsford in November: stays 13.5f: acts on polytrack and tapeta: often travels strongly: will go on improving. *Chris Wall*

KRISTOFF (IRE) 2 b.c. (Apr 23) Frozen Power (IRE) 108 – Easter Girl (Efisio 120) **46**
[2015 6g 6g p8g p7g² Dec 10] compact colt: poor maiden: best effort at 7f. *Jim Boyle*

KRYSTALLITE 2 ch.f. (Feb 15) Kheleyf (USA) 116 – Chrystal Venture (IRE) 71 **74**
(Barathea (IRE) 127) [2015 t5.1g² 5d⁴ 5m² 6m t5.1f³ p5g² t5.1f* Dec 21] fourth foal: half-
sister to 5f-7f winner Wimboldsley (by Milk It Mick): dam, 7f winner (including at 2 yrs),
half-sister to useful winner up to 6f Noverre To Go: fair performer: won maiden at
Wolverhampton in December: best form at 5f: acts on polytrack and tapeta: front runner/
races prominently. *Scott Dixon*

KTCLOUSEAU (IRE) 3 b.f. Notnowcato 128 – Prithee 74 (Barathea (IRE) 127) [2015 **57**
p8m 7g 7d 8g 10s 8g p10f⁶ p12g Nov 20] fourth foal: half-sister to 1½m winner Aficionado
(by Halling): dam 11f-13f winner: modest maiden: left Paul Cole after first start: stays
1¼m: acts on polytrack: often races in rear. *John Joseph Murphy, Ireland*

KUALA QUEEN (IRE) 4 b.f. Kodiac 112 – See Nuala (IRE) 73 (Kyllachy 129) [2015 **62**
63: p6f⁵ 6g p6g 6m Aug 10] sturdy filly: modest maiden: stays 6f: acts on polytrack and
good to firm going. *Denis Coakley*

KUANTAN 2 b.g. (Mar 21) Acclamation 118 – Gay Mirage (GER) 75 (Highest Honor **76 p**
(FR) 124) [2015 8.3d² Oct 14] 140,000Y: first foal: dam maiden (stayed 1½m), half-sister
to useful 11.5f-1¾m winner Amerigo out of useful 2-y-o 7f winner Geminiani: 7/1, did
well under circumstances when second in maiden at Nottingham (2½ lengths behind
Mainstream) in October, caught further back than ideal: sure to progress. *Roger Charlton*

KUANYAO (IRE) 9 b.g. American Post 121 – Nullarbor (Green Desert (USA) 127) **53 §**
[2015 85: f6g f6g f5s f6g³ 7g⁶ f5g³ t7.1m⁶ p5m³ t6g 5.3g² 6m⁵ 5.7m p5g⁴ 5.3g⁶ 5f⁵ 7v⁵
5s⁶ 6s p5f³ f5g p6f⁵ f6g Dec 22] sturdy gelding: modest handicapper: left Conor Dore after
third start: stays 7f: acts on polytrack, fibresand and firm going: often wears headgear:
unreliable. *Ann Stokell*

KUBEBA (IRE) 4 b.g. Kodiac 112 – Brillano (FR) 75 (Desert King (IRE) 129) [2015 76: **71**
7.6d² p8g⁴ 8.3m 9s³ p8f 10s⁴ f8g Nov 12] sturdy gelding: fair maiden: stays 1¼m: acts on
polytrack, tapeta and soft going: often in cheekpieces in 2015: often races prominently.
Paul Cole

KUMANAVSUMFUN 2 b.f. (May 19) Captain Gerrard (IRE) 113 – Samadilla (IRE) 83 **64**
(Mujadil (USA) 119) [2015 6g³ 6d³ 6m* 6d² 6d³ 6.1g 6g Aug 31] sister to 2-y-o 6f winner
Three Pips and half-sister to 7f winner We're Delighted (by Tobougg) and winner up to 6f
Studfarmer (2-y-o 5f winner, by Multiplex): dam 2-y-o 5f/6f winner: modest performer:
won seller at Windsor in June: raced only at 6f: acts on good to firm and good to soft going:
front runner/races prominently. *David Evans*

KUMMIYA 2 b.g. (Feb 20) Dansili 127 – Balisada 115 (Kris 135) [2015 8s p8m* Nov 17] **90 p**
half-brother to several winners, including very smart 1¼m-1½m winner Galactic Star and
smart 1½m-2m winner (stays 21.5f) El Salvador (both by Galileo) and useful 7f-9f winner
Blues Ballad (by Singspiel): dam winner up to 1m (2-y-o 7f winner): better effort when
winning maiden at Lingfield (by 1¾ lengths from Always Welcome) in November: will
stay 1¼m: likely to progress further. *Roger Charlton*

KUNG HEI FAT CHOY (USA) 6 b.g. Elusive Quality (USA) – Lady Succeed (JPN) **74**
(Brian's Time (USA)) [2015 65, a91: f7d² f7g* f7d⁴ p8f p8g⁴ f8g* f7d³ p8f⁶ 7m 7s 8g³ **a86**
7.1m* 7m 7m 7.6g f7g p7m Dec 31] fairly useful handicapper: won at Southwell in
January and March and Musselburgh in June: stays 1m: acts on polytrack, fibresand, good
to firm and heavy going: usually wears headgear. *James Given*

KURIOSA (IRE) 3 ch.f. Rip Van Winkle (IRE) 134 – Kite Mark 58 (Mark of Esteem **73 p**
(IRE) 137) [2015 10.3m p10f³ Dec 21] closely related to very smart winner up to 15.5f
Kite Wood (2-y-o 1m winner) and smart 9f winner (stays 1½m) Odeon (both by Galileo)
and half-sister to 1¼m-15f winner Daylami Dreams (by Daylami): dam ran once: better
effort when third in maiden at Chelmsford in December, needing stiffer test: will be suited
by 1½m: remains open to improvement. *Marco Botti*

KURLAND (IRE) 2 gr.f. (Mar 18) Kheleyf (USA) 116 – Bunditten (IRE) 92 (Soviet Star **90**
(USA) 128) [2015 5g* 5f⁴ 6m 5g³ 5m⁵ 5g⁶ Oct 9] €15,500F: neat filly: half-sister to several
winners, including 5f/6f winner Star Fire (by Dark Angel) and winner up to 9f Airborne
Again (2-y-o 5f winner, by Acclamation): dam ungenuine 2-y-o 5f winner: fairly useful
performer: won maiden at Newmarket in April: third in listed race at York (length behind
Shadow Hunter) in August: may prove better at 5f than 6f: acts on firm going: front runner/
races prominently. *Martyn Meade*

KUWAIT STAR 6 ch.g. Resplendent Glory (IRE) 115 – Mofeyda (IRE) 70 (Mtoto 134) **57**
[2015 78: p10g f8g Dec 12] modest handicapper: left Sarah Humphrey after first start:
stays 9.5f: acts on polytrack, good to firm and heavy going: often races prominently.
Charlie Wallis

KWANTO 5 b.m. Piccolo 121 – Craic Sa Ceili (IRE) 83 (Danehill Dancer (IRE) 117) [2015 **–**
t5.1f Sep 19] modest maiden: stays 7f: acts on firm going: tried in headgear/tongue tie:
temperament under suspicion. *Ken Wingrove*

KYLACH ME IF U CAN 3 b.g. Kyllachy 129 – Raskutani (Dansili 127) [2015 78: **82**
7.5m⁴ 8g⁶ 7d² 7g² 7d² 8g³ 7.2g⁶ 8.5m² Oct 1] fairly useful handicapper: good second at
Beverley final start in Britain: stays 8.5f: acts on good to firm and good to soft going: often
in headgear in 2015: front runner/races prominently: sold 20,000 gns, won minor event
over 6f at Syracuse in November. *Kevin Ryan*

KYLEA (IRE) 2 b.f. (Feb 28) Iffraaj 127 – Pitrizza (IRE) (Machiavellian (USA) 123) **56**
[2015 7s⁶ 6g Sep 19] 70,000F, 300,000Y: half-sister to several winners, including 7f/7.4f
(including at 2 yrs) winner Snow Watch and winner up to 1m Vilasol (2-y-o 6f winner)
(both useful and by Verglas): dam 11.5f winner: better effort when sixth in maiden at
Salisbury in September. *Richard Hannon*

KYLE OF BUTE 9 ch.g. Kyllachy 129 – Blinding Mission (IRE) 70 (Marju (IRE) 127) **42**
[2015 61: t9.5g t8.6g t9.5g Jul 23] good-quartered gelding: poor handicapper: stays 1¼m:
acts on polytrack, firm and good to soft going: tried in headgear prior to 2015: often races
towards rear. *Richard Ford*

KYLIES WILD CARD 3 b.f. Aussie Rules (USA) 123 – Jemiliah 64 (Dubai Destination **55**
(USA) 127) [2015 41: p6g⁴ p7f p6m⁶ 16m⁴ 6m 6d² 6d² 6g² 5.1d⁵ 6v³ 6v⁶ t7.1f Oct 23] leggy **a38**
filly: modest maiden: stays 6f: acts on good to soft going. *Simon Hodgson*

KYLLA 2 b.f. (Mar 4) Kyllachy 129 – Mamounia (IRE) 101 (Green Desert (USA) 127) **–**
[2015 5m⁶ 6m Aug 8] seventh foal: half-sister to 6f-7f winner Medam (by Medicean): dam,
7f-9f winner, half-sister to smart winner up to 12.5f Maroussies Wings: well held in
maiden/seller. *Shaun Harris*

KYLLACH ME (IRE) 3 b.g. Kyllachy 129 – Good For Her 72 (Rock of Gibraltar (IRE) **69**
133) [2015 44: f7g⁵ f5d⁴ f6d³ t6m* t6f* 6m⁴ 6d⁵ 6d⁵ 6m³ 5.9s t6f² Nov 13] fair
handicapper: won at Wolverhampton in February and March: stays 6f: acts on tapeta and
good to firm going: usually in blinkers in 2015. *Bryan Smart*

KYLLACHYKOV (IRE) 7 ch.g. Kyllachy 129 – Dance On 93 (Caerleon (USA) 132) **52**
[2015 63: f12g² f11g⁶ f11g⁶ t12.2f t12.2f f12g⁴ f11g Dec 29] modest handicapper: stays
8.5f: acts on polytrack and good going: tried in headgear: usually leads, tends to find little.
Rebecca Bastiman

KYLLACHY QUEEN (IRE) 3 b.f. Kyllachy 129 – Queen Sensazione (IRE) (King **105**
Charlemagne (USA) 120) [2015 8d² 8g 7m* 8g² 8g⁴ t7.1g² Nov 27] useful performer: won
listed race at Milan (by 1¾ lengths from Aury Touch) in May: second in listed race at Milan
(½ length behind Reset In Blue) in September and, having left Stefano Botti, Italy, minor
event at Wolverhampton (½ length behind Lamar) in November: stays 1m: acts on tapeta
and good to firm going: often races towards rear. *Marco Botti*

KYLLACHY SPIRIT 7 b.g. Kyllachy 129 – Cartuccia (IRE) (Doyoun 124) [2015 p11f **60 §**
p12m p11g⁶ 10.2m² 9g p10g² p12g Jul 2] good-topped gelding: fair handicapper: stays 11f:
acts on polytrack, soft and good to firm going: tried in cheekpieces prior to 2015: usually
races close up: not one to rely on. *Gary Moore*

KYLLA INSTINCT 2 b.f. (Mar 26) Kyllachy 129 – Craighall 66 (Dubawi (IRE) 129) **82**
[2015 p6g⁶ 7g 6g³ t6f² Oct 31] 20,000Y: close-coupled filly: second foal: dam maiden
half-sister to smart 1¼m-1½m winner (stays 1¾m) Connecticut: fairly useful maiden: third
in maiden at Windsor and second in nursery at Wolverhampton in October: stays 6f.
Philip McBride

KYLLARNEY 3 b.f. Kyllachy 129 – Hurricane Harriet 81 (Bertolini (USA) 125) [2015 **61 +**
60: p6m p6f² Feb 3] fair maiden: acts on polytrack, best turf form on soft going: sent to
France, where won 6 times in Provinces at up to 9.2f. *Charles Hills*

KYLLUKEY 2 b.g. (Jan 30) Kyllachy 129 – Money Note 68 (Librettist (USA) 124) [2015 **78**
5m⁴ 5f³ 5.1g² 6m 6g² 6d³ p6g⁵ Oct 27] strong gelding: fair maiden: stays 6f: acts on firm
going. *Charles Hills*

KYRENIA CASTLE (GER) 3 b.g. Dashing Blade 117 – Key To Win (FR) (Halling **73** (USA) 133) [2015 75: 5g 6.1s 7m* 7m 7g³ 7g* 8m* 7.5m⁴ Aug 12] fair performer: won seller at Redcar in May and claimers at Catterick in July and Redcar in August: stays 1m: acts on tapeta and good to firm going: often wears cheekpieces: front runner/races prominently: none too reliable. *David Nicholls*

L

LAAFIRAAQ (FR) 2 b.c. (Feb 22) Cape Cross (IRE) 129 – Zaaqya 94 (Nayef (USA) **87** 129) [2015 p8g p8g⁵ 8.3m* 9g² 7g Dec 29] sturdy colt: third foal: dam winner up to 1½m (2-y-o 7f-1m winner): fairly useful performer: won maiden at Hamilton (by 7 lengths from Head High) in September: creditable second to Southdown Lad in nursery at Newmarket next time: will be suited by at least 1¼m: acts on good to firm going: left Mark Johnston after fourth start. *Mohammed Jassim Ghazali, Qatar*

LAAHIJ 3 b.g. Arcano (IRE) 122 – Acicula (IRE) 96 (Night Shift (USA)) [2015 p8g Dec **–** 20] 33/1, very green when tailed off in maiden at Lingfield. *Jamie Poulton*

LA ASOMADA 2 b.f. (Feb 21) Arabian Gleam 122 – Morristown Music (IRE) 71 (Distant **60** Music (USA) 126) [2015 5m 5g² 5m⁴ Sep 8] £2,000Y: second foal: dam 5f winner: modest maiden: best effort when second at Musselburgh (¾ length behind Searanger) in August. *David Barron*

LA BACOUETTEUSE (FR) 10 b.g. Miesque's Son (USA) 117 – Toryka (Vettori (IRE) **77** 119) [2015 78: 14g⁴ 16.1d 14.1v⁴ 16m 15.8g⁶ 15.8m³ 15s² 16d* 15.8g⁵ 17.1d⁴ 15g* Sep 29] fair handicapper: won at Ripon in August and Ayr in September: stays 2m: acts on good to firm and heavy going: usually wears headgear: sometimes slowly away, often races in rear, often races lazily. *Iain Jardine*

LA BOHEME (GER) 3 b.f. Montjeu (IRE) 137 – La Reine Noir (GER) (Rainbow Quest **85** (USA) 134) [2015 10d² 9.9d⁴ 10m³ Jun 11] €260,000Y: lengthy, attractive filly: second foal: dam, placed at 1m/9f in Germany, half-sister to Prix de l'Opera winner Lady Marian: fairly useful maiden: best effort when second at Sandown (neck behind Brandybend) in April: will stay 1½m: sent to USA. *Luca Cumani*

LA BRAVA 5 ch.m. Kheleyf (USA) 116 – La Belga (ARG) (Roy (USA)) [2015 –: t12.2g **–** Apr 11] no form. *Steve Flook*

LACAN (IRE) 4 b.c. New Approach (IRE) 132 – Invincible Isle (IRE) 89 (Invincible **99** Spirit (IRE) 121) [2015 104: p8m⁶ p8g* 8m³ 7m⁴ 7m p8f⁵ p8f⁴ p8g Dec 10] well-made colt: useful handicapper: won at Chelmsford (by ¾ length from God Willing) in May: ran creditably most other starts in 2015: stays 8.5f: acts on polytrack, tapeta and good to firm going: in cheekpieces last 2 starts. *Marco Botti*

LA CELEBS VILLE (IRE) 2 b.f. (Feb 1) Sea The Stars (IRE) 140 – Bryanstown (IRE) **75** 69 (Galileo (IRE) 134) [2015 7m 8d³ 8d⁵ Sep 26] 40,000F, 70,000Y: close-coupled filly: first foal: dam, ran once, out of sister to Derby winner Commander In Chief and half-sister to Warning: fair maiden: best effort when third at Haydock (2½ lengths behind Peru) in September, slowly away: tried in cheekpieces. *Tom Dascombe*

LACERTA 4 b.g. Astronomer Royal (USA) 121 – Rubber (IRE) 88 (Namid 128) [2015 63: **66** 7.9v⁶ 12.5m⁶ 10m⁶ 12g 12d 12.4g* 12.1m² 13.8v Oct 17] fair handicapper: won at Newcastle in September: stayed 12.5f: acted on good to firm going: dead. *Micky Hammond*

LACEY 6 b.g. Rail Link 132 – Shamana (USA) (Woodman (USA) 126) [2015 66: t13.9g³ **68** t13.9g⁴ t13.9f² t16.5m⁴ t16.5g⁵ t16.5g³ t13.9g⁴ t13.9g² t13.9g t16.5g³ t13.9m t16.5f² t16.5f* t16.5f⁴ Nov 16] fair handicapper: won at Wolverhampton in October: left Andrew Hollinshead after second start: stays 16.5f: acts on polytrack and tapeta: often wears headgear: often races towards rear. *Sarah Hollinshead*

LACING 3 b.f. Equiano (FR) 127 – Lacework 91 (Pivotal 124) [2015 95: 7m⁵ 6.1s 6.9g **92** 6m⁵ 7s³ 6m² 6g Oct 10] workmanlike filly: fairly useful performer: second in handicap at Hamilton in September: stays 7f: acts on good to firm going. *Richard Fahey*

LACKADAY 3 gr.g. Kyllachy 129 – Day Creek (Daylami (IRE) 138) [2015 82: p5g² p6g⁵ **80** 5m 5m⁶ 5d⁴ 6g⁵ 6m p6f⁶ p6g f6g² Dec 18] rather leggy, close-coupled gelding: fair performer: stays 6f: acts on polytrack, fibresand, good to firm and heavy going: tried in cheekpieces. *William Jarvis*

LACOCK 4 b.g. Compton Place 125 – Puya 88 (Kris 135) [2015 p8g p8f Feb 11] modest **56**
maiden: stays 1¼m: acts on polytrack, good to firm and heavy going: tried in headgear:
front runner/races prominently, tends to find little. *Sean Curran*

LAC SACRE (FR) 6 b.g. Bering 136 – Lady Glorieuse (FR) (Le Glorieux 127) [2015 **53**
16.2s³ t16.5f Oct 27] modest handicapper: stays 2m: acts on heavy going: sometimes wears
headgear/tongue tie. *John Flint*

LA CUESTA (IRE) 3 b.f. Showcasing 117 – Dowager 102 (Groom Dancer (USA) 128) **79**
[2015 86: 5m 5d 5f⁵ t5.1f⁶ p5g Oct 20] tall filly: fair handicapper: best form at 5f: acts on
tapeta, good to firm and good to soft going: sold 22,000 gns, sent to Spain. *Jamie Osborne*

LA DANZA 5 b.m. Country Reel (USA) 113 – Freedom Song 74 (Singspiel (IRE) 133) **36**
[2015 65, a54: f7g t6g f6d f7g Mar 3] poor maiden: stays 1m: acts on all-weather: tried in
headgear. *Shaun Harris*

LA DONACELLA 3 b.f. Sir Percy 129 – Tessie (Tiger Hill (IRE) 127) [2015 : 9g⁷ 10m³ **79**
Jul 21] fair maiden: better effort in 2015 when second at Goodwood in June. *Daniel Kubler*

LA DOROTEA (IRE) 3 ch.f. Lope de Vega (IRE) 125 – Nawal (FR) 103 (Homme de Loi **101**
(IRE) 120) [2015 p7g³ t8.6g² p8g² t8.6m³ p8f⁴ f8g* 10.4g⁵ 8m 8g* 8.1m 7.6m⁶ 8m⁵ 8.9d⁴
9.9d⁴ p9.4g Dec 2] €100,000 2-y-o: lengthy filly: half-sister to several winners, including
US Grade 1 1¼m winner Mast Track (by Mizzen Mast) and useful French 7f/1m winner
Redbrook (by Raven's Pass): dam 2-y-o 7f/7.5f winner: useful performer: won maiden at
Southwell in April and handicap at Pontefract in June: left Richard Fahey after twelfth
start: good efforts when fourth in listed races after, at Chantilly (best effort, 1¾ lengths
behind Thank You Bye Bye) and Saint-Cloud: stays 1¼m: acts on polytrack/fibresand and
good to soft going. *Francis-Henri Graffard, France*

LADURELLI (IRE) 3 b.g. Mastercraftsman (IRE) 129 – Chanter (Lomitas 129) [2015 **96 p**
8m p10f* p11m³ Oct 28] €50,000F, 120,000Y: sturdy gelding: fourth foal: half-brother to
1¼m winner Music Man (by Oratorio) and temperamental 2-y-o 7f winner Edge (by
Acclamation): dam unraced half-sister to King George VI & Queen Elizabeth Stakes
winner Belmez: useful performer: won maiden at Chelmsford (by 2 lengths from Tartoor)
in October: further improvement when third in handicap at Kempton (¾ length behind
Revision) in October, needing stronger gallop: left Roger Varian after first start: will stay
1½m: remains with potential. *Paul Cole*

LADWEB 5 ch.g. Bertolini (USA) 125 – Adweb 88 (Muhtarram (USA) 125) [2015 96: 5m **85**
5m⁵ 6m 6.1m⁵ 5m⁶ 5m 5d⁶ 6s 5s² 5.3s⁴ Oct 15] leggy gelding: fairly useful handicapper:
second at Sandown in September: stays 5.5f: acts on good to firm and heavy going: tried in
visor in 2015: often starts slowly. *John Gallagher*

LADY ANTONIOS (IRE) 3 b.f. Bushranger (IRE) 119 – Rahika Rose 91 (Unfuwain **–**
(USA) 131) [2015 –: p6g⁵ t6g Jun 4] no form: in hood in 2015. *Chris Dwyer*

LADY ARGENTUM (IRE) 2 b.f. (Feb 1) Kodiac 112 – Silver Dip 90 (Gulch (USA)) **64**
[2015 5g⁴ 5m 6m³ 6m² 7g 6d³ 6.3d t7.1f⁶ t6f Oct 23] €8,000F, €16,000Y: fifth foal: closely
related to a winner in Spain by Tiger Hill and half-sister to 2-y-o 6f winner Bellechance (by
Acclamation) and 1m-1¼m winner Piccadilly Jim (by Royal Applause): dam 7f winner
(including at 2 yrs): modest maiden: stays 6f: acts on good to firm going. *Richard Fahey*

LADY ATLAS 3 ch.f. Dutch Art 126 – Paquerettza (FR) 96 (Dr Fong (USA) 128) [2015 **70**
60: 6m³ p6g* t6g 7d 6g 7m⁵ p8f⁵ p8f⁴ 7.2g² 7s³ t7.1f³ t6f⁵ Nov 13] fair handicapper: won
at Chelmsford in April: will be suited by a return to 7f+: acts on polytrack and good to firm
going. *David Brown*

LADY BACCHUS 2 b.f. (Apr 24) Compton Place 125 – Beauty (IRE) 74 (Alzao (USA) **–**
117) [2015 7.5g 6d 6g 7s Oct 26] 7,000Y: sixth foal: half-sister to 3 winners, including 6f
winner (including at 2 yrs) Ishibee (by Ishiguru) and 2-y-o 1m winner Fabiello (by
Indesatchel), later successful in Spain: dam maiden (stayed 1¼m): no form. *Richard Guest*

LADY BAYSIDE 7 ch.m. Ishiguru (USA) 114 – Seldemosa 67 (Selkirk (USA) 129) [2015 **72**
79: 10.2f⁴ 8m⁵ 8.1m³ 8.1m³ 8.1m⁵ 8.1m⁵ 8.1d 7.1s² 8s⁵ 8g⁵ Oct 18] fair handicapper: stays
1¼m: acts on any turf going: tried in headgear in 2015. *Malcolm Saunders*

LADY BEE (IRE) 3 b.f. Lawman (FR) 121 – Rainbow Lyrics (IRE) (Rainbow Quest **–**
(USA) 134) [2015 –: p7g 7g p10m 9g⁶ 10.2f⁶ p6f t7.1m Nov 28] sturdy filly: no form:
sometimes in headgear in 2015. *George Baker*

LADY BLANCO (USA) 2 b.f. (Feb 17) Cape Blanco (IRE) 130 – War Clan (USA) (War **54 p**
Front (USA) 119) [2015 p8g Oct 6] first foal: dam US 1m winner: 25/1, seventh in maiden
at Kempton (9½ lengths behind Nessita) in October: should do better in time.
Andrew Balding

LADY BLING 3 b.f. Showcasing 117 – Bling Bling (IRE) 70 (Indian Ridge 123) [2015 –: **35** p6m p7f p8f t6g t5.1g 6d⁶ f6d⁵ 7m 6d f7s Aug 6] poor maiden: stays 7f: acts on fibresand, tapeta, good to firm and good to soft going: in headgear in 2015. *Michael Attwater*

LADY BRAMBLETYE (IRE) 3 b.f. Lawman (FR) 121 – Steeple (Selkirk (USA) 129 **–** [2015 p7g p6f⁶ Apr 15] 20,000Y, £18,000 2-y-o: half-sister to several winners, including 9.3f-1½m winner Arturius (by Anabaa) and 1¼m winner Hunting Country (by Cape Cross), both useful: dam French 9f winner: well held in 2 maidens. *Simon Dow*

LADY BRIGID (IRE) 4 b.f. Holy Roman Emperor (IRE) 125 – Brigids Cross (IRE) **69** (Sadler's Wells (USA) 132) [2015 89: p6g p7g f8g 20] lengthy, rather unfurnished filly: fair handicapper: stays 6f: acts on polytrack, best turf form on ground softer than good (acts on heavy): usually races close up. *Olly Stevens*

LADY CANFORD (IRE) 2 b.f. (Mar 8) Canford Cliffs (IRE) 133 – Soul Mountain **74** (IRE) 88 (Rock of Gibraltar (IRE) 133) [2015 6m 6d² 7v³ p8m² p8g Dec 15] 55,000F, 42,000Y: half-sister to several winners, including 6f winner Hills And Dales (by Acclamation) and 1m winner Caliso Day (by High Chaparral): dam, 1¼m/10.6f winner, half-sister to US Grade 2 8.5f winner Girl Warrior: fair maiden: stays 7f: acts on polytrack. *James Bethell*

LADY CHARA 2 b.f. (Jan 16) Stimulation (IRE) 121 – Noble Nova 69 (Fraam 114) [2015 **–** 6d May 27] £18,000Y: fifth foal: half-sister to 3 winners, including useful 6f (including at 2 yrs) winner New Bidder (by Auction House) and 5f-7f winner (including in Germany) Captain Noble (by Captain Rio): dam winner up to 1m (2-y-o 6f winner): 22/1, well held in maiden at Hamilton. *Ann Duffield*

LADY CHARLIE 3 b.f. Myboycharlie (IRE) 118 – Fancy Rose (USA) (Joyeux Danseur **61** (USA) 123) [2015 63: p7f p8g t7.1m 8f⁶ 8m³ 10.2f 11.7f¹⁴ t8.6g³ 8g Aug 21] modest handicapper: stays 11.5f: acts on tapeta and firm going: sold £1,500, sent to Germany. *Jo Hughes*

LADY CLAIR (IRE) 2 b.f. (Mar 11) Canford Cliffs (IRE) 133 – Queen of Carthage **93** (USA) (Cape Cross (IRE) 129) [2015 5g* 5g* 6g⁴ 6g 6s⁵ Oct 31] €13,000Y, €55,000 2-y-o: first foal: dam unraced daughter of Prix de l'Opera winner Satwa Queen: fairly useful performer: won maiden at Catterick and nursery at Thirsk by ¾ length from New Road Side), both in July: good fourth in Lowther Stakes at York (5½ lengths behind Besharah) in August: left David Barron, well held in listed race on softer ground at Maisons-Laffitte final start: stays 6f. *Francis-Henri Graffard, France*

LADY CLITICO (IRE) 4 b.f. Bushranger (IRE) 119 – Villa Nova (IRE) 55 (Petardia **79** 113) [2015 81: 10s² 12.5m 12m* 13.1g⁴ 13.1d⁶ 12d t9.5f Dec 21] fair handicapper: won at Ripon in June: stays 1½m: acts on good to firm and heavy going: sometimes wears cheekpieces. *Rebecca Menzies*

LADY CORDIE 3 b.f. Monsieur Bond (IRE) 120 – Lady Benjamin 81 (Spinning World **52** (USA) 130) [2015 –: 6g⁴ 5g⁶ 6g 7.2g 5d 6m Aug 20] modest maiden: best effort at 6f. *Jim Goldie*

LADY CORRESPONDENT (USA) 3 b.f. War Front (USA) 119 – Fanzine (USA) **88** (Cozzene (USA)) [2015 84P: 7m⁶ 7m 6g Sep 24] lengthy, attractive filly: fairly useful form: sixth of 8 to Osaila in Nell Gwyn Stakes at Newmarket, best effort of 2015: should stay 1m. *John Gosden*

LADY CROSSMAR (IRE) 4 b.f. Duke of Marmalade (IRE) 132 – Rekindled Cross **84** (IRE) (Cape Cross (IRE) 129) [2015 85: 7d⁶ 8m³ Apr 6] angular filly: fairly useful handicapper: stays 1m: acts on polytrack, tapeta and good to firm going. *Brian Ellison*

LADY DESIRE (IRE) 3 b.f. Lookin At Lucky (USA) 127 – Princess Desire (IRE) **71** (Danehill (USA) 126) [2015 86: 7.9v 6.9g⁵ 6g⁶ 6m⁴ 6g³ 6g t7.1m t7.1f Oct 30] fair handicapper: left Keith Dalgleish after sixth start: stays 7f: acts on good to firm going: tried in cheekpieces. *David O'Meara*

LADYDOLLY 7 b.m. Kyllachy 129 – Lady Pekan 87 (Sri Pekan (USA) 117) [2015 –: **–** t5.1f Jan 12] modest handicapper in 2012: lightly raced and out of sorts since: best effort at 5f: acts on fibresand and firm going: wears headgear. *Roy Brotherton*

LADY DRAGON (IRE) 4 b.f. Galileo (IRE) 134 – Spinola (FR) 103 (Spinning World **108** (USA) 130) [2015 12.9g* 14.9d³ 14m⁵ 14.9d⁵ 11.9g⁶ Oct 7] half-sister to several winners, including useful French performer up to 1¼m Eldandy (2-y-o 1m winner, by Danehill Dancer) and useful French 7f/1m winner (including at 2 yrs) Kirkinola (by Selkirk): dam 2-y-o 6f/7f winner: useful performer: won minor event at Fontainebleau in May: third in listed race at Chantilly (1½ lengths behind Fly With Me) in June: seemed unsuited by track but ran respectably when 4¼ lengths fifth to Simple Verse in Lillie Langtry Stakes at Goodwood on third outing: below form last 2 starts: stays 15f: acts on soft and good to firm going. *M. Delzangles, France*

LADY D'S ROCK (IRE) 3 gr.f. Aussie Rules (USA) 123 – Za Za 64 (Barathea (IRE) 127) [2015 –: 10.2m3 10.2m6 8g p12g3 p11g* Dec 3] modest handicapper: won at Kempton in December: stays 1½m: acts on polytrack and good to firm going: often in tongue tie in 2015. *Clive Cox* **60**

LADY DUTCH 4 b.f. Dutch Art 126 – Monjouet (IRE) (Montjeu (IRE) 137) [2015 p8f* p8g* 9F4 8g 8.1m 7m Oct 3] strong filly: third foal: half-sister to Italian 2-y-o 7.5f winner Wiston (by Hawk Wing) and Italian 1m and (at 2 yrs) 8.5f winner Capitan Jack (by Dubawi): dam Italian maiden: useful performer: left B. Grizzetti, Italy, won minor event at Kempton in February and listed race at same course (by 1¼ lengths from Solar Magic) in April: stays 1¼m: acts on polytrack, firm and good to soft going: has worn tongue tie, including on final start. *Marco Botti* **103**

LADY ELIZABETH (IRE) 2 b.f. (Mar 10) Dandy Man (IRE) 123 – Disarm (IRE) (Bahamian Bounty 116) [2015 5g 5m6 6g4 5s3 5d f5g4 f5g5 Dec 18] €18,000F: seventh foal: half-sister to 3 winners, including useful 5f (including at 2 yrs) winner Sir Geoffrey and winner up to 7f Caprio (2-y-o 6f winner) (both by Captain Rio): dam unraced: modest maiden: stays 6f: acts on fibresand: often in cheekpieces: races prominently. *Scott Dixon* **62**

LADY EMMA 2 b.f. (Mar 2) Mount Nelson 125 – Songbook (Singspiel (IRE) 133) [2015 8v Oct 24] seventh foal: dam unraced half-sister to smart 7f-1¼m performer Two-Twenty-Two: 40/1, last of 10 in maiden at Newbury. *Steph Hollinshead* **–**

LADY ESTELLA (IRE) 3 b.f. Equiano (FR) 127 – Lady Scarlett (Woodman (USA) 126) [2015 69: 7g4 7d5 8d5 t7.1g* p7g5 t7.1m t7.1f6 p8m2 Nov 21] fair handicapper: won at Wolverhampton in August: stays 1m: acts on polytrack and tapeta. *Marco Botti* **62 + a78**

LADY FONTENAIL 2 b.f. (Jan 23) Compton Place 125 – Nina Fontenail (FR) 66 (Kaldounevees (FR) 118) [2015 5.7f5 6g 7.4d6 p8g Dec 2] fifth foal: half-sister to 1m-1½m winner Poetic Verse (by Byron): dam 1½m winner: fair maiden: best effort at 7.5f. *Rod Millman* **65**

LADY GEMINI 3 b.f. Myboycharlie (IRE) 118 – Gemini Gold (IRE) 97 (King's Best (USA) 132) [2015 84: 5g2 5d 5.7f* 6m4 p6g t5.1g Nov 27] fair performer: won maiden at Bath in September: stays 6f: acts on firm going: tried in cheekpieces in 2015. *Jo Hughes* **78**

LADY GERONIMO (IRE) 6 b.m. Hawk Wing (USA) 136 – Birthday (IRE) (Singspiel (IRE) 133) [2015 p10f6 p12f Apr 15] maiden: no form in 2015: stays 1¼m: acts on firm and good to soft going: in hood first start in 2015. *Conrad Allen* **–**

LADY GIBRALTAR 6 b.m. Rock of Gibraltar (IRE) 133 – Lady Adnil (IRE) (Stravinsky (USA) 133) [2015 81: p7f6 5.5g 5m* 5f3 5m* 5f 5g Jul 28] strong mare: useful handicapper: won at Goodwood and Haydock (by 1½ lengths from By Rights) in June: stays 6f: acts on polytrack, soft and good to firm going: has worn headgear: usually races prominently, often travels strongly. *Timothy Jarvis* **96**

LADY HARE (IRE) 3 b.f. Approve (IRE) 112 – Peaceful Kingdom (USA) (King of Kings (IRE) 125) [2015 63: t8.6g6 p8f3 9g p10f 9.9s Oct 15] modest maiden: left David Simcock after fourth start: should stay 1¼m: acts on polytrack: tried in cheekpieces in 2015: temperament under suspicion. *Richard Hughes* **55**

LADY HEIDI 4 b.f. High Chaparral (IRE) 132 – Water Feature (Dansili 127) [2015 –: p8m Mar 5] useful winner at 2 yrs, well held both starts since: best effort at 1m: acts on heavy going: sold 200,000 gns in December. *Alison Hutchinson* **–**

LADY HORATIA 4 gr.f. Mount Nelson 125 – Lady Xara (IRE) (Xaar 132) [2015 92: 6m6 6.1g2 6m3 6g 6g5 6.1g p7g2 Oct 14] good-topped filly: fairly useful handicapper: stays 7f: acts on polytrack, tapeta, soft and good to firm going: tried in headgear in 2015: usually races close up. *William Muir* **88**

LADY IBROX 5 b.m. Ishiguru (USA) 114 – Last Impression 69 (Imp Society (USA)) [2015 80: t5.1f3 f5d2 f6s5 5g 5d2 6d 5d3 5g5 5g 5.1d 6d Oct 26] tall mare: fair handicapper: stays 6f: acts on all-weather, good to firm and heavy going: tried in headgear: tried in tongue tie: front runner/races prominently: untrustworthy. *Alan Brown* **76 § a66 §**

LADY IN WHITE (IRE) 3 ro.f. Zebedee 113 – Alexander Phantom (IRE) (Soviet Star (USA) 128) [2015 –: p6m2 p6m3 Mar 5] good-topped filly: modest maiden: stays 6f: often in hood prior to 2015. *Roger Varian* **56**

LADY JOANNA VASSA (IRE) 2 ch.f. (Mar 1) Equiano (FR) 127 – Lady Natilda 64 – (First Trump 118) [2015 5.1g 5.1g⁶ 5m Aug 10] 21,000Y: half-sister to several winners, including useful 2-y-o 5f winner Primo Lady (by Lucky Story) and 6f winner Zhiggy's Stardust (by Zafeen): dam 2-y-o 6f winner: little form: tried in tongue tie. *Richard Guest*

LADY KASHAAN (IRE) 6 b.m. Manduro (GER) 135 – Lady's Secret (IRE) 111 (Alzao 96 (USA) 117) [2015 97: 16s* 16g⁶ 18.7d May 6] useful handicapper: won at Musselburgh (by 7 lengths from Handiwork) in April: stays 2m: acts on soft and good to firm going: sold 17,000 gns. *Alan Swinbank*

LADY KATHERINE 2 b.f. (Feb 3) Dick Turpin (IRE) 127 – Vax Star 96 (Petong 126) – [2015 p6g 6m 6d⁵ p7g⁶ 5.7m Jul 31] 8,000Y: half-sister to several winners, including 2-y-o 6f winner Negligee (by Night Shift) and 5f/6f winner (including at 2 yrs) Yurituni (by Bahamian Bounty): dam 2-y-o 5f winner: no form: sometimes in blinkers. *Eve Johnson Houghton*

LADY KHELEYF 2 bl.f. (Mar 22) Kheleyf (USA) 116 – Mosa Mine 61 (Exceed And 57 + Excel (AUS) 126) [2015 5m 5g³ p5g* 5d⁴ p5f p5m⁵ t5.1g Nov 27] 5,000F, £9,000Y, a64 £34,000 2-y-o: workmanlike filly: first foal: dam, maiden (best at 5f), half-sister to smart 7f winner Sirocco Breeze: modest performer: won maiden at Lingfield in August: raced only at 5f: acts on polytrack: front runner/races prominently. *George Margarson*

LADY KNIGHT (IRE) 4 b.f. Champs Elysees 124 – Knight's Place (IRE) 72 (Hamas 49 (IRE) 125) [2015 –: 17.2f⁵ 16.2s⁴ p16g 13.1m Sep 28] angular filly: poor handicapper: won at Bath in April: left Sean Curran after third start: stays 17f: acts on firm and soft going: tried in headgear prior to 2015. *Natalie Lloyd-Beavis*

LADY KYLLAR 3 b.f. Kyllachy 129 – Miss Otis 78 (Danetime (IRE) 121) [2015 70: p5f* 90 5m² 5g* 5m³ 5m² 5d Jul 24] rather leggy filly: fairly useful handicapper: won at Lingfield in March and Windsor in May: good second at Windsor in July: raced only at 5f: acts on polytrack and good to firm going: usually responds generously to pressure. *George Margarson*

LADY LEKKI (IRE) 3 b.f. Champs Elysees 124 – One Zero (USA) 73 (Theatrical) 75 [2015 8g* 12.1g⁴ 14.1d⁴ Oct 26] €7,000Y: second foal: dam, maiden (stayed 13f), half-sister to dam of high-class performer around 1¼m Byword and very smart US Grade 1 1m/9f winner Proviso: fair performer: won maiden at Wetherby in April: best effort when fourth in handicap at Redcar final start: stays 1¾m. *Ben Haslam*

LADY LISA JAYNE 5 b.m. Moss Vale (IRE) 126 – Mimic 83 (Royal Applause 124) – [2015 5g Aug 29] third foal: dam, 6f winner, half-sister to smart winner up to 1½m Naked Welcome: 40/1 and in hood, well held in maiden at Beverley, slowly away. *Clive Mulhall*

LADY LIZ 4 b.f. Byron 117 – Sister Rose (FR) (One Cool Cat (USA) 123) [2015 60: 6s – 8m Aug 10] maiden: no form in 2015: stays 7f: acts on soft going: sometimes wears blinkers. *George Moore*

LADY LLOYD 2 b.f. (Feb 5) Paco Boy (IRE) 129 – Carafe 85 (Selkirk (USA) 129) [2015 67 6g⁶ 6m⁶ p6f² p8f⁵ p7g⁶ t7.1g³ p8g⁴ p7m Dec 31] 10,000Y: seventh foal: half-sister to useful 1¼m winner Next Approach (by New Approach) and a winner in Qatar by Oasis Dream: dam 7f winner out of Falmouth/Nassau Stakes winner Caramba: fair maiden: stays 1m: acts on polytrack, tapeta and good to firm going. *William Jarvis*

LADY LUNCHALOT (USA) 5 b.m. More Than Ready (USA) 120 – Betty Johanne 72 (USA) (Johannesburg (USA) 127) [2015 84: p10f p10g* p10f⁵ p12g p10m⁵ p10f³ 10g⁵ p10m⁴ 10m² 11.6m⁶ p12g p12f³ p12g⁴ p12f⁴ p10f⁶ p12m⁴ p12g² p12f² p12m³ p12g⁴ Dec 30] angular mare: fair handicapper: won at Lingfield in February: stays 1½m: acts on polytrack and good to firm going: sometimes wears cheekpieces: usually races close up. *Laura Mongan*

LADY LYDIA (IRE) 4 b.f. Kheleyf (USA) 116 – Piece Unique (Barathea (IRE) 127) 83 [2015 78: p8g² p7f² p8f 8g p7f² p7f t7.1f² p7g* t7.1m⁶ Dec 26] big, good-topped mare: fairly useful handicapper: won at Kempton (by 1½ lengths from Be Royale) in December: stays 1m: acts on polytrack, tapeta, soft and good to firm going: sometimes in headgear prior to 2015: sometimes slowly away. *Conrad Allen*

LADY MACAPA 2 b.f. (Feb 7) Equiano (FR) 127 – Brazilian Style 67 (Exit To Nowhere 90 (USA) 122) [2015 6m³ 6m* 6d³ p7m⁶ Nov 21] useful-looking filly: fourth foal: half-sister to 3 winners, including 6f winner Smidgen (by Bahamian Bounty) and unreliable 7f winner Loving Thought (by Oasis Dream): dam placed all 3 starts at 5f at 2 yrs: fairly useful performer: won maiden at Newmarket (by 2¾ lengths from White Witch) in June: third in listed race at Newmarket (4½ lengths behind Only Mine) in October: worth a try at 5f. *William Knight*

LADY MAESMOR 3 b.f. Kyllachy 129 – Pulsate 52 (Inchinor 119) [2015 68: 7m⁵ 6g⁵ **64** Jul 22] modest handicapper: stays 7f: acts on polytrack, good to firm and good to soft going. *Martyn Meade*

LADY MANDEVILLE (IRE) 3 b.f. Strategic Prince 114 – My Causeway Dream (IRE) **52** 62 (Giant's Causeway (USA) 132) [2015 72: p7g p6g⁴ 7d p6g⁶ p5g p8g p8g t6m Dec 30] modest handicapper: stays 7f: acts on polytrack, soft and good to firm going: sometimes wears headgear: sometimes slowly away, usually races towards rear. *Adrian McGuinness, Ireland*

LADY MARGAEUX (IRE) 5 b.m. Redback 116 – Storm Lady (IRE) (Alhaarth (IRE) **–** 126) [2015 t7.1f p10g⁶ Feb 5] maiden: well held both starts since 2013: stays 7f: acts on good to soft going: tried in blinkers. *Alan Brown*

LADY MARL 4 b.f. Duke of Marmalade (IRE) 132 – Empress Anna (IRE) (Imperial **89** Ballet (IRE) 110) [2015 75: p8g⁴ p8f* p8g⁴ p8m* 9.9d 8.3m* 8.3m* 9g 8.3m Aug 17] well-made filly: fairly useful handicapper: won at Lingfield in March and April and Windsor in June and July: stays 8.5f: acts on polytrack, soft and good to firm going: often wears hood: held up. *Gary Moore*

LADY MASCOT (IRE) 3 ch.f. Zebedee 113 – Tradmagic (IRE) (Traditionally (USA) **64** 117) [2015 64: 7g⁴ 8.3g⁶ 7m⁵ p6gᵖᵘ Jun 24] sturdy filly: modest maiden: stays 7f: acts on good to firm going. *Richard Hannon*

LADY MCGUFFY (IRE) 2 b.f. (Mar 19) Holy Roman Emperor (IRE) 125 – Fountain **59** of Honour (IRE) 84 (Sadler's Wells (USA) 132) [2015 5m⁶ 6g⁴ 6d⁴ 6s 7s* f7g³ t7.1g⁵ f7g⁴ Dec 18] €8,000Y: first foal: dam 1m winner who stayed 10.5f: modest performer: won claimer at Redcar in October: stays 7f: acts on fibresand and soft going. *Michael Dods*

LADY NAHEMA (IRE) 2 b.f. (Mar 26) Zoffany (IRE) 121 – Jamary (IRE) (Grand **60** Reward (USA) 112) [2015 6g⁶ 7.5g⁴ 6.9m Sep 9] €31,000F: second foal: dam once-raced half-sister to dam of high-class performer up to 12.5f Cherry Mix: modest maiden: best effort when fourth at Beverley, having run of race. *Ann Duffield*

LADY NAYEF 2 b.f. (Mar 8) Nayef (USA) 129 – Luck Will Come (IRE) 82 (Desert Style **78** (IRE) 121) [2015 p5g³ 5g⁴ 6m p6g⁶ 7f 6g⁵ 5v² 6g⁵ p6f² p6f* t5.1f⁴ Oct 16] rather leggy filly: third foal: dam, 6f-1¼m winner, half-sister to useful winner up to 7f B Fifty Two: fair performer: won maiden at Chelmsford in October: best effort at 6f: acts on polytrack and any turf going: front runner/races prominently. *John Ryan*

LADY OF DUBAI 3 b.f. Dubawi (IRE) 129 – Lady of Everest (IRE) (Montjeu (IRE) 137) **110** [2015 95p: 9.9g* 12g³ 9.9m⁶ 12d 10d⁴ Sep 13] useful-looking filly: smart performer: won listed race at Goodwood (by 3¼ lengths from Encore L'Amour) in May: further improvement when 2½ lengths third to Qualify in Oaks at Epsom in June: respectable fourth of 9 to Ribbons in Blandford Stakes at the Curragh final start: will prove suited by a return to 1½m: acts on good to firm and good to soft going: joined Roger Varian. *Luca Cumani*

LADY OF ILLUSION 3 b.f. Compton Place 125 – Doric Lady 91 (Kyllachy 129) [2015 **–** –: p6m t5.1g Jun 4] no form. *Mark Usher*

LADY OF YUE 5 b.m. Manduro (GER) 135 – Desert Royalty (IRE) 96 (Alhaarth (IRE) **75** 126) [2015 78, a71: 12g⁴ 11.8d³ 11.6p² 11.8g⁵ 14g³ 14.1m² 16.2d⁴ 16d⁶ Oct 30] sturdy mare: fair handicapper: stays 2m: acts on good to firm and heavy going: consistent. *Eugene Stanford*

LADY PERCY (IRE) 6 b.m. Sir Percy 129 – Genuinely (IRE) 43 (Entrepreneur 123) **56** [2015 60: 12.1m 12.1m 11.9d⁴ 11.9s³ Oct 6] leggy mare: modest handicapper: stays 1½m: acts on polytrack, good to firm and heavy going. *Mark Usher*

LADY PERIGNON 2 b.f. (Feb 3) Poet's Voice 126 – Amallna (Green Desert (USA) 127) **– p** [2015 7m Jul 30] €185,000Y: first foal: dam unraced half-sister to Musidora/Nassau Stakes winner Zahrat Dubai: 8/1, shaped as if needed experience when ninth in maiden at Goodwood won by Notary: will improve. *Andrew Balding*

LADY PINNACLE 3 b.f. Zamindar (USA) 116 – Lady Donatella 57 (Last Tycoon 131) **71** [2015 72: 8.3m⁶ 8g⁴ 7m 7.1m t8.6m⁴ t7.1g* p8g⁴ Dec 30] rather leggy filly: fair performer: won maiden at Wolverhampton in December: stays 1m: acts on polytrack and tapeta: sometimes in hood in 2015. *Andrew Balding*

LADY POPPY 5 b.m. Kyllachy 129 – Poppets Sweetlove 73 (Foxhound (USA) 103) **69** [2015 71§: 5d⁴ 5g⁴ 5s⁶ 5g⁴ 5.5m 5m 5m Sep 27] leggy mare: fair handicapper: won at Catterick in April: best form at 5f: acts on firm and soft going: inconsistent. *George Moore*

LADY PRESIDENT (IRE) 2 b.f. (Apr 22) Fast Company (IRE) 126 – Lovere (St Jovite **48**
(USA) 135) [2015 t7.1g t7.1g p8f⁶ t9.5f³ t9.5f t9.5f² t9.5f Dec 11] €3,000Y: seventh foal:
half-sister to winner up to 8.6f Miami Gator (2-y-o 6f/7f winner, by Titus Livius): dam, ran
once in Italy, half-sister to smart performer up to 1m Flashy Wings: poor maiden: best
effort at 9.5f: acts on tapeta in cheekpieces. *J. S. Moore*

LADY RANGER (IRE) 4 b.f. Bushranger (IRE) 119 – Annus Iucundus (IRE) 67 (Desert **77**
King (IRE) 129) [2015 64, a58: 5.8d² 6s 7g² 8g 7d⁴ 6m⁴ 7m 7.2g² 7d 7.2d² 8d⁴ p8g p7g
Oct 16] fair handicapper: won at Roscommon in June: left A. P. Keatley after eleventh start:
stays 7f: acts on heavy going: tried in headgear: often races towards rear. *Peter McCreery,
Ireland*

LADY ROCKA 2 ch.f. (Mar 25) Rock of Gibraltar (IRE) 133 – Tap Dance Way (IRE) 77 **61**
(Azamour (IRE) 130) [2015 7s⁶ 7d² 8s⁵ p7g Oct 27] 7,500Y: first foal: dam, 1m winner,
half-sister to smart Japanese miler Live Concert: modest maiden: stays 1m. *Amanda Perrett*

LADY SPANGLES (IRE) 3 b.f. Starspangledbanner (AUS) 128 – Lady of Garmoran **– §**
(USA) 65 (Mr Greeley (USA) 122) [2015 –: t9.5f¹¹ Jan 5] no form: refused to race only
outing in 2015: one to avoid. *J. S. Moore*

LADY SUGARFOOT (IRE) 3 b.f. Naaqoos 117 – Fire Finch 83 (Halling (USA) 133) **–**
[2015 6s⁶ 8.3g⁴ 9.8d 8s⁶ Oct 6] €6,500Y: fourth foal: half-sister to winner up to 1m
Fieldgunner Kirkup (2-y-o 6f winner, by Acclamation): dam 1½m/13f winner: no form:
sold 800 gns, sent to Germany. *K. R. Burke*

LADY SYLVIA 6 ch.m. Haafhd 129 – Abide (FR) 85 (Pivotal 124) [2015 83: 8m⁵ 8m⁵ **68**
8.3m Jun 27] angular mare: fair handicapper: stays 8.5f: acts on polytrack, soft and good
to firm going: tried in cheekpieces prior to 2015: often races in rear. *Joseph Tuite*

LADY TATIANA 3 b.f. Sakhee (USA) 136 – Telori 72 (Muhtarram (USA) 125) [2015 **–**
p6m t8.6g t6g t9.5g Apr 21] third foal: half-sister to 6f winner Piddie's Power (by Starcraft):
dam 7f winner: no form. *Ian Williams*

LADY TIANA 4 b.f. Sir Percy 129 – Cartoon 81 (Danehill Dancer (IRE) 117) [2015 111: **111**
9.9g⁶ 11.9d³ 11.9g* 10d 12d Oct 17] lengthy, rather sparely-made mare: smart performer:
won Lancashire Oaks at Haydock in July by ¾ length from Lustrous: well held both
subsequent starts: stays 1½m: acts on good to firm and heavy going. *Lucy Wadham*

LADY TURPIN (IRE) 2 gr.f. (May 18) Arakan (USA) 123 – Proficiency 68 (El Prado **42**
(IRE) 119) [2015 6g t5.1g⁶ 6.9m 8g 8.3s Oct 13] first foal: dam 1¼m winner: poor maiden:
best effort at 7f: acts on good to firm going. *Richard Fahey*

LADY VELLYN 3 gr.f. Hellvelyn 118 – Alvarinho Lady 72 (Royal Applause 124) [2015 **–**
–: f5d⁵ Jan 22] no form: tried in hood. *Derek Haydn Jones*

LADY WOOTTON 2 b.f. (Apr 14) Wootton Bassett 119 – Killer Class 72 (Kyllachy 129) **67**
[2015 6g 5g³ 5d² 5g 6g 6g³ Oct 8] third foal: half-sister to 5f winner Orient Class (by
Orientor): dam 5f winner: fair maiden: stays 6f: acts on good to soft going. *Keith Dalgleish*

LADY WULFRUNA 2 ch.f. (Apr 11) Dutch Art 126 – My Girl Jode 70 (Haafhd 129) **74**
[2015 5g 6g 6m* 6s⁵ p6.5g⁶ p6.5g⁶ Nov 30] £52,000Y, £5,000 2-y-o: third foal: half-sister
to 2-y-o 7f winner Xanthos (by Medicean): dam, 1¼m winner, half-sister to useful 1½m
winner Kassiopeia: fair performer: won seller at York in June, then left Alan McCabe: stays
6.5f: acts on polytrack, soft and good to firm going. *F. Chappet, France*

LADY YEATS 4 b.f. Yeats (IRE) 128 – Oblique (IRE) 102 (Giant's Causeway (USA) 132) **82**
[2015 86: 16v⁵ 16d⁴ 16m⁴ 15.9m³ 16.4g Sep 6] leggy filly: fairly useful handicapper: stays
2m: acts on good to firm and heavy going: sometimes in headgear in 2015: signs of
temperament. *George Moore*

LADY ZODIAC (IRE) 3 br.f. Kodiac 112 – Treacle Noir (IRE) 53 (Raise A Grand (IRE) **55**
114) [2015 57: 5g 6g 5.7f³ 6m² 5.7m⁴ 6d² 7g⁶ 5f p6f Oct 1] modest maiden: left Ruth Carr
after second start: stays 6f: acts on good to firm and good to soft going: usually in headgear
in 2015. *James Unett*

LA ESTATUA 3 b.f. Lope de Vega (IRE) 125 – Statua (IRE) 98 (Statoblest 120) [2015 69: **66**
t7.1f³ t7.1g⁴ f6s t7.1g t7.1f³ Feb 16] fair maiden: stays 1m: acts on tapeta and good to firm
going: tried in visor in 2015: often leads. *David Evans*

LA ESTRELLA (USA) 12 b.g. Theatrical – Princess Ellen 114 (Tirol 127) [2015 85: **85**
p15.8m* f12g² t16.5f⁵ t13.9f⁶ f14m⁴ f16g* Dec 29] lengthy, useful-looking gelding:
fairly useful performer: won claimer at Lingfield in January and handicap at Southwell in
December, latter his 16th course success and a record 27th victory overall on the all-
weather: stayed 2½m: acted on all-weather and good to firm going: had worn headgear:
reportedly retired. *Don Cantillon*

LA FRITILLAIRE 3 b.f. Champs Elysees 124 – Generous Diana 90 (Generous (IRE) **57** 139) [2015 10.2m 12g⁴ p12g⁵ 16.1g⁵ p13.3f² p16f³ p16g Nov 4] seventh foal: closely related to very smart 9f-13.5f winner (stays 2m) Dandino (by Dansili): dam 9f-10.3f winner: modest maiden: stays 2m: acts on polytrack: races prominently. *James Given*

LAGENDA 2 b.c. (Feb 28) Dick Turpin (IRE) 127 – Whirly Dancer 93 (Danehill Dancer **84** (IRE) 117) [2015 6m⁶ t7.1g³ 7m* 7m³ 6.5m Sep 10] 28,000F, £32,000Y: first foal: dam, 7f winner, half-sister to smart winner up to 1m Malabar: fairly useful performer: won maiden at Wetherby in July: stays 7f: acts on good to firm going. *Kevin Ryan*

LA HAVRESE (FR) 4 ch.f. Le Havre (IRE) 124 – La Buena (IRE) (Big Shuffle (USA) **65** 122) [2015 76: 8.3d⁶ 8.3s⁵ 7m⁴ 7.1m⁶ 7.5f⁶ 7g² 7g 7g 7g³ 7.2g⁵ t7.1f⁵ Oct 16] fair handicapper: stays 1m: acts on tapeta, good to firm and good to soft going: often wears headgear. *Ann Duffield*

LAHAYEB 3 b.f. High Chaparral (IRE) 132 – Tea Break (Daylami (IRE) 138) [2015 61: **104** p7m⁶ p10f² 8.3s* 10.2m³ 8.3s* 10.2v² 10.2d* 10.3v p11g Dec 3] useful performer: left Richard Hannon after second start: won handicaps at Nottingham in April, May and (by 3 lengths from Aleator) in October: well below form last 2 starts, including listed race on first occasion: stays 1¼m: best form on heavy going. *Michael Appleby*

LAHENT 3 b.c. Makfi 130 – Misty Waters (IRE) (Caerleon (USA) 132) [2015 –: 8.5g⁴ **65** 10m p10g⁴ 8.3m Jun 25] good-topped colt: fair maiden on Flat: stays 1¼m: acts on polytrack and good to firm going: sold 10,000 gns, sent to Italy and won over hurdles at Milan in October. *Charlie Fellowes*

LA HOOFON 3 b.f. Mastercraftsman (IRE) 129 – Polish Lake (Polish Precedent (USA) **–** 131) [2015 –: 12m⁴ f14s Aug 6] no form. *Mike Sowersby*

LAIDBACK ROMEO (IRE) 3 b.g. Kodiac 112 – Belmora (USA) (Scrimshaw (USA)) **93** [2015 89p: 8m³ 9g 8.3g* 8d 8.3m² 8.1g⁴ Sep 11] tall gelding: fairly useful handicapper: won at Windsor in June: stays 8.5f: acts on good to firm going: often races prominently. *Clive Cox*

LAILA HONIWILLOW 2 b.f. (Apr 4) Bahamian Bounty 116 – Anatase (Danehill **58** (USA) 126) [2015 5.9m 6m³ p6f Sep 24] 38,000F: half-sister to very smart 5f performer Hamish McGonagall (by Namid) and useful winner up to 15f Steelwolf (2-y-o 1m winner, by Fraam): dam unraced: modest maiden: best effort when third in maiden at Redcar (1¾ lengths behind Tikthebox) in August. *Jedd O'Keeffe*

LAJATICO 2 b.f. (Feb 14) Equiano (FR) 127 – Italian Connection (Cadeaux Genereux **57 p** 131) [2015 p7g⁵ Jul 22] third foal: half-sister to 7f winner I'vegotafeeling (by Rock of Gibraltar) and useful 1m/9f winner Talyani (by Halling): dam unraced half-sister to dam of King George VI & Queen Elizabeth Stakes winner Postponed: 12/1, better than result when fifth of 11 to Sakada in maiden at Lingfield, considerably handled: will improve. *Ed Vaughan*

LAJJAH (IRE) 3 b.f. Invincible Spirit (IRE) 121 – Idilic Calm (IRE) 78 (Indian Ridge **–** 123) [2015 p5m⁵ Jun 1] €320,000Y: half-sister to several winners, including very smart winner up to 1m Calming Influence (2-y-o 6f winner, by King's Best) and smart winner up to 1m in North America Steel Light (2-y-o 5f-7f winner, by Stravinsky): dam 7f winner: 4/1, well-held fifth of 7 in maiden at Lingfield on debut: sent to France. *Richard Hannon*

LAKE PLACID 2 b.c. (Apr 12) Champs Elysees 124 – Phantom Wind (USA) 111 (Storm **72 p** Cat (USA)) [2015 8.3d Oct 5] half-brother to 5f/6f winner Fujin (by Oasis Dream): dam winner up to 7f (2-y-o 6f winner) who stayed 9f: 10/1, weakened over 1f out when eighth in maiden at Windsor (5¼ lengths behind Top Beak): should do better. *Charles Hills*

LAKE SHORE DRIVE (IRE) 3 b.g. Thewayyouare (USA) 117 – Labrusca 58 (Grand **80** Lodge (USA) 125) [2015 10m⁶ 11.8d³ 12d⁵ 15g⁶ 12d⁶ Oct 24] €4,000F, €3,800Y, €20,000 2-y-o: half-brother to useful 7f/1m winner Great Huzzar and temperamental 6f winner Delaware Dancer (both by Danehill Dancer): dam once-raced half-sister to Yorkshire Oaks winner Catchascatchcan, herself dam of very smart/unreliable miler Antonius Pius: fairly useful maiden: stays 1½m: acts on good to soft going. *J. J. Feane, Ireland*

LA MANGA (IRE) 2 b.f. (Feb 2) Kodiac 112 – Good Shot Noreen (IRE) 87 (Sleeping **50 p** Indian 122) [2015 p8f t7.1f p6g⁵ Dec 2] £12,000Y: first foal: dam, 7f winner, closely related to smart/unreliable 6f-8.6f winner Dabbers Ridge: modest maiden: best effort when fifth at Kempton final start, left with too much to do: remains open to improvement. *Jamie Osborne*

LAMAR (IRE) 4 b.f. Cape Cross (IRE) 129 – Deveron (USA) 105 (Cozzene (USA)) [2015 100: t9.5f* p8g* p10f² p7f² 9f⁶ 9.9g³ 8.5g 8f p8g* t7.1g* p10g³ Dec 19] big filly: useful handicapper: won minor events at Wolverhampton and Chelmsford in January, listed race at Lingfield (by ½ length from Very Special) in October and minor event at Wolverhampton (by ½ length from Kyllachy Queen) in November: also placed in 2 listed races at Lingfield, on final start beaten ¾ length when third to Don't Be: stays 1¼m: acts on polytrack, tapeta and firm going: tried in hood prior to 2015: usually races prominently. *James Tate* — **100 a109**

L'AMI LOUIS (IRE) 7 b.g. Elusive City (USA) 117 – Princess Electra (IRE) 69 (Lake Coniston (IRE) 131) [2015 67: 7.1m 6g 5s 5.1f Oct 31] lengthy gelding: modest handicapper nowadays: well held in 2015; stays 6f: acts on firm going: has worn headgear. *Ian Semple* — **–**

L'AMIRAL DAVID (FR) 5 b.g. My Risk (FR) 120 – Mme La Vicomtesse (FR) (Baroud d'Honneur (FR) 117) [2015 p12g³ t12.2g⁶ Dec 5] fair form: better effort when third in maiden at Lingfield in November, barely adequate test: will stay further than 1½m *Alan King* — **77**

LA MORTOLA (IRE) 2 b.f. (Apr 13) Dubawi (IRE) 129 – Claba di San Jore (IRE) (Barathea (IRE) 127) [2015 8.3g⁶ 8d 8d⁶ Oct 23] half-sister to several winners, including high-class 9.5f-13.5f winner (stayed 2m) Jakkalberry (by Storming Home), very smart Italian winner up to 11f Crackerjack King (2-y-o 9f winner, by Shamardal) and smart Italian winner up to 1½m Kidnapping (2-y-o 1m winner, by Intikhab): dam Italian 1¼m winner: fair maiden: best effort when sixth at Doncaster (6 lengths behind Zest) on final outing, slowly away: should stay at least 1¼m: remains with potential. *John Gosden* — **69 p**

LAMPS 8 b.g. Dynaformer (USA) – Conspiring (USA) 98 (Grand Slam (USA) 120) [2015 t16.5f p16g⁶ p16g Dec 16] modest maiden: stays 16.5f: acts on polytrack and tapeta: temperamental. *Michael Blake* — **59 §**

LAMPS OF HEAVEN (IRE) 3 b.f. Invincible Spirit (IRE) 121 – Star Studded (Cadeaux Genereux 131) [2015 73: 5m² 5g p6g⁵ 6m³ f5g* t5.1g⁶ Nov 27] fair performer: won maiden at Southwell in November: stays 6f: acts on all-weather and good to firm going. *Olly Stevens* — **72**

LAMSA (IRE) 3 b.f. Invincible Spirit (IRE) 121 – Golden Flyer (FR) (Machiavellian (USA) 123) [2015 –54: t1.71f² 6m² Jun 13] fair maiden: better effort in 2015 when second at Wolverhampton: off 3 months, not given hard time once held on final outing: should stay 1m: remains open to improvement. *Ed Dunlop* — **67 p**

LAMYAA 3 ch.f. Arcano (IRE) 122 – Divine Grace (IRE) (Definite Article 121) [2015 –: p7f⁶ 7.5m³ 8.3g* 8.1d⁵ 10.2d² 10g⁶ t8.6f³ Oct 3] fairly useful performer: won maiden at Nottingham in July: placed in handicaps at Bath and Wolverhampton after: stays 1¼m: acts on tapeta and good to soft going: front runner/races prominently. *Charles Hills* — **83**

LANAI (IRE) 3 b.f. Camacho 118 – Stately Princess 70 (Robellino (USA) 127) [2015 67p: f5d² p5g* Feb 7] poor performer: won maiden at Lingfield in February: likely to stay 6f. *David Barron* — **47**

LANCELOT DU LAC (ITY) 5 b.g. Shamardal (USA) 129 – Dodie Mae (USA) (Capote (USA)) [2015 110, a117: 5g² 5g 5g⁴ 5g 5f 6f³ 6f 6m p6g* 6d 6v³ p6g* Nov 25] good-topped gelding: very smart performer: won at Kempton in October (minor event, by 1¼ lengths from Horsted Keynes) and November (handicap, by 1¼ lengths from Intransigent): third of 25 to Interception in Wokingham Stakes (Handicap) at Royal Ascot and third of 14 to Jack Dexter in listed race at Doncaster: stays 7f: acts on polytrack and heavy going: tried in hood prior to 2015: front runner/races prominently, usually travels strongly. *Dean Ivory* — **121**

LANCEUR (FR) 6 b.g. Rail Link 132 – Lanciana (IRE) (Acatenango (GER) 127) [2015 p10g* 8f 10.4m Jul 11] useful handicapper: won at Chelmsford (by 2¼ lengths from Latin Charm) in April: stays 1¼m: acts on polytrack, best turf form on good going: fairly useful hurdler. *Lucy Wadham* — **99**

LANDING NIGHT (IRE) 3 b.g. Kodiac 112 – Night Delight (IRE) 86 (Night Shift (USA)) [2015 72: f5g* p5m⁵ 5d³ 5m³ 5g* 5m* 5f⁴ 5.5g 5m 5s 5g Sep 18] fairly useful performer: won maiden at Southwell in January and handicaps at Catterick in May and June: best form at 5f: acts on fibresand, good to firm and good to soft going: often in cheekpieces in 2015. *Ann Duffield* — **85**

LANDOFHOPEANDGLORY (IRE) 2 b.c. (Apr 5) High Chaparral (IRE) 132 – Wurfklinge (GER) (Acatenango (GER) 127) [2015 8.3d* 8d² 10g² 9s² Oct 25] €120,000F, 260,000Y: good sort: sixth foal: half-brother to 3 winners, including 2-y-o 7f winner Nora — **103 p**

Mae (by Peintre Celebre), later successful abroad, and 7f winner Sir Fredlot (by Choisir): dam, German 2-y-o 1m winner (useful up to 1¾m), sister to smart dam of Deutsches Derby Waldpark and grandam of St Leger winner Masked Marvel: useful form: won maiden at Galway in August on debut: second in nursery at Naas (head behind Mint Chai) and in listed races at Newmarket (1¼ lengths behind Glamorous Approach) and Leopardstown (¾ length behind Moonlight Magic): stays 1¼m: remains open to improvement. *Aidan O'Brien, Ireland*

LANDWADE LAD 3 b.g. Dansili 127 – Sell Out 107 (Act One 124) [2015 84p: 9.9m⁴ 9.8g³ 10.2m² 10d² p11g* p11d² 10.3d⁶ p11g Nov 9] compact gelding: useful handicapper: won at Kempton (by 3¼ lengths from Soluble) in August: stays 11f: acts on polytrack. *James Fanshawe* **96**

LANGHAM 2 b.f. (Apr 6) Royal Applause 124 – Three Ducks 89 (Diktat 126) [2015 p6g² Dec 16] 11,000Y: second foal: half-sister to winner up to 7.5f Three Gracez (2-y-o 7f winner, by Kyllachy). dam 1m winner (including at 2 yrs) who stayed 1¼m: 5/1, promise when 2 lengths second of 8 to Soofiah in maiden at Kempton, keeping on after conceding first run: sure to progress. *Martyn Meade* **71 p**

LANGLAUF (USA) 2 gr.f. (Mar 28) Raven's Pass (USA) 133 – Emirates Girl (USA) (Unbridled's Song (USA) 125) [2015 7f⁴ 7g² 8g² 7.5g³ p7g⁴ p8g Nov 4] fourth foal: dam, useful French 1m winner, sister to useful 7f/1m winner Paper Talk: fair maiden: stays 1m: best form on good going: tried in cheekpieces: temperament under suspicion. *Charlie Appleby* **78**

LANGLEY VALE 6 b.g. Piccolo 121 – Running Glimpse (IRE) 84 (Runnett 125) [2015 86: 6g² 6m⁴ 6mʳ 7m 6m 6s⁴ 5g Sep 11] good-topped gelding: fairly useful handicapper: stays 6f: acts on polytrack, firm and good to soft going: sometimes wears cheekpieces. *Roger Teal* **82**

LANKAN RUPEE (AUS) 6 b.g. Redoute's Choice (AUS) – Estelle Collection (NZ) (Stravinsky (USA) 133) [2015 132: 5g* 6g⁶ 6s 5.5g³ Oct 10] top-class performer: the highest rated performer in Australia for second successive year in 2015, but suffered injury problems: won Lightning Stakes at Flemington (by 2¾ lengths from Brazen Beau, leading inside final 1f) in February: fair sixth to same rival in Newmarket Handicap on same course next time, but well below form last 2 starts, including when (off over 6 months) 1½ lengths third to Alpha Miss in Group 2 Schillaci Stakes at Caulfield final outing (reportedly suffered ligament damage and underwent surgery on off-hind): stays 6f: acts on heavy going: used to wear headgear. *Mick Price, Australia* **130**

LA PAIVA (FR) 4 b.f. Milk It Mick 120 – Cora Pearl (IRE) 51 (Montjeu (IRE) 137) [2015 47: t12.2f 10.3d f6g⁵ Dec 15] maiden: no form in 2015: often wears headgear: front runner/races prominently. *Scott Dixon* **–**

L'APOGEE 2 ch.g. (May 2) Rip Van Winkle (IRE) 134 – Pappas Ruby (USA) 63 (Red Ransom (USA)) [2015 6m⁴ 5.9g⁵ Jun 24] better effort when fourth in maiden at Newcastle (5½ lengths behind Red Artist) in June. *Richard Fahey* **64**

LA PYLE (FR) 4 b.f. Le Havre (IRE) 124 – Lidana (IRE) 87 (King's Best (USA) 132) [2015 12.1s Sep 15] second foal: half-sister to French 2-y-o 1m/9f winner Lillebonne (by Danehill Dancer): dam, 2-y-o 7f winner who stayed 10.7f, half-sister to very smart winner up to 1¼m Linngari: fairly useful performer: won handicap at Le Lion-d'Angers and claimer at Saint-Cloud in 2014: well held at Chepstow only outing on Flat in 2015: stays 1½m: acts on soft going: usually wore headgear in France. *Philip Hobbs* **–**

LARA CARBONARA (IRE) 3 b.f. The Carbon Unit (USA) 106 – Janna's Jewel (IRE) (Traditionally (USA) 117) [2015 12g 8m 9.5m 9.2s* 12.1g³ 9s Sep 16] fourth foal: sister to 1m winner (stayed 1½m) Dolce N Karama and half-sister to 7f winner Rominintheglomin (by Whipper) and 1m-1¼m winner (stays 1½m) Hold The Line (by Ivan Denisovich), both useful: dam largely fair performer: won handicap at Hamilton in July: stays 1½m: acts on soft going. *John Patrick Shanahan, Ireland* **73**

LARA LIPTON (IRE) 4 b.f. Excellent Art 125 – Dyness (USA) (Dynaformer (USA)) [2015 –: p10g p13.3g⁴ 11.5d p11g 8m p10f 10.1g Aug 30] maiden: no form in 2015: tried in headgear prior to 2015. *Jane Chapple-Hyam* **–**

LARCH (IRE) 3 b.f. Acclamation 118 – Shady Nook (IRE) (Key of Luck (USA) 126) [2015 –: 6f⁵ t6g 8m 6d 8.5d² 8.5s* Aug 31] useful-looking filly: modest handicapper: left Richard Hannon, won at Les Landes in August: stays 8.5f: acts on soft going: usually races prominently, tends to find little: not straightforward. *Mrs A. Malzard, Jersey* **60**

LA RIOJA 2 b.f. (Feb 4) Hellvelyn 118 – Talampaya (USA) (Elusive Quality (USA)) [2015 6g² 6m* 6s* Sep 3] 27,000F, 50,000Y: strong filly: fourth foal: half-sister to 3 winning sprinters, including 2-y-o 6f winner Pastoral Girl and useful 2-y-o 5f winner **112 p**

Lilbourne Lass (both by Pastoral Pursuits): dam unraced: smart form: won maiden at Newbury (by 5 lengths from Greenfyre) in July: further marked improvement when winning Dick Poole Fillies' Stakes at Salisbury in September by 4½ lengths from Whatdoiwantthatfor, travelling strongly before quickening to lead over 1f out: raced only at 6f: should do better still. *Henry Candy*

LARMOR (FR) 4 bl.g. Green Tune (USA) 125 – Mia's Baby (USA) (Rahy (USA) 115) **71** [2015 7.1m² 8m 10m⁵ Jul 21] fair maiden: stays 10.5f: acts on good to firm and good to soft going: sold £10,000, sent to Italy. *Micky Hammond*

LA ROUMEGUE (USA) 4 b.f. Henrythenavigator (USA) 131 – Chandrina (USA) **66** (Trempolino (USA) 135) [2015 p10f p8m Nov 19] $37,000Y, €25,000 2-y-o: sixth foal: half-sister to winners abroad by Bernstein (in USA) and Quiet American (in Sweden): dam unraced: fair ex-French-trained maiden: stays 9.5f: acts on soft going. *Ed Walker*

LASER BLAZER 7 b.g. Zafeen (FR) 123 – Sashay 72 (Bishop of Cashel 122) [2015 **79** t12.2f⁴ p12g⁵ Dec 20] angular gelding: fair handicapper: stays 17f: acts on polytrack, tapeta and firm going: usually wears headgear: often races in rear. *Alan King*

LASHKAAL 3 b.f. Teofilo (IRE) 126 – Mudaaraah 106 (Cape Cross (IRE) 129) [2015 80p: **71** p10g³ t8.6g² t9.5m Apr 2] fair maiden: stays 1¼m: acts on polytrack, firm and good to soft going: often in cheekpieces in 2015: usually races close up. *John Gosden*

LAST MINUTE LISA (IRE) 5 b.m. Strategic Prince 114 – Bradwell (IRE) 76 (Taufan **63** (USA) 119) [2015 79: 11.6m Apr 13] modest handicapper: stays 13f: acts on polytrack, tapeta, soft and good to firm going: tried in headgear prior to 2015: races well off pace. *Sylvester Kirk*

LAST STAR FALLING (IRE) 2 b.f. (Apr 3) Acclamation 118 – Star Port (Observatory **67** (USA) 131) [2015 p6g⁶ 7.5g⁵ 7s³ Oct 6] €20,000Y: fourth foal: half-sister to French winner up to 9.5f Grimillier (2-y-o 1m winner, by Dylan Thomas): dam unraced: fair maiden: best effort when third at Brighton final start: likely to prove best up to 1m. *Henry Spiller*

LAST SUPPER 6 b.m. Echo of Light 125 – Scotland The Brave 82 (Zilzal (USA) 137) **66** [2015 f11g* 11.1d³ May 27] fair performer: won maiden at Southwell in January: worth a try at 1½m+: acts on fibresand and heavy going: often wears headgear: fairly useful hurdler. *James Bethell*

LAST TANGO INPARIS 2 ch.f. (Feb 9) Aqlaam 125 – Strictly Lambada 77 (Red **89 p** Ransom (USA)) [2015 9d³ 8v* Oct 24] second foal: half-sister to 1½m-1¾m winner Sleep Easy (by Rip Van Winkle): dam, maiden (stayed 1½m), half-sister to smart performer up to 2m Yankee Doodle: better effort when winning maiden at Newbury (by 1¾ lengths from High Hopes) in October, suited by emphasis on stamina: will stay 1¼m+: open to further improvement. *Hughie Morrison*

LASTUCE (FR) 5 b.m. Orpen (USA) 116 – Labamba (FR) (Green Tune (USA) 125) **95** [2015 6.1s³ 6g 6m Jul 10] sixth foal: half-sister to 3 winners in France, including 1¼m winner Labepi (by Vettori) and 11.5f winner Shocking (by Starborough): dam French 8.5f winner: useful performer: won 7 times in France in 2012-14: easily best effort of 2015 when third in listed race at Nottingham (1¾ lengths behind Newsletter) in May: stays 6.5f: acts on viscoride and soft going. *Chris Wall*

LAST WISH (IRE) 4 b.g. Raven's Pass (USA) 133 – Quiet Dream (USA) (Seattle Slew **68** (USA)) [2015 8m⁴ 8g³ 8g⁵ 11.1g⁴ 12.2g Oct 13] fair maiden: stays 11f: best form on good going: in headgear: often races in rear. *Richard Guest*

LA SUPERBA (IRE) 3 ch.f. Medicean 128 – La Spezia (IRE) 94 (Danehill Dancer (IRE) **95** 117) [2015 58: p8m p8g² 8g⁴ 7m⁴ 8.3m⁴ 10d⁴ 8.5m* 8.3d* 8.1v* 8.3g² Sep 30] third foal: half-sister to useful 1¼m-1½m winner Thomas Hobson (by Halling): dam 8.6f winner: useful handicapper: much improved and won at Beverley and Windsor in August and Sandown (by 3¾ lengths from Belle Travers) in September: should prove as effective at 1¼m: acts on polytrack, good to firm and heavy going: in headgear last 5 starts: usually races nearer last than first: has looked quirky on occasions. *David Elsworth*

LATENIGHTREQUEST 4 b.f. Major Cadeaux 121 – Love Quest (Pursuit of Love 124) **99** [2015 105: 10s 10g 10g 10d 12s⁴ 10.3v² p12g Nov 25] plain filly: useful performer: best effort of 2015 when second in listed race at Doncaster (1½ lengths behind Princess Loulou) in November: stays 1½m: acts on good to firm and heavy going: tried in cheekpieces prior to 2015: often races in rear: sold 29,000 gns, sent to Saudi Arabia. *Richard Fahey*

LATE SHIPMENT 4 b.g. Authorized (IRE) 133 – Time Over 76 (Mark of Esteem (IRE) **86** 137) [2015 93: 14m⁴ 14m⁶ p16g t12.2g³ 16.1m 15.9m 13.1f⁶ 12.1s² t12.2f Nov 16] lengthy **a65** gelding: fairly useful handicapper: left Jamie Osborne after fourth start: stays 13f: acts on polytrack, soft and good to firm going: often wears cheekpieces: has shown signs of temperament. *Nikki Evans*

LATE SHOW 2 br.f. (Feb 24) Authorized (IRE) 133 – Hydro Calido (USA) 117 (Nureyev **–** (USA) 131) [2015 p7g 8.3g p8g p8f Nov 12] half-sister to numerous winners, including smart Japanese performer up to 11f Shinko Calido (by Silver Hawk) and useful French 7f/1m winner Espero (by Forty Niner): dam, French 7.5f/1m (Prix d'Astarte) winner, half-sister to Machiavellian and Exit To Nowhere: no form: tried in cheekpieces. *Sir Mark Prescott Bt*

LATHARNACH (USA) 3 b.c. Iffraaj 127 – Firth of Lorne (IRE) 112 (Danehill (USA) **119** 126) [2015 98p⁺ 7f² 8f² 8m³ Jul 31] lengthy colt. smart performer: progressed again when second in St James's Palace Stakes at Royal Ascot (2½ lengths behind Gleneagles) in June: disappointing third to Malabar in Thoroughbred Stakes at Goodwood final start, seeming not to knuckle down fully: stays 1m: acts on firm going. *Charlie Appleby*

LAT HAWILL (IRE) 4 b.g. Invincible Spirit (IRE) 121 – Arbella 106 (Primo Dominie **110** 121) [2015 102: 8g 7d² 9.5m* 8.3d 9s Sep 16] sturdy, attractive gelding: smart performer: won 3-runner minor event at Gowran (by ¾ length from Clonard Street) in June: best form previous start when second in listed race at Naas (½ length behind Heaven's Guest): stays 9.5f: acts on good to firm and good to soft going: tried in cheekpieces in 2015: often races prominently. *G. M. Lyons, Ireland*

LATHOM 2 b.c. (Apr 19) Compton Place 125 – Wigan Lane 66 (Kheleyf (USA) 116) **99** [2015 5g* 5m² 5f 5.2m* 5g⁵ 6g 5g Sep 18] 21,000F, £39,000Y: good-topped colt: second foal: half-brother to German 2-y-o 6f winner Woomera (by Strategic Prince): dam, 2-y-o 6f winner, half-sister to smart sprinter Hoh Hoh Hoh: useful performer: won maiden at Beverley in May and 22-runner Super Sprint at Newbury (by neck from Mr Lupton) in July: respectable fifth to Kachy in Molecomb Stakes at Goodwood next start, well held last 2: best form at 5f: acts on good to firm going: often races prominently. *Richard Fahey*

LATIN CHARM (IRE) 4 b.g. Cape Cross (IRE) 129 – Di Moi Oui 111 (Warning 136) **93** [2015 97: p11g p10g² Apr 28] fairly useful handicapper: second at Chelmsford in April: should prove suited by a return to 11f+: acts on polytrack, best turf form on soft/heavy going: usually wears cheekpieces. *Marco Botti*

LATIN REBEL (IRE) 8 b.g. Spartacus (IRE) 107 – Dance To The Beat 58 (Batshoof **65** 122) [2015 64: 11.1s² 11.1d² 11.1m* 12.1g⁵ 11.1s⁵ 9.1g³ 8d³ 8d⁴ 9.2g 9.2m 8g 13.1g⁵ Oct 8] fair handicapper: won at Hamilton in June: stays 13f: acts on soft and good to firm going: sometimes wears headgear: often races towards rear. *Jim Goldie*

LAUGHALOUD 2 ch.f. (Mar 26) Dubawi (IRE) 129 – Opera Comique (FR) 100 (Singspiel **64 p** (IRE) 133) [2015 p8g⁶ Dec 15] half-sister to several winners, including very smart 1¼m-12.3f winner Debussy (by Diesis) and useful 1m winner (stays 1½m) Entertainment (by Halling): dam, 2-y-o 9f winner, half-sister to King George VI & Queen Elizabeth Stakes winner Belmez: evens, below expectations when sixth in maiden at Kempton (4¼ lengths behind Cajoled) in December, finding little: in tongue tie sole start: entitled to do better. *John Gosden*

LAUGHARNE 4 b.g. Authorized (IRE) 133 – Corsican Sunset (USA) 102 (Thunder **75** Gulch (USA) 129) [2015 68: p12g 16s t13.9f p16g Dec 9] good-topped gelding: fair handicapper: stays 2m: acts on heavy going: tried in blinkers prior to 2015. *Graham Mays*

Weatherbys Super Sprint, Newbury—Richard Fahey saddles three of the first four as outsiders fill the frame in this valuable contest, with Lathom (No.2) beating Mr Lupton (far side), Field of Vision (striped sleeves) and David's Duchess (No.16)

LAUGHING JACK 7 b.g. Beat Hollow 126 – Bronzewing 103 (Beldale Flutter (USA) **75** 130) [2015 87: 16m 14.1m⁶ 14m⁴ 11.9g p15.8g⁶ 12v⁴ 12s⁴ Sep 13] good-bodied gelding: fair handicapper: stays 1¾m: acts on polytrack, firm and good to soft going: tried in eyeshields prior to 2015: often in tongue tie in 2015: sold 800 gns, sent to Italy. *Tony Carroll*

LAUGHING ROCK (IRE) 5 b.m. Rock of Gibraltar (IRE) 133 – The Last Laugh 78 **52** (Kyllachy 129) [2015 62: f7g⁵ 6d⁵ 5m p6f⁴ t6f p6g p7g Dec 10] modest handicapper: stays 7f: acts on polytrack, fibresand and good to firm going: often wears headgear. *Michael Appleby*

LAUGHTON 2 b.c. (Mar 28) Acclamation 118 – Peach Pearl (Invincible Spirit (IRE) 121) **76 p** [2015 6m⁴ 6g⁵ 5m⁵ 5m* Sep 27] €8,000Y, €150,000 2-y-o: third foal: half brother to French 11.5f winner Altaira (by Dubawi): dam useful French 6.5f and (at 2 yrs) 7f winner: fair performer: won nursery at Musselburgh in September: best effort at 5f: open to further improvement. *Kevin Ryan*

LAURA B 3 b.f. Acclamation 118 – New Design (IRE) 93 (Bluebird (USA) 125) [2015 63: **62** p6m p7m³ t6g² p6m⁵ t6g 5m⁴ p6g³ Aug 19] modest maiden: stays 7f: acts on polytrack, tapeta and good to firm going: often races prominently: sent to Greece. *Chris Wall*

LAUREL CREEK (IRE) 10 b.g. Sakura Laurel (JPN) – Eastern Sky (AUS) (Danehill **50** (USA) 126) [2015 t13.9f⁶ p16g p12g⁶ 14g Jun 25] modest handicapper: effective at 1½m to 16.5f: acts on polytrack, tapeta and good to firm going: tried in cheekpieces: tried in tongue tie prior to 2015. *M. C. Grassick, Ireland*

LAURENCE 3 b.g. Dubawi (IRE) 129 – Victoire Celebre (USA) (Stravinsky (USA) 133) **97** [2015 66p: 8m³ 8f* 10m² 9.9g⁵ 8f⁵ 10g³ 9.9g* 10s 10.3d⁵ Oct 23] useful-looking gelding: useful performer: won maiden at Newmarket in May and handicap at Beverley (by 1¼ lengths from Sealife) in August: stays 1¼m: acts on firm going: often races towards rear. *Luca Cumani*

LAVENDER LANE (IRE) 4 ch.f. Shamardal (USA) 129 – Alix Road (FR) 112 (Linamix **100** (FR) 127) [2015 114: p9.4g⁴ 9.9g³ 8g 8.9d⁶ Oct 18] second foal: dam French 1¼m-1½m winner: smart performer at 3 yrs, winning minor event at Chantilly and third in 2 pattern races: just useful form in listed races in 2015: last of 10 at Newmarket on third outing: stays 1½m: acts on polytrack, good to firm and good to soft going: has worn hood: often races towards rear. *J. E. Hammond, France*

LAVETTA 3 b.f. Peintre Celebre (USA) 137 – Card Games 89 (First Trump 118) [2015 6g **85** 7m³ 6.9m³ 10g 7s⁵ 7v* Nov 3] seventh foal: half-sister to 3 winners, including very smart 5f-7f winner Tiddliwinks and 5f-8.6f winner Pelmanism (both by Piccolo): dam 5f and (at 2 yrs) 6f winner: fairly useful performer: won handicap at Redcar in November: will stay 1m: acts on heavy and good to soft going: often races prominently. *Alan Swinbank*

LA VIEN ZEN (IRE) 3 b.f. Dylan Thomas (IRE) 132 – Se La Vie (FR) (Highest Honor **–** (FR) 124) [2015 –: 10g 9.2d 12g 14.1g Jul 9] no form: often in headgear in 2015. *Jim Goldie*

LAVINIA ROSE 2 ch.f. (Feb 11) Compton Place 125 – Lavinia's Grace (USA) 66 (Green **69** Desert (USA) 127) [2015 5m⁶ 6m² 6.1s³ 6.5m p6f⁴ t5.1m⁵ Dec 12] 25,000Y: good-topped filly: fifth foal: closely related to useful 7f-8.4f winner Justoneforthuroad (by Domedriver) and half-sister to 6f winner Jubilante (by Royal Applause): dam French 2-y-o 7f winner: fair performer: stays 6f: acts on polytrack and good to firm going: usually races close up. *Ralph Beckett*

LAWMAKING 2 b.c. (Apr 19) Zamindar (USA) 116 – Canada Water (Dansili 127) [2015 **106** 6d³ 7g² 7g⁵ Sep 24] first foal: dam, French maiden (stayed 10.5f), sister to Prix de l'Arc de Triomphe winner Rail Link and half-sister to very smart French 1¼m-1½m winner Crossharbour (by Zamindar): useful maiden: best effort when head second to Attendu in Prix La Rochette at Longchamp in September: respectable 2 lengths fifth of 6 to Sanus Per Aquam in Somerville Tattersall Stakes at Newmarket next time: will stay 1m. *A. Fabre, France*

LAWMAN'S JUSTICE (IRE) 2 b.c. (May 5) Lawman (FR) 121 – Brazilian Bride **–** (IRE) 103 (Pivotal 124) [2015 7g 6g Sep 4] behind in maidens at Doncaster and Newcastle. *Michael Dods*

LAWMANS THUNDER 5 b.g. Lawman (FR) 121 – Rhapsodize (Halling (USA) 133) **95** [2015 105: p8g⁴ 8d⁴ p10g Jun 18] good-topped gelding: useful handicapper: stays 1m: acts on polytrack and good to soft going: tongue tie once in 2013: sold 30,000 gns, sent to Saudi Arabia. *Ismail Mohammed*

LAWSONG (IRE) 4 b.g. Lawman (FR) 121 – Flaming Song (IRE) (Darshaan 133) [2015 **64** 71p: p8f⁵ Sep 17] showed a little ability in 2 maidens 20 months apart: dead. *Jamie Osborne*

LAWYER (IRE) 4 b.g. Acclamation 118 – Charaig (Rainbow Quest (USA) 134) [2015 **88** 93: 8g³ 8g³ 8g² 10.3g⁵ 7.6f 8m 8d³ 7.9g³ p8g 7g f7f t9.5m Dec 30] good-topped gelding: fairly useful handicapper: stays 8.5f: acts on polytrack, good to firm and good to soft going: tried in blinkers in 2015: usually races nearer last than first. *David Barron*

LAXFIELD ROAD (USA) 2 b.f. (Apr 3) Quality Road (USA) 131 – Katori (USA) **95** (Dixie Union (USA) 121) [2015 a4.5f* 6f 5.5f³ Aug 19] $130,000Y: second foal: closely related to a winner in USA by Elusive Quality: dam, second at around 6f in USA, half-sister to smart US Grade 1 9f winner Monba: made all to win maiden at Keeneland in April by 11 lengths from Sombree: well held in Albany Stakes at Royal Ascot next time, doing too much too soon: ran respectably in non-graded event at Saratoga final outing: will prove best short of 6f: wears blinkers. *Wesley A. Ward, USA*

LAYERTHORPE (IRE) 3 b.g. Vale of York (IRE) 117 – Strobinia (IRE) 45 (Soviet Star **55** (USA) 128) [2015 61. t9.5f⁵ p7m p11g 8f Apr 23] modest maiden: stays 11f: acts on polytrack and tapeta: tried in visor in 2015: often races prominently: temperament under suspicion. *David Brown*

LAYLA'S HERO (IRE) 8 b.g. One Cool Cat (USA) 123 – Capua (USA) (Private Terms **83** (USA)) [2015 88: 6g⁴ f6d 6m⁶ 7.5m* 7.5g* 7d 8g* t6m⁴ p6f⁴ p7g⁶ Dec 9] good-topped **a69** gelding: fairly useful performer: won 2 claimers at Beverley in August and seller at Redcar in September: stays 1m: acts on polytrack, fibresand, good to firm and heavy going: often wears headgear: tried in tongue tie prior to 2015: sometimes slowly away, often races in rear: quirky sort. *David Nicholls*

LAYLA'S KING 7 b.g. Dubawi (IRE) 129 – Top Jem 85 (Damister (USA) 123) [2015 **55** 8.5g⁴ 9.9m³ 9.3d³ 10.2d³ p12g p10f t9.5f² Oct 16] lengthy gelding: modest handicapper: stays 1½m: acts on all-weather, good to firm and good to soft going: tried in headgear prior to 2015: usually races close up. *David C. Griffiths*

LAYLINE (IRE) 8 b.g. King's Best (USA) 132 – Belle Reine (King of Kings (IRE) 125) **68** [2015 75, a83: f12d³ p12m⁶ t13.9g³ f16d⁵ f14d² t12.2g⁶ f14s² p14g⁴ f14g³ p15.8f⁵ p13.3m t12.2g* t12.2g t12.2g* f12d² p12g⁶ t12.2m⁴ Sep 5] lengthy gelding: fair performer: won at Wolverhampton in June (seller) and July (claimer): stayed 16.5f: acted on all-weather and any turf going: had worn headgear: usually raced nearer last than first: dead. *Gay Kelleway*

LAZARUS BELL 5 ch.g. Bahamian Bounty 116 – Snake's Head 81 (Golden Snake **75** (USA) 127) [2015 91: 7.1g⁶ 10.1d⁵ 6.9m³ 8m⁵ 8g² 9.3s 8m³ 8m⁴ 7m 8g⁵ 7.9m³ 10g 8.5m³ Oct 1] good-topped gelding: fair handicapper: stays 9f: acts on any turf going: has worn headgear. *Alan Brown*

LAZIZAH 2 b.f. (Jan 16) Medicean 128 – Atyaab 78 (Green Desert (USA) 127) [2015 7s **67** 7s⁶ 7g Oct 9] compact filly: first foal: dam, ungenuine maiden (stayed 1m), out of sister to Breeders' Cup Juvenile/Preakness Stakes winner Timber Country: fair maiden: best effort when sixth at Newbury (7 lengths behind Tabarrak) in September, faring best of those held up. *Marcus Tregoning*

LAZY DAYS IN LOULE (IRE) 3 b.f. Approve (IRE) 112 – Lazy Lady (Selkirk (USA) **67** 129) [2015 54: t7.1g 7g³ 7.1s⁵ 7.1m⁴ 6d² 6m* 6d³ 6g⁵ 6g 6d 5g³ 5m⁵ 6d⁴ Oct 26] fair handicapper: won at Ripon (apprentice) in June: stayed 6f: acted on good to firm and good to soft going: tried in hood: dead. *Noel Wilson*

LAZY SIOUX 4 b.f. Sleeping Indian 122 – Aimee's Delight 85 (Robellino (USA) 127) **67** [2015 60: t5.1f² t6g t5.1g⁵ t6f⁵ t5.1f* 5d* f5g³ 5g⁶ 5m³ 5m 5f* 5.5m³ 5d 5d⁴ 5d 5g⁴ 5m **a57** Oct 1] fair handicapper: won at Wolverhampton in March, Catterick (apprentice) in April and Beverley in July: left Richard Guest after thirteenth start: stays 6f: acts on tapeta, firm and good to soft going: tried in visor: front runner/races prominently: sold £800, sent to Belgium. *Karen Tutty*

LAZZAM 2 ch.c. (Mar 25) Archipenko (USA) 127 – Empire Rose (ARG) (Sunray Spirit **95** (USA) 108) [2015 6m³ p7g² p8g* p8m² 8s⁶ Oct 19] finely-made colt: first foal: dam, 2-y-o 5f/7f winner in South Africa, half-sister to Argentinian Group 2 1m winner Empire Aztec: useful performer: easily landed odds in maiden at Chelmsford in August: good second in minor event at Chelmsford (¾ length behind Dragon Mall) in September: stays 1m: acts on polytrack. *Marco Botti*

LEAD A MERRY DANCE 4 b.f. Bertolini (USA) 125 – Green Supreme (Primo **79** Dominie 121) [2015 73: 5.7f* 6g* 6m³ 6m³ 5.7g³ 6g⁵ p6g² 5f Sep 12] fair handicapper: won at Bath and Goodwood (apprentice) in May: stays 6f: acts on polytrack and firm going: front runner/races prominently. *Sylvester Kirk*

LEADERENE 4 b.f. Selkirk (USA) 129 – La Felicita (Shareef Dancer (USA) 135) [2015 **93**
89, a81: 12.1m 9.9m³ 10m* 9.9g 12.3g* 12g³ 14.1d 13g Aug 29] big filly: fairly useful
handicapper: won at Newmarket in May and Chester (by nose from Energia Fox) in July:
stays 12.5f: acts on polytrack and good to firm going: usually leads, often races freely.
Mark Johnston

LEADING DESIGN (IRE) 3 b.f. Dubawi (IRE) 129 – Watership Crystal (IRE) **–**
(Sadler's Wells (USA) 132) [2015 10d 12m May 15] €380,000Y: sturdy filly: fifth foal:
half-sister to 3 winners, including useful 2-y-o 7f winner Cocozza and French 9.5f winner
Black Crystal (both by Elusive Quality): dam twice-raced sister to smart performer up to
1¼m Dubai Success and closely related to Fillies' Mile winner Crystal Music: behind in
maidens at Sandown and Newmarket (visored). *Saeed bin Suroor*

LEAH FREYA (IRE) 4 b.f. Aussie Rules (USA) 123 – A Woman In Love 87 (Muhtarram **97**
(USA) 125) [2015 p12g³ p10f p13g⁵ p13f⁶ 11.5d* 11.6m⁶ 12m* 12g⁴ 10.1v* 12d* 12m
Oct 3] angular filly: third foal: dam 7f/1m winner: useful handicapper: won at Lingfield in
May and at Epsom in July, August and September (apprentice, by 10 lengths from
El Campeon): stays 1½m: acts on good to firm and heavy going. *Pat Phelan*

LEAN BURN (USA) 9 b.g. Johannesburg (USA) 127 – Anthelion (USA) (Stop The **51**
Music (USA)) [2015 t13.9f⁵ 16.2s² 14.1g³ t16.5m Nov 21] modest maiden: stays 2m: acts
on tapeta, fibresand and soft going: tried in blinkers: usually wears tongue tie. *Barry Leavy*

LEAN ON PETE (IRE) 6 b.g. Oasis Dream 129 – Superfonic (FR) (Zafonic (USA) 130) **80**
[2015 83: t12.2f f11g⁶ t8.6m* 9.5m³ f11g³ f8s⁵ t9.5g² t8.6f t9.5f t9.5g⁵ t9.5f³ Dec 14]
good-topped gelding: fairly useful handicapper: won at Wolverhampton in February: stays
11f: acts on all-weather, good to firm and heavy going: tried in cheekpieces. *Ollie Pears*

LEAP 2 ch.f. (Jan 12) Pounced (USA) 112 – Liel 58 (Pivotal 124) [2015 p6g⁴ Jun 4] second **66 p**
foal: dam, maiden (stayed 7f), half-sister to useful winner up to 1½m Tall Ship out of
Cheveley Park Stakes winner Magical Romance, herself closely related to Oaks winner
Alexandrova: 9/2, fourth in maiden at Kempton (3½ lengths behind Azhar) in June: will
improve. *Richard Hannon*

LEARNING CURVE (IRE) 2 b.g. (Mar 30) Monsieur Bond (IRE) 120 – Existentialist **–**
78 (Exceed And Excel (AUS) 126) [2015 p6g 6.1d 6g p6f Oct 1] no form. *John Quinn*

LEAR'S ROCK (IRE) 3 b.g. Rock of Gibraltar (IRE) 133 – Cordelia 71 (Green Desert **100**
(USA) 127) [2015 83: p8g* 8.3m* 8.5g² 8m⁵ p8g 8s* Oct 23] useful performer: won
maiden at Lingfield in February and handicaps at Windsor in April and Newbury (by head
from Predominance) in October: stays 8.5f: acts on polytrack, soft and good to firm going:
front runner/races prominently: sold 38,000 gns, sent to Saudi Arabia. *Ralph Beckett*

LEAVE IT TO ARNO 3 ch.g. Paco Boy (IRE) 129 – Presto Vento 103 (Air Express **59**
(IRE) 125) [2015 7d f7g⁴ 8d t7.1g 10m⁶ 10.2g 10.1g 6m Aug 29] modest maiden: should
prove best at sprint trips: acts on fibresand, good to firm and good to soft going: tried in
blinkers. *Michael Easterby*

LE CHAT D'OR 7 b.g. One Cool Cat (USA) 123 – Oh So Well (IRE) (Sadler's Wells **94**
(USA) 132) [2015 99: 8d⁵ 8.3s³ 8d 8d 8.3s³ Oct 28] fairly useful handicapper: stays 9f: acts
on heavy going: often wears headgear: usually wears tongue tie: often starts slowly, often
races in rear. *Michael Dods*

LEDBURY (IRE) 3 b.g. Lawman (FR) 121 – Truly Magnificent (USA) 62 (Elusive **71**
Quality (USA)) [2015 t9.5f⁶ 10.3d t12.2g³ p12g f12g³ Dec 22] fair maiden: left Charles
Hills after third start: stays 1½m: acts on all-weather: tried in blinkers: front runner/races
prominently. *Lee Carter*

LE DELUGE (FR) 5 b.g. Oratorio (IRE) 128 – Princess Sofia (UAE) (Pennekamp (USA) **65**
130) [2015 76: f11g* f12g⁴ p10g⁵ 10s 12g 12g 12g³ 12.1m 9.3g 10.4f⁶ p10m* f8g² Nov **a72**
24] strong gelding: fair handicapper: won at Southwell (apprentice) in March and Lingfield
(apprentice) in November: stays 1½m: acts on polytrack, fibresand, good to firm and good
to soft going: sometimes wears tongue tie: front runner/races prominently. *Heather Dalton*

LEE BAY 2 b.c. (Apr 30) Cacique (IRE) 124 – Bantu 80 (Cape Cross (IRE) 129) [2015 **50 p**
8.3s⁶ Nov 4] 100,000Y: second foal: half-brother to 2-y-o 8.3f winner Banzari (by
Motivator): dam, maiden (stayed 1¼m), half-sister to Craven Stakes winner Adagio and
US Grade 2 1½m winner Arvada: 7/1, looked in need of experience and never a threat
when sixth of 10 in maiden at Nottingham won by Wajeez: should do better. *John Gosden*

LEEDORA 2 b.f. (Apr 26) Sir Percy 129 – Alizadora 76 (Zilzal (USA) 137) [2015 6m 7m **35** 5.9m 8g 10d⁵ Oct 5] 10,000F, 8,500Y: fourth foal: sister to useful Spanish winner up to 11f Madrileno (2-y-o 1m winner) and half-sister to 1¼m winner Alzavola (by With Approval): dam, 2-y-o 5f winner, out of close relative to smart stayer Alleluia: poor maiden: stays 1m: acts on good to firm going. *Karen Tutty*

LEE'S HALL (IRE) 2 b.g. (Apr 18) Invincible Spirit (IRE) 121 – Russian Roubles (IRE) **79 p** (Sadler's Wells (USA) 132) [2015 5g⁵ 6d 7s⁵ p7g³ p8m⁴ Nov 19] €48,000Y, 70,000 2-y-o: sturdy gelding: sixth foal: half-brother to 2 winners in Italy, including useful winner up to 1½m Russianduke (2-y-o 9f winner, by Duke of Marmalade): dam, of little account, half-sister to very smart 1¼m-1¾m winner Dr Johnson: fair maiden: shaped better than result on handicap debut final start: should stay 1m: acts on polytrack: should do better. *Gary Moore*

LEFORTOVO (FR) 2 b.c. (Mar 18) Arcano (IRE) 122 – Lorientaise (IRE) (Xaar 132) **71** [2015 t7.1g 6g² 7s⁴ Sep 5] fair maiden: best effort when second in maiden at Deauville (2 lengths behind Attendu) in August, responding well: should be better suited by 7f than 6f. *Jo Hughes*

LEGAL ART 3 ch.f. Dutch Art 126 – Sosumi 101 (Be My Chief (USA) 122) [2015 p6g⁶ **58** p7g² p6g² 7s 7.9g⁵ 7d⁶ p6f⁴ Oct 10] closely related to winner abroad by Medicean and half-sister to several winners, including useful 7f-8.3f winner Tevez (by Sakhee) and 11.5f winner Edward Whymper (by Bahamian Bounty): dam 2-y-o 5f winner who stayed 1¼m: modest maiden: left Mark H. Tompkins after sixth start: stays 7f: acts on polytrack. *Brian Ellison*

LEGAL SHARK (IRE) 4 b.g. Lawman (FR) 121 – Sea Searcher (USA) (Theatrical) **67** [2015 t8.6g p6m⁵ p7g t8.6g⁶ f8d⁵ p8f* p8f² p10f p10f Oct 1] fair handicapper: won at Lingfield in August: will be suited by 1¼m: acts on polytrack: usually in hood. *Sir Mark Prescott Bt*

LEGATISSIMO (IRE) 3 b.f. Danehill Dancer (IRE) 117 – Yummy Mummy 86 **122** (Montjeu (IRE) 137) [2015 93p: 7v⁴ 9.5g* 8f* 12g² 10m² 9.9m* 8g* 9.5g² Oct 31]
The top three-year-old fillies in Ireland were an outstanding collection and enjoyed a striking run of success at the highest level in the latest season. Both fillies' classics in Britain fell to Irish fillies (Legatissimo and Qualify) and the Irish One Thousand Guineas was kept at home (Pleascach); with the help of Diamondsandrubies and Curvy, the classic winners added other Group 1s in Britain (Nassau and Yorkshire Oaks), Ireland (Pretty Polly and Matron) and North America (E. P. Taylor Stakes). A late-season victory by Found put the icing on the cake when she beat Derby and Arc winner Golden Horn in the Breeders' Cup Turf at Keeneland, after previously finishing runner-up in the Irish One Thousand Guineas, the Coronation Stakes and the Champion Stakes in both Ireland and Britain. Found ended up the best of this illustrious sextet on merit, but it would be unfair for Legatissimo not to share the limelight with her. Like Found, Legatissimo had a full campaign—eight races which culminated in an appearance at the Breeders' Cup—and only once finished out of the first two. Whereas the Breeders' Cup Turf was the only Group 1 that Found won, Legatissimo won three, the One Thousand Guineas, the Nassau Stakes (the richest race for fillies and mares in Britain, having overtaken the British Champions Fillies' And Mares' and the Oaks) and the Matron Stakes. Legatissimo also finished second in three other Group 1s, and a judiciously spread length and a half in those three races would have taken her to six Group 1 successes for the season. She was beaten a short head in both the Oaks and the Pretty Polly Stakes and a length and a quarter in the Breeders' Cup Filly & Mare Turf after stumbling at the start and having to be switched wide in the straight to get into a challenging position.

Legatissimo won a seven-furlong maiden at Galway from three starts as a two-year-old and managed only fourth of eight in the Leopardstown One Thousand Guineas Trial on her reappearance. She got off the mark as a three-year-old in a listed event at Gowran in late-April, forging clear to win by three and three quarter lengths from Wedding Vow. At this point, Legatissimo was still a virtual unknown, though her trainer David Wachman said after the Gowran race that he had 'not ruled out a tilt at the Irish One Thousand Guineas.' It was generally expected anyway that her owners, the Coolmore partners, would be represented in the One Thousand Guineas by the ante-post favourite Found (Legatissimo could be backed at 40/1 for the Guineas a week before the race). However, when Found was scratched and Ryan Moore was switched to Legatissimo, her odds tumbled and she started second favourite at 13/2, only two points longer than the Rockfel Stakes winner Lucida, who had finished second in the Moyglare, a place in front of Found who had gone on to win France's top race for two-year-old fillies, the Prix Marcel Boussac. The absence of Found (a beaten favourite in the Athasi Stakes at the Curragh instead twenty-four hours later) and the Moyglare winner Cursory Glance, who had been ruled out with a fetlock injury over the winter, weakened the One Thousand Guineas field, but Legatissimo was a very good winner in a strongly-run race on firm going which produced one of the fastest winning times ever for the race, 1m 34.60sec, the fastest that can be found in records going back to 1900 with the exception of Ghanaati's 1m 34.22sec in 2009 when there was a strong wind behind the runners. A fast time in itself is not necessarily significant—often indicating only that the prevailing conditions were favourable—but the *time value* of Legatissimo's performance, which produced a timefigure of 0.77 fast (equivalent to a timerating of 119), backed up the assessment of the form as being above standard for the race. There were no stamina worries about Legatissimo beforehand—her win at Gowran had come over a furlong and a half further—but the One Thousand Guineas was her third race in as many weeks, an unorthodox preparation for a classic to say the least. Patiently ridden at Newmarket, Legatissimo saw her stamina brought into play by the strong gallop as she cut down her rivals over the last two furlongs. Still with ground to make up entering the final furlong, she pegged back Lucida in the final fifty yards to beat her by three quarters of a length, with first and second both seeing out the mile well. The Lowther and Cheveley Park winner Tiggy Wiggy and Malabar, who had come fourth in both the Moyglare and the Marcel Boussac, completed the frame, beaten a further four and a half lengths and a length and a quarter after being handy throughout. The Rockfel runner-up Fadhayyil finished fifth and Irish Rookie, who was runner-up next time in the Poule d'Essai des Pouliches, came sixth in the thirteen-runner line-up.

Ryan Moore's victory on Legatissimo strengthened his closer, more formal links with the Coolmore partners just twenty-four hours after he won the Two Thousand Guineas on Gleneagles for the same owners. Moore was the first jockey to complete the Guineas double since Kieren Fallon did so on Footstepsinthesand and Virginia Waters ten years earlier, also for Coolmore, though that pair were both handled by the same trainer, Aidan O'Brien. When Lester Piggott won both races in 1970, he also did so on horses trained by different trainers, Nijinsky by Vincent O'Brien and Humble Duty by Peter Walwyn, that particular pair also in different ownership. Legatissimo was the first British classic winner for her trainer David Wachman and came six years after he won the Irish One Thousand Guineas with Again, also a daughter of Legatissimo's sire Danehill Dancer owned by the Coolmore partners (probably the one fact everyone knows about the self-effacing Wachman, who gives very few interviews, is that he is the son-in-law of Coolmore supremo John Magnier).

Qipco 1000 Guineas Stakes, Newmarket—in an up-to-scratch renewal, Legatissimo (right) finds plenty to get past Lucida in the final fifty yards; Tiggy Wiggy (armlets) holds on for third ahead of Malabar (rail) and Fadhayyil (striped cap); it's a Guineas double for the Coolmore partners and jockey Ryan Moore after the victory of Gleneagles the day before

Qatar Nassau Stakes, Goodwood—several disappoint but Legatissimo is right on her game as she bags a second Group 1, beating Wedding Vow and Arabian Queen; the winner earned just over £340,000 in prize money, treble that for the 2014 renewal

Ballydoyle saddled three Oaks runners and Sir Michael Stoute had the second favourite Crystal Zvezda, but Ryan Moore maintained his partnership with Legatissimo at Epsom. The One Thousand Guineas form was the best on offer—though the field featured the winners of most of the key trials—and given that Legatissimo's dam is a sister to the Irish Derby and Gold Cup winner Fame And Glory she seemed sure to get the trip. Legatissimo was narrowly denied a One Thousand Guineas/Oaks double (last achieved by Kazzia in 2002) by the rank outsider Qualify, who had finished last in the One Thousand Guineas. In a rough race, Legatissimo, who started from stall one, was shuffled back in the field early on as others cut across and had only four behind her at Tattenham Corner. Switched wide in the home straight, she barged her way past eventual third Lady of Dubai and into the lead over a furlong out—Ryan Moore picking up a one-day ban for careless riding—but, after looking to have the race won, was caught right on the post by 50/1-shot Qualify. Irish fillies filled three of the first four places, with Qualify's stablemate Diamondsandrubies rallying to finish fourth after being baulked by the third Ballydoyle runner Together Forever in serious scrimmaging about a furlong and a half out. Diamondsandrubies inflicted a second Group 1 short-head defeat on Legatissimo when the pair met later in the month in the Pretty Polly Stakes at the Curragh, which provides the first opportunity of the season for the top fillies of the classic generation to take on the best of their elders who have remained in training. The Irish One Thousand Guineas winner Pleascach was also in the field, having won the Ribblesdale Stakes ten days earlier at Royal Ascot (where Lucida upheld the One Thousand Guineas form when a close third in the Coronation Stakes). Pleascach ran as if feeling the effects of her Royal Ascot exertions but Diamondsandrubies and Legatissimo made it a one, two for the three-year-olds, Legatissimo just failing to peg back her front-running rival and looking a shade unlucky not to prevail, with the mares Ribbons and Secret Gesture third and fourth.

The Qatar Nassau Stakes at Goodwood, worth £340,260 to the winner, was next for both Legatissimo and Diamondsandrubies, in a field also including the Prix de Diane winner Star of Seville (who had been one of those who suffered serious interference in the Oaks). The Oaks third and fifth, Lady of Dubai and Jazzi Top, were also in the line-up, along with a second Ballydoyle runner, Wedding Vow, who had continued to run well in pattern company since her early-season defeat by Legatissimo at Gowran. The sole French challenger, the four-year-old Cladocera, had run well in Dubai in the early part of the year and had most recently finished a creditable third to Amazing Maria in the Duke of Cambridge Stakes at Royal Ascot. With Diamondsandrubies and Star of Seville both failing to run anywhere near their best, Legatissimo gained handsome consolation for her narrow defeats in the Oaks and the Pretty Polly with a ready two-and-a-quarter-length victory from Wedding Vow, with 25/1-shot Arabian Queen a further length and a half away third. Cladocera, Jazzi Top and Lady of Dubai completed the first six, the two last-named suffering trouble in running. The pace in the Nassau was muddling and the bare form was difficult to rate so highly as that produced by some of the best winners of the race (it was below the form shown by three-times winner Midday for her victories, for example).

Having been dropped back to a mile and a quarter for her first two races after the Oaks, Legatissimo reverted to a mile in the Coolmore Matron Stakes at Leopardstown on Irish Champions' Weekend in September. The Matron produced an eagerly-anticipated meeting with the four-year-old Amazing Maria, who was seeking a four-timer after following up wins in the Duke of Cambridge at Royal Ascot and the Falmouth at Newmarket with a victory over the Coronation Stakes winner Ervedya in the Prix Rothschild at Deauville. The Matron looked a two-horse race—7/4 Legatissimo, 15/8 Amazing Maria, 8/1 and upwards the rest—but such contests have a habit of failing to live up to their billing. The story of the Matron Stakes was different from the one widely anticipated, with Amazing Maria giving a tame display which left Legatissimo to cement her claims to being the season's leading filly over a mile with another impressive victory. Cruising through from mid-field to challenge entering the straight, Legatissimo quickened into the lead over a furlong out and forged clear to win by two and a quarter lengths and the same from Cladocera and the smart three-year-old Ainippe who was tackling Group 1 company for the first time. Legatissimo's trainer revealed afterwards that he had come close to not running Legatissimo after overnight rain—conditions which resulted in Gleneagles being taken out of the Irish Champion Stakes on the same card (Wachman had apparently given serious thought to taking on Golden Horn in that race but connections had decided on the Matron once the Irish Champion became a target for Gleneagles).

Legatissimo's career so far has been restricted to races against her own sex and she completed her three-year-old campaign in the Breeders' Cup Filly & Mare Turf at Keeneland at the end of October, reunited with Ryan Moore after Wayne Lordan had stood in over the summer while Moore was injured. Legatissimo had the best form in the ten-runner contest and started odds-on but she wasn't quite at her best and, although stumbling leaving the stalls and then having to come four horses wide in the home straight to make her challenge, it couldn't be said that she was in any way an unlucky loser. Legatissimo beat the other European challengers, the Prix Saint-Alary winner Queen's Jewel and the older duo Secret Gesture (first past the post in the Beverly D Stakes at Arlington) and Miss France (the 2014 One Thousand Guineas winner), but six-year-old Stephanie's Kitten, second in the race

Coolmore Fastnet Rock Matron Stakes, Leopardstown—the drop back to a mile is no problem for Legatissimo who wins in clear-cut fashion; Cladocera (striped cap) and Ainippe (rail) fill the places

M. Tabor, Mrs J. Magnier & D. Smith's "Legatissimo"

the previous year, kept the prize at home, getting a clear run on the inside and holding off Legatissimo by a length and a quarter, with Queen's Jewel third, Secret Gesture seventh and Miss France eighth.

Legatissimo (IRE)
(b.f. 2012)
- Danehill Dancer (IRE)
  (b 1993)
  - Danehill
    (b 1986)
    - Danzig
    - Razyana
  - Mira Adonde
    (b or br 1986)
    - Sharpen Up
    - Lettre d'Amour
- Yummy Mummy
  (b 2005)
  - Montjeu
    (b 1996)
    - Sadler's Wells
    - Floripedes
  - Gryada
    (b 1993)
    - Shirley Heights
    - Grimpola

The lengthy Legatissimo, by the now-pensioned versatile Coolmore stallion Danehill Dancer, cost 350,000 guineas as a yearling, a year after her Sea The Stars half-brother Royal Battalion had made 575,000 guineas (he didn't make the grade on the Flat and has gained his only win so far—after being sold on for just 21,000 guineas—in a handicap hurdle at Fontwell). Legatissimo is the third foal out of Yummy Mummy, who won a mile and a quarter maiden at Sligo and stayed a mile and a half; her first foal Another Cocktail (by Dalakhani) was a useful staying handicapper, runner up in the Ascot Stakes over two and a half miles. Yummy Mummy has paid her way for Newsells Park Stud since being purchased at the 2009 December Sales, the year Fame And Glory won the Irish Derby, for 460,000 guineas (carrying Another Cocktail who made 85,000 guineas as a yearling). Her latest yearling to reach the sale-ring, a close relative to Legatissimo by Redoute's Choice, was knocked down to M. V. Magnier for 725,000 guineas at the Newmarket October Sales Book 1.

Legatissimo's grandam Gryada, who won at seven furlongs and a mile as a two-year-old but didn't train on, would have had a distinguished record as a broodmare even without producing Fame And Glory. As well as Yummy Mummy, Gryada has bred numerous other winners, the latest of them Grace And Favour, a sister to Fame And Glory and Yummy Mummy. Gryada's other winners include the useful Guaranda, who has bred the smart stayer Gravitation, successful in the Lillie Langtry Stakes at Goodwood, while a close relative of Fame And Glory and Yummy Mummy, the German mile and a quarter winner Gaze, is herself the dam of the smart Greatwood who stayed a mile and three quarters. Legatissimo's great grandam Grimpola—who was imported by Plantation Stud in the late-'eighties—was also a classic winner, successful in the Schwarzgold-Rennen, at the time regarded as the German One Thousand Guineas (also placed in the German Oaks), and she is also the dam of the unraced Gonfalon, a three-parts sister to Gryada (both sired by Derby-winning sons of Mill Reef, Gonfalon being by Slip Anchor). Gonfalon is the dam of the dual Group 1-winning German mare Gonbarda who was purchased to race for Godolphin. Gonbarda didn't reach the racecourse for Godolphin but proved a valuable addition to the Darley broodmare band, becoming the dam of the Champion Stakes winner Farhh.

The thoroughly genuine Legatissimo has proved herself in races at the highest level at a mile, a mile and a quarter and a mile and a half, which gives her connections plenty of options for her four-year-old campaign, in which she will presumably again be kept apart from the same connections' Found who showed herself to be similarly versatile so far as distance is concerned. Legatissimo acts on firm going and a dry summer would suit her. *David Wachman, Ireland*

LEGEND'S GATE (IRE) 3 b.g. New Approach (IRE) 132 – Arthur's Girl 103 (Hernando (FR) 127) [2015 86p: p10g³ 12m² May 2] good-topped gelding: fair maiden: should stay 1¼m+. *Charlie Appleby* — **78**

LEGERITY (IRE) 3 b.f. Dubawi (IRE) 129 – Much Faster (IRE) 113 (Fasliyev (USA) 120) [2015 –: p8m³ t8.6g p8g⁵ Feb 26] modest maiden: stays 1m: blinkered final start. *Charlie Appleby* — **56**

LEIA ORGANA (IRE) 2 ch.f. (Feb 26) Mastercraftsman (IRE) 129 – Fancy Vivid (IRE) 69 (Galileo (IRE) 134) [2015 7m³ 6g⁶ 7.5g⁵ t7.1f Oct 13] £12,500Y: second foal: closely related to 7f winner Double Fast (by Fast Company): dam, maiden (placed up to 1½m in France), out of sister to smart sprinter Land of Dreams, herself dam of top-class 6f/7f performer Dream Ahead: fair maiden: stays 7f: sold 4,500 gns, sent to Sweden. *Richard Fahey* — **67**

LEIGHTERTON 3 ch.c. Halling (USA) 133 – Dawnus (IRE) 103 (Night Shift (USA)) [2015 p10m³ 10g³ 11.5d² 12g* 12m⁵ 14m³ p12g⁴ Aug 24] 26,000Y: sturdy colt: seventh foal: brother to useful winner up to 1m in USA Longhunter (2-y-o 6f/7f winner) and half-brother to useful 1m-1¼m winner Initiator (by Motivator) and 2-y-o 6f/7f winner Beedee (by Beat Hollow): dam 1m-1¼m winner: fairly useful handicapper: won at Ripon in June: stays 1¾m: acts on polytrack, good to firm and good to soft going. *Martyn Meade* — **86**

LEITH BRIDGE 3 b.g. Avonbridge 123 – Ishibee (IRE) 64 (Ishiguru (USA) 114) [2015 p6g³ f5g⁵ p6m³ t6f³ Dec 21] modest maiden: stays 6f. *Mark Usher* — **55**

LEITRIM PASS (USA) 5 ch.g. Raven's Pass (USA) 133 – Santolina (USA) 101 (Boundary (USA) 117) [2015 82: t9.5g 7s p8g Jun 17] rangy gelding: fairly useful at best, no form in 2015: tried in cheekpieces/tongue tie. *Tony Carroll* — **–**

LEITRIM TRAVELLER (USA) 2 b.g. (Mar 24) Henrythenavigator (USA) 131 – Purple (USA) (Royal Academy (USA) 130) [2015 6g⁶ 6m 6m p6g⁵ p6f p6f³ p7f³ p6dᵘʳ Nov 30] modest maiden: stays 7f: acts on polytrack: in headgear. *Jamie Osborne* — **55**

LE LAITIER (FR) 4 b.g. Milk It Mick 120 – La Brigitte 92 (Tobougg (IRE) 125) [2015 79: 6g 5m 6g⁵ 6m 7m² 7m 7g⁴ 7m² p7f Nov 12] fair handicapper: stays 7f: acts on firm going. *Scott Dixon* — **67**

LE MAITRE CHAT (USA) 4 b.g. Tale of The Cat (USA) 113 – Bedside Story 104 (Mtoto 134) [2015 98: 14.1m⁴ 14g⁴ 16.4m³ 16s 18g⁶ p16g⁶ Nov 18] workmanlike gelding: useful handicapper: third at York (¾ length behind Eshtiaal) in July: left Clive Cox after fourth start: stays 2¼m: acts on soft going: usually in cheekpieces in 2015: not straightforward. *Ian Williams* — **102**

LE MANEGE ENCHANTE (IRE) 2 gr.g. (Mar 20) Zebedee 113 – Beth 79 (Deportivo **74**
116) [2015 5.1m 5g⁶ p5f⁴ 5.1d³ p6f t5.1g³ t5.1f* p6g⁵ Dec 20] fair performer: won nursery
at Wolverhampton in December: best effort at 5f: acts on tapeta. *Derek Shaw*

LEMBIT AND BUTLER (IRE) 2 b.g. (Apr 7) Lilbourne Lad (IRE) 111 – Fathoming **–**
(USA) (Gulch (USA)) [2015 t7.1m t7.1f Oct 20] down field both starts in maidens: wears
hood. *Tom Dascombe*

LEMONCETTA (USA) 3 ch.f. Lemon Drop Kid (USA) 131 – Excelente (IRE) 99 **83**
(Exceed And Excel (AUS) 126) [2015 68p: 8.3g³ 8m³ 8.3m³ 10d* 10g⁴ 11.6g* 12m³ t9.5f
p12g⁶ Nov 25] rather leggy filly: fairly useful performer: won handicaps at Newmarket in
July and Windsor (by ¾ length from Silver Quay) in September: 40/1, ran as well as could
be expected when sixth of 10 to Fire Fighting in listed race at Kempton final start: stays
1½m: acts on polytrack and good to soft going: temperament under suspicion: sold
30,000 gns, sent to Saudi Arabia. *John Gosden*

LENDAL BRIDGE 4 ch.g. Avonbridge 123 – Dunloe (IRE) 54 (Shaadi (USA) 126) **63**
[2015 59: f7d³ t8.6f* f7g t9.5f 7.1s* 8d⁴ 8.3d⁴ 8.5d 7s 7s³ f7g f8g Nov 24] modest **a56**
handicapper: won at Wolverhampton (amateur) in February and Musselburgh in May:
stays 8.5f: acts on tapeta and soft going: tried in headgear. *Tony Coyle*

LENIENCE (IRE) 2 b.f. (May 2) Oasis Dream 129 – Acts of Grace (USA) 109 (Bahri **64 p**
(USA) 125) [2015 6m 8d⁵ t8.6g Sep 29] €65,000Y: good-topped filly: fifth foal: sister to
9f/1¼m winner Damascene and half-sister to 6f winner Blaugrana (by Exceed And Excel)
and 1¼m winner Contradict (by Raven's Pass): dam, 1¼m-1½m winner, half-sister to very
smart sprinter Invincible Spirit out of Prix de Diane winner Rafha: modest form in
maidens: slowly away second outing, not knocked about once held final start: should do
better in time. *Martyn Meade*

LE NOTRE 3 b.g. Champs Elysees 124 – Millistar 88 (Galileo (IRE) 134) [2015 t8.6g³ **85**
t9.5g* p11g^pu t9.5m p12g² Dec 9] 105,000Y: fourth foal: closely related to
1¼m-1½m winner Syncopate (by Oratorio) and half-brother to 9f/1¼m winner Familliarity
(by Nayef): dam 1¼m winner: fairly useful performer: won maiden at Wolverhampton in
July: left Marco Botti after fifth start: stays 1½m: acts on polytrack and tapeta: tried in
cheekpieces: front runner/races prominently. *Jeremy Noseda*

LEONARDO (GER) 3 ch.g. Areion (GER) 115 – Lolli Pop (GER) (Cagliostro (GER)) **–**
[2015 68: 10m Jul 18] angular gelding: lightly-raced maiden, well held only outing in 2015.
James Fanshawe

LEONARD THOMAS 5 b.g. Singspiel (IRE) 133 – Monawara (IRE) 73 (Namaqualand **66**
(USA)) [2015 87: p9g⁵ t9.5g⁶ t9.5f⁶ 7d 10.2s 8.1s 7m⁶ 11.6g⁶ 8.3m t8.6m⁶ 8g³ 7s³ 7s² p8m⁶ **a77**
p10g Dec 15] fair handicapper: left David Lanigan after third start: stays 1¼m: acts on
polytrack, tapeta, soft and good to firm going: tried in headgear in 2015: tried in tongue tie
in 2015: usually races nearer last than front. *Tony Carroll*

LEONCAVALLO (IRE) 3 b.g. Cape Cross (IRE) 129 – Nafura 95 (Dubawi (IRE) 129) **75**
[2015 54p: p8f⁶ p10g² t12.2m* 12.1m⁴ 11.6g⁴ Apr 27] rather unfurnished gelding: fair
handicapper: won at Wolverhampton (apprentice) in April: stays 1½m: acts on polytrack
and tapeta: sometimes in cheekpieces in 2015: often starts slowly: useful hurdler for John
Ferguson. *Charlie Appleby*

LE ROCK (IRE) 3 b.g. Rock of Gibraltar (IRE) 133 – Reine Violette (FR) (Fly To The **76**
Stars 124) [2015 13.1m³ 14.9d³ 14m⁵ 14.4s² 14.9s Nov 17] fair maiden on balance of form:
stays 15f: acts on soft and good to firm going. *J. S. Moore*

LE ROI DU TEMPS (USA) 2 ch.g. (Mar 8) Leroidesanimaux (BRZ) 127 – Minute **80**
Limit (IRE) 78 (Pivotal 124) [2015 6g 7m³ 7d* 8g⁶ 8d Oct 23] £19,000Y: first foal: dam,
6f (at 2 yrs) to 8.5f (in USA) winner, out of useful 7f/1m winner Magic Cove: fairly useful
performer: won maiden at Leicester in August: stays 1m: acts on good to soft going: often
races prominently. *Tom Tate*

LE ROUQUIN (FR) 3 ch.g. Siyouni (FR) 122 – Tenue d'Amour (FR) (Pursuit of Love **75**
124) [2015 69: t9.5f⁵ p8f* p8f* p8m² 9.9m³ 8m⁵ p8g² 8d p8f^bu Sep 24] fair handicapper:
won at Kempton and Lingfield in January: stays 1m: acts on polytrack: tried in visor: tried
in tongue tie: often races in rear. *Michael Bell*

L'ES FREMANTLE (FR) 4 b.g. Orpen (USA) 116 – Grand Design 64 (Danzero (AUS)) **–**
[2015 –: 7g 6m 10m 12g 16.5m⁶ 11.8m 11.9d Aug 5] no form: tried in headgear. *Michael
Chapman*

LES GAR GAN (IRE) 4 b.f. Iffraaj 127 – Story (Observatory (USA) 131) [2015 73, a66: p10g* t8.6f t9.5f 10.2m t8.6g t9.5g t0g t9.5m 8v² t8.6f⁴ t9.5f⁴ t9.5m⁵ t8.6f* p10g⁵ Dec 30] angular filly: modest handicapper: won at Lingfield in January (subsequently left Keith Dalgleish) and Wolverhampton in December: stays 13f: acts on polytrack, tapeta, soft and good to firm going: tried in headgear. *Daniel Loughnane*   **57 a63**

LESHA (IRE) 4 b.g. Amadeus Wolf 122 – Dane Blue (IRE) 97 (Danehill Dancer (IRE) 117) [2015 98: t9.5f 8d 9.8d 8g 8.1m 8.5g Jun 5] tall gelding: useful handicapper: below form last 4 starts in Britain: stays 10.5f: acts on fibresand, tapeta, good to firm and heavy going: has worn hood/cheekpieces: sent to Qatar, and won 1¼m handicap at Doha in December. *Kevin Ryan*   **96**

LESSON IN LIFE 4 b.f. Duke of Marmalade (IRE) 132 – Vanity (IRE) 75 (Thatching 131) [2015 61: f11d⁵ f11g³ Jan 8] modest maiden: stays 12.5f: acts on fibresand, tapeta and good to soft going: in cheekpieces first start in 2015. *David O'Meara*   **50**

LETBYGONESBEICONS 2 b.g. (Apr 29) Sixties Icon 125 – Composing (IRE) 71 (Noverre (USA) 125) [2015 6d 7.5m⁶ 6m⁴ 6s² 6v* 5.9m 6g Oct 8] fair performer: won nursery at Ffos Las in August: best effort at 6f: acts on heavy going: front runner/races prominently. *Ann Duffield*   **72**

LETHAL LEGACY (IRE) 3 b.c. Alfred Nobel (IRE) 110 – Cafe Creme (IRE) (Catrail (USA) 123) [2015 83: 7m p8g 7.1f⁶ 7v⁶ Aug 24] maiden: no form in 2015: usually races prominently. *Richard Hannon*   **–**

LE TISSIER 2 ch.g. (Apr 6) Sir Percy 129 – Incarnation (IRE) 72 (Samum (GER) 126) [2015 7g⁶ Sep 30] 13,500F, €17,000Y: third foal: half-brother to 1½m winners Impertinent and Al (both by Halling): dam, 1¼m winner, half-sister to high-class/temperamental performer up to 1½m Norse Dancer: 14/1, sixth of 13 in maiden at Salisbury (4¾ lengths behind Royal Reserve) in September: will be suited by 1m+: entitled to progress. *Andrew Balding*   **58 p**

LET IT GO 3 b.f. Halling (USA) 133 – Kisses (Sakhee (USA) 136) [2015 10m 7s p7g⁵ Nov 25] second foal: dam unraced: no form. *Tony Carroll*   **–**

LE TORRENT 3 ch.g. Sir Percy 129 – Cinnas Ransom (Red Ransom (USA)) [2015 62: p8f 10.2f⁵ 10m 12.1m³ 11.7f* 13.1f* p13.3f* Oct 10] fair handicapper: won at Bath in July (subsequently left Henry Candy) and September and Chelmsford in October: stays 13.5f: acts on polytrack, best turf form on firm going: often in headgear in 2015. *Simon Dow*   **76**

LET RIGHT BE DONE 3 gr.g. Lawman (FR) 121 – Cheerfully 67 (Sadler's Wells (USA) 132) [2015 59: f7g⁶ t9.5f* p10m³ t9.5f 8m² 10.2m⁴ 10d* 8m³ 8s² 9.2d³ 7.2d 8d⁶ 8g⁵ 7.2g⁴ 8g 8g² 7.2g Oct 13] fair performer: won handicap at Wolverhampton in January and claimer at Leicester in June, then left Ed McMahon: stays 1¼m: acts on tapeta, soft and good to firm going: usually in headgear in 2015. *Linda Perratt*   **69 a62**

LET'S CONFER 6 ch.m. Doyen (IRE) 132 – Vrennan 74 (Suave Dancer (USA) 136) [2015 –: p12g p12g p16m⁶ p15.8g 11.5d⁴ p11g p12g 13.1d p12g⁶ Oct 27] poor maiden: probably stays 2m: acts on polytrack and good to soft going: often wears cheekpieces: tried in tongue tie in 2015. *Michael Attwater*   **46**

LET'S GO (USA) 3 b.g. Street Cry (IRE) 130 – Lady Darshaan (IRE) 109 (High Chaparral (IRE) 132) [2015 7.6g* t9.5g* 8d⁶ p9.2m² p10m* Nov 14] 300,000Y: first foal: dam, 2-y-o 5f winner who stayed 1m, half-sister to very smart sprinter Total Gallery: smart performer: won maiden at Lingfield (by 2¼ lengths from Mister Brightside) in June, handicap at Wolverhampton (by 9 lengths from Fiftyshadesfreed) in July and listed race at Lingfield (by ¾ length from Grendisar) in November: also good ½-length second to Tryster in minor event at Chelmsford: stays 1¼m: acts on polytrack and tapeta: tracks pace. *Saeed bin Suroor*   **117**

LET'S TWIST 3 ch.g. Piccolo 121 – Takes Two To Tango 69 (Groom Dancer (USA) 128) [2015 7g 7g* 7m⁶ 7.5d* Sep 22] fair performer: won maiden at Catterick in July and handicap at Beverley in September: will stay 1m: tried in blinkers. *Kevin Ryan*   **75**

LETTERS OF NOTE (IRE) 3 b.f. Azamour (IRE) 130 – Boo Boo Bear (IRE) 81 (Almutawakel 126) [2015 77p: p7g* 8d 6.9g⁵ 6m² 6m* 6g⁵ Aug 22] €80,000Y, €13,500 2-y-o: good-topped filly: first foal: dam, 1m winner, sister to smart winner up to 1m Eddie Jock: useful performer: won maiden at Dundalk (by 5 lengths from Period Piece) in January and listed race at Naas (by head from Byzantium) in July: probably stays 1m: acts on polytrack, good to firm and good to soft going. *M. D. O'Callaghan, Ireland*   **105**

LET THERE BE LIGHT 2 ch.g. (Feb 28) Phoenix Reach (IRE) 124 – Pink Supreme 70 (Night Shift (USA)) [2015 6g⁵ p6g 7.2m⁵ 7s Oct 26] fair maiden: best effort at 6f: tried in cheekpieces. *Gay Kelleway*   **65**

LETTUCE SNOW (IRE) 3 b.f. Clodovil (IRE) 116 – Lola Rosa (IRE) (Peintre Celebre **56** (USA) 137) [2015 –: p7g 6m 8m² 10.2f³ 12.1s p8g² p10f⁴ Oct 29] modest maiden: best effort at 1m: acts on polytrack and firm going. *Geoffrey Deacon*

LEWAMY (IRE) 5 b.g. Amadeus Wolf 122 – Thai Dye (UAE) (Jade Robbery (USA) 121) **54** [2015 45, a64: f7g² p7m⁶ p8g Feb 1] modest handicapper: stays 1m: acts on polytrack, fibresand, best turf form on good to soft/soft going: tried in headgear prior to 2015: sent to Greece. *Michael Bell*

LEWISHAM 5 b.g. Sleeping Indian 122 – Almunia (IRE) (Mujadil (USA) 119) [2015 **53 §** 84§: p6f Jan 31] sturdy gelding: modest handicapper: stays 6f: acts on polytrack, soft and good to firm going: tried in headgear: usually slowly away, often races in rear: ungenuine. *Luke Dace*

LEWIS VALENTINE (IRE) 3 b.g. Rip Van Winkle (IRE) 134 – Full of Love (IRE) 88 **54 p** (Hawk Wing (USA) 136) [2015 78: 8.3s⁶ May 3] thrice-raced maiden: fair form at 2 yrs, slowly away and shaped as if in need of race only outing in 2015: bred to stay 1m: remains with potential. *Bryan Smart*

LEXI GRADY ALICE 3 b.f. Royal Applause 124 – Missoula (IRE) 95 (Kalanisi (IRE) **42** 132) [2015 43: p13.3m p12g⁴ 14d⁵ Jul 26] poor maiden: stays 1½m: acts on polytrack and tapeta. *Suzy Smith*

LEXINGTON ABBEY 4 b.g. Sleeping Indian 122 – Silvereine (FR) (Bering 136) [2015 **105** 100: 6d⁴ 6g 5m 6.1m* 6.1m² 6g 6s Oct 10] sturdy gelding: useful handicapper: won at Nottingham (by ½ length from Greeb) in June: good second on same course (short head behind Greeb) in July: stays 6f: acts on good to firm and good to soft going: tried in cheekpieces in 2015. *Kevin Ryan*

LEXINGTON BAY (IRE) 7 b.g. High Chaparral (IRE) 132 – Schust Madame (IRE) 46 **79 §** (Second Set (IRE) 127) [2015 83: f11g⁵ f16d² f14g² t12.2f⁶ f16g² t16.5g³ 12s³ f14d* f12g f16g Dec 29] compact gelding: fair performer: won claimer at Southwell in May, left Richard Fahey after: stays 16.5f: acts on polytrack, fibresand, good to firm and heavy going: tried in headgear: unreliable. *Philip Kirby*

LEXINGTON BLUE 5 b.g. Bertolini (USA) 125 – Jasmine Breeze 61 (Saddlers' Hall **47** (IRE) 126) [2015 t9.5g⁶ p10f p11f 8.3g⁶ t8.6g 10.2m⁵ t12.2g 12.1m Jul 16] poor handicapper: left Seamus Mullins after third start: stays 1¼m: acts on all-weather and good to firm going: often wears headgear: usually races close up, tends to find little. *Steve Flook*

LEXINGTON PLACE 5 ch.g. Compton Place 125 – Elidore 95 (Danetime (IRE) 121) **97** [2015 90: t5.1f³ 5d 5g 5g² 5.1m* 5f* 5m* 5g³ 5g⁴ 5m² 5g* 5d⁴ 5s⁵ 5s Oct 9] useful handicapper: won at Nottingham in May, Haydock and Ayr in June and Musselburgh (by neck from Compton Heights) in August: good fourth to Maljaa at Haydock in September: has won over 6f, races mainly at 5f: acts on fibresand, tapeta, firm and soft going: has worn headgear, including last 2 starts: usually travels strongly. *Ruth Carr*

LEXINGTON ROSE 4 b.f. Captain Gerrard (IRE) 113 – Silca Destination 65 (Dubai **59** Destination (USA) 127) [2015 72: t5.1g⁴ Jan 19] good-topped filly: modest handicapper: stays 6f: acts on polytrack, tapeta, good to firm and good to soft going: tried in headgear: often races prominently. *Bryan Smart*

LEXINGTON TIMES (IRE) 3 b.c. Paco Boy (IRE) 129 – Fuaigh Mor (IRE) 68 (Dubai **104** Destination (USA) 127) [2015 99: p7g* p8f³ p8g² 8g 7g⁶ 8f 7s 7s⁵ p7g Oct 29] rather unfurnished colt: useful performer: won listed race at Lingfield (by neck from Angelic Lord) in March: second in listed race on same course (neck behind Fanciful Angel) in April: stays 1m: acts on polytrack and good to soft going. *Richard Hannon*

LEXI'S HERO (IRE) 7 b.g. Invincible Spirit (IRE) 121 – Christel Flame (Darshaan 133) **99** [2015 95: 5.1s* 5g 5m 5g² 6.1g⁴ 6m⁵ 6m 6g⁶ 5.5m 6g 5d 5s Oct 9] big, strong gelding: useful handicapper: won at Chester (by 1¼ lengths from Confessional) in May: good second at Newcastle (length behind Northgate Lad) in June: stays 6f: acts on polytrack, soft and good to firm going: often wears headgear. *Richard Fahey*

LEX TALIONIS (IRE) 2 b.c. (Mar 3) Thewayyouare (USA) 117 – Dawn Air (USA) 53 **64** (Diesis 133) [2015 7s⁴ 7d⁶ 8d 8d⁵ Oct 21] modest maiden: stays 1m. *J. F. Levins, Ireland*

LEYLAND (IRE) 6 b.g. Peintre Celebre (USA) 137 – Lasting Chance (USA) (American **– §** Chance (USA) 117) [2015 66§: f16g p16m 14d⁴ Jul 26] fairly useful at best, no form in 2015: sometimes wears blinkers: temperamental. *Natalie Lloyd-Beavis*

L GE R 4 b.f. Pastoral Pursuits 127 – Cashbar 81 (Bishop of Cashel 122) [2015 p16g⁵ 10m **46** 10.1g⁴ p10f Oct 29] poor maiden: stays 1¼m: acts on good to firm going. *Peter Charalambous*

L'HIRONDELLE (IRE) 11 b.g. Anabaa (USA) 130 – Auratum (USA) 93 (Carson City (USA)) [2015 54: p10g p11g Jun 4] workmanlike gelding: fairly useful at best, no form in 2015: stays 9f: acts on polytrack and soft going: tried in headgear prior to 2015: often starts slowly, usually finds little. *Michael Attwater* –

LIAM'S MAP (USA) 4 gr.c. Unbridled's Song (USA) 125 – Miss Macy Sue (USA) (Trippi (USA) 121) [2015 a8f* a9f² a9f* a8f* Oct 30] $800,000Y: second foal: dam smart US Grade 3 6f winner: top-class performer: won 6 of his 8 starts, including optional claimer at Belmont in June, Woodward Stakes at Saratoga (by 4¾ lengths from Coach Inge) in September and Breeders' Cup Dirt Mile at Keeneland (by 2½ lengths from Lea, leading inside final 1f) in October: neck second to Honor Code in Whitney Stakes at Saratoga on second outing, clear off home turn but caught late on: was effective at 1m/9f: raced only on dirt: to stand at Lane's End Farm, Kentucky, fee $25,000 (live foal). *Todd A. Pletcher, USA* 130

LIBBARD 3 ch.f. Galileo (IRE) 134 – Clouded Leopard (USA) 81 (Danehill (USA) 126) [2015 70p: 12m² 9g³ p12f² 13.1m² p12g³ Sep 22] unfurnished filly: fair maiden: stays 13f: acts on polytrack, soft and good to firm going: in hood last 3 starts: front runner/races prominently: sold 10,000 gns, sent to France. *Roger Charlton* 78

LIBERAL ANGEL (FR) 3 b.f. Librettist (USA) 124 – Angel Voices (IRE) 81 (Tagula (IRE) 116) [2015 70: 8.3s³ 8.3s⁶ 8.3d⁴ 8g³ 7m² 7d* 7d⁴ 7.2g³ 8s³ p8g p7.5g⁴ Dec 16] fair performer: won handicap at Newcastle in August: left K. R. Burke after ninth start: stays 1m: acts on good to firm and good to soft going: usually races close up. *D. de Waele, France* 70

LIBERALITY 3 b.f. Shamardal (USA) 129 – Charity Belle (USA) 107 (Empire Maker (USA) 129) [2015 t9.5g³ 10m² 10.2g² t9.5g³ 10.3g² Sep 12] second foal: half-sister to 1¼m winner Caridadi (by Invincible Spirit): dam 1¼m winner, including Prix de la Nonette: fairly useful maiden: stays 1¼m: acts on tapeta, best turf form on good going: usually races prominently. *John Gosden* 81

LIBERTY JACK (IRE) 5 b.g. Sakhee (USA) 136 – Azeema (IRE) 82 (Averti (IRE) 117) [2015 94: 6m 6m 7m* 7g⁵ 7g³ p7g⁵ p7g 7d* Sep 27] workmanlike gelding: fairly useful handicapper: won at Epsom in July and September (by neck from Gold Hunter): stays 1m: acts on polytrack, good to firm and good to soft going: usually wears headgear. *Jim Boyle* 91

LIBERTY RED (GER) 4 b.g. Dubawi (IRE) 129 – Late Night (GER) (Groom Dancer (USA) 128) [2015 89: 9.8v⁴ 9.8d⁴ 10g* 12f⁵ 12g⁴ 14.1m⁴ 12.8m⁴ t12.2f Oct 17] compact gelding: fairly useful handicapper: won at Pontefract (by ¾ length from Chadic) in June: stays 13f: acts on polytrack and good to firm going: sold £17,000, sent to Saudi Arabia. *James Given* 90

LIBERTY RULES (IRE) 3 b.g. Aussie Rules (USA) 123 – Polynesian Queen (IRE) (Statue of Liberty (USA) 115) [2015 –: t9.5g t8.6g 6d⁵ 5.1d⁶ p6g Aug 26] no form. *Malcolm Saunders* –

LIBERTY SKY (IRE) 3 b.f. Rip Van Winkle (IRE) 134 – High Spot 73 (Shirley Heights 130) [2015 67p: 8.5m⁶ 9.8d 8.3d³ 8.3g³ 9.2s⁵ 10d² 9.2d* 9.2m⁵ 10s p10g Nov 25] fair handicapper: won at Hamilton in September: stays 1¼m: acts on good to soft going: often in headgear in 2015: front runner/races prominently. *Richard Fahey* 67

LIBRAN (IRE) 4 b.g. Lawman (FR) 121 – True Crystal (IRE) 94 (Sadler's Wells (USA) 132) [2015 90: 8g 9.9g* 12g* 10m 12f⁴ 12d* 9s⁶ Nov 5] smart handicapper: won at Beverley (by 6 lengths from Next Stop) and York (by length from Pressure Point) in May and at York (dead-heated with Memorial Day) in August: left Alan Swinbank before final outing: stays 1½m: acts on firm and good to soft going: usually races prominently, usually responds generously to pressure. *Chris Waller, Australia* 112

LIBRISA BREEZE 3 gr.g. Mount Nelson 125 – Bruxcalina (FR) (Linamix (FR) 127) [2015 p8f² p10f* 10g⁶ 10.3m⁵ p8g* 8.9s² Oct 10] 60,000Y: first foal: dam, useful French 1¼m winner, half-sister to smart French 9.5f/10.5f winner Baraan: useful performer: won maiden at Lingfield in March and handicap at Kempton (by neck from Commodore) in September: further improvement when second in handicap at York (head behind Arthenus, outbattled) in October: stays 1¼m: acts on polytrack and soft going: often races in rear. *Jeremy Noseda* 102

LICENCE TO TILL (USA) 8 b.g. War Chant (USA) 126 – With A Wink (USA) (Clever Trick (USA)) [2015 87: 9g⁵ 9.2s 7.9d 7.9m 5.9g 7g⁶ t6m Sep 25] well-made gelding: fairly useful handicapper in 2014, out of sorts in 2015: stays 9.5f: acts on polytrack, good to firm and heavy going: tried in cheekpieces. *Alan Berry* –

LIDO LADY (IRE) 2 b.f. (Mar 13) Danehill Dancer (IRE) 117 – Showbiz (IRE) 89 **75** (Sadler's Wells (USA) 132) [2015 6g* 6m⁵ 7m Jul 30] €30,000, 26,000Y: rather unfurnished filly: sixth foal: sister to 3 winners, including 5f/6f winner Harwoods Star and useful 6f (at 2 yrs)/1m (in USA) winner Conniption: dam, 2-y-o 7f winner, half-sister to smart Scandinavian 6f-1m winner Hanzano: fair performer: best effort when winning maiden at Goodwood (by 1¾ lengths from Star Jeanie) in June: should stay 7f. *Mark Johnston*

LIEUTENANT GENERAL (IRE) 2 b.c. (Jan 23) Fastnet Rock (AUS) 127 – Lady **95** Lupus (IRE) 105 (High Chaparral (IRE) 132) [2015 7m² 6m³ 7g³ 7g* 7d 6g 7d⁴ Oct 24] second foal: dam, 2-y-o 1m winner and third in Irish Oaks, half-sister to smart winner up to 1m Furner's Green: useful performer: won maiden at Leopardstown in August: back to form when fourth of 7 to Blue de Vega in Killavullan Stakes at Leopardstown final start: likely to stay 1m: acts on good to firm and good to soft going: blinkered last 3 starts, in tongue tie last 4: has hinted at temperament. *Aidan O'Brien, Ireland*

LIFE KNOWLEDGE (IRE) 3 ch.g. Thewayyouare (USA) 117 – Rosa Bellini (IRE) **69** (Rossini (USA) 118) [2015 –: 8g³ 10g⁴ 8.3g⁶ 10m³ 9.8m³ 9.2d² 8.5d Sep 22] fair maiden: stays 1¼m: acts on good to firm and good to soft going: tried in cheekpieces in 2015. *Patrick Holmes*

LIFE LESS ORDINARY (IRE) 3 b.g. Thewayyouare (USA) 117 – Dont Cross Tina **85** (IRE) 76 (Cape Cross (IRE) 129) [2015 78p: 11.6f* 10.4g⁶ 12m 10.2m² 10g Aug 21] big, lengthy gelding: fairly useful handicapper: won at Windsor in May: stays 11.5f: acts on tapeta and firm going: often races in rear. *Jamie Osborne*

LIFE OF FAME 2 b.f. (Jan 28) Equiano (FR) 127 – Fame Is The Spur 81 (Motivator 131) **67** [2015 5g⁵ 6d³ 6g⁵ 6d Oct 26] 16,000F, £25,000Y: second foal: sister to 2-y-o 5f winner Lightning Stride: dam, 1¼m winner, half-sister to smart winner up to 1¼m Battle of Hastings: fair maiden: stays 6f. *Bryan Smart*

LIGHT AND SHADE 3 b.f. Aqlaam 125 – Tara Moon (Pivotal 124) [2015 79p: 10.3m² **99** 10m 8m* 8.3m² t8.6g³ 8g* 8g 8d Oct 31] useful handicapper: won at Haydock in June and Ascot (by 3½ lengths from Iconic) in September: stays 10.5f: acts on polytrack and good to firm going: in cheekpieces last 4 starts: usually races towards rear: may not be straightforward. *James Tate*

LIGHT BREAKS (IRE) 3 b.g. Dylan Thomas (IRE) 132 – Anywaysmile (IRE) 87 **74 p** (Indian Ridge 123) [2015 62p: 10g⁴ t12.2g⁴ 11.7f* 11.7f⁴ Jul 1] fair handicapper: won at Bath in June: best effort at 11.5f, should stay further: acts on firm going: in headgear last 3 starts: sold to Nigel Twiston-Davies 16,000 gns: remains with potential. *Sir Mark Prescott Bt*

LIGHT FROM MARS 10 gr.g. Fantastic Light (USA) 134 – Hylandra (USA) (Bering **81** 136) [2015 93: t6g⁵ 16f⁴ p6m² p6m t7.1m³ p7f 6m⁴ 6m 6g 6g p6g² 6.1m³ t7.1g p6g³ p7m⁵ **a88** t5.1m⁴ t5.1f⁶ Dec 21] good-topped gelding: fairly useful handicapper: stays 8.5f: acts on polytrack, tapeta, good to firm and good to soft going: sometimes wears cheekpieces: tried in tongue tie prior to 2015. *Ronald Harris*

LIGHT MUSIC 2 b.f. (Mar 1) Elusive Quality (USA) – Medley 102 (Danehill Dancer **101 p** (IRE) 117) [2015 7s² 7s* 7v* Oct 24] third foal: sister to useful 1m winner Sea Shanty: dam, 6f (at 2 yrs) to 1m (in USA) winner, half-sister to smart performer up to 8.5f in USA Green Line: useful form when winning maiden at Leicester (by 14 lengths from Permera) and listed race at Newbury (by neck from Make Fast, leading on bridle 2f out), both in October: raced only at 7f: should do better still. *William Haggas*

LIGHTNING CHARLIE 3 b.g. Myboycharlie (IRE) 118 – Lighted Way 66 (Kris 135) **82** [2015 81p: 6g⁴ 7g⁴ 6g⁵ 5.7s² 6s⁶ p6g⁴ Oct 6] close-coupled gelding: fairly useful handicapper: stays 6f: acts on polytrack and soft going: often leads. *Amanda Perrett*

LIGHTNING MOON (IRE) 4 b.c. Shamardal (USA) 129 – Catch The Moon (IRE) **112** (Peintre Celebre (USA) 137) [2015 122p: 6g 7d 6d 6v² Nov 7] good-topped colt: smart performer: not quite at best and failed to win in 2015, though looked unlucky when head second to Jack Dexter in listed race at Doncaster final start (tongue tied first time), held up and left with too much to do: stays 6f: acts on soft going: tried in tongue tie in 2015. *Ed Walker*

LIGHTNING SPEAR 4 ch.c. Pivotal 124 – Atlantic Destiny (IRE) 99 (Royal Academy **119** (USA) 130) [2015 100p: p8m* 8m* 8f² 8d⁴ 8g³ 10d Oct 17] rangy colt: smart performer: won handicaps at Lingfield (by ½ length from Sacred Act) in April and Salisbury (by 2 lengths from Saigon City) in June: better form when second in Summer Mile Stakes at

Ascot (1½ lengths behind Arod) in July and fourth in Prix Jacques le Marois at Deauville (3 lengths fourth to Esoterique) in August: stays 8.5f: acts on polytrack, firm and good to soft going: often races towards rear: joined David Simcock. *Olly Stevens*

LIGHTNING SPREE (IRE) 3 gr.g. Jeremy (USA) 122 – Spree (IRE) 93 (Dansili 127) **74**
[2015 –p: f7g² 6m⁵ 7.5g 9.2s² 8g⁶ 8g 8.3m Sep 28] fair maiden: best effort at 9f: acts on fibresand and soft going: often starts slowly, often races towards rear: temperament under suspicion. *Kevin Ryan*

LIGHTNING STEPS 3 b.g. Champs Elysees 124 – Fairy Steps (Rainbow Quest (USA) **50**
134) [2015 11.9d 12d 8g⁶ 9.9g 14.1s⁴ Sep 15] modest maiden: best effort at 1¾m: acts on soft going: usually races towards rear. *Declan Carroll*

LIGHTNING THUNDER 4 b.f. Dutch Art 126 – Sweet Coincidence 69 (Mujahid **97**
(USA) 125) [2015 111: 7s 8f⁶ 7g⁶ 9.9m Aug 12] strong filly: useful performer: not at best in 2015: stays 1m: acts on soft and good to firm going: tried in blinkers: sold 420,000 gns in December. *Olly Stevens*

LIGHT OF ASIA (IRE) 4 b.g. Oratorio (IRE) 128 – Lucy Cavendish (USA) (Elusive **82**
Quality (USA)) [2015 82: 12d³ 11.6g⁴ 10.1d* 11.9d³ 12m² 10g⁶ 12d⁵ 12g⁴ Sep 19] tall, attractive gelding: fairly useful handicapper: won at Newcastle in May: stays 1½m: acts on good to firm and good to soft going: blinkered once in 2014: sold 28,000 gns, sent to Saudi Arabia. *Alan Swinbank*

LIGHT OF LOVE 3 b.f. Dylan Thomas (IRE) 132 – May Light 62 (Midyan (USA) 124) **67**
[2015 –p: 8.3g 7g⁶ 8g³ 10m⁵ p12g 10g³ 10m 7.1s 8f² 8v Oct 6] rather unfurnished filly: fair maiden: stays 1¼m: acts on firm going: sometimes slowly away, often races in rear. *Henry Candy*

LIGHT OF THE WORLD (IRE) 3 b.f. Fastnet Rock (AUS) 127 – Gassal 69 (Oasis **57**
Dream 129) [2015 66: p10f⁶ t9.5f⁶ Jan 29] modest maiden: stays 9.5f: acts on polytrack and tapeta: often races prominently: sent to Greece. *Jamie Osborne*

LIGHT ROSE (IRE) 5 b.m. Cape Cross (IRE) 129 – Laureldean Lady (IRE) (Statue of **73**
Liberty (USA) 115) [2015 75: t6g⁴ p7f² p8g p7f⁴ p8g³ p7g* p7g² 7s 7g t7.1g⁴ t7.1m⁵ t7.1f³ t7.1f p7g⁵ Dec 2] rather leggy mare: fair handicapper: won at Lingfield in April: stays 1¼m: acts on polytrack, tapeta, soft and good to firm going: tried in headgear: front runner/races prominently. *Jeremy Gask*

LIGHTSCAMERACTION (IRE) 3 ch.g. Pastoral Pursuits 127 – Silca Boo 99 (Efisio **100 +**
120) [2015 93: p5g⁴ p5m⁴ t6f⁴ p5f* 6f 5m 5m⁶ 5g p6m p5g* Dec 2] smart performer: won **a117**
AW 3YO Sprint Championships Stakes at Lingfield (by neck from Blue Aegean) in April and handicap on same course (by 1¾ lengths from Brother Tiger) in December: raced at 5f/6f: acts on polytrack and good to firm going: sometimes in headgear in 2015: tried in tongue tie in 2015. *Gay Kelleway*

LIGHTSOME 2 b.f. (Mar 26) Makfi 130 – Aunty Mary 82 (Common Grounds 118) [2015 **81**
7.4v² 8s⁴ 8.3d⁴ p7g² p7g² t7.1m Dec 18] sister to 2-y-o 6f winner Mary McPhee and half-sister to several winners, including 2-y-o 5f/6f winner Mary's Daughter (by Royal Applause) and winner up to 1¼m Scrutiny (2-y-o 6.5f winner, by Aqlaam): dam, 2-y-o 5f winner, half-sister to 1000 Guineas winner Attraction: fairly useful maiden: worth a try at 5f/6f: acts on polytrack and good to soft going: front runner/races prominently. *Clive Cox*

LIGHTSTREAM (IRE) 3 b.f. Shamardal (USA) 129 – Lurina (IRE) 111 (Lure (USA) **69 p**
131) [2015 9.9d⁵ May 14] half-sister to several winners, including smart winner up to 1½m Centennial (2-y-o 1m winner, by Dalakhani) and useful 1¼m winner Siren's Song (by Azamour): dam, 7f winner, half-sister to high-class 1¼m-1½m performer Croco Rouge: 6/1, some encouragement when fifth in maiden at Salisbury (6½ lengths behind Bateel) in May: should do better. *John Gosden*

LIGHT THE CITY (IRE) 8 b.g. Fantastic Light (USA) 134 – Marine City (JPN) 77 **–**
(Carnegie (IRE) 129) [2015 63: f14s Mar 25] fair handicapper at best: stays 2m: acts on polytrack, fibresand, good to firm and heavy going: tried in blinkers prior to 2015. *Ruth Carr*

LIGHT UP LIFE (IRE) 2 b.g. (Mar 9) Acclamation 118 – Golden Destiny (IRE) 116 **60**
(Captain Rio 122) [2015 5d 6.1m⁶ 5g⁶ 8g Aug 21] lengthy gelding: modest maiden: stays 6f. *Clive Cox*

LIGHT UP OUR WORLD (IRE) 2 b.f. (Feb 12) Zoffany (IRE) 121 – Shine Like A **97**
Star 60 (Fantastic Light (USA) 134) [2015 7g² 7g* 7s³ 8m⁴ 7g³ 7g Oct 9] rather unfurnished filly: fourth foal: half-sister to 3 winners, including useful 2-y-o 6f/7f winner Light Up My Life (by Zamindar) and 13f winner The Kid (by High Chaparral): dam, maiden (best effort at 1¼m), half-sister to Coronation Stakes winner Fallen For You: useful performer: won

maiden at Newmarket in August: much better form after, third in Prestige Stakes at Goodwood (1½ lengths behind Hawksmoor) and in nursery at Newmarket (3½ lengths behind Drifting Spirit): stays 1m: acts on soft and good to firm going: usually races close up. *Richard Hannon*

LIGHT WAVE (IRE) 3 b.c. Echo of Light 125 – Meynell 78 (Sakhee (USA) 136) [2015 **85** t8.6f⁵ p10g² p10g³ p12g⁴ 10g* t9.5m p10g² Oct 27] fourth foal: half-brother to a winner in Italy by Iffraaj: dam, maiden (placed at 1m), half-sister to smart winner up to 1m Ahla Wasahl: fairly useful handicapper: won at Windsor in September: stays 1¼m: acts on polytrack: usually races close up. *James Tate*

LIKE A DIAMOND (IRE) 5 b.g. Antonius Pius (USA) 123 – Silk Law (IRE) 80 **–** (Barathea (IRE) 127) [2015 89: f8sᵖᵘ Mar 25] handicapper, fairly useful at best: pulled up only outing in 2015: stays 1½m: acts on polytrack: tried in hood. *Heather Dalton*

LIKE A PRAYER 4 b.g. Compton Place 125 – Floating (Oasis Dream 129) [2015 73: 10s **67** 8g² 7d p8g 8.7m 8m⁴ p8d p8g 7d⁴ 8s² 7.2g² 7.2g Oct 8] sturdy gelding: fair handicapper: **a58** stays 8.5f: acts on polytrack, tapeta, soft and good to firm going: sometimes in headgear in 2015: usually races close up. *Garvan Donnelly, Ireland*

LIKELY (GER) 3 ch.f. Exceed And Excel (AUS) 126 – La Pilaya (GER) (Pivotal 124) **–** [2015 103p: 5m Jun 13] lengthy filly: useful form when successful sole start at 2 yrs, then reportedly suffered hairline fracture of pelvis: well held in listed race at Sandown on return: raced only at 5f. *David Barron*

LIKE NO OTHER 2 b.c. (Feb 26) Approve (IRE) 112 – Blue Beacon 68 (Fantastic Light **73** (USA) 134) [2015 6.1v⁴ t7.1f⁶ p8f⁵ t8.6f² Dec 14] fair maiden: will be suited by 1¼m: in tongue tie last 2 starts. *William Haggas*

LILBOURNE PRINCE (IRE) 2 b.g. (Apr 19) Lilbourne Lad (IRE) 111 – Defensive **81** Boast (USA) (El Gran Senor (USA) 136) [2015 6m 6g* 8s⁵ 7s⁴ 8.3g⁵ p8g t8.6m² Dec 26] €45,000F, £30,000 2-y-o: half-brother to 3 winners in USA: dam, US 1m winner, half-sister to high-class sprinter Les Arcs: fairly useful performer: won maiden at Ffos Las in July: stays 8.5f: acts on tapeta and soft going: often races towards rear. *David Evans*

LILIAN BAYLIS (IRE) 3 b.f. Shamardal (USA) 129 – Kiyra Wells (IRE) 85 (Sadler's **83 p** Wells (USA) 132) [2015 –p: 8.3s³ 8m³ 10d* 12g² 9.9s² Aug 23] fairly useful handicapper: won at Pontefract (apprentice) in July: worth another try at 1½m: acts on soft going: remains with potential. *Luca Cumani*

LILIARGH (IRE) 6 b.m. Acclamation 118 – Discover Roma (IRE) (Rock of Gibraltar **53** (IRE) 133) [2015 58: t7.1g 7d⁵ 7m Aug 5] modest handicapper: stays 1m: acts on heavy going: sometimes wears headgear: often races in rear. *Ben Haslam*

LILLY BONBON (IRE) 2 ch.f. (May 15) Zoffany (IRE) 121 – Simonda 95 (Singspiel **60** (IRE) 133) [2015 p6g³ 7v⁶ 7d⁴ p7g t9.5f Dec 11] €5,000F, €5,000Y, £5,500 2-y-o: sixth foal: half-sister to 8.5f-1¼m winner Jane Lachatte (by Doyen) and 2-y-o 7f winner Emperor Bob (by Big Bad Bob): dam, 1¼m-11.6f winner, half-sister to useful French winner up to 1½m Lady's Purse: modest maiden: left Ronald Thompson after first start: stays 7f: acts on heavy going. *Gary Moore*

LILLY VEGA (IRE) 2 ch.f. (Mar 26) Lope de Vega (IRE) 125 – Salpiglossis (GER) **74** (Monsun (GER) 124) [2015 7g 7vᵘʳ p8f² p8g* Nov 26] 13,000F, 30,000Y: workmanlike filly: half-sister to several winners in Italy: dam, Italian maiden, half-sister to useful Italian 7.5f-9f winner Sadowa: fair performer: won maiden at Chelmsford in November: stays 1m. *K. R. Burke*

LILOZZA (IRE) 2 ro.f. (Apr 1) Lilbourne Lad (IRE) 111 – Vanozza (FR) (Dylan Thomas **–** (IRE) 132) [2015 6d⁶ 6d 6d Oct 26] €20,000F: good-bodied filly: first foal: dam once-raced half-sister to very smart French miler Vahorimix: no form. *Tim Easterby*

LIL ROCKERFELLER (USA) 4 ch.g. Hard Spun (USA) 124 – Layoune (USA) (Mt **89** Livermore (USA)) [2015 86: 14.1f² May 23] tall gelding: fairly useful handicapper: second at Salisbury in May: stays 1¾m: acts on firm and good to soft going: in cheekpieces sole start in 2015: smart hurdler. *Neil King*

LIL'S JOY (IRE) 2 b.f. (Jan 27) Lilbourne Lad (IRE) 111 – Eman's Joy 68 (Lion Cavern **101** (USA) 117) [2015 p5g⁴ 5.1d² 5m⁶ 5g⁵ 5g* 5m* 5g² 5d² Oct 9] closely related to winners around 1m Exalted and Joyful Sound (both by Acclamation) and half-sister to 3 winners, including useful 2-y-o 7f/1m winner Blitzkrieg (by Barathea): dam 6f winner: useful performer: left Noel Quinlan after first start: won nursery at Lingfield in July and minor event at Musselburgh in August: better form when second in Prix d'Arenberg at

Longchamp (1¼ lengths behind Yakaba) and listed race at Chantilly (neck behind Fine Blend) last 2 starts: raced only at 5f: acts on good to firm and good to soft going: front runner/races prominently. *Giles Bravery*

LIL SOPHELLA (IRE) 6 ch.m. Indian Haven 119 – Discotheque (USA) 73 (Not For **84** Love (USA)) [2015 74: 8.5m⁵ 8g⁴ 8m² 8.3d* 7.6f³ 8.3d* 8m³ 8m 8d² 8.3d² 8d 8m* 7s Oct 9] fairly useful handicapper: won at Hamilton in May (awarded race) and June and Musselburgh in September: stays 8.5f: acts on good to firm and good to soft going: tried in hood prior to 2015. *Patrick Holmes*

LILVANITA (IRE) 2 b.f. (Mar 31) Lilbourne Lad (IRE) 111 – Miss Vanita (IRE) (Refuse **71** To Bend (IRE) 128) [2015 5g t5.1g² t6g⁶ Jul 23] €5,500Y, £9,000 2-y-o: third foal: dam unraced half-sister to 2000 Guineas winner Island Sands: fair maiden: best effort when second at Wolverhampton (½ length behind Encantar) in July, hampered: tried in hood. *Brian Ellison*

LILY ASH (IRE) 2 b.f. (Apr 22) Lilbourne Lad (IRE) 111 – Ashdali (IRE) (Grand Lodge **63** (USA) 125) [2015 t6g⁵ p6g⁵ 7.1f Nov 20] €24,000F: fourth foal: half-sister to 1m winner Wot A Shot (by Refuse To Bend): dam unraced half-sister to dam of Derby/Arc winner Sinndar: modest form in maidens. *Mike Murphy*

LILY EDGE 6 b.m. Byron 117 – Flaming Spirt 78 (Blushing Flame (USA) 109) [2015 68: **62** p12g p10g p12f p10m² p10g p10g⁴ 11.6g³ 11.5g⁵ p10f p10g 11.6m 10m⁴ p12g⁶ 9.9d⁶ p10f p12g⁴ p12g p12g⁴ p10g Dec 30] modest handicapper: stays 1½m: acts on polytrack and good to firm going: often wears headgear: often races prominently. *John Bridger*

LILY MORETON (IRE) 3 b.f. Kodiac 112 – Hollow Haze (USA) 90 (Woodman (USA) **67** 126) [2015 70: 6g 5m³ 6m⁵ 5g³ 5g⁵ 5d⁵ Aug 14] fair maiden: best form at 5f: acts on soft and good to firm going: tried in headgear. *Noel Wilson*

LILY RULES (IRE) 4 br.f. Aussie Rules (USA) 123 – Causeway Charm (USA) 60 **88** (Giant's Causeway (USA) 132) [2015 101: 10.4m 10.2m 10g 10.4d 10.3v Nov 7] leggy, close-coupled filly: fairly useful performer: stays 1½m: acts on good to firm and good to soft going: sometimes in headgear in 2015: often races towards rear. *Tony Coyle*

LILY TRICKS 2 b.f. (Mar 8) Authorized (IRE) 133 – Trick of Ace (USA) (Clever Trick **68** (USA)) [2015 8.3g⁵ 8.3g Oct 20] sister to 1½m winner Ace of Valhalla and half-sister to 3 winners, including useful 1¼m-1¾m winner Trick Or Treat (by Lomitas): dam US 1m/8.5f winner: better effort when fifth in maiden at Nottingham (2½ lengths behind Stoney Broke) in September. *Marco Botti*

LIMATO (IRE) 3 b.g. Tagula (IRE) 116 – Come April 77 (Singspiel (IRE) 133) **126** [2015 121p: 6f* 6d² 6f² 7d* 7m² Oct 4]

There may have been no Group 1 success for connections of Limato to celebrate in 2015 but the gelding still more than played his part in what was a fine campaign overall for the Henry Candy yard (more details of which can be found in the essay on Twilight Son). Limato finished in the first two on all five of his starts, which included two wins in pattern company as well as good efforts in defeat behind Muhaarar in the Commonwealth Cup at Royal Ascot and Make Believe in the Prix de la Foret at Longchamp. The Candy yard have plenty to look forward to in 2016 with Limato and Twilight Son, who landed the Sprint Cup at Haydock as well as finishing a good second to champion sprinter Muhaarar in the British Champions Sprint Stakes. It is unlikely the pair will meet, certainly in the first half of the season, with connections of Limato reportedly keen on stepping him up to a mile.

Limato ended 2014 as Timeform's joint top-rated two-year-old (with the filly Tiggy Wiggy) after an unbeaten four-race campaign, which included an impressive success in Redcar's richly-endowed Two-Year-Old Trophy (which carries listed status). He looked an obvious contender for the inaugural Commonwealth Cup at Royal Ascot—as a gelding he was barred from the classics and could not have run in the Two Thousand Guineas—and he started the season over the course and distance in the Group 3 Merriebelle Stable Pavilion Stakes at Ascot in late-April. Limato started an uneasy favourite after his trainer voiced concerns in the build-up ('he's not quite as brilliant on the gallops as he was last year') but he won readily by a length and a half and the same from Tendu and Adaay. Limato took a bit of time to warm to his task but was travelling sweetly on the bridle by halfway and stormed clear after being produced to lead entering the final furlong. Limato's Commonwealth Cup credentials took a dent on his next outing, however, when he surprisingly lost his

Saint Gobain Weber Park Stakes, Doncaster—
Limato slams his fourteen rivals with a high-class effort; Markaz (striped cap) finishes second,
ahead of Breton Rock (hidden by runner-up) and Naadirr (white face)

unbeaten record in the Sandy Lane Stakes at Haydock. Limato had every chance but couldn't get past Adaay in the final furlong, going down by a length. The Pavilion Stakes and the Group 2 Sandy Lane were among races upgraded in the latest season as part of the changes to the programme for Europe's top sprinters (the Sandy Lane making the leap from listed status) with the aim of providing a clear programme of races for good-class three-year-old sprinters in the early months of the turf season before the Commonwealth Cup. Connections of Limato were among those who embraced the venture (Candy stated later in the year that 'we started him off in April to get him into the new sprint scheme'), though, ironically, the first winner of the Commonwealth Cup was a Guineas contender dropping back in trip. Limato was beaten nearly four lengths by Muhaarar at Royal Ascot but emerged with plenty of credit all the same, especially as he and third-placed Anthem Alexander raced away from the main pace, which turned out to be towards the far side.

After missing intended engagements in the Lennox Stakes and Hungerford Stakes because of concerns over soft ground (among the six-day declarations for the latter but withdrawn the day before the race), Limato eventually made the step up to seven furlongs in the Saint Gobain Weber Park Stakes on the St Leger card at Doncaster in mid-September. He was sent off 9/2 favourite ahead of another three-year-old, 11/2-shot Home of The Brave, who had finished first past the post in the Minstrel Stakes on his previous outing (he was stripped of that success much later in the year having failed a post-race drugs test). The Godolphin-owned pair Lightning Moon, making only the second appearance of a disjointed campaign, and Safety Check, a close third in the Lennox on his previous outing, came next in the betting ahead of Ivawood, third in both the Two Thousand Guineas and Irish equivalent before going off the boil. They were the only ones at single-figure odds in a field of fifteen. What looked a competitive Group 2 was turned into anything but as Limato produced a high-class effort to slam his rivals. After travelling well held up, he stormed clear over the final furlong and had almost four lengths to spare over runner-up Markaz, with a further length and a quarter back to Breton Rock. Limato achieved a timefigure of 1.01 fast (equivalent to a timerating of 125) in the Park Stakes, a performance on the clock that was bettered only by Muhaarar, Golden Horn and Mecca's Angel in the latest season. Breton Rock franked the form when beaten a neck by Cable Bay in the Challenge Stakes at Newmarket four weeks later. Limato had also seemed set to end his campaign in the Challenge but he concluded it instead stepped back to Group 1 company in the Prix de la Foret on Arc day at Longchamp. Limato was deemed by some to be an unlucky loser after going down by a length and a quarter to the Poule d'Essai des Poulains winner Make Believe in a strongly-run Foret. Although he made up significant late ground from a poor position under Ryan Moore, however, his troubles early in the race were of his own making (he was soon pushed along in rear) and it is hard to be dogmatic about whether he would have beaten the winner (who travelled easily throughout) had he not become detached. On form, it was a creditable effort anyway, not far off the performance that Limato gave at Doncaster.

	Tagula (IRE) (b 1993)	Taufan (b 1977)	Stop The Music Stolen Date
Limato (IRE) (b.g. 2012)		Twin Island (ch 1989)	Standaan Jolly Widow
	Come April (b 2004)	Singspiel (b 1992)	In The Wings Glorious Song
		So Admirable (b 1998)	Suave Dancer Sumoto

As stated in *Racehorses of 2014*, Limato isn't bred to be simply a sprinter, which was borne out by events in the latest season when he showed that he clearly stays seven furlongs well. In the Foret in particular, Limato left the impression that a mile will be within his range as a four-year-old, an avenue which his trainer is seemingly keen to explore ('It looks as though he wants a mile now' was among the trainer's comments after the race). Limato's pedigree was outlined in last year's Annual and there are only a couple of minor updates. His dam Come April's third foal (Limato is the second) Limonata (by Bushranger) didn't achieve much for the same connections on her racecourse debut in a juvenile maiden at Windsor in September, shaping as if needing the run. Come April also has a yearling filly by Arcano and a colt foal by the same sire, the latter sold for 60,000 guineas at the December Sales. Despite connections' concerns over softish ground—he was also withdrawn from

Mr Paul G. Jacob's "Limato"

the Mill Reef as a juvenile because it was soft—his performance in the Park Stakes was achieved on going that was good to soft by Timeform's reckoning. He has also won on firm ground and polytrack. A compact sort in appearance, Limato didn't grow much from two to three but clearly trained on well. He should win more good races as a four-year-old, when adding a Group 1 to his tally is certainly within his compass. *Henry Candy*

LIME AND LEMON (IRE) 2 b.f. (Feb 2) Makfi 130 – Nimboo (USA) (Lemon Drop – Kid (USA) 131) [2015 8v Oct 24] €40,000Y: first foal: dam unraced half-sister to very smart 7f/1m performer Lord Shanakill and Fillies' Mile winner Together Forever: 8/1, ninth of 10 in maiden at Newbury (11 lengths behind Chastushka), never a threat. *Charles Hills*

LIMERICK LORD (IRE) 3 b.g. Lord Shanakill (USA) 121 – Hollow Green (IRE) 90 **75** (Beat Hollow 126) [2015 54p: p7m p/f³ p5g* p7f³ p8m⁵ 7m⁵ 5m⁴ t6g³ 5m³ 6m⁵ t6g⁴ 5f⁵ p6f⁴ f8g* Dec 12] neat gelding: fair performer: won maiden at Lingfield in February and handicap at Southwell in December: left Stuart Williams after sixth start: stays 1m: acts on polytrack, fibresand, tapeta and good to firm going: tried in headgear in 2015: usually races prominently. *Julia Feilden*

LIMONATA (IRE) 2 b.f. (Jan 28) Bushranger (IRE) 119 – Come April 77 (Singspiel – p (IRE) 133) [2015 6g Sep 7] 90,000Y: third foal: half-sister to high-class winner up to 7f Limato (2-y-o 6f winner, by Tagula): dam 1¼m winner: 10/1, eighth of 10 in maiden at Windsor (7¾ lengths behind Sunflower), weakening 2f out: should do better in time. *Henry Candy*

LINCOLN (IRE) 4 b.g. Clodovil (IRE) 116 – Gilt Linked 85 (Compton Place 125) [2015 **111** 102: 8d 7g³ 7m² 8f 7m³ 7d 8m 7d 7s 8g Sep 19] tall gelding: smart handicapper: easily best efforts of 2015 when second in Victoria Cup at Ascot (½ length behind Speculative Bid) in May and third in Criterion Stakes at Newmarket (2½ lengths behind Markaz) in June: stays 7.5f: acts on polytrack, soft and good to firm going: usually races towards rear. *Mick Channon*

LINCOLN ROCKS 2 b.f. (Feb 12) Rock of Gibraltar (IRE) 133 – Redskin Dancer (IRE) – 90 (Namid 128) [2015 7m 8.1g Aug 2] £20,000Y, resold £12,500Y: first foal: dam, 2-y-o 6f winner, sister to smart 7f/1m winner Redstone Dancer: well held in 2 maidens. *Alan McCabe*

LINDART (ITY) 4 ch.g. Dutch Art 126 – Linda Surena (ARG) (Southern Halo (USA)) **54 §** [2015 79: p10g⁵ p8g⁴ t7.1m t9.5g* t9.5g 10m⁴ 10m p12g 13.1m 12.1s Jul 24] strong **a64 §** gelding: modest performer: won seller at Wolverhampton in March: left Richard Hannon after second start, Sylvester Kirk after fourth, John Spearing after fifth: stays 1¼m: acts on polytrack, tapeta, firm and good to soft going: usually wears blinkers: often races towards rear, often races lazily: unreliable. *John Flint*

LINDSAY'S DREAM 9 b.m. Montjeu (IRE) 137 – Lady Lindsay (IRE) 105 (Danehill **56** Dancer (IRE) 117) [2015 9.9v⁴ 9.9s² 9.9m⁶ 9.9s⁶ Oct 15] modest maiden: stays 11.5f: acts on firm and soft going: sometimes wears cheekpieces. *Zoe Davison*

LINEMAN 5 b.g. Rail Link 132 – Shamana (USA) (Woodman (USA) 126) [2015 82: **71** t13.9g² t12.2g t16.5g 17.2f⁶ Apr 17] fair handicapper: left Andrew Hollinshead after first start: stays 16.5f: acts on polytrack, tapeta and good to firm going: sometimes wears headgear: tried in tongue tie in 2015. *Sarah Hollinshead*

LINE OF REASON (IRE) 5 br.g. Kheleyf (USA) 116 – Miss Party Line (USA) (Phone **118** Trick (USA)) [2015 111: 5g 6g⁶ 5g⁶ 6g 5g 5f* 6m³ 5m⁴ 5m⁴ 5g 5g² 5d 5d⁵ Sep 22] compact gelding: smart performer: won listed race at Cork (by 2¼ lengths from Ardhoomey) in June: good second in similar event at Beverley (neck behind Maarek) in August: stays 6.5f: acts on polytrack and firm going: tried in cheekpieces prior to 2015. *Paul Midgley*

L'INGANNO FELICE (FR) 5 br.g. Librettist (USA) 124 – Final Overture (FR) 57 **79** (Rossini (USA) 118) [2015 84: f12g² 11.9d 10.1m* 9.8m³ 10.2g⁶ 10g 10d⁵ t9.5f Nov 13] big gelding: fair handicapper: won at Newcastle in June: left Iain Jardine after first start: likely to prove best up to 1½m: acts on fibresand, tapeta, good to firm and heavy going: often wears hood. *John Mackie*

L'INGENUE 3 b.f. New Approach (IRE) 132 – Green Room (FR) 108 (In The Wings 128) **90** [2015 75p: 11.5d* 12.3g⁵ 11.6d³ 14.1g Aug 13] rather leggy filly: fairly useful performer: won maiden at Lingfield in May: third in handicap at Windsor in July: stays 11.5f: acts on good to soft going. *Ralph Beckett*

LINGER (IRE) 2 b.c. (Feb 19) Cape Cross (IRE) 129 – Await So (Sadler's Wells (USA) **74**
132) [2015 7.5m 7s p8g⁴ Oct 27] fair maiden: best effort when fourth at Lingfield (10
lengths behind Von Blucher), having run of race. *Mark Johnston*

LINGFIELD LASS 2 b.f. (Feb 28) Mullionmileanhour (IRE) 116 – Hannah's Dream **45**
(IRE) 69 (King's Best (USA) 132) [2015 p5g⁴ p5g⁵ 6d⁶ 6g⁶ p7g p8g p7g Oct 29] smallish,
plain filly: fourth foal: half-sister to 2-y-o 1m winner Excel Best (by Exceed And Excel):
dam 1¼m-1½m winner in Scandinavia: poor maiden: stays 6f: acts on polytrack and good
to soft going: usually races towards rear. *John Best*

LINGUINE (FR) 5 ch.g. Linngari (IRE) 124 – Amerissage (USA) (Rahy (USA) 115) **–**
[2015 98: p15.8g Dec 28] good-topped gelding: useful handicapper: in cheekpieces, well
held only outing in 2015: stays 14.5f: acts on any turf going: tried in tongue tie: usually
leads. *Seamus Durack*

LINGUIST (FR) 2 ch.g. (Apr 22) Linngari (IRE) 124 – Western Bowl (USA) (Gone West **75**
(USA)) [2015 7g⁵ 7.6g p8f⁴ 8.9g⁶ Oct 1] fair maiden: best effort when fourth at Chelmsford.
Harry Dunlop

LINGUISTIC (IRE) 2 b.c. (Jan 16) Lope de Vega (IRE) 125 – Dazzle Dancer (IRE) 84 **98 p**
(Montjeu (IRE) 137) [2015 8m² 8g² Sep 24] 650,000Y: second foal: dam, 1½m winner
who stayed 1¾m, half-sister to useful 9f/1¼m winner Lunduv out of smart French winner
up to 1½m Another Dancer: useful form when second in maidens at Doncaster (3¾ lengths
behind Very Talented) and Newmarket (2 lengths behind Mustajeer), both in September:
will be well suited by 1¼m+: open to further improvement. *John Gosden*

LINKS BAR MARBELLA (IRE) 2 ch.g. (May 1) Intense Focus (USA) 117 – Silesian **–**
(IRE) (Singspiel (IRE) 133) [2015 6m 7g⁵ 7.1g p7g 7s⁵ 8s Oct 23] tall gelding: no form.
Eric Wheeler

LINKS DRIVE LADY 7 br.m. Striking Ambition 122 – Miskina 67 (Mark of Esteem **94**
(IRE) 137) [2015 100: 6d 7s 6g* 6m 6m⁵ p6g⁶ 6d 6g² 6g³ 6d⁶ p6f 6v⁵ Nov 7] sturdy mare:
fairly useful handicapper: won at Goodwood (by 2¼ lengths from My Call) in June: stays
7f: acts on any turf going: tried in headgear prior to 2015: sometimes slowly away.
Dean Ivory

LINTON (AUS) 9 gr.g. Galileo (IRE) 134 – Heather (NZ) (Centaine (AUS)) [2015 102: **84**
p8m t9.5f³ Jan 16] very smart performer at his best, last in minor events both starts in 2015:
stays 1¼m: acts on polytrack and good to soft going: usually in headgear. *Marco Botti*

LIONS CHARGE (USA) 8 ch.g. Lion Heart (USA) 124 – Fellwaati (USA) (Alydar **70**
(USA)) [2015 66: t8.6g 12g⁵ t8.6f² t9.5f* p12g* Dec 2] fair performer: won minor event
at Wolverhampton in November and handicap at Kempton in December: stays 1½m: acts
on polytrack and tapeta: tried in headgear: often wears tongue tie. *Neil Mulholland*

LIPSTICKANDPOWDER (IRE) 3 gr.f. Mastercraftsman (IRE) 129 – Raphimix (FR) **–**
(Linamix (FR) 127) [2015 51: f8s f8s Feb 3] maiden: no form in 2015: stays 8.5f: acts on
tapeta, heavy turf form on good to firm going: usually in hood prior to 2015. *William Jarvis*

LISALA (FR) 2 b.f. (Mar 19) Siyouni (FR) 122 – Lilac Charm (IRE) (Marju (IRE) 127) **56**
[2015 p8g Dec 15] €33,000Y: fifth foal: half-sister to French 1½m winner Luminosite (by
Motivator) and French 7.5f-9.5f winner Lagoa (by Dark Angel): dam unraced half-sister to
very smart/ungenuine 1m-11f winner Tam Lin: 66/1 and wearing hood, seventh in maiden
at Kempton (7¼ lengths behind Cajoled) on debut. *George Peckham*

LISAMOUR (IRE) 4 b.f. Azamour (IRE) 130 – Lisa de La Condra (IRE) 56 (Galileo **87**
(IRE) 134) [2015 85: 10.2s³ 10.3g⁶ 9.9m 8d⁵ 10.3m⁶ p12g³ p12g t9.5f Nov 10] fairly useful **a78**
handicapper: stays 1½m: acts on polytrack, good to firm and heavy going: tried in headgear:
usually races prominently. *Paul Cole*

LITIGANT 7 b.g. Sinndar (IRE) 134 – Jomana (IRE) 113 (Darshaan 133) [2015 110: **121**
14g* 16d 12v* Nov 7]
     The tannoy announcement after the Ebor Handicap that the jockeys had
'weighed in' was followed not long afterwards by another one—'The Jackpot has
not been won.' Not too many York racegoers, or off-course punters, could claim to
have known much about the winning horse or his trainer, let alone claim to have
had a winning bet. Seven-year-old Litigant had only seven career starts behind him
and was having his first outing for small-scale Lambourn trainer Joseph Tuite after
an absence of four hundred and ninety-two days. He had scraped into Europe's
richest handicap at the foot of the weights with the Ascot Stakes winner Clondaw
Warrior, the pair of them on a BHA mark of 99 (Clondaw Warrior squeezing in
by virtue of a 4-lb penalty after another big handicap win at the Galway Festival).

Betfred Ebor (Heritage Handicap), York—a remarkable training performance from Joseph Tuite as Litigant makes a successful debut for his small yard in the most valuable handicap of the season after a 492-day absence; Irish raider Wicklow Brave (behind winner), Suegioo (left) and Toe The Line (right) complete the frame

The Betfred Ebor was hotly contested as usual, with the overall quality of the field probably as high as it has ever been, indicated by the fact that the only three-year-old in the line-up Fields of Athenry, who came a good fifth, went on to finish a very creditable third in the St Leger. Litigant's most recent racecourse appearance had been on Good Friday in April 2014 when winning the inaugural All-Weather Marathon Championship Stakes for Seamus Durack on the polytrack at Lingfield. That was only his fourth start in two years, and before joining Durack he had been off the course altogether for two and a half years, since winning twice at Maisons-Laffitte (ten and a half furlongs and a mile and three quarters) for Andre Fabre as a three-year-old. Litigant carried the colours of Sheikh Mohammed in those days but he was weeded out by Darley at the Doncaster January Sales as a five-year-old when his present owner acquired him for just £18,500. To say that Joseph Tuite's stable did an excellent job to produce Litigant better than ever to win the Ebor is an understatement, and the horse showed even better form when going on to win the Betfred November Handicap, the final big prize of the turf season, putting up a very smart performance to defy top weight of 9-10. Provided the clearly fragile Litigant can be kept in one piece, he looks like making a significant impact in pattern company in the next season.

Litigant was a 33/1-shot in the Ebor but he travelled well from the start in a strongly-run race and took the lead over a furlong out, after making headway early in the home straight, and he kept going well to win by a length and a half and a neck from Clondaw Warrior's well-fancied stablemate Wicklow Brave and the smart Suegioo (subsequently third in the Doncaster Cup). The run of good form enjoyed by Clondaw Warrior, 5/1 joint favourite with another Irish raider the smart handicapper and recent Galway Hurdle winner Quick Jack, came to an end when he finished down the field. Litigant's trainer, who branched out on his own in 2011 after lengthy spells with Charlie Egerton and Mick Channon, was keen to give the credit to his staff for Litigant's performance, saying that 'the last two months have all been about the Ebor and I've kicked the cat plenty of times as I've walked out of his stable as things have gone wrong … he's been lame so many times, we tried swimming him to get him here but we nearly drowned him!' Both Oisin Murphy, who rode Litigant, and Wicklow Brave's claiming rider Jack Kennedy incurred whip bans (four days and nine days respectively), reflecting the importance of an occasion that Joe Tuite described as 'not your average race, you go into the history books when you win the Ebor'.

The next part of the plan for Litigant involved a tilt at the Prix du Cadran at Longchamp, but connections took him out on the day because of the good to firm going. Rerouted to British Champions' Day, Litigant managed only ninth of thirteen behind Flying Officer in the Long Distance Cup, clearly not in the same form as he

Betfred November Handicap, Doncaster—a second notable handicap success for Litigant who stretches clear of Buonarroti and Esteaming in typically testing conditions for the final turf fixture of the year

had been for the Ebor. He soon banished the memory of that first venture into pattern company with an easy win in the twenty-two-runner November Handicap, run on heavy going on the last day of the turf season. Racing off a handicap mark 7 lb higher than in the Ebor, Litigant was ridden at Doncaster by freelance George Baker (credited with doing a lot of work for the Tuite stable) and the pair cruised home by four and a half lengths from Buonarroti and Hayley Turner. Until the latest season, Doncaster was the scene of the traditional Flat finale but the jockeys' championship had concluded on British Champions' Day at Ascot where Silvestre de Sousa was feted as the new champion. Doncaster did keep up its tradition, though, of crowning the 'Cock of the North' who, in the latest season, was Graham Lee. A presentation was also made, surrounded by her fellow jockeys, to Hayley Turner who retired from the saddle on November Handicap day. Britain's leading female jockey—who had

Mr A. A. Byrne's "Litigant"

received an award as joint champion apprentice on the equivalent day in 2005—rode 761 winners in Britain, including Group 1 wins on Dream Ahead in the July Cup and Margot Did in the Nunthorpe (she also won the Beverly D Stakes on I'm A Dreamer). Turner was the first woman jockey to ride a hundred winners in a calendar year, which she achieved in 2008, but she was said to have become frustrated at her lack of opportunities, her winning total down in the forties in her last two years. She was a member of the all-female team which won the annual Shergar Cup international jockeys' competition at Ascot for the first time in the latest season.

Litigant (b.g. 2008)	Sinndar (IRE) (b 1997)	Grand Lodge (ch 1991)	Chief's Crown
			La Papagena
		Sinntara (b 1989)	Lashkari
			Sidama
	Jomana (IRE) (b 1998)	Darshaan (br 1981)	Shirley Heights
			Delsy
		Kerenza (ch 1993)	Seattle Dancer
			Home Love

The good-topped Litigant was bred by Darley and sired by the Aga Khan's Derby and Arc winner Sinndar, who has been an influence for stamina at stud. On the distaff side, Litigant is out of the Prix Corrida and Prix Exbury winner Jomana who has bred a couple of other minor winners for Darley, including Metternich (by Machiavellian) who won a maiden over nine and a half furlongs at Wolverhampton on his only start for Mark Johnston before being sold to Sweden. Litigant's great grandam Home Love was purchased as an unraced four-year-old in North America for 375,000 dollars (she was a half-sister to the very smart stakes winner Sportin' Life and the good filly Folk Art) and was a success at stud, the best of her winners being the Mill Reef winner Local Suitor and the Prix Jean Prat winner Local Talent, both of whom carried the colours of Sheikh Mohammed. Home Love also bred Homage who was unraced but became the dam (covered as a three-year-old) of Mark of Esteem who won the Two Thousand Guineas for Godolphin. Litigant stays two miles but travels strongly in his races and is fully effective at a mile and a half when the emphasis is on stamina. He acts on polytrack and heavy going. *Joseph Tuite*

LITMUS (USA) 6 ch.m. Latent Heat (USA) 118 – Fairy Glade (USA) (Gone West (USA)) – [2015 63: p10m Jan 9] modest performer: stays 1½m: acts on polytrack and good to firm going: usually wears headgear. *Simon Dow*

LITTLE 3 b.f. Paco Boy (IRE) 129 – Wafeira 86 (Dansili 127) [2015 70: f6s⁴ t6g 5.7m t6g 59 p6g 6g³ p6g 5.7m⁵ 5f Sep 13] modest handicapper: stays 7f: acts on all-weather and good to firm going. *Jamie Osborne*

LITTLE AVON 2 b.f. (Feb 10) Makfi 130 – Bahamamia 92 (Vettori (IRE) 119) [2015 73 p 8.3s* Oct 13] fifth foal: half-sister to useful 2-y-o 6f winners Switcher (by Whipper) and Marine Boy (by One Cool Cat) and winner up to 13f Jeanie Johnston (2-y-o 6f winner, by One Cool Cat): dam French 2-y-o 7.5f winner: 9/4, won 10-runner maiden at Leicester by ½ length from So Celebre, staying on to lead 1f out: will improve. *Ralph Beckett*

LITTLE BELTER (IRE) 3 gr.g. Dandy Man (IRE) 123 – On Thin Ice (IRE) (Verglas 62 (IRE) 118) [2015 71: 6g 5s² 5m⁶ 5d⁰ 6tft¹ 7.1g 5m⁷ 6g⁷ 5m⁴ Sep 20] neat gelding: modest maiden: stays 6f: acts on good to firm and good to soft going: in cheekpieces last 2 starts. *Linda Perratt*

LITTLE BIG MAN 4 b.g. Sleeping Indian 122 – Doris Souter (IRE) 81 (Desert Story 57 (IRE) 115) [2015 75: p7m p8f p6g² 6m 6m 7g f7d t6m⁶ t7.1f⁴ t7.1m p7g Dec 30] compact a69 gelding: fair handicapper: stays 1m: acts on polytrack and fibresand: often wears headgear: tried in tongue tie in 2015: sometimes slowly away. *Brendan Powell*

LITTLE CHOOSEY 5 ch.m. Cadeaux Genereux 131 – Little Nymph 89 (Emperor 56 Fountain 112) [2015 55: t6g* t6f⁴ p6g f6d t7.1f⁵ f7g² t7.1g⁶ 5g 6m 8.3m² 10.2m* 10g 8.5d⁶ t9.5f⁴ f8g³ p6g f7m t8.6f² t8.6f⁵ Dec 21] smallish mare: modest handicapper: won at Wolverhampton in January and Nottingham (apprentice event) in August: stays 1¼m: acts on all-weather, firm and soft going: usually wears headgear: wears tongue tie. *Roy Bowring*

LITTLECOTE LADY 6 b.m. Byron 117 – Barefooted Flyer (USA) 67 (Fly So Free 50 (USA) 122) [2015 61: p7g p6f³ p6g p7g Mar 25] sturdy mare: modest handicapper: stays 6f: acts on polytrack and tapeta: sometimes wears visor: sometimes slowly away. *Mark Usher*

LITTLE DANIELLE (IRE) 3 b.f. Dansant 118 – Sacha Wild (Kheleyf (USA) 116) –
[2015 –: p6g p5g⁴ Feb 5] well held in maidens. *Phil McEntee*

LITTLE ELI 5 b.g. Green Desert (USA) 127 – Princess Ellis 97 (Compton Place 125) **59**
[2015 75: t5.1g t5.1m⁵ 5m⁵ May 25] modest handicapper: stays 6f: acts on polytrack,
tapeta and good to firm going: sometimes wears headgear: usually leads. *Eric Alston*

LITTLE EVEREST 5 b.g. Kayf Tara 130 – Ski Run 112 (Petoski 135) [2015 p12g –
Feb 20] 66/1, tailed off in maiden at Lingfield. *Jimmy Fox*

LITTLE FLO 4 ch.f. Midnight Legend 118 – Sweet Robinia (IRE) (Bob Back (USA) 124) **60**
[2015 58: p10f p10f f14g⁴ t12.2f² Dec 21] stocky filly: modest maiden: left Brendan
Powell after second start: should stay 1¼m: acts on tapeta and good to firm going.
William Stone

LITTLE INDIAN 5 b.g. Sleeping Indian 122 – Once Removed 65 (Distant Relative 128) **65**
[2015 66: p8g* p8f² p8m p8m⁵ 8s⁴ 7m 10g 7.6s⁶ p8f p8f⁵ p10f 8s⁵ p8f p8g² t8.6t Dec 11]
compact gelding: fair handicapper: won at Chelmsford in April: stays 1m: acts on polytrack,
firm and soft going: tried in headgear: usually races towards rear. *J. R. Jenkins*

LITTLE KIPLING 2 b.f. (Mar 31) Royal Applause 124 – Victoria Sponge (IRE) 96 **68 p**
(Marju (IRE) 127) [2015 7m⁶ 7d⁴ p6f⁵ p7g* Oct 20] second foal: sister to useful 1m winner
Royal Albert Hall: dam winner up to 7f (2-y-o 6f winner) who stayed 1¼m: fair performer:
won maiden at Lingfield in October: stays 7f: should do better still. *Stuart Williams*

LITTLE LADY KATIE (IRE) 3 b.f. Lord Shanakill (USA) 121 – Akarita (IRE) 92 **87**
(Akarad (FR) 130) [2015 91: 8d⁶ 7g 8g⁵ 8m² 8m 8.3g³ 8s⁶ Oct 23] compact filly: fairly
useful handicapper: first past the post at Ayr in June (demoted after causing interference):
stays 8.5f: acts on good to firm and good to soft going: front runner/races prominently.
K. R. Burke

LITTLE LORD NELSON 3 b.g. Mount Nelson 125 – Cactus Curtsey 54 (Royal **77**
Applause 124) [2015 66p: t6f* t7.1f³ 8.3m² 8.5g p7g p8g p8f Dec 21] fair performer: won
maiden at Wolverhampton in January: stays 8.5f: acts on tapeta and good to firm going:
sometimes in hood in 2015: races in rear. *Stuart Williams*

LITTLE LOTTE (IRE) 2 b.f. (Apr 15) Kodiac 112 – Dancing Steps (Zafonic (USA) **62**
130) [2015 5m 5m⁶ 6g p7g⁴ p8g⁵ 8.9g² 8.4s² 8d Oct 13] €20,000Y: small, leggy filly: sister
to 1½m winner Dance For Livvy and winner up to 8.4f Strictly Glitz (2-y-o 7f winner), and
half-sister to winner up to 1¼m Dance For Julie (2-y-o 6f winner, by Redback): dam
unraced half-sister to smart performer up to 1½m Firebet: modest maiden: ran in France
last 3 starts: will stay 1¼m: acts on soft going: in cheekpieces last 2 starts: used to race
towards rear, but made running last 2 outings. *K. R. Burke*

LITTLE MISS MIGHTY 3 b.f. Mighty 117 – Spia (USA) (Diesis 133) [2015 54: t9.5f³ **53**
p8f Jan 21] modest maiden: stays 9.5f: acts on tapeta, raced only on good going on turf.
Nick Littmoden

LITTLEMISSPARTON 3 b.f. Sir Percy 129 – Miss Prism 60 (Niniski (USA) 125) **55**
[2015 –: 8m⁶ 10.3g p14g³ 14.1m p14f Sep 17] modest maiden: stays 1¾m: acts on
polytrack: sometimes in cheekpieces in 2015. *Denis Quinn*

LITTLEMISSPOSITIVE 3 b.f. Pastoral Pursuits 127 – Spirito Libro (USA) 89 (Lear –
Fan (USA) 130) [2015 55: p8f 8f Apr 23] maiden: no form in 2015: likely to prove best at
short of 1m. *Martin Smith*

LITTLE ORCHID 2 b.f. (Mar 7) Observatory (USA) 131 – Bushy Dell (IRE) 81 (King –
Charlemagne (USA) 120) [2015 7d p8g Nov 11] first foal: dam winner up to 1¾m (2-y-o
8.6f winner): well held in 2 maidens. *Julia Feilden*

LITTLE PALAVER 3 b.g. Showcasing 117 – Little Nymph 89 (Emperor Fountain 112) **98**
[2015 75: p6m* p6f² 6s³ 6m 6m⁶ 7m 6m³ 6.1s² 6g* Sep 30] close-coupled gelding: useful
handicapper: won at Lingfield in February and Salisbury (by ¾ length from Memories
Galore) in September: stays 6f: acts on polytrack and good to firm going. *Clive Cox*

LITTLE PEBBLES 2 ch.f. (May 6) Compton Place 125 – Pain Perdu (IRE) (Waajib 121) **50 p**
[2015 6g⁴ 6g t6m Sep 14] 17,000Y, 35,000 2-y-o: half-sister to several winners, including
2-y-o 7f winner Sister Bluebird (by Bluebird) and useful 6f-1½m winner Tifernati (by
Dansili): dam 1¼m winner: modest form: well held in maidens, though not given at all a
hard time when always behind at Wolverhampton final start (reportedly in season): type to
do better. *Jamie Osborne*

LITTLE PIPPIN 2 b.f. (Apr 26) Sir Percy 129 – Lady Le Quesne (IRE) 78 (Alhaarth **56** (IRE) 126) [2015 7g³ 7m⁵ 7s⁶ 8.3s* Oct 28] £2,000Y: seventh foal: half-sister to winner up to 1m in Qatar Excuse To Linger (2-y-o 6f winner, by Compton Place) and a winner abroad by Iceman: dam 2-y-o 5f/6f winner who probably stayed 1m: modest performer: won seller at Nottingham in October: best effort at 8.5f. *Tony Coyle*

LITTLE POLYANNA 3 b.f. Indesatchel (IRE) 120 – Simianna 101 (Bluegrass Prince – (IRE) 110) [2015 –: 5g 5m 5g Aug 3] no form. *Alan Berry*

LITTLE PRAIRIE 3 ch.f. Exceed And Excel (AUS) 126 – Chetwynd (IRE) (Exit To **85** Nowhere (USA) 122) [2015 7m² 7m⁴ 7g⁴ p10g⁴ p8f⁵ p7g Oct 14] 105,000Y: good-topped filly: half-sister to several winners, including useful 1¼m/11f winner Wickwing (by In The Wings) and 7f/1m winner Dance For Georgie (by Motivator): dam unraced half-sister to dam of Irish 2000 Guineas winner Roderic O'Connor: fairly useful performer: won maiden at Lingfield in May: stays 1¼m: acts on polytrack and good to firm going: tried in headgear: sometimes in tongue tie. *Hughie Morrison*

LITTLE RIGGS 3 b.g. Cape Cross (IRE) 129 – Craighall 66 (Dubawi (IRE) 129) [2015 **67** 73: 8.1m⁴ 8.3m³ Jul 4] fair maiden: stays 8.5f: acts on heavy going: often races prominently: sold 8,000 gns, sent to Italy. *Ed Walker*

LITTLE SALAMANCA 2 ch.g. (Apr 18) Sakhee's Secret 128 – Little Nymph 89 (Emperor – Fountain 112) [2015 p7g p7g⁶ Dec 16] behind in 2 maidens at Kempton. *Clive Cox*

LITTLE STAMPY (IRE) 4 ch.f. Artan (IRE) 119 – Gold Stamp (Golden Act (USA)) **63** [2015 75: 13g 14m⁵ p12g⁵ p12g t12.2m* Dec 18] modest handicapper: won at Wolverhampton in December: stays 2m: acts on polytrack, tapeta, good to firm and good to soft going: usually wears headgear. *D. Broad, Ireland*

LITTLE SWIFT (IRE) 2 b.f. (Mar 2) Kodiac 112 – Admire The View (IRE) 94 (Dubawi **73** (IRE) 129) [2015 6g⁴ 6m² 6m² p6f³ p6f² p6f² Oct 22] €10,000F, £18,000Y: second foal: dam winner up to 1m (2-y-o 7f winner) out of useful 1m-1¼m winner Miss Honorine: fair maiden: raced only at 6f: acts on polytrack and good to firm going. *David Simcock*

LITTLE VOICE (USA) 2 b.f. (Mar 28) Scat Daddy (USA) 120 – Excelente (IRE) 99 **78** (Exceed And Excel (AUS) 126) [2015 5f⁴ 5m² 5f⁶ 6m² 5.1d* 5.2s⁶ Aug 14] €160,000Y: compact filly: second foal: half-sister to 1¼m/11.6f winner Lemoncetta (by Lemon Drop Kid): dam, 2-y-o 7f winner (later 5f/1m winner in USA), closely related to winner up to 11f Prince Nureyev: fair performer: won maiden at Chepstow in August: best form at 5f: acts on firm and good to soft going. *Charles Hills*

LIVE DANGEROUSLY 5 b.g. Zamindar (USA) 116 – Desert Lynx (IRE) 79 (Green **84** Desert (USA) 127) [2015 75§: 6f 8s* 8g* 8m² 7g⁶ 8.1g⁴ 7d* 7v² 7g* 7d³ 8d⁶ p8m Oct 21] rather leggy gelding: fairly useful handicapper: won at Brighton (twice) in June, Goodwood in August and Epsom in September: stays 1¼m: acts on good to firm and heavy going: has worn headgear/tongue tie. *John Bridger*

LIVELLA FELLA (IRE) 2 b.f. (Mar 16) Strategic Prince 114 – Ardent Lady 79 **70** (Alhaarth (IRE) 126) [2015 6d 6g² 5.9g² 7.1m² 7.2g² t7.1g² 7.9m³ 7.2g³ p8f 7s Oct 16] £12,000Y: half-sister to several winners, including 1m winner Gatamalata (by Spartacus) and 2-y-o 5f winner First Choice (by Choisir): dam 9.3f winner: fair maiden: stays 7f: acts on tapeta and good to firm going: usually races prominently. *Keith Dalgleish*

LIVING LEADER 6 b.g. Oasis Dream 129 – Royal Jade 82 (Last Tycoon 131) [2015 81: **78** p7g p8f p7m* 8.3m⁴ 8f 7.6d 7.1m* 8g 8.1m² 7.1m⁵ 7.4d⁴ 6d t7.1f Oct 13] leggy gelding: fair handicapper: won at Lingfield in April and Chepstow in June: stays 9f: acts on polytrack and good to firm going: wears headgear: usually wears tongue tie: usually slowly away, often races in rear. *Grace Harris*

LIZZY'S DREAM 7 ch.g. Choisir (AUS) 126 – Flyingit (USA) 90 (Lear Fan (USA) 130) **51** [2015 60: t6f t5.1f⁴ 5v³ f5g 5m⁶ 5f⁶ 5m⁵ 5g² 5g⁴ 5.1g⁶ 5g⁵ 5d³ 5m t6m Dec 30] modest handicapper: best form at 5f: acts on polytrack, tapeta and good to firm going: tried in blinkers: often races towards rear. *Rebecca Bastiman*

LLAMADAS 13 b.g. Josr Algarhoud (IRE) 118 – Primulette 82 (Mummy's Pet 125) [2015 – p13f p15.8f Sep 22] rather leggy, close-coupled gelding: handicapper: well held both starts in 2015: stays 2m: acts on polytrack, fibresand and good to soft going: has worn headgear. *Helen Nelmes*

LLEWELLYN 7 b.g. Shamardal (USA) 129 – Ffestiniog (IRE) 96 (Efisio 120) [2015 83d: **76** 7.9v³ t7.1g 5.9s⁵ f7d² 6m⁵ 7g⁵ 6d* 6s⁵ 7v³ f7g* f6g³ f6g Dec 15] rather leggy gelding: fair handicapper: won at Catterick in August and Southwell in November: stays 7.5f: acts on fibresand, good to firm and heavy going: tried in headgear prior to 2015: front runner/races prominently. *Declan Carroll*

LLYN 3 ch.f. Dutch Art 126 – Makara (Lion Cavern (USA) 117) [2015 7.5m⁴ Oct 1] **51 p**
65,000Y: sister to useful 2-y-o 5f winner Graphic Guest and half-sister to 3 winners,
including smart winner up to 1m Fourpenny Lane (2-y-o 5f/6f winner, by Efisio): dam
unraced: 20/1, ran green when fourth in maiden at Beverley (12½ lengths behind Afjaan)
in October: should do better. *Michael Appleby*

LLYRICAL 4 b.g. Firebreak 125 – One of The Family 73 (Alzao (USA) 117) [2015 58, **62**
a64: f7g p8f p8g³ t7.1g⁴ 8.3m² p8g⁴ t8.6g⁴ t8.6g⁴ t9.5g⁵ t8.6g⁵ Aug 6] workmanlike
gelding: modest handicapper: won at Wolverhampton in June and July: left Derek Haydn
Jones after first start: best around 1m: acts on tapeta and good to firm going: tried in hood
prior to 2015: front runner/races prominently, often travels strongly. *Mike Murphy*

LOADED (IRE) 2 b.c. (Apr 22) Kodiac 112 – Fikrah 92 (Medicean 128) [2015 6s⁶ Sep **– p**
18] €85,000Y: second foal: dam 2-y-o 1m winner: 16/1, held back by inexperience when
sixth in maiden at Newbury (10 lengths behind Christchurch) in September: should do
better *Andrew Balding*

LOADING (IRE) 2 b.c. (Feb 8) Arcano (IRE) 122 – Sally Wood (CAN) (Woodman **80**
(USA) 126) [2015 8.3d⁵ 8.3s³ p8f² t8.6f* t7.1m⁵ Dec 18] £44,000Y: sixth foal: half-brother
to 3 winners, including 8.4f winner Maknificent (by Makfi) and winner up to 15f Santo
Prince (2-y-o 7f winner, by Henrythenavigator): dam unraced: fairly useful performer: won
maiden at Wolverhampton in October: stays 8.5f: acts on polytrack, tapeta and good to soft
going: usually races prominently. *Richard Hannon*

LOAVES AND FISHES 3 b.f. Oasis Dream 129 – Miracle Seeker 104 (Rainbow Quest **95**
(USA) 134) [2015 75P: 11.4d 9.9g⁴ 10m⁴ 12g p13g Oct 29] rather leggy filly: useful
performer: best effort when fourth in listed race at Newbury (1½ lengths behind Speedy
Boarding) in June on third start: should prove suited by 1½m: acts on good to firm going:
often races freely: sold 40,000 gns in December. *Clive Cox*

LOBSTER POT 4 b.f. Dylan Thomas (IRE) 132 – Classical Flair (Distant Music (USA) **–**
126) [2015 77: 10g p8g Jul 8] fair at best, no form in 2015: stays 1¼m: acts on heavy going:
tried in blinkers: often wears tongue tie: front runner/races prominently, tends to find little.
Hugo Palmer

LOCAL TIME 3 b.f. Invincible Spirit (IRE) 121 – Marie de Medici (USA) 104 (Medicean **105**
128) [2015 103: a7f* a8f* a9.4f* 8f 8f 9d 8g* 10g Oct 9] sturdy filly: useful performer:
successful at Meydan first 3 starts, in minor event (by short head from Ad Idem) in January
and listed UAE 1000 Guineas (by 3¼ lengths from Good Place) and UAE Oaks (by 4¾
lengths from Shahrasal) in February: back to form to win Istanbul Trophy at Veliefendi (by
½ length from Rekdhat) in September: stays 9.5f: acts on polytrack/dirt, best turf form on
good going: in cheekpieces last 2 starts. *Saeed bin Suroor*

LOCKEDOUTAHEAVEN (IRE) 4 ch.g. Rock of Gibraltar (IRE) 133 – Second Burst **55**
(IRE) (Sadler's Wells (USA) 132) [2015 76: 10s May 5] maiden, fair form at best: would
have stayed 1¼m+: dead. *Maurice Barnes*

LOCKRAM (USA) 2 b.c. (Feb 2) Lonhro (AUS) 128 – Silk Blossom 107 (Barathea **82**
(IRE) 127) [2015 6s⁴ t6g* p5gᵖᵘ Jun 17] fairly useful form: won maiden at Wolverhampton
in June: pulled up in minor event at Chelmsford, going wrong over 1f out: dead. *Mark
Johnston*

LOCOMOTION 3 gr.g. Proclamation (IRE) 130 – Miss Madame (IRE) 74 (Cape **60**
Cross (IRE) 129) [2015 –p: p8f⁴ 5m 6g 7g³ p7.5g p8g 5.7g Oct 18] fair maiden: stays 7.5f: **a79**
acts on polytrack: tried in headgear. *Jo Hughes*

LOGANS LAD (IRE) 5 b.g. Baltic King 120 – Lulu Island (Zafonic (USA) 130) [2015 **79**
68, a74: 16g² t6m⁵ t6m⁴ t7.1g* t6g² 6m t6g² 7g t7.1m* t7.1f⁶ t7.1f³ t7.1f t7.1m Nov
21] fair performer: won at Wolverhampton in April (handicap) and September (claimer):
stays 7f: acts on tapeta and good to firm going: often wears headgear: usually wears tongue
tie: often races towards rear. *Daniel Loughnane*

LOGARITHM (USA) 2 br.f. (Feb 26) Lonhro (AUS) 128 – Lophorina (King's Best **–**
(USA) 132) [2015 p7g Dec 3] $170,000Y: second foal: dam, French maiden (placed up to
10.5f), half-sister to smart 1m-1¼m winner Marhoob out of smart winner up to 1¼m
Flagbird: 8/1, tenth of 13 in maiden at Kempton on debut. *John Gosden*

LOGORRHEIC 3 b.g. Thewayyouare (USA) 117 – Thousandkissesdeep (IRE) 79 (Night **82**
Shift (USA)) [2015 p7p: p8g³ t9.5f* 10.3d⁶ p8f 9.9m May 3] fairly useful handicapper:
won at Wolverhampton in March: stays 9.5f: acts on polytrack and tapeta: often races
prominently: temperament under suspicion. *Ralph Beckett*

totepool Two-Year-Old Trophy, Redcar—Log Out Island beats Mr Lupton (No.7) and Delizia in this long-standing valuable contest in which the weights are based on the median price of the sires' yearlings

LOG OUT ISLAND (IRE) 2 b.c. (Feb 18) Dark Angel (IRE) 113 – White Daffodil **113** (IRE) 76 (Footstepsinthesand 120) [2015 5f* 5f² 6m³ 6m 5d² 5m³ 6s² 6g* 6d⁵ Oct 16] £95,000Y: good-topped colt: second foal: dam, winner up to 6f (2-y-o 5f winner), half-sister to useful 6f winner Lady Links: smart performer: won minor event at Ascot (by 4½ lengths from Handytalk) in April and listed Two-Year-Old Trophy at Redcar (by 2 lengths from Mr Lupton) in October: best efforts otherwise when second in Norfolk Stakes at Royal Ascot (½ length behind Waterloo Bridge), third in Flying Childers Stakes at Doncaster (neck behind Gutaifan) and second in Mill Reef Stakes at Newbury (1¼ lengths behind Ribchester) second/sixth/seventh starts: stays 6f: acts on firm and soft going: usually leads (refused to settle held up fourth outing). *Richard Hannon*

LOLAMOTION 2 ch.f. (Mar 27) Equiano (FR) 127 – Ocean View (USA) 109 (Gone **51** West (USA)) [2015 5m 5m⁴ 6d 5m* 5m⁵ 6m 6g Jul 31] £6,000Y: half-sister to several winners, including US Grade 3 2-y-o 1m winner Officer Rocket (by Officer) and 1¼m winner Miss Lucy Jane (by Aqlaam): dam US winner up to 6.5f (2-y-o 5.5f winner): modest performer: won claimer at Beverley in June: best form at 5f: acts on good to firm going: often in headgear. *Ann Duffield*

LOLITA 3 ch.f. Sir Percy 129 – Miss Ippolita 84 (Diktat 126) [2015 63: p6g⁴ 6.1m* 6d* **79** 5.7g 6.1m³ 6g⁴ 6.1g² 6g* 6d Oct 12] fair handicapper: won at Chepstow and Lingfield in May and Lingfield in September: stays 6f: acts on good to firm and good to soft going: front runner/races prominently. *J. R. Jenkins*

LOLLA FINCESS (FR) 2 gr.f. (Apr 1) Dark Angel (IRE) 113 – Screen Legend (IRE) 62 **81 p** (Invincible Spirit (IRE) 121) [2015 p6g² 6g* Jun 9] €40,000Y: first foal: dam maiden (third at 7f in France): fair form in 2 maidens at Lingfield, winning by ½ length from La Rioja in June: sold 24,000 gns, sent to Bahrain: open to improvement. *Richard Hannon*

LONDON CITIZEN (USA) 5 ch.h. Proud Citizen (USA) 122 – Sally Bowles (SAF) **91** (London News (SAF) 120) [2015 10m⁴ 10m 10g³ 10.1dᵖᵘ Sep 27] good-topped horse: fairly useful handicapper nowadays: missed 2014, best effort of 2015 when third at Newmarket in August: stays 1¼m: acts on polytrack and good to firm going. *Chris Wall*

LONDONIA 3 gr.g. Paco Boy (IRE) 129 – Snowdrops (Gulch (USA)) [2015 63: 10.2m⁴ **63** 10.2f May 13] modest maiden: stays 1¼m: acts on polytrack and good to firm going: often races prominently. *Paul Cole*

LONDON PROTOCOL (FR) 2 ch.g. (Apr 7) Muhtathir 126 – Troiecat (FR) (One Cool **91** Cat (USA) 123) [2015 6g³ 6d² 6.5g* 8d⁶ 7.1s³ Sep 16] €17,000Y: third foal: half-brother to French 2-y-o 5f winner Super Ale (by Elusive City): dam French maiden: fairly useful performer: won minor event at Deauville (by length from Omar Bradley) in August: third in minor event at Sandown in September: stays 7f: acts on soft going: in cheekpieces third/fourth starts: usually races close up. *K. R. Burke*

LONE ANGEL (IRE) 2 gr.f. (Mar 16) Dark Angel (IRE) 113 – The Hermitage (IRE) 83 **52** (Kheleyf (USA) 116) [2015 p5g² 5m Apr 20] 9,000Y: smallish, angular filly: second foal: sister to 6f winner Where's Sue: dam, 2-y-o 5f winner who stayed 7f, half-sister to Oaks third Crown of Light: better effort when second in maiden at Chelmsford (5 lengths behind Ample) in April. *James Tate*

594

LONEOS 2 b.c. (Mar 12) Raven's Pass (USA) 133 – Halle Bop 92 (Dubai Millennium 140) **– p**
[2015 p7g Oct 7] sixth foal: half-brother to 7f winner Highest Level (by Invincible Spirit):
dam, 2-y-o 6f winner, out of useful half-sister to Derby winner Oath: 5/1, badly needed
experience when last of 13 in maiden at Kempton, slowly away: should do better.
Charlie Appleby

LONE STAR BOY (IRE) 3 b.g. Starspangledbanner (AUS) 128 – Pascali 61 (Compton **76**
Place 125) [2015 60: 7g⁵ 7d³ 8.3g 7m t7.1g* t7.1m² Oct 2] fair handicapper: won at
Wolverhampton in August: stays 7f: acts on tapeta: usually in headgear in 2015: tried in
tongue tie in 2015: temperament under suspicion. *Tom Dascombe*

LONG AWAITED (IRE) 7 b.g. Pivotal 124 – Desertion (IRE) 92 (Danehill (USA) 126) **96 §**
[2015 99§: p5g³ t5.1f 5m² 5g⁶ 5m² 5m⁵ 5s⁶ 5m Jun 13] sturdy, good-bodied gelding: useful
handicapper: second at Beverley (½ length behind Pipers Note) in April and second at
Goodwood (½ length behind Humidor) in May: races at 5f: acts on any turf going: often
wears headgear: no battler and one to be wary of. *David Barron*

LONG CALL 2 b.g. (Apr 4) Authorized (IRE) 133 – Gacequita (URU) (Ride The Rails **71**
(USA) 116) [2015 9s 8m⁶ 8s⁴ 9d⁴ Oct 26] well-made colt: fair maiden: stays 9f. *Charlie
Appleby*

LONGINA (GER) 4 ch.f. Monsun (GER) 124 – Love Academy (GER) 103 (Medicean **107**
128) [2015 110: 9f 8m³ 9.9g³ 8.9g³ Aug 8] second foal: half-sister to German 9f-11f winner
Letro (by Montjeu): dam, German 2-y-o 7.5f/1m (Preis der Winterkonigin) winner, half-
sister to smart German performer up to 1½m Lauro (by Monsun): useful performer: won
Diana-Trial at Hoppegarten in 2014: possibly unsuited by firm conditions when well held
in Dahlia Stakes at Newmarket on reappearance: creditable third after, beaten 1¾ lengths
by Wake Forest in Hamburg Trophy at Hamburg and 2¾ lengths by Wildpark in listed race
at Hoppegarten on last 2 occasions: stays 11f: acts on soft going: usually races close up.
P. Schiergen, Germany

LONG ISLAND 2 b.f. (Mar 11) Firebreak 125 – Fakhuur 88 (Dansili 127) [2015 7g 7v² **64**
8m 7s⁴ p8m⁴ Nov 21] first foal: dam, 1m winner, out of close relative to top-class 1½m
performer Old Vic: modest maiden: stays 7f: acts on heavy going: sometimes slowly away,
often races towards rear. *James Eustace*

LONGSHADOW 5 ch.g. Monsun (GER) 124 – La Felicita (Shareef Dancer (USA) 135) **91**
[2015 87: 16.5m* 16.1g⁴ 21.7f 16.4m 15.8g³ 16.1m⁵ 16d³ 16.4g² 16.5f² p16g t16.5f²
t16.5m⁶ Dec 12] sturdy gelding: fairly useful handicapper: won at Doncaster in April:
second at York and Wolverhampton (twice): stays 16.5f: acts on tapeta, soft and good to
firm going: sometimes wears headgear: front runner/races prominently. *Jason Ward*

LONGSHAW 5 ch.m. Firebreak 125 – Sharpe Image (IRE) (Bluebird (USA) 125) [2015 **51**
10d t12.2m 12s t12.2m Nov 21] first foal: dam little form: modest maiden: best effort at
1¼m. *Ollie Pears*

LONGSIDE 3 b.g. Oasis Dream 129 – Hypoteneuse (IRE) 86 (Sadler's Wells (USA) 132) **68**
[2015 78: t7.1f⁴ f6s⁶ t6g⁵ 8.3m² 8d 8m p10g⁶ p12g p12g³ Dec 19] fair maiden: left Charles
Hills after third start: stays 1½m: acts on polytrack, tapeta and good to firm going: tried in
blinkers/tongue tie in 2015: temperament under suspicion. *James Eustace*

LOOK HERE'S AL 4 gr.g. Alhaarth (IRE) 126 – Look Here's Dee (Dansili 127) [2015 **55**
69, a62: t8.6g⁴ 7.1m t8.6f⁶ t8.6g t8.6g⁴ 10.2m² 10.2m* 9.9m 10.2m⁶ 10.2d t12.2m⁶ t12.2f
10g³ 10.2s³ 10.2s Nov 4] modest handicapper: won at Chepstow in June: left Andrew
Hollinshead after first start: stays 1¼m: acts on polytrack, tapeta, good to firm and good to
soft going: wears cheekpieces. *Sarah Hollinshead*

LOOKING GOOD 3 b.f. Makfi 130 – Primo Heights 87 (Primo Valentino (IRE) 116) **72**
[2015 72: 8.3s² 8.3d⁴ 8.3g 8s³ Sep 5] fair maiden: left David Brown after third start: stays
8.5f: acts on soft going. *David O'Meara*

LOOM OF LIFE (IRE) 3 b.g. Rip Van Winkle (IRE) 134 – Feeling Wonderful (IRE) 73 **67**
(Fruits of Love (USA) 127) [2015 62: 8g³ 9g⁶ 12m⁶ 11.9m 8.3m⁴ Jul 4] good-topped
gelding: fair maiden: stays 9f: best form on good going: tried in visor in 2015. *Richard Fahey*

LOPES DANCER (IRE) 3 b.g. Lope de Vega (IRE) 125 – Ballet Dancer (IRE) 77 **77**
(Refuse To Bend (IRE) 128) [2015 7.1s⁴ 8s³ 8g⁴ 9.2m² 8m⁵ Jun 27] fair maiden: stays 9f:
acts on soft and good to firm going. *Alan Swinbank*

LOPITO DE VEGA (IRE) 3 ch.g. Lope de Vega (IRE) 125 – Athenian Way (IRE) 104 **77**
(Barathea (IRE) 127) [2015 –p: 8m 8g* 7m 7.2g⁶ 8.5d* 9.9s² p10f Oct 24] rather leggy
gelding: fair handicapper: won at Salisbury in August and Beverley in September: stays
1¼m: acts on soft going. *David C. Griffiths*

LORAINE 5 b.m. Sir Percy 129 – Emirates First (IRE) 77 (In The Wings 128) [2015 82: **77**
p10g p10g* p10f² t8.6m⁶ p10g⁵ 10m⁶ Aug 17] fair handicapper: won at Lingfield in
February: left Jamie Osborne after fourth start: stays 1¼m: acts on polytrack and tapeta.
Stuart Kittow

LORD ARATAN (GER) 8 b.g. Tiger Hill (IRE) 127 – Luce (IRE) 59 (Sadler's Wells **50**
(USA) 132) [2015 t12.2g f12g⁵ Dec 22] modest form in maidens. *Patrick Holmes*

LORD ASLAN (IRE) 2 b.c. (Feb 13) Thewayyouare (USA) 117 – Lunar Lustre (IRE) –
(Desert Prince (IRE) 130) [2015 p8g Nov 11] 16/1, green when well held in maiden at
Kempton on debut. *Andrew Balding*

LORD AVONBROOK 5 b.g. Avonbridge 123 – Miss Brookie 70 (The West (USA) 107) –
[2015 –: 7.9d Sep 15] lightly-raced handicapper, no form since 2012: stays 6f: acts on
fibresand and soft going: sent to Germany. *Andrew Crook*

LORD BEN STACK (IRE) 3 b.g. Dylan Thomas (IRE) 132 – Beringold (Bering 136) **96**
[2015 88p: 10m⁴ 10.4m⁵ 10.4g² Jul 4] big, unfurnished gelding: useful performer: best
effort when second in handicap at Haydock (neck behind Cymro) in July: stays 10.5f: acts
on good to firm going: usually races close up. *K. R. Burke*

LORD BUFFHEAD 6 br.g. Iceman 117 – Royal Pardon 61 (Royal Applause 124) [2015 **55 §**
66§, a55§: t5.1f 5v⁴ 6g 5s 6s 6s⁶ 5d May 21] modest handicapper: stays 6f: acts on polytrack
and heavy going: often wears headgear: often races in rear: unreliable. *Richard Guest*

LORD FRANKLIN 6 ch.g. Iceman 117 – Zell (IRE) 65 (Lend A Hand 124) [2015 85: 8g **86**
8g 8m 9.2d 10.2m³ 9g* 8.3s* 9.2g⁶ 8d 8.3m⁴ 10.2g* 10.4s Oct 10] tall, leggy gelding:
fairly useful handicapper: won at Wetherby in July, Hamilton in August and Nottingham in
September: stays 10.5f: acts on good to firm and heavy going: tried in cheekpieces prior to
2015: usually races close up. *Eric Alston*

LORD GEORGE (IRE) 2 gr.c. (Feb 22) Sir Percy 129 – Mahima (FR) (Linamix (FR) **85 p**
127) [2015 8m³ t8.6m* Oct 2] €25,000Y: fifth foal: half-brother to useful French 1m-9.5f
winner Persiste Et Signe (by With Approval) and French 7.5f winner Tres Honore (by
Muhtathir): dam French 2-y-o 6f-1m winner: better effort when winning maiden at Wolverhampton in October by neck from Hepplewhite, just pushed out: likely to stay beyond 1m:
open to further improvement. *James Fanshawe*

LORD HUNTINGDON 2 b.g. (Jan 12) Lord of England (GER) 119 – Marajuana 82 **63**
(Robellino (USA) 127) [2015 p7g⁶ p8m⁴ Dec 16] better effort when fourth in maiden at
Lingfield (8 lengths behind Hombre Rojo) in December. *Andrew Balding*

LORD KELVIN (IRE) 2 br.g. (Jan 29) Iffraaj 127 – Eastern Appeal (IRE) 110 (Shinko **75**
Forest (IRE)) [2015 6m 7.1m⁴ 8.3m* 7m Sep 9] good-quartered gelding: fair performer:
won maiden at Windsor in August: best effort at 8.5f. *Charles Hills*

LORD MCGUFFY (IRE) 2 b.g. (Mar 15) Frozen Power (IRE) 108 – La Herradura –
(Hernando (FR) 127) [2015 7m 7m Jul 25] well held in 2 maidens: in cheekpieces latter
start. *Ann Duffield*

LORD OF THE ROCK (IRE) 3 b.g. Rock of Gibraltar (IRE) 133 – La Sylphide 94 **100**
(Rudimentary (USA) 118) [2015 86p: 8s⁴ 7m² 7g* 7g Aug 15] useful performer: won
maiden at Newcastle (by 8 lengths from Madame Butterfly) in June: stays 7f: acts on good
to firm going: usually races close up. *Michael Dods*

LORD OFTHE SHADOWS (IRE) 6 ch.g. Kyllachy 129 – Golden Shadow (IRE) 77 **78**
(Selkirk (USA) 129) [2015 93, a82: p8g⁵ p8g² p8g p8f³ Mar 4] lengthy gelding: fair
handicapper: stays 8.5f: acts on polytrack, soft and good to firm going: tried in blinkers:
usually races prominently. *Richard Hannon*

LORD OF THE STORM 7 b.g. Avonbridge 123 – Just Run (IRE) 45 (Runnett 125) **65**
[2015 70: t9.5f³ t9.5f³ p10g⁶ Feb 24] lengthy gelding: fair handicapper: stays 1½m: acts
on polytrack, tapeta, good to firm and heavy going: tried in cheekpieces: tried in tongue tie
prior to 2015. *Bill Turner*

LORD OF WORDS (IRE) 3 b.g. Thousand Words 113 – Dame Laura (IRE) 100 (Royal –
Academy (USA) 130) [2015 58: 8s 10g 8d 9m 8.3g 9.9g Aug 30] maiden: no form in 2015:
tried in visor in 2015. *Patrick Holmes*

LORD REASON 3 b.g. Sixties Icon 125 – Luck Will Come (IRE) 82 (Desert Style (IRE) **78**
121) [2015 8g 8.3m² p7g² p8m³ 10m t8.6g³ 8.3g⁵ 8g p8f² p10f⁴ p10g t8.6f⁵ p8f⁴ Nov 12]
fair maiden: stays 8.5f: acts on polytrack and tapeta. *John Ryan*

LORD ROB 4 b.g. Rob Roy (USA) 122 – First Grey (Environment Friend 128) [2015 7s **62**
12m 7g² 7s 7g 8g 10s 8v Nov 3] modest maiden: best effort at 7f: usually in hood.
David Thompson

LORD YATESBURY 3 b.c. Bertolini (USA) 125 – Sachiko 54 (Celtic Swing 138) [2015 **50** p6g p7f 8.3m⁴ 8.3m p8g 7m⁶ 6g⁵ Jun 20] modest maiden: best effort at 8.5f: acts on good to firm going: usually races close up, often races freely. *W. de Best-Turner*

LORD YEATS 2 b.c. (Feb 22) Yeats (IRE) 128 – Bogside Theatre (IRE) 102 (Fruits of **–** Love (USA) 127) [2015 8g 9d Oct 26] well held in 2 maidens. *George Moore*

LORELEI 3 b.f. Excellent Art 125 – Light Dreams 70 (Fantastic Light (USA) 134) [2015 **55** p7f p8m t8.6f⁶ p11g³ 11.7f p12g² p12g 16g⁴ p15.8g² p15.8g² Aug 26] 10,500F, £20,000Y: second foal: dam, maiden (best at 1m), half-sister to smart sprinters Vision of Night and Struggler and smart German performer up to 1½m Baroon: modest maiden: left Rod Millman after seventh start: stays 2m: acts on polytrack: tried in cheekpieces. *William Muir*

LORELINA 2 b.f. (May 9) Passing Glance 119 – Diktalina 61 (Diktat 126) [2015 7g⁴ 8g⁴ **75** p8g p7m Dec 31] first foal: dam, ungenuine 11.6f winner who stayed 1¾m, also won over hurdles: fair performer: won maiden at Epsom in July: best effort at 7f. *Andrew Balding*

LORIMER'S LOT (IRE) 4 ch.f. Camacho 118 – Alwiyda (USA) (Trempolino (USA) **61** 135) [2015 77: 5g⁴ 5d 5m 6m⁶ 5g³ 5m² 5d² 5s 5m² 5g⁶ 5m 5s² 5s t5.1f Nov 13] modest handicapper: stays 6f: acts on soft and good to firm going: sometimes wears headgear. *Mark Walford*

LOS BARBADOS (IRE) 3 b.c. Galileo (IRE) 134 – Milanova (AUS) (Danehill (USA) **94** 126) [2015 81p: 10d³ 10d⁶ 11g* 10g⁴ Oct 13] fairly useful performer: won maiden at Wexford in August: will stay 1½m: best form on good going: blinkered/tongue tied last 2 starts: sent to UAE. *Aidan O'Brien, Ireland*

LOS NADIS (GER) 11 ch.g. Hernando (FR) 127 – La Estrella (GER) (Desert King (IRE) **–** 129) [2015 16.1g May 29] fairly useful handicapper at best, has shown little in 4 runs since 2012: stays 17.5f: acts on good to firm and heavy going: tried in cheekpieces. *Jim Goldie*

LOSTOCK HALL (IRE) 3 b.g. Lord Shanakill (USA) 121 – Cannikin (IRE) 82 (Lahib **86** (USA) 129) [2015 90: 10g⁴ 10f 10.1m p12g p11g p10g⁵ Dec 20] close-coupled gelding: fairly useful handicapper: stays 1½m: acts on polytrack and firm going. *K. R. Burke*

LOTHAIR (IRE) 6 b.g. Holy Roman Emperor (IRE) 125 – Crafty Example (USA) (Crafty **75** Prospector (USA)) [2015 80: 7m 6s³ 7.2s* 6d 7.9g 6g 7g 8m 7s Oct 16] fair handicapper: won at Ayr in May: stays 7f: acts on good to firm and heavy going. *Alan Swinbank*

LOTI 3 ch.f. Monsieur Bond (IRE) 120 – Bond Platinum Club 59 (Pivotal 124) [2015 p7g **58** p5g⁴ t6g⁵ p5g⁴ t5.1f⁵ f5d Mar 11] 3,500Y: third foal: closely related to 6f (including at 2 yrs) winner Bond Club (by Misu Bond): dam once-raced half-sister to smart sprinter Lord Kintyre: modest maiden: best effort at 5f: acts on polytrack: often races prominently. *Rod Millman*

LOTTE LENYA (FR) 2 ch.f. (Apr 24) Peintre Celebre (USA) 137 – Tricoteuse (Kris **–** 135) [2015 t7.1m Dec 18] €22,000Y: sister to French 2-y-o 9f winner Boudin and half-sister to 3 winners, including 11f-16.5f winner Riguez Dancer (by Dansili) and 1¼m winner Emotional Dream (by Shirocco): dam unraced: 50/1, very green when well held in maiden at Wolverhampton. *Mike Murphy*

LOUD 5 ch.g. Dutch Art 126 – Applauding (IRE) (Royal Applause 124) [2015 80: p8g⁵ **56** 8.3m f8d⁵ p8g⁶ 7m⁴ 7g p7g Oct 7] angular gelding: modest handicapper: stays 8.5f: acts on **a47** all-weather, good to firm and heavy going: usually wears headgear. *Denis Quinn*

LOUDLY (USA) 3 gr.f. War Front (USA) 119 – T K O Lady (USA) (Two Punch (USA)) **–** [2015 –p: 8.3g 8g 6m Aug 29] no form: tried in headgear. *George Peckham*

LOUIS THE PIOUS 7 b.g. Holy Roman Emperor (IRE) 125 – Whole Grain 72 (Polish **101** Precedent (USA) 131) [2015 117: 6s⁴ 7g 6f 7f Jul 11] big gelding: smart handicapper in 2014, not at best in 2015: stays 7f: acts on good to firm and heavy going: wears headgear. *David O'Meara*

LOUIS VEE (IRE) 7 b.g. Captain Rio 122 – Mrs Evans (IRE) 97 (College Chapel 122) **66** [2015 66: t5.1m⁵ t6f t5.1f⁴ f6g⁶ t5.1g 5.1m t5.1f p5g t7.1m p6f* t6m* Dec 30] fair handicapper: won at Chelmsford and Wolverhampton in December: left Roy Brotherton after sixth start: stays 6f: acts on polytrack, tapeta and soft going: tried in cheekpieces in 2015: often in tongue tie prior to last 5 starts. *John O'Shea*

LOUMARIN (IRE) 3 b.f. Bushranger (IRE) 119 – Masela (IRE) 71 (Medicean 128) **58 +** [2015 77: p5g⁴ 5m⁵ 5f⁵ 5g⁶ 5.1m t6f⁵ 5.1d p5f⁵ t5.1m* p5g³ f5g t5.1f Dec 21] rather leggy **a72** filly: fair handicapper: won at Wolverhampton in November: left Martyn Meade after second start, Heather Dalton after fifth: best form at 5f: acts on polytrack, tapeta and good to firm going: tried in tongue tie in 2015. *Michael Appleby*

LOURDES LADY 2 b.f. (May 16) Arabian Gleam 122 – Wenden Belle (IRE) (Brave Act **58**
119) [2015 6d p5g⁵ p6g p6f* p5f⁴ Oct 24] fourth foal: half-sister to 6f/7f winner My Own
Way Home (by Danbird): dam unraced half-sister to useful 5f winner Calm Bay: modest
performer: won nursery at Chelmsford in October: stays 6f: acts on polytrack: sometimes
in blinkers. *Chris Dwyer*

LOURES (IRE) 2 ch.c. (May 18) Shamardal (USA) 129 – Lura (USA) 67 (Street Cry   **– p**
(IRE) 130) [2015 p8d Sep 4] second foal: brother to smart 2-y-o 6f/7f (Rockfel Stakes)
winner Lucida, runner-up in 1000 Guineas: dam once-raced half-sister to Breeders' Cup
Turf winner English Channel: 5/1, very green when well held in maiden at Kempton:
should do better in time. *Charlie Appleby*

LOUVE REINE (FR) 2 b.f. (May 15) King's Best (USA) 132 – Louve Solitaire (USA)   **–**
(Our Emblem (USA) 114) [2015 t8.6g Dec 5] €36,000Y: third foal: half-sister to French
1½m-15f winner Lorenzo Boy (by Sabiango): dam, maiden (stayed 11f), half-sister to
high-class French winner up to 1¼m Loup Sauvage: 66/1, shaped as if amiss when well
held in maiden at Wolverhampton. *Ralph Beckett*

LOVE IN THE DARK 2 b.f. (Mar 30) Sleeping Indian 122 – Love In The Park 78   **49**
(Pivotal 124) [2015 5.7d 7g Sep 30] first foal: dam 9f/1¼m winner: better effort when ninth
of 13 in maiden at Salisbury (5¾ lengths behind Royal Reserve) second start. *Nikki Evans*

LOVE ISLAND 6 b.m. Acclamation 118 – Sally Traffic 57 (River Falls 113) [2015 101:   **101**
6m² 6g⁵ 6m 6m² 6m⁶ 5mᵖᵘ 5g³ 6d 6.5m⁶ 6g 6d Oct 23] angular mare: useful handicapper:
third at Doncaster (½ length behind Maljaa) in August: stays 6.5f: acts on good to firm and
heavy going: tried in headgear: in tongue tie last 5 starts. *Richard Whitaker*

LOVEISRECKLESS (IRE) 2 b.f. (Apr 17) Mount Nelson 125 – Sassari (IRE) 76   **–**
(Darshaan 133) [2015 6g Oct 20] 18,000Y: half-sister to several winners, including useful
5f-7f winner Sassaway (by Bertolini) and winner up to 1¼m Janet's Pearl (2-y-o 7f winner,
by Refuse To Bend): dam maiden (stayed 1¼m): 66/1, badly needed experience when last
of 14 in maiden at Windsor. *William Muir*

LOVELL 2 b.c. (Feb 13) Dubawi (IRE) 129 – Cosmodrome (USA) 108 (Bahri (USA) 125)   **86**
[2015 7m 7.1g² 7s* Sep 5] 725,000Y: good-topped colt: fourth foal: dam, 9.5f/1¼m winner,
half-sister to useful winners up to 1¼m Splashdown and Boogie Shoes: fairly useful
performer: landed odds in maiden at Thirsk in September: better form when second in
similar event at Sandown (2¼ lengths behind Stormy Antarctic): will stay 1m+.
Charlie Appleby

LOVELY MEMORY (IRE) 3 b.f. Shamardal (USA) 129 – Folk Opera (IRE) 117   **98**
(Singspiel (IRE) 133) [2015 87: p8f* 8d³ p8f⁴ p10f⁴ Nov 5] useful performer: won maiden
at Chelmsford in September: good third in handicap at Pontefract (1¾ lengths behind
Pallister) in October: bred to stay 1¼m+: acts on polytrack and good to soft going: in
cheekpieces last 2 starts. *Saeed bin Suroor*

LOVELYN (GER) 3 b.f. Tiger Hill (IRE) 127 – Laurella (Acatenango (GER) 127) [2015   **118**
10.4g* 10.9m* 11.9g* 10.9g 11.9s* Oct 18] sister to German 1¼m/11f winner Larello and
half-sister to 3 winners in Germany, including useful 1m winner Labrice (by Dubawi):
dam, German 11f winner, sister/half-sister to Deutsches Derby winners Lando and
Laroche: smart performer: won maiden at Cologne in April, Oaks d'Italia at Milan (by a
head from dead-heaters Full of Beauty and Joyful Hope) in May, Grosser Hansa-Preis at
Hamburg in June and Gran Premio del Jockey Club at Milan (beat Dylan Mouth 3 lengths)
in October: well below form when ninth to Turfdonna in Preis der Diana at Dusseldorf on
fourth start: stays 1½m: acts on soft and good to firm going. *P. Schiergen, Germany*

LOVELY SURPRISE (IRE) 3 ch.f. Shamardal (USA) 129 – Dubai Surprise (IRE) 115   **87**
(King's Best (USA) 132) [2015 69p: 8.3s² 8.3g* 8f 8s⁵ 8s Oct 23] well-made, attractive
filly: fairly useful performer: won maiden at Nottingham (by ½ length from Rive Gauche)
in May: stays 8.5f: acts on soft going. *Ismail Mohammed*

LOVE MARMALADE (IRE) 5 ch.g. Duke of Marmalade (IRE) 132 – Green Castle   **83**
(IRE) 101 (Indian Ridge 123) [2015 88: t12.2f 14m² 12.5m 16m 13.1g³ 10.4f⁵ 11.9m³
12.2g² 12g⁴ 12.8m³ t12.2f⁴ t12.2f³ Nov 16] fairly useful handicapper: stays 1¾m: acts on
tapeta, firm and good to soft going: tried in cheekpieces in 2015. *Alistair Whillans*

LOVE ON THE ROCKS (IRE) 2 ch.f. (Feb 8) Exceed And Excel (AUS) 126 – My   **80**
Love Thomas (IRE) 84 (Cadeaux Genereux 131) [2015 5.1m⁴ 5m⁵ 6g⁴ 5f* 5m Sep 11]
90,000Y: good-quartered filly: third foal: sister to smart 5f/6f winner Double Up and half-
sister to winner up to 1m Full Support (2-y-o 5f winner, by Acclamation): dam, 2-y-o 6f
winner, half-sister to high-class sprinter G Force: fairly useful performer: won maiden at
Bath in August: best effort at 5f: acts on firm going: often in hood. *Charles Hills*

LOVE OR FEAR 2 b.f. (Apr 23) Holy Roman Emperor (IRE) 125 – Fame Game (IRE) **59 p**
64 (Fasliyev (USA) 120) [2015 6m 6g 5.9m⁴ 6d⁵ Aug 28] £28,000Y: fourth foal: half-sister
to a winner in Japan by Royal Applause: dam, maiden (stayed 6f), half-sister to dam of
Grand Prix de Paris winner Gallante: modest maiden: shaped better than result final start:
raced only at 6f: remains open to improvement. *K. R. Burke*

LOVER MAN (IRE) 6 b.g. Lawman (FR) 121 – Seltitude (IRE) 114 (Fairy King (USA)) **86**
[2015 –: p5g 6g 7d⁶ 7d 6d⁴ 5g 8m 6.9s⁵ Sep 15] fairly useful handicapper: stays 7f: acts on
viscoride and good to soft going: tried in cheekpieces/tongue tie: usually races towards
rear: sold 4,000 gns, sent to Belgium. *Keith Dalgleish*

LOVE THE KITTEN (USA) 2 ch.f. (Mar 17) Kitten's Joy (USA) 128 – Anura (IRE) **77**
(Giant's Causeway (USA) 132) [2015 a4.5m² p4.5f² 7f 8.5f⁵ 8.5f⁶ 8.5g³ 8f² Dec 30]
strong filly: sister to several winners in USA, including smart 2-y-o 1m winner and
Breeders' Cup Juvenile Turf runner-up Luck of The Kitten: dam US 8.5f/9f winner: fair
maiden: placed 4 times in North America: in rear in Chesham Stakes at Royal Ascot on
third start: stays 8.5f: acts on dirt: blinkered first 4 outings. *Wesley A. Ward, USA*

LOVING SPIRIT 7 b.g. Azamour (IRE) 130 – Lolla's Spirit (IRE) 68 (Montjeu (IRE) **106**
137) [2015 106: 8m⁵ 8m 7.6g* 10.4m 8m Jul 31] rangy gelding: useful handicapper: won
at Chester (by ½ length from Jallota) in May: stayed 8.5f: acted on polytrack, firm and soft
going: successful with/without headgear: often raced towards rear: quirky sort: dead.
Richard Fahey

LOVING THINGS 3 b.f. Pivotal 124 – Fallen In Love 104 (Galileo (IRE) 134) [2015 **103**
9.9s* 10.4d² 10g Oct 9] angular filly: second foal: half-sister to 1½m winner Loving Home
(by Shamardal): dam, 2-y-o 1m winner, half-sister to Coronation Stakes winner Fallen For
You: useful performer: won maiden at Salisbury (by 1½ lengths from Dizzey Heights) in
May: best effort when second in handicap at Haydock (head behind Polar Eyes) in
September: stays 10.5f. *John Gosden*

LOVING YOUR WORK 4 b.g. Royal Applause 124 – Time Crystal (IRE) 83 (Sadler's **68**
Wells (USA) 132) [2015 77: 12g² t13.9g⁶ 11.8m⁶ 11.6m³ p12g³ 10.2m⁵ 9.9s² 11.6g² Oct
19] rather unfurnished gelding: fair handicapper: stays 1½m: acts on polytrack, soft and
good to firm going: tried in headgear: often races towards rear. *George Baker*

LOW KEY (IRE) 8 b.g. Pentire 132 – La Capilla (Machiavellian (USA) 123) [2015 91: **96**
18g* 18g Oct 10] sturdy gelding: useful handicapper: fit from jumps (useful hurdler), won
in good style at Newmarket in September: 13/2, below expectations when mid-field in
34-runner Cesarewitch there: stays 2¼m: acts on polytrack and heavy going: has worn
headgear. *David Pipe*

LOYALTY 8 b.g. Medicean 128 – Ecoutila (USA) (Rahy (USA) 115) [2015 93: p8g⁵ p8m* **87**
p8m⁵ p7g³ p8g* f7s⁶ p8m⁴ p7g⁵ p8f p7d⁵ p8g⁵ p8m⁴ Dec 27] compact gelding: fairly
useful handicapper: won at Lingfield in January and Chelmsford in March: stays 1¼m: acts
on polytrack: usually wears visor: front runner/races prominently. *Derek Shaw*

LOZAH 2 b.f. (Feb 6) Lawman (FR) 121 – Princess Luna (GER) (Grand Lodge (USA) **63**
125) [2015 8g t8.6g³ p7g Oct 14] 25,000Y: sixth foal: half-sister to useful 7f-8.6f winner
Space War (by Elusive City) and 7f winner Lunette (by Teofilo): dam German 1m winner:
modest maiden: best effort when third at Wolverhampton in September: in tongue tie last 2
starts. *John Gosden*

LUATH 2 ch.g. (Mar 29) Archipenko (USA) 127 – Delaware Dancer (IRE) 68 (Danehill **70**
Dancer (IRE) 117) [2015 6m³ 7g⁶ 8g⁶ t9.5f f8m⁵ f8g* Dec 29] fair performer: won nursery
at Southwell in December: best effort at 1m: acts on fibresand: tried in visor. *David Brown*

LUCIA SCIARRA 2 ch.f. (Apr 23) Monsieur Bond (IRE) 120 – Oke Bay 62 (Tobougg **–**
(IRE) 125) [2015 6m 6g 7g Sep 26] third foal: half-sister to a winner in Hungary by Three
Valleys: dam maiden (stayed 1¾m): no form. *Giles Bravery*

LUCIDA (IRE) 3 b.f. Shamardal (USA) 129 – Lura (USA) 67 (Street Cry (USA) 130) **119**
[2015 112: 8f² 8f³ 8m⁶ Jul 10] robust, good-topped filly: smart performer: second in 1000
Guineas at Newmarket (¾ length behind Legatissimo, leading from over 1f out until last
50 yds) in May and third in Coronation Stakes at Royal Ascot (¾ length behind Ervedya,
finishing strongly) in June: better than result when 1¼ lengths sixth to Amazing Maria in
Falmouth Stakes at Newmarket final start, left poorly placed even before impeded final 1f
and finishing with running left: likely to stay further than 1m: acts on firm and good to soft
going. *J. S. Bolger, Ireland*

LUCIE RIE (IRE) 3 b.f. Excellent Art 125 – Farthingale (IRE) 67 (Nashwan (USA) 135) **65**
[2015 57: 7.2s⁵ 10d⁵ 10g 10.5g⁴ 9.5m³ 11.9m⁶ 12.1v⁴ f14g³ Dec 12] fair maiden: left David
Wachman after fifth start: seems to stay 1¾m: acts on fibresand, soft and good to firm
going: in headgear in 2015. *K. R. Burke*

LUCK OF THE KITTEN (USA) 3 ch.c. Kitten's Joy (USA) 128 – Anura (IRE) **106**
(Giant's Causeway (USA) 132) [2015 113: 8.5s² 8.5f⁴ 7f Jun 17] good-quartered colt:
fourth foal: brother to 3 winners in USA, including useful 7.5f and (including at 2 yrs) 1m
winner Empire Builder: dam US 8.5f/9f winner: useful performer: successful in 2014 in
maiden at Arlington and non-graded event at Santa Anita, and also second in Breeders' Cup
Juvenile Turf on latter course: not in same form in 2015, though neck second to Night
Prowler in Grade 3 Transylvania Stakes at Keeneland: 8¼ lengths eleventh to Dutch
Connection in Jersey Stakes at Royal Ascot final outing: stays 1m: acts on firm going: wore
blinkers at 2 yrs, not in 2015: front runner/races prominently. *Wesley A. Ward, USA*

LUCKY BEGGAR (IRE) 5 gr.g. Verglas (IRE) 118 – Lucky Clio (IRE) 59 (Key of Luck **100**
(USA) 126) [2015 112: 6d⁶ 5.2m⁴ 5.1s⁴ 5g⁵ 5.4g 5.6d 5d⁵ Oct 24] strong gelding: useful
handicapper: one of better efforts in 2015 when 1½ lengths fifth of 18 to Easy Road at
Doncaster final start: stays 6f: acts on good to firm and heavy going: has been gelded.
Charles Hills

LUCKY BOO (IRE) 6 b.m. Kodiac 112 – Lucky April 62 (Whittingham (IRE) 104) **45**
[2015 –: p5g p6g p7g⁶ t7.1f Mar 23] poor maiden: stays 7f: acts on polytrack: usually
wears headgear: often races in rear: has carried head awkwardly.
Muredach Kelly, Ireland

LUCKY BRIDLE (IRE) 6 b.g. Dylan Thomas (IRE) 132 – Auction Room (USA) 90 **–**
(Chester House (USA) 123) [2015 103: 10g⁶ Sep 24] useful handicapper: left W. P. Mullins,
well held only start in 2015: stays 1½m: acts on good to firm and good to soft going: has
worn hood. *Chris Grant*

LUCKY CLOVER 4 ch.f. Lucky Story (USA) 128 – Willisa 67 (Polar Falcon (USA) **66**
126) [2015 50: t6g⁵ t5.1m* 5m² 5.1m* 5m² 5.1m⁴ p5g² 5m³ 5g* 5.1d³ p5g³ 5.3d 5m Sep
28] fair handicapper: won at Wolverhampton in April, Chepstow in May and Ffos Las in
July: best form at 5f: acts on polytrack, tapeta, good to firm and good to soft going: tried in
headgear: front runner/races prominently: largely consistent. *Malcolm Saunders*

LUCKY DI 5 br.m. Araafa (IRE) 128 – Lucky Date (IRE) 91 (Halling (USA) 133) [2015 **73**
78: p7g p6g⁵ p7f⁵ p7f⁵ p6f p6f* 5.7f⁴ p6g⁵ 6g* p7g 6g 6g t6g* t7.1f² t7.1g t7.1f Dec 21] **a81**
sturdy mare: fairly useful handicapper: won at Lingfield in April, Leicester in July and
Wolverhampton (apprentice) in September: stays 7f: acts on polytrack, tapeta and good to
firm going: usually races towards rear: has shown signs of temperament. *Peter Hedger*

LUCKY DIVA 8 ch.m. Lucky Story (USA) 128 – Cosmic Countess (IRE) 74 (Lahib **61**
(USA) 129) [2015 66: 13.1m⁶ 16.2m 13.1m³ 13.1m⁴ 17.2f³ 13.1d p15.8f Sep 22] modest
handicapper: stays 17f: acts on polytrack, firm and good to soft going: often wears
headgear: usually races in rear. *Bill Turner*

LUCKY DOTTIE 4 b.f. Lucky Story (USA) 128 – Auntie Dot Com 70 (Tagula (IRE) **60**
116) [2015 66: p12g² p13g* p12g* p12f p11f p12g Dec 2] modest handicapper: won at
Lingfield in January and February: stays 13f: acts on polytrack: tried in hood in 2015: often
races towards rear. *Pat Phelan*

LUCKY HENRY 6 br.g. Lucky Story (USA) 128 – Seldemosa 67 (Selkirk (USA) 129) **80**
[2015 10m⁴ 10.4f⁴ p11g³ 11.8g³ p12g⁵ 10.2f⁴ p11g⁶ t12.2f Oct 23] rather leggy, attractive
gelding: fairly useful handicapper: stays 1½m: acts on polytrack and firm going: tried in
headgear prior to 2015. *Clive Cox*

LUCKY KRISTALE 4 b.f. Lucky Story (USA) 128 – Pikaboo 62 (Pivotal 124) [2015 99: **110**
6g⁵ 6g 6m² 6f 6m² 6g³ 6g* 7m 7m Oct 3] strong, compact filly: smart performer: won listed
race at York (by ½ length from Fort Del Oro) in September: second in listed race at
Windsor (½ length behind Tropics) in June and in Summer Stakes at York (head behind
New Providence) in July: stays 6f: acts on firm going: often in headgear in 2015: held up.
George Margarson

LUCKY LEYF 3 b.f. Kheleyf (USA) 116 – Lucky Dice (Perugino (USA) 84) [2015 65: **65**
7d 7.1m t6g⁵ p6g⁵ 6g Sep 7] fair maiden: stays 7f: acts on polytrack and tapeta: in
cheekpieces/tongue tie final start: often races towards rear. *Gary Moore*

LUCKY LODGE 5 b.g. Lucky Story (USA) 128 – Melandre 74 (Lujain (USA) 119) **79**
[2015 73: t7.1g* t7.1f² 7m² 6d⁴ 7g² 7m 7.5m 7.5d t7.1f t7.1f⁵ Dec 21] leggy gelding: fair
handicapper: won at Wolverhampton in January: stays 7f: acts on tapeta, good to firm and
heavy going: often wears blinkers: often races towards rear. *Antony Brittain*

LUCKY MARK (IRE) 6 b.g. Moss Vale (IRE) 126 – Vracca 82 (Vettori (IRE) 119) **69**
[2015 61, a69: f6d* f6g⁴ f6g³ f6s³ f6g⁶ 5g⁵ 6d² 5g 6d f6g f5m⁴ Dec 8] close-coupled
gelding: fair handicapper: won at Southwell in January: will prove suited by a return to 6f:
acts on polytrack, fibresand and good to soft going: often wears headgear: front runner/
races prominently. *John Balding*

LUCKY PRIZE 5 b.m. Lucky Story (USA) 128 – Mana Pools (IRE) 76 (Brief Truce **–**
(USA) 126) [2015 t7.1f Jan 5] no form. *Mel Brittain*

LUCKY STARS 5 ch.m. Lucky Story (USA) 128 – Cosmic Countess (IRE) 74 (Lahib **–**
(USA) 129) [2015 –: t8.6g 12.1m 8d Jun 23] no form: tried in cheekpieces. *Bill Turner*

LUCKY SURPRISE 4 b.f. Lucky Story (USA) 128 – Bella Bertolini 67 (Bertolini (USA) **–**
125) [2015 59: f7g 5m 6d Jun 23] close-coupled filly: maiden: no form in 2015: often
wears blinkers: often races towards rear/races lazily. *Jeremy Gask*

LUCKY TIMES 4 b.f. Lucky Story (USA) 128 – Paradise Eve 81 (Bahamian Bounty 116) **65**
[2015 72: f5d³ f5d Jan 22] fair handicapper: best form at 5f: acts on fibresand and soft
going. *Mel Brittain*

LUCYMAI 2 b.f. (Apr 5) Multiplex 114 – Miss Lesley 80 (Needwood Blade 117) [2015 **75**
p6g* 7m⁴ Jun 26] third foal: sister to Spanish 7f winner Horsetracker: dam temperamental
2-y-o 6f winner: better effort when winning maiden at Kempton (by neck from Taqwaa) in
June. *Dean Ivory*

LUCY PARSONS (IRE) 4 ch.f. Thousand Words 113 – Consensus (IRE) 91 (Common **–**
Grounds 118) [2015 t5.1f 5m Jun 20] fair winner at 2 yrs: missed 2014, well held only start
in 2015: raced only at 5f. *David Barron*

LUCY THE PAINTER (IRE) 3 b.f. Excellent Art 125 – Royal Bounty (IRE) 80 **81**
(Generous (IRE) 139) [2015 67: 6s² t7.1g 6g* 6g⁶ 6v² p6d⁶ 6s⁶ 6g³ Oct 20] fairly useful
handicapper: won at Ffos Las in July: stays 6f: acts on tapeta and heavy going. *Peter Makin*

LUGANO 2 b.c. (Mar 2) Galileo (IRE) 134 – Swiss Lake (USA) 115 (Indian Ridge 123) **57 p**
[2015 8.3s t8.6f⁴ p8f Nov 25] 250,000Y: half-brother to several winners, including smart
sprinters Swiss Diva (by Pivotal), Swiss Spirit (by Invincible Spirit) and Swiss Dream (by
Oasis Dream): dam 5f winner (including at 2 yrs): modest form in maidens, showing a little
promise: should do better in time. *Sir Mark Prescott Bt*

LUIS VAZ DE TORRES (IRE) 3 b.g. Tagula (IRE) 116 – Tekhania (IRE) (Dalakhani **91**
(IRE) 133) [2015 77p: p5g³ 6m⁶ 5d⁶ 5.4m 6g 5g 5s³ f5g p6g² p6g⁶ t5.1f p6g* Dec 28]
fairly useful handicapper: won at Pontefract in July and Lingfield in December: stays 6f:
acts on polytrack, tapeta and soft going. *Richard Fahey*

LUJEANIE 9 br.g. Lujain (USA) 119 – Ivory's Joy 109 (Tina's Pet 121) [2015 64, a75: **65**
p6m² p6m⁵ p6f⁶ p6m p6f³ p7m p5f⁵ May 1] good-topped gelding: fair handicapper: stays
6f: acts on polytrack, firm and good to soft going: often wears headgear. *Peter Crate*

LULANI (IRE) 3 b.f. Royal Applause 124 – Louveriaux (IRE) (Verglas (IRE) 118) [2015 **75**
86p: 10f 9.9g 8.3d⁶ Aug 29] lengthy filly: fair performer: best effort at 1m: acts on heavy
going: tried in hood in 2015. *Harry Dunlop*

LULU THE ZULU (IRE) 7 ch.m. Danroad (AUS) 112 – Timbervati (USA) 91 **106**
(Woodman (USA) 126) [2015 106: 7m 6g⁴ 6m⁴ 7m² 7f Jul 11] medium-sized mare: useful
handicapper: second at Newcastle (head behind Zarwaan) in June: stays 7.5f: acts on good
to firm and heavy going. *Michael Appleby*

LULWORTH (IRE) 2 b.g. (Apr 30) Canford Cliffs (IRE) 133 – Aitch (IRE) (Alhaarth **59 p**
(IRE) 126) [2015 p7g t7.1m⁶ p7g⁵ Dec 28] 22,000Y: fifth foal: half-brother to 7f winner
Sabratha (by Hawk Wing) and useful winner up to 10.3f Stellar Express (2-y-o 7f-8.3f
winner, by Royal Applause): dam once-raced half-sister to smart 1¼m-17f winner Galileo's
Choice: modest maiden: best effort when fifth at Lingfield, not knocked about: left James
Toller after first start: tried in cheekpieces: remains open to improvement. *William Jarvis*

LUMIERE 2 gr.f. (Mar 10) Shamardal (USA) 129 – Screen Star (IRE) 110 (Tobougg **115 p**
(IRE) 125) [2015 6m* 6g² 6g* Sep 26]

Mark Johnston's Kingsley Park training base was the first to send out two
hundred winners in Britain in a calendar year. That was in 2009 and another double
century in 2015 meant that the Johnston string has now reached two hundred winners
in six of the last seven years (a century has been chalked up in each of the last
twenty-two). Johnston himself believed before the season started that it would be 'a
daunting task' to amass another double century, given the significant change to the
make-up of his string which included a much-enlarged raft of Darley two-year-olds.

Connolly's Red Mills Cheveley Park Stakes, Newmarket—the grey Lumiere looks a leading One Thousand Guineas contender as she beats Illuminate (closest to rail), Besharah (between winner and runner-up) and Alice Springs (third right) in a strong renewal

Four-fifths of the stable's wins in 2014 were recorded by three-year-olds and older horses but, with two-year-olds making up two-thirds of the string in the latest season, there was a near fifty-fifty split in the stable's winners between the juveniles and their elders. The one hundred and twenty two-year-olds, as a group, exceeded their trainer's expectations and the Cheveley Park winner Lumiere and Coventry Stakes winner Buratino also ended the year as the stable's two leading earners overall. Lumiere's win in the Cheveley Park Stakes gave Kingsley Park its first Group 1 victory since Jukebox Jury dead-heated as a five-year-old in the 2011 Irish St Leger, and its first domestic Group 1 win since Awzaan in the 2009 Middle Park Stakes. Awzaan was well held in the following year's Two Thousand Guineas and was eventually shipped off to stud in Uruguay after failing to win another race after the Middle Park. There is plenty of confidence, however, that Lumiere's three-year-old career will blossom into something much better. Her trainer has compared her to his 2004 One Thousand Guineas winner Attraction (the last British classic winner he had) and reportedly told Lumiere's owner just before the Cheveley Park that 'I don't know whether she will win this, but I think she'll win the Guineas.' The good news for Johnston, whose job for Darley has long been seen as developing talent for Godolphin (he trained Lumiere's Dewhurst-winning sire Shamardal as a two-year-old), is that Lumiere will remain at his Middleham stable. New Godolphin supremo John Ferguson confirmed at the end of the season that 'we are not transferring horses like we used to and Mark is a Godolphin trainer now.'

The Johnston two-year-olds, even the very good ones, usually start in the bargain basement—Awzaan's first race was a maiden at Hamilton, Shamardal's was at Ayr and Attraction's at Nottingham—but Lumiere was different. Rumours that Lumiere had been catching pigeons on the Middleham gallops proved well founded when she skated home, backed as if defeat was out of the question, by six lengths from Sharja Queen on her debut in a division of a valuable maiden fillies race at the Newmarket July meeting (her time was nearly a second faster than the winner of the first division thirty-five minutes earlier). Lumiere was clearly a pattern performer in the making and she was sent straight to York for the Lowther Stakes at the Ebor meeting, a race for which she had to be supplemented. In another good renewal of that race, which York is pushing for promotion into a summer Group 1 for juvenile

Sheikh Hamdan Bin Mohammed Al Maktoum's "Lumiere"

fillies, Lumiere found only the much more experienced Besharah too good for her. Lumiere travelled enthusiastically in the lead for a long way—she had made all at Newmarket—but she wandered under pressure through greenness when tackled by Besharah who forged ahead to beat her by two and a quarter lengths, with the Queen Mary runner-up Easton Angel the same distance further away in third.

Lumiere looked sure to derive plenty from the experience in the Lowther Stakes but her trainer's slight reluctance to go overboard about her chance in the Connolly's Red Mills Cheveley Park on her next start, at Newmarket in September, was centred around the fact that she had started to go in her coat in the lead up to the race ('I've only got three two-year-olds who are losing their coat and she would happen to be one of them'). Johnston need not have worried. Among the opposition were Besharah and unbeaten Illuminate, who had met previously (involved in a very close finish) in the Duchess of Cambridge—formerly the Cherry Hinton—the day after Lumiere made her debut. Alice Springs, third in the Moyglare behind stablemates Minding and Ballydoyle, represented the strongest Irish form lines. Lumiere got home in a tight finish with her three main rivals, winning by half a length, a head and three quarters of a length from Illuminate, Besharah and Alice Springs, with the first four pulling away from the rest. Lumiere made all and had to fight hard for her victory, displaying battling qualities when challenged that bode well for her three-year-old prospects. She was edging away again from Illuminate as the line was reached, suggesting that she will certainly stay seven furlongs and will probably get the Guineas trip (she is 8/1 third favourite at the time of writing).

The Cheveley Park was contested at a good gallop with Lumiere's time only marginally slower than that recorded by Shalaa when beating Lumiere's stablemate Buratino by half a length in the Middle Park on the same day.

```
                          ┌ Giant's Causeway ┌ Storm Cat
            ┌ Shamardal (USA) │   (ch 1997)     └ Mariah's Storm
            │ (b 2002)        └ Helsinki        ┌ Machiavellian
Lumiere     │                    (b 1993)       └ Helen Street
(gr.f. 2013)│                  ┌ Tobougg        ┌ Barathea
            │ Screen Star (IRE)│  (b 1998)      └ Lacovia
            └ (gr 2005)        └ Actoris         ┌ Diesis
                                  (ro 1994)      └ Avice Caro
```

Lumiere's speed and style of racing—she is a front runner like her sire—have led some to conclude that she will turn out to be a sprinter purely and simply. However, her make and shape—she was lean and rather unfurnished as a two-year-old—are not typical of a sprinting type. As has been said, Lumiere is by the very successful Darley stallion Shamardal whose feat of winning both the Poule d'Essai des Poulains and the Prix du Jockey Club was replicated five years later by his son Lope de Vega, who is also now a successful stallion. Lumiere's dam Screen Star also started her racing career with Mark Johnston, making a remarkable front-running debut in a seven-furlong minor event at Redcar and winning by eleven lengths, earning an exceptional Timeform rating for a debutante of 110p. She looked sure to prove a force at pattern level as a three-year-old but, transferred to Godolphin, she never ran again. Screen Star was by the Derby third Tobougg and would certainly have stayed a mile. Lumiere is her fourth foal and her only previous winner the fairly useful Silent Movie (by Cape Cross) successful at a mile and a half for Mark Johnston. Lumiere's grandam Actoris was a useful winner at a mile in France and her great grandam Avice Caro, twice successful at Brighton over a mile and a quarter, was a half-sister to the smart miler Sensation who won the Falmouth Stakes in Sheikh Mohammed's colours (Lumiere's fourth dam is Outstandingly, winner of the Breeders' Cup Juvenile Fillies). Sensation went on to produce the Cumberland Lodge and Ormonde Stakes winner Systematic for the Johnston stable. Lumiere, incidentally, was the last foal produced for Darley by Screen Star who was bought by Mark Johnston for 52,000 guineas (in foal to Exceed And Excel) at the 2013 December Sales. The resulting colt was initially sold for 70,000 guineas as a foal but bought back by Mark Johnston Racing for 105,000 guineas at Newmarket in December. *Mark Johnston*

LUNA MARE (IRE) 2 b.f. (Mar 11) Galileo (IRE) 134 – Pale Moon Rising (IRE) **75 p** (Kingmambo (USA) 125) [2015 8.5m⁵ p8f³ Nov 12] second foal: dam unraced half-sister to useful stayers Min Alemarat and Beyond Conceit (both by Galileo): better effort when third in maiden at Chelmsford (2½ lengths behind Khaleesy) in November, barely adequate test: will prove suited by at least 1¼m: likely to progress further. *Richard Fahey*

LUNA MISSION (IRE) 3 b.f. Acclamation 118 – Bowness 84 (Efisio 120) [2015 79: **75** t6m⁵ t7.1g 7v⁵ p7f⁶ Dec 17] fair handicapper: stays 7f: acts on polytrack, tapeta and heavy going. *Marco Botti*

LUNA MOON 3 b.f. Equiano (FR) 127 – Luanshya 78 (First Trump 118) [2015 71p: p7m* **77** 8g⁶ 7g p7g Oct 14] lengthy filly: fair handicapper: won at Lingfield in April: stays 1m: acts on polytrack and soft going. *Jeremy Noseda*

LUNAR DEITY 6 b.g. Medicean 128 – Luminda (IRE) (Danehill (USA) 126) [2015 86: **90** p8g* p8g² p8f* p7f p8g* p8f⁶ 7m 7m⁴ 7m 7m 8d p8f p8g⁶ Dec 10] strong, good-topped **a99** gelding: useful handicapper: won at Lingfield in January (twice) and March: stays 8.5f: acts on polytrack, good to firm and good to soft going: tried in headgear prior to 2015. *Stuart Williams*

LUNAR KNOT 3 b.f. Stimulation (IRE) 121 – Moon Bird 71 (Primo Dominie 121) [2015 **–** 50: f6d 6m 8.5d Sep 22] maiden: no form in 2015: tried in headgear. *John Balding*

LUNAR LOGIC 3 b.g. Motivator 131 – Moonmaiden 71 (Selkirk (USA) 129) [2015 11m **56** p10m⁶ 11.5d⁴ 11.6g Jun 22] good-topped gelding: modest maiden: stays 11.5f. *Andrew Balding*

LUNAR SON 2 gr.g. (Mar 20) Medicean 128 – Moon Empress (FR) 84 (Rainbow Quest **56 §**
(USA) 134) [2015 6m 5.1d⁴ 7v 8.3s³ p8g t9.5f⁶ p8m² Nov 21] rather leggy gelding: modest
maiden: stays 8.5f: acts on polytrack and soft going: tried in cheekpieces: temperamental.
Mick Channon

LUNASEA (IRE) 4 b.c. Sea The Stars (IRE) 140 – Musical Treat (IRE) 98 (Royal **83**
Academy (USA) 130) [2015 90p: 10m⁶ 12g⁴ May 14] fairly useful handicapper, lightly
raced: may prove best at short of 1½m: sold 32,000 gns, sent to Saudi Arabia. *Luca Cumani*

LUNGARNO PALACE (USA) 4 b.g. Henrythenavigator (USA) 131 – Good Time **94**
Sally (USA) (Forestry (USA) 121) [2015 97: p12g⁵ 10.3d⁵ 12g* 12f 12m 11.9g 10g⁵ 12m⁶
16.4d³ 18g Sep 19] fairly useful handicapper: won at Epsom (by ½ length from Jakey) in
April: third at York in August: stays 16.5f: acts on polytrack, good to firm and good to soft
going: tried in blinkers: tried in tongue tie prior to 2015. *John Gallagher*

LUPO D'ORO (IRE) 6 b.g. Amadeus Wolf 122 – Vital Laser (USA) (Seeking The Gold **76**
(USA)) [2015 79, a70: p5f² p5f* p5m² p6g² p6f⁴ p6f p8d³ p8m⁴ Dec 31] sparely-made
gelding: fair handicapper: won at Kempton in February: may prove best short of 1m: acts
on polytrack, soft and good to firm going: tried in visor prior to 2015. *John Best*

LU'S BUDDY (GR) 4 b.g. Reel Buddy (USA) 118 – Papality 76 (Giant's Causeway **84**
(USA) 132) [2015 82: p11g 10m³ 8m³ 9.9s⁵ 8m* 8m³ 10.1m² 10g⁵ 9s⁹ 9.9g⁵ 8.3s³ t9.5m⁵
p8m² Oct 21] lengthy gelding: fairly useful handicapper: won at Newmarket (apprentice)
in June: stays 1¼m: acts on polytrack, tapeta, soft and good to firm going: usually in
headgear in 2015: tried in tongue tie: front runner/races prominently: sold 26,000 gns.
Amanda Perrett

LUSO GOLD 2 b.f. (Apr 16) Poet's Voice 126 – Bezant (IRE) 51 (Zamindar (USA) 116) **72 p**
[2015 8g 7g⁵ Aug 28] 31,000F, 50,000Y: sturdy filly: seventh foal: half-sister to smart 6f
(at 2 yrs) and 7f (in Hong Kong) winner Deposer (by Kheleyf): dam maiden (stayed 1m):
better effort when fifth in maiden at Newmarket (5½ lengths behind Promising Run) in
August, nearest finish: will benefit from return to 1m: should do better. *Clive Brittain*

LUSTROUS 4 b.f. Champs Elysees 124 – Tamzin (Hernando (FR) 127) [2015 106: 12m **110**
11.9d 11.9g² 14m⁴ 12d 12.3s² Sep 12] angular filly: smart performer: second in Lancashire
Oaks at Haydock (¾ length behind Lady Tiana) in July and in listed race at Chester (neck
behind Secret Number) final start: stays 1¾m: acts on soft and good to firm going.
Richard Hannon

LUTINE CHARLIE (IRE) 8 br.g. Kheleyf (USA) 116 – Silvery Halo (USA) 68 (Silver **53**
Ghost (USA)) [2015 63: p7m⁴ t7.1f⁶ p8g t7.1m⁴ p6m⁵ 8g⁵ 7.1m 7g³ 8g p8f t7.1f t7.1m⁴
Dec 30] compact gelding: modest handicapper: trained by Pat Eddery until after tenth start:
stays 8.5f: acts on all-weather, soft and good to firm going: sometimes wears headgear.
Emma Owen

LUVLY 2 b.g. (Feb 1) Multiplex 114 – Luv U Too 82 (Needwood Blade 117) [2015 f5g³ **60**
f5g³ Apr 27] better effort when third in maiden at Southwell (5¼ lengths behind New Road
Side) on debut. *Brian Baugh*

LUVLYLYNNTHOMAS 3 gr.f. Equiano (FR) 127 – Dansa Queen 89 (Dansili 127) **–**
[2015 –: 8d Apr 16] no form. *Micky Hammond*

LUV U 3 b.f. Royal Applause 124 – Love Roi (ITY) 102 (Roi Danzig (USA)) [2015 54: **58**
t9.5f⁴ f8g⁴ p8d* 7.1m² 8.9m⁴ Jul 31] modest handicapper: won at Chelmsford in March:
left Ed Dunlop after first start: stays 9.5f: acts on polytrack, tapeta and good to firm going:
tried in blinkers in 2015. *Michael Appleby*

LUV U LUCKY 3 b.g. Multiplex 114 – Lady Suesanne (IRE) 66 (Cape Cross (IRE) 129) **61**
[2015 f7g³ f7g³ 10.2m f6g³ Dec 15] modest maiden: stays 7f. *Michael Appleby*

LUV U WHATEVER 5 b.g. Needwood Blade 117 – Lady Suesanne (IRE) 66 (Cape **103**
Cross (IRE) 129) [2015 87: f11s* f12s* f12g* t12.2g² t12.2m³ p15.8f 12g t12.2m⁶
t9.5m t9.5m² Dec 26] useful handicapper: much improved in 2015 and won 3 times at
Southwell in January: placed 3 times at Wolverhampton after, good second to Second Wave
final start: stays 2m: acts on all-weather: tried in blinkers: front runner/races prominently.
Michael Appleby

LYCIDAS (GER) 6 b.g. Zamindar (USA) 116 – La Felicita (Shareef Dancer (USA) 135) **102**
[2015 f12g² t16.5f* p16g³ p14g³ 16.4m* 20f 14m⁴ Jul 11] workmanlike gelding: useful
performer: won handicaps at Wolverhampton in March and York (by ¾ length from
Moscato) in May: third in minor event at Chelmsford (length behind Pinzolo) fourth start:
stays 16.5f: acts on polytrack, tapeta and good to firm going: wears headgear: has joined
James Ewart. *Charlie Fellowes*

LYDIA'S PLACE 2 ch.f. (Mar 2) Equiano (FR) 127 – Peace And Love (IRE) 75 (Fantastic **89**
Light (USA) 134) [2015 5.1s 5m* 5f* 5m* t5.1f Oct 30] 3,750Y: third foal: half-sister to
7f/1m winner Dimitar (by Mizzen Mast): dam, 2-y-o 5f winner, out of useful half-sister to
Melbourne Cup winner Jeune: fairly useful performer: won maiden at Catterick in May and
minor event at Beverley and nursery at York in July: raced only at 5f: acts on firm going:
usually races close up. *Richard Guest*

LYDIATE (IRE) 2 b.f. (Mar 19) Acclamation 118 – Maid To Order (IRE) 83 (Zafonic **73**
(USA) 130) [2015 6g⁴ 6g² t5.1m* f5g⁶ Dec 18] £50,000Y: sister to winner up to 1m Jibaal
(2-y-o 7f winner) and 2-y-o 5f winner Storm Trooper and half-sister to 3 winners: dam 1m
winner: fair performer: won maiden at Wolverhampton in November: stays 6f.
Richard Fahey

LYDIATE LADY 3 b.f. Piccolo 121 – Hiraeth 76 (Petong 126) [2015 43, a52: 5d² 5g* 5g **67**
t3.1g⁵ 5.1m² 5g⁵ 5m⁵ 6g⁴ 5.9g² 6g⁵ 5.9s 5.1d³ Oct 14] fair handicapper: won at Catterick
in April and Haydock in August: stays 6f: acts on good to soft and good to firm going: tried
in cheekpieces. *Paul Green*

LYFKA 3 ch.f. Kheleyf (USA) 116 – Tarkamara (IRE) 80 (Medicean 128) [2015 48, a94: **93**
7m 7m³ 7g² 7m p6g p7m Oct 21] compact filly: fairly useful performer: second in handicap
at Goodwood in June: stays 6f: acts on polytrack and tapeta. *Paul Cole*

LYNNGALE 4 b.f. Myboycharlie (IRE) 118 – Belle Annie (USA) (Aptitude (USA) 128) **62**
[2015 74: t9.5g t8.6f² 8.5m⁶ 7.5g 10.2g 8.5g⁶ t9.5g² t9.5m⁶ t9.5m³ t9.5f² t9.5f⁴ t12.2m **a69**
p10g Dec 7] fair handicapper: stays 1¼m: acts on polytrack, tapeta and firm going: often
wears hood: front runner/races prominently. *Kristin Stubbs*

LYSANDER THE GREEK 3 b.g. Exceed And Excel (AUS) 126 – Hector's Girl 99 **67**
(Hector Protector (USA) 124) [2015 70: f8g* f8d² 8.5f 8.3f 8f Oct 10] good-quartered
gelding: fair performer: won handicap at Southwell in January: left Ralph Beckett, last all
3 starts in USA: stays 1m: acts on fibresand and good to firm going: tried in headgear. *Niall
Saville, USA*

LYSSIO (GER) 8 b.g. Motivator 131 – Lysuna (GER) 105 (Monsun (GER) 124) [2015 –: **–**
p11f Feb 25] lengthy gelding: useful performer at one time, behind both starts on Flat since
2012: stays 11f: acts on synthetics, soft and good to firm going: has worn headgear.
Jim Best

LYTHAM ST ANNES (IRE) 2 b.c. (Feb 4) Bahamian Bounty 116 – Kerrys Requiem **88**
(IRE) 94 (King's Best (USA) 132) [2015 5.9g 7m² 7g* 6g³ Sep 30] 70,000Y: first foal: dam
ungenuine winner up to 6f (2-y-o 5f winner) who stayed 1m: fairly useful performer: won
maiden at Epsom (by 3½ lengths from Regality) in September: stays 7f: sent to UAE.
David Simcock

M

MAAREK 8 b.g. Pivotal 124 – Ruby Rocket (IRE) 113 (Indian Rocket 115) [2015 123: 5s³ **117**
5g⁴ 6g² 6g⁵ 5g* 5d² 5m 6d 6s Nov 19] neat gelding: smart performer: won listed race at
Beverley (by neck from Line of Reason) in August: also ran well when runner-up twice at
the Curragh, in Greenlands Stakes (length behind Mustajeeb) in May and Flying Five
Stakes (head behind Sole Power) in September: stays 6f: has form on good to firm going,
best efforts under more testing conditions (acts on heavy): sometimes slowly away, usually
races in rear. *Miss Evanna McCutcheon, Ireland*

MACARTHURS PARK (IRE) 3 b.f. Equiano (FR) 127 – La Tintoretta (IRE) 88 **§§**
(Desert Prince (IRE) 130) [2015 5s⁶ 5d⁶ 5m⁶ 5g⁴ 5.9s⁶ Aug 24] good-topped filly: poor
maiden: stays 5.5f: acts on polytrack, tapeta and soft going: tried in headgear: most
temperamental (flashes tail repeatedly), and one to leave well alone. *Alan Berry*

MACBETH (IRE) 6 b.g. Acclamation 118 – Filandre (Cadeaux Genereux 131) [2015 **–**
103: 14m Jun 12] strong gelding: useful at best. well held only outing in 2015: stays 2m:
acts on heavy going: often in headgear/tongue tie prior to 2014. *Michael Appleby*

MACCUS (IRE) 2 b.c. (Mar 10) Fast Company (IRE) 126 – Raven One (IRE) 45 (Titus **94 p**
Livius (FR) 115) [2015 6m* 6f 7m² Aug 7] €9,000F, £28,000Y: third foal: dam, maiden
(stayed 1¼m), sister to smart winner up to 1m Sehrezad: fairly useful performer: won
maiden at Windsor (by 3 lengths from Arlecchino's Rock) in May: best effort when second
in nursery at Newmarket (short head behind Montsarrat) in August, clear of rest: stays 7f:
should do better still. *Brian Meehan*

MACDILLON 9 b.g. Acclamation 118 – Dilys 84 (Efisio 120) [2015 82: 5m⁵ 5m* 5.2s* **85** 5g⁵ 6g 5s Oct 19] well-made gelding: fairly useful handicapper: won at Sandown in July and Newbury in August: stays 6f: acts on polytrack, soft and good to firm going: tried in headgear/tongue tie prior to 2015. *Stuart Kittow*

MACHIAVELIAN STORM (IRE) 3 gr.f. Dark Angel (IRE) 113 – Terri's Charmer **53** (USA) (Silver Charm (USA) 132) [2015 59: 8m⁶ 7m 8d t9.5f⁶ 10.2s f8g³ t7.1m⁶ Dec 30] modest maiden: left Ollie Pears after fifth start: stays 1m: acts on polytrack and good to firm going: tried in cheekpieces/tongue tie in 2015: often races towards rear. *Michael Herrington*

MACHINE LEARNER 2 b.g. (Feb 11) Sir Percy 129 – My First Romance 61 (Danehill **84** (USA) 126) [2015 7.1m⁴ 7m³ 7.6g* 8g³ 9v³ Oct 7] sturdy gelding: half-brother to numerous winners, including smart 1m-1½m winner Chapter Seven (by Excellent Art) and useful 2-y-o 5f winners Romantic Liason (by Primo Dominie) and Romantic Myth (by Mind Games): dam ran twice: fairly useful performer: won maiden at Lingfield in August: third in nurseries at Newmarket and Nottingham last 2 starts: stays 9f: acts on heavy going. *Michael Bell*

MACHO MAC 2 ch.g. (Apr 18) Pastoral Pursuits 127 – Clarice Orsini (Common Grounds **65** 118) [2015 6m⁵ 5.1g⁵ 6.5s Oct 23] fair form when fifth in maidens at Windsor and Nottingham. *Hughie Morrison*

MACK'S SISTER 8 ch.m. Pastoral Pursuits 127 – Linda's Schoolgirl (IRE) (Grand **42** Lodge (USA) 125) [2015 42: p6f Jan 30] poor handicapper: stays 7f: acts on polytrack: tried in cheekpieces prior to 2015. *Michael Madgwick*

MACMIDNIGHT 3 b.f. Mawatheeq (USA) 126 – Rehlaat (USA) (Swain (IRE) 134) **–** [2015 9.2d 9.3d Jul 26] third foal: closely related to winner up to 9f Piergiorgio (2-y-o 1m winner, by Elnadim): dam unraced out of useful 6f (including at 2 yrs) winner Judhoor: tailed off in 2 maidens. *Donald Whillans*

MAC'S POWER (IRE) 9 b.g. Exceed And Excel (AUS) 126 – Easter Girl (Efisio 120) **71 §** [2015 86§: p6g p7g t7.1f p7g⁵ p7g⁴ p6g p7g⁵ 7d⁴ p6g p7g² Dec 28] lengthy gelding: fair handicapper: stays 1m: acts on polytrack, good to firm and good to soft going: tried in hood prior to 2015: often wears tongue tie: hard to win with: one to be wary of. *Willie Musson*

MAC'S SUPERSTAR (FR) 5 b.g. Elusive City (USA) 117 – Diamond Light (USA) 70 **–** (Fantastic Light (USA) 134) [2015 86: 7.6d³ 7m⁶ 9.9s⁶ Jun 2] good-bodied gelding: fairly useful handicapper in 2014, no form in 2015: acted at 7f: acted on polytrack: wore hood in 2014, blinkered final start: dead. *Alan Coogan*

MAC TIERNAN (IRE) 8 b.g. Minashki (IRE) 106 – Softly Softly (IRE) 80 (Lucky **–** Guest 109) [2015 f8g t9.5f f11g Dec 29] smallish gelding: fair at best, no form in 2015. *Philip Kirby*

MADAKHEEL (USA) 4 b.f. Mr Greeley (USA) 122 – Manaal (USA) 93 (Bahri (USA) **53** 125) [2015 –: t8.6g⁵ t9.5g⁵ f8d 7m 7d 7.9s Aug 24] modest maiden: stays 1¼m: acts on tapeta and good to soft going. *Simon West*

MADAME BARKER (IRE) 2 ch.f. (Feb 5) Frozen Power (IRE) 108 – Shadow **46 +** Mountain (Selkirk (USA) 129) [2015 5.9g 5.9g 5g⁵ 5d⁶ t5.1m² t6f* 5m⁵ t6f⁴ t5.1g⁵ t6f³ **a64** Dec 22] £18,000Y: sixth foal: half-sister to 5f/6f winner Mountain Excel (by Exceed And Excel) and useful 6f winner Dickie's Lad (by Diamond Green): dam 7f winner: modest performer: won seller at Wolverhampton in September: stays 6f: acts on tapeta: tried in blinkers. *Bryan Smart*

MADAME BUTTERFLY (IRE) 3 b.f. Rip Van Winkle (IRE) 134 – Messias da Silva **78 p** (USA) 89 (Tale of The Cat (USA) 113) [2015 7g² 7g² Jun 26] third foal: half-sister to very smart winner up to 1m Amazing Maria (2-y-o 7f winner, by Mastercraftsman): dam 2-y-o 6f winner: fair form when runner-up in maidens at Thirsk (better effort) and Newcastle: should stay 1m: remains with potential. *David O'Meara*

MADAME CHIANG 4 b.f. Archipenko (USA) 127 – Robe Chinoise 103 (Robellino **110** (USA) 127) [2015 117: 10.4m⁵ 12d⁴ 9.9d 12d Oct 17] tall, rather leggy filly: smart performer: not at best in 2015, though respectable effort when 5¾ lengths fourth of 7 to Postponed in King George VI and Queen Elizabeth Stakes at Ascot in July: stays 1½m: acts on good to firm and heavy going: often races in rear. *David Simcock*

MADAME CLAUD 2 ch.f. (May 6) Champs Elysees 124 – Change Partners (IRE) 79 **56 p** (Hernando (FR) 127) [2015 9d p8g p8m Nov 17] seventh foal: half-sister to 2-y-o 7f winner Zingana (by Zamindar): dam, 1½m winner, half-sister to useful 2-y-o 6f winner (stayed 1m) Total Love: modest form in maidens: should do better given time and longer distances. *Hughie Morrison*

MADAME LAFITE 3 b.f. Dutch Art 126 – Poppo's Song (CAN) (Polish Navy (USA)) **69**
[2015 10d 12m 10m p13f Jul 25] 42,000F, 46,000Y: good-topped filly: half-sister to several
winners, including useful winner up to 9.5f Nabbaash (2-y-o 7.5f-9f winner, by Aqlaam)
and 17f winner Petaluma (by Teofilo): dam 1m (minor Canadian stakes) winner: fair
maiden: stays 13f. *Jonathan Portman*

MADAME MIRASOL (IRE) 4 b.f. Sleeping Indian 122 – Confidentiality (IRE) 93 **–**
(Desert Style (IRE) 121) [2015 68, a83: f7g⁶ f7g Jan 13] angular filly: fairly useful at best,
no form in 2015: stays 1m: acts on all-weather, good to firm and good to soft going: often
wears cheekpieces: tried in tongue. *Kevin Ryan*

MADAME THUNDER (IRE) 2 gr.f. (Mar 24) Zebedee 113 – Cuca Vela (USA) **77**
(Devil's Bag (USA)) [2015 5s* 7g⁵ 5.2s 5g 6g p6g⁵ p7g⁴ 8g Oct 11] €17,000Y: seventh
foal: half-sister to 6f-11f winner Blackleyf (by Kheleyf) and winner up to 9.5f Makin (by
Shirocco): dam unraced: fair performer: won maiden at Naas in April: stays 7f: acts on
polytrack and soft going: sometimes in headgear. *Darren Bunyan, Ireland*

MADAM LILIBET (IRE) 6 b.m. Authorized (IRE) 133 – Foxilla (IRE) 68 (Foxhound **72 §**
(USA) 103) [2015 71: 18s³ 21.6g⁴ 17.1d⁶ 18d⁴ 18s³ 16d Oct 30] good-bodied mare:
handicapper: stays 2¼m: acts on heavy going: lazy: best treated with caution. *Sharon Watt*

MADAM MAI TAI 3 ch.f. Compton Place 125 – Dash of Lime 67 (Bold Edge 123) [2015 **39**
–: 7g⁶ 8g⁵ 7m 6g⁶ Sep 4] poor maiden: stays 1m: acts on good to firm going.
Rebecca Bastiman

MADAM MIDNIGHT 3 ch.f. Shamardal (USA) 129 – Miss Marvellous (USA) 78 **69**
(Diesis 133) [2015 68: t9.5f³ p8g⁴ t8.6g 11.6m³ Jun 29] angular filly: fair maiden: stays
11.5f: acts on tapeta and good to firm going: sold 11,000 gns, sent to Sweden. *David Simcock*

MADDYS DREAM 2 b.g. (Apr 27) Arabian Gleam 122 – Group Force (IRE) 64 **75 p**
(Montjeu (IRE) 137) [2015 d6³ Jul 13] leggy, close-coupled gelding: fourth foal: dam 2-y-o
1m winner who stayed 2m: 80/1, promise when third in maiden at Windsor (1½ lengths
behind Essenaitch) in July: should do better. *Lydia Pearce*

MAD ENDEAVOUR 4 b.g. Muhtathir 126 – Capefly 71 (Cape Cross (IRE) 129) [2015 **68**
65: 6m 6.1s⁵ t6g* 6g² 6.1m³ 6g⁴ p6g⁶ Aug 7] compact gelding: fair handicapper: won at
Wolverhampton in June: stays 6f: acts on tapeta and good to firm going: tried in headgear:
tried in tongue tie prior to 2015: front runner/races prominently. *Stuart Kittow*

MADE WITH LOVE 4 b.g. Exceed And Excel (AUS) 126 – Maid To Perfection 102 **92**
(Sadler's Wells (USA) 132) [2015 90: p8g⁴ 10.3m⁵ 8g p8g Nov 9] rather leggy gelding:
fairly useful handicapper: left John Gosden after second start: stays 1m: acts on polytrack
and good to firm going: tried in hood in 2015: usually leads. *David O'Meara*

MADHATTEN (IRE) 2 b.f. (Mar 19) Dream Ahead (USA) 133 – Traou Mad (IRE) 107 **71**
(Barathea (IRE) 127) [2015 6g 5.1g³ p5f³ 5.7m³ Sep 28] tall, angular filly: half-sister to
several winners, including useful 7.5f winner Roscoff (by Daylami) and 1¼m-1½m winner
Honoured (by Mark of Esteem): dam 2-y-o 5f winner: fair maiden: should stay at least 6f.
Richard Hannon

MADINAT JUMEIRAH (IRE) 2 b.c. (Jan 29) Bernardini (USA) 132 – Tizdubai **–**
(USA) 114 (Cee's Tizzy (USA)) [2015 7s Oct 13] seventh foal: half-brother to useful
6f-7.5f winner Dragon Falls (by Distorted Humor) and 6f winner Gratitude (by Elusive
Quality): dam 3-y-o 5.5f-6.5f winner, sister to dual Breeders' Cup Classic winner Tiznow:
16/1, possibly unsuited by ground when last of 10 in maiden at Leicester: sold 3,000 gns,
sent to Bahrain. *Mark Johnston*

MADRASA (IRE) 7 b.g. High Chaparral (IRE) 132 – Shir Dar (FR) (Lead On Time **58**
(USA) 123) [2015 75: 11.8d⁴ t12.2g t13.9m t16.5f Oct 17] smallish, leggy gelding: modest
handicapper: stays 2m: acts on good to firm and good to soft going: often wears headgear:
often in tongue tie prior to 2015: usually races nearer last than first. *Tony Forbes*

MADRINHO (IRE) 2 ch.c. (Feb 24) Frozen Power (IRE) 108 – Perfectly Clear (USA) **95**
(Woodman (USA) 126) [2015 6.5m⁴ 6f* 6g² 6.1g² 6m² 6g 7v Oct 24] €25,000F, £55,000Y:
useful-looking colt: half-brother to several winners, including winner up to 1¼m Safari
Team (2-y-o 1m winner, by Pleasantly Perfect) and 7f-1½m winner Jenniings (by Jeremy):
dam 1m/9f winner: useful maiden: won maiden at Ascot in July by neck from Race Day:
second in listed race at Newbury (neck behind Tasleet) and minor events at Chester (1¼
lengths behind King Robert) and Doncaster (½ length behind Venturous): should stay 7f:
acts on firm going: often races prominently. *Richard Hannon*

MAER ROCKS (IRE) 2 br.f. (Jan 23) Dream Ahead (USA) 133 – Dream of The Hill **–**
(IRE) (Tiger Hill (IRE) 127) [2015 p8g p8m p7g Dec 16] 50,000F: first foal: dam, ran

twice, closely related to smart winner up to 1¼m Dream Peace out of smart 1¼m-1½m winner Truly A Dream: down the field in maidens. *Marcus Tregoning*

MAESTRO MAC (IRE) 2 b.c. (Mar 21) Roderic O'Connor (IRE) 119 – Union City Blues (IRE) 59 (Encosta de Lago (AUS)) [2015 p8g⁴ 7g t8.6f* Sep 19] €22,000F, 44,000Y: first foal: dam lightly-raced half-sister to smart 13f winner (stayed 2m) Road To Mandalay: fairly useful performer: best effort when winning maiden at Wolverhampton (by ¾ length from Change The Game) in September: likely to stay 1¼m: should do better still. *Hughie Morrison* **83 p**

MAFTOOL (USA) 3 b.g. Hard Spun (USA) 124 – With Intention (USA) (Mr Greeley (USA) 122) [2015 113: a7f³ a8f* a9.4f² 8g 10f⁶ 11.1s p8g³ 11.9g² Sep 6] attractive gelding: smart performer: won UAE 2000 Guineas at Meydan (by head from Mubtaahij) in February: second in UAE Derby at Meydan (8 lengths behind Mubtaahij) in March, third in minor event at Chelmsford (1½ lengths behind Algaith) in August and second in Bosphorus Cup at Veliefendi (½ length behind Connecticut) in September: stays 1½m: acts on polytrack, dirt and firm going: usually in headgear in 2015. *Saeed bin Suroor* **113**

MAFTOON (IRE) 3 gr.g. Dark Angel (IRE) 113 – Chincoteague (IRE) 75 (Daylami (IRE) 138) [2015 85: p8g* 8m⁵ Apr 25] rather leggy, medium-sized gelding: fairly useful handicapper: won at Chelmsford (by ¾ length from Flashy Memories) in March: stays 9f: acts on polytrack and good to firm going: tried in blinkers prior to 2015: sent to UAE. *Richard Hannon* **85**

MAGGIE PINK 6 b.m. Beat All (USA) 120 – Top Notch (Alderbrook 120) [2015 98: p7m⁶ p8g² p8f² p8f⁵ p7f 7.2m³ 7d* 7m⁶ 7v* 7v t7.1g p7g⁴ Dec 7] useful handicapper: won at Chester (by 2¼ lengths from Pearl Ice) in September and Newbury (by 1¾ lengths from Breakable) in October: stays 1m: acts on polytrack, good to firm and heavy going: usually leads. *Michael Appleby* **105 a92**

MAGH MEALL 3 b.f. Monsieur Bond (IRE) 120 – Tibesti (Machiavellian (USA) 123) [2015 68: 6d³ 6.5m⁴ 6g 6g⁵ Aug 1] fair handicapper: stays 6.5f: acts on soft and good to firm going: front runner/races prominently. *David Nicholls* **68**

MAGICAL DAZE 3 b.f. Showcasing 117 – Poulaine Bleue 44 (Bertolini (USA) 125) [2015 71p: t6g² 6d 5m³ 5.7g³ p6g* 5m* 5.7s³ 6g⁵ Sep 7] angular filly: fairly useful handicapper: won at Kempton in June and Windsor in August: stays 6f: acts on polytrack, tapeta, soft and good to firm going. *Sylvester Kirk* **80**

MAGICAL EFFECT (IRE) 3 ch.g. New Approach (IRE) 132 – Purple Glow (IRE) 96 (Orientate (USA) 127) [2015 74p: p6m⁴ 7s³ Aug 20] fair form all 3 starts in maidens: raced freely when upped to 7f final outing. *Charlie Appleby* **71**

MAGICAL LASSO (IRE) 2 ch.g. (Mar 26) Monsieur Bond (IRE) 120 – How Sweet It Is (IRE) 65 (Kodiac 112) [2015 7.5m⁴ 7.2m² Sep 27] 28,000F, 20,000Y, £26,000 2-y-o: first foal: dam maiden sister to useful 2-y-o 6f winner Sweet Cecily: better effort when fourth in maiden at Beverley (3½ lengths behind Drifting Spirit) in August, never nearer: remains with potential. *Kevin Ryan* **71 p**

MAGICAL MACEY (USA) 8 ch.g. Rossini (USA) 118 – Spring's Glory (USA) (Honour And Glory (USA) 122) [2015 87: f5s³ Jan 20] tall, rather sparely-made gelding: fairly useful handicapper: best form at 5f: acted on polytrack, fibresand, heavy and good to firm going: wore blinkers: was a front runner/raced prominently: dead. *David Barron* **91**

MAGICAL MEMORY (IRE) 3 gr.g. Zebedee 113 – Marasem 86 (Cadeaux Genereux 131) [2015 88: 6m⁴ 6m³ 6m* 6g³ 6m* 6m* 6d³ Sep 5] compact gelding: very smart performer, much improved in 2015: won handicaps at Leicester in May, Newmarket in July and Stewards' Cup at Goodwood (by ¾ length from Toofi) in August: 14/1, further progress **121**

Qatar Stewards' Cup (Heritage Handicap), Goodwood—the only three-year-old Magical Memory becomes the first of his age to win this valuable prize since Danetime in 1997;
Toofi (third left), Rivellino (right) and Dinkum Diamond (No.7) complete the frame

Kennet Valley Thoroughbreds I's "Magical Memory"

when ¾-length third of 15 to Twilight Son in Sprint Cup at Haydock final start, challenging from 1f out: stays 6f: acts on good to firm and good to soft going: often races towards rear, usually travels strongly. *Charles Hills*

MAGICAL MISCHIEF 5 b.m. Rob Roy (USA) 122 – Magical Flute 75 (Piccolo 121) **54** [2015 60: 8m⁵ 8g 7.9s⁶ 7.9d 7.2g Sep 29] modest maiden: stays 1m: acts on good to firm going: front runner/races prominently. *Chris Fairhurst*

MAGICAL SPRING (IRE) 2 b.g. (Apr 18) Zebedee 113 – Appletreemagic (IRE) 72 **60** (Indian Danehill (IRE) 121) [201f 5m⁴ 6r⁵ 5m⁶ 5g³ 6s Oct 6] modest maiden: stays 6f: acts on soft going: sold £6,500, sent to Sweden. *David Barron*

MAGICAL THOMAS 3 ch.g. Dylan Thomas (IRE) 132 – Magical Cliche (USA) 86 **86** (Affirmed (USA)) [2015 62p: 9.9m³ 9.9f⁵ p11g* p12g⁶ 12d² 12d p12g² p12g³ p12g⁴ p11g⁶ Nov 9] fairly useful handicapper: won at Kempton in June: good efforts there eighth/ninth starts: stays 1½m: acts on polytrack: usually races freely. *Marcus Tregoning*

MAGIC ARTIST (IRE) 4 br.c. Iffraaj 127 – Artisti (Cape Cross (IRE) 129) [2015 114: **120** 9.9g* 9.9m² 10g⁵ 9.9g⁵ 9.9d⁴ 8d⁴ 8.9s Dec 5] 105,000Y: second foal: half-brother to useful 1m (at 2 yrs) and 11f (including Austrian Derby) winner Magic Art (by Nayef): dam unraced half-sister to St Leger winner Mastery and very smart winner up to 1½m Kirklees: very smart performer: won Premio Ambrosiano at Milan (by short head from Cleo Fan) in April: mostly creditable efforts after, including in Premio Presidente della Repubblica at Rome (neck second to Cleo Fan, finishing strongly), Mackinnon Stakes at Flemington (first start after leaving W. Figge, length fourth to Gailo Chop, short of room for much of final 1½f) and Emirates Stakes (Handicap) at Flemington (length fourth to Turn Me Loose): below form final outing: stays 1¼m: acts on soft and good to firm going: often races towards rear. *A. Wohler, Germany*

MAGIC BUCKS (IRE) 3 ch.g. Zebedee 113 – Bon Expresso (IRE) 96 (Spectrum (IRE) **52**
126) [2015 p6g⁵ 5.7f⁵ 6m 5.7f 5.7f p8g p7m³ Oct 21] modest maiden: stays 7f: acts on
polytrack and firm going. *Jo Hughes*

MAGIC CIRCLE (IRE) 3 b.g. Makfi 130 – Minkova (IRE) (Sadler's Wells (USA) 132) **97 p**
[2015 59p: 12d* 14.1m⁴ 13d* 16.2d* 14.6d* Oct 23] big, rather unfurnished gelding:
useful handicapper: won at Doncaster in May, Newmarket in July and Haydock in October:
8/15, improved again when winning at Doncaster on final start by 2½ lengths from
Craggaknock, responding well: will be suited by a return to 2m+: acts on good to firm and
good to soft going: usually responds generously to pressure: likely to progress further.
Ralph Beckett

MAGIC CITY (IRE) 6 b.g. Elusive City (USA) 117 – Annmarie's Magic (IRE) 28 **106**
(Flying Spur (AUS)) [2015 111: p7f 8g⁴ 8m 7s 7g 8.3s⁵ 7s Oct 12] tall gelding: useful
handicapper: stays 1m: acts on polytrack, good to firm and good to soft going: sometimes
slowly away. *Richard Hannon*

MAGIC DANCER 3 b.g. Norse Dancer (IRE) 127 – King's Siren (IRE) 77 (King's Best **105**
(USA) 132) [2015 88p: 11.5s² 12f⁶ 11.1s 12m⁶ 13g 18g 11.8s Oct 26] useful-looking
gelding: useful performer: second in Derby Trial at Lingfield (1¼ lengths behind
Kilimanjaro) in May: little impact subsequently: stays 1½m: acts on soft and good to firm
going: often in headgear in 2015: joined Charlie Longsdon. *Ralph Beckett*

MAGIC EMPRESS (IRE) 3 b.f. Baltic King 120 – Red Trance (IRE) 79 (Soviet Star **–**
(USA) 128) [2015 55: f8s Jan 20] modest performer: best effort at 1m: acts on fibresand:
often races in rear. *Tony Coyle*

MAGIC ESCAPADE (IRE) 3 b.f. Azamour (IRE) 130 – Esclarmonde (IRE) 79 (In The **–**
Wings 128) [2015 12d Jun 14] €4,000F, 12,000Y: fourth foal: dam maiden sister to smart
winner up to 10.5f (stayed 12.5f) Trumbaka: 66/1, very green when tailed off in maiden at
Doncaster. *William Knight*

MAGIC GARDEN (IRE) 2 b.f. (Mar 19) Zebedee 113 – Sisal (IRE) 84 (Danehill (USA) **66**
126) [2015 6g³ 6m t6m³ Dec 30] 7,000 2-y-o: seventh foal: half-sister to 3 winners,
including 2-y-o 5f winner (stays 7f) Small Fury (by Windsor Knot) and ungenuine 6f-1m
winner (stayed 1½m) High 'N Dry (by Halling): dam 2-y-o 6f winner: fair maiden: best
effort when third at Wolverhampton final start: should prove suited by 7f. *Jonathan Portman*

MAGICIAN COUTINHO 3 b.g. Misu Bond (IRE) 114 – Chez Cherie 108 (Wolfhound **51 p**
(USA) 126) [2015 7g⁶ 7m⁴ 7m⁴ Aug 8] sixth foal: closely related to smart 7f-9.5f winner
Alfred Hutchinson (by Monsieur Bond) and half-brother to 8.5f winner Chez La Sammana
(by Proud Citizen): dam winner up to 11f (2-y-o 7f winner): showed a little ability in
maidens: should do better in time. *Geoffrey Oldroyd*

MAGIC ICE 5 b.m. Royal Applause 124 – Winter Ice (Wolfhound (USA) 126) [2015 –: **42**
p7g⁶ t6f Jan 16] poor maiden: stays 6f: acts on polytrack: tried in cheekpieces prior to 2015.
John Berry

MAGIC MAGNOLIA (IRE) 4 b.f. Azamour (IRE) 130 – Royal Aly (USA) (Royal **–**
Academy (USA) 130) [2015 67: p12g⁵ Jan 21] maiden: no form since debut in 2014: tried
in headgear/tongue tie. *Mark Gillard*

MAGIC MAISIE 4 b.f. Tiger Hill (IRE) 127 – Silcasue (Selkirk (USA) 129) [2015 –: 9.2s **–**
12g Jun 8] no form. *Alistair Whillans*

MAGIC ROUND (IRE) 3 gr.g. Zebedee 113 – Street Kitty (IRE) (Tiger Hill (IRE) 127) **39**
[2015 –: t5.1f p6g⁶ t7.1m⁴ p7m Jun 1] poor maiden: stays 7f: acts on tapeta: often wears
headgear. *Bill Turner*

MAGIC SECRET 7 b.g. Trade Fair 124 – Just Devine (IRE) 69 (Montjeu (IRE) 137) **–**
[2015 6d Mar 29] useful handicapper in 2013: off 18 months, well held only outing in
2015: raced only at 6f: best form on soft/heavy going. *William Muir*

MAGIC SKYLINE (IRE) 5 b.m. Refuse To Bend (IRE) 128 – Grecian Air (FR) (King's **–**
Best (USA) 132) [2015 53: 10.3d 12.4g Apr 11] maiden: no form in 2015: stays 12.5f: acts
on good to soft going: tried in cheekpieces: sometimes in tongue tie: fair hurdler.
Brian Ellison

MAGIC STRIKE (IRE) 2 b.c. (Apr 15) Zebedee 113 – Artemis Culture (USA) (Smart **66 p**
Strike (CAN) 121) [2015 6m⁴ 6g⁶ 5.7m⁴ Jul 31] €26,000Y: second foal: dam 5f winner: fair
maiden: fourth of 10 at Bath final start, not knocked about: remains with potential.
Clive Cox

MAGISTRAL 5 b.g. Manduro (GER) 135 – Tamalain (USA) 80 (Royal Academy (USA) **86**
130) [2015 13m 13.1g 12d Oct 24] well-made gelding: fairly useful handicapper: stays 13f:
acts on soft and good to firm going: tried in headgear prior to 2015. *J. J. Lambe, Ireland*

MAGNIFIED 5 b.g. Passing Glance 119 – Scrutinize (IRE) (Selkirk (USA) 129) [2015 **54** 72: p12g⁴ Jan 21] maiden: sold £800, sent to Germany, second twice from 17 starts there. *David O'Meara*

MAGNOLIA RIDGE (IRE) 5 b.g. Galileo (IRE) 134 – Treasure The Lady (IRE) 95 **60** (Indian Ridge 123) [2015 10.3d 10m³ 10d 10g 12m 10.2s⁶ t12.2m⁵ Nov 21] smallish gelding: modest handicapper: left Kristin Stubbs after fifth start: stays 12.5f: acts on polytrack, good to firm and good to soft going: usually wears headgear: tends to find little. *Tony Coyle*

MAGNUM (IRE) 2 gr.g. (Apr 1) Lawman (FR) 121 – Coventina (IRE) 108 (Daylami **82 p** (IRE) 138) [2015 8g³ 8s² Oct 23] 47,000Y: sixth foal: half-brother to 3 winners, including smart 9f-1½m winner Conduct (by Selkirk) and 2m winner Aiyana (by Indian Haven): dam winner up to 2m (2-y-o 1m winner): fairly useful form when placed in maidens at Salisbury and Newbury: length second to Midterm in latter, barely adequate test: will be suited by 1¼m+: remains with potential. *Brian Meehan*

MAGNUS MAXIMUS 4 b.g. Holy Roman Emperor (IRE) 125 – Chanrossa (IRE) 72 **95** (Galileo (IRE) 134) [2015 108: p6g⁶ p6m³ p6g 6g 6g 6m 5g 6d⁴ 6g³ p6f³ p6f⁴ p6m³ Nov 14] dipped-backed gelding: useful performer: won handicap at Ascot in September by ¾ length from Spring Loaded: third in listed race at Lingfield (1½ lengths behind Goken) final start: stays 6f: acts on polytrack and good to soft going: tried in blinkers in 2015. *Nick Littmoden*

MAHICAN (IRE) 5 b.g. Cape Cross (IRE) 129 – Dark Indian (IRE) (Indian Ridge 123) **67** [2015 14mᵘʳ 16m 14.6m 12g⁶ 10g Aug 14] lengthy gelding: fair handicapper: stays 10.5f: acts on polytrack, soft and good to firm going: sometimes in headgear. *Denis Quinn*

MAHSOOB 4 b.c. Dansili 127 – Mooakada (IRE) 104 (Montjeu (IRE) 137) [2015 94p: **116** 10m* 10.4g* 10f* 12m⁶ 8.9g⁵ Aug 22] well-made, attractive colt: smart performer: won handicaps at Newbury in April and York in May, then showed further improvement to complete his hat-trick in Wolferton Handicap at Royal Ascot (by ½ length from Sennockian Star) in June: below best after in Princess of Wales's Stakes at Newmarket and Strensall Stakes at York, finding less than looked likely: should stay 1½m: acts on polytrack and firm going: often races towards rear. *John Gosden*

MAHSOOBA (USA) 3 b.f. Hard Spun (USA) 124 – Ishraak (USA) (Sahm (USA) 112) **69** [2015 77: 8g⁵ 8.3s⁵ 8.3d⁵ 8g Jun 8] fair handicapper: stays 1m: acts on firm going: usually in headgear in 2015. *Ed Dunlop*

MAIDEN APPROACH 4 b.f. New Approach (IRE) 132 – Ivowen (USA) 104 **84** (Theatrical) [2015 85: t8.6g⁴ p8f* t9.5f* p7f 8g 8.3m⁴ 7.9m² p8g p7g Dec 7] fairly useful handicapper: won at Lingfield and Wolverhampton in February: stays 9.5f: acts on polytrack, tapeta, good to firm and good to soft going: tried in visor. *Richard Fahey*

MAID IN A HORSEBOX 3 b.f. Myboycharlie (IRE) 118 – Why Nee Amy 66 (Tipsy **–** Creek (USA) 115) [2015 7v Sep 2] first foal: dam 1m-1¼m winner: 10/1, tailed off in maiden at Lingfield. *Rae Guest*

MAID IN RIO (IRE) 4 ch.f. Captain Rio 122 – Silver Whale (FR) (Highest Honor (FR) **107** 124) [2015 108: p14g⁴ 14f 14g 11.9f* Jun 10] useful performer: won handicap at Haydock (by 2¼ lengths from Tahira) in June: stays 2m: acts on firm and good to soft going: usually races close up. *Mark Johnston*

MAID OF KENT 3 br.f. Halling (USA) 133 – First Fantasy 97 (Be My Chief (USA) 122) **63** [2015 –: p10g³ p12g⁶ 10v p11g Oct 7] modest maiden: should stay at least 1½m: acts on polytrack: tried in visor in 2015. *James Fanshawe*

MAID OF MEDINA 2 b.f. (Apr 6) Pastoral Pursuits 127 – La Pantera 86 (Captain Rio **–** 122) [2015 6m 7.1m Sep 10] 7,000Y: sturdy filly: second foal: half-sister to 2-y-o 7f/1m winner Pertinace (by Kheleyf): dam 2-y-o 6f winner: tailed off in 2 maidens. *Michael Blanshard*

MAID OF THE GLENS (IRE) 4 b.f. The Carbon Unit (USA) 106 – There's A Light **95** (IRE) 70 (Fantastic Light (USA) 134) [2015 101: 12g⁵ 12v³ 12m⁴ 12g⁶ 10.9g⁶ a9.9f Dec 3] useful handicapper: third at Leopardstown (2 lengths behind Ballybacka Queen) in May: left John Patrick Shanahan after second start, P. J. Prendergast after fourth: stays 1½m: acts on good to firm and heavy going. *S. Seemar, UAE*

MAID OF TUSCANY (IRE) 4 b.f. Manduro (GER) 135 – Tuscania (USA) (Woodman **55** (USA) 126) [2015 10.2s⁵ 10.2m Sep 28] angular filly: modest maiden: stays 13f: acts on polytrack and any turf going: in headgear last 3 starts. *Neil Mulholland*

MAIMARA (FR) 3 b.f. Makfi 130 – Hideaway Heroine (IRE) 100 (Hernando (FR) 127) **114** [2015 9.9s* 8g 8.9g² 8g* 8d* 8s⁴ 8m Oct 3] angular filly: smart performer: won minor event at Saint-Cloud in April, listed race at Maisons-Laffitte in July and Prix de Lieurey at Deauville (by 2½ lengths from subsequently disqualified Akatea) in August: creditable 2 lengths fourth to Ervedya in Prix du Moulin at Longchamp next time: respectable seventh to Esoterique in Sun Chariot Stakes at Newmarket final outing: stays 1¼m: acts on soft going. *M. Delzangles, France*

MAINSTREAM 2 b.c. (May 4) Dansili 127 – Golden Stream (IRE) 110 (Sadler's Wells (USA) 132) [2015 7g⁴ 8.3d* Oct 14] second foal: dam, 7f winner (including at 2 yrs), sister to Oaks runner-up Flight of Fancy: landed odds in maiden at Nottingham (by 2½ lengths from Kuantan) in October: better form when fourth at Leicester (2 lengths behind Move Up) on debut: stays 1m: in hood both starts: remains with potential. *Sir Michael Stoute* **84 p**

MAISON BRILLET (IRE) 8 b.g. Pyrus (USA) 106 – Stormchaser (IRE) (Titus Livius (FR) 115) [2015 72: t13.9g⁶ p12g³ p13g² p12f* p15.8m⁵ Dec 16] good-topped gelding: fair handicapper: won at Kempton in March: stays 2m, effective at shorter: acts on polytrack and good to firm going: usually wears headgear: usually races towards rear. *Clive Drew* **72**

MAIZIN 8 b.g. Danroad (AUS) 112 – Haunt The Zoo 86 (Komaite (USA)) [2015 f7d⁶ t7.1g t6f f5g Mar 10] no form. *Derek Shaw*

MAJDOOL (IRE) 2 b.g. (Feb 6) Acclamation 118 – Maany (USA) 62 (Mr Greeley (USA) 122) [2015 6.1d⁵ 6.1g² t7.1g* 7f⁴ 6.5m 7g* Sep 30] first foal: dam lightly-raced half-sister to smart US Grade 2 9f winner Adonis: useful performer: won maiden at Wolverhampton in June and nursery at Kempton (by ½ length from Vibrant Chords) in September: stays 7f: acts on polytrack and tapeta: usually races prominently. *Roger Varian* **97**

MAJEED (IRE) 3 b.g. Mount Nelson 125 – Clever Millie (USA) 81 (Cape Canaveral (USA) 115) [2015 p10g* p11g* 12m⁵ p12g³ 12m⁴ p11d* p10m* Sep 26] strong, useful-looking gelding: useful handicapper: progressed well in 2015 and won at Chelmsford in March, Kempton in May and September and Chelmsford (by length from Bint Dandy) later in September: stays 12.5f: acts on polytrack and good to firm going: held up. *David Simcock* **107**

MAJENSKI (IRE) 3 b.g. Camacho 118 – D'addario (IRE) 72 (Galileo (IRE) 134) [2015 –: t6g⁶ t5.1g³ f5s³ t5.1f Feb 23] poor maiden: best form at 5f: acts on fibresand and tapeta: front runner/races prominently. *Jamie Osborne* **42**

MAJESTICA 2 b.f. (Feb 1) Royal Applause 124 – Snake's Head 81 (Golden Snake (USA) 127) [2015 6m 6m⁵ p7g 8.1m Sep 10] 3,500Y: fourth foal: half-sister to 2-y-o 7f winner (stays 9f) Lazarus Bell (by Bahamian Bounty) and winner up to 6f Classic Pursuit (2-y-o 6f winner, by Pastoral Pursuits): dam, 12.4f winner, half-sister to smart winner up to 6f Flyman: no form. *Michael Blanshard* **–**

MAJESTIC BOND 2 b.f. (Jan 22) Misu Bond (IRE) 114 – Bond Royale 89 (Piccolo 121) [2015 5g³ 5g³ 5m 5m³ 5m Jul 25] €24,000Y: sister to winner up to 6f Master Bond and closely related to 5f (including at 2 yrs) winner Lady Royale and 6f (including at 2 yrs) winner Monsieur Royale (both by Monsieur Bond): dam 2-y-o 6f winner: fair maiden: raced only at 5f: acts on good to firm going. *Geoffrey Oldroyd* **74**

MAJESTIC GIRL (IRE) 2 b.f. (Apr 30) Royal Applause 124 – Pretty Majestic (IRE) 92 (Invincible Spirit (IRE) 121) [2015 p6g⁶ p6f⁴ Oct 29] fifth foal: half-sister to 1m winner Gold Falcon (by Iffraaj): dam 2-y-o 6f winner: better effort when fourth in maiden at Chelmsford (8½ lengths behind Saucy Spirit) in October. *Robert Cowell* **51**

MAJESTIC HERO (IRE) 3 b.g. Majestic Missile 118 – Xena (IRE) (Mull of Kintyre (USA) 114) [2015 88: t5.1g³ 6d⁵ 5m⁶ 5m 5m² 5g³ 6g t5.1f 5.1d Nov 4] strong gelding: fairly useful handicapper: best form at 5f: acts on tapeta, good to firm and heavy going: often races prominently. *Ronald Harris* **88**

MAJESTIC MANANNAN (IRE) 6 b.g. Majestic Missile 118 – Miraculous (IRE) (Marju (IRE) 127) [2015 76: 6m⁴ 5m⁵ 5.9g 5.5m 6g² 5d⁵ 5g 5m² 5m² 5g Oct 3] fair handicapper: stays 6f: acts on good to firm going: tried in cheekpieces prior to 2015: often leads: inconsistent. *David Nicholls* **72**

MAJESTIC MOON (IRE) 5 b.g. Majestic Missile 118 – Gala Style (IRE) (Elnadim (USA) 128) [2015 103: 7m⁴ 7m 7g⁶ 7m⁴ 7g⁶ 7d 7m⁶ 7g* 6g 7m Oct 3] good-topped gelding: useful handicapper: won at Newmarket (by 1¼ lengths from Mr Win) in June and Ascot (by ½ length from Suzi's Connoisseur) in September: stays 7f: acts on soft and good to firm going: tried in headgear: usually leads. *John Gallagher* **108**

MAJESTIC MOUNT 5 b.h. Exceed And Excel (AUS) 126 – Our Poppet (IRE) 58 (Warning 136) [2015 5g⁶ 7g⁴ 7d 8m Oct 3] useful-looking horse: useful performer: won minor event and listed race at Deauville in late-2014: best effort in 2015 when 3¼ lengths fourth to Baghadur in Prix de la Porte Maillot at Longchamp: below form in Hungerford **106**

Stakes at Newbury next time: stays 1m: acts on polytrack, viscoride and good to firm going: tried in cheekpieces. *Rodolphe Collet, France*

MAJESTIC MYLES (IRE) 7 b.g. Majestic Missile (IRE) 118 – Gala Style (IRE) **97** (Elnadim (USA) 128) [2015 99: 7g 6d 7g⁶ 7.2g* p7g⁶ 7v Nov 7] tall gelding: useful handicapper: won at Ayr (by 1¾ lengths from Edgar Balthazar) in October: stays 7f: acts on good to firm and heavy going: tried in eyeshields prior to 2015. *Richard Fahey*

MAJESTIC QUEEN (IRE) 5 b.m. Kheleyf (USA) 116 – Night Fairy (IRE) 89 (Danehill **113** (USA) 126) [2015 108: 7d 7s* 6g³ 7g² 6.5g⁶ 7m Sep 10] well-made mare: smart performer: better than ever in 2015 and won Chartwell Stakes at Lingfield (by 2 lengths from New Providence) in May: third in Greenlands Stakes at the Curragh (1½ lengths behind Mustajeeb) and, after being sold £825,000 Goffs London Sale in June, second in Brownstown Stakes at Fairyhouse (1½ lengths behind Ainippe) next 2 starts: stayed 1m: acted on polytrack, soft and good to firm going: stud. *Tracey Collins, Ireland*

MAJESTIC SUN (IRE) 4 b.g. King's Best (USA) 132 – Shining Vale (USA) (Twilight **63** Agenda (USA) 126) [2015 12g 12d⁴ t13.9f⁽ʳ Oct 13] sturdy gelding: modest handicapper: stays 1½m: acts on tapeta, good to firm and heavy going: often wears hood. *Jim Boyle*

MAJESTIQUE (IRE) 2 br.f. (Apr 14) High Chaparral (IRE) 132 – Germane 100 (Distant **77 p** Relative 128) [2015 7d⁶ 8.3g⁶ Oct 20] €49,000Y: sister to smart 2-y-o 7f winner Lucky Chappy and half-sister to several winners, including useful 1m/8.3f winner Granted and 7.4f/1m winner Robema (both by Cadeaux Genereux): dam 2-y-o 7f winner: 25/1, improved from debut when 3 lengths sixth to So Mi Dar in maiden at Windsor, taking strong hold and no extra final 100 yds: open to further improvement. *Marco Botti*

MAJEYDA (USA) 4 b.f. Street Cry (IRE) 130 – Alzerra (UAE) 108 (Pivotal 124) [2015 **85** 104: p8g³ Jan 22] useful filly: useful performer: in first-time cheekpieces, below form only start in 2015, not looking keen: stays 1m: acts on tapeta, soft and good to firm going. *Charlie Appleby*

MAJOR ATTITUDE 3 b.g. Major Cadeaux 121 – Alexander Ballet 86 (Mind Games **39** 121) [2015 –: 6m p6g Jul 14] poor maiden: best effort at 5.5f: acts on good to soft going. *Mark Hoad*

MAJOR CRISPIES 4 b.g. Pastoral Pursuits 127 – Nellie Melba 82 (Hurricane Sky **94** (AUS)) [2015 101: p6f⁵ p6g p7g⁴ p6f² p7g⁵ 6m³ 6m* 7g 6m⁵ 6m 7m² 7f⁵ 7m³ 7g⁶ t6f Oct 3] good-quartered gelding: fairly useful handicapper: won at Windsor in May: stays 7f: acts on polytrack and firm going: tried in headgear: often races towards rear: has awkward head carriage. *James Eustace*

MAJOR FRANKO 3 ch.g. Major Cadeaux 121 – Royal Future (IRE) (Royal Academy **54** (USA) 130) [2015 10m 9.9v³ 9.9m p13.3f p12g Nov 4] workmanlike gelding: modest maiden: stays 1½m: acts on polytrack, good to firm and heavy going. *Michael Attwater*

MAJOR JACK 4 b.g. Kheleyf (USA) 116 – Azeema (IRE) 82 (Averti (IRE) 117) [2015 **99** 105: 6m² 6g⁴ 6m³ 6m⁵ 6m p6f⁵ᵘ Aug 18] strong gelding: useful handicapper: second at Ascot (head behind Basil Berry) in May: raced only at 6f: acted on polytrack and good to firm going: in cheekpieces last 3 starts: usually raced towards rear: dead. *Roger Charlton*

MAJOR MAC 3 ch.g. Shirocco (GER) 129 – Spring Fashion (IRE) 54 (Galileo (IRE) **77** 134) [2015 74: f12g⁴ 12d² 12.1s² 14.1g 12.1v* 12g Sep 24] fair handicapper: won at Chepstow in August: best effort at 1½m: acts on heavy going: often in cheekpieces in 2015: front runner/races prominently. *Hughie Morrison*

MAJOR MUSCARI (IRE) 7 ch.g. Exceed And Excel (AUS) 126 – Muscari 68 (Indian **71** Ridge 123) [2015 62, a72: p8g³ p7f* f6g² p6f² 5d⁶ 7g² 6g⁴ p8g³ p6g⁴ 7d t5.11f⁶ t6g² p6m² Dec 16] lengthy gelding: fair handicapper: won at Lingfield (apprentice) in January: stays 7f: acts on all-weather and firm going: often wears headgear: usually races nearer last than first. *Shaun Harris*

MAJOR PUSEY 3 ch.g. Major Cadeaux 121 – Pusey Street Lady 103 (Averti (IRE) 117) **84** [2015 –: 7d⁶ 5.7f⁴ 6d³ 5g* 6d 5g² 5m² 5m⁶ 5g⁴ 5.2m⁶ Sep 15] close-coupled gelding: fairly useful handicapper: won at Goodwood in May: good second at Windsor and Sandown: best form at 5f: acts on good to firm going. *John Gallagher*

MAJOR ROWAN 4 b.g. Captain Gerrard (IRE) 113 – Julie's Gift (Presidium 124) [2015 **62** 63: f8s⁴ f12d⁴ f8g³ 9.2d f12d⁵ f14g* Dec 12] modest handicapper: left Bryan Smart/off 5 months, won at Southwell in December: stays 1m: acts on fibresand: has worn blinkers. *John Davies*

MAJOR VALENTINE 3 b.g. Major Cadeaux 121 – Under My Spell 80 (Wizard King **76** 122) [2015 p7g⁵ p8f⁶ 5m⁵ 5.7g⁴ 6.1m p6g* p6g* p6g⁴ 5.7m³ Sep 28] fourth foal: dam, **a86** winner up to 6f (2-y-o 5f winner) who stayed 1m, half-sister to useful winner up to 1m

Ardbrae Lady: fairly useful handicapper: won twice at Kempton in August, by 7 lengths on latter occasion: stays 6f: acts on polytrack and good to firm going. *John O'Shea*

MAJROOH (IRE) 3 b.c. Acclamation 118 – Neve Lieve (IRE) 89 (Dubai Destination (USA) 127) [2015 t7.1g* 7m⁴ 8g⁶ 10g* 10v⁶ 10d³ Oct 12] 45,000Y: lengthy colt: second foal: dam 11f-2m winner out of smart 2-y-o 6f/7f winner Love of Silver: fairly useful performer: won maiden at Wolverhampton in June and handicap at Newmarket in August: good third in handicap at Windsor in October: stays 1¼m: acts on tapeta and good to soft going: often starts slowly, often races in rear: not straightforward: sent to UAE. *George Peckham*   **87**

MAKBULLET 8 gr.g. Makbul 104 – Gold Belt (IRE) 61 (Bellypha 130) [2015 14.4g⁴ 16.1g Sep 4] tall, good-topped gelding: modest handicapper: stays 14.5f: acts on soft and good to firm going. *Michael Smith*   **63**

MAKE BELIEVE 3 b.c. Makfi 130 – Rosie's Posy (IRE) 86 (Suave Dancer (USA) 136) [2015 7s² 8g* 8f⁵ 7m* 8g⁵ Oct 31]   **127**

Gleneagles was not the only Guineas winner to be on the 'missing' list for much of the season. His French counterpart Make Believe, winner of the Poule d'Essai des Poulains, was also absent between Royal Ascot and the autumn. Unlike Gleneagles, though, when Make Believe was seen out again, he came back better than ever, adding a second Group 1 at Longchamp to his record when winning the Prix de la Foret. Make Believe was supplemented for the St James's Palace Stakes at Royal Ascot, looking the biggest threat to odds-on Gleneagles in a field of just five, after his stable-companion Territories, runner-up to Gleneagles at Newmarket, was forced to miss the race with a stone bruise. But Make Believe ran by far the worst race of his career, failing to settle behind the leader and weakening from two furlongs out to return a detached last as Gleneagles readily completed a hat-trick of Group 1 wins after his Two Thousand Guineas victories at Newmarket and the Curragh.

While Gleneagles was thwarted by unsuitable ground in the interim, Make Believe's lengthy absence after the St James's Palace was an enforced one. No injury was reported, but he was said to have been very tired after his first race on

Poule d'Essai des Poulains - Prix le Parisien, Longchamp—
Make Believe is a clear-cut winner from stable-companion New Bay who finishes strongly on the wide outside from a much less favourable draw

very firm ground and was given plenty of time to recover before finally returning to action on the Arc card. Make Believe faced a dozen rivals in the Qatar-sponsored Foret, five of them from Britain in addition to Gordon Lord Byron from Ireland who had won the race in 2012 and finished runner-up both years since. The pick of Make Believe's British rivals was fellow three-year-old Limato who had yet to finish worse than second in his career and had been an impressive winner of the Park Stakes at Doncaster last time out on his first try at seven furlongs, while Toormore, winner of the Lennox Stakes at Goodwood and more recently successful in Turkey, represented the Richard Hannon stable successful with Olympic Glory twelve months earlier. Make Believe appeared to have less to fear from his French rivals, though they included the only horse to have got the better of him on home soil. A race-fit Ride Like The Wind had beaten Make Believe a head in the Prix Djebel at Maisons-Laffitte in April but had failed to add to that success subsequently, finishing only in mid-division behind Gleneagles in the Two Thousand Guineas and, more recently, third over the Foret course and distance in the Prix du Pin behind Taniyar and La Berma who were both also in the Foret line-up.

Although back at seven furlongs for the first time since the Djebel, and on much firmer going, Make Believe had no trouble laying up behind a strong pace set by the British-trained outsider Salateen who flew out from his stall next to the rail. Limato, the 6/5 favourite, on the other hand, was soon detached from the main body of the field after a sluggish start and was being pushed along to stay in touch. Salateen had run his race with two furlongs still to go where Toormore briefly took over in front, but Make Believe was still on the bridle between that pair and quickly settled matters over a furlong out. Meanwhile, Limato had been pulled out widest of all to make his run from the rear and stormed home, whilst edging to his right, but only succeeded in reducing Make Believe's advantage to a length and a quarter at the line, with Toormore emerging best in a bunched finish for third another length and a half behind. Gordon Lord Byron could only keep on in mid-division for sixth while the David O'Meara-trained stable-companions Custom Cut and G Force were well beaten, and Salateen paid for his exertions coming back tailed off in last. The strong pace and firmish ground resulted in the track record being broken in the Foret for the second year running, Make Believe bettering Olympic Glory's 1m 17.73sec with a time of 1m 17.05sec. Those are incredibly, if not impossibly, quick times and it could be said that Make Believe is an appropriately-named record-holder for Longchamp's so-called seven furlongs (or its metric equivalent, fourteen hundred metres). It is well established that Longchamp's 'seven-furlong' course, which starts in a chute before joining the main round track and finishes at the second winning post, beyond the main one, is, in fact, some way short (around forty-three yards by our reckoning) of the advertised distance. By way of comparison, the official North American record time for a turf race over seven furlongs, set at Woodbine in 2004 by the Canadian champion Soaring Free, stands at 1m 19.38sec! Discrepancies in race distances at jumps courses in Britain have recently been addressed, but it is bizarre that the anomaly of the seven-furlong course at France's premier racecourse has not been addressed. The Foret, is, after all, currently Europe's only Group 1 over seven

Qatar Prix de la Foret, Longchamp—Make Believe returns from three and a half months off to put up a high-class performance, beating his fellow three-year-old Limato (finishing strongly down the outside) and Toormore (third left) among others

furlongs for older horses. Perhaps the closure of Longchamp for modernisation work on the stands will be an opportunity to make the necessary alterations. If that proves impractical, races over that particular trip simply need to be advertised over the true distance.

Make Believe had already demonstrated plenty of speed, with the help of a good draw, when making all in the Poule d'Essai des Poulains - Prix Le Parisien at Longchamp in May. At the time, the field he beat looked to have more in the way of quantity (there were eighteen runners) than quality. But, by the autumn, it was evident that Make Believe had taken some notable scalps in the Poulains, even though he was clearly better suited by a mile than New Bay, Highland Reel or Muhaarar. The last-named finished only eighth (having the worst of the draw) at Longchamp before going on to prove himself the best sprinter in Europe later in the season, while Make Believe's stable-companion New Bay, another drawn wide and left with too much to do before eating up ground in the straight, developed into the top French three-year-old colt over middle distances, winning the Prix du Jockey Club and Prix Niel before finishing third in the Prix de l'Arc de Triomphe. Make Believe, who was sent off the 6/1 second favourite for the Poule d'Essai des Poulains behind Gleneagles' stablemate Highland Reel (another who proved suited by longer trips later in the year, winning the Hong Kong Vase), impressed with the way he travelled in front before going clear from two furlongs out when shaken up in the straight, never looking in danger from then on. New Bay was beaten three lengths, with another length and a half to the third Mr Owen.

The French have an excellent record in the Breeders' Cup Mile and, three weeks after the Foret, Make Believe headed a four-strong team at Keeneland which also comprised his stable-companion Esoterique, winner of the Prix Jacques le Marois and Sun Chariot Stakes, the previous season's Poule d'Essai des Poulains winner Karakontie, who was bidding to win the Breeders' Cup Mile for the second year running, and the improving three-year-old filly Impassable, winner of the Prix Daniel Wildenstein at the Arc meeting. Make Believe was sent off favourite ahead of Esoterique (as is customary for their stable, the Fabre pair ran without lasix, as did Time Test from Britain) but his chances were dealt an early blow when he missed the break, meaning he was never able to adopt his usual handy pitch as a result. With the Canadian filly Tepin running out a clear-cut winner from the other British runner Mondialiste, who finished strongly for second, Make Believe could only keep on for fifth, although he still fared best of the French ahead of Impassable in sixth, Esoterique in seventh and Karakontie, who was in rear throughout.

The useful-looking Make Believe looked likely to win more good races as a four-year-old, having had only seven starts all told, but he has been retired to stud. He won both his races late in the year as a two-year-old, a newcomers race at Deauville and a minor event at Saint-Cloud, both in testing ground over seven and a half furlongs. Make Believe has been bought to stand at Ballylinch Stud in Ireland, where his fee will be €20,000, alongside another Foret winner, Dream Ahead, and Lope de Vega who also won the Poule d'Essai des Poulains for Andre Fabre. Make Believe comes from the first crop of Makfi who went one better than Make Believe in the Djebel before causing a 33/1 upset in the Two Thousand Guineas and then beating Goldikova in the Prix Jacques le Marois. Like his son, however, Makfi underperformed in the St James's Palace Stakes in between and flopped again back at Ascot when only fifth when starting even-money favourite for the Queen Elizabeth II Stakes. Makfi had also been due to end his career in the Breeders' Cup Mile but contracted ringworm and was unable to take part. Makfi had famously been bought as an unraced two-year-old for just 26,000 guineas when culled by his breeders Shadwell. As a stallion, he has made the same journey from Britain to France, starting out at Tweenhills Stud in Gloucestershire after being bought by Qatar's Sheikh Fahad Al Thani for a reported £12m. However, for the second season running, Makfi will be standing at the Aga Khan's Haras de Bonneval in Normandy in a joint venture between the two breeding operations which will also involve Charm Spirit in 2016. Makfi has also successfully shuttled to the southern hemisphere where Marky Mark in New Zealand became his first Group 1 winner before Make Believe followed suit in France.

If Makfi was 'one that got away', then the same could also be said of Make Believe's dam Rosie's Posy. She proved disappointing after what looked a promising start to her career when winning a maiden at Bath on her debut at two over an extended five furlongs. Sold out of Barry Hills' stable for just 2,200 guineas at the end of the following season, Rosie's Posy has had much more success as a broodmare. Make Believe is her second top-flight winner after the filly Dubawi Heights, by Makfi's sire Dubawi. Although placed in the Lowther Stakes at two, Dubawi Heights was still a maiden when she was among the horses her trainer Simon Callaghan took with him when he moved to the States. Dubawi Heights won five races there, notably the Grade 1 Gamely Stakes and Yellow Ribbon Stakes, and was sold to Japan at the end of her racing career for 1,600,000 dollars. Rosie's Posy had also produced the useful winner up to a mile Generous Thought (by Cadeaux Genereux) by the time Make Believe was sold as a foal at the December Sales for 180,000 guineas. Rosie's Posy changed hands herself at Newmarket a week later, this time fetching 400,000 guineas in foal to Oasis Dream. The colt she was carrying became her fourth winner when, named Estikmaal, he made a successful debut in a newcomers race at Chantilly in October for Freddie Head in the colours of Hamdan Al Maktoum. Estikmaal had himself been bought for 400,000 guineas as a yearling, and, coincidentally, Rosie's Posy's yearling half-sister by Redoute's Choice fetched the same price at Newmarket in October.

Make Believe (b.c. 2012)	Makfi (b 2007)	Dubawi (b 2002)	Dubai Millennium
			Zomaradah
		Dhelaal (b 2002)	Green Desert
			Irish Valley
	Rosie's Posy (IRE) (b 1999)	Suave Dancer (b 1988)	Green Dancer
			Suavite
		My Branch (b 1993)	Distant Relative
			Pay The Bank

Rosie's Posy is among seven winners (all of them fillies, incidentally) to date produced by her smart dam My Branch whose wins included the Firth of Clyde Stakes and Sceptre Stakes (when those races had only listed status) and who was also second in the Cheveley Park Stakes and third in the Irish One Thousand Guineas. Much the best of My Branch's winners is Tante Rose who ended her racing career with a high-class effort to win the Sprint Cup at Haydock, though she was also successful over seven furlongs in the Fred Darling Stakes. Like Rosie's Posy and My Branch, Make Believe's great grandam Pay The Bank, a mile winner at two, was also trained by Barry Hills. As well as My Branch, Pay The Bank's other notable winner was Celestial Halo who was also smart on the Flat for the same stable before making a name for himself as a high-class hurdler. *A. Fabre, France*

MAKE FAST 2 b.f. (Mar 10) Makfi 130 – Raymi Coya (CAN) 100 (Van Nistelrooy (USA) 108) [2015 6s* 7g⁵ 7v² 7.5g⁶ Nov 8] rather leggy filly: third foal: dam winner up to 1m (2-y-o 5f-7f winner): useful form: won maiden at Ffos Las in September: further improvement when second in listed race at Newbury (neck behind Light Music) in October: well below form in similar event at Rome final start: will stay 1m: acts on heavy ground. *Andrew Balding* **97**

MAKE IT UP 3 b.c. Halling (USA) 133 – American Spirit (IRE) (Rock of Gibraltar (IRE) 133) [2015 103: 7g² 8f 7.6m* 7d⁴ 7g* 7m⁵ Oct 3] smart performer: won apprentice handicap at Chester in July and minor event at Lingfield (by 3¼ lengths from Zarwaan) in September: creditable fifth of 17 to Buckstay in handicap at Ascot final start, not settling fully: stays 7.5f: acts on good to firm going: front runner/races prominently: sent to UAE. *Andrew Balding* **116**

MAKE MISCHIEF 2 b.c. (Mar 16) Makfi 130 – Northern Mischief (USA) (Yankee Victor (USA) 121) [2015 8.3d 8s Oct 23] sixth foal: half-brother to minor US winner by Ghostzapper: dam, 1m winner (2-y-o 7f winner), half-sister to US Grade 1 8.5f/9f winner Gourmet Girl: better effort when seventh in maiden at Newbury (5¼ lengths behind Algometer) latter start, not knocked about: sold 17,000 gns, sent to Italy: open to further improvement. *Stuart Williams* **74 p**

MAKE MUSIC 2 b.f. (Mar 1) Acclamation 118 – Come What May 67 (Selkirk (USA) 129) [2015 7g 6.5s² t7.1f² p7g³ Nov 26] 11,000F, €40,000Y: rangy filly: fifth foal: half-sister to winner up to 6f Woodlandsway (2-y-o 6f winner, by Oasis Dream) and 1¼m winner Inevitable (by Dubawi): dam, 5f winner, sister to very smart winner up to 7f Etlaala: fair maiden: stays 7f. *Andrew Balding*

MAKE ON MADAM (IRE) 3 b.f. Captain Rio 122 – Rye (IRE) 75 (Charnwood Forest (IRE) 125) [2015 75: t7.1g 7.5m⁶ 7.5g² 8d² 8g 8.3g³ 7.5g* 7.5m⁶ 7.5m⁴ 7m⁵ 7.9d⁵ 7.5d⁶ 7.5m² 7.2g⁴ Oct 13] fair handicapper: won at Beverley in July: stays 7.5f: acts on fibresand, good to firm and good to soft going: usually in headgear in 2015: tried in tongue tie in 2015: often races prominently. *Les Eyre* **71**

MAKHFAR (IRE) 4 b.g. Bushranger (IRE) 119 – Let Me Shine (USA) 79 (Dixie Union (USA) 121) [2015 79: p8g 7d 8.1g⁶ 7g⁵ 7.2g Oct 13] fair handicapper: probably stays 1m: acts on good to firm going: tried in hood in 2015: often races in rear. *Kevin Morgan* **65**

MAKIN A STATEMENT (IRE) 3 b.g. Bahamian Bounty 116 – Star Now 69 (Librettist (USA) 124) [2015 77: f6g⁴ 5.9m 5d 5g⁴ Oct 3] fair maiden: should be suited by 6f: acts on good to firm going: usually races prominently: sent to Greece. *David O'Meara* **70**

MAKING SHAPES 3 b.g. Makfi 130 – Danceabout 110 (Shareef Dancer (USA) 135) [2015 79p: 10m³ 10.1d* 10g⁵ 11.9m³ 12s⁵ 10.1g p10g Oct 20] tall, attractive gelding: fair performer: won maiden at Newcastle in May: stays 1½m: acts on good to firm and good to soft going: tried in cheekpieces in 2015. *Peter Chapple-Hyam* **77**

MAKIN THE RULES (IRE) 4 b.g. Lawman (FR) 121 – Shinto Duchess (IRE) 59 (Bachelor Duke (USA) 122) [2015 87: 6d 8m⁶ 10m⁴ 8.3g⁴ 8g 6m Jul 24] fair handicapper: stays 1¼m: acts on soft and good to firm going: usually in headgear in 2015: sometimes slowly away. *David O'Meara* **74**

MAKIN TROUBLE (IRE) 3 b.g. Lawman (FR) 121 – Crafty Notion (IRE) 61 (Viking Ruler (AUS)) [2015 –: 6v 8g May 29] no form. *David O'Meara* **–**

MAKZON (USA) 3 b.g. Henrythenavigator (USA) 131 – Fab's Melody (USA) (Devil's Bag (USA)) [2015 –p: p8f 10.2d⁴ 10g⁴ 12g⁵ a9.9f² Dec 17] fair maiden: left Sir Michael Stoute after fourth start: should be suited by 1½m: acts on dirt and good to soft going: in headgear last 3 starts, also tongue tied final one. *A. bin Harmash, UAE* **78**

MALABAR 3 b.f. Raven's Pass (USA) 133 – Whirly Bird 101 (Nashwan (USA) 135) [2015 106: 8f⁴ 8g 10.4g 8m* 9g 8m Oct 3] attractive, rather unfurnished filly: smart performer: fourth in 1000 Guineas (6½ lengths behind Legatissimo): won Thoroughbred Stakes at Goodwood (by 3 lengths from Kool Kompany) in July: below form both subsequent starts, at Belmont on first occasion: stays 10.5f: acts on firm going: in headgear last 3 starts. *Mick Channon* **111**

MALAF (USA) 3 b.g. Elusive Quality (USA) – Holy Wish (USA) (Lord At War (ARG)) [2015 82p: 8.3m⁴ t8.6g* 8f 8m Oct 2] fairly useful handicapper: won at Wolverhampton (by 7 lengths from Yamllik) in June: stays 8.5f: acts on tapeta: in cheekpieces last 3 starts: sent to UAE. *John Gosden* **92**

MALAIKA 2 b.f. (May 4) Sixties Icon 125 – Evanesce 72 (Lujain (USA) 119) [2015 7.4v⁴ Aug 19] sister to winner up to 1m Yorkshire Icon (2-y-o 7f/7.4f winner) and 2-y-o 5f winner Amahoro and half-sister to winner up to 2m Alfraamsey (2-y-o 6f winner, by Fraam): dam 2-y-o 6f winner: 20/1, green when fourth of 5 to Sharja Queen in maiden at Ffos Las. *Mick Channon* **51**

MALAKKY (IRE) 2 b.c. (Apr 23) Tamayuz 126 – Safiya Song (IRE) (Intikhab (USA) 135) [2015 6.5m Jun 11] 170,000Y: second foal: half-brother to 2-y-o 6f winner Fuwairt (by Arcano): dam unraced half-sister to smart winner up to 6f Tajasir: 16/1, 8¼ lengths eighth of 15 to Twin Sails in maiden at Newbury on debut, no extra inside final 1f: open to improvement. *Brian Meehan* **65 p**

MALAYSIAN BOLEH 5 ch.g. Compton Place 125 – Orlena (USA) (Gone West (USA)) [2015 62, a81: p8g p8g⁶ p7g* t5.1f² p6m* p6g⁴ 6f⁴ 5.9g 8m⁶ p6g t6g p8f Dec 21] fairly useful performer: won claimer at Lingfield in February and handicap at Chelmsford March: left Simon Dow after third start: stays 1m: acts on polytrack, tapeta and firm going: tried in headgear: tried in tongue tie in 2015: sometimes slowly away, usually races nearer last than first: quirky. *Shaun Lycett* **63 a85**

MALEFICENT QUEEN 3 b.f. Mount Nelson 125 – Manila Selection (USA) (Manila (USA)) [2015 8.3s² 9.2s* 7.9m* 10g* Sep 17] half-sister to several winners, including 7f-8.3f winner Danski (by Dansili) and 7f-9f winner Balata (by Averti): dam unraced: useful performer: won maiden at Hamilton and handicap at Carlisle in May and handicap at Ayr in September, beating Next Stop a neck when completing the hat-trick: stays 1¼m: acts on soft and good to firm going: open to further improvement. *Keith Dalgleish* **96 p**

MALEKOV (IRE) 6 b.g. Dansili 127 – Young And Daring (USA) (Woodman (USA) **90**
126) [2015 11.9g³ a9.9f 10.9g² 10.9g 12g² 12.1d⁶ p12g⁵ Sep 23] big, strong gelding: fairly
useful handicapper: won at Meydan in 2014: left Salem Al Ketbi after fourth start in 2015:
stayed 1¾m: acted on polytrack, tapeta and good to soft going: wore headgear: often raced
in rear: temperament was under suspicion: dead. *Hugo Palmer*

MALICE 3 b.f. Makfi 130 – Shemriyna (IRE) (King of Kings (IRE) 125) [2015 58: 10m **57**
7.1s⁵ 10.2g p10g³ p11g Aug 24] sturdy filly: modest maiden: stays 1¼m: acts on polytrack
and soft going: often in cheekpieces in 2015. *Kevin Frost*

MALIH 6 b.g. Echo of Light 125 – Sultry Lass (USA) (Private Account (USA)) [2015 50: **62**
p6f t6f⁶ p8f⁵ t7.1f⁵ p8m⁵ 9.9m p7m⁴ 7.6g² 8d* t8.6g³ 8g³ t8.6m⁶ 8d 8m⁵ p10g² Dec 30]
modest handicapper: won at Brighton in June: stays 1¼m: acts on polytrack, tapeta, firm
and soft going: often in hood in 2015: often races towards rear. *Eric Wheeler*

MALIMBI (IRE) 3 b.g. Cape Cross (IRE) 129 – Mirina (FR) (Pursuit of Love 124) [2015 **62**
–: p8g 8.3d p11g⁶ 10.2m* 10.2g³ t12.2m t9.5f Oct 17] modest handicapper: won at **a55**
Nottingham in July: left Mark Johnston after: stays 1¼m: acts on good to firm going: tried
in cheekpieces in 2015: usually races close up. *Brian Ellison*

MALJAA 3 ch.g. Paco Boy (IRE) 129 – Kerry's Dream 84 (Tobougg (IRE) 125) [2015 92p: **117**
5g³ 5m² 5m² 5g* 5d* 5d³ 5s² Oct 13] smart handicapper: much improved and won at
Doncaster in August and twice at Haydock (by neck from Confessional latter occasion) in
September: 5/6, not seen to best effect but still showed his form when length second to
Demora at Leicester final start, needing stronger gallop: stays 5.5f: acts on soft and good
to firm going: in blinkers last 4 starts: often races prominently, often travels strongly.
Roger Varian

MALLYMKUN 3 b.f. Kheleyf (USA) 116 – Harriet's Girl 88 (Choisir (AUS) 126) [2015 **64**
77: 7d 7f⁴ 8m⁶ 7g 7d³ 6g⁴ t6g³ t7.1m² t7.1f³ t7.1f* Oct 23] fair handicapper: won at **a77**
Wolverhampton in October: stays 1m: acts on tapeta, firm and soft going: tried in
cheekpieces in 2015: often races prominently. *K. R. Burke*

MALMOOSA (IRE) 2 b.f. (Mar 9) Shamardal (USA) 129 – Mohafazaat (IRE) 77 **72 p**
(Sadler's Wells (USA) 132) [2015 7g 8v⁴ Oct 24] fifth foal: half-sister to 3 winners, including
10.5f winner Mutebah and 9.7f-1½m winner Estedaama (both useful and by Marju): dam,
1¼m winner, half-sister to smart 7f-1¼m winner Makderah: better effort when fourth in
maiden at Newbury (7 lengths behind Last Tango Inparis) in October: open to further
improvement. *Brian Meehan*

MALMOSTOSA 2 b.f. (Mar 2) Intikhab (USA) 135 – Tell Mum (Marju (IRE) 127) [2015 **72 p**
7g⁵ Oct 21] 20,000F, 75,000Y: good-topped filly: second foal: sister to 2-y-o 5f winner
Granny Alice: dam unraced, half-sister to useful winner up to 1m Tell Dad: 16/1, fifth in
maiden at Newmarket (5¼ lengths behind Farandine) in October, weakening final 1f: will
improve. *Marco Botti*

MALTA BADIA (IRE) 3 b.f. Fastnet Rock (AUS) 127 – M'oubliez Pas (USA) (El **75**
Corredor (USA) 123) [2015 p7g p8g⁵ 8g⁶ p9.4g⁵ 10.9g⁶ p9.4g 8.3d⁴ t8.6f⁵ Oct 30] first
foal: dam, 2-y-o 5.5f/6f winner, half-sister to very smart 1m winner Riviera: fair maiden:
left Y. Barberot after sixth start: stays 9.5f: acts on polytrack. *William Jarvis*

MALTEASE AH 6 br.m. Librettist (USA) 124 – Manic 67 (Polar Falcon (USA) 126) **50**
[2015 –: f5g 6d⁴ 7m 6m jun 10] compact mare: modest handicapper: stays 6f: acts on
fibresand, soft and good to firm going: tried in headgear/tongue tie. *Ron Haslam*

MALVIA 3 b.g. Exceed And Excel (AUS) 126 – Always On My Mind 91 (Distant Relative **64**
128) [2015 –p: 7m 5g² 6s Oct 6] modest maiden: best effort at 5f. *Michael Bell*

MAMBO FEVER 4 b.f. Footstepsinthesand 120 – Mambo's Melody (Kingmambo **71**
(USA) 125) [2015 72p: 8g³ 7g² 7.2g⁴ 6g² 7g f7g⁴ Nov 26] fair handicapper: stays 1m: acts
on fibresand, raced only on good going on turf: tried in cheekpieces final start: usually
races close up. *David C. Griffiths*

MAMBO PARADISE 3 b.f. Makfi 130 – Mambo Halo (USA) (Southern Halo (USA)) **101**
[2015 79: t6m* 7g p6m* 7.6f² 6g 6.1g 7.6m² 7m* 7m² 7m Aug 8] leggy, angular filly:
useful handicapper: won at Wolverhampton in April, Chelmsford in June and Doncaster in
July: good second at Goodwood (¾ length behind Enlace) in August: stays 7.5f: acts on
polytrack, tapeta, good to firm and good to soft going. *Mark Johnston*

MAMBO RHYTHM 4 b.f. Authorized (IRE) 133 – Mambo Halo (USA) (Southern Halo **74**
(USA)) [2015 85: p11f⁶ 12d 10.2m⁴ 12.5s² 14d May 20] plain, rather sparely-made
filly: fair handicapper: stays 1¾m: acts on soft and good to firm going: wears headgear
nowadays. *Mark Johnston*

MAMBO SPIRIT (IRE) 11 b.g. Invincible Spirit (IRE) 121 – Mambodorga (USA) (Kingmambo (USA) 125) [2015 74: f6d p7m⁶ t5.1f⁴ t7.1f⁶ 6m² 6f 5.7m* 5.7f* 5.7d⁶ 5.7m 5.7g p6g t7.1g p7g Dec 28] tall, good-topped gelding: fair handicapper: won at Wolverhampton in February and at Bath in July and August: stays 1m: acts on polytrack, tapeta, firm and soft going: tried in blinkers/tongue tie prior to 2015: sometimes slowly away, usually races nearer last than first. *Tony Newcombe* **79 a69**

MAMILLIUS 2 b.c. (Mar 4) Exceed And Excel (AUS) 126 – Laika Lane (USA) (Street Cry (IRE) 130) [2015 6g² Jul 27] €16,000F, €32,000Y, 70,000 2-y-o: first foal: dam, unraced, out of half-sister to smart Canadian performer up to 1½m Windward Islands: 25/1, shaped well when second in maiden at Windsor (½ length behind Shakerattlenroll) in July: should do better. *George Baker* **68 p**

MAMOO 2 ch.c. (Apr 1) Sir Percy 129 – Meredith (Medicean 128) [2015 7g p8d⁶ p8g p8g Dec 15] form (modest) only when sixth to Kasseopia in maiden at Kempton in September. *Mike Murphy* **64**

MANAAFIDH (IRE) 2 b.c. (Feb 19) Zebedee 113 – Starring (FR) 74 (Ashkalani (IRE) 128) [2015 7m* 7d³ 7.1m² 8d³ Sep 5] €330,000Y: useful-looking colt: half-brother to several winners, including 7f-8.6f winner Spinning (by Pivotal), 6f-1m (including at 2 yrs) winner (stayed 1¼m) Letsgoroundagain (by Redback) and winner up to 1½m Goodwood Starlight (2-y-o 7f-1m winner, by Mtoto), all useful: dam placed at 1¼m: useful form: won maiden at Newmarket (by head from Muntazah) in July: second in Solario Stakes at Sandown (½ length behind First Selection) in August: just respectable third of 5 to Foundation in listed race at Haydock final outing: best form at 7f. *Richard Hannon* **101**

MANALAPAN (IRE) 5 b.g. Six Sense (JPN) 117 – Mia Mambo (USA) (Affirmed (USA)) [2015 111: 12s⁴ 10g⁶ 12.4d 15.9g Nov 14] smart performer at best: just useful form when sixth in listed race at Ayr on second outing, then left D. Weld: below form in Australia last 2 starts: stays 1¾m: acts on synthetics and good to firm going: has worn tongue tie: front runner/races prominently. *Ciaron Maher, Australia* **98**

MANATEE 4 b.c. Monsun (GER) 124 – Galatee (FR) 115 (Galileo (IRE) 134) [2015 113p: 11.9s⁴ 11.9g* 11.9m⁴ 11.9m 15.4d⁵ Oct 25] third foal: half-brother to useful French 1½m-15.5f winner Gaterie (by Dubai Destination) and French 14.5f winner Galleria (by Dalakhani): dam 9.5f/1¼m winner out of half-sister to Breeders' Cup Classic winner Arcangues: high-class performer: won Grand Prix de Chantilly (by ¾ length from Prince Gibraltar) in May: just respectable efforts at best after, in Grand Prix de Saint-Cloud (fourth to Treve), Prix de l'Arc de Triomphe at Longchamp (eleventh to Golden Horn) and Prix Royal-Oak at Saint-Cloud (fifth to Vazirabad): stays 15f: acts on polytrack, soft and good to firm going: often races prominently. *A. Fabre, France* **125**

MANATEE BAY 5 b.g. Royal Applause 124 – Dash of Lime 67 (Bold Edge 123) [2015 77: 6g⁴ 6s* 6g⁶ 5.9m* 6m⁶ 6d⁵ 6d 7d³ 7v⁵ 6s Oct 27] fairly useful handicapper: won at Thirsk and Carlisle in May: stays 7f: acts on soft and good to firm going: often wears headgear: often starts slowly. *David Nicholls* **85**

MANCHESTAR 5 b.g. Elusive City (USA) 117 – Grande Terre (IRE) 71 (Grand Lodge (USA) 125) [2015 92: 8m² 8d⁵ 8m⁴ 8g 8m² 7.9m 8d 8d Oct 16] fairly useful handicapper: second at Thirsk in May and Haydock in August: stays 10.5f, effective at shorter: acts on good to firm and good to soft going: sometimes wears hood: has raced freely. *Richard Fahey* **90**

MANCINELLO (IRE) 2 b.g. (Mar 21) Bushranger (IRE) 119 – Queen Cobra (IRE) 80 (Indian Rocket 115) [2015 7.4v³ t7.1m t7.1f⁶ p8m Nov 19] modest maiden: stays 7.5f. *Brian Meehan* **60**

MANDALAY KING (IRE) 10 b.g. King's Best (USA) 132 – Mahamuni (IRE) (Sadler's Wells (USA) 132) [2015 75: 6d 6m 6s Jul 29] smallish, close-coupled gelding: fair handicapper: well below form in 2015: stays 7f: acts on any turf going: often wears headgear: often races in rear. *Marjorie Fife* **–**

MANDRELL (USA) 2 b.f. (Apr 23) Dubawi (IRE) 129 – Country Star (USA) 116 (Empire Maker (USA) 129) [2015 p8g* Dec 15] second foal: dam US 2-y-o Grade 1 8.5f winner: 6/1, looked good prospect when winning 8-runner maiden at Kempton on debut by 3 lengths from Shypen, slowly away, switched and quickened to lead over 1f out: open to improvement. *Charlie Appleby* **87 p**

MANDRIA (IRE) 3 b.f. Duke of Marmalade (IRE) 132 – Albertine Rose 89 (Namid 128) [2015 53: 6g p7g³ t8.6m* p8f⁶ t8.6f⁷ t9.5f t8.6f Nov 14] workmanlike filly: modest handicapper: won at Wolverhampton in September: stays 8.5f: acts on polytrack and tapeta: often in hood in 2015. *Daniel Kubler* **63 §**

MANDY LAYLA (IRE) 5 ch.m. Excellent Art 125 – Chervil 80 (Dansili 127) [2015 67: **64** f6g³ t6g⁶ f6g Jan 29] leggy mare: modest handicapper: stays 6f: acts on polytrack, fibresand, good to firm and good to soft going: often races prominently, tends to find little. *Bryan Smart*

MANDY'S BOY (IRE) 5 b.g. Kyllachy 129 – African Queen (IRE) (Cadeaux Genereux **54** 131) [2015 11.6g⁶ p10f Sep 22] modest handicapper: stays 1¼m: acts on good to firm and heavy going: tried in cheekpieces prior to 2015. *Ralph Smith*

MANDY THE NAG (USA) 5 b.m. Proud Citizen (USA) 122 – Storm To Glory (USA) **–** (Storm Bird (CAN) 134) [2015 68: t9.5g t8.6f Jan 29] fair handicapper: well held in 2015: stays 8.5f: acts on fibresand, tapeta, good to firm and heavy going. *Nikki Evans*

MANGE ALL 4 b.g. Zamindar (USA) 116 – Blancmange (Montjeu (USA) 137) [2015 **97** 106p: 8d⁵ 8d 10s 9.9g⁶ Sep 30] good-topped gelding: useful handicapper: fifth in Lincoln at Doncaster (5 lengths behind Gabrial) on reappearance, best effort of 2015: stays 10.5f: acts on good to firm and good to soft going: in cheekpieces final outing: has suspect attitude. *William Haggas*

MANGO CHUTNEY 2 b.g. (Apr 30) Sleeping Indian 122 – Crimson Topaz 75 **61** (Hernando (FR) 127) [2015 6g 6g 7m⁶ 7m⁶ f7g³ Nov 3] modest maiden: will stay at least 1m: acts on fibresand. *John Davies*

MANHATTAN SKYLINE (IRE) 2 gr.f. (Apr 15) Clodovil (IRE) 116 – Rainbow **86 §** Above You (IRE) 53 (Mujadil (USA) 119) [2015 t5.1g⁵ 5g³ 6g⁵ t6g* 7g³ 7s p8g³ Dec 19] lengthy filly: third foal: dam maiden: fairly useful performer: won maiden at Wolverhampton in July: third in listed race at Deauville (1¼ lengths behind Aktoria) in August: stays 7f: acts on tapeta: temperamental (flashes tail/sometimes hangs). *J. S. Moore*

MANHATTAN SWING (IRE) 5 b.g. Invincible Spirit (IRE) 121 – Bluebell Park **96** (USA) 60 (Gulch (USA)) [2015 12g² 12g³ 12g⁵ 12m⁵ 12d 12v Nov 7] useful handicapper: mostly creditable efforts in 2015: stays 1½m: acts on good to firm and heavy going: wears blinkers: useful hurdler. *Brian Ellison*

MAN IN THE ARENA 5 b.g. Bertolini (USA) 125 – Torver 58 (Lake Coniston (IRE) **–** 131) [2015 45: p8f Mar 19] poor maiden: stays 1m: acts on soft going: in headgear last 5 starts. *Dr Jon Scargill*

MANIPULATION (IRE) 4 b.g. Elnadim (USA) 128 – Intriguing (IRE) 87 (Fasliyev **71** (USA) 120) [2015 p8g t8.6f² 10m Apr 13] fair handicapper: left David Simcock after second start: best at 7f/1m: acts on tapeta and good to soft going. *Tony Carroll*

MANIPURA 2 gr.f. (Feb 6) Sleeping Indian 122 – Ming Meng (IRE) 85 (Intikhab (USA) **63** 135) [2015 5.1g t5.1f⁴ 6s p5g³ t5.1f⁵ Dec 21] first foal: dam, 6f winner, sister to useful winner up to 9f Fine Silver out of useful 2-y-o 5f/6f winner Petula: modest maiden: best form at 5f: acts on polytrack and tapeta. *Derek Shaw*

MANJAAM (IRE) 2 ch.c. (May 14) Tamayuz 126 – Priory Rock (IRE) 79 (Rock of **71** Gibraltar (IRE) 133) [2015 8.1g⁶ 7.5m⁵ 10.2g⁶ Oct 18] fair maiden: best effort when sixth at Sandown on debut: should stay at least 1¼m. *Ed Dunlop*

MAN LOOK 3 b.g. Nayef (USA) 129 – Charlecote (IRE) (Caerleon (USA) 132) [2015 –: **73** p10g* 11g 12m⁴ 12m 12.1g³ 12v³ 13.1f⁴ 11.9d Sep 25] tall gelding: fair performer: won maiden at Lingfield in February: stays 13f: acts on polytrack and firm going: in hood last 2 starts. *Andrew Balding*

MANNDAWI (FR) 5 gr.g. Dalakhani (IRE) 133 – Mintly Fresh (USA) (Rubiano (USA)) **106** [2015 10g³ 14d⁶ 11.6d 12g³ Oct 21] smart performer in France at 3 yrs: missed 2014: best effort in 2015 when 5 lengths third to Almoonqith in Group 3 Geelong Cup (Handicap) at Geelong final start, short of room over 1f out: should stay 1¾m: acts on soft and good to firm going. *Ed Dunlop*

MAN OF HARLECH 4 b.g. Dansili 127 – Ffestiniog (IRE) 96 (Efisio 120) [2015 95p: **109** 8m 8.1m⁴ p8g² 8d* 8d² 9g⁴ p10f* p10g Dec 19] attractive gelding: useful handicapper: won at Ffos Las (by 2¼ lengths from Peak Storm) in August and Lingfield (by 1¼ lengths from Aleator, showing himself better than ever) in November: stays 1¼m: acts on polytrack and soft going. *Andrew Balding*

MAN OF LA MANCHA (IRE) 2 b.g. (Apr 30) Zoffany (IRE) 121 – Sarella Loren **–** (USA) 69 (Theatrical) [2015 7g Sep 23] 7/1, ninth of 12 in maiden at Redcar on debut. *Ben Haslam*

MAN OF MUSIC 4 b.g. Piccolo 121 – Blue Goddess (IRE) 94 (Blues Traveller (IRE) 119) **54** [2015 –: 7.6g⁵ 6.1m⁵ 7.1m⁶ t6g² p6f² Oct 1] good-topped gelding: modest maiden: stays 7.5f: acts on polytrack, tapeta and good to firm going: blinkered last 2 starts. *Tony Carroll*

MAN OF TIME (IRE) 2 ch.c. (Apr 20) Dandy Man (IRE) 123 – She's Our Rock (IRE) **53** (Rock of Gibraltar (IRE) 133) [2015 5g 6g 6m 6m Aug 8] workmanlike colt: modest maiden: best effort second start: tried in headgear. *Ismail Mohammed*

MANOLITO 3 b.g. High Chaparral (IRE) 132 – Break Time (Dansili 127) [2015 76p: 10m **85** 8.3m³ 7m⁶ t7.1m⁴ p8f⁷ t8.6g* t8.6f³ t9.5g⁴ Nov 27] good-bodied gelding: fairly useful handicapper: won at Chelmsford and Wolverhampton in September: stays 8.5f: acts on polytrack, tapeta and good to firm going: usually wears tongue tie: usually travels strongly. *Hughie Morrison*

MANOMINE 6 b.g. Manduro (GER) 135 – Fascinating Hill (FR) (Danehill (USA) 126) **70** [2015 81: 11m⁶ p11g p10g⁵ p10f Oct 1] lengthy gelding: fair handicapper: stays 2m: acts on polytrack, tapeta and good to firm going: tried in blinkers: front runner/races prominently. *Clive Brittain*

MANSFIELD 2 b.g. (Apr 11) Exceed And Excel (AUS) 126 – Jane Austen (IRE) 104 **91** (Galileo (IRE) 134) [2015 p6g 7d* 8d³ p7g² p7f³ p8g¹ Dec 2] 130,000F: fourth foal: closely related to 1½m winner Just Darcy (by Danehill Dancer) and half-brother to 11f winner Queen's Novel (by King's Best): dam 1½m-1¾m winner: fairly useful performer: won maiden at Brighton in August: better form when placed in 3 nurseries: stays 1m: acts on polytrack and good to soft going. *Charlie Appleby*

MANSHAA (IRE) 3 ch.g. Dubawi (IRE) 129 – Ghizlaan (USA) (Seeking The Gold **74** (USA)) [2015 75: 7.5m³ 7.6m Jun 26] fair maiden: stays 7.5f: acts on good to firm going: front runner/races prominently: sold 30,000 gns, sent to Qatar. *Mark Johnston*

MANSON 2 ch.c. (Apr 3) Equiano (FR) 127 – Swain's Gold (USA) (Swain (IRE) 134) **86** [2015 6m² 7g⁴ 7g⁶ p7g* Nov 18] 40,000Y: sixth foal: half-brother to 3 winners, including Irish Derby winner Jack Hobbs (2-y-o 8.6f winner, by Halling) and smart 9f-11f winner Niceofyoutotellme (by Hernando): dam 6f/6.5f winner: fairly useful performer: won maiden at Kempton in November, making all: will stay 1m. *Dominic Ffrench Davis*

MANSURI 4 ch.g. Piccolo 121 – Antonia's Choice 73 (Music Boy 124) [2015 p8f t8.6g **–** Jun 26] fairly useful at best, no form in 2015: left Warren Greatrex after first start: stays 9.5f: acts on polytrack and good to firm going: sometimes wears headgear: sold 8,000 gns, sent to Saudi Arabia. *Tom Dascombe*

MANTON GRANGE 2 b.c. (Mar 30) Siyouni (FR) 122 – Emulate 81 (Alhaarth (IRE) **82** 126) [2015 7g⁵ p7f 7g³ 8s⁶ Sep 18] £50,000Y, 60,000 2-y-o: lengthy colt: has scope: fourth foal: half-brother to 1m winner Sandra (by Three Valleys): dam, 2-y-o 7f winner who stayed 1¼m, half-sister to useful winner up to 1m Coastline: fair form: third in maiden at Ascot (3 lengths behind Knife Edge) in September: 20/1, shaped much better than distance beaten suggests when 8½ lengths sixth of 8 to Stormy Antarctic in minor event at Newbury final start: best effort at 7f: may yet do better. *George Baker*

MANUKA (IRE) 6 ch.g. Galileo (IRE) 134 – Honey Gold (IRE) (Indian Ridge 123) [2015 **71** 74: p10.7d 13.8d t16.5g* Dec 5] fair handicapper: left M. D. O'Callaghan, won at Wolverhampton in December: stays 16.5f: acts on polytrack, tapeta, good and soft going: sometimes wears headgear: in tongue tie last 3 starts. *Karl Thornton, Ireland*

MANY DREAMS (IRE) 2 b.f. (Apr 26) Kodiac 112 – Deeday Bay (IRE) 78 (Brave Act **73** 119) [2015 p6g³ 6d⁵ 7s³ 7d² p7m² 6d p7g⁶ p7g⁴ Dec 28] £40,000 2-y-o: lengthy, rather unfurnished filly: fifth foal: half-sister to winner up to 1¼m El Torbellino (2-y-o 1m winner, by Chineur): dam 2-y-o 6f winner: fair maiden: stays 7f: acts on polytrack: often races towards rear. *Mark Usher*

MAOI CHINN TIRE (IRE) 8 b.g. Mull of Kintyre (USA) 114 – Primrose And Rose 72 **79** (Primo Dominie 121) [2015 85: 14m 17.1g⁶ 16m⁵ 14f⁴ 13.9m 15.8s* Oct 27] sturdy gelding: fair handicapper: won at Catterick in October: stays 2m: acts on polytrack, firm and soft going: has worn headgear: wears tongue tie: often races freely. *Jennie Candlish*

MAONTRI (IRE) 8 b.m. Catcher In The Rye (IRE) 115 – Arabian Dream (IRE) (Royal **93** Academy (USA) 130) [2015 107: p10.7g⁶ p8g⁵ 7m* 6.9g* 7m⁴ 6m 7g³ 7d⁴ p7g 8s p8g p8g **a86** p7g⁴ p8g⁴ Dec 4] tall mare: fairly useful handicapper: won at Leicester in May and Sligo in June: stays 1m: acts on polytrack, good to firm and good to soft going: usually wears headgear: front runner/races prominently. *M. J. Tynan, Ireland*

MAPLE STIRRUP (IRE) 3 b.f. Duke of Marmalade (IRE) 132 – Street Shaana (FR) **65** 111 (Darshaan 133) [2015 12.1g⁶ 9.3m⁶ 12d 12d t13.9f⁴ t16.5m⁴ p16g³ Dec 16] sixth foal: closely related to 11.6f winner Yeah Baby (by Danehill Dancer) and half-sister to 2 winners, including 12.5f winner Sourabad (by Halling): dam 10.5f-15f (French Group 3) winner: fair maiden: stays 16.5f: acts on polytrack and tapeta: often in hood. *Patrick Holmes*

MAP

MAPPIN TIME (IRE) 7 b.g. Orientate (USA) 127 – Different Story (USA) (Stravinsky (USA) 133) [2015 102: p6g⁴ t5.1f* t6m p5g² p5g² 5.1s 5g² 5g⁵ 5m 6d 5g t6f⁵ p5f f5g² Dec 12] sturdy gelding: fairly useful handicapper on turf, useful on all-weather: won at Wolverhampton (by neck from Basil Berry) in February: good 2 lengths second to Meadway at Southwell final start, faring best of those held up: stays 6f: acts on all-weather, firm and good to soft going: wears headgear: often races in rear. *Tim Easterby* **92 a103**

MARAAKIB (IRE) 3 b.g. Dark Angel (IRE) 113 – Mrs Cee (IRE) 71 (Orpen (USA) 116) [2015 93: 8m 9g p8g⁶ 8d³ 7d² 8d⁴ 8.3g⁶ 10s* 10.3d* 10d⁶ 10v* Nov 3] tall gelding: useful handicapper: left Brian Meehan after third start: won at Leicester and Doncaster (amateur) in October and Redcar (by length from Empress Ali, making all) in November: stays 10.5f: acts on heavy going: often travels strongly. *David O'Meara* **95**

MARASIM 3 ch.g. Exceed And Excel (AUS) 126 – Muffled (USA) 67 (Mizaaya 104) [2015 –: p6g³ 6g³ 6m² p6g Jun 10] fair maiden: raced only at 6f: acts on good to firm going. *Roger Varian* **72**

MARAWEH (IRE) 5 b.g. Muhtathir 126 – Itqaan (USA) 83 (Danzig (USA)) [2015 16s⁵ Apr 5] lengthy gelding: modest maiden: best effort at 1½m: acts on soft going. *Lucinda Russell* **55**

MARCANO (IRE) 3 b.g. Arcano (IRE) 122 – Aquatint (Dansili 127) [2015 89: p8g 8d⁶ 6d 10m 10m⁴ 10g 8g⁶ Aug 21] well-made gelding: fair handicapper: stays 1m: acts on good to firm going: tried in cheekpieces in 2015. *Rod Millman* **74**

MARCEL (IRE) 2 b.c. (Mar 25) Lawman (FR) 121 – Mauresmo (IRE) (Marju (IRE) 127) [2015 7f⁵ 7g* 8d* Oct 24] **118**

'Even though I don't have many good horses, you know when a good one comes along.' Marcel gave trainer Peter Chapple-Hyam his third win in the Racing Post Trophy, following Commander Collins in 1998 and Authorized in 2006. Authorized went on to win the Derby, but, while Marcel is 25/1 in most lists for the Epsom classic, he does not currently hold an entry and his trainer has warned that the race will not necessarily be Marcel's biggest priority. Marcel is set to return to action in either the Two Thousand Guineas (for which he is generally 25/1) or the Poule d'Essai des Poulains, which will in 2016 be run over the straight mile at Deauville while work is carried out at Longchamp, which should at least minimise the draw bias that often manifests itself over the round mile course at Longchamp. Chapple-Hyam is also keen to run Marcel in his 'favourite race', the Dante Stakes, which he won with Authorized, with the Prix du Jockey Club perhaps Marcel's more likely target after that given his breeding, which suggests he isn't sure to stay a mile and a half. Marcel gave jockey Andrea Atzeni his third straight win in the Racing Post Trophy, following Kingston Hill and Elm Park. In October Atzeni announced he was leaving his role as number-one jockey for Qatar Racing to ride as retained jockey for Sheikh Mohammed Obaid, a position he occupied in 2014. Atzeni, incidentally, has won the last five Group 1 races run at Doncaster, having also won the St Leger in 2014 on Kingston Hill and in 2015 on Simple Verse.

Racing Post Trophy, Doncaster—rank outsider Marcel gallops on strongly to win from Johannes Vermeer (who won in Group 1 company next time) and the unlucky Foundation; it was trainer Peter Chapple Hyam's third win in the race

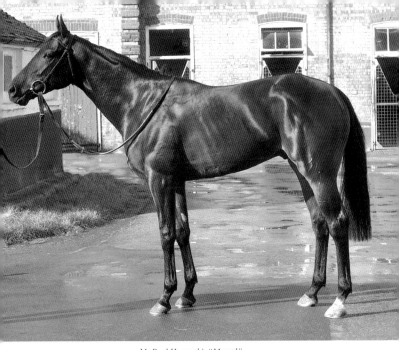

Mr Paul Hancock's "Marcel"

Marcel finished an encouraging seven lengths fifth of thirteen to Ray's The Bar on firm ground at Ascot in July on his debut, and he left that form well behind after eight weeks off when winning an eight-runner maiden on good ground at Newcastle (starting joint favourite) in August, scoring by three and three quarter lengths from Heir To A Throne. Marcel was apparently being lined up to run in nurseries until the official handicapper refused him a mark, and he also appeared among the entries for the Horris Hill Stakes at Newbury on the same day as the Racing Post Trophy at Doncaster. 'He's a nice horse, but he's not Authorized,' said Chapple-Hyam before the seven-runner Racing Post Trophy, for which Marcel was sent off the 33/1 rank outsider. The betting was headed at 11/10-on by undefeated Foundation who had beaten second favourite Deauville (7/2) by three quarters of a length in the Royal Lodge Stakes. Deauville, wearing first-time cheekpieces, was joined in the Racing Post Trophy by stablemates Johannes Vermeer (7/1) and Port Douglas (20/1), with the field completed by Mengli Khan (8/1) and Tony Curtis (14/1). In the event it turned out to be nothing like the race that was anticipated as neither Foundation nor Deauville were involved in the finish, with Deauville fading out of it and proving part of the trouble Foundation found himself in, pocketed with no way out at a crucial stage two furlongs out. Although the race was therefore unsatisfactory in some respects—chiefly because of the difficulties that put paid to the chances of Foundation—Marcel was certainly in the right place at the right time as he swept down the outside of the field, which had converged on the stand rail, and galloped on strongly to beat Johannes Vermeer by a length and a half. The first two were patiently ridden in a race run at a good gallop on good to soft ground, though they still got first run on the unlucky Foundation who finished a further two and a half lengths back in third, not knocked about at all. After the race, Peter Chapple-Hyam joked: 'I did say he was no Authorized, but that was because this lad had already won a maiden!' While Group 1 races from now on are likely to be harder to win for Marcel, the Racing Post Trophy form was franked when Johannes Vermeer won the Criterium International eight days later.

			Invincible Spirit	Green Desert
		Lawman (FR)	(b 1997)	Rafha
		(b 2004)	Laramie	Gulch
Marcel (IRE)			(b 1994)	Light The Lights
(b.c. 2013)			Marju	Last Tycoon
		Mauresmo (IRE)	(br 1988)	Flame of Tara
		(b 2004)	Absaar	Alleged
			(b 1987)	My Nord

Marcel made €50,000 as a foal and was resold for only 26,000 guineas as a yearling, but he is a useful-looking colt related to some smart horses. Marcel is by the Prix du Jockey Club winner Lawman, who has sired the three-year-old Group 1-winning milers Most Improved and Just The Judge, and is the second foal out of Mauresmo after the ill-fated maiden First Serve. Mauresmo is an unraced sister to the smart winner at up to six furlongs Munjiz and the useful two-year-old seven-furlong winner Mutawaffer, who stayed a mile and a half. Marcel's grandam, the eleven-furlong winner Absaar, is a half-sister to the Grand Prix de Paris/Melbourne Cup winner At Talaq and the Grade 1 winner in the States at up to nine furlongs Annoconnor. Mauresmo has a yearling colt by Lope de Vega. Marcel was broken in as a yearling by former Flat jockey Robyn Brisland who was granted a trainer's licence in December and has taken over the Newmarket yard formerly occupied by the now-retired Nick Littmoden. Marcel isn't sure to stay much further than a mile and a quarter on pedigree but probably isn't likely to prove quite good enough to win a Derby anyway. *Peter Chapple-Hyam*

MARCIANO (IRE) 5 b.g. Pivotal 124 – Kitty Matcham (IRE) 102 (Rock of Gibraltar (IRE) 133) [2015 70: f7d* 8s f8g* 7d May 11] fairly useful handicapper: won at Southwell in February and April: stayed 1m: best form on fibresand: often in headgear: dead. *Michael Appleby* **85**

MARCLE (IRE) 2 b.g. (Apr 17) Kodiac 112 – Mark One 85 (Mark of Esteem (IRE) 137) [2015 6.1m 6g p6g t7.1m² p7g² t7.1f* Oct 13] fair performer: won nursery at Wolverhampton in October: stays 7f: acts on tapeta. *Ed de Giles* **72**

MARCRET (ITY) 8 b.g. Martino Alonso (IRE) 113 – Love Secret (USA) 94 (Secreto (USA) 128) [2015 102: 7g 7.6v⁵ 7.6g 8.5g⁶ 8d⁵ 7.6g² 7.6m⁶ 8d⁴ 7.6s* 7d⁴ 8.3s Oct 26] quite attractive gelding: useful handicapper: won at Chester (by 2¼ lengths from Jack's Revenge) in September: left Ruth Carr after fifth start: stays 10.5f: acts on polytrack, good to firm and heavy going: tried in hood: tried in tongue tie prior to 2015: often races in rear. *James Unett* **100**

MAREEF (IRE) 5 b.g. Oasis Dream 129 – Katayeb (IRE) (Machiavellian (USA) 123) [2015 –: p10gᵖᵘ Mar 12] twice-raced maiden: dead. *Kevin Morgan* **–**

MARENGO 4 gr g. Verglas (IRE) 118 – Cloudchaser (IRE) (Red Ransom (USA)) [2015 77: 12.1m 12g⁵ 10.2m⁴ 12.1m* 11.5d 12.1d¹ 12s³ 12d³ 8.9p 27] fairly useful handicapper: won at Chepstow in July (apprentice) and August: stays 1½m: acts on good to firm and heavy going: often wears cheekpieces. *Bernard Llewellyn* **80**

MARENKO 2 b.f. (Mar 7) Exceed And Excel (AUS) 126 – Safina 100 (Pivotal 124) [2015 6m 7g* 7m³ 7g² 8m² 8g Oct 9] lengthy filly: second foal: half-sister to 2-y-o 6f winner Vesnina (by Sea The Stars): dam, 7f winner, half-sister to useful 7f/1m winner Russian Realm out of 1000 Guineas winner Russian Rhythm: useful performer: won maiden at Ascot in July in good style: better form when third in Sweet Solera Stakes at Newmarket (length behind Blue Bayou), and second in Prix du Calvados at Deauville (neck behind Great Page) and May Hill Stakes at Doncaster (¾ length behind Turret Rocks): well held in Fillies' Mile at Newmarket final start: stays 1m: acts on good to firm going: usually leads. *Richard Hannon* **102**

MARGARET'S MISSION (IRE) 4 b.f. Shamardal (USA) 129 – Wimple (USA) 101 (Kingmambo (USA) 125) [2015 66p: 8s 8g* 8g* 8m* 7m³ 7d 10.3m 7.2g 9g Sep 26] fairly useful handicapper: won at Newcastle in May and June and Doncaster in July: stays 1m: acts on good to firm going: often in tongue tie prior to 2015: usually races in rear. *Jim Goldie* **92**

MARGOT ROSE 3 b.f. Kheleyf (USA) 116 – Sanjuna (Tiger Hill (IRE) 127) [2015 53: **52** t6f⁴ p8f p6g f5g³ p6m⁵ f5d² p5g³ 6d t5.1g³ 6d⁶ t6g⁵ 5g⁶ 5m 5s⁴ 5g t5.1m Dec 18] modest maiden: left Harry Dunlop after third start, Gay Kelleway after twelfth, Victor Dartnall after fifteenth: stays 6f: acts on all-weather, soft and good to firm going: often wears headgear. *Alan Berry*

MARGRETS GIFT 4 ch.f. Major Cadeaux 121 – Its Another Gift 64 (Primo Dominie **84** 121) [2015 79: 5g⁴ 5m 5m⁴ 5g³ 5s 5.1g⁵ 5g* 5g Sep 26] fairly useful handicapper: won at Ayr in April and Beverley in August: stays 6f: acts on good to firm and heavy going: often wears cheekpieces. *Tim Easterby*

MARIET 6 ch.m. Dr Fong (USA) 128 – Medway (IRE) 60 (Shernazar 131) [2015 f16g Jan **–** 6] rather leggy mare: maiden, modest at best: stays 1½m: acts on polytrack, good to firm and good to soft going: wears hood nowadays. *Suzy Smith*

MARIGOLD HOTEL (IRE) 3 gr.f. Galileo (IRE) 134 – Hotelgenie Dot Com 107 **70** (Selkirk (USA) 129) [2015 7m 8g⁴ p10g⁵ Aug 4] 350,000Y: sister to 1¼m winner Loch Ma Naire and half-sister to smart winner up to 1m Simply Perfect (by Danehill) and 1½m winner (stays 1¾m) Allied Answer (by Danehill Dancer): dam 2-y-o 7f winner: fair form in maidens at Newmarket and Chelmsford last 2 starts. *M. F. de Kock, South Africa*

MARIGOT BAY 3 b.f. Paco Boy (IRE) 129 – Mamma Morton (IRE) 79 (Elnadim (USA) **–** 128) [2015 78: f5g Feb 26] rather leggy filly: maiden, fair at best: best effort at 5f: acts on good to soft going. *Gay Kelleway*

MARILYN MON 3 b.f. Multiplex 114 – Future Regime (IRE) 56 (Xaar 132) [2015 71: **58** f6g³ Jan 13] modest maiden: stays 7f: acts on polytrack and tapeta. *Jo Hughes*

MARINA BALLERINA 7 b.m. Ballet Master (USA) 92 – Marinaite 82 (Komaite **–** (USA)) [2015 73: f11g 11.8m⁶ Jul 16] fair at best, no form in 2015: stays 11f: acts on fibresand: sometimes wears headgear. *Roy Bowring*

MARINERS MOON (IRE) 4 ch.g. Mount Nelson 125 – Dusty Moon 78 (Dr Fong **62** (USA) 128) [2015 81: 12d⁶ 14.1m 11.5m⁵ 8g⁵ 8.9g 9.3m⁶ Sep 9] modest handicapper: stays 1½m: acts on good to firm and good to soft going: tried in cheekpieces prior to 2015. *Patrick Holmes*

MARITAL (IRE) 4 b.g. Montjeu (IRE) 137 – Fleeting Affair (USA) (Gone West (USA)) **63** [2015 8.3s 12m 10d t8.6g² t8.6g² t9.5g* t8.6g⁶ t8.6m⁴ Sep 5] modest handicapper: won at Wolverhampton in July: stays 9.5f: acts on tapeta and good to firm going: in cheekpieces/ tongue tie last 6 starts: front runner: sold 8,000 gns, sent to Italy. *Michael Dods*

MARJONG 5 b.m. Mount Nelson 125 – Vermilliann (IRE) 98 (Mujadil (USA) 119) [2015 **82** 83: p7g⁵ p6f² p6g⁴ p6f 5.7g⁶ Jul 14] fairly useful handicapper: stays 7f: acts on polytrack, soft and good to firm going: often wears hood: sometimes slowly away, often races towards rear. *Simon Dow*

MARJU'S QUEST (IRE) 5 b.g. Marju (IRE) 127 – Queen's Quest (Rainbow Quest **–** (USA) 134) [2015 12g⁶ May 14] fairly useful at best, well held only start in 2015: stays 1½m: best form on ground firmer than good: fairly useful hurdler. *David Dennis*

MARKABAH (IRE) 3 b.f. Dubawi (IRE) 129 – Ghaidaa (IRE) 105 (Cape Cross (IRE) **84 p** 129) [2015 10d 9.9s 8m² p10f* Nov 23] good-bodied filly: third foal: half-sister to useful 10.4f/11f winner Tajheez (by Raven's Pass) and 8.6f-1¼m winner Thurayaat (by Tamayuz): dam, 1¼m winner, half-sister to Oaks winner Eswarah: fairly useful performer: won maiden at Chelmsford (by 5 lengths from U S Navy Seal) in November: stays 1¼m: open to further improvement. *Roger Varian*

MARKAMI (FR) 5 ch.g. Medicean 128 – Marque Royale 107 (Royal Academy (USA) **–** 130) [2015 p15.8g 16d May 19] fairly useful at best, no form in 2015: best effort at 13f: acts on polytrack: tried in headgear/tongue tie. *Johnny Farrelly*

MARKAZ (IRE) 3 gr.c. Dark Angel (IRE) 113 – Folga 104 (Atraf 116) [2015 105: 6f⁴ 7f³ **116** 6d⁴ 7m* 7d⁶ 7d² 7g⁵ Oct 9] athletic colt: smart performer: won Criterion Stakes at Newmarket (by 1¾ lengths from Hors de Combat) in June: good efforts last 2 starts, in Park Stakes at Doncaster (3¾ lengths second to Limato) and Challenge Stakes at Newmarket (length fifth to Cable Bay): stays 7f: acts on good to firm and good to soft going: front runner/races prominently. *B. W. Hills*

MARKET CHOICE 2 b.g. (Mar 14) Majestic Missile (IRE) 118 – Ron's Secret **85** 92 (Efisio 120) [2015 5.9g² 5.9g* 7g⁴ 6g Oct 3] €23,000Y: half-brother to several winners, including smart 1¼m-1½m winner Agent Secret (by Pyrus) and 7f-1½m winner Acteur Secret (by Captain Rio): dam 1m/9f winner: fairly useful form: won maiden at Carlisle (by 1½ lengths from Another Touch) in July, easily best effort: stays 6f: has been gelded. *Michael Dods*

MARKET FRESH 2 b.f. (Mar 13) Sir Percy 129 – Laverre (IRE) 81 (Noverre (USA) **40** 125) [2015 7.5m⁶ 7.5g⁵ 7d 8g t9.5f Nov 3] 2,500Y: first foal: dam 9f-13f winner: poor maiden: bred to be suited by middle distances: acts on good to firm going: often in hood. *Tim Easterby*

MARKET PUZZLE (IRE) 8 ch.g. Bahamian Bounty 116 – Trempjane 71 (Lujain **–** (USA) 119) [2015 51: 10g‡ Jul 8] lengthy, workmanlike gelding: modest handicapper: stays 10.5f: acts on polytrack and any turf going: often wears headgear. *Mark Brisbourne*

MARKET SHARE 5 b.g. Zamindar (USA) 116 – Winter Solstice 104 (Unfuwain (USA) **94** 131) [2015 112: 8.3f⁵ 8.3m⁶ 8m 7.6g⁵ 6g 7.2g p8f Oct 24] sturdy gelding: fairly useful handicapper: stays 9f: acts on polytrack, soft and good to firm going: often in hood in 2015: sent to Greece. *David O'Meara*

MARK HOPKINS 3 b.g. Mount Nelson 125 – Halska (Unfuwain (USA) 131) [2015 **97 p** 10m² 12s* 14.1s² Oct 12] 15,000Y: strong gelding: seventh foal: half-brother to 9f-1¼m winner Smooth Jazz (by Zafonic) and 1m winner Fakhour (by Dansili): dam, unraced, closely related to Prix du Jockey Club/Irish Derby winner Old Vic: useful performer: won maiden at Newmarket (by 6 lengths from Mishghar) in July: best effort when second in handicap at Salisbury (neck behind Faithful Mount) in October, sticking to task: stays 1¼m: acts on soft going: will go on improving. *David Elsworth*

MARKSTEIN (IRE) 3 ch.c. Raven's Pass (USA) 133 – Manerbe (USA) (Unbridled's **80** Song (USA) 125) [2015 8g 8f⁴ p7g⁴ 8.3m² 9.9m³ Jun 30] €70,000Y: second foal: half-brother to useful 7f (including at 2 yrs) winner Marbre Rose (by Smart Strike): dam, 7.5f winner, half-sister to Canadian Grade 1 8.5f winner Zoftig: fairly useful maiden in Britain: sold 62,000 gns, sent to Qatar, and won 8.5f maiden at Doha in December. *John Gosden*

MARMAJUKE BAY 2 b.g. (Apr 23) Duke of Marmalade (IRE) 132 – Shimoni 90 (Mark **72** of Esteem (IRE) 137) [2015 7g⁶ 8.3d⁴ Oct 14] fair form in maidens at Ascot and Nottingham: bred to stay middle distances: in cheekpieces. *Mark Usher*

MARMALAD (IRE) 3 b.g. Duke of Marmalade (IRE) 132 – Primissima (GER) (Second **74** Set (IRE) 127) [2015 70, a83: p7m⁵ t8.6g³ 8.3m 7.1m⁶ 7g p8g⁴ p8g⁴ t7.1g⁶ p8g* t7.1m4 p8f² **a80** p10f³ p10g⁵ t9.5f² Dec 11] close-coupled gelding: fairly useful performer: won claimer at Lingfield in August: left Tom Dascombe after eleventh start: stays 1¼m: acts on polytrack, tapeta and good to firm going: tried in headgear in 2015: races prominently. *Shaun Lycett*

MARMALADY (IRE) 5 ch.m. Duke of Marmalade (IRE) 132 – Grecian Glory (IRE) 88 **80** (Zafonic (USA) 130) [2015 100, a91: 6m p6g⁶ 5m 6g Oct 20] angular mare: fairly useful handicapper: stays 6f: acts on polytrack, firm and good to soft going. *Gary Moore*

MARMANDE (IRE) 4 ch.f. Duke of Marmalade (IRE) 132 – Roselyn 66 (Efisio 120) **–** [2015 58: p8f t7.1f Mar 13] maiden: no form in 2015: best effort at 7f: acts on polytrack: in blinkers final start. *Daniel Kubler*

MARMARUS 4 b.g. Duke of Marmalade (IRE) 132 – Polly Perkins (IRE) 100 (Pivotal **62** 124) [2015 64, a86: 7.2g 7m 8g 7.2g t7.1f Dec 21] modest handicapper: stays 7f: acts on polytrack and tapeta: often races freely. *David Nicholls*

MARMA'S BOY 3 ch.g. Duke of Marmalade (IRE) 132 – Graduation 102 (Lomitas 129) **97** [2015 80: t9.5g* 10f* 12f³ Jun 18] useful performer: won maiden at Wolverhampton in April and handicap at Newmarket (by 2 lengths from Azraff) in May: improved again when 2 lengths third to Space Age in King George V Stakes (Handicap) at Royal Ascot final outing, coming from further back than other principals: stays 1½m: acts on tapeta and firm going: in cheekpieces last 2 starts: sent to Hong Kong, where renamed Gannet. *Ralph Beckett*

MARMION 3 b.g. Cape Cross (IRE) 129 – Margarula (IRE) 120 (Doyoun 124) [2015 **88** p12m² 12m² 12m* 12g² 12m 12s p11m Oct 28] tall, unfurnished gelding: half-brother to several winners, including winner up to 2m (Australian Group 1 event) Magog (2-y-o 1m winner, by Dansili) and useful 1¼m-2m winner Rosslyn Castle (by Selkirk): dam won Irish Oaks, also 2-y-o 1m winner: fairly useful performer: won maiden at Catterick in June: left John Gosden after first start: stays 1½m: acts on polytrack and good to firm going. *Les Eyre*

MARMOOZ 3 ch.f. Piccolo 121 – Aegean Mystery (Dr Fong (USA) 128) [2015 7f t8.6m **44** p8g t8.6f p7m f5g⁶ f7m f6g⁴ Dec 29] £2,000Y: first foal: dam unraced: poor maiden: stays 8.5f, may prove suited by shorter: acts on fibresand, tapeta and firm going. *Michael Appleby*

MARMOT 3 b.c. Champs Elysees 124 – Winter Bloom (USA) 89 (Aptitude (USA) 128) **85** [2015 69p: p7g² 10.4d 9.9m* 12m⁴ 10.1g⁴ p10g⁵ Sep 2] fairly useful performer: won maiden at Lingfield in April and handicap at Brighton in June: stays 1½m: acts on polytrack and good to firm going: in headgear last 4 starts: sold 22,000 gns, sent to UAE. *Roger Charlton*

MAROC 2 b.c. (Apr 29) Rock of Gibraltar (IRE) 133 – Zietory 107 (Zieten (USA) 118) **69 p**
[2015 8.3s⁵ t9.5f⁶ Oct 23] half-brother to several winners, including 7f winner Ziekhani (by Dalakhani) and winner up to 7f Ziefhd (by Haafhd): dam winner up to 1m (2-y-o 6f winner): better effort when fifth in maiden at Leicester (4 lengths behind Little Avon) on debut: remains open to improvement. *Paul Cole*

MARRON 2 ch.f. (Mar 18) Raven's Pass (USA) 133 – Morzine 84 (Miswaki (USA) 124) **64 p**
[2015 6g⁵ p7g Oct 29] good-topped filly: fourth foal: half-sister to 1½m winner Try Out (by Rail Link) and 9f-1¼m winner Ski Lift (by Pivotal): dam, 2-y-o 6f winner, half-sister to smart 2-y-o 6f winner (stayed 8.5f) Three Valleys: better effort when fifth in maiden at Haydock (3¾ lengths behind Balance) in October, hampered: should be suited by 7f: remains open to improvement. *John Gosden*

MARSHA (IRE) 2 b.f. (Mar 16) Acclamation 118 – Marlinka 95 (Marju (IRE) 127) [2015 **105 p**
p6d² 6g* p5g* p5g³ Oct 23] second foal: second foal: half-sister to useful 5f (including at 2 yrs) winner Judicial (by Iffraaj): dam 2-y-o 5f winner: useful form· won maiden at Catterick in September and minor event at Dundalk (by 3¼ lengths from Go Kart) in October: upped in grade and against older horses, respectable 2¾ lengths third to Take Cover in listed race at Dundalk final start: stays 6f: remains with potential. *Sir Mark Prescott Bt*

MARSHAL DAN TROOP (IRE) 2 b.c. (Mar 3) Lawman (FR) 121 – Corrozal (GER) **81 p**
(Cape Cross (IRE) 129) [2015 7g 6g⁴ 6v* Sep 2] 35,000Y: sturdy colt: fourth foal: dam, 1m winner who stayed 10.5f, half-sister to useful 12.2f winner Cabimas out of useful 1¼m-1¾m winner Casanga: fairly useful performer: best effort when winning maiden at Lingfield (by neck from Cautious Optimism) in September, slowly away: stayed by emphasis on stamina: will stay at least 1m: should do better still. *Peter Chapple-Hyam*

MARSH DAISY 4 ch.f. Pivotal 124 – Bella Lambada 87 (Lammtarra (USA) 134) [2015 **105**
107: 12d 9.9g* 9.5s⁶ 10.4s Nov 1] leggy filly: useful performer: won listed race at Fontainebleau (by length from Alzubra) in September: stays 12.5f: acts on soft going. *Hughie Morrison*

MARSHGATE LANE (USA) 6 b.g. Medaglia d'Oro (USA) 129 – Louvain (IRE) 105 **–**
(Sinndar (IRE) 134) [2015 102: 10s Sep 19] sturdy gelding: useful at best: showed nothing only start in 2015: stays 11f: acts on polytrack and soft going. *Neil Mulholland*

MARSH HAWK 3 b.f. Invincible Spirit (IRE) 121 – Asaawir 97 (Royal Applause 124) **105**
[2015 105: 7m 8g 7d⁶ 7m 7s⁵ Sep 18] rangy filly: useful performer: little impact in 2015, well positioned in steadily-run race when seeming to show her form in listed event at Newbury (fifth of 11 to Hathal) final outing: stays 1m: acts on soft going: front runner/races prominently. *Richard Hannon*

MARSH PRIDE 3 b.f. Stimulation (IRE) 121 – Peneia (USA) (Nureyev (USA) 131) **94**
[2015 81p: 6.9g 7.2s⁴ 8m⁶ 8.3d* 8g³ 8.9s⁴ Oct 10] fairly useful handicapper: won at Hamilton (by 1½ lengths from Lil Sophella) in September: will prove suited by a return to 1m: acts on soft going: front runner/races prominently. *Ann Duffield*

MARSOOMAH 3 b.f. Aqlaam 125 – Bukhoor (IRE) (Danehill (USA) 126) [2015 –: **61**
t7.1g² Jan 19] modest maiden: likely to have stayed 1m: acted on tapeta: in hood last 2 starts: often started slowly/raced in rear: dead. *Richard Fahey*

MARTHAMBLES 2 ch.f. (May 10) Sixties Icon 125 – Ribbons And Bows (IRE) 91 (Dr **–**
Devious (IRE) 127) [2015 7.6g 8m Oct 3] narrow filly: sixth foal: half-sister to 3 winners, including useful 1¼m/11f winner Brindos (by Singspiel) and 5f/6f winner Time Medicean (by Medicean): dam winner up to 9.5f (2-y-o 6f winner) who stayed 1½m: well held in 2 maidens. *Luke Dace*

MARTINIQUAISE 3 b.f. Mawatheeq (USA) 126 – Maria di Scozia 90 (Selkirk (USA) **86**
129) [2015 t9.5f² f8g* 9.9g⁶ 12m* 12m² 12f 10d⁶ 12m 12mᵖᵘ Oct 3] lengthy, angular filly: second foal: dam 1¼m-1½m winner: fairly useful performer: won maiden at Southwell in March and handicap at Newmarket in June: stays 1½m: acts on tapeta, fibresand and good to firm going: front runner/races prominently. *Mark Johnston*

MARTINI TIME (IRE) 2 b.f. (Apr 1) Pivotal 124 – Naadrah (Muhtathir 126) [2015 6g² **83**
6g 6d* 7m* 7m 8s³ 8g 7g Oct 10] leggy filly: fairly useful performer: won maiden at Hamilton in June and nursery at Leicester in July: stayed 1m: acted on soft and good to firm going: suspected temperament: dead. *Mark Johnston*

MARTLET 3 b.f. Dansili 127 – Marywell 87 (Selkirk (USA) 129) [2015 76p: p10g* 10m **109**
p10g* 12d* 12.4m⁶ Oct 3] tall filly: useful performer: won maiden at Chelmsford in April: much better form when successful in handicap at Chelmsford (by 4 lengths) and 16-runner

listed race at York (going away by 2¼ lengths from Koora), both in August: respectable sixth to Candarliya in Prix de Royallieu at Longchamp final start: suited by 1½m: acts on polytrack and good to soft going: often races towards rear. *John Gosden*

MARY ANN BUGG (IRE) 3 b.f. Bushranger (IRE) 119 – Shobobb (Shamardal (USA) **63** 129) [2015 –: p5g² p5g² f5g⁶ p6m⁴ p5g⁵ p6g⁶ t6g⁵ p6m² p6m⁴ p6m⁵ 6g⁴ 6d p6g p6f* p6f p6f p6m³ p5m Dec 31] modest handicapper: won at Chelmsford in October: best effort at 6f: acts on polytrack: tried in visor/tongue tie prior to 2015: usually leads. *Phil McEntee*

MARY ANNING 2 b.f. (Feb 28) Dutch Art 126 – Grasshoppergreen (IRE) (Barathea **–** (IRE) 127) [2015 f7m f7f t8.6m Dec 30] 18,500F, 23,000Y: fourth foal: dam unraced half-sister to very smart winner up to 1m Indian Ink: no form. *Michael Easterby*

MARYLEBONE 2 b.c. (Mar 24) Shamardal (USA) 129 – Mary Boleyn (IRE) 108 **84 p** (King's Best (USA) 132) [2015 7s⁶ p7g* Nov 9] 80,000Y: second foal: dam, 9f/1¼m winner, sister to smart 6f winner Kaldoun Kingdom: much better effort when winning maiden at Kempton (by ½ length from Cape Banjo) in November: will stay 1m+: open to further improvement. *Ed Walker*

MARY LE BOW 4 b.f. Sir Percy 129 – Bermondsey Girl 69 (Bertolini (USA) 125) [2015 **73** 71: 10.2g t8.6f* t9.5g³ t9.5f⁴ Dec 11] fair handicapper: won at Wolverhampton in November: stays 1½m, effective at shorter: acts on polytrack and tapeta: often wears headgear: usually in tongue tie in 2015. *Victor Dartnall*

MARY MCPHEE 3 ch.f. Makfi 130 – Aunty Mary 82 (Common Grounds 118) [2015 78: **72** p7m⁴ 7m 6g⁵ 7g⁵ 7v⁴ t7.1m Sep 25] tall filly: fair handicapper: stays 7f: acts on polytrack: sometimes wears hood. *Charles Hills*

MARY PARMENTER (IRE) 2 b.f. (Jan 22) Dick Turpin (IRE) 127 – Umniya (IRE) 95 **–** (Bluebird (USA) 125) [2015 p6g⁶ p6g Aug 7] seventh foal: half-sister to 2-y-o 7f winner Pat Mustard (by Royal Applause): dam, 2-y-o 6f winner who stayed 1m, half-sister to useful 6f winner Lady Links: well held in claimer and seller (blinkered) at Lingfield. *J. S. Moore*

MARY'S PRAYER 4 b.f. Champs Elysees 124 – Phi Phi (IRE) 66 (Fasliyev (USA) 120) **42** [2015 51, a44: t8.6g t8.6g 9.9m 8.3g 8.1d 10.9g Aug 31] poor maiden: stays 1¼m: acts on polytrack, good to firm and heavy going: tried in headgear. *John Holt*

MARZOCCO (USA) 4 b.g. Kitten's Joy (USA) 128 – Dynamia (USA) (Dynaformer **106** (USA)) [2015 116: p16g* 15.9g 21.7f⁵ 14s⁶ Aug 29] useful-looking gelding: useful performer: won minor event at Chelmsford (by neck from John Reel) in March: tailed-off last of 6 in listed race at Goodwood final outing: stays 2m: acts on polytrack, soft and good to firm going: usually races prominently, tends to find little: best treated with some caution. *John Gosden*

MASAMAH (IRE) 9 gr.g. Exceed And Excel (AUS) 126 – Bethesda 91 (Distant Relative **84** 128) [2015 109: t5.1f³ p5m³ p5g⁴ p5g 5.1s³ 5m 5f Jul 3] good-topped gelding: useful **a105** performer: fourth in listed race at Lingfield (2¾ lengths behind Pretend) in March: well below form subsequently: stays 6f: acts on polytrack, tapeta, firm and soft going: wears headgear: tried in tongue tie. *Marco Botti*

MASARZAIN (IRE) 2 br.g. (Mar 29) Kodiac 112 – Cache Creek (IRE) 104 (Marju (IRE) **78** 127) [2015 7m⁵ 7.1g⁵ Aug 2] useful-looking gelding: better effort when fifth in maiden at Newmarket (6½ lengths behind Ibn Malik) on debut. *B. W. Hills*

MASHKOOR APPROACH 3 ch.c. New Approach (IRE) 132 – Winners Chant (IRE) **74** 75 (Dalakhani (IRE) 133) [2015 9.9m⁶ 10d² p12g³ 14.1g Aug 13] good-bodied colt: fair maiden: best effort at 1½m: usually in visor. *Sir Michael Stoute*

MASH POTATO (IRE) 5 b.g. Whipper (USA) 126 – Salva 73 (Grand Lodge (USA) **77** 125) [2015 82: f11g 8g⁶ 9.1g 10s³ 9.3s* Aug 24] fair handicapper: won at Carlisle in August: stays 10.5f: acts on heavy going: usually wears cheekpieces. *Michael Dods*

MASIPA (IRE) 3 b.f. Lawman (FR) 121 – Barconey (IRE) (Danehill Dancer (IRE) 117) **37** [2015 57p: p6g f5g⁶ p5g⁶ 6d³ p7m Apr 29] poor maiden: stays 6f: acts on polytrack and good to soft going: usually wears headgear: sometimes slowly away, usually races nearer last than first. *Michael Squance*

MASKED DANCE (IRE) 8 gr.g. Captain Rio 122 – Brooks Masquerade (Absalom 128) **40 §** [2015 60§: f8s⁵ f8g⁶ t6g 6m f7d 6d⁶ 7g Sep 19] close-coupled gelding: poor handicapper: stays 7f: acts on polytrack, fibresand, best turf form on good going or softer (acts on heavy): usually wears headgear: tried in tongue tie prior to 2015: best treated with caution. *Scott Dixon*

MASQUERADED (USA) 2 ch.c. (Apr 28) Drosselmeyer (USA) 126 – Maudie May **71**
(USA) (Gilded Time (USA)) [2015 7s⁴ t8.6f³ t8.6f³ t9.5f* f8f* Dec 17] fair performer:
in cheekpieces, won claimer at Wolverhampton in November and seller at Southwell in
December: stays 9.5f: acts on fibresand, tapeta and soft going: front runner/races
prominently. *Gay Kelleway*

MASSAAT (IRE) 2 b.c. (Feb 20) Teofilo (IRE) 126 – Madany (IRE) 94 (Acclamation **114 p**
118) [2015 7.1m² 7d* 7g² Oct 10] tall, good sort: first foal: dam, 2-y-o 6f winner, half-sister
to useful 2-y-o 5f/6f winner Dolled Up: smart form: odds-on, confirmed debut promise
when easily winning maiden at Leicester in September: 20/1, further marked improvement
when 3¼ lengths second of 7 to Air Force Blue in Dewhurst Stakes at Newmarket final
start, leading briefly 2f out: will stay 1m: type to make an even better 3-y-o. *B. W. Hills*

MASS RALLY (IRE) 8 b.g. Kheleyf (USA) 116 – Reunion (IRE) 108 (Be My Guest **101**
(USA) 126) [2015 119: 6g⁴ 6g⁵ 6s 6g 6g 5.4g 6g 7.2g⁴ 7.2g³ 6g⁴ 6d² 7v Nov 7] strong
gelding: smart performer in 2014: useful handicapper in 2015, best efforts at Pontefract and
York first 2 starts: best at 6f/7f nowadays. acts on polytrack, soft and good to firm going:
wears headgear: has worn tongue tie: races towards rear: quirky sort. *Michael Dods*

MASTER APPRENTICE (IRE) 3 gr.c. Mastercraftsman (IRE) 129 – Lady Hawkfield **105**
(IRE) (Hawk Wing (USA) 136) [2015 99: 10d* Apr 24] workmanlike colt: useful
performer: further improvement when winning 4-runner Classic Trial at Sandown (by ½
length from Cape Clear Island, having run of race) on only start in 2015: stays 1¼m: acts
on good to firm and good to soft going: front runner/races prominently: sold privately and
sent to Hong Kong, where renamed Master Ceramibo. *Andrew Balding*

MASTER BLUEYES (IRE) 2 gr.g. (May 1) Mastercraftsman (IRE) 129 – Miss Blueyes **73 p**
(IRE) 77 (Dushyantor (USA) 123) [2015 p8g p8g⁵ 8.3d⁶ Oct 5] €18,000Y, 42,000 2-y-o:
workmanlike colt: fifth foal: dam 10.4f-1½m winner: fair maiden: best effort when sixth at
Windsor (5 lengths behind Top Beak) on final start: will stay at least 1¼m: remains with
potential. *Alan King*

MASTER BOND 6 b.g. Misu Bond (IRE) 114 – Bond Royale 89 (Piccolo 121) [2015 94: **92**
5m⁴ 5m² 5s³ 5m² 5m* 5m 5m² 6m 5s Sep 21] good-bodied gelding: fairly useful
handicapper: won at Leicester (by ½ length from Noodles Blue Boy) in June: best at 5f:
acts on tapeta, good to firm and heavy going: tried in visor/tongue tie prior to 2015. *David
O'Meara*

MASTER BURBIDGE 4 b.g. Pasternak 111 – Silver Sequel (Silver Patriarch (IRE) 125) **–**
[2015 p10f t12.2g⁵ 7.1s Sep 15] no form. *Neil Mulholland*

MASTER CARPENTER (IRE) 4 ch.c. Mastercraftsman (IRE) 129 – Fringe 93 (In **117**
The Wings 128) [2015 110: 8m 7d 8m³ 8.1m³ 10.4m* 10.4m² 10d 8d⁵ 9g Sep 26] smallish,
good-quartered colt: smart performer: won John Smith's Cup (Handicap) at York in July by
neck from Kelinni: also ran well when third in handicap at Sandown (½ length behind
Basem) and second in Rose of Lancaster Stakes at Haydock (5 lengths behind Intilaaq)
fourth/sixth starts: stays 10.5f: acts on soft and good to firm going: front runner/races
prominently. *Rod Millman*

*John Smith's Cup (Heritage Handicap), York—Master Carpenter (right) just beats
Kelinni in a typically competitive renewal of this valuable event*

MASTER CLOCKMAKER (IRE) 4 gr.g. Mastercraftsman (IRE) 129 – Mairead **62**
Anne (USA) (Elusive Quality (USA)) [2015 8.3m 8.3g⁴ 8m² 7.9d⁶ 7g⁶ 7.2g Oct 8] modest
maiden: stays 1¼m: acts on good to firm and good to soft going: tried in headgear.
Ann Duffield

MASTER DANCER 4 gr.g. Mastercraftsman (IRE) 129 – Isabella Glyn (IRE) 75 **–**
(Sadler's Wells (USA) 132) [2015 p12g Dec 20] workmanlike gelding: modest
handicapper: stays 1¼m: acts on polytrack, tapeta, soft and good to firm going: has worn
headgear. *Tim Vaughan*

MASTERFUL ACT (USA) 8 ch.g. Pleasantly Perfect (USA) 130 – Catnip (USA) **86**
(Flying Paster (USA)) [2015 t13.9g f11g* Dec 15] tall, workmanlike gelding: fairly useful
performer: won claimer at Southwell in December: stays 2m: acts on polytrack and
fibresand: tried in tongue tie prior to 2015. *David O'Meara*

MASTER GUNNER (USA) 2 b.c. (Apr 30) War Front (USA) 119   Queen of The Night **68 p**
76 (Sadler's Wells (USA) 132) [2015 7m⁵ Sep 16] third foal: dam, ran once (would have
stayed 1½m), closely related to top-class winner up to 1½m Falbrav: 12/1, some
encouragement when fifth in maiden at Yarmouth (3½ lengths behind Banksea) in
September, not knocked about: open to improvement. *Sir Michael Stoute*

MASTER MIRASOL (IRE) 2 b.g. (May 9) Arcano (IRE) 122 – Hidden Meaning 66 **79**
(Cadeaux Genereux 131) [2015 6g⁴ 6m⁵ 6m⁵ 6s* 7d² 6v Nov 7] fair performer: won
nursery at Hamilton in August: stays 7f: acts on good to soft going. *Kevin Ryan*

MASTER OF DISGUISE 9 b.g. Kyllachy 129 – St James's Antigua (IRE) 79 (Law **54**
Society (USA) 130) [2015 66: t6g⁶ t6g⁴ f6d t5.1f⁵ t5.1m t5.1f⁵ t6g Apr 27] compact
gelding: modest handicapper: stays 7f: acts on all-weather, soft and good to firm going:
tried in headgear: sometimes wears tongue tie. *Brian Baugh*

MASTER OF FINANCE (IRE) 4 ch.g. Mastercraftsman (IRE) 129 – Cheal Rose **104**
(IRE) 83 (Dr Devious (IRE) 127) [2015 95: 10s* 9.8d 10.3s³ 10.4g² 10.1g³ 10.3f⁵ 10.4m
10s² 10.4g 11.9d⁶ 10g⁵ Sep 24] strong gelding: useful handicapper: won at Pontefract (by
3½ lengths from Silvery Moon) in April: good second at York (½ length behind Mahsoob)
and Ascot (length behind Great Park) fourth/eighth starts: stays 10.5f: acts on firm and soft
going: blinkered final outing: front runner/races prominently. *Mark Johnston*

MASTER OF HEAVEN 2 b.g. (Jan 22) Makfi 130 – Maid In Heaven (IRE) 99 (Clodovil **– p**
(IRE) 116) [2015 p8m p8g Dec 9] 22,000F, 40,000Y: first foal: dam, 6f-7f winner, half-
sister to useful winner up to 7f Delphie Queen: looked in need of experience when well
held in maidens at Lingfield and Kempton: likely to do better in time. *Jim Boyle*

MASTER OF IRONY (IRE) 3 b.g. Makfi 130 – Mother of Pearl (IRE) 113 (Sadler's **91**
Wells (USA) 132) [2015 78p: 8d² 8d* 8g⁶ Aug 21] useful form: won handicap at Doncaster
(by 3¼ lengths from Ziggys Star) in June: will stay 1¼m: acts on good to soft going.
Ralph Beckett

MASTER OF SONG 8 ch.g. Ballet Master (USA) 92 – Ocean Song 61 (Savahra Sound **60**
111) [2015 48, a64: f12d⁴ p10g⁵ 8.3m f8g⁴ Dec 12] modest handicapper: stays 1½m: acts
on fibresand, polytrack, good to firm and good to soft going: usually wears headgear: tried
in tongue tie prior to 2015. *Roy Bowring*

MASTER OF SPEED (IRE) 3 ch.g. Mastercraftsman (IRE) 129 – Mango Groove **87**
(IRE) 67 (Unfuwain (USA) 131) [2015 68p: 10m* 12g³ 13.3s⁶ 14d⁶ Sep 5] tall, rather
unfurnished gelding: fairly useful performer: won maiden at Sandown in June: stays 1⅝m:
acts on good to firm going: often races towards rear: sold 50,000 gns and joined Gary
Moore. *Roger Varian*

MASTERPAVER 4 gr.g. Mastercraftsman (IRE) 129 – Most-Saucy 86 (Most Welcome **71**
131) [2015 p12f² p15.8m⁶ p12f⁵ p15.8f12g p11g⁴ p10g² 12.3m⁵ 10g Jul 5] fair handicapper **a100**
on turf, useful on all-weather: second at Lingfield in January and Chelmsford in June: stays
easy 2m, effective over much shorter: acts on polytrack, tapeta and good to firm going: has
worn headgear, including on last 4 starts. *Alan Bailey*

MASTER PEKAN 2 b.g. (Mar 29) Piccolo 121 – Lady Pekan 87 (Sri Pekan (USA) 117) **–**
[2015 5.1m 5s t5.1f⁶ Dec 21] no form. *Roy Brotherton*

MASTERSON (IRE) 2 gr.g. (May 2) Lawman (FR) 121 – Indian Dumaani 51 (Indian **69**
Ridge 123) [2015 7m 8.1g⁵ 8g² 8g³ 10.2f* 10.2g⁶ Sep 30] fair performer: won nursery at
Bath in September: best effort at 1¼m: acts on firm going. *Mick Channon*

MASTER THE WORLD (IRE) 4 gr.g. Mastercraftsman (IRE) 129 – Zadalla 68 (Zaha **113**
(CAN) 106) [2015 101: 8g³ 8m⁴ 8.1m⁴ 8.1m³ 10m* 9.9g 8m 9g² 9g 8d³ 8d⁵ Oct 31] good-
topped gelding: smart performer: better than ever in 2015 and won handicap at Newmarket
(by 1¼ lengths from Azmaam) in June: good efforts subsequently when second in

34-runner Cambridgeshire Handicap at Newmarket (short head behind Third Time Lucky) and third in 20-runner Balmoral Handicap at Ascot (3¼ lengths behind Musaddas): stays 1¼m: acts on soft and good to firm going: usually wears headgear: usually races prominently. *David Elsworth*

MASTER WIZARD 5 b.g. Motivator 131 – Enchanted 99 (Magic Ring (IRE) 115) [2015 **51** f5s 8.3m 7m⁶ Jun 13] modest maiden, very lightly raced: may prove best at sprint distances: acts on good to firm going: tried in cheekpieces prior to 2015. *David C. Griffiths*

MASTER ZAIN (IRE) 3 b.c. Mastercraftsman (IRE) 129 – Tafseer (IRE) (Grand Lodge **76 p** (USA) 125) [2015 8d³ Oct 5] 40,000Y: fourth foal: half-brother to 9.5f-1½m winner Saint Helena (by Holy Roman Emperor): dam unraced half-sister to 1½m-1¾m winner (stayed 2¼m) Ta-Lim and winner up to 1¾m (stayed 2m) Tholjanah, both smart: 12/1, some encouragement when third in maiden at Pontefract (9 lengths behind Somethingthrilling) on debut: will be suited by further than 1m: should do better. *Robert Cowell*

MASTER ZEPHYR 3 b.c. Shirocco (GER) 129 – Missy Dancer (Shareef Dancer (USA) **110** 135) [2015 71p: 10.2f² 11.7m² 12g⁴ 12m* 11m⁴ 12.4g³ 12.4g* 12.4g* Nov 28] angular gelding: smart handicapper: won at Newbury in July and twice at Moonee Valley in November: left Roger Charlton after fifth start, A. de Watrigant after sixth: stays 12.4f: acts on tapeta and firm going: often races in rear/travels strongly. *Darren Weir, Australia*

MATCH MY FIRE (IRE) 2 ch.g. (Apr 14) Makfi 130 – High Lite 54 (Observatory **72** (USA) 131) [2015 7d 8.3d⁴ 8.3s⁴ Nov 4] fair form when fourth in maidens at Nottingham last 2 starts: will be suited by further than 1m. *Ralph Beckett*

MATEKA 4 ch.f. Nayef (USA) 129 – Marakabei 98 (Hernando (FR) 127) [2015 –: p12g **–** Apr 27] tailed off in 2 maidens, in hood sole start in 2015. *Roger Charlton*

MATERIALISTIC 2 b.f. (Mar 6) Oasis Dream 129 – Pongee 110 (Barathea (IRE) 127) **82 p** [2015 7g* Oct 9] rather leggy filly: half-sister to several winners, including smart winner up to 1¾m Pinzolo (2-y-o 1m winner, by Monsun) and useful 2-y-o 1m winner Poplin (by Medicean): dam 1¼m-1½m winner: 16/1, won 17-runner maiden at Newmarket on debut by ½ length from Colonial Classic, leading 1f out: will stay at least 1m: will improve. *Luca Cumani*

MATIDIA 2 ch.f. (Feb 4) Manduro (GER) 135 – Caesarea (GER) (Generous (IRE) 139) **65** [2015 7m 7.4d⁴ 7.6g⁵ 10.2g Sep 30] closely related to 1¼m-1¾m winner Carion (by Monsun) and half-sister to several winners, including smart 1¼m-1½m winner Corriolanus (by Zamindar) and useful 11f-14.6f winner Ashbrittle (by Rainbow Quest): dam 11f/1½m winner: fair maiden: should stay at least 1¼m. *Ralph Beckett*

MATILDA GLEAM 2 b.f. (Feb 2) Arabian Gleam 122 – Matilda Peace (Namaqualand **64** (USA)) [2015 p5g⁶ 6.1v p6g⁴ t5.1f Dec 11] sixth foal: half-sister to winner up to 9.5f Poppy Bond (2-y-o 5f winner, by Misu Bond): dam unraced half-sister to useful sprinter Blue Iris, herself grandam of smart sprinters Swiss Spirit and Swiss Diva: modest maiden: takes keen hold, may prove best at 5f. *Lisa Williamson*

MATILDA'S LAW 2 b.f. (Apr 3) Aussie Rules (USA) 123 – Oatey 68 (Master Willie **62** 129) [2015 6d⁴ p6g³ 7d Sep 14] 5,500Y: half-sister to several winners, including winner up to 6f Alternative (2-y-o 5f winner, by Dr Fong) and winner up to 1½m Spiritual Art (2-y-o 6f winner, by Invincible Spirit): dam 5f winner: modest maiden: best effort when fourth at Leicester on debut. *Chris Wall*

MATRAASH (USA) 9 b.h. Elusive Quality (USA) – Min Alhawa (USA) 108 (Riverman **66** (USA) 131) [2015 78: p10g² t9.5f² p10g³ t9.5f* t9.5g⁴ t9.5f⁶ t12.2m⁴ 10m³ 10m⁶ p10g **a73** p10g* 10.2m t9.5g p10m³ Dec 16] big, deep-girthed horse: fair handicapper: won at Wolverhampton in March and Lingfield in August: stays 1½m: acts on polytrack, tapeta, good to firm and good to soft going: often wears headgear: tried in tongue tie in 2015: often races towards rear. *Daniel Loughnane*

MATTMU 3 b.c. Indesatchel (IRE) 120 – Katie Boo (IRE) 92 (Namid 128) [2015 113: 6g² **118** 6d⁵ 6m² 6g* 5g³ 6d Sep 5] tall colt: smart performer: won Phoenix Sprint Stakes at the Curragh (by short head from Toscanini) in August: second in Duke of York Stakes at York (head behind Glass Office) and Chipchase Stakes at Newcastle (½ length behind Aeolus), and third in Nunthorpe Stakes at York (4 lengths behind Mecca's Angel): stays 6f: acts on good to firm and heavy going: wears cheekpieces nowadays: front runner/races prominently. *Tim Easterby*

MAULESDEN MAY (IRE) 2 b.f. (Feb 14) Dark Angel (IRE) 113 – Jemima's Art 61 **59** (Fantastic Light (USA) 134) [2015 6m 6g 7.2m⁵ 8d² 8d Oct 19] €43,000Y: small filly: third foal: sister to 2-y-o 1m winner (stays 1½m) Shalimah: dam, 1¼m winner, half-sister to smart winner up to 1¼m Battle of Hastings: modest maiden: stays 1m: acts on good to soft going. *Keith Dalgleish*

*Longines Hong Kong Mile, Sha Tin—the Ryan Moore-ridden Maurice (No.2)
produces a high-class performance to win his third Group 1 from the grey Giant Treasure;
favourite Able Friend (cheekpieces), who was found to be lame and had to pass the vet
before being declared fit to run, finishes only third*

MAUREB (IRE) 3 br.f. Excellent Art 125 – Almost Blue (USA) (Mr Greeley (USA) 122)   **77**
[2015 58p: 6s⁴ 7g* 8g⁵ 6.9g* 5.9g 7g⁵ 7m³ 7.6g 6d Sep 17] fair performer: won maiden at
Redcar in April and handicap at Carlisle in June: stays 7f: acts on good to firm going: often
in cheekpieces in 2015. *Tony Coyle*

MAURICE (JPN) 4 b.c. Screen Hero (JPN) 124 – Mejiro Frances (JPN) (Carnegie (IRE)   **126**
129) [2015 8f* 8.9g* 8f* 8f* 8f* 8g* Dec 13] high-class performer: named Horse of the
Year in Japan in 2015 after winning non-graded events at Nakayama in January and
March, Group 3 Lord Derby Challenge Trophy on same course in April, Yasuda Kinen at
Tokyo (by neck from Vincennes) in June, Mile Championship at Kyoto (by 1¼ lengths
from Fiero) in November and Hong Kong Mile at Sha Tin (beat Giant Treasure ¾ length,
leading inside final 1f) in December: stays 9f: acts on firm going: has worn tongue tie.
Noriyuki Hori, Japan

MAURITIUS 3 b.g. Zamindar (USA) 116 – Mascarene (USA) 82 (Empire Maker (USA)   **–**
129) [2015 p8g p10g⁶ p8g Dec 28] no form. *Lee Carter*

MAVEN 7 b.m. Doyen (IRE) 132 – Bollin Jeannie 74 (Royal Applause 124) [2015 97: 10s⁶   **92**
9.8v² 10.3g² 9.9m* 10.4m⁵ t9.5g Jul 8] fairly useful handicapper: won at Beverley in May:
best form at 1¼m: acts on polytrack and any turf going: front runner/races prominently.
Tim Easterby

MAVERICK WAVE (USA) 4 ch.c. Elusive Quality (USA) – Misty Ocean (USA)   **118**
(Stormy Atlantic (USA)) [2015 111: p10m* p10f⁵ p10g* 10.3s* 10d 10d p10m⁶ Nov 14]
sturdy colt: smart performer: won handicaps at Lingfield in January and Chelmsford (by 10
lengths from Barye) in March and Huxley Stakes at Chester (by ½ length from Cannock
Chase) in May: only form in 3 subsequent starts when respectable sixth to Let's Go in listed
race at Lingfield: stays 10.5f: acts on polytrack, tapeta, soft and good to firm going: usually
leads. *John Gosden*

MAVERIK 7 ch.g. Iceman 117 – Nouvelle Lune (Fantastic Light (USA) 134) [2015 8.1m   **84**
7m 8m⁴ 8.3m⁶ 8.1m Aug 22] lengthy gelding: fairly useful handicapper: stays 9f: acts on
polytrack, snow, good to firm and good to soft going: sometimes in cheekpieces in 2015:
often leads. *Ali Stronge*

MAWAANY (IRE) 2 gr.g. (Apr 10) Teofilo (IRE) 126 – Middle Persia 76 (Dalakhani   **–**
(IRE) 133) [2015 8g Sep 30] 16/1, very green when well held in maiden at Salisbury. *Sir
Michael Stoute*

MAWAQEET (USA) 6 b.g. Dynaformer (USA) – Lady Ilsley (USA) (Trempolino (USA)   **92**
135) [2015 16.4m 16.1g* 21.7f 21g t13.9g⁵ Dec 5] well-made gelding: fairly useful
handicapper: won at Newcastle (by head from King of The Picts) in May: stays 2m: acts on
good to firm and heavy going: often wears headgear. *Michael Appleby*

MAWASEEL 4 ch.g. Sea The Stars (IRE) 140 – Kareemah (IRE) (Peintre Celebre (USA)   **69**
137) [2015 74: 10m² 10s⁴ 9.9m Aug 12] strong, lengthy gelding: fair maiden: stays 1¼m:
acts on soft and good to firm going: tried in tongue tie prior to 2015: often races prominently.
B. W. Hills

MAWJOOD 3 b.c. Dubawi (IRE) 129 – Gile Na Greine (IRE) 117 (Galileo (IRE) 134)   **96**
[2015 7g 10m² 9.8m² 9.2d* 12d⁴ 7g 9.2g⁶ 9.9g Dec 30] well-made colt: first foal: dam,
2-y-o 7f winner, sister to smart 1m/9f winner (stayed 1½m) Scintillula: useful performer:

won maiden at Hamilton in September: left William Haggas after fifth start: best effort in minor event at Doha seventh outing: should stay beyond 1¼m: acts on good to firm and good to soft going: in hood/tongue tie final outing. *Majed Seifeddine, Qatar*

MAX BEDDOW (IRE) 2 b.c. (Feb 20) Tagula (IRE) 116 – Copper Harbour (IRE) **53** (Foxhound (USA) 103) [2015 6d p6g⁴ Dec 16] better effort when fourth in maiden at Kempton (8¼ lengths behind Soofiah). *Geoffrey Deacon*

MAX DYNAMITE (FR) 5 b.g. Great Journey (JPN) – Mascara (GER) (Monsun **124** (GER) 124) [2015 16.1m² 16.4d* 15.9g² Nov 3]

Trained in Ireland, owned by the wife of an American based in England, ridden by an Italian, bred in France, by a Japanese stallion out of a German mare, Max Dynamite would have had the most international make-up yet of any winner of Australia's greatest race, the Melbourne Cup. As it was, he finished second, something of an unlucky runner-up at that, though it could be said that his performance was a revelation, given that less than twelve months earlier he had made a successful debut for connections better known for their jumpers in a maiden hurdle at Thurles. With Frankie Dettori in the saddle, Max Dynamite was fourth choice in the betting for the Melbourne Cup at 12/1 and, with the Japanese-trained favourite Fame Game down the field, it was the 100/1-shot Prince of Penzance who got the better of Max Dynamite, the winner's rider Michelle Payne making history as the first female jockey to win the race. Both Prince of Penzance and Max Dynamite were in touch behind the leaders as the tightly-packed field swung for home but Dettori twice had to switch Max Dynamite to get a clear run in the straight, on the second occasion having to pull out from behind the eventual winner just as Prince of Penzance was hitting top gear over a furlong out. That left Max Dynamite with a couple of lengths to make up on Prince of Penzance and, while he finished strongly, he succeeded only in reducing the gap to half a length at the line. Dettori's manoeuvring came at a cost, however, as he was deemed guilty of careless riding that caused interference to several other horses and picked up a month's ban and a fine of A$20,000 (he had incurred a similar suspension for the same offence when seventh on Mamool for Godolphin in 2004). Jamie Spencer on fifth-placed Big Orange was also found guilty of careless riding but given a less severe suspension. Dettori also finished a half-length second in the Melbourne Cup in 1999, on 50/1-shot Central Park for Godolphin and Saeed bin Suroor, and at the time that was the best placing in the race for a horse trained in Britain, one that has been matched several times but not bettered by any of the many British challengers since.

Max Dynamite's trainer Willie Mullins is no stranger to winning big races much further afield than Cheltenham and Punchestown, or even Auteuil. In 2013 he became the first European trainer to win Japan's hugely valuable international jumps race, the Nakayama Grand Jump, with Blackstairmountain who was owned, like Max Dynamite, by Rich and Susannah Ricci. Present as a spectator when the Dermot Weld-trained Vintage Crop won the Melbourne Cup in an historic win for Ireland and Europe in 1993, Mullins had been less successful with his own first Melbourne Cup challenger Holy Orders in 2003. Holy Orders was a smart dual-purpose performer who won a total of twelve races for Mullins, including two Grade 1s over hurdles, and he beat Weld's Media Puzzle on the Flat before that horse won the 2002 Melbourne Cup. Holy Orders was none too reliable, though, and finished only seventeenth at Flemington after proving reluctant in his work in Australia. Max Dynamite's much better showing came two years after a good run from stable-companion Simenon, another smart dual-purpose horse who finished fourth to Fiorente.

Given his connections, Max Dynamite was doubtless acquired first and foremost with a jumping career in mind for him, but he had already shown himself to be at least useful on the Flat in France as a three-year-old and, rather than being bought privately as many of the stable's jumpers are, he was purchased at public auction. The Mullins team had to go to €200,000 to buy him out of John van Handenhove's stable at the 2013 Arc Sale. Max Dynamite's only win had come in a maiden at Fontainebleau early that season but he had not been discredited at long odds when taking on some of the best three-year-old colts subsequently. He

Weatherbys Hamilton Lonsdale Cup, York—Max Dynamite draws right away in an up-to-scratch renewal of this Group 2; Mizzou (striped sleeves) wins the race for second

finished eighth of nineteen in the Prix du Jockey Club, for example, and on his final start in France was beaten just over three lengths when seventh in the Prix Niel at Longchamp. Derby winner Ruler of The World lost out by a nose to the Japanese Derby winner Kizuna in that contest in which Max Dynamite was ridden by Dettori for the first time.

It was more than a year before Max Dynamite made his debut for his new connections at Thurles (a performance promising enough to earn him a Timeform 'large P') and the following spring, on just his fourth start over hurdles, he emerged with plenty of credit when fourth to stable-companion Wicklow Brave in the ultra-competitive County Hurdle at the Cheltenham Festival. Max Dynamite's next two starts over hurdles resulted in a fall, and then a poor run at pattern level at the Punchestown Festival, but his first Flat start for Mullins was considerably better. Stepping up to two miles on the Flat for the first time in the Northumberland Plate at Newcastle, Max Dynamite kept on to be beaten a length and quarter by Quest For More who went on to finish ninth in the Melbourne Cup. Before his next outing on the Flat, Max Dynamite took in another competitive handicap over hurdles, the Galway Hurdle, and ran another good race when staying on strongly to take second behind Quick Jack who had also finished a place in front of him at Cheltenham.

Max Dynamite's final run before Australia saw him reunited with Dettori in the Weatherbys Hamilton Lonsdale Cup at York in August. Simenon had been beaten a head in the same race before his Melbourne Cup bid two years earlier and was also in the field again. With the Gold Cup winner Trip To Paris, the Goodwood Cup winner Big Orange and the Sagaro Stakes winner Mizzou also among his rivals, Max Dynamite faced a number of stayers already proven at pattern level. Favourite though was the three-times course winner Clever Cookie, himself an ex-hurdler who had been successful in the Ormonde Stakes at Chester earlier in the year. Only sixth choice in the betting at 8/1 in a field of eight, Max Dynamite stepped up again on his Newcastle effort with a thoroughly dominant display, given that the race was modestly run. With little covering the whole field three furlongs out, Max Dynamite showed the best speed and stretched clear in the final furlong to beat Mizzou by four and a half lengths. Clever Cookie was touched off for third by the Godolphin filly Hidden Gold, while Trip To Paris and Big Orange finished a well-held fifth and seventh respectively. That Melbourne-bound pair finished much closer to Max Dynamite when fourth and fifth at Flemington.

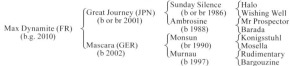

		Great Journey (JPN) (b or br 2001)	Sunday Silence (b or br 1986)	Halo
Max Dynamite (FR) (b.g. 2010)				Wishing Well
			Ambrosine (b 1988)	Mr Prospector
				Barada
		Mascara (GER) (b 2002)	Monsun (br 1990)	Konigsstuhl
				Mosella
			Murnau (b 1997)	Rudimentary
				Bargouzine

Oddly, the pedigree of the New Zealand-bred Melbourne Cup winner probably has more familiar names in it from a European point of view than Max Dynamite's. Prince of Penzance is by the Geoff Wragg-trained King George winner Pentire and is a grandson of Only Royale who won the Yorkshire Oaks twice for

Luca Cumani. As for Max Dynamite's sire, Great Journey, he was a smart performer in Japan where he contested all three legs of the triple crown. His best placing in those races came when eighth in the equivalent of the St Leger (won by Japan's future Melbourne Cup winner Delta Blues) over fifteen furlongs, but Great Journey did all his racing afterwards at much shorter trips, gaining his most important wins in Group 3 contests over a mile and over nine furlongs. From the same family as Green Desert, Great Journey stood his first season in France in 2008 at the Haras de Lonray where he replaced Divine Light, another son of Sunday Silence, who had been moved on to Turkey. Divine Light left behind Natagora in France, winner of the 2007 Cheveley Park Stakes and the following year's One Thousand Guineas, but there was little reason to regret Great Journey's export to Tunisia at the end of 2014 until Max Dynamite's exploits in the latest season.

Max Dynamite's dam Mascara won at seven furlongs and a mile at two in Germany, and again over a mile as a four-year-old, and has bred two other winners to date in France besides Max Dynamite. Kizzy Nizzy (by Anabaa Blue) won over thirteen furlongs, while three-year-old Somebody To Love (by Fuisse) was a winner over ten and a half furlongs in the latest season. The sales catalogues credit Mascara with a fourth winner but, despite earning 'black type' from a third place in a listed race at Maisons-Laffitte, Gold For Tina (by Lando) never actually won a race. Mascara didn't stay anything like so well as most by her sire Monsun who has been responsible for the two Melbourne Cup winners before the latest one, Fiorente and Protectionist. Max Dynamite's grandam Murnau also won three times in Germany, her successes including a listed race over nine furlongs. Among her winning siblings was the tough winner at up to a mile Muchea who was smart in his prime, finishing second in the Phoenix Stakes and Middle Park Stakes at two and third in the Prix Maurice de Gheest at four. Coincidentally, this is also the family of Frankie Dettori's other Melbourne Cup runner-up Central Park whose fourth dam Pelting appears as the fifth dam in Max Dynamite's pedigree. Pelting was a five-furlong winner, though another good stayer to descend from her was Braashee who dead-heated in the Prix Royal-Oak. With his owner having plenty of good horses over jumps, it would be no surprise to see Max Dynamite kept to the Flat from now on in a bid to go one better in the next Melbourne Cup. He is a smart hurdler but, at least as good on the Flat, clearly has the potential to go for much bigger prizes. Max Dynamite stays two miles well and acts on soft and good to firm ground. *W. P. Mullins, Ireland*

MAXIE T 4 b.g. Dalakhani (IRE) 133 – Ballet Ballon (USA) 81 (Rahy (USA) 115) [2015 14.1f May 23] compact gelding: fairly useful handicapper at best, well held only start in 2015: stays 1¾m: acts on polytrack and heavy going: useful hurdler. *Jonjo O'Neill* –

MAXWELL (IRE) 3 b.g. Big Bad Bob (IRE) 118 – Gladiole (GER) 71 (Platini (GER) 126) [2015 79: t8.6g* 9.9m* 12f 12f* 14g 13.7g⁶ Sep 12] unfurnished gelding: useful performer: won maiden at Wolverhampton in March and handicaps at Salisbury in May and Newmarket (by 2¾ lengths from Endless Credit) in July: stays 1½m: acts on tapeta and firm going: tried in cheekpieces. *Ralph Beckett* **97**

MAYASA (IRE) 2 ch.f. (Mar 23) Iffraaj 127 – Lanzana (IRE) (Kalanisi (IRE) 132) [2015 p7g p8f 18.6g³ f8g* Dec 18] €31,000F, €90,000Y: sturdy filly: fifth foal: half-sister to 3 winners, including 8.7f winner Gallope (by Lope de Vega) and 6f/7f winner Heyaaraat (by Lawman): dam unraced half-sister to smart winner up to 1½m Ebaziya: fairly useful performer: won maiden at Southwell in December: stays 8.5f: in blinkers last 2 starts. *James Tate* **80**

MAYBE DEFINITELY 3 ch.g. Bahamian Bounty 116 – Celestial Princess 84 (Observatory (USA) 131) [2015 8m 8d² 8.3d⁶ 8.3m² 7m* 6g⁴ 6d 8d Oct 11] 8,500F, €25,000Y: good-quartered gelding: sixth foal: half-brother to winner up to 1m (stays 1¼m) Bloodsweatandtears (2-y-o 7f winner, by Barathea) and 2m winner Story Writer (by Sakhee): dam 2-y-o 7f winner: fairly useful performer: won maiden at Newmarket in July: stays 8.5f: acts on good to firm and good to soft going: usually races close up. *Martyn Meade* **87**

MAYBELATER 3 b.f. Mount Nelson 125 – Muscovado (USA) 71 (Mr Greeley (USA) 122) [2015 p10g* 10.3m³ 11.5s 9.9m* 10m³ 10g* 9.9m 10m² 10g Oct 9] good-topped filly: third foal: half-sister to 1m winner (stays 1½m) Monsieur Rieussec (by Halling): dam twice-raced daughter of dual Yorkshire Oaks winner Only Royale: useful performer: won **95**

maiden at Lingfield in March and handicaps at Salisbury in June and Newbury in July: good second in a handicap at Newmarket (1½ lengths behind Shell Bay) in October: stays 1¼m: acts on polytrack and good to firm going. *Jonathan Portman*

MAYBEME 9 b.m. Lujain (USA) 119 – Malvadilla (IRE) 77 (Doyoun 124) [2015 82: 9.9g May 4] sparely-made mare: fairly useful at best, well held only start in 2015: acts on any turf going: wears headgear: sometimes slowly away, often races towards rear. *Neville Bycroft* –

MAYBE NOW BABY (IRE) 3 b.f. Kodiac 112 – Slow Jazz (USA) 106 (Chief's Crown (USA)) [2015 67: 8g 8.1m³ 8v² p11g 10.2s⁶ Oct 28] close-coupled filly: modest maiden: stays 1m: acts on good to firm and heavy going. *David Simcock* 57

MAYBERAIN (IRE) 2 b.f. (Jan 21) Acclamation 118 – Luckbealadytonight (IRE) 53 (Mr Greeley (USA) 122) [2015 6m Sep 15] €72,000F: first foal: dam, maiden (stayed 6f), half-sister to smart 2-y-o 6f/7f winner Maybe out of useful 2-y-o 5f winner Sumora: 20/1, ninth of 10 in maiden at Yarmouth: sent to France. *Rae Guest* –

MAY BE SOME TIME 7 ch.g. Iceman 117 – Let Alone 78 (Warning 136) [2015 11.6m³ 12.1m⁴ 12.1m* 12m² 14g³ 14.1g⁵ 13.1f⁴ Sep 12] compact gelding: fair handicapper: won at Chepstow in May: stays 1¾m: acts on any turf going: tried in blinkers prior to 2015: often wears tongue tie. *Stuart Kittow* 75

MAYBE TOMORROW 3 b.f. Zamindar (USA) 116 – Appointed One (USA) (Danzig (USA)) [2015 63: 10.3m 8d* 7v Oct 24] fairly useful performer: won maiden at Ffos Las in August: best effort at 1m: acts on good to soft going: often races in rear. *David Simcock* 83

MAYFAIR LADY 2 b.f. (Feb 19) Holy Roman Emperor (IRE) 125 – Lady Luachmhar (IRE) 94 (Galileo (IRE) 134) [2015 5m³ 5m² 5g* 6g* 6s⁴ 6g⁵ Oct 3] first foal: dam 9f-10.4f winner who stayed 13f: closely related to winner up to 13f: half-sister to smart 2-y-o 5f winner who stayed 13f: dam 9f-10.4f winner who stayed 13f: closely related to winner up to 13f: half-sister to top-class winner up to 7f Strong Suit: no form. *Richard Hannon* 105

MAYFAIR MAGIC 2 b.f. (Apr 14) Dick Turpin (IRE) 127 – B Berry Brandy (USA) (Event of The Year (USA) 125) [2015 7m 7m p7g 8.1m p6f Oct 10] fifth foal: half-sister to 3 winners, including 7f (including at 2 yrs) winner (stays 1¼m) Cricklewood Green (by Bob And John): dam lightly-raced half-sister to top-class winner up to 7f Strong Suit: no form. *Richard Hannon* –

MAYFIELD BOY 4 b.g. Authorized (IRE) 133 – Big Pink (IRE) (Bigstone (IRE) 126) [2015 82: 8m⁶ 9g Jul 13] fairly useful at best, no form in 2015: stays 1m: acts on good to firm and heavy going: in cheekpieces final start. *Antony Brittain* –

MAYFIELD GIRL (IRE) 5 br.m. One Cool Cat (USA) 123 – Rose of Mooncoin (IRE) 99 (Brief Truce (USA) 126) [2015 75: t6f⁴ 5m⁶ t6f t5.1f Nov 10] small, angular mare: modest handicapper: stays 6f: acts on tapeta, soft and good to firm going. *Antony Brittain* 58

MAY HAY 5 b.m. Dubai Destination (USA) 127 – Trounce (Barathea (IRE) 127) [2015 f16d* Jan 2] fair handicapper: won at Southwell (amateur) in January: stays 16.5f: acts on all-weather and good to soft going: often races prominently. *Anthony Carson* 71

MAYMYO (IRE) 4 b.g. Invincible Spirit (IRE) 121 – Lady Windermere (IRE) (Lake Coniston (IRE) 131) [2015 77: p7g⁶ 6m p6g³ 6.1m* t6g* 6g⁴ p6g⁴ p6d⁴ p6g Dec 16] good-quartered gelding: fair handicapper: won at Chepstow in June and Wolverhampton in August: stays 6f: acts on polytrack, tapeta and good to firm going: tried in tongue tie in 2015. *Sylvester Kirk* 79

MAY QUEEN 4 ch.f. Shamardal (USA) 129 – Mango Lady 80 (Dalakhani (IRE) 133) [2015 72: t9.5g* p10m* p12g⁴ p10g* p10g³ Aug 17] fairly useful handicapper: won at Wolverhampton in April and Lingfield in June and July: stays 1¼m: acts on polytrack and tapeta: front runner/races prominently: sent to Saudi Arabia. *Chris Wall* 88

MAY ROSE (IRE) 2 b.f. (Mar 24) Lawman (FR) 121 – Rose de France (IRE) (Diktat 126) [2015 p7g Dec 3] €520,000Y: fourth foal: closely related to 5f winner Tanghan and smart winner up to 7f Cable Bay (2-y-o 6f winner) (both by Invincible Spirit) and half-sister to winner up to 7f Sea Wolf (by Amadeus Wolf): dam lightly-raced half-sister to very smart 5f winner Ahtoug: 7/2, some encouragement when ninth in maiden at Kempton (8¾ lengths behind Kakashan) in December, not knocked about: will improve. *Marco Botti* – p

MAY'S BOY 7 gr.h. Proclamation (IRE) 130 – Sweet Portia (IRE) 61 (Pennekamp (USA) 130) [2015 12.5m May 22] compact horse: handicapper, no form in 2 starts since 2013: stays 1m: acts on polytrack and good to firm going: usually wears cheekpieces: fair hurdler. *James Moffatt* –

MAZAAHER 5 b.g. Elnadim (USA) 128 – Elutrah (Darshaan 133) [2015 76, a86: 7g⁵ 7g⁴ 7m² 8.3s Sep 21] lengthy gelding: fair handicapper: stays 8.5f: acts on tapeta and good to firm going: often races towards rear. *B. W. Hills* **78**

MAZIJ 7 b.m. Haafhd 129 – Salim Toto 107 (Mtoto 134) [2015 54, a61: t12.2f* p13g⁶ t12.2m t12.2m⁵ t12.2f 11.9g 12.1m May 30] lengthy mare: modest handicapper: won at Wolverhampton in January: stayed 13f: acted on all-weather and good to firm going: tried in blinkers: dead. *Peter Hiatt* **57**

MAZOVIAN (USA) 7 b.g. E Dubai (USA) 124 – Polish Style (USA) (Danzig (USA)) [2015 f16g⁶ f11s f16d⁴ f14g⁴ f14s f11g* Dec 29] stocky gelding: modest handicapper: won at Southwell in December: left Michael Chapman after fifth start: stays 11f: acts on polytrack, fibresand, good to firm and good to soft going: tried in cheekpieces: often races lazily. *Neil Mulholland* **58**

MAZZINI 2 ch.c. (Feb 26) Exceed And Excel (AUS) 126 – Firenze 109 (Efisio 120) [2015 p6g² Dec 3] fourth foal: half-brother to ungenuine 6f winner Isola Verde (by Oasis Dream) and 5f-6f winner Green Monkey (by Green Desert): dam, 6f winner, sister to very smart 5f/6f winner Frizzante: 6/1, shaped with promise and looked unlucky not to win when neck second of 7 to Tailwind in maiden at Kempton, caught further back than ideal before finishing strongly: sure to progress. *James Fanshawe* **84 p**

MBOTO GORGE 3 b.g. Sixties Icon 125 – Spring Bouquet (IRE) 60 (King's Best (USA) 132) [2015 p10g Jun 20] 4/1, well held in seller at Lingfield. *Mick Channon* **–**

MCCARTHY MOR (IRE) 4 b.g. Bushranger (IRE) 119 – Alexander Anapolis (IRE) 94 (Spectrum (IRE) 126) [2015 63: f6d⁴ f6g⁶ Dec 22] modest maiden: left Richard Fahey after first start: stays 7f: acts on good to firm and heavy going: sometimes wears visor. *Heather Dalton* **51**

MCCOOLS GOLD 2 b.c. (Feb 6) Yeats (IRE) 128 – Gold Reef (Double Trigger (IRE) 123) [2015 8.3s Oct 28] 66/1, last of 8 in maiden at Nottingham. *Robert Mills* **–**

MCCREERY 3 b.g. Big Bad Bob (IRE) 118 – Dolma (FR) 116 (Marchand de Sable (USA) 117) [2015 93p: 7f³ 8.1g* 8d² Sep 26] useful form: won handicap at Sandown (by 3 lengths from Alkawn) in September: 1½ lengths second to Dancetrack in similar event at Haydock final start, staying on: stays 1m: sent to Australia: open to further improvement. *Roger Charlton* **108 p**

MCDELTA 5 b.g. Delta Dancer – Mcnairobi 89 (Josr Algarhoud (IRE) 118) [2015 p7m⁵ 10g p7g 8.3m⁶ Aug 10] sturdy gelding: modest handicapper: stays 8.5f: acts on polytrack, soft and good to firm going. *Geoffrey Deacon* **55**

MC DIAMOND (IRE) 3 b.g. Windsor Knot (IRE) 118 – Vinesgrove (IRE) 54 (Danetime (IRE) 121) [2015 71: 6d 5.1s 6d 5.6m⁶ 6.1g 6g 5.7m⁴ 5f³ p6m² p6g⁴ Dec 2] fair maiden: stays 6f: acts on polytrack, firm and good to soft going: tried in headgear: front runner/races prominently. *Michael Mullineaux* **68**

MCELLIGOTT (IRE) 2 b.g. (Apr 14) Dark Angel (IRE) 113 – Nina Blini 90 (Bertolini (USA) 125) [2015 7m 6d Aug 17] tailed off in 2 maidens: has been gelded. *K. R. Burke* **–**

MCLOVIN RIVERDANCE 3 b.g. Lawman (FR) 121 – Electric Dream (Royal Applause 124) [2015 –: 5g³ t6g 8.5g p5g p6g Dec 11] modest maiden: left Ann Duffield after second start: should be suited by further than 5f. *T. G. McCourt, Ireland* **50**

MEADOW CROSS (IRE) 3 b.f. Cape Cross (IRE) 129 – Hovering (IRE) 100 (In The Wings 128) [2015 –: 8v 9s⁶ 11d 11.8g³ 12v p12g Dec 4] fair maiden: stays 1½m: acts on polytrack: often in headgear in 2015. *Denis Hogan, Ireland* **69**

MEADWAY 4 b.g. Captain Gerrard (IRE) 113 – Tibesti (Machiavellian (USA) 123) [2015 98: 5m² 5f 5.1m⁵ 5.4g 5m⁴ 5d f5g* p5m⁴ Dec 27] sturdy gelding: useful handicapper: won at Southwell (by 2 lengths from Mappin Time) in December: stays 5.5f: acts on polytrack, fibresand, good to firm and good to soft going: usually in headgear nowadays. *Bryan Smart* **103**

MEANDMYSHADOW 7 ch.m. Tobougg (IRE) 125 – Queen Jean 73 (Pivotal 124) [2015 78§: 6g 6m² 6s 6g 7m 6g 6g² 6m 5.9m³ 6g⁶ 5.9s* t6f* t6f 6s Oct 27] plain, leggy mare: fairly useful handicapper: won at Carlisle in September and Wolverhampton in October: stays 6f: acts on tapeta and any turf going: tried in headgear: often races lazily: unreliable. *Alan Brown* **84 §**

MECADO (IRE) 3 ch.c. Compton Place 125 – Corryvreckan (IRE) 70 (Night Shift (USA)) [2015 74: p7m² p6f² Apr 30] fair performer: acts on polytrack and good to firm going: sent to Sweden, where won at 1m on dirt at Taby in June. *Richard Hannon* **79**

MECCA'S ANGEL (IRE) 4 gr.f. Dark Angel (IRE) 113 – Folga 104 (Atraf 116) **129**
[2015 121: 5g* 5m² 5g* Aug 21]

It was certainly a breakthrough year for County Durham-based trainer Michael Dods. Mecca's Angel's success in the Nunthorpe Stakes at the York Ebor meeting gave Dods his first Group 1 winner, twenty-five years after first taking out a training licence, and the £175,801 she won for connections that day also played a big part in the yard passing its previous best prize money total, amassing over £575,000 in first-three prize money. Mecca's Angel herself only made it to the track three times but her performance in the Nunthorpe was the best over five furlongs in Europe all season. At a time when it is widely perceived that jumps racing in the North is struggling—a subject dealt with in *Chasers & Hurdlers 2014/15*—2015 was another successful year on the Flat for northern-based trainers. The Yorkshire-based pair of Richard Fahey and Mark Johnston both finished high up in the trainers' championship, with each sending out over two hundred winners in the calendar year, and it was also a particularly good campaign for Yorkshire-based David O'Meara, who continued his ascent with another century of winners (his third in a row). There was quality to go with the quantity too. As well as Mecca's Angel's success in the Nunthorpe, the Johnston and O'Meara yards also landed domestic Group 1s with Lumiere (Cheveley Park) and Amazing Maria (Falmouth), the latter also winning the Prix Rothschild in France among other notable wins abroad for the likes of the Karl Burke-trained Odeliz, successful in Group 1 races in France and Italy, and O'Meara's Mondialiste, who followed victory in the Woodbine Mile with a second in the Breeders' Cup Mile.

There were three Group 1 winners in the field for the Nunthorpe, the previous year's winner Sole Power, the King's Stand winner Goldream and the O'Meara-trained 2014 Prix de l'Abbaye winner Move In Time. However, the market—and most of the pre-race discussion—was dominated by the two-year-old filly Acapulco, who had been tremendously impressive on her only previous start in Britain when slamming the Dods-trained Easton Angel in the Queen Mary Stakes at Royal Ascot. In receipt of 24 lb weight-for-age allowance from the eventual winner, Acapulco was sent off at 13/8, with the King George Stakes winner Muthmir next at 13/2, and Mecca's Angel (15/2) and Sole Power (8/1) the only others at single-figure odds in a field of nineteen. On the face of it, the official weight-for-age scale is overly-generous at the time of the Nunthorpe—the allowance for juveniles over five furlongs in the second half of August is 16 lb on the Timeform scale—though there can be no such thing as a perfect weight-for-age scale, given it can take no account of the fact that individual horses mature at different rates. It is particularly difficult to be dogmatic about weight-for-age so far as two-year-olds are concerned, since the allowance comes into play so infrequently. Lyric Fantasy in 1992 and Kingsgate Native in 2007 are the only two juveniles to have landed the Nunthorpe in the last half century and Acapulco was the eighth juvenile to have tried and failed since

Coolmore Nunthorpe Stakes, York—Mecca's Angel wins a cracking edition from the trailblazing American-trained two-year-old Acapulco and the three-year-old Mattmu (right); the King's Stand winner Goldream (stars on sleeves) finishes fifth

Kingsgate Native, though she certainly mounted a very strong challenge. As at Royal Ascot, Acapulco showed plenty of speed and made the running towards the far side (after the start had been delayed by Take Cover who burst through his stall and had to be withdrawn). Approaching the final furlong, it was apparent that Mecca's Angel, who had been prominent throughout down the centre of the course, was the only one likely to challenge Acapulco. Acapulco maintained her lead over the rest of the field but couldn't hold off Mecca's Angel, who got to the front in the final fifty yards. The winning margin was two lengths, with the same distance back to the third Mattmu, another who raced close up. With a wind behind the runners on the day, it wasn't easy for those more patiently ridden, and Sole Power did best of them to finish fourth. Mecca's Angel achieved a Timeform rating of 129, a figure matched only by Oasis Dream (2003) among Nunthorpe winners since the outstanding runaway success of Dayjur in 1990 although, as a filly, Mecca's Angel received a 3-lb sex allowance. Confirmation of the quality of her performance is provided by the clock. Mecca's Angel recorded a timefigure of 1.16 fast (equivalent to a timerating of 129), which was the second highest recorded in 2015, only just behind Muhaarar's in the British Champions Sprint at Ascot.

Mecca's Angel was useful as a juvenile, winning a maiden and a nursery and finishing in the frame on three occasions in listed company, but it was as a three-year-old that she really started to make a name for herself. She won four of her five outings in 2014, starting off with facile wins against lesser opposition in a handicap at Thirsk and a minor event at Hamilton in the spring before landing the Scarbrough Stakes at Doncaster's St Leger meeting and the World Trophy at Newbury after returning from a mid-season break. Mecca's Angel's win at Newbury was only her trainer's second at pattern level, following Barney McGrew's success in the 2010 Chipchase Stakes. Mecca's Angel returned in the latest season with another Group 3 success in the Prix de Saint-Georges at Longchamp in May, which she won from French-trained Robert Le Diable by a comfortable two lengths, with Hot Streak and Maarek completing the frame. The King's Stand at Royal Ascot was the obvious next step for Mecca's Angel but she was declared a non-runner on the day because of concerns over the firm ground. It was a similar story at Sandown three weeks later when Mecca's Angel was withdrawn from the Coral Charge. Conditions were officially good when Mecca's Angel next appeared, in the Sapphire Stakes on Irish Oaks day at the Curragh later in July. An analysis of the race times suggested the ground was riding firmer than the official description and Timeform called it good to firm. Odds-on Mecca's Angel suffered a reverse, beaten a neck by Stepper Point after having every chance but never travelling with her usual zest. Drying conditions were also behind her withdrawal from the Prix de l'Abbaye after she had been among the declared runners, and when it was decided not to supplement her (at a cost of £40,000) for the British Champions Sprint, her campaign ended without her running again after the Nunthorpe.

Mecca's Angel's dam Folga was a useful sprinter, winning five handicaps (including one over five furlongs at the Ebor meeting) and also being placed in listed company in a career spanning four seasons. Yeomanstown Stud purchased Folga for 33,000 guineas at the end of her racing days and she turned out to be an inspired purchase. She has produced two foals of racing age, both by the stud's headline sire Dark Angel. The first was Mecca's Angel—clearly a bargain purchase herself having been picked up for just 16,000 guineas by Michael Dods as a yearling—and the second was her year-younger half-brother Markaz, who was purchased as a yearling for 200,000 guineas by Shadwell and has developed into a smart performer over seven furlongs, winning the Criterion Stakes in the latest season. Folga's latest yearling through the ring, another filly by Dark Angel, was sold for 825,000 guineas to Fawzi Abdulla Nass at Newmarket in October and has been sent into training with George Peckham in Newmarket (Folga also has a filly foal by Dark Angel). Dark Angel was retired after winning four races at two, including the Mill Reef and the Middle Park Stakes (he too won at the Ebor meeting, in a valuable sales race) with his commercial success taking off in recent seasons, such that his fee has been more than doubled to €60,000 for 2016 (having started out at €10,000). Mecca's Angel is the best of her sire's progeny judged strictly on form, just 1 lb ahead of Lethal Force, the top-rated sprinter in Britain and Ireland in 2013 when he completed the Diamond Jubilee-July Cup double. Bred for speed (Folga's sire Atraf won the Cork And Orrery and her dam Desert Dawn was a smart five-furlong performer although down the field in a Nunthorpe), it's no surprise that Mecca's Angel has excelled at five furlongs. Folga won six races in all, equally spread between five and six furlongs, but it remains to be seen if Mecca's Angel will prove so effective over six, an avenue connections seem keen to explore in 2016 (she has failed to see her race out on both attempts beyond a bare mile, the latest of them when meeting her only defeat in the 2014 season). Mecca's Angel will clearly be the one to beat in the big five-furlong events, though ground conditions are always likely to dictate her running plans, with connections unlikely to risk her on anything firmer than good (her defeat in the Sapphire Stakes in the latest season was her only outing under such conditions). For the record, Mecca's Angel has won on fibresand and soft ground, though both her wins in 2015 came on good and she clearly doesn't need a soft surface. Mecca's Angel's owner David Metcalfe has stated that 2016 will be her final season ('I'll sell her then, I've no interest in breeding from her so somebody else can do that'). Mecca's Angel usually races prominently, and can make the running if required. *Michael Dods*

MECCA'S MISSUS (IRE) 2 b.f. (Feb 19) Lilbourne Lad (IRE) 111 – Silk Dress (IRE) **71** 91 (Gulch (USA)) [2015 5d² 6g² 6m* 6f 6.1m⁴ 5g⁶ 6g 7s⁴ Oct 16] £11,000Y: fourth foal: closely related to 7f-1¼m winner Top Frock (by Acclamation) and half-sister to 9f/1¼m winner Sureness (by Hurricane Run) and 2-y-o 1m winner (stays 11f) Billy Blue (by High Chaparral): dam maiden: fair performer: won maiden at Thirsk in July: stays 6f: acts on good to firm going: in headgear last 3 starts. *Michael Dods*

MEDAL OF VALOUR (JPN) 7 b.g. Medaglia d'Oro (USA) 129 – Tres Tres Joli (USA) **56** (Gone West (USA)) [2015 p12f t9.5g³ t9.5m³ t8.6f Dec 21] lengthy gelding: modest performer: left Mark Gillard after third start: stays 1¼m: acts on polytrack, tapeta and firm going: often wears headgear: usually wears tongue tie: usually races prominently. *Roy Brotherton*

MEDAM 6 b.m. Medicean 128 – Mamounia (IRE) 101 (Green Desert (USA) 127) [2015 – 64, a73: t6f p6g p8g⁵ 7m Jun 27] leggy, smallish mare: fair at best, no form in 2015: tried in headgear/tongue tie prior to 2015. *Shaun Harris*

MEDBURN CUTLER 5 ch.g. Zafeen (FR) 123 – Tiegs (IRE) 55 (Desert Prince (IRE) **75** 130) [2015 65: 16.2m² 16.2s* 16.2m* 16g 12.1s³ 18g 16d⁴ 16s³ p16f⁵ Nov 23] plain gelding: fair handicapper: won at Chepstow in May and June: stays 2¼m: acts on polytrack, good to firm and heavy going: usually wears headgear: often races prominently. *Paul Henderson*

MEDBURN DREAM 2 b.c. (Mar 17) Showcasing 117 – Tiegs (IRE) 55 (Desert Prince **59** (IRE) 130) [2015 6g⁶ 6.5s⁶ p6g⁶ Nov 11] modest maiden: best effort when sixth at Kempton (5½ lengths behind Consulting) on final start. *Paul Henderson*

MEDDLESOME 2 b.g. (Mar 5) Medicean 128 – Meddle (Diktat 126) [2015 t7.1g p8f **62 p** 7.5g Sep 16] 20,000Y: half-brother to several winners, including 2-y-o 6f winner (stays 8.5f) Anastazia (by Kyllachy) and winner up to 1m Darnathean (2-y-o 6f winner, by Librettist): dam, of little account, closely related to smart winner up to 7f Pan Jammer: modest maiden: best effort when seventh at Beverley (4¼ lengths behind Billy Roberts) final start: remains with potential. *Sir Mark Prescott Bt*

MEDDLING 5 ch.m. Halling (USA) 133 – Piffling (Pivotal 124) [2015 74: p8g⁶ p8f p8g⁴ **65** t7.1g² t7.1g⁵ 8m t7.1g p8f⁶ Nov 19] fair handicapper: stays 1¼m: acts on all-weather and good to firm going: tried in hood prior to 2015: usually races close up. *Julia Feilden*

MEDIA BOOK (IRE) 2 b.f. (Feb 22) Shamardal (USA) 129 – Catchline (USA) – (Bertolini (USA) 125) [2015 6s Oct 15] second foal: half-sister to useful 1m winner Emirates Skycargo (by Iffraaj): dam unraced half-sister to smart 1m-1¼m winner Ancient

World: 4/1, badly needed experience when down the field in maiden at Brighton: sold 8,000 gns, sent to Qatar. *Mark Johnston*

MEDIA DAY (IRE) 3 b.f. Footstepsinthesand 120 – Mathuna (IRE) (Tagula (IRE) 116) **76 p**
[2015 6.9m² Aug 11] €21,000Y, 42,000 2-y-o: third foal: half-sister to useful winner up to 1m Caledonian Spring (by Amadeus Wolf) and 7f winner Eusepio (by One Cool Cat): dam, 2-y-o 7.5f winner, half-sister to useful 1m/9f winner Wilside: 6/1, promise when neck second of 6 to Jillanar in maiden at Carlisle, responding well and just failing: open to improvement. *Richard Fahey*

MEDIA HYPE 8 b.h. Tiger Hill (IRE) 127 – Hyperspectra 91 (Rainbow Quest (USA) **86**
134) [2015 93: t13.9g² t16.5m⁶ f12g* Mar 5] good-topped horse: fairly useful performer: won seller at Southwell in March: stays 1¾m: acts on all-weather and good to firm going: tried in headgear. *K. R. Burke*

MEDIATE 4 ch.g. New Approach (IRE) 132 – Miss Prim (Case Law 113) [2015 66p: 9.8d⁶ **76**
11.7f³ 11.5s² 10d² p10g Dec 20] fair maiden: left Mark Johnston after fourth start: stays 11.5f: acts on firm and soft going. *Richard Rowe*

MEDIATION 3 b.f. Azamour (IRE) 130 – Macleya (GER) 115 (Winged Love (IRE) 121) **85 p**
[2015 10s² 10s³ p10f* Nov 7] third foal: dam, 1¼m-15f (including French Group 2 12.5f) winner, half-sister to smart 1½m winner Montclair: fairly useful performer: won maiden at Chelmsford (by 4 lengths from Fair's Fair) in November: will be suited by 1½m+: remains open to improvement. *Roger Varian*

MEDIA WORLD (IRE) 2 ch.g. (Feb 22) Medicean 128 – Panoptic 89 (Dubawi (IRE) **71**
129) [2015 8.5g³ 7.5d⁶ Sep 22] better effort in maidens at Beverley when 2¼ lengths third of 6 to Anabel on debut. *Rae Guest*

MEDICEAN BLISS (IRE) 3 b.f. Medicean 128 – So Blissful (IRE) 77 (Cape Cross **81 §**
(IRE) 129) [2015 70: t6f* p7g⁴ 16m⁴ p7g* 7d⁴ p8g 8g⁶ p7g p8f Oct 22] fairly useful performer: won maiden at Wolverhampton in March and handicap at Lingfield in May: stays 7f: acts on polytrack and tapeta: tried in cheekpieces in 2015: all but refused to race last 2 starts, best treated with caution. *Jeremy Gask*

MEDICEAN MAN 9 ch.g. Medicean 128 – Kalindi 102 (Efisio 120) [2015 118: 5g⁵ 5g⁵ **119**
6g 5g 5f² 5g 5m⁶ 5m p6m⁶ p5f* Nov 23] good-topped gelding: smart performer: won handicap at Chelmsford in November by length from Brother Tiger, staying on well to lead last 50 yds: in frame in 3 of last 4 runnings of King's Stand Stakes at Royal Ascot, showing himself at least as good as ever when short-head second to Goldream on latest occasion in June: effective at 5f to 7f: acts on polytrack, tapeta, firm and good to soft going: wears headgear/tongue tie. *Jeremy Gask*

MEDICEAN MELODY 3 br.f. Royal Applause 124 – Meredith (Medicean 128) [2015 **57**
–: p8f⁴ p10g³ p10g 7s* 8m 7v³ 7s⁵ Oct 6] modest handicapper: won at Brighton in June: stays easy 1¼m: acts on polytrack and soft going: in hood last 4 starts. *David Simcock*

MEDICIMAN 2 b.c. (Apr 7) Medicean 128 – Quintrell 92 (Royal Applause 124) [2015 **78**
7m³ 7m⁵ 8g³ Oct 21] compact colt: fair form all 3 starts in maidens: seems to stay 1m. *Henry Candy*

MEDICINE HAT 4 b.g. Multiplex 114 – Blushing Heart 62 (Observatory (USA) 131) **71**
[2015 10g 18d* Oct 5] fair handicapper: won at Pontefract in October: stays 2¼m: acts on heavy going: fairly useful hurdler. *George Moore*

MEDIEVAL BISHOP (IRE) 6 b.g. Bachelor Duke (USA) 122 – On The Backfoot **69**
(IRE) 69 (Bob Back (USA) 124) [2015 73, a56: t13.9g⁴ t16.5f⁵ t13.9g² t13.9f⁴ t13.9g² t12.2g* t13.9g³ 11.8m² t13.9g⁶ t12.2g t13.9m² Dec 30] fair handicapper: won at Wolverhampton (amateur) in May: stays 14.5f: acts on tapeta, good to firm and good to soft going: often wears headgear: usually races close up. *Tony Forbes*

MEDINA SIDONIA (IRE) 3 b.g. Montjeu (IRE) 137 – Valdara (Darshaan 133) [2015 **84**
12m⁵ 12m³ 12g* 16.2m³ 14d⁶ 13.8g⁴ Sep 19] fairly useful ex-French-trained handicapper: won at Thirsk in July: stays 2m: acts on good to firm and good to soft going: usually races towards rear, often races lazily. *Tim Easterby*

MEDRANO 3 b.c. Archipenko (USA) 127 – Trick Or Treat 108 (Lomitas 129) [2015 99: **113**
10.4s² 9.9s³ 12.3s³ 11g³ 11.1s* 12g⁴ 12d⁵ 14.6d⁶ Sep 12] good-topped colt: smart performer: won listed race at Hamilton (by 6 lengths from Prince Gagarin, somewhat flattered on testing ground) in July: struggled in better company after, again raced freely (wore hood) when well-held sixth of 7 to Simple Verse in St Leger at Doncaster final outing: should stay at least 1½m: acts on soft going. *David Brown*

MEEBO (IRE) 4 b.f. Captain Rio 122 – Abbeyleix Lady (IRE) (Montjeu (IRE) 137) [2015 **58**
62, a71: f6s⁶ p6g⁶ f5s* f5g⁵ 5.1m⁴ 6.1m 6g 5.1d f6g Nov 24] modest handicapper: won at **a64**
Southwell in March: stays 6f: acts on fibresand, tapeta, soft and good to firm going: usually
wears headgear: sometimes wears tongue tie: front runner/races prominently. *J. R. Jenkins*

MEETINGS MAN (IRE) 8 gr.g. Footstepsinthesand 120 – Missella (IRE) 63 (Danehill **77**
(USA) 126) [2015 11.6m⁶ 10m 13g⁴ p15.8g 13.1m* 13.1f p16fᵇᵘ Oct 8] leggy gelding: fair
handicapper: won at Bath in August: stays 2m: acts on polytrack, firm and soft going:
usually wears cheekpieces: front runner/races prominently. *Ali Stronge*

MEGALALA (IRE) 14 b.g. Petardia 113 – Avionne 59 (Derrylin 115) [2015 71: 9.9d⁵ **62**
11.5d⁴ 9.9s⁴ 10m* 9.9m³ 10g³ 10.1g⁴ p10g 11.9d³ 11.9s* 9.9s⁴ Oct 15] lengthy gelding:
modest handicapper: won at Lingfield in June and Brighton (apprentice) in October: stays
1½m: acts on polytrack and any turf going: tried in headgear: front runner/races
prominently. *John Bridger*

MEGALEKA 5 b.m. Misu Bond (IRE) 114 – Peyto Princess 85 (Bold Arrangement 127) **80**
[2015 97: p5g² t5.1f p5m⁴ p5g⁶ 5.1d⁴ 5f t5.1d p10g⁴ 5.5m 5d 5g Sep 18] small mare: fairly **a90**
useful handicapper: lost her form after third start: best at 5f: acts on polytrack, tapeta, good
to firm and heavy going: tried in hood. *Alan Bailey*

MEGAMUNCH (IRE) 5 b.g. Camacho 118 – Liscoa (IRE) 81 (Foxhound (USA) 103) **74**
[2015 66: f8d² f8d³ p8g⁶ f8g* t9.5f f11g⁴ f11g* f11g³ p10m⁶ p10g⁴ p12g t12.2g p10g p8f
f8g f12g Nov 24] leggy gelding: fair performer: won claimer at Southwell in March
(subsequently left Kristin Stubbs) and handicap there in April: stays 11f: acts on fibresand,
good to firm and heavy going: often wears headgear: often races towards rear. *Conor Dore*

MEGARA 3 ch.g. Medicean 128 – Alicante 80 (Pivotal 124) [2015 t9.5f t9.5f⁶ t8.6f⁵ p10g⁵ **69 p**
Dec 9] second foal: dam, 11f/11.5f winner, half-sister to 2m winner (stays 2¼m) Moscato
and winner up to 1½m Hernandoshideaway, both useful: fair maiden: should prove suited
by further than 1¼m: in cheekpieces last 2 starts: remains with potential. *Sir Mark
Prescott Bt*

MEGHWAR (IRE) 2 gr.g. (Apr 1) Zebedee 113 – Champion Tipster (Pursuit of Love 124) **63**
[2015 5m⁴ 5m 5m³ May 25] good-topped gelding: modest form in maidens. *Roger Varian*

MEHDI (IRE) 6 b.g. Holy Roman Emperor (IRE) 125 – College Fund Girl (IRE) 76 **95**
(Kahyasi 130) [2015 102: 7g⁶ 6g³ 6m⁵ 7m² 7m 6.1g 7d 5.5m 7g 6d Sep 26] big, well-made
gelding: useful handicapper: placed at York in May (2 lengths third to Algar Lad) and June
(length second to Regal Dan): stays 1m: acts on polytrack, tapeta, good to firm and good to
soft going: tried in blinkers prior to 2015: wears tongue tie. *Richard Fahey*

MEHRONISSA 3 ch.f. Iffraaj 127 – Miss University (USA) (Beau Genius (CAN)) [2015 **98**
83p: p7f 8m 7m⁵ 6g* 6m² 6g* Sep 19] useful handicapper: won at Windsor (by 2 lengths
from Heartsong) in July and Newmarket (by ½ length from Stake Acclaim) in September:
winner at 7f, likely to prove best at shorter: acts on good to firm going: often in hood: often
races freely. *Ed Vaughan*

MEISTER (IRE) 2 b.c. (Apr 11) Mastercraftsman (IRE) 129 – Dash Back (USA) 91 **57**
(Sahm (USA) 112) [2015 6m 7.2s 8d⁴ 8g Sep 23] modest maiden: stays 1m: tried in
cheekpieces. *Michael Dods*

MELADI (IRE) 2 b.g. (Mar 19) Oasis Dream 129 – Bridiette (IRE) 112 (Sadler's Wells **83**
(USA) 132) [2015 6m⁴ 6m* 7m 7g⁵ 7m Oct 3] 250,000Y: attractive gelding: sixth foal:
half-brother to 5f-8.3f winner Point North (by Danehill Dancer) and 2-y-o 1m winner
(stayed 13f) Thomasgainsborough (by Dansili), both useful: dam, 1¼m-1½m winner, half-
sister to top-class 1¼m-1½m winner Pilsudski: fairly useful performer: won maiden at
Doncaster (by ¾ length from Ribchester) in July: best effort at 6f: acts on good to firm
going: in blinkers final start: sometimes slowly away. *William Haggas*

MELBOURNE SHUFFLE (USA) 3 b.f. Street Cry (IRE) 130 – Liffey Dancer (IRE) **75**
(Sadler's Wells (USA) 132) [2015 77p: p8g³ p8m² p8f⁴ 8g p8.9g 9.9g5³ 10d* 10.5s a10.7g
Dec 9] fair performer: left John Gosden after fourth start: won maiden at Durtal in
November: stays 1¼m: acts on polytrack and good to soft going. *Francis-Henri Graffard,
France*

MELFIT (IRE) 2 b.c. (Feb 1) Sea The Stars (IRE) 140 – Alshahbaa (IRE) 91 (Alhaarth **86 p**
(IRE) 126) [2015 f8g* Nov 26] €42,000F, 240,000Y: first foal: dam, 2-y-o 6f winner, half-
sister to useful 9f/1½m winner Daymooma: 11/2, knew job when winning 10-runner
maiden at Southwell by 1¼ lengths from Mystic Blaze, making all: open to improvement.
Richard Hannon

MELGATE MELODY 2 b.g. (Feb 13) Royal Applause 124 – Maeander (FR) 101 – p
(Nashwan (USA) 135) [2015 5.9m 5.9g⁵ 6m Aug 29] 9,000F, £18,000Y: seventh foal: half-
brother to winner abroad by Sulamani: dam, 1½m winner, half-sister to useful 6f-1½m
winner Massey and 1m-9f winner Tessa Reef: no form, but hasn't been knocked about and
may well do better. *Michael Easterby*

MELODICA 3 b.f. Dansili 127 – Maganda (IRE) 84 (Sadler's Wells (USA) 132) [2015 69: **79**
8m 10.2f² t9.5g³ p12g² p11g 11.6g² 12d⁶ Oct 30] tall, rather unfurnished filly: fair maiden:
stays 1½m: acts on polytrack, tapeta and firm going: often races freely. *Roger Charlton*

MELODIOUS 3 b.f. Cape Cross (IRE) 129 – Gower Song 114 (Singspiel (IRE) 133) [2015 **108**
72p: 8.3s* 10.2d* 10.4g⁶ 12m² 12m⁴ 12d⁵ 14.1s² 14.6m² 12g⁴ 12v² Oct 24] sturdy filly:
useful performer: won maiden and handicap (by ¾ length from Graceland) at Nottingham
in May: much better form later in season, notably when neck second to Gretchen in Park
Hill Stakes at Doncaster: respectable 1½ lengths second to Koora in St Simon Stakes at
Newbury final start (hampered 2f out): stays 14.5f: acts on soft and good to firm going.
David Elsworth

MELROSE ABBEY (IRE) 4 ch.f. Selkirk (USA) 129 – Villa Carlotta 110 (Rainbow –
Quest (USA) 134) [2015 100: 9g 12m Aug 15] tall, rather unfurnished filly: useful at best,
no form in 2015: stays 1½m: acts on heavy going: often races in rear. *Ralph Beckett*

MELTING ICE (IRE) 3 gr.f. Verglas (IRE) 118 – Burn The Breeze (IRE) 115 (Beat –
Hollow 126) [2015 8m⁶ 10.1d⁶ Sep 27] second foal: dam, 1¼m/10.5f winner who stayed
12.5f, half-sister to smart 1m winner Lethals Lady: well held both starts in maidens.
Ed Vaughan

MELVIN THE GRATE (IRE) 5 b.g. Danehill Dancer (IRE) 117 – Hawala (IRE) 97 **103**
(Warning 136) [2015 93+, a104: p8f³ p8g⁴ t8.6m p8f 8.1m⁶ 8d⁴ 8g² 8.3s⁴ p8f p8g³ Dec 28]
lengthy gelding: useful handicapper: several creditable efforts in 2015: stays 8.5f: acts on
polytrack, tapeta, good to firm and good to soft going: tried in hood: usually slowly away,
often races towards rear. *Andrew Balding*

MEMORIA 4 b.f. Teofilo (IRE) 126 – Midnight Shift (IRE) 73 (Night Shift (USA)) [2015 **85**
84: 8.3m⁵ 10g⁷ 9d³ 10.1g 10.2v⁵ Oct 7] fairly useful handicapper: won at Windsor (by 2
lengths from Ttainted Love) in July: stays 1¼m: acts on tapeta and good to soft going: front
runner/races prominently. *Rae Guest*

MEMORIAL DAY (IRE) 4 b.g. Cape Cross (IRE) 129 – Reunite (IRE) 111 (Kingmambo **103**
(USA) 125) [2015 78p: 8m² 8m* 10g* 12d* 12s² 10.4s⁴ Oct 10] useful performer: won
maiden at Haydock and handicap at Newmarket in July, and handicap at York (dead-heated
with Libran) in August: creditable efforts in handicaps last 2 starts: stays 1½m: acts on soft
and good to firm going: usually races prominently. *Saeed bin Suroor*

MEMORIES GALORE (IRE) 3 b.g. Invincible Spirit (IRE) 121 – Persian Memories **93**
(IRE) 78 (Indian Ridge 123) [2015 –: 7g t6g⁴ t6g* p6f⁵ 6g² 6g Oct 20] rather leggy
gelding: fairly useful handicapper: won at Wolverhampton in July and Lingfield in August:
good second at Salisbury in September: stays 6f: acts on polytrack and tapeta: front runner/
races prominently. *Harry Dunlop*

MEMORY CLOTH 8 b.g. Cape Cross (IRE) 129 – Gossamer 118 (Sadler's Wells (USA) **82**
132) [2015 89: 10.1g⁴ 10.4g⁵ 9.8d³ 10.1m³ 10d Oct 30] big, lengthy, rather leggy gelding:
fairly useful handicapper: stays 11.5f: acts on good to firm and heavy going: tried in
blinkers prior to 2015. *Brian Ellison*

MEMPHIS MAGIC (GER) 5 b.g. Tertullian (USA) 115 – Maltage (USA) (Affirmed **58**
(USA)) [2015 10.2m⁵ 13.1d² 15.8s Oct 6] modest maiden: stays 13f: acts on good to firm
going: often wears tongue tie. *Brendan Powell*

MEMYSELFIE (IRE) 2 b.f. (Apr 14) Kodiac 112 – Cool Tarifa (IRE) 80 (One Cool Cat **46 §**
(USA) 123) [2015 p5g⁵ 5m 5.1g p5g⁶ 5d p5f³ p5m Nov 17] £35,000Y: neat filly: third foal:
sister to useful/ungenuine winner up to 6f Smoothtalkinrascal (2-y-o 5f winner): dam 2-y-o
5f winner: poor maiden: raced only at 5f: acts on polytrack: usually slowly away:
temperamental. *Derek Shaw*

MENAI (IRE) 2 b.c. (Feb 7) Dark Angel (IRE) 113 – Glisten 95 (Oasis Dream 129) [2015 **73**
6g² 6m² Jun 8] well-made colt: fair form when runner-up in maidens at Haydock and
Windsor. *Charles Hills*

MENDACIOUS HARPY (IRE) 4 b.f. Dark Angel (IRE) 113 – Idesia (IRE) 78 (Green **63**
Desert (USA) 127) [2015 77: 7.1s⁴ 7m⁴ 7d² 6s 7s Oct 13] compact filly: modest
handicapper: stays 8.5f: acts on any turf going: sometimes wears headgear: usually in
tongue tie in 2015: usually slowly away. *George Baker*

MENDELITA 4 ch.f. Archipenko (USA) 127 – Dame de Noche 102 (Lion Cavern (USA) 117) [2015 72: 12.4g 10.3d May 11] fair at best, no form in 2015: stays 1½m: acts on soft and good to firm going. *Richard Fahey* —

MENELIK (IRE) 6 b.g. Oasis Dream 129 – Chica Roca (USA) 49 (Woodman (USA) 126) [2015 74: p11m p10f⁶ p10f p8f p8f³ t8.6f³ p8f t8.6g⁶ p7g⁵ p7g Dec 30] attractive gelding: modest handicapper: stays 1½m: acts on polytrack and tapeta: usually wears headgear: tried in tongue tie prior to 2015: often starts slowly. *Des Donovan* **64**

MENGLI KHAN (IRE) 2 b.c. (Feb 18) Lope de Vega (IRE) 125 – Danielli (IRE) 79 (Danehill (USA) 126) [2015 8g³ 8.3v* 8d Oct 24] 150,000Y: sixth foal: brother to useful winner up to 1m Very Special (2-y-o 6f winner) and half-brother to useful winner up to 1m Janicellaine (2-y-o 7f winner, by Beat Hollow) and smart 2-y-o 7f/1m (including Fillies' Mile and Breeders' Cup Juvenile Fillies Turf) winner Chriselliam (by Iffraaj): dam maiden who stayed 13f: useful form: won maiden at Nottingham (by 3¼ lengths from Across The Stars) in October: 8/1, off the bridle by halfway when last of 7 to Marcel in Racing Post Trophy at Doncaster final start: stays 8.5f: should still improve. *Hugo Palmer* **97 p**

MEN UNITED (FR) 2 b.c. (Apr 30) Acclamation 118 – Moore's Melody (IRE) (Marju (IRE) 127) [2015 5g 5m p5f² 5g⁴ p5m* t5.1g⁵ p5m³ Dec 27] fair performer: won nursery at Lingfield in November: raced only at 5f: acts on polytrack: front runner/races prominently. *James Given* **72**

MERCERS ROW 8 b.g. Bahamian Bounty 116 – Invincible 76 (Slip Anchor 136) [2015 77: 7g³ 7g 7s* 6.9m² 7.9g* 8m⁶ 8.5s 7m² 7d⁴ 6m* 5.9s⁶ 5s* 5.1d Nov 4] leggy gelding: fairly useful handicapper: won at Thirsk in May, Carlisle in June, Redcar in September and Pontefract in October: left Karen Tutty after seventh start: effective from 5f to 1m: acts on soft and good to firm going: tried in cheekpieces prior to 2015. *Michael Herrington* **88**

MERCHANT OF DUBAI 10 b.g. Dubai Destination (USA) 127 – Chameleon 79 (Green Desert (USA) 127) [2015 80: 12m³ 14m 12m³ 10g⁵ 10.3m² 10m³ 12.2g⁴ Sep 12] good-bodied gelding: fair handicapper: best at around 1¼m-1¾m: acts on polytrack, fibresand, good to firm and heavy going: tried in headgear prior to 2015: usually leads. *Jim Goldie* **76**

MERCHANT OF MEDICI 8 b.g. Medicean 128 – Regal Rose 110 (Danehill (USA) 126) [2015 72: t12.2f⁴ f12d 10.4g* 11.9m* 11.9f* 12g² 12d⁴ 10m 12g⁴ 16.2d Oct 16] good-topped gelding: fair handicapper: won twice at Haydock in May (latter amateur event), and also successful in apprentice race there in June: stays 1½m: acts on polytrack, firm and soft going: has worn headgear. *Micky Hammond* **73**

MERCIFILLY (FR) 2 b.f. (Apr 19) Whipper (USA) 126 – Coco (USA) 105 (Storm Bird (CAN) 134) [2015 6g t7.1f³ Nov 20] €28,000Y: half-sister to several winners, including useful 2-y-o 6f winner Maramba (by Hussonet) and 9f-13f winner Coco In Love (by Hurricane Run): dam 8.2f winner: better effort when third in maiden at Wolverhampton (1¼ lengths behind Rebel Lightning) in November: open to further improvement. *Ed Walker* **63 p**

MERCURY 3 ch.g. Showcasing 117 – Miss Rimex (IRE) 84 (Ezzoud (IRE) 126) [2015 58: 7g 8s 8g 8.3m 9.9m* 9.2s 9.9m⁵ 9.9g t9.5f* t9.5f² p10f t9.5m⁴ Dec 18] modest handicapper: won at Beverley in July and Wolverhampton in October: stays 1¼m: acts on tapeta, soft and good to firm going: usually in headgear in 2015: usually leads: none too reliable. *Kevin Ryan* **61**

MERCURY MAGIC 4 b.g. Oratorio (IRE) 128 – Lochridge 110 (Indian Ridge 123) [2015 66, a59: p8f⁶ t8.6f⁵ t8.6f 9.9m⁵ p10m 8.3m 12.1m⁴ p12g Aug 5] poor maiden: stays 1½m: acts on polytrack, tapeta, good to firm and heavy going: often wears headgear. *David Menuisier* **48**

MERCY ME 3 b.f. Mawatheeq (USA) 126 – Fantastic Santanyi (Fantastic Light (USA) 134) [2015 –: p12g* 11.8m* 11.5s 12g 16f 12g⁵ 10g p12g 11.7g Oct 18] tall filly: fair performer: won maiden at Lingfield in March and handicap at Leicester in April: stays 1½m: acts on polytrack and good to firm going: often races towards rear. *John Ryan* **75**

MERDON CASTLE (IRE) 3 b.g. Acclamation 118 – Siren's Gift 104 (Cadeaux Genereux 131) [2015 97: p6g² p5g* p5m² p5f³ 6f 5m 6m 6d 6m Aug 15] lengthy gelding: useful performer: won minor event at Chelmsford (by neck from Apache Storm) in February: placed in similar contests at Kempton and Lingfield (twice): stays 6f: acts on polytrack and good to firm going: sometimes slowly away. *David Elsworth* **88 a98**

MERE ANARCHY (IRE) 4 b.g. Yeats (IRE) 128 – Maracana (IRE) (Glacial Storm (USA) 127) [2015 t12.2f Oct 31] bumper winner: left Kim Bailey £125,000/off 6 months, 10/1, well beaten in maiden at Wolverhampton. *Robert Stephens* —

MERHOOB (IRE) 3 b.g. Cape Cross (IRE) 129 – Lady Slippers (IRE) 65 (Royal Academy (USA) 130) [2015 75p: p8f⁶ 7d⁶ 7s² 6s Oct 16] fair maiden: best effort at 7f: acts on soft going. *Marco Botti* **78**

MERITOCRACY (IRE) 4 br.g. Kheleyf (USA) 116 – Chiosina (IRE) (Danehill Dancer (IRE) 117) [2015 92: p6g² p6g⁶ 6m³ p5g⁴ p6g⁵ 6.1m⁵ Jun 25] workmanlike gelding: fairly useful handicapper: stays 6.5f: acts on polytrack and good to firm going: sometimes in headgear: tried in tongue tie. *Paul Cole* **82**

MERMAID (IRE) 2 b.f. (Apr 9) Kodiac 112 – Ma Vie En Rose (IRE) 63 (Red Ransom (USA)) [2015 5m³ 6.5m 5m³ Jun 27] £8,000Y: third foal: dam, maiden (seemed to stay 7f), closely related to useful 6f/7f winner Saint Etienne: fair form when third in maidens at Leicester and Lingfield: sold 3,000 gns, sent to Sweden. *Richard Hannon* **68**

MEROULA (FR) 2 b.f. (Apr 16) Vision d'Etat (FR) 127 – Laureldean Desert 60 (Green Desert (USA) 127) [2015 7g⁴ 7s Oct 12] €28,000Y: unfurnished filly: first foal: dam lightly-raced half-sister to very smart/ungenuine 7f/1m winner Salselon: better effort in maidens at Salisbury when fourth on debut (well positioned). *Harry Dunlop* **59 ?**

MERRIMENT 2 ch.f. (Mar 8) Makfi 130 – Trianon 80 (Nayef (USA) 129) [2015 8v Oct 24] fourth foal: half-sister to useful 2-y-o 6f winner Touchline (by Exceed And Excel): dam, 2-y-o 1m winner who stayed 1½m, half-sister to smart winner up to 13f Phantom Gold and useful 1m-1¼m winner Fictitious: 50/1, well held in maiden at Newbury. *Michael Bell* **–**

MERRITT ISLAND 3 b.f. Exceed And Excel (AUS) 126 – Moon Crystal 77 (Fasliyev (USA) 120) [2015 58p: 8m* t8.6g² 8.1m² 8m⁵ 8.5g⁴ 8.3g* 10.2f* 9.4g² p10f² p10f³ p9.4g⁶ Dec 2] strong filly: useful performer: won minor event at Bath in May and handicaps at Nottingham and Bath in August: good efforts when second in minor event at Chelmsford (2 lengths behind Fire Fighting) and third in handicap at Chelmsford ninth/tenth starts: stays 1¼m: acts on polytrack, tapeta and firm going: front runner/races prominently. *Sir Mark Prescott Bt* **103**

MERRY DANCER (IRE) 3 ch.f. Duke of Marmalade (IRE) 132 – Starlit Sky (Galileo (IRE) 134) [2015 63p: 10m 10m p11g 11.6g* p12g⁴ Dec 2] workmanlike filly: modest handicapper: won at Windsor (amateur) in October: stays 1½m: acts on polytrack: often races prominently. *Paul Webber* **64**

MERRY ME (IRE) 4 b.f. Invincible Spirit (IRE) 121 – Thought Is Free 88 (Cadeaux Genereux 131) [2015 103: 8m 8.5g² 8d² 8g² 8d Oct 17] small, sturdy filly: useful performer: second in handicap at Epsom (neck behind Gratzie), listed race at Pontefract (length behind Nakuti) and Oettingen-Rennen at Baden-Baden (5 lengths behind Vadamos): stays 10.5f: acts on polytrack, good to firm and heavy going. *Andrew Balding* **103**

MERTESACKER (GER) 6 b.g. Lord of England (GER) 119 – Monalind (GER) (Park Romeo 121) [2015 t9.5m⁵ 8.3g⁵ May 18] fair performer at best, winning twice at Dusseldorf in 2013, in minor event and a handicap: left V. Rohrig, well beaten both starts on Flat in Britain: best effort at 8.5f. *Robin Dickin* **47**

MESHARDAL (GER) 5 b.g. Shamardal (USA) 129 – Melody Fair (IRE) (Montjeu (IRE) 137) [2015 84: f6s² 6d* 6g* 6m* 6m² 6g⁵ 6m* 6m⁶ 6s 6m 6m² 6g 6d 6m Sep 10] well-made gelding: fairly useful handicapper: won at Catterick and Thirsk in April, Doncaster in May and Catterick (by ½ length from Native Falls) in June: best form at 6f: acts on fibresand, soft and good to firm going: often races in rear. *Ruth Carr* **94**

MESSILA STAR 5 ch.h. Pivotal 124 – Jamboretta (IRE) 102 (Danehill (USA) 126) [2015 89: p8m Jan 24] smallish, angular horse: fair handicapper: stays 1m: acts on polytrack: wears visor: tried in tongue tie prior to 2015: usually races prominently: sold 16,000 gns, sent to Saudi Arabia. *Jeremy Noseda* **71**

MESTI BOLEH 4 b.g. Cape Cross (IRE) 129 – Miss Meltemi (IRE) 100 (Miswaki Tern (USA) 120) [2015 t8.6g 10.2m⁶ Jun 25] better effort in maidens when sixth at Nottingham. *Michael Scudamore* **56**

METROPOL (GER) 4 b.c. Holy Roman Emperor (IRE) 125 – Monetary (GER) 107 (Winged Love (IRE) 121) [2015 p9.4g³ p9.4g² 8s 8.9s⁴ p9.4g* 8d p9.4g* 9.9g³ p9.4g p10m³ p10g⁵ Dec 19] €32,000Y, €42,000 2-y-o: fourth foal: half-brother to 11.5f/1½m winner Malibran (by Dubawi): dam winner up to 12.5f (2-y-o 9.5f winner): smart performer: won handicaps at Chantilly in May and Deauville (by ¾ length from Lexceed) in August: best effort when third in listed race at Lingfield (¾ length behind Let's Go) on penultimate start: respectable 1¼ lengths fifth to Don't Be in similar race on same course final outing: left A. & G. Botti after fourth start: stays 1¼m: acts on polytrack. *Mme Pia Brandt, France* **111**

METTE 2 b.f. (Mar 22) Virtual 122 – Regal Gallery (IRE) 76 (Royal Academy (USA) 130) – [2015 5m May 21] rather unfurnished filly: sixth foal: sister to 2-y-o 1m winner Gilded Lace and half-sister to 1¼m winner Suntrap (by Desert Sun): dam 1¼m-1½m winner: 100/1, badly needed experience when seventh of 8 in maiden at Sandown. *Rod Millman*

MEXICAN JIM 3 ch.g. Dubai Destination (USA) 127 – Artic Bliss (Fraam 114) [2015 10m Jul 20] 100/1, down the field in maiden at Windsor, slowly away. *Tony Carroll*

MEXICAN MICK 6 ch.g. Atraf 116 – Artic Bliss (Fraam 114) [2015 t9.5f t12.2m f12g⁵ **55** t16.5m⁴ 11.8m⁵ 12.1m⁴ p12g⁶ 12.1s² 14.1s⁵ Sep 15] modest maiden: stays 1½m: acts on tapeta, soft and good to firm going: in blinkers last 3 starts. *Peter Hiatt*

MEY BLOSSOM 10 ch.m. Captain Rio 122 – Petra Nova 51 (First Trump 118) [2015 65: – t6g Jan 9] fair handicapper: stays 6f: acts on polytrack and any turf going: sometimes wears headgear. *Richard Whitaker*

MEYDAN STYLE (USA) 9 b.g. Essence of Dubai (USA) 118 – Polish Ruby (USA) **33** (Polish Pro (USA)) [2015 : t7.1m t8.6f Feb 23] poor handicapper: best effort at 7f: acts on polytrack: tried in headgear: often races prominently. *Brian Baugh*

MEZAJY (IRE) 3 b.g. Makfi 130 – Maidin Maith (IRE) 91 (Montjeu (IRE) 137) [2015 **89** 76p: 8.3s³ 8.5g⁴ 8g³ 10.1m⁵ 10d⁶ 10.1g² 12.1g³ p11g Oct 7] rather leggy gelding: fairly useful performer: won maiden at Epsom in April: good second in handicap at Yarmouth in August: stays 1½m: best form on good going. *Ed Walker*

MEZEL 4 b.g. Tamayuz 126 – Mumayeza 80 (Indian Ridge 123) [2015 92: 7m 8d² Oct 11] **90** fairly useful handicapper: improved when ½-length second to Ifwecan at Goodwood: stays 1m: acts on polytrack, good to firm and good to soft going. *B. W. Hills*

MEZZOTINT (IRE) 6 b.g. Diamond Green (FR) 121 – Aquatint (Dansili 127) [2015 93: **90** 7m 7m⁶ 7f 7m 7m⁴ 7g 7m 7s⁴ p7g 7d p8f* t7.1f⁴ p8f³ p7f p8f* Dec 21] robust gelding: fairly useful handicapper: won at Chelmsford in October and December (by ½ length from Exceeding Power): left Stuart Williams after thirteenth start: stays 1m: acts on polytrack, tapeta, soft and good to firm going: tried in headgear/tongue tie in 2015: often races towards rear, usually travels strongly. *Lee Carter*

MFIFTYTHREEDOTCOM (IRE) 4 ch.g. Tamayuz 126 – Pearl Trader (IRE) 67 **73** (Dubai Destination (USA) 127) [2015 78: 8.5m 8d 8.9g 8m² 8.3s 8.3g³ 9.8d* 10.3s 10.2v **a50** 10d⁴ p10f p10g⁵ t9.5m Dec 26] fair performer: won seller at Ripon in August: stays 1¼m: acts on firm and good to soft going: often wears headgear: front runner/races prominently. *Richard Fahey*

MHEELAH (IRE) 2 b.f. (Apr 27) Kodiac 112 – Red Remanso (IRE) (Redback 116) – p [2015 6d 6g Oct 20] €48,000Y: second foal: dam twice-raced sister to winner up to 1m Redolent and 2-y-o 1m winner Qatar Dance, both useful: better effort in maidens when tenth of 14 at Windsor latter start, meeting some trouble over 1f out and not knocked about: remains open to improvement. *Richard Hannon*

MIA ECCELLENZA 3 b.c. Exceed And Excel (AUS) 126 – Mia Diletta 90 (Selkirk **90** (USA) 129) [2015 8s² 8.4m² 7.5g⁴ 8s⁵ t9.5g Sep 29] sturdy colt: fairly useful performer: second in minor event at Milan on reappearance, best effort in 2015: left Stefano Botti after third start: stays 1m: acts on soft and good to firm going: sent to Bahrain. *Marco Botti*

MIAMI GATOR (IRE) 8 ch.g. Titus Livius (FR) 115 – Lovere (St Jovite (USA) 135) **51** [2015 65: f8s³ p8o⁵ p8o⁶ p8m³ Feb 18] lengthy gelding: modest handicapper: stays 8.5f: acts on polytrack, soft and good to firm going: wears visor: usually leads: sold £1,800, sent to Germany. *K. R. Burke*

MIA SAN TRIPLE 4 b.f. Invincible Spirit (IRE) 121 – Atlantide (USA) (Southern Halo **74** (USA)) [2015 93: p5g p6m 6m⁴ 6m⁶ Jul 17] fair handicapper: stays 7f: acts on good to firm going: front runner/races prominently. *Jeremy Noseda*

MIA'S BOY 11 b.g. Pivotal 124 – Bint Zamayem (IRE) 95 (Rainbow Quest (USA) 134) **80** [2015 95: t8.6g³ t9.5f Jan 30] compact gelding: fairly useful handicapper: stays 1¼m: acts on polytrack, tapeta, soft and good to firm going: sometimes slowly away, usually races nearer last than first. *Chris Dwyer*

MIA TESORO (IRE) 2 b.f. (Apr 14) Danehill Dancer (IRE) 117 – Souter's Sister (IRE) **63** 103 (Desert Style (IRE) 121) [2015 6m⁶ t6g⁶ 6d p6f p7g Oct 27] second foal: dam 2-y-o 6f-7f winner: modest maiden: stays 6f: acts on good to firm and good to soft going: sometimes slowly away. *Jamie Osborne*

MICA MIKA 7 ch.g. Needwood Blade 117 – Happy Talk (IRE) 74 (Hamas (IRE) **95** 125) [2015 88: f11s⁴ p10g⁶ t12.2g 10.3d* 10.1g* 10.3s* 10.3g³ 10m² 10.3g⁵ 10d² 10s 10.1d² 10.2d 10v Oct 24] useful handicapper: won at Doncaster in March, Newcastle in

April and Chester in May: good second at Epsom (2¼ lengths behind Quest For Wonder) on twelfth start: stays 16.5f: acts on polytrack, good to firm and heavy going: tried in headgear: tough. *Richard Fahey*

MICHAELA 3 ch.f. Sholokhov (IRE) 121 – La Capilla (Machiavellian (USA) 123) [2015 **54** 60: 7m⁶ p7g t12.2m Nov 21] modest maiden: bred to be suited by 1m+. *Paul Webber*

MICHAEL DIVINE 3 b.g. Calcutta 112 – Divine Miss-P 90 (Safawan 118) [2015 5m 5g 7s Jul 29] no form. *Ollie Pears*

MICHAEL'S MISSILE (IRE) 4 ch.f. Majestic Missile (IRE) 118 – Glenviews Big Bird **67** (USA) (Danehill (USA) 126) [2015 57: p6g 6g⁵ 7d³ 8m 6g* 6m 6d⁴ 6d Aug 30] fair handicapper: won at Ayr in July: stays 6f: acts on good to soft going: usually in headgear in 2015. *A. P. Keatley, Ireland*

MICHAEL'S MOUNT 2 ch.g. (Apr 14) Mount Nelson 125 – Dumnoni 97 (Titus Livius **74** (FR) 115) [2015 7.1g⁵ 8.3g Sep 7] sturdy gelding: fair form in maidens at Sandown and Windsor (still looked in need of experience): should stay 1m. *Ed Dunlop*

MICK DUGGAN 5 ch.g. Pivotal 124 – Poppy Carew (Danehill (USA) 126) **83** [2015 90: p15.8m³ Dec 16] angular gelding: fairly useful handicapper: stays easy 2m: acts on polytrack: tried in cheekpieces prior to 2015. *Michael Blake*

MICK DUNDEE (IRE) 5 b.g. Aussie Rules (USA) 123 – Lucky Oakwood (USA) 75 – (Elmaamul (USA) 125) [2015 –: t7.1g t7.1f p8m Apr 8] fair at best, no form in 2015: often wears headgear: usually wears tongue tie: front runner/races prominently, usually finds little. *Richard Ford*

MICKEY HALLER (IRE) 3 b.g. Approve (IRE) 112 – Miss Assertive 88 (Zafonic **77** (USA) 130) [2015 67p: 7g³ 7.1d² Aug 5] fair form: off 3 months and gelded, improved when 1½ lengths second to Flying Hammer in maiden at Chepstow final start. *Brian Meehan*

MICKEY (IRE) 2 b.c. (Apr 15) Zoffany (IRE) 121 – Enchantment 108 (Compton Place **87** 125) [2015 6g⁴ 6g⁶ Aug 20] £18,000Y: fourth foal: half-brother to 6f winner Heroic Endeavour (by Ishiguru) and 5f winner Dream Sika (by Elnadim): dam 5f winner (including at 2 yrs): 40/1, much improved from debut when 2½ lengths sixth of 18 to Tasleet in valuable sales race at York. *Tom Dascombe*

MICRAS 4 b.f. Medicean 128 – Purple Heather (USA) 93 (Rahy (USA) 115) [2015 93: – 11.6m⁵ 10d Oct 21] quite attractive filly: fairly useful at best, no form in 2015: left Tim Vaughan after first start: stays 1¼m: acts on good to firm and heavy going: sometimes wears visor: often races prominently. *P. A. Fahy, Ireland*

MIDAS HAZE 3 ch.f. Pivotal 124 – Eva's Request (IRE) 115 (Soviet Star (USA) 128) **70** [2015 –p: 8.3g⁵ 7.5m⁶ 10.2d⁶ p10f p10m⁴ Oct 28] sturdy filly: fair maiden: stays 1¼m: acts on polytrack and good to firm going. *Michael Bell*

MIDDLE EAST PEARL 3 b.f. Equiano (FR) 127 – Zia (GER) (Grand Lodge (USA) **78** 125) [2015 69: p5m³ p5g* p5g³ p6g t5.1g² Jun 22] fair handicapper: won at Chelmsford in April: best form at 5f: acts on polytrack and tapeta: often races prominently. *James Tate*

MIDDLE ENGLAND (IRE) 3 b.f. Dubawi (IRE) 129 – Mannington (AUS) 118 **77** (Danehill (USA) 126) [2015 73p: p7f* t7.1g⁴ 7mᵖᵘ May 26] fair form: won maiden at Lingfield in January: raced only at 7f: dead. *Charlie Appleby*

MIDDLEMAN 2 b.g. (Feb 10) Oasis Dream 129 – Sense of Pride 88 (Sadler's Wells **54 p** (USA) 132) [2015 6.1g⁵ Jul 30] well-made gelding: first foal: dam, 10.3f winner, sister to very smart 1¼m-13.4f winner Day Flight out of smart winner up to 1½m (2-y-o 1m winner) Bonash: bolted when withdrawn on intended debut in June: 5/2, considerate introduction on actual debut when 5½ lengths fifth of 10 to Dream Mover in maiden at Nottingham, taking strong hold: gelded after: capable of better *John Gosden*

MIDHMAAR 2 b.c. (May 3) Iffraaj 127 – Merayaat (IRE) 80 (Darshaan 133) [2015 6m **92** 7g⁴ p7g³ 8m* 8d⁵ 8g² Sep 26] well-made colt: seventh foal: half-brother to smart winner up to 13.3f Hawaafez (2-y-o 1m winner, by Nayef) and 1¾m-15f winner Nateeja (by Shamardal): dam 1¾m winner who should have stayed 2m: fairly useful performer: won nursery at Salisbury in August: good second to Move Up in similar event at Ripon final start (twice met trouble): stays 1m: acts on polytrack and good to firm going. *B. W. Hills*

MIDLANDER (IRE) 3 b.c. Shamardal (USA) 129 – Mille (Dubai Millennium 140) **100** [2015 84: 6s 6g 7d 6g 5.3d* 5f* 5.1g* 5d* 5m 6m 5.4g 5d 5s* Sep 21] sturdy colt: useful handicapper: completed 4-timer in June/July, winning at Brighton, Sandown, Chester and Ascot: back to form when also won at Leicester on final start by ¾ length from Apache Storm: has won at 6f, best form at 5f: acts on polytrack, firm and soft going: sent to UAE. *Mark Johnston*

MIDLIGHT 3 b.g. Elusive City (USA) 117 – My Heart's Deelite (USA) (Afternoon **75** Deelites (USA) 122) [2015 f8s² t8.6m² 10g² p10g⁴ 8m 10g f8g⁴ f8m Dec 8] fair maiden: left David Simcock after fourth start: stays 1¼m: acts on tapeta: tried in blinkers: sometimes slowly away. *Richard Whitaker*

MIDNIGHT CROSSING (IRE) 2 b.f. (Apr 5) Dark Angel (IRE) 113 – Line Ahead **88** (IRE) (Sadler's Wells (USA) 132) [2015 7m 7g² 8m⁶ Sep 11] €65,000Y: half-sister to 3 winners, including smart 1¼m-1¾m winner Excellent Result (by Shamardal) and 2-y-o 7f winner (stayed 11f) Goldenveil (by Iffraaj): dam ran once: fairly useful maiden: similar form when second in minor event at the Curragh and 6 lengths sixth of 8 to Turret Rocks in May Hill Stakes at Doncaster. *Edward Lynam, Ireland*

MIDNIGHT DANCE (IRE) 3 b.f. Danehill Dancer (IRE) 117 – Dark Missile 114 **89** (Night Shift (USA)) [2015 60: 6s* p6g p6f* p7d⁴ Nov 30] fairly useful performer: won maiden at Pontefract in April and handicap at Chelmsford in October: stays 6f: acts on polytrack and soft going. *Ralph Beckett*

MIDNIGHT DESTINY (IRE) 3 ro.f. Dark Angel (IRE) 113 – Cappella (IRE) 75 **55** (College Chapel 122) [2015 57: p5g² 5d 5g⁵ 5.1g t5.1g² 5g² 5g f5g t5.1m⁶ Dec 18] workmanlike filly: modest maiden: best form at 5f: acts on polytrack, tapeta, best turf form on good going: often wears visor. *Derek Shaw*

MIDNIGHT GAME 8 b.g. Montjeu (IRE) 137 – Midnight Angel (GER) 108 (Acatenango **–** (GER) 127) [2015 16g 12g May 30] useful at best, well held both starts in 2015: best effort at 13f: acts on soft and good to firm going: fairly useful hurdler/chaser: sold £5,500 in November, sent to Germany. *Brian Ellison*

MIDNIGHT MACCHIATO (IRE) 2 b.c. (Apr 12) Dark Angel (IRE) 113 – Lathaat 72 **78** (Dubai Destination (USA) 127) [2015 7m⁴ 7m* 8g Sep 26] fair form: didn't need to run up to debut form to land odds in maiden at Thirsk in August by length from Dark Confidant: well held final outing: stays 7f. *David Brown*

MIDNIGHT MALIBU (IRE) 2 b.f. (Mar 5) Poet's Voice 126 – Midnight Martini 100 **84** (Night Shift (USA)) [2015 5v⁵ 5m⁴ 6g⁶ 5.1m* 5.2m 5m* 5g³ Aug 30] €18,000Y: close-coupled filly: first foal: dam 2-y-o 5f/6f winner: fairly useful performer: won maiden at Nottingham in July and nursery at Haydock: best form at 5f: acts on good to firm going: usually races close up. *Tim Easterby*

MIDNIGHT MOJITO 3 b.f. Azamour (IRE) 130 – Shaken And Stirred (Cadeaux **65** Genereux 131) [2015 8g⁵ 6g² 7.5m 6m⁴ Jun 27] £23,000Y: fifth foal: closely related to useful 2-y-o 5f/6f winner Midnight Martini (by Night Shift): dam unraced: fair maiden: best efforts at 6f. *Tim Easterby*

MIDNIGHT RIDER (IRE) 7 b.g. Red Ransom (USA) – Foreplay (IRE) 86 (Lujain **92 §** (USA) 119) [2015 88§: 7d 5m* 5.1m⁴ 6g 6m³ 5m⁶ 6f 6.1m* 6m² 6.1g* 6m⁶ 6v⁴ 6.1s⁵ 7.1s³ 6g⁵ 7s Oct 9] lengthy gelding: fairly useful handicapper: won at Windsor in April and Chepstow in July and August: stays 7f: acts on good to firm and heavy going: tried in cheekpieces prior to 2015: one to treat with caution. *Rod Millman*

MIDNIGHT ROBBERY 2 br.g. (Mar 5) Dick Turpin (IRE) 127 – Zietunzeen (IRE) 99 **61** (Zieten (USA) 118) [2015 6g 5.9m⁵ 5.9s 6s 5g⁴ t5.1f Oct 31] modest maiden: stays 6f: acts on good to firm going. *Bryan Smart*

MIDNIGHT WARRIOR 5 b.g. Teofilo (IRE) 126 – Mauri Moon 104 (Green Desert **64** (USA) 127) [2015 65: 12g⁶ 14.1m* 12m⁶ 12.1f³ 14.1m 12.8m³ 16d 12.1g 14.1m⁴ 12g 13.8v Oct 17] modest handicapper: won at Redcar in May: stays 1¾m: acts on firm going: often wears hood. *Ron Barr*

MIDNIGHT WHISTLER (USA) 3 b.g. Henrythenavigator (USA) 131 – Ball Gown **74** (USA) (Silver Hawk (USA) 123) [2015 p12g⁴ p10f Sep 24] better effort when fourth in maiden at Lingfield in September, best work finish. *Martyn Meade*

MIDNITE MOTIVATION 6 b.m. Motivator 131 – Tamise (USA) 113 (Time For A **–** Change (USA)) [2015 10.2m May 21] no form: tried in hood. *Derek Shaw*

MIDNITEMUDCRABS (IRE) 2 ch.f. (Apr 14) Arcano (IRE) 122 – Ma Nikitia (IRE) **67** (Camacho 118) [2015 p6g⁶ 7g p7f⁵ Nov 12] €40,000Y: rather unfurnished filly: second foal: half-sister to 2-y-o 5f winner Zebelini (by Zebedee): dam, unraced, closely related to useful winner up to 1m Dimenticata: fair maiden: likely to prove suited by return to 6f. *Marco Botti*

MIDNITE RIDE (IRE) 3 b.f. Footstepsinthesand 120 – Takaliyda (IRE) 65 (Azamour **65** (IRE) 130) [2015 67: 9.9m⁶ 8g Sep 12] fair maiden: stays 1¼m: acts on good to firm going. *Richard Fahey*

MIDTECH STAR (IRE) 3 b.g. Kodiac 112 – Royal Rival (IRE) (Marju (IRE) 127) **65**
[2015 78: 7g 10.4d 10.3d 7.6g 12d⁴ 12.1m⁴ 13.4d⁶ Sep 26] fair handicapper: stays 1½m:
acts on tapeta, good to firm and good to soft going: in headgear last 4 starts: often races
lazily. *Ian Williams*

MIDTERM 2 b.c. (Jan 16) Galileo (IRE) 134 – Midday 126 (Oasis Dream 129) [2015 8s* **91 P**
Oct 23] first foal: dam winner 6 times in Group 1s up to 1½m (2-y-o 1m winner): 8/1,
looked good prospect when winning 17-runner maiden at Newbury by length from
Magnum, overcoming inexperience to lead close home under mainly hands and heels: will
stay 1¼m+: impeccably bred, and sort to improve markedly. *Sir Michael Stoute*

MIGHTY BOND 3 b.g. Misu Bond (IRE) 114 – Mighty Flyer (IRE) (Mujtahid (USA) **56**
118) [2015 –: 8d 6d 6s 7g 6s⁶ f6g Dec 29] modest maiden: best effort at 6f: acts on soft
going: often races towards rear. *Tracy Waggott*

MIGHTY MAMBO 8 b.g. Fantastic Light (USA) 134 – Mambo's Melody (Kingmambo **69**
(USA) 125) [2015 p15.8g⁴ p15.8f⁴ t16.5g* Jul 28] compact gelding: fair handicapper: won
at Wolverhampton in July: stays 16.5f: acts on polytrack, tapeta and good to soft going: in
cheekpieces/tongue tie nowadays: sent to Italy. *Lawney Hill*

MIGHTY MISSILE (IRE) 4 ch.g. Majestic Missile (IRE) 118 – Magdalene (FR) **67**
(College Chapel 122) [2015 17.2f⁴ 18d⁶ Oct 5] fair maiden on Flat: stays 17f: acts on firm
and good to soft going: tried in cheekpieces: in tongue tie in 2015: quirky sort: fairly useful
hurdler. *Warren Greatrex*

MIGHTY THOR 5 b.g. Norse Dancer (IRE) 127 – Leyaaly 45 (Night Shift (USA)) [2015 **65**
p12g² p13f p15.8g* Dec 21] lengthy gelding: fair handicapper: won at Lingfield (amateur)
in December: best effort at 2m: acts on polytrack. *Lydia Richards*

MIGHTY WHITEY (IRE) 9 b.g. Sesaro (USA) 81 – Deeco Valley (IRE) (Satco (FR) **59 ?**
114) [2015 12m³ 12g 12.2f Dec 21] modest performer nowadays: stays 1½m: acts on good
to firm and heavy going: has worn headgear: wears tongue tie: front runner/races
prominently. *Noel C. Kelly, Ireland*

MIGHTY YAR (IRE) 5 gr.g. Teofilo (IRE) 126 – Karaliyfa (IRE) 89 (Kahyasi 130) **96**
[2015 111: 10m³ 12m 13.7m⁴ 12d Aug 21] tall, good-topped gelding: useful handicapper:
best efforts of 2015 when third at Newmarket and fourth at Musselburgh: stays 1½m: acts
on polytrack and good to firm going: tried in blinkers in 2015. *Lady Cecil*

MIGHTY ZIP (USA) 3 ch.g. City Zip (USA) 112 – Incredulous (FR) 95 (Indian Ridge **89**
123) [2015 –p: t5.1f³ 16g* p7g³ 6.1g³ 6m 6m p6f t7.1f p6f* p6g² Dec 7] fairly useful
performer: won maiden at Wolverhampton in April and handicap at Chelmsford in
November: stays 6f: acts on polytrack and tapeta: in headgear last 6 starts: front runner/
races prominently. *Kevin Ryan*

MIGNOLINO (IRE) 3 b.g. Kodiac 112 – Caterina di Cesi (Cape Town (IRE) 119) [2015 **89**
86: t5.1m* t5.1f³ p5f² p5f 5s⁴ 6g 7m p6.5g⁶ Dec 21] close-coupled gelding: fairly useful
performer: won handicap at Wolverhampton in February: left David Barron after seventh
start: best form at 5f: acts on polytrack, tapeta and soft going: wears blinkers. *J. Reynier,
France*

MIGUELA MCGUIRE 4 b.f. Sir Percy 129 – Miss McGuire 72 (Averti (IRE) 117) **–**
[2015 42: 8d 8.3d May 27] small filly: maiden: no form in 2015: acts on soft
and good to firm going: tried in headgear: sometimes slowly away. *Eric Alston*

MIGWAR (IRE) 3 b.c. Sea The Stars (IRE) 140 – Katyusha (USA) (Kingmambo (USA) **120**
125) [2015 9.9s* 11.9s² 11.9s³ 11.9d² Oct 18] £180,000Y: first foal: dam unraced sister to
St Leger winner Rule of Law: very smart performer: won minor event at Saint-Cloud (by
5 lengths from Zafiro) in March: subsequently off nearly 6 months: placed after in listed
race at Clairefontaine, Prix Niel at Longchamp (4¼ lengths third to New Bay) and Prix du
Conseil de Paris at Chantilly (1¼ lengths second to Ming Dynasty, finishing strongly):
stays 1½m: acts on soft going. *F. Head, France*

MIKANDY (IRE) 3 b.f. Arcano (IRE) 122 – Belle de Cadix (IRE) 82 (Law Society **87**
(USA) 130) [2015 61, a78: 10.2m* 10g² 11.6m² 13.1f³ p12g Oct 6] fairly useful
handicapper: won at Nottingham in June: stays 13f: acts on polytrack, tapeta and firm
going: races prominently. *Clive Cox*

MIKITERI (IRE) 2 gr.f. (Apr 2) Zebedee 113 – Lina Story (Linamix (FR) 127) [2015 **58**
6m⁶ 6m p7g⁶ p6g⁴ p6m p7.5g Dec 17] €16,000Y, £28,000 2-y-o: workmanlike filly: fifth
foal: half-sister to 3 winners, including 1m-1½m winner (stayed 1¾m) Eton Fable (by Val
Royal) and 2-y-o 5f winner Armero (by Baltic King): dam placed at 7.5f at 2 yrs: modest
maiden: left Robert Mills 4,000 gns after fifth start: should be suited by 7f+: acts on
polytrack: often races towards rear. *N. Caullery, France*

MIKMAK 2 b.c. (Mar 5) Makfi 130 – Rakata (USA) 83 (Quiet American (USA)) [2015 **83**
8.1g 7.4v* 7v Oct 24] 14,000Y: fourth foal: half-brother to 6f-1m winner (stays 1¼m)
Magma (by Singspiel): dam 7f-8.3f winner out of useful 13.4f winner Haleakala: fairly
useful form: won maiden at Ffos Las in August by 6 lengths: 8/1, shaped better than
distance beaten suggests when 7 lengths eighth of 9 to Crazy Horse in Horris Hill Stakes at
Newbury last start, weakening when hampered final 1f and eased: stays 7.5f. *William Muir*

MIKRO POLEMISTIS (IRE) 2 b.f. (Mar 15) Big Bad Bob (IRE) 118 – Kristal Xenia –
(IRE) 75 (Xaar 132) [2015 t6m f5g t6f Nov 14] €26,000Y: second foal: sister to 2-y-o 7f
winner Cherie Good: dam 5f winner: no form. *Brian Ellison*

MILADY 3 b.f. Shamardal (USA) 129 – Lady Grace (IRE) 110 (Orpen (USA) 116) [2015 **89 p**
6m⁵ 6m* 6d⁵ p6f² p7g⁴ Oct 14] fourth foal: half-sister to 1m winner Darling Grace (by
Nayef) and useful 5.5f-7f winner Penmaen (by Pivotal): dam, 6f 7f winner (including at
2 yrs), sister to useful 6f/7f winner Gracefully: fairly useful performer: won maiden at
Lingfield in August: stays 7f: acts on polytrack, good to firm and good to soft going: often
starts slowly, usually races towards rear: remains with potential. *Roger Charlton*

MILADY EILEEN (IRE) 3 ch.f. Footstepsinthesand 120 – Arazena (USA) (Woodman **58**
(USA) 126) [2015 55: 6m⁵ 5m* 5g² 5d³ 5d² 5d⁴ 6g 5.9s⁵ t5.1f Oct 27] modest handicapper:
won at Hamilton in June: stays 6f: acts on fibresand, soft and good to firm going. *Richard Fahey*

MILDMAY ARMS 3 b.g. Kheleyf (USA) 116 – Akathea (Barathea (IRE) 127) [2015 –: –
8f May 13] lightly-raced maiden: best effort at 6f: in hood sole start in 2015. *Simon Hodgson*

MILE HIGH 3 b.f. Fastnet Rock (AUS) 127 – Crinolette (IRE) (Sadler's Wells (USA) **75**
132) [2015 p8m⁴ 8.5g² 11.4d⁵ 10m³ 10m⁵ 10s 10.3g⁶ p10f Sep 24] 105,000Y: sturdy filly:
half-sister to several winners, including useful 2-y-o 6f winner Cedarberg (by Cape Cross)
and useful winner up to 1m (stays 1¼m) Cravat (2-y-o 5f-7f winner, by Dubai Destination):
dam ran once: fair maiden: barely stays 11.5f: acts on polytrack, good to firm and good to
soft going: front runner/races prominently. *Charles Hills*

MILETAKETHEBALL (IRE) 2 b.g. (Mar 8) Vale of York (IRE) 117 – Carrauntoohil **67 p**
(IRE) 49 (Marju (IRE) 127) [2015 p8f⁴ Oct 15] 9,500Y: second foal: dam lightly raced:
20/1, late headway (green and off bridle long way out) when 3½ lengths fourth of 7 to
Richie McCaw in maiden at Chelmsford: will stay beyond 1m: entitled to progress. *Marco Botti*

MILITARY MUSIC 3 b.f. Captain Gerrard (IRE) 113 – Cumbrian Concerto 44 (Petong **40**
126) [2015 47: p6g p5g Feb 14] poor maiden: stays 6f: acts on polytrack and tapeta: tried
in visor. *Mark Usher*

MILKY WAY (IRE) 3 b.c. Galileo (IRE) 134 – Beauty Bright (IRE) 113 (Danehill (USA) **80 p**
126) [2015 80p: 10.1m³ p12g² Aug 8] useful-looking colt: fairly useful handicapper: better
effort in 2015 (just third race all told) when length second to Azilian at Lingfield: stays
1½m: likely to progress further. *Gary Moore*

MILLAR ROSE (IRE) 3 b.f. Vale of York (IRE) 117 – Barbera (GER) (Night Shift –
(USA)) [2015 66: t6g Jan 26] fair at best: best form at 5f: acts on tapeta, good to firm and
good to soft going: usually races close up, often races freely: sold £2,000, sent to the
Netherlands. *K. R. Burke*

MILLE ET MILLE 5 b.g. Muhtathir 126 – Quezon Sun (GER) (Monsun (GER) 124) **119**
[2015 15.4g* 15.4m² 15.4g* 15.4s 19.9m* 15.4d³ Oct 25] smart performer: won handicap
at Saint-Cloud in April, listed race at Maisons-Laffitte in July and Prix du Cadran at
Longchamp (by 1½ lengths from Kicky Blue) in October: also second in Prix Vicomtesse
Vigier at Longchamp (2½ lengths behind Bathyrhon) and third in Prix Royal-Oak at Saint-
Cloud (6 lengths behind Vazirabad): stays 2½m: acts on soft and good to firm going: front
runner/races prominently. *C. & Y. Lerner, France*

Qatar Prix du Cadran, Longchamp—
Mille Et Mille dictates things in front to win from Kicky Blue and British-trained Fun Mac

MILLENNIUM FALCON 2 ch.f. (Mar 28) Kheleyf (USA) 116 – Musical Twist (USA) **67**
97 (Woodman (USA) 126) [2015 5d⁶ 5m* 6d p5g³ 6f⁵ 5m⁴ 5m² 5d Sep 25] £13,000Y: half-
sister to several winners, including 11.6f winner Dance Tempo (by Dansili) and 2-y-o 5f
winner Northern Water (by Pastoral Pursuits): dam maiden (stayed 1m): fair performer:
won maiden at Thirsk in May: best form at 5f: acts on good to firm going: tried in
cheekpieces: usually races prominently. *K. R. Burke*

MILLIONAIRES ROW (USA) 4 b.f. Dynaformer (USA) – Ladue (USA) (Demons **67**
Begone (USA)) [2015 64: p12m² p11f⁶ Jan 21] good-bodied filly: fair maiden: best effort
at 1½m. *John Gosden*

MILLKWOOD 5 b.g. Millkom 124 – Wedgewood Star 74 (Bishop of Cashel 122) [2015 **78**
84: 7m 7m⁵ 8d 7m³ 7m 7m 7.9m f7g Nov 3] big, workmanlike gelding: fair handicapper:
stays 1m: acts on good to firm and heavy going: usually wears headgear: tried in tongue tie
prior to 2015. *John Davies*

MILLPIKE (USA) 3 b.g. Fastnet Rock (AUS) 127 – Forever Beautiful (USA) (Giant's **–**
Causeway (USA) 132) [2015 8.3s p8f 9.9m Jun 7] no sign of ability. *Ed Walker*

MILL POINT 3 b.f. Champs Elysees 124 – Marching West (USA) 99 (Gone West (USA)) **79**
[2015 p8g³ 9.9s³ p10f* 10s Oct 23] lengthy filly: sixth foal: half-sister to 3 winners,
including useful winner up to 1m Marching Time (2-y-o 7f winner, by Sadler's Wells) and
13f/1¼m winner Giovanni Jack (by Three Valleys): dam, 2-y-o 5.5f winner, sister to top-
class winner up to 1m Zafonic: fair performer: won maiden at Lingfield in September: will
be suited by 1½m. *Amanda Perrett*

MILL SPRINGS 3 b.f. Shirocco (GER) 129 – Mezzogiorno 108 (Unfuwain (USA) 131) **100**
[2015 p10g³ 12m⁵ 12.1m² 12.1m* 12g² 14.6m 14m* Oct 2] tall filly: sister to 1½m winner
Suhaili and half-sister to several winners, including smart 1m–1¼m winner Moturani (by
Indian Ridge) and useful 6f-7f winner Monnavanna (by Machiavellian): dam winner up to
1¼m (2-y-o 7f winner): useful performer: won maiden at Chepstow in June and listed race
at Ascot (by 2¼ lengths from Secateur) in October: stays 14.5f: acts on good to firm going:
front runner/races prominently, often travels strongly. *John Gosden*

MILLY ROYALE 3 b.f. Royal Applause 124 – Milly Fleur 67 (Primo Dominie 121) **39**
[2015 –: 6d t5.1f p6g⁶ p6g Dec 3] poor maiden: left Peter Makin after second start: stays
6f: acts on polytrack and tapeta. *Michael Blanshard*

MILLY'S GIFT 5 b.m. Trade Fair 124 – Milly's Lass 79 (Mind Games 121) [2015 110: **83**
5f 5m p6m Nov 14] angular mare: fairly useful performer: stays 6f: acts on polytrack and
good to firm going. *Clive Cox*

MILLY'S SECRET (IRE) 4 ch.f. Sakhee's Secret 128 – Swan Sea (USA) (Sea Hero **59**
(USA) 124) [2015 76, a63: t6f t8.6g³ t9.5f⁴ p10g³ Feb 5] modest handicapper: stays 8.5f:
acts on fibresand, tapeta, best turf form on good going or firmer (acts on firm): sometimes
wears headgear. *David O'Meara*

MILROW (IRE) 2 b.c. (Apr 15) Tamayuz 126 – Cannikin (IRE) 82 (Lahib (USA) 129) **75**
[2015 p8f p8g⁵ Nov 26] better effort in maidens at Chelmsford when 1¼ lengths fifth to
Lilly Vega: likely to stay 1¼m. *Martyn Meade*

MILU MAC 4 b.f. Milk It Mick 120 – Efipetite 54 (Efisio 120) [2015 7.5m⁶ 5g³ Jul 31] **–**
half-sister to several winners, including 9f-1¼m winner (stayed 16.5f) Dium Mac and
winner up to 1m Efidium (2-y-o 5f winner), both by Presidium: dam 1m winner: 25/1, 1½
lengths third of 4 to Art World in maiden at Thirsk: will prove suited by 6f+. *Neville Bycroft*

MILYAAR (IRE) 2 b.c. (Mar 30) Vale of York (IRE) 117 – Central Force 82 (Pivotal 124) **53**
[2015 t9.5f Dec 14] 66/1, well held in maiden at Wolverhampton. *Roger Teal*

MIME DANCE 4 b.g. Notnowcato 128 – Encore My Love 68 (Royal Applause 124) **91**
[2015 89: 7m³ 7.6s 7.1m* 7g³ 7.1m* 7g⁶ 7m 8.1s⁶ 7.6s⁵ 7d⁴ 7s Oct 9] sturdy gelding: fairly
useful handicapper: won at Chepstow in May and July: stays 1m: acts on soft and good to
firm going: wears cheekpieces nowadays. *Andrew Balding*

MIMI LUKE (USA) 4 b.f. U S Ranger (USA) 124 – Hard As Nails (USA) (Holy Bull **52**
(USA) 134) [2015 67: p6f p5m⁶ f6s p6m f6g² t6g p5m p7m 6m 6.1m p8f Nov 19] leggy
filly: modest handicapper: stays 7f: acts on polytrack, fibresand, soft and good to firm
going: often wears visor: sometimes slowly away. *Alan Bailey*

MIN ALEMARAT (IRE) 4 ch.g. Galileo (IRE) 134 – Baraka (IRE) 106 (Danehill **98**
(USA) 126) [2015 105: p13.3f³ 12.1s 16.1m Jun 27] useful handicapper: third at
Chelmsford (3¼ lengths behind Nabatean), only form in 2015: stays 15f: acts on polytrack
and soft going: tried in cheekpieces in 2015: usually races prominently. *Marco Botti*

MINALISA 6 b.m. Oasis Dream 129 – Mina 73 (Selkirk (USA) 129) [2015 114: 6m 6m³ **78**
6m 6g 6g Oct 10] sturdy mare: fair performer: stays 6f: acts on soft and good to firm going.
Rae Guest

MINDBENDER 2 b.c. (Feb 28) Acclamation 118 – Magic Eye (IRE) 103 (Nayef (USA) **62**
129) [2015 8g 8.3d p8f Oct 22] first foal: dam, 7f-8.5f winner, half-sister to smart/
unreliable 6f-8.8f winner Dabbers Ridge: modest maiden: sold 3,500 gns, sent to Sweden.
Mick Channon

MINDING (IRE) 2 b.f. (Feb 10) Galileo (IRE) 134 – Lillie Langtry (IRE) 120 **120 p**
(Danehill Dancer (IRE) 117) [2015 7g² 6g* 7g² 7d* 8g* Oct 9]

Minding is the highest-rated two-year-old filly trained so far by Aidan
O'Brien. In fact, she's one of the highest-rated two-year-old fillies trained in Europe
in recent decades. A rating of 120 is very rarely achieved by a two-year-old filly
nowadays and only Queen's Logic (125 in 2001), Hooray and Tiggy Wiggy (both
121, in 2010 and 2014 respectively) have been rated more highly this century (Six
Perfections was also rated 120p in 2002); the American-trained Songbird is rated
125p after demolishing her opponents in the Breeders' Cup Juvenile Fillies at
Keeneland. Minding reversed the form of her Debutante Stakes second to stablemate
Ballydoyle when winning the Moyglare Stud Stakes, and she further enhanced her
classic claims with a comprehensive victory over a good field in the Dubai Fillies'
Mile at Newmarket. Minding produced one of the best performances in the Fillies'
Mile for many a year and she has merely to reproduce that to be very much the
one to beat in the One Thousand Guineas, for which she is 7/2 favourite at the
time of writing. Only three fillies this century have run to 120 in the first classic,
Finsceal Beo in 2007, the Aidan O'Brien-trained Homecoming Queen in 2012 and
Legatissimo in the latest season.

Minding made a promising debut when two and a half lengths second to
Tanaza in a seven-furlong maiden at Leopardstown and she landed the odds from
three rivals in a similar event over six furlongs there later in June, winning by five
and a half lengths. Tanaza had gone on to win the Silver Flash Stakes (from another
Ballydoyle filly, Alice Springs) by the time Minding appeared next in the Debutante
Stakes at the Curragh. Minding showed much improved form, finishing two lengths
second of eight to Ballydoyle, keeping on well without troubling the winner.

The nine-runner Moyglare Stud Stakes at the Curragh in September was
monopolised by Ballydoyle fillies, Aidan O'Brien saddling the first three finishers in
a race he had won six times previously. The trio did not finish in the order anticipated,
with 15/2-shot Minding winning by three quarters of a length from 5/4 favourite
Ballydoyle and 20/1-shot Alice Springs (Tanaza finished fourth). The domination
was more a reflection of the depth of talent among O'Brien's juvenile fillies, rather
than a slight on the race itself, with Minding rated an above-average winner. The

Moyglare Stud Stakes, the Curragh—a 1, 2, 3 for Aidan O'Brien,
though not in the order anticipated as Minding beats the favourite Ballydoyle and Alice Springs

Dubai Fillies' Mile, Newmarket—Minding produces an effort right out of the top drawer as she draws away from Nathra, giving Aidan O'Brien his fourth win in this Group 1

prominently-ridden Minding finally got the better of Ballydoyle, who set a good gallop, well inside the final furlong and the winning time was over a second quicker than that of Air Force Blue over the course and distance in the National Stakes later the same afternoon. Minding looked a little ungainly, carrying her head slightly high (as she did for her maiden win) with her rider Seamus Heffernan resorting only to hands and heels, but she stayed on well, in the manner of a filly sure to stay a mile. The previous year's switch to a mid-October date had seemed to impact on the quality of the field for the traditionally strong Fillies' Mile which had been run at Ascot before 2011. The 2014 race was won by Together Forever who gave Aidan O'Brien his third Fillies' Mile win. The 2015 edition produced a much better line-up thanks to a combination of a slightly earlier date in the latest season and more than doubling the prize money, as the Fillies' Mile became part of a new two-day Dubai Future Champions' Festival (the Dewhurst and the Fillies' Mile are now the two richest two-year-old events in Europe). Minding started at 5/4, ahead of the unbeaten minor event winner Nathra, representing the Gosden stable, at 4/1, with a second runner from Ballydoyle, the C. L. Weld Park Stakes winner Coolmore, sharing third favouritism with the Rockfel Stakes winner Promising Run, representing Godolphin who had won the race three times in the last five years. The six other fillies started at 14/1 or longer.

Minding led two furlongs out, relishing the extra furlong in a truly-run race and winning by four and a half lengths from Nathra, producing a performance better even than that produced by the likes of Rainbow View, Listen (for Ballydoyle) and Nannina in the Fillies' Mile; Listen had only a brief three-year-old campaign, but Rainbow View (Matron Stakes) and Nannina (Coronation Stakes) both went on to win Group 1s. Minding recorded the joint highest timefigure of the season by a two-year-old filly—0.68 fast, equivalent to a timerating of 117—and also the best timefigure in the Fillies' Mile since Bosra Sham (won the One Thousand Guineas and Champion Stakes at three); not only does the form show that Minding is a high-class filly but the clock says so too. Two and a quarter lengths behind Nathra (who may yet have more to offer herself) in third was Hawksmoor, who finished a head in front of Coolmore. Coolmore still has potential, as does the fifth Beautiful Morning, while Promising Run in seventh is clearly not herself for some reason and is best judged on her previous form.

Minding (IRE) (b.f. 2013)	Galileo (IRE) (b 1998)	Sadler's Wells (b 1981)	Northern Dancer Fairy Bridge
		Urban Sea (ch 1989)	Miswaki Allegretta
	Lillie Langtry (IRE) (b or br 2007)	Danehill Dancer (b 1993)	Danehill Mira Adonde
		Hoity Toity (br 2000)	Darshaan Hiwaayati

Minding is the second foal out of Lillie Langtry who won three of her seven races as a two-year-old, including the Debutante Stakes. She reportedly suffered a small fracture in a knee when down the field in the Breeders' Cup Juvenile Fillies Turf. Lillie Langtry raced only in Group 1s at three, improving on a close fifth in the Irish One Thousand Guineas when winning the Coronation Stakes at Royal Ascot and then bouncing back from a laboured effort in the Falmouth Stakes to win the Matron Stakes at Leopardstown. Lillie Langtry stayed a mile (she did not race over any further) and acted on firm ground (only third when odds-on in the Moyglare on heavy ground, her only outing on going softer than good). Lillie Langtry's first foal Kissed By Angels was unraced at two but showed useful form when winning the One Thousand Guineas Trial over a mile at Leopardstown in April. She was well beaten in the Irish One Thousand Guineas and the Irish Oaks on her two subsequent starts. Lillie Langtry is closely related to the smart winner at up to a mile and a quarter Count of Limonade, and is the third foal out of the unraced Hoity Toity, who was a Maktoum two-year-old cast-off from Gainsborough Stud at the 2002 December Sales (made only 15,000 guineas). Lillie Langtry cost 230,000 guineas as a yearling, and three of her siblings have sold for plenty of money as yearlings but have failed to make the track; they include her three-year-old brother Patronising who cost 300,000 guineas and is in training with David Lanigan, who also trains Hoity Toity's two-year-old filly Danilovna (closely related to Lillie Langtry) who made a winning debut in November. Another daughter of Hoity Toity is the once-raced Lady Hawkfield, the dam of Master Apprentice, winner of the Sandown Classic Trial on his only start in the latest season. Hoity Toity herself is a half-sister to the useful mile winner Sweet Emotion (dam of the smart performer at up to a mile and a quarter Winged Cupid) out of a half-sister to the very smart six/seven-furlong performers, the brothers Lead On Time and Great Commotion who won the Prix Maurice de Gheest and the Cork And Orrery respectively. Minding, a strong filly, is likely to stay a mile and a quarter, though she isn't guaranteed to stay much further, despite her sire being a strong influence for stamina. She acts on good to soft ground (Kissed By Angel's sole win to date came on heavy going) and usually responds generously to pressure. Most progressive and open to further improvement, Minding is a very exciting prospect. *Aidan O'Brien, Ireland*

MINDUROWNBUSINESS (IRE) 4 b.c. Cape Cross (IRE) 129 – Whos Mindin Who **120** (IRE) (Danehill Dancer (IRE) 117) [2015 100: p8f² p8g* t8.6m* p8f p8m* p8f* p10g³ Dec 2] sturdy colt: very smart handicapper: won at Lingfield and Wolverhampton early in year: off over 7 months, further improvement to win at Lingfield and Chelmsford (by 1¼ lengths from Big Whiskey) in November: 8/11, excuses when only third of 4 in minor event at Lingfield final start: should be suited by a return to 1m: acts on polytrack, tapeta and good to firm going: often races prominently/travels strongly. *Roger Varian*

MINGALABAR 4 b.g. Shirocco (GER) 129 – Veenwouden 107 (Desert Prince (IRE) – 130) [2015 11.5g 12g⁶ p12g Aug 17] no form. *Ian Williams*

MING DYNASTY (FR) 3 b.c. King's Best (USA) 132 – Memoire (FR) (Sadler's Wells **122** (USA) 132) [2015 11.9g* 11.9g* 11.9s* 11.9s⁶ 11.9d* 11.9g⁴ Dec 13] half-brother to 9f-1½m winner Montagne Lointaine (by Numerous) and 13f winner Moscow Nights (by Peintre Celebre): dam, 1¼m winner, out of Prix Saint-Alary winner Moonlight Dance: very smart performer: won newcomers race at Maisons-Laffitte in April, minor event at Clairefontaine in July, listed race on latter course in August and Prix du Conseil de Paris at Chantilly (by 1¼ lengths from Migwar) in October: creditable 4½ lengths fourth to Highland Reel in Hong Kong Vase at Sha Tin final outing: raced only at 1½m: acts on soft going: wore hood last 2 starts: reportedly worked up beforehand when well below form in Prix Niel at Longchamp fourth start. *M. Delzangles, France*

MINIATURIST (FR) 2 b.g. Shamardal (USA) 129 – Herboriste (Hernando **83** (FR) 127) [2015 5g² 5d² 6g⁵ 7.1f* 7.1m 7g 8g Sep 26] €180,000Y: good-bodied gelding: fourth foal: half-brother to 1½m winner Heron Lake (by Danehill Dancer): dam, US Grade 2 1½m winner, half-sister to smart winner up to 1½m Fast And Furious: fairly useful performer: won maiden at Sandown (by 1¼ lengths from Taqwaa) in July: best effort at 7f: acts on firm going: usually leads. *Mark Johnston*

MINI MINSTREL 3 br.f. Pastoral Pursuits 121 – Bruma (IRE) (Footstepsinthesand 120) – [2015 –: 5g⁵ 5.7f⁵ 7g Sep 19] no form. *Colin Teague*

MININGGOLD 2 b.f. (Apr 10) Piccolo 121 – Rosein 86 (Komaite (USA)) [2015 5m⁶ 5v⁴ **69** 6g 5m³ 5s* 5m⁵ 5.2m 5m⁴ 6s 5g* 5g⁵ Oct 16] £21,000Y: good-topped filly: fifth foal: sister to 5f winner Picc of Burgau and half-sister to 2-y-o 5f winner Molly Mylenis (by Needwood Blade) and 6f-7f winner Signorina Roseina (by Captain Gerrard): dam winner up to 7f, 2-y-o 5f winner: fair performer: won maiden at Carlisle in July and nursery at Catterick in September: best form at 5f: acts on soft and good to firm going. *Tim Easterby*

MININGROCKS (FR) 3 b.g. Lawman (FR) 121 – Fashion School (Shamardal (USA) 129) [2015 f7s⁶ f7g⁶ 8.5m 8s⁵ 8g 8g⁴ 8.3g⁶ 8m 8m 7g* 8g² 8m 7d⁵ 9.2d 8.5d Sep 22] modest handicapper: won at Thirsk in July: stays 1m: best form on good going: sometimes slowly away, often races in rear. *Ruth Carr* **62**

MINIONETTE (IRE) 4 b.f. Manduro (GER) 135 – La Vita E Bella (IRE) 105 (Definite Article 121) [2015 60p: 12.5s f8g Apr 23] maiden: no form in 2015: stays 11f: acts on heavy going. *Alan Swinbank* **–**

MINISKIRT 4 b.f. Naaqoos 117 – Minnola 58 (Royal Applause 124) [2015 86: t8.6g f8d* p8f³ f8g⁴ p8g³ f8d² 8d⁶ 8v p8f Oct 1] fairly useful handicapper: won at Southwell in February: stays 1m: acts on polytrack, fibresand and heavy going: usually races prominently: sold 3,500 gns, sent to Saudi Arabia. *Rae Guest* **83**

MINISTER OF FUN 4 b.g. Pastoral Pursuits 127 – Diane's Choice 95 (Komaite (USA)) [2015 77: f6s t6g 6d⁶ 6g 6m t6g Aug 27] fair winner at 2 yrs, poor form since: best effort at 6f on fibresand. *Scott Dixon* **48**

MINNEAPOLIS 10 b.g. Sadler's Wells (USA) 132 – Teggiano (IRE) 108 (Mujtahid (USA) 118) [2015 12.1m 16.2m Jun 12] good-topped, quite attractive gelding: once useful performer, has deteriorated markedly: in tongue tie last 2 starts. *Sophie Leech* **–**

MINNIE (IRE) 3 b.f. Sakhee's Secret 128 – Numerus Clausus (FR) (Numerous (USA)) [2015 65: t6g 6m⁵ p7g t9.5f p8g⁶ p7m⁶ Oct 21] modest maiden: left Ian Williams after second start: stays 1m: acts on polytrack, tapeta and good to firm going: often in headgear in 2015: front runner/races prominently. *Phil McEntee* **53**

MINNIE THE MOOCHER 3 b.f. Cockney Rebel (IRE) 127 – Compose (Anabaa (USA) 130) [2015 10s p10g 10.2m⁶ 12g p14g p8f t9.5f Oct 16] lengthy filly: sister to useful 1¼m-13f winner Cockney Sparrow and half-sister to 3 winners, including 1½m winner Dino Mite (by Doctor Dino) and 1m/9f winner Sarbola (by Dubai Destination): dam lightly raced: fair maiden at best: stays 1¼m: acts on polytrack and soft going: sometimes in cheekpieces. *Dave Morris* **65 d**

MINORITY INTEREST 6 ch.g. Galileo (IRE) 134 – Minority 106 (Generous (IRE) 139) [2015 p10g Dec 9] good-topped gelding: fair handicapper in 2013, well held on return to Flat in December: stays 13f: acts on polytrack, raced only on good going or firmer on turf: usually in headgear: one to treat with some caution. *Daniel O'Brien* **–**

MINOT STREET (CAN) 5 b.g. Van Nistelrooy (USA) 108 – Just Outta Here (USA) (Rahy (USA) 115) [2015 49, a81: p12g⁵ 10d 12.5s 10s 12g t12.2m* Dec 12] fair handicapper: won at Wolverhampton in December: stays 1½m: acts on polytrack, tapeta and good to firm going: often wears headgear: usually wears tongue tie. *John McConnell, Ireland* **78**

MINSTREL LAD 7 ch.g. Where Or When (IRE) 124 – Teal Flower (Pivotal 124) [2015 75, a66: f12s⁵ 10.4g² 10m 10g 10g 10.1v⁴ 10g⁴ 10s² t9.5f⁶ 10.2s Nov 4] sturdy, lengthy gelding: fair handicapper: stays 1½m: acts on polytrack, tapeta, soft and good to firm going. *Lydia Pearce* **76**

MINTY JONES 6 b.h. Primo Valentino (IRE) 116 – Reveur 69 (Rossini (USA) 118) [2015 55§, a43§: f6d⁵ t6f 5.1d³ 5.1m 5m 5m* 6m⁵ 5s 5d² 5s 6g 5s³ 5.1d⁴ Nov 4] modest handicapper: won at Beverley in July: stays 7.5f: acts on polytrack, tapeta, good to firm and heavy going: usually wears headgear: front runner/races prominently: inconsistent. *Michael Mullineaux* **62 §**

MIRACLE GARDEN 3 ch.g. Exceed And Excel (AUS) 126 – Sharp Terms (Kris 135) [2015 t6g⁵ 6.1s⁴ 5m⁶ 5.1g⁴ 5.1m 5.1g 16m* p5g* t5.1f* Nov 30] 175,000Y, £4,000 3-y-o: brother to smart 2-y-o 5f/6f winner Best Terms and half-brother to 3 winners, including 1¼m/11f winner Sunsemperchi (by Montjeu) and useful 1¼m winner Hevelius (by Polish Precedent): dam unraced: fairly useful handicapper: won at Wolverhampton in September, Kempton in October and Wolverhampton in November: stays 6f: acts on polytrack and tapeta: usually in cheekpieces: front runner/races prominently. *Roy Brotherton* **85**

MIRACLE NINETYNINE (IRE) 3 b.c. Big Bad Bob (IRE) 118 – Scrumptious 69 (Sakhee (USA) 136) [2015 76p: 7d³ 8.1m² p8m² 8f² 7.1m¹ 7g⁴ Aug 13] compact colt: fairly useful maiden: stays 1m: acts on polytrack, good to firm and good to soft going: tried in blinkers in 2015. *Richard Hannon* **84**

MIRACLE OF MEDINAH 4 ch.g. Milk It Mick 120 – Smart Ass (IRE) 91 (Shinko Forest (IRE)) [2015 104: p8f⁵ t8.6m⁵ 8.1m⁵ 7g 7g³ 7.6m² 7g⁵ p7g Oct 29] neat gelding: useful performer: second in handicap at Chester (¾ length behind Sound Advice) in August: stays 7.5f: acts on polytrack and firm going: usually races towards rear. *Mark Usher* **104 a97**

MIRAGE (IRE) 2 b.f. (Mar 1) Oasis Dream 129 – Applauded (IRE) 83 (Royal Applause 124) [2015 6s* 8f² 8d 8f⁴ 8f⁶ Dec 27] 150,000Y: fourth foal: closely related to winner up to 1m Amnesia (2-y-o 6f winner, by Invincible Spirit) and half-sister to 1¼m/10.5f winner Arthur The King (by Medicean): dam, 2-y-o 7f winner, half-sister to winner up to 1m Power (by Oasis Dream) and winner up to 1½m Curvy, both smart: useful performer: won maiden at Brighton in June: left Jamie Osborne, good efforts in US next 2 starts, particularly in Breeders' Cup Juvenile Fillies Turf at Keeneland (4½ lengths eighth to Catch A Glimpse): below form last 2 outings: stays 1m: acts on firm and soft going. *Simon Callaghan, USA* **100**

MIRAMONTE DANCER (IRE) 2 b.f. (Apr 19) Fast Company (IRE) 126 – Bonne 72 (Namid 128) [2015 6g 6f 5m⁶ Aug 12] €5,000Y: second foal: dam, 6f winner, half-sister to smart 6f winner Rising Shadow and winner up to 9f Espumanti: well held in maidens. *David C. Griffiths* **–**

MIRO (IRE) 3 b.g. Rock of Gibraltar (IRE) 133 – Mission Secrete (IRE) (Galileo (IRE) 134) [2015 8.3m³ 10.2d³ p10f³ p7g² p8g² Dec 28] first foal: dam, 14.5f winner, half-sister to 1000 Guineas winner Miss France out of smart 2-y-o 1m winner (stayed 1½m) Miss Tahiti: fairly useful maiden: stays 1¼m: acts on polytrack, good to firm and good to soft going. *James Fanshawe* **83**

MIRROR CITY 2 b.f. (Feb 17) Street Cry (IRE) 130 – Ama (USA) (Storm Cat (USA)) [2015 p7g³ p8g* Aug 26] third foal: half-sister to 9f winner Nightster (by Raven's Pass): dam maiden half-sister to high-class miler and top sire Kingmambo and very smart winner up to 1¼m East of The Moon out of Miesque: 13/8, confirmed debut promise when winning maiden at Kempton by 5 lengths from Street Duel, making all, eased near finish: open to further improvement. *Charlie Appleby* **84 p**

MIRSAALAH 2 b.f. (Apr 30) Sir Percy 129 – Lyric Art (USA) 65 (Red Ransom (USA)) [2015 7m⁵ 8.1g² 8g* 8g⁴ Aug 21] 20,000Y: third foal: sister to 1½m winner Knight Music: dam, 7f winner, closely related to smart 1½m-14.6f winner Meeznah out of useful 1¼m-12.5f winner String Quartet: fair performer: won maiden at Brighton in August: bred to be suited by middle distances. *James Tate* **76**

MIRSAALE 5 ch.g. Sir Percy 129 – String Quartet (IRE) 109 (Sadler's Wells (USA) 132) [2015 105: 12m 12m⁵ 8v p10f⁶ 8g Sep 23] well-made gelding: useful at best, no form in 2015: often wears headgear: usually in tongue tie in 2015. *Mrs Ilka Gansera-Leveque* **–**

MIRZA 8 b.g. Oasis Dream 129 – Millyant 114 (Primo Dominie 121) [2015 117: 5g 5g 5g⁶ 5f⁵ 5d* 5g 5s³ 5m⁶ Oct 4] good-topped gelding: smart performer: as good as ever when winning listed race at Deauville (by 1¼ lengths from Muharaaj) in July: respectable 2¾ lengths sixth to Goldream in Prix de l'Abbaye at Longchamp final start: effective at 6f, races mostly at 5f nowadays: acts on good to firm and heavy going: wears cheekpieces. *Rae Guest* **117**

MISCHIEF MAISY (IRE) 2 gr.f. (Apr 10) Clodovil (IRE) 116 – Maise And Blue (USA) (Distant View (USA) 126) [2015 p7m Dec 31] €27,000F, 25,000Y: second foal: dam 1m winner in US: 20/1, very green when eighth of 12 in maiden at Lingfield. *Amanda Perrett* **–**

MISE EN ROSE (USA) 2 b.f. (Mar 5) War Front (USA) 119 – Buy The Barrel (USA) (E Dubai (USA) 124) [2015 p7g³ p7g* 8g³ 7g⁴ Oct 10] $240,000Y: useful-looking filly: second foal: dam US Grade 2 8.5f winner: fairly useful form: won maiden at Kempton in August: better form subsequently in nurseries at Pontefract and Newmarket (2½ lengths fourth of 15 to Mix And Mingle): stays 1m. *Charlie Appleby* **93**

MISHAAL (IRE) 5 ch.g. Kheleyf (USA) 116 – My Dubai (IRE) 76 (Dubai Millennium 140) [2015 97: p6f³ p6g p6g² t7.1g 5g 6.1m⁵ Jul 17] useful handicapper: third at Lingfield (head behind History Book) in January and second at Kempton (head behind History Book) in March, well held otherwise in 2015: stays 1m: acts on polytrack and good to firm going: sometimes wears headgear: usually leads. *Michael Herrington* **96**

MISHAM 3 ch.f. Shamardal (USA) 129 – Mi Anna (GER) (Lake Coniston (IRE) 131) [2015 60p: 8.3g t7.1g² t7.1g⁵ 7m Aug 5] rather leggy filly: fair maiden: should stay 1m: acts on tapeta: usually in blinkers in 2015: often races towards rear. *Marco Botti* **69**

MISHGHAR 3 b.c. Galileo (IRE) 134 – Akdarena 113 (Hernando (FR) 127) [2015 8f⁶ 11.5g⁶ 12s² p12g⁵ p12g³ 12v⁵ Sep 1] rather leggy colt: fair maiden: stays 1½m: acts on polytrack and soft going: sold 14,000 gns, sent to Italy. *Richard Hannon* **77**

MISHRIF (USA) 9 b.g. Arch (USA) 127 – Peppy Priscilla (USA) (Latin American (USA) 120) [2015 84: f8d⁴ f8d⁵ f12d⁵ a8g³ p8g* f11g⁵ p8f⁶ p8g p8g p8m Dec 27] close-coupled gelding: fair handicapper: won at Chelmsford (apprentice) in March: stays 11f: acts on polytrack, fibresand, soft and good to firm going: usually wears headgear: tried in tongue tie prior to 2015. *J. R. Jenkins* **66**

MISLEADING 3 ch.g. Footstepsinthesand 120 – Danny's Choice 88 (Compton Place — 125) [2015 82: 7g May 13] fairly useful winner at 2 yrs: 25/1, well held in handicap at York only outing in 2015, finding little. *Peter Chapple-Hyam*

MISSANDEI 3 b.f. Red Rocks (IRE) 124 – Onda Chiara (ITY) (Dane Friendly 108) [2015 **61** 60: t8.6f² t9.5f t7.1f⁶ p8g 9.9m² 9.9g⁵ 10.2m⁴ 10g 10.2m⁵ t12.2f t9.5m t12.2m⁴ Dec 18] close-coupled filly: modest maiden: stays 1½m: acts on tapeta and good to firm going: usually in headgear in 2015, also in tongue last 2 starts. *Steph Hollinshead*

MISS BALLYGALLY (IRE) 5 b.m. Ramonti (FR) 126 – Miss Gally (IRE) (Galileo **65** (IRE) 134) [2015 10.5s³ 8.3g⁶ 10.2s Oct 28] fair maiden: best effort at 10.5f: acts on soft going: in tongue tie in 2015. *Mark McNiff, Ireland*

MISS BLONDELL 2 ch.f. (Apr 12) Compton Place 125 – Where's Broughton 77 **65** (Cadeaux Genereux 131) [2015 7m⁵ p7g* 7m Sep 11] 7,500Y: fourth foal: half-sister to 1¼m winner Where's Tiger (by Tiger Hill): dam, 9.5f winner, sister to very smart 1m-1¼m winner Desert Deer: fair performer: won maiden at Kempton in August: likely to stay 1m. *Marcus Tregonning*

MISS BUCKAROO (IRE) 3 b.f. Acclamation 118 – Pearl Trader (IRE) 67 (Dubai **50** Destination (USA) 127) [2015 p6f⁶ f8f³ Dec 17] €18,000Y, resold 22,000Y: third foal: half-sister to 6f-1m winner Bamurru (by Kheleyf) and 1¼m winner Mfiftythreedotcom (by Tamayuz): dam 12.2f winner out of Irish Oaks winner Vintage Tipple: better effort when third in maiden at Southwell: left Ralph Smith after first start. *James Given*

MISS BUCKSHOT (IRE) 4 b.f. Tamayuz 126 – Miss Bellbird (IRE) (Danehill (USA) **89** 126) [2015 80, a90: p10g² p10g⁴ p8m* 8m⁶ 8.5g⁶ 8d p8g Sep 5] fairly useful handicapper: won at Kempton in April: stays 1¼m: acts on polytrack and good to firm going: often races towards rear. *Rae Guest*

MISS BURNETT (USA) 4 ch.f. Mr Greeley (USA) 122 – Tink So (USA) (Meadowlake **57** (USA)) [2015 7g 7s 8s⁵ 10d⁵ May 21] modest form: well held both starts in bumpers: just modest form in 4 starts on Flat: stayed 1¼m: dead. *Alan Swinbank*

MISS DUSKY DIVA (IRE) 3 gr.f. Verglas (IRE) 118 – Dispol Veleta 83 (Makbul 104) **58** [2015 p6g t7.1f⁵ t7.1g 9d² 9.9m 9.9m⁵ t9.5f Oct 3] third foal: dam 1m/8.3f winner who stayed 10.3f: modest maiden: stays 1¼m: acts on good to firm and good to soft going: sometimes slowly away. *John Spearing*

MISSED CALL (IRE) 5 b.m. Authorized (IRE) 133 – Incoming Call (USA) 61 (Red **105** Ransom (USA)) [2015 95: 12g³ 14g⁶ 12m* 13.4m⁵ 12m² p12g* Nov 4] workmanlike mare: useful performer: won handicap at Ascot (by short head from Elbereth) in August and listed race at Kempton (by neck from Hamelin) in November: also ran well when second in Cumberland Lodge Stakes at Ascot (2¾ lengths behind Star Storm): stays 13.5f: acts on polytrack and good to firm going. *James Fanshawe*

MISS EXCELLENCE 3 b.f. Exceed And Excel (AUS) 126 – Hunter's Fortune (USA) **49** (Charismatic (USA) 127) [2015 p6g⁵ t7.1f p7g³ p6g⁶ f7g⁶ 6s 7.1m⁶ Jun 6] fourth foal: half-sister to 2-y-o 5f winner Miss Rosie (by Librettist): dam 5.5f (including at 2 yrs)/6f winner out of US Grade 2 2-y-o 6.5f winner Salty Perfume: poor maiden: stays 7f: acts on polytrack. *Mark Johnston*

MISS FORTUNE 2 ch.f. (Jan 23) Notnowcato 128 – Rowan Flower (IRE) 67 (Ashkalani **53** (IRE) 128) [2015 p6g 7.1m⁶ f7s⁶ 7.1g t9.5f⁶ Dec 11] 3,500Y: close-coupled filly: half-sister to winner up to 1m Boy Blue (2-y-o 7f winner, by Observatory) and 2m winner Aldreth (by Champs Elysees): dam, 7f winner, half-sister to smart 1¼m winner Muakaad: modest maiden: best effort at 7f: acts on good to firm going. *Mark Usher*

MISS FRANCE (IRE) 4 b.f. Dansili 127 – Miss Tahiti 127 (Tirol 127) [2015 119: **117** 8g² 8m² 9.5g Oct 31] unfurnished filly: smart performer: won 1000 Guineas at Newmarket in 2014: suffered from a splint problem in spring of 2015 and didn't return until September: showed she retained most of her ability when second to Impassable in Prix Daniel Wildenstein at Longchamp on second outing: below form when 8¼ lengths eighth to Stephanie's Kitten in Breeders' Cup Filly & Mare Turf at Keeneland on final outing, not settling over longer trip: best around 1m: acts on good to firm going. *A. Fabre, France*

MISS FRIDAYTHORPE 2 b.f. (Mar 29) Pastoral Pursuits 127 – Cosmic Destiny (IRE) **54 p** 79 (Soviet Star (USA) 128) [2015 5m⁴ Jun 13] third foal: sister to 6f winner Costa Filey and useful winner up to 6f Primrose Valley (2-y-o 5f winner): dam 5f/5.3f winner: 4/1, 5½ lengths fourth of 6 to Fine Blend in maiden at Lingfield, not knocked about: should progress. *Ed Vaughan*

MISS GILER 3 b.f. High Chaparral (IRE) 132 – Funday 93 (Daylami (IRE) 138) [2015   **72**
–p: p10g² p12f³ p10g³ 11.5s⁴ 9.9g⁵ 10m p10f² p10f³ p10f⁴ p10f⁵ Dec 21] fair maiden:
stays 1½m: acts on polytrack and soft going: sometimes wears tongue tie. *John Gosden*

MISS GOLDSMITH (IRE) 2 gr.f. (May 7) Mastercraftsman (IRE) 129 – Golden   **61 p**
Legacy (IRE) 107 (Rossini (USA) 118) [2015 t7.1f⁵ t6f⁴ Dec 22] €55,000F, €80,000Y:
fifth foal: sister to useful 7f (including at 2 yrs) winner Roachdale House and half-sister to
useful winner up to 6f Stake Acclaim (by Acclamation): dam 2-y-o 6f winner: better effort
when fourth at Wolverhampton, nearest finish: will be suited by a return to 7f+:
remains with potential. *Richard Fahey*

MISS INGA SOCK (IRE) 3 ch.f. Tagula (IRE) 116 – Support Fund (IRE) 83 (Intikhab   **80**
(USA) 135) [2015 57: 8f² t8.6g 7s* 8m³ 7.1m² 8s⁴ 8.5m² 7v⁵ Aug 25] fairly useful
handicapper: won at Brighton in June: stays 8.5f: acts on soft and good to firm going. *Eve
Johnson Houghton*

MISSION IMPOSSIBLE 10 gr.g. Kyllachy 129 – Eastern Lyric 93 (Petong 126) [2015   **80**
74: 6g 6d* Aug 14] tall gelding: fairly useful handicapper: won at Newcastle in August:
stays 6f: acts on polytrack, good to firm and heavy going: sometimes in cheekpieces prior
to 2015: often races towards rear. *Tracy Waggott*

MISSION MARS 2 b.g. (Apr 22) Kyllachy 129 – Ashraakat (USA) 105 (Danzig (USA))   **53 p**
[2015 7m 6.1g⁶ 6.1d Aug 14] 65,000Y: half-brother to several winners, including 5f-1¼m
winner El Dececy (by Seeking The Gold) and winner up to 12.3f Hezaam (2-y-o 7f winner,
by Red Ransom): dam 6f/7f winner (including at 2 yrs): modest form in maidens: likely to
do better at 3 yrs. *Luca Cumani*

MISSISSIPPI 6 b.g. Exceed And Excel (AUS) 126 – Ruby Rocket (IRE) 113 (Indian   **93**
Rocket 115) [2015 94: 6d³ 6v² 6m⁶ 6d* 6d⁵ 6.3m 6g 6g 6m³ 6g Oct 16] fairly useful
handicapper: won at Ripon (by neck from Barkston Ash) in June: stays 1m: acts on
polytrack, good to firm and heavy going: has worn headgear, including often of late: often
races towards rear. *Paul Midgley*

MISS JONH (FR) 3 ch.f. Deportivo 116 – Flower 82 (Zamindar (USA) 116) [2015 52:   **–**
t5.1g Jan 26] lightly-raced maiden, modest form at best: raced only at 5f: tried in hood.
Martyn Meade

MISS LILLIE 4 b.f. Exceed And Excel (AUS) 126 – Never Lose 95 (Diktat 126) [2015   **66**
64, a83: 7.1g p8g p8f⁶ p8f⁵ t8.6f p7m³ p7g Dec 16] workmanlike filly: fair handicapper:
stays 8.5f: acts on polytrack, tapeta, soft and good to firm going: sometimes in headgear
prior to 2015: tends to find little. *Roger Teal*

MISS LUCY JANE 4 ch.f. Aqlaam 125 – Ocean View (USA) 109 (Gone West (USA))   **73**
[2015 84: 10.2s 9.9m⁵ 12.3f⁴ 9.9m⁶ Jun 23] fair handicapper: stays 1½m: acts on firm
going. *Richard Fahey*

MISS MACNAMARA (IRE) 6 b.m. Dylan Thomas (IRE) 132 – Kincob (USA) 63   **76**
(Kingmambo (USA) 125) [2015 82: 13.8d⁴ 13g 16m 15.8d⁶ 15.9m 13.8d Sep 15] fair
handicapper: stays 2m: acts on soft and good to firm going: tried in headgear.
Martin Todhunter

MISS MARINA BAY 2 ch.f. (Feb 3) Galileo (IRE) 134 – Miss Corniche 104 (Hernando   **50 p**
(FR) 127) [2015 7.6v⁵ 8.1v⁴ 8d Sep 4] sister to 1¾m-16.5f winner (stays 21f) Italian
Riviera and half-sister to 3 winners, including smart 1m-1¾m winner Moyenne Corniche
(by Selkirk) and winner up to 7f Miss Eze (2-y-o 6f winner, by Danehill Dancer): dam
winner up to 1¼m (2-y-o 7f winner): modest form in maidens: will be suited by 1¼m+:
should do better in time. *Sir Mark Prescott Bt*

MISS MARJURIE (IRE) 5 b.m. Marju (IRE) 127 – Kazatzka 62 (Groom Dancer (USA)   **114**
128) [2015 103: 12m* 11.9d* 11.9g³ 12d⁵ Aug 20] rangy mare: smart performer: won
listed race at Goodwood (by neck from Dream Child) and Pinnacle Stakes at Haydock (by
short head from Wonderstruck), both in May: length third to Lady Tiana in Lancashire
Oaks at Haydock, then career-best effort when 1¼ lengths fifth to Pleascach in Yorkshire
Oaks at York, despite being left poorly placed: stays 13f: acts on polytrack, good to firm
and good to soft going: often races towards rear/travels strongly. *Denis Coakley*

MISS MAYFLOWER 3 b.f. Monsieur Bond (IRE) 120 – Scrooby Baby 66 (Mind   **–**
Games 121) [2015 6d Jun 4] third foal: half-sister to 5f winner (stayed 7f) Sandy Toes (by
Footstepsinthesand) and 2-y-o 6f winner Scrooby Doo (by Kheleyf): dam, maiden (stayed
6f), half-sister to very smart winner up to 1m (stayed 1¼m) Milk It Mick: 25/1, eighth of
9 in maiden at Hamilton. *Scott Dixon*

MISS MINUTY 3 gr.f. Verglas (IRE) 118 – Miss Provence 88 (Hernando (FR) 127) [2015 **88**
62: t8.6f* p10f* t9.5g³ p10m² t9.5m² 10.3m 8.3m⁵ t8.6g⁵ 10.2f* 10d t9.5f² t12.2f³ Dec 11]
fairly useful performer: won seller at Wolverhampton and handicap at Lingfield in January
and handicap at Bath in September: left Sir Mark Prescott after first start, David Evans after
fourth, John Gallagher after eighth: stays 1½m: acts on polytrack, tapeta and firm going:
blinkered first 7 starts in 2015: often races towards rear. *Tony Newcombe*

MISS MITTENS 3 b.f. Shirocco (GER) 129 – River of Silence (IRE) (Sadler's Wells **–**
(USA) 132) [2015 8.1s 10m 11.7f⁶ Jun 24] 6,500Y: first foal: dam ran once: no form.
Peter Makin

MISS MONEYPENNY (IRE) 2 b.f. (Apr 14) Kodiac 112 – Pearly Brooks 77 (Efisio **79**
120) [2015 5g³ 5f* 6m⁴ 6f 6g Aug 1] €15,000F, £42,000Y: neat filly: closely related to 1m
(including at 2 yrs) winner Classic Voice (by Oratorio) and half-sister to useful 2-y-o 5f
winners Fine 'N Dandy (by Dandy Man) and Pearl's Azinger (by Zebedee): dam, 6f
winner, sister to smart winner up to 1m Pips Pride: fair performer: won maiden at Windsor
in May: best effort at 5f: acts on polytrack: sold 23,000 gns, sent to Spain. *Ralph Beckett*

MISS MOPPET 4 b.f. Nayef (USA) 129 – So Blissful (IRE) 77 (Cape Cross (IRE) 129) **–**
[2015 63: p8g Jul 8] maiden: well held only start on Flat in 2015 (wore hood): best effort
at 7f: acts on polytrack. *J. R. Jenkins*

MISS MOZAICO 2 b.f. (Apr 11) Pastoral Pursuits 127 – Grin (Key of Luck (USA) 126) **–**
[2015 6g 7m 6m 7.2g 7s t9.5f t8.6f Nov 30] £3,500Y: second foal: dam unraced: no form:
tried in blinkers. *Richard Guest*

MISS MULLBERRY 3 b.f. Kodiac 112 – Chaenomeles (USA) 74 (Fusaichi Pegasus **91 §**
(USA) 130) [2015 86: p5m 5m 5g⁶ 5m⁴ 5m 6m⁵ 5.4m 5g³ 5s* 5g 5s 5s Oct 19] leggy filly:
fairly useful handicapper: won at Thirsk (by ¾ length from Straightothepoint) in
September: best form at 5f: acts on soft and good to firm going: often wears hood:
unreliable. *David O'Meara*

MISS PHILLYJINKS (IRE) 2 b.f. (Feb 2) Zoffany (IRE) 121 – Smoken Rosa (USA) **69**
(Smoke Glacken (USA) 120) [2015 p5g² 6g⁵ 6.9g⁴ 6.3d t6m² t6m* Dec 30] €12,000Y:
fourth foal: half-sister to 7f winner Refusetolisten and 1m winner Bosstime (both by
Clodovil): dam maiden half-sister to US Grade 3 8.5f/9f winner Snowdrops: fair performer:
won maiden at Wolverhampton (dead-heated with Murdanova) in December: left M.
Halford after fourth start: stays 6f: acts on tapeta: tried in headgear. *Paul D'Arcy*

MISS PIMPERNEL (IRE) 2 b.f. (Mar 31) Clodovil (IRE) 116 – Mrs Seek (Unfuwain **78**
(USA) 131) [2015 6g⁴ 7d⁴ 7.4g³ 8.3m⁴ 8.1s⁴ p8f* p8g Dec 15] 60,000Y: lengthy filly:
closely related to 9.5f-2m winner L'Avenue (by Champs Elysees) and half-sister to 3
winners, including smart winner up to 1½m Change The World (2-y-o 9f winner, by
Sakhee): dam 1m-1¼m winner: fair performer: won nursery at Chelmsford in October:
stays 1m: acts on polytrack and good to firm going: front runner/races prominently.
Charles Hills

MISS POPOV 2 b.f. (Apr 30) Monsieur Bond (IRE) 120 – Priti Fabulous (IRE) 92 **38**
(Invincible Spirit (IRE) 121) [2015 5m 6g 5d⁶ 6f Nov 10] 3,500Y: third foal: half-sister to
7f winner Myboydaniel (by Myboycharlie): dam, 7f/1m winner, half-sister to useful 2-y-o
5.5f/6f winner Black Amber: poor maiden: stays 6f. *Noel Wilson*

MISS RANGER (IRE) 3 gr.f. Bushranger (IRE) 119 – Remiss (IRE) (Indian Ridge 123) **70**
[2015 61: 7g 8m 9.5m⁵ 9.3m³ 8.3g* 9.2d⁴ 9.3g² 9.9d² p10f* Oct 8] fair handicapper: won
at Hamilton (apprentice) in August and Chelmsford in October: left Cecil Ross after third
start: stays 1¼m: acts on polytrack, good to soft and good to firm going: tried in tongue tie
in 2015. *John Wainwright*

MISS RUBY ROYALE 3 ch.f. Monsieur Bond (IRE) 120 – Amoureuse 54 (Needwood **–**
Blade 117) [2015 –: 6g 6g 5f Jul 3] no form. *Paul Midgley*

MISSTEMPER (IRE) 4 b.f. Diamond Green (FR) 121 – Legnani 75 (Fasliyev (USA) **53**
120) [2015 72: p6f p6f³ p6m 6m 6m t7.1g⁵ p6g t6g 7g p6g Aug 22] angular filly: modest **a62**
handicapper: best effort at 6f: acts on fibresand: often wears headgear: often races lazily.
Jose Santos

MISS TEMPLE CITY (USA) 3 b.f. Temple City (USA) – Glittering Tax (USA) (Artax **115**
(USA) 126) [2015 8f³ 8g² 8.5f* 8f⁴ 9g³ 9f² Oct 10] well-made filly: fifth foal: half-
sister to 3 winners: dam US 5f and (including at 2 yrs) 6.5f winner: smart performer: won
non-graded event at Pimlico in May: good efforts 3 of last 4 starts, in Coronation Stakes at
Royal Ascot (2 lengths fourth to Ervedya), Grade 2 Lake Placid Stakes at Saratoga (1¼
lengths second to Sentiero Italia) and Queen Elizabeth II Challenge Cup at Keeneland

(looked unlucky loser when head second to Her Emmynency, hampered and losing momentum over 1f out, finishing strongly): stays 9f: acts on firm going: has worn tongue tie. *H. Graham Motion, USA*

MISS UNDERSTOOD (IRE) 3 b.f. Excellent Art 125 – Puck's Castle 92 (Shirley **83** Heights 130) [2015 64: p10f* Dec 17] fairly useful handicapper: upped in trip, much improved when winning at Chelmsford on only outing in 2015: stays 1¼m: acts on polytrack and good to soft going. *David Simcock*

MISS UPPITY 2 ch.f. (Mar 14) Notnowcato 128 – Instructress 66 (Diktat 126) [2015 5g3 **50** p5g6 p6g Dec 16] first foal: dam unreliable 5f winner (including at 2 yrs): modest form first 2 starts in maidens. *Robert Cowell*

MISS VAN GOGH 3 b.f. Dutch Art 126 – Accede 88 (Acclamation 118) [2015 67: 8.3d2 **89** 8d* 8d* 8m5 10g 8.3d2 8d* Oct 30] workmanlike filly: fairly useful handicapper: first past the post at Hamilton in May (demoted to second after causing interference), Ripon in June, Haydock in July and Newmarket in October: stays 8.5f: acts on soft going: tried in visor prior to 2015: usually races close up. *Richard Fahey*

MISS VICTORY (IRE) 2 b.f. (Apr 26) Mount Nelson 125 – Wars (IRE) 60 (Green **38** Desert (USA) 127) [2015 6.1m 5.7m6 p6d p6g4 p6f5 p6d t8.6f5 f7g Dec 18] half-sister to several winners, including winner up to 6f Deeds Not Words (by Royal Applause) and winner up to 1m Heroes (2-y-o 7f winner, by Diktat), both useful: dam maiden sister to very smart winner up to 8.5f Gabr: poor maiden: stays 6f: acts on polytrack and good to firm going. *Mark Usher*

MISSY BLUE EYES 2 b.g. (Mar 21) Kyllachy 129 – Sapphire Bracelet (IRE) 77 **83** (Sadler's Wells (USA) 132) [2015 6.1d3 6d* 7s2 p7g3 6s6 Oct 23] 30,000F, 18,000 2-y-o: second foal: dam, lightly raced, closely related to useful 12.5f/13f winner Quel Avantage out of smart 2-y-o 7f winner Necklace: fairly useful performer: won maiden at Windsor in August: better form when placed in 2 nurseries after: will stay 1m: acts on polytrack and soft going. *William Muir*

MISS YORK 2 ch.f. (May 2) Monsieur Bond (IRE) 120 – Knavesmire (IRE) 91 (One Cool **–** Cat (USA) 123) [2015 5g 6g Sep 19] £800Y: second foal: dam 2-y-o 5f winner: well held in maidens. *Antony Brittain*

MISTAKEN LADY 2 b.f. (Mar 30) Multiplex 114 – Sharoura 90 (Inchinor 119) [2015 **–** 5m 6m p6g5 5d5 p6g4 Jul 22] sixth foal: dam 5f-7f winner: no form: often in headgear. *Jo Hughes*

MISTAMEL (IRE) 3 b.g. Rip Van Winkle (IRE) 134 – Without Precedent (FR) (Polish **75** Precedent (USA) 131) [2015 74p: p8g 8.3f6 8d5 8d6 12.1d3 11.7f* 11.9s2 16d2 13.1f5 11.6d6 Oct 12] fair handicapper: won at Bath in August: stays 2m: acts on firm and soft going: usually in headgear in 2015. *Eve Johnson Houghton*

MISTER ARCHIE 3 b.g. Archipenko (USA) 127 – Zooming (IRE) (Indian Ridge 123) **–** [2015 –: 9.2gpu Jun 17] poor maiden: dead. *Alistair Whillans*

MISTERAY 5 ch.g. Singspiel (IRE) 133 – Hannda (IRE) 74 (Dr Devious (IRE) 127) [2015 **47** 16m5 Aug 10] poor maiden: best effort at 2m: acts on good to firm going: usually wears tongue tie. *Bill Turner*

MISTER BOB (GER) 6 ch.g. Black Sam Bellamy (IRE) 121 – Mosquera (GER) 108 **76** (Acatenango (GER) 127) [2015 83: t16.5g2 Jan 23] fair handicapper: stays 16.5f: acts on all-weather: usually wears headgear: races towards rear. *James Bethell*

MISTER BRIGHTSIDE (IRE) 3 b.c. Lord Shanakill (USA) 121 – Lamh Eile (IRE) 93 **106** (Lend A Hand 124) [2015 80: 8.3g2 7.6g2 6g* 7m* 6g3 7g* 7m3 9f2 9f 8f6 Dec 26] sturdy colt: useful performer: won maiden at Lingfield in June then handicaps at Newmarket in July and August, last-named by 2 lengths from Easy Tiger: placed next 2 starts, in handicap at Doncaster (½-length third to Sulaalaat) and Grade 2 Twilight Derby at Santa Anita (good 2¼ lengths second to Om): effort best forgiven when ninth to Chiropractor in Hollywood Derby at Del Mar on penultimate start, never really getting any room to challenge and not persevered with: left Jeremy Noseda, respectable 7¼ lengths sixth to Om in Grade 2 Mathis Brothers Mile at Santa Anita final outing: stays 9f: acts on firm going: often travels strongly. *Patrick Gallagher, USA*

MISTER FIZZ 7 b.g. Sulamani (IRE) 130 – Court Champagne (Batshoof 122) [2015 94: **83** 12msu 14.1s5 12m 13.3s4 16d Oct 11] fairly useful handicapper: stays 1¾m: acts on polytrack, soft and good to firm going: tried in cheekpieces in 2015: front runner/races prominently: useful hurdler. *Miss Imogen Pickard*

MISTER GREEN (FR) 9 b.g. Green Desert (USA) 127 – Summertime Legacy 109 **44**
(Darshaan 133) [2015 –: t7.1f p12f⁶ p7f t8.6f p8f p8f t8.6g p11f p5g p10g p11g p12g⁵
p12g⁶ p7g 7g p6f p10f Sep 17] good-topped gelding: poor handicapper: stays 1¼m: acts on
polytrack, soft and good to firm going: often wears headgear: often wears tongue tie: often
starts slowly. *David Flood*

MISTERIOSO (IRE) 3 b.c. Iffraaj 127 – Roystonea (Polish Precedent (USA) 131) [2015 **97**
93: p8g⁵ 7m² 7f⁵ 8m 7.6m 8m⁵ 7d 7m⁶ 7d⁵ Sep 26] rangy colt: useful handicapper: second
at Doncaster (¾ length behind Realtra) in May: stays 1m: acts on polytrack and good to
firm going: in blinkers last 4 starts. *Richard Hannon*

MISTER MARCASITE 5 gr.g. Verglas (IRE) 118 – No Rehearsal (FR) (Baillamont **66**
(USA) 124) [2015 70, a58: t12.2g² t12.2f² t12.2m⁴ t12.2g⁶ t13.9g³ Jul 8] fair handicapper:
will benefit from return to 1½m: acts on tapeta, good to firm and heavy going: tried in visor
prior to 2015: front runner/races prominently. *Antony Brittain*

MISTER MAYDAY (IRE) 4 br.g. Kheleyf (USA) 116 – Soxy Doxy (IRE) 51 (Hawk **83**
Wing (USA) 136) [2015 77, a66: 8.3m 10g³ 9d* 10.2m³ 10.1m 10.2d⁴ 8d² 8.3s* 8.3d Oct
5] sturdy gelding: fairly useful handicapper: won at Lingfield in June and Leicester in
September: stays 1¼m: acts on good to firm and heavy going: often wears headgear:
usually races nearer last than first. *George Baker*

MISTER MISCHIEF 2 b.g. (Jan 13) Makfi 130 – Bluebelle Dancer (IRE) 70 (Danehill **72 p**
Dancer (IRE) 117) [2015 6s³ 6g² Aug 15] 16,000F, €11,000Y: fourth foal: half-brother to
6f-1m winner Moody Dancer (by Cape Cross): dam, maiden (stayed 1m), half-sister to
useful 6f winner Catch A Glimpse: fair form when placed in maidens at Redcar and Ripon:
will be suited by 7f+: remains with potential. *Paul Midgley*

MISTER MUSIC 6 b.g. Singspiel (IRE) 133 – Sierra 65 (Dr Fong (USA) 128) [2015 91: **90**
8d 8m 7s⁴ 8f 8g* 10m⁴ 9s⁶ 10s 8d⁵ Oct 11] attractive gelding: fairly useful handicapper:
won at Goodwood in July: stays 1¼m: acts on any turf going: usually wears headgear:
often races towards rear. *Robert Eddery*

MISTER MUSICMASTER 6 b.g. Amadeus Wolf 122 – Misty Eyed (IRE) 112 (Paris **91**
House 123) [2015 86: p6g t7.1g² 8m* 7d⁴ 8m* 8g³ 8m 8f⁵ 8.3m⁶ t7.1m⁴ Sep 5] compact **a81**
gelding: fairly useful handicapper: won at Bath in May and Newbury in June: stays 1m:
acts on polytrack, firm and soft going: tried in blinkers prior to 2015. *Ron Hodges*

MISTER PARMA (IRE) 2 ch.c. (Apr 29) Iffraaj 127 – Annee Lumiere (IRE) (Giant's **–**
Causeway (USA) 132) [2015 p8m Oct 21] 25/1, green when seventh of 8 in maiden at
Kempton: sent to UAE. *Ian Williams*

MISTER ROCKANDROLL 3 b.g. Rock of Gibraltar (IRE) 133 – Cruel Sea (USA) 94 **87**
(Mizzen Mast (USA) 121) [2015 77: p12f² p10g* 12.1m⁵ 9.9m² 10.2s⁴ 11.7m⁴ 11.5g⁴ 12g⁵
10.1g² 9.9m³ 11.9g* 11.5m* 9.9g⁵ 14.1m³ 13.7g³ 12g Oct 9] close-coupled gelding: fairly
useful performer: won maiden at Chelmsford in March and handicaps at Brighton and
Carlisle in August: stays 1¾m: acts on polytrack and good to firm going: tried in headgear
in 2015: front runner/races prominently: sold 24,000 gns, sent to Saudi Arabia.
Mark Johnston

MISTER UNIVERSE 3 br.c. Cape Cross (IRE) 129 – Miss Ivanhoe (IRE) 107 (Selkirk **107**
(USA) 129) [2015 94: 8s 8.1d⁵ 7m* 7g⁵ 7g² 7f 8.1m 7m² 7g⁶ 7m Oct 3] sturdy colt: useful
performer: won handicap at Ascot (by 2 lengths from Capel Path) in May: second in listed
race at Epsom (1¼ lengths behind Code Red) and handicap at Newbury (length behind
Windfast): stays 7f: acts on firm and good to soft going. *Mark Johnston*

MISTER UNO (IRE) 4 b.c. Tamayuz 126 – Starlight Smile (USA) (Green Dancer (USA) **64 §**
132) [2015 72: 10.1d 10.2m⁶ 9.9v⁵ 9.9m⁵ 10g t12.2g⁴ 12g⁶ 12.2m⁶ 12.1m Aug 13] modest
handicapper: stays 13f: acts on tapeta, good to firm going: often wears headgear:
tried in tongue tie in 2015: not one to rely on. *Ann Duffield*

MISTER YORK 3 b.g. Monsieur Bond (IRE) 120 – Knavesmire (IRE) 91 (One Cool Cat **–**
(USA) 123) [2015 60: 7.5m Jul 20] modest maiden: best effort at 5f: acts on good to firm
going. *Antony Brittain*

MISTER ZOFF (FR) 2 b.c. (Mar 2) Zoffany (IRE) 121 – Maureenda (FR) (Shamardal **38**
(USA) 129) [2015 6g 7m 7m⁶ 7.2g⁴ 8g Sep 23] poor maiden: stays 7f: acts on good to firm
going: sold 8,000 gns, sent to Switzerland. *Richard Fahey*

MISTIROC 4 br.g. Rocamadour 116 – Mistinguett (IRE) 77 (Doyoun 124) [2015 96p: 14s **97**
12.1s⁴ 10.4m² 10m⁵ 12m 10d⁴ 12d 10.4d⁵ 10g* 9g 12d² 12v⁴ Nov 7] useful handicapper:
won by 1¼ lengths from Salieris Mass at Ayr in September: second at York (1½ lengths
behind Donny Rover) in June and Doncaster (½ length behind Argus) in October: stays
1½m: acts on good to firm and good to soft going: often in cheekpieces in 2015. *Jim Goldie*

MISTRAL 3 b.f. Multiplex 114 – Song of The Desert (Desert Sun 120) [2015 56: t7.1m p8f   **47**
10.2m 12f⁵ t13.9g⁵ 12.1m⁴ 14.1m t12.2f Sep 19] smallish filly: poor maiden: stays 1¾m:
acts on tapeta and good to firm going: usually wears hood: often races prominently.
Steph Hollinshead

MISTRUSTING (IRE) 3 b.f. Shamardal (USA) 129 – Misheer 109 (Oasis Dream 129)   **110**
[2015 85p: 6m² 7g* 7d* 7m 6g* Oct 10] sturdy filly: smart performer: progressed well in
2015 and won handicaps at Newmarket (by 2½ lengths from Wordcraft) and York (by neck
from Dusky Queen) in August and listed race at Newmarket (by 1½ lengths from Terror) in
October: stays 7f: acts on good to soft going. *Charlie Appleby*

MISTRY 2 b.f. (Apr 29) Mullionmileanhour (IRE) 116 – Smart Ass (IRE) 91 (Shinko   **–**
Forest (IRE)) [2015 p7g Oct 7] half-sister to several winners, including useful 2-y-o 6f/7f
winner Miracle of Medinah (by Milk It Mick) and 2-y-o 6f winner Al Gharrafa (by Dutch
Art): dam 7f/1m winner: 66/1, down the field in maiden at Kempton, slowly away.
Mark Usher

MISTY EYES 6 b.m. Byron 117 – Wax Eloquent 67 (Zaha (CAN) 106) [2015 42: t6f Jan   **–**
16] poor maiden: best effort at 7f: acts on polytrack: wears headgear. *Geoffrey Harker*

MISTYMOISTYMORNING (IRE) 2 gr.f. (Mar 17) Alhaarth (IRE) 126 – Bermuxa   **74**
(FR) 60 (Linamix (FR) 127) [2015 f5g² 5d² f5d³ 7.5g* 7d⁴ 8m⁶ p8f Oct 10] €14,000Y:
fourth foal: half-sister to useful winner up to 1m Intermix (2-y-o 7.5f winner, by Intikhab):
dam maiden sister to 7f-15.5f winner Miraculous and winner up to 13.5f Bernimixa, both
smart: fair performer: won maiden at Beverley in July: stays 7.5f: acts on fibresand and
good to soft going: front runner/races prominently. *Mark Johnston*

MISTY SECRET (IRE) 5 b.m. Clodovil (IRE) 116 – Villafranca (IRE) (In The Wings   **–**
128) [2015 t8.6f t7.1f p10g⁴ p10f p8f Mar 19] narrow mare: poor maiden: in headgear last
4 starts. *Lisa Williamson*

MISU MAC 5 b.m. Misu Bond (IRE) 114 – Umbrian Gold (IRE) 83 (Perugino (USA) 84)   **77**
[2015 –: f8g f6g* f6g² f5g* f6g* f6d* May 18] fair performer: won maiden in March and
3 handicaps in April/May, all at Southwell: stays 6f: acts on fibresand: usually travels
strongly. *Neville Bycroft*

MISU MONEYPENNY 2 b.f. (May 2) Misu Bond (IRE) 114 – Watersilk (IRE) (Fasliyev   **68**
(USA) 120) [2015 f5d* f5g⁶ 5g³ p5f* 5.1d⁴ p5f⁴ Nov 19] £800Y: fourth foal: closely
related to 5f winner Crosse Fire (by Monsieur Bond): dam unraced out of useful 2-y-o 6f
winner Dances With Dreams: fair performer: won maiden at Southwell in May and nursery
at Chelmsford in September: likely to prove best at bare 5f: acts on polytrack and fibresand:
front runner/races prominently. *Scott Dixon*

MISU PETE 3 b.g. Misu Bond (IRE) 114 – Smart Ass (IRE) 91 (Shinko Forest (IRE))   **66**
[2015 –: p6g* p6f³ t6f⁶ p7g² t7.1f² Dec 22] fair handicapper: won at Kempton in January:
stays 7f: acts on polytrack and tapeta: tried in visor prior to 2015: often races prominently.
Mark Usher

MITCHUM 6 b.g. Elnadim (USA) 128 – Maid To Matter (Pivotal 124) [2015 62: 7m⁶ 8d   **53**
7g⁶ 8s⁴ 6g² 5s⁵ Oct 6] close-coupled gelding: modest handicapper: stays 1m: acts on
fibresand, good to firm and heavy going: usually wears headgear. *Ron Barr*

MITCHUM SWAGGER 3 b.g. Paco Boy (IRE) 129 – Dont Dili Dali 102 (Dansili 127)   **115 p**
[2015 7g* 8d* 8d² 8d² Oct 31] 40,000F, 46,000Y: useful-looking gelding: third foal: half-
brother to 13f winner Surrey Storm (by Montjeu) and useful 12.2f-14.5f winner Andry
Brusselles (by Hurricane Run): dam, 1m winner (including at 2 yrs) who barely stayed
1½m, sister to useful 7f-8.3f winner Balducci: smart performer: won maiden at Newbury
(by head from Time Flies) in May and handicap at Haydock (by 1½ lengths from Ghinia)
in September: improved again when head second to Big Baz in listed race at Newmarket
final start: will stay 1¼m: will continue to progress. *David Lanigan*

MITHQAAL (USA) 2 ch.c. (Mar 15) Speightstown (USA) 124 – Bestowal (USA)   **52**
(Unbridled's Song (USA) 125) [2015 6.5m 6m⁴ p7g Nov 4] modest maiden: best effort
when fourth at Leicester (8 lengths behind Academy House) in June. *B. W. Hills*

MITRAAD (IRE) 4 ch.g. Aqlaam 125 – Badweia (USA) 83 (Kingmambo (USA) 125)   **111 p**
[2015 8m* p8g² Aug 4] neat gelding: smart form: won handicap at Newmarket in July by
length from Express Himself: 6/5, improved and looked unlucky not to win when
½-length second to Hakka in handicap at Chelmsford, finishing well after meeting trouble
home turn: stays 1m: should progress further. *William Haggas*

MITRE PEAK 3 ch.f. Shamardal (USA) 129 – Milford Sound (Barathea (IRE) 127) [2015   **85**
p9.4g³ 10.4g³ 8g³ 8.4g⁴ p7.5g³ 8s⁴ f7g² Dec 29] second foal: half-sister to 10.5f winner
(stays 15f) Quebec (by Dansili): dam, 1m winner, half-sister to Prix de l'Arc de Triomphe

winner Rail Link: fairly useful form in maidens and minor event in France for P. Bary: below-form second in maiden event at Southwell on British debut, finding less than looked likely: stays 10.5f: acts on polytrack and soft going. *Richard Fahey*

MIX AND MINGLE (IRE) 2 ch.f. (Feb 25) Exceed And Excel (AUS) 126 – Mango Lady 80 (Dalakhani (IRE) 133) [2015 7g³ 7.6g* 7g* Oct 10] rather unfurnished filly: third foal: sister to 7f winner Semai and half-sister to 9.5f/1¼m winner May Queen (by Shamardal): dam, 1½m winner, closely related to very smart winner up to 1½m (stayed 1¾m) High Accolade: quickly developed into a useful performer and won maiden at Lingfield (by 3¾ lengths from Heartstone) in September and nursery at Newmarket in October, quickening to lead final 1f when beating Summer Icon 1¼ lengths in latter: will stay 1m: open to further improvement. *Chris Wall* — **100 p**

MIXED MESSAGE (IRE) 5 b.m. Kodiac 112 – Berenica (IRE) 101 (College Chapel 122) [2015 76: 10.2m 10.2m 14g 10m 10s⁴ t9.5f Nov 20] small mare: modest handicapper: stays 1¼m: acts on fibresand, good to firm and heavy going: tried in headgear: often races towards rear. *Mandy Rowland* — **52**

MIXOLOGY (IRE) 2 b.c. (Feb 8) Cape Cross (IRE) 129 – Margarita (IRE) 72 (Marju (IRE) 127) [2015 7d 6g⁵ 7.2g⁵ 7d⁴ Oct 16] fair form in maiden and nursery last 2 starts: will stay 1m: sold 12,000 gns, sent to Italy. *Mark Johnston* — **71**

MIZZEN HEAD (IRE) 3 b.g. Fastnet Rock (AUS) 127 – Chaussons (IRE) 68 (Indian Ridge 123) [2015 8.1f⁴ Jul 23] 9/1, looked in need of experience when last of 4 in maiden at Sandown, very slowly away. *Brian Meehan* — **–**

MIZZOU (IRE) 4 b.c. Galileo (IRE) 134 – Moments of Joy 113 (Darshaan 133) [2015 114p: 16f* 20f 16.4d² Aug 21] attractive colt: smart performer: won Sagaro Stakes at Ascot in April by 2 lengths from Vent de Force: creditable efforts both subsequent starts, when 3½ lengths seventh of 12 to Trip To Paris in Gold Cup at Royal Ascot and 4½ lengths second of 8 to Max Dynamite in Lonsdale Cup at York: stays 2½m: acts on firm and soft going: usually races towards rear. *Luca Cumani* — **117**

MOBSTA (IRE) 3 b.c. Bushranger (IRE) 119 – Sweet Nicole 54 (Okawango (USA) 115) [2015 94p: 5d³ 7s² 7d⁴ 6d* 6v Nov 7] tall, useful-looking colt: useful performer: won minor event at Newmarket (by neck from Apache Storm) in October: good second of 7 to Wet Sail in similar contest at Salisbury earlier, and better than result when eighth of 14 to Jack Dexter in listed race at Doncaster final start (not clear run from over 1f out): effective at 6f/7f: best form on soft/heavy going. *Mick Channon* — **104**

MOCCASIN (FR) 6 b.g. Green Tune (USA) 125 – Museum Piece (Rainbow Quest (USA) 134) [2015 82: f12s⁴ t12.2f³ t12.2f* 12.5s⁵ 9g* 9.8v³ 9.9m⁴ 10s 9.3g⁵ 10m⁵ 10.4g 10g* 10.2g 10.3d t12.2f t9.5f t12.2f Dec 22] fairly useful handicapper: won at Wolverhampton in March, Wetherby in April and Redcar in September: stays 1¾m: acts on polytrack, tapeta, good to firm and heavy going: tried in headgear. *Geoffrey Harker* — **80 a70**

MOCKINBIRD (IRE) 2 b.f. (Mar 27) Makfi 130 – Littlefeather (IRE) 107 (Indian Ridge 123) [2015 p6g³ p7f² Dec 17] half-sister to several winners, including 6f winner Bee Eater (by Green Desert) and 2-y-o 6.7f winner Expedition (by Oasis Dream), both useful: dam, 5f/6f winner (including at 2 yrs), half-sister to very smart miler Marling: better effort when second in maiden at Chelmsford (neck behind Silk Gem) in December: sticking to task: open to further improvement. *Sir Mark Prescott Bt* — **67 p**

MOCKINGBIRD HILL 3 b.g. Cockney Rebel (IRE) 127 – Claws 63 (Marju (IRE) 127) [2015 7d² 6v⁵ 7m³ t8.6g⁵ Jul 8] fair maiden: best effort on debut: stays 7f. *Tim Easterby* — **76**

MODELLO (IRE) 2 b.f. (Apr 1) Intikhab (USA) 135 – Precious Citizen (USA) 57 (Proud Citizen (USA) 122) [2015 6m 8.3m³ 8.5v² p8m⁴ 8.3g⁶ t8.6f Nov 30] €65,000Y: third foal: half-sister to useful winner up to 1¼m Bronze Maquette (2-y-o 5f-7f winner, by Dark Angel): dam maiden: fair maiden: left Gary Moore after fifth start: stays 8.5f: acts on good to firm and heavy going: tried in cheekpieces. *Giles Bravery* — **65**

MODERAH 3 b.f. Makfi 130 – Meetyouthere (IRE) (Sadler's Wells (USA) 132) [2015 –p: 10.3m⁵ 11.8s* 12v³ Oct 24] useful performer: won maiden at Leicester (by 5 lengths from Champagne Ceri) in September: improved again when 2 lengths third of 9 to Koora in St Simon Stakes at Newbury: stays 1½m. *James Fanshawe* — **103**

MODERNISM 6 b.g. Monsun (GER) 124 – La Nuit Rose (FR) 109 (Rainbow Quest (USA) 134) [2015 97: 10.3s 12m* 12m⁶ 12g⁶ 11.5g⁶ 10.3g² 12.3g⁴ 9.9m² 10.4g⁵ 10.4d 12.2f p10m⁴ p10g³ p10g* Dec 20] sturdy gelding: fairly useful handicapper: won at Pontefract in May and Lingfield (by ½ length from Giantstepsahead) in December: stays 12.5f: acts on polytrack and firm going: tried in cheekpieces prior to 2015. *Richard Fahey* — **91**

MODERN TUTOR 6 b.g. Selkirk (USA) 129 – Magical Romance (IRE) 110 (Barathea **77**
(IRE) 127) [2015 86: p7g p6m 6m p6g³ p6g 7.4g⁶ p10.7g Dec 4] well-made gelding: fair
handicapper: left Andrew Balding after sixth start: stays 8.5f: acts on polytrack, soft and
good to firm going: often wears hood: sometimes in tongue tie in 2015. *J. J. Lambe, Ireland*

MODEST 2 b.f. (Mar 24) Kyllachy 129 – Coy (IRE) 112 (Danehill (USA) 126) [2015 6m³ **76**
5.1m⁶ 6m⁵ 5m⁵ p6g² 6s* 5g² 6v Nov 7] 28,000Y: sturdy filly: closely related to 3 winners
by Pivotal, including winner up to 9f Resolute (2-y-o 7f winner) and 1m winner What
Asham: dam, winner up to 1m (2-y-o 6f winner), half-sister to smart winner up to 1m Il
Warrd: fair performer: won nursery at Catterick in October: stays 6f: acts on soft going.
Michael Bell

MOHAB 2 b.c. (Feb 23) Sir Percy 129 – Princess Aurora (USA) (Mr Greeley (USA) 122) **99**
[2015 7m³ 7m* 7d⁵ 7m³ Sep 11] 28,000Y, 90,000 2-y-o: second foal: dam unraced: useful
form: won maiden at Catterick (by 8 lengths from Hollywood Ken) in August: similar form
both subsequent starts, when fifth of 10 to Recorder in Acomb Stakes at York and 2½
lengths third of 6 to Tashweeq in listed race at Doncaster: will stay 1m. *Kevin Ryan*

MOHAIR 6 b.m. Motivator 131 – Cashmere 86 (Barathea (IRE) 127) [2015 45: t12.2m –
t12.2f t9.5f t16.5g Apr 10] workmanlike mare: maiden: no form in 2015: wears headgear:
often races towards rear. *Steph Hollinshead*

MOHATEM (USA) 3 ch.c. Distorted Humor (USA) 117 – Soul Search (USA) 116 (A P **82**
Indy (USA) 131) [2015 90p: 10g 10m May 16] attractive, rather unfurnished colt: fairly
useful handicapper, very lightly raced: stays 1¼m. *B. W. Hills*

MOHAWK RIDGE 9 b.g. Storming Home 128 – Ipsa Loquitur 69 (Unfuwain (USA) –
131) [2015 14.1v Nov 3] leggy, useful-looking gelding: fairly useful handicapper in 2013
for Michael Dods: well held only outing on Flat since: stays 17.5f: acts on polytrack, good
to firm and heavy going: has worn cheekpieces. *James Moffatt*

MOHEET (IRE) 3 b.c. High Chaparral (IRE) 132 – Abunai 100 (Pivotal 124) [2015 92P: **104 p**
8g³ 8m 12m 8m⁶ Jul 31] strong, well-made colt: type to carry plenty of condition: useful
performer: best efforts in 2015 at Newmarket first 2 starts, finishing 3¼ lengths third to
Kool Kompany in Craven Stakes and 2¾ lengths eighth of 18 to Gleneagles in 2000
Guineas: not seen to best effect when sixth of 10 to Malabar in Thoroughbred Stakes at
Goodwood final start, short of room throughout: should be suited by further than 1m (never
a threat last at 1½m in Derby at Epsom): acts on good to firm going: usually races nearer
last than first: remains open to improvement. *Richard Hannon*

MO HENRY 3 b.g. Monsieur Bond (IRE) 120 – Mo Mhuirnin (IRE) 94 (Danetime (IRE) **72**
121) [2015 81: 5g⁶ 6g⁴ 6d⁵ 6m⁵ t7.1g² 6g³ t7.1g⁴ 6m⁵ t6f Sep 19] fairly useful handicapper: **a80**
stays 7f: acts on tapeta and good to firm going: tried in cheekpieces in 2015: front runner/
races prominently. *Richard Whitaker*

MOI AUSSIE 2 gr.f. (Apr 19) Aussie Rules (USA) 123 – Oceana Blue 89 (Reel Buddy **56**
(USA) 118) [2015 7m⁵ 7.5s⁴ p7f t7.1m p7g Oct 6] third foal: closely related to 6f/7f winner
Gold Club (by Multiplex): dam 6f/7f winner: modest maiden: will prove best up to 7f: acts
on soft and good to firm going. *Ed McMahon*

MOIETY 4 b.f. Myboycharlie (IRE) 118 – Millinsky (USA) 85 (Stravinsky (USA) 133) **66**
[2015 72: p6g³ p6f Feb 11] fair performer: raced only at 6f: acts on polytrack: has worn
tongue tie: sent to Belgium. *Rae Guest*

MOJAWIZ 3 b.g. Dubawi (IRE) 129 – Zayn Zen 107 (Singspiel (IRE) 133) [2015 76: **71 §**
p10t⁴ p8g³ Feb 4] fair maiden: stays 1¼m: acts on polytrack, tapeta and good to soft going:
sometimes wears cheekpieces: temperamental. *Charlie Appleby*

MOJOLATION 2 b.f. (Mar 2) Stimulation (IRE) 121 – Demolition Jo 89 (Petong 126) –
[2015 6d 6d⁶ Sep 15] £2,500Y: half-sister to 3 winners, including 5f winner Select
Committee (by Fayruz) and 10.5f-1¼m winner (including in Belgium) Zinnobar (by
Ishiguru): dam 6f/7f winner (including at 2 yrs): no form. *Edwin Tuer*

MOLANS MARE (IRE) 5 ch.m. Shirocco (GER) 129 – Devious Diva (IRE) 94 (Dr –
Devious (IRE) 127) [2015 t8.6f Nov 3] poor form in maidens/handicap in 2013: left C.
Moore/off 26 months, well held in minor event at Wolverhampton: best effort at 1¾m: acts
on good to soft going. *Emmet Michael Butterly, Ireland*

MOLIVIAS GEM 2 b.f. (Mar 26) Baltic King 120 – Mississippi Millie (IRE) (Tagula **53**
(IRE) 116) [2015 6m⁶ 6g 6.1v³ 6s 5d⁶ Oct 26] second foal: dam unraced half-sister to smart
7f winner Glen Moss: modest maiden: best effort at 6f: acts on soft going. *David Thompson*

MOLIVIAS LAD 4 b.g. Monsieur Bond (IRE) 120 – Mississippi Millie (IRE) (Tagula **52**
(IRE) 116) [2015 12m 10g 7.9g⁵ 7g⁶ 6s t6f Nov 20] modest maiden: best effort at 6f: acts
on soft going. *David Thompson*

MOLLASSES 4 b.f. Authorized (IRE) 133 – Muscovado (USA) 71 (Mr Greeley (USA) **74**
122) [2015 76: p12f³ Sep 12] sturdy filly: fair maiden: likely to stay 1¼m: acts on
polytrack, soft and good to firm going: tried in hood prior to 2015. *Harry Whittington*

MOLLIE'S GIRL (IRE) 2 b.f. (Apr 17) Elusive Pimpernel (USA) 117 – Ebony Star **73**
(Desert Prince (IRE) 130) [2015 p6g⁶ 5s⁴ p6g f7g* f8m⁶ f8g² Dec 29] €12,000Y: fourth
foal: half-sister to Italian 7.5f/1m winner Leis An Athair (by Indian Haven): dam, unraced,
closely related to smart winner up to 1m Yamal: fair performer: won nursery at Southwell
in November: stays 1m: acts on fibresand. *Michael Appleby*

MOLLY APPROVE (IRE) 3 b.f. Approve (IRE) 112 – Kathleen Rafferty (IRE) (Marju **55**
(IRE) 127) [2015 –: 6m 7d³ f6d⁶ 6g 8g 7g³ 5s 7d Oct 26] modest maiden: stays 7f: acts on
good to soft going: often races prominently. *Tony Coyle*

MOLLY CAT 5 ch.m. Dylan Thomas (IRE) 132 – Pentatonic 100 (Giant's Causeway **68**
(USA) 132) [2015 77: p10f⁴ p10g⁶ 12.1v Aug 25] fair maiden: stays 12.5f: acts on
polytrack, good to firm and good to soft going. *Neil Mulholland*

MOLLY DOLLY (IRE) 3 b.f. Exceed And Excel (AUS) 126 – Garra Molly (IRE) 77 **101**
(Nayef (USA) 129) [2015 p7g* 7.6m* 7m³ 8s³ 8.1m 9.2s Sep 27] tall, lengthy filly: second
foal: half-sister to 2-y-o 7f winner Dr Phibes (by Dr Fong), later successful in New
Zealand: dam, maiden (stayed 1¾m), closely related to smart winner up to 1m Swift
Gulliver: useful performer: won maiden at Kempton in January and handicap at Chester
(apprentice) in June: best effort when third in listed race at Ascot (2 lengths behind Evita
Peron) in July: stays 1m: acts on polytrack, soft and good to firm going: tried in cheekpieces:
usually slowly away. *Sir Mark Prescott Bt*

MOLLYOW (IRE) 7 ch.m. Iceman 117 – Corryvreckan (IRE) 70 (Night Shift (USA)) **47**
[2015 –: 116.5g⁶ Feb 9] smallish mare: poor handicapper: stays 17f: acts on polytrack, soft
and good to firm going: tried in headgear prior to 2015. *Dai Burchell*

MOLTEN GOLD 2 b.c. (Mar 29) New Approach (IRE) 132 – Flash of Gold 76 (Darshaan **– p**
133) [2015 8g Oct 21] rather unfurnished colt: closely related to useful winner up to 2m
Moidore (2-y-o 8.3f winner, by Galileo) and half-brother to several winners, including
useful winner up to 1½m Mustard (2-y-o 1m winner, by Motivator): dam, maiden (stayed
1½m), half-sister to smart winner up to 13f Phantom Gold: 25/1, badly needed experience
when ninth of 12 in maiden at Newmarket, not knocked about: should do better in time.
Andrew Balding

MOLTEN LAVA (IRE) 3 b.g. Rock of Gibraltar (IRE) 133 – Skehana (IRE) 69 **82**
(Mukaddamah (USA) 125) [2015 69: p10g⁵ p8g⁴ 8m² p10g⁵ 8.3m* 8.3m* p11g⁶ p8m⁶
p10g p8g Dec 7] tall gelding: fairly useful handicapper: won at Windsor (by head from Hot
Mustard) in July and Leicester in August: stays 8.5f: acts on good to firm going: often races
freely. *Paul Cole*

MOMENT TO DREAM 3 b.f. Halling (USA) 133 – Pretty Majestic (IRE) 92 (Invincible **59**
Spirit (IRE) 121) [2015 8g p8g⁶ t9.5f⁵ Oct 27] £5,500 2-y-o: sturdy filly: fourth foal: half-
sister to 1m winner Gold Falcon (by Iffraaj): dam 2-y-o 6f winner: modest maiden: best
effort when fifth at Wolverhampton. *Julia Feilden*

MOMENTUS (IRE) 4 b.f. Montjeu (IRE) 137 – Race For The Stars (USA) 113 (Fusaichi **98**
Pegasus (USA) 130) [2015 99: 12m 10.2m⁵ 11.9g 12g⁵ 9.9g⁴ 11.9g Oct 7] big, good-
looking filly: useful performer: stays 1½m: acts on good to firm and heavy going: front
runner/races prominently. *David Simcock*

MONACO ROSE 2 b.f. (Apr 3) Sir Percy 129 – Pallas (Statue of Liberty (USA) 115) **64**
[2015 8.3g 8s³ Oct 15] 17,000Y: second foal: dam unraced half-sister to dam of smart
performer up to 1m Trumpet Major: better effort when third in maiden at Brighton (3
lengths behind Albe Back) in October. *Richard Fahey*

MONALEEN (IRE) 4 b.f. High Chaparral (IRE) 132 – Dawn Air (USA) 53 (Diesis 133) **91**
[2015 p10f² t9.5f* t9.5f² 10.3g* 10.2m 10.4m⁶ 12g 11.9d 10g⁴ p13g⁵ p12g⁵ Nov 25] tall **a98**
filly: fifth foal: half-sister to ungenuine 7f winner Sunrise Lyric (by Rock of Gibraltar):
dam, maiden (third at 1½m), half-sister to smart performer up to 1½m Midnight Line:
useful performer: won maiden at Wolverhampton in March and handicap at Doncaster in
May: better form last 2 starts when fifth in listed races won by Urban Castle at Lingfield
and Fire Fighting at Kempton: stays 13f: acts on polytrack and tapeta: sometimes slowly
away. *Ian Williams*

MONARCH MAID 4 b.f. Captain Gerrard (IRE) 113 – Orange Lily (Royal Applause **80**
124) [2015 78: p6g² 6s 6m* 6g 6m² 6g³ 6m⁶ 5.3s³ 6m 6d Sep 14] compact filly: fairly
useful handicapper: won at Catterick in May: stays 6f: acts on polytrack and firm going:
front runner/races prominently. *Peter Hiatt*

MONASADA 3 b.f. Nayef (USA) 129 – Asawer (IRE) 110 (Darshaan 133) [2015 t12.2g² **92**
12m² 12m³ 10.2g* 10g* p10g* 10.4d⁴ Sep 26] fifth foal: half-sister to useful 2-y-o 1m
winner Ghaawy (by Teofilo) and a winner in Scandinavia by Authorized: dam, 1¼m winner
who stayed 1½m, half-sister to dam of high-class US Grade 1 9f/1¼m winner Questing:
fairly useful performer: won maiden at Nottingham and handicap at Sandown in August
and handicap at Lingfield in September: should prove suited by a return to 1½m: acts on
polytrack, best turf form on good going: usually races close up. *Sir Michael Stoute*

MONASHKA BAY (IRE) 4 b.g. Kodiac 112 – River Style (IRE) 53 (Desert Style (IRE) **41**
121) [2015 59: p6g p7m Jan 18] lengthy gelding: poor handicapper: stays 6f: acts on
polytrack: tried in blinkers prior to 2015. *Michael Blanshard*

MON BEAU VISAGE (IRE) 2 br.g. (Mar 27) Footstepsinthesand 120 – Hurricane Lily **80**
(IRE) 61 (Ali-Royal (IRE) 127) [2015 6g* 6g³ 6m 6d² 7g Sep 19] €41,000Y: sixth foal:
brother to Swiss 1m winner Sea Cloud and half-brother to winner up to 7f Moscow Eight
(2-y-o 5f winner, by Elusive City) and winner up to 6f Kool Henry (2-y-o 5f winner, by
One Cool Cat), both useful: dam, lightly raced, closely related to very smart stayer Aaim
To Prosper and half-sister to smart 1m/9f performer Hurricane Alan: fairly useful
performer: won maiden at Redcar in May: third in minor event at Pontefract and second in
nursery at Catterick: stays 6f: acts on good to soft going: tried in cheekpieces: temperament
under suspicion. *David O'Meara*

MON BRAV 8 b.g. Sampower Star 118 – Danehill Princess (IRE) 62 (Danehill (USA) 126) **86**
[2015 91: 7d 7d³ 5g³ 7m 6m 6g³ 6m* 6m³ 6s³ 6.1g 7v 5d Oct 24] rather leggy gelding:
fairly useful handicapper: won at York (by length from Ad Vitam) in July: stays 7f: acts on
soft and good to firm going: tried in headgear: usually races towards rear. *Brian Ellison*

MONCARNO 5 b.g. Lucarno (USA) 121 – Sparkling Jewel 77 (Bijou d'Inde 127) [2015 **–**
p10f p11g p12g Oct 14] no form. *John Best*

MON CIGAR (IRE) 4 b.g. Bushranger (IRE) 119 – Practicallyperfect (IRE) 82 (King **74**
Charlemagne (USA) 120) [2015 67, a79: p8g p7g³ 7g 8.1g³ 9s⁵ Aug 14] fair maiden: stays
1m: acts on polytrack. *Denis Coakley*

MONDAY CLUB 2 ch.g. (Mar 27) Strategic Prince 114 – Support Fund (IRE) 83 **63**
(Intikhab (USA) 135) [2015 7g 7s⁶ 8m⁵ 10.2g⁵ t9.5f⁶ t8.6f³ t9.5f Dec 11] modest maiden:
stays 8.5f: acts on tapeta, soft and good to firm going: tried in cheekpieces. *Dominic
Ffrench Davis*

MONDIAL (IRE) 2 b.f. (May 18) Shamardal (USA) 129 – Mannington (AUS) 118 **73 p**
(Danehill (USA) 126) [2015 p6g⁴ t6f² Dec 22] half-sister to 7f winner Middle England (by
Dubawi) and several winners abroad, including smart Australian Group 1 12.5f winner
Benicio (by More Than Ready): dam, Australian 2-y-o Group 3 5.5f winner, half-sister to
Australian Group 1 7.5f winner Bollinger: better effort when second in maiden at
Wolverhampton (1¾ lengths behind Go On Go On Go On) in December, clear of rest: will
go on improving. *Charlie Appleby*

MONDIALISTE (IRE) 5 b.h. Galileo (IRE) 134 – Occupandiste (IRE) 123 **122**
(Kaldoun (FR) 122) [2015 112: 8d² 9g³ 8f³ 8f 8d* 8.9g* 8d* 8g² 8g Dec 13]
    The rise of trainer David O'Meara, who has moved his Yorkshire base
over the winter from Arthington Barn Stables in Nawton to a new yard in Upper
Helmsley with more scope for expansion, continued unabated in the latest season
and he will have a string of one hundred and forty in 2016. For the second year
running, the yard broke through the million-pound mark in winning prize money
domestically after another century of winners (its third in a row), which included
two pattern-race wins for Amazing Maria at Royal Ascot (Duchess of Cambridge
Stakes) and the Newmarket July meeting (Falmouth Stakes). Another pattern winner
for the yard was So Beloved in Goodwood's Supreme Stakes in September (he also
finished first past the post in the valuable Betfred Mile at the same track in August
before being disqualified after a prohibited substance—bute—was discovered in
his system). One of the yard's star performers the previous season, Custom Cut,
landed the Group 2 Mile at Sandown in April. O'Meara's success wasn't confined to
the domestic scene. Custom Cut landed the Boomerang Stakes, a valuable Group 2
event at Leopardstown on Irish Champions' Weekend, whilst Amazing Maria (Prix
Rothschild) and 2014 Abbaye winner Move In Time (Prix du Petit Couvert) both
recorded pattern wins in France. O'Meara's horizons were broadened even further
with the campaigning of Mondialiste, a big-money recruit from France in the

summer of 2014 who had a fine first season for the stable. Following two wins in Britain, including in York's Strensall Stakes at the Ebor meeting, Mondialiste became the first runner for O'Meara in North America when he won the Woodbine Mile in September, taking home £295,647 in prize money and capping off a fine weekend for the yard after Custom Cut's win in Ireland and Move In Time's in France. Mondialiste gave his owners, long-standing O'Meara patrons Geoff and Sandra Turnbull, another good payday when runner-up in the Breeders' Cup Mile on his next outing, faring best of a strong European challenge. As mentioned in the essay on Amazing Maria, O'Meara has become renowned for his handling of horses recruited from other yards, and the achievements of both Amazing Maria and Mondialiste in the latest season reflect great credit on him and his team.

Unraced at two, Mondialiste was trained by Freddie Head as a three- and four-year-old, when his most notable effort from eight starts was a third, beaten a length and three quarters, behind the Hannon-trained Havana Gold in the 2013 Prix Jean Prat when acting as a pacemaker for the same connections' Anodin. Mondialiste failed to build on that effort in lesser company before belatedly getting off the mark in a minor event at Saint-Cloud eleven months later on what turned out to be his final start for Head. He was sold six weeks later by owner-breeders the Wertheimer brothers for €190,000 at the Deauville Summer Sale and wasn't seen on the track again in 2014. After a ten-month absence, Mondialiste was a 25/1-shot when making his debut for new connections in the Lincoln at Doncaster where he almost got off to the perfect start in Britain, going down by just a neck to Gabrial after making headway to lead a furlong out. From a BHB mark of 105, that performance represented a career best from Mondialiste, one he failed to match on his next three outings; he wasn't disgraced when third to French Navy in the Earl of Sefton Stakes at Newmarket but was below par under much firmer conditions in a listed race at Ascot and in handicap company in the Royal Hunt Cup. Encountering softish ground for the first time since the Lincoln, Mondialiste routed his five rivals in a listed race at Pontefract in late-July, winning by ten lengths from Short Squeeze. The winning margin was a lot tighter when Mondialiste followed up in the nine-runner Strensall Stakes, a Group 3 at the Ebor meeting, in which, starting favourite, he found plenty under pressure to reel in Mutakayyef well inside the final furlong and win by a neck, with the in-form pair Basem and Top Notch Tonto completing the frame.

Trade Storm's success in the 2014 Woodbine Mile on turf was a first in the race for a horse trained in Europe, and Mondialiste crossed the Atlantic for the latest renewal along with French-trained Mr Owen, third in the Poule d'Essai des Poulains and successful in a listed race at Deauville. The betting was headed by Lea, successful in the Grade 1 Donn Handicap the previous year and third in the latest Dubai World Cup, and Obviously, who was making his first start since finishing fifth

Ricoh Woodbine Mile Stakes, Woodbine—up-and-coming David O'Meara's first runner in North America, Mondialiste, improves again as he collars Lea (second left) close home in a race run at a strong pace thanks to Obviously (right)

in the 2014 Breeders' Cup Mile. In what is generally a weak Grade 1 by European standards, 38/10-shot Mondialiste didn't need to improve a great deal to gain his first success at the top level. In a strongly-run affair, more patient tactics than usual were employed on Mondialiste, who was ridden by Fergal Lynch with regular jockey Daniel Tudhope aboard Move In Time at Longchamp earlier in the day. The long straight at Woodbine played into Lynch's hands as he produced Mondialiste with a strong late run to lead well inside the final furlong, getting up to beat Lea by half a length, with front-running Obviously finishing third (beaten a further length and a quarter). Mr Owen was a disappointment in sixth. After some deliberation by connections, who were reportedly concerned that the shorter straight at Keeneland wouldn't suit Mondialiste, he took his chance in the Breeders' Cup Mile six weeks later (the Woodbine Mile is part of the 'Win and You're In' series, which offers the winner an all-expenses-paid berth in the Breeders' Cup Mile). Despite being the outsider in a six-strong European challenge, which included the favourite Make Believe and the 2014 winner Karakontie, Mondialiste fared much the best of the raiders and might even have given the winner Tepin more to do under different circumstances. Dropped out once again, despite an inside draw, Mondialiste travelled well but was left with too much ground to make up in the straight after Obviously set a much steadier pace this time. Finishing strongly, Mondialiste was two and a quarter lengths adrift of Tepin at the line, with a further length and a half back to the third Grand Arch. Make Believe fared best of the other European runners in fifth. Mondialiste appeared once more in 2015, running well below form when twelfth of fourteen in the Hong Kong Mile at Sha Tin in December.

	Galileo (IRE) (b 1998)	Sadler's Wells (b 1981)	Northern Dancer Fairy Bridge
Mondialiste (IRE) (b.h. 2010)		Urban Sea (ch 1989)	Miswaki Allegretta
	Occupandiste (IRE) (b 1993)	Kaldoun (gr 1975)	Caro Katana
		Only Seule (ch 1988)	Lyphard Elle Seule

Mondialiste was bred by Gerard and Alain Wertheimer from their Kaldoun mare Occupandiste, who was a very smart racemare over six and seven furlongs for Criquette Head-Maarek, winning the Prix Maurice de Gheest and Prix de la Foret. Occupandiste has proved just as successful at stud, producing seven winners from nine foals who have raced, including four at listed and pattern level. That quartet includes Mondialiste's year-younger brother Planetaire, who landed a listed race over nine furlongs in France in 2014 before being transferred to the States in the latest season. Mondialiste is the first Group 1 winner out of Occupandiste, though she also bred the smart miler Impressionnante (by Danehill) who was successful in the Group 2 Prix de Sandringham as a three-year-old when she also twice finished runner-up at Group 1 level (promoted from third in the Poule d'Essai des Pouliches having been hampered by first past the post Price Tag). Another half-sister to Mondialiste, Only Answer (by Green Desert) landed the Prix de Saint-Georges and the Prix du Petit Couvert over five furlongs as a four-year-old, while Only Answer's sister Desertiste is the dam of one of the leading French two-year-old fillies Sasparella, winner of the Prix Eclipse. Impressionnante has gone on to make a further impression as the dam of the 2013 Prix du Jockey Club winner Intello, who is by Mondialiste's sire Galileo (more background information on the family—Mondialiste's great grandam Elle Seule is a daughter of Fall Aspen—can be found in the essay on Intello in *Racehorses of 2013*). The latest progeny of Occupandiste to make it to the track is three-year-old Attentif (by Oasis Dream), successful in a maiden over six and a half furlongs in February. Mondialiste clearly possesses more stamina than the majority of his siblings—he saw out the nine furlongs thoroughly when winning the Strensall Stakes—and like his dam, who went well with cut in the ground, Mondialiste himself seems best on good ground or softer, his win at York and his second in the Breeders' Cup both coming on good. The game Mondialiste is tactically versatile, making the running on occasions, though he was ridden much more patiently on his later runs in 2015. *David O'Meara*

MONEIN (USA) 3 ch.g. New Approach (IRE) 132 – Spring Oak 113 (Mark of Esteem (IRE) 137) [2015 p10g* t9.5g* p10f² 11g t9.5m² Dec 30] compact gelding: half-brother to several winners in France, including useful winner up to 11.5f Castlereagh (2-y-o 6f winner, by Machiavellian) and useful 12.5f winner Manjakani (by Barathea): dam French winner up to 10.5f (2-y-o 1m winner): fairly useful performer: won maiden at Lingfield and handicap at Wolverhampton in January: second in handicap at Wolverhampton in December: bred to stay 1½m: acts on polytrack and tapeta. *Charlie Appleby* **91**

MONEL 7 ch.g. Cadeaux Genereux 131 – Kelucia (IRE) 101 (Grand Lodge (USA) 125) [2015 74: 6g⁴ 6d 6g⁴ 7.2s⁶ 7.2g⁴ 6g⁵ 7.2d 6g⁴ 6g² 7.2g 6g Oct 8] fair handicapper: stays 7f: acts on good to firm and heavy going: tried in hood prior to 2015: usually races nearer last than first. *Jim Goldie* **69**

MONEYPENNIE 4 b.f. Captain Gerrard (IRE) 113 – Snoozy (Cadeaux Genereux 131) [2015 55: p8f 8m Sep 28] maiden: no form in 2015: probably stays 1m: acts on polytrack and good to firm going: tried in cheekpieces: sometimes wears tongue tie: often races prominently, often races freely. *Marcus Tregoning* **–**

MONEY PRINTER (IRE) 3 b.g. Intense Focus (USA) 117 – Biasca (Erhaab (USA) 127) [2015 p10g 10m Aug 7] tailed off in 2 maidens. *Paul D'Arcy* **–**

MONEY TEAM (IRE) 4 b.g. Kodiac 112 – Coral Dawn (IRE) 67 (Trempolino (USA) 135) [2015 98: p6g⁵ p6g² p7f p6d⁶ 6g⁶ 6m 5m 6m⁶ 5m 5g⁵ 6m⁴ 5m³ 5d 5m⁴ 5g p6m⁵ p6f³ Dec 17] plain, leggy gelding: fairly useful handicapper: stays 6f: acts on polytrack, tapeta and good to firm going: often races prominently. *David Barron* **83 a90**

MON GRIS (IRE) 3 gr.g. Falco (USA) 122 – Turpitude (Caerleon (USA) 132) [2015 –: 7d 8g³ 10g³ 8m³ 8.9g 7d⁸ Sep 21] modest performer: won seller at Leicester in September: should stay at least 1m: acts on good to firm and good to soft going: races prominently. *Kristin Stubbs* **64**

MONJENI 2 b.g. (Feb 7) Montjeu (IRE) 137 – Polly's Mark (IRE) 112 (Mark of Esteem (IRE) 137) [2015 p8m t8.6f t8.6g⁵ Dec 5] 650,000Y: first foal: dam, 1¼m-1½m winner, out of half-sister to 1000 Guineas winner Ameerat: fair maiden: best effort on debut: bred to be suited by 1¼m+: remains with potential. *Sir Mark Prescott Bt* **67 p**

MONNA VALLEY 3 ch.g. Exceed And Excel (AUS) 126 – Monnavanna (IRE) 109 **68**
(Machiavellian (USA) 123) [2015 –p: 7d⁴ 6m⁵ 7m⁴ t7.1m* t7.1f⁵ Sep 19] fair handicapper:
won at Wolverhampton in September: stays 7f: acts on tapeta and good to firm going.
Stuart Williams

MONOPOLI 6 ch.m. Cadeaux Genereux 131 – Jump Ship 74 (Night Shift (USA)) [2015 **63**
64: 8.3d 9.9m 9.9m² 9.9s⁴ 10m² 10g⁶ t12.2g³ 10.2s⁴ Oct 28] compact mare: modest
handicapper: stays 1½m: acts on tapeta and any turf going: sometimes wears cheekpieces:
sometimes slowly away. *Ivan Furtado*

MONOTYPE (IRE) 3 b.g. Makfi 130 – Mill Guineas (USA) (Salse (USA) 128) [2015 **97 p**
10.2d³ 12d* 13m⁵ Jul 9] 300,000Y: half-brother to several winners, including Scandinavian
winner up to 9f Mill Rahm (2-y-o 5f winner, by Pivotal) and French 2-y-o 7f/7.5f winner
Olvia (by Giant's Causeway), both useful: dam, useful French maiden (stayed 1¼m), half-
sister to smart winner up to 1m Ronda: useful performer: won maiden at Doncaster (by ½
length from She Is No Lady) in June: better form when last of 5 in Bahrain Trophy at
Newmarket (6½ lengths behind Mr Singh) only subsequent start: stays 13f: has been
gelded: probably capable of better still. *Luca Cumani*

MON PETIT FLEUR 3 b.f. Arabian Gleam 122 – Mon Petit Diamant 54 (Hector **63**
Protector (USA) 124) [2015 61: t5.1f⁵ t6m² t6f³ t6g Nov 27] modest maiden: left Chris
Dwyer after first start: stays 6f: acts on tapeta: often in hood in 2015. *Lydia Pearce*

MONSART (IRE) 3 b.g. Echo of Light 125 – Monet's Lady (IRE) 51 (Daylami (IRE) **–**
138) [2015 –: t12.2g⁶ Mar 24] has shown little in 3 maidens: sold £2,600 in October.
Jo Hughes

MONSEA (IRE) 4 gr.g. Manduro (GER) 135 – Sea Drift (FR) 72 (Warning 136) [2015 83: **76 §**
t9.5g³ t12.2f⁵ 10.3d 9.9m³ 10.1d 9.9m³ 9.8m⁵ 12m³ 9.9m 12v³ p9.4g⁵ Dec 21] fair
performer: left Brian Ellison 6,000 gns after tenth start: stays 1½m: acts on polytrack,
tapeta, good to firm and heavy going: sometimes in cheekpieces: not one to trust. *Mlle M.
Henry, France*

MONSIEUR CHABAL 4 b.g. Avonbridge 123 – Coup de Torchon (FR) 61 (Namid 128) **53**
[2015 50: t8.6f³ p10g⁴ p12m⁴ p10m⁴ t9.5m⁴ t8.6g⁵ p10f Mar 18] modest maiden: stays
1½m: acts on polytrack and tapeta: in cheekpieces last 4 starts. *Jamie Osborne*

MONSIEUR CHEVALIER (IRE) 8 b.g. Chevalier (IRE) 115 – Blue Holly (IRE) 83 **88**
(Blues Traveller (IRE) 119) [2015 94: f8d³ t9.5f* t8.6f* t9.5m⁶ 7g⁵ 8m⁵ 7.1m⁵ 8.3m³
t8.6g* 7g t7.1g³ p8g⁴ t8.6g⁵ p8g² 7.5g* p8g t9.5m Dec 30] smallish, well-made gelding:
fairly useful performer: won claimers at Wolverhampton in January and March
(subsequently left Jamie Osborne) and handicaps in Warwick in June and Beverley
in August: stays 9.5f, effective at shorter: acts on polytrack, tapeta, soft and good to firm
going: wears headgear: often races towards rear. *James Given*

MONSIEUR GLORY 2 ch.g. (Apr 15) Monsieur Bond (IRE) 120 – Chushka 81 (Pivotal **64 p**
124) [2015 7m t8.6f 8d Sep 26] 12,000F, £40,000Y: strong gelding: second foal: dam, 6f
winner, half-sister to July Stakes winner Captain Hurricane: modest maiden: best effort
when eighth at Haydock final start, not knocked about: capable of better. *Tom Dascombe*

MONSIEUR JAMIE 7 b.g. Monsieur Bond (IRE) 120 – Primula Bairn 77 (Bairn (USA) **78**
126) [2015 76: f5g³ p6f 5g 6s² 5s* 6g 5s⁵ 5g f6m⁴ Dec 8] sturdy, good-bodied gelding: fair **a68**
handicapper: won at Lingfield in August: stays 6f: acts on fibresand and heavy going:
wears headgear: sometimes slowly away: inconsistent, has refused to race. *J. R. Jenkins*

MONSIEUR JIMMY 3 ch.g. Monsieur Bond (IRE) 120 – Artistic License (IRE) 94 **51**
(Chevalier (IRE) 115) [2015 52: 6m f7g* 7.5g 6.1d 6.9v 5g⁵ 5s⁵ 5m 6s 7m 5m 6g⁵ f7g⁶ **a75**
f7g⁶ f8m⁵ f7g² Dec 15] compact gelding: fair handicapper: won at Southwell in April:
stays 7f: acts on fibresand, good to firm and heavy going: tried in headgear in 2015.
Declan Carroll

MONSIEUR JOE (IRE) 8 b.g. Choisir (AUS) 126 – Pascali 61 (Compton Place 125) **116**
[2015 114: 5g⁶ 6g 5g 5g 5m⁴ 5m³ 5g* 5m² 5f⁴ 5m² 5m⁶ 5d* 5m 5m Oct 4] sturdy gelding:
smart performer: won handicap at York (by ½ length from Red Baron) in May and listed
race at Tipperary (by 1½ lengths from Iffranesia) in August: runner-up in between at 'Dash'
(Handicap) at Epsom (length behind Desert Law) and listed race at York (neck behind Out
Do): best form at 5f: acts on polytrack, soft and good to firm going: tried in visor prior to
2015. *Paul Midgley*

MONSIEUR RIEUSSEC 5 bl.g. Halling (USA) 133 – Muscovado (USA) 71 (Mr **80**
Greeley (USA) 122) [2015 91: 10m 10m⁵ 10.2m⁵ Jul 4] good-topped gelding: fairly useful
handicapper: stays 1½m: acts on soft and good to firm going: usually travels strongly.
Jonathan Portman

MONSIEUR ROYALE 5 ch.g. Monsieur Bond (IRE) 120 – Bond Royale 89 (Piccolo **58**
121) [2015 63: p8g p8f⁵ p7g⁴ Mar 25] modest handicapper: stays 1m: acts on polytrack and
good to firm going: usually in headgear prior to 2015. *Clive Drew*

MONSIEUR VALENTINE 3 ch.g. Monsieur Bond (IRE) 120 – Minnina (IRE) (In The **66**
Wings 128) [2015 –p: 7d⁴ 7.6s³ 7.1s* 8.3g f7g p8d Nov 30] fair handicapper: won at
Chepstow in August: stays 7.5f: acts on soft going. *Tony Carroll*

MONTAFF 9 b.g. Montjeu (IRE) 137 – Meshhed (USA) 102 (Gulch (USA)) [2015 68§:
f14g⁵ Apr 14] rather leggy gelding: one-time smart performer, very much on the
downgrade: has worn headgear: often starts slowly, *Richard Guest*

MONTAGUE WAY (IRE) 2 b.g. (Mar 12) Rock of Gibraltar (IRE) 133 – Shanghai Lily **–**
(IRE) 98 (King's Best (USA) 132) [2015 7.1m 8.1g Aug 2] well held in maidens at
Sandown and Chepstow, racing too freely both occasions. *Andrew Balding*

MONTALCINO (IRE) 3 b.f. Big Bad Bob (IRE) 118 – Fair Sailing (IRE) 62 (Docksider **106**
(USA) 124) [2015 92: 8f⁶ 10m² 8.1m² 7m³ 8.1m⁴ 7s Sep 18] useful-looking filly: useful
performer: second in listed races at Newbury and Sandown (neck behind Blond Me) in
July, third in Oak Tree Stakes at Goodwood (1¾ lengths behind Amy Eria) and fourth in
Atalanta Stakes at Sandown (length behind Nakuti): stays 1m: acts on good to firm going:
usually races nearer last than first: sent to USA. *Brian Meehan*

MONTALY 4 b.g. Yeats (IRE) 128 – Le Badie (IRE) (Spectrum (IRE) 126) [2015 104: **104**
p14g⁵ 12m⁶ 14m Jul 11] useful handicapper: stays 1½m: acts on any turf going: often in
hood in 2015: usually races nearer last than first. *Andrew Balding*

MONT D'ARGENT 3 gr.c. Montjeu (IRE) 137 – Ayla (IRE) 101 (Daylami (IRE) 138) **71**
[2015 p10f³ Mar 20] 90,000Y: third foal: half-brother to 1¼m-11.6f winner Ayla's Emperor
(by Holy Roman Emperor): dam, 1½m winner who stayed 1¾m, half-sister to Prix du
Cadran winner Alandi: 4/1, shaped well when third in maiden at Lingfield (7¼ lengths
behind Librisa Breeze) on debut, not knocked about: bred to be suited by 1½m+: sold 4,500
gns, sent to Sweden. *Mark Johnston*

MONTE CASSINO (IRE) 10 ch.g. Choisir (AUS) 126 – Saucy Maid (IRE) 69 (Sure **–**
Blade (USA) 130) [2015 61: 8s Apr 5] big, workmanlike gelding: modest handicapper:
stays 7f: acts on polytrack and fibresand: has worn headgear, including often of late: often
races towards rear. *Bryan Smart*

MONTEFALCON (IRE) 3 b.g. Footstepsinthesand 120 – Gwyllion (USA) 71 (Red **81**
Ransom (USA)) [2015 65p: 7.5m* 8m⁵ 8d⁴ 10.2m⁶ 8.9m⁶ 8.5d⁵ Sep 22] attractive gelding:
has scope: fairly useful handicapper: won at Beverley in April: stays 8.5f: acts on good to
firm and good to soft going: often starts slowly, often races freely: sold 5,500 gns, sent to
Bahrain. *Richard Fahey*

MONTEFELTRO 7 ch.g. Medicean 128 – Bustling 106 (Danehill (USA) 126) [2015 **100**
13.4v 16.2g 16.1m 14g 14.1d⁶ 14d 18g⁶ 18gᵖᵘ Oct 10] strong gelding: useful handicapper:
in first-time cheekpieces (on Flat), pulled up in Cesarewitch final outing: stays 2¼m: acts
on good to firm and good to soft going. *Brian Ellison*

MONTEVERDI (FR) 2 b.c. (May 16) Kyllachy 129 – West of Saturn (USA) (Gone West **84 p**
(USA)) [2015 6.5s* Oct 23] €72,000Y, 57,000 2-y-o: second foal: half-brother to French
1m winner Bartavelle (by Makfi): dam twice-raced daughter of Prix Marcel Boussac
winner Amonita: 9/2, won 9-runner maiden at Newbury by 1¾ lengths from Silca Star,
slowly away, staying on to lead final 1f and well on top finish: sure to stay at least 7f: open
to improvement. *Jamie Osborne*

MONT FEU (IRE) 3 b.f. Montjeu (IRE) 137 – I'm In Love (USA) 88 (Zafonic (USA) **–**
130) [2015 10m 12m May 15] third foal: half-sister to US Grade 3 2-y-o 1m winner More
Than Love (by More Than Ready) and 2-y-o 6f winner Masai (by Oasis Dream), both
useful: dam, 7f and (at 2 yrs) 1m winner, later 8.5f winner in USA: last in maidens at
Newbury and Newmarket. *Alan McCabe*

MONT KIARA (FR) 2 b.g. (Mar 30) Kendargent (FR) 112 – Xaarienne (Xaar 132) [2015 **97**
6m² 6g³ 6g* 6d Oct 16] €135,000 2-y-o: second foal: half-brother to useful French 7f
winner Xaarina (by Aussie Rules): dam French 2-y-o 5.5f winner: useful performer: 2¾
lengths third to Tourny in Prix de Cabourg at Deauville in August: 2/7, didn't need to run
anywhere near that form to win maiden at Newcastle in September: below form in
Criterium de Maisons-Laffitte final outing: gelded after: raced only at 6f. *Kevin Ryan*

MONT RAS (IRE) 8 ch.g. Indian Ridge 123 – Khayrat (IRE) (Polar Falcon (USA) 126) **105**
[2015 110: 8m 7m 8d 7.9m³ 7.2g p8f p8g² t8.6m² p8g² Dec 10] good-topped gelding:
useful handicapper: several creditable efforts in 2015, including when second at
Chelmsford (1¼ lengths behind Realize) final start: stays 8.5f: acts on polytrack, tapeta and
good to firm going: tried in tongue tie in 2015. *David O'Meara*

MONTSARRAT (IRE) 2 br.c. (Mar 19) Poet's Voice 126 – Flying Flag (IRE) **91**
(Entrepreneur 123) [2015 7m* 7g* 7m² 7m* 8d Sep 12] 45,000F: half-brother to several
winners in Italy, including useful winner up to 9f Laguna Salada (2-y-o 7.5f winner, by
Invincible Spirit) and 9f-11f winner Daring Life (by Cape Cross): dam ran once in Italy:
fairly useful performer: won maiden at Salisbury in June and nurseries at Catterick in July
and Newmarket (by short head from Maccus) in August: should stay 1m: acts on good to
firm going: races prominently. *Mark Johnston*

MONUMENTAL MAN 6 b.g. Vital Equine (IRE) 121 – Spark Up 81 (Lahib (USA) 129) **93**
[2015 90: t5.1g⁴ 5g* 5m 5m t6g 5.5m 5v⁵ Aug 31] big gelding: fairly useful handicapper:
won at Epsom (by 3¾ lengths from Secret Missile) in April: stays 6f: acts on polytrack and
good to firm going: usually wears cheekpieces: tried in tongue tie prior to 2015. *James Unett*

MONUMENT ROCKS (IRE) 2 b.g. (Apr 10) Rock of Gibraltar (IRE) 133 – Be Glad **56**
105 (Selkirk (USA) 129) [2015 7m 8.1g 8.3d⁶ Oct 5] good-topped gelding: modest maiden:
best effort when sixth at Windsor final start. *Ian Williams*

MONZINO (USA) 7 b.g. More Than Ready (USA) 120 – Tasso's Magic Roo (USA) **54 §**
(Tasso (USA)) [2015 54§, a63§: f16d t12.2g f11s f12d* f12d⁶ f12g f14s 10.2m 11.6m⁵
16m Jul 1] tall gelding: modest handicapper: won at Southwell in February: stays 1½m:
acts on polytrack, fibresand and good to firm going: sometimes wears headgear: usually
races nearer last than first: untrustworthy. *Michael Chapman*

MOOHAARIB (IRE) 4 b.g. Oasis Dream 129 – Evita 76 (Selkirk (USA) 129) [2015 **116**
107: 8d³ 8f* 8m 8g 8d Sep 5] tall gelding: smart performer: much improved when winning
listed race at Ascot in April impressively by 1¼ lengths from Hors de Combat: only
creditable effort in 4 other starts in 2015 when third of 22 to Gabrial in Lincoln (Handicap)
at Doncaster: stays 1m: acts on firm and soft going: in cheekpieces final start: races towards
rear, often travels strongly, tends to find little: has been gelded. *Marco Botti*

MOOIZO (IRE) 2 b.f. (Apr 27) Rock of Gibraltar (IRE) 133 – Skid (IRE) (Montjeu (IRE) –
137) [2015 7g t8.6f 8m p8g Dec 15] good-topped filly: first foal: dam, unraced, closely
related to National Stakes runner-up Berenson and and half-sister to useful 1m winner
Pollen: no form. *Paul D'Arcy*

MOOJANED (IRE) 4 b.g. Raven's Pass (USA) 133 – Mufradat (IRE) 93 (Desert Prince **80**
(IRE) 130) [2015 –: 11.5d* 9.9m⁴ 11.8m² 13.3m* 11.6m* 11.6m³ 12d⁵ 11.6g³ 10.3d*
10.2s⁵ p12g f12f⁶ Dec 17] fairly useful handicapper: successful at Lingfield in June and in
amateur events at Newbury in July, Windsor in August and Doncaster in October: stays
13.5f: acts on soft and good to firm going: usually races close up. *David Evans*

MOONADEE (IRE) 3 gr.g. Haatef (USA) 117 – Again Royale (IRE) (Royal Academy **75**
(USA) 130) [2015 62: 7d² 8.3d* 8.3m⁴ 11.1d⁵ Sep 1] lengthy gelding: fair performer: won
minor event at Nottingham in May: stays 8.5f: acts on good to firm and good to soft going:
usually races towards rear. *Michael Appleby*

MOON ARC (IRE) 3 b.g. Arcano (IRE) 122 – Moon Unit (IRE) 119 (Intikhab (USA) **70**
135) [2015 41p: f8g⁶ f8d² p10g⁴ 8g⁴ 10g³ 7d⁶ 9.2d* 10d 11.5g² 10g 14.1g⁵ 11.1s* 11.1s
12.2m Aug 7] fair handicapper: won at Hamilton in May and July (awarded race): stays
11.5f: acts on soft going: sometimes in headgear in 2015. *Keith Dalgleish*

MOON ARROW (IRE) 2 b.c. (Mar 27) Authorized (IRE) 133 – Moon Sister (IRE) 100 –
(Cadeaux Genereux 131) [2015 7s 9d Oct 26] second foal: dam, 9.7f-11f winner, out of
close relative to King George VI & Queen Elizabeth Stakes winner Pentire: green when
well held in 2 maidens. *Ismail Mohammed*

MOONBI CREEK (IRE) 8 b.g. Fasliyev (USA) 120 – Moonbi Range (IRE) 85 **68**
(Nordico (USA)) [2015 72: 6s 7.2d⁶ t8.6m⁴ t8.6m t7.1f* t7.1m⁵ t7.1f³ Dec 22] fair
handicapper: won at Wolverhampton in October: stays 1¼m: acts on polytrack, tapeta,
sand, good to firm and good to soft going: tried in headgear prior to 2015: tried in tongue
tie: sometimes slowly away. *Richard Ford*

MOONDAY SUN (USA) 6 gr.g. Mizzen Mast (USA) 121 – Storm Dove (USA) 108 **81**
(Storm Bird (CAN) 134) [2015 95, a101: p10g p8m p8g² p8g t8.6g p8g p8m Oct 21]
fairly useful handicapper: second at Chelmsford in March: left John Butler after third start:
stays 1m: best form on good going: tried in cheekpieces prior to 2015: usually races nearer
last than first, usually finds little. *Phil McEntee*

MOONDYNE JOE (IRE) 2 b.g. (Apr 22) Bushranger (IRE) 119 – Golden Shine 80 **75 p** (Royal Applause 124) [2015 5g* 5.2m Jul 18] £13,000Y: well-made gelding: second foal: half-brother to 2-y-o 6f winner Arthur Martinleake (by Alfred Nobel): dam, 2-y-o 5f winner, half-sister to useful sprinter Falcon Hill: won maiden at Carlisle on debut in June: 20/1, still needed experience when 5¼ lengths sixteenth of 22 to Lathom in Super Sprint at Newbury, also on wrong side as it developed: remains with potential. *K. R. Burke*

MOON EYES 3 b.f. Oasis Dream 129 – Enticing (IRE) 116 [2015 –p: t8.6g⁵ **73** 6g² 5.7f³ p7g³ t7.1f² p6f⁴ Nov 25] fair maiden: stays 7f: acts on polytrack, tapeta and firm going: tried in blinkers in 2015: usually races prominently. *William Haggas*

MOONFAARID 4 b.g. Dubawi (IRE) 129 – Manoeuvre (IRE) (Galileo (IRE) 134) [2015 **74** 78: p7g² p7f^bu Mar 25] good-topped gelding: fair maiden: stayed 1m: acted on polytrack and tapeta: usually raced close up, often raced freely, tended to find little: dead. *Jane Chapple-Hyam*

MOONLIGHT GIRL (IRE) 2 ch f (Mar 22) Arcano (IRE) 122 – Moonlight Red (IRE) **57 §** (Kheleyf (USA) 116) [2015 6g⁵ 6g 6g 7m 8.3g 7d^rr Aug 24] £19,000Y: first foal: dam Italian 2-y-o 7f/7.5f winner: modest maiden: best effort at 6f: best treated with caution (refused to race final start). *Tim Easterby*

MOONLIGHTNAVIGATOR (USA) 3 b.c. Henrythenavigator (USA) 131 – Victorica **92** (USA) (Exbourne (USA) 125) [2015 92p: 8s* 8g 8g 9.9g Aug 29] good-topped colt: fairly useful handicapper: won at Musselburgh (by ¾ length from Spring Offensive) in April: stays 1m: acts on soft and good to firm going. *John Quinn*

MOONLIGHT SONATA 3 b.f. Galileo (IRE) 134 – Blue Rhapsody 79 (Cape Cross **89** (IRE) 129) [2015 81p: 10d³ p12f* 10.2d³ 12m⁵ Oct 3] rather leggy filly: fairly useful performer: won maiden at Lingfield in August: third in handicap at Bath in September: stays 1½m: acts on polytrack and good to soft going. *Sir Michael Stoute*

MOONLIGHT VENTURE 4 ch.g. Tobougg (IRE) 125 – Evening 75 (Mark of Esteem **78 §** (IRE) 137) [2015 80: f8g⁴ 8s² 10m⁵ 8d² 9.2d 8m⁶ 8m⁴ 10.3s⁶ p8f⁵ f7g³ f8m⁶ Dec 8] fair handicapper: stays 1m: acts on polytrack, fibresand, soft and good to firm going: usually in headgear in 2015: temperamental. *Kevin Ryan*

MOON OVER MOBAY 2 b.f. (Mar 24) Archipenko (USA) 127 – Slew The Moon **65 p** (ARG) (Kitwood (USA) 119) [2015 8g p8g⁵ Nov 18] seventh foal: half-sister to 3 winners, including useful winner up to 2m Bowdler's Magic (2-y-o 8.6f winner, by Hernando) and 2-y-o 1m winner Luz de La Luna (by Cozzene): dam Argentinian Group 1 1m winner: better effort when fifth in maiden at Kempton (8¾ lengths behind Predilection) in November, inadequate test: will be suited by 1¼m+: open to further improvement. *Andrew Balding*

MOON OVER RIO (IRE) 4 b.f. Captain Rio 122 – Moonchild (GER) (Acatenango **66** (GER) 127) [2015 64: f12g⁶ 12d⁴ 11.1m 12g⁵ 11.5d³ 10.4d Sep 25] fair handicapper: won at Ripon in June: stays 1½m: acts on good to soft going: front runner/races prominently. *Ben Haslam*

MOONRAKER 3 ch.c. Starspangledbanner (AUS) 128 – Licence To Thrill 83 (Wolfhound **111** (USA) 126) [2015 100: 6m* 5g⁴ 6g⁶ 6m⁵ 6s Oct 10] rangy colt: smart performer: much improved when winning handicap at Ascot in August by 1¼ lengths from Squats: not in same form afterwards: stays 6f: acts on good to firm and good to soft going. *Mick Channon*

MOONRISE LANDING (IRE) 4 gr.f. Dalakhani (IRE) 133 – Celtic Slipper (IRE) 102 **106** (Anabaa (USA) 130) [2015 88: 13.1f³ 16.1g 12m² 12m⁴ 12m 12g⁴ 12d* p16g* t16.5m* Dec 12] good-topped filly: useful performer: won handicaps at Newmarket (by ½ length from More Mischief) in October and Kempton (by 4½ lengths from Percy Veer) in November, and completed hat-trick in minor event at Wolverhampton (by 4½ lengths from Anglophile) in December: stays 16.5f: acts on polytrack, tapeta and good to soft going: tried in headgear in 2015: often races towards rear, often travels strongly. *Ralph Beckett*

MOON RIVER (IRE) 3 b.f. Exceed And Excel (AUS) 126 – Dame Blanche (IRE) 67 **69** (Be My Guest (USA) 126) [2015 71p: f5g* f5s² 5.1d⁴ 6.1d⁶ 5g t7.1g⁴ t7.1f⁶ p10f Dec 17] **a76** fair handicapper: won at Southwell in February: stays 7f: acts on all-weather: sometimes in blinkers prior to 2015. *Michael Appleby*

MOONSTONE LADY 3 ch.f. Observatory (USA) 131 – Force In The Wings (IRE) (In **–** The Wings 128) [2015 8.3m 7g⁵ 7d³ 8g p8g⁵ Aug 15] 1,000F: smallish filly: fifth foal: sister to a winner in Spain and half-sister to a winner in Italy by Bertolini: dam unraced half-sister to useful sprinter Nights Cross: no form: usually in cheekpieces. *John Bridger*

MOONTOWN 4 ch.g. Sea The Stars (IRE) 140 – Eva's Request (IRE) 115 (Soviet Star – (USA) 128) [2015 78: 12g Apr 22] good-topped gelding: fair maiden at best: stays 1½m: acts on polytrack and good to firm going: often races towards rear: sold 6,500 gns. *Charles Hills*

MOON TRIP 6 b.g. Cape Cross (IRE) 129 – Fading Light 103 (King's Best (USA) 132) **55** [2015 75: p16g⁶ p12f 11.6m 18d Aug 20] strong gelding: modest handicapper: stays 2m: best form on good going or firmer (acts on firm): tends to find little. *Geoffrey Deacon*

MOORSHOLM (IRE) 4 b.g. High Chaparral (IRE) 132 – Arctic Freedom (USA) 75 – (War Chant (USA) 126) [2015 –: 8.3s 12.5m Jun 13] no form. *Alan Swinbank*

MOORSIDE 2 b.f. (Apr 30) Champs Elysees 124 – Marching West (USA) 99 (Gone West **82 p** (USA)) [2015 8.3g³ p8g³ Nov 4] sister to 1¼m winner Mill Point and half-sister to 3 winners, including useful winner up to 1m Marching Time (2-y-o 7f winner, by Sadler's Wells) and 13f/1¾m winner Giovanni Jack (by Three Valleys): dam, French 2-y-o 5.5f winner, sister to Zafonic and Zamindar: fairly useful form when third in maidens at Windsor in October and Kempton (length behind Persuasive) in November: should still improve. *Charles Hills*

MOOTAHARER (IRE) 2 b.c. (Mar 20) Dubawi (IRE) 129 – Tahrir (IRE) 100 (Linamix **92 p** (FR) 127) [2015 7g² 7g* Oct 21] rangy, good sort: half-brother to several winners, including top-class winner up to 7f Muhaarar (2-y-o 5.6f/6f winner, by Oasis Dream), smart 6f/7f winner Tamaathul (by Tiger Hill) and useful 1m winner Raasekha (by Pivotal): dam 7f winner: better effort when winning maiden at Newmarket (by 4½ lengths from Symbolic) in October, kept up to work: likely to stay 1m: sure to progress. *Charles Hills*

MOPS ANGEL 4 b.f. Piccolo 121 – Tanning 60 (Atraf (116) [2015 72: t6f⁴ t7.1g⁵ p6f⁵ p6f **69** 7m 6s 6g⁵ 7m² t8.6g³ t7.1f³ t9.5m² Dec 26] fair handicapper: won at Wolverhampton in January: stays 9.5f: acts on tapeta, soft and good to firm going: often in headgear in 2015. *Michael Appleby*

MORACHE MUSIC 7 b.g. Sleeping Indian 122 – Enchanted Princess 82 (Royal **90** Applause 124) [2015 112: 6m 7g 7g 7g 6g 7s⁶ Oct 12] sturdy gelding: fairly useful handicapper: stays 7f: acts on polytrack, good to firm and heavy going: tried in headgear: usually races nearer last than first. *Peter Makin*

MORE DRAMA (IRE) 3 b.f. Thewayyouare (USA) 117 – Our Drama Queen (IRE) 76 **47** (Danehill Dancer (IRE) 117) [2015 55: p8f p10g⁵ 18.6m p10m³ Feb 18] poor handicapper: stays 1¼m: acts on polytrack and tapeta: often races prominently. *Sylvester Kirk*

MORE KUDOS (USA) 2 ch.g. (Apr 21) Exchange Rate (USA) 111 – Marquise Quest **– p** (USA) (Coronado's Quest (USA) 130) [2015 6m 5.9s 5g Sep 16] $100,000Y: sixth foal: half-brother to several winners in USA: dam, US 1m winner, half-sister to high-class US Grade 1 7f-9f winner Left Bank: no form in 3 maidens: should do better. *John Quinn*

MORE MISCHIEF 3 b.f. Azamour (IRE) 130 – Mischief Making (USA) 101 (Lemon **92** Drop Kid (USA) 131) [2015 10.3d⁶ 8.3s* 10.4g² 12.1g* 11.5d* 12m 11.8s² 12d² Oct 30] 28,000Y: lengthy filly: second foal: half-sister to useful winner up to 11f Devilment (2-y-o 1¼m winner, by Cape Cross): dam, 9.5f-13f winner who stayed 2m, half-sister to smart 7f winner That Is The Spirit: fairly useful performer: won at Hamilton in May (maiden) and June (handicap) and at Carlisle (handicap) in July: better form when second in handicaps at Leicester and Newmarket last 2 starts: stays 1½m: acts on soft going: front runner/races prominently. *Jedd O'Keeffe*

MORE SPICE (IRE) 3 b.g. Exceed And Excel (AUS) 126 – High Spice (USA) 92 **58 p** (Songandaprayer (USA) 118) [2015 50p: t6f⁴ f5g⁴ f5f⁵ Dec 17] lightly-raced maiden, modest form: best effort at 5f: remains open to improvement. *Robert Cowell*

MORE TO COME 2 b.c. (Mar 12) Sea The Stars (IRE) 140 – Magic Tree (UAE) 52 **83 p** (Timber Country (USA) 124) [2015 7.1g 8g⁴ Aug 14] sturdy colt: fifth foal: half-brother to 3 winners, including high-class 1m-10.4f winner Mukhadram (by Shamardal) and useful 1½m-16.5f winner Entihaa (by Tiger Hill): dam once-raced half-sister to St Leger winner Mastery and very smart 1¼m-1½m winner Kirklees: better effort when fourth in maiden at Newmarket (5 lengths behind Ventura Storm) in August, needing stiffer test: will stay 1¼m: will go on improving. *Saeed bin Suroor*

MORNA'S GLORY 6 b.m. Resplendent Glory (IRE) 115 – Tipsy Cake (Tipsy Creek – (USA) 115) [2015 –: p7g Jan 14] maiden: lightly raced and no form since 2012. *Sarah Humphrey*

MORNING MIX (IRE) 3 b.g. Teofilo (IRE) 126 – Fainne (IRE) (Peintre Celebre (USA) **99** 137) [2015 80: 10d⁵ 12g² 10g* 12g⁴ 12g⁴ Oct 11] useful performer: won maiden at the Curragh (by 7½ lengths from Here For The Craic) in June: better subsequent effort when fourth in Ballyroan Stakes at Leopardstown (6½ lengths behind Fields of Athenry) on next start: stays 1½m: best form on good going: tried in tongue tie: usually races close up: sent to Australia. *J. S. Bolger, Ireland*

MORNINGTON 2 b.g. (Mar 4) Aussie Rules (USA) 123 – Giusina Mia (USA) (Diesis 133) [2015 7m Aug 1] 20,000Y: rather unfurnished gelding: half-brother to several winners, including 2-y-o 5f winner Tia Mia (by Dr Fong) and 1m winner Perfect Practice (by Medicean): dam Italian 1¼m winner: 50/1, needed experience when eleventh of 17 to Folkswood in maiden at Goodwood, not unduly punished: should do better. *Marcus Tregoning*   **– p**

MOROCCO 6 b.g. Rock of Gibraltar (IRE) 133 – Shanghai Lily (IRE) 98 (King's Best (USA) 132) [2015 10.1g 12s 11.9m 10g 9.3g 7.9m⁵ 8.5m⁵ 12.4g³ 12s⁶ 12.2g 10.3d⁶ Oct 23] tall, attractive gelding: fair handicapper: stays 12.5f: acts on good to firm and good to soft going. *Karen Tutty*   **66**

MORUADII (IRE) 3 b.f. Fastnet Rock (AUS) 127 – Olympienne (IRE) (Sadler's Wells (USA) 132) [2015 –p: 9.9g⁴ 11.8m* 13.4m⁴ 12g⁶ 11.8d³ 12g Sep 21] fair performer: won maiden at Leicester in June: stays 1½m: acts on good to firm and good to soft going: often in visor in 2015. *Sir Michael Stoute*   **78**

MOSCATO 4 gr.g. Hernando (FR) 127 – Alba Stella 92 (Nashwan (USA) 135) [2015 96p: 16m* 16.4m² 18g 18g Oct 10] rangy gelding: useful handicapper: won at Ascot (apprentice) in May by length from Arty Campbell: creditable 2¼ lengths seventh of 34 to Grumeti in Cesarewitch at Newmarket final start: stays 2¼m: acts on good to firm going: usually in cheekpieces: front runner/races prominently. *Sir Mark Prescott Bt*   **104**

MOSHE (IRE) 4 b.g. Dansili 127 – Rosinka (IRE) 116 (Soviet Star (USA) 128) [2015 90: 14.1s 14.1f 12g 12m² 11.8d* 12v² t16.5f² p16f⁶ f16g⁴ Dec 18] sturdy gelding: fairly useful handicapper: won at Leicester in August: left Hughie Morrison after seventh start: stays 16.5f: acts on all-weather, good to firm and heavy going: front runner: has looked hard ride. *Philip Kirby*   **86 §**

MOSSGO (IRE) 5 b.g. Moss Vale (IRE) 126 – Perovskia (USA) (Stravinsky (USA) 133) [2015 52, a64: p5m² p5m* t5.1g⁶ p5f* p5g* p5g* 5m⁶ 5m³ p5g* 5g⁵ 5.1s⁵ p5g² p5fᵇᵘ p5m³ p5g³ Dec 10] lengthy, angular gelding: fairly useful handicapper: won at Lingfield in February, May (twice) and June and at Kempton in August: best form at 5f: acts on polytrack, good to firm and good to soft going: tried in cheekpieces prior to 2015: wears tongue tie. *John Best*   **81**

MOSTASHREQAH 2 ch.f. (Apr 30) Equiano (FR) 127 – China Cherub 94 (Inchinor 119) [2015 t7.1g⁵ t7.1f* p8g⁴ p7m Dec 31] 3,500Y, €26,000 2-y-o: fourth foal: half-sister to 2-y-o 5f winner (stays 7.5f) Dad's Girl (by Sakhee's Secret): dam 6f winner: fair performer: won maiden at Wolverhampton in November: barely stays 1m: should do better. *Simon Crisford*   **79 p**

MOST BEAUTIFUL 2 b.f. (Feb 13) Canford Cliffs (IRE) 133 – Saphira's Fire (IRE) 111 (Cape Cross (IRE) 129) [2015 5s⁴ 5.8g* 6m* 7g³ Aug 22] 70,000F, 120,000Y: second foal: dam 8.6f-1¼m winner who stayed 1½m: useful performer: won maiden at Navan (by 1¾ lengths from Waterloo Bridge) in May and Grangecon Stud Stakes at the Curragh (by ¾ length from Only Mine) in June: further improvement when third in Debutante Stakes at the Curragh (2¼ lengths behind Ballydoyle) in August: likely to stay 1m. *David Wachman, Ireland*   **106**

MOST TEMPTING 3 ch.f. Showcasing 117 – La Carot (Motivator 131) [2015 62: t6g⁵ p5m* t5.1g³ 5g³ p5g p5g³ t5.1m t5.1f Nov 10] fair performer: won maiden at Lingfield in June: stays 6f: acts on polytrack and tapeta: usually in visor in 2015: sometimes slowly away. *Robert Cowell*   **65**

MOTDAW 2 b.f. (Apr 28) Motivator 131 – Dawnus (IRE) 103 (Night Shift (USA)) [2015 5.7f 6s⁴ 7.6g⁴ 7s³ 7g Oct 21] 30,000Y: rather unfurnished filly: sister to useful 1m-1¼m winner Initiator and half-sister to 3 winners, including useful winner up to 1m in USA Longhunter (2-y-o 6f/7f winner) and 1½m winner Leighterton (both by Halling): dam 1m-1¼m winner: fair maiden: will stay 1m+: acts on soft going. *Mick Channon*   **72**

MOTHERS FINEST (IRE) 3 ch.f. Tamayuz 126 – Sheer Glamour (IRE) 57 (Peintre Celebre (USA) 137) [2015 8m² 8g* 8m⁵ 8f 8g⁵ 8g⁵ Sep 25] €70,000Y: angular filly: fifth foal: half-sister to 1¼m-1½m winner (stays 16.5f) Dame Lucy (by Refuse To Bend): dam lightly-raced half-sister to dam of Derby runner-up Libertarian: useful performer: won maiden at Haydock (by length from Gold Sands) in April: better form when fifth in listed races at York, Longchamp and Newmarket, beaten 3¾ lengths by Solar Magic on last-named course: raced only at 1m: acts on good to firm going. *K. R. Burke*   **98**

MOTION PICTURE 3 b.f. Motivator 131 – Starshine 71 (Danehill Dancer (IRE) 117) **70**
[2015 t8.6g³ p10g⁵ t8.6g² 12g⁵ Jul 15] first foal: dam maiden (stayed 2m) out of useful
close relative to very smart 1¼m-1½m performer Kutub: fair maiden: stays 1¼m: in hood:
temperament under suspicion. *Michael Bell*

MOUEENN 2 ch.g. (Jan 23) Lope de Vega (IRE) 125 – Quesada (IRE) (Peintre Celebre **63 p**
(USA) 137) [2015 p8g Dec 9] 180,000Y: first foal: dam useful German winner up to 1m
(2-y-o 7f winner): 10/1, some encouragement when 5½ lengths seventh of 12 to Graceful
James in maiden at Kempton on debut, not unduly punished but making late headway: sure
to progress. *Roger Varian*

MOULIN ROUGE (DEN) 4 ch.f. Zambezi Sun 121 – Embattle (FR) (Dernier Empereur **60**
(USA) 125) [2015 60: p12f⁴ t9.5f* p10g⁴ t9.5g⁵ 9m⁶ May 21] rangy filly: modest
handicapper: won at Wolverhampton in February: stays 1¼m: acts on polytrack and tapeta:
often races prominently. *Ian Williams*

MOUNTAIN BELL 2 b.f. (Apr 23) Mount Nelson 125 – Shenir (Mark of Esteem (IRE) **86 p**
137) [2015 8.3d² Oct 5] €46,000Y: second foal: dam unraced: 11/4, promise when head
second of 11 to Top Beak in maiden at Windsor, hanging left and headed inside final
100yds: open to improvement. *Ralph Beckett*

MOUNTAIN MAN 3 b.g. Hellvelyn 118 – Jane Jubilee (IRE) 91 (Mister Baileys 123) **71**
[2015 62: 5.1m² 6.1d 6g³ 6g² 5g 6m t6g t5.1m⁵ Dec 30] good-topped gelding: fair maiden:
first past the post in handicap at Nottingham in April (demoted to second after causing
interference): stays 7f: acts on tapeta and good to firm going: tried in blinkers in 2015: in
tongue tie in 2015. *Michael Easterby*

MOUNTAIN MUSIC 3 b.f. Three Valleys (USA) 119 – Meadow Floss 59 (Cyrano de **70**
Bergerac 120) [2015 p6m t8.6g⁵ 8.3m⁴ p7g 7d* 6g 8s³ t7.1m³ Sep 5] close-coupled filly:
third foal: dam twice-raced half-sister to dam of smart sprinters Fire Up The Band, Strike
Up The Band and Sampower Star: fair performer: won maiden at Lingfield in July: stays
1m: acts on tapeta and soft going. *Sylvester Kirk*

MOUNTAIN RANGE (IRE) 7 b.g. High Chaparral (IRE) 132 – Tuscany Lady (IRE) **64**
(Danetime (IRE) 121) [2015 73: t12.2f p12g⁴ p12m* Jan 18] rather leggy gelding: modest
handicapper: won at Kempton in January: stays 1½m: acts on polytrack and soft going:
often in tongue tie in 2015: usually races nearer last than first. *Willie Musson*

MOUNTAIN RESCUE (IRE) 3 b.g. High Chaparral (IRE) 132 – Amber Queen (IRE) **87**
92 (Cadeaux Genereux 131) [2015 82p: t8.6g⁵ 11g⁵ t12.2g² p11m Oct 28] close-coupled
gelding: fairly useful handicapper: stays 1½m: acts on polytrack and tapeta: often races
prominently. *Roger Charlton*

MOUNT CHEIRON (USA) 4 b.g. Henrythenavigator (USA) 131 – Chalamont (IRE) **59**
88 (Kris 135) [2015 62: p8f t8.6g⁴ f7g* 8d⁶ 8.3m⁵ 8.3d⁵ 7.9m⁵ 8g⁴ 7g 8.3g⁴ 7.9d t8.6f² f7g
t8.6g Dec 1] modest performer: won minor event at Southwell in April: stays 9.5f: acts on
fibresand, tapeta and good to firm going: tried in headgear: often races towards rear.
Richard Ford

MOUNT HOLLOW 10 b.g. Beat Hollow 126 – Lady Lindsay (IRE) 105 (Danehill **54**
Dancer (IRE) 117) [2015 69: 16g 6g t8.6g⁶ 7g p6g p7g t7.1f Oct 23] modest handicapper:
stays 1m: acts on all-weather, good to firm and good to soft going: usually wears headgear.
Simon Hodgson

MOUNT LOGAN (IRE) 4 ch.c. New Approach (IRE) 132 – Vistaria (USA) (Distant **119**
View (USA) 126) [2015 110: 10.1g 10f⁴ 10.4m³ 9.9g* 10m² Aug 22] small colt: smart
handicapper: won at Goodwood (by 1¼ lengths from Elhaame) in July: third of 17 to
Master Carpenter in John Smith's Cup at York previous start and good 2¼ lengths second
of 13 to Exosphere at Sandown final one: stays 1½m: acts on good to firm and good to soft
going: joined Roger Varian. *Luca Cumani*

MOUNT SHAMSAN 5 b.g. Danehill Dancer (IRE) 117 – Shamaiel 113 (Lycius **64**
(USA) 124) [2015 85: 10m 8v* Nov 3] modest performer: won seller at Redcar in
November: stays 1¼m: acts on good to firm and heavy going: races prominently.
Gary Moore

MOUNT TAHAN (IRE) 3 b.g. Lope de Vega (IRE) 125 – Sorpresa (USA) (Pleasant Tap **94**
(USA)) [2015 79p: 7g* 7g 7g⁵ p8g² 6m² 7g* 8g 6g 7m³ Oct 2] fairly useful performer: won
maiden at Wetherby in April and handicap at Newmarket in August: good third in handicap
at Ascot final start: stays 1m: acts on polytrack and good to firm going: front runner.
Kevin Ryan

MOUSKERSIZE (IRE) 4 b.f. Lawman (FR) 121 – Sesenta (IRE) 105 (King's Theatre **57**
(IRE) 128) [2015 74: 9.5g 11g p10.7g t8.6f Dec 11] modest maiden: left W. McCreery after
second start: stays 11f: acts on polytrack, soft and good to firm going: tried in cheekpieces/
tongue tie in 2015. *John McConnell, Ireland*

MOVEABLE ASSET (IRE) 7 b.g. Trans Island 119 – Mica Male (ITY) (Law Society **–**
(USA) 130) [2015 p15.8m Dec 16] one-time fairly useful performer: stays 2m: acts on
polytrack, good to firm and heavy going: tried in blinkers. *Henry Tett*

MOVE IN TIME 7 ch.g. Monsieur Bond (IRE) 120 – Tibesti (Machiavellian (USA) 123 **118**
[2015 119: 5g* 5m⁵ 5g 5s* 5m⁵ Oct 4] stocky gelding: smart performer: won minor event
at Hamilton (by 3½ lengths from Addictive Dream) in June and Prix du Petit Couvert at
Longchamp (by 1¼ lengths from Gengis) in September: third in King George Stakes at
Goodwood (½ length behind Muthmir) in between, and fifth of 18 to Goldream when going
for repeat win in Prix de l'Abbaye at Longchamp final start: stays 6f, races at 5f nowadays:
acts on firm and soft going: tried in headgear in 2012. *David O'Meara*

MOVE UP 2 b.c. (May 14) Dubawi (IRE) 129 – Rosinka (IRE) 116 (Soviet Star (USA) **99 p**
128) [2015 p7f⁵ 7g* 8g* 10g³ Oct 10] well-made colt: fourth foal: half-brother to 1½m
winner Moshe (by Dansili) and 1m-1¼m winner Jam Jar (by Duke of Marmalade): dam, 6f
(at 2 yrs) to 11f (US Grade 3) winner, half-sister to smart French/US performer up to 1½m
King's Drama: useful performer: won maiden at Leicester and nursery at Ripon in
September: further improvement when third in listed race at Newmarket (2½ lengths
behind Glamorous Approach): stays 1¼m: should continue to progress. *Saeed bin Suroor*

MOVIE MAGIC 4 b.f. Multiplex 114 – Alucica 64 (Celtic Swing 138) [2015 55: p8f⁵ 7s⁶ **55**
p8g p10g 10g³ 10m 10d⁵ 14.1g⁶ p8g⁶ p10f 10d p8g⁴ p10m⁵ p8f Dec 17] sturdy filly: modest
maiden: left John Bridger after twelfth start: stays 1¼m: acts on polytrack and good to soft
going: often wears visor: front runner/races prominently. *Mark Hoad*

MOVIE SET (USA) 3 b.g. Dubawi (IRE) 129 – Short Skirt 117 (Diktat 126) [2015 10s* **96 p**
p12g² Nov 4] fourth foal: half-brother to useful 2-y-o 7f winner Minidress (by Street Cry),
stayed 1¼m: dam, winner up to 1½m (2-y-o 7f winner), including St Simon Stakes, closely
related to very smart winner up to 15f Little Rock: won maiden at Ascot in September by
1¼ lengths from Prendergast Hill: upped in trip, improved when neck second to Osipova
in handicap at Kempton, having run of race and sticking to task: stays 1½m: remains with
potential. *Saeed bin Suroor*

MOVIESTA (USA) 5 b.g. Hard Spun (USA) 124 – Miss Brickyard (USA) (A P Indy **118**
(USA) 131) [2015 120: 5g 6f 5m³ 5m 6g* 5d Sep 13] robust gelding: smart performer: left
Bryan Smart after reappearance: won Renaissance Stakes at the Curragh by ¾ length from
Toscanini) in August: easily best other effort in 2015 when third in Sapphire Stakes at the
Curragh (length behind Stepper Point): stays 6f: acts on polytrack, good to firm and good
to soft going: tongue tied third/fourth starts. *Edward Lynam, Ireland*

MOVING UPWARDS 3 ch.g. Bahamian Bounty 116 – Rainbow End 101 (Botanic **52**
(USA)) [2015 57: 8s 6.1m⁵ f8d 7g Aug 6] modest maiden: stays 6f: acts on polytrack and
good to firm going: tried in cheekpieces in 2015: sometimes slowly away. *Kevin Ryan*

MOWHOOB 5 b.g. Medicean 128 – Pappas Ruby (USA) 63 (Red Ransom (USA)) [2015 **63**
79: 7m 8g⁵ 8s⁴ 8m⁶ 7.1m⁴ 7.1m⁵ 8.3d⁴ 7.2m³ 8m² 8.9g 7s Sep 21] sturdy gelding: modest
handicapper: left Jim Goldie after tenth start: stays 1m: acts on polytrack, good to firm and
heavy going: tried in headgear: tried in tongue tie prior to 2015: sometimes slowly away.
Graeme McPherson

MO WONDER 2 b.f. (May 22) Monsieur Bond (IRE) 120 – Mo Muhirnin (IRE) 94 **–**
(Danetime (IRE) 121) [2015 5m 5d Aug 26] £800Y: second foal: sister to 2-y-o 5f winner
(stays 7f) Mo Henry: dam 6f/7f winner: well held in maidens at Beverley and Catterick.
Richard Whitaker

MOXEY 4 ch.g. Nayef (USA) 129 – Emily Blake (IRE) 115 (Lend A Hand 124) [2015 51: **–**
t8.6f Feb 7] angular gelding: modest maiden: stays 1m: acts on fibresand: wears headgear:
tried in tongue tie: not straightforward. *Danielle McCormick*

MOYDIN 3 b.g. Motivator 131 – Yding (IRE) (Danehill (USA) 126) [2015 63p: t12.2m⁶ **–**
10m 8f⁶ 10.2m⁶ Jun 5] behind in maidens/handicaps. *Mick Channon*

MOZIMBA 2 ch.f. (May 6) Monsieur Bond (IRE) 120 – Mozayada (USA) 85 (Street Cry **–**
(IRE) 130) [2015 5m 5v⁶ 6m 7d⁶ Aug 14] £800Y: first foal: dam 7f/1m winner: no form:
often in headgear. *Antony Brittain*

MR BISSTO 3 b.g. High Chaparral (IRE) 132 – Senta's Dream (Danehill (USA) 126) **63**
[2015 67: 10.2m³ 12m 14m⁴ 16g 12.1m⁵ Sep 10] modest maiden: stays 1¾m: acts on
polytrack, tapeta and good to firm going. *Ian Williams*

MR BOSS MAN (IRE) 7 b.g. Beneficial 117 – Sarah Massini (IRE) (Dr Massini (IRE) **75**
117) [2015 69: p12g 12.5m³ 13.8d 16g² 15g³ p16g⁵ p12g⁵ t13.9m* Dec 30] fair
handicapper: won at Wolverhampton in December: stays 2m: acts on polytrack, tapeta and
good to firm going: often travels strongly. *Adrian McGuinness, Ireland*

MR BOSSY BOOTS (IRE) 4 b.g. Teofilo (IRE) 126 – Zelding (IRE) 108 (Warning 136) **98**
[2015 91p: p7g* p7g⁴ p8m⁴ p6g p7m* Oct 21] compact gelding: useful handicapper: won
at Lingfield in January and Kempton (dead-heated with Elemraan) in October: stays 1m:
acts on polytrack and tapeta: sometimes in tongue tie in 2015: often races prominently,
often races freely. *Ralph Beckett*

MR BURBIDGE 7 b.g. Midnight Legend 118 – Twin Time 77 (Syrtos 106) [2015 96: **–**
t16.5f Jan 2] fairly useful performer: well held sole start in 2015: stays 16.5f: acts on
polytrack and fibresand: wears blinkers: front runner/races prominently: fairly useful
hurdler/chaser. *Neil Mulholland*

MR CHOCOLATE DROP (IRE) 11 b.g. Danetime (IRE) 121 – Forest Blade (IRE) **54**
(Charnwood Forest (IRE) 125) [2015 54: t9.5m t8.6g* t8.6m² 8.3m p8g 8.3m⁶ t8.6m⁵ t9.5f
t8.6f⁵ t8.6g⁶ t8.6f³ Dec 21] modest handicapper: won at Wolverhampton (apprentice) in
April: stays 1¼m: acts on all-weather and any turf going: tried in headgear: wears tongue
tie: usually races towards rear. *Mandy Rowland*

MR CHRISTOPHER (IRE) 3 b.g. Bahamian Bounty 116 – Embassy Pearl (IRE) 80 **75**
(Invincible Spirit (IRE) 121) [2015 –: 8g t8.6g⁵ 10m t6f t6f³ t7.1m* t7.1f⁶ Dec 22] fair
handicapper: won at Wolverhampton in November: left Noel Wilson after third start: stays
7f: acts on tapeta. *Tom Dascombe*

MR CHUCKLES (IRE) 2 b.c. (Apr 28) Arcano (IRE) 122 – Caribbean Escape (Pivotal **75**
124) [2015 6d 5d* 6g⁶ 6.1g⁵ 6g 6d Oct 5] fair performer: won maiden at Hamilton in July:
best effort at 5f: acts on good to soft going: often races towards rear. *Philip Kirby*

MR CONUNDRUM 2 b.g. (Mar 27) Paco Boy (IRE) 129 – Folly Drove 71 (Bahri (USA) **50**
125) [2015 7.5m 6g 7.2m⁶ 8g t8.6f Oct 3] modest maiden: left Ann Duffield after second
start: stays 1m: acts on good to firm going: sometimes in hood. *David O'Meara*

MR COOL CASH 3 b.g. Firebreak 125 – Cashleen (USA) 73 (Lemon Drop Kid (USA) **76**
131) [2015 –p: f8g 7.2g² 7.2d² 8g* 7d* 7.9s³ 8g⁴ 7s³ Oct 16] fair handicapper: left Ann
Duffield, won at Ayr and Thirsk in July and Thirsk in August: stays 1m: acts on soft going.
Richard Guest

MR CRIPPS 3 b.g. Sir Percy 129 – Pella 71 (Hector Protector (USA) 124) [2015 10.3d² **88 p**
11m⁴ p13g* Aug 7] 10,000F, 70,000Y: compact gelding: sixth foal: dam, 1m-1¼m winner
who stayed 1½m, half-sister to smart winner up to 1m Sugarfoot: fairly useful performer:
won maiden at Lingfield (by 3½ lengths from Etibaar) in August: better form when fourth
to Mr Singh in similar event at Newbury previous start: stays 13f: remains open to
improvement. *Ralph Beckett*

MR DANDY MAN (IRE) 4 ch.g. Dandy Man (IRE) 123 – Boudica (IRE) (Alhaarth **64 §**
(IRE) 126) [2015 81§: 5m⁶ 5d⁴ 5.2m⁵ t6f t5.1f⁵ Oct 31] workmanlike gelding: modest
handicapper: left Ronald Harris after third start: stays 5.5f: acts on good to firm and good
to soft going: tried in headgear: sometimes in tongue tie in 2015: front runner/races
prominently: unreliable. *Daniel Loughnane*

MR FICKLE (IRE) 6 b.g. Jeremy (USA) 122 – Mamara Reef 71 (Salse (USA) 128) **79**
[2015 62: 9.9g⁴ p16g* p12g* 12g³ 16d² Oct 11] sturdy, quite attractive gelding: fair
handicapper: won at Chelmsford and Kempton in August: stays 2m: acts on polytrack and
soft going: often wears headgear: previously not straightforward. *Gary Moore*

MR FRANKIE 4 b.g. Sleeping Indian 122 – Shes Minnie 90 (Bertolini (USA) 125) [2015 **81**
74: 8.1s² 8d³ 9s² 8g³ 10.2f² 9.9g³ t8.6f² 11.6g³ t9.5g t7.1g⁶ Dec 5] fairly useful maiden: left **a74**
Ed de Giles after eighth start: will benefit from return to 1m+: acts on firm and soft going:
tried in cheekpieces in 2015. *Richard Phillips*

MR GALLIVANTER (IRE) 4 ch.g. Heliostatic (IRE) 115 – Purepleasureseeker (IRE) **91**
(Grand Lodge (USA) 125) [2015 89: 12d* p12g* Jul 1] fairly useful handicapper: won at
Catterick in April and Kempton (by head from Noble Gift) in July: stays 1½m: acts on
polytrack, good to firm and heavy going: tried in cheekpieces prior to 2015: front runner/
races prominently: sold 40,000 gns in July, sent to Germany, where won at 11f at Cologne
in September. *John Quinn*

MR GATSBY 4 b.g. Lucky Story (USA) 128 – Otylia 57 (Wolfhound (USA) 126) [2015 **–**
73: 8g 7m Jul 1] maiden: no form in 2015: often wears blinkers. *Mark Walford*

Weatherbys Hamilton £300,000 2-Y-O Stakes, Doncaster—
Mr Lupton (left), narrowly beaten in the Super Sprint two months earlier, goes one better
in another valuable contest as he comes with a strong run to beat Humphrey Bogart

MR GLOBETROTTER (USA) 2 b.g. (Feb 16) Henrythenavigator (USA) 131 – **67**
Sunshine For Life (USA) (Giant's Causeway (USA) 132) [2015 6g⁴ 6m⁴ 7d Oct 23] fair
maiden: best effort when fourth at Newcastle (1½ lengths behind Prince Hellvelyn) on
second start, unsuited by emphasis on speed: should be suited by 7f. *Michael Dods*

MR GRUMPY 2 b.g. (Apr 4) Sir Percy 129 – Panna 106 (Polish Precedent (USA) 131) **–**
[2015 8.3m⁵ Sep 20] 11/2, fifth of 6 in maiden at Hamilton on debut. *Keith Dalgleish*

MR KHALID 2 b.c. (Jan 9) Pour Moi (IRE) 125 – Island Dreams (USA) 71 (Giant's **86 p**
Causeway (USA) 132) [2015 p8f³ 8.3d* Oct 14] 135,000Y: second foal: half-brother to
2-y-o 1m winner Who'sthedude (by Duke of Marmalade): dam once-raced half-sister to
very smart 1m-1¼m performer Rob Roy: better effort when winning maiden at Nottingham
(by 7 lengths from Hammer Gun) in October, having run of race: likely to stay 1¼m: will
go on improving. *Marco Botti*

MR KITE 4 b.g. Sixties Icon 125 – Mar Blue (FR) 75 (Marju (IRE) 127) [2015 12g⁴ 12d³ **82**
11.9d⁴ 18d⁵ 14.1s⁶ Oct 28] sixth foal: dam 9f winner: fairly useful maiden: likely to prove
best up to 2m: acts on good to soft going: front runner/races prominently. *Mick Channon*

MR LUCAS (IRE) 2 b.g. (May 11) Le Cadre Noir (IRE) 113 – Maripova (IRE) (Marju **45**
(IRE) 127) [2015 5g 5m⁶ 5g 7.5m⁵ 8g⁴ t8.6f⁵ f7g Nov 3] poor maiden: stays 1m: best form
on good going: sometimes in visor: temperament under suspicion. *Peter Niven*

MR LUPTON (IRE) 2 ch.g. (Apr 29) Elnadim (USA) 128 – Chiloe Wigeon (IRE) 55 **106**
(Docksider (USA) 124) [2015 5m² 6g⁶ 5m* 6m³ 5.2m² 6.1g³ 6g 6.5m* 6g² Oct 3] €6,500F,
£15,000Y: strong gelding: fourth foal: half-brother to a winner in Italy by Kheleyf: dam,
maiden, out of half-sister to smart sprinter Tipsy Creek: useful performer: won maiden at
Haydock (by neck from Mayfair Lady) in June and Weatherbys Hamilton £300,000 2-Y-O
Stakes at Doncaster (by head from Humphrey Bogart) in September: good 2 lengths second
of 20 to Log Out Island in listed Two-Year-Old Trophy at Redcar final start: stays 6.5f: acts
on good to firm going. *Richard Fahey*

MR MARBIN (IRE) 2 b.c. (Mar 25) Raven's Pass (USA) 133 – Ultra Finesse (USA) 107 **57**
(Rahy (USA) 115) [2015 6.1m 7.1m 8g³ 7s p7g⁵ p10f⁵ Oct 22] modest maiden: best effort
at 7f: acts on polytrack and good to firm going: tried in blinkers: often races towards rear:
sold 5,000 gns, sent to Hungary. *Harry Dunlop*

MR MARCHWOOD 2 gr.c. (Mar 9) Medicean 128 – Crocus Rose 89 (Royal Applause **70**
124) [2015 t8.6m⁶ t8.6f⁴ t7.1f⁴ Nov 3] fair form in maidens at Wolverhampton.
Sylvester Kirk

MR MO JO 7 b.g. Danbird (AUS) – Nampara Bay 50 (Emarati (USA) 74) [2015 76: t5.1g **48**
t5.1g t5.1g 5g⁵ 5.1m Apr 18] sturdy gelding: poor handicapper: raced only at 5f: acts on
tapeta, good to firm and good to soft going: often wears headgear: front runner/races
prominently: none too reliable. *Les Eyre*

681

MR MOROCCO 3 b.g. Shirocco (GER) 129 – Moxby (Efisio 120) [2015 –: t8.6f t9.5m[6] **49**
Nov 28] modest maiden, lightly raced: stays 9.5f: tried in blinkers/tongue tie. *Giles Bravery*

MR MORSE 2 ro.g. (May 19) Hellvelyn 118 – Songsheet 74 (Dominion 123) [2015 5v[6] **64**
5m[3] May 2] better effort when third in maiden at Doncaster (2½ lengths behind Birchwood)
in May. *Brian Ellison*

MR ORANGE (IRE) 2 b.g. (Feb 4) Paco Boy (IRE) 129 – Shirley Blake (IRE) 101 **64**
(Acclamation 118) [2015 6g[4] 6d[5] 6v[6] Nov 7] strong gelding: modest maiden: best effort
when fourth at Pontefract on debut. *Paul Midgley*

MR PICKWICK 3 b.g. Mount Nelson 125 – Never Lose 95 (Diktat 126) [2015 10g **83**
10.3g[5] 10s[5] 8.3v[4] p10g Oct 29] 18,000Y: good-topped gelding: second foal: half-brother to
winner up to 8.6f Miss Lillie (2-y-o 7f winner, by Exceed And Excel): dam, 6f/7f winner,
half-sister to smart winner up to 7f Morache Music: fairly useful maiden: may prove best
at short of 1¼m: acts on heavy going. *James Fanshawe*

MR POTTER 2 ch.g. (Feb 16) Assertive 121 – Enclave (USA) (Woodman (USA) 126) **66**
[2015 6m 6g[6] 6g[5] 7m[2] 7d[6] t7.1f[6] Oct 27] unfurnished gelding: fair maiden: best effort at 7f:
acts on good to firm going: usually in eyeshields. *Richard Guest*

MR QUICKSILVER 3 gr.c. Dansili 127 – Last Second (IRE) 121 (Alzao (USA) 117) **83**
[2015 –p: 8.5g[3] 10.3s[3] 10m[2] 10.3g[3] 10v[2] 10.3d[2] p10m[3] p8g p8g* Dec 28] good-topped
colt: fairly useful performer: in first-time tongue strap, won maiden at Lingfield final start:
stays 10.5f: acts on polytrack, good to firm and good to soft going: usually in hood: usually
leads, often races freely: temperament under suspicion. *Andrew Balding*

MR RED CLUBS (IRE) 6 b.g. Red Clubs (IRE) 125 – Queen Cobra (IRE) 80 (Indian **80**
Rocket 115) [2015 86: t8.6g p8m[4] p10f[6] p8g[3] p10g[2] 9s[2] 8.3s[6] p8g 8g[3] 10.1m p8g Dec 16]
rather leggy gelding: fairly useful handicapper: stays 1¼m: acts on polytrack, soft and
good to firm going: sometimes wears headgear: usually races towards rear. *Michael Appleby*

MR ROCK (IRE) 4 b.g. Galileo (IRE) 134 – Kitza (IRE) 113 (Danehill (USA) 126) **77**
[2015 92: p11g p11g 12.1d t9.5m p10g[6] t12.2f[6] Nov 16] fair handicapper: stays 1½m: acts
on polytrack and good to firm going: in cheekpieces prior to 2015: often starts slowly.
George Baker

MRS BIGGS 3 ch.f. Paco Boy (IRE) 129 – Hoh Chi Min 103 (Efisio 120) [2015 63: 6m **73**
8m[3] 7.5m[2] 7.9v[5] 6.9s[5] 7g[4] 7.5m 7m[2] 7m 7m 7g[2] 7.5m[4] Oct 1] fair handicapper: stays 1m:
acts on good to firm going: tried in blinkers in 2015: front runner/races prominently.
Declan Carroll

MRS BOJANGLES 2 b.f. (Feb 27) Sakhee's Secret 128 – Dimakya (USA) 83 (Dayjur **69**
(USA) 137) [2015 6g 5.7f[4] 6g[4] 6d 7s[2] t7.1f[3] t8.6f[6] Oct 27] compact filly: closely related to
useful winner up to 7f Red Seventy (2-y-o 6f/6.5f winner, by Sakhee) and half-sister to
several winners, including useful French 2-y-o 5.5f winner Mpumalanga (by Observatory):
dam French 7.5f winner who stayed 1¼m: fair maiden: stays 7f: acts on tapeta and soft
going: front runner/races prominently: sent to Greece. *Charles Hills*

MRS BUBBLES (IRE) 3 b.f. Lord Shanakill (USA) 121 – Champagne Blitz (IRE) 75 **73**
(Viking Ruler (AUS)) [2015 p6m[5] p6f[6] t5.1f[3] t7.1m* p6.5g Dec 21] €2,800 2-y-o: first
foal: dam 6f winner: won maiden at Wolverhampton in December: stays 7f:
acts on tapeta: in hood. *J. S. Moore*

MRS BURBIDGE 5 b.m. Pasternak 111 – Twin Time 77 (Syrtos 106) [2015 –: p12g[4] **57**
p10g[6] 10g* 10g* t12.2f* Dec 21] modest handicapper: won at Les Landes in June, Les
Landes (amateur) in July and Wolverhampton in December: stays 1½m: acts on polytrack
and tapeta: often in cheekpieces in 2015: usually in tongue tie in 2015. *Neil Mulholland*

MRS EVE (IRE) 3 ch.f. Bahamian Bounty 116 – Catbells (IRE) 80 (Rakti 130) [2015 66: **65**
t6f[5] t7.1g[4] 6d[4] 8d[2] p10g 7.6g[6] 7.2g 8g t7.1f Oct 23] smallish, rather leggy filly: fair maiden:
stays 1m: acts on tapeta, good to firm and good to soft going: sometimes in hood in 2015.
Alan Bailey

MR SINGH 3 b.c. High Chaparral (IRE) 132 – Sundari (IRE) 103 (Danehill (USA) 126) **112**
[2015 71p: 11m* 11g[5] 12f[2] 13m* Jul 9] good-topped colt: smart performer: won maiden at
Newbury (by neck from Scottish) in April and Bahrain Trophy at Newmarket (by 2½
lengths from Future Empire) in July: good 1¼ lengths second to Balios in King Edward VII
Stakes at Royal Ascot in between: among leaders in St Leger ante-post betting when ruled
out for rest of season with an infection: likely to stay 1¾m: acts on firm going. *John Gosden*

MRS MAGS 2 b.f. (Apr 25) Sleeping Indian 122 – Esteraad (IRE) 90 (Cadeaux Genereux –
131) [2015 6g 6d Sep 25] 7,000Y: half-sister to several winners, including 2-y-o 7f winner
Press Baron (by King's Best), later useful winner up to 9f in USA, and 1m-1¾m winner

Noora (by Bahhare): dam 2-y-o 6f winner who stayed 1¼m: well held in maidens at Newcastle and Haydock. *Ben Haslam*

MR SNOOZY 6 b.g. Pursuit of Love 124 – Hard To Follow (Dilum (USA) 115) [2015 89: **71** 16s⁴ 16.5m³ 16d³ f14m⁶ Dec 8] tall, good-topped gelding: fair handicapper: stays 16.5f: acts on soft and good to firm going: wears headgear. *Mark Walford*

MR SOPRANO 4 ch.g. Halling (USA) 133 – Rima Baciata (Fantastic Light (USA) 134) **74** [2015 61p: p8g² t9.5f⁶ 10.3d p8m⁴ p8g* 8g p8f³ t8.6m³ p8f² p8g Dec 18] rather leggy gelding: fair handicapper: won at Kempton in July: left Stuart Williams after ninth start: stays 8.5f: acts on polytrack and tapeta: tried in hood in 2015, in tongue tie last 5 starts: often races towards rear. *Miss Hilary McLoughlin, Ireland*

MR STANDFAST 2 b.c. (Feb 23) Mullionmileanhour (IRE) 116 – Phantom Ridge (IRE) **–** 72 (Indian Ridge 123) [2015 p6g t7.1f Dec 22] well held both starts in maidens. *Alan Phillips*

MR STRAVINSKY (IRE) 2 b.g. (Mar 29) Zebedee 113 – Galvano (IRE) (Galileo (IRE) **56** 134) [2015 6g⁵ 6g⁵ Jun 17] modest form in maidens at Thirsk and Hamilton (in cheekpieces): has been gelded. *Ann Duffield*

MR SUNDOWNER (USA) 3 b.g. Scat Daddy (USA) 120 – Bold Answer (USA) **70** (Dynaformer (USA)) [2015 50: t9.5g⁴ p12m⁶ t8.6m f8g⁵ 8m 9.8d³ 8.9g³ 9.2d³ 8.5g² 7.2g* 7.2g³ 7v² Nov 3] fair handicapper: won at Ayr in September: left Noel Quinlan after fourth start: stays 7f: acts on heavy going: tried in blinkers in 2015: often in tongue tie in 2015. *Wilf Storey*

MRS WARREN 5 b.m. Kyllachy 129 – Bold Bunny 57 (Piccolo 121) [2015 79, a70: p7f² **72** p7f 7.6d 7.1m⁶ t6g 7d 6s³ 7.1s³ 7s 6g⁴ Oct 19] fair handicapper: stays 7f: acts on polytrack, soft and good to firm going: tried in headgear. *George Baker*

Lady Bamford's "Mr Singh"

MR TURNER 2 b.c. (Mar 14) Nayef (USA) 129 – Seasonal Blossom (IRE) (Fairy King (USA)) [2015 8.3v 8g Oct 21] good-bodied colt: half-brother to several winners, including useful 6f-1½m winner Brushing (by Medicean) and 1¼m-1¾m winner Wee Charlie Castle (by Sinndar): dam of little account: improved from debut when seventh of 12 in maiden at Newmarket won by Prize Money: likely to progress further. *Mark H. Tompkins* **52 p**

MR VENDMAN (IRE) 5 b.g. Whipper (USA) 126 – So Precious (IRE) 86 (Batshoof 122) [2015 46: 116.5m Nov 21] modest maiden: stays 2m: acts on good to soft going: often in headgear. *Ian Williams* **–**

MR WIN (IRE) 4 b.g. Intikhab (USA) 135 – Midnight Oasis 49 (Oasis Dream 129) [2015 101: 6m 7g² 7m² 7m* 7g* 7g³ 7g* 7m⁴ Oct 3] good-quartered gelding: smart handicapper: continued progress in 2015, winning at Newmarket in July, August and September (by ¾ length from Scottish Glen): looked unlucky not to finish closer when 4 lengths fourth of 17 to Buckstay at Ascot final start, shuffled back over 1f out: effective at 6f/7f: acts on good to firm and good to soft going: usually races prominently: sent to UAE. *Chris Wall* **113**

MR WIZARD 2 b.c. (Jan 11) Major Cadeaux 121 – Yearbook 56 (Byron 117) [2015 6m* 7.1m³ Aug 22] 9,000Y, 8,000 2-y-o: lengthy colt: first foal: dam, sprint maiden, half-sister to useful 2-y-o 7f/1m winner Day of Conquest (by Major Cadeaux): won maiden at Windsor in August by 2 lengths from This Is For You: 25/1, upped in trip and better form when 2 lengths third of 10 to First Selection in Solario Stakes at Sandown: useful. *Nick Littmoden* **97**

MS EBORACUM (IRE) 3 b.f. Vale of York (IRE) 117 – Ms Victoria (IRE) 90 (Fasliyev (USA) 120) [2015 55: t7.1g² f6d² t7.1g 5f p7g⁵ p6g² p6g³ p6g⁴ t6m 6s³ f5g⁵ p6g⁵ p7g⁴ p6f⁶ Dec 17] modest maiden: stays 7f: acts on all-weather and soft going: tried in headgear in 2015. *Michael Appleby* **59**

MU'AJIZA 5 ch.m. Pivotal 124 – Siyasa (USA) 81 (Rahy (USA) 115) [2015 91: 6.1s 6g⁶ 6m⁶ Jun 12] fairly useful performer: effective at 6f to 1¼m: acts on good to firm and good to soft going. *Paul Midgley* **94**

MUATADEL 2 b.c. (Feb 21) Exceed And Excel (AUS) 126 – Rose Blossom 113 (Pastoral Pursuits 127) [2015 p5m³ 6m³ 5m² 5.9m³ Sep 9] fair maiden: stays 6f. *Mark Johnston* **78**

MUBARAZA (IRE) 6 ch.g. Dalakhani (IRE) 133 – Mokaraba 86 (Unfuwain (USA) 131) [2015 110: p16g⁵ 18.7d May 6] useful-looking gelding: useful handicapper: stays 2½m: acts on polytrack, good to firm and good to soft going: held up. *Ed Dunlop* **97**

MUBTAAHIJ (IRE) 3 b.c. Dubawi (IRE) 129 – Pennegale (IRE) (Pennekamp (USA) 130) [2015 93p: a7f* a8f² a9.4f* a9.4f* a10f a12f⁴ Jun 6] lengthy, good-topped colt: very smart performer: vastly improved in 2015, successful at Meydan in minor event in January, then listed race and UAE Derby (very impressively by 8 lengths from Maftool, leading 1½f out and quickening clear), both in March: head second to Maftool in UAE 2000 Guineas there on second outing: below form in Kentucky Derby at Churchill Downs on penultimate start, but ran creditably when 7¾ lengths fourth to American Pharoah in Belmont Stakes at Belmont final outing: probably stays 1½m: acts on dirt. *M. F. de Kock, South Africa* **120**

MUBTADI 7 b.g. Dr Fong (USA) 128 – Noble Peregrine (Lomond (USA) 128) [2015 88: p10g* p10f⁵ 10m⁶ p11g Jun 24] tall, good-bodied gelding: fairly useful handicapper: won at Lingfield in January: stays 1¼m: acts on polytrack, soft and good to firm going: tried in headgear: tried in tongue tie prior to 2015: often races towards rear. *Ismail Mohammed* **87**

MUBTAGHAA (IRE) 3 b.g. Acclamation 118 – Mabalane (IRE) (Danehill (USA) 126) [2015 104: 7g 6m 6m 6m* 6g³ Sep 6] smart performer: improved to win handicap at Newmarket in August by neck from Burnt Sugar: respectable third in listed race at York (2¼ lengths behind Lucky Kristale) on final start: stays 6f: acts on good to firm and good to soft going: front runner/races prominently: sent to UAE. *William Haggas* **112**

MUDAMMERA (IRE) 3 b.f. Dubawi (IRE) 129 – Fatanah (IRE) 103 (Green Desert (USA) 127) [2015 t8.6g³ 7g⁶ 8.3g⁶ 8.3m⁴ Jun 23] first foal: dam, 1¼m winner, closely related to smart US Grade 2 1¼m winner Makderah: modest maiden: stays 8.5f: usually in hood. *Roger Varian* **61**

MUFFARREH (USA) 3 b.c. First Samurai (USA) 119 – Sarayir (USA) 104 (Mr Prospector (USA)) [2015 77p: 8m⁶ 8.3m 7.4g⁴ 10.2f Sep 13] fair maiden: stays 1m: acts on good to firm going: tried in blinkers in 2015: often races towards rear. *B. W. Hills* **71**

MUFFIN THE MULE (IRE) 2 b.c. (Apr 18) The Carbon Unit (USA) 106 – Mad Madam Mym 75 (Hernando (FR) 127) [2015 8d p7g⁶ p7g f7g² Nov 26] modest maiden: stays 7f. *John Patrick Shanahan, Ireland* **62**

MUFFRI'HA (IRE) 3 b.f. Iffraaj 127 – Grecian Dancer 114 (Dansili 127) [2015 92p: 8m² **102** 7g⁶ 8f 7m² 7.6g* 7m 8g⁴ 7m⁴ 6g Oct 10] lengthy filly: useful performer: won minor event at Lingfield (by 4 lengths from Third Time Lucky) in July: similar form when second in handicap at Newmarket and fourth in listed race at Ascot fourth/eighth starts: stays 1m: acts on good to firm going. *William Haggas*

MUGHARRED (USA) 3 gr.g. Bernardini (USA) 132 – Wid (USA) 100 (Elusive Quality **56** (USA)) [2015 –: 7g⁴ p7g 7m 8f⁶ Sep 12] modest maiden: stays 7f: acts on polytrack and good to firm going: usually races towards rear. *B. W. Hills*

MUHAAFIZ (IRE) 3 br.g. Lord Shanakill (USA) 121 – Yasmin Satine (IRE) (Key of **83** Luck (USA) 126) [2015 73: p8m⁵ 7g⁶ 8g² 10.3m² 10m² 10d³ Sep 17] fairly useful maiden: stays 10.5f: acts on good to firm going. *David Brown*

MUHAARAR 3 b.c. Oasis Dream 129 – Tahrir (IRE) 100 (Linamix (FR) 127) [2015 **132** 111: 7m* 8g 6f* 6f* 6.5g* 6d* Oct 17]

'Every so often comes an occasion on a racecourse when those present count themselves fortunate to have been there.' Nothing could live with Dayjur in the 1990 Nunthorpe Stakes, when he ran to a Timeform rating of 137 and recorded an exceptional timefigure of 1.69 fast (equivalent to a timerating of 142), drawing the comment reproduced from *Racehorses*. In the latest season Muhaarar, representing the same owner Hamdan Al Maktoum, earned the highest rating for a British-trained sprinter since Dayjur. Dayjur won the King's Stand, the Nunthorpe, the Sprint Cup and the Prix de l'Abbaye on successive outings and Muhaarar won four straight Group 1s, becoming only the second horse to win three Group 1 sprints in succession since Dayjur won the Nunthorpe, Sprint Cup and Prix de l'Abbaye (the King's Stand was then Group 2).

Excluding two-year-olds, nineteen horses in the quarter of a century since Dayjur (also including Goldream in the latest season) have won two Group 1 sprints in Europe (up to and including six and a half furlongs) in the same year, among them the tough mare Lochsong (who achieved it in 1993), those two fine champions named after the composers Stravinsky (1999) and Mozart (2001) and Muhaarar's sire Oasis Dream (who won the July Cup and the Nunthorpe in 2003 after coming third against older horses in the King's Stand), but only one other has won three in succession, the French-trained five-year-old Marchand d'Or who won the July Cup, Prix Maurice de Gheest (a race he won three years running) and Prix de l'Abbaye in 2008. Marchand d'Or won the edition of the Abbaye that was rerun nearly five hours after the void race won by Overdose, in which Marchand d'Or was pulled up at halfway, and Overdose was not asked to take part in the rerun. Dream Ahead won three Group 1s at up to seven furlongs (July Cup, Sprint Cup and the Prix de la Foret) in 2011. Also worth a special mention are Sheikh Albadou, who added the Breeders' Cup Sprint in 1991 (the year after Dayjur's unfortunate defeat when he hurdled a shadow) to his earlier success in the Nunthorpe; and Choisir, whose Royal Ascot double in 2003 was achieved while the King's Stand was a Group 2.

Admittedly, Muhaarar's record included two Group 1s that were in their first year as Group 1s, the inaugural Commonwealth Cup for three-year-olds which was run at Royal Ascot and the British Champions Sprint which was upgraded

Commonwealth Cup, Royal Ascot—Muhaarar produces a performance verging on top class in the inaugural running of this Group 1 for three-year-olds over six furlongs; Limato proves best of the rest, ahead of Anthem Alexander and Salt Island (far side)

from Group 2, but there's no doubt at all that he was a top-class performer who ranks with the best sprinters of recent times. Just like Dayjur—who spent his stud career in Kentucky—and Oasis Dream, Muhaarar will not be seen at four having been retired to stand at a fee of £30,000 (his sire stands at £75,000) which had breeders falling over themselves to use him (he was fully booked well before Christmas). Muhaarar is the best son of Oasis Dream, who has sired fourteen Group 1 winners—including the King's Stand and Prix de l'Abbaye winner Goldream—from his first eight crops. Oasis Dream is also responsible for the promising young sire Showcasing, who won the Gimcrack like Muhaarar.

Muhaarar's new home is Shadwell's Nunnery Stud in Norfolk, one of eight Sheikh Hamdan-owned stud farms worldwide (which house over two hundred mares and numerous stallions). Muhaarar will stand alongside Mukhadram, Nayef and Sakhee at the stud which had Oasis Dream's sire Green Desert for his entire stallion career until he was put down due to the infirmities of old age at thirty-two in September (he had been pensioned from covering duties since 2011). Green Desert, who carried the colours of Sheikh Hamdan's brother Maktoum Al Maktoum, became one of the most influential sires of the past twenty-five years, and was also responsible for such as Cape Cross (sire of Sea The Stars and Golden Horn) and the Irish National Stud's flagship stallion Invincible Spirit (sire of Kingman). Green Desert was one of the first sons of North American sire Danzig (Dayjur's sire, about whom there is more in the essay on Air Force Blue) to stand in Europe. As discussed in the essay on Oaks winner Taghrooda in *Racehorses of 2014*, Sheikh Hamdan built his breeding empire on the success of North American-based stallions; he also owns Shadwell Farm in Lexington, Kentucky, set up in 1985, which has a stallion division called Nashwan Stud (named after the owner's Nashwan who was by North American-based sire Blushing Groom). Green Desert covered a full book of mares at £25,000 during his first season and the largest book he covered was eighty-eight in 2003—the year after Oasis Dream was crowned champion two-year-old. Green Desert produced a number of smart performers for Sheikh Hamdan, including Sandown Mile winner Gabr, Al Quoz Sprint winner Mutamarres and Princess Royal Stakes winner Itnab, while Muhaarar joins other Group 1-winning sons of Oasis Dream, Arcano, Naaqoos and Aqlaam to have become Shadwell stallions (the last-named died aged eight in 2013) after carrying the owner's royal blue, white epaulets, striped cap. Sheikh Hamdan has enjoyed a major renaissance as an owner, after something of a lull, and he was champion owner in Britain in 2014 with three Group 1 wins from Taghrooda (two) and Mukhadram, after not having had a Group 1 win in Britain since 2009. He finished runner-up to Godolphin in the 2015 standings on both first-three earnings and number of wins, with his team spearheaded by Muhaarar whose name means 'liberated' in Arabic.

Muhaarar was a smart two-year-old, winning two of his five starts, including the Gimcrack at York, and finishing third on the three others including the Middle Park. He looked likely to prove a sprinter but returned to action in the Greenham Stakes at Newbury in April when, at 16/1, he was the longest-priced of the three horses owned by Sheikh Hamdan, behind Estidhkaar (ridden by first jockey Hanagan) and Fannaan (ridden by second jockey O'Neill), with Frankie Dettori wearing a distinguishing pink cap on Muhaarar. The favourite was Estidhkaar's stablemate Ivawood, who had been unbeaten as a two-year-old until going down by a nose when odds-on for the Middle Park; the Dewhurst winner Belardo was also in the field. The Greenham has always been one of the principal Two Thousand Guineas trials in recent times, and four of the five previous winners had landed Group 1s over a mile subsequently, among them Frankel, Olympic Glory and Kingman (who beat the subsequent Guineas winner Night of Thunder in the 2014 renewal).

The latest Greenham field looked every bit as strong as usual, and the finish was fought out by Muhaarar and Estidhkaar who both looked candidates for top mile honours, Muhaarar staying on to lead well inside final furlong and win by a neck. The pair finished four and a half lengths clear of Ivawood, who was a further three and a quarter lengths ahead of another two-year-old Group 1 winner Dick Whittington. Muhaarar looked much improved with a winter on his back, with the step back up in trip and the good pace at which the Greenham was run both

Darley July Cup, Newmarket—in what is now the first opportunity for the generations to clash in a six-furlong Group 1, Muhaarar collars the seven-year-old Tropics, who finishes runner-up for the second year running; 50/1-shot Eastern Impact (No.6) grabs third, ahead of Sole Power and Danzeno

appearing to favour him. Muhaarar's time of 1m 20.8sec broke the seven-furlong course record by some margin (previously 1m 21.50sec) and, while the prevailing good to firm ground and the truly-run race were the main reason that Muhaarar broke the record by the best part of a second, his performance—and that of runner-up Estidhkaar—made the time and form students sit up. Muhaarar was open to further improvement and certainly looked the type to win more good races, with the Poule d'Essai des Poulains somewhat surprisingly preferred for his next target, despite the claims he would have held in the Two Thousand Guineas. Estidhkaar was aimed at Newmarket instead and the owner also supplemented the impressive Newbury maiden winner Intilaaq, neither of whom figured. Muhaarar looked sure to give a good account of himself in the Poule d'Essai des Poulains at Longchamp eight days later but he managed only eighth of eighteen to Make Believe, an explanation for his performance, back under Paul Hanagan, found in the fact that he had the worst draw and, after being still in the rear on the home turn, had to come widest of all in the straight.

Muhaarar reverted to six furlongs next for the Commonwealth Cup, which was run on the Friday at Royal Ascot and was incorporated into the British Champions Series. The three-year-old sprint programme in the first part of the season was changed for the better, with the Pavilion Stakes at Ascot in April upgraded to Group 3 status and the Sandy Lane Stakes at Haydock in May made into a Group 2 (having previously had only listed status), the changes marking out a natural path to the Commonwealth Cup. Similar events in France and Ireland were also upgraded. Muhaarar, however, was a Guineas horse turned sprinter (Oasis Dream had been thought of as a classic colt but failed to come to himself early enough at three, while Green Desert finished runner-up to Dancing Brave in the Two Thousand Guineas before being dropped back down in trip). The Commonwealth Cup attracted a representative field and had an outstanding first winner in Muhaarar who looked champion sprinter material as he stretched three and three quarter lengths clear of the previous year's leading male two-year-old Limato, who had won the Pavilion Stakes on his return before finishing second to Adaay in the Sandy Lane. Anthem Alexander finished less than a length behind Limato in third in the Commonwealth Cup, closely followed by Salt Island and Profitable, who were

LARC Prix Maurice de Gheest, Deauville—Muhaarar gets the better of a good battle with Esoterique (rail); Irish challenger Gordon Lord Byron (No.3) wins the race for third, ahead of British-trained Watchable (cheekpieces)

ahead of Home of The Brave. Adaay, carrying Sheikh Hamdan's first colours, came next in seventh, a place ahead of front-running French challenger Goken, with the American-trained favourite Hootenanny only eleventh. The previous year's leading two-year-old filly Tiggy Wiggy, who was also dropping back in trip after finishing third in the One Thousand Guineas, managed only sixteenth of the eighteen runners.

The strong pace that seemed assured in the Commonwealth Cup never really materialised among the stand-side runners (which included Tiggy Wiggy and Hootenanny) with the strongest pace towards the far side, also putting such as Limato and Profitable, perhaps even Anthem Alexander (stall nine), at some disadvantage as well, though, given Muhaarar's clear superiority, none of them could be said in any way to have been unlucky. Ridden by Dane O'Neill for the second time (he had ridden him when third to Ivawood in the July Stakes)—Paul Hanagan having chosen Adaay—Muhaarar was waited with from stall eight and travelled well until being switched to come widest of all towards the far side (Adaay had tracked him but couldn't keep up). Muhaarar made good headway and hit the front from Salt Island, Goken and Home of The Brave over a furlong out, before staying on strongly to record a performance that was verging on top class (he broke twenty-three seconds for the last two furlongs, very good even on firm going). Muhaarar was the first horse aged three or older to win a Group 1 sprint for Sheikh Hamdan since Malhub (only third string for the owner on the day) was successful in the 2002 Golden Jubilee Stakes (in its first year as a Group 1 after formerly being known as the Cork And Orrery Stakes). There are some in British horseracing who seem opposed to any change, but it was difficult to find anyone bemoaning the creation of the Commonwealth Cup which, along with the revamped three-year-old sprint programme, had been needed for some time and will quickly prove its worth.

The new three-year-old sprint programme means that the Diamond Jubilee at Royal Ascot is no longer open to three-year-olds and the Darley July Cup at Newmarket (also part of the British Champions Series, as well as being part of the Global Sprint Challenge) is now the first opportunity for a clash of the generations in a six-furlong Group 1. The latest renewal was dominated by Muhaarar and the Australian-trained four-year-old (in the northern hemisphere) Brazen Beau. They were sent off 2/1 joint favourites, the latter representing the Diamond Jubilee form in the absence of the American-trained winner of that race, Undrafted. The Sheikh Hamdan-owned Muthmir, successful in the Prix du Gros-Chene and a close third in the King's Stand Stakes on his two previous starts and carrying the owner's black cap, was next in the betting at 9/1, ahead of Danzeno and Anthem Alexander (the only other three-year-old in the field apart from Muhaarar) both at 12/1, with Sole Power at 16/1 and the eight other runners at 20/1 or longer. Brazen Beau was close up for a long way before weakening rather tamely, and Muhaarar didn't have to match the form he had shown in the Commonwealth Cup to get home by a nose from 25/1-shot Tropics, who made the running for the first time and still held a clear lead inside the final furlong. Muhaarar had to find plenty to battle his way to the front late on, after looking in trouble. Tropics set just a fair pace for the opening couple of furlongs and it was an advantage to race in touch, as Muhaarar did, travelling in second among a group of eight that raced near the stand-side rail headed by Astaire,

688

as Tropics led the rest more towards the centre of the track. The patiently-ridden Sole Power and Danzeno were probably a little better than their result (fourth and fifth respectively, just behind 50/1-shot Eastern Impact). The form on the day was towards the lower end of the range that might be called average for a July Cup, although firm ground and a following wind made for some notably quick times on the day, with Muhaarar just 0.23sec outside Lethal Force's course record set in the 2013 July Cup. With a stronger early pace, the record might well have gone.

Muhaarar made his next appearance in the Prix Maurice de Gheest and justified even-money favouritism in another close finish, winning by half a length from the French mare Esoterique. British- and Irish-trained runners had already won the Maurice de Gheest seven times this century and made up six of the twelve in the field; of those, Gordon Lord Byron finished third (half a length behind Esoterique), Watchable fourth, Majestic Queen sixth, Ivawood seventh and Coulsty eighth. Muhaarar won despite reportedly losing a front shoe, taking a keen hold in touch until being pushed along two furlongs out and leading inside the final furlong. Muhaarar's connections opted to bypass both the Sprint Cup at Haydock and the Foret at Longchamp to give Muhaarar plenty of time (ten weeks) to recover from his three summer races (the stable took second and third in the Sprint Cup with Strath Burn and Magical Memory).

The first running of the Qipco British Champions Sprint Stakes as a Group 1 attracted a twenty-strong field that was thoroughly representative of the available British- and Irish-trained sprinters, as well as the 33/1-shot Emperor Max from Singapore. The line up included two previous winners, Maarek (2012) and Gordon Lord Byron (2014), but the market was dominated by Muhaarar (who started at 5/2) and the unbeaten three-year-old Twilight Son (4/1) who had won the Sprint Cup at Haydock. Twilight Son convincingly beat the rest who were headed by Danzeno (12/1) and another progressive three-year-old The Tin Man (10/1), who had been supplemented for the race after winning a few days after being taken out at the previous forfeit stage. Twilight Son proved no match though for Muhaarar who put up the best performance of his career on his final start, surpassing even the pick of the sterling efforts on the racecourse of his sire Oasis Dream, who was probably the best European-trained sprinter since Mozart and probably Stravinsky. As the Commonwealth Cup had shown, Ascot suited Muhaarar down to the ground and he travelled well close behind outsider Lancelot du Lac in the centre of the track as that horse helped set the pace with 20/1-shot Eastern Impact who raced towards the far side with just Lightning Moon for company until halfway. Muhaarar quickened to lead over a furlong out and kept on well inside the final furlong to win by two lengths from Twilight Son, who raced mostly near the stand-side rail before drifting towards the centre of the track late on. In the absence of electronic sectionals, Timeform took manual ones and Muhaarar's win was the timing highlight of the day as he clocked 1m 13.34sec on good to soft ground. Muhaarar's time performance, as measured by an overall timefigure of 1.17 fast (equivalent to a timerating of 127), was the fastest by any horse all year in Britain over any distance, challenged only by Mecca's Angel's 1.16 fast in the Nunthorpe Stakes.

Qipco British Champions Sprint Stakes, Ascot—
Muhaarar rounds off his career with a sparkling performance in the first running of this race
as a Group 1, beating the previously unbeaten Sprint Cup winner Twilight Son by two lengths,
with Danzeno (No.3, partly hidden) third and The Tin Man (crossed noseband) fourth

Mr Hamdan Al Maktoum's "Muhaarar"

			Danzig
	Oasis Dream	Green Desert	Foreign Courier
	(b 2000)	(b 1983)	Dancing Brave
Muhaarar		Hope	Bahamian
(b.c. 2012)		(b 1991)	Mendez
	Tahrir (IRE)	Linamix	Lunadix
	(gr 2002)	(gr 1987)	Last Tycoon
		Miss Sacha	Heaven High
		(b 1991)	

Muhaarar doesn't hail from a particularly distinguished family—at least compared to most of the horses owned (and bred) by Sheikh Hamdan—and the closest Group 1 winner on his dam's side is his great grandam Heaven High's half-sister Timarida who won the Irish Champion Stakes for the Aga Khan and John Oxx. That said, Muhaarar's dam Tahrir, who was trained by Barry Hills, father of Muhaarar's trainer, was rated 100 by the time of her retirement and Muhaarar became the fourth of her first five offspring to better that rating: the others are the smart winner at up to seven furlongs Tamaathul (by Tiger Hill) and the useful performers Raasekha (mile winner by Pivotal) and the ill-fated Sajwah (listed winner at two by Exceed And Excel who broke her pelvis in the Cheveley Park). Tahrir's two-year-old colt Mootaharer (by Dubawi) has a rating of 92p after just two starts in maidens and he was staying on well at the end of seven furlongs when winning at Newmarket. Tahrir also has a colt foal by Dubawi. Tahrir was herself campaigned mostly over seven furlongs (she won twice at that trip and was also tried at a mile) though her best performance was over six furlongs on heavy ground, when runner-up in the listed Wentworth Stakes at Doncaster on her tenth and final start. Tahrir was purchased by Shadwell for 350,000 guineas as a yearling—the most expensive Linamix yearling sold that year at auction—and is out of Miss Sacha who won one of her eight races at three and four, her success coming in the listed Topaz Stakes over five furlongs on heavy ground at Tipperary. Miss Sacha ran her best race when fifth in the Irish One Thousand Guineas on her next start after the Topaz, and she also finished fourth in the King's Stand. Miss Sacha was well held on both her outings as a four-year-old after being switched to Britain, and she made just 25,000 guineas when sold as a prospective broodmare at the end of that season.

Miss Sacha's best produce is the smart French performer at up to nine furlongs (would have stayed ten) Mister Sacha, and Miss Sacha is a half-sister to several winners out of the lightly-raced Heaven High, who, along with her half-sister Timarida, is a granddaughter of the smart sprinter-miler Pugnacity who became the backbone of one of the successful families developed by Major Lionel Holliday (Pugnacity was the dam of Benson & Hedges Gold Cup winner Relkino). Muhaarar stayed seven furlongs (there was talk at one stage of running him in the Breeders' Cup Mile) but his best efforts came over shorter and he acted on any turf going (won on heavy and firm) and was thoroughly genuine. Muhaarar's retirement in the same year as Green Desert's death could not have been better timed to bring the story of Nunnery Stud, best known for stallions who made their names at middle distances, nearly full circle. Muhaarar's grandsire was the first stallion to stand under the Shadwell banner at Nunnery after also being acclaimed as the champion sprinter of his year. Muhaarar might just turn out to be the high-class commercial stallion prospect that Shadwell has been looking for since Green Desert's retirement; he will also provide a source of speed for Sheikh Hamdan's broodmare band, though, because of demand, only a dozen of the hundred and ten or so mares to visit Muhaarar in his first season will be Shadwell mares. *Charles Hills*

MUHADATHAT 2 b.f. (Apr 11) Showcasing 117 – Cavallo da Corsa (Galileo (IRE) 134) **93**
[2015 5v³ 5m* 5.1m² 5g² 5.1m* 5g⁴ 5.2s 6g Aug 31] 800F, €20,000Y, £26,000 2-y-o: rather unfurnished filly: fourth foal: dam unraced half-sister to useful 6f/7f winner Cansili Star: fairly useful performer: won maiden at Musselburgh in June and nursery at Chester in July: should be suited by 6f: acts on good to firm going. *Mark Johnston*

MUHAZWARA (IRE) 3 b.f. Fastnet Rock (AUS) 127 – Carn Lady (IRE) 52 (Woodman –
(USA) 126) [2015 7g Sep 19] £72,000Y: fourth foal: closely related to 1m winner War Lord (by Aussie Rules) and half-sister to 2-y-o 7f winner Tradition (by Footstepsinthesand) and 6f/7f winner Lana (by Amadeus Wolf): dam maiden (best at 5f/6f): 6/1, well held in maiden at Catterick on debut. *George Peckham*

MUHDIQ (USA) 6 b.g. Hard Spun (USA) 124 – Enfiraaj (USA) (Kingmambo (USA) **83**
125) [2015 91: p5f⁵ p5m⁵ p6f⁴ Mar 20] strong gelding: fairly useful handicapper: stayed 6f: acted on polytrack and good to firm going: dead. *Ed de Giles*

MUHTARIS (IRE) 5 b.g. Teofilo (IRE) 126 – Fann (USA) 96 (Diesis 133) [2015 p12g –
Oct 6] fairly useful handicapper: stays 1½m: acts on polytrack, fibresand, best turf form on heavy going: fair hurdler. *James Evans*

MUIR LODGE 4 ch.g. Exceed And Excel (AUS) 126 – Miss Chaussini (IRE) 76 (Rossini **98**
(USA) 118) [2015 89: 6m⁴ 6m⁴ 7g 7f³ 7g 6m* 6v⁴ 6g 6g² Oct 16] useful-looking gelding: useful handicapper: won at Newmarket in August: good second at Haydock (1¼ lengths behind Mukaynis) final start: stays 7f: acts on polytrack and firm going: tried in headgear: often wears tongue tie: temperament under suspicion (wears net muzzle). *George Baker*

MUJAAHER (IRE) 4 ch.g. Nayef (USA) 129 – Raaya (USA) (Giant's Causeway (USA) **73**
132) [2015 10m⁵ 8d⁵ 7m⁵ 8.3d³ 9.3gᵖᵘ Sep 15] fair maiden: should have been suited by 1¼m: acted on good to soft going: dead. *Alan Swinbank*

MUJAAMIL 2 b.c. (Apr 10) Dansili 127 – Muwakleh 115 (Machiavellian (USA) 123) **68 p**
[2015 7d Oct 30] tall colt: brother to useful 6f/7f winner Ghasabah and half-brother to winner up to 1m Manaal (2-y-o 7f winner, by Bahri) and 1m winner Tawaasul (by Haafhd): dam, UAE 1m winner (including UAE 1000 Guineas) and second in 1000 Guineas, sister to Dubai World Cup winner Almutawakel: 7/1, green when 3¼ lengths ninth of 13 to Chelsea Lad in maiden at Newmarket on debut, not unduly knocked about: will improve. *William Haggas*

MUJASSAM 3 ch.g. Kyllachy 129 – Naizak 73 (Medicean 128) [2015 92: 7m 7g 7g* 7d 7g* Aug 30] good-topped gelding: useful handicapper: improved to win at Salisbury (by 8 lengths from Upstaging) in July and Yarmouth (visored, by 2 lengths from Fieldsman) in August: stays 7f: acts on heavy going. *Roger Varian* **106**

MUJAZIF (IRE) 5 br.g. Shamardal (USA) 129 – Red Bandanna (IRE) 80 (Montjeu (IRE) 137) [2015 102: 8d 7g 8m 8.5g⁶ 7.9d⁴ 7.5g 8g 7s 8.3s f8g Dec 22] useful-looking gelding: fairly useful handicapper: stays 10.5f, effective at shorter: acts on good to firm and heavy going: often in tongue tie prior to 2015. *David Nicholls* **83**

MUKAYNIS (IRE) 4 b.g. Tamayuz 126 – Wild Ways (Green Desert (USA) 127) [2015 86, a76: p5g⁴ t5.1g* t5.1f⁴ 6g* 6g 6g² 5m² 6g³ 5.5m 6g 6.1g⁴ 6g* Oct 16] useful handicapper: won at Wolverhampton in January, Doncaster in May and Haydock (by 1¼ lengths from Muir Lodge) in October: stays 7.5f: acts on tapeta and good to firm going: sometimes in headgear: often races towards rear. *Kevin Ryan* **100**

MUKHAYYAM 3 b.g. Dark Angel (IRE) 113 – Caster Sugar (USA) 87 (Cozzene (USA)) [2015 94: 8.1d 8m⁴ 7g 8s⁴ Sep 5] good-topped gelding: useful handicapper, generally disappointing in 2015, best effort when fourth at Ayr (½ length behind Little Lady Katie) second start: stays 1m: acts on good to firm going: visored final outing. *Sir Michael Stoute* **98**

MUKHMAL (IRE) 3 ch.g. Bahamian Bounty 116 – May Day Queen (IRE) 79 (Danetime (IRE) 121) [2015 97: t5.1f⁵ 5d 6f⁶ 6m* 6g⁶ 6m 5d³ 6f² 6g³ Sep 5] strong gelding: useful handicapper: won at Newmarket (by 2¼ lengths from Barracuda Boy) in May: second at Chelmsford (2 lengths behind Golden Amber) and third at Ascot (1¼ lengths behind Right Touch) last 2 starts: stays 6f: acts on polytrack and good to firm going: often wears hood: usually races close up. *Mark Johnston* **105**

MULAASEQ 3 b.g. Showcasing 117 – Lonely Heart 101 (Midyan (USA) 124) [2015 7d* 8d⁵ May 11] £60,000Y: half-brother to several winners, including winner up to 1m Leitrim House (2-y-o 6f winner, by Cadeaux Genereux) and 7f-9f winner Ace of Hearts (by Magic Ring), both smart: dam 1¼m winner: better effort when winning maiden at Doncaster (by short head from Nortron) in March, conceding first run: should stay 1m: remains with potential. *Marcus Tregoning* **87 p**

MULHAAM (IRE) 3 gr.g. Fast Company (IRE) 126 – Park Approach (IRE) 77 (Indian Ridge 123) [2015 7d 7.1d⁵ 6g⁴ 7v³ p7g t6g t7.1f Oct 9] fair maiden: stays 7f: acts on heavy going: tried in cheekpieces. *Ed Dunlop* **72 a62**

MULLED WINE 2 b.c. (Feb 21) Mullionmileanhour (IRE) 116 – Numanthia (IRE) 56 (Barathea (IRE) 127) [2015 p7g Oct 7] 50/1, last of 10 in maiden at Kempton on debut. *John Best* **–**

MULLIONDOLLAR 2 b.g. (Feb 26) Mullionmileanhour (IRE) 116 – Dolly Parton (IRE) 79 (Tagula (IRE) 116) [2015 p6g p6g 6.1s⁶ Sep 12] no form. *John Best* **–**

MULLIONHEIR 3 b.g. Mullionmileanhour (IRE) 116 – Peyto Princess 85 (Bold Arrangement 127) [2015 57: p6g* p6f* 6d⁴ 7g³ 6g* 6m⁴ 7d* Aug 15] lengthy gelding: useful handicapper: thrived in 2015 and won 5 of 7 starts, at Chelmsford and Kempton in April, Lingfield in May, Windsor in June and Newbury (beat Czech It Out by neck) in August: stays 7f: acts on polytrack, good to firm and good to soft going. *John Best* **101**

MULLOVER 2 b.f. (Mar 22) Mullionmileanhour (IRE) 116 – Daughters World 48 (Agnes World (USA) 123) [2015 p6g p6g⁴ p7m Dec 21] third foal: dam maiden: poor maiden. *John Best* **44**

MULTELLIE 3 b.g. Multiplex 114 – Bollin Nellie 98 (Rock Hopper 124) [2015 67p: 9.9g³ 11.9m⁴ 10g² 12g² 12m⁵ 12g* 12d² 10.3g 12s² Oct 27] fairly useful handicapper: won at Haydock in May and Ripon in August: good second at Catterick final start: stays 1½m: acts on soft and good to firm going: front runner/races prominently. *Tim Easterby* **90**

MULTIDEAL 2 b.g. (May 19) Multiplex 114 – Elusive Deal (USA) 59 (Elusive Quality (USA)) [2015 5m 7m³ p7.5g² 7g⁵ 8g⁴ 8g⁵ 7d 8.4s Oct 6] fourth foal: brother to 2-y-o 7.5f winner Chester Deal and half-brother to a winner in Greece by Captain Gerrard: dam maiden (stayed 1¼m): fairly useful maiden: second in claimer at Deauville in August (left Jo Hughes after): should stay 1m: acts on polytrack, best turf form on good going: tried in cheekpieces. *D. Windrif, France* **81**

MULTIGIFTED 2 b.f. (Apr 2) Multiplex 114 – Attlongglast (Groom Dancer (USA) 128) [2015 5m⁶ 6g 6m⁴ 7m p8g⁶ p6g* 7s³ 6g Oct 20] workmanlike filly: fourth foal: sister to useful 7f/1m winner Multi Bene and winner up to 7f Multitask (2-y-o 5f winner): dam unraced: modest performer: won nursery at Kempton in September: stays 6f: acts on polytrack and good to firm going: often races towards rear. *Michael Madgwick* **63**

MULTI GRAIN 3 b.f. Sir Percy 129 – Grain Only (Machiavellian (USA) 123) [2015 69p: 72
9.9g⁶ 8g⁴ 8.5m⁵ 6g⁶ 10.4g 9.8g⁶ Aug 31] fair handicapper: won at Thirsk in May: left Brian
Ellison after fifth start: stays 1m: acts on good to firm going. *Micky Hammond*

MULTILINGUAL 3 b.f. Dansili 127 – Zenda 115 (Zamindar (USA) 116) [2015 7m⁶ Apr 75 p
17] well-made filly: sister to 7f winner Panzanella and smart 1m-1¼m winner Remote and
half-sister to top-class miler Kingman (2-y-o 7f winner, by Invincible Spirit): dam 1m/8.5f
winner, including Poule d'Essai des Pouliches, half-sister to high-class sprinter Oasis
Dream: 2/1, sixth in maiden at Newbury (3½ lengths behind Yasmeen) in April: will be
suited to 1m: sent to USA: sure to progress. *John Gosden*

MULTI QUEST 3 b.f. Multiplex 114 – Ryan's Quest (IRE) 67 (Mukaddamah (USA) 125) 56
[2015 62, a53: p5f³ p5m⁶ p5f⁶ p6f³ 6d⁵ p5g⁶ 6g² 6g⁵ 6g⁵ p5g⁶ p6g⁵ p6f⁴ Dec 17] modest
handicapper: left Jo Hughes after second start: stays 6f: acts on polytrack, firm and good to
soft going: usually in headgear in 2015. *John E. Long*

MULTI REGIME 2 b.c. (Apr 19) Multiplex 114 – Future Regime (IRE) 56 (Xaar 132) –
[2015 7g 6d 7g Sep 23] no form. *Tony Coyle*

MULTISTAR 3 b.f. Multiplex 114 – Express Logic (Air Express (IRE) 125) [2015 65: 7d 54
7s⁴ 7t.7f 7s⁴ 8s Oct 15] modest maiden: should stay 1m: acts on soft going: often starts
slowly/races in rear: sold 1,800 gns, sent to Germany. *Chris Wall*

MULTITASK 5 b.g. Multiplex 114 – Attlongglast (Groom Dancer (USA) 128) [2015 75, 73
a87: p6g* p6f⁶ p5g⁶ p7g* p6f⁵ p6g 6m⁴ 6m 6g⁴ p7g⁴ p6g p6g⁶ Dec 28] good-topped a82
gelding: fairly useful handicapper: won at Lingfield in January and February: stays 1m:
acts on polytrack, good to firm and good to soft going: often wears headgear: often races
towards rear. *Michael Madgwick*

MULZAMM (IRE) 3 b.g. Cape Cross (IRE) 129 – Vine Street (IRE) 88 (Singspiel (IRE) 112
133) [2015 90p: t7.1g² 7g⁶ 6m² p7g² 7g p8f² p8m² p8g* Dec 28] lengthy gelding: smart
handicapper: further improvement when winning at Lingfield on final start easily by 3¼
lengths from Bravo Zolo: stays 1m: acts on polytrack, tapeta and good to firm going:
usually wears hood, not last outing: in tongue tie last 4 starts: usually leads. *Charlie Appleby*

MUMARASAAT (USA) 4 b.f. Elusive Quality (USA) – Reefaljamal (USA) (Dixieland –
Band (USA)) [2015 –: p7g t8.6g Mar 6] no form. *Michael Squance*

MUMBLES MAGIC (IRE) 2 b.f. (Mar 19) Thousand Words 113 – Chaguaramas (IRE) –
93 (Mujadil (USA) 119) [2015 6g 7g p7g⁶ Jul 22] €7,500Y: half-sister to several winners,
including winner up to 1½m Jersey Bull (2-y-o 6f winner, by Clodovil): dam 2-y-o 5f
winner who stayed 1m: no form. *Jo Hughes*

MUMFORD 3 b.c. Stimulation (IRE) 121 – Noble Nova 69 (Fraam 114) [2015 75p: 7g³ 66
Apr 30] strong, attractive colt: fair maiden: stays 7f. *Geoffrey Harker*

MUNAASER 4 b.g. New Approach (IRE) 132 – Safwa (IRE) 85 (Green Desert (USA) 113
127) [2015 106: 8m 8f8.1m² 8m⁴ 10.4g Aug 22] useful-looking gelding: smart handicapper:
best effort when second at Sandown (½ length behind Basem) in July: stays 9f: acts on
good to firm and good to soft going: sent to UAE. *Sir Michael Stoute*

MUNAAWIB 7 b.g. Haafhd 129 – Mouwadh (USA) 64 (Nureyev (USA) 131) [2015 77: 68
t7.1g² f7g⁵ t7.1f t7.1f t7.1f 7.5m² 10m 7.5s⁴ 7.1m 8.5d* 8.5m⁶ f7g⁴ f7g f7g Dec 15] a77
fair handicapper: won at Beverley in September: stays 8.5f: acts on all-weather, soft and
good to firm going: often wears headgear: usually wears tongue tie: often starts slowly/
races in rear. *Deborah Sanderson*

MUNFALLET (IRE) 4 b.g. Royal Applause 124 – Princess Mood (GER) (Muhtarram 93
(USA) 125) [2015 90: 7m⁶ 6g⁴ 6m* 6m⁴ 6sᵘʳ 6m⁶ 5g Sep 5] well-made gelding: fairly
useful handicapper: won at Hamilton (by 3 lengths from Jacob's Pillow) in June: stays 6f:
acts on good to firm and good to soft going: tried in headgear prior to 2015: front runner/
races prominently: consistent. *David Brown*

MUNFARRID 3 b.rg. Showcasing 117 – Thankful 55 (Diesis 133) [2015 p7f* 8.3m² 8m⁶ 82
May 8] 55,000F, 150,000Y: compact gelding: third foal: half brother to useful 2-y-o 6.5f
winner Morning Post (by Acclamation), later 1m winner in Qatar: dam maiden (stayed
1m): fairly useful performer: won maiden at Kempton in March: best effort when second
in handicap at Nottingham (½ length behind Stardrifter) in April: stays 8.5f: sold 1,000 gns
in October, sent to Italy. *Richard Hannon*

MUNIRA EYES (USA) 2 ch.c. (Mar 9) Cape Blanco (IRE) 130 – Desert Sky (IRE) 97 83
(Green Desert (USA) 127) [2015 6m³ 6m³ p6g³ p6f² t6f² Oct 20] 78,000Y: smallish colt:
sixth foal: half-brother to 3 winners, including smart US Grade 2 1m winner No Jet Lag

(2-y-o 7f winner, by Johar): dam, 2-y-o 6f/7f winner, later 5f winner in USA: fairly useful maiden: raced only at 6f: acts on polytrack and good to firm going: front runner/races prominently: sold 30,000 gns, sent to Qatar. *Roger Varian*

MUNJALLY 4 b.g. Acclamation 118 – Parabola 72 (Galileo (IRE) 134) [2015 84: t9.5f³ **67** 10.3d 8g⁵ 7.5g 6g⁶ 6d* 6g⁵ 6g 6d⁴ 6s³ 6g⁵ 6d³ 6d⁴ 6g Sep 23] rangy gelding: fair handicapper: won at Hamilton in June: stays 9.5f, effective at shorter: acts on polytrack, tapeta, soft and good to firm going: often wears headgear. *Patrick Holmes*

MUNSARIM (IRE) 8 b.g. Shamardal (USA) 129 – Etizaaz (USA) 117 (Diesis 133) **72 §** [2015 82§: p10f* p10g⁴ p13g³ p10g p8f* p8g⁶ 10m* 8.3m 10m p12g p10g⁶ p8f p8f² p10f³ p10f p10m Dec 16] lengthy, good-topped gelding: fair performer: won at Lingfield in February (handicap) and May (seller) and Windsor (claimer) in June: stays 1¼m: acts on polytrack and good to firm going: wears headgear: best treated with caution. *Lee Carter*

MUNSTEAD PRIDE 3 ch.g. Sir Percy 129 – Memsahib (Alzao (USA) 117) [2015 83p: **83** 12f³ 14f⁴ 14f⁵ 16.1m⁶ p16g⁵ 14d⁶ Sep 25] smallish, angular gelding: fairly useful handicapper: stays 1¾m: acts on fibresand, raced mainly on good or firmer on turf: in cheekpieces last 2 starts: often races towards rear: temperament under suspicion: has joined Gordon Elliott. *Andrew Balding*

MUNTADAB (IRE) 3 b.g. Invincible Spirit (IRE) 121 – Chibola (ARG) (Roy (USA)) **88** [2015 –p: p8g* 10m* 10m 8.1g p7m Oct 21] good-bodied gelding: fairly useful performer: won maiden at Lingfield in May and handicap at Sandown (by ½ length from Banditry) in June: stays 1¼m: acts on polytrack and good to firm going. *Sir Michael Stoute*

MUNTAZAH 2 b.c. (Feb 2) Dubawi (IRE) 129 – Rumoush (USA) 114 (Rahy (USA) 115) **106** [2015 7m² 7d⁵ 7g* 8g³ Sep 26] second foal: dam, winner up to 9f (2-y-o 1m winner) who stayed 14.6f, half-sister to high-class 1m-1½m winner Mawatheeq and 1000 Guineas winner Ghanaati: useful performer: easily landed odds in maiden at Leicester in September: up in class, 10/1, improved form when 3 lengths third of 6 to Foundation in Royal Lodge Stakes at Newmarket final start, leading from over 2f out until over 1f out: stays 1m. *B. W. Hills*

MUQARRED (USA) 3 b.g. Speightstown (USA) 124 – Bawaara (FR) (Quiet American **85** (USA)) [2015 77: 7m* 7d⁶ p8g Jul 8] compact gelding: fairly useful handicapper: won at Leicester in April: likely to prove best up to 7f: acts on good to firm going, probably on polytrack: tried in cheekpieces in 2015. *Saeed bin Suroor*

MUQTASER (USA) 3 b.g. Distorted Humor (USA) 117 – Life Well Lived (USA) **94** (Tiznow (USA) 133) [2015 94p: 10g³ 10f³ 10g* 12g Sep 5] well-made gelding fairly useful handicapper: won at Sandown (by 2¼ lengths from Zamperini) in August: likely to prove best at around 1¼m: acts on firm and good to soft going: sometimes slowly away, often travels strongly: sent to USA. *Roger Varian*

MURAABIT 3 ch.g. Makfi 130 – Ho Hi The Moon (IRE) (Be My Guest (USA) 126) [2015 **84** p8g p8g⁴ p7g³ 8.5s 10g* 10.5m² 8d³ 9d* 10d Sep 17] 37,000Y: sixth foal: half-brother to smart winner up to 9f Latin Love (2-y-o 1m winner) and useful 1m-1¼m winner Stand To Reason (both by Danehill Dancer): dam, French 11f winner, half-sister to Irish Oaks winner Moonstone: fairly useful handicapper: won at Navan in May and Ffos Las in August: left David Marnane after sixth start: stays 10.5f: acts on good to firm and good to soft going: tried in cheekpieces. *Ismail Mohammed*

MURAAQABA 3 b.f. Dubawi (IRE) 129 – Nufoos 110 (Zafonic (USA) 130) [2015 105: **–** 7m Apr 15] useful performer at 2 yrs: well held in Nell Gwyn Stakes at Newmarket only outing in 2015: stays 7f: acts on soft going: front runner/races prominently, often races lazily. *Mark Johnston*

MURAD KHAN (FR) 2 b.c. (Mar 16) Raven's Pass (USA) 133 – Lady Elgar (IRE) **72 p** (Sadler's Wells (USA) 132) [2015 p8m³ Oct 21] €110,000Y: closely related to French 1¼m winner Lamazonia (by Elusive City) and half-brother to several winners, including very smart French/US winner up to 1½m Grand Couturier (2-y-o 9f/1¼m winner, by Grand Lodge) and smart 1m winner Ascription (by Dansili): dam raced once: 2/1, showed plenty when 1¾ lengths third of 8 to Bluebeard in maiden at Kempton, not knocked about: will improve. *Hugo Palmer*

MURDANOVA (IRE) 2 gr.c. (Apr 10) Zebedee 113 – Agnista (IRE) (Iffraaj 127) [2015 **76 p** 6m⁶ 5.4m³ p5f² p6f³ t6m² p6g⁴ t6m* Dec 30] €8,500F, £17,000Y, £16,000 2-y-o: first foal: dam unraced: fair performer: won maiden at Wolverhampton (dead-heated) in December: left Ronald Thompson after fifth start: will be suited by 7f: acts on tapeta: will go on improving. *Kevin Frost*

MURGAN 3 b.c. Galileo (IRE) 134 – Approach 105 (Darshaan 133) [2015 79p: 11m⁵ 11g² **99 p** 11.9d² 10.2d* Oct 14] tall, useful-looking gelding: useful performer: second in handicap at Newbury (¾ length behind King Bolete) in May: off 5 months, 8/13, made most of good opportunity in 3-runner maiden at Nottingham final start, winning easily by 1¾ lengths from Signed Sealed: stays 11f: acts on good to soft going: remains with potential. *Peter Chapple-Hyam*

MUROOR 2 ch.g. (Mar 30) Nayef (USA) 129 – Raaya (USA) (Giant's Causeway (USA) 132) [2015 7s 7s⁴ Oct 13] third foal: dam unraced close relative to high-class miler Aljabr: 12/1, much improved when 2 lengths fourth of 10 to Vincent's Forever in maiden at Leicester: will stay 1m: wears hood. *Marcus Tregoning* **79**

MUSAAID (IRE) 3 br.g. Lawman (FR) 121 – Fonda (USA) 46 (Quiet American (USA)) [2015 8m 7m* 7m⁴ Jul 17] well-made gelding: fair performer: best effort when winning maiden at Newmarket (by 1¼ lengths from Holland Park) in June: stays 7f. *Roger Varian* **77**

MUSADDAS 5 b.g. Exceed And Excel (AUS) 126 – Zuleika Dobson 106 (Cadeaux Genereux 131) [2015 97: 8m* 8m² 8d⁶ 9g 8d* Oct 13] rangy gelding: smart handicapper: further improvement to win at Newmarket (by 2 lengths from Jacob Black) in May and 20-runner Balmoral Handicap at Ascot (by 1½ lengths from GM Hopkins) in October: stays 8.5f: acts on polytrack, tapeta, soft and good to firm going: usually in headgear nowadays. *Saeed bin Suroor* **112**

MUSCADELLE 3 b.f. Azamour (IRE) 130 – Sauterne 98 (Rainbow Quest (USA) 134) [2015 –: p10f p10g⁴ t12.2m⁵ t12.2g 14.1m⁶ Apr 18] rather unfurnished filly: poor maiden: best effort at 1¼m: acts on polytrack: sometimes in blinkers in 2015. *Eve Johnson Houghton* **49**

MUSHARRIF 3 b.g. Arcano (IRE) 122 – Cefira (USA) 66 (Distant View (USA) 126) [2015 8g 7g³ 7d* 7s t6m⁵ Dec 12] 77,000F, 300,000Y: sturdy gelding: half-brother to 5f (including at 2 yrs) winner Sirenuse (by Exceed And Excel) and 2-y-o 5f/6f winner Forty Proof (by Invincible Spirit): dam, 6f winner, closely related to Gimcrack Stakes winner Abou Zouz: fairly useful performer: won maiden at Catterick in August: left Sir Michael Stoute after fourth start: will prove suited by a return to 7f: acts on tapeta and good to soft going: remains with potential. *Declan Carroll* **86 p**

MUSICAL COMEDY 4 b.g. Royal Applause 124 – Spinning Top 105 (Alzao (USA) 117) [2015 112: 5s² 6g 5d⁶ 6g³ 6.1g⁶ 5g⁴ 5.2s Sep 19] good-topped gelding: smart performer: second in listed race at Naas (¾ length behind Great Minds) in April: disappointing subsequently, in blinkers final start: stays 6f: acts on heavy going: usually races prominently. *Richard Hannon* **113**

MUSICAL MOLLY (IRE) 4 gr.f. Mastercraftsman (IRE) 129 – Park Approach (IRE) 77 (Indian Ridge 123) [2015 79: f6d⁴ f6d² f8d⁴ Feb 8] unfurnished filly: modest handicapper: stays 6f: acts on fibresand, best turf form on good to firm going: tried in cheekpieces prior to 2015: front runner/races prominently. *Brian Ellison* **62**

MUSICAL TASTE 2 b.f. (Apr 24) Makfi 120 – Blas Ceoil (USA) 97 (Mr Greeley (USA) 122) [2015 p6g³ 6m 6d² 6s⁴ 7d³ t7.1f* Oct 20] fourth foal: half-sister to 7f winner Rapid Approach (by New Approach), later successful abroad: dam, 2-y-o 5f/6f winner, half-sister to useful/unreliable 6f winner Radharcnafarraige: fair performer: won nursery at Wolverhampton in October: likely to stay 1m: acts on tapeta and good to soft going: in tongue tie last 2 starts. *Philip McBride* **79**

MUSIC AND DANCE 3 b.f. Galileo (IRE) 134 – Jamboretta (IRE) 102 (Danehill (USA) 126) [2015 84p: 8.1m³ 10.4g 8m³ p10g⁴ Aug 4] rather unfurnished filly: fairly useful handicapper: stays 1m: acts on polytrack and good to firm going: often races towards rear. *Sir Michael Stoute* **88**

Balmoral Handicap (Sponsored by Qipco), Ascot—
Musaddas delivers the big effort he'd promised earlier in the season as he beats
the Royal Hunt Cup winner GM Hopkins and the grey Master The World

MUSIC HALL (FR) 5 gr.g. Stormy River (FR) 123 – Aaliyah (GER) (Anabaa (USA) **56**
130) [2015 f8g 10.3d t9.5g⁶ f8d 9.1g⁶ 8d f7s 8.5d Sep 22] modest ex-French-trained
handicapper: stays 10.5f: acts on all-weather: in headgear last 2 starts: often races towards
rear. *Shaun Harris*

MUSIC LOVER 8 b.g. Piccolo 121 – Ligne d'Amour (Pursuit of Love 124) [2015 7v⁵ **51**
p7m² 7m⁵ p5g⁵ p6g Jul 14] sturdy gelding: modest maiden: stays 7f: acts on polytrack and
good to firm going: tried in blinkers prior to 2015. *Michael Madgwick*

MUSIC MASTER 5 b.h. Piccolo 121 – Twilight Mistress 84 (Bin Ajwaad (IRE) 119) **114**
[2015 122: 6g³ 5d 6f⁴ 5d³ 5g 6m³ Sep 15] leggy horse: smart performer: best efforts of
2015 when third in Abernant Stakes at Newmarket (1¾ lengths behind Astaire) on
reappearance, fourth in Diamond Jubilee Stakes at Royal Ascot (3½ lengths behind
Undrafted) and third in listed race at Deauville (1¼ lengths behind Mirza) on fourth start:
winner at 7f earlier in career, raced mostly at 5f/6f: acted on firm and good to soft going:
tried in tongue tie in 2013: to stand at Throckmorton Court Stud, Pershore, Worcestershire,
fee £4,000. *Henry Candy*

MUSICORA 4 b.f. Acclamation 118 – Belladera (IRE) 82 (Alzao (USA) 117) [2015 96: **86**
5f⁶ 6g p6g 6m 5g⁴ 6g⁶ Sep 12] workmanlike filly: fairly useful handicapper: stays 7f: acts
on polytrack, soft and good to firm going: tried in headgear: tried in tongue tie in 2015:
front runner/races prominently. *Clive Cox*

MUSIC THEORY (IRE) 4 b.g. Acclamation 118 – Key Girl (IRE) 48 (Key of Luck **110**
(USA) 126) [2015 113: 7g³ 8g 7g a7f Feb 28] good-topped gelding: smart handicapper:
raced only at Meydan in 2015, best efforts first 2 starts: stays 7f: acts on polytrack and good
to firm going: in hood in 2015. *Charlie Appleby*

MUSTAAQEEM (USA) 3 b.g. Dynaformer (USA) – Wasseema (USA) 111 (Danzig **95 p**
(USA)) [2015 8g² 8d* 9m⁴ Jun 13] well-made gelding: fourth foal: half-brother to 7f
winner Qaffaal (by Street Cry): dam 1m winner: useful form: won maiden at Doncaster in
May by ½ length from Maybe Definitely: improved when 3¾ lengths fourth to Awesome
Power in handicap at Sandown, well positioned: stays 9f: has been gelded: may well do
better still. *Sir Michael Stoute*

MUSTADAAM (IRE) 4 br.g. Dansili 127 – Sundus (USA) 80 (Sadler's Wells (USA) **69** 132) [2015 89: 10.4m 12g⁵ 10.2m Aug 22] good-topped gelding: fair handicapper: likely to prove best up to 1¼m: acts on good to firm going: often in tongue tie in 2015: races prominently. *Simon Crisford*

MUSTADEEM (IRE) 3 b.g. Arcano (IRE) 122 – Hureya (USA) 82 (Woodman (USA) **113** 126) [2015 93p: 9m⁶ 10m² 10f³ 10m⁶ 8g 8f³ Sep 13] attractive gelding: has scope: smart performer: third in Tercentenary Stakes at Royal Ascot (4 lengths behind Time Test) in June: stays 1¼m: acts on firm going: tried in blinkers in 2015: sometimes slowly away, usually races close up: sent to UAE. *Brian Meehan*

MUSTAFIZ (USA) 4 ch.g. Distorted Humor (USA) 117 – Somethinaboutbetty (USA) **–** (Forestry (USA) 121) [2015 65: f8g Jan 6] lightly-raced maiden, fair form in 2014: in first-time tongue strap, well held only outing in 2015. *Noel Quinlan*

MUSTAJEEB 4 ch.c. Nayef (USA) 129 – Rifqah (USA) (Elusive Quality (USA)) [2015 **119** 121: 6g* 6f⁵ Jun 20] stocky colt: smart performer: won Greenlands Stakes at the Curragh (by length from Maarek) in May: not so good when 4 lengths fifth of 15 to Undrafted in Diamond Jubilee Stakes at Royal Ascot, barely adequate test: stayed 1m, fully effective at 6f: acted on good to firm and good to soft going: often raced prominently: to stand at Overbury Stud, Tewkesbury, Gloucestershire, fee £5,000. *D. K. Weld, Ireland*

MUSTAJEER 2 b.c. (Apr 17) Medicean 128 – Qelaan (USA) 93 (Dynaformer (USA)) **106 p** [2015 8m⁴ 8g* Sep 24] third foal: half-brother to useful Qatari 1m-1¼m winner Makruma (by Dubawi) from 11.5f/1½m winner: 7/1, confirmed debut promise/much improved when winning 14-runner maiden at Newmarket in September by 2 lengths from Linguistic, asserting final 1f: bred to stay at least 1¼m: open to further improvement. *B. W. Hills*

MUSTAQBAL (IRE) 3 b.g. Invincible Spirit (IRE) 121 – Alshamatry (USA) (Seeking **77** The Gold (USA)) [2015 65: p6f³ 7.5m² 7.1m* 8m⁶ 8m⁴ 7.9s 7.5m² 7d⁵ 7.2m⁶ Sep 27] fair handicapper: won at Musselburgh in May: stays 1m: acts on good to firm going: front runner/races prominently. *Mark Johnston*

MUSTAQQIL (IRE) 3 b.g. Invincible Spirit (IRE) 121 – Cast In Gold (USA) 92 (Elusive **86** Quality (USA)) [2015 8.3m p8g* 8.1g⁵ p8d² Sep 4] 42,000F, 110,000Y: third foal: closely related to useful 6f/7f winner (including at 2 yrs) Wedding Ring (by Oasis Dream) and half-brother to 7f winner Golden Causeway (by Giant's Causeway): dam, 2-y-o 7f winner, half-sister to St Leger winner Rule of Law: fairly useful performer: won maiden at Kempton in August: blinkered, second in apprentice handicap there final start: raced only at 1m. *John Gosden*

MUSTARD 3 b.g. Motivator 131 – Flash of Gold 76 (Darshaan 133) [2015 83p: 10d³ 10f⁵ **108** 10f² 9.9m³ 11.9m* 12g* Oct 9] lengthy gelding: useful handicapper: won at Haydock (by ½ length from Captain Navarre) in August: well ridden though full value for improvement when following up at Newmarket by length from Goathland: will probably stay 1¾m: acts on good to firm going: signs of temperament, but usually responds generously to pressure. *Sir Michael Stoute*

MUSTASHRY 2 b.c. (Mar 9) Tamayuz 126 – Safwa (IRE) 85 (Green Desert (USA) 127) **73 p** [2015 p8m⁴ Oct 21] fourth foal: closely related to 1¼m winner Radhaadh (by Nayef) and half-brother to smart 1m winner Munaaser (by New Approach): dam, 1m winner, half-sister to high-class winner up to 1½m Maraahel: 7/1, held back by inexperience when 3¾ lengths fourth of 10 to Southern Gailes in maiden at Kempton: capable of better. *Sir Michael Stoute*

Vision Old Rowley Cup (Heritage Handicap), Newmarket—Mustard responds well in the royal colours to beat Goathland and Justice Belle (right) in this valuable event

Qatar King George Stakes, Goodwood—even though some big names are missing—Sole Power, Goldream and Mecca's Angel among them—Muthmir (left) defies a 4-lb penalty to take this enriched sprint from Take Cover (No.10) and Move In Time (stars on cap)

MUSTATRIF 2 b.c. (Apr 7) Bahamian Bounty 116 – Little Annie 43 (Compton Place 125) [2015 7m p8g Aug 22] well held in 2 maidens, blinkered in latter: sent to Italy. *Ed Dunlop* —

MUST HAVE (FR) 3 ch.g. Le Havre (IRE) 124 – Belle Et Brave (FR) (Falbrav (IRE) 133) [2015 76: 7m⁴ 7g³ 8d³ 8.3g⁵ Aug 3] fair maiden: stays 8.5f: acts on firm and good to soft going: tried in cheekpieces in 2015: often races prominently. *William Jarvis* **75**

MUSTIQUE DANCER (IRE) 3 b.f. Rip Van Winkle (IRE) 134 – Cilium (IRE) 102 (War Chant (USA) 126) [2015 –: 7.9m Aug 11] lightly-raced maiden, no form. *Richard Fahey* —

MUSTIQUE (IRE) 2 b.f. (Apr 19) Danehill Dancer (IRE) 117 – Blessing (USA) 79 (Pulpit (USA) 117) [2015 6g* 6g Sep 19] third foal: dam, maiden (stayed 1¼m), half-sister to dam of very smart US Grade 2 1½m winner Redeemed: won maiden at Ripon in August by 1¼ lengths from Prying Pandora: 16/1, stiff task and run probably best overlooked when well held in Firth of Clyde Stakes at Ayr final start: remains with potential. *Richard Fahey* **78 p**

MUSTN'T GRUMBLE (IRE) 2 ch.g. (Apr 30) Intense Focus (USA) 117 – Lough Mist (IRE) 93 (Captain Rio 122) [2015 5.3m⁵ 5.1s 6g* t6g³ 5m² 6s³ 6v³ p7g 5.7m⁵ p6g³ p5m⁴ t6g p6g⁶ Dec 7] fair performer: won seller at Ripon in May: stays 6f: acts on polytrack: tried in headgear: usually races close up. *Bill Turner* **66**

MUTAFAAKIR (IRE) 6 b.g. Oasis Dream 129 – Moon's Whisper (USA) (Storm Cat (USA)) [2015 95: 5m 5g 6d 5.1s³ 6.1d t6f⁵ Oct 9] strong, close-coupled gelding: fair handicapper: stays 7f: acts on good to firm and heavy going: often in headgear/tried in tongue tie prior to 2015. *Ruth Carr* **79**

MUTAKAYYEF 4 ch.g. Sea The Stars (IRE) 140 – Infallible 114 (Pivotal 124) [2015 117: 8.9g² 10g² 9g³ Oct 10] lengthy gelding: smart performer: second in Strensall Stakes at York (neck behind Mondialiste) and listed race at Ayr (neck behind Scottish) in September: below form tried in blinkers final start, doing too much too soon: stays 1¼m: acts on soft going: usually races close up, strong traveller: has been gelded. *William Haggas* **119**

MUTAMAKKIN (USA) 3 b.g. War Front (USA) 119 – La Laja (USA) (El Prado (IRE) 119) [2015 87p: 7f⁶ May 16] useful-looking gelding: fairly useful winner at 2 yrs, possibly unsuited by conditions when well held in listed race at Newmarket only outing in 2015: raced only at 7f: has been gelded. *Sir Michael Stoute* —

MUTAMID 3 b.c. Medicean 128 – Inchberry 110 (Barathea (IRE) 127) [2015 70: 8.3m 8m p7g³ p7g³ 18.6g* p8g² p8f⁴ Sep 22] sturdy colt: fairly useful handicapper: won at Wolverhampton in July: stays 8.5f: acts on polytrack and tapeta: often travels strongly. *Ismail Mohammed* **82**

MUTARAJJIL (IRE) 2 b.g. (Apr 8) Acclamation 118 – Rouge Noir (USA) (Saint Ballado (CAN)) [2015 6.5s p6g² Nov 11] 105,000Y: half-brother to several winners, including 2-y-o 5f winner Light The Fire (by Invincible Spirit), later successful in Scandinavia, and 2-y-o 7f winner Cadley Road (by Elusive City), both useful: dam US 6f winner: much better effort when second in maiden at Kempton (nose behind Consulting) in November, finishing well: will go on improving. *Roger Varian* **79 p**

MUTARAKEZ (IRE) 3 ch.g. Fast Company (IRE) 126 – Nightswimmer (IRE) 75 (Noverre (USA) 125) [2015 91: 8.1d* 8g* 8f Jun 18] sturdy gelding: useful handicapper: improved to win at Sandown (by 2¾ lengths from Shaakis) in April and Haydock (by ¾ length from Goring) in May: below form in Britannia Stakes at Royal Ascot final outing: stays 1m: acts on good to firm going: has been gelded. *Brian Meehan* **107**

MUTASAYYID 3 ch.c. Bahamian Bounty 116 – Clear Voice (USA) (Cryptoclearance (USA)) [2015 91p: 8m* 8g 8f³ 8d² 8m⁴ 8g* 8.9s Oct 10] sturdy colt: useful handicapper: won at Newmarket in May and Ayr (by head from Melvin The Grate) in September: stays 1m: acts on firm and good to soft going: front runner/races prominently: sent to UAE. *Richard Hannon* **102**

MUTATIS MUTANDIS (IRE) 4 gr.f. Mastercraftsman (IRE) 129 – Amathia (IRE) 105 **110**
(Darshaan 133) [2015 100: 12m 11.6g* 10.2m* 10m⁶ 9d p12g⁴ 10s³ 12f⁴ Nov 7]
workmanlike filly: smart performer: won handicap at Windsor (by neck from dead-heaters
Warrior of Light and Captain Morley) in May and listed race at Nottingham (by ½ length
from Dream Child) in June: creditable efforts last 2 starts, in Flower Bowl Stakes at
Belmont (4¾ lengths third to Stephanie's Kitten) and Grade 3 Long Island Handicap (2¼
lengths fourth to Goldy Espony): stays 1½m: acts on polytrack, firm and soft going: in
hood in 2013: sometimes slowly away, usually races in rear. *Ed Walker*

MUTAWAALY (IRE) 2 b.c. (Apr 2) Cape Cross (IRE) 129 – Sana Abel (IRE) 78 **84 p**
(Alhaarth (IRE) 126) [2015 18.6g* Dec 5] third foal: half-brother to useful 1¼m winner
(stayed 1½m) Reesha (by Teofilo): dam, 1¾m winner, closely related to Oaks winner
Eswarah: 11/4, looked useful prospect when winning 12-runner maiden at Wolverhampton
on debut by 3¾ lengths from Canford Crossing, well positioned before forging clear final
1f: bred to stay middle distances: should progress. *Roger Varian*

MUTAWATHEA 4 b.g. Exceed And Excel (AUS) 126 – Esteemed Lady (IRE) 96 (Mark **106**
of Esteem (IRE) 137) [2015 89: p8f* p8g p8g* 8f³ 7g² p8g⁶ Sep 5] unfurnished gelding:
useful handicapper: won at Kempton in April (by 1¼ lengths from Tommy's Secret) and
July (by 4½ lengths from Arthenus): stays 1m: acts on polytrack and good to firm going: in
cheekpieces last 4 starts: front runner/races prominently. *Simon Crisford*

MUTHMIR (IRE) 5 b.g. Invincible Spirit (IRE) 121 – Fairy of The Night (IRE) 107 **122**
(Danehill (USA) 126) [2015 125p: 6g⁵ 5g* 5f³ 6f 5m* 5g⁶ 5m³ Oct 4] good-topped
gelding: very smart performer: won Prix du Gros-Chene at Chantilly (by short head from
Catcall) in May and King George Stakes at Goodwood (by head from Take Cover) in July:
third to Goldream in King's Stand Stakes at Royal Ascot (beaten a neck) in between, and
in Prix de l'Abbaye at Longchamp (beaten 2 lengths) final start: has won at 6f, probably
best at 5f: acts on firm going. *William Haggas*

Mr Hamdan Al Maktoum's "Muthmir"

MUTHRAAB ALDAAR (IRE) 2 b.c. (Mar 31) Baltic King 120 – Vertigo On Course **75** (IRE) 69 (Anabaa (USA) 130) [2015 8d⁴ 8s Oct 9] better effort in maidens when fourth of 11 to Ormito at Haydock on debut. *Mick Channon*

MUWAFFAK (FR) 3 b.c. Shamardal (USA) 129 – Dancing Lady (FR) 106 (Dansili 127) **–** [2015 8g⁶ Jun 20] 16/1, very green when sixth of 8 in maiden at Newmarket, slowly away: sent to France. *Marco Botti*

MUWALAAH (USA) 3 b.f. Smart Strike (CAN) 121 – Almoutezah (USA) 65 (Storm Cat **82** (USA)) [2015 8.3d 8.3g⁵ 10.3m² 11.5g³ p12g³ t12.2m⁴ Oct 2] lengthy filly: third foal: half-sister to 1m winner Deglet Noor (by New Approach) and useful 10.3f winner Almashooqa (by Dubawi): dam twice-raced close relative to very smart US Grade 1 1¼m winner Summer Colony: fairly useful maiden: likely to prove best at short of 1½m: acts on good to firm going: front runner/races prominently. *Roger Varian*

MUZAAHIM (IRE) 4 ch.g. Tamayuz 126 – Elizabeth Swann 95 (Bahamian Bounty 116) **70** [2015 76: p7g p7g³ p8g⁶ p8m⁵ Dec 27] fair maiden: stays 1m: acts on polytrack and good to soft going: sometimes slowly away. *Kevin Morgan*

MUZDAWAJ 2 b.c. (Apr 16) Dansili 127 – Shabiba (USA) 103 (Seeking The Gold **90 p** (USA)) [2015 8g⁴ 8s² Oct 16] fourth foal: half-brother to 3 winners, including smart winner up to 7f Ertijaal (2-y-o 6f winner, by Oasis Dream) and useful 2-y-o 6f winner Odooj (by Pivotal): dam winner up to 1m (2-y-o 6f winner): promising fourth to Mustajeer in maiden at Newmarket in September: 8/13, below that form on soft ground when second in similar event at Redcar: remains open to improvement. *William Haggas*

MY AMIGO 2 gr.c. (Feb 1) Stimulation (IRE) 121 – Blue Crest (FR) (Verglas (IRE) 118) **76 p** [2015 6g* 7m⁴ Jul 30] £38,000Y: first foal: dam French 7.5f winner: won maiden at Newcastle in May by ½ length from Blue Humor: off 9 weeks, fourth of 16 to Jaadu in nursery at Goodwood only subsequent start: remains with potential. *Ann Duffield*

MY ANCHOR 4 b.g. Mount Nelson 125 – War Shanty 66 (Warrshan (USA) 117) [2015 **64** p12m⁶ p12f p10f⁵ p10f⁴ p10f t8.6f p10g t12.2g³ t12.2g* t12.2g⁴ p10g² t12.2g* 11.5d³ 11m⁵ Jun 25] modest handicapper: won at Wolverhampton in April and June (apprentice): stays 1½m: acts on polytrack, tapeta and heavy going: front runner/races prominently. *Sylvester Kirk*

MY BEST SONG (USA) 2 ch.f. (Apr 24) Songandaprayer (USA) 118 – Great Look **69** (USA) (Giant's Causeway (USA) 132) [2015 6m⁵ 5.7m² 5.3s² p6f⁵ p6f² Nov 5] $3,000F, $12,000Y: first foal: dam unraced sister to smart US Grade 3 1m/9f winner Winning Cause: fair maiden: will stay 7f: acts on polytrack. *Jamie Osborne*

MY BETHANY (USA) 3 b.f. Bernstein (USA) 115 – Euroslew (USA) (Seattle Slew **88 p** (USA)) [2015 p8g* Nov 9] $95,000Y: second foal: sister to US 5f winner B For Baba: dam second at 6.5f in USA on only start: 33/1, looked smart prospect when winning 10-runner maiden at Kempton by 6 lengths from Karmadal, in touch and quickening clear approaching final 1f in impressive fashion: open to improvement. *Paul Fitzsimons*

MYBOYALFIE (USA) 8 b.g. Johannesburg (USA) 127 – Scotchbonnetpepper (USA) **72 §** (El Gran Senor (USA) 136) [2015 93: p8m² p8f p10g 7g 7.1v⁴ 7.1s⁵ 8d 8d Oct 30] smallish **a80 §** gelding: fair handicapper: stayed 8.5f: acted on polytrack, fibresand and heavy going: wore headgear: was unreliable: dead. *J. R. Jenkins*

MYBOYDANIEL 7 b.g. My Boy Charlie (IRE) 118 – Prim Fabulous (IRE) 92 (Invincible **82** Spirit (IRE) 121) [2015 –p: 7s⁴ 6m² 7m* 7g⁶ 7g 5g 7.2m⁴ Sep 27] fairly useful handicapper: won at Newcastle in June: best effort at 7f: acts on good to firm going. *Brian Ellison*

MY BUBBA 3 b.g. Dutch Art 126 – Moyoko (IRE) 64 (Mozart (IRE) 131) [2015 57p: 6g **56** 6g³ 7.1g⁶ p7g t8.6f Dec 21] modest maiden: left John Gallagher after second start: stays 7f: acts on soft going: tried in hood in 2015. *Michael Blanshard*

MY CALL 3 b.f. Shamardal (USA) 129 – Hush Money (CHI) (Hussonet (USA)) [2015 **106 p** 6m* 6g² 16m* Dec 12] lengthy filly: has scope: fourth foal: half-sister to 1m winner Samedi (by Any Given Saturday): dam Chilean Oaks/Derby winner: useful performer: won maiden at Pontefract (by 7 lengths from Marasim) in May: off 6 months, best effort when winning handicap at Wolverhampton by 1½ lengths from Anonymous John: likely to stay 7f: will go on improving. *Saeed bin Suroor*

MY DAD SYD (USA) 3 b.g. Acclamation 118 – Weekend Fling (USA) 68 (Forest **87 p** Wildcat (USA) 120) [2015 6g* 6g² 6g 6d Oct 12] $90,000Y: fourth foal: half-brother to 6f winner Royal Empress (by Holy Roman Emperor) and useful 2-y-o 7f winner Craftsman (by Mastercraftsman), later 7.5f winner in USA: dam, 6f winner who stayed 1m, half-sister to very smart US Grade 1 9f winner Archarcharch: fairly useful form: won maiden at

Doncaster in August by 2½ lengths from Moon Eyes: best effort after when second to Dragon King in handicap at Newmarket: raced only at 6f: has been gelded: remains open to improvement. *Richard Fahey*

MY DESTINATION (IRE) 6 b.g. Dubai Destination (USA) 127 – Gossamer 118 **67** (Sadler's Wells (USA) 132) [2015 79: 12s 16d^{pu} 14.1v^5 14.6d^4 16m t13.9g^2 p16g^6 t16.5g^6 17.2d 12.1m 16d 15.8d 16.1g 14.1m 12.1g^5 Sep 21] fair handicapper: stays 16.5f: acts on tapeta, good to firm and heavy going: often wears headgear. *Declan Carroll*

MY DREAM BOAT (IRE) 3 b.c. Lord Shanakill (USA) 121 – Betty Burke 65 (Choisir **115** (AUS) 126) [2015 77: 7g* 7g^4 7.1m^2 8f 8g* 9g 8d* 8s* Nov 1] sturdy colt: smart performer: won handicaps at Doncaster (by 2½ lengths from Pensax Boy) in May and York (by 2¼ lengths from Hathal) in August, listed race at Chantilly (by 2½ lengths from Leader Writer) in October and Prix Perth at Saint-Cloud in November: further improvement when beating Momayyaz by 1½ lengths in last-named, finding plenty to lead well inside final 1f: will stay 1¼m: acts on soft going. *Clive Cox*

MY ESCAPADE (IRE) 4 ch.f. Tamayuz 126 – Highly Respected (IRE) 57 (High Estate **–** 127) [2015 58: 16m Apr 6] small filly: maiden: modest form at best: stays 2m: acts on soft and good to firm going: front runner/races prominently. *Simon Waugh*

MY FAVOURITE THING 2 b.f. (Mar 21) Oasis Dream 129 – The Sound of Music **74** (IRE) (Galileo (IRE) 134) [2015 7m 7s^3 Aug 23] compact filly: third foal: half-sister to useful Qatari 1m-1½m winner Seema (by Dubawi): dam, unraced, closely related to St Leger winner Scorpion: fair form in maidens at Newmarket and Brighton, third of 7 to Goodwood Zodiac in latter. *Luca Cumani*

MY GIRL JO (FR) 3 b.f. Whipper (USA) 126 – Prairie Moon 47 (Halling (USA) 133) **47** [2015 –p: 7d 9.2g^5 8.3g^5 Jul 22] poor maiden: stays 9f: acts on good to firm going: often races towards rear. *David O'Meara*

MY GUARDIAN ANGEL 6 b.g. Araafa (IRE) 128 – Angels Guard You (Bahamian **61** Bounty 116) [2015 73: 12m^2 Jun 25] workmanlike gelding: modest handicapper: probably stays 1½m: acts on soft and good to firm going: tried in headgear prior to 2015. *Mark H. Tompkins*

MY ISLA 2 br.f. (Jan 29) Makfi 130 – Islandia (USA) (Johar (USA) 130) [2015 7.6g Sep **–** 12] 20,000Y: second foal: dam, US 7.5f/8.5f winner, half-sister to US Grade 3 6.5f winner Ten Meropa: 16/1, very green when well held in maiden at Lingfield. *Clive Brittain*

MYJESTIC MELODY (IRE) 7 b.m. Majestic Missile (IRE) 118 – Bucaramanga (IRE) **–** (Distinctly North (USA) 115) [2015 41: t6f f7g Mar 3] small mare: poor maiden: stays 7f: acts on polytrack, good to firm and good to soft going: tried in headgear/tongue tie prior to 2015: sometimes slowly away. *Shaun Harris*

MY LORD 7 br.g. Ishiguru (USA) 114 – Lady Smith (Greensmith 121) [2015 79: p13f^3 **–** Jan 23] workmanlike gelding: fair performer: stays 13.5f: acts on polytrack, soft and good to firm going: sometimes wears headgear: tried in tongue tie. *Luke Dace*

MY MAJOR (IRE) 4 b.g. Holy Roman Emperor (IRE) 125 – Greek Easter (IRE) 85 **77** (Namid 128) [2015 5.7f^2 Apr 17] 77,000Y: well-made gelding: first foal: dam, 7f-1¼m winner who stayed 1½m, half-sister to US Grade 3 1m winner Doc Holiday: in hood, 7/1, promise when ¾-length second of 7 to Frostman in maiden at Bath, green when shaken up 2f out and nearest finish: sent to Germany. *Clive Cox*

MYMATECHRIS (IRE) 4 br.g. High Chaparral (IRE) 132 – Splendeur (FR) (Desert **108** King (IRE) 129) [2015 104p: p12f^3 p15.8f* 18.7d 12f Jun 19] useful performer: won AW Marathon Championships Stakes at Lingfield (by head from Anglophile) in April: stays 2m: seems best on polytrack: tried in tongue tie prior to 2015. *Andrew Balding*

MY MATE (IRE) 3 ch.c. Approve (IRE) 112 – Date Mate (USA) (Thorn Dance (USA) **75** 107) [2015 74: 7.5m^5 t7.1g^4 6.1m^6 7m^5 6.1m^2 t6g 7g^2 6g^5 p7g^3 8.5d^5 Sep 27] good-topped colt: fair maiden: stays 1m: acts on polytrack, tapeta and good to firm going: front runner/races prominently: sold 10,000 gns, sent to the Netherlands. *Clive Brittain*

MY METEOR 8 b.g. Bahamian Bounty 116 – Emerald Peace (IRE) 103 (Green Desert **61** (USA) 127) [2015 72: f6d^6 p6m t5.1f^4 6m 6f 5m 5f^3 5m 5.7f 5m p5g Oct 14] small gelding: modest handicapper: stays 5.5f: acts on tapeta, firm and soft going: often starts slowly. *Tony Newcombe*

MY MISTRESS (IRE) 3 ch.f. Mastercraftsman (IRE) 129 – Majestic Eviction (IRE) 94 **–** (King's Theatre (IRE) 128) [2015 80: 8g^5 10d p10g^6 8g p8g p8g^6 p8f p13.3m t9.5f p10f Nov 12] handicapper: fair winner sole start in 2014, no impact since: best effort at 7f: acts on polytrack: has worn headgear/tongue tie. *Phil McEntee*

MY MO (FR) 3 b.g. Silver Frost (IRE) 122 – Anna Ivanovna (FR) (Fasliyev (USA) 120)   **75**
[2015 58: p8d³ t7.1g² p8f* 8f⁴ 8m 7m⁶ 8m p7g p6g² p8f³ p10f* t9.5m* 9.9s⁴ p10f* Oct
24] angular gelding: fair handicapper: won at Kempton in April, Chelmsford and
Wolverhampton in September and Chelmsford in October: stays 1¼m: acts on polytrack,
tapeta and soft going: often in cheekpieces in 2015: front runner/races prominently.
David Dennis

MY MY (IRE) 4 b.g. Iffraaj 127 – Yin 58 (Dansili 127) [2015 –: p8g p7m 5g⁶ 8.7m 6m³   **49**
6m 7.5s 8s p10f Oct 29] poor maiden: best effort at 6f: acts on good to firm going: tried in
blinkers in 2015: often in tongue tie in 2015. *J. J. Feane, Ireland*

MY NAME IS RIO (IRE) 5 ch.g. Captain Rio 122 – Walk In My Shadow (IRE) 71   **95**
(Orpen (USA) 116) [2015 98: 6g 6g² 6d⁵ 5g* 5g 6d 5d⁵ 6g 5s Oct 9] useful handicapper:
won at Ayr (by neck from Gowanharry) in July: stays 6f: acts on fibresand, soft and good
to firm going: tried in cheekpieces in 2015. *Michael Dods*

MY NEW ANGEL (IRE) 6 gr.m. Dark Angel (IRE) 113 – Mynu Girl (IRE) (Charnwood   **–**
Forest (IRE) 125) [2015 57, a50: f8gᵖᵘ Jan 6] fair handicapper at best: stayed 1¼m: acted
on polytrack, fibresand, best turf form on good going or firmer: wore headgear on
occasions: dead. *Daniel Loughnane*

MYOPIC 2 b.f. (Apr 6) Teofilo (IRE) 126 – Blinking (Marju (IRE) 127) [2015 8.3g² Sep   **78 p**
8] fourth foal: half-sister to 1¼m winner Maracuja (by Medicean) and useful 1½m winner
Twitch (by Azamour): dam unraced sister to high-class Hong Kong performer up to 1½m
Viva Pataca: 20/1, showed plenty when ½-length second of 12 to Sepal in maiden at
Leicester on debut, leading from over 1f out until final 50 yds: should progress.
Luca Cumani

MY PAINTER (IRE) 4 b.f. Jeremy (USA) 122 – Last Cry (FR) (Peintre Celebre (USA)   **74**
137) [2015 p10.7g 10s 8v² p8g 8v³ 7d 7v Oct 17] strong filly: fair maiden: stays 1m: acts
on polytrack, good to firm and heavy going: tried in tongue tie in 2015: winning hurdler.
Denis Hogan, Ireland

MY RENAISSANCE 5 b.g. Medicean 128 – Lebenstanz 66 (Singspiel (IRE) 133) [2015   **56**
64: p12m³ t8.6g⁵ p10g p8g Oct 14] rather leggy gelding: modest handicapper: stays 1½m:
acts on polytrack and tapeta: tried in cheekpieces in 2015, in tongue tie last 3 starts.
Ben Case

MY REWARD 3 b.g. Rail Link 132 – Tarot Card 100 (Fasliyev (USA) 120) [2015 94:   **100**
10.3d 10m⁶ 10d³ 12m⁵ 10g t12.2f Oct 17] useful handicapper: good fifth at Ascot (2 lengths
behind Shell Bay) in August: stays 1½m: acts on polytrack, good to firm and good to soft
going: front runner/races prominently: has been gelded. *Charles Hills*

MY SECRET DREAM (FR) 4 b.f. Stormy River (FR) 123 – Aventure Secrete (FR)   **–**
(Polish Precedent (USA) 131) [2015 61: p10g p7g Feb 24] lengthy filly: maiden: no form
in 2015: stays 1¼m: acts on good to firm and good to soft going: in cheekpieces last start:
often races freely. *Charlie Wallis*

MY SINGLE MALT (IRE) 7 b.g. Danehill Dancer (IRE) 117 – Slip Dance (IRE) 108   **77**
(Celtic Swing 138) [2015 88, a82: 7v⁵ 7g⁴ 7.6f 8g³ 7.6g 8m 8m⁵ 8d Aug 17] rangy gelding:
fair handicapper: stays 8.5f: acts on polytrack and any turf going: has worn headgear.
Julie Camacho

MY SON MAX 7 b.g. Avonbridge 123 – Pendulum 82 (Pursuit of Love 124) [2015 78,   **73**
a86: t7.1f³ t7.1f* p8f p7f⁵ 8m⁶ 10.2m³ 7.1m⁴ 8.1m⁴ 10.2m² 7.1g² 10.2d⁰ 10.2v³ 8d⁴ 10.2s   **a83**
Sep 15] tall, angular gelding: fairly useful handicapper: won at Wolverhampton in March:
stays 1¼m, effective at shorter: acts on all-weather, good to firm and heavy going: wears
headgear: often starts slowly. *Nikki Evans*

MY SONNY BOY 4 b.g. Imperial Dancer 123 – Lily of Tagula (IRE) (Tagula (IRE) 116)   **–**
[2015 –: p12m⁵ Jan 24] tailed off both starts in maidens, including in visor/tongue tie.
Lisa Williamson

MY SPIRIT (IRE) 4 b.f. Invincible Spirit (IRE) 121 – My Renee (USA) 109 (Kris S   **93**
(USA)) [2015 106: 10.2m⁶ 10.1g 10.4m⁴ 12m Aug 8] small, rather sparely-made filly:
fairly useful handicapper: stays 1½m: acts on good to soft going. *William Haggas*

MYSTERIAL 5 b.g. Invincible Spirit (IRE) 121 – Diamond Dilemma (IRE) (Sinndar   **79**
(IRE) 134) [2015 74: 10.3d 7g 7.5g⁶ 7s 8.3m⁶ 10.2m² 10.2m* 10.1m* 10g⁶ 11.8m* 12g⁴
12.3g⁴ 12m⁴ 13m² 12g³ 16.4s Oct 10] fair handicapper: won at Nottingham and Newcastle
in June, Leicester in July and Chester in August: stays 13f: acts on soft and good to firm
going: tried in blinkers prior to 2015: front runner, often travels strongly. *Declan Carroll*

MYSTERIOUS GLANCE 2 b.f. (Mar 26) Cacique (IRE) 124 – Largo (IRE) 94 (Selkirk **69** (USA) 129) [2015 6f⁵ 6m⁵ 7g 6d t5.1f³ Oct 13] 800F: half-sister to 3 winners, including 11.5f-13f winner Afro (by Araafa): dam, 11.6f/1½m winner, half-sister to useful performers Coventina (stayed 2m) and Ladies Best (up to 1½m), latter ungenuine: fair maiden: should stay at least 7f: acts on tapeta and firm going: often races prominently. *Ed McMahon*

MYSTERIOUS LOOK 2 ch.f. (Feb 3) Sakhee's Secret 128 – Look Here's Carol (IRE) **66** 102 (Safawan 118) [2015 5.1m p6g 6d t5.1g² t5.1f³ t6f² Dec 22] 2-y-o winner up to 6f Secret Look (2-y-o 5f/5.5f winner) and half-sister to 3 winners, including 2-y-o 5f winner Look Whos Next (by Compton Place) and 2-y-o 1m winner Imperial Look (by Royal Applause): dam, 6f/7f winner, half-sister to smart 6f/7f winner Now Look Here: fair maiden: effective at 5f/6f: acts on tapeta: front runner/races prominently. *Ed McMahon*

MYSTERIOUS STAR (FR) 3 b.c. Iron Mask (USA) 117 – Red Star (IRE) (Lure (USA) **62** 131) [2015 62: t7.1f⁵ 10.9d³ 11s 9.5m* a10g⁴ a10g Dec 22] modest performer: left Martyn Meade after first start: won maiden at Nimes in November: stays 11f: acts on tapeta/ polytrack, good to firm and good to soft going. *J. Reynier, France*

MYSTERY CODE 3 b.f. Tobougg (IRE) 125 – Mystery Lot (IRE) 87 (Revoque (IRE) **85** 122) [2015 63p: 11.5d² p10g* 11.6m³ 11.8g⁵ 10d Oct 12] fairly useful performer: won maiden at Chelmsford in June: stays 1½m: acts on polytrack and good to firm going. *Alan King*

MYSTERY DRAMA 5 b.m. Hernando (FR) 127 – Mystery Lot (IRE) 87 (Revoque (IRE) **84** 122) [2015 87: p13.3m* 16m⁴ p13.3g⁵ 14m⁶ 12g⁵ Aug 13] sturdy mare: fairly useful handicapper: won at Chelmsford in May: stays 2m: acts on polytrack, fibresand and good to firm going: usually races nearer last than first. *Alan King*

MYSTICAL KING 5 b.g. Notnowcato 128 – Mystical Ayr (IRE) 76 (Namid 128) [2015 **54** -: 7.2d 9.2g 7.2g 8g³ 7.2d 6s³ 6d 5d⁵ 5m⁵ 5m³ Sep 28] modest maiden: best effort at 5f: acts on good to firm going: usually in headgear in 2015: often races prominently. *Linda Perratt*

MYSTICAL MAZE 4 b.f. Multiplex 114 – Musical Maze 70 (Distant Music (USA) 126) **–** [2015 47: t12.2g⁵ 9.8v⁶ 9.9s⁶ Jun 2] maiden: no form in 2015: tried in cheekpieces. *Mark Brisbourne*

MYSTICAL MOMENT 5 ch.m. Dutch Art 126 – Tinnarinka 84 (Observatory (USA) **61** 131) [2015 73: 8d 8g 8m 7.5m² 7d³ 7g⁶ 5.9m⁶ 7g⁶ 7.5m⁵ 6v Nov 3] rather leggy mare: modest handicapper: stays 1m: acts on any turf going: tried in headgear. *Edwin Tuer*

MYSTICAL SAPPHIRE 5 b.m. Sakhee's Secret 128 – Nadyma (IRE) (Daylami (IRE) **83** 138) [2015 93: 7g⁶ p8g⁵ 7.4g⁴ p7g⁶ p7m* p7f p7m⁴ Dec 31] lengthy mare: fairly useful handicapper: won at Kempton in October: stays 8.5f: acts on polytrack. *Jo Crowley*

MYSTICAL SPIRIT (FR) 3 ch.g. Spirit One (FR) 122 – Miss Maguilove (FR) (Dyhim **86** Diamond (IRE) 117) [2015 p8g² p8f³ 8.3s⁵ 7m³ 7g* 7m⁵ 8.3d³ 7g² Sep 19] €12,000Y: fourth foal: half-brother to French 6f/7f winner Mystical Power (by Tomorrows Cat): dam French 2-y-o 6f winner: fairly useful performer: won maiden at Lingfield in July: good second in handicap at Newmarket in September: stays 8.5f: acts on polytrack, good to firm and good to soft going: front runner/races prominently. *Martyn Meade*

MYSTIC AND ARTIST 3 b.f. Excellent Art 125 – Mystical Spirit (IRE) 48 (Xaar 132) **68** [2015 79: 8s⁵ 8.3g 8.1v 7s Oct 16] angular filly: fair handicapper: should stay 1m: acts on soft and good to firm going: tried in cheekpieces in 2015: often leads, tends to find little: sold 4,000 gns, sent to Greece. *K. R. Burke*

MYSTIC BLAZE (IRE) 2 ch.c. (Apr 19) Arcano (IRE) 122 – Star Approval (IRE) **83** (Hawk Wing (USA) 136) [2015 7g p7f³ f8g² Nov 26] 50,000Y: good-quartered colt: fourth foal: half-brother to 5f (including at 2 yrs) winner Katchy Lady (by Kyllachy) and useful Italian 2-y-o 1m winner Kocna (by Aussie Rules): dam unraced half-sister to Moyglare Stud Stakes winner Mail The Desert: fairly useful maiden: best effort when second at Southwell (1¼ lengths behind Melfit) in November, clear of rest: left Clive Brittain after first start. *Andrew Balding*

MYSTIC MIRAAJ 3 ch.g. Iffraaj 127 – Salsa Brava (IRE) 106 (Almutawakel 126) [2015 **87** 64p: 8g⁶ 9g² 8d* 8g³ 8d² 7d 8.5g⁴ 7.2g⁴ 8g² 7d² Oct 24] fairly useful performer: won minor event at Newcastle in May: second in handicaps at Redcar and Doncaster (apprentice) last 2 starts: stays 1m: acts on good to soft going: tried in blinkers in 2015. *Tim Easterby*

MYSTIC PRINCESS (IRE) 4 ch.f. Manduro (GER) 135 – Granny Kelly (USA) 60 **57** (Irish River (FR) 131) [2015 12.1g⁴ 13.1g Oct 8] modest maiden: stays 1½m: best form on soft/heavy going: tried in cheekpieces prior to 2015: often races prominently. *Mark McNiff, Ireland*

MYSTIKANA 2 ch.f. (Mar 21) Sir Percy 129 – Peintre d'Argent (IRE) 84 (Peintre Celebre **71** (USA) 137) [2015 7s⁴ 7s⁴ 7s⁴ Oct 12] 13,000Y: leggy filly: second foal: half-sister to 2-y-o 7f winner Father Stone (by Winker Watson): dam, 11.5f/1½m winner, half-sister to smart/ ungenuine stayer Winged d'Argent: fair maiden: best effort when fourth at Newbury (4¾ lengths behind Tabarrak) on second start: will be suited by at least 1m. *Marcus Tregoning*

MYSTIQUE HEIGHTS 2 b.g. (Apr 6) High Chaparral (IRE) 132 – Musique Magique **– p** (IRE) 89 (Mozart (IRE) 131) [2015 p8m t8.6f t9.5f Nov 14] fifth foal: half-brother to 1m winner Mia Madonna (by Motivator) and useful 1m-1¼m winner Dinvar Diva (by Dalakhani): dam, 2-y-o 7f winner (on only start), half-sister to smart French 1¼m-1½m winner Magadan (by High Chaparral): down the field in maidens: bred to do better at 1¼m+. *Sir Mark Prescott Bt*

MY STRATEGY (IRE) 3 b.g. Strategic Prince 114 – Mythie (FR) (Octagonal (NZ) 126) **81** [2015 66p: p8g* p8g² 10.2s³ 8d³ 8.5g³ 8.3g³ 8g⁶ 8g⁴ 8.3v³ Oct 7] strong gelding: fairly useful handicapper: won at Chelmsford in April: stays 1¼m: acts on polytrack and heavy going: sold 21,000 gns, sent to Saudi Arabia. *Michael Bell*

MY TARGET (IRE) 4 b.g. Cape Cross (IRE) 129 – Chercheuse (USA) 110 (Seeking The **94** Gold (USA)) [2015 90: p8g⁶ 7d 6g⁶ p7g² t7.1m* Dec 26] fairly useful handicapper: better won at Wolverhampton (by ¾ length from Dougan) in December: stays 1m: acts on polytrack and tapeta. *Michael Wigham*

MYTH CYCLE 3 b.g. Cape Cross (IRE) 129 – Princesse Dansante (IRE) 109 (King's **–** Best (USA) 132) [2015 t9.5fᵇᵘ Jan 12] pulled up around halfway in maiden at Wolverhampton, only outing: dead. *Charlie Appleby*

MYTHICAL CITY (IRE) 3 b.f. Rock of Gibraltar (IRE) 133 – Rainbow City (IRE) 85 **87** (Rainbow Quest (USA) 134) [2015 72: p12f⁴ 10.4g* 9.8d³ 10.3m* 10m 10.4m⁶ Jul 25] fairly useful handicapper: won at Haydock in May and Ripon and Chester (by neck from First Dream) in June: should stay at least 1½m: acts on good to firm and good to soft going. *Mark Johnston*

MYTHICAL MADNESS 4 b.g. Dubawi (IRE) 129 – Miss Delila (USA) (Malibu Moon **105** (USA)) [2015 91: 10m* 10m³ 10.3f 10m⁶ 10d³ p8g² Dec 7] useful handicapper: won at Windsor (by 1½ lengths from Red Warrior) in May: good head second to Volunteer Point at Chelmsford in December: stays 1¼m: acts on polytrack and good to firm going: in headgear in 2015: front runner/races prominently: temperament under suspicion. *Charlie Appleby*

MYTHICAL MAID (IRE) 3 ch.f. Arakan (USA) 123 – Bonne 72 (Namid 128) [2015 –: **–** p7f 8.3d⁶ f8g Nov 3] no form. *Seamus Mullins*

MYTHICAL MOMENT 3 b.f. Authorized (IRE) 133 – Dancing Fire (USA) (Dayjur **84 p** (USA) 137) [2015 64p: 11.5d³ p12g² 14.1g* 14m* Jul 15] fairly useful handicapper: won at Carlisle and Sandown in July: stays 1¾m: acts on good to firm going: often in hood in 2015: open to further improvement. *William Haggas*

MYTHMAKER 3 b.c. Major Cadeaux 121 – Mythicism 80 (Oasis Dream 129) [2015 81: **101** 6s² 6d⁵ 6.9s⁴ 6m* 6m* 6m 6d p6m² t6g⁵ p6g² Dec 30] useful handicapper: won at Haydock and Newcastle in July: twice good second at Lingfield subsequently, beaten neck by Boomerang Bob latter occasion: stays 6f: acts on polytrack and good to firm going: front runner/races prominently. *Bryan Smart*

MY TIME 6 b.g. Mind Games 121 – Tick Tock 68 (Timeless Times (USA) 90) [2015 ⁺: t6f Oct 23] modest handicapper: raced mainly at 5f: has worn headgear: often starts slowly, often races in rear. *Michael Mullineaux*

MYTIMEHASCOME 2 b.f. (Jan 30) Montjeu (IRE) 137 – Vital Statistics 102 (Indian **77 p** Ridge 123) [2015 7g⁵ p8d² Nov 30] rather unfurnished filly: third foal: half-sister to useful winner up to 7f Ashaadd (2-y-o 6f winner, by Dansili): dam 2-y-o 6f winner: fair form in maidens, not ideally placed when length second to Diamonds Pour Moi at Kempton: remains open to improvement. *Roger Varian*

MY TITANIA (IRE) 4 b.f. Sea The Stars (IRE) 140 – Fairy of The Night (IRE) 107 **102** (Danehill (USA) 126) [2015 109p: 8g⁴ 9.5g³ 9d Aug 30] attractive filly: useful performer: best effort in 2015 when third in listed race at Gowran (2½ lengths behind Easter) in August: stays 9f: acts on good to firm going: usually races close up, often races freely. *John M. Oxx, Ireland*

MY TRINGALING (IRE) 3 ch.f. Summer Bird (USA) 126 – Lady Amira (USA) **57** (Langfuhr (CAN) 124) [2015 8.3g t9.5g 10m p10f⁴ p12g⁶ Dec 15] 60,000Y: first foal: dam, US 6f winner, half-sister to dam of Dubai World Cup winner Prince Bishop: modest maiden: best effort at 1¼m: acts on polytrack: sometimes slowly away. *Stuart Williams*

MY TWO SCOOPS 2 ch.g. (Feb 21) Showcasing 117 – Miss Beaudacious (IRE) 73 (Antonius Pius (USA) 123) [2015 7.2s⁶ 7m⁴ 5.9s³ 5.9m⁵ 7g⁴ 7s⁴ 8d⁶ Oct 19] strong gelding: fair maiden: will be suited by a return to 6f/7f: acts on soft and good to firm going: tried in cheekpieces: usually races close up. *Ann Duffield*

MY VALENTINO (IRE) 2 ch.g. (Apr 5) Duke of Marmalade (IRE) 132 – Nadwah 70 (USA) 107 (Shadeed (USA) 135) [2015 6s⁵ 5.9g⁴ 7m⁴ 7m 7m Aug 5] fair maiden: best effort at 6f: tried in cheekpieces. *Dianne Sayer*

MYWAYALWAYS (IRE) 3 b.g. Baltic King 120 – Goose Island (IRE) 85 (Kahyasi 130) 79 [2015 77: 8.3m 9.9m 10.4m² 10g³ 14.4g⁵ 10m³ 8.3m⁴ 8.1g⁴ 10g 10d⁴ 10g Oct 19] fair handicapper: stays 10.5f: acts on good to firm and heavy going: blinkered final start: sold 4,000 gns, sent to Bahrain. *David Evans*

MYWAYISTHEONLYWAY (IRE) 2 b.c. (Feb 11) Tamayuz 126 – Soul Custody 76 p (CAN) 100 (Perfect Soul (IRE) 122) [2015 p6g⁵ p6g* Nov 25] 30,000F, £25,000Y: first foal: dam US winner up to 1m (2-y-o 6f winner): off 9 weeks, 2/1, improved from debut when winning maiden at Kempton in November by ¾ length from The Commendatore, leading from over 1f out: will stay 7f: open to further improvement. *Martyn Meade*

MYWAY QUEEN 2 b.f. (Mar 12) Stimulation (IRE) 121 – Ellway Queen (USA) 71 57 (Bahri (USA) 125) [2015 6m 6m 6m⁴ 6g⁴ 7m Sep 8] modest maiden: stayed 6f: dead. *Tom Tate*

N

NAABEGHA 8 ch.g. Muhtathir 126 – Hawafiz (Nashwan (USA) 135) [2015 83, a90: f6d – f7g 7m Apr 6] useful at best, no form in 2015: tried in headgear prior to 2015: tried in tongue tie in 2015: often races towards rear: quirky. *John Balding*

NAADIRR (IRE) 4 b.g. Oasis Dream 129 – Beach Bunny (IRE) 114 (High Chaparral 116 § (IRE) 132) [2015 116: 6d* 6g 6m 6g² 7d⁴ 6m² 6d⁵ Oct 17] robust gelding: smart performer: won listed race at Doncaster (by 1¼ lengths from Astaire) in March: second in listed race at Newmarket (length behind Polybius) in August and in Bengough Stakes at Ascot (neck behind Eastern Impact) in October, and fifth of 20 to Muhaarar in Champions Sprint Stakes at Ascot final outing: stays 7f: acts on polytrack, good to firm and good to soft going: sometimes wears headgear: often travels strongly: one to be wary of. *Marco Botti*

NAADY 3 b.f. Mawatheeq (USA) 126 – Al Tamooh (IRE) 84 (Dalakhani (IRE) 133) [2015 68 62: t8.6m² 10g⁶ 8d⁴ p10f Jul 25] fair maiden: best effort at 8.5f: acts on tapeta. *Ed Dunlop*

NABATEAN (IRE) 4 b.g. Rock of Gibraltar (IRE) 133 – Landinium (ITY) 109 (Lando 113 (GER) 128) [2015 102p: p13.3f* 14g² May 30] good-bodied gelding: smart performer: won handicap at Chelmsford in April by 2 lengths from The Quarterjack: upped in grade, further improvement when 2¾ lengths second of 10 to Clever Cookie in listed race at York: stays 1¾m: acts on polytrack and good to soft going: often races prominently, usually travels strongly. *Andrew Balding*

NACHI FALLS 2 ch.c. (Mar 3) New Approach (IRE) 132 – Lakuta (IRE) (Pivotal 124) – [2015 p8f Nov 25] 16/1, well held in maiden at Lingfield. *Charlie Appleby*

NADDER 3 ch.f. Notnowcato 128 – Tavy (Pivotal 124) [2015 83p: 10m May 16] angular – filly: ran only twice, winning maiden at 2 yrs and finishing down the field in listed race at Newbury in May: dead. *Andrew Balding*

NAFAQA (IRE) 3 b.g. Sir Percy 129 – Maghya (IRE) 96 (Mujahid (USA) 125) [2015 107: 106 8g² 10.4m⁴ 10m⁴ 10f 10.3m³ 9g Sep 26] big, strong gelding: useful performer: second in Craven Stakes at Newmarket (1¼ lengths behind Kool Kompany) in April: mainly disappointing subsequently: stays 10.5f: acts on good to firm going: sent to UAE. *B. W. Hills*

NAFLA (USA) 3 gr.f. Unbridled's Song (USA) 125 – Our Dani (USA) (Homebuilder 73 (USA)) [2015 10s⁴ p10g⁶ p8g⁵ p10f³ Sep 24] $200,000Y: tall filly: sister to 7.5f winner You Make Me Sing and half-sister to several winners, including very smart US Grade 1 7f-8.5f winner You (by You And I): dam winning sprinter: fair maiden: stays 1¼m: in cheekpieces last 2 starts: sent to Saudi Arabia. *John Gosden*

NAGGERS (IRE) 4 ch.g. Excellent Art 125 – Trika (First Trump 118) [2015 84: 6g May 69 p 16] fairly useful performer: off 10 months, shaped well when 6 lengths eighth of 18 to Mukaynis in handicap at Doncaster only outing in 2015: stays 6f: acts on soft going: remains open to improvement. *Paul Midgley*

NAG'S WAG (IRE) 2 b.f. (Jan 20) Approve (IRE) 112 – Street Kitty (IRE) (Tiger Hill **74** (IRE) 127) [2015 5f* 5m⁴ 5.1d⁶ 5g³ 6.3d 5.5d p6g* Oct 7] rather leggy filly: second foal: dam unraced: fair performer: won maiden at Bath in April and claimer at Kempton in October: stays 6f: acts on polytrack and firm going. *David Evans*

NAIZAH (IRE) 3 b.f. Tamayuz 126 – Etizaaz (USA) 117 (Diesis 133) [2015 58p: 7m⁶ **77** p8g² p10g⁶ Oct 27] fair maiden: should stay 1¼m. *Ed Dunlop*

NAKEETA 4 b.g. Sixties Icon 125 – Easy Red (IRE) (Hunting Lion (IRE) 115) [2015 87: **100** 12m 12.5m⁴ 11.5g 10g³ 10.3m⁶ 12m⁵ 12.3g² 12.1d² 14d* 14d⁵ Sep 26] useful handicapper: won Old Borough Cup at Haydock (by neck from Pearl Castle) in September: further improvement when following up in 17-runner event at same course later in month by ½ length from Hassle, leading entering final 1f: likely to stay 2m: acts on soft and good to firm going: wears hood: usually responds generously to pressure. *Iain Jardine*

NAKUTI (IRE) 4 b.f. Mastercraftsman (IRE) 129 – Sheba Five (USA) 73 (Five Star Day **109** (USA) 120) [2015 99: p8g⁴ 7m⁵ 8m⁶ 8d* 7d 8m⁵ 8.1m* 10g⁶ Oct 18] tall filly: useful performer: won listed race at Pontefract (by length from Merry Me) and Atalanta Stakes at Sandown (by neck from Blond Me) in August: creditable 2½ lengths sixth of 12 to Curvy in E. P. Taylor Stakes at Woodbine final start: stays 1¼m: acts on soft and good to firm going: often races towards rear. *Sylvester Kirk*

NAMED ASSET 3 b.g. Invincible Spirit (IRE) 121 – Sabria (USA) (Miswaki (USA) 124) **62** [2015 65: 7m t6g 6m⁶ 6d 6g* 6v 5.7f Sep 12] modest handicapper: won at Ffos Las in July: stays 6f: acts on good to soft going: in cheekpieces last 3 starts: front runner/races prominently. *Martin Bosley*

NAMEITWHATYOULIKE 6 b.g. Trade Fair 124 – Emma Peel 113 (Emarati (USA) **110** 74) [2015 89: 6v* 6g 6d² 6d* 6g³ 6g² 6g 6g² 6s³ 6d* 6v Nov 7] lengthy, good-topped gelding: smart handicapper: won at Ripon (by ½ length from Mississippi) in May, Pontefract (by 1¾ lengths from Sunraider) in July and Doncaster (by 1½ lengths from Mass Rally) in October: has form at 8.5f, but at least as effective over shorter: acts on good to firm and heavy going: tried in blinkers prior to 2015: usually leads. *Bryan Smart*

NAME THAT TOON 2 b.f. (Apr 3) Paco Boy (IRE) 129 – Saktoon (USA) 60 (El Prado **50** (IRE) 119) [2015 p6g⁶ p5g⁴ 5m 5.1m p6g² p5f⁶ t5.1f⁵ p5f* Nov 7] £14,000Y: first foal: dam maiden (best effort at 6f): modest performer: won nursery at Chelmsford in November: stays 6f: acts on polytrack: often in visor: front runner/races prominently. *Derek Shaw*

NAM HAI (IRE) 4 b.g. Fastnet Rock (AUS) 127 – Bowstring (IRE) 105 (Sadler's Wells **73** (USA) 132) [2015 77: 16.2d Oct 16] well-made gelding: fair handicapper: should prove fully effective at 2m: acts on polytrack. *Kim Bailey*

NAMHROODAH (IRE) 3 br.f. Sea The Stars (IRE) 140 – Independant (Medicean 128) **96** [2015 77p: 10f⁴ 10m⁵ 12g³ Sep 25] useful form: best effort when 8¼ lengths third of 12 to Journey in listed race at Newmarket final start: stays 1½m. *James Tate*

NAM MA PROW 4 ch.g. Bahamian Bounty 116 – Charlotte Vale 84 (Pivotal 124) [2015 **44** 58: t12.2g f11d 15.8m⁶ t12.2g⁵ Jun 2] poor maiden: stays 2m: acts on good to firm and good to soft going: often wears headgear: often races prominently. *Simon West*

NANCY ASTOR 3 b.f. Shamardal (USA) 129 – Summers Lease 92 (Pivotal 124) [2015 **75** 75: p8m² p7m³ 8.5g 6g p5g 8g* p7m⁵ Nov 25] fair handicapper: won at Gowran in **a67** October: left John Gosden after second start, Patrick J. Flynn after fifth: stays 1m: acts on polytrack: races freely. *Ross O'Sullivan, Ireland*

NANCY FROM NAIROBI 4 b.f. Sixties Icon 125 – Madame Hoi (IRE) 89 (Hawk **102** Wing (USA) 136) [2015 97: 10m² 10s² 10.1g⁴ 12g² 11.9g 10f 10.3m⁶ 9g² 8m* 8f² Dec 30] tall filly: useful handicapper: won at Newmarket (by ¾ length from Wordcraft) in August: second at Goodwood (½ length behind Tazffin) in July: left Mick Channon after ninth start: stays 1¼m: acts on soft and good to firm going: in visor last 3 starts in Britain. *John W. Sadler, USA*

NANNY MAKFI 2 b.f. (Mar 6) Makfi 130 – Pan Galactic (USA) 105 (Lear Fan (USA) **53** 130) [2015 p7g 6d⁵ 6d t8.6g 7s² Oct 26] sturdy filly: closely related to 7f winner Panoptic (by Dubawi) and half-sister to several winners, including 1m-12.4f winner Emerging (by Mount Nelson) and 1m winner (stays 1½m) Engrossing (by Tiger Hill): dam 1m winner: modest maiden: will be suited by a return to 1m: acts on soft going. *Stuart Kittow*

NANTON (USA) 13 gr.g. Spinning World (USA) 130 – Grab The Green (USA) (Cozzene **–** (USA)) [2015 89: 14.6m⁶ 12g May 13] good-bodied gelding: fairly useful handicapper who has been a grand servant to his stable over the years (very tough and versatile): well held both starts in 2015: stayed 14.5f: acted on polytrack, firm and good to soft going: usually raced in rear: retired. *Jim Goldie*

NAOISE (IRE) 7 ch.g. Stormy Atlantic (USA) – Machinale (USA) (Kingmambo (USA) **84** 125) [2015 85: t7.1f⁵ t9.5f⁵ 8.5g 8m⁶ 7g⁵ 7.5m* 8.3g⁵ 7.5f³ 8.5m² 6g⁴ 7.5g t8.6f⁴ t8.6f³ t7.1m Nov 21] fairly useful handicapper: won at Beverley in June: best at 7f/1m: acts on polytrack, tapeta and any turf going: tried in cheekpieces prior to 2015: usually wears tongue tie: sometimes slowly away, often races towards rear. *Ollie Pears*

NAPOLEONIC (USA) 4 b.g. War Front (USA) 119 – High Savannah 77 (Rousillon **65** (USA) 133) [2015 t7.1g t9.5m⁴ t12.2f⁵ 8v⁶ p10m Nov 17] fair maiden: stays 9.5f: acts on tapeta, viscoride and firm going: tried in blinkers prior to 2015: usually races prominently. *Ed de Giles*

NAPOLEON SOLO 3 b.g. Cockney Rebel (IRE) 127 – Trump Street 77 (First Trump **77** 118) [2015 66p: 7v² 6m⁴ p7f t6f² Nov 20] fair maiden: should prove suited by a return to 7f: acts on tapeta and heavy going. *Dave Morris*

NARBOROUGH 4 b.g. Winker Watson 118 – Solmorin (Fraam 114) [2015 68§, a61§: **56 §** t6g⁴ 5d 5m 5.1s 5m 5.1m p5g⁶ 5.1m⁶ Jul 10] small, angular gelding: modest maiden in Britain: acts on polytrack, tapeta, soft and good to firm going: irresolute: sold £1,800, sent to Germany, where won twice from 8 starts, 6.5f maiden at Bad Doberan in August and 7.5f handicap on sand at Neuss in November. *Mick Channon*

NARVLA (IRE) 2 br.f. (Feb 1) Kheleyf (USA) 116 – Perino (IRE) 84 (Speightstown **59** (USA) 124) [2015 6d 6g⁴ 6d 6g Sep 21] €40,000Y: first foal: dam, 5f winner, half-sister to smart winner up to 7f Whaileyy: modest maiden: raced only at 6f. *John Quinn*

NASHVILLE (IRE) 6 b.g. Galileo (IRE) 134 – Brown Eyes 86 (Danehill (USA) 126) **–** [2015 91§: 16s 16.4m 16.1g 17.1g 14.1s Oct 16] fairly useful at best, no form in 2015: tried in headgear: often races towards rear/lazily. *Andrew Crook*

NASRI 9 b.g. Kyllachy 129 – Triple Sharp 80 (Selkirk (USA) 129) [2015 p7g p7g⁶ p6g* **69** p6g 6g p6g⁵ 7s Oct 26] well-made gelding: fair handicapper: won at Kempton in August: stays 7f: acts on polytrack, firm and soft going: tried in headgear prior to 2015. *Pat Eddery*

NASSUVIAN PEARL 2 br.f. (Apr 15) Bahamian Bounty 116 – Melody Maker 62 **69 p** (Diktat 126) [2015 p6g* Sep 22] fourth foal: half-sister to 3 winners, including useful winner up to 1m Haaf A Sixpence (2-y-o 7f winner, by Haafhd) and winner up to 8.3f Hard To Handel (2-y-o 7f winner, by Stimulation): dam ran twice: 10/1, won 12-runner maiden at Kempton on debut by ½ length from Yosemite, leading final ½f: open to improvement. *Ralph Beckett*

NATALIA 6 ch.m. Dutch Art 126 – Pintle 103 (Pivotal 124) [2015 55: t6f³ t6f³ t7.1g⁵ 6g⁵ **51** t6g⁶ t6g³ t6g Aug 27] modest maiden: stays 7f: acts on tapeta and good to firm going: sometimes wears headgear: usually races towards rear. *Sarah Hollinshead*

NATHRA (IRE) 2 b.f. (Mar 25) Iffraaj 127 – Rada (IRE) 52 (Danehill (USA) 126) [2015 **107** 7s* 7s* 8g² Oct 9] 270,000Y: compact filly: fifth foal: half-sister to 3 winners, including useful winner up to 9f Angelic Upstart (2-y-o 7f/1m winner, by Singspiel) and useful winner up to 1m Tickle Time (2-y-o 6f/7f winner, by Kheleyf): dam, lightly raced, closely related to very smart 6f winner Owington: useful form: won maiden at Salisbury and 5-runner minor event (by 7 lengths from Alqubbah) at Newbury in September: 4/1, confirmed previous promise when 4½ lengths second of 10 to Minding in Fillies' Mile at Newmarket, keeping on well: stays 1m. *John Gosden*

NATIONAL SERVICE (USA) 4 b.g. War Chant (USA) 126 – Cotton Club Ballet **66** (USA) (Street Cry (IRE) 130) [2015 77: 5m 5m 6m 5.8m⁴ 6d 7.2g⁴ 5d p6g⁶ p7g² p7g² p6m⁶ p7g Dec 11] fair handicapper: stays 7f: acts on polytrack, tapeta and firm going: sometimes wears headgear: often wears tongue tie: usually races nearer last than first, usually travels strongly. *Gordon Elliott, Ireland*

NATIVE FALLS (IRE) 4 ch.g. Elnadim (USA) 128 – Sagrada (GER) (Primo Dominie **85** 121) [2015 83: 5m 6d* 6m² 6m 6d⁶ 6g² 6m 6g Aug 1] neat gelding: fairly useful handicapper: won at Ayr in May: second at Catterick in June and July: has won at 7f, better form over shorter: acts on good to firm and good to soft going: front runner/races prominently. *Alan Swinbank*

NATURAL BEAUTY 2 b.f. (Jan 25) Oasis Dream 129 – Maskunah (IRE) (Sadler's Wells **80** (USA) 132) [2015 7m 8v p8m* Nov 19] sturdy filly: closely related to very smart 1¼m-1½m winner Laaheb and smart 6f-7f winner Ruwaiyan (both by Cape Cross) and half-sister to several winners, including 7f winner Guarantia (by Selkirk): dam unraced: fairly useful performer: best effort when winning maiden at Lingfield (by 2½ lengths from Chelabella) in November, having run of race: stays 1m: tried in tongue tie. *John Gosden*

NATURAL NINE (IRE) 3 b.g. Shamardal (USA) 129 – Source of Life (IRE) (Fasliyev **93** (USA) 120) [2015 79: 7.5m* p8f³ p8g³ p7f* Nov 23] rather leggy gelding: fairly useful performer: won maiden at Beverley in June and handicap at Chelmsford (by neck from Be Royale) in November: will stay beyond 1m: acts on polytrack and good to firm going. *Roger Varian*

NATURAL SCENERY 2 b.f. (Feb 10) Dubawi (IRE) 129 – Argentina (IRE) 116 **73 p** (Sadler's Wells (USA) 132) [2015 7f⁵ Jul 11] third foal: half-sister to 1½m-2m winner Bordoni (by Bernardini): dam winner up to 10.5f (2-y-o 9f winner): 10/1, some encouragement when fifth in maiden at Newmarket (9 lengths behind Ballydoyle) in July, slowly away: will be suited by 1m+: open to improvement. *Saeed bin Suroor*

NATURAL WONDER 2 ro.f. (Apr 6) Paco Boy (IRE) 129 – Galapagar (USA) (Miswaki **79** (USA) 124) [2015 8d⁶ 7d³ 7g⁴ 8v⁴ Oct 24] 75,000Y: workmanlike filly: half-sister to several winners, including smart winner up to 7f (stays 1¼m) Emirates Flyer (2-y-o 5f/6f winner, by Acclamation) and 7f winner Tajathub (by Bahamian Bounty): dam winner up to 9f (2-y-o 1m winner): fair maiden: best effort at 7f. *Richard Hannon*

NAUGHTY SPICE 4 b.f. Three Valleys (USA) 119 – Milldown Story 69 (Lucky Story **64** (USA) 128) [2015 6m⁴ 7m⁴ 6m p8g Jul 8] modest maiden: stays 7f: acts on firm going. *Rod Millman*

NAVAJO CHIEF 8 b.g. King's Best (USA) 132 – Navajo Rainbow (Rainbow Quest **96** (USA) 134) [2015 105: 7.6g⁵ 8f⁶ 8m 10.4g 10.4d 10s³ 10.4s Oct 10] workmanlike gelding: useful handicapper: well below form after reappearance: stays 10.5f: acts on polytrack, soft and good to firm going: tried in visor prior to 2015: none too consistent. *Timothy Jarvis*

NAVAJO DREAM 4 ch.f. Selkirk (USA) 129 – Rubies From Burma (USA) 104 (Forty **54** Niner (USA)) [2015 58: t9.5g t8.6g² p10m Feb 4] modest maiden: stays 8.5f: acts on tapeta: in cheekpieces last 2 starts. *Michael Appleby*

NAVAJO STORM (IRE) 2 gr.f. (Apr 30) Dark Angel (IRE) 113 – Strike Lightly **63** (Rainbow Quest (USA) 134) [2015 6g⁴ 7d f7g p7g Dec 9] 10,000Y: half-sister to 1¼m/11f winner (stays 1¾m) Significant Move (by Motivator) and 10.5f winner Triumvirate (by Rail Link): dam unraced sister to very smart 8.4f-1½m winner Ulundi: modest maiden: stays 7f. *Michael Appleby*

NAVAJO WAR DANCE 2 b.c. (Mar 10) Makfi 130 – Navajo Rainbow (Rainbow Quest **91** (USA) 134) [2015 7m 8v² 7g⁵ 8s³ 8d⁵ Oct 16] fifth foal: half-brother to smart/unreliable winner up to 9f Navajo Chief (2-y-o 5f winner, by King's Best) and 1¼m winner Flyfong (by Dr Fong): dam unraced half-sister to very smart winner up to 1¼m (stayed 1½m) Jammaal: fairly useful maiden: easily best efforts at Newbury, when second in maiden and third in minor event: will stay beyond 1m: best form on soft/heavy going. *Timothy Jarvis*

NAVAL ACTION 3 b.g. Lawman (FR) 121 – Dance of The Sea (IRE) (Sinndar (IRE) 134) **51** [2015 46: t9.5f* t12.2g² p12m⁵ 8g 11.5g⁵ t12.2f^{bu} 10g 10d Oct 26] modest handicapper: won at Wolverhampton in January: left Sir Mark Prescott after third start, Sandy Thomson after fifth: best effort at 9.5f: acts on tapeta: often wears headgear: temperament under suspicion. *Kenny Johnson*

NAVIGATE (IRE) 3 b.g. Iffraaj 127 – Dorothy Dene (Red Ransom (USA)) [2015 80p: **96** 6m⁵ 6.1s* 7g³ 6m 6.5m Sep 11] rangy gelding: useful handicapper: much improved when winning at Chester (by length from Northgate Lad) in May: shaped as if amiss last 2 starts (reportedly bled first time): likely to prove best at sprint trips: acts on soft going: has been gelded. *Martyn Meade*

NAWAASY (USA) 3 ch.f. Distorted Humor (USA) 117 – Stormin Maggy (USA) (Storm **66** Cat (USA)) [2015 76p: p10g³ Apr 1] 15/8, failed to improve from debut when third of 7 to Giantouch in maiden at Chelmsford. *Charles Hills*

NAWKHATHA (USA) 2 ch.f. (Feb 24) Tapit (USA) 118 – Lear's Princess (USA) 118 **74 p** (Lear Fan (USA) 130) [2015 7g³ Sep 30] third foal: dam US Grade 1 9f winner: 25/1, showed plenty when third in maiden at Salisbury (½ length behind Tafteesh) in September, sticking to task: will be suited by 1m+: should do better. *Brian Meehan*

NAYEL (IRE) 3 b.c. Acclamation 118 – Soliza (IRE) 93 (Intikhab (USA) 135) [2015 79p: **90 p** 8.3m⁴ 8f* 8.3m* Jul 17] fairly useful performer: won maiden at Bath and handicap at Nottingham (by ¾ length from Light And Shade) in July: will stay at least 1¼m: should continue to progress. *Richard Hannon*

NAZIBA (IRE) 2 gr.f. (Apr 19) Zebedee 113 – Nashaat (Redoute's Choice (AUS)) [2015 **61** 5f 6m 5.1m⁴ 5.7m³ 5m Sep 8] 11,000Y: first foal: dam unraced half-sister to useful 1½m winner Rewaaya: modest maiden: should be suited by 6f+: acts on good to firm going. *David Menuisier*

NEARLY CAUGHT (IRE) 5 b.g. New Approach (IRE) 132 – Katch Me Katie 77 **113** (Danehill (USA) 126) [2015 112: p14g2 16.2g³ 16.1m³ 14g 18g⁵ 18s* Oct 19] strong gelding: smart performer: easily landed odds in minor event at Pontefract in October: good efforts when 1½ lengths third of 19 to Quest For More in Northumberland Plate (Handicap) and 1¼ lengths fifth of 34 to Grumeti in Cesarewitch (Handicap) third/fifth starts: stays 2¼m: acts on polytrack, good to firm and heavy going: races prominently. *Hughie Morrison*

NEATH ABBEY 3 ch.f. Notnowcato 128 – Ewenny 71 (Warrshan (USA) 117) [2015 –: **–** 8.3m⁶ p10f p10f t9.5f Oct 3] no form. *William Muir*

NEBULA STORM (IRE) 8 b.g. Galileo (IRE) 134 – Epping 81 (Charnwood Forest **65** (IRE) 125) [2015 78: p14f p13g³ 11.6m 14m 11.5d³ p12g² 11.6m⁵ 11.6m² 11.6m* 11.6g⁶ Sep 7] ex-Irish gelding: fair performer: won seller at Windsor in August: stays 13f: acts on polytrack, soft and good to firm going: often wears visor: often races towards rear. *Gary Moore*

NED'S INDIAN (IRE) 7 b.g. Sleeping Indian 122 – Zanella (IRE) 87 (Nordico (USA)) **84** [2015 93: p10.7g⁴ p12g³ p10.7g p10.7g 11g 10.3m⁵ 10s 10g p10.7g Dec 18] fairly useful handicapper: stays 1½m: acts on polytrack, good to firm and heavy going: tried in headgear: usually races prominently, tends to find little. *Sabrina J. Harty, Ireland*

NEEDLESS SHOUTING (IRE) 4 b.g. Footstepsinthesand 120 – Ring The Relatives **79** 75 (Bering 136) [2015 86: 14.1m⁵ 16d⁴ 14.1m² 15.9m⁴ 16m² 21g 15.9m 14.1m⁵ Sep 15] useful-looking gelding: fair handicapper: stays 2m: acts on soft and good to firm going: tried in visor prior to 2015: usually races close up. *Mick Channon*

NEFETARI 2 b.f. (Feb 15) Kodiac 112 – Town And Gown 72 (Oasis Dream 129) [2015 **44** 5m 5g 5m 5g⁶ 7.5g 6g Sep 23] 28,000F, £32,000Y: third foal: sister to 5f winner Kassbaan and half-sister to 2-y-o 5f winner Oasis Town (by Sleeping Indian): dam, maiden (stayed 6f), half-sister to smart 2-y-o 6f winner Auditorium: poor maiden: best form at 5f: acts on good to firm going: tried in blinkers. *Alan Brown*

NELLIES QUEST 6 b.m. Rainbow High 121 – Dream Seeker (IRE) (Kahyasi 130) [2015 **63** 54§: 12.1m⁴ 11.9f³ 11.6mᵖᵘ Jun 29] smallish mare: modest handicapper: won at Chepstow in May: stayed 1½m: acted on firm going: was often in hood: front runner/raced prominently: dead. *Brendan Powell*

NELLIE THE ELEGANT 4 b.f. Mount Nelson 125 – Mexican Hawk (USA) 98 (Silver Hawk (USA) 123) [2015 66: p10m⁵ Dec 27] fair winner in 2014: in blinkers and tongue strap, well held only outing in 2015: best effort at 8.5f. *Tim Vaughan*

NELSON QUAY (IRE) 5 b.g. Holy Roman Emperor (IRE) 125 – Frippet (IRE) 87 (Ela- **70** Mana-Mou 132) [2015 59, a78: p11g⁵ Jan 7] strong gelding: fair handicapper: stays 11f: acts on polytrack: sometimes wears headgear. *Jeremy Gask*

NELSON'S BAY 6 b.g. Needwood Blade 117 – In Good Faith (USA) 74 (Dynaformer **70** (USA)) [2015 71: 8s* 8g* 8g⁵ 7m⁶ 10.1m⁴ 9.3g 8.9g⁵ 8m³ 8m 7.2g³ 9.2m 12.2g⁶ 10.3d Oct 23] tall gelding: fair handicapper: won at Musselburgh in April and May: probably stays 1½m, effective at shorter: acts on tapeta, firm and soft going: tried in tongue tie prior to 2015: often races in rear. *Wilf Storey*

NELSON'S HILL 5 b.g. Mount Nelson 125 – Regal Step 85 (Royal Applause 124) [2015 **–** –: p8f p8g⁶ May 28] no form. *W. de Best-Turner*

NELSON'S PRIDE 4 b.f. Mount Nelson 125 – Bandanna 98 (Bandmaster (USA) 97) **44** [2015 63: p5g³ 6m 6m⁶ 6m 5.7f 8m p6m Oct 21] workmanlike filly: poor maiden: stays 6f: acts on polytrack, tapeta and firm going: often wears headgear: front runner/races prominently. *Roger Ingram*

NELSPRUIT (IRE) 2 ch.c. (Feb 27) Makfi 130 – Mpumalanga 98 (Observatory (USA) **86** 131) [2015 6g² 5g* 6m² 5f Jun 16] €44,000F: compact colt: third foal: half-brother to 2-y-o 7f winner Tea In Transvaal (by Teofilo): dam, 2-y-o 5.5f winner, half-sister to useful winner up to 7f (stayed 1¼m) Red Seventy: fairly useful performer: won maiden at Goodwood in May: second in listed race at Epsom (6 lengths behind Buratino) in June: will be suited by a return to 6f+: sold £100,000 later in June, sent to Qatar. *Richard Hannon*

NEMORALIA (USA) 2 b.f. (Mar 25) More Than Ready (USA) 120 – Alina (USA) **112 p** (Came Home (USA) 122) [2015 6m⁵ 7f² p7g* 6.5m* a8s² 8d³ Oct 30] $140,000F, $170,000 2-y-o: third foal: half-sister to minor US winners by Sky Mesa and Stormy Atlantic: dam US winner up to 8.5f (2-y-o 5.6f winner): smart performer: won maiden at

Kempton in August and 19-runner nursery at Doncaster (value for plenty extra when beating Sharaakah by a length, travelling strongly and just pushed out) in September: good efforts last 2 starts, in Frizette Stakes at Belmont (3½ lengths second to Nickname, steadied off pace and keeping on nicely) and Breeders' Cup Juvenile Fillies Turf at Keeneland (length third to Catch A Glimpse, finishing well after being left with plenty to do): stays 1m: acts on dirt (effective in the wet) and on good to firm and good to soft going: still open to improvement. *Jeremy Noseda*

NESSITA 2 ch.f. (Mar 21) Shamardal (USA) 129 – Neshla 49 (Singspiel (IRE) 133) [2015 **79 p** 8.3g³ p8g* Oct 6] fourth foal: sister to 2-y-o 6f winner (stayed 1m) Wahylah and useful 1m winner Muhtaram and half-sister to 2-y-o 7f winner Faraajh (by Iffraaj): dam maiden half-sister to useful 7f winner (stayed 1¼m) Sueboog: fairly useful form: improved from debut when winning maiden at Kempton by length from Percy's Romance, giving trouble at start but straightforward in the race: should progress further. *Hugo Palmer*

NEUF DES COEURS 4 b.f. Champs Elysees 124 – Intervene (Zafonic (USA) 130) **74** [2015 67: 8d 9.2d* 8.3d 12.5m* 13.1g⁵ 15 8g 12,2g 12.2g 9.2m Sep 28] rather unfurnished filly: fair handicapper: won at Hamilton in May and Musselburgh in June: stays 12.5f: acts on good to firm and good to soft going: tried in blinkers prior to 2015: often races in rear. *Keith Dalgleish*

NEUTRON BOMB (IRE) 3 ch.f. Lope de Vega (IRE) 125 – Neutrina (IRE) (Hector **78** Protector (USA) 124) [2015 7d³ 7v³ 6m² 7.6m² t7.1g 8g² 8m t7.1m Oct 2] €48,000Y: half-sister to several winners, including 1m/9f winner Neutrafa (by Araafa) and 2-y-o 7f winner Three Gems (by Jeremy), both useful: dam unraced half-sister to Breeders' Cup Mile winner Domedriver: fair maiden: stays 1m: acts on heavy going: often in headgear. *Tom Dascombe*

NEVER CHANGE (IRE) 3 b.f. New Approach (IRE) 132 – Auspicious 103 (Shirley **77** Heights 130) [2015 91p: t7.1f* Nov 16] fairly useful form sole start at 2 yrs: left Saeed bin Suroor £5,800/off 12 months, fair form when winning maiden at Wolverhampton only outing in 2015: should prove suited by a return to 1m. *David Evans*

NEVER EASY (IRE) 3 gr.c. Zebedee 113 – Silk Point (IRE) (Barathea (IRE) 127) [2015 **59 §** 63: f6s³ f7g³ Jan 13] modest maiden: stays 7f: acts on fibresand: in visor last start: looks a hard ride, best treated with caution. *Richard Fahey*

NEVER GIVE IN 2 b.c. (Mar 28) Alfred Nobel (IRE) 110 – Mad Annie (USA) (Anabaa **76 p** (USA) 130) [2015 6m 6.5s⁴ Oct 23] half-brother to several winners, including 6f/7f winner Another Try (by Spinning World) and 7f-1¼m winner (stayed 2m) Oetzi (by Iceman): dam unraced: better effort when fourth in maiden at Newbury (2¾ lengths behind Bedrock) in October, not knocked about: open to further improvement. *Timothy Jarvis*

NEVER IN DOUBT 3 b.g. (May 12) Royal Applause 124 – African Breeze 79 (Atraf **74** 116) [2015 6g 5s⁵ 6d² Oct 26] 40/1, easily best effort (fair form) when short-head second of 14 to Captain Dion in maiden at Redcar final start. *Richard Whitaker*

NEVER SAY (IRE) 2 b.f. (Mar 8) Monsieur Bond (IRE) 129 – Wong Again 62 (Araafa **46** (IRE) 128) [2015 5.1m 5m 6m² 6g⁶ 6g f7g⁵ Nov 26] €3,000Y, £19,000 2-y-o: first foal: dam maiden half-sister to smart winner up to 13.4f Buccellati: poor maiden: left Ann Duffield after fourth start: best effort at 6f: acts on good to firm going: tried in cheekpieces. *Jason Ward*

NEVER TO BE (USA) 4 b.g. Thewayyouare (USA) 117 – Kitty Foille (USA) (Black **78** Minnaloushe (USA) 123) [2015 93: p7g⁵ p8m⁶ Mar 5] fair handicapper: stays 1m: acts on polytrack and good to firm going: wears tongue tie. *David O'Meara*

NEW ABBEY ANGEL (IRE) 2 gr.g. (Mar 10) Dark Angel (IRE) 113 – Alinda (IRE) 86 **–** (Revoque (IRE) 122) [2015 7g t7.1g p8f⁶ Oct 28] no form. *Gay Kelleway*

NEW ABBEY DANCER (IRE) 3 b.f. Thewayyouare (USA) 117 – Brave Cat (IRE) **– §** (Catrail (USA) 123) [2015 49: t9.5f 11.7f⁶ 9.2d 9.2g Jun 17] untrustworthy handicapper: left Gay Kelleway after second start: usually in headgear. *Keith Dalgleish*

NEW BAY 3 ch.c. Dubawi (IRE) 129 – Cinnamon Bay 107 (Zamindar (USA) 116) **128** [2015 8g* 8g² 10.4g* 9.9d* 11.9s* 11.9m³ Oct 4]
There may have been a familiar ring to the campaign of France's top three-year-old New Bay who finished strongly from a poor draw to be placed in the Poule d'Essai des Poulains, then enjoyed his biggest win in the Prix du Jockey Club, and ended the year with a good third in the Prix de l'Arc de Triomphe. In those respects, New Bay's season exactly mirrored that of Intello for the same stable two years earlier. It is now ten years since the Prix du Jockey Club was shortened from a

mile and a half to ten and a half furlongs, whilst at the same time the Grand Prix de Paris, previously run over a mile and a quarter, became France's Group 1 mile and a half contest for three-year-old colts, making it the new 'French Derby' in terms of distance, if not name. Those alterations were controversial at the time and the failure of any of the Prix du Jockey Club winners over the last ten years to go on to success in the Prix de l'Arc de Triomphe has done little to assuage the critics who opposed altering the traditional 'classic' Derby distance of the Prix du Jockey Club. Six winners of the Jockey Club in its current form have gone on to contest the Prix de l'Arc de Triomphe and Intello and New Bay have fared much the best of those by finishing third. The record of recent Grand Prix de Paris winners in the Arc is scarcely better, though. Rail Link won both races in 2006 for New Bay's trainer Andre Fabre and owner Khalid Abdullah, but Cavalryman (Fabre again), third three years later, is the only other Grand Prix de Paris winner to have been placed in the Arc since 2005. Fabre won the 2005 Arc with Hurricane Run who was beaten a neck by Shamardal in the first new-look Jockey Club.

The record of France's three-year-old colts in the Arc over the past ten years or so is less than flattering, perhaps, but it would be hard to prove that the altered programme for classic colts is to blame. The plain fact is that France has not had a genuinely top-notch three-year-old colt in that period to compare with the likes of Peintre Celebre, Montjeu and Dalakhani who all completed the Jockey Club-Arc double in a seven-year period around the turn of the century. There have been top-class French-trained three-year-old winners of the Arc in more recent seasons, but they have been fillies—Zarkava and Treve—and the Derby winners that have been successful—Workforce, Sea The Stars and now Golden Horn—have come from Epsom rather than Chantilly. Whatever impact it has had on the Arc, if any, one definite consequence of reducing the trip of the Prix du Jockey Club has been to tie it much more closely to the major colts' classic that precedes it, the Poule d'Essai des Poulains. Shamardal won both races in 2005, as did that horse's son Lope de Vega for Andre Fabre five years later. Intello was unlucky not to win the Poulains, beaten a neck and a head into third after being left with a lot to do from stall seventeen, and Fabre must have rued his luck again when New Bay was drawn sixteen in another eighteen-runner field for the latest renewal. At least he had the consolation of training the winner as well, Make Believe succeeding in making all from a much lower draw, but it was New Bay who caught the eye after turning for home at the back of the field. Only finding his stride out wide from over a furlong out, New Bay stormed home but was able only to reduce his stable-companion's advantage to three lengths at the line. New Bay's effort was all the more praiseworthy given that he was having just the third run of his life and taking a big step up in class from the two minor events, both also over a mile, that he had previously contested. He had been beaten by the filly Urjuwaan on the polytrack at Chantilly in November on his only start at two and then made a successful reappearance over the Poulains course and distance in April.

The extra distance of the Prix du Jockey Club at Chantilly at the end of May looked certain to suit New Bay and he was the pick on form, though it was the Aga Khan's comfortable winner of the Prix Noailles, Karaktar, who was slightly the more favoured of the two in the betting. The field of fourteen was on the small side for the Prix du Jockey Club in its current form and, unusually, lacked any runners from Britain, though it had originally been the target for Golden Horn before his Dante win prompted his owner to go for Epsom instead; the 2014 Dante winner The Grey Gatsby had followed up his York win at Chantilly. There were, though, three challengers from Aidan O'Brien's stable, including Highland Reel who had started favourite on his reappearance in the Poulains and had finished a keeping-on sixth. Although the Jockey Club field contained several winners of the dedicated trials, they were all found wanting as New Bay and Highland Reel took the first two places. Patiently ridden and delivering his challenge wide again, New Bay quickened smartly to lead a furlong out and kept on well to beat Highland Reel by half a length with War Dispatch, who had run up a winning sequence of six, beaten another length and three quarters into third. Karaktar had briefly looked dangerous but finished only eighth and was found to have sustained an injury after slipping on the turn for home.

Surprisingly, the Prix du Jockey Club in its old guise had not been a particularly successful race for France's master trainer, Peintre Celebre being the only Fabre-trained winner prior to 2005, but New Bay's success, added to those of Lope de Vega and Intello, means that Fabre has now won three of the last six renewals. It had also been a long time—twenty-five years to be precise—since Khalid Abdullah's silks were last carried to victory in the race. That was by Sanglamore, ridden by Pat Eddery for Roger Charlton, three days before owner, trainer and jockey were also successful with Quest For Fame in the Derby at Epsom. Eddery enjoyed plenty of success as retained rider to Khalid Abdullah (Juddmonte also supported him when he took up training), including partnering consecutive Arc winners in Rainbow Quest and Dancing Brave before a third win in a row on Fabre's first Arc winner Trempolino in 1987. There is more about Eddery's career in the Introduction which reports his sad death at only sixty-three.

New Bay's Chantilly victory went a long way to cementing the new association between his connections and twenty-one-year-old jockey Vincent Cheminaud. More than that, it set the seal on a significant change of direction in Cheminaud's career. The son of a successful jump jockey, Cheminaud became champion over jumps in France in 2014 when his wins included the Grand Steeple-Chase de Paris—*Chasers & Hurdlers* praised his 'superbly-judged' ride on Storm of Saintly who was produced to lead in the shadow of the post. Later the same year, he rode a Group 1 winner for Paul Nicholls at Auteuil when Zarkandar won the Grand Prix d'Automne. Andre Fabre, himself a former jump jockey, was evidently also impressed with Cheminaud's talent and provided the rider with a first pattern-race success on the Flat (from his first ride in a pattern race on the level) when Khalid Abdullah's Mexican Gold won the Prix de la Grotte at Longchamp in April. Just a week after the Prix du Jockey Club, Cheminaud, who began the year still entitled to draw a claim on the Flat, returned to Auteuil for what were to be his last rides over jumps before concentrating full-time on the Flat, and he rode a treble which included a Group 1 success on the top French four-year-old hurdler Blue Dragon. With generally lighter weights carried over jumps in France than in Britain, there is a long history of French jockeys winning at the highest level under both codes. Guy Chancelier, for example, who won the 1959 Prix du Jockey Club on Herbager, had won the Grand Steeple-Chase de Paris two years earlier on Bonosnap. Joseph O'Brien, who rode the Jockey Club runner-up Highland Reel, himself had a handful of rides over hurdles earlier in the year, though they were prompted by his ongoing struggle with his weight which had caused him to miss the start of the Irish Flat season in March.

It looked as though a first meeting between the Derby winners Golden Horn and New Bay might take place in the Eclipse Stakes, but New Bay was spared the ordeal of travelling from France in a heatwave as temperatures soared in early-July and his next appearance came instead at Deauville in August. Intello had contested the Prix Jacques le Marois over a mile at the same meeting, but there was no temptation to bring New Bay back in trip. Instead he contested the Prix Guillaume d'Ornano - Haras du Logis Saint Germain over a mile and a quarter, a valuable Group 2 contest which is run without penalties, earmarking it for a possible upgrade to Group 1 in the future. New Bay faced a fairly straightforward task in the latest edition against five rivals and quickened into the lead in the straight to beat the smart pair Dariyan and Ampere by a length and a half and two and a half lengths. The runner-up had beaten the Jockey Club third War Dispatch in the Prix Eugene Adam last time out, while New Bay's stablemate Ampere had finished second to Erupt in the Grand Prix de Paris. Erupt was now unbeaten in four starts and looked a serious rival to New Bay as the pair dominated the betting in a field of seven for the following month's Qatar Prix Niel at Longchamp.

New Bay was stepping up in trip in the Niel which was also run on softer ground than he had encountered previously. A son of Dubawi, like Erupt, New Bay was out of a mare who had failed to stay (in the Prix de Diane) on her only start beyond a mile, but there was no shortage of stamina a little further back in his pedigree. However, despite New Bay having the services of a pacemaker, Countermeasure, who had also done duty for him at Deauville, the Niel was the most slowly-run of the three Arc trials on the card and therefore wasn't the test it might have been. Proven at the trip, Erupt kicked on at the entrance to the straight to try to expose any flaws in New Bay's stamina, but New Bay moved past him on the bridle under two furlongs out and quickened away inside the final furlong as Erupt weakened disappointingly to finish a well-held fourth. Silverwave, only ninth in the Jockey Club and fourth in the Grand Prix de Paris, kept on for second, two and a half lengths behind the winner, with Migwar another length and three quarters back in third.

Whilst the Niel might not have been a true test, New Bay still put up a very good effort on his first try at the Arc trip, showing high-class form. Fabre had won the Niel ten times previously, with Trempolino, Carnegie, Sagamix, Hurricane Run and Rail Link all going on to win the Arc three weeks later. Another of the stable's Niel winners, Subotica, won the Arc a year later, while Peintre Celebre suffered an unlucky defeat in the race prior to his Arc win. New Bay therefore had the typical profile of a three-year-old Arc winner from his stable, even if his form still left him something to find with Golden Horn, not to mention the hat-trick-seeking Treve. New Bay was one of three from his stable in the Arc field who also included Khalid Abdullah's five-year-old Flintshire, contesting the race for the third time and runner-up to Treve the year before, while the third runner was the Godolphin-owned four-year-old Manatee. Treve was odds on, with New Bay preferred to Golden Horn as second favourite on the pari-mutuel. The Arc delivered a clear-cut verdict on which of the two Derby winners was the better. The Abdullah pair were always well positioned to the fore, just behind Golden Horn, with New Bay the first to throw down his challenge on Golden Horn's inner at the two-furlong pole. Unable to do any more, New Bay only just held on to deprive Treve of third, beaten two lengths and a neck behind Golden Horn and Flintshire.

Just a year after Kingman, this particular Juddmonte family has come up trumps again with another top three-year-old colt. Like Timeform's 2014 Horse of the Year, New Bay is a great grandson of the Lingfield Oaks Trial winner Bahamian. Her considerable influence as a foundation mare for Khalid Abdullah's

Prix du Jockey Club, Chantilly—New Bay confirms the considerable promise of his second from an unfavourable draw to the same yard's Make Believe in the Poulains as he beats Ballydoyle's Highland Reel and the grey War Dispatch; the win gives dominant French trainer Andre Fabre only his fourth Jockey Club but his third in six years, following Lope de Vega and Intello

breeding operation was detailed in Kingman's essay in *Racehorses of 2014*. Her daughters Wemyss Bight, Coraline and Hope have all been important broodmares for Juddmonte, and now a fourth daughter, New Bay's grandam Trellis Bay, can be added to that list. Wemyss Bight was the pick of them on the track, winning the Irish Oaks for the Fabre stable and then producing the Grand Prix de Paris and Arlington Million winner Beat Hollow at stud. Coraline was very much a staying influence as she became the dam of Martaline, Reefscape and Coastal Path, the latter pair both placed in the Gold Cup for Fabre. Although a sister to Wemyss Bight, Hope has been responsible for the family's speedier members, being the dam of Oasis Dream and Kingman's dam Zenda who won the Poule d'Essai des Pouliches. As for New Bay's grandam Trellis Bay, a sister to Coraline, she was very much a stayer, winning a maiden at Doncaster over a mile and a half and running her best race over two miles on her final start when second in a listed handicap at Newmarket. The best of Trellis Bay's five winners at stud also stayed well, the smart Bellamy Cay winning the Prix Maurice de Nieuil over a mile and three quarters and finishing second in the Prix Royal-Oak. Andre Fabre trained both Bellamy Cay and his half-sister Cinnamon Bay but, as has been said, the latter, New Bay's dam, by Zenda's sire Zamindar, didn't stay beyond a mile (all three of her wins, including one in a listed race, came over that trip at Chantilly). No better than useful, it should be said that Cinnamon Bay faced an uphill task in the Diane. New Bay is Cinnamon Bay's third foal after Margate (by Mizzen Mast), a mile winner at Lingfield from just two starts on the all-weather, and another filly, Iowa Falls (by Dansili) who finished fourth on all three of her outings for Fabre, showing fairly useful form at around nine furlongs. The two-year-old filly Spice Trail (by Champs Elysees) is yet to make her debut for the same stable. Besides Bahamian in the bottom half of New Bay's pedigree, another Juddmonte foundation mare features in the top half of his pedigree as Dubawi's dam was by Deploy, a son of Slightly Dangerous. Along with Sanglamore and Quest For Fame mentioned earlier, Deploy was the third member of a trio of Derby colts for Khalid Abdullah and Roger Charlton in 1990, Deploy earning the highest rating of the three when going down to the top-class filly Salsabil in the Irish Derby.

New Bay (ch.c. 2012)	Dubawi (IRE) (b 2002)	Dubai Millennium (b 1996)	Seeking The Gold
			Colorado Dancer
		Zomaradah (b 1995)	Deploy
			Jawaher
	Cinnamon Bay (ch 2004)	Zamindar (b 1994)	Gone West
			Zaizafon
		Trellis Bay (b 1996)	Sadler's Wells
			Bahamian

With only seven starts behind him, the robust, close-coupled New Bay, who is the type to carry plenty of condition, seems sure to win more good races at four when there will be plenty of options open to him. He has the speed to prove as effective back at around a mile and a quarter, as well as at a mile and a half, and has shown he acts on both soft and good to firm ground. He has a good turn of foot but is normally ridden prominently, and he has a particularly determined way of galloping with his ears flat back, as illustrated in the photo accompanying this essay. *A. Fabre, France*

NEW BIDDER 4 b.g. Auction House (USA) 120 – Noble Nova 69 (Fraam 114) [2015 92:   **95** 7d 6g 5.9v⁶ 6g⁶ 6g* 6g* 6g³ 6g³ 6d Oct 11] sturdy gelding: useful handicapper: won at Ayr (twice, by head from Exotic Guest latter occasion) in July: good third at Ayr and Pontefract next 2 starts: stays 6f: acts on heavy going: wears headgear nowadays: front runner. *Jedd O'Keeffe*

NEW CALEDONIA (IRE) 2 b.c. (May 2) Cape Cross (IRE) 129 – Tessa Reef (IRE)   **90** (Mark of Esteem (IRE) 137) [2015 7.2s 7m* 8.3m² 7g² 7s Oct 6] sturdy colt: half-brother to several winners, including winner up to 1m Second Wave (2-y-o 7f winner, by New Approach) and 9f/1¼m winner Samana Cay (by Authorized), both useful: dam 1m-9f winner: fairly useful performer: won maiden at York in July: best effort when second in nursery at Newmarket fourth start: will benefit from return to 1m: acts on good to firm going. *Mark Johnston*

NEW COLOURS 4 gr.g. Verglas (IRE) 118 – Briery (IRE) 66 (Salse (USA) 128) [2015 **73** 75: 9s 10g 12.5m⁵ 11.1d⁵ 12.5m² 12.5m² 12.5m⁴ 13.1g⁶ 11.1s 12.8m⁵ 11.5d⁶ 12.2m⁵ 15.8g 13.7m³ 12.2g 13.1g 13.1g 12.2g⁴ 10d Oct 26] tall gelding: fair handicapper: stays 12.5f: acts on polytrack, good to firm and heavy going: usually wears headgear: usually races nearer last than first. *Linda Perratt*

NEW DECADE 6 ch.g. Pivotal 124 – Irresistible 98 (Cadeaux Genereux 131) [2015 74: **31** f6g p6f t6g⁶ t6g t5.1m Apr 29] strong, good-topped gelding: poor handicapper: stays 1m: acts on all-weather, good to firm and heavy going: in headgear in 2015: sometimes wears tongue tie: sometimes slowly away. *Milton Bradley*

NEWERA 3 ch.g. Makfi 130 – Coming Home (Vettori (IRE) 119) [2015 –: 8.3s 10g* **90** 10.4f* 10.4m³ 10.4g* 10.4m* 11m⁵ 10.3g³ 10.3d Oct 23] angular gelding: fairly useful handicapper: won at Redcar in May and at Haydock in June and July (twice): should stay 1½m: acts on firm going: wears headgear: front runner/races prominently: has been gelded. *Tom Dascombe*

NEWGATE PRINCESS 3 gr.f. Bahri (USA) 125 – Arctic Queen (Linamix (FR) 127) **–** [2015 57: 12d Aug 17] maiden, modest form at best: best effort at 1m: sometimes slowly away. *Tony Coyle*

NEWGATE QUEEN 4 gr.f. Phoenix Reach (IRE) 124 – Arctic Queen (Linamix (FR) **–** 127) [2015 65: 12.5s f12g⁴ 16s 13d Jun 4] small filly: fair at best, no form in 2015: tried in cheekpieces. *Tony Coyle*

NEWHOLM (IRE) 3 b.g. Acclamation 118 – Benedicte (IRE) 77 (Galileo (IRE) 134) **72** [2015 f6s² p6g² p7f⁴ t6f² 6.1m³ 6g² 6m³ Jun 26] fair maiden in Britain: stays 6f: acts on tapeta and good to firm going: often races prominently: sold 18,000 gns, sent to Qatar, where won 6f maiden at Doha in December. *David Brown*

NEW HOPE (IRE) 2 b.g. (Apr 5) Exceed And Excel (AUS) 126 – Great Hope (IRE) 87 **68** (Halling (USA) 133) [2015 6g 7.2s⁴ 8m⁶ 8g t8.6f³ Oct 9] fair maiden: stays 8.6f: acts on tapeta and soft going: sold 26,000 gns, sent to Qatar. *Kevin Ryan*

NEW IDENTITY (IRE) 4 b.g. Rock of Gibraltar (IRE) 133 – Zaafran 86 (Singspiel **78** (IRE) 133) [2015 81: p7g 6m² Aug 18] fair maiden: stays 1m: acts on soft and good to firm going. *Denis Coakley*

NEW LEASE OF LIFE 6 b.g. Orientor 118 – Primo Heights 87 (Primo Valentino (IRE) **71** 116) [2015 71: 6s³ 5d³ 6d⁴ 5.9s² 6d⁶ 6s 6d* 5.9s⁵ 6m⁴ f7g Nov 3] medium-sized gelding: fair handicapper: won at Hamilton in August: stays 6f: acts on soft going: often wears cheekpieces: often races towards rear. *Keith Dalgleish*

NEW LEYF (IRE) 9 b.g. Kheleyf (USA) 116 – Society Fair (FR) (Always Fair (USA) **70** 121) [2015 72, a83: p6m⁴ p7f⁴ p6f* p6f* p6f⁶ p7f⁴ p7m³ p6f³ 6g² 5.1d⁵ 5.2m² 5.1m⁴ p7g **a82** p6g³ p6g* t6f² p7m t7.1f t5.1f Dec 21] stocky gelding: fairly useful handicapper: won at Kempton in February (twice) and September: stays 7f: acts on polytrack, tapeta, good to firm and good to soft going: often wears headgear: tried in tongue tie in 2015. *Jeremy Gask*

NEW LOOK (IRE) 5 b.g. New Approach (IRE) 132 – Lady Miletrian (IRE) 103 **48** (Barathea (IRE) 127) [2015 p8g p6f⁵ p8g⁶ Dec 20] poor form in maidens. *Ralph Smith*

NEWMARCH 3 ch.g. New Approach (IRE) 132 – Vallericca (USA) (Dynaformer (USA)) **109** [2015 p8g* 10.3g* t12.2m* Sep 5] useful form: unbeaten in 3 starts, in maiden at Lingfield in March and handicaps at Doncaster (by 4 lengths from Taper Tantrum) in August and Wolverhampton (by 5 lengths from Hamelin) in September: stayed 1½m: dead. *Charlie Appleby*

NEWMARKET WARRIOR (IRE) 4 b.g. Dalakhani (IRE) 133 – Heavens Peak 64 **71** (Pivotal 124) [2015 8g 8d⁴ 8d 8g 10.4d 8g³ 7s⁴ Oct 16] leggy gelding: fair maiden: stays 1m: acts on soft and good to firm going: tried in headgear: sometimes slowly away, often races in rear: quirky sort. *Iain Jardine*

NEW PROVIDENCE 3 ch.f. Bahamian Bounty 116 – Bayja (IRE) (Giant's Causeway **108** (USA) 132) [2015 104: 7m² 7s² 6d³ 6f 6m* 7m⁴ 8.5f Aug 29] smallish filly: useful performer: won Summer Stakes at York (by head from Lucky Kristale) in July: second in Chartwell Stakes at Lingfield (2 lengths behind Majestic Queen) and third in Sandy Lane Stakes at Haydock (length behind Adaay) second/third starts, and also ran creditably when fourth to Amy Eria in Oak Tree Stakes at Goodwood: stays 7f: acts on firm and soft going: usually races prominently. *Hugo Palmer*

NEW REVIVE 3 b.g. New Approach (IRE) 132 – Dance Lively (USA) (Kingmambo **–** (USA) 125) [2015 10m p8g⁶ Aug 24] workmanlike gelding: well held in 2 maidens. *Amanda Perrett*

NEW RICH 5 b.g. Bahamian Bounty 116 – Bling Bling (IRE) 70 (Indian Ridge 123) [2015 **73**
73: p6g⁶ p6f p6f⁶ 6g⁴ 7m² 6m⁵ 7g² p6g p7g⁶ p6f* p6m³ p6f³ p6m⁵ Dec 16] fair handicapper:
won at Chelmsford in November: stays 6f: acts on polytrack and firm going: usually wears
headgear: races towards rear. *Eve Johnson Houghton*

NEW ROAD SIDE 2 b.f. (Mar 11) Paco Boy (IRE) 129 – Spring Green 86 (Bahamian **83**
Bounty 116) [2015 f5g* 5m⁵ 5m⁵ 5m* 5f 5g² 5g⁰ʳ 5d Sep 25] £1,000Y: rather
unfurnished filly: second foal: half-sister to useful 2-y-o 6f winner Byzantium (by Dutch
Art): dam, 5f winner, closely related to smart 5f/6f winner Texas Gold: fairly useful
performer: won maiden at Southwell in April and minor event at Musselburgh in June:
raced only at 5f: acts on fibresand and good to firm going. *Tony Coyle*

NEWSLETTER (IRE) 3 b.f. Sir Percy 129 – Payphone (Anabaa (USA) 130) [2015 101: **103**
5f³ 6.1s* 6g² 6m⁵ 6m³ 7.5s⁵ Aug 27] good-topped filly: useful performer: won listed race
at Nottingham (by 1¼ lengths from Pastoral Girl) in May: better form after when second in
Ballyogan Stakes at the Curragh (½ length behind Ainippe) and third in listed race at Naas
(1½ lengths behind Letters of Note): stays 6f: acts on soft and good to firm going:
sometimes wears tongue tie. *K. J. Condon, Ireland*

NEWSPEAK (IRE) 3 b.g. New Approach (IRE) 132 – Horatia (IRE) 106 (Machiavellian **–**
(USA) 123) [2015 –: 10m Aug 3] tall gelding: well held both starts in maidens.
Charlie Appleby

NEWSTEAD ABBEY 5 b.g. Byron 117 – Oatcake 68 (Selkirk (USA) 129) [2015 105: **108**
7g⁶ 7.6v* May 8] well-made gelding: useful handicapper: won at Chester (by 1¾ lengths
from Rene Mathis) in May: stays 1m: acts on polytrack and any turf going: usually races
prominently. *David Barron*

NEW STORY 4 b.c. New Approach (IRE) 132 – Al Hasnaa (Zafonic (USA) 130) [2015 **–**
108p: p10g Mar 14] well-made colt: useful performer in 2014: badly needed run when last
of 11 in Winter Derby at Lingfield, only outing in 2015: stays 10.5f: acts on good to firm
going. *Ismail Mohammed*

NEW STRATEGY (IRE) 3 b.g. Lawman (FR) 121 – Kate The Great 79 (Xaar 132) **92**
[2015 79p: 8.5g⁴ 7g 7d² 6g³ 7.5m* p7g* p7g² Sep 5] sturdy gelding: fairly useful
handicapper: won at Beverley in July and Kempton in August: stays 8.5f: acts on polytrack,
good to firm and good to soft going: often in cheekpieces in 2015: sometimes in tongue tie
in 2015. *Saeed bin Suroor*

NEW STREAM (IRE) 4 b.c. New Approach (IRE) 132 – Shimna 62 (Mr Prospector **66**
(USA)) [2015 –: 8d³ 7.1s² t8.6g p12g Oct 6] fair maiden: should be suited by 1¼m+: acts
on polytrack and soft going. *Clive Brittain*

NEW STYLE (USA) 3 b.f. Street Cry (IRE) 130 – Land of Dreams 115 (Cadeaux **58 p**
Genereux 131) [2015 –: p7f³ p8g³ May 28] lightly-raced maiden: modest form when third
at Kempton and Lingfield: should do better. *Saeed bin Suroor*

NEW TARABELA 4 ch.g. New Approach (IRE) 132 – Tarabela (CHI) (Hussonet (USA)) **63 §**
[2015 86: p13g⁴ p12g 11.6d 17.1d f14g⁵ Dec 12] strong, short-backed gelding: modest
maiden: stays 1¾m: acts on polytrack, fibresand, soft and good to firm going: tried in
headgear: tried in tongue tie in 2015: usually let down by attitude and one to be wary of.
Tony Carroll

NEWTON BOMB (IRE) 3 b.f. Fast Company (IRE) 126 – Athlumney Dancer (Shareef **–**
Dancer (USA) 135) [2015 62: f5g p8f Jan 21] maiden: no form in 2015: stays 6.5f: tried in
hood prior to 2015: often leads: temperament under suspicion. *Conrad Allen*

NEWTON'S LAW (IRE) 4 b.g. Lawman (FR) 121 – Royal Alchemist 109 (Kingsinger **92**
(IRE) 94) [2015 84: 6m² 5f² 5m* 6m 5g 5m 5m p5m⁵ p5g t6m Dec 12] sturdy gelding:
fairly useful handicapper: won at Newmarket (by 1½ lengths from Sandfrankskipsgo) in
June: stays 6f: acts on firm and good to soft going: often wears hood: wears tongue tie:
often starts slowly, often races in rear. *Brian Meehan*

NEWTOWN CROSS (IRE) 5 ch.g. Kheleyf (USA) 116 – Sacred Pearl (IRE) (Daylami **53**
(IRE) 138) [2015 71: t13.9m⁶ p16m⁴ Feb 18] strong, lengthy gelding: modest handicapper:
stays 2m: acts on polytrack and good to firm going: tried in headgear. *Jimmy Fox*

NEW YEAR'S NIGHT (IRE) 4 ch.g. Raven's Pass (USA) 133 – Nightime (IRE) 113 **101**
(Galileo (IRE) 134) [2015 91: p8m t9.5f² t12.2g* p12g* p11g⁶ 12m² May 9] rather leggy
gelding: useful handicapper: won at Wolverhampton and Lingfield in March: best effort
when second at Ascot (short head behind Penhill) final start: stays 1½m: acts on polytrack,
tapeta and good to firm going: tried in hood in 2014. *Charlie Appleby*

NEXT APPROACH 3 ch.c. New Approach (IRE) 132 – Carafe 85 (Selkirk (USA) 129) **97 p**
[2015 10m³ 10m* Jun 19] 165,000 2-y-o: sixth foal: half-brother to 5f-7f winner Amphora
(by Oasis Dream): dam 7f winner out of smart 1m/1¼m (Nassau Stakes) winner Caramba:
useful form: 5/6, confirmed debut promise when winning 6-runner maiden at Newmarket
impressively by 6 lengths from Star Storm, making running: wears hood: open to further
improvement. *John Gosden*

NEXT BEND (IRE) 4 b.g. Azamour (IRE) 130 – Polite Reply (IRE) 96 (Be My Guest **–**
(USA) 126) [2015 76: 13.1d Jun 8] maiden, fair form for D. K. Weld in 2014: well held
only start in 2015: stays 1¼m: acts on good to firm and good to soft going: tried in
headgear/tongue tie. *John McConnell, Ireland*

NEXT EDITION (IRE) 7 b.g. Antonius Pius (USA) 123 – Starfish (IRE) (Galileo (IRE) **73**
134) [2015 89: 10g 10d 12g 12s t13.9f⁵ t12.2f⁵ t13.9f³ t13.9f² t12.2f Dec 22] fair
handicapper: stays 1¾m: acts on tapeta, firm and soft going: often races freely. *Philip Kirby*

NEXT GENERATION (IRE) 3 b.f. Royal Applause 124 – Gazebo 68 (Cadeaux **52**
Genereux 131) [2015 –: p7g⁵ Feb 11] neat filly: lightly-raced maiden, modest form at best.
Olly Stevens

NEXT LIFE 2 b.f. (Apr 3) Oasis Dream 129 – Silkwood 116 (Singspiel (IRE) 133) [2015 **86 p**
p6g* Sep 30] fourth foal: half-sister to 8.5f winner Ghostflower (by Dansili): dam,
9.5f-1½m (Ribblesdale Stakes) winner, half-sister to smart winner up to 1m Kavango: 3/1,
looked useful prospect when winning 10-runner maiden at Kempton on debut by 2 lengths
from Jameerah, quickening to lead after hampered entering final 1f: sure to progress. *Saeed bin Suroor*

NEXT STAGE 2 ch.c. (Feb 26) Dubawi (IRE) 129 – Dash To The Front 105 (Diktat 126) **92 p**
[2015 p8f* Nov 25] 800,000Y: fourth foal: half-brother to 3 winners, including smart 1¼m
winner Speedy Boarding (by Shamardal) and useful 8.6f-1½m winner Miss Dashwood (by
Dylan Thomas): dam, 8.6f-11f winner, half-sister to smart/ungenuine winner up to 1¼m
(stayed 1½m) Dash To The Top: 2/1, won maiden at Lingfield on debut by 1¾ lengths from
Always Welcome, travelling well and asserting final 1f: will stay 1¼m: likely to improve.
Saeed bin Suroor

NEXT STOP 4 b.f. Rail Link 132 – Reaching Ahead (USA) (Mizzen Mast (USA) 121) **77**
[2015 76: 10.3d 8.5m³ 9.9m* 9.9g² 10m² 12g⁴ 9.2s⁴ 9.3d² 9.9m⁴ 8m² 10g² 10g³ 12v⁶ Oct
17] fair handicapper: won at Beverley in April: stays 1½m: acts on polytrack, good to firm
and heavy going: often races prominently: consistent. *David Nicholls*

NEXT TRAIN'S GONE 2 b.g. (Mar 16) Rail Link 132 – Coh Sho No 59 (Old Vic 136) **–**
[2015 p8g Dec 9] 100/1, well held in maiden at Kempton. *James Eustace*

NEYMAR 3 ch.g. New Approach (IRE) 132 – Just Like A Woman 96 (Observatory (USA) **87**
131) [2015 10m 10g⁴ 12m³ 10.1m* 12f 12f⁵ Jul 11] useful-looking gelding: third foal:
half-brother to winner up to 8.6f (stays 10.5f) Rainbow Beauty (by Manduro) and 7f
winner Zain Empire (by Dubawi): dam 7f winner (including at 2 yrs): fairly useful
performer: won maiden at Newcastle (by 2¾ lengths from Bank of Gibraltar) in June: stays
1½m: acts on firm going: usually in hood: temperament under suspicion. *Michael Bell*

NEZAR (IRE) 4 ch.g. Mastercraftsman (IRE) 129 – Teddy Bears Picnic (Oasis Dream **88**
129) [2015 93: 6d 6m⁵ 6g 6.1f 7m⁵ 6m⁴ 6m² 6d⁴ 6g 6.1g⁶ t7.1f³ p6g⁴ t7.1m⁶ Dec 26]
angular gelding: fairly useful handicapper: stays 1m, usually races over 6/7f: acts on
polytrack, tapeta and firm going: often wears headgear. *John Quinn*

NGORONGORO (USA) 2 ch.c. (Mar 20) Giant's Causeway (USA) 132 – Firey Red **57 p**
(IRE) 99 (Pivotal 124) [2015 7g 8s Oct 23] $65,000Y: second foal: dam winner up to 1m
(2-y-o 6f winner): some encouragement when seventh in maiden at Salisbury on debut:
well held in similar event at Newbury next time: worth another chance. *Joseph Tuite*

NIBLAWI (IRE) 3 b.g. Vale of York (IRE) 117 – Finnmark (Halling (USA) 133) [2015 **77**
69p: 8.1s² 8.3g² p10g³ t8.6m² 8.1m⁶ Sep 10] fair maiden: stays 1¼m: acts on tapeta,
soft and good to firm going: in headgear last 3 starts. *Michael Bell*

NICARRA (IRE) 2 b.f. (Feb 16) Kodiac 112 – Nassma (IRE) 95 (Sadler's Wells (USA) **70 p**
132) [2015 7s⁴ Oct 12] 80,000F: rather unfurnished filly: half-sister to numerous winners,
including smart winner up to 7.4f Lady Wingshot (2-y-o 7f winner, by Lawman) and useful
winner up to 1m Bahama Mama (2-y-o 5f/6f winner, by Invincible Spirit): dam 1¼m-13f
winner: 20/1, promise amidst inexperience when 3¾ lengths fourth of 10 to Dutch Destiny
in maiden at Salisbury: sure to progress. *Henry Candy*

NICE FUTURE (IRE) 2 b.c. (Feb 23) Dubawi (IRE) 129 – Comic (IRE) 87 (Be My **81 p**
Chief (USA) 122) [2015 7s³ 8.5v* 9g⁶ Oct 21] 1,400,000Y: well-made colt: half-brother to
several winners, including smart US Grade 1 9f/1¼m winner Laughing (by Dansili) and

high-class Hong Kong performer up to 1½m Viva Pataca (by Marju, 2-y-o 6f-8.5f winner in Britain as Comic Strip): dam 1¼m-11.5f winner: fairly useful form: won 4-runner maiden at Epsom in September by neck from Modello: sixth to Southdown Lad in nursery at Newmarket final start, not persevered with once held: stays 8.5f: remains with potential. *Saeed bin Suroor*

NICE NAME (IRE) 2 b.c. (Feb 26) Royal Applause 124 – Grand Zafeen 86 (Zafeen (FR) 123) [2015 7g 6d³ 6s Oct 16] fair maiden: best form when eighth at Leicester on debut: will be suited by a return to 7f: sold 23,000 gns, sent to Italy. *Richard Fahey* **77**

NICEOFYOUTOTELLME 6 b.g. Hernando (FR) 127 – Swain's Gold (USA) (Swain (IRE) 134) [2015 107: 9g⁴ 10m³ 10f 12m⁶ p12g⁶ p9.2m p10f p10m Nov 14] smallish, leggy gelding: smart performer: better than ever in 2015, but only placing when ½-length third of 5 to Western Hymn in Brigadier Gerard Stakes at Sandown: seemingly stays 1½m: acts on polytrack, firm and good to soft going: sometimes wears hood: held up (sometimes slowly away). *Ralph Beckett* **114**

NICEONEMYSON 6 b.g. Misu Bond (IRE) 114 – Kungfu Kerry (Celtic Swing 138) [2015 68§: 5m³ 5m 5m² 5m⁵ 6s⁵ 5s⁶ 6g 6v Nov 3] modest handicapper: stays 7f: acts on any turf going: tried in headgear/tongue tie: unreliable. *Christopher Wilson* **62 §**

NICE STORY (IRE) 5 ch.m. Suave (USA) 123 – Royal Aly (USA) (Royal Academy (USA) 130) [2015 10.9s 11.9m⁴ 12m* 10.9d* 11.9g* 11.4g³ 13.9g* 11.9g t12.2f* Nov 3] unfurnished mare: fair handicapper: won at L'Ancresse in May, Hoppegarten and Bremen in June, Baden-Baden in September and Wolverhampton in November: stays 1¾m: acts on tapeta, heavy and good to firm going. *R. Storp, Germany* **67**

NICE THOUGHTS (IRE) 3 b.g. Shamardal (USA) 129 – Zacheta (Polish Precedent (USA) 131) [2015 8d⁶ 8.3m³ 8m³ 10.4f² 10.3m³ 8.1g³ 8g³ 8.3d* 8.1m² 7.2g t9.5m p8g* Oct 27] sturdy gelding: seventh foal: half-brother to 11.5f winner Dawn Sky (by Fantastic Light) and very smart winner up to 9f Ransom Note (2-y-o 7f winner, by Red Ransom): dam unraced half-sister to Prix de l'Arc de Triomphe winner Marienbard: fairly useful performer: won maiden at Hamilton in August and handicap at Lingfield (by 1½ lengths from Real Smart) in October: stays 10.5f: acts on tapeta, polytrack, firm and good to soft going: tried blinkered, in cheekpieces last 5 starts: front runner/races prominently: hasn't always looked straightforward. *James Tate* **93**

NICKSCREAMCRACKER (IRE) 3 b.g. Fast Company (IRE) 126 – Golden Ora (ITY) (Nordance (USA)) [2015 –: 7.5m 9g 10g 14.1g 12.1f 9.9m⁶ 12.1s* 12.1m³ 14.1m⁵ 14.1s⁶ t13.9m Oct 2] modest handicapper: won at Beverley in July: stays 1¾m: acts on soft and good to firm going. *Ruth Carr* **61**

NICKY NUTJOB (GER) 9 b.g. Fasliyev (USA) 120 – Natalie Too (USA) (Irish River (FR) 131) [2015 11.7g⁶ Jun 13] close-coupled gelding: poor maiden: seems to stay 13f: acts on firm and soft going: has worn headgear, including last 5 starts. *John O'Shea* **–**

NIDNOD 2 b.f. (Feb 4) Myboycharlie (IRE) 118 – Littlemisstutti (IRE) (Noverre (USA) 125) [2015 5g 5g³ p5m³ 6g* 6g 5.9m 6d 5d p6f⁴ p5m p6g³ Dec 7] 30,000Y: smallish, angular filly: second foal: dam unraced half-sister to smart winner up to 6f Guinea Hunter and useful 6f winner Dhanyata: fair performer: won nursery at Lingfield in July: left Hugo Palmer after eighth start: stays 6f: acts on polytrack and good to soft going: often races prominently. *John Bridger* **69**

NIETZSCHE 2 ch.g. (Apr 10) Poet's Voice 126 – Ganga (IRE) 94 (Generous (IRE) 139) [2015 6g⁴ 7m⁶ 6.1m 8.3d⁵ p10f⁴ t9.5f³ Nov 16] fair maiden: left William Haggas after fifth start: stays 1¼m: acts on polytrack and tapeta: sometimes slowly away, usually races nearer last than first, often races freely. *Brian Ellison* **66**

NIFTY KIER 6 b.g. Kier Park (IRE) 114 – Yeldham Lady 52 (Mujahid (USA) 125) [2015 61§: p10f³ p8g⁶ p10g⁵ p8m² p8m⁶ 8m* 9.9d³ 10.2m⁴ p10f⁶ 10.1g t8.6g⁵ p8f⁶ Dec 17] compact gelding: modest handicapper: won at Bath in July: stays 1¼m: acts on polytrack, firm and soft going: tried in visor/tongue tie prior to 2015: front runner/races prominently: unreliable. *Phil McEntee* **57 §** **a51 §**

NIGEL 3 b.c. New Approach (IRE) 132 – Deirdre 101 (Dubawi (IRE) 129) [2015 10m 12m³ p12g² 12m² 14g 12g³ p13.3f² Oct 8] strong colt: first foal: dam, 2-y-o 1m winner, half-sister to very smart 1¼m-1¾m winner (stayed 2m) Duncan: fairly useful maiden: second at Kempton and Newbury: should stay 1¾m: acts on polytrack and good to soft going: sometimes slowly away. *John Gosden* **85**

NIGEL'S DESTINY (USA) 4 b.c. Giant's Causeway (USA) 132 – Ticket To Seattle (USA) (Capote (USA)) [2015 93: p8f* p7g⁴ p8m⁵ 7g³ 7m Jun 7] useful handicapper: won at Lingfield in February: stays 1m: acts on polytrack: visored final start: sent to USA. *Jeremy Noseda* **96**

NIGHTFLOWER (IRE) 3 ch.f. Dylan Thomas (IRE) 132 – Night of Magic (IRE) 106 **118**
(Peintre Celebre (USA) 137) [2015 9.9s² 10.4g² 9.9g* 10.4g 10.9g² 11.9g² 11.9s* 11.9f
Nov 29] first foal: dam, won Oaks d'Italia, sister to dam of Deutsches Derby winner Nutan:
smart performer: won Diana-Trial at Hoppegarten in May and Preis von Europa at Cologne
(by 2 lengths from Sirius, leading over 1f out) in September: second in Preis der Diana at
Dusseldorf (¾ length behind Turfdonna) and Grosser Preis von Baden at Baden-Baden
(1¾ lengths behind Prince Gibraltar) in between: short of room final 1f and not persevered
with when eleventh behind Shonan Pandora in Japan Cup at Tokyo final outing: suited by
1½m: acts soft going, probably on firm. *P. Schiergen, Germany*

NIGHT GENERATION (GER) 3 ch.g. Sholokhov (IRE) 121 – Night Woman (GER) **89**
(Monsun (GER) 124) [2015 –p: p10m⁵ 11.5g* p15.8f* 16.2m* 16.2d⁵ Oct 16] fairly useful
handicapper: won at Carlisle in June, Lingfield in September and Beverley in October:
stays 2m: acts on polytrack and good to firm going: in cheekpieces last 3 starts: usually
races close up. sold 62,000 gns, and has joined Noel Meade. *Sir Mark Prescott Bt*

NIGHT OF THUNDER (IRE) 4 ch.c. Dubawi (IRE) 129 – Forest Storm 99 **123**
(Galileo (IRE) 134) [2015 127: 8m* 8f⁵ 8g⁶ Jul 29]

    Night of Thunder won one of the strongest editions of the Two Thousand
Guineas in recent memory during a three-year-old campaign that also saw him finish
placed in the St James's Palace Stakes, the Prix du Moulin and the Queen Elizabeth
II Stakes. Alas, he became the latest British classic winner to fail to enhance his
standing at four. Since the start of the century, six Two Thousand Guineas winners
have stayed in training for a further year, but only three of them—Golan, Refuse
To Bend and Frankel—went on to show improved form, with Night of Thunder
(rated 127 in *Racehorses of 2014*) joining George Washington (who reappeared in
the June of his four-year-old year after a failed spell at stud) and Camelot (who
recovered from surgery after suffering an attack of colic after running in the Arc as a
three-year-old) as those that failed. Night of Thunder made a successful return in the
Lockinge Stakes at Newbury in May, when carrying the Godolphin colours for the
first time, but he didn't need to improve to win by a neck from stablemate Toormore
(who had finished a close third in the Queen Elizabeth II Stakes). Poor efforts
afterwards behind Solow in both the Queen Anne Stakes and the Sussex Stakes saw
Night of Thunder retired to stud before the end of August. Night of Thunder was the
only horse to beat the top-class miler Kingman (in the Guineas) which is a claim
to fame sure to be highlighted as he becomes one of five new stallions for Darley's
European arm in 2016 when he will stand at a fee of €30,000 at Kildangan Stud in
County Kildare, which once stood his sire Dubawi.

    Al Shaqab's sponsorship of the latest Lockinge Stakes came with a massive
increase in prize money, up by over £130,000 from the 2014 edition won by
Al Shaqab Racing-owned Olympic Glory trained by Richard Hannon. The big prize

Al Shaqab Lockinge Stakes, Newbury—
Night of Thunder (right) beats the largest field in the race's history—thanks to a massive increase in
prize money—headed by his stablemate Toormore (light silks), Arod (rail) and the mare Integral

attracted an original declaration of eighteen, which, even after the seven-year-olds Tullius and Trade Storm were withdrawn on the day, the former on account of the ground which was good to firm by Timeform calculations, left the largest field in the race's history. The field was more about quantity than quality, with genuine Group 1 performers in short supply. Night of Thunder himself set the standard and started 11/4 joint favourite with the five-year-old mare Integral whose connections have a particularly good record in the Lockinge. Custom Cut had won the Mile at Sandown on his reappearance and started at 7/1, with Toormore at 10/1 and the rest at 11/1 or longer. Night of Thunder travelled well in mid-field and hit the front inside the two-furlong marker and was ridden out from there by new jockey James Doyle. As it turned out, with Arod in third and Integral in fourth, the form among the principals passed muster at least, even if the winning performance itself was a little below recent standards for the race. Night of Thunder still looked the leading British contender for top miling honours among the older horses and he started at 4/1 for the Queen Anne Stakes at Royal Ascot, behind only French-trained Solow and Able Friend from Hong Kong. Night of Thunder finished out of the places for the first time in six outings in Group 1 races over a mile, managing just a one-paced fifth of eight, a place behind Toormore who was also purchased privately by Godolphin before he won the Lennox Stakes at Goodwood, where Night of Thunder was beaten in the Sussex by the same margin as in the Queen Anne—four and three quarters lengths—when sixth of eight to Solow, still travelling just about best two and a half furlongs out but not really responding when asked.

Night of Thunder (IRE) (ch.c. 2011)	Dubawi (IRE) (b 2002)	Dubai Millennium (b 1996)	Seeking The Gold / Colorado Dancer
		Zomaradah (b 1995)	Deploy / Jawaher
	Forest Storm (ch 2006)	Galileo (b 1998)	Sadler's Wells / Urban Sea
		Quiet Storm (b 2000)	Desert Prince / Hertford Castle

Night of Thunder's pedigree was discussed in detail in *Racehorses of 2014*. He was the only foal out of Forest Storm who died the year after Night of Thunder was foaled, while Forest Storm herself had only three known siblings (the youngest now six), which helps to explain why there are no significant updates on Night of Thunder's immediate family. However, Night of Thunder's fourth dam, the champion two-year-old filly of 1986 Forest Flower, is a half-sister to the grandam of the Canadian-trained Catch A Glimpse, winner of the Breeders' Cup Juvenile Fillies Turf in October. Night of Thunder wasn't expensive as a yearling—he cost 32,000 guineas—but his pedigree brings together two of the top modern-day stallions, Dubawi and Galileo, and he certainly has the credentials to become a successful stallion himself. The early promise shown by Dubawi's other Two Thousand Guineas-winning son Makfi as a stallion (his first crop contained Make Believe) might be taken as auguring well for Night of Thunder's prospects. Night of Thunder is a useful-looking colt in appearance but he is not the best of walkers. He was usually held up, stayed a mile and acted on heavy and good to firm going. *Richard Hannon*

NIGHT'S WATCH 5 b.h. Authorized (IRE) 133 – Nachtigall (GER) (Danehill (USA) – 126) [2015 68: f8g t8.6g t8.6g⁴ Apr 18] fair at best, no form in 2015: front runner/races prominently. *Dai Burchell*

NIGHT TO REMEMBER (IRE) 2 b.g. (Apr 28) Dark Angel (IRE) 113 – Night Club 68
60 (Mozart (IRE) 131) [2015 7g³ 7d p7g p7g Dec 9] fair maiden: will stay 1m+: in headgear last 2 starts. *Ralph Beckett*

NIGHT TRADE (IRE) 8 b.m. Trade Fair 124 – Compton Girl (Compton Place 125) 35
[2015 62, a42: t6f⁵ t6f Feb 20] sturdy mare: poor performer: stays 7f: acts on polytrack, fibresand, good to firm and heavy going: often wears headgear: usually races nearer last than first. *Ronald Harris*

NIMBLE KIMBLE 4 ch.f. Kirkwall 118 – Lovely Lyca 76 (Night Shift (USA)) [2015 79: 69
p10g p8g⁶ p8f⁴ 10.3d² 9m p8g⁴ Jun 18] fair handicapper: barely stays 10.5f: acts on polytrack and soft going. *James Eustace*

NIMR 2 b.c. (May 3) Shamardal (USA) 129 – Riberac 110 (Efisio 120) [2015 5.9s* 6g⁴ 7m⁵ Oct 3] 200,000Y: sturdy colt: half-brother to several winners, including winner up to 11.5f Dordogne (2-y-o 9f winner, by Singspiel) and winner up to 1¼m Gothic (2-y-o 8.3f winner, by Danehill Dancer), both useful: dam winner up to 1¼m (2-y-o 5f winner): fairly useful form: won maiden at Carlisle in August by 3¼ lengths from Cheeky Angel: creditable fifth of 14 to Gifted Master in valuable sales race at Newmarket final start, late headway: will be suited by 1m+. *Richard Fahey* **88**

NINEPINS (IRE) 3 b.f. Rip Van Winkle (IRE) 134 – Cland di San Jore (IRE) (Lando (GER) 128) [2015 68: 10.2m⁶ 8.3f p11g 9.9m⁴ 14g 12v³ t13.9m⁴ 17.2g³ Oct 18] sturdy filly: fair maiden: stays 17f: acts on polytrack, tapeta and good to firm going: in blinkers last 5 starts: usually races towards rear: sold 10,000 gns. sent to Italy. *Richard Hannon* **70**

NINEPOINTSIXTHREE 5 b.g. Bertolini (USA) 125 – Armada Grove 75 (Fleetwood (IRE) 107) [2015 55: t12.2f⁶ t12.2f* t12.2f* t16.5m* t12.2g 16.2m 12.1s³ 12d⁴ 13.1m⁶ 12.1s* 13.1d⁴ 16d Oct 11] fair handicapper: won at Wolverhampton in March (twice) and April, and at Chepstow in August and Bath in September: stays 16.5f: acts on tapeta and soft going: sometimes wears cheekpieces: usually slowly away. *John O'Shea* **75 a64**

NINETEENTH HOLE (IRE) 3 b.g. Dark Angel (IRE) 113 – Kingpin Delight (Emarati (USA) 74) [2015 t8.6f⁴ t9.5g³ Dec 4] better effort (fair form) in maidens at Wolverhampton when fourth in November on debut. *Michael Wigham* **71**

NINE TENTHS 3 b.g. Shamardal (USA) 129 – Possession (USA) (Belong To Me (USA)) [2015 7.5m³ 8.3d⁶ Oct 12] modest form in maidens: dead. *Mark Johnston* **56**

NINETTA (IRE) 2 b.f. (Feb 17) New Approach (IRE) 132 – Pine Chip (USA) (Nureyev (USA) 131) [2015 7.5g² 7.9d* 7m³ Oct 3] 60,000Y: close-coupled filly: half-sister to several winners, including 1½m winner (stayed 2½m) Pouvoir Absolu (by Sadler's Wells) and 9f-11f winner Perfect Murder (by Desert King), both smart: dam third at 1m sole start: fairly useful performer: won maiden at Carlisle (by 4 lengths) in September: improved again when 5½ lengths third to Alice Springs in valuable sales race at Newmarket: will be suited by further than 1m. *Ann Duffield* **84**

NINETY MINUTES (IRE) 4 b.g. Oratorio (IRE) 128 – Fleeting Mirage (USA) (Afleet Alex (USA) 128) [2015 74: p8g t7.1g p7f p10g⁵ t9.5f³ p12f³ p10g* p10g⁶ 10.4g² 10g² 12m 10.4m⁴ 10m² 12g* 12.3g p11g² Sep 5] sturdy gelding: fairly useful handicapper: won at Chelmsford in April and Epsom in July: stays 12.5f: acts on polytrack and good to firm going: often races towards rear, often travels strongly: sold 31,000 gns. sent to Saudi Arabia. *John Best* **84**

NINJAGO 5 b.g. Mount Nelson 125 – Fidelio's Miracle (USA) 108 (Mountain Cat (USA)) [2015 117: 6g a6f⁶ p7g* p7g⁶ 7m⁶ 7m 6g³ 6f 6m 6g 6g 6g³ 6m Oct 3] good-topped gelding: smart performer: won minor event at Kempton in March by head from American Hope: best effort of 2015 when ½ -length third of 25 to Don't Touch in Ayr Gold Cup (Handicap) at Ayr on penultimate start: stays 7f: acts on polytrack, firm and soft going: wears blinkers: often races in rear: has been gelded. *Richard Hannon* **112 a105**

NIQNAAQPAADIWAAQ 3 b.g. Aqlaam 125 – Aswaaq (IRE) 74 (Peintre Celebre (USA) 137) [2015 7.1s⁵ t7.1g⁴ 10.3s⁵ 9.2d⁶ 7m 6s* 6g 6m 7v Nov 3] fair performer: won maiden at Hamilton in August: best effort at 6f: acts on soft going: usually races close up, tends to find little. *Eric Alston* **75**

NISSER 2 b.c. (Feb 28) Dream Ahead (USA) 133 – Poppy Seed 103 (Bold Edge 123) [2015 6m³ 6f⁴ 5g* Jul 27] £130,000Y: useful-looking colt: first foal: dam 6f winner out of sister to very smart sprinter Pipalong: fairly useful form: dropped in trip, 3/10, easily won 5-runner maiden at Windsor in July by 3¾ lengths from Dream Destination, disputing lead before going clear over 1f out, then coasting home: best effort at 5f: will go on improving. *Richard Hannon* **90 p**

NIXYBA 4 b.f. Cockney Rebel (IRE) 127 – Hisaronu (IRE) 75 (Stravinsky (USA) 133) [2015 65: 7.5m 8.3g 7g t8.6f⁶ Oct 13] modest maiden: left Les Eyre after third start: stays 8.5f: acts on polytrack and tapeta: in hood in 2015. *David Evans* **54**

NO BACKCHAT (IRE) 3 b.g. Dutch Art 126 – Brilliana 92 (Danehill Dancer (IRE) 117) [2015 –: 8f⁵ 10.2m⁵ 10m² 11.1s⁴ 12.2g* 12.1g⁶ Sep 16] fair handicapper: won at Musselburgh in August: best effort at 1½m: acts on good to firm going: in cheekpieces last 2 starts: usually races close up: sent to Saudi Arabia. *Kevin Ryan* **78**

NOBLE ALAN (GER) 12 gr.g. King's Theatre (IRE) 128 – Nirvavita (FR) (Highest Honor (FR) 124) [2015 91: 12s⁴ 11.5g Jun 24] fairly useful handicapper: has form at 16.5f, probably ideally suited by well-run 1½m: acts on good to firm and heavy going: often races towards rear. *Nicky Richards* **80**

NOBLE ASSET 4 ch.g. Compton Place 125 – Chance For Romance 81 (Entrepreneur 123) [2015 90: 5v 5m2 5g 5m 5.1m3 5m6 5g 5g3 5d4 5g Sep 18] fairly useful handicapper: best form at 5f: acts on good to firm and good to soft going: tried in hood. *John Quinn* **91**

NOBLE CAUSE 3 b.f. Showcasing 117 – Noble Peregrine (Lomond (USA) 128) [2015 –: p6f p6m 8d 6g Jul 15] compact filly: no form: visored last 2 starts. *Luke Dace* **–**

NOBLE CITIZEN (USA) 10 b.g. Proud Citizen (USA) 122 – Serene Nobility (USA) (His Majesty (USA)) [2015 106: p8f5 f7s3 p8g5 p10m May 19] good-topped gelding: useful handicapper: third at Southwell (3 lengths behind Pearl Nation) in March: stays 8.5f: acts on polytrack, fibresand, dirt and firm going: often wears headgear: sometimes slowly away, often races in rear. *David Simcock* **99**

NOBLE DEED 5 ch.g. Kyllachy 129 – Noble One 107 (Primo Dominie 121) [2015 95: p6g 6m 6m 7g p6g p6gur p6d2 p6g6 Dec 16] smallish, sturdy gelding: fair handicapper: stays 6f: acts on polytrack and firm going: tried in blinkers in 2015. *Michael Attwater* **76**

NOBLE GIFT 5 ch.g. Cadeaux Genereux 131 – Noble Penny 64 (Pennekamp (USA) 130) [2015 97§: p12g3 p12g* p12f3 t12.2m4 p11g* 12m4 p12g2 9.9g4 10m3 10s 11.8s* Oct 26] workmanlike gelding: useful performer: reformed character in 2015, winning minor event at Lingfield (by short head from Anglophile) in January and handicaps at Kempton (by nose from Fire Fighting) in March and Leicester (by 2¼ lengths from Kinema) in October: stays 1½m: acts on polytrack, good to firm and heavy going: tried in hood prior to 2015: suited by front-running tactics. *William Knight* **106 a99**

NOBLE MASTER 3 b.g. Sir Percy 129 – Eurolinka (IRE) (Tirol 127) [2015 –: 8f p10m 8m6 8.3m 10m5 11.7g4 p10g4 p12g 10.2f 11s5 p10m Oct 21] rather leggy gelding: poor maiden: stays 11.5f: acts on polytrack, good to firm and good to soft going: tried in cheekpieces and sometimes in tongue tie in 2015. *Sylvester Kirk* **48**

NOBLE PEACE 2 b.g. (Mar 5) Kyllachy 129 – Peace Concluded 72 (Bertolini (USA) 125) [2015 6g2 6d5 6m2 6g3 6d2 p6g4 Nov 11] £15,000Y, £14,000 2-y-o: good-topped gelding: first foal: dam maiden (seemed to stay easy 9.5f): fairly useful maiden: second in nursery at Pontefract in October: will be suited by 7f: acts on good to soft going. *Henry Candy* **90**

NOBLE REACH 4 b.f. Phoenix Reach (IRE) 124 – Comtesse Noire (CAN) 67 (Woodman (USA) 126) [2015 57: 10.1d5 f11d3 12.4g6 11.1m 14.1m2 16.1m3 15.8m3 14.1m3 16d6 Aug 18] modest maiden: stays 2m: acts on tapeta, good to firm and good to soft going: sometimes wears headgear: front runner/races prominently. *Lawrence Mullaney* **57**

NOBLE SILK 6 gr.g. Sir Percy 129 – Tussah (Daylami (IRE) 138) [2015 104: 16.2g 20f4 16.4d 14.6m3 18g p12g Dec 19] workmanlike gelding: useful handicapper: third in Mallard Stakes at Doncaster (3 lengths behind Curbyourenthusiasm) in September: stays 2½m: acts on polytrack, tapeta, firm and good to soft going: usually wears headgear. *Lucy Wadham* **101**

NOBLEST 3 ch.f. Pivotal 124 – Noble One 107 (Primo Dominie 121) [2015 59p: 7m3 8.1m3 t7.1f3 8.3d2 f7g* f8g6 Dec 15] fairly useful performer: left William Haggas, won maiden at Southwell in November: stays 8.5f: acts on fibresand, good to firm and good to soft going: front runner/races prominently. *Jamie Osborne* **80**

NOBLE STORM (USA) 9 b.g. Yankee Gentleman (USA) – Changed Tune (USA) (Tunerup (USA)) [2015 95: 5.2m6 5.1s 5g6 5m 5m 5m5 5g2 5g 5s4 5s6 Oct 9] well-made gelding: useful handicapper: second at Sandown (2¼ lengths behind Chilworth Icon) in August: stays 6f: acts on fibresand, soft and good to firm going: usually races close up. *Ed McMahon* **99**

NOBLE VISION (IRE) 3 b.f. Teofilo (IRE) 126 – Rafting (IRE) 87 (Darshaan 133) [2015 –p: t8.6g 8.3s 12.1m Jun 10] modest maiden: left John Gosden after first start. *Ismail Mohammed* **50**

NO BODY'S FOOL 2 ch.f. (Mar 27) Sixties Icon 125 – Leleyf (IRE) 78 (Kheleyf (USA) 116) [2015 5.3m4 p5g p6g p5m Nov 17] first foal: dam 2-y-o 5f/5.5f winner: no form. *Michael Madgwick* **–**

NOCTURN 6 b.g. Oasis Dream 129 – Pizzicato 64 (Statoblest 120) [2015 91: p6g t6m 6d 6m6 6m 5m* 5m2 5g Jul 28] good-bodied gelding: fairly useful handicapper: won at Windsor in July: stays 6f: acts on polytrack, good to firm and good to soft going: usually wears cheekpieces: usually races close up: often hangs. *Ronald Harris* **89**

NODACHI (IRE) 2 b.c. (Apr 25) Rip Van Winkle (IRE) 134 – Jabroot (IRE) 71 (Alhaarth (IRE) 126) [2015 7g 10.2g2 Oct 18] 170,000Y: third foal: dam maiden (stayed 1½m), closely related to smart 1¼m/10.4f winner Zahrat Dubai: 25/1, 1¾ lengths second of 7 to Wapping in maiden at Bath final start: open to further improvement. *Andrew Balding* **76 p**

NO DELUSION (USA) 3 b.f. Street Cry (IRE) 130 – Dream Empress (USA) 114 **90**
(Bernstein (USA) 115) [2015 73p: p8m* 8.3m² 8.3m² 8g* 8m* 8.1g Sep 11] fairly useful
performer: won maiden at Lingfield in February and handicaps at Newmarket in June and
Newbury (by 1¼ lengths from Sharqeyih) in July: stays 8.5f: acts on polytrack and good to
firm going: in cheekpieces last 3 starts: usually responds generously to pressure: sent to
USA. *Charlie Appleby*

NO EDUCATION 2 b.c. (Apr 12) Showcasing 117 – Ceilidh Band (Celtic Swing 138) **108**
[2015 6g⁴ 6g² 6.5g* 7.5g⁴ 8d² 8m 7s⁵ Nov 11] €18,000Y, £30,000 2-y-o: stocky colt: fifth
foal: half-brother to 8.6f winner Robero (by Piccolo): dam unraced half-sister to very smart
9f-13.5f winner (stays 2m) Dandino: useful performer: won minor event at Deauville (by
1½ lengths from Valdaya) in August: much better form last 3 starts, when neck second to
Robin of Navan in listed race at Deauville, ninth of 11 to Ultra in Prix Jean-Luc Lagardere
at Longchamp and fifth of 8 to Johannes Vermeer in Criterium International at Saint-Cloud:
stays 1m: acts on soft and good to firm going. *Jo Hughes*

NOFIZZOPHOBIA 2 ch.f. (Jan 31) Bahamian Bounty 116 – Croeso Cusan 75 (Diktat **–**
126) [2015 7v t6f Nov 14] second foal: dam 1m winner: showed nothing in maidens at
Redcar and Wolverhampton. *Derek Shaw*

NOGUCHI (IRE) 10 ch.g. Pivotal 124 – Tuscania (USA) (Woodman (USA) 126) [2015 **78**
75§, a81§: f12s³ p12f⁴ t13.9g* p12f⁴ t12.2g⁵ p16g³ p16d² p13.3f³ 12d p14g* p13.3g*
p13.3f⁶ p13.3m⁵ p13.3m⁴ t12.2g* t12.2g⁵ t13.9g* t12.2g⁵ p16f² 12v p14f⁴ t13.9g⁵ t9.5f⁴
p13.3m⁴ Dec 27] fair performer: won claimer at Wolverhampton in January, 2 handicaps at
Chelmsford in April, claimer at Wolverhampton in June and handicap at Wolverhampton in
July: stays 2m: acts on all-weather and good to firm going: usually wears headgear.
Chris Dwyer

NOKHADA (IRE) 2 b.c. (Mar 20) Lilbourne Lad (IRE) 111 – Silverdreammachine (IRE) **88**
51 (Marju (IRE) 127) [2015 p6d⁴ t7.1m² 8g* p8g³ t8.6m* Dec 26] €28,000, 70,000Y:
third foal: half-brother to 2-y-o 6.5f winner Aimee (by Alfred Nobel): dam maiden sister to
smart 6f winner Stormont: fairly useful performer: won maiden at Musselburgh in October
(subsequently left William Haggas) and nursery at Wolverhampton in December: stays
8.5f: acts on tapeta. *David Simcock*

NO LEAF CLOVER (IRE) 4 b.g. Kodiac 112 – Rajmahal (UAE) (Indian Ridge 123) **–**
[2015 102: 6g 6m Jun 27] compact gelding: useful at best, no form in 2015: stays 6f: acts
on good to firm going: tried in cheekpieces prior to 2015. *Ollie Pears*

NOLECCE 8 ch.g. Reset (AUS) 124 – Ghassanah 73 (Pas de Seul 133) [2015 62, a68: **66**
t12.2g³ t13.9g t12.2m² t12.2m⁶ f12g t12.2f⁵ t12.2g* t13.9g³ 11.8m² 11.9f⁵ t12.2f⁵ t12.2f*
t13.9f t12.2f⁶ Dec 22] close-coupled, workmanlike gelding: fair handicapper: won at
Wolverhampton in April and in October: stays 15f: acts on polytrack, tapeta, good to firm
and heavy going: often in headgear prior to 2015: often races prominently. *Tony Forbes*

NOMADIC (IRE) 2 ch.c. (Apr 7) Raven's Pass (USA) 133 – Turkana Girl 67 (Hernando **65**
(FR) 127) [2015 6m⁶ 6g⁵ p6f 7g p7g³ Nov 18] well-made colt: fair maiden: likely to stay
1m: acts on polytrack. *John Gosden*

NOMENKLATURA 3 b.f. Archipenko (USA) 127 – Ninotchka (USA) 110 (Nijinsky **74**
(CAN) 138) [2015 t8.6g² 10g³ f8g³ 12d⁶ p12g⁶ 12d* 12.2g² f12g p12mᵖᵘ Dec 16] fair **a67**
handicapper: won at Pontefract in October: stayed 1½m: acted on tapeta and good to soft
going: often raced prominently: dead. *Mark Johnston*

NONA BLU 3 b.g. Diktat 126 – Shivering 80 (Royal Applause 124) [2015 81: 8g p11g⁶ **67**
8.1m⁶ Jun 22] fair handicapper: stays 1m: acts on polytrack: tried in blinkers in 2015:
usually races towards rear. *Harry Dunlop*

NONAGON 4 b.g. Pastoral Pursuits 127 – Nine Red 63 (Royal Applause 124) [2015 –: f8g **63**
9.8v 8d² 10.1m⁵ 9m 9.3d⁴ 8.5d³ 10d³ 10.2s* Oct 28] modest handicapper: won at
Nottingham (amateur) in October: stays 1¼m: acts on soft going: usually in tongue tie in
2015. *Wilf Storey*

NONCHALANT 4 gr.g. Oasis Dream 129 – Comeback Queen 91 (Nayef (USA) 129) **92**
[2015 97: 9.8d 10.4g 8d 10d 11.5g 10g 12m² 10.3m⁵ 13.8m⁴ 12m⁵ 12g Sep 6] fairly useful
handicapper: stays 1½m: acts on good to firm and good to soft going: tried in headgear:
usually races towards rear. *David O'Meara*

NONEEDTOTELLME (IRE) 2 gr.f. (Mar 5) Fast Company (IRE) 126 – Gemma's **–**
Delight (IRE) 71 (Clodovil (IRE) 116) [2015 t6g Jul 13] €7,000Y: first foal: dam, 7f/7.6f
winner, half-sister to useful winner up to 1½m Fortun: 50/1, well held in maiden at
Wolverhampton, slowly away. *James Unett*

NONIOS (IRE) 3 b.g. Oasis Dream 129 – Young And Daring (USA) (Woodman (USA) **86 p** 126) [2015 t8.6f² t9.5g² Dec 4] 2,000 3-y-o: half-brother to useful 2-y-o 1m winner (stayed 2m) Daring Ransom (by Red Ransom) and 11f-1¾m winner Malekov (by Dansili): dam 6f-9f (including minor US stakes) winner: progressed from debut when ½-length second of 5 to Fallen For A Star in maiden at Wolverhampton (would have benefited from stronger gallop): wears hood: open to further improvement. *David Simcock*

NONNO GIULIO (IRE) 4 ch.g. Halling (USA) 133 – Contrary (IRE) 79 (Mark of **80** Esteem (IRE) 137) [2015 94, a75: p7g t1.1g p8g* t7.1m Sep 5] rather leggy gelding: fairly useful performer: won claimer at Lingfield in July: stays 1¼m: acts on polytrack, soft and good to firm going: sometimes in hood, including on last 2 starts: front runner/races prominently. *Simon Dow*

NO NO CARDINAL (IRE) 6 ch.g. Touch of Land (FR) 122 – Four Moons (IRE) **–** (Cardinal Flower 101) [2015 10.2m⁴ May 1] lengthy gelding: well held in 3 maidens: tried in hood. *Mark Gillard*

NOODLES BLUE BOY 9 b.g. Makbul 104 – Dee Dee Girl (IRE) 60 (Primo Dominie **81** 121) [2015 82: 5d² 5g⁴ 5g³ 5m³ 5m² 5m³ 5g 5m 5g6 6m 5g 5m² 5m* 5g Oct 3] neat gelding: fairly useful handicapper: won at Musselburgh (apprentice) in September: stays 6f: acts on soft and good to firm going: tried in headgear: front runner/races prominently. *Ollie Pears*

NOOR AL HAYA (IRE) 5 b.m. Tamayuz 126 – Hariya (IRE) 99 (Shernazar 131) [2015 **66** p16g⁵ 16g* p15.8f⁵ 17.2f 12g p16g Dec 16] quite attractive mare: fair handicapper: won at **a57** Lingfield in July: stays 17f: acts on polytrack and any turf going: usually wears hood: often races towards rear. *Laura Mongan*

NOOSHANA (GER) 3 ch.f. Lando (GER) 128 – Noosham (IRE) (Daylami (IRE) 138) **–** [2015 p12g t9.5g 7d Jul 29] showed fair form on debut (in Germany in 2014), no form since. *Andrew Reid*

NOOZHOH CANARIAS (SPA) 4 b.c. Caradak (IRE) 121 – Noozhah (Singspiel (IRE) **110** 133) [2015 125: 6g³ 6g³ 7g³ 6.5g 7g6 6g² Oct 25] good-topped colt: high-class form at 3 yrs: disappointing in 2015, best effort when third in Prix de la Porte Maillot at Longchamp (beaten 1¾ lengths by Baghadur): left C. Laffon-Parias before final outing: stays 7f: acts on soft and good to firm going: usually free-going front runner. *J.-A. Remolina Diez, Spain*

NO PLEASING YOU (IRE) 2 b.f. (Apr 30) Frozen Power (IRE) 108 – Villafranca (IRE) (In The Wings 128) [2015 7.5g f7s Aug 6] 3,200F, 6,000Y: half-sister to several winners, including winner up to 7f Villa Sciarra (by Elnadim) and useful winner up to 9f Eternal Ruler (2-y-o 1m winner, by Aussie Rules): dam 1¼m winner: tailed off in 2 maidens. *Bill Turner*

NO POPPY (IRE) 7 b.m. Chineur (FR) 123 – Capetown Girl 71 (Danzero (AUS)) [2015 **97** 95: 8g⁴ 8m³ 8d* 8g³ 8m 8g 8d 8m Aug 8] lengthy, sparely-made mare: useful handicapper: won at Haydock (by 3½ lengths from Altharoos) in May: stays 1m: acts on good to firm and heavy going: wears headgear: usually races nearer last than first. *Tim Easterby*

NORA BATTY 4 b.f. Zamindar (USA) 116 – Soolaimon (IRE) 71 (Shareef Dancer (USA) **60** 135) [2015 45: p10m p12g³ t12.2m⁶ 12.1m* 13.1g⁴ 14.1g² 17.2f⁵ 13.1d⁴ p15.8f t16.5f⁶ Oct 17] modest handicapper: won at Chepstow in June: stays 1¾m: acts on good to firm going: tried in blinkers in 2015: usually races prominently. *Rod Millman*

NORAB (GER) 4 b.g. Galileo (IRE) 134 – Night Woman (GER) (Monsun (GER) 124) **97** [2015 93: p13.3g* 16g⁴ 14f⁵ 18g 11.8g6 Oct 26] workmanlike gelding: useful handicapper: won at Chelmsford in April: left Marco Botti 82,000 gns/off 5 months, well held last twice, including in Cesarewitch first occasion: stays 2m: acts on polytrack, tapeta and heavy going: has worn cheekpieces, including last start: often leads. *Bernard Llewellyn*

NORDIC BEAT 3 ch.g. Norse Dancer (IRE) 127 – Florida Heart 78 (First Trump 118) **–** [2015 11.5d 11.7f⁵ Jun 24] green when well held in maidens: sold 1,000 gns. *Andrew Balding*

NO REFUND (IRE) 4 b.g. Invincible Spirit (IRE) 121 – Evangeline (Sadler's Wells **–** (USA) 132) [2015 66: 7d 7m⁵ Jun 1] fair at best, no form in 2015: stays 1m: acts on polytrack: often races towards rear. *Martin Smith*

NORFOLK SKY 6 ch.m. Haafhd 129 – Cayman Sound 72 (Turtle Island (IRE) 123) **67** [2015 86: 12m⁵ Jul 23] rather leggy mare: fair handicapper: stays 2m: acts on polytrack and soft going. *Brian Barr*

NORMAL EQUILIBRIUM 5 b.g. Elnadim (USA) 128 – Acicula (IRE) 96 (Night Shift **104**
(USA)) [2015 100: p5g* 5.2m² 5.1s² 5g 5m 5m 5f 5m 5s⁴ p5g⁶ p5m⁶ Dec 27] sturdy
gelding: useful handicapper: won at Chelmsford (by 1¼ lengths from Mappin Time) in
April: stays 6f: acts on polytrack, soft and good to firm going: often wears headgear: front
runner/races prominently. *Robert Cowell*

NORMANDY BARRIERE (IRE) 3 b.g. Rock of Gibraltar (IRE) 133 – Ma Paloma **86**
(FR) (Highest Honor (FR) 124) [2015 49: 6m* 6m* 7g² 6g² Jun 8] fairly useful
handicapper: won at Redcar and Pontefract in April: good second at York and Pontefract
last 2 starts: stays 7f: acts on good to firm going. *Nigel Tinkler*

NORMANDY KNIGHT 3 b.g. Acclamation 118 – Prayer (IRE) 83 (Rainbow Quest **76**
(USA) 134) [2015 71: 7d⁴ 7.5m³ 8g⁵ 8.3m* 8.5g* 8.9m 8d² 8d Sep 3] fair handicapper:
won at Leicester in June and Beverley in July: stays 8.5f: acts on good to firm and good to
soft going: often races prominently. *Richard Fahey*

NORMAN'S STAR 4 b.g. Tiger Hill (IRE) 127 – Canis Star (Wolfhound (USA) 126) **51**
[2015 t12.2g 11.8m³ 11.9m⁴ t12.2g⁴ Jun 26] modest maiden: left Chris Dwyer after first
start: stays 1½m: acts on tapeta and good to firm going: often wears headgear: front runner/
races prominently. *Denis Quinn*

NORO LIM (IRE) 3 b.g. Thewayyouare (USA) 117 – Rohain (IRE) (Singspiel (IRE) **89**
133) [2015 76p: 10.2s³ p10g* 12g² t12.2m⁶ 11.8s Oct 6] fairly useful handicapper: won at
Chelmsford in April: good second at Goodwood in June: stays 1½m: acts on polytrack: sent
to Australia. *Luca Cumani*

NORPHIN 5 b.g. Norse Dancer (IRE) 127 – Orphina (IRE) 63 (Orpen (USA) 116) [2015 **–**
p8g Nov 25] maiden: no form in 2015: stays 8.5f: acts on good to firm and heavy going:
tried in headgear prior to 2015. *Simon Hodgson*

NORSE BLUES 7 ch.g. Norse Dancer (IRE) 127 – Indiana Blues 90 (Indian Ridge 123) **79**
[2015 94: t8.6g² p8g⁶ f7d⁶ Feb 8] tall gelding: fairly useful handicapper: stayed 8.5f: acted
on tapeta, good to firm and heavy going: dead. *David Barron*

NORSE CASTLE 2 b.c. (Apr 18) Norse Dancer (IRE) 127 – Hursley Hope (IRE) **–**
(Barathea (IRE) 127) [2015 p7g Nov 4] 50/1, well held in maiden at Kempton on debut.
David Elsworth

NORSE MAGIC 2 b.f. (Feb 18) Norse Dancer (IRE) 127 – Gift of Love (IRE) 72 **79**
(Azamour (IRE) 130) [2015 7m⁴ 7f⁶ 8.3g² 8v² Oct 24] first foal: dam, maiden (stayed
1¼m), half-sister to smart 1½m-15f winner Gold Medallist out of useful 2-y-o 5f winner
(stayed 1½m) Spot Prize: fair maiden: stays 8.5f. *Sylvester Kirk*

NORTH AMERICA 3 b.g. Dubawi (IRE) 129 – Northern Mischief (USA) (Yankee **88**
Victor (USA) 121) [2015 –: t9.5g² 10.2m² 9.8d⁴ 10.1m⁴ 10g³ Aug 21] fairly useful maiden:
best effort when third in handicap at Sandown: stays 1¼m: acts on good to firm going: in
cheekpieces last 2 starts: front runner/races prominently. *Charlie Appleby*

NORTH BAY LADY (IRE) 3 b.f. Fast Company (IRE) 126 – Straight Sets (IRE) 80 **–**
(Pivotal 124) [2015 51: 14.1g 12.1m 9.9g 16.2m p14f p16f t16.5f Oct 17] maiden: no form
in 2015: often wears cheekpieces. *John Wainwright*

NORTH CREEK 2 b.c. (Mar 19) Iffraaj 127 – Maine Rose (Red Ransom (USA)) [2015 **73 p**
6d t7.1f p6g⁵ p7m* Dec 31] €82,000F, 80,000Y: third foal: half-brother to 1m-1½m winner
Gentle Maine (by Muhtathir) and 6.5f winner Mads' Dream (by Footstepsinthesand): dam,
11f-1¾m winner, half-sister to useful 2m winner Sunley Peace: fair performer: won
nursery at Lingfield in December: best effort at 7f: should do better still. *Chris Wall*

NORTHERN BEAU (IRE) 2 b.f. (Apr 10) Canford Cliffs (IRE) 133 – View (IRE) 56 **–**
(Galileo (IRE) 134) [2015 6g 7m 8d Sep 4] €10,000Y: first foal: dam ran twice: no form.
Ronald Harris

NORTHERN MEETING (IRE) 5 b.m. Dylan Thomas (IRE) 132 – Scottish Stage **84**
(IRE) 112 (Selkirk (USA) 129) [2015 12m² 12m⁶ Jul 23] fairly useful handicapper: stays
1½m: acts on polytrack and good to firm going. *Robert Stephens*

NORTHGATE LAD (IRE) 3 gr.g. Dark Angel (IRE) 113 – Canosa (IRE) 53 (Catrail **98**
(USA) 123) [2015 82p: 5g² 6.1s² 6g⁴ 5g* 5d⁵ 5g 6g 5d Sep 26] good-topped gelding: useful
handicapper: won at Newcastle (by length from Lexi's Hero) in June: stays 6f: acts on
heavy going: sometimes in cheekpieces: often races prominently. *Brian Ellison*

NORTHMAN (IRE) 2 b.g. (Apr 10) Frozen Power (IRE) 108 – Chifney Rush (IRE) **–**
(Grand Lodge (USA) 125) [2015 7.1g 7d p8g p10g⁶ Nov 26] compact gelding: no form.
Jim Boyle

NORTHSIDE PRINCE (IRE) 9 b.g. Desert Prince (IRE) 130 – Spartan Girl (IRE) 91 **80**
(Ela-Mana-Mou 132) [2015 12.1g^4 11.1s^3 13d^3 13.1d^4 12.2g^6 12g^3 13.1g 12v^6 f11g^3 f12g^2
f14m^3 f16g^2 Dec 29] lengthy, angular gelding: fairly useful handicapper: stays 2m: acts on
fibresand, firm and soft going: usually races prominently, often travels strongly.
Alan Swinbank

NORTH SPIRIT (IRE) 2 b.g. (Mar 23) Zebedee 113 – Zara's Girl (IRE) 57 (Tillerman **64**
123) [2015 5m 5g^3 f5g^5 t5.1g Nov 27] modest maiden: left Keith Dalgleish after first start:
raced only at 5f. *David O'Meara*

NORTRON (IRE) 3 b.c. Makfi 130 – Nessa (FR) (Marchand de Sable (USA) 117) [2015 **85**
74: 7d^2 7m 6.1g^2 6m* 6m 6.1s^3 p7m^2 p7d Nov 30] lengthy colt: fairly useful performer:
won maiden at Lingfield in June: stays 7f: acts on polytrack, soft and good to firm going:
front runner/races prominently. *Andrew Balding*

NO RUM (IRE) 3 b.g. Alfred Nobel (IRE) 110 – Common Rumpus (IRE) 87 (Common **60**
Grounds 118) [2015 t7.1f^4 t7.1m^4 p7m^5 10m Aug 29] modest maiden: left Ralph Beckett
after third start: best effort at 7f: tried in hood. *Olly Williams*

NORVILLE (IRE) 8 b.g. Elusive City (USA) 117 – Saraposa (IRE) 66 (Ahonoora 122) **72**
[2015 81, a72: p8g* 8s 6s^2 p8g^5 7.2d^3 8m p8d^3 7m 7.2d p8g p8g p8g Dec 11] close-coupled
gelding: fair handicapper: won at Dundalk in January: stays 1m: acts on polytrack, soft and
good to firm going: usually wears headgear. *L. Smyth, Ireland*

NORWEGIAN REWARD (IRE) 7 ch.g. Hernando (FR) 127 – Stay Behind 97 **54**
(Elmaamul (USA) 125) [2015 43: p8m^6 t8.6g^4 p10m p10g^6 p10g 8d^4 8g^4 8g p10f^4 Aug 18]
rather leggy gelding: modest handicapper: stays 1¼m: acts on polytrack, tapeta, best turf
form on good going: sometimes wears headgear/tongue tie. *Conrad Allen*

NOSEY BARKER (IRE) 3 b.c. Rip Van Winkle (IRE) 134 – Cold Cold Woman 93 **79**
(Machiavellian (USA) 123) [2015 p8g^2 8.3m^3 8g^2 9d^5 p10f^5 t8.6f^3 f8g^2 f12g^3 p10g* Dec
30] rather unfurnished colt: fair performer: won maiden at Lingfield in December: stays
1½m: acts on all-weather and good to firm going: tried in cheekpieces: front runner/races
prominently. *Richard Hannon*

NOT AGAIN 3 b.g. Notnowcato 128 – Royal Bloom (IRE) 52 (Royal Applause 124) **–**
[2015 –: 7g 11.5g 8g Jul 13] no form: tried in blinkers. *Tim Easterby*

NOTARISED 4 b.g. Authorized (IRE) 133 – Caribbean Dancer (USA) 76 (Theatrical) **110**
[2015 93: p12g^5 12g 13s^3 12m* 12m 14g* 16.1m 11.9g* 14g^6 14g 14d 12s^3 Sep 23]
smallish, workmanlike gelding: smart handicapper: won at York in May, Goodwood in
June and Old Newton Cup at Haydock (by ½ length from Watersmeet) in July: creditable
third to Scrutinise at Goodwood final start: stays 1¾m: acts on soft and good to firm going:
often leads. *Mark Johnston*

bet365 Old Newton Cup (Heritage Handicap), Haydock—
a 1, 2 for the Mark Johnston stable in this valuable event as Notarised beats Watersmeet

NOTARY 2 b.f. (Mar 27) Lawman (FR) 121 – Purity (Pivotal 124) [2015 7m³ 7m* Jul 30] **82 p**
third foal: dam unraced sister to very smart 7f-9f winner Virtual: 5/4, confirmed debut
promise when winning 14-runner maiden at Goodwood by short head from Anabel, keen/
wide to begin with but leading 1f out and finding extra when pressed: will go on improving.
Roger Varian

NOTEBOOK 4 b.g. Invincible Spirit (IRE) 121 – Love Everlasting 112 (Pursuit of Love **59**
124) [2015 80d: p10g⁴ p12g p10g 10.3d Mar 28] modest maiden: stays 1¼m: acts on
polytrack and good to firm going: often wears headgear: often races prominently.
Martin Smith

NOT NEVER 3 ch.g. Notnowcato 128 – Watchoverme (Haafhd 129) [2015 80p: 12.3s* **103**
11.9g⁴ 14g² 14.6m 12g² 12g Oct 9] good-topped gelding: useful handicapper: won at
Chester (by 5 lengths from Hernandoshideaway) in May: good second at York (Melrose
Stakes, head behind Polarisation) and Newmarket (4 lengths behind Rare Rhythm): stays
1¾m: acts on soft going: usually races close up. *Hugo Palmer*

NOT SO GENTLE (IRE) 2 b.g. (May 14) Dylan Thomas (IRE) 132 – Sliding Scale **71**
(Sadler's Wells (USA) 132) [2015 p7g 7m 7.5s⁶ 8d⁵ 10.2f³ 10.2g⁴ p8f⁵ Oct 8] fair maiden:
best effort at 1¼m: acts on firm going: in blinkers last 3 starts: usually races prominently.
Sir Mark Prescott Bt

NOT SO SLEEPY 3 ch.g. Beat Hollow 126 – Papillon de Bronze (IRE) (Marju (IRE) **108**
127) [2015 88p: 10.3v* 10f 10d⁴ 9.9s³ 9.9g 8s Nov 1] compact gelding: useful performer:
won listed race at Chester (by short head from Disegno) in May: fourth in Winter Hill
Stakes at Windsor (2¾ lengths behind Racing History) and third in Prix du Prince d'Orange
at Longchamp (7¼ lengths behind Karaktar): stays 10.3f: acts on heavy going: has worn
tongue tie: often races freely. *Hughie Morrison*

NOT TOUCH 2 ch.c. (May 2) Dream Ahead (USA) 133 – Umlilo 64 (Mtoto 134) [2015 **80 p**
7.1g³ 7g⁵ Sep 30] 16,000Y, 52,000 2-y-o: lengthy colt: seventh foal: half-brother to smart
winner up to 9f Fantastic Pick (2-y-o 1m winner, by Fantastic Light) and 1m winner Gigi
Balla (by Araafa): dam maiden half-sister to smart 1m-10.4f winner Miss Keller: fair form
in maidens at Sandown and Salisbury, length fifth behind Tafteesh in latter: open to further
improvement. *Richard Hannon*

NOTTS SO BLUE 4 b.f. Pastoral Pursuits 127 – Blue Nile (IRE) 70 (Bluebird (USA) **50**
125) [2015 58: 10g 8d⁵ 8.5g 9.9s 10.2s⁴ f7g⁵ p10g Dec 30] modest handicapper: stays
1¼m: acts on fibresand and soft going: tried in headgear. *Shaun Harris*

NOT YOUR CALL (IRE) 4 b.g. Balmont (USA) 117 – Cafe Lassere (USA) (Giant's **52**
Causeway (USA) 132) [2015 84: p10.7m p8g p7g p7g p6g p6m Dec 31] modest
handicapper: left Edward Lynam after second start: stays 1m: acts on polytrack: usually
wears headgear. *Lee Carter*

NOUVEAU FORET 3 b.f. Myboycharlie (IRE) 118 – Forest Express (AUS) (Kaaptive **59**
Edition (NZ)) [2015 77: 8g 7m 8.3m 10m 8s⁵ 10g 8.3d t7.1f⁴ p8f² p8f² p7f Dec 17] lengthy **a75**
filly: fair handicapper: left Ed Walker after fourth start: stays 1m: acts on polytrack and
tapeta: tried in headgear in 2015. *Willie Musson*

NOUVELLE ERE 4 b.g. Archipenko (USA) 127 – Sinister Ruckus (USA) (Trippi (USA) **66**
121) [2015 59: p10g* p8m* t12.2m² p10f* t12.2g⁵ 10.3d 10m⁶ p11g t12.2g⁴ p12g p12g⁵
10.2d* p10f 10.2g p10g* p10d p10m³ Dec 27] fair handicapper: won at Chelmsford
(apprentice) and Kempton (apprentice) in February, Kempton in March, Bath in September
and Kempton in November: stays 1½m: acts on polytrack, tapeta and good to soft going:
often wears headgear: usually in tongue tie in 2015: usually leads. *Tony Carroll*

NOUVELLI DANCER (IRE) 2 b.f. (Apr 1) Lilbourne Lad (IRE) 111 – Kiralik 100 **40**
(Efisio 120) [2015 5m 5.9m 5m t8.6f⁴ Oct 9] 3,500F, £10,000Y: seventh foal: half-sister to
9f winner Adlington (by Dansili): dam, winner up to 1m (2-y-o 5f-7f winner), half-sister to
winner up to 1m River Belle and unreliable 7.4f/1m winner (stayed 1¼m) Rio Riva, both
smart: poor maiden: left Brian Ellison after third start: best effort at 8.5f. *Ivan Furtado*

NOVABRIDGE 7 ch.g. Avonbridge 123 – Petrovna (IRE) 78 (Petardia 113) [2015 75: **62**
p5f⁶ p5m⁶ p5f⁵ 6.1d p6g t6g p5f² p6f t5.1f p5g Dec 2] modest handicapper: left John
Butler after third start: stays 6f: acts on polytrack and any turf going: usually wears
headgear. *Phil McEntee*

NOVALIST 7 ch.g. Avonbridge 123 – Malelane (IRE) 48 (Prince Sabo 123) [2015 49, a66: **68**
f7g⁵ f8s³ t7.1g f7g³ f8g 7.1s* 8g 7s 6v 7g f7g Dec 12] leggy gelding: fair handicapper: **a60**
won at Musselburgh in April: stays 1m: acts on fibresand, soft and good to firm going:
wears blinkers. *Rebecca Bastiman*

NOVANCIA (IRE) 3 b.f. Fastnet Rock (AUS) 127 – Ceoil An Aith (IRE) 81 (Accordion) **85**
[2015 9.3m* 10g⁶ 10g² 12s* 12m 14.1g Aug 19] angular filly: first foal: dam, 1½m winner,
sister to very smart 7f-15.5f winner Yavana's Pace and smart winner up to 1¼m
Littlepacepaddocks: fairly useful performer: won maiden at Carlisle in May and handicap
at Newmarket in July: stays 1½m: acts on soft and good to firm going: front runner/races
prominently. *Mark Johnston*

NOVANTAE 2 b.f. (Apr 19) Pivotal 124 – Etive (USA) (Elusive Quality (USA)) [2015 **76**
6m⁶ 6g³ 5m⁵ 6v⁶ 6d² p6f⁴ Oct 8] close-coupled filly: first foal: dam, 7.5f winner (including
at 2 yrs), half-sister to smart performer up to 1m Latharnach: fair maiden: stays 6f: acts on
good to soft going. *Charlie Appleby*

NOVEL DANCER 7 b.g. Dansili 127 – Fictitious 100 (Machiavellian (USA) 123) [2015 **60**
p12g* p12f⁶ p12f p12g⁵ 11.5d p12g Oct 20] leggy gelding: modest handicapper: won at
Kempton in January: stays 1½m: acts on polytrack and good to firm going: sometimes
wears headgear: tried in tongue tie prior to 2015: often starts slowly. *Lydia Richards*

NOVEMBER (IRE) 2 b.f. (Mar 5) Kodiac 112 – Pale Light (USA) (Lemon Drop Kid **65**
(USA) 131) [2015 p6g⁵ 5f³ 6d 5.2v⁴ 5g 6d p5g Oct 14] 7,000F: strong filly: first foal: dam
lightly raced out of useful 1m (including at 2 yrs) winner On A Cloud: fair maiden: stays
6f: acts on polytrack and firm going: sent to Greece. *Richard Hannon*

NOVERRE TO GO (IRE) 9 ch.g. Noverre (USA) 125 – Ukraine Venture 96 (Slip **78**
Anchor 136) [2015 84: p6g t6f t5.1g² t5.1g 6.1s² 6v* 5.3s⁵ 6m 6.1m 6g² 5.7f⁶ 6s³ 6s 6d⁴ **a70**
t6m 5.3s 6g⁵ 5.1d² p6d Nov 30] sturdy gelding: fair handicapper: won at Brighton in May:
stays 6f: acts on polytrack, tapeta and any turf going: often wears headgear: sometimes in
tongue tie prior to 2015. *Ronald Harris*

NOVINOPHOBIA 2 ch.c. (Apr 9) Showcasing 117 – Malelane (IRE) 48 (Prince Sabo **81 p**
123) [2015 6g 7.1m³ 6m 7m⁵ 7.2g* 7s² 7s² Oct 6] 90,000Y: fifth foal: half-brother to 3
winners, including useful winner up to 6f Secret Missile (2-y-o 5f winner, by Sakhee's
Secret) and 5f/6f winner Compton Prince (by Compton Place): dam maiden who stayed 6f:
fairly useful performer: won nursery at Musselburgh in August: second in nurseries at
Salisbury and Catterick last 2 starts: stays 7f: acts on soft going: front runner/races
prominently: remains with potential. *Richard Fahey*

NO WIN NO FEE 5 b.g. Firebreak 125 – Milliscent 49 (Primo Dominie 121) [2015 88, **73**
a76: 10.3d 10.4g⁶ 10.2s⁴ 11m Jun 7] fair handicapper: left Michael Appleby after third
start: stays 1¼m: acts on polytrack, fibresand, good to firm and heavy going: tried in
cheekpieces: often races prominently. *Dr Richard Newland*

NOWREYNA 4 gr.f. Notnowcato 128 – Kryena 72 (Kris 135) [2015 8g 7g 6g 8.3s 6g —
10.1m⁶ Jun 6] £1,000 3-y-o: fifth foal: half-sister to 5f/6f winner Luckyreno (by Kyllachy)
and winner up to 1m Haafkry (2-y-o 6f winner, by Haafhd): dam maiden: no form: tried in
cheekpieces/tongue tie. *Kenny Johnson*

NOW SAY BOOOOM 3 b.f. Proclamation (IRE) 130 – Grezie 63 (Mark of Esteem (IRE) —
137) [2015 –: p8m Jan 10] angular filly: no form: often wears hood. *Luke Dace*

NOW WHAT 8 ch.m. Where Or When (IRE) 124 – Vallauris 94 (Faustus (USA) 118) **68**
[2015 68: 12g 11.6m 11.6g³ Oct 19] fair handicapper: stays 13f: acts on polytrack, firm and
soft going. *Jonathan Portman*

NUBAR BOY 8 ch.g. Compton Place 125 – Out Like Magic 82 (Magic Ring (IRE) 115) **75**
[2015 78: p8g³ Dec 30] sturdy gelding: fair handicapper: stays 1¼m: acts on polytrack, soft
and good to firm going: often wears headgear: tried in tongue tie: front runner/races
prominently. *Ronald Thompson*

NUCKY THOMPSON 2 b.g. (Apr 16) Cockney Rebel (IRE) 127 – Vino Veritas (USA) **72**
72 (Chief's Crown (USA)) [2015 6m 7g* 7m⁴ 8g⁵ 8m⁵ p8f Nov 23] strong gelding: fair
performer: won maiden at Lingfield in July: stays 1m: acts on good to firm going: usually
leads: has been gelded. *Dave Morris*

NUFOOTH (IRE) 3 b.f. Elnadim (USA) 128 – Sahaayeb (IRE) 77 (Indian Haven 119) **65**
[2015 71: p8g⁵ p8f 8v⁵ 10.2g Oct 18] fair maiden: stays 1m: acts on polytrack, firm and
good to soft going. *James Eustace*

NUMBER ONE LONDON (IRE) 5 b.g. Invincible Spirit (IRE) 121 – Vadorga (Grand **78**
Lodge (USA) 125) [2015 92: 21g Jul 29] good sort: fair handicapper: stays 21f: acts on soft
and good to firm going: sometimes in headgear prior to 2015. *Tim Vaughan*

NUNO TRISTAN (USA) 3 b.g. Henrythenavigator (USA) 131 – Saintly Speech (USA) **90**
103 (Southern Halo (USA)) [2015 81p: 6m 6m 6m⁶ 6g p6f* Oct 15] lengthy gelding: fairly
useful handicapper: won at Chelmsford (by ¾ length from Spring Loaded) in October:
raced only at 6f: acts on polytrack: often races prominently. *William Jarvis*

NUSANTARA 4 b.f. New Approach (IRE) 132 – Pentatonic 100 (Giant's Causeway (USA) 132) [2015 61: 7g 11.1d⁴ 12g⁵ May 29] fair maiden: stayed 1½m: acted on good to soft going: dead. *Alan Swinbank* **70**

NUTAN (IRE) 3 b.c. Duke of Marmalade (IRE) 132 – Neele (IRE) 102 (Peintre Celebre (USA) 137) [2015 10.9g² 10.9g* 10.9g³ 11.9g* 11.9g³ Aug 9] third foal: closely related to smart German 1¼m-1½m (Grosser Preis von Berlin) winner Nymphea (by Dylan Thomas) and German 1¼m/11f winner Nocturne (by Rock of Gibraltar): dam, German winner up to 1¼m (2-y-o 6.5f winner), sister to Oaks d'Italia winner Night of Magic: very smart performer: won maiden at Cologne (by 7 lengths) in May and Deutsches Derby at Hamburg (by 5 lengths from Palace Prince, leading 1½f out) in July: creditable 1½ lengths third to Second Step in Grosser Preis von Berlin at Hoppegarten final outing: stayed 1½m: raced only on good going: to stand at Gestut Lindenhof, Germany, fee on application. *P. Schiergen, Germany* **120**

NUTBOURNE LAD (IRE) 2 b.g. (Mar 2) Lilbourne Lad (IRE) 111 – Cape Sydney (IRE) 52 (Cape Cross (IRE) 129) [2015 6d 6g 6g³ p8f Oct 10] workmanlike gelding: fair maiden: best effort at 6f. *Amanda Perrett* **68**

NUTCRACKER PRINCE 4 b.g. Rail Link 132 – Plum Fairy (Sadler's Wells (USA) 132) [2015 p12f⁶ p11g t12.2m Oct 2] fair maiden: best effort second start: in tongue tie. *Shaun Lycett* **71**

NUTZMA 2 b.f. (May 24) Multiplex 114 – Nut (IRE) 65 (Fasliyev (USA) 120) [2015 p7g f7g⁵ p7g⁵ Dec 10] 4,000Y: sixth foal: sister to 1½m winner Captain Caroline and half-sister to winner up to 1m Rex Kalejs (2-y-o 5f/6f winner, by Captain Gerrard): dam maiden who should have stayed 7f: modest maiden. *Mike Murphy* **52**

NYANZA (GER) 4 b.f. Dai Jin 123 – Nouvelle Fortune (IRE) 107 (Alzao (USA) 117) [2015 12.4s p12g³ p16g⁴ Jul 1] fairly useful handicapper: likely to prove best up to 2m: acts on polytrack, tapeta, best turf form on good to firm going. *Alan King* **86**

O

OAKBANK (USA) 4 b.g. Empire Maker (USA) 129 – Summer Shower (Sadler's Wells (USA) 132) [2015 56: p14g p15.8f* p13.3m p16g p12g p15.8g Dec 2] modest handicapper: won at Lingfield in April: stays 16.5f: acts on polytrack and tapeta: front runner/races prominently. *Brett Johnson* **54**

OAK BLUFFS (IRE) 4 b.g. Royal Applause 124 – Key Stage (IRE) (King's Best (USA) 132) [2015 66: t7.1f² t7.1g⁴ 7g² 7.2g* 7.2g⁵ p7f⁵ f7g p8g⁴ f8g⁴ Dec 22] fair handicapper: won at Ayr in September: stays 8.5f: acts on polytrack, tapeta, best turf form on good going: tried in cheekpieces prior to 2015: consistent. *Richard Fahey* **70**

OAK FOREST 2 b.g. (Mar 8) Mullionmileanhour (IRE) 116 – Lady Royal Oak (IRE) 67 (Exceed And Excel (AUS) 126) [2015 5v⁵ t6f⁶ Sep 19] well held in maiden and seller. *Michael Attwater* **–**

OAKLEY GIRL 3 b.f. Sir Percy 129 – Pivotting (Pivotal 124) [2015 –: 8.3g⁵ 8m³ p10g* 10g⁵ 8.5d³ 8g⁴ p10g* Nov 13] sturdy filly: fairly useful performer: won at Lingfield in August (maiden) and November (handicap): stays 1¼m: acts on polytrack, good to firm and good to soft going: waited with. *Stuart Williams* **90**

OAKLEY STAR 3 b.f. Multiplex 114 – Star Welcome 62 (Most Welcome 131) [2015 –: p8f⁵ p8g⁴ 9.9g p8g² 10d² 10.2g p10g p10g³ p10m⁶ Nov 17] modest maiden: stays 1¼m: acts on polytrack and good to soft going: often in headgear in 2015. *Gay Kelleway* **63**

OAKWELL (IRE) 7 b.g. Antonius Pius (USA) 123 – Cindy's Star (IRE) 68 (Dancing Dissident (USA) 119) [2015 12s⁶ May 5] modest maiden: in cheekpieces, tailed off in claimer at Catterick on first start for 2 years. *Andrew Crook* **–**

OASIS FANTASY (IRE) 4 br.g. Oasis Dream 129 – Cara Fantasy (IRE) 84 (Sadler's Wells (USA) 132) [2015 96: 12g 12m³ 14g² 12m³ 16.1m 14g 16.4d⁴ 14d 14d 12d Oct 24] tall, attractive gelding: useful handicapper: placed at Ascot, Goodwood and Epsom: stays 16.5f: acts on firm and good to soft going: tried in cheekpieces: often races freely. *Ed Dunlop* **106**

OASIS ROSE (FR) 3 b.f. Naaqoos 117 – Dream Rose (IRE) 80 (Anabaa (USA) 130) [2015 t7.1m⁵ t6f⁶ Dec 21] fifth foal: half-sister to 5f winner Eland Ally and 7f/1m winner Striking Rose (both by Striking Ambition): dam 1m winner out of useful 2-y-o 7f winner (stayed 14.6f) Hiddnah: well held in 2 maidens at Wolverhampton. *Jeremy Gask* **–**

OASIS SPEAR 3 b.g. Oasis Dream 129 – Sunspear (IRE) (Montjeu (IRE) 137) [2015 **88 p**
10.2d 10m³ 10m³ t9.5g* Aug 27] workmanlike gelding: second foal: dam unraced sister
to Derby winner Motivator: fairly useful performer: won maiden at Wolverhampton (by
¾ length from High Baroque) in August: will be suited by 1½m: should do better still.
Chris Wall

OASIS SPIRIT 5 b.m. Oasis Dream 129 – Fearless Spirit (USA) 74 (Spinning World **75**
(USA) 130) [2015 77: t6f² t7.1m⁵ 6m⁶ p6g⁶ Jun 24] useful-looking mare: fair handicapper:
stays 7f: acts on polytrack, tapeta and good to firm going: often wears visor. *Andrew Balding*

OAT COUTURE 3 b.f. Kyllachy 129 – Oat Cuisine 92 (Mujahid (USA) 125) [2015 p7g **75**
7m 6g² 6m⁶ 7.1s 5.7f² Sep 12] angular filly: second foal: half-sister to 13.3f winner (stays
2m) Born To Reign (by Sir Percy): dam, 1m-1¼m winner, half-sister to useful 2-y-o 5f
winner Pyman's Theory: fair maiden: stays 6f: acts on firm going. *Henry Candy*

OBBOORR 6 b.g. Cape Cross (IRE) 129 – Felawnah (USA) 111 (Mr Prospector (USA)) **69**
[2015 74: p10g⁶ t12.2m⁵ Dec 26] fair handicapper: stays 1½m: acts on polytrack, tapeta
and good to firm going: tried in cheekpieces prior to 2015. *Tim Fitzgerald*

OBSIDIAN ROCK (USA) 3 b.g. More Than Ready (USA) 120 – Balletomaine (IRE) 65 **–**
(Sadler's Wells (USA) 132) [2015 –: p12.4g Dec 21] well held both starts, in claimer at
Deauville in 2015. *J. S. Moore*

OBSIDIAN (USA) 4 br.c. Street Cry (IRE) 130 – Latice (IRE) 121 (Inchinor 119) [2015 **95**
94: 10m⁴ 8s* 7d³ 8.5g⁴ 8g⁵ 8d⁴ 8m* 8g³ 8d 9g 8g³ t8.6f³ Oct 20] sturdy colt: useful
performer: won maiden at Thirsk in May and handicap at Redcar in August: effective at 1m
to 1¼m: acts on tapeta, soft and good to firm going: sold 60,000 gns, sent to Australia.
Richard Fahey

OBSTACLE 5 ch.g. Observatory (USA) 131 – Stage Left 57 (Nashwan (USA) 135) [2015 **–**
11.6g Apr 27] strong gelding: maiden: behind in handicaps at Windsor only 2 Flat starts
since 2013. *Paul Webber*

OCCULT 3 b.g. Oasis Dream 129 – Trojan Queen (USA) (Empire Maker (USA) 129) **73**
[2015 7d³ 8.3s 8.3g⁴ 8.3g⁵ p8g⁵ p8g⁵ Dec 20] strong, attractive gelding: fair maiden: left
John Gosden after fourth start: stays 8.5f: acts on polytrack and good to soft going.
Simon Dow

OCEAN APPLAUSE 5 b.g. Royal Applause 124 – Aldora 109 (Magic Ring (IRE) 115) **88**
[2015 86: 10m 10m³ p10m⁵ 10m³ 10.1m⁶ 10f 12g 10m⁵ p10f* 10.1m Sep 16]
rather leggy gelding: fairly useful handicapper: won at Newmarket in August and
Chelmsford in September: stays 1½m: acts on polytrack, good to firm and good to soft
going: tried in headgear prior to 2015: wears tongue tie: usually races nearer last than first:
sent to Saudi Arabia. *John Ryan*

OCEAN BENTLEY (IRE) 3 b.g. Amadeus Wolf 122 – Bentley's Bush (IRE) 96 **44**
(Barathea (IRE) 127) [2015 –: p8f p10g⁶ p10g⁶ p11g 12.1s⁵ p10g⁴ t13.9g⁴ Jul 13] poor
maiden: stays 1¾m: acts on polytrack and tapeta: often races freely. *Tony Carroll*

OCEAN CRYSTAL 3 b.f. Stimulation (IRE) 121 – Crystal Gale (IRE) 71 (Verglas (IRE) **63**
118) [2015 62, a49: p6g⁴ 8m⁶ p7m² 7.6d⁴ 7s³ p8g⁶ 7m⁶ 7m² 7m³ 9g⁵ 7g⁴ 10m³ 7g³ 7d⁶ 8.5s **a57**
Aug 31] modest performer: won claimer at Lingfield in May: left John Ryan after thirteenth
start: stays 7.5f: acts on good to firm and good to soft going. *Mrs A. Malzard, Jersey*

OCEANE (FR) 3 b.g. Kentucky Dynamite (USA) 118 – Zahrana (FR) (Zamindar (USA) **95**
116) [2015 12m³ 12f 12s³ Sep 18] compact gelding: useful performer: left K. Borgel,
France, after final 2014 start: easily best effort in 2015 when third in handicap at Salisbury
(¾ length behind Simple Verse) on first start: stays 1½m: acts on soft and good to firm
going. *Alan King*

OCEAN ELEVEN 2 b.g. (Feb 14) Equiano (FR) 127 – Fittonia (FR) 66 (Ashkalani (IRE) **77**
128) [2015 6g³ 6f 5f 6m⁶ 6d³ p6f³ Nov 7] lengthy gelding: fair maiden: stays 6f: acts on
soft and good to firm going. *John Ryan*

OCEANELLA (IRE) 2 b.f. (Mar 18) Canford Cliffs (IRE) 133 – Mundus Novus (USA) **58 p**
(Unbridled's Song (USA) 125) [2015 6d⁵ 7d⁵ 6g Oct 16] €17,000F, £17,000Y: half-sister
to several winners, including very smart winner up to 1m (stays 1¼m) Consort (2-y-o 7f
winner, by Lope de Vega) and useful 2-y-o 6f/7f winner (stayed 1¼m) Steer By The Stars
(by Pivotal): dam 1m winner: modest maiden: best effort when seventh at Haydock final
start, never dangerous but not knocked about: remains open to improvement. *K. R. Burke*

OCEAN GALE 2 b.f. (Mar 6) Shirocco (GER) 129 – Ocean Transit (IRE) 89 (Trans – Island 119) [2015 6s Oct 26] first foal: dam, winner up to 1¼m (2-y-o 6f winner) who stayed 2m, also won over hurdles, half-sister to useful winner up to 11f Titus Awarded: 66/1, tailed off in maiden at Leicester. *Richard Price*

OCEAN JIVE 2 b.c. (Apr 5) Norse Dancer (IRE) 127 – Kaylianni 101 (Kalanisi (IRE) **89 p** 132) [2015 7g 8d* 8s⁴ 9.9s Nov 1] fourth foal: half-brother to 13f winner Crimson Knight (by Zafeen) and 1½m winner Picalily (by Piccolo): dam, 1¼m winner who stayed 1½m, half-sister to smart winner up to 1m Diamond Diva: fairly useful performer: won maiden at Goodwood (by 1¼ lengths from Swift Response) in August: far from discredited when 14 lengths ninth of 10 to Robin of Navan in Criterium de Saint-Cloud final outing: will be suited by 1½m: should improve further. *Brian Meehan*

OCEAN LEGEND (IRE) 10 b.g. Night Shift (USA) – Rose of Mooncoin (IRE) 99 **81** (Brief Truce (USA) 126) [2015 81: p7m* t6m* p8f⁵ t8.6f³ p7m* p6m⁴ 7d³ p8g p7g⁶ 6m* 7g³ p6g* 6g t7.1f³ p7d p6g³ Dec 16] workmanlike gelding: fairly useful performer: won handicap at Kempton in January, seller at Wolverhampton (dead-heated) in February, handicap at Kempton in April, seller at Windsor in June and claimer at Kempton in September: stays 1m: acts on all-weather, good to firm and good to soft going: tried in visor/tongue tie prior to 2015. *Tony Carroll*

OCEANOGRAPHER 3 b.g. Sea The Stars (IRE) 140 – Que Puntual (ARG) (Contested **111** Bid (USA) 120) [2015 79p: 10d⁶ p10f* p11g* Dec 3] useful handicapper: won at Chelmsford (by 8 lengths from Sarsted) in November: upped in trip, further improvement when following up at Kempton in December by 4½ lengths from Barye, dictating and staying on strongly: will stay at least 1½m: acts on polytrack and soft going: in cheekpieces last 2 starts: front runner/races prominently: may do better still. *Charlie Appleby*

OCEAN READY (USA) 2 b.g. (Mar 4) More Than Ready (USA) 120 – Tjinouska **69 p** (USA) 86 (Cozzene (USA)) [2015 p7f⁶ p8g⁶ p8g⁶ Aug 26] $110,000Y: good-topped gelding: brother to useful 6.5f-1m (including at 2 yrs) winner In The Slips and half-brother to several winners, including 1¼m winner Straits of Hormuz (by War Chant) and 2-y-o 7f winner Delta Diva (by Victory Gallop): dam 1½m winner: fair form when sixth in maidens at Kempton last 2 starts, not knocked about: remains with potential. *Sir Mark Prescott Bt*

OCEAN SHERIDAN (IRE) 3 b.g. Starspangledbanner (AUS) 128 – Endless Night **90** (GER) (Tiger Hill (IRE) 127) [2015 75: 5.1m³ 6m⁵ 6g³ 6d* 6s* 6g 5s 7s³ 7v Nov 7] fairly useful handicapper: won at Hamilton in July (twice) and August (by 1¼ lengths from Especial): stays 7f: acts on heavy going: often races towards rear. *Michael Dods*

OCEAN TEMPEST 6 gr.g. Act One 124 – Ipsa Loquitur 69 (Unfuwain (USA) 131) **114** [2015 118: a8f 9.9g⁵ 8.9g² 8.9g a8f⁵ a8f 8d 8m Jul 31] plain, leggy gelding: smart handicapper at best: second at Meydan (1¼ lengths behind Umgiyo) in January: below form after (off 4 months before final outing): stays 8.5f: acts on polytrack, tapeta, good to firm and heavy going: tried in cheekpieces. *John Ryan*

OCHOS RIOS 2 b.g. (Mar 3) Shirocco (GER) 129 – Society Rose 88 (Saddlers' Hall **55** (IRE) 126) [2015 6m 7m 8.1g⁶ Aug 2] modest maiden: best effort when sixth at Chepstow final start. *David Evans*

O'CONNOR'S GIRL 2 b.f. (Feb 15) Roderic O'Connor (IRE) 119 – Dollar Bird (IRE) **63 p** 103 (Kris 135) [2015 p7g⁴ Dec 20] half-sister to several winners, including useful 6f-1½m winner (stays 2m) Buckland (by Oratorio) and useful winner up to 9.4f (stayed 1½m) Dollar Chick (2-y-o 7f winner, by Dansili): dam 2-y-o 8.2f winner who stayed 1¾m: 16/1, some encouragement when fourth in maiden at Lingfield (2¾ lengths behind Foxinthehenhouse) on debut, left poorly placed: will improve. *Sir Mark Prescott Bt*

OCTOBER STORM 2 br.c. (Jan 25) Shirocco (GER) 129 – Cyber Star 66 (King's Best **53 p** (USA) 132) [2015 8g⁶ Oct 21] 85,000Y: angular colt: first foal: dam, maiden, half-sister to Oaks second Shirocco Star (by Shirocco): 25/1, green when sixth of 12 to Prize Money in maiden at Newmarket on debut, late headway: should do better. *Mick Channon*

ODD BALL (IRE) 8 b.g. Redback 116 – Luceball (IRE) 56 (Bluebird (USA) 125) [2015 **36** 45: p8m t8.6g t8.6g 10g 8.1g t8.6g 7.4d⁴ 8.1v⁴ p8f⁶ p8f Sep 17] lengthy gelding: poor **a44** handicapper: stays 8.5f: acts on polytrack: tried in headgear: often races freely. *Lisa Williamson*

ODDSOCKS (IRE) 3 b.f. Tagula (IRE) 116 – Datura 74 (Darshaan 133) [2015 6d p6m – p6m p6g⁵ Dec 2] half-sister to 3 winners, including winner up to 1¼m Daedal (2-y-o 6f winner, by Dr Fong) and 7f winner Blistering Dancer (by Moss Vale): dam 1m winner: no form. *Ralph Smith*

O DEE 3 ch.g. Iffraaj 127 – Queen's Grace 107 (Bahamian Bounty 116) [2015 p5g⁴ p5f⁵ **63**
p6g³ 5m p6g Dec 16] modest maiden: best effort at 6f: acts on polytrack: often in headgear.
Dean Ivory

ODELIZ (IRE) 5 ch.m. Falco (USA) 122 – Acatama (USA) (Efisio 120) [2015 111: **118**
8v 10.4m⁴ 8.5g³ 8g* 8g⁴ 9.9d* 9.9m 9.9g* Oct 25]

The last Derby winner trained in the North, Dante who won a wartime
substitute at Newmarket in 1945, was trained in Middleham by Matt Peacock,
one of many fine trainers that the historic North Yorkshire town has had down the
centuries. By the time Mark Johnston arrived there in the late-'eighties, though, he
found 'a poverty of ambition' that was common in northern Flat racing at the time.
Mark Johnston set about putting Middleham back on the racing map almost single-
handedly and the achievements of such as the Two Thousand Guineas winner Mister
Baileys and that very fine stayer Double Trigger in the 'nineties launched a career
that has seen Johnston firmly establish himself at the top of his profession over the
past two decades. Although the bulk of the nation's wealth and the lion's share of
Government investment is still in the London area, no-one could now say that there
is 'a poverty of ambition' in northern Flat racing. It is thriving like never before in
the period since the end of World War II—just look at the sizes of the strings trained
by Yorkshire trainers Johnston, Richard Fahey ('I train 200 but I wish I had 300'),
Kevin Ryan and David O'Meara, for example—and, given the right material, the
leading northern trainers have certainly proved they can deliver the goods.

Middleham itself celebrated three Group 1 victories in the latest season,
the Cheveley Park Stakes success of the Johnston-trained Lumiere and victories
in France (Prix Jean Romanet) and Italy (Premio Lydia Tesio) by the Karl Burke-
trained mare Odeliz. Burke's yard Spigot Lodge, which will house a string of a
hundred in 2016, has a long history and was the home of the winner of the 1849
Derby and St Leger winner The Flying Dutchman. The yard sent out the runner-up
in the 2013 Derby, Libertarian, during a brief period when Burke's wife Elaine held
the licence (she was the first woman to saddle a horse to finish in the first three in
the Derby). Karl Burke had saddled the last Group 1 winner from the yard in 2009,
when Lord Shanakill won the Prix Jean Prat at Chantilly, and the two successes of
Odeliz were not the stable's only pattern wins in the latest season, Odeliz herself
also winning a Group 3 in Germany, while the stable's fifty-seven domestic victories
included three for the smart sprinting two-year-old filly Quiet Reflection who was a
ready winner of the Group 3 Cornwallis Stakes at Newmarket (the smart four-year-
old handicapper You're Fired also won three times).

Unraced at two, Odeliz has progressed with each of her three campaigns and
has been a fine servant for her stable. She won in listed company at Longchamp as
a three-year-old, when she was successful three times and finished in the frame in

Premio Longines Lydia Tesio, Rome—
the British-trained Odeliz adds to her earlier Group 1 win in the Prix Jean Romanet at Deauville

Mrs Barbara M. Keller's "Odeliz"

pattern company at Toulouse on her final start. Then, at four, she showed further improvement and was a shade unfortunate not to add to her winning tally, posting good placed efforts in the Middleton Stakes at York, the Princess Elizabeth Stakes at Epsom and the Atalanta Stakes at Sandown, topping even those performances when going down by half a length to Just The Judge in the Grade 1 E.P. Taylor Stakes at Woodbine on her final appearance. The Middleton Stakes and the Princess Elizabeth Stakes were again among the targets for Odeliz in the first part of the latest season and she ran creditably in both, fourth behind Secret Gesture at York and third behind Arabian Queen (the only three-year-old in the field) at Epsom. The Princess Elizabeth was the last time Odeliz appeared on a British racecourse. She was found a good opportunity in the Franz-Gunther von Gaertner Gedachtnisrennen Hamburger Meile, a Group 3 at Hamburg, where Dutch-born, German-based Adrie de Vries rode her for the first time. In first-time cheekpieces, Odeliz beat fellow British challenger Evita Peron in a close finish, quickening well in the final furlong after her jockey had to wait for a gap before he could launch his challenge.

The consistent Odeliz seemed to be just a notch below the very best fillies and mares and, after finishing a good fourth behind Amazing Maria, Ervedya and Bawina in the Prix Rothschild at Deauville, she was sent off at 35/1 in the Darley Prix Jean Romanet (over two furlongs further) on the same course three weeks later. Adrie de Vries, who kept the ride for the rest of the season after winning on Odeliz at Hamburg, sent her to the front from the start in a smart field in the Romanet and, turning round the Rothschild form with Bawina, Odeliz put up a career-best effort, battling back after being headed a furlong out to win by a neck, with Avenir Certain three quarters of a length further back in third, ahead of We Are, Fate and British-trained Ribbons who had won the race twelve months earlier (also causing a surprise). Bawina was subsequently disqualified from second place after testing positive for a prohibited substance. Ribbons had gone on to finish second in the Prix de l'Opera on Arc day but Odeliz failed by a long way to emulate her, never threatening after reportedly getting upset in the stalls and trailing home last of thirteen. Given the opportunity to redeem herself in the Premio Longines Lydia Tesio at Rome three weeks later, Odeliz narrowly justified favouritism from Sound of Freedom and Via Pisa, idling after quickening into a two-length lead entering the final furlong. Connections announced her retirement straight after the race and she changed hands for 1,000,000 guineas (in a private sale) at the December Sales, sold to begin her career as a broodmare in Kentucky.

		Pivotal (ch 1993)	Polar Falcon / Fearless Revival
	Falco (USA) (b 2005)	Icelips (b 1999)	Unbridled / Sea Hill
Odeliz (IRE) (ch.m. 2010)		Efisio (b 1982)	Formidable / Eldoret
	Acatama (USA) (b or br 2005)	Tanzania (b 1994)	Alzao / Triple Couronne

The big, quite attractive Odeliz is by the 2008 Poule d'Essai des Poulains winner Falco who stood at a fee of just €2,500 in the latest season. On the distaff side, Odeliz is from the wider family of the dual Arc winner Treve and her brilliant French-trained contemporary Moonlight Cloud. All three are distant descendants of the tough and very smart American mare Margarethen (the fourth dam of Moonlight Cloud and the fifth dam of Treve and Odeliz, and also the grandam of Derby winner Generous and Oaks winner Imagine). Like Treve, Odeliz is descended from the best racemare that Margarethen produced, the tough and genuine Trillion who had only four foals, among them the great grandam of Odeliz, Triple Couronne, who was a sister to Trillion's outstanding daughter Triptych. Odeliz is easily the best of four winners out of the unraced Acatama (who is herself a half-sister to the smart Grade 1 scorer at nine furlongs in the States, Amorama, the dam of 2015 Grand Prix de Paris runner-up Ampere). Odeliz stayed ten and a half furlongs and acted on soft and good to firm going. She wore cheekpieces on her last five outings. *K. R. Burke*

ODEON 4 b.g. Galileo (IRE) 134 – Kite Mark 58 (Mark of Esteem (IRE) 137) [2015 110: 12m⁴ 14g 10m 10.4m 10.2d 12s Oct 27] very big gelding: smart at 3 yrs: disappointing in 2015: stays 1½m: acts on good to soft going, probably on good to firm: tried in tongue tie in 2015: front runner/races prominently, tends to find little. *James Given* **88**

ODE TO EVENING 2 ch.g. (Mar 24) Poet's Voice 126 – Ever Love (BRZ) (Nedawi 126) [2015 6m⁵ 6d* 6f⁵ 6g Aug 22] close-coupled gelding: third foal: half-brother to useful winner up to 1¼m Torchlighter (2-y-o 6f winner, by Shamardal): dam 7f winner: useful form: won maiden at Ripon (by 9 lengths from Flying Pursuit) in June: creditable fifth in Coventry Stakes at Royal Ascot (5½ lengths behind Buratino) next start, well held in Gimcrack Stakes at York only subsequent outing: will stay 7f. *Mark Johnston* **96**

OEIL DE TIGRE (FR) 4 b.g. Footstepsinthesand 120 – Suerte 55 (Halling (USA) 133) [2015 93: p6g⁴ t7.1m p6g⁶ 6m³ May 15] fairly useful handicapper: best form at 5.5f: acts on polytrack, tapeta and soft going. *Tony Carroll* **80**

OFCOURSEWECAN (USA) 5 b.g. Elusive Quality (USA) – Valid Warning (USA) (Valid Appeal (USA)) [2015 21.7f t16.5g Jul 28] lengthy gelding: fair performer in 2013, well held both starts on Flat since: stays 1½m: acts on good to firm going: tried in blinkers. *Mark Gillard* **–**

OFF ART 5 ch.g. Dutch Art 126 – Off Camera (Efisio 120) [2015 101: 8m² 8m 8d³ 8m⁴ 8m 10.3g 10.4g³ 10.3m⁵ 10g⁶ 10.4s² 12v Nov 7] useful handicapper: good 2¼ lengths second to Chancery at York on penultimate start: stays 10.5f: acts on soft and good to firm going: sometimes in headgear in 2015. *Tim Easterby* **102**

OFFBEAT SAFARIS (IRE) 7 b.g. Le Vie dei Colori 126 – Baywood (Emarati (USA) 74) [2015 58: 7g f8g t9.5f t8.6f⁶ t7.1m Dec 30] lengthy gelding: poor handicapper: left John Joseph Hanlon after first start: stays 1¼m: acts on polytrack, fibresand, good to firm and heavy going: sometimes wears cheekpieces: temperamental. *John Mackie* **47**

OFFICER IN COMMAND (USA) 9 b.g. Officer (USA) 120 – Luv To Stay N Chat **61**
(USA) (Candi's Gold (USA)) [2015 79: t8.6f⁵ t8.6g* p10f⁵ t12.2g p10f⁵ p10f² Dec 21]
lengthy, angular gelding: modest handicapper: won at Wolverhampton in January: left John
Butler after third start, Denis Quinn after fifth: stays 1¼m: acts on polytrack, tapeta and
good to firm going: usually wears headgear: tried in tongue tie. *Alan Bailey*

OFFICER SYDNEY (IRE) 3 b.g. Lawman (FR) 121 – Morena Park 105 (Pivotal 124) **76**
[2015 –: 10m 7.6g 8.3g³ 8d² Jul 7] tall, rather unfurnished gelding: fair maiden: stays
8.5f: acts on good to soft going: often races prominently: has joined Gordon Elliott.
Brian Meehan

OFFSHORE 3 gr.c. Iffraaj 127 – Ronaldsay 108 (Kirkwall 118) [2015 66, a74: f11g² **77**
p10f³ t9.5f³ 12.1m⁶ 9.9f⁴ p10g* 11.9m⁵ Jun 30] fair handicapper: won at Lingfield in June:
stays 11f: acts on all-weather and firm going: often wears cheekpieces: often races lazily.
James Tate

OFF THE PULSE 5 b.g. Araafa (IRE) 128 – Off By Heart (Royal Applause 124) [2015 **59**
90: t9.5g4 t9.5f* t9.5g* t9.5m³ 8.5g⁶ 8d t9.5g³ 8d t9.5f4 t9.5f t9.5f³ Dec 21] fairly useful **a83**
handicapper: won at Wolverhampton in January and February: stays 9.5f: acts on polytrack,
tapeta, good to firm and heavy going. *John Mackie*

OFF THE SCALE (IRE) 3 b.g. Strategic Prince 114 – Vanilla Delight (IRE) 76 (Orpen **77**
(USA) 116) [2015 t6f f7s⁴ 6g⁶ 8g 6g* 6m⁴ 6m² Aug 5] fair handicapper: won at Newcastle
in June: should be suited by 7f: acts on good to firm going: usually races towards rear.
Brian Ellison

OGBOURNE DOWNS 5 b.g. Royal Applause 124 – Helen Sharp (Pivotal 124) [2015 **90**
95: 8m⁶ 8.1m 8g* 8.3g³ 8m⁴ 7d⁶ p8d⁵ 7m t7.1f⁵ Nov 16] lengthy, angular gelding: fairly
useful handicapper: won at Bath (by nose from Starlit Cantata) in June: stays 8.5f: acts on
polytrack, good to firm and good to soft going: often races towards rear: consistent.
Charles Hills

OH MY TINKERBELL 3 b.f. Piccolo 121 – Indian Girl 59 (Erhaab (USA) 127) [2015 **–**
p7g 8g 5g Jun 13] long-backed filly: third foal: dam maiden half-sister to useful winner up
to 6f Connect: no form. *Mick Channon*

OH SO SASSY 5 b.m. Pastoral Pursuits 127 – Almasi (IRE) 96 (Petorius 117) [2015 101: **95**
p6g⁶ p6f⁶ p6m p6g* 6f⁶ 5g 5g³ 5m³ Oct 3] compact mare: useful handicapper: won at
Kempton (by 2 lengths from Plucky Dip) in June: third at Ascot last 2 starts: stays 6f: acts
on polytrack and firm going: usually races close up. *Chris Wall*

OHSOSECRET 3 ch.f. Sakhee's Secret 128 – Warden Rose 61 (Compton Place 125) **69**
[2015 –: p7f 7g 6s 6g⁶ 5.3g¹ p5g⁴ 5s² p5f* 5s⁶ p5f³ t5.1f* t5.1m⁶ p5g⁵ p5g⁴ Dec 19] fair
handicapper: won at Chelmsford in September and Wolverhampton in November: best
form at 5f: acts on polytrack, tapeta and soft going. *Stuart Williams*

OH THIS IS US (IRE) 2 b.c. (Mar 12) Acclamation 118 – Shamwari Lodge (IRE) 114 **78**
(Hawk Wing (USA) 136) [2015 6m p8m t8.6m³ Dec 30] lengthy colt: fair maiden: best
effort when 1¾ lengths third to Disobedience at Wolverhampton. *Richard Hannon*

OH WHAT A SPECIES (IRE) 2 b.f. (Mar 18) Captain Rio 122 – Aspired (IRE) 57 **64**
(Mark of Esteem (IRE) 137) [2015 t7.1m t6m⁴ Dec 30] €4,500Y: sixth foal: sister to winner
up to 1m Janeiro (2-y-o 7f winner) and half-sister to 7f winner Yes I Am and 1m winner
Arakan Aspired (both by Arakan): dam twice-raced half-sister to useful 9.7f/10.5f winner
First Fantasy: better effort when fourth in maiden at Wolverhampton (length behind dead-
heaters Miss Phillyjinks and Murdanova) in December: in tongue tie. *Alan Berry*

OIL STRIKE 8 b.g. Lucky Story (USA) 128 – Willisa 67 (Polar Falcon (USA) 126) [2015 **67**
59: t5.1g³ 5g⁴ 5m⁵ 5v² 5g 6g p6f t5.1f* t5.1f² t6m² f5f³ Dec 17] tall, angular gelding: fair **a75**
handicapper: won at Wolverhampton in October: stays 7f: acts on all-weather and any turf
going: has worn blinkers, including last 4 starts: in tongue tie last 4 starts: front runner/
races prominently. *Michael Easterby*

OJAI (IRE) 2 br.f. (Feb 18) Big Bad Bob (IRE) 118 – Femme Fatale 102 (Fairy King **63**
(USA)) [2015 p5g⁵ p5g⁴ t5.1g⁵ 5d⁵ 5.3d* 6v⁶ 5.5m Sep 28] €16,000Y: half-sister to several
winners, including smart 7f/1m winner Temptress (by Shirocco) and useful 6f winner
Shahzan (by Dansili): dam 6f winner (including at 2 yrs): modest performer: won nursery
at Brighton in August: stays 5.5f: acts on good to soft going. *Dean Ivory*

OLD FASHION 3 b.f. Shirocco (GER) 129 – Oriental Dance (Fantastic Light (USA) 134) **67**
[2015 50, a65: 10.2s 10m⁵ 12g² 11.5g³ 12.1f² 11.1s⁶ f12s 12.1m* Aug 12] fair handicapper:
won at Beverley in August: stays 1½m: acts on polytrack and firm going: front runner/races
prominently. *Michael Appleby*

OLDJOESAID 11 b.g. Royal Applause 124 – Border Minstral (IRE) 69 (Sri Pekan (USA) **73**
117) [2015 84: 5d 5m 6s⁵ 5g⁵ 5g⁶ 5.5m 5s⁴ 5d⁵ 5g 5g⁴ 5g 5m⁴ 5s* Oct 27] rather leggy
gelding: fair handicapper: won at Catterick in October: stays 6f: acts on polytrack,
fibresand, good to firm and heavy going: tried in blinkers/tongue tie prior to 2015: usually
races nearer last than first. *Paul Midgley*

OLD MAN CLEGG 5 b.g. Pastoral Pursuits 127 – Stolen Melody 74 (Robellino (USA) **71**
127) [2015 71: 7g² 7g² 7s⁶ 6.9m⁴ 8m⁶ 7m 7g Jun 20] fair handicapper: stayed 1m: acted on
good to firm and good to soft going: tried in blinkers: wore tongue tie: often raced towards
rear: dead. *Michael Easterby*

OLD TOWN BOY 4 b.c. Myboycharlie (IRE) 118 – Native Ring (FR) (Bering 136) [2015 **93**
101: p14g⁶ 12m 13g Aug 29] fairly useful handicapper: stays 1¾m: acts on polytrack, good
to firm and heavy going: often races prominently. *Philip McBride*

OLIVER'S GOLD 7 b.g. Danehill Dancer (IRE) 117 – Gemini Gold (IRE) 97 (King's **51**
Best (USA) 132) [2015 48. 12g⁵ 16m³ Aug 10] modest maiden: stays 2m: acts on soft and
good to firm going: has worn headgear, including often of late: tried in tongue tie: fairly
useful hurdler/useful chaser. *Mark Walford*

OLIVERS MOUNT 5 ch.g. Mount Nelson 125 – Phoebe Woodstock (IRE) 76 (Grand **59**
Lodge (USA) 125) [2015 68: p8g p8m⁴ t12.2f⁴ t12.2g⁶ Apr 11] modest handicapper: stays
1½m: acts on polytrack and tapeta: tried in headgear: often wears tongue tie. *Ed Vaughan*

OLIVIA FALLOW (IRE) 3 b.f. Vale of York (IRE) 117 – Spinning Maid (USA) **95**
(Forestry (USA) 121) [2015 71: 5m² 5.1f* 5.4m⁴ 5g² 5m* Aug 10] useful handicapper:
progressed well and won at Chester (by neck from Roudee) in June and Thirsk (by 1¼
lengths from Bowson Fred) in August: best form at 5f: acts on firm going. *Paul Midgley*

OLIVIA POPE (IRE) 2 b.f. (Feb 26) Lilbourne Lad (IRE) 111 – Flash And Dazzle (IRE) **–**
64 (Bertolini (USA) 125) [2015 5s⁶ p6g 5g Jun 13] €28,000F, 26,000Y: fifth foal: half-
sister to useful 2-y-o 5.5f-7f winner Ascot Memory (by Iffraaj): dam, maiden (stayed 7f),
half-sister to smart 5f/6f winner Balmont Mast: no form. *Dominic Ffrench Davis*

OL' MAN RIVER (IRE) 3 b.c. Montjeu (IRE) 137 – Finsceal Beo (IRE) 123 (Mr **108**
Greeley (USA) 122) [2015 110p: 8m 10.4m⁶ 12f⁴ 11.9s⁵ Sep 13] looked top prospect at 2
but turned out to be just a useful performer: first form in 2015 when creditable 3½ lengths
fourth to Balios in King Edward VII Stakes at Royal Ascot: off nearly 3 months, fifth of 7
behind New Bay in Prix Niel at Longchamp, soon beaten after edging left under 2f out:
may prove best at short of 1½m: acts on firm going: has worn tongue tie. *Aidan O'Brien,
Ireland*

OLNEY LASS 8 b.m. Lucky Story (USA) 128 – Zalebe 52 (Bahamian Bounty 116) [2015 **61**
70, a53: p8f³ t7.1f⁴ p8m² t8.6g p8f³ p8m 8s 7g⁴ 8d⁵ 7m⁵ 7g⁵ 8v⁴ 7d 6s Oct 15] compact **a51**
mare: modest handicapper: stays 1¼m: acts on polytrack, tapeta, soft and good to firm
going: usually races towards rear. *Lydia Pearce*

OLYMNIA 4 b.f. Teofilo (IRE) 126 – Diotima (High Estate 127) [2015 65: f16d p12g **–**
p15.8f⁴ p13.3g⁴ 11.9d Sep 14] angular filly: maiden: no form in 2015: left Robert Eddery
after fourth start: sometimes wears headgear: usually races towards rear. *Gary Moore*

OLYMPIAD (IRE) 7 b.g. Galileo (IRE) 134 – Caumshinaun (IRE) 114 (Indian Ridge **–**
123) [2015 16d⁵ 13m Sep 20] tall, leggy gelding: useful handicapper in 2012, lightly raced
and no form in That since. *Martin Todhunter*

OLYMPIC CHARM 3 b.g. Invincible Spirit (IRE) 121 – Super Sleuth (IRE) 113 (Selkirk **55 §**
(USA) 129) [2015 61: p5g³ p6f⁴ t5.1m t5.1g⁶ 5g 5g 5d t5.1g⁵ t6g Aug 6] quite good-topped
gelding: modest maiden: stays 6f: acts on polytrack, tapeta and good to firm going: in visor
last 5 starts: often races towards rear: not one to trust. *Derek Shaw*

OLYMPIC RUNNER 2 ch.f. (Feb 4) Exceed And Excel (AUS) 126 – Lochridge 110 **76 p**
(Indian Ridge 123) [2015 6d³ 6g⁶ p5m* Nov 21] sixth foal: closely related to 2-y-o 6f
winner Echo Ridge (by Oratorio) and half-sister to useful 6f (including at 2 yrs) winner
City Girl (by Elusive City): dam, 6f/7f winner, half-sister to 5f winner Loch Verdi and 5f/6f
winner Swan Song, both useful: fair performer: best effort when winning maiden at
Lingfield (by length from Belle Mare Plage) in November, overcoming positional bias:
stays 6f: remains open to improvement. *William Haggas*

OLY'ROCCS (IRE) 4 b.g. Tagula (IRE) 116 – Orpendonna (IRE) 75 (Orpen (USA) 116) **58**
[2015 60: t12.2g⁴ t12.2m² t12.2g* t12.2g² t13.9g⁵ t12.2g³ Jun 2] modest handicapper: won
at Wolverhampton in March: stays 1½m: acts on polytrack and tapeta: often in cheekpieces
in 2015: front runner/races prominently. *Philip Kirby*

OMAR KHAYYAM 6 b.h. Pivotal 124 – Kithanga (IRE) 117 (Darshaan 133) [2015 p12g – Jan 7] smallish, good-quartered horse: fairly useful handicapper in 2013: in hood, well held only subsequent start: stayed 1½m: acted on polytrack, best turf form on ground softer than good: wore tongue tie: dead. *Andrew Balding*

OMEED 2 b.f. (Feb 2) Equiano (FR) 127 – Manaaber (USA) 80 (Medicean 128) [2015 6g – Aug 30] 5,000Y: first foal: dam, 2-y-o 6f winner, half-sister to useful 1m winner Cornrow out of smart 1m/9f winner Needlecraft: 40/1, tailed off in maiden at Yarmouth. *George Margarson*

OMEGA OMEGA 6 b.m. Halling (USA) 133 – In Luck 72 (In The Wings 128) [2015 54: – 14m⁴ May 4] poor handicapper: stays 1¾m: acts on fibresand and any turf going: often wears headgear: tried in tongue tie. *Liam Corcoran*

OMID 7 b.g. Dubawi (IRE) 129 – Mille Couleurs (FR) (Spectrum (IRE) 126) [2015 51§: – § 16.1m Jul 25] big gelding: poor handicapper: stays 2m: acts on fibresand, soft and good to firm going: wears headgear: usually in tongue tie: one to leave alone. *Dianne Sayer*

OMINOTAGO 3 ch.f. Aqlaam 125 – Sharp Dresser (USA) 80 (Diesis 133) [2015 12d⁶ **73 p** t9.5g⁵ 12v⁶ Aug 25] third foal: half-sister to 1½m winner Deinonychus (by Authorized): dam, 1¼m winner, also won over hurdles: fair maiden: best effort when sixth at Doncaster on debut, should way away: should do better. *William Knight*

OMOTESANDO 5 b.g. Street Cry (IRE) 130 – Punctilious 117 (Danehill (USA) 126) **78** [2015 44, a59: t8.6g 8d t8.6g² t8.6g⁶ 8m² t8.6g⁴ t8.6m* p10g* t8.6m⁵ t12.2f⁶ 10.4d* 10.2v* Oct 7] fair handicapper: won at Wolverhampton (apprentice) and Lingfield in August, Haydock (apprentice) in September and Nottingham (apprentice) in October: stays 10.5f: acts on polytrack, tapeta and heavy going: tried in cheekpieces prior to 2015. *Mark Brisbourne*

ON A PAR 3 b.g. Major Cadeaux 121 – Dancing Loma (FR) (Danehill Dancer (IRE) 117) **67** [2015 7g⁶ 7.5m⁴ 7m 8d⁴ 9.3d³ 12.2m³ 12d 9.9g 7.9d⁴ 8.5d² Sep 22] fair maiden: stays 1½m: acts on good to firm and good to soft going: tried in cheekpieces. *Tim Easterby*

ON A WHIM 3 b.f. Tamayuz 126 – Love Me Tender 78 (Green Desert (USA) 127) [2015 **46** t8.6f⁴ t9.5g⁶ 7v t8.6g t8.6f Dec 11] 27,000Y: fifth foal: half-sister to 6f-8.3f winner Limit Up (by Shamardal): dam maiden who stayed 7f: poor maiden: stays 9.5f: acts on tapeta. *Daniel Loughnane*

ON BUDGET (IRE) 2 b.g. (Apr 25) Duke of Marmalade (IRE) 132 – Henties Bay (IRE) – (Cape Cross (IRE) 129) [2015 6g Jul 31] 33/1, very green when tailed off in maiden at Newmarket. *Anthony Carson*

ONDA DISTRICT (IRE) 3 b.g. Oasis Dream 129 – Leocorno (IRE) 108 (Pivotal 124) **77** [2015 p8g 8m² 8g* t9.5g Sep 29] fair form: won maiden at Newcastle (by 3¼ lengths from American Hustle) in September: well held on handicap debut final start: will be suited by 1¼m. *Sir Michael Stoute*

ON DEMAND 4 ch.f. Teofilo (IRE) 126 – Mimisel 92 (Selkirk (USA) 129) [2015 73: – p10g f12d³ Feb 8] maiden: no form in 2015: stays 1½m: acts on polytrack, fibresand, good to firm and heavy going: sometimes in headgear prior to 2015: usually races close up, often races freely. *Simon Hodgson*

ONE BIG SURPRISE 3 b.f. Kier Park (IRE) 114 – Cloridja (Indian Ridge 123) [2015 – p6g⁶ Feb 13] fifth foal: dam unraced half-sister to smart 1¼m/10.5f winner Colombian out of smart 1m-9.2f winner Clodora: 50/1, well held in maiden at Lingfield. *Joseph Tuite*

ONE BOY (IRE) 4 ch.g. Captain Gerrard (IRE) 113 – Paris Song (IRE) 69 (Peintre **84** Celebre (USA) 137) [2015 89: 5m 5m³ 5m⁴ 5g 5g³ 5m 5d² 5d 5g 5s⁶ Oct 19] sturdy gelding: fairly useful handicapper: best form at 5f: acts on good to firm and good to soft going: in cheekpieces last 4 starts: often races prominently. *Michael Dods*

ONE CHANCE (IRE) 4 b.f. Invincible Spirit (IRE) 121 – Towards (USA) (Fusaichi **106** Pegasus (USA) 130) [2015 98: 5m 6m⁴ 5d 6g Sep 6] close-coupled filly: useful performer: fourth in Summer Stakes at York (length behind New Providence) in July: stays 6f: acts on firm and soft going: in cheekpieces last 5 starts: races prominently. *James Fanshawe*

ONEFOURSEVEN (IRE) 2 b.g. (May 10) Lilbourne Lad (IRE) 111 – Easy To Thrill – (Soviet Star (USA) 128) [2015 5.9g 7m 7m⁶ 7.5gᵖᵘ Sep 16] no form: dead. *Rebecca Menzies*

ONEHELLUVATOUCH 2 gr.f. (Mar 13) Hellvelyn 118 – Soft Touch (IRE) 78 (Petorius **59 p** 117) [2015 8.1s⁵ Sep 16] 5,500F: closely related to 3 winners, including useful winner up to 6f Gentle Guru and useful 6f (including at 2 yrs) winner Gentle Lord (both by Ishiguru) and half-sister to 3 winners, including 3-y-o 6f/7f winner Basantee (by Lucky

Story): dam, 1m winner, also won over hurdles: 33/1, showed a bit when fifth in maiden at Sandown (8¼ lengths behind Taskeen) in September, finishing with running left: should do better. *Philip Hide*

ONE LAST DREAM 6 ch.g. Resplendent Glory (IRE) 115 – Pip's Dream 52 (Glint of **49** Gold 128) [2015 61: p6m p12g t12.2m³ t12.2f³ t8.6f⁵ p12g³ 8f⁵ t12.2g 13.1m t12.2f⁴ **a56** 11.6g⁶ t12.2f⁴ t12.2f p10g² Dec 30] modest handicapper: stays 1½m: acts on polytrack, tapeta and heavy going: sometimes wears headgear: front runner/races prominently. *Ron Hodges*

ONELASTFLING 3 b.f. Paco Boy (IRE) 129 – Goodie Twosues 91 (Fraam 114) [2015 – 51p: 11.7f p8g 8g 10.2f Aug 12] maiden: no form in 2015. *Sylvester Kirk*

ONE LIFE LIVE IT 3 b.g. Holy Roman Emperor (IRE) 125 – Lacandona (USA) 71 **82** (Septime Ciel (USA) 123) [2015 p7g* p7f* 8g 7.1m⁵ p8g Aug 5] 17,000F: good-topped gelding: half-brother to 3 winners, including useful 2-y-o 1m winner (stayed 1½m) Baranova (by Caerleon) and 12.3f winner Perigeo (by Sadler's Wells): dam maiden who stayed 1¼m: fairly useful performer: won maiden at Lingfield in March and handicap there in April: stays 7f: acts on polytrack and good to firm going: tried in blinkers: often races prominently: sent to Hong Kong, where renamed Golden Kid. *Nick Littmoden*

ONE MAN ARMY 3 b.g. Mount Nelson 125 – Hms Pinafore (IRE) (Singspiel (IRE) 133) **71** [2015 p6g⁶ f7g* 7d 7.1m 7m⁵ 8g Jul 31] fair performer: won maiden at Southwell in April: best effort at 7f: acts on fibresand: tried in hood. *Michael Bell*

ONE MOMENT 3 ch.f. Notnowcato 128 – Two Step 60 (Mujtahid (USA) 118) [2015 75: **53** p5f⁵ Jan 23] modest maiden: stays 6f: acts on polytrack, tapeta, soft and good to firm going: tried in headgear prior to 2015: usually leads. *Robert Cowell*

ONE MORE GO (IRE) 4 b.g. Papal Bull 128 – Enchanted Wood (IRE) (Hawk Wing **95** (USA) 136) [2015 11.9g³ 12m⁵ 9.2s³ 11.5m³ 16d* 16m 16m⁵ 14.1g* 16d* 17.5g⁴ 18g Oct 10] €8,000: good-bodied gelding: first foal: dam unraced: useful handicapper: won at Ripon in June and Carlisle and Thirsk in August: stays 2¼m: acts on good to soft going: sold 40,000 gns and joined Dr Richard Newland. *Alan Swinbank*

ONE MORE PUSEY 3 b.f. Hellvelyn 118 – Pusey Street Girl 87 (Gildoran 123) [2015 – 6d⁵ May 5] £12,000Y: half-sister to several winners, including 5f winner Mornin Reserves (by Atraf) and 6f winner Pusey Street Lady (by Averti), both useful: dam 7f winner: 9/1, very green when well held in maiden at Brighton. *John Gallagher*

ONEOFAPEAR 9 b.g. Pyrus (USA) 106 – Whitegate Way 46 (Greensmith 121) **46** [2015 t16.5g⁴ t13.9g⁶ 12.1m Aug 13] good-topped gelding: poor handicapper: stays 16.5f: good to firm and heavy going: tried in headgear. *Mike Sowersby*

ONE PEKAN (IRE) 5 b.g. Hard Spun (USA) 124 – Stormy Blessing (USA) (Storm Cat **92** (USA)) [2015 94: 10s⁵ 10.3f³ 12.3g⁴ 10.2g² 10.1g 10s³ 10.1d p10f² p10m⁶ t8.6m⁶ p10g⁵ p8m³ Dec 27] rangy gelding: fairly useful handicapper: stays 10.5f: acts on polytrack, tapeta and any turf going: often wears headgear: tried in tongue tie prior to 2015: sometimes slowly away. *Roger Varian*

ONE PURSUIT (IRE) 7 br.g. Pastoral Pursuits 127 – Karinski (USA) (Palace Music **78** (USA) 129) [2015 101: 12.1s⁵ May 15] leggy, workmanlike gelding: fair handicapper: stays 13f: acts on fibresand and heavy going: usually races prominently. *Brendan Powell*

ONE WORD MORE (IRE) 5 b.g. Thousand Words 113 – Somoushe (IRE) (Black **111** Minnaloushe (USA) 123) [2015 99: 7g* 7.6m 7g⁴ 7g² 7f² 7d 8d⁵ 7d⁵ 8g⁶ Sep 19] sturdy gelding: smart handicapper: won at Thirsk (by ½ length from So Beloved) in April: good second of 17 at York (head behind Jallota) in June and Newmarket (Bunbury Cup, length behind Rene Mathis) in July: stays 1m: acts on polytrack and any turf going: in headgear last 2 starts. *Tim Easterby*

ON FIRE 2 b.c. (Mar 14) Olden Times 121 – La Notte 88 (Factual (USA) 108) [2015 7g⁵ **56** 7s⁵ Oct 10] modest form in maidens at Newcastle and York. *James Bethell*

ON HIGH 3 b.f. Exceed And Excel (AUS) 126 – Kirk 79 (Selkirk (USA) 129) [2015 73: – 7v 8g 6m⁵ 7.1m Jun 22] tall, rather unfurnished filly: maiden: no form in 2015: blinkered final start: front runner/races prominently, tends to do little. *Richard Hannon*

ONLINE ALEXANDER (IRE) 4 b.f. Acclamation 118 – Dance Club (IRE) 71 **106** (Fasliyev (USA) 120) [2015 108: 5m 5m⁴ 5m⁶ 5m⁶ 6m² 6g 5m⁶ p5g Oct 23] rather leggy filly: useful performer: second in listed race at Pontefract (neck behind Divine) in August: stays 6f: acts on good to firm going: front runner/races prominently. *Kevin Ryan*

ONLY FOR YOU 5 b.m. Elusive City (USA) 117 – Enlisted (IRE) 83 (Sadler's Wells **43**
(USA) 132) [2015 –: f7g f7d p6g⁶ t5.1f Feb 20] poor maiden: best effort at 6f: acts on
polytrack, fibresand and good to firm going: tried in headgear: tried in tongue tie prior to
2015. *Alan Brown*

ONLY JOKING 3 b.f. Aussie Rules (USA) 123 – Cliche (IRE) 108 (Diktat 126) [2015 82: **83**
p8g* p8g³ 9g p8f³ 8.3d Oct 12] leggy filly: fairly useful handicapper: won at Lingfield in
May: stays 1m: acts on polytrack and good to soft going: tried in cheekpieces in 2015: sold
27,000 gns, sent to Saudi Arabia. *Hugo Palmer*

ONLY JUST (IRE) 3 b.g. Bushranger (IRE) 119 – Inter Madera (IRE) (Toca Madera 111) **86**
[2015 5m 6m⁶ 5g⁴ 6s 6g² Aug 31] €23,000F: closely related to 7f winner Time In Madera
(by Danetime) and half-brother to several winners, including useful 2-y-o 7f winner
(stayed 1½m) Sandton City (by Daggers Drawn) and winner up to 7f Sanbenito (2-y-o
5f/6f winner, by Elbio): dam unraced: fairly useful performer: won maiden at Beverley in
July: second in handicap at Ripon in August: stays 6f: best form on good going: usually
races towards rear: sold 2,500 gns, sent to Italy. *Kevin Ryan*

ONLY MINE (IRE) 2 b.f. (Jan 20) Pour Moi (IRE) 125 – Truly Mine (IRE) 98 (Rock of **104**
Gibraltar (IRE) 133) [2015 6g⁴ 6m² 6g* 7g 6g² 6d* Oct 30] €80,000Y: workmanlike filly:
fifth foal: half-sister to 3 winners, including smart winner up to 1½m Miner's Lamp (2-y-o
1m-1¼m winner, by Shamardal) and useful 1¼m winner (stays 2m) Truthwillsetufree (by
Dalakhani): dam 9f-10.7f winner: useful performer: won maiden at Cork in August and
listed race at Newmarket (by head from Squash) in October: neck second to Shaden in Firth
of Clyde Stakes at Ayr in between: stays 6f: acts on soft going. *Joseph G. Murphy, Ireland*

ONLY ORSENFOOLSIES 6 b.g. Trade Fair 124 – Desert Gold (IRE) 97 (Desert Prince **90**
(IRE) 130) [2015 89: 12d² 12.1s⁴ 12g³ 13.4m 12g⁵ 12d⁴ 12v⁵ Nov 7] fairly useful
handicapper: won at Hamilton (by neck from Dark Ruler) in May: stays 1½m: acts on
heavy going: usually races close up. *Micky Hammond*

ONLY TEN PER CENT (IRE) 7 b.g. Kheleyf (USA) 116 – Cory Everson (IRE) (Brief **67**
Truce (USA) 126) [2015 78, a86: f5g p6g⁴ p5g⁵ p6f f6g p6f² p6f⁵ p6f⁶ p6g³ 5.1d⁵ 5.1m⁴ **a74**
6s⁴ p6g p6m⁵ p6g* f7g⁵ Dec 15] fair handicapper: won at Kempton in December: stays 7f:
acts on polytrack, fibresand, good to firm and good to soft going: sometimes wears
headgear. *J. R. Jenkins*

ONORINA (IRE) 3 b.f. Arcano (IRE) 122 – Miss Honorine (IRE) 109 (Highest Honor **71**
(FR) 124) [2015 –: 9.9g 10m 11.5g* 12g⁵ p12g⁴ Sep 22] sturdy filly: fair handicapper: won
at Lingfield in July: stays 1½m: acts on polytrack: tried in hood. *Jim Boyle*

ON THE CUSP (IRE) 8 b.g. Footstepsinthesand 120 – Roman Love (IRE) (Perugino **61**
(USA) 84) [2015 72: f8g t9.5f t12.2g f11d p10f* Sep 10] leggy gelding: modest
handicapper: won at Chelmsford (apprentice) in September: stays 1½m: acts on polytrack,
fibresand, good to firm and heavy going: usually wears headgear: tried in tongue tie prior
to 2015: front runner, sometimes finds little. *Heather Dalton*

ON THE HUH 3 b.g. Avonbridge 123 – Red Sovereign 81 (Danzig Connection (USA)) **62 §**
[2015 64: f5s p6f 7d² 7m 6.1m 6m⁶ 7g⁶ t6m p7g⁴ p8g³ Oct 14] modest maiden: stays 7f:
acts on polytrack, good to firm and good to soft going: often in headgear in 2015: one to
treat with caution. *Michael Bell*

ON THE TILES 3 gr.g. Royal Applause 124 – Secret Night 99 (Dansili 127) [2015 58: **68**
p7f f7d⁵ t8.6m³ t7.1f² t7.1g* 7.5g 8m⁶ 7m⁴ Jun 18] compact gelding: fair handicapper:
won at Wolverhampton in April: stays 7f: acts on tapeta and good to firm going: usually in
headgear in 2015: front runner/races prominently. *David Brown*

OOTY HILL 3 gr.c. Dubawi (IRE) 129 – Mussoorie (FR) 108 (Linamix (FR) 127) [2015 **104**
95p: 10m² 11s⁵ 9g Oct 10] lengthy, well-made colt: useful form: 3½ lengths second to Star
of Seville in minor event at Newbury, disappointing both subsequent starts (lost action in
Darley Stakes final outing): stays 1¼m. *Roger Charlton*

OPAL TIARA (IRE) 2 b.f. (Mar 18) Thousand Words 113 – Zarafa (Fraam 114) [2015 **98**
t5.1g* 5m² 5f 6g⁴ 7m⁴ 8g² 8m³ 8g Oct 9] rather leggy filly: useful performer: won maiden at
Wolverhampton in May: good efforts in Sweet Solera Stakes at Newmarket, listed race at
Salisbury and May Hill Stakes at Doncaster (2¼ lengths third of 8 to Turret Rocks, unable
to sustain effort) fifth to seventh starts: well held in Fillies' Mile at Newmarket final outing:
stays 1m: acts on tapeta and good to firm going: often races prominently. *Mick Channon*

OPEN THE RED 3 b.g. Lawman (FR) 121 – Acquainted 98 (Shamardal (USA) 129) **87**
[2015 75p: 9.9m* 10m⁴ 10m 12m³ p12g⁵ Sep 21] strong gelding: fairly useful handicapper:
won at Goodwood in May: stays 1½m: acts on polytrack and good to firm going: often
travels strongly. *Amanda Perrett*

OPERA BARON 2 b.g. (Mar 31) Equiano (FR) 127 – Opera Dancer 79 (Norse Dancer **96** (IRE) 127) [2015 6g 6m⁴ 6m⁶ t7.1m* t8.6f* 8.3d* 7v⁶ 7g⁴ Dec 29] compact gelding: useful performer: won nurseries at Wolverhampton in September and October, and Nottingham (by 2¼ lengths from Toboggan's Fire) later in October: 25/1, possibly flattered when 2½ lengths sixth of 9 to Crazy Horse in Horris Hill Stakes at Newbury next time, allowed uncontested lead: left Sylvester Kirk 60,000 gns before final outing: stays 8.6f: acts on tapeta and heavy going: often leads. *Jassim Al Ghazali, Qatar*

OPERA BUFF 6 b.g. Oratorio (IRE) 128 – Opera Glass 88 (Barathea (IRE) 127) [2015 88: **70** f14d³ t13.9f p15.8g p13g² p15.8g⁶ Apr 7] stocky, deep-girthed gelding: fair handicapper: stays 2m: acts on polytrack, good to firm and heavy going: often wears cheekpieces: tried in tongue tie prior to 2015: front runner/races prominently. *Jose Santos*

OPERA BUFFA (IRE) 2 b.f. (Feb 25) Exceed And Excel (AUS) 126 – Dubai Opera – (USA) (Dubai Millennium 140) [2015 p6f⁴ p7g p7m Dec 16] sixth foal: half-sister to useful winner up to 9.5f Rebel Song (by Refuse To Bend) and 2-y-o 7f/1m winner Grigolo (by Shamardal): dam unraced half-sister to smart 1¼m winner Nabucco out of 1000 Guineas winner Cape Verdi: well held in maidens. *Mark Johnston*

OPERA LAD (IRE) 3 b.g. Teofilo (IRE) 126 – Opera Glass 88 (Barathea (IRE) 127) **78** [2015 p10g³ p12f* 14g 14.1g⁵ 15.9s⁵ Sep 12] workmanlike gelding: fair performer: won maiden at Lingfield in February: stays 1¾m: acts on polytrack, best turf form on good going. *Andrew Balding*

OPERATEUR (IRE) 7 b.g. Oratorio (IRE) 128 – Kassariya (IRE) (Be My Guest (USA) **62** 126) [2015 12.4g 12g 11.1m⁶ 13d 11.5d Aug 3] modest handicapper: stays 1¾m: acts on good to firm and heavy going: tried in cheekpieces/tongue tie prior to 2015: often races towards rear. *Ben Haslam*

OPERATIC HEIGHTS (IRE) 6 b.g. Golan (IRE) 129 – Opera Lover (IRE) 97 – (Sadler's Wells (USA) 132) [2015 11.8s p12g Oct 6] placed in bumper: well beaten in 2 maidens. *Alan Phillips*

OPERATIVE 2 ch.c. (Apr 2) Pastoral Pursuits 127 – Gilt Linked 85 (Compton Place 125) **85** [2015 5f² 6m³ 6g⁴ 6g 6d² 6s² Sep 18] £44,000Y: strong, compact colt: fifth foal: half-brother to smart 7f (including at 2 yrs) winner Lincoln (by Clodovil): dam, 2-y-o 5f winner, half-sister to smart winner up to 1m (stays 1¼m) Chil The Kite: fairly useful maiden: runner-up at Salisbury, Ascot (head behind Taurean Star) and Newbury: best effort at 6f on good to soft going: in cheekpieces last 2 starts. *Ed de Giles*

OPHIR 4 b.g. Nayef (USA) 129 – Ermine (IRE) 86 (Cadeaux Genereux 131) [2015 66: **60** p13.3m⁴ May 19] lengthy, useful-looking gelding: modest maiden: stays 13.5f: acts on polytrack and soft going: often races towards rear. *William Muir*

OPITO BAY (IRE) 3 ch.f. Bahamian Bounty 116 – Reveuse de Jour (IRE) 79 (Sadler's **66** Wells (USA) 132) [2015 t8.6f³ p10g 9.9m⁶ p10m Sep 26] 170,000Y: half-sister to several winners, including smart winner up to 9f Nova Hawk (2-y-o 7f winner, by Hawk Wing): dam lightly raced: fair maiden: best effort at 8.5f. *Charles Hills*

OPPORTUNA 3 b.f. Rock Hard Ten (USA) 126 – Veiled Beauty (USA) (Royal Academy **48** (USA) 130) [2015 71: 8g 6.9g f8d 7.5m t6f Nov 20] poor maiden: left Tom Dascombe after second start: stays 7.5f: acts on soft and good to firm going: tried in cheekpieces in 2015. *Michael Appleby*

OPPOSITION 2 gr.g. (Mar 18) Dalakhani (IRE) 133 – Censored 79 (Pivotal 124) [2015 **67** 8v⁶ 8.3x 8s Oct 23] fair maiden: will stay 1¼m. *Ed Dunlop*

OPTIMA PETAMUS 3 gr.g. Mastercraftsman (IRE) 129 – In A Silent Way (IRE) 102 **88** (Desert Prince (IRE) 130) [2015 10g⁶ t8.6g³ 8.3m⁴ p10g 8g⁵ 8.3d* Oct 12] 30,000Y, 52,000 2-y-o: lengthy gelding: sixth foal: half-brother to 3 winners, including useful 2-y-o 1m winner Crecy (by Refuse To Bend) and 9f-10.5f winner Driven Snow (by Linamix): dam, winner up to 1¼m (2-y-o 6f winner), half-sister to smart winner up to 1m (stayed 1¼m) Bon Nuit: fairly useful performer: won maiden at Windsor (by 1¼ lengths from Noblest) in October: worth another try at 1¼m: acts on good to soft going: races prominently. *Luca Cumani*

OPTIMYSTIC (IRE) 3 ch.f. Exceed And Excel (AUS) 126 – Psychic (IRE) 72 (Alhaarth **58** (IRE) 126) [2015 54: p6m⁶ p6g² t5.1g³ 5.1m 5.7f 6m Jul 7] modest maiden: best effort at 6f: acts on polytrack: in hood/tongue tie last 5 starts. *Andrew Balding*

OPT OUT 5 ch.g. Pivotal 124 – Easy Option (IRE) 115 (Prince Sabo 123) [2015 72: 7.1s 6g⁵ 6g 7.1m* 7.1m³ 6m 6g⁵ 7.2g³ 8m* 7.2d 8.9g⁶ 8m* 7.2g 8.3g⁴ 7.2g² 7.2g⁴ 7.2g* Oct 13] lengthy, angular gelding: fair handicapper: won at Musselburgh in June, August and October: stays 9f: acts on good to firm and good to soft going: wears headgear: often races towards rear. *Alistair Whillans*   **72**

OPUS DEI 8 b.g. Oasis Dream 129 – Grail (USA) (Quest For Fame 127) [2015 55§: t7.1f² t8.6g t7.1m 8g Sep 23] good-bodied gelding: modest handicapper: left Fred Watson after third start: stays 1m: acts on all-weather and good to firm going: often in headgear prior to 2015: sometimes slowly away, often races towards rear: irresolute. *Garry Moss*   **53 §**

OPUS TOO (IRE) 4 b.g. Lawman (FR) 121 – Jerez (IRE) 58 (Lake Coniston (IRE) 131) [2015 –: t12.2g⁵ p13.3m p16g² p13.3m 16g p16g p12g⁴ p13f 11.9s Oct 6] modest maiden: best effort at 2m: acts on polytrack: tried in blinkers: sometimes in tongue tie in 2015: front runner/races prominently. *John Ryan*   **56**

ORACLE BOY 4 b.g. Mount Nelson 125 – Snow Princess (IRE) 111 (Ela-Mana-Mou 132) [2015 72: 14d³ 14.1g 13g³ 15.8g p15.8f Sep 22] sturdy gelding: fair handicapper: stays 1¾m: acts on tapeta and good to soft going: often wears cheekpieces: front runner/races prominently. *William Muir*   **72**

ORACOLO (IRE) 3 b.g. Cape Cross (IRE) 129 – Illuminise (IRE) 109 (Grand Lodge (USA) 125) [2015 79p: 8g⁵ 8m* 8m* 8f Jul 11] useful handicapper: won twice at Doncaster (by 2½ lengths from Azraff latter occasion) in June: left poorly placed when below best final start: stays 1m: acts on tapeta and good to firm going: sometimes slowly away, often races towards rear: should do better still if all is well. *David Simcock*   **97 p**

ORANGE BLOOM 3 ch.f. New Approach (IRE) 132 – Fleur de Lis (Nayef (USA) 129) [2015 10.2m³ p13.3g⁵ 8.3g p12g Jun 18] third foal: half-sister to 1m (including at 2 yrs) winner Cekath (by Medicean): dam, ran once, out of smart performer who stayed 1½m Melodist: no form. *Michael Bell*   **–**

ORANGECHERIE (IRE) 2 b.f. (Apr 10) Duke of Marmalade (IRE) 132 – Ochre (IRE) 82 (Diktat 126) [2015 8.1s p8g Dec 15] €15,000Y, 26,000 2-y-o: second foal: half-sister to winner up to 1m La Reine de Pearls (2-y-o 7f winner, by Dubawi): dam, 1m/8.6f winner, sister to useful 7f/1m winner Vista Bella out of useful 2-y-o 7f winner Cox Orange: tailed off in 2 maidens. *Mike Murphy*   **–**

ORATORIO'S JOY (IRE) 5 b.m. Oratorio (IRE) 128 – Seeking The Fun (USA) (Alhaarth (IRE) 126) [2015 83: p11g⁴ t12.2f² p13.3g² p13.3g² p16m² t13.9m⁴ 14.1f⁶ t12.2g* 11.8d 11.9m⁵ 16m⁵ 16g⁶ 13.1m⁴ 17.2f⁴ t16.5f⁴ f11g Dec 22] sturdy mare: fairly useful handicapper: won at Wolverhampton in June: stays 17f: acts on polytrack, tapeta, firm and soft going: often races in rear. *Jamie Osborne*   **75 a82**

ORBIT THE MOON (IRE) 7 b.g. Oratorio (IRE) 128 – Catch The Moon (IRE) (Peintre Celebre (USA) 137) [2015 84: 6g² 6s 6g² 6g 6m⁵ 6g 7g² 7g t6g t7.1f Oct 13] tall, lengthy gelding: fair handicapper: left Michael Dods after eighth start: stays 7f: acts on soft and good to firm going: often wears headgear: usually wears tongue tie: inconsistent. *Grace Harris*   **77 §**

ORCRAIG 5 b.g. Royal Applause 124 – Our Faye 106 (College Chapel 122) [2015 p8f⁵ Feb 25] 33/1, green when fifth of 9 to Townsville in maiden at Kempton. *Sylvester Kirk*   **58**

ORDER OF SERVICE 5 ch.g. Medicean 128 – Choir Gallery (Pivotal 124) [2015 78, a88: 7.2g 7.2s 7m 7m³ 6g³ 6d* 7m* 7m 6d⁴ 7s p6g Dec 7] fairly useful handicapper: won at Ayr and Newcastle in July: left Jim Goldie after tenth start: stays 1m: acts on polytrack, tapeta, good to firm and good to soft going: tried in visor/tongue tie: sometimes slowly away, races well off pace. *Shaun Harris*   **88**

ORDER OF ST GEORGE (IRE) 3 b.c. Galileo (IRE) 134 – Another Storm (USA) (Gone West (USA)) [2015 102: 14m² 12.9m* 14s* 14d* Sep 13]   **129**

When Ballydoyle went into the winter with six of the first eight in the Derby ante-post betting, it was hard to envisage the eventual paucity of good three-year-old colts in the yard that led to talk of pressing the Two Thousand Guineas winner Gleneagles, or the stable's top filly Found, into service to try to win a fourth successive Derby. Gleneagles was virtually a one-man show among the Ballydoyle colts at the time, although Highland Reel's classic campaign in France yielded a good second in the Prix du Jockey Club. The three colts who came through the auditions to represent Ballydoyle at Epsom—Giovanni Canaletto, Kilimanjaro and Hans Holbein—all finished ten lengths or more behind the Derby winner Golden

Palmerstown House Estate Irish St Leger, the Curragh—
the only three-year-old in the line-up Order of St George routs the opposition as he becomes the
first of his age to land the prize since Vinnie Roe in 2001; Agent Murphy (light star on cap) finishes
second, ahead of Wicklow Brave (seams), Second Step (rail) and Forgotten Rules (noseband)

Horn. Gleneagles was seen out only twice after he had completed a splendid Anglo/ Irish Guineas and St James's Palace treble, by which time one of the stablemates who was to usurp his position as the highest-rated horse at Ballydoyle, another blue-blooded son of Galileo, Order of St George, had not even made his seasonal reappearance.

Order of St George wasn't on the radar as a potential Derby candidate for Ballydoyle. In five appearances as a two-year-old, he won once—picking up a maiden at Leopardstown on his third start—and was beaten in pattern and listed company on his last two outings. There were no excuses when he finished five lengths fifth behind Commemorative in what was not a strong renewal of the Group 3 Autumn Stakes, his only outing in pattern company. Order of St George simply didn't look good enough, tending to run around at Newmarket when he came under pressure, having spoiled his appearance beforehand by sweating. Although bred to come into his own over longer distances as a three-year-old, and clearly not the finished article physically as a two-year-old, it was hard to see Order of St George making the sort of progress that he made between the end of June and the middle of September in the latest season. Reappearing in the Curragh Cup over a mile and three quarters (and again sweating beforehand), he stepped up markedly on his two-year-old form to fight out a close finish with stablemate Bondi Beach, who beat him by a short head despite that horse's jockey dropping his whip in the closing stages. The target for both Order of St George and Bondi Beach was said afterwards to be the St Leger but, while Bondi Beach contested the main trial for that race, finishing second in the Great Voltigeur Stakes at York, Order of St George had his lines cast in calmer waters. After landing odds of 5/1-on in a minor event at Down Royal in July, he bypassed the Voltigeur and contested the Palmerstown House Estate Irish St Leger Trial at the Curragh four days later. Starting at 6/4-on, up against his stable's Gold Cup runner-up Kingfisher and three others, Order of St George followed up with another wide-margin success, this time beating the 2012 Hardwicke winner Sea Moon (who had been returned to Europe after an unsuccessful stint in Australia) by seven and a half lengths, with Kingfisher a further eight and a half further back in third.

Order of St George was 3/1 ante-post favourite for the St Leger after the final deadline for scratchings reduced the St Leger field to just a dozen (six of them trained by Aidan O'Brien). He was still in the field—9/4 joint favourite with Voltigeur winner Storm The Stars—when the Ballydoyle team was trimmed to three at the six-day stage and, although among the eight final declarations on the Thursday, Order of St George was rerouted the following day to the Curragh on Sunday, the day after the St Leger. Aidan O'Brien explained that connections 'wouldn't be happy running him on good to firm [the state of the Doncaster going on the first three days].' As it happens, the going eased for the St Leger which was run on good to soft, the same as for the Palmerstown House Estate Irish St Leger, for which Order of St George started 5/4 favourite in a field of eleven in which he was the only three-year-old. The opposition included the 2014 Long Distance Cup winner Forgotten

742

Rules, the Geoffrey Freer Stakes winner Agent Murphy, the winner of the race the previous year Brown Panther, and the Jockey Club Stakes and Grosser Preis von Berlin winner Second Step, those four the only others to start at shorter than 20/1. The Curragh crowd was treated to one of the best performances—on a par with those of Kayf Tara in 1999 and Septimus in 2008—seen in the Irish St Leger since it was opened up to horses above the age of three in 1983, a performance that, if it had been repeated at Doncaster, would have seen Order of St George run out a clear-cut winner of the St Leger itself. Order of St George didn't quite equal the thirteen-length margin of victory at the Curragh by Septimus but, in a strongly-run race marred by the fatal injury suffered by Brown Panther, he annihilated his rivals, quickening to lead over two furlongs out and storming clear, despite edging right, to beat Agent Murphy by eleven lengths, with the Ebor runner-up Wicklow Brave and Second Step a neck and half a length further back, just ahead of Forgotten Rules.

Order of St George's Irish St Leger form was the best in a staying event in Europe all year and there was talk of his being sent for the Melbourne Cup, after Australian owner Lloyd Williams bought into him, as part of a deal including shares in Bondi Beach and Kingfisher. While that pair did make the trip to Flemington, Order of St George suffered what was described as 'a minor training setback' and was put away for a four-year-old campaign in which the Gold Cup at Royal Ascot seems likely to be on the agenda. Order of St George's trainer is already the most successful in the long history of that race (he has won it six times) and, in Order of St George, he has the ideal contender to put him further clear in the

Michael Tabor/Derrick Smith/Mrs Magnier's "Order of St George"

all-time list. Order of St George was Aidan O'Brien's third Irish St Leger winner (he also won the race with four-times Gold Cup winner Yeats) and took his total of Irish classic victories to thirty-four—if the Irish St Leger can still be counted as a 'classic', given that most of the runners nowadays are four-year-olds and above and the race has become almost the exclusive preserve of the older stayers (Order of St George was the first of his age to win it since Vinnie Roe gained the first of his four victories in the race in 2001). Aidan O'Brien's achievements since succeeding his illustrious namesake Vincent at Ballydoyle are phenomenal. He was champion trainer in Ireland for the eighteenth time in the latest season (including seventeen in a row) and Gleneagles and the Oaks winner Qualify took his total of British classic victories to twenty-three, moving him into second place—only two short of Henry Cecil's record—in the list of the most successful trainers in the British classics since 1900. Vincent O'Brien, incidentally, who operated with a much smaller string, won twenty-seven Irish classics, sixteen British classics (including the Derby six times) and was champion trainer in Ireland thirteen times.

		Sadler's Wells	Northern Dancer
	Galileo (IRE)	(b 1981)	Fairy Bridge
	(b 1998)	Urban Sea	Miswaki
Order of St George (IRE)		(ch 1989)	Allegretta
(b.c. 2012)		Gone West	Mr Prospector
	Another Storm (USA)	(b 1984)	Secrettame
	(b 1999)	Storm Song	Summer Squall
		(b 1994)	Hum Along

If Order of St George's trainer is building an exceptional legacy, then the same can be said about Order of St George's sire Galileo, the most successful stallion of the last decade (he topped the general sires' table in Britain and Ireland for the seventh time in eight years). Aside from his own achievements, Galileo—whose fee is advertised as 'private'—is making a very big name for himself as a sire of sires. With Gleneagles joining Galileo at Coolmore at a fee of €60,000, Galileo will have no fewer than five sons at stud in 2016 who stand at a fee of at least €50,000 (or the sterling equivalent), the others being Frankel (£125,000), New Approach (€60,000), Teofilo (€50,000) and the stallion promoted by Coolmore as 'the heir apparent to Galileo' Australia (€50,000). New Approach and Teofilo are the only pair old enough to have had runners but they have quickly made their mark. Teofilo has sired winners of the Irish One Thousand Guineas, the Irish Derby and the Irish St Leger, and New Approach has already had winners of the Two Thousand Guineas and Oaks in Britain, along with runners-up in the Derby and St Leger. Order of St George was purchased as a yearling at Keeneland for 550,000 dollars and is a half-brother to four winners, three of whom have also won at pattern or listed level. Asperity (by War Chant) won the Prix Paul de Moussac at Chantilly and was a smart miler; Sehoy (by Menifee) was a fairly useful performer at a mile and a half for Asperity's trainer John Gosden before going on to win in listed company in Scandinavia; and Angel Terrace (by Ghostzapper) won the Pin Oak Valley View Stakes, a Grade 3 race over an extended mile for fillies run at Keeneland, before going on to show that she stayed a mile and a half. Order of St George's dam Another Storm won only once, over eight and a half furlongs as a two-year-old in the States, but she was a million-dollar yearling, reflecting the fact that her own dam Storm Song was the champion juvenile filly of 1996 when she completed a Grade 1 double in the Frizette Stakes and the Breeders' Cup Juvenile Fillies (Timeform rated her the best two-year-old, of either sex, in the northern hemisphere). Order of St George's two-year-old brother Kellstorm, a Derby entry who cost 875,000 guineas as a yearling, proved too green to show anything in a back-end maiden at Gowran but can be expected to prove a different proposition for Ballydoyle at three. Order of St George stays a mile and three quarters and should get further if tried. He acts well on soft going and has won on good to firm and, despite usually getting in a sweat before his races, is thoroughly genuine. *Aidan O'Brien, Ireland*

ORDINAL 2 b.c. (Mar 28) Shamardal (USA) 129 – Mille (Dubai Millennium 140) [2015 – 6s 6d Oct 26] well held in maidens at Redcar. *Mark Johnston*

Queen Alexandra Stakes, Royal Ascot—Oriental Fox, fifth (promoted) in the Gold Cup at this meeting in 2014, makes an impressive return from a year off as he wins by seven lengths

OREGON GIFT 3 b.g. Major Cadeaux 121 – Dayville (USA) 86 (Dayjur (USA) 137) **69** [2015 70, a84: p8g 8g⁶ 8d⁵ 8m⁶ 10s⁵ 10s⁵ 10m³ 7.9g 12s Oct 6] fair handicapper: stays 1m: acts on polytrack and soft going: tried in blinkers in 2015: usually races prominently. *Mark Johnston*

ORIENTAL DREAM (IRE) 4 b.g. Shamardal (USA) 129 – Oriental Melody (IRE) 72 **50** (Sakhee (USA) 136) [2015 –: 8s 7g⁴ 7.1s⁵ 8d⁶ 6g⁴ t7.1g⁵ 9m Jul 19] modest maiden: stays 7f: acts on tapeta, best turf form on good going: often wears headgear. *Nigel Tinkler*

ORIENTAL FOX (GER) 7 ch.g. Lomitas 129 – Oriental Pearl (GER) (Big Shuffle **117** (USA) 122) [2015 112: 21.7f* 16m 14.9d² 15.4s² 18g² 13.9s³ Oct 24] leggy gelding: smart performer, better than ever in 2015: won Queen Alexandra Stakes at Royal Ascot by 7 lengths from Taws: second after in Prix Kergorlay at Deauville (2½ lengths behind Alex My Boy), Prix Gladiateur at Longchamp (promoted after finishing 2¼ lengths third to Fly With Me) and Cesarewitch Handicap at Newmarket (short head behind Grumeti): stays 21.7f: acts on firm and soft going: waited with. *Mark Johnston*

ORIENTAL GRACE (IRE) 2 ch.f. (May 20) Strategic Prince 114 – Asian Lady 68 **62** (Kyllachy 129) [2015 5m* 5m² 6.1m⁶ p6g 6v Sep 2] modest performer: won maiden at Bath in May: best form at 5f: acts on good to firm going. *Roger Charlton*

ORIENTAL HEIGHTS 4 b.f. Orientor 118 – Harrken Heights (IRE) (Belmez (USA) **–** 131) [2015 39: 6g 5d 5g 7.2d⁶ 6g Jul 6] poor maiden: tried in hood: usually races nearer last than first. *Jim Goldie*

ORIENTAL RELATION (IRE) 4 gr.g. Tagula (IRE) 116 – Rofan (USA) (Cozzene **93** (USA)) [2015 78, a95: f6d² f5g⁴ f6s⁴ p6f* p6f² f5g* p5g p6d* p5g p6f p6f⁴ p6g⁵ t6m t5.1f p6g⁵ Dec 30] good-topped gelding: fairly useful handicapper: won at Chelmsford in February and Southwell and Chelmsford in March: stays 6f: acts on all-weather, firm and soft going: usually wears headgear: usually leads. *James Given*

ORIENTAL SPLENDOUR (IRE) 3 b.g. Strategic Prince 114 – Asian Lady 68 **76** (Kyllachy 129) [2015 76: p6g⁴ 5m⁴ 5.7f² 5.7g² Oct 18] sturdy gelding: fair maiden: stays 6f: acts on polytrack, best turf form on good going: tried in cheekpieces in 2015: often travels strongly. *Roger Charlton*

ORIENTAL TIGER 4 b.g. Tiger Hill (IRE) 127 – Cal Norma's Lady (IRE) 87 (Lyphard's **76** Special (USA) 122) [2015 9.2s 9.2d⁶ 10g³ 12d 12.1g² 11.9d³ 13m⁶ 10g⁴ 10g⁴ Oct 8] fair maiden: stays 1½m: acts on good to soft going: usually in hood: often starts slowly, often races in rear. *Jim Goldie*

ORIENT CLASS 4 ch.g. Orientor 118 – Killer Class 72 (Kyllachy 129) [2015 80: 5s⁵ 5s **50** 5s⁴ Aug 1] modest handicapper: best form at 5f: acts on good to firm and heavy going: often wears visor: front runner/races prominently. *Paul Midgley*

ORIENT SKY 4 b.g. Orientor 118 – Sister Eugenie (IRE) 55 (Indian Lodge (IRE) 127) **69** [2015 57: 6s⁵ 6d³ 6g⁵ 6g⁶ 6d² 7.2d⁴ 6g⁶ 8g⁶ 6g² 6s⁵ Oct 16] fair maiden: stays 7f: best form on good going: sometimes wears headgear. *Paul Midgley*

ORIGINALITY (IRE) 2 b.g. (Mar 12) Roderic O'Connor (IRE) 119 – Original **–** (Caerleon (USA) 132) [2015 8g⁴ 7.4v⁵ 8m Sep 11] no form. *Seamus Mullins*

ORINOCCO 6 b.g. Shirocco (GER) 129 – Norcroft Joy 82 (Rock Hopper 124) [2015 12s **–** Oct 19] tailed off in minor event at Newmarket and maiden at Pontefract 4 years apart. *David C. Griffiths*

ORION'S BOW 4 ch.g. Pivotal 124 – Heavenly Ray (USA) 97 (Rahy (USA) 115) [2015 **83** 87: 8m 7m² 6g² 7m 7m⁶ 7m⁴ 7d 7g⁵ 6s² 6m* 7v Oct 17] fairly useful handicapper: won at Hamilton in September: stays 8.5f, effective at shorter: acts on polytrack, tapeta and good to firm going: sometimes wears blinkers: usually in tongue tie prior to 2015: usually travels strongly. *David Nicholls*

ORLANDO ROGUE (IRE) 3 b.g. Bushranger (IRE) 119 – Boston Ivy (USA) (Mark of **77** Esteem (IRE) 137) [2015 82: 8.3m p7m* 7s² 7m² 7.1m² 7m⁴ 6g⁴ t7.1m t7.1m 7v p7g⁵ f8g⁶ p8g² p7g* Dec 9] sturdy gelding: fair performer: won claimer at Lingfield in April and handicap at Kempton in December: left George Baker after sixth start: stays 1m: acts on polytrack and good to firm going: usually in cheekpieces in 2015: usually races prominently. *Conor Dore*

ORMANUMPS (IRE) 2 b.g. (Feb 16) Elnadim (USA) 128 – Tawjeeh (Haafhd 129) **50** [2015 6m⁶ 6d t7.1m p6m t6f² t7 1f t5,1f Dec 11] modest maiden: should be suited by 7f: acts on tapeta: tried in cheekpieces. *Daniel Loughnane*

ORMERING 2 b.f. (Feb 27) Kyllachy 129 – Lihou Island 89 (Beveled (USA)) [2015 6m **–** 5f 7.6g p6g Sep 22] 25,000Y: seventh foal: sister to smart winner up to 7f Horseradish (2-y-o 6f winner) and half-sister to 1m winner Hot Mustard (by Pastoral Pursuits): dam 2-y-o 6f winner: no form. *Roger Teal*

ORMITO (GER) 2 b.c. (Feb 13) Mamool (IRE) 124 – Ormita (GER) (Acatenango (GER) **99** 127) [2015 8s² 8d* 10g⁴ 9.9s Nov 1] €24,000Y: good-topped colt: fifth foal: brother to useful 11f-15f winner Orluna and half-brother to 1m winner Orotouch (by Touch Down): dam 1½m winner: useful form: won maiden at Haydock (by 7 lengths from Replenish) in September: fourth in listed race at Newmarket (2½ lengths behind Glamorous Approach) next time, disappointing final start: bred to stay at least 1½m. *Andrew Balding*

ORMSKIRK 2 gr.c. (Feb 27) Hellvelyn 118 – River Song (USA) (Siphon (BRZ) 130) **80** [2015 7m² 7d⁵ 6d* 6s³ Oct 9] £11,000Y, £60,000 2-y-o: fifth foal: dam, 5.5f winner, half-sister to very smart miler Allied Forces: fairly useful performer: won maiden at Catterick in September: should prove suited by a return to 7f. *Richard Fahey*

ORNATE 2 b.c. (Apr 16) Bahamian Bounty 116 – Adorn 105 (Kyllachy 129) [2015 6m⁴ **114** 5m* 5g⁴ 5m² t5.1g³ Dec 5] useful-looking colt: has scope: third foal: half-brother to 2-y-o 5f/6f winner Saayerr (by Acclamation) and 2-y-o 5f winner Fendale (by Exceed And Excel), both useful: dam 2-y-o 6f winner: smart performer: won maiden at Ripon (by 5 lengths from Crombay) in July: best effort when head second to Gutaifan in Flying Childers Stakes at Doncaster: best form at 5f on good to firm going: front runner/races prominently. *William Haggas*

OROBAS (IRE) 3 b.g. Dark Angel (IRE) 113 – Miss Mujadil (IRE) (Mujadil (USA) 119) **47** [2015 38: 8g⁴ 8g⁶ 8g⁶ 7d Aug 26] poor maiden: stays 1m: best form on good going: tried in cheekpieces prior to 2015. *Ron Barr*

ORSIPPUS (USA) 9 b.g. Sunday Break (JPN) 121 – Mirror Dancing (USA) (Caveat **–** (USA)) [2015 16.4s Oct 10] good-topped gelding: fairly useful handicapper: well held only outing on Flat in 2015: stays 2¼m: acts on good to firm and heavy going: has worn visor: fairly useful hurdler/chaser. *Michael Smith*

OR SO (USA) 3 ch.g. Rock Slide (USA) – Miss Santa Anita (CAN) (Ide (USA) 119) [2015 **59** a8.2f⁶ a8.2f a5.5f⁵ 8.5f⁶ a8.5s² a8.3s* p10mᵘʳ Oct 28] modest performer: won maiden claimer at Delaware in June, subsequently left Steve Epley: unseated rider after 2f in handicap at Kempton in October: stays 8.5f: acts on dirt: sometimes in headgear. *Phil Middleton*

ORTAC ROCK (IRE) 6 b.g. Aussie Rules (USA) 123 – Fashion Guide (IRE) 87 **71** (Bluebird (USA) 125) [2015 81, a71: t7.1f* 7.1f⁴ p7g² t7.1f t7.1f* 6s² 5.9g⁴ 5g² 6m⁵ 5.1d⁶ 6d p6m Nov 17] well-made gelding: fair performer: won claimer at Wolverhampton in January: stays 7f: acts on tapeta, soft and good to firm going: usually wears tongue tie: often races towards rear. *Richard Fahey*

ORTHODOX LAD 7 ch.g. Monsieur Bond (IRE) 120 – Ashantiana 64 (Ashkalani (IRE) **–** 128) [2015 t12.2f Dec 22] angular gelding: fair handicapper in 2012 for Ed de Giles: fit from jumps, well held at Wolverhampton on return: stays 1¼m: acts on polytrack, good to firm and heavy going: tried in blinkers. *Grace Harris*

ORVAR (IRE) 2 b.c. (Mar 5) Dandy Man (IRE) 123 – Roskeen (IRE) (Grand Lodge **99** (USA) 125) [2015 5f* 5f⁶ 6m⁵ 6d² 6g⁵ 6g* 6g Oct 3] €40,000F, £60,000Y: good-quartered colt: sixth foal: half-brother to 3 winners, including 2-y-o 7f winner Dark Kingdom (by Lord Shanakill) and 6f/7f winner Great Crested (by Clodovil): dam unraced half-sister to useful winner up to 6f Roker Park: useful performer: won maiden at Salisbury in May and minor event at Veliefendi (by length from Graystorm) in September: stays 6f: acts on firm and good to soft going. *Richard Hannon*

ORWELLIAN 6 b.g. Bahamian Bounty 116 – Trinny (Rainbow Quest (USA) 134) [2015 **60 §** 79, a61: 7m 6m 6s 7s 6d Oct 26] modest handicapper: best at 7f: acts on fibresand, good to firm and heavy going: tried in headgear prior to 2015: sometimes slowly away, usually races towards rear. *Bryan Smart*

OSAILA (IRE) 3 b.f. Danehill Dancer (IRE) 117 – Mennetou (IRE) (Entrepreneur 123) **115** [2015 106: 7m* 8f 8f* 7m² 9g⁵ 8.5f Dec 17] useful-looking fr: smart performer: won Nell Gwyn Stakes at Newmarket (by short head from New Providence) in April and listed Sandringham Handicap at Royal Ascot (by nose from Always Smile): respectable ½-length second to Amy Eria in Oak Tree Stakes at Goodwood in July, unsuited by drop in trip: below form in USA last 2 starts, leaving Richard Hannon before final outing: suited by 1m: acts on firm going. *Todd A. Pletcher, USA*

OSARUVEETIL (IRE) 4 b.g. Teofilo (IRE) 126 – Caraiyma (IRE) 84 (Shahrastani **82 p** (USA) 135) [2015 91p: 12g May 13] fairly useful form: won maiden on sole start in 2014, seventh of 16 to Libran in handicap at York only outing in 2015: sold 13,500 gns in July: remains with potential. *William Haggas*

OSCAR HUGHES (IRE) 2 br.g. (May 5) Frozen Power (IRE) 108 – Pedra Ona (IRE) **–** (Mark of Esteem (IRE) 137) [2015 7g Oct 3] 66/1, well held in maiden at Redcar. *Julie Camacho*

OSCARS JOURNEY 5 ch.g. Dubai Destination (USA) 127 – Fruit of Glory 106 (Glory **78** of Dancer 121) [2015 76: f5g⁶ p6f² p6g* 5.1s³ 5m⁴ 5.1g* 5d⁶ 5.1v⁴ 5.1d f5g Dec 15] quite good-topped gelding: fair handicapper: won at Chelmsford in April and Nottingham in July: stays 6f: acts on polytrack, good to firm and heavy going: often wears headgear: usually races close up: inconsistent. *J. R. Jenkins*

OSGOOD 8 b.g. Danehill Dancer (IRE) 117 – Sabreon 85 (Caerleon (USA) 132) [2015 54: **47** p12g Aug 26] tall gelding: poor handicapper: stays 1½m: acts on polytrack, good to firm and heavy going: tried in visor. *Gary Moore*

OSIPOVA 3 b.f. Makfi 130 – Barynya 77 (Pivotal 124) [2015 8.3s p10g² p12g* 12s⁶ p11g² **95** p12g* p12g Nov 25] second foal: dam, maiden, (stayed 1m), half-sister to useful 7f-1m winner Russian Realm out of very smart winner up to 1¼m (2-y-o 6f winner) Russian Rhythm): useful performer: won maiden in August and handicap (by neck from Movie Set) in November, both at Kempton: below form in listed race at same course final start: stays 1½m: acts on polytrack: usually races prominently. *James Fanshawe*

OSKAR DENARIUS (IRE) 4 b.g. Authorized (IRE) 133 – Elizabethan Age (FR) 78 **83** (King's Best (USA) 132) [2015 68p: p10g⁶ 10.2s* 11.6g* 12.1d Aug 28] fairly useful handicapper: won at Chepstow (awarded race) in May and Windsor (by 8 lengths from Khee Society) in July: stays 11.5f: acts on soft going: usually in hood in 2015: often races towards rear. *Marcus Tregoning*

OSTEOPATHIC REMEDY (IRE) 11 ch.g. Inchinor 119 – Dolce Vita (IRE) 85 (Ela- **87** Mana-Mou 132) [2015 98: 8.3s 7g 8m³ 8g 7.9g 8d 8g 8g⁶ 8g Sep 17] sparely-made gelding: fairly useful handicapper: stays 8.5f: acts on good to firm and heavy going: often in tongue tie. *Michael Dods*

OSTRALEGUS 5 b.g. Choisir (AUS) 126 – Midnight Pearl (USA) 59 (Woodman (USA) **55** 126) [2015 71: p10g (7.1g⁴ Feb 9] modest handicapper: stays 1m: acts on polytrack, tapeta and soft going: tried in headgear: weak finisher. *John Gallagher*

OST WIND 3 b.g. Oasis Dream 129 – Maroussies Wings (IRE) 111 (In The Wings 128) **63** [2015 p8g⁴ Aug 24] workmanlike gelding: fair maiden: twice raced in France at 2 yrs: left H-A. Pantall, below-form fourth of 9 to Power Game in maiden at Kempton. *Michael Attwater*

OTTAVINO (IRE) 6 b.g. Piccolo 121 – Indian's Feather (IRE) 98 (Indian Ridge 123) **–** [2015 –: 7g Jul 22] lightly-raced maiden, modest at best: best effort at 6f: acts on polytrack and good to firm going: tried in cheekpieces. *Jane Chapple-Hyam*

OUR BOY JACK (IRE) 6 b.g. Camacho 118 – Jina (IRE) 36 (Petardia 113) [2015 96: **91 §** 7g 8m⁶ 7.2s⁴ 8d⁴ 7.2d 7.9g³ 10g 10.3m⁴ 8.5g² 8d 8d* 8g 8d⁴ 8.3s p8g Nov 13] good-topped gelding: fairly useful handicapper: won at Thirsk (by 1¼ lengths from Lil Sophella) in August: stays 8.5f: acts on good to firm and heavy going: tried in cheekpieces: quirky sort, one to be wary of. *Richard Fahey*

OUR CHANNEL (USA) 4 ch.g. English Channel (USA) 126 – Raw Gold (USA) 108 **107**
(Rahy (USA) 115) [2015 110: 8.9g⁶ 8g a8f p8g² Dec 19] useful handicapper: easily best
effort of 2015 when sixth at Meydan on first start: stays 1¼m: acts on polytrack, good to
firm and good to soft going: tried in cheekpieces: front runner/races prominently.
William Haggas

OUR ELTON (USA) 2 ch.g. (Feb 22) Speightstown (USA) 124 – Warsaw Ballet (CAN) –
(El Prado (IRE) 119) [2015 6g Aug 6] 40/1, last of 12 in maiden at Haydock. *Tom Dascombe*

OUR FOLLY 7 b.g. Sakhee (USA) 136 – Regent's Folly (IRE) 101 (Touching Wood **74**
(USA) 127) [2015 82: 16m 16g 17.2m² 18d² Aug 20] sturdy gelding: fair handicapper:
stays 2¼m: acts on any turf going: tried in headgear: often wears tongue tie: often races
towards rear. *Stuart Kittow*

OUR GABRIAL (IRE) 8 b.g. Rock of Gibraltar (IRE) 133 – Jojeema (Barathea (IRE) **92 §**
127) [2015 97: 10.3s 12g 14m³ 15.9m² 16.4m 16m⁶ 13g 15.9g 14d t12.2f³ 16d Oct 30]
lengthy gelding: fairly useful handicapper: stays 2m: acts on all-weather and any turf
going: tried in headgear prior to 2015: usually slowly away, often races in rear: best treated
with caution. *Richard Fahey*

OUR GREY LADY 4 gr.f. Proclamation (IRE) 130 – Just Run (IRE) 45 (Runnett 125) –
[2015 59: 5v⁴ t5.1g Aug 27] lightly-raced maiden, modest form at best: raced mainly at 5f:
tried in hood. *Bill Turner*

OUR JOY (IRE) 2 b.f. (Feb 2) Kodiac 112 – Great Joy (IRE) (Grand Lodge (USA) 125) **87**
[2015 5m² 6f t6g⁴ 6.5m³ 7g³ p7g* Oct 29] rather leggy filly: half-sister to very smart
winner up to 1m (stays 1¼m) Xtension (2-y-o 6f/7f winner, by Xaar) and useful 6f winner
A Huge Dream (by Refuse To Bend): dam 7f winner: fairly useful performer: won maiden
at Lingfield (by 2¼ lengths from Intermittent) in October: stays 7f: acts on polytrack and
good to firm going. *Clive Cox*

OUR KYLIE (IRE) 3 b.f. Jeremy (USA) 122 – Prakara (IRE) 53 (Indian Ridge 123) **65**
[2015 66: 10.2m⁶ 12d 9.8d³ 9.9g 10m Jul 21] fair handicapper: stays 1¼m: acts on good to
soft going: often races prominently. *Tony Coyle*

OURLITTLE SENORITA 3 b.f. Fantastic Spain (USA) – Our Little Missy (Sadler's –
Way 74) [2015 12g Jul 30] first foal: dam unraced: 100/1, tailed off in maiden at Ffos Las
on debut. *Miss Imogen Pickard*

OUR LORD 3 gr.g. Proclamation (IRE) 130 – Lady Filly 92 (Atraf 116) [2015 6m p5m⁴ **71**
5g² 5.1m³ Jun 25] fair maiden: best effort at 5f on good ground. *Bill Turner*

OUR MAN PHIL (IRE) 3 ch.c. Dandy Man (IRE) 123 – Drumcliffe Dancer (IRE) 66 **40**
(Footstepsinthesand 120) [2015 64: p8g p8g 7d p8g 7.2d 8m 5.8m⁵ 6g 5.8m 6d p6g p7g **a49**
Nov 6] poor maiden: stays 1m: acts on polytrack and good to firm going: often wears
headgear: tried in tongue tie in 2015: usually races nearer last than first. *John McConnell,
Ireland*

OUR PHYLLI VERA (IRE) 6 b.m. Motivator 131 – With Colour (Rainbow Quest –
(USA) 134) [2015 p13.3m May 12] useful-looking mare: fair handicapper at one time:
blinkered, well held sole start in 2015: stays 10.5f: acts on soft going: sold £4,000 and
joined Joanne Foster. *Alan King*

OUR PLACE IN LOULE 2 ch.g. (Apr 29) Compton Place 125 – Show Off 56 (Efisio **56**
120) [2015 6g 5m 5d Sep 22] modest form at best in maidens. *Noel Wilson*

OUR QUEENIE (IRE) 4 ch.f. Strategic Prince 114 – Matibibi (ITY) (Barathea (IRE) **84 §**
127) [2015 95: 7d p7f⁵ 7.6d p10m² 10.2m⁴ 10g⁶ 8.1g⁴ 8.1m* 9.9g⁵ p7g⁶ Oct 14] smallish
filly: fairly useful handicapper: won at Chepstow in September: stays 1m: acts on polytrack,
good to firm and heavy going: worth a try in headgear: often races lazily: sold 8,000 gns,
sent to Saudi Arabia. *Richard Hannon*

OUR THOMAS (IRE) 3 b.g. Dylan Thomas (IRE) 132 – Sinamay (USA) (Saint Ballado **82**
(CAN)) [2015 9.8g³ 12d² 11.9d³ 12g² Sep 26] fourth foal: half-brother to winner up to 2m
Deepsand (2-y-o 6f winner, by Footstepsinthesand): dam once-raced out of useful 2-y-o
1m/9f winner Chenille: fairly useful maiden: should be suited by further than 1½m: fairly
useful hurdler. *Tim Easterby*

OUR TIME WILL COME (IRE) 3 b.f. Rock of Gibraltar (IRE) 133 – Signorina **76**
Cattiva (USA) 117 (El Gran Senor (USA) 136) [2015 53p: 7s* 8m 9.9g* 10g⁵ 10.3d p11g
Nov 11] fair performer: won maiden at Catterick in May and handicap at Beverley in
August: stays 1¼m: acts on soft going: often races towards rear. *John Quinn*

OUT AND ABOUT (IRE) 2 b.g. (Mar 25) Fastnet Rock (AUS) 127 – Starship (IRE) 89 **96 p**
(Galileo (IRE) 134) [2015 7s⁴ 7g* Oct 3] closely related to several winners, including
smart winner up to 1¼m (stays 1½m) Alexander Pope (2-y-o 7f/1m winner, by Danehill
Dancer) and useful winner up to 1m Bilimbi (2-y-o 7f winner, by Duke of Marmalade):
dam winner up to 8.3f (2-y-o 7f winner): better effort when winning maiden at Redcar (by
1¼ lengths from Colour Me Happy) in October, forging clear: bred to be suited by 1m+:
will go on improving. *William Haggas*

OUTBACK BLUE 2 gr.c. (Mar 2) Aussie Rules (USA) 123 – Beautiful Lady (IRE) 77 **80**
(Peintre Celebre (USA) 137) [2015 6d t8.6m t6f⁴ t7.1f⁶ t7.1f⁴ t7.1g⁴ t7.1m* p7g⁶ Dec 28]
€22,000 2-y-o: third foal: half-brother to 1m winner Practising (by Rail Link): dam, 1½m
winner, half-sister to useful winner up to 8.6f (stayed 1½m) Putra Sas: fairly useful
performer: won maiden at Wolverhampton in December: should stay 1m: acts on tapeta.
David Evans

OUTBACK PRINCESS 2 gr.f. (Jan 21) Aussie Rules (USA) 123 – Royal Assent 56 **51**
(Royal Applause 124) [2015 6d 7.6g 7.6v⁴ Aug 13] 8,000F: second foal: half-sister to 2-y-o
8.6f winner (stays 11.5f) Royal Altitude (by Zamindar): dam once-raced half-sister to
smart winner up to 8.3f Banknote: modest maiden: best effort when fourth at Lingfield.
Gary Moore

OUTBACK RULER (IRE) 3 gr.g. Aussie Rules (USA) 123 – My American Beauty 93 **93**
(Wolfhound (USA) 126) [2015 76: 8.3s⁵ 8.1m* 7d* 7g⁴ 6.1g⁴ 7g⁴ 7m Oct 2] fairly useful
handicapper: won at Chepstow and Haydock (by 1¼ lengths from Swift Approval) in May:
stays 1m: acts on good to firm and good to soft going: has been gelded. *Clive Cox*

OUTBACK TRAVELLER (IRE) 4 b.g. Bushranger (IRE) 119 – Blue Holly (IRE) 83 **110**
(Blues Traveller (IRE) 119) [2015 116: p7g² 7m 7m⁵ 6g³ 7g 7g⁴ 7m Oct 3] compact
gelding: smart handicapper: second at Kempton (head behind Speculative Bid) in April
and fourth at Ascot (2½ lengths behind Majestic Moon) in September: stays 7f: acts on
polytrack and firm going: often races prominently: sold 65,000 gns, then gelded. *Jeremy
Noseda*

OUT DO 6 ch.g. Exceed And Excel (AUS) 126 – Ludynosa (USA) 98 (Cadeaux Genereux **118**
131) [2015 107: 6g* 5m* 5d² 5m⁴ 5m* 5m Jul 31] strong gelding: smart performer: won
handicaps at Pontefract (by 2 lengths from Barkston Ash) in April and York (by neck from
Red Baron) in May and listed race at York (by neck from Monsieur Joe) in July: stays 6f:
acts on polytrack, soft and good to firm going: usually wears visor: held up: often travels
strongly. *David O'Meara*

OUTER SPACE 4 b.g. Acclamation 118 – Venoge (IRE) (Green Desert (USA) 127) [2015 **101**
97: 7m 8m 7m⁴ 7m⁴ 8g 7m p7g* 7g 7g⁵ p8f³ p8g⁴ p7f⁶ p8f³ p7g³ p7f³ Dec 21] strong,
compact gelding: useful performer: won handicap at Kempton (by length from Mulzamm)
in August: held form well, good 3 lengths third to Cold As Ice in minor event at Chelmsford
final start: stays 1m: acts on polytrack, good to firm and good to soft going: often races
towards rear, usually responds generously to pressure. *Jamie Osborne*

OUTLAW KATE (IRE) 3 b.f. Bushranger (IRE) 119 – Diosper (IRE) 64 (Diesis 133) **52**
[2015 –: f6d⁶ 7g 6g 8.3m⁵ 8.1m⁴ 7.1s² 7.4d* Aug 13] modest handicapper: won at Ffos Las
in August: best effort at 7.4f: acts on soft and good to firm going: in cheekpieces last 4
starts. *Michael Mullineaux*

OUTLAW TORN (IRE) 6 ch.g. Iffraaj 127 – Touch And Love (IRE) (Green Desert **75**
(USA) 127) [2015 75: 10.3d 7g 8d 8.3s⁶ 8d 8g* 7m³ 10.1m⁵ 7.9g⁴ 10.1m* 9g⁴ 8m⁴
10.1m³ 8m³ 8.5m² 9.3s² 9.3g⁶ 8.3g³ 9.2m⁶ 10.2v⁴ t9.5f* Oct 23] fair handicapper: won at
Redcar in May, Newcastle in June and Wolverhampton in October: stays 1¼m: acts on
all-weather, firm and soft going: usually wears eyeshields: front runner/races prominently.
Richard Guest

OUT OF ACES 3 ch.c. Piccolo 121 – Subtle Move (USA) 60 (Known Fact (USA) 135) **45**
[2015 34: f7g⁴ p6g t7.1m³ t6m Feb 27] workmanlike colt: poor maiden: in cheekpieces last
2 starts: dead. *Kevin Ryan*

OUT OF THE DARK (IRE) 2 b.f. (Feb 20) Kyllachy 129 – Assumption (IRE) 57 **– p**
(Beckett (IRE) 116) [2015 7m Jun 25] 30,000F, 72,000Y: fourth foal: half-sister to 7f
winners Quan and Elaysa (both by Shamardal): dam, 7f winner, half-sister to very smart
winner up to 6f Kingsgate Native: 9/2, held back by inexperience when tenth of 13 in
maiden at Newbury on debut, not knocked about: will improve. *Richard Hannon*

OUTRAGE 3 ch.g. Exceed And Excel (AUS) 126 – Ludynosa (USA) 98 (Cadeaux Genereux **78 p**
131) [2015 6g 5m* 5d³ Sep 2] 65,000F, 80,000Y: strong gelding: brother to smart 5f-6f
winner Out Do and half-brother to 3 winners, including 6f winner Siren Party (by Pivotal)

and 6f-9f winner Arabian Moonlight (by Barathea): dam 6f/7f winner: fair performer: won maiden at Windsor (by short head from Regal Miss) in August: improved again when third in handicap at Bath, slowly away: best form at 5f: remains with potential. *Daniel Kubler*

OUTRANK 2 ch.c. (Mar 24) Exceed And Excel (AUS) 126 – Lane County (USA) (Rahy (USA) 115) [2015 6g 6.1m⁶ 6s⁴ 6d⁶ 7d* 7m³ p7g t7.1f Oct 20] strong colt: fair performer: won nursery at Leicester in August: stays 7f: acts on good to firm and good to soft going: usually races close up: unreliable. *Mark Johnston* **74 §**

OUTSPOKEN (IRE) 3 b.g. Galileo (IRE) 134 – Riskaverse (USA) 119 (Dynaformer (USA)) [2015 10g* 12g² p10.7d* 14g³ Aug 22] fifth foal: brother to 1½m winner Pink Damsel and smart 9f-1½m winner Say and closely related to useful/moody winner up to 1½m Sadler's Risk (2-y-o 8.3f winner, by Sadler's Wells): dam US Grade 1 9f/1¼m winner: smart form: won maiden at Navan in May and minor event at Dundalk (by 4¼ lengths from Xebec) in July: in first-time cheekpieces, good ½-length third of 18 to Polarisation in Melrose Stakes (Handicap) at York, taking strong hold but keeping on well: stays 1¾m: has been gelded. *Aidan O'Brien, Ireland* **110**

OUTSTANDING (IRE) 3 b.f. Galileo (IRE) 134 – Absolutelyfabulous (IRE) 105 (Mozart (IRE) 131) [2015 80: 8d⁴ 10m* 10f³ 12d 9d 10d⁶ 9.5s³ 8s⁴ Oct 3] smart performer: won maiden at Naas in May and listed race on same course (by 2¾ lengths from Stellar Glow) in June: good 3½ lengths third to Lady Eli in Belmont Oaks in July and creditable 2½ lengths third to Jack Naylor in Denny Cordell Stakes at Gowran in September, carrying head bit awkwardly: excuses when fourth of 11 to Tepin in First Lady Stakes at Keeneland final start, rearing at start and missing break: stays 1¼m: acts on firm and soft going: wore hood sixth/seventh starts: often races towards rear. *Aidan O'Brien, Ireland* **111**

OUTSTRIP 4 gr.c. Exceed And Excel (AUS) 126 – Asi Siempre (USA) 123 (El Prado (IRE) 119) [2015 116: a8f 8g Feb 26] angular colt: smart at best: won Champagne Stakes at Doncaster and Breeders' Cup Juvenile Turf at Santa Anita at 2 yrs: well held in 2015 in Maktoum Challenge Round 1 and Zabeel Mile, both at Meydan: stayed 1m: acts on firm and good to soft going: to stand at Dalham Hall Stud, Newmarket, fee £5,000. *Charlie Appleby* **–**

OVERAGE 3 b.g. Medicean 128 – Quiet Elegance 96 (Fantastic Light (USA) 134) [2015 t6f⁶ f7s⁵ 8m 6g Apr 27] no sign of ability: tried in blinkers (had looked hard ride): dead. *Eric Alston* **–**

OVERHAUGH STREET 2 b.g. (Mar 27) Bahri (USA) 125 – Bom Chicka Wah Wah (USA) (Dynaformer (USA)) [2015 7.2m⁴ 8g 6d³ Oct 26] fair form: dropped in trip, improved when ¾-length third of 13 to Gowanless in maiden at Redcar final start. *Keith Dalgleish* **69**

OVERHEARD (IRE) 3 b.f. Lope de Vega (IRE) 125 – Gutter Press (IRE) 51 (Raise A Grand (IRE) 114) [2015 7g 9g⁴ 8g⁵ 10g 10v⁴ p10f Oct 1] €30,000Y, resold 35,000Y: sturdy filly: fourth foal: half-sister to 7f winner Jackie Love (by Tobougg): dam twice-raced half-sister to very smart winner up to 6f Inxile: fair maiden: stays 1¼m: acts on heavy going: often races prominently. *Jeremy Noseda* **73**

OVERLORD 3 b.g. Lawman (FR) 121 – Hip 88 (Pivotal 124) [2015 53: 8s⁴ 8.3m* 9d 10.4f³ 8.3m 7.1s t9.5f² Oct 3] modest handicapper: won at Nottingham in May: stays 10.5f: acts on tapeta, firm and soft going: tried in blinkers prior to 2015: temperamental. *Mark Rimell* **64 §**

OVERRIDER 5 b.g. Cockney Rebel (IRE) 127 – Fustaan (IRE) 71 (Royal Applause 124) [2015 65: t9.5g p8f⁵ p8m⁴ p8f t9.5m⁶ t12.2f t12.2f⁶ t9.5m⁴ p8g Dec 15] close-coupled gelding: modest handicapper: stays 1¼m: acts on polytrack, tapeta and good to firm going: tried in headgear: usually wears tongue tie: usually leads: not straightforward. *Shaun Lycett* **53**

OVERSTONE LASS (IRE) 3 b.f. Excellent Art 125 – Clinging Vine (USA) 60 (Fusaichi Pegasus (USA) 130) [2015 –: 9.9g 8m 8g 8g 8s Oct 15] poor maiden: best effort at 1m. *John Spearing* **39**

OWER FLY 2 b.g. (Apr 8) Pastoral Pursuits 127 – Contrary Mary 85 (Mujadil (USA) 119) [2015 p5g² 5f* 5m³ 6.1m 5g⁶ Jul 8] fair performer: won maiden at Bath in April: best form at 5f: acts on firm going. *Richard Hannon* **73**

OYSTER PEARL (IRE) 2 gr.f. (Apr 30) Thousand Words 113 – Rectify (IRE) (Mujadil (USA) 119) [2015 7m⁵ t7.1g³ p7g t7.1f t9.5f t9.5f⁵ Nov 30] €3,500Y: sixth foal: half-sister to winner up to 7f Transfixed (by Trans Island) and 6f winner Red Tide (by Tamayuz): dam unraced half-sister to useful winner up to 9f Holtye: modest maiden: best effort at 7f: acts on good to firm going: tried in visor. *David Evans* **59**

P

PABUSAR 7 b.g. Oasis Dream 129 – Autumn Pearl 102 (Orpen (USA) 116) [2015 81: p6m **82** f5g⁵ t6f⁵ f6g⁴ f5g² f5s³ f6g⁶ 5g³ 5m⁴ p5m* p6g⁵ 6d 5g* 5g* 6d⁵ 5m⁴ p5g 5v 5g 5g 5.3s **a73** p5f p6m f5g Dec 15] well-made gelding: fairly useful handicapper: won at Chelmsford in May, Hamilton in June and Ayr in July: left Richard Guest after fourth start: stays 6f: acts on polytrack, good to firm and good to soft going: wears headgear: wears tongue tie: sometimes slowly away, often races in rear. *Heather Dalton*

PACABAG 2 b.f. (Feb 20) Paco Boy (IRE) 129 – Veronica Franco 90 (Darshaan 133) **–** [2015 p7g Dec 20] half-sister to several winners, including useful/temperamental 9.7f-11f winner Franco Is My Name (by Namid) and 7f/1m winner Franco's Secret (by Sakhee's Secret): dam 1½m-2m winner: 33/1/in hood, last of 8 in maiden at Lingfield. *Peter Hedger*

PACCHES (IRE) 2 b.f. (Apr 7) Clodovil (IRE) 116 – Ringarooma 61 (Erhaab (USA) 127) **75** [2015 5f⁷ 5m⁴ 5.2m Jul 18] 23,000Y: rather unfurnished filly: fifth foal: half-sister to winners abroad by Kyllachy and Fast Company: dam 1¼m winner: fair maiden: best effort when second at Windsor on debut. *Mick Channon*

PACHARANA 2 b.f. (Feb 22) Oasis Dream 129 – Cascata (IRE) 86 (Montjeu (IRE) 137) **– p** [2015 8.3g 7d Oct 31] second foal: sister to useful 1¼m-1½m winner Richard of Yorke: dam, 2-y-o 1m winner who stayed 1½m, sister to high-class winner up to 13.4f St Nicholas Abbey (behind in maidens at Windsor and Newmarket (still needed experience): should do better in time. *Luca Cumani*

PACIFICA (IRE) 2 b.f. (Feb 3) Aqlaam 125 – Raggiante (IRE) (Rock of Gibraltar (IRE) **43** 133) [2015 5f p5m⁶ 6g 7g p8g Nov 11] 14,000Y: first foal: dam, Italian 6f winner, half-sister to high-class 1m-1¼m winner Arod: poor maiden: stays 1m: acts on polytrack: often races prominently. *Nick Littmoden*

PACIFIC SALT (IRE) 2 gr.c. (Jan 23) Zebedee 113 – Villa Nova (IRE) 55 (Petardia 113) **– p** [2015 6d Oct 12] 210,000Y: half-brother to several winners, including 1¼m winner Six of Diamonds (by Redback), later successful in Hong Kong, and winner up to 8.5f Prince of Denmark (2-y-o 5f-1m winner, by Danetime), both useful: dam maiden (best at 1m/9f): 7/2, well held in maiden at Windsor won by Fighting Temeraire: will prove different proposition in time. *Roger Charlton*

PACIFY 3 b.g. Paco Boy (IRE) 129 – Supereva (IRE) (Sadler's Wells (USA) 132) [2015 **103** 79p: 8.3g² 9m³ 10m² 10m* 10.4g⁴ 10s⁵ 10.3d² Oct 23] useful-looking gelding: useful handicapper: won at Newmarket (by 10 lengths from Resonant) in July: best effort when 2¾ lengths second to Classic Collection at Doncaster final start: worth a try at 1½m: acts on polytrack, soft and good to firm going. *Ralph Beckett*

PACKED HOUSE 3 b.f. Azamour (IRE) 130 – Riotous Applause 104 (Royal Applause **58** 124) [2015 57p: p7m p7f³ p8g⁴ Feb 26] modest maiden: stays 1m: acts on polytrack: visored last 2 starts, also in tongue tie in latter: often starts slowly: temperament under suspicion. *Ralph Beckett*

PACKING EMPIRE (IRE) 2 b.g. (Mar 21) Holy Roman Emperor (IRE) 125 – Ceoil An **–** Aith (IRE) 81 (Accordion) [2015 f7m p7f p7g Dec 28] 66/1, well held in 3 maidens in December. *Jamie Osborne*

PACKING (IRE) 2 b.c. (Mar 25) Lilbourne Lad (IRE) 111 – Elegant Ridge (IRE) 102 **58 p** (Indian Ridge 123) [2015 p6g p6g p6g⁵ t5.1m Dec 12] 32,000Y: half-brother to very smart winner up to 1m Montiridge (2-y-o 7f winner, by Ramonti) and a winner in USA by High Yield: dam German/US 6.5f-8.5f winner: modest form in maidens: unsuited by drop in trip final start: remains capable of better. *Jamie Osborne*

PACK IT IN (IRE) 2 br.g. (Mar 14) Big Bad Bob (IRE) 118 – Evening Dress 65 **–** (Medicean 128) [2015 7g 7g 8s Oct 23] behind in maidens at Newbury (2) and Doncaster: should stay at least 1m. *Brian Meehan*

PACK LEADER (IRE) 4 b.g. Hurricane Run (IRE) 134 – Bright Enough 78 (Fantastic **90** Light (USA) 134) [2015 p11g⁶ 12m 14g 10f⁶ 12.1d⁴ 10.1v⁵ 12d Sep 27] lengthy gelding: fairly useful handicapper: stays 1½m: acts on polytrack, good to firm and heavy going: tried in headgear: often races prominently: sold 7,000 gns, sent to Italy. *Amanda Perrett*

PACK TOGETHER 3 b.f. Paco Boy (IRE) 129 – New Assembly (IRE) 99 (Machiavellian **105** (USA) 123) [2015 96p: 8m⁶ 8f 8.1m⁶ 8g³ 7m² p8g⁵ 7s³ p7.5g Dec 27] sturdy filly: useful performer: raced in listed company in 2015, placed at Newmarket, Ascot and Fontainebleau (close third to Siyoushake, leading till last 50 yds): below form at Deauville final outing: stays 1m: acts on soft and good to firm going: used to race towards rear, but more prominent last 2 starts. *Richard Hannon*

PACNGO 3 b.f. Paco Boy (IRE) 129 – Orange Pip 89 (Bold Edge 123) [2015 62: 5g 6d 5g⁴ **70** 5g* 5m³ 5.1d² 5s* 5d⁵ 5g Sep 17] fair handicapper: won at Thirsk (apprentice) in July and Carlisle in August: best form at 5f: acts on soft and good to firm going: in hood last 5 starts: tried in tongue tie in 2015: often races towards rear. *Tim Easterby*

PACOLITA (IRE) 3 ch.f. Paco Boy (IRE) 129 – Clara (IRE) (In The Wings 128) [2015 **77** 69: p7m⁶ 8.3f 7g* 7.1g² 8.1g² 10.1g³ 7s* 7g p8f⁴ p7g p6m p7g* Dec 28] good-topped filly: fair handicapper: won at Epsom in July, Leicester (apprentice) in September and Lingfield in December: should stay 1m: acts on polytrack, tapeta and soft going. *Sylvester Kirk*

PACOMMAND 2 b.c. (Apr 28) Paco Boy (IRE) 129 – Indian Story (IRE) (Indian Ridge **72** 123) [2015 p7g⁶ t7.1g⁴ p8f⁴ Dec 21] fair maiden: best effort when fourth at Chelmsford (5 lengths behind Cape Speed) final start. *Marco Botti*

PACO PAT 2 b.c. (Feb 12) Paco Boy (IRE) 129 – Tanwir 76 (Unfuwain (USA) 131) [2015 **48 p** p8g p8g p6g⁴ Dec 16] half-brother to several winners, including useful Italian/Slovakian 1m-1¼m winner Sakheart (by Sakhee) and 8.6f winner Libritish (by Librettist): dam, 1½m winner, out of half-sister to 1000 Guineas winner Harayir: showed a little ability in maidens: will benefit from return to at least 1m: capable of better. *Richard Hannon*

PACO'S DREAM 3 b.f. Paco Boy (IRE) 129 – Isle of Flame (Shirley Heights 130) [2015 **42** 51: p10g p10d⁴ p10g³ 11.7f Apr 23] angular filly: poor maiden: stays 1¼m: acts on polytrack and good to firm going: often in headgear prior to 2015: often races towards rear. *Harry Dunlop*

PACO'S SUNSHINE (IRE) 3 b.f. Paco Boy (IRE) 129 – Nuage Irise (Rainbow Quest **60** (USA) 134) [2015 68: 6g⁵ 5g 5.1g⁶ 5g 6d³ 5g 5s Oct 27] modest maiden: stays 6f: acts on good to firm and good to soft going: tried in hood. *Brian Ellison*

PACT 3 b.f. Paco Boy (IRE) 129 – Jade Pet 90 (Petong 126) [2015 –: 6m 7s⁵ p6f⁵ Nov 6] – angular filly: no form: in cheekpieces final start. *Lee Carter*

PACTOLUS (IRE) 4 b.g. Footstepsinthesand 120 – Gold Marie (IRE) 92 (Green Desert **88** (USA) 127) [2015 79: p7g⁴ p7g* p7f p8g⁵ 7.1g⁴ p8g* p8f⁵ p8g⁶ t9.5g* p10g* Dec 10] tall, useful-looking gelding: fairly useful handicapper: won at Lingfield in February, Chelmsford in August and at Wolverhampton (apprentice) and Chelmsford in December: stays 1¼m: acts on polytrack and tapeta: usually in hood in 2015, also in tongue tie last 3 starts: races towards rear. *Stuart Williams*

PADDY POWER (IRE) 2 ch.g. (Apr 7) Pivotal 124 – Rag Top (IRE) 101 (Barathea **87** (IRE) 127) [2015 5m⁶ 5d⁵ 5m² 5m³ Aug 10] €40,000F: smallish, good-quartered gelding: seventh foal: half-brother to 3 winners, including 2-y-o 6f winners Brick Tops (by Danehill Dancer) and Ragsta (by Key of Luck): dam 2-y-o 5f-7f winner: fairly useful maiden: easily best effort when second at Newcastle in June: raced only at 5f. *Richard Fahey*

PADDYS MOTORBIKE (IRE) 3 ch.g. Fast Company (IRE) 126 – Saffa Garden (IRE) **97** 49 (King's Best (USA) 132) [2015 83: 10d* 8.9s 10.3d⁴ p11g⁴ p12g² Dec 19] useful handicapper: won at Leicester (by 3¾ lengths from Belgrade) in April: stays 1½m: acts on polytrack and heavy going. *David Evans*

PADDY'S ROCK (IRE) 4 b.g. Whipper (USA) 126 – Hedera (USA) 90 (Woodman **76** (USA) 126) [2015 73: t12.2f⁶ 12.4g 11.1s⁶ 8.3d² 9.3s² 8.3s² Jul 11] rangy, quite attractive gelding: fair handicapper: stays 1¼m: acts on soft going: often wears headgear. *Lynn Siddall*

PADDYS RUNNER 3 gr.g. Sir Percy 129 – Frosty Welcome (USA) 105 (With Approval **85** (CAN)) [2015 –: 11.5d⁴ 10m⁶ 14.1m³ 12.1m² p14f⁵ 16d⁴ Oct 30] good-topped gelding: fairly useful maiden: barely stays 2m: acts on soft and good to firm going: fairly useful hurdler. *Alan King*

PADLOCK (IRE) 3 br.c. Key of Luck (USA) 126 – Rumuz (IRE) 67 (Marju (IRE) 127) **92** [2015 83: a7f⁶ a8f 6d a6f² Dec 3] fairly useful performer: second in handicap at Meydan in December: left David Simcock after third start: will benefit from return to 7f: acts on fibresand and dirt: tried in headgear in 2015. *D. Watson, UAE*

PAGEANT BELLE 4 ch.f. Bahamian Bounty 116 – Procession 72 (Zafonic (USA) 130) **76** [2015 86: p7f 7g⁵ 8m⁴ 7m⁵ 7g* 7g³ 8g⁶ 7s Oct 16] fair handicapper: won at Doncaster in August: stays 1m: acts on polytrack and good to firm going: sometimes slowly away, often races in rear. *Kristin Stubbs*

PAGE OF WANDS 2 b.f. (Mar 30) Multiplex 114 – No Page (IRE) 81 (Statue of Liberty – (USA) 115) [2015 t8.6g Dec 5] second foal: sister to 7f/1m winner Rocco's Delight: dam 2-y-o 6f winner: 100/1, well held in maiden at Wolverhampton. *Karen McLintock*

PAINTED CLIFFS (IRE) 2 b.c. (Jan 25) Canford Cliffs (IRE) 133 – Lulawin (Kyllachy **107**
129) [2015 6g 6g* 6m* 6g⁴ 7d⁵ Sep 13] 100,000€, €200,000Y: angular colt: second foal:
half-brother to winner up to 1m Rockaroundtheclock (2-y-o 7f winner, by Starspangledbanner): dam unraced close relative to high-class miler Excellent Art: useful performer:
won maiden at Leopardstown and Railway Stakes at the Curragh (by 2¾ lengths from
Rockaway Valley) in June: not disgraced behind Air Force Blue in Phoenix Stakes and
National Stakes at the Curragh last 2 starts: may prove best at sprint trips: acts on good to
firm and good to soft going: in blinkers last 4 starts: usually races close up. *Aidan O'Brien,
Ireland*

PAINT THE STAR (IRE) 3 b.f. Acclamation 118 – Art Work 83 (Zafonic (USA) 130) **84**
[2015 79p: 6m³ 6d³ 6f² p6m* 6g* 6g⁶ Jul 27] sturdy filly: fairly useful performer: won
maiden at Lingfield and minor event at Pontefract in June: stays 6f: acts on polytrack and
firm going: usually leads. *Richard Hannon*

PALACE MOON 10 b.g. Fantastic Light (USA) 134 – Palace Street (USA) 103 (Secreto **70 §**
(USA) 128) [2015 91§: p8g p7g⁵ p8g 6m p10g p7g p8g Dec 30] tall, lengthy gelding: fair
handicapper: left William Knight after fifth start: stays 1m: acts on polytrack and good to
firm going: usually wears tongue tie: unreliable. *Michael Attwater*

PALACE PRINCE (GER) 3 b.c. Areion (GER) 115 – Palace Princess (GER) (Tiger Hill **116**
(IRE) 127) [2015 8g⁶ 9.9g* 11.9g² 10.2g* 11.9g⁴ 10d Oct 17] useful-looking colt: second
foal: closely related to German 9.5f winner Palace Secret (by Big Shuffle): dam, German
1m/8.5f winner, half-sister to smart German milers Pepperstorm and Peppercorn: smart
performer: won listed race at Compiegne (awarded race after finishing ½-length second to
demoted Zafira) in June and Grosser Preis der Sparkasse Krefeld at Krefeld (by head from
Iquitos) in August: second in Deutsches Derby at Hamburg (5 lengths behind Nutan) in
between: good fourth in Grosser Preis von Baden at Baden-Baden (3½ lengths behind
Prince Gibraltar) in September: stiff task when 1¼ lengths ninth to Fascinating Rock in
Champion Stakes at Ascot final outing: stays 1½m: acts on good to soft going. *Andreas
Lowe, Germany*

PALADIN (IRE) 6 b.g. Dubawi (IRE) 129 – Palwina (FR) (Unfuwain (USA) 131) [2015 **77**
f8d² f8d² t7.1g² 7.4d* 8.5v 8.1m Sep 10] quite attractive gelding: fair handicapper: won at
Ffos Las in August: stays 1m: acts on fibresand and good to soft going: front runner/races
prominently. *Dominic Ffrench Davis*

PALAWAN 2 b.c. (Feb 22) Mount Nelson 125 – Apple Sauce 70 (Prince Sabo 123) [2015 **103**
6m⁵ 7f⁴ 7m* 7m³ 7g³ 7d³ 7s* 7d³ Sep 12] 6,500F, €27,000Y: rather unfurnished colt: half-
brother to 3 winners, including winner up to 6f Steelcut (2-y-o 5f winner, by Iron Mask):
dam, 5f winner, half-sister to smart sprinter Sizzling Melody: useful performer: won
maiden at Salisbury in July and 3-runner minor event at Goodwood (by 5 lengths) in
September: best effort when ¾-length third to Galileo Gold in Vintage Stakes at Goodwood
fifth outing: will stay 1m: acts on soft and good to firm going. *Richard Hannon*

PALENVILLE (IRE) 2 ch.f. (Apr 21) Rip Van Winkle (IRE) 134 – Faithful Duchess **76**
(IRE) 70 (Bachelor Duke (USA) 122) [2015 5m 6m* 6f Jun 19] £22,000F: workmanlike
filly: second foal: half-sister to a winner in Poland by Cockney Rebel: dam, ungenuine
maiden (stayed 6f), half-sister to very smart winner up to 7f Etlaala: fair performer: best
effort when winning maiden at Newmarket (by 1¼ lengths from Blossomtime) in May:
stiff task/met some trouble final outing: will be suited by 7f+. *Richard Hannon*

PALERMA 4 b.f. Shamardal (USA) 129 – West Lorne (USA) 60 (Gone West (USA)) **85**
[2015 86: 10.2f* 12g⁶ 9.9m³ 9.9m⁴ 12.4m⁴ Jul 25] tall filly: fairly useful handicapper:
won at Bath in April: stays 1½m: acts on firm going: front runner/races prominently.
Mick Channon

PALIMONY (IRE) 3 b.f. Oasis Dream 129 – Palmeraie (USA) (Lear Fan (USA) 130) **70**
[2015 8g⁴ 19.5g⁴ Aug 27] half-sister to numerous winners, including 1¼m-12.5f winner
Policy Maker (by Sadler's Wells), winner up to 15.5f Pushkin (2-y-o 1m winner, by
Caerleon) and 1¼m-1½m winner Place Rouge (by Desert King), all smart: dam once-raced
half-sister to dam of Peintre Celebre: fair form when fourth in maidens at Salisbury and
Wolverhampton. *David Lanigan*

PALING 2 b.c. (Feb 21) Zamindar (USA) 116 – Solar Pursuit (Galileo (IRE) 134) [2015 **87 p**
p8d p7g* Oct 7] first foal: dam, French 13f winner on only start, half-sister to very smart
French 1¼m-13f winner Polish Summer and to dam of very smart performer up to 14.6f
Snow Sky: better effort when winning maiden at Kempton (beaten nose by Blue Humor but
awarded race after carried left final 1f) in October: bred to stay at least 1¼m: open to
further improvement. *Roger Charlton*

Qatar Racing Limited's "Pallasator"

PALISADE 2 b.c. (Apr 12) Fastnet Rock (AUS) 127 – Portal 108 (Hernando (FR) 127) **66 p**
[2015 t8.6f⁶ 8.5m 8.3d Oct 14] fourth foal: half-brother to 1½m-16.5f winner Porcini (by
Azamour) and smart winner up to 1½m Windshear (2-y-o 1m winner, by Hurricane Run):
dam winner up to 1¼m (2-y-o 7f winner) who stayed 1½m: fair maiden: best effort when
sixth at Wolverhampton on debut: bred to be suited by 1¼m+: should do better. *Sir Mark
Prescott Bt*

PALLASATOR 6 b.g. Motivator 131 – Ela Athena 119 (Ezzoud (IRE) 126) [2015 121: **115**
16f 16m⁴ 13.3d⁴ 18m* 16d⁴ Oct 17] big gelding: smart performer: won Doncaster Cup
at Doncaster in September by ¾ length from Clondaw Warrior: creditable efforts when
3 lengths fourth to Big Orange in Goodwood Cup second start and 4¾ lengths fourth to
Flying Officer in Long Distance Cup at Ascot (hampered 2f out) final outing: stays 2¼m:
acts on polytrack, soft and good to firm going: tends to prove troublesome in preliminaries/
on way to post. *Sir Mark Prescott Bt*

PALLISTER 3 b.g. Pivotal 124 – Punctilious 117 (Danehill (USA) 126) [2015 90: 10d⁶ **105**
8.1m 8.1g³ 8d³ 8d* Oct 5] well-made gelding: useful handicapper: further improvement
when winning by 1¼ lengths from Volunteer Point at Pontefract in October: should stay
1¼m: acts on good to firm and good to soft going. *Charlie Appleby*

PALMERSTON 2 b.c. (Jan 12) Oasis Dream 129 – Marywell 87 (Selkirk (USA) 129) **77**
[2015 p7g⁴ p8f³ p8f Dec 21] fair maiden: best effort when third in maiden at Lingfield (6¼
lengths behind Brave Hero) in November: should be suited by 1¼m+. *John Gosden*

PALMETTO DUNES (USA) 2 b.c. (Jan 25) First Defence (USA) 119 – Gainful (USA) **85**
(Gone West (USA)) [2015 7g³ 7d² 7g Aug 21] third foal: half-brother to useful French
winner up to 8.5f Dornoch (2-y-o 6f winner) and French 9f winner Re Employ (both by

Mizzen Mast): dam, useful French 2-y-o 1m winner, half-sister to smart Australian performer up to 1½m Index Linked: fairly useful form: second to Whiskey Sour in maiden at Galway in July: well held in similar event at York final start. *D. K. Weld, Ireland*

PALMINA 2 ch.f. (Apr 20) Bahamian Bounty 116 – Starfleet 66 (Inchinor 119) [2015 t6f Nov 14] £17,000Y: sister to useful winner up to 1m (US Grade 2) Mr Napper Tandy (2-y-o 7f winner) and half-sister to 3 winners, including useful 1m-1¼m winner Wind Star (by Piccolo): dam maiden: 16/1, shaped as if needed experience when eighth in maiden at Wolverhampton (5 lengths behind Prisom) in November: should do better. *Dean Ivory*   **51 p**

PAL OF THE CAT 5 ch.g. Choisir (AUS) 126 – Evenstorm (USA) 60 (Stephen Got Even (USA) 125) [2015 90: 6g p5g Dec 10] lengthy gelding: fairly useful at best, no form in 2015: best form at 5f: acts on firm going: usually wears headgear: sometimes wears tongue tie: usually leads. *Brian Gubby*   **–**

PALOMA DANCER 3 b.f. Refuse To Bend (IRE) 128 – Anapola (GER) (Polish Precedent 131) [2015 57: f8g3 7.1m6 p6g 5g5 8.2g4 7m 7d 7d 8d p12.4g p12.4g Dec 27] modest maiden: left Harry Dunlop after fourth start, Mme G. Rarick after ninth: stays 1m: acts on fibresand and soft going. *Mlle C. Comte, France*   **59**

PALPITATION (IRE) 2 b.g. (May 10) Fast Company (IRE) 126 – Sensation 114 (Soviet Star (USA) 128) [2015 5g5 6.1m p6g6 5m 5g5 p6f3 7d6 Oct 16] modest maiden: should stay at least 7f: acts on polytrack and good to firm going: tried in cheekpieces. *David Brown*   **62**

PALUS SAN MARCO (IRE) 6 b.g. Holy Roman Emperor (IRE) 125 – Kylemore (IRE) (Sadler's Wells (USA) 132) [2015 80, a66: 11.9f6 Jun 11] close-coupled gelding: fair handicapper: in first-time cheekpieces, ran moody race only outing in 2015: stays 1½m: acts on soft going: sometimes in hood: has worn tongue tie: often starts slowly, usually races in rear. *Jennie Candlish*   **–**

PAMONA (IRE) 3 b.f. Duke of Marmalade (IRE) 132 – Palanca 99 (Inchinor 119) [2015 96p: 10m3 12f3 10.4m3 9.9m 9.9d2 11.9v Nov 21] lengthy, useful-looking filly: useful performer: third in listed race at Newbury (4 lengths behind Crystal Zvezda) in May, Ribblesdale Stakes at Royal Ascot (5 lengths behind Curvy) in June and in listed race at York (6 lengths behind French Dressing) in July, and second in listed race at Saint-Cloud (2½ lengths behind Stone Roses) in November: stays 1½m: acts on firm and good to soft going. *Luca Cumani*   **103**

PAMUSHANA (IRE) 3 b.f. Teofilo (IRE) 126 – Singitta (Singspiel (IRE) 133) [2015 71: 8g2 10.4g4 10d4 10.4m3 9.3d* 10.2d3 10.4g 10g3 12g2 10d4 Oct 19] rather sparely-made filly: fairly useful performer: won maiden at Carlisle in July: stays 1½m: acts on good to firm and good to soft going: tried in visor in 2015: front runner/races prominently: consistent. *Richard Fahey*   **82**

PANAMA HAT 4 ch.g. Medicean 128 – Street Style (IRE) 83 (Rock of Gibraltar (IRE) 133) [2015 120: 14d5 14g2 14m6 12g* 13.5f2 12d2 p10.7g* Oct 2] smart performer: won listed race at Roscommon (by length from Altesse) in July and Diamond Stakes at Dundalk (by length from Carla Bianca) in October: second in listed race at Leopardstown (½ length behind Kingfisher), American St Leger Stakes at Arlington (¾ length behind Lucky Speed) and Enterprise Stakes at Leopardstown (6 lengths behind Fascinating Rock): stays 1¾m: acts on polytrack, firm and good to soft going: usually wears headgear. *Andrew Oliver, Ireland*   **113**

PANCAKE DAY 3 b.c. Mullionmileanhour (IRE) 116 – Fangfoss Girls 68 (Monsieur Bond (IRE) 120) [2015 53, a60: t5.1f4 f5g4 f6d* f6d5 5d 5g3 f6d 5.1g 5d* 6m 5d4 6g 6d p6f2 6d f6g6 t6m6 Dec 12] fair handicapper: won at Southwell in January and Leicester in June: stays 6f: acts on polytrack, fibresand and good to soft going: sometimes in visor. *Jason Ward*   **69 a62**

PANDAR 6 b.g. Zamindar (USA) 116 – Pagnottella (IRE) (Dansili 127) [2015 92: 5.3d5 6g 5m5 5m5 p6g 6m 6.1m6 5.1s6 6d 5.1d 6s5 6s6 Aug 24] good-topped gelding: fair handicapper: stays 7.5f: acts on polytrack, good to firm and heavy going: tried in headgear/tongue tie: sometimes slowly away. *Milton Bradley*   **71**

PANDA SPIRIT (USA) 3 b.f. Invincible Spirit (IRE) 121 – Towanda (USA) 65 (Dynaformer (USA)) [2015 89: 7m 8.3g4 7m6 Jul 23] fairly useful handicapper: stays 8.5f: acts on polytrack and good to firm going: often races prominently. *Sir Michael Stoute*   **82**

PANDORA (IRE) 3 ch.f. Galileo (IRE) 134 – Song of My Heart (IRE) 107 (Footstepsinthesand 120) [2015 10.3d* 10.4g3 12f 12g Aug 1] first foal: dam, 2-y-o 6f winner, closely related to very smart 6f winner Lightning Moon: useful form: won maiden at Doncaster in March by 1¼ lengths from Captain Navarre: easily best effort when third in Musidora Stakes at York (2¾ lengths behind Star of Seville): raced freely last 2 starts, and should prove suited by a return to 1¼m. *Charles Hills*   **100**

PANDORICA 7 b.m. Indesatchel (IRE) 120 – Hope Chest 70 (Kris 135) [2015 10.2m³ **56** May 1] leggy mare: modest handicapper: stays 12.5f: acts on good to firm and heavy going: often wears cheekpieces. *Bernard Llewellyn*

PANKO (IRE) 2 b.c. (Apr 8) Iffraaj 127 – Engraving (Sadler's Wells (USA) 132) [2015 **– p** 7.1s p7g p7g Oct 29] €58,000F, 70,000Y: tall, useful-looking colt: fifth foal: half-brother to 6f (at 2 yrs) and 1m (in France) winner Ladykin (by Holy Roman Emperor) and useful Italian winner up to 11f Virtual Game (2-y-o 7.5f/1m winner, by Kheleyf): dam, unraced, closely related to smart French winner up to 1½m Kocab: no form in maidens: looks type to do better at 3 yrs. *Ed de Giles*

PANOPTICON 4 ch.f. Lucky Story (USA) 128 – Barnacla (IRE) 83 (Bluebird (USA) 125) [2015 t8.6m Aug 21] sister to 6f winner Milldown Story and half-sister to 3 winners, including useful 2-y-o 6f winner Dutch Supreme (by Dutch Art), later successful abroad: dam 6f winner: well beaten in bumpers, and in maiden at Wolverhampton. *Giles Bravery*

PANTHER PATROL (IRE) 5 b.g. Tagula (IRE) 116 – Quivala (USA) (Thunder Gulch **82** (USA) 129) [2015 92: 6m² 6m 6gᶠ May 23] smallish gelding: fairly useful handicapper: stays 6f: acts on polytrack and firm going: often wears headgear. *Eve Johnson Houghton*

PAPA LUIGI (IRE) 2 b.c. (Apr 18) Zoffany (IRE) 121 – Namaadhej (USA) (Swain (IRE) **80** 134) [2015 6.1d² 6.5m⁶ 6m³ 6g² 7g 6d² 6s⁴ Sep 13] €51,000F, €85,000Y: good-topped colt: first foal: dam, French maiden, sister to French/US 1m winner Makaan and French winner up to 1½m Almail (both useful): fairly useful maiden: stays 6f: acts on good to firm going. *Richard Hannon*

PAPOU TONY 2 b.g. (Mar 20) Raven's Pass (USA) 133 – Lukrecia (IRE) 104 (Exceed **–** And Excel (AUS) 126) [2015 7g p8d Sep 4] useful-looking gelding: behind in maidens at Salisbury and Kempton. *George Baker*

PARADISE FOUND 4 b.f. Pastoral Pursuits 127 – Crochet (IRE) (Mark of Esteem (IRE) **–** 137) [2015 p8g⁴ Jan 22] £400Y: fifth foal: half-sister to useful winner up to 1¼m Gworn (2-y-o 8.6f winner, by Aussie Rules): dam unraced sister to 1m/9f winner Needlecraft and half-sister to 1m-10.5f winner Fractional (both smart in France): 66/1, last of 4 in minor event at Chelmsford. *Pat Eddery*

PARADISE PALM 2 ch.f. (Jan 29) Sakhee's Secret 128 – Akathea (Barathea (IRE) 127) **60** [2015 t6m⁵ Dec 30] 2,000Y: fifth foal: dam, of little account, half-sister to smart performer up to 1½m Ela-Aristokrati: 66/1, green when fifth in maiden at Wolverhampton (1¾ lengths behind dead-heaters Miss Phillyjinks and Murdanova) on debut, never nearer. *Andi Brown*

PARADISE SPECTRE 8 b.g. Firebreak 125 – Amber's Bluff 80 (Mind Games 121) **59** [2015 56, a69: t7.1m⁵ 7pg t6g⁶ 6m⁴ 6g⁵ p6g 8g t7.1f t7.1m Dec 30] strong, good-bodied gelding: modest handicapper: seemingly stays 1m: acts on polytrack, tapeta, good to firm and heavy going: wears headgear: sometimes slowly away, often races towards rear: none too reliable. *Zoe Davison*

PARAFIN YOUNG 2 ch.g. (Mar 11) Cape Blanco (IRE) 130 – Hasty (IRE) 90 (Invincible **–** Spirit (IRE) 121) [2015 6g 5m⁶ 7g p7g Sep 23] rather unfurnished gelding: well held in maidens/nursery. *Peter Chapple-Hyam*

PARANORMAL (IRE) 2 b.c. (Feb 21) Pivotal 124 – Clairvoyance (IRE) 107 (Shamardal **– p** (USA) 129) [2015 p8m⁵ Dec 16] first foal: dam 6f-8.5f winner: 7/1, 13 lengths fifth of 8 to Hombre Rojo in maiden at Lingfield on debut, no extra after short of room 2f out: open to improvement. *Saeed bin Suroor*

PARIS CARVER (FR) 3 b.f. Monsieur Bond (IRE) 120 – Rose of Coma (IRE) 60 **–** (Kheleyf (USA) 116) [2015 61: p7m Jan 14] modest maiden: well held in claimer only start in 2015: best effort at 7f: acts on tapeta: often races in rear. *Jonathan Portman*

PARISH HALL (IRE) 6 b.h. Teofilo (IRE) 126 – Halla Siamsa (IRE) 89 (Montjeu (IRE) **115** 137) [2015 116: p10.7g² 10d* 10v² 10.5g² 10g² 10m² Jun 28] quite attractive horse: smart performer: won listed race at the Curragh in April by 2 lengths from Loch Garman: runner-up 3 times at the Curragh subsequently, in Mooresbridge Stakes (1¼ lengths behind Fascinating Rock), listed race (neck behind Postulation) and International Stakes (3 ran, beaten 1¼ lengths by Air Pilot): stays 1½m: acts on polytrack, good to firm and heavy going: often in tongue tie in 2014: often races towards rear/travels strongly. *J. S. Bolger, Ireland*

PARISH (IRE) 3 b.g. Dark Angel (IRE) 113 – Penicuik (Hernando (FR) 127) [2015 68p: **66**
8.3g⁶ 8.3d⁶ 8d⁵ Jul 7] good-topped gelding: fair maiden: stays 8.5f: acts on heavy going:
tried in cheekpieces in 2015. *Roger Varian*

PARISIANNA 2 b.f. (Apr 17) Champs Elysees 124 – Simianna 101 (Bluegrass Prince **–**
(IRE) 110) [2015 5.1m p7g t6m⁶ Dec 18] 5,000Y: sixth foal: closely related to useful 2-y-o
6f winner Mortitia (by Dansili): dam winner up to 6f (2-y-o 5f winner): no form: left David
Barron after first start. *Richard Fahey*

PARISIAN PYRAMID (IRE) 9 gr.g. Verglas (IRE) 118 – Sharadja (IRE) (Doyoun 124) **63**
[2015 81: f7d⁶ t6g⁶ f6g⁴ 5.1m 9g p7m Nov 21] sturdy gelding: modest handicapper: left Jo
Hughes after fifth start: stays 7f: acts on good to firm and heavy going: usually in headgear:
tried in tongue tie: often races towards rear. *Lee Carter*

PARIS MAGIC 2 b.c. (Feb 15) Champs Elysees 124 – Belgooree 51 (Haafhd 129) [2015 **88 p**
t9.5f² p8g³ Dec 16] 22,000F, 20,000G: second foal: dam, lightly raced, out of half-sister to
very smart 1¼m-1½m performer Imperial Dancer: ¾ length second to Soldier In Action in
maiden at Wolverhampton in November, sticking to task and clear of rest: dropped in trip,
below debut form when third in similar event at Kempton, caught out wide throughout: will
stay 1¼m: remains open to improvement. *Hugo Palmer*

PARIS PROTOCOL 2 b.c. (Mar 14) Champs Elysees 124 – Island Vista 92 (Montjeu **98 p**
(IRE) 137) [2015 7.1g³ 7g² 8g* Sep 30] 55,000Y: second foal: dam, 1¼m winner, out of
half-sister to Irish Oaks winner Colorspin, herself dam of Opera House and Kayf Tara:
useful form: upped in trip, improved again when winning maiden at Salisbury in September
by 2¾ lengths from Stargazer, leading approaching final 1f and responding well: will stay
1¼m+: likely to progress further. *Richard Hannon*

PARIS SNOW 5 b.g. Montjeu (IRE) 137 – Snow Key (USA) 103 (Cozzene (USA)) [2015 **85**
88d: t9.5f p12f² t12.2g⁶ 12g³ 14.6m* 14.6d* 13g* 13d* 14.9g⁴ 12v⁴ Aug 31] fairly useful **a67**
handicapper: won 4 times in June, at Doncaster (twice, latter apprentice event), Newmarket
and Hamilton (amateur): stays 14.5f: acts on polytrack, soft and good to firm going: usually
in headgear of late: tried in tongue tie. *Ian Williams*

PARKES AND RIDE (IRE) 2 b.g. (Feb 3) Pivotal 124 – Kaabari (USA) 89 (Seeking **77**
The Gold (USA)) [2015 6g⁵ 6m³ 6g* 7g Dec 29] heat form: third in seller at York in June:
left K. R. Burke, won maiden at Doha in December: stays 6f: tried in headgear. *M. Al Yaqout,
Qatar*

PARKOUR (IRE) 2 b.c. (Feb 5) Holy Roman Emperor (IRE) 125 – School Holidays **91**
(USA) 90 (Harlan's Holiday (USA) 124) [2015 6.1g⁴ p6g⁴ 6d t6f* t6f* Nov 14] 55,000Y:
first foal: dam, 7f winner, half-sister to smart 6f-8.4f winner One More Round: fairly useful
performer: won at Wolverhampton in October (maiden) and November (nursery, further
improvement when beating Rockley Point 3 lengths): raced only at 6f: acts on tapeta.
Jeremy Noseda

PARK PLACE 5 b.g. Beat Hollow 126 – Blend 73 (Zafonic (USA) 130) [2015 t9.5g⁶ **78**
t8.6f³ 8g 8.5g⁵ 8.9g⁵ 10d t9.5f Nov 13] fair handicapper: stays 1½m: acts on tapeta and
heavy going. *John Quinn*

PARLIAMENTARIAN (IRE) 2 b.g. (Feb 14) Dubawi (IRE) 129 – Forum Floozie (NZ) **78 p**
(Danasinga (AUS)) [2015 9d³ Oct 26] fifth foal: half-brother to smart French 1½m winner
Lawspeaker (by Singspiel) and 1¼m winner Controversy (by Elusive Quality): dam,
Australian 6f-1m winner, half-sister to high-class 7f-1½m winner Starcraft: 9/2, shaped
well when 2½ lengths third of 10 to Play Gal in maiden at Redcar, well positioned: has
been gelded: open to improvement. *Charlie Appleby*

PARNELL'S DREAM 3 b.f. Oasis Dream 129 – Kitty O'Shea 115 (Sadler's Wells **82**
(USA) 132) [2015 10m⁶ 10m 10s 11.6g⁵ 11.9d* Sep 25] closely related to 1¼m winner
Lunar Spirit (by Invincible Spirit) and half-sister to several winners, including smart
winner up to 1½m Kissable (2-y-o 7f winner, by Danehill Dancer): dam, 1m winner
(including at 2 yrs), sister to St Leger winner Brian Boru and to dam of Derby/Prix de l'Arc
de Triomphe winner Workforce: fairly useful performer: won handicap at Haydock in
September: likely to stay further than 1½m: acts on good to soft going. *Ralph Beckett*

PAROLE (IRE) 3 ch.g. Mastercraftsman (IRE) 129 – Leniency (IRE) (Cape Cross (IRE) **79**
129) [2015 71p: 10.2s* p11g⁵ 10.2m³ Jul 4] fair handicapper: won at Nottingham in May:
worth another try at beyond 1¼m: acts on soft and good to firm going: front runner/races
prominently. *Hughie Morrison*

PAR THREE (IRE) 4 b.g. Azamour (IRE) 130 – Little Whisper (IRE) 95 (Be My Guest 68
(USA) 126) [2015 p13.3m² p16m* p13f⁴ t16.5g⁴ t16.5g⁴ 14m* 16.2s⁶ 14g* p16g* p12g⁶
p14f² t13.9f Oct 13] fair handicapper: won at Kempton in February, L'Ancresse in May,
Les Landes in May and Chelmsford in June: stays 2m: acts on polytrack, tapeta and good
to firm going: tried in headgear: tried in tongue tie prior to 2015. *Tony Carroll*

PARTNER'S GOLD (IRE) 5 b.g. Red Clubs (IRE) 125 – Unfortunate 55 (Komaite 46
(USA)) [2015 51: 7d 6g⁶ t6g 6d 5s f7m Dec 8] poor maiden: stays 7f: acts on polytrack,
fibresand, good to firm and good to soft going: often wears blinkers: usually slowly away,
often races in rear. *Alan Berry*

PARTY ANIMAL 2 b.f. (Jan 31) Makfi 130 – Party (IRE) 97 (Cadeaux Genereux 131) 57
[2015 t8.6g Sep 29] 60,000Y: third foal: half-sister to 1½m-1¾m winner (stayed 16.4f)
Party Line (by Montjeu) and 1m (in Australia)/11f winner Observational (by Galileo), both
useful: dam 2-y-o 6f/7f winner who stayed 1¼m: 40/1, shaped as if needed experience
when tenth of 11 in maiden at Wolverhampton (5¾ lengths behind Dubai Fashion) in
September. *James Tate*

PARTY PALACE 11 b.m. Auction House (USA) 120 – Lady-Love 70 (Pursuit of Love 41
124) [2015 t13.9f⁵ t16.5g⁶ 13.1m 14.1g⁶ 13.1d⁵ Sep 2] small, sparely-made mare: poor
handicapper: stays 17f: acts on polytrack and tapeta, best turf form on good going or
firmer: tried in cheekpieces prior to 2015. *Stuart Howe*

PARTY ROYAL 5 b.g. Royal Applause 124 – Voliere 102 (Zafonic (USA) 130) [2015 92: 80
p8g t8.6f p10m* 9g 10m 8g* 10g³ 9s t9.5f⁶ Dec 14] tall, angular gelding: fairly useful a74
handicapper: won at Chelmsford in March and Salisbury (amateur) in July: left John Butler
after third start: stays 1¼m: acts on polytrack, good to firm and good to soft going: often in
headgear in 2015: often races towards rear: none too consistent. *Nick Gifford*

PARTY THYME 2 ch.f. (Feb 6) Medicean 128 – Thymesthree (IRE) 63 (Galileo (IRE) 68
134) [2015 6d 7m⁶ 7.5g² 7g⁵ Oct 21] £3,000Y: rather unfurnished filly: first foal: dam
maiden (best effort at 8.6f): fair form in maiden at Beverley and nursery at Newmarket last
2 starts: will be suited by 1m. *Chris Wall*

PASHAN GARH 6 b.g. Anabaa (USA) 130 – Mimisel 92 (Selkirk (USA) 129) [2015 76: –
p8g p11g 7.1g 8.1v⁶ 8v⁴ 10.3d⁵ 7s^bd Oct 12] market leggy gelding: modest maiden on turf,
poor on all-weather: stayed 8.5f: acted on polytrack and heavy going: sometimes wore
headgear: none too consistent: dead. *Pat Eddery*

PASSING DREAM 2 b.f. (Feb 28) Passing Glance 119 – Violet's Walk (Dr Fong (USA) –
128) [2015 p8m p8g Dec 9] third foal: sister to 1m winner Reedcutter and half-sister to 7f
winner Tunnager Grove (by Piccolo): dam unraced: signs of ability in maidens at Lingfield
and Kempton: may do better in time. *Hughie Morrison*

PASSING STAR 4 b.c. Royal Applause 124 – Passing Hour (USA) 80 (Red Ransom –
(USA)) [2015 107: 7g 7g May 30] useful at best, no form in 2015: stays 1m: acts on
polytrack: blinkered final start. *Charles Hills*

PASSIONADA 6 b.m. Avonbridge 123 – Lark In The Park (IRE) 57 (Grand Lodge (USA) 46
125) [2015 66: t6g⁵ 6g t6g² t6g⁴ 5d 6g 6g t5.1f⁵ p5g⁵ Sep 30] modest handicapper: stays a59
6f: acts on polytrack, tapeta, good to firm and good to soft going: tried in headgear: front
runner/races prominently. *Richard Ford*

PASSIONATE APPEAL 3 b.g. Lawman (FR) 121 – Amaryllis (IRE) 71 (Sadler's Wells –
(USA) 132) [2015 58: 14.1g 11.5g⁶ Jun 15] modest maiden: well held in handicaps in
2015: should stay beyond 1¾m: tried in cheekpieces. *Ann Duffield*

PASSIONATEPRINCESS (IRE) 2 b.f. (Mar 29) Elnadim (USA) 128 – Romany 49
Princess (IRE) 97 (Viking Ruler (AUS)) [2015 5d 5m 5m⁴ t6f⁶ t5.1g⁶ Nov 27] €17,000Y:
third foal: half-sister to 2-y-o 7f winner Muradif (by Zebedee): dam winner up to 8.3f
(2-y-o 7f winner): poor maiden: stays 6f: acts on tapeta and good to firm going: tried in
hood. *Ann Duffield*

PASS MUSTER 8 b.g. Theatrical (IRE) 128 – Morning Pride (IRE) 113 (Machiavellian 77
(USA) 123) [2015 16m 16.4m 15.8g² Jul 21] fair handicapper: stays 2m: acts on firm
going. *Philip Kirby*

PASSOVER 4 b.g. Passing Glance 119 – Floriana 61 (Selkirk (USA) 129) [2015 9d⁵ 99
10.2m* 10.1g* 10g* 10.1v⁴ 10.1m⁴ 10v* Oct 24] tall gelding: useful gelding: won at
Nottingham (amateur) and Epsom (apprentice) in July, Sandown (amateur) in August and
Newbury (by 8 lengths from Silvery Moon, easily best effort) in October: stays 1¼m: acts
on good to firm and heavy going: in hood last 6 starts: often wears tongue tie: front runner/
races prominently. *Andrew Balding*

PASS THE MOON (IRE) 2 ch.f. (Mar 12) Raven's Pass (USA) 133 – Dubai Moon   **64**
(USA) 77 (Malibu Moon (USA)) [2015 p5m² 5g³ p6g⁵ 6d⁴ 6.1m⁶ p7f⁴ p8g t7.1m Sep 14]
20,000Y: smallish filly: first foal: dam, third at 7f at 2 yrs on only start, sister to smart
US Grade 1 1¼m winner Funny Moon: modest maiden: stays 7f: acts on polytrack:
sometimes in hood: tried in tongue tie: often races prominently. *Hugo Palmer*

PAST MASTER 2 gr.c. (Apr 26) Mastercraftsman (IRE) 129 – Millestan (IRE) 91   **86**
(Invincible Spirit (IRE) 121) [2015 7.1g³ 8g⁴ Sep 30] compact colt: third foal: half-brother
to 6f winner Seraphima (by Fusaichi Pegasus) and 8.3f winner Weetles (by High
Chaparral): dam, 1m (at 2 yrs)/8.5f (in USA) winner, half-sister to smart winner up to 7f
Seeking Magic: promising third of 10 to Stormy Antarctic in maiden at Sandown in August
on debut, finishing well: upped in trip, disappointing in similar event at Salisbury next
time: should stay 1m. *Henry Candy*

PASTORAL DANCER 6 b.g. Pastoral Pursuits 127 – Dancing Flame 60 (Groom Dancer   –
(USA) 128) [2015 51: p7m p8g p6g p6g Aug 18] plain gelding: poor maiden: stays 7f: acts
on polytrack: tried in tongue tie. *Richard Rowe*

PASTORAL GIRL 3 b.f. Pastoral Pursuits 127 – Talampaya (USA) (Elusive Quality   **93**
(USA)) [2015 93: 6.1s² 8g 6f 6m 6.1g 6m Aug 16] unfurnished filly: fairly useful
performer: easily best effort of 2015 when second in listed race at Nottingham (1¼ lengths
behind Newsletter) in May: stays 6f: acts on soft and good to firm going: tried in blinkers
in 2015. *James Given*

PASTORAL PLAYER 8 b.g. Pastoral Pursuits 127 – Copy-Cat 60 (Lion Cavern (USA)   **95 §**
117) [2015 97: 7m² 8m³ 8.1m⁶ 7m 8m⁶ 7g* 7d⁶ 7s 7.2g³ 7g 7s Oct 13] well-made gelding:
useful handicapper: won at Goodwood (by ½ length from Mutawathea) in July: several
creditable efforts in defeat, including when third at Ayr (½ length behind Right Touch) in
September: stays 1m: acts on firm and good to soft going: races towards rear: tricky ride
and one to be wary of. *Hughie Morrison*

PASTORAL STAR 2 ch.f. (Feb 3) Pastoral Pursuits 127 – Movie Star (IRE) (Barathea   **64**
(IRE) 127) [2015 7m 7d⁵ p8f 7s⁴ Sep 23] £19,000Y: half-sister to several winners,
including useful 9f-1½m winner Demolition (by Starborough) and French 2-y-o 1m winner
Dame Helen (by Royal Applause): dam ran once: modest maiden: best effort at 7f: twice
blinkered. *Hughie Morrison*

PASTUREYES 5 ch.m. Milk It Mick 120 – Veils of Salome (Arkadian Hero (USA) 123)   **67**
[2015 75: 5m⁴ 5.3g⁴ 6m 5g 5f⁶ 5g Oct 3] small mare: fair handicapper: stays 6f: acts on
firm and soft going: often wears cheekpieces: often races prominently. *Scott Dixon*

PATANJALI (IRE) 2 b.f. (Mar 10) Poet's Voice 126 – Penang (IRE) 57 (Xaar 132) [2015   **60**
6m⁴ 6m⁴ 7s p7g⁶ Sep 23] €31,000F: fourth foal: half-sister to 1m winners Chrissycross
(including at 2 yrs) and Carenza (both by Cape Cross): dam lightly-raced half-sister to
useful winner up to 7f Badminton: modest maiden: should prove suited by 7f+. *Eve
Johnson Houghton*

PATAVIUM (IRE) 12 b.g. Titus Livius (FR) 115 – Arcevia (IRE) 85 (Archway (IRE) 115)   –
[2015 12g 12d Aug 17] good-topped gelding: fairly useful at best, no form in 2015: stays
13f: acts on firm and good to soft going: tried in headgear. *Edwin Tuer*

PATENTAR (FR) 4 b.c. Teofilo (IRE) 126 – Poppets Sweetlove 73 (Foxhound (USA)   **108 d**
103) [2015 112: 7g³ 7m 7.6g 8f 9f³ 8f Nov 22] attractive colt: useful performer: third in
minor event at Thirsk (2¼ lengths behind Heaven's Guest) in April, below form
subsequently: left Marco Botti after third start: stays 7f: acts on polytrack and good to firm
going: often in headgear in 2015: often wears tongue tie. *Simon Callaghan, USA*

PATHWAY TO HONOUR 3 ch.g. New Approach 132 – Cheerleader 84 (Singspiel   **89**
(IRE) 133) [2015 90p: p8m² p8g* 8.3m⁴ 9.8m⁴ Jul 18] angular gelding: fairly
useful performer: won maiden at Lingfield (by 3¾ lengths from Reetaj) in February: bred
to be suited by 1¼m: acts on polytrack: in hood final start. *Charlie Appleby*

PAT MUSTARD 3 b.g. Royal Applause 124 – Umniya (IRE) 95 (Bluebird (USA) 125)   **?**
[2015 67: t8.6f⁴ 8.9m Apr 30] fair at best, well held only outing in Britain in 2015: stays
7f: acts on polytrack and fibresand: tried in cheekpieces: often in tongue tie in 2015: sent
to Qatar. *Jamie Osborne*

PATRICK (IRE) 3 b.g. Acclamation 118 – Red Liason (IRE) 103 (Selkirk (USA) 129)   **94**
[2015 p6m* p6g³ f5g⁴ 6m³ 6.1m* 6.1m⁴ 5g* 5m⁴ Jul 30] €32,000F: half-brother to 8.4f   **a78**
winner Thoroughly Red (by King's Best) and 2-y-o 7f winner Dimander (by Namid): dam,
winner up to 7f (2-y-o 6f winner), half-sister to smart 7f/1m winner Redstone Dancer:

fairly useful performer: won maiden at Lingfield in January and handicaps at Nottingham in May and Carlisle (by 2¾ lengths from Soie d'Leau) in July: stays 6f: acts on polytrack and good to firm going. *Richard Fahey*

PATRIOTIC (IRE) 7 b.g. Pivotal 124 – Pescara (IRE) 108 (Common Grounds 118) **93**
[2015 78, a96: f8d³ p8g³ f8d² t9.5f⁵ p8m⁵ f7s² p10g³ p10g p10f t9.5f t8.6m⁶ f7f³ Dec 17] leggy gelding: fairly useful handicapper: stays 1¼m: acts on all-weather and soft going: wears headgear. *Chris Dwyer*

PATRON OF EXPLORES (USA) 4 b.g. Henrythenavigator (USA) 131 – India Halo **54**
(ARG) (Halo Sunshine (USA) 118) [2015 54: t7.1f⁶ t7.1f⁵ t8.6f⁴ t8.6f* t7.1f⁴ t8.6f* 8.3g⁵ 8.5g t9.5f⁵ t8.6g⁵ t8.6f t7.1m³ Dec 30] modest handicapper: won at Wolverhampton in March: should prove suited by a return to 1m: acts on tapeta: tried in hood in 2015: sometimes wears tongue tie: usually races nearer last than first. *Patrick Holmes*

PAT'S LEGACY (USA) 9 ch.g. Yankee Gentleman (USA) – Sugars For Nanny (USA) **60**
(Brocco (USA) 124) [2015 76: f7g³ f8d 11.6m⁴ 11.6g⁴ 9s⁴ 9.9v⁶ Aug 24] lengthy gelding: modest handicapper: left Marjorie Fife after second start: stays 11.5f: acts on fibresand, soft and good to firm going: tried in headgear: tried in tongue tie prior to 2015. *Pat Phelan*

PAVERS STAR 6 ch.g. Pastoral Pursuits 127 – Pride of Kinloch 80 (Dr Devious (IRE) **63**
127) [2015 70: 5g 5g 5m 5g⁵ 5d⁶ 5g⁶ 5m* 5d³ 5g 5s t5.1f⁶ f5m Dec 8] modest handicapper: won at Newcastle in July: best form at 5f: acts on good and good to firm going: usually wears headgear: front runner/races prominently. *Noel Wilson*

PEACE AND WAR (USA) 3 b.f. War Front (USA) 119 – More Oats Please (USA) **107**
(Smart Strike (CAN) 121) [2015 114p: a8.5f a8f a8.3g² a8.5f² a8.5f³ a9f a9f⁵ 9f Dec 27] neat filly: useful performer: won Alcibiades Stakes at Keeneland at 2 yrs: left Olly Stevens after second start in 2015: placed after in non-graded event and Grade 3 Delaware Oaks (1¾ lengths second to Calamity Kate), both at Delaware, and Cotillion Stakes at Parx (4¼ lengths third behind I'm A Chatterbox): stays 8.5f: acts on dirt, has won on polytrack. *H. Graham Motion, USA*

PEACEFUL JOURNEY 2 ch.f. (Jan 28) Exceed And Excel (AUS) 126 – Dove (IRE) 83 **79**
(Sadler's Wells (USA) 132) [2015 p8d⁴ p7m² Dec 16] third foal: dam, 1¼m winner, half-sister to smart winner up to 11.6f Naheef: 6/4, similar form to debut when 2 lengths second of 12 to Auntinet in maiden at Lingfield, no extra final 100 yds. *Saeed bin Suroor*

PEACE LILLY (USA) 3 b.f. Distorted Humor (USA) 117 – Julia Tuttle (USA) (Giant's **69**
Causeway (USA) 132) [2015 p6g t7.1f⁶ 8g³ t9.5g⁶ 10.1v⁶ 8m² 8g f7g² f8g Dec 12] second **a57**
foal: half-sister to a winner in USA by Smart Strike: dam, US 1m/9f winner, out of sister to top-class US Grade 1 1¼m winner Candy Ride: fair maiden: left Kevin Ryan after third start, Michael Attwater after eighth: best effort at 1m: acts on good to firm going: sometimes in headgear. *Michael Appleby*

PEACE PRIZE (IRE) 3 b.f. Alfred Nobel (IRE) 110 – Applaud (USA) 105 (Rahy (USA) **87**
115) [2015 p7f⁵ p7m p8f⁵ 10.2s* 11.6f⁴ 10m* 10m³ 11.6m⁵ Jul 20] 20,000F, £30,000Y: rather leggy filly: half-sister to numerous winners, including useful winner up to 1½m (in USA) Jazz Jam (2-y-o 1m winner, by Pivotal): dam 2-y-o 5f/6f (Cherry Hinton Stakes) winner: fairly useful handicapper: won at Nottingham in April and Newmarket (by length from Polarisation) in June: stays 1¼m: acts on soft and good to firm going: sold 11,000 gns, sent to USA. *Hugo Palmer*

PEACE SEEKER 7 b.g. Oasis Dream 129 – Mina 73 (Selkirk (USA) 129) [2015 96: **95**
p5g* p6g Sep 21] sturdy gelding: useful performer: won seller at Lingfield (by 4½ lengths from Dangerous Age) in June: left Anthony Carson, well held both subsequent starts: stays 6f: acts on polytrack, good to firm and good to soft going: tried in cheekpieces prior to 2015: usually races prominently. *Ronald Harris*

PEACOCK 3 b.c. Paco Boy (IRE) 129 – Rainbow's Edge 85 (Rainbow Quest (USA) 134) **115**
[2015 104: p8g* 9m² 10m* 10f² Jun 18] smart performer: won minor event at Kempton (by 2¾ lengths from Azraff) in April and listed race at Newmarket (by 1¼ lengths from Mustadeem) in May: second in listed race at Newmarket (1½ lengths behind Golden Horn) and in Tercentenary Stakes at Royal Ascot (3¼ lengths behind Time Test) on other starts: will probably stay 1½m: acts on polytrack and firm going: sent to Hong Kong. *Richard Hannon*

PEAK HILL 2 ch.g. (Apr 1) Bahamian Bounty 116 – River Naiad (Nayef (USA) 129) **79**
[2015 6m 7.4g* 7m³ 6v² 6g⁴ Sep 18] fair performer: won maiden at Ffos Las in July: will prove suited by a return to 7f: acts on good to firm and heavy going: front runner/races prominently. *David Evans*

PEAK STORM 6 b.g. Sleeping Indian 122 – Jitterbug (IRE) (Marju (IRE) 127) [2015 74: **85** t7.1f⁵ p8g 7m 8g⁶ 8f³ 8.1m* 7.1m² 8.1s* 7.1g* 10.2d² 8d² 9s* 9s 8.1s² 7.1s⁶ Sep 15] fairly useful handicapper: won at Chepstow in July (twice) and at Chepstow and Newbury (apprentice) in August: stays 9f: acts on polytrack, good to firm and heavy going: often wears headgear: usually races towards rear. *John O'Shea*

PEARL ACCLAIM (IRE) 5 b.g. Acclamation 118 – With Colour (Rainbow Quest (USA) **95** 134) [2015 98: 5m 5m⁶ 5m 5m* 5g⁵ 5f 5m⁶ 5m 5g 5v 5d p5g⁵ Dec 2] compact gelding: useful handicapper: won at Musselburgh (by head from Meadway) in June: stays 6f: acts on firm and good to soft going: tried in headgear. *David Nicholls*

PEARL BLUE (IRE) 7 b.m. Exceed And Excel (AUS) 126 – Sanfrancullinan (IRE) 89 **89** (Bluebird (USA) 125) [2015 102: p6g³ p5g⁴ p6g p6g p6f* 6g* 6.1g⁴ 6m 5g⁶ 5m 5g⁵ 6g 6dᵖᵘ **a82** 6d Sep 17] compact mare: fairly useful performer: won claimers at Lingfield in April and Windsor in May, then left Jamie Osborne: stays 6f: acts on polytrack and heavy going: tried in headgear in 2015: usually races nearer last than first. *David O'Meara*

PEARL CASTLE (IRE) 5 b.g. Montjeu (IRE) 137 – Ghurra (USA) 91 (War Chant **98** (USA) 126) [2015 101: 12.1s³ 12g 12d⁵ 14d² 14d 12d⁶ 12v p12g³ Dec 19] tall, attractive gelding: useful handicapper: good efforts when second in Old Borough Cup at Haydock (neck behind Nakeeta) in September and third at Lingfield (2½ lengths behind Barye) on final outing: left John Quinn after second start: will prove suited by a return to 1¾m: acts on polytrack, good to firm and good to soft going: usually races prominently: useful hurdler. *K. R. Burke*

PEARL EARING (IRE) 4 b.f. Excellent Art 125 – Triple Axel (IRE) 72 (Danehill **–** Dancer (IRE) 117) [2015 92: 6g 8g⁵ 6d Aug 28] fairly useful at best, no form in 2015: sometimes wears cheekpieces. *K. R. Burke*

PEARL ICE 7 b.g. Iffraaj 127 – Jezebel 104 (Owington 123) [2015 82: p8g 8m p8g* p8g⁴ **97** p8g 8m³ p8g 7d² p8m⁴ Nov 14] robust gelding: useful handicapper: held form well after winning at Kempton in May by neck from Anya, 2¾ lengths fourth to Mindurownbusiness at Lingfield final start: stays 1m: acts on polytrack, soft and good to firm going: tried in headgear. *Charlie Fellowes*

PEARL NATION (USA) 6 b.g. Speightstown (USA) 124 – Happy Nation (USA) (Lear **110** Fan (USA) 130) [2015 94, a106: f8d² t8.6f* t8.6m f7s* a8.6g⁶ f7g⁵ Dec 12] big, strong gelding: smart handicapper: won at Wolverhampton (by short head from Energia Flavio) in January and Southwell (by 1¼ lengths from Patriotic) in March: off 7 months, creditable effort at Southwell final start: stays 8.5f: acts on fibresand, tapeta and firm going: wears hood. *Michael Appleby*

PEARL NOIR 5 b.g. Milk It Mick 120 – Cora Pearl (IRE) 51 (Montjeu (IRE) 137) [2015 **79** 63, a73: p6g² p5m⁵ p6f³ p5m* p5f⁵ p5g⁵ p5f² p5f 5m² 6m⁵ p6g 5f* 5m* 5g 5m p5f⁶ p5m p5g Dec 7] fair handicapper: won at Kempton in February, Doncaster (apprentice) in July and Beverley in August: stays 6f: acts on all-weather and firm going: wears headgear: tried in tongue tie prior to 2015: usually leads. *Scott Dixon*

PEARL OF PHOENIX 5 b.m. Phoenix Reach (IRE) 124 – Pearl's Girl 86 (King's Best **–** (USA) 132) [2015 p10g Mar 27] thrice-raced maiden, no form. *Simon Hodgson*

PEARL RANSOM (IRE) 5 b.g. Intikhab (USA) 135 – Massada 106 (Most Welcome **58** 131) [2015 74: p8g⁴ p8g⁴ t9.5f² f7g³ t7.1f² 8.3g² t8.6g⁵ 7.5m⁶ 8m p8g⁵ Jul 18] fair **a72** handicapper: stays 9.5f: acts on polytrack, tapeta and good to firm going: wears visor: front runner/races prominently: consistent. *Alan Bailey*

PEARL SECRET 6 ch.h. Compton Place 125 – Our Little Secret (IRE) 104 (Rossini **116** (USA) 118) [2015 119: 5g 5g* 5f⁴ 6f 5g 6d 5d⁶ 5m⁴ Oct 4] strong, lengthy horse: smart performer: won Temple Stakes at Haydock in May by neck from Jack Dexter: creditable efforts when fourth behind Goldream subsequently, beaten ¾ length in King's Stand Stakes at Royal Ascot (finished strongly) and 2¾ lengths in Prix de l'Abbaye at Longchamp (dropped in from wide draw, had to pick way through and never nearer): best at 5f: acts on firm and soft going: often races in rear: tends to sweat in preliminaries. *David Barron*

PEARL SPECTRE (USA) 4 ch.g. Street Cry (IRE) 130 – Dark Sky (USA) (Storm Cat **78** (USA)) [2015 t6f⁵ p8g Dec 16] fair performer: left Bob Baffert after first start (blinkered) and returned to former trainer: stays 1m: acts on polytrack and good to soft going. *Andrew Balding*

761

PEARLY PRINCE 3 b.g. Cockney Rebel (IRE) 127 – Princess Raya 58 (Act One 124) **59 p**
[2015 p10g⁴ Dec 30] £400Y: third foal: half-brother to 9f-11.6f winner First Sargeant (by
Dutch Art): dam, maiden, closely related to useful performer up to 1¾m Princess Taylor:
33/1, 6¼ lengths fourth of 7 to Nosey Barker in maiden at Lingfield on debut, travelling
better than most and not knocked about once held: capable of better. *Peter Hedger*

PEARLY STEPH (FR) 3 b.f. Oasis Dream 129 – Pearl Banks 112 (Pivotal 124) [2015 **106**
p7.5g² 8s* 8g⁵ 8s² 8g* 8.9g² 7m⁶ Sep 10] first foal: dam French 10.5f-1½m winner out of
Prix Vermeille winner Pearly Shells: useful performer: won minor event at Saint-Cloud in
March and listed race at Longchamp (by neck from Zaridiya) in June: shaped better than
result (not clear run when 3½ lengths sixth of 20 to Realtra) in Sceptre Stakes at Doncaster
final outing: stays 9f: acts on soft going. *F. Head, France*

PEA SHOOTER 6 b.g. Piccolo 121 – Sparkling Eyes 80 (Lujain (USA) 119) [2015 92: **86**
f6s⁶ f5g⁵ 6m⁵ 5g* 5g 5m 6m p6g⁶ 5g² 5g t6m² 5g* p6f Nov 7] tall gelding: fairly useful **a78**
handicapper: won at Ripon in June and Musselburgh (by ¾ length from Economic Crisis)
in October: left David Nicholls after second start, Marjorie Fife after sixth, David Nicholls
after tenth: stays 6f: acts on soft and good to firm going: tried in headgear: tried in tongue
tie prior to 2015. *Brian Ellison*

PEBBLES PLACE 2 b.f. (May 5) Oasis Dream 129 – Lavender And Lace 55 (Barathea **–**
(IRE) 127) [2015 p8f p7g Nov 26] 28,000Y: first foal: dam, maiden, closely related to Prix
Saint-Alary winner Wavering and half-sister to Criterium de Saint-Cloud winner
Mandaean: well held in maidens at Chelmsford: sold 5,000 gns. *Jamie Osborne*

PECKING ORDER (IRE) 3 b.f. Fastnet Rock (AUS) 127 – Shemaya (IRE) 99 **90**
(Darshaan 133) [2015 t9.5g³ 12g² p12g² 12g* Sep 26] closely related to 2 winners in
France, including useful 1m/9f winner Shendaya (by Danehill Dancer), and half-sister to 3
winners, including smart French 1¼m winner Shamkiyr (by Sea The Stars): dam, French
9f/1¼m winner, out of Prix de Diane winner Shemaka: fairly useful form: improved to win
maiden at Ripon in September by 9 lengths from Our Thomas, drawing clear final 1f: stays
1½m. *James Fanshawe*

PEEPS 3 ch.f. Halling (USA) 133 – Twelfth Night (IRE) 67 (Namid 128) [2015 57: p7g **64**
p12g⁴ p10f⁵ 10.1g⁵ p10m p13.3f⁴ t13.9f² p16g⁴ Nov 26] modest maiden: stays 1¾m: acts
on polytrack and tapeta. *Mark H. Tompkins*

PELAGIAN (USA) 4 b.g. Henrythenavigator (USA) 131 – Japon (Alzao (USA) 117) **–**
[2015 62: 8v⁵ 8d Sep 14] modest at best, no form in 2015: best effort at 1m: acts on
polytrack: in hood in 2015, also in tongue tie final start: often races freely. *Dean Ivory*

PELERIN (IRE) 4 ch.f. Shamardal (USA) 129 – Fragrancy (IRE) 106 (Singspiel (IRE) **104**
133) [2015 107: 8g⁶ 8d³ 8m⁵ 7m² 7m* 7s² Oct 31] useful performer: won listed race at
Ascot in October by ½ length from Pack Together: also second in Sceptre Stakes at
Doncaster (2¼ lengths behind Realtra) and Premio Chiusura at Milan (just respectable
effort, beaten 1¼ lengths by Pensierieparole): effective at 7f to 1¼m: acts on polytrack,
good to firm and good to soft going: usually wears cheekpieces nowadays. *Marco Botti*

PELOPONNESE (FR) 2 b.f. (Feb 17) Montjeu (IRE) 137 – Mimalia (USA) (Silver **68 p**
Hawk (USA) 123) [2015 7g 7.5g³ 8.3d Oct 14] lengthy filly: seventh foal: half-sister to
smart winner up to 1¼m Unnefer (2-y-o 7f winner) and French 2-y-o 1m winner Varega
(both by Danehill Dancer): dam, French maiden (stayed 1¼m), closely related to Derby
winner Kris Kin: fair maiden: best effort when third at Beverley: will prove suited by
1¼m+: remains with potential. *Sir Michael Stoute*

PENALTY SCORER 3 ch.f. Captain Gerrard (IRE) 113 – Mindfulness (Primo Dominie **43**
121) [2015 52: t5.1f⁴ t5.1g f5s⁴ t5.1g⁶ t5.1f Feb 23] smallish, sturdy filly: poor maiden:
stays 6f: acts on tapeta, good to firm and good to soft going: sometimes in headgear prior
to 2015. *Richard Guest*

PENANG PAPARAJA (IRE) 3 b.c. Dansili 127 – Penang Pearl (FR) 106 (Bering 136) **68**
[2015 60: 7d 8g 9d⁴ 9.9g² 11.7f² 11.7m⁵ p12g p11g p10g Oct 27] fair maiden: best effort **a58**
at 11.5f: acts on firm going. *Michael Bell*

PENCAITLAND 3 b.f. Champs Elysees 124 – Anthea 66 (Tobougg (IRE) 125) [2015 –: **48**
14.1g 9.9m⁴ 9.9g⁶ t12.2f Oct 16] poor maiden: best effort at 1¾m: acts on good to firm
going. *Noel Wilson*

PENDO 4 b.g. Denounce 89 – Abundant 96 (Zafonic (USA) 130) [2015 77: 8m⁴ 10.2m⁶ **77**
8.3g⁵ p8g⁶ 8g⁶ 8g² 7.6s² 8v² 8.3g⁶ t8.6g² p8g* Dec 30] fair handicapper: won at Lingfield
in December: stays 8.5f: acts on polytrack, tapeta, soft and good to firm going: tried in
headgear: usually responds generously to pressure. *Paul Cole*

PENELOPE PITSTOP 3 b.f. Captain Gerrard (IRE) 113 – Obsessive Secret (IRE) **56**
(Grand Lodge (USA) 125) [2015 59: t6f p8f⁶ p7g p6g 5d 7.2d⁶ 8.3g² 8.3d² 9.2s⁶ 7.2d 7.2d⁵
8.3g³ p8g Dec 11] modest maiden: left Keith Dalgleish after second start: stays 8.5f: acts
on fibresand, tapeta and good to soft going: sometimes slowly away. *L. Smyth, Ireland*

PENHILL 4 b.g. Mount Nelson 125 – Serrenia (IRE) (High Chaparral (IRE) 132) [2015 **106**
97: 12m* 12m 11.9g⁴ 12g² 11.9d* 12v⁶ Nov 7] workmanlike gelding: useful handicapper:
won at Ascot (by short head from New Year's Night) in May and Haydock (by ½ length
from Buonarroti) in September: stays 1½m: acts on soft and good to firm going: free-going
sort. *Luca Cumani*

PENIAPHOBIA (IRE) 4 b.g. Dandy Man (IRE) 123 – Umlani (IRE) (Great Commotion **128**
(USA) 123) [2015 125: 5m* 6g⁴ 5g² 6m⁴ 5g 6m³ 6g² 6g* Dec 13] strong, quite good-
topped gelding: high-class performer: won Centenary Sprint Cup at Sha Tin in January and
Hong Kong Sprint on same course (by ½ length from Gold-Fun, quickening 2f out) in
December: respectable ½-length second to Sole Power in Al Quoz Sprint at Meydan on
third outing: stays 6f: acts on firm going: wears cheekpieces/tongue tie: usually races close
up. *A. S. Cruz, Hong Kong*

PENITENT 9 b.g. Kyllachy 129 – Pious 74 (Bishop of Cashel 122) [2015 114: 8d⁴ 7m 7s³ **104**
7g 7f³ 8d 8g⁴ 8d 8.5s Oct 9] sturdy, compact gelding: won 11 races during career, including
3 pattern races and 4 listed races: just useful in 2015, best efforts when third in listed races
at Doncaster and Haydock first/third starts, 3¼ lengths third to That Is The Spirit in latter:
stayed 9f: acted on polytrack, good to firm and heavy going: tried in headgear: retired.
David O'Meara

PENMAEN (IRE) 5 b.m. Pivotal 124 – Lady Grace (IRE) 110 (Orpen (USA) 116) [2015 **105**
6g* 6g⁶ 6g* 7m 6s³ 6s Nov 19] second foal: half-sister to 1m winner Darling Grace (by
Nayef): dam 6f to (at 2 yrs) 1m winner: useful performer: won minor event at Maisons-
Laffitte in May and listed race at Hoppegarten (by 2 lengths from Daring Match) in August:
creditable third in Prix de Seine-et-Oise at Maisons-Laffitte (2¼ lengths behind Gammarth)
in October: below form in Sceptre Stakes at Doncaster in between: stays 7f: acts on soft
going. *J. E. Hammond, France*

PENNERLEY 2 b.f. (Feb 10) Aqlaam 125 – Penelewey 97 (Groom Dancer (USA) 128) **–**
[2015 8d Oct 23] seventh foal: half-sister to 3 winners, including smart winner up to 1¼m
Jedediah (2-y-o 1m winner, by Hernando) and 7f-8.6f winner Marksbury (by Mark of
Esteem): dam 6f/7f winner: 100/1, 8½ lengths eighth of 11 to Zest in maiden at Doncaster
on debut. *James Eustace*

PENNINE PANTHER 4 b.g. Notnowcato 128 – Kozmina (IRE) (Sadler's Wells (USA) **75**
132) [2015 80: 12m⁵ 10d⁶ Jul 29] sturdy gelding: fair handicapper: stays 1½m: acts on soft
and good to firm going. *Henry Candy*

PENNINE WARRIOR 4 b.g. Lucky Story (USA) 128 – Discoed 38 (Distinctly North **77**
(USA) 115) [2015 83: 6s 6v⁶ 6g* f6d 6m⁵ p6f² f6g⁵ Nov 26] good-topped gelding: fair
handicapper: won at Hamilton in June: stays 6f: acts on polytrack, fibresand, good to firm
and good to soft going: wears headgear: none too reliable. *Scott Dixon*

PENNOCK 2 b.c. (Mar 30) Pivotal 124 – Persinette (USA) (Kingmambo (USA) 125) **68**
[2015 6d⁶ 7.2g⁶ 6d⁴ 6g 6v⁶ Nov 7] fair maiden: should stay at least 7f: acts on good to soft
going. *Mark Johnston*

PENNY BOO (IRE) 3 b.f. Acclamation 118 – Daqtora 70 (Dr Devious (IRE) 127) [2015 **56**
f7d 7.1s⁶ 9.9m⁶ 12.1g⁵ 12.1m 10.1m Jul 25] £24,000Y: sister to French 1m winner Hearts
of Stone (later successful in Qatar) and 5f/6f winner Royal Brave and half-sister to several
winners, including 2-y-o 5.7f winner (stayed 1m) Qalahari (by Bahri): dam 11f winner:
modest maiden: best effort at 1½m: tried in cheekpieces. *Brian Ellison*

PENNY DREADFUL 3 b.f. Piccolo 121 – Trina's Pet 65 (Efisio 120) [2015 –: t6g² 6m **82**
t6g³ 6m* 6g² 6.1g⁶ 5m 6g⁶ p6f* p6f⁴ t6f Oct 9] fairly useful performer: won maiden at
Catterick in May and handicap at Chelmsford in September: stays 6f: acts on polytrack and
good to firm going: in cheekpieces in 2015: usually leads. *Scott Dixon*

PENNY POT LANE 2 b.f. (Mar 25) Misu Bond (IRE) 114 – Velvet Band 73 (Verglas **70**
(IRE) 118) [2015 5g 5g³ 5m* 5f⁴ 5m³ 5.9m⁶ 6v⁵ Nov 7] £1,000Y: second foal: dam, 2-y-o
6f winner, half-sister to useful winner up to 1½m Jazz Jam out of Cherry Hinton Stakes
winner Applaud: fair performer: won maiden at Ripon in June: best form at 5f: acts on good
to firm going. *Richard Whitaker*

PENNY PURSUITS 4 b.f. Pastoral Pursuits 127 – Sattelight (Fraam 114) [2015 –: 7.1s **37**
8.3d 10d 8.3d⁶ 8d⁶ 7.2d 8.3g 10d 10v⁴ Nov 3] poor maiden: stays 1m: acts on good to soft
going: tried in blinkers in 2015. *Alan Berry*

PENNY ROYALE 3 b.f. Monsieur Bond (IRE) 120 – Royal Punch (Royal Applause 124) **79**
[2015 70: 6m⁵ 5g⁴ 5m⁴ 6d³ 5g⁴ 5.4m⁵ 5g⁵ 5m³ 6g³ 5g⁵ 5g² Oct 3] unfurnished filly: fair
handicapper: won at Musselburgh in May: stays 6f: acts on good to firm and good to soft
going: in headgear nowadays: often races prominently. *Tim Easterby*

PENNYS ANGEL (IRE) 4 b.g. Dark Angel (IRE) 113 – The Good Life (IRE) (Rainbow **– §**
Quest (USA) 134) [2015 60§: 10d 11g 9.3d⁶ 10.5s Aug 18] modest maiden at best: left J.
T. Gorman, well held in handicaps in 2015: stays 10.5f: usually in headgear/tongue tie
nowadays: one to treat with caution (has refused to race). *Mark McNiff, Ireland*

PENNY'S BOY 4 ch.g. Firebreak 125 – Sunderland Echo (IRE) 87 (Tagula (IRE) 116) **54**
[2015 77: p10g p8g 8f 9.9m⁵ 10.2m⁶ t9.5f⁶ Oct 16] sturdy gelding: modest handicapper:
left Simon Hodgson after fifth start: stays 1¼m: acts on polytrack, good to firm and heavy
going: tried in headgear in 2015: usually wears tongue tie. *Daniel Loughnane*

PENSAX BOY 3 b.g. Rail Link 132 – Cyclone Connie 98 (Dr Devious (IRE) 127) [2015 **89**
71: 7m² 7g² 8.3m³ 9m⁵ 8m² 7.5m² t8.6g⁴ Dec 1] sturdy gelding: fairly useful performer:
1/7, didn't need to improve to win maiden at Wolverhampton on final start by 6 lengths:
stays 8.5f: acts on tapeta and good to firm going. *Ian Williams*

PENSAX LAD (IRE) 4 gr.g. Verglas (IRE) 118 – Betelgeuse 86 (Kalaglow 132) [2015 **76**
79: p5m* t5.1f* p5g p5f 5m 6g 6m⁵ 6m⁶ 6s² 6d⁶ 6g f5g p5g² p5g* t5.1f² p6g³ Dec 30] **a93**
rather leggy gelding: fairly useful handicapper: won at Lingfield and Wolverhampton in
January and Chelmsford (by ½ length from Doctor Parkes) in December: stays 6f: acts on
all-weather, soft going and good to firm going: often races prominently. *Ronald Harris*

PENSIONNAT (IRE) 3 b.f. Cape Cross (IRE) 129 – Surval (IRE) 91 (Sadler's Wells **75**
(USA) 132) [2015 55p: p10g⁴ 12.1m³ 12m³ 11.6m 9.9g² 9.9g 11.6d⁴ Oct 12] tall filly: fair
maiden: stays 1½m: acts on good to firm and good to soft going: often races prominently.
Ralph Beckett

PENWORTHAM (IRE) 2 b.g. (Apr 14) Dandy Man (IRE) 123 – Portofino Bay (IRE) **78**
74 (Montjeu (IRE) 137) [2015 6m⁶ 6m⁴ t5.1g* 5g 6d Oct 5] fair performer: won maiden at
Wolverhampton in August: best effort at 5f: acts on tapeta: has been gelded. *Richard Fahey*

PEONY ROSE (IRE) 3 br.f. Makfi 130 – Rose Briar (IRE) 60 (Grand Lodge (USA) 125) **51**
[2015 –: p7g 9s 7g⁶ 10g⁶ 7.5s³ p8g p10.7g Nov 27] €11,500Y: fourth foal: dam, maiden
(stayed 1m), half-sister to Sprint Cup winner Tante Rose and to dam of high-class French
7f/1m winner Make Believe (by Makfi): modest maiden: best effort at 7.5f: acts on soft
going: sometimes in blinkers in 2015: often races towards rear. *John Joseph Murphy,
Ireland*

PEPPARD 2 b.f. (Apr 22) Dansili 127 – Arum Lily (USA) (Woodman (USA) 126) [2015 **65 p**
7s Oct 12] sturdy filly: seventh foal: sister to useful 1m-9.5f winner Premium and half-
sister to very smart winner up to 1½m Redwood (2-y-o 1m winner, by High Chaparral) and
useful/untrustworthy winner up to 1½m (stays 2m) Perennial (2-y-o 1m winner, by
Motivator): dam French 1m/9f winner: 20/1, green and given a considerate introduction
when 5¼ lengths seventh of 10 to Dutch Destiny in maiden at Salisbury: will stay at least
1m: will improve. *Charles Hills*

PEPPERING (USA) 2 b.f. (Feb 12) Bernardini (USA) 132 – Joharra (USA) (Kris S **59**
(USA)) [2015 p7g⁵ p8g⁶ Oct 6] half-sister to 10.3f winner Caprivi (by Cape Cross) and
useful French 10.5f/11f winner Royal Bengali (by Tiger Hill): dam, maiden (stayed 9f),
half-sister to very smart winner up to 1¼m Equerry and Breeders' Cup Juvenile Fillies
winner Tempera: modest form in maidens at Kempton: better effort when fifth on debut
(slowly away): should stay at least 1m. *Charlie Appleby*

PEPPY MILLER 2 b.f. (Mar 23) Cockney Rebel (IRE) 127 – Solar Crystal (IRE) 110 **–**
(Alzao (USA) 117) [2015 6d Jun 4] half-sister to several winners, including smart 2-y-o 6f
winner (stayed 1½m) Feared In Flight (by Hawk Wing) and useful 2-y-o 7f winner Lunar
Crystal (by Shirley Heights): dam 2-y-o 6f-1m (May Hill Stakes) winner who stayed 1¼m:
25/1, green when well held in maiden at Lingfield: will prove suited by further than 6f.
George Margarson

PERARDUA 3 ch.f. Cockney Rebel (IRE) 127 – Quiquillo (USA) 73 (Cape Canaveral **81**
(USA) 115) [2015 82: 6d 6d³ 5g² 5g³ 5s⁴ 5g³ t6f Oct 17] fairly useful handicapper: best
form at 5f: acts on soft and good to firm going: front runner/races prominently.
Richard Fahey

PERCEIVED 3 ch.f. Sir Percy 129 – New Light 56 (Generous (IRE) 139) [2015 69p: **74**
10.2s⁵ 9.9m² 10.2d⁴ 10.2g² p10g⁴ 10s* Sep 13] fair handicapper: won at Ffos Las in
September: stays 1¼m: acts on polytrack, good to firm and heavy going: front runner/races
prominently. *Henry Candy*

PERCELLA 3 b.f. Sir Percy 129 – Temple of Thebes (IRE) 92 (Bahri (USA) 125) [2015 **63**
62: p8g 10m* t12.2g³ 10d³ t9.5m⁶ Dec 18] modest performer: won seller at Leicester in
May: left Hughie Morrison after: stays 1½m: acts on polytrack, tapeta and good to firm
going: sometimes wears tongue tie. *Ian Williams*

PERCEUS 3 b.g. Sir Percy 129 – Lady Hestia (USA) 82 (Belong To Me (USA)) [2015 80: **92**
10f⁴ 12.3g 12g³ 12s* 11.5m³ 12d⁵ Oct 11] tall gelding: fairly useful handicapper: won at
Goodwood (by 7 lengths from Silver Quay) in August: stays 1½m: acts on soft and good to
firm going: tried in hood: usually races prominently: sold 22,000 gns to join James Eustace.
Marcus Tregoning

PERCEYSVIVACE 2 b.f. (Mar 18) Sir Percy 129 – Calico Moon (USA) (Seeking The **70 p**
Gold (USA)) [2015 7m⁴ t7.1g 8s⁴ Oct 9] 5,000Y: sixth foal: half-sister to a winner in Saudi
Arabia by Giant's Causeway: dam, ran once in France, out of smart sister to Oaks winner
Imagine and half-sister to Generous: fair maiden: 50/1, up in trip, best effort when 3¼
lengths fourth of 13 to Dolphin Vista at York final start: should be suited by 1¼m: better
still to come. *Richard Fahey*

PERCHE 3 ch.g. New Approach (IRE) 132 – Persian Filly (IRE) (Persian Bold 123) [2015 **82**
70: 10d⁵ p12g² p12g² Oct 14] fairly useful form when runner-up in maidens at Kempton
last 2 starts: likely to stay beyond 1½m: acts on polytrack. *Charlie Appleby*

PERCY ALLELINE 3 b.g. Sir Percy 129 – Dominica 115 (Alhaarth (IRE) 126) [2015 **66**
90: p7.5g 7g 8.3m⁶ p8g² t7.1m⁶ p6g Sep 9] leggy gelding: fair performer: left Ralph
Beckett after first start: stays 1m: acts on polytrack, good to firm and heavy going: often
wears headgear. *Harry Dunlop*

PERCY'S GAL 4 ch.f. Sir Percy 129 – Galette 94 (Caerleon (USA) 132) [2015 83: 6g **83**
5.9v* 5.9g 6s⁵ f6s² 5.9s³ 7d 5g⁶ Oct 13] fairly useful handicapper: won at Carlisle in June:
stays 7f: acts on fibresand, good to firm and heavy going: tried in cheekpieces in 2015.
Karen Tutty

PERCY'S LASS 3 gr.f. Sir Percy 129 – Brave Mave 83 (Daylami (IRE) 138) [2015 61p: **60**
7m⁵ 8.3g 10.4f 7m Jun 25] modest maiden: stays 7f: acts on good to firm going:
temperament under suspicion. *Brian Ellison*

PERCYS PRINCESS 4 b.f. Sir Percy 129 – Enford Princess 89 (Pivotal 124) [2015 81: **81**
f12d⁴ t9.5g⁵ t13.9f² t12.2g³ t13.9g⁵ 14.1m³ 14.1s 11.6m² t9.5f⁴ p12g⁵ f11g⁶ Dec 22] fairly
useful handicapper: stays 1¾m: acts on tapeta and good to firm going. *Michael Appleby*

PERCY'S ROMANCE 2 ch.f. (Apr 29) Sir Percy 129 – Top Romance (IRE) 105 **76 p**
(Entrepreneur 123) [2015 p7g 7.6g² p8g² Oct 6] half-sister to several winners, including
useful winner up to 1¼m (stays 1½m) Top Tug (2-y-o 1m winner, by Halling) and useful
1m-11f winner Top Diktat (by Diktat): dam, 2-y-o 7f winner, half-sister to smart 1¼m
performer National Anthem: fair maiden: best effort when second at Kempton (length
behind Nessita) final start: will be suited by 1¼m+: open to further improvement. *Sir
Michael Stoute*

PERCY STREET 2 br.c. (Mar 1) Sir Percy 129 – Star of Gibraltar 88 (Rock of Gibraltar **97 p**
(IRE) 133) [2015 7s⁵ 8g* 8s³ Oct 19] 10,000Y: leggy colt: third foal: dam, 1½m winner,
closely related to Coronation Stakes winner Fallen For You: useful performer: won maiden
at Pontefract in September by 6 lengths from Dot Green: further progress when 1½ lengths
third to Thanksfortellingme in listed race at same course: will be suited by 1¼m+: should
continue to improve. *K. R. Burke*

PERCY VEER 3 ch.g. Sir Percy 129 – Fandangerina 81 (Hernando (FR) 127) [2015 68: **79 +**
p8g 10.2f³ 12f³ 14.1m p12g* p12g* 12m⁶ p16g³ p12g⁴ p14f* p16g² t13.9g³ p15.8g³ Dec **a96**
28] useful handicapper: improved to win at Lingfield in June and July and Chelmsford in
November: even better form after, when second at Kempton and third at Wolverhampton
and Lingfield in December: stays 2m: acts on polytrack and tapeta. *Sylvester Kirk*

PERDURABLE 3 br.f. Sakhee's Secret 128 – Pain Perdu (IRE) (Waajib 121) [2015 –: **–**
8.3g May 31] no form in 2 maidens (9 months apart). *Charlie Fellowes*

PERENNIAL 6 ch.g. Motivator 131 – Arum Lily (USA) (Woodman (USA) 126) [2015 **70 §**
12d 14g³ 16s² 14m 16.1m³ 15.8d t13.9f³ t13.9f³ Oct 31] well-made gelding: fair handicapper: stays 2m: acts on polytrack, tapeta, soft and good to firm going: in headgear
nowadays: sometimes slowly away: untrustworthy. *Philip Kirby*

PERESTROIKA 3 b.f. Sir Percy 129 – Lekka Ding (IRE) 60 (Raise A Grand (IRE) 114) **94**
[2015 –: 10g⁶ 12m 10m* 11.8m³ 11.6m* 12m² Aug 8] lengthy, rather unfurnished filly:
fairly useful performer: won at Windsor in June (maiden) and July (handicap): stays 1½m:
acts on good to firm going. *Henry Candy*

PERFECT ALCHEMY (IRE) 4 b.f. Clodovil (IRE) 116 – Desert Alchemy (IRE) 103   **79** (Green Desert (USA) 127) [2015 88: p6g 6g f6s⁶ 6g p7g³ p8d⁵ p7g⁵ Dec 16] quite attractive mare: fair handicapper: left Ralph Beckett after third start: may prove best up to 7f: acts on polytrack, good to firm and good to soft going: tried in blinkers in 2015. *Patrick Chamings*

PERFECT BLESSINGS (IRE) 4 b.f. Kheleyf (USA) 116 – Yxenery (IRE) 101 (Sillery   **101** (USA) 122) [2015 98: 6d³ 6.1s 6g 6g Sep 5] lengthy filly: useful performer: good third in listed race at Doncaster (2 lengths behind Naadirr) on return in March: well below form after, in first-time tongue strap final start: stays 6f: acts on soft going: tried in cheekpieces. *Clive Cox*

PERFECT BOUNTY 3 ch.f. Bahamian Bounty 116 – Perfect Cover (IRE) 48 (Royal   **68** Applause 124) [2015 51p: t6g* p6m³ 7m* 5.7f² 7m p7g⁵ p7m⁵ Nov 21] fair handicapper: won at Wolverhampton in April and Salisbury in June: stays 7f: acts on polytrack, tapeta and firm going: sometimes slowly away. *Clive Cox*

PERFECT CRACKER 7 ch.g. Dubai Destination (USA) 127 – Perfect Story (IRE) 95   **84** (Desert Story (IRE) 115) [2015 89, a83: p10g⁵ t9.5f³ t9.5g³ t9.5f* t9.5f* t9.5m² 10m 10f⁶   **a91** 10m⁶ t9.5f³ t9.5f⁴ Nov 20] sturdy gelding: fairly useful handicapper: won at Wolverhampton in February and March: stays 1¼m: acts on polytrack and tapeta, raced only on good going or firmer on turf (acts on firm). *Clive Cox*

PERFECT FIT (IRE) 3 ch.f. Teofilo (IRE) 126 – Queen of Lyons (USA) 61 (Dubai   **77** Destination (USA) 127) [2015 82: 7dᵘʳ 6.9g² 7g² p7d³ 7g⁵ p7g⁶ 8s² p8m³ p10.7g p8g² p8g³ Dec 28] sparely-made filly: second foal: dam twice-raced half-sister to high-class sprinter Benbaun: fair maiden: stays 1m: acts on polytrack and soft going: often wears cheekpieces: usually races prominently. *David Wachman, Ireland*

PERFECT GLANCE (USA) 3 b.f. Rock Hard Ten (USA) 126 – Brief Look 94 (Sadler's   **76** Wells (USA) 132) [2015 74p: 10m⁵ 9.9m³ 9.9m* Jun 30] fair form: won maiden at Brighton in June, making all: stays 1¼m: raced only on good to firm going: sold 28,000 gns in July, sent to Bahrain. *Sir Michael Stoute*

PERFECT LEGEND 4 b.g. Norse Dancer (IRE) 127 – Flamjica (USA) 81 (Real Quiet   **–** (USA) 131) [2015 –: 12m⁶ 12.1m⁶ 14.1g Aug 4] maiden: well held in handicaps in 2015. *Andrew Balding*

PERFECTLY FAIR 2 b.f. (Mar 22) Invincible Spirit (IRE) 121 – She Storm (IRE)   **61** (Rainbow Quest (USA) 134) [2015 p6f⁵ t7.1m⁵ Sep 25] 150,000F: third foal: half-sister to 1¼m-1½m winner Stormin Tom (by Dylan Thomas): dam unraced half-sister to useful Italian 7f/1m winner She Breeze: showed promise in maiden at Chelmsford on debut: upped in trip, disappointing in similar event at Wolverhampton: should stay at least 7f. *Saeed bin Suroor*

PERFECT MISSION 7 b.g. Bertolini (USA) 125 – Sharp Secret (IRE) 69 (College   **68** Chapel 122) [2015 74: p7f⁶ p8m* p8f⁴ 7m 7.6g⁴ Jun 20] lengthy gelding: fair handicapper: won at Lingfield in February: stays 8.5f: acts on polytrack, firm and soft going: wears headgear. *Andrew Balding*

PERFECT MUSE 5 b.m. Oasis Dream 129 – Perfect Echo 81 (Lycius (USA) 124) [2015   **92** 97: 5m³ 5m 5m⁵ 5f 5g 5g² 5s³ 5m 5.1d Oct 14] sturdy mare: fairly useful handicapper: best form at 5f: acts on any turf going: tried in blinkers in 2015. *Clive Cox*

PERFECT ORANGE 3 ch.f. Sir Percy 129 – La Peinture (GER) (Peintre Celebre (USA)   **68** 137) [2015 74: 8.3d³ 9g p7g³ 8s⁵ p12f 10.2m 9.9s Oct 12] angular filly: fair maiden: stays 1m: acts on polytrack and good to soft going: often in headgear in 2015. *Marcus Tregoning*

PERFECT OUTCOME 4 b.f. Echo of Light 125 – Cautiously (USA) 77 (Distant View   **48** (USA) 126) [2015 61: p12g⁵ Feb 7] rather unfurnished filly: poor maiden: stays 1½m: acts on polytrack: front runner/races prominently. *Patrick Chamings*

PERFECT PASTIME 7 ch.g. Pastoral Pursuits 127 – Puritanical (IRE) (Desert King   **77** (IRE) 129) [2015 76, a66: p6g⁴ p6f⁵ 6g⁶ 6m p6g³ 5v⁴ 6s⁵ 5.3d* 6s⁵ 5.3s 5g⁵ Oct 19] sturdy   **a67** gelding: fair handicapper: won at Lingfield in August and Brighton in September: effective from 5f to 7f: acts on polytrack and any turf going: wears headgear: sometimes slowly away, usually races towards rear. *Jim Boyle*

PERFECT PASTURE 5 b.g. Pastoral Pursuits 127 – Word Perfect 87 (Diktat 126) [2015   **101** 111: p6g f5s* p6g 5m 5g 5m 6g 6g 5s³ 5d⁴ p5f Nov 23] useful handicapper: won by 1¼   **a108** lengths from Royal Bajan at Southwell in January: generally well below form subsequently: stays 6f: acts on polytrack, fibresand and good to soft going: wears visor. *Michael Easterby*

PERFECT PEAK 3 ch.f. Distant Peak (IRE) – Word Perfect 87 (Diktat 126) [2015 –: 5d³ **68**
6d⁶ 5.1g 5m 5d² 5d⁵ 5g* 5g⁶ 5d 5d⁴ 6g 5s⁴ 6v f6g f5m² Dec 8] fair handicapper: won at
Catterick in July: best form at 5f: acts on fibresand and good to soft going: in tongue tie in
2015, also blinkered last 2 starts: sometimes slowly away. *Michael Easterby*

PERFECT QUEST 2 br.f. (Feb 12) Bushranger (IRE) 119 – Love Quest (Pursuit of Love **64**
124) [2015 7g 7s 6s⁴ Oct 26] rather unfurnished filly: sixth foal: half-sister to 3 winners,
including useful winner up to 1½m Latenightrequest (2-y-o 7f/1m winner, by Major
Cadeaux) and 5f-7f winner La Zamora (by Lujain): dam unraced half-sister to smart 2-y-o
sprinter Orpen Grey: modest maiden: best effort when seventh at Salisbury second start.
Clive Cox

PERFECT RHYTHM 4 b.f. Halling (USA) 133 – Bassinet (USA) 84 (Stravinsky (USA) **77**
133) [2015 74: 11.7f³ 13.1m⁴ p12g* p12g* 13.1m² 11.6g 12d Sep 27] fair handicapper:
won at Lingfield in July (apprentice) and August: stays 13f: acts on polytrack and good to
firm going: often races towards rear. *Patrick Chamings*

PERFECT SUMMER (IRE) 5 b.m. High Chaparral (IRE) 132 – Power of Future **84**
(GER) 104 (Definite Article 121) [2015 88: 12s⁶ p13.3g² 12g⁶ t13.9g Dec 1] good-topped
mare: fairly useful handicapper: left Lady Cecil after third start: stays 1¾m: acts on
polytrack, soft and good to firm going: often in visor in 2015. *Ian Williams*

PERFECT WORDS (IRE) 5 ch.g. Thousand Words 113 – Zilayah (USA) 79 (Zilzal **67**
(USA) 137) [2015 77: 5g 5m 5.5m 5.5m⁵ 6d⁵ 5d⁶ 5g⁶ 5m 5s² t5.1f* p5g Dec 2]
fair handicapper: won at Wolverhampton in November: has form at 7f, races mainly at
5f/6f: acts on tapeta, heavy and good to firm going: wears headgear: front runner/races
prominently. *Marjorie Fife*

PERFORMER 2 b.f. (Mar 23) New Approach (IRE) 132 – Annalina (USA) (Cozzene **57 p**
(USA)) [2015 6f Jun 10] half-sister to several winners, including useful 2-y-o 6f winner
Dr No (by Aussie Rules) and 1½m winners Sagamore (by Azamour) and Hepworth (by
Singspiel): dam unraced: 9/1, some encouragement when seventh in maiden at Haydock
(5½ lengths behind Blue Bayou) in June: will improve. *Richard Hannon*

PERGAMINO 2 b.g. (Mar 28) Dubawi (IRE) 129 – Pryka (ARG) (Southern Halo (USA)) **83**
[2015 6m 8d³ p8m² Oct 21] third foal: brother to 1m winner Pacquita: dam prolific
Argentinian 5f (Grade 1 winner) to 7f winner: fairly useful form: progressed again when
short-head second to Southern Gailes in maiden at Kempton final start, headed post: may
do better still: has been gelded. *Charlie Appleby*

PERICLES (IRE) 2 ch.g. (Apr 14) Danehill Dancer (IRE) 117 – Althea Rose (IRE) **–**
(Green Desert (USA) 127) [2015 7g 6g 7d Oct 30] well held in 2 maidens and a valuable
sales race: has been gelded. *Peter Chapple-Hyam*

PERIGEE 2 b.c. (Mar 19) Cacique (IRE) 124 – Purissima (USA) 88 (Fusaichi Pegasus **73**
(USA) 130) [2015 7.1g 8.3s³ Oct 28] rangy, attractive colt: third foal: closely related to 7f
winner Ramshackle (by Dansili): dam, 2-y-o 6f winner, closely related to smart French/US
6.5f-8.5f winner Etoile Montante: improved from debut when 4¼ lengths third of 8 to
Rainbow Dreamer in maiden at Nottingham, disputing lead until over 1f out. *John Gosden*

PERIL 4 ch.g. Pivotal 124 – Portodora (USA) 92 (Kingmambo (USA) 125) [2015 82p: **100**
t7.1g* 7d* p8g 7d* 8d Sep 12] useful handicapper: won at Wolverhampton in June, Ascot
(amateur) in July and Haydock (by ½ length from Exchequer) in September: stays 7f: acts
on tapeta and good to soft going. *Simon Crisford*

PERIOD PIECE (IRE) 3 br.f. Intikhab (USA) 135 – Babberina (IRE) 75 (Danehill **81**
Dancer (IRE) 117) [2015 78p: p7g² p7g² p7g* p7m² 8.3m⁵ 8.1m 7d 7.1g p6f⁵ p7g t7.1f
p8m⁵ Nov 14] third foal: half-sister to 6f winner Barbeque (by Elusive City) and a winner
in Italy by Marju: dam maiden (stayed 8.5f): fairly useful performer: won maiden claimer
at Dundalk in March: left Mrs J. Harrington after third start: stays 8.5f: acts on polytrack
and good to firm going: tried in cheekpieces in 2015. *Jamie Osborne*

PERKUNAS (IRE) 2 b.g. (Apr 13) Baltic King 120 – Zafine 67 (Zafonic (USA) 130) **103**
[2015 7m² 7g⁵ 7g* 7v⁴ 7g* Dec 29] 42,000 2-y-o: seventh foal: half-brother to 5f/6f winner
(including at 2 yrs) Kodafine (by Kodiac) and a winner abroad by Chevalier: dam, 2-y-o 5f
winner, half-sister to smart winner up to 7f Tremar: useful form: won maiden at Brighton
(by 1¼ lengths from Bluebeard) in September and 16-runner minor event at Doha (beat
Astley Hall by 2 lengths, storming run to lead final ½f) in December: good head fourth of
9 to Crazy Horse in Horris Hill Stakes at Newbury in between: raced only at 7f.
Brian Meehan

PERLE EXPRESS 3 b.f. Rail Link 132 – Perle d'Or (IRE) 89 (Entrepreneur 123) [2015 **–**
–: 7f⁶ p9.2g⁵ 7s Oct 6] no form: usually wears hood. *Michael Appleby*

PERMAISURI (IRE) 2 b.f. (Apr 21) Sea The Stars (IRE) 140 – Puteri Wentworth 88 – (Sadler's Wells (USA) 132) [2015 p7g Oct 29] rather unfurnished filly: half-sister to several winners, including useful winner up to 8.6f Putra Sas (2-y-o 1m winner, by Sri Pekan) and useful 1¾m-16.4f winner (stayed 2½m) Bukit Tinggi (by Peintre Celebre): dam 1½m-2½m winner: 25/1, well held in maiden at Lingfield on debut. *Kevin Ryan*

PERMERA 2 b.f. (Apr 13) Sir Percy 129 – Four Miracles 96 (Vettori (IRE) 119) [2015 6g⁵ **60** 7.5g⁴ 7s² 8d Oct 19] compact filly: second foal: half-sister to 8.6f winner Hold Firm (by Refuse To Bend): dam 1¼m-2¼m winner: modest maiden: stays 7.5f. *Mark H. Tompkins*

PERMITTED 4 b.f. Authorized (IRE) 133 – Discerning 96 (Darshaan 133) [2015 –: p15.8f Jan 30] lightly-raced maiden, no form: usually slowly away. *Lee Carter*

PERNICKETY 2 b.f. (Feb 14) Sir Percy 129 – Nicola Bella (IRE) 98 (Sadler's Wells **– p** (USA) 132) [2015 7g Aug 28] rather unfurnished filly: sister to 1¼m winners Beau Knight, Pernica and Scarlet Belle (all stay/stayed at least 1½m) and half-sister to several winners, including very smart German winner up to 1¼m Neatico (2-y-o 1m/8.5f winner, by Medicean): dam 9.6f winner: 33/1 and in hood, better for run when 8½ lengths ninth of 11 to Diploma in maiden at Newmarket on debut: should do better given time/longer distances. *Lucy Wadham*

PERRAULT (IRE) 3 gr.c. Rip Van Winkle (IRE) 134 – La Persiana 112 (Daylami (IRE) **92** 138) [2015 7p: 10.2m* 10g³ 12s⁶ 12g Sep 24] tall colt: fairly useful performer: won maiden at Chepstow in May: form after only when third in handicap at Sandown: should be suited by 1½m: acts on good to firm going: blinkered final start. *Ralph Beckett*

PERSEPOLIS (IRE) 5 gr.g. Dansili 127 – La Persiana 112 (Daylami (IRE) 138) [2015 **87** 80, a90: p8m⁴ p10g⁴ p12g* t12.2g⁶ p12f⁶ 10g³ 7.6s p11g³ Jun 24] lengthy, quite attractive gelding: fairly useful handicapper: won at Lingfield in February: stays 1½m: acts on polytrack and good to firm going: tried in headgear prior to 2015: sometimes slowly away, often races freely: sold 58,000 gns, sent to Saudi Arabia. *Lee Carter*

PERSEVERENT PETE (USA) 5 b.g. Johannesburg (USA) 127 – Indian Halloween **51** (USA) (Sunday Break (JPN) 121) [2015 55: t9.5f⁶ p10f² p10g² p10g⁶ p10m⁶ p10m³ 11.5d⁵ 11.5d Jun 4] lengthy gelding: modest maiden: stays 1¼m: acts on polytrack, tapeta, soft and good to firm going: tried in cheekpieces prior to 2015. *Christine Dunnett*

PERSIAN BREEZE 3 b.f. Pivotal 124 – Persian Jasmine 79 (Dynaformer (USA)) [2015 **78** 10.2m³ 10s³ p12g³ p12g² 12s⁵ p10g⁶ Nov 13] second foal: half-sister to 2-y-o 6f winner Warm Breeze (by Oasis Dream): dam 2-y-o 7f winner (only start) out of US Grade 2 9f winner Rumpipumpy: fair maiden: stays 1½m: acts on polytrack, soft and good to firm going. *John Gosden*

PERSIAN HERALD 7 gr.g. Proclamation (IRE) 130 – Persian Fortune 53 (Forzando **62** 122) [2015 13.8m³ Jun 5] workmanlike gelding: modest performer: fit from jumping, respectable third in seller at Catterick on rare Flat outing: stays 1¾m: acts on polytrack, best turf form on good going or softer: has worn headgear. *Dianne Sayer*

PERSIFLAGE 3 b.f. Sir Percy 129 – Emirates First (IRE) 77 (In The Wings 128) [2015 **66** p8m⁶ 8g⁵ p10m³ 10m 9.9g⁴ Jul 4] 10,000Y: sister to 1m-1¼m winner Loraine and 7f winner Cornborough and half-sister to 7f winner Arabian Flight (by Exceed And Excel): dam, 9.5f winner, sister to very smart winner up to 2m Mamool: fair maiden: stays 1¼m: acts on polytrack: sometimes in blinkers: has joined Gordon Elliott. *Hugo Palmer*

PERSONA GRATA 4 b.f. Sir Percy 129 – Kaldounya (Kaldoun (FR) 122) [2015 92p: **107** t9.5g² 8.3m³ 10m* p9.4g² 9.9g² 9.9d 8.9d* 10.4s³ Nov 1] lengthy filly: useful performer: improved and won handicap at Windsor (by 1½ lengths from Tears of The Sun) in June and listed race at Maisons-Laffitte (by 1½ lengths from Deauville Shower) in September: second in listed races at Deauville and Maisons-Laffitte in between, and third in Prix de Flore at Saint-Cloud (2¼ lengths behind Si Luna) final start: stays 10.4f: acts on polytrack, tapeta, soft and good to firm going: wears headgear nowadays. *Ed Walker*

PERSONAL OPINION 4 ch.g. New Approach (IRE) 132 – Sentimental Value (USA) **–** 107 (Diesis 133) [2015 104: p12g⁴ Jan 3] useful handicapper: stumbled and fell at Lingfield only outing in 2015: stayed 1¾m: acted on polytrack, tapeta and good to firm going: tried in cheekpieces: often raced prominently: dead. *Charlie Appleby*

PERSONAL TOUCH 6 ch.g. Pivotal 124 – Validate (Alhaarth (IRE) 126) [2015 88: **91** p6g* 7d 6d 6g³ t7.1g* 7.2g* p6g 7g 6v² Aug 28] smallish gelding: fairly useful performer: won handicap at Chelmsford in March, claimer at Wolverhampton in June (subsequently left Richard Fahey) and handicap at Ayr in July: stays 7f: acts on polytrack, tapeta, good to firm and heavy going: tried in cheekpieces in 2015: front runner/races prominently. *Heather Dalton*

PERSUASIVE (IRE) 2 gr.f. (Mar 16) Dark Angel (IRE) 113 – Choose Me (IRE) 109 **88 p**
(Choisir (AUS) 126) [2015 p8g* Nov 4] €180,000Y: second foal: half-sister to useful 6f/7f
winner Amazour (by Azamour): dam winner up to 1¼m (2-y-o 6f/7f winner): 16/1, won
maiden at Kempton on debut by neck from Secret Sense, shaken up 2f out, leading soon
after and driven out: should progress. *John Gosden*

PERSUN 3 ch.f. Sir Percy 129 – Sunley Shines (Komaite (USA)) [2015 85: 8g⁵ 8g* 8.5d* **87**
8.9s 7v Oct 24] sparely-made filly: fairly useful performer: won maiden at Newmarket in
August and handicap at Epsom (by 1½ lengths from Cosmic Ray) in September: stays 8.5f:
acts on good to soft going: front runner/races prominently. *Mick Channon*

PERTUIS (IRE) 9 gr.g. Verglas (IRE) 118 – Lady Killeen (IRE) 60 (Marju (IRE) 127) **68**
[2015 79: 12g* 12g³ 12g 10g⁵ 12g³ 12g* 12g 12d⁵ 12g⁶ 12g Sep 24] angular gelding: fair
handicapper: won at Catterick in April and July (apprentice): stays 1½m: acts on polytrack,
good to firm and heavy going: usually wears headgear: races towards rear. *Micky Hammond*

PERU 2 b.f. (Mar 25) Motivator 131 – Bolsena (USA) (Red Ransom (USA)) [2015 7g⁴ **90**
p7g⁷ 8d* 8g² 8d Oct 31] 20,000F: rather leggy filly: half-sister to 3 winners, including
useful 1m winner Cactus Rose (by Zamindar) and 2-y-o 6f winner Wolf Slayer (by Diktat):
dam unraced out of US Grade 1 winner up to 1½m Waya: fairly useful performer: won
maiden at Haydock by neck from Combe Hay) in September: second in nursery at
Pontefract (nose behind Rioca) next time, well held in listed race at Newmarket final start:
stays 1m. *Hugo Palmer*

PERUSAL (IRE) 2 b.f. (Feb 17) Sir Percy 129 – Overlook 60 (Generous (IRE) 139) **–**
[2015 p8g Dec 16] €6,000Y, 11,000Y: fifth foal: half-sister to 1¼m winner Black Minstrel
(by Dylan Thomas): dam, maiden (stayed 2m), half-sister to smart miler Passing Glance:
100/1, well held in maiden at Kempton on debut, slowly away. *Jonathan Portman*

PETER ANDERS 6 b.h. Pivotal 124 – Astorg (USA) 106 (Lear Fan (USA) 130) [2015 **109**
10.9g a8.9g* 10.9g a9.4g⁴ 11.9g³ 10.9g* 11.9m* 10.9m² 12m May 16] leggy, close-
coupled horse: useful performer: won minor events at Doha in January, March and April
(by nose from Ponfeigh): third in H. H. The Emir's Trophy on same course (¾ length
behind Dubday) on fifth start: well below form in listed race at Newbury final outing: stays
1½m: acts on fibresand, dirt, soft and good to firm going. *Zuhair Mohsen, Qatar*

PETERGATE 4 b.g. Alhaarth (IRE) 126 – Shamayel 85 (Pivotal 124) [2015 63: t8.6f 7m **48**
10g⁵ 10d⁵ 12d³ 10s⁴ 10.1g 16d 11.5s Aug 24] poor maiden: stays 1½m: acts on good to firm
and heavy going: often wears headgear: usually races prominently. *Brian Rothwell*

PETERHOF 3 b.c. Dansili 127 – Spinning Queen 118 (Spinning World (USA) 130) [2015 **94**
91p: 11g³ 10m³ 9.9s² 12g³ Sep 24] strong, attractive colt: fairly useful handicapper: placed
all 4 starts in 2015, best effort when 1¼ lengths second to Royal Toast at Goodwood: stays
1½m: acts on polytrack, soft and good to firm going: sold 120,000 gns, sent to UAE.
Sir Michael Stoute

PETERHOUSE (USA) 3 ch.g. Elusive Quality (USA) – Dynaire (USA) (Dynaformer **88**
(USA)) [2015 65p: p10m* 9.9m* 12m 10.4d⁴ 10g² 12m⁴ 8.9m² 9.9m* 9.9g⁴ 10.3m³
Sep 11] fairly useful handicapper: won at Lingfield in January and Beverley in April and
August: left John Gosden after first start: stays 10.5f: acts on polytrack and good to firm
going. *Jason Ward*

PETER ISLAND (FR) 12 b.g. Dansili 127 – Catania (USA) (Aloma's Ruler (USA)) **60**
[2015 6m³ 5.3m⁶ 5.3g Aug 7] smallish, strong gelding: modest handicapper: stays 7f: acts
on polytrack and firm going: usually wears headgear. *John Gallagher*

PETER PARK 2 b.c. (Mar 30) Kheleyf (USA) 116 – Go Go Gurl 74 (Pivotal 124) [2015 **76**
6.5m⁵ 6m³ 7s 7m⁵ t7.1f⁶ Oct 20] compact colt: fair maiden: stays 7f: acts on tapeta and
good to firm going. *Clive Cox*

PETER'S FRIEND 6 b.g. Gentleman's Deal (IRE) 114 – Giffoine 79 (Timeless Times **–**
(USA) 99) [2015 79: t9.5g Jan 19] fair handicapper: well held sole outing in 2015: stays
1m: acts on fibresand. *Michael Herrington*

PETHER'S MOON (IRE) 5 b.h. Dylan Thomas (IRE) 132 – Softly Tread (IRE) **121**
111 (Tirol 127) [2015 119: 12m² 12m³ 12m* Jun 6]
British-trained winners of the Investec Coronation Cup, the main supporting
race on Derby Day since being moved from its Friday slot in 2012, are becoming
an endangered species. Ask, who won the race for Sir Michael Stoute in 2009, and
the latest winner Pether's Moon are the only home-trained winners in the last eleven
runnings, seven of which have been farmed by Aidan O'Brien, with two others going
to French raiders. With no O'Brien-trained challenger for the latest edition, the prize

Investec Coronation Cup, Epsom—an upset as Pether's Moon (No.3) defeats market leaders Dolniya and Flintshire in this four-runner affair

looked destined for France with six-times winning trainer Andre Fabre saddling the previous year's Prix de l'Arc runner-up Flintshire (second in the Coronation Cup in 2014) and Alain de Royer Dupre represented by Dolniya, fifth in the previous year's Arc but twice triumphant since over Flintshire, including in the Dubai Sheema Classic on World Cup night in Dubai. The pair stood out on form with Dolniya sent off at 11/8-on and Flintshire at 7/4. The Coronation Cup's first prize of £212,663 befits its status as the premier mile and a half event for older horses in Britain in the early-summer, and it seems to be repelling what looked at one time likely to prove a strong challenge for that title from the Hardwicke Stakes, Royal Ascot's mile and a half contest for older horses. Although the quality of the Hardwicke has been improving, attempts to elevate it to Group 1 status—it is run without penalties—have not succeeded and it remains a Group 2, the first prize for the latest running, which was an all-domestic affair, being just a little over half that for the Coronation Cup. The Epsom authorities cannot afford to be complacent, though, with the home-trained defence sometimes chronically weak in recent years for a race of the importance of the Coronation Cup. Firmish conditions were the reason for the late withdrawal of the previous year's Derby third Romsdal from the latest edition which, with the exodus of outsider Ayrad too, was left with a field of four, the consistent Pether's Moon and globe-trotting Sheikhzayedroad, who had finished fifth in the Sheema Classic on his most recent outing, both having something to find on their overseas opponents and starting at 11/1 and 12/1 respectively.

Pether's Moon is as reliable as they come and, after progressing into a smart performer at three, he made the breakthrough to pattern level as a four-year-old with wins in the Glorious Stakes at Goodwood, the Bosphorus Cup at Veliefendi and the Cumberland Lodge Stakes at Ascot (he also came third in the Hardwicke). It was still seemingly asking plenty of him to win a Coronation Cup, especially after a rare poor run when a well-beaten third of four in the Jockey Club Stakes on his most recent outing. There seemed no obvious reason for Pether's Moon's performance at Newmarket but, in a move seemingly instigated by the horse's owner, Pat Dobbs replaced champion jockey Richard Hughes at Epsom. Dobbs rides as a freelance but has been an important part of the Hannon set-up over the years and, with Hughes set to retire from the saddle to take up training (he eventually hung up his saddle after Goodwood), more of the rides for the Hannon yard were being shared out as Richard Hannon managed the transition. Dobbs enjoyed the best campaign of his career, riding sixty-four winners in spite of having to sit out the end of the turf season as he served a sixteen-day ban after being referred to the BHA for a fifth whip offence of between two and six days during the season. After 'working around

Richard, covering the second meetings', Dobbs will be hoping for more big days like the one he enjoyed on Pether's Moon at Epsom. In a muddling affair, Dobbs took his chance to shine, extricating Pether's Moon from a tight spot on the rail in the home straight, and bringing him with a late run to head Dolniya close home after the favourite had looked to have things under control. 'He has loads of speed but just pulls up when he gets to the front, he was very good there,' said Dobbs afterwards. Pether's Moon beat Dolniya by a neck, with Flintshire a length and a half back in third. Pether's Moon seemed to put up a career-best effort, though the form couldn't be taken literally, with Dolniya's performance leaving the distinct impression that she was probably asked to start the sprint for home a shade sooner than was ideal, given the fairish rise to the winning post in the last furlong at Epsom. Pether's Moon didn't get the chance to show whether he could repeat his Coronation Cup form, as he wasn't seen again. He has been retired to stud at Yorton Farm in Powys where he will stand at £1,500 in 2016.

		Danehill (b 1986)	Danzig Razyana
	Dylan Thomas (IRE) (b 2003)		
		Lagrion (ch 1989)	Diesis Wrap It Up
Pether's Moon (IRE) (b.h. 2010)			
		Tirol (br 1987)	Thatching Alpine Niece
	Softly Tread (IRE) (b 1998)		
		Second Guess (b 1986)	Ela-Mana-Mou Warning Sound

The big, good-topped Pether's Moon is by Dylan Thomas, a top-class racehorse (winner of the Arc and the Irish Derby, and two renewals of the Irish Champion) but nowhere near so successful as a sire, having started out at a fee of

Mr John Manley's "Pether's Moon"

€50,000 in 2008 but now languishing as a member of Coolmore's National Hunt team, costing just €5,000 in 2015. Dylan Thomas probably had his most successful year so far, with the very smart Dylan Mouth winning two Group 1s in Italy, Nightflower winning the Preis von Europa and Blazing Speed winning in Group 1 company in Hong Kong. Softly Tread, the dam of Pether's Moon, won the Gladness Stakes over seven furlongs and finished seventh in Imagine's Irish One Thousand Guineas. Pether's Moon is her second winner, following his fair year-older sister Mona Brown who won twice at a mile and once at a mile and a quarter for Jim Bolger. Pether's Moon's grandam Second Guess was a fairly useful performer in Ireland, successful at a mile and a quarter, and is a half-sister to the Moyglare runner-up Heed My Warning. Pether's Moon stayed a mile and a half and acted on polytrack, soft and good to firm going. He often travelled strongly in his races and usually raced prominently. To see such a consistent type fitted with blinkers in the 2014 Geoffrey Freer Stakes at Newbury (just after he had won the Glorious Stakes) came as a surprise at the time; he didn't show his form in them and never wore headgear again. *Richard Hannon*

PETITE MADAME (IRE) 4 b.f. Champs Elysees 124 – Seeking The Fun (USA) – (Alhaarth (IRE) 126) [2015 –: 8d f14d⁶ 16.1m Jun 6] maiden: no form in 2015: often wears headgear: tried in tongue tie: has looked none too keen. *David Thompson*

PETIT TRIANON 3 b.f. Dansili 127 – Jolie Etoile (USA) (Diesis 133) [2015 6f³ 6m² Jun 29] rather leggy filly: sixth foal: sister to useful winner up to 12.5f Preferential (2-y-o 1m winner) and half-sister to 2-y-o 6f winner Rule of Nature (by Oasis Dream): dam maiden half-sister to smart French/US 6.5f-8.5f winner Etoile Montante: fair form when placed in maidens at Salisbury and Windsor (found nothing, reportedly bled). *Roger Charlton* **73**

PETRIFY 5 b.g. Rock of Gibraltar (IRE) 133 – Frigid (Indian Ridge 123) [2015 55: t12.2g⁵ 13.1m³ 11.5d⁵ 10.2m² 12.1m³ 12.1m² 12.1s⁴ 11.9d² 10.2d⁶ 13.1d³ 13.1m⁵ 11.9s Oct 6] modest maiden: stays 13f: acts on polytrack, good to firm and good to soft going: sometimes wears cheekpieces: often wears tongue tie: often starts slowly/races in rear: irresolute. *Bernard Llewellyn* **54 §**

PETRUCCI (IRE) 3 b.c. Azamour (IRE) 130 – Spring Symphony (IRE) 94 (Darshaan 133) [2015 10m p10f* 10g³ Oct 19] brother to Australian 1m-1½m winner Fruehling and half-brother to 3 winners, including winner up to 11f Glass Harmonium (2-y-o 7f winner, by Verglas) and 1¼m-1½m winner Arab Spring (by Monsun), both very smart: dam, 1½m winner, sister to Great Voltigeur winner Hard Top and closely related to top-class 1½m performer and St Leger winner Conduit: fairly useful form: won maiden at Chelmsford (by ½ length from Tartoor) in September: best effort when ½-length third to Wild Storm in handicap at Windsor final start: should be suited by 1½m: open to further improvement. *Sir Michael Stoute* **91 p**

PETTICOATED PIRATE 2 ch.f. (Feb 26) Bahamian Bounty 116 – Rosy Alexander 73 (Spartacus (IRE) 107) [2015 7g t7.1f⁵ p8g⁶ Nov 26] useful-looking filly: has scope: second foal: dam 2-y-o 7f winner: modest form in maidens, not knocked about: remains with potential. *David Simcock* **63 p**

PETTOCHSIDE 6 b.g. Refuse To Bend (IRE) 128 – Clear Impression (IRE) 103 (Danehill (USA) 126) [2015 83: 5m³ 6m⁴ 6g 6g⁶ 6g³ 6m 6d⁴ 6s⁴ 6g⁵ 6g² p6f p6d Nov 30] useful-looking gelding: fair handicapper: won at Goodwood in August (apprentice) and September: left Chris Gordon after tenth start: stays 6f: acts on polytrack, soft and good to firm going: sometimes in tongue tie prior to 2015. *John Bridger* **78**

PHANTASMAGORIC (IRE) 3 b.f. Dansili 127 – Sacred Song (USA) 116 (Diesis 133) [2015 60p: 9.9d 10m⁵ 11.7m³ 10g* Jul 30] fair performer: won handicap at Ffos Las in July: will stay 1½m: acts on good to firm going: often races prominently: likely to progress further. *Sir Michael Stoute* **71 p**

PHANTOM FLIPPER 2 ch.c. (Mar 10) Bahamian Bounty 116 – Artistic License (IRE) 94 (Chevalier (IRE) 115) [2015 6g³ 6m 6g² 7g² 8.1s³ t8.6g⁶ f7f² p7g³ Dec 28] sturdy colt: fair maiden: stays 7f: acts on polytrack and fibresand, best turf form on good going: often races prominently. *Richard Hannon* **74**

PHANTOM RIVER 3 b.f. Observatory (USA) 131 – Madam'x 51 (Xaar 132) [2015 t9.5g³ 10s⁵ p12g t8.6f³ t8.6f Nov 20] first foal: dam maiden (stayed 1½m): fair maiden: will prove suited by a return to 1¼m+: acts on soft going. *Alan King* **73**

PHANTOM SPIRIT 4 b.f. Invincible Spirit (IRE) 121 – Jackie's Opera (FR) (Indian – Ridge 123) [2015 –: f7g⁴ f8s Jan 20] poor maiden: often in headgear: sometimes slowly away. *Rae Guest*

PHARADELLE (IRE) 3 ch.f. Lope de Vega (IRE) 125 – Pharaoh's Delight 112 (Fairy **69** King (USA)) [2015 8d 7.2s³ p8g² Dec 2] half-sister to several winners, including 2-y-o 6f winner Pharmacist (by Machiavellian), herself dam of Breeders' Cup Turf winner Red Rocks, and 2-y-o 7f winner Phariseek (by Rainbow Quest), both useful: dam 2-y-o 5f/6f winner, including Phoenix Stakes: fair maiden: best effort when second at Lingfield final outing (carried head awkwardly): stays 1m: in tongue tie last 2 starts. *K. J. Condon, Ireland*

PHARAOH 2 b.c. (Feb 4) Paco Boy (IRE) 129 – Royal Circles (Royal Applause 124) **75** [2015 6g⁵ 6g 5s* Aug 26] £20,000Y: second foal: dam unraced sister to useful 6f/7f winner Right Touch and half-sister to useful 1m winner Forgive: fair performer: best effort when winning maiden at Bath in August by length from Belledesert: should stay at least 6f: sold 4,500 gns, sent to Italy. *Richard Hannon*

PHARMACEUTICAL (IRE) 3 b.g. Invincible Spirit (IRE) 121 – Pharmacist (IRE) 108 **94** (Machiavellian (USA) 123) [2015 p7m* t7.1g⁵ p7f⁴ p7g⁴ 8m³ 7m² 7.4g⁵ 7s² 6.1m⁶ 6g t7.1f* Oct 13] €100,000Y: half-brother to several winners, including very smart 1¼m-1½m (Breeders' Cup Turf) winner Red Rocks and smart French 1¼m/11f winner Galvaun (both by Galileo): dam 2-y-o 6f winner: fairly useful performer: won maiden at Lingfield in January and handicap at Wolverhampton (by length from Seychelloise) in October: stays 7f: acts on polytrack and tapeta, soft and good to firm going: sometimes in hood: often races towards rear, usually travels strongly. *Charles Hills*

PHAROH JAKE 7 ch.g. Piccolo 121 – Rose Amber (Double Trigger (IRE) 123) [2015 **63** 73: p6m⁶ p5f⁴ p5f³ p5m² p5m⁵ p5f² p5g⁶ p5g⁴ 5.3g⁶ p6g³ p5g² 5m⁵ p5g⁵ 5s⁴ 5.3d⁵ p5f **a71** Sep 22] smallish gelding: fair handicapper: stays 6f: acts on polytrack, good to firm and heavy going: tried in visor prior to 2015. *John Bridger*

PHILADELPHIA (IRE) 2 b.g. (Feb 26) Roderic O'Connor (IRE) 119 – Harvest Joy **74 p** (IRE) 89 (Daggers Drawn (USA) 114) [2015 7d³ Oct 23] €52,000Y: third foal: half-brother to 5f-6.5f (including at 2 yrs) winner Andhesontherun (by Captain Rio) and 2-y-o 6f winner (stays 1¼m) Don Sigfredo (by Majestic Missile): dam temperamental winner up to 1¼m (2-y-o 6f winner): 16/1, encouragement when 7 lengths third of 13 to Royal Artillery in maiden at Doncaster on debut, effort flattening out: should prove as effective at 6f: has been gelded: will improve. *Roger Varian*

PHILBA 3 b.g. Cockney Rebel (IRE) 127 – Hisaronu (IRE) 75 (Stravinsky (USA) 133) **71 +** [2015 66: 9.9m⁵ 10.2s 11.9m 14.1m 7m* 7d 7m³ f8g² f8g* f7f* Dec 17] fairly useful **a91** handicapper: won at Catterick in August: much improved when also successful at Southwell in November and December (by 2¼ lengths from Shootingsta): stays 1m: acts on fibresand and good to firm going: sometimes wears headgear, also in tongue tie last 3 starts. *Michael Appleby*

PHILHARMONIC HALL 7 b.g. Victory Note (USA) 120 – Lambast 70 (Relkino 131) **64** [2015 12.1v² 11.9d⁵ Sep 25] good-topped gelding: modest maiden: stays 1½m: acts on good to firm and heavy going: sometimes in headgear prior to 2015. *Peter Hiatt*

PHOENIX PHIL 3 ch.g. Phoenix Reach (IRE) 124 – Pearl's Girl 86 (King's Best (USA) – 132) [2015 –: 7s 6g May 16] little form. *Shaun Harris*

PHOIBE 3 b.f. Royal Applause 124 – Polish Belle (Polish Precedent (USA) 131) [2015 85: **92** 6.5m* 7s 6g⁵ 7g 6.5g² 6.5g* 7g⁶ 7d² a7.5g² p7.5g Dec 27] fairly useful performer: won maiden at Magdeburg in April and handicap on same course in August: well below form in Chartwell Fillies' Stakes at Lingfield on second outing: stays 7.5f: acts on sand, good to firm and good to soft going. *P. Schiergen, Germany*

PHOSPHORESCENCE (IRE) 5 b.g. Sakhee (USA) 136 – Eccentricity (USA) 75 – (Kingmambo (USA) 125) [2015 83: 10.4g p11g Jul 8] fairly useful at best, no form in 2015: stays 1½m: acts on polytrack and good to soft going: in cheekpieces first start in 2015. *Lady Cecil*

PHOTO OPPORTUNITY 8 b.g. Zamindar (USA) 116 – Fame At Last (USA) 98 (Quest – For Fame 127) [2015 t9.5g Jan 19] useful performer in 2010: very lightly raced and well held since. *John Norton*

PHYLLIS MAUD (IRE) 3 ch.f. Halling (USA) 133 – Debonnaire 82 (Anabaa (USA) **82** 130) [2015 69: 10.2m² 10.2f* 9.9g⁴ t12.2g* 12.2m* t13.9m p10g Dec 19] fairly useful handicapper: won at Bath in July, Wolverhampton (amateur) in August and Musselburgh in September: stays 1½m: acts on tapeta and firm going: front runner/races prominently. *Simon Crisford*

PIANOLA (USA) 3 b.f. Arch (USA) 127 – Firey Red (IRE) 99 (Pivotal 124) [2015 7d⁵ **62** 10d⁶ 8.3g³ 10g 14.1d t16.5f Nov 16] first foal: dam 6f (at 2 yrs) to 8.5f (in USA) winner: modest maiden: left D. K. Weld after second start: best effort at 7f: acts on good to soft going: in headgear last 3 starts. *Rebecca Menzies*

PIAZON 4 br.g. Striking Ambition 122 – Colonel's Daughter 61 (Colonel Collins (USA) **91 §** 122) [2015 97: 5g 5.1s⁶ 6d 6g³ 6d³ 6g 5s⁵ 6g Oct 20] good-topped gelding: fairly useful handicapper: best efforts in 2015 when third at Ripon and Haydock: reportedly bled final outing: stays 6f: acts on firm and soft going: often races towards rear: tends to hang left: unreliable. *Kevin Ryan*

PIAZZA SAN PIETRO 9 ch.g. Compton Place 125 – Rainbow Spectrum (FR) 57 **–** (Spectrum (IRE) 126) [2015 t6f p6g Dec 3] sparely-made gelding: fairly useful handicapper in 2013, little encouragement in 2 runs since: stays 7f: acts on polytrack and any turf going: usually wears headgear. *Zoe Davison*

PICANSORT 8 b.g. Piccolo 121 – Running Glimpse (IRE) 84 (Runnett 125) [2015 69, **64** a92: p5g⁵ p5m² p5m⁶ p5g p5f⁴ p5g⁶ p5g³ 5m³ 6m² p5g 5.3g* 6g² 5g⁵ p5g⁶ p5g⁴ p5g² Dec **a77** 19] good-topped gelding: fair handicapper: won at Brighton in August: stays 6f: acts on polytrack, good to firm and good to soft going: often wears headgear: tried in tongue tie prior to 2015. *Peter Crate*

PICCACARD 2 b.f. (Feb 19) Piccolo 121 – All Business 92 (Entrepreneur 123) [2015 5g⁴ **55** 6g 5m⁵ 7g⁴ 6m⁴ 6g² 6m⁵ 6d p6f⁶ f7g² f6g³ f7g² f8g⁵ f7g⁵ Dec 18] half-sister to useful winner up to 1m The Kyllachy Kid (2-y-o 6f winner, by Kyllachy) and a winner abroad by Zafeen: dam 1½m winner who stayed 15f: modest maiden: left Nigel Tinkler after eighth start: should stay 1m: acts on fibresand: sometimes in visor. *Michael Appleby*

PICCADILLY JIM (IRE) 4 gr.g. Royal Applause 124 – Silver Dip 90 (Gulch (USA)) **81** [2015 74: 6g 8g³ 8g* 9.3g² 9.1g⁶ 8.3s³ 9.2g² 9.2g⁴ 10g* 10v* t8.6m⁵ Nov 21] fairly useful performer: won handicap at Pontefract in June, seller at Redcar in October and claimer at Redcar in November: stays 1¼m: acts on heavy going: tried in visor in 2015: usually races prominently, often travels strongly. *Richard Fahey*

PICCARDO 2 ch.g. (Apr 14) Piccolo 121 – Billiard 73 (Kirkwall 118) [2015 6g 6m⁵ p6g **62** Nov 11] modest maiden: best effort when fifth at Hamilton: still looked green final start. *Richard Fahey*

PICC OF BURGAU 5 b.m. Piccolo 121 – Rosein 86 (Komaite (USA)) [2015 69: p5g Jul **–** 14] quite attractive mare: fair handicapper: well held only outing in 2015: stays 5.5f: acts on soft and good to firm going: often races towards rear. *Geoffrey Deacon*

PICCOLO EXPRESS 9 b.g. Piccolo 121 – Ashfield 67 (Zilzal (USA) 137) [2015 56: **52** t7.1f³ t7.1g³ t7.1f t7.1m t7.1f 7.1m 7g 7g Sep 19] modest maiden: stays 8.5f: acts on polytrack, tapeta, firm and good to soft going: tried in cheekpieces: front runner/races prominently. *Brian Baugh*

PICENO (IRE) 7 b.g. Camacho 118 – Ascoli (Skyliner 117) [2015 91§: f8g 7d³ 7g⁵ 7d **79 §** f7g³ f8g f8g f7g Dec 15] sturdy, close-coupled gelding: fair handicapper: stays 1m: acts **a68 §** on fibresand, good to firm and heavy going: usually wears headgear: front runner/races prominently: unreliable. *Scott Dixon*

PICK A LITTLE 7 b.g. Piccolo 121 – Little Caroline (IRE) (Great Commotion (USA) **83** 123) [2015 75: p6g p7m t1.1m³ f7g⁴ 7m* 8d* 8v⁵ 8g² 8.1m* 8.1m* 8d² Aug 5] close-coupled gelding: fairly useful handicapper: won at Brighton in April and May and at Chepstow in June and July: stays 1m: acts on polytrack, fibresand, firm and good to soft going: tried in cheekpieces prior to 2015: usually races close up. *Michael Blake*

PICKAPOCKET (IRE) 2 b.c. (Mar 23) Fast Company (IRE) 126 – Ann's Annie (IRE) **68** 78 (Alzao (USA) 117) [2015 6.1m 6m⁵ 6.1m⁵ 7d⁵ p8f³ Nov 23] well-made colt: fair maiden: left Charles Hills after third start: will be suited by at least 1¼m: acts on polytrack and good to firm going. *Andrew Balding*

PICKET LINE 3 b.g. Multiplex 114 – Dockside Strike (Docksider (USA) 124) [2015 60: **78** p6f² 7s p6f² p6g² t5.1f* Dec 11] fair performer: won maiden at Wolverhampton in December: will be suited by a return to 6f: acts on polytrack and tapeta. *Geoffrey Deacon*

PICKETT'S CHARGE 2 b.g. (Mar 29) Clodovil (IRE) 116 – Chelsea Morning (USA) **74** 80 (Giant's Causeway (USA) 132) [2015 6g 7.5g³ 7m* 8g⁵ 8g⁵ Sep 17] fair performer: won maiden at Newcastle in August: stays 7.5f: acts on good to firm going. *Tony Coyle*

PICKLE LILLY PEARL 3 b.f. Captain Gerrard (IRE) 113 – Branston Jewel (IRE) 95 **58** (Prince Sabo 123) [2015 62: 6m 6g⁶ 5g³ 5m² 5d⁵ 5s 6g² t6m⁵ t6m⁶ p7m⁵ t7.1f⁶ Oct 23] modest maiden: stays 6f: acts on tapeta and good to soft going: tried in headgear: often starts slowly, often races towards rear. *David C. Griffiths*

PICKS PINTA 4 b.g. Piccolo 121 – Past 'N' Present (Cadeaux Genereux 131) [2015 81: **77** p7g² t6g⁴ t7.1g⁴ 7m⁶ 6s³ Aug 15] fair handicapper: left Jo Hughes after first start: stays 1m: acts on polytrack, tapeta and firm going: wears headgear nowadays: often starts slowly, often races towards rear. *Patrick Morris*

PICK YOUR CHOICE 3 b.g. Elusive Quality (USA) – Enticement 102 (Montjeu (IRE) **96** 137) [2015 72p: p8m³ p8m* 8d Jul 25] tall, good-topped gelding: useful form: easily landed odds in maiden at Chelmsford in June: disappointing in handicap at Ascot only subsequent start: stays 1m. *William Haggas*

PICTOGRAPH (USA) 2 b.c. (Feb 13) Lonhro (AUS) 128 – Puppet Queen (USA) **83 p** (Kingmambo (USA) 125) [2015 7g t7.1f⁴ t7.1f³ Dec 22] second foal: dam unraced half-sister to high-class Hong Kong performer up to 1½m Vengeance of Rain: fairly useful maiden: best effort when third in maiden at Wolverhampton (2¼ lengths behind Always Welcome) in December: will be suited by 1m+: open to further improvement. *Charlie Appleby*

PICTURE DEALER 6 b.g. Royal Applause 124 – Tychy 102 (Suave Dancer (USA) 136) **94** [2015 98: p6m² p6g² 6d 6f⁴ p6g* 6m p6f Aug 18] useful handicapper: won at Chelmsford **a102** (by 2¾ lengths from Golden Amber) in July: stays 6.5f: acts on polytrack, soft and good to firm going: often races in maiden. *Lydia Pearce*

PICTURE PAINTER (IRE) 2 gr.g. (Apr 19) Zoffany (IRE) 121 – Sisceal (Dalakhani **78** (IRE) 133) [2015 6g⁶ 7.2g⁶ 6g³ 6d⁵ Oct 26] fair form: third in maiden at Ayr (½ length behind Cheeky Angel) in October: should stay at least 7f. *Jim Goldie*

PIDDIE'S POWER 8 ch.m. Starcraft (NZ) 128 – Telori 72 (Muhtarram (USA) 125) **67** [2015 73: t7.1g⁶ t7.1g t7.1g⁴ 7g⁴ Aug 15] lengthy mare: fair handicapper: stays 1m: acts on tapeta, firm and soft going: tried in cheekpieces/tongue tie prior to 2015. *Kevin Frost*

PIETRAFIORE (IRE) 2 ch.f. (Mar 11) Dubawi (IRE) 129 – Porto Roca (AUS) **70 p** (Barathea (IRE) 127) [2015 p8g⁴ Dec 15] sister to 2 winners, notably high-class 1m-12.4f winner (including Dubai World Cup) Monterosso, and half-sister to several winners, including useful winner up to 1½m Expert Fighter (2-y-o 1m winner, by Dubai Destination): dam smart Australian winner up to 1m, including Group 1 7.5f event: 10/3, always prominent when 1¾ lengths fourth to Cajoled in maiden at Kempton on debut: should do better. *Charlie Appleby*

PIKE CORNER CROSS (IRE) 3 b.g. Cape Cross (IRE) 129 – Smart Coco (USA) 98 **73** (Smarty Jones (USA) 134) [2015 7m 7d³ 8m⁵ 10g⁶ p10g Nov 25] fair maiden: best effort at 1m: acts on good to firm going: tried in tongue tie. *Joseph Tuite*

PILGRIM 3 ch.f. Bahamian Bounty 116 – Deep Bleu (Kyllachy 129) [2015 –: 6d⁴ 6d p6g⁵ **–** Aug 19] no form. *Eve Johnson Houghton*

PILGRIMS PATH 2 b.g. (Apr 29) Sakhee (USA) 136 – Scrooby Baby 66 (Mind Games **61** 121) [2015 6g⁴ 6s⁵ 6d⁵ 6s f6g f6g⁴ Dec 15] modest maiden: raced only at 6f: acts on soft going: in cheekpieces last 3 starts. *Scott Dixon*

PILGRIMS REST (IRE) 6 ch.g. Rock of Gibraltar (IRE) 133 – Holly Blue 107 **88** (Bluebird (USA) 125) [2015 96: 11.6g⁵ 13.4g⁴ 21.7f 21g 12v Aug 31] workmanlike gelding: fairly useful handicapper: stays 13.5f: acts on good to firm and heavy going: tried in cheekpieces in 2015: front runner/races prominently. *George Baker*

PILLAR 2 b.g. (Mar 5) Rock of Gibraltar (IRE) 133 – Ceilidh House 107 (Selkirk (USA) **65** 129) [2015 8.3s t8.6m p8g f8f² Dec 17] fair maiden: stays 8.5f: tried in blinkers. *Ralph Beckett*

PILLAR BOX (IRE) 3 ch.g. Sakhee's Secret 128 – Red Red Rose (Piccolo 121) [2015 **78** 82: 6g⁵ 5f⁴ 5m⁵ p5g 5f⁶ 5s p5g Oct 20] fair handicapper: best effort at 5f: acts on good to firm going: tried in blinkers in 2015: front runner/races prominently. *William Haggas*

PIMPERNELLA (IRE) 2 b.f. (Feb 5) Elusive Pimpernel (USA) 117 – Soviet Belle **–** (IRE) 85 (Soviet Star (USA) 128) [2015 7.6g⁶ 8.3g p8m Nov 19] sixth foal: half-sister to German 7f/1m winner Lonely Star (by Bachelor Duke) and 1m winner Bellini Bliss (by Big Bad Bob): dam, 2-y-o 6f winner, sister to smart winner up to 1¼m Eva's Request: no form. *Ed Dunlop*

PIM STREET (USA) 5 b.m. Street Sense (USA) 128 – Crown of Jewels (USA) (Half A **62** Year (USA) 130) [2015 73: t12.2f⁵ t8.6f⁴ Jan 29] rather unfurnished mare: modest handicapper: seems to stay 1½m: acts on polytrack, tapeta, best turf form on good going: tried in headgear: often races towards rear. *David O'Meara*

PINA 2 b.f. (Jan 27) Dansili 127 – Bourbonella (Rainbow Quest (USA) 134) [2015 p8m⁵ **71** p8g⁶ Dec 15] half-sister to several winners, including high-class 7f/1m winner Aqlaam (by Oasis Dream) and smart 1m winner Nine Realms (by Green Desert): dam unraced half-sister to very smart stayer Persian Punch: better effort when fifth in maiden at Lingfield in November: hung left home turn then faltered 2f out at Kempton on next start. *Roger Charlton*

PINCH A KISS 2 ch.f. (Mar 24) Sakhee's Secret 128 – Pin Cushion 85 (Pivotal 124) **65**
[2015 t5.1g³ p6g³ 5m t6g⁴ 7s 7d* 7s⁴ Oct 6] 4,000F, 7,000Y: workmanlike filly: first foal: dam, 6f winner, out of July Cup winner Frizzante: fair performer: won maiden at Brighton in September: stays 7f: acts on tapeta and soft going. *Jonathan Portman*

PINE RIDGE 2 b.f. (Apr 26) Elusive City (USA) 117 – Fisadara 69 (Nayef (USA) 129) **83 p**
[2015 5m⁴ 6m 5g* Oct 18] sturdy filly: third foal: half-sister to 7f winner Royal Connection (by Bahamian Bounty): dam, 11.6f winner, half-sister to smart 5.4f-7f winner Barney McGrew: fairly useful performer: much improved when winning maiden at Bath (by ¾ length from Summer Chorus) in October: should stay 6f: open to further improvement. *Clive Cox*

PINK AND BLACK (IRE) 4 b.f. Yeats (IRE) 128 – Raysiza (IRE) (Alzao (USA) 117) **–**
[2015 65: f11d⁶ p12g p12g Aug 26] rather leggy filly: maiden: no form in 2015: tried in hood: usually races freely. *William Muir*

PINK ANGEL (IRE) 2 gr.f. (Mar 10) Dark Angel (IRE) 113 – Xarzee (IRE) (Xaar 132) **61 p**
[2015 p6g* May 20] £22,000Y: fifth foal: half-sister to 3 winners, including useful 7f/1m winner Skaters Waltz (by Verglas) and 2-y-o 7.4f winner Magical Rose (by Elusive City): dam twice-raced half-sister to high-class 7f/1m winner Paco Boy: 7/1, won maiden at Kempton on debut by neck from Rial: open to improvement. *Paul Cole*

PINK DIAMOND 4 b.f. Champs Elysees 124 – Fairy Dance (IRE) (Zafonic (USA) 130) **60**
[2015 73: 10m 11.5d⁶ 10m⁴ 9.9m⁴ 10.2m 13.1d⁶ Sep 2] good-topped filly: modest handicapper: stays 13f: acts on good to firm and good to soft going: tried in headgear in 2015: usually races close up. *Eve Johnson Houghton*

PINK ICE 2 br.f. (May 21) Monsieur Bond (IRE) 120 – Ice Girl 49 (Iceman 117) [2015 6g 5.1g 6m 7g⁵ Jun 19] no form: tried in blinkers: dead. *Michael Easterby*

PINK LIPS 7 b.m. Noverre (USA) 125 – Primrose Queen (Lear Fan (USA) 130) [2015 **58 §**
69§: t8.6g t9.5m⁵ p12f² 11.8m p10f⁶ p12g Dec 2] modest handicapper: stays 1½m: acts on polytrack, soft and good to firm going: wears headgear nowadays: sometimes slowly away, lazy. *Neil Mulholland*

PINK MARTINI (IRE) 2 b.f. (Apr 2) Tagula (IRE) 116 – Ohwhatalady (IRE) (Invincible **61**
Spirit (IRE) 121) [2015 t6m⁶ t5.1f⁶ Oct 13] €4,000Y, €28,000 2-y-o: first foal: dam of little account: sixth in 2 maidens at Wolverhampton, better effort second start. *Joseph Tuite*

PINK RIBBON (IRE) 3 b.g. Dark Angel (IRE) 113 – My Funny Valentine (IRE) 105 **77**
(Mukkadamah (USA) 125) [2015 62: 10m p8f⁴ 10.2m⁵ 8m² 9g² 8.3g² 7g⁴ p10g* 8s⁴ p8f* 9.9s⁵ p10g² Nov 25] lengthy gelding: fair handicapper: won at Lingfield in August and September: stays 1¼m: acts on polytrack: usually in cheekpieces in 2015: front runner/races prominently. *Sylvester Kirk*

PINKY PROMISE (IRE) 2 b.f. (Mar 9) Zoffany (IRE) 121 – Promise of Love 75 (Royal **76**
Applause 124) [2015 7m 6m³ p6g³ 6s* 6.5m 5g p8g a7.5g p6.5g Dec 28] €10,000F, **a71**
£100,000Y: unfurnished filly: third foal: half-sister to 5f winner Where The Boys Are (by Dylan Thomas): dam, maiden (stayed 7f), half-sister to very smart sprinter Captain Rio: fair performer: won maiden at Brighton in August: left Richard Hannon 4,000 gns after sixth start: best effort at 6f: acts on soft going: tried in headgear: front runner/races prominently. *P. Monfort, France*

PINOTAGE 7 br.g. Danbird (AUS) – Keen Melody (USA) 60 (Sharpen Up 127) [2015 68: **56**
12d 12d 13.7m⁶ Sep 4] workmanlike gelding: modest handicapper: stays 1¾m: acts on polytrack, soft and good to firm going: often in headgear: quirky (flashes tail). *Peter Niven*

PINSTRIPE 2 br.c. (May 25) Dansili 127 – Paisley 80 (Pivotal 124) [2015 t7.1f p8f⁴ p8g⁶ **76 p**
Dec 9] third foal: brother to 8.3f winner Patterned and half-brother to 6f winner Duffel (by Shamardal): dam, 1¼m winner, half-sister to smart winner up to 1¾m Pinzolo out of Lancashire Oaks winner Pongee: fair maiden: best effort when fourth at Lingfield, considerably handled: bred to stay at least 1¼m: remains with potential. *Luca Cumani*

PINTLE'S IMAGE 3 b.f. Paco Boy (IRE) 129 – Pintle 103 (Pivotal 124) [2015 6d⁶ p7m **–**
Oct 28] third foal: half-sister to a winner abroad by Dutch Art: dam 5f-1m winner: behind in maidens at Windsor (signs of ability) and Kempton. *John Spearing*

PINTURA 8 ch.g. Efisio 120 – Picolette 56 (Piccolo 121) [2015 90: 8d² 8f 8g⁶ 8g³ 7d² 8d 8d 7.2g 8.3s² 8.3s³ Nov 4] neat gelding: useful handicapper: best efforts in 2015 when second at Galway (neck behind Baraweez) and Leicester (2¾ lengths behind Storm Rock) fifth/ninth starts: stays 9f: acts on good to firm and heavy going: usually in headgear: often races prominently. *Alistair Whillans* **101**

PIN UP (IRE) 3 b.f. Lookin At Lucky (USA) 127 – All My Loving (IRE) 113 (Sadler's Wells (USA) 132) [2015 79: p10g⁶ 12g³ 12d² 12g* 12d² 14d* 14m³ Oct 2] useful performer: won maiden at Ripon in August and handicap at Haydock (by nose from Dawn Missile) in September: good third in listed race at Ascot (3½ lengths behind Mill Springs) in October: will stay 2m: acts on fibresand, tapeta, good to firm and good to soft going: in cheekpieces last 2 starts: sent to USA. *Richard Fahey* **95**

PINZOLO 4 b.g. Monsun (GER) 124 – Pongee 110 (Barathea (IRE) 127) [2015 113: a9.9f⁶ p12f* 12g⁵ p14g* May 6] strong, good-topped gelding: smart performer: won handicap at Lingfield (by 3 lengths from First Mohican) in March and minor event at Chelmsford (by ½ length from Nearly Caught) in May: stays 1¾m: acts on polytrack, good to firm and good to soft going: usually in cheekpieces in 2015: usually races close up. *Charlie Appleby* **117**

PIPER BILL 4 b.g. Halling (USA) 133 – Murielle 68 (Diktat 126) [2015 –: 8m 10.1mᵖᵘ Jun 6] no form. *Jim Goldie* **–**

PIPERS NOTE 5 ch.g. Piccolo 121 – Madam Valentine (Primo Valentino (IRE) 116) [2015 106: 5m* 6g* 6g 5m* 5m⁵ 6m 5.6d 5d² 6g⁴ 6s Oct 10] strong gelding: smart performer: won handicaps at Beverley (by ½ length from Long Awaited) and Ripon (by ½ length from Another Wise Kid) in April and minor event at Beverley (by ½ length from Willbeme) in June: stays 6f: acts on soft and good to firm going: usually races prominently. *Richard Whitaker* **110**

PIPERS PIPING (IRE) 9 b.g. Noverre (USA) 125 – Monarchy (IRE) (Common Grounds 118) [2015 67: t9.5f⁶ p8f⁴ p10m t8.6g⁶ t8.6f² t7.1g³ t8.6m³ t7.1g* t8.6m t8.6f t7.1f Oct 16] leggy gelding: modest handicapper: won at Wolverhampton in June: stays 8.5f: acts on all-weather and good to soft going: sometimes in headgear/tried in tongue tie prior to 2015: often races towards rear. *Mandy Rowland* **59**

PIPPIN STREET 2 b.f. (Apr 8) Assertive 121 – Selkirk Rose (IRE) 74 (Pips Pride 117) [2015 5v² 5m⁴ 6m⁴ 6d 6g⁴ 7g² Dec 30] £3,000Y: half-sister to 3 winners, including useful winner up to 7f Miss Meggy (2-y-o 5f winner, by Pivotal) and 1m/8.6f winner Sir Lancelott (by Piccolo): dam winner up to 6f (2-y-o 5f winner): fair maiden: left Richard Fahey after fourth start: stays 7f. *Jassim Al Ghazali, Qatar* **69**

PIRATE COVE (IRE) 5 b.m. Lawman (FR) 121 – Uncharted Haven (Turtle Island (IRE) 123) [2015 82: p12m⁴ p10g⁴ f11g⁵ Feb 26] fair maiden: stays 1½m: acts on polytrack, soft and good to firm going: tried in headgear prior to 2015: tends to find little. *Mark Johnston* **67**

PIRATE'S TREASURE 2 b.c. (Mar 1) Iffraaj 127 – Musical Sands (Green Desert (USA) 127) [2015 t7.1m³ p7g⁴ Dec 16] fair form when in frame in maidens at Wolverhampton and Kempton. *James Tate* **68**

PIRI WANGO (IRE) 6 ch.g. Choisir (AUS) 126 – Zoldan (Deploy 131) [2015 115: 7d² 8v⁴ 8f 9d⁴ 7d 8g 8d 10d Sep 13] strong gelding: smart performer in 2014: useful form in 2015, second in Gladness Stakes at the Curragh (1¼ lengths behind Flight Risk) and fourth in Amethyst Stakes (to Onenightidreamed) and Meld Stakes (to Carla Bianca) at Leopardstown: stays 1¼m: acts on polytrack, good to firm and heavy going: sometimes in headgear. *G. M. Lyons, Ireland* **106**

PIROUETTE 2 ch.f. (Apr 19) Pivotal 124 – Passiflora 75 (Night Shift (USA)) [2015 p7g² p7g⁴ p8f² Nov 12] 40,000Y: lengthy filly: half-sister to several winners, including US Grade 2 1m winner Passified (2-y-o 6f winner, by Compton Place) and useful winner up to 7f Zomerlust (2-y-o 6f winner, by Josr Algarhoud): dam 2-y-o 6f winner: fair maiden: best effort when second at Chelmsford (1¾ lengths behind Flyweight) in November, not ideally placed: still unexposed. *Hughie Morrison* **74 p**

PISCES 3 b.f. Halling (USA) 133 – Optimistic 90 (Reprimand 122) [2015 54: p10g³ t12.2m³ Feb 17] modest maiden: should stay 1½m: acts on polytrack: in cheekpieces in 2015: often races towards rear. *David Elsworth* **56**

PISTON (IRE) 3 b.g. Paco Boy (IRE) 129 – Fairy Contessa (IRE) 63 (Fairy King (USA)) [2015 t7.1g⁶ 6m May 3] well held in maidens at Wolverhampton and Salisbury. *Clive Cox* **–**

PISTYLL RHAEADR 3 ch.f. Mount Nelson 125 – Sukuma (IRE) 55 (Highest Honor –
(FR) 124) [2015 t9.5g t8.6m⁵ 7.1m t9.5f t12.2f Oct 16] half-sister to several winners,
including 1m winner Geordan Murphy (by Firebreak) and 2-y-o 6f winner Bottle Blonde
(by Indesatchel), later winner up to 8.5f in USA: dam maiden (stayed 1m): no form: tried
in visor. *Ed McMahon*

PITT RIVERS 6 br.g. Vital Equine (IRE) 121 – Silca Boo 99 (Efisio 120) [2015 61: 6g **60**
7.1s 6s 7.2d² 7.2g 6d 7.2d⁵ 8.3g 6d 6g⁵ 7.2g⁵ 6g 7.2g⁶ 7.2g Oct 13] close-coupled gelding:
modest handicapper: stays 7f: acts on good to firm and heavy going: tried in headgear:
sometimes slowly away: none too consistent. *Linda Perratt*

PITY CASH (IRE) 2 b.f. (Apr 30) Approve (IRE) 112 – Farthing (IRE) 73 (Mujadil **79**
(USA) 119) [2015 5g³ 5f 5f* 5.1g³ 5g 5.2s³ 6.1m⁶ 6s⁶ 6.3d Sep 13] €4,000Y: small,
sparely-made filly: fifth foal: half-sister to 1m winner (stayed 1¼m) Misleading Promise
(by Refuse To Bend) and a winner in Italy by Kheleyf: dam, maiden (stayed 7f), half-sister
to very smart performer up to 1m Kalahari Gold: fair performer: won maiden at Bath in
July: best form at 5f: acts on firm and soft going. *David Evans*

PIVOTAL DREAM (IRE) 2 br.f. (Feb 14) Excellent Art 125 – Oasis Fire (IRE) 85 **57**
(Oasis Dream 129) [2015 5m t5.1g 6g⁶ 7m 8.3g 8g⁶ t8.6g 8.3s³ t9.5f t9.5f⁴ t8.6f² t9.5f²
Dec 11] 4,000Y: second foal: half-sister to 2-y-o 6f winner Secret Friend (by Royal
Applause): dam 1m winner: modest maiden: stays 9.5f: acts on tapeta, soft and good to firm
going: often races prominently. *Mark Brisbourne*

PIVOTIQUE 3 b.f. Pivotal 124 – Suba (USA) 85 (Seeking The Gold (USA)) [2015 –p: **69 p**
8m⁴ 10s⁶ Aug 14] lengthy, rather unfurnished filly: second foal: dam, 8.3f winner, closely
related to high-class miler Dubawi: lightly-raced maiden: left John Oxx, fair form at
Haydock and Newbury in 2015: remains open to improvement. *Luca Cumani*

PIVOTMAN 7 ch.g. Pivotal 124 – Grandalea 85 (Grand Lodge (USA) 125) [2015 72, a86: **75**
p12g* t9.5g⁵ 10.4m 11.5g 8f³ 10.4m 10m³ 8g³ t7.1g³ 8m Sep 9] rangy gelding: fair **a87**
handicapper on turf, fairly useful on all-weather: won at Kempton (amateur) in January:
stays 1½m: acts on polytrack, tapeta and any turf going: usually in blinkers: wears tongue
tie: sometimes slowly away. *Michael Easterby*

PIVOT POINT (IRE) 3 b.g. Excellent Art 125 – Lily of Laguna (IRE) 70 (Zafeen (FR) **66**
123) [2015 72: 8.3m 8m 7.1m⁴ 10g Jul 22] fair maiden: likely to prove best up to 1m: acts
on good to firm going: tried in blinkers prior to 2015. *Brian Meehan*

PIXELEEN 3 b.f. Pastoral Pursuits 127 – Ballyalla 90 (Mind Games 121) [2015 71: 5.7f **86**
5m* 5.1m² 5m* 5m³ 5g³ 6d³ 5f⁴ 6g³ Sep 30] lengthy, rather unfurnished filly: fairly useful
handicapper: won at Salisbury in June and Bath in July: stays 6f: acts on good to firm and
good to soft going: usually races close up. *Malcolm Saunders*

PIXEY PUNK 3 gr.f. Mount Nelson 125 – Mosquera (GER) 108 (Acatenango (GER) 127) –
[2015 –: t8.6g 12g Jun 8] no form. *Tim Easterby*

PIXIE CUT (IRE) 5 b.m. Chineur (FR) 123 – Fantastic Cee (IRE) 71 (Noverre (USA) **66**
125) [2015 79: 8.3d⁴ 11.1m⁴ 16m⁵ 11.1s⁴ 15.8m⁵ 9.8g⁴ 11.5s Aug 24] lengthy mare: fair
handicapper: stays 13f: acts on good to firm and heavy going: sometimes in headgear in
2015. *Alistair Whillans*

PLAGIARISM (USA) 2 b.f. (May 3) Lonhro (AUS) 128 – Journalist (IRE) 102 (Night **86**
Shift (USA)) [2015 5m* 6g³ 5m³ 6.1m⁵ Aug 22] compact filly: half-sister to several
winners, including 7f/1m winner Paper Talk (by Unbridled's Song) and 2-y-o 6f winner La
Presse (by Gone West), both useful: dam, 2-y-o 6f winner, half-sister to useful sprinter
Sheer Viking: fairly useful performer: won maiden at Newcastle in June: third in listed race
at Newbury (½ length behind Tasleet) next start: stays 6f. *Mark Johnston*

PLAIN STRIKING 6 b.m. Striking Ambition 122 – Daphne's Doll (IRE) 72 (Polish
Patriot (USA) 128) [2015 –: p7g Jan 7] showed nothing in 2 maidens at Kempton: dead. *Dr
Jeremy Naylor*

PLAISIR (IRE) 3 b.f. Elusive City (USA) 117 – Sea Sex Sun (Desert Prince (IRE) 130) **70**
[2015 71: p8g² p8f⁴ t7.1g² t7.1g 7.6m⁵ Jun 26] fair maiden: stayed 1m: acted on polytrack,
tapeta and good to firm going: tried in headgear: dead. *Marco Botti*

PLANE SONG (IRE) 3 ch.g. Nayef (USA) 129 – Kitty Hawk 88 (Danehill Dancer (IRE) **84**
117) [2015 10m³ 9.8d³ 9.9m* 12d⁴ 12d⁶ Aug 26] third foal: half-brother to ungenuine 1m
winner (stays 1¼m) Tercel (by Monsun): dam, 6f (at 2 yrs) and 1m (in USA) winner,
closely related to useful performer up to 1½m Pamona: fairly useful performer: won
maiden at Salisbury in June: should stay 1½m: acts on good to firm and good to soft going:
tried in visor: temperament under suspicion. *Sir Michael Stoute*

PLANETARIA (IRE) 2 b.g. (Mar 3) Lilbourne Lad (IRE) 111 – Red Planet (Pivotal 124)   **72**
[2015 7g 6m 7g² 6g⁴ 8g* 7.2g³ p8f⁵ f7g³ f8m² Dec 8] fair performer: left Tony Coyle, won
nursery at Redcar in September: stays 1m: acts on fibresand, best turf form on good going:
tried in blinkers: front runner/races prominently. *Garry Moss*

PLANETOID (IRE) 7 b.g. Galileo (IRE) 134 – Palmeraie (USA) (Lear Fan (USA) 130)   **76**
[2015 14.1m Apr 28] rangy gelding: fairly useful handicapper in 2014, probably needed
run only outing in 2015: stays 2m: acts on polytrack and good to firm going: wears
headgear. *Jim Best*

PLANTATION (IRE) 2 b.g. (Apr 10) Invincible Spirit (IRE) 121 – Matula (IRE) 86   **–**
(Halling (USA) 133) [2015 6m 6v 5g⁶ 5d Oct 26] well held in 3 maidens (subsequently
gelded) and a nursery. *Roger Varian*

PLATINUM PROOF (USA) 5 b.g. Smart Strike (CAN) 121 – Keeper Hill (USA) 122   **–**
(Deputy Minister (CAN)) [2015 p10m 11.5d⁴ 14.1g t12.2f Dec 21] maiden: no form in
2015: often wears headgear: tried in tongue tie prior to 2015. *John Berry*

PLATITUDE 2 b.c. (Mar 21) Dansili 127 – Modesta (IRE) 105 (Sadler's Wells (USA)   **100**
132) [2015 7m* 7d² 8g³ p8m⁵ Sep 26] strong, compact colt: brother to useful winner up to
1m Intense (2-y-o 7f winner) and 1½m winner Archive and half-brother to 3 winners,
including smart 1¼m-1½m winner Model Pupil (by Sinndar): dam, 11.5f-1¾m winner,
closely related to Oaks winner Reams of Verse: useful performer: won maiden at Doncaster
in June: better form when placed in listed races at Ascot (1¼ lengths second of 4 to Sixth
Sense) and Salisbury (3¼ lengths third of 5 to Tony Curtis): in cheekpieces when well
below best on all-weather debut final start: will be suited by 1¼m+. *Sir Michael Stoute*

PLATONIC LOVE (IRE) 2 b.f. (May 10) Danehill Dancer (IRE) 117 – Cat Belling   **–**
(IRE) 109 (Catrail (USA) 123) [2015 6g May 29] third foal: dam winner up to 1m (2-y-o
5f winner): 20/1, well held in maiden at Newcastle. *John Patrick Shanahan, Ireland*

PLAUSEABELLA 4 b.f. Royal Applause 124 – Ellablue 63 (Bahamian Bounty 116)   **67**
[2015 55: 7g* 7v 7m* 8.1m² 7.1s³ Jul 24] fair handicapper: won at Brighton in April and
Lingfield in June: stays 1m: acts on good to firm going: often in headgear nowadays: front
runner/races prominently. *Stuart Kittow*

PLAYBOY BAY 3 b.g. Indesatchel (IRE) 120 – Dim Ofan 80 (Petong 126) [2015 68§:   **65**
9.8d 10g 7.5f 8g³ 7m 7g⁴ 7d² 7v Nov 3] lengthy gelding: fair maiden: stays 10.5f: acts on
good to soft going: tried in headgear: none too consistent. *Ron Barr*

PLAY GAL 2 b.f. (Feb 8) Multiplex 114 – Plead (FR) (Bering 136) [2015 8.3d 9d* Oct 26]   **80 p**
half-sister to several winners, including 2-y-o 6f winner Adele Blanc Sec (by Marchand de
Sable) and French 1½m winner Quart de Cidre (by Hernando): dam, French 11f winner,
half-sister to smart French/US performer up to 12.5f Playact: 9/1, showed benefit of
experience when winning maiden at Redcar in October by head from Soldier In Action,
well positioned: sure to stay at least 1¼m: likely to do better still. *David Evans*

PLAYMAKER (IRE) 3 b.g. Dubawi (IRE) 129 – Playful Act (IRE) 113 (Sadler's Wells   **–**
(USA) 132) [2015 p10f p8g⁵ Feb 14] well held in 2 maidens at Lingfield, in cheekpieces in
latter. *Charlie Appleby*

PLAY NICELY 3 ch.g. Naaqoos 117 – Aalya (IRE) 65 (Peintre Celebre (USA) 137) [2015   **66**
–: f5s⁴ t6g⁵ f6s³ f7d² p8g³ f7d* t7.1g t7.1g⁵ 7.5m 10s Oct 16] fair performer: first past the
post in maiden at Southwell in March and, having left James Given, handicap at Redcar
(disqualified after saddle came off, weighing in 21 lb light as a result) on final outing: stays
1m: acts on all-weather: often in cheekpieces in 2015: front runner/races prominently:
temperament under suspicion (has hung/carried head high). *David Barron*

PLAY THE BLUES (IRE) 8 gr.m. Refuse To Bend (IRE) 128 – Paldouna (IRE)   **57**
(Kaldoun (FR) 122) [2015 51: p8m² p8f* p8g⁴ 8.3g t8.6g³ t7.1g p8g⁴ t9.5f Oct 27] lengthy,
angular mare: modest handicapper: won at Lingfield in May: stays 8.5f, effective at shorter:
acts on polytrack, tapeta and good to firm going: often in headgear prior to 2015: wears
tongue tie: sometimes slowly away, often races freely. *Henry Tett*

PLAY THE FIELD (IRE) 3 ch.c. Fast Company (IRE) 126 – Tarakana (USA) 101   **73**
(Shahrastani (USA) 135) [2015 p6.5g p6.5g p8g⁵ p9.4g p9.4g* 10.4s² p9.4g p9.4g Dec 11]
fair performer: left Gay Kelleway after third start: won handicap at Deauville in August:
stays 10.4f: acts on polytrack and soft going. *Mlle M. Henry, France*

PLAYTOTHEWHISTLE 4 b.g. Sakhee's Secret 128 – Prima Ballerina 73 (Pivotal 124)   **79**
[2015 67: f8s⁵ f8d* f7g* 7d⁴ f8g 8.3s f8d⁵ f7g² Nov 3] fair handicapper: won at Southwell
(twice) in March: stays 1m: acts on fibresand and good to soft going: usually in visor in
2015: tends to find little. *Bryan Smart*

PLEASANT VALLEY (IRE) 4 b.f. Shamardal (USA) 129 – Poughkeepsie (IRE) **98**
(Sadler's Wells (USA) 132) [2015 100p: 10m* 10.2m 10.1g 10.1m 9.9g⁵ Oct 14] useful
performer: won handicap at Pontefract (by 9 lengths from Easy Terms) in April: creditable
4 lengths fifth of 8 to Alzubra in listed race at Saint-Cloud final start: stays 10.5f: acts on
good to firm going: front runner/races prominently. *Luca Cumani*

PLEASCACH (IRE) 3 b.f. Teofilo (IRE) 126 – Toirneach (USA) 103 (Thunder **117**
Gulch (USA) 129) [2015 98p: 10d² 10d* 8g* 12f² 10m⁵ 12d* 10g⁴ Sep 12]
     In the mould of numerous good Jim Bolger-trained fillies before her, the
genuine and resilient Pleascach came through a searching and varied programme
as a three-year-old with flying colours. Brought back in distance to win the Irish
One Thousand Guineas, she seemed at one time to be heading for an ambitious
attempt to land the Irish Derby/Irish Oaks double, a plan shelved only after she was
sold to Godolphin (who went on to win the Irish Derby with Epsom runner-up Jack
Hobbs). After he had put Pleascach in the Irish Derby at the second entry stage—just
before the Irish One Thousand Guineas took place—Bolger said the move 'wasn't
so much what I thought about her, it was really what I thought about the colts, with
all due respect to our neighbours.' The reference to Ballydoyle's struggle to uncover
a top three-year-old middle-distance colt coincided with talk that the stable's top
filly, Found, might eventually be supplemented for the Derby. After an interrupted
preparation, Found missed the One Thousand Guineas at Newmarket, for which she
had been the long-time ante-post favourite, and, despite being beaten in her warm-up
in the Athasi Stakes, she started a heavily-backed 5/4-shot for the eighteen-runner
Tattersalls Irish One Thousand Guineas towards the end of May.
     Pleascach was sent off the 11/2 second favourite at the Curragh after looking
all over a potential Group 1 filly when recording an eight-and-a-half-length success
in the Group 3 Blue Wind Stakes at Naas just eleven days earlier. After winning a
seven-furlong maiden at Leopardstown on the second of two outings as a juvenile
(she had made a promising debut in a Group 3 contest at the Curragh just four
days earlier), Pleascach began her three-year-old campaign at a mile and a quarter,
finishing second to Bocca Baciata in Navan's listed Salsabil Stakes (in which
Diamondsandrubies came third before running in the Blue Wind). The Blue Wind
usually serves more as an Oaks trial, though its most recent Bolger-trained winner
Banimpire had also run next in the Irish One Thousand Guineas (fifth to Misty For
Me) before being stepped up to a mile and a half, over which, in a long campaign
in which she won six times, she was successful in the Ribblesdale at Royal Ascot (a
race also won by the 2012 Blue Wind winner Princess Highway). Found's stablemate
Kissed By Angels, successful in the Leopardstown One Thousand Guineas Trial on

Tattersalls Irish 1000 Guineas, the Curragh—Pleascach (left) has to survive a stewards' inquiry
after narrowly defeating 5/4 favourite Found, having jinked left inside the final 100yds; Devonshire
(No.2, partly hidden) finishes third ahead of Jack Naylor, who stays on strongly from off the pace

Darley Yorkshire Oaks, York—a first success in the Godolphin silks for Pleascach who gets home in a tight finish from Covert Love (blaze), French challenger Sea Calisi (No.11) and the visored Curvy

just her second start, and Bocca Baciata were the only other Irish One Thousand Guineas runners to start at single-figure odds. Ballydoyle also saddled 50/1-shot Qualify (last of thirteen in the Newmarket version) who, along with Malabar (fourth at Newmarket), were the only runners to line up from the One Thousand Guineas.

Qualify ran a little more encouragingly to finish tenth at the Curragh but Malabar couldn't uphold the Newmarket form, managing only eighth behind Pleascach and Found who fought out a close finish—Pleascach crossing the line half a length in front—though the stewards held an inquiry into possible interference between the first two before the result was confirmed. Two of Pleascach's stablemates, rank outsiders Mainicin and Steip Amach, were in the race to ensure the strong pace that seemed likely to be needed to play to Pleascach's strengths. Pleascach had to be rousted along to take up a prominent position and kept on gamely after moving past Steip Amach into the lead over a furlong out. Pleascach jinked left inside the final hundred yards, taking the challenging Found with her (though there was no contact between the pair), and was holding on to her advantage as the line was reached. The 33/1-shot Devonshire justified her connections' decision to supplement her by taking third, beaten a further length and a half, just ahead of the fast-finishing Jack Naylor, who had come third to Found the previous autumn in France's top two-year-old race for fillies the Prix Marcel Boussac. Bocca Baciata came a creditable fifth, while Kissed By Angels was a disappointment, beating only one home.

'She is not a miler, she's a relentless galloper with a turn of foot, the Guineas was a bonus,' was the frank post-race summing up of Pleascach by her trainer, for whose Coolcullen yard she was a second Irish One Thousand Guineas winner. Pleascach followed Finsceal Beo who won in 2007 when coming close to landing an unprecedented Guineas treble, also winning the One Thousand Guineas at Newmarket and going down by a head in the Poule d'Essai des Pouliches before winning at the Curragh when contesting her third classic in three weeks! Home-bred Pleascach ran in the colours of Mrs Jim Bolger in the Irish One Thousand Guineas but her next appearance, in the Ribblesdale Stakes at Royal Ascot, was in the Godolphin royal blue. Pleascach is a daughter of champion two-year-old Teofilo, one of three ex-Bolger performers (he also trained New Approach and Dawn Approach) now plying their trade as stallions under the Darley banner in what has become a very successful line-up. Pleascach looked a ready-made Royal Ascot winner for Godolphin. She was a classic winner without a penalty, since only winners of Group 1 and 2 races over a mile and a quarter or more incur penalties in the Group 2 Ribblesdale. Hot favourite Pleascach would have been a clear-cut winner without Curvy in the line-up but she couldn't hold the late challenge of her main rival and went down by a length. Pleascach turned in a rather flat display ten days later when only fifth to Diamondsandrubies in the Pretty Polly Stakes at the Curragh the day after the Irish Derby, and she bypassed the Irish Oaks to wait for the Darley Yorkshire Oaks in August.

Freshened up by a seven-week break, Pleascach beat the Irish Oaks winner Covert Love and also took her revenge on Curvy in a close finish at York, in which runner-up Covert Love and fourth-placed Curvy were split by another three-year-old, the French-trained challenger Sea Calisi. The Yorkshire Oaks showed Pleascach in a good light as she rallied in most determined fashion (her jockey picking up a two-day suspension for overuse of the whip), after being a little tapped for speed when first asked to quicken, and she finally collared front-running Covert Love in the last fifty yards to win by a neck, little over a length separating the first five with 25/1-shot Miss Marjurie, a five-year-old, finishing best of all in fifth. It was a game win in a somewhat muddling affair that couldn't be called a vintage edition from a form point of view. The only other appearance by Pleascach, who presumably remains in training (her trainer mentioning an Arc challenge as a four-year-old after the Yorkshire Oaks), came against Golden Horn, Found and Free Eagle in the Irish Champion Stakes in which Pleascach turned in another good effort to come fourth in her first race outside those confined to her own sex, finishing three and a half lengths behind Golden Horn.

Pleascach (IRE) (b.f. 2012)	Teofilo (IRE) (b 2004)	Galileo (b 1998)	Sadler's Wells
			Urban Sea
		Speirbhean (b 1998)	Danehill
			Saviour
	Toirneach (USA) (b 2005)	Thunder Gulch (ch 1992)	Gulch
			Line of Thunder
		Wandering Pine (b 1997)	Country Pine
			Wandering Lace

Pleascach is a big filly with plenty of scope and, all things being equal, she should train on well as a four-year-old and contribute further to the burgeoning reputation of her sire. Teofilo, a son of Galileo, was unable to race because of

Godolphin's "Pleascach"

injury as a three-year-old when, after an unbeaten five-race campaign at two, he was regarded by his trainer as a 'triple crown horse', Bolger calling him at the time potentially the best he had trained (his champion three-year-old of 1992 St Jovite, who died in retirement in early-2016, was rated 135). Teofilo has now had four three-year-old crops and is already a 'triple crown' sire of sorts in Ireland, also having an Irish Derby winner (Trading Leather) and an Irish St Leger winner (four-year-old Voleuse de Coeurs) to his name, as well as Pleascach's Irish One Thousand Guineas. The Bolgers, who retained ownership of Teofilo on his retirement, have done as much as any breeders to support him and they were rewarded with the Dewhurst winner Parish Hall from his first crop and Trading Leather from his second. Teofilo's fee had fallen to €15,000 from an initial €40,000 when the Bolgers sent him the Thunder Gulch mare Toirneach, whom Jim Bolger trained to win at seven furlongs as a two-year-old and a mile and a quarter at three. The result was Pleascach, foaled the year after Parish Hall's Dewhurst victory, a victory that saw Teofilo's fee raised to €25,000. It has continued to rise and he now stands at €50,000, the highest advertised fee (not counting Shamardal whose fee is 'private') of any of the Darley stallions at Kildangan Stud in Ireland. The versatile Teofilo is also the sire of Oaks runner-up Tarfasha and has had success in Australia with Group 1 winners Sonntag and the high-class miler Kermadec, the last-named winning the Doncaster Mile in April and the George Main Stakes in September. Wandering Pine, the grandam of Pleascach, won only a mile maiden event in the States but Toirneach was one of five winners she bred and, more importantly, Wandering Pine is a half-sister to Drina, the dam of the Breeders' Cup Distaff winner Spain who was also a daughter of Thunder Gulch. Pleascach is Toirneach's second foal and only winner to date, her two-year-old Brontide (a gelded son of Vocalist) unsuccessful in six starts, including in a nursery, for Jim Bolger in the latest season. Pleascach wasn't raced over shorter than a mile and a quarter after winning the Irish One Thousand Guineas, and she stays a mile and a half. She acts on firm and good to soft going and usually races prominently. *J. S. Bolger, Ireland*

PLEASURE DOME 2 b.f. (Apr 28) Makfi 130 – Nouvelle Lune (Fantastic Light (USA) 134) [2015 p8f⁴ Nov 12] fourth foal: closely related to 6f and (including at 2 yrs) 7f winner Glossy Posse (by Dubawi), later successful in Qatar, and half-sister to 2 winners, including useful 7f-9f winner Maverik (by Iceman): dam unraced half-sister to smart dam of St Leger winner Kingston Hill: 12/1, shaped well when 2¾ lengths fourth of 10 to Khaleesy in maiden at Chelmsford on debut, keeping on: will improve. *Peter Chapple-Hyam* **76 p**

PLEIADES 3 b.c. Galileo (IRE) 134 – Angara 119 (Alzao (USA) 117) [2015 86p: 7.5m³ 7.6s⁴ 8f⁶ 10m⁴ Jul 4] close-coupled colt: fairly useful handicapper: best effort on final outing: stays 1¼m: acts on firm going: wore hood last 2 starts: sold 35,000 gns, sent to Qatar. *Sir Michael Stoute* **87**

PLENARY (USA) 2 ch.c. (Jan 6) Kitten's Joy (USA) 128 – Southern Alibi (USA) (Elusive Quality (USA)) [2015 8g t9.5f² Nov 14] €300,000Y: fourth foal: brother to a winner in USA and half-brother to a winner there by Defer: dam, US maiden (second at 6f), half-sister to useful US Grade 2 1m winner Nefertini: left Marco Botti, better effort when second in maiden at Wolverhampton (1½ lengths behind City of Ideas) in November: likely to progress further. *Jeremy Noseda* **77 p**

PLOVER 5 b.m. Oasis Dream 129 – Short Dance (USA) 105 (Hennessy (USA) 122) [2015 78: p8g⁴ p10g p10f p8f p10g p8g p8g⁵ p8g p8g p10g⁶ Dec 30] good-topped mare: modest handicapper: stays 1¼m: acts on polytrack and firm going: tried in headgear. *Michael Attwater* **56**

PLUCKY DIP 4 b.g. Nayef (USA) 129 – Plucky 93 (Kyllachy 129) [2015 67, a97: p8g p6g³ p6g⁴ 6m⁶ 6m⁶ p6g² 7g² 7m⁵ 7f⁴ 7m² Jul 18] angular gelding: fairly useful handicapper: stays 1m: acts on polytrack, tapeta and good to firm going. *John Ryan* **91**

PLUNDER 5 ch.g. Zamindar (USA) 116 – Reaching Ahead (USA) (Mizzen Mast (USA) 121) [2015 66: 9.3d 5.9g t6m 6m t6m⁶ t6m⁶ Dec 30] poor handicapper: stays 8.5f: acts on polytrack: often wears headgear. *Alan Berry* **48**

PLUTOCRACY (IRE) 5 b.g. Dansili 127 – Private Life (FR) (Bering 136) [2015 104: p12g⁴ p11d³ 10g⁴ Sep 24] useful-looking gelding: useful handicapper: third at Kempton (½ length behind Majeed) in September: stays 1½m: acts on polytrack and tapeta: tried in cheekpieces prior to 2015: often races towards rear. *David Lanigan* **98**

PLYMOUTH SOUND 3 b.g. Fastnet Rock (AUS) 127 – Shardette (IRE) (Darshaan 133) **91**
[2015 85: 8.1d³ 10m 10.3m⁵ 8m³ 8.1g 10d⁵ Oct 12] leggy gelding: fairly useful handicapper:
third at Sandown and Salisbury: stays 1¼m: acts on good to firm and good to soft going:
tried in cheekpieces. *Eve Johnson Houghton*

POCKET 2 b.f. (Feb 14) Paco Boy (IRE) 129 – Take The Plunge 46 (Benny The Dip **–**
(USA) 127) [2015 6m t7.1f p6g Dec 2] 1,000F, 5,000Y: third foal: half-sister to a winner
in Denmark by Royal Applause: dam maiden half-sister to useful sprinter River Falcon:
little form. *James Eustace*

POETIC CHOICE 4 b.f. Byron 117 – Ennobling 62 (Mark of Esteem (IRE) 137) [2015 **79**
85, a78: p6g p7f⁶ t6f³ 6m⁴ p8g³ p7g p7g⁵ p8g² Dec 18] lengthy filly: fair handicapper: left
Nick Littmoden after fourth start: stays 1m: acts on polytrack, tapeta, good to firm and
good to soft going: tried in headgear in 2015. *Keith Henry Clarke, Ireland*

POETIC LICENSE (IRE) 3 b.g. Dylan Thomas (IRE) 132 – Bright Bank (IRE) **– §**
(Sadler's Wells (USA) 132) [2015 –: p10g⁵ t13.9g f14s⁴ t12.2m f12g Nov 26] no form,
taking little interest last 2 starts after having left Sir Mark Prescott: tried in blinkers: held
back by attitude and isn't one to trust. *James Grassick*

POETIC VERSE 5 gr.m. Byron 117 – Nina Fontenail (FR) 66 (Kaldounevees (FR) 118) **87**
[2015 12d⁴ 13g³ 12m² 12.3f² 15.9m 12g² 12s Oct 27] compact mare: fairly useful
handicapper: stays 1¾m: acts on polytrack, fibresand, firm and good to soft going: tried in
cheekpieces in 2015: fairly useful hurdler. *John Quinn*

POET MARK (IRE) 3 b.g. Vale of York (IRE) 117 – Attanagh (IRE) 74 (Darnay 117) **55**
[2015 –: 12.1m⁴ 16.2m 14.1m⁴ 14.1s Sep 15] modest maiden: should stay 2m: acts on good
to firm going: usually wears blinkers: often races towards rear. *Tim Easterby*

POET'S BEAUTY (IRE) 2 ch.g. (May 3) Poet's Voice 126 – Extreme Beauty (USA) 89 **78**
(Rahy (USA) 115) [2015 6g⁵ 6.1m 6g³ 7.4d³ 8g 8s² 7d⁵ Oct 16] good-topped gelding: fair
maiden: stays 1m: acts on soft going: in visor last 2 starts. *Ismail Mohammed*

POET'S PRIZE 2 b.c. (Feb 5) Compton Place 125 – La Gessa 69 (Largesse 112) [2015 **100 p**
5g⁴ 5.4g² 5g* 6m* Oct 3] 22,000Y: well-made colt: fourth foal: half-brother to 3 winners,
including winner up to 1m Tommy's Secret (2-y-o 5f/6f winner, by Sakhee's Secret) and
winner up to 9f Wordismybond (2-y-o 7f winner, by Monsieur Bond): dam 1¼m-12.6f
winner: useful form: won maiden at Beverley (by 2¼ lengths from Extortion) in September:
progressed again when following up in 26-runner quite valuable sales race at Newmarket
by ½ length from Receding Waves, quickening to lead 1f out: stays 6f: open to further
improvement. *David Barron*

POET'S SONG (IRE) 2 b.g. (Mar 17) Poet's Voice 126 – Bee Eater (IRE) 105 (Green **80**
Desert (USA) 127) [2015 6g⁶ p6g⁶ 6g⁶ 6v² Aug 24] 64,000F, €130,000Y: angular gelding:
fourth foal: half-brother to French 1m-1¼m winner Picking Up Pieces (by Montjeu) and 7f
winner Leafcutter (by Shamardal): dam, 6f winner, out of useful half-sister to very smart
miler Marling: fairly useful maiden: second in nursery at Brighton in August: worth a try
at 5f. *Marcus Tregoning*

POET'S WORD (IRE) 2 b.c. (Apr 5) Poet's Voice 126 – Whirly Bird 101 (Nashwan **76 p**
(USA) 135) [2015 7g⁴ Oct 21] 300,000Y: lengthy colt: half-brother to several winners,
including smart winner up to 1m Malabar (2-y-o 7f winner, by Raven's Pass) and useful
1¼m-11.5f winner (stayed 2m) Clowance Estate (by Teofilo): dam, 9.5f-11f winner, half-
sister to smart winner up to 1¾m Ursa Major: 16/1, very much caught eye when 5 lengths
fourth of 10 to Mootaharer in maiden at Newmarket on debut, not knocked about but
finishing well: will stay 1m+: sure to progress. *Sir Michael Stoute*

POINT NORTH (IRE) 8 b.g. Danehill Dancer (IRE) 117 – Briolette (IRE) 112 (Sadler's **77**
Wells (USA) 132) [2015 78: t6f³ t6m² 5g* 6.1m 5.1g⁴ 5g⁶ 5g⁴ 5.1d⁶ f6g Nov 26] well-
made gelding: fair handicapper: won at Beverley in May: stays 8.5f: acts on polytrack,
tapeta and heavy going: wears headgear: tried in tongue tie prior to 2015. *John Balding*

POINT OF WOODS 2 b.g. (Feb 27) Showcasing 117 – Romantic Myth 105 (Mind **94**
Games 121) [2015 5m⁶ 6m⁴ 6m² 5m* 5g 5d² t5.11f* 6d⁶ Oct 24] 110,000Y: closely related
to 2-y-o 6f winner Mythicism (by Oasis Dream) and half-brother to several winners,
including 7f winner Headache (by Cape Cross): dam 2-y-o 5f winner, including Queen
Mary Stakes: fairly useful performer: won maiden at Thirsk in August and nursery at
Wolverhampton by ¾ length from Sign of The Kodiac in October: should prove best at
5f: acts on tapeta and good to firm going. *Ralph Beckett*

POINT THE TOES (IRE) 10 b.m. Atraf 116 – Fern Fields (IRE) 81 (Be My Native 76
(USA) 122) [2015 79: p12g 21.6g* 16.5d⁵ 17.1g⁵ Jun 8] fair handicapper: won at Pontefract
in April: stays long distances: acts on good to soft going: sometimes wears headgear: tried
in tongue tie prior to 2015: sometimes slowly away, usually races in rear. *Mark Fahey,
Ireland*

POLAR EYES 4 b.f. Dubawi (IRE) 129 – Everlasting Love 100 (Pursuit of Love 124) 102
[2015 89: 10m 10.3s⁴ 10.3m⁶ 9g 10.4d* 9.9g⁴ 10.3v⁵ Nov 7] compact filly: useful
handicapper: won at Haydock (by head from Loving Things) in September: good fourth in
listed race at Saint-Cloud (1½ lengths behind Alzubra) next start: stays 10.5f: acts on heavy
going: wears cheekpieces: often races prominently. *Tom Dascombe*

POLAR FOREST 5 br.g. Kyllachy 129 – Woodbeck 90 (Terimon 124) [2015 81, a74: 9s* 95
8g³ 8.3s* 8m 8g 8g* 10.4g 8.1s⁴ 8.5s 8.3s³ 8d⁶ 10v⁴ Nov 3] useful handicapper: won at
Musselburgh in April, Nottingham in May and Ripon (by head from Green Howard) in
August: stays 1½m: acts on polytrack, tapeta, good to firm and heavy going: wears
headgear. *Richard Guest*

POLARISATION 3 b.g. Echo of Light 125 – Concordia (Pivotal 124) [2015 81: p7f⁶ 8m² 104
10m³ 10m² 12m² 14d* 12f⁶ 13d* 12m⁵ 12m 14g* 12.1d* 12g³ 14.6m Sep 11] tall, angular
gelding: useful handicapper: successful in July at Haydock and Hamilton and in August at
York (18-runner Melrose Stakes by head from Not Never, going in snatches but finding
plenty to lead late on) and Hamilton (by 1½ lengths from Nakeeta): good third at Ascot (2¾
lengths behind dead-heaters Wonder Laish and Duretto) in September: should stay beyond
1¾m: acts on good to firm and good to soft going: has joined John Ferguson. *Mark Johnston*

POLAR KITE (IRE) 7 b.g. Marju (IRE) 127 – Irina (IRE) 91 (Polar Falcon (USA) 126) 76
[2015 81: p7m² p7g³ p6f⁴ p7m⁶ p7g 7d⁵ 7g⁵ p6d p7g p7g² p7m² p7g⁵ Dec 28] tall, lengthy
gelding: fair handicapper: stays 1m: acts on polytrack, good to firm and good to soft going:
wears hood: usually slowly away/races in rear. *Michael Attwater*

POLDARK (IRE) 2 b.c. (Apr 10) Rip Van Winkle (IRE) 134 – Maybe I Will (IRE) 77 76
(Hawk Wing (USA) 136) [2015 5.1s⁴ p6g⁵ 7g² 7f 8g⁶ 7s⁵ p7g* Sep 22] sturdy colt: fair
performer: won claimer at Kempton in September: stays 7f: acts on polytrack: front runner/
races prominently: sold 7,000 gns, sent to Morocco. *Richard Hannon*

POLITBUREAU 8 b.g. Red Ransom (USA) – Tereshkova (USA) 113 (Mr Prospector 70
(USA)) [2015 56: 16m* 15.8s² 15s* 16d³ 13d² 13.1g² 15.8d⁶ Aug 26] fair handicapper:
won at Redcar in April and Ayr in May: stays 2m: acts on good to firm and heavy going:
tried in headgear: often races towards rear. *Micky Hammond*

POLITICO 3 ch.f. Medicean 128 – Tafawut 80 (Nayef (USA) 129) [2015 52: 10.1g Aug –
6] modest maiden: very slowly away only outing in 2015: probably stays 1¼m: acts on
tapeta and soft going. *Marjorie Fife*

POLLY GARTER 3 b.f. Dylan Thomas (IRE) 132 – Esteemed Lady (IRE) 96 (Mark of
Esteem (IRE) 137) [2015 t7.1f p10m⁵ Nov 19] closely related to useful 6f-1m winner
Mutawathea (by Exceed And Excel) and half-sister to 3 winners, including 5f/6f winner
Sleepy Blue Ocean (by Oasis Dream) and winner up to 1m Edgewater (2-y-o 6f winner, by
Bahamian Bounty): dam twice-raced half-sister to useful winner up to 7f Revenue: well
held both starts in maidens. *Chris Wall*

POLLY JACKSON 3 b.f. Sir Percy 129 – Fly In Style (Hernando (FR) 127) [2015 66: 59
10m 8g 8m 7.5s⁶ 9.3m⁶ 9.9g⁴ Aug 30] modest maiden: stays 1¼m: acts on good to soft
going: tried in hood in 2015. *Karen Tutty*

POLSKI MAX 5 b.g. Kyllachy 129 – Quadrophenia 63 (College Chapel 122) [2015 92: 79
6g 6d⁵ 6d 5m Jul 10] sturdy, good-bodied gelding: fair handicapper: stays 6f: acts on
fibresand and heavy going: in cheekpieces nowadays. *Brian Ellison*

POLYBIUS 4 b.g. Oasis Dream 129 – Freedonia 117 (Selkirk (USA) 129) [2015 110p: 6g 115
6f 6g² 6g* 6m³ p6m Nov 14] well-made gelding: smart performer: won listed race at
Newmarket in August by length from Naadirr: creditable third in Bengough Stakes at Ascot
(¾ length behind Eastern Impact) next start: stays 6f: acts on polytrack and good to firm
going: held up. *David Lanigan*

POLYDAMOS 6 b.g. Nayef (USA) 129 – Spotlight 110 (Dr Fong (USA) 128) [2015 60§: 55 §
p8f³ p8f⁶ 9.9d 8.5g² p11g 10m 9.9d Aug 5] good-topped gelding: modest maiden: stays
11f: acts on polytrack, tapeta, soft and good to firm going: sometimes in headgear/tongue
tie: unreliable. *Tony Carroll*

POLYMNIA 2 br.f. (Apr 19) Poet's Voice 126 – Lucky Token (IRE) 77 (Key of Luck **66** (USA) 126) [2015 7s p7g³ p6g p7g Oct 27] 115,000Y: fourth foal: half-sister to a winner in Hong Kong by Exceed And Excel: dam, 8.6f winner, half-sister to 1000 Guineas winner Sky Lantern: fair maiden: best effort at 7f on polytrack. *Richard Hannon*

POMME DE GUERRE (IRE) 3 b.g. Kodiac 112 – Lucky Apple (IRE) (Key of Luck **60** (USA) 126) [2015 69p: p6g⁵ p7f⁴ p7g 8.3m Jun 25] modest maiden: stays 7f: acts on polytrack. *Eve Johnson Houghton*

POMME DE TERRE (IRE) 3 ch.g. Sakhee's Secret 128 – Suzie Quw 83 (Bahamian **84** Bounty 116) [2015 62: 6g³ 6g⁵ 7.2d⁵ 5.9s² 6m* 6g² Sep 29] fairly useful performer: blinkered last 2 starts and showed improved form, winning maiden at Redcar in September then finishing good second in handicap at Ayr: stays 6f: acts on good to firm and soft going: front runner/races prominently. *Michael Dods*

PONGO TWISTLETON 2 b.g. (Apr 1) Champs Elysees 124 – Pretty Girl (IRE) 103 – (Polish Precedent (USA) 131) [2015 7d 8s Oct 23] tailed off in 2 maidens. *Jonjo O'Neill*

PONIATOWSKI 3 ch.g. Dubawi (IRE) 129 – Lady Jane Digby 118 (Oasis Dream 129) **83** [2015 10d⁴ 10.3d* 10g p10f Nov 6] first foal: dam, winner up to 11f (2-y-o 7f winner), closely related to smart winner up to 9f Gateman: fairly useful performer: won maiden at Chester (by ¾ length from Mr Quicksilver) in September: likely to stay 1½m: sent to Saudi Arabia. *Mark Johnston*

PONIEL 3 b.g. Bahri (USA) 125 – Rafta (IRE) 83 (Atraf 116) [2015 –: 10m 12.1d p15.8g – 12.1s 11.9g Sep 7] no form. *Dai Williams*

PONTY ROYALE (IRE) 2 b.f. (Feb 9) Royal Applause 124 – Sodashy (IRE) 71 **65** (Noverre (USA) 125) [2015 5m 6m⁴ 5m³ 6d³ 6g* 5d² Oct 26] first foal: dam, maiden (stayed 1m), half-sister to useful 2-y-o 5f winner Ponty Acclaim: fair performer: won nursery at Redcar in September: will prove suited by a return to 6f: best form on good going: in hood last 3 starts, in tongue tie last 2: sometimes slowly away. *Tim Easterby*

PONY (IRE) 2 b.f. (May 3) Holy Roman Emperor (IRE) 125 – Little Match Girl (IRE) **35** (Fantastic Light (USA) 134) [2015 7g³ 7m 7d⁵ Aug 14] €1,700Y, €7,000 2-y-o: third foal: half-sister to a winner in Italy by Invincible Spirit: dam maiden daughter of smart performer up to 1¼m Calando: poor maiden. *Nigel Tinkler*

POOLE HARBOUR (IRE) 6 b.g. Elusive City (USA) 117 – Free Lance (IRE) 69 **63** (Grand Lodge (USA) 125) [2015 –: 7m 7d⁵ 7.5m⁶ Aug 12] compact gelding: modest handicapper: stays 7f: acts on polytrack, best turf form on ground firmer than good. *K. R. Burke*

POOL HOUSE 4 b.g. Sakhee's Secret 128 – Gitane (FR) (Grand Lodge (USA) 125) [2015 **83** 99: p8m⁶ p7f f7d⁵ p7g 7s³ 7.6d⁵ 6m² 8.3m⁶ t7.1g⁵ p8g³ 7m⁴ p7g p8f² t7.1f⁵ Nov 16] fairly useful performer: left Andrew Balding after seventh start: stays 8.5f: acts on all-weather and soft going: sometimes in headgear in 2015. *Mike Murphy*

POOLSTOCK 3 b.g. Equiano (FR) 127 – Pure Speculation 80 (Salse (USA) 128) [2015 **65** 65: f5g⁵ t7.1g⁵ 8g⁴ 8s 6m⁵ 5m³ 6g 5f³ 7.5m² 6g 7d⁴ 7g³ 5.9s³ 7.2g⁵ 6v Nov 3] fair maiden: effective at 6f to 1m: acts on tapeta, firm and soft going: sometimes in hood in 2015. *Les Eyre*

POOR DUKE (IRE) 5 b.g. Bachelor Duke (USA) 122 – Graze On Too (IRE) 54 **61** (Rainbow Quest (USA) 134) [2015 65, a76: t8.6g⁶ t12.2g t9.5g 10.2m 8.3g* t8.6g 8.5m t8.6m f8g t8.6g t7.1m⁵ Dec 30] sparely-made gelding: modest handicapper: won at Leicester in July: stays 8.5f: acts on polytrack, tapeta, firm and good to soft going: sometimes wears headgear: often races towards rear: none too consistent. *Michael Mullineaux*

POP CULTURE 2 ch.f. (Mar 14) Equiano (FR) 127 – Naizak 73 (Medicean 128) [2015 **64 p** 6g⁴ 6m* Jul 9] 10,000Y: angular filly: third foal: half-sister to winners up to 7f Smart Salute (2-y-o 6f winner, by Royal Applause) and Mujassam (2-y-o 6.5f winner, by Kyllachy), latter useful: dam maiden (stayed 7f): 16/1, improved from debut to win maiden at Newbury in July by ½ length from Lavinia Rose: should continue to progress. *Jonathan Portman*

POPESWOOD (IRE) 3 b.g. Haatef (USA) 117 – Binfield (IRE) 77 (Officer (USA) 120) **91** [2015 89: 7m 7g 7.1m 7.6m⁴ 7.6g 6s² 6g⁶ 7s 8s 7d* Oct 31] angular gelding: fairly useful handicapper: better than ever when winning at Newmarket (by ½ length from Jan Van Hoof) in October: stays 7.5f: acts on soft and good to firm going. *Mick Channon*

POPLAR 2 b.c. (Apr 4) Hellvelyn 118 – Amelie Pouliche (FR) (Desert Prince (IRE) 130) – [2015 5m p6g p6g Nov 11] no form. *Nick Littmoden*

POPLAR CLOSE (IRE) 2 b.f. (May 6) Canford Cliffs (IRE) 133 – Magena (USA) **74** (Kingmambo (USA) 125) [2015 6.5m⁶ 7.5m² 7.5g² 7.2g* 7.2m² 7m 8g Sep 24] €17,000Y: first foal: dam, unraced, out of half-sister to high-class performer up to 1½m Hernando: fair performer: won maiden at Musselburgh in July: stays 7.5f: acts on good to firm going. *David O'Meara*

POPPET ROCKET (IRE) 3 b.f. Myboycharlie (IRE) 118 – Zacchera 82 (Zamindar – (USA) 116) [2015 61p: 8.3g May 31] lightly-raced maiden, modest form at best. *Brian Meehan*

POPPY BOND 5 b.m. Misu Bond (IRE) 114 – Matilda Peace (Namaqualand (USA)) **82** [2015 64: f7d* t9.5g³ f8d² f7g⁴ t7.1m* f6s* p6g³ Apr 1] fairly useful handicapper: won at Southwell in January and Wolverhampton and Southwell in March: stays 9.5f: acts on all-weather, best turf form on soft/heavy going. *Alan Bailey*

POPPY IN THE WIND 3 b.f. Piccolo 121 – Vintage Steps (IRE) 76 (Bahamian Bounty **68** 116) [2015 57, a41: 6m 6.1m⁴ 5m* 5g 5.9s⁴ 6g⁴ 5m² 6g Oct 8] fair handicapper: won at Newcastle in August: stays 6f: acts on soft and good to firm going: wears headgear nowadays: often races towards rear. *Alan Brown*

POPPYPICCOLINA 2 b.f. (Apr 7) Piccolo 121 – Popocatepetl (FR) 66 (Nashwan **54** (USA) 135) [2015 6g 6m⁵ 5g⁶ 6f⁶ 7.5m⁴ 5.9m 7s Oct 16] 4,000F: half-sister to several winners, including useful winners up to 1m Mariachi Man (2-y-o 6f/1m winner, by Haafhd) and Guacamole (2-y-o 7f winner, by Inchinor): dam maiden (probably stayed 1¾m): modest maiden: stays 6f: acts on good to firm going: tried in headgear: sent to Greece. *Tim Easterby*

POPSIES JOY (IRE) 2 b.f. (Apr 23) Alfred Nobel (IRE) 110 – Senzate (Lujain (USA) **70** 119) [2015 6g⁵ 6g⁶ 6m² 7.5g³ 8s⁵ Oct 9] fourth foal: half-sister to 2 winners in Italy by Strategic Prince: dam Italian 2-y-o 7.5f winner: fair maiden: stays 1m: acts on soft and good to firm going. *Tim Easterby*

PORCUPINE CREEK (IRE) 2 b.g. (Mar 19) Zebedee 113 – Daanaat (IRE) 51 **57** (Kheleyf (USA) 116) [2015 6m⁶ 5.1g⁴ 6m 5m 6s⁵ p5f Oct 24] modest maiden: best effort at 5f: often in hood: usually races towards rear. *Ronald Thompson*

PORT 3 b.c. Hurricane Run (IRE) 134 – Captain's Paradise (IRE) (Rock of Gibraltar (IRE) **67** 133) [2015 –p: 8.3d 9.9m⁵ 8.3g 10g³ Jul 8] fair maiden: stays 1¼m: acts on good to firm going. *Richard Hannon*

PORTAGE (IRE) 3 b.c. Teofilo (IRE) 126 – Galley (Zamindar (USA) 116) [2015 94p: 8g **110** 8f 8d* 8d² 9g⁵ Sep 26] well-made colt: smart handicapper: improved form when winning by 1¼ lengths from Mutasayyid at Ascot in July: good efforts both subsequent starts, 1¾ lengths second to Hint of A Tint in Irish Cambridgeshire at the Curragh then better than result when fifth of 34 to Third Time Lucky in Cambridgeshire at Newmarket, challenging away from main action: stays 9f: acts on good to firm and good to soft going. *M. Halford, Ireland*

PORTAMENTO (IRE) 3 gr.c. Shamardal (USA) 129 – Octave (USA) 119 (Unbridled's **111** Song (USA) 125) [2015 102: p5f⁶ 6.1g⁴ 6m² 6.1g⁴ 6g Aug 29] well-made colt: smart performer: won handicap at Chester in July by 1¼ lengths from Anonymous John: creditable second in Hackwood Stakes at Newbury (length behind Strath Burn) next time: stays 6f: acts on polytrack, tapeta, soft and good to firm going. *Charlie Appleby*

PORTA ROSA (USA) 2 b.f. (Apr 2) Street Cry (IRE) 130 – Sander Camillo (USA) 116 **85** (Dixie Union (USA) 121) [2015 7g p7g³ p7g⁴ p6g² p6g* Dec 2] attractive filly: fifth foal: sister to winner up to 8.5f Vociferous (2-y-o 1m winner): dam 2-y-o 6f (Albany/Cherry Hinton Stakes) winner: fairly useful performer: won maiden at Kempton (by 4½ lengths from Go On Go On Go On) in December: stays 7f: acts on polytrack. *Charlie Appleby*

PORT DOUGLAS (IRE) 2 b.c. (Mar 25) Galileo (IRE) 134 – Walzerkoenigin (USA) **104** 116 (Kingmambo (USA) 125) [2015 7g* 7g² 7.5s⁴ 8d* 8d⁴ Oct 24] closely related to smart German 1½m-15.5f winner Walzertakt (by Montjeu) and half-brother to several winners, including very smart 10.5f-1½m (including Deutsches Derby) winner Wiener Walzer (by Dynaformer): dam German winner up to 1¼m (2-y-o 7f winner): useful performer: won maiden at Leopardstown in June and Beresford Stakes at the Curragh (by short head from True Solitaire) in September: 20/1, 5½ lengths fourth of 7 to Marcel in Racing Post Trophy at Doncaster final start: bred to stay at least 1¼m: acts on good to soft going: in blinkers last 2 starts: usually races close up. *Aidan O'Brien, Ireland*

PORT GAVERNE (IRE) 2 b.g. (Apr 10) Lord Shanakill (USA) 121 – Jillian (USA) **68** (Royal Academy (USA) 130) [2015 5m⁵ 5f³ 5.3g³ May 6] fair form when third in 2 maidens at Bath: has been gelded. *Marcus Tregoning*

PORT LAIRGE 5 b.g. Pastoral Pursuits 127 – Stylish Clare (IRE) 77 (Desert Style (IRE) **77** 121) [2015 62, a51: t7.1f 7m⁴ 7g² 7v* 7g* 7g² 7.4v³ 7v* 7g³ 7.1s⁴ 7s⁵ 8d Oct 30] fair handicapper: won at Brighton in May, June and August: should stay 1m: acts on heavy going: wears headgear. *John Gallagher*

PORT PARADISE 2 gr.g. (Mar 10) Paco Boy (IRE) 129 – Yacht Woman (USA) (Mizzen **70** Mast (USA) 121) [2015 6m⁴ 6d⁶ 6g⁶ 6m p7g p5g⁵ t6f p5m⁴ Dec 27] rather leggy gelding: **a63** fair maiden: stays 6f: acts on good to firm going: often races towards rear. *William Jarvis*

POSH BOUNTY 4 ch.f. Bahamian Bounty 116 – Fission 77 (Efisio 120) [2015 60: t6g³ **69** 5.9g 6v* 7s⁴ 6v 7s⁵ 6g³ 6v* Nov 3] plain filly: fair handicapper: won at Brighton in August and Redcar in November: stays 6f: best form on heavy going: front runner/races prominently. *Joseph Tuite*

POSSIBLE FUTURE 2 b.g. (May 8) Compton Place 125 – Lalectra (King Charlemagne **73** (USA) 120) [2015 7.2g⁶ 7m³ 7g⁵ Oct 3] fair maiden: best effort when third at Yarmouth (1¾ lengths behind Banksea) in September. *Ismail Mohammed*

POSTBAG 3 b.f. Three Valleys 119 – Postage Stampe 95 (Singspiel (IRE) 133) **91** [2015 73p: 7d⁴ 8g³ 8.3m² 8.1v⁶ Sep 16] lengthy, useful-looking filly: fairly useful performer: won maiden at Leicester in April: second in handicap at Windsor in August: should stay 1¼m: acts on good to firm and good to soft going: usually responds generously to pressure. *Henry Candy*

POSTER GIRL 2 b.f. (Apr 1) Excellent Art 125 – Accede 88 (Acclamation 118) [2015 **81** 6m* 6g 7m⁵ 8g⁴ Sep 24] £12,000Y: third foal: half-sister to winner up to 1m Miss Van Gogh (2-y-o 7f winner, by Dutch Art): dam 2-y-o 6f winner who stayed 1¼m: fairly useful form: won maiden at Newbury in June: improved when 2½ lengths fourth to Rioca in nursery at Pontefract: stays 1m. *Jonathan Portman*

POSTILLION (IRE) 7 b.h. Sleeping Indian 122 – Princess of Eden (GER) (Eden Rock **36** (GER) 113) [2015 57: f6d⁶ f7g Mar 3] poor handicapper: stays 1m: acts on sand and soft going: tried in headgear. *Richard Ford*

POSTPONED (IRE) 4 b.c. Dubawi (IRE) 129 – Ever Rigg 83 (Dubai Destination **126** (USA) 127) [2015 125: 10d² 10.5g³ 12f³ 12d* 11.9s* Sep 13]
The epic clash between Grundy and Bustino in the King George VI and Queen Elizabeth Stakes has become a staple of highlight reels, usually with the soundtrack of Peter O'Sullevan's commentary … 'Bustino on the far side, Grundy on the near side, the three-year-old and the four-year-old as they race into the final one hundred and fifty yards, and it's Grundy going on from Bustino … Bustino's fighting his way back but Grundy's holding him.' O'Sullevan, who was dubbed 'The Voice of Racing', earned immortality by providing the accompanying commentary to so many of racing's great TV moments during fifty years working for the BBC. He died at the age of ninety-seven the week after the latest King George which marked the fortieth anniversary of 'the race of the century' in which the Derby winner Grundy had his stamina put to the sternest of tests by the previous year's decisive St Leger winner Bustino who was provided with not one pacemaker but two. Bustino himself set sail for home half a mile out, with Grundy, whose rising young jockey Pat Eddery was fully alive to his opponent's well-laid plans, moving into second when Bustino went ahead. Grundy and Bustino provided a pulsating exhibition of horse racing at its best. Grundy was within two lengths of Bustino at the two-furlong pole, under pressure and chasing hard, and a furlong from home the pair were level. Both horses gave their all and the race could have gone either way in the closing stages until Grundy edged ahead in the last fifty yards to win by half a length. Under conditions ideal for the setting of a fast time—the going was firm and the race was truly run thanks to the pacemakers—Grundy easily beat the course record. Five lengths behind Bustino in third was Dahlia, winner of the two previous renewals, who was also inside the existing record (which, incidentally, had been set the previous year at Royal Ascot by Dakota in the three-year-old handicap the King George V Stakes; Dakota became temperamental and erratic, picking up a Timeform squiggle, but he did finish fourth in the King George VI and Queen Elizabeth as a five-year-old).

Forty years on, Ascot racegoers may not have expected to see a battle comparable to that between Grundy and Bustino, but the eleventh-hour withdrawal of the unbeaten Derby winner Golden Horn, after heavy rain the previous day and overnight, certainly gave the latest King George a more open look. Odds-on Golden Horn was set to be the only three-year-old in the line-up but there was no Bustino against him. It takes at least two to make a horse race and Golden Horn looked a cut above the nine older horses declared against him in the richest King George VI and Queen Elizabeth Stakes in history, its first prize of £689,027 consolidating its place as the third most valuable race in the British calendar behind the Derby and the Champion Stakes. The withdrawal three hours before the race of Golden Horn—added to that of the previous year's Arc runner-up Flintshire (also on account of the going)—left a substandard, purely domestic field, with the exception of Italy's top horse Dylan Mouth who had been well beaten on his only previous visit to Britain, behind Eagle Top in the King Edward VII Stakes at Royal Ascot the previous year. With the Prince of Wales's Stakes fourth The Corsican also a ground-related absentee, the Hardwicke Stakes represented the best form on offer, with the runner-up in that race Eagle Top, a stablemate of Golden Horn, starting 5/2 favourite for the King George, with the Hardwicke winner Snow Sky at 3/1, ahead of the Ormonde Stakes winner Clever Cookie at 4/1 (gambled on after the rain came) and the Hardwicke third Postponed at 6/1.

Snow Sky had been allowed to dictate affairs in the Hardwicke in which neither Eagle Top nor Postponed had been seen to best advantage in a tactical race. The Hardwicke was Postponed's third outing of the season, on all of which he had been ridden by the owner's retained jockey Adam Kirby, who incurred the wrath of Eagle Top's trainer after the Hardwicke when he accused him of 'all-weather winter tactics' after Postponed bumped Eagle Top, ridden by Frankie Dettori, shortly after the start and Kirby then kept Dettori hemmed in early in the home straight, forcing him to switch before just getting the better of Postponed for second. The Royal Ascot stewards did not hold an inquiry as 'Adam Kirby held his line which he was entitled to do', according to a BHA media release. However, Dettori later revealed that the incidents had led to a fall out with Kirby. After partnering Postponed when second to Western Hymn (ridden by Dettori) in the Gordon Richards Stakes at Sandown on his reappearance and then when third in both the Tattersalls Gold Cup at the Curragh (beaten a neck and a short head by Al Kazeem and Fascinating Rock) and in the Hardwicke, Kirby found himself replaced for the King George. The ride on Postponed went to Andrea Atzeni who had ridden for Postponed's owner the previous year, when Postponed looked a horse with a bright future when beating Snow Sky in the Great Voltigeur Stakes at York (after which he was put away for a four-year-old campaign). Postponed's owner Sheikh Mohammed Obaid, whose decision it was to replace Kirby, said that the jockey 'wasn't lucky with the horse.'

Postponed's connections at one time discussed running a pacemaker for him in the King George, his trainer saying 'Ideally what we'd like to see is a Grundy/ Bustino pace.' Luca Cumani, who first took out a training licence the year after Grundy's King George, may have been concerned about the prevailing softish ground (Postponed's best form had been on good to firm), but he need not have worried about getting a truly-run race. Eagle Top's stablemate Romsdal, third in the previous year's Derby and second in the St Leger, was ridden to make his stamina count, which suited both Eagle Top and Postponed, probably in equal measure. Romsdal came under pressure early in the home straight and was headed by the always prominent Postponed two furlongs out. Staying on strongly, Eagle Top joined battle with Postponed in the final furlong. If the closing stages bore some visual resemblance to the famous finish of forty years earlier, the outcome was in the balance for even longer this time. Grundy always looked like winning his race over the final fifty yards, but the tussle between Postponed and Eagle Top wasn't settled until the very last stride. Dettori looked to have timed his run to perfection as Eagle Top edged to the front in the final hundred yards, but Postponed rallied in most willing fashion to get back up on the line. The photo-finish showed that Postponed had prevailed by a nose, the shortest margin possible. Romsdal kept on for third, three and three quarter lengths behind the principals, with the previous

year's winner of the British Champions Fillies' And Mares' Stakes Madame Chiang
a never dangerous fourth, Clever Cookie fifth after being detached for much of the
race, Snow Sky sixth and Dylan Mouth last.

The race between Postponed and Eagle Top did much to rescue the King
George VI and Queen Elizabeth Stakes from anti-climax after the withdrawal of
Golden Horn but, in form terms, it was in the lower echelon among King Georges.
Postponed's victory was the first in the race for his trainer, after second places with
Celestial Storm and Derby winner High-Rise and a third with Tolomeo. Cumani
was understandably reluctant to get involved in speculation about what the outcome
would have been had Golden Horn been in the field. 'None of us will ever know,
it's all ifs and buts,' Cumani said, though anyone fancying Postponed or Eagle
Top for the Prix de l'Arc de Triomphe, the next main target announced for them
both afterwards, were able to avail themselves of ante-post odds of 25/1 and 33/1
respectively immediately after the King George.

There was a sting in the tail after the King George for the jockeys on the
first two, both of whom were adjudged to have breached the whip rules. In a driving
finish to a race in which the stakes were high and the finish very tight, both Atzeni
and Dettori used their whip a little above the permitted level, Dettori receiving a
four-day suspension and Atzeni six days, as he also used the whip down Postponed's
shoulder in breach of the rules. Neither jockey's breach was serious enough to
warrant the seven-day ban or longer which would have resulted in them also being
fined a proportion of their winning prize money, but the suspensions still figured
prominently in stories about the race (especially as the charismatic Dettori was ruled
out of Ascot's international jockeys' competition the Shergar Cup, at which he had
captained the winning team the previous year).

Discussion of the whip rules in these pages must be becoming tedious for
readers and anyone wanting a fuller exposition of Timeform's view is referred to
the essays on Leading Light and Noble Mission in *Racehorses of 2014*. Eight whip
strikes currently triggers a review by the stewards on the Flat, but the specifying of
a numerical limit gives them little room for manoeuvre and often results in needless
suspensions like the ones imposed on Atzeni and Dettori in the King George. Only
just over half a per cent of all rides in 2015 incurred a penalty for improper whip
use but such offences in big races are always 'newsworthy' and unfortunately serve
only to foster the false impression that racing has a welfare issue with the whip. The
cushioned whips now used in racing encourage horses but do not hurt them—neither
Postponed nor Eagle Top suffered undue distress from the use of the whip—and
whip abuse in Britain is largely a thing of the past. Even if whip abuse does exist, it
certainly cannot be accurately calculated by counting the number of hits. Horses are
different and react differently, and, as has been said before in *Racehorses*, it cannot
be right to have rules that apply equally to a jockey riding a fully mature racehorse,
perhaps with a lazy streak, and a jockey on an inexperienced and immature two-
year-old, for example.

The rules need to be flexible enough to fit individual cases and should place more emphasis on *incorrect* use of the whip, rather than on how often it is used. The current numerical limit is at the heart of most of the problems and the next review of the whip rules needs to consider dropping the 'norm' and giving stewards more discretion, such as they are required to exercise in so many other areas of the *Rules of Racing*. This is not to say that the jockeys should be given free rein; the stewards should be given the ultimate power—which they do not have at present—to disqualify horses in extreme cases of improper whip use, as, for example, when Frankie Dettori struck Rewilding twenty-four times in the last two furlongs of the 2011 Prince of Wales's Stakes. Disqualifications would be certain to create controversy, as well as risking the alienation of punters and racegoers, and stewards would have to use such powers carefully if they were given them.

To return to Postponed, he appeared once more for Bedford House Stables, apparently putting himself on course for the Arc when again showing his battling qualities to win a strongly-run Prix Foy at Longchamp (in which he had a pacemaker). However, within days of Postponed's Prix Foy victory, it became known that Sheikh Mohammed Obaid was going to withdraw his thirty-five-strong string of horses from the care of Luca Cumani, whom he had employed for twenty years (Derby winner High-Rise belonged to him). No reason for the decision was made public and Cumani himself—who had been informed in early-August that the split was coming—said he was not told why the association had been ended. 'Owners have that prerogative. They buy the horses and they can choose who trains them,' he said. Owners take horses away from trainers all the time, but Sheikh Obaid's horses made up a third of the Cumani string and the timing of the move was puzzling, given the successful campaign the Obaid horses had had. Another Newmarket trainer Roger Varian took over the sheikh's string but Postponed did not take his place in the Arc field. He does, however, stay in training as a five-year-old.

But for the untimely death of Dubai Millennium from grass sickness, Postponed's sire Dubawi would almost certainly have raced in Sheikh Mohammed Obaid's yellow, large black spots and spots on cap, and been trained by Luca Cumani (who had trained Dubawi's home-bred dam Zomaradah who won the Oaks d'Italia and the E. P. Taylor Stakes in the Obaid silks the same year that High-Rise won the Derby). Sheikh Mohammed Obaid is a cousin of the ruler of Dubai, Sheikh Mohammed, who gathered up most of the fifty-six foals from Dubai Millennium's sole crop. Dubawi was one of twenty-eight who went into training with Godolphin and was his sire's first pattern winner, in the Superlative Stakes at Newmarket's July meeting. After also winning the National Stakes at the Curragh to end a three-race juvenile campaign unbeaten, Dubawi became Dubai Millennium's only classic winner when successful in the Irish Two Thousand Guineas (after being a beaten favourite in the Two Thousand Guineas at Newmarket). Dubawi finished third in Motivator's Derby before making a successful return to a mile in the Prix Jacques le Marois, a race his sire had won after failing to stay in the Derby. Dubai Millennium went on to even greater things as a four-year-old but Dubawi was retired to Dalham Hall Stud after his three-year-old season and has gone on to prove himself an even better sire than he was a racehorse. He ran Coolmore stalwart Galileo close in the race to be champion sire in Britain and Ireland in the latest season and, having embarked on his stallion career at a fee of £25,000 in 2006, he will be standing at £225,000 in 2016.

Al Kazeem, Arabian Queen and Night of Thunder were among Dubawi's other principal winners in Britain and Ireland, while Prince Bishop won the world's richest race, the Dubai World Cup, and New Bay (Prix du Jockey Club) and Erupt (Grand Prix de Paris) were major winners for Dubawi in France, and Red Dubawi won the Group 1 Premio Vittorio di Capua in Italy (there were Group 1 successes in Australia too with Srikandi and Shamal Wind). The successes of seven- and eight-year-olds Al Kazeem, Prince Bishop, Red Dubawi and Hunter's Light (Group 1 Jebel Hatta in Dubai) indicate the durability of Dubawi's progeny, while the fact that, at the end of his seventh year with runners, he has had the winners of no fewer than eighty-five European pattern races is a remarkable testament to the overall quality of his offspring. Only thirteen stallions have sired the winners of a hundred

Sheikh Mohammed Obaid Al Maktoum's "Postponed"

or more European pattern races since the official pattern was inaugurated in 1971 and Dubawi will soon be joining them at his current rate of progress (fourteen wins in 2014, twenty in 2015). The average distance of the races won by Dubawi's three-year-olds and upwards is nine furlongs but Postponed is among a number of his offspring who have scored in pattern company at a mile and a half, an essential requirement for any stallion with pretensions to winning the sires' championship.

	Dubawi (IRE) (b 2002)	Dubai Millennium (b 1996)	Seeking The Gold
			Colorado Dancer
		Zomaradah (b 1995)	Deploy
Postponed (IRE) (b.c. 2011)			Jawaher
	Ever Rigg (b 2005)	Dubai Destination (b 1999)	Kingmambo
			Mysterial
		Bianca Nera (b 1994)	Salse
			Birch Creek

Postponed's dam Ever Rigg won a maiden as a three-year-old over a mile and a half at Kempton, her only success, but she was by the miler Dubai Destination which added to doubts, after his Great Voltigeur win, about whether Postponed would have the stamina for the St Leger (Dubai Destination is also the sire of the dam of Golden Horn, about whom there were also stamina doubts for the Derby at one time). Postponed is Ever Rigg's second foal and the only winner bred by her so far, her first foal the filly Neamour (by Oasis Dream) showing fair form at two and three (when she was placed at a mile and a half) before being sold at the end of her three-year-old season at the 2013 December Sales for 34,000 guineas (she was resold in May for 72,000 guineas in foal to a covering to southern hemisphere time by Archipenko). Ever Rigg, who has a yearling filly by Nathaniel—who will be in training in 2016 for her breeder—and a colt foal by Makfi, went through the sale-ring at the 2015 December Sales, in foal again to Dubawi, but was bought back for

792

1,500,000 guineas (Ever Rigg had made only 26,000 guineas ten years earlier as a foal at the same sale before fetching €360,000 at the following year's Goffs Million Sale). Postponed's grandam Bianca Nera won the Lowther and the Moyglare Stud Stakes for Sheikh Mohammed and is a half-sister to Hotelgenie Dot Com (the dam of Fillies' Mile and Falmouth Stakes winner Simply Perfect), who was placed in the Moyglare and the Fillies' Mile. Hotelgenie Dot Com is the grandam of the latest St Leger runner-up Bondi Beach, in whose essay a little more can be found about the family. Postponed's great grandam Birch Creek failed to win from six starts in France but scraped some 'black type' when third in a Group 3 mile event at Turin. The strong, close-coupled Postponed, built in similar mould to his sire who was also not very big, stays a mile and a half and acts on soft going and good to firm. He has made the running but usually tracks the pace. Thoroughly genuine, he looks sure to train on and win more good races as a five-year-old. *Luca Cumani*

POSTSCRIPT (IRE) 7 ch.g. Pivotal 124 – Persian Secret (FR) 101 (Persian Heights 129) [2015 97: 10.3g 7.6f⁵ 7m⁶ Jun 27] sturdy gelding: fairly useful handicapper: stays 9.5f: acts on polytrack, tapeta, good to firm and good to soft going. *Richard Fahey* **82**

POSTULANT 3 b.f. Kyllachy 129 – Pious 74 (Bishop of Cashel 122) [2015 6g³ 7.1m² 7g³ 6g* 6m⁵ Jul 17] sister to very smart 7f/1m winner Penitent and useful 2-y-o 5f/6f (including Mill Reef Stakes) winner Supplicant and closely related/half-sister to several winners, including useful 5f winner Solemn (by Pivotal): dam 6f winner (including at 2 yrs): fair performer: won maiden at Hamilton in June: stays 7f: acts on good to firm going. *Richard Fahey* **68**

POTTERNELLO (IRE) 3 b.f. Captain Marvelous (IRE) 114 – Purepleasureseeker (IRE) (Grand Lodge (USA) 125) [2015 7m 8.3m⁴ 7v⁴ 10m 8.1m³ 7g³ 7m* 7d³ 7g 6g⁴ 5.7m² 6v* 6m³ t7.1m⁴ 6s⁶ p6g Oct 20] 7,000Y, €33,000 2-y-o: compact filly: seventh foal: half-sister to 3 winners, including winner up to 1½m Mr Gallivanter (2-y-o 8.3f winner, by Heliostatic) and winner up to 10.4f Evervescent (2-y-o 6f winner, by Elnadim): dam lightly raced: fair performer: won seller at Leicester in July and handicap at Epsom in August: stays 7f: acts on good to firm and heavy going: often in visor. *Mick Channon* **76**

POULICHE 2 b.f. (May 14) Monsieur Bond (IRE) 120 – Tarneem (USA) 87 (Zilzal (USA) 137) [2015 6m t6g³ t5.1g² 5d Oct 12] 4,000F, €6,000Y: half-sister to numerous winners, including very smart winner up to 1¼m (stayed 1½m) Enforcer (2-y-o 7f winner, by Efisio) and useful 1¼m winner Canaveral (by Cape Cross): dam 1m winner: fair maiden: stays 6f. *Harry Dunlop* **69**

POUNCING TIGER 4 b.f. Tiger Hill (IRE) 127 – Ipsa Loquitur 69 (Unfuwain (USA) 131) [2015 49: p8f p8f p10f⁶ Mar 18] modest maiden: worth a try at 1½m: acts on polytrack: tried in visor in 2015: sometimes slowly away: covered by Sun Central, sold 2,000 gns, sent to Saudi Arabia. *Stuart Williams* **53**

POUND NOTE 3 b.g. Top Line Dancer (IRE) 72 – Avondale Girl (IRE) 73 (Case Law 113) [2015 5.9s⁴ Aug 24] 25/1, very green when fourth in maiden at Carlisle (6¾ lengths behind Ki Ki) on debut. *Michael Mullineaux* **52**

POUR L'AMOUR (IRE) 2 b.f. (Feb 27) Aqlaam 125 – Passion Fruit 91 (Pursuit of Love 124) [2015 6.5m 7m⁶ t7.1g Jul 7] £18,000Y: third foal: dam, 6f/7f winner, half-sister to useful winner up to 1½m King's Welcome: modest maiden: best effort when sixth at Chester. *Alan McCabe* **59**

POUR LA VICTOIRE (IRE) 5 b.g. Antonius Pius (USA) 123 – Lady Lucia (IRE) 51 (Royal Applause 124) [2015 72, a80: p5g² p5m⁴ t5.1m* p6m⁶ p6m⁶ 5m 5m⁶ 5.3g⁴ 6g* 5.3s² 6s 5.3s³ 6g p6g⁵ p8g³ Dec 16] workmanlike gelding: fairly useful handicapper: won at Wolverhampton in February and Brighton in August: stays 1m, effective at shorter: acts on polytrack, tapeta, soft and good to firm going: usually wears headgear: usually races towards rear. *Tony Carroll* **82**

POUR PAVOT (IRE) 2 b.f. (Apr 16) Pour Moi (IRE) 125 – Lake Windermere (IRE) 84 (Oasis Dream 129) [2015 6d 6m 7m Jul 30] £32,000 2-y-o: rather unfurnished filly: third foal: half-sister to 1¼m winner Van Schaick (by Rip Van Winkle): dam, 7f winner, out of smart 1¼m winner Spinnette: modest maiden. *Harry Dunlop* **62**

POURQUOI NON (IRE) 2 b.g. (Mar 11) Pour Moi (IRE) 125 – Anyuta 71 (Singspiel (IRE) 133) [2015 8g p7g³ p8m⁵ Nov 17] fair maiden: best effort when third at Lingfield (¾ length behind Little Kipling) in October: stays 1m. *Denis Coakley* **70**

POWDERHORN (IRE) 2 b.c. (Apr 25) Raven's Pass (USA) 133 – Innclassic (IRE) 72 **92** (Stravinsky (USA) 133) [2015 5.4m⁶ 7m³ 7g³ p7f* p7g² 7g* 7g⁵ Sep 19] €50,000F: compact colt: half-brother to several winners, including 2-y-o 9f winner Mahaazen (by Cape Cross): dam, 6f winner, half-sister to very smart US Grade 1 1m/1¼m winner Daytona: fairly useful performer: won maiden at Lingfield in August and nursery at Chester (by head from Kingston Kurrajong) in September: stays 7f: acts on polytrack and good to firm going: front runner/races prominently. *Mark Johnston*

POWDERONTHEBONNET (IRE) 7 b.g. Definite Article 121 – Zuhal 67 (Busted **64** 134) [2015 12v⁴ 10.3d⁶ p12g Oct 6] modest maiden: best effort when fourth at Newbury on belated Flat debut: fair hurdler/chaser. *Richard Phillips*

POWDER SNOW (USA) 2 ch.f. (Mar 30) Dubawi (IRE) 129 – Snow Ballerina 61 **75** (Sadler's Wells (USA) 132) [2015 7g⁶ 7g⁴ 7.5g² 10.2g³ Sep 30] useful-looking filly: fifth foal: half-sister to 3 winners, including useful winner up to 13f Snow Squall (2-y-o 7f winner, by Dansili) and 2-y-o 1m winner Equity Card (by Dubai Destination): dam, maiden (stayed 1½m), closely related to top-class winner up to 1½m Lammtarra: fair maiden: stays 1¼m. *Charlie Appleby*

POWERALLIED (IRE) 2 b.c. (Apr 30) Camacho 118 – Kaplinsky (IRE) 75 (Fath **84** (USA) 116) [2015 5v* 5.2m 6.1g⁴ 5g⁴ 5.5s* 5.5d⁴ 6g Oct 3] €11,500Y, resold £16,000Y: stocky colt: second foal: dam 7f winner: fairly useful performer: won maiden at Musselburgh in April and nursery at Chester in September: stays 6f: acts on heavy going. *Richard Fahey*

POWERED (IRE) 2 b.g. (Feb 2) Frozen Power (IRE) 108 – Confirm (IRE) 62 (In The **69** Wings 128) [2015 7m⁵ 7.1m 6g⁴ p6.5g⁴ 7g 8m f7g³ f8f⁴ Dec 17] lengthy gelding: fair maiden: stays 1m: acts on polytrack and good to firm going: tried in cheekpieces: often races towards rear. *Jo Hughes*

POWERFUL DREAM (IRE) 2 b.f. (Mar 23) Frozen Power (IRE) 108 – Noble View **59** (USA) 68 (Distant View (USA) 126) [2015 5g⁴ 5.1m 6d 5g* 5g⁵ Jul 30] €22,000Y: lengthy filly: half-sister to several winners, including useful 5f-7f winner (including at 2 yrs) Corporal Maddox and useful 6f-1m winner Silver Hotspur (both by Royal Applause): dam maiden (stayed 9f): modest performer: won nursery at Bath in July: best effort at 5f: often races towards rear. *Ronald Harris*

POWERFUL PIERRE 8 ch.g. Compton Place 125 – Alzianah 102 (Alzao (USA) 117) – [2015 70, a87: t7.1f⁶ Jan 12] close-coupled gelding: fair performer: stayed 7f: acted on polytrack, fibresand and good to firm going: was usually in headgear: had worn tongue tie: often started slowly, often raced towards rear: dead. *Noel Quinlan*

POWERFUL PRESENCE (IRE) 9 ch.g. Refuse To Bend (IRE) 128 – Miss A Note **73** (USA) (Miswaki (USA) 124) [2015 91: f7d t7.1m⁶ 7d⁶ 7s⁵ 8m May 16] lengthy gelding: fair handicapper: stays 8.5f: acts on fibresand, good to firm and heavy going: tried in headgear. *David O'Meara*

POWERFULSTORM 3 b.f. Bertolini (USA) 125 – Frisson (Slip Anchor 136) [2015 54: **50** t6f³ f6d t6f³ t7.1g p6m³ t7.1f⁶ t7.1g Apr 10] workmanlike filly: modest maiden: stays 7f: acts on polytrack, tapeta and good to soft going: often wears headgear: usually leads. *Ronald Harris*

POWERFUL WIND (IRE) 6 ch.g. Titus Livius (FR) 115 – Queen of Fools (IRE) (Xaar **85** 132) [2015 90: t5.1m² p5f² f5g t5.1f 5.1m* 5m 5d 6g f5g² f5g³ Dec 29] stocky gelding: fairly useful handicapper: won at Chepstow in May: left Ronald Harris after eighth start: stays 5.5f: acts on polytrack, fibresand, firm and good to soft going: tried in cheekpieces/tongue tie prior to 2015: front runner/races prominently. *Charlie Wallis*

POWER GAME 3 ch.g. Shamardal (USA) 129 – Counterclaim 98 (Pivotal 124) [2015 **101 p** 78: p8g² p8g* p8g* Sep 21] good-topped gelding: useful performer: won at Kempton in August (maiden, by 4 lengths) and September (handicap, by ½ length from Si Senor): will stay 1¼m: raced only on polytrack: will go on improving. *Saeed bin Suroor*

POWER UP 4 b.f. Rail Link 132 – Melpomene 95 (Peintre Celebre (USA) 137) [2015 73: **71** p10m* p10g* 10.2m⁴ 11.6m p10f³ 9.9d³ p10m⁵ p12m p10g* p10m⁴ Dec 27] fair handicapper: won at Chelmsford (amateur) in May, Lingfield (amateur) in June and Chelmsford in December: left Jane Chapple-Hyam after sixth start: stays 1½m: acts on all-weather, soft and good to firm going: tried in headgear prior to 2015: tried in tongue tie in 2015: usually races prominently. *Robert Eddery*

POYLE JESSICA 3 b.f. Royal Applause 124 – Poyle Caitlin (IRE) 62 (Bachir (IRE) 118) **79** [2015 67: 7m⁴ 7.1s* 7.4d² 7.4v⁶ t7.1f Oct 30] useful-looking filly: fair handicapper: won at Chepstow in July: stays 7.5f: acts on soft going: in cheekpieces last 2 starts. *Ralph Beckett*

POYLE SOPHIE 4 b.f. Teofilo (IRE) 126 – Lost In Lucca 72 (Inchinor 119) [2015 p10g **71**
9.9m⁵ 10m⁶ p12g² 12.1m t13.9m Oct 2] lengthy filly: half-sister to several winners,
including useful 11.6f-15f winner Poyle Thomas (by Rail Link) and 8.3f-1¼m winner
Poyle Meg (by Dansili): dam unreliable 1½m winner: fair maiden: should stay beyond
1½m: acts on polytrack. *Ralph Beckett*

POYLE TOBY (IRE) 5 b.g. Bahamian Bounty 116 – Lost In Lucca 72 (Inchinor 119) –
[2015 67p: f8d p8mᵖᵘ Feb 12] very lightly-raced maiden, fair form at best: dead.
Ralph Beckett

POYLE VINNIE 5 b.g. Piccolo 121 – Poyle Dee Dee 72 (Oasis Dream 129) [2015 107: **114**
f5s⁵ 5m 5m⁵ 6s* 6m 6g 6g⁵ 6g² 6s Oct 10] sturdy gelding: smart handicapper: improved
form when winning by 2¾ lengths from Tatlisu at Hamilton in July: also ran well when
½ -length second of 25 to Don't Touch in Ayr Gold Cup at Ayr in September: stays 6f: acts
on polytrack, fibresand, soft and good to firm going: usually races close up. *Michael Appleby*

PRAIRIE HAWK (USA) 10 b.g. Hawk Wing (USA) 136 – Lady Carla 122 (Caerleon **47**
(USA) 132) [2015 t16.5m⁵ Nov 21] good-topped gelding: poor handicapper: stays 16.5f:
acts on polytrack, tapeta and good to firm going: often wears tongue tie. *Adrian Wintle*

PRAIRIE IMPULSE 2 b.f. (Mar 26) Major Cadeaux 121 – Prairie Sun (GER) 81 (Law **52**
Society (USA) 130) [2015 6d 7.5m Jun 16] fourth foal: dam, 1½m-2m winner, also won
over hurdles: modest form in maidens at Ripon and Beverley. *Ann Duffield*

PRAIRIE TOWN (IRE) 4 b.g. High Chaparral (IRE) 132 – Lake Baino (Highest Honor **80**
(FR) 124) [2015 p11f² 11m³ 12m⁵ 10s⁶ Sep 18] fairly useful maiden: left N. Clement after
final 2014 start: stays 15f: acts on polytrack, good to firm and good to soft going: has worn
cheekpieces: fairly useful hurdler. *Tony Carroll*

PRAISE N GLORY 4 ch.f. Resplendent Glory (IRE) 115 – Tapsalteerie (Tipsy Creek –
(USA) 115) [2015 p7g f6s Jan 20] tall filly: no form: tried in visor. *Linda Jewell*

PRAVDA STREET 10 ch.g. Soviet Star (USA) 128 – Sari 83 (Faustus (USA) 118) [2015 **42**
52: f12d⁵ t8.6f t9.5f t8.6g t8.6g⁶ p8m t8.6g Jun 4] tall gelding: poor handicapper: stays 9f:
acts on all-weather, good to firm and heavy going: tried in headgear/tongue tie.
Christopher Kellett

PRAYER TIME 3 ch.g. Pastoral Pursuits 127 – Nice Time (IRE) 74 (Tagula (IRE) 116) **66**
[2015 –: p8g⁶ f8g* t9.5f⁴ f8s² 8m 8.3m Jun 25] fair handicapper: won at Southwell in
March: stays 1m: acts on fibresand and good to firm going: often races towards rear. *Mark
H. Tompkins*

PRECARIOUS (IRE) 3 gr.g. Iffraaj 127 – Screen Star (IRE) 110 (Tobougg (IRE) 125) –
[2015 10g 10d⁴ 12g Aug 3] well held all 3 starts in maidens: gelded after. *Mark Johnston*

PRECAST 3 ch.f. Halling (USA) 133 – Preceder (Polish Precedent (USA) 131) [2015 66p: **66**
p8f⁵ p8m⁴ p8g Apr 27] fair maiden: best effort at 1m: acts on polytrack: sometimes slowly
away. *David Simcock*

PRECISION FIVE 6 b.m. Proclamation (IRE) 130 – Sashay 72 (Bishop of Cashel 122) **94**
[2015 63, a74: p10g* p13.3g* p12m² t12.2g² t12.2g² p12g* 11.9m² 13.3s p12g² Nov 18]
fairly useful handicapper: won at Lingfield (dead-heated) in January, Chelmsford in
February and Lingfield in June: good second at Kempton in November: stays 13.5f: acts on
polytrack, tapeta and firm going: wears cheekpieces: often races towards rear, usually
responds generously to pressure. *Alan King*

PRECISION STRIKE 5 b.g. Multiplex 114 – Dockside Strike (Docksider (USA) 124) –
[2015 t13.9m 16s Apr 5] sturdy gelding: fairly useful at best, no form in 2015: stays 2m:
acts on polytrack, fibresand, good to firm and heavy going: wears headgear: tried in tongue
tie prior to 2015: usually races in rear. *Richard Guest*

PREDILECTION (USA) 2 b.c. (Jan 30) First Defence (USA) 119 – Summer Shower **93 p**
(Sadler's Wells (USA) 132) [2015 6g² p8g* Nov 18] well-made colt: fifth foal: half-brother
to 3 winners, including smart winner up to 10.3f Starboard (2-y-o 7f winner, by Zamindar)
and 1¾m winner All Rounder (by Mizzen Mast): dam, French 1½m/12.5f winner, sister to
very smart winner up to 12.3f Doctor Fremantle: off 6 months, much better effort when
winning maiden at Kempton in November by 5 lengths from Van Dyke, forging clear: will
stay at least 1¼m: will go on improving. *John Gosden*

PREDOMINANCE (IRE) 3 b.g. Danehill Dancer (IRE) 117 – Gilded Vanity (IRE) 83 **104 p**
(Indian Ridge 123) [2015 7.1s* 8s² 7v⁴ Nov 7] 155,000Y: seventh foal: brother to smart
winner up to 1m Birdman (2-y-o 6f winner), closely related to 2-y-o 6f winner Roman Seal
(by Holy Roman Emperor) and half-brother to 6f (including at 2 yrs) winner Desert Icon
(by Desert Style): dam, 5f winner, sister to smart 7f/1m performer Fa-Eq: useful form: won

maiden at Chepstow in September by 6 lengths: head second to Lear's Rock in handicap at Newbury (best effort) next time, then 3¾ lengths fourth of 21 to Withernsea in similar event at Doncaster, needing stiffer test: stays 1m: still unexposed. *William Haggas*

PREFECT 3 b.c. Paco Boy (IRE) 129 – Oshiponga 72 (Barathea (IRE) 127) [2015 p7f² 7g 7m² p7g 7.1s² 7.1d⁴ p6d⁴ Sep 4] lengthy colt: fair maiden: stays 7f: acts on polytrack and good to firm going: tried in blinkers: often races prominently. *Richard Hannon* **73**

PREMIER CURRENCY (IRE) 2 b.c. (Mar 30) Elusive Pimpernel (USA) 117 – Zeena 61 (Unfuwain (USA) 131) [2015 6m 6m⁵ 7.1m p7g² p8g* p8g* 7m³ 8g Sep 24] good-topped colt: fair performer: won 2 nurseries at Kempton in August: stays 1m: acts on polytrack and good to firm going: front runner/races prominently. *Richard Hannon* **73**

PREMIER JACK'S 4 b.g. Tobougg (IRE) 125 – Arabellas Homer 49 (Mark of Esteem (IRE) 137) [2015 p15.8g Feb 11] of little account: tried in hood. *Nikki Evans* **–**

PRENDERGAST HILL (IRE) 3 b.g. Raven's Pass (USA) 133 – Daraliya (IRE) (Kahyasi 130) [2015 10m⁴ 10s² 10.1d* Sep 27] 40,000Y: half-brother to several winners, including smart 1¼m winner Attercliffe (by Alhaarth), smart 11.5f-2m winner Circassian (by Groom Dancer) and useful 1¼m-1½m winner Vulcanite (by Dubawi): dam French 12.5f winner: fairly useful performer: best effort when winning maiden at Epsom in September by 1¼ lengths from Swashbuckling: likely to stay beyond 1¼m: open to further improvement. *Ed de Giles* **90 p**

PRESBURG (IRE) 6 b.g. Balmont (USA) 117 – Eschasse (USA) (Zilzal (USA) 137) [2015 98: 10.1g p11g 10.3g⁵ 10f² 9m 10m p11g 10s p12g Dec 2] rather leggy gelding: fairly useful handicapper: effective from 1¼m to 2m: acts on polytrack and any turf going: often starts slowly, often races in rear. *Joseph Tuite* **87**

PRESCIENCE (IRE) 3 b.c. Kyllachy 129 – Clear Vision 71 (Observatory (USA) 131) [2015 10m⁶ 11.5g² p12f³ p12g² p11g⁵ 12s⁴ Sep 18] 70,000F: rangy colt: fifth foal: half-brother to 9.5f winner (stayed 1½m) Shestheman (by Manduro): dam, maiden (stayed 1½m), half-sister to smart winner up to 11.5f Cassydora: fairly useful maiden: good second in handicap at Kempton fourth start: stays 1½m: acts on polytrack: sold 22,000 gns, sent to Australia. *Richard Hannon* **90**

PRESS GANG 2 b.g. (Feb 5) Mount Nelson 125 – Rutba 74 (Act One 124) [2015 p8d 8.1g p10g² 10.2m³ 10.2g⁵ Oct 18] fair maiden: best effort at 1¼m: acts on polytrack: sometimes slowly away. *Richard Hannon* **72**

PRESSURE 3 ch.g. Equiano (FR) 127 – Classical Dancer 98 (Dr Fong (USA) 128) [2015 71: 7m⁶ 7d⁶ 7m⁴ 8.1s⁴ 7m³ t7.1m³ t7.1m³ 7s Oct 15] good-topped gelding: fair maiden: stays 1m: acts on tapeta, soft and good to firm going: in headgear last 3 starts: sold 13,000 gns, sent to Germany. *Clive Cox* **74**

PRESSURE POINT 5 b.g. Oasis Dream 129 – Arrive 109 (Kahyasi 130) [2015 81: 12.5s⁴ 12.4g* 12g² 12g* 12m⁴ 12m* 13.7m* 14d 14.6m⁴ Sep 11] useful-looking gelding: useful handicapper: won at Newcastle in April, York in May, Ripon in July and Musselburgh (by neck from Future Empire) in August: looked unlucky not to finish closer when 4¼ lengths fourth to Curbyourenthusiasm in Mallard Stakes at Doncaster final start, short of room under 3f out: stays 14.5f: acts on good to firm and good to soft going: usually races prominently. *Keith Dalgleish* **102**

PRESTO BOY 3 b.g. Compton Place 125 – Presto Levanter 69 (Rock of Gibraltar (IRE) 133) [2015 67: p6f⁴ 6g 5m t6g⁴ t7.1f t6f² t5.1f⁵ t6f p8g Dec 9] modest maiden: left James Fanshawe after fourth start: stays 6f: acts on polytrack and tapeta: tried in hood in 2015: sometimes in tongue tie prior to 2015. *Richard Hughes* **61**

PRESUMIDO (IRE) 5 b.g. Iffraaj 127 – Miss Megs (IRE) 81 (Croco Rouge (IRE) 126) [2015 63, a83: p8g p8m* p8f⁴ p8m 6m⁵ p7g 8.5v⁶ p8g³ p8f³ p8m p8m* p8g² Dec 7] workmanlike gelding: fairly useful handicapper: won at Kempton in February and Lingfield in November: stays 1m: acts on polytrack, soft and good to firm going: wears hood: often races towards rear. *Simon Dow* **88**

PRETEND (IRE) 4 b.g. Invincible Spirit (IRE) 121 – Fafinta (IRE) (Indian Ridge 123) [2015 110: p6g t6m* p5g* p6f* 6m Jun 1] very smart performer: won handicap at Wolverhampton (by 1¼ lengths from Boomerang Bob) in March, listed race at Lingfield (by 1¼ lengths from Alben Star) in March and AW Sprint Championships Stakes at Lingfield (by length from Alben Star) in April: well held in listed race at Windsor final start: has won at 7f, best at sprint trips: acts on polytrack and tapeta: sometimes wears hood: often travels strongly. *Charlie Appleby* **123**

PRETTY BUBBLES 6 b.m. Sleeping Indian 122 – Willmar (IRE) 53 (Zafonic (USA) **93**
130) [2015 89: f7d³ p7g* f7d⁵ p8f² p7f³ p7f³ 7.6d³ 7m² 7s² 7.6f² 7m* 7.6g⁴ p7g² 7.2m²
6d² 8m⁶ 7v³ p7g⁵ p8m Dec 27] angular mare: fairly useful handicapper: won at Kempton
in January and Newbury (by 3 lengths from Gen I Am) in July: stays 1m: acts on polytrack,
fibresand, good to firm and good to soft going: wears cheekpieces nowadays: often races
towards rear. *J. R. Jenkins*

PRETTY JEWEL 2 b.f. (Feb 14) Aqlaam 125 – Highland Jewel (IRE) 58 (Azamour **63**
(IRE) 130) [2015 p6g⁶ 7.6g³ t8.6g⁵ 6m Oct 3] 10,000Y: rather leggy filly: second foal: dam,
maiden (best effort 8.6f), half-sister to useful Slovakian winner up to 15f Ryan: modest
maiden: stays 8.5f. *Clive Brittain*

PRICELESS 2 b.f. (Mar 9) Exceed And Excel (AUS) 126 – Molly Brown 95 (Rudimentary **102**
(USA) 118) [2015 6d* 6g³ 6d⁵ Oct 30] 70,000Y: rather leggy filly: half-sister to several
winners, including smart 2-y-o 6f winner Doctor Brown (by Dr Fong), later successful in
Hong Kong, and useful winner up to 8.3f Insaaf (2-y-o 6f winner, by Averti): dam winner
up to 6f (2-y-o 5f winner): useful form: won maiden at Haydock in September by 7 lengths
from Evangelical: much better subsequent effort, shaping well, when 3 lengths third of 14
to Shaden in Firth of Clyde Stakes at Ayr, short of room after 1f and left poorly placed:
raced only at 6f. *Clive Cox*

PRIGSNOV DANCER (IRE) 10 ch.g. Namid 128 – Brave Dance (IRE) (Kris 135) **79**
[2015 69, a62: f5d t6g⁶ t5.1g³ t5.1f t6f 6.1d⁴ 5g⁶ 5m* 5m 6g* 5m⁵ 5d³ 6g 5.1d* 5s⁵ t6f Nov **a53**
13] small, strong, close-coupled gelding: fair handicapper: won at Beverley in June, Thirsk
(apprentice) in July and Nottingham in October: stays 7f: acts on polytrack, tapeta, good to
firm and good to soft going: sometimes wears headgear: tried in tongue tie prior to 2015:
often races prominently. *Deborah Sanderson*

PRIM AND PROPER 4 b.f. Sleeping Indian 122 – Quite Fantastic (IRE) (Fantastic **72**
Light (USA) 134) [2015 8f² 7s² 10.2m 8.1m* 10.2m² 8.5m⁴ 8.1m² 8m⁴ 8.1m⁵ Sep 10]
workmanlike filly: fair handicapper: won at Chepstow in June: stays 1¼m: acts on
polytrack, good to firm and soft going: tried in cheekpieces prior to 2015: has hinted at
temperament. *Dai Burchell*

PRIMA PAGINA 3 ch.f. Showcasing 117 – La Gazzetta (IRE) 59 (Rossini (USA) 118) **49**
[2015 –: t7.1g² Aug 6] poor maiden: best effort at 7f: acts on tapeta: often races towards
rear. *Dr Jon Scargill*

PRIME EXHIBIT 10 b.g. Selkirk (USA) 129 – First Exhibit (Machiavellian (USA) 123) **63**
[2015 81: t8.6f³ t7.1m* t8.6m⁴ t8.6f⁴ t8.6f⁴ t8.6m⁵ t8.6g 7.6g⁴ 8.3d 7d 8m⁵ 7.1s⁴ t8.6g Dec **a70**
5] rangy gelding: fair performer: won seller at Wolverhampton in February: stays 8.5f: acts
on polytrack, tapeta, firm and soft going: tried in headgear prior to 2015: often wears
tongue tie. *Daniel Loughnane*

PRIMITIVO 2 b.g. (Feb 20) Excellent Art 125 – Dolcetto (IRE) 83 (Danehill Dancer **86 p**
(IRE) 117) [2015 t7.1g⁶ 7m⁶ p8d³ 10.2g² 8.3g* Oct 19] 10,000Y: first foal: dam 1¼m-1½m
winner: fairly useful performer: won nursery at Windsor (by 2 lengths from Deodoro) in
October: will prove suited by a return to 1¼m: best form on good going: usually races
towards rear: will go on improving. *Alan King*

PRIMOBELLA 2 ch.f. (Apr 8) Duke of Marmalade (IRE) 132 – Arbella 106 (Primo **– p**
Dominie 121) [2015 7s⁵ 8.3d t7.1f Nov 10] fifth foal: closely related to useful 1¾m-2m
winner Chocala (by Rock of Gibraltar) and half-sister to useful winner up to 9.4f Lat
Hawill (2-y-o 7f winner, by Invincible Spirit) and 13.3f winner Bellajeu (by Montjeu):
dam, 1½m winner, half-sister to smart stayer/top-class hurdler Overturn: no form, but may
yet do better given time/longer distances. *Mark Johnston*

PRIMOGENITURE (IRE) 4 b.g. Glory of Dancer 121 – Jacqueline (IND) (King **95**
Charlemagne (USA) 120) [2015 93: 12g 16.1g 10.4f⁵ 9.9m² 10.4m² 9.8m² 9.8g* 9.9m
10.2d Oct 14] sturdy, angular gelding: useful handicapper: won at Ripon (by 2 lengths from
Cooper) in August: stays 2m, effective at much shorter: acts on good to firm and good to
soft going: sometimes wears headgear (visored last 6 starts): usually races prominently.
David O'Meara

PRIMROSE BROWN 4 b.f. Indian Danehill (IRE) 124 – Royal Tango (Petoski 135) **53**
[2015 p10f p8g² Dec 20] fifth foal: dam unraced: placed in bumper: better effort in maidens
when second at Lingfield, showing modest form. *Conrad Allen*

PRIMROSE VALLEY 3 b.f. Pastoral Pursuits 127 – Cosmic Destiny (IRE) 79 (Soviet **109**
Star (USA) 128) [2015 91: p6f* p6g* p5m* t5.1f* p5f 6m³ 6m⁴ 6m 7m 6g Oct 10] has
scope: useful performer: won handicaps at Kempton in January and Lingfield in February

and minor events at Lingfield later in February and at Wolverhampton in March: good third in handicap at Newmarket (2 lengths behind Magical Memory) in July: stays 6f: acts on polytrack, tapeta and good to firm going: often wears headgear: held up. *Ed Vaughan*

PRINCE ALZAIN (USA) 6 b.h. Street Sense (USA) 128 – Monaassabaat (USA) 105 – (Zilzal (USA) 137) [2015 92: a8f Jan 22] sturdy horse: smart performer at best: well held all 3 outings since 2013: stays 1½m: acts on polytrack: tried in headgear. *Robert Cowell*

PRINCE ART (IRE) 4 b.g. Art Connoisseur (IRE) 121 – Princess Misty (IRE) 56 – § (Invincible Spirit (IRE) 121) [2015 53§: 8d May 13] poor maiden: stays 1¼m: acts on polytrack and good to firm going: has worn headgear: tried in tongue tie: temperamental. *Derek Shaw*

PRINCE BALLYGOWEN 4 b.g. Prince Arch (USA) 119 – Ball Gown 98 (Jalmood – (USA) 126) [2015 –: p10m⁵ 7m 10.2m t12.2g Jun 26] smallish gelding: no form: dead. *Clifford Lines*

PRINCE BISHOP (IRE) 8 ch.g. Dubawi (IRE) 129 – North East Bay (USA) **126** (Prospect Bay (CAN) 117) [2015 125: a9.4f² a9.9g² a9.9f* Mar 28]
　　　　Winners should always receive the credit they are due. In normal circumstances, Prince Bishop's achievement in beating the two high-class North American challengers in the Dubai World Cup would have been met almost universally with the same enthusiasm with which it was greeted by the partisan home crowd at Meydan. The style of the victory was stunning, with Prince Bishop sweeping into the lead over a furlong out, after labouring in the rear, at least five lengths adrift at one time, and being in danger of becoming tailed off (he was given reminders). After coming from a long way back and challenging wide, Prince Bishop strode clear, edging left as he did so, to win by two and three quarter lengths and a length and a quarter from the previous year's Kentucky Derby and Preakness winner California Chrome, who started 5/4 favourite at Meydan, and the lightly-raced Lea (4/1 second favourite) who had been sidelined for much of the previous season after winning his first two starts. Those included the Donn Handicap at Gulfstream Park, in the latest edition of which he had shown himself to be in good form when a keeping-on second (the Donn has been used regularly as a preparatory race by American challengers, while California Chrome had finished second in the San Antonio Invitational at Santa Anita, a race also previously used by American World Cup challengers as a warm-up).
　　　　There was a gap after the first three in the Dubai World Cup of five and a quarter lengths to Candy Boy, who had shown smart form in North America (sixth in the Breeders' Cup Classic) as a three-year-old and was having his first start for new Middle Eastern connections. Japanese challenger Hokko Tarumae, one of the top dirt performers in his own country and successful in his last three races, came fifth and the previous year's World Cup winner African Story sixth. The only British-trained challenger Side Glance, who had been fourth in the two previous editions, managed only eighth of the nine runners, patently not taking to the dirt which had replaced

Dubai World Cup Sponsored by Emirates Airline, Meydan—
a seventh success in the world's richest race for Saeed bin Suroor as Prince Bishop
lands the spoils in the first renewal run on dirt since 2009; the two US-trained runners,
Kentucky Derby winner California Chrome (right) and Lea, fill the places

the synthetic tapeta surface used for the five previous editions of the Dubai World Cup run at Meydan (the last World Cup contested on traditional dirt had been in 2009 at Nad Al Sheba where American dirt horses had enjoyed plenty of success over the years).

The importance of having worthy North American challengers for a race calling itself the World Cup had prompted the change of surface at Meydan and, had Prince Bishop not been in the line-up, there would undoubtedly have been plenty of stories about the Dubai World Cup having 'recaptured its magic.' To an impartial observer it was hard to escape the conclusion that some of the negative media coverage stemmed from the fact that the Emirates Airline-sponsored World Cup did not produce the outcome so widely anticipated. 'Unbelievable' was the first word that appeared in the report of the race in the *Racing Post*; 'unsatisfactory and hard to fathom' was the initial reaction to the result in the *Timeform* analysis. Did Prince Bishop's Dubai World Cup victory really defy logic, as some of the reaction implied? Although he was a 14/1-shot, sixth in the betting, Prince Bishop had shown himself to be a high-class performer at his best, successful the previous year in two rounds of the Maktoum Challenge (beating African Story in the first of them), stepping stones at Meydan in February and March to the World Cup in which he started joint third favourite in a field of sixteen. Prince Bishop went on to win a second September Stakes at Kempton—putting up the best performance on the all-weather in Britain all year—on his only other outing. Prince Bishop had a rating of 125 in *Racehorses of 2014*, in which California Chrome was rated 127, Lea 123 and Candy Boy 121 (African Story had a rating of 128 and Hokko Tarumae 124).

The reservations about Prince Bishop's World Cup chances—as with those of 8/1-shot African Story for that matter—arose from his performances in both Maktoum Challenges that he had won the previous year. Prince Bishop probably should have won the first of those races, failing to adapt to the change of surface and dropping back into a poor position before finishing best of all and being beaten only a head by Frankyfourfingers. African Story didn't seem to take to the dirt either, managing only seventh, and neither he nor Prince Bishop seemed completely at home on the surface when they fought out a close finish to the Maktoum Challenge Round 3, pulling clear of the remainder, with Prince Bishop's performance remarkably similar to his reappearance, shying from the kickback in the early stages and again getting going all too late, failing by a neck after coming with a wet sail once switched wide out of the kickback. On those two performances, Prince Bishop made limited appeal for the World Cup—it was his fourth appearance in the race and he had yet to finish in the first six—but attempts afterwards to explain away his win, as some did, by saying that California Chrome was taken along too quickly and forfeited ground by racing wide, were not fair to Prince Bishop. California Chrome was kept off the rail but he covered no more ground than Prince Bishop who was moved wide in the back straight to avoid the kickback. There were no complaints afterwards from California Chrome's connections, his trainer saying 'No excuses, he was just second best today and that's what happens in this game, the horse you think is going to win doesn't always.' Prince Bishop produced a career-best effort on the day and California Chrome lost little in defeat, only a shade below his best in the end after moving up to have every chance over a furlong out.

Prince Bishop (IRE) (ch.g. 2007)	Dubawi (IRE) (b 2002)	Dubai Millennium (b 1996)	Seeking The Gold
			Colorado Dancer
		Zomaradah (b 1995)	Deploy
			Jawaher
	North East Bay (USA) (b or br 2001)	Prospect Bay (b 1992)	Crafty Prospector
			Baltic Sea
		Wassifa (b 1988)	Sure Blade
			Rye Tops

The Dubai World Cup turned out to be the final race for the eight-year-olds Prince Bishop and African Story, both geldings who were retired shortly afterwards. They were returned to Britain where they were eventually placed with Retraining of Racehorses, the official charity partly funded by racing and its participants and set up for the welfare of retired racehorses, with the aim of finding alternative careers or pastimes for them. The charity says that over 10,000 ex-racehorses are currently

Sheikh Hamdan bin Mohammed Al Maktoum's "Prince Bishop"

registered in Britain as active in other disciplines; care is also provided for former racehorses who became 'vulnerable or unwanted.' The well-made Prince Bishop is the second Dubai World Cup winner sired by Dubawi, following Monterosso in 2012 (when Prince Bishop finished seventh), and, like African Story, Prince Bishop began his career in France with Andre Fabre for whom he showed smart form as a three-year-old, winning the Prix du Prince d'Orange and the Prix du Conseil de Paris at Longchamp, before joining Saeed bin Suroor for whom he did much of his racing over the years at the Dubai Racing Carnival where he built up a good record. Prince Bishop's pedigree is of only academic interest now, but he was bought as a foal for 80,000 guineas at the Newmarket Sales, and is out of once-raced North East Bay, a half-sister to the smart miler Hold To Ransom, who won the Sandringham Handicap at Royal Ascot, and to the smart mile and a quarter performer Gulf Express. Prince Bishop's grandam Wassifa was an eleven-furlong winner in Britain who subsequently won at up to nine furlongs in the States; she was out of a half-sister to the Derby runner-up Most Welcome. The pick of North East Bay's three other winners is Strategic Mission (by Red Ransom) who was useful at his best when he won at a mile and a quarter. Prince Bishop was effective at a mile and a quarter to a mile and a half, and acted on dirt, synthetic surfaces and heavy going. He wore a visor. *Saeed bin Suroor*

PRINCE CONNOISSEUR (IRE) 4 ch.g. Art Connoisseur (IRE) 121 – Brewing Storm **85** (IRE) (King Charlemagne (USA) 120) [2015 95: 5d 5m p5d⁵ p5g² p5g 5d p5f Oct 29] fairly useful handicapper: stays 6f: acts on polytrack and good to firm going: tried in blinkers: front runner/races prominently. *J. J. Feane, Ireland*

PRINCE GAGARIN (IRE) 3 b.c. Dubawi (IRE) 129 – Cara Fantasy (IRE) 84 (Sadler's **104**
Wells (USA) 132) [2015 104: 10.3v³ 10g³ 11.1s² 12g 8.1v⁴ 9g Sep 26] strong, deep-girthed
colt: useful performer: third in Dee Stakes at Chester (2 lengths behind Not So Sleepy) and
Gallinule Stakes at the Curragh (1¾ lengths behind Curvy), and second in listed race at
Hamilton (6 lengths behind Medrano): well below form subsequently: stays 11f: acts on
good to firm and heavy going: sent to USA. *Ed Dunlop*

PRINCE GIBRALTAR (FR) 4 ch.c. Rock of Gibraltar (IRE) 133 – Princess Sofia **125**
(UAE) (Pennekamp (USA) 130) [2015 124: 10.4s⁶ 11.9g² 10.4m³ 11.9g* 11.9m 11.9s²
9.9g⁵ Nov 8] big, rangy colt: high-class performer: won Grosser Preis von Baden at Baden-
Baden (by 1¾ lengths from Nightflower) in September: placed in Grand Prix de Chantilly
(¾-length second to Manatee), York Stakes at York (1¼ lengths third to Tullius) and
Grosser Preis von Bayern at Munich (4 lengths second behind Ito): also ran well when 4
lengths seventh to Golden Horn in Prix de l'Arc de Triomphe at Longchamp on fifth
outing: below form in Premio Roma at Rome final appearance: stayed 1½m: acted on good
to firm and heavy going: blinkered once in 2014 and last 4 starts in 2015: often raced
towards rear: to stand at Haras de Reboursiere et de Montaigu, France, fee €5,000. *Jean-
Claude Rouget, France*

PRINCE HELLVELYN 2 b.g. (Mar 11) Hellvelyn 118 – Queens Jubilee 71 (Cayman **77**
Kai (IRE) 114) [2015 6g³ 6m* 7g³ 7mᵖᵘ Sep 9] fair performer: won maiden at Newcastle
in June: stayed 7f: dead. *Brian Ellison*

PRINCE JAI 2 ch.g. (Mar 31) Showcasing 117 – Play Around (IRE) 105 (Niniski (USA) **65**
125) [2015 5.1g 6m 6g⁵ p7g⁴ p7g³ p7g⁴ a7f Dec 18] angular gelding: fair maiden: left Ian
Williams after sixth start: will stay 1m: acts on polytrack: tried in cheekpieces. *S. Seemar,
UAE*

PRINCE OF ARRAN 2 b.c. (Mar 28) Shirocco (GER) 129 – Storming Sioux 79 **84**
(Storming Home 128) [2015 7m⁶ 7g² 7s⁴ 8d² 8s² p8g* Nov 11] third foal: dam, maiden
(best form at 1m), closely related to very smart winner up to 1¼m Best of The Bests: fairly
useful performer: won maiden at Kempton in November: stays 1m: acts on polytrack and
soft going: in headgear last 3 starts. *Charlie Fellowes*

PRINCE OF CARDAMOM (IRE) 3 b.g. Nayef (USA) 129 – Tiger Spice 68 (Royal **70**
Applause 124) [2015 60: p12m³ 11.6m⁴ 12.3s 10m⁴ 13.1f Sep 12] sturdy gelding: fair
maiden: left Andrew Balding after fourth start: stays 1½m: acts on polytrack and good to
firm going: often races freely: temperament under suspicion. *Jonathan Geake*

PRINCE OF JOHANNE (IRE) 9 gr.g. Johannesburg (USA) 127 – Paiute Princess **–**
(FR) (Darshaan 133) [2015 108: 8g 8m May 14] good-topped gelding: useful handicapper:
below form both starts in 2015: stays 10.5f: acts on firm and good to soft going: wears
cheekpieces. *Tom Tate*

*Longines - Grosser Preis von Baden, Baden-Baden—the late withdrawal of Ito leaves the way clear
for France's Prince Gibraltar (left) to beat the remainder of the home-trained runners
with some authority; Nightflower (out of picture to the right), Sirius (second left) and
Palace Prince (striped cap) complete the frame*

PRINCE OF PARIS 3 b.c. Champs Elysees 124 – Cool Kitten (IRE) 65 (One Cool Cat **85**
(USA) 123) [2015 85: p8g⁴ p10f* p8m⁴ p12g² 10d 11g May 15] sturdy colt: fairly useful
handicapper: won at Lingfield in January: stays 1½m, effective at shorter: acts on polytrack.
Roger Ingram

PRINCE OF PASSION (CAN) 7 ch.g. Roman Ruler (USA) 122 – Rare Passion (CAN) –
(Out of Place (USA)) [2015 70: f6d Jan 4] compact gelding: modest handicapper: stays 7f:
acts on all-weather, good to firm and good to soft going: usually in headgear: tried in
tongue tie. *Derek Shaw*

PRINCE OF TIME 3 ch.g. Bahamian Bounty 116 – Touching (IRE) 89 (Kheleyf (USA) –
116) [2015 65p: 6.5m May 2] fair maiden: well held only outing in 2015: stays 7.5f: acts
on good to soft going: usually races close up. *Mark Johnston*

PRINCE REGAL 5 ch.g. Cockney Rebel (IRE) 127 – Wachiwi (IRE) 67 (Namid 128) **75**
[2015 80: p6f 6g⁴ 6.1m² 6m² 6m 6m⁵ 6g 6g⁵ 6g Oct 19] sturdy gelding: fair handicapper:
stays 7f: acts on polytrack, soft and good to firm going: tried in cheekpieces in 2015: front
runner/races prominently. *Timothy Jarvis*

PRINCE ROFAN (IRE) 3 gr.g. Strategic Prince 114 – Rofan (USA) (Cozzene (USA)) –
[2015 –: t6f f6d⁴ f8s Feb 3] no form: visored in 2015. *Derek Shaw*

PRINCESS COOKIE 2 b.f. (Feb 3) Sakhee's Secret 128 – Rouge Dancer (Elusive City **54 p**
(USA) 117) [2015 t7.1m⁶ Dec 18] 1,600F, 1,800Y: third foal: half-sister to 1¼m winner
Durand (by Motivator): dam unraced: 7/2, showed ability when 5 lengths sixth of 11 to
Outback Blue in maiden at Wolverhampton on debut: will improve. *Philip McBride*

PRINCESSES VOICE (IRE) 2 br.f. (Apr 9) Poet's Voice 126 – Hear My Cry (USA) **69**
(Giant's Causeway (USA) 132) [2015 7m⁶ 7m⁶ p7g⁴ Aug 24] €47,000Y: useful-looking
filly: second foal: half-sister to Italian 7f/1m winner (including at 2 yrs) Magia Nera
(by Bellamy Road): dam, ran once in Italy, half-sister to dam of Dubai World Cup winner
Prince Bishop: fair maiden: best effort when fourth at Kempton: sent to Argentina.
Marco Botti

PRINCESS GUEST (IRE) 3 b.f. Iffraaj 127 – Princess Speedfit (FR) 77 (Desert Prince –
(IRE) 130) [2015 7d⁵ 8.3s 7m 8d p8f Dec 17] 150,000Y: half-sister to several winners,
including smart winner up to 7f Imperial Guest (2-y-o 6f winner, by Imperial Dancer) and
useful winner up to 1m Excellent Guest (2-y-o 6f winner, by Exceed And Excel): dam 8.3f
winner: no form. *George Margarson*

PRINCESS KODIAC (IRE) 2 b.f. (Apr 3) Kodiac 112 – Silver Cache (USA) 59 (Silver **62 p**
Hawk (USA) 123) [2015 6g⁴ Sep 26] 42,000Y, 45,000 2-y-o: seventh foal: sister to 2-y-o
5f winner Ko Cache, closely related to 7f/1m winner Barbary (by Rock of Gibraltar) and
half-sister to useful Italian performer up to 1¼m Diva Cattiva (2-y-o 5f-7.5f winner, by
Lujain): dam maiden (stayed 1¼m): 7/1, better for run when fourth in maiden at Ripon (3¾
lengths behind Bobby's Babe) on debut, slowly away: sure to progress. *Richard Fahey*

PRINCESS KODIA (IRE) 2 b.f. (Mar 25) Kodiac 112 – Pixie's Blue (IRE) 89 (Hawk **85**
Wing (USA) 136) [2015 p5g⁴ 5m 5m 5g* 5.2m 5g⁶ p6g p6f⁴ Oct 15] €22,000F, £20,000Y:
angular filly: third foal: dam, French 1m winner, half-sister to smart French 9f/1¼m winner
Thattinger: fairly useful performer: won maiden at Bath in June: stays 6f: acts on polytrack,
best turf form on good going. *Brian Meehan*

PRINCESS LOULOU (IRE) 5 ch.m. Pivotal 124 – Aiming 76 (Highest Honor (FR) **102**
124) [2015 115: 12.4d 11.6d 10.3v* Nov 7] useful-looking mare: useful performer: off 10
weeks, back to form when winning listed race at Doncaster in November by 1½ lengths
from Latenightrequest, leading 2f out: stays 10.5f: acts on heavy going: usually wears
hood: races prominently. *Roger Varian*

PRINCESSOFTHESTARS (IRE) 3 ch.f. Sea The Stars (IRE) 140 – Wadud 59 **90 §**
(Nashwan (USA) 135) [2015 10m⁵ 10.3m* 10.2d² 12s² 12g⁵ 10g Oct 9] well-made filly:
sixth foal: half-sister to 3 winners, including smart 1¼m-1½m winner Ice Queen (by
Danehill Dancer) and French 1½m winner Wonderous Light (by Montjeu): dam maiden
(stayed 1½m): fairly useful performer: won maiden at Doncaster in June: second in
handicaps at Nottingham and Goodwood: stays 1½m: acts on soft and good to firm going:
in cheekpieces last 3 starts: front runner/races prominently: flashes tail and best treated
with caution: sent to Japan. *John Gosden*

PRINCESS ONE MUCH (IRE) 2 b.f. (Apr 28) Approve (IRE) 112 – So Blissful (IRE) –
77 (Cape Cross (IRE) 129) [2015 5f 6m 5m t6g p5g p7g p6g⁵ 5.1m p5g Nov 25] €6,000F,
5,000Y: rather leggy filly: third foal: half-sister to temperamental 6f/7f winner Medicean
Bliss (by Medicean): dam 7f winner who stayed 1¼m: no form: tried in blinkers: front
runner/races prominently. *Michael Blanshard*

PRINCESS PEACHES 3 ch.f. Notnowcato 128 – Miss Apricot 48 (Indian Ridge 123) [2015 8m^{6} 7g^{2} t8.6g 6.9g 8.5d p8f^{4} t8.6f f8f* Dec 17] third foal: half-sister to 5f/6f winner Apricot Sky (by Pastoral Pursuits) and 8.6f winner Charlcot (by Monsieur Bond): dam ran twice: fair performer: won maiden at Southwell in December: best effort at 1m: acts on fibresand: often races towards rear. *James Bethell* **70**

PRINCESS RAIHANA 2 br.f. (Mar 17) Cape Cross (IRE) 129 – Raihana (AUS) 117 (Elusive Quality (USA)) [2015 8d Oct 23] first foal: dam 7f-9.5f winner in South Africa/UAE, including UAE Oaks: 16/1, very green when 10¾ lengths ninth of 11 to Zest in maiden at Doncaster on debut, hanging left under pressure: should do better. *Marco Botti* **– p**

PRINCESS TANSY 3 b.f. Equiano (FR) 127 – Tanasie (Cadeaux Genereux 131) [2015 t7.1f^{5} p6g^{4} t6f^{4} 5m^{2} 5m* 5.7g^{5} 5d^{2} 5d* Sep 2] 26,000F: half-sister to several winners, including 5f/6f winner Doric Lady (by Kyllachy) and 1m-1½m winner Jamhoori (by Tiger Hill): dam French 1m winner: fairly useful handicapper: won at Newmarket in June and Bath in September: best form at 5f: acts on good to firm and good to soft going: often travels strongly. *David Simcock* **82**

PRIORS BROOK 4 b.g. Champs Elysees 124 – Dyanita 76 (Singspiel (IRE) 133) [2015 75: 11.6m^{2} 10.2m* 12s^{5} p11g p12g Nov 18] fairly useful handicapper: won at Chepstow in June: stays 11.5f: acts on polytrack and good to firm going. *Andrew Balding* **85**

PRIORS GATE (IRE) 3 b.g. Acclamation 118 – Key Rose (IRE) 88 (Key of Luck (USA) 126) [2015 –p: 6m^{3} 7m 6g^{4} 8m^{4} 9.9s Oct 15] modest maiden: best effort at 1m: acts on good to firm going. *Marcus Tregoning* **64**

PRIORY 2 b.f. (Apr 16) Mullionmileanhour (IRE) 116 – Alectrona (FR) (Invincible Spirit (IRE) 121) [2015 p5g* 5m^{4} 5m^{6} 6m^{3} p6g^{4} p7g 5.7m p6f p6g^{4} p6g^{5} Dec 19] third foal: dam once-raced half-sister to useful French winner up to 9f Darjeeling: modest performer: won maiden at Lingfield in April: left Robert Eddery after fifth start: stays 6f: acts on polytrack and good to firm going. *Martin Smith* **64 d**

PRISOM (IRE) 2 b.f. (Apr 1) Zebedee 113 – Crystal Theatre (IRE) 72 (King's Theatre (IRE) 128) [2015 t6f* p6g p6g Dec 30] €30,000 2-y-o: seventh foal: half-sister to 3 winners, including 1¼m-11.3f winner Breenainthemycra (by Jeremy): dam, maiden (stayed 1½m), out of May Hill Stakes winner Solar Crystal: fair performer: best effort when winning maiden at Wolverhampton in November, well positioned: raced only at 6f. *Gay Kelleway* **71**

PRIVATE DONALD 2 ch.c. (Apr 18) Sakhee's Secret 128 – Excello 94 (Exceed And Excel (AUS) 126) [2015 t6m^{3} Dec 18] second foal: half-brother to 5f winner Ernest (by Showcasing): dam, 2-y-o 5f winner, half-sister to smart UAE sprinter Rafeej: 7/1, green when 5 lengths third of 9 to Tesoro in maiden at Wolverhampton on debut, nearest finish without being knocked about: sure to progress. *Robert Cowell* **59 p**

PRIVILEGED (IRE) 3 b.f. Exceed And Excel (AUS) 126 – Almaviva (IRE) 93 (Grand Lodge (USA) 125) [2015 7m p7f^{3} 7g^{2} 6.9g^{4} p8g* 8g^{4} 8.3d^{2} 7.1g^{2} t8.6f^{2} Oct 3] 75,000Y: smallish filly: fifth foal: half-sister to useful winner up to 1¼m Indian Jack (2-y-o 7f winner) and 8.6f winner Indian Trifone (both by Indian Haven): dam 2-y-o 7f winner: fairly useful performer: won maiden at Chelmsford in July: stays 8.5f: acts on polytrack, tapeta and good to soft going: front runner/races prominently: sold 42,000 gns, sent to UAE. *Roger Varian* **92**

PRIZE MONEY 2 b.c. (Apr 4) Authorized (IRE) 133 – Dresden Doll (USA) 78 (Elusive Quality (USA)) [2015 8g* Oct 21] good-topped colt: third foal: half-brother to 6f/7f winner Role Player (by Exceed And Excel): dam, 2-y-o 5f winner, half-sister to very smart winner up to 1¼m Crimplene: 11/8, looked smart prospect when winning 12-runner maiden at Newmarket on debut by 4½ lengths from Hepplewhite, staying on strongly and well on top finish: will be suited by 1¼m: sure to progress. *Saeed bin Suroor* **94 p**

PROCESS 3 b.c. Nayef (USA) 129 – Intense 99 (Dansili 127) [2015 p11g* p12g* 12f^{2} 12m^{6} 14f^{3} 13.3s Aug 14] second foal: dam, winner up to 1m (2-y-o 7f winner), half-sister to US Grade 3 9f winner Button Down and 1¼m-1½m winner Model Pupil, both smart: fairly useful performer: won maiden at Kempton in March and handicap on same course in April: stays 1½m: acts on polytrack and firm going: tried in hood: usually races close up: sold 25,000 gns, sent to Saudi Arabia. *Amanda Perrett* **92**

PROCUREMENT 4 b.f. Zamindar (USA) 116 – Acquisition 94 (Dansili 127) [2015 80?: p8g p8g t8.6f Mar 23] lightly-raced maiden, little form in Britain: stays 1¼m: acts on synthetics. *Simon Dow* **–**

PROFESSOR 5 ch.h. Byron 117 – Jubilee 66 (Selkirk (USA) 129) [2015 119: 8g 7g 6g 7g^{2} 6g 7m^{6} 8d Oct 17] strong horse: useful handicapper: second at Haydock (3¼ lengths behind Emell) in April: stays 7f: best form on good going or firmer (acts on firm): tried in visor in 2015. *Michael Attwater* **105**

PROFILE STAR (IRE) 6 b.g. Kodiac 112 – Fingal Nights (IRE) 81 (Night Shift (USA)) **69** [2015 80: p6m⁵ p6m t5.1f* Feb 6] sturdy gelding: fair handicapper: won at Wolverhampton in February: stays 6f: acts on polytrack, tapeta, good to firm and good to soft going: tried in headgear prior to 2015. *Violet M. Jordan*

PROFITABLE (IRE) 3 b.c. Invincible Spirit (IRE) 121 – Dani Ridge (IRE) 92 (Indian **109** Ridge 123) [2015 100: 5d⁵ 5m* 5m² 6f⁵ 5g 5s⁵ Sep 13] well-made colt: useful performer: won listed race at York (by neck from Tendu) in May: good fifth in Commonwealth Cup at Royal Ascot (5¼ lengths behind Muhaarar) and respectable fifth in Prix du Petit Couvert at Longchamp (4¼ lengths behind Move In Time) fourth/final starts: stays 6f: acts on firm and good to soft going: usually travels strongly. *Clive Cox*

PROHIBITION (IRE) 9 b.g. Danehill Dancer (IRE) 117 – Crumpetsfortea (IRE) **47** (Henbit (USA) 130) [2015 65: t9.5g⁵ t8.6g t9.5m⁴ t8.6g 8f⁵ Jul 3] close-coupled gelding: poor performer: left Mandy Rowland after third start: stays 1¼m: acts on polytrack, good to firm and heavy going: tried in headgear/tongue tie: sometimes slowly away, often races in rear. *Alan Berry*

PROJECTION 2 b.g. (Feb 24) Acclamation 118 – Spotlight 110 (Dr Fong (USA) 128) **98** [2015 6m 6m* 6g 6.5m⁴ 6g* Sep 30] £90,000Y: lengthy gelding: half-brother to useful 1m winner Up In Lights (by Makfi): dam, 2-y-o 7f/1m winner, later Grade 2 9f winner in USA: useful performer: won maiden at Windsor in August and minor event at Salisbury (by neck from Tabarrak) in September: will stay 7f: acts on good to firm going: has been gelded. *Roger Charlton*

PROMINNA 5 ch.g. Proclamation (IRE) 130 – Minnina (IRE) (In The Wings 128) [2015 **66** –: t5.1m p6g³ p7g 7.6d p6g⁶ 5s* 5.1d* p5g³ p5m² Dec 31] lengthy, plain gelding: fair handicapper: won at Bath in August and Nottingham in November: best form at 5f: acts on soft going: often races prominently. *Tony Carroll*

PROMISED MONEY (IRE) 2 b.f. (Mar 29) Dark Angel (IRE) 113 – Hartstown House **94** (IRE) 83 (Primo Dominie 121) [2015 5d 5g* 6d³ 5g* 5g⁶ 5g³ 5g⁴ Oct 9] 35,000Y: good-topped filly: half-sister to several winners, including useful 7f-8.3f winner Hacienda (by Kheleyf) and 2-y-o 5f winner Beldale Memory (by Camacho): dam 2-y-o 5f winner: fairly useful performer: won maiden at Cork in May and listed race at Tipperary (by ½ length from Independence Day) in July: respectable fourth to Quiet Reflection in Cornwallis Stakes at Newmarket final start: worth another try at 6f: best form on good going: tongue tied last 2 outings. *Edward Lynam, Ireland*

PROMISING RUN (USA) 2 b.f. (Feb 7) Hard Spun (USA) 124 – Aviacion (BRZ) **110** (Know Heights (IRE) 118) [2015 6g³ 7g* 7g* 8g Oct 9] rangy filly: fifth foal: sister to 2-y-o 7f winner Kunooz and half-sister to 2 winners, including smart 1m-1½m winner Arabian Comet (by Dubawi): dam Brazilian Grade 1 1¼m winner: smart performer: won maiden at Newmarket in August and Rockfel Stakes there in September, in latter leading approaching final 1f and staying on stoutly to beat Thetis 1¾ lengths: should stay 1m (disappointing when tried at trip in Fillies' Mile at Newmarket). *Saeed bin Suroor*

Shadwell Rockfel Stakes, Newmarket—a pair stepping out of maidens come to the fore as Promising Run stays on stoutly to beat Thetis, with favourite Hawksmoor (third right) back in third

PROOFREADER 6 b.g. Authorized (IRE) 133 – Blixen (USA) 90 (Gone West (USA)) **95**
[2015 p10f³ p11f* p11g⁵ Mar 28] useful-looking gelding: useful handicapper: won at
Kempton in March: stays 11f: acts on polytrack and soft going: fairly useful hurdler.
Neil Mulholland

PROPERUS (IRE) 3 b.g. Lord Shanakill (USA) 121 – Amistad (GER) (Winged Love **86**
(IRE) 121) [2015 84: 6m² 6f 7.6m 7s Oct 27] fairly useful handicapper: left William
Haggas after third start: stays 6f: acts on good to firm and good to soft going. *Keith Dalgleish*

PROPOSED 3 b.c. Invincible Spirit (IRE) 121 – On A Soapbox (USA) 119 (Mi Cielo **104**
(USA)) [2015 63: 10g⁶ 12.3s⁵ 10m* 12f 12g⁶ 13g 14.6d Sep 12] tall, lengthy colt: useful
performer: won maiden at Sandown in May: struggled in better company after, last of 7 in
St Leger at Doncaster final start: stays 1½m: acts on firm going: sold 40,000 gns, sent to
Bahrain. *Richard Hannon*

PROSECUTE (FR) 2 b.c. (Feb 23) Lawman (FR) 121 – Dissitation (IRE) 77 (Spectrum **71 p**
(IRE) 126) [2015 7f 8.3g 8.3d Oct 5] €50,000Y: strong, compact colt. fourth foal: dam,
maiden (stayed 8.5f), sister to useful winner up to 7f Rum Charger, herself dam of very
smart US performer up to 1½m Winchester: fair maiden: best effort when ninth at Windsor
(5¾ lengths behind Top Beak) final start, not knocked about: open to further improvement.
David Simcock

PROSPECTUS 2 b.g. (Mar 20) Sakhee (USA) 136 – Some Sunny Day 89 (Where Or **69 p**
When (IRE) 124) [2015 p8g⁶ f8g Nov 26] 40,000Y: second foal: dam, 1¼m-11.6f winner,
half-sister to July Cup winner Sakhee's Secret (by Sakhee): sixth of 13 to D'niro in maiden
at Kempton in November, running on late: well held at Southwell next time: has been
gelded: worth another chance. *Hughie Morrison*

PROSPERITEE 2 b.f. (Apr 22) Paco Boy (IRE) 129 – Goodie Twosues 91 (Fraam 114) **–**
[2015 7g 8s⁶ 7.6g Sep 12] 7,000Y: half-sister to several winners, including 1½m winners
Communicator (useful up to 2¼m, by Motivator) and Craggaknock (by Authorized): dam
2-y-o 6f winner who stayed 8.5f: no form. *Michael Blanshard*

PROSTATE AWARENESS (IRE) 4 b.g. Camacho 118 – Genuinely (IRE) 43 (Entre- **56**
preneur 123) [2015 64: 8s 10.1d 12m 12.1f⁴ 14g⁶ 16.1m⁵ 12.1g 13.8v Oct 17] modest
maiden: stays 2m: acts on firm going: sometimes wears headgear. *Patrick Holmes*

PROTEST (IRE) 2 b.g. (Apr 20) Fastnet Rock (AUS) 127 – Phrase 72 (Royal Anthem **75**
(USA) 135) [2015 6g p8f⁴ 8s p7g⁵ Nov 13] rather unfurnished gelding: fair maiden: will
benefit from return to 1m+. *Sylvester Kirk*

PROUD OF YOU (IRE) 3 b.g. Fast Company (IRE) 126 – Shambodia (IRE) (Petardia **63**
113) [2015 64: 7d 6g 7.5g 8g⁶ 7.2d⁴ 8.5m³ 7.5g⁴ 8m 7.5m⁴ 8.9m 8.5m 9.2d Sep 1] modest
maiden: stays 8.5f: acts on good to firm and good to soft going: tried in cheekpieces in
2015. *Nigel Tinkler*

PROUD TIMES (USA) 9 b.g. Proud Citizen (USA) 122 – Laura's Pistolette (USA) (Big **–**
Pistol (USA)) [2015 57: f14s⁶ Mar 25] rangy gelding: modest handicapper: probably stays
2m: acts on polytrack, fibresand and heavy going: wears headgear: temperament under
suspicion. *Ali Stronge*

PROVATO (IRE) 3 ch.g. Approve (IRE) 112 – Sagemacca (IRE) (Danehill Dancer (IRE) **70**
117) [2015 8.3m⁶ 10f⁶ 10.2m⁴ 12m 11.6g 12g Jul 31] useful-looking gelding: fair maiden:
best effort at 1½m: acts on good to firm going: tried in cheekpieces: sold £1,400, sent to
Germany. *Amanda Perrett*

PROVENANCE 4 b.f. Galileo (IRE) 134 – Echelon 120 (Danehill (USA) 126) [2015 108: **108**
8m³ 10f⁵ 10f² 9.9m⁵ Aug 12] lengthy, attractive filly: useful performer: best efforts when
length fifth to Mahsoob in Wolferton Handicap at Royal Ascot (edgy and sweating, finished
well after not clear run over 2f out) and 2½ lengths second of 4 to Tha'ir in listed race at
Sandown: stays 1¼m: acts on polytrack and firm going: often in hood prior to 2015:
usually in tongue tie in 2015: often races towards rear. *Sir Michael Stoute*

PROVIDENT SPIRIT 4 b.g. Invincible Spirit (IRE) 121 – Port Providence (Red **92**
Ransom (USA)) [2015 92: 7.2d 7.9g² 8d⁵ 8g 7g² 6g 7v Nov 7] sturdy gelding: fairly useful
handicapper: second at Carlisle in June and Leicester in September: stays 1m: acts on good
to soft going: tried in blinkers prior to 2015. *David O'Meara*

PROVOKING (USA) 2 b.g. (Mar 11) Any Given Saturday (USA) 128 – Fair And Lively **73**
(USA) (Lively One (USA)) [2015 7.4g 8.3d 8.3d³ t7.1f Oct 30] fair maiden: stays 8.5f.
David Evans

PRUSSIAN BLUE 3 ch.c. New Approach (IRE) 132 – Agata Laguna (IRE) (Elnadim **80**
(USA) 128) [2015 p10f³ p8f³ Feb 25] fair form in maidens at Lingfield and Kempton, in
latter keeping on when breaking down near finish: dead. *Charlie Appleby*

805

PRYERS PRINCESS 3 ch.f. Medicean 128 – Opening Ceremony (USA) 89 (Quest For **74** Fame 127) [2015 40p: t6f² 7g³ 6g⁴ t6g 6m 6g⁶ 6g* 7.2m⁴ 6g³ 6m t7.1m⁶ Sep 25] fair handicapper: won at Doncaster in August: stays 6f: best form on good going: sometimes in tongue tie in 2015: usually races towards rear. *Michael Herrington*

PRYING PANDORA (FR) 2 b.f. (Mar 18) Dark Angel (IRE) 113 – Leniency (IRE) **77** (Cape Cross (IRE) 129) [2015 6g³ 6g² 7.2g² 7s² Oct 10] €85,000Y: sturdy filly: fourth foal: half-sister to 1¼m winner Parole (by Mastercraftsman): dam unraced half-sister to high-class winner up to 1m Court Masterpiece: fair form: improved when length second to Garcia in maiden at York final start, making running, quickening clear over 2f out but headed last 50 yds: stays 7f: acts on soft going. *Richard Fahey*

PTOLOMEOS 12 b.g. Kayf Tara 130 – Lucy Tufty 44 (Vin St Benet 109) [2015 53: **49** 10.2m 10d⁴ 10.2s Oct 28] poor handicapper: stays 1¼m: best form on going softer than good (acts on heavy): tried in cheekpieces prior to 2015: sometimes slowly away, often races towards rear. *Sean Regan*

PUBLILIA 3 b.f. Makfi 130 – Terentia 108 (Diktat 126) [2015 91: 8m p7g Dec 9] fairly – useful performer in 2014: showed nothing in 2 starts in 2015: stays 7f: acts on good to firm going. *Mark Johnston*

PUCON 6 b.m. Kyllachy 129 – The Fugative 94 (Nicholas (USA) 111) [2015 80: p5f⁶ p5g **80** 5.3m³ 5m* 5m² 5.3g⁵ 5d Aug 21] fairly useful handicapper: won at Lingfield in June: stays 6f: acts on polytrack and good to firm going: in cheekpieces last 4 starts: front runner. *Roger Teal*

PUDDING (IRE) 3 b.f. Bushranger (IRE) 119 – Kahyasi Moll (IRE) 35 (Brief Truce **51** (USA) 126) [2015 –: 8g³ 8m⁵ 8v Aug 24] modest maiden: best effort at 1m: in tongue tie in 2015, also visored final start: often starts slowly. *Lady Cecil*

PUISSANT (IRE) 3 b.g. Galileo (IRE) 134 – Elletelle (IRE) 106 (Elnadim (USA) 128) **104** [2015 93p: 9m⁵ 8g⁵ 8d² 8.2g³ Sep 21] useful performer: gelded and in cheekpieces, improved form last 2 starts, second in handicap at Ascot (½ length behind Energia Davos) and third in listed race at Craon (4¼ lengths behind Chika Dream): bred to stay middle distances: acts on good to soft going: front runner/races prominently. *Marco Botti*

PULCINELLA (IRE) 3 b.f. Dubawi (IRE) 129 – Petrushka (IRE) 126 (Unfuwain (USA) **101** 131) [2015 97p: 8f³ 10.4g³ 8f⁶ Jul 11] sturdy filly: useful handicapper: third at York (4¼ lengths behind Covert Love) in May: will benefit from return to 1¼m: acts on good to firm going: often travels strongly. *Charlie Appleby*

PULL THE PIN (IRE) 6 b.g. Kheleyf (USA) 116 – Inscribed (IRE) 55 (Fasliyev (USA) **67** 120) [2015 64, a74: f6s⁴ f6g³ 5.1m² 5d⁶ 6s² 5g⁴ 5v³ p6f² f6g⁵ p5g⁴ f5m Dec 8] fair handicapper: stays 7f: acts on polytrack, fibresand, good to firm and heavy going: wears headgear/tongue tie: front runner/races prominently. *Heather Dalton*

PULL THE PLUG (IRE) 4 b.f. Sleeping Indian 122 – Babylonian 66 (Shamardal (USA) **85** 129) [2015 74: 6m* t7.1g* 7m 5.9g⁴ 7g² 6.1g³ 6d³ 6m⁵ Sep 20] fairly useful handicapper: won at Doncaster and Wolverhampton in April: stays 7f: acts on polytrack, tapeta, good to firm and good to soft going. *Declan Carroll*

PUMAFLOR (IRE) 3 b.g. Aussie Rules (USA) 123 – Krasotka (IRE) (Soviet Star (USA) **85** 128) [2015 70: 8g 7m* 7m² 8d* 7.5m⁵ 8.9m³ 8m⁶ 8d² 7d⁵ 8d³ Oct 30] plain, rather leggy gelding: fairly useful handicapper: won at Thirsk in June and Pontefract in July: stays 9f: acts on good to firm and good to soft going: sometimes slowly away, often races towards rear: worth try in headgear. *Richard Guest*

PUMPKIN SPICE (IRE) 2 ch.f. (Feb 16) Mastercraftsman (IRE) 129 – Chaibia (IRE) **– p** 111 (Peintre Celebre (USA) 137) [2015 8s Oct 16] €40,000Y: sister to French 1¼m winner Primus Incitatus and half-sister to 3 winners in France, including 1¼m winner Manuka (by Mr Greeley) and 10.5f winner Jawaher (by Fastnet Rock): dam, French winner up to 1¼m (2-y-o 1m winner), out of close relative to Derby winner Erhaab: 14/1, well held in maiden at Redcar: sold 12,000 gns, sent to Qatar: should do better. *Mark Johnston*

PUNK ROCKER (IRE) 3 b.f. Fastnet Rock (AUS) 127 – Cape Vintage (IRE) 91 (Cape **78** Cross (IRE) 129) [2015 74: 5g⁴ 6g* 6g⁴ 6.1d² 6g⁵ 5g⁴ Sep 24] fair handicapper: won at Thirsk in July: stays 6f: acts on good to firm and good to soft going: often races towards rear, often travels strongly. *Michael Dods*

PURANA 4 ch.f. Pastoral Pursuits 127 – Arruhan (IRE) 87 (Mujtahid (USA) 118) [2015 – 52: p8f Dec 17] maiden, modest form at best: best effort at 1m: acts on polytrack: tried in hood prior to 2015: usually races freely. *Ms N. M. Hugo*

PURA VIDA 3 b.f. Stimulation (IRE) 121 – Coffee Ice 92 (Primo Dominie 121) [2015 7g – 7d⁵ p6f⁴ Nov 6] half-sister to several winners, including 1¼m-1¾m winner Ebony Express and 2-y-o 6f winner Premium Coffee (both by Superior Premium): dam 5f (at 2 yrs) and 6f (in USA) winner: little form. *Tim Etherington*

PURE DIAMOND 2 b.f. (Feb 18) Street Cry (IRE) 130 – White Rose (GER) 105 (Platini **99 p** (GER) 126) [2015 7m p8g* 8m p8g* Sep 30] rather unfurnished filly: half-sister to several winners, including smart winner up to 1½m Elite Army (2-y-o 1m winner, by Authorized) and useful French/German 1¼m winner Promesse de L'Aube (by Galileo): dam 2-y-o 7f (Prix Miesque) winner who stayed 11f: useful performer: won at Kempton in August (maiden, by 6 lengths) and September (minor event, by ¾ length from Zodiakos): stays 1m: likely to progress further. *Saeed bin Suroor*

PURE DRAMA (IRE) 3 b.f. Azamour (IRE) 130 – Distant Drama (USA) 73 (Distant **66** View (USA) 126) [2015 6.7s⁵ p7g 9.5m 9.5d³ 7.5s² 7s 10s 7.2s 7g² p8d⁶ Nov 30] €12,000Y: fourth foal: dam, 8.6f winner, sister to smart Japanese sprinter Keeneland Swan: fair maiden: left John Joseph Murphy after ninth start: stays 1m: acts on polytrack and soft going: sometimes in blinkers: tried in tongue tie. *Giles Bravery*

PURE FANTASY 2 b.f. (Mar 30) Fastnet Rock (AUS) 127 – Fictitious 100 (Machiavellian **72 p** (USA) 123) [2015 8.3d p8m⁴ p8d³ Nov 30] closely related to 3 winners, including useful winner up to 1m (stayed 1¼m) Quadrille (2-y-o 6f/7f winner) and useful 6f/7f (including at 2 yrs) winner Free Verse (both by Danehill Dancer) and half-sister to 2 winners, including winner up to 2m Hunting Tower (2-y-o 1m winner, by Sadler's Wells): dam 1m-1¼m winner, including in USA: fair form in maidens: will be suited by 1¼m+: remains open to improvement. *Roger Charlton*

PURE HAPPINESS (USA) 2 b.f. (Mar 2) Kitten's Joy (USA) 128 – Brickyard Gal **70** (USA) (Proud Citizen (USA) 122) [2015 6m p7g² 6.9m Sep 9] $110,000F, $190,000Y: rather unfurnished filly: fourth foal: sister to 2 winners in USA and half-sister to winner there by Talent Search: dam, US maiden, half-sister to very smart sprinter Moviesta: fair maiden: easily best effort when second at Kempton: will stay 1m. *Saeed bin Suroor*

PURE LINE 3 b.f. Zamindar (USA) 116 – Pure Grain 121 (Polish Precedent (USA) 131) **75** [2015 76p: 10s³ p12g² 10s⁴ t12.2m³ p10f⁵ Oct 28] useful-looking filly: fair maiden: stays 1½m: acts on polytrack, tapeta and soft going: front runner/races prominently. *Ralph Beckett*

PURE SOUL 2 b.c. (Mar 15) Iffraaj 127 – Spiritual Healing (IRE) 64 (Invincible Spirit – (IRE) 121) [2015 6d Oct 26] 33/1, very green when well held in maiden at Redcar. *Ismail Mohammed*

PURE VANITY 2 b.f. (Feb 1) New Approach (IRE) 132 – Miss Pinkerton 104 (Danehill **63 p** (USA) 126) [2015 8g⁵ t8.6g⁴ Sep 29] sister to useful 8.6f winner (stayed 1½m) Vanity Rules and half-sister to several winners, including useful 1¼m/10.4f winner This Is The Day (by Footstepsinthesand): dam winner up to 1m (2-y-o 6f winner) out of Coronation Stakes winner Rebecca Sharp: modest form in maidens at Ascot and Wolverhampton: will stay 1¼m: likely to do better at 3 yrs. *Roger Charlton*

PURFORD GREEN 6 ch.m. Kyllachy 129 – Mo Stopher 47 (Sharpo 132) [2015 47: p7g⁴ **53** p8g p7g⁴ Dec 30] modest maiden: stays 7f: acts on polytrack: often wears headgear: often races towards rear. *Michael Attwater*

PURPLE BELLE 2 br.f. (May 8) Assertive 121 – Stunning In Purple (IRE) 70 (Kheleyf – (USA) 116) [2015 5g p6g p6g Nov 11] first foal: dam 2-y-o 5f winner: no form. *Jimmy Fox*

PURPLE LANE (IRE) 4 ch.g. Danehill Dancer (IRE) 117 – Big Heart (Mr Greeley **63** (USA) 122) [2015 74: 7.6d⁵ 10m⁶ p8f Aug 11] good-topped gelding: modest maiden: stays 1m: acts on good to firm and good to soft going: often races towards rear: temperament under suspicion. *Graham Mays*

PURPLE MAGIC 2 b.f. (May 3) Rip Van Winkle (IRE) 134 – Discerning 96 (Darshaan **72 p** 133) [2015 8.3g³ p8f* Nov 6] half-sister to 3 winners, including useful 1¼m winner Phillipina (by Medicean) and 2m winner Star of Pompey (by Hernando): dam, 11.5f winner, half-sister to very smart 7f-8.4f winner Cesare: off 5 weeks, 11/10, didn't need to progress much to win maiden at Chelmsford by head from With Pleasure, leading close home: will be suited by at least 1¼m: will go on improving. *Michael Bell*

PURPLE 'N GOLD (IRE) 6 b.g. Strategic Prince 114 – Golden Dew (IRE) 72 (Montjeu – (IRE) 137) [2015 81: 12g Jul 30] fairly useful handicapper: well held only start in 2015: stays 1¼m: acts on polytrack and firm going: wears headgear: fairly useful hurdler/winning chaser. *David Pipe*

PURPLE RAVEN 2 b.f. (Feb 24) Poet's Voice 126 – Juniper Girl (IRE) 108 (Revoque **68 p** (IRE) 122) [2015 8d⁴ 8.3d⁶ 7d⁶ Oct 31] fluid foal: half-sister to winner up to 13f Forced Family Fun (2-y-o 1¼m winner, by Refuse To Bend) and 2-y-o 1¼m winner Kifaaya (by Intikhab): dam, winner up to 2¼m (2-y-o 7.4f winner), sister to smart Italian performer up to 1m Golden Nepi: fair form first 2 starts in maidens: will stay at least 1¼m: remains with potential. *Michael Bell*

PURPLE ROCK (IRE) 3 b.g. Fastnet Rock (AUS) 127 – Amethyst (IRE) 111 (Sadler's **89** Wells (USA) 132) [2015 82p: 8.1d⁴ 9.9m⁶ 8f⁵ 8.3m² 8f 8s Oct 23] rangy gelding: fairly useful handicapper: stays 8.5f: acts on firm and good to soft going: in blinkers last 3 starts. *Charles Hills*

PURPLE SAGE (IRE) 9 b.m. Danehill Dancer (IRE) 117 – Kylemore (IRE) (Sadler's **73** Wells (USA) 132) [2015 91: p12f⁵ p12g p8g Mar 12] good-topped mare: just fair form at best in handicaps in 2015: best up to 1m: acts on polytrack and good to firm going. *Brendan Powell*

PURPLE SPECTRUM 4 gr.g. Verglas (IRE) 118 – Rainbow's Edge 85 (Rainbow Quest **99** (USA) 134) [2015 94: t16.5f* p13.3g⁶ 14.1m³ 10m 14m⁴ p16g* 16s 16m Aug 8] useful-looking gelding: useful handicapper: won at Wolverhampton in January and Kempton (by 2¾ lengths from High Secret) in July: stays 16.5f: acts on polytrack, tapeta, good to firm and good to soft going: sometimes wears headgear: usually races in rear. *J. R. Jenkins*

PURPLE SURPRISE 3 b.f. Teofilio (IRE) 93 – Manic 67 (Polar Falcon (USA) 126) **–** [2015 55: t6g⁶ p6f 7d Sep 21] maiden: no form in 2015. *Andrew Reid*

PURSUITOFTHESTARS (IRE) 2 b.f. (Apr 28) Sea The Stars (IRE) 140 – Pursuit of **84 p** Life (Pursuit of Love 124) [2015 7d⁵ 7g⁴ 7m⁴ Oct 3] 320,000Y: useful-looking filly: closely related to Italian winner up to 8.5f Lapistanera (2-y-o 7f winner, by Cape Cross) and half-sister to 3 winners, including smart Italian 8.5f-1½m winner Gimmy (by Lomitas) and useful Italian/French winner up to 1m Stay Alive (2-y-o 6f/7.5f winner, by Iffraaj): dam Italian 5f-7.5f winner (including at 2 yrs): fairly useful maiden: best effort when fourth in valuable sales race at Newmarket (5½ lengths behind Alice Springs) final start, nearest finish: will be suited by 1m+: remains with potential. *John Gosden*

PURSUIT OF TIME 2 br.f. (Mar 31) Pastoral Pursuits 127 – Pressed For Time (IRE) 64 **–** (Traditionally (USA) 117) [2015 p6g 7f Jul 16] second foal: dam 5f winner (including at 2 yrs): well held in maidens at Chelmsford and Doncaster. *Michael Appleby*

PUSEY'S SECRET 2 b.f. (May 2) Sakhee's Secret 128 – Pusey Street Lady 103 (Averti **63** (IRE) 117) [2015 5g⁵ 6d⁵ Sep 25] second foal: half-sister to 5f winner Major Pusey (by Major Cadeaux): dam, 6f winner, half-sister to useful 5f winner Mornin Reserves: better effort in maidens when fifth over 5f at Sandown: stamina possibly stretched over testing 6f next time. *John Gallagher*

PUSHAQ (IRE) 2 b.g. (Mar 13) Roderic O'Connor (IRE) 119 – Et Dona Ferentes 61 **73** (Green Desert (USA) 127) [2015 8g p8m⁵ Oct 21] 33/1, improved from debut when 3¾ lengths fifth to Southern Gailes in maiden at Kempton: has been gelded. *Marco Botti*

PUSHINGMYPATIENCE (IRE) 3 b.f. Azamour (IRE) 130 – Whos Mindin Who **72** (IRE) (Danehill Dancer (IRE) 117) [2015 7g² 7g² 7m⁴ 8d² 8.3d 8g³ p10f f8g Nov 24] 2,000Y: third foal: half-sister to very smart 7f-8.6f winner Mindurownbusiness (by Cape Cross): dam unraced sister to smart winner up to 1½m Westphalia: fair maiden: stays 1m: acts on good to soft going: tried in visor: usually races close up. *K. R. Burke*

PUSH ME (IRE) 8 gr.m. Verglas (IRE) 118 – Gilda Lilly (USA) 80 (War Chant (USA) **79** 126) [2015 85: 7.9m⁴ 8.5m 8m t9.5f⁵ Nov 10] good-topped mare: fair handicapper: stays 9.5f: acts on polytrack, tapeta, good to firm and heavy going: tried in hood prior to 2015. *Iain Jardine*

PUSHY LADY 2 b.f. (Jan 9) Piccolo 121 – Jane's Payoff (IRE) 72 (Danetime (IRE) 121) **64 p** [2015 6g⁶ Jul 25] 8,000Y: third foal: half-sister to 6f winner Bold Max (by Assertive): dam 5f winner: 33/1, some encouragement when sixth in maiden at Salisbury (3 lengths behind Steel of Madrid) in July: may well do better. *Rod Millman*

PUSS MOTH 3 b.f. Paco Boy (IRE) 129 – Seeking Dubai 93 (Dubawi (IRE) 129) [2015 **– p** 6d p6m⁶ 6m³ Jun 13] 1,200 2-y-o: first foal: dam, 2-y-o 6f winner, half-sister to useful winner up to 7f Presto Vento: well held in maidens: wears hood: has joined Brian Ellison: type to do better in handicaps *Zoe Davison*

PUTARINGONIT (IRE) 3 ch.f. Peintre Celebre (USA) 137 – Virginias Best (King's **80** Best (USA) 132) [2015 p8g⁴ t8.6f³ p8g³ p10f* p10g² Dec 15] 28,000Y: third foal: half-sister to 2 winners by Westerner, including useful winner up to 8.3f Tobacco Road (2-y-o

7f winner): dam twice-raced half-sister to Deutsches Derby winner Lavirco: fairly useful performer: won handicap at Lingfield in November: stays 1¼m: acts on polytrack: usually in hood. *Jeremy Gask*

PUTEMINTHEBOOT (IRE) 2 b.f. (Jan 26) Medicean 128 – Tiger Royale 61 (Tiger Hill (IRE) 127) [2015 5d 5m⁵ 5m 6g p7g f6g⁴ p6d f6g* f7g Dec 18] €8,000Y, £9,000 2-y-o: lengthy filly: first foal: dam twice-raced half-sister to smart winner up to 7f Prime Defender: modest performer: won nursery at Southwell in December: will benefit from return to 6f: acts on fibresand. *David Evans* — 51

PUTIN (IRE) 7 b.g. Fasliyev (USA) 120 – Consignia (IRE) 67 (Definite Article 121) [2015 78: f6d⁶ f8g² f8d³ f8g⁵ p8m* p6f⁴ p10m p6f p6f⁶ f7g⁴ p8g⁵ p8f* p8f³ f8d p8g⁵ p8g⁶ 7m f7d* 6s⁶ p8g t7.1g a6g* p6f⁶ p6f p7f Nov 12] lengthy, useful-looking gelding: fair handicapper: won at Chelmsford in February and April, Southwell in July and Laytown in September: stays 1½m, races over much shorter nowadays: acts on all-weather, good to firm and good to soft going: usually wears headgear: usually wears tongue tie. *Phil McEntee* — 70

PUTMEINTHESWINDLE 5 ch.g. Monsieur Bond (IRE) 120 – Birthday Belle 70 (Lycius (USA) 124) [2015 p10g Mar 12] no form. *Peter Hedger* — —

PUT THE BOOT IN (IRE) 3 ch.g. Duke of Marmalade (IRE) 132 – Mubkera (IRE) 100 (Nashwan (USA) 135) [2015 10.4s⁶ 8g⁵ 10.5m⁵ 9.9s⁴ Sep 1] fair maiden: left Andrew Oliver after third start: stays 10.5f: acts on good to firm going: sometimes slowly away. *Barry Brennan* — 70

PUTTING GREEN 3 ch.g. Selkirk (USA) 129 – Ryella (USA) (Cozzene (USA)) [2015 78: p10g* 10d⁵ 10m² 9.9g³ 12f 12g* 11.9m³ 14g 12g⁵ Sep 24] big, lengthy gelding: useful performer: won maiden at Lingfield in April and handicap at Doncaster (by 4½ lengths from Lilian Baylis) in August: likely to prove best short of 1¾m: acts on polytrack and good to firm going: sold 90,000 gns, joined. *Richard Hannon* — 98

PUZZLED LOOK 2 b.f. (Feb 4) Sakhee's Secret 128 – Funny Enough 64 (Dansili 127) [2015 7m² 7.1m* 6m⁵ Oct 3] 20,000Y: close-coupled filly: first foal: dam lightly-raced half-sister to 1m-1¼m winner Smart Enough and winner up to 1m Oasis Dancer (both smart): fairly useful form: landed odds in maiden at Chepstow in September: 4 lengths fifth of 26 to Poet's Prize in quite valuable sales race at Newmarket final start, unsuited by drop in trip: stays 7f: sent to USA: remains open to improvement. *Ralph Beckett* — 79 p

PUZZLE TIME 5 b.m. Araafa (IRE) 128 – Puzzling (Peintre Celebre (USA) 137) [2015 93, a87: t9.5f⁴ p10f* p11f p10g⁵ 9.8d² 9.9d⁶ 9.9m² 9.9m⁶ 10m⁶ 10m³ 9.8d² 9.9g² Sep 3] rather leggy mare: useful performer: won handicap at Kempton (by 1½ lengths from Scottish Star) in February: better than ever when second in listed race at Longchamp (went down by short neck to Zipzip) final start: stays 1½m: acts on polytrack, good to firm and good to soft going: sometimes slowly away, often travels strongly: sent to Saudi Arabia. *Giles Bravery* — 104

PYJAMA PARTY (IRE) 3 b.c. Rip Van Winkle (IRE) 134 – Dancing Eclipse (IRE) (Danehill Dancer (IRE) 117) [2015 8.3g³ 9.2s² 8.3m² 8m* 8.1g² 8g* 8g⁵ 8d Oct 5] useful-looking colt: third foal: half-brother to a winner in Spain by Footstepsinthesand: dam, French maiden (placed at 9.5f), half-sister to smart performer up to 1½m Etoile: useful performer: won maiden at Ripon in July and handicap at Haydock (by neck from Glad Tidings) in August: good second in handicap at Sandown in between: stays 1m: acts on good to firm going, probably on soft: usually races close up: sold 55,000 gns, sent to USA. *William Haggas* — 97

PYLA (IRE) 3 b.f. Footstepsinthesand 120 – Beautiful Hill (IRE) 74 (Danehill (USA) 126) [2015 58: p8g⁴ t9.5g⁵ 9d³ 7.6m* 8f* 7.5m⁶ 8g p7f⁶ Nov 12] fair handicapper: won at Lingfield in August and Bath in September: left Ed Dunlop after seventh start: stays 1m: acts on polytrack and firm going: usually in cheekpieces in 2015. *Denis Quinn* — 71

PYROCLASTIC (IRE) 3 b.g. Tagula (IRE) 116 – Gypsy Royal (IRE) 54 (Desert Prince (IRE) 130) [2015 61: 16g* p6g 6.1m³ 7d⁵ p7g⁶ p7g p7g⁶ p7g³ Dec 28] fair performer: won minor event at Wolverhampton in April: stays 7f: acts on polytrack, tapeta and firm going: sometimes in headgear in 2015. *Jim Boyle* — 71

PYROCUMULUS (IRE) 3 b.g. Kodiac 112 – Dry Lightning 63 (Shareef Dancer (USA) 135) [2015 50, a60: t7.1m* t7.1f* 7m t7.1g⁵ 8.3m* 7g⁵ t7.1g* 8d* 8.5v* Aug 31] lengthy, rather sparely-made gelding: fairly useful handicapper: much improved in 2015 and won at Wolverhampton (twice) in March, Windsor in June, Wolverhampton in July and at Epsom in August: stays 8.5f: acted on fibresand, tapeta, good to firm and heavy going: tried in headgear: was usually slowly away, often raced towards rear: dead. *Tony Carroll* — 87

PYTHIUS (IRE) 2 b.c. (Feb 20) Lord Shanakill (USA) 121 – Silicon Star (FR) (Starborough 126) [2015 8d* 7.1m 8g³ Sep 17] rangy colt: has scope: half-brother to several winners, including 6f/7f winner Sacha Park (by Iffraaj) and 10.5f winner Park Rebel (by Cockney Rebel): dam French maiden half-sister to smart French 5f-7f winner Latona: fairly useful performer: won maiden at Ayr (by ¾ length from Cape Love) in August: best effort when third in minor event at Ayr (3 lengths behind Speed Company) in September: stays 1m: sold 40,000 gns, sent to Italy. *K. R. Burke* **86**

Q

QAFFAAL (USA) 4 b.g. Street Cry (IRE) 130 – Wasseema (USA) 111 (Danzig (USA)) [2015 f8g⁴ f8d⁴ f7s 8m⁵ 6g⁶ 7m* f7d³ 7g⁵ 7.2g² t8.6g 7s⁴ Oct 26] fair handicapper: won at Thirsk in July: stays 7f: acts on good to firm going: tried in blinkers. *Michael Easterby* **71**

QAMARAIN (USA) 2 ch.f. (Mar 21) Hard Spun (USA) 124 – Emtyazat (Gone West (USA)) [2015 7g³ Oct 9] well-made filly: fourth foal: half-sister to a winner in USA by Tapit: dam, US 1m/8.5f winner, half-sister to very smart US Grade 1 1m winner Corinthian: 6/1, shaped as if needed experience when ¾-length third of 17 to Materialistic in maiden at Newmarket on debut, staying on from further back than first 2: sure to progress. *Brian Meehan* **80 p**

QANAN 6 b.g. Green Desert (USA) 127 – Strings (Unfuwain (USA) 131) [2015 96, a88: 10m p11g p11g⁴ 12g⁵ 13.3s 13g 10.1m² p11g³ Sep 30] tall gelding: fairly useful handicapper: second at Yarmouth and third at Kempton in September: stays 1½m: acts on polytrack, soft and good to firm going: often wears hood. *Chris Wall* **92**

QASSER (IRE) 6 b.g. Intikhab (USA) 135 – Surrender To Me (USA) (Royal Anthem (USA) 135) [2015 73: p10f² t9.5g* t9.5g³ 10.2s⁴ May 19] fair handicapper: won at Wolverhampton in April: stays 1½m: acts on tapeta and any turf going: tried in hood prior to 2015: often races prominently. *Harry Whittington* **79**

QATAR FALCON (IRE) 3 ch.c. Mastercraftsman (IRE) 129 – Nouveau Riche (IRE) 84 (Entrepreneur 123) [2015 –: p10f⁶ p10g³ 12.1m Apr 15] fair maiden in Britain: best effort at 1¼m: in cheekpieces final start: sent to Qatar, where won 9.2f maiden at Doha in November. *Kevin Ryan* **68**

QATAR PRINCESS (IRE) 4 b.f. Marju (IRE) 127 – Bridal Dance (IRE) 62 (Danehill Dancer (IRE) 117) [2015 60: t5.1g⁶ p5g⁵ t5.1f² Mar 26] rather unfurnished filly: modest maiden: stays 6f: acts on polytrack, tapeta and good to firm going: wears visor: front runner/races prominently: sent to Malaysia. *J. R. Jenkins* **51**

QATAR SUCCESS 3 b.f. Kyllachy 129 – Cherokee Stream (IRE) 72 (Indian Ridge 123) [2015 –: f8s Feb 3] well held in maidens/handicap: usually in blinkers: twice in tongue tie: sold 1,500 gns in February, sent to Germany. *Olly Stevens* **–**

QEMAH (IRE) 2 b.f. (Feb 19) Danehill Dancer (IRE) 117 – Kartica 108 (Rainbow Quest (USA) 134) [2015 7.5g² 8.4g* 8m³ Oct 4] €200,000Y: first foal: dam, French 2-y-o 1m winner, stayed 10.5f: useful form: won minor event at Longchamp (easily by 3 lengths from Doha Dream) in September: good third in Prix Marcel Boussac at Longchamp (1½ lengths behind Ballydoyle, keeping on well) final start: stays 8.5f: likely to progress further. *Jean-Claude Rouget, France* **107 p**

QEYAADAH (IRE) 2 b.g. (Feb 28) Acclamation 118 – Effervesce (IRE) 84 (Galileo (IRE) 134) [2015 6g⁸ 6f 7m² 6g⁴ 6.5m Sep 10] 65,000F, 160,000Y: good-topped gelding: has scope: first foal: dam, improved maiden 10.3f winner, half-sister to smart sprinters Hitchens and Tanzeel: fairly useful performer: won maiden at Newbury in May: fourth in nursery at York in August: stays 7f: acts on good to firm going: has been gelded. *Ed Dunlop* **86**

QIBTEE (FR) 5 b.g. Antonius Pius (USA) 123 – Embers of Fame (IRE) (Sadler's Wells (USA) 132) [2015 66: p13g³ t13.9f p13g⁶ 12g 10m⁵ 10g* 12g³ 10g⁴ 12.4g⁶ 10.4d⁶ 13.8v 10.2s* p12m f12g⁴ Dec 22] quite attractive gelding: fair handicapper: won amateur events at Pontefract in June and Nottingham in October: stays 1¼m: acts on soft and good to firm going: tried in headgear: quirky sort and one to treat with caution. *Les Eyre* **70 §**

QORTAAJ 2 b.g. (Jan 28) Kyllachy 129 – Cardrona 66 (Selkirk (USA) 129) [2015 6v⁴ Nov 7] 33,000F, 130,000Y: first foal: dam lightly-raced sister to smart/moody performer up to 1¼m Selinka: 6/1, promise when 2¾ lengths fourth of 8 to Times Legacy in maiden at Doncaster, pushed along over 2f out then keeping on: will improve. *William Haggas* **73 p**

Q TEN GIRL (IRE) 2 ch.f. (Apr 13) Zebedee 113 – Regresa A Mi (IRE) 84 (Spartacus (IRE) 107) [2015 5g 6m⁶ 6m⁶ p7g² p6g³ p7g t6f² t7.1f* t7.1f 8.3s⁴ t8.6f² f8g t7.1g* t8.6f⁶ Dec 14] €3,800Y: compact filly: first foal: dam 1½m-2m winner: modest performer: won sellers at Wolverhampton in October (left Mark Usher after) and December: stays 8.5f: acts on polytrack and tapeta: often in headgear: often races towards rear. *James Unett* **51 +**
a63

Q TWENTY GIRL (IRE) 3 b.f. Fast Company (IRE) 126 – Extravagance (IRE) 80   **49**
(King's Best (USA) 132) [2015 54: t7.1g f8s⁶ t8.6m⁶ t8.6g⁴ 8g⁶ t8.6g t8.6g 10m 12.4g⁶
Aug 31] poor maiden: left Mark Usher after third start: stays 8.5f: acts on tapeta, best turf
form on good going: often wears headgear. *John Norton*

QUADRIGA (IRE) 5 b.g. Acclamation 118 – Turning Light (GER) 108 (Fantastic Light   **73**
(USA) 134) [2015 62: p8f⁵ t8.6f² f8g* f7g* p8f⁴ f7d² 8.3s f8d³ f8s⁴ 7.2g t7.1f t9.5f⁶
t8.6f⁴ t12.2m f8g Dec 12] strong, lengthy gelding: fair handicapper: won at Southwell in
March and April: left Paul Burgoyne after sixth start: stays 9.5f: acts on polytrack, fibresand
and good to firm going: tried in visor prior to 2015: tried in tongue tie in 2015. *Philip Kirby*

QUADRILLER (FR) 8 b.g. Lando (GER) 128 – Tabachines (FR) (Art Francais (USA)   **68**
120) [2015 75: 17.2m³ Jul 31] fair handicapper: stays 17f: acts on good to firm going: often
wears tongue tie: fair hurdler/chaser. *Philip Hobbs*

QUAE SUPRA 3 b.g. Exceed And Excel (AUS) 126 – Noodle Soup (USA) (Alphabet   **44**
Soup (USA) 126) [2015 56: 8m 10.2m 7s⁴ 5d t8.6g 7m Aug 9] poor maiden: left Richard
Hannon after third start: stays 8.5f: acts on heavy going: often in headgear in 2015.
Michael Appleby

QUALIFY (IRE) 3 b.f. Fastnet Rock (AUS) 127 – Perihelion (IRE) 105 (Galileo   **114**
(IRE) 134) [2015 104: 8f 8g 12g* 12m⁶ Jun 27]
    The Oaks [Oakes] was first run in 1779, the year before the first Derby, and
is the second oldest of the five classics behind the St Leger. There were seventeen
subscribers at fifty guineas each for the inaugural Oaks, and twelve took part in a
race for a prize of £840 on Epsom Downs won by the favourite Bridget, owned by
the twelfth Earl of Derby whose leased country house on the outskirts of Epsom had
given its name to the race for three-year-old fillies over a mile and a half. By the
end of the eighteenth century, the Derby, the Oaks and the St Leger, all confined to
three-year-olds, were regarded as 'the three great races' on the turf and remained so
for a further half century, even after the Two Thousand Guineas and One Thousand
Guineas, also confined to three-year-olds, had become established features of the
spring racing calendar in the early part of the nineteenth century. The term 'classics'
was coined some time just after the mid-1800s by which time it seemed to have
become widely accepted that the five races made up a set. The prestige attached to
winning one of the five classics was enormous and they became the races that every
owner, trainer and jockey wanted to win more than any others. The classics still
confer great prestige but they no longer dominate the racing landscape, the Oaks,
for example, having been overtaken in value in Britain in recent years by both the
British Champions Fillies' And Mares' Stakes and the Nassau Stakes, both races
open to fillies and mares above the age of three. Even so, it is a virtual certainty that
Simple Verse and Legatissimo, the three-year-olds who won those two big prizes,
will be remembered much longer for their victories in the St Leger and the One
Thousand Guineas respectively. The Oaks winner Qualify did not win another race
as a three-year-old but, along with Simple Verse and Legatissimo, her name will
endure because she is a 'classic winner'.
    There has never been an Oaks winner at longer odds than Qualify who started
at 50/1, the third winner of the race to do so, following Vespa in 1833 and Jet Ski
Lady in 1991, the latter's feat made the more extraordinary by the fact that she won
by ten lengths! Like Jet Ski Lady, Qualify was the rank outsider in the field but there
was no wide margin victory for her—and she might not have won at all if one of
her better-fancied stablemates Together Forever had not become unbalanced on the
camber and badly baulked the third Ballydoyle runner Diamondsandrubies on her
inside about a furlong and a half out, in the process forcing Diamondsandrubies
into long-time leader on the rails Star of Seville who also lost all chance. That trio
were the most serious sufferers in the incident which unfortunately occurred at a
point where there were plenty still in with a chance, meaning that there had to be
reservations about the value of the form. The finish eventually involved Qualify and
the 5/2 favourite Legatissimo, the latter barging her way past Lady of Dubai (Ryan
Moore picked up a one-day suspension after 'creating a gap') and briefly looking to
have the race in the bag until pegged back and just short-headed by Qualify who led
right on the post.

Investec Oaks, Epsom—stamina wins the day as Qualify (right), seemingly the Ballydoyle third string, misses trouble in a rough race to spring a surprise at 50/1; she stays on strongly from off the pace to get up on the post to beat Legatissimo, the pair clear of Lady In Dubai and the badly hampered Diamondsandrubies (hidden)

The patiently-ridden Qualify missed the trouble, beginning to make headway under pressure two furlongs from home and enjoying a clear run. She tracked the eventual third Lady of Dubai (who was beaten two and a half lengths) and Legatissimo towards the middle of the course, and then challenged on the inside of Legatissimo to close her down over the last furlong, needing every inch of the trip to get up. Diamondsandrubies lost all momentum and a fair bit of ground when baulked and she deserved plenty of credit for recovering to finish fourth, three and a quarter lengths further back, with Jazzi Top and Jack Naylor, both caught up less seriously in the scrimmaging, coming fifth and sixth. Together Forever dropped back to seventh and the heavily-eased Star of Seville finished ninth of the eleven runners. The 7/2 second favourite Crystal Zvezda ruined her chance by pulling far too hard for the first half mile and French challenger Al Naamah, a 5,000,000-guinea sister to the 2012 Oaks winner Was, didn't seem to adapt to the course and lost a prominent position early in the home straight.

The Epsom stewards held an inquiry afterwards and deemed that none of the interference a furlong and a half out had involved a riding offence. Leaving aside whether she was lucky or not, Qualify, who gave Ballydoyle stalwart Colm O'Donoghue his first winning ride in an English classic, is rated a substandard Oaks winner, the lowest rated winner of the race since Casual Look (114) in 2003. It was, however, still the best performance of Qualify's career by some margin. She won twice from seven starts as a two-year-old, showing useful form and winning in pattern company in the Group 3 C. L. Weld Park Stakes at the Curragh and then, on her final outing, meeting trouble herself when shaping better than her eighth in the Breeders' Cup Juvenile Fillies Turf at Santa Anita might suggest.

Qualify's three other appearances as a three-year-old also came in classics, beaten forty-one lengths behind Legatissimo when last in the One Thousand Guineas (in which she was Ballydoyle's only representative), faring better in the Irish One Thousand Guineas but still below the pick of her juvenile form when tenth of eighteen behind Pleascach, and then, on her only outing after Epsom, finishing sixth of eight behind Jack Hobbs in the Irish Derby. Qualify was the only filly in the line-up, her supplementary entry fee of €100,000 funded by the Curragh under an incentive scheme to try to boost the field for Ireland's richest race. Waiting tactics were used with Qualify in all her races at three but she never landed a blow in the Irish Derby after being dropped out and she proved no match for the colts who had finished second, third, fourth and sixth in the Derby at Epsom. A projected fifth classic appearance, in the Irish Oaks in July, was scrapped when connections decided that the prevailing going would be too firm for her. Qualify's next public appearance came at the December Sales when she changed hands for 1,600,000 guineas, knocked down to John Ferguson and bound for the Darley broodmare band. Qualify's Spanish owner had bought her from the O'Briens before the Breeders' Cup Juvenile Fillies Turf.

The big, close-coupled Qualify was home bred by her trainer—who has now saddled five winners of the Oaks—and by his wife under their Whisperview Trading banner. O'Brien was fined £3,000 by the Epsom stewards for being late saddling his three runners for the Oaks, having still been saddling Together Forever when the signal for the jockeys to mount was given (he admitted to the stewards that he had failed to allow sufficient time). Nothing would have spoiled the feeling of satisfaction, though, of having both bred and trained a classic winner. Arthur Budgett achieved the feat twice in four years in the Derby, with Blakeney and Morston, but it was over a century since it had last happened in the Oaks. Signorinetta, owned, bred and trained by Edoardo Ginistrelli, who had come to England from Italy in the 1880s, won the 1908 Oaks two days after triumphing at 100/1 in the Derby, one of three 100/1-shots who have won the greatest classic. The O'Briens were joint-breeders (with father-in-law Joe Crowley) of the Two Thousand Guineas winner Rock of Gibraltar and Whisperview Trading Ltd had previously enjoyed Group 1 success as breeders with the Dewhurst winner Beethoven (the operation also bred the latest Gold Cup runner-up Kingfisher).

Qualify's dam Perihelion, a daughter of Galileo, was a useful performer for Aidan O'Brien, winning a maiden over an extended mile and a half and finishing second in the Park Hill Stakes. Her first four foals to reach the racecourse have all been successful. Her first foal Saltanat (by Duke of Marmalade) won the Czech Oaks in 2013 and was sold for 170,000 guineas at the December Sales, having changed hands for only €20,000 at Deauville twelve months earlier; her second, the useful

Mrs C. C. Regalado-Gonzalez's "Qualify"

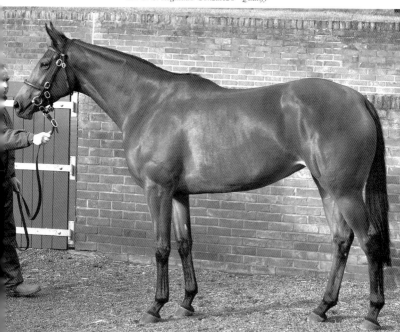

Satellite (by Danehill Dancer and therefore closely related to Qualify), stays a mile and three quarters and won at Newbury for William Haggas in the latest season; Qualify is her third foal; and her fourth is Qualify's two-year-old brother Shogun, a €400,000 yearling who won a maiden at the Curragh in July for Aidan O'Brien and ran in the Prix Jean-Luc Lagardere (sixth) and the Breeders' Cup Juvenile Turf (tenth). Perihelion has a yearling filly by Henrythenavigator.

	Fastnet Rock (AUS) (b 2001)	Danehill (b 1986)	Danzig Razyana
Qualify (IRE) (b.f. 2012)		Piccadilly Circus (b 1995)	Royal Academy Gatana
	Perihelion (IRE) (ch 2005)	Galileo (b 1998)	Sadler's Wells Urban Sea
		Medicosma (ch 1986)	The Minstrel Media Luna

Naturally enough, Coolmore stallions are chosen for most of the Whisperview Trading mares and Qualify's sire Fastnet Rock, a son of Danehill and already very successful in Australia where he was champion sire in 2014/15, began shuttling to Ireland in 2010 and his first two Irish-conceived crops are headed by the four-year-old Champion Stakes winner Fascinating Rock and the three-year-old fillies Qualify and Diamondsandrubies. Fastnet Rock was a sprinter brought to Europe principally as an outcross for mares from the stouter Sadler's Wells line (Diamondsandrubies is out of a mare by Sadler's Wells) and many of his European progeny stay a mile and a quarter or more. Qualify's pedigree has plenty of stamina on the distaff side. Her grandam Medicosma, culled by Juddmonte and picked up for just 16,000 guineas at the 1989 December Sales, won at up to two miles and her great grandam Media Luna was runner-up (starting at 66/1) in the 1984 Oaks and was bought privately at the end of her three-year-old days to join the Juddmonte broodmare band for whom she did sterling service (one of her granddaughters bred the 2010 Derby and Arc winner Workforce and one of her daughters bred the 2001 Kentucky Oaks and Alabama Stakes winner Flute, both of whom raced for Juddmonte, and Media Luna is also the grandam of the 2003 Aidan O'Brien-trained St Leger winner Brian Boru). Qualify stayed a mile and a half and acted on polytrack and good to firm going. She was best held up. *Aidan O'Brien, Ireland*

QUALITY ART (USA) 7 b.g. Elusive Quality (USA) – Katherine Seymour 107 (Green **77** Desert (USA) 127) [2015 53§, a70§: p5m² t5.1f* t5.1f* p5m² p5f* t5.1g* t5.1g* p5g⁶ Apr 16] strong, attractive gelding: fair handicapper: formerly unreliable, but in good form in first few months of year, winning at Wolverhampton in January and February, Lingfield in March and Wolverhampton in March/April: best form at 5f: acts on all-weather and good to firm going: tried in headgear/tongue tie prior to 2015: often travels strongly. *Simon Hodgson*

QUALITY SONG (USA) 3 b.g. Elusive Quality (USA) – Run In (USA) (Dynaformer **85** (USA)) [2015 59p: 8f 9.9m⁵ t9.5g⁴ t12.2f* t12.2m² t13.9f³ Dec 14] fairly useful handicapper: left Peter Chapple-Hyam, won at Wolverhampton in November: good placed efforts there subsequently: stays 1¾m: acts on tapeta. *Richard Hughes*

QUALITY TIME (IRE) 2 b.f. (Feb 17) Exceed And Excel (AUS) 126 – Crinoline **87 p** (USA) (Street Cry (IRE) 130) [2015 p7g* Nov 26] first foal: dam unraced half-sister to Phoenix/Moyglare Stud Stakes winner Saoirse Abu: 5/6, had plenty to spare when winning maiden at Chelmsford by 2 lengths from Hidden Treasures: sure to progress. *Saeed bin Suroor*

QUANTATIVE 3 b.c. Selkirk (USA) 129 – Star Cluster 106 (Observatory (USA) 131) **71** [2015 t8.6g⁶ 7g May 15] well-made colt: fifth foal: half-brother to 1½m winner Asterism (by Motivator) and 5.7f/6f winner Encapsulated (by Zamindar): dam, winner up to 1m (2-y-o 7f winner), half-sister to US Grade 2 8.5f winner Didina: better effort in maidens when sixth at Wolverhampton: became upset in stalls next time: sold £1,600. *Lady Cecil*

QUANTUM DOT (IRE) 4 ch.g. Exceed And Excel (AUS) 126 – Jeed (IRE) 86 **60 §** (Mujtahid (USA) 118) [2015 56: t6f⁶ p6f p6f⁵ p5m* t5.1f⁵ p5g* p5g⁶ Dec 2] modest handicapper: won at Kempton in February and November: best form at 5f: acts on polytrack: wears headgear: tried in tongue tie prior to 2015: front runner/races prominently: unreliable. *Ed de Giles*

QUARTERBACK (GER) 3 b.c. American Post 121 – Quebra (GER) 106 (Surumu (GER)) [2015 7g^4 7g^4 a9.4f^5 10.7g^4 11.9g* 14.1d^2 10d^2 9.9g Dec 30] €26,000Y: half-brother to several winners abroad, including 8.5f-1½m winner Quiron (by Desert King): dam German 9f/10.5f winner: smart performer: won listed Norsk Derby at Ovrevoll (by 2½ lengths from Icecapada) in August: second on next 2 starts, in minor event at Ovrevoll (½ length behind Bokan) and listed race at Newmarket (beaten 1½ lengths by Restorer): stays 1¾m: acts on soft going: in headgear last 4 starts: has worn tongue tie. *Rune Haugen, Norway* **112**

QUASQAZAH 4 ch.g. Bahamian Bounty 116 – Rock Lily 81 (Rock of Gibraltar (IRE) 133) [2015 68: f7g t7.1g Apr 21] poor maiden: stays 1m: acts on soft going: tried in blinkers prior to 2015: usually races freely. *Ruth Carr* **43**

QUATORZE (FR) 5 b.g. Elusive City (USA) 117 – Queseraisjesanstoi (FR) (Rainbow Quest (USA) 134) [2015 p8g* t7.1m 7s 8g 8d* 6g^6 10g^2 Dec 14] smart performer: won listed race at Cagnes-sur-Mer (by 1½ lengths from Skaters Waltz) in February and handicap at Deauville (by ¾ length from Caointiorn) in August: respectable eighth to Sovereign Debt in listed race at Wolverhampton on second outing: left Francois Rohaut after fifth start: ¾-length second to Ponfeigh in minor event at Doha final appearance: stays 1¼m: acts on polytrack, viscoride and good to soft going. *A. de Mieulle, Qatar* **111**

QUATRIEME AMI 2 b.c. (Feb 6) Equiano (FR) 127 – Hundred Year Flood (USA) (Giant's Causeway (USA) 132) [2015 p5g^4 6g 5g* t5.1f* t5.1g* Dec 5] 45,000F, 12,000Y: sixth foal: half-brother to useful 1½m-2m winner Castilo del Diablo (by Teofilo): dam, US 2-y-o 8.5f winner, half-sister to useful US Grade 3 6f winner Sweet Hope: useful performer: won maiden at Windsor in October, nursery at Wolverhampton in November and minor event at Wolverhampton (by neck from Sign of The Kodiac, showing good attitude) in December: best form at 5f: acts on tapeta: often races prominently: open to further improvement. *Philip McBride* **101 p**

QUEBEE 2 b.f. (Mar 6) Sir Percy 129 – Tintac 53 (Intikhab (USA) 135) [2015 p7g^3 Oct 29] leggy filly: fourth foal: sister to 1m (including at 2 yrs) winner Emmuska: dam, maiden (stayed 9.5f), half-sister to useful performer up to 1½m Balladonia, herself dam of smart 2-y-o 6f/7f winner Wootton Bassett: 50/1, shaped as if needed experience when third in maiden at Lingfield (4½ lengths behind Vaunting) in October, nearest finish: will stay at least 1m: will improve. *Clive Cox* **75 p**

QUEEN AGGIE (IRE) 5 b.m. Elnadim (USA) 128 – Catfoot Lane 50 (Batshoof 122) [2015 66, a81: p7g^3 t7.1g^6 t7.1f^6 p7f^2 p6g^3 t7.1f^2 p8g^3 p8m^5 t7.1g^3 7m^6 7.6f^6 t6g^4 t8.6g^5 7d* 8s^4 7v^6 t7.1m^6 t7.1m* 7m t6f^3 t7.1f t7.1f f6g^6 Dec 15] workmanlike mare: fairly useful handicapper: won at Brighton in August and Wolverhampton in September: stays 8.5f: acts on polytrack, tapeta and heavy going: tried in headgear: often races in rear. *Tony Carroll* **73 a81**

QUEEN ATHENA (IRE) 2 b.f. (Apr 24) Royal Applause 124 – Olimpic Girl (IRE) (Darshaan 133) [2015 p8d Nov 30] half-sister to several winners, including French 13.5f winner Mandore (by Rock of Gibraltar): dam useful French 1¼m-11.5f winner: 33/1, well held in maiden at Kempton on debut. *Roger Charlton*

QUEEN CATRINE (IRE) 4 b.f. Acclamation 118 – Kahira (IRE) 80 (King's Best (USA) 132) [2015 112: p8g 6.1s^4 7m* 8m^2 8d 8m 7d 8g* Oct 18] tall, unfurnished filly: useful performer: won minor event at Leicester (by 1¾ lengths from Risen Sun) in June and listed race at Naas (by 1¾ lengths from Assume) in October: second in listed race at Milan (4 lengths behind Testa O Croce) in between: left Charles Hills after seventh start: stays 1m: acts on good to firm and good to soft going: blinkered sixth outing. *G. M. Lyons, Ireland* **105**

QUEEN CEE 4 b.f. Royal Applause 124 – Tee Cee 77 (Lion Cavern (USA) 117) [2015 –: t7.1f t9.5f Feb 7] little sign of ability (including in headgear). *Simon Hodgson* **–**

QUEEN NEFERTITI (IRE) 3 b.f. Galileo (IRE) 134 – Chintz (IRE) 112 (Danehill Dancer (IRE) 117) [2015 94p: p8g^3 8f 7g^3 9d^5 7g Jul 30] second foal: sister to 2-y-o 7.5f winner Illinois: dam 2-y-o 7f winner: useful performer: best effort when third in Brownstown Stakes at Fairyhouse (2¼ lengths behind Ainippe) in July: stays 1m: acts on good to soft going: front runner/races prominently: sent to USA. *David Wachman, Ireland* **101**

QUEEN OF EPIRUS 7 ch.m. Kirkwall 118 – Andromache 66 (Hector Protector (USA) 124) [2015 t12.2f Feb 16] angular mare: maiden, modest form at best: stays 1½m: acts on firm and soft going: poor hurdler. *Brian Rothwell* **–**

QUEEN OF ICE 4 ch.f. Selkirk (USA) 129 – Ice Palace 100 (Polar Falcon (USA) 126) [2015 109: 11.9d 11.9g 12m Oct 3] well-made filly: useful at 3 yrs, no form in pattern races in 2015: tongue tied final start: front runner/races prominently, tends to find little. *William Haggas* **–**

John Smith's Northumberland Plate (Heritage Handicap), Newcastle—the end of an era as blinkered Quest For More wins the last 'Pitmen's Derby' to be run on turf following the decision to replace Newcastle's Flat turf course with an all-weather track over the winter; Max Dynamite (third right) follows the winner through from off the pace for second, with Nearly Caught (second left) and Angel Gabrial (between winner and runner-up) completing the frame

QUEEN OF NORWAY (IRE) 4 b.f. Papal Bull 128 – Fanacanta (IRE) 62 (Olden Times 121) [2015 –: p7f p6m Feb 28] maiden: no form in 2015: stays 1m: acts on good to firm and good to soft going: tried in hood prior to 2015. *Paddy Butler* —

QUEEN OF SKIES (IRE) 6 b.m. Shamardal (USA) 129 – Attractive Crown (USA) 105 (Chief's Crown (USA)) [2015 75: f7g⁴ f8d⁴ f8d² t9.5f² f11g⁴ f8g² 8m⁶ 10m⁵ May 29] strong mare: fair handicapper: stays 11f: acts on fibresand and tapeta: tried in cheekpieces in 2015. *Michael Appleby* **67**

QUEENSBURY ODYSSEY 2 ch.c. (Apr 21) Poet's Voice 126 – Russian Spirit 105 (Falbrav (IRE) 133) [2015 7g 6g 6m⁶ 8.3g⁵ p8g⁵ Aug 17] modest maiden: should stay 1m: acts on polytrack and good to firm going: tried in blinkers. *Ed Dunlop* **52**

QUEEN'S ESTATE (GER) 6 b.g. Hurricane Run (IRE) 134 – Questabelle (Rainbow Quest (USA) 134) [2015 59: p10m May 12] modest handicapper: stays 1½m: acts on good to firm and heavy going: tried in cheekpieces. *Miss Joey Ellis* —

QUEEN'S JEWEL 3 ch.f. Pivotal 124 – Safari Queen (ARG) (Lode (USA)) [2015 9.9s* 10.4g* 9.9m* 10.4g 9.9m 9.5g³ Oct 31] fourth foal: half-sister to useful French winner up to 9f Royalmania (2-y-o 7.5f/1m winner, by Elusive Quality): dam, champion 2-y-o filly in Argentina, later Grade 2 1½m winner in USA: smart performer: won newcomers race at Saint-Cloud in March, Prix Penelope at Saint-Cloud in April and Prix Saint-Alary at Longchamp (by 3 lengths from Wekeela) in May: respectable third in Breeders' Cup Filly & Mare Turf at Keeneland (3½ lengths behind Stephanie's Kitten, never nearer) final start: beaten just over 4 lengths in Prix de Diane at Chantilly and Prix de l'Opera at Longchamp on other starts: stays 10.4f: acts on soft and good to firm going. *F. Head, France* **118**

QUEEN'S NOVEL 3 b.f. King's Best (USA) 132 – Jane Austen (IRE) 104 (Galileo (IRE) 134) [2015 p11g* Oct 7] 10,000Y: third foal: half-sister to French 1½m winner Just Darcy (by Danehill Dancer): dam 1½m-1¾m winner: 20/1, overcame greenness when winning maiden at Kempton by 1¾ lengths from Ballynanty, better placed than most and leading entering final 1f: will stay 1½m+: capable of better. *James Tate* **84 p**

QUEENS PARK (FR) 4 b.f. King's Best (USA) 132 – Anna Deesse (FR) (Anabaa (USA) 130) [2015 82: 8m⁴ 8.5g 8m⁶ 9.8g Aug 15] fair handicapper: stays 1¼m: acts on good to firm going: tried in tongue tie in 2015. *John Davies* **73**

QUEEN'S PEARL (IRE) 3 b.f. Exceed And Excel (AUS) 126 – Gimasha 105 (Cadeaux Genereux 131) [2015 83p: 6m² 6m* 6.1g* 6m⁵ 6g⁶ Sep 24] useful handicapper: won at Newmarket (by ½ length from Secret Hint) in July and Nottingham (by 6 lengths from Lady Horatia) in August: raced only at 6f: acts on good to firm going: often travels strongly. *Roger Varian* **105**

QUEEN'S TRUST 2 b.f. (Mar 4) Dansili 127 – Queen's Best 110 (King's Best (USA) 132) [2015 p7g* 7g⁵ Oct 9] tall, attractive filly: fourth foal: sister to useful 7f winner Royal Seal: dam, winner up to 1½m (2-y-o 6f winner), half-sister to smart French 1½m winner Reverie Solitaire: won maiden at Kempton in September by 3¼ lengths from Gravity Flow: 9/4, still needed experience and possibly unsuited by track when 4 lengths fifth of 12 to First Victory in Oh So Sharp Stakes at Newmarket next time: remains open to improvement. *Sir Michael Stoute* **90 p**

QUEEN ZAIN (IRE) 3 b.f. Lawman (FR) 121 – Tropical Lady (IRE) 117 (Sri Pekan 47
(USA) 117) [2015 49p: t6g⁵ t6g³ p7g Oct 7] poor maiden: should stay at least 7f.
Robert Cowell

QUERIDO (GER) 11 b.g. Acatenango (GER) 127 – Quest of Fire (FR) (Rainbow Quest 43
(USA) 134) [2015 46: 7d p10m⁶ p10g p8g p10f⁶ 11.9s p8g p10g Dec 30] leggy gelding:
poor handicapper: stays 1¼m: acts on polytrack and heavy going: wears headgear/tongue
tie: sometimes slowly away. *Paddy Butler*

QUEST FOR MORE (IRE) 5 b.g. Teofilo (IRE) 126 – No Quest (IRE) (Rainbow Quest 116
(USA) 134) [2015 99: 12f² 14g⁴* 16.1m* 16m² 12g 15.9g Nov 3] tall, useful-looking
gelding: smart performer: further progress in 2015 and won handicaps at Goodwood in
May and Newcastle (Northumberland Plate, beat Max Dynamite 1¼ lengths, showing a
good turn of foot) in June: ran well when neck second to Big Orange in Goodwood Cup
next time, off nearly 3 months after: creditable 4 lengths ninth of 24 to Prince of Penzance
in Melbourne Cup (Handicap) at Flemington final start, bit short of room 2f out: stays 2m:
acts on firm going: wears blinkers. *Roger Charlton*

QUEST FOR WONDER 3 b.f. Makfi 130 – Sinndiya (IRE) 84 (Pharly (FR) 130) [2015 96
71p: f11g* f12g² 11.9v* 14d³ 12m⁴ 12s⁴ 10.1d* Sep 27] useful handicapper: won at
Southwell in January and Brighton (by 11 lengths) in May: better than ever when also won
at Epsom final start by 2¼ lengths from Mica Mika: left James Tate after fourth outing:
effective at 1¼m and stays 1¾m: acts on polytrack, fibresand, good to firm and heavy
going. *Pat Phelan*

QUESTO 3 ch.g. Monsieur Bond (IRE) 120 – Ex Gracia (Efisio 120) [2015 6d⁴ 6m² 6m⁴ 75
Jun 17] fair maiden: best effort when second at Redcar in May. *Tracy Waggott*

QUEST OF COLOUR (IRE) 4 b.f. Iffraaj 127 – With Colour (Rainbow Quest (USA) 72
134) [2015 75p: 10d 10.1m 10.4f³ 12g⁴ 9.3g⁴ 9.3g⁴ 10.2g⁴ Sep 30] fair handicapper: stays
10.5f: acts on firm going: often in hood in 2015. *Richard Fahey*

H.R.H. Sultan Ahmad Shah's "Quest For More"

Dubai Cornwallis Stakes, Newmarket—a comfortable win for short-priced favourite Quiet Reflection, who beats Field of Vision and Shadow Hunter (second left)

QUICKASWECAN 4 b.g. Shamardal (USA) 129 – Arctic Air 79 (Polar Falcon (USA) **84**
126) [2015 80: p6g p6f t8.6m f7g⁶ p6m⁶ p7g 6g* 6g* 6g⁵ 6d⁵ Sep 14] leggy gelding: fairly
useful handicapper: left Mark Johnston, won at Catterick in July and Lingfield in August:
stays 7f: acts on polytrack, good to firm and heavy going: tried in blinkers in 2015: usually
races close up. *Ivan Furtado*

QUICK DEFENCE (USA) 3 b.c. First Defence (USA) 119 – Quickfire 100 (Dubai **93**
Millennium 140) [2015 84p: p10g² 10f² 8.3m* 8f 8f 8g⁵ Aug 31] angular colt: fairly useful
performer: won maiden at Leicester (by 4½ lengths from Stars And Stripes) in June: stays
8.5f: acts on firm going. *Sir Michael Stoute*

QUICK JACK (IRE) 6 ch.g. Footstepsinthesand 120 – Miss Polaris 93 (Polar Falcon **111**
(USA) 126) [2015 18.7d² 14g 18g³ Oct 10] strong, lengthy gelding: smart handicapper:
better than ever in 2015 and good efforts when second in Chester Cup at Chester (¾ length
behind Trip To Paris) in May and third in Cesarewitch at Newmarket (length behind
Grumeti) in October: stays 2¼m: acts on soft and good to firm going: tried in headgear
prior to 2015: smart hurdler (won Galway Hurdle in July). *A. J. Martin, Ireland*

QUICK LOOK 2 b.g. (Mar 4) Kheleyf (USA) 116 – Weqaar (USA) 83 (Red Ransom **77 p**
(USA)) [2015 6d⁵ Jun 23] 10,000F: half-brother to 3 winners, including 2-y-o 1¼m winner
Cherry Street (by Alhaarth) and 9.5f winner Fadhaa (by Bahri): dam, 1¼m winner, half-
sister to Prix de l'Arc de Triomphe winner Sakhee: 16/1, knew job when winning maiden
at Brighton by 1¼ lengths from Al Dallah on debut, staying on to lead final 1f under hands-
and-heels ride: subsequently joined Michael Banks: bred to stay beyond 6f: should do
better. *William Jarvis*

QUICK MARCH 2 b.f. (Mar 31) Lawman (FR) 121 – Strut 103 (Danehill Dancer (IRE) **85 p**
117) [2015 6m 6s³ 6g* Sep 7] sturdy filly: fifth foal: half-sister to 3 winners, including very
smart 6f (including at 2 yrs) winner Mince (by Medicean) and useful 6f winner Stomp (by
Nayef): dam 2-y-o 5f winner: fairly useful performer: best effort when winning maiden at
Windsor (by 5 lengths from Heroic Heart) in September: raced only at 6f: will go on
improving. *Roger Charlton*

QUICK N QUIRKY (IRE) 2 b.f. (Apr 4) Lilbourne Lad (IRE) 111 – Beseech (IRE) **86**
(Danehill (USA) 126) [2015 6g* 6m² 6g 6.5m 7g³ 8g 6g Oct 3] €10,000Y: third foal: dam
once-raced half-sister to E. P. Taylor Stakes winner Fraulein: fairly useful performer: won
maiden at Thirsk in June: best effort when second in minor event at Newcastle: stays 6f:
acts on good to firm going: often in tongue tie. *Tim Easterby*

QUICK RUSH 3 b.f. Stimulation (IRE) 121 – Aziz Presenting (IRE) 86 (Charnwood **–**
Forest (USA) 125) [2015 7m Jul 11] sixth foal: dam, 2-y-o 5f winner, half-sister to smart
7f/1m performer Camp Commander: 50/1, looked hard ride when well held in maiden at
Salisbury, slowly away. *Mick Channon*

QUICK WIT 8 b.g. Oasis Dream 129 – Roo 97 (Rudimentary (USA) 118) [2015 106: **109**
a9.4f 8.9g 8.1s³ 10.3m³ 8.5s² Oct 9] strong gelding: useful handicapper: visored first time,
best effort of 2015 when ½ -length second to You're Fired at York final start: stays 1¼m:
acts on polytrack, soft and good to firm going: usually wears cheekpieces: often races
towards rear. *Saeed bin Suroor*

QUICK WITTED 2 b.f. (Apr 11) Poet's Voice 126 – Fastback (IRE) 93 (Singspiel (IRE) **56**
133) [2015 p8g Dec 16] third foal: dam, 9.7f-11f winner, half-sister to useful performers up
to around 1¼m Kings Quay and Milne Graden: 50/1, seventh of 13 behind Ballard Down
in maiden at Kempton: will be suited by further than 1m. *Harry Dunlop*

QUIET BEAUTY 3 b.f. Acclamation 118 – Upperville (IRE) 79 (Selkirk (USA) 129) **–**
[2015 –: 7g 5g t6g 7v Aug 25] has shown little in maidens/handicaps, including in
cheekpieces, *Robert Cowell*

QUIET REFLECTION 2 b.f. (Feb 19) Showcasing 117 – My Delirium 83 (Haafhd 129) **112 p**
[2015 5g* 6g⁵ 5g* 5g* Oct 9] £32,000Y, £44,000 2-y-o: workmanlike filly: first foal: dam
2-y-o 6f winner: smart performer: won maiden at Hamilton (by 5 lengths from Farkle
Minkus) in July, listed race at Ayr (by 4 lengths from Field of Vision) in September and
Cornwallis Stakes at Newmarket (by 2½ lengths from Field of Vision) in October: best
form at 5f: open to further improvement. *K. R. Burke*

QUIET WARRIOR (IRE) 4 b.g. Kodiac 112 – Pretty Woman (IRE) 45 (Night Shift **78 §**
(USA)) [2015 86: p0g⁶ t7.1m 6m⁶ 6m⁴ 6.1m 6d 7.5g 5g 5d Oct 21] smallish, good-
quartered gelding: fair handicapper: left Marco Botti after fifth start: stays 7f: acts on
polytrack, tapeta, good to firm and good to soft going: sometimes wears headgear: tried in
tongue tie in 2015: often starts slowly: unreliable. *Adrian McGuinness, Ireland*

QUILL ART 3 b.g. Excellent Art 125 – Featherweight (IRE) 89 (Fantastic Light (USA) **72**
134) [2015 64p: t9.5f⁵ t8.6f² Jan 30] fair maiden: all 3 runs at Wolverhampton, best effort
when runner-up final start: likely to stay 1¼m. *Richard Fahey*

QUINA BROOK (IRE) 2 b.f. (Apr 28) Peintre Celebre (USA) 137 – Barconey (IRE) **60**
(Danehill Dancer (IRE) 117) [2015 6f p6g⁴ 6g Aug 10] €6,000Y, €82,000 2-y-o: fifth foal:
half-sister to 6f-8.6f winner Bint Alzain (by Marju) and a winner in Italy by Nayef: dam
unraced half-sister to smart winner up to 1m Brunel: modest maiden: best effort when
fourth at Kempton. *Ronald Thompson*

QUINTA FEIRA (IRE) 4 gr.g. Medicean 128 – Bunditten (IRE) 92 (Soviet Star (USA) **67 d**
128) [2015 p8f p7g⁵ p6f⁵ p7g p6m 8f* p8f⁶ 8m 8g 8f⁵ 8.3g 8.9m⁶ 8.4s 10d p9.4g p9.4g⁶
p7.5g Dec 28] fair handicapper at best: won at Bath in April: left Ed de Giles after eleventh
start: stays 1m: acts on polytrack and firm going: sometimes in headgear in 2015. *S. Cerulis,
France*

QUINTUS CERIALIS (IRE) 3 b.g. Vale of York (IRE) 117 – Red Fox (IRE) (Spectrum **83**
(IRE) 126) [2015 79: 6d 7m 7m⁵ 7.1m⁶ p7g* t7.1f Dec 11] close-coupled gelding: fairly
useful performer: won maiden at Kempton (by 11 lengths from Miro) in November: best
effort at 7f: acts on polytrack: often in headgear in 2015. *Clive Cox*

QUITE A STORY 3 ch.f. Equiano (FR) 127 – Perfect Story 95 (Desert Story (IRE) **78**
115) [2015 5.7m² 6m* 6g³ 6gᵘʳ 5.7m³ Aug 22] 46,000Y: leggy filly: fourth foal: half-sister
to 7f-1¼m winner Perfect Cracker (by Dubai Destination) and useful 2-y-o 6f winner
(stays 1¼m) Tanseeb (by Royal Applause): dam 6f/7f winner: fair performer: won maiden
at Windsor in June: stays 6f: acts on good to firm going: usually races prominently.
Clive Cox

QUITE SMART (IRE) 3 b.f. Arcano (IRE) 122 – Lyca Ballerina 76 (Marju (IRE) 127) **75**
[2015 72: 7m² 7g* p6m 6g³ 7m⁶ p7g Dec 2] fair performer: won maiden at Redcar in May:
stays 7f: acts on good to firm going. *Robert Cowell*

QUITE SPARKY 8 b.g. Lucky Story (USA) 128 – Imperialistic (IRE) 99 (Imperial Ballet **55**
(IRE) 110) [2015 64: f8g⁵ t13.9m³ t12.2m³ t12.2m t8.6f⁴ t12.2f⁵ t9.5m³ t9.5m³ Dec 26]
leggy gelding: modest handicapper: left Geoffrey Harker after fourth start: stays 1¾m: acts
on tapeta, soft and good to firm going: wears headgear. *Lucinda Egerton*

QUOTELINE DIRECT 2 ch.g. (Apr 28) Sir Percy 129 – Queen's Pudding (IRE) 84 **78**
(Royal Applause 124) [2015 6m* 6g 7m³ 7s⁶ Oct 6] fair performer: won maiden at
Pontefract in July: stays 7f. *Micky Hammond*

R

RAAQY (IRE) 2 gr.f. (Mar 30) Dubawi (IRE) 129 – Natagora (FR) 116 (Divine Light **88**
(JPN)) [2015 6.5m* 7.1f³ 8m Sep 11] fourth foal: half-sister to 2-y-o 6f winner Rayaheen
(by Nayef): dam won 1000 Guineas, also 2-y-o 5f/6f winner who stayed 10.5f: fairly useful
performer: won maiden at Doncaster in June, better form when 4¾ lengths third to
Fireglow in listed race at Sandown: 14/1, seventh of 8 to Turret Rocks in May Hill Stakes
at Doncaster final outing, weakening 2f out: stays 7f. *B. W. Hills*

RAASMAAL 2 b.g. (Apr 4) Poet's Voice 126 – Luminda (IRE) (Danehill (USA) 126) – [2015 p7g Nov 4] 50/1, shaped as if in need of experience when well held in maiden at Kempton. *Ed Dunlop*

RAAS (USA) 3 b.f. Iffraaj 127 – Sarmad (USA) 56 (Dynaformer (USA)) [2015 7g 7s May – 9] first foal: dam lightly-raced half-sister to smart 2-y-o 6f winner Woodborough and useful 5f-1m winner Performing Magic: well held in maiden at Newmarket and Chartwell Stakes at Lingfield: sold £600 in December. *Clive Brittain*

RACE DAY (IRE) 2 ch.c. (Mar 5) Dubawi (IRE) 129 – Nadia 116 (Nashwan (USA) 135) **105** [2015 7g 6f² p6f³ p7g* p8m* p7m* Nov 21] stocky colt: half-brother to several winners, including winner up to 9f Namecheck (2-y-o 7.4f winner, by Shamardal) and 5f/6f winner Shipyard (by Pivotal), both useful: dam, 1¼m (Prix Saint-Alary) winner, also 1¼m winner at 2 yrs: useful performer: successful at Lingfield last 3 starts, in maiden in October and minor events in November, in cheekpieces and best effort when beating Special Season by ½ length on final outing: stays 1m: acts on polytrack: usually leads, often travels strongly. *Saeed bin Suroor*

RACE TO GLORY (FR) 4 b.g. Montjeu (IRE) 137 – Cawett (IRE) (Danehill Dancer – (IRE) 117) [2015 14g 11.8d 14.1g Sep 30] fairly useful maiden in 2014, well held in handicaps in 2015: stays 13f: best effort on good to firm going: in cheekpieces last 2 starts: sent to France. *David Pipe*

RACING ANGEL (IRE) 3 b.f. Dark Angel (IRE) 113 – Roclette (USA) 76 (Rock of **71** Gibraltar (IRE) 133) [2015 –p: 6d 5g³ 5g* 5m* 5m² Aug 9] fair handicapper: won at Leicester and Redcar in July: best form at 5f: acts on good to firm going: usually races close up. *Mick Quinn*

RACING HISTORY (IRE) 3 b.c. Pivotal 124 – Gonbarda (GER) 117 (Lando (GER) 128) **120 p** [2015 –p: 8g* 10.3m* 10d* 10d⁴ Oct 17] well-made colt: very smart performer: progressed extremely well in 2015 and won first 3 starts, namely maiden at Haydock in May, handicap at Chester in July and Winter Hill Stakes at Windsor (by length from Cannock Chase) in August: 16/1, excellent effort when 3¼ lengths fourth of 13 to Fascinating Rock in Champion Stakes at Ascot final outing, ridden over 3f out and responding well: will probably stay 1½m: acts on good to firm and good to soft going: open to further improvement. *Saeed bin Suroor*

RACING KNIGHT (IRE) 3 b.g. Sir Percy 129 – Salydora (FR) (Peintre Celebre (USA) **72 p** 137) [2015 63p: 7.5g 10m² 12g⁴ Jun 29] fair maiden: shaped well when fourth in handicap at Pontefract final start, left with too much to do: stays 1½m: acts on good to firm going: often races towards rear: open to further improvement. *John Quinn*

RACING'S DREAM 4 b.g. Iffraaj 127 – There's Two (IRE) 85 (Ashkalani (IRE) 128) **83** [2015 70: p6m² t7.1g⁵ 7.6g* Jun 20] fairly useful performer: won handicap at Lingfield in June, sold 40,000 gns in July and joined Gordon Elliott: stays 7.5f: acts on polytrack and heavy going. *Brian Meehan*

RACING SPIRIT 3 ch.g. Sir Percy 129 – Suertuda (Domedriver (IRE) 128) [2015 –p: – 10g 14.1g May 26] no form: tried in blinkers. *John Quinn*

RACING VENTURE (IRE) 2 b.c. (Apr 30) Lilbourne Lad (IRE) 111 – Tagula Mon **40** (IRE) (Tagula (IRE) 116) [2015 5g⁵ 6g⁶ May 17] showed little in maiden at Pontefract and seller at Ripon (in cheekpieces), *John Quinn*

Unibet Winter Hill Stakes, Windsor—
a decidedly smart effort from up-and-coming three-year-old Racing History on his pattern debut as he beats Cannock Chase (spotted cap) and Battalion (noseband); Irish challenger Fascinating Rock is a short-priced favourite but performs as if needing the run

RACQUET 2 br.c. (Apr 10) Pastoral Pursuits 127 – Billie Jean 65 (Bertolini (USA) 125) **88**
[2015 5d⁴ 6m* 6m⁴ 5.2m 6.1m² Aug 11] €11,000F, £13,000Y: smallish colt: third foal:
half-brother to 5f/6f winner Petit Arc En Ciel (by Footstepsinthesand) and 7f (including
at 2 yrs) winner Celestine Abbey (by Authorized): dam, 2-y-o 5f winner, half-sister to 2000
Guineas winner Cockney Rebel: fairly useful performer: won maiden at Salisbury (by 7
lengths from Swanton Blue) in June: second in minor event at Nottingham in August: stays
6f: acts on good to firm going. *Richard Hannon*

RADDEH 3 gr.f. Shamardal (USA) 129 – Hathrah (IRE) 113 (Linamix (FR) 127) [2015 **86 p**
57p: 10d⁶ 9.9d⁶ 8m² 8.3m* Jul 4] well-made filly: fairly useful performer: won handicap at
Nottingham in July: stays 8.5f: acts on good to firm going: will go on improving. *Sir
Michael Stoute*

RADHAADH (IRE) 3 b.f. Nayef (USA) 129 – Safwa (IRE) 85 (Green Desert (USA) **88**
127) [2015 61p: 10m⁴ 11.5s³ p10g² p10f* p11d⁶ 9.9g Sep 30] fairly useful performer: won
maiden at Chelmsford in August: stays 11f: acts on polytrack: front runner/races
prominently. *Sir Michael Stoute*

RADMORES EXPRESS 6 b.g. Primo Valentino (IRE) 116 – Emma Lilley (USA) 53 **58**
(Theatrical (IRE) 128) [2015 t12.2m⁴ t12.2g⁶ Feb 9] placed in bumpers: better effort in
maidens at Wolverhampton when fourth of 8. *John O'Shea*

RAFAAF (IRE) 7 b.g. Royal Applause 124 – Sciunfona (IRE) (Danehill (USA) 126) **71**
[2015 50: t6f² t6g² t8.6g² t7.1m² t8.6g³ 7.6g² 10.3g⁶ Aug 2] strong gelding: fair
handicapper: left Richard Phillips after first start: stays 10.5f: acts on polytrack, tapeta and
heavy going: tried in headgear: usually responds generously to pressure. *James Unett*

RAFFERS 3 b.g. Calcutta 112 – Deserted Island (IRE) (Desert Style (IRE) 121) [2015 8g **–**
10.3g 8m⁶ 7.5g⁶ Aug 30] no form. *David C. Griffiths*

RAGDOLLIANNA 11 b.m. Kayf Tara 130 – Jupiters Princess 54 (Jupiter Island 126) **61**
[2015 56: p15.8f⁴ p15.8g³ p15.8g 14.1g³ p12g* p13f Sep 12] leggy mare: modest
handicapper: won at Kempton in August: stays 2m: acts on polytrack, good to firm and
good to soft going: races towards rear. *Mark Hoad*

RAGING BEAR (USA) 5 b.g. Leroidesanimaux (BRZ) 127 – Gliding Light (USA) **§§**
(Always A Classic (CAN) 124) [2015 78: t12.2f f12s t8.6f² t8.6g⁴ 10.3g⁴ t9.5mʳʳ
10.2mʳʳ 9gʳʳ Jul 13] fair handicapper: left James Evans after sixth start: stays 11f: acts on
all-weather, good to firm and heavy going: sometimes wears headgear: refused to race last
4 starts, and one to leave well alone. *Jennie Candlish*

RAGTIME DANCER 3 ch.f. Medicean 128 – Honky Tonk Sally 86 (Dansili 127) [2015 **52**
66: p7m⁵ p7f⁶ Jan 23] modest performer: stays 7f: acts on polytrack: tried in headgear.
Jonathan Portman

RAHMAH (IRE) 3 b.c. Vale of York (IRE) 117 – Sweet Home Alabama (IRE) 56 (Desert **84**
Prince (IRE) 130) [2015 77: t5.1g* 6m 5f² 5g³ 8.3d³ p8g Dec 7] fairly useful performer:
won maiden at Wolverhampton in April: left Robert Cowell after fourth start: stays 8.5f:
acts on tapeta, firm and good to soft going: sometimes wears cheekpieces. *Geoffrey Deacon*

RAH RAH 2 b.f. (Mar 18) Lonhro (AUS) 128 – Rahiyah (USA) 113 (Rahy (USA) 115) **98**
[2015 p5g* 5.1d* 5f 6m⁵ 6d⁴ Jul 25] angular filly: fifth foal: half-sister to 8.5f-1¼m winner
Hellenistic (by Street Cry) and useful winner up to 1m Decathlete (2-y-o 6f winner, by
Medaglia d'Oro): dam, 2-y-o 6f winner, also third in Poule d'Essai des Pouliches: useful
performer: won maiden at Kempton in March and minor event at Chester in May: best
effort when fifth (demoted from fourth) to Illuminate in Duchess of Cambridge Stakes at
Newmarket: stays 6f: acts on polytrack, good to firm and good to soft going: front runner/
races prominently. *Mark Johnston*

RAHYAH 2 b.f. (Mar 26) Acclamation 118 – Kahlua Kiss 103 (Mister Baileys 123) [2015 **69 p**
p7g⁵ p7g² Dec 20] 75,000Y: fourth foal: half-sister to very smart winner up to 1¼m
Windhoek (2-y-o 6f winner, by Cape Cross) and 1½m winner Spiritoftheunion (by
Authorized): dam winner up to 10.4f (2-y-o 7f winner): better effort when second in
maiden at Lingfield (½ length behind Foxinthehenhouse) in December, nearest finish:
remains with potential. *William Haggas*

RAINBOW BEAUTY 5 ch.m. Manduro (GER) 135 – Just Like A Woman 96 (Observatory **79**
(USA) 131) [2015 10.3m⁴ Jun 26] angular mare: fair handicapper: stays 10.5f: acts on
polytrack, soft and firm going: often wears cheekpieces: tried in tongue tie prior to
2015. *Richard Ford*

RAINBOW DREAMER 2 b.c. (Mar 26) Aqlaam 125 – Zamhrear 73 (Singspiel (IRE) **91 p**
133) [2015 8.3d⁵ 8.3s* Oct 28] 4,200Y, 8,000 2-y-o: fifth foal: half-brother to 7f winner
Capelita (by Cape Cross): dam, 7f/1m winner, half-sister to very smart winner up to 11f

Blue Monday: much improved from debut and value for extra when winning maiden at Nottingham by 4 lengths from Twobeelucky, quickening clear over 1f out: open to further progress. *Alan King*

RAINBOW LAD (IRE) 2 b.g. (Mar 6) Lilbourne Lad (IRE) 111 – Carmona 65 (Rainbow — Quest (USA) 134) [2015 f6s³ 6m 7.5g Sep 16] no form. *Michael Appleby*

RAINBOW LOLLIPOP 4 b.f. Dubawi (IRE) 129 – Cross Section (USA) 76 (Cape Cross (IRE) 129) [2015 p8f f8g Nov 3] ex-French-trained maiden, modest form at best: left C. Laffon-Parias €10,000, tailed off in 2 handicaps (in cheekpieces/tongue tie) in 2015. *Tom Gretton*

RAINBOW ORSE 3 b.g. Zebedee 113 – Khafayif (USA) 62 (Swain (IRE) 134) [2015 59: **78** 5s* 5g 5.1m* 5d⁵ p6f Oct 22] fair performer: won maiden at Musselburgh in May and handicap at Nottingham in June: best form at 5f: acts on soft and good to firm going: in cheekpieces last 3 starts. *Robert Cowell*

RAINBOW PRIDE (IRE) 3 gr.g. Clodovil (IRE) 116 – Rahila (IRE) (Kalanisi (IRE) **79 p** 132) [2015 62p: 10.2m⁵ p10f 12d⁵ p16f* Oct 15] fair handicapper: won at Chelmsford in October: best effort at 2m: acts on polytrack: will go on improving. *Sir Mark Prescott Bt*

RAINBOW REBEL (IRE) 2 b.g. (Apr 25) Acclamation 118 – Imperial Quest 61 **70** (Rainbow Quest (USA) 134) [2015 f5g² 5l.1g² 6.1s⁴ 6g⁶ t7.1f³ t7.1f³ Oct 27] fair maiden: stays 7f: acts on tapeta: often races prominently. *Mark Johnston*

RAINFORD GLORY (IRE) 5 ch.g. Rock of Gibraltar (IRE) 133 – My Dolly Madison **66** 77 (In The Wings 128) [2015 69: t12.2f t8.6f p13g⁴ p12g⁴ p12f³ t12.2g² 14.1m⁴ 13.1d³ t12.2g⁶ 10.2m³ 12g⁴ 9.9s³ 10.2d⁶ 9.9g² 9.9d⁴ 10s* 10.3d p12m⁵ Nov 19] fair handicapper: won at Redcar (amateur, awarded race) in October: stays 1¾m, effective at shorter: acts on polytrack, soft and good to firm going: tried in cheekpieces. *Tim Fitzgerald*

RAIN GOD (USA) 5 b.g. Henrythenavigator (USA) 131 – Lotta Dancing (USA) (Alydar **69** (USA)) [2015 –: p8g p10f p6m² 6m² 7s 6g⁴ p7g 6s⁶ Aug 15] tall, rather unfurnished gelding: fair handicapper: stays 1m: acts on polytrack and firm going: usually wears headgear: tongue tied last 4 starts: front runner/races prominently: sold £800, sent to Germany. *Gary Moore*

RAIN IN THE FACE 2 b.g. (Apr 26) Naaqoos 117 – Makaaseb (USA) 100 (Pulpit **67 p** (USA) 117) [2015 p8f p8g⁵ Dec 16] second foal: dam, 2-y-o 1m winner who stayed 10.4f, half-sister to US 8.5f (minor stakes) winner Sirpa: 33/1, improved from debut when 4½ lengths fifth of 13 to Ballard Down in maiden at Kempton, pushed along 2f out and keeping on: still better to come. *Ralph Beckett*

RAIN WIND AND FIRE (USA) 3 ch.g. Eskendereya (USA) 126 – Call Mariah (USA) **80** (Dixie Union (USA) 121) [2015 p7g* p7g* 7m p8g⁴ Aug 5] lengthy, angular gelding: third foal: half-brother to useful 2-y-o 6f winner (stays 8.5f) Califante (by Kyllachy): dam unraced half-sister to Breeders' Cup Dirt Mile winner Albertus Maximus: fairly useful performer: won maiden at Lingfield in February and minor event at Kempton in April: stays 1m: tried in cheekpieces. *Jeremy Noseda*

RAISE A BILLION 4 b.g. Major Cadeaux 121 – Romantic Destiny 90 (Dubai Destination **61** (USA) 127) [2015 60: 6s 6s⁴ 7.2d³ 7.2d³ 6d⁴ 6g³ 6g* 7.2g 6v Nov 3] modest handicapper: won at Hamilton in September: stays 7f: acts on soft going: often races towards rear. *Alan Berry*

RAISED HOPE 4 b.g. Byron 117 – Wax Eloquent 67 (Zaha (CAN) 106) [2015 t9.5g⁶ — t7.1g 8s May 9] no form. *Shaun Harris*

RAISE THE GAME (IRE) 2 b.g. (Feb 23) Bushranger (IRE) 119 – Fancy Feathers (IRE) — 79 (Redback 116) [2015 f5g⁴ Apr 9] 7/1, well-held fourth of 5 in maiden at Southwell. *Bill Turner*

RAISING SAND 3 b.g. Oasis Dream 129 – Balalaika 108 (Sadler's Wells (USA) 132) — **p** [2015 p10f Sep 24] closely related to very smart 7f-1¼m winner Alkaadhem (by Green Desert) and half-brother to 3 winners, including useful 1m-1¼m winner Lookalike (by Rainbow Quest) and winner up to 1¼m Doctor Zhivago (2-y-o 1m winner, by Shamardal): dam 9f winner who stayed 1½m: 6/1, very green when tailed off in maiden at Chelmsford on debut: should do better. *Roger Varian*

RAJADAMRI 2 gr.g. (Apr 4) Hellvelyn 118 – Crofters Ceilidh 101 (Scottish Reel 123) **66** [2015 6d 5g p7g³ 7d Oct 11] fair maiden: stays 7f. *Rod Millman*

RAJAPUR 2 gr.g. (Mar 31) Dalakhani (IRE) 133 – A Beautiful Mind (GER) (Winged Love **74** (IRE) 121) [2015 7m⁵ 8m⁵ 7m 7g 8.5g⁵ t7.1f Dec 22] fair maiden: left D. K. Weld after fifth start: stays 1m: acts on good to firm going: tried in blinkers. *Philip Kirby*

RAJEH (IRE) 12 b.g. Key of Luck (USA) 126 – Saramacca (IRE) 54 (Kahyasi 130) [2015 **48** 54: p13g⁵ p15.8f³ Jan 30] sturdy gelding: poor handicapper: stays 2m: acts on polytrack, firm and soft going. *Peter Grayson*

RAJ TO RICHES (IRE) 2 ch.c. (Mar 3) Iffraaj 127 – Moriches (IRE) 68 (Alhaarth **75** (IRE) 126) [2015 5m² 5.1m² 5.1s⁶ 5m³ 6s⁴ 5m² 6g⁴ 5g⁴ Jul 8] fair maiden: stays 6f: acts on soft and good to firm going: usually leads: sold 12,000 gns, sent to Qatar. *David Evans*

RAKAAN (IRE) 8 ch.g. Bahamian Bounty 116 – Petite Spectre 74 (Spectrum (IRE) 126) **71 §** [2015 76, a87: p10g³ p10m³ p8m p10f* p7m 10m p8g⁶ p10g 8m⁶ p10g⁴ p10g 8m* p10f⁵ p8m p7m p8g⁵ Dec 30] compact gelding: fair performer: won claimer at Lingfield in March and handicap at Bath in August: stays 1¼m: acts on polytrack, tapeta and good to firm going: often in headgear: usually slowly away, often races towards rear: quirky and one to be wary of. *Brendan Powell*

RALPH MCTELL 3 b.g. Tobougg (IRE) 125 – Alashaan 73 (Darshaan 133) [2015 –: **43** 8.3m f6d 7s⁵ 6m⁶ 5d⁶ 5.7f⁶ Jun 24] poor maiden: tried in blinkers: dead. *Alan Coogan*

RALPHY BOY (IRE) 6 b.g. Acclamation 118 – Silcasue (Selkirk (USA) 129) [2015 84: **85** 9s 7.1g* 7m 7.1m 7.6f 7.1m⁴ 7.2s 7m 8g* 7.9g² 7.2g* 7.9m 7.2g³ 7v Oct 17] fairly useful handicapper: won at Musselburgh in May and Pontefract and Musselburgh in August: stays 8.5f: acts on good to firm and good to soft going: tried in cheekpieces prior to 2015. *Alistair Whillans*

RALPHY LAD (IRE) 4 b.g. Iffraaj 127 – Hawattef (IRE) (Mujtahid (USA) 118) [2015 **85** 73: 8m f11g* 11.1s* 12.5s* 12g 11.5g 12s 10d 12g f12f f11g² Dec 22] big, lengthy, good-topped gelding: fairly useful handicapper: won at Southwell in April and Hamilton and Musselburgh in May: stays 12.5f: acts on fibresand, soft and good to firm going: often races towards rear. *Alan Swinbank*

RAMBO WILL 7 b.g. Danbird (AUS) – Opera Belle 77 (Dr Fong (USA) 128) [2015 71, **69** a81: f5d p5f p6g 6m 5m 5m⁴ 6g* 5v³ 5g 5g⁶ Oct 5] sturdy gelding: fair handicapper: won at Lingfield in July: stays 6f: acts on polytrack, fibresand, good to firm and heavy going: tried in blinkers prior to 2015: front runner/races prominently. *J. R. Jenkins*

RAMPERS (IRE) 2 b.g. (Jan 21) Thewayyouare (USA) 117 – Korresia (IRE) (Elnadim **72** (USA) 128) [2015 p5f⁵ 5m³ f5d² p6g⁶ t5.1g³ f5g² 5.3d³ t5.1g⁴ p6g⁴ p5f Sep 22] fair maiden: best form at 5f: acts on fibresand and tapeta: often starts slowly. *Jamie Osborne*

RANCHER (IRE) 5 b.g. High Chaparral (IRE) 132 – Shot of Redemption (Shirley **57** Heights 130) [2015 t9.5f t9.5m⁶ p10f² Mar 4] modest handicapper: stays 1½m: acts on polytrack, tapeta and heavy going: tried in blinkers prior to 2015. *Tony Carroll*

RANDALL'S ALANNAH (IRE) 5 b.m. High Chaparral (IRE) 132 – Randall's Diana **–** (IRE) 63 (Monashee Mountain (USA) 115) [2015 f8g⁶ Jan 6] handicapper: off 14 months, well held only outing in 2015: stays 1m: acts on heavy going: in blinkers last 4 starts. *Seamus Fahey, Ireland*

RANDALL'S REBECCA (IRE) 4 b.f. Excellent Art 125 – Randall's Diana (IRE) 63 **–** (Monashee Mountain (USA) 115) [2015 –: f7g 6.3s Sep 18] well held in maidens/handicaps: tried in cheekpieces. *Seamus Fahey, Ireland*

RANDOM SUCCESS (IRE) 5 b.m. Shamardal (USA) 129 – Foreplay (IRE) 86 (Lujain **82** (USA) 119) [2015 90: p5g² p5f⁴ t5.1f⁴ Mar 20] fairly useful handicapper: stays 6f: acts on polytrack, firm and good to soft going: sometimes wears hood: usually races nearer last than first. *Roger Charlton*

RANGALI 4 ch.g. Namid 128 – Tejaara (USA) (Kingmambo (USA) 125) [2015 120: 5g 5f **122** 5d⁴ 5s 5m² Oct 4] close-coupled gelding: very smart performer: in first-time blinkers, back to form when second in Prix de l'Abbaye at Longchamp (for second year in succession, beaten short neck by Goldream) on final outing, headed close home having quickened to lead 1f out: gelded after: has won at 7f, best form at shorter: acts on polytrack, soft and good to firm going: in cheekpieces penultimate start. *H-A. Pantall, France*

RANSOM NOTE 8 b.g. Red Ransom (USA) – Zacheta (Polish Precedent (USA) 131) **93** [2015 12s⁴ 12d 10.4d⁴ Sep 4] sturdy, compact gelding: one-time smart performer, fairly useful handicapper nowadays: effective at 1m to 10.5f: acts on firm and good to soft going: tried in cheekpieces/tongue tie. *Nigel Twiston-Davies*

RANTAN (IRE) 2 b.g. (Feb 25) Kodiac 112 – Peace Talks (Pivotal 124) [2015 5m⁵ 6s* 6g **80** p6g⁶ Dec 30] £65,000Y: first foal: dam unraced: fairly useful performer: won maiden at Redcar in July: best effort at 6f on soft ground: tried in tongue tie. *David Barron*

RAPID WATER 9 b.g. Anabaa (USA) 130 – Lochsong 129 (Song 132) [2015 –: p7g p8f **38** Jan 21] good-quartered gelding: poor handicapper: stays 1m: acts on polytrack, soft and good to firm going: often wears headgear: quirky sort. *Pat Eddery*

RARE RHYTHM 3 b.c. Dubawi (IRE) 129 – Demisemiquaver 82 (Singspiel (IRE) 133) **101 p**
[2015 93p: 10m 12g* Sep 24] useful form: best effort when winning handicap at
Newmarket in September by 4 lengths from Not Never, driven clear final 1f: stays 1½m:
lightly raced and open to further improvement. *Charlie Appleby*

RAS AL MAL (IRE) 2 ch.c. (Mar 6) Tamayuz 126 – Midnight Glimmer (IRE) 70 (Dr –
Devious (IRE) 127) [2015 p8m Dec 16] 33/1, very green when last of 8 in maiden at
Lingfield. *Ed Dunlop*

RASAMAN (IRE) 11 b.g. Namid 128 – Rasana 74 (Royal Academy (USA) 130) [2015 **82**
91: t6g 6m 5.9m² 6d³ 6m³ 7.1m* 7.2g² 6d⁶ 7.2g⁵ 7d 7.2g⁵ Sep 29] sturdy gelding: fairly
useful handicapper: won at Musselburgh in June: stays 7f: acts on all-weather, soft and firm
going: sometimes wears headgear: tried in tongue tie prior to 2015. *Jim Goldie*

RASASEE (IRE) 2 gr.c. (Apr 16) Rip Van Winkle (IRE) 134 – Gleaming Silver (IRE) 86 **74 p**
(Dalakhani (IRE) 133) [2015 t9.5f³ Nov 14] 60,000F, 26,000Y, £55,000 2-y-o: second
foal: half-brother to 1m winner Silversmith (by Mastercraftsman): dam, ungenuine 1m
winner who stayed 10.7f, half-sister to smart 1m/9f winner Tiz The Shot: 11/1, shaped well
when 2¾ lengths third of 10 to City of Ideas in maiden at Wolverhampton, staying on close
home from unpromising position: better to come. *Marco Botti*

RASEEL 3 b.f. Aqlaam 125 – Waafiah 57 (Anabaa (USA) 130) [2015 –: 6g⁶ 6f May 23] –
well held in maidens: sold 1,500 gns. *Peter Chapple-Hyam*

RASHA (IRE) 3 b.f. Zebedee 113 – Sonny Sunshine (Royal Applause 124) [2015 –: p5g³ **– p**
Aug 17] compact filly: thrice-raced maiden: off 15 months, shaped as if needed run only
outing in 2015: should do better. *Roger Varian*

RASHASH (IRE) 3 b.g. Kyllachy 129 – Labisa (IRE) 80 (High Chaparral (IRE) 132) **75**
[2015 55p: p6m³ 5g² 5g* 6m³ 6v⁴ Aug 31] fair performer: won maiden at Leicester in July:
stays 6f: acts on good to firm going: often races prominently: sold 15,000 gns, sent to
Sweden. *Roger Varian*

RASHEEQ (IRE) 2 b.c. (Jan 24) Vale of York (IRE) 117 – Limber Up (IRE) (Dansili 127) **95**
[2015 t6g² p6g² f6s* 8d³ 6m³ 5g 6s⁴ Oct 9] first foal: dam unraced half-sister to smart
1m-1¼m winner Moneycantbuymelove: useful performer: won maiden at Southwell (by
15 lengths) in August: creditable fourth of 9 in nursery at York final start: stays 6f: acts on
fibresand and soft going: usually races close up. *Ismail Mohammed*

RASIKH (IRE) 2 b.c. (Apr 29) Thewayyouare (USA) 117 – Ann Kastan 55 (Red Ransom **79**
(USA)) [2015 t8.6m p8f⁵ t8.6f² 7g* Dec 30] fair performer: won minor event at Doha in
December: worth a try at 1¼m: blinkered second/third starts: has joined Zuhair Mohsen,
Qatar. *Marco Botti*

RASKOVA (USA) 5 b.m. Henrythenavigator (USA) 131 – Diamond Necklace (USA) 99 **91**
(Unbridled's Song (USA) 125) [2015 104: 10.1g⁶ 10.2m Jun 3] tall mare: fairly useful
performer: stays 10.5f: acts on any turf going: tried in blinkers prior to 2015: often races
towards rear. *William Jarvis*

RASSELAS (IRE) 8 b.g. Danehill Dancer (IRE) 117 – Regal Darcey 67 (Darshaan **67 §**
133) [2015 77§: 8d⁴ 9.2d 8m* 7.9g 8m 9.3g 7.2g⁶ 7g Aug 6] compact gelding: fair
handicapper: won at Newcastle in June: stays 9.5f: acts on polytrack, firm and soft going:
wears headgear: hard to catch right. *Ruth Carr*

RAT CATCHER (IRE) 5 b.g. One Cool Cat (USA) 123 – Molly Marie (IRE) 75 (Fasliyev **60**
(USA) 120) [2015 57: t5.1f³ t5.1m² t5.1g* t5.1f² t5.1g 5m t5.1g t5.1f⁵ t5.1m t5.1f⁵ t5.1f²
t5.1f t5.1m* Dec 18] leggy gelding: modest handicapper: won at Wolverhampton in
February and December: stays 6f: acts on tapeta, best turf form on good going: wears
headgear. *Lisa Williamson*

RATEEL (IRE) 2 b.g. (Mar 25) Arcano (IRE) 122 – Spanish Pride (IRE) 78 (Night Shift **72**
(USA)) [2015 5m 7.1m 7m⁴ p8f³ p8f p8f* p5g Dec 11] good-topped gelding: fair
performer: won nursery at Chelmsford in October: left James Tate after: stays 1m: acts on
polytrack: sometimes in hood. *J. F. Levins, Ireland*

RATHAATH (IRE) 3 b.f. Oasis Dream 129 – Jamaayel 99 (Shamardal (USA) 129) [2015 **106**
87p: 6.1g⁶ 5.7g⁶ 5m 5g* 5.2s 5m³ Oct 3] useful performer: won handicaps at Bath (by neck
from Snap Shots) in July and Ascot (by 1½ lengths from Perfect Muse) in September: good
third in listed race at Ascot (¾ length behind Dutch Masterpiece) final start: stays 5.5f: acts
on firm going. *Brian Meehan*

RATHEALY (IRE) 4 b.g. Baltic King 120 – Baltic Belle (IRE) 86 (Redback 116) [2015 –
10m May 28] angular gelding: fair handicapper: stays 1¼m: acts on heavy going: tried in
hood/cheekpieces: fairly useful hurdler. *David Pipe*

RATHVALE 2 b.f. (Apr 15) Prime Defender 118 – Frabrofen 59 (Mind Games 121) [2015 **52** 6g⁵ t7.1f⁶ Nov 10] fourth foal: half-sister to 5f winner Tabiet (by Danroad): dam sprint maiden: showed a little ability in maidens at Ayr and Wolverhampton. *Ann Duffield*

RATTLING JEWEL 3 b.g. Royal Applause 124 – Mutoon (IRE) 64 (Erhaab (USA) 127) – [2015 87: 7g⁶ Jul 25] fairly useful form in 2014, well held only outing in 2015: best effort at 7f: acts on polytrack: sold £5,000 and joined J. J. Lambe. *Andrew Balding*

RAUCOUS 2 b.c. (Mar 23) Dream Ahead (USA) 133 – Shyrl 98 (Acclamation 118) [2015 **109** 5m* 6d* 6g³ 6s³ Sep 19] 100,000Y: well-made colt: fourth foal: dam 2-y-o 5f winner, also runner-up in Queen Mary Stakes: useful performer: won maiden at Sandown (by 3¾ lengths from A Momentofmadness) in June and minor event at Newmarket (by neck from Orvar) in July: subsequently third in Gimcrack Stakes at York (3¼ lengths behind Ajaya, third effort) and Mill Reef Stakes at Newbury (5¾ lengths behind Ribchester): stays 6f. *William Haggas*

RAVELIN (USA) 2 ch.f. (Feb 21) Congrats (USA) 118 – Rouwaki (USA) (Miswaki – (USA) 124) [2015 7d Oct 31] closely related to smart winner up to 1m (stayed 1¼m) Critical Moment (2-y-o 7f winner, by Aptitude) and half-sister to several winners, including very smart winner up to 7f (stays 9f) Rerouted (by Stormy Atlantic) and useful 1m winner (stayed 13f) Rattan (by Royal Anthem): dam maiden: 20/1, showed little in maiden at Newmarket. *Charles Hills*

RAVENHOE (IRE) 2 ch.g. (Mar 25) Bahamian Bounty 116 – Breathless Kiss (USA) 101 **89** (Roman Ruler (USA) 122) [2015 5d* 5m⁴ 5d* 5g² 6m⁴ 5f 5m⁴ 5m⁶ 5g⁴ 5m⁴ 5.5s 6s⁴ Oct 23] €25,000F, £16,000Y: first foal: dam 5f winner, including at 2 yrs: fairly useful performer: won minor events at Doncaster in March and Newcastle in April: best form at 5f: acts on firm and good to soft going: tried in blinkers. *Mark Johnston*

RAVENOUS 4 b.g. Raven's Pass (USA) 133 – Supereva (IRE) (Sadler's Wells (USA) 132) **84** [2015 10m³ p10g⁵ 8.1m³ 8s⁶ 8.5v⁴ 7g⁵ 8.3d⁶ p10g⁴ p8m Nov 19] compact, attractive gelding: fairly useful handicapper: stays 1¼m: acts on polytrack, good to firm and heavy going: tried in cheekpieces in 2015. *Luke Dace*

RAVENS QUEST 2 ch.c. (Mar 13) Raven's Pass (USA) 133 – Seradim 95 (Elnadim **70** (USA) 128) [2015 f8g⁶ p8g⁴ p8f⁶ Dec 21] fair form in maidens at Kempton and Chelmsford (did too much too soon) last 2 starts. *Hughie Morrison*

RAWAKI (IRE) 7 b.g. Phoenix Reach (IRE) 124 – Averami 68 (Averti (IRE) 117) [2015 **108** 116: 12m⁴ 12g² 14s⁵ 12v Oct 24] angular gelding: smart performer: creditable efforts in listed races at Ascot and Goodwood (second, beaten ½ length by Ayrad) in May: off 3 months, well below form both subsequent starts: stays 2m: acts on polytrack, good to firm and heavy going: tried in cheekpieces. *Andrew Balding*

RAW IMPULSE 3 b.c. Makfi 130 – Marika 103 (Marju (IRE) 127) [2015 8m⁶ 10.2d* **97 p** 10g² 9s³ 9.9g² Sep 30] 50,000Y: well-made colt: half-brother to several winners, including smart 5.5f/6f (including at 2 yrs) winner Sabratah (by Oasis Dream) and winner up to 1m (stayed 1¼m) Folly Lodge (2-y-o 7f winner, by Grand Lodge): dam 6f-1m winner: useful performer: won maiden at Nottingham in May: second in handicaps at Newmarket (½ length behind Memorial Day) and Salisbury (2¾ lengths behind Think Ahead): stays 1¼m: acts on good to soft going: sometimes slowly away: sent to Australia: remains with potential. *Clive Cox*

RAYAA 2 b.f. (Jun 4) Virtual 122 – Winsa (USA) 80 (Riverman (USA) 131) [2015 7m* 7m **69** Aug 15] £13,000Y: half-sister to several winners, including useful 2-y-o 7f/7.6f winner Mutahayya (by Peintre Celebre) and useful 1¼m winner (stayed 1½m) Elmaleeha (by Galileo): dam 1½m winner: fair form when winning maiden at Wetherby in July on debut: well held in nursery at Newmarket: should stay further than 7f. *David Evans*

RAYADOUR (IRE) 6 b.g. Azamour (IRE) 130 – Rayyana (IRE) 102 (Rainbow Quest **63** (USA) 134) [2015 68: 18s 16.1d³ 14.1v³ 14g⁴ 16.1m³ 15.8s Oct 27] modest handicapper: stays 2m: acts on good to firm and heavy going: often wears headgear: tried in tongue tie prior to 2015. *Micky Hammond*

RAYAK (IRE) 5 b.g. Invincible Spirit (IRE) 121 – Rayyana (IRE) 102 (Rainbow Quest **78** (USA) 134) [2015 –: 10m 10.2d* 10m 10.2v Oct 7] strong gelding: fair handicapper: won at Chepstow in August: best effort at 1¼m: best form on good to soft/soft going: tried in tongue tie in 2015: usually races nearer last than first. *Jonjo O'Neill*

RAYDARA (IRE) 3 b.f. Rock of Gibraltar (IRE) 133 – Raydiya (IRE) 102 (Marju (IRE) **108** 127) [2015 110p: 8g 9d⁴ 8g² 8g⁴ 8m Oct 3] rather leggy, close-coupled filly: useful performer: mainly creditable efforts in 2015 including at Leopardstown third/fourth starts, second in Desmond Stakes (¾ length behind Cougar Mountain) and fourth in Matron Stakes (5 lengths behind Legatissimo): should stay beyond 1m: acts on good to firm going. *M. Halford, Ireland*

RAYMOND'S DREAM 5 br.m. Lightning Lad – Spirit of Song (IRE) 75 (Selkirk (USA) — 129) [2015 p6g p6g Feb 26] compact mare: no form. *Phil McEntee*

RAY'S THE BAR 2 b.c. (Mar 18) Exceed And Excel (AUS) 126 – Cosmic Fire (FR) **101** (Dalakhani (IRE) 133) [2015 7f* 8.5f³ 8d Oct 30] €42,000Y, 37,000 2-y-o: useful-looking colt: third foal: half-brother to 1½m winner Cosmic City (by Elusive City): dam, 11.5f winner, half-sister to very smart 1¼m/11f winner Smoking Sun out of useful 7f/1m winner Burning Sunset: useful performer: won maiden at Ascot (by head from Bernie's Boy) in July: left Michael Bell, better form when third to Isotherm (beaten 2 necks) in Grade 3 Pilgrim Stakes at Belmont next time: eleventh of 14 to Hit It A Bomb in Breeders' Cup Juvenile Turf at Keeneland final outing: stays 8.5f. *Chad C. Brown, USA*

RAY WARD (IRE) 5 b.g. Galileo (IRE) 134 – Kentucky Warbler (IRE) 77 (Spinning **99** World (USA) 130) [2015 106: 10m 20f⁵ Jun 16] tall, useful-looking gelding: useful handicapper: in first-time cheekpieces, creditable 4 lengths fifth of 19 to Clondaw Warrior in Ascot Stakes at Royal Ascot: stays 21f: acts on polytrack and firm going: usually races towards rear. *David Simcock*

RAZIN' HELL 4 b.g. Byron 117 – Loose Caboose (IRE) 82 (Tagula (IRE) 116) [2015 68, — a81: 6f 6.1m Jun 11] fair handicapper: well held both starts in 2015: stays 6f: acts on fibresand and good to firm going. *Alan McCabe*

RAZOR WIND (IRE) 4 b.g. Dubawi (IRE) 129 – Tender Is Thenight (IRE) (Barathea **106** (IRE) 127) [2015 102: p10m² p10g⁶ 10.3m* Apr 25] good-topped gelding: useful handicapper: improved form when winning at Doncaster in April by neck from Ajman Bridge: stays 10.5f: acts on polytrack, tapeta and good to firm going: has been gelded. *Charlie Appleby*

RAZZLE DAZZLE 'EM 6 b.g. Phoenix Reach (IRE) 124 – Rasmani 40 (Medicean **41** 128) [2015 16m⁶ p10g Dec 30] unfurnished gelding: poor maiden: best effort at 2m: acts on good to firm going: tried in tongue tie prior to 2015. *Shaun Harris*

R BAR OPEN (FR) 2 b.g. (May 6) Orpen (USA) 116 – Bahama Love (USA) (Hennessy **62** (USA) 122) [2015 p7g p6g 6d Oct 11] modest maiden: best effort when seventh at Kempton second start. *Dean Ivory*

REACHFORMYHEART 3 ch.f. Phoenix Reach (IRE) 124 – Miles (Selkirk (USA) — 129) [2015 7m 7gᵘʳ Aug 28] no impact in maidens, jinked and unseated rider at start final outing: dead. *Shaun Harris*

REACH THE BEACH 6 ch.m. Phoenix Reach (IRE) 124 – Comtesse Noire (CAN) 67 — (Woodman (USA) 126) [2015 70: p16gᵖᵘ Jan 22] fair handicapper: pulled up only outing in 2015: stays 13f: acts on fibresand and any turf going: usually wears headgear/tongue tie: front runner/races prominently. *Brendan Powell*

READY (IRE) 5 ch.g. Elnadim (USA) 128 – Fusili (IRE) 100 (Silvano (GER) 126) [2015 **99** 88: t8.6f* p8g 7d t9.5g⁴ 10.2v* t9.5f² Nov 20] lengthy gelding: useful handicapper: won at Wolverhampton in February (subsequently left Garry Moss) and Nottingham in October: good second at Wolverhampton final outing: stays 1¼m: acts on polytrack, tapeta, good to firm and heavy going: wears headgear. *Ivan Furtado*

READY STEADY (USA) 2 b.f. (Mar 16) More Than Ready (USA) 120 – Medal Winner **58** (USA) (Medaglia d'Oro (USA) 129) [2015 p7g⁶ t6f Dec 22] 45,000Y: first foal: dam,1m winner, half-sister to US Grade 3 6.5f/7f winner Skip To The Stone: better effort in maidens (modest form) when sixth of 13 to Kakashan at Kempton. *Richard Hannon*

REAL ART 2 ch.f. (Feb 11) Dutch Art 126 – Castaway Queen (IRE) 76 (Selkirk (USA) — p 129) [2015 5m⁵ May 26] 75,000Y: closely related to winner up to 8.6f Tuscan King and 6f-1m winner Macchiara (both by Medicean) and half-sister to 5f/6f winner Quick Queen (by Singspiel): dam, maiden (stayed 1¼m), half-sister to useful winner up to 9f Mister Fire Eyes: 14/1, better for run when fifth in maiden at Leicester won by Jersey Breeze, not knocked about: will improve. *Kevin Ryan*

REAL DOMINION (USA) 2 b.c. (Feb 3) Cape Blanco (IRE) 130 – Real Doll (USA) **79 p** (Known Fact (USA) 135) [2015 7.1g⁴ 7g 8.1g³ Sep 11] $50,000F, 60,000Y: seventh foal: half-brother to 3 winners, including 6f-1m winner Cocico (by Henrythenavigator) and 1m/8.5f winner Barbies M (by Afleet Alex): dam 5f (minor Canadian stakes) winner: fair form: 3½ lengths third to Valitop in maiden at Sandown final start, hampered over 1f out: likely to stay beyond 1m: remains with potential. *Andrew Balding*

REALITY SHOW (IRE) 8 b.g. Cape Cross (IRE) 129 – Really (IRE) 97 (Entrepreneur **63**
123) [2015 72: p12g⁶ Dec 30] modest handicapper: stays 1½m: acts on polytrack and good
to firm going. *Shaun Harris*

REALIZE 5 b.g. Zafeen (FR) 123 – Relkida 76 (Bertolini (USA) 125) [2015 77, a90: p6g⁵ **96 +**
p7g* p7m* f7d² p8g* 8g t7.1g² 7m 7d³ p8f⁶ p8g* p7f² Dec 21] lengthy gelding: useful
performer: won handicaps at Lingfield (2, apprentice event first time) in February,
Kempton in April and Chelmsford (by 1¾ lengths from Mont Ras) in December: good
¾-length second to Cold As Ice in minor event at Chelmsford final outing: stays 1m: acts
on all-weather, firm and good to soft going: has worn cheekpieces: wears tongue tie.
Stuart Williams

REAL SMART (USA) 3 gr.f. Smart Strike (CAN) 121 – Rose Diamond (IRE) 103 **97**
(Daylami (IRE) 138) [2015 7.1d³ 7.1m³ t7.1f² p8g² p10m* p10g Dec 19] first foal: dam 6f
winner (including at 2 yrs) who stayed 1m out of high-class winner up to 7f (2-y-o 6f
winner) Tante Rose: useful performer: won maiden at Lingfield (by 1½ lengths from Fallen
For A Star) in November: 25/1, improved despite not seen to best effect when 4 lengths
seventh to Don't Be in listed race there final start, left poorly placed: stays 1¼m: acts on
polytrack: sometimes slowly away, often travels strongly. *David Lanigan*

REALT NA MARA (IRE) 12 b.g. Tagula (IRE) 116 – Dwingeloo (IRE) 83 (Dancing **–**
Dissident (USA) 119) [2015 7s⁵ p8f Nov 7] strong gelding: poor handicapper nowadays:
stays 7f: acts on polytrack, fibresand, good to firm and good to soft going: has worn
headgear. *Hughie Morrison*

REALTRA (IRE) 3 gr.f. Dark Angel (IRE) 113 – Devious Diva (IRE) 94 (Dr Devious **116**
(IRE) 127) [2015 94: 7m* 8m³ 7g⁵ 8f 8m* 7m* 8m⁵ Oct 3] lengthy filly: smart performer:
won handicap at Doncaster in May, listed race at Haydock in August and Sceptre Stakes
at Doncaster (by 2¼ lengths from Pelerin) in September: further improvement when

Mr Yasushi Kubota's "Realtra"

2¾ lengths fifth to Esoterique in Sun Chariot Stakes at Newmarket final start, left poorly placed and not clear run: left Richard Fahey after fourth start: stays 1m: acts on good to firm going. *Roger Varian*

REASSERT 3 b.g. Assertive 121 – Zonta Zitkala 76 (Daylami (IRE) 138) [2015 53: f8g³ **59** 8m Aug 10] modest maiden: best effort at 1m: acts on fibresand: tried in blinkers prior to 2015. *Roy Bowring*

REAVER (IRE) 2 b.c. (Feb 3) Sabiango (GER) 120 – Mattinata (Tiger Hill (IRE) 127 **56** [2015 7s p7g Nov 9] showed ability when seventh of 12 in maiden at Kempton latter start, though was better placed than most. *Eve Johnson Houghton*

REBEL COLLINS (IRE) 4 gr.g. Jeremy (USA) 122 – Million All Day (IRE) 57 **78** (Daylami (IRE) 138) [2015 p12g p12g⁴ p13.3f³ t16.5f⁶ f12g² t13.9g* Nov 27] fair performer: won maiden at Wolverhampton in November: possibly stays 16.5f: acts on all-weather. *David Evans*

REBELLE SOURIANTE 3 br.f. Cockney Rebel (IRE) 127 – Happy Omen (Warning – 136) [2015 t7.1m Feb 27] half-sister to 1m winner Kassuta and winner up to 1m Woteva (2-y-o 7.4f winner) (both by Kyllachy): dam once-raced half-sister to smart 2-y-o 6f winner (stayed 1m) First Trump: 7/1, badly needed experience when last of 7 in maiden at Wolverhampton, very slowly away. *Michael Appleby*

REBEL LIGHTNING (IRE) 2 gr.c. (Mar 17) Zebedee 113 – Bellechance 56 **75 p** (Acclamation 118) [2015 p6f³ t7.1f* Nov 20] £20,000Y: first foal: dam 2-y-o 6f winner: upped in trip, didn't need to improve to win maiden at Wolverhampton in November by neck from Zauffaly, pushed along 3f out then leading close home: will stay 1m: remains open to improvement. *Dave Morris*

REBELLIOUS GUEST 6 b.g. Cockney Rebel (IRE) 127 – Marisa (GER) (Desert Sun **101** 120) [2015 97, a105: p10g p10g p10f² p11g³ p10f⁶ 12m 10m May 25] useful-looking gelding: useful handicapper: stays 11f: acts on polytrack, good to firm and good to soft going: tried in cheekpieces. *George Margarson*

REBEL RAISER 2 b.g. (Feb 25) Kheleyf (USA) 116 – Trump Street 77 (First Trump 118) **68** [2015 6m 7m 6v⁴ Sep 2] fair form: 50/1, improved/seen to advantage when 2¼ lengths fourth to Marshal Dan Troop in maiden at Lingfield, having benefit of rail: has been gelded. *Dave Morris*

REBEL SMILE 3 b.f. Cockney Rebel (IRE) 127 – Velma Kelly 63 (Vettori (IRE) 119 **54** [2015 p7g 8.3m p7g⁵ t8.6g 8.3m t13.9g p10f³ p10g³ p10g⁴ 9.9d t9.5f⁴ Oct 3] third foal: half-sister to 1¼m winner Kitty Baxter (by Leporello): dam 9.5f winner: modest maiden: stays 1¼m: acts on polytrack: sometimes in eyeshields: often starts slowly, usually races in rear, often travels strongly. *Mark Usher*

REBEL STATE (IRE) 2 b.c. (Mar 2) Zoffany (IRE) 121 – Stately Princess 70 (Robellino **65** (USA) 127) [2015 7g 8g p7f Nov 12] lengthy colt: fair maiden: best effort when seventh at Chelmsford (4½ lengths behind Jufn) final start. *Dave Morris*

REBEL SURGE (IRE) 2 b.f. (Mar 22) Kodiac 112 – Face The Storm (IRE) 72 (Barathea **86** (IRE) 127) [2015 5m 5.1m² 5f 6g* 6g 6s² 6.5m⁴ 6g Sep 26] 35,000Y: angular filly: sister to 6f (including at 2 yrs) winner Kojak and half-sister to 3 winners, including smart winner up to 7f Roi de Vitesse (2-y-o 5f/6f winner, by Chineur) and winner up to 8.6f Cavort (2-y-o 6f winner, by Vettori): dam 2-y-o 1m winner: fairly useful performer: won maiden at Lingfield in July: in frame in 2 nurseries: out of depth final start: will stay 7f: acts on good to firm going. *Dave Morris*

REBEL YELL 3 b.g. Shamardal (USA) 129 – Solaia (USA) 110 (Miswaki (USA) 124) – [2015 8m 8d⁵ 7m 10g 10m Aug 18] angular gelding: no form: tried in visor. *Mick Channon*

RECEDING WAVES 2 b.c. (Apr 12) Dick Turpin (IRE) 127 – Welanga (Dansili 127) **102** [2015 5.7f³ 6m* 5.1m* 5.2m 6g 6d* 6m² Oct 3] 22,000Y: compact colt: fourth foal: half-brother to 2-y-o 5f winner Chasing Dreams (by Pastoral Pursuits) and 10.7f/11f winner Udogo (by Lucky Story): dam unraced half-sister to useful winner up to 1m Out of Reach: useful performer: won maiden at Redcar in June, minor event at Chepstow in July and nursery at Haydock (by short head from Donjuan Triumphant) in September: good second of 26 to Poet's Prize in quite valuable sales race at Newmarket final start: should stay 7f: acts on good to firm and good to soft going: usually responds generously to pressure: sold £80,000, sent to Qatar. *Richard Hannon*

RECENTLY ACQUIRED 3 b.g. Beat Hollow 126 – Acquisition 94 (Dansili 127) [2015 **91** 70p: f8g³ 12.3s 10m³ 10.3g Aug 15] fairly useful performer: won maiden at Southwell in April: third in handicap at Leicester in June: stays 1¼m: acts on fibresand and good to firm going: tried in blinkers in 2015. *Lady Cecil*

RECKLESS AMBITION (USA) 2 gr.c. (Feb 24) Exchange Rate (USA) 111 – Chapala 55
(USA) (Meadowlake (USA)) [2015 7d⁶ t8.6f 8.5m p6m³ p7f t7.1f Nov 30] modest maiden:
best effort at 6f: acts on polytrack: often in headgear. *John Quinn*

RECKLESS BLUE 3 ch.f. Bahamian Bounty 116 – Framboise (Diesis 133) [2015 –: –
t6g⁶ 6m Jun 17] no form. *Michael Easterby*

RECKLESS WAVE (IRE) 2 b.f. (Apr 27) Cape Cross (IRE) 129 – Fairybook (USA) 54 p
(El Prado (IRE) 119) [2015 8.3g p8f⁶ p8f⁴ Oct 28] 3,500Y: fourth foal: dam, 1¼m winner,
half-sister to very smart winner up to 12.5f Penglai Pavilion: modest maiden: best effort
when fourth at Chelmsford: likely to stay 1¼m: remains with potential. *Ed Walker*

RECOGNITION (IRE) 2 gr.c. (Feb 28) Rip Van Winkle (IRE) 134 – Bali Breeze (IRE) 68
85 (Common Grounds 118) [2015 7.1f⁶ 7m 8.5v³ 8m⁴ 8.3d t8.6f⁴ p10g⁵ Nov 26] good-
bodied colt: fair maiden: stays 8.5f: acts on good to firm and heavy going: tried in headgear.
Roger Varian

RECONCILLIATION 2 b.g. (Feb 8) Aqlaam 125 – Gretna 77 (Groom Dancer (USA) –
128) [2015 p8g Dec 16] 100/1, very green when well held in maiden at Kempton.
Ed Vaughan

RECORDER 2 ch.c. (Jan 28) Galileo (IRE) 134 – Memory (IRE) 112 (Danehill Dancer 111 p
(IRE) 117) [2015 7g³ 7d* 7d* Aug 19] lengthy, useful-looking colt: first foal: dam, 2-y-o
6f (including Albany and Cherry Hinton Stakes) winner who stayed 1m, half-sister to
useful 2-y-o 7f winner Remember Alexander: useful form: won maiden at Newmarket in
July and 10-runner Acomb Stakes at York in August, further marked improvement when
beating Bing Bang Bong by 1¼ lengths in latter (moved smoothly into contention): will
stay 1m: should go on progressing. *William Haggas*

RECTITUDE 4 b.f. Virtual 122 – Evasive Quality (FR) (Highest Honor (FR) 124) [2015 54
p10g Dec 30] modest maiden: stays 1¼m. *Henry Tett*

RED AGGRESSOR (IRE) 6 b.g. Red Clubs (IRE) 125 – Snap Crackle Pop (IRE) 87 79
(Statoblest 120) [2015 88: 6m 6g t7.1g⁵ Jun 3] tall, leggy gelding: fair handicapper: stays
7f: acts on polytrack, tapeta, good to firm and good to soft going: often wears headgear.
Clive Brittain

REDALANI (IRE) 5 b.m. Redback 116 – Zafaraya (IRE) 68 (Ashkalani (IRE) 128) 55
[2015 58: t6g⁴ t5.1m⁴ t5.1f 5s t5.1f t5.1f⁵ t5.1m² t6m² Dec 30] modest maiden: stays 6f:
acts on tapeta and good to firm going: often wears headgear: tried in tongue tie: front
runner/races prominently. *Alan Brown*

RED ARTIST 2 b.g. (Apr 21) Archipenko (USA) 127 – Danceatdusk (Desert Prince (IRE) 81
130) [2015 6m* 7f 6f⁶ Jul 10] 800F, €21,000Y, 82,000 2-y-o: rather unfurnished gelding:
fourth foal: half-brother to 3 winners, including 2-y-o 7f winner Ninita (by Storming
Home) and 2-y-o 5f winner Speed The Plough (by Kyllachy): dam unraced half-sister to
winner up to 1¼m Island Sound and 1m winner Fair Trade, both smart: fairly useful
performer: best effort when winning maiden at Newcastle (by length from Dawaa) in June:
will benefit from return to 7f: has been gelded. *Simon Crisford*

*Tattersalls Acomb Stakes, York—a smooth transition to pattern company
for the Queen's promising colt Recorder (No.10) who just needs to be kept up to his work to beat
the equally unexposed Bing Bang Bong; Cymric (No.3) edges out Humphrey Bogart for third*

RED AVENGER (USA) 5 b.g. War Front (USA) 119 – Emotional Rescue (USA) (Smart **102**
Strike (CAN) 121) [2015 106: p8g⁶ p10g⁶ 8m⁶ 7m 8m 8m* 8m 8m p10f Oct 8] well-made
gelding: useful handicapper: won at Newcastle (dead-heated with Eutropius) in June: left
Ed Dunlop after eighth start: stays 10.5f: acts on good to firm and good to soft going:
sometimes wears headgear: inconsistent. *Gary Moore*

RED BARON (IRE) 6 b.g. Moss Vale (IRE) 126 – Twinberry (IRE) (Tagula (IRE) 116) **111**
[2015 99: t5.1f 5v⁵ t5.1g* t5.1g* 5m² 5m* 5g² 5m* 5m 5s 5m² Sep 27] smart handicapper:
won at Wolverhampton (twice) in April, Thirsk in May and Musselburgh (by 1½ lengths
from Fast Track) in June: best form at 5f: acts on tapeta, soft and good to firm going: tried
in headgear prior to 2015: front runner, often travels strongly. *Eric Alston*

RED CADEAUX 9 ch.g. Cadeaux Genereux 131 – Artisia (IRE) (Peintre Celebre **121**
(USA) 137) [2015 124: 9.9g⁵ 9.9s² 9.9m 12f 13.3d³ 15.9gᵖᵘ Nov 3]
    Red Cadeaux's death from complications, following surgery on an injury
sustained on his fifth appearance in the Melbourne Cup at Flemington in November,
was a very sad conclusion to an amazing career. The bold way in which he was
campaigned over the years by his owner Ronnie Arculli and trainer Ed Dunlop
(whose stable is known for producing tough and genuine international performers)
saw him race in eight countries and accumulate £5,002,767 in total prize money
(Timeform uses exchange rates at the time of the individual race, rather than
calculating prize money at a fixed annual level as other publications do). Red
Cadeaux is the first British-trained horse to earn five million but, had he survived,
he would have spent his retirement in Australia rather than Britain, alongside other
leading retired racehorses at Living Legends, a tourist attraction near Melbourne.
Few horses can have become so popular by virtue of their performances in a race
they never won—Red Cadeaux was second three times in the Melbourne Cup,
beaten just a nose on the first occasion—and he has been buried at Flemington
racecourse. He also enjoyed particularly memorable days in Hong Kong, winning
the Hong Kong Vase in 2012, and in Dubai, where he was runner-up (earning his
single biggest purse) in the World Cup in 2013, but, in all, he won only seven of his
fifty-four races and over four fifths of his prize-money came in place money. The
only pattern race he won in Britain was the Yorkshire Cup in 2012 when he also
finished second in the Coronation Cup and third in the Hardwicke Stakes before
resuming his globe-trotting.
    Red Cadeaux's final season began with his being targeted at 'The
Championships' at the Sydney Autumn Carnival, a two-day event at Randwick
on consecutive Saturdays in April which has been revitalised to try to attract
international competition. His target was the Queen Elizabeth Stakes, the richest
race at the meeting and a race that is now Australia's most valuable weight-for-age
event (chosen in preference to the two-mile Sydney Cup) and he was warmed up in
the Australian Cup over a mile and a quarter at Flemington in mid-March, finishing
a staying-on fifth to Spillway. The Queen Elizabeth Stakes is also over a mile and a
quarter but overnight rain turned the going soft to put the emphasis more on stamina
and Red Cadeaux finished in his now-familiar runner-up spot, coming a good second
to Criterion after being stuck behind a wall of horses a furlong and a half out and not
getting a clear run until the winner had flown.
    After calling in at Hong Kong, where he ran below form in the Queen
Elizabeth II Cup, Red Cadeaux was returned to Britain for the summer when the
excellent posed portrait of him was taken which accompanies this essay. He ran
twice on home soil, well held in the Hardwicke Stakes and a respectable third in
the Geoffrey Freer Stakes at Newbury in August before setting off on his travels
again and that fateful final appearance in the Melbourne Cup. In mid-division on
the home turn, Red Cadeaux was beaten when pulled up inside the final furlong and
dismounted by Gerald Mosse (who was praised afterwards for his quick reaction),
his regular jockey in recent years though partnering him for the first time in the
latest season. It transpired that Red Cadeaux had sustained serious damage to the
sesamoid bone in his near-fore and he underwent surgery which at first looked as if
it was going to save him. Regular bulletins were published and pictures were issued
of him recuperating, but seventeen days after the surgery the decision was taken to
put him down.

The Hon R. J. Arculli's "Red Cadeaux"

Red Cadeaux (ch.g. 2006)	Cadeaux Genereux (ch 1985)	Young Generation (b 1976)	Balidar
			Brig O'Doon
		Smarten Up (ch 1975)	Sharpen Up
			L'Anguissola
	Artisia (IRE) (ch 2000)	Peintre Celebre (ch 1994)	Nureyev
			Peinture Bleue
		Almaaseh (b 1988)	Dancing Brave
			Al Bahathri

The lengthy Red Cadeaux has had essays in earlier editions of *Racehorses*, in which his pedigree has been covered. Odd as it may seem now, he was bred for speed, by the top-class sprinter Cadeaux Genereux out of Artisia, who didn't show much on the racecourse but was closely related to the smart five-furlong performer Almaty (Artisia is also a half-sister to Hong Kong champion Military Attack). Red Cadeaux showed in races like the Dubai World Cup and the Queen Elizabeth Stakes that he was capable of showing his form at a mile and a quarter, but he seemed ideally suited by the two miles of the Melbourne Cup (he was second in the Cesarewitch Trial over two and a quarter miles at Newmarket as a four-year-old and ran in the Cesarewitch itself, tried in blinkers for the only time in his career). He acted on polytrack, tapeta and any turf going. *Ed Dunlop*

RED CAPE (FR) 12 b.g. Cape Cross (IRE) 129 – Muirfield (FR) (Crystal Glitters (USA) **56** 127) [2015 61, a74: t5.1m t5.1g t6g 6.1d 6s⁴ 6g 16g³ 6.1m⁶ t7.1g 6m 16g* 6g 6s² 6g 6m 6g **a67** t6m t6m* Sep 25] big, rangy gelding: fair handicapper: won at Wolverhampton in July and September: stays 7f: acts on polytrack, tapeta, firm and soft going: often wears headgear: often races in rear: inconsistent. *Ruth Carr*

RED CARDINAL (IRE) 3 b.c. Montjeu (IRE) 137 – Notable (Zafonic (USA) 130) **83 p**
[2015 t12.2m² t12.2f² Oct 31] sixth foal: brother to smart 1¼m-12.5f winner (stayed 2½m)
Maria Royal: dam unraced: fairly useful form when runner-up in maidens at Wolverhampton
won by Bess of Hardwick and Good Judge: remains with potential. *David Simcock*

RED CHARMER (IRE) 5 b.g. Red Clubs (IRE) 125 – Golden Charm (IRE) 63 **84**
(Common Grounds 118) [2015 83: 8s 8.5m² 8m² 8.5m* 9.8m² 8m² 8.5m⁵ 8g 7.2g 8d² 8.5d
7v 8.3s Oct 28] fairly useful handicapper: won at Beverley in June: barely stays 1½m: acts
on good to firm and good to soft going: tried in cheekpieces prior to 2015: often races in
rear. *Ann Duffield*

RED COSSACK (CAN) 4 ch.g. Rebellion 117 – Locata (USA) (Stravinsky (USA) 133) **76**
[2015 64: p6f⁶ p6m³ p7g⁵ p7g⁵ 7m⁵ p7g* p8m³ Oct 28] fair handicapper: won at Kempton
in September: stays 1m: acts on polytrack: often wears headgear: tried in tongue tie in
2015: sometimes slowly away. *Paul Webber*

RED CURRENT 11 b.m. Soviet Star (USA) 128 – Fleet Amour (USA) (Afleet (CAN)) **§**
[2015 45§: p13.3g⁶ Feb 26] leggy, close-coupled mare: poor handicapper: stays 17f: acts
on all-weather, good to firm and heavy going: has worn headgear: has worn tongue tie: not
one to be interested in. *Michael Scudamore*

RED DRAGON (IRE) 5 b.g. Acclamation 118 – Delphie Queen (IRE) 104 (Desert Sun **66**
120) [2015 74, a81: p10d³ p10g Dec 15] smallish gelding: fair handicapper: stays 2m,
effective at shorter: acts on polytrack, soft and good to firm going. *Michael Blanshard*

RED DUBAWI (IRE) 7 ch.h. Dubawi (IRE) 129 – Maredsous (FR) 109 (Homme de Loi **116**
(IRE) 120) [2015 118: 8s 8g 8d³ 8g⁴ 8g* 8g Dec 13] smart performer: best effort of year
when winning Premio Vittorio di Capua at Milan (by 2 lengths from Bookrunner,
quickening to lead inside final 1f) in September: last of 14 behind Maurice in Hong Kong
Mile at Sha Tin final outing: won at 1¼m, raced at 1m in latter part of career: acted on soft
going: tried in cheekpieces: sometimes slowly away, often raced in rear: to stand at Haras
des Sablonnets, France, fee €2,000. *Frau E. Mader, Germany*

RED EXPLORER (USA) 5 b.h. Henrythenavigator (USA) 131 – Remote (USA) –
(Seattle Slew (USA)) [2015 58: f7g Mar 10] lengthy horse: handicapper, fairly useful at
best: stayed 7f: acted on polytrack, firm and soft going: sometimes in headgear: tried in
tongue tie: front runner/raced prominently: dead. *Heather Dalton*

RED FLUTE 3 ch.g. Piccolo 121 – Fee Faw Fum (IRE) (Great Commotion (USA) 123) **57**
[2015 –: p7m p6g t6f⁶ p5g* t5.1g p5m 5.3g 5.7f p6m p5g⁵ f7g p6f Dec 17] well-made
gelding: modest handicapper: won at Lingfield in March: best effort at 5f: acts on polytrack:
often wears visor: often in tongue tie in 2015: sometimes slowly away, usually races
towards rear. *Denis Quinn*

RED FOREVER 4 ch.g. Major Cadeaux 121 – Spindara (IRE) 64 (Spinning World **57**
(USA) 130) [2015 68: 5.1s⁵ 5d 5f 5g⁵ 5g⁵ 5m⁵ 5d 5d⁴ 5m³ 5s³ 5.1d⁵ t5.1m Dec 18] modest
handicapper: stays 5.5f: acts on tapeta, soft and good to firm going. *Alan Berry*

RED GALILEO 4 b.g. Dubawi (IRE) 129 – Ivory Gala (FR) 101 (Galileo (IRE) 134) **110**
[2015 113: p10g⁵ 12m⁶ 12m² 14g⁴ 12g⁴ 12g4⁶ 10.3m² 12g 12m⁵ Oct 3] useful-looking
gelding: smart performer: second in listed race at Ascot (3 lengths behind Agent Murphy)
in May and minor event at Doncaster (short head behind Elhaame) in September: stays
1½m: acts on polytrack, good to firm and good to soft going: tried in tongue tie prior to
2015: sold 155,000 gns, sent to UAE. *Ed Dunlop*

RED HARRY (IRE) 3 ch.g. Manduro (GER) 135 – Iktidar 80 (Green Desert (USA) 127) **79**
[2015 80p: 6g* 6g f6g t7.1f² Dec 11] fair performer: won maiden at Redcar in June: stays
7f: acts on tapeta, best turf form on good going: often races prominently. *Tom Tate*

RED HOT CHILLY (IRE) 2 ch.g. (Apr 19) Frozen Power (IRE) 108 – She's Got The –
Look (Sulamani (IRE) 130) [2015 6m 6m Jul 6] rather unfurnished gelding: well held in 2
maidens. *Joseph Tuite*

REDHOTRAVEN 3 ch.f. Raven's Pass (USA) 133 – Blast Furnace (IRE) 74 (Sadler's **56**
Wells (USA) 132) [2015 t8.6f⁵ p10g 10s⁶ Apr 7] first foal: dam, maiden (stayed 1m),
closely related to very smart winner up to 7f King Charlemagne and smart winner up to 7f
Meshaheer: modest maiden. *Tom Dascombe*

RED HOT SECRET 6 ch.m. Three Valleys (USA) 119 – Princess Miletrian (IRE) 80 –
(Danehill (USA) 126) [2015 t9.5g Jan 23] maiden, modest form at best: stays 7f: best form
on good going: tried in blinkers prior to 2015. *Dai Burchell*

RED HOUSE REBEL (IRE) 3 b.g. Cockney Rebel (IRE) 127 – Avril Rose (IRE) (Xaar **61 p**
132) [2015 –: 10s p10g 8d p8f³ Nov 7] modest maiden: best effort final start, shaping well:
stays 1m: acts on polytrack: tried in tongue tie in 2015: capable of better. *Stuart Williams*

RED INCA 7 ch.g. Pivotal 124 – Magicalmysterykate (USA) (Woodman (USA) 126) **70 §**
[2015 8.3s³ 10.2g³ 12g⁴ 10.1m² Jun 27] small, compact gelding: fair handicapper: stays
1½m: acts on good to firm and heavy going: tried in cheekpieces: sometimes slowly away,
usually races in rear: best treated with caution. *Brian Ellison*

RED INVADER (IRE) 5 b.g. Red Clubs (IRE) 125 – Tifariti (USA) (Elusive Quality **77**
(USA)) [2015 68: t8.6f t6g 7m 7d 5.1m⁴ 6m⁴ p5g* 5m* 5g³ 5d* 5g² p5f⁴ 5s³ 5.1g t5.1f³
Dec 21] angular gelding: fair handicapper: won at Chelmsford and Leicester (amateur) in
June and Carlisle (amateur) in August: stays 7f: acts on all-weather, good to firm and good
to soft going: tried in headgear. *Paul D'Arcy*

RED LEGACY 7 ch.m. Distant Music (USA) 126 – Emma May (Nicholas Bill 125) [2015 **–**
–: 8d Aug 1] no form. *Sean Regan*

RED MAJESTY 3 b.g. Acclamation 118 – Red Shareef (Marju (IRE) 127) [2015 53: p8f⁵ **56**
8g 8g Apr 26] modest maiden in Britain: stays 1m: acts on polytrack: sometimes wears
headgear: usually races prominently: sold 16,000 gns, sent to Qatar, where won 6f maiden
at Doha in October. *Kevin Ryan*

REDMANE 2 b.c. (Apr 5) Bahamian Bounty 116 – Miss Villefranche 69 (Danehill Dancer **65 p**
(IRE) 117) [2015 p7g t7.1m⁵ p7m⁶ Dec 31] 42,000F, 48,000Y: first foal: dam,
temperamental 8.6f winner, half-sister to smart 1m-1¾m winner (stayed 2m) Moyenne
Corniche out of useful winner up to 1¼m (2-y-o 7f winner) Miss Corniche: fair maiden:
best effort when sixth at Lingfield (5 lengths behind Shypen) final start: should do better.
Jamie Osborne

RED PALADIN (IRE) 5 b.g. Red Clubs (IRE) 125 – Alexander Goldmine 74 (Dansili **82**
127) [2015 81: 7m⁶ 7m⁵ 8g² 8g⁵ 8m* 8m³ 7.9g⁶ 7m 8.3m² 8d p8m³ Oct 21] fairly useful
handicapper: won at Doncaster in June: stays 1m: acts on polytrack, soft and good to firm
going: usually wears headgear: usually slowly away, often races in rear: not straightforward.
Kristin Stubbs

RED PERDITA (IRE) 3 b.f. Approve (IRE) 112 – Bakewell Tart (IRE) 92 (Tagula (IRE) **66**
116) [2015 68: p8g 7m⁴ 7m⁴ 8.1m⁵ 7d Jul 25] fair handicapper: stays 1m: acts on polytrack,
tapeta and good to firm going: sometimes in cheekpieces in 2015. *George Baker*

RED PIKE (IRE) 4 ch.g. Kheleyf (USA) 116 – Fancy Feathers (IRE) 79 (Redback 116) **107**
[2015 105: 6m⁴ 6m⁴ 7m 6g* 5g 6g 6s Oct 10] good-topped gelding: useful performer: won
minor event at Doncaster (by short head from Polybius) in August: stays 6f: acts on soft
and good to firm going: tried in visor prior to 2015: races prominently. *Bryan Smart*

RED PRIMO (IRE) 4 b.g. Iffraaj 127 – Testa Unica (ITY) (Nordance (USA)) [2015 –, **66**
a84: f7g⁵ f7g⁶ Jan 29] fair handicapper: stays 7f: acts on polytrack and fibresand.
Tony Coyle

RED REFRACTION (IRE) 5 b.h. Red Clubs (IRE) 125 – Dreamalot (Falbrav (IRE) **95**
133) [2015 97, a90: 8g⁴ 7m 8m 6m 6d 7g⁴ Jul 4] sturdy horse: useful performer: stays
1m: acts on polytrack, soft and good to firm going. *Richard Hannon*

RED RIVERMAN 7 b.g. Haafhd 129 – Mocca (IRE) 99 (Sri Pekan (USA) 117) [2015 **67**
9.9d⁴ 12d³ 8v⁶ Aug 28] fair maiden: stays 1½m: acts on good to firm and good to soft
going: sometimes in headgear: fairly useful hurdler/chaser. *Nigel Twiston-Davies*

RED ROBIN (SWE) 4 ch.g. Fraam 114 – Robin Lane 98 (Tenby 125) [2015 a8g* a8.6g⁴ **83**
8.3m a8g* a8.6g* a8.6g² a8g² a8.6g a8g² a8g³ Nov 15] fairly useful performer: won minor
events at Jagersro in April and July (2): well held in claimer at Leicester third start: stays
8.6f: acts on dirt and good to firm going. *Jessica Long, Sweden*

RED ROZEN 3 ch.f. Aqlaam 125 – Red Zinnia (Pivotal 124) [2015 7mᵖᵘ Aug 8] 7/2, **–**
pulled up in maiden at Redcar on debut: dead. *David Barron*

RED RUBLES (IRE) 3 b.g. Soviet Star (USA) 128 – Shantalla Peak (IRE) 68 (Darshaan **78**
133) [2015 82: p8f* 9g 10m⁶ Jun 19] big, strong gelding: fair performer: won maiden at
Lingfield in April: stays 1m: acts on polytrack, good to firm and good to soft going: often
wears hood. *Andrew Balding*

RED RUFFIAN (IRE) 2 ch.g. (Jan 24) Tamayuz 126 – Hatria (IRE) (Royal Applause **57**
124) [2015 p7g⁵ p8g Dec 16] showed a little ability in 2 maidens at Kempton. *Dean Ivory*

RED SEVENTY 6 b.g. Sakhee (USA) 136 – Dimakya (USA) 83 (Dayjur (USA) 137) **60**
[2015 55: p10m Feb 18] good-topped gelding: modest handicapper: stays 1¼m: acts on
polytrack, good to firm and heavy going: tried in headgear prior to 2015. *Sarah Humphrey*

RED SHADOW 6 b.m. Royal Applause 124 – Just A Glimmer 93 (Bishop of Cashel 122) **47**
[2015 61: t8.6f t6f⁵ f6g Dec 22] close-coupled mare: poor handicapper: stays 7f: acts on
polytrack, tapeta, good to firm and heavy going: often wears headgear. *Alan Brown*

RED SHUTTLE 8 b.g. Starcraft (NZ) 128 – Red Azalea 95 (Shirley Heights 130) [2015 **80** 86: t9.5g⁴ i9.5f⁴ t9.5f 10m⁵ t9.5g Sep 29] fairly useful handicapper: stays 1¼m: acts on polytrack, tapeta and firm going: tried in hood/tongue tie prior to 2015. *Andi Brown*

RED SKIPPER (IRE) 10 ch.g. Captain Rio 122 – Speed To Lead (IRE) 90 (Darshaan **–** 133) [2015 52: p12f⁶ t16.5g⁶ Apr 27] strong, compact gelding: fair at best, no form in 2015: stays 1½m: acts on polytrack, good to firm and heavy going: tried in headgear prior to 2015. *John O'Shea*

REDSTART 3 b.f. Cockney Rebel (IRE) 127 – Ecstasy 81 (Pursuit of Love 124) [2015 **106** 82p: 7m* 8f May 3] attractive filly: useful form: won Fred Darling Stakes at Newbury (by ¾ length from Jellicle Ball) in April: 16/1, possibly unsuited by conditions when well held in 1000 Guineas at Newmarket, seemed amiss: should stay at least 1m. *Ralph Beckett*

RED STRIPES (USA) 3 b.g. Leroidesanimaux (BRZ) 127 – Kaleidoscopic (USA) **93** (Fortunate Prospect (USA)) [2015 49, a60: f6s* f5g² p5m² p6g* t5.1m² p6f⁵ p5f t5.1g⁶ p5g² p6f³ p5g* 5f² p6g⁶ 6m p6f³ p6f³ f5g² p5g⁵ t5.1f⁶ p5m* Dec 27] fairly useful handicapper: won at Southwell in January and at Chelmsford in February, August and December (by ½ length from Waseem Faris): effective at 5f/6f: acts on polytrack, fibresand and firm going: often wears headgear. *Brian Meehan*

RED TEA 2 ch.f. (Mar 3) Sakhee (USA) 136 – Maimoona (IRE) 96 (Pivotal 124) [2015 **68** 7.5m² 6d³ t7.1f⁵ Nov 20] £4,000Y: fourth foal: half-sister to winner up to 1m Sahra Al Khadra (2-y-o 7f winner, by Green Desert): dam 5f/6f winner: fair maiden: left Tony Coyle after second start. *Peter Hiatt*

RED TIDE (IRE) 4 gr.g. Tamayuz 126 – Rectify (IRE) (Mujadil (USA) 119) [2015 77: **72** f6d* f7g f6s 6sᵖᵘ May 9] fair handicapper: won at Southwell in January: stays 7.5f: acts on fibresand and good to firm going: often wears cheekpieces: front runner/races prominently. *Marjorie Fife*

RED TORNADO (FR) 3 ch.g. Dr Fong (USA) 128 – Encircle (USA) (Spinning World **94** (USA) 130) [2015 97: 9.9d 11.5s⁴ 11.1s³ 8.9s⁵ Oct 6] sturdy gelding: fairly useful performer: third in listed race at Hamilton (12 lengths behind Medrano) in July: stays 9f: acts on soft going. *Harry Dunlop*

RED TOUCH (USA) 3 b.g. Bluegrass Cat (USA) 120 – Touchnow (CAN) (Pleasant Tap **76** (USA)) [2015 72: t8.6g* t7.1g⁶ t8.6g³ 10g⁴ 10.2m p10g 8m³ Aug 8] fair performer: won maiden at Wolverhampton in January: stays 1¼m: acts on polytrack and tapeta: tried in headgear in 2015. *Tony Coyle*

RED TYCOON (IRE) 3 b.g. Acclamation 118 – Rugged Up (IRE) (Marju (IRE) 127) **89** [2015 73: t6f² t7.1m⁵ 6g² 6g* 6d² 6m⁴ 6m 7v² t7.1f⁶ Nov 16] neat gelding: fairly useful performer: won maiden at Ayr in April: second in handicaps at Haydock and Catterick: stays 7f: acts on heavy going: blinkered once in 2014: in tongue tie last 2 starts. *David Barron*

RED UNICO (IRE) 3 b.g. Vale of York (IRE) 117 – Testa Unica (ITY) (Nordance (USA)) **76** [2015 –: f7g² f8s³ f8s³ f7d⁶ f8g² f8s³ 8g² 8s 10g³ 8g⁴ p10m⁴ 7m* 7.4d² 7g² t8.6g⁴ p10f³ p10f⁶ Oct 24] fair handicapper: won at Catterick in August: left David C. Griffiths after eleventh start: stays 1¼m: acts on polytrack, tapeta and good to firm going: often in headgear in 2015. *Michael Appleby*

RED VERDON (USA) 2 ch.c. (Mar 24) Lemon Drop Kid (USA) 131 – Porto Marmay **85 p** (IRE) 92 (Choisir (AUS) 126) [2015 t8.6m² t8.6g* Dec 5] $85,000Y, 90,000 2-y-o: second foal: dam, winner up to 6f (2-y-o 5f winner), half-sister to useful winner up to 7f Orpsie Boy: fairly useful form: promising debut at Wolverhampton in November, then won maiden there by head from Vizier, showing good attitude: remains open to improvement. *Ed Dunlop*

REDVERS (IRE) 7 br.g. Ishiguru (USA) 114 – Cradle Brief (IRE) (Brief Truce (USA) **91** 126) [2015 108: 7m 6m 7m 7m⁵ 7g Sep 26] good-topped gelding: fairly useful handicapper: stays 7.5f: acts on polytrack, firm and soft going: usually wears headgear. *Ed Vaughan*

RED WARRIOR (IRE) 5 ch.h. Iffraaj 127 – Wiolante (GER) (Lagunas) [2015 94: 10m² **88** 10.1d⁶ 10m 10m² 10.3m⁴ 8.3m² 10m⁵ i9.5g Sep 29] good-topped horse: fairly useful handicapper: stays 1¼m: acts on polytrack and good to firm going: sometimes in cheekpieces: usually races towards rear. *Ismail Mohammed*

RED WORDS (IRE) 3 b.f. Intikhab (USA) 135 – Literacy (USA) 74 (Diesis 133) [2015 **66** 66: 8m⁴ 10m 8d⁶ p8g p8g² 8g⁴ p8g² p8g² p8g² p8g Dec 11] fair maiden: left George Margarson after second start: stays 1m: acts on polytrack, best turf form on good going: tried in cheekpieces in 2015: may not be entirely straightforward. *Miss Elizabeth Doyle, Ireland*

REETAJ 3 b.g. Medicean 128 – Bakhoor (IRE) 88 (Royal Applause 124) [2015 86p: f8d² **81**
p8g² 9.9m² 10.3d³ 12s³ Oct 19] fairly useful maiden: stays 1½m: acts on polytrack,
fibresand, soft and good to firm going: temperament under suspicion: has been gelded.
Peter Chapple-Hyam

REET PETITE (IRE) 3 b.f. Fast Company (IRE) 126 – Damjanich (IRE) 78 (Mull of **–**
Kintyre (USA) 114) [2015 43: t6g Apr 18] poor maiden: stays 8.5f: acts on tapeta, good to
firm and good to soft going: has worn headgear: usually races nearer last than first.
James Evans

REFLATION 3 b.g. Stimulation (IRE) 121 – Miss Poppy 68 (Averti (IRE) 117) [2015 66: **72**
p7m⁴ p8m⁶ 6.1m² 5m⁵ 6g⁴ 6.1m 5.7m⁶ 6.1v* 6g³ 5.1d Oct 14] fair performer: won maiden
at Chepstow in August: stays 6f: acts on good to firm and heavy going: tried in headgear in
2015: often races prominently. *Richard Hannon*

REFLECTION 4 ch.f. Major Cadeaux 121 – River Song (USA) (Siphon (BRZ) 130) **–**
[2015 –: 8f⁶ 7.2d 8d 7.1m Jul 16] poor maiden: stays 1m: acts on firm going: has worn
headgear: often races towards rear. *Brian Baugh*

REFLEKTOR (IRE) 2 ch.g. (Apr 10) Bahamian Bounty 116 – Baby Bunting 63 **85**
(Wolfhound (USA) 126) [2015 f5gᵖᵘ 6d⁶ t6f⁶ 6s* Oct 26] €31,000F, £45,000Y: brother to
3 winning sprinters, including to Bahamian Babe and Victorian Bounty and half-brother to 6f
winner (including at 2 yrs) Nova Champ (by Intikhab): dam, sprint maiden, half-sister to
smart sprinter Atraf: stayed 7f: fairly useful form: 16/1, much improved when winning
maiden at Leicester in October by 3½ lengths from Hillside Dream, making all: stays 6f.
Tom Dascombe

REFRESHESTHEPARTS (USA) 6 ch.m. Proud Citizen (USA) 122 – St Francis Wood **56**
(USA) 95 (Irish River (FR) 131) [2015 72: p10g Jan 3] good-topped mare: modest
handicapper: stayed 1¼m: acted on polytrack and tapeta: had worn tongue tie: dead.
George Baker

REFULGENCE (FR) 2 b.f. (Feb 27) Azamour (IRE) 130 – Ares Flight (IRE) (Hernando **62**
(FR) 127) [2015 p6g⁵ p7g p7g 6v² 6d⁵ 7s Oct 26] first foal: dam 2-y-o 6f winner: modest
maiden: stays 6f: acts on polytrack and heavy going: in hood last 3 starts. *Marco Botti*

REFUSE COLETTE (IRE) 6 ch.m. Refuse To Bend (IRE) 128 – Roclette (USA) 76 **81**
(Rock of Gibraltar (IRE) 133) [2015 87: p8f⁵ p6f⁶ f6g 6m⁵ 7.6d² 7m⁴ 6m⁵ p8g³ 6m⁵ 7m **a70**
6.1d* p6g³ 6g 6g⁵ 8g 7d⁶ Oct 31] rather leggy mare: fairly useful handicapper: won at
Nottingham in August: stays 1m: acts on soft and good to firm going: sometimes in
headgear prior to 2015: usually races prominently. *Mick Quinn*

REGAL BOND 4 b.g. Misu Bond (IRE) 114 – Bond Royale 89 (Piccolo 121) [2015 t7.1g **56**
t6f⁴ t6g⁵ 7m 6g t7.1g⁴ f7d 6m Aug 29] modest maiden: stays 7f: acts on tapeta: often in
visor: often races lazily. *Geoffrey Oldroyd*

REGAL DAN (IRE) 5 b.g. Dark Angel (IRE) 113 – Charlene Lacy (IRE) 77 (Pips Pride **98**
117) [2015 92: 7g² 7.1g² 7.2s⁵ 7m 7m* 7f⁴ 7m³ 6m² 7.2g 6g Sep 26] small gelding: useful
handicapper: won at York (by length from Mehdi) in June: good neck second of 20 to Rex
Imperator at Doncaster in September: stays 7f: acts on polytrack, firm and good to soft
going: tried in visor: often races prominently. *David O'Meara*

REGAL GAIT (IRE) 2 b.g. (May 2) Tagula (IRE) 116 – Babylonian 66 (Shamardal **– p**
(USA) 129) [2015 6g Jul 27] £45,000Y: second foal: half-brother to winner up to 7f Pull
The Plug (2-y-o 5f/6f winner, by Sleeping Indian): dam lightly-raced half-sister to smart
11f/1½m winner Counterpunch out of useful 1m-1½m winner Evil Empire: 12/1, badly
needed experience when last of 15 in maiden at Windsor: should do better. *Henry Candy*

REGAL GALAXY 2 b.f. (Mar 22) Royal Applause 124 – Astromancer (USA) 62 (Silver **–**
Hawk (USA) 123) [2015 7m 7.5g 6m p10f Oct 22] 2,000Y: lengthy filly: seventh foal:
half-sister to 11.5f winner Cotton Grass (by Medicean): dam 1¾m winner who stayed easy
2m: no form. *Mark H. Tompkins*

REGALITY (IRE) 2 b.f. (Apr 3) Lord Shanakill (USA) 121 – Regalline (IRE) 79 (Green **72**
Desert (USA) 127) [2015 6m p7g³ 7g³ 8s² Oct 15] third foal: half-sister to useful 7f
(including at 2 yrs) winner Reglisse (by Verglas): dam, 1m winner, closely related to smart
winner up to 8.4f Recharge out of very smart winner up to 10.5f (2-y-o 1m winner)
Rebelline: fair maiden: stays 1m: sold 45,000 gns, sent to Qatar. *William Haggas*

REGAL MISS 3 b.f. Royal Applause 124 – Pretty Miss 85 (Averti (IRE) 117) [2015 6m⁴ **72**
5m² 5.7f⁴ p6g² p6f⁴ f6f⁴ Nov 6] smallish filly: third foal: dam, 5f winner, half-sister to
high-class 5f winner Kyllachy: fair maiden: stays 6f: acts on polytrack and good to firm
going. *Patrick Chamings*

REGAL MISSILE (IRE) 3 b.g. Royal Applause 124 – Leenane (IRE) (Grand Lodge **66** (USA) 125) [2015 77: 8g⁵ 8g 8d³ 7m 10.4g 7.9d Sep 15] fair maiden: stays 1m: acts on heavy going: often in cheekpieces in 2015. *Mark Walford*

REGAL MONARCH 2 b.g. (Jan 31) Notnowcato 128 – Regal Fairy (IRE) (Desert King **69** (IRE) 129) [2015 f7g⁴ f8g⁴ t9.5f⁶ Dec 14] fair maiden: fourth to Davey Boy at Southwell in November on debut: below that form over longer trips subsequently. *Mark Johnston*

REGAL PARADE 11 ch.g. Pivotal 124 – Model Queen (USA) 76 (Kingmambo (USA) **91** 125) [2015 95: p6f³ p6g² p6m³ 6g 6m² 6g³ 6v⁵ 6g 6g t7.1f t7.1f Nov 16] strong, lengthy gelding: fairly useful handicapper: below form after sixth start: has form at 9f, races at shorter: acts on polytrack, fibresand and any turf going: wears tongue tie. *Charlie Wallis*

REGAL PARK (IRE) 8 b.g. Montjeu (IRE) 137 – Classic Park 115 (Robellino (USA) **62** 127) [2015 68: 16m 15.8s⁴ 14.1m³ May 21] lengthy gelding: modest handicapper: stays 2m: acts on soft and good to firm going: tried in cheekpieces prior to 2015. *Miss Imogen Pickard*

REGAL RESPONSE (IRE) 2 b.c. (Feb 2) Acclamation 118 – Qalahari (IRE) 92 (Bahri **74 p** (USA) 125) [2015 6g⁴ 6s² Oct 16] 52,000F, €105,000Y: first foal: dam 2-y-o 5.7f winner who stayed 1m: improved from debut when 2½ lengths second to Explosive Power in maiden at Redcar: should progress further. *Michael Dods*

REGAL WAYS (IRE) 3 b.f. Royal Applause 124 – Step This Way (USA) 93 (Giant's **77** Causeway (USA) 132) [2015 68: p10g² 8.3s 9.8g² 10.4g 10.3g⁶ 8m 11.1g³ 12.1m* 12v⁵ Oct 17] unfurnished filly: fair handicapper: won at Hamilton in September: stays 1½m: acts on polytrack, good to firm and heavy going: signs of temperament. *Mark Johnston*

REGARDS (IRE) 3 ch.g. Shamardal (USA) 129 – Truly Yours (IRE) (Barathea (IRE) **68** 127) [2015 t7.1g⁵ p7g³ p8g² 8.3m Apr 13] fair maiden: stays 8.5f. *Charlie Appleby*

REGGIE BOND 5 ch.g. Monsieur Bond (IRE) 120 – Triple Tricks (IRE) 70 (Royal **71 +** Academy (USA) 130) [2015 76: t8.6f* t8.6f⁴ 8m 8.5g t8.6g* 8.9g t8.6g* t8.6m⁵ t8.6f Nov 3] fairly useful handicapper: won at Wolverhampton in January, June and August: stays 8.5f: acts on polytrack, tapeta, best turf form on good going: wears headgear: sent to Saudi Arabia. *Geoffrey Oldroyd*

REGINALD CLAUDE 7 b.g. Monsieur Bond (IRE) 120 – Miller's Melody 86 (Chief **66** Singer 131) [2015 68: p6m p6f p6g t6g* 6m² 6f⁶ 6m 6d* p6g³ 16m² t6g⁵ t6f⁴ p7g t7.1g Dec 4] good-topped gelding: fair handicapper: won at Wolverhampton in March and Windsor (apprentice) in July: stays 7f: acts on polytrack, tapeta, soft and good to firm going: tried in headgear prior to 2015: often races towards rear. *Mark Usher*

REGINA PHALANGE (IRE) 2 b.f. (Feb 5) Clodovil (IRE) 116 – Campbellite (Desert **–** Prince (IRE) 130) [2015 7s 6d Oct 26] 7,500F, 5,500Y: sixth foal: closely related to 7f winner Choral Clan (by Oratorio) and half-sister to 2-y-o 7f winner Martin Mount (by Ramonti): dam unraced: well held in claimer and maiden at Redcar. *Declan Carroll*

REGULATION (IRE) 6 br.g. Danehill Dancer (IRE) 117 – Source of Life (IRE) **102** (Fasliyev (USA) 120) [2015 105: p8m³ p8g³ 8.5g⁵ p11g⁶ Dec 3] useful handicapper: third at Lingfield (2 lengths behind Halation) and Kempton (length behind Realize): stays 1¼m: acts on polytrack, soft and good to firm going: tried in headgear: fairly useful hurdler. *Neil King*

REHEARSE (IRE) 2 b.c. (Mar 3) Big Bad Bob (IRE) 118 – And Again (USA) 83 (In The **– p** Wings 128) [2015 7.1s⁴ Sep 16] €170,000Y: third foal: half-brother to 1½m/12.5f winner Dylanelle (by Dylan Thomas): dam, 1¼m-1½m winner, half-sister to very smart 9f winner Olden Times out of useful 6f winner Garah: 13/2, stiff task when well-held last of 4 to Cymric in minor event at Sandown: should do better. *Andrew Balding*

REIGNING 3 b.f. Sakhee's Secret 128 – Raindrop 59 (Primo Dominie 121) [2015 –: 8m⁴ **–** 8f⁴ 11s⁴ 9.9v Oct 6] poor maiden. *Michael Blanshard*

REINFORCED 2 ch.g. (Feb 2) Equiano (FR) 127 – Fonnie (IRE) 58 (Barathea (IRE) 127) **50** [2015 5.9s⁶ 6g 6s Oct 16] modest form at best in maidens. *Michael Dods*

REJAAH 3 b.f. Authorized (IRE) 133 – Dhan Dhana (IRE) 79 (Dubawi (IRE) 129) [2015 **81** p10g* 11.8m⁴ 12m⁶ Jul 6] first foal: dam, 9.7f/1¼m winner who barely stayed 1½m, half-sister to useful dam of Middle Park Stakes winner Charming Thought: fairly useful performer: best effort when winning maiden at Lingfield in May: stays 1½m: sold £23,000 in August and joined Nigel Hawke. *William Haggas*

REKDHAT (IRE) 4 b.f. Shamardal (USA) 129 – Taarkod (IRE) (Singspiel (IRE) 133) **103**
[2015 98p: 8m³ 8d⁴ 8m² 8g² p8g Oct 29] sturdy filly: useful performer: third in handicap at
Salisbury (2 lengths behind Lightning Spear), and second in handicap at Newbury (short
head behind Forest Maiden) and Istanbul Trophy at Veliefendi (½ length behind Local
Time): worth a try at 1¼m: acts on polytrack and firm going: sometimes wears hood: often
races towards rear. *Roger Varian*

RELATED 5 b.g. Kheleyf (USA) 116 – Balladonia 103 (Primo Dominie 121) [2015 102: **104**
p7f⁶ p7f⁶ p6d⁴ p6g* 6f⁴ 7f⁴ 6m Aug 1] useful handicapper: won at Kempton in March:
good fourth to Interception in Wokingham Stakes at Royal Ascot and to Rene Mathis in
Bunbury Cup at Newmarket fifth/sixth starts: better than result when ninth of 27 to Magical
Memory in Stewards' Cup at Goodwood final start, making running in less-favoured
group: stays 1m, races at 6f/7f nowadays: acts on polytrack and firm going: wears headgear:
front runner/races prominently: sold 65,000 gns. *David Simcock*

RELIGHT MY FIRE 5 ch.g. Firebreak 125 – Making Music 72 (Makbul 104) [2015 79: **77**
7.5g⁵ 7.5m* 7.5f⁴ 7.5m⁵ 8.5s² 8m 8d 7.5g 8m⁶ 7.5d⁵ Sep 22] fair handicapper: won at
Beverley in June: stays 8.5f: acts on firm and soft going: usually wears headgear. *Tim
Easterby*

REMAAN 2 ch.c. (Apr 22) Footstepsinthesand 120 – Scorn (USA) 84 (Seeking The Gold **66**
(USA)) [2015 7m 6g⁶ 6g⁵ 6m 7f.1f⁶ p7g f8g Dec 29] workmanlike colt: fair maiden: stays
7f: acts on tapeta: tried in eyeshields: usually races towards rear. *Stuart Williams*

REMARKABLE 2 b.c. (Mar 25) Pivotal 124 – Irresistible 98 (Cadeaux Genereux 131) **– p**
[2015 7d Sep 21] brother to several winners, including 6f winner Watchable and 7f
(including at 2 yrs) winner Infallible (both smart) and useful 7f (including at 2 yrs) winner
Thrill: dam 6f winner, including at 2 yrs: 11/2, some encouragement when well held in
maiden at Leicester, unable to sustain effort and not knocked about: sure to progress.
John Gosden

REMBRANDT 3 b.c. Dutch Art 126 – Authoritative (Diktat 126) [2015 66p: 8m⁴ 7g⁴ 9m **86**
8m³ p8g⁴ 8g 10g⁶ 10.2s² a8.5g 9.7g 10.4d⁶ Nov 9] heavy-topped colt: fairly useful maiden:
left Richard Hannon after eighth start: best form at 1m: acts on polytrack and good to firm
going: hung badly left eighth outing. *A. de Royer Dupre, France*

REMBRANDT VAN RIJN (IRE) 4 b.g. Peintre Celebre (USA) 137 – Private Life (FR) **110**
(Bering 136) [2015 90§: t12.2g* 10.3g* 10m* 10.4m* 10d Aug 29] compact gelding:
smart performer: won maiden at Wolverhampton in April and handicaps at Chester in May,
Sandown in June and Haydock (completed four-timer, by 2 lengths from The Character) in
August: excuses when seventh of 8 in Winter Hill Stakes at Windsor final start, having
hopeless task from position: stays 1½m: acts on tapeta and good to firm going: often races
in rear, often travels strongly: not straightforward (has reacted badly to whip): sold 400,000
gns, sent to UAE. *David Lanigan*

REMEDIO (IRE) 5 b.g. Ramonti (FR) 126 – Cant Hurry Love (Desert Prince (IRE) 130) **–**
[2015 f11g⁵ f12g⁴ 11.9g 10.1m Jun 6] no form: tried in blinkers. *Andrew Crook*

REMEMBERANCE DAY 4 ch.f. Major Cadeaux 121 – Today's The Day 72 (Alhaarth **76**
(IRE) 126) [2015 77: t7.1g² p7g² p7f³ 7m³ 7m t7.1f⁵ p8m⁴ p8g t7.1f Dec 21] fair
handicapper: stays 1m: acts on polytrack and good to firm going: wears tongue tie. *Les Eyre*

REMEMBER ME 2 b.f. (Feb 12) Acclamation 118 – Forgotten Me (IRE) (Holy Roman **71 p**
Emperor (IRE) 125) [2015 6d 7s p6g³ Sep 30] 55,000Y: strong, compact filly: first foal:
dam, unraced, closely related to useful winner up to 1m Dimenticata: fair form: 33/1,
improved when 6¼ lengths third to Bounce at Kempton, keeping on and never nearer:
should prove suited by a return to 7f: should do better still. *Hughie Morrison*

REMEMBER ROCKY 6 ch.g. Haafhd 129 – Flower Market 68 (Cadeaux Genereux **69**
131) [2015 71: 10g³ 10.1d³ 11.1d 10s² 7.9m 9.3d³ 9.2g Aug 20] fair handicapper: stays
1¼m: acts on soft and good to firm going: usually wears headgear: often races prominently.
Lucy Normile

REMOTE 5 b.h. Dansili 127 – Zenda 115 (Zamindar (USA) 116) [2015 9.9g⁵ May 23] **–**
strong, useful-looking horse: smart performer in 2013: off 23 months, 6/4, shaped well for
long way when 11¼ lengths fifth of 6 to The Corsican in listed race at Goodwood on only
outing in 2015, weakening final 1f (reportedly bled): stays 1¼m: acts on firm going: sent to
Argentina. *John Gosden*

RENEGE 2 ch.f. (Feb 14) Firebreak 125 – Today's The Day 72 (Alhaarth (IRE) 126) [2015 **–**
t7.1g Dec 4] £5,000Y: fourth foal: half-sister to 7f winner Rememberance Day (by Major
Cadeaux): dam, maiden (stayed 7f), half-sister to useful 2-y-o 7f/1m winner Day of
Conquest: 50/1, well held in maiden at Wolverhampton. *Ed McMahon*

*bet365 Bunbury Cup, Newmarket—Rene Mathis makes it three wins in the last five years in this race
for trainer Richard Fahey, who also saddles the third home, 2014 winner Heaven's Guest (blaze);
runner-up One Word More (far side) and Related (near rail) are the others to make the frame*

RENE MATHIS (GER) 5 ch.g. Monsieur Bond (IRE) 120 – Remina (GER) (Erminius 113
(GER) 111) [2015 108: 7g 7.6v² 7g⁵ 6f 7f* 7d 7m 7s* 6g 7m 8d Oct 17] workmanlike
gelding: smart handicapper: won 17-runner Bunbury Cup at Newmarket in July by length
from One More Word and 19-runner event at Goodwood in August by 1½ lengths from
Jallota: stays 7.5f: acts on polytrack and any turf going: often races prominently.
Richard Fahey

RENEWING 4 b.g. Halling (USA) 133 – Electric Society (IRE) 107 (Law Society (USA) 65
130) [2015 –: t12.2m⁵ t12.2g² t13.9g⁵ 13.1m p16g t12.2g t12.2m p12g Dec 15] fair
maiden: best effort at 1½m: acts on tapeta: sometimes wears headgear. *Roy Brotherton*

RENFREW STREET 2 br.f. (Mar 23) Iffraaj 127 – Malpas Missile (IRE) 78 (Elusive 80
City (USA) 117) [2015 8s² 7.5g* 7g⁴ 7g p7g⁴ Nov 4] 37,000F, 38,000Y: lengthy, angular
filly: first foal: dam 2-y-o 6f winner: fairly useful performer: won maiden at Beverley (by
4½ lengths from Powder Snow) in September: stays 7.5f: best form on good going.
Mark Johnston

RENNETI (FR) 6 b.g. Irish Wells (FR) 122 – Caprice Meill (FR) (French Glory 118) 100
[2015 14d 18g⁴ Oct 10] strong gelding: useful handicapper: trained in France in 2012: only
second run on Flat since when good 1¼ lengths fourth of 34 to Grumeti in Cesarewitch
Handicap at Newmarket, keeping going very well considering he raced freely for long way:
stays 2¼m: acts on soft going: smart hurdler. *W. P. Mullins, Ireland*

RENNIE MACKINTOSH (IRE) 3 b.g. Excellent Art 125 – Mac Melody (IRE) 91 68
(Entrepreneur 123) [2015 65: f7d* t6g³ p6g⁵ 8d p10f⁴ 11.6d⁵ p10g p7g p12g Dec 19] fair
handicapper: won at Southwell in February: left Mark Johnston after sixth start: stays
1½m: acts on all-weather and good to soft going. *John Bridger*

RENOUNCE (IRE) 3 b.c. Elnadim (USA) 128 – Relinquished 80 (Royal Applause 124) 86
[2015 p6m² p6f* p6g⁵ Dec 28] 37,000Y: second foal: dam, 2-y-o 7f/7.4f winner, half-sister
to smart 7f/1m winner Green Line: fairly useful performer: best effort when winning
maiden at Lingfield (by 1¼ lengths from Picket Line) in November: raced only at 6f.
Jeremy Noseda

REPEAT OFFENDER (IRE) 2 b.g. (Apr 4) Thewayyouare (USA) 117 – Dame 78
Rochelle (IRE) 49 (Danehill Dancer (IRE) 117) [2015 t6g* 6.5m³ p6g³ 6f 7.5g⁶ p8g⁴ 8.3d
p8.9g³ p8g⁶ Dec 2] sturdy gelding: fair performer: won minor event at Wolverhampton in
June: probably stays 7.5f: acts on polytrack, tapeta and good to firm going: tried in blinkers.
J. S. Moore

REPECHAGE (FR) 4 ch.f. Gold Away (IRE) 125 – Acola (FR) 59 (Acatenango (GER) 62
127) [2015 t7.1g⁴ 6m 7m⁶ p8g 8.3m 10.2m³ t9.5g 10.2d² 11.9s⁶ p10g Dec 7] modest
handicapper: stays 10.5f, often over shorter recently: acts on polytrack, tapeta and good to
soft going: usually in cheekpieces in 2015: often races towards rear. *Robert Cowell*

REPETITION 5 b.g. Royal Applause 124 – Uno 81 (Efisio 120) [2015 94: f7d⁶ f7g 7.2g –
Apr 27] fairly useful handicapper: stayed 1m: acted on fibresand, tapeta, firm and soft
going: tried in cheekpieces: dead. *Kristin Stubbs*

REPLENISH (FR) 2 ch.c. (Apr 1) Le Havre (IRE) 124 – Brambleberry 79 (Cape Cross **89**
(IRE) 129) [2015 7m 8d² 8d² p7m* Oct 21] €3,500Y, resold €26,000Y, 65,000 2-y-o:
second foal: dam 2-y-o 5f winner out of Prix Jacques le Marois winner Miss Satamixa:
fairly useful performer: won nursery at Kempton in October: stays 1m. *James Fanshawe*

REPOSER (IRE) 7 br.g. Kheleyf (USA) 116 – Tragic Point (IRE) 89 (Tragic Role (USA)) **79**
[2015 86: 6d⁴ f7g⁶ 7g 7.1m 6m 6m Aug 16] tall, lengthy gelding: fair handicapper: stays
1m: acts on polytrack and good to soft going: tried in cheekpieces/tongue tie prior to 2015.
Keith Dalgleish

REPUTATION (IRE) 2 b.g. (Apr 7) Royal Applause 124 – Semaphore (Zamindar (USA) **89**
116) [2015 6m⁶ 6m* 6g 7g² 8g³ Sep 19] £70,000Y: half-brother to several winners,
including 2-y-o 7f winner Annie's Fortune (by Montjeu) and 1m winner Semaral (by
High Chaparral), both useful: dam unraced: fairly useful performer: won maiden at York
in July: second in nursery there in September: stays 7f: acts on good to firm going: tried in
cheekpieces. *John Quinn*

RESILIENCY (IRE) 4 ch.g. Mastercraftsman (IRE) 129 – Euroceleb (IRE) 76 (Peintre **96**
Celebre (USA) 137) [2015 94: p16g⁴ 14f⁴ 16.1m 16.4d Aug 19] useful handicapper: ran
creditably first 3 starts: seems to stay 2m: acts on polytrack and firm going. *Michael Appleby*

RESONANT (IRE) 3 b.g. Cape Cross (IRE) 129 – Last Rhapsody (IRE) 108 (Kris 135) **107**
[2015 72p: 8g³ 10g* 9g* 10.1m 8f 10m* 10m² 9.9m Jul 30] good-topped gelding: useful
performer: won maiden at Newmarket (by 10 lengths from Fallen For A Star) and handicap
at Goodwood (by 1¼ lengths from Darshini) in May and handicap at Newmarket (by 3¾
lengths from Gibeon) in July: stays 1¼m: acts on good to firm going: usually leads: sent to
UAE. *Mark Johnston*

RESONATOR 2 b.g. (Apr 8) Compton Place 125 – Saddlers Bend (IRE) 90 (Refuse To **–**
Bend (IRE) 128) [2015 6m 7m 7d 7s⁶ Oct 6] good-quartered gelding: little form: tried in
blinkers. *Peter Chapple-Hyam*

RESPECTABILITY 3 b.f. Echo of Light 125 – Respectfilly (Mark of Esteem (IRE) 137) **–**
[2015 8.3g May 18] tall filly: first foal: dam unraced half-sister to smart winner up to 1¾m
Quiz Mistress: 20/1, badly needed experience when well held in maiden at Windsor.
Hughie Morrison

RESPONSE 5 ch.g. New Approach (IRE) 132 – Spotlight 110 (Dr Fong (USA) 128) [2015 **73**
67: 9.9m⁶ 9.9v² 10.3s⁴ 9.2m³ 8.3v⁶ p8f p10g Nov 18] fair maiden: left Steve Gollings
after first start: stays 1¼m: acts on good to firm and heavy going: tried in headgear.
Michael Appleby

RESSURRETO (IRE) 2 b.f. (Apr 11) Frozen Power (IRE) 108 – Silver Whale (FR) **41**
(Highest Honor (FR) 124) [2015 5s⁶ 6d⁶ 6m⁶ Jun 20] €16,000Y: fourth foal: half-sister to
useful winner up to 2m Maid In Rio (2-y-o 7f winner, by Captain Rio): dam, 2-y-o 1¼m
winner, sister to very smart winner up to 2m (stayed 2¾m) Double Honour: poor maiden:
will be suited by further than 6f. *Keith Dalgleish*

REST EASY 3 b.f. Rip Van Winkle (IRE) 134 – Early Evening 84 (Daylami (IRE) 138) **–**
[2015 9.9g 11.5d⁵ 9g 9.9m Jul 11] 4,000Y: fifth foal: half-sister to 3 winners, including
winner up to 8.5f Early Emperor (2-y-o 7f/7.5f winner, by Araafa) and 1m winner (stays
1¼m) Early Applause (by Royal Applause): dam 9f/1¼m winner: no form: tried in
blinkers. *Amanda Perrett*

RESTORER 3 gr.c. Mastercraftsman (IRE) 129 – Moon Empress (FR) 84 (Rainbow Quest **113**
(USA) 134) [2015 106: 10d* Oct 31] medium-sized, good-topped colt: off 12 months,
improved form (smart) when winning 6-runner listed race at Newmarket by 1½ lengths
from Quarterback, finding plenty to lead final 100 yds: stays 1¼m: acts on soft going.
William Muir

RETIREMENT PLAN 5 b.h. Monsun (GER) 124 – Passage of Time 115 (Dansili 127) **–**
[2015 110: 13g Aug 29] big, well-made bay: smart handicapper: off 12 months and in
first-time cheekpieces, shaped as if retaining some ability despite well held at Newmarket,
racing closer to pace than ideal: stayed 2m: acted on good to firm going: usually raced
prominently: to stand at Tullaghansleck Stud, Co. Westmeath, Ireland, fee on application.
Lady Cecil

RETRO VALLEY (IRE) 3 b.g. Vale of York (IRE) 117 – Retrato (USA) 67 (Fusaichi **78**
Pegasus (USA) 130) [2015 51: p8f³ t9.5f³ t8.6m⁴ p8g² p8f p10g⁵ 8f⁵ 10.2f* 10g* 10m⁵
11.9m³ 11.6g⁶ 11.9m* Jun 30] small, close-coupled gelding: fair handicapper: won at Bath
and Redcar in May and Brighton in June: stays 1½m: acts on firm going: in cheekpieces
nowadays. *David Dennis*

RETURN ACE 3 b.f. Zamindar (USA) 116 – Match Point (Unfuwain (USA) 131) [2015 **94 p**
t9.5g² p12g* p12g* 12d³ Oct 30] 8,500Y: rather leggy filly: fifth foal: half-sister to 3
winners, including useful 11f-1¾m winner Deuce Again (by Dubawi) and 9f/1¼m winner
Bend Point (by Refuse To Bend): dam unraced half-sister to very smart 11f-2¾m winner
San Sebastian and smart winner up to 1½m Noushkey: fairly useful performer: won
maiden in August and handicap in September, both at Kempton: will stay beyond 1½m:
remains open to further improvement. *James Fanshawe*

RETURN OF THE MAK 2 b.c. (Mar 25) Makfi 130 – Tell The Wind (IRE) 98 (Mujadil **103 p**
(USA) 119) [2015 7g* 7v³ Oct 24] 72,000F: first foal: dam, 7f winner (including at 2 yrs),
half-sister to smart winner up to 1¼m Coupe de Ville: won maiden at Redcar in October by
3½ lengths from Rivers of Asia: better form when very close third to Crazy Horse in Horris
Hill Stakes at Newbury, edged out close home: sent to Hong Kong: already useful, and
likely to progress further. *Richard Fahey*

REUTLINGEN (FR) 2 b.f. (Jan 19) Elusive City (USA) 117 – Distant Dreamer (USA) –
(Rahy (USA) 115) [2015 p6g 6v⁵ t7.1f p6g Dec 7] €8,000F: third foal: half-sister to 1¼m
winner Distant High (by High Chaparral): dam, of little account, half-sister to useful 2-y-o
6f winner (stayed 1¼m) Jaish: no form: tried in cheekpieces. *Rae Guest*

REVE DE NUIT (USA) 9 ch.g. Giant's Causeway (USA) 132 – My Dream Castles **95**
(USA) (Woodman (USA) 126) [2015 101: f12s² f12s³ f11g* Apr 14] good-topped gelding:
useful performer: won claimer at Southwell in April: stays 1½m: acts on polytrack,
fibresand, soft and good to firm going: tried in headgear prior to 2015: usually leads. *K. R.
Burke*

REVERENT (IRE) 3 b.f. Teofilo (IRE) 126 – Wadaat 102 (Diktat 126) [2015 p10f⁶ t12.2f⁶ **61**
Oct 31] 205,000Y: second foal: dam, 1m winner who stayed 11f, half-sister to useful 2-y-o
7.5f winner Mrs Snow: modest form in maidens at Chelmsford and Wolverhampton.
James Tate

REVISION (FR) 3 b.g. Vision d'Etat (FR) 127 – Karmibola (FR) (Persian Bold 123) **96**
[2015 –: 10g³ 10m* p10g⁵ p12g* 11s* 12d² p11m* p11g² Nov 9] useful handicapper: won
at Leicester in July and August and at Kempton and Goodwood in September: good second
to The Steward at Kempton final start: stays 1½m: acts on polytrack, soft and good to firm
going: often races towards rear, usually responds generously to pressure. *John Best*

REVOLUTIONIST (IRE) 3 b.c. Pivotal 124 – Mysterial (USA) (Alleged (USA) 138) **101**
[2015 66p: p8f* 8.3d* t8.6f* p8m Nov 14] big, strong colt: useful performer: won maiden
at Lingfield in March and handicaps at Windsor and Wolverhampton in October: stays 8.5f:
acts on polytrack, tapeta and good to soft going. *Mark Johnston*

REWRITTEN 3 b.g. Dubawi (IRE) 129 – Portrayal (USA) 114 (Saint Ballado (CAN)) **65**
[2015 63: p10g³ t12.2m⁶ 10g Oct 3] fair maiden: left Charlie Appleby after second start:
will stay 1½m: acts on polytrack: tried in visor in 2015: often wears tongue tie. *Alan Berry*

REX BELL (IRE) 2 b.c. (Mar 19) Dubawi (IRE) 129 – Clara Bow (IRE) 84 (Sadler's **82 p**
Wells (USA) 132) [2015 8.3s 8s³ Oct 23] fifth foal: half-brother to 11.5f/1½m winner
(stays 2m) Angus Glens (by Dalakhani): dam, 7f winner, sister to Fillies' Mile winner
Listen and Moyglare Stud Stakes winner Sequoyah, latter dam of Henrythenavigator: 8/1,
improved from debut (when badly in need of experience) when 2¼ lengths third of 15 to
Algometer in maiden at Newbury, soon handy and keeping on: open to further improvement.
John Gosden

REX IMPERATOR 6 b.g. Royal Applause 124 – Elidore 95 (Danetime (IRE) 121) [2015 **97**
112d: 6m 6m 7g³ 7m⁴ 6m* 6m 6d 6m* Sep 10] angular gelding: useful handicapper: won
at Thirsk in July and Doncaster (by neck from Regal Dan) in September: stays 7f: acts on
good to firm and good to soft going: sometimes wears headgear. *David O'Meara*

REX WHISTLER (IRE) 5 b.g. Tamayuz 126 – Dangle (IRE) 102 (Desert Style (IRE) **75**
121) [2015 83: t12.2f⁵ 12.4g³ Apr 11] fair handicapper: stays 12.5f: acts on tapeta and good
to firm going: tried in hood. *Julie Camacho*

REZWAAN 8 b.g. Alhaarth (IRE) 126 – Nasij (USA) 101 (Elusive Quality (USA)) [2015 **69**
62: p11f* t8.6f³ p8f p8g p11g* p10f p10m p11g p8d f8g Dec 18] good-bodied gelding: fair
handicapper: won at Kempton in March and June: stays 11f: acts on polytrack, good to firm
and good to soft going: wears headgear. *Murty McGrath*

RHOMBUS (IRE) 5 b.g. Authorized (IRE) 133 – Mathool (IRE) (Alhaarth (IRE) 126) **103**
[2015 106: 14g⁵ 20f 14.1d* 16s³ Sep 1] tall gelding: useful handicapper: won at Nottingham
(by head from Kinema) in August: stays 2m: acts on good to firm and heavy going: tried
in hood prior to 2015: often races towards rear: temperament under suspicion. *Ismail
Mohammed*

RHYTHM EXCEL 3 b.f. Exceed And Excel (AUS) 126 – Caldy Dancer (IRE) 97 (Soviet   **– p**
Star (USA) 128) [2015 p7f p7f 6m⁶ Sep 15] sixth foal: sister to smart 6f-1m winner
Rewarding Hero and half-sister to smart 7f-8.5f winner Dance And Dance (by Royal
Applause) and 8.6f winner On With The Dance (by Byron): dam 2-y-o 5f winner who
stayed 7f: well held in maidens at Kempton, Lingfield and Yarmouth (first run for 6
months): remains open to improvement. *Ed Vaughan*

RHYTHMICAL 3 b.f. Halling (USA) 133 – Caribbean Dancer (USA) 76 (Theatrical)   **89**
[2015 10m* 11m² 12m² 14d⁵ 12g⁴ Sep 24] tall filly: fourth foal: half-sister to 1m winner
Reggae Star (by Cape Cross) and smart winner up to 1½m Notarised (2-y-o 1¼m winner,
by Authorized): dam 1¼m winner who stayed 1½m: fairly useful performer: won maiden
at Leicester in July: second in handicaps at Goodwood and Newmarket: stays 1¾m: acts on
good to firm and good to soft going. *Mark Johnston*

RIAL (IRE) 2 b.f. (Jan 31) Dark Angel (IRE) 113 – Coin Box 74 (Dubai Destination   **74**
(USA) 127) [2015 5m⁶ 5m³ p6g² p6g² Jun 17] €33,000Y: rather unfurnished filly: first foal:
dam maiden who stayed 7f: fair maiden: best effort at 5f. *Marco Botti*

RIALTO MAGIC 3 b.f. Monsieur Bond (IRE) 120 – Discover Roma (IRE) (Rock of   **66**
Gibraltar (IRE) 133) [2015 65: t7.1f² p6f³ t6f² p6m⁴ t6g⁴ p7g² p7g³ p6f f7g⁵ t7.1g⁶ t7.1g
p7g⁶ p6f* p6f p6m t7.1f Dec 22] fair handicapper: won at Chelmsford in October: stays 7f:
acts on polytrack and tapeta: sometimes in cheekpieces in 2015: often starts slowly/races
in rear. *Jamie Osborne*

RIBBING (USA) 2 ch.f. (Feb 14) Distorted Humor (USA) 117 – Contentious (USA) 107   **79 p**
(Giant's Causeway (USA) 132) [2015 p7g⁴ 7g² Jul 24] 85,000 2-y-o: third foal: half-sister
to 6f winner Carolina South (by Dixie Union): dam, 1m winner, half-sister to smart
US Grade 2 9f winner Gone Astray: better effort when second in maiden at Thirsk
(neck behind Gold Merlion) in July, left poorly placed: open to further improvement.
David Simcock

RIBBLEHEAD (USA) 4 b.g. Arch (USA) 127 – Moolakaya (FR) (Alzao (USA) 117)   **88**
[2015 89p: 12g 11.9d 9.8m* 10.4m 8d³ Sep 25] fairly useful handicapper: won at Ripon in
June: stays 10.5f: acts on good to firm and good to soft going: in headgear last 2 starts: sold
11,000 gns, sent to Saudi Arabia. *Tim Easterby*

RIBBONS 5 ch.m. Manduro (GER) 135 – Sister Act 85 (Marju (IRE) 127) [2015 119:   **115**
10.4m³ 10m³ 9.9d⁵ 10d* 10d Oct 17] rather leggy mare: smart performer: won Blandford
Stakes at the Curragh in September by ½ length from Tapestry: creditable third in
Middleton Stakes at York (1¾ lengths behind Secret Gesture) and Pretty Polly Stakes at the
Curragh (neck behind Diamondsandrubies): stays 1¼m: acts on polytrack, soft and good to
firm going: often races towards rear: sold, and to continue career in USA. *James Fanshawe*

Moyglare "Jewels" Blandford Stakes, the Curragh—
still in training at the age of five, Ribbons beats the reappearing Tapestry (No.4) and Bocca Baciata

RIBCHESTER (IRE) 2 b.c. (Mar 24) Iffraaj 127 – Mujarah (IRE) 59 (Marju (IRE)   **115**
127) [2015 6m² 6g² 6s* Sep 19]

Godolphin broke new ground in the latest season when having its first horses with Malton trainer Richard Fahey, whose two hundred and thirty-five wins equalled the record for the most winners trained in Britain in a calendar year (set by Richard Hannon Snr in 2013). Godolphin purchased Birchwood privately from David Armstrong in May after he had won his first two starts, and before he won the Superlative Stakes at Newmarket in July and finished third in the National Stakes and the Breeders' Cup Juvenile Turf. Godolphin purchased Ribchester from the same owner in September after he had come second in the Gimcrack Stakes on only his second start. Ribchester won the Mill Reef Stakes at Newbury on his first start in the royal blue, beating the Hannon-trained Log Out Island, another colt Godolphin had bought after he made a bright start to his career. For a horse to lose its maiden status in a pattern race is relatively rare, and Acapulco in the Queen Mary was the only other example in Britain in the latest season; more famously, Authorized achieved the feat in the 2006 Racing Post Trophy and so did Kingsgate Native as a two-year-old in the 2007 Nunthorpe Stakes. Richard Fahey's only previous Two Thousand Guineas runners were Fishforcompliments (200/1 when eighteenth in 2007) and Garswood (12/1 when seventh in 2013) and he must have Guineas aspirations for Ribchester who is bred to stay at least seven furlongs. Ribchester is a 33/1-shot for the Newmarket classic but his Mill Reef performance was as good as any in the race in recent times (his stable also won the 2013 renewal with Supplicant) and, as that was only his third start, he may have further improvement in him.

Ribchester made a pleasing first appearance when three quarters of a length second of eight to Melabi in a maiden at Doncaster in July, and he was the 25/1 outsider of eight when stepping up considerably to fill the same spot behind Ajaya, who beat him by a length and a quarter, in the very valuable Gimcrack at York the following month (Ribchester earned more for his second in the Gimcrack than he did for winning the Mill Reef). Ribchester was still only seventh over a furlong out at York before finally being called upon for his effort and he was still gaining on the winner late on. Although still a maiden, Ribchester had the best form going into the six-runner Dubai Duty Free Mill Reef Stakes at Newbury in September, and he started 13/8 favourite ahead of 11/4-shot Raucous, who had finished two lengths behind him when third in the Gimcrack, with Log Out Island third favourite at 9/2. The prevailing soft ground took its toll on the runners and only Ribchester and Log Out Island gave their running, Ribchester travelling smoothly to lead approaching the final furlong and being driven out to score by a length and a quarter under James Doyle (taking over from Tony Hamilton). There was no reason to doubt the

Dubai Duty Free Mill Reef Stakes, Newbury—
testing conditions take their toll as only two give their true running, but it still requires a smart
effort from Gimcrack runner-up Ribchester to get the better of Log Out Island

Godolphin's "Ribchester"

performances of the first two, however, with Log Out Island running to a similar level as when he had been placed in the Flying Childers Stakes eight days earlier. Log Out Island produced a career-best effort when franking the form in the listed Two-Year-Old Trophy at Redcar two weeks later, while Ribchester's efforts in both the Gimcrack and Mill Reef were supported by good times too. The Middle Park Stakes came too soon for Ribchester, just seven days after the Mill Reef, and he was never entered for the Dewhurst Stakes.

Ribchester (IRE) (b.c. 2013)	Iffraaj (b 2001)	Zafonic (b 1990)	Gone West Zaizafon
		Pastorale (ch 1988)	Nureyev Park Appeal
	Mujarah (IRE) (b 2008)	Marju (br 1988)	Last Tycoon Flame of Tara
		Tanaghum (b 2000)	Darshaan Mehthaaf

Ribchester cost €78,000 as a foal and €105,000 as a yearling. Given that he is now owned by Godolphin, it is ironic that many of his family have carried the colours of Sheikh Hamdan. These include Ribchester's dam Mujarah who finished well held in five starts at up to a mile and a half for John Dunlop before being culled by Shadwell Estates, sold for only 18,000 guineas as a three-year-old in 2011. Ribchester is her first foal and her second, a colt by Arcano, was bought by Ribchester's trainer for 85,000 guineas at the latest Newmarket October Sales Book 2. Mujarah was bred by Shadwell and is a half-sister to the very smart winner at up to a mile and three quarters Tactic (also trained by John Dunlop before being sent to Australia) and the smart eleven-furlong winner Yaazy, among other winners, including another trained by John Dunlop, Zahoo, who showed useful form at up to twelve furlongs and is the dam of the smart Irish three-year-old seven furlong/mile performer Convergence. Mujarah is out of the useful ten-furlong winner Tanaghum, who stayed twelve furlongs, and Tanaghum in turn is out of the very smart Mehthaaf who won the Irish One Thousand Guineas and the Celebration Mile for Sheikh Hamdan and John Dunlop. Mehthaaf is a daughter of Elle Seule who showed smart form at up to ten and a half furlongs and was bought carrying Mehthaaf for 1,500,000 dollars. Elle Seule is also the dam of July Cup winner Elnadim, among numerous other winners. There is more about the family, that of renowned broodmare Fall Aspen, in the essay on Mondialiste. *Richard Fahey*

RIB RESERVE (IRE) 3 b.g. Azamour (IRE) 130 – Fringe Success (IRE) 61 (Selkirk   **94**
(USA) 129) [2015 –p: 10m³ 10.2m* 12f 10.3g⁵ 10m* 9.9g³ 10.1d Sep 27] useful-looking gelding: fairly useful performer: won maiden at Bath in May and handicap at Leicester (by 3¼ lengths from Cayuga) in August: stays 1¼m: acts on firm going: sold 60,000 gns. *Sir Michael Stoute*

RICH AGAIN (IRE) 6 b.g. Amadeus Wolf 122 – Fully Fashioned (IRE) 75 (Brief Truce   **88**
(USA) 126) [2015 72, a85: t6g* t6f* p7m³ p6d³ p6g⁵ t7.1g³ 6d⁶ 6g p6f t7.1f⁵ t7.1m⁴ t5.1f⁵ Dec 22] fairly useful handicapper: won at Wolverhampton (twice) in January: stays 7f: acts on polytrack, tapeta and good to firm going: wears headgear. *James Bethell*

RICHARD OF YORKE 3 b.c. Oasis Dream 129 – Cascata (IRE) 86 (Montjeu (IRE)   **96**
137) [2015 10g* 10m⁴ 10m⁴ 12s* 14d³ Sep 25] well-made colt: first foal: dam, 2-y-o 1m winner who stayed 1½m, sister to high-class winner up to 13.4f St Nicholas Abbey: useful performer: won maiden at Windsor in April and handicap at Ascot (by ¾ length from Aussie Andre) in September: stays 1¾m: acts on soft and good to firm going: sold 120,000 gns, joined Chris Waller in Australia. *Luca Cumani*

RICHARD PANKHURST 3 ch.c. Raven's Pass (USA) 133 – Mainstay 86 (Elmaamul   **108**
(USA) 125) [2015 107p: 7d* p8g Nov 18] useful performer: won minor event at Haydock (by short head from Dark Emerald) in September: run best excused final start, unsuited by way race developed: should stay 1m: acts on good to firm and good to soft going: in hood for both wins. *John Gosden*

RICH HARVEST (USA) 10 b.g. High Yield (USA) 121 – Mangano (USA) (Quiet   **46**
American (USA)) [2015 –: t6g 6.1m 5.1m t5.1m Dec 18] good-bodied, attractive gelding: poor handicapper: stays 7f: acts on good to firm and good to soft going: tried in tongue tie prior to 2015: usually races close up. *Ray Peacock*

RICHIE MCCAW 2 b.c. (Feb 12) Zamindar (USA) 116 – Cochin (USA) (Swain (IRE)   **84 p**
134) [2015 7.5g⁵ p8f* Oct 15] €12,000Y: half-brother to 11f-1¾m winner Permit (by Dansili) and 11f-1½m winner Seaport (by Champs Elysees), both useful: dam, 1¼m winner, half-sister to very smart winner up to 1¼m Senure and smart 7f-8.2f winner Dexterity: 7/2, much improved from debut when winning maiden at Chelmsford by 2 lengths from Gold Trade, making running and finding extra when pressed: should progress further. *Mark Johnston*

RICHTER SCALE (IRE) 2 gr.f. (Mar 19) Lilbourne Lad (IRE) 111 – Danamight (IRE)   **82**
72 (Danetime (IRE) 121) [2015 5d³ 5m* 5m⁶ 5g⁴ Jul 31] €50,000Y: third foal: closely related to 1m winner Octavia (by Acclamation) and half-sister to useful 7f winner Queen of Power (by Medicean): dam maiden who stayed 1¼m: fairly useful performer: won maiden at Thirsk (by 3 lengths from Krystallite) in May: raced only at 5f. *Michael Dods*

RIDE LIKE THE WIND (IRE) 3 b.c. Lope de Vega (IRE) 125 – Biswa (USA) 48   **115**
(Kafwain (USA) 118) [2015 p7.5g² 7s* 8m 7g⁴ 7g⁵ 7g³ 7m 8s Nov 1] €180,000Y: second foal: half-brother to French 6f winner Royale du Buisson (by Invincible Spirit): dam twice raced, half-sister to smart 8.4f winner Ariege out of smart 9.5f winner Kostroma: smart performer: won Prix Djebel at Maisons-Laffitte (by head from Make Believe) in April: short of room under 2f out when ninth of 18 in 2000 Guineas at Newmarket next time: good efforts when third in Prix du Pin at Longchamp (1¼ lengths behind Taniyar) and seventh in Prix de la Foret on same course (4 lengths behind Make Believe) sixth/seventh starts: stays 7f: acts on soft and good to firm going: has worn tongue tie: often races towards rear. *F. Head, France*

RIDEONASTAR (IRE) 4 b.g. Manduro (GER) 135 – Capestar (IRE) 78 (Cape Cross   **77**
(IRE) 129) [2015 85p: 12g⁵ 13.3m³ 14.1g⁴ Jul 25] close-coupled gelding: fair handicapper: worth a try at further than 1¾m: acts on heavy going: often races prominently. *Brendan Powell*

RIDE THE LIGHTNING 2 b.c. (Apr 5) Dalakhani (IRE) 133 – Bright Halo (IRE)   **73**
(Bigstone (IRE) 126) [2015 7g⁶ 8.1g² p8g³ 10.2g⁴ Oct 18] attractive colt: fair maiden: stays 1m. *Brian Meehan*

RIDGE RANGER (IRE) 4 b.f. Bushranger (IRE) 119 – Dani Ridge (IRE) 92 (Indian **114**
Ridge 123) [2015 84: 5.5g* 6g² 6.1g* 6m 5g* 5g³ 5.2s² Sep 19] smart performer: won
handicaps at Wetherby (by 1½ lengths from Secret Hint) in April, Chester (by short head
from Gran Canaria Queen) in May and Goodwood (by 1½ lengths from Double Up) in
July: further improvement when second in World Trophy at Newbury (nose behind Steps)
in September: stays 6f: acts on soft going: front runner/races prominently. *Eric Alston*

RIDGEWAY STORM (IRE) 5 b.g. Hurricane Run (IRE) 134 – Hesperia (Slip Anchor **95**
136) [2015 89: t16.5f³ p16m³ p16g* p16f⁴ 14m² 21g 16.4d p16g³ p15.8g⁶ Dec 28] rangy
gelding: useful handicapper: won at Kempton in April: second at York (¾ length behind
Saved By The Bell) in June and third at Kempton (5¾ lengths behind Moonrise Landing)
in November: stays 2m: acts on polytrack and good to firm going: sometimes slowly away,
races towards rear. *Alan King*

RIFLE RANGE (IRE) 3 b.g. Shamardal (USA) 129 – Ratukidul (FR) 79 (Danehill **96**
(USA) 126) [2015 p8m² 8m* 8f* 8g 8g⁶ Sep 24] €230,000Y: well-made gelding: sixth
foal: half-brother to useful winner up to 1½m Kithonia (2-y-o 7f winner, by Sadler's Wells)
and 1m winner Maximum Velocity (by Muhtathir): dam, 2-y-o 7f winner, half-sister to
high-class 1¼m-1½m winner Hernando: useful performer: won maiden at Haydock in June
and handicap at Ascot (by neck from Dutch Law) in July: should prove suited by further
than 1m: acts on firm going: sent to Australia. *Roger Varian*

RIFLESCOPE (IRE) 2 b.c. (Jan 25) Raven's Pass (USA) 133 – Red Intrigue (IRE) 80 **97**
(Selkirk (USA) 129) [2015 5.1m³ 5s* 6m 5f⁴ 5f* 6m⁶ 5g⁶ 5.5d⁵ Sep 26] 52,000F,
130,000Y: good-topped colt: first foal: dam, 1¼m winner, half-sister to smart 7f/1m winner
Redstone Dancer out of useful 1¼m winner Red Affair: useful performer: won maiden at
Lingfield in May and listed race at Sandown (by length from Ejaazah) in July: should be
suited by 6f: acts on firm and soft going. *Mark Johnston*

RIGHTCAR 8 b.g. Bertolini (USA) 125 – Loblolly Bay 99 (Halling (USA) 133) [2015 55: **33**
t6g t5.1f p6f t5.1g Feb 9] lengthy gelding: poor handicapper: stays 7f: acts on polytrack and
tapeta: tried in headgear: often starts slowly, usually races in rear. *Peter Grayson*

RIGHT MADAM (IRE) 3 b.f. Jeremy (USA) 122 – Mawaared 61 (Machiavellian **57**
(USA) 123) [2015 52: 8.3m 8.3m 7m t6g⁵ 7m³ 7m t8.6m² t9.5m t9.5f³ t9.5f⁶ t9.5f⁶ t9.5f²
t12.2m⁶ Nov 21] modest maiden: stays 9.5f: acts on tapeta: usually in headgear in 2015:
often races in rear. *Sarah Hollinshead*

RIGHT TOUCH 5 b.g. Royal Applause 124 – Amira 70 (Efisio 120) [2015 97: 6g 6d 6d* **104**
6g⁴ 6g⁵ 6g* 7.2g* Sep 19] lengthy gelding: useful handicapper: won at Pontefract in July
and at Ascot (by ½ length from Charles Molson) and Ayr (by neck from Al Khan) in
September: stays 7f: acts on good to firm and good to soft going. *Richard Fahey*

RIGHTWAY (IRE) 4 b.g. Cockney Rebel (IRE) 127 – Caeribland (IRE) 90 (Namaqualand **–**
(USA)) [2015 82: p8g Jan 11] fairly useful handicapper: well held only start in 2015: stays
8.5f: acts on polytrack, tapeta and good to firm going. *Tony Carroll*

RIGOLLETO (IRE) 7 b.g. Ad Valorem (USA) 125 – Jallaissine (IRE) (College Chapel **72**
122) [2015 80: p6m² p6f⁵ p6g⁵ 6.1m 6d² 5.9d⁶ 6s 6d² 16g 6g² p6f⁴ p6g³ p6m p6m⁴
Dec 31] lengthy gelding: fair handicapper: stays 1m: acts on polytrack, good to firm and
heavy going: tried in headgear prior to 2015: often races prominently: none too consistent.
Anabel K. Murphy

RI NA SI 5 b.g. Green Horizon – Luisa Miller (IRE) 56 (Entrepreneur 123) [2015 –: f7d
Jan 27] poor maiden: in cheekpieces last 2 starts. *Michael Appleby*

RING EYE 7 b.g. Definite Article 121 – Erins Lass (IRE) (Erins Isle 121) [2015 **66**
71: 11.9f⁶ 9.9m⁶ 12.1m⁵ 12.1m* 16.2s² 12.1g 12.1m³ 12s⁵ 12v t13.9f Oct 31] fair
handicapper: won at Chepstow (apprentice) in July: best effort at 1½m: acts on polytrack,
soft and good to soft going. *John O'Shea*

RING OF ART 2 b.g. (Mar 11) Dutch Art 126 – Katimont (IRE) 90 (Montjeu (IRE) 137) **– p**
[2015 t7.1f f7m Dec 8] 155,000F, €115,000 2-y-o: fourth foal: closely related to winner up
to 1¼m Kramer Drive (2-y-o 1m winner, by Medicean): dam, 8.3f winner, half-sister to
smart 1½m-1¾m winner Katiykha: well held in maidens at Wolverhampton and Southwell:
sent to France: should do better. *Richard Fahey*

RING OF FIRE (GER) 6 ch.g. Tertullian (USA) 115 – Rowina (GER) (Hamond (GER) **–**
116) [2015 16.1d 14.1m May 25] modest at best, no form in 2015: stays 12.5f: acts on dirt
and good to soft going: tried in cheekpieces. *Tony Coyle*

RING OF TRUTH 2 b.f. (Apr 27) Royal Applause 124 – Spinning Top 105 (Alzao (USA) **83**
117) [2015 5.2m² 6g* 5f 6.1m⁴ 5.7d⁴ Sep 2] good-topped filly: sister to smart 6f (including
at 2 yrs) winner Musical Comedy and half-sister to several winners, including 7f/1m

(including at 2 yrs) winner Humdrum (by Dr Fong) and winner up to 12.4f Full Toss (2-y-o 7f winner, by Nayef), both useful: dam 1¼m winner: fairly useful performer: won maiden at Haydock in May: stays 6f: acts on good to firm going: front runner/races prominently: sold 40,000 gns, sent to USA. *Richard Hannon*

RIOCA (IRE) 2 b.f. (Feb 14) Jeremy (USA) 122 – Rising Wind (IRE) 99 (Shirocco (GER) **89** 129) [2015 7.5m³ 7m² 7m³ 8s* 8g* 9v⁴ 8d² Oct 31] first foal: dam 2-y-o 1m winner who stayed 2m out of useful winner up to 1¾m (2-y-o 7f winner) Right Key: fairly useful performer: won nurseries at Ffos Las and Pontefract (by nose from Peru) in September: creditable efforts in cheekpieces after, second in listed race at Newmarket (4 lengths behind Fireglow) final start: stays 9f: acts on heavy going: front runner/races prominently. *Sir Mark Prescott Bt*

RIO COBOLO (IRE) 9 b.g. Captain Rio 122 – Sofistication (IRE) 68 (Dayjur (USA) **–** 137) [2015 54, a74: f8g Jan 13] good-bodied gelding: handicapper: well held only start in 2015: stays 7.5f: acts on fibresand and any turf going: usually in headgear. *Keith Reveley*

RIO DEVA (IRE) 2 b.f. (Apr 11) Captain Rio 122 – Kenema (IRE) 88 (Petardia 113) **61** [2015 5m 5m³ 5d⁴ t5.1g³ 5d t5.1m⁶ 5m² Sep 27] €3,000Y, €6,000 2-y-o: half-sister to smart winner up to 6f Kingsgate Choice (by Choisir) and winner up to 7f Aris Terz (2-y-o 5f winner, by Monashee Mountain): dam 5f-6.5f winner: modest maiden: raced only at 5f: acts on tapeta and good to firm going: tried in cheekpieces: usually leads. *Keith Dalgleish*

RIO FALLS (IRE) 3 b.g. Captain Rio 122 – Swallow Falls (IRE) 52 (Lake Coniston **77** (IRE) 131) [2015 p8m⁴ p8f² t8.6g* t9.5m Dec 30] fair performer: won maiden at Wolverhampton in May: left Noel Quinlan after first start, Giles Bravery after third: stays 8.5f. *Jennie Candlish*

RIO GLAMOROUS 2 b.g. (Mar 14) Aussie Rules (USA) 123 – Glamorous Spirit (IRE) **63** 109 (Invincible Spirit (IRE) 121) [2015 5m 5.7f 5.1m⁶ 5.3s⁴ 7d f5g⁶ Nov 3] sturdy gelding: modest maiden: left Ronald Harris after fourth start: best effort at 5f: acts on fibresand: sometimes in blinkers/tongue tie: sometimes slowly away: has looked hard ride. *Roy Bowring*

RIOJA DAY (IRE) 5 b.g. Red Clubs (IRE) 125 – Dai E Dai (USA) (Seattle Dancer (USA) **70 §** 119) [2015 65: 8s⁴ 8g² 8d² 9.1s⁶ 8.3d³ 7.1m² 8.3g³ 8.3s³ 7.2d* 8d⁷ 8m⁵ 7.2g 9.2m 7.2g Oct 13] sturdy gelding: fair handicapper: won at Ayr in July: stays 1¼m: acts on any turf going: often wears headgear: often races lazily and is one to be wary of. *Jim Goldie*

RIO RONALDO (IRE) 3 b.g. Footstepsinthesand 120 – Flanders (IRE) 110 (Common **91** Grounds 118) [2015 80: p5f⁴ 6m* 6m⁵ 5.6m⁴ 6g 5m* 5g p6f Oct 28] good-topped gelding: fairly useful handicapper: won at Windsor in April and August (by ¾ length from Majestic Hero): stays 6f: acts on tapeta and good to firm going: tried in blinkers in 2015: sometimes slowly away, often races freely: temperament under suspicion. *Mike Murphy*

RIO'S CLIFFS 2 b.f. (Feb 8) Canford Cliffs (IRE) 133 – What's Up Pussycat (IRE) 100 **80** (Danehill Dancer (IRE) 117) [2015 6m⁴ 6g6 7g³ 7.5d* 9g⁴ Oct 21] good-topped filly: first foal: dam 2-y-o 6f winner who stayed 1m: fairly useful performer: won maiden at Beverley in September: stays 9f: acts on good to soft going: often races freely. *Martyn Meade*

RIO YUMA (ITY) 4 b.f. Gold Sphinx (USA) – Selsey 72 (Selkirk (USA) 129) [2015 60: **47** t8.6f⁴ Jan 2] poor maiden: stays 8.5f: acts on polytrack and tapeta: in cheekpieces sole start in 2015. *Kristin Stubbs*

RIPINTO (IRE) 3 ch.g. Rip Van Winkle (IRE) 134 – For Evva Silca 60 (Piccolo 121) **83** [2015 70: p7g² 8m 7m³ 7m 7v⁴ p7g p8f t7.1m p6f² p7g³ Dec 2] rather unfurnished gelding: fairly useful handicapper: stays 7f: acts on polytrack and good to firm going: in headgear last 4 starts: often races freely. *Jim Boyle*

RIP N ROAR (IRE) 3 b.g. Rip Van Winkle (IRE) 134 – Aine (IRE) 105 (Danehill Dancer **53 p** (IRE) 117) [2015 8.3s Apr 8] 100,000F, 115,000Y: first foal: dam, 5f/6f winner, half-sister to useful 6f-1m winner Aranel: 25/1, some encouragement when seventh of 14 in maiden at Nottingham on only start, not knocked about: should do better. *William Haggas*

RIPOLL (IRE) 2 b.g. (Apr 2) Alfred Nobel (IRE) 110 – Lahu Lady (Red Ransom (USA)) **69** [2015 t7.1g⁴ p7g 7d t9.5f⁵ p8g* t8.6f² t8.6f⁴ Nov 30] fair performer: won nursery at Kempton in November: stays 8.5f: acts on polytrack and tapeta: often in tongue tie: usually races close up. *Sylvester Kirk*

RIPONIAN 5 ch.g. Trade Fair 124 – Dispol Katie 90 (Komaite (USA)) [2015 48: 10.1d³ **58** 8d* 10.1m⁶ 9.3g³ 8.3g* 8.3d³ 8m 9.2s⁴ 8.3g Aug 20] modest handicapper: won at Newcastle in May and Hamilton in June: best around 1m: acts on soft and good to firm going: front runner/races prominently. *Susan Corbett*

RIPTIDE 9 b.g. Val Royal (FR) 127 – Glittering Image (IRE) (Sadler's Wells (USA) 132) **75 §**
[2015 84§: 18s 21.6g⁵ 17.1g 18g² 16.2m⁴ 17.1m³ 17.1d⁴ 18d³ 18s⁴ Oct 19] good-bodied
gelding: fair handicapper: stays 21.5f: acts on any turf going: usually wears headgear:
unreliable. *Michael Scudamore*

RIP VAN SUZY (IRE) 2 b.f. (Apr 14) Rip Van Winkle (IRE) 134 – Suzy Bliss 105 **60 p**
(Spinning World (USA) 130) [2015 t6f t6m Dec 30] €20,000Y: half-sister to
2-y-o 6f winner (stays 10.5f) Goodnightsuzy (by Azamour): dam, 2-y-o 7f winner who
stayed 1½m, half-sister to useful 1½m winner Cutting Crew: better effort when seventh in
maiden at Wolverhampton second start, needing stiffer test: should do better in time.
David Evans

RISEN SUN 3 b.f. Shamardal (USA) 129 – Bright Morning 95 (Dubai Millennium 140) **97**
[2015 96: 7m² 8f 7d² 7d 6g⁴ Sep 24] rangy filly: useful performer: second in minor event
at Leicester and handicap at Newmarket, and also ran creditably when 2½ lengths fourth to
Golden Amber in handicap at Newmarket final outing: stays 7f: acts on good to firm and
good to soft going: usually races close up. *Charlie Appleby*

RISE TO GLORY (IRE) 7 b.h. King's Best (USA) 132 – Lady At War (Warning 136) **69**
[2015 78: t5.1f p6f⁶ p6f p5f⁴ t5.1m⁶ 6g p5f² 6.1d² 6s 5d² t5.1g⁶ 6.1f 5.1d 7s t6f Nov 13]
fair handicapper: stays 7f: acts on polytrack, tapeta, soft and good to firm going: has worn
headgear, including often of late: has worn tongue tie: front runner/races prominently.
Shaun Harris

RISE UP SINGING 2 b.f. (Jan 24) Showcasing 117 – Sambarina (IRE) 70 (Victory Note **47**
(USA) 120) [2015 6d 6d⁶ 5g⁴ 6s⁴ 7s Oct 16] fifth foal: half-sister to 2-y-o 7f-8.6f
winner Lea Valley Black (by Three Valleys) and winner up to 1¼m Zafeen Plus (2-y-o 9f
winner, by Zafeen): dam, lightly raced, closely related to winner up to 1m Meanya: poor
maiden: stays 6f: acts on soft going: tried in cheekpieces: front runner/races prominently.
Karen Tutty

RISING BREEZE (FR) 4 b.g. Shirocco (GER) 129 – Moon Tree (FR) (Groom Dancer **–**
(USA) 128) [2015 85: 10m May 28] handicapper: no worthwhile form in 2015: stays 10.5f:
acts on good to firm and good to soft going: has worn hood, including often of late:
temperament under suspicion. *Tom George*

RISK ADJUSTED (IRE) 2 b.c. (May 8) Bushranger (IRE) 119 – Silk Fan (IRE) 100 **89**
(Unfuwain (USA) 131) [2015 5g² 5g² 6g² 5d* 7m⁶ 7.1m² 7m⁶ 7.1s² p8g⁴ 7g³ 7g⁵ Dec 29]
€15,000Y: lengthy, rather unfurnished colt: half-brother to several winners, including 5f/6f
(including at 2 yrs) winner Haikbidiac (by Kodiac) and 1½m-16.4f winner Eagle Rock (by
High Chaparral), both useful: dam 7f winner (including at 2 yrs) who stayed 1¼m: fairly
useful performer: won maiden at Hamilton in June: placed after in nursery and minor event
at Sandown, and minor event at Newmarket: left Ann Duffield after fourth start, Conrad
Allen after tenth (for 42,000 gns): stays 1m: acts on polytrack, soft and good to firm going.
Dhafi Al Marri, Qatar

RISK 'N' REWARD (IRE) 4 ch.g. Dandy Man (IRE) 123 – Sharp Diversion (USA) 42 **75**
(Diesis 133) [2015 66: f7d* f6g* t6f f7g⁵ f7g 7m* 7g 6g* 5.9m 6d 6g⁶ 6d 6g⁵ t7.1g 6g
7.2g f7m Dec 8] fair performer: won 2 handicaps at Southwell in January and seller and
claimer at Redcar in April: subsequently left David O'Meara: stays 7f: acts on fibresand
and good to firm going: often wears headgear: often starts slowly, usually races in rear.
Alan Berry

RISKY RIZKOVA 5 b.g. Sleeping Indian 122 – Tri Pac (IRE) (Fairy King (USA)) [2015 **59**
p6f t5.1m p5f³ p5g p5g⁴ p5g³ p5g* p5g² p6g² p6g⁴ p5f⁵ p5g Oct 14] sturdy gelding:
modest handicapper: won at Lingfield in July: stays 6f: acts on polytrack and good to firm
going: often wears headgear: usually races close up. *Peter Hedger*

RITA'S BOY (IRE) 3 b.g. Captain Rio 122 – The Oldladysays No (IRE) 85 (Perugino **90**
(USA) 84) [2015 67, a85: f6d² p5g⁵ p5m⁶ f5s³ 5.1d² 5g² 5.1v² 5m 5d 5g⁵ 5.1d* f5g⁴ f5g
Dec 12] fairly useful handicapper: won at Nottingham (by ¾ length from Keep It Dark) in
November: best form at 5f: acts on fibresand and good to soft going: usually in visor in
2015. *K. R. Burke*

RITASUN (FR) 2 b.g. (Mar 25) Monsun (GER) 124 – Baselga (GER) (Second Set (IRE) **75**
127) [2015 7g⁴ 8.3m⁵ 8g t8.6f* t8.6m⁶ Dec 26] fair performer: won nursery at
Wolverhampton in November: best effort at 8.5f: acts on tapeta: often races towards rear.
Richard Hannon

RITE TO REIGN 4 b.g. Tiger Hill (IRE) 127 – Magical Cliche (USA) 86 (Affirmed **98**
(USA)) [2015 95p: p13.3g³ 16.4m⁴ 16.2g⁵ 16.1m 16s 18g 18g 16d⁵ Oct 30] rangy, useful-
looking gelding: useful handicapper: didn't win in 2015 but often shaped better than bare

result: probably stays 2¼m: acts on polytrack, good to firm and good to soft going: in cheekpieces last 2 starts: often starts slowly, usually races nearer last than first. *Philip McBride*

RIVE GAUCHE 3 b.f. Fastnet Rock (AUS) 127 – Raysiza (IRE) (Alzao (USA) 117) **98** [2015 69P: 8m⁴ 8.3g² 8f 10.2m² 8g* 10.1m⁶ 10g p8g Oct 29] sturdy filly: useful performer: won maiden at Salisbury (by 3¼ lengths from Saguna) in August: 25/1, respectable 3 lengths eighth to Lamar in listed race at Lingfield final start, better placed than most: stays 1¼m: acts on good to firm going: in headgear last 4 outings. *William Haggas*

RIVELLINO 5 b.g. Invincible Spirit (IRE) 121 – Brazilian Bride (IRE) 103 (Pivotal 124) **114** [2015 116: p6f* p6f 6g 6f 6.1g³ 6m³ 6g p6m⁵ p6g⁵ Nov 25] athletic gelding: smart performer: won listed race at Lingfield in February by head from Glen Moss: length third of 27 to Magical Memory in Stewards' Cup at Goodwood sixth start: stays 6f: acts on polytrack and good to firm going. *K. R. Burke*

RIVERBOAT LADY (IRE) 2 gr.f. (Apr 15) Zebedee 113 – Tomanivi (Caerleon (USA) – 132) [2015 6g 7s 6s p5f⁵ Nov 7] €8,500Y: rather unfurnished filly: half-sister to 1m winner Krakatau (by Noverre) and 1m-1¼m winner Tucciano (by Observatory): dam once-raced half-sister to smart winner up to 1m Barricade: no form: tried in tongue tie. *Gay Kelleway*

RIVER DART (IRE) 3 ch.g. Dutch Art 126 – Sky Galaxy (USA) 84 (Sky Classic (CAN)) **87** [2015 74: 9.9g* 10f* 12m 10m³ p10m³ Sep 26] tall gelding: fairly useful handicapper: won at Goodwood in June and Ascot (by ¾ length from Mustard) in July: stays 1½m: acts on polytrack and firm going: tried in cheekpieces in 2015. *Marcus Tregoning*

RIVER DREAMER (IRE) 4 ch.f. Intense Focus (USA) 117 – Guard Hill (USA) 87 **50** (Rahy (USA) 115) [2015 51: t6g f6g² f6d⁴ f7g⁴ 7m 5.1m 5.7m Jul 8] modest handicapper: stays 6f: acts on polytrack and fibresand: tried in blinkers in 2015: usually wears tongue tie. *Robert Stephens*

RIVER DU NORD (FR) 8 b.m. Voix du Nord (FR) 119 – Palala River (Colmore Row **50** 111) [2015 45: 12g² 12m 12g⁵ 12d⁵ 12d Aug 31] modest handicapper: ran only at Les Landes in 2015, winning there in April: stays 16.5f: acts on polytrack, firm and good to soft going: tried in cheekpieces prior to 2015. *Susan Gardner*

RIVER ECHO 2 br.c. (Apr 29) Equiano (FR) 127 – Day Creek (Daylami (IRE) 138) **82** [2015 7s² 7g⁴ Sep 30] second foal: half-brother to 2-y-o 6f winner Lackaday (by Kyllachy): dam unraced half-sister to smart winner up to 1¼m With Interest out of smart 2-y-o 6f winner With Fascination: fairly useful form in maidens when second to Tabarrak at Newbury and fourth to Tafteesh at Salisbury: sent to USA. *Mick Channon*

RIVER GLASS (IRE) 4 gr.g. Verglas (IRE) 118 – Spartan Girl (IRE) 91 (Ela-Mana-Mou – 132) [2015 –: p12g 10m t13.9m Oct 2] little impact in maidens/handicap: dead. *Alan King*

RIVERLYNX (IRE) 3 b.f. Holy Roman Emperor (IRE) 125 – Banba (IRE) 87 (Docksider **41** (USA) 124) [2015 –: t6g t7.1m² f7g⁴ 9.2d May 27] poor maiden: best effort at 7f: acts on tapeta: sometimes slowly away, often races prominently. *Ben Haslam*

RIVER OF DREAMS (IRE) 3 br.g. Big Bad Bob (IRE) 118 – Toberanthawn (IRE) 87 **67 §** (Danehill Dancer (IRE) 117) [2015 71: f8d³ f7d³ f7d⁴ 7.1s⁶ 7d May 11] fair maiden: stays 1m: acts on fibresand and tapeta: often wears headgear: ungenuine. *Kevin Ryan*

RIVERS OF ASIA 2 ch.c. (Mar 23) Medicean 128 – Aliena (IRE) (Grand Lodge (USA) **75** 125) [2015 7m p7g³ 7g² Oct 3] fair form in maidens/minor event: will stay beyond 7f. *Philip McBride*

RIVERS OF BABYLON (IRE) 3 b.f. Holy Roman Emperor (IRE) 125 – Sweet Times **94** 60 (Riverman (USA) 131) [2015 74: 8.2g³ 7v² 9.5g* 8m* 10m⁵ 8.5g 7g 11g⁴ 9s³ Aug 27] fairly useful performer: won maiden at Gowran in May and minor event at Navan in June: stays 9.5f: acts on soft and good to firm going: sometimes slowly away. *W. McCreery, Ireland*

RIVERS RUN (IRE) 3 b.f. High Chaparral (IRE) 132 – Quiet Waters (USA) (Quiet **76 p** American (USA)) [2015 t12.2g³ Dec 5] 65,000Y: fourth foal: sister to 9f-1½m winner Hi Finn: dam lightly-raced half-sister to useful dam of smart performers up to 1¼m Mandaean and Wavering: 8/1, third in maiden at Wolverhampton (4¾ lengths behind Sign of A Victory) on debut: should progress. *Ralph Beckett*

RIVER THAMES 2 b.c. (May 4) Bernardini (USA) 132 – River Street (Machiavellian – (USA) 123) [2015 7.1m p7g Jun 24] attractive colt: well held in maidens at Sandown and Kempton. *Mark Johnston*

RIZAL PARK (IRE) 4 b.g. Amadeus Wolf 122 – Imelda (USA) (Manila (USA)) [2015 **78** 85: p8g p8m⁶ p8m³ p8g² t8.6g 8d 10s p8g p10g p8g Dec 3] useful-looking gelding: fair handicapper: left Andrew Balding after fourth start: best at 1m: acts on polytrack and good to firm going: often wears hood: tried in tongue tie. *James Evans*

RIZEENA (IRE) 4 b.f. Iffraaj 127 – Serena's Storm (IRE) 87 (Statue of Liberty (USA) **114** 115) [2015 115: 9f 8f² 8g⁶ Aug 2] attractive filly: smart performer: 2 lengths second of 6 to Amazing Maria in Duke of Cambridge Stakes at Royal Ascot: also ran creditably when sixth of 8 to Amazing Maria in Prix Rothschild at Deauville final start, left poorly placed: stayed 1m: acted on firm and soft going: was inclined to hang left: retired. *Clive Brittain*

ROAD MAP (IRE) 4 b.g. Saville Road 102 – Lauren Eria (Singspiel (IRE) 133) [2015 **–** 58: t8.6g Jun 29] maiden, modest form at best: stays 9.5f: acts on polytrack and tapeta: sometimes slowly away, often races towards rear. *Daniel Loughnane*

ROARING FORTIES (IRE) 2 b.g. (Feb 8) Invincible Spirit (IRE) 121 – Growling **87** (IRE) (Celtic Swing 138) [2015 6.1d 6g⁴ 6g² 7m³ 6.1g* p6g* 6g Aug 19] 220,000F: first foal: dam unraced half-sister to very smart 1m-11f winner Pressing: fairly useful performer: won 6f nurseries at Chester and Kempton in August: will prove as effective at 7f: acts on polytrack. *Charlie Appleby*

ROARING RORY 2 ch.g. (Mar 4) Sakhee's Secret 128 – Barbieri (IRE) 91 (Encosta de **64** Lago (AUS)) [2015 5d⁵ 5m³ 5g⁵ 5d² 5s⁴ t5.1g* 5m Sep 27] modest performer: won claimer at Wolverhampton in August: raced only at 5f: acts on tapeta, good to firm and good to soft going: in cheekpieces last 2 starts: front runner/races prominently. *Ollie Pears*

ROAYH (USA) 7 ch.g. Speightstown (USA) 124 – Most Remarkable (USA) (Marquetry **85** (USA) 121) [2015 86⁵ 8g 8s* 8d 8.9g 8m 9.8g⁶ 8g 8m⁶ 8d 8.3v 7s Oct 16] tall gelding: fairly useful handicapper: won at Musselburgh in May: left Richard Guest after fifth start: stays 1¼m: acts on polytrack, soft and good to firm going: tried in cheekpieces: sold £2,000, sent to Belgium. *Nigel Tinkler*

ROBANNE 2 b.f. (Apr 29) Paco Boy (IRE) 129 – Arctic Song (Charnwood Forest (IRE) **98** 125) [2015 7s* 7g³ Oct 9] 37,000Y: lengthy filly: sixth foal: half-sister to 3 winners, including useful 2-y-o 6f winner (stayed 1m) Hartley (by Lucky Story) and useful 1¼m winner Peacock's Pride (by Groom Dancer): dam unraced half-sister to smart/untrustworthy winner up to 6f Andronikos: useful form: won maiden at Salisbury in September by 3 lengths from Carenot: 14/1, better form when 1½ lengths third of 12 to First Victory in Oh So Sharp Stakes at Newmarket, keeping on well: will stay 1m. *William Knight*

ROBBEN 3 b.g. Dutch Art 126 – Little Greenbird (Ardkinglass 114) [2015 58: t9.5f² **67** t12.2g⁵ 10.2s 9.9g² 10m³ 10.4f⁶ t12.2m³ t12.2g⁴ 12d³ Oct 5] fair maiden: stays 1½m: acts on tapeta, good to firm and good to soft going: usually wears headgear: often starts slowly, often races towards rear. *John Mackie*

ROBBIAN 4 b.g. Bertolini (USA) 125 – Crathes 53 (Zilzal (USA) 137) [2015 53: f6g⁵ 8.3s **55** 10m 6m⁴ 5m f7d 5.1d³ 7s² 5.1d⁶ Nov 4] modest handicapper: stays 7f: acts on heavy going. *Charles Smith*

ROBBIE ROO ROO 2 br.f. (Apr 5) Kheleyf (USA) 116 – Haiti Dancer 64 (Josr **54** Algarhoud (IRE) 118) [2015 7m 6g 7g p6f Oct 10] tall, rather unfurnished filly: fifth foal: sister to 1m winner Hungry Heidi: dam, 2-y-o 7f winner who stayed 1¼m, half-sister to useful 1m-1¼m winner Park Charger: modest maiden: stays 7f. *Giles Bravery*

ROBERO 3 b.c. Piccolo 121 – Ceilidh Band (Celtic Swing 138) [2015 f7s³ p6g⁴ t9.5g⁴ **76** t8.6m* 10.4g 8d p8g p8g⁵ p8d Nov 30] fair performer: won maiden at Wolverhampton in August: left Brian Barr after second start, Ms N. M. Hugo after fifth: stays 9.5f: acts on polytrack and tapeta: front runner/races prominently. *John E. Long*

ROBERT LE DIABLE (FR) 6 ch.g. Dutch Art 126 – Red Begonia (Pivotal 124) [2015 **112** 7s* 6g² 5g² 7g² 6f² 6.5g Aug 9] compact gelding: smart performer: won minor event at Longchamp (by 1½ lengths from Complimentor) in April: second on next 4 starts, in Prix de Saint-Georges at Longchamp (2 lengths behind Mecca's Angel), Prix du Palais-Royal at Longchamp (beaten short head by Rosso Corsa) and Wokingham Stakes (Handicap) at Royal Ascot (1¼ lengths behind Interception) on last 3 occasions: in rear in Prix Maurice de Gheest at Deauville final outing: stays 7f: acts on polytrack, viscoride, firm and soft going: tried in headgear prior to 2015: usually races close up. *D. Prod'homme, France*

ROBERTO LOPEZ 2 b.g. (Apr 5) Royal Applause 124 – The Fugitive 94 (Nicholas **–** (USA) 111) [2015 5m⁶ Jun 6] 25/1, last of 6 in maiden at Lingfield. *Roger Teal*

ROBERT THE PAINTER (IRE) 7 b.g. Whipper (USA) 126 – Lidanna 113 (Nicholas **99** (USA) 111) [2015 106: a9.9f 9.9g 8d t8.6g 8d² 8m² 8.3s⁵ p8g p7f² p10g⁵ Dec 7] useful **a93** handicapper: second in minor events at Ascot in September (½ length behind Arthenus) and October (1¾ lengths behind Sir Robert Cheval): stays 1¼m: acts on polytrack and any turf going: usually wears headgear: often leads. *Lee Carter*

ROBIN HILL 3 b.f. Misu Bond (IRE) 114 – Enchanting Eve 67 (Risk Me (FR) 127) [2015 **52** 67: f5s* f5s⁶ t5.1f⁶ p5f³ 6d⁴ 5.1m 5m t5.1g Jun 26] sparely-made filly: modest performer: won maiden at Southwell in January: stays 6f: acts on all-weather, firm and soft going: sometimes in headgear in 2015. *William Muir*

ROBIN HOOD (IRE) 7 b.g. Galileo (IRE) 134 – Banquise (IRE) (Last Tycoon 131) **51** [2015 72, a60: p8f⁶ p10m Apr 29] leggy gelding: modest handicapper: stays 13f: acts on polytrack and soft going: often in headgear prior to 2015. *Philip Mitchell*

ROBINNIELLY (IRE) 2 b.g. (Feb 7) Approve (IRE) 112 – Beauty And Style (AUS) **84** (King of Kings (IRE) 125) [2015 6d 6m⁴ 7.2s⁵ 7.2g* 8g² Sep 19] €16,000F, £21,000Y: third foal: dam unraced half-sister to smart winner up to 1¼m (stayed 16.4f) Linney Head: fairly useful performer: won nursery at Musselburgh in September: best effort when second in similar event at Ayr final start: stays 1m: best form on good going. *Keith Dalgleish*

ROBIN OF NAVAN (FR) 2 ch.c. (Apr 18) American Post 121 – Cloghran (FR) **114** (Muhtathir 126) [2015 p7g⁶ 7g* 7.5g² 8d* 8.9g* 9.9s* Nov 1]

Ed Dunlop's first pattern winner came in a French Group 1 when Ta Rib landed the 1996 Poule d'Essai des Pouliches, and his younger brother Harry emulated him when Robin of Navan took the Criterium de Saint-Cloud in November. Harry Dunlop worked for Nicky Henderson, Sir Henry Cecil (who was his godfather) and his father John Dunlop before setting up as a trainer in 2006, and his first runner Situla was successful at Wolverhampton. The following year, Festoso finished in the frame in three two-year-old pattern races for the trainer, including the Cheveley Park, while Classic Remark landed a listed race in 2008. Festoso won a listed race herself in 2009 and Dunlop also trained Green Moon to win three races in 2010, including a listed race, before he went on to win the 2012 Melbourne Cup when trained in Australia. There was also Sir Patrick Moore who won his first two starts as a two-year-old in 2012 before finishing runner-up in a listed race and the Greenham Stakes on his return at three. French-bred Sir Patrick Moore had been bought for €16,000 as a yearling with the lucrative French system of owners' premiums in mind, and his success in a minor event at Compiegne covered his purchase price. Sir Patrick Moore was later sold to Australia where he was renamed Weary and won a Group 2 in January.

It's not hard to see why Dunlop, along with a clutch of other British-based trainers, routinely send horses to compete in the lesser, mid-week races in France. A two-year-old maiden at a non-premier track in Britain may be worth around £3,000 to the winner, whereas its equivalent in France could be worth around £10,000 to the winner, with winners there aged two, three and four sometimes eligible for a sixty-four per cent bonus (the bonus is forty-three per cent for horses aged five and older) on top of already generous prize money. There are also premiums worth €20m a year

Criterium de Saint-Cloud, Saint-Cloud—a stiff test of stamina for two-year-olds, especially on soft ground, and Robin of Navan copes best as he wins unchallenged, giving his trainer Harry Dunlop a first Group 1 winner; Cloth of Stars is a clear second, with Notte Bianca (stripes) third

Cross, Deal, Foden, Sieff's "Robin of Navan"

for breeders in France. Dunlop saddled Flambeuse (rated in the 60s by the BHA) to win a handicap at Chantilly in July, collecting the equivalent of over £7,300 in the process, and when French-bred Red Tornado won a maiden and a minor event as a two-year-old in 2014, his connections collected almost £25,000. Robin of Navan made his debut in Britain but raced in France on his five subsequent starts, winning four times and earning the equivalent of something like £300,000, when bonuses are taken into account, for his connections. Robin of Navan may do better still next year, though he is not entered in the Derby, with his trainer suggesting he will be aimed at the Prix du Jockey Club.

Robin of Navan finished in the middle of the field in a maiden on the polytrack at Kempton in June and then won a minor event at Compiegne in July and a very valuable listed race at Deauville (by a neck from another British-trained colt No Education) in August, either side of finishing second to George Patton in a minor event at Deauville. Robin of Navan matched the form of his second win when landing the five-runner Group 3 Prix de Conde at Chantilly in October by two and a half lengths from Millfield, with odds-on Cloth of Stars, winner of the Prix des Chenes, third. Three horses dominated the pari-mutuel betting on the Criterium de Saint-Cloud—Ballydoyle's once-raced brother to Highland Reel, Idaho (22/10), Cloth of Stars (26/10) and Robin of Navan (27/10). On softer ground than he had encountered previously and stepping up another furlong in trip, Robin of Navan improved again to win by two and a half lengths from the headstrong Cloth of Stars, with another three lengths back to the filly Notte Bianca who edged out Idaho (possibly the best long-term prospect in the field) for third. Robin of Navan set a sound pace, brought the field wide into the straight and was ridden clear soon

851

afterwards, just having to be kept up to his work to maintain his advantage to the line. Robin of Navan was ridden by Tony Piccone who partnered him on all of his starts in France. Piccone has been steadily climbing the jockey ranks in France and he recorded more than eighty wins for the third year running in 2015, which placed him inside the top ten in the French jockeys' championship for the second successive year. Robin of Navan was reportedly Piccone's first pattern winner. The Criterium de Saint-Cloud over a mile and a quarter, with its November date virtually guaranteeing ground on the soft side, provides a stiff test for two-year-olds and its winners have met with varying degrees of success subsequently, with Voix du Nord (2003), Fame And Glory (2008) and Prince Gibraltar (2013) the last three to go on to win again at Group 1 level.

Robin of Navan (FR) (ch.c. 2013)	American Post (br 2001)	Bering (ch 1983)	Arctic Tern Beaune
		Wells Fargo (b 1996)	Sadler's Wells Cruising Height
	Cloghran (FR) (b 2008)	Muhtathir (ch 1995)	Elmaamul Majmu
		The Wise Lady (b 2000)	Ganges Miller's Lily

The rangy Robin of Navan cost only €10,000 as a yearling before making €47,000 at the Saint-Cloud Breeze-Up Sale which took place less than seven weeks before his debut. He is the first foal out of the lightly-raced French middle-distance maiden Cloghran who is a half-sister to the useful pair Ming Zhi Cosmos, a winner at up to a mile, and the two-year-old sprinter Melodyman. Robin of Navan's grandam The Wise Lady was a useful winner in France over six furlongs and his great grandam Miller's Lily won two of her twenty-four starts at up to seven furlongs in France. Miller's Lily's listed race-winning daughters Liliside, who stayed nine furlongs, and Lily America, who stayed a mile, are both by Robin of Navan's sire American Post. Liliside was denied a much bigger prize when demoted for causing interference after passing the post first in the 2010 Poule d'Essai des Pouliches. American Post failed to stay a mile and a half in the Derby but was bred to stay middle distances, being out of a half-sister to St Leger second High And Low and the smart stayer Corradini. Robin of Navan should stay beyond a mile and a quarter and acts on soft going. *Harry Dunlop*

ROBIN PARK 3 b.f. Invincible Spirit (IRE) 121 – Haigh Hall 84 (Kyllachy 129) [2015 **82** 64: 6.1d* 6m* 6.1g³ 6m 6m Jul 23] rather leggy filly: fairly useful handicapper: won at Nottingham and Newmarket in May: acts on good to firm and good to soft going: tried in hood in 2015: front runner/races prominently, often races freely. *Richard Fahey*

ROBINS PEARL (FR) 3 ch.f. Linngari (IRE) 124 – Fire Sale (ARG) (Not For Sale **86** (ARG)) [2015 60p: p8f³ 9m* 8g⁵ t9.5m* t8.6f² Dec 14] plain filly: fairly useful handicapper: won at Sandown in May and Wolverhampton in September: left Olly Stevens after: will stay 1¼m: acts on tapeta and good to firm going. *Harry Dunlop*

ROBOT BOY (IRE) 5 ch.g. Shamardal (USA) 129 – Pivotal's Princess (IRE) 107 **113** (Pivotal 124) [2015 114: 5v³ 5.2m* 5g 5f 5f⁴ 6m 5.4g 5.6d 5d⁴ 6s 5d Oct 24] strong gelding: useful handicapper: won at Newbury (by length from Normal Equilibrium) in April: best subsequent effort when fourth of 18 to Double Up at Ascot on fifth start: stays 6f: acts on firm and soft going. *David Barron*

ROBOTIC 4 b.g. Oasis Dream 129 – Bionic 105 (Zafonic (USA) 130) [2015 6m 5g⁵ 7g⁵ – p6f Dec 17] little form: wears tongue tie. *Michael Easterby*

ROB'S LEGACY 2 ch.g. (May 19) Phoenix Reach (IRE) 124 – Clumber Pursuits – (Pastoral Pursuits 127) [2015 7.2g 7d Oct 23] well held in 2 maidens. *Shaun Harris*

ROCAVERDE (IRE) 2 b.f. (Mar 20) Rock of Gibraltar (IRE) 133 – Green Room (FR) **58 p** 108 (In The Wings 128) [2015 8g Sep 30] fifth foal: closely related to 16.5f winner Dukes Den (by Duke of Marmalade) and half-sister to 11.5f winner L'Ingenue (by New Approach): dam 11f-1½m winner: 20/1, modest form when seventh of 12 in maiden at Salisbury, looking in need of experience: should do better. *Ralph Beckett*

ROCCO'S DELIGHT 3 b.g. Multiplex 114 – No Page (IRE) 81 (Statue of Liberty **81** (USA) 115) [2015 60: t7.1g f8g* 7d* 6.9v* 7.2g 7v³ Nov 3] fairly useful handicapper: won at Southwell in April, Doncaster in May and Carlisle in June: stays 1m: acts on fibresand and heavy going: tried in cheekpieces: usually races close up. *Tony Coyle*

ROC DE PRINCE 6 b.g. Shirocco (GER) 129 – Louella (USA) (El Gran Senor (USA) 66
136) [2015 12.4g⁶ 16s* 16.1d 15s 16.1g Sep 4] fair handicapper: won at Musselburgh
(amateur) in May: stays 2m: acts on good to firm and heavy going: tried in headgear/tongue
tie: usually races towards rear. *James Ewart*

ROCETTE 2 ch.f. (Mar 19) Prime Defender 118 – Makindi 63 (Makbul 104) [2015 6g Sep –
24] first foal: dam lightly raced on Flat/over hurdles: 100/1, seventh of 10 in maiden at
Pontefract, slowly away. *Michael Appleby*

ROCHAMBEAU (IRE) 4 b.g. Sir Percy 129 – Tableau Vivant (IRE) 87 (Pivotal 124) 68
[2015 75: f11g⁶ 12.4g 12g⁵ 12g² 12g² 12m⁵ 12g 12m⁶ Aug 4] lengthy, rather unfurnished
gelding: fair handicapper: stays 1½m: acts on polytrack and good to firm going: often wears
blinkers: usually races freely: temperament under suspicion. *Ruth Carr*

ROCKABILLY RIOT (IRE) 5 br.g. Footstepsinthesand 120 – Zawariq (IRE) 62 68
(Marju (IRE) 127) [2015 13.8d 12.4d* 11.5m² 13.1g 12g⁴ 14.4g² 12d⁶ 12d⁶ Sep 15] fair
handicapper: won at Newcastle in April: stays 14.5f: acts on polytrack, firm and soft going:
sometimes in headgear prior to 2015: in tongue tie final start: often races towards rear.
Martin Todhunter

ROCK A DOODLE DOO (IRE) 8 b.g. Oratorio (IRE) 128 – Nousaiyra (IRE) (Be My –
Guest (USA) 126) [2015 12d Mar 29] good-bodied gelding: one-time fairly useful
handicapper: stays 1¾m: acts on polytrack, soft and good to firm going: has worn headgear,
including last 4 starts. *Sally Hall*

ROCKAROUNDTHECLOCK (IRE) 3 ch.c. Starspangledbanner (AUS) 128 – 83
Lulawin (Kyllachy 129) [2015 70, a76: t7.1f⁴ p7.5g* 8s² 8d⁴ 8g³ 8s* p8g⁵ 8.3d p8g p8f⁵
Dec 17] strong colt: fairly useful performer: won claimers at Chantilly in February
(apprentices) and May: stays 1m: acts on polytrack and soft going: tried in blinkers/tongue
tie. *Paul Cole*

ROCKAWANGO (FR) 9 b.g. Okawango (USA) 115 – Janou La Belle (FR) (Shining 70
Steel 123) [2015 12.5s³ 12.4g 14g⁶ 12.5s³ May 11] fair handicapper: stays 2m: acts on
viscoride and soft going: sometimes wears headgear: tried in tongue tie. *James Ewart*

ROCKCANDY MOUNTAIN (IRE) 3 b.g. Captain Rio 122 – Over The Ridge (IRE) 69
(Indian Ridge 123) [2015 7m³ 5.9s³ 7g³ 8g Sep 18] fair maiden: stayed 7f: dead.
David Barron

ROCK CANYON (IRE) 6 b.g. Rock of Gibraltar (IRE) 133 – Tuesday Morning 72
(Sadler's Wells (USA) 132) [2015 59: 5v 6g² 7.1s⁴ 6s* 5d* 6d⁵ 6d² 6m 6d 6g⁵ 6g 5s³ 6d³
6d² 5d⁵ 5m 5g* 6g 6g Sep 29] compact gelding: fair handicapper: won at Ayr in May
(twice) and September: best at 5f/6f: acts on good to firm and heavy going: often in
cheekpieces prior to 2015. *Linda Perratt*

ROCK CHARM 4 b.g. Araafa (IRE) 128 – Evening Charm (IRE) (Bering 136) [2015 62: 64
p12m⁶ p8g* p8f³ f8g³ p8f³ 8s 9.9g² 8s 10.1m 8.3g 18.6g f7g⁶ Dec 18] good-topped
gelding: modest handicapper: won at Chelmsford in February: left Stuart Williams after
seventh start: stays 1¼m: acts on polytrack: often in headgear in 2015: usually in tongue tie
in 2015. *Ronald Thompson*

ROCKET PUNCH (IRE) 3 b.g. Makfi 130 – Crystal Reef (King's Best (USA) 132) 90
[2015 8g⁵ 8g* p8g* 8d 9g 10.4s⁴ Oct 10] 120,000F: compact gelding: second foal: dam,
maiden (stayed 14.5f), half-sister to smart/very smart stayers Coastal Path and Reefscape:
fairly useful performer: won maiden at Goodwood in June and handicap at Kempton in
July: in first-time blinkers, good 2¾ lengths fourth of 20 to Empress Ali in handicap at York
final start: worth a try at 1½m: acts on polytrack and soft going: has joined Gordon Elliott.
Andrew Balding

ROCKET ROB (IRE) 9 b.g. Danetime (IRE) 121 – Queen of Fibres (IRE) 65 (Scenic 75 §
128) [2015 81§, a69§: p6f p6f⁶ 6g 5m 5m⁴ 5d² 6d⁵ 5s³ 5.1g⁶ p5f⁵ t6f⁴ p5g² p5m³ Dec 31] **a64 §**
good-quartered gelding: fair handicapper: stays 7f: acts on polytrack, firm and good to soft
going: tried in headgear prior to 2015: sometimes slowly away, often races towards rear:
unreliable. *Willie Musson*

ROCKET RONNIE (IRE) 5 b.g. Antonius Pius (USA) 123 – Ctesiphon (USA) 55 80
(Arch (USA) 127) [2015 83: p8m t7.1f⁵ 8g⁴ 8m⁴ 8d⁶ 8.3g* 8.3v* 8d p8d⁴ t8.6f⁴ Dec 14]
strong, good-bodied gelding: fairly useful handicapper: won at Hamilton in September and
Nottingham in October: stays 1¼m: acts on polytrack and any turf going: in headgear last
6 starts. *Ed McMahon*

ROCKFAST 3 b.g. Fastnet Rock (AUS) 127 – Empress Anna (IRE) (Imperial Ballet (IRE) **68**
110) [2015 74p: p8f³ p10g* 10d 9.9g t8.6g⁴ 9.9g³ 10g Sep 7] lengthy gelding: fair **a75**
performer: won maiden at Chelmsford in February: stays 1¼m: acts on polytrack and
tapeta: tried in blinkers in 2015: often races prominently, often races freely. *Gary Moore*

ROCKFELLA 9 ch.g. Rock of Gibraltar (IRE) 133 – Afreeta (USA) (Afleet (CAN)) [2015 **–**
88: 14.1m 14.1g p16d Sep 4] compact gelding: fairly useful at best, no form in 2015 (in
cheekpieces final start). *Denis Coakley*

ROCKFIELD LAST (IRE) 2 b.f. (Apr 3) Frozen Power (IRE) 108 – Speckled Hen **81**
(IRE) 60 (Titus Livius (FR) 115) [2015 5m⁴ 5g* 5.5g² 6g* 6g 6s⁴ Oct 20] €3,200F, 5,500Y:
fourth foal: half-sister to useful winner up to 8.2f Baba O'Riley (2-y-o 6f winner, by
Whipper) and smart 7f-9f winner Third Time Lucky (by Clodovil): dam maiden who
stayed 7f: fairly useful performer: won seller at Redcar in April and, having left Giles
Bravery €19,666 after third start, claimer at Chantilly (despite putting head in air) in July,
then left P. Sogorb: stays 6f: tried in cheekpieces. *N. Clement, France*

ROCK FOLLIES 3 b.f. Rock of Gibraltar (IRE) 133 – Ashraakat (USA) 105 (Danzig **73**
(USA)) [2015 67: 6s² p6f³ 6m⁴ May 27] fair maiden: best effort at 6f: acts on soft going:
front runner/races prominently. *Lady Cecil*

ROCK HEROINE 3 gr.f. Rock of Gibraltar (IRE) 133 – Kinetix 78 (Linamix (FR) 127) **82**
[2015 –: t7.1m³ f8g² t12.2g³ 8.5g² 9.9g⁴ Dec 29] fairly useful maiden: left Hughie
Morrison after third start: stays 1¼m: acts on fibresand. *Jassim Al Ghazali, Qatar*

ROCK ICON 2 b.g. (Apr 6) Sixties Icon 125 – Monashee Rock (IRE) 78 (Monashee **42**
Mountain (USA) 115) [2015 t9.5f⁶ t8.6f⁴ Dec 14] poor form in claimers at Wolverhampton.
Heather Main

ROCKIE ROAD (IRE) 4 b.g. Footstepsinthesand 120 – Roclette (USA) 76 (Rock of **65**
Gibraltar (IRE) 133) [2015 62: p12g⁵ p10f 8m² 8.3m 9d 8d* 8g³ 8v* Aug 24] rather
unfurnished gelding: fair handicapper: won at Brighton in June and August: stayed 1½m:
acted on polytrack, good to firm and heavy going: tried in cheekpieces: was sometimes
slowly away: dead. *Mick Quinn*

ROCKING RUDOLPH (USA) 2 b.f. (Jan 22) Discreetly Mine (USA) 120 – Empire **79 p**
Spring (USA) (Empire Maker (USA) 129) [2015 f5g* 5.2s 5.2v⁵ Aug 25] $40,000Y: first
foal: dam 8.5f winner: fair form: won maiden at Southwell in July by 3 lengths from Sea of
Uncertainty: switched to turf, below that form on soft/heavy last 2 starts: raced only at 5f:
remains with potential. *Robert Cowell*

ROCKLEY POINT 2 b.c. (Apr 14) Canford Cliffs (IRE) 133 – Statua (IRE) 98 **81**
(Statoblest 120) [2015 6m³ 7f³ 6g⁴ p6g² 6g p8f⁵ t6f² t6m³ Nov 21] £31,000Y: workmanlike
colt: half-brother to several winners, including smart 7f-1¼m winner St Moritz (by
Medicean), 2-y-o 5f winner Dance Anthem (by Royal Academy) and 6f-1m winner
Annemasse (by Anabaa), latter 2 useful: dam 6f-1m winner: fairly useful maiden: good
second in nursery at Wolverhampton penultimate start: worth another try at 7f: acts on
polytrack, tapeta and firm going. *Paul D'Arcy*

ROCKLEY (USA) 2 b.c. (Feb 2) Speightstown (USA) 124 – African Skies 99 **70**
(Johannesburg (USA) 127) [2015 7g³ 7g⁵ p7f p8g³ p8f⁶ Sep 3] fair maiden: stays 1m: acts
on polytrack: in cheekpieces final start: sent to UAE. *Charlie Appleby*

ROCKLIFFE 2 b.g. (Mar 8) Notnowcato 128 – Hope Island (IRE) 69 (Titus Livius (FR) **69**
115) [2015 5m⁵ 6g³ 6m 7m³ 7g⁵ p7m Dec 31] rather unfurnished gelding: fair maiden:
should stay 7f: acts on good to firm going: usually races prominently. *Mick Channon*

ROCK LOBSTER 3 ch.g. Bahamian Bounty 116 – Reeling N' Rocking (IRE) 82 (Mr **85**
Greeley (USA) 122) [2015 68p: 10m⁵ 10.2s⁵ 8.3m⁵ 10.4g⁴ p10g* 10.2s⁴ 10.2g p8f² Oct 22]
fairly useful handicapper: won at Chelmsford in August: stays 1¼m: acts on polytrack and
good to firm going: sometimes in cheekpieces in 2015: usually races prominently.
Ed Dunlop

ROCK MONTJEU (IRE) 3 b.g. Rock of Gibraltar (IRE) 133 – Leala (IRE) (Montjeu **64**
(IRE) 137) [2015 p7g 8m⁶ 7d⁶ 7g f8g⁴ Dec 18] modest maiden: left C. W. J. Farrell after
fourth start: stays 1m: acts on good to firm and good to soft going, probably fibresand:
sometimes in headgear. *A. P. Keatley, Ireland*

ROCKMOUNT 3 b.c. Major Cadeaux 121 – Fisher Island (IRE) 59 (Sri Pekan (USA) **55**
117) [2015 –: 6g t7.1g 6m 5.7m⁵ t6g⁴ t6m p6f⁵ Oct 1] modest maiden: stays 6f: acts on **a44**
good to firm going: often in hood in 2015. *Ed McMahon*

ROCK 'N RED (IRE) 2 b.f. (Jan 20) Fastnet Rock (AUS) 127 – Red Fantasy (IRE) 98 **54**
(High Chaparral (IRE) 132) [2015 7.4v⁵ p7g Sep 21] first foal: dam, 1¼m winner, half-
sister to smart 6f/7f winner Desert Fantasy out of smart 5f/6f winner Petite Fantasy: better
effort when seventh of 14 in maiden at Kempton second start, fading 1f out. *Ed Dunlop*

ROCK 'N' ROLL STAR 4 b.g. Cockney Rebel (IRE) 127 – Sweet Afton (IRE) 98 **–**
(Mujadil (USA) 119) [2015 79: p7g May 27] well-made gelding: fair handicapper: well
held only outing in 2015: stays 8.5f: acts on polytrack and firm going: usually slowly away,
races well off pace. *Lee Carter*

ROCK OF AGES 6 ch.g. Pivotal 124 – Magic Peak (IRE) 78 (Danehill (USA) 126) [2015 **64**
f16d³ f16g* f16dᵖᵘ 12g t13.9m t16.5f f16g⁶ t16.5f Nov 16] modest handicapper: won at
Southwell in January: left Neil King after third start: stays 2m: acts on fibresand: usually
wears blinkers: sometimes slowly away, often races lazily. *Steve Flook*

ROCK OF LEON 4 b.g. Rock of Gibraltar (IRE) 133 – Leonica 92 (Lion Cavern (USA) **–**
117) [2015 12d Mar 29] modest handicapper at best: stays 16.5f: acts on tapeta and good
to firm going: often in headgear: tried in tongue tie: front runner/races prominently: fairly
useful hurdler. *Dan Skelton*

ROCK OF MAX 3 b.g. Royal Applause 124 – Poldhu (Cape Cross (IRE) 129) [2015 8g **78**
p10g p8g t8.6m⁵ 10g³ 10.4d 12d⁴ 14.1d³ p16g² Nov 26] fair maiden: seems to stay 2m: acts
on polytrack and good to soft going: tried in cheekpieces: front runner/races prominently.
Michael Bell

ROCK OF MONACO 2 b.f. (May 1) Monsieur Bond (IRE) 120 – Melandre 74 (Lujain **62**
(USA) 119) [2015 5m 5m t6f⁵ t7.1f* Nov 30] £3,200Y: fifth foal: sister to 5f winner
Stanghow and half-sister to 2-y-o 6f winner First Phase (by First Trump) and winner up to
7f Lucky Lodge (2-y-o 5f winner, by Lucky Story): dam 2-y-o 5f winner: modest
performer: won nursery at Wolverhampton in November: best effort at 7f. *Antony Brittain*

ROCK ON BOLLINSKI 5 b.g. Bollin Eric 125 – Bred For Pleasure (Niniski (USA) **80**
125) [2015 12s 17.1g 12.1m⁵ 12g⁶ 15.8d³ 16.1g* 15g⁵ 14.1s* 15.8s³ Oct 27] fairly useful
handicapper: won at Newcastle in September and Redcar in October: stays 2m: acts on soft
going: usually races towards rear: in cheekpieces in 2015: often races towards rear: has carried head high.
Brian Ellison

ROCK ON CANDY 6 b.m. Excellent Art 125 – Rock Candy (IRE) (Rock of Gibraltar **–**
(IRE) 133) [2015 73: p6m Jan 18] handicapper, fair at best: best form at 5f: acts on good to
firm and heavy going: often races towards rear. *John Spearing*

ROCK ON (IRE) 2 ch.c. (Mar 27) Rock of Gibraltar (IRE) 133 – Spectacular Show (IRE) **–**
79 (Spectrum (IRE) 126) [2015 7m Jul 25] €34,000Y, resold £42,000Y: fourth foal:
half-brother to smart 6f/7f winner Valbchek and 5.5f winner Premier Acclaim (both by
Acclamation): dam, 2-y-o 5f winner who stayed 7f, half-sister to Prix de Diane winner Star
of Seville: 11/1, shaped better than result when well held in maiden at Newcastle on debut:
sold only £3,000 in September, sent to Sweden. *Tim Easterby*

ROCK ON RODNEY 3 b.g. Cockney Rebel (IRE) 127 – Intriguing Glimpse 100 **–**
(Piccolo 121) [2015 p6g p8g 7s⁶ Aug 20] no form. *Roger Teal*

ROCK OPERA 2 b.f. (Mar 21) Fastnet Rock (AUS) 127 – Opera Glass 88 (Barathea **– p**
(IRE) 127) [2015 8v Oct 24] seventh foal: closely related to 1¾m winner (stays 2m) Opera
Buff (by Oratorio) and half-sister to useful 1¼m-11.6f winner Opera Gal (by Galileo) and
1½m winner (stays 1¾m) Opera Lad (by Teofilo): dam, 8.4f winner, sister to smart winner
up to 7f Opera Cape: 33/1, in need of experience when eighth of 12 in maiden at Newbury,
slowly away: should do better in time. *Andrew Balding*

ROCK ROYALTY 3 ch.g. Kyllachy 129 – Mayaar (USA) 64 (Grand Slam (USA) 120) **75**
[2015 6g³ p6f² 6d⁴ Oct 5] fair form when placed in maidens at Doncaster and Chelmsford:
did too much too soon final start: sold 5,500 gns, sent to Italy. *George Peckham*

ROCKSAVAGE (IRE) 2 b.f. (May 2) Fastnet Rock (AUS) 127 – Magnificent Style **– p**
(USA) 107 (Silver Hawk (USA) 123) [2015 8.3g p8g Nov 4] closely related to 9f winner
Distinctive Look (by Danehill) and half-sister to numerous winners, including King
George VI & Queen Elizabeth Stakes winner Nathaniel (by Galileo) and very smart
11.5f-1¾m winner (stayed 2m) Percussionist (by Sadler's Wells): dam 1¼m winner: well
held in maidens at Nottingham and Kempton (still green): should do better in time.
John Gosden

ROCK SONG 6 b.g. Rock of Gibraltar (IRE) 133 – Jackie's Opera (FR) (Indian Ridge **63**
123) [2015 10d⁵ Jul 29] tall gelding: modest handicapper: stays 1½m: acts on polytrack,
firm and good to soft going. *John Mackie*

ROCKSPIRIT (IRE) 2 b.c. (May 8) Fastnet Rock (AUS) 127 – Phillippa (IRE) (Galileo **76 p**
(IRE) 134) [2015 p8f⁴ Oct 22] 28,000Y: fifth foal: closely related to useful 1¼m-12.3f
winner Naseem Alyasmeen (by Clodovil) and winner up to 8.3f Starlight Symphony (2-y-o
7f winner, by Oratorio) and half-brother to 2-y-o 8.6f winner (stays 10.5f) Aabir (by
Invincible Spirit): dam unraced: 20/1, better for run when 1¾ lengths fourth of 10 to
Thikriyaat in maiden at Chelmsford, keeping on well/nearest finish under hands-and-heels
ride: sure to progress. *Marco Botti*

ROCK STEADY (IRE) 2 ch.g. (Mar 30) Intikhab (USA) 135 – Mannsara (IRE) (Royal **81 p**
Academy (USA) 130) [2015 6d 7.1s⁴ 6.1v² t7.1f* Oct 27] €25,000F, €66,000 2-y-o: half-
brother to several winners, including useful 5f-1m winner Manzila (by Cadeaux Genereux)
and 1m-10.4f winner (stays 16.5f) Russian George (by Sendawar): dam maiden: fairly
useful performer: won nursery at Wolverhampton in October: stays 7f: will go on
improving. *Roger Charlton*

ROCKTHERUNWAY (IRE) 6 ch.g. Nayef (USA) 129 – Femme Fatale 102 (Fairy **81**
King (USA)) [2015 14.1s³ 13d⁵ 16d⁴ 12g 14.1s⁶ Oct 16] sturdy gelding: fairly useful
handicapper: barely stays testing 17.5f: acts on good to firm and heavy going: often wears
cheekpieces: often starts slowly. *Michael Dods*

ROCK WARBLER (IRE) 2 ch.g. (Feb 25) Raven's Pass (USA) 133 – Rare Tern (IRE) **76 p**
96 (Pivotal 124) [2015 7g⁴ 7.6g³ p7g² Sep 23] 62,000F, €170,000Y: first foal: dam, 8.5f
winner, half-sister to 6f winner Bee Eater and 6.7f winner Expedition (both useful) out
of useful winner up to 6f (including at 2 yrs) Littlefeather: fair form: 7/4, improved when
1¼ lengths second of 9 to Gold Faith in maiden at Kempton, clear of rest: has been gelded:
likely to progress further. *Charlie Appleby*

ROCKWEILLER 8 b.g. Rock of Gibraltar (IRE) 133 – Ballerina Suprema (IRE) 87 **64**
(Sadler's Wells (USA) 132) [2015 68, a57: 12d p12g 10d² 12.4g⁴ 12g 10g 10m 11.6m
t9.5m Nov 28] neat gelding: modest handicapper: stays 13f: acts on polytrack, soft and
good to firm going: sometimes wears headgear: often races prominently, tends to find little.
Shaun Harris

ROCKWOOD 4 b.g. Rock of Gibraltar (IRE) 133 – Hannah Frank (IRE) (High Chaparral **62**
(IRE) 132) [2015 8m 8d⁵ f11d⁵ 8.3d 10.2mᵖᵘ 10g⁶ 8.9g³ 10.1g⁴ 10m 9.9g* 9.9d⁶ t9.5f
t9.5f⁴ t9.5f⁵ t8.6g² Dec 5] fair handicapper: left David C. Griffiths after fourteenth start:
stays 1¼m: acts on tapeta: has worn headgear, including last 2 starts: tried in tongue tie:
sometimes slowly away. *Karen McLintock*

ROCKY HILL RIDGE 4 b.g. Auction House (USA) 120 – Amwell Star (USA) 46 **–**
(Silver Buck (USA)) [2015 53: t6g f7s⁶ f7m f6g Dec 22] maiden: no form in 2015: often
wears headgear: front runner/races prominently. *John Balding*

ROCKY REBEL 7 b.g. Norse Dancer (IRE) 127 – Gulchina (USA) 72 (Gulch (USA)) **57**
[2015 71: f12g³ t12.2m Apr 29] big gelding: modest handicapper nowadays: stays 2m: acts
on polytrack and soft going: has worn headgear: fair hurdler. *Michael Blake*

ROCKY RIDER 3 b.c. Galileo (IRE) 134 – Blue Symphony 73 (Darshaan 133) [2015 **109**
89p: p10f* 10g³ 10m⁴ 12f⁵ Jun 18] tall colt: useful performer: won handicap at Chelmsford
(by 6 lengths from Monein) in March: 33/1, shaped well when 2½ lengths fifth of 17 to
Space Age in King George V Stakes (Handicap) at Royal Ascot final start, finishing well
after meeting trouble and having to go wide: stays 1½m: acts on polytrack, firm and good
to soft going: often races freely. *Andrew Balding*

ROCKY'S PRIDE (IRE) 9 b.g. Rock of Gibraltar (IRE) 133 – L'Animee (Green Tune **55**
(USA) 125) [2015 62: 7m⁴ 7.5f 8m Aug 10] modest handicapper: stays 1¼m: acts on
polytrack and firm going: sometimes in headgear/tongue tie prior to 2015: front runner/
races prominently. *Richard Whitaker*

ROCKY TWO (IRE) 5 ch.g. Rock of Gibraltar (IRE) 133 – Toorah Laura La (USA) **44**
(Black Minnaloushe (USA) 123) [2015 14g 12.5m 11.6m⁶ 12g 13.7g⁵ Aug 26] poor
handicapper: stays 13f: acts on soft and good to firm going: tried in cheekpieces: front
runner/races freely, often races freely, tends to find little. *Philip Kirby*

ROCOCOA (IRE) 2 b.f. (Apr 5) Zebedee 113 – Nightbird (IRE) 108 (Night Shift (USA)) **69 p**
[2015 p7g³ Dec 20] £38,000Y: half-sister to several winners, including 1¼m winner Silent
Hawk (by Halling) and 1m/8.3f winner Border Owl (by Selkirk): dam, 6f winner (including
at 2 yrs), half-sister to smart 6f-1m winner Edinburgh Knight: 33/1, raced freely when third
of 8 in maiden at Lingfield (½ length behind Foxinthehenhouse) on debut: should progress.
Ed Walker

RODERIC'S SECRET (IRE) 2 ch.g. (Mar 20) Roderic O'Connor (IRE) 119 – Midris (IRE) 97 (Namid 128) [2015 8.3d⁶ p8g Nov 26] fair maiden: similar form to debut when 3¾ lengths seventh of 9 to Lilly Vega at Chelmsford. *David Menuisier* **65**

ROD OF IRON 2 br.g. (Jun 10) Alkaased (USA) 127 – Leading Star 47 (Motivator 131) [2015 8s⁶ p7g Nov 9] well held in 2 maidens. *Michael Madgwick* **–**

RODRIGO DE TORRES 8 ch.g. Bahamian Bounty 116 – Leonica 92 (Lion Cavern (USA) 117) [2015 76: t6f 7m⁴ 6g³ 6s 6d⁶ 7d* 7.2g* 7m* 8g 6g 7.2g⁶ Sep 29] lengthy, good-topped gelding: fairly useful handicapper: left Fred Watson: won at Catterick and Musselburgh in July and Redcar in August: stays 8.5f: acts on tapeta, good to firm and heavy going: usually wears headgear: usually leads. *Garry Moss* **90**

ROGER THORPE 6 b.g. Firebreak 125 – Nunthorpe 79 (Mystiko (USA) 124) [2015 73: t9.5g⁵ f8d⁶ t7.1g 10g 8.5d f8g² f8g* f8g Dec 12] fair handicapper: won at Southwell (amateur) in November: stays 1¼m: acts on fibresand, tapeta and heavy going: sometimes slowly away, often races prominently. *Deborah Sanderson* **65**

ROGUE RUNNER (GER) 3 b.c. King's Best (USA) 132 – Rosa di Brema (ITY) 103 (Lomitas 129) [2015 8g* 9.9s⁵ 12m 11.9g⁵ 10.2g 11.9g* p9.4g 9.9g* Dec 30] €55,000Y: lengthy colt: eighth foal: closely related to useful winner up to 1¼m (2-y-o 6f winner) Rosa del Dubai (by Dubai Destination) and half-brother to several minor winners abroad: dam, winner up to 1¼m (2-y-o 7f winner), second in Oaks d'Italia: useful performer: won minor event at Hoppegarten in April and Qatar Derby at Doha (dead-heated with Tannaaf): well held in Derby at Epsom on third appearance, but good efforts on fourth and sixth starts, 7½ lengths fifth to Nutan in Deutsches Derby at Hamburg and 2 lengths fourth to Connecticut in Bosphorus Cup at Veliefendi: left A. Wohler after sixth outing: stays 1½m: in headgear 5 of last 6 starts: too free on fifth outing. *M. Hofer, Germany* **107**

ROGUES' GALLERY (IRE) 2 ch.c. (Apr 24) Fast Company (IRE) 126 – Melpomene 95 (Peintre Celebre (USA) 137) [2015 p5g³ 5f² 5m² 5.1s² 5d* 5f⁵ 5.1g² 6.3m⁴ 6.1gᵖᵘ Aug 2] angular colt: fairly useful performer: won maiden at Ayr (by 6 lengths) in May: fifth in Norfolk Stakes at Royal Ascot (2½ lengths behind Waterloo Bridge) next start: best form at 5f: acted on firm and good to soft going: front runner/raced prominently: dead. *Mark Johnston* **93**

ROGUE WAVE (IRE) 4 b.g. Iffraaj 127 – Lady Naomi (USA) (Distant View (USA) 126) [2015 83: p8f 8m³ 7f⁶ 8g⁵ 7g³ Sep 12] useful-looking gelding: fairly useful handicapper: stays 1m: acts on polytrack, firm and soft going: sold 8,500 gns, sent to Bahrain. *Timothy Jarvis* **83**

ROJINA (IRE) 2 ch.f. (Apr 7) Intense Focus (USA) 117 – Hurricane Havoc (IRE) 106 (Hurricane Run (IRE) 134) [2015 t6m Dec 30] 13,000Y: first foal: dam winner up to 1¼m, also 2-y-o 7f winner: 50/1, ninth of 10 in maiden at Wolverhampton (4½ lengths behind dead-heaters Miss Phillyjinks and Murdanova) on debut. *Joseph Tuite* **55**

ROKBAAN 3 b.g. Camacho 118 – Salinia (IRE) (Rainbow Quest (USA) 134) [2015 –: t7.1f⁵ f8d p8f⁵ p11g t9.5g⁶ p8f⁵ p10m 5.7f Jun 24] modest maiden: left Roger Varian after second start: stays 1m: acts on polytrack and tapeta: in visor last 3 starts. *Mark Usher* **51**

ROKEBY 4 b.g. Byron 117 – Scarlet Royal 43 (Red Ransom (USA)) [2015 58: 12d 16g⁶ 15.8m Aug 4] small, leggy gelding: maiden: no form in 2015: tried in blinkers: often races towards rear, often races lazily. *George Moore* **–**

ROKERBY HALL 2 b.f. (Mar 21) Dutch Art 126 – Royal Punch (Royal Applause 124) [2015 6m 6s 6d Oct 26] 60,000Y: half-sister to several winners, including useful 2-y-o winners Royal Rascal (6f, by Lucky Story) and Cocktail Charlie (5f, by Danbird): dam once-raced half-sister to smart 1m/9f winner Tigah: poor maiden: blinkered last 2 starts. *Tim Easterby* **49**

ROLEN SLY 6 b.g. Tillerman 123 – Feiticeira (USA) 79 (Deposit Ticket (USA)) [2015 7g 6m⁶ 8.5d⁵ 10.2s⁵ Oct 28] modest maiden: probably stays 1½m: acts on good to firm and good to soft going: tried in cheekpieces. *Neville Bycroft* **53**

ROLL ON RORY 2 b.g. (Apr 6) Mullionmileanhour (IRE) 116 – Fangfoss Girls 68 (Monsieur Bond (IRE) 120) [2015 5m² 5m* 5f 5s⁴ Oct 27] compact gelding: second foal: brother to winner up to 6f (including at 2 yrs) Pancake Day: dam 2-y-o 5f winner: fairly useful performer: won maiden at Carlisle in May: raced only at 5f. *Jason Ward* **80**

ROLY TRICKS 4 b.f. Pastoral Pursuits 127 – Freya Tricks 72 (Noverre (USA) 125) [2015 64: p8g⁶ 12mᵘʳ f11d⁴ 12.1m⁴ 14.1g p8g² 10g⁵ 8.5s⁵ 9.9d* p10f 9.9v* 9.9s* Oct 15] fair handicapper: won at Brighton in September (apprentice) and October (twice): stays 1¼m: acts on polytrack and heavy going: tried in headgear. *Natalie Lloyd-Beavis* **75**

ROMANCINGTHESTONE 2 b.f. (May 2) Bertolini (USA) 125 – Diamond Vanessa **47** (IRE) (Distinctly North (USA) 115) [2015 6m 6m t6g p6g² 6g p7g p8f 7g³ 6.1s 7s³ f7g⁵ **a55** p5f⁴ t7.1f⁴ p6g² t6f Dec 22] seventh foal: half-sister to winner up to 7f Gaby North (by Puissance): dam of little account: modest maiden: stays 7f: acts on all-weather, best turf form on good going: in headgear nowadays. *J. S. Moore*

ROMAN DE BRUT (IRE) 3 ch.g. Rock of Gibraltar (IRE) 133 – Nesmeh (USA) (More **67** Than Ready (USA) 120) [2015 52: t9.5f³ t8.6f* t8.6f² t9.5m* Dec 26] fair handicapper: won twice at Wolverhampton in December: stays 9.5f: acts on tapeta. *Ronald Thompson*

ROMAN FLIGHT (IRE) 7 b.g. Antonius Pius (USA) 123 – Flight Sequence 88 (Polar **87** Falcon (USA) 126) [2015 80: p11f⁵ 12.3v⁵ May 8] fairly useful handicapper: stays 1½m: acts on polytrack and good to soft going: sometimes wears visor: useful jumper. *David Dennis*

ROMAN HOLIDAY (IRE) 2 b.f. (May 9) Holy Roman Emperor (IRE) 125 – Burn The **67 p** Breeze (IRE) 115 (Beat Hollow 126) [2015 7g⁶ Oct 21] rather unfurnished filly: third foal: dam, 1¼m/10.5f winner who stayed 12.5f, half-sister to winner 1m winner Lethals Lady: 66/1, shaped as if needed experience when 6¾ lengths sixth of 11 to Farandine in maiden at Newmarket on debut, not knocked about: will improve. *Ed Vaughan*

ROMAN MAGIC (IRE) 2 b.f. (Feb 22) Holy Roman Emperor (IRE) 125 – Folle **–** Blanche (USA) (Elusive Quality (USA)) [2015 6m p7g⁶ Jul 14] €32,000F, €80,000Y: good-topped filly: first foal: dam, second at 1¼m at 2 yrs, out of smart winner up to 1m (including at 2 yrs) Always Loyal: well held in 2 maidens: sold only £1,600 in December. *Richard Hannon*

ROMANTIC ANGEL (USA) 2 b.f. (Mar 23) Macho Uno (USA) 124 – Non Sibi (USA) **– p** (Wild Deputy (USA)) [2015 p7g Oct 29] $80,000Y: rather unfurnished filly: fifth foal: half-sister to 2 winners, notably smart Canadian Grade 2 7f winner Lookout (by Limehouse): dam winning sprinter, including at 2 yrs: 66/1, 8¼ lengths eighth of 12 to Vaunting in maiden at Lingfield on debut: should do better. *Ismail Mohammed*

ROMANTIC BLISS (IRE) 4 b.f. Holy Roman Emperor (IRE) 125 – Thea di Bisanzio **–** (IRE) 57 (Dr Fong (USA) 128) [2015 62: t7.1f Jan 29] compact filly: modest handicapper: well held only outing in 2015: sold €13,000 in November: stays 1m: acts on polytrack: wears headgear. *K. R. Burke*

ROMANTIC COMEDY (IRE) 2 ch.f. (Apr 27) Equiano (FR) 127 – Gay Romance 71 **64** (Singspiel (IRE) 133) [2015 5m t5.1g⁶ p6f p7g p7g³ f7g² f8g⁴ Dec 29] 30,000F, 10,000Y: sixth foal: half-sister to 1½m winner (stays 2m) Layla's Boy (by Sakhee) and smart winner up to 1m (stays 1¼m) Belgian Bill (2-y-o 7f winner, by Exceed And Excel): dam, 7f winner who stayed 9.5f, half-sister to high-class 7f-11f winner Hawksley Hill: modest maiden: stays 1m: acts on fibresand: tried in cheekpieces. *James Tate*

ROMANTICISED (USA) 3 b.g. Street Sense (USA) 128 – Delighted (IRE) 74 (Danehill **–** (USA) 126) [2015 t8.6f f8d⁵ Mar 11] well held in maiden and a seller. *Tony Coyle*

ROMAN TIMES (IRE) 2 b.f. (Mar 28) Holy Roman Emperor (IRE) 125 – Timeless **57** Dream 79 (Oasis Dream 129) [2015 5m 6m 5.1g⁴ 5m⁴ 6.1m⁵ 6s⁶ 16f² t5.1m⁶ Dec 26] third foal: half-sister to 6f winner Zain Dream (by Mastercraftsman): dam, 6f winner, half-sister to very smart winner up to 7f Welsh Emperor and smart 5f/6f winner Majestic Times: modest maiden: left Tom Dascombe after seventh start: stays 6f: acts on tapeta and good to firm going: tried in cheekpieces. *Alan Berry*

ROMSDAL 4 ch.g. Halling (USA) 133 – Pure Song 75 (Singspiel (IRE) 133) [2015 121: **117** p10g* 12m³ 14m⁴ 12d³ 13.3d⁶ 12m⁴ 12v Oct 24] leggy gelding: smart performer: won listed race at Kempton in March by 2½ lengths from Afonso de Sousa: third in John Porter Stakes at Newbury (1¾ lengths behind Arab Spring) and King George VI and Queen Elizabeth Stakes at Ascot (3¾ lengths behind Postponed): well below form last 3 starts: stays 14.6f: acts on polytrack, good to firm and good to soft ground: front runner/races prominently: has been gelded. *John Gosden*

RONALD GEE (IRE) 8 ch.g. Garuda (IRE) 116 – Panache Lady (IRE) (Cyrano de **76** Bergerac 120) [2015 74: 10.3d 10.1d⁶ 12.5m² 12m 12m³ 12.8m² 12d* 12g* 13.1g 10g Sep 29] fair handicapper: won at Thirsk in August and York (apprentice) in September: stays 13f: acts on firm and soft going: tried in hood in 2015: sometimes slowly away, often races in rear. *Jim Goldie*

RONALDINHO (IRE) 5 b.g. Jeremy (USA) 122 – Spring Glory 73 (Dr Fong (USA) –
128) [2015 81: 11.9d 10.4m⁶ 7.9d 12.2g Aug 27] angular gelding: fairly useful at best, no
form in 2015: tried in headgear/tongue tie. *Dianne Sayer*

RONALDJAMESSACH (IRE) 2 ch.g. (Apr 17) Lord Shanakill (USA) 121 – –
Boschendal (IRE) (Zamindar (USA) 116) [2015 f7f⁶ Dec 17] 10/1, shaped as if needed run
for fitness/experience when 9¼ lengths sixth of 9 to Autumn Blossom in maiden at
Southwell, unable to sustain effort. *James Bethell*

RONNIE BAIRD 2 ch.g. (Mar 5) Poet's Voice 126 – Fleur de Lis (Nayef (USA) 129) **78**
[2015 7m⁵ 8.1g⁵ 7s³ 8g³ 7d⁴ p7m⁶ Oct 21] useful-looking gelding: fair maiden: will prove
suited by a return to 1m: acts on polytrack and good to soft going: in headgear last 3 starts.
Hugo Palmer

RON'S BALLAD 2 ch.g. (Mar 13) Sakhee's Secret 128 – Nom de La Rosa (IRE) 67 –
(Oratorio (IRE) 128) [2015 6m p7g p6g⁶ 6m⁶ Aug 8] angular gelding: no form.
Michael Madgwick

RON WAVERLY (IRE) 5 ch.g. Haatef (USA) 117 – Mermaid Beach (Slew O' Gold **53**
(USA)) [2015 10m⁶ 10m 8.3g 10.1m⁴ 10.1g p12g 10.1v³ 11.9d³ 11.9s⁵ p12g³ Dec 15]
smallish gelding: modest maiden: left Pat Phelan after ninth start: stays 1½m: acts on
polytrack, good to firm and heavy going: often in tongue tie: usually races towards rear.
Paddy Butler

RONYA (IRE) 4 b.f. Bushranger (IRE) 119 – Beenablaw (IRE) 76 (Alzao (USA) 117) **64**
[2015 69: 9.8v² 10m 10g⁴ 9m* 9.3m 9.8g⁶ 10m 10d² Oct 26] modest handicapper: won at
Redcar in July: left K. R. Burke after second start: stays 1¼m: acts on soft and good to firm
going: tried in blinkers in 2015: usually races close up. *Tracy Waggott*

ROOKERY (IRE) 4 b.g. Raven's Pass (USA) 133 – Zacheta (Polish Precedent (USA) –
131) [2015 74: p13g Jan 21] fair maiden at best: has lost way: stays 1½m: acts on polytrack
and good to firm going: tried in blinkers: front runner/races prominently, usually finds
little: sold £600 in June. *Michael Attwater*

ROOM KEY 3 ch.c. Mount Nelson 125 – Saturday Girl (Peintre Celebre (USA) 137) [2015 **104**
98: 8m 8.1m⁴ 8f 8m⁵ 10m⁶ 10.3d Sep 26] plain colt: useful performer: best efforts when 4
lengths fifth of 10 to Malabar in Thoroughbred Stakes at Goodwood and sixth of 13 to
Exosphere in handicap at Sandown fourth/fifth starts: stays 1¼m: acts on good to firm and
good to soft going: tried in cheekpieces: usually races towards rear. *Eve Johnson Houghton*

ROOSSEY (IRE) 3 b.c. Acclamation 118 – Tatiana Romanova (USA) 81 (Mr Greeley **99**
(USA) 122) [2015 93: 6g 6m² 6m 6g⁴ 6m a6f² Dec 11] tall, useful-looking colt: useful
performer: good second to Magical Memory at Newmarket in July: left William Haggas
after fifth start: stays 6f: acts on good to firm going. *D. J. Selvaratnam, UAE*

RORING SAMSON (IRE) 4 b.g. Art Connoisseur (IRE) 121 – Marju Guest (IRE) 67 **64**
(Marju (IRE) 127) [2015 63: 6g³ 6s⁵ 6v⁴ 5s* p5f 5.1d Oct 14] smallish gelding: modest
handicapper: won at Ffos Las in September: stays 7f: acts on soft going: tried in cheekpieces
prior to 2015: usually in tongue tie in 2015: often races towards rear. *George Baker*

ROSAIRLIE (IRE) 7 ch.m. Halling (USA) 133 – Mrs Mason (IRE) 90 (Turtle Island **83**
(IRE) 123) [2015 88: 13.8d 16v 21g 16.4g 16.4s Oct 10] lengthy mare: fairly useful
handicapper: first past the post at Ripon in May on second start, later disqualified due to
prohibited substance: stays 2¼m: acts on polytrack, best turf form on good going or softer
(acts on heavy): tried in headgear prior to 2015. *Micky Hammond*

ROSALIE BONHEUR 3 ch.f. Siyouni (FR) 122 – Crozon 68 (Peintre Celebre (USA) **87**
137) [2015 84p: 7m⁶ p7g⁴ 8.3m* 8.1v⁴ Sep 16] fairly useful handicapper: won at Windsor
in August: stays 8.5f: acts on polytrack and good to firm going. *Clive Cox*

ROSAMARIA (IRE) 2 gr.f. (Mar 17) Rip Van Winkle (IRE) 134 – Rosa Grace 106 **72**
(Lomitas 129) [2015 8g⁴ 8.1v² 8g⁴ 8g⁴ Oct 13] 16,000Y: second foal: dam winner up to
1¼m (2-y-o 7f winner): fair maiden: raced only at 1m. *Mark Johnston*

ROSA'S CANTINA (IRE) 3 b.f. Paco Boy (IRE) 129 – Mountain Law (USA) (Mountain **64**
Cat (USA)) [2015 7f⁵ p8g⁶ 7m³ 7v⁶ 7.1m Sep 5] lengthy filly: half-sister to several
winners, including 7f-1m winner Law of The Range (by Alhaarth) and 7f-9f winner High
Court Drama (by Theatrical), both useful: dam unraced: modest maiden: best effort at 7f:
acts on good to firm going. *Marco Botti*

ROSE ABOVE 3 b.f. Yeats (IRE) 128 – Sabah 91 (Nashwan (USA) 135) [2015 65p: 9g **66**
8.3m⁵ 9g Jul 29] good-topped filly: fair maiden: will be suited by 1¼m+: looked
temperamental tried in hood final start, reluctant leaving stalls and swishing tail.
Andrew Balding

ROSE ACCLAIM (IRE) 3 b.f. Acclamation 118 – Carmona 65 (Rainbow Quest (USA) **53**
134) [2015 58: 8g 8g⁵ 7.2d⁵ 8g⁶ 6g⁴ 7m⁴ 6d 5.9s² 5s Oct 6] modest maiden: will prove best
at sprint trips: acts on soft going: often in headgear in 2015: usually races close up. *David O'Meara*

ROSEALEE (IRE) 2 gr.f. (Feb 28) Zebedee 113 – Why Now 81 (Dansili 127) [2015 **77**
p5g* 5f p5m² Dec 27] £32,000Y: compact filly: half-sister to several winners, including
2-y-o 6f winner What About You (by Statue of Liberty) and winner up to 6f Here Now And
Why (2-y-o 5f winner, by Pastoral Pursuits): dam 5f/6f winner: fair performer: won maiden
at Kempton in April: off 6 months, best effort when second in nursery at Chelmsford: raced
only at 5f. *Jeremy Gask*

ROSEBURG (IRE) 4 ch.g. Tamayuz 126 – Raydaniya (IRE) 78 (In The Wings 128) **115**
[2015 111: 10.3g² 10.4g² 11.9s⁶ Sep 13] sturdy gelding: smart performer: second in
handicaps at Doncaster and York, improved form when beaten a neck by Elhaame in latter
(hung left but finished well): acted as pacemaker for Postponed in Prix Foy at Longchamp
final start: should stay 1½m: acts on good to firm and good to soft going: often races
towards rear: has been gelded. *Luca Cumani*

ROSECOMB (IRE) 2 b.f. (Mar 19) Rip Van Winkle (IRE) 134 – Malyana 89 (Mtoto **60**
134) [2015 6m 7d 6g 7m Aug 7] €50,000Y: rather unfurnished filly: fourth foal: half-sister
to 2-y-o 7f winner Bint Malyana (by Bahamian Bounty): dam, winner up to 1¼m (2-y-o
1m winner), sister to smart winner up to 1¼m Tarfshi and half-sister to Cheveley Park
Stakes winner Embassy: modest maiden: should prove suited by 7f+. *Michael Bell*

ROSE ECLAIR 2 b.f. (Mar 24) Major Cadeaux 121 – Katie Boo (IRE) 92 (Namid 128) **67**
[2015 6g⁶ 6.5m 6g³ 6d⁶ 7m 5g⁴ 6v Nov 7] fourth foal: half-sister to winner up to 7f Penny
Garcia (2-y-o 6f winner) and smart 6f (including at 2 yrs) winner Mattmu (both by
Indesatchel): dam 5f/6f winner, including at 2 yrs: fair maiden: stays 6.5f: acts on good to
firm going. *Tim Easterby*

ROSE MARMARA 2 ch.f. (Mar 10) Exceed And Excel (AUS) 126 – Show Rainbow 97 **70 p**
(Haafhd 129) [2015 6g³ 5.1g² 5g* Oct 13] first foal: dam 6f winner, including at 2 yrs: fair
performer: won maiden at Musselburgh (by neck from Sunnyside Bob) in October: stays
6f: remains with potential. *Richard Fahey*

ROSENBAUM 3 b.g. Dubawi (IRE) 129 – Rave Reviews (IRE) 112 (Sadler's Wells **83 +**
(USA) 132) [2015 64: p10g⁴ t12.2g* f12g* 12m⁵ 14f⁴ t12.2g* p11g² 13d⁶ p11m⁴ t16.5f⁵ **a95**
Nov 30] useful handicapper: won at Wolverhampton in March, Southwell in April and
Wolverhampton in June: will benefit from return to around 1½m: acts on all-weather,
probably on firm going: in blinkers in 2015, also in tongue tie last 5 starts: front runner/
races prominently. *Charlie Appleby*

ROSES WILD 3 b.f. Halling (USA) 133 – Rose Show (Belmez (USA) 131) [2015 p13.3g⁶ **–**
12.1m⁶ 8m⁶ 10.2m 12.1s t12.2g Sep 29] half-sister to several winners, including smart
1¼m/10.3f winner Prize Winner and 8.2f winner (stayed 1½m) Show Winner (both by
Mtoto): dam unraced: no form: left Andrew Balding after second start: often in headgear.
Simon Hodgson

ROSE ZAFONIC 2 b.f. (Mar 29) Poet's Voice 126 – With Distinction 59 (Zafonic (USA) **53**
130) [2015 p6g 7m³ Aug 4] 32,000Y: half-sister to several winners, including useful 2-y-o
6f-7f winner Talking Hands (by Mujahid) and unreliable winner up to 1m Herbert Crescent
(2-y-o 7f winner, by Averti): dam maiden who stayed 1½m: better effort in maidens when
13 lengths third of 8 to Mohab at Catterick: sold 2,000 gns, sent to Qatar. *Robert Cowell*

ROSIE CROWE (IRE) 3 b.f. Approve (IRE) 112 – Tolzey (USA) 94 (Rahy (USA) 115) **59**
[2015 56: t7.1g³ 7g⁵ 8g* 8g² 8g⁶ 8g 8m⁴ 10.3m t7.1g 7s p8f* p8f p8f⁵ t8.6g⁵ Dec 5] modest
handicapper: won at Redcar in April and Chelmsford in October: stays 8.5f: acts on
polytrack, tapeta, best turf form on good going: sometimes in visor in 2015: front runner/
races prominently. *Shaun Harris*

ROSIE HALL (IRE) 5 ch.m. Lion Heart (USA) 124 – Baltic Dip (IRE) 95 (Benny The **50**
Dip (USA) 127) [2015 –: t12.2m⁴ t12.2f⁵ t12.2f⁶ 8.5m t8.6g t12.2f t9.5m Nov 28] modest
maiden: left Les Eyre after fifth start: stays 1½m: acts on tapeta and firm going: often wears
headgear: often races towards rear. *John Wainwright*

ROSIE PROSPECTS 4 b.f. Byron 117 – Sea Jade (IRE) 56 (Mujadil (USA) 119) [2015 **52**
57: p10g⁶ p10f p10f p8f⁴ p10g⁴ p8f⁶ p10g⁵ 10m 10d² p10g p10g Aug 15] modest maiden:
stays 1¼m: acts on polytrack and good to soft going: usually wears headgear. *Roger Ingram*

ROSIE ROYALE (IRE) 3 gr.f. Verglas (IRE) 118 – Fearn Royal (IRE) 103 (Ali-Royal (IRE) 127) [2015 67: p8m p8f 8m 10.1m⁵ 7.6m⁵ 7.4d⁴ 8g* 10v* 9.9s Oct 12] sturdy filly: fair handicapper: won at Brighton and Sandown in September: likely to stay 1½m: acts on polytrack and heavy going: tried in headgear in 2015. *Roger Teal* **66**

ROSIE ROYCE 2 b.f. (Feb 5) Acclamation 118 – Rebecca Rolfe 109 (Pivotal 124) [2015 5f 5.1d³ 6m⁴ 5d Oct 12] first foal: dam 5f/6f winner: fair maiden: stays 6f. *Henry Candy* **69**

ROSIE'S PREMIERE (IRE) 3 b.f. Showcasing 117 – Golden Rosie (IRE) 74 (Exceed And Excel (AUS) 126) [2015 96: 6d 5f 5m 5m 6m³ 6m* 6g 6d Oct 11] small, close-coupled filly: useful handicapper: won at Leicester (by neck from Mulzamm) in August: stays 6f: acts on soft and good to firm going: in tongue tie final start. *Dean Ivory* **95**

ROSIE'S VISION 2 b.f. (May 5) Passing Glance 119 – Bold Rose 69 (Bold Edge 123) [2015 p7g 7s p7g Oct 29] lengthy filly: second foal: dam, 5f-7f winner, half-sister to smart winner up to 9f Wise Dennis: no form. *Mark Usher* **–**

ROSINA 2 b.f. (Feb 8) Showcasing 117 – Mondovi 97 (Kyllachy 129) [2015 5m⁵ 5m³ 5m* 5g* 5g⁶ 6s⁵ Oct 10] 5,000F, £17,000Y, £41,000 2-y-o: second foal: half-sister to 6f winner Dont Have It Then (by Myboycharlie): dam 5f-7f winner: fairly useful performer: won maiden at York in June and nurseries at Ripon and Beverley (by 2 lengths from Sunnyside Bob) in August: creditable 4¼ lengths fifth to Donjuan Triumphant in listed race at York final start: stays 6f: acts on soft and good to firm going: usually races towards rear. *Ann Duffield* **92**

ROSSINGTON 6 b.g. Gentleman's Deal (IRE) 114 – Ettrbee (IRE) (Lujain (USA) 119) [2015 f7d⁵ t9.5f f7s t8.6g 9.9m 9.9m t8.6g⁴ t8.6f Dec 21] modest maiden: best effort at 8.5f: acts on tapeta: in headgear: often races towards rear. *John Wainwright* **51**

ROSSLARE (IRE) 3 b.f. Fastnet Rock (AUS) 127 – Waterways (IRE) 99 (Alhaarth (IRE) 126) [2015 –: 7g⁶ 7m 8.3g* 10g⁵ 9g Jul 29] sturdy filly: fair performer: won maiden at Windsor in June: stayed 1¼m: best form on good going: dead. *Charles Hills* **78**

ROSSO CORSA 4 b.c. Footstepsinthesand 120 – Lady Scarlett (Woodman (USA) 126) [2015 7g* 8g p7g 8m⁵ 7g* May 30] leggy colt: smart performer: mostly trained by Mick Channon at 2 yrs: successful once from 15 starts at Doha in 2014: won handicap on same course in February and Prix du Palais-Royal at Longchamp (by short head from Robert Le Diable) in May: respectable 6 lengths fifth to Spark Plug in handicap at Newbury on fourth outing: left Majid Safedeen after second start: stays 1¼m: acts on polytrack and good to firm going. *G. E. Mikhalides, France* **112**

ROSTOVA (USA) 2 b.f. (Apr 5) Arch (USA) 127 – Tsar's Pride (Sadler's Wells (USA) 132) [2015 7g⁴ 7s* Oct 12] lengthy filly: sister to useful 7f/1m winner Pavlosk and half-sister to several winners, including smart 1¼m-1½m winner Exhibit One (by Silver Hawk) and 7f/1m winner Signal Fire (by Mizzen Mast): dam 1¼m winner: better effort when winning maiden at Salisbury in October by 2 lengths from Secret Sense, suited by emphasis on stamina: will be suited by at least 1m: sure to go on improving. *Sir Michael Stoute* **88 p**

ROSY BLUSH 3 b.f. Youmzain (IRE) 131 – Sweet Lilly 107 (Tobougg (IRE) 125) [2015 p11g 8.9s³ 8g⁴ 8s* 9.9s⁶ Nov 19] fairly useful performer: won maiden at Dusseldorf in 2014: left A. Wohler, well held in handicap at Kempton on reappearance, only outing for Mike Murphy: won minor event at Maisons-Laffitte in October: stays 1¼m: acts on soft going. *Mme Pia Brandt, France* **90**

ROSY MORNING (IRE) 2 b.f. (Mar 14) Exceed And Excel (AUS) 126 – Bright Morning 95 (Dubai Millennium 140) [2015 6g² p6g* 6.5m t6f Oct 31] seventh foal: half-sister to useful 2-y-o 6f winner Risen Sun (by Shamardal) and 7f-9f winner Incorruptible (by Cape Cross): dam, 2-y-o 6.5f winner, half-sister to high-class winner up to 1½m Desert King: fairly useful performer: won maiden at Chelmsford (by 4½ lengths from Aqua Libre) in August, easily best effort. *Mark Johnston* **82**

ROSY RYAN (IRE) 5 b.m. Tagula (IRE) 116 – Khaydariya (IRE) (Akarad (FR) 130) [2015 56: 8.5g³ 8m* 7.9m² 8d² 8g 8.3d⁵ 8.5d 7.5m Oct 1] modest handicapper: won at Wetherby in July: stays 1m: acts on soft and good to firm going. *Tina Jackson* **64**

ROTHERWICK (IRE) 3 ch.c. Starspangledbanner (AUS) 128 – Pivotalia (IRE) 74 (Pivotal 124) [2015 91: 10d² 8f⁵ 10m⁴ 9.9m 10.3g⁴ p10m⁴ p10f t12.2m⁵ p12g Dec 19] sturdy colt: useful handicapper: creditable fourth at Chester in September, below best in 4 subsequent starts: stays 10.5f: acts on firm and good to soft going. *Paul Cole* **99**

ROTHESAY CHANCER 7 ch.g. Monsieur Bond (IRE) 120 – Rhinefield Beauty (IRE) 52 (Shalford (IRE) 124) [2015 84: 5g⁵ 5m³ 5m* 5m 5m⁴ 5d² 5g 5g⁶ Jul 21] fairly useful handicapper: won at Musselburgh in May: stays 6f: acts on good to firm and heavy going: tried in cheekpieces: often races towards rear. *Jim Goldie* **90**

ROUDEE 3 b.g. Kodiac 112 – Eau Rouge 77 (Grand Lodge (USA) 125) [2015 93: t7.1g⁴ **99** 8m 6.1s³ 5.1v* 5.1f² 6.1g⁶ 5m⁵ 6m 5.5m⁶ 6g 5d³ 5s Oct 9] useful handicapper: won at Chester (by 1¼ lengths from Rita's Boy) in May: fifth at Goodwood in July, below form after: best form at 5f: acts on any turf going: has worn headgear, including last 2 starts: usually races prominently: has hinted at temperament. *Tom Dascombe*

ROUGE NOIR 2 b.f. (Apr 3) Showcasing 117 – Vive Les Rouges 91 (Acclamation 118) **53** [2015 p7g⁴ p6g Dec 2] 68,000Y: third foal: half-sister to useful 6f winner Speedfiend (by Bahamian Bounty) and 6f/7f winner Dougan (by Dutch Art): dam, 2-y-o 6f winner, half-sister to smart 6f winner Bounty Box: fourth of 9 to Manson in maiden at Kempton in November, better effort. *Jeremy Noseda*

ROUGE NUAGE (IRE) 5 ch.g. Indian Haven 119 – Nom Francais 39 (First Trump 118) **80** [2015 77, a84: p7g⁶ p8g t7.1f⁶ p6f⁵ p6m⁴ p6f³ t7.1g* p6g t7.1g⁴ 6m t7.1g² p7g⁵ t7.1g³ 7g³ **a90** 7.1f³ t7.1g* 7g³ t7.1f* Nov 3] lengthy gelding: fairly useful handicapper: won at Wolverhampton in March, August and November (by head from Foreign Diplomat): stays 1¼m: acts on polytrack, tapeta and firm going: tried in headgear. *Conrad Allen*

ROUGH COURTE (IRE) 4 b.f. Clodovil (IRE) 116 – Straight Sets (IRE) 80 (Pivotal **69** 124) [2015 80: 8.3s⁵ 8.5m p8g⁶ 8.1m² p8g⁵ 8.3g Jul 4] small, sparely-made filly: fair handicapper: stays 1¼m: acts on polytrack, soft and good to firm going. *Mick Channon*

ROUGHLYN 6 ch.g. Haafhd 129 – Dime Bag 87 (High Line 125) [2015 t16.5m⁵ p12f **49** t13.9g p13.3m² p13.3m⁶ p16g⁵ p16g p16g³ 16.1m² Jul 25] poor handicapper: stays 2m: acts on polytrack, good to firm and good to soft going: wears headgear. *Lisa Williamson*

ROULEAU 2 b.c. (Feb 12) Exceed And Excel (AUS) 126 – Rachelle (IRE) (Mark of **104** Esteem (IRE) 137) [2015 6.1m⁴ t6g* 6f* 5g³ 5g² p6g* 6g⁵ Sep 26] good-quartered colt: seventh foal: closely related to very smart 6f (including at 2 yrs) winner Amadeus Wolf (by Mozart), 7f/1m winner Always A Rock (by Rock of Gibraltar) and half-brother to 10.3f winner Benedicte (by Galileo): dam 7f winner: useful performer: won maiden at Wolverhampton in June, nursery at Ascot in July and Sirenia Stakes at Kempton (by ½ length from Dream Destination) in September: stays 6f: acts on polytrack, tapeta and firm going: races prominently. *Charlie Appleby*

ROUNDABOUT TIME (IRE) 2 gr.c. (Jan 7) Zebedee 113 – Brosna Time (IRE) 61 – (Danetime (IRE) 121) [2015 6v Oct 17] 10/1, seventh of 8 in maiden at Catterick on debut, hanging left from 2f out. *Ann Duffield*

ROUNDSMAN 2 b.c. (Apr 9) Pivotal 124 – Forgotten Dreams (IRE) 44 (Olden Times **88 p** 121) [2015 7v* Nov 3] 220,000Y: third foal: half-brother to useful winner up to 7f Remember (by Selkirk) and 1¼m winner (stays 1½m) Fiesole (by Montjeu): dam, twice-raced half-sister to Oaks d'Italia winner Zomaradah, herself dam of Dubawi: 5/4, won 16-runner maiden at Redcar on debut by 3 lengths from Just Fab, always prominent and keeping on well: will stay 1m: sure to go on to better things. *Charlie Appleby*

ROUND THE ISLAND 2 b.g. (May 9) Royal Applause 124 – Luanshya 78 (First Trump **55** 118) [2015 5g p6g Nov 11] 100/1, modest form when 6½ lengths seventh of 12 to Consulting in maiden at Kempton latter start: has been gelded. *Richard Whitaker*

ROUND TWO (IRE) 2 b.c. (Mar 27) Teofilo (IRE) 126 – Khazina (USA) 72 (Kingmambo **107 p** (USA) 125) [2015 6d* 5g* 6f Jun 16] compact colt: first foal: dam, 6f winner who barely stayed 1m, out of US Grade 1 1m winner Easy Now, herself half-sister to Belmont Stakes winner Easy Goer: useful form: won minor event at Naas and 10-runner listed race at the Curragh, both in May, latter by 2 lengths from Washington DC: 9/4, seemed unsuited by firm ground when well held in Coventry Stakes at Royal Ascot only subsequent start: stays 6f: remains with potential. *J. S. Bolger, Ireland*

ROUSAYAN (IRE) 4 b.g. Invincible Spirit (IRE) 121 – Rose Quartz 85 (Lammtarra **85** (USA) 134) [2015 80: 8g² 8.5g* 7m³ 8.9g⁴ 8.5m³ 8d 7.5g⁴ 7.6g t8.6f³ Oct 13] fairly useful handicapper: won at Beverley in May: stays 8.5f: acts on tapeta, soft and good to firm going: sometimes in headgear. *David O'Meara*

ROWAN RIDGE 7 ch.g. Compton Place 125 – Lemon Tree (USA) (Zilzal (USA) 137) **72** [2015 79: p12m² Jan 9] fair handicapper: stays 13f: acts on polytrack, best turf form on good to soft/soft going: often wears headgear: front runner/races prominently. *William Knight*

ROWELLIAN (IRE) 3 b.g. High Chaparral (IRE) 132 – Steam Cuisine 104 (Mark of – Esteem (IRE) 137) [2015 8g p8f p8m⁶ Jun 3] no form. *Lydia Pearce*

ROWLESTONE LASS 5 b.m. Hernando (FR) 127 – Charmante Femme 53 (Bin Ajwaad **84** (IRE) 119) [2015 62, a83: t16.5f² 16d t12.2g⁴ 12.3f* 12.3m² 12f⁶ 16m⁴ 14g⁶ 15.9m* 15.9g³ Sep 11] rather leggy mare: fairly useful handicapper: won at Chester in June and August: stays 16.5f: acts on tapeta and firm going: sometimes in hood prior to 2015: often travels strongly. *Richard Price*

ROXIE LOT 3 b.f. Exceed And Excel (AUS) 126 – Orlena (USA) (Gone West (USA)) **68** [2015 70: 8g 7d 7m⁵ t7.1g⁶ 6m⁵ p7g⁴ p8f* p8f p8f² t8.6f⁶ Nov 3] fair handicapper: won at Chelmsford in September: stays 8.5f: acts on polytrack, tapeta and good to soft going: sometimes in blinkers, including for win. *Pam Sly*

ROXY HART 4 ch.f. Halling (USA) 133 – Possessive Artiste 73 (Shareef Dancer (USA) **48** 135) [2015 72: t8.6g² p7m t7.1f t7.1f 8m⁵ Apr 21] poor maiden: stays 11.5f, usually over shorter: acts on polytrack and good to firm going: tried in headgear: tends to find little. *Robert Cowell*

ROXY LANE 6 b.m. Byron 117 – Comme Ca (Cyrano de Bergerac 120) [2015 60: 8.3m **55** 10.2m⁶ 8d⁴ 8m³ 8m 8g* 8.1d 8g⁵ 8m t8.6f Oct 20] stocky mare: modest handicapper: won at Brighton in August: stays 1m: acts on good to firm going. *Peter Hiatt*

ROXY MADAM 6 br.m. Generous (IRE) 139 – Masouri Sana (IRE) (Broken Hearted **50** 124) [2015 –: t8.6g⁵ t9.5f t8.6f t12.2m⁶ t12.2m Dec 12] modest maiden: best effort at 1½m: acts on tapeta: often in hood, also in tongue last 3 starts. *Mandy Rowland*

ROXY STAR (IRE) 3 b.f. Fastnet Rock (AUS) 127 – Sweet Dreams Baby (IRE) **99** (Montjeu (IRE) 137) [2015 83p: 8.3m* 8f* 8m 8.1m 10.3m² 8m Oct 2] rangy filly: useful performer: won handicaps at Nottingham in June and Ascot in July: group second to California in handicap at Doncaster in September: stays 10.5f: acts on polytrack and firm going: tried in blinkers final start: usually races towards rear. *William Haggas*

ROYAL ACCLAIM (IRE) 3 b.g. Acclamation 118 – Top Row 64 (Observatory (USA) **–** 131) [2015 7m⁴ Jun 22] 8/1, shaped as if needed experience when fourth of 6 in maiden at Wetherby, slowly away. *Rebecca Bastiman*

ROYAL ACQUISITION 5 b.g. Royal Applause 124 – Flavian 94 (Catrail (USA) 123) **86** [2015 82: p5g⁴ p5g³ p5g² t5.1g p5g⁵ p5g t5.1g³ 5g* p5g* p5g⁶ t5.1f Dec 22] fairly useful handicapper: left Robert Cowell, won at Redcar in September and Lingfield in October: raced only at 5f: acts on polytrack: often wears headgear (not for last 5 starts). *Ivan Furtado*

ROYAL ALBERT HALL 3 b.g. Royal Applause 124 – Victoria Sponge (IRE) 96 (Marju **104** (IRE) 127) [2015 84: p8m* 8f 8f² 9f² 8f⁴ 8f³ 8.5f³ 9f² 9s⁶ 9f³ 9f Nov 28] useful performer: won handicap at Lingfield in January: left Olly Stevens after: several good efforts in USA subsequently, including when placed behind Om in Grade 2 events at Del Mar (2¼ lengths second in Del Mar Derby) and Santa Anita (2¾ lengths third in Twilight Derby) on eighth/ tenth starts: in rear in Hollywood Derby at Del Mar final outing: stays 9f: acts on polytrack/ tapeta and firm going, below form on soft. *Doug F. O'Neill, USA*

ROYAL ALSTROEMERIA 2 b.f. (Apr 5) Intikhab (USA) 135 – Delta Diva (USA) 78 **–** (Victory Gallop (CAN) 130) [2015 7s Oct 12] fourth foal: half-sister to 3 winners, including 1m winner Monlora de Luna (by Doctor Dino) and 1¼m-1½m winner Delegation (by Mount Nelson): dam, 2-y-o 7f winner, half-sister to useful 6.5f-1m winner In The Slips: 100/1, shaped as if needed experience when eighth of 11 in maiden at Salisbury. *Stuart Kittow*

ROYAL ALTITUDE 3 b.g. Zamindar (USA) 116 – Royal Assent 56 (Royal Applause **85** 124) [2015 82: 8d⁴ 8g⁴ 11.6d² 10.2g⁵ 10.1g⁶ p8f* Oct 22] tall gelding: fairly useful handicapper: won at Chelmsford in October: stays 11.6f: acts on polytrack, tapeta and good to soft going: usually races prominently: sold 50,000 gns, sent to Saudi Arabia. *Chris Wall*

ROYAL ARTILLERY (USA) 2 b.c. (Jan 30) War Front (USA) 119 – Masseuse (USA) **95 P** (Dynaformer (USA)) [2015 7d* Oct 23] $450,000F: third foal: dam North American 1m/9f winner, including Canadian Grade 2 event: evens, looked excellent prospect when winning 13-runner maiden at Doncaster on debut by 2½ lengths from Wild Hacked, still full of running when moving through to lead over 1f out and just kept up to his work: will stay at least 1m: open to plenty of improvement. *John Gosden*

ROYAL BAJAN (USA) 7 gr.g. Speightstown (USA) 124 – Crown You (USA) (Two **79** Punch (USA)) [2015 77, a96: f5s⁴ p5g³ f5s² p5g* t5.1f p5m p5g⁶ p5g* p5g⁵ 5m 5.1s⁵ **a95** 5.1m⁵ 5m⁵ f5g p5m Dec 27] workmanlike gelding: fair handicapper on turf, useful on all-weather: won at Chelmsford in February and March (by 1½ lengths from Mappin Time): off 6 months, well held last 2 starts: stays 5.5f: acts on polytrack, fibresand and good to firm going, probably on soft: wears headgear. *James Given*

ROYAL BARGE (IRE) 5 b.m. Shirocco (GER) 129 – Sahara Lady (IRE) (Lomitas 129) – [2015 t12.2f⁵ Jan 5] sturdy mare: has shown little in maidens/handicaps. *Alex Hales*

ROYAL BATTALION 4 b.g. Sea The Stars (IRE) 140 – Yummy Mummy 86 (Montjeu 76 (IRE) 137) [2015 68: t12.2f⁴ p13.3g⁴ Jan 22] fair maiden: stays 1¾m: acts on tapeta: winner over hurdles. *Stuart Williams*

ROYAL BIRTH 4 b.g. Exceed And Excel (AUS) 126 – Princess Georgina 78 (Royal 93 p Applause 124) [2015 86: t5.1f² p5g² Dec 15] strong gelding: fairly useful handicapper, lightly raced: good second at Wolverhampton and Kempton 9 months apart in 2015: best form at 5f: acts on polytrack, tapeta and firm going: in tongue tie in 2015: often races towards rear: still unexposed. *Stuart Williams*

ROYAL BLESSING 3 b.g. Royal Applause 124 – Zuleika Dobson 106 (Cadeaux 68 Genereux 131) [2015 59: t7.1g 8.3m⁶ p10g 8.3g* p8f⁴ t8.6m t9.5m⁵ 10s⁶ Oct 13] fair performer: won seller at Leicester in July: stays 8.5f: acts on polytrack and tapeta: in visor last 5 starts: sometimes slowly away, usually races towards rear. *George Peckham*

ROYAL BRAVE (IRE) 4 b.g. Acclamation 118 – Daqtora 70 (Dr Devious (IRE) 127) 84 [2015 88: 6m⁵ 6.1m 6m² 5m* 5m³ 6.1m⁴ 5m⁵ t5.1f Oct 9] lengthy gelding: fairly useful handicapper: won at Sandown in June: stays 6f: acts on firm going. *William Muir*

ROYAL CAPER 5 b.g. Royal Applause 124 – Ukraine (IRE) (Cape Cross (IRE) 129) 65 [2015 66: p7g* 8m p7g p8f p8f² p8f Oct 1] angular gelding: fair handicapper: won at Kempton in May: stays 1m: acts on polytrack and good to firm going: tried in headgear prior to 2015: tried in tongue tie prior to 2015: none too consistent. *Miss Joey Ellis*

ROYAL CONNOISSEUR (IRE) 4 b.g. Art Connoisseur (IRE) 121 – Valferno (IRE) 76 83 (Val Royal (FR) 127) [2015 86§: 7d 6d² 6s⁴ 6g 6m⁵ 6g 6g 6g 6g⁴ t6f³ t6f⁵ t6g⁴ Nov 27] a71 fairly useful handicapper: second at Ripon in April, below form after: stays 6f: acts on tapeta, soft and good to firm going: tried in headgear prior to 2015: has looked none too genuine. *Richard Fahey*

ROYAL DISPLAY 2 ch.g. (Mar 20) Showcasing 117 – Amouage Royale (IRE) (Mr 66 Greeley (USA) 122) [2015 6g⁶ 6g⁵ 6s⁶ 7m 6g t7.1f⁴ Oct 3] fair form when fifth in maiden at Haydock, showed little subsequently: in headgear last 3 starts: usually races prominently. *Kevin Ryan*

ROYAL DUCHESS 5 b.m. Dutch Art 126 – Royal Citadel (IRE) 75 (City On A Hill 79 (USA) 114) [2015 66: 8g⁴ 7.2d* 7.2d* 8g⁴ 6.9d² 7d³ 7g² 7.2g⁵ 7.2g Sep 29] fair handicapper: won at Ayr in May and June: stays 7f: acts on soft going: sometimes slowly away. *Lucy Normile*

ROYAL ETIQUETTE (IRE) 8 b.g. Royal Applause 124 – Alpine Gold (IRE) 86 66 (Montjeu (IRE) 137) [2015 70: p12f³ 11.6m 10d⁴ 10.9g² 9.9d p12m⁴ t13.9f Nov 30] angular gelding: fair handicapper: stays 1½m: acts on polytrack, good to firm and good to soft going: wears headgear/tongue tie: usually slowly away. *Lawney Hill*

ROYAL FLAG 5 b.g. New Approach (IRE) 132 – Gonbarda (GER) 117 (Lando (GER) 90 128) [2015 92: 11.6m² p10m⁴ May 19] fairly useful maiden, very lightly raced: stays 11.5f: acts on polytrack and good to firm going: in visor final start: sold £12,000. *Saeed bin Suroor*

ROYAL HISTORY 4 b.g. New Approach (IRE) 132 – Tessa Reef (IRE) (Mark of Esteem 92 (IRE) 137) [2015 p12g² 11.5d⁵ p9.2g² 12g Sep 10] sixth foal: half-brother to 3 winners, including useful 9f/1¼m winner Samana Cay (by Authorized) and 7f (including at 2 yrs) winner (stays 9.5f) Destination Aim (by Dubai Destination): dam 1m-9f winner: fairly useful maiden: first season in 2015, runner-up at Kempton and Chelmsford: stays 1½m. *Saeed bin Suroor*

ROYAL HOLIDAY (IRE) 8 ch.g. Captain Rio 122 – Sunny Slope 77 (Mujtahid (USA) 73 118) [2015 80: f8g² f8d⁵ f8g³ 8s⁶ 8d⁵ 7.5m⁵ 8m 9.3g 7.9s* 8g² 7.9m⁶ 9.2m³ 7s⁴ f8m* f8g³ a82 Dec 22] fairly useful handicapper: won at Carlisle in August and Southwell in December: stays 9.5f: acts on polytrack, fibresand and heavy going: wears headgear: front runner/races prominently. *Marjorie Fife*

ROYAL IRISH HUSSAR (IRE) 5 b.g. Galileo (IRE) 134 – Adjalisa (IRE) 65 – (Darshaan 133) [2015 –: 20f May 16] compact gelding: useful performer at best (raced only 5 times on Flat): fit from hurdling, went as if amiss when well held in Ascot Stakes (Handicap) at Royal Ascot: stays 1¾m: acts on good to firm going: in cheekpieces last 4 starts: useful hurdler. *Nicky Henderson*

ROYAL MAHOGANY (IRE) 2 b.c. (Apr 22) Kodiac 112 – Chiba (UAE) (Timber – Country (USA) 124) [2015 p8m⁶ Nov 17] 14/1, 7½ lengths sixth of 9 to Baydar in maiden at Lingfield: one for the longer term. *Luca Cumani*

ROYAL MARSKELL 6 b.g. Multiplex 114 – Socialise 69 (Groom Dancer (USA) 128) **87**
[2015 78, a88: f11s⁵ f12g³ p14f³ f12g* 11.8g p12g p11g f12f⁴ Dec 17] workmanlike
gelding: fairly useful handicapper: won at Southwell in February: left Alison Hutchinson
after fourth start, Clare Ellam after fifth: stays 1¾m: acts on polytrack, fibresand, soft and
good to firm going: tried in cheekpieces: often races towards rear. *Gay Kelleway*

ROYAL MEMORY 4 b.f. Invincible Spirit (IRE) 121 – Entre Nous (IRE) (Sadler's Wells **81**
(USA) 132) [2015 94p: p8g Apr 4] fairly useful performer: won maiden at Leopardstown
in 2014: left John M. Oxx/off 8 months and in first-time tongue strap, eighth of 10 in listed
race at Kempton only outing in 2015: stays 1m: acts on good to firm going: in hood first 3
starts (in 2014): sent to France. *Hugo Palmer*

ROYAL MEZYAN (IRE) 4 b.g. Royal Applause 124 – Rice Mother (IRE) 69 (Indian **87**
Ridge 123) [2015 98: 6m 5m 6m⁶ 6m 6m* 6g p6g p6f p7d t5.1f Dec 22] sturdy gelding: **a74**
fairly useful handicapper: won at Leicester in August: stays 6f: acts on polytrack and good
to firm going: tried in headgear/tongue tie. *Henry Spiller*

ROYAL MIGHTY 2 b.f. (Apr 11) Mighty 117 – Royal Hush 79 (Royal Applause 124) **45**
[2015 p6g 6m 7m p7g⁵ p8g Oct 20] £5,300Y. first foal: dam 1m winner out of useful 2-y-o
1m winner Sablonne: poor maiden: stays 7f: acts on polytrack: usually in hood. *Jane
Chapple-Hyam*

ROYAL MIZAR (SPA) 5 b.g. What A Caper (IRE) – Zahaadid (FR) (Limpid 119) [2015 **54**
58: p12g² t12.2f⁵ p13g⁵ Mar 27] workmanlike gelding: modest maiden: stays 1½m: acts on
polytrack, tapeta and any turf going: tried in cheekpieces. *Ralph Smith*

ROYAL NAVY SHIP (USA) 3 b.c. War Front (USA) 119 – Indy Punch (USA) (Pulling **107 §**
Punches (USA)) [2015 102: 9.5g² 10.9g⁴ 8m⁵ p10.7g² Aug 16] useful performer: second in
minor event at Gowran (½ length behind Zafilani) in April and handicap at Dundalk
(4 lengths behind Intisari) in August: stays 10.5f: acts on polytrack and good to soft going:
tried in blinkers/tongue tie: not one to trust: joined P. V. Lafferty, South Africa. *Aidan
O'Brien, Ireland*

ROYAL NORMANDY 3 b.g. Royal Applause 124 – Border Minstral (IRE) 69 (Sri **77**
Pekan (USA) 117) [2015 –: 6m 6g⁵ 7m² 7m* p7g² 7.1f* 7.1g p7g² p7f p7g⁶ p6g* Dec 16] **a84**
good-topped gelding: fairly useful handicapper: won at Leicester in June, Sandown in July
and Kempton in December: stays 7f: acts on polytrack and firm going: usually in headgear:
front runner/races prominently. *Andrew Balding*

ROYAL PARTY 3 b.f. Royal Applause 124 – Foxtrot Alpha (IRE) 82 (Desert Prince (IRE) **44**
130) [2015 –: p7m⁶ 7m p8g 6g⁶ 7d p10f p10f p8f 7s p12g p12g Nov 4] lengthy filly: poor
maiden: left William Knight after first start, John E. Long after eighth: best effort at 1½m:
acts on polytrack: in headgear last 6 starts. *Denis Quinn*

ROYAL PEARL 2 gr.f. (Apr 22) Aussie Rules (USA) 123 – Gower Diva (Sakhee (USA) **69**
136) [2015 7m 6s p7g⁴ p8f* p8f⁴ t8.6f⁴ Nov 16] compact filly: first foal: dam of little
account: fair performer: won claimer at Chelmsford in October: likely to stay beyond 1m:
acts on polytrack: often starts slowly. *Jonathan Portman*

ROYAL PECULIAR 7 b.g. Galileo (IRE) 134 – Distinctive Look (IRE) 86 (Danehill **78 §**
(USA) 126) [2015 f11g³ f12g⁴ f12g² Mar 10] useful-looking gelding: fair handicapper:
stays 1½m: acts on polytrack, fibresand and good to firm going: tried in headgear/tongue
tie: ungenuine. *Michael Appleby*

ROYAL PRESERVE 4 ch.g. Duke of Marmalade (IRE) 132 – Castaway Queen (IRE) 76 **71**
(Selkirk (USA) 129) [2015 85: 8m 7g⁶ 6.1m 7.2g t13.9f 10s Oct 16] good-topped gelding:
fair handicapper: stays 1m: acts on polytrack: often in headgear in 2015. *Tim Easterby*

ROYAL RAZALMA (IRE) 3 ch.f. Lope de Vega (IRE) 125 – Twiggy's Sister (IRE) 100 **–**
(Flying Spur (AUS)) [2015 105: 7m 8g 6m Jul 10] angular filly: useful performer in 2014,
well held all 3 starts in 2015: likely to prove best at 5f/6f: acts on good to firm and good to
soft going: often races prominently. *Jonathan Portman*

ROYAL REEF (IRE) 3 b.g. Duke of Marmalade (IRE) 132 – Bintalreef (USA) 99 **66 p**
(Diesis 133) [2015 10v⁴ p12g 11.8s⁶ Sep 21] 40,000Y: closely related to useful 1m winner
Epic Encounter and winner up to 8.3f Ejadah (both by Clodovil) and half-brother to useful
1½m winner (stayed 16.5f) Buxted (by Dynaformer): dam 2-y-o 7f winner: fair maiden:
best effort when sixth of 14 at Leicester: should continue to progress. *William Knight*

ROYAL REGENT 3 b.g. Urgent Request (IRE) 120 – Royal Citadel (IRE) 75 (City On A **74**
Hill (USA) 114) [2015 75: 8d 10d⁶ Jun 8] fair handicapper, lightly raced: likely to stay
1½m. *Lucy Normile*

ROYAL RESERVE 2 b.c. (Apr 20) Duke of Marmalade (IRE) 132 – Lady Hawkfield **77**
(IRE) (Hawk Wing (USA) 136) [2015 7g⁴ 7g* 7v Oct 24] fair form: won 13-runner maiden
at Salisbury in September by length from Mootaharer: well held in Horris Hill Stakes at
Newbury final start, probably unsuited by heavy ground: raced only at 7f. *William Muir*

ROYAL RETTIE 3 b.f. Royal Applause 124 – Bended Knee 83 (Refuse To Bend (IRE) **68**
128) [2015 65p: 6m² 7m⁴ p7g⁵ p8f⁶ p6g⁵ f8f² Dec 17] fair maiden: left Chris Wall after
fourth start: stays 1m: acts on polytrack, fibresand and good to firm going: wears hood:
often races freely. *Heather Dalton*

ROYAL ROSLEA 3 b.f. Royal Applause 124 – Roslea Lady (IRE) 63 (Alhaarth (IRE) **66**
126) [2015 –: p7m 7m³ 9.9g⁴ 10.2f* 10g² 10.2m³ 9.9s Oct 12] angular filly: fair handicapper: won at Bath in August: stays 1¼m: acts on firm going: often races towards rear.
Marcus Tregoning

ROYAL SEA (IRE) 6 b.g. Refuse To Bend (IRE) 128 – Janayen (USA) 97 (Zafonic **–**
(USA) 130) [2015 t12.2g⁶ 11.9m³ 12.5m⁶ 12g 11.9d Sep 3] fair at best, little form in 2015:
often wears headgear: tried in tongue tie in 2015. *Michael Mullineaux*

ROYAL SEAL 4 b.f. Dansili 127 – Queen's Best 110 (King's Best (USA) 132) [2015 101: **100**
7m² 7g² 7m⁶ 7m⁴ 7d⁵ Sep 26] rangy filly: useful handicapper: second at York (1¼ lengths
behind Dusky Queen) and Haydock (¾ length behind Above The Rest) first 2 starts, and
also ran creditably when fourth at Newmarket: should stay 1m: acts on good to firm going:
often wears headgear: usually races prominently, often travels strongly. *Sir Michael Stoute*

ROYAL SIGNALLER 5 b.g. Dylan Thomas (IRE) 132 – Whirly Bird 101 (Nashwan **93**
(USA) 135) [2015 t16.5f³ 16s p13.3f⁴ 14m² 14.6m* 16m* 13g⁵ 14.6m⁶ Sep 11] rather
leggy gelding: fairly useful handicapper: won at Doncaster in July and Ascot (by length
from Buckland) in August: stays 2m: acts on good to firm going: has worn cheekpieces,
including last 5 starts: usually races prominently. *Michael Appleby*

ROYAL SILK 3 b.f. Royal Applause 124 – Silky Dawn (IRE) 100 (Night Shift (USA)) **83**
[2015 87p: 8g* 8.1m 8g p8f⁴ Oct 22] well-made filly: fairly useful handicapper: won at
Goodwood in May: stays 1m: acts on polytrack. *Roger Charlton*

ROYAL STREET 3 b.g. Street Cry (IRE) 130 – Touch My Soul (FR) 109 (Tiger Hill **–**
(IRE) 127) [2015 –: 10.2m³ 12f May 23] well-made gelding: no form: tried in tongue tie.
Warren Greatrex

ROYAL SUPREME (IRE) 5 br.g. Royal Anthem (USA) 135 – Supreme Baloo (IRE) **–**
(Supreme Leader 123) [2015 11.9d⁶ 11.8s Sep 21] well held both starts in maidens: bumper
winner/poor hurdler. *Alex Hales*

ROYAL TOAST (IRE) 3 b.g. Duke of Marmalade (IRE) 132 – Ripalong (IRE) 68 **91**
(Revoque (IRE) 122) [2015 8m 7g 8m³ 9.9g³ 8f³ 10m² 10g² 9.9s* p11g Sep 23] 40,000Y:
sturdy gelding: closely related to smart winner up to 1m Imperial Rome (by Holy Roman
Emperor) and half-brother to 3 winners, including smart winner up to 1m Shamwari Lodge
(2-y-o 6f winner, by Hawk Wing) and 1¼m-1½m winner Shamardal Phantom (by
Shamardal): dam maiden: fairly useful handicapper: won at Goodwood (by 1¼ lengths
from Peterhof) in August: likely to stay 1½m: acts on soft and good to firm going: often
races prominently. *Richard Hannon*

ROYAL TROOPER (IRE) 9 b.g. Hawk Wing (USA) 136 – Strawberry Roan (IRE) 113 **§§**
(Sadler's Wells (USA) 132) [2015 t13.9gᵗ Jan 9] good-topped gelding: fairly useful at best:
stays 15f: acts on polytrack, tapeta, good to firm and heavy going: tried in headgear/tongue
tie prior to 2015: thoroughly temperamental (has refused to race last 3 outings).
Mark Brisbourne

ROYAL WARRANTY 4 ch.f. Sir Percy 129 – Royal Patron 78 (Royal Academy (USA) **94**
130) [2015 87: 11.7m² 14g p13.3g³ 12s² 11.6d³ p10m⁵ p11g² Dec 9] fairly useful
handicapper: stays 1½m: acts on polytrack, firm and good to soft going: usually races
towards rear. *Andrew Balding*

ROYAL WARRIOR 4 b.g. Royal Applause 124 – Tiana 99 (Diktat 126) [2015 86: 5.3d³ **60**
6g 6v⁵ May 29] quite good-topped gelding: fair handicapper: stayed 6f: acted on fibresand,
good to firm and good to soft going: tried in cheekpieces: showed signs of temperament:
dead. *Lydia Richards*

ROY ROCKET (FR) 5 gr.g. Layman (USA) 121 – Minnie's Mystery (FR) (Highest **67**
Honor (FR) 124) [2015 53: p8f⁴ p8m⁵ 9.9m* 11.9g* 14d² 11.9m* 9.9d² 12m³ 11.9g³ 11.9s⁵
Aug 23] workmanlike gelding: fair handicapper: won at Brighton in April (twice) and June:
stays 1½m: acts on good to firm and good to soft going: usually races in rear, often travels
strongly. *John Berry*

ROY'S LEGACY 6 b.h. Phoenix Reach (IRE) 124 – Chocolada (Namid 128) [2015 72, **72**
a80: t6f³ p5g⁶ p6f p5f³ 15.1f p5f³ p5d⁴ 5v² 5.1m² 5.1f³ p5g⁵ 5s⁶ 5d³ 5g³ 5m⁶ p5g⁶ 5g 5m 5m t5.1f²
p5g* p5m* Dec 31] smallish horse: fair handicapper: won at Kempton and Lingfield in
December: best form at 5f: acts on polytrack, tapeta, good to firm and heavy going: tried in
headgear: often in tongue tie prior to 2015: usually races close up. *Shaun Harris*

ROZENE (IRE) 4 b.f. Sleeping Indian 122 – Few Words (Fraam 114) [2015 81: 5g* 5g **85**
5g² 5m⁴ Jun 13] fairly useful handicapper: won at Ripon (apprentice) in May: best form at
5f: acts on good to soft going: front runner/races prominently. *David Barron*

RUBAN (IRE) 6 ch.g. Dubawi (IRE) 129 – Piece Unique (Barathea (IRE) 127) [2015 77: **87**
f8g* p8m⁵ p8g² f8d⁴ p8m* p8f² p10g⁴ 9m⁶ p8g p8g⁵ 7g³ 8.5g⁵ 7s⁵ Aug 29] workmanlike
gelding: fairly useful performer: won maiden at Southwell in January and handicap at
Chelmsford in March: stays 1m: acts on polytrack, fibresand and soft going: tried in hood
in 2015: often wears tongue tie. *Stuart Williams*

RUBENSIAN 2 ch.c. (Feb 28) Medicean 128 – Hymnsheet 93 (Pivotal 124) [2015 8.3v⁶ **63 p**
t8.6f⁵ Oct 31] 48,000Y: second foal: half brother to 1¼m winner Rocksheet (by Rock of
Gibraltar). dam, 2-y-o 1m winner who stayed 11f, sister to very smart 1m-1¼m winner
Chorist: similar form to debut when 4½ lengths fifth of 9 to Loading in maiden at
Wolverhampton: remains open to improvement. *David Simcock*

RUBHEIRA 3 ch.f. Arkadian Hero (USA) 123 – Devon Ruby 51 (Zilzal (USA) 137) [2015 **44**
–: p6g⁶ 6m⁵ 8m p6f Nov 6] poor maiden: best effort at 6f: acts on good to firm going.
Hugo Froud

RUBIS 2 ch.f. (May 5) Monsieur Bond (IRE) 120 – Princess Cocoa (IRE) 86 (Desert Sun **64**
120) [2015 t7.1f⁴ f8g³ p7g Dec 20] third foal: dam 8.6f-10.3f winner: modest form in
maidens. *Richard Fahey*

RUBY HIND 3 b.f. Firebreak 125 – Linden's Lady 82 (Compton Place 125) [2015 8g⁶ **–**
9.3d⁶ 7m t9.5f Nov 13] second foal: dam winner up to 1m, also 2-y-o 6f winner: no form.
John Weymes

RUBY LOOKER 4 b.c. Bertolini (USA) 125 – Ellcon (IRE) 71 (Royal Applause 124) **–**
[2015 67p: p5g Aug 17] won maiden at Southwell in 2014: only outing prior to shaping as
if amiss in handicap at Chelmsford 20 months later. *J. R. Jenkins*

RUBY NOTION (USA) 2 b.f. (Mar 19) Great Notion (USA) – Modena Bay (NZ) **101**
(Volksraad 109) [2015 a4.5f* 5f⁵ 5f* a5.5s* 8d Oct 30] strong filly: third foal: half-sister
to 6.5f/7f winner Wild Pearl (by Kitten's Joy) and winner up to 9f Loophole (by Perfect
Soul): dam US/New Zealand 6f-8.5f winner: useful performer: won maiden claimer at
Churchill Downs in May, then non-graded stakes at Monmouth in August and Laurel (by 8
lengths from Look Who's Talking) in September: respectable 3¾ lengths fifth to
Washington DC in listed Windsor Castle Stakes at Royal Ascot on second outing, doing too
much too soon: will prove best at 5f/6f (beat only one home in 14-runner Breeders' Cup
Juvenile Fillies Turf over 1m at Keeneland final outing): acts on dirt and firm going:
blinkered first 4 starts. *Wesley A. Ward, USA*

RUBY'S DAY 6 ch.m. Vital Equine (IRE) 121 – Isabella's Best (IRE) 53 (King's Best **80**
(USA) 132) [2015 87: 5d⁵ 5f* 5g² 5f 5g 5s Oct 19] fairly useful handicapper: won at
Doncaster (by head from Fredricka) in July: stays 6f: acts on polytrack and firm going:
tried in headgear: usually races nearer last than first. *David Brown*

RUBY WEDNESDAY 2 b.f. (May 8) Mullionmileanhour (IRE) 116 – Cheap N Chic 79 **62**
(Primo Valentino (IRE) 116) [2015 p7g⁵ Aug 26] fifth foal: half-sister to 1½m winner Caldi
Mill (by Indesatchel): dam, 2-y-o 6f winner, half-sister to useful winner up to 6.5f Golden
Nun: 16/1, some encouragement when 3¼ lengths fifth of 10 to Shufoog in maiden at
Lingfield on debut. *John Best*

RUFFORD (IRE) 4 b.g. Invincible Spirit (IRE) 121 – Speedy Sonata (USA) (Stravinsky **86**
(USA) 133) [2015 101: p6g p6g p6g p6f* p7g p7g p6f³ 6d 7g 6g* 7s Oct 26] leggy
gelding: fairly useful performer: won handicap at Lingfield in May and claimer at Windsor
in October: stays 6f: acts on polytrack, soft and good to firm going: tried in headgear: front
runner/races prominently. *Lee Carter*

RUGGERO 5 b.g. Tiger Hill (IRE) 127 – Bergamask (USA) (Kingmambo (USA) 125) **–**
[2015 –: t12.2f p12g p12g p16m f12g⁵ t12.2f t8.6m Nov 21] useful handicapper in 2013,
has totally lost way: has worn headgear. *Roy Brotherton*

RULER OF THE NILE 3 b.g. Exceed And Excel (AUS) 126 – Dinka Raja (USA) **72**
(Woodman (USA) 126) [2015 p7g³ p8g⁴ p7g 7m p12g t16.5g³ Dec 5] fair maiden: left
David Simcock after second start: best effort at 16.5f: acts on tapeta. *Robert Stephens*

RUM

RUMBLE OF THUNDER (IRE) 9 b.g. Fath (USA) 116 – Honey Storm (IRE) 73 **69** (Mujadil (USA) 119) [2015 74: t16.5g³ 16.5m⁴ 16v² 13.1g⁶ Sep 17] leggy, close-coupled gelding: fair handicapper: stays 16.5f: acts on tapeta, good to firm and heavy going: in headgear in 2015. *Philip Kirby*

RUM SWIZZLE 3 b.f. Mawatheeq (USA) 126 – Port Providence (Red Ransom (USA)) **77** [2015 54: 11.6g⁶ p13.3m 10.2m² 11.7f² 9.9m³ p12g² p12g* t12.2m⁵ t12.2g² 11.6g* t16.5f Nov 16] lengthy filly: fair handicapper: won at Lingfield in August and Windsor (amateur) in October: stays 1½m: acts on polytrack, tapeta and firm going: often races prominently. *Harry Dunlop*

RUNAIOCHT (IRE) 5 ch.g. Teofilo (IRE) 126 – Julie Girl (USA) (Jules (USA) 110) **61** [2015 63: p10m² p10m² p10f p11f² 11.7f⁵ p10m* p11g 10m p10d p10g Dec 15] modest handicapper: won at Lingfield in April: probably stays 11.5f: acts on polytrack, good to firm and heavy going: sometimes wears headgear, including on last 5 starts: often races prominently. *Paul Burgoyne*

RUN FAT LASS RUN 5 b.m. Sakhee (USA) 136 – Feolin 75 (Dr Fong (USA) 128) [2015 **68** 76, a70: f8d f7d² f8d⁵ f6d⁵ f7g f6g* f8g² 6g 7g 8m² 7.9m* 8s³ 8g Aug 6] fair handicapper: **a57** won at Southwell in March and Carlisle in July: left Conor Dore after seventh start: stays 1¼m: acts on fibresand, good to firm and heavy going: often wears headgear (not on last 6 starts). *Brian Ellison*

RUN FOUR YOUR LIFE 4 ch.g. Bertolini (USA) 125 – Pick A Nice Name 85 (Polar **46** Falcon (USA) 126) [2015 10s 8.3d p7m p7g³ p7g Dec 10] poor maiden: best effort at 7f: acts on polytrack: usually in hood. *Peter Hedger*

RUNNER RUNNER (IRE) 3 gr.f. Dark Angel (IRE) 113 – Distant Piper (IRE) 85 **98** (Distant Music (USA) 126) [2015 92: a7f³ a8f⁵ a9.4f³ 9.9d³ 8.5f³ 10f⁴ 8.5f⁴ a9s⁵ Dec 2] useful performer: in cheekpieces, best efforts when third on third/fourth starts, beaten 4¾ lengths by Local Time in UAE Oaks at Meydan and ½ length by Princess Charm in listed race at Saint-Cloud: left George Baker, just fair efforts at best in USA last 4 outings: stays 1¼m: acts on dirt/tapeta, soft and good to firm going: blinkered final start: often races prominently. *Chad C. Brown, USA*

RUN RIO RUN (IRE) 2 ch.g. (Mar 20) Captain Rio 122 – Anklesocks (IRE) (Night Shift **72** (USA)) [2015 5g⁶ 6m² 6g⁵ 6g⁶ Aug 6] standout effort (fair form) when second of 9 to Prince Hellvelyn in maiden at Newcastle in June. *Michael Dods*

RUN RIOT (IRE) 2 b.g. (Apr 4) Kodiac 112 – Three Gems (IRE) 100 (Jeremy (USA) **–** 122) [2015 6g 5d Sep 11] well held both starts in maidens: has been gelded. *John Joseph Murphy, Ireland*

RUN WITH PRIDE (IRE) 5 b.g. Invincible Spirit (IRE) 121 – Zibilene 101 (Rainbow **89** Quest (USA) 134) [2015 91: p6g² p6f² 6f p6g⁵ p6g 7g 7g 6m⁶ t6m f7g Dec 22] fairly useful handicapper: stays 7f: acts on polytrack and good to firm going. *Derek Shaw*

RUPERT BOY (IRE) 2 ch.g. (Apr 20) Frozen Power (IRE) 108 – Curious Lashes (IRE) **51** (Footstepsinthesand 120) [2015 5d 6g 6m f6s⁴ p6f⁴ p6f² p6g³ f6g² Dec 15] modest maiden: stays 6f: acts on polytrack and fibresand: usually in blinkers: front runner/races prominently. *Scott Dixon*

RURAL AFFAIR 4 b.f. Pastoral Pursuits 127 – Torcross 96 (Vettori (IRE) 119) [2015 **59** t7.1f 10.2f⁵ f8d³ 9.2d 10.2m⁶ Jun 11] modest handicapper: missed 2014: stays 9f: acts on polytrack and soft going: wore hood once in 2013. *Michael Appleby*

RURAL CELEBRATION 4 b.f. Pastoral Pursuits 127 – Queens Jubilee 71 (Cayman **95** Kai (IRE) 114) [2015 94: 5m 6g⁵ 5g* 5m³ 6d 6g 5s⁵ 5v³ Oct 17] useful handicapper: won at Ayr (by ½ length from Gowanharry) in July: stays 6f: acts on any turf going. *David O'Meara*

RUSSIAN BOLERO (GER) 4 ch.g. Tertullian (USA) 115 – Russian Samba (IRE) **75** (Laroche (GER) 123) [2015 11.8s t12.2g⁴ Dec 5] fair maiden: left David Bridgwater after first start: stays 11f: acts on good to soft going: sometimes wears headgear: tried in tongue tie. *David Dennis*

RUSSIAN BREEZE (IRE) 3 b.g. Shirocco (GER) 129 – Kirov 87 (Darshaan 133) **–** [2015 10.1d⁶ 11.9d 10d 10.2s Oct 28] no form. *Tom Tate*

RUSSIAN GEORGE (IRE) 9 ch.g. Sendawar (IRE) 129 – Mannsara (IRE) (Royal **–** Academy (USA) 130) [2015 14.1g 9.9d t12.2g Sep 29] stocky gelding: fairly useful at best, no form in 2015: left Steve Gollings after first start: tried in cheekpieces/tongue tie. *Alan Berry*

RUSSIAN HEROINE 3 b.f. Invincible Spirit (IRE) 121 – Russian Rhythm (USA) 123 **94** (Kingmambo (USA) 125) [2015 78: 7.5m 7m⁵ 6d* 6m* Jun 17] close-coupled filly: fairly useful handicapper: won twice at Ripon in June, further improvement when beating George Dryden 2¾ lengths in latter event: best efforts at 6f: acts on good to firm and good to soft going. *Sir Michael Stoute*

RUSSIAN ICE 7 ch.m. Iceman 117 – Dark Eyed Lady (IRE) 82 (Exhibitioner 111) [2015 **57** 73: p7m* p7g⁶ p8f⁶ Feb 3] quite good-topped mare: modest handicapper: won at Kempton in January: stays 7f: acts on polytrack, tapeta and good to firm going: often wears headgear: tried in tongue: front runner/races prominently. *Dean Ivory*

RUSSIAN PUNCH 3 b.f. Archipenko (USA) 127 – Punch Drunk 77 (Beat Hollow 126) **92** [2015 98: 7m 8g 8.1m 10.4m 8m 7.2m⁴ Sep 4] compact filly: fairly useful performer: stays 1m: acts on good to firm and heavy going. *James Given*

RUSSIAN RADIANCE 3 ch.f. Paco Boy (IRE) 129 – Russian Ruby (FR) 85 (Vettori **91** (IRE) 119) [2015 7m⁵ 7g⁵ 6f⁴ 6d p8g t7.1m⁴ t7.1f* t7.1f* Nov 30] £18,000Y: sturdy filly: sixth foal: half-sister to 3 winners, including useful 6f-7f winner Russian Rave (by Danehill Dancer) and 6f-1¾m winner (stays 2m) Russian Royale (by Royal Applause): dam 2-y-o 6f/7f winner: fairly useful handicapper: won at Wolverhampton in October and November: stays 7f: acts on tapeta and good to firm going: in hood last 3 starts. *Jonathan Portman*

RUSSIAN RASCAL 2 b.g. (Apr 8) Kyllachy 129 – Russian Ruby (FR) 85 (Vettori (IRE) – 119) [2015 7s 6s Oct 26] well held in maidens at Newbury and Leicester. *Stuart Kittow*

RUSSIAN REALM 5 b.g. Dansili 127 – Russian Rhythm (USA) 123 (Kingmambo **106** (USA) 125) [2015 105: 7m 8d 7m² 7m⁶ 7g* 8d 7s⁶ p8g⁵ Dec 19] compact gelding: useful performer: won minor event at Thirsk (by ½ length from Hawkesbury) in July: left David O'Meara after seventh start: stays 1m: acts on soft and good to firm going: usually in hood in 2015: tends to find little. *Richard Hughes*

RUSSIAN REMARQUE 4 b.g. Archipenko (USA) 127 – Accede 88 (Acclamation 118) **77** [2015 76: 10g 10m⁴ 9g³ 11.6m² 11m² Jun 25] useful-looking gelding: fair maiden: stays 11.5f: acts on soft and good to firm going. *Jonathan Portman*

RUSSIAN REWARD (IRE) 3 b.g. Iffraaj 127 – Forever Times 98 (So Factual (USA) **82** 120) [2015 74: 7g³ t7.1g² 8g³ 8f² p8f* p8g Dec 7] good-topped gelding: fairly useful performer: won maiden at Chelmsford in November: stays 1m: acts on polytrack, tapeta and firm going: in tongue tie last 4 starts: usually races close up. *Paul Cole*

RUSSIAN ROYALE 5 b.m. Royal Applause 124 – Russian Ruby (FR) 85 (Vettori (IRE) **75** 119) [2015 16.1m³ 13.8d Sep 15] fair handicapper: stays 2m: acts on tapeta and firm going: tried in cheekpieces: fair hurdler. *Micky Hammond*

RUSSIAN SOUL (IRE) 7 b.g. Invincible Spirit (IRE) 121 – Russian Hill 116 (Indian **106** Ridge 123) [2015 119: a6f⁵ a7f 6g p6g* 5d 5g² 6g³ 5f³ 6m⁴ 5m p5d* 5m 6g p6g⁴ 6d 5d **a115** p6g⁴ p5g⁶ Oct 23] useful on turf, smart on all-weather: won minor event in March and handicap in July (by 2 lengths from Master Speaker), both at Dundalk: has won at 1m but races at shorter nowadays (effective at 5f): acts on polytrack, tapeta and good to firm going: wears headgear. *M. Halford, Ireland*

RUSTIQUE 3 ch.f. Pastoral Pursuits 127 – Nihal (IRE) 94 (Singspiel (IRE) 133) [2015 52: **73** 7d⁶ p10m² 10m t9.5g* p10g³ 10v p10m³ Oct 28] fair handicapper: won at Wolverhampton in July: stays 1¼m: acts on polytrack and tapeta: often races prominently. *Ed Walker*

RUSTY ROCKET (IRE) 6 ch.h. Majestic Missile (IRE) 118 – Sweet Compliance 71 **90** (Safawan 118) [2015 94: t5.1f t5.1g⁵ 5s* 5m³ 5.1g⁴ 6m⁵ 6.1f⁶ 5.1m² 5g³ 5m⁵ 5m* 6m 5g 5.1d⁵ 5s 5.1d Nov 4] fairly useful handicapper: won at Catterick in May and Musselburgh (by 1½ lengths from Master Bond) in July: stays 7f: acts on polytrack, soft and good to firm going: tried in visor in 2015. *Paul Green*

RUTLAND PANTHER 3 b.g. Alhaarth (IRE) 126 – Desert Lynx (IRE) 79 (Green Desert – (USA) 127) [2015 50: 7g 5g May 12] poor maiden: best effort at 7f: acts on good to firm going: front runner/races prominently: blinkered final start. *Declan Carroll*

RUWAIYAN (USA) 6 b.h. Cape Cross (IRE) 129 – Maskunah (IRE) (Sadler's Wells **113** (USA) 132) [2015 115: 6f 6g* 6m⁵ 6f 6m 7g Oct 3] compact horse: smart performer: won handicap at Goodwood in May by 2½ lengths from Zanetto, best effort of 2015: stays 7f: acts on polytrack, soft and good to firm going: wears headgear: carries head awkwardly. *James Tate*

RUZEIZ (USA) 6 b.g. Muhtathir 126 – Saraama (USA) (Bahri (USA) 125) [2015 77: **55 +** 9.9m⁶ 11s⁴ p12g 11.6g p12m² t13.9f Nov 30] workmanlike gelding: fair handicapper: stays 1½m: acts on polytrack and soft going, probably on heavy: tried in cheekpieces/tongue tie in 2015: often races prominently. *Peter Hedger*

RYAN STYLE (IRE) 9 b.g. Desert Style (IRE) 121 – Westlife (IRE) 32 (Mind Games **57** 121) [2015 54: p5m⁵ p5g⁴ 6m² 5.1m⁵ p6g⁵ 5d⁴ 6g³ 5m² p6f² p6f³ 6g⁵ Sep 21] strong gelding: modest handicapper: stays 7f: acts on polytrack, firm and good to soft going: often wears headgear: tried in tongue. *Lisa Williamson*

RYAN THE GIANT 2 b.c. (Feb 19) Fastnet Rock (AUS) 127 – Comeraincomeshine **58** (IRE) 67 (Night Shift (USA)) [2015 6d 8.5v⁴ 8.3d⁴ p10f f7g⁴ f8f Dec 17] modest maiden: best effort at 8.5f: acts on good to soft going: tried in cheekpieces. *Richard Hannon*

RYDAN (IRE) 4 ch.g. Intense Focus (USA) 117 – Lough Mewin (IRE) (Woodman (USA) **101** 126) [2015 95, a110: 10.3s 9.9g⁶ 12m⁵ 10g⁵ 12s⁶ p12g³ p12g Nov 25] tall gelding: useful handicapper: third at Kempton (1½ lengths behind Osipova) in November: stays 1½m: acts on polytrack, soft and good to firm going: often in visor in 2015: often races towards rear. *Gary Moore*

RYEDALE LASS 7 b.m. Val Royal (FR) 127 – First Dawn 68 (Dr Fong (USA) 128) **35** [2015 55: t7.1g t9.5g t8.6g t12.2g t8.6g 7.1m 9.9v Aug 24] poor handicapper: stays 1½m: acts on soft going: usually wears headgear: temperament under suspicion. *Nikki Evans*

RYEDALE MIST 3 b.f. Equiano (FR) 127 – Alhufoof (USA) 100 (Dayjur (USA) 137) **–** [2015 –: 7g 5g May 18] little form in maidens/handicaps: wore hood in 2015: sold 10,000 gns, sent to France. *Tim Easterby*

RYEOLLIEAN 4 ch.g. Haafhd 129 – Brave Mave 83 (Daylami (IRE) 138) [2015 82: **–** 11.6m⁴ 12g Jun 5] rather leggy gelding: fairly useful at best, no form in 2015: stays 12.5f: acts on heavy going: tried in cheekpieces: often leads: fairly useful hurdler. *Gary Moore*

RYLEE MOOCH 7 gr.g. Choisir (AUS) 126 – Negligee 94 (Night Shift (USA)) [2015 **79 §** 75§: f5d f6g t5.1f* t5.1g² t5.1g 5.1d* 5m⁴ 5m 6m 5g⁶ Aug 29] workmanlike gelding: fair handicapper: won at Wolverhampton in February and Nottingham in May: stays 6f: acts on polytrack, tapeta, good to firm and good to soft going: usually wears headgear: usually leads: unreliable. *Richard Guest*

RYTON RUNNER (IRE) 7 b.g. Sadler's Wells (USA) 132 – Love For Ever (IRE) **–** (Darshaan 133) [2015 66: 13.1g Sep 17] leggy gelding: fair maiden: well held only start in 2015: stays 13f: acts on soft going: tried in cheekpieces/tongue tie. *Keith Dalgleish*

S

SAAB ALMANAL 4 b.g. Dubawi (IRE) 129 – Caribbean Pearl (USA) 86 (Silver Hawk **90** (USA) 123) [2015 107: 11.8s⁵ p16g Nov 18] big, strong gelding: fairly useful handicapper: stays 1½m: acts on soft and good to firm going: has been gelded. *James Fanshawe*

SABAANI 2 b.c. (May 8) Aqlaam 125 – Sabaweeya (Street Cry (IRE) 130) [2015 t9.5f⁴ **67 p** Dec 14] first foal: dam unraced half-sister to Prix de l'Arc de Triomphe winner Marienbard: 14/1, some encouragement when 11 lengths fourth of 11 to Every Chance in maiden at Wolverhampton: better to come. *James Tate*

SABATO (IRE) 2 ch.c. (Mar 6) Shamardal (USA) 129 – Mondalay (Monsun (GER) 124) **64** [2015 t7.1m t7.1f p6g⁴ t6f⁴ Dec 22] modest form: improved when ¾-length fourth to Hold On Magnolia in nursery at Wolverhampton final start, inadequate test: should prove suited by at least 7f. *Charlie Appleby*

SABHA (IRE) 3 b.f. Thewayyouare (USA) 117 – Genipabu (IRE) (Danetime (IRE) 121) **57** [2015 54: 10m 11.9f⁴ 9.9m 10.2g 10v Sep 16] lengthy filly: modest maiden: best effort at 1½m: acts on firm going. *Timothy Jarvis*

SABORIDO (USA) 9 gr.g. Dixie Union (USA) 121 – Alexine (ARG) (Runaway Groom **88** (CAN)) [2015 94: p16g² p16g⁴ p16f³ 17.2m³ p16g⁶ p16g⁵ p16g⁴ Aug 26] big, useful-looking gelding: fairly useful handicapper: stays 17f: acts on polytrack and any turf going: tried in headgear. *Amanda Perrett*

SABRE ROCK 5 b.g. Dubawi (IRE) 129 – Retainage (USA) (Polish Numbers (USA)) **84** [2015 70: p10m* p10g* p10f* Mar 4] fairly useful handicapper: successful at Lingfield on last 2 starts in 2014 and unbeaten in 3 races there in 2015, in January (2) and March: stays 10.5f: acts on polytrack, tapeta, good to firm and good to soft going: wears tongue tie nowadays: usually responds generously to pressure. *Julia Feilden*

SABRE SQUADRON (IRE) 2 b.g. (Mar 2) Lope de Vega (IRE) 125 – Caravan of **71 p** Dreams (IRE) 74 (Anabaa (USA) 130) [2015 8s Oct 23] 75,000Y: third foal: half-brother to useful 12.5f-1¾m winner (stays 2m) Weather Watch (by Hurricane Run): dam, maiden (stayed 1m), half-sister to very smart/ungenuine winner up to 2m Royal And Regal: 33/1, some encouragement when 5¼ lengths ninth of 17 to Midterm in maiden at Newbury, ideally needing stiffer test: has been gelded: capable of better. *Peter Chapple-Hyam*

SACRAMENT (IRE) 2 b.f. (Feb 4) Acclamation 118 – Alstemeria (IRE) 103 (Danehill (USA) 126) [2015 6s³ 6g p6g³ p5m Dec 27] 75,000Y: sixth foal: half-sister to smart winner up to 7f Kitty Kiernan (2-y-o 6f winner, by Pivotal) and 7f winner Fernando Torres (by Giant's Causeway): dam, 6f winner (stayed 1m), sister to smart winner up to 11f Johan Cruyff and half-sister to dam of high-class Hong Kong performer up to 1½m Blazing Speed: fair maiden: left Ralph Beckett after third start: best effort at 6f on debut. *David Evans* **75**

SACRED ACT 4 b.g. Oasis Dream 129 – Stage Presence (IRE) 95 (Selkirk (USA) 129) [2015 95p: 8.3s p8m² Apr 29] rangy gelding, lightly raced: best effort (useful form) when ½-length second to Lightning Spear in steadily-run handicap at Lingfield in April: gelded after: stays 8.5f. *John Gosden* **97**

SACRED BOND 3 ch.f. Exceed And Excel (AUS) 126 – Gay Romance 71 (Singspiel (IRE) 133) [2015 68: t5.1f⁴ 7.2g² 7v Nov 3] fair maiden: worth a try over 1m+: acts on heavy going: usually races prominently. *Richard Fahey* **70**

SACRED HARP 2 b.f. (Feb 13) Oasis Dream 129 – Zabeel Park (USA) 94 (Medicean 128) [2015 6m 6g 5m⁶ Aug 13] smallish filly: first foal: dam, 2-y-o 6f winner, half-sister to 1000 Guineas winner Finsceal Beo: down the field in maidens, still green final start (started slowly). *Charlie Appleby* **–**

SACRED SQUARE (GER) 5 ch.g. Peintre Celebre (USA) 137 – Square The Circle (Second Empire (IRE) 124) [2015 10.4m 10g⁴ 10g³ f11g⁶ Dec 15] fair handicapper: left Donald McCain after third start: stays 1¾m: acts on good to firm going: often wears headgear: has looked temperamental. *Conor Dore* **74 §**

SACRED TRUST 2 b.c. (Mar 30) Acclamation 118 – Paracel (USA) (Gone West (USA)) [2015 p8f³ p8m² Dec 16] 39,000Y, 55,000 2-y-o: fourth foal: half-brother to 3 winners, including smart winner up to 9.5f I'm Back (2-y-o 6f-1m winner, by Exceed And Excel) and 1½m-2m winner Yorkindred Spirit (by Sea The Stars): dam, French 8.5f winner, half-sister to smart 1¼m-1½m winner Nabucco out of 1000 Guineas winner Cape Verdi: improved from debut when ½-length second to Hombre Rojo in maiden at Lingfield, sticking to task and clear of rest: open to further progress. *Hugo Palmer* **84 p**

SACRIFICIAL (IRE) 3 ch.g. Showcasing 117 – Armanda (GER) (Acatenango (GER) 127) [2015 87: 8s⁸ 8.5s* 8d³ 8f³ 8.3d* 8.5m³ 8d Oct 17] smart performer: won maiden at Leopardstown in April and handicaps at Killarney (by neck from Liffey View) in May and Galway (by 2¾ lengths from Lily's Rainbow) in July: third in Britannia Stakes (Handicap) at Royal Ascot and listed race at Killarney (length behind Algonquin) fourth/sixth starts: stays 8.5f: acts on polytrack, firm and soft going: blinkered last 4 starts: sold 130,000 gns, sent to Hong Kong. *G. M. Lyons, Ireland* **112**

SADIE BABES (IRE) 2 b.f. (Mar 10) Iffraaj 127 – Daffodil Walk (IRE) 93 (Captain Rio 122) [2015 5g² 5m 5s³ t6m⁴ Nov 21] second foal: dam winner up to 6f (2-y-o 5f winner) who stayed 8.5f: fair maiden: should be suited by a return to 5f. *Richard Fahey* **69**

SAEEDAN (IRE) 2 b.c. (Apr 18) Tagula (IRE) 116 – Sharadja (IRE) (Doyoun 124) [2015 p6f Sep 10] €20,000F, £36,000 2-y-o: half-brother to several winners, including useful 6f (including at 2 yrs) winner Parisian Pyramid (by Verglas) and 7f-1¼m winner She's Our Lass (by Orpen): dam unraced: 20/1, green when well held in maiden at Chelmsford: should do better in time. *Marco Botti* **– p**

SAFE INVESTMENT (USA) 11 b.g. Gone West (USA) – Fully Invested (USA) 99 (Irish River (FR) 131) [2015 50: p12g Jun 27] small gelding: modest handicapper nowadays: stays 1½m: acts on good to firm and good to soft going: usually in headgear/tongue tie. *Lawney Hill* **–**

SAFETY CHECK (IRE) 4 ch.c. Dubawi (IRE) 129 – Doors To Manual (USA) (Royal Academy (USA) 130) [2015 115: 7g* 7g* 8g* 7g³ 7d Sep 12] sturdy colt: very smart performer: improved again in 2015 and successful at Meydan first 3 starts, in handicap (by 2¾ lengths from Another Party) and Al Fahidi Fort (by 4 lengths from Eastern Rules) in January, and Zabeel Mile in February (by length from Dark Emerald): much the better effort after when third in Lennox Stakes at Goodwood (¾ length behind Toormore): stays 1m: acts on firm and good to soft going. *Charlie Appleby* **123**

SAFE VOYAGE (IRE) 2 b.g. (Apr 15) Fast Company (IRE) 126 – Shishangaan (IRE) (Mujadil (USA) 119) [2015 5m⁶ Apr 29] £52,000Y: fourth foal: dam 2-y-o 6f winner in Italy: 12/1, considerate introduction when sixth in maiden at Pontefract (13 lengths behind Sixth Sense) in April: should do better in time. *John Quinn* **– p**

SAFFIRE SONG 4 ch.f. Firebreak 125 – Saffwah (IRE) 86 (King's Best (USA) 132) **58** [2015 66, a80: t6f p6g f6g³ p5m³ 5g⁶ t6g² 5d⁵ t5.1g t6m⁵ p5g⁵ Oct 14] sturdy filly: modest handicapper: stays 7f: acts on all-weather, good to firm and good to soft going: tried in visor: front runner/races prominently: sold 800 gns, sent to Italy. *Alan Bailey*

SAFIRA MENINA 3 b.f. Paco Boy (IRE) 129 – Isla Azul (IRE) 74 (Machiavellian (USA) **72** 123) [2015 p7m⁵ p7f⁶ p6g p8d⁴ p11g⁶ t9.5g⁴ t13.9g⁶ t12.2g⁶ 11.9s³ 11.9g* 10v³ 9.9v³ Oct 6] 15,000Y: half-sister to several winners, including useful winner up to 9f North Star Boy (2-y-o 5f winner, by Acclamation) and 9f winner Wellingrove (by Cape Cross): dam, maiden (stayed 1¼m), sister to Coronation Stakes winner Rebecca Sharp and half-sister to dam of Golden Horn: fair handicapper: won at Brighton in September: left Ed Vaughan after sixth start: stays 1½m: acts on polytrack and heavy going: tried in headgear: often in tongue tie. *Alison Hutchinson*

SAGACIOUSLY (IRE) 3 b.f. Lawman (FR) 121 – Saga Celebre (FR) 104 (Peintre **92** Celebre (USA) 137) [2015 89: 12f 12s² 13.3s 14m⁴ 12d⁴ Oct 30] rangy filly: fairly useful handicapper: stays 1½m: acts on firm and soft going: often races prominently. *Ed Dunlop*

SAGELY (IRE) 2 b.f. (Apr 26) Frozen Power (IRE) 108 – Saga Celebre (FR) 104 (Peintre **64 p** Celebre (USA) 137) [2015 8.3g t8.6g² Sep 29] €35,000Y: third foal: half-sister to 2-y-o 8.3f winner (stays 1½m) Sagaciously (by Lawman): dam, 9f/1¼m winner (including in USA) who stayed 1½m, out of sister to Prix de l'Arc de Triomphe winner Sagamix: 66/1, improved from debut when 2¾ lengths second to Dubai Fashion in maiden at Wolverhampton, though no match for winner: will be suited by 1¼m+: capable of better still. *Ed Dunlop*

SAGUNA (FR) 3 b.f. Le Havre (IRE) 124 – Sandy Winner (FR) (Priolo (USA) 127) [2015 **80** 7m 7f² 8g² p7g* Aug 12] €30,000Y: useful-looking filly: second foal: dam, French maiden (third at 8.5f), half-sister to very smart French miler Spirito del Vento: fairly useful form: 3/10, won 4-runner maiden at Kempton final start by 6 lengths from Tafolau, making all and forging clear despite edging left: stays 1m. *Charles Hills*

SAHAAFY (USA) 3 b.c. Kitten's Joy (USA) 128 – Queen's Causeway (USA) (Giant's **111** Causeway (USA) 132) [2015 77p: 8m* 8g² 8m* 8f 8.1m 8g⁴ Aug 21] useful-looking colt: smart performer: won maiden at Newbury in April and handicap at Newmarket (by 5 lengths from Angel Vision) in May: best subsequent effort when fourth of 19 to My Dream Boat in handicap at York final start: stays 1m: acts on good to firm going: often races prominently: sent to UAE. *B. W. Hills*

SAHALIN 2 b.f. (Jan 15) Red Rocks (IRE) 124 – Tamathea (IRE) (Barathea (IRE) 127) **67** [2015 t8.6g p8g* p8m t8.6f* Dec 14] second foal: sister to Italian 2-y-o 1m winner Lady Honoria: dam, Italian 6f winner, half-sister to smart French 1¼m-1½m winner Coroner: fair performer: won maiden at Lingfield in October and claimer at Wolverhampton in December: stays 8.5f. *Marco Botti*

SAHARA DESERT (IRE) 4 b.g. Montjeu (IRE) 137 – Festoso (IRE) 102 (Diesis 133) **53** [2015 56: p8m p10g p12f 10.3d f11g³ 6g p10g Jun 6] modest maiden: best effort at 8.5f: acts on heavy going: usually wears headgear: left Jane Chapple-Hyam after fifth start. *Denis Quinn*

SAHARA (IRE) 3 b.f. Clodovil (IRE) 116 – Celtic Lynn (IRE) 83 (Celtic Swing 138) **81** [2015 54p: 8.3s⁴ 9.9g t9.5g² 9g* 10g³ 8.1v³ Sep 16] attractive filly: fairly useful handicapper: won at Sandown in July: stays 1¼m: acts on tapeta and soft going: usually races prominently. *Chris Wall*

SAHRAWI (GER) 4 b.f. Pivotal 124 – Sand River (IRE) (High Chaparral (IRE) 132) **109** [2015 10.4s³ 11.9g³ 12g² 11.9g⁴ 13.9g* 15.4d Oct 25] first foal: dam, French 1¼m winner, half-sister to useful French 1¼m-1½m winner Sano di Pietro: useful performer: won listed race at Saint-Cloud (by ¾ length from Sweeping Up) in October: creditable efforts in similar events all previous starts, nose second to Gretchen at Newmarket: far from discredited when ninth to Vazirabad in Prix Royal-Oak at Saint-Cloud final outing: probably stays 15f: acts on soft going: wore cheekpieces first outing. *M. Delzangles, France*

SAHREEJ (IRE) 2 gr.c. (Mar 13) Zebedee 113 – Petite Boulangere (IRE) (Namid 128) **95** [2015 5f⁴ 6g² 5.1m* 5f 5g² 5.2v* 6g⁵ Sep 18] 160,000Y: well-grown colt: fifth foal: half-brother to 6f winner Ficelle (by Chineur) and 2-y-o 5f winner She's A Worldie (by Kodiac): dam lightly-raced half-sister to smart sprinter Guinea Hunter: useful performer: won maiden at Chepstow in May and nursery at Newbury (by 4½ lengths from Fashionable Spirit) in August: best form at 5f: acts on good to firm and heavy going: often travels strongly. *Charles Hills*

SAIGON CITY 5 b.g. Mount Nelson 125 – Hoh Chi Min 103 (Efisio 120) [2015 94: 8f² **98 §** 7m⁵ 8m² 8d Aug 1] well-made gelding: useful handicapper: second at Ascot (apprentice) in April and Salisbury (2 lengths behind Lightning Spear) in June: stays 1¼m: acts on any turf going: usually wears headgear: usually travels strongly but a hard ride and one to be wary of. *Luca Cumani*

SAIL HOME 8 b.m. Mizzen Mast (USA) 121 – Bristol Channel 113 (Generous (IRE) 139) **61** [2015 61: p10g p10f³ p10f² p10f* p10g³ Apr 1] modest handicapper: won at Chelmsford in March: stays 1½m: acts on polytrack, fibresand, good to firm and good to soft going: tried in cheekpieces: often races prominently. *John E. Long*

SAILOR MALAN 3 b.g. Mount Nelson 125 – Flying Hi (Kyllachy 129) [2015 10s 12m⁶ **61** p10g⁴ Dec 9] workmanlike gelding: modest maiden: left Peter Fahey after first start. *Gay Kelleway*

SAILORS WARN (IRE) 8 b.g. Redback 116 – Coral Dawn (IRE) 67 (Trempolino **77** (USA) 135) [2015 89: 12.5m⁴ 12g⁵ p10g t12.2g⁶ Aug 10] fair handicapper: left E. J. O'Grady after second start: stays 15f: acts on soft and good to firm going: tried in cheekpieces/tongue tie. *Ronald Thompson*

SAILOR'S WAY 2 b.g. (Apr 18) Dubawi (IRE) 129 – Sail (IRE) 101 (Sadler's Wells **72** (USA) 132) [2015 8m⁶ p10g 8.3s⁴ t9.5f* Nov 16] fair performer: won nursery at Wolverhampton in November: best effort at 9.5f. *Charlie Appleby*

SAIL WITH SULTANA 4 ch.f. Black Sam Bellamy (IRE) 121 – Strathtay 60 (Pivotal **59** 124) [2015 57: t13.9g⁶ 16.2s* 14.1m t13.9f t16.5f Oct 27] modest handicapper: won at Chepstow in May: stays 2m: acts on tapeta and soft going: often races prominently. *Mark Rimell*

SAINGLEND 10 b.g. Galileo (IRE) 134 – Verbal Intrigue (USA) (Dahar (USA) 125) **–** [2015 t13.9f t16.5m³ Apr 2] tall gelding: fairly useful at best, no form in 2015: stays 2m: acts on firm and soft going: tried in cheekpieces. *Sean Curran*

SAINTED 2 ch.f. (Mar 8) Dutch Art 126 – Blithe 91 (Pivotal 124) [2015 6v* Nov 7] third **79 p** foal: sister to smart 6f winner Telmeyd: dam, 2-y-o 7f winner, closely related to very smart 7f/1m winner Penitent: 5/1, won 7-runner maiden at Doncaster by ¾ length from Udontdodou, asserting late on: better to come. *William Haggas*

SAINT HELENA (IRE) 7 b.m. Holy Roman Emperor (IRE) 125 – Tafseer (IRE) (Grand **66** Lodge (USA) 125) [2015 p10g p12g⁴ p10g³ p12f⁵ 10.2f⁵ t12.2g p11g² 14.1g p12m p12g Dec 2] rather leggy mare: fair handicapper: left Jim Best after fourth start: stays 1½m: acts on polytrack and good to firm going: usually wears headgear. *Mark Gillard*

SAINT HONORE 3 b.f. Champs Elysees 124 – Gwyneth 62 (Zafonic (USA) 130) [2015 **74** 61: p11g⁴ p11g³ 9m³ 9.9g⁵ p12f⁶ 10v 7s p10m* p12f* p12g³ Dec 3] lengthy filly: fair handicapper: won twice at Lingfield in November, latter apprentice event: stays 1½m: acts on polytrack and good to soft going: often races towards rear, usually travels strongly. *Pat Phelan*

SAINT LUCY 4 b.f. Selkirk (USA) 129 – Sister Maria (USA) 89 (Kingmambo (USA) **75** 125) [2015 74p: 11.5g 12.1g 13.1m³ 17.2f* 18d t13.9f Oct 13] big filly: fair handicapper: won at Bath in September: stays 17f: acts on polytrack and firm going: in cheekpieces/ tongue tie nowadays: usually races close up. *Brendan Powell*

SAINT POIS (FR) 4 b.g. Le Havre (IRE) 124 – Our Dream Queen 68 (Oasis Dream 129) **81** [2015 89, a96: p7f p8m p7m³ p7f t6g⁵ 7m⁴ 8m² 8.1m³ 8m⁵ 8.1m³ 7s⁶ Oct 15] fairly useful handicapper: will prove suited by a return to 1m+: acts on polytrack, good to firm and good to soft going: sometimes in tongue tie in 2015. *Tony Carroll*

SAINT THOMAS (IRE) 8 b.g. Alhaarth (IRE) 126 – Aguilas Perla (IRE) (Indian Ridge **71** 123) [2015 75: 9.9m⁵ 9.9m² 9.9m 9.3g 11.8g⁶ 11.8d⁶ Aug 24] close-coupled gelding: fair handicapper: stays 1½m: acts on polytrack, firm and good to soft going: tried in blinkers. *John Mackie*

SAIRAAM (IRE) 9 b.m. Marju (IRE) 127 – Sayedati Eljamilah (USA) 64 (Mr Prospector **44** (USA)) [2015 49: t7.1f f7g⁶ 7d 7m⁴ 6.1m⁵ 5m⁶ 6m 7g⁵ 6.1m 5.1d Nov 4] close-coupled mare: poor handicapper: stays 1¼m, races over much shorter nowadays: acts on polytrack, tapeta, firm and soft going: tried in headgear: inconsistent. *Charles Smith*

SAKADA 2 ch.c. (Mar 11) Sakhee's Secret 128 – Nevada Princess (IRE) (Desert Prince **88** (IRE) 130) [2015 6m p7g* 7s² p7g p7m Oct 21] 4,000F, £26,000Y: fifth foal: half-brother to Italian 5f/6f winner Nuracale (by Compton Place): dam, French 8.5f winner, half-sister to smart winner up to 1m Atlantis Prince: fairly useful performer: won maiden at Lingfield (by 8 lengths) in July: stays 7f: acts on polytrack: tried in blinkers: sold 10,000 gns, sent to Bahrain. *Richard Hannon*

SAKASH 5 b.h. Sakhee (USA) 136 – Ashwell Rose 63 (Anabaa (USA) 130) [2015 83: f7g **85**
p7m² 7f 7g* Jul 17] sturdy horse: fairly useful handicapper: won at Newbury (by head from
Exceeding Power) in July: stays 7f: acts on polytrack, fibresand and good to firm going:
usually in cheekpieces: usually races towards rear: sent to Saudi Arabia. *J. R. Jenkins*

SAKHALIN STAR (IRE) 4 ch.g. Footstepsinthesand 120 – Quela (GER) (Acatenango **80**
(GER) 127) [2015 78: 7g⁴ 7.5g³ 7s² 8.3s² 7.9v⁴ 9.2d² 8.3s* 9.1g 8.3g⁵ 10s³ 10.3d⁴ 10.2s
f8m Dec 8] fairly useful handicapper: won at Hamilton in July: stays 10.5f: acts on good
to firm and heavy going: wears headgear: consistent. *Richard Guest*

SAKHASTIC 2 b.g. (Apr 8) Sakhee's Secret 128 – Rutland Water (IRE) (Hawk Wing **44**
(USA) 136) [2015 5g t6g t6g t8.6f⁶ f7g t8.6f p7g⁵ Dec 10] poor maiden: best effort at 7f:
acts on polytrack: in headgear. *Christine Dunnett*

SAKHEE'S CITY (FR) 4 b.g. Sakhee (USA) 136 – A Lulu Ofa Menifee (USA) (Menifee **–**
(USA) 124) [2015 12m May 16] well held in maiden at Thirsk only outing on Flat: placed
in bumpers. *Philip Kirby*

SAKHEE'S JEM 2 ch.f. (Jan 22) Sakhee's Secret 128 – Amandian (IRE) 84 (Indian **69**
Ridge 123) [2015 5g² p5f³ 5m 5m³ 6m⁴ 6m⁵ 6m 7g p6f⁵ p6f⁶ Nov 19] 5,000Y: rather leggy
filly: half-sister to several winners, including 2-y-o 7f winner (stayed 1¼m) Graceful Star
(by Soviet Star) and 1m/9f winner Bahamian C (by Bahamian Bounty): dam 6f winner: fair
maiden: stays 6f: acts on good to firm going: tried in headgear. *Gay Kelleway*

SAKHEE'S RETURN 3 b.g. Sakhee's Secret 128 – Sofia Royale 61 (Royal Applause **94**
124) [2015 77: 8d³ 7g³ 7f* 7m² 7m* 7m⁵ 8d⁵ p7f Nov 19] fairly useful handicapper: won
at Haydock in June and York (apprentice, by ¾ length from Heartbreak Hero) in July: stays
7f: acts on firm going: usually races prominently. *Tim Easterby*

SAKHEE'S ROSE 5 b.m. Sakhee's Secret 128 – Isobel Rose (IRE) 73 (Royal Applause **75**
124) [2015 74: t7.1f* p6f² p6g⁴ t6f⁵ p6g* 6g⁶ 6g⁴ 6g t7.1m p7g Dec 16] sturdy mare: fair
handicapper: won at Wolverhampton in January and Kempton in April: stays 7f: acts on
polytrack and tapeta: wears blinkers. *Ed McMahon*

SAKHRA 4 b.g. Nayef (USA) 129 – Noble Desert (FR) (Green Desert (USA) 127) [2015 **49**
68: t12.2g⁵ t12.2g³ 11.8m⁴ 14.1g⁶ 16g⁶ 11.8m⁵ p12g³ 11.9g⁴ p12g t12.2m 11.9d² t12.2g⁶ **a56**
11.9s⁴ t16.5f⁴ t16.5f⁵ t13.9f Nov 10] modest maiden: stays 16.5f: acts on polytrack, tapeta,
good to firm and good to soft going: sometimes in headgear in 2015. *Mark Brisbourne*

SALATEEN 3 ch.c. Dutch Art 126 – Amanda Carter 92 (Tobougg (IRE) 125) [2015 103: **114**
8g 7m* 7g³ 7m 7d³ Oct 24] tall, unfurnished colt: smart performer: won handicap at York
in July by 3½ lengths from Captain Bob: creditable third to Fadhayyil in listed race there
next time: left Kevin Ryan before final outing: stays 7f: acts on soft and good to firm going:
usually leads. *David O'Meara*

SALFORD DREAM 6 ch.g. Halling (USA) 133 – Spitting Image (IRE) 84 (Spectrum **59**
(IRE) 126) [2015 49: f16g² f12d⁶ 16m² 21.6g⁶ 15s³ 14.1m⁴ 16m⁶ Jun 29] good-topped
gelding: modest maiden: stays 2m: acts on soft and good to firm going: usually races
prominently. *Pauline Robson*

SALIENT 11 b.g. Fasliyev (USA) 120 – Savannah Belle 84 (Green Desert (USA) 127) **65**
[2015 67: p12m³ p13g² p12g* p12f⁶ p12g⁵ 11m⁵ p12g⁴ p12g 11s* 12d p12m² p12g p12g
p16g Dec 16] sturdy, compact gelding: fair handicapper: won at Lingfield (apprentice) in
April and Goodwood in September: stays 13f: acts on polytrack, good to firm and heavy
going: tried in headgear. *Michael Attwater*

SALIERIS MASS 3 b.g. Mount Nelson 125 – Sunley Gift 70 (Cadeaux Genereux 131) **94**
[2015 9.8g* 10g⁵ 11.9d⁴ 10g² 10.2d Oct 14] 17,000F, 50,000Y: fourth foal: half-brother to
2-y-o 5f winner Senator Bong (by Dutch Art): dam 2-y-o 5f winner: fairly useful performer:
won maiden at Ripon in April: stays 1½m: acts on good to soft going: usually races close
up: has been gelded. *Mark Johnston*

SALLABEH 3 b.f. Showcasing 117 – Clincher Club 77 (Polish Patriot (USA) 128) [2015 **80**
71: p7f³ p8m 7.5g³ 8.3g⁴ 8g* 8.3d Sep 1] fairly useful handicapper: won at Haydock in
August: stays 1m: acts on polytrack and good to firm going. *David O'Meara*

SALMA GONDIS (IRE) 3 b.f. Kodiac 112 – Rainbowskia (FR) (Rainbow Quest (USA) **71**
134) [2015 71: t8.6g³ 8.3d³ 8.3g⁴ 8.5m⁴ 7.2g 7m* 7.9s Aug 24] fair handicapper: won at
Newcastle in August: stays 8.5f: acts on good to firm and good to soft going: usually wears
hood: front runner/races prominently. *David O'Meara*

SALMON SUSHI 4 ch.g. Dalakhani (IRE) 133 – Salsa Steps (USA) 103 (Giant's **86 §**
Causeway (USA) 132) [2015 84: p11g t9.5f² t9.5f p11g 10.3m³ 10.3g² 10m⁴ Aug 22]
strong, close-coupled gelding: fairly useful handicapper: stays 10.5f: acts on polytrack,
tapeta and good to firm going: wears hood: often starts slowly, often races in rear:
ungenuine: sold £20,000 and joined Tim Easterby. *David Lanigan*

SALOON DAY (GER) 5 b.h. Dai Jin 123 – Saloon Rum (GER) (Spectrum (IRE) 126) **–**
[2015 14f Jul 3] fairly useful performer in Germany in 2013, successful in maiden at
Dortmund: left M. Hofer/off 24 months, behind in handicap at Sandown on only outing in
2015: stays 1½m: acts on good to soft going. *Ian Williams*

SALTARELLO (IRE) 3 b.g. Fast Company (IRE) 126 – Step Dancing 62 (Distant Music **70**
(USA) 126) [2015 70: t7.1g² t7.1f⁵ t7.1g⁶ 7.1s⁴ 7g* 6.5m 7m² 6g³ 7.9g 7d³ 7g³ 8d³ 7.2g⁴
8.3g 7.2g Oct 13] fair performer: won maiden at Redcar in April: left John Quinn after
eighth start: stays 1m: acts on tapeta and good to soft going: sometimes in headgear in
2015. *Marjorie Fife*

SALT ISLAND 3 b.c. Exceed And Excel (AUS) 126 – Tiana 99 (Diktat 126) [2015 91p: **112**
6m* 6m³ 6d⁶ 6f⁴ 5m 5m Jul 31] sturdy colt: smart performer: won handicap at Newmarket
in April by 3¼ lengths from Properus: good fourth in Commonwealth Cup at Royal Ascot
(4½ lengths behind Muhaarar): stayed 6f: acted on firm going: dead. *Charles Hills*

SALT LAKE SOOTY 2 gr.c. (Apr 28) Arabian Gleam 122 – Kilmovee 59 (Inchinor 119) **51**
[2015 5m⁶ 5m⁵ 6m p6g⁵ 7s 6s⁶ 5s Oct 6] modest maiden: best form at 5f: acts on good to
firm going: tried in cheekpieces: front runner/races prominently. *Denis Quinn*

SALUTAMASORETA (USA) 4 b.f. U S Ranger (USA) 124 – My Little Dragon (USA) **–**
(Cactus Ridge (USA) 109) [2015 t7.1m⁶ t6f Mar 20] $6,000Y: first foal: dam US 9f winner:
well held in 2 maidens. *David O'Meara*

SALVADO (IRE) 5 b.g. Invincible Spirit (IRE) 121 – Easter Fairy (USA) (Fusaichi **53**
Pegasus (USA) 130) [2015 72, a63: p6m⁵ p5g³ t5.1f³ p6m⁶ 6m t6g 6m 8v t6m³ t6m⁵ p8g
p5g p6g* p7g t7.1m Dec 30] workmanlike gelding: modest handicapper: won at
Chelmsford (apprentice) in November: stays 1m, usually over shorter: acts on polytrack,
tapeta and good to firm going: often wears hood: tried in tongue tie. *Tony Carroll*

SALVATORE FURY (IRE) 5 b.g. Strategic Prince 114 – Nocturnal (FR) 71 (Night Shift **79**
(USA)) [2015 81, a89: p6m p6g⁵ p6f³ p6g* 6m 6m 5.9m⁶ 5m 6g t6g⁴ 5.9m² 6m⁴ p6g² **a91**
Oct 6] sturdy gelding: fairly useful handicapper: won at Lingfield in April: head second to
Elis Eliz at Kempton final start (outbattled): stays 6f: acts on polytrack and firm going:
wears headgear. *Keith Dalgleish*

SALVO 2 b.f. (Mar 6) Acclamation 118 – Passe Passe (USA) 78 (Lear Fan (USA) 130) **84**
[2015 6m* 6d⁵ 6.5m Sep 10] lengthy, rather unfurnished filly: closely related to winner up
to 11f Ryedale Ovation (2-y-o 5f winner, by Royal Applause) and half-sister to several
winners, including useful winner up to 1¼m Cabinet (2-y-o 7f winner, by Grand Lodge)
and ungenuine 7f-1½m winner Magic Instinct (by Entrepreneur): dam maiden (stayed
1½m): won maiden at Newmarket in July by 1¾ lengths from Cosmopolitan Girl: below
that form in Princess Margaret Stakes at Ascot and nursery at Doncaster (slowly away).
Charlie Fellowes

SAMAAWY 2 b.c. (Mar 25) Alhaarth (IRE) 126 – Tasheyaat 86 (Sakhee (USA) 136) [2015 **81 p**
7s⁵ Oct 13] first foal: dam, 1¼m winner, half-sister to useful 6f winner Judhoor (by
Alhaarth) out of half-sister to 2000 Guineas/Champion Stakes winner Haafhd (also by
Alhaarth): 7/2, shaped very well when 2¾ lengths fifth of 10 to Vincent's Forever in
maiden at Leicester, going strongly and stretching the field from 2f out (did too much too
soon): will improve. *Mark Johnston*

SAMEEK (IRE) 3 b.g. Acclamation 118 – Varenka (IRE) 91 (Fasliyev (USA) 120) [2015 **?**
8.3d May 19] 175,000Y: fifth foal: half-brother to 7f winner (including at 2 yrs) Meezaan
(by Medicean) and 1m-10.4f winner Whispering Warrior (by Oasis Dream), both useful:
dam, 2-y-o 7.5f winner, half-sister to smart performer up to 1¼m Steinbeck (known as Pure
Champion in Hong Kong): eleventh of 12 in maiden at Nottingham on debut: sent to
Sweden, winning maiden at Taby (6.7f on dirt) in October and handicap (1m on dirt) in
November. *Ed Dunlop*

SAMHAIN 4 b.g. Compton Place 125 – Athboy Nights (IRE) 64 (Night Shift (USA)) **53 +**
[2015 80: f5g* 5m 5v⁵ 5g f5g⁶ Nov 12] fairly useful handicapper: won at Southwell in **a86**
March: best form at 5f: easily best form on fibresand: front runner/races prominently.
David Brown

SAMMY'S CHOICE 3 ch.g. Pastoral Pursuits 127 – Diane's Choice 95 (Komaite – (USA)) [2015 57: p6g p7g p6g Dec 3] lightly-raced maiden, no form since debut (in 2014). *Paul Burgoyne*

SAMMY'S WARRIOR 3 b.g. Myboycharlie (IRE) 118 – Tahfeez (IRE) 61 (Alhaarth **84** (IRE) 126) [2015 71p: t8.6f* t8.6g⁵ t9.5f 10v² Nov 3] fairly useful performer: won maiden at Wolverhampton in March: stays 9.5f: acts on tapeta: tried in blinkers once in 2015. *Marco Botti*

SAM NOMBULIST 7 ch.g. Sleeping Indian 122 – Owdbetts (IRE) 69 (High Estate 127) **63** [2015 t8.6g⁵ t9.5g⁶ Apr 28] leggy gelding: modest handicapper: stays 8.5f: best form on good to soft/soft going: often wears headgear: tried in tongue tie: quirky sort. *Muredach Kelly, Ireland*

SAMPERA (IRE) 3 b.f. Iffraaj 127 – Al Cobra (IRE) 70 (Sadler's Wells (USA) 132) **79** [2015 69: 10.2s⁵ 12d 10m* 10.3d⁴ 9.9g* 10g⁶ 10s⁴ Sep 13] lengthy filly: fair handicapper: won at Leicester in May and Beverley in July: stays 10.5f: acts on good to firm going: visored last 5 starts: sold 30,000 gns, sent to Saudi Arabia. *Michael Bell*

SAMPLE (FR) 3 b.f. Zamindar (USA) 116 – Sanabyra (FR) (Kahyasi 130) [2015 50: **66** p7m⁴ p8f³ p10m² t8.6f⁴ Mar 14] fair maiden: stays 1¼m: acts on polytrack: wears hood. *Roger Charlton*

SAMSAMSAM 3 b.g. Sakhee's Secret 128 – Greenfly (Green Desert (USA) 127) [2015 **58** –: 6g 5.1g⁴ 5g³ t6g² 6g Jul 22] modest maiden: stays 6f: acts on tapeta: in cheekpieces last 4 starts: sent to UAE. *Robert Cowell*

SAMSON 4 ch.g. Black Sam Bellamy (IRE) 121 – Riverine (Risk Me (FR) 127) [2015 – p13.3g⁵ Dec 10] won bumper in October on debut: 5/4, last of 5 in maiden at Chelmsford. *Hughie Morrison*

SAMSONITE (IRE) 3 ch.g. Pivotal 124 – Silca's Sister 112 (Inchinor 119) [2015 7d⁶ 7g⁴ **79** 7.5g⁵ 8d³ 10g* 10.4g 8d 10.3d Oct 23] fair performer: won handicap at Pontefract (amateur) in August: stays 1¼m: acts on good to soft going. *Tony Coyle*

SAM SPADE (IRE) 5 gr.g. Clodovil (IRE) 116 – Red Empress 88 (Nashwan (USA) 135) **47** [2015 76: p8g t9.5f t8.6f t9.5f⁶ p8g 8d 7m 8.3g⁶ 10m Jun 22] rather leggy gelding: poor handicapper: stays 1¼m: acts on all-weather: wears headgear. *Derek Shaw*

SAMTU (IRE) 4 b.g. Teofilo (IRE) 126 – Samdaniya 79 (Machiavellian (USA) 123) **86** [2015 79: f14d² f16d⁶ f14g* f14g⁴ 14.6m² 16g² 18gᵖᵘ 16.2m⁵ Jul 14] fairly useful **a74** handicapper: won at Southwell in March and Doncaster in May: left Brian Ellison after sixth start: stays 2m: acts on fibresand and good to firm going: in hood final start: usually leads: fairly useful hurdler. *Tony Coyle*

SANAADH 2 ch.c. (Apr 28) Exceed And Excel (AUS) 126 – Queen's Logic (IRE) 125 **54 p** (Grand Lodge (USA) 125) [2015 5g⁵ 6.1v² Oct 7] half-brother to several winners, including very smart 5f/6f winner (including at 2 yrs) Lady of The Desert (by Rahy) and useful 1¼m winner Prince of Stars (by Sea The Stars): dam, winner up to 7f (2-y-o 5f/6f winner) including Cheveley Park and Fred Darling Stakes, half-sister to top-class 1¼m-1½m performer Dylan Thomas and 1000 Guineas winner Homecoming Queen: better effort when 9 lengths second to Scrutineer in maiden at Nottingham: should continue to progress. *Richard Fahey*

SAN CASSIANO (IRE) 8 b.g. Bertolini (USA) 125 – Celtic Silhouette (FR) (Celtic **77** Swing 138) [2015 96: 10.3d 9.8d 10.4g 9.9g³ 10s⁶ 9.8d⁶ 10g* 10.1m 10s⁶ 10g² 9.8g⁵ 10.3g 12.1g⁵ 12.2g³ 11.9d Sep 25] good-topped gelding: fair handicapper: won at Redcar in June: stays 1½m: acts on polytrack, good to firm and heavy going: in blinkers last 6 starts. *Ruth Carr*

SANDACRES 2 b.c. (Mar 9) Frozen Power (IRE) 108 – Lady Golan (IRE) (Golan (IRE) **69** 129) [2015 p7g⁵ p7g³ Dec 16] fair maiden: similar form to debut when 4¼ lengths third to Severini at Kempton. *Jo Crowley*

SANDAHL (IRE) 2 b.g. (Apr 4) Footstepsinthesand 120 – Little Scotland 92 (Acclamation **86 d** 118) [2015 5.1g⁴ 6g* 6m 6g p7g Sep 30] €68,000F, €80,000Y: useful-looking gelding: second foal: dam 6f/7f winner: fairly useful performer at best: won maiden at York (by ¾ length from Fast And Furious) in June: went wrong way after, folding final start: best effort at 6f: blinkered fifth start: sold 11,500 gns, sent to Italy. *Ralph Beckett*

SAND BY ME 2 b.g. (Mar 11) Piccolo 121 – Marysienka 78 (Primo Dominie 121) [2015 – 5g Oct 19] 100/1, very green when well held in maiden at Windsor. *Peter Crate*

SANDFRANKSKIPSGO 6 ch.g. Piccolo 121 – Alhufoof (USA) 100 (Dayjur (USA) **95** 137) [2015 96: p5g⁴ 5g³ p5f² 5m 5m² 5m⁵ 5m² p5g³ p5g³ t5.1f³ Dec 22] rather leggy gelding: useful handicapper: creditable third at Kempton (twice) and Wolverhampton last 3 starts: stays 5.5f: acts on polytrack, tapeta and firm going: tried in tongue. *Peter Crate*

SANDGATE 3 ch.g. Compton Place 125 – Jump Ship 74 (Night Shift (USA)) [2015 65p: **68** 8m 9.8d⁵ 9.2g⁴ 10.4g* 10s³ 10.4g⁶ 11.5s³ 9.8g⁴ Aug 31] fair handicapper: won at Haydock in July: stays 11.5f: acts on soft going: in cheekpieces final start: often travels strongly. *Richard Fahey*

SANDRA'S SECRET (IRE) 2 gr.f. (Feb 5) Zebedee 113 – Good For Her 72 (Rock of **69** Gibraltar (IRE) 133) [2015 5g 5m* 5g⁶ 5g 8g⁶ 6g⁵ t5.1f⁶ Oct 30] €22,000Y: second foal: half-sister to 6f winner Kyllach Me (by Kyllachy): dam, maiden (stayed 1m), closely related to very smart performer up to 1m Zoffany: fair performer: won maiden at Beverley in July: best effort at 5f: acts on good to firm going: tried in blinkers. *Les Eyre*

SANDS CHORUS 3 b.g. Footstepsinthesand 120 – Wood Chorus 97 (Singspiel (IRE) **79** 133) [2015 65: f7d² p10g 10.2m⁴ 8s² t9 5u³ 8g* 9.3d³ t9.3g* p8g³ 8.5g³ t9.5m Sep 25] good-topped gelding: fair handicapper: won at Thirsk in July and Wolverhampton in August: stays 9.5f: acts on tapeta and good to soft going: front runner. *James Given*

SANDS OF FORTUNE (IRE) 6 ch.g. Shamardal (USA) 129 – Shell Garland (USA) 80 **92** (Sadler's Wells (USA) 132) [2015 11.9d 12d³ 15.8d² 21g* 18gᵖᵘ Sep 19] strong, sturdy gelding: fairly useful handicapper: won at Goodwood (by 6 lengths from Taws) in July: pulled up final outing: stays 21f. *Nigel Twiston-Davies*

SANDY CAY (USA) 3 gr.f. Mizzen Mast (USA) 121 – Camanoe (USA) 63 (Gone West **–** (USA)) [2015 89: 8m May 30] fairly useful form at 2 yrs: in first-time hood, well held in handicap only outing in 2015: best effort at 7f: sold 62,000 gns in December. *Sir Michael Stoute*

SANDY COVE 4 br.g. Oasis Dream 129 – Maganda (IRE) 84 (Sadler's Wells (USA) 132) **73** [2015 76, a65: p12f* p12f* t12.2f² 12g⁵ 14m⁶ 11.9m³ 10m⁴ 12g p12g⁴ t12.2f* t12.2f⁶ p10g Oct 20] compact gelding: fair handicapper: won at Kempton in January and February and Wolverhampton in September: stays 1½m: acts on polytrack, tapeta and good to firm going: tried in hood prior to 2015: often races prominently. *James Eustace*

SAN QUENTIN (IRE) 4 gr.g. Lawman (FR) 121 – In The Soup (USA) (Alphabet Soup **67** (USA) 126) [2015 p12g p12g t12.2f⁶ p11f⁴ 12g² t12.2g 11.5d p11g⁴ p12g³ t12.2m* t12.2g* t12.2f* p11g⁶ t12.2m⁴ Dec 12] good-topped gelding: fair handicapper: left Tony Carroll after eighth start, won at Wolverhampton in September (twice) and October: stays 1½m: acts on polytrack, tapeta and good to firm going: often wore cheekpieces and also tried in tongue tie for previous trainer: usually races towards rear, usually travels strongly. *Dean Ivory*

SANTADELACRUZE 6 b.g. Pastoral Pursuits 127 – Jupiters Princess 54 (Jupiter Island **64** 126) [2015 71: p10g p10g p10g p12f⁴ 11.5d³ 10m³ 10g² p10g³ p11g⁶ 9.9s Oct 15] workmanlike gelding: modest handicapper: stays 1¼m: acts on polytrack and good to firm going: often wears headgear: often travels strongly. *Mark Hoad*

SANTAYANA (GER) 6 ch.m. Manduro (GER) 135 – Saderlina (IRE) (Sadler's Wells **57** (USA) 132) [2015 f11s² t12.2f² t13.9f* f14d⁴ t13.9g⁴ 13.1m² 13.1g³ 16.2s⁶ 13.1d³ p13.3m⁴ t16.5f⁶ t16.5f Oct 30] modest handicapper: won at Wolverhampton in February: stays 1¾m: acts on polytrack, tapeta, good to firm and good to soft going: tried in headgear. *David Evans*

SANTEFISIO 9 b.g. Efisio 120 – Impulsive Decision (IRE) 71 (Nomination 125) [2015 **97** 109: t8.6f³ p8g p7f t8.6m² t8.6g⁵ 8m⁴ 7m 8.1m 8m² 7m 7.9m t8.6m³ 7.2g⁴ p7g Oct 29] good-topped gelding: useful handicapper: stays 8.5f: acts on polytrack, tapeta and firm going: wears headgear: often races in rear: hard to win with. *Keith Dalgleish*

SANT'ELIA 3 b.f. Authorized (IRE) 133 – Trew Class 99 (Inchinor 119) [2015 p10g⁶ 10m **63** 10.3g Aug 1] fifth foal: closely related to 11.5f winner Jennifer J (by Motivator) and half-sister to 11.5f/1½m winner Kathleen Frances (by Sakhee): dam 1¼m winner: seemed to show modest form on first of 3 starts in maidens, well held on turf otherwise. *Mark H. Tompkins*

SANTIBURI SPRING 2 b.f. (Mar 21) Mullionmileanhour (IRE) 116 – Santiburi Girl 77 **67 p** (Casteddu 111) [2015 p7g p7g Nov 26] half-sister to several winners, including winner up to 1m Mr Willis (2-y-o 7f winner, by Desert Sun) and 7f-1½m winner Samsons Son (by Primo Valentino), both useful: dam winner up to 11f (2-y-o 7f winner) who stayed 1¾m: off 4 months, 50/1, much improved from debut when 2 lengths seventh of 10 to Crowning Glory in maiden at Chelmsford, not unduly punished: open to further improvement. *John Best*

Somerville Tattersall Stakes, Newmarket—Sanus Per Aquam (rail) is one of the first under pressure but finds plenty to gain a narrow verdict over Tasleet (striped cap), who hangs off the rail; Adventurous (No.3) and Zonderland complete the frame

SANUS PER AQUAM (IRE) 2 b.c. (Apr 8) Teofilo (IRE) 126 – Fainne (IRE) (Peintre **108 p**
Celebre (USA) 137) [2015 7m* 7g* 7g² 8d³ 7g* 7g³ Oct 10] big, unfurnished colt: fifth
foal: brother to useful 1¼m winner Morning Mix: dam once-raced half-sister to 2000
Guineas winner Dawn Approach: useful performer: won maiden at the Curragh (by 1¼
lengths from Lieutenant General) in June, minor event at Leopardstown (by 4¾ lengths
from Port Douglas) in July and Somerville Tattersall Stakes at Newmarket (by nose from
Tasleet) in September: creditable efforts when placed all other starts, second in Tyros Stakes
at Leopardstown (½ length behind Deauville) and third in Willis Champions Juvenile Stakes
at Leopardstown (2 lengths behind Johannes Vermeer) and Dewhurst Stakes at Newmarket
(6 lengths behind Air Force Blue): should be suited by a return to 1m: acts on good to firm
going: races prominently: remains with potential. *J. S. Bolger, Ireland*

SAOI (USA) 8 ch.g. Wiseman's Ferry (USA) 117 – Careyes (IRE) (Sadler's Wells (USA) **97**
132) [2015 100: p12g4 p11g 10s³ 12m⁴ 11.6m⁴ 14f⁶ Jul 10] workmanlike gelding: useful
handicapper: stays 1½m: acts on polytrack, soft and good to firm going: wears hood.
William Knight

SAPTAPADI (IRE) 9 ch.g. Indian Ridge 123 – Olympienne (IRE) (Sadler's Wells (USA) **66**
132) [2015 96: f12s t12.2g⁵ 12d 13s⁵ 12m* May 23] well-made gelding: just fair performer
in 2015: won claimer at Catterick final start: stayed 16.5f: acted on polytrack, soft and good
to firm going: tried in blinkers: was often in tongue tie: dead. *Brian Ellison*

SARABI 2 b.f. (Jan 30) Rip Van Winkle (IRE) 134 – Xaphania (Sakhee (USA) 136) [2015 **69**
5m p6f⁵ p5g⁵ f5g* Dec 18] 17,000Y: second foal: half-sister to 6f and (at 2 yrs) 7f winner
Cape Xenia (by Cape Cross): dam, unraced, out of half-sister to very smart performer up to
1½m Imperial Dancer: fair performer: in first-time cheekpieces, won nursery at Southwell
in December: will prove suited by a return to 6f. *Scott Dixon*

SARAFINA 3 b.f. Mullionmileanhour (IRE) 116 – Nala (USA) (Lion Heart (USA) 124) **48**
[2015 –: p7m p7m p12g³ p10g² p10m p12g⁵ p10g² 10m⁶ 10.1m⁶ 8m⁶ 8.3g t12.2m t13.9g
Nov 27] smallish filly: poor maiden: left John Best after eighth start, Dianne Sayer after
eleventh: stays 1½m: acts on polytrack and good to firm going: in cheekpieces final start:
often starts slowly, usually races nearer last than first. *David Thompson*

SARAHA 3 b.f. Dansili 127 – Kareemah (IRE) (Peintre Celebre (USA) 137) [2015 69p: **79 p**
8d⁴ p8g² p12f* Sep 12] useful-looking filly: fairly useful form: value for extra when
winning handicap at Lingfield in September by ½ length from Whoopsy Daisy: stays 1½m:
in hood last 3 starts: will go on improving. *William Haggas*

SARAH JOYCE (IRE) 3 b.f. The Carbon Unit (USA) 106 – The Real Thing (IRE) 84 **80**
(Traditionally (USA) 117) [2015 83: 8.5v⁶ 10.5v⁴ 8g² 8g⁴ 9.2d* 8.3d⁶ 9.5v⁶ Sep 20] fairly
useful handicapper: won at Hamilton in July: stays 9f: acts on soft going: tried in visor in
2015. *John Patrick Shanahan, Ireland*

SARANGOO 7 b.m. Piccolo 121 – Craic Sa Ceili (IRE) 83 (Danehill Dancer (IRE) 117) **88**
[2015 84: p7f* 7d⁵ 7.1m² 7s* 7m 7.1m⁴ 6g⁴ 7.1v* 7.1g⁴ 7.1s Sep 15] workmanlike mare:
fairly useful handicapper: won at Kempton in April, Brighton in June and Chepstow in
August: stays 7f: acts on polytrack and any turf going: tried in cheekpieces: front runner.
Malcolm Saunders

SARHAAN 3 b.g. New Approach (IRE) 132 – Coveted (Sinndar (IRE) 134) [2015 p8g – Mar 28] 16/1, tailed-off last of 8 in maiden at Chelmsford on debut: sold 3,500 gns, sent to Italy. *B. W. Hills*

SARISTA (IRE) 3 b.f. Kodiac 112 – Suffer Her (IRE) (Whipper (USA) 126) [2015 88: 6m – 6g 5g Jun 20] fairly useful performer in 2014, no form in 2015: best effort at 5f: acts on good to firm and good to soft going. *Richard Fahey*

SARK (IRE) 2 b.c. (Apr 29) Zoffany (IRE) 121 – Breezeway (IRE) 70 (Grand Lodge 71 (USA) 125) [2015 7.4d 7.4v⁴ 8.3g⁶ p8f t9.5f* Nov 3] fair performer: won nursery at Wolverhampton in November: stays 9.5f: acts on tapeta. *David Evans*

SARLAT 4 b.f. Champs Elysees 124 – Midnight Sky 52 (Desert Prince (IRE) 130) [2015 61 57, a65: t9.5f⁴ t8.6g² t9.5g* t9.5f⁵ t9.5m t9.5m Sep 25] modest handicapper: won at Wolverhampton (apprentice) in January: stays 9.5f: acts on tapeta. *Mark Brisbourne*

SARPECH (IRE) 4 b.g. Sea The Stars (IRE) 140   Sadima (IRE) 103 (Sadler's Wells 81 (USA) 132) [2015 70p: t12.2m² 16v p13.3g⁶ t12.2g⁵ Jul 7] fairly useful maiden: best effort at 1½m: acts on tapeta: blinkered final start: sold 30,000 gns, joined Charlie Longsdon. *Sir Mark Prescott Bt*

SARSTED 3 b.g. Paco Boy (IRE) 129 – Red Blooded Woman (USA) 71 (Red Ransom 84 (USA)) [2015 82p: 8m⁴ 11g⁴ p10g* 9.9s⁶ 10s t8.6f⁶ p10f² Nov 5] well-made gelding: fairly **a90** useful handicapper: won at Chelmsford in July: stays 1¼m: acts on polytrack and tapeta and soft going: front runner/races prominently. *Hughie Morrison*

SARTORI 4 b.g. Elnadim (USA) 128 – Little Caroline (IRE) (Great Commotion (USA) 70 § 123) [2015 73: 6g 6g 6s 5d⁵ 5m* 6g⁶ 5d² 5m 5s f5f Dec 17] smallish gelding: fair handicapper: won at Catterick in August: stays 6f: acts on good to firm and good to soft going: tried in visor, in cheekpieces last 7 starts: front runner/races prominently: quirky and is one to treat with caution. *Marjorie Fife*

Mrs J. S. Bolger's "Sanus Per Aquam"

SASKIA'S DREAM 7 b.m. Oasis Dream 129 – Swynford Pleasure 72 (Reprimand 122) **65**
[2015 65: p6g³ p6m⁴ p6g³ p6g⁵ 7m³ 6.1d p7m² 7m² 7m⁴ p6g⁴ 6g³ 7v Aug 25] sturdy,
well-made mare: fair handicapper: stays 9f: acts on polytrack, firm and good to soft going:
often wears headgear: often races in rear/travels strongly. *Jane Chapple-Hyam*

SASPARELLA (FR) 2 b.f. (Apr 9) Shamardal (USA) 129 – Desertiste (Green Desert **110**
(USA) 127) [2015 6d* 7g⁴ 6d* Sep 21] third foal: dam, French 5f/8.7f winner, closely
related to smart dam of high-class performer up to 1½m Intello and half-sister to very smart
1m/9f performer Mondialiste: smart form: won newcomers race at Deauville (by 4 lengths)
in July and Prix Eclipse at Chantilly (5 ran, by 1¼ lengths from Tourny) in September:
favourite when 1¾ lengths fourth of 5 to Great Page in Prix du Calvados at Deauville in
between: bred to stay beyond 6f: acts on good to soft going. *C. Laffon-Parias, France*

SATANIC BEAT (IRE) 6 br.g. Dark Angel (IRE) 113 – Slow Jazz (USA) 106 (Chief's **81**
Crown (USA)) [2015 89: 10.3d 12s 12m³ 9.9m⁵ 12m⁶ 12.3g 12.1g³ 12vᵘʳ Oct 24] close-
coupled gelding: fairly useful handicapper: left Jedd O'Keeffe after seventh start: stays
1½m: acts on good to firm and heavy going: front runner/races prominently: fairly useful
hurdler. *Phil Middleton*

SATANIC MILLS (IRE) 3 b.g. Dark Angel (IRE) 113 – Few Are Chosen (IRE) 97 –
(Sulamani (IRE) 130) [2015 –: 6m⁶ 7.5m⁵ 9.9m Jun 23] no form. *Nigel Tinkler*

SATCHVILLE FLYER 4 ch.g. Compton Place 125 – Palinisa (FR) 106 (Night Shift **76**
(USA)) [2015 54: p6g* p6m* p6f² p5d² p6g* 6g⁵ p6g² 6g⁶ p6f⁵ p7g p6g Dec 16] fair
handicapper: won at Chelmsford (twice) in February and at Kempton in May: stays 6f: acts
on polytrack: front runner/races prominently. *Brett Johnson*

SATELLITE EXPRESS (IRE) 4 ch.f. Observatory (USA) 131 – Composition 82 –
(Wolfhound (USA) 126) [2015 61: f7d Jan 2] smallish, angular filly: modest performer:
looked hard ride when well held only outing in 2015: stays 7f: acts on all-weather: in visor
last 2 starts. *David Evans*

SATELLITE (IRE) 4 b.g. Danehill Dancer (IRE) 117 – Perihelion (IRE) 105 (Galileo **109**
(IRE) 134) [2015 104: 10.4g 11.9f⁶ 12.3g⁵ 14m² 13.3s* 12s² Sep 18] useful-looking gelding:
useful handicapper: won at Newbury (by 4 lengths from Faithful Mount) in August: career-
best effort when neck second to Keep In Line there final start: stays 13.5f: acts on soft
going: has worn hood: sold 105,000 gns and joined Tim Vaughan. *William Haggas*

SATIN AND LACE (IRE) 3 b.f. Mawatheeq (USA) 126 – Katayeb (IRE) (Machiavellian **72**
(USA) 123) [2015 8.3g t8.6m 8s⁴ f12g⁶ p12f Nov 25] €14,000F: sturdy filly: sixth foal:
closely related to 1¼m winner Tahkeem (by Green Desert) and half-sister to 1¾m winner
Juwireya (by Nayef): dam once-raced half-sister to high-class 1¼m-1½m winner White
Muzzle and to dam of Dubai World Cup winner Almutawakel: fair maiden: should be
suited by further than 1m: acts on soft going: often starts slowly. *Rae Guest*

SATIN CHIC 2 ch.f. (Mar 17) Monsieur Bond (IRE) 120 – Satin Doll 68 (Diktat 126) **75**
[2015 5v⁴ 6d* 5f⁵ 6d 6d⁶ 6g² t6f Nov 14] £800Y: second foal: half-sister to useful 6f
(including at 2 yrs) winner Seal Rock (by Ishiguru): dam maiden (stayed 1m): fair
performer: won maiden at Hamilton in May: stays 6f: acts on good to soft going: in
cheekpieces last 2 starts. *Bryan Smart*

SATIN WATERS 4 b.f. Halling (USA) 133 – Velvet Waters 80 (Unfuwain (USA) 131) –
[2015 57: p14g Apr 9] big filly: maiden, modest form at best: stays 11f: acts on polytrack
and good to soft going: often in headgear prior to 2015. *Christine Dunnett*

SATISH 2 b.c. (Apr 28) Dansili 127 – Maycocks Bay 100 (Muhtarram (USA) 125) [2015 **93 p**
7g⁴ Sep 5] half-brother to 3 winners, including high-class winner up to 1½m (including
Oaks) Sariska (2-y-o 7f winner, by Pivotal), useful winner up to 1¾m Gull Wing (2-y-o
8.6f winner, by In The Wings), herself dam of high-class 1½m performer Eagle Top, and
useful 1½m-2m winner Zigato (by Azamour): dam 1¼m-1¾m winner: 16/1, not seen to
best effect when encouraging 2½ lengths fourth of 10 to Culturati in maiden at Ascot,
caught further back than ideal and running on having been forced to switch: sure to
progress. *John Gosden*

SATTELAC 2 b.f. (Feb 24) Kodiac 112 – Sattelight (Fraam 114) [2015 6g⁵ 6s⁴ 5.9m⁶ 7.2g³ **61 p**
Aug 27] £23,000Y: sixth foal: half-sister to winners abroad by Royal Applause and
Bahamian Bounty: dam, third in bumper, half-sister to useful sprinter Ajigolo: modest
maiden: upped in trip, better than result when third in nursery at Musselburgh final start:
best effort at 6f: remains open to improvement. *Keith Dalgleish*

SATURATION POINT 4 b.f. Beat Hollow 126 – Query (USA) (Distant View (USA) 73 §
126) [2015 72: p10g* 10m⁴ 10g p10m⁵ t9.5g p10f t9.5f Oct 20] fair handicapper: won at
Lingfield in April: stays 1¼m: acts on polytrack and tapeta: in blinkers last 2 starts: often
starts slowly/races in rear: ungenuine. *James Toller*

SATURN LACE (IRE) 2 b.f. (Mar 26) Kodiac 112 – Atishoo (IRE) 70 (Revoque (IRE) 92
122) [2015 5m³ 6g⁴ 5m⁴ 6m³ 6f² 6g⁴ 6d* 7s* 8f² Dec 20] £42,000Y: sixth foal: sister to
2-y-o 5f winner Kodatish and half-sister to 2 winners, including winner up to 1¼m Sonoran
Sands (2-y-o 6f/7f winner, by Footstepsinthesand): dam maiden (stayed 1m): fairly useful
performer: won nurseries at Catterick in August and October, improved form upped in trip
in latter: left John Quinn 40,000 gns before final start: probably stays 1m: acts on firm and
soft going: often races prominently. *Roy S. Lerman, USA*

SAUCY MINX (IRE) 5 b.m. Dylan Thomas (IRE) 132 – Market Day 105 (Tobougg 98 §
(IRE) 125) [2015 100: p8g 7m* 7g⁵ 8.5g 8.1m 7g 7.6v³ 8d⁴ 7g⁴ 8m p8g⁴ p7g Dec 9]
big, good-topped mare: useful handicapper: won at Salisbury (by neck from Ishiamber) in
May: stays 1m: acts on polytrack, soft and good to firm going: usually wears headgear:
often races prominently: irresolute. *Amanda Perrett*

SAUCY SPIRIT 2 b.f. Invincible Spirit (IRE) 121 – Salsa Steps (USA) 103 83 p
(Giant's Causeway (USA) 132) [2015 p6f* Oct 29] fourth foal: half-sister to useful 8.3f
winner (stayed 1½m) Spicy Dal and ungenuine 1¼m winner Salmon Sushi (both by
Dalakhani): dam 6f winner out of Irish Oaks winner Dance Design: 9/2, green when
winning 8-runner maiden at Chelmsford by 1½ lengths from Gale Song, hanging right
before asserting close home: should progress. *Hughie Morrison*

SAUMUR 3 b.f. Mawatheeq (USA) 126 – Sparkling Montjeu (IRE) 63 (Montjeu (IRE) 76
137) [2015 57: p7g⁴ p10g⁴ 10.2m² p12g* p12g 11.8s³ Oct 6] good-topped filly: fair
handicapper: won at Kempton in August: stays 1½m: acts on polytrack and soft going:
races towards rear. *Denis Coakley*

SAUTTER 2 b.c. (May 3) Kyllachy 129 – Regency Rose (Danehill (USA) 126) [2015 7g – p
Oct 21] 60,000F, 220,000Y: leggy colt: fifth foal: half-brother to 3 winners, including
useful 2-y-o 6.3f/7f winner Regional Counsel and 8.3f winner Regal Salute (both by
Medicean): dam unraced sister to Cheveley Park Stakes winner Regal Rose: 25/1, showed
something when 8¾ lengths ninth of 10 to Mootaharer in maiden at Newmarket on debut,
eased final 1f: should do better. *Peter Chapple-Hyam*

SAVANNAH BEAU 3 b.f. Major Cadeaux 121 – Mancunian Way (Green Desert (USA) 89
127) [2015 66: 6.5m 5d* 5.9g² 5g* 5.5g³ 5.4m² 5m⁶ 5g³ 6m Sep 10] fairly useful
handicapper: won at Newcastle in May and Newcastle in June: stays 6f: acts on good to
firm and good to soft going: often races towards rear. *Marjorie Fife*

SAVANNAH STAR 2 b.f. (Apr 18) Haafhd 129 – Mitsuki 91 (Puissance 110) [2015 6g –
6.1v Oct 7] sixth foal: half-sister to French 9f winner Nevaeh (by Firebreak): dam 5f/6f
winner (at 2 yrs): tailed off in 2 maidens. *Nick Kent*

SAVED BY THE BELL (IRE) 5 b.g. Teofilo (IRE) 126 – Eyrecourt (IRE) 64 (Efisio 97
120) [2015 100: 12.1m⁴ 16.4m 12g 14m* 16.4m 16.4d² 16.4m² 16.4d Oct 10]
lengthy gelding: useful handicapper: won by ¾ length from Ridgeway Storm at York in
June: second at York in July (length behind Big Thunder) and August (2½ lengths behind
Heartbreak City): stays 16.5f: acts on good to firm and good to soft going. *David O'Meara*

SAVED MY BACON (IRE) 4 b.f. Camacho 118 – Sally Green (IRE) 79 (Common 77
Grounds 118) [2015 56: f5d⁵ t5.1f p5m⁴ p6m³ p6g* p6g* f5g² p5f* p5m⁵ p6g p5g f6s*
6m⁴ p6f f5g³ f6g Dec 15] fair handicapper: won at Chelmsford in February, March and
April and at Southwell in August: stays 6f: acts on polytrack, fibresand and good to firm
going: tried in cheekpieces, in hood last 5 starts: usually races nearer last than first.
Chris Dwyer

SAVE THE BEES 7 b.g. Royal Applause 124 – Rock Concert 71 (Bishop of Cashel 122) 82
[2015 86: 10.3d 9g 12g 10.4g 12g⁴ 9.3g² 10m⁴ 9.3s* 10.3g* 9.8m* 10g³ 10m⁶ 9.8d⁴ 10.4g
10.3s³ 10g⁵ 10.2g⁶ Sep 30] sparely-made gelding: fairly useful handicapper: won at
Carlisle, Chester and Ripon in July: stays 1½m: acts on polytrack, good to firm and heavy
going: usually in headgear: front runner. *Declan Carroll*

SAVOY SHOWGIRL (IRE) 3 ch.f. Kyllachy 129 – The Strand (Gone West (USA)) 77
[2015 86: p8g 7m 8g Jun 20] fair handicapper: stays 7f: acts on firm and good to soft going.
Michael Bell

SAVVY (IRE) 3 gr.f. Verglas (IRE) 118 – Alikhlas 81 (Lahib (USA) 129) [2015 9.9g 10m⁶ 69
10.2g⁴ p12g² p13f³ p13.3f⁶ t12.2m* Nov 21] €24,000F, €38,000Y: sister to useful 2-y-o
7f/1m winner Cest Notre Gris and half-sister to several winners, including useful 7f

(including at 2 yrs) winner Silk Fan (by Unfuwain): dam 1m winner: fair handicapper: won at Wolverhampton in November: stays 13f: acts on polytrack and tapeta: often in hood (not when successful). *Jeremy Noseda*

SAWWALA 5 b.m. Sakhee (USA) 136 – Jawwala (USA) 84 (Green Dancer (USA) 132) **43**
[2015 57: f12g f11s p13.3m Sep 26] poor maiden: stays 13f: acts on polytrack, fibresand and firm going: tried in visor in 2015: front runner/races prominently. *J. R. Jenkins*

SAXONETTE 7 b.m. Piccolo 121 – Solmorin (Fraam 114) [2015 63: 5g⁶ 5d² 5d⁴ 5m³ 6g³ **73**
5d⁴ 5g⁶ 5g* 5g 5m² 5d² 5g* 5m 5g 6g⁴ 5m* 6g 6g⁵ Oct 8] fair handicapper: won at Musselburgh in July, August and September (apprentice): has form at 7f, races mainly over shorter: acts on polytrack, good to firm and heavy going: tried in headgear prior to 2015. *Linda Perratt*

SAXON GOLD (IRE) 2 ch.f. (Mar 17) Zoffany (IRE) 121 – Apple Brandy (USA) (Cox's **62**
Ridge (USA)) [2015 6m⁶ 6m 7m⁵ 8g⁵ Sep 23] 9,000Y: half-sister to several winners, including 13f winner Flavian Dynasty (by Titus Livius) and ungenuine 6f (including at 2 yrs) winner Applesnap (by Clodovil): dam ran once: modest maiden: stays 1m. *John Davies*

SAYEDAATI SAADATI (IRE) 2 b.c. (Feb 7) Montjeu (IRE) 137 – Guessing (USA) 52 **61 p**
(Kingmambo (USA) 125) [2015 6m⁴ Aug 20] first foal: dam once-raced half-sister to Prix Jean-Luc Lagardere winner Horatio Nelson and very smart 1m-1¼m performer Viscount Nelson out of Irish 1000 Guineas and Oaks winner Imagine: evens, green when 5¾ lengths fourth of 5 to Al Shahaniya in maiden at Hamilton on debut, slowly away and hanging right approaching final 1f: will be well suited by at least 1m: clearly thought capable of better. *Kevin Ryan*

SAYEURI 3 b.f. Siyouni (FR) 122 – Nalear (FR) (Lear Fan (USA) 130) [2015 f8f⁴ Dec 17] **– p**
fourth foal: half-sister to useful French 9.5f-14.5f winner Norashman (by Sinndar): dam French 1¼m/10.5f winner: 7/4, fourth of 5 on debut in maiden at Southwell won by Princess Peaches: will stay further than 1m: should do better. *Rae Guest*

SBRAASE 4 ch.c. Sir Percy 129 – Hermanita 64 (Hernando (FR) 127) [2015 86: t9.5g² **90**
t9.5f³ t12.2f* p10g² Apr 9] compact colt: fairly useful handicapper: won at Wolverhampton in March: will be suited by a return to 1½m: acts on polytrack and tapeta: tried in headgear prior to 2015. *James Tate*

SCALZO 3 ch.g. Paco Boy (IRE) 129 – Cruinn A Bhord 107 (Inchinor 119) [2015 71p: **108**
6m* 6g* 6g Jun 13] useful form: won maiden at Doncaster and handicap at Haydock (by 7 lengths from Straighttothepoint), both in May: well below form final start (fractured off-hind pastern): raced only at 6f: has been gelded. *Martyn Meade*

SCARBOROUGH (IRE) 4 ch.f. Dandy Man (IRE) 123 – Alchimie (IRE) (Sri Pekan **92**
(USA) 117) [2015 90: f5g* f5s⁶ 5d 5.1d³ p5g⁶ f5g Dec 12] fairly useful handicapper: won at Southwell (by 1½ lengths from Extreme Supreme) in January: stays 6f: acts on fibresand and good to firm going: tried in cheekpieces prior to 2015. *Michael Appleby*

SCARLET BOUNTY (IRE) 3 b.f. Bahamian Bounty 96 – Red Kyte 91 (Hawk Wing **67**
(USA) 136) [2015 77: 5.9s t7.1m 7s t5.1f p6g f7g* p7g Dec 28] fair performer: won minor event at Southwell in December: stays 7f: acts on fibresand and good to firm going: in hood last 2 starts. *Richard Fahey*

SCARLET DRAGON 2 b.g. (Mar 1) Sir Percy 129 – Welsh Angel (Dubai Destination **84**
(USA) 127) [2015 6g³ 7m* 7d⁴ 6.5m 7d⁵ 8d⁴ Oct 23] 38,000F, 32,000Y: sturdy gelding: second foal: dam unraced half-sister to winner up to 1m Nantyglo and winner up to 1½m Resplendent Light (both useful): fairly useful performer: won maiden at Leicester in August: should stay 1m+: acts on good to firm going: in hood last 3 starts. *Eve Johnson Houghton*

SCARLET MINSTREL 3 b.g. Sir Percy 129 – Sweet Mandolin (Soviet Star (USA) 128) **86**
[2015 65: 10m³ 10f⁵ 12.3g⁶ p12g³ 11s⁴ p13.3f⁴ p13.3f* p16g³ Dec 9] angular gelding: fairly useful performer: won handicap at Chelmsford in November: stays 2m: acts on polytrack, soft and good to firm going: often races towards rear/travels strongly. *Andrew Balding*

SCARLET PIMPERNEL 2 b.f. (Mar 1) Sir Percy 129 – Sweet Pea 94 (Persian Bold **64**
123) [2015 8m⁵ 8.3g⁶ Sep 30] half-sister to 3 winners, including winner up to 7f Scarlet Runner (2-y-o 6f winner, by Night Shift) and winner up to 1m Bronze Prince (2-y-o 7f winner, by Oasis Dream), both useful: dam 1m winner: better effort when fifth in maiden at Salisbury on debut. *Hughie Morrison*

SCARLET PURSUITS (IRE) 2 b.f. (Mar 12) Pastoral Pursuits 127 – Red Blooded **43**
Woman (USA) 71 (Red Ransom (USA)) [2015 5d⁶ 5.1m 6m² t7.1g Jul 28] 6,000Y: fourth
foal: half-sister to 3 winners, including 10.7f winner Automated (by Authorized) and
winner up to 1¼m Sarsted (2-y-o 1m winner, by Paco Boy): dam, 7.5f winner, half-sister
to useful performer up to 1¼m Drumbeat: poor maiden: left Richard Fahey after third start.
Declan Carroll

SCARLET SASH 4 b.f. Sir Percy 129 – Scarlet Buttons (IRE) (Marju (IRE) 127) [2015 **81**
76p: 10.2m² 10m³ 11.6m* 12m⁶ 10g 11.8d⁴ 10.2f³ 10.2v² Oct 7] compact filly: fairly
useful handicapper: won at Windsor (apprentice) in June: stays 1½m: acts on polytrack,
heavy and firm going: sold 5,000 gns, sent to Saudi Arabia. *Henry Candy*

SCARPETA (FR) 2 b.g. (Apr 4) Soldier of Fortune (IRE) 131 – Sanada (IRE) (Priolo **–**
(USA) 127) [2015 p8f t9.5f p8g t9.5f Dec 11] no form. *Mark Johnston*

SCENT OF POWER 3 b.f. Authorized (IRE) 133 – Aromatherapy 96 (Oasis Dream 129) **57**
[2015 57: p7f t7.1m² 10s² t9.5f Oct 16] modest maiden: left Anthony Carson after second
start: stays 1¼m: acts on polytrack, tapeta and soft going: usually races prominently.
Barry Leavy

SCENT OF SUMMER (USA) 3 b.f. Rock Hard Ten (USA) 126 – Wild Forest (USA) **85**
(Forest Wildcat (USA) 120) [2015 72p: 5g* 5g 5s 5f Sep 13] quite attractive filly: fairly
useful performer: won maiden at Thirsk in July: best form at 5f: acts on soft going.
William Haggas

SCHMOOZE (IRE) 6 b.m. One Cool Cat (USA) 123 – If Dubai (USA) (Stephen Got **67**
Even (USA) 125) [2015 61: 12.5m⁶ 13d² 11.1m³ 12.1g² 13d⁶ 12.1g* 13.1g 11.1g² 12.1m⁶
13.1g⁶ 12.2g Oct 13] fair handicapper: won at Hamilton in August: stays 13f: acts on
polytrack, good to firm and good to soft going: tried in headgear: usually races towards
rear. *Linda Perratt*

SCHOOLBOY ERROR (IRE) 2 ch.g. (Apr 19) Roderic O'Connor (IRE) 119 – La **50 p**
Grande Zoa (IRE) 50 (Fantastic Light (USA) 134) [2015 p8f t7.1f t7.1g Dec 4] 16,500F:
fifth foal: half-brother to very smart winner up to 2½m (Gold Cup) Trip To Paris (2-y-o 7f
winner, by Champs Elysees): dam lightly raced: modest maiden: will prove suited by a
return to 1m+: should do better. *Jamie Osborne*

SCHOOL FETE (IRE) 2 b.c. (Jan 22) Authorized (IRE) 133 – Local Spirit (USA) 101 **75 p**
(Lion Cavern (USA) 117) [2015 8d 8d⁴ Oct 16] sixth foal: brother to smart winner up to
1½m Al Saham (2-y-o 7f winner) and half-brother to 6f winner Active Spirit (by Pivotal)
and useful winner up to 1¼m Classic Collection (2-y-o 7f winner, by Cape Cross): dam,
temperamental 1¼m winner who stayed 1½m, sister to very smart winner up to 1¼m
Crimplene: 33/1, much sharper when 4½ lengths fourth to Gershwin in maiden at Haydock,
staying on: will be suited by at least 1¼m: likely to progress further. *Michael Bell*

SCHOTTISCHE 5 ch.m. Pastoral Pursuits 127 – Calligraphy 79 (Kris 135) [2015 67: **63**
f8g³ f8d* f8d⁶ f8g⁶ t8.6g⁶ p10m⁶ 9.1g³ p8f³ t8.6f t8.6f³ f8g² p10m f8g⁴ p8f Dec 17]
modest handicapper: won at Southwell in January: left Derek Haydn Jones after third start:
stays 9f: acts on all-weather and good to soft going: usually wears headgear: none too
consistent. *Alan Bailey*

SCHUBERT (USA) 2 b.c. (May 17) War Front (USA) 119 – Score (USA) (A P Indy **93**
(USA) 131) [2015 7d⁴ 8m² 6g⁴ Oct 18] $1,300,000Y: lengthy colt: fourth foal: half-brother
to 3 winners in USA, including smart 2-y-o 8.5f winner Timely Tally (by Mr Greeley):
dam, ran twice, out of US Grade 1 1m (including at 2 yrs) winner Educated Risk: fairly
useful form: 2¾ lengths second to Carntop in maiden at Newmarket in October: 4/5,
disappointing in similar event at Naas final start: will benefit from return to 7f+. *Aidan
O'Brien, Ireland*

SCIMITARRA 3 gr.f. Motivator 131 – Scrupulous 70 (Dansili 127) [2015 –: p10g Jan 3] **–**
no form. *Paul Cole*

SCIUSTREE 3 b.c. Royal Applause 124 – Tia Mia 92 (Dr Fong (USA) 128) [2015 63p: **72**
t7.1f³ t7.1g² t7.1g⁶ p7g Aug 5] fair maiden: raced only at 7f: acts on tapeta: in cheekpieces
last 2 starts: front runner/races prominently. *Marco Botti*

SCOONER (USA) 3 ch.c. Mizzen Mast (USA) 121 – Palisade (USA) 87 (Gone West **92**
(USA)) [2015 81p: t8.6g* 9.9g² 8.3g⁵ 9.9m⁴ 12g⁴ p10m⁶ Sep 26] fairly useful performer:
won maiden at Wolverhampton in April: second in handicap at Goodwood in June:
stays 1¼m: acts on tapeta and good to firm going: sold 30,000 gns, sent to Australia.
Roger Charlton

SCOPPIO DEL CARRO 4 b.g. Medicean 128 – Sadie Thompson (IRE) 79 (King's Best — (USA) 132) [2015 10.1m 10g⁶ 8.5s⁶ 9.9m 12d p12m Nov 19] rather leggy gelding: fairly useful at best, no form in 2015: often wears tongue tie. *John Quinn*

SCORELINE 4 b.g. Captain Gerrard (IRE) 113 – Waterline Twenty (IRE) 89 (Indian **76** Danehill (IRE) 124) [2015 79: t6f⁴ t5.1f⁶ f5d³ t5.1g⁶ t5.1m* p5d³ f6s⁴ 5g⁴ 5m² 5g⁴ 6g⁴ 5g 5g² 5d³ 5g³ 6m 5d² 5d* 5g³ p6f⁶ Oct 29] fair performer: won claimer at Wolverhampton in March and handicap at Catterick in September: best form at 5f: acts on all-weather, soft and good to firm going: tried in headgear prior to 2015. *David O'Meara*

SCOT DADDY (USA) 3 ch.g. Scat Daddy (USA) 120 – Flor de Oro (USA) (Out of Place **71** (USA)) [2015 p7g 6g 6m⁴ 7.1m p8g t7.1g⁴ t8.6f⁵ Dec 22] lengthy, rather unfurnished gelding: fair maiden: worth a try beyond 1m: acts on polytrack, tapeta and good to firm going: tried in hood: often starts slowly/races nearer last than first. *David Dennis*

SCOTLAND (GER) 4 b.g. Monsun (GER) 124 – Sqillo (IRE) (Bachelor Duke (USA) **113** 122) [2015 111: 12m⁵ 12m⁴ 20f⁶ Jun 18] tall gelding: smart performer: 20/1, possibly flattered when 3¼ lengths sixth of 12 to Trip To Paris in Gold Cup at Royal Ascot final start, never nearer: stays 2½m: acts on firm and good to soft going. *Andrew Balding*

SCOTS FERN 3 b.f. Selkirk (USA) 129 – Ushindi (IRE) 73 (Montjeu (IRE) 137) [2015 **71** 69: p10g 8g⁶ 8f⁴ 8m* 8g p11g⁴ p12f⁴ Nov 25] fair handicapper: won at Bath in September: stays 11f: acts on polytrack and firm going: in visor last 5 starts. *Andrew Balding*

SCOTS GAELIC (IRE) 8 ch.g. Tomba 119 – Harmonic (USA) 80 (Shadeed (USA) 135) — [2015 12g 12m Jul 18] useful handicapper at best: lightly raced since 2012, well held in 2015: stays 2¼m: acts on soft and good to firm going: has worn headgear: fairly useful hurdler/chaser. *Rebecca Menzies*

SCOTTISH COMMAND 2 b.g. (Feb 28) Kyllachy 129 – Angel Song 68 (Dansili 127) **63** [2015 6m⁴ 5m 6m⁶ 6.1m⁴ p7g p6g p5m⁶ Dec 27] good-topped gelding: modest maiden: stays 6f: acts on good to firm going: tried in hood. *Richard Hannon*

SCOTTISH GLEN 9 ch.g. Kyllachy 129 – Dance For Fun 74 (Anabaa (USA) 130) [2015 **99** 87: 7g² 7g* 7f* p8d⁴ 7g² Sep 26] sturdy gelding: useful handicapper: better than ever and won at Goodwood (apprentice) in June, Ascot in July and Kempton (apprentice) in September: excellent ¾-length second of 13 to Mr Win at Newmarket final start: stays 1m: acts on polytrack, firm and good to soft going: tried in cheekpieces. *Patrick Chamings*

SCOTTISH (IRE) 3 b.g. Teofilo (IRE) 126 – Zeiting (Zieten (USA) 118) [2015 **117** –p: 11m² 10g* 12f² 12g² 12.4d⁵ 10g* Sep 19] rangy gelding: smart performer: won maiden at Newbury (by 1¾ lengths from Keble) in May and listed race at Ayr (by neck from Mutakayyef) in September: also ran well when 1½ lengths second to Highland Reel in Gordon Stakes at Goodwood fourth start: stays 1½m: acts on firm ground: often travels strongly. *Andrew Balding*

SCOTTISH STAR 7 gr.g. Kirkwall 118 – Child Star (FR) 58 (Bellypha 130) [2015 90: **84** p10f² Feb 11] good-topped gelding: fairly useful handicapper: stays 13f: acts on polytrack, best turf form on good going or firmer (acts on firm). *James Eustace*

SCOTTISH SUMMIT (IRE) 2 b.c. (Feb 16) Shamardal (USA) 129 – Scottish Stage **73 p** (IRE) 112 (Selkirk (USA) 129) [2015 t8.6m⁴ Nov 21] half-brother to several winners, including 2-y-o 7f winner (stayed 1½m) Festival Theatre (by Danehill Dancer) and 1½m winner Northern Meeting (by Dylan Thomas): dam, winner up to 1¼m (2-y-o 7f winner) and second in Irish Oaks, half-sister to smart performer up to 1½m Eleanora Duse: 12/1, some encouragement when 2¾ lengths fourth of 10 to Coherent in maiden at Wolverhampton, running on: likely to improve. *Sir Michael Stoute*

SCRAFTON 4 b.g. Leporello (IRE) 118 – Some Diva 75 (Dr Fong (USA) 128) [2015 18s **76 §** 13.1g⁵ 14.1s⁵ t13.9g³ p15.8m⁴ Dec 16] fair handicapper: left John Quinn after third start: stays 2m: acts on polytrack, tapeta, soft and good to firm going: often races towards rear, often travels strongly: one to treat with caution. *Tony Carroll*

SCRAPPER SMITH (IRE) 9 b.g. Choisir (AUS) 126 – Lady Ounavarra (IRE) (Simply **88** Great (FR) 122) [2015 16s⁶ 13s² 13d⁴ 13.1d² 12s² Sep 5] smallish, compact gelding: fairly useful handicapper: stays 13.5f: best form on good going or softer (acts on heavy): tried in visor: sometimes slowly away, often races towards rear. *Alistair Whillans*

SCRIBE (IRE) 7 b.g. Montjeu (IRE) 137 – Crafty Example (USA) (Crafty Prospector **61** (USA)) [2015 f14d³ t12.2g³ 16g⁵ 15s⁴ Aug 8] just modest performer in 2015: stayed 17f: acted on all-weather, soft and good to firm going: wore headgear: wore tongue tie: dead. *Richard Ford*

SCRUFFY MCGUFFY 2 b.g. (Apr 20) Firebreak 125 – Eloquent Isle (IRE) (Mull of Kintyre (USA) 114) [2015 8.3d^5 6d^5 6g^6 6g Oct 8] modest maiden: will be suited by a return to 7f+. *Ann Duffield* **64**

SCRUTINEER (IRE) 2 br.c. (Mar 19) Intense Focus (USA) 117 – Royal Esteem (Mark of Esteem (IRE) 137) [2015 6g^3 6.1v* 7d* 7s Nov 1] £48,000Y: fourth foal: half-brother to 1m winner (stays 10.5f) Hostile Fire (by Iffraaj) and a winner abroad by Ramonti: dam US 6f winner: useful form: won maiden at Nottingham and nursery at Doncaster (by 6 lengths from General Alexander), both in October: off 8 days/stiff task, ran to similar level when 4¾ lengths last of 8 to Johannes Vermeer in Criterium International at Saint-Cloud: stays 7f. *Mick Channon* **103**

SCRUTINISE 3 b.g. Intense Focus (USA) 117 – Tetravella (IRE) (Groom Dancer (USA) 128) [2015 73p: t9.5g^2 p10g^2 p10m* p11g^2 12s* 12s* 14.1s^3 Oct 12] angular gelding: useful performer: won maiden at Chelmsford in May and handicaps at Thirsk and Goodwood (by ½ length from First Mohican) in September: again ran well when 1½ lengths third to Faithful Mount in handicap at Salisbury, not ideally placed: stays 1¾m: acts on polytrack and soft going: usually responds generously to pressure. *Ed Dunlop* **102**

SCRUTINY 4 b.g. Aqlaam 125 – Aunty Mary 82 (Common Grounds 118) [2015 68: 9.8v^4 10.1d^2 10d^3 9.9m^2 7.5f^3 9.9m^2 9.9s* 8s* 10m^4 10g 7s* Oct 16] lengthy gelding: fairly useful handicapper: won amateur events at Beverley and Redcar in July: better form when successful again at Redcar (by 1¼ lengths from What Could She Be) on final start: stays 1¼m: best form on soft/heavy going: sometimes wears headgear. *David O'Meara* **88**

SCULPTURED (FR) 3 b.f. Archipenko (USA) 127 – Kelang (Kris 135) [2015 73: p7m^2 p7m^6 p8f^2 t8.6m^5 f7d^2 p8g^3 f7g* p7m^5 8.1m t7.1g* 8g^5 8d p8f^4 p8g^5 Sep 22] fair performer: won maiden at Southwell in April and handicap at Wolverhampton in July: stays 1m: acts on all-weather, firm and soft going: usually in headgear in 2015: usually leads: sold 18,000 gns, sent to Saudi Arabia. *Jo Hughes* **79**

SCURR MIST (IRE) 4 gr.g. Aussie Rules (USA) 123 – Stratospheric (Slip Anchor 136) [2015 –: 10s 8.3d 9.3m* 10.3g^2 t9.5m* t9.5m^2 t12.2f^2 Oct 23] fairly useful handicapper: left Iain Jardine after second start and returned to previous trainer: won at Carlisle and Wolverhampton in August: stays 1½m: acts on tapeta, soft and good to firm going: tried in headgear in 2015: often races prominently: has high head carriage. *Keith Dalgleish* **83**

SEA CALISI (FR) 3 b.f. Youmzain (IRE) 131 – Triclaria (GER) (Surumu (GER)) [2015 10.9g^3 10.9g* 11.9g^2 11.9m* 12d^3 11.9s^3 12d Oct 17] good-topped filly: closely related to French 1¼m/11f winner Sea Claria (by Sinndar) and half-sister to numerous winners, including smart 10.5f-12.5f winner Timos (by Sholokhov) and smart German 1¼m-1½m winner Tareno (by Saddlers' Hall): dam German 1m-11f winner: smart performer: won maiden at Lyon Parilly in May and Prix de Malleret at Saint-Cloud (by 1½ lengths from Kataniya) in June: good efforts when third in Yorkshire Oaks at York (½-length behind Pleascach) and Prix Vermeille at Longchamp (6½ lengths behind Treve): below form when 6½ lengths seventh to Simple Verse in Fillies' And Mares' Stakes at Ascot final outing: stays 1½m: acts on soft and good to firm going: often races towards rear. *Francois Doumen, France* **118**

SEA FANTASY 3 b.f. Paco Boy (IRE) 129 – Takarna (IRE) 70 (Mark of Esteem (IRE) 137) [2015 –: 5.7m^3 Jun 5] well held in 2 maidens in Britain (9 months apart): sold 1,200 gns in July, sent to France. *Jo Crowley* **–**

SEAGULL STAR 4 b.g. Sea The Stars (IRE) 140 – Dash To The Top 116 (Montjeu (IRE) 137) [2015 101: 10.1g 11.6m 12s Jul 24] rather leggy, medium-sized gelding: useful performer in 2014: disappointing in 2015, in cheekpieces final start: should stay 1½m: acts on good to firm going: sometimes slowly away, often races towards rear. *William Haggas* **87**

SEAHAM HALL HOTEL 4 b.f. Tiger Hill (IRE) 127 – Molly Mello (GER) 106 (Big Shuffle (USA) 122) [2015 t9.5f t7.1m^5 t8.6m^6 Mar 10] sixth foal: half-sister to 3 winners, including useful 1m-1½m winner Brunston (by High Chaparral) and 6f-8.3f winner Serenity Spa (by Excellent Art): dam German 7f winner (including at 2 yrs): modest maiden. *Tony Carroll* **51**

SEALED (USA) 4 b.g. Speightstown (USA) 124 – Sinister Sister (USA) (Formal Dinner (USA)) [2015 84: p9.9g^5 p9.9g p9.4g^4 p9.4g p10g p9.4g 7g p7.5g Aug 30] fair maiden: stays 1¼m: acts on polytrack and tapeta: often wears headgear. *Gay Kelleway* **73**

SEALIFE (IRE) 3 b.f. Sea The Stars (IRE) 140 – Bitooh (Diktat 126) [2015 8.3m* 8m 10.2d* 9.9g^2 Aug 29] €125,000Y: attractive filly: third foal: half-sister to French 9.5f-11.5f winner Speed Pack (by King's Best): dam, French 1¼m winner who stayed 1½m, half-sister to very smart winner up to 1½m Golden Sword and to dam of Oaks winner Alexandrova: useful form: won maiden at Windsor in July and handicap at Nottingham (by **101 p**

1¾ lengths from Princessofthestars) in August: shaped very well when 1¼ lengths second to Laurence in handicap at Beverley final start, nearest finish: should prove suited by 1½m: will go on improving. *William Haggas*

SEA MOON 7 b.h. Beat Hollow 126 – Eva Luna (USA) 114 (Alleged (USA) 138) [2015   **110** 14s² 14d 12g³ Oct 11] useful-looking horse: high-class performer at best for Sir Michael Stoute: trained by Robert Hickmott in Australia in 2013 and 2014, winning Group 2 Herbert Power Handicap at Caulfield: returned to Europe in 2015, best effort when second in Irish St Leger Trial at the Curragh (7½ lengths behind Order of St George): below form on same course after, in Irish St Leger and listed race (8½ lengths third to Variable): stays 1¾m: acts on good to firm and heavy going: tried in blinkers. *John M. Oxx, Ireland*

SEAMOOR SECRET 3 b.f. Sakhee's Secret 128 – Labaqa (USA) 92 (Rahy (USA) 115)   **48** [2015 58, a49: t7.1g⁶ p6g⁵ f7d p7m 9.9g 11.7f⁶ 10d⁴ 10.2g 7.1s 7s t5.1f⁶ p6m t5.1m t6m⁶ Dec 30] poor maiden: wears headgear/tongue tie. *Alex Hales*

SEAMOUR (IRE) 4 b.g. Azamour (IRE) 130 – Chifney Rush (IRE) (Grand Lodge (USA)   **109** 125) [2015 87: 12g⁶ 16.2g* 16.1m⁶ 16s* 18m⁶ 12v Nov 7] lengthy gelding: useful handicapper: won at Haydock in May and Ascot in July, latter by short head from High Secret: creditable sixth of 11 to Pallasator in Doncaster Cup penultimate start: favourite, reportedly inhaled mud when last in November Handicap at Doncaster, final outing: stays 2m: acts on polytrack, soft and good to firm going: useful hurdler. *Brian Ellison*

SEAMSTER 8 ch.g. Pivotal 124 – Needles And Pins (IRE) 104 (Fasliyev (USA) 120)   – [2015 83: f6g Dec 15] fairly useful at best, well held only start in 2015: stays 7f: acts on all-weather, sand: usually in headgear/tongue tie prior to 2015: sometimes slowly away. *David O'Meara*

SEAMUS THE PAVER (IRE) 3 ch.g. Fast Company (IRE) 126 – Bent Al Fala (IRE)   – 59 (Green Desert (USA) 127) [2015 8d⁵ Oct 5] 20/1, very green when well held in maiden at Pontefract on debut. *Alan Bailey*

SEANIE (IRE) 6 b.g. Kodiac 112 – Cakestown Lady (IRE) 100 (Petorius 117) [2015 108:   **106** p6g⁴ 8s⁵ 8m² 8g⁶ 8.5m⁶ 7g³ 7.5g* p8g p6g³ p7g⁴ Dec 18] compact gelding: useful performer: won handicap at Tipperary (by ½ length from Bubbly Bellini) in October: stays 1m: acts on polytrack, good to firm and good to soft going: tried in blinkers prior to 2015: in tongue tie last 5 starts. *David Marnane, Ireland*

SEA OF FLAMES 2 ch.g. (Mar 30) Aqlaam 125 – Hidden Fire 82 (Alhaarth (IRE) 126)   – [2015 6m Jul 23] sturdy gelding: 25/1, shaped as if needed experience when eighth of 10 in maiden at Newbury, slowly away. *David Elsworth*

SEA OF GREEN 3 b.f. Iffraaj 127 – Sea of Leaves (USA) 103 (Stormy Atlantic (USA))   **69 §** [2015 6g⁵ 7g³ 7g 6g 7g⁶ 6m² 6g 6g⁴ 6s 6d Oct 26] 65,000Y: first foal: dam, winner up to 6f (2-y-o 5f winner), half-sister to useful 9.5f-1½m winner Distinctive Image: fair maiden: stays 7f: acts on good to firm going: wears hood: usually races nearer last than first: temperamental. *Jim Goldie*

SEA OF HEAVEN (IRE) 3 b.g. Sea The Stars (IRE) 140 – Maid of Killeen (IRE) 97   **98** (Darshaan 133) [2015 64p: p8m p12g² 14m² 16.1m* 16.2m² 15.9s* Sep 12] useful handicapper: progressed well and won at Newcastle in August and Chester (by 2¼ lengths from Yorkidding) in September: stays 2m: acts on soft and good to firm going: usually races prominently and finds plenty. *Sir Mark Prescott Bt*

SEA OF HOPE 2 b.f. (May 9) Rock of Gibraltar (IRE) 133 – Labrusca 58 (Grand   **59** Lodge (USA) 125) [2015 p6g⁴ p6g⁵ Oct 14] €8,500Y, £55,000 2-y-o: closely related to useful 7f/1m winner Great Huzzar and unreliable 6f winner Delaware Dancer (both by Danehill Dancer): dam once-raced half-sister to Yorkshire Oaks winner Catchascatchcan, herself dam of very smart/unreliable miler Antonius Pius: modest form in 2 maidens at Kempton, better effort on debut. *Jeremy Gask*

SEA OF RED 3 b.g. Duke of Marmalade (IRE) 132 – Abandon (USA) 94 (Rahy (USA)   **68** 115) [2015 64p: p10g⁵ p8g⁴ p11g 7s 9.9g t8.6f³ t8.6f² Oct 23] fair maiden: will be suited by a return to 1¼m: acts on polytrack and tapeta: often in cheekpieces in 2015. *J. S. Moore*

SEA OF UNCERTAINTY 2 b.g. (May 4) Kyllachy 129 – Moving Sea (IRE) (Rock of   **63** Gibraltar (IRE) 133) [2015 6m f5g² f6s² 5g² f5g² t6f⁶ Dec 22] modest maiden: left Alan McCabe after fourth start: best form at 5f: acts on fibresand: often in visor: usually races close up. *Michael Appleby*

SEAPERLE 2 b.f. (Apr 30) Firebreak 125 – Ocean Grove (IRE) 84 (Fairy King (USA)) – [2015 5.9g 7m 5.9s⁵ 7m Sep 8] 24,000Y: half-sister to several winners, including 5f-7f winner Silaah (by Mind Games) and winner up to 7f Sea Hunter (2-y-o 5f winner, by Lend A Hand), both smart: dam 2-y-o 6f winner who stayed 1m: no worthwhile form. *Tim Easterby*

SEA PRIDE (IRE) 4 b.f. Sea The Stars (IRE) 140 – Claxon 110 (Caerleon (USA) 132) **101 p** [2015 p12g* 14d² 16g³ Oct 11] half-sister to several winners, including smart winner up to 11.5f Cassydora (2-y-o 7f winner, by Darshaan) and useful 1¼m winner Classic Remark (by Dr Fong): dam winner up to 1¼m (2-y-o 1m winner): bumper winner in March: useful performer: won maiden at Kempton (by 6 lengths from Pecking Order) in September: best effort when 1¼ lengths third of 20 to Digeanta in handicap at the Curragh final start (would have benefited from stronger gallop): stays 2m: will go on improving. *Sir Mark Prescott Bt*

SEARANGER (USA) 2 b.g. (Feb 21) U S Ranger (USA) 124 – Baby Lets Cruise (USA) **71** (Tale of The Cat (USA) 113) [2015 5.9g⁵ 5s² 5d³ 5m 5g* 5m³ Sep 20] fair performer: won maiden at Musselburgh in August: best form at 5f: acts on soft going: often races prominently. *Ann Duffield*

SEARCHING (IRE) 3 ro.g. Mastercraftsman (IRE) 129 – Miracolia (IRE) (Montjeu **83** (IRE) 137) [2015 73: 12.3g* 12g⁴ 10.3g⁴ 14g⁵ 12s Sep 15] fairly useful handicapper: won at Chester in May: stays 1¾m: best form on good going: usually in blinkers in 2015: sold 18,000 gns, joined Gary Moore. *Roger Varian*

SEARCHLIGHT 4 b.g. Kyllachy 129 – Baralinka (IRE) 93 (Barathea (IRE) 127) [2015 **84** 93: p5f² t5.1f* 6g p6g 5g 6d 5g⁶ 5m 5g 5s p5g⁶ Dec 15] lengthy gelding: useful **a95** handicapper: won at Wolverhampton (by neck from Royal Birth) in March: left Kevin Ryan after tenth start: stays 6f: acts on polytrack, tapeta, firm and soft going: tried in headgear: tried in tongue tie prior to 2015: usually races nearer last than first. *Jim Boyle*

SEA REBELLE 6 b.m. Cockney Rebel (IRE) 127 – Bianca Sforza (Anabaa (USA) 130) **48** [2015 –: p8f p8m May 12] poor maiden: best effort at 1½m: acts on polytrack: tends to find little. *Jo Crowley*

SEA SCENT (USA) 3 ch.f. Mizzen Mast (USA) 121 – July Jasmine (USA) 103 (Empire **74** Maker (USA) 129) [2015 8.3g⁴ 10.2m⁴ Jun 25] first foal: dam, 2-y-o 7f winner who stayed 1½m, half-sister to very smart 1m-1¼m performer Rob Roy: in hood, fair form when fourth in 2 maidens at Nottingham, carrying head awkwardly and flashing tail in latter: sold 11,000 gns, sent to Qatar. *Sir Michael Stoute*

SEASIDE SIZZLER 8 ch.g. Rahy (USA) 115 – Via Borghese (USA) 116 (Seattle Dancer **87** (USA) 119) [2015 95: p14f² Nov 7] tall, lengthy gelding: fairly useful handicapper, lightly raced: stays 21.5f: acts on polytrack and good to soft going: usually wears headgear/tongue tie: quirky sort. *William Knight*

SEA SILK 3 b.g. Shamardal (USA) 129 – Ocean Silk (USA) 119 (Dynaformer (USA)) – [2015 t7.1m⁶ Dec 12] 25/1 and in cheekpieces, well held in maiden at Wolverhampton. *Dean Ivory*

SEA SOLDIER (IRE) 7 b.g. Red Ransom (USA) – Placement (Kris 135) [2015 65: p8g* **71** p8g* Feb 1] strong, attractive gelding: fair handicapper: won apprentice events at Lingfield in January and Chelmsford in February: stays 1m: acts on polytrack, good to firm and good to soft going: tried in headgear. *Andrew Balding*

SEASTROM 2 b.g. (Apr 30) Oasis Dream 129 – Seta 113 (Pivotal 124) [2015 5.1m⁴ 6m* **84** 8s⁴ 6g³ 6d p7m Oct 21] 425,000Y: angular gelding: first foal: dam, winner up to 1m (2-y-o 7f winner) who stayed 1¼m, half-sister to smart winners up to 1½m Gravitas and Berlin Berlin and smart winner up to 15.5f Armure: fairly useful performer: won maiden at York in May: third in valuable sales race at Newmarket in September: stays 6f: acts on good to firm going. *Charlie Appleby*

SEA THE SKIES 4 b.g. Sea The Stars (IRE) 140 – Model Queen (USA) 76 (Kingmambo **89 p** (USA) 125) [2015 10g* 10m 12m⁵ 12m* Jul 18] strong gelding: fairly useful handicapper: won at Leicester in May and Ripon (by head from Endless Credit) in July: stays 1½m: acts on firm going: likely to do better still. *Mark Johnston*

SEA TIGER 5 b.g. Tiger Hill (IRE) 127 – Possessive Artiste 73 (Shareef Dancer (USA) **47** 135) [2015 60: p8g⁴ p10f⁴ p10f p10g⁶ p12g p10g p10g Jul 18] poor maiden: stays 1½m: acts on polytrack, tapeta and heavy going: in cheekpieces last 3 starts. *Chris Gordon*

SEA VISION (IRE) 5 b.g. Haatef (USA) 117 – Fantastic Account (Fantastic Light (USA) – 134) [2015 76: 16m 12g⁵ 14g⁶ p13f⁴ Sep 12] maiden: fair form in 2014, little impact in handicaps in 2015: stays 13f: acts on polytrack: in visor 2 starts: sold 800 gns, sent to the Netherlands. *Jo Crowley*

Grosser Preis von Berlin, Hoppegarten—only a second success in the last 11 runnings of this race for Britain as Second Step (right of leading pair) overhauls Ito, who raced in a clear lead for much of the way; Deutsches Derby winner Nutan (hidden by runner-up), the only three-year-old in the race, finishes third

SEA WHISPER 4 ch.f. Compton Place 125 – Starfleet 66 (Inchinor 119) [2015 51: f7g Jan 6] modest maiden: stays 7f: acts on fibresand: front runner/races prominently. *Ann Stokell* —

SEA WOLF (IRE) 3 b.g. Amadeus Wolf 122 – Rose de France (IRE) (Diktat 126) [2015 91: 8m⁶ 7m 7d⁶ 6g⁶ 7s⁵ 7d* 7v⁴ Nov 7] fairly useful handicapper: won at Doncaster (apprentice, by nose from Mystic Miraaj) in October: stays 7f: acts on good to firm and good to soft going: in cheekpieces last 2 starts. *Michael Dods* **93**

SEAWORTHY (IRE) 3 b.f. Sea The Stars (IRE) 140 – Night Fairy (IRE) 89 (Danehill (USA) 126) [2015 10d 10s 9.9g t7.1g Jun 3] €120,000Y: rather unfurnished filly: fourth foal: sister to useful 1m winner Stars So Bright and half-sister to smart 6f-1m winner Majestic Queen (2-y-o 7f winner, by Kheleyf): dam, 1¼m winner, sister to useful dam of very smart sprinter Muthmir: modest maiden: best effort at 1¼m: tried in blinkers. *Ed Dunlop* **63**

SEBASTIAN BEACH (IRE) 4 b.g. Yeats (IRE) 128 – Night Club 60 (Mozart (IRE) 131) [2015 90: 16g 14m Jun 13] attractive gelding: fairly useful at best, no form in 2015: stays 1¾m: acts on firm going: fairly useful hurdler. *Jonjo O'Neill* —

SEBASTIAN'S WISH (IRE) 2 b.g. (Apr 21) Aqlaam 125 – Swish (GER) (Monsun (GER) 124) [2015 7d 7m⁵ 8.3s⁵ Oct 28] 13,000F: fourth foal: half-brother to useful German 1¼m/11f winner Swacadelic (by Adlerflug) and German 8.5f winner Short Cut (by Tertullian): dam unraced sister to high-class 1½m performer Shirocco: modest form: fifth of 7 to Zoffanys Pride in maiden at Nottingham final start, shuffled back over 2f out but sticking to task without being knocked about: remains with potential. *Richard Whitaker* **59 p**

SEBS SENSEI (IRE) 4 ch.g. Art Connoisseur (IRE) 121 – Capetown Girl 71 (Danzero (AUS)) [2015 68: p8g p8g⁶ 13.1m⁴ p16g⁶ 16g⁴ p16f⁵ Dec 21] useful-looking gelding: modest maiden: stays 2m: acts on polytrack, good to firm and good to soft going: tried in headgear. *Mark Hoad* **60**

SECATEUR 3 b.g. Danehill Dancer (IRE) 117 – Rose Cut (IRE) (Montjeu (IRE) 137) [2015 80p: 10s² 12m* 12.3s⁴ 13m* 14f² 14.1d⁵ 14d⁴ 14m² Oct 2] rangy, attractive gelding: useful performer: won maiden at Doncaster in April and handicap at Newmarket in June: better form when second in handicap at Sandown (head behind Who Dares Wins) in July and listed race at Ascot (2¼ lengths behind Mill Springs) in October: stays 1¾m: acts on firm and soft going: in cheekpieces nowadays: front runner: sold 65,000 gns, sent to Australia. *John Gosden* **102**

SECOND CUT (IRE) 3 b.g. Acclamation 118 – Morality (Elusive Quality (USA)) [2015 t5.1f⁶ 5d⁴ 6v⁶ 6m³ 6d² 6m 7.2g² 7g⁴ 6g 7s⁶ Oct 16] fair handicapper: won at Newcastle in August: best effort at 7f: acts on good to firm and good to soft going. *David O'Meara* **71**

SECOND GUEST 3 b.f. Refuse To Bend (IRE) 128 – Impeccable Guest (IRE) 60 (Orpen (USA) 116) [2015 t9.5g f12g⁶ Nov 24] second foal: dam, maiden on Flat (stayed 1¾m), winning hurdler: tailed off in 2 maidens. *John Mackie* —

SECONDO (FR) 5 b.g. Sakhee's Secret 128 – Royal Jade 82 (Last Tycoon 131) [2015 95, **82** a103: p6g Jan 3] attractive gelding: fairly useful handicapper: raced only at 6f: acts on tapeta, best turf form on good going or firmer: tried in headgear: usually races in rear. *Robert Stephens*

SECOND SERVE (IRE) 2 b.c. (Apr 17) Cape Cross (IRE) 129 – Aguinaga (IRE) 76 **50 p** (Machiavellian (USA) 123) [2015 7m⁵ Aug 4] €32,000Y: seventh foal: brother to useful 2-y-o 7f winner Storm Force and closely related to 2 winners by Invincible Spirit, including smart/unreliable 5f/6f (including at 2 yrs) winner Conquest: dam, 12.5f winner, half-sister to very smart 6f/7f winner Iktamal: 9/2, very green when fifth of 8 to Mohab in maiden at Catterick, outpaced and merely closing up late: will improve. *Mark Johnston*

SECOND STEP (IRE) 4 b.g. Dalakhani (IRE) 133 – My Dark Rosaleen 84 (Sadler's **124** Wells (USA) 132) [2015 110p: 12m* 12m² 11.9g* 14d⁴ 12g Oct 18] useful-looking gelding: very smart performer: won Jockey Club Stakes at Newmarket in May by head from Telescope and Grosser Preis von Berlin at Hoppegarten in August by ¾ length from Ito: ½-length second to Big Orange in Princess of Wales's Stakes at Newmarket in between: below form last 2 starts, when 11¾ lengths fourth to Order of St George in Irish St Leger at the Curragh (no match for winner but shaped second best for much of straight) and ninth of 11 to Cannock Chase in Canadian International at Woodbine: should stay 1¾m: acts on good to firm and heavy going. *Luca Cumani*

SECOND WAVE (IRE) 3 b.g. New Approach (IRE) 132 – Tessa Reef (IRE) (Mark of **109** Esteem (IRE) 137) [2015 80p: 8g* 8.3m³ 8d² p8f* 8s³ p8g* p8g⁴ t9.5m* Dec 26] smart handicapper: won at Redcar in April, Chelmsford in October, Kempton (by neck from Afjaan) in November and Wolverhampton in December: further improvement when beating Luv U Forever 2¼ lengths on last-named course, suited by way race developed: stays 9.5f, worth a try over further: acts on polytrack, tapeta, best turf form on good going: often races prominently. *Charlie Appleby*

SECRET AMBITION 2 b.c. (Apr 13) Exceed And Excel (AUS) 126 – Inner Secret **71** (USA) 85 (Singspiel (IRE) 133) [2015 5g⁵ 5m² 5m⁴ 6d⁵ p6g⁴ p5g² 5m³ 7s* 7g p7g Nov 13] angular colt: fair performer: won nursery at Brighton in October: stays 7f: acts on polytrack, soft and good to firm going. *Mark Johnston*

Merry Fox Stud Limited's "Second Step"

SECRETAN 2 ch.g. (Mar 29) Monsieur Bond (IRE) 120 – Real Diamond 74 (Bertolini – (USA) 125) [2015 5d⁴ 5g 7.5m⁵ 6s 7s Oct 16] no form: tried in cheekpieces. *Ollie Pears*

SECRET ART (IRE) 5 ch.g. Excellent Art 125 – Ivy Queen (IRE) (Green Desert (USA) **99** 127) [2015 98, a104: p8g p8m p8g⁶ 8m 7.6s³ 8.1m² 8.3g* 8m⁵ 8m⁶ p8g 8g* Sep 24] tall, rangy gelding: useful handicapper: won at Windsor (by ¾ length from Directorship) in June and Newmarket (by ½ length from Ansaab) in September: stays 8.5f: acts on polytrack, soft and good to firm going: tried in cheekpieces: usually races close up. *William Knight*

SECRET ASSET (IRE) 10 gr.g. Clodovil (IRE) 116 – Skerray 71 (Soviet Star (USA) **83** 128) [2015 93: p6g³ p5g⁴ p6m⁶ t6g⁵ 6m 6m³ 5g 5d⁵ 5g³ 5.7m t6f⁴ 5.7g² p5f* p6f t5.1m t5.1f⁵ t6m⁵ Dec 26] sturdy gelding: fairly useful handicapper: won at Chelmsford in October: left Jane Chapple-Hyam after third start: stays 6f: acts on polytrack, tapeta, good to firm and good to soft going: usually wears headgear. *Lisa Williamson*

SECRET BANTA 2 b.f. (Mar 24) Sakhee's Secret 128 – Atnab (USA) 64 (Riverman (USA) **50** 131) [2015 5m⁵ 6g 7.5m³ 7m 6d 7s Oct 16] 5,000F: half-sister to several winners, including useful 6f and (at 2 yrs) 7f winner Seeking Magic (by Haafhd) and useful French winner up to 15f Grey Mystique (2-y-o 9.5f winner, by Linamix): dam 1½m winner: modest maiden: will be suited by 1m+: acts on good to firm going: sold £900, sent to Denmark. *Tim Easterby*

SECRET BAY (IRE) 3 ch.f. Arcano (IRE) 122 – Caribbean Escape (Pivotal 124) [2015 **69** 8.3g 8g 8m t9.5g Jul 8] €35,000F, £22,000Y: sturdy filly: half-sister to several winners, including 2-y-o 5f winner Knavesmire (by One Cool Cat) and 7f/1m winner Pilates (by Shamardal): dam unraced half-sister to smart sprinter Splice: fair maiden: best effort at 1m: usually in headgear. *Jonathan Portman*

SECRET BIRD (IRE) 3 br.g. Arcano (IRE) 122 – Asfurah (USA) 108 (Dayjur (USA) **68** 137) [2015 p7m 6m⁴ 6.1v² 6g* p6g Oct 6] fair performer: won handicap at Windsor in September: should stay 7f: acts on heavy going. *Dean Ivory*

SECRET BRIEF (IRE) 3 b.g. Shamardal (USA) 129 – Discreet Brief (IRE) 113 **108** (Darshaan 133) [2015 106: 10g 8.1m² 7g³ 8m⁶ 7m 7g 7g³ 8d³ Sep 4] strong gelding: useful performer: second in listed race at Sandown (2½ lengths behind Consort) in May and third in handicap at Ascot (length behind Energia Davos) final start, best efforts: stays 1m: acts on soft and good to firm going: tried in cheekpieces: sometimes slowly away. *Charlie Appleby*

SECRET CITY (IRE) 9 b.g. City On A Hill (USA) 114 – Secret Combe (IRE) 81 **72 §** (Mujadil (USA) 119) [2015 69§: 7m² 7g 7.1g 6g³ 7m 6m* 6m 6d³ 6d⁶ 6g³ 7s Oct 16] good-bodied gelding: fair handicapper: won at Thirsk in July: stays 7f: acts on good to firm and heavy going: usually wears headgear: untrustworthy. *Rebecca Bastiman*

SECRET CLAUSE 2 b.c. (Mar 7) Sakhee's Secret 128 – Claws 63 (Marju (IRE) 127) **66** [2015 5d 5m⁵ 5m f5g³ 5.3v* 5g² Aug 28] fair performer: won nursery at Brighton in August: worth a try at 6f: acts on heavy going. *Michael Appleby*

SECRET CONVOY 3 b.g. Hellvelyn 118 – Tee Cee 77 (Lion Cavern (USA) 117) [2015 **66** 8.3m 10m⁵ p10f⁶ p12g Sep 9] fair maiden: best effort at 1¼m. *Clive Brittain*

SECRET EMOTION 2 ch.f. (Feb 14) Dutch Art 126 – Agony And Ecstasy 100 (Captain **52** Rio 122) [2015 6m 6g 6d 8.3g⁵ p7g⁶ Oct 6] 65,000F, £115,000Y: rather unfurnished filly: first foal: dam, 7.6f/1m winner (including at 2 yrs), half-sister to useful UAE sprinter Doctor Hilary: modest maiden: stays 8.5f: best form on good going: sometimes in tongue tie: sold 6,500 gns, sent to Sweden. *Ralph Beckett*

SECRETFACT 2 br.c. (Feb 10) Sakhee's Secret 128 – Matterofact (IRE) 83 (Bold Fact – (USA) 116) [2015 7m 6.1m 5g² Jul 27] no form. *Malcolm Saunders*

SECRET GESTURE 5 b.m. Galileo (IRE) 134 – Shastye (IRE) 108 (Danehill (USA) **117** 126) [2015 115: 10.4m* 10m⁴ 9.5d³ 9.5g Oct 31] close-coupled mare: smart performer: won Middleton Stakes at York in May by 1½ lengths from Talmada: first past post in Beverly D Stakes at Arlington (1¼ lengths ahead of Watsdachances, leading inside final 1f before edging right) in August, but demoted to third: below-form seventh to Stephanie's Kitten in Breeders' Cup Filly & Mare Turf at Keeneland final start: stays 1½m: acts on any turf going: usually races close up. *Ralph Beckett*

SECRET GLANCE 3 b.g. Sakhee's Secret 128 – Look Here's Dee (Dansili 127) [2015 **86** 81: 6m³ t6g⁴ 6m 6.1m* 6g* Aug 5] fairly useful handicapper: won at Nottingham in July and Pontefract (by neck from Eternitys Gate) in August: stays 6f: acts on polytrack, tapeta and good to firm going: front runner/races prominently: sold £24,000. *Ed McMahon*

SECRET HINT 4 b.f. Oasis Dream 129 – Teeky 89 (Daylami (IRE) 138) [2015 97: 5.5g^2 **103** 6g 6f^3 6m^2 7d^3 t7.1g^5 p7g^3 Dec 7] useful handicapper: best effort when ½-length second to Queen's Pearl at Newmarket fourth start: stays 7f: acts on polytrack and firm going. *Andrew Balding*

SECRET INSIDER (USA) 2 b.f. (Jan 23) Elusive Quality (USA) – Fashion Insider **68** (USA) 76 (Indian Charlie (USA) 126) [2015 6m^4 6m^6 7.5g Sep 16] $150,000Y: lengthy filly: first foal: dam, US 1m winner, sister to smart US Grade 2 winners Bwana Charlie (6f) and My Pal Charlie (9f): fair maiden: best effort when fourth at Newmarket on debut. *Hugo Palmer*

SECRET INTERLUDE (IRE) 2 b.f. (Feb 5) Clodovil (IRE) 116 – Elouges (IRE) **59** (Dalakhani (IRE) 133) [2015 6m 6.1s^6 5.7m 6m t6f* t7.1f^3 p6g^5 Dec 7] £23,000Y: fifth foal: half-sister to French 9.5f-10.5f winner Indiakhani (by Indian Haven) and 2-y-o 8.6f winner (stays 11.5f) Dragoon Guard (by Jeremy): dam, French maiden (third at 12.5f), half-sister to very smart winner up to 1½m Mons: modest performer: won nursery at Wolverhampton in November: stays 7f: acts on tapeta: sometimes slowly away. *Jamie Osborne*

SECRETINTHEPARK 5 ch.g. Sakhee's Secret 128 – Lark In The Park (IRE) 57 (Grand **101** Lodge (USA) 125) [2015 103: 6f 6g^5 6m^3 5f 6m 5m* 5.4g p5m Sep 26] tall gelding: useful handicapper: won at Ascot (by short head from Dutch Masterpiece) in August: stays 7f, races mostly at 5f/6f: acts on polytrack and firm going: usually in cheekpieces in 2015: often races prominently. *Robert Cowell*

SECRET JOURNEY (IRE) 3 ch.g. Sakhee's Secret 128 – Hinokia (IRE) (Forestry **76** (USA) 121) [2015 68p: p7g* p7f f8d p7g p6g Sep 22] fair performer: won maiden at Kempton in April: stays 7f: acts on polytrack: tried in cheekpieces in 2015: usually races prominently. *Hughie Morrison*

Qatar Racing Ltd & Newsells Park Stud's "Secret Gesture"

SECRET LIGHTNING (FR) 3 ch.f. Sakhee's Secret 128 – Dimelight 74 (Fantastic **74** Light (USA) 134) [2015 65: 8g 8s* 9.2d² 9.8d² 8.3m⁵ 10g⁴ 10d³ 8m* 9.8g³ 8.3d⁴ 8.3m Sep 28] tall, unfurnished filly: fair handicapper: won at Thirsk in May and Ripon in August: stays 1¼m: acts on soft and good to firm going. *Michael Appleby*

SECRET LOOK 5 ch.g. Sakhee's Secret 128 – Look Here's Carol (IRE) 102 (Safawan **75** 118) [2015 97: 6m 7g 6g t6g 6s p6f t6f 6g t6g⁵ f6g Dec 18] fair handicapper: stays 6f: acts on tapeta, good to firm and heavy going: often in headgear in 2015. *Ed McMahon*

SECRET MILLIONAIRE (IRE) 8 b.g. Kyllachy 129 – Mithl Al Hawa 99 (Salse **76** (USA) 128) [2015 85, a78: p6g⁵ p5g t6m³ t6f t5.1m³ p5f⁶ 5v⁴ t6g 5.1m 6g 5g⁶ 5m 5g 5.1d⁵ Nov 4] quite attractive gelding: fair handicapper: left Luke Dace after third start: stays 6f: acts on polytrack and good to firm going: tried in headgear: usually races prominently. *Shaun Harris*

SECRET MISSILE 5 b.g. Sakhee's Secret 128 – Malelane (IRE) 48 (Prince Sabo 123) **101** [2015 94: 5g² 5d⁵ 5m p5m² 6d p6f* p5f⁶ Nov 23] rangy gelding: useful handicapper: won at Chelmsford (by 2¼ lengths from Elis Eliz) in October: stays 6f: acts on polytrack, good to firm and heavy going: often wears headgear: front runner/races prominently. *Gary Moore*

SECRET NUMBER 5 b.h. Raven's Pass (USA) 133 – Mysterial (USA) (Alleged (USA) **116** 138) [2015 114: 12.3s* 12.9d² Nov 7] useful-looking horse: smart performer, lightly raced in recent years: won listed race at Chester in September by neck from Lustrous: creditable 1¾ lengths second to Dandino in Group 3 Queen's Cup (Handicap) at Flemington final start: probably stays 14.6f: acts on polytrack, tapeta and soft going. *Saeed bin Suroor*

SECRET OF DUBAI 3 ch.f. Sakhee's Secret 128 – Dubai Legend 83 (Cadeaux Genereux – 131) [2015 49: 7.5m p6g t5.1f p8g Oct 14] poor maiden: in headgear last 2 starts. *Shaun Harris*

SECRET PALACE 3 ch.f. Pastoral Pursuits 127 – Some Sunny Day 89 (Where Or When **54** (IRE) 124) [2015 t6f 7g² t6g⁴ 7.6m 7v⁴ 7d² p8g Oct 14] 18,000Y: first foal: dam, 1¼m-11.6f winner, half-sister to July Cup winner Sakhee's Secret: modest maiden: stays 7f: acts on good to soft going. *Rae Guest*

SECRET PATTERN 3 b.g. Sakhee's Secret 128 – Saddlers Bend (IRE) 90 (Refuse To – Bend (IRE) 128) [2015 –: 6g 7.5f 10m 8.5m t6m Sep 14] no form: tried in cheekpieces. *Ollie Pears*

SECRET PURSUIT (IRE) 4 b.f. Lawman (FR) 121 – Secret Melody (FR) 106 (Inchinor **86** 119) [2015 105: 9.5s⁵ 9.9d⁵ 10.4s Nov 1] useful performer at 3 yrs: below form in 2015 in Denny Cordell Lavarack & Lanwades Stud Fillies Stakes at Gowran, Premio Verziere at Milan and Prix de Flore at Saint-Cloud: stays 1¼m: acts on polytrack and soft going: front runner/races prominently. *Marcus Tregoning*

SECRET RECIPE 5 ch.g. Sakhee's Secret 128 – Fudge (Polar Falcon (USA) 126) [2015 **79** 79: f8g 8.2f* 8.9g⁶ 9d³ 9.9m* 8s⁵ a11.9g² Dec 9] formerly useful performer: left David Nicholls after first outing: won claimer at Amiens in June and amateurs event at Lyon Parilly in September: stays 1¼m: acts on any turf going: tried in blinkers. *J. Bossert, France*

SECRET SENSE (USA) 2 b.f. (Feb 14) Shamardal (USA) 129 – Shastye (IRE) 108 **86 p** (Danehill (USA) 126) [2015 p7g 7s² p8g² Nov 4] useful-looking filly: sixth foal: half-sister to 3 winners, including winner up to 11.5f Secret Gesture (2-y-o 1m winner) and 7f winner Sir Isaac Newton (both smart and by Galileo): dam, 1½m/13f winner, half-sister to Prix de l'Arc de Triomphe winner Sagamix: fairly useful maiden: second in maidens at Salisbury (2 lengths behind Rostova) and Kempton (neck behind Persuasive): will prove suited by at least 1¼m: still unexposed. *Ralph Beckett*

SECRET SINNER (IRE) 2 b.f. (Apr 17) Lawman (FR) 121 – Mamela (GER) 106 **36** (Protektor (GER) 120) [2015 p8f p8m⁶ t9.5f⁴ Nov 30] €30,000F, €25,000Y: fourth foal: sister to 2-y-o 5f winner Boom And Bloom: dam 7f/1m winner (including at 2 yrs): poor maiden. *Jamie Osborne*

SECRET SOBRIETY (IRE) 2 b.g. (Apr 21) Arcano (IRE) 122 – No Tippling (IRE) 72 – (Unblest 117) [2015 6m 7.4g 8g⁵ Aug 6] no form. *David Dennis*

SECRET SPIRIT 3 b.f. Sakhee's Secret 128 – Naayla (IRE) 85 (Invincible Spirit (IRE) **77** 121) [2015 76: 6.5m² 6.1d² 6d 5.9g⁶ 6g⁴ 5.7s⁶ p6g⁶ t7.1f⁴ Oct 13] neat filly: fair maiden: stays 6.5f: acts on polytrack, good to firm and good to soft going: often in headgear in 2015: sold 6,000 gns, sent to Italy. *Clive Cox*

SECRETS SAFE (IRE) 3 b.g. Arcano (IRE) 122 – Keritana (FR) (One Cool Cat (USA) **65** 123) [2015 53: f8s* p10g² 8g 10m 8.3d Jul 31] fair handicapper: won at Southwell in February: left David Brown after third start: stays 1¼m: acts on polytrack and fibresand: in cheekpieces final start: front runner/races prominently. *John Joseph Hanlon, Ireland*

SECRET TALE (IRE) 2 b.f. (Apr 27) Zoffany (IRE) 121 – Intimate Secret (IRE) 75 **79**
(Invincible Spirit (IRE) 121) [2015 5m⁴ 5g² 5m* 5f Jun 17] €7,000Y: strong filly: third
foal: half-sister to Italian 6f winner Wedding Night (by Alhaarth): dam maiden (stayed 7f):
fair performer: won maiden at Lingfield in June: sold £120,000, sent to Qatar, where won
6f nursery at Doha in December. *Jamie Osborne*

SECRET WITNESS 9 ch.g. Pivotal 124 – It's A Secret 95 (Polish Precedent (USA) 131) **76 §**
[2015 102d: f6d⁶ 6g 6g 6m⁶ 6.1m⁴ 6.1m 6g⁶ p6g⁶ Nov 13] big, strong, lengthy gelding: fair
handicapper: races mainly at 6f: acts on polytrack and any turf going: usually wears
headgear: unreliable. *Ronald Harris*

SECULAR SOCIETY 5 b.g. Royal Applause 124 – Fantastic Santanyi (Fantastic Light **78**
(USA) 134) [2015 84: p11f² 10.2f² 10.2f⁵ May 13] sturdy gelding: fair handicapper: stays
11f: acts on polytrack and firm going: sometimes wears cheekpieces: usually races close
up: none too consistent. *George Baker*

SEE AND BE SEEN 5 b.g. Sakhee's Secret 128 – Anthea 66 (Tobougg (IRE) 125) [2015 **85**
87, a78: 16m⁴ 16g 16g⁶ p15.8g³ 18g⁴ 21g 16g 16d Oct 30] good-bodied gelding: fairly
useful handicapper: won at Pontefract in June: stays 2¼m: acts on polytrack and any turf
going: usually wears cheekpieces: often races prominently. *Sylvester Kirk*

SEEBEEDEE 3 b.f. Multiplex 114 – Border Ballet (IRE) (Noverre (USA) 125) [2015 65: **76**
8.3f² 10.2m* 10.2m³ 10m* 9.9g Sep 7] sturdy filly: fair performer: won minor event at
Bath in June and handicap at Windsor in August: stays 1¼m: acts on polytrack and firm
going: usually leads. *Harry Dunlop*

SEEKING MAGIC 7 b.g. Haafhd 129 – Atnab (USA) 64 (Riverman (USA) 131) [2015 **101**
111: 6f 5m⁵ 6m⁵ 6m 6m p6g* t6f² p6g³ t6m³ Dec 18] stocky, close-coupled gelding: useful
handicapper: won at Kempton (by head from Acolyte) in September: creditable efforts
when placed all 3 starts after: stays 7f: acts on polytrack, tapeta, firm and good to soft
going: wears hood/tongue tie: usually races prominently, often races freely. *Clive Cox*

SEEK THE FAIR LAND 9 b.g. Noverre (USA) 125 – Duchcov 101 (Caerleon (USA) **79**
132) [2015 67, a84: p7g² p7g⁴ p7g p7m⁶ p7f⁴ p8f² p6g⁴ t7.1g³ p6g* t6g⁶ t7.1f p8f⁶ p7g*
Dec 9] workmanlike gelding: fair performer: won handicap at Kempton (apprentice) in
July and seller at Lingfield in December: best at 6f/7f: acts on polytrack, good to firm and
heavy going: wears headgear. *Lee Carter*

SEE NO SHIPS 4 b.f. Compton Place 125 – Queen of Havana (USA) (King of Kings **45**
(IRE) 125) [2015 52: p7g³ p8g p8f p8f⁵ t9.5f Mar 23] poor maiden: stays 7f: acts on
polytrack, soft and good to firm going: tried in headgear: often races towards rear.
Mark Usher

SEE THE STORM 7 b.g. Statue of Liberty (USA) 115 – Khafayif (USA) 62 (Swain **82**
(IRE) 134) [2015 85, a64: 7v 7f 7m 7.6f⁴ 6.1m⁶ 7m 7.6g 7d 6g² 6s² 6m 6s⁴ Sep 23] fairly
useful handicapper: has form at 9f, but races mainly at 6f/7f nowadays: acts on polytrack
and any turf going: tried in headgear. *Ian Williams*

SEE THE SUN 4 ch.g. Assertive 121 – Cocabana 69 (Captain Rio 122) [2015 104: 6g⁶ 5m **95**
6d 5m 6m² 6m 5m 6d 6g Sep 26] sturdy, close-coupled gelding: useful handicapper: second
at Newcastle (1¼ lengths behind Bushcraft) in June: stays 6f: acts on soft and good to firm
going: tried in headgear: tried in tongue tie in 2015: front runner/races prominently: none
too consistent. *Tim Easterby*

SEE VERMONT 7 b.g. Kyllachy 129 – Orange Lily (Royal Applause 124) [2015 56: t6f* **72**
t6g⁶ 5m* 6g⁵ 5m² 5m⁴ 5f² 5.1m* 5.5m⁴ 5m³ 5g⁵ Aug 29] fair handicapper: won at
Wolverhampton in March, Bath in May and Chepstow in July: stays 6f: acts on tapeta, firm
and soft going: wears cheekpieces: often races prominently. *Rebecca Bastiman*

SEE YOU WHEN (IRE) 2 b.c. (Feb 27) Acclamation 118 – Lighthouse 92 (Warning **82 p**
136) [2015 7.1m³ Jun 12] 70,000Y: sturdy colt: half-brother to several winners, including
7f/1m winner Kehaar and 2-y-o 5f winner All For Laura (both useful, by Cadeaux
Genereux): dam, 8.3f winner, half-sister to Middle Park Stakes winner First Trump: 25/1,
promise when 2¼ lengths third of 12 to Albernathy in maiden at Sandown on debut, staying
on final 1f: will improve. *Richard Hannon*

SEISMOS (IRE) 7 ch.g. Dalakhani (IRE) 133 – Sasuela (GER) (Dashing Blade 117) **–**
[2015 120: 16f Apr 29] rather leggy gelding: very smart performer at best: run best excused
when well held in Sagaro Stakes at Ascot only outing in 2015, possibly unsuited by
conditions/needing race: stays 13.5f: acts on sand and heavy going: tried in cheekpieces:
often races prominently. *Marco Botti*

SEKURAS GIRL (IRE) 3 b.f. Approve (IRE) 112 – Alinda (IRE) 86 (Revoque (IRE) **60**
122) [2015 52: 6m 7m³ t6g⁴ 6m 8m 7.5m* 7m⁴ 8.5d⁴ Sep 22] modest handicapper: won at
Beverley in July: left Michael Dods after second start: stays 8.5f: acts on good to firm and
good to soft going: sometimes wears headgear: usually leads. *Clive Mulhall*

SELDOM HEARD 3 br.g. Bahri (USA) 125 – Turtle Dove 65 (Tobougg (IRE) 125) –
[2015 p8g May 28] 16/1, slowly away when well held in maiden at Lingfield. *Henry Candy*

SELENA ROSE 2 b.f. (Feb 28) Stimulation (IRE) 121 – Dot Hill (Refuse To Bend (IRE) –
128) [2015 5.1d 6m 8d t8.6g Sep 29] second foal: sister to useful 5f (including at 2 yrs)
winner Union Rose: dam unraced half-sister to smart sprinter Taajub: no form. *Ronald
Harris*

SELFRESPECT 3 b.f. Thewayyouare (USA) 117 – Self Esteem (Suave Dancer (USA) –
136) [2015 –: 10m 10m May 25] no form. *Henry Candy*

SELINA KYLE 2 b.f. (Feb 13) Acclamation 118 – Shim Sham (IRE) 91 (Danehill Dancer –
(IRE) 117) [2015 5m 5g 5m 5d 5d⁵ 6g Sep 23] €16,000Y: first foal: dam, 2-y-o 7f winner,
sister to smart winner up to 9f Decado: no form. *David O'Meara*

SELLINGALLTHETIME (IRE) 4 ch.g. Tamayuz 126 – Anthyllis (GER) (Lycius **88**
(USA) 124) [2015 84§: f11g² f12s² f11g³ 10s 12g* 12g² 12m* 10g 12g³ 12v* 12s⁵ Oct 27]
lengthy gelding: fairly useful handicapper: not one to trust in the past, but won at Doncaster
(apprentice) in May, York (apprentice) in June and Catterick in October: stays 1½m: acts
on firesand, good to firm and heavy going: wears headgear. *Michael Appleby*

SEMARAL (IRE) 4 b.f. High Chaparral (IRE) 132 – Semaphore (Zamindar (USA) 116) **92**
[2015 74, a93: p8f⁵ p8f* p8g⁶ 8m⁵ 10.2m p9.4g Jun 27] fairly useful performer: won
handicap at Lingfield in March: stays 10.5f: acts on polytrack, good to firm and good to soft
going: wears cheekpieces: often races in rear: carries head awkwardly. *Chris Wall*

SEMILLE OBON 3 b.g. Royal Applause 124 – Starparty (USA) 76 (Cozzene (USA)) –
[2015 t8.6f⁶ p10g Dec 30] well held in 2 maidens, in cheekpieces in latter. *Jamie Poulton*

SENATOR BONG 5 ch.g. Dutch Art 126 – Sunley Gift 70 (Cadeaux Genereux 131) –
[2015 65: p5m Jan 9] close-coupled gelding: fair handicapper: well held only outing in
2015: stays 7f: acts on polytrack, best turf form on ground softer than good: tried in
blinkers. *Peter Grayson*

SENATOR MATT 5 b.h. Joe Bear (IRE) 109 – Anytime Anywhere 77 (Daring March –
116) [2015 –: p8m p8f 12.1m 14.1g Aug 4] no form. *John Berry*

SENDIYM (FR) 8 b.g. Rainbow Quest (USA) 134 – Seraya (FR) (Danehill (USA) 126) **53**
[2015 52: t16.5g 16s⁵ 17.2d⁶ 16d⁴ Aug 18] modest maiden: stays 17f: acts on tapeta and
heavy going: often in headgear prior to 2015. *Dianne Sayer*

SENNOCKIAN SONG 2 ch.g. (Apr 24) New Approach (IRE) 132 – Chorist 120 **71 p**
(Pivotal 124) [2015 8.3v p8f p7g Nov 9] 52,000Y: closely related to very smart 1¼m-1¾m
(Yorkshire Cup) winner Gospel Choir (by Galileo) and half-brother to 3 winners, including
smart winner up to 1¼m Sennockian Star (2-y-o 7f winner, by Rock of Gibraltar): dam
1m-1¼m winner: fair maiden: likely to stay at least 1¼m: should do better in time.
Mark Johnston

SENNOCKIAN STAR 5 ch.g. Rock of Gibraltar (IRE) 133 – Chorist 120 (Pivotal 124) **105**
[2015 113: 9.9g⁶ 9.9g 9.9g 9.9g p10g³ 10s 10.1g 10.3s p10m* 10.1g 10.3f* 10f² 10.4m
9.9g 10.4m³ 10m 10d 12s⁴ 10.4s Oct 10] workmanlike gelding: useful handicapper: won at
Chelmsford (by neck from Angelic Upstart) in May and Chester (by 1¼ lengths from Spirit
of The Law) in June: good efforts when second in Wolferton Handicap at Royal Ascot (½
length behind Mahsoob) in June and third at Haydock (3 lengths behind Rembrandt Van
Rijn) in August: stays 1½m: acts on polytrack, firm and good to soft going: usually wears headgear:
front runner/races prominently. *Mark Johnston*

SENORA LOBO (IRE) 5 b.m. Amadeus Wolf 122 – Valencia (FR) (Croco Rouge (IRE) **51**
126) [2015 49: p7g p7g p6m⁶ p6g² p5g² p6f f6g p5m 6s May 15] modest handicapper:
stays 6f: acts on polytrack, good to firm and heavy going: usually wears headgear: often
races towards rear. *Lisa Williamson*

SENOR FIRECRACKER (IRE) 3 b.g. Acclamation 118 – Miss Eze 92 (Danehill **47**
Dancer (IRE) 117) [2015 –: p7g⁵ p6g³ 8m³ p10m 8d⁵ 9.9m⁶ p8g⁶ Jul 14] poor maiden: stays
1m: acts on polytrack and good to firm going. *Brett Johnson*

SENOR GEORGE (IRE) 8 b.g. Traditionally (USA) 117 – Mrs St George (IRE) 87 **68**
(Orpen (USA) 116) [2015 71: t8.6f f11g³ f8g⁵ t9.5f³ t12.2g 8f³ 10m² 8m⁵ 11.9m² 11.8m³
13.1g* 13.1m 11.7s⁵ Aug 26] fair handicapper: won at Bath in July: left Daniel Loughnane
after fifth start: stays 13f: acts on fibresand, tapeta, firm and good to soft going: usually
wears headgear: often races towards rear. *Simon Hodgson*

SENRIMA (IRE) 3 b.g. High Chaparral (IRE) 132 – Alexander Divine (Halling (USA) **89**
133) [2015 10m² 12m* 14m* 12m Aug 1] 31,000F, 35,000Y: lengthy gelding: fourth
foal: dam once-raced half-sister to smart winner up to 1½m Ambivalent and to dam of
Prix de l'Abbaye winner Total Gallery: fairly useful performer: won maiden at Newbury
and handicap at Haydock (by 3 lengths from Joseph Jefferson) in July: stays 1¾m.
Brian Meehan

SENSATIONAL SECRET 2 ch.f. (Apr 25) Sakhee's Secret 128 – Eolith 99 (Pastoral **55**
Pursuits 127) [2015 5g² 6s t5.1g³ 6d⁴ 5d Sep 15] £5,000Y: second foal: half-sister to useful
7f winner Harry Hurricane (by Kodiac): dam 2-y-o 7f winner: modest maiden: best effort
at 5f: sold £4,000, sent to Germany. *Ollie Pears*

SENSE OF FUN (USA) 2 b.f. (Apr 21) Distorted Humor (USA) 117 – Abhisheka (IRE) **67**
108 (Sadler's Wells (USA) 132) [2015 5g p6g p6g⁴ p7f² 6d³ Sep 21] fourth foal: sister to
very smart winner up to 1m (Prix Jean Prat) Aesop's Fables (2-y-o 6f winner): dam,
1m-1¼m winner, closely related to top-class winner up to 1½m Lammtarra: fair maiden:
stays 7f: acts on polytrack. *Charlie Appleby*

SENSES OF DUBAI 2 b.c. (Feb 11) Royal Applause 124 – Umseyat (USA) 92 (Arch **73 p**
(USA) 127) [2015 7.2m² Sep 4] €20,000Y: first foal: dam, ungenuine 2-y-o 1m winner who
stayed 1¼m, half-sister to very smart performer up to 1½m Alwaary: 7/2, knew job when
1½ lengths second of 6 to Daleelak in maiden at Musselburgh, no match for winner: should
progress. *Simon Crisford*

SENSES OF EMIRATES (USA) 2 b.f. (Mar 6) Bernardini (USA) 132 – Harmony **–**
Lodge (USA) 120 (Hennessy (USA) 122) [2015 p7g p7g Sep 21] $55,000Y, 50,000 2-y-o:
lengthy filly: seventh foal: closely related to 2 winners in USA by A P Indy, including smart
US Grade 3 5.5f winner Stratford Hill: dam US Grade 1 7f winner: well held in maidens at
Kempton: sold 60,000 gns in December, sent to USA. *Simon Crisford*

SENSIBLE WAY (USA) 4 b.f. Street Sense (USA) 128 – Nasheej (USA) 112 (Swain **–**
(IRE) 134) [2015 82: p10m Jan 10] good-topped filly: fairly useful handicapper: well held
only start in 2015: stays 1m: acts on polytrack and good to firm going: front runner/races
prominently. *Richard Hannon*

SENSOR (USA) 6 b.g. Street Sense (USA) 128 – Minister Wife (USA) 119 (Deputy **–**
Minister (CAN)) [2015 t8.6m f7g t16.5g Mar 24] won maiden at Gulfstream from 4 starts
in USA in 2012: subsequently left Tom Albertrani and missed 2013 and 2014: well held all
3 starts in Britain, in hood final one. *Tony Coyle*

SENZA UNA DONNA 2 b.g. (Apr 4) Sir Percy 129 – Sensationally 77 (Montjeu (IRE) **71**
137) [2015 7m 7.1g f7s³ 8.1m* 8g⁴ p8f Oct 1] fair performer: won nursery at Chepstow in
September: will stay beyond 1m: acts on good to firm going: often races towards rear.
Hughie Morrison

SEPAL (USA) 2 b.f. (Feb 14) Afleet Alex (USA) 128 – Faraway Flower (USA) 98 (Distant **79 p**
View (USA) 126) [2015 7m⁶ 8.3g* 8g⁵ Sep 24] good-topped filly: third foal: dam, 2-y-o 6f
winner, half-sister to dam of very smart US Grade 1 8.5f/9f winner Close Hatches: fair
form: won maiden at Leicester in September by ½ length from Myopic: excuses (worst of
draw) when well held in nursery final start: stays 8.5f: remains with potential. *Charles Hills*

SEPTEMBER ISSUE 2 b.g. (Apr 29) Dutch Art 126 – Alexander Ballet 86 (Mind Games **84**
121) [2015 p6.5g⁵ 5g² p6g³ Oct 27] 30,000Y, £65,000 2-y-o: half-brother to 3 winners,
including smart 2-y-o 5f-1m winner Hearts of Fire (by Firebreak) and useful 7f winner
Kenny Powers (by Vital Equine): dam 5f winner: fairly useful form in maidens: in
cheekpieces second start: has been gelded. *Gay Kelleway*

SEPTEMBER STARS (IRE) 2 ch.f. (Apr 7) Sea The Stars (IRE) 140 – Altesse **87 p**
Imperiale (IRE) (Rock of Gibraltar (IRE) 133) [2015 8d³ Oct 23] 260,000Y: fourth foal:
closely related to useful 2-y-o 7f winner (stayed 1½m) Altruistic (by Galileo) and half-
sister to 11.6f winner Pitchoun (by Street Cry): dam, French 9.5f winner, closely related to
smart French 9f-10.5f winner Actrice and half-sister to smart French/US 9f-1½m winner
Angara: 10/1, shaped well when length third of 11 to Zest in maiden at Doncaster on debut,
left poorly placed but finishing well: bred to be suited by middle distances: sure to improve.
Brian Meehan

SEQUESTER 4 ch.f. Selkirk (USA) 129 – Al Theraab (USA) 81 (Roberto (USA) 131) **95**
[2015 83: t9.5g* 10.2f* 9m⁴ 9.9g* 10.2m⁶ p9.4g p10g Dec 19] useful handicapper: won at
Wolverhampton in April, Bath in May and Brighton (by ½ length from Shasag) in August:
stays 1¼m: acts on polytrack, tapeta and firm going: wears cheekpieces: often races
towards rear, usually races freely. *David Lanigan*

SERAFFIMO 3 ch.g. Monsieur Bond (IRE) 120 – Hula Ballew 90 (Weldnaas (USA) 112) **51** [2015 43: f8s 10g² 12.1g 12.1s 14.1s³ Sep 15] modest maiden: stays 1¾m: acts on heavy going: tried in hood: often races prominently. *Sharon Watt*

SERAPHIMA 5 b.m. Fusaichi Pegasus (USA) 130 – Millestan (IRE) 91 (Invincible Spirit **56** (IRE) 121) [2015 47: p7g t6f* t6f⁶ p6m t6f t6g 5.1g 7.4d t6g p8f t5.1f⁶ p6g t5.1m⁵ t6m Dec 30] leggy mare: modest handicapper: won at Wolverhampton in January: stays 6f: acts on tapeta and good to firm going: wears headgear: often races towards rear: has looked awkward. *Lisa Williamson*

SERENADE 3 b.f. Oratorio (IRE) 128 – After You 92 (Pursuit of Love 124) [2015 –: p7f p10g⁵ Feb 13] no form in maidens. *Kevin Ryan*

SERENA GRAE 4 gr.f. Arakan (USA) 123 – Success Story 60 (Sharrood (USA) 124) [2015 **91** 93: 9g 12s³ 12g⁶ p11g³ Dec 3] tall mare: fairly useful handicapper: stays 1½m: acts on polytrack, soft and good to firm going: wears hood: usually races close up. *Marcus Tregoning*

SERENDIB'S GLORY (IRE) 2 b.f. (Mar 27) Holy Roman Emperor (IRE) 125 – Rose of Mooncoin (IRE) 99 (Brief Truce (USA) 126) [2015 p8d Nov 30] closely related to useful winner up to 1¼m Emma's Gift (2-y-o 5f winner, by Aussie Rules) and half-sister to several winners, including smart winner up to 8.6f Russki (2-y-o 7f winner, by Fasliyev): dam 2-y-o 6f winner: 100/1, possibly flattered when 8¾ lengths ninth of 10 to Diamonds Pour Moi in maiden at Kempton. *Julia Feilden*

SERENE BEAUTY (USA) 3 b.f. Street Cry (IRE) 130 – Divine Dixie (USA) (Dixieland **102** Band (USA)) [2015 t8.6g* 10.4d² 10.3m* 9.9m² 12m³ 10.2d⁵ Aug 14] sister to smart 2-y-o 6f/7f (Sweet Solera Stakes) winner Discourse and half-sister to several winners, including very smart US Grade 1 9f winner Bandini (by Fusaichi Pegasus): dam US 6f-8.5f winner: useful performer: won maiden at Wolverhampton in March and handicap at Chester (by 2½ lengths from Shasag) in June: placed in handicaps at Salisbury and Newbury: stays 1½m: acts on tapeta, good to firm and good to soft going: free-going sort, often races prominently. *Charlie Appleby*

SERENITY NOW (IRE) 7 b.g. Key of Luck (USA) 126 – Imdina (IRE) 70 (Soviet Star **83** (USA) 128) [2015 f8d f8d⁴ t9.5f f12g² f12g* f12s³ f14g² f11g² 12g⁴ 12m 14.1m* f12d* 14.1m² 12g⁵ f14m² f12f⁵ Dec 17] fairly useful handicapper: won at Southwell (apprentice) in March and Redcar (apprentice) and Southwell in July: stays 1¾m: acts on fibresand and good to firm going: often races towards rear, often travels strongly: fairly useful hurdler. *Brian Ellison*

SERENITY SPA 5 gr.m. Excellent Art 125 – Molly Mello (GER) 106 (Big Shuffle (USA) **85** 122) [2015 94: p5g t6f p6f⁵ 6.1s 7s⁵ 6m⁵ 5m² 6m⁴ Jun 26] sparely-made mare: fairly useful performer: seems best at 6f nowadays: acts on polytrack, firm and good to soft going: often in headgear prior to 2015. *Tony Carroll*

SERGEANT PINK (IRE) 9 b.g. Fasliyev (USA) 120 – Ring Pink (USA) 111 (Bering **62** 136) [2015 67: t12.2m 12g 11.5d* 13.7g Aug 26] tall, lengthy gelding: modest handicapper: won at Carlisle (amateur) in August: stays 17f, effective at shorter: acts on heavy going: has worn headgear. *Dianne Sayer*

SERIOUS (IRE) 4 b.f. Camacho 118 – Tobar Suil Lady (IRE) 74 (Statue of Liberty **33** (USA) 115) [2015 6.9g 6m 5m 5d 5s⁵ 6d Sep 23] first foal: dam ungenuine winner up to 7f (2-y-o 6f winner): poor maiden: stays 6f: acts on soft and good to firm going: sometimes in headgear. *David Christie, Ireland*

SERRADURA (IRE) 2 b.f. (Feb 14) Acclamation 118 – Days of Summer (IRE) 80 **74** (Bachelor Duke (USA) 122) [2015 6g* 6d Sep 21] €100,000Y: lengthy filly: first foal: dam, 2-y-o 6f winner, half-sister to useful dam of Breeders' Cup Turf winner Red Rocks out of Phoenix Stakes winner Pharaoh's Delight: won maiden at Newbury in July by 1½ lengths from Fataawy: well held in nursery only other start, still green/seeming unsuited by conditions. *Charles Hills*

SERVERY 3 b.g. Sir Percy 129 – Heat of The Night 98 (Lear Fan (USA) 130) [2015 76: 10f 9.9m 12m⁶ 12m 10g⁵ Jul 21] rather leggy gelding: maiden: no impact in 2015, in headgear last 3 starts: tried in blinkers. *Richard Hannon*

SET TO GO 8 b.g. Reset (AUS) 124 – Golubitsa (IRE) (Bluebird (USA) 125) [2015 p6g⁶ **45** t6m Dec 30] angular gelding: poor handicapper: stays 7f: acts on polytrack and good to firm going: wears headgear. *Mark Usher*

SEVE 3 ch.g. Exceed And Excel (AUS) 126 – Flamenco Dancer (Mark of Esteem (IRE) **103** 137) [2015 87p: 5m⁵ 6d 5.1m⁴ 5m* 5m 5d 5m t6g t5.1f* Dec 22] useful handicapper: won at Sandown in July and Wolverhampton (by 2¼ lengths from Pensax Lad) in December:

best form at 5f: acts on tapeta and good to firm going: tried in cheekpieces in 2015: front runner/races prominently. *Tom Dascombe*

SEVEN BELLE 5 b.m. Septieme Ciel (USA) 123 – Auction Belle 47 (Auction House (USA) 120) [2015 t12.2g⁶ Apr 11] first foal: dam lightly raced: well held in bumpers and maiden at Wolverhampton. *Jo Hughes*   –

SEVEN CLANS (IRE) 3 b.g. Cape Cross (IRE) 129 – Cherokee Rose (IRE) 122 (Dancing Brave (USA) 140) [2015 6d p7m³ p8f² p8g* Dec 9] fair form: didn't need to improve to win maiden at Kempton on final start: stays 1m. *Neil Mulholland*   74

SEVEN COLOURS (IRE) 3 b.f. Thewayyouare (USA) 117 – Stamatina (Warning 136) [2015 7m Apr 17] neat filly: half-sister to several winners, including 1m winner Just A Martian (by Marju) and 2-y-o 1m winner Turn Left (by Xaar): dam Italian 7f-9f winner: 66/1, well held in maiden at Newbury. *Rod Millman*   –

SEVEN LUCKY SEVEN 4 b.g. Avonbridge 123 – Moon Bird 71 (Primo Dominie 121) [2015 74§: p6g⁵ t7.1g³ p8g³ 5.9g t6g 7g⁴ Jul 22] fair handicapper: stays 1m: acts on polytrack, tapeta, soft and good to firm going: tried in headgear: sometimes slowly away, often races towards rear: not straightforward, and one to treat with caution. *Michael Herrington*   67 §

SEVENTH HEAVEN (IRE) 2 b.f. (Mar 29) Galileo (IRE) 134 – La Traviata (USA) 112 (Johannesburg (USA) 127) [2015 7d 7g⁴ Sep 26] fifth foal: half-sister to 3 winners, including smart 6f (including at 2 yrs) winner Cristoforo Colombo (by Henrythenavigator) and smart 2-y-o 6f winner (including Middle Park Stakes) Crusade (by Mr Greeley): dam US Grade 3 6f winner: fair form in maidens: shaped well on debut (behind Anamba) at the Curragh, and better than result when 8 lengths fourth of 11 to First Victory at Newmarket, left poorly placed and finishing with running left: will improve. *Aidan O'Brien, Ireland*   78 p

SEVERAL (USA) 3 b.g. Rock Hard Ten (USA) 126 – Proud Fact (USA) 108 (Known Fact (USA) 135) [2015 p11g⁴ p13.3f⁶ t13.9g Nov 27] fair maiden: best effort when fourth at Kempton on debut: left Amanda Perrett after second start. *Kevin Frost*   76

SEVERINI (IRE) 2 b.c. (Apr 15) Shamardal (USA) 129 – Ballerina Blue (IRE) (High Chaparral (IRE) 132) [2015 p8f² p7g* Dec 16] €60,000Y: fourth foal: half-brother to French 7.5f-12.5f winner Ar Poulgwenn (by Nayef): dam, French 2-y-o 7.5f winner, half-sister to Prix du Jockey Club winner Blue Canari: dropped in trip, 4/7, didn't need to improve on debut form to win maiden at Kempton by 2¼ lengths from winners from Cambodia, prominent throughout and scoring readily: may do better still. *Richard Hughes*   82

SEVERNWIND (IRE) 4 b.g. Diamond Green (FR) 121 – Zeena 61 (Unfuwain (USA) 131) [2015 t13.9g⁴ Feb 13] maiden: well held only start in 2015: stays 7f: acts on all-weather: has worn headgear. *David Evans*   –

SEWN UP 5 ch.g. Compton Place 125 – Broughton Bounty 68 (Bahamian Bounty 116) [2015 59, a76: t7.1f² t7.1f⁵ t6f 7.1s⁵ 7g 6d⁵ 7.2d⁵ 5.9g⁵ 8.3g 6s⁶ 8d t6m⁵ 5m³ 7.2g³ t7.1f t7.1f² t6f* t7.1f⁴ Dec 11] big, strong gelding: fair handicapper: won at Wolverhampton in November: stays 7f: acts on all-weather, soft and good to firm going: wears headgear: tried in tongue tie: one to treat with caution. *Keith Dalgleish*   56 a74

SEXTON BLAKE (IRE) 2 b.g. (Apr 15) Rip Van Winkle (IRE) 134 – Soviet Treat (IRE) 92 (Ashkalani (IRE) 128) [2015 6d Sep 4] £20,000 2-y-o, resold €28,000 2-y-o: fifth foal: half-brother to French 9.5f-1½m winner Blue Verglas (by Verglas) and 7f winner Moscow Treat (by Fasliyev): dam 7f winner: 66/1, considerate introduction when well held in maiden at Ascot, not knocked about: will do better. *Gary Moore*   – p

SEXY SECRET 4 b.g. Sakhee's Secret 128 – Orange Walk (IRE) 88 (Alzao (USA) 117) [2015 65, a72: p11m p10g² t9.5m⁵ t9.5f² t8.6g³ t9.5g³ p10g² 10m 9.9v² p10g⁶ 8m 10d p10g 9.9d p10f p10f³ p10m p10d Nov 30] leggy, plain gelding: fair handicapper: stays 1½m: acts on all-weather and heavy going: often wears headgear. *Lydia Pearce*   66

SEYCHELLOISE 3 b.f. Pivotal 124 – Starlit Sands 104 (Oasis Dream 129) [2015 71: f6g² f6s⁵ p8f t7.1f* t7.1f² t7.1f² t7.1m* p6f² p7g² Dec 7] useful handicapper: won at Wolverhampton in October, and at Wolverhampton and Lingfield in November: good second at Lingfield (neck behind Tempting) final start: stays 7f: acts on polytrack and tapeta: usually in headgear in 2015: front runner/races prominently. *Sir Mark Prescott Bt*   102

SGT RECKLESS 8 b.g. Imperial Dancer 123 – Lakaam 57 (Danzero (AUS)) [2015 p12m* 10.1m⁵ Sep 16] second foal: dam lightly raced: won maiden at Lingfield in January by 5 lengths from Millionaires Row: not seen to best effect only subsequent start, and remains with potential on the Flat: useful hurdler/chaser. *Mick Channon*   86 p

SHAAKIS (IRE) 3 gr.g. Dark Angel (IRE) 113 – Curious Lashes (IRE) (Footstepsinthesand 120) [2015 83: p8g* 8.1d² 10.1m 8m⁶ 8m* 9.9m 8m² 9s⁵ Aug 29] useful-looking gelding: 95

useful handicapper: won at Chelmsford in April and Newbury in July: good second at Pontefract (neck behind Swift Emperor) in August: stays 1¼m: acts on polytrack, good to firm and good to soft going: in cheekpieces last 4 starts: sent to UAE. *Marcus Tregoning*

SHAAN (IRE) 2 b.f. (Mar 8) Iffraaj 127 – Evening Time (IRE) 117 (Keltos (FR) 132) **86 p** [2015 p8d² Nov 30] 300,000Y: fourth foal: half-sister to 3 winners, including useful French winner up to 6.5f Morning Frost (2-y-o 6f winner, by Duke of Marmalade) and 6f winner Penny Pepper (by Fast Company): dam 6f winner (including at 2 yrs): 14/1, shaped well on debut when head second of 10 to Zaakhir in maiden at Kempton, leading briefly final 1f: sure to improve. *Richard Hannon*

SHABBAH (IRE) 2 br.c. (Apr 8) Sea The Stars (IRE) 140 – Alizaya (IRE) (Highest **63** Honor (FR) 124) [2015 7g 8d⁶ p7g Nov 9] modest maiden: best effort on debut: will be suited by 1¼m+. *Sir Michael Stoute*

SHABEEB (USA) 2 b.c. (Apr 3) Smart Strike (CAN) 121 – Sortita (GER) 98 (Monsun **76 P** (GER) 124) [2015 8s⁶ Oct 23] fourth foal: half-brother to smart winner up to 1¼m Mutashaded (2-y-o 1m winner, by Raven's Pass) and 2-y-o 7f winner Baarez (by Hard Spun): dam, 9.7f/10.3f winner, sister to Samum and Schiaparelli and to dam of Sea The Moon, all Deutsches Derby winners: 5/1, shaped with promise when 3½ lengths sixth of 17 to Midterm in maiden at Newbury, finishing with running left and not at all knocked about: type to do much better. *Roger Varian*

SHACKLED N DRAWN (USA) 3 b.g. Candy Ride (ARG) 133 – Cajun Flash (USA) **81** (Bertrando (USA) 127) [2015 77: 5m 5m² 5m⁵ p5g⁵ Aug 22] strong gelding: fairly useful handicapper: raced only at 5f: acts on polytrack and good to firm going: in cheekpieces last 5 starts: wears tongue tie: often races towards rear. *Olly Stevens*

SHADAD (IRE) 2 b.g. (Apr 29) Zamindar (USA) 116 – Tender Morn (USA) (Dayjur **66 p** (USA) 137) [2015 p6g⁶ Aug 17] 100,000€, €200,000Y: useful French 2-y-o 7.5f/1m winner Zantenda, closely related to useful French 2-y-o 7f winner Elusif (by Elusive Quality) and half-brother to 2 winners in France, including useful 1m winner Single (including at 2 yrs, by Singspiel): dam French 2-y-o 5f winner: 4/1 and in hood, better for run when 2½ lengths sixth of 12 to Valko in maiden at Kempton, not unduly punished: has been gelded: should improve. *Ralph Beckett*

SHADARPOUR (IRE) 6 b.g. Dr Fong (USA) 128 – Shamadara (IRE) 114 (Kahyasi 130) **71** [2015 p15.8g p15.8g⁵ 17.2g⁵ Oct 18] fair maiden: stays 17f: acts on polytrack: has worn blinkers, including last 5 starts: often races prominently: fairly useful hurdler. *Alan King*

SHADELE (IRE) 2 b.f. (Apr 7) Rip Van Winkle (IRE) 134 – Zadalla 68 (Zafra (CAN) **–** 106) [2015 7g Oct 9] €50,000F, 50,000 2-y-o: useful-looking filly: third foal: half-sister to smart winner up to 1¼m Master The World (2-y-o 1m winner, by Mastercraftsman): dam, 2-y-o 5f winner, half-sister to useful performer up to 2m Hearthstead Wings: 33/1, lacked sharpness when well held in maiden at Newmarket on debut. *Ed Walker*

SHADEN (IRE) 2 b.f. (Feb 19) Kodiac 112 – Lady Avenger (IRE) 92 (Namid 128) [2015 **105** 5.1m* 5f 5g* 5.7d² 6g* Sep 19] 40,000Y: sparely-made filly: second foal: half-sister to useful 1¼m/10.5f winner I'll Be Your Clown (by Aqlaam): dam 2-y-o 5f winner: useful performer: won maiden at Nottingham (by ½ length from Rebel Surge) in June, nursery at Ffos Las (by 1¾ lengths from Sahreej) in July and Firth of Clyde Stakes at Ayr (by neck from Only Mine) in September: stays 6f: acts on good to firm going. *Lady Cecil*

SHADES OF GREY 8 gr.m. Dr Fong (USA) 128 – Twosixtythreewest (FR) 69 (Kris 135) **–** [2015 77: 12g 13.3m 17.2g Oct 18] leggy mare: handicapper: no form in 2015: stays 1½m: acts on good to firm and heavy going: tried in blinkers. *Clive Cox*

SHADES OF SILK 4 b.f. Bahamian Bounty 116 – Terentia 108 (Diktat 126) [2015 78: **75** f6d³ p6g⁴ p6f² 5g⁵ t6f⁵ f6g Nov 26] angular filly: fair handicapper: stays 6f: acts on all-weather, good to firm and good to soft going: tried in cheekpieces: front runner. *James Given*

SHADES OF SILVER 5 b.g. Dansili 127 – Silver Pivotal (IRE) 113 (Pivotal 124) [2015 **97** 77: p13.3f³ 12.1m² 16d* p16g* 16s² Sep 1] well-made, attractive gelding: useful handicapper: won at Nottingham in May (subsequently left Michael Scudamore) and Kempton (by length from King Calypso) in June: good second to Gale Force at Goodwood final start: stays 2m: acts on polytrack, soft and good to firm going: usually races close up. *Ed de Giles*

SHADOW GAME 2 b.c. (Apr 18) Shamardal (USA) 129 – Victoria Star (IRE) (Danehill **78** (USA) 126) [2015 6g p6g³ 7g³ 7g³ t6g² 6m* 6g Sep 18] fair performer: won maiden at Newmarket in August: stays 7f: acts on polytrack, tapeta and good to firm going: usually races close up. *Mark Johnston*

SHADOW HUNTER (IRE) 2 b.f. (Mar 20) Arcano (IRE) 122 – Sweet Irish (Shamardal **94**
(USA) 129) [2015 6m³ 5.2s⁴ 5g* 5m 6g 5g³ Oct 9] €5,000F, €38,000 2-y-o: lengthy filly:
second foal: dam, Danish 1m winner, half-sister to 1000 Guineas third Super Sleuth: useful
performer: won listed race at York (33/1, by neck from Rouleau) in August: creditable 3¾
lengths third of 11 to Quiet Reflection in Cornwallis Stakes at Newmarket final start: may
prove best at 5f: best form on good going: tried in hood. *Paul D'Arcy*

SHADOW OF THE DAY 8 b.g. Sugarfoot 118 – She Who Dares Wins 56 (Atraf 116) **43**
[2015 –: 12g 6d Aug 17] poor maiden: best effort at 6f: acts on good to soft going: in
blinkers/tongue tie final start: often starts slowly. *Lee James*

SHADOW ROCK (IRE) 3 gr.g. Verglas (IRE) 118 – Ice Rock (IRE) (Rock of Gibraltar **81**
(IRE) 133) [2015 80: 9.9m² 10f⁴ 14d⁴ 11.8s⁵ 16.2d p14f p12g Dec 3] well-made gelding:
fairly useful handicapper: stays 1¼m: acts on good and good to firm going: sometimes in
blinkers in 2015: races prominently, lazy. *Richard Hannon*

SHADOWS OFTHENIGHT (IRE) 4 b.f. Fastnet Rock (AUS) 127 – Madaen (USA) **76**
(Nureyev (USA) 131) [2015 77: p12m⁴ t16.5f⁴ t16.5g⁴ 18s⁵ 16.2m* 16m⁵ 16d⁶ 16m⁴
16.5m⁵ p15.8f³ 17.2m⁴ 16d³ p16f⁶ 17.2g 15.8s⁶ Oct 27] rather leggy filly: fair handicapper:
won at Chepstow in May: stays 17f: acts on polytrack, tapeta, soft and good to firm going:
often races prominently. *Mick Channon*

SHADOW SPIRIT 2 b.f. (Apr 5) Makfi 130 – Highland Shot 91 (Selkirk (USA) 129) **73**
[2015 7v⁵ p7g 8.3g² Sep 30] seventh foal: half-sister to smart 1m/9f winner Highland
Knight (by Night Shift) and 1m winner Great Shot (by Marju): dam 7f-8.5f winner: fair
form: 33/1, much improved when head second to Stoney Broke in maiden at Nottingham
final start, though having run of race. *James Eustace*

SHADOWTIME 10 b.g. Singspiel (IRE) 133 – Massomah (USA) 90 (Seeking The Gold **65**
(USA)) [2015 90: 8m⁵ 7m⁵ 8g 7.5g⁴ 8.5d 8d Oct 5] smallish gelding: fair handicapper:
stays 8.5f: acts on firm and good to soft going. *Tracy Waggott*

SHADY MCCOY (USA) 5 b.g. English Channel (USA) 126 – Raw Gold (USA) 108 **95**
(Rahy (USA) 115) [2015 –: 6f* 6g* 6m³ 7s* 7g* 7m² Oct 2] sturdy gelding: useful
handicapper: won at Salisbury in May, Goodwood in June, Leicester in August and
Newmarket in September: further improvement when second at Ascot (nose behind
Cricklewood Green) final start: stays 7f: acts on firm and soft going: often starts slowly/
races towards rear. *Ian Williams*

SHAFAFYA 2 b.f. (Feb 26) Shamardal (USA) 129 – Tanaghum 104 (Darshaan 133) [2015 **76 p**
7g 8.3g⁴ p8g⁵ Nov 4] good-topped filly: half-sister to several winners, including very smart
1½m-1¾m winner Tactic (by Sadler's Wells) and smart French 11f/1½m winner Yaazy (by
Teofilo) and to dam of Mill Reef Stakes winner Ribchester: dam 1¼m winner who stayed
1½m: fair form in maidens: will stay at least 1¼m: remains with potential. *Ed Dunlop*

*William Hill Firth of Clyde Stakes, Ayr—a useful effort from all-the-way winner Shaden
(second right) who is a final winner at pattern level for both jockey Hayley Turner and trainer
Lady Cecil, who both retired at the end of the season; Only Mine is outbattled in second,
with Priceless (left) and Whatdoiwantthatfor (armlets) completing the frame*

SHAFT OF LIGHT 4 b.g. Exceed And Excel (AUS) 126 – Injaaz 99 (Sheikh Albadou **62** 128) [2015 67: t5.1m³ p6g f5g p6m 5d t5.1f 5.1d t5.1f Nov 13] strong gelding: modest handicapper: best effort at 5f: acts on tapeta: wears headgear: often starts slowly, often races towards rear. *Derek Shaw*

SHAGAH (IRE) 3 b.f. Invincible Spirit (IRE) 121 – Propaganda (IRE) 76 (Sadler's Wells **–** (USA) 132) [2015 100: p8g⁴ 8f Apr 29] strong filly: useful at 2 yrs: well held in minor events in 2015: stays 1m: acts on good to firm and heavy going: sent to France. *Richard Hannon*

SHAHBAR 2 b.g. (Mar 2) Champs Elysees 124 – Dahama 66 (Green Desert (USA) 127) **86** [2015 6m² 8.1g* 8g³ Aug 31] 160,000F, 320,000Y: good-bodied gelding: third foal: half-brother to useful 6f/7f winner (including at 2 yrs) Al Thakhira (by Dubawi): dam, maiden, closely related to smart French 7f winner Bezrin and half-sister to dam of smart Australian sprinter Shamal Wind: fairly useful form: won maiden at Sandown (by ½ length from Ride The Lightning) in August: in cheekpieces, creditable third to Turn Tide in nursery at Newcastle (went in snatches): stays 1m: has been gelded. *Marco Botti*

SHAHDAROBA (IRE) 5 b.g. Haatef (USA) 117 – Gold Script (FR) (Script Ohio (USA)) **86** [2015 92: 7g⁴ 8.3m* 8d 8.3m³ 8.3m⁶ 8g⁵ 8g⁴ 7s Oct 27] good-topped gelding: fairly useful handicapper: won at Nottingham in May: stays 8.5f: acts on any turf going: wears headgear: sold 7,000 gns, sent to Bahrain. *David O'Meara*

SHAHRAZAD (IRE) 6 b.m. Cape Cross (IRE) 129 – Khulasah (IRE) 78 (Darshaan 133) **62** [2015 67: 7.6g 6m 6d p8f⁵ p7g* Oct 7] leggy mare: modest handicapper: won at Kempton in October: stays 1½m: acts on polytrack and firm going: often in tongue tie prior to 2015: often leads. *Miss Joey Ellis*

SHAIYEM (IRE) 2 b.c. (Apr 12) Starspangledbanner (AUS) 128 – Shaanbar (IRE) 53 **78** (Darshaan 133) [2015 7.4d* p7g⁵ Sep 5] fair form: won maiden at Ffos Las in August by 1¼ lengths from Valitop: disappointing when last of 5 in minor event at Kempton only other start. *Richard Hannon*

SHAKA ZULU (IRE) 2 b.g. (Mar 14) Holy Roman Emperor (IRE) 125 – High Figurine **91** (IRE) 88 (High Chaparral (IRE) 132) [2015 6m³ p5g⁴ 5m² 6d* Sep 15] first foal: dam, 11f-1½m winner, half-sister to smart sprinter Fyodor: fairly useful form: blinkered, improved when winning maiden at Catterick final start by 3 lengths from Geno, making all: stays 6f: in cheekpieces third start: sold 15,000 gns, sent to Qatar. *William Haggas*

SHAKERATTLENROLL (IRE) 2 b.c. (May 6) Intikhab (USA) 135 – Carolxaar (IRE) **86** (Xaar 132) [2015 6d³ t7.1g⁶ 6g* 6g⁶ 6g⁴ p7g* Nov 4] €14,000Y, 18,000 2-y-o: second foal: dam unraced half-sister to smart 1m-1¼m performer Ferneley: fairly useful performer: won maiden at Windsor in July and nursery at Kempton (by 3¾ lengths from Mansfield) in November: stays 7f: acts on polytrack and good to soft going. *Paul Cole*

SHAKOPEE 3 b.g. High Chaparral (IRE) 132 – Tentpole (USA) 85 (Rainbow Quest **90 p** (USA) 134) [2015 86p: 10g² Apr 16] fairly useful form: shaped well when head second to Dissolution in handicap at Newmarket only outing in 2015, getting to front before winner pounced: subsequently gelded: will stay 1½m: will go on improving. *Luca Cumani*

SHALAA (IRE) 2 b.c. (Feb 23) Invincible Spirit (IRE) 121 – Ghurra (USA) 91 (War **123 p** Chant (USA) 126) [2015 6m 6m* 6m* 6m* 6d* 6g* Sep 26]
      Clarehaven isn't a yard renowned for producing top two-year-olds and, when it does so, it is rarely the end of the story. Oasis Dream and Raven's Pass were the last two John Gosden-trained performers before Shalaa to feature in the top three two-year-olds of their year—the exciting Kingman ended his juvenile season with a rating of 112P—and both did even better at three, winning two Group 1s each, respectively the July Cup and the Nunthorpe Stakes and the Queen Elizabeth II Stakes and Breeders' Cup Classic. Gosden also trained the 119p-rated two-year-old filly Rainbow View who went on to win the Group 1 Matron Stakes at three. Shalaa had an outstanding two-year-old campaign, winning four pattern races including the Prix Morny, in which he recorded the best performance by a two-year-old over six furlongs in Europe, and the Middle Park Stakes. He was his trainer's second Middle Park winner, following the 2002 victory of Oasis Dream, with whom John Gosden compares Shalaa who looks set to be kept to sprinting as a three-year-old. Tall and attractive and under the care of a master trainer, Shalaa is just the type to train on well, with the Commonwealth Cup at Royal Ascot (for which he is 4/1 favourite at the time of writing) likely to be his first major target. Beyond that, he looks champion sprinter material and could well emulate Oasis Dream in that regard.

Darley Prix Morny, Deauville—three of the five runners are trained in Britain and the spoils duly go across the Channel for the fifth time in seven years as Shalaa wins readily from Gutaifan; Tourny (left) proves the better of the two French-trained runners in a well-held third

Shalaa was well backed on his debut in a valuable minor event at Newbury in mid-May, which carried the name of his owner Al Shaqab Racing's stallion Olympic Glory and also featured the Al Shaqab-owned Eltezam. Shalaa was slowly into his stride and then failed to settle fully before coming home last of eight to Birchwood (Eltezam finished third). Shalaa was a totally different proposition on his next start two weeks later, clearly having learned plenty from his first racecourse experience, and he won an eleven-runner maiden at Newmarket, beating Fang by two lengths. Shalaa still carried his owner's second colours in the Arqana July Stakes back at Newmarket, with Al Shaqab's retained rider Frankie Dettori (who had ridden Shalaa on both his starts) choosing Eltezam who had won a Haydock maiden and finished third in the Coventry Stakes at Royal Ascot (under Dettori) since Newbury. Shalaa had bypassed Royal Ascot because of 'a nervous nature last time at Newmarket,' according to Gosden. The trainer added 'I've brought him down here a few times to school and he's learning.' The Robert Havlin-ridden Shalaa started at 14/1 for the July Stakes, with only one of his eight rivals at longer odds (Eltezam was one of three co-favourites at 9/2). The July Stakes seems a race that is regaining some of its former importance—Muhaarar finished third to Ivawood in 2014—and the latest field included several who had done well at Royal Ascot (including Areen and Steady Pace, second and third in the Windsor Castle, who were the other co-favourites). Not all the runners from Royal Ascot repeated their form three weeks on, however, and it paid to side with the upgraded maiden winners in the line-up, with Shalaa and the third Elronaq coming into that category. The four lowest drawn—including Shalaa—raced slightly apart from the others, with Shalaa disputing the lead overall with Elronaq and Eltezam (who came fourth) in the larger group. The field went a good gallop and Shalaa established himself as just about the top juvenile colt around as he beat Steady Pace by a length, being the last to come off the bridle before being shaken up to take command approaching the final furlong. The only sign of immaturity came when Shalaa veered left a hundred yards out, but he was still well in control at the line.

Shalaa enhanced his claims to be one of the season's top juveniles when he followed up in the eight-runner Qatar Richmond Stakes at Goodwood in late-July, a race that had its prize money raised significantly in 2015. Starting 11/8 favourite, Shalaa faced some of those he had beaten in the July Stakes—Steady Pace was second favourite at 4/1, whilst Elronaq was also in the field—and he was even more impressive, under a 3-lb penalty too. Shalaa always had things well under control, even when Steady Pace headed him at around halfway, and only the Newbury listed winner Tasleet emerged as any sort of threat out of the pack, Shalaa eventually having two and three quarter lengths to spare, with Steady Pace in third. Shalaa was clearly getting better all the time, and looking more the finished article, and it was after the Richmond that John Gosden first said that Shalaa reminded him a lot of Oasis Dream, adding at that stage that Shalaa would be kept to sprinting, both in the short and the long term.

Juddmonte Middle Park Stakes, Newmarket—Shalaa (second right) confirms his status as the top sprinting two-year-old of 2015 with a victory over Buratino (right) in a race moved back to its traditional position in the calendar; Steady Pace (white cap) finishes third ahead of Ajaya (left)

The Darley Prix Morny at Deauville in late-August was the next target and it also featured the winners of the Prix Robert Papin (Gutaifan) and the Prix de Cabourg (Tourny). Shalaa and Gutaifan, the latter representing the same owner as Shalaa but a different trainer in Richard Hannon, were among three runners from Britain in the five-runner field (the other was rank outsider Zebstar). Victory went to a British-trained runner for the fifth time in seven years as Shalaa won by a length and three quarters from Gutaifan, who finished five lengths clear of the third Tourny. Shalaa confirmed himself the top two-year-old in Europe with another very smart performance, quickening past the leader Gutaifan over a furlong out and just pushed out to win readily. It was a second successive Prix Morny win for Al Shaqab Racing and Frankie Dettori, following The Wow Signal, while Shalaa registered John Gosden's first win in the race. With one Group 1 in the bag, it was on to Newmarket for the Juddmonte Middle Park Stakes at Newmarket in late-September, with Shalaa taken on by the Coventry winner Buratino and the Gimcrack winner Ajaya. Shalaa started at 2/1-on, with Ajaya at 6/1, Buratino at 13/2 and the four others (which included Steady Pace) at 12/1 or longer. Shalaa was soon sent to the front by Dettori and he stayed there all the way, quickening after being ridden over a furlong out and going a length clear before edging left and having to work in the end to hold off Buratino by half a length. Shalaa was by no means all out in the finish, eased in the final strides and also winning with a bit in hand. With Steady Pace third and Ajaya fourth, the form was better than for most recent editions of the Middle Park, only Dream Ahead (2010) and Dutch Art (2006) putting up better winning performances in the ten previous years. For Shalaa, it was his third very smart performance in a row and there was no doubt that he deserved to be regarded as the best two-year-old colt seen all season up to that point, though his form was bettered by Air Force Blue's pulsating performance in the Dewhurst a fortnight later.

Like Gutaifan, Shalaa is out of a Shadwell-bred mare, and Shalaa became his family's second Middle Park winner after Hayil who won a much more modest edition of the race in 1997. By Sheikh Hamdan's brilliant sprinter but disappointing

sire Dayjur, Hayil was one of nine winners out of Shalaa's grandam Futuh who had been a $200,000 yearling purchase by Shadwell. Futuh failed to add to her success in a Redcar maiden (when she broke the six-furlong juvenile track record), but as a broodmare no fewer than seven of her own offspring earned 'black type'. Shalaa's dam Ghurra—a close relative to Hayil, she too being by a son of Danzig in War Front—won over six furlongs as a two-year-old (on her debut at Yarmouth) but failed to win again for her original owner. Sold for 90,000 guineas at the end of her three-year-old season, she was, however, successful twice more at around a mile in the States where she also finished third in a Grade 3 contest. Shalaa, who fetched 100,000 guineas as a foal and 170,000 guineas as a yearling, is his dam's fifth foal and second winner on the Flat after the useful winner up to a mile and a half Pearl Castle. By Montjeu, Pearl Castle is also a useful hurdler, a sphere in which his brother Dai Bando has also been successful, though Shalaa, by Invincible Spirit, will surely prove best at sprint trips. Indeed, his pedigree unusually features speed influence Danzig twice among his great grandsires, while his other two great grandsires are the full brothers Kris and Diesis, the latter also a Middle Park winner. Shalaa races prominently, and he acts on good to firm and good to soft going. *John Gosden*

SHALABINA 3 b.f. Nayef (USA) 129 – Shibina (IRE) 95 (Kalanisi (IRE) 132) [2015 76p: 10.2m* 12m 10.4g 12g⁶ 12f³ 16.2m⁴ 13.1g p13.3f Nov 19] fair performer: won maiden at Nottingham in April: stays 1½m: acts on good to firm going: often races prominently. *Richard Fahey*

SHALAMAN (IRE) 6 b.g. Oratorio (IRE) 128 – Shalama (IRE) 91 (Kahyasi 130) [2015 **107** 96: p10.7g* p10.7g* p10f⁴ p10f⁴ 12g 10m³ 10d.6g⁶ Aug 16] useful performer: won handicap at Dundalk (by neck from Whipper's Boy) in February and minor event there (by head from Parish Hall) in March: good third in handicap at Navan (head behind I'll Be Your Clown) in July: stays 1½m: acts on polytrack and good to firm going: sometimes wears cheekpieces: usually wears tongue tie: usually races in rear. *Matthew J. Smith, Ireland*

SHALAMBAR (IRE) 9 gr.g. Dalakhani (IRE) 133 – Shalama (IRE) 91 (Kahyasi 130) **74** [2015 74: p12g* p15.8f² 12d p10g⁶ Nov 25] tall, lengthy gelding: fair handicapper: won at Kempton in January: stays 2m: acts on polytrack and good to soft going: usually wears headgear. *Tony Carroll*

SHALAMZAR (FR) 6 ch.g. Selkirk (USA) 129 – Shamalana (IRE) (Sinndar (IRE) 134) **83** [2015 93: 9v⁵ 8g 8.3g² p10.7g 10d 9s⁵ p14f⁶ t9.5f Dec 14] fairly useful handicapper: left A. J. Martin after sixth start: stays 9f: acts on good to firm going: tried in cheekpieces/tongue tie in 2015: often races towards rear. *Heather Dalton*

SHALIANZI (IRE) 5 b.g. Azamour (IRE) 130 – Shalama (IRE) 91 (Kahyasi 130) [2015 **–** 11.6g⁵ Jul 27] fair performer: well held only outing in 2015: stays 15f: acts on polytrack, best turf form on good going: in blinkers last 4 starts. *Gary Moore*

SHALIMAR (IRE) 3 br.g. Dark Angel (IRE) 113 – Jemima's Art 61 (Fantastic Light **74** (USA) 134) [2015 80: 10d 11.7m⁵ 12m⁴ 10.2f³ 11.6g⁴ Sep 7] smallish gelding: fair handicapper: stays 1½m: acts on firm going: in visor last 2 starts. *Clive Cox*

SHALL WE (IRE) 2 b.f. (May 2) Dansili 127 – Insight (FR) 115 (Sadler's Wells (USA) **73 p** 132) [2015 p8f² Nov 12] closely related to useful 1¼m-14.6f winner Stomachion (by Duke of Marmalade) and half-sister to 3 winners, including smart French/US winner up to 9f Ershaad (2-y-o 6.5f winner, by Kingmambo): dam, winner up to 1¼m (2-y-o 9f winner) including Prix de l'Opera and E. P. Taylor Stakes, sister to Irish 2000 Guineas winner Saffron Walden: 5/1, better for run when 2½ lengths second of 10 to Khaleesy in maiden at Chelmsford on debut: likely to stay 1¼m: sure to progress. *Sir Michael Stoute*

SHAMAHAN 6 b.g. Shamardal (USA) 129 – Hanella (IRE) 91 (Galileo (IRE) 134) [2015 **73** 79: p6f³ p6g p5m³ p6f p6g5⁵ p6f³ 6g² 6g 6m 6m⁴ p7g 5.7g t6f Nov 13] good-topped gelding: fair handicapper: left Luke Dace after tenth start: stays 7f: acts on polytrack and firm going: sometimes in hood in 2015. *Richard Hughes*

SHAMAHEART (IRE) 5 b.g. Shamardal (USA) 129 – Encouragement 76 (Royal **79** Applause 124) [2015 81: 7m³ 7g⁴ 7.5g² 8.5m³ 7m 8.5m⁴ 8m 7.5s 7.9m* 8m³ 7.5d³ 8g⁴ 8d⁴ Oct 30] compact gelding: fair handicapper: won at Carlisle in August: stays 1½m: acts on good to firm and good to soft going: usually wears headgear: sometimes slowly away, often races towards rear. *Geoffrey Harker*

SHAMALAD 5 b.g. Shamardal (USA) 129 – Steam Cuisine 104 (Mark of Esteem (IRE) **64** 137) [2015 p11f⁵ Jan 21] close-coupled gelding: modest form in 2 maidens: dead. *Lydia Pearce*

SHAMAL WIND (AUS) 6 b.m. Dubawi (IRE) 129 – Firemaid (USA) (Machiavellian **118** (USA) 123) [2015 5g* 5.5g* 5fJun 16] strong mare: first foal: dam, Australian 5f-7f winner, half-sister to smart French 7f winner Bezrin: smart performer: won listed race at Sandown (Australia) in January and Group 1 Oakleigh Plate (Handicap) at Caulfield (by ¾ length from Under The Louvre, strong run to lead final 50 yds) in February: well below form in King's Stand Stakes at Royal Ascot final outing: stayed 6f: acted on soft going: wore tongue tie: visited Sea The Stars to southern hemisphere time. *Robert Smerdon, Australia*

SHAMIANA 5 b.m. Manduro (GER) 135 – Camp Riverside (Forest Camp (USA) **43** 114) [2015 58: f8s⁴ f7g⁶ Mar 3] poor maiden: stays 9.5f: acts on all-weather: often in headgear/tried in tongue tie prior to 2015: sometimes slowly away. *Daniel Kubler*

SHAMKHANI 3 b.g. Mullionmileanhour (IRE) 116 – Matilda Peace (Namaqualand **–** (USA)) [2015 32: 5m 5g² 5m 5g⁶ Sep 4] little impact in maidens/handicaps. *Alan Berry*

SHAMLAN (IRE) 3 br.g. Shamardal (USA) 129 – Atamana (IRE) 82 (Lahib (USA) 129) **79** [2015 8m⁴ 7g* t7.1f² t8.6g t7.1f⁴ Dec 21] fair performer: won maiden at Catterick in September: left Roger Varian after third start: stays 7f: acts on tapeta. *Kevin Frost*

SHAMROCK SHEILA (IRE) 3 ch.f. Fast Company (IRE) 126 – Green Vision (IRE) **76** (Green Desert (USA) 127) [2015 72, a66: t5.1g 5f* 5g³ 5.3m² 5m⁴ 5m 5m⁴ 5d³ Aug 28] light-framed filly: fair handicapper: won at Bath in June: stays 6f: acts on polytrack and firm going: usually in hood prior to 2015. *J. S. Moore*

SHANGHAI GLORY (IRE) 2 ch.g. (Mar 7) Exceed And Excel (AUS) 126 – Hecuba **80** 93 (Hector Protector (USA) 124) [2015 5g³ 6.1d* 5f 6m⁶ p7m Oct 21] €115,000Y: lengthy, good-quartered gelding: closely related to useful winner up to 1m Aeronwyn Bryn (2-y-o

7f winner, by Dylan Thomas) and half-brother to 3 winners, including winner up to 1¼m Choose Me (2-y-o 6f/7f winner, by Choisir) and 1¼m/10.5f winner Spirit of Cuba (by Invincible Spirit), both useful: dam 1¼m winner: fairly useful performer: won maiden at Nottingham in May: stays 6f: acts on good to soft going. *Charles Hills*

SHANGHAI SUNRISE 4 b.f. Royal Applause 124 – Duchcov 101 (Caerleon (USA) 132) [2015 –: t12.2f Jan 5] workmanlike filly: no form: has worn headgear. *Keiran Burke* — **–**

SHANTI 5 b.g. Dansili 127 – Maycocks Bay 100 (Muhtarram (USA) 125) [2015 –: p10g p8g² Dec 9] fair maiden: stays 1¼m: acts on polytrack: has sometimes looked temperamental. *Dean Ivory* — **66**

SHARAAKAH (IRE) 2 b.f. (Feb 24) Roderic O'Connor (IRE) 119 – Lanark Belle (Selkirk (USA) 129) [2015 7g⁴ 7m* 7m² 6.5m² 7g Oct 9] €22,000Y: useful-looking filly: fifth foal: half-sister to 3 winners, including 2-y-o 7f winner Diamond Geezah (by Diamond Green), later 6f-8.5f winner in USA, and 6f winner Aledaid (by Acclamation): dam, ran 3 times, half-sister to smart winner up to 1¼m Adiemus: fairly useful performer: won maiden at Newmarket (by ½ length from Puzzled Look) in July: good second in nursery at Doncaster (length behind Nemoralia) penultimate start: stays 7f: acts on good to firm going: often travels strongly. *Ed Dunlop* — **93**

SHARARA 2 ch.g. (Mar 29) Dutch Art 126 – Tafawut 80 (Nayef (USA) 129) [2015 6g⁶ 6g t6g³ 5d³ 7m⁶ Sep 11] lengthy gelding: fair maiden: best effort at 6f on tapeta: often in blinkers: sold 10,000 gns, sent to Italy. *Brian Meehan* — **70**

SHARED BELIEF (USA) 4 b.g. Candy Ride (ARG) 133 – Common Hope (USA) (Storm Cat (USA)) [2015 130: a9f* a10f* a9fᵖᵘ Apr 18] top-class performer: won 10 of his 12 starts, including Grade 2 San Antonio Invitational (beat California Chrome 1½ lengths) in February and Santa Anita Handicap (beat Moreno easily by 4¼ lengths, leading on home turn and going clear without being asked a serious question) in March: odds on, pulled up in back straight in Grade 2 Charles Town Classic won by Moreno at Charles Town final outing (reportedly suffered fractured pelvis): was effective at 7f to 1¼m: acted on dirt/synthetics: died of colic in December. *Jerry Hollendorfer, USA* — **132**

SHARED EQUITY 4 b.g. Elnadim (USA) 128 – Pelican Key (IRE) 80 (Mujadil (USA) 119) [2015 100: 6d³ 7d³ 6d³ 6s³ 7g⁴ 7s³ 6g 6s* 6v Nov 7] lengthy gelding: smart handicapper: easily best effort when winning 19-runner Coral Sprint Trophy at York in October by 3 lengths from Go Far: stays 7f: acts on soft and good to firm going: usually races prominently, often travels strongly. *Jedd O'Keeffe* — **114**

SHARENI (IRE) 6 b.g. Azamour (IRE) 130 – Sharesha (IRE) 93 (Ashkalani (IRE) 128) [2015 t16.5g⁶ f16g⁵ Apr 9] fairly useful maiden on Flat for A. de Royer Dupre, placed in minor events all 3 starts in 2012: left David Rees, tailed off last 2 starts: best effort at 8.5f. *Zoe Davison* — **–**

SHARISSIMA 3 ch.f. Shamardal (USA) 129 – Purissima (USA) 88 (Fusaichi Pegasus (USA) 130) [2015 65p: 7g t1.1g⁵ 7.5d 8g⁵ 7s⁵ 5.5v⁵ 7s² Nov 29] fair maiden: left Lady Cecil after second start: stays 7f: acts on soft going: has worn hood. *H-A. Pantall, France* — **69**

Coral Sprint Trophy, York—a smart effort from clear-cut winner Shared Equity, who lands a gamble in this valuable autumn prize; the places are filled by Go Far (right), Nameitwhatyoulike (left) and Tatlisu (partly hidden by winner)

SHARJA QUEEN 2 b.f. (Feb 6) Pivotal 124 – Dubai Queen (USA) 103 (Kingmambo **77 p** (USA) 125) [2015 6m² 7.4v* Aug 19] first foal: dam, 1m winner, half-sister to high-class miler Dubawi out of Oaks d'Italia winner Zomaradah: upped in trip, 1/4, won 5-runner maiden at Ffos Las in August comfortably by 3¼ lengths from Lightsome: will be suited by 1m: will go on improving. *Luca Cumani*

SHARP JACK 2 ch.c. (Mar 20) Pivotal 124 – Sharp Terms (Kris 135) [2015 t6m Dec 18] **– p** 50,000Y: half-brother to several winners, including smart 2-y-o 5f/6f (including Queen Mary/Lowther Stakes) winner Best Terms and 5f/6f winner Miracle Garden (both by Exceed And Excel): dam unraced half-sister to smart performer up to 2m First Charter: 3/1, very green but hinted at ability when seventh of 9 to Tesoro in maiden at Wolverhampton on debut: should do better. *Tom Dascombe*

SHARP RISE (IRE) 8 b.g. Croco Rouge (IRE) 126 – Missusan (IRE) (King's Ride 88) **64** [2015 12s⁶ Oct 19] 13/2, 10¼ lengths sixth of 15 to Blue Sea of Ibrox in maiden at Pontefract: fairly useful hurdler/chaser. *Pauline Robson*

SHARP SAILOR (USA) 3 b.c. Henrythenavigator (USA) 131 – Lady Ilsley (USA) **106** (Trempolino (USA) 135) [2015 94: p8m³ 10.1g³ 10.3f⁶ 10f³ 10m* Aug 8] well-made colt: useful performer: won handicap at Newmarket in August by neck from Solo Hunter: good third of 4 to Tha'ir in listed event at Sandown previous start: stays 10.5f: acts on polytrack and firm going: sent to Hong Kong. *Marco Botti*

SHARP SWORD (IRE) 4 ch.g. King's Best (USA) 132 – Pictavia (IRE) 115 (Sinndar **76** (IRE) 134) [2015 t12.2g* t13.9m⁶ p11f⁴ 8m 10m Jun 8] fair performer: won maiden at Wolverhampton in February: stays 1½m: acts on polytrack and tapeta: in hood last 3 starts: sometimes slowly away, often races in rear, races freely. *Neil Mulholland*

SHARQEYIH 3 br.f. Shamardal (USA) 129 – Shabiba (USA) 103 (Seeking The Gold **88** (USA)) [2015 81p: 8g³ 9.3m³ 7.5m* 8m² 8m² Jul 23] fairly useful performer: won maiden at Beverley in June: in cheekpieces, second in handicaps at Doncaster and Newbury last 2 starts: stays 1m: acts on good to firm going. *William Haggas*

SHASAG (IRE) 3 b.f. Arcano (IRE) 122 – Popolo (IRE) 66 (Fasliyev (USA) 120) [2015 **89** –p: p8m⁴ t8.6g* 10.3m² 8f⁵ 9.9g² 9.9s* 10.4d Sep 26] leggy filly: fairly useful performer: won maiden at Wolverhampton in January and handicap at Brighton in August: stays 1¼m: acts on tapeta and soft going: often in hood in 2015: sold 35,000 gns, sent to Saudi Arabia. *Roger Varian*

SHAUNAS SPIRIT (IRE) 7 b.m. Antonius Pius (USA) 123 – Shaunas Vision (IRE) 88 **62** (Dolphin Street (FR) 125) [2015 75: p7g p7m p8f p7f³ p7f p7f⁵ p6g³ 6m p7g May 20] rather leggy mare: modest handicapper: stays 1m, effective at shorter: acts on polytrack and heavy going: usually wears headgear: front runner/races prominently, tends to find little. *Dean Ivory*

SHAVAUGHN 3 b.f. Kheleyf (USA) 116 – Shannon Falls (FR) 55 (Turgeon (USA) 123) **55** [2015 p8m⁶ p10f⁵ p12f⁶ p11g Apr 8] first foal: dam, maiden on Flat, winning hurdler/ chaser in France: modest maiden: best effort at 1¼m. *Jo Crowley*

SHAWAAHID (IRE) 2 b.c. (Apr 20) Elnadim (USA) 128 – Vexatious (IRE) (Shamardal **89** (USA) 129) [2015 5.1g* 6m² 7d⁴ 6g⁵ 8g⁴ Sep 19] 42,000F, 100,000Y: first foal: dam unraced half-sister to smart 1m-1¼m winner Mango Diva out of smart winner up to 10.3f Mango Mischief: fairly useful performer: won maiden at Nottingham in June and nursery at Newmarket in July: should stay 1m: acts on good to firm and good to soft going. *Richard Hannon*

SHAWKANTANGO 8 b.g. Piccolo 121 – Kitty Kitty Cancan 73 (Warrshan (USA) 117) **67** [2015 78: f5g² t5.1g f5d⁵ f5g⁴ t5.1g 5g⁴ 5g⁶ 5g 5.1d f5m⁵ f5g* Dec 12] big, workmanlike gelding: fair handicapper: won at Southwell in December: stays 6f: acts on all-weather and heavy going: wears headgear: usually races nearer last than first. *Derek Shaw*

SHAW TING 3 b.f. Winker Watson 118 – Shawhill 93 (Dr Fong (USA) 128) [2015 74: **74** 9m⁵ 10.3d² 12f⁴ p12g⁶ 10v⁶ t9.5f t12.2f⁴ Dec 14] sturdy filly: fair maiden: stays 10.5f: acts on tapeta and good to soft going: sometimes in cheekpieces in 2015: front runner/races prominently. *Tom Dascombe*

SHEARIAN 5 b.g. Royal Applause 124 – Regal Asset (USA) (Regal Classic (CAN)) **71** [2015 66: f7g* f7g³ 7d² 8d² 8g⁵ f7d⁴ 7g² 8m² 7g 8g² 8g Sep 23] strong gelding: fair **a65** handicapper: won at Southwell in March: stays 1¼m: acts on polytrack, fibresand, good to firm and good to soft going: usually in cheekpieces: usually races prominently. *Tracy Waggott*

SHEDED (IRE) 2 b.c. (Mar 6) Rip Van Winkle (IRE) 134 – Amhooj 77 (Green Desert **71** (USA) 127) [2015 8.3d p8m⁴ p8f Nov 25] fair form: fourth of 8 to Bluebeard at Kempton, best effort. *Richard Hannon*

SHEER HONESTY 3 b.f. Hellvelyn 118 – Honesty Pays (Dr Fong (USA) 128) [2015 p8f **79** 8.3g⁴ 8d² 8v* 8.3d Oct 12] £10,000Y: third foal: closely related to winner up to 7f Ishi Honest (2-y-o 5f winner, by Ishiguru): dam unraced: fair performer: won maiden at Ffos Las in August: stays 1m: acts on heavy going. *Andrew Balding*

SHEIKH THE REINS (IRE) 6 b.g. Iffraaj 127 – Wychwood Wanderer (IRE) 88 **65** (Barathea (IRE) 127) [2015 76: p7g p7m a6.5g² a8g⁵ a6.5g⁶ p7g⁵ p7f⁵ p7g⁴ 7.6g p8g⁴ p10g⁴ Aug 15] strong, close-coupled gelding: fair handicapper: stays 1¼m: acts on polytrack, snow and good to firm going: sometimes wears headgear: tried in tongue tie in 2015: often races towards rear. *John Best*

SHEIKHZAYEDROAD 6 b.g. Dubawi (IRE) 129 – Royal Secrets (IRE) 78 (Highest **116** Honor (FR) 124) [2015 118: 12g² 12g⁵ 12m⁴ 12f⁴ 12m 16m⁶ 12.3s³ 12g³ Oct 18] leggy gelding: smart performer: ran creditably at Meydan first 2 starts, and back to form when 2½ lengths third to Cannock Chase in Canadian International at Woodbine final outing: seems to stay 2m: acts on any turf going: wears hood: held up: suited by strong pace: not straightforward. *David Simcock*

SHEILA'S BUDDY 6 ch.g. Reel Buddy (USA) 118 – Loreto Rose 76 (Lahib (USA) 129) **90** [2015 88: p10g⁴ t9.5f⁶ 10s⁴ 9g t9.5g* p10m² Dec 16] workmanlike gelding: fairly useful handicapper: won at Wolverhampton in November: stays 1¼m: acts on polytrack, tapeta, soft and good to firm going: tried in hood: often races towards rear. *J. S. Moore*

SHEILA'S HEART 5 ch.g. Dubai Destination (USA) 127 – Sefemm (Alhaarth (IRE) **–** 126) [2015 69: t12.2f p16f Sep 10] fair maiden: well held in 2015, left John E. Long after first start: stays 1¾m: acts on fibresand and tapeta: tried in cheekpieces. *Julia Feilden*

SHEILA'S STEPS (IRE) 3 b.g. Excellent Art 125 – Positive Step (IRE) 74 **–** (Footstepsinthesand 120) [2015 t8.6g 10m p12g⁴ p13.3f Sep 24] big gelding: no form: tried in cheekpieces. *J. S. Moore*

SHEILA'S TREAT (IRE) 2 b.g. (Feb 22) Frozen Power (IRE) 108 – Bonny Rose 79 **74** (Zaha (CAN) 106) [2015 6m 7g⁶ p7g t8.6f* p8g* Dec 2] fair performer: won nurseries at Wolverhampton in October and Kempton in December: stays 8.5f: acts on polytrack and tapeta. *Denis Coakley*

SHE IS NO LADY 3 b.f. Lope de Vega (IRE) 125 – Capestar (IRE) 78 (Cape Cross (IRE) **93** 129) [2015 79: 9.9s³ 12d² 11.5s* 12m* 12g⁶ 12g⁵ Oct 9] sturdy filly: fairly useful performer: won maiden at Carlisle in July and handicap at Newmarket in August: stays 1½m: acts on good to firm going: sometimes slowly away. *Ralph Beckett*

SHELL BAY (USA) 3 b.g. Hard Spun (USA) 124 – Rebel Account (USA) (Dixieland **94** Band (USA)) [2015 74p: 7g⁶ p7g⁴ 7m⁵ 8m* 10m² 11m³ 12m* 12g* 12g p11g³ 10m* 12d Oct 11] good-topped gelding: fairly useful handicapper: won at Newbury in June, Ascot and Salisbury in August and Newmarket (by 1½ lengths from Maybelater) in October: stays 1½m: acts on polytrack and good to firm going: often races towards rear. *Richard Hannon*

SHE LOVES YOU 4 b.f. Lawman (FR) 121 – On Fair Stage (IRE) 103 (Sadler's Wells **82** (USA) 132) [2015 11.7d² 9.4g² 8.9g* t9.5f p8g⁶ Dec 16] half-sister to several winners, including high-class French/Australian 1¼m-1½m winner Reliable Man (by Dalakhani) and very smart winner (including in Australia) up to 10.4f I'm Imposing (2-y-o 1m winner, by Danehill Dancer): dam 1m-1½m winner: fairly useful performer: won minor event at Le Croise-Laroche in May: left A. de Royer Dupre after: stays 9f: acts on good to soft going: in cheekpieces third/fourth starts. *Roger Charlton*

SHEMAY 3 b.f. Shirocco (GER) 129 – Shemanikha (FR) (Sendawar (IRE) 129) [2015 **54** t8.6g⁴ t9.5f⁴ t8.6g 8s 10s 9.8g 8.5g 15.8s Oct 6] 15,500 2-y-o: third foal: half-sister to winner up to 9.5f Berlusca (2-y-o 6f winner, by Holy Roman Emperor): dam unraced half-sister to smart French 1¼m-15f winner Shemima out of Prix de Diane winner Shemaka: modest maiden: stays 1¼m: acts on tapeta and soft going: tried in hood. *Tom Tate*

SHEPHERD'S BUSH (USA) 2 ch.c. (Apr 28) Shamardal (USA) 129 – Infinite Spirit **61** (USA) 108 (Maria's Mon (USA) 121) [2015 6.1g 7m 6g⁵ 6s Oct 6] modest maiden: stays 7f. *Mark Johnston*

SHERIFF OF NAWTON (IRE) 4 b.g. Lawman (FR) 121 – Pivotal Role 66 (Pivotal **88** 124) [2015 79: t9.5g t8.6f⁵ t12.2f² t12.2g³ 10.3d* 10.1g² 12m* 12m 10.3g 12.1d 10.3m⁶ 10.4s t12.2f⁶ t16.5f³ Nov 30] fairly useful handicapper: won apprentice events at Doncaster in March and May: stays 16.5f: acts on tapeta, good to firm and heavy going. *David O'Meara*

SHERMAN MCCOY 9 ch.g. Reset (AUS) 124 – Naomi Wildman (USA) (Kingmambo **76** (USA) 125) [2015 77: 13.8d* 14.6m⁵ 12s 13.8d 12s Oct 6] lengthy gelding: fair handicapper: won at Catterick in April: stays 1¾m: acts on polytrack, fibresand and any turf going: tried in cheekpieces: races prominently. *Marjorie Fife*

SHERRY 4 b.f. Tobougg (IRE) 125 – Vino 73 (Efisio 120) [2015 12m⁴ 12m* 12.1m² **87** 12.4m³ 12m Aug 16] second foal: half-sister to 1½m winner Fly Solo (by Soviet Star): dam 7f winner: fairly useful performer: won maiden at Thirsk in May: stays 12.5f: acts on good to firm going. *Micky Hammond*

SHE'S ALL MINE 2 b.f. (Mar 17) Sakhee's Secret 128 – I'm All Yours (IRE) (High **65** Chaparral (IRE) 132) [2015 p6g⁵ 7d² 6m 6v⁴ 5.7m⁶ Sep 28] lengthy filly: first foal: dam, Italian 1¼m winner, half-sister to useful winner up to 10.4f Im Spartacus: fair maiden: will prove suited by a return to 6f: acts on good to soft going. *Richard Hannon*

SHE'S ELECTRIC (IRE) 2 b.f. (Apr 10) Roderic O'Connor (IRE) 119 – Maundays **71** Bay (IRE) 80 (Invincible Spirit (IRE) 121) [2015 5d⁶ 7.2m³ 7.9d⁴ 7.2g⁶ 6g* Oct 8] €10,500F, €45,000Y: first foal: dam 2-y-o 7f winner: fair performer: won nursery at Ayr in October: stays 7f: often races towards rear. *Keith Dalgleish*

SHE'S GOLDEN 2 gr.f. (Mar 12) Sakhee's Secret 128 – Actionplatinum (IRE) (Act One **61** 124) [2015 8.3g 7d⁵ 7s⁴ Oct 6] second foal: dam unraced: modest form in maidens last 2 starts. *Michael Appleby*

SHE'S GORGEOUS (IRE) 4 b.f. Acclamation 118 – Acquiesced (IRE) 85 (Refuse To **87** Bend (IRE) 128) [2015 77: p8g 10m³ p8g* t8.6g⁴ p8d 8d Oct 31] sturdy filly: fairly useful handicapper: won at Lingfield in June: barely stays 1¼m: acts on polytrack and heavy going: often wears visor: races prominently. *James Fanshawe*

SHE'S INVINCIBLE (IRE) 3 b.f. Invincible Spirit (IRE) 121 – White And Red (IRE) **59** 93 (Orpen (USA) 116) [2015 –: 5.8d⁵ 5.8g 5m 6m 5.1s⁴ 6d 8m⁴ t8.6m⁵ Sep 5] 200,000Y: first foal: dam, 6.5f winner, half-sister to useful German performer up to 1¾m Wild Passion: modest maiden: left John Patrick Murtagh after fourth start: stays 1m: acts on soft and good to firm going: front runner/races prominently. *Mark Johnston*

SHE'S LATE 5 ch.g. Pivotal 124 – Courting 108 (Pursuit of Love 124) [2015 16.2g 14m **–** Jun 12] strong gelding: useful handicapper in 2013: missed 2014 and well below form in 2015: stays 1½m: acts on good to firm and good to soft going: has worn headgear: fairly useful hurdler. *Jonjo O'Neill*

SHE'S MY PRINCESS (IRE) 2 b.f. (Mar 15) Kodiac 112 – Aguilas Perla (IRE) (Indian **– p** Ridge 123) [2015 p5g⁶ Aug 1] 57,000F, 100,000Y: closely related to 6f winner Hazelwood Ridge (by Mozart), later successful abroad, and 2-y-o 5f-6.5f winner Spirit of Pearl (by Invincible Spirit) and half-sister to several winners, including 1¼m-1½m winner Saint Thomas (by Alhaarth): dam unraced: 5/1, 7¾ lengths sixth of 8 to Cherry Kool in maiden at Lingfield: should do better in time. *Robert Cowell*

SHE'S NO BIMBO 3 ch.f. Recharge (IRE) 116 – Senorita Parkes 50 (Medicean 128) **57** [2015 p7g⁴ p7g⁶ p8f p8g t8.6g Dec 1] £2,200Y: second foal: dam, maiden (stayed 6f), half-sister to useful sprinter Doctor Parkes out of useful 5f performer Lucky Parkes: modest maiden: best effort at 7f: acts on polytrack. *Anthony Carson*

SHESNOTFORTURNING (IRE) 5 b.m. Refuse To Bend (IRE) 128 – Diplomats **57** Daughter 81 (Unfuwain (USA) 131) [2015 7d² 6g³ 6m² 6g* 7m⁴ 6g t6f Oct 23] modest performer: won maiden at Hamilton in July: stays 7f: acts on good to firm and good to soft going. *Ben Haslam*

SHEWEARSTHETROWZAS (IRE) 2 br.f. (Mar 18) Bushranger (IRE) 119 – Dubai **–** Princess (IRE) 105 (Dubai Destination (USA) 127) [2015 7.5g 6g 7s Oct 16] €10,000Y: fourth foal: half-sister to 3 winning sprinters, including 5f/6f winner Taquka (by Kodiac): dam, 5f/6f winner (including at 2 yrs), half-sister to smart 5f winner Swiss Lake, herself dam of smart sprinters Swiss Spirit and Swiss Diva: no form. *Nigel Tinkler*

SHIFTING MOON 3 b.f. Kheleyf (USA) 116 – Fleeting Moon 70 (Fleetwood (IRE) **73** 107) [2015 –: p11g⁶ p13.3m* p12g³ 12.1s⁴ p15.8g⁴ p14g* p16f* p13.3f* p16f⁴ Oct 8] good-bodied filly: fair handicapper: won at Chelmsford in June, August and September (twice): stays 2m: acts on polytrack: wears blinkers. *Hughie Morrison*

SHIFTING POWER 4 ch.c. Compton Place 125 – Profit Alert (IRE) 97 (Alzao (USA) **114** 117) [2015 118: 8.1d³ 8.3f* 8.5gᵖᵘ 8g 8g⁴ Sep 6] tall, quite attractive colt: smart performer: won listed race at Windsor in May by 1¾ lengths from Complicit: best other effort in 2015 when third in Mile at Sandown (3¼ lengths behind Custom Cut) on reappearance: reportedly lame when pulled up at Epsom (didn't handle track) third outing: stays 8.5f: acts on firm and soft going: usually races prominently: sold 72,000 gns. *Richard Hannon*

SHIFTING STAR (IRE) 10 ch.g. Night Shift (USA) – Ahshado 70 (Bin Ajwaad (IRE) 79
119) [2015 76, a69: p8g⁵ p8g⁴ p8m² p8f³ p7g⁶ 8.3m³ 8g* 8v³ 8.3m² 7.6d² 8d⁶ 8.3m³ 8.5v²
p8f² 8.3g* p8f p8m³ p8d Nov 30] strong, sturdy gelding: fair handicapper: won at Brighton
in April and Windsor in October: stays 8.5f: acts on polytrack and any turf going: wears
headgear/tongue tie: front runner/races prominently. *John Bridger*

SHIMBA HILLS 4 b.g. Sixties Icon 125 – Search Party 78 (Rainbow Quest (USA) 134) 82
[2015 p12g⁶ t12.2m² Dec 26] rather unfurnished gelding: fairly useful handicapper: stays
1½m: acts on polytrack and tapeta, best turf form on good going or softer. *Lawney Hill*

SHINE 2 ch.f. (May 16) Exceed And Excel (AUS) 126 – Sensational Mover (USA) 68 – p
(Theatrical) [2015 7g Sep 30] sister to useful 2-y-o 6f/6.5f winner Shamandar and half-
sister to 2 winners, including useful 2-y-o 7f winner Hung Parliament (by Numerous): dam
second at 1½m: 25/1, very green when well held in maiden at Salisbury, not knocked about:
should do better. *Ralph Beckett*

SHINE LIKEADIAMOND 2 ch.f. (Jan 17) Atlantic Sport (USA) 115 – Solmorin 70
(Fraam 114) [2015 5m p5g⁴ 5m³ 5s³ t5.1m² 5d² 5d² 5.4s² t5.1f² 5g² 6s p5m³ p5g² t5.1f⁴
Dec 21] well-grown filly: half-sister to several winners, including useful 5f (including at
2 yrs) winner Lucky Leigh and 5f and (including at 2 yrs) 6f winner Saxonette (both by
Piccolo): dam well held in bumper/maiden: fair maiden: stays 5.5f: acts on polytrack,
tapeta, soft and good to firm going: usually leads. *Mick Channon*

SHINGLE 4 b.g. Oasis Dream 129 – Orford Ness 107 (Selkirk (USA) 129) [2015 87: p7f⁶ 96
p7m² t6g* 6m 6m² 6.1m³ 6m Jul 2] sturdy gelding: useful handicapper: won at
Wolverhampton (by 4½ lengths from Vincentti) in April: stays 7f, at least as effective over
6f: acts on polytrack, tapeta and good to firm going: in cheekpieces final start: often races
prominently, usually travels strongly: sold 50,000 gns, sent to Qatar. *Ed de Giles*

SHINING EMERALD 4 gr.g. Clodovil (IRE) 116 – Janayen (USA) 97 (Zafonic (USA) 117
130) [2015 104: 6s* 6.5s* 7g² 6g* 7g Oct 9] well-made gelding: smart performer: trained
in Ireland at 2 and 3 yrs: won minor event at Bremen in April, Silberne Peitsche at Munich
(by 7 lengths from Amy Eria) in May and Goldene Peitsche at Baden-Baden (by head from
Son Cesio) in August: second in listed race at Munich (½ length behind Fly First) in July:
respectable 3 lengths seventh to Cable Bay in Challenge Stakes at Newmarket final outing,
not handling the Dip well (wandered): stays 7f: acts on soft going: tried in headgear prior
to 2015. *A. Wohler, Germany*

SHINING GLITTER (IRE) 4 b.f. Shamardal (USA) 129 – Lune Rose (High Chaparral 79
(IRE) 132) [2015 83: p10m² 13.1f⁴ t12.2g³ Jun 4] tall filly: has scope: fair handicapper:
stays 1½m: acts on polytrack and tapeta: sold 37,000 gns in July, sent to Saudi Arabia.
James Fanshawe

SHINOOK 3 ch.f. Teofilo (IRE) 126 – La Vida Loca (IRE) 102 (Caerleon (USA) 132) –
[2015 t9.5g p12g Aug 5] closely related to 1½m winner Brigh (by Galileo) and half-sister
to several winners, including 8.6f winner Fitzgerald (by Duke of Marmalade) and
9.5f-1½m winner El Mansour (by Rahy): dam, 2-y-o 5f winner, later 1m winner in USA:
well held in maidens at Wolverhampton (reportedly bled) and Kempton: sold £800.
David Simcock

SHIPSHAPE MYFOOT 2 b.f. (Mar 19) Bahamian Bounty 116 – Rise 84 (Polar Falcon 56
(USA) 126) [2015 p7g⁵ p7g Oct 14] sixth foal: sister to 2-y-o 6f winner Seemenomore and
half-sister to 2 winners by Green Desert, including 1m/8.6f winner Join Up: dam 6f and (at
2 yrs) 7f winner: little impact in 2 maidens at Kempton. *Andrew Reid*

SHIPWRIGHT (IRE) 3 b.g. Shamardal (USA) 129 – Shinko Hermes (IRE) (Sadler's 57
Wells (USA) 132) [2015 77: p8f⁴ t6f⁴ p8g⁴ p7g p8f⁶ 8g 7.5m Jun 23] modest maiden: stays
1m: acts on polytrack, tapeta, soft and good to firm going: tried in blinkers twice in 2015:
front runner/races prominently, weak finisher: sold 2,500 gns, sent to Italy. *Mark Johnston*

SHIPYARD (USA) 6 ch.g. Pivotal 124 – Nadia 116 (Nashwan (USA) 135) [2015 95: 6d⁵ 97
6s 5d 5.8m⁴ 5m² 6g³ 5g* 5m⁵ 6m² 6g* 5m* 6d⁶ p5f f5g⁵ Dec 12] useful handicapper: left
Andrew Oliver, won at Musselburgh in July, Ripon in August and Ascot (by neck from
Vimy Ridge) in October: stays 1m, raced only at 5f/6f in 2015: acts on soft and good to firm
going: tried in headgear/tongue tie. *Michael Appleby*

SHIRATAKI (IRE) 7 b.g. Cape Cross (IRE) 129 – Noodle Soup (USA) (Alphabet Soup 59
(USA) 126) [2015 65: p12g p12g p12g 11.9d t12.2f p12g⁴ p11g p12g p12m² Dec 16]
modest handicapper: stays 1½m: acts on polytrack, firm and good to soft going: tried in
hood/tongue tie prior to 2015: sometimes slowly away. *Peter Hiatt*

SHIRLS SON SAM 7 b.g. Rambling Bear 115 – Shirl 52 (Shirley Heights 130) [2015 53: **58**
f16g³ f14d⁴ t13.9g³ f14s⁴ 16m f14g⁶ 15.8d⁵ 16.1g² 15.8s⁶ t16.5f² Oct 30] modest maiden:
stays 17f: acts on fibresand, tapeta, soft and good to firm going: none too consistent.
Chris Fairhurst

SHIROCCO PASSION 4 b.f. Shirocco (GER) 129 – Pete's Passion (Rock of Gibraltar **67**
(IRE) 133) [2015 66: 10m⁴ 10g² 10d⁶ 9.9m⁵ Jul 14] fair handicapper: stays 1¼m: acts on
soft going: often starts slowly, often races towards rear. *Tony Coyle*

SHKHARA (IRE) 2 b.f. (Feb 20) Dubawi (IRE) 129 – Mount Elbrus 106 (Barathea (IRE) **–**
127) [2015 7g 8.3g Sep 8] sturdy, attractive filly: half-sister to several winners, including
2-y-o 7f/1m winner Strobilus (by Mark of Esteem), French 9.7f-11f winner Lava Flow (by
Dalakhani) and winner up to 1½m Hunterview (2-y-o 7.4f winner, by Reset), all useful:
dam 1¼m-13f winner: well held in maidens at Newmarket and Leicester. *Charlie Appleby*

SHOAL 3 b.f. Oasis Dream 129 – Midsummer 99 (Kingmambo (USA) 125) [2015 10m **81**
10.2m* 10g² sturdy filly: sister to 2 winners, notably high-class winner up to 1½m
Midday (2-y-o 1m winner), and half-sister to 2 winners, including smart 7f (Nell Gwyn
Stakes) and 1m (at 2 yrs) winner Hot Snap (by Pivotal): dam, 11f winner, half-sister to
Oaks winner Reams of Verse: fairly useful form: won maiden at Nottingham in July by
head from Rive Gauche: well held in listed race at York final start: should stay at least
1½m. *Sir Michael Stoute*

SHOGUN (IRE) 2 b.c. (Apr 28) Fastnet Rock (AUS) 127 – Perihelion (IRE) 105 (Galileo **112**
(IRE) 134) [2015 7m 7m* 7s³ 8m⁶ 8d Oct 30] €400,000Y: fourth foal: brother to Oaks
winner Qualify (2-y-o 7f winner) and closely related to 2 winners, including useful
1¼m-13f winner Satellite (by Danehill Dancer): dam 12.7f winner: smart performer: won
maiden at the Curragh in July: improved form when 1½ lengths sixth to Ultra in Prix Jean-
Luc Lagardere at Longchamp in October: only tenth of 14 behind stable-companion Hit It
A Bomb in Breeders' Cup Juvenile Turf at Keeneland final outing: will be suited by 1¼m+:
blinkered last 4 starts. *Aidan O'Brien, Ireland*

SHOOTINGSTA (IRE) 3 b.g. Fast Company (IRE) 126 – Kiva (Indian Ridge 123) **90**
[2015 78: 6m* 6g⁶ 7g³ 7m 7.2m* t7.1f² f7f² Dec 17] tall gelding: has scope: fairly useful
performer: won maiden at Redcar in May and handicap at Musselburgh in September:
good second in handicap at Southwell final start: stays 7f: acts on fibresand, tapeta and
good to firm going: in in cheekpieces last 3 starts. *Bryan Smart*

SHORE STEP (IRE) 5 br.g. Footstepsinthesand 120 – Chatham Islands (USA) 77 **100**
(Elusive Quality (USA)) [2015 99: 6f 6m 6m² 6m⁴ 5.4g⁶ 6.5m³ Sep 11] strong gelding:
useful handicapper: good efforts when in frame at York, Goodwood and Doncaster: stays
6.5f: acts on firm and soft going: front runner/races prominently: consistent. *Mick Channon*

SHORT DISTANCE (USA) 2 b.c. (Jan 30) Smart Strike (CAN) 121 – Ransomed Bride **73 p**
97 (Cape Cross (IRE) 129) [2015 p8g⁴ t8.6m⁵ Dec 30] $200,000Y: second foal: half-
brother to French 1½m winner Shotgun Wedding (by Champs Elysees): dam 1¼m/10.7f
winner: fourth of 12 to Towerlands Park in maiden at Kempton in December: disappointing
in similar event at Wolverhampton next time: remains capable of better. *Saeed bin Suroor*

SHORT SQUEEZE (IRE) 5 b.g. Cape Cross (IRE) 129 – Sunsetter (USA) 94 (Diesis **116**
133) [2015 118: 7g 8g² 8g 8.3m² 8d² 7g Aug 21] sturdy gelding: smart performer: second
in handicap at Meydan (neck behind Samurai Sword) in February: best subsequent effort
when ¾-length second to Kodi Bear in listed race at Windsor fourth start: stays 1m: acts on
good to firm and good to soft going: usually in headgear/tongue tie: usually races nearer
last than first. *Hugo Palmer*

SHORT WORK 2 ch.g. (Apr 23) Kyllachy 129 – Agony Aunt 81 (Formidable (USA) 125) **84**
[2015 6d³ 6.1d⁵ 6d⁴ 7s 7g² Oct 21] 21,000F, 26,000Y: rather unfurnished gelding: closely
related to 3 winners by Captain Rio, including winner up to 7f Captain Revelation (2-y-o
6f winner) and useful 7.6f/1m winner (including at 2 yrs) Agony And Ecstasy, and half-
brother to several winners, including useful sprinter Doctor Hilary (by Mujahid): dam 1¼m
winner: fairly useful maiden: in cheekpieces when second in nursery at Newmarket: likely
to stay 1m: sometimes slowly away, often races prominently. *Ralph Beckett*

SHOTGUN START 5 b.g. Kyllachy 129 – Fly In Style (Hernando (FR) 127) [2015 80: **75**
t7.1g³ p7m⁵ Jan 18] fair handicapper: stays 7f: acts on tapeta, best turf form on good to firm
going: in cheekpieces final start: sold 2,000 gns, sent to Greece. *Michael Wigham*

SHOWBIRD 3 b.f. Showcasing 117 – Dancing Feather 72 (Suave Dancer (USA) 136) **–**
[2015 p7f 7.6g⁶ 7m f8d 8g⁶ Aug 13] 23,000Y: rather leggy filly: half-sister to numerous
winners, including 7f winner Carniolan (by Royal Applause) and 1m/8.5f winner Wagtail
(by Cape Cross), both useful: dam 1m winner: no form. *Ed Walker*

SHOWBIZZY 2 ch.f. (Feb 13) Showcasing 117 – Nellie Ellis (IRE) 63 (Compton Place **64**
125) [2015 5d⁴ 5.4g⁶ 5.1g³ 5d Oct 12] first foal: dam, 2-y-o 5f winner, out of half-sister to
Prix de l'Abbaye winner Gilt Edge Girl: modest maiden: best form at 5f. *Richard Fahey*

SHOW BOAT 3 b.g. Showcasing 117 – Bluegrass Gal (USA) (Cape Canaveral (USA) **58**
115) [2015 54: t6g 5d³ Apr 8] modest maiden: will benefit from return to 6f+. *Ann Duffield*

SHOWBOATING (IRE) 7 b.g. Shamardal (USA) 129 – Sadinga (IRE) 85 (Sadler's **96**
Wells (USA) 132) [2015 98: f7g⁴ f7g* 7v³ 7m⁵ f8d* f8s² 7.6m 8d⁵ 8d 7v f7g⁶ f7g⁴
Dec 22] useful handicapper: won at Southwell in April and July: will benefit from return to
1m: acts on polytrack, fibresand, good to firm and heavy going: usually in headgear/tongue
tie prior to 2015: formerly quirky. *John Balding*

SHOWDAISY 2 ch.f. (May 13) Showcasing 117 – Darling Daisy (Komaite (USA)) [2015 **58**
t5.1m⁴ t5.1m⁵ Dec 26] third foal: dam unraced sister/half-sister to useful 6f/7f winners
Kostar and Ishiamber: fourth of 9 to Lydiate in maiden at Wolverhampton in November,
better effort: carried head awkwardly next time. *Andrew Balding*

SHOW DAY (IRE) 2 b.f. (Feb 12) Shamardal (USA) 129 – Monday Show (USA) **–**
(Maria's Mon (USA) 121) [2015 5g Apr 16] second foal: sister to useful French 1m/9.5f
winner Usheride: dam, useful French winner around 1¼m, sister to smart US Grade 2 11f
winner Expansion: 5/1, green and not knocked about when well held in maiden at
Newmarket. *Charlie Appleby*

SHOWING OFF (IRE) 2 ch.g. (Jan 25) Notnowcato 128 – Walk On Water 99 (Exceed **77 p**
And Excel (AUS) 126) [2015 7g Sep 25] first foal: dam 2-y-o 6f winner: 50/1, shaped as if
better for run when 4¾ lengths seventh of 16 to Crazy Horse in maiden at Newmarket on
debut, travelling well but no extra final 1f: sure to progress. *Henry Candy*

SHOW LEGEND 2 ch.c. (Apr 23) Showcasing 117 – Dubai Legend 83 (Cadeaux **78**
Genereux 131) [2015 6m 6m² 6.1m³ 7m* 7d Sep 27] fair performer: won nursery at
Doncaster in September: best effort at 7f: acts on good to firm going. *Michael Bell*

SHOW ME AGAIN 2 ch.g. (May 4) Showcasing 117 – Broughtons Revival 88 (Pivotal **89**
124) [2015 6.1m* 6f 7m⁴ p8f⁶ p8m³ p8f* p8g² Dec 2] 24,000Y, £50,000 2-y-o: compact
gelding: fifth foal: half-brother to 3 winners, including smart Scandinavian winner up to
1m Easy Road (2-y-o 5.5f winner, by Compton Place) and 6f winner Walk With An Angel
(by Myboycharlie): dam 11.5f-1¾m winner: fairly useful performer: won maiden at
Nottingham in June and nursery at Chelmsford in November: stays 1m: acts on polytrack
and good to firm going: has been gelded. *David Dennis*

SHOW ME BAILEYS (FR) 3 b.g. Naaqoos 117 – Exhibitor (USA) 68 (Royal Academy **–**
(USA) 130) [2015 –: f7g p10g May 6] offered little in 3 maidens. *James Given*

SHOW ME THE BAR 3 b.g. Showcasing 117 – Barboukh 95 (Night Shift (USA)) [2015 **61**
–: p7g 10.2f³ 11.9g 8.3g Oct 20] modest maiden: will benefit from return to around 1¼m:
acts on firm going: often leads. *Jo Hughes*

SHOWMETHEWAYAVRILO 2 ch.c. (Feb 22) Showcasing 117 – Avrilo 78 (Piccolo **65**
121) [2015 5.1m 6m⁵ 6.1m⁵ 5g⁴ 6v⁵ 5.1m⁴ p5g² p6m* Oct 28] fair performer: won nursery
at Kempton in October: stays 6f: acts on polytrack and good to firm going. *Malcolm Saunders*

SHOW PALACE 2 ch.c. (Apr 8) Showcasing 117 – Palais Polaire 65 (Polar Falcon **67**
(USA) 126) [2015 5.9g 6m 6m 5d* 5d* 6s³ 5d* Oct 26] fair performer: won nurseries at
Newcastle in August, Catterick in September and Redcar in October: best form at 5f: acts
on good to soft going: usually travels strongly. *Jennie Candlish*

SHOW STEALER 2 ch.f. (Apr 15) Showcasing 117 – Winifred Jo 52 (Bahamian Bounty **88**
116) [2015 6g⁴ 6d* 6.1m² 6g³ 7s Aug 29] 8,500F, €48,000Y, 40,000 2-y-o: sturdy filly:
second foal: half-sister to Swedish 2-y-o 1m winner Dutch Heart (by Dutch Art): dam,
sprint maiden, half-sister to smart winner up to 11f Mantoba: fairly useful performer: won
maiden at Brighton in June and nursery at Pontefract in July: stays 6f: acts on good to firm
and good to soft going. *Rae Guest*

SHOWSTOPPA 3 ch.f. Showcasing 117 – Harryana 79 (Efisio 120) [2015 78: t5.1g² 5d* **94**
6s⁵ 5m⁵ 5m⁵ 6m* 5d² 5m³ 6g 5v Aug 31] fairly useful handicapper: won at Newcastle in
April and Ripon in July: good second at Ascot after: effective at 5f/6f: acts on soft and good
to firm going: often races prominently. *Mark Johnston*

SHOWTIME BLUES 3 b.g. Showcasing 117 – Night Symphonie (Cloudings (IRE) 112) **78**
[2015 82: p8g⁴ p7g⁶ 7.1m p8g p7g² p8g⁵ 7d p7g² p6f⁴ t7.1m 7s p7g p8d p7g Dec 28]
tall gelding: fair handicapper: left Amanda Perrett after eleventh start: stays 7f: acts on
polytrack: often blinkered: often races towards rear: none too reliable. *Jim Boyle*

SHOWTIME STAR 5 b.g. Byron 117 – Piddies Pride (IRE) 75 (Indian Lodge (IRE) 127) **80**
[2015 85: f6d* p6.5g p6.5g³ p6.5g f5g⁴ f6g* p6g³ p6g² p6g⁵ p6g⁶ 6m⁶ 5d⁵ 6m 6.1g² p6f² **a92**
p6g* 5.3s p6m² t6g⁶ t6m Dec 12] fairly useful handicapper: won at Southwell in January
and March and Lingfield in August: stays 6f: acts on polytrack, fibresand, good to firm and
good to soft going: usually wears hood. *Gay Kelleway*

SHREWD 5 b.g. Street Sense (USA) 128 – Cala (FR) 98 (Desert Prince (IRE) 130) [2015 **91**
95: 14.6m² 12.9m⁴ 13.7m 17.5g⁵ 10.4s 12s³ 12v t12.2f⁴ Dec 11] sturdy gelding: fairly
useful handicapper: left L. Smyth after third start: stays 17f: acts on tapeta, good to firm
and heavy going: tried in cheekpieces: often races towards rear: fairly useful hurdler.
Iain Jardine

SHRILL 2 b.f. (Apr 14) Shamardal (USA) 129 – Wood Vine (USA) (Woodman (USA) 126) **97**
[2015 5f* 5g³ 5.2s 5m* Sep 5] half-sister to several winners, including smart 9.5f-1½m
(Ribblesdale Stakes) winner Silkwood (by Singspiel), smart French winner up to 1m
Kavango (2-y-o 7f winner, by Cape Cross) and useful 2-y-o 6f (including Cherry Hinton
Stakes) winner Silent Honor (by Sunday Silence): dam unraced: useful performer: won
maiden at Cork in June and nursery at Navan (by length from Blood Moon) in September:
raced only at 5f. *W. McCreery, Ireland*

SHUDBEME 2 ch.g. (Apr 23) Monsieur Bond (IRE) 120 – Oomph 83 (Shareef Dancer –
(USA) 135) [2015 7s 7g Sep 23] well held in maidens at Thirsk and Redcar. *Neville Bycroft*

SHUFOOG 2 b.f. (Feb 11) Mawatheeq (USA) 126 – Hamloola 91 (Red Ransom (USA)) **78 p**
[2015 p7g* Aug 26] second foal: dam, 7f/1m winner, half-sister to useful 7f/1m winner
Grand Inquisitor: 11/4, won 10-runner maiden at Lingfield on debut by 1¼ lengths from If
Winter Comes, keeping on well to lead final ½f: sure to progress. *William Haggas*

SHU LEWIS (IRE) 9 b.m. Pyrus (USA) 106 – Poppy Lewis (IRE) 69 (Paris House 123) **103**
[2015 105: 14d² 18.7d 14g⁴ 16d³ 12g Oct 18] useful performer: third in listed race at the
Curragh (1¾ lengths behind Silwana) in September: stays 2m, often over shorter: acts on
soft and good to firm going: in headgear last 3 starts: has worn tongue tie, including last 2
starts. *Mrs M. Dowdall Blake, Ireland*

SHURFAH (IRE) 3 ch.f. Sea The Stars (IRE) 140 – Cap Coz (IRE) 110 (Indian Ridge –
123) [2015 p10g May 26] 400,000Y: half-sister to winner up to 1½m Indian Days (2-y-o 7f
winner, by Daylami), winner up to 6f Biniou (2-y-o 5f winner, by Mozart) and winner up
to 7f Reply (2-y-o 6f/6.5f winner, by Oasis Dream), all smart: dam French 2-y-o 5.5f-7f
winner: 5/1, showed only greenness when well held in maiden at Lingfield on debut.
Ed Dunlop

SHURIKEN (IRE) 4 b.f. Hurricane Run (IRE) 134 – Wurfklinge (GER) (Acatenango **57**
(GER) 127) [2015 70: t12.2f⁵ 13d Apr 18] modest maiden: left Peter Chapple-Hyam after
first start: stays 1½m: acts on polytrack, tapeta, best turf form on soft/heavy going:
sometimes slowly away. *W. McCreery, Ireland*

SHWAIMAN (IRE) 5 br.g. Authorized (IRE) 133 – Blue Lightning (Machiavellian – §
(USA) 123) [2015 110§: 20f Jun 16] useful-looking gelding: smart performer at best: tailed
off in Ascot Stakes at Royal Ascot only outing in 2015: stays 2½m: acts on polytrack, good
to firm and good to soft going: tried in blinkers: far from straightforward: fairly useful
hurdler. *William Jarvis*

SHWAIMSA (IRE) 2 b.f. (Mar 4) Canford Cliffs (IRE) 133 – Sharp Point (IRE) 105 **87 p**
(Royal Academy (USA) 130) [2015 6d* 7m² Sep 11] half-sister to several winners,
including smart French 1m-10.5f winner Fractional (by Manduro) and smart French
winner up to 9f Needlecraft (2-y-o 1m winner, by Mark of Esteem): dam 5f-1m winner
(2-y-o 6f winner): fairly useful form: won maiden at Haydock in September by 1¼ lengths
from Cancan Katy: off just 7 days, 8/11, still green when ½-length second of 3 to Flying
Empress in minor event at Salisbury: remains with potential. *Richard Hannon*

SHYPEN 2 b.f. (Feb 6) Archipenko (USA) 127 – Coconut Shy 88 (Bahamian Bounty 116) **79**
[2015 6s p8g³ p8g² p7m* Dec 31] second foal: half-sister to useful winner up to 7f Shyron
(2-y-o 6f winner, by Byron): dam 2-y-o 5.5f/6f winner: fair performer: won maiden at
Lingfield in December: likely to stay 1¼m. *George Margarson*

SHYRON 4 b.g. Byron 117 – Coconut Shy 88 (Bahamian Bounty 116) [2015 102: p7f* p7f **96**
7m 7.6g p8m p7g p6g⁴ Dec 30] useful-looking gelding: useful handicapper: won at
Lingfield (by length from Grey Mirage) in January: will benefit from return to around 7f:
acts on polytrack, tapeta and good to firm going: tried in cheekpieces in 2015: sometimes
slowly away, usually races nearer last than first. *George Margarson*

SIBERIAN POWER (IRE) 2 b.c. (Apr 15) Frozen Power (IRE) 108 – Novosibirsk (USA) –
(Distant View (USA) 126) [2015 6g 7m 7f⁴ Jul 18] well held in 3 maidens. *Jennie Candlish*

SICILIANO (IRE) 2 b.f. (Apr 23) Tagula (IRE) 116 – Akatib (IRE) (Lahib (USA) 129) **58**
[2015 6m 5m⁶ 6g Sep 26] 15,000 2-y-o: sixth foal: half-sister to 2-y-o 6f winner
Concealment (by Iron Mask), later successful in Greece, and a winner in Greece by Golan:
dam of little account: modest maiden: best effort when sixth at Redcar. *James Bethell*

SIDE GLANCE 8 b.g. Passing Glance 119 – Averami 68 (Averti (IRE) 117) [2015 124: –
a9.9f Mar 28] useful-looking gelding: very smart at best, winner of Mackinnon Stakes at
Flemington in 2014 and in frame in numerous other pattern races, including Dubai World
Cup at Meydan twice: in blinkers and eyeshields, well held in latter race on only outing in
2015: stayed 11f: acted on synthetics, good to firm and good to soft going: reported in June
to have been retired. *Andrew Balding*

SIEGE OF BOSTON (IRE) 2 ch.c. (Mar 19) Starspangledbanner (AUS) 128 – Milton **72**
of Campsie 83 (Medicean 128) [2015 6.1d 5.9s 6m⁵ 6m³ Sep 28] fair form: length third to
Extortion in maiden at Hamilton final start: raced only at 6f. *Deborah Sanderson*

SIGHORA (IRE) 4 b.f. Royal Applause 124 – Singitta (Singspiel (IRE) 133) [2015 91: **90**
p8g³ p8g³ Jun 4] tall filly: has scope: useful handicapper: stays 1m: acts on polytrack
and good to firm going: usually leads. *Ismail Mohammed*

SIGHTLINE 2 b.f. (Jan 29) Rock of Gibraltar (IRE) 133 – Look So 92 (Efisio 120) [2015 **79 p**
8d⁴ Oct 23] third foal: closely related to smart winner up to 1¼m Regardez (2-y-o 1m
winner), by Champs Elysees) and half-sister to useful winner up to 7f Compton (2-y-o 6f
winner, by Compton Place): dam, 7f/1m winner, half-sister to Oaks winner Look Here:
14/1, promise when 2½ lengths fourth of 11 to Zest in maiden at Doncaster on debut,
keeping on without being unduly punished: sure to progress. *Ralph Beckett*

SIGNED AND SEALED 2 b.g. (Feb 20) Authorized (IRE) 133 – Broken Peace (USA) **73**
(Devil's Bag (USA)) [2015 8g 10d³ 8.3s³ Oct 28] fair form: best effort when third in
maiden at Pontefract second start: has been gelded. *Mark Johnston*

SIGNED SEALED (USA) 3 ch.c. Giant's Causeway (USA) 132 – Latice (IRE) 121 **82**
(Inchinor 119) [2015 8g² p8f⁴ 10.2d² p10f⁴ p10f⁴ Dec 28] useful-looking colt: fourth foal:
closely related to a winner in USA by Forestry and half-brother to smart/ungenuine winner
up to 1m Fencing (2-y-o 7f winner) and 1m winner Obsidian (both by Street Cry): dam,
winner up to 1½m (2-y-o 1m/9f winner), including Prix de Diane, half-sister to Prix du
Jockey Club winner Lawman: fairly useful maiden: second at Newmarket and Nottingham:
stays 1¼m: acts on good to soft going. *John Gosden*

SIGN OF A VICTORY (IRE) 6 b.g. Kayf Tara 130 – Irish Wedding (IRE) (Bob Back **88 p**
(USA) 124) [2015 t12.2g* Dec 5] 4/6, won 9-runner maiden at Wolverhampton on Flat
debut easily by 3½ lengths from U S Navy Seal: open to improvement: smart hurdler.
Nicky Henderson

SIGN OF THE KODIAC (IRE) 2 b.c. (May 13) Kodiac 112 – Summer Magic (IRE) **76 +**
90 (Desert Sun 120) [2015 5m⁵ t6g² 6f 6g³ 5m³ p5g* 6g 5m t5.1f² t5.1f* t5.1f² t5.1g² **a99**
Dec 5] £50,000Y: fourth foal: brother to useful winner up to 1m Vector Force (2-y-o 7f
winner): dam winner up to 8.5f (2-y-o 6f winner): fair on turf, useful on all-weather: won
nurseries at Chelmsford in August and Wolverhampton in October: further improvement
when neck second to Quatrieme Ami in minor event at Wolverhampton final start: stays 6f:
acts on polytrack, tapeta and firm going: usually races close up. *James Given*

SIGN OF THE TIMES 3 b.f. Medicean 128 – Still Small Voice (Polish Precedent (USA) **52**
131) [2015 p12g p10f p12g p12g f14f³ Dec 17] 15,000Y: third foal: dam unraced sister to
Irish/Yorkshire Oaks winner Pure Grain: modest maiden: best effort at 1¾m: acts on
fibresand. *J. R. Jenkins*

SIGNORE PICCOLO 4 b.g. Piccolo 121 – Piccolo Cativo 67 (Komaite (USA)) [2015 **93**
96: 5d⁵ 5m³ 5m⁶ 6m² 6g 6m⁶ 6g* 7d⁴ 6g 6g Oct 16] fairly useful handicapper: won at
Ripon (apprentice) in April and Catterick in July: stays 7f: acts on good to firm and good to
soft going: usually in hood in 2015. *David O'Meara*

SIGNORET (IRE) 3 ch.f. Naaqoos 117 – Katelyns Kiss (USA) (Rahy (USA) 115) [2015 **73**
70: 6d² 5d⁴ 6m* 6m 6m³ 7.6m⁵ 5.9g⁶ 6d⁶ 6gᵖᵘ Oct 8] fair performer: won maiden at Thirsk
in May: stays 6f: acts on good to firm and good to soft going. *Richard Fahey*

SIGNORINA ROSEINA 3 b.f. Captain Gerrard (IRE) 113 – Rosein 86 (Komaite **73**
(USA)) [2015 50: 6m* 5d⁴ 6m⁴ 7d² 7.5m⁶ 7m³ 7d⁵ 7.2g⁶ 7g⁴ 7s* t7.1f f6g⁶ f7g* Dec 15]
fair handicapper: won at Catterick in June, Leicester (apprentice) in October and Southwell
in December: stays 7f: acts on fibresand, soft and good to firm going: sometimes in
cheekpieces in 2015: front runner/races prominently, often travels strongly. *David O'Meara*

SIGNS AND SIGNALS (IRE) 3 b.f. Kodiac 112 – Larrocha (IRE) 116 (Sadler's Wells **–**
(USA) 132) [2015 –: t8.6g 11.9s Oct 6] well held in 4 maidens and a handicap. *Ed Vaughan*

SIGURD (GER) 3 ch.g. Sholokhov (IRE) 121 – Sky News (GER) (Highest Honor (FR) **50**
124) [2015 9.2d⁵ 10m 10.3g 14.1d Oct 26] modest form in maidens and a handicap.
Kevin Ryan

SIKANDAR (IRE) 3 ch.g. Medicean 128 – Siniyya (IRE) 70 (Grand Lodge (USA) 125) **89**
[2015 10g 13g⁶ 12m² 10.3m* 10.3g³ 10.4g Aug 22] fifth foal: half-brother to 13f winner
(stays 2m) Sinakar (by Manduro): dam, maiden (stayed 2m), sister to Derby/Arc winner
Sinndar: fairly useful performer: left M. Halford, won handicap at Doncaster in July:
stays 1½m: acts on good to firm going: tried in cheekpieces: sometimes slowly away.
Brian Ellison

SILAS R (IRE) 2 b.g. (Apr 9) Pour Moi (IRE) 125 – Playwithmyheart (Diktat 126) [2015 **67**
p7g⁵ p7g⁶ p7g p10g* t8.6f Nov 30] leggy gelding: fair performer: won nursery at
Chelmsford in November: best effort at 1¼m: acts on polytrack: in cheekpieces last 2
starts. *Sir Mark Prescott Bt*

SILCA STAR 2 ch.c. (Mar 29) Medicean 128 – Silca Chlave 106 (Pivotal 124) [2015 6.5s² **78 p**
Oct 23] fourth foal: half-brother to 6f-1m winner Strictly Silca (by Danehill Dancer): dam,
2-y-o 6f winner, half-sister to Prix Morny winner Silca's Sister and smart performers Green
Manalishi (sprinter) and Golden Silca (best at 1m-1¼m): 7/1, shaped well when 1¾ lengths
second of 9 to Monteverdi in maiden at Newbury, finishing well under hands and heels
having run green: sure to progress. *Mick Channon*

SILCA WINGS 2 b.f. (Apr 29) Multiplex 114 – Silca Destination 65 (Dubai Destination **73 p**
(USA) 127) [2015 p8g p8g³ Dec 15] fourth foal: half-sister to 3 winners, including 2-y-o
1m winner Lizzie Tudor (by Tamayuz) and 5f (including at 2 yrs) winner Lexington Rose
(by Captain Gerrard): dam, 7f/1m winner, out of smart 1m-1¼m performer Golden Silca:
better effort when fifth in maiden at Kempton (2 lengths behind Cajoled) in December:
should do better. *James Fanshawe*

SILENCE IN COURT (IRE) 3 b.g. Invincible Spirit (IRE) 121 – Hammrah (Danehill **38**
(USA) 126) [2015 –: 8.3g 6g⁵ t6g⁶ 6m⁴ 11s⁶ Aug 30] poor maiden: probably stays 8.5f: acts
on tapeta, best turf form on good going: tried in cheekpieces in 2015. *Eve Johnson Houghton*

SILENT AMBITION 6 b.m. Striking Ambition 122 – Hi Rock 55 (Hard Fought 125) **–**
[2015 10.2m t9.5f Oct 23] no sign of ability in varied events. *Steph Hollinshead*

SILENT ATTACK 2 b.c. (Mar 14) Dream Ahead (USA) 133 – Chanterelle (FR) **69 p**
(Trempolino (USA) 135) [2015 p6d Sep 4] €60,000Y, 150,000 2-y-o: second foal: half-
brother to useful winner up to 11f King Bolete (2-y-o 8.3f winner, by Cape Cross): dam
once-raced sister to US Grade 3 8.5f/9f winner Cox Orange and half-sister to Prix Marcel
Boussac winner Amonita: 10/11, showed more temperament than ability when 6½ lengths
seventh of 11 to Zhui Feng in maiden at Kempton, losing race at the start: clearly though
capable of better. *Saeed bin Suroor*

SILENT DIVA 2 gr.f. (Apr 2) Sakhee's Secret 128 – Silent Waters (Polish Precedent **38**
(USA) 131) [2015 7m 5.9s 7s⁶ 8g Sep 23] 18,000Y: half-sister to 3 winners around 1½m,
including Silver Waters (by Fantastic Light) and Phase Shift (by Iceman): dam, little form,
half-sister to smart 1¼m-1½m winner Gower Song: poor maiden: bred to be suited by at
least 1m: usually in hood. *Tim Easterby*

SILENT DREAMER 2 b.f. (Feb 18) Dream Ahead (USA) 133 – In A Silent Way (IRE) **69**
102 (Desert Prince (IRE) 130) [2015 6g 7.5m³ 6s² 7.2g⁶ 7d³ p6f p8f⁶ Oct 29] 3,000Y:
unfurnished filly: seventh foal: half-sister to 3 winners in France, including useful 2-y-o 1m
winner Crecy (by Refuse To Bend) and 9f-10.5f winner Driven Snow (by Linamix): dam
winner up to 1¼m (2-y-o 6f winner): fair maiden: stays 7.5f: acts on good to firm and good
to soft going. *Mark Johnston*

SILENT PURSUIT 4 br.f. Pastoral Pursuits 127 – Lay A Whisper 72 (Night Shift (USA)) **59**
[2015 59: p6g p7g³ p8f⁶ p6m³ Feb 28] modest maiden: stays 1m: acts on polytrack: in
headgear last 2 starts. *Philip Hide*

SILENT THUNDER (IRE) 3 b.c. Sea The Stars (IRE) 140 – Speed Song 92 (Fasliyev **68**
(USA) 120) [2015 74: t9.5f⁴ p8f² Feb 2] fair maiden in Britain, lightly raced: sold 18,000
gns in February, sent to Qatar, where won 9.2f maiden at Doha in December. *William Haggas*

SILHOUETTE (IRE) 2 ch.g. (Feb 19) Frozen Power (IRE) 108 – Missalonghi (IRE) 67 **–**
(In The Wings 128) [2015 p6g t7.1g Jul 28] well held in maidens at Chelmsford and
Wolverhampton: has been gelded. *Daniel Kubler*

SILHUETTE (IRE) 2 b.f. (Mar 24) Canford Cliffs (IRE) 133 – Lisfannon 68 (Bahamian **92**
Bounty 116) [2015 5.9m* 6g* 6g Sep 19] £18,000Y: fifth foal: half-sister to 2-y-o 5f
winner Dress Up (by Noverre) and 2-y-o 6f winner Mironica (by Excellent Art): dam,
maiden (stayed 7.5f), half-sister to useful sprinter Dazed And Amazed: fairly useful form:

won maiden at Carlisle in July and minor event at Ripon (by 1¾ lengths from Unilit) in August: well below form in Firth Of Clyde Stakes at Ayr final start: raced only at 6f. *Ann Duffield*

SILJAN'S SAGA (FR) 5 bl.m. Sagamix (FR) 129 – Humoriste (FR) (Saint Cyrien (FR) 128) [2015 118: 9.9g 10.4g⁵ 9.9d* 12.4d* 11.9m 15.4d² Oct 25] very smart performer: won minor event at Vichy in August and Grand Prix de Deauville (by ¾ length from Cocktail Queen) in August: good eighth in Prix de l'Arc de Triomphe at Longchamp (4¼ lengths behind Golden Horn) in October: creditable length second to Vazirabad in Prix Royal-Oak at Saint-Cloud final outing, clear of rest: stays 15.4f: acts on soft and good to firm going. *J-P. Gauvin, France* **121**

SILK BOW 2 b.f. (Mar 12) Elusive City (USA) 117 – Ishraaqat 82 (Singspiel (IRE) 133) [2015 5d p5g* 5m² 5f 6m 6g⁵ Aug 1] 10,000F, £31,000Y: rather leggy filly: second foal: dam, 1m winner, half-sister to useful performer up to 9f Taqseem: fairly useful performer: won maiden at Chelmsford in April: creditable efforts when second in listed race at York (1½ lengths behind Delizia) and fifth of 20 in nursery at Newmarket: stays 6f: acts on polytrack and good to firm going: usually races close up, usually travels strongly. *James Given* **82**

SILK CRAVAT 2 ch.g. (Apr 3) Kyllachy 129 – Polly Floyer 66 (Halling (USA) 133) [2015 7g⁵ Sep 8] 38,000Y: second foal: dam, 7f winner, half-sister to 1¼m-11.6f Fairmile and 1m-11f winner Marzelline (both smart): 50/1, shaped well when 2 lengths fifth of 14 to Move Up in maiden at Leicester on debut: has been gelded: sure to progress. *Simon Crisford* **84 p**

SILKEN OCEAN 3 b.f. Dynaformer (USA) – Mambo Jambo (USA) (Kingmambo (USA) 125) [2015 –: 12m May 15] no form in 2 maidens (5 months apart). *Ralph Beckett* **–**

SILKEN SKIES (IRE) 2 ch.f. (Apr 2) Zoffany (IRE) 121 – Sky Red 75 (Night Shift (USA)) [2015 5f 6m³ 6d* 6s Oct 23] £25,000Y: sturdy filly: half-sister to several winners, including smart 2-y-o 5f/6f winner Orpen Grey (by Orpen) and useful 6f winner Dawn's Early Light (by Starspangledbanner): dam 5f winner: fairly useful performer: won maiden at Haydock (by short head from Ice Dream) in September: stays 6f. *Clive Cox* **82**

SILK GEM (IRE) 2 b.c. (Feb 20) Roderic O'Connor (IRE) 119 – Fine Silk (USA) 69 (Rahy (USA) 115) [2015 t7.1f p7f p7f* Dec 17] fair performer: best effort when winning maiden at Chelmsford (by neck from Mockinbird) in December: raced only at 7f. *William Haggas* **73**

SILK HALL (UAE) 10 b.g. Halling (USA) 133 – Velour 94 (Mtoto 134) [2015 81: 17.5g Sep 18] rather leggy gelding: fair handicapper: stays 2m: acts on polytrack, soft and good to firm going: has worn headgear, including often of late. *J. J. Lambe, Ireland* **–**

SILK TRAIN 5 b.m. Rail Link 132 – Monsoon Wedding 75 (Monsun (GER) 124) [2015 80: p10m⁶ 10.2m⁶ May 1] sturdy mare: modest handicapper: stays 1½m: acts on polytrack and good to firm going: in tongue tie in 2015. *Alexandra Dunn* **59**

SILLY BILLY (IRE) 7 b.g. Noverre (USA) 125 – Rock Dove (IRE) 77 (Danehill (USA) 126) [2015 62, a78: f8g t7.1m⁶ Feb 2] rather leggy gelding: fair handicapper at best: has lost his way: usually in headgear: has worn tongue tie: tends to find little. *John Balding* **–**

SILVA ECLIPSE 2 gr.c. (Mar 26) Multiplex 114 – Linen Line (Double Eclipse (IRE) 122) [2015 8s 9d⁵ Oct 26] still needed experience when fifth of 10 to Play Gal in maiden at Redcar latter start. *Kevin Ryan* **53**

SILVALA DANCE 5 b.m. Kyllachy 129 – Bride of The Sea (Cape Cross (IRE) 129) [2015 62: 6.1d t6g⁶ t7.1g⁶ 6m* 6m* 6m² Aug 10] strong mare: fair handicapper: won apprentice events at Windsor and Leicester in July: stays 6f: acts on good to firm and heavy going. *Chris Wall* **71**

SILVANUS (IRE) 10 b.g. Danehill Dancer (IRE) 117 – Mala Mala (IRE) 104 (Brief Truce (USA) 126) [2015 101: 5m 5.1s* 5m 5m 5m⁶ 5g³ 5m⁴ 5m* 5m* 5.4g³ 5d 5d⁴ Sep 22] angular, useful-looking gelding: useful performer: won minor event at Chester in May and handicaps at Pontefract (by ¾ length from Mukaynis) in July and Ripon (by length from Lexington Place) in August: third in handicap at York (1½ lengths behind Caspian Prince) later in August: stays 6f, races mainly at 5f: acts on polytrack, soft and good to firm going: tried in headgear prior to 2015: often travels strongly. *Paul Midgley* **106**

SILVER ALLIANCE 7 gr.g. Proclamation (IRE) 130 – Aimee Vibert 76 (Zilzal (USA) 137) [2015 84: p10d³ 10s 10.2f³ 9.9s* 10m 10g⁴ 10.1m⁶ 8.3m⁵ t9.5f⁶ t9.5f Nov 13] good-topped gelding: fair handicapper: won at Brighton in June: stays 1¼m: acts on polytrack, tapeta, soft and good to firm going: wears headgear. *Julia Feilden* **78**

SILVER DETAIL (IRE) 3 b.f. Youmzain (IRE) 131 – Ayam Zainah 62 (Pivotal 124) **41**
[2015 6d 7g 5m⁶ 7s⁵ 9.9g p8f p13.3g⁵ Dec 7] £6,000Y: first foal: dam, maiden (best at
6f/7f), half-sister to smart performer up to 10.7f Prince of All: poor maiden. *Alan Coogan*

SILVER DIXIE (USA) 5 br.g. Dixie Union (USA) 121 – More Silver (USA) 90 (Silver **82**
Hawk (USA) 123) [2015 83, a77: p10f² 10.2f 11m 10m* p11g 10.1g* 10d⁴ 10g p10f⁴ **a72**
Nov 6] useful-looking gelding: fairly useful handicapper: won at Newbury (amateur) in
June and Epsom in July: stays 11f: acts on polytrack, good to firm and good to soft going:
often wears headgear: often races towards rear. *Peter Hedger*

SILVER DUKE (IRE) 4 gr.g. Papal Bull 128 – Dumaani's Dream (USA) (Dumaani **79**
(USA) 115) [2015 79: 9s⁴ 10g² 11.1s⁴ 10s⁵ 8g 8.9m⁵ 10.3g⁴ 8g 12.2g³ Oct 13] sturdy
gelding: fair maiden: stays 1¼m: best form on good going: often races towards rear.
Jim Goldie

SILVER GHOST (IRE) 2 gr.c. (Apr 15) Dark Angel (IRE) 113 – Aqualina (IRE) 104 **69 p**
(King's Theatre (IRE) 128) [2015 7g 7s⁵ Sep 19] €42,000F, 26,000Y: fifth foal: half-
brother to 1m winner Mister Ross (by Medicean): dam, winner up to 1m (2-y-o 7f winner)
who stayed 12.3f, half-sister to smart stayer Biennale: 66/1, improved from debut when 7
lengths fifth of 17 to Tabarrak in maiden at Newbury: open to further progress. *Peter Makin*

SILVER GLAZE (IRE) 3 gr.g. Verglas (IRE) 118 – Tullawadgeen (IRE) (Sinndar (IRE) **–**
134) [2015 t7.1g⁵ f7g⁶ Dec 29] down field in bumper/both starts in Flat maidens.
Brian Ellison

SILVERHEELS (IRE) 6 gr.g. Verglas (IRE) 118 – Vasilia (Dansili 127) [2015 95: p8m² **90**
p7.5g² p8m² p8f⁶ p8g⁶ 8.3m² 8.3m p8d p8g* p8g Dec 9] strong gelding: fairly useful
performer: won claimer at Chantilly in October: stays 8.5f: acts on polytrack, viscoride,
good to firm and heavy going: often wears headgear: tried in tongue tie prior to 2015.
Paul Cole

SILVER HEIGHTS 2 gr.f. (Feb 10) Hellvelyn 118 – Tintean (IRE) 79 (Clodovil (IRE) **–**
116) [2015 6s⁵ Oct 26] 1,200F: second foal: dam 2-y-o 7f winner: 100/1, knew job when 7
lengths fifth of 12 to Flowing Clarets in maiden at Leicester. *Dr Jon Scargill*

SILVER LINING (IRE) 3 gr.g. Dark Angel (IRE) 113 – Out of Woods (USA) (Woodman **67**
(USA) 126) [2015 p6f⁵ 7d p7g⁴ 8.3f 7m³ 7m 7.1g p7g⁶ 9.9v² 8g⁵ p11g⁴ 11.6g⁴ p10m p12g³
p12g² Dec 19] useful-looking gelding: fair maiden: stays 1½m: acts on polytrack, good to
firm and heavy going: usually in tongue tie: sometimes slowly away. *Marcus Tregoning*

SILVER MOUNTAIN 4 gr.g. Sir Percy 129 – Pearl Bright (FR) 80 (Kaldoun (FR) 122) **80**
[2015 f12d p13f* p15.8f* p16f⁶ p16g⁵ 12.3m p16g Jul 8] fairly useful handicapper: won
twice at Lingfield in March: stays 2m: acts on polytrack: sometimes slowly away, often
races in rear. *J. R. Jenkins*

SILVER QUAY (IRE) 3 gr.c. Dark Angel (IRE) 113 – She Runs (FR) (Sheyrann) [2015 **84 +**
83: 9g⁴ 10m⁵ 10m 8m⁶ p12g³ 12s² 11.6g² 11s 10d t12.2f³ p12g* p12g³ Dec 9] rangy colt: **a96**
useful handicapper: improved form when winning at Lingfield in December by 8 lengths
from Daisy Boy: creditable third there final start: stays 1½m: acts on polytrack, tapeta, soft
and good to firm going: often races towards rear. *Richard Hannon*

SILVER RAINBOW (IRE) 3 gr.f. Starspangledbanner (AUS) 128 – Enchanting Way **92**
(Linamix (FR) 127) [2015 82p: 7m 5.6m* 5.7g⁵ 6m⁴ p6m⁵ Nov 19] lengthy, useful-looking
filly: fairly useful handicapper: won at Doncaster (by ¾ length from Bahamian Sunrise)
in June: has won at 7f, raced around 6f lately: acts on tapeta and good to firm going.
Charles Hills

SILVERRICA (IRE) 5 gr.m. Ad Valorem (USA) 125 – Allegorica (IRE) (Alzao (USA) **84**
117) [2015 83: t5.1g 5.7m⁴ 5.7g³ 5g* 5m⁵ 5g⁴ 5.7f⁴ 6d³ Oct 12] sturdy mare:
fairly useful handicapper: won at Lingfield in June and at Bath (apprentice) and Sandown
in September: likely to prove best at short of 6f: acts on firm and good to soft going: usually
leads. *Malcolm Saunders*

SILVER RIME (FR) 10 gr.g. Verglas (IRE) 118 – Severina (Darshaan 133) [2015 92: **87**
7.2g 8d 7.1m⁶ 8.3g 7.1m³ 7.2g⁶ 8.5m⁴ 9.1g 8d⁶ 7.2m⁶ 7.9d* 8g² 7.9m² 8d 7.2g 7.2g
Oct 8] leggy gelding: fairly useful handicapper: won at Carlisle (amateur) in August:
stays 8.5f: acts on soft and good to firm going: sometimes slowly away, often races in rear.
Linda Perratt

SILVER SANDS (IRE) 2 gr.g. (Mar 29) Zebedee 113 – Eloquent Rose (IRE) 83 **64**
(Elnadim (USA) 128) [2015 6m 6d⁴ 6d Oct 26] modest maiden: easily best effort when
fourth at Thirsk. *Tim Easterby*

SILVER SECRET 4 gr.g. Moss Vale (IRE) 126 – Alphilda 83 (Ezzoud (IRE) 126) [2015 **64**
60: p8g⁵ Mar 26] twice-raced maiden, modest form: still green when fifth of 8 at
Chelmsford only outing in 2015. *Miss Joey Ellis*

SILVER SHUFFLE (IRE) 8 ch.g. Big Shuffle (USA) 122 – Silvetta (Lando (GER) 128) **71**
[2015 52: 12.2g³ 15.8m* 16d² 15.8g² 12d³ 15.8s² 15.8g³ Oct 13] fair handicapper: won at
Catterick in August: acts on polytrack, soft and good to firm going: sometimes in
headgear prior to 2015: often races towards rear. *Dianne Sayer*

SILVERSMITH (IRE) 3 gr.g. Mastercraftsman (IRE) 129 – Gleaming Silver (IRE) 86 **68 p**
(Dalakhani (IRE) 133) [2015 p8f² p8m* Feb 12] €40,000Y: first foal: dam, 1m winner
(stayed 1¼m), half-sister to smart 2-y-o 1m/9f winner Tiz The Shot: improved to win
maiden at Chelmsford in February: will stay beyond 1m: should do better still: sold 11,500
gns in July, sent to Bahrain. *Rae Guest*

SILVER SPRINGS (IRE) 2 gr.f. (Mar 26) Zebedee 113 – Charming Vista (Josr **60**
Algarhoud (IRE) 118) [2015 5m 6m² 5m 5g⁶ 6m* 5d⁶ 6d 5d 5d t6f¹ p6d p6g* p6g⁶ p5m⁵
Dec 27] €8,000V: quite attractive filly: fourth foal: dam unraced half-sister to Rockfel
Stakes winner Distant Valley: fair performer: won nurseries at Lingfield in August and
Chelmsford in December: will be suited by a return to 6f: acts on polytrack and good to
firm going. *David Evans*

SILVER STREAK (IRE) 2 gr.g. (Apr 16) Dark Angel (IRE) 113 – Happy Talk (IRE) 74 **80**
(Hamas (IRE) 125) [2015 7.5s² 7.5m⁶ 7g³ 8d⁶ Oct 23] €45,000Y: brother to 2-y-o 6f winner
Evoke, later successful in Greece, and half-brother to several winners, including useful
2-y-o 5f winner Nagham (by Camacho) and winner up to 12.3f Mica Mika (2-y-o 7f
winner, by Needwood Blade): dam 1¼m winner: fairly useful maiden: in hood, best effort
when third at Newcastle: will stay 1m. *Ann Duffield*

SILVERWARE (USA) 7 b.g. Eurosilver (USA) 118 – Playing Footsie (USA) (Valiant **69**
Nature (USA) 118) [2015 92: t8.6f⁵ p8g t8.6f³ t8.6m⁴ 7g t8.6g⁶ 7.5m 7.5f Jul 3] good-
topped gelding: fair handicapper: stays 8.5f: acts on polytrack, tapeta, good to firm and
good to soft going: tried in visor in 2015. *Kristin Stubbs*

SILVERWAVE (FR) 3 b.c. Silver Frost (IRE) 122 – Miss Bio (FR) (River Mist (USA) **123**
119) [2015 9.9g* 9.9s* 10.4g 11.9m⁴ 11.9s² 11.9m Oct 4] closely related to 3 winners in
France by Verglas, notably very smart winner up to 1m (including Prix Jean Prat) Stormy
River (2-y-o 7f winner), and half-brother to 3 winners, including useful 7f/1m winner Line
Drummer (by Galileo): dam unraced: very smart performer: won minor event at Angers (by
7 lengths) in March and Prix La Force at Longchamp (by 4 lengths from Epicuris) in April:
good efforts on latter course last 2 starts, second in Prix Niel (2½ lengths behind New Bay)
and tenth of 17 in Prix de l'Arc de Triomphe (4¾ lengths behind Golden Horn, last into
straight and staying on well): stays 1½m: acts on viscoride, soft and good to firm going:
often races in rear: joined P. Bary. *A. Couetil, France*

SILVER WINGS (IRE) 2 gr.g. (Mar 24) Zebedee 113 – Daisy Hill (Indian Ridge 123) **90**
[2015 5g* 5.1d² 5g² 5m⁵ 5f 5.1m³ 5.1m³ 5m³ 6g 5.7d³ p6f t5.1f⁶ p6g⁶ p6g Dec 30] sturdy **a80**
gelding: seventh foal: half-brother to winner up to 8.6f Soviet Palace (2-y-o 6f winner, by
Jade Robbery) and 9f-10.3f winner Frontline Phantom (by Noverre): dam French 1m
winner: fairly useful performer: won maiden at Windsor in April: second in minor events
at Chester and Windsor: left David Evans after twelfth start: stays 5.5f: acts on tapeta, good
to firm and good to soft going: tried in blinkers. *Roger Ingram*

SILVERY MOON (IRE) 8 gr.g. Verglas (IRE) 118 – Starry Night 89 (Sheikh Albadou **101**
128) [2015 96: 10s² 9.8d³ 12g⁶ 10.4g⁶ 10m⁴ 10.4m³ 8m 8g⁴ 10.4m 7.9g* 7.9m⁴ 10g² 8.5s⁵
10v² 10v⁶ Nov 3] big, lengthy gelding: useful handicapper: won at Carlisle in August:
second at Pontefract (head behind This Is The Day) in September: stays 10.5f: acts on good
to firm and heavy going. *Tim Easterby*

SILWANA (IRE) 4 b.f. Peintre Celebre (USA) 137 – Simawa (IRE) 99 (Anabaa (USA) **115**
130) [2015 103p: 16g 16m* 14d² 14d* 16d* Sep 27] first foal: dam, 2-y-o 1m winner who
stayed 1½m, half-sister to Derby/Arc winner Sinndar: smart performer: won handicaps at
the Curragh (by neck from Hurricane Ridge) in June and Leopardstown (by 4¾ lengths
from Western Boy) in September and listed race at the Curragh (by neck from Toe The
Line) later in September: stays 2m: acts on soft and good to firm going: visored last 3 starts:
often races prominently. *D. K. Weld, Ireland*

SIMENON (IRE) 8 b.g. Marju (IRE) 127 – Epistoliere (IRE) (Alzao (USA) 117) [2015 **116**
118: 16.4m⁵ 20f⁴ 16m 16.4d 18m⁵ 19.9m 16d Oct 17] angular gelding: smart performer:
best effort of 2015 when 2 lengths fourth of 12 to Trip To Paris in Gold Cup at Royal Ascot:
stays 21.5f: acts on firm and good to soft going: has worn hood. *W. P. Mullins, Ireland*

SIMPLE ATTACK 2 b.g. (Apr 13) Invincible Spirit (IRE) 121 – Princess Taise (USA) **82 p** 100 (Cozzene (USA)) [2015 6.1g⁴ 7d* 8g⁶ 7d⁴ Sep 27] fourth foal: half-brother to useful winner up to 9f Elkhart (2-y-o 7.4f winner, by Refuse To Bend): dam 2-y-o 7f winner: fairly useful form: won maiden at Newcastle (by neck from Ikerrin Road) in August: shaped well when fourth in nursery at Epsom final start (left with too much to do): should stay 1m: has been gelded: remains with potential. *Saeed bin Suroor*

SIMPLE ELEGANCE (USA) 3 b.f. Street Cry (IRE) 130 – Rutherienne (USA) 115 **73** (Pulpit (USA) 117) [2015 75: p6g² t7.1f⁴ t8.6m² p8f* Mar 19] fair performer: won maiden at Chelmsford in March: stays 8.5f: acts on polytrack, tapeta and good to firm going: front runner/races prominently. *Charlie Appleby*

SIMPLE VERSE (IRE) 3 b.f. Duke of Marmalade (IRE) 132 – Guantanamera (IRE) **121** (Sadler's Wells (USA) 132) [2015 p10g⁶ p11g³ p12m² 12g² 12m* 14m* 14.6d* 12d* Oct 17]

The limited powers of the International Federation of Horseracing Authorities are alluded to in the essay on Hit It A Bomb when discussing the permissive attitude of North America to the use of raceday medication. The IFHA is not responsible for staging racing's major international occasions, such as the Breeders' Cup or the Prix de l'Arc de Triomphe meeting, and can only advise and encourage from the sidelines (although, in that regard, it isn't doing enough). A governing body such as FIFA, for example, which organises football's World Cup, is in a position to enforce and implement changes to a set of rules that already apply worldwide. As with drug use, horse racing has no accepted worldwide set of rules governing interference and disqualification, inevitably leading to confusion and friction at times which affects the integrity of a sport that has become increasingly international (there were over a thousand British-trained runners on foreign soil in 2015).

The Qatar Racing team found itself at the centre of cases concerning controversial disqualifications on both sides of the Atlantic in the latest season which helped to illustrate the need for the sport to move more quickly towards closer harmonisation of its rules, even if only in the major international events. The five-year-old mare Secret Gesture (owned in partnership with Newsells Park and runner-up in the 2013 Oaks) was demoted to third after passing the post first in the Beverly D Stakes at Arlington in August. The rules in Illinois—American racing is run on a state-by-state basis—are strict, with any horse crossing in front of another, so as to impede it in any way, liable to disqualification. Secret Gesture was clearly the best horse in the race on the day and, under British or Irish (but not French) rules, would not have been in the slightest danger of disqualification. However, the Arlington stewards adjudged that when Secret Gesture drifted off a true line she impeded the 'blameless' third-placed Stephanie's Kitten and made herself liable to disqualification under the rules. The runner-up Watsdachances suffered no interference herself but was promoted to first when Secret Gesture was placed behind Stephanie's Kitten. The Arlington stewards have made headlines in Europe before with disqualifications, including that of Powerscourt (ridden, like Secret Gesture, by Jamie Spencer) in the 2004 Arlington Million. Stephanie's Kitten's jockey Irad Ortiz came in for plenty of criticism in the British media for 'play acting' when standing up in his irons, and Secret Gesture's connections, irritated that the stewards took evidence only from Ortiz and did not call Spencer, decided to appeal.

While waiting for that appeal (which eventually upheld the Arlington stewards' decision), another Qatar Racing filly also trained by Ralph Beckett, the three-year-old Simple Verse, found herself at the centre of a similar debate when she was demoted from first place in the final classic, the Ladbrokes St Leger. In Britain, the first past the post nearly always keeps the race unless interference has been caused by dangerous or reckless riding (other riding offences, such as careless riding or improper use of the whip, are dealt with separately from any judgement made about the equity of the result). Simple Verse's winning margin over Bondi Beach was a head and she lost the race on the day when the Doncaster stewards deemed that she had 'improved her position' in two incidents of interference between the pair, firstly when she edged out and bumped Bondi Beach at the two-furlong pole and then when they came together half a furlong out when duelling for the lead. The jockeys' evidence to the stewards' inquiry was televised by Channel

Ladbrokes St Leger Stakes, Doncaster—
controversy as Simple Verse edges out Bondi Beach (left), after some interference between the pair
in the final two furlongs, only to be demoted by the stewards at an inquiry in which the evidence
given by the jockeys is televised by Channel 4; the Doncaster stewards' decision is later overturned
by a BHA disciplinary panel on appeal; Bondi Beach's stablemate Fields of Athenry gets up for
third ahead of the non-staying Storm The Stars (rail)

4, as discussed in the essay on Bondi Beach, and the BHA's head of stewarding Paul Barton explained later in front of the TV cameras that 'The stewards don't have to be satisfied beyond all reasonable doubt, but they have to leave the room feeling comfortable that the decision they have made is the correct one.' The connections of Simple Verse disagreed with that decision and mounted an appeal to have the filly reinstated (Jacqueline Quest, in the 2010 One Thousand Guineas, had been the last horse to lose a British classic in the stewards' room). The Simple Verse appeal, held eleven days later at High Holborn before a BHA panel chaired by Tim Charlton QC, with both sides legally represented, was successful. After three hours of evidence and cross-examination of witnesses, including the two jockeys, Simple Verse became the first classic winner in British racing history to be disqualified and then reinstated, a decision that the successful QC for Simple Verse's owners said afterwards was probably a 'fifty-fifty call'. In a good piece of public relations, the presentation of the St Leger trophies was re-enacted at Doncaster on Racing Post Trophy day, though the best-known face of Qatar Racing, Sheikh Fahad, missed the occasion as he was in America.

The result of the St Leger appeal was accepted with good grace by the connections of Bondi Beach and was soon forgotten, in contrast to a similar case in 1981 in Ireland when the Irish Two Thousand Guineas winner Kings Lake, trained by Vincent O'Brien, was reinstated by the stewards of the Turf Club after an appeal against his relegation to second for hampering main rival To-Agori-Mou, the winner of the Two Thousand Guineas at Newmarket. Kings Lake and To-Agori-Mou stood out from the rest of the three-year-old milers in Europe and their rivalry—they met four times in all—became one of the highlights of the season, with their clash in the Irish Two Thousand Guineas a continuing talking point. The decision to reinstate Kings Lake, after a six-hour hearing, was controversial, with the senior officiating steward at the Curragh on Guineas day resigning from the Turf Club in protest (he later withdrew his resignation), while the British and Irish racing Press, almost to a man, felt the appeal result had been a travesty. The two Timeform racereaders who had been at the Curragh gave evidence in support of O'Brien's appeal, having been of the strong opinion that the interference had not affected the result. Some of the anger over the appeal decision was directed at the time against Timeform for giving evidence at the appeal hearing, but the brunt of it was reserved for Ballydoyle whose relations with the Press at the time had become strained in preceding weeks by Vincent O'Brien's placing an embargo on the release of the stable's running plans following a row about ante-post favourite Storm Bird missing the Two Thousand Guineas (Ballydoyle had reportedly confirmed to a reporter that the horse would run, only for an announcement to be made two or three hours later that Storm Bird had coughed at exercise that same morning and would miss the race).

That Simple Verse should even make the field for the St Leger could hardly have been envisaged when she was beaten off a BHA handicap mark of just 77 by Endless Time in a fillies handicap at Goodwood in May. Not seen out at two, it had already taken her three attempts to get off the mark in maiden company (which she did against four rivals at Lingfield in early-April) but she really began to blossom in the summer. After winning the Ashbrittle Stud Bibury Cup, a fairly useful handicap for three-year-olds at Salisbury at the end of June, in a close finish with Polarisation and Oceane, Simple Verse seemed to surprise even her own connections when stepped up in both class and distance in the Markel Insurance Fillies' Stakes (registered as the Lillie Langtry) at the newly-branded Qatar Goodwood Festival at the end of July. Apparently the second string (ridden by Harry Bentley) behind the Qatar Racing-owned French-trained challenger Lady Dragon, and the only three-year-old in the line-up, Simple Verse started at 11/1 and improved markedly on her previous form to pick her way through the field in the home straight and score a shade cosily by a length and a half from the useful Hidden Gold and twelve others. While the Park Hill Stakes, the so-called 'fillies St Leger', looked the next likely target, Simple Verse continued to show at home that she was a fast-improving filly and connections paid £50,000 to supplement her for the St Leger.

Only a dozen remained in the final classic—for a winner's purse of £393,738—at the last deadline for scratchings and six of those were trained by Aidan O'Brien, with the hard-working Derby third Storm The Stars (who had won the Great Voltigeur from Bondi Beach on his eighth start of the campaign) the pick of the home-trained colts still left in. The Ballydoyle contingent was reduced to three at the final declaration stage, before one of the trio, Order of St George, was rerouted on the Friday to the Irish St Leger after fears that the going might be too firm for him at Doncaster, leaving a team of seven for the St Leger. Bondi Beach and Storm The Stars were sent off 2/1 joint favourites, with the Ballydoyle second string, the Ebor third (under 9-3) Fields of Athenry, next at 100/30. Simple Verse started at 8/1, the first filly to run in the race since the same stable's Oaks winner Talent finished runner-up two years earlier. Although no filly had won the St Leger since User Friendly in 1992, a number of fillies had run well in the race since, High And Low, Ramruma, Quiff and Unsung Heroine the others who had finished second (Ralph Beckett had also run his 2008 Oaks winner Look Here in the race and she had come third). With the St Leger attracting a crowd of over 30,000 to Doncaster for the fourth year in a row, the only sour note was the 'disappointing' late decision taken by the organisers of Irish Champions' Weekend (without consulting Doncaster) to move the time of the Irish Champion Stakes forward by sixty-five minutes to run it on fresh ground at 5.45 because of a forecast of rain. The decision meant that the charismatic Frankie Dettori, riding Derby winner Golden Horn in the Irish Champion, had to abandon plans to ride Bondi Beach in the St Leger ('The helicopter was booked but it would have been a disaster if I'd got held up and missed Golden Horn'). Mike Dillon of Ladbrokes was particularly critical: 'We were unhappy about the introduction of Irish Champions' Weekend in 2013 but they offered an olive branch, saying they didn't want to affect the Leger and that they wanted the races to work concurrently rather than in opposition, which is why this is so disappointing.'

The St Leger turned into a thorough test of stamina on the prevailing good to soft going, with Fields of Athenry setting a good gallop. Storm The Stars moved like the best horse in the race for most of the way and was a couple of lengths to the good approaching the final furlong after Bondi Beach, covering the forward move by Storm The Stars, had been bumped by Simple Verse as she pushed her way out from a pocket two furlongs out. Storm The Stars ran out of stamina inside the final

Qipco British Champions Fillies' And Mares' Stakes, Ascot—dropping back in trip, Simple Verse (second left) revels in a good test of stamina as she stays on to overhaul Journey; Beautiful Romance (No.5) and a below-par Covert Love (blaze) complete the frame

furlong where the race came down to a duel between Simple Verse and Bondi Beach who brushed together again about a hundred yards from the line before Simple Verse scrambled home by a head, with Fields of Athenry staying on to pip Storm The Stars for third, a length and three quarters behind. The first four finished clear of the others, who were headed by French challenger Vengeur Masque, a 16/1-shot who had really not done enough to warrant a tilt at a classic. While the Doncaster stewards evidently concluded that both incidents involving Simple Verse and Bondi Beach had been caused by Simple Verse, and, taken together, had 'improved her placing', that wasn't the way Timeform saw it. Bondi Beach may have been on the wrong end of the bumping two furlongs out but it wasn't all one way traffic, with Simple Verse also being leaned on by her rival at one stage, and it was at least debatable whether the interference Bondi Beach suffered then, and again half a furlong out, had affected the result. Simple Verse kept finding extra, most responsive to the urgings of Andrea Atzeni, and Bondi Beach never really looked like getting past her. To that extent, the decision of the stewards on the day to reverse the placings looked harsh, especially given the benefit of the doubt to the winner that is implied in the rules, and justice was almost certainly done by the BHA disciplinary panel when it reinstated Simple Verse who became the forty-second filly to win the St Leger. Both jockeys involved in the St Leger finish incurred suspensions, Atzeni picking up a three-day ban for careless riding when pushing his way out, and Colm O'Donoghue receiving two days for using his whip above the permitted level.

Simple Verse's owners are behind the Qipco sponsorship of Britain's richest raceday, British Champions' Day at Ascot in October, and Simple Verse finished her three-year-old campaign in what was still a good renewal of the British Champions Fillies' And Mares' Stakes, despite the absence of three Irish fillies who had won Group 1s in Britain, the Oaks winner Qualify, the Nassau winner Legatissimo and the Yorkshire Oaks winner Pleascach, while the Irish-trained Ribblesdale winner Curvy went for the E. P. Taylor in Canada instead. Dropping back to a mile and a half didn't inconvenience Simple Verse and, in a strongly-run affair on good to soft going, she repeated her St Leger form to win by three quarters of a length and two lengths from Journey and Beautiful Romance, with the Irish Oaks winner Covert Love, who started favourite, completing the frame. Simple Verse was ridden handily by Andrea Atzeni, who had announced that he was ending his association with Qatar Racing after only a year to ride for Sheikh Obaid and trainer Roger Varian. Simple Verse stayed on strongly to bring her jockey's spell as Qatar Racing's number-one to a successful conclusion. With the first four in the Fillies' And Mares' all staying in training, it looks as though there will be other meetings between them to look forward to. Simple Verse herself is said to have the King George VI and Queen Elizabeth Stakes as her main target and she wouldn't have to make much improvement to have a good chance against the colts in that race, especially if conditions put the emphasis on stamina.

Simple Verse (IRE)
(b.f. 2012)

Duke of Marmalade (IRE) (b 2004)	Danehill (b 1986)	Danzig
		Razyana
	Love Me True (ch 1998)	Kingmambo
		Lassie's Lady
Guantanamera (IRE) (b 2004)	Sadler's Wells (b 1981)	Northern Dancer
		Fairy Bridge
	Bluffing (b 1992)	Darshaan
		Instinctive Move

The fine season enjoyed by Simple Verse's sire Duke of Marmalade, after being banished to South Africa, is covered in the essay on Star of Seville. The big, lengthy Simple Verse, who carries plenty of condition, was bought for €240,000 at Goffs as a yearling and is the third winner out of her unraced dam Guantanamera, a Sadler's Wells daughter of the useful Irish mile and a half performer Bluffing. Guantanamera's first two winners were both milers by Holy Roman Emperor, the fairly useful Irish maiden winner Lord Jim and the useful Maxentius who was in the frame in the Superlative Stakes and the Champagne as a two-year-old. Guantanamera's two-year-old daughter Even Song (by Mastercraftsman) made a very promising start to her career for Aidan O'Brien in the autumn, readily winning a maiden at Leopardstown on her second start. Simple Verse's great grandam Instinctive Move was a half-sister to the Irish Derby winner Law Society. Simple Verse stays an extended mile and three quarters and acts on polytrack, good to firm and good to soft going. She usually races prominently and finds plenty under pressure. *Ralph Beckett*

SIMPLY BLACK (IRE) 4 br.f. Kheleyf (USA) 116 – Tashyra (IRE) 59 (Tagula (IRE) **49** 116) [2015 61, a72: t5.1g t5.1f⁶ t5.1f f5g⁶ Apr 14] poor handicapper: left David O'Meara after first start: raced only at 5f: acts on polytrack, tapeta and good to firm going: sometimes wears headgear: often races towards rear. *Ann Stokell*

SIMPLY CLEVER 2 ch.f. (Feb 14) Stimulation (IRE) 121 – Well of Echoes 68 (Diktat —
126) [2015 f5g⁴ f5d⁵ 5.1m p8g⁶ p7g Aug 26] second foal: dam 8.6f winner: no form in
maidens/nurseries. *David Brown*

SIMPLY ME 2 b.f. (Mar 27) New Approach (IRE) 132 – Ego 107 (Green Desert (USA) **65 p**
127) [2015 7g Oct 9] 90,000Y: good-topped filly: half-sister to several winners, including
useful winner up to 1m (stayed 1¼m) Chef (2-y-o 7f winner, by Selkirk) and 2-y-o 7f
winner Self Centred (by Medicean): dam 2-y-o 6f winner: 50/1, 5½ lengths ninth of 17 to
Materialistic in maiden at Newmarket on debut: should do better. *Tom Dascombe*

SIMPLY ROUGE 5 b.m. Croco Rouge (IRE) 129 – Simply Mystic (Simply Great (FR) **79**
122) [2015 12m 12d⁴ 8m³ 12.4m⁵ Jul 25] first foal: dam, winning hurdler, half-sister to
very smart 10.4f-1¼m winner Clever Cookie: fair maiden: best effort at 1½m. *Peter Niven*

SIMPLY SHINING (IRE) 5 ch.m. Rock of Gibraltar (IRE) 133 – Bright Smile (IRE) 83 **88**
(Caerleon (USA) 132) [2015 83§: 8m* 8m* 8m 8f⁴ 8m⁴ 8d² 8m⁵ 8m⁵ 8d⁶ Sep 26] angular
mare: fairly useful handicapper: won at Doncaster in April and Thirsk in May: stays 8.5f:
acts on firm and soft going: tried in cheekpieces prior to 2015: front runner/races
prominently. *Richard Fahey*

SINAKAR (IRE) 4 br.g. Manduro (GER) 135 – Siniyya (IRE) 70 (Grand Lodge (USA) **81**
125) [2015 9.2d³ 10d 13.1g* 15.8s² f14m p13.3m⁵ Dec 27] fairly useful ex-French-trained
handicapper: won at Ayr in October: stays 2m: acts on soft going: often races lazily. *David
O'Meara*

SINBAD THE SAILOR 10 b.g. Cape Cross (IRE) 129 – Sinead (USA) (Irish River (FR) **69**
131) [2015 57: 16g t16.5m* t16.5g Dec 5] strong, compact gelding: fair handicapper: won
at Wolverhampton in November: stays 16.5f: acts on polytrack, tapeta, firm and soft going:
often wears headgear: often in tongue tie in 2015. *George Baker*

SINEMA 3 gr.g. Compton Place 125 – Dictatrix 91 (Diktat 126) [2015 p6m p6g⁴ p7f⁵ p7g² **68**
6g⁴ 7m² p8g p7g p7f f7g f6g⁶ Dec 29] good-bodied gelding: fair maiden: stays 7f: acts on
polytrack, fibresand and good to firm going: in headgear last 3 starts: races prominently,
tends to find little. *Christine Dunnett*

SINFONIETTA (FR) 3 b.g. Sinndar (IRE) 134 – Final Whistle (IRE) (Rossini (USA) **79**
118) [2015 7s⁵ 8g² 7.6m⁶ 8g² p10f² 7s⁴ p8g Oct 18] fair maiden on balance of form at 3 yrs:
left F. Chappet after second start: stays 9.5f: acts on polytrack and soft going. *David
Menuisier*

SINGAPORE DREAM (IRE) 3 b.g. Teofilo (IRE) 126 – Rainbow Desert (USA) 86 **53**
(Dynaformer (USA)) [2015 p8m⁵ 8.3g⁵ 7m 10m⁵ p10g p8f Sep 3] angular-looking gelding:
modest maiden: stays 9f: acts on polytrack: tried in headgear. *Charlie Wallis*

SINGEUR (IRE) 8 b.g. Chineur (FR) 123 – Singitta (Singspiel (IRE) 133) [2015 98: 5m **94**
5g⁶ 5m 5g* 6m² 5g² 5m³ 5m⁴ 6g⁶ 5.4g⁵ 6m 5g² 5s 5s⁵ Oct 19] lengthy gelding: fairly
useful handicapper: won at Redcar in May: good second at Ripon in September: stays 6f:
acts on fibresand, firm and soft going: sometimes in headgear, including last 3 starts.
Rebecca Bastiman

SINGING STAR (IRE) 4 b.f. Iffraaj 127 – Seven Sing (USA) 83 (Machiavellian (USA) **49**
123) [2015 57: 16g⁴ t6f 5g 6m Jul 1] poor maiden: stays 6f: acts on tapeta and soft going:
usually leads. *Antony Brittain*

SINGLE LENSE (IRE) 3 b.c. Kodiac 112 – Undulation (Alhaarth (IRE) 126) [2015 p7f² **79**
t8.6f* p8m⁴ 8.3m⁵ 8m⁶ Jun 19] fair performer: won maiden at Wolverhampton in February:
worth a try at 7f: acts on tapeta and good to firm going. *Ed Walker*

SINGLE SUMMIT 3 b.c. Hellvelyn 118 – Once Removed 65 (Distant Relative 128) **—**
[2015 p5g⁴ 7v p6f³ p6f f5g t5.1f⁴ p6m⁵ Dec 27] no form: tried in visor. *J. R. Jenkins*

SINGOALLA 3 b.f. Arch (USA) 127 – Songerie 115 (Hernando (FR) 127) [2015 62p: **69**
p10g⁶ 13.1f⁵ p16g Nov 4] fair maiden: best effort at 13f: acts on firm going: tried in
blinkers in 2015: usually races prominently. *Sir Mark Prescott Bt*

SING SOMETHING 2 gr.c. (Feb 8) Paco Boy (IRE) 129 – Rock Ace (IRE) 82 (Verglas **67**
(IRE) 118) [2015 5g⁵ 5m³ p5m⁴ 6d³ 5g² 5g⁴ 6v⁴ 5.7m t7.1f² Oct 20] fair maiden: stays 7f:
acts on polytrack, tapeta and good to firm going: sold 5,000 gns, sent to France.
David Brown

SINGULAR QUEST 3 ch.g. Dalakhani (IRE) 133 – Singuliere (IRE) (Singspiel (IRE) **80**
133) [2015 70p: p10g² p10f⁴ 12.1m³ 14m² 14f⁵ 14f⁵ 12d⁵ p16g⁶ Sep 5] angular gelding:
fairly useful maiden: stays 1¾m: acts on firm going: tried in cheekpieces: front runner/
races prominently: sold 2,000 gns and joined Kevin Frost. *Ralph Beckett*

SINGYOURSONG (IRE) 2 b.f. (Feb 1) Aqlaam 125 – Dhan Dhana (IRE) 79 (Dubawi **86 p**
(IRE) 129) [2015 p8g³ Dec 15] second foal: half-sister to 1¼m winner Rejaah (by
Authorized): dam, 9.7f/1¼m winner, half-sister to useful 1m-1¼m winner Annabelle's
Charm, herself dam of Middle Park Stakes winner Charming Thought: 20/1, shaped as if
needed experience when third in maiden at Kempton (1¾ lengths behind Cajoled) in
December, not having run of race: will stay 1¼m: sure to progress. *David Simcock*

SINGZAK 7 ch.g. Singspiel (IRE) 133 – Zakuska 96 (Zafonic (USA) 130) [2015 68, a85: **72**
12g 12g f12g⁵ f14g² f16g³ Dec 29] fair handicapper: stays 16.5f: acts on polytrack,
fibresand and good to firm going: usually leads. *David C. Griffiths*

SI NON OSCILLAS (IRE) 3 b.f. Fastnet Rock (AUS) 127 – Playboy Mansion (IRE) **–**
(Grand Lodge (USA) 125) [2015 p10g p10f⁶ Mar 20] 42,000Y: fourth foal: half-sister to
useful 1¼m-1½m winner Cape Caster (by Cape Cross): dam, US 1m winner, sister to
US Grade 2 8.5f winner Grande Melody: well held in 2 maidens at Lingfield. *Ralph Beckett*

SIOUX CHIEFTAIN (IRE) 5 b.g. Mount Nelson 125 – Lady Gin (USA) (Saint Ballado **81**
(CAN)) [2015 88: p14g⁵ t12.2f² 12.4g⁵ 12s³ May 9] fairly useful handicapper: stays 12.5f:
acts on tapeta and heavy going: usually races prominently. *Michael Appleby*

SIOUXPERHERO (IRE) 6 b.g. Sleeping Indian 122 – Tintern (Diktat 126) [2015 79§: **68 §**
8f 8.1s⁶ 9d⁶ 8.3m⁵ 8m³ Jun 30] compact gelding: fair handicapper: stays 9f: acts on tapeta,
firm and good to soft going: wears headgear: tried in tongue tie prior to 2015: front runner/
races prominently: not one to trust. *William Muir*

SIRAJIAH (IRE) 2 ch.f. (Apr 15) Exceed And Excel (AUS) 126 – Miss Honorine (IRE) **76 p**
109 (Highest Honor (FR) 124) [2015 6d² 5.1d² Aug 5] 85,000Y: seventh foal: half-sister to
3 winners, including useful winner up to 7f in Scandinavia Master Chef (2-y-o 6f winner,
by Oasis Dream) and winner up to 1m Admire The View (2-y-o 7f winner, by Dubawi):
dam 1m-1¼m winner: dropped in trip, improved from debut when ½-length second of 7 to
Little Voice in maiden at Chepstow, clear of rest: likely to stay at least 7f: should do better
still. *William Haggas*

SIR BILLY WRIGHT (IRE) 4 b.g. High Chaparral (IRE) 132 – Lure of The Moon **91**
(USA) (Lure (USA) 131) [2015 75: t6m* p5g² 5m⁵ p5g² p6m⁶ 6.1f⁵ 6g⁵ t6g³ 5d* 5v* 6v³
6.1g⁵ 5s 5.1d⁶ f5g³ Nov 12] lengthy gelding: fairly useful handicapper: won at
Wolverhampton in March and twice at Ffos Las in August: stays 6f: acts on fibresand,
tapeta and heavy going: tried in visor in 2015. *David Evans*

SIR CHAUVELIN 3 b.g. Authorized (IRE) 133 – Jabbara (IRE) 65 (Kingmambo (USA) **81**
125) [2015 75: 10d³ 12.4g² 14m⁴ 13.1d³ 10.3g⁵ 13.1g* 14s⁵ Oct 9] fairly useful handicapper:
won at Ayr (by 1¾ lengths from Carpe Vita) in September: stays easy 1¾m: acts on firm
and good to soft going: signs of temperament: useful hurdler. *Jim Goldie*

SIRDAAB (USA) 3 b.g. City Zip (USA) 112 – Stormy Union (USA) (Dixie Union (USA) **55**
121) [2015 68p: 7d 5.7f⁶ 5.7m t5.1f⁶ f5g t6f p6f p6m⁴ Dec 27] modest maiden: left
B. W. Hills after third start: stays 6f: acts on polytrack and good to firm going: tried in
hood/tongue tie. *Ann Stokell*

SIRDAAL (USA) 2 b.c. (Mar 16) Medaglia d'Oro (USA) 129 – Sarayir (USA) 104 **– p**
(Mr Prospector (USA)) [2015 7g Sep 25] half-brother to several winners, including
high-class 1m-1½m winner Mawatheeq (by Danzig) and 1000 Guineas/Coronation Stakes
winner Ghanaati (2-y-o 7f winner, by Giant's Causeway): dam, winner up to 1¼m (2-y-o
7f winner), closely related to Nayef and Unfuwain: 25/1, very
green when down the field in maiden at Newmarket: should do better. *B. W. Hills*

SIR DOMINO (FR) 3 b.g. Evasive 116 – Domino Queen (IRE) 68 (Primo Dominie 121) **82**
[2015 82p: 6s³ 7.2d 7g⁴ 6.1s 5.1d⁴ Oct 28] fairly useful handicapper: stays 6f: acts on soft
going: in cheekpieces final start. *Kevin Ryan*

SIR DUDLEY (IRE) 2 b.c. (Feb 10) Arcano (IRE) 122 – Rosy Dudley (IRE) 72 (Grand **75**
Lodge (USA) 125) [2015 5d⁵ 5.1m* 6m⁵ p5g² 6m⁵ 5g⁵ t5.1g⁴ p6g⁴ Dec 30] £52,000Y: **a85**
half-brother to several winners, including useful winner up to 1m Apostle (2-y-o 6f winner,
by Dark Angel) and 1m winner Shafrah (by Acclamation): dam, 8.4f winner, half-sister to
smart 2-y-o sprinter Deadly Dudley: fairly useful performer: won maiden at Nottingham in
April: second in minor event at Chelmsford in June: may prove best at bare 5f: acts on
polytrack and good to firm going: front runner/races prominently. *James Given*

SIR DYLAN 6 b.g. Dylan Thomas (IRE) 132 – Monteleone (IRE) (Montjeu (IRE) 137) **52 §**
[2015 11.7f t12.2g² Apr 28] modest handicapper: stays 1½m: acts on polytrack, tapeta and
good to soft going: usually wears headgear: irresolute. *Polly Gundry*

SIREN'S COVE 3 b.f. Sir Percy 129 – Siren Sound 80 (Singspiel (IRE) 133) [2015 70: **89**
p7m⁶ p7m⁶ p10g* f12g² 12d p12g² p10g³ p12g* t9.5g² p12g⁶ p12g⁶ p13g t9.5f⁶ p11g⁵
p10m⁴ Dec 16] angular filly: fairly useful handicapper: won at Chelmsford in March and
Lingfield in June: left James Tate after ninth start, Ed Walker after twelfth: stays 13f: acts
on polytrack and tapeta: tried in hood in 2015. *Richard Fahey*

SIR GEOFFREY (IRE) 9 b.g. Captain Rio 122 – Disarm (IRE) (Bahamian Bounty 116) **63**
[2015 73, a80: p5g⁴ f5d⁴ f5g³ p5d⁶ 5d p5f⁴ f6d³ 5d² t5.1m⁴ 5s* 5.1d⁵ 5s⁵ f6g f5m f5f Dec
17] sturdy gelding: modest handicapper: won at Catterick (amateur) in October: stays 6f:
acts on all-weather, firm and soft going: wears headgear: tried in tongue tie. *Scott Dixon*

SIRHEED (IRE) 3 ch.g. Rip Van Winkle (IRE) 134 – Rozella (IRE) (Anabaa (USA) 130) **89**
[2015 72: 7m* 8m² t9.5g 7g² 10.3g⁶ 8d⁴ Sep 3] fairly useful performer: won maiden at
Salisbury in June: better form in handicaps: stays 1m: acts on good to firm and good to soft
going: races prominently: sold 18,000 gns, sent to Bahrain. *Richard Hannon*

SIR HENRY RAEBURN (IRE) 3 b.g. Henrythenavigator (USA) 131 – La Traviata **78**
(USA) 112 (Johannesburg (USA) 127) [2015 71: p7g* 8.3m p7f² p7g⁵ Jun 4] useful-
looking gelding: fair handicapper: won at Kempton in April: stays 7f: acts on polytrack:
often wears tongue tie. *Paul Cole*

SIRI 2 br.f. (Mar 20) Atlantic Sport (USA) 115 – Search Party 78 (Rainbow Quest (USA) **75 p**
134) [2015 7.1m² Sep 10] half-sister to several winners, including 1¼m-16.5f winner
Foster's Road (by Imperial Dancer) and 1m winner (including at 2 yrs) Shimba Hills
(by Sixties Icon), stays 1½m: dam maiden (stayed 1¼m): 12/1, 1¼ lengths second of 8 to
Puzzled Look in maiden at Chepstow: entitled to progress. *Mick Channon*

SIR ISAAC NEWTON 3 b.c. Galileo (IRE) 134 – Shastye (IRE) 108 (Danehill (USA) **115**
126) [2015 97P: 10.3s² 7g* 7f⁶ 8g⁴ Sep 12] useful-looking colt: smart performer: won
maiden at Gowran (by 3¼ lengths from Stop And Linger) in May: refused to settle/hung
right throughout (also met some trouble) when 2 lengths sixth of 16 to Dutch Connection
in Jersey Stakes at Royal Ascot next start: should stay at least 1m: temperament under suspicion. *Aidan O'Brien, Ireland*

SIRIUS (GER) 4 ch.c. Dashing Blade 117 – Saratina (IRE) (Monsun (GER) 124) [2015 **118**
116: 11.9g⁶ 11.9g² 11.9g⁴ 11.9g³ 11.9s² 11.9s⁴ Nov 1] smart performer: won Grosser Preis
von Berlin at Hoppegarten at 3 yrs: in frame last 5 starts in 2015, including in Grosser
Hansa-Preis at Hamburg (head second to Lovelyn), Grosser Preis von Baden at Baden-
Baden (2¼ lengths third behind Prince Gibraltar) and Preis von Europa at Cologne
(2 lengths second to Nightflower): below form when 10 lengths fourth to Ito in Grosser
Preis von Bayern at Munich final outing: stays 1½m: acts on soft going: wears blinkers.
Andreas Löwe, Germany

SIRIUS MOVE 2 b.g. (Mar 14) Monsieur Bond (IRE) 120 – Lady Paris (IRE) 96 **58**
(Invincible Spirit (IRE) 121) [2015 6d 5d⁶ 5.4s t6f t7.1f Nov 30] modest maiden: best effort
at 5f: acts on good to soft going: sometimes in headgear. *Geoffrey Oldroyd*

SIRIUS PROSPECT (USA) 7 b.g. Gone West (USA) – Stella Blue (FR) 106 (Anabaa **107**
(USA) 130) [2015 119: a7f⁵ 7g a8f 8d³ 8.3f⁴ 8f 7f 7d Jul 25] good-topped gelding: useful
performer: third in listed race at Doncaster (¾ length behind Tullius) in March: stays 1m:
acts on polytrack, dirt, firm and good going: sometimes in headgear prior to 2015: quirky.
Dean Ivory

SIR JACK LAYDEN 4 b.g. Sir Percy 129 – Barawin (IRE) 87 (Hawk Wing (USA) 136) **87**
[2015 55: 8f 10.4g 10m 12m³ 12m⁴ 10m⁴ 13.1f p12g* Oct 6] good-topped gelding: fairly
useful handicapper: in first-time cheekpieces, won at Kempton in October: stays 1½m: acts
on polytrack, tapeta, good to firm and good to soft going: sold 35,000 gns, sent to Saudi
Arabia. *David Brown*

SIR JAMIE 2 ch.c. (Feb 16) Monsieur Bond (IRE) 120 – First Dawn 68 (Dr Fong (USA) **–**
128) [2015 7g 6d Oct 12] well held in maidens at Salisbury and Windsor. *Geoffrey Deacon*

SIR KEATING 3 b.g. Sir Percy 129 – Moiava (FR) 112 (Bering 136) [2015 t7.1g* t7.1g* **78 p**
Mar 24] 35,000Y: half-brother to several winners, including useful winner up to 7f
Indignant (2-y-o 6f winner) and French 1m winner Intolerance (both by Gold Away): dam
2-y-o 7f (including Criterium de Maisons-Laffitte) winner: successful debut in maiden at
Wolverhampton in January, and followed up in handicap at same course in March by 1½
lengths from Plaisir: will stay 1m: sent to Hong Kong, where renamed Beauty Connection:
open to further improvement. *Kevin Ryan*

SIR KELTIC BLUE 3 b.g. Sir Percy 129 – Bougainvilia (IRE) 89 (Bahamian Bounty **–**
116) [2015 73: 6g⁶ 8.3m 7d Sep 21] maiden: no form in 2015. *Daniel Loughnane*

SIR LANCELOTT 3 b.g. Piccolo 121 – Selkirk Rose (IRE) 74 (Pips Pride 117) [2015 61: **75** t8.6g* f8s² 8g* 9g³ 8g 9.3d⁵ 8m⁴ 9.3g t9.5m t8.6f⁶ t8.6f t9.5m³ t8.6f* Dec 22] workmanlike gelding: fair handicapper: won at Wolverhampton in February, Newcastle in April and Wolverhampton (apprentice) in December: left Keith Dalgleish after seventh start: stays 9.5f: acts on tapeta, best turf form on good going: in cheekpieces final start. *David O'Meara*

SIR MAXIMILIAN (IRE) 6 b.g. Royal Applause 124 – Nebraska Lady (IRE) 87 **117** (Lujain (USA) 119) [2015 113: 5g 5g³ 5g 6g⁵ 5g* 5g⁶ t6m² Dec 26] good-topped gelding: smart performer: won 16-runner Meydan Sprint in March by short head from Ahtoug: off 9 months, respectable second in minor event at Wolverhampton final start: best form at 5f: acts on polytrack, good to firm and good to soft going. *Ian Williams*

SIR PASS I AM 2 b.g. (Feb 28) Passing Glance 119 – Orbital Orchid 63 (Mujahid (USA) **56 p** 125) [2015 8.1s Sep 16] first foal: dam, temperamental staying maiden on Flat, winning hurdler; 10/1, some encouragement when 11½ lengths seventh of 12 to Taskeen in maiden at Sandown, penny dropping late: has been gelded: will improve. *Andrew Balding*

SIRPERTAN 4 b.g. Sir Percy 129 – Tanwir 76 (Unfuwain (USA) 131) [2015 62: f16d – Jan 2] smallish, strong gelding: modest handicapper at best: stays 1¾m: acts on heavy going: tried in headgear: usually races close up. *Marjorie Fife*

SIRRAH STAR (IRE) 7 gr.m. Great Palm (USA) 119 – Simply Deep (IRE) (Simply – Great (FR) 122) [2015 11.7f⁴ Apr 23] showed nothing in 3 maidens on Flat: placed in bumper/modest hurdler. *Neil Mulholland*

SIR RENOS SANTI 2 b.g. (Feb 26) Observatory (USA) 131 – Diamond Reef (Alzao – (USA) 117) [2015 7f 8.3g 8.5m Oct 1] small, compact gelding: well held in 3 maidens: has been gelded. *Ian Williams*

SIR ROBERT CHEVAL 4 b.g. Green Desert (USA) 127 – Aunt Ruby (USA) 67 **101** (Rubiano (USA)) [2015 104: 6m⁶ 7d⁴ 7m⁴ 7g⁵ 7d 7g⁴ 8m* p8f Oct 24] useful-looking gelding: useful performer: won minor event at Ascot (by 1¼ lengths from Robert The Painter) in October: stays 1m: acts on polytrack, good to firm and good to soft going: often races towards rear. *Marco Botti*

SIR RODERIC (IRE) 2 b.g. (Apr 21) Roderic O'Connor (IRE) 119 – Begin The Beguine **71** (IRE) 72 (Peintre Celebre (USA) 137) [2015 6m 6d⁴ 7g⁵ 8.3d⁵ Oct 5] maiden, fair form second/third starts: should stay 1m. *Rod Millman*

SIR ROGER MOORE (IRE) 2 b.g. (Apr 1) Kodiac 112 – Truly Magnificent (USA) 62 **78** (Elusive Quality (USA)) [2015 6m³ 6f 6g 6g p6m² p7g⁵ t5.1m* Dec 26] smallish gelding: fair performer: won maiden at Wolverhampton in December: stays 7f: acts on polytrack, tapeta and good to firm going. *Charles Hills*

SIR THEODORE (IRE) 2 b.g. (Apr 29) Arcano (IRE) 122 – Key Rose (IRE) 88 (Key **72** of Luck (USA) 126) [2015 6g 5.1m² 5f 5g⁵ 6.1m³ 6v* 6g⁵ t6f Nov 14] compact gelding: fair performer: won nursery at Lingfield in September: stays 6f: acts on good to firm and heavy going. *Dave Morris*

SI SENOR (IRE) 4 b.g. Dansili 127 – Kotsi (IRE) 103 (Nayef (USA) 129) [2015 100: **97** p8g⁶ 8m⁴ p8g p8g² 7m⁵ Oct 2] sturdy gelding: useful handicapper: good second at Kempton (½ length behind Power Game) in September: stays 1m: acts on polytrack: tried in cheekpieces in 2015. *Ed Vaughan*

SISTER DUDE 2 ch.f. (Mar 16) Notnowcato 128 – Inaminute (IRE) 86 (Spectrum (IRE) **67 p** 126) [2015 8d 7.2g⁴ Sep 18] third foal: half-sister to useful winner up to 1m Hay Dude (2-y-o 7f winner, by Dubawi): dam 7f winner: better effort when fourth in maiden at Ayr (2½ lengths behind Constantino) in September, considerably handled: open to further improvement. *K. R. Burke*

SISYPHUS 3 b.g. Halling (USA) 133 – Cape Dancer (IRE) 66 (Cape Cross (IRE) 129) **78** [2015 10.1d⁵ 9.3g³ 10m⁶ 10g² 12.2m² 12g Sep 26] rather leggy gelding: fair maiden: stays 1½m: acts on good to firm going. *Ollie Pears*

SIX SILVER LANE 7 gr.g. Aussie Rules (USA) 123 – Aurelia 80 (Rainbow Quest (USA) **72** 134) [2015 81: p8g⁶ 8m⁴ p8g p8g* p8g³ 8g⁵ p8d⁵ 8.3d⁵ 8.9g* 8g* p8g Oct 16] fair handicapper: won at Dundalk in April, Musselburgh in August and Ayr (apprentice) in September: stays 1¼m: acts on polytrack, sand, soft and good to firm going: usually wears headgear: tried in tongue tie: often races prominently. *J. J. Feane, Ireland*

SIXTH SENSE (IRE) 2 ch.c. (Apr 23) Shamardal (USA) 129 – Shinko Hermes (IRE) **104** (Sadler's Wells (USA) 132) [2015 5v³ 5.2m³ 5m* 6m⁵ 7f³ 6m 7d⁴ 6g 8g³ 8g⁶ Sep 26] strong, well-grown colt: half-brother to numerous winners, including smart winner up to 11f Lake Toya (2-y-o 1¼m winner, by Darshaan) and useful 1m winner Glen Innes (by Selkirk): dam, ran once in Japan, sister to Oaks winner Imagine and half-sister to Generous:

useful performer: won maiden at Pontefract in April and listed race at Ascot (by 1¼ lengths from Platitude) in July: third in Chesham Stakes at Royal Ascot (1¼ lengths behind Suits You) and in Prix des Chenes at Longchamp (3½ lengths behind Cloth of Stars) in September: probably stays 1m: acts on firm and good to soft going: usually leads. *Mark Johnston*

SIXTIES GROOVE (IRE) 2 b.c. (Feb 14) Sixties Icon 125 – Gift Dancer (Imperial **64 p** Dancer 123) [2015 p8g⁵ Nov 11] 45,000F, 80,000Y: first foal: dam unraced half-sister to Irish 1000 Guineas/US Grade 1 9f winner Samitar: 8/1, shaped well when 7¼ lengths fifth of 13 to Prince of Arran in maiden at Kempton, very green/late headway: sure to progress. *Jeremy Noseda*

SIXTIES LOVE 4 b.f. Sixties Icon 125 – Love Always 81 (Piccolo 121) [2015 75: p10g³ **80** p10g 8g² 8d² 7.6d 8v⁶ 7m⁴ 7m² 6g 7g⁴ 9.9g² p12g* p12g² p14f³ p12g Dec 2] fairly useful handicapper: won at Kempton in September: stays 1¾m: acts on polytrack: tried in cheekpieces in 2015: often races in rear/travels strongly. *Simon Dow*

SIXTIES PILGRIM 2 b.f. (Feb 23) Sixties Icon 125 – Sweet Pilgrim 74 (Talkin Man **66** (CAN) 120) [2015 6d 7m* Aug 7] 1,000F: second foal: sister to Swedish 1m winner Run By Faith: dam 6f winner: improved from debut when winning seller at Newmarket by 3½ lengths from Broughtons Fancy: sold 9,000 gns after, sent to Sweden. *Mick Channon*

SIXTIES QUEEN 5 b.m. Sixties Icon 125 – Lily of Tagula (IRE) (Tagula (IRE) 116) **51** [2015 61: t8.6g⁴ t8.6g³ t9.5f⁶ p10f⁵ t8.6g² t8.6g⁵ p8m³ p8m³ t8.6g p8g t8.6g p8f t8.6f p8g⁵ t8.6f Dec 21] modest handicapper: left Alan Bailey after fifth start: stays 1¼m: acts on polytrack, tapeta, good to firm and good to soft going: sometimes in headgear in 2015: usually races close up. *Lisa Williamson*

SIXTIES SUE 2 gr.f. (Mar 17) Sixties Icon 125 – Rose Cheval (USA) 74 (Johannesburg **94** (USA) 127) [2015 5m³ 5m⁵ 6d* 6.1m³ 7f 6m⁴ 6m 5m² 6g 6.1m* 5.2s 6.1m³ 6s² p6g⁵ 5.5d² 6s 6d⁴ 6d⁴ Oct 30] smallish, leggy filly: third foal: sister to 2-y-o 5f-7f winner Scargill: dam maiden (stayed 8.6f): fairly useful performer: won maiden at Lingfield in June and minor event at Nottingham in August: second in nurseries at Goodwood and Chester in September: stays 6f: acts on soft and good to firm going: often races towards rear. *Mick Channon*

SIX WIVES 8 b.m. Kingsalsa (USA) 118 – Regina 97 (Green Desert (USA) 127) [2015 73, **–** a84: f5g f6d³ Jan 27] sturdy mare: fairly useful at best, no form in 2015: best form at 5f: acts on polytrack, fibresand, good to firm and good to soft going: wears headgear. *Scott Dixon*

SKATE 3 gr.g. Verglas (IRE) 118 – Strut 103 (Danehill Dancer (IRE) 117) [2015 85p: 5.7g* **94** 7g* 8g⁴ 7g⁵ Dec 3] fairly useful performer: won handicap at Bath (by 1¼ lengths from Dominium) in June (left Roger Charlton 85,000 gns after) and minor event at Doha in November: stays 7f: front runner/races prominently. *S. Ibido, Qatar*

SKEAPING 2 b.c. (Jan 25) Excellent Art 125 – Gale Green 78 (Galileo (IRE) 134) [2015 **84** 6m⁶ 7m² 7g³ 8s² 6m⁴ Oct 3] 8,500F, 24,000Y: strong colt: first foal: dam 1¼m winner: fairly useful maiden: second at Salisbury and Goodwood: will prove best at 7f+: acts on soft and good to firm going: often leads. *Richard Hannon*

SKELL GILL 3 b.g. Multiplex 114 – Socceroo 65 (Choisir (AUS) 126) [2015 t6f⁶ t6f **–** t7.1m³ t7.1g Mar 24] little impact in maidens/handicap at Wolverhampton. *James Unett*

SKI BLAST 4 ch.g. Three Valleys (USA) 119 – Chasing Stars 103 (Observatory (USA) **78** 131) [2015 5m 6m² 5g⁵ 7g* 7m⁶ Sep 8] fair performer: won maiden at Newcastle in August: stays 7f: acts on good to firm going. *Ivan Furtado*

SKIDBY MILL (IRE) 5 b.m. Ramonti (FR) 126 – Glasnas Giant 60 (Giant's Causeway **71** (USA) 132) [2015 70: p7g³ p7m⁵ p7f³ p8f* p7f³ p8f³ p8g* p8m² 7m² p8f² p8g* p8g² 8.3m³ p7g p8f⁴ 8v⁴ Aug 25] workmanlike mare: fair handicapper: won at Kempton in February and at Lingfield in March and May: stays 8.5f: acts on polytrack, good to firm and heavy going: tried in headgear prior to 2015: often races prominently: quirky. *Laura Mongan*

SKIDDAW VALLEYS 3 ch.g. Three Valleys (USA) 119 – Skiddaw Wolf 74 (Wolfhound **78** (USA) 126) [2015 10g² 8.3s 10g⁴ 10g 9.3g* 11.5d⁵ 12m 9.8g³ 13.8g* 13.4d⁴ Sep 26] fair handicapper: won at Carlisle in July and Catterick in September: stays 1¾m: acts on good to firm going. *Alan Swinbank*

SKINNY LOVE 4 b.f. Holy Roman Emperor (IRE) 125 – Lady Mickataine (USA) 71 **88** (Speightstown (USA) 124) [2015 69: p6g* p7f* p7f² 7m* 8f 8m 8.1m⁶ 7.1g* 7.1g² p7g* p6m⁴ t7.1g t6m⁴ Dec 26] smallish, close-coupled filly: fairly useful handicapper: improved and won at Lingfield (twice) in February, Redcar in April, Sandown in August and at Kempton (by nose from Lady Horatia) in October: stays 7f: acts on polytrack and good to firm going: tried in cheekpieces: usually races close up. *K. R. Burke*

SKIP AND JUMP (USA) 3 b.f. Elusive Quality (USA) – Skip A Dare (USA) (Skip Away –
(USA) 134) [2015 72: p8m⁴ Jan 14] tall, quite attractive filly: lightly-raced maiden, fair form at best: stays 8.5f: tried in hood: sold 13,000 gns, sent to Kazakhstan. *Roger Varian*

SKI SLOPE 3 b.f. Three Valleys (USA) 119 – Danehurst 118 (Danehill (USA) 126) [2015 **74**
82p: 7m⁵ p7g⁶ Jun 10] fairly useful winner in 2014, below form both starts in 2015: stays 7f. *Richard Hannon*

SKY CAPE 3 b.g. Cape Cross (IRE) 129 – Green Swallow (FR) 107 (Green Tune (USA) **99**
125) [2015 8g³ 8m* p10f² t9.5g² p11g* Oct 7] fifth foal: half-brother to 1¼m winner (stayed 2m) Hayzoom (by Anabaa) and smart 1½m (Prix de Malleret) winner Yellow And Green (by Monsun): dam French 2-y-o 6f/7f (Prix du Calvados) winner: useful performer: won maiden at Pontefract (by 8 lengths) in August and handicap at Kempton (by short head from The Steward) in October: stays 11f: acts on polytrack, tapeta and good to firm going: usually races close up, often travels strongly. *Charlie Appleby*

SKYE MORNING 3 b.f. Invincible Spirit (IRE) 121 – Bright Morning (USA) (Storm Cat **59**
(USA)) [2015 p8f⁶ p7f⁵ 6g² 8g⁶ 7.4d³ t6m p7g Oct 7] second foal: dam unraced half-sister to top-class winner up to 9f Observatory: modest maiden: best effort at 7.5f: acts on good to soft going: usually in hood. *Harry Dunlop*

SKY FERRY 2 br.g. (Mar 10) Captain Gerrard (IRE) 113 – Ellovamul 62 (Elmaamul **62**
(USA) 125) [2015 6m 6m 7m⁶ p7g⁴ 7m³ 8g⁶ 8s² p8f⁵ t8.6g 7s⁵ 8.3s² p9.4g Nov 2] modest **a40 +**
maiden: stays 8.5f: acts on soft and good to firm going: tried in hood. *J. S. Moore*

SKYFIRE 8 ch.g. Storm Cat (USA) – Sunray Superstar 101 (Nashwan (USA) 135) [2015 –
8.3m Jul 17] leggy gelding: modest handicapper: stays 1m: acts on soft and good to firm going: often in cheekpieces: usually races prominently. *Nick Kent*

SKY HUNTER 5 b.g. Motivator 131 – Pearl Kite (USA) 106 (Silver Hawk (USA) 123) **121**
[2015 121: 12g* 11s² 15.9g Nov 3] good-bodied gelding: very smart performer: won Dubai City of Gold at Meydan (by 1¾ lengths from Sheikhzayedroad) in March: off 7 months, good 1½ lengths second of 5 to The Corsican in Arc Trial at Newbury next time: appeared not to stay when in rear in 24-runner Melbourne Cup (Handicap) at Flemington final outing, weakening over 2f out: stays 1½m: acts on heavy and good to firm going: in hood nowadays. *Saeed bin Suroor*

SKYLARK LADY (IRE) 2 ch.f. (Apr 2) Tamayuz 126 – Allegrissimo (IRE) 48 **54**
(Redback 116) [2015 t7.1g⁶ p7m Dec 16] 17,000Y: first foal: dam French 2-y-o 1m winner: modest form in maidens at Wolverhampton and Lingfield. *Rae Guest*

SKYMASTER 3 gr.g. Aussie Rules (USA) 123 – Last Slipper (Tobougg (IRE) 125) [2015 – **p**
8.3m 10m 8d⁵ Aug 11] tall, rather unfurnished gelding: third foal: half-brother to useful French 1m winner Slippers Best (by Mount Nelson): dam unraced half-sister to smart 1m-1½m winner Dansili Dancer: little impact in maidens: looks type to do better. *Henry Candy*

SKY OF STARS (IRE) 2 b.c. (Feb 1) Frozen Power (IRE) 108 – So So Lucky (IRE) 68 **71**
(Danehill (USA) 126) [2015 7.1g 8g Aug 14] rather unfurnished colt: 33/1, better effort in maidens when 9¾ lengths eighth of 10 to Ventura Storm at Newmarket second start. *Richard Hannon*

SKY ROSE 3 b.f. Sakhee (USA) 136 – Intersky High (USA) (Royal Anthem (USA) 135) **66**
[2015 61p: 12d t9.5g⁶ 12.1d⁶ 16d⁵ p13.3m³ t16.5f³ Oct 17] fair maiden: stays 16.5f: acts on polytrack, tapeta and heavy going. *William Knight*

SKY SHIP 2 ch.c. (Mar 31) Raven's Pass (USA) 133 – Angara 119 (Alzao (USA) 117) **80 p**
[2015 7g p7g⁴ t7.1m* Nov 28] half-brother to several winners, including useful 10.3f winner Space Ship and 2-y-o 7.5f winner Pleiades (both by Galileo): dam, French 1¼m/10.5f winner, later US Grade 1 9f/9.5f winner: fairly useful form: 4/6, didn't need to improve to win maiden at Wolverhampton by 3½ lengths from Hutton, eased close home: will stay at least 1m: remains open to improvement. *Sir Michael Stoute*

SKY STEPS (IRE) 3 ch.g. Strategic Prince 114 – Best Dancing (GER) (Keos (USA) 120) **49 §**
[2015 56: t5.1f⁶ t6g⁵ t5.1g² Jan 26] smallish, close-coupled gelding: poor maiden: stays 7f: acts on tapeta: wears headgear: tried in tongue tie: usually races nearer last than first: flashes tail, one to treat with caution. *Philip McBride*

SKYWARDS MILES (IRE) 3 b.f. New Approach (IRE) 132 – Park Twilight (IRE) **67**
(Bertolini (USA) 125) [2015 p10g p10g4 t12.2g3 12s 10.3d p12m t16.5g t13.9m6 Dec 30]
150,000Y: first foal: dam unraced close relative to Cheveley Park Stakes winner Seazun:
fair maiden: left Charlie Appleby after third start: stays 1¼m: acts on polytrack: tried in
cheekpieces. *Tim Fitzgerald*

SLEEP EASY 3 b.g. Rip Van Winkle (IRE) 134 – Strictly Lambada 77 (Red Ransom **88**
(USA)) [2015 73: p12f3 14m4 p13f6 f12s* p12g* 14d5 14d* Sep 25] useful-looking
gelding: fairly useful handicapper: won at Southwell and Lingfield in August and Haydock
in September: stays 1¾m: acts on polytrack, fibresand and good to soft going: in blinkers
last 4 starts: usually responds generously to pressure: has been gelded. *Hughie Morrison*

SLEEPING APACHE (IRE) 5 ch.g. Sleeping Indian 122 – Remedy 72 (Pivotal 124) **87**
[2015 77: 5g* 5s2 5g2 5g2 5m4 6m Jul 24] fairly useful handicapper: won at Pontefract in
April: best effort when second there on fourth start: stays 6f: best form on good going.
Michael Dods

SLEEPING STAR 4 ch.f. Sleeping Indian 122 – Silver Purse 67 (Interrex (CAN)) [2015 **46**
60: f8g4 t8.6f Dec 21] poor maiden: stays 7f: acts on fibresand and heavy going.
Antony Brittain

SLEEPY BLUE OCEAN 9 b.g. Oasis Dream 129 – Esteemed Lady (IRE) 96 (Mark of **76**
Esteem (IRE) 137) [2015 82, a91: f5g5 f5g2 5m 5m6 5m3 5.1m* 5.1g f5g f5g f5g4 Dec 29] **a88**
compact gelding: fairly useful handicapper: won at Nottingham in August: stays 6f: acts on
polytrack, fibresand and any turf going: wears cheekpieces: often races prominently: has
raced moodily. *John Balding*

SLEEPY DUST (IRE) 3 b.f. Rip Van Winkle (IRE) 134 – Knockatotaun 65 (Spectrum **73**
(IRE) 126) [2015 81: 7g p7g4 7v t7.1m 7s3 p8f6 Oct 22] good-topped filly: fair handicapper:
stays 7f: acts on polytrack and soft going. *Sylvester Kirk*

SLEEPY SIOUX 4 b.f. Sleeping Indian 122 – Bella Chica (IRE) 95 (Bigstone (IRE) 126) **93 §**
[2015 104: f5s3 p5g f5s 5.1g 6m 5f3 6g 5g p5m 5m 5.1d Oct 14] good-topped filly: **a84 §**
unreliable handicapper: stays 5.5f: acts on polytrack, firm and good to soft going: wears
headgear: usually races nearer last than first: sold 16,000 gns, sent to Spain. *David Elsworth*

SLEET (IRE) 4 b.g. Amadeus Wolf 122 – Secret Justice (USA) 125 (Lit de Justice (USA) 125) **58 §**
[2015 65: f7d3 f8g4 f6s3 f6d2 f7g3 f6g2 t7.1f2 f7g5 7m5 f7g4 f7g4 f6g4 f6g5 Dec 29]
modest maiden: stays 7f: acts on fibresand and tapeta: usually wears headgear: sometimes
slowly away: one to treat with caution. *Michael Appleby*

SLEMY (IRE) 4 b.g. Raven's Pass (USA) 133 – Wolf Cleugh (IRE) 65 (Last Tycoon 131) **79**
[2015 85: 8g 8.5g 8d 7.2d5 7m4 7.2g4 7m* 7m4 Aug 8] fair handicapper: won at Wetherby
in July: stays 8.5f: acts on polytrack and good to firm going: usually races towards rear.
Ruth Carr

SLIDE SHOW 7 b.m. Galileo (IRE) 134 – First Exhibit (Machiavellian (USA) 123) [2015 **–**
12m4 13.8m4 10.1m Jun 25] fair at best, no form in 2015: tried in headgear. *David Thompson*

SLIM CHANCE (IRE) 6 b.m. Clodovil (IRE) 116 – Valluga (IRE) (Ashkalani (IRE) **74**
128) [2015 85: 6d 5.5g 6d5 6d4 5.9v3 6m5 6g6 5d6 5s 5.9s t6f Sep 19] fair handicapper: stays
8.5f: acts on tapeta, good to firm and heavy going: tried in headgear/tongue tie: sometimes
slowly away, often races prominently. *Simon West*

SLINGSBY 4 b.g. Dutch Art 126 – Ballet Fame (USA) 79 (Quest For Fame 127) [2015 62, **83**
a68: 6g* t6g* 6g 7m3 6m 7d 7d5 6.1d 7v Oct 17] fairly useful handicapper: won at Redcar
(amateur) in May and Wolverhampton in June: stays 8.5f: acts on tapeta, good to firm and
good to soft going: often wears blinkers: sometimes slowly away. *Michael Easterby*

SLINKY MCVELVET 4 ch.f. Refuse To Bend (IRE) 128 – Rania (GER) (Paolini (GER) **–**
121) [2015 76: f8d t8.6m6 Feb 5] fair at best, no form in 2015: stays 8.5f: acts on polytrack,
fibresand, soft and good to firm going: tried in cheekpieces: front runner/races prominently,
usually finds little. *Garry Moss*

SLIPPER SATIN (IRE) 5 b.m. Excellent Art 125 – In The Ribbons 88 (In The Wings **73**
128) [2015 –: t9.5f5 t9.5f6 t9.5g6 14.1g4 14.1m* 14g* 14.1m2 15.8d 13.7m4 13m3 16.2m3 **a54**
Oct 1] fair handicapper: won at Redcar in June and Wetherby in July: stays 2m: acts on
good to firm going: tried in blinkers: in tongue tie nowadays: front runner/races
prominently. *Simon West*

SLIP SLIDING AWAY (IRE) 8 b.g. Whipper (USA) 126 – Sandy Lady (IRE) 91 **92**
(Desert King (IRE) 129) [2015 97: 6m5 5m3 6g4 5f5 6m* 6m 5g6 6gpu Sep 30] rather leggy
gelding: fairly useful handicapper: won at Windsor in July: stayed 6f: acted on soft and
good to firm going: usually raced in rear: dead. *Peter Hedger*

SLOANE AVENUE (USA) 4 ch.c. Candy Ride (ARG) 133 – Apt (USA) (A P Indy **121** (USA) 131) [2015 113: a8f² Mar 28] very smart performer: second in Godolphin Mile at Meydan (short head behind Tamarkuz) only outing in 2015: stays 1m: acts on dirt/ polytrack: often starts slowly. *Jeremy Noseda*

SLOVAK (IRE) 3 ch.f. Iffraaj 127 – Bratislava 54 (Dr Fong (USA) 128) [2015 69p: 7g⁴ **64 +** 8.3s 8g⁴ p8g t7.1m* t7.1m⁴ p8f* Oct 22] fairly useful handicapper: won at Wolverhampton **a82** in September and Chelmsford in October: stays 1m: acts on polytrack and tapeta: front runner/races prominently. *James Tate*

SLUNOVRAT (FR) 4 b.g. Astronomer Royal (USA) 121 – Slewmamba (FR) (Kingsalsa **80** (USA) 118) [2015 70: 12d² 14.1m⁵ 14.1m* 14.1mᵘʳ 14.6m³ 16g 12.4g* 11.9d² Sep 25] workmanlike gelding: fairly useful handicapper: won at Nottingham in May and Newcastle in August: good second at Haydock final start: stays 1¾m: acts on firm and good to soft going: front runner/races prominently. *David Menuisier*

SMAIH (GER) 3 b.c. Paco Boy (IRE) 129 – Solola (GER) (Black Sam Bellamy (IRE) **92** 121) [2015 102: 8g 7g 7g 8.1s Aug 31] attractive colt: useful at 2 yrs, just fairly useful form at best in 2015: stays 7f: acts on heavy going. *Richard Hannon*

SMALLJOHN 9 ch.g. Needwood Blade 117 – My Bonus 79 (Cyrano de Bergerac 120) **68** [2015 75: t7.1g t7.1g⁴ t7.1f t7.1m⁵ 7.1s² 7g* 7.1g² 7d 7.9m 7.2g⁵ t7.1f⁶ Dec 22] close- **a62** coupled gelding: fair handicapper: won at Catterick (apprentice) in April: stays 7f: acts on polytrack, tapeta, good to firm and good to soft going: usually wears visor: front runner/ races prominently. *Bryan Smart*

SMART DAISY K 5 b.m. Pastoral Pursuits 127 – Katy-Q (IRE) 58 (Taufan (USA) 119) **77** [2015 101: t6g 5g t6g Dec 4] fair handicapper: best form at 5f: acts on polytrack, tapeta, firm and soft going: tried in tongue tie in 2015: usually races towards rear. *Sarah Hollinshead*

SMART DJ 4 ch.g. Major Cadeaux 121 – Katy-Q (IRE) 58 (Taufan (USA) 119) [2015 60: **65** 5.1m⁵ 5.1g² 5m* t5.1f² t5.1m⁶ t6f* t6f⁵ t6m Dec 12] fair performer: won handicap at Bath in August and minor event at Wolverhampton in October: stays 6f: acts on tapeta and good to firm going: often races towards rear. *Sarah Hollinshead*

SMARTIE ARTIE (IRE) 4 b.c. Smart Strike (CAN) 121 – Green Room (USA) **88** (Theatrical) [2015 8g³ 10g⁵ 10m* 10m³ p11d⁴ p10m Sep 26] lengthy colt: fifth foal: half- brother to very smart winner up to 1m Lord Shanakill (2-y-o 6f winner, by Speightstown) and 7f/1m winner Brannagh (by Hennessy): dam unraced half-sister to US Grade 1 1¼m winner Spanish Fern: fairly useful performer: won maiden at Windsor in July: stays 11f: acts on polytrack and good to firm going: in hood: often starts slowly/races freely/leads: quirky sort: sold 24,000 gns, sent to UAE. *Jeremy Noseda*

SMART MOTIVE 5 b.g. Motivator 131 – Santana Lady (IRE) 72 (Blakeney 126) [2015 **81** t12.2g³ t12.2g² 11.5d² p16g³ Jun 4] fairly useful maiden: stays 2m. *Alan King*

SMART MOVER (IRE) 2 b.f. (Feb 2) Fast Company (IRE) 126 – Alltherightmoves **77** (IRE) 45 (Namid 128) [2015 5v⁵ 5d⁵ 6g² 6m⁵ 5m* 5m⁶ t5.1m⁵ 6g⁵ 6s² 7s* Oct 26] €35,000Y: first foal: dam maiden half-sister to Oaks third Crown of Light: fair performer: won seller at Musselburgh in June and nursery at Leicester in October: stays 7f: acts on soft and good to firm going: tried in visor. *John Quinn*

SMART RULER (IRE) 9 ch.g. Viking Ruler (AUS) – Celebrated Smile (IRE) (Cadeaux **73** Genereux 131) [2015 72: 12g³ 14m May 22] fair maiden: stays 1½m: acts on firm and good to soft going. *James Moffatt*

SMART SALUTE 4 b.g. Royal Applause 124 – Naizak 73 (Medicean 128) [2015 84: 6g⁵ **84** 6m² 7m* Jun 27] well-made gelding: fairly useful handicapper: won at Doncaster in June: stays 7f: acts on polytrack and good to firm going: often wears headgear: sent to Hong Kong. *Ed Walker*

SMASH WILLIAMS (IRE) 2 ch.c. (Jan 23) Fracas (IRE) 116 – Take Flight (IRE) 85 **111** (Pivotal 124) [2015 6g* 6d* 6d³ Oct 16] first foal: dam, 2-y-o 5f winner, sister to Irish 1000 Guineas winner Saoire: won maiden at the Curragh (24 ran, by 6½ lengths) and 5-runner Round Tower Stakes at same course (beat Rockaway Valley 1¼ lengths, leading over 1f out), both in August: 1/1 favourite, below form when 6¼ lengths third of 7 to Donjuan Triumphant in Criterium de Maisons-Laffitte: raced only at 6f. *J. S. Bolger, Ireland*

SMIDGEN (IRE) 4 b.g. Bahamian Bounty 116 – Brazilian Style 67 (Exit To Nowhere **88** (USA) 122) [2015 77: p6g⁶ t6f* t6m p6g* 6m³ 6m 6m 6m 5v⁶ 6d t6f t6m⁶ Oct 2] tall gelding: fairly useful handicapper: won at Wolverhampton and Lingfield in March: stays 6f: acts on polytrack, tapeta, good to firm and good to soft going: front runner/races prominently: sold 1,500 gns, sent to Belgium. *Ed de Giles*

SMILE OF APPROVAL (IRE) 2 b.f. (Apr 30) Approve (IRE) 112 – Min Asl Wafi **60**
(IRE) 75 (Octagonal (NZ) 126) [2015 p7g 7s⁶ p8f⁵ Nov 6] 4,500F, 6,000Y: smallish filly:
half-sister to several winners, including 9f/1¼m winner Flawless Filly (by Clodovil) and 5f
winner Texas Queen (by Shamardal): dam once-raced half-sister to very smart miler
Zafeen: modest maiden. *Jonathan Portman*

SMILE THAT SMILE 3 b.f. Champs Elysees 124 – Tenpence 60 (Bob Back (USA) 124) **68**
[2015 63: 10f⁵ t12.2g⁵ 10g⁵ 14.1v² p12g⁶ Nov 13] sturdy filly: fair handicapper: stays
1¾m: acts on heavy going. *Mark H. Tompkins*

SMILEY BAGEL (IRE) 2 b.g. (Apr 27) Kyllachy 129 – Epistoliere (IRE) (Alzao (USA) **–**
117) [2015 6m 8m 8.3s Oct 28] no form. *Ed Walker*

SMILEY MILEY (IRE) 7 ch.m. Danroad (AUS) 112 – Music Teacher 66 (Piccolo 121) **–**
[2015 7.1m 7.1g Aug 2] no form: tried in visor. *Dai Burchell*

SMILING STRANGER (IRE) 4 br.g. Nayef (USA) 129 – Carraigoona (IRE) 76 (Rock **92**
of Gibraltar (IRE) 133) [2015 94: p11g² p10g² 10g² 10.2m⁴ Aug 22] fairly useful
handicapper: won at Bath (by ½ length from Cornish Path) in August: stays 11f: acts on
polytrack and good to firm going: front runner/races prominently. *Andrew Balding*

SMIRFY'S SILVER 11 b.g. Desert Prince (IRE) 130 – Goodwood Blizzard 97 (Inchinor **49**
119) [2015 –: 8m p10m⁶ p11g Dec 3] short-backed gelding: poor handicapper: stays 1½m:
acts on polytrack, good to firm and good to soft going: tried in cheekpieces prior to 2015.
Michael Mullineaux

SMOKER 5 b.g. Motivator 131 – Request 87 (Rainbow Quest (USA) 134) [2015 89: **57**
12.1m⁶ 10.2s⁵ 16.2m p10g Aug 7] leggy, useful-looking gelding: modest handicapper:
stays 1¼m: acts on soft going: tried in headgear/tongue: usually races prominently: sent to
Belgium. *Tim Vaughan*

SMOKE RING (USA) 3 gr.g. Smoke Glacken (USA) 120 – With This Ring (USA) **–**
(Green Dancer (USA) 132) [2015 –: 7d Oct 26] well held in 2 maidens 13 months apart.
Jennie Candlish

SMOKETHATTHUNDERS (IRE) 5 gr.g. Elusive City (USA) 117 – Zinstar (IRE) **82**
(Sinndar (IRE) 134) [2015 83, a89: t7.1g⁴ 6.1f t7.1g² 7g⁴ 7d³ 6m 7.6g³ 6d Oct 12] fairly
useful handicapper: will benefit from return to 7f: acts on polytrack, tapeta and soft going:
tried in headgear/tongue tie. *James Unett*

SMOKY HILL (IRE) 6 gr.g. Galileo (IRE) 134 – Danaskaya (IRE) 106 (Danehill (USA) **63**
126) [2015 p15.8g⁶ 12d 10m 12g 14m 14g 11.6d⁵ 11.9d 11.6g⁶ Oct 19] strong, close-
coupled gelding: useful performer at best in France (for M. Delzangles), no impact in
Britain (in hood final start): stays 15.5f: acts on heavy going. *Tony Carroll*

SMOOTH OPERATOR 3 b.g. Azamour (IRE) 130 – Teggiano (IRE) 108 (Mujtahid **71**
(USA) 118) [2015 10g⁵ 10g³ 10d⁶ Jul 7] maiden, fair form first 2 starts: raced at 1¼m: has
joined A. J. Martin. *James Fanshawe*

SMOOTHTALKINRASCAL (IRE) 5 b.g. Kodiac 112 – Cool Tarifa (IRE) 80 (One **88 §**
Cool Cat (USA) 123) [2015 107: p6g p5g⁶ p5m 5g 5d⁴ 6g⁶ 5m⁶ 5m 5f⁴ 5d 5.3s⁴ 5g t5.1f
Oct 9] sturdy, close-coupled gelding: fairly useful handicapper: stays 6f: acts on polytrack,
firm and soft going: tried in visor prior to 2015: often in tongue tie in 2015: not one to trust.
Peter Crate

SMUGGLER'S COVE (IRE) 3 b.c. Fastnet Rock (AUS) 127 – Chenchikova (IRE) 96 **96**
(Sadler's Wells (USA) 132) [2015 115: 7d⁶ 10.3v⁴ 8g May 23] deep-girthed colt: won
listed race at Dundalk at 2 yrs (smart form): just useful in 2015: in first-time cheekpieces,
33/1, 7½ lengths eighth of 11 to Gleneagles in Irish 2000 Guineas at the Curragh final start:
stayed 1m: acted on polytrack and good to soft going: to stand at Track Supreme Stud,
India. *Aidan O'Brien, Ireland*

SMUGGLERS LANE (IRE) 3 b.g. Bushranger (IRE) 119 – Finty (IRE) (Entrepreneur **50**
123) [2015 46: t9.5f⁴ p10g* p10g² t9.5f² t12.2g 11.7f⁵ 10.2f⁶ 11.5d³ p12g* 11.7f 10m⁴ **a56**
p10g p10g p11g t13.9m⁴ Dec 30] lengthy gelding: modest performer: won at Lingfield in
February (handicap) and June (seller): stays 1¾m: acts on polytrack, tapeta, good to firm
and heavy going: tried in visor in 2015. *David Evans*

SMUGGLER'S MOON 2 b.g. (Mar 16) Danehill Dancer (IRE) 117 – Alchemilla (Dubai **– p**
Destination (USA) 127) [2015 6.5m Jun 11] 60,000Y: second foal: closely related to
winner up to 9.3f Stardrifter (2-y-o 7f winner, by Rock of Gibraltar): dam unraced half-
sister to July/Vintage Stakes winner Strategic Prince: 10/1, considerate introduction when
tenth in maiden at Newbury won by Twin Sails, not knocked about: should do better.
Brian Meehan

SNAN (IRE) 2 b.c. (Mar 28) High Chaparral (IRE) 132 – Slow Sand (USA) (Dixieland **70** Band (USA)) [2015 7m 8g⁴ Oct 21] rather unfurnished colt: better effort when seventh of 12 to Ibn Malik in maiden at Newmarket: off 4 months after: will stay 1m. *Richard Hannon*

SNAPPY GUEST 3 b.g. Kodiac 112 – Golden Shadow (IRE) 77 (Selkirk (USA) 129) **76** [2015 63: 8g* 8.3f⁵ 8.3g³ 8.3m² 7.5g⁵ 10g⁵ 8.3g* 8.3g⁵ Oct 19] compact gelding: fair handicapper: won at Wetherby in April and Windsor in July: stays 1¼m: acts on good to firm going: in cheekpieces last 3 starts: consistent. *George Margarson*

SNAP SHOTS (IRE) 3 b.g. Kodiac 112 – Refuse To Give Up (IRE) (Refuse To Bend **99** (IRE) 128) [2015 93: 5g⁴ 5.1v⁴ 5g² 5g⁴ 5.7g² 6g² 6d 5d t6f⁶ Oct 3] compact, quite attractive gelding: useful handicapper: second at Haydock, Bath and Ripon: stays 6f: best form on good going or firmer (acts on firm): usually in headgear/tongue tie nowadays: usually races prominently. *Tom Dascombe*

SNEAKING BUDGE 3 b.g. Nayef (USA) 129 – Ikat (IRE) 100 (Pivotal 124) [2015 –p: **67** p12g⁵ p10f⁶ 11.6d p16g Nov 26] fair maiden: left David Lanigan after third start: best effort at 1½m: acts on polytrack: tried in blinkers in 2015. *Stuart Edmunds*

SNEAKIN'PETE 2 b.c. (Mar 18) Frozen Power (IRE) 108 – Jillolini 40 (Bertolini (USA) – 125) [2015 7.2g 6m 6g Oct 8] no form. *Linda Perratt*

SNOANO 3 b.g. Nayef (USA) 129 – White Dress (IRE) (Pivotal 124) [2015 101: 10d³ **99** 10m⁶ 8f Jul 11] close-coupled gelding: useful performer: third in Classic Trial at Sandown (3½ lengths behind Master Apprentice) in April: well below form both subsequent starts: stays 1¼m: acts on soft and good to firm going: often races prominently: has been gelded. *John Gosden*

SNOOZING INDIAN 3 ch.g. Sleeping Indian 122 – Balnaha 67 (Lomond (USA) 128) **79** [2015 f8g² p8g² Sep 23] off 5 months, 4/11, improved from debut when 1½ lengths second of 10 to Bastille Day in maiden at Kempton. *Andrew Balding*

SNOW CLOUD (IRE) 3 b.f. Kodiac 112 – Thistlestar 64 (Lion Heart (USA) 124) **101** [2015 80: 5m* 6d⁶ 5.1f 5.6m³ 5g² 5g 6.1d⁶ 5s³ 6d⁴ 5s³ 5.1d³ f5g* p5m* Nov 21] useful handicapper: won at Redcar in May and Southwell and Lingfield (by ⅓ length from Jebediah Shine, well on top finish) in November: best form at 5f: acts on polytrack, fibresand and good to firm going: sold 55,000 gns in December. *David O'Meara*

SNOW CONDITIONS 4 b.f. Aussie Rules (USA) 123 – Snow Gonal (FR) (Octagonal **72** (NZ) 126) [2015 14d⁴ 12g⁴ 11.9d² 16g³ 17.2f* 17.2f 17.2g Oct 18] good-topped filly: fair handicapper: won at Bath in August: stays 17f: acts on firm going: tried in hood prior to 2015: sometimes slowly away. *Philip Hide*

SNOW COVER 3 gr.f. Verglas (IRE) 118 – Cover Look (SAF) (Fort Wood (USA) 117) – [2015 –: p7g p10g Apr 28] no form: tried in blinkers. *Roger Varian*

SNOW DANCER (IRE) 11 b.m. Desert Style (IRE) 121 – Bella Vie (IRE) (Sadler's **53** Wells (USA) 132) [2015 63: t8.6f t9.5g t9.5f⁴ t12.2m⁵ t9.5m² t12.2f* t12.2f t12.2g t12.2g⁶ t12.2g⁶ 12.1g* t12.2g 12g⁵ 14.1m t12.2f t12.2f Nov 3] leggy mare: modest handicapper: won at Wolverhampton in March and Hamilton (apprentice) in June: stays 1½m: acts on polytrack, tapeta, firm and good to soft going: usually in headgear: sometimes slowly away. *John David Riches*

SNOWED IN (IRE) 6 gr.g. Dark Angel (IRE) 113 – Spinning Gold 45 (Spinning World – (USA) 130) [2015 11.5d 12d Aug 14] sturdy gelding: fair at best, no form in 2015: stays 1½m: acts on polytrack and soft going: in cheekpieces first start in 2015. *Dianne Sayer*

SNOW KING (USA) 5 ch.g. Elusive Quality (USA) – Cloudspin (USA) (Storm Cat **62** (USA)) [2015 66: p11m 6g p5g p6g⁵ 8g p7g p6m* p6m³ p5g⁵ Dec 19] lengthy, well-made gelding: modest handicapper: won at Lingfield in November: stays 1½m: acts on polytrack and firm going. *Ted Powell*

SNOWMANE (IRE) 4 b.g. Galileo (IRE) 134 – Tree Tops 77 (Grand Lodge (USA) 125) **86** [2015 98, a106: p12g 10.4g 12g 10.2g* 10.1m 10.4m 16.4m 11.9g² p13.3f⁶ Aug 18] fairly useful handicapper: won at Nottingham in June: stays 16.5f: acts on polytrack, tapeta and good to firm going: usually in headgear/tongue tie: front runner/races prominently. *James Given*

SNOW MOON 2 b.f. (Feb 25) Oasis Dream 129 – Sariska 125 (Pivotal 124) [2015 8.3d³ **83 p** Oct 14] second foal: dam 7f (at 2 yrs) to 1½m (Oaks) winner: 7/1, encouragement when 1¾ lengths third of 17 to Architecture in maiden at Nottingham on debut, running on without being knocked about: will improve. *John Gosden*

SNOW PEARL 3 b.f. Nayef (USA) 129 – Snow Gretel (IRE) 101 (Green Desert (USA) **57** 127) [2015 t9.5f⁴ p8f⁵ Mar 19] showed a little ability in maidens: dead. *Marco Botti*

Hardwicke Stakes, Royal Ascot—a ninth win in the race for trainer Sir Michael Stoute courtesy of Snow Sky, who is seen to good effect as jockey Pat Smullen dictates in a tactical affair; Eagle Top (third right) stays on well to snatch second from Postponed close home

SNOW PRINCE 4 gr.g. Royal Applause 124 – Snowdrops (Gulch (USA)) [2015 12s⁴ **73** p13.3f⁴ Nov 5] better effort in maidens when fourth of 15 to Blue Sea of Ibrox at Pontefract on debut: unplaced in bumpers. *Steve Gollings*

SNOW SKY 4 b.c. Nayef (USA) 129 – Winter Silence (Dansili 127) [2015 121: 14m* 12f* **124** 12d⁶ 11.9g⁵ 15.9g Nov 3] well-made colt: very smart performer: more progress in 2015, winning Yorkshire Cup at York (by ½ length from Brown Panther) in May and Hardwicke Stakes at Royal Ascot (dictated, beat Eagle Top by 3¾ lengths) in June: creditable 4¾ lengths fifth of 18 to Mongolian Khan in Caulfield Cup (Handicap) in October: in rear in 24-runner Melbourne Cup (Handicap) at Flemington final start, disputing lead 2f out but fading when bumped and snatched up just inside final 1f: stayed 14.6f: acted on any turf going: to stand at Ballycurragh Stud, Co. Carlow, Ireland, fee on application. *Sir Michael Stoute*

SNOW TROUBLE (USA) 4 gr.c. Tapit (USA) 118 – Smara (USA) (Storm Cat (USA)) **96** [2015 94: p8m³ p8g⁵ 8f³ 8.5f* 8.5f Nov 27] workmanlike colt: useful performer: left Marcus Tregoning after second start: won allowance race at Gulfstream Park West in October by ¾ length from Oklahoma Den: stays 8.5f: acts on polytrack: tried in cheekpieces/tongue tie: often starts slowly/races towards rear. *Todd A. Pletcher, USA*

SNOWY DAWN 5 gr.g. Notnowcato 128 – Tereyna 58 (Terimon 124) [2015 85: 14.1f **74** 14.1g 15.9m⁵ 15.9g Sep 11] good-topped gelding: fair handicapper: stays 2m: acts on polytrack, good to firm and heavy going: sometimes wears cheekpieces. *Ben Case*

SOAPY AITKEN 2 b.c. (Feb 11) Pastoral Pursuits 127 – Littlemisssunshine (IRE) 93 **96** (Oasis Dream 129) [2015 5m* 5g* 5f⁴ 5f³ 5.2m 5g2 Aug 22] 25,000Y: rather leggy colt: second foal: half-brother to 2-y-o 5f winner Littlemissblakeney (by Sir Percy): dam 5f winner (including at 2 yrs): useful performer: won maiden at Leicester in April and minor event at Windsor in May: raced only at 5f: acts on firm going: often travels strongly. *Clive Cox*

SOARING SPIRITS (IRE) 5 ch.g. Tamayuz 126 – Follow My Lead 72 (Night Shift **79** (USA)) [2015 87: p6g p7g⁴ p6g³ t7.1g 6m⁶ 7.1v⁵ t7.1m 6g p6g⁵ p7g Dec 2] good-topped gelding: fair handicapper: stays 8.5f: acts on polytrack and any turf going: wears headgear. *Dean Ivory*

SO BELOVED 5 b.g. Dansili 127 – Valencia 79 (Kenmare (FR) 125) [2015 99: 7g2 7m **117** 7g* 7g 8m 7g 7s* 7g2 7g4 8d³ Oct 31] big, well-made gelding: smart performer: won handicap at York (by 1½ lengths from Alfred Hutchinson) in May and Supreme Stakes at Goodwood (by head from Here Comes When) in August: also first past post in Betfred Mile (Handicap) at latter course on fifth start but disqualified due to prohibited substances: placed in listed races at Redcar (¾-length second to Zarwaan) and Newmarket (¾ length third behind Big Baz), and fourth in Challenge Stakes at Newmarket (beaten ¾ length by Cable Bay), all in October: stays 1m: acts on polytrack, firm and soft going: often in headgear prior to 2015: often travels strongly. *David O'Meara*

SOBER UP 3 b.f. Kheleyf (USA) 116 – Morning After 84 (Emperor Jones (USA) 119) **–** [2015 7g f8g⁶ 18.6g³ Dec 1] 10,000Y: compact filly: fifth foal: half-sister to 1m winner Dazzled (by Starcraft) and 7f winner Elizona (by Pastoral Pursuits): dam, 2-y-o 5.7f winner who stayed 1m, half-sister to smart performer up to 1¼m Royal Prince: little form: left Roger Charlton after first start. *Ivan Furtado*

SO CELEBRE (GER) 2 ch.g. (Feb 13) Peintre Celebre (USA) 137 – Saldennahe (GER) **77** 105 (Next Desert (IRE) 122) [2015 8.1s⁶ 8.3s2 8.3s2 Oct 28] fair form: best effort when second of 10 to Little Avon in maiden at Leicester in October on second start: will be suited by 1¼m+. *Ian Williams*

SOCIAL CLIMBER (IRE) 3 b.g. Strategic Prince 114 – Ivy Queen (IRE) (Green Desert **70**
(USA) 127) [2015 62: p8g 10.5g² 9.5m* 10g² 12g⁴ f16g⁵ Nov 3] fair handicapper: won at
Gowran in June: left Kevin Prendergast after fifth start: stays 10.5f: acts on good to firm
going: often in headgear in 2015: often races prominently. *Fergal O'Brien*

SOCIALITES RED 2 ch.f. (Apr 11) Sakhee's Secret 128 – Tipsy Girl 79 (Haafhd 129) **73**
[2015 t5.1g² 5m³ 5f t6g⁵ 5m* 5g⁶ 5.5s³ 5g³ Sep 19] 4,000Y: neat filly: first foal: dam 2-y-o
5.7f winner who stayed 1m: fair performer: won maiden at Leicester in August: stays 5.5f:
acts on soft and good to firm going: usually races prominently. *Scott Dixon*

SOCIALITES ZERO 2 b.g. (Mar 8) Milk It Mick 120 – Cora Pearl (IRE) 51 (Montjeu **–**
(IRE) 137) [2015 f5g Nov 3] 12/1, last of 13 in maiden at Southwell. *Scott Dixon*

SOCIOLOGA INC (ARG) 5 b.m. Include (USA) 121 – Stormy Sober (Bernstein (USA) **105**
115) [2015 8.9g⁶ 11.9g 14 9d 12.9d 9.9g Sep 4] useful performer: won 3 pattern races for
Roberto Bullrich in Argentina in 2014, including Grade 1 Gran Premio Criadores at
Palermo: ran at Meydan first 2 starts in 2015 (not discredited first outing), then left Takashi
Kodama: stays 12.4f: acts on dirt and soft going: in headgear last 2 starts. *S. Kobayashi,
France*

SOCIOPATH (IRE) 3 b.g. Fastnet Rock (AUS) 127 – Nancy Spain (IRE) (Sadler's Wells **75**
(USA) 132) [2015 51p: 9.9m⁵ 10m 12.4g* 11.9g⁴ Sep 7] attractive gelding: fair performer:
won handicap at Newcastle in August: best effort at 12.5f: temperament under suspicion:
sold 8,000 gns, sent to Switzerland. *Peter Chapple-Hyam*

SOFIAS NUMBER ONE (USA) 7 b.g. Silver Deputy (CAN) – Storidawn (USA) **63 §**
(Hennessy (USA) 122) [2015 79§: f12d⁵ f11g t12.2g 10.2m⁴ f12d⁴ t9.5m f8g³ f11g⁴ Dec
29] modest handicapper: stays 11f: acts on all-weather and good to firm going: usually
wears headgear: tried in tongue tie prior to 2015: untrustworthy. *Roy Bowring*

SOFT LOVE (IRE) 3 b.f. Kodiac 112 – Appley Bridge (IRE) (One Cool Cat (USA) 123) **49**
[2015 66: p5g² p5g³ p5f⁴ 5g 5.7m⁵ 5m 6v t5.1f Oct 31] sturdy filly: modest maiden: left **a59**
Kevin Ryan after fifth start: best form at 5f: acts on polytrack, tapeta and good to firm
going: temperament under suspicion (often pulls hard). *Seamus Mullins*

SOFTLY SHE TREADS (IRE) 4 b.f. Azamour (IRE) 130 – Lady Lucre (IRE) 73 (Last **64**
Tycoon 131) [2015 59, a73: p12g⁵ p12g 16d p12m Oct 28] lengthy filly: modest
handicapper: stays 1½m: acts on polytrack, best turf form on good going: often wears
headgear. *Pat Phelan*

SOFTSONG (FR) 7 b.g. Singspiel (IRE) 133 – Soft Gold (USA) (Gulch (USA)) [2015 **89**
93: p12g 9.9g 14.9g* p16.9g² 15.9s 13.9s 10.4d⁵ p12.4g p12.4g⁶ Dec 21] tall, good-topped
gelding: fairly useful performer: won amateurs event at Maisons-Laffitte in July: left David
Pipe after first start: stays 2¼m: acts on polytrack, good to firm and heavy going: tried in
headgear. *Mlle A. Rosa, France*

SOGNO D'AMORE (USA) 2 b.c. (Apr 14) Bernardini (USA) 132 – Love Dancing **–**
(ARG) (Salt Lake (USA)) [2015 8.3d Oct 14] 25/1, last of 11 in maiden at Nottingham,
dropping away 2f out. *Mark Johnston*

SOHCAHTOA (IRE) 9 b.g. Val Royal (FR) 127 – Stroke of Six (IRE) 84 (Woodborough **–**
(USA) 112) [2015 53: 16d Aug 18] good-topped gelding: modest handicapper: stays 16.5f:
acts on polytrack, soft and good to firm going: has worn headgear. *Andrew Crook*

SOIE D'LEAU 3 b.g. Monsieur Bond (IRE) 120 – Silky Silence (High Chaparral (IRE) **90**
132) [2015 61: 6m⁶ 5d² 5g² 5d* 5g⁵ 5g² 5g² 5s⁶ 5g* 5.5m* 6g Sep 6] fairly useful
performer: won maiden at Newcastle in May and handicaps at Newcastle and Chester in
August: stays 5.5f: acts on good to firm and good to soft going: front runner/races
prominently. *Kristin Stubbs*

SOIREE 2 b.f. (Feb 25) Piccolo 121 – Nightunderthestars (Observatory (USA) 131) [2015 **–**
5.1m⁵ 6g 7s p6g Sep 22] rather unfurnished filly: first foal: dam unraced half-sister to smart
sprinter Definightly: well held in maidens/nursery. *Eve Johnson Houghton*

SO IT'S WAR (FR) 4 b.g. Orpen (USA) 116 – Impulsive Decision (IRE) 71 (Nomination **80**
125) [2015 68: 10.1d⁶ 8.5m* 8g* 8m⁴ 7.9g 8s³ t8.6g² t8.6g⁴ t8.6m² 8m⁶ 7.2g⁶ Sep 17] fairly
useful handicapper: won at Beverley and Redcar in May: stays 8.5f: acts on tapeta, soft and
good to firm going: in cheekpieces last 4 starts: often travels strongly. *Keith Dalgleish*

SOJOURNA 2 b.f. (Jan 28) Equiano (FR) 127 – Sceilin (IRE) 69 (Lil's Boy (USA) 109) **53**
[2015 5.1m 6g⁶ p7g Oct 20] £5,500Y: first foal: dam 1¼m/11f winner: modest maiden: best
effort when sixth at Windsor. *Martyn Meade*

SOLAR DEITY (IRE) 6 b.h. Exceed And Excel (AUS) 126 – Dawn Raid (IRE) 94 **114**
(Docksider (USA) 124) [2015 114: t9.5f² t8.6m⁴ t9.5g² t8.6m³ p10g³ p10f⁵ p9.2m p10f³
p10m t9.5m⁴ t9.5m³ Dec 26] good-topped horse: smart performer: best efforts of 2015

when third in handicaps at Wolverhampton and Chelmsford fourth/eighth starts: stays 1¼m: acts on polytrack, tapeta, good to firm and good to soft going: has worn headgear: not straightforward. *Marco Botti*

SOLAR FLAIR 3 b.c. Equiano (FR) 127 – Air Biscuit (IRE) 84 (Galileo (IRE) 134) [2015 **102** 77p: 8.3m⁶ 8.1m⁵ 9g⁵ 7m⁴ 7m* p7g* 7m Aug 1] sturdy colt: useful handicapper: won at Newmarket in June and Lingfield (by 4 lengths from Royal Normandy) in July: stays 7f: acts on polytrack and good to firm going: front runner/races prominently, often travels strongly. *William Knight*

SOLAR MAGIC 4 ch.f. Pivotal 124 – Moon Goddess 98 (Rainbow Quest (USA) 134) **108** [2015 95p: p8g² 8m² 10.2m 10.1g 8s² 8g* Sep 25] rather leggy filly: useful performer: won 10-runner listed race at Newmarket final start by ½ length from Black Cherry, well ridden and leading over 1f out: stays 1m: acts on polytrack, soft and good to firm going. *John Gosden*

SOLARMAITE 6 b.m. Needwood Blade 117 – Marinaite 82 (Komaite (USA)) [2015 75: **75** f8g* 7s 10.2m⁴ 10.2m Jun 11] fair handicapper: won at Southwell in April: stays 11f, effective at shorter: acts on fibresand, soft and good to firm going: wears headgear. *Roy Bowring*

SOLAR SPIRIT (IRE) 10 b.g. Invincible Spirit (IRE) 121 – Misaayef (USA) 82 (Swain **77** (IRE) 134) [2015 85: 6d⁶ 6g 7s⁴ 6m³ 6m³ 6m⁴ 6g⁵ 6m⁵ 6m 7v⁴ f7g Nov 3] tall, good-topped gelding: fair handicapper: stays 1m: acts on polytrack, tapeta and any turf going: tried in headgear prior to 2015. *Tracy Waggott*

SOLDIER IN ACTION (FR) 2 b.c. (Mar 16) Soldier of Fortune (IRE) 131 – Ripley **85** (GER) (Platini (GER) 126) [2015 8g² 9d² †9.5f* p8f⁶ Nov 23] €40,000Y: half-brother to several winners abroad, including useful German 1m winner Rubber Duck (by Big Shuffle) and useful German/French 9f-1½m winner Red Ghost (by Dai Jin): dam German 8.5f winner: fairly useful form: won maiden at Wolverhampton (by ¾ length from Paris Magic) in November: disappointing final start: will stay 1¼m+. *Mark Johnston*

SOLE BAY STAR 2 ch.f. (Feb 15) Dutch Art 126 – Celebrity 90 (Pivotal 124) [2015 6m **–** p6g Oct 14] £20,000Y, £15,000 2-y-o: first foal: dam 2-y-o 6f winner: well held in 2 maidens: sent to France. *James Toller*

SOLE POWER 8 b.g. Kyllachy 129 – Demerger (USA) (Distant View (USA) 126) **123** [2015 128: 5g 5g* 6g⁶ 5f⁵ 6f⁴ 5g⁴ 5d* 5m 6g Dec 13]

Even at the ripe old age of eight, there was still new ground to conquer for the popular Irish sprinter Sole Power who managed a first win in Dubai, at the ninth time of asking, when landing the Al Quoz Sprint on World Cup night at Meydan in March. It was Sole Power's fifth attempt at that particular race, his best effort previously being a second to Ortensia in the 2012 renewal. The best horse in Europe over five furlongs in 2014, when he won both the King's Stand and Nunthorpe, both for a second time, Sole Power wasn't quite the same force in Europe in the latest season after his return from Dubai. He did, however, still manage a noteworthy success in the Flying Five Stakes at the Curragh on Irish Champions' Weekend, recording his first win on home soil since 2010, and, surprisingly, also a first success on turf in Ireland, with his two previous 'home' wins both coming on the polytrack at Dundalk. Sole Power is making his seventh appearance in the *Racehorses* annual, stretching back to 2009, and it is the fourth occasion that his achievements have brought him an extended entry (the first essay was in the 2010 edition, covering his 100/1 success in that year's Nunthorpe). With no speculation about retirement coming from his connections, the likelihood is that Sole Power will be making an eighth appearance in these pages in *Racehorses of 2016*.

As in the four previous seasons, Sole Power started his latest campaign with a preparatory run in Dubai ahead of his tilt at the Al Quoz Sprint, finishing down the field (after meeting trouble) in the Group 3 Meydan Sprint in early-March. With that run under his belt, Sole Power bounced back to near his best to land what looked a high-quality renewal of the Al Quoz Sprint three weeks later. A strongly-run race suited Sole Power, who came through to lead late on after being patiently ridden as usual, beating the Hong Kong-trained Peniaphobia (runner-up in the Hong Kong Sprint the previous year) by half a length, with Wesley Ward's US raider Green Mask beaten a further half a length in third. Sixth-placed Sir Maximilian fared best of the seven British-trained runners. Sole Power was a surprising absentee from

Newmarket's Palace House Stakes, a race he landed in both 2013 and 2014, and he wasn't seen in Europe until contesting the six-furlong Greenlands Stakes at the Curragh later in May. Running in Ireland for the first time in over three and a half years, Sole Power managed only sixth of nine behind Mustajeeb, though he didn't shape badly all things considered and the run seemed likely to put him spot on for Royal Ascot and his bid for an unprecedented third win in the King's Stand Stakes. However, Sole Power couldn't produce his trademark turn of foot and came only fifth—beaten a length and a quarter—behind Goldream. It was a similar story for Sole Power in both the July Cup and the Nunthorpe on his next two outings, although he ran respectably to make the frame on each occasion. He fared best of those held up when fourth to Muhaarar at Newmarket, not seeming at a disadvantage over a stiffish six furlongs for once, before filling the same position behind Mecca's Angel at York, where he never threatened to get to the leaders.

Sole Power was returned to Ireland for the Flying Five Stakes, a five-furlong event at the Curragh held on the second day of Irish Champions' Weekend. The lack of opportunities on home soil for good-class Irish-trained sprinters—as amply demonstrated by Sole Power's very infrequent runs in Ireland—was the subject of comment in last year's *Racehorses*. As part of a series of changes to the European sprint programme, instituted by the European Pattern Committee, the Flying Five was one of three events in Ireland upgraded from Group 3 to Group 2 in the latest season, the others being the Sapphire Stakes, another five-furlong event at the Curragh, and the Greenlands Stakes over six. The Sapphire was also given a new position in the calendar, moving from the Irish Derby card in late-June to Irish Oaks day in mid-July. The Flying Five had been moved from its traditional late-August slot to form part of the inaugural Irish Champions' Weekend in 2014. Given that the meeting hosts five Group 1 races, it's likely that the organisers of Irish Champions' Weekend will be pushing for an upgrade to Ireland's first Group 1 sprint for the Flying Five, which had a total prize fund in the latest season of getting on for double that for the Greenlands Stakes and Sapphire Stakes in 2015. A strong field for the Flying Five's inaugural running as a Group 2 was clearly a boon for the powers that be who have decided to run the Flying Five without penalties in 2016, another sign of the ambition to turn it into a Group 1. Sole Power and 2013 Abbaye winner Maarek gave the race two Group 1 winners and, in an open market, they were joined at the head of the betting by Sole Power's stablemate Moviesta. That trio were among the seven pattern winners in the twelve-runner field which also had a strong British contingent headed by Stepper Point, who had landed the Sapphire Stakes, and the Temple Stakes winner Pearl Secret. Conceding upwards of 3 lb all around, Sole Power showed very smart form to prevail by a head from the fast-finishing Maarek,

Al Quoz Sprint Empowered by IPIC, Meydan—
a first success in this race at the fifth attempt for Sole Power, who comes with his customary
late run to beat Peniaphobia (fourth right), Green Mask (right) and Amber Sky (third right);
it is a final Group 1 win in the saddle for Richard Hughes, who retires in the middle of the season

Derrinstown Stud Flying Five Stakes, the Curragh—a belated first win on turf in Ireland for the veteran Sole Power, who just holds on from the fast-finishing Maarek (spotted silks) and Take Cover (rail) in a race earmarked to become Ireland's first all-aged Group 1 sprint

just holding on after racing a bit closer to the pace than usual in mid-division and taking the lead inside the last furlong. Take Cover was beaten a further length into third, doing best of the British runners. Not only was the Flying Five Sole Power's first success on turf in Ireland, it was also the first among ten career wins on turf that has been gained on ground softer than good. Chris Hayes became the tenth different jockey to partner Sole Power, Frankie Dettori having taken the ride in the Nunthorpe following the retirement of Richard Hughes, Sole Power's regular jockey since the 2014 King's Stand. Hayes retained the ride for Sole Power's two subsequent outings, both back at Group 1 level. Following a ninth in the Abbaye—a race he hasn't won in five attempts—Sole Power ended his campaign in the Hong Kong Sprint at Sha Tin in December. He finished second in the 2013 renewal but hasn't figured in two attempts since, beating only two home in the latest renewal won by Peniaphobia.

		Pivotal	Polar Falcon
Sole Power (b.g. 2007)	Kyllachy (b 1998)	(ch 1993)	Fearless Revival
		Pretty Poppy	Song
		(b 1988)	Moonlight Serenade
	Demerger (USA) (b 1997)	Distant View	Mr Prospector
		(ch 1991)	Seven Springs
		Merida	Warning
		(b 1991)	Metair

Sole Power's pedigree has been covered extensively in previous editions of *Racehorses*. The only update of note is that his dam Demerger's latest yearling (by Sepoy) was bought back for 550,000 guineas at Newmarket in October. The durable Sole Power has a handful of placed efforts over six furlongs on his record but five furlongs—over which all twelve of his career wins have been gained—is his optimum distance. He acts well on firm ground, though his win on good to soft in the Flying Five suggests that a bit of cut isn't necessarily a hindrance to him nowadays (he also won on polytrack in his younger days). Usually held up, Sole Power can still produce a good turn of foot when on song and is ideally suited by a well-run race. *Edward Lynam, Ireland*

SOLIANA 3 ch.f. Dutch Art 126 – Pink Stone (FR) (Bigstone (IRE) 126) [2015 p8m[5] **59** t8.6f[3] p7g[6] 9s 10g 8m t9.5f t7.1m Nov 28] 36,000F, 85,000Y: half-sister to several winners, including useful 2-y-o 7f winner Tiger Eye (by Danehill Dancer) and 1½m-2m winner Battleoftrafalgar (by Galileo): dam French maiden (stayed 10.5f): modest maiden: left Roger Varian after third start: stays 8.5f: acts on polytrack and tapeta: tried in headgear: usually races nearer last than first. *John O'Shea*

SOLIDARITY 4 b.g. Dubawi (IRE) 129 – Assabiyya (IRE) 91 (Cape Cross (IRE) 129) **92** [2015 112: f12s[5] Jan 20] compact, attractive gelding: smart handicapper at best: stayed 11.5f: acted on polytrack, tapeta and acted on any turf going: often travelled strongly: dead. *Charlie Appleby*

SOLID JUSTICE (IRE) 4 b.g. Rock of Gibraltar (IRE) 133 – Burnin' Memories (USA) **65** (Lit de Justice (USA) 125) [2015 76, a60: 10.1d 10.4g 12g 12.1m[4] 11.8m[3] 9.9s[5] 10g[4] 10s 10d 14.1v f6g Dec 22] good-topped gelding: fair handicapper: left Jason Ward after sixth start: stays 1½m: acts on soft going: often in headgear in 2015: usually races nearer last than first. *Kenny Johnson*

SOLO HUNTER 4 b.g. Sleeping Indian 122 – Night Owl 73 (Night Shift (USA)) [2015 **93** 8.3d* 10m[2] 10f 10m[2] 10.2m[4] 10m[5] Oct 3] compact gelding: fairly useful handicapper: won at Leicester in April: stays 1¼m: acts on tapeta, soft and good to firm going: often wears headgear: often leads. *Martyn Meade*

SOLOW 5 gr.g. Singspiel (IRE) 133 – High Maintenance (FR) 103 (Highest Honor **129** (FR) 124) [2015 121: p8g* 8.9g* 9.2m* 8f* 8g* 8d* Oct 17]
The Flat racing year was certainly not short of star performers, with an American Triple Crown winner and an outstanding Derby winner, both campaigned in the true spirit of the sport, topping the bill on either side of the Atlantic. Those two were among a number of the season's top horses who had still to experience defeat in the campaign by the end of July—the milers Gleneagles and Solow, and the dual Arc-winning mare Treve included—but, by the end of the year, Solow was the only champion who still remained unbeaten. He won all six of his races in 2015, the last five of them Group 1s, and extended a winning sequence that now stretches to nine as he took his career earnings (prize money converted at the prevailing exchange rate) to £4,140,588, all bar £189,853 accumulated in the latest season. Solow's victories included a spectacular Group 1 hat-trick over a mile in the Queen Anne Stakes at Royal Ascot, the newly-enriched Sussex Stakes at the Qatar Goodwood Festival and the richly-endowed Queen Elizabeth II Stakes on British Champions' Day, a programme at least partly dictated by the continuing nonsensical ban on geldings in most of the Group 1 races in his native France. Solow contested only one such race all year in his own country, the Prix d'Ispahan in which he met another French-trained gelding who has become familiar to British racegoers because of the same circumstances, the highest earner in the history of European racing Cirrus des Aigles whose record now looks in serious danger of being overtaken by Solow.

Dubai Turf Sponsored by DP World, Meydan—a most impressive success for five-year-old Solow, his first at Group 1 level; The Grey Gatsby stays on down the outside for second, with Mshawish (No.3) and Euro Charline (noseband, rail) completing the frame

Prix d'Ispahan, Longchamp—a disappointing effort from Cirrus des Aigles (who was found to have lost half of one of his shoes afterwards) leaves a straightforward task for Solow, who beats the two remaining runners, Gailo Chop (rail) and Sparkling Beam, with something to spare

It was the legendary West Ilsley trainer Jack Colling who said 'Give me a stable full of geldings and I'll have the bookies crying for mercy.' Betting shop punters wouldn't have become rich backing Solow, who started a short-priced favourite (on three occasions odds on) on five of his six outings, but his reliability and straightforwardness supports Colling's maxim. Solow was gelded as a three-year-old, his trainer recalling that he was 'nervous' as a young horse and it had been 'very difficult travelling him to the racecourse.' Solow was a heavy horse as a youngster with some leg problems which was another reason he was 'cut'. Castrated animals lose some of the characteristics of colts, such as the condition in the crest of the neck, and they tend to lose some weight which happened with Solow, helping to alleviate the leg problems from which he suffered. Being a gelding certainly made Solow into a better racehorse, though it took a little longer before connections discovered that a mile was his optimum distance. Before the middle of his four-year-old year, after Solow had begun the season with wins in minor events at around a mile and a quarter at Longchamp and Saint-Cloud, a plan was formed to step him up further in trip, significantly further in fact to nearly two miles in the Prix Vicomtesse Vigier at Longchamp in late-May. He finished only sixth of eight, though beaten only four lengths or so behind Fly With Me, and was brought back to around a mile for his last three races, all of which he won, including the Prix Quincey at Deauville (by five lengths) and the Prix Daniel Wildenstein at Longchamp on Arc weekend.

Clearly very smart now, Solow was aimed at the Dubai Turf Sponsored by DP World (formerly the Duty Free) on World Cup night at Meydan at the end of March. He was warmed up in a minor event on the polytrack at Chantilly before the Dubai Turf, which was the only race for which he did not start favourite in 2015. The previous year's Prix du Jockey Club and Irish Champion Stakes winner The Grey Gatsby started at 6/4, with Solow at 9/4 in a field of ten in which the other runners started at odds varying from 9/1 to 50/1. The steady pace favoured Solow more than The Grey Gatsby over nine furlongs and he beat his rival by four and a quarter lengths after quickening to lead over a furlong out. It was Solow's first tilt at a Group 1 but it looked unlikely to be his last success at the highest level. After adding the Prix d'Ispahan over nine furlongs at Longchamp in May (from another French gelding who became a Group 1 winner, Gailo Chop, with Cirrus des

Queen Anne Stakes, Royal Ascot—Able Friend (out of picture) and Night of Thunder (right) fail to come up to expectations in the Royal Ascot curtain raiser as Solow beats fellow French raider Esoterique (hidden by winner) and the strong-finishing Cougar Mountain (striped cap); Toormore (second right) finishes fourth

Aigles last of four after losing half of one of his shoes), Solow started at 11/8 in an international field for the Queen Anne Stakes, including Hong Kong's top miler Able Friend. Some of his opponents, including Able Friend, were below their best on the day but Solow's triumph from fellow French challenger Esoterique and Ballydoyle's representative Cougar Mountain whetted the appetite for the forthcoming clashes with the leading three-year-old milers, particularly Gleneagles who added to his Anglo/Irish Guineas double by winning the St James's Palace Stakes later on the opening day at Royal Ascot. The proposed meeting between Solow and Gleneagles in the Sussex Stakes looked likely to be the clash of the Qatar Goodwood Festival but the potentially engrossing duel had to wait when Gleneagles was scratched at the forty-eight-hour stage after more rain than forecast fell at Goodwood the weekend before the meeting.

New sponsorship, effectively from the hugely-rich Qatar government which is also the source of the vast prize money lavished on Longchamp's Prix de l'Arc weekend, led to the rebranding of Glorious Goodwood (racegoers were met with an array of Qatari flags which some thought spoiled the 'feel' of what has been one of the quintessentially English race meetings). The five-day meeting carried an extra £2m in prize money, with a significant slice of it going to the Sussex Stakes whose first prize of £560,200 moved it into fifth place on the list of the most valuable races in the British calendar, behind only the Derby, the Champion Stakes, the King George VI and Queen Elizabeth Stakes, and the Queen Elizabeth II Stakes. Goodwood appropriately featured the first winner in Britain to be trained in Qatar, Dubday winning the Glorious Stakes ridden by Frankie Dettori. Although the Australian-trained sprinter Ortensia won the 2012 King George Stakes (another race to have its prize money raised substantially in 2015), Goodwood's feature meeting has not been a strong draw for international challengers over the years, something which the windfall of prize money through the ten-year contract with Qatar should slowly change. There were two French-trained winners at the meeting in the latest season, 33/1-shot Amy Eria in the Oak Tree Stakes, who beat the Hannon-trained and Dettori-ridden joint favourite Osaila to give Sheikh Joaan's Al Shaqab Racing a one, two, and Solow, sent off at 5/2-on in a field of eight for the Sussex.

Solow became the first winner ever saddled at the main Goodwood meeting by Freddie Head (whose father Alec won the 1960 Sussex with Venture VII) and he was also the first French-trained winner of the Sussex since Bigstone in 1993, a year in which all but one of Britain's Group 1 races over a mile for three-year-olds and upwards were won by horses trained in France (the Sussex runner-up Sayyedati had kept the One Thousand Guineas at home). Solow started at the same odds as the previous year's Sussex winner Kingman and was the seventh winning favourite (six of them at odds-on, including Frankel at 20/1-on) in the last eight years. Given a well-judged ride by Maxime Guyon, riding at Goodwood for the first time, Solow had the leader Arod, carrying the colours of Qatar Racing, in his sights all the way and kept on well after being shaken up to lead over a furlong out, winning with something in hand by half a length and two and a quarter from Arod and 50/1-shot Gabrial, with the two other Group 1 winners in the line-up, Lockinge winner Night of Thunder (one of the disappointments in the Queen Anne) and Belardo only sixth and seventh. Ineligible to contest either the Jacques le Marois or the Prix du Moulin, Solow was given a break before his final start in the Queen Elizabeth II Stakes nearly three months later. Winning the Sussex entitled Solow to a guaranteed place in the field for the Breeders' Cup Mile, a race that the record-breaking racemare Goldikova won three times in the Wertheimer et Frere royal blue, white seams, sleeves and cap. Goldikova was trained by Freddie Head who also won the Breeders' Cup Mile twice as a jockey on Miesque but he made it clear at Goodwood that Solow would not be going to Keeneland ('He is easy to ride but the course might be too tight').

Bigstone followed up his Sussex Stakes win in 1993 by also taking the Queen Elizabeth II Stakes (finishing a very close third in the Prix du Moulin in between). Solow's appearance in the latest Queen Elizabeth II Stakes (first prize £623,810) gave British Champions' Day one of its headline acts, along with champion sprinter-elect Muhaarar in the British Champions Sprint, which had Group 1 status for the first time. It was the fifth running of British Champions' Day, the richest raceday of the year in Britain, which now boasts four Group 1s. Bankrolled by Qatari money, British Champions' Day and the associated thirty-five-race British Champions' Series between May and October is not funded by the Qatar government like Goodwood, but by Qipco, a private investment vehicle belonging to Sheikh Fahad and his five brothers which has diverse interests including property, construction and oil and gas trading. Qipco's backing for British Champions' Day is contracted until 2024 and is reported to be worth over £50m (Qipco also has official partner status with Ascot racecourse, including the Royal meeting).

Starting earlier than usual with the first race at 12.45, British Champions' Day tried to avoid a clash with a televised Rugby World Cup quarter final by squeezing in its pattern races (the Long Distance Cup remains Group 2) by 3.15. The Channel 4 viewing figures nonetheless fell to just 367,000, with Qipco racing representative David Redvers saying that the broadcaster was 'shrinking' racing's television audience. Channel 4's audience for the Derby was also at a record low and ITV's potential to raise the viewing figures for racing helped in its successful bid for the new four-year terrestrial contract to cover racing from 2017. The switch to ITV—which last showed racing regularly in the mid-'eighties—will end Channel 4's association with the sport which stretches back over thirty years. ITV is said to have paid in the region of £30m to secure coverage of racing, which will be split between ITV (for the thirty-four major racedays) and the backwater of ITV4. The principal attraction for Britain's largest commercial broadcaster was the multi-million-pound market created since the relaxation of regulations which used to prevent bookmakers and betting organisations from advertising on television. Sheikh Fahad stressed in an interview before British Champions' Day that Qipco's long-term commitment to British racing was 'a business decision,' based on 'building the Qipco brand'. The level of exposure is an important factor in that—the crowd on course was 30,967—and the move to ITV will be welcomed by Qipco and all the sport's major sponsors, though the backers of races on the sixty days being banished to ITV4 are unlikely to be so happy.

Qatar Sussex Stakes, Goodwood—with the top three-year-old miler Gleneagles absent for the first million-pound Sussex Stakes, Solow lands the odds from Arod (rail), the pair clear of Gabrial (noseband) and Here Comes When (right)

Queen Elizabeth II Stakes Sponsored by Qipco, Ascot—the grey Solow caps a tremendous campaign with his fifth Group 1 success in a row, stretching a winning run to nine; Belardo (white cap) and Gabrial (noseband) come through from off the pace to fill the places with Integral (centre, still just ahead of Gabrial) fourth, whilst Gleneagles (left), only given the go-ahead to run at the last minute, fails to pick up on the softened ground, finishing sixth

Misgivings remain over some aspects of British Champions' Day, including its place in the calendar which makes it more vulnerable to the weather, but no-one could complain about the standard of the racing itself at the latest renewal. Hot on the heels of Muhaarar cementing his position as champion sprinter with a brilliant performance, and St Leger winner Simple Verse winning a good renewal of the British Champions Fillies' And Mares', Solow confirmed himself the best miler around with a crowning victory in the Queen Elizabeth II Stakes from a field which included Gleneagles who was allowed to run despite reservations that the going might prove too soft for him. Conditions were not ideal for Gleneagles, with his four-month absence probably relevant too, and he managed only a below-form sixth in a fairly bunched finish, on his first racecourse appearance since Royal Ascot. Solow was well placed all the way and didn't have to be at his best to win by three quarters of a length and a length and a half from Belardo, who fared best of the five three-year-olds, and 66/1-shot Gabrial, both of whom came through to be nearest at the finish after being dropped out at the back of the field. While Muhaarar's appearance on British Champions' Day was his final one on a racecourse before taking up stallion duties, Solow looks set to become something of a regular at the fixture. Connections announced after the Queen Elizabeth II Stakes that his programme for 2016 would be the same as that followed in the most recent season.

	Singspiel (IRE) (b 1992)	In The Wings (b 1986)	Sadler's Wells / High Hawk
Solow (gr.g. 2010)		Glorious Song (b 1976)	Halo / Ballade
	High Maintenance (FR) (gr 2004)	Highest Honor (gr 1983)	Kenmare / High River
		Fabulous Hostess (ch 1988)	Fabulous Dancer / Young Hostess

The big, strong, lengthy Solow, a phlegmatic individual who was notably relaxed in the preliminaries on British Champions' Day, is from the penultimate crop of the now-deceased Singspiel whose record on Dubai World Cup night he enhanced when winning the Dubai Turf. Singspiel himself included a Dubai World Cup on dirt among a string of big-race wins as a racehorse and he sired a winner of that race, Moon Ballad, as well as two winners of the Sheema Classic, Eastern Anthem and Dar Re Mi. Singspiel also has a Gold Cup winner at Royal Ascot to his name in Papineau, and Solow's dam High Maintenance was a useful stayer, successful at up to fifteen furlongs and third in the Prix Gladiateur, all of which helps to explain why Solow himself was tried at long distances ('I find pedigrees fascinating and love delving into the origins of a given horse,' says his trainer, 'but from time to time you just have to ignore what they tell you, it's mad how Solow has turned out'). Solow is High Maintenance's first foal and his grandam Fabulous Hostess also possessed the stamina to win a soft-ground Prix de Royallieu over an extended mile and a half for Criquette Head in the Wertheimer silks. Solow's great grandam Young Hostess was also Wertheimer-bred and trained by Criquette Head and showed useful form

Wertheimer et Frere's "Solow"

at her best, winning over nine furlongs as a two-year-old. Young Hostess was a half-sister to several winners including Yamuna who won only in minor company but became the grandam of Prix Saint-Alary winner Reve d'Oscar (sired by Highest Honor, the sire of Solow's dam) and the great grandam of the Irish One Thousand Guineas winner Bethrah (who was out of a daughter of Highest Honor who was champion sire in France three times). Young Hostess is also the great grandam of the tough mile- to mile-and-a-quarter racemare Thistle Bird who finally gained an elusive Group 1 victory at the age of six in the Pretty Polly Stakes at the Curragh in 2014. The genuine and consistent Solow has won at up to a mile and a half but is best at around a mile. He acts on polytrack, firm and soft going. *F. Head, France*

SOLSTALLA 3 b.f. Halling (USA) 133 – Solstice 84 (Dubawi (IRE) 129) [2015 68p: p7m⁶ p8f³ 10.2s⁴ 10.2m⁵ t9.5g⁵ 11s* 13.8g³ 11.6d Oct 12] fair performer: won seller at Goodwood in August: left William Jarvis after: stays 1¾m: acts on soft and good to firm going: front runner/races prominently. *William Muir* — **72**

SOLUBLE (GER) 3 b.g. Galileo (IRE) 134 – So Squally (GER) (Monsun (GER) 124) [2015 t9.5f* 9.9m³ 10m³ 10m³ p11g² 14d³ Sep 5] 400,000Y: well-made, attractive gelding: third foal: dam unraced sister to high-class 1½m performer Shirocco: fairly useful performer: won maiden at Wolverhampton in February: better form when placed in handicaps last 4 starts: stays 1¾m: acts on polytrack, tapeta, good to firm and good to soft going: usually races close up: has been gelded: sent to USA. *Marco Botti* — **92**

SOLVEIG'S SONG 3 b.f. Norse Dancer (IRE) 127 – Ivory Lace 96 (Atraf (116) [2015 –: p7m 8g 6g⁵ 7m² 6d⁴ 8g 8s p8g⁶ p8g⁴ p10g³ Dec 30] modest maiden: stays 1¼m: acts on polytrack and good to firm going: tried in cheekpieces in 2015. *Steve Woodman* — **56**

SOME CHARACTER (IRE) 3 b.g. Fast Company (IRE) 126 – Puerto Oro (IRE) 70 – (Entrepreneur 123) [2015 61: p6g⁵ p7g 10m⁶ 8.7m Jun 14] maiden: no form in 2015. *M. J. Tynan, Ireland*

SOMEDAYSRDIAMONDS 3 b.f. Equiano (FR) 127 – Good Health 78 (Magic Ring 64 (IRE) 115) [2015 67: 5.1m⁴ 5m 5g⁴ 5m⁶ Jul 22] smallish, angular filly: modest handicapper: best form at 5f: acts on polytrack, tapeta and good to firm going: often wears headgear: usually races close up. *J. S. Moore*

SOMEONE EXCITING 2 b.f. (Feb 7) Notnowcato 128 – Quite Something 69 48 (Footstepsinthesand 120) [2015 6d 7s⁵ 6d⁶ p6m⁵ p7g Nov 18] first foal: dam ran once: poor maiden: stays 7f: acts on polytrack. *Alexandra Dunn*

SOMERS LAD (IRE) 2 b.c. (Feb 24) Lilbourne Lad (IRE) 111 – Somaggia (IRE) – (Desert King (IRE) 129) [2015 6d 6m p10g⁶ p8f Oct 8] no form, including in claimer· in blinkers last 2 starts. *Richard Hannon*

SOME SHOW 3 ch.f. Showcasing 117 – Dancing Nelly 52 (Shareef Dancer (USA) 135) 76 [2015 71: 5.7f⁵ 6d⁴ 5g⁶ 6s Oct 6] fair handicapper: stays 6f: acts on polytrack, firm and good to soft going: sold 4,000 gns, sent to Belgium. *Henry Candy*

SOME SITE (IRE) 4 b.f. Nayef (USA) 129 – Horatia (IRE) 106 (Machiavellian (USA) 86 123) [2015 82p: 9g⁴ 12.3s⁶ Sep 12] fairly useful performer: stays 12.5f: acts on heavy going. *David Simcock*

SOMETHING LUCKY (IRE) 3 gr.g. Clodovil (IRE) 116 – Lucky Leigh 96 (Piccolo 92 121) [2015 94: p6g⁵ 5s³ 5m 5g⁵ 5g 5g 5g⁶ 5g⁵ 5s 6d Oct 12] fairly useful handicapper: stays 6.5f: acts on polytrack and soft going: tried in blinkers in 2015. *Kristin Stubbs*

SOMETHINGTHRILLING 3 b.f. Makfi 130 – Something Exciting 114 (Halling 91 p (USA) 133) [2015 8d* Oct 5] fifth foal: half-sister to 1½m winner Fascinating (by Cape Cross): dam winner up to 1¼m (2-y-o 1m winner) and second in Oaks: 6/1, promising start when winning 6-runner maiden at Pontefract by 9 lengths from Dinaria, leading over 2f out, drawing clear soon after then staying on strongly: capable of better. *David Elsworth*

SO MI DAR 2 b.f. (Mar 14) Dubawi (IRE) 129 – Dar Re Mi 124 (Singspiel (IRE) 133) 84 P [2015 8.3g* Oct 20] second foal: half-sister to smart French winner up to 9.7f De Treville (2-y-o 7f winner, by Oasis Dream): dam, 1¼m-12.5f winner (including Yorkshire Oaks and Dubai Sheema Classic), half-sister to top-class winner up to 1½m Rewilding: 6/1, won 12-runner maiden at Windsor by neck from Golden Stunner, shaken up 2f out and staying on to lead late on under a mostly hands-and-heels ride: likely to progress considerably. *John Gosden*

SO MUCH FUN (IRE) 2 b.f. (Apr 8) Iffraaj 127 – Seminole Lass (USA) (Indian Charlie 74 (USA) 126) [2015 p7g⁴ 6.9m⁴ p7g³ 7s⁶ Oct 6] €15,000F, 85,000Y: rather leggy filly: third foal: half-sister to 1½m winner Bold Henmie (by Henrythenavigator): dam US 5.5f (including at 2 yrs) to 1m winner: fair form second/third starts in maidens: possibly unsuited by soft ground final outing: raced only at 7f. *Ismail Mohammed*

SONG AND DANCE MAN 5 b.g. Danehill Dancer (IRE) 117 – Song (IRE) (Sadler's 66 Wells (USA) 132) [2015 72: p10f Feb 2] fair maiden: stays 1½m: acts on polytrack and good to soft going: sometimes wears headgear. *Gary Moore*

SONGBIRD (USA) 2 b.f. (Apr 30) Medaglia d'Oro (USA) 129 – Ivanavinalot (USA) 111 125 p (West Acre (USA)) [2015 a6f¹ a7f* a8.5f* a8.5f* Oct 31] $400,000Y: half-sister to US 5.5f-1m winner Bolting Brown (by Big Brown) and US 6.5f/1m winner Ivana Beat Yabad (by More Than Ready): dam US Grade 2 9f winner: high-class form: unbeaten in 4 races, namely maiden at Del Mar in July, the Del Mar Debutante Stakes on same course and Chandelier Stakes at Santa Anita (by 4½ lengths from Land Over Sea), both in September, and Breeders' Cup Juvenile Fillies at Keeneland (dominated from the front when beating Rachel's Valentina impressively by 5¾ lengths) in October: stays 8.5f: has more improvement in her, and is a most exciting prospect. *Jerry Hollendorfer, USA*

SONG LIGHT 5 b.g. Echo of Light 125 – Blue Lullaby (IRE) 82 (Fasliyev (USA) 120) 84 [2015 76: 14.1g* 16.1m Aug 8] tall, lengthy gelding: fairly useful handicapper: won at Nottingham in May: stays 1¾m: acts on heavy going: sometimes slowly away, usually races towards rear. *Seamus Mullins*

SONG OF NORWAY 4 b.f. Halling (USA) 133 – Amarullah (FR) (Daylami (IRE) 138) 87 [2015 71§: 7.5g⁴ 7g* 7.1m³ 7g* p8g² p7g³ Oct 7] fairly useful performer: won maiden at Catterick in May and handicap at Brighton in September: left Ann Duffield after third start: stays 1m: acts on polytrack and firm going: sometimes in cheekpieces prior to 2015: often travels strongly, usually responds generously to pressure. *Chris Wall*

SONG OF PARADISE 2 ch.f. (Feb 19) Kyllachy 129 – Merry Diva 81 (Bahamian **73** Bounty 116) [2015 6m 6m 6g p5g³ p6g² t6m⁶ Dec 30] 18,000Y: third foal: half-sister to 7f winner Concrete Mac (by Mastercraftsman) and 2-y-o 6f winner Belvoir Diva (by Exceed And Excel): dam, 2-y-o 6f winner, sister to smart sprinter Paradise Isle: fair maiden: best effort at 6f on polytrack. *Chris Wall*

SONG OF SHADOWS 2 b.g. (Feb 9) Invincible Spirit (IRE) 121 – Lyrique (IRE) (Iffraaj **78 p** 127) [2015 6g 6m² Jun 23] lengthy gelding: first foal: dam, French 1m winner, half-sister to very smart 1¼m-12.3f winner Debussy: 3/1, much sharper when ½-length second of 6 to Academy House in maiden at Leicester, staying on/clear of rest: will stay at least 7f: has been gelded: will go on improving. *Charlie Appleby*

SONGSMITH 7 b.g. Librettist (USA) 124 – Venus Rising (Observatory (USA) 131) **75** [2015 p11g³ p11g p16g* p16g² p15.8g⁴ 16d⁶ Oct 11] big gelding: fair handicapper: won at Kempton in June: stays 2m: acts on polytrack and good to soft going: tried in headgear: usually races prominently. *Lucy Wadham*

SONIC RAINBOW (GR) 3 ch.f. Harmonic Way 121 – Rainbow Way (High Chaparral **57** (IRE) 132) [2015 –: p8m p11g⁴ 11.7f² p12g 13.1f³ 16.2m⁴ f14s⁶ 11.9s⁶ 11s³ 11.9d Sep 14] modest maiden: stays 13f: acts on firm going: usually in headgear in 2015. *Amanda Perrett*

SONNETATION (IRE) 5 b.m. Dylan Thomas (IRE) 132 – Southern Migration (USA) **87** (Kingmambo (USA) 125) [2015 77, a71: t8.6f² t8.6f² t9.5m² p8f⁴ t9.5f* p8g* 8f³ 8.1m² 8.3m p8d Sep 4] workmanlike mare: fairly useful handicapper: won at Wolverhampton in March and Chelmsford in April: stays 9.5f: acts on polytrack, tapeta and firm going: tried in cheekpieces prior to 2015. *Jim Boyle*

SONNOLENTO (IRE) 3 b.c. Rip Van Winkle (IRE) 134 – Dreams Come True (FR) 106 **90** (Zafonic (USA) 130) [2015 74: 10.3d⁴ 10d⁵ p11g* 9.9g⁴ 10g⁴ p11g⁴ Sep 30] fairly useful handicapper: won at Kempton in May: stays 11f: acts on polytrack and soft going: often in tongue tie in 2015: sometimes slowly away, often races towards rear: sold 25,000 gns, sent to Morocco. *Andrew Balding*

SONNYTHENAVIGATOR (USA) 3 b.g. Henrythenavigator (USA) 131 – Lady **61** Simpson (Yankee Victor (USA) 121) [2015 t9.5g³ t8.6g³ 8d p12g p12g t9.5m⁶ Dec 26] modest maiden: should stay 1¼m: acts on polytrack and tapeta: tried in cheekpieces. *David Simcock*

SON OF AFRICA 3 b.g. Equiano (FR) 127 – Generously Gifted (Sakhee (USA) 136) **103** [2015 94: 6m⁴ 5g⁴ 5m 5f Jul 11] strong gelding: useful handicapper: won at Newmarket (by 3 lengths from Union Rose) in June: stays 6f: acts on good to firm going: often starts slowly. *Henry Candy*

SON OF FEYAN (IRE) 4 ch.g. Nayef (USA) 129 – Miss Penton 66 (Primo Dominie **–** 121) [2015 65: 11.1m Jun 10] lengthy gelding: fair maiden at best, looked none too keen only outing in 2015: stays 1½m: acts on polytrack and good to firm going: tried in hood. *Lucy Normile*

SONORAN SANDS (IRE) 7 b.g. Footstepsinthesand 120 – Atishoo (IRE) 70 (Revoque **56** (IRE) 122) [2015 10.3g 8m 7.9m 9.3d 8.5m 10.9g p13f⁶ Sep 12] lengthy, angular gelding: modest handicapper: stays 11f: acts on polytrack, firm and good to soft going: tried in headgear: sometimes slowly away. *Alan Berry*

14 Hands Winery Breeders' Cup Juvenile Fillies, Keeneland—
the best performance by a juvenile in North America in 2015 from all-the-way winner Songbird;
Rachel's Valentina is a distant second ahead of Dothraki Queen

SOOFIAH 2 b.f. (Apr 3) King's Best (USA) 132 – Anaamil (IRE) 85 (Darshaan 133) [2015 **78 p**
p7g⁴ p6g* Dec 16] seventh foal: sister to very smart 1m-10.4f winner Sajjhaa and closely
related to useful 7f winner Momaris (by Dubai Destination): dam 10.6f winner out of
Lancashire Oaks winner Noushkey: 11/10, improved when winning maiden at Kempton by
2 lengths from Langham, making all and eased close home: should stay 1m+: open to
further improvement. *Saeed bin Suroor*

SOOQAAN 4 bl.g. Naaqoos 117 – Dream Day (FR) (Spectrum (IRE) 126) [2015 68, a74: **75**
f8g⁵ f8g⁴ f7g² 8s 8g f6m⁶ t7.1f Dec 21] fair handicapper: stays 9.5f: acts on fibresand,
tapeta and heavy going. *Antony Brittain*

SOPHISTICA (IRE) 2 b.f. (Mar 22) Thousand Words 113 – Texas Queen 76 (Shamardal **64**
(USA) 129) [2015 5.1d⁵ 5.1s⁶ 6g 6g⁴ p6f* p6f² Oct 10] €20,000Y: first foal: dam, 5f
winner who stayed 7f, out of half-sister to very smart miler Zafeen: modest performer: won
nursery at Chelmsford in October: stays 6f: acts on polytrack: often in hood. *Mick Channon*

SOPHISTICATED HEIR (IRE) 5 b.g. New Approach (IRE) 132 – My Girl Sophie **85**
(USA) 99 (Danzig (USA)) [2015 88: 8g² 9.8v⁶ 8g 8g 9.2d⁴ 8.5s⁴ 8d 7.2g² 8d⁶ 7s⁵ Oct 27]
fairly useful handicapper: stays 1¼m: acts on good to firm and heavy going: usually wears
headgear: front runner/races prominently. *David O'Meara*

SOQOTRA 3 b.f. King's Best (USA) 132 – Yemen Desert (IRE) 73 (Sadler's Wells (USA) **–**
132) [2015 –: 9g p12g 7m Aug 9] no form. *Peter Chapple-Hyam*

SO STROPPY POPPY 3 ch.f. Phoenix Reach (IRE) 124 – Toy Girl (IRE) (Cadeaux **–**
Genereux 131) [2015 7.1m t8.6f Oct 30] fifth foal: dam unraced: tailed off in 2 maidens.
Shaun Harris

SOTERIA (IRE) 2 b.f. (Feb 21) Acclamation 118 – Roo 97 (Rudimentary (USA) 118) **70**
[2015 6g³ 6d⁴ 7m Oct 3] 300,000Y: half-sister to several winners, including smart winner
up to 7f Gallagher (2-y-o 6f winner, by Bahamian Bounty) and smart winner up to 1¼m
Quick Wit (2-y-o 7f winner, by Oasis Dream): dam 2-y-o 5f/6f winner: fair maiden: in
first-time cheekpieces, 50/1, excelled herself when 10¼ lengths eighth of 12 to Alice
Springs in sales race at Newmarket final start: sent to France. *Roger Varian*

SO THE STORY GOES 2 b.f. (Apr 5) Equiano (FR) 127 – Stylish Dream (USA) 66 **–**
(Elusive Quality (USA)) [2015 6s t7.1f Nov 20] 16,000Y: first foal: dam, ran twice, out of
half-sister to high-class 1¼m-1½m performer Nathaniel and Irish Oaks winner Great
Heavens: well held both starts in maidens: wears tongue tie. *Paul Fitzsimons*

SOUK AL TAHAB (IRE) 3 b.g. Arcano (IRE) 122 – Quiet Dream (USA) (Seattle Slew **53**
(USA)) [2015 75: p7f⁵ p7g Jul 2] modest maiden: stays 7f: acts on polytrack and tapeta:
often races freely. *Ed Dunlop*

SOUL BROTHER (IRE) 4 b.g. Captain Rio 122 – Goodwood March 66 (Foxhound **89 §**
(USA) 103) [2015 93: 6d 5g³ 5g³ 5.9v⁵ 6g 6m 5g* 6.1g 5s Oct 19] strong, close-coupled
gelding: fairly useful handicapper: won at Pontefract (by ¾ length from Imperial Legend)
in September: best at 5f: acts on soft and good to firm going: usually in cheekpieces in
2015: tried in tongue tie prior to 2015: usually races towards rear: unreliable. *Tim Easterby*

SOUL INSTINCT 4 b.g. Myboycharlie (IRE) 118 – However (IRE) (Hector Protector **60**
(USA) 124) [2015 56, a63: p8g p7m³ p6f p6g² p6m⁴ t7.1f⁶ t7.1f p7m* t7.1g⁴ Jun 22]
modest handicapper: won at Lingfield in June: stays 7f: acts on polytrack, good to firm and
good to soft going: tried in headgear prior to 2015. *Simon Dow*

SOUL SEARCHER (IRE) 3 b.f. Motivator 131 – Israar (Machiavellian (USA) 123) **90**
[2015 t12.2g³ p12f* 12.1m* 12m³ t12.2g* 12g⁴ t13.9m² t12.2f Oct 23] €240,000Y: fourth
foal: half-sister to 3 winners, including smart winner up to 1m Rutland Boy (2-y-o 7f
winner, by Bertolini) and 5f winner Exceed Power (by Exceed And Excel), later successful
in Greece: dam unraced: fairly useful performer: won maiden at Kempton in March and
handicaps at Beverley in April and Wolverhampton in July: stays 1¾m: acts on polytrack,
tapeta and good to firm going. *Charles Hills*

SOUND ADVICE 6 b.g. Echo of Light 125 – Flylowflylong (IRE) 74 (Danetime (IRE) **107**
121) [2015 99: 10m 8m* 8g³ 8f³ 8m⁶ 8g² 7.6g* 7.6m* 6g Sep 19] good-topped gelding:
useful handicapper: won at Thirsk in May and twice at Chester in August (by ¾ length from
Miracle of Medinah latter occasion): stays 8.5f: acts on fibresand, soft and good to firm
going: tried in blinkers: usually races prominently, often travels strongly. *Keith Dalgleish*

SOUND OF FREEDOM (IRE) 3 ch.f. Duke of Marmalade (IRE) 132 – Paint In Green **113**
(IRE) 102 (Invincible Spirit (IRE) 121) [2015 8d* 8g* 8g* 10.9m² 10.4g⁶ 9.9d³ 9.9g²
Oct 25] €55,000Y: third foal: sister to useful Italian 1m-9.5f winner Collateral Risk and
half-sister to useful Italian 1m-1¼m winner Drive To Hell (by Manduro): dam Italian 7.5f
(at 2 yrs) to 11f winner: smart performer: won her first 4 starts, including minor event at

Rome in March, and listed race at Milan and Premio Regina Elena at Rome (by 4 lengths from Anchise, leading over 2f out and going clear last ½f), both in April: placed after in Derby Italiano at Rome (3 lengths second to Goldstream), Premio Verziere at Milan (3¾ lengths third to Loritania) and Premio Lydia Tesio at Rome (good neck second to Odeliz): probably stays 11f: acts on good to soft going, probably good to firm: often races prominently: has joined Marco Botti. *Stefano Botti, Italy*

SOUND REFLECTION (USA) 4 b.f. Street Cry (IRE) 130 – Echoes In Eternity (IRE) **100** 111 (Spinning World (USA) 130) [2015 96: 10.3g³ 12m* 10.4m Jul 24] big filly: useful performer: won handicap at Newmarket (by head from Moonrise Landing) in June: stays 1½m: acts on polytrack and good to firm going: in hood last 5 starts: tends to find little. *Charlie Appleby*

SOUNDS OF THUNDER 8 b.m. Tobougg (IRE) 125 – Distant Music (Darshaan 133) – [2015 13g 12.5m 17g f12g Nov 26] compact mare: fair at best, no form in 2015: tried in headgear. *Adrian McGuinness, Ireland*

SOUTHDOWN LAD (IRE) 2 b.c. (Apr 23) Lilbourne Lad (IRE) 111 – Elizabelle (IRE) **93** 63 (Westerner 130) [2015 6d* p7g⁴ 8g² 9g* Oct 21] 34,000Y: good-topped colt: second foal: half-brother to 2-y-o 6f-1m winner Power Play (by Zebedee): dam lightly-raced half-sister to smart 2-y-o 6f/7f winner Orizaba: fairly useful performer: won maiden at Ffos Las in August and nursery at Newmarket (by 2 lengths from Laafiraaq) in October: stays 9f. *William Knight*

SOUTHERLY BUSTER 3 b.g. Shirocco (GER) 129 – Appleby 72 (Anabaa (USA) 130) **69** [2015 12s t12.2f⁴ t13.9g⁴ Nov 27] fair maiden: best effort when fourth at Wolverhampton final start. *Nigel Twiston-Davies*

SOUTHERN BELLE (IRE) 2 b.f. (May 12) Aqlaam 125 – Areyaam (USA) 75 (Elusive **89** Quality (USA)) [2015 5f² p5g³ 5g* 5g Oct 9] tall filly: fourth foal: half-sister to 3 winners, including useful 2-y-o 6.5f-1m winner Go Angellica (by Kheleyf) and 2-y-o 6f winner My Lucky Liz (by Exceed And Excel): dam maiden (stayed 8.6f): fairly useful form: won maiden at Sandown (by 2½ lengths from September Issue) in September: below form in Cornwallis Stakes at Newmarket final start: raced only at 5f. *Robert Cowell*

SOUTHERN CROSS 4 ch.f. Mount Nelson 125 – Bread of Heaven 79 (Machiavellian **49** (USA) 123) [2015 64: p10g 17.2f 10.2d Sep 2] poor maiden: left Andy Turnell after first start: stays 1¼m: acts on polytrack, tapeta, firm and good to soft going: tried in headgear/tongue tie: often races towards rear: temperament under suspicion. *Dai Williams*

SOUTHERN GAILES (IRE) 2 ch.c. (Apr 20) Frozen Power (IRE) 108 – Pardoned **90 p** (IRE) 74 (Mujadil (USA) 119) [2015 p7g³ p8m* p8m² Nov 14] €5,000F, €10,000Y, €39,000 2-y-o: half-brother to 3 winners, including useful winner up to 1¼m River Captain (2-y-o 7f/1m winner, by Captain Rio) and winner up to 11f Proper (2-y-o 6f winner, by Rossini): dam maiden (stayed 7f): fairly useful form: won maiden at Kempton in October by short head from Pergamino: better form when 1¼ lengths second of 4 to Race Day in minor event at Lingfield: likely to stay 1¼m: will go on improving. *K. R. Burke*

SOUTHERN SEAS 2 ch.f. (Apr 17) Archipenko (USA) 127 – Sourire 97 (Domedriver **64** (IRE) 128) [2015 7g³ 8g 7v³ f8g² f8m Dec 8] fourth foal: half-sister to a winner abroad by Hernando: dam, winner up to 8.6f (2-y-o 7f winner), half-sister to smart performers up to around 1¾m Songerie and Souvenance: modest maiden: should prove suited by further than 1m: acts on fibresand: tried in visor: usually races close up. *Ann Duffield*

SOUTHERN STARS 2 b.f. (Feb 9) Smart Strike (CAN) 121 – Stacelita (FR) 123 **73 P** (Monsun (GER) 124) [2015 8d⁵ Oct 23] first foal: dam winner up to 1½m (2-y-o 9f winner), including Prix de Diane and Prix Vermeille: 9/1, promise when 4½ lengths fifth of 11 to Zest in maiden at Doncaster on debut, good headway over 2f out and not knocked about as effort flattened out: type to make well above average improvement. *John Gosden*

SOUTHERN STORM (IRE) 3 b.f. Cape Cross (IRE) 129 – Stormy Blessing (USA) **73** (Storm Cat (USA)) [2015 8.3g⁴ 8m⁴ Jun 14] angular filly: second foal: half-sister to 8.5f-1¼m winner One Pekan (by Hard Spun): dam, ran twice in USA, sister to smart performer up to 9f Brave Tin Soldier out of sister to Kentucky Derby winner Fusaichi Pegasus: fair form in maidens at Windsor and Salisbury: should be suited by 1¼m. *Ralph Beckett*

SOUTHFIELDS (IRE) 2 ch.g. (Mar 15) New Approach (IRE) 132 – Southern House **74 p** (IRE) 100 (Paris House 123) [2015 8.1s⁴ 10.2m² 9d⁶ Oct 11] half-brother to several winners abroad, including Japanese Group 3 1¼m winner Cosmo Phantom (by Stephen Got Even): dam Italian/US 6.5f-1m winner (7.5f winner at 2 yrs): fair form: best effort in maidens when second to Calvinist at Bath in September: has been gelded: remains open to improvement. *Charlie Appleby*

SOUTHVIEW LADY 3 b.f. Misu Bond (IRE) 114 – Salalah 62 (Lion Cavern (USA) **58**
117) [2015 –: 8g 7g⁶ 8m⁴ 8g³ 8g 9.3m 7.9m⁵ 8.5d 12d Oct 5] modest maiden: stays 1m: acts
on good to firm going: usually in headgear in 2015. *Mark Walford*

SOUVILLE 4 b.f. Dalakhani (IRE) 133 – Royale Danehill (IRE) (Danehill (USA) 126) **96**
[2015 96: 6m 6m* 7f⁴ 6d p6g 6g⁶ p6f Oct 28] good-topped filly: useful handicapper: won
at Windsor (by 1¼ lengths from Tamayuz Star) in June: stays 6f: acts on polytrack and
good to firm going: sometimes in hood prior to 2015. *Chris Wall*

SOVEREIGN BOUNTY 3 ch.g. Bahamian Bounty 116 – Sovereign Abbey (IRE) 68 **79**
(Royal Academy (USA) 130) [2015 70: 7.5m³ 7.5m* 7m⁵ 8g Jul 14] fair handicapper: won
at Beverley in May: best effort at 7.5f: acts on good to firm going: tried in hood prior to
2015. *Jedd O'Keeffe*

SOVEREIGN DEBT (IRE) 6 gr.g. Dark Angel (IRE) 113 – Kelsey Rose 97 (Most **116**
Welcome 131) [2015 p8g² p7f³ t1.1m* p8f² 7d⁵ 7g³ 8m* 7d² 8d² 7.5g* 9g² 7s* p8g⁴ p7.5g²
Dec 12] compact gelding: smart performer: won listed races at Wolverhampton (by 1¼
lengths from Chookie Royale) in March and the Curragh (by 4¾ lengths from Flight Risk)
in June, and Concorde Stakes at Tipperary (awarded race after going down by short head
to Tested) and listed race at Leopardstown (by ½ length from Iveagh Gardens) in October:
creditable second in handicap at Lingfield (¾ length behind Mindurownbusiness), Superior
Mile at Haydock (1½ lengths behind Balty Boys), Darley Stakes at Newmarket (¾ length
behind Energia Davos) and listed race at Deauville (short neck behind Ross) first/ninth/
eleventh/final starts: stays 9f: acts on polytrack, tapeta, soft and good to firm going: tried in
cheekpieces prior to 2015: often races prominently: consistent. *David Nicholls*

SOVEREIGN TREATY 3 b.c. Mawatheeq (USA) 126 – Katya Kabanova (Sadler's **59**
Wells (USA) 132) [2015 8d p8g 10m p10g² p10g³ Aug 20] modest maiden: stays 1¼m:
acts on polytrack: in blinkers last 2 starts: usually races nearer last than first. *David Lanigan*

SOV (IRE) 4 gr.g. Duke of Marmalade (IRE) 132 – Exotic Mix (FR) (Linamix (FR) 127) **–**
[2015 64p: 10.2m 14.1g f11g Dec 22] fair form when successful only start in 2014, well
held in 2015 (left Alan McCabe after second start): best effort at 1¼m: acts on good to firm
going: tried in visor. *John Balding*

SPACE AGE (IRE) 3 ch.g. New Approach (IRE) 132 – Historian (IRE) (Pennekamp **104**
(USA) 130) [2015 84p: 10m⁵ 10m* 12f* 12f² 12g⁵ Jul 29] compact gelding: useful
handicapper: won at Newmarket in May and Royal Ascot (King George V Stakes, made all
to beat Scottish by 1¼ lengths) in June: good efforts last 2 starts, up in grade when 8¾
lengths fifth of 9 to Highland Reel in Gordon Stakes at Goodwood: stays 1½m: acts on firm
and good to soft going: usually leads: has been gelded. *Charlie Appleby*

SPACE ARTIST (IRE) 5 b.g. Captain Marvelous (IRE) 114 – Dame Laura (IRE) 100 **82**
(Royal Academy (USA) 130) [2015 88: 5d 5m 5g p5f* t5.1m⁵ t5.1g⁴ Nov 27] fairly useful
performer: won seller at Chelmsford in October: stays 6f: acts on polytrack, tapeta, good to
firm and good to soft going: sometimes in visor, including on last 4 starts. *Nigel Tinkler*

SPACELAB 4 b.f. Champs Elysees 124 – Shuttle Mission (Sadler's Wells (USA) 132) **94**
[2015 93: 12g 12m* 12g⁶ 12s 12m⁴ t12.2f⁶ Oct 17] lengthy filly: fairly useful handicapper:
won at Newbury (by short head from Melodious) in July: stays 13f: acts on polytrack,
tapeta and good to firm going: often races towards rear. *Amanda Perrett*

SPACE MOUNTAIN 2 b.c. (Jan 29) Sea The Stars (IRE) 140 – Ripples Maid 109 **70**
(Dansili 127) [2015 7f 8d⁵ 10.2m⁵ Sep 28] fair form: best effort when fifth at Haydock
second start. *Mark Johnston*

SPACE WAR 8 b.g. Elusive City (USA) 117 – Princess Luna (GER) (Grand Lodge (USA) **72**
125) [2015 75: 7.1g⁴ f8d* 8g⁶ 7.5m⁶ 8m⁵ 7.6g* 7.9m⁶ 9.3g 7.2g 7m⁴ 7.5d 7s t8.6f Nov 20]
useful-looking gelding: fair handicapper: won at Southwell in May and Chester (amateur)
in July: stays 8.5f: acts on all-weather and good to firm going: tried in blinkers prior to
2015: tried in tongue tie: none too consistent. *Michael Easterby*

SPANGLED 3 ch.f. Starspangledbanner (AUS) 128 – Zykina (Pivotal 124) [2015 7g 7m* **105**
7m* 7d⁴ 8g Sep 25] tall filly: first foal: dam unraced half-sister to useful 7f/1m winner
Russian Realm out of 1000 Guineas winner Russian Rhythm: useful performer: won
maiden at Lingfield (by 6 lengths from Arc Cara) in June and handicap at Newmarket (by
length from Muffri'ha) in July: should stay 1m: acts on good to firm going: sometimes
slowly away. *Roger Varian*

SPANISH BOY (IRE) 2 b.c. (Apr 27) Lope de Vega (IRE) 125 – Iuturna (USA) 94 **73**
(Intidab (USA) 115) [2015 7g⁴ p8g³ 7g t7.1f Oct 20] tall, attractive colt: fair maiden: stays
1m. *Richard Hannon*

SPANISH CITY 2 ch.c. (Jan 30) Exceed And Excel (AUS) 126 – Annabelle's Charm **80 p**
(IRE) 107 (Indian Ridge 123) [2015 6g³ 6g² Sep 4] second foal: half-brother to smart 2-y-o
6f winner (including Middle Park Stakes) winner Charming Thought (by Oasis Dream):
dam 1m-1¼m winner: better effort in maidens when third of 12 to Firedanser at Haydock
on debut: remains with potential. *Roger Varian*

SPANISH DANSER (IRE) 3 ch.f. Lord Shanakill (USA) 121 – Highwater Dancer (IRE) **56**
(Sadler's Wells (USA) 132) [2015 –: t8.6g⁴ t9.5g p10g t9.5f Oct 3] modest maiden: best
effort at 8.5f: acts on tapeta: in tongue tie final start. *George Baker*

SPANISH ROMANCE (IRE) 2 b.f. (Apr 23) Rip Van Winkle (IRE) 134 – Utr (USA) **98**
(Mr Prospector (USA)) [2015 5d* 5g* 6f⁶ Jun 19] compact filly: half-sister to several
winners, including smart performer up to 1¼m Bonnard (2-y-o 6f winner, by Nureyev),
later successful abroad, and useful 2-y-o 1m winner Sundrenched (by Desert King): dam,
probably temperamental, out of smart half-sister to 2000 Guineas/Champion Stakes winner
Haafhd: useful form: won newcomers race at Chantilly (by 5 lengths) in April and minor
event on same course (by 1¼ lengths from Du Pyla) in May: made effort earlier than ideal
when 6 lengths sixth of 18 to Illuminate in Albany Stakes at Royal Ascot final outing: best
form at 5f. *E. J. O'Neill, France*

SPANISH SQUEEZE (IRE) 3 ch.g. Lope de Vega (IRE) 125 – Appetina 76 (Perugino **108**
(USA) 84) [2015 91p: p8g⁴ p10f² p12g Nov 25] lengthy, unfurnished gelding: useful
performer: comfortably best effort when second of 7 in handicap at Chelmsford (nose
behind Bancnuanaheireann) in November: stays 1¼m: acts on polytrack. *Hugo Palmer*

SPARBROOK (IRE) 3 b.f. Kodiac 112 – Summer Sunshine (Dubai Destination (USA) **–**
127) [2015 44, a65: 6m Jul 7] compact filly: fair handicapper in 2014, well held only outing
in Britain in 2015: stays 6f: acts on polytrack: tried in visor: usually races close up: sent to
Belgium. *Simon Dow*

SPARKLE FACTOR (IRE) 4 b.f. Arch (USA) 127 – Thoughtless Moment (IRE) 102 **98**
(Pivotal 124) [2015 101: 7g² 7m 8.5g⁴ 8d³ Jul 19] leggy, angular filly: useful handicapper:
second at Gowran (2¼ lengths behind Duchess Andorra) in April: stays 8.5f: acts on soft
and good to firm going: often in headgear in 2015: tried in tongue tie prior to 2015: usually
races prominently: sent to USA. *D. K. Weld, Ireland*

SPARKLING ICE (IRE) 4 gr.f. Verglas (IRE) 118 – Sand Crystal (IRE) (Singspiel **–**
(IRE) 133) [2015 58, a69: f12g t9.5f Feb 7] fair at best, no form in 2015: stays 1½m: acts
on polytrack, firm and soft going: often wears headgear: usually races close up. *Zoe Davison*

SPARKLING SAPPHIRE 3 ro.f. Monsieur Bond (IRE) 120 – Velvet Band 73 (Verglas **47**
(IRE) 118) [2015 50: f7g⁵ 5g⁶ 6g 6g⁴ 7g 5g³ 6d 6m t5.1f⁴ 5m⁶ Oct 1] poor maiden: stays
7f: acts on fibresand, tapeta and good to firm going: often wears headgear: usually races
close up. *Richard Whitaker*

SPARK PLUG (IRE) 4 b.g. Dylan Thomas (IRE) 132 – Kournikova (SAF) (Sportsworld **113**
(USA) 121) [2015 106: 8m² 8m* 8fᶠ 8.1m 10m 8d⁶ 8d⁵ Oct 17] smallish gelding: smart
handicapper: won at Newbury (by neck from GM Hopkins) in May: in first-time
cheekpieces, 25/1, better than result when 5¾ lengths fifth of 20 to Musaddas in Balmoral
Handicap at Ascot final start: stays 1¼m: acts on good to firm going, probably on good to
soft: tried in blinkers: usually races nearer last than first. *Brian Meehan*

SPARKS (IRE) 3 br.f. Elusive City (USA) 117 – Hambye 97 (Distant Relative 128) [2015 **–**
10d Apr 24] €14,000Y, €50,000 2-y-o: angular filly: half-sister to several winners abroad,
including smart Italian winner up to 9f Marbye (2-y-o 5f/6f winner, by Marju): dam Italian
5f/6f winner (including at 2 yrs): 40/1, very green when tailed off in maiden at Sandown.
Jonathan Portman

SPARKY (GER) 4 ch.g. Sholokhov (IRE) 121 – Simply Red (GER) (Dashing Blade 117) **–**
[2015 8m f8g p10m p10f Dec 21] no form: left Keith Dalgleish after second start: tried in
hood. *Ali Stronge*

SPARKY JACK 2 b.c. (Mar 17) Holy Roman Emperor (IRE) 125 – Prospectress (USA) **72**
87 (Mining (USA)) [2015 5.2m 5g⁵ 6g May 14] workmanlike colt: fair form at best in
maidens: dead. *Brendan Powell*

SPARRING (IRE) 3 b.g. Teofilo (IRE) 126 – Henties Bay (IRE) (Cape Cross (IRE) 129) **100**
[2015 66p: p10f* 11.6m* 12m* t12.2m* Nov 28] useful-looking gelding: useful performer:
won maiden at Lingfield in January and handicaps at Windsor and Pontefract in April: off
7 months and gelded, completed 4-timer in handicap at Wolverhampton by short head from
Brandon Castle: stays 1½m: acts on polytrack, tapeta and good to firm going: often races
prominently, usually responds generously to pressure. *Charlie Appleby*

K. Quinn/ C. Benham/ I. Saunders' "Speculative Bid"

SPARRING QUEEN (USA) 2 b.f. (Mar 25) War Front (USA) 119 – Spa Break (USA) **50**
(Giant's Causeway (USA) 132) [2015 p7g p7g Sep 21] second foal: half-sister to a winner
in USA by Arch: dam, US 1m winner, half-sister to smart 1¼m performer Sabre d'Argent
and smart US Grade 2 7f winner Exchange Rate: showed only a little ability in maidens at
Kempton, in tongue tie latter occasion. *Ralph Beckett*

SPA'S DANCER (IRE) 8 b.g. Danehill Dancer (IRE) 117 – Spa (Sadler's Wells (USA) **95**
132) [2015 109: 8d 10.3s⁴ 8.3m³ 9.9g 10v Oct 24] good-bodied gelding: useful handicapper:
third at Nottingham in June: stays 10.5f: acts on polytrack, soft and good to firm going:
tried in headgear prior to 2015: often starts slowly, often races in rear. *James Eustace*

SPECIAL CODE (IRE) 3 b.g. Iffraaj 127 – Najmati (Green Desert (USA) 127) [2015 **63**
65: p8g⁴ f8d⁴ p5g⁴ 6d⁶ 5g⁴ t6g 5g* 5g⁵ 6g 7.4v p6f f6g Nov 24] modest performer: left
John Gosden after first start: won seller at Beverley in May: stays 6f: acts on polytrack,
tapeta, best turf form on good going: wears tongue tie: front runner/races prominently.
Heather Dalton

SPECIAL MISS (IRE) 4 b.f. Authorized (IRE) 133 – Whatamiss (USA) (Miswaki (USA) 124) **77**
[2015 80: 10.2f³ 9.9d⁴ 11.6m* 12m⁶ 10f⁴ 11.9g⁵ 10m⁶ p10g p10g p10f⁶ Dec 17] rather
leggy filly: fair handicapper: won at Windsor in May: stays 1½m: acts on polytrack, good
to firm and good to soft going: tried in cheekpieces in 2015. *Ali Stronge*

SPECIAL REPORT (IRE) 5 b.g. Mujadil (USA) 119 – Ellistown Lady (IRE) (Red **–**
Sunset 120) [2015 42: p8f 8.5g Apr 6] poor maiden: stayed 1½m: acted on firm and soft
going: in blinkers last 3 starts, also tongue tied last 2: fair hurdler: dead. *Neil Mulholland*

SPECIAL SEASON 2 ch.c. (Feb 12) Lope de Vega (IRE) 125 – Keep Dancing (IRE) 77 **103**
(Distant Music (USA) 126) [2015 7.1g* 8s² 8g⁴ p7m² p8g* Dec 19] 95,000Y: well-made
colt: first foal: dam, 5.5f winner, half-sister to smart performers Humidor (sprinter) and
Alhebayeb (stayed 1m): useful performer: won maiden at Sandown in August and minor
event at Lingfield (by 2½ lengths from Good Trip) in December: stays 1m: acts on
polytrack and soft going: in cheekpieces for second win: often races towards rear.
William Haggas

SPECIAL VENTURE (IRE) 3 b.c. Azamour (IRE) 130 – La Reine Mambo (USA) **86** (High Yield (USA) 121) [2015 80: 7.5m 6m² 7g⁶ 7.6m³ 6.9s² 7.6g³ Jul 11] fairly useful handicapper: stays 7.5f: acts on soft going: tried in visor in 2015: front runner/races prominently: sent to Macau. *Tim Easterby*

SPECIALV (IRE) 2 br.f. (Apr 22) Big Bad Bob (IRE) 118 – Montbretia 105 (Montjeu **66 p** (IRE) 137) [2015 6.1v f5g² t5.1m f8g⁵ Dec 28] €40,000Y: second foal: dam 1¼m winner: fair maiden: stays 1m: remains capable of better. *Brian Ellison*

SPECTATOR 4 br.g. Passing Glance 119 – Averami 68 (Averti (IRE) 117) [2015 99: **90** 14.1m⁶ 12g³ 16.4m 14.1d 13g 13.1g 14.1s⁵ Oct 12] good-topped gelding: fairly useful handicapper: third at York in May: stays 14.5f: acts on heavy going: wears headgear: often travels strongly. *Andrew Balding*

SPECULATIVE BID (IRE) 4 b.g. Excellent Art 125 – Barzah (IRE) 98 (Darshaan 133) **118** [2015 88; p7f* p7g* 7m* 8f⁵ 7d 7g³ 7g² Aug 21] angular gelding: smart handicapper: successful at Kempton in March and April and in 26-runner Victoria Cup at Ascot (in good style by ½ length from Lincoln, quickening to lead final 100 yds) in May: good ½-length second of 14 to Fadhayyil in listed race at York final start, no extra close home: stays 1m: acts on polytrack and any turf going: sometimes slowly away, usually races nearer last than first. *David Elsworth*

SPECULATOR 3 gr.c. Bahamian Bounty 116 – Swift Dispersal 87 (Shareef Dancer **71** (USA) 135) [2015 –: 6m⁵ 7m⁴ 7m⁴ 7g⁵ 10.2g² p10g* p10f* p10f⁵ Oct 8] fair handicapper: won at Lingfield in August and September: stays 1¼m: acts on polytrack and good to firm going: tried in cheekpieces in 2015. *David Menuisier*

SPEED COMPANY (IRE) 2 b.c. (Feb 13) Fast Company (IRE) 126 – Trentini (IRE) **96 p** (Singspiel (IRE) 133) [2015 7.5m² 7.2g* 8g* Sep 17] £48,000Y: second foal: dam, French 1¼m winner, out of sister to very smart miler No Excuse Needed and close relative to high-class performer up to 1¼m Capponi: useful form: won maiden at Musselburgh in August by 2¾ lengths from Bay Mirage and minor event at Ayr in September by 1¾ lengths from Euchen Glen: stays 1m: open to further improvement. *John Quinn*

SPEED HAWK (USA) 4 b.g. Henny Hughes (USA) 125 – Cosmic Wing (USA) (Halo **115** (USA)) [2015 111: 5g a6f² 5g a6f³ a6f³ a6f 5d⁵ 5g⁴ 5m 5d⁵ 5m³ 5m² p5g² Oct 23] lengthy, good-quartered gelding: smart performer: raced at Meydan first 6 starts, best efforts when third in Al Shindagha Sprint (1½ lengths behind Reynaldothewizard) and in Mahab Al Shimaal (¾ length behind Shaishee): subsequently second in listed races at Ascot (neck behind Dutch Masterpiece) and Dundalk (1½ lengths behind Take Cover): stays 6f: acts on polytrack, dirt, firm and good to soft going: usually in cheekpieces in 2015. *Robert Cowell*

SPEED THE PLOUGH 4 b.g. Kyllachy 129 – Danceatdusk (Desert Prince (IRE) 130) **67** [2015 p7f⁶ p6f p6g⁶ 6g³ p6g 6.1m⁴ 5.2m⁶ 5m 5s⁵ Aug 20] compact gelding: fair handicapper: stays 6f: acts on firm going: usually in headgear in 2015. *Dean Ivory*

SPEEDY BOARDING 3 b.f. Shamardal (USA) 129 – Dash To The Front 105 (Diktat **111** 126) [2015 74p: 9.9g* 10m* 12m⁵ 10.1m² 12d Oct 17] tall filly with plenty of scope: smart performer: won maiden at Goodwood (by ½ length from Journey) in May and listed race at Newbury (by ¾ length from Hot Sauce) in June: best effort when second in listed race at Yarmouth (½ length behind Talmada) in September: stays 1¼m: acts on good to firm going. *James Fanshawe*

SPEEDY MOVE (IRE) 3 b.c. Iffraaj 127 – Beautiful Filly 78 (Oasis Dream 129) [2015 **90** 86: 6.1s⁵ 5m⁶ 6m* 6g⁶ 6d Sep 26] close-coupled colt: fairly useful handicapper: won at Haydock (by neck from Nezar) in August: stays 7f: acts on polytrack and good to firm going: sent to UAE. *Ismail Mohammed*

SPEEDY STAR (IRE) 6 b.g. Authorized (IRE) 133 – North Sea (IRE) 60 (Selkirk (USA) **–** 129) [2015 –: 16.1g Sep 4] workmanlike gelding: no form, including over hurdles: tried in cheekpieces. *Tina Jackson*

SPEIGHTOWNS KID (USA) 7 gr.g. Speightstown (USA) 124 – Seize The Wind **66** (USA) (Maria's Mon (USA) 121) [2015 74: f6d² f6g⁶ f5g⁶ f6s f6g f5m⁶ Dec 8] well-made gelding: fair handicapper: stays 6f: acts on polytrack, fibresand and good to soft going: usually in headgear: often races towards rear. *Ann Stokell*

SPELLMAKER 6 b.g. Kheleyf (USA) 116 – Midnight Spell 79 (Night Shift (USA)) **67** [2015 79, a85: p6m* p6g⁴ p6f⁵ p6g² p6g³ p6m p6f⁶ 5.7d 5.7m 5.7g p6g t7.1f p6g Dec 28] **a81 d** fairly useful handicapper at best: won at Lingfield in January: stays 6f: acts on polytrack, soft and good to firm going: tried in eyeshields. *Tony Newcombe*

SPEND A PENNY (IRE) 3 b.g. Acclamation 118 – Coachhouse Lady (USA) 81 (Rahy **63**
(USA) 115) [2015 67: 5d⁵ 5m³ 6g⁶ 5g 5g² 5g⁶ 5g Sep 23] modest maiden: stays 6f: acts on
good to firm going: tried in headgear in 2015: usually leads. *John Quinn*

SPENNITHORNE (IRE) 2 b.f. (Mar 26) Shamardal (USA) 129 – Two Marks (USA) 73 **89 p**
(Woodman (USA) 126) [2015 6m³ 7g³ 10g⁶* p5f² p6f* Sep 24] 65,000Y, 200,000 2-y-o: tall
filly: half-sister to several winners, including ungenuine 1m and (at 2 yrs) 10.4f winner
Framley Garth (by Clodovil); dam, 8.4f-1½m winner, half-sister to smart US Grade 1
9f/1¼m winner Alpha: fairly useful performer: won maiden at Wolverhampton in August
and nursery at Chelmsford (by neck from Lady Nayef) in September: will prove suited by
a return to 7f: acts on polytrack and tapeta: front runner/races prominently: will go on
improving. *Charlie Appleby*

SPERRIN (IRE) 3 b.c. Dubawi (IRE) 129 – Speciosa (IRE) 115 (Danehill Dancer (IRE) **63**
117) [2015 67. p8f¹ Feb 2] lightly-raced maiden, fair form at best: will stay 1¼m.
Charlie Appleby

SPERRY (IRE) 3 b.f. Shamardal (USA) 129 – Badee'a (IRE) (Marju (IRE) 127) [2015 **111**
90p: 8f³ 8m* 8f⁶ Jun 19] good-topped filly: smart performer: won minor event at Ascot in
April and listed race at York (by ½ length from Yasmeen) in May: 16/1, best effort when
2½ lengths sixth of 9 to Ervedya in Coronation Stakes at Royal Ascot final start: stays 1m:
acts on tapeta and firm going: front runner/races prominently, often travels strongly.
John Gosden

SPES NOSTRA 7 b.g. Ad Valorem (USA) 125 – Millagros (IRE) 86 (Pennekamp (USA) **92**
130) [2015 98: p10g⁵ t9.5g⁴ t9.5f⁴ 10.1g 9.8v* 12.1s 9g⁴ 10m Jun 20] fairly useful
handicapper: won at Ripon (by 12 lengths from Maven) in May: acts on
polytrack, tapeta, good to firm and heavy going: usually wears blinkers. *David Barron*

SPICE BOAT 3 ch.g. Shamardal (USA) 129 – Frizzante 121 (Efisio 120) [2015 8.3g 6m⁶ **59**
6d p7m p10g² p10m p10m p15.8g⁵ p10g Dec 30] compact gelding: modest maiden: left
Richard Hannon after second start: best effort at 1¼m: acts on polytrack: tried in
cheekpieces: tried in tongue tie. *Paddy Butler*

SPICE FAIR 8 ch.g. Trade Fair 124 – Focosa (ITY) (In The Wings 128) [2015 a86: 14g **89**
14m⁵ 14f 16g² 14g* p16g⁶ 14.1s Oct 28] sturdy gelding: fairly useful handicapper: won at
Haydock in August: stays 2½m: acts on polytrack, soft and good to firm going: races well
off pace: fairly useful hurdler. *Mark Usher*

SPICEUPYOURLIFE (IRE) 4 b.f. Sakhee's Secret 128 – Tiger Spice 68 (Royal **–**
Applause 124) [2015 84: 10.2f⁶ 11.9mᵖᵘ 9.9g⁵ p12g Dec 11] fairly useful at best, no form
in 2015: left David Evans after third start: tends to find little. *J. J. Feane, Ireland*

SPIC 'N SPAN 10 b.g. Piccolo 121 – Sally Slade 80 (Dowsing (USA) 124) [2015 51§: **37 §**
t5.1f⁶ p5m Feb 4] good-topped gelding: poor handicapper nowadays: best form at 5f: acts
on all-weather and any turf going: wears headgear: has worn tongue tie: sometimes slowly
away, often races prominently: unreliable. *Ronald Harris*

SPICY JAM 3 b.f. Holy Roman Emperor (IRE) 125 – Jalys (IRE) (Sri Pekan (USA) 117) **102**
[2015 6g² 6m³ 6g* 5g² 6d⁵ p6g⁴ t6m Dec 18] €25,000Y: sixth foal: dam useful Italian
winner up to 1¼m (2-y-o 7.5f/1m winner): useful performer: successful 3 times in Italy at
2 yrs, including in 2 listed races: won minor event at Milan (by head from Trust You) in
May: left Stefano Botti after fifth start, creditable efforts in handicaps at Kempton (wore
hood) and Wolverhampton last 2: should stay 7f: acts on polytrack, tapeta and firm going.
Marco Botti

SPIDER BAY 6 gr.m. Almaty (IRE) 113 – Severance (USA) (Dispersal (USA)) [2015 45: **36**
p7g p7g p8m 7g 7v May 29] angular mare: poor maiden: stays 7f: acts on polytrack: often
wears headgear: often starts slowly/races in rear. *Lydia Richards*

SPIDER LILY 4 b.f. Sleeping Indian 122 – Scarlett Ribbon 104 (Most Welcome 131) **68**
[2015 77, a56: 6f 5m³ 5.2m⁴ 5m⁶ Aug 3] close-coupled filly: fair handicapper: stays 6f: acts
on firm going. *Peter Makin*

SPIEGEL (IRE) 2 b.g. (Feb 12) Oasis Dream 129 – Kirinda (IRE) 106 (Tiger Hill (IRE) **69**
127) [2015 9d t9.5f⁴ p8g Dec 9] fair maiden: best effort when fourth at Wolverhampton:
has awkward head carriage and temperament under suspicion. *Charlie Appleby*

SPIELBERG (JPN) 6 b.h. Deep Impact (JPN) 134 – Princess Olivia (USA) (Lycius **120**
(USA) 124) [2015 123: 9.9s⁴ 10f⁶ 8.9f 9.9f Nov 1] well-made horse: brother to very smart
Japanese performer up to 2m Tosen Ra and half-brother to several winners, including high-
class US Grade 1 1¼m winner Flower Alley (by Distorted Humor): dam US 2-y-o 5.5f/6.5f
winner: very smart performer: successful at Tokyo in 2014 in minor event and Tenno Sho
(Autumn): best effort in 2015 when respectable 4 lengths sixth to Free Eagle in Prince of

Wales's Stakes at Royal Ascot on second outing, hanging right: just fair efforts last 2 starts, in Tenno Sho (Autumn) (tenth behind Lovely Day) on final appearance: stays 1½m: acts on firm going: usually held up. *Kazuo Fujisawa, Japan*

SPIFER (IRE) 7 gr.g. Motivator 131 – Zarawa (IRE) (Kahyasi 130) [2015 85: 10.3d 10.1g 12m⁴ 12g 12.5m⁶ 12m⁵ 13d⁶ 12m* 12.2g Aug 27] compact gelding: fairly useful performer: won claimer at Catterick in August: stays 12.5f: acts on polytrack, good to firm and good to soft going: often wears headgear: sometimes slowly away: not straightforward: sold £9,000 and joined Julia Brooke. *David Nicholls* **82 §**

SPIKE (IRE) 2 b.g. (Feb 10) Lilbourne Lad (IRE) 111 – Vintage Allure (IRE) (Barathea (IRE) 127) [2015 6g 5d² 5d* 5.1v⁵ Oct 7] fair performer: won maiden at Pontefract in September: best effort previous start when short-head second to Baby Ballerina in similar event at Catterick: best form at 5f. *David Barron* **79**

SPINATRIX 7 b.m. Diktat 126 – Shrink 75 (Mind Games 121) [2015 117: 5.1d* 6.1s⁵ 5m⁴ 6m 6g Aug 15] smart performer: won minor event at Nottingham (by 3¼ lengths from Blithe Spirit) in April: below form after: stays 6f: acts on good to firm and heavy going: wears cheekpieces: front runner/races prominently. *Michael Dods* **106**

SPINDLE (IRE) 3 b.f. Dubai Destination (USA) 127 – Phantom Turtle (IRE) 50 (Turtle Island (IRE) 123) [2015 73: f8g² Jan 6] fair handicapper: stays 8.5f: acts on fibresand, tapeta and heavy going. *Mark Usher* **72**

SPINNING COBBLERS 4 b.g. Royal Applause 124 – Tychy 102 (Suave Dancer (USA) 136) [2015 57, a74: p7g³ p6g³ p7m⁶ p6g* p6m² Dec 31] tall, angular gelding: fair handicapper: won at Lingfield in December: stays 7f: acts on polytrack and tapeta: wears headgear: front runner/races prominently, often travels strongly. *Stuart Williams* **76**

SPINNING PEARL (IRE) 2 b.f. (Apr 26) Dylan Thomas (IRE) 132 – Spinning Gold 45 (Spinning World (USA) 130) [2015 p8g p8g Nov 18] fourth foal: half-sister to 2-y-o 5f-1m winner Snowed In (by Dark Angel) and 5f/6f winner (including at 2 yrs) Sylvia Pankhurst (by Antonius Pius): dam maiden: better effort when seventh of 13 in maiden at Kempton on debut. *Eve Johnson Houghton* **57**

SPINNING ROSE 3 ch.f. Pivotal 124 – Aqua Rose (USA) (Redoute's Choice (AUS)) [2015 p8g⁶ Dec 9] £7,500 3-y-o: first foal: dam, unraced, out of sister to Dubai World Cup winner Street Cry: modest form: 20/1, very green when sixth of 10 to Seven Clans in maiden at Kempton on debut: should do better. *Dean Ivory* **53 p**

SPIRAEA 5 ch.m. Bahamian Bounty 116 – Salvia (Pivotal 124) [2015 82: 7m 7m⁵ 6g² 6g³ 6d* 6g 7v⁴ 6v Nov 7] sturdy mare: fairly useful handicapper: won at Pontefract in September: stays 6f: acts on good to firm and heavy going. *Mark Rimell* **86**

SPIRITED ACCLAIM (IRE) 3 b.f. Acclamation 118 – Lafleur (IRE) 75 (Grand Lodge (USA) 125) [2015 72: 8.3g⁴ 8m² 8.3m² 8s² 8g* 10g 8.1v⁵ 8.3d Oct 12] lengthy, angular filly: fairly useful handicapper: won at Newmarket in August: stays 1m: acts on soft going: in blinkers final start. *David Elsworth* **84**

SPIRITED GIRL (IRE) 2 b.f. (Feb 1) Invincible Spirit (IRE) 121 – Albarouche 89 (Sadler's Wells (USA) 132) [2015 6d 8d Sep 26] compact filly: third foal: sister to ungenuine French 1¼m/11f winner Nibbling: dam, 1¼m winner, sister to Derby runner-up Dragon Dancer: well held in maidens at Newbury (green) and Haydock (went with little fluency). *Richard Hannon* **–**

SPIRITING (IRE) 3 b.g. Invincible Spirit (IRE) 121 – Gold Bubbles (USA) 105 (Street Cry (IRE) 130) [2015 95: 6m³ 6m³ 8m³ 8.3m* 8m⁵ Jul 10] useful performer: won handicap at Leicester (by 3½ lengths from Silverheels) in June: stays 8.5f: acts on good to firm going: front runner/races prominently: has been gelded. *Luca Cumani* **91**

SPIRIT IN TIME (IRE) 3 b.f. Vale of York (IRE) 117 – Star Port (Observatory (USA) 131) [2015 54: t6g 6.1m 7s² 7.1m³ 7.1m⁵ 17.1g 5f Aug 12] modest maiden: stays 7f: acts on soft and good to firm going: often wears hood: front runner/races prominently. *Malcolm Saunders* **50**

SPIRITJIM (FR) 5 b.h. Galileo (IRE) 134 – Hidden Silver (Anabaa (USA) 130) [2015 122: 15.4s⁶ 11.9g⁴ 13.9m⁴ 12.4d 11.9s² 11.9m 11.9d⁴ Oct 18] tall, leggy horse: very smart performer: back to best when second in Prix Foy at Longchamp (¾ length behind Postponed) in September: respectable efforts last 2 starts, in Prix de l'Arc de Triomphe on same course (twelfth behind Golden Horn) and Prix du Conseil de Paris at Chantilly (5¼ lengths fourth to Ming Dynasty): left P. Bary after second (2015) start: stays 12.5f: acts on soft and good to firm going: genuine: to continue career with Chris Waller in Australia. *A. Couétil, France* **122**

SPIRIT OF ARAKAN (IRE) 3 b.f. Arakan (USA) 123 – Angel Rays 68 (Unfuwain — (USA) 131) [2015 6m³ 7g Jun 8] 7,000Y: second foal: dam, maiden (stayed 7f), half-sister to smart 5.4f-7f winner Barney McGrew: offered little both starts in maidens. *Ben Haslam*

SPIRIT OF GONDREE (IRE) 7 b.g. Invincible Spirit (IRE) 121 – Kristal's Paradise **73** (IRE) 100 (Bluebird (USA) 125) [2015 72: t7.1g² t7.1f* t7.1g t7.1f⁴ t8.6g⁵ p7g p8g p7g t7.1f p8d⁴ t8.6g* p8m³ Dec 27] fair handicapper: won at Wolverhampton in January and December: best up to 1¼m: acts on polytrack, tapeta, best turf form on good to soft/soft going: wears headgear: usually races towards rear: quirky sort. *Milton Bradley*

SPIRIT OF MAYFAIR (IRE) 2 b.c. (Feb 21) Dandy Man (IRE) 123 – Masakira (IRE) **52** 58 (Royal Academy (USA) 130) [2015 6g 6d Oct 11] better effort in maidens when seventh of 12 to Above N Beyond at Kempton on debut: sold 6,500 gns, sent to Switzerland. *Olly Stevens*

SPIRIT OF ROSANNA 3 gr.f. Hellvelyn 118 – Tharwa (IRE) 63 (Last Tycoon 131) **58** [2015 –: 6d* 7m 7d⁵ 6m 7.5g 7.1m 6v³ 6s* 6v t7.1m Nov 28] rather leggy filly: modest performer: won seller at Leicester in April and handicap at Brighton in October: stays 6f: acts on good to soft going: usually wears headgear: wears tongue tie: often races prominently. *Steph Hollinshead*

SPIRIT OF SOUND (FR) 3 b.f. Invincible Spirit (IRE) 121 – Sound of Summer (USA) **64** (Fusaichi Pegasus (USA) 130) [2015 –p: 6m⁴ 5d³ 5m⁶ May 27] modest maiden: best effort at 6f. *Hugo Palmer*

SPIRIT OF THE LAW (IRE) 6 b.g. Lawman (FR) 121 – Passion Bleue (In The Wings **93** 128) [2015 105: p10g 9.8d⁴ 9m 10.4g 10.1g 10.3f² 10d² 10m 10.4g 10.1d 8.5s 8.3s t8.6m³ **a79** p8g p10.7g Dec 18] fairly useful handicapper: left Richard Fahey after thirteenth start: stays 10.5f: acts on polytrack, firm and soft going: has worn cheekpieces: in tongue tie last 2 starts: usually races nearer last than first. *James McAuley, Ireland*

SPIRIT OF THE SEA (IRE) 3 b.f. Invincible Spirit (IRE) 121 – Cedar Sea (IRE) **65** (Persian Bold 123) [2015 54p: 7.1s 7.1m 8.3g 8m⁵ 9.1g² 12g² 12g 10d³ t9.5g⁴ t12.2m³ Dec 18] fair maiden: left Jim Goldie after eighth start: stays 1½m: acts on tapeta and good to soft going: often races towards rear. *Iain Jardine*

SPIRIT OF THE VALE (IRE) 2 b.f. (Mar 13) Royal Applause 124 – Nesmeh (USA) **54** (More Than Ready (USA) 120) [2015 6g 7m⁵ 7g⁵ 7.2g⁵ 5.9m⁴ p6g 7d 7s⁴ p8g t8.6f³ **a48** Nov 14] €16,000F, 25,000Y: second foal: dam unraced daughter of useful performer up to 8.5f Freefurracing: modest maiden: stays 7f: acts on soft and good to firm going: tried in visor. *Tom Dascombe*

SPIRITOFTOMINTOUL 6 gr.g. Authorized (IRE) 133 – Diamond Line (FR) (Linamix **89** (FR) 127) [2015 93: t16.5g³ p16g⁵ p16g 14.1s² 11.9d² 12s⁵ 14d 14.1s 10d p12g Nov 18] good-topped gelding: fairly useful handicapper: stays 16.5f: acts on polytrack, tapeta, soft and good to firm going: usually races in rear. *Tony Carroll*

SPIRIT OF WEDZA (IRE) 3 b.g. Footstepsinthesand 120 – Sampers (IRE) 94 (Exceed **76** And Excel (AUS) 126) [2015 79: 6g² 7sᵘʳ 6v 6.1m² 6g³ 6.1m 6d⁴ 6.1g⁵ 8.3g² 7.9m³ 8.5m³ 8.5g 9.3g Sep 15] fair maiden: stays 8.5f: acts on good to firm and good to soft going: in blinkers last 2 starts: usually leads. *Mark Johnston*

SPIRIT OF ZEBEDEE (IRE) 2 gr.c. (Mar 29) Zebedee 113 – Sampers (IRE) 94 **60** (Exceed And Excel (AUS) 126) [2015 5g 7m⁴ 7d 6g² 6s⁶ p6g⁶ Dec 7] modest maiden: best effort at 6f: tried in cheekpieces. *John Quinn*

SPIRIT OF ZEB (IRE) 3 ch.g. Zebedee 113 – Miss Glitters (IRE) 91 (Chevalier (IRE) **81** 115) [2015 74: 6d* 6m³ 6s³ 6m⁶ 7.2g 6d⁵ 6s⁶ p6f f6g* f5g Dec 29] small, rather leggy **a92** gelding: fairly useful handicapper: won at Hamilton in June and Southwell (by 3½ lengths from Split The Atom) in November: stays 6f: acts on fibresand, soft and good to firm going. *Richard Fahey*

SPIRIT QUARTZ (IRE) 7 b.g. Invincible Spirit (IRE) 121 – Crystal Gaze (IRE) **114** (Rainbow Quest (USA) 134) [2015 118: 5g⁶ 5g³ 5f 5m³ 5d⁶ Jul 30] good-bodied gelding: smart performer: creditable third in Prix du Gros-Chene at Chantilly (1¼ lengths behind Muthmir) in May: 2½ lengths third to Waady in Sprint Stakes at Sandown on fourth start: stays 6f: acts on polytrack, soft and good to firm going: wears headgear: has worn tongue tie: rejoined Robert Cowell. *X. Nakkachdji, France*

SPIRIT RAISER (IRE) 4 b.f. Invincible Spirit (IRE) 121 – Macadamia (IRE) 115 **97 +** (Classic Cliche (IRE) 128) [2015 88p: 8m⁴ p8g* 8m² 8m³ p8g* p8g² 8g⁶ Sep 25] sturdy **a106** filly: useful handicapper: won at Kempton in June and August (by 1¾ lengths from

Certificate): good second to Georgian Bay at Kempton in September: stays 1m: acts on polytrack and good to firm going: in visor last 3 starts: usually races prominently. *James Fanshawe*

SPIRIT RAPPING (IRE) 3 b.g. Azamour (IRE) 130 – Snowpalm (Halling (USA) 133) [2015 –: f12g Nov 24] well held 3 starts in maidens. *Sarah Hollinshead* –

SPIRIT RIDER (USA) 5 b.g. Candy Ride (ARG) 133 – Teenage Queen (USA) (Regal Classic (CAN)) [2015 54: p10f p10g Jun 20] fairly useful form in 2013, little impact since: best effort at 9.5f: acts on polytrack: tried in blinkers/tongue tie. *Giles Bravery* –

SPIRITUAL ACCLAIM (IRE) 3 b.f. Acclamation 118 – Sister Clement (IRE) 85 (Oasis Dream 129) [2015 –: 9g⁵ 7m⁶ 7g Jul 24] no impact in maidens/handicap: tried in blinkers. *John Weymes* –

SPIRITUAL JOURNEY (IRE) 3 gr.f. Zebedee 113 – Daneville (IRE) (Danetime (IRE) 121) [2015 50: 6g t5.1g⁵ 5m⁴ t5.1f Oct 17] poor maiden: best form at 5f: acts on tapeta and good to firm going: tried in hood in 2015: often races prominently. *Ann Duffield* **48**

SPIRITUAL STAR (IRE) 6 b.g. Soviet Star (USA) 128 – Million Spirits (IRE) 90 (Invincible Spirit (IRE) 121) [2015 91, a97: p10m³ p10m⁴ p8f* p8g⁵ p8m⁵ p8g⁴ p8g 8m 8.1m 8.3m² 6m⁶ 6m 7g p8f* p8f⁴ t8.6m⁵ p8g² p8g Dec 28] strong, well-made gelding: useful performer: won handicap at Lingfield in January and claimer at Chelmsford in October: stays 8.5f: acts on polytrack, tapeta and good to firm going: tried in blinkers in 2015: usually wears tongue tie: often travels strongly. *Anthony Carson* **82 a95**

SPITFIRE 10 b.g. Mujahid (USA) 125 – Fresh Fruit Daily 92 (Reprimand 122) [2015 76§: f6d² f6g² p6g² p6m⁵ f6g* f6g⁵ p6f³ Nov 5] tall, good-topped gelding: fair performer: won seller at Southwell in April: stays 7f: acts on polytrack, fibresand, good to firm and heavy going: tried in headgear prior to 2015: wears tongue tie: ungenuine. *J. R. Jenkins* **73 §**

SPLASH OF VERVE (IRE) 3 b.g. Fast Company (IRE) 126 – Ellistown Lady (IRE) 71 (Red Sunset 120) [2015 58, a66: 9g 8g t8.6g⁶ 8.5m⁶ 9.9m* t9.5g³ 9.9m² 10g⁵ 9.3g t12.2f³ Oct 3] fair handicapper: won at Beverley in July: stays 1½m: acts on tapeta and good to firm going: sometimes slowly away, usually races nearer last than first, usually travels strongly. *Philip Kirby* **71**

SPLIT THE ATOM (IRE) 3 ch.g. The Carbon Unit (USA) 106 – The Mighty Atom 91 (USA) 78 (Sky Mesa (USA) 116) [2015 83: 6.9v p7g 6g² 7d³ 6s 8g⁴ 6d p7g³ p7g² f6g² p7g* p7g² Dec 18] fairly useful handicapper: won at Dundalk (apprentice) in December: trained for third start only by P. J. Prendergast: stays 1m: acts on polytrack, fibresand, best turf form on good going: front runner/races prominently: consistent. *John Patrick Shanahan, Ireland* **91**

SPOKEN WORDS 6 b.m. Fruits of Love (USA) 127 – Jerre Jo Glanville (USA) 52 (Skywalker (USA)) [2015 58: t7.1f t6g² t7.1g t9.5g 7.9g² t8.6g 6s 6s⁵ 6g⁵ 9.3d t8.6f 6m³ t7.1m Dec 30] modest handicapper: stays 1m: acts on tapeta and good to firm going: often wears headgear: usually races towards rear: none too reliable. *John David Riches* **52**

SPOKESPERSON (USA) 7 b.g. Henny Hughes (USA) 125 – Verbal (USA) (Kingmambo 66 (USA) 125) [2015 56: t8.6f² t8.6g⁶ t9.5m³ 8d² 8d⁵ 9.9m⁴ 10.1m² 10g* 12.2g* 12.2m 12d Aug 17] fair handicapper: won at Ayr (dead-heated) and Musselburgh in July: stays 1½m: acts on tapeta and good to firm going: often wears headgear: races prominently. *Fred Watson* **66**

SPONGY (IRE) 2 b.c. (Feb 10) Zoffany (IRE) 121 – Eminence Gift 60 (Cadeaux 88 Genereux 131) [2015 p5m⁴ 6.1g³ 7m* 7f² 7m⁴ 8m² 7g Dec 29] 7,000F, £35,000Y: workmanlike colt: fourth foal: half-brother to 3 winners, including winner up to 1m Saint Jerome (2-y-o 6f winner, by Jeremy): dam, 1¼m winner, half-sister to smart Italian/US performer up to 1¼m Lucky Chappy: fairly useful performer: won maiden at Leicester in June: second in nurseries at Newmarket and Salisbury: left Richard Hannon after sixth start: stays 1m: acts on firm going. *Mohammed Jassim Ghazali, Qatar* **88**

SPORTING BOB 3 b.c. Mawatheeq (USA) 126 – Tanwir 76 (Unfuwain (USA) 131) 40 [2015 –: t9.5f t12.2g³ p12m Feb 4] workmanlike colt: poor maiden: stays 1½m: acts on polytrack and tapeta: tried in visor prior to 2015. *Robert Eddery* **40**

SPORTING PRINCE 3 b.g. Pastoral Pursuits 127 – Queen of Iceni 81 (Erhaab (USA) 50 127) [2015 –: t8.6g⁴ p8f p12g 14.1m Jun 3] modest maiden: should stay at least 1¼m: acts on tapeta: tried in blinkers: often starts slowly/races lazily. *Ed Dunlop* **50**

SPORTY YANKEE (USA) 2 g.r.c. (Apr 11) Paddy O'Prado (USA) 121 – I Insist (USA) 69 p (Green Dancer (USA) 132) [2015 7m⁵ 8.3g⁵ 8s Oct 9] $14,000Y: half-brother to several winners in USA: dam US 8.5f winner: best effort in maidens when fifth of 14 to Four On Eight at Windsor second start: not knocked about at York final outing: remains with potential. *K. R. Burke* **69 p**

SPOT THE PRO (IRE) 6 b.g. Barathea (IRE) 127 – Truly Precious (IRE) (Pennekamp (USA) 130) [2015 75: 7.2g t8.6g f12s⁵ Aug 6] maiden: no form in 2015: in tongue tie in 2015: often starts slowly. *Rebecca Menzies* –

SPOWARTICUS 6 ch.g. Shamardal (USA) 129 – Helen Bradley (IRE) 85 (Indian Ridge 123) [2015 53, a66: p6g² p6m⁶ t6f* p6m³ f6d* f6s³ f6g³ 6.1m 6m p6g² f6g⁴ p6g Dec 7] fair handicapper: won at Wolverhampton in February and Southwell in March: stays 6f: acts on all-weather: wears headgear. *Scott Dixon* **70**

SPRAY TAN 5 b.m. Assertive 121 – Even Hotter 63 (Desert Style (IRE) 121) [2015 68: p5f⁵ t5.1m t5.1f t5.1g 5m 5.1m 6m 5.1m³ 5.7m⁶ 5.1m³ t5.1m t6m Dec 30] lengthy mare: modest handicapper: stays 6f: acts on polytrack, tapeta and firm going: tried in blinkers/tongue tie in 2015. *Tony Carroll* **56 a49**

SPREADABLE (IRE) 4 br.g. Duke of Marmalade (IRE) 132 – Spring View (Fantastic Light (USA) 134) [2015 75, a88: p8g t8.6g⁵ p7g⁵ p7g⁶ t9.5m⁶ t7.1g 7m⁶ p10f⁵ t12.2g⁴ Jun 3] sturdy gelding: fair handicapper: stays 1m: acts on polytrack, tapeta and good to soft going: often wears headgear: often races towards rear. *Nick Littmoden* **76**

SPRING BIRD 6 b.m. Danbird (AUS) – Dolphin Dancer 45 (Dolphin Street (FR) 125) [2015 72: 5d² 5g² 5g⁶ 5g 5g 5s Jul 28] fair handicapper: best form at 5f: acts on fibresand, soft and good to firm going: usually races prominently. *David Nicholls* **75**

SPRING DIXIE (IRE) 3 gr.f. Zebedee 113 – Dixie Jazz 51 (Mtoto 134) [2015 73: 9.9m³ 11.9v² 12g² 11.5g² 10g² 12.2g² p10g p13.3g⁴ p10f Dec 17] fair maiden: left Rae Guest after sixth start: stays 1½m: acts on good to firm going. *John Ryan* **74 a55**

SPRING FLING 4 b.f. Assertive 121 – Twilight Mistress 84 (Bin Ajwaad (IRE) 119) [2015 92: p6g⁴ 6v⁶ Nov 7] strong filly: fairly useful performer: stays 6f: acts on polytrack, good to firm and heavy going: front runner/races prominently. *Henry Candy* **91**

SPRING LOADED (IRE) 3 gr.g. Zebedee 113 – Nisriyna (IRE) (Intikhab (USA) 135) [2015 84: 6m 7g⁴ 6d² p6g* p6f² 6g* p6f t6m* Dec 18] useful handicapper: won at Kempton and Windsor in October and Wolverhampton (by neck from Anonymous John, showing further improvement) in December: best at 6f: acts on polytrack, tapeta and good to soft going: usually responds generously to pressure. *Paul D'Arcy* **100**

SPRING OFFENSIVE (IRE) 3 b.g. Iffraaj 127 – Night Sphere (IRE) 74 (Night Shift (USA)) [2015 86p: 8s² 8.1d⁶ 8m⁵ 9.9m⁵ 8m³ 8g* 8g⁴ 8.9s Oct 10] good-topped gelding: fairly useful handicapper: won at Musselburgh (by ¾ length from Silver Rime) in August: stays 1m: acts on soft and good to firm going: in cheekpieces final start. *Richard Fahey* **92**

SPRING OVERTURE 3 ch.f. Pastoral Pursuits 127 – April Stock 97 (Beveled (USA)) [2015 7m 8.3g Jun 28] sixth foal: half-sister to 1½m-1¾m winner Stock Hill Fair (by Sakhee) and 1¼m-1½m winner Stockhill Diva (by Haafhd): dam 11.6f/1½m winner: well held in maidens. *Rod Millman* –

SPRING SERAPH (IRE) 3 gr.g. Dark Angel (IRE) 113 – Saffron Crocus 83 (Shareef Dancer (USA) 135) [2015 –: p8f Jan 17] well held in 2 maidens: sold 1,500 gns. *Olly Stevens* –

SPRINGSTRIDE 3 b.f. Jeremy (USA) 122 – Stoney Cove (IRE) (Needwood Blade 117) [2015 59: 7g⁵ 10.4s 7g 8m⁵ 6m 7.2d Aug 10] €10,000Y: second foal: half-sister to ungenuine 5f/6f winner Gentlemen (by Ad Valorem): dam unraced half-sister to smart Italian winner up to 1m Golden Nepi: modest maiden: stays 1m: acts on good to firm going. *Mrs Prunella Dobbs, Ireland* **50**

SPRINGTIME WINNIE 3 b.f. Multiplex 114 – Springtime Parkes (Medicean 128) [2015 7m 6m⁵ 8g⁴ 5s⁴ Oct 6] second foal: dam, of little account, half-sister to useful sprinters Lucky Parkes and Summerhill Parkes: poor maiden: best effort at 5f. *Eric Alston* **42**

SPRYT (IRE) 3 b.g. Invincible Spirit (IRE) 121 – Out of Thanks (IRE) 89 (Sadler's Wells (USA) 132) [2015 78: 8m² 7.5m² 8g² 7g⁴ 8m 8.3g* 7m³ 8m 8s⁶ t7.1g² 7.2m 7s Oct 9] fairly useful performer: won maiden at Hamilton in June: stays 8.5f: acts on tapeta and good to firm going: usually in headgear prior to 2015. *David O'Meara* **88**

SQUASH 2 b.f. (Feb 15) Pastoral Pursuits 127 – Super Midge 50 (Royal Applause 124) [2015 6m⁴ t6g* 6g⁴ 7m⁵ 7m⁴ 7g⁶ 6d² Oct 30] rather unfurnished filly: second foal: half-sister to 2-y-o 5f winner Frozen Princess (by Showcasing): dam twice-raced sister to smart winner up to 7f Tremar: useful performer: won maiden at Wolverhampton (by 3¼ lengths from Company Asset) in July: best effort when head second of 8 to Only Mine in listed race at Newmarket final start: stays 7f: acts on tapeta and soft going. *Philip McBride* **103**

SQUATS (IRE) 3 b.g. Dandy Man (IRE) 123 – Light Sea (IRE) 59 (King's Best (USA) 132) [2015 102: p5g⁶ p5m⁵ t6f⁵ p5f⁴ 6g⁵ 6m 6m² 6g⁴ Sep 5] close-coupled gelding: useful handicapper: best efforts at Ascot last 2 starts, on latter occasion finishing well when 1¼ lengths fourth of 17 to Right Touch: stays 6f: acts on firm going: tried in cheekpieces/tongue tie: often races towards rear. *William Haggas* **107 a95 +**

SQUIGGLEY 2 b.f. (Apr 20) Sir Percy 129 – Oat Cuisine 92 (Mujahid (USA) 125) [2015 7s⁴ Sep 3] third foal: sister to ungenuine 13.3f winner Born To Reign: dam 1m-1¼m winner: 18/1, some encouragement when 12¼ lengths fourth of 11 to Nathra in maiden at Salisbury on debut, very slowly away: should do better. *Henry Candy* **57 p**

SQUIRE 4 b.g. Teofilo (IRE) 126 – Most Charming (FR) (Darshaan 133) [2015 71p: p10f⁴ p10m⁴ p12g⁶ 8.3m* p8g³ 10g* 10m² 10m³ 10f 10f³ 9g² 10g⁶ Oct 19] sturdy gelding: fairly useful handicapper: won at Windsor in April and Newmarket in May: stays 1¼m: acts on polytrack and firm going. *Michael Attwater* **86**

SR SWING 4 b.f. Passing Glance 119 – Wigman Lady (IRE) 64 (Tenby 125) [2015 57: t13.9g 14.1m⁵ 16.1m⁶ Jun 6] poor maiden: stays 1¾m: acts on good to firm going. *Peter Niven* **48**

SRUTHAN (IRE) 5 b.g. Arakan (USA) 123 – Giveupyeraulsins (IRE) (Mark of Esteem (IRE) 137) [2015 116: 7d⁴ 8v² 7.5g 8.5g⁵ 10d⁵ Oct 24] compact gelding: useful performer: second in Amethyst Stakes at Leopardstown (nose behind Onenightidreamed) in May: stays 8.5f: acts on polytrack, good to firm and heavy going: sometimes wears headgear: often races prominently. *P. D. Deegan, Ireland* **107**

SS VEGA 2 b.f. (Feb 12) Kheleyf (USA) 116 – Annie Gee (Primo Valentino (IRE) 116) [2015 6d⁵ Oct 26] fourth foal: dam unraced: 10/1, 6 lengths fifth of 14 to Captain Dion in maiden at Redcar on debut: should do better in time. *James Bethell* **44 p**

STADIUM OF LIGHT (IRE) 8 b.g. Fantastic Light (USA) 134 – Treble Seven (USA) 58 (Fusaichi Pegasus (USA) 130) [2015 f12s⁶ t12.2m⁶ Aug 21] useful-looking gelding: poor handicapper nowadays: well beaten both starts in 2015: has worn cheekpieces/tongue tie. *Christopher Kellett* **–**

STADIUS (IRE) 2 b.c. (Feb 28) Cape Cross (IRE) 129 – Sherifa (GER) (Monsun (GER) 124) [2015 t8.6f⁵ Dec 9] 68,000F: fifth foal: half-brother to 2 winners abroad, including useful German 1m winner Cherry Danon (by Rock of Gibraltar): dam unraced: 50/1, still green when 6½ lengths eighth of 12 to Graceful James in maiden at Kempton: remains capable of better. *Mark Johnston* **61 p**

STAFFORD CHARLIE 9 ch.g. Silver Patriarch (IRE) 125 – Miss Roberto (IRE) 63 (Don Roberto (USA)) [2015 –: 13.1d Sep 2] poor maiden: best effort at 13f: acts on good to soft going: tried in cheekpieces. *John O'Shea* **40**

STAFF SERGEANT 8 b.g. Dubawi (IRE) 129 – Miss Particular (IRE) 86 (Sadler's Wells (USA) 132) [2015 87: 10.1m p12g⁵ f12g Nov 12] strong gelding: modest handicapper: stays 1½m: acts on fibresand, soft and good to firm going: tried in headgear. *Jim Best* **54**

STAGE GIRL 4 b.f. Tiger Hill (IRE) 127 – Primavera 65 (Anshan 119) [2015 54: p7g p8f p6f⁴ f7g 7mᵖᵘ Apr 21] poor maiden: stayed 1m: acted on polytrack: in headgear last 3 starts: dead. *Mark Hoad* **55**

STAG HILL (IRE) 6 ch.g. Redback 116 – Counting Blessings 53 (Compton Place 125) [2015 p12f³ 11.7f t12.2g May 11] modest handicapper: stays 1½m: acts on polytrack and good to firm going: wears headgear: has worn tongue tie, including often of late: often starts slowly. *Bernard Llewellyn* **55**

STAGS LEAP (IRE) 8 b.g. Refuse To Bend (IRE) 128 – Swingsky (IRE) (Indian Ridge 123) [2015 12.4g² 12.2g³ Oct 13] lengthy gelding: fair handicapper: stays 2m: acts on soft and good to firm going: often wears headgear. *Julia Brooke* **71**

STAINTONDALE LASS (IRE) 2 b.f. (Apr 20) Bushranger (IRE) 119 – Siphon Melody (USA) (Siphon (BRZ) 130) [2015 p6g⁴ p6f* p7g Oct 27] €800Y, €20,000 2-y-o: half-sister to several winners, including useful 1m-10.4f winner Shamdarley (by Shamardal) and 10.3f winner Betty The Thief (by Teofilo): dam, US 5f-8.5f winner, half-sister to very smart performer up to 1½m Talloires: fair performer: won maiden at Chelmsford in October: should prove suited by at least 7f. *Ed Vaughan* **68**

STAKE ACCLAIM (IRE) 3 b.g. Acclamation 118 – Golden Legacy (IRE) 107 (Rossini (USA) 118) [2015 91p: p7g 6m⁵ 5g* 6g² Sep 19] rather leggy gelding: useful handicapper: won at Newmarket in August by length from Red Invader: good second at Newmarket (½ length behind Mehronissa) final start: stays 6f: acts on good to firm and heavy going: front runner/races prominently, usually travels strongly: should do better still. *Dean Ivory* **96 p**

STAMP DUTY (IRE) 7 b.g. Ad Valorem (USA) 125 – Lothian Lass (IRE) 67 (Daylami **53**
(IRE) 138) [2015 57: t8.6f t9.5m³ t9.5f⁴ t12.2g 12g⁵ 12g 10.1m⁴ 9m⁴ Jul 19] workmanlike
gelding: modest handicapper: stays 12.5f: acts on polytrack, tapeta, good to firm and heavy
going: tried in cheekpieces prior to 2015: often races towards rear. *Suzzanne France*

STAMPEDE (IRE) 4 b.g. High Chaparral (IRE) 132 – Summerhill Parkes 105 (Zafonic **78**
(USA) 130) [2015 88: p10m⁶ May 19] lengthy gelding: fairly useful handicapper in 2014,
just respectable effort only outing in 2015: stays 1¼m: acts on good to soft going: usually
races towards rear. *Sir Michael Stoute*

STAMP HILL (IRE) 2 b.g. (Apr 25) Zoffany (IRE) 121 – Edelfa (IRE) (Fasliyev (USA) **79**
120) [2015 6v⁴ 6g⁵ 5f 5g² 6.1s* Sep 12] lengthy gelding: fair performer: won maiden at
Chester in September: stays 6f: acts on firm and soft going: has been gelded. *Richard Fahey*

STAMP OF APPROVAL (IRE) 3 b f Approve (IRE) 112 – Wassendale 59 (Erhaab **50**
(USA) 127) [2015 –: t7.1f t8.6f³ p7g Dec 30] modest maiden: stays 8.5f: acts on tapeta.
Chris Wall

STAMP OF AUTHORITY (IRE) 3 b.g. Invincible Spirit (IRE) 121 – Silver Bracelet **75**
92 (Machiavellian (USA) 123) [2015 65: t6g³ p6f p6g⁴ p6g² Nov 27] fair maiden: left
James Tate after second start: worth another try at 7f: acts on polytrack and tapeta: in
headgear in 2015, also tried in tongue tie. *T. G. McCourt, Ireland*

STANARLEY PIC 4 b.g. Piccolo 121 – Harlestone Lady (Shaamit (IRE) 127) [2015 86: **80**
13g⁶ 12s⁵ 12m⁵ 12m⁴ 12.1g³ 10d 12.8m⁴ 11.5m² 12.4g² 13.8d³ 15g² 16.4s Oct 10] fairly
useful handicapper: stays 15f: acts on good to firm and heavy going: tried in cheekpieces
in 2015: often races prominently. *Alan Swinbank*

STANDING STRONG (IRE) 7 b.g. Green Desert (USA) 127 – Alexander Three D **57**
(IRE) 108 (Pennekamp (USA) 130) [2015 p11m p12f⁴ p10g t8.6g t12.2m⁵ p10g p10g Dec
30] workmanlike gelding: modest handicapper: stays 1¼m: acts on polytrack and good to
firm going: wears headgear: often races towards rear. *Zoe Davison*

ST ANDREWS (IRE) 2 ch.g. (Mar 13) Rip Van Winkle (IRE) 134 – Stellavera (FR) **76 p**
(Anabaa (USA) 130) [2015 7g⁴ Aug 31] first foal: dam unraced half-sister to useful winner
up to 1½m Peligroso: 7/4, some encouragement when 4¾ lengths fourth of 8 to Marcel in
maiden at Newcastle, green under pressure but keeping on: has been gelded: will improve.
Richard Fahey

STAND TO REASON (IRE) 7 ch.g. Danehill Dancer (IRE) 117 – Ho Hi The Moon **72**
(IRE) (Be My Guest (USA) 126) [2015 –: p12g⁴ t13.9f⁶ 10.3d⁴ p13.3g² 12g May 16]
lengthy gelding: fair handicapper: stays 13.5f: acts on polytrack and heavy going:
sometimes in headgear prior to 2015. *Tony Carroll*

STANGHOW 3 b.g. Monsieur Bond (IRE) 120 – Melandre 74 (Lujain (USA) 119) [2015 **87**
69: 5d² 5g* 5.1g* 5g² 5.5g⁴ 5.4m 5g² 5.1d⁶ Oct 14] fairly useful handicapper: won at
Beverley in May and Nottingham in June: best form at 5f: acts on good to soft going.
Antony Brittain

STANLEY BRIDGE 8 b.g. Avonbridge 123 – Antonia's Folly 64 (Music Boy 124) [2015 **–**
9.3d Aug 3] no form on Flat. *Barry Murtagh*

STANLOW 5 b.g. Invincible Spirit (IRE) 121 – Ghazal (USA) 103 (Gone West (USA)) **58**
[2015 66: p10m³ t8.6g³ t9.5g⁴ t9.5f f8g t12.2g⁵ p10m 9.9m³ p16g t12.2g⁵ 8.1d* 10.3d t8.6g
t8.6f⁵ Dec 21] modest handicapper: left Daniel Loughnane, won at Chepstow in August:
stays 1¼m: acts on polytrack, tapeta, firm and good to soft going: usually wears headgear:
tried in tongue tie: often races towards rear. *Michael Mullineaux*

STAN NINETEEN (IRE) 4 b.g. Kodiac 112 – Redwood Forest (IRE) (Barathea (IRE) **39**
127) [2015 –: p7g p10m Feb 4] poor maiden: stays 1¼m: acts on polytrack: in tongue tie
in 2015. *Simon Hodgson*

STAR ANISE (FR) 4 b.f. Astronomer Royal (USA) 121 – Sasicha (IRE) (Montjeu (IRE) **72**
137) [2015 81: p12m 10.2m p12m⁴ 11.7g⁵ t12.2g* p12g p12g p12g⁵ p12g t13.9m Oct 2]
fair performer: won seller at Wolverhampton in July: left Harry Dunlop after first start,
George Baker after sixth: stays 1½m: acts on polytrack and tapeta: usually wears hood:
tried in tongue tie in 2015: often starts slowly, often races in rear: quirky. *Paddy Butler*

STAR ASCENDING (IRE) 3 ch.g. Thousand Words 113 – Sakaka (Tobougg (IRE) 125) **67**
[2015 61: 8.3s 8g⁵ 7.5m⁴ 9.9g² 9.3g* 9.9d 10s Oct 16] fair handicapper: won at Carlisle in
September: stays 1¼m: acts on good to firm and heavy going: often races towards rear.
Les Eyre

STAR ASSET 3 b.g. Dutch Art 126 – Black Belt Shopper (IRE) 82 (Desert Prince (IRE) **98 p**
130) [2015 p7g* p8g⁶ 7g* 7g* Aug 7] 66,000Y: closely related to 2 winners by Medicean,

including 1½m winner Black Label, and half-brother to several winners, including 2-y-o 7f winner Cheque Book (by Araafa): dam 2-y-o 6f winner who stayed 1m: useful form: won maiden at Lingfield in February: much improved when successful in handicaps at Epsom (by 2½ lengths from Guiding Light) in July and Brighton (by 3 lengths from Port Lairge) in August: stays 7f: in hood first 2 starts: sent to Hong Kong, where renamed Golden Sun: open to further improvement. *Michael Wigham*

STARBOARD 6 b.g. Zamindar (USA) 116 – Summer Shower (Sadler's Wells (USA) 132) **101** [2015 102: 10s 8.1s* 8d⁵ 8.3s² p10f Oct 28] useful handicapper: won at Chepstow (by 3¾ lengths from Peak Storm) in August: stays 11f: acts on tapeta and soft going. *David Simcock*

STAR CITIZEN 3 b.g. New Approach (IRE) 132 – Faslen (USA) 92 (Fasliyev (USA) – 120) [2015 91p: 6d May 30] fairly useful winner in 2014 (ran twice): slowly away when well held in handicap only outing in 2015: will be suited by 7f. *Charlie Appleby*

STAR CRACKER (IRE) 3 ch.g. Starspangledbanner (AUS) 128 – Champagne Cracker **76** 74 (Up And At 'Em 109) [2015 76: 5d 5m⁵ 5m² 5g⁵ 6d³ 6d⁴ 5g⁵ 6g³ 7s Oct 16] fair handicapper: left Michael Dods after fifth start: stays 6f: acts on good to firm and good to soft going: often in cheekpieces in 2015. *Jim Goldie*

STARCROSSED 3 b.g. Cape Cross (IRE) 129 – Gretna 77 (Groom Dancer (USA) 128) **77** [2015 10m p12f⁴ 13.1m⁴ p12g³ p13.3f* p16g Dec 9] good-topped gelding: fair performer: won maiden at Chelmsford in November: stays 2m: acts on polytrack and good to firm going: front runner/races prominently. *Eve Johnson Houghton*

STARDANSE 4 b.f. High Chaparral (IRE) 132 – Danse Spectre (IRE) 70 (Spectrum (IRE) – 126) [2015 –: p7g p7m p10fᵇᵘ p10m 10m Jun 13] has shown little in maidens/handicaps. *John Bridger*

STARDRIFTER 3 b.g. Rock of Gibraltar (IRE) 133 – Alchemilla (Dubai Destination **82** (USA) 127) [2015 71: 8.3m* 8m 8m⁵ 8.5f³ 9.3d* 7.9g² 8.5g² 8.3s 8d⁵ Oct 5] fairly useful handicapper: won at Nottingham in April and Carlisle in July: stays 9.5f: acts on firm going and good to soft going: usually races towards rear. *Richard Fahey*

STARFIELD 6 b.g. Marju (IRE) 127 – Sister Moonshine (FR) 99 (Piccolo 121) [2015 **96** f8d* f8d 18.6m⁴ 8.3s p8g³ p8g Jun 4] well-made gelding: useful handicapper: won at Southwell (by 1¼ lengths from Pearl Nation) in January: left Michael Appleby after second start: stays 9.5f: acts on all-weather: wears headgear. *Mike Murphy*

STAR FIRE 3 b.f. Dark Angel (IRE) 113 – Bunditten (IRE) 92 (Soviet Star (USA) 128) **91** [2015 65p: 5.1m* 5g⁴ 5m² 5.7g* 5m² 5m⁵ 5f³ p6g⁵ 5.7g* p6m* Nov 17] fairly useful handicapper: won at Nottingham (awarded race) in April, Bath in June and October and Lingfield (by neck from Showtime Star) in November: stays 6f: acts on polytrack and good to firm going: in hood in 2015: often races towards rear. *Roger Charlton*

STAR FOCUS (IRE) 2 b.f. (May 4) Intense Focus (USA) 117 – Star of Siligo (USA) **75** (Saratoga Six (USA)) [2015 6d³ 6m² 7.5m* 6d³ 6g 6.3d Sep 13] €16,000Y: half-sister to several winners, including useful Italian winner up to 1m Magritte (2-y-o 5f/6f winner, by Modigliani) and 1¼m-1½m winner Estibdaad (by Haatef): dam Italian maiden: fair performer: won maiden at Beverley in June: stays 7.5f: acts on good to firm and good to soft going: front runner/races prominently. *Mark Johnston*

STAR FOR LIFE (USA) 6 b.g. Giant's Causeway (USA) 132 – Clerical Etoile (ARG) – (The Watcher (USA)) [2015 7.1s 12.5s⁶ May 11] maiden: no form in 2015: best effort at 10.5f: acts on soft going: usually wears headgear: in tongue tie in 2015. *Dianne Sayer*

STARGAZER (IRE) 2 b.c. (Feb 26) Canford Cliffs (IRE) 133 – Star Ruby (IRE) 109 **91 p** (Rock of Gibraltar (IRE) 133) [2015 7.1g⁴ 7g³ 8g² Sep 30] lengthy colt: second foal: half-brother to smart winner up to 1¼m Stravagante (2-y-o 1m winner, by Rip Van Winkle): dam 1¼m winner: fairly useful form: upped in trip, improved again when 2¾ lengths second of 12 to Paris Protocol in maiden at Salisbury: stays 1m: will continue to progress. *Sir Michael Stoute*

STAR GLIMMER (IRE) 2 b.f. (Apr 1) Kodiac 112 – Skyscape 89 (Zafonic (USA) 130) **68** [2015 p7g⁵ p7g⁴ 5.7d⁵ p6f⁴ 6s p6f⁵ Nov 12] €17,000Y: fourth foal: sister to 7f winner Marcus Caesar (by Antonius Pius): dam 1m-9.4f winner who stayed 1½m: fair maiden: bred to be suited by at least 7f: acts on polytrack: tried in blinkers. *Henry Spiller*

STAR JEANIE 2 b.f. (Mar 2) Kyllachy 129 – Floating (Oasis Dream 129) [2015 6g² 6g* **77 p** Jul 8] £20,000Y: third foal: half-sister to 1m winner Like A Prayer (by Compton Place): dam French maiden: 11/8, improved from debut when winning maiden at Lingfield by 1¼ lengths from Kidmenever, quickening to lead over 1f out and having bit in hand: open to further improvement. *Henry Candy*

STARLETINA (IRE) 3 b.f. Sea The Stars (IRE) 140 – Favourable Terms 120 (Selkirk **79** (USA) 129) [2015 t8.6g* 10.3m⁵ Apr 25] fifth foal: half-sister to French 5.5f winner Derivatives (by Dansili) and useful French 11f winner Semester (by Monsun): dam 7f-1¼m winner, including Nassau Stakes: won maiden at Wolverhampton in April by 4½ lengths from Nomenklatura: well held in handicap at Doncaster only other start: sold 90,000 gns in December. *Charlie Appleby*

STARLEYF 2 b.f. (Apr 27) Kheleyf (USA) 116 – Satin Braid 78 (Diktat 126) [2015 5d p6f – Oct 1] third foal: closely related to 5f/6f winner Ada Lovelace (by Byron): dam 1m winner: well held in maidens. *Ben Haslam*

STARLIGHT BANNER (IRE) 3 b.f. Starspangledbanner (AUS) 128 – Dromod Mour **48** (IRE) (Azamour (IRE) 130) [2015 p7m t8.6g⁶ 7g 8g t8.6m t9.5m t9.5f⁶ p12g⁵ t12.2m Nov 21] first foal: dam unraced half-sister to smart 2-y-o 1m/9f winner Tiz The Shot: poor maiden: stays 9.5f. acts on tapeta. *Daniel Loughnane*

STARLIGHT GENIE 3 b.f. Hellvelyn 118 – Anneliina 80 (Cadeaux Genereux 131) **67** [2015 t7.1f² t7.1m² t7.1f⁴ 7d t8.6g t9.5f⁶ Dec 11] £14,000Y: half-sister to several winners, including useful winner up to 6f Cadeaux Pearl (2-y-o 5f winner, by Acclamation) and 2-y-o 6f winner Cheap Street (by Compton Place): dam maiden (stayed 7f): fair maiden: left Jonathan Portman after fourth start: stays 9.5f: acts on tapeta. *Richard Phillips*

STARLIGHT JUNE 3 gr.f. Hellvelyn 118 – Pelican Key (IRE) 80 (Mujadil (USA) 119) **48** [2015 55: t7.1g t9.5g 10s⁴ Oct 6] poor maiden: left Jonathan Portman after third start: stays 1¼m: acts on tapeta, firm and soft going. *Jim Boyle*

STARLIGHT SYMPHONY (IRE) 5 b.m. Oratorio (IRE) 128 – Phillippa (IRE) **75** (Galileo (IRE) 134) [2015 83: p10m⁴ p8f³ p8g² p8f² 8.3m⁶ 8.1m 8.1m⁵ 8m⁵ 8m² 7g² p8f⁴ 7.5m² p8g⁵ Oct 27] compact mare: fair handicapper: stays 1¼m: acts on polytrack and firm going: wears headgear: often travels strongly. *Eve Johnson Houghton*

STAR LINKS (USA) 9 b.g. Bernstein (USA) 115 – Startarette (USA) (Dixieland Band **79** (USA)) [2015 96: p10m⁶ p10.7g p7m p8g t8.6g⁴ 8d 8g 8m p8g t8.6g t8.6g p8f t8.6f⁶ p8g Dec 30] leggy gelding: fair handicapper at best nowadays: stays 9.5f: acts on polytrack, tapeta, good to firm and heavy going: wears headgear/tongue tie: starts slowly, usually races nearer last than first: none too reliable. *Sylvester Kirk*

STARLIT CANTATA 4 b.f. Oratorio (IRE) 128 – Starlit Sky (Galileo (IRE) 134) [2015 **89** 79: p10m* p10f* 9.9m³ 8g² 8.3d² p10g* p10m³ p10g Dec 19] sturdy mare: fairly useful handicapper: won at Lingfield in April (twice) and October: stays 1¼m: acts on polytrack, firm and good to soft going: tried in cheekpieces. *Eve Johnson Houghton*

STARLIT NIGHT 3 b.f. Nayef (USA) 129 – Perfect Night 79 (Danzig Connection – (USA)) [2015 p11g t12.2f Oct 31] seventh foal: half-sister to smart 5f to (at 2 yrs) 7f winner Definightly (by Diktat) and 1m winner Why Not Now (by Notnowcato): dam 6f/7f winner: well held in 2 maidens: sold £1,200 in December. *Roger Charlton*

STARLUCK (IRE) 10 gr.g. Key of Luck (USA) 126 – Sarifa (IRE) (Kahyasi 130) [2015 **88** 12g* 10g³ Sep 24] fairly useful handicapper: won at Epsom (by neck from Golden Jubilee) in September: stays 1½m: acts on polytrack, soft and good to firm going: tried in cheekpieces. *David Arbuthnot*

STAR OF LOMBARDY (IRE) 2 b.f. (Feb 28) Cape Cross (IRE) 129 – Million Waves **73** (IRE) 92 (Mull of Kintyre (USA) 114) [2015 7m² 7g 7.9m⁶ p7g² Nov 26] 57,000Y: sixth foal: half-sister to 3 winners, including smart winner up to 1¾m Blue Wave (2-y-o 1m winner, by Raven's Pass) and 1m-1¼m winner Waveguide (by Dubawi): dam, 2-y-o 7f winner who stayed 1¼m, half-sister to very smart French miler Elusive Wave: fair maiden: second at Leicester and Chelmsford: stays 7f. *Mark Johnston*

STAR OF SEVILLE 3 b.f. Duke of Marmalade (IRE) 132 – Stage Presence (IRE) **116** 95 (Selkirk (USA) 129) [2015 97p: 10m* 10.4g* 12g 10.4g* 9.9m 9.9m Oct 4]

A third of France's Group 1 races in 2015 were won by British challengers, with the lion's share of the £6m prize money won by British-trained horses on French soil being claimed by Clarehaven Stables who landed the biggest prize of all, the Prix de l'Arc de Triomphe, with Golden Horn. Shalaa's triumph at odds on in the Prix Morny at Deauville in August and Star of Seville's surprise victory at Chantilly in the Prix de Diane Longines, Europe's richest race for fillies, helped to lift Britain's champion trainer John Gosden into third place in the trainers' championship in France. Star of Seville's victory in the Prix de Diane—the first in the race by a British-trained filly since another outsider Confidential Lady in 2006—came only eight days after Golden Horn's Derby win at Epsom, and only nine days after Star

Prix de Diane Longines, Chantilly—Star of Seville, badly hampered and heavily eased in the Oaks, makes a quick reappearance to become the first British-trained winner since Confidential Lady in 2006; Physiocrate justifies the decision to supplement her for €66,000 by finishing second, with Little Nightingale, the strong-finishing Desiree Clary and Sainte Amarante also in the picture

of Seville herself had run in the Oaks. Front-running Star of Seville was one of the worst sufferers in a roughhouse Oaks, badly hampered when the cannoned-into Diamondsandrubies forced her against the rail soon after she had been headed about a furlong and a half out. With all chance gone, Star of Seville's jockey William Buick wisely eased her, and her finishing position, ninth of eleven, gave a false indication of how she had shaped. It still came as a surprise, however, to see her in the starting line-up at Chantilly but, ridden by Frankie Dettori (who had been on stablemate Jazzi Top at Epsom), Star of Seville fully vindicated the decision of her trainer to turn her out again so quickly, a decision that the filly's owner Lady Bamford (at whose insistence she had reportedly run in the Oaks) admitted afterwards she had thought 'was crazy'. Star of Seville's success in the Prix de Diane was followed thirteen days later by the victory of Jack Hobbs in the Irish Derby which gave Clarehaven a major classic victory in three different countries in June. Like Jack Hobbs, Star of Seville will be in training again as a four-year-old.

Star of Seville is a home bred and the second classic-winning filly to carry the all-maroon colours of Lady Bamford, also owner-breeder of the 2009 Oaks and Irish Oaks winner Sariska who is now among twenty broodmares at her Daylesford Stud in the Cotswolds. Among the other Daylesford home breds in training at Clarehaven in the latest season were the King George VI and Queen Elizabeth Stakes runner-up Eagle Top (out of a half-sister to Sariska) and the King Edward VII Stakes runner-up Mr Singh (out of Cherry Hinton third Sundari, one of the first mares, along with Sariska's dam Maycocks Bay, to carry Lady Bamford's colours with some distinction on the racecourse before being retired to Daylesford). Mr Singh was among the leaders in the St Leger ante-post market before being ruled out with an infection. Star of Seville's dam the Selkirk mare Stage Presence was added to the Daylesford broodmare band at the 2007 December Sales (at a cost of 475,000 guineas) and among the other recent additions are the 950,000-guinea purchase at the 2010 December Sales, Soinlovewithyou, a half-sister to Ruler of The World and Duke of Marmalade, the last-named coincidentally the sire of Star of Seville.

Star of Seville ran twice as a two-year-old and was an impressive winner of a back-end maiden at Doncaster on her second start. Clearly open to further improvement, she followed up, making all, on her reappearance in a five-runner minor event at Newbury and then emulated Sariska by winning the Tattersalls Musidora Stakes over an extended mile and a quarter at York in May. Sariska was a clear-cut winner, but Star of Seville got home only by a head from the Fillies' Mile winner Together Forever, who had to concede 4 lb. Star of Seville again made the running but only just held on, with neither her style of racing nor her pedigree suggesting she would improve when stepped up further in distance. The fact that Dettori, who rode Star of Seville at both Newbury and York, chose the winner of the

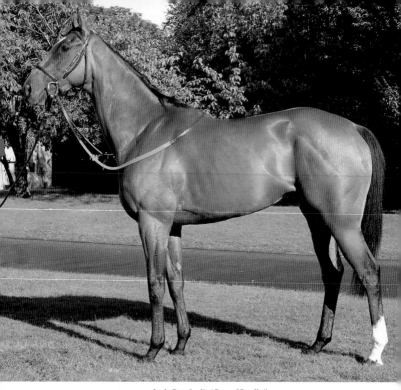

Lady Bamford's "Star of Seville"

listed Pretty Polly Stakes, Jazzi Top, at Epsom might partly have been a reflection of that view. John Gosden seemed to favour running Star of Seville in the Prix de Diane rather than the Oaks, though, in the event, she ran in both.

There was a field of seventeen for the Prix de Diane Longines for which Queen's Jewel, the winner of the main trial the Prix Saint-Alary, started a hot favourite, ahead of another unbeaten winner the Jean-Claude Rouget-trained Mojo Risin whose biggest win had come in a listed event at Toulouse. Physiocrate and Desiree Clary were both supplemented for €66,000 after finishing first and second in a minor event over the course the previous month and they were the only others to start at shorter than 13/1, the odds at which the Prix Cleopatre winner Little Nightingale was sent off. Star of Seville and the One Thousand Guineas fourth Malabar, the first British challengers since 2009, started at 17/1 and 27/1 respectively. Both Maxime Guyon on Queen's Jewel and Dettori on Star of Seville were drawn high and, while Queen's Jewel was settled in mid-field and couldn't reproduce her Prix Saint-Alary form (managing only eleventh), Star of Seville was kept wide from her high draw, away from the main pack, until converging on Queen's Jewel's pacemaker Clarmina before taking up the running early in the home straight (in hindsight, this was the blueprint for Dettori's winning ride on Golden Horn in the Arc!). Star of Seville kept on well to win by a length and three quarters of a length, with Physiocrate and Little Nightingale filling the places, just ahead of Desiree Clary in a bunched finish in which Desiree Clary and Mojo Risin were among those to encounter trouble in running (fifth-placed Sainte Amarante's objection to Physiocrate was unsuccessful). While Star of Seville was John Gosden's first Prix de Diane winner, it was Frankie Dettori's second, following West Wind in 2007, the year he won the Derby for the first time, on Authorized. On her two subsequent starts Star of Seville was prominent as usual but faded rather tamely and cut little ice, managing only seventh of nine in the Nassau Stakes and eighth of thirteen in the Prix de l'Opera (in which she was again passed over by Dettori in favour of Jazzi Top who went on to finish a very close second).

Star of Seville (b.f. 2012)	Duke of Marmalade (IRE) (b 2004)	Danehill (b 1986)	Danzig
			Razyana
		Love Me True (ch 1998)	Kingmambo
			Lassie's Lady
	Stage Presence (IRE) (ch 1998)	Selkirk (ch 1988)	Sharpen Up
			Annie Edge
		Park Charger (b 1992)	Tirol
			Haitienne

The tall, useful-looking Star of Seville is by the top-notch middle-distance performer Duke of Marmalade who was sold to South Africa in May 2014 after standing six seasons at Coolmore. As so often seems to happen when a stallion is banished abroad, Duke of Marmalade's fortunes have taken a distinct turn for the better. Star of Seville's triumph at Chantilly was quickly followed by another classic triumph when Nutan won the Deutsches Derby, while the St Leger win of Simple Verse and the Goodwood Cup win of Big Orange further illustrated that commercial breeders had probably been hasty in discarding Duke of Marmalade. After covering a full book of 170 mares in his first season at €40,000, Duke of Marmalade covered 160, 184 and 138 in the next three years but was sent only 37 and 41 mares in each of his last two years at Coolmore. Star of Seville's dam Stage Presence won at up to a mile and the best of her four winners before Star of Seville, close relative English Ballet (by Danehill Dancer), won the Sweet Solera Stakes and was placed in the Fillies' Mile as a two-year-old, her only season to race. A half-sister to Stage Presence, the useful Rum Charger, who won the Athasi Stakes and the Ballycorus Stakes over seven furlongs, is the dam of Winchester whose Grade 1 wins over middle distances in the States included the Turf Classic and the Sword Dancer Invitational, both over a mile and a half on turf (Winchester won the Secretariat Stakes while still with Dermot Weld). Star of Seville stays ten and a half furlongs and acts on soft and good to firm. *John Gosden*

STAR OF SPRING (IRE) 3 b.f. Iffraaj 127 – Gift of Spring (USA) (Gilded Time (USA)) **77** [2015 71: 7m³ 7m³ 8s³ 8.1d⁴ 8.3d⁴ 7.1m² 8g³ Oct 18] fair maiden: stays 8.5f: acts on soft and good to firm going: sometimes wears hood. *Charles Hills*

STAR OF THE STAGE 3 b.g. Invincible Spirit (IRE) 121 – Enact 104 (Kyllachy 129) **73** [2015 77: t7.1g² 7f⁵ t7.1f⁶ p7g p7f p8g Dec 5] fair handicapper: left Richard Fahey after second start: stays 7f: acts on polytrack and tapeta. *Julia Feilden*

STAR PURSUITS 3 b.f. Pastoral Pursuits 127 – Garter Star 56 (Mark of Esteem (IRE) **50** 137) [2015 51: t7.1m p7g Dec 9] modest maiden: stays 7f: acts on polytrack and good to firm going: often races towards rear. *Jimmy Fox*

STAR RIDER 3 gr.f. Cape Cross (IRE) 129 – Starfala 108 (Galileo (IRE) 134) [2015 10m³ **94** p13.3g* 12g⁴ 16f 14f⁴ 14.1g³ p14f 16.2d³ 16d* Oct 30] angular filly: first foal: dam, 1½m winner, closely related to useful 1½m-1¾m winner Sweeping Up and half-sister to useful performer up to 2¼m Under The Rainbow: fairly useful performer: won maiden at Chelmsford in May and handicap at Newmarket (by ¾ length from Wind Place And Sho, showing further improvement in first-time cheekpieces) in October: stays 2m: acts on polytrack, firm and soft going: front runner/races prominently. *Hughie Morrison*

STARS AND STRIPES 3 ch.g. Selkirk (USA) 129 – Capannina 72 (Grand Lodge (USA) **79** 125) [2015 81p: 10m⁵ 8.3m² 8.3g³ 8g 10g Aug 21] tall, well-made gelding: fair maiden: stays 8.5f: acts on good to firm and good to soft going: tried in blinkers in 2015: front runner/races prominently. *Luca Cumani*

STARS AT NIGHT (IRE) 2 b.f. (Jan 18) Galileo (IRE) 134 – Miarixa (FR) (Linamix (FR) **77 p** 127) [2015 p8m⁴ p8g⁴ Dec 15] half-sister to several winners, including Irish/Yorkshire Oaks winner Blue Bunting (also 2-y-o 1m and 1000 Guineas winner, by Dynaformer) and

2m-2¼m winner Descaro (by Dr Fong): dam unraced: better effort when fourth in maiden at Kempton (3¾ lengths behind Mandrell) on second start, barely adequate test: will be suited by 1¼m+: should do better still. *John Gosden*

STARSHAPED (IRE) 3 b.g. The Carbon Unit (USA) 106 – Nawshewisnae (IRE) 61 **61** (Hawk Wing (USA) 136) [2015 8.2g 10.5v 8.5s 8g* 8m⁴ 11.1s⁵ 9.2s³ 7.2g⁵ 9.2d⁵ Sep 1] modest handicapper: won at Newcastle in May: stayed 1m: acted on good to firm going: tried in cheekpieces: dead. *John Patrick Shanahan, Ireland*

STARS N ANGELS (IRE) 2 gr.f. (Mar 16) Dark Angel (IRE) 113 – Passage To India **62** (IRE) 74 (Indian Ridge 123) [2015 6m 6g 7d³ 7m⁶ 8.3g Aug 3] third foal: sister to a winner in Greece and half-sister to 5f (including at 2 yrs) winner Appleberry (by Approve): dam, maiden (best at 7f), sister to smart Italian/French 5f-7f winner Rosendhal: modest maiden: stays 7f: acts on good to soft going. *Michael Appleby*

STAR STORM (IRE) 3 b.c. Sea The Stars (IRE) 140 – Sayyedati Storm (USA) 52 **116** (Storm Cat (USA)) [2015 10.2d⁶ 10m² 10m² 11.1s⁴ 10.3g⁴ 11.9d* 11.5m* 12m* Oct 3] useful-looking colt: first foal: dam temperamental half-sister to Champagne Stakes winner Almushahar out of 1000 Guineas winner Sayyedati: smart performer: won maiden at Haydock and handicap at Yarmouth in September and Cumberland Lodge Stakes at Ascot in October: much improved when beating Missed Call by 2¾ lengths in last-named, leading over 1f out and quickening clear, impressive: stays 1½m: acts on good to firm and good to soft going: often travels strongly: may do better still. *James Fanshawe*

STAR SYSTEM (USA) 3 b.g. Whipper (USA) 126 – Beiramar (IRE) (Monsun (GER) **95** 124) [2015 f8s* 9.8g* 9m 10g⁴ 9.9s⁵ 10s* 10.3d⁴ Sep 26] $14,000Y: good-topped gelding: fourth foal: half-brother to French 1¼m-15f winner Montesquieu (by Silvano): dam, useful German 1¼m winner, sister to smart French stayer Bathyrhon: useful performer: won maiden at Southwell in March and handicaps at Ripon in May and Newbury in September: good fourth to Erik The Red in handicap at Chester final start: stays 10.5f: acts on fibresand and soft going: in hood since debut: free-going sort, often starts slowly/races in rear: sold 48,000 gns, sent to Saudi Arabia. *Andrew Balding*

START SEVEN 3 br.g. Dilum (USA) 115 – Dancingintheclouds (IRE) 67 (Rainbow Quest **65 p** (USA) 134) [2015 p8g p10g³ Dec 30] fifth foal: brother to French 1f-13.5f winner King Wood and half-brother to 1m winner On My Own (by Rock of Gibraltar): dam lightly-raced sister to St Leger winner Millenary: better effort when third in maiden at Lingfield in December (still green): will stay at least 1½m: open to further improvement. *Joseph Tuite*

START TIME (IRE) 2 b.g. (Mar 13) Invincible Spirit (IRE) 121 – Silca's Sister 112 **103** (Inchinor 119) [2015 7d² 7s² 7s* 8.3d* 7v² Oct 24] fifth foal: half-brother to 3 winners, including 2-y-o 7f/1m winner Tender Emotion and 1¼m winner Samsonite (both by Pivotal): dam, 2-y-o 6f winner (including Prix Morny) who stayed 9f, sister to smart 1m-1¼m performer Golden Silca: useful performer: won maiden at Thirsk in September and nursery at Windsor (by 4½ lengths from Triassic) in October: 5/1, probably should have also won when nose second of 9 to Crazy Horse in Horris Hill Stakes at Newbury final start, leading over 2f out, wandering in front and headed post: stays 8.5f: acts on heavy going: in headgear last 4 starts: often races prominently, often races freely: quirky sort. *Saeed bin Suroor*

STARVING FAITHFUL 3 ch.f. Makfi 130 – Sensational Mover (USA) 68 (Theatrical) **69** [2015 p12g⁵ f12g² Dec 12] seventh foal: half-sister to 3 winners, including 2-y-o 6f/6.5f winner Shamandar (by Exceed And Excel) and 2-y-o 7f winner Hung Parliament (by Numerous), both useful: dam second at 1½m: fair form in maidens, second of 5 at Southwell. *Ralph Beckett*

STARWATCH 8 b.g. Observatory (USA) 131 – Trinity Reef 80 (Bustino 136) [2015 96, **93** a83: 7.6s 11.6m⁵ 8.5m* 8.1m 8.3d⁵ 10.1v² 10.1d⁴ 11.6d⁵ Oct 5] rather leggy gelding: fairly useful handicapper: won at Epsom in July: stays 11.5f: acts on polytrack, good to firm and heavy going: tried in visor: often races prominently. *John Bridger*

STATE OF THE UNION (IRE) 3 ch.g. Approve (IRE) 112 – First Lady (IRE) (Indian **78 §** Ridge 123) [2015 80: t5.1m⁵ p6f³ t6f 5d 5g³ 5.1m 6d 5s⁶ p6g* p6g⁴ p6g Dec 28] fair performer: won seller at Lingfield in October: left David O'Meara after eighth start: stays 6f: acts on polytrack: tried in headgear in 2015: tried in tongue tie in 2015: has looked temperamental. *Lee Carter*

STATSMINISTER 4 b.f. Champs Elysees 124 – Sailing Days 67 (Kris 135) [2015 85: **79** 14m⁵ 17.1g³ 16g 14.1m⁵ 13.1f³ 12m⁶ Oct 3] tall filly: fair handicapper: stays 17f: acts on firm going: tried in cheekpieces in 2015: front runner/races prominently. *Luke Dace*

STATUESQUE 2 b.f. (Feb 24) Sea The Stars (IRE) 140 – Kahara 100 (Sadler's Wells (USA) 132) [2015 8.3g⁴ Sep 30] 375,000Y: fourth foal: closely related to smart German winner up to 8.5f Karpino (2-y-o 7f winner, by Cape Cross) and half-sister to 2 winners in Germany, including useful 7f winner Karpina (by Pivotal): dam, 1¼m-1¾m winner, sister to St Leger winner Milan: 9/2, promising 7½ lengths fourth of 10 to Andastra in maiden at Nottingham on debut, running green but staying on not knocked about: will be suited by at least 1¼m: open to plenty of improvement. *Sir Michael Stoute* — **64 P**

STATUS QUO (IRE) 2 br.g. (Apr 8) Thewayyouare (USA) 117 – Again Royale (IRE) (Royal Academy (USA) 130) [2015 7g⁶ 7.5g⁴ 17.1g* Sep 29] €28,000Y: half-brother to 3 winners, including useful 1m-11f winner Super Say (by Intikhab) and useful 2-y-o 5f/6f winner Sacred Aspect (by Haatef): dam unraced sister to smart 5f/6f winner Tiger Royal: fairly useful form: 14/1, improved when winning maiden at Wolverhampton in September by ½ length from Theos Lolly, staying on to lead close home: should be suited by 1m+: has been gelded: will go on improving. *Sir Mark Prescott Bt* — **81 p**

STATUTORY (IRE) 5 b.g. Authorized (IRE) 133 – Mialuna (Zafonic (USA) 130) [2015 106: 20f Jun 16] strong gelding: useful handicapper: well held but shaped as if retaining ability in Ascot Stakes at Royal Ascot only outing in 2015: stays 2¼m: acts on soft and good to firm going: front runner/races prominently. *Saeed bin Suroor* — **–**

STAY IN MY HEART (IRE) 6 ch.m. Medicean 128 – Christmas Cracker (FR) (Alhaarth (IRE) 126) [2015 p15.8f⁵ Jan 30] maiden: left Charlie Swan, well held on first start on Flat since 2013: best effort at 1½m: best form on soft going: tried in blinkers: modest hurdler. *Laura Mongan* — **–**

STAY STRONG (GER) 3 b.g. Monsun (GER) 124 – Sasuela (GER) (Dashing Blade 117) [2015 70p: 8m⁶ 9.9m⁶ Apr 23] fair form in 2014, well held both outings in Britain in 2015: sold £18,500 in June, sent to Germany, where won maiden at Mannheim in September and handicap at Baden-Baden (1½m) in October. *Saeed bin Suroor* — **70**

ST DUNSTAN (IRE) 2 b.c. (Jan 15) Zoffany (IRE) 121 – Box of Frogs (IRE) 50 (One Cool Cat (USA) 123) [2015 7.2g⁵ 7s 7v Nov 3] modest maiden: best effort when fifth at Ayr on debut. *John Quinn* — **60**

STEADY MAJOR (IRE) 3 b.g. Invincible Spirit (IRE) 121 – Combust (USA) (Aptitude (USA) 128) [2015 76: p10m² p10f² f8d* p10m* 9.9m⁴ 8.1m 10.1m 12m 10.1m⁴ 10d³ p8f⁴ Oct 15] good-topped gelding: fair performer: won maiden at Southwell and claimer at Lingfield in February: left David Simcock after fourth start: stays 1½m: acts on polytrack, fibresand and good to firm going: tried in blinkers in 2015. *Simon Dow* — **73 a79**

STEADY PACE 2 b.c. (Apr 6) Dark Angel (IRE) 113 – Cool Kitten (IRE) 65 (One Cool Cat (USA) 123) [2015 5m* 5m³ 5f³ 6m² 6m³ 6g⁵ 6g³ Sep 26] 80,000F: compact, attractive colt: second foal: half-brother to winner up to 1¼m Prince of Paris (2-y-o 1m winner, by Champs Elysees): dam, 7f/1m winner, half-sister to smart winner up to 1m Atlantis Prince: smart performer: won maiden at Ascot in May by 2¾ lengths from Beaverbrook: best efforts when placed behind Shalaa at Newmarket fourth/final starts, in July Stakes (second, beaten a length) and in Middle Park Stakes (third, beaten 2½ lengths): should stay 7f: acts on good to firm going. *Saeed bin Suroor* — **111**

STEALING THE SHOW 3 b.g. Makfi 130 – Belle Reine (King of Kings (IRE) 125) [2015 9.9m³ Jun 24] 75,000Y: half-brother to several winners, including useful winner up to 16.5f Layline (2-y-o 1m winner, by King's Best) and useful 2-y-o 5f/6f winner Ishbelle (by Invincible Spirit): dam unraced half-sister to 1m/9f winner Smart Enough and winner up to 1m Oasis Dancer (both smart): 6/1, shaped as if needed experience when 6 lengths third of 7 to Plane Song in maiden at Salisbury on debut: has been gelded: open to improvement. *Andrew Balding* — **72 p**

STEAL THE SCENE (IRE) 3 b.c. Lord Shanakill (USA) 121 – Namoos (USA) 74 (Sahm (USA) 112) [2015 74: 8.3s⁵ 7m* 8f² 7m p8f³ 7f³ p7d* Nov 30] well-made colt: fairly useful handicapper: won at Leicester in May and Kempton (by 1¼ lengths from Trucanini) in November: stays 1m: acts on polytrack, firm and good to soft going: races prominently. *Richard Hannon* — **94**

STEEL BLAZE 3 b.f. Striking Ambition 122 – Ocean Blaze 91 (Polar Prince (IRE) 117) [2015 –: 5.7f Sep 12] well held all 3 starts in maidens, *Nikki Evans* — **–**

STEEL CITY BOY (IRE) 12 b.g. Bold Fact (USA) 116 – Balgren (IRE) (Ballad Rock 122) [2015 50: f5d² t5.1f⁶ t6f² t6g t6g p6g² p6g p6m² t6f⁵ p6g⁵ f6g⁵ t7.1f f7g Apr 9] lengthy, good-bodied gelding: modest handicapper: stays 6f: acts on all-weather, good to firm and heavy going: tried in cheekpieces: front runner/races prominently. *Ann Stokell* — **51**

STEEL OF MADRID (IRE) 2 b.c. (Apr 6) Lope de Vega (IRE) 125 – Bibury 80 (Royal **108 p**
Applause 124) [2015 6g* p8g² Sep 9] 120,000Y: second foal: dam, 7f winner who stayed
10.7f, half-sister to Gold Cup winner Rite of Passage: won maiden at Salisbury in July on
debut: upped in trip, much better form when head second of 4 to Hawkbill in minor event
at Kempton, finishing strongly having conceded first run: will stay 1¼m: open to further
improvement. *Richard Hannon*

STEEL RAIN 7 b.g. Striking Ambition 122 – Concentration (IRE) (Mind Games 121) –
[2015 72§: 6g⁶ 6.1s Aug 31] modest handicapper: well held in 2015: stays 5.5f: acts on
good to firm and heavy going: tried in blinkers. *Nikki Evans*

STEELRIVER (IRE) 5 b.g. Iffraaj 127 – Numerus Clausus (FR) (Numerus (USA)) **95**
[2015 106: p8f⁴ p6g³ t5.1f⁵ t6m 6d 7g 7g 6g 6m³ 5m 6m⁵ t6g⁴ p8g⁶ p6g³ t6f³ p6g³ Oct 7] **a103**
close-coupled gelding: useful performer: good third in handicap at Wolverhampton (length
behind Kasbah) and minor event at Kempton (2¾ lengths behind Lancelot du Lac) last 2
starts: stays 7f: acts on polytrack, tapeta, good to firm and good to soft going: tried in
headgear: often races towards rear. *Michael Herrington*

STEEL STOCKHOLDER 9 b.g. Mark of Esteem (IRE) 137 – Pompey Blue 71 (Abou **68**
Zouz (USA) 109) [2015 73: t8.6f⁶ t8.6g 8m² 9g 7g Sep 19] close-coupled gelding: fair
handicapper: stays 8.5f: acts on polytrack, tapeta, soft and good to firm going: in
cheekpieces last 2 starts. *Antony Brittain*

STEEL TRAIN (FR) 4 b.g. Zafeen (FR) 123 – Silent Sunday (IRE) (Testa Rossa (AUS) **94**
128) [2015 7d 7g* 7m 7d² 7g⁴ 7.2g Sep 19] fairly useful handicapper: won at Thirsk in
May: good second there in August: stays 7.5f: acts on soft going: tried in cheekpieces:
often races towards rear. *David O'Meara*

STEEVO (IRE) 3 b.g. Dark Angel (IRE) 113 – Moriches (IRE) 68 (Alhaarth (IRE) 126) **55**
[2015 57p: 8f³ 9d p10g⁶ 8v⁶ 8g⁴ 6v Oct 6] modest handicapper: acts on polytrack, firm and
good to soft going: often wears headgear: usually races freely: sold 1,500 gns, sent to
Spain, where won twice at up to 11f at Dos Hermanas in December. *Gary Moore*

STEIPAMACH (IRE) 3 b.f. Vocalised (USA) 114 – Celst Elle (IRE) /2 (Noverre (USA) **100**
125) [2015 101: 8v⁶ 7v⁵ 8g 6g³ 7m 8g³ 7.5s⁴ 8g⁶ 7.5g³ 7s⁴ Oct 25] good-topped filly: useful
performer: third in Ballyogan Stakes at the Curragh (3¼ lengths behind Ainippe), listed
race at Cork (head behind Eshera) and Concorde Stakes at Tipperary (1¾ lengths behind
Tested): stays 1m: acts on soft going: tried in cheekpieces/tongue tie. *J. S. Bolger, Ireland*

STELLA ETOILE (IRE) 3 b.f. Duke of Marmalade (IRE) 132 – Sangita 47 (Royal **68**
Academy (USA) 130) [2015 74p: 8.3s⁶ 8.3g⁶ 8.3g⁶ 9.2d² 10g⁴ 8g⁵ p8g⁵ t8.6f⁶ Nov 14] fair
maiden: left Richard Fahey after fifth start: stays 9f: acts on soft going: tried in visor.
Ian Williams

STELLAIRE 3 b.f. Archipenko (USA) 127 – Summer Night 94 (Nashwan (USA) 135) **69**
[2015 p8f⁵ 8g* 10.4f⁵ Jun 11] half-sister to numerous winners, including smart performer
up to 14.6f Songerie (2-y-o 7f/1m winner) and smart winner up to 1¾m Souvenance (2-y-o
7f winner) (both by Hernando): dam 6f winner: fair performer: won maiden at Redcar in
May: should be suited by at least 1¼m. *Ed Walker*

STELLARTA 4 b.f. Sakhee's Secret 128 – Torgau (IRE) 109 (Zieten (USA) 118) [2015 **89**
87: p6f* 6m⁵ 6m² 6m 7g³ 7m⁶ 6m⁴ 6m* 6g³ 5m p6g⁴ Nov 26] angular filly: fairly useful
handicapper: won at Kempton in February and Windsor in August: stays 7f: acts on
polytrack and good to firm going: often races prominently. *Michael Blanshard*

STENCIVE 6 b.g. Dansili 127 – Madeira Mist (IRE) 80 (Grand Lodge (USA) 125) [2015 **91**
p10f p10f⁴ p12g Dec 19] strong gelding: fairly useful handicapper: stays 1½m: best form
on good going or firmer. *Charlie Wallis*

STENID 3 ch.g. Exceed And Excel (AUS) 126 – Indian Mystery (IRE) 69 (Indian Ridge **60**
123) [2015 –: p7f t6f 6m 6g t6g 6m² 6g³ 6d⁴ 6d 6m⁶ Aug 29] modest maiden: stays 6f: acts
on good to firm going: usually in headgear: tried in tongue tie: sold £3,800, sent to Sweden.
Kevin Ryan

STENTORIAN (IRE) 7 ch.g. Street Cry (IRE) 130 – Nomistakeaboutit (CAN) (Affirmed –
(USA)) [2015 14m 9.2g Aug 20] well-made gelding: handicapper: stayed 1¾m: acted on
polytrack, fibresand and good to firm going: wore headgear: modest hurdler: dead.
Linda Perratt

STEPHEN HERO (IRE) 5 br.g. Celtic Swing 138 – Albaiyda (IRE) (Brief Truce (USA) –
126) [2015 t16.5f⁶ Sep 19] fair handicapper: well held only outing in 2015: stays 1½m:
acts on soft and good to firm going: sometimes in cheekpieces: tried in tongue tie.
Brian Barr

STEP ON IT (IRE) 3 b.g. Footstepsinthesand 120 – Woodyousmileforme (USA) **73**
(Woodman (USA) 126) [2015 67: 10.2s⁶ t9.5m 10.2m t12.2f² t12.2g² Dec 4] lengthy,
useful-looking gelding: fair maiden: left Eve Johnson Houghton after first start: best effort
at 1½m: acts on tapeta: often in cheekpieces in 2015. *Daniel Loughnane*

STEPPE DAUGHTER (IRE) 4 b.f. Steppe Dancer (IRE) 117 – Carmencita (Rock of **88**
Gibraltar (IRE) 133) [2015 79: p10m⁴ 10.2f* 9.9g* 10g⁶ 10m⁵ 9.9g⁵ p12g⁴ Nov 4] rather
leggy filly: fairly useful performer: won maiden at Bath in May and handicap at Brighton
in June: stays 1½m: acts on polytrack and firm going: sometimes slowly away, usually
races nearer last than first. *Denis Coakley*

STEPPER POINT 6 b.g. Kyllachy 129 – Sacre Coeur 90 (Compton Place 125) [2015 **118**
123: 5g 5m⁴ 5g 5f 5m⁴ 5m* 5gᵖᵘ 5d 5m Oct 4] sturdy, good-quartered gelding: smart
performer: won Sapphire Stakes at the Curragh in July by neck from Mecca's Angel, best
effort of 2015: stays 5.5f: acts on polytrack, good to firm and good to soft going: wears
headgear. *William Muir*

STEPPING AHEAD (FR) 5 ch.g. Footstepsinthesand 120 – Zghorta (USA) 106 (Gone **80**
West (USA)) [2015 105: 10s 12s* 11.9g* Jul 16] fairly useful performer: won claimers at
Catterick in May (left K. R. Burke after) and Compiegne in July: stays 1½m: acts on
polytrack, fibresand, good to firm and heavy going: tried in headgear: usually races close
up. *Ian Williams*

STEPS (IRE) 7 gr.g. Verglas (IRE) 118 – Killinallan 70 (Vettori (IRE) 119) [2015 120: **122**
5.2m 5m⁴ 5f 6f 5m 5.6d* 5.2s* 5m 5d Oct 24] close-coupled gelding: very smart performer:
better than ever and won 20-runner Portland Handicap at Doncaster by 1¼ lengths from
Harry Hurricane and World Trophy at Newbury by nose from Ridge Ranger, both in
September: stays 6f: acts on polytrack, good to firm and heavy going: wears headgear:
sometimes slowly away, often races towards rear. *Roger Varian*

Mr Michael Hill's "Steps"

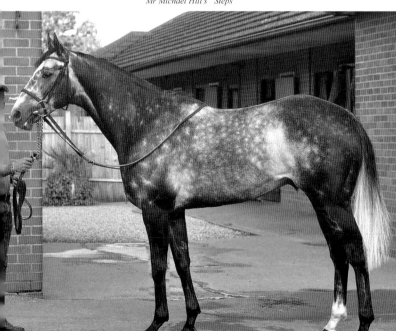

STERLING LINES 2 b.c. (Mar 18) Equiano (FR) 127 – Owdbetts (IRE) 69 (High Estate **72** 127) [2015 6g p7g 7g³ 5.7m² 5g⁶ p5f³ a8.5g p9.4g² Dec 16] angular colt: fair maiden: left Peter Chapple-Hyam after sixth start: stays 5.5f: acts on polytrack and good to firm going: usually races close up. *P. Monfort, France*

STERLING WORK (IRE) 2 b.c. (Feb 8) Invincible Spirit (IRE) 121 – Drama Class **79** (IRE) 102 (Caerleon (USA) 132) [2015 7g⁶ 7m⁴ 7d⁵ 8g² 8.3d³ Oct 5] compact colt: brother to 1¼m winner Debating Society, closely related to useful 1¼m winner Namibian Orator (by Cape Cross) and half-brother to several winners, including smart winner up to 1¼m (stayed 1½m) Eleanora Duse (2-y-o 1m winner, by Azamour): dam 1¼m winner: fair maiden: second in nursery at Newmarket (¾ length behind Bathos) in August, best effort: stays 1m: sold 40,000 gns, sent to Qatar. *Sir Michael Stoute*

STETCHWORTH (IRE) 4 ch.g. New Approach (IRE) 132 – Hallowed Park (IRE) **93** (Darathea (IRE) 127) [2015 95p: p10g³ 12g⁴ p10g⁴ 12.1s 10.3g² 8d 10v Oct 24] big gelding: fairly useful handicapper: stays 10.5f: acts on soft going: usually races towards rear. *Mark Johnston*

STETCHWORTH PARK 2 b.g. (Apr 27) Duke of Marmalade (IRE) 132 – Perseida – (IRE) (Galileo (IRE) 134) [2015 8.3d Oct 14] 25/1, badly needed experience when well held in maiden at Nottingham, slowly away. *Michael Bell*

STEUBEN (GER) 9 ch.g. Monsun (GER) 124 – Schwarzach (GER) (Grand Lodge – (USA) 125) [2015 f12g f14g f11g Apr 23] fair handicapper: well held in 2015: stays 1½m: acts on fibresand and soft going: tried in cheekpieces: often races in rear. *Des Donovan*

STEVENTON STAR 4 b.g. Pastoral Pursuits 127 – Premiere Dance (IRE) (Loup **81** Solitaire (USA) 117) [2015 99: p7f t9.5g⁶ p8f t8.6f⁶ p6f³ p6g⁴ 7m 7m 7m⁵ 6s² 6m² 5.9d³ 6m³ 6s⁵ 6g Aug 31] good-topped gelding: fairly useful handicapper: left Michael Scudamore after sixth start: stays 8.5f: acts on polytrack, tapeta, good to firm and good to soft going: wears headgear: tried in tongue tie: often starts slowly, usually races in rear. *Kevin Ryan*

STEVE PRESCOTT 3 gr.g. Dutch Art 126 – Toy Top (USA) 86 (Tactical Cat (USA) **98** 116) [2015 87: 6.1s 6f² 7m 6m 6d⁵ 6m* 6m¹ 6g 6g Sep 19] useful handicapper: won at Newmarket (by 2¼ lengths from Meshardal) in August: stays 6f: acts on good to firm going: tried in blinkers. *Richard Fahey*

STEVE ROGERS (IRE) 4 b.g. Montjeu (IRE) 137 – Three Owls (IRE) 79 (Warning **96 p** 136) [2015 –p: t12.2f* t13.9f* 14.1m* 16.4m⁵ 14m* 14f³ 15.9g* 18g Oct 10] good-topped gelding: useful handicapper: won at Wolverhampton in January and February, Nottingham in April, Sandown in June and Chester (by ½ length from Be Perfect) in September: finished well with lot to do (dropped out from poor draw) when 3 lengths ninth of 34 to Grumeti in Cesarewitch at Newmarket final start: stays 2¼m: acts on tapeta and any turf going: should improve further. *Roger Varian*

ST GEORGES CROSS 2 b.c. (Apr 8) Showcasing 117 – Garter Star 56 (Mark of Esteem **69** (IRE) 137) [2015 6.1m² 6g³ 6.1m⁵ 6g⁵ 7m⁴ p8f 8.3d p7g Oct 27] fair maiden: stays 7f: acts on good to firm going: often races prominently: sold 4,500 gns, sent to Italy. *Richard Fahey*

ST GEORGES ROCK (IRE) 3 b.g. Camacho 118 – Radio Wave 78 (Dalakhani (IRE) **72 §** 133) [2015 76: 8.3m 9.9m⁵ 12m 11.6g⁵ 10m⁵ p10f Nov 25] compact gelding: fair maiden: stays 11.5f: acts on good to soft going: usually in headgear in 2015: often races prominently: not one to trust: has been gelded. *Clive Cox*

STHENIC (FR) 3 b.g. Fastnet Rock (AUS) 127 – Ela's Giant (Giant's Causeway (USA) **68** 132) [2015 p12g⁶ 10m 11.8m⁴ Jun 18] fair maiden: should be suited by at least 1½m. *Andrew Balding*

STICKLEBACK 6 ch.m. Manduro (GER) 135 – The Stick 61 (Singspiel (IRE) 133) **62 §** [2015 18s⁴ 21.6g² 14.1v⁶ Jun 1] modest maiden: stays 21.5f: acts on heavy going: sometimes wears headgear: temperamental. *Micky Hammond*

STILL ON TOP 2 b.c. (Jan 25) Royal Applause 124 – Poulaine Bleue 44 (Bertolini (USA) **96** 125) [2015 6g* 6g³ 6g³ 6g⁴ 8s⁴ Oct 19] 15,000F, £12,000Y: strong colt: second foal: half-brother to 5f/6f winner Magical Daze (by Showcasing): dam, maiden (stayed 1m), half-sister to useful winner up to 9f Genre: useful performer: won maiden at Pontefract in August: much better form subsequently, including when third in valuable sales race at York (¾ length behind Tasleet) on second start and fourth in listed race at Pontefract (1¾ lengths behind Thanksfortellingme) on final one: stays 1m: acts on soft going: wore hood last 4 starts. *Tim Easterby*

STIMULATOR 2 b.g. (Feb 6) Motivator 131 – Fleeting Echo 99 (Beat Hollow 126) [2015 – 7s 6.5s Oct 23] showed nothing in 2 maidens at Newbury: has been gelded. *Mark Usher*

ST LAWRENCE GAP (IRE) 3 ch.g. Tagula (IRE) 116 – Kannon 72 (Kyllachy 129) **77**
[2015 57: p12g p12g⁶ 14m³ 14g² 14.1g p16g² 14d⁵ p12g⁵ Oct 6] fairly useful maiden: stays **a83**
2m: acts on polytrack: tried in visor: sometimes in tongue tie. *Robert Mills*

ST MICHEL 2 b.c. (Feb 25) Sea The Stars (IRE) 140 – Miss Provence 88 (Hernando (FR) **74 p**
127) [2015 7.5m³ 7s p8m⁴ Nov 17] half-brother to several winners, including useful 2-y-o
7f winner Oasis Cannes (by Oasis Dream), later successful abroad, and 1¼m-1½m winner
Miss Aix (by Selkirk): dam 9.5f winner who stayed 1½m: fair maiden: best effort when
fourth at Lingfield: will be suited by 1¼m+: should do better still. *Sir Mark Prescott Bt*

STOCKHILL DIVA 5 ch.m. Haafhd 129 – April Stock 97 (Beveled (USA)) [2015 76: **82**
10g² 9.9m⁵ 10g³ 12g* 11.8g 10s³ Oct 23] workmanlike mare: fairly useful handicapper:
won at Salisbury in August: stays 1½m: acts on soft going. *Brendan Powell*

STOCK HILL FAIR 7 b.g. Sakhee (USA) 136 – April Stock 97 (Beveled (USA)) [2015 **90**
84: p12g² 12g³ 14f³ 12g* 13.3s³ Aug 14] tall gelding: fairly useful handicapper: won at
Newmarket (by 3 lengths from Malekov) in August: stays 1¾m: acts on polytrack, firm and
soft going: wears tongue tie: front runner/races prominently. *Brendan Powell*

STOCKING 3 gr.f. Acclamation 118 – Red Boots (IRE) 66 (Verglas (IRE) 118) [2015 77: **95**
5m⁶ t5.1g* 5g³ p5g⁵ 5f² 5f.11f* p6m p5f⁵ p5m³ Dec 27] useful handicapper: won at
Wolverhampton in June and October (by 1¼ lengths from Doctor Parkes): best form at 5f:
acts on polytrack and tapeta: tried in headgear: often races towards rear. *Roger Varian*

STOIC BOY 3 ch.g. Paco Boy (IRE) 129 – Dramatic Turn 87 (Pivotal 124) [2015 p8f 7s⁶ **68 p**
p6m³ Oct 21] first foal: dam, 2-y-o 5f winner (later 4.5f-5.5f in France/Spain), out of very
smart 5f performer Eveningperformance: fair form: much improved when head third to
Emperors Warrior in maiden at Kempton: should continue to progress. *Henry Candy*

STOKED (IRE) 3 b.g. Fast Company (IRE) 126 – Es Que (Inchinor 119) [2015 85: 11g **74**
7.9s 10s⁶ Jul 29] handicapper, just fair form at best in 2015: should stay 1¼m+: acts on
heavy going: usually races close up: has been gelded. *Ed Walker*

STOLEN STORY (IRE) 3 b.c. Kodiac 112 – Mirwara (Darshaan 133) [2015 70: **80**
8.3m⁴ 11.6g* 11.6f⁵ 11.6g 11.6d⁵ Jul 13] compact colt: fairly useful handicapper: won at
Windsor in April: stays 11.5f: acts on firm and good to soft going: in cheekpieces final start:
sold £20,000, sent to Qatar. *George Margarson*

STOMACHION (IRE) 5 b.g. Duke of Marmalade (IRE) 132 – Insight (FR) 115 (Sadler's
Wells (USA) 132) [2015 109: 16f⁶ Apr 29] lengthy gelding: useful handicapper in 2014:
run best excused when sixth of 8 to Mizzou in Sagaro Stakes at Ascot only outing of 2015,
possibly unsuited by conditions and not persevered with once held: stays 14.5f: acts on
heavy going: sold 12,000 gns in October, sent to France. *Sir Michael Stoute*

STONEACRE OSKAR 6 b.m. Echo of Light 125 – Keidas (FR) 77 (Lomitas 129) [2015 –
46: f7g Jan 16] poor handicapper: probably stays 1m, races mainly at shorter: acts on
polytrack, fibresand and good to firm going. *Peter Grayson*

STONEBOAT BILL 3 ch.g. Virtual 122 – Applauding (IRE) (Royal Applause 124) [2015 **79**
56: 8s³ 8g* 8.3m² 10.2m³ 8g⁵ 8.9m⁵ 7.9g³ t9.5m³ 11.8s⁴ Oct 6] fair handicapper: won at
Thirsk in June: stays 1¼m: acts on tapeta and good to firm going. *Declan Carroll*

STONECOLDSOBA 2 b.g. (Apr 14) Aqlaam 125 – Aswaaq (IRE) 74 (Peintre Celebre –
(USA) 137) [2015 p8g Dec 7] 100/1, well held in maiden at Lingfield. *Paul Morgan*

STONECUTTER (IRE) 4 gr.g. Mastercraftsman (IRE) 129 – Sparkle of Stones (FR) **88**
(Sadler's Wells (USA) 132) [2015 91p: p14g* p14f² 14.6d Oct 23] fairly useful
handicapper: won at Chelmsford in January: left Marco Botti after first start, James Unett
after second: stays 1¾m: acts on polytrack and fibresand: usually races prominently.
Gay Kelleway

STONEFIELD FLYER 6 b.g. Kheleyf (USA) 116 – Majestic Diva (IRE) (Royal **88**
Applause 124) [2015 94: p7g³ p6g* p6g 7g⁴ 7.2g⁵ 6m 5.9m⁵ 5g³ 6g* 6d² 6g² 6d 6g² 6m 6d
t6m³ Oct 2] fairly useful performer: won claimer at Lingfield in January and handicap at
Hamilton in June: effective at 5f to 7f: acts on polytrack, tapeta, good to firm and good to
soft going: wears headgear: sometimes slowly away, often races in rear: sent to Sweden.
Keith Dalgleish

STONEHAM 4 b.f. Sixties Icon 125 – Cibenze 74 (Owington 123) [2015 t16.5g³ t16.5g² **63**
t16.5m² t16.5g* 17.2f² 13.1m³ t13.9g⁵ t16.5g² 12.1s⁵ Aug 31] rather leggy filly: modest
handicapper: won at Wolverhampton in April: will prove suited by a return to 1¾m+: acts
on tapeta, firm and soft going: tried in visor prior: often travels strongly. *Mick Channon*

STONE OF FOLCA 7 b.g. Kodiac 112 – Soyalang (FR) (Alydeed (CAN) 120) [2015 83: **85**
p5g p6f² 6g⁵ May 6] leggy gelding: fairly useful handicapper: will prove suited by a return
to 5f: acts on polytrack, good to firm and good to soft going: often wears hood: usually
races close up. *John Best*

STONE QUERCUS (IRE) 2 b.g. (Mar 23) Rock of Gibraltar (IRE) 133 – Redglow **68**
(IRE) (Fasliyev (USA) 120) [2015 6.1g³ p8g⁵ 7g⁴ Sep 23] fair form at best in maidens: has
been gelded. *James Given*

STONE ROSES (IRE) 3 gr.f. Zebedee 113 – Blanche Dubois (Nashwan (USA) 135) **76**
[2015 66: t6g⁶ 8m⁴ 8.3m³ 8.1m* 8.1d³ p8f⁶ t7.1m Sep 25] leggy filly: fair handicapper: **a63**
won at Chepstow in July: stays 8.5f: acts on good to firm going: usually races freely.
Michael Bell

STONEY BROKE 2 b.f. (Apr 2) Dansili 127 – Alvee (IRE) 75 (Key of Luck (USA) 126) **76 p**
[2015 8.3g* Sep 30] second foal: dam, maiden (stayed 2m), half-sister to smart stayer
Allegretto: 7/1, won 9-runner maiden at Nottingham on debut by head from Shadow Spirit,
running green but leading post without being knocked about: will be well suited by 1¼m+:
sure to progress. *James Fanshawe*

STOPPED OUT 10 gr.g. Montjoy (USA) 122 – Kiomi 65 (Niniski (USA) 125) [2015 **79**
14.1s⁶ May 9] fairly useful handicapper in 2014, just respectable effort only outing in 2015:
stays 2m: acts on soft and good to firm going: wears cheekpieces: front runner: useful
hurdler/chaser. *Philip Kirby*

STORM AHEAD (IRE) 2 b.g. (Apr 5) Iffraaj 127 – Loose Julie (IRE) (Cape Cross (IRE) **85 p**
129) [2015 p7g⁶ p7g⁵ p7g* Dec 28] 40,000F: third foal: half-brother to useful winner up to
6f Banaadeer (2-y-o 5f winner, by Tamayuz) and 7f winner Crystalin (by Arcano), later
successful abroad: dam, unraced, closely related to useful 5f/6f winner Moonis: fairly
useful performer: best effort when winning maiden at Lingfield (by neck from Bernie's
Boy) in December, overcoming positional bias: raced only at 7f: will go on improving.
Marcus Tregoning

STORMBOUND (IRE) 6 b.g. Galileo (IRE) 134 – A Footstep Away (USA) (Giant's **72**
Causeway (USA) 132) [2015 79: p8g³ p8g* p8g p8g³ 8g³ 8m³ 8f⁶ 8m⁶ Aug 22] strong, **a79**
lengthy gelding: fair handicapper: won at Lingfield (apprentice) in February: stays 8.5f:
acts on polytrack and firm going: often in headgear nowadays: tried in tongue: usually
races prominently. *Paul Cole*

STORM CHECK 3 b.g. New Approach (IRE) 132 – Lunda (IRE) 60 (Soviet Star (USA) **65**
128) [2015 8m 8g 10m⁵ f12s⁴ Aug 6] fair maiden: stays 1¼m: visored final start: has been
gelded. *Saeed bin Suroor*

STORMFLOWER 2 gr.f. (Apr 11) Arcano (IRE) 122 – Someone's Angel (USA) **77**
(Runaway Groom (CAN)) [2015 5m³ 5m⁶ 5g⁵ 5m³ 5m² 5g 5v* 6v⁴ p5f 6g 5d* Oct 12]
2,000F, 4,200Y: rather leggy filly: seventh foal: half-sister to useful/ungenuine winner up
to 7f Ghostwing (2-y-o 6f winner, by Kheleyf) and 1m winner That Boy David (by Kodiac):
dam of little account: fair performer: won maiden at Lingfield in August and nursery at
Windsor in October: best form at 5f: acts on heavy going: usually leads. *John Bridger*

STORM FORCE TEN 4 b.g. Shirocco (GER) 129 – Stravinsky Dance (Stravinsky **90**
(USA) 133) [2015 p12g⁴ 12.3v* 12d 12v Nov 7] lengthy, useful-looking gelding: fairly
useful handicapper: won at Chester (apprentice) in May: stays 12.5f: acts on polytrack and
heavy going: races prominently. *Andrew Balding*

STORM HAWK (IRE) 8 b.g. Hawk Wing (USA) 136 – Stormy Larissa (IRE) 79 (Royal **– §**
Applause 124) [2015 76§: f14d Jan 27] compact gelding: fair handicapper: stays 2m: acts
on polytrack, fibresand, good to firm and good to soft going: wears headgear: usually
slowly away, usually races in rear: unreliable. *Pat Eddery*

STORMING AMBITION 2 b.g. (Mar 23) Captain Gerrard (IRE) 113 – Lady Roxanne **–**
65 (Cyrano de Bergerac 120) [2015 t7.1f Nov 3] 25/1, well held in maiden at
Wolverhampton: has been gelded. *Conrad Allen*

STORMING HARRY 3 ch.g. Assertive 121 – Miss Pebbles (IRE) 82 (Lake Coniston **57**
(IRE) 131) [2015 –: 10.2f⁵ t12.2g 16g⁵ p15.8g* Aug 13] sturdy gelding: modest
handicapper: won at Lingfield in August: stays 2m: acts on polytrack and firm going: tried
in tongue tie: often starts slowly, usually races in rear. *Robin Dickin*

STORMIN TOM (IRE) 3 b.g. Dylan Thomas (IRE) 132 – She Storm (IRE) (Rainbow **71**
Quest (USA) 134) [2015 –: 10.2m* 12d 9.8d 10g⁵ 9.9m* 9.9m² 12g* 14.1g⁵ 12.1g⁵ 16.2m⁵
Oct 1] fair handicapper: won at Nottingham in April, Beverley in June and Ripon in August:
stays 1½m: acts on good to firm going: often races prominently. *Tim Easterby*

STORM LIGHTNING 6 b.g. Exceed And Excel (AUS) 126 – All For Laura 99 (Cadeaux **85** Genereux 131) [2015 80: t5.1g⁴ 5.3g* 5.1s² 5.1m² 5.7m 5.3d⁵ 5.1m* 5m⁶ p5g 6g² 5.3s⁵ **a72** 5.1s 6d⁶ 6.1d t5.1f Oct 9] workmanlike gelding: fairly useful handicapper: won at Brighton in April and Chester in June: stays 6f: acts on polytrack, good to firm and heavy going: sometimes in headgear prior to 2015. *Mark Brisbourne*

STORM MELODY 2 b.g. (Apr 22) Royal Applause 124 – Plume 88 (Pastoral Pursuits **81** 127) [2015 5d 5g³ 5g⁶ 5d³ 5.1v³ Oct 7] 22,000F, £60,000 2-y-o: compact, good-quartered gelding: first foal: dam 2-y-o 6f winner: fairly useful maiden: raced only at 5f: acts on heavy going: sometimes slowly away: has been gelded. *Jonjo O'Neill*

STORMONT BRIDGE 7 b.g. Avonbridge 123 – Stormont Castle (USA) (Irish River **50** (FR) 131) [2015 8d 7s³ 6m 7d⁵ 8.9g Jul 21] modest maiden: stays 1m: acts on soft and good to firm going: usually in visor in 2015: wears tongue tie. *Maurice Barnes*

STORM RIDER (IRE) 4 b.g. Fastnet Rock (AUS) 127 – On The Nile (IRE) 103 **–** (Sadler's Wells (USA) 132) [2015 80: 10m May 25] rangy, attractive gelding: fair handicapper in 2014, well held only outing in 2015: stays 11.5f: best effort on good to firm going: tried in blinkers. *David Nicholls*

STORM RISING (IRE) 2 b.c. (Feb 27) Canford Cliffs (IRE) 133 – Before The Storm 78 **97** (Sadler's Wells (USA) 132) [2015 7s* 7s* 7g⁵ Oct 21] 60,000Y: good-topped colt: sixth foal: half-brother to winner up to 1m Mr Majeika (2-y-o 5f winner, by Oasis Dream) and 9.5f/1¼m winner (stays 1¾m) Landau (by Aussie Rules): dam, maiden (stayed 1m), half-sister to useful performer up to 14.6f Valentine Girl: useful form: won at Newbury in August (maiden, by 1¾ lengths from In The Red) and September (nursery, by 3 lengths from Missy Blue Eyes): well held in minor event at Newmarket final start: raced only at 7f. *Richard Hannon*

STORM ROCK 3 b.c. Rock of Gibraltar (IRE) 133 – Seasonal Cross 80 (Cape Cross **110** (IRE) 129) [2015 85p: 10.3d³ 8s³ 8g 8g⁵ 8.3s* 8.3s² t8.6m Nov 28] smart handicapper: won at Leicester in October by 2¾ lengths from Pintura: improved again when second at Nottingham (neck behind You're Fired) in November: stays 8.5f: acts on soft going. *Harry Dunlop*

STORM RUNNER (IRE) 7 b.g. Rakti 130 – Saibhreas (IRE) 83 (Last Tycoon 131) **47** [2015 70: p8g⁴ t8.6f³ p8m⁵ t8.6g² p10m 8.3g⁵ p10g⁶ 9.9d⁴ 10.1g p10m² t8.6g⁴ p8g* Dec 9] **a68** fair handicapper: won at Lingfield (apprentice) in December: stays 1¼m: acts on polytrack and good to soft going: tried in headgear. *George Margarson*

STORM THE STARS (USA) 3 b.c. Sea The Stars (IRE) 140 – Love Me Only (IRE) **123** (Sadler's Wells (USA) 132) [2015 103p: 10m⁵ 10m* 12.3s² 11g* 12m³ 12m² 11.9m³ 12d* 14.6d⁴ Sep 12]

The racing character of Gleneagles was frequently likened in the first part of the season to that of 'The Iron Horse' Giant's Causeway by the man who trained them both at Ballydoyle. Giant's Causeway ran ten times for Aidan O'Brien as a three-year-old, recording five Group 1 victories, and there wasn't a top horse that season who could outscore him for toughness. However, while Gleneagles eventually ended up spending most of the latest summer on the sidelines, Giant's Causeway had kept his form for the best part of seven months in 2000 without a break and without a single easy race. The making of comparisons between Gleneagles and Giant's Causeway stemmed originally from the fact that You'resthrilling, the dam of Gleneagles, is a sister to Giant's Causeway. However, there was another relative of Giant's Causeway who, in terms of resilience at least, was a closer parallel. Storm The Stars, whose dam is an unraced half-sister to Giant's Causeway and You'resthrilling, may not have been in the same league as Gleneagles or Giant's Causeway as a racehorse but he was as tough as teak and in similar mould to Giant's Causeway when it came to holding his form through a testing campaign.

Storm The Stars appeared nine times between mid-April, when fifth in a Newmarket maiden, and mid-September, when he finished a non-staying fourth behind Simple Verse in the St Leger. In between, he was never out of the first three in pattern and listed company, showing himself to be thoroughly genuine and consistent and gaining the most important of his three victories in the Great Voltigeur Stakes at York in August, after reaching a place in three of the season's top races for middle-distance three-year-olds, the Derby, the Irish Derby and the Grand Prix de Paris. The fact that he held every chance at one stage in all of those races, but proved no match for the winner in any of them, illustrated the gap between him and the top middle-distance horses. It was undoubtedly one of the reasons behind the decision to send Storm The Stars to Australia to continue his racing career with Chris Waller. He showed himself completely at home on firmish going at Epsom, the Curragh and Longchamp, which will stand him in good stead Down Under where he should do well.

After a comfortable victory in a maiden at Leicester on his second outing of the season, Storm The Stars earned his place in the Derby field with a staying-on second to the O'Brien-trained Hans Holbein in the Chester Vase, followed by victory in a tactical Cocked Hat Stakes (once the Predominate Stakes) at Goodwood. Interestingly, Storm The Stars and Golden Horn had already met as two-year-olds in a maiden at Nottingham when pulling a long way clear, with Storm The Stars sent off at even money after a promising debut at Newmarket and going down by a head to newcomer Golden Horn. Ideally positioned from the start in a truly-run Derby, Storm The Stars had every chance and put up a fine effort to finish third to Golden Horn and Jack Hobbs, albeit beaten eight lengths by the outstanding winner. A repeat of that form saw him finish a clear-cut runner-up to Jack Hobbs at the Curragh where he again finished ahead of Ballydoyle's selected representatives. Having his third outing in Group 1 company in a little over five weeks, Storm The Stars didn't quite match his Derby and Irish Derby form when third to Erupt and Ampere in the Grand Prix de Paris, but he kept himself firmly in the St Leger picture with a game victory over Bondi Beach and five others in the Betway Great Voltigeur Stakes at what turned out to be a splendid York Ebor meeting for his stable, which had five winners and completed the big Gimcrack/Lowther two-year-old double with Ajaya and Besharah (every race at the four-day fixture carried at least £50,000 in prize money and attendances were up ten per cent). Storm The Stars had to survive a stewards' inquiry before being confirmed the winner of the Voltigeur in which he carried Bondi Beach across the track inside the final furlong, beating him by half a length with the pair clear (Pat Cosgrave was given a three-day suspension for careless riding on the

Betway Great Voltigeur Stakes, York—Derby third Storm The Stars (left) has to survive a televised stewards' inquiry after carrying Bondi Beach across the track inside the final furlong; the pair finish clear of the latter's stablemate Giovanni Canaletto (striped cap) and Tashaar

Sheikh Juma Dalmook Al Maktoum's "Storm The Stars"

winner). Storm The Stars started joint favourite for the St Leger with Bondi Beach but, after moving like the best horse in the race for most of the way, his stamina ran out in the final furlong after he had briefly stretched a couple of lengths clear. He lost third, behind Simple Verse and Bondi Beach, to Fields of Athenry right on the line.

		Sea The Stars (IRE) (b 2006)	Cape Cross (b 1994)	Green Desert
Storm The Stars (USA) (b.c. 2012)				Park Appeal
			Urban Sea (ch 1989)	Miswaki
				Allegretta
		Love Me Only (IRE) (b 2008)	Sadler's Wells (b 1981)	Northern Dancer
				Fairy Bridge
			Mariah's Storm (b 1991)	Rahy
				Immense

The sturdy Storm The Stars kept his sire's name in lights, although the much smaller second crop of three-year-olds by Sea The Stars to reach the racecourse produced nothing to compare with the pick of his first crop, the classic winners Taghrooda and Sea The Moon. The fluctuations in the number of mares Sea The Stars has covered since being retired to stud in 2010 illustrate the part played by fashion—he covered 136 mares in his first year, 83 in his second, 138 in his third, 96 in his fourth, 118 in his fifth and 159 in his sixth (after Taghrooda's and Sea the Moon's three-year-old achievements). Storm The Stars is the first foal out of the Sadler's Wells mare Love Me Only and there is more about her family in the essay on Gleneagles. Storm The Stars has shown his best form at around a mile and a half, and he acts on good to firm and good to soft going. He races prominently.
William Haggas

STORMY ANTARCTIC 2 ch.c. (Feb 24) Stormy Atlantic (USA) – Bea Remembered **115**
105 (Doyen (IRE) 132) [2015 6g³ 6f³ 7.1g* 8s* 7s² Nov 1] 68,000F, 200,000 2-y-o: well-
made colt: first foal: dam 1m-10.3f winner: smart form: won maiden at Sandown (by 2¼
lengths from Lovell) in August and minor event at Newbury (by 1½ lengths from Special
Season, slowly away, quickening to lead final 1f) in September: further improvement when
head second of 8 to Johannes Vermeer in Criterium International at Saint-Cloud final start,
not settling fully but keeping on well: stays 1m: acts on soft going. *Ed Walker*

STORMY ART (IRE) 2 b.g. (Apr 11) Excellent Art 125 – Maybe Grace (IRE) 104 **64**
(Hawk Wing (USA) 136) [2015 5m⁶ 6d Oct 19] leggy, close-coupled gelding: better effort
in maidens when sixth of 10 at Haydock. *Michael Dods*

STORMY MORNING 9 ch.g. Nayef (USA) 129 – Sokoa (USA) (Peintre Celebre (USA) **–**
137) [2015 57, a70: t13.9g Jun 3] sturdy gelding: modest handicapper: stays 16.5f: acts on
polytrack, tapeta and any turf going: wears cheekpieces. *Philip Kirby*

STORMY PARADISE (IRE) 4 br.g. Excellent Art 125 – Stormy Larissa (IRE) 79 **–**
(Royal Applause 124) [2015 –: p8f⁵ p8g p10g Mar 12] compact gelding: useful at 2 yrs,
little impact in just 4 outings since: stays 1m: acts on polytrack, good to firm and good to
soft going: tried in blinkers. *Brian Meehan*

STORYTALE 3 ch.g. Rip Van Winkle (IRE) 134 – Night Haven 99 (Night Shift (USA)) **49**
[2015 –p: p7g⁶ 6g 10.2f⁴ Aug 12] poor maiden: stays 1¼m: tried in hood. *Michael Bell*

STOSUR (IRE) 4 b.f. Mount Nelson 125 – Jules (IRE) 76 (Danehill (USA) 126) [2015 98: **90**
p7m p7f 8.3m² 9.9d⁵ 10.3g⁵ 8g⁶ 8m⁵ 11.9m³ 8m* 8g³ 8m t12.2m p10m³ Dec 16] sturdy
mare: fairly useful handicapper: won at Bath in July: stays 1½m: acts on polytrack,
tapeta, good to firm and heavy going: wears headgear: front runner/races prominently.
Gay Kelleway

STOUT CORTEZ 4 b.g. Hernando (FR) 127 – Zooming (IRE) (Indian Ridge 123) [2015 **67 §**
70§: 11.9d⁴ Sep 25] fair maiden: creditable fourth in handicap at Haydock only outing in
2015: stays 1¾m: acts on good to firm and heavy going: front runner/races prominently:
has awkward head carriage, best treated with caution. *Malcolm Jefferson*

ST PATRICK'S DAY (IRE) 3 b.c. Fastnet Rock (AUS) 127 – Race For The Stars (USA) **75**
113 (Fusaichi Pegasus (USA) 130) [2015 75p: p10f t8.6f* Dec 14] fair performer: in first-
time visor, won maiden at Wolverhampton in December: stays 8.5f: acts on tapeta and good
to firm going: signs of temperament. *J. R. Jenkins*

ST PAUL'S SQUARE (IRE) 3 b.g. Amadeus Wolf 122 – Swynford Lady (IRE) **58**
(Invincible Spirit (IRE) 121) [2015 –: t8.6f p7m² t7.1f⁵ p7m⁵ p6f⁴ t6g³ t7.1m³ t6f⁴ p6g² 8f
7m⁵ 8m Jul 22] modest maiden: left Jamie Osborne after eighth start: stays 7f: acts on
polytrack, tapeta and good to firm going: often in blinkers: often races prominently.
Chris Gordon

STRADATER (IRE) 6 b.g. Catcher In The Rye (IRE) 115 – Starring Role (IRE) (Glenstal **51**
(USA) 118) [2015 64: f8d* f8g⁴ p10m⁶ 8g 8d⁵ 9.9g 10g Sep 8] fair handicapper: won at **a70**
Southwell in January: left Richard Guest after fifth start: stays 1m: acts on fibresand and
good to soft going: sometimes in headgear: front runner/races prominently. *Nigel Tinkler*

STRADUFF (IRE) 2 b.g. (Jan 14) Kodiac 112 – She's A Minx (IRE) (Linamix (FR) 127) **–**
[2015 5.3s⁴ May 29] 10/1, green when fourth of 6 to Art Collection in maiden at Brighton:
has been gelded. *J. S. Moore*

STRAIGHT ARROW 3 b.g. Refuse To Bend (IRE) 128 – Spring Goddess (IRE) 89 **68**
(Daggers Drawn (USA) 114) [2015 p7g⁶ 8g 8.3g 8m* 8.3g⁶ Aug 3] close-coupled gelding:
fair performer: won handicap at Wetherby in July: should stay further than 1m: acts on
good to firm going: sometimes slowly away. *Timothy Jarvis*

STRAIGHT GIN 4 b.g. Major Cadeaux 121 – Nee Lemon Left 60 (Puissance 110) [2015 **–**
50: 5s³ 6g May 26] poor maiden: best form at 5f: acts on heavy going: sometimes wears
headgear/tongue tie: front runner/races prominently. *Alan Berry*

STRAIGHTOTHEPOINT 3 b.g. Kyllachy 129 – Choisette 75 (Choisir (AUS) 126) **89**
[2015 79: 6g² 6d* 5.5g² 5.4m⁶ 6m⁴ 5.5m² 5s² 6g 6m² 6g 6s⁵ p6m Nov 17] small gelding:
fairly useful handicapper: won at Leicester in June: stays 6f: acts on soft and good to firm
going: sometimes wears headgear: front runner/races prominently. *Bryan Smart*

STRAIT OF MAGELLAN (IRE) 3 ch.g. Captain Rio 122 – Golden (FR) (Sanglamore **89**
(USA) 126) [2015 –: p10m² 10.2m² 12m 11.5g² p12g² 12.1d² p12f² 10.1g² 12s* 12v³
Oct 17] tall gelding: fairly useful handicapper: won at Bath in June and Catterick in
October: stays 1½m: acts on polytrack, good to firm and heavy going: usually in headgear
in 2015: often travels strongly. *Michael Bell*

STRAIT RUN (IRE) 4 ch.g. Rock of Gibraltar (IRE) 133 – Gentlemen's Guest (USA) **57**
(Gentlemen (ARG) 136) [2015 81: 12g 12m 10m 8m 12m 11.1s³ 12d 10m 13.8v Oct 17]
well-made handicapper: modest handicapper: stays 11f: acts on good to firm and heavy going:
often races in rear. *Micky Hammond*

STRAITS OF MALACCA 4 ch.g. Compton Place 125 – Cultural Role 95 (Night Shift **85 §**
(USA)) [2015 78: 6d² 6m 6m* p6g 6m 6m 5g⁵ 6m 5d 5g 5g⁶ 5s Oct 19] lengthy, good-
quartered gelding: fairly useful handicapper: won at Thirsk in May: stays 6f: acts on soft
and good to firm going: often in headgear in 2015: untrustworthy. *Kevin Ryan*

STRANDS OF SILK (IRE) 2 b.f. (Mar 19) Kodiac 112 – Saldenaera (GER) (Areion **75**
(GER) 115) [2015 5g* 5m 6f 5.1m⁴ 5g³ 5g* 5g p5f⁵ f5g Dec 18] €11,000F, £24,000Y:
rather leggy filly: first foal: dam German 5f winner: fair performer: won maiden at
Doncaster in May and nursery at Newcastle in August: best form at 5f on good going: in
hood last 4 starts: sometimes slowly away. *James Given*

STRATEGIC FORCE (IRE) 4 b.g. Strategic Prince 114 – Mooching Along (IRE) **91**
(Mujahid (USA) 125) [2015 79, a95: t6g⁴ p6m³ 7.1m³ 7m 6m³ 6m² 6m p6g³ p6f⁴ p6g⁵ p7g⁶
p6g⁵ Dec 11] tall, quite attractive gelding: fairly useful handicapper: effective at 6f/7f: acts
on polytrack, tapeta and good to firm going: often wears headgear: not straightforward.
G. O'Leary, Ireland

STRATEGIC ORDER (IRE) 3 b.g. Strategic Prince 114 – Glencoagh Order (IRE) **53**
(Danehill (USA) 126) [2015 53: 6s⁴ 5m 6g⁴ 6s⁴ 6s⁶ 7g⁴ 7m⁶ 9.9g⁶ Aug 30] modest maiden:
stays 7f: acts on soft and good to firm going: often in headgear in 2015: consistent.
Paul Midgley

STRATEGISE (IRE) 3 ch.f. Strategic Prince 114 – Fikrah 92 (Medicean 128) [2015 53: **–**
t8.6f Jan 5] poor maiden: stays 6f: acts on tapeta, soft and good to firm going: in cheekpieces
of late. *Daniel Loughnane*

STRATH BURN 3 b.c. Equiano (FR) 127 – Irish Light (USA) 91 (Irish River (FR) 131) **123**
[2015 106: 6f 5m³ 6m* 6m* 6d² 6d Oct 17] good-topped colt: very smart performer: won
maiden at Doncaster (by ¾ length from Tap Shoes) and Hackwood Stakes at Newbury (by
length from Portamento), both in July: further marked improvement when short-head

Qatar Racing Limited & R A Bartlett's "Strath Burn"

second of 15 to Twilight Son in Sprint Cup at Haydock, keeping on well from off the pace (drifted left): reportedly finished lame when well held final outing: stays 6f: acts on good to firm and good to soft going. *Charles Hills*

STRATHEARN (IRE) 2 b.g. (Feb 25) Halling (USA) 133 – Polska (USA) 103 (Danzig **70** (USA)) [2015 7m 7.4g² 7.5m⁵ 8.3g⁴ 8g⁵ 9g p8f² Nov 23] rather unfurnished gelding: fair maiden: should stay 1¼m: acts on polytrack, best turf form on good going: often races prominently. *Michael Bell*

STRATUM 2 b.c. (Feb 19) Dansili 127 – Lunar Phase (IRE) 79 (Galileo (IRE) 134) [2015 **70 p** 7d Oct 30] close-coupled colt: first foal: dam, 8.3f winner who stayed 1½m, closely related to useful French 1¼m-13f winner Messager du Roi: 14/1, green when 2½ lengths eighth of 13 to Chelsea Lad in maiden at Newmarket on debut, keeping on without being knocked about: will be suited by 1m: sure to progress. *John Gosden*

STRAVAGANTE (IRE) 3 b.c. Rip Van Winkle (IRE) 134 – Star Ruby (IRE) 109 (Rock **106** of Gibraltar (IRE) 133) [2015 86p: 10d³ 10.1m* 12fᵖᵘ Jun 19] good-topped colt: useful performer: won handicap at Epsom (by 3¼ lengths from Gibeon, value extra) in June: 11/4, pulled up in King Edward VII Stakes at Royal Ascot: stayed 1¼m: acted on good to firm going: sometimes slowly away, usually raced nearer last than first: dead. *Sir Michael Stoute*

STRAWBERRYFIELDS 3 ch.f. Three Valleys (USA) 119 – Crossed Wire 77 (Lycius **–** (USA) 124) [2015 6m⁶ t7.1f p8g⁴ Dec 2] fifth foal: half-sister to useful 5f/6f winner Liberty Lady (by Statue of Liberty): dam, 10.5f-15f winner, sister to useful winner up to 7.5f winner Roman Maze: no form. *Des Donovan*

STRAWBERRY MARTINI 4 ch.f. Mount Nelson 125 – Strawberry Lolly 89 (Lomitas **91** 129) [2015 81, a89: 12m⁵ 14m* 12g 13.4m 17.5g 14.1s⁶ p14f⁵ Nov 7] tall filly: fairly useful handicapper: won at Sandown (by 6 lengths from Satellite) in July: stays 2m: acts on polytrack, tapeta, soft and good to firm going: front runner/races prominently. *William Muir*

STRAWBERRY SORBET 2 b.f. (Mar 27) Street Cry (IRE) 130 – Strawberrydaiquiri **75 p** 119 (Dansili 127) [2015 p7g⁶ 8.3g p7g³ p8g³ Dec 15] 125,000Y: first foal: dam 1m/9f winner: fair maiden: best effort at 1m: open to further improvement. *Clive Cox*

STREAM OF LIGHT 4 b.f. Multiplex 114 – Flawspar (Montjoy (USA) 122) [2015 t9.5f **–** Feb 7] poor maiden. *John Mackie*

STREET ART (IRE) 3 ch.g. Excellent Art 125 – Via Aurelia (IRE) 66 (Antonius Pius **62** (USA) 123) [2015 8.3m t8.6g p10g⁵ p12g p12g* t12.2m² Dec 18] modest performer: won handicap at Kempton in November: stays 1½m: acts on polytrack and tapeta: tried in tongue tie. *Mike Murphy*

STREET ARTIST (IRE) 5 ch.g. Street Cry (IRE) 130 – Portrayal (USA) 114 (Saint **97** Ballado (CAN)) [2015 94: f12s* t13.9g* Jan 15] useful performer: won claimers at Southwell (by 3 lengths from Reve de Nuit) and Wolverhampton (by 2½ lengths from Media Hype) in January: stays 1¾m: acts on all-weather (best efforts on fibresand) and good to soft going: tried in blinkers: front runner/races prominently. *David Nicholls*

STREET DUEL (USA) 2 b.c. (Apr 23) Street Cry (IRE) 130 – Fifth Avenue Doll (USA) **78** (Marquetry (USA) 121) [2015 7g⁴ 7m² 7m² p8g² Aug 26] fair maiden: runner-up at Brighton, Newcastle and Kempton: stays 1m. *Mark Johnston*

STREET ENTERTAINER (IRE) 8 br.g. Danehill Dancer (IRE) 117 – Opera Ridge **80** (FR) (Indian Ridge 123) [2015 14.1m³ 14.1g² Aug 21] lengthy gelding: fairly useful handicapper: stays 1¾m: acts on polytrack and good to firm going: wears headgear/tongue tie: quirky: useful hurdler. *David Pipe*

STREET FORCE (USA) 4 b.c. Street Cry (IRE) 130 – Maskunah (IRE) (Sadler's Wells **71** (USA) 132) [2015 –: f8d f6s³ f7d* f6g³ 8g 7d⁶ 17.1g⁶ 6.1m f8d⁶ t8.6g* t7.1g* f7f t7.1m³ **a91** Dec 26] good-topped colt: fairly useful performer: won maiden at Southwell in February and handicaps at Wolverhampton in November and December: stays 8.5f: acts on fibresand, tapeta and firm going: usually wears headgear/tongue tie. *Michael Appleby*

STREET OUTLAW (IRE) 2 b.g. (Apr 22) Haatef (USA) 117 – Helen Wells (IRE) 72 **–** (Sadler's Wells (USA) 132) [2015 7.2g Sep 18] 80/1, last of 8 in maiden at Ayr, slowly away. *Ronald Thompson*

STREETS OF NEWYORK 8 b.g. Dalakhani (IRE) 133 – Minute Waltz (Sadler's Wells **76** (USA) 132) [2015 16s³ Apr 5] well-made gelding: fair handicapper: stays 2m: acts on fibresand, good to firm and good to soft going: tried in cheekpieces. *Brian Ellison*

STRICTLY ART (IRE) 2 b.g. (Mar 17) Excellent Art 125 – Sadinga (IRE) 85 (Sadler's **68** Wells (USA) 132) [2015 p6f⁶ f7g* Nov 24] fair form: much better effort when winning claimer at Southwell in November: will be suited by at least 1m. *Alan Bailey*

STRICTLY CARTER 2 b.g. (Mar 22) Multiplex 114 – Compolina (Compton Place 125) **66**
[2015 t6g5 f5g4 6m2 6g 6m p5m3 t5.1f6 Dec 11] sturdy gelding: fair maiden: acts
on polytrack, tapeta and good to firm going: tried in cheekpieces: sometimes slowly away,
often races prominently. *Alan Bailey*

STRICTLY GLITZ (IRE) 4 b.f. Kodiac 112 – Dancing Steps (Zafonic (USA) 130) **–**
[2015 8.3g6 8d f8g Dec 12] fair at best, no form in 2015: tried in cheekpieces. *Mike Sowersby*

STRICTLY THE ONE (IRE) 5 b.g. Robin des Pres (FR) – Rita's Charm (IRE) (Arctic **63**
Lord 114) [2015 13.1m* 13.1m 13.1m Sep 28] modest handicapper: won at Bath in July:
stays 13f: acts on polytrack and good to firm going: in blinkers/tongue tie in 2015: often
races towards rear. *Neil Mulholland*

STRIDING OUT (IRE) 3 b.f. Cape Cross (IRE) 129 – Honours Stride (IRE) 81 (Red **73**
Ransom (USA)) [2015 79p: 12m6 9.2d* 9f Oct 11] fair performer: won maiden at Hamilton
in June: left David Simcock 30,000 gns after: should prove suited by 1¼m. *Simon
Callaghan, USA*

STRIKE A LIGHT 4 gr.f. Dutch Art 126 – Bridal Path 75 (Groom Dancer (USA) 128) **–**
[2015 81: 7.6d6 7d 7s Oct 15] fairly useful at best, no form in 2015: stays 7f: acts on soft
going. *Rae Guest*

STRIKEMASTER (IRE) 9 b.g. Xaar 132 – Mas A Fuera (IRE) (Alzao (USA) 117) [2015 **54**
15.8m4 16m 15.8m 16m2 16.1g Sep 4] leggy gelding: modest handicapper: stays 2¼m: acts
on polytrack, good to firm and heavy going: wears tongue tie: often starts slowly, often races towards rear. *Lee James*

STRIKING STONE 3 ch.g. Archipenko (USA) 127 – Lady Le Quesne (IRE) 78 (Alhaarth **43**
(IRE) 126) [2015 –: f7g p7f4 t6m5 f8s4 8m 7s t6g Jun 29] smallish gelding: poor maiden:
left Jo Hughes after second start: stays 7f: acts on polytrack and fibresand: often wears
headgear. *Michael Appleby*

STROBE 11 ch.g. Fantastic Light (USA) 134 – Sadaka (USA) 77 (Kingmambo (USA) 125) **–**
[2015 12.1g 15s Aug 8] good-bodied gelding: modest handicapper: stays 17f: acts on
polytrack and good to firm going: wears cheekpieces: front runner/races prominently.
Lucy Normile

STROKE OF MIDNIGHT (IRE) 2 b.f. (Jan 29) Dark Angel (IRE) 113 – Timbre **70**
(Dubai Destination (USA) 127) [2015 5g6 5m2 5g2 6g2 6.1s2 6d 6d 5d6 t7.1f Oct 20]
€45,000Y: angular filly: first foal: dam unraced half-sister to useful performer up to 1½m
Ustura out of smart performer up to 1¼m Calando: fair maiden: stays 6f: acts on soft and
good to firm going: tried in blinkers: front runner/races prominently: sold 8,000 gns, sent
to France. *Richard Hannon*

STROLL PATROL 3 b.f. Mount Nelson 125 – Maid For Winning (USA) (Gone West **109**
(USA)) [2015 100: 7v 7m 6.3m* 6m4 6g4 p6g5 6g Oct 10] strong filly: useful performer:
won handicap at the Curragh in July by ¾ length from Your Pal Tal: good fourth to
Moviesta in Renaissance Stakes at the Curragh fifth start: stays 6.5f: acts on good to firm
going. *John Patrick Murtagh, Ireland*

STRONG CHALLENGE (IRE) 2 ch.c. (Apr 20) Exceed And Excel (AUS) 126 – Miss **98 p**
Brief (IRE) 72 (Brief Truce (USA) 126) [2015 5s2 6g* 7g Jul 28] 200,000F: good sort:
seventh foal: brother to useful winner up to 7f Crown Prosecutor (2-y-o 6f winner), closely
related to smart 5f/6f winner Riskit Fora Biskit (by Kodiac) and half-brother to useful
2-y-o 6f winner Fox Trotter (by Bushranger): dam, sprint maiden, half-sister to smart
sprinter Guinea Hunter: useful form: won maiden at Goodwood in June by 1¾ lengths from
Gutaifan: run best excused when well held in Vintage Stakes at Goodwood final start,
pulling too hard upped in trip: will prove best at sprint distances: remains open to
improvement. *Saeed bin Suroor*

STRONG CHEMISTRY 3 b.g. Oasis Dream 129 – Mambo Light (USA) 105 **104 §**
(Kingmambo (USA) 125) [2015 100p: 7m2 7m4 8m 7m Jul 18] good-topped gelding: useful
handicapper: good second to Desert Force at Newbury on reappearance: subsequently lost
his way, looking temperamental, and gelded after final start: stays 7f: acts on polytrack and
good to firm going: in hood last 2 starts: headstrong: one to avoid. *Charlie Appleby*

STRONG CONVICTION 5 ch.g. Piccolo 121 – Keeping The Faith (IRE) 88 (Ajraas **–**
(USA) 88) [2015 7.6s Aug 15] good-quartered gelding: modest handicapper nowadays:
stays 1¼m: acts on polytrack, good to firm and heavy going: has worn headgear: front
runner/races prominently. *Simon Hodgson*

STRONG MAN 7 b.g. Gentleman's Deal (IRE) 114 – Strong Hand 99 (First Trump 118) **87** [2015 82: 7m⁵ 8.5g² 8.5m 7.9g³ 8.5m* Jul 14] fairly useful handicapper: won at Beverley in July: stays 8.5f: acts on polytrack, fibresand, soft and good to firm going: often in blinkers prior to 2015: tried in tongue tie: front runner/races prominently: consistent. *Michael Easterby*

STRONG STEPS 3 br.g. Aqlaam 125 – Wunders Dream (IRE) 107 (Averti (IRE) 117) **97** [2015 p8g² p8f* 8.1m⁵ 10d² p8g² 8g³ 8g p8g⁴ p10m⁵ 8d Oct 16] 50,000F, 40,000Y: good-topped gelding: closely related to winner abroad by Oasis Dream and half-brother to several winners, including useful winner up to 6.5f Inyordreams (2-y-o 6f winner by Teofilo) and useful 2-y-o 5f winner Fire Eyes (by Exceed And Excel): dam 2-y-o 5f winner, including Flying Childers Stakes: useful performer: won maiden at Chelmsford (by short head from Yamllik) in April: better form in handicaps, particularly when third at Goodwood and fourth at Kempton: stays 1m: acts on polytrack: wears headgear: front runner/races prominently: has been gelded. *Hugo Palmer*

STRUCTURED NOTE (IRE) 3 b.c. Acclamation 118 – Saik (USA) (Riverman (USA) **63** 131) [2015 67: 7d 7d⁴ 7.9v⁶ t9.5g Jun 26] modest maiden: stays 1m: acts on heavy going. *Jedd O'Keeffe*

STRUMMER (IRE) 2 b.g. (Feb 22) Frozen Power (IRE) 108 – Question (USA) 56 **70** (Coronado's Quest (USA) 130) [2015 5.9g⁶ 6g² 5.9g² 7m⁵ 6g⁵ Oct 8] fair maiden: stays 7f: acts on good to firm going. *Kevin Ryan*

ST SAVIOUR 3 b.g. Danehill Dancer (IRE) 117 – Titivation 83 (Montjeu (IRE) 137) **89** [2015 –p: 10g³ 9g³ 8.1g⁴ 9.9v* 10v⁵ 10d⁶ Oct 12] tall gelding: fairly useful performer: won maiden at Brighton in August: stays 1¼m: acts on heavy going: front runner/races prominently: sold 20,000 gns and joined Philip Hobbs: useful hurdler. *Andrew Balding*

STUBBINS 3 b.f. Rip Van Winkle (IRE) 134 – Skimmia (Mark of Esteem (IRE) 137) **82** [2015 54: 10m² 12.1g² 11.8m² 12d 12m* 11.9g 11.9d² Dec 11] good-topped filly: fairly useful performer: won maiden at Epsom in July: left John Gosden after fifth start: stays 1½m: acts on good to firm and good to soft going: sometimes in cheekpieces: usually races close up. *H-A. Pantall, France*

STUDFARMER 5 b.g. Multiplex 114 – Samadilla (IRE) 83 (Mujadil (USA) 119) [2015 **53** 56: t6g⁶ p6f* p5m³ p6m t7.1f³ 7m⁶ 5.1m⁵ May 30] rather leggy gelding: modest handicapper: won at Kempton in January: best at 5f/6f: acts on polytrack, soft and good to firm going: often wears headgear: sold £1,800, sent to Germany, where won 6f handicap at Hamburg in July. *Polly Gundry*

STUDIO STAR 3 ch.g. Showcasing 117 – Forrest Star 57 (Fraam 114) [2015 66: t6m f5d⁴ **54** 5d 5g³ 6m 5m 5f 5g² 5s Oct 6] modest handicapper: stays 6f: acts on fibresand, good to firm and good to soft going: usually wears cheekpieces: tried in tongue tie in 2015. *Ollie Pears*

STUN GUN 5 b.g. Medicean 128 – Tapas En Bal (FR) (Mille Balles (FR) 124) [2015 63: **60 §** p7g f6d³ f7g² f7g* t7.1f f7g⁶ 7m⁶ 7.5g 7d 7m* 7m 7d⁶ 8m² 7g⁶ f8g³ f7g p8g⁶ t8.6g⁴ t8.6f⁴ t8.6f Dec 21] modest handicapper: won at Southwell in March and Leicester in June: stays 8.5f: acts on all-weather and good to firm going: wears headgear: unreliable. *Derek Shaw*

STUNNED 4 b.g. Shamardal (USA) 129 – Amazed 58 (Clantime 101) [2015 p5g* p6g³ **96** p5m³ p5g² 5m⁶ 6f a6f² Dec 11] strong gelding: useful performer: won maiden at Chelmsford in April: placed in handicaps after, on same course (3 times) and Jebel Ali: left Robert Cowell after sixth start: races mainly at 6f: acts on polytrack: in cheekpieces last 4 starts in Britain. *D. Watson, UAE*

STYLISH BOY 2 b.c. (Mar 27) Paco Boy (IRE) 129 – Black Baroness (Ishiguru (USA) **76** 114) [2015 6m³ 7.2s² 7m³ 7.2g⁴ 6.3d Sep 13] fair maiden: will stay 1m: acts on soft and good to firm going: tried in blinkers. *Richard Fahey*

STYLISH MINERVA 2 b.f. (Apr 19) Paco Boy (IRE) 129 – Lady In The Bath (Forzando **67** 122) [2015 6g³ 6d⁵ 6d t6f Oct 16] lengthy, rather unfurnished filly: third foal: half-sister to 6f winner Especial (by Misu Bond): dam ran once on Flat/over hurdles: fair maiden, best effort on debut: raced only at 6f. *Richard Hannon*

STYLISTIK 2 ch.f. (Apr 12) Sakhee's Secret 128 – Passing Hour (USA) 80 (Red Ransom **73** (USA)) [2015 6m³ 6m* 7m² 7g Oct 10] leggy filly: fifth foal: half-sister to 5f (including at 2 yrs)/6f winner Sixty Minutes (by Compton Place) and 7f/1m winner Passing Star (by Royal Applause), both useful: dam, 1m winner, sister to Queen Mary Stakes winner Shining Hour: fair performer: won maiden at Windsor in August: stays 7f. *Luke Dace*

STYNES (IRE) 5 b.g. Aussie Rules (USA) 123 – Magic Princess 62 (Bahhare (USA) 122) **50**
[2015 p10.7g p12.7g p10f Dec 21] modest maiden: left John McConnell after second start:
stays 1½m: acts on polytrack, good to firm and good to soft going: tried in headgear prior
to 2015: wears tongue tie. *Ali Stronge*

SUBCONTINENT (IRE) 3 b.g. Dubawi (IRE) 129 – Saree 95 (Barathea (IRE) 127) **97**
[2015 80: t9.5f² t8.6m* 10.3m* 10f* 11.9g⁶ 10.3m² 10.4g³ p10m Sep 26] useful-looking
colt: useful performer: won maiden at Wolverhampton in March and handicaps at
Doncaster in April and at Windsor in May: best effort when second in minor event at
Doncaster (2¼ lengths behind Exosphere) in June: stays 10.5f: acts on tapeta and firm
going: usually races close up. *Charlie Appleby*

SUBLIMATION (IRE) 5 ch.g. Manduro (GER) 135 – Meon Mix 61 (Kayf Tara 130) **71**
[2015 –: 10m² 9d⁴ 8.3m⁵ 8.3m⁴ 10s⁶ 10d* Oct 26] small gelding: fair performer: won seller
at Redcar in October: left Ian Williams after first start: stays 1¼m: acts on good to firm and
heavy going: often races prominently. *Steve Gollings*

SUBSTANTIVO (IRE) 5 b.g. Duke of Marmalade (IRE) 132 – Damson (IRE) 113 **62 §**
(Entrepreneur 123) [2015 71§: p7f³ p7g³ p7g 8.3g Jun 15] strong gelding: modest maiden:
stays 1m: acts on polytrack and good to firm going: often races towards rear: quirky.
Timothy Jarvis

SUBTLE KNIFE 6 ch.m. Needwood Blade 117 – Northern Bows (Bertolini (USA) 125) **91**
[2015 85: p8g² p8g⁵ p8g³ p8g³ p8g² f8g⁴ p8g* 7.6d* 7m⁶ p8m³ p8g⁶ 8g⁴ 7.6v* 7d 8g 8d **a84**
p8g Dec 7] rather leggy mare: fairly useful handicapper: won at Chelmsford in April and at
Lingfield in May and August (by 5 lengths from Alfajer): stays 1m: acts on polytrack, good
to firm and heavy going: often races in rear. *Giles Bravery*

SUBVERSIVE (IRE) 3 b.g. Invincible Spirit (IRE) 121 – Persian Secret (FR) 101 **87**
(Persian Heights 129) [2015 76: t6g* p6g* t7.1g³ 6m⁵ 6f 6d² 6g² 6m² 7m⁴ 7m³ 6m⁶ 6.1m³
t6g⁶ p6f⁵ 7.1s p7g² p6f Oct 15] workmanlike gelding: fairly useful handicapper: won at
Wolverhampton and Lingfield in March: raced at 6f/7f: acts on polytrack, tapeta, good to
firm and good to soft going: tried in blinkers. *Mark Johnston*

SUCCESS DAYS (IRE) 3 gr.c. Jeremy (USA) 122 – Malaica (FR) 103 (Roi Gironde **114**
(IRE) 104) [2015 86: 8.5v* 10v* 10v* 12m 11.9s Nov 1] good-topped colt: third foal: dam
French winner up to 6f (2-y-o 5f/5.5f winner): smart performer: won minor event at Cork
and 3-runner Ballysax Stakes at Leopardstown (by 4½ lengths from Zafilani) in April, and
4-runner Derrinstown Stud Derby Trial at Leopardstown (by 10 lengths from Summaya) in
May: well below form last 2 starts, in Derby at Epsom (reportedly suffered a stress fracture
of near-fore) and Grosser Preis von Bayern at Munich (blinkered when last of 7 behind
Ito): stays 1¼m: acts on heavy going. *K. J. Condon, Ireland*

SUDDEN WISH (IRE) 6 b.m. Jeremy (USA) 122 – Fun Time 64 (Fraam 114) [2015 63: **60**
p10g p10m⁵ t12.2g⁶ 11.5d² p10m⁴ p12g⁵ p10g³ Dec 30] good-bodied mare: modest
handicapper: left Gary Moore after fourth start: stays 1½m: acts on polytrack, tapeta, soft
and good to firm going: has worn headgear, including often of late. *Paul Burgoyne*

SUDDYAN (IRE) 3 b.g. Holy Roman Emperor (IRE) 125 – Raydaniya (IRE) 78 (In The **96**
Wings 128) [2015 83p: 10f⁵ 7g⁵ 8.1g² Aug 21] good-topped gelding: useful form: left
Sir Michael Stoute after reappearance: in first-time cheekpieces, improved form when
head second to Chevallier in handicap at Sandown final start: stays 1m: sold 45,000 gns,
gelded and sent to Hong Kong, where renamed Best Reward. *Stuart Williams*

*P. W. McGrath Memorial Ballysax Stakes, Leopardstown—the first of two wide-margin successes
in classic trials for Success Days, who revels in the testing conditions; the two other runners
are Zafilani and the very disappointing, long odds-on favourite John F Kennedy*

SUEGIOO (FR) 6 ch.g. Manduro (GER) 135 – Mantesera (IRE) (In The Wings 128) [2015 **113** 110: 12g⁴ 18.7d 16.2g⁴ 16.1m⁵ 16.4m⁴ 14g³ 18m³ 16d⁶ Oct 17] angular gelding: smart performer: several creditable efforts in 2015, including when fifth in Northumberland Plate (Handicap) at Newcastle (1½ lengths behind Quest For More) and third in Ebor (Handicap) at York (1¾ lengths behind Litigant) and Doncaster Cup at Doncaster (1½ lengths behind Pallasator): stays 2¼m: acts on polytrack, good to firm and good to soft going: wears headgear: usually races nearer last than first: quirky sort. *Marco Botti*

SUFFOLK SKY 3 b.f. Pastoral Pursuits 127 – Charlevoix (IRE) 78 (King Charlemagne **61** (USA) 120) [2015 –: p6f⁴ p7g f7s p7g p8f² p8f⁴ Sep 17] modest maiden: stayed 1m: acted on polytrack: tried in blinkers: in tongue tie last 4 starts: often raced freely: dead. *Ed Vaughan*

SUFFUSED 3 ch.f. Champs Elysees 124 – Scuffle 106 (Daylami (IRE) 138) [2015 85p: **106** 8m⁴ 10m² 10m* 9.9m* 9.9m² 12d⁴ 10.1m⁴ Sep 16] sturdy filly: useful handicapper: won at Newbury (by 2¼ lengths from Dreamlike) in June and Salisbury (by 6 lengths from Serene Beauty) in July: good second in listed race at Salisbury (2¼ lengths behind Journey) in August: stays 1¼m: acts on good to firm going: front runner/races prominently, often travels strongly: sent to USA. *Roger Charlton*

SUGAR BOY (GER) 3 b.c. Areion (GER) 115 – Sugar Baby Love (GER) 99 (Second **92** Empire (IRE) 124) [2015 73p: t7.1m* 7m⁴ p7f³ 8.1m* 8f 7g Aug 1] useful-looking colt: fairly useful performer: won maiden at Wolverhampton in April and handicap at Sandown (dead-heated with Critical Risk) in May: well below form both subsequent starts: stays 1m: acts on tapeta and good to firm going: sent to UAE. *John Gosden*

SUGARFORMYHONEY (IRE) 6 ch.m. Dutch Art 126 – Sweetsformysweet (USA) **–** 63 (Forest Wildcat (USA) 120) [2015 73: 8g 8.3sʳʳ May 9] tall mare: fairly useful handicapper at best: well held on reappearance, in first-time blinkers when refused to race in apprentice event next time: stays 1m: acts on polytrack: has worn cheekpieces. *Jo Hughes*

SUGAR LUMP 3 b.g. Sakhee's Secret 128 – Icing 74 (Polar Falcon (USA) 126) [2015 **78 §** 78p: 6m⁶ 6f 7m 7g* 7g⁵ 7.6m 6s¹ 7m⁵ 7.2g 7d Oct 24] fair performer: won claimer at Redcar in June: left Richard Hannon after: stays 7.5f: acts on good to firm going: not one to trust. *Eric Alston*

SUGAR TOWN 5 b.m. Elusive City (USA) 117 – Sweetsformysweet (USA) 63 (Forest **55** Wildcat (USA) 120) [2015 61: 7m⁵ 7g³ t7.1f f7g⁵ f6g⁴ Nov 24] modest handicapper: stays 7f: acts on good to firm going: tried in cheekpieces: front runner/races prominently. *Peter Niven*

SUITOR 3 ch.g. Dutch Art 126 – Entreat 87 (Pivotal 124) [2015 8m⁴ 8.3m⁴ 7m⁵ 10.4g Sep **76** 6] tall colt: fair maiden: left Richard Hannon after second start: best effort at 8.5f. *Brian Ellison*

SUITSUS 4 b.g. Virtual 122 – Point Perfect (Dansili 127) [2015 71, a78: p6g⁶ p6g⁶ 6m 6g⁶ **69** 6s³ 7d⁵ Sep 14] fair handicapper: stays 6f: acts on polytrack, tapeta, soft and good to firm going: sometimes wears cheekpieces. *Peter Makin*

SUITS YOU (FR) 2 b.c. (Mar 29) Youmzain (IRE) 131 – Lady Fashion 107 (Oasis Dream **108 p** 129) [2015 6g* 7f* Jun 20] €12,000Y: good-topped colt: first foal: dam 7f winner: won maiden at Maisons-Laffitte (by 1½ lengths from Wootton's Walk) in May: better effort when winning Chesham Stakes at Royal Ascot (by short head from Ballydoyle) in June: will be suited by 1m: sent to Hong Kong, where renamed Sunny Way: open to further improvement. *E. J. O'Neill, France*

SULAALAAT 3 b.f. New Approach (IRE) 132 – Danehill Dreamer (USA) (Danehill **99** (USA) 126) [2015 96: 6m⁵ 8f⁵ 7m 7m* 7m Oct 3] good-topped filly: useful handicapper: won at Doncaster (by short head from Caprior Bere) in September: stays 7f: acts on firm going: blinkered last 2 starts: front runner/races prominently. *Brian Meehan*

SULTANA BELLE (IRE) 7 b.m. Black Sam Bellamy (IRE) 121 – Sultana (GER) (Law **–** Society (USA) 130) [2015 15s⁵ May 20] poor maiden, lightly raced on Flat: stays 15f: acts on heavy going: sometimes in cheekpieces: fair hurdler/chaser. *Stuart Crawford, Ireland*

SUMBAL (IRE) 3 b.c. Danehill Dancer (IRE) 117 – Alix Road (FR) 112 (Linamix (FR) **117** 127) [2015 9.9s* 9.9s* 9.9s* 10.4g⁵ 12.4d⁶ 9.9s² 10d Oct 17] €180,000Y: good-topped colt: third foal: half-brother to smart French 1m winner (stays 1½m) Lavender Lane (by Shamardal): dam French 1¼m-1½m winner: smart performer: won newcomers race at Saint-Cloud in March, minor event at Compiegne in April and Prix Greffulhe at Saint-Cloud (by 6 lengths from Untold Secret) in May: good second in Prix du Prince d'Orange at Longchamp (neck behind Karaktar) in September: below form when tenth to Fascinating Rock in Champion Stakes at Ascot final outing: should stay 1½m: acts on soft going. *Francis-Henri Graffard, France*

SUMEIDA (USA) 3 b.g. Street Sense (USA) 128 – Camargue (USA) (Mineshaft (USA) 132) [2015 –: p8f⁶ p8g⁶ 8.3m p7g p7g p8g⁶ t9.5f Oct 17] leggy gelding: modest maiden: stays 1m: acts on polytrack: in tongue tie last 4 starts. *Jeremy Noseda* **59**

SUMMER CHORUS 2 b.f. (Mar 11) Exceed And Excel (AUS) 126 – Soviet Terms (Soviet Star (USA) 128) [2015 5g² p5g* Nov 13] 58,000F: fourth foal: closely related to French 2-y-o 9.8f winner Dolce La Hulpe (by Kodiac) and half-sister to 6f winner Pirate's Song (by Bahamian Bounty) and 7.6f winner It's My Time (by Green Desert), both also successful abroad: dam twice-raced half-sister to Queen Mary/Lowther Stakes winner Best Terms (by Exceed And Excel): fairly useful form: didn't need to run up to debut form to win maiden at Lingfield (by ¾ length from Entertaining Ben) in November: will be suited by 6f: hooded both starts: open to improvement. *Andrew Balding* **80 p**

SUMMER DOVE (USA) 2 gr.f. (Feb 2) Super Saver (USA) 121 – No Foul Play (CAN) (Great Gladiator (USA)) [2015 7g p7g⁶ Oct 14] $160,000Y: seventh foal: half-sister to several winners in North America, including US Grade 3 9f winner Temporary Saint (by Awesome Again): dam Canadian winner up to 1¼m (2-y-o 6f/7f winner), including minor stakes: better effort when sixth in maiden at Kempton (3 lengths behind Desiderada) in October: sent to UAE. *George Peckham* **67**

SUMMER ICON 2 b.f. (Apr 17) Sixties Icon 125 – Summer Cry (USA) (Street Cry (IRE) 130) [2015 6.1m⁶ 7g⁵ 6g³ 7.1m⁵ 8m³ 7g² 7v⁶ Oct 24] 800F: rather leggy filly: fourth foal: half-sister to a winner abroad by Kodiac: dam unraced: fairly useful maiden: best effort when second in nursery at Newmarket in October: should stay beyond 7f: acts on good to firm going: sometimes slowly away. *Mick Channon* **85**

SUMMERINTHECITY (IRE) 8 ch.g. Indian Ridge 123 – Miss Assertive 88 (Zafonic (USA) 130) [2015 70: t7.1g⁴ p6m⁶ t5.1m⁴ f6g⁴ t6m⁵ t6f* f6m Dec 8] sturdy gelding: fair handicapper: left Richard Fahey/off 8 months, won at Wolverhampton in November: stays 7f: acts on all-weather, soft and good to firm going: tried in cheekpieces in 2015: often races prominently. *Patrick Morris* **76**

SUMMER ISLES 5 b.m. Exceed And Excel (AUS) 126 – Summers Lease 92 (Pivotal 124) [2015 p5g p6g p5g⁶ 5d 5s 5s* p5g⁴ t5.1m* Dec 30] fair handicapper: left Patrick J. Flynn, won at Catterick (amateur) in October and Wolverhampton in December: stays 6f: acts on polytrack, tapeta and soft going: tried in headgear/tongue tie: often leads. *Paul Midgley* **79**

SUMMERLING (IRE) 4 br.f. Excellent Art 125 – Sun Seasons (IRE) 99 (Salse (USA) 128) [2015 66: p8g p13.3g⁵ p10f 8g² 8.1d² 10.1g⁶ 8.5d t9.5f Oct 16] modest maiden: stays 1½m: acts on polytrack and good to soft going: tried in cheekpieces: usually races nearer last than first. *Phil McEntee* **57**

SUN'AQ (IRE) 2 b.f. (Mar 2) Kodiac 112 – Zingeeyah 63 (Singspiel (IRE) 133) [2015 t6g* 6v* p7d² 7g² 7d p5f* t6g⁵ p6g Dec 20] £24,000Y, 67,000 2-y-o: third foal: closely related to 7f-8.4f winner Reckless Lad (by Chevalier): dam maiden half-sister to smart 6f winner Kaldoun Kingdom: fairly useful performer: won maiden at Wolverhampton in August, and nursery at Ffos Las in August, and nursery at Chelmsford in November: stays 6f: acts on polytrack, tapeta and heavy going: in headgear last 2 starts. *Sir Mark Prescott Bt* **89**

SUNBAKED (IRE) 2 b.f. (Apr 22) Kodiac 112 – Bronze Baby (USA) (Silver Charm (USA) 132) [2015 p6g t5.1f 5g p6f p7g² p6d Nov 30] 10,000 2-y-o: fourth foal: sister to 2-y-o 7f winner Scutum and half-sister to 1¼m winner Redlorryellowlorry (by Bushranger): dam lightly-raced half-sister to 1000 Guineas runner-up Arch Swing: fair maiden: best effort at 7f: acts on polytrack: in cheekpieces last 2 starts. *Eve Johnson Houghton* **67**

SUNBIRD 3 b.f. Echo of Light 125 – Sundrop (JPN) 115 (Sunday Silence (USA)) [2015 t8.6f* Jan 30] fifth foal: half-sister to useful 7f winner Volcanic Wind (by Distorted Humor) and French 9f winner Quenching (by Street Cry): dam winner up to 1¼m (2-y-o 7f winner): 11/4, won 9-runner maiden at Wolverhampton on debut by 1½ lengths from Quill Art, well positioned: sold 25,000 gns: looked sure to progress. *John Gosden* **71 p**

SUNBLAZER (IRE) 5 gr.g. Dark Angel (IRE) 113 – Damask Rose (IRE) 100 (Dr Devious (IRE) 127) [2015 89: t13.9m² t13.9g² 16s 16.4d⁶ 16m⁵ t16.5f* t16.5m⁴ Dec 12] angular gelding: fairly useful handicapper: won at Wolverhampton in November: stays 16.5f: acts on polytrack, tapeta and firm going: tried in headgear: wears tongue tie: often races towards rear. *Kim Bailey* **87**

SUNDAY ROYAL (FR) 3 b.g. Sunday Break (JPN) 121 – Princess d'Orange (FR) **81**
(Anabaa (USA) 130) [2015 72p: p10f⁵ 8.3g⁵ 10.4g³ 7.9v⁴ 8.3g² 8d⁴ 14.1g⁵ 10.3d² t13.9g
Nov 27] close-coupled gelding: fairly useful maiden: stays 10.5f: acts on good to soft
going: usually races prominently. *Harry Dunlop*

SUNFLOWER 2 ch.f. (Feb 24) Dutch Art 126 – Swan Wings 89 (Bahamian Bounty 116) **93 p**
[2015 6g* 6g⁶ Sep 26] second foal: dam, 2-y-o 5f winner, closely related to smart sprinter
Texas Gold: won maiden at Windsor in September by neck from Gravity Flow: 33/1,
improved form (but no threat) when 6¼ lengths sixth of 8 to Lumiere in Cheveley Park
Stakes at Newmarket: should do better still. *Andrew Balding*

SUNI DANCER 4 b.f. Captain Gerrard (IRE) 113 – Sunisa (IRE) 87 (Daggers Drawn **57**
(USA) 114) [2015 61: t7.1m⁵ t8.6g t8.6g² t8.6g⁶ 8g 8m³ 7.9v⁵ t8.6g 7g⁴ 8.1d³ 10.2d⁴ 8d⁶
t9.5f t9.5m Nov 28] modest handicapper: left Paul Green after ninth start: stays 10.5f: acts
on tapeta, good to firm and good to soft going: sometimes in cheekpieces/tongue tie in
2015: often races freely. *Tony Carroll*

SUN IN HIS EYES 3 ch.g. Compton Place 125 – Sunset Lady (IRE) 75 (Red Sunset 120) **–**
[2015 7g 8g p8g⁵ Dec 28] well held in 3 maidens, left Paul Midgley before final start.
Ed de Giles

SUNLIT WATERS 2 ch.f. (Mar 2) New Approach (IRE) 132 – Faraway Waters 102 **64 p**
(Pharly (FR) 130) [2015 p8g⁵ p8d⁵ Nov 30] half-sister to smart winner up to 1¼m/Oaks
runner-up Something Exciting (2-y-o 1m winner, by Halling) and 1¼m winner Golden
Waters (by Dubai Destination): dam, 2-y-o 6f winner, half-sister to smart performer up to
1¾m Gower Song: showed more than on debut when 6 lengths fifth of 10 to Diamonds
Pour Moi in maiden at Kempton, running on late: will prove suited by 1¼m+: open to
further improvement. *Eve Johnson Houghton*

SUN LOVER 2 b.c. (Apr 16) Oasis Dream 129 – Come Touch The Sun (IRE) (Fusaichi **86 p**
Pegasus (USA) 130) [2015 7m⁶ 7g³ Aug 28] 360,000Y: good-topped colt: second foal:
dam, US 6f winner, half-sister to very smart winner up to 1¼m Misty For Me and Prix
Marcel Boussac winner Ballydoyle: improved from debut when 2¾ lengths third of 16 to
Tashweeq in maiden at Newmarket, keeping on until final 50 yds: has joined Roger Varian:
will go on improving. *Luca Cumani*

SUNNUA (IRE) 2 gr.f. (Mar 31) Dark Angel (IRE) 113 – Island Sunset (IRE) 98 (Trans **82**
Island 119) [2015 5s³ 6g² 5.2m 6g⁶ 6.3d 6g² 7v* Oct 17] €35,000Y: compact filly: second
foal: dam winner up to 1¼m (2-y-o 7f winner): fairly useful performer: won maiden at
Catterick in October: good second in nursery at Ayr previous start: stays 7f: acts on heavy
going. *Richard Fahey*

SUNNY BANK 6 b.g. Notnowcato 128 – Sweet Mandolin (Soviet Star (USA) 128) [2015 **–**
f11d 16g Jul 8] modest maiden at best, tailed off in handicaps in 2015: sometimes wears
tongue tie. *Alan Coogan*

SUNNY FUTURE (IRE) 9 b.g. Masterful (USA) 119 – Be Magic 57 (Persian Bold 123) **84**
[2015 84: 10.2f³ 17.2m* 14.1f⁴ 12m² 14.1m³ 16m p16g⁶ 14.1s⁴ 13.1f² Sep 12] big, rangy
gelding: fairly useful handicapper: won at Bath in May: stays 17f: acts on any turf going:
wears hood. *Malcolm Saunders*

SUNNYHILLS BELFORD 2 ch.f. (Feb 12) Monsieur Bond (IRE) 120 – Zamindari **45**
(Zamindar (USA) 116) [2015 5g⁴ 5s 6g 5g Aug 28] 900F, 4,500Y: third foal: half-sister to
6f winner Mr Bounty (by Bahamian Bounty) and a winner in Italy by Pastoral Pursuits:
dam unraced half-sister to useful 6f winner Fast Shot: poor maiden. *Noel Wilson*

SUNNY MONDAY 3 br.g. Manduro (GER) 135 – Sunray Superstar 101 (Nashwan (USA) **–**
135) [2015 10d 7s Oct 6] tailed-off last in 2 maidens: has been gelded. *Pat Eddery*

SUNNYSIDE BOB (IRE) 2 b.g. (Apr 10) Big Bad Bob (IRE) 118 – Jinxy Jill (Royal **79**
Applause 124) [2015 5.9g⁴ 6m⁵ 5.9m³ 5g² 5d⁶ 5g² t5.1f² Oct 30] fair maiden: should prove
suited by a return to 6f: acts on tapeta and good to firm going: often races prominently.
Geoffrey Oldroyd

SUNNY SPIRIT (IRE) 2 b.f. (Feb 19) Zebedee 113 – Chingford (IRE) 64 (Redback 116) **63**
[2015 5.7f⁶ 6g⁴ 6g 7d 5.7m Sep 28] smallish filly: fourth foal: half-sister to 2-y-o 5f winner
Courtland Avenue (by Kodiac) and 5.7f winner Connaught Sunny (by Aussie Rules): dam
maiden (stayed 7f): modest maiden: best effort at 6f. *Jonathan Portman*

SUNNY YORK (IRE) 3 b.f. Vale of York (IRE) 117 – Alexander Ridge (IRE) 77 (Indian **61**
Ridge 123) [2015 74: t5.1m³ t6g⁵ Mar 27] modest performer: best effort at 5f: acts on good
to firm going: sometimes slowly away. *James Tate*

SUN ODYSSEY 3 b.f. Mastercraftsman (IRE) 129 – Penolva (IRE) 65 (Galileo (IRE) **60**
134) [2015 61p: 10d 12f 11.9v³ 11.7f⁵ 13.1f⁵ 10d Oct 15] useful-looking filly: modest
maiden: stays 1f: acts on firm and good to soft going: tried in visor in 2015. *Luke Dace*

SUNRAIDER (IRE) 8 b.g. Namid 128 – Doctrine 97 (Barathea (IRE) 127) [2015 100: 6g **90**
6m 7d 6g 7m 6d² 6d² 6m⁴ 6m 6m 6g⁵ 7s Oct 9] well-made gelding: fairly useful
handicapper: stays 6f: acts on good to firm and good to soft going: tried in headgear.
Paul Midgley

SUNRISE DANCE 6 ch.m. Monsieur Bond (IRE) 120 – Wachiwi (IRE) 67 (Namid 128) **54**
[2015 58§: 6m 5m 5m⁴ 6d³ 6m² t6m⁶ t5.1f 5s Oct 6] lengthy mare: modest handicapper:
stays 6f: acts on polytrack, firm and good to soft going: tried in headgear: front runner/
races prominently: quirky. *Kenny Johnson*

SUNSCAPE (IRE) 2 ch.f. (Feb 12) Roderic O'Connor (IRE) 119 – Opatja (Nashwan **74**
(USA) 135) [2015 t8.6m 7s⁴ p8f* Oct 28] €18,000F, 14,000Y: lengthy filly: second foal:
dam, Italian 9f-11f winner (also won over hurdles), half-sister to smart 9f/1¼m winner
Moving On Up: fair performer: best effort when winning maiden at Chelmsford (by length
from Lilly Vega) in October, having run of race: stays 1m. *Hughie Morrison*

SUNSET DREAM (IRE) 2 b.f. (Apr 10) Acclamation 118 – Oasis Sunset (IRE) 82 **–**
(Oasis Dream 129) [2015 7m Jul 30] 130,000Y: third foal: dam, 2-y-o 7f winner, half-sister
to Cheveley Park Stakes winner Seazun: 12/1, badly needed experience when last of 14 in
maiden at Goodwood. *Richard Hannon*

SUNSET SAIL (IRE) 3 b.c. Arcano (IRE) 122 – Mythologie (FR) (Bering 136) [2015 93: **89**
5g 6g⁴ 5m⁴ 6m 6d Oct 11] good-topped colt: fairly useful handicapper: stays 7f: acts on
polytrack and any turf going: sold 7,000 gns, sent to Germany. *Richard Hannon*

SUNSHINE ALWAYS (IRE) 9 b.g. Verglas (IRE) 118 – Easy Sunshine (IRE) 96 **59**
(Sadler's Wells (USA) 132) [2015 p7m⁴ Apr 8] modest handicapper: stays 1m: acts on
polytrack and soft going: tried in cheekpieces. *Michael Attwater*

SUNSHINEANDBUBBLES 2 b.f. (Apr 19) Multiplex 114 – Dockside Strike (Docksider **52**
(USA) 124) [2015 t8.6f Sep 19] £8,500Y: seventh foal: sister to 3 winners, including 5f
winner Picket Line and winner up to 2m Precision Strike (2-y-o 8.3f winner) and half-sister
to winner up to 6f Under Approval (2-y-o 5f winner, by Captain Gerrard): dam unraced
half-sister to July Stakes winner Winker Watson: 100/1, green when 10¾ lengths seventh
of 11 to Maestro Mac in maiden at Wolverhampton, very slowly away. *Daniel Loughnane*

SUNSHINE BAND 3 ch.f. Compton Place 125 – Precedence (IRE) 88 (Polish Precedent **–**
(USA) 131) [2015 t7.1f⁶ p8g Dec 2] £1,300 2-y-o: half-sister to useful 2-y-o 1m winner
(stayed 1½m) Wingman (by In The Wings) and 9f winner (stayed 11f) Charlie Tango (by
Desert Prince): dam maiden (stayed 9f): well held in 2 maidens. *Phil McEntee*

SUPA SEEKER (USA) 9 b.g. Petionville (USA) – Supamova (USA) 88 (Seattle Slew **53**
(USA)) [2015 58: p8g⁵ t8.6g⁶ p10f⁶ t12.2f⁵ t9.5m t12.2f³ p11f⁴ 8.5g* 8m² 12.1m⁴ 9.9g* **a44**
11.6m⁴ 9.9v³ 9.9d⁴ 9.9s p8g⁴ p10f⁶ Dec 21] angular gelding: modest handicapper: won at
Les Landes in April and Brighton (amateur) in August: stays 1½m: acts on polytrack, good
to firm and heavy going: tried in headgear/tongue tie: sometimes slowly away. *Tony Carroll*

SUPER ICON 3 b.g. Sixties Icon 125 – Brigadiers Bird (IRE) (Mujadil (USA) 119) [2015 **62**
7g p7g 7g 7d⁶ t7.1g³ Aug 6] good-topped gelding: modest maiden: raced only at 7f: acts on
tapeta: often races towards rear. *Ed Walker*

SUPER KID 3 b.g. Exceed And Excel (AUS) 126 – Crimson Year (USA) (Dubai **93 +**
Millennium 140) [2015 98: p8g³ 7m 7m⁵ p8g p10g² 10.3m² 10m³ p11m² p10g* t9.5m⁵ **a104**
Dec 12] useful-looking gelding: useful handicapper: won at Lingfield (by 2¾ lengths from
Brocklebank) in December: stays 11f: acts on polytrack, tapeta and good to firm going:
tried in cheekpieces in 2015: often races towards rear. *Saeed bin Suroor*

SUPERLATIVE (IRE) 3 ch.f. Iffraaj 127 – Slieve Mish (IRE) 105 (Cape Cross (IRE) **69**
129) [2015 64p: 8.3g³ p8g 11.9g⁶ t8.6f a7.5g² p7.5g Dec 11] fair maiden: left James Tate
after fourth start (blinkered): best effort at 8.3f. *Priscilla Peelman, Belgium*

SUPER MOON 3 b.g. Black Sam Bellamy (IRE) 121 – Aussie Deal (IRE) (Flemensfirth **–**
(USA) 122) [2015 t7.1g Jan 26] 100/1/in hood, ninth of 12 in maiden at Wolverhampton.
Richard Phillips

SUPER MOON (JPN) 6 b.h. Brian's Time (USA) – Fairy Ballade (IRE) (Sadler's Wells **106**
(USA) 132) [2015 9.9g³ 10f 9.9f 12.4d⁵ 9.9f² Dec 20] rangy horse: half-brother to 3
winners in Japan: dam, ran twice in Japan, sister to very smart US Grade 1 1½m winner
Sligo Bay: smart performer in 2014: placed in 2015 in listed races at Tokyo (2½ lengths

third to Azuma Shuttle) and Nakayama (neck second to Tosen Reve): tenth of 13 behind Mahsoob in listed Wolferton Handicap at Royal Ascot on second start: stays 12.5f: acts on firm going. *Kazuo Fujisawa, Japan*

SUPER QUICK (IRE) 3 b.f. Rip Van Winkle (IRE) 134 – Public Ransom (IRE) (Red — Ransom (USA)) [2015 69: 10.3d Jun 14] lightly-raced maiden, fair form at best: should stay at least 1m: in tongue tie only outing in 2015. *Richard Fahey*

SUPERSTA 4 ch.g. Pivotal 124 – Resort 97 (Oasis Dream 129) [2015 77: t7.1f⁵ p6f t7.1f³ **69 +** 6m 6.1m⁶ 7g⁶ 7.1g⁵ 6g 5m⁵ 6g t7.1f² t8.6f* p8g* p8g* p8f⁵ p8m⁶ Dec 27] lengthy gelding: **a89** fairly useful handicapper: won at Wolverhampton in October and at Chelmsford in November and December: left Ronald Harris after eighth start: stays 8.5f: acts on polytrack, tapeta, good to firm and good to soft going: usually wears headgear: often starts slowly: often races in rear/travels strongly. *Michael Appleby*

SUPERYACHT (IRE) 2 b.c. (Mar 13) Fastnet Rock (AUS) 127 – Olympienne (IRE) **– p** (Sadler's Wells (USA) 132) [2015 8.1g Sep 11] brother to 1½m winner Moruadh and half-brother to 3 winners, including very smart winner up to 2m/Gold Cup runner-up Patkai (2-y-o 1m winner, by Indian Ridge) and smart 9.7f-1½m winner (stayed 1¾m) Modun (by King's Best): dam unraced sister to very smart 1¼m-1½m performer Islington: 16/1, badly needed experience when 11½ lengths ninth of 10 to Valitop in maiden at Sandown: should do better. *Sir Michael Stoute*

SUPPLICANT 4 b.c. Kyllachy 129 – Pious 74 (Bishop of Cashel 122) [2015 105: 6g⁵ 6f **92** 7g 6m⁵ 6s 6g⁶ 6g 8d⁴ Oct 11] useful performer at best (won Mill Reef Stakes at Newbury at 2 yrs): fairly useful handicapper in 2015: suited by 6f (finished weakly over 7f/1m): acted on firm and soft going: often in visor in 2015: to stand at Petches Farm Stud, Finchingfield, Essex, fee £3,000. *Richard Fahey*

SUPREME BELLE (IRE) 3 b.f. Tamayuz 126 – Final Opinion (IRE) 92 (King's **33** Theatre (IRE) 128) [2015 37: t6f p5g t5.1g 6d May 20] strong filly: poor maiden: should prove suited by 7f+: acts on tapeta and good to firm going: sometimes slowly away. *Derek Shaw*

SUPREME OCCASION (IRE) 3 b.f. Teofilo (IRE) 126 – Pirie (USA) (Green Dancer **95** (USA) 132) [2015 96: 11.5s⁶ 10m 8f² 10.4m⁴ 8m⁴ 8g 8d⁵ Sep 4] angular filly: useful handicapper: best efforts when second at Ascot and fourth at Newmarket third/fifth starts: stays 1m: acts on firm and good to soft going. *David O'Meara*

SUPRISE VENDOR (IRE) 9 ch.g. Fath (USA) 116 – Dispol Jazz 70 (Alhijaz 122) **67** [2015 65: 18s* 21.6g 16s³ May 11] fair handicapper: won at Pontefract in April (successful in same event 12 months earlier): stays 2¼m: acts on heavy going. *Stuart Coltherd*

SUQOOR 2 b.g. (Apr 5) Equiano (FR) 127 – Ukraine (IRE) (Cape Cross (IRE) 129) [2015 6.1m p6g Aug 17] well held in maidens at Nottingham and Kempton: has been gelded. *Richard Hannon*

SURAJ 6 ch.g. Galileo (IRE) 134 – Maid of Killeen (IRE) 97 (Darshaan 133) [2015 99§: **– §** 14s f11g⁴ Apr 14] leggy gelding: useful handicapper at best: well below form both starts in 2015, latter in claimer on fibresand debut): stays 2½m: acts on soft and good to firm going: ungenuine. *Keith Dalgleish*

SURBETT (IRE) 2 b.c. (Feb 5) Rock of Gibraltar (IRE) 133 – Causeway Queen (IRE) **93** (Giant's Causeway (USA) 132) [2015 6m 6m² 6m* p5g⁴ 6g³ 7.5d² 6d² Nov 7] €85,000Y: useful-looking colt: second foal: dam unraced half-sister to Derby third Astrology out of Prix Saint-Alary winner Ask For The Moon: fairly useful form: won maiden at Epsom (by neck from Goodwood Zodiac) in July: placed last 3 starts, in listed race at Milan (good effort, 1¾ lengths third to Zapel, left Marco Botti after) and minor events at Rome and Milan (beaten favourite both times): stays 7.5f: acts on good to firm going: has hung left/carried head awkwardly. *A. & S. Botti, Italy*

SUR EMPIRE 3 b.f. Equiano (FR) 127 – Shersha (IRE) 105 (Priolo (USA) 127) [2015 71: **77** 7g⁶ 7.1m* 7.1m⁵ 6.1g⁵ 7m⁵ 6.9s 7.5m 7m 7d⁶ p6g⁶ 9.3m* 9.2m² 9.2m² 8.5m⁴ 10s⁴ p10f⁵ Oct 24] angular filly: fair performer: won maiden at Musselburgh in May and handicap at Carlisle in September: stays 9.5f: acts on good to firm going: usually races close up. *Mark Johnston*

SURETY (IRE) 4 b.c. Cape Cross (IRE) 129 – Guarantia 92 (Selkirk (USA) 129) [2015 **67** 81: p8m 7.1m⁵ p6g* p6g³ 7g³ 7g Aug 7] fairly useful handicapper: won at Kempton (by ½ **a80** length from Satchville Flyer) in July: stays 8.5f: acts on polytrack, good to firm and good to soft going: front runner/races prominently. *Clive Brittain*

SUREWECAN 3 b.g. Royal Applause 124 – Edge of Light 94 (Xaar 132) [2015 94: 7g 7g **87** p8g³ 6m⁶ 7m⁶ 8m 8m⁶ 7m 6m⁶ 7s⁵ 8s⁶ 8.3m p6f p6g⁵ Oct 20] rather leggy gelding: fairly useful handicapper: stays 1m: acts on polytrack, firm and soft going: in headgear last 3 starts. *Mark Johnston*

SURPRISE CALL 3 ch.c. New Approach (IRE) 132 – Calakanga 90 (Dalakhani (IRE) **–** 133) [2015 10g Apr 27] smallish, angular colt: 7/1, well held in maiden at Windsor: sold 3,500 gns. *Sir Michael Stoute*

SURPRISE ME THEN 3 b.f. Cockney Rebel (IRE) 127 – Xandra (IRE) 55 (Xaar 132) **–** [2015 p8gᵖᵘ Sep 23] first foal: dam, maiden, half-sister to smart performer (best at 6f/7f) Ceremonial Jade: 66/1, shaped as if amiss in maiden at Kempton on debut. *Mark Hoad*

SURPRISE US 8 b.g. Indian Ridge 123 – Pingus (Polish Precedent (USA) 131) [2015 52: **55** 16.2s⁵ 12.1m² 12.1m 12.1m⁶ 11.6m² p11g Dec 3] modest maiden: stays 1½m: acts on firm going: usually wears headgear: front runner/races prominently. *Mark Gillard*

SURROUND SOUND 5 b.g. Multiplex 114 – Tintera (IRE) (King's Theatre (IRE) 128) **73** [2015 72: f7d⁶ t9.5f⁴ t12.2g t12.2g* f11d 12.5m⁴ t12.2g² 12.5m* 13d⁵ 16.5m⁴ 12g² 11.5d⁵ t12.2g⁵ 11.9d Sep 3] workmanlike gelding: fair handicapper: won amateur events at Wolverhampton in May and Musselburgh in June: stays 16.5f: acts on tapeta, good to firm and heavy going: wears headgear/tongue tie: often races towards rear, usually travels strongly. *Tim Easterby*

SURSPENDERS (FR) 4 b.g. Whipper (USA) 126 – Lanciana (IRE) (Acatenango (GER) **75** 127) [2015 p11g Sep 30] fair handicapper: won maiden at Lisieux and claimer at Argentan in 2014: left S. Wattel, respectable effort at Kempton only outing in Britain in 2015: stays 1¼m: acts on polytrack, soft and good to firm going: wears cheekpieces: sold 3,500 gns, returned to France. *Lucy Wadham*

SUSTAINABLE 3 b.f. Sulamani (IRE) 130 – Attainable 72 (Kalanisi (IRE) 132) [2015 **48** p12g⁴ p11g 12s p16g⁶ t13.9m Dec 30] first foal: dam maiden (stayed 1½m): poor maiden: best effort at 2m: acts on polytrack. *Nigel Twiston-Davies*

SUSURRO 2 ch.f. (Jan 31) Rip Van Winkle (IRE) 134 – Heavenly Whisper (IRE) 105 **–** (Halling (USA) 133) [2015 8g 8g Sep 19] 24,000Y: half-sister to several winners, including useful 1m winner River Tiber (by Danehill) and useful 2-y-o 1m/8.6f winner Premier Banker (by Cape Cross), later successful abroad: dam 1m winner (including at 2 yrs): down the field in maidens at Ascot and Newmarket. *David Simcock*

SUTTONBUSINESSPACE 3 b.f. Myboycharlie (IRE) 118 – Marah 93 (Machiavellian **–** (USA) 123) [2015 p8g Feb 20] half-sister to 3 winners, including 7f winner Marah Music (by Royal Applause) and 1½m winner Remaal (by Unfuwain): dam 2-y-o 7f winner: in first-time hood, 25/1, well held in maiden at Lingfield. *Pat Phelan*

SUTTON SID 5 ch.g. Dutch Art 126 – Drastic Measure 73 (Pivotal 124) [2015 75: p15.8f **– §** Jan 30] quite attractive gelding: fair handicapper: well held only outing in 2015: stays 11.5f: acts on polytrack, fibresand, good to firm and heavy going: wears headgear: has worn tongue tie: often starts slowly, usually races in rear: one to avoid. *Paddy Butler*

SUUKI 2 ch.f. (Mar 22) Major Cadeaux 121 – Smooth As Silk (IRE) 73 (Danehill Dancer **–** (IRE) 117) [2015 6f⁶ 7.6g 6m p8g Oct 20] rather unfurnished filly: third foal: dam, maiden (stayed 1¾m), half-sister to smart/moody winner up to 1¼m Humungous and useful performer up to 1½m Amazing Beauty: no form: tried in tongue tie. *Robert Mills*

SUZI ICON 3 ch.f. Sixties Icon 125 – Suzi Spends (IRE) 94 (Royal Applause 124) [2015 **72** 12.1g⁴ 12m⁵ 10g³ 12g t12.2g³ 8.5m 9.9g⁴ 14.1m t12.2g Sep 29] second foal: half-sister to useful winner up to 7f Suzi's Connoisseur (2-y-o 5f/6f winner, by Art Connoisseur): dam winner up to 1¼m (2-y-o 8.3f winner): fair maiden: stays 1½m: acts on good to firm going: in headgear last 4 starts: front runner/races prominently: temperament under suspicion. *Mark Johnston*

SUZI'S CONNOISSEUR 4 b.g. Art Connoisseur (IRE) 121 – Suzi Spends (IRE) 94 **106** (Royal Applause 124) [2015 109: 6f 7m 6f 7f⁶ 7d⁵ 6m 7s 7g² 5.6d⁶ 6s Oct 10] angular gelding: useful performer: creditable efforts in several well-contested handicaps in 2015, though only placing when ½-length second of 16 to Majestic Moon at Ascot in September: stays 7f: acts on good to firm and heavy going: usually wears headgear. *Stuart Williams*

SWAHEEN 3 b.g. Lawman (FR) 121 – Whole Grain 72 (Polish Precedent (USA) 131) **96** [2015 71: 9g* 12m³ 12.5m⁵ 12g⁴ 12d³ 13.7g⁴ 14s* Oct 9] useful handicapper: won at Redcar in April and Ripon (by 7 lengths from Adele) in July: better than ever when also won 6-runner event at York final start by 1½ lengths from Brandon Castle, responding well: stays 1¾m: acts on soft and good to firm going: in hood last 3 starts: usually races nearer last than first, often travels strongly. *Julie Camacho*

SWAMPFIRE (IRE) 7 b.g. Anabaa (USA) 130 – Moonfire 76 (Sadler's Wells (USA) –
132) [2015 65: t16.5f 12.1g Aug 20] one-time useful performer: stayed 1½m: acted on soft
going: had worn headgear: fair hurdler: dead. *Linda Perratt*

SWAN LAKES (IRE) 4 gr.f. Dalakhani (IRE) 133 – Rock Salt (Selkirk (USA) 129) **83**
[2015 65: t16.5f 12.1g Aug 9] angular filly: fairly useful handicapper: worth a try at further
than 1½m: acts on polytrack and good to firm going: front runner/races prominently: sent
to France. *David Simcock*

SWANSWAY 2 ch.c. (Mar 16) Showcasing 117 – Spring Stroll (USA) (Skywalker (USA)) **53 p**
[2015 6g 6.1v⁴ Oct 7] €55,000Y: fifth foal: half-brother to useful French winner up to 9.5f
Dinner's Out (2-y-o 7f/1m winner, by War Front): dam placed up to 11f in USA: better
effort in maidens when seventh of 12 to Firedanser at Haydock in August: still green next
start: remains with potential. *Tom Dascombe*

SWANTON BLUE (IRE) 2 b.c. (Apr 28) Kodiac 112   Cabopino (IRE) 58 (Captain Rio **77**
122) [2015 6.1d 6m² 5.7m⁵ 6g² p6f² 6g Oct 8] fair maiden: stays 6f: acts on polytrack. *Ed
de Giles*

SWASHBUCKLING (IRE) 3 b.g. Raven's Pass (USA) 133 – Hazarayna 70 (Polish **88**
Precedent (USA) 131) [2015 8g³ 10.1d² t9.5f³ Oct 20] 40,000Y: fourth
foal: dam, maiden (stayed 1¼m), half-sister to smart performer up to 1½m Hazarista: fairly
useful maiden: best effort when second at Epsom (1¼ lengths behind Prendergast Hill) in
September. *Michael Wigham*

SWEEPING UP 4 b.f. Sea The Stars (IRE) 140 – Farfala (FR) 106 (Linamix (FR) 127) **104**
[2015 86: 14.1m⁴ 14f* 14m 16.4d⁵ p12g² 13.9g² p13g⁴ Oct 29] good-topped filly: useful
performer, much improved in 2015: won handicap at Sandown in July: good second in
September Stakes at Kempton (3¼ lengths behind Jack Hobbs) and in listed race at Saint-
Cloud (¾ length behind Sahrawi): stays 16.5f: acts on polytrack, firm and good to soft
going: usually wears tongue tie. *Hughie Morrison*

SWEEP OF DIAMONDS 2 br.c. (Feb 10) Mawatheeq (USA) 126 – Apple Blossom –
(IRE) 81 (Danehill Dancer (IRE) 117) [2015 7g 8.3s Nov 4] well held in 2 maidens.
Denis Quinn

SWEET DANCER (IRE) 3 ch.c. Danehill Dancer (IRE) 117 – Thinking Positive 80 **69**
(Rainbow Quest (USA) 134) [2015 t8.6g⁵ 8d⁶ p8g t9.5g⁶ p10g⁴ p8g⁵ Sep 9] fair maiden:
stays 1¼m: acts on polytrack and tapeta: tried in blinkers. *David Lanigan*

SWEET DREAM 3 b.f. Oasis Dream 129 – Sweet Stream (ITY) 117 (Shantou (USA) **78**
125) [2015 87: 11.4d⁶ 12m 12s Sep 18] rather leggy filly: fair performer: stays 1½m: acts
on good to firm and heavy going. *Ralph Beckett*

SWEET DREAM LADY (IRE) 2 b.f. (Mar 8) Rip Van Winkle (IRE) 134 – Visite **62**
Royale (USA) 81 (Danehill Dancer (IRE) 117) [2015 6s 7s p8g⁶ Oct 27] €43,000 2-y-o:
sturdy filly: third foal: half-sister to 8.3f winner Kalahari Kingdom (by Footstepsinthesand),
later 9f winner in Qatar, and a winner in Italy by Excellent Art: dam 9.3f winner: modest
maiden: bred to stay 1m: tried in hood. *Gary Moore*

SWEETHEART ABBEY 4 b.f. Dancing Spree (USA) – Hinton Pearl (Loch Pearl 81) **84**
[2015 85, a92: 12mᵘʳ 12g⁵ p12g⁴ 11.9m⁴ 10.1g⁵ t12.2g² p12g 12g⁴ 16m³ Oct 2] rather leggy
filly: fairly useful handicapper: stays 2m: acts on polytrack, tapeta, and good to firm going:
often wears cheekpieces. *William Knight*

SWEETLY DOES IT 3 ch.f. Shirocco (GER) 129 – Sweetness Herself 106 (Unfuwain **51**
(USA) 131) [2015 –: 10m p7g 16g³ 16d⁴ p13f Sep 12] modest maiden: best effort at 2m:
sometimes in visor: often races prominently. *Stuart Williams*

SWEET MARTONI 5 b.m. Dubawi (IRE) 129 – Sweetness Herself 106 (Unfuwain **74**
(USA) 131) [2015 84: 10.3d 10g⁶ 10g⁴ 12g⁶ 10.2g² Jun 15] leggy mare: fair handicapper:
stays 1¼m: acts on heavy going. *William Knight*

SWEET MIDNIGHT 3 b.f. Mawatheeq (USA) 126 – Sweet Reply 84 (Opening Verse **46**
(USA) 126) [2015 –: f8g⁶ 12.1g 12f 10.2g 12v⁵ Aug 19] poor maiden: stays 1½m: acts on
heavy going: often races prominently. *John Holt*

SWEET MISSI (IRE) 3 b.f. Thousand Words 113 – Touch And Love (IRE) (Green **67**
Desert (USA) 127) [2015 58: 6g² 6m 6m² 6g 6m t7.1m⁶ 7g⁴ 7.2g Sep 29] fair maiden: stays
6f: acts on good to firm going: tried in cheekpieces: usually races towards rear. *Brian Ellison*

SWEET P 4 b.f. Sir Percy 129 – Desert Run (IRE) (Desert Prince (IRE) 130) [2015 77: **98**
10m* 12.4m* 11.6d* p12g Nov 4] leggy filly: useful handicapper: won at Windsor and
Newcastle in July and again at Windsor (by 1¾ lengths from Classic Collection) in
October: ran creditably upped in grade final start: stays 12.5f: acts on polytrack, good to
firm and good to soft going: wears hood. *Marcus Tregoning*

SWEET PERSUASION 3 ch.f. Motivator 131 – Sweet Lemon (IRE) (Oratorio (IRE) – 128) [2015 p7g Jan 7] 19,000F: second foal: dam unraced half-sister to Racing Post Trophy winner Kingsbarns: 25/1, well held in maiden at Kempton. *Gary Moore*

SWEET PICCOLO 5 ch.g. Piccolo 121 – Quality Street 86 (Fraam 114) [2015 52, a41: **41** p6f⁶ p5m⁵ t6f 7g 6s 7v p6f⁶v Oct 6] poor maiden: stays 6f: acts on polytrack, tapeta and good to soft going: sometimes wears headgear: often races towards rear. *Paddy Butler*

SWEET SELECTION 3 b.f. Stimulation (IRE) 121 – Sweet Coincidence 69 (Mujahid **77** (USA) 125) [2015 62p: 9.9m⁴ 9.9m⁴ 11.6m⁴ 11m 12s³ 10s p10f p16g* Nov 26] sturdy filly: fair handicapper: won at Goodwood in May and Chelmsford in November: stays 2m: acts on polytrack and good to firm going: tried in blinkers. *Hughie Morrison*

SWEETS'N'SHEETS (IRE) 2 b.f. (Apr 5) Fast Company (IRE) 126 – Casandra – Crossing (IRE) (High Chaparral (IRE) 132) [2015 6g 6m Jun 12] €3,000Y: first foal: dam unraced: well held in maiden/seller, in visor final start. *Paul Midgley*

SWEET TABOO (IRE) 2 b.f. (Apr 28) Approve (IRE) 112 – Silca Boo 99 (Efisio 120) **52** [2015 5f⁵ 6g⁴ 6.1d⁴ 7s 5.1m⁵ 6.1s p6f Oct 1] €14,000Y: half-sister to several winners, including useful 5f (including at 2 yrs) winner Lightscameraction (by Pastoral Pursuits) and useful winner up to 6f Fast Track (2-y-o 5f winner, by Rail Link): dam 2-y-o 5f/6f winner: modest performer: won seller at Leicester in July: stays 6f: acts on good to soft going: front runner/races prominently: sold 1,500 gns, sent to Spain. *David Evans*

SWEET TEMPTATION (IRE) 2 b.f. (May 20) Amadeus Wolf 122 – Summer Spice **72 p** (IRE) 88 (Key of Luck (USA) 126) [2015 p7g* Dec 10] €9,000Y, 15,000 2-y-o: sister to 1m winner Ivors Involvement and half-sister to 3 winners, including useful winner up to 1½m Anice Stellato (2-y-o 7f winner, by Dalakhani) and 1¾m winner (stays 2m) Winter Spice (by Verglas): dam, 2-y-o 6f winner who stayed 1m, half-sister to very smart performer up to 1½m Definite Article: 9/1, won 6-runner maiden at Chelmsford on debut by 3 lengths from Zauffaly, staying on to lead final 1f: will stay 1m: will improve. *Stuart Williams*

SWEET WORLD 11 b.g. Agnes World (USA) 123 – Douce Maison (IRE) 67 (Fools **54** Holme (USA)) [2015 12.1m³ 12.1s⁶ 11.9d⁵ 10.2d Aug 20] lengthy gelding: modest handicapper: missed 2013 and 2014: stays 1½m: acts on all-weather, best turf form on good going or softer: tried in headgear. *Bernard Llewellyn*

SWENDAB (IRE) 7 b.g. Trans Island 119 – Lavish Spirit (USA) 80 (Southern Halo **81** (USA)) [2015 83§, a55§: t5.1f³ p6m³ p6m* p5f t7.1m p6f⁶ t6g² t6g 5.1m 5.7m 5.7g⁶ 5m² **a59** 5.2m⁴ 5.1mᵘʳ 5.7m⁵ 5.1s² 5m* 5.1d* 5d⁶ 5d⁴ 5.7d Sep 2] good-topped gelding: fairly useful handicapper: won at Kempton in January, Bath in July and Chepstow in August: stays 7f: acts on polytrack, firm and good to soft going: wears headgear: usually slowly away, front runner/races prominently: not one to trust implicitly. *John O'Shea*

SWIFT ACT 6 b.m. Act One 124 – Lasting Image (Zilzal (USA) 137) [2015 –: t12.2f **38** t12.2m t12.2f 12.1s t12.2g f12g Nov 26] poor maiden: stays 9.5f: wears headgear. *Nikki Evans*

SWIFT APPROVAL (IRE) 3 ch.g. Approve (IRE) 112 – Tiltili (IRE) 51 (Spectrum **89** (IRE) 126) [2015 85: 8.5g 7d² 6g⁴ 7m 7.5m⁶ 7d³ 7.2m³ Sep 27] fairly useful handicapper: stays 7f: acts on good to firm and good to soft going: usually races nearer last than first. *Kevin Ryan*

SWIFT BLADE (IRE) 7 ch.g. Exceed And Excel (AUS) 126 – Gold Strike (IRE) **77 §** (Rainbow Quest (USA) 134) [2015 82§: p12g⁶ p12g³ 11.6m⁵ 14m⁶ 12g p12g⁴ p15.8g 11.6g³ t13.9f⁴ p12g Dec 9] workmanlike gelding: fair handicapper: stays 1½m: acts on polytrack, firm and soft going: often wears headgear: quirky, not one to rely on. *Graham Mays*

SWIFT CEDAR (IRE) 5 ch.g. Excellent Art 125 – Ravish 58 (Efisio 120) [2015 93, a79: **86** p10m⁶ 8.6f t8.6m³ t9.5g³ 10m* 10.4d* 9g⁵ 8.3m³ 7.6m⁵ 10d³ 10.4f* 10.3g⁴ 12d² 10.4g 12g² t12.2f 14.1s⁵ f12g* t13.9f f14m⁵ f11g* Dec 22] rather leggy gelding: fairly useful handicapper: won at L'Ancresse and Haydock (apprentice) in May, Haydock in July and at Southwell in November and December: stays 1½m: acts on polytrack, fibresand, firm and soft going: has worn headgear. *David Evans*

SWIFT EMPEROR (IRE) 3 b.g. Holy Roman Emperor (IRE) 125 – Big Swifty (IRE) **92** (Intikhab (USA) 135) [2015 84p: 7g 8f* 8m* Aug 16] fairly useful form: won handicaps at Haydock (by head from Steal The Scene) in June and Pontefract (by neck from Shaakis) in August: stays 1m, should prove as effective at 7f. *David Barron*

SWIFTLY DONE (IRE) 8 b.g. Whipper (USA) 126 – Ziffany 68 (Taufan (USA) 119) **69** [2015 96: 8d 8.5g 8d⁵ May 21] angular, attractive gelding: fair handicapper: stays 1m: acts on heavy going: sometimes wears headgear. *Declan Carroll*

SWIFT RESPONSE (USA) 2 b.c. (Mar 14) Hat Trick (JPN) 121 – Promptly (IRE) 88 **79**
(Lead On Time (USA) 123) [2015 p7g 7g³ 8d² 8g⁴ 9g⁵ Oct 21] useful-looking colt: fair
maiden: stays 9f: acts on good to soft going: often races prominently. *Sir Michael Stoute*

SWIFT SUSIE 3 b.f. Kheleyf (USA) 116 – Overwing (IRE) 84 (Fasliyev (USA) 120) **38**
[2015 –: t5.1g⁵ p5g⁴ 5.1g t5.1g p5g Jul 21] poor maiden: raced only at 5f: acts on polytrack:
sometimes in headgear/tongue tie: often races prominently. *Stuart Williams*

SWILKEN 4 ch.g. Halling (USA) 133 – Azure Mist 79 (Bahamian Bounty 116) [2015 67:
8m p5m⁶ 7m 6g⁶ Jun 9] sturdy gelding: maiden: no form in Britain in 2015: tried in
headgear: front runner/races prominently, tends to find little: sold 9,000 gns, sent to Italy.
Mark H. Tompkins

SWILLY SUNSET 2 b.g. (Feb 8) Kyllachy 129 – Spanish Springs (IRE) 69 (Xaar 132) **76**
[2015 6d⁵ 6s t7.1f* p7g⁴ Nov 13] fair performer: won maiden at Wolverhampton in
October: stays 7f. *Charles Hills*

SWINFORD LASS 3 b.f. Dutch Art 126 – Tidal 94 (Bin Ajwaad (IRE) 119) [2015 p10f –
p8g Nov 9] sixth foal: sister to 5f/6f winner Tidal's Baby and half-sister to winner up to
1¼m Faldal (2-y-o 1m winner, by Falbrav) and 6f winner Tidal Beauty (by Verglas): dam
1¼m-1½m winner: tailed off in 2 maidens. *Lee Carter*

SWING ALONE (IRE) 6 b.g. Celtic Swing 138 – Groupetime (USA) 69 (Gilded Time **87**
(USA)) [2015 101: f11s⁶ p10g⁴ p10g⁵ p8m p10g³ t12.2f³ p10g⁴ p10g⁶ 10g p10g⁵ Aug 17]
lengthy gelding: fairly useful handicapper: stays 2m: acts on polytrack, tapeta, soft and
good to firm going: usually wears headgear: often races prominently. *Gay Kelleway*

SWING EASY 5 b.g. Zamindar (USA) 116 – Shahmina (IRE) 78 (Danehill (USA) 126) **96**
[2015 12s 10.2d⁴ 10v p10f⁵ Nov 25] useful handicapper: missed 2014: easily best effort in
2015 on second start: stays 1¼m: acts on polytrack, good to firm and good to soft going:
blinkered final outing. *Gary Moore*

SWINGING HAWK (GER) 9 ch.g. Hawk Wing (USA) 136 – Saldenschwinge (GER) –
108 (In The Wings 128) [2015 85: t13.9g Dec 5] rather leggy gelding: fairly useful
handicapper: well held only outing in 2015: stays 2¼m: acts on viscoride, good to firm and
heavy going: has worn tongue tie: fairly useful hurdler. *Ian Williams*

SWIRRAL EDGE 2 b.f. (Feb 15) Hellvelyn 118 – Pizzarra 62 (Shamardal (USA) 129) **74 p**
[2015 5m⁵ 5.1d 5m⁵ 5d⁴ 6g* Oct 8] £10,500Y: first foal: dam, maiden (best at 5f), half-
sister to smart 5f-1m winner Grecian Dancer and useful sprinters Nocturn and Wunders
Dream: fair performer: won nursery at Ayr in October: will stay 7f: open to further
improvement. *David Brown*

SWISS AFFAIR 3 b.f. Pivotal 124 – Swiss Lake (USA) 115 (Indian Ridge 123) [2015 6m² **82 p**
6d² 6d* Oct 5] sister to smart 5f and (including at 2 yrs) 6f winner Swiss Diva and half-
sister to several winners, including smart sprinters Swiss Spirit (by Invincible Spirit) and
Swiss Dream (by Oasis Dream): dam 5f winner (including at 2 yrs): fairly useful form: off
5 months, didn't need to reproduce best to land odds in 15-runner maiden at Windsor final
start by 2 lengths from Dream Bounty, quickening clear over 1f out: raced only at 6f: useful
sprinter in the making. *John Gosden*

SWISS CROSS 8 b.g. Cape Cross (IRE) 129 – Swiss Lake (USA) 115 (Indian Ridge 123) **87**
[2015 96, a104: p5g p7g 5g⁴ 6f p6m p5m⁶ 6m⁴ 6.1m⁶ 5.3d 6m³ 7g² 7g 8d t7.1g⁶ a7g³ p6f³
p6f p6f⁶ p6g t7.1f p7m Dec 31] useful-looking gelding: fairly useful handicapper: stays 7f:
acts on polytrack, tapeta and good to firm going: tried in headgear: usually wears tongue
tie: often races prominently. *Phil McEntee*

SWISS LAIT 4 b.f. Milk It Mick 120 – Matilda Peace (Namaqualand (USA)) [2015 63: **57**
8.5m⁶ 7.9g³ 7g⁵ 8m 7d⁶ 7d³ 8.5g⁴ 9.2m⁴ t9.5f t8.6g Dec 5] lengthy filly: modest maiden:
stays 9f: acts on tapeta, soft and good to firm going: tried in headgear: often starts slowly,
usually races nearer last than first: signs of temperament. *Patrick Holmes*

SWISS RANGE 2 b.f. (Apr 14) Zamindar (USA) 116 – Spanish Sun (USA) 119 (El Prado **86 p**
(IRE) 119) [2015 7d² Oct 31] half-sister to 11f winner Cordoba and 7f winner Solar Verde
(both by Oasis Dream): dam, 7f (at 2 yrs) and 1½m (Ribblesdale Stakes winner), sister to
high-class winner up to 1½m Spanish Moon: 5/4, shaped well when 1½ lengths second of
9 to Tiptree in maiden at Newmarket, clear of rest: will improve. *John Gosden*

SWNYMOR (IRE) 6 b.g. Dylan Thomas (IRE) 132 – Propaganda (IRE) 76 (Sadler's –
Wells (USA) 132) [2015 108: 13s 16.1m 14.1s Oct 12] strong, good-topped gelding: useful
handicapper at best: well held in 2015 (left John Quinn after second start): stays 2m: acts
on good to firm and heavy going. *Kevin Frost*

SWORDBEARER 4 ch.g. Selkirk (USA) 129 – Isis (USA) 71 (Royal Academy (USA) **79**
130) [2015 79: t8.6m³ p8g³ 9g³ 10g 8m⁴ p8g³ p8g Oct 6] angular gelding: fair maiden:
stays 9f: acts on polytrack: tried in visor: suspect attitude. *James Fanshawe*

SWORD OF THE LORD 5 b.g. Kheleyf (USA) 116 – Blue Echo 97 (Kyllachy 129) **75 §**
[2015 83: 8.1s⁴ 10m³ 10.2s² 10v* 11s² Sep 1] compact gelding: fair handicapper: won at
Ffos Las in August: stays 11f: acts on polytrack, good to firm and heavy going: tried in
cheekpieces/tongue tie: travels strongly: quirky sort, not one to rely on. *Nigel Twiston-Davies*

SWORDS 13 b.g. Vettori (IRE) 119 – Pomorie (IRE) 67 (Be My Guest (USA) 126) [2015 **40**
–: t12.2f p12f f11s⁵ t12.2f⁶ t13.9f 11.9m t12.2g Aug 27] sturdy gelding: poor handicapper:
stays 16.5f: acts on polytrack, fibresand and good to firm going: tried in headgear.
Ray Peacock

SWOT 3 b.g. Exceed And Excel (AUS) 126 – House Point 59 (Pivotal 124) [2015 77: 7s* **77**
8.5g t7.1f Oct 13] quite attractive gelding: fair performer: won maiden at Lingfield in
August: stays 7f: acts on soft and good to firm going. *John Gosden*

SYDNEY HEIGHTS (IRE) 3 ch.c. Lord Shanakill (USA) 121 – Ashdali (IRE) (Grand **46**
Lodge (USA) 125) [2015 p8g⁶ 8m 10m Jul 6] rather unfurnished colt: poor form in
maidens/claimer: sold 4,000 gns, sent to Italy. *Charles Hills*

SYDNEY RUFFDIAMOND 3 b.g. Equiano (FR) 127 – Pirouetting 81 (Pivotal 124) **93**
[2015 72: 7m 5m* 5g⁴ 6g⁴ 5g* 6g⁴ 5d* 5g 5g Sep 5] strong gelding: fairly useful
handicapper: won at Windsor in May, Redcar in June and Ascot (by neck from Showstoppa)
in July: best form at 5f: acts on good to firm and good to soft going. *Richard Hannon*

SYLVETTE 3 ch.f. Selkirk (USA) 129 – Souvenance 110 (Hernando (FR) 127) [2015 66: **64**
p12g p16f⁴ Dec 21] modest maiden: stays 2m: acts on polytrack, tapeta and soft going:
tried in cheekpieces/tongue tie: front runner/races prominently. *Roger Varian*

SYMBOLIC 2 b.c. (Feb 2) Shamardal (USA) 129 – Resort 97 (Oasis Dream 129) [2015 **78 p**
7g² Oct 21] well-made colt: third foal: half-brother to 6f-8.6f winner Supersta (by Pivotal):
dam, 7f/1m winner, closely related to smart performer up to 1m Byron out of Cheveley
Park Stakes winner Gay Gallanta: 7/2, promising 4½ lengths second of 10 to Mootaharer
in maiden at Newmarket on debut: will improve. *John Gosden*

SYMBOLIC STAR (IRE) 3 b.g. New Approach (IRE) 132 – Epitome (IRE) 71 **77**
(Nashwan (USA) 135) [2015 83p: t7.1f* 8m⁶ Apr 25] good-topped gelding: fairly useful
form: 4/9, easily won 12-runner maiden at Wolverhampton in January: disappointing in
handicap only subsequent start: should stay at least 1m: sold only £7,500. *Charlie Appleby*

SYMBOLIST (IRE) 3 b.f. Yeats (IRE) 128 – Pescia (IRE) 98 (Darshaan 133) [2015 10m **65**
p12g³ p12g p15.8f⁴ Sep 22] €10,000F: lengthy, well-made filly: closely related to several
winners, including useful/unreliable 1¼m winner Stately Home (by Montjeu) and 11f
winner Tri Na Ceile (by Galileo): dam French 1¼m-1½m winner: fair maiden: stays 15f.
Richard Hannon

SYMPHONY OF KINGS 4 b.g. Lucarno (USA) 121 – Flying Lion 58 (Hunting Lion **85**
(IRE) 115) [2015 t12.2g² p12g² p12m* 11.6m 12.1m⁵ 10m² p12g 10.1m³ 10g³ 9.9v* 10g²
Sep 11] workmanlike gelding: fourth foal: dam 2-y-o 7f winner: fairly useful performer:
won maiden at Lingfield in February and handicap at Brighton in August: left Tony Carroll
after sixth start: stays 1½m: acts on polytrack, good to firm and heavy going: in cheekpieces
last 4 starts. *Michael Attwater*

SYMPOSIUM 2 ch.f. (Feb 27) Exceed And Excel (AUS) 126 – Soodad (King's Best **78**
(USA) 132) [2015 6d⁴ 16m* 7g Oct 10] 70,000Y: lengthy, good-quartered filly: second
foal: half-sister to a winner in Spain by Azamour: dam, ran 3 times in France, out of half-
sister to 1000 Guineas winner Virginia Waters: fairly useful form: won maiden at
Wolverhampton in September: below expectations in nursery at Newmarket final start,
carrying head awkwardly: should stay 7f. *William Haggas*

SYNAESTHESIA (FR) 4 b.f. High Chaparral (IRE) 132 – I'm Sensational 83 (Selkirk **57**
(USA) 129) [2015 67: t8.6f⁴ 10.3d p8g⁶ Jun 18] modest maiden: stays 1¼m: acts on
polytrack and tapeta: tried in hood. *Lady Cecil*

SYNCOPATE 6 b.g. Oratorio (IRE) 128 – Millistar 88 (Galileo (IRE) 134) [2015 85: **86**
10.3g² p10f⁴ 12g³ 12v* p12g Nov 18] fairly useful handicapper: won at Doncaster
(apprentice) in August and Newbury (amateur) in October: stays 1½m: acts on polytrack
and heavy going. *Pam Sly*

SYNODIC (USA) 3 br.c. Henrythenavigator (USA) 131 – Seven Moons (JPN) (Sunday **73**
Silence (USA)) [2015 –: 8d³ 8d 8m⁵ Jun 20] tall colt: fair maiden: best effort on
reappearance: wears tongue tie. *David Lanigan*

SYNONYM (ITY) 4 ch.f. Haatef (USA) 117 – Shatarah 79 (Gulch (USA)) [2015 63: f6d p7m 5f⁴ 6g³ 6.1m p5g⁵ Aug 17] poor handicapper: stays 7f: acts on polytrack and firm going: often in hood in 2015: usually slowly away: best treated with caution. *Michael Appleby* **47 §**

SYNOPSIS 3 b.f. Azamour (IRE) 130 – Censored 79 (Pivotal 124) [2015 10m⁴ 9g* Oct 11] good-topped, attractive filly: third foal: half-sister to 2-y-o 1m winner Dutchartcollector (by Dutch Art): dam, 1m winner who stayed 10.3f, half-sister to Prix de Diane winner Confidential Lady: fairly useful form: better effort when winning maiden at the Curragh (by 1½ lengths from Melanna) in October: left Roger Varian after first start: will stay at least 1¼m: open to further improvement. *G. M. Lyons, Ireland* **82 p**

SYNOPTIC DREAM (USA) 3 b.f. Medicean 128 – Specific Dream (Danehill Dancer (IRE) 117) [2015 p8m 8.3m 7m f8d t9.5g p14g p10f Sep 10] 45,000Y: first foal: dam unraced sister to 1000 Guineas winner Speciosa: no form. *Derek Shaw* **–**

SYRDARYA 3 ch.f. Galileo (IRE) 134 – Rock Salt (Selkirk (USA) 129) [2015 9.9g³ 10m³ 12m² 12g⁵ p10f² p12g⁶ Oct 14] closely related to smart 2-y-o 7f (including Moyglare Stud Stakes) winner Termagant (by Powerscourt) and half-sister to several winners, including useful winner up to 1½m Splinter Cell (2-y-o 1m winner, by Johannesburg): dam placed up to 11f in France: fair maiden: left Ralph Beckett after fourth start: stays 1½m: acts on polytrack and good to firm going: often in hood: front runner/races prominently. *Roger Varian* **78**

SYRIAN 8 b.g. Hawk Wing (USA) 136 – Lady Lahar 106 (Fraam 114) [2015 64§: t8.6f 9.9d 10s Oct 16] rangy gelding: modest handicapper: well held in amateur events in 2015: stays 1¼m: acts on polytrack, tapeta, good to firm and heavy going: has worn tongue tie: starts slowly, often races in rear: ungenuine. *Alan Berry* **– §**

SYRIAN PEARL 4 gr.f. Clodovil (IRE) 116 – Syrian Queen 82 (Slip Anchor 136) [2015 90, a83: 6m 6.1m⁶ 6g² 6m⁴ 6g 6g⁴ 6.1g² Sep 30] fairly useful handicapper: stays 7f: acts on polytrack and good to firm going. *Chris Wall* **90**

T

TAAJUB (IRE) 8 b.g. Exceed And Excel (AUS) 126 – Purple Tiger (IRE) (Rainbow Quest (USA) 134) [2015 100: p6f p5f³ 6m 5f³ 6m 5f² 5f² 5d⁴ 5g⁵ p5g Dec 15] good-bodied gelding: fairly useful handicapper: stays 6f: acts on polytrack, firm and good to soft going: tried in headgear. *Peter Crate* **93**

TAAQAH (USA) 3 b.f. Arch (USA) 127 – Classic West (USA) (Gone West (USA)) [2015 93p: 7g p8m² 6.9g 8f⁴ p10g⁵ 8d² p8g Oct 29] medium-sized filly: useful performer: best effort when second in listed race at Hanover (2 lengths behind Amabelle) on penultimate start: stays 1m: acts on polytrack, good to firm and good to soft going: in headgear nowadays: *James Tate* **99**

TAARESH (IRE) 10 b.g. Sakhee (USA) 136 – Tanaghum 104 (Darshaan 133) [2015 p13.3g² p12g Oct 6] rather leggy gelding: fair handicapper: stays 1½m: acts on polytrack, soft and good to firm going: tried in cheekpieces. *Kevin Morgan* **70**

TABARRAK (IRE) 2 b.c. (Jan 22) Acclamation 118 – Bahati (IRE) 99 (Intikhab (USA) 135) [2015 7g² 7s* 6g² Sep 30] €85,000F, £180,000Y: strong colt: first foal: dam, 2-y-o 6f winner who stayed 1m, half-sister to useful 5f-7f winner Zero Money: fairly useful form: won maiden at Newbury in September by 3½ lengths from River Echo: improved again when neck second of 8 to Projection in minor event at Salisbury, sticking to task: stays 7f. *Richard Hannon* **97**

TABIKAT ELLE (IRE) 2 ch.f. (Apr 21) Showcasing 117 – Mansiya 65 (Vettori (IRE) 119) [2015 7f⁶ 7.2d⁶ 6g³ 6g Oct 20] €34,000Y, £45,000 2-y-o: fifth foal: half-sister to 7f winner Hunt (by Dark Angel) and a winner abroad by Oratorio: dam maiden (stayed 9.5f): fair maiden: stays 7f. *K. R. Burke* **69**

TABLA 3 b.f. Rail Link 132 – Questa Nova (Rainbow Quest (USA) 134) [2015 p12f⁵ p10f⁴ 8.3g p12g p10g p8g* Dec 2] 13,000 2-y-o: well-made filly: sixth foal: sister to useful French 7f winner Eurozone and half-sister to 2-y-o 7f winner Paint Splash (by Beat Hollow) and French 1m winner Straight Six (by Starcraft): dam once-raced half-sister to smart 6f-1m performer Danger Over: fair performer: won maiden at Lingfield in December: stays 1½m: acts on polytrack: front runner/races prominently. *Lee Carter* **70**

TABLEFORTEN 4 ch.g. Pastoral Pursuits 127 – Twitch Hill 67 (Piccolo 121) [2015 60§: **63 §** t6g⁵ p7g² t7.1f t7.1m² p7g Feb 24] rather leggy gelding: modest handicapper: acts on polytrack/tapeta and any turf going: often in headgear prior to 2015: temperamental: sent to Germany, where won handicaps at Hamburg (1m) in June and Cologne (7f) in September. *J. S. Moore*

TAC DE BOISTRON (FR) 8 gr.g. Take Risks (FR) 116 – Pondiki (FR) (Sicyos (USA) **122** 126) [2015 124: 13.4v² 20f Jun 18] good-topped gelding: very smart performer: won Prix Royal-Oak at Longchamp in 2013 and 2014: second in Ormonde Stakes at Chester (1¼ lengths behind Clever Cookie) in May: 8/11, unsuited by ground when held in Gold Cup at Royal Ascot only subsequent start: stayed 2½m: best form on good going or softer (acted on heavy): first in cheekpieces: often raced towards rear/travelled strongly: retired in September. *Marco Botti*

TACTICAL STRIKE 4 ch.g. Pivotal 124 – Alvee (IRE) 75 (Key of Luck (USA) 126) **–** [2015 p15.8f Jan 30] fair maiden: well held in handicap only outing in 2015: stays 1¾m: acts on good to soft going: tried in headgear/tongue tie. *Shaun Harris*

TACTICUS (USA) 4 b.c. A P Indy (USA) 131 – Visions of Clarity (IRE) (Sadler's Wells **114** (USA) 132) [2015 80: p12g³ f12g* f12s* p13.3g⁵ 10.3m⁶ a9f⁴ a14f* a13f* Sep 12] smart performer: successful in 2 handicaps at Southwell in March: left Lady Cecil after fifth outing: improved form last 2 starts, winning listed race at Saratoga in August and non-graded stakes at Belmont (beat V. E. Day by 3¾ lengths) in September: stayed 1¾m: acted on dirt, polytrack and fibresand, probably on good to firm going: wore headgear: usually raced prominently: fractured a leg in training in early-October and put down. *H. Graham Motion, USA*

TADAAWOL 2 b.c. (Apr 13) Kyllachy 129 – Bright Edge 102 (Danehill Dancer (IRE) **76 p** 117) [2015 7s² 7s⁴ Oct 10] 35,000F, £82,000Y: seventh foal: half-brother to 3 winners, including useful 5f-8.6f winner Arthur's Edge (by Diktat) and 2-y-o 5f winner Edge of Light (by Xaar): dam 6f winner (including at 2 yrs): fair form in maidens at Goodwood (second to Inn The Bull) and York (fourth to Garcia, keeping on well without being knocked about): likely to do better. *Richard Hannon*

TADALAVIL 10 gr.g. Clodovil (IRE) 116 – Blandish (USA) (Wild Again (USA)) [2015 **51** 62: 5d⁶ 5d 7.1m⁵ 5d⁵ 5m⁵ 6g² 5d⁵ 5g 5g⁵ 5m³ 5d 5g⁶ 5m⁶ 6g 5m² Sep 27] small, strong, close-coupled gelding: modest handicapper: stays 6f: acts on good to firm and heavy going: front runner/races prominently: none too consistent. *Linda Perratt*

TADARROK 3 ch.c. Elusive Quality (USA) – Don't Forget Faith (USA) 102 (Victory **82** Gallop (CAN) 130) [2015 p6g² 6g p8m p8g a6f² a7f* Nov 27] 75,000Y: first foal: dam 6f (at 2 yrs) and 11f (in USA) winner out of US Grade 1 2-y-o 7f winner Contredance: fairly useful performer: left Mark Johnston after fourth start: won maiden at Jebel Ali in November: stays 7f: acts on sand: races prominently. *D. Watson, UAE*

TADPOLE 3 b.f. Sir Percy 129 – Frog 84 (Akarad (FR) 130) [2015 79p: p12g³ 11.9v³ **82** 13.1f⁶ Sep 12] fairly useful handicapper: stays 1½m: acts on polytrack and soft going. *William Haggas*

TADQEEQ 3 b.g. Makfi 130 – Perfect Spirit (IRE) (Invincible Spirit (IRE) 121) [2015 84: **90** 8s³ 8d² 8s⁴ 10.1m p8g⁴ Jul 1] tall gelding: fairly useful handicapper: worth another try at 1¼m: acts on tapeta and good to soft going: sometimes in headgear: usually races close up: sold 54,000 gns, sent to Qatar. *William Haggas*

TAEXALI (IRE) 2 ch.c. (Feb 11) Raven's Pass (USA) 133 – Enchanted Evening (IRE) **87** 105 (High Chaparral (IRE) 132) [2015 5v⁵ 5.3m* 5g⁵ May 23] stocky colt: first foal: dam, 7f/1m winner, half-sister to smart 5f-1m winner King Jock out of smart 6f/7f winner Glen Kate: fairly useful form: won 5-runner maiden at Brighton in April: 33/1, improved again when 4½ lengths fifth of 10 to Round Two in listed race at the Curragh: stays 5.3f: sent to UAE. *John Patrick Shanahan, Ireland*

TAFAHOM (IRE) 3 b.g. Acclamation 118 – Dance Set (Selkirk (USA) 129) [2015 68: **80** 9.8g⁴ 8m⁴ 8.3m* 8m⁶ Jun 26] good-topped gelding: fairly useful performer: won maiden at Nottingham in June: best effort at 8.5f: acts on good to firm going: sometimes slowly away: has been gelded. *B. W. Hills*

TAFFETTA 3 ch.f. Paco Boy (IRE) 129 – Tarneem (USA) 87 (Zilzal (USA) 137) [2015 **71** 53: 6s³ 6g⁴ 5d³ 5m* 5.9g 5d³ 5m³ 7m⁶ Aug 5] fair performer: won maiden at Beverley in May: stays 6f: acts on good to firm and good to soft going. *Tony Coyle*

TAFOLAU (IRE) 3 b.f. Dylan Thomas (IRE) 132 – Sliding Scale (Sadler's Wells (USA) **71**
132) [2015 p7g² t8.6m⁶ t9.5g⁵ p13.3f³ p16f p13.3f³ Oct 24] fourth foal: closely related to
1m winner Scala Romana and a winner in Sweden (both by Holy Roman Emperor): dam
unraced daughter of St Leger runner-up High And Low: fair maiden: stays 13.5f: acts on
polytrack: tried in blinkers: often races lazily. *Sir Mark Prescott Bt*

TAFTEESH (IRE) 2 b.g. (Apr 12) Kodiac 112 – Mudalalah (IRE) 70 (Singspiel (IRE) **84**
133) [2015 7s³ 7g* p8f⁴ Nov 23] €35,000F, €120,000Y: second foal: dam, maiden (stayed
1½m), half-sister to smart winner up to 1¼m Moiqen: fairly useful form: won maiden at
Salisbury in September by neck from Galvanize: upped in trip and in first-time tongue
strap, disappointing in nursery at Chelmsford final start, looking awkward: should be suited
by 1m+: has been gelded. *Simon Crisford*

TAGHREEB 4 b.g. Dubawi (IRE) 129 – Ghaneema (USA) 82 (Forestry (USA) 121) [2015 **89 p**
80p: 8g* 10.1d⁴ May 19] fairly useful form: won handicap at Redcar in April by head from
Dubai Hills: upped in trip, raced freely when fourth of 9 in similar event at Newcastle only
subsequent start: will benefit from return to 1m: in blinkers last 2 starts: has been gelded:
should still do better. *Brian Meehan*

TAGTALE (IRE) 3 b.f. Tagula (IRE) 116 – Story (Observatory (USA) 131) [2015 54: 5m **–**
6s 7.2d 7.2g Sep 29] modest performer at best, well held in 2015: stays 6f: acts on heavy
going: has worn blinkers. *Alistair Whillans*

TAGULA NIGHT (IRE) 9 ch.g. Tagula (IRE) 116 – Carpet Lady (IRE) 70 (Night Shift **92**
(USA)) [2015 89: p7f⁵ 7v p6g⁴ p6g⁴ 5f⁶ p6g⁴ p7g 6m⁴ 6g⁴ 5s Oct 19] workmanlike
gelding: fairly useful handicapper: won at Kempton (by 2 lengths from Picture Dealer) in
May: stays 6f: acts on polytrack, firm and soft going: wears headgear/tongue tie: front
runner/races prominently. *Dean Ivory*

TAHAF (IRE) 5 b.g. Authorized (IRE) 133 – Lady Zonda 95 (Lion Cavern (USA) 117) **55**
[2015 75: 8m 9.9d⁶ Jun 23] lengthy, useful-looking gelding: modest handicapper: stays
8.5f: acts on good to firm and heavy going: wears headgear: usually in tongue tie prior to
2015. *Mark Brisbourne*

TAHCHEE 4 ch.g. Sleeping Indian 122 – Neyraan 53 (Lujain (USA) 119) [2015 82: 5m **74**
6m⁵ p6g p6g 7m* 7v p7g p8g Oct 6] lengthy gelding: fair performer: won seller at Leicester
in August: stays 7f: acts on polytrack and good to firm going: sometimes in headgear in
2015: tried in tongue tie in 2015. *Seamus Durack*

TAHIRA (GER) 5 ch.m. Doyen (IRE) 132 – Tennessee Queen (GER) (Big Shuffle (USA) **103**
122) [2015 108: 10.3s⁶ 11.9f² 12m Jun 27] lengthy mare: useful handicapper: best effort of
2015 when second at Haydock (2¼ lengths behind Maid In Rio) in June: stays 1½m: acts
on firm and good to soft going: in hood last 2 starts. *John Quinn*

TAHITI ONE 2 b.f. (Apr 19) Bertolini (USA) 125 – Club Tahiti 92 (Hernando (FR) 127) **59**
[2015 5m⁵ p6g* p7g⁵ p6g* 7v² 7d Oct 11] first foal: dam, 2-y-o 6.5f winner who stayed 9f,
half-sister to smart performer up to 1¾m Clowance: modest performer: won sellers at
Lingfield in July and August: stays 7f: acts on polytrack and heavy going: sometimes
slowly away. *Tony Carroll*

TAILORMADE 3 b.g. Josr Algarhoud (IRE) 118 – Victoriana 53 (Wolfhound (USA) 126) **61**
[2015 t8.6g⁴ p10g p10g⁶ 10m 7d Jun 23] modest maiden: best effort at 8.5f: acts on tapeta:
often races prominently, has found little. *Lydia Pearce*

TAILWIND 2 b.c. (Feb 4) Dubawi (IRE) 129 – Time Saved 89 (Green Desert (USA) 127) **80 p**
[2015 t7.1f² p6g* Dec 3] half-brother to several winners, including 7f-1¼m winner Lay
Time (by Galileo) and winner up to 1½m Plea Bargain (2-y-o 7f winner, by Machiavellian),
both smart: dam 1¼m winner out of top-class 1¼m-1½m performer Time Charter: dropped
in trip, 100/30-on, didn't need to improve on debut form to win 7-runner maiden at
Kempton by neck from Mazzini, going clear over 1f out but just holding on: better to come.
Roger Varian

TAJATHUB 3 gr.g. Bahamian Bounty 116 – Galapagar (USA) (Miswaki (USA) 124) **74**
[2015 88p: p7g* 7d⁶ p7g Sep 5] won maiden at Kempton in May: raced only at 7f: dead.
Ed Dunlop

TAKAFOL (IRE) 3 b.g. Fast Company (IRE) 126 – Jamary (IRE) (Grand Reward (USA) **67 §**
112) [2015 64p: t6g⁶ 5g² 5g⁴ 8g³ 8d 6m 6m⁵ 7g² 6g 6d³ Oct 26] fair maiden: stays 7f: acts
on good to soft going: usually in headgear: often starts slowly: unreliable. *David O'Meara*

TAKAHIRO 3 b.c. Kyllachy 129 – Marliana (IRE) (Mtoto 134) [2015 –: t7.1f p5g⁵ p6f⁶ **57**
t7.1m⁶ t8.6f⁵ 6d⁵ p7m³ Apr 29] modest maiden: stays 7f: acts on tapeta: tried in blinkers in
2015. *Richard Hannon*

TAKE A BREAK 4 b.f. Josr Algarhoud (IRE) 118 – Waterpark 75 (Namaqualand (USA)) – [2015 7m May 25] no sign of ability. *Ray Craggs*

TAKE A NOTE 6 b.g. Singspiel (IRE) 133 – Ela Paparouna 85 (Vettori (IRE) 119) [2015 **97** 98: 7g 7m³ 7m 7.6g³ p7g² 7g 8m Oct 2] sturdy gelding: useful performer: third in handicap at Goodwood (2¼ lengths behind Donncha), minor event at Lingfield (4½ lengths behind Muffri'ha) and handicap at Kempton (1½ lengths behind Outer Space): stays 1m: acts on polytrack and firm going: usually wears headgear: front runner/races prominently. *Patrick Chamings*

TAKE CHARGE 2 b.c. (Apr 2) Showcasing 117 – Be Decisive 65 (Diesis 133) [2015 7m⁵ **78 p** 7g⁶ 7g³ Sep 23] 9,500F, £41,000Y: half-brother to 3 winners, including winner up to 9f Be Fantastic (2-y-o 6f winner, by Fantastic Light) and 2-y-o 5f winner To The Point (by Refuse To Bend): dam 1m winner: fair form in maidens at Doncaster and Redcar first/final starts, 2 lengths third to Dark Devil in latter (wandered): remains with potential. *David Brown*

TAKE COVER 8 b.g. Singspiel (IRE) 133 – Enchanted 99 (Magic Ring (IRE) 115) [2015 **119** 121: 5g 5f⁶ 5m 5m² 5d³ 5m p5g* Oct 23] big, strong, lengthy gelding: developed into very smart performer in 2014: almost as good in 2015, and won listed race at Dundalk in October by 1½ lengths from Speed Hawk: best other efforts when head second to Muthmir in King George Stakes at Goodwood (had won race 12 months earlier) and length third to Sole Power in Flying Five Stakes at the Curragh: winner at 7f, best form at 5f: acts on polytrack, fibresand, soft and good to firm going: front runner/races prominently. *David C. Griffiths*

TAKE IN TIME 2 b.g. (Apr 29) Hellvelyn 118 – Barnacla (IRE) 83 (Bluebird (USA) 125) – [2015 6g 6g Sep 19] tailed-off last in 2 maidens. *Michael Easterby*

TAKEITFROMALADY (IRE) 6 b.g. Intikhab (USA) 135 – Pinheiros (IRE) (Rock of **69** Gibraltar (IRE) 133) [2015 71: p15.8g² p13g⁵ p15.8g² p15.8f⁴ p16g³ p15.8g* p16g⁶ p15.8g 12v³ Sep 1] workmanlike gelding: fair handicapper: won at Lingfield in June: stays 2m: acts on polytrack, good to firm and heavy going: wears headgear. *Lee Carter*

TAKE NOTE (IRE) 3 b.f. Azamour (IRE) 130 – Lolla's Spirit (IRE) 68 (Montjeu (IRE) **54** 137) [2015 66: 7g t8.6g⁶ t9.5g p10g² p10f⁵ p12m⁴ Dec 16] modest maiden: left James Toller after fifth start: stays 1¼m: acts on polytrack: often in headgear. *Seamus Mullins*

TAKE THE HELM 2 ch.g. (Mar 12) Monsieur Bond (IRE) 120 – Oasis Breeze 88 (Oasis **88** Dream 129) [2015 5m⁵ 6.5s⁵ t7.1g* t7.1m⁵ t8.6m³ Dec 26] £33,000Y: strong, compact gelding: third foal: half-brother to 6f/7f winner Dutch Breeze (by Dutch Art) and 2-y-o 5f winner Don't Tell Annie (by Royal Applause): dam, 2-y-o 5f/6f winner, closely related to smart winner up to 1¼m Familiar Territory: fairly useful performer: won maiden and nursery at Wolverhampton in December: stays 8.5f: acts on tapeta. *Brian Meehan*

TAKE THE LEAD 5 ch.m. Assertive 121 – My Dancer (IRE) 79 (Alhaarth (IRE) 126) – [2015 57, a72: t5.1f 5.9s Aug 24] handicapper, fair at best: well held in 2015: stays 6f: acts on fibresand and soft going: tried in blinkers. *John Weymes*

TAKE TWO 6 b.g. Act One 124 – Lac Marmot (FR) (Marju (IRE) 127) [2015 p11g² **78** t12.2f³ p12g³ Feb 14] unfurnished gelding: fair handicapper: stays 1½m: acts on polytrack, tapeta, soft and good to firm going: fairly useful form over hurdles. *Alex Hales*

TAKING LIBERTYS 2 b.g. (Apr 14) Makfi 130 – Liberty Chery (Statue of Liberty **89** (USA) 115) [2015 5m* 6m* 7g⁶ 7.1m⁶ 8g⁵ Sep 19] £18,000Y: rather unfurnished gelding: third foal: dam, useful French 1m winner, half-sister to useful French performer up to 10.5f Fauvelia: fairly useful performer: won maiden at Beverley in April and minor event at Pontefract (by ½ length from Carrington) in May: best effort after when sixth of 10 to First Selection in Solario Stakes at Sandown penultimate start: gelded after final outing: should stay 1m: acts on good to firm going. *Kevin Ryan*

TALAWAT 3 b.f. Cape Cross (IRE) 129 – Queen of Mean 79 (Pivotal 124) [2015 p10g⁴ **83** t9.5g* p10g² p10g³ p8f Sep 10] 260,000Y: first foal: dam, 6f winner, half-sister to very smart performer up to 1m Zoffany: fairly useful performer: won maiden at Wolverhampton in July: stays 1¼m: acts on polytrack and tapeta: races prominently. *Marco Botti*

TALENT SCOUT (IRE) 9 b.g. Exceed And Excel (AUS) 126 – Taalluf (USA) 82 **81** (Hansel (USA)) [2015 89: 8m 7m³ 8m t7.1g 7.9g 7.5m² 6.9d 8g 7.9g³ 7.5g³ 8g⁴ 8d³ Oct 5] sturdy gelding: fairly useful handicapper: stays 1m: acts on polytrack, good to firm and good to soft going: usually wears headgear: usually leads. *Karen Tutty*

TALKSALOT (IRE) 4 b.g. Thousand Words 113 – Lady Piste (IRE) 67 (Ali-Royal (IRE) **66** 127) [2015 –: t7.1g⁵ p6g 8.3m⁶ Jul 20] fair handicapper: stays 7f: acts on polytrack and tapeta: tried in cheekpieces. *J. S. Moore*

TALLULAH FLEUR 2 b.f. (Feb 25) Royal Applause 124 – Topflightcoolracer 89 —
(Lujain (USA) 119) [2015 6d Oct 26] £10,000Y: second foal: half-sister to 2-y-o 6f winner
Topflight Princess (by Cockney Rebel): dam 5f winner: 20/1, better for run when 8 lengths
ninth of 13 to Gowanless in maiden at Redcar on debut. *Ann Duffield*

TALLY'S SONG 2 b.f. (Feb 18) Piccolo 121 – Talamahana 66 (Kyllachy 129) [2015 5m —
5m Jun 5] first foal: dam, temperamental 6f/7f winner, half-sister to useful 2-y-o 7f/7.6f
winner Captain Saif: well held in 2 maidens. *Milton Bradley*

TALMADA (USA) 4 b.f. Cape Cross (IRE) 129 – Aryaamm (IRE) 94 (Galileo (IRE) 134) **110**
[2015 104: 10.4m² 11.9d⁴ 10.1g² 9d⁵ 8.1m⁵ 10.1m* 10g² Oct 18] big, rangy filly: smart
performer: won listed race at Yarmouth in September by ½ length from Speedy Boarding:
second in Middleton Stakes at York (1½ lengths behind Secret Gesture), listed race at
Newcastle (length behind Covert Love) and E. P. Taylor Stakes at Woodbine (best effort,
beaten 1½ lengths by Curvy). stays 1½m: acts on good to firm and good to soft going:
usually races prominently. *Roger Varian*

TALYANI 3 ch.g. Halling (USA) 133 – Italian Connection (Cadeaux Genereux 131) [2015 **98**
8d* p8g³ 8.9m* 8g* 8g Aug 21] 40,000Y: second foal: half-brother to 7f winner
I'vegotafeeling (by Rock of Gibraltar): dam unraced half-sister to dam of King George VI
& Queen Elizabeth Stakes winner Postponed: useful performer: won maiden at Ripon in
June and handicaps at York (apprentice) and Newmarket (by 3½ lengths from Estikhraaj)
in July: met trouble when well below form final outing: stays 9f: acts on good to firm and
good to soft going: usually travels strongly: sent to UAE. *William Haggas*

TAMARA LOVE (IRE) 2 b.f. (Feb 9) Tamayuz 126 – Lovers Peace (IRE) 87 (Oratorio —
(IRE) 128) [2015 6m May 26] 85,000Y: first foal: dam, 1½m/13f winner, half-sister to
useful 5f performer Emerald Peace: 50/1, very green when well held in maiden at Leicester
on debut. *Stuart Williams*

TAMARIN 3 ch.f. Paco Boy (IRE) 129 – Les Hurlants (IRE) (Barathea (IRE) 127) [2015 **57**
68: f6d5 t6g² t5.1f² 6.1m 7s⁶ 6d⁶ t6g t7.1m t6m t9.5m p8g t7.1f⁵ p6g² t7.1m p6f Dec 17]
has no near-side eye: modest maiden: left David Evans after seventh start: stays 7f: acts on
polytrack, tapeta, good to firm and good to soft going: usually in headgear in 2015: front
runner/races prominently. *Lisa Williamson*

TAMARKUZ (USA) 5 ch.h. Speightstown (USA) 124 – Without You Babe (USA) **123**
(Lemon Drop Kid (USA) 131) [2015 a7f² a8f* a8f* a8f* a8f* a8f⁴ a7f⁶ a8s⁴ Oct 3] tall
horse: very smart performer: in good form at Meydan early in year, winning handicap in
January, Firebreak Stakes in February, then Burj Nahaar and Godolphin Mile (beat Sloane
Avenue by short head, slowly into stride but responding well to lead last 100 yds), both in
March: left M. Al Muhairi after: just fair efforts at best subsequently, including when fourth
to Appealing Tale in Grade 2 Kelso Handicap at Belmont final outing: will probably stay
bit beyond 1m: acts on dirt/synthetics: wore hood final outing in 2014 (unseated rider at
start): has worn tongue tie: strong traveller: often races prominently. *Kiaran P. McLaughlin,
USA*

TAMASHA 4 ch.f. Sea The Stars (IRE) 140 – Tamarind (IRE) 107 (Sadler's Wells (USA) **95**
132) [2015 94p: 11.9f⁴ 11.6m Jun 27] useful form: only third start when creditable fourth
of 7 in handicap at Haydock, much better effort in 2015: stays 13f. *Ralph Beckett*

TAMAYUZ MAGIC (IRE) 4 b.g. Tamayuz 126 – Anne Tudor (IRE) 79 (Anabaa (USA) **82**
130) [2015 73: 10.3d³ 10.1d* 8s³ 12m² 12g⁴ 10.4g⁶ Sep 6] fairly useful handicapper: won
at Newcastle in April: stays 1½m: acts on any turf going: wears headgear. *Michael Easterby*

TAMAYUZ STAR (IRE) 5 ch.g. Tamayuz 126 – Magical Peace (IRE) 80 (Magical **91**
Wonder (USA) 125) [2015 92: 6m² 6m² 6m 6f⁵ 6m 7m³ 7g^ro Sep 26] smallish, strong
gelding: just fairly useful handicapper in 2015: stayed 7f: acted on firm going: dead.
George Margarson

TAMUJIN (IRE) 7 b.g. Elusive City (USA) 117 – Arabian Princess (Taufan (USA) 119) **51**
[2015 51: p10g⁶ 9.9m² 9.9d⁶ 11.5d⁶ 9.9m⁶ p10m² p10g⁵ Dec 30] modest maiden: stays **a61**
1¼m: acts on polytrack and good to firm going: sometimes in headgear/tongue tie prior to
2015. *Ken Cunningham-Brown*

TANAASUB (IRE) 2 ch.f. (Apr 23) Lope de Vega (IRE) 125 – Corryvreckan (IRE) 70 **74**
(Night Shift (USA)) [2015 6g² 6v⁶ Nov 7] £10,000Y, £52,000 2-y-o: half-sister to several
winners, including 2-y-o 5f winner Leftontheshelf (by Namid) and 2m winner Mollyow
(by Iceman): dam maiden (stayed 1m): second of 10 to Balance in maiden at Haydock in
October: well below that form on heavy ground in similar event at Doncaster: may yet do
better. *Robert Cowell*

TAN ARABIQ 2 b.c. (Apr 2) Arabian Gleam 122 – Tanning 60 (Atraf 116) [2015 f5g⁵ 7g **62** 7.5m⁴ Oct 1] 66/1, first form (modest) when 9 lengths fourth of 10 to Column in maiden at Beverley final start. *Michael Appleby*

TANASOQ (IRE) 2 b.c. (Feb 7) Acclamation 118 – Alexander Youth (IRE) 98 (Exceed **78 p** And Excel (AUS) 126) [2015 6.5s³ 7.1f³ Nov 13] 180,000Y: third foal: half-brother to smart 6f/7f winner Almargo (by Invincible Spirit) and winner up to 7.4f Denzille Lane (2-y-o 6f winner, by Iffraaj): dam, 6f winner, half-sister to high-class sprinter Moss Vale: third in maidens at Newbury (behind Monteverdi) in October and Wolverhampton in November, below debut form upped in trip in latter: may prove best at sprint distances: remains with potential. *B. W. Hills*

TANAWAR (IRE) 5 b.g. Elusive City (USA) 117 – Parakopi (IRE) 53 (Green Desert **75** (USA) 127) [2015 70: t.1g 7d⁵ 7g 8g⁴ 7s⁵ 7.2d 7.2d 8.3m* 7m⁶ 8.3m⁵ 7.2d² 8d⁵ 7d² 7d⁵ 7m* 7.9d* 8d Oct 5] fair handicapper: won at Nottingham (apprentice) in June and Redcar (apprentice) and Carlisle in September: effective at 7f to 1¼m: acts on polytrack, soft and firm going: wears headgear: often travels strongly. *Ruth Carr*

TANCRED (IRE) 4 b.g. Oratorio (IRE) 128 – Mythologie (FR) (Bering 136) [2015 –: **70** 5.3m⁵ p6g⁴ 6m⁴ f8d 7.6s p6g 6s* 6v⁶ 6g³ p6f 6v* t7.1f 6d⁶ Nov 13] leggy gelding: **a56** fair handicapper on turf, modest on all-weather: won at Brighton in August and October: stays 6f: acts on heavy going: wears headgear: often races in rear: none too consistent. *Conor Dore*

TANEEN (USA) 2 b.c. (Feb 18) Speightstown (USA) 124 – Moon And Sun (USA) **92 p** (Malibu Moon (USA)) [2015 6m³ 6g* Aug 29] $350,000Y: well-made colt: third foal: dam, US 2-y-o 5.5f winner from 2 starts, half-sister to US Grade 3 6f winner Palanka City: 5/2, confirmed debut promise when winning maiden at Newmarket by 2 lengths from Fighting Temeraire, quickening clear under hands-and-heels: will go on improving. *Roger Varian*

TANGERINE TREES 10 b.g. Mind Games 121 – Easy To Imagine (USA) (Cozzene **100** (USA)) [2015 103: 5v* 5m 5m 5m⁵ 5g⁴ 6m⁴ 5.4g 5g⁶ 5.6d 5s Oct 9] big, strong gelding: useful performer: won minor event at Musselburgh (by 1¼ lengths from Borderlescott) in April: stays 7f: acts on polytrack, good to firm and heavy going: wears headgear: front runner/races prominently. *Bryan Smart*

TANGO SKY (IRE) 6 b.g. Namid 128 – Sky Galaxy (USA) 84 (Sky Classic (CAN)) **77** [2015 82: p6g⁴ t7.1f* t7.1g⁴ t8.6f t7.1f* t7.1f⁶ t7.1f t7.1g³ 7s⁴ 7m² 7m⁵ 7m³ 7m t7.1g⁴ **a70** 6s* 6m⁴ 6m⁵ 6g² 6m² Sep 28] lengthy, useful-looking gelding: fair handicapper: won at Wolverhampton in January (apprentice) and February and at Redcar in July: stays 7f: acts on polytrack, tapeta, good to firm and heavy going: sometimes wears headgear. *Paul Midgley*

TANGO TURNER (IRE) 3 ch.c. Excellent Art 125 – Kassyderia (IRE) (Docksider **60** (USA) 124) [2015 –: p8f⁵ p8f p8f³ Mar 25] modest maiden: best effort when third at Kempton on handicap debut: will stay beyond 1m. *Jamie Poulton*

TANGRAMM 3 b.g. Sakhee's Secret 128 – Tripti (IRE) 72 (Sesaro (USA) 81) [2015 50: **74** p8g² t8.6f* t9.5f* t9.5m* Dec 18] fair performer: won minor event and handicap at Wolverhampton in November and another handicap there in December: stays 9.5f: acts on tapeta: usually responds generously to pressure. *Dean Ivory*

TANIYAR (IRE) 3 b.g. Shamardal (USA) 129 – Tanoura (IRE) 109 (Dalakhani (IRE) **117** 133) [2015 8s* 8g³ 8g* 8g⁴ 7g* 7m⁵ Oct 4] first foal: dam, 7f (at 2 yrs) and 1½m winner, half-sister to smart performers up to 1½m Takali and Takarian: smart performer: won minor events at Saint-Cloud in May and Deauville in June, and Prix du Pin at Longchamp (readily, by 1¼ lengths from La Berma) in September: good 3 lengths fifth to Make Believe in Prix de la Foret on last-named course final outing: stays 1m: acts on soft and good to firm going: gelded and sent to Hong Kong, where renamed Magpies Bridge. *A. de Royer Dupre, France*

TANNAAF (IRE) 3 b.c. High Chaparral (IRE) 132 – Wanna (IRE) 95 (Danehill Dancer **107** (IRE) 117) [2015 86p: 7g 10g⁴ 12.3s⁴ 10m³ 9.9g* Dec 30] useful performer: won Qatar Derby at Doha (dead-heated with Rogue Runner) in December: third in listed race at Newmarket (1¼ lengths behind Peacock) in May: stays 12.3f: acts on soft and good to firm going. *M. F. de Kock, South Africa*

TANNERON (IRE) 3 b.f. Elnadim (USA) 128 – Valbonne (IRE) 76 (Refuse To Bend **60** (IRE) 128) [2015 58: p7g 7.5s 7g² 7g 7v 6.1m 8m 7.5s* 7g p6m Nov 25] first foal: dam, 2-y-o 7f winner, half-sister to smart 2-y-o 6f winner Big Time: modest handicapper: won at Tipperary (apprentice) in August: stays 1m: acts on soft going: tried in blinkers. *John Joseph Murphy, Ireland*

TANZEEL (IRE) 4 b.g. Elusive City (USA) 117 – Royal Fizz (IRE) (Royal Academy **111** (USA) 130) [2015 102: 6m⁴ 6m* 7g 6g 7m Oct 3] sturdy gelding: smart handicapper: improved form when winning 20-runner event at York in July by 2 lengths from Shore Step, leading final 1f: well held all 3 subsequent starts: stays 6f: acts on good to firm going: wears tongue tie: sometimes slowly away. *Charles Hills*

TANZINA 3 b.f. Equiano (FR) 127 – Pilcomayo (IRE) (Rahy (USA) 115) [2015 7m 7.4g³ **59** p7g⁵ 7s Oct 12] lengthy filly: fourth foal: half-sister to 5f/6f winner Princess Dayna (by Green Desert) and a winner abroad by Rail Link: dam unraced daughter of US Grade 1 9f winner Link River: modest maiden: raced only around 7f. *Jo Crowley*

TAOPIX 3 b.g. Rip Van Winkle (IRE) 134 – Sinister Ruckus (USA) (Trippi (USA) 121) **60** [2015 9.2m⁵ 10m 10.1d⁴ 7g 7g Sep 19] modest maiden: best effort at 1¼m: acts on good to soft going: tried in blinkers: often races freely. *Karen McLintock*

TAPER TANTRUM (IRE) 3 b.g. Azamour (IRE) 130 – Maramba (USA) 97 (Hussonet **90** (USA)) [2015 81: 10.1m³ 12f 10m 8.1g³ 10.3g² p11g⁵ 10g Oct 19] sturdy gelding: fairly useful handicapper: good second at Doncaster in August: stays 10.5f: acts on good to firm and good to soft going: tried in hood in 2015. *Michael Bell*

TAPESTRY (IRE) 4 b.f. Galileo (IRE) 134 – Rumplestiltskin (IRE) 116 (Danehill (USA) **113** 126) [2015 123: 10d² 11.9m 12d Oct 17] tall, leggy, angular filly: very smart performer in 2014, winner of Yorkshire Oaks at York: not so good in 2015, best effort when second in Blandford Stakes at the Curragh (½ length behind Ribbons) in September: stays 1½m: acts on good to firm and good to soft going. *Aidan O'Brien, Ireland*

TAPIS LIBRE 7 b.g. Librettist (USA) 124 – Stella Manuela (FR) (Galileo (IRE) 134 **87** [2015 71: 12.4g 10.1d² 12g² 12.5m* 13.3m⁵ 12.8m* 15.8m* 12d* 12s⁵ 10g 16.4s 14.1s Oct 28] workmanlike gelding: fairly useful handicapper: won at Musselburgh in May, amateurs there in July and August, and Catterick (amateur, by short head from Hubertas) also in August: stays 2m: acts on polytrack, tapeta, good to firm and heavy going: has worn headgear. *Michael Easterby*

TAP SHOES 3 ch.f. Equiano (FR) 127 – Ruff Shod (USA) (Storm Boot (USA)) [2015 6m⁵ **59** 6m⁷ 6g⁶ p7g 5.7f¹ 6v Oct 6] angular filly: sixth foal: half-sister to French 13f winner Rock of Deauville (by Rock of Gibraltar) and 1½m winner Unex Picasso (by Galileo): dam unraced half-sister to US Grade 1 8.5f winner Hail Atlantis: modest maiden: should prove suited by 7f: acts on firm going: often races prominently. *Henry Candy*

TAP THE HONEY 2 b.g. (May 1) Fastnet Rock (AUS) 127 – Balladonia 103 (Primo **73 p** Dominie 121) [2015 8d 8d⁵ Sep 26] 92,000F: half-brother to numerous winners, including smart 2-y-o 6f/7f winner Wootton Bassett and useful 2-y-o 6f winner Glenalmond (both by Iffraaj) and useful winner up to 7.6f Mister Hardy (2-y-o 5f winner, by Kyllachy): dam 9f winner who stayed 1½m: 50/1, much improved from debut when 9 lengths fifth of 11 to Ormito in maiden at Haydock: subsequently gelded: open to further improvement. *K. R. Burke*

TAQDEER (IRE) 2 ch.c. (Jan 29) Fast Company (IRE) 126 – Brigantia (Pivotal 124) **80 p** [2015 t7.1g² Dec 4] €42,000F, £140,000Y: first foal: dam unraced half-sister to useful French/German 11f/1½m winner Britannic: well-backed 5/4, probably should have won when ½-length second of 9 to Take The Helm in maiden at Wolverhampton on debut, green early and forced to switch 1f out but closing all way to line: will be suited by 1m+: sure to progress. *John Gosden*

TAQDEES (IRE) 2 ch.f. (Mar 28) Sea The Stars (IRE) 140 – Aquarelle Bleue (Sadler's **69 p** Wells (USA) 132) [2015 8d 8.3s³ Nov 4] 400,000Y: fourth foal: closely related to smart 7f-9f winner Barawez (by Cape Cross): dam, placed at 11f-12.5f in France, out of very smart French 1¼m-1½m winner Aquarelliste: off 6 weeks, 10/1, left debut form well behind when 4¼ lengths third of 11 to Good Trip in maiden at Nottingham, despite being slowly into stride: open to further improvement. *John Gosden*

TAQNEEN (IRE) 4 b.g. Cape Cross (IRE) 129 – Badee'a (IRE) (Marju (IRE) 127) [2015 **81** 87: p8f⁵ 9.8v t8.6g 10.1m⁶ 8m² Aug 5] fairly useful handicapper: probably stays 1¼m: acts on polytrack, good to firm and heavy going: tried in blinkers: sent to UAE. *Ed Dunlop*

TAQNEYYA (IRE) 3 b.f. Raven's Pass (USA) 133 – Misdaqeya 106 (Red Ransom **82** (USA)) [2015 88p: 7m 7d³ 8d⁵ Aug 11] tall, lengthy, attractive filly: has plenty of scope: fairly useful handicapper: should stay at least 1m: acts on good to firm and good to soft going: usually races close up. *Charles Hills*

TAQWAA (IRE) 3 ch.c. (Mar 19) Iffraaj 127 – Hallowed Park (IRE) (Barathea (IRE) 127) **87 p** [2015 p6g² 7.1f² 7g³ 8.1s* Aug 31] 140,000Y: fourth foal: half-brother to 6f and (including at 2 yrs) 7f winner Shamrocked (by Rock of Gibraltar) and 9f/1¼m winner Stetchworth (by

New Approach): dam, unraced, closely related to Derby runner-up Walk In The Park: fairly useful form: third in maiden at York (1¼ lengths behind Beautiful Morning) in August: 2/7, won 3-runner maiden at Chepstow next time by 9 lengths, heavily eased: stays 1m: remains with potential. *Richard Hannon*

TARAKKOM (FR) 3 ch.g. Naaqoos 117 – Sahabah (USA) (Swain (IRE) 134) [2015 8g 12.4g t12.2m t9.5f f12g⁶ f14g⁵ Dec 12] modest maiden: left F. Head after second start: best effort at 12.4f: blinkered first 2 outings. *Peter Hiatt* — **58**

TARANDO 3 b.f. Equiano (FR) 127 – Christmas Tart (IRE) 74 (Danetime (IRE) 121) [2015 63: 6d 5g² p5g⁵ 5g⁵ 5.1d⁶ 5.9s⁶ 5m* 6g² 5s* f6g Nov 26] unfurnished filly: fair handicapper: won at Hamilton in September and at Ayr and Catterick in October: left Michael Bell after fifth start: stays 6f: acts on soft and good to firm going: in hood last 5 starts. *Keith Dalgleish* — **74**

TARA'S QUEST 2 b.f. (Feb 18) Makfi 130 – Gaditana (Rainbow Quest (USA) 134) [2015 6g /g Aug 31] 50,000Y: first foal: dam once-raced sister to Racing Post Trophy winner/ St Leger runner-up Armiger: modest form when seventh of 13 to Mustique in maiden at Ripon, better effort: pulled hard next time: sold 1,000 gns, sent to Portugal. *Michael Dods* — **52**

TARAZ 3 b.g. Oasis Dream 129 – Tamarind (IRE) 107 (Sadler's Wells (USA) 132) [2015 58: 8.3s 9.8d 10m* 10.1m* 11m 10.3g² Sep 11] good-topped gelding: fairly useful handicapper: won at Windsor in June and Epsom in July: should be suited by 1½m: acts on good to firm going: often leads. *Roger Varian* — **90**

TARGET FIXATION 2 b.g. (Mar 10) Assertive 121 – My Dancer (IRE) 79 (Alhaarth (IRE) 126) [2015 5f⁴ 6g⁶ t5.1g⁶ Aug 10] well held in maiden, seller and a claimer: has been gelded. *Tony Carroll* — **–**

TARLETON (IRE) 3 b.g. Invincible Spirit (IRE) 121 – Aguinaga (IRE) 76 (Machiavellian (USA) 123) [2015 t7.1g t7.1m⁴ t6fʰᵘ Feb 23] modest form in maidens at Wolverhampton first 2 outings: blinkered, pulled up soon after start there next time: gelded after. *Richard Fahey* — **61**

TARNEND LASS 2 b.f. (Mar 22) Equiano (FR) 127 – Valjarv (IRE) 97 (Bluebird (USA) 125) [2015 5f⁴ 5v May 8] 6,500F, £16,000Y: sixth foal: half-sister to 5f winner Val C (by Dubawi) and 9.7f/1¼m winner Destiny of Dreams (by Dubai Destination): dam, ungenuine 2-y-o 6f winner, half-sister to useful winner up to 7f Qadar: 14/1, green and well held in maiden at Ripon. *Tim Easterby* — **–**

TARONEESH 2 b.g. (Apr 12) Canford Cliffs (IRE) 133 – Blur 62 (Oasis Dream 129) [2015 6.1g t6g p5f Aug 18] well held in 3 maidens. *Derek Shaw* — **–**

TAROOQ (USA) 9 b.g. War Chant (USA) 126 – Rose of Zollern (IRE) 111 (Seattle Dancer (USA) 119) [2015 115: p6m⁵ p7f² p5m* t6m³ p6m³ p6f* f6g* 5.1m³ 7f³ 6g⁶ 6m³ 6g t7.1g² 7.6g³ 6m⁴ Jul 23] quite good-topped gelding: fair on turf, useful on all-weather: won claimers at Lingfield in February and March and Southwell (by neck from Abi Scarlet) in April: best at up to 7f nowadays: acts on all-weather and any turf going: has worn headgear/ tongue tie. *Tom Dascombe* — **76 a103**

TARO TYWOD (IRE) 6 br.m. Footstepsinthesand 120 – Run To Jane (IRE) (Doyoun 124) [2015 81: t9.5g⁵ t9.5g⁴ t9.5g⁴ 10m³ 9.9s⁴ 9.9g³ 10.3m² 10.2f³ t9.5g⁴ 9.9g⁶ Aug 6] fair handicapper: won at Wolverhampton in April: stays 12.5f: acts on polytrack, tapeta, fibresand and good to soft going: tried in headgear. *Mark Brisbourne* — **73**

TARPORLEY 2 b.c. (Mar 30) Bushranger (IRE) 119 – Labisa (IRE) 80 (High Chaparral (IRE) 132) [2015 6g 6d Jun 3] well held in maidens at Haydock and Ripon: dead. *George Moore* — **–**

TARRAGON 3 b.g. Compton Place 125 – Hennalaine (IRE) 59 (Lujain (USA) 119) [2015 62: 7m p6g t8.6g³ 7.4d p8g Sep 9] modest maiden: stays 8.5f: acts on polytrack and tapeta: sometimes in headgear: sent to Greece. *Jeremy Gask* — **58**

TARTAN BUTE 2 b.c. (Mar 14) Azamour (IRE) 130 – On A Soapbox (USA) 119 (Mi Cielo (USA)) [2015 t8.6f Oct 31] €70,000Y: half-brother to several winners, including very smart 9.5f-2m winner Soapy Danger (by Danzig) and useful 1¼m winner (stays 1½m) Proposed (by Invincible Spirit): dam US Grade 1 1½m winner: 18/1, very green but hinted at ability in maiden at Wolverhampton on debut: should do better in time. *Mark Johnston* — **– p**

TARTAN GIGHA (IRE) 10 b.g. Green Desert (USA) 127 – High Standard 83 (Kris 135) [2015 63: t8.6f t9.5g⁶ Mar 19] good-topped gelding: useful in his prime: stayed 1½m: acted on synthetics, best turf form on good going or firmer (acted on firm): sometimes wore headgear: dead. *Geoffrey Harker* — **47**

TARTAN JURA 7 b.g. Green Desert (USA) 127 – On A Soapbox (USA) 119 (Mi Cielo —
(USA)) [2015 84: f16g Nov 3] tall, good-topped gelding: fairly useful handicapper at best,
well held only outing in 2015: stays 2m: acts on fibresand, firm and soft going: wears
headgear. *David Thompson*

TARTAN TRIP 8 b.g. Selkirk (USA) 129 – Marajuana 82 (Robellino (USA) 127) [2015   76
79: f8d⁴ p8m² f7g* f8s³ 8m⁴ f8g⁶ Dec 22] good-topped gelding: fair handicapper: won at
Southwell in March: stays 9f: acts on polytrack, fibresand, soft and good to firm going:
wears headgear: tried in tongue tie. *Michael Appleby*

TARTOOR (GER) 3 br.g. Oasis Dream 129 – Templerin (GER) 104 (Acatenango (GER)   85
127) [2015 8g 10.1d² 9.9m³ p10f² p10f² t9.5f² Oct 20] €90,000Y: half-brother to smart/
ungenuine 1¼m-2m winner Toughness Danon (by Tiger Hill) and German 11f winner
Traumprinz (by Manduro): dam German 1¼m winner: fairly useful maiden: stays 1¼m:
acts on polytrack: front runner/races prominently: sent to UAE. *Ed Dunlop*

TASAABOQ 4 b.g. Aqlaam 125 – Seldemosa 67 (Selkirk (USA) 129) [2015 66: 8g⁴ 7.6g⁶   55
7m 8g⁵ p8f 7v 7g³ p6f⁶ t7.1f³ p7g² p6f Dec 17] modest maiden: stays 1¼m: acts on
polytrack, tapeta and good to firm going: wears headgear/tongue tie: usually slowly away:
temperament under suspicion. *Phil McEntee*

TASHAAR (IRE) 3 b.c. Sea The Stars (IRE) 140 – Three Moons (IRE) 104 (Montjeu   115
(IRE) 137) [2015 8m* 11m* 12d⁴ 12g² Sep 25] 380,000Y: lengthy, attractive colt: first foal:
dam, 9.7f winner, half-sister to smart French 6f/7f winner The Right Man: smart performer:
won maiden at Haydock (by 4½ lengths from Count Montecristo) in May and handicap at
Goodwood (by 1½ lengths from Rhythmical, heavily eased) in July: further improvement
when 5¼ lengths fourth to Storm The Stars in Great Voltigeur Stakes at York and 3¾
lengths second to Cannock Chase in listed race at Newmarket: may prove best at short of
1½m. *Richard Hannon*

TASHWEEQ (IRE) 2 b.c. (Jan 10) Big Bad Bob (IRE) 118 – Dance Hall Girl (IRE) 81   109
(Dansili 127) [2015 7s² 7g* 7m* 7g⁴ 7s⁶ Nov 1] £150,000Y: well-made colt: second foal:
half-brother to useful winner up to 6f Kasbah (2-y-o 5f winner, by Acclamation): dam, 6.7f
winner, closely related to smart performer up to 1¼m Solar Deity: useful performer: won
maiden at Newmarket in August and listed race at Doncaster (by 1½ lengths from Haalick)
in September: 6 lengths fourth of 7 to Air Force Blue in Dewhurst Stakes at Newmarket
and 3¼ lengths sixth of 8 to Johannes Vermeer in Criterium International at Saint-Cloud
last 2 starts: raced only at 7f: acts on soft and good to firm going. *John Gosden*

TASKEEN (IRE) 2 b.c. (Feb 21) Lilbourne Lad (IRE) 111 – Lola Rosa (IRE) (Peintre   83
Celebre (USA) 137) [2015 7.1g 8.1s* 10g Oct 10] 65,000F, 140,000Y: strong colt: third
foal: dam unraced daughter of smart French/US performer up to 11f Snow Polina: fairly
useful form: won maiden at Sandown in September by nose from Yensir: 28/1, stiff task but
seemed amiss in listed race at Newmarket final start: stays 1m. *Richard Hannon*

TASLEET 2 b.c. (Mar 19) Showcasing 117 – Bird Key (Cadeaux Genereux 131) [2015 6g⁴   107
6.1m* 6g* 6m² 6g* 7g² Sep 24] £52,000Y: good-topped colt: sixth foal: half-brother to
useful 7f winner Makaamen (by Selkirk), later succesful in Spain, and 2-y-o 7f winner Face
The Future (by Green Desert): dam once-raced half-sister to very smart winner up to 7f
Etlaala: useful performer: won maiden at Chepstow (by 3 lengths from Bear Faced) in
June, listed race at Newbury (by neck from Madrinho) in July and valuable sales race at
York (by ½ length from Ferryover) in August: also ran well when second in Richmond
Stakes at Goodwood (2¾ lengths behind Shalaa) and Somerville Tattersall Stakes at
Newmarket (nose behind Sanus Per Aquam): stays 7f: acts on good to firm going: usually
responds generously to pressure. *William Haggas*

TASRIH (USA) 6 b.g. Hard Spun (USA) 124 – Rare Gift (USA) (Unbridled's Song (USA) —
125) [2015 90: f7d Jan 2] fairly useful handicapper at best, well held only outing in 2015:
stays 1m: acts on polytrack and fibresand: tried in cheekpieces: usually leads: sold 1,000
gns. *David C. Griffiths*

TASSELLED 3 b.f. Tobougg (IRE) 125 – Roseum 102 (Lahib (USA) 129) [2015 t9.5g⁵ Jul   64
13] fifth of 7 to Le Notre in maiden at Wolverhampton on only start: dead. *Ralph Beckett*

TASTE THE WINE (IRE) 9 gr.g. Verglas (IRE) 118 – Azia (IRE) 71 (Desert Story   66
(IRE) 115) [2015 72: 16.2m⁵ 16.2m⁵ 16.2m* 17.2m⁵ 18d Aug 20] rather leggy gelding: fair
handicapper: won at Chepstow in June: stays 2m: acts on polytrack, good to firm and heavy
going: has worn cheekpieces: usually wears tongue tie. *Bernard Llewellyn*

TATHQEEF (USA) 2 b.c. (Apr 17) Tapit (USA) 118 – Foxy Danseur (USA) (Mr Greeley   84 P
(USA) 122) [2015 t9.5f* Oct 23] $1,100,000Y: third foal: half-brother to a winner in USA
by Tiznow: dam useful US 6f-8.5f winner (including at 2 yrs/minor stakes): 4/9, overcame

difficulties when winning 7-runner maiden at Wolverhampton on debut readily by 2¼ lengths from Templier, slowly away and green but finding plenty to lead 1f out: open to significant improvement. *John Gosden*

TATIANI 3 ch.f. Refuse To Bend (IRE) 128 – Tech Zinne (Zinaad 114) [2015 –: 8m 8d **49** 9.9m⁶ 8m⁴ 10.2f 8.1d² 7.1m⁵ 8m⁶ 7s³ t8.6f⁵ t7.1m Nov 28] poor maiden: stays 1m: acts on good to firm and good to soft going: wears headgear: tried in tongue tie: front runner/races prominently. *Jose Santos*

TATLISU (IRE) 5 b.g. Red Clubs (IRE) 125 – Zwadi (IRE) 74 (Docksider (USA) 124) **111** [2015 104: 6d* 6g³ 6g⁴ 6f 6s² 6m 6g³ 7s 6g* 7m 6s⁴ Oct 10] compact gelding: smart handicapper: won at Doncaster (21 ran, by ½ length from Farlow) in March and Ayr (25 ran, by head from George Bowen, showing himself better than ever) in September: successful at 7f, races mostly at 6f nowadays: acts on any turf going: tried in headgear: often races towards rear. *Richard Fahey*

TATTING 6 ch.g. Street Cry (IRE) 130 – Needlecraft (IRE) 113 (Mark of Esteem (IRE) **82** 137) [2015 89: f8d⁵ p10g⁶ p8g⁴ p8m* p8g⁵ p8g 10m 8m³ t8.6g² 8f⁴ 8.5g 10g 8.1g⁵ p8f t8.6f⁵ 8d² t9.5f⁵ t8.6g* Dec 4] tall gelding: fairly useful performer: won handicap at Chelmsford in February and claimer at Wolverhampton in December: left Chris Dwyer after seventh start: stays 9.5f: acts on all-weather and any turf going: tried in blinkers prior to 2015: tried in tongue tie in 2015. *Mark Hoad*

TAUREAN BEAUTY 4 b.f. Firebreak 125 – La Belle Katherine (USA) (Lyphard (USA) – 132) [2015 8gʳᵒ Jul 3] £700Y: half-sister to several winners, including winner up to 8.6f Aventura (2-y-o 5f winner, by Sri Pekan) and winner up to 1m Stevedore (2-y-o 7f winner, by Docksider): dam ran twice in France: 33/1, ran out in maiden at Haydock on debut. *Alan Berry*

TAUREAN STAR (IRE) 2 b.g. (Feb 10) Elnadim (USA) 128 – Marhaba 73 (Nayef **85** (USA) 129) [2015 7g⁴ 7m⁴ 6d* 6s⁵ Oct 23] €18,500Y, 43,000 2-y-o: sturdy gelding: first foal: dam once-raced daughter of Prix de Diane winner Sil Sila: fairly useful form: won maiden at Ascot (by head from Operative) in September: slowly away when disappointing in nursery final start: best effort at 6f: has been gelded. *Michael Bell*

TAURIAN 4 b.f. Central Park (IRE) 123 – Emma-Lyne 65 (Emarati (USA) 74) [2015 8g **75** 9g⁵ 7.6m³ 10.1m⁶ 8.1d³ p8f t9.5m 10s p12m* p12g⁴ Dec 20] lengthy filly: eighth foal: dam maiden (best efforts at 6f/7f at 2 yrs): fair handicapper: won at Lingfield (amateur) in November: stays 1½m: acts on polytrack and good to soft going. *Ian Williams*

TAUTOLOGY 2 b.c. (Feb 12) Dubawi (IRE) 129 – Portmanteau 96 (Barathea (IRE) 127) **76 p** [2015 8d⁴ 8g⁵ Sep 24] fifth foal: brother to 2 winners, notably high-class 9f-11f winner Hunter's Light, and half-brother to useful French 9.5f-1½m winner Linda Radlett (by Manduro): dam 1¼m winner: fourth of 11 to Dal Harraild in maiden at Haydock in September: disappointing in similar event at Pontefract next time, leading on bridle 2f out but folding approaching final 1f: remains with potential. *Charlie Appleby*

DBS Premier Yearling Stakes, York—form choice Tasleet (striped cap) justifies favouritism in workmanlike fashion as he gives trainer William Haggas his third win in a row in this valuable sales event; the strong-finishing Ferryover (noseband), Still On Top (No.18) and Delizia (No.5) fill the frame

TAVENER 3 b.c. Exceed And Excel (AUS) 126 – Sea Chorus 82 (Singspiel (IRE) 133) **79**
[2015 61p: p5g p5g² 7.5m t6g² 6g* 6m² 6d⁵ 6m² 5.1g Sep 30] fair handicapper: won at
Thirsk in June: left William Jarvis after: should stay 7f: acts on good to firm going: in
cheekpieces at Thirsk. *David O'Meara*

TAWAASHEEH (IRE) 3 b.c. New Approach (IRE) 132 – Sana Abel (IRE) 78 (Alhaarth **67**
(IRE) 126) [2015 84: 9.9m⁵ Apr 15] tall colt: lightly-raced maiden: fairly useful form on
debut, well below that both outings since: bred to stay at least 1½m: tried in hood: sold
£6,000, sent to Italy. *Roger Varian*

TAWAKKOL 2 b.c. (Feb 15) Firebreak 125 – Dayville (USA) 86 (Dayjur (USA) 137) **84**
[2015 p5g⁴ 5g² 6m² 6g³ 7.5m² 7m² Jul 13] 25,000F, £70,000Y: brother to 5f/6f winner
Daylight and half-brother to several winners, including useful 2-y-o 7f/1m winner Day of
Conquest (by Major Cadeaux) and useful 5f/6f winner Day By Day (by Kyllachy): dam 6f
winner (including at 2 yrs): fairly useful maiden: stays 7.5f: acts on good to firm going.
Mark Johnston

TAWAYNA (IRE) 2 b.f. (Apr 23) Invincible Spirit (IRE) 121 – Bratislava 54 (Dr Fong **71**
(USA) 128) [2015 6m 5m⁴ 5d* Aug 18] €300,000Y: close-coupled filly: sixth foal: closely
related to a winner in USA by Diamond Green and half-sister to 3 winners, including smart
6f (including at 2 yrs) winner Katla (by Majestic Missile) and 1m-1¼m winner Derulo
(by Arakan): dam lightly-raced half-sister to smart 2-y-o 6f/7f winner Wootton Bassett: fair
form: improved when winning maiden at Ripon final start, making all: should stay 6f.
William Haggas

TAWDEEA 3 b.c. Intikhab (USA) 135 – Sharedah (IRE) 94 (Pivotal 124) [2015 57p: 8.1f² **87 p**
8.3d³ Aug 14] well-made colt: fairly useful maiden: better effort in 2015 when second at
Sandown (¾ length behind Franklin D) in July: bred to stay further than 1m: remains open
to improvement. *Richard Hannon*

TAWDHEEF (IRE) 2 br.g. (Mar 12) Zebedee 113 – Duchess of Foxland (IRE) 107 **99**
(Medecis 119) [2015 5.7f* 5m 6.1m* 7f³ 7m 6s* Oct 23] €37,000F, £92,000Y: good-
topped gelding: first foal: dam winner up to 9.4f (2-y-o 6f winner): useful performer: won
maiden at Bath in May, minor event at Chepstow in June and nursery at Newbury (by neck
from Ground Control, showing improved form) in October: stays 7f: acts on firm and soft
going. *Brian Meehan*

TAWEYLA (IRE) 4 b.f. Teofilo (IRE) 126 – Qasirah (IRE) 97 (Machiavellian (USA) 123) **65**
[2015 71: p11f³ t12.2m² p12g⁵ t12.2g³ Apr 11] fair maiden: stays 1½m: acts on polytrack,
tapeta and good to soft going: in cheekpieces last 2 starts: usually leads: fair hurdler.
Pam Sly

TAWS 4 b.f. Hernando (FR) 127 – Reaf (In The Wings 128) [2015 87: t16.5g* p16g⁶ 16g⁵ **98**
16m³ 16.2g 21.7f² 16.4m 21g² 16.4d 18m Sep 11] sparely-made filly: useful handicapper:
won at Wolverhampton in March: better than ever when second in Queen Alexandra Stakes
at Royal Ascot (7 lengths behind Oriental Fox) and Goodwood Stakes (beaten 6 lengths by
Sands of Fortune): stays 21f: acts on tapeta, good to firm and heavy going: usually races
prominently. *Rod Millman*

TAWWAAQ (IRE) 2 gr.f. (Mar 24) Zebedee 113 – Killinallan 70 (Vettori (IRE) 119) **83**
[2015 5.1d⁴ 6m² 5f* 6g² 6d⁵ Sep 5] £120,000Y: fourth foal: half-sister to very smart winner
up to 6f Steps (2-y-o 5f winner, by Verglas): dam ran once: fairly useful performer: won
maiden at Sandown in July: stays 6f: acts on firm going. *Roger Varian*

TAX REFORM (IRE) 5 b.g. Namid 128 – Happy Flight (IRE) (Titus Livius (FR) 115) **60 §**
[2015 63, a73: 9.9v³ 8g³ f8d⁴ p10g 9.9v⁵ 8g 8s p5g² t6f⁴ f5g t6m⁵ Dec 30] modest maiden:
left Gary Moore after seventh start: stays 1m: acts on polytrack, tapeta and heavy going:
wears headgear: ungenuine. *Natalie Lloyd-Beavis*

TAYSH (USA) 3 b.g. Bernstein (USA) 115 – Normandy's Nell (USA) (Mt Livermore **88**
(USA)) [2015 83p: t8.6g² p10g Dec 7] fairly useful handicapper: easily better effort in
2015 when second at Wolverhampton, subsequently left John Gosden £7,000 and gelded:
stays 8.5f: tried in blinkers/tongue tie. *Michael Appleby*

TAZAAYUD 2 b.g. (Apr 27) Kodiac 112 – Esteemed Lady (IRE) 96 (Mark of Esteem (IRE) **–**
137) [2015 6g 6.1g May 30] well held in 2 maidens: has been gelded. *Marcus Tregoning*

TAZFFIN (IRE) 3 b.f. Iffraaj 127 – Tarfshi 111 (Mtoto 134) [2015 81p: 8.3g* 10.4g² 8f **103**
9g* 9.9m³ Aug 12] lengthy, dipped-backed filly: useful performer: won maiden at Windsor
in May and handicap at Goodwood (by ½ length from Nancy From Nairobi) in July:
creditable third in listed race at Salisbury (4¾ lengths behind Journey) final start: stays
10.5f: acts on good to firm going: in headgear first 3 starts in 2015. *Roger Varian*

TEA BLOSSOM 4 b.f. Rail Link 132 – Snow Blossom (Beat Hollow 126) [2015 p8f⁴ p8g⁵ 8f⁵ 10.1g⁵ 10.4m⁶ 12d⁶ 12g 12v⁴ Oct 24] second foal: dam, French 9f/1¼m winner, half-sister to 7f to 8.6f winner Vortex: useful performer: won newcomers event at Maisons-Laffitte for Mme C. Head-Maarek on debut at 3 yrs: 20/1, best effort though seen to advantage when 2½ lengths fourth of 9 to Koora in St Simon Stakes at Newbury final start in 2015, dictating: stays 1½m: acts on heavy going: often travels strongly. *James Eustace* — **102**

TEA GOWN (IRE) 4 ch.f. Iffraaj 127 – Dignify (IRE) 105 (Rainbow Quest (USA) 134) [2015 8d² 7.9m³ 7.5m 6g⁶ 10.3g³ 8.3d 10s⁴ t9.5f Nov 10] closely related to winner up to 1¼m Personify (2-y-o 6f winner, by Zafonic) and half-sister to 7f-8.4f winner Declamation (by Shamardal) and a winner in USA by Refuse To Bend: dam French 2-y-o 7f/1m (Prix d'Aumale) winner: fairly useful ex-French-trained maiden: left Paul Midgley after fourth start: likely to prove best at around 1m: acts on soft and good to firm going: tried in blinkers prior to 2015. *Ed de Giles* — **81**

TEAJAN (IRE) 2 gr.c. (Apr 11) Dandy Man (IRE) 123 – Red Riddle (IRE) 66 (Verglas (IRE) 118) [2015 p5g³ 5g Oct 18] third of 10 to Teresar at Kempton in September on debut: shaped as if amiss when well held in similar event at Bath. *James Tate* — **73**

TEAJAYBE (USA) 7 b.g. Street Cry (IRE) 130 – Wild Heaven (IRE) 106 (Darshaan 133) [2015 85: f14d* p16m⁴ f12g³ f16g⁴ Apr 9] useful-looking gelding: fairly useful handicapper: won at Southwell in January: stays 2m: acts on polytrack, fibresand, good to firm and good to soft going: sometimes in headgear/tried in tongue tie prior to 2015: often races prominently. *Michael Appleby* — **88**

TEAK (IRE) 8 b.g. Barathea (IRE) 127 – Szabo (IRE) 88 (Anabaa (USA) 130) [2015 95: p16g 16g⁴ 16m² 21.7f³ 21g⁵ 16m³ 18g p16g Nov 18] smallish, good-bodied gelding: useful handicapper: third in Queen Alexandra Stakes at Royal Ascot (7½ lengths behind Oriental Fox) on third start: stays 21.5f: acts on polytrack and firm going: wears headgear: tried in tongue tie. *Ian Williams* — **99**

TEARS IN MY EYES (IRE) 2 b.f. (Mar 5) Lilbourne Lad (IRE) 111 – Genuine Charm (IRE) 77 (Sadler's Wells (USA) 132) [2015 5f p7g⁶ 7m² 7m⁶ p8f p8m Nov 19] 130,000Y: rather unfurnished filly: half-sister to several winners, including 2-y-o 1m winner Rich Tapestry (later very smart sprinter in Hong Kong, by Holy Roman Emperor): dam, maiden (stayed 1½m), sister to high-class winner up to 1¼m Refuse To Bend: fair maiden: stays 7f: acts on good to firm going: in cheekpieces final start. *Jeremy Noseda* — **74 a62**

TEARS OF THE SUN 4 b.f. Mastercraftsman (IRE) 129 – Perfect Star 107 (Act One 124) [2015 89: p11f 10.2f² 9.9d* 10m² 10m* 9g⁵ 11.6d⁶ 10g⁵ p11g⁵ Nov 9] smallish, angular filly: fairly useful handicapper: won at Brighton in May and Windsor in June: stays 1½m: acts on polytrack, fibresand, good to firm and good to soft going. *Clive Cox* — **94**

TEA WITH ELEANOR (IRE) 3 b.f. Duke of Marmalade (IRE) 132 – Ms Sophie Eleanor (USA) 70 (Grand Slam (USA) 120) [2015 11.7f⁴ 12g Sep 26] €32,500Y: second foal: dam, 7f winner, half-sister to Racing Post Trophy/Dante Stakes winner Saratoga Springs: better effort when fourth in maiden at Bath. *Charles Hills* — **58**

TEBA MATEBA (FR) 2 b.c. (Mar 7) Wootton Bassett 119 – Misty Heights 105 (Fasliyev (USA) 120) [2015 7m⁴ 6s 7.2g³ 7.5d³ Sep 22] fair maiden: third at Musselburgh and Beverley: will stay 1m: sold 30,000 gns, sent to France. *David O'Meara* — **75**

TECHNICOLOUR 2 b.g. (Apr 29) Dubawi (IRE) 129 – Many Colours 112 (Green Desert (USA) 127) [2015 p8g⁶ t8.6f³ t9.5f³ t9.5f⁶ Nov 14] fair maiden: stays 9.5f: in blinkers last 2 starts. *Charlie Appleby* — **79**

TECTONIC (IRE) 6 b.g. Dylan Thomas (IRE) 132 – Pine Chip (USA) (Nureyev (USA) 131) [2015 77: 8s 8.3s³ 9.2d⁵ 10d⁴ 9.3g* 8.3g⁶ 9.3s⁵ 9.3g³ 9.1g² 7.9m⁴ 8d³ 8.3s⁵ 10s⁴ 9.3g² 11.1d³ 7.9m 9.3g³ 11.1g⁶ Sep 21] fair handicapper: won at Carlisle in June: stays 11f: acts on soft and good to firm going: wears headgear: none too resolute (carries head high). *Keith Dalgleish* — **79 §**

TECUMSEH (IRE) 3 br.g. Danehill Dancer (IRE) 117 – Absolute Music (USA) 98 (Consolidator (USA) 121) [2015 74: 7.1s³ 6gᵖᵘ May 22] good-topped gelding: fair handicapper: stayed 7f: acted on soft going: sometimes wore hood: dead. *K. R. Burke* — **66**

TED DOLLY (IRE) 11 b.g. Bob's Return (IRE) 123 – Little Pearl (IRE) 55 (Bigstone (IRE) 126) [2015 70: t12.2f⁶ t13.9g⁶ Jan 23] modest performer: stays 1¾m: acts on tapeta and good to soft going: tried in cheekpieces. *Tom Symonds* — **58**

TEDHKAAR (IRE) 3 b.f. Teofilo (IRE) 126 – Merayaat (IRE) 80 (Darshaan 133) [2015 **70 p**
12.3m⁴ p12g³ p12g⁴ Oct 14] sixth foal: half-sister to smart winner up to 13.3f Hawaafez
(2-y-o 1m winner, by Nayef) and 1¾m/15f winner Nateeja (by Shamardal): dam 1¾m
winner: fair maiden: bred to be suited by at least 1¾m: type to do better. *B. W. Hills*

TED LARKIN (IRE) 3 b.g. Dandy Man (IRE) 123 – Shewillifshewants (IRE) (Alzao **–**
(USA) 117) [2015 –: t7.1m⁶ 7d May 13] well held in maidens/handicaps: in headgear last
2 starts. *Richard Guest*

TED'S BROTHER (IRE) 7 b.g. Fath (USA) 116 – Estertide (IRE) (Tagula (IRE) 116) **70**
[2015 82: 7m 8.3m⁴ 7g 8d⁶ 7.2g⁶ 8g 7.9d⁶ 7.2g⁶ 8.3g² 7s⁶ Oct 26] fair handicapper: stays
8.5f: acts on polytrack, good to firm and heavy going: wears headgear: tried in tongue tie:
sometimes slowly away, often races towards rear. *Richard Guest*

TED SPREAD 8 b.g. Beat Hollow 126 – Highbrook (USA) 88 (Alphabatim (USA) 126) **–**
[2015 103: t16.5m Feb 2] good-topped gelding: useful handicapper in 2014, well held only
outing in 2015: stays 16.5f: acts on polytrack, tapeta, soft and good to firm going: wears
tongue tie: front runner/races prominently. *Suzy Smith*

TED'S SECRET 4 b.g. Sakhee's Secret 128 – Sinduda (Anabaa (USA) 130) [2015 p8g **–**
May 28] 25/1, well held in maiden at Lingfield on only start, not knocked about. *Ed Dunlop*

TEE IT UP TOMMO (IRE) 6 gr.g. Clodovil (IRE) 116 – Lamh Eile (IRE) 93 (Lend A **74**
Hand 124) [2015 90: 8.3g⁶ p8g 8m⁶ p8m Nov 19] long-backed gelding: fair handicapper:
stays 8.5f: acts on polytrack, tapeta and good to firm going: not straightforward.
Sheena West

TEENAGE DREAM (IRE) 7 b.g. Antonius Pius (USA) 123 – Lucayan Star (IRE) 77 **60**
(First Trump 118) [2015 73: 14.1g 14g⁵ 16g 12g f12g² f14g³ f11g⁶ Dec 29] modest
maiden: stays 2m: acts on polytrack and fibresand: often wears headgear/tongue tie.
Brian Ellison

TEEN AGER (FR) 11 b.g. Invincible Spirit (IRE) 121 – Tarwiya (IRE) 103 (Dominion **69**
123) [2015 67: p7m p8f³ p7g⁴ p7g* p7g³ p7g p7g³ p8g² 7m³ Jun 13] strong, compact
gelding: fair handicapper: won at Lingfield in March: stays 1m: acts on polytrack and good
to firm going: wears cheekpieces: front runner/races prominently. *Paul Burgoyne*

TEEPEE TIME 2 b.f. (Jan 16) Compton Place 125 – Deora De (Night Shift (USA)) [2015 **51**
6g 6g⁶ 6g⁴ p8g 7.2g 7.2g 8g Sep 29] 20,000F, £30,000Y: second foal: sister to a winner
abroad: dam once-raced half-sister to useful sprinter Prolific (by Compton Place): modest
maiden: best effort at 6f: tried in headgear. *Ann Duffield*

TEETOTAL (IRE) 5 ch.g. Footstepsinthesand 120 – Tea Service (USA) (Atticus (USA) **71**
121) [2015 84: 7d 6g 6s⁶ 6m 6m⁴ 6m³ 6m³ 6m³ 6m⁶ 6g 6d³ 6g Sep 23] close-coupled
gelding: fair handicapper: stays 6f: acts on soft and good to firm going: tried in cheekpieces:
sometimes slowly away. *Nigel Tinkler*

TEGARA 2 ch.f. (Mar 14) Hard Spun (USA) 124 – Damaniyat Girl (USA) 108 (Elusive **75 p**
Quality (USA)) [2015 7g³ Sep 26] third foal: half-sister to 1m winner Baynunah (by Medaglia
d'Oro): dam, 6f winner (including at 2 yrs), half-sister to smart 1m-1¼m performer
Magellan out of 1000 Guineas runner-up Dabaweyaa: 33/1, promise when 3½ lengths third
of 13 to Aljuljalah in maiden at Newmarket: open to improvement. *James Fanshawe*

TEIDE PEAK (IRE) 6 b.g. Cape Cross (IRE) 129 – Teide Lady 75 (Nashwan (USA) **61**
135) [2015 62, a69: t9.5f p12f p10f³ p10f⁶ t9.5m⁵ t12.2g* t12.2g⁴ t12.2m³ 13.1m t12.2g⁴
12.1m t12.2g⁵ 14.1g⁵ 11.6m⁴ t12.2m Dec 18] lengthy gelding: modest handicapper: won at
Wolverhampton in April: stays 1¾m: acts on polytrack, tapeta and good to firm going:
wears headgear/tongue tie. *Grace Harris*

TEKFA (IRE) 3 b.c. Makfi 130 – Night Club 60 (Mozart (IRE) 131) [2015 7g⁶ 8g p8f t9.5f **–**
Oct 3] rather leggy colt: no form: sold 1,000 gns, sent to Sweden. *Charlie Fellowes*

TELEGRAM 2 b.c. (Feb 24) Dream Ahead (USA) 133 – Miss Chaussini (IRE) 76 **– p**
(Rossini (USA) 118) [2015 p8f Sep 22] 36,000F, 42,000Y: half-brother to several winners,
including winner up to 1¼m Strictly Silver (2-y-o 7f winner, by Dalakhani) and winner up
to 6f Muir Lodge (2-y-o 5f winner, by Exceed And Excel), both useful: dam 7f winner:
25/1, in need of run for both fitness and experience when eighth of 10 in maiden at
Lingfield on debut: will do better. *Richard Hannon*

TELEGRAPH (IRE) 4 b.g. Bushranger (IRE) 119 – Vampire Queen (IRE) 54 (General **65 d**
Monash (USA) 107) [2015 68, a59: p6g p6g t7.1f³ t7.1m⁶ t7.1g* t7.1m⁶ t7.1m 6m 7m³
p5m 6.1s t7.1g t7.1g 6s⁴ 7.1s Aug 31] rather leggy gelding: fair handicapper at best: won
at Wolverhampton in February: stays 7f: acts on tapeta and soft going: wears headgear:
often leads. *David Evans*

TELESCOPE (IRE) 5 b.h. Galileo (IRE) 134 – Velouette (Darshaan 133) [2015 127: 12m² 12m* 12f⁶ Jun 20] good sort: high-class performer at best: successful in Great Voltigeur Stakes at York in 2013 and Hardwicke Stakes at Royal Ascot in 2014: won listed race at Newbury (by 6 lengths from Dubday) in May: second in Jockey Club Stakes at Newmarket (head behind Second Step) previous start: below form in Hardwicke Stakes (missed King George VI and Queen Elizabeth through injury and not seen again): stayed 1½m: acted on firm going: often raced prominently: to stand at Shade Oak Stud, Bagley, Shropshire, fee £3,000. *Sir Michael Stoute* **123**

TELL ME ANOTHER 3 b.g. Royal Applause 124 – Silver Rhapsody (USA) 115 (Silver Hawk (USA) 123) [2015 p8f⁴ p8g p8g t8.6g⁶ 8.3g⁷ 7.4d Aug 13] modest maiden: bred to stay at least 1¼m: acts on polytrack. *Rae Guest* **54**

TELL ME WHEN 4 b.f. Monsieur Bond (IRE) 120 – Giffoine 79 (Timeless Times (USA) 99) [2015 55: p7g f8f⁵ Dec 17] maiden: no form in 2015: tried in headgear. *Tony Coyle* **–**

TELLOVOI (IRE) 7 b.g. Indian Haven 119 – Kloonlara (IRE) 73 (Green Desert (USA) 127) [2015 99: 7.1m⁶ 7.2g⁵ 8g 7g 7d 7.2g 8.3v 7s f8g³ f6g² f7g³ Dec 15] fairly useful handicapper: stays 8.5f, effective at shorter: acts on polytrack, fibresand, good to firm and heavy going: wears headgear: sometimes slowly away, front runner/races prominently. *Richard Guest* **81 a74**

TEME TRIXIE 5 b.m. Needwood Blade 117 – Castanet 78 (Pennekamp (USA) 130) [2015 7.4g⁶ 7.1d⁶ 8v² 10s⁵ p7g Oct 7] fourth foal: dam, staying maiden on Flat (winning hurdler), half-sister to smart 7f/1m winner Priors Lodge: modest maiden: best effort at 1m: acts on heavy going. *Andrew Price* **53**

TEMPLE ROAD (IRE) 7 b.g. Street Cry (IRE) 130 – Sugarhoneybaby (IRE) 104 (Docksider (USA) 124) [2015 84: p5g* p5f* p5f p6f³ t5.1f 5.1m⁶ p5g 5.7m p6g⁵ p6g⁴ t6g p5g⁴ t5.1m t5.1g* p5g* p5g³ 5.1f Dec 22] fairly useful handicapper: won at Lingfield in January and February (dead-heated), Wolverhampton in November and Lingfield again in December: stays 6f: acts on polytrack, tapeta and good to firm going: wears headgear/tongue tie: often races prominently, usually travels strongly. *Milton Bradley* **81**

TEMPLIER (IRE) 2 b.g. (May 6) Mastercraftsman (IRE) 129 – Tigertail (FR) 112 (Priolo (USA) 127) [2015 7.2m² 8d³ 7m² t8.6f⁵ 19.5f² Oct 23] fair maiden: stays 9.5f: acts on tapeta, good to firm and good to soft going: has been gelded. *Mark Johnston* **79**

TEMPTING 3 ch.f. Pivotal 124 – Entrap (USA) 106 (Phone Trick (USA)) [2015 7g³ 7g* 6.9g⁶ 7v p8f⁵ p7g* Dec 7] fifth foal: sister to 7f-9f winner Ensnare: dam 6f winner (including at 2 yrs): useful performer: won maiden at Thirsk in June and handicap at Lingfield (by neck from Seychelloise, showing further improvement) in December: best effort at 7f: acts on polytrack: often races prominently. *William Haggas* **103**

TEMPTRESS (IRE) 4 ch.f. Shirocco (GER) 129 – Femme Fatale 102 (Fairy King (USA)) [2015 101: 8m* 8f² 8d⁶ Jul 7] smart leggy filly: smart handicapper: won at Ascot in May by 2 lengths from Solar Magic: excellent neck second of 30 to GM Hopkins in Hunt Cup at Royal Ascot in June: disappointing in listed race at Pontefract final start: stays 1m: acts on firm and good to soft going: wore hood first 3 starts in 2014: usually races nearer last than first, often travels strongly: remains capable of better. *Roger Charlton* **110 p**

TEMPURAN 6 b.g. Unbridled's Song (USA) 125 – Tenderly (IRE) (Danehill (USA) 126) [2015 66: 9.9d* 10.2m² 10m 10.2f⁴ p12g 11.7g³ p12m* t13.9f² t16.5g² p16f² Dec 21] tall gelding: fair handicapper: won at Brighton in June and Kempton in October: stays 16.5f: acts on polytrack, tapeta and good to soft going: tried in cheekpieces prior to 2015. *David Bridgwater* **68 a75**

TEMPUS TEMPORIS (USA) 3 b.g. Dynaformer (USA) – Tempus Fugit (USA) (Alphabet Soup (USA) 126) [2015 87p: p8g* p8f² 10m³ p10m Nov 14] good-topped gelding: useful performer: won minor event at Chelmsford in January by 5 lengths from Anonymous John: good third in listed race at Newmarket (3½ lengths behind Best of Times) in May, subsequently off over 6 months and well held on return: stays 1¼m: acts on polytrack and good to firm going: wears blinkers. *John Gosden* **104**

TENDU 3 b.f. Oasis Dream 129 – Arabesque 100 (Zafonic (USA) 130) [2015 105: 6f³ 5m² 6f Jun 19] strong, well-made filly: smart performer: second in Pavilion Stakes at Ascot (best effort, 1½ lengths behind Limato) and listed race at York (neck behind Profitable): stays 6f: acts on polytrack and firm going: sometimes slowly away, often travels strongly: temperament under suspicion. *John Gosden* **111**

TENHOO 9 b.g. Reset (AUS) 124 – Bella Bambina 45 (Turtle Island (IRE) 123) [2015 –: **59** t13.9g t8.6f 12.4g⁶ 12.4d 10.4g⁶ 11.9m² 10.1m³ 9.3d 10.2m 10m⁶ 12.4g t8.6m t9.5m t9.5f **a49** f11g⁶ Nov 3] modest handicapper: left Eric Alston after seventh start: stays 13f: acts on good to firm and heavy going: tried in headgear. *Alan Berry*

TENOR (IRE) 5 b.g. Oratorio (IRE) 128 – Cedar Sea (IRE) (Persian Bold 123) [2015 118: **113** 8.9g³ a9.9f a9.9f² p10g p8f 8f Jun 17] sturdy gelding: smart performer: creditable efforts when placed in handicaps at Meydan early in year, 2¼ lengths third to Umgiyo and 3¾ lengths second to Henry Clay: below form back in Britain last 3 starts: stays 1¼m: acts on polytrack, dirt and any turf going: wears tongue tie. *John Ryan*

TEN ROCKS 2 b.g. (Feb 12) Kheleyf (USA) 116 – Exultate Jubilate (USA) (With **60** Approval (CAN)) [2015 5f⁵ p6f⁶ p6g⁶ p6d⁶ p7g⁴ t6m Dec 30] modest maiden: stays 7f: acts on polytrack: tried in hood. *Brian Meehan*

TENZING NORGAY 2 gr.g. (May 13) Aussie Rules (USA) 123 – Miss Katmandu (IRE) **67** (Rainbow Quest (USA) 134) [2015 p6g p8g 7v 7.1s⁵ t8.6g² t8.6f² p10f² Oct 22] fair maiden: stays 1¼m: acts on polytrack and tapeta: tried in cheekpieces. *Sir Mark Prescott Bt*

TEOLAGI (IRE) 5 ch.g. Teofilo (IRE) 126 – Satulagi (USA) 98 (Officer (USA) 120) **77** [2015 92: p12gᵘʳ t12.2g⁴ p12g⁵ 8m p10.4g 10.2m 8f⁶ p8g² Jul 18] angular gelding: fair handicapper: stays 1½m, effective at shorter: acts on polytrack, tapeta, firm and good to soft going: in headgear in 2015: often races towards rear. *J. S. Moore*

TEOSROYAL (IRE) 3 br.f. Teofilo (IRE) 126 – Fille de Joie (IRE) 68 (Royal Academy **91** (USA) 130) [2015 71p: p8g² 10f 11.9d 8.1m* 8.1m t8.6g² 8g⁴ Sep 5] sturdy filly: fairly useful performer: won maiden at Chepstow in June: stays 8.5f: acts on tapeta and good to firm going: usually races close up. *Clive Brittain*

TEPELENI 3 b.f. Teofilo (IRE) 126 – Bronwen (IRE) 93 (King's Best (USA) 132) [2015 **71** 46: 10d⁴ 11.4d 12.1m⁵ p12g p12g⁶ Sep 9] angular filly: fair maiden: stays 1½m: acts on polytrack, good to firm and good to soft going. *Clive Brittain*

TEPUTINA 3 ch.f. Teofilo (IRE) 126 – West Lorne (USA) 60 (Gone West (USA)) [2015 **52** p8f² p10g⁶ Dec 30] 17,000Y, 800 3-y-o: third foal: half-sister to 1m-1¼m winner Palerma (by Shamardal): dam, maiden (stayed 1¾m), out of half-sister to Lammtarra: better effort when second in claimer at Chelmsford in December, never nearer. *Julia Feilden*

TEQUILA SLAMMER (IRE) 3 b.f. Papal Bull 128 – No Tippling (IRE) 72 (Unblest – 117) [2015 7g 8m 8g⁶ 9.9g 8d⁶ 10d Oct 26] half-sister to several winners, including 1m winner Cothrom Na Feinne (by Invincible Spirit) and 2-y-o 6f/7f winner Bay of Fires (by Iffraaj): dam 9f winner: no form: tried in cheekpieces. *Karen Tutty*

TERCEL (IRE) 4 b.g. Monsun (GER) 124 – Kitty Hawk 88 (Danehill Dancer (IRE) 117) **73 §** [2015 88§: 10m⁶ May 4] fair handicapper: in first-time tongue strap, refused to settle when well held only outing on Flat in 2015: stays 1¼m: acts on soft and good to firm going: has worn hood: temperamental: fairly useful form over hurdles: sold £11,000 in September. *Paul Nicholls*

TERESAR (IRE) 2 ch.f. (Apr 22) Dandy Man (IRE) 123 – High Chart 67 (Robellino **85 p** (USA) 127) [2015 5m³ p5g* 5g⁵ Oct 9] €7,000F, £20,000Y: smallish, good-quartered filly: fourth foal: dam winner up to 1m (2-y-o 5f winner): fairly useful form: won maiden at Kempton in September by 1½ lengths from Equinette: 16/1, improved when 5¾ lengths fifth of 11 to Quiet Reflection in Cornwallis Stakes at Newmarket: best kept to 5f: likely to do better still. *Henry Candy*

TERHAAL (IRE) 3 b.g. Raven's Pass (USA) 133 – Silk Trail 81 (Dubai Destination **85 p** (USA) 127) [2015 83p: 7.2m 7v³ 8d³ Oct 30] fairly useful form: 5¾ lengths third of 12 to Greenside in handicap at Newmarket final start, meeting some trouble: stays 1m: lightly raced and type to do better still. *David O'Meara*

TERRITORIES (IRE) 3 b.c. Invincible Spirit (IRE) 121 – Taranto 111 (Machiavellian **123** (USA) 123) [2015 11p: 8g* 8m² 8g* 8d² Oct 17] strong-quartered, attractive colt: very smart performer: won Prix de Fontainebleau at Longchamp in April and Prix Jean Prat at Chantilly (by ½ length from Dutch Connection, soon detached in last but well on top at line) in July: creditable second in 2000 Guineas at Newmarket (2¼ lengths behind Gleneagles, keeping on) and Prix Jacques le Marois at Deauville (1½ lengths behind Esoterique): not ideally placed when 3¼ lengths seventh of 9 to Solow in Queen Elizabeth II Stakes at Ascot final outing: stays 1m: acts on firm and good to soft going: usually races towards rear. *A. Fabre, France*

TERROR (IRE) 3 b.f. Kodiac 112 – Baltic Belle (IRE) 86 (Redback 116) [2015 105: 8f **105** 8d 7m³ 6g² 6g⁵ Oct 18] close-coupled filly: useful performer: placed in Sceptre Stakes at Doncaster (2¾ lengths third of 20 to Realtra, despite meeting trouble) and listed race at

Newmarket (1½ lengths second of 16 to Mistrusting): respectable fifth of 10 to Bye Bye Bernie in Grade 2 Nearctic Stakes at Woodbine final outing, short of room over 1f out: probably best short of 1m: acts on good to firm and good to soft going: sold 300,000 gns in December. *David Simcock*

TERSE 3 b.f. Dansili 127 – Cut Short (USA) 86 (Diesis 133) [2015 70: p7m⁶ Apr 29] **64 p** lightly-raced maiden: 16/1, still green when 4¼ lengths sixth of 8 to Francisco at Lingfield only outing in 2015, not knocked about: sold 22,000 gns in December: remains with potential. *David Lanigan*

TERUNTUM STAR (FR) 3 ch.g. Dutch Art 126 – Seralia 95 (Royal Academy (USA) **101** 130) [2015 99: 6s p6m 6d* 6m 6g Sep 19] quite attractive gelding with scope: useful handicapper: easily best effort of 2015 when winning at Newmarket in July by 1½ lengths from Bond's Girl: stays 6f: acts on good to firm and good to soft going: has been gelded. *Kevin Ryan*

TESORO (IRE) 2 b.f. (Apr 13) Galileo (IRE) 134 – Theann 111 (Rock of Gibraltar (IRE) **71** 133) [2015 6m 8.3g p7g p6f³ t6m* Dec 18] 200,000 2-y-o: fifth foal: sister to smart 7f-1¼m (US Grade 1) winner Photo Call and 1½m winner Pincode: dam, 6f winner (including at 2 yrs), half-sister to winner up to 1¼m Halfway To Heaven and 5f/6f winner Tickled Pink (both smart): fair performer: won maiden at Wolverhampton in December: should stay 7f: acts on polytrack and tapeta: tried in hood: often races prominently. *Dean Ivory*

TESSELLATE (IRE) 2 b.f. (Apr 1) Acclamation 118 – Sterope (FR) 76 (Hernando (FR) **59** 127) [2015 5.7m 6g t6m p6f⁴ p5g⁶ p6m Oct 28] €9,000Y: fourth foal: half-sister to French winner around 1¼m Kareman (by Zamindar): dam, French 11f winner, half-sister to very smart 1m-10.6f winner Multidimensional: modest maiden: best effort at 6f on polytrack. *Sylvester Kirk*

TESTA ROSSA (IRE) 5 b.g. Oratorio (IRE) 128 – Red Rita (IRE) 97 (Kefaah (USA) **66** 124) [2015 69: 10.1m 10g³ 10s* 10s⁶ 12.4g³ 11.9d 10g³ 10s³ t9.5f⁵ Nov 20] fair handicapper: won at Ayr in July: stays 12.5f: acts on polytrack, soft and good to firm going: usually wears headgear: none too consistent. *Jim Goldie*

TESTED 4 b.f. Selkirk (USA) 129 – Prove 109 (Danehill (USA) 126) [2015 112: 7g² 6m⁶ **115** 7g² 7.5s* 7.5g² 7s Oct 25] leggy filly: smart performer: first past the post in Fairy Bridge Stakes (for second successive year, by 1½ lengths from Military Angel) at Tipperary in August and Concorde Stakes (beat Sovereign Debt by short head, demoted to second after bumping that rival) at same course in October: second in Ballycorus Stakes at Leopardstown (neck behind Convergence) on reappearance: stays 7.5f: acts on soft and good to firm going: in visor final outing: often travels strongly. *D. K. Weld, Ireland*

TESTING (FR) 4 gr.f. New Approach (IRE) 132 – Testama (FR) 106 (Testa Rossa (AUS) **54** 128) [2015 –: 7g⁶ 10.3d⁵ 10.1m 7m 7g 16.1g⁴ 14.1s t16.5f Oct 27] unfurnished filly: modest maiden: stays 2m: acts on good to firm going: tried in headgear: temperament under suspicion. *David Thompson*

TETE ORANGE 4 ch.f. Pastoral Pursuits 127 – Imperialistic (IRE) 99 (Imperial Ballet **56 §** (IRE) 110) [2015 72: p11m t9.5f⁵ Feb 7] angular filly: modest handicapper: stays 11f: acts on polytrack, tapeta and good to firm going: tried in headgear: in tongue tie in 2015: not one to trust. *Stuart Williams*

TETRADRACHM 2 b.c. (Mar 11) Holy Roman Emperor (IRE) 125 – Dahlia's Krissy **75** (USA) (Kris S (USA)) [2015 8.3s⁴ p8g³ Oct 27] 4/1, similar form to debut when 9½ lengths third of 10 to Von Blucher in maiden at Lingfield. *David Lanigan*

Prix Jean Prat, Chantilly—with no Gleneagles in opposition this time, Territories goes one better than in the Two Thousand Guineas as he beats Dutch Connection, one of three British challengers; Sir Andrew and Kodi Bear (left) are a distant third and fourth

TETRATINA (USA) 3 b.f. Medaglia d'Oro (USA) 129 – Trepidation (USA) (Seeking **72 p**
The Gold (USA)) [2015 8.3g 8g⁶ 9g p10f⁶ Nov 23] $340,000Y: sturdy filly: half-sister to
several winners, including smart US/UAE 7f/1m winner Tiz Now Tiz Then (by Tiznow)
and useful winner up to 7f Maoineach (2-y-o 6f winner, by Congaree): dam unraced: fair
maiden: should prove suited by a return to 1m: tried in tongue tie: should do better.
David Lanigan

TEVERSHAM 2 b.g. (Apr 17) Kheleyf (USA) 116 – Snow Shoes 84 (Sri Pekan (USA) **64**
117) [2015 5d⁶ 5s⁴ t6g² f5g 5m Aug 18] modest maiden: stays 6f: acts on tapeta and soft
going: in headgear: sometimes slowly away. *Chris Dwyer*

TEVEZ 10 b.g. Sakhee (USA) 136 – Sosumi 101 (Be My Chief (USA) 122) [2015 72: p7g **51**
May 20] strong gelding: modest handicapper: stays 8.5f: acts on polytrack, fibresand, good
to firm and heavy going: wears headgear: tried in tongue tie: sometimes slowly away, often
races towards rear. *Des Donovan*

TEXAS SCRAMBLE 3 b.g. Nayef (USA) 129 – Footlight Fantasy (USA) 68 (Nureyev **61 p**
(USA) 131) [2015 f10f 8.3d⁵ t7.1m⁴ Dec 12] 15,000Y: half-brother to numerous winners,
including smart 7f/1m winner Unscrupulous (by Machiavellian) and useful 2-y-o 6f winner
Dominant Dancer (by Primo Dominie): dam 7f winner: modest maiden: should be suited
by 1m+: open to further improvement. *Michael Wigham*

THACKERAY 8 b.g. Fasliyev (USA) 120 – Chinon (IRE) (Entrepreneur 123) [2015 69: **52**
f11g³ t12.2g⁴ 13.1d⁴ 14g f12d³ 14.1v t12.2m⁴ f14f⁴ Dec 17] modest handicapper: stays
13f: acts on fibresand, tapeta and heavy going. *Chris Fairhurst*

THAHAB IFRAJ (IRE) 2 ch.g. (Mar 28) Frozen Power (IRE) 108 – Penny Rouge (IRE) **60 p**
59 (Pennekamp (USA) 130) [2015 6g p6f 8.3s⁴ Oct 28] €60,000F, 110,000Y: sixth foal:
half-brother to 1¼m winner Heddwyn (by Bahri) and smart winner up to 1¼m
Elleval (2-y-o 7f winner, by Kodiac): dam maiden half-sister to smart 7f winner Redstone
Dancer: modest form: 50/1, 7¾ lengths fourth of 7 to Zoffanys Pride in maiden at
Nottingham, closing up late and again not knocked about: has been gelded: remains with
potential. *Ismail Mohammed*

THAHAB (IRE) 3 ch.c. Dubawi (IRE) 129 – Mise (IRE) (Indian Ridge 123) [2015 79p: **92**
p6g⁴ 5d³ 5m p6m⁴ Jun 3] sturdy colt: fairly useful performer: won maiden at Chelmsford
in April: stays 6f: acts on polytrack: often leads, usually travels strongly: sent to Qatar,
where won 6f handicap at Doha in December. *Richard Hannon*

THAI NOON (IRE) 3 b.f. Dansili 127 – Alsace Lorraine (IRE) 109 (Giant's Causeway **67 p**
(USA) 132) [2015 8.3d p8g⁴ p8g³ p8g* Dec 20] first foal: dam, 1m-1¼m winner, half-sister
to smart 1m winner Hot Bed: fair form: 5/6, won maiden at Lingfield final start by
3½ lengths from Primrose Brown, easily: stays 1m: remains open to improvement.
James Fanshawe

THA'IR (IRE) 5 b.h. New Approach (IRE) 132 – Flashing Green (Green Desert (USA) **115**
127) [2015 112: a9.9f 9.9g* 9.9g² 10f* 10.4m a9.9g* Sep 5] compact horse: smart
performer: won handicap at Meydan in February, listed race at Sandown (by 2½ lengths
from Provenance) in July and Anatolia Trophy at Veliefendi (by 2 lengths from Tumbaga)
in September: stays 11f: acts on polytrack/tapeta, firm and good to soft going: tried in
cheekpieces: front runner/races prominently. *Saeed bin Suroor*

THAMES KNIGHT 3 b.g. Sir Percy 129 – Bermondsey Girl 69 (Bertolini (USA) 125) **83**
[2015 64p: 8.3m 10m² 10m⁵ 10m³ 10.4g³ 10.2m* 10.2s* 11s³ 10d⁴ Oct 12] sturdy gelding:
fairly useful handicapper: won twice at Bath in August: stays 1¼m: acts on soft and good
to firm going: in headgear nowadays. *Marcus Tregoning*

THANAAYA (IRE) 3 b.f. Haatef (USA) 117 – Mejala (IRE) 74 (Red Ransom (USA)) **63**
[2015 61p: t7.1m⁴ p8f⁵ 7m 7m Jul 7] modest maiden: stays 1m: acts on polytrack and good
to soft going: sometimes slowly away. *Ed Dunlop*

THANE OF CAWDOR (IRE) 6 b.g. Danehill Dancer (IRE) 117 – Holy Nola (USA) **72**
(Silver Deputy (CAN)) [2015 64, a76: p11m p12f t12.2m⁶ p11g* p11g⁴ t12.2g t9.5g p12g⁵
p11g⁵ 8s p11g² p10d* p10m⁶ Dec 27] big, rangy gelding: fair handicapper: won at
Kempton in May (apprentice) and November: stays 1½m: acts on polytrack and tapeta:
tried in cheekpieces: often races towards rear. *Joseph Tuite*

THANKSFORTELLINGME (IRE) 2 b.g. (Apr 12) Notnowcato 128 – Red Blossom **104 p**
70 (Green Desert (USA) 127) [2015 8s⁸ 8.5d⁸ 8s⁴ Oct 19] €20,000Y: fifth foal: half-
brother to a winner in Hong Kong by Medicean: dam, temperamental 8.6f winner, half-
sister to winner up to 1¼m Red Bloom and 1¼m-13.4f winner Red Gala (both smart):
useful performer: won maiden at Goodwood (by short head from Skeaping) in August,

minor event at Epsom (by 3 lengths from Kingston Kurrajong) in September and listed race at Pontefract (by ¾ length from Beast Mode) in October: will stay at least 1¼m: sent to Hong Kong: will go on improving. *Ralph Beckett*

THANKSGIVING DAY (IRE) 3 b.c. Thewayyouare (USA) 117 – Cozzene's Pride (USA) (Cozzene (USA)) [2015 80: p8m² p8g* 8f 8f a8f⁴ 11f⁴ 11f Nov 29] fairly useful performer: won handicap at Chelmsford in February: left Jamie Osborne after: stays 11f: acts on polytrack and firm going: usually in headgear nowadays: usually leads. *Neil Drysdale, USA* — **90**

THANKSTOMONTY 3 b.g. Dylan Thomas (IRE) 132 – Beldarian (IRE) 101 (Last Tycoon 131) [2015 71p: 9.9m² 9g⁴ 8.5m² 8.5f* 8g Jul 14] fair handicapper: won at Beverley in July: stays 1¼m: acts on firm going: in cheekpieces final start: front runner/races prominently. *David O'Meara* — **77**

THAQAFFA (IRE) 2 b.c. (Apr 17) Kodiac 112 – Incense 73 (Unfuwain (USA) 131) [2015 5.2m³ 6m³ 6m¹ Jun 14] compact colt: fair maiden: best effort when fourth at Salisbury. *Marcus Tregoning* — **67**

THATABOY (IRE) 4 b.g. Green Desert (USA) 127 – Hawas 93 (Mujtahid (USA) 118) [2015 85: p6f⁶ p6g² t7.1m² p6g⁶ 6m⁶ 6g t7.1f t7.1m t7.1f³ t7.1f⁶ Dec 21] strong gelding: fair handicapper: stays 7f: acts on polytrack and tapeta: tried in cheekpieces/tongue tie. *Tom Dascombe* — **79**

THAT BE GRAND 4 b.f. Firebreak 125 – Manila Selection (USA) (Manila (USA)) [2015 67: 15s 14.1m⁶ 15.8g⁶ t12.2m 13.8v² 14.1v⁵ Nov 3] modest handicapper: best effort at 1¾m: acts on heavy going. *Shaun Harris* — **53**

THATCHEREEN (IRE) 4 ro.f. Mastercraftsman (IRE) 129 – Roof Fiddle (USA) 95 (Cat Thief (USA) 126) [2015 82: t12.2g⁴ 10m⁵ Jul 17] useful-looking filly: fair handicapper: probably stays 1½m: acts on good to firm and heavy going: sent to Saudi Arabia. *Michael Bell* — **71**

THATCHERITE (IRE) 7 gr.g. Verglas (IRE) 118 – Damiana (IRE) (Thatching 131) [2015 84: t7.1g 6g⁶ 5m³ 5g* 6m⁵ 5g³ 5g 5m⁵ 5.5m⁵ 5g 5m⁵ 5m⁶ 5m⁶ 5g³ 6m 5g³ 5g* Oct 3] angular gelding: fair handicapper: won at Beverley in May and Redcar in October: has won over 8.5f, best at sprint trips: acts on polytrack, tapeta, good to firm and good to soft going: tried in headgear prior to 2015: usually wears tongue tie: often races in rear: temperament under suspicion. *Tony Coyle* — **79**

THAT IS THE SPIRIT 4 b.g. Invincible Spirit (IRE) 121 – Fraulein 117 (Acatenango (GER) 127) [2015 109: 7d 7s* 7d⁶ 6m⁶ 7d Aug 15] tall, good-topped gelding: smart performer: won listed race at Haydock (by 1¾ lengths from Dusky Queen) in May, best effort of 2015: stays 7f: acts on soft and good to firm going: usually leads. *David O'Meara* — **113**

THAT'LL HAPPEN 2 b.g. (Feb 20) Atlantic Sport (USA) 115 – Musiara 46 (Hunting Lion (IRE) 115) [2015 5f³ 5g³ 6.1g Aug 3] modest form when third in maidens at Bath and Beverley, well held in similar event final start. *Mick Channon* — **64**

THAT MAN OF MINE (IRE) 3 ch.g. Thewayyouare (USA) 117 – Do The Deal (IRE) 67 (Halling (USA) 133) [2015 –: t12.2g* p12m* t12.2g p11g⁵ 14.1m Apr 18] modest handicapper: won at Wolverhampton in January and Kempton in February: stays 1½m: acts on polytrack and tapeta: in headgear in 2015. *Jamie Osborne* — **54**

THATSALLIMSAYING (IRE) 2 br.f. (Apr 26) Dandy Man (IRE) 123 – Model Looks (IRE) (Majestic Missile (IRE) 118) [2015 5m⁴ 5.1g² 6.1s* 5.2s² 6s 5g Sep 18] €37,000 2-y-o: first foal: dam unraced half-sister to useful winner up to 7f Master Robbie: fairly useful performer: won maiden at Chepstow in July: second in listed race at Newbury (½ length behind Whatdoiwantthatfor) next time: stays 6f: acts on soft going: front runner/races prominently. *David Evans* — **89**

THAWRAAT 3 b.f. Cape Cross (IRE) 129 – Raaya (USA) (Giant's Causeway (USA) 132) [2015 79p: 7g² p8f⁶ Oct 10] modest maiden: best effort at 1m: in cheekpieces final outing. *Saeed bin Suroor* — **59**

THE ALAMO (IRE) 4 b.g. High Chaparral (IRE) 132 – Inner Strength (FR) (Take Risks (FR) 116) [2015 83: p10g⁶ 10m⁴ 10.2f⁴ 10m 10g* 12.1g t12.2m⁴ 10.2s³ Aug 31] lengthy gelding: fair performer: won seller at Ffos Las in July: stays 11.5f: acts on polytrack and any turf going: in headgear last 6 starts: front runner/races prominently, tends to find little: sold £5,500, sent to Italy. *David Dennis* — **75**

THE ARMED MAN 2 b.g. (Apr 3) Misu Bond (IRE) 114 – Accamelia 67 (Shinko Forest (IRE)) [2015 5s 6d⁶ Oct 26] 100/1, showed more than on debut when 4½ lengths sixth of 13 to Gowanless in maiden at Redcar. *Chris Fairhurst* — **54**

THE AULD KIRK 2 b.g. (May 5) Millkom 124 – Lady Counsellor (Turbo Speed 99) – [2015 7.1m 7.9m Sep 9] tailed off in 2 maidens: has been gelded. *Susan Corbett*

THE BAY BANDIT 8 b.g. Highest Honor (FR) 124 – Pescara (IRE) 108 (Common 49 Grounds 118) [2015 67: p10f⁶ Mar 4] modest handicapper: stays 9.5f: acts on polytrack and soft going: wears headgear: fair hurdler/chaser. *Neil Mulholland*

THE BIG GUY 2 br.g. (Jan 31) Atlantic Sport (USA) 115 – Linda Green 82 (Victory Note – (USA) 120) [2015 p8g p8g t7.1f Dec 22] well held in 3 maidens. *Mick Channon*

THE BIG LAD 3 ch.g. Kheleyf (USA) 116 – Cultured Pride (IRE) 81 (King's Best (USA) 86 p 132) [2015 p6m* p6d* Nov 30] first foal: dam 2-y-o 6f winner who stayed 8.3f: won maiden at Lingfield in November on debut: much better form when following up in handicap at Kempton by length from Noble Deed, staying on to lead final 1f: likely to stay 7f: will go on improving. *Richard Hughes*

THE BLACK PRINCESS (FR) 2 b.f. (Jan 25) Iffraaj 127 – Larceny (IRE) (Cape Cross 79 P (IRE) 129) [2015 p8g* Nov 4] €170,000Y: second foal: half-sister to French 11.5f/1½m winner Lucelle (by High Chaparral): dam, ran once in France, closely related to Prix du Jockey Club winner Lawman and half-sister to Prix de Diane winner Latice: 11/4, value for extra when winning 11-runner maiden at Kempton in good style by 2 lengths from Bombilate, progressing to lead over 1f out despite slow start: type to go on to much better things. *John Gosden*

THE BLUE BANANA (IRE) 6 b.g. Red Clubs (IRE) 125 – Rinneen (IRE) 67 (Bien 59 § Bien (USA) 125) [2015 66§: 7g 7g⁵ 7s 8.5m⁴ 9.9m 10.1m³ 9.9m 9.3m 9.9d Sep 22] close-coupled gelding: modest handicapper: stays 1¼m: acts on good to firm and good to soft going: wears headgear: temperamental. *Edwin Tuer*

THE BLUE DOG (IRE) 8 b.m. High Chaparral (IRE) 132 – Jules (IRE) 76 (Danehill 61 (USA) 126) [2015 79: t12.2g³ p13.3g³ t12.2f² p13.3m⁵ p12f Mar 11] sturdy, good-bodied mare: modest handicapper: stays 1¾m: acts on all-weather and good to firm going: tried in headgear: in tongue tie in 2015: front runner/races prominently. *Phil McEntee*

THE BOSS OF ME 4 ch.g. Bahamian Bounty 116 – Orange Pip 89 (Bold Edge 123) – [2015 46: t7.1g Jan 15] poor maiden: should prove best up to 7f: acts on polytrack: tried in headgear, tongue tied last 4 starts: often leads. *Sean Curran*

THE BURNHAM MARE (IRE) 2 b.f. (Apr 1) Kodiac 112 – Courte Paille (IRE) 74 (Common Grounds 118) [2015 5m 5.1s 6m² 6m⁶ 6f⁴ 6g² 5g³ 6v² 6.3d p5g* p5f* t5.1f* t5.1f⁴ t6g⁴ Dec 1] €8,000Y: angular filly: fifth foal: half-sister to German 8.5f/9f winner Naaqueen (by Naaqoos): dam French 1m/8.5f winner: fair performer: won nurseries at Kempton, Chelmsford and Wolverhampton in October: best form at 5f: acts on polytrack, tapeta and any turf going: usually in cheekpieces: front runner/races prominently. *J. S. Moore*

THE CARBONATOR (IRE) 3 b.c. The Carbon Unit (USA) 106 – There's A Light 80 (IRE) 70 (Fantastic Light (USA) 134) [2015 77: 9s⁵ 8.5g 8v⁴ 8.5s 7m³ 10m⁵ 12.2g⁴ 11.1d² 10s p12g Dec 18] fairly useful maiden: trained by P. J. Prendergast fifth/sixth starts, then returned to former trainer: stays 1½m: acts on good to firm and heavy going: tried in cheekpieces in 2015. *John Patrick Shanahan, Ireland*

THE CASHEL MAN (IRE) 3 b.g. High Chaparral (IRE) 132 – Hadarama (IRE) 86 94 (Sinndar (IRE) 134) [2015 63: 14.1g⁴ 14.1m* 16g² 16.1m* 16m⁶ Oct 2] attractive, good-topped gelding: fairly useful handicapper: won at Redcar in May, Nottingham in June and Newmarket (by 5 lengths from Amour de Nuit) in August: will be suited by further than 2m: acts on good to firm going: usually races nearer last than first. *David Simcock*

THE CASH GENERATOR (IRE) 7 b.g. Peintre Celebre (USA) 137 – Majestic – Launch 85 (Lear Fan (USA) 130) [2015 71: 10m 10m t9.5m Aug 21] rangy gelding: maiden: no form in 2015. *Ralph Smith*

THE CHARACTER (IRE) 4 b.g. Bushranger (IRE) 119 – Operissimo (Singspiel (IRE) 89 133) [2015 90: 8g⁶ 10.3s 12.3v 11.9d⁶ 10.4f* 10g⁵ 10.3g⁴ 10.3m² 12.3g⁶ 10.4m² 10.1m t12.2f Oct 17] fairly useful handicapper: won at Haydock in June: second at Chester in July and Haydock in August: stays 12.5f: acts on tapeta and firm going: in cheekpieces last 5 starts. *Tom Dascombe*

THE COFFEE HUNTER (FR) 3 gr.g. Doctor Dino (FR) 123 – Mamamia (FR) (Linamix 72 (FR) 127) [2015 p9.4g 15.9g² Apr 12] ran both times in France, better effort when second in maiden at Saumur in April, no match for winner. *Nick Williams*

THE COMMENDATORE 2 b.c. (Mar 12) Starspangledbanner (AUS) 128 – Donna **73**
Giovanna 74 (Mozart (IRE) 131) [2015 p6g³ p6g³ p6g² p6g³ Dec 9] fair form when placed in 3
maidens, all at Kempton: blinkered final start. *John Gosden*

THECORNISHBARRON (IRE) 3 b.g. Bushranger (IRE) 119 – Tripudium (IRE) **75**
(Night Shift (USA)) [2015 p12f⁶ p12g t9.5f⁶ t8.6f Nov 3] fair maiden: best effort at 9.5f.
John Ryan

THECORNISHCOCKNEY 6 bl.g. Cockney Rebel (IRE) 127 – Glittering Image (IRE) –
(Sadler's Wells (USA) 132) [2015 98: 16g Sep 24] tall gelding: useful handicapper at best:
shaped as if amiss when well held in listed race at Newmarket only outing in 2015: stays
16.5f: acts on polytrack and good to soft going: usually in headgear/tongue tie: quirky.
John Ryan

THECORNISHCOWBOY 6 b.g. Haafhd 129 – Oriental Dance (Fantastic Light (USA) **78**
134) [2015 95, a80: p12m³ t12.2f⁵ p10g⁴ p10g⁴ t12.2f⁵ p12g⁴ 11.6m 12m 12g⁵ p11g p12g³
p12m* p12g⁶ 12m³ 12m³ 12m⁶ 10g 11.6m* t12.2g⁴ 12d⁶ t12.2m³ Aug 21] angular gelding:
fair handicapper: won at Lingfield in June and Windsor (amateur) in August: stayed 13f:
acted on polytrack, good to firm and heavy going: had worn headgear: wore tongue tie:
usually raced nearer last than first: dead. *John Ryan*

THE CORSICAN (IRE) 4 b.c. Galileo (IRE) 134 – Walklikeanegyptian (IRE) 77 **122**
(Danehill (USA) 126) [2015 109p: 9.9g* 10f⁴ 12m² 11s* 10d⁶ Oct 17] attractive colt: very
smart performer: continued his progress in 2015 and won listed race at Goodwood (by 2
lengths from Educate) in May and Arc Trial at Newbury (by 1½ lengths from Sky Hunter)
in September: also ran well when 3¼ lengths fourth to Free Eagle in Prince of Wales's
Stakes at Royal Ascot, ¾-length second to Dubday in Glorious Stakes at Goodwood and
4½ lengths sixth to Fascinating Rock in Champion Stakes at Ascot (raced closer to pace
than ideal): stays 1½m: acts on polytrack, firm and soft going: usually travels strongly.
David Simcock

Mrs Fitri Hay's "The Corsican"

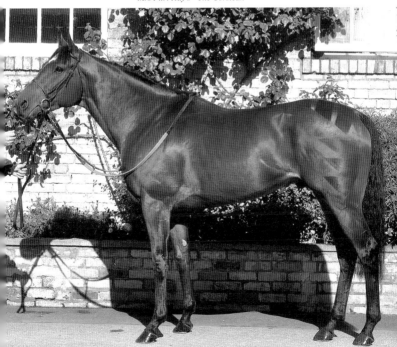

THE DANCING LORD 6 br.g. Imperial Dancer 123 – Miss Brookie 70 (The West **84**
(USA) 107) [2015 70, a82: p8g* p8g³ p8g³ p8g* 8g⁴ 8g⁶ 8m⁵ p10.7g t7.1m t9.5m³ p8f p10g⁵
t9.5f Nov 13] sturdy gelding: fairly useful performer: won handicap at Dundalk in January
and minor event there in March: left John Geoghegan after seventh start: stays 1¼m: acts
on polytrack, tapeta and good to firm going: has worn headgear: wears tongue tie.
Robert Mills

THE DANDY YANK (IRE) 4 b.g. Dandy Man (IRE) 123 – Bronze Queen (IRE) **77**
(Invincible Spirit (IRE) 121) [2015 82: p6f p6g* f5d p6f p5f³ p5g³ t5.1g⁵ p5g⁵ p5f⁶ p5f⁶
5.1d⁶ 5.3s p5g³ Jun 18] sturdy gelding: fair handicapper: won at Chelmsford in January:
stays 6f: acts on polytrack and good to firm going: often wears headgear. *Jamie Osborne*

THE DAPPER TAPPER (IRE) 3 b.g. Dandy Man (IRE) 123 – Sound Tap (IRE) **79**
(Warning 136) [2015 71: p6m² p6f⁵ p7f* t7.1g* p7f⁶ 8m 8.3g⁶ Jun 22] leggy gelding: fair
handicapper: won at Lingfield in March and Wolverhampton in April: stayed 7f: acted on
polytrack and tapeta: wore visor: was sometimes slowly away, often raced towards rear:
dead. *Eve Johnson Houghton*

THE DREAM FAST 3 b.g. Sleeping Indian 122 – Past 'N' Present (Cadeaux Genereux **52**
131) [2015 83p: p8m 6m⁴ 6g³ Jun 20] lightly-raced maiden, just modest form in 2015: will
benefit from return to 7f: sold 6,000 gns in July. *Rae Guest*

THE DUCKING STOOL 8 ch.m. Where Or When (IRE) 124 – Dance Sequel 54 **75**
(Selkirk (USA) 129) [2015 78: 10g⁵ 10m⁴ 13g⁵ 12f⁵ 13.3m³ 12d 11.9d² 11.9d³ 16s* Oct
23] big mare: fair handicapper: won at Newbury (apprentice) in October: stays 2m: acts on
polytrack, good to firm and heavy going: tried in cheekpieces. *Julia Feilden*

THE DUKKERER (IRE) 4 b.f. Footstepsinthesand 120 – Saffron Crocus 83 (Shareef **66**
Dancer (USA) 135) [2015 74: 7d 7m 8.3m 7m 8.3g³ t8.6g³ 8m t8.6g² 10.2d⁴ p8f³ p10f*
p10f Oct 8] fair handicapper: won at Chelmsford in September: stays 1¼m: acts on all-
weather, soft and good to firm going. *James Given*

THEE AND ME (IRE) 2 b.c. (Apr 16) Canford Cliffs (IRE) 133 – Lake Ladoga (Green **74**
Desert (USA) 127) [2015 5m⁶ t5.1g* 5.1d⁵ 5m⁴ 6.1m⁵ 6m⁶ 5g⁵ t5.1g² 6d p6g⁵ 6d
Oct 24] fair performer: won maiden at Wolverhampton in April: left Bill Turner after eighth
start: stays 6f: acts on polytrack, tapeta, good to firm and good to soft going: tried in
cheekpieces. *Brian Ellison*

THE EXCEL QUEEN (IRE) 2 br.f. (Feb 22) Excellent Art 125 – Gypsie Queen (IRE) **59**
83 (Xaar 132) [2015 7.5m⁴ 7m 8g⁵ 8g³ 10d⁶ Oct 5] £13,000Y: first foal: dam, 2-y-o 7f
winner who stayed 1¾m, half-sister to useful winner up to 9f Sikeeb: modest maiden: best
efforts at 1m. *Tony Coyle*

THE FENLAND MAN 4 b.g. Rob Roy (USA) 122 – Spark Up 81 (Lahib (USA) 129) **–**
[2015 –: t7.1m³ Dec 12] very lightly-raced maiden, modest form: raced only at 7f: tried in
cheekpieces. *James Unett*

THE FIRM (IRE) 6 b.g. Acclamation 118 – Aspen Falls (IRE) 78 (Elnadim (USA) 128) **69**
[2015 77: t9.5g⁶ p10g⁶ t8.6f 9m p10g t8.6f* t9.5f f8g t8.6g Dec 4] fair handicapper: won
at Wolverhampton in October: stays 10.5f: acts on polytrack, tapeta and good to firm going:
often in headgear in 2015: front runner/races prominently. *Daniel Loughnane*

THE FRENCH GREY (FR) 4 gr.f. Stormy River (FR) 123 – Khaliyna (IRE) 109 **58**
(Danehill (USA) 126) [2015 –: t7.1f² p7g t8.6g⁵ t12.2g³ p13.3m t9.5g⁴ p11g⁵ 11.9d Jun 23]
modest maiden: stays 1½m: acts on polytrack and tapeta: tried in cheekpieces in 2015:
usually races prominently. *Charlie Wallis*

THE FULWELL END 3 b.g. Amadeus Wolf 122 – Green Silk (IRE) (Namid 128) [2015 **54**
–: 7d 10g⁵ 8g 9m⁵ 10.1m 8g⁵ 7.9d² 7.2g Sep 29] modest maiden: left Noel Wilson after first
start: best effort at 1m: acts on good to firm and good to soft going: tried in visor in 2015:
often in tongue tie in 2015: sent to Greece. *Tracy Waggott*

THE GAY CAVALIER 4 b.g. Henrythenavigator (USA) 131 – Dear Daughter 111 (Polish **76**
Precedent (USA) 131) [2015 72: p10g² p10m* 19.5g p10m* p11f* p10f⁴ p12g p11g p11g **a87**
p11g⁶ 10d⁵ 9m⁵ 11.9g p10g⁴ 9s p8f 8.3g p10f⁴ p10g p10g* 19.5g Dec 1] fair handicapper
on turf, fairly useful on all-weather: won at Lingfield in January and at Kempton in
February (twice) and November: stays 1½m: acts on polytrack and good to firm going:
wears tongue tie: often starts slowly, often races in rear: quirky. *John Ryan*

THE GINGER BERRY 5 ch.g. First Trump 118 – Dolly Coughdrop (IRE) 72 (Titus **73**
Livius (FR) 115) [2015 75: p12f⁴ p12f⁴ p11g⁵ p11g² p11g p12g² p12g p12g Oct 6] fair
handicapper: stays 1½m: acts on polytrack: usually wears hood. *Dr Jon Scargill*

THE GRADUATE (IRE) 2 gr.c. (Feb 18) Mastercraftsman (IRE) 129 – Ballyvarra (IRE) (Sadler's Wells (USA) 132) [2015 8s 8.3s Nov 4] €165,000F, 100,000Y: third foal: half-brother to French 9.5f-12.5f winner Eponyme (by Zamindar): dam unraced half-sister to dam of Cheveley Park Stakes winner/1000 Guineas runner-up Wannabe Grand: signs of ability in maidens at Newbury and Nottingham: will be suited by 1¼m+: sure to do better. *Andrew Balding* – p

THE GREEDY BOY 2 b.g. (Feb 12) Atlantic Sport (USA) 115 – Indian Girl 59 (Erhaab (USA) 127) [2015 7s 8d⁶ p8d Sep 4] well held in maidens. *Mick Channon* –

THE GREEN OGRE 5 b.g. Dubai Destination (USA) 127 – Takegawa (Giant's Causeway (USA) 132) [2015 p12m⁴ Feb 27] workmanlike gelding: fair form in maidens in 2013, well held only start on Flat since: best effort at 8.5f: fairly useful hurdler. *Gary Moore* –

THE GREY GATSBY (IRE) 4 gr.c. Mastercraftsman (IRE) 129 – Marie Vison (IRE) 103 (Entrepreneur 123) [2015 128: 8.9g² 10.5g⁴ 10f² 10m² 10.4d³ 10g⁶ Sep 12] **128**

The Prix du Jockey Club and Irish Champion Stakes winner The Grey Gatsby failed to win in six starts in the latest season, but he showed himself to be as good as ever when runner-up in the Prince of Wales's Stakes at Royal Ascot and the Eclipse Stakes at Sandown, unlucky not to win at the Royal meeting after meeting trouble and just failing to catch Free Eagle. It may seem a little surprising that The Grey Gatsby stays in training, given that he is already a dual Group 1 winner with a good pedigree, but there is plenty to suggest that he can find another Group 1 provided he maintains the same level of form as a five-year-old. The Grey Gatsby is set to be given another chance over a mile and a half—his only previous run over the trip was an inconclusive sixth on soft ground in the 2014 Grand Prix de Paris—with the Dubai Sheema Classic on World Cup night pencilled in as his first port of call.

The Grey Gatsby started favourite for the nine-furlong Dubai Turf at Meydan on his reappearance at four, in a race previously run as the Dubai Duty Free, and he caught a tartar in the shape of Solow who was having his first tilt at a Group 1 and beat The Grey Gatsby by four and a quarter lengths. The Grey Gatsby was below his very best that day and he didn't show his true form on his next outing either, starting a short-priced favourite but managing only fourth of six to Al Kazeem, albeit beaten just a length and three quarters, in the Tattersalls Gold Cup at the Curragh in May, with interference suffered when bumped over a furlong out (when upsides front-running Postponed) not enough of an explanation for his defeat.

The Grey Gatsby was equipped with first-time cheekpieces in the Prince of Wales's Stakes at Royal Ascot and bounced back to his best to finish a short-head second of nine to Free Eagle, almost getting up after being penned in behind the winner from the two-furlong pole until inside the final furlong. With his regular rider Ryan Moore required to ride Cannock Chase for Sir Michael Stoute, The Grey Gatsby was ridden by Jamie Spencer for the first time since the Two Thousand Guineas and he retained the mount for the rest of the campaign. The pair gave the unbeaten Derby winner Golden Horn and Frankie Dettori a good race in the Eclipse on their next start after Royal Ascot. The Grey Gatsby gave his all as he challenged Golden Horn from early in the straight, the pair locked together until Golden Horn forged clear inside the final furlong. The Grey Gatsby was just not good enough against a rival of Golden Horn's quality on weight-for-age terms but he acquitted himself admirably before eventually going down by three and a half lengths. 'The winner is very special but we gave him a real race and the Arc is on the agenda now,' said The Grey Gatsby's trainer Kevin Ryan afterwards.

The Grey Gatsby never made it to the Arc, though, as he didn't show his very best form, either when three and a half lengths third of seven to Arabian Queen in a muddling race for the International at York in August, or when four and three quarter lengths sixth of seven to Golden Horn in the Irish Champion Stakes at Leopardstown on what proved to be his final start (the Breeders' Cup Turf was also said to have been under consideration until connections decided to give him a long rest with a five-year-old campaign in mind). Perhaps The Grey Gatsby's tremendous efforts in the Prince of Wales's and the Eclipse left something of a mark—it would hardly be a surprise if they had—but his performances afterwards certainly were not quite of the same calibre.

		Danehill Dancer	Danehill
	Mastercraftsman (IRE)	(b 1993)	Mira Adonde
	(gr 2006)	Starlight Dreams	Black Tie Affair
The Grey Gatsby (IRE)		(gr 1995)	Reves Celestes
(gr.c. 2011)		Entrepreneur	Sadler's Wells
	Marie Vison (IRE)	(b 1994)	Exclusive Order
	(ch 2001)	Metisse	Kingmambo
		(ch 1995)	Maximova

The Grey Gatsby's pedigree was covered in detail in *Racehorses of 2014*. He has a three-year-old half-sister by Fastnet Rock named Marie Rock who is unraced in Ireland, and a two-year-old brother named Master Vison who is unraced in Morocco (where the colt was foaled; Marie Vison's yearling colt is by Jan Vermeer who stands there). Marie Vison was due to visit Galileo in 2015. Marie Vison's dam Metisse won in France and has produced eight winners, including the Falco three-year-old Arms of Mine who was successful three times at around a mile and a quarter in France during the year. The Grey Gatsby, who remains the highest-rated performer by his sire Mastercraftsman, is a strong, compact colt and the type to carry plenty of condition. He stays an extended mile and a quarter and has good prospects of proving fully effective at a mile and a half. He acts on firm and good to soft going, but his best form (including his fine efforts in the Prince of Wales's and Eclipse) has come on ground firmer than good. He wore cheekpieces on his last four starts but is a tough and reliable sort, though he was uncharacteristically mulish at the start on his final outing and eventually had to be loaded into the stalls without his rider. *Kevin Ryan*

THE HAPPY HAMMER (IRE) 9 b.g. Acclamation 118 – Emma's Star (ITY) (Darshaan 133) [2015 50, a72: p7g p8f² p8g³ t7.1m⁴ p8m p8f* p8f⁴ p8f³ Oct 15] workmanlike gelding: fair handicapper: won at Chelmsford in September: stays 1m: acts on polytrack, tapeta, best turf form on good going: tried in headgear: often races towards rear. *Eugene Stanford* — **70**

THE HAPPY PRINCE (IRE) 3 b.c. Rip Van Winkle (IRE) 134 – Maid To Dream 72 (Oasis Dream 129) [2015 84p: 6.7s* p8g² 6d* 6d² 7.5g⁴ 6g² 7s³ Oct 25] smart performer: won maiden at Limerick in April and handicap at Naas (by ½ length from Penny Pepper) in May: second in Lacken Stakes at Naas (length behind Anthem Alexander) in June and listed race at the Curragh (1½ lengths behind Fort Del Oro) in October: best form at 6f: acts on soft going: in tongue tie last 2 starts. *Aidan O'Brien, Ireland* — **114**

THE HOLYMAN (IRE) 7 ch.g. Footstepsinthesand 120 – Sunset (IRE) (Polish Precedent (USA) 131) [2015 82: 12.1m p12g 11.9m⁶ Jun 30] quite good-topped gelding: fairly useful at best, no form in 2015: in visor final start: front runner/races prominently. *Jo Crowley* — **–**

THE HOODED CLAW (IRE) 4 ch.g. Dandy Man (IRE) 123 – Changari (USA) 90 (Gulch (USA)) [2015 93: 6m² 6m 6g t6f Oct 3] fairly useful handicapper: stays 6f: acts on good to firm and heavy going: tried in headgear. *Simon Crisford* — **93**

THE JUGGLER 2 b.c. (Jan 30) Archipenko (USA) 127 – Oblige 101 (Robellino (USA) 127) [2015 8g 8g⁶ 7s² Oct 12] useful-looking colt: fair maiden: 2¾ lengths second of 9 to Hermarna at Salisbury final start: will prove best at 1m+. *William Knight* — **66**

THE KID 4 b.g. High Chaparral (IRE) 132 – Shine Like A Star 60 (Fantastic Light (USA) 134) [2015 80: 14f² 14g⁵ 14.1g⁶ 16.4g Sep 6] fairly useful handicapper: stays 1¾m: acts on any turf going: often wears cheekpieces/tongue tie: often races towards rear. *John Quinn* — **80**

THE KING'S STEED 2 b.g. (Feb 4) Equiano (FR) 127 – King's Siren (IRE) 77 (King's Best (USA) 132) [2015 7g⁶ p8g Nov 11] sturdy gelding: second foal: half-brother to useful 2-y-o 8.3f winner (stays 1½m) Magic Dancer (by Norse Dancer): dam 2-y-o 7f winner out of smart winner up to 7f Blue Siren: fair form when sixth of 10 to Mootaharer in maiden at Newmarket in October: shaped as if something wrong next time, subsequently gelded: worth another chance. *Ralph Beckett* — **74 p**

THE KNAVE (IRE) 2 b.g. (Feb 20) Dick Turpin (IRE) 127 – Bayswater 76 (Caerleon (USA) 132) [2015 7.2s f7s⁴ 8.3d³ p8m⁶ 8.3s⁵ 7s⁶ Oct 26] modest maiden: stays 8.5f: acts on polytrack and soft going: tried in cheekpieces: front runner/races prominently. *Scott Dixon* — **60**

THE KURATOR (IRE) 3 ch.g. Art Connoisseur (IRE) 121 – A L'Aube (IRE) (Selkirk (USA) 129) [2015 –: f8g⁵ 7.5g May 4] little impact in maidens/handicaps: tried in cheekpieces. *Ann Duffield* —

THE LAMPO GENIE 3 b.g. Champs Elysees 124 – Samar Qand 59 (Selkirk (USA) 129) [2015 74: 11.9g* 11.9g 12.5m 10.4g⁴ 11.9m⁵ 10m Aug 29] fairly useful performer: won maiden at Haydock in April: stays 1½m: best form on good going: tried in visor. *K. R. Burke* **80**

THE LILLSTER 2 b.f. (Mar 24) Kodiac 112 – Wind Surf (USA) (Lil's Lad (USA) 121) [2015 6m 6.5s p6g² p6g⁵ Dec 30] 42,000Y: sturdy filly: fourth foal: dam 1m/8.5f winner in USA/Canada: fair maiden: best effort when second at Kempton. *Brian Meehan* **68**

THELLO 3 b.g. Arcano (IRE) 122 – Silca Destination 65 (Dubai Destination (USA) 127) [2015 7.5m 7s⁵ 7s³ p8g f8g* Dec 22] modest performer: won handicap at Southwell in December: stays 1m: acts on fibresand and soft going: sometimes slowly away. *Nigel Tinkler* **64**

THE LOCK MASTER (IRE) 8 b.g. Key of Luck (USA) 126 – Pitrizza (IRE) (Machiavellian (USA) 123) [2015 98: f11s² f12s⁴ f12g⁴ p14f⁵ p10d 10.3d⁴ p10g⁵ 12g⁶ 12g* 14.6m⁴ 11.8d 12f⁴ 11.9m² 12.4g 12g f11g³ Dec 22] fairly useful handicapper: won at Thirsk in May and Doncaster in July: stays 1¾m: acts on all-weather and any turf going: tried in headgear (wears cheekpieces nowadays): often races prominently. *Michael Appleby* **75 a83**

THE LYNCH MAN 2 b.c. (Apr 13) Sakhee's Secret 128 – Diliza 65 (Dilum (USA) 115) [2015 6g 6g² 7g⁴ 8s⁵ Oct 16] fair maiden: stays 1m. *John Quinn* **71**

THE MAJOR 2 b.g. (Apr 22) Major Cadeaux 121 – Ballerina Suprema (IRE) 87 (Sadler's Wells (USA) 132) [2015 7g³ 7.1m⁴ 7m⁴ Aug 5] fair maiden: best effort when fourth at Newcastle final start. *Michael Bell* **65**

THEM AND US (IRE) 3 ch.c. Rock of Gibraltar (IRE) 133 – Sagrada (GER) (Primo Dominie 121) [2015 80: p7m³ 8.5g* 8g² 8m 7g* 8f⁴ 7g³ 6g⁵ 7m² Oct 2] useful handicapper: won at Epsom in April and Newmarket (by neck from Use Your Filbert) in June: good second at Ascot (head behind Flying Hammer) final start: stays 8.5f: acts on firm going: often races towards rear: sold 78,000 gns, sent to USA. *Michael Bell* **101**

THE NAB (USA) 3 ch.g. Lookin At Lucky (USA) 127 – Moon's Tune (USA) (Dixieland Band (USA)) [2015 f7d⁶ f7s* 8m p11g f8d⁴ 10g p8f 8.3g Oct 19] strong, lengthy gelding: fair performer: won maiden at Southwell in March: best effort at 7f: acts on fibresand: in headgear. *Michael Attwater* **75**

THE NAME'S BOND 3 ch.g. Monsieur Bond (IRE) 120 – Fairlie 70 (Halling (USA) 133) [2015 –: 6m 8g 10g⁵ May 18] poor maiden: stays 1¼m: best form on good going: often races in rear, often races lazily. *Keith Reveley* **39**

THE NAME'S PAVER 2 ch.g. (Apr 21) Monsieur Bond (IRE) 120 – Pride of Kinloch 80 (Dr Devious (IRE) 127) [2015 5g 6g⁴ 6g⁵ 6g 6s⁵ Oct 16] fair maiden: stays 6f: acts on soft going. *Noel Wilson* **67**

THE NEW PHARAOH (IRE) 4 b.g. Montjeu (IRE) 137 – Out West (USA) 103 (Gone West (USA)) [2015 56: 11.5g p12g⁶ 15.8sʳᵒ 16s⁴ Oct 23] tall gelding: fair maiden: much improved in handicap at Catterick penultimate start (clear final 1f when crashed through rail and unseated rider): shaped well when length fourth to The Ducking Stool in apprentice handicap at Newbury next time, left with too much to do: stays 2m: acts on soft going: not straightforward but remains capable of better. *Chris Wall* **70 p**

THEOS LOLLY (IRE) 2 b.c. (Mar 31) Kodiac 112 – Aluana (IRE) 67 (Alzao (USA) 117) [2015 5g⁶ 5d⁵ 6g³ 6g³ t7.1g² 7d⁴ t7.1f² Nov 20] 18,000 2-y-o: second foal: dam 13f winner who stayed 2m: fairly useful maiden: stays 7f: acts on tapeta: often races prominently. *Richard Fahey* **81**

THE OSTEOPATH (IRE) 12 ch.g. Danehill Dancer (IRE) 117 – Miss Margate (IRE) 60 (Don't Forget Me 127) [2015 82: 8s⁵ 9g⁶ 10.1d⁴ 9.9m⁴ 9.3g⁶ 10s* 8g⁴ 8g⁶ 12v⁵ Oct 17] leggy gelding: fair performer: won claimer at Newcastle in May and seller at Redcar in July: will benefit from return to 1¼m: acts on any turf going: tried in headgear. *John Davies* **69**

THE OTMOOR POET 2 b.g. (Feb 13) Yeats (IRE) 128 – Kristalette (IRE) 95 (Leporello (IRE) 118) [2015 t8.6g Dec 5] 100/1, better for run when ninth of 11 in maiden at Wolverhampton. *Alan King* —

THE PERFECT SHOW 2 ch.g. (Feb 5) Showcasing 117 – Nizhoni (USA) 65 (Mineshaft (USA) 132) [2015 6g⁶ 6d 6d² Sep 25] 55,000Y, 240,000 2-y-o: third foal: half-brother to 6f (including at 2 yrs) winner Ayasha (by Indesatchel): dam, maiden (stayed 6f), half-sister to **76 p**

useful 7f winner Lady Fashion: fair form: 20/1, much improved when ¾-length second to King of Swing in maiden at Haydock final start, leading briefly final 100 yds: has been gelded: will go on improving. *Ed Walker*

THE PLOUGH (IRE) 2 gr.g. (Apr 28) Sea The Stars (IRE) 140 – Chinese White (IRE) **69** 118 (Dalakhani (IRE) 133) [2015 p8f 8.3d⁶ t9.5f⁵ Nov 14] 40,000Y: third foal: closely related to winner up to 1m Chinese Jade (2-y-o 7f winner, by Cape Cross): dam winner up to 1¼m (2-y-o 7f winner), including Pretty Polly Stakes: fair form in maidens: has been gelded. *Martyn Meade*

THE QUARTERJACK 6 b.g. Haafhd 129 – Caressed 92 (Medicean 128) [2015 78: **81** p13.3f² f14g² p13.3f² p13.3m p13.3f⁵ p14f 16s f16g* f16g⁵ f16g Dec 29] leggy gelding: fairly useful handicapper: won at Southwell in November: stays 17f: acts on all-weather, good to firm and heavy going: tried in cheekpieces. *Charlie Wallis*

THE RECTIFIER (USA) 8 b.g. Langfuhr (CAN) 124 – Western Vision (USA) (Gone **106** West (USA)) [2015 112: p8f⁶ 8f 8m⁵ 8m² 8f² p7g t8.6m Nov 28] compact gelding: useful **a100** handicapper: second in Betfred Mile at Goodwood (promoted from third when beaten 3¼ lengths by subsequently-disqualified So Beloved) in July and in minor event at Bath (neck behind Algaith) in September: stays 8.5f: acts on polytrack and firm going: often wears tongue tie: front runner/races prominently. *Seamus Durack*

THE REEL WAY (GR) 4 br.f. Reel Buddy (USA) 118 – Nephetriti Way (IRE) 92 **54** (Docksider (USA) 124) [2015 50: 7g³ p7m⁵ 7.1m⁴ 7.1g³ Aug 2] tall, narrow filly: modest maiden: stays 7f: best form on good going. *Patrick Chamings*

THE RESDEV WAY 2 b.g. (Feb 13) Multiplex 114 – Lady Duxyana 54 (Most Welcome **56** 131) [2015 7m 6.1g f7s⁵ 7.2g² 8.1m 8g Sep 23] modest maiden: best effort at 7f. *Richard Guest*

THERMAL COLUMN (IRE) 3 b.g. Vale of York (IRE) 117 – Swiss Roll (IRE) 96 **74** (Entrepreneur 123) [2015 63: f8g⁶ t7.1f³ f8g³ p10g⁶ f12g⁵ f8g 8.6f³ t9.5f⁴ t8.6f² p8f³ t9.5g** p10g² Dec 7] fair handicapper: won at Wolverhampton in October and December: left Richard Fahey after second start, Heather Dalton after sixth: stays 1¼m: acts on polytrack and tapeta. *Michael Appleby*

THERTHAAR 2 b.c. (Feb 11) Kyllachy 129 – Red Tiara (USA) 60 (Mr Prospector **–** (USA)) [2015 6d 6g 6s Oct 26] wel held in maidens. *Ismail Mohammed*

THE SALMON MAN 3 b.c. Showcasing 117 – Donna Vita 85 (Vettori (IRE) 119) [2015 **72 p** 7g⁵ p8g⁵ 8.3d³ Oct 12] compact colt: fifth foal: half-brother to 1¼m-11.6f winner Dark Amber (by Sakhee): dam, 2-y-o 7f winner, half-sister to useful performer up to 2m Sentinel: fair maiden: best effort when third at Windsor final start, inadequate test: will stay at least 1¼m: capable of better. *Brendan Powell*

THESME 3 b.f. Exceed And Excel (AUS) 126 – Final Dynasty 104 (Komaite (USA)) **98 p** [2015 5d⁶ 5m² 5m³ 5g* 5.1m⁴ 5.4m* 5g* Aug 22] 80,000Y: second foal: closely related to 6f winner Crazee Diamond (by Rock of Gibraltar): dam 5f winner (including at 2 yrs): useful handicapper: won at Redcar in June and York (by 1½ lengths from Savannah Beau) in July: improved again when following up in apprentice event on latter course by 1¾ lengths from Imtiyaaz: stays 5.5f: acts on good to firm going: usually leads, often travels strongly: should continue to progress. *Nigel Tinkler*

THE SOCIETY MAN (IRE) 8 ch.g. Moscow Society (USA) 110 – Redruth (IRE) 60 **–** (Sri Pekan (USA) 117) [2015 f12g Dec 22] tailed off in maiden at Southwell only outing on Flat: winning hurdler/modest chaser. *Michael Chapman*

THE SPECIAL HOUSE (IRE) 3 ro.g. Dalakhani (IRE) 133 – Noble Galileo (IRE) 99 **63** (Galileo (IRE) 134) [2015 8m p10g⁴ 12m⁶ 12g 10.3m⁵ Jul 16] modest maiden: left Mark Johnston after fourth start: stays 1½m: acts on polytrack and good to firm going: often starts slowly. *Brian Ellison*

THE SPECIAL ONE (IRE) 2 br.f. (Mar 29) Cape Cross (IRE) 129 – Capote West **57** (USA) (Capote (USA)) [2015 6m 6g⁶ 6g⁶ Sep 7] €45,000F, 30,000Y: rather unfurnished filly: fourth foal: sister to 2-y-o 1m winner Capeslew, closely related to 7f/1m winner Sister Slew (by Kheleyf) and half-sister to 7f winner Lady Sparkler (by Tamayuz): dam US 5.5f/6f winner: modest maiden. *Clive Cox*

THE STEWARD (USA) 4 b.g. Street Cry (IRE) 130 – Candlelight (USA) (Kingmambo **102** (USA) 125) [2015 87p: p10g⁵ p11g² t12.2f² p11g* t12.2m³ p12g⁶ Dec 19] useful handicapper: won at Kempton in November: good third at Wolverhampton (neck behind Sparring) next time: stays 1½m: acts on polytrack and tapeta: in headgear last 3 starts. *Sir Mark Prescott Bt*

THE TEMPEST 3 gr.f. Mastercraftsman (IRE) 129 – Virginia Hall 107 (Medicean 128) **84**
[2015 64p: 12.1g* 10.4d⁶ 12.1m³ 12f² 12m⁴ 14g⁶ 14d Sep 4] £85,000Y: first foal: dam,
winner up to 1m (2-y-o 5f/6f winner), half-sister to Nell Gwyn Stakes winner Silca's Gift:
fairly useful performer: won maiden at Beverley in May: second in handicap at Doncaster
in July: will benefit from return to around 1½m: acts on firm going: usually leads. *David
O'Meara*

THE THIRD MAN 4 gr.g. Dalakhani (IRE) 133 – Spinning Queen 118 (Spinning World **78**
(USA) 130) [2015 85: p8m⁶ p10m³ p10f⁴ 10g 10m⁵ 10g² 11.8d 9.5m⁴ t9.5f* t9.5m⁴ Dec **a86**
30] leggy gelding: fairly useful handicapper: won at Wolverhampton in November: stays
1¼m: acts on polytrack, tapeta and good to firm going: tried in hood in 2015: often travels
strongly. *Henry Spiller*

THE TICHBORNE (IRE) 7 b.g. Shinko Forest (IRE) – Brunswick (Warning 136) **–**
[2015 75: p8g p8m Dec 31] strong gelding: handicapper, lightly raced nowadays: stays 8.5f:
acts on polytrack, soft and good to firm going: usually in headgear nowadays. *Roger Teal*

THE TIN MAN 3 b.g. Equiano (FR) 127 – Persario 96 (Bishop of Cashel 122) [2015 6m⁶ **120**
6m* 6m* 6g 6m* 6d⁴ Oct 17] 80,000Y: robust gelding: fifth foal: half-brother to top-class
5f/6f winner Deacon Blues (by Compton Place) and useful sprinters Holley Shiftwell (by
Bahamian Bounty) and If So (by Iffraaj): dam 6f/7f winner: very smart performer: won
maiden at Doncaster in June and handicaps at Doncaster in July and Ascot (by 4½ lengths
from Dawn's Early Light) in October: 10/1, further improvement when 3¾ lengths fourth
of 20 to Muhaarar in Champions Sprint Stakes at Ascot final start: raced only at 6f: acts on
good to firm and good to soft going: strong traveller. *James Fanshawe*

THETIS (IRE) 2 b.f. (Feb 10) Invincible Spirit (IRE) 121 – Serres (IRE) (Daylami (IRE) **105 p**
138) [2015 7m³ 6.9m* 7g² Sep 25] attractive filly: has scope: fourth foal: sister to 1¼m
winner Indelible Ink and half-sister to 2 winners, including useful winner up to 10.4f
(Musidora Stakes) Liber Nauticus (2-y-o 1m winner, by Azamour): dam unraced half-sister
to top-class 1½m performer and St Leger winner Conduit: useful form: won maiden at
Carlisle in September by 2 lengths from Golden Stunner: 7/1, much improved when 1¾
lengths second of 7 to Promising Run in Rockfel Stakes at Newmarket final start, keeping
on: likely to stay at least 1m: open to further progress. *Sir Michael Stoute*

THE TWISLER 3 b.g. Motivator 131 – Panna 106 (Polish Precedent (USA) 131) [2015 **110**
65: 11.7f² 12d⁴ 14.1m² 16f 14g⁴ 14.1g* 14s* 14.9m⁵ 15.4v⁵ t16.5m⁵ Dec 12] rather leggy
gelding: smart performer: left Charles Hills after reappearance: won handicap at Salisbury
and listed race at Goodwood, both in August, improved form when beating Fun Mac 3
lengths in latter: stays 15.5f: acts on heavy going. *Jane Chapple-Hyam*

THE WALLACE LINE (IRE) 4 b.g. Mastercraftsman (IRE) 129 – Surval (IRE) 91 **64**
(Sadler's Wells (USA) 132) [2015 –: t16.5f³ Oct 30] tall, unfurnished gelding: modest
maiden: stays 16.5f: acts on polytrack and tapeta, best turf form on good going or softer:
tried in cheekpieces. *Tim Vaughan*

THE WARRIOR (IRE) 3 b.c. Exceed And Excel (AUS) 126 – Aymara 85 (Darshaan **96**
133) [2015 103: 6v* 6m³ 7v³ 8g 7g Jun 18] useful-looking colt: useful performer: won
25-runner maiden at the Curragh in March: third in £150,000 Tattersalls Millions 3-Y-O
Sprint at Newmarket (3¼ lengths behind Bossy Guest) and in listed race at the Curragh
(5¼ lengths behind Tombelaine): stays 7f: acts on good to firm and heavy going: tried in
headgear: often races in rear. *Aidan O'Brien, Ireland*

THEWAYITELLUM (IRE) 2 b.f. (Mar 3) Kodiac 112 – Christmas Cracker (FR) **70**
(Alhaarth (IRE) 126) [2015 5.1g⁴ t6g 6d t5.1f³ p6f p6g Dec 7] €22,000Y, £50,000 2-y-o:
fifth foal: closely related to 6f winner Christmas Aria (by Oratorio), later successful in
Qatar, and half-sister to 1¼m winner Avocadeau (by Lawman): dam, French 2-y-o 7.5f
winner, half-sister to useful winner up to 1½m in France/Qatar Hamriya: fair maiden: best
form at 5f: acts on tapeta. *James Given*

THE WAY YOU DANCE (IRE) 3 b.g. Thewayyouare (USA) 117 – Beautiful Dancer **66**
(IRE) 50 (Danehill Dancer (IRE) 117) [2015 –: 8.3m⁵ 8f p11g 10.4g⁴ 9.9g⁶ 9.9g⁵ 8.5g⁶ **a74**
t9.5f* t9.5f² Oct 23] compact gelding: fair performer: won minor event at Wolverhampton
in October: stays 11f: acts on tapeta, polytrack and good to firm going: tried in cheekpieces
in 2015: temperament under suspicion. *Ismail Mohammed*

THE WEE BARRA (IRE) 3 b.f. Rock of Gibraltar (IRE) 133 – Gamra (IRE) 73 (Green **71**
Desert (USA) 127) [2015 68: 8g 8g 9.9m⁵ 9.9m⁴ 12g⁵ 9.3g* 9.8g* 10g Oct 8] fair
handicapper: won at Carlisle and Ripon in August: stays 1¼m: best form on good going: in
cheekpieces last 2 starts: usually leads. *Kevin Ryan*

Betfred Cambridgeshire (Heritage Handicap), Newmarket—a fifth success of the season for the thriving Third Time Lucky (nearest camera), who gets back up on the line to edge out Master The World (cheekpieces); Examiner (partly hidden by first 2) does best of the stand-side/centre group in third; the riderless horse is Brendan Brackan who unseated his jockey at the start

THE WEE CHIEF (IRE) 9 ch.g. King Charlemagne (USA) 120 – La Belle Clare (IRE) 61 (Paris House 123) [2015 44§: p6f* 5m⁴ 6f May 23] lengthy, rather sparely-made gelding: modest handicapper: won at Lingfield in January: stays 6f: acts on polytrack and good to firm going: tried in headgear/tongue tie prior to 2015: usually races towards rear, often travels strongly: one to treat with caution (finds little/carries head high). *Jimmy Fox* **63 §**

THEWESTWALIAN (USA) 7 b.g. Stormy Atlantic (USA) – Skies of Blue (USA) (Ogygian (USA)) [2015 62, a42: 7m⁴ 6m* 6m 7g 5.9m 5.9g⁵ Aug 19] modest handicapper: won at Hamilton (amateur) in June: stays 6f: acts on polytrack and good to firm going: tried in hood prior to 2015. *Peter Hiatt* **61**

THE WINNINGTIPSTER 2 ch.g. (Apr 4) Kheleyf (USA) 116 – Freedom Song 74 (Singspiel (IRE) 133) [2015 7.9m 7.2m⁶ Sep 27] tailed off in maidens. *Susan Corbett* **–**

THE WISPE 3 ch.f. Kyllachy 129 – Twitch Hill 67 (Piccolo 121) [2015 73: 5.1m³ 5g² 5m⁶ 5g⁶ 5d² 5.1g² 5m⁵ 5.1g⁵ 5g p5f p5g⁶ Dec 7] rather leggy filly: fair handicapper: best form at 5f: acts on good to firm and good to soft going: tried in cheekpieces in 2015: often races prominently. *Robert Cowell* **73**

THE YANK 6 b.g. Trade Fair 124 – Silver Gyre (IRE) 65 (Silver Hawk (USA) 123) [2015 59: t12.2f² p12m² t13.9m* t16.5g* p13.3m* p13g⁶ t12.2g⁴ p12m³ Nov 19] tall gelding: fair handicapper: won Wolverhampton (twice, apprentice event first time) and Chelmsford in February: left Tony Carroll after ninth outing: stays 2m: acts on polytrack and tapeta: tried in tongue tie: winning chaser. *David Bridgwater* **75**

THEYDON BOIS 3 b.f. Three Valleys (USA) 119 – Velvet Waters 80 (Unfuwain (USA) 131) [2015 64: 8g* 8.1m⁶ 13m⁶ Jun 26] rather leggy filly: fair handicapper: won at Newmarket in May: should be suited by further than 1m: acts on tapeta, soft and good to firm going: in hood/tongue tie: usually races towards rear. *Peter Charalambous* **66**

THEYDON GREY 2 gr.g. (Jan 18) Champs Elysees 124 – Cheerfully 67 (Sadler's Wells (USA) 132) [2015 8g⁵ p8f* 8g⁶ 8.5d* Sep 27] 9,000Y: lengthy gelding: second foal: half-brother to 9.5f/1¼m winner Let Right Be Done (by Lawman): dam maiden (best effort at 1¼m): fairly useful performer: won maiden at Chelmsford in September: stays 1m: has awkward head carriage. *Peter Charalambous* **81**

THEYDON THUNDER 3 b.g. Virtual 122 – Lady Agnes 53 (Singspiel (IRE) 133) [2015 51: f8g Mar 5] modest maiden: well held in handicap only outing in 2015: best effort at 7f: acts on fibresand. *Peter Charalambous* **–**

THEY SEEK HIM HERE (IRE) 2 b.c. (Mar 20) Elusive Pimpernel (USA) 117 – Spiritville (IRE) 59 (Invincible Spirit (IRE) 121) [2015 p7g* 7f⁴ 7.1m⁴ Aug 22] €50,000Y: lengthy, attractive colt: first foal: half-brother to 1½m winner Officer Drivel (by Captain Rio): dam maiden (stayed 9.5f): useful performer: won 14-runner maiden at Kempton in June by ¾ length from Jayjinski: better form when 3½ lengths fourth of 8 to Birchwood in Superlative Stakes at Newmarket and 3 lengths fourth of 10 to First Selection in Solario Stakes at Sandown: will stay at least 1m. *Hugo Palmer* **99**

THIEF OF HEARTS 2 br.f. (Apr 10) Dick Turpin (IRE) 127 – Constant Craving 82 **52**
(Pastoral Pursuits 127) [2015 7.4g 6dᵀᵀ p6g² p6g⁵ Dec 7] first foal: dam 8.3f winner: modest
maiden: should stay 7f. *Bill Turner*

THIKRIYAAT (IRE) 2 b.g. (Feb 4) Azamour (IRE) 130 – Malaspina (IRE) (Whipper **81 p**
(USA) 126) [2015 p8f* Oct 22] 70,000Y: second foal: half-brother to 1¾m winner Cahill
(by Lawman): dam, French maiden (placed at 7.5f/1m), half-sister to smart winner up to
1m Johnny Barnes: 16/1, overcame lack of experience when winning 10-runner maiden at
Chelmsford by ½ length from Loading, headway out wide over 1f out then staying on to
lead close home: likely to stay 1¼m: type to improve, and likely win handicaps. *Sir Michael Stoute*

THIMAAR (USA) 7 b.g. Dynaformer (USA) – Jinaan (USA) 72 (Mr Prospector (USA)) **76**
[2015 –: t16.5f t12.2m Dec 26] big, rangy gelding: one-time smart performer, just fair
nowadays: stays 16.5f: acts on polytrack, soft and good to firm going: tried in headgear
prior to 2015. *Sarah Hollinshead*

THINK AHEAD 4 b.g. Shamardal (USA) 129 – Moonshadow 75 (Diesis 133) [2015 **107**
10m* 10f³ p8g³ 10.4d³ 9.9g* Sep 30] well-made gelding: useful performer: won maiden at
Windsor (by 2 lengths from Senrima) in June and handicap at Salisbury (by 2¾ lengths
from Raw Impulse) in September: stays 10.5f: acts on polytrack, firm and soft going: in
cheekpieces final start: usually leads. *Saeed bin Suroor*

THIRD DIMENSION 4 b.g. Dubawi (IRE) 129 – Round The Cape 94 (Cape Cross **112**
(IRE) 129) [2015 99: 8v³ 9v³ 8.5d⁵ 8.3d⁴ 8d 7s* 8s* Oct 10] smart handicapper: won at
Listowel (by 2½ lengths from Bubbly Bellini) in September and Limerick in October,
improving again but very much having run of race when beating Canary Row by 1½
lengths in latter: stays 1m: acts on soft going: sold 55,000 gns, sent to Qatar. *G. M. Lyons, Ireland*

THIRD ROCK (IRE) 2 b.g. (Mar 15) Hat Trick (JPN) 121 – Rochitta (USA) (Arch **68**
(USA) 127) [2015 6g 7m⁶ p7g⁵ Nov 18] fair maiden: best effort when sixth of 9 at
Yarmouth (3¾ lengths behind Banksea) on second start. *Sir Michael Stoute*

THIRD STRIKE 4 b.g. Tertullian (USA) 115 – Shaabra (IRE) (Rainbow Quest (USA) **69**
134) [2015 61: p12g⁶ p10m* p10f³ p10f* p10g* p11g 10m⁵ 8m³ 10d⁶ Jul 13] small
gelding: fair handicapper: won at Kempton (twice, latter apprentice event) and Chelmsford
in February and at Lingfield in April: stays 1¼m: acts on polytrack and good to firm going:
tried in blinkers prior to 2015: usually races nearer last than first, often travels strongly:
sold £5,000, sent to Italy. *Gary Moore*

THIRD TIME LUCKY (IRE) 3 gr.g. Clodovil (IRE) 116 – Speckled Hen (IRE) 60 **110**
(Titus Livius (FR) 115) [2015 82: 7.1s* 8.3g* 8m* 7.6g² 8g⁴ 8s* 9g*] workmanlike
gelding: smart performer: flourished through 2015 and won maiden at Musselburgh in
April and handicaps at Leicester in May, Musselburgh in June and Thirsk in September (by 3½ lengths
from Father Bertie) and Newmarket (34-runner Cambridgeshire, by short head from
Master The World) in September: will probably stay 1¼m: acts on soft and good to firm
going: front runner/races prominently. *Richard Fahey*

THIS IS FOR YOU 2 b.g. (Mar 6) Paco Boy (IRE) 129 – Waypoint 95 (Cadeaux **80**
Genereux 131) [2015 5d 6g 6m² 5.1d* 5.5s² 5.5d Sep 26] £10,000Y: good-topped gelding:
half-brother to several winners, including smart 5f-7f winner Jonny Mudball (by Oasis
Dream) and useful 2-y-o 5f/5.5f (Prix Robert Papin) winner Never A Doubt (by Night
Shift): dam, 6f/7f winner, half-sister to smart sprinter Acclamation: fairly useful performer:
won maiden at Chepstow in August: stays 5.5f: acts on soft going: usually races close up.
Andrew Balding

THIS IS THE DAY 4 b.f. Footstepsinthesand 120 – Miss Pinkerton 104 (Danehill (USA) **107**
126) [2015 99: 10s⁶ 10.2m³ 10.1g⁴ 9.9g 9.9m⁶ 10g* p10f⁵ p10m⁴ Nov 14] sturdy filly:
useful handicapper: won by head from Silvery Moon at Pontefract in September: creditable
fourth of 14 to Let's Go in listed race at Lingfield final start: stays 10.5f: acts on polytrack
and good to firm going: tried in hood. *Charlie Fellowes*

THOLEN (USA) 2 b.f. (May 1) Lonhro (AUS) 128 – Zelanda (IRE) 108 (Night Shift **76**
(USA)) [2015 5g⁶ 5.1f⁵ 7m² 7m³ 7.2m⁴ Aug 7] useful-looking filly: half-sister to several
winners, including smart French/UAE 5.5f-1m winner Time Prisoner (by Elusive Quality)
and useful 2-y-o 5f/6f winner Pearl Grey (by Gone West): dam 5f and (including at 2 yrs)
6f winner: fair maiden: stays 7f: acts on good to firm going: usually races close up.
Mark Johnston

THOMAS BLOSSOM (IRE) 5 b.g. Dylan Thomas (IRE) 132 – Woman Secret (IRE) **73** (Sadler's Wells (USA) 132) [2015 61: t12.2f* p12g³ p12m* t13.9g³ t12.2g⁵ 14d⁵ 13.1m⁵ t13.9f² t13.9f⁵ Dec 14] fair handicapper: won at Wolverhampton in January and Lingfield in February: left Patrick Chamings after eighth start: stays 1¾m: acts on polytrack and tapeta: sometimes wears visor: often races towards rear: consistent. *Ali Stronge*

THOMAS SENSAZIONE 4 b.g. Dylan Thomas (IRE) 132 – Queen Sensazione (IRE) **91 d** (King Charlemagne (USA) 120) [2015 8.9m 11.9m⁵ t9.5g p8g 10d⁵ p8f⁵ Oct 24] fairly useful ex-Italian-trained handicapper: left Stefano Botti after second start: disappointing in Britain: stays 1½m: acts on good to firm going: wore cheekpieces last 2 starts: often leads. *Marco Botti*

THORKHILL STAR (IRE) 3 b.g. Equiano (FR) 127 – Reine de Romance (IRE) **84** (Vettori (IRE) 119) [2015 76: p8g⁵ 8.5g 7.5g* 8.5m* Jun 16] fairly useful performer: won maiden at Beverley in May and handicap there in June: stays 8.5f: acts on good to firm going. *Richard Fahey*

THORNABY NASH 4 br.g. Kheleyf (USA) 116 – Mistress Twister 83 (Pivotal 124) **87** [2015 6g 6d² 8d⁵ 8m* 8g² 8m⁶ 8m⁶ 8m 10.4g Sep 6] fairly useful handicapper: missed 2014: won at Wetherby in June: stays 10.5f: acts on soft and good to firm going. *David O'Meara*

THORNABY PRINCESS 4 b.f. Camacho 118 – Ingleby Princess 78 (Bold Edge 123) **64** [2015 73: 5d 5m 5s³ 5m³ 6g³ 6d 5s 5m⁴ 16f Oct 23] modest handicapper: left Marjorie Fife after seventh start: stays 6f: acts on good to firm and good to soft going: tried in cheekpieces in 2015. *Colin Teague*

THORNADO (IRE) 2 b.c. (Feb 28) Scat Daddy (USA) 120 – Oui Say Oui (IRE) 100 **– p** (Royal Applause 124) [2015 7m Jul 10] €280,000Y: second foal: dam, 6f (at 2 yrs) and 8.5f (in USA) winner, half-sister to winner up to 1m Satchem and winner up to 2m Eye of The Storm (both smart): 33/1, 9¼ lengths ninth of 13 to Manaafidh in maiden at Newmarket, weakening 1f out: sent to USA: should do better. *Ed Walker*

THORNTOUN CARE 4 b.g. Rail Link 132 – Thorntoun Piccolo 64 (Groom Dancer **78** (USA) 128) [2015 87: 13s 14m⁶ 12g 12.2g⁵ 10.4g Sep 6] fair handicapper: stays 13f: acts on soft and good to firm going: sometimes slowly away, often races in rear. *Jim Goldie*

THORNTOUN LADY (USA) 5 b.m. Henrythenavigator (USA) 131 – Valery Lady **85** (ARG) (Roy (USA)) [2015 76: 6m 5m* 5f* 5m 5d² 5g 5d Sep 26] fairly useful handicapper: won at Musselburgh in June and Haydock in July: has form over as far as 1m, should prove best at 5f/6f: acts on firm and good to soft going: usually races in rear. *Jim Goldie*

THORPE BAY 6 b.g. Piccolo 121 – My Valentina 84 (Royal Academy (USA) 130) [2015 **84** 66, a83: f6d³ f5s* f5d² Jan 22] fairly useful performer: won seller at Southwell in January: stays 6f: acts on fibresand, tapeta, soft and good to firm going: sometimes in headgear/tried in tongue tie prior to 2015: usually races prominently, usually responds generously to pressure: sent to the Netherlands, and won 6f handicap at Dortmund in December. *Michael Appleby*

THOU SWELL (IRE) 3 b.g. Tiznow (USA) 133 – Kamarinskaya (USA) 105 (Storm Cat **71** (USA)) [2015 10.5g 10g 13g 14.1d f12g³ f12g⁴ p10g² Dec 30] fair maiden: left John M. Oxx after third start: will benefit from return to at least 1½m: acts on polytrack and fibresand: tried in blinkers: often races prominently. *Shaun Harris*

THOWAR (USA) 3 gr.g. Exchange Rate (USA) 111 – Elusive Fancy (USA) (Elusive **55** Quality (USA)) [2015 70: 7.5m p7g 8.3g 8.5f⁵ Jul 3] modest maiden in Britain: stays 1m: acts on polytrack: sometimes wears headgear: sold 1,500 gns, sent to Sweden, where won maiden at Taby (1m, dirt) in December. *Kevin Ryan*

THRAYA QUEEN 2 ch.f. (Apr 15) Shamardal (USA) 129 – Samira Gold (FR) 107 (Gold **59** Away (IRE) 125) [2015 7.5g 8g⁵ t8.6g f8g Dec 29] fourth foal: half-sister to 1¼m winner Paris Rose (by Cape Cross) and 11.5f winner Gold Approach (by New Approach): dam 1m-1¼m winner who stayed 13f: modest maiden: will stay 1¼m: wears hood. *Richard Fahey*

THREAT ASSESSED (IRE) 2 b.c. (Mar 24) Holy Roman Emperor (IRE) 125 – High **66 p** Reserve 95 (Dr Fong (USA) 128) [2015 8s Oct 23] €32,000Y: sixth foal: closely related to ungenuine 9.4f winner Pedantic (by Danehill Dancer) and half-brother to useful 1m winner Critical Risk (by Pivotal): dam, 1m-1¼m winner, half-sister to very smart 1m-10.4f winner Poet: 28/1, green when 8¼ lengths eighth of 15 to Algometer in maiden at Newbury: should do better. *Clive Cox*

THREAVE 7 b.m. Diktat 126 – Bianca Sforza (Anabaa (USA) 130) [2015 81: 5.1m f6d⁴ **97** 6g² 6g⁶ 5s* 5s* 5s* 5s Oct 9] lengthy mare: useful handicapper: improved and won at Goodwood in August and Sandown and Goodwood (apprentice, by 4½ lengths from By Rights) in September: stays 6f: acts on soft and good to firm going: tried in tongue tie prior to 2015: front runner/races prominently. *Jo Crowley*

THREEBAGSUE (IRE) 2 ch.f. (Mar 24) Lord Shanakill (USA) 121 – Feet of Flame **76** (USA) 59 (Theatrical) [2015 p6g³ 6m⁶ 6m t7.1g⁵ p7f³ p7.5g² 8s⁶ p8f³ t8.6f² t8.6f³ t8.6f* p7g* Dec 28] £10,000Y: workmanlike filly: half-sister to 3 winners, including useful 7f-8.6f winner Kinky Afro (by Modigliani) and 2-y-o 8.6f winner Fullback (by Redback): dam maiden (third at 1¼m): fair performer: won nurseries at Wolverhampton in November and Lingfield in December: stays 8.5f: acts on polytrack, tapeta and good to firm going: usually in blinkers: consistent. *J. S. Moore*

THREE BROTHERS (FR) 2 gr.c. (Mar 28) Slickly (FR) 128 – Vivartic (FR) (Verglas – (IRE) 118) [2015 8.3s Nov 4] 16/1, well held in maiden at Nottingham. *Harry Dunlop*

THREE GRACEZ 3 b.f. Kyllachy 129 – Three Ducks 89 (Diktat 126) [2015 69p: p8g³ **90** p8f² 7.5g* 7d⁴ 7m² 6.9g³ 8g⁴ 7d⁶ 8g² p7.5g Dec 12] fairly useful performer: won handicaps at Beverley (apprentices) and Doncaster in May: left Noel Quinlan after reappearance and Philip McBride after sixth start: several good efforts in France after, including when second in minor event at Bordeaux: stays 1m: acts on polytrack, tapeta, good to firm and good to soft going: often travels strongly. *C. Gourdain, France*

THREEINONEDAY (IRE) 2 b.g. (Apr 30) Bushranger (IRE) 119 – Star Studded **54** (Cadeaux Genereux 131) [2015 6g 7m 7g 8d 7s p8g Nov 11] modest maiden: best effort at 7f: tried in visor: sometimes slowly away. *Nigel Tinkler*

THREES GRAND 5 b.m. Milk It Mick 120 – Ginger Cookie 47 (Bold Edge 123) [2015 **69** 74: 5d⁶ 5s⁴ 5g³ 5m 5g 5g Jul 5] workmanlike mare: fair handicapper: stays 6f: acts on good to firm and heavy going: tried in headgear. *Scott Dixon*

THREE TIMES A LORD 3 b.c. Three Valleys (USA) 119 – Sesmen 106 (Inchinor 119) – [2015 p8f⁶ Feb 3] 20/1, green when 10 lengths last of 6 to Virtual Reality in maiden at Kempton. *John Butler*

THRILLED (IRE) 2 b.f. (Mar 19) Kodiac 112 – Fuerta Ventura (IRE) 102 (Desert Sun **67 p** 120) [2015 6g⁶ p7g⁶ p7g Oct 14] 460,000Y: fourth foal: half-sister to useful winner up to 7f The Gold Cheongsam (2-y-o 6f/6.5f winner, by Red Clubs) and 6f winner Hope And Faith (by Zebedee): dam, 1m-9.4f winner who stayed 1¾m, half-sister to useful 5.7f-7f winner Redvers: fair maiden: best effort when seventh of 12 at Kempton (3 lengths behind Desiderada) on final start, not knocked about: capable of better. *David Lanigan*

THRTYPOINTSTOTHREE (IRE) 4 b.g. Kodiac 112 – Miss Taken (IRE) 58 (Dubai **59** Destination (USA) 127) [2015 42: t8.6g t9.5g³ t9.5f³ t9.5f⁶ t9.5m² p10f⁵ t9.5f² t8.6g⁶ 12d t8.6m t8.6m t9.5m Sep 25] small, close-coupled gelding: modest maiden: stays 1¼m: acts on polytrack and tapeta: tried in blinkers in 2015: often races prominently. *Nikki Evans*

THRUST CONTROL (IRE) 8 ch.g. Fath (USA) 116 – Anazah (USA) (Diesis 133) – [2015 59: f7g⁵ f8g 7.1s⁶ 7g f8d May 18] sturdy gelding: modest handicapper: no form in 2015: stays 9f: acts on fibresand, soft and good to firm going: wears headgear. *Tracy Waggott*

THUNDERBIRD 3 b.f. Sakhee (USA) 136 – Trustthunder 87 (Selkirk (USA) 129) [2015 **54** f6g⁶ f5g² f6g² f7g² f6d³ p6f f7g f7m f7g Dec 12] half-sister to 3 winners, including 6f to (including at 2 yrs) 1m winner Thunderball (by Haafhd) and winner up to 1¼m Thunderstruck (2-y-o 7.5f winner, by Bertolini): dam 6f winner (including at 2 yrs): modest maiden: stays 7f: acts on fibresand: usually in headgear: usually races prominently. *Scott Dixon*

THUNDERING HOME 8 gr.g. Storming Home 128 – Citrine Spirit (IRE) 76 (Soviet **66** Star (USA) 128) [2015 61: p16m² Feb 18] leggy gelding: fair handicapper: stays 2m: acts on polytrack, fibresand, firm and soft going: tried in cheekpieces/tongue tie: fairly useful hurdler. *Richard Mitchell*

THUNDER IN MYHEART (IRE) 3 gr.f. Mastercraftsman (IRE) 129 – Happy Land **77** (IRE) (Refuse To Bend (IRE) 128) [2015 72: 8.5m² 8.3s 8g⁶ 8.1m⁵ p10f* t9.5m p10f Oct 28] unfurnished filly: fair handicapper: won at Lingfield in August: stays 1¼m: acts on polytrack and good to firm going: in hood last 3 starts: often races towards rear. *Michael Bell*

THUNDER PASS 4 b.g. High Chaparral (IRE) 132 – Hadarama (IRE) 86 (Sinndar **92** (IRE) 134) [2015 78: 14m⁴ 13.4g⁶ 14g² 16m 14.1d 14.1m* Sep 9] sturdy gelding: fairly useful handicapper: won at Goodwood in May and Carlisle (by nose from Cool Sky) in September: stays 1¾m: acts on firm and soft going: front runner/races prominently. *Hughie Morrison*

TICKING AWAY 2 gr.g. (Feb 15) Monsieur Bond (IRE) 120 – Pendulum 82 (Pursuit of 67
Love 124) [2015 6m 5g³ 6g 7d³ 5.9m 6m⁶ 7s Oct 26] tall, leggy gelding: fair maiden: stays
7f: acts on good to soft going: tried in hood. *David Brown*

TICKS THE BOXES (IRE) 3 ch.g. Fast Company (IRE) 126 – Swan Sea (USA) (Sea 91
Hero (USA) 124) [2015 96: 6m 7g² 7g⁶ 7m 7d t8.6m⁶ 8.3g Sep 30] workmanlike gelding:
fairly useful handicapper: stays 8.5f: acts on tapeta, best turf form on good going: often
races freely. *Clive Cox*

TIDAL MOON 3 b.f. Sea The Stars (IRE) 140 – Miss Riviera Golf 106 (Hernando (FR) 77
127) [2015 p10g⁴ 10m³ 11.5s 10m 9.9s² 11.8s 12s t9.5g Nov 27] 110,000Y: angular filly:
half-sister to several winners, including 7f-1½m winner Hotel du Cap (by Grand Lodge),
2-y-o 8.3f winner Mont Agel (by Danehill Dancer) and winner up to 1¾m (stayed 2m)
Gassin Golf (2-y-o 1m winner, by Montjeu), all useful: dam 6f winner: fair maiden: stays
1¼m: acts on soft and good to firm going. *Mick Channon*

TIDAL'S BABY 6 b.g. Dutch Art 126 – Tidal 94 (Bin Ajwaad (IRE) 119) [2015 82, a73: 67
p6m p6g p6m p6f 6m 6f³ 7v⁶ 6m⁵ 6g⁶ 6d² 6g p6g² 6g² p7g Dec 2] workmanlike gelding: a59
fair handicapper: stays 1m, effective at shorter: acts on polytrack, firm and soft going: tried
in headgear prior to 2015: sometimes slowly away, often races towards rear. *Lee Carter*

TIDAL WAVE 2 b.c. (Apr 7) Canford Cliffs (IRE) 133 – Lady Links 100 (Bahamian 90
Bounty 116) [2015 7m³ 7m* 7m⁴ 6s Oct 9] 55,000Y: useful-looking colt: half-brother to 3
winners, including smart/moody winner up to 1m Selinka (2-y-o 6f/7f winner, by Selkirk)
and 2-y-o 7f winner Swanky Lady (by Cape Cross): dam 6f winner (including at 2 yrs):
fairly useful performer: won maiden at Newmarket in August by short head from Bernie's
Boy: stays 7f: acts on good to firm going, ran poorly on soft final start. *Richard Hannon*

TIDAL WAY (IRE) 6 gr.g. Red Clubs (IRE) 125 – Taatof (IRE) (Lahib (USA) 129) [2015 75
12v⁶ t16.5f² p16g t13.9f⁴ Dec 14] fair handicapper: stays 16.5f: acts on polytrack, tapeta,
good to firm and heavy going: wears headgear. *Shaun Lycett*

TIERCEL 2 b.c. (Apr 14) Olden Times 121 – Sharp Mode (USA) (Diesis 133) [2015 8.1s³ 82 p
8g Oct 10] sturdy colt: half-brother to several winners, including smart winner up to 1½m
Annalah (2-y-o 7f winner, by Teofilo) and useful French winner up to 1¼m Eternal (2-y-o
1m winner, by New Approach): dam unraced: promising third to Taskeen in maiden at
Sandown on debut: stiff task, 16/1, well held in Autumn Stakes at Newmarket: should still
progress. *Roger Varian*

TIFAWT 2 b.f. (Feb 21) High Chaparral (IRE) 132 – Native Picture (IRE) 79 (Kodiac 112) –
[2015 6m Sep 15] first foal: dam, 6f winner (including at 2 yrs), half-sister to very
smart sprinter Kingsgate Native: in blinkers, 50/1, well held in maiden at Yarmouth.
George Margarson

TIGA TUAN (FR) 2 b.f. (Apr 21) Le Havre (IRE) 124 – Ramita (Fasliyev (USA) 120) –
[2015 6.9m 7d Sep 26] €4,000F, €14,000Y, €85,000 2-y-o: fourth foal: dam, French 6.5f
winner, half-sister to smart French 1m-1¼m winner Reggane: well held in maidens at
Carlisle and Chester. *Kevin Ryan*

TIGER HEIGHTS 4 b.g. Tiger Hill (IRE) 127 – Primo Heights 87 (Primo Valentino –
(IRE) 116) [2015 –: 9.1g 12g 8d⁶ 8.3g 7.2g Sep 29] well held in maidens/handicaps: in
cheekpieces last 4 starts. *Jim Goldie*

TIGER JIM 5 b.g. Tiger Hill (IRE) 127 – Quintrell 92 (Royal Applause 124) [2015 86: 95
6m³ 6g³ 6d* 6s 7g⁶ 6g² 6g 6d 7v Nov 7] useful handicapper: won at Ayr (by 2¼ lengths
from Nameitwhatyoulike) in June: good second of 25 to Go Far there in September: stays
7f: acts on good to soft going: usually races in rear. *Jim Goldie*

TIGER LILLY (IRE) 4 b.f. Galileo (IRE) 134 – Banquise (IRE) (Last Tycoon 131) –
[2015 86: 16.4m 14.6m⁶ Jun 26] fairly useful handicapper in 2014, well held both starts in
2015: stays 1¾m: acts on good to firm and good to soft going. *Richard Fahey*

TIGER'S HOME 5 b.m. Tiger Hill (IRE) 127 – Homeward (IRE) 49 (Kris 135) [2015 57: 51 +
6m 6g 7.2d⁴ 7.2d 8.3g² t9.5f⁵ f8g* f7g* f8m² f8g² Dec 15] fair handicapper: won twice at
Southwell (latter apprentice event) in November: stays 1m: acts on fibresand, good to firm
and good to soft going: tried in cheekpieces, usually wears hood: usually races prominently,
usually travels strongly. *Iain Jardine*

TIGERS TALE (IRE) 6 b.g. Tiger Hill (IRE) 127 – Vayenga (FR) (Highest Honor (FR) 98
124) [2015 97, a105: p8f² p8g³ p8f⁴ 7.6s⁴ 8.1m³ 8.1m⁵ 8m⁴ 8.1m* Jul 15] sturdy gelding: a106
useful handicapper: in first-time cheekpieces (was usually visored), won by neck from
Ifwecan at Sandown: stayed 1¼m: acted on polytrack, firm and soft going: usually raced
prominently: dead. *Roger Teal*

TIGER STONE 4 b.f. Tiger Hill (IRE) 127 – Lacandona (USA) 71 (Septieme Ciel (USA) **36**
123) [2015 –: p8g p8f⁶ p10f Feb 11] poor maiden: stays 1½m: acts on polytrack.
Michael Blanshard

TIGER TWENTY TWO 4 b.g. Authorized (IRE) 133 – Collette's Choice 72 (Royal **–**
Applause 124) [2015 87: 7m 10.1d 10m 9.3s⁶ Aug 24] close-coupled gelding: fairly useful
at best, no form in 2015: left Richard Fahey after first start. *Brian Rothwell*

TIGERWOLF (IRE) 2 br.c. (Apr 26) Dream Ahead (USA) 133 – Singing Field (IRE) **94**
(Singspiel (IRE) 133) [2015 7m 7m⁴ 7g⁴ Oct 21] 45,000F, 120,000Y: good-topped colt:
fourth foal: half-brother to 1m-10.7f winner Marise (by Azamour) and a winner abroad by
Orientate: dam unraced sister to smart French/US winner up to 1½m Fast And Furious:
useful form: best effort when fourth of 14 to Gifted Master in Tattersalls Millions 2-y-o
Trophy at Newmarket in October on second start. *Mick Channon*

TIGGY WIGGY (IRE) 3 b.f. Kodiac 112 – Kheleyf's Silver (IRE) 86 (Kheleyf (USA) **106**
116) [2015 121: 7m³ 8f³ 6f 6d Sep 5] small, rather leggy filly: very smart performer at
2 yrs, winner of 6 races, including Cheveley Park Stakes: didn't recapture that form in
2015, best effort when 5¼ lengths third to Legatissimo in 1000 Guineas at Newmarket on
second start: subsequently well held in Commonwealth Cup at Royal Ascot and Sprint Cup
at Haydock, then retired: best at 5f/6f: acted on polytrack, firm and soft going: front runner/
raced prominently: sold 2,100,000 gns in December. *Richard Hannon*

TIGHT LIPPED (IRE) 6 gr.g. Dark Angel (IRE) 113 – Kayoko (IRE) 74 (Shalford **68**
(IRE) 124) [2015 81: p12g p10g³ p8m t9.5f⁵ p10g² f11gᵖᵘ Apr 14] sturdy gelding: fair
handicapper: stayed 1¼m: acted on polytrack, tapeta, soft and good to firm going: had
worn headgear: front runner/raced prominently: dead. *Julia Feilden*

TIGRILLA (IRE) 3 gr.f. Clodovil (IRE) 116 – Lisieux Orchid (IRE) 88 (Sadler's Wells **–**
(USA) 132) [2015 101: 8m 7d Oct 16] small, narrow filly: useful performer at 2 yrs: well
held both starts in 2015: stays 1m: acts on soft and good to firm going. *Roger Varian*

TIGSERIN (IRE) 2 ch.f. (Jan 24) Approve (IRE) 112 – Mairead Anne (USA) (Elusive **55**
Quality (USA)) [2015 8g⁶ t7.1g⁶ p6f⁶ Oct 10] 16,000F: third foal: half-sister to a winner in
Italy by Verglas: dam, US 1m winner, half-sister to useful French 7f-9f winner Quittance:
modest maiden. *Giles Bravery*

TIHANA 2 b.f. (Feb 21) Lawman (FR) 121 – La Bocca (USA) 70 (Latent Heat (USA) 118) **58**
[2015 6m⁴ 6m³ 7m p7f t6f⁵ 5g³ Oct 13] 4,000Y: first foal: dam, lightly raced (second at 5f),
closely related to smart US Grade 1 9f winner Monzante: modest maiden: left Brian
Meehan after fifth start: stays 6f: acts on good to firm going: tried in blinkers: front runner/
races prominently. *Alan Berry*

TIJAN (IRE) 4 b.g. Shamardal (USA) 129 – Cherry Orchard (IRE) (King's Best (USA) **81**
132) [2015 82p: f7s² p7g 6m Apr 25] smallish gelding: fairly useful maiden in Britain:
stays 7f: acts on polytrack and fibresand: often wears hood: front runner/races prominently:
temperament under suspicion: sold £20,000, sent to Qatar, where won 6f handicap at Doha
in December. *Saeed bin Suroor*

TIJORI (IRE) 7 b.g. Kyllachy 129 – Polish Belle (Polish Precedent (USA) 131) [2015 **68**
16.2m⁴ 16.2s² 17.2d 18d Aug 20] strong, sturdy gelding: fair handicapper: stays 2m: acts
on polytrack and any turf going: wears headgear. *Bernard Llewellyn*

TIJUCA (IRE) 6 b.m. Captain Rio 122 – Some Forest (IRE) (Charnwood Forest (IRE) **70**
125) [2015 69: p10f t8.6f t8.6g* p8g³ Dec 15] workmanlike mare: fair handicapper: won
at Wolverhampton in December: stays 1¼m: acts on polytrack and tapeta: tried in
cheekpieces/tongue tie: often races towards rear. *Ed de Giles*

TIKTHEBOX (IRE) 2 b.g. (Apr 22) Approve (IRE) 112 – Nicene (USA) (Pulpit (USA) **82**
117) [2015 5m³ 5v⁵ 5m 5m 6g 5m² 6m* 6g Oct 5] €22,000Y: rather
unfurnished gelding: sixth foal: half-brother to 10.7f winner Shisha Threesixty (by High
Chaparral) and 1½m winner Katniss (by Champs Elysees): dam US maiden: fairly useful
performer: won maiden at Redcar in August and nursery at Hamilton in September: stays
6f: acts on good to firm going. *David Brown*

TILSTARR (IRE) 5 b.m. Shamardal (USA) 129 – Vampire Queen (IRE) 54 (General **72**
Monash (USA) 107) [2015 80: p11m p8g p10m⁴ p10g² p12f⁵ 11.5d² 9.9v* 11m⁴ 10g⁴
11.5g⁴ 12g³ 10.1g² p10f⁶ 11s⁵ 9.9v⁶ Oct 6] good-topped mare: fair handicapper: won at
Brighton in May: stays 1½m: acts on polytrack, good to firm and heavy going: wears
cheekpieces: sometimes slowly away, usually races nearer last than first. *Roger Teal*

TILSWORTH ANNALISA 4 br.f. Observatory (USA) 131 – Tilsworth Charlie 70 **–**
(Dansili 127) [2015 –: f5s⁶ Jan 1] no form: tried in visor. *J. R. Jenkins*

Shadwell Joel Stakes, Newmarket—Time Test gets back on track with a comfortable victory from 2014 winner Custom Cut, the pair clear of the two other runners Decorated Knight and Tupi (left)

TILSWORTH MICKY 3 br.g. Kheleyf (USA) 116 – Tilsworth Charlie 70 (Dansili 127) **75 p** [2015 p6m² Dec 27] third foal: dam 5.7f-7f winner: 7/1, ½-length second of 6 to Desert Morning in maiden at Chelmsford, slowly away: should do better. *J. R. Jenkins*

TIMBA 3 b.f. Oasis Dream 129 – Teeky 89 (Daylami (IRE) 138) [2015 94p: 8m³ Aug 7] **99 p** useful form: won first of 2 starts at 2 yrs, and shaped encouragingly when third of 7 to Nancy From Nairobi in handicap at Newmarket only outing in 2015: will stay beyond 1m: open to further improvement. *John Gosden*

TIME AGAIN 2 b.f. (Mar 12) Kyllachy 129 – Record Time 69 (Clantime 101) [2015 f5g **48** p6m t5.1m Nov 28] half-sister to 3 winners, including very smart 5f winner Moorhouse Lad (by Bertolini) and smart winner up to 6f Off The Record (2-y-o 5f winner, by Desert Style): dam 5f winner: poor maiden. *David Brown*

TIME AND PLACE 5 ch.g. Compton Place 125 – Forthefirstime 99 (Dr Fong (USA) **85** 128) [2015 90: t6f² f7d³ Feb 10] fairly useful handicapper: stays 7f: acts on all-weather, good to firm and good to soft going: tried in blinkers prior to 2015. *Richard Fahey*

TIME CONTINUUM 3 b.f. Monsieur Bond (IRE) 120 – Primum Tempus 49 (Primo **–** Dominie 121) [2015 –p: 6g⁶ Jun 20] no form in 2 maidens (11 months apart). *Eric Alston*

TIME FLIES 3 b.g. Exceed And Excel (AUS) 126 – Simply Times (USA) 64 (Dodge **100** (USA)) [2015 62p: 7g² p8g² 6m² p6f* p7g³ Oct 29] good sort: useful performer: won maiden at Chelmsford in September by 5 lengths from Rock Royalty: improved again when length third to Crazy Chic in handicap at Lingfield: stays 7f: acts on polytrack: in tongue tie last 3 starts: often travels strongly: has high head carriage: sent to UAE. *John Gosden*

TIMELESS ART (IRE) 2 b.c. (Apr 28) Medicean 128 – Bellona (IRE) 105 (Bering 136) **80 p** [2015 6d 7s³ Oct 10] €40,000Y: half-brother to several winners, including useful French 10.5f winner Brave Impact (by Montjeu) and to dam of very smart Hong Kong performer up to 1½m Dominant and smart performer up to 1m Es Que Love: dam, French winner up to 10.5f (2-y-o 1m winner), half-sister to smart 1m-10.5f winner In Clover, herself dam of Prix de l'Opera winner We Are: improved from debut when 1¼ lengths third of 10 to Garcia in maiden at York: likely to improve further. *K. R. Burke*

TIME MEDICEAN 9 gr.g. Medicean 128 – Ribbons And Bows (IRE) 91 (Dr Devious **74** (IRE) 127) [2015 68: 6m t6g 6m⁵ 6s² 5.3d³ 5g² 7s Oct 26] lightly-made gelding: fair handicapper: stays 7f, best form at 5f/6f these days: acts on polytrack, good to firm and heavy going: tried in blinkers/tongue tie: sometimes slowly away. *Tony Carroll*

TIME OF MY LIFE (IRE) 6 b.g. Galileo (IRE) 134 – In My Life (IRE) (Rainbow Quest **48** (USA) 134) [2015 58: 16m Apr 6] poor handicapper: stays 1¾m: acts on good to soft going: tried in cheekpieces: often wears tongue tie: front runner/races prominently. *Patrick Holmes*

TIMES LEGACY 2 b.c. (Mar 28) Cape Cross (IRE) 129 – Simply Times (USA) 64 **82 p** (Dodge (USA)) [2015 6s 6v* Nov 7] closely related to 2 winners by Oasis Dream, including smart 6f-1m winner Brave Prospector, and half-brother to several winners, including very smart winner up to 7f Welsh Emperor (2-y-o 5f/6f winner, by Emperor Jones): dam ran twice: 16/1, much improved when winning 8-runner maiden at Doncaster in November by length from Abaco Ridge, leading over 1f out and kept up to work: open to further improvement. *Peter Chapple-Hyam*

TIME SPACE (CAN) 3 b.f. Arch (USA) 127 – Tiz My Time (USA) 95 (Sharp Humor (USA) 118) [2015 p7m 9.3m⁴ 8m⁶ Jul 1] $110,000Y: first foal: dam US maiden (third in Albany Stakes only start in Britain): fair maiden: best effort when fourth at Carlisle. *K. R. Burke* **72**

TIME SQUARE (FR) 8 b.g. Westerner 130 – Sainte Parfaite (FR) (Septieme Ciel (USA) 123) [2015 62, a70: 10.4d 11.6g p11g p10g p12g Dec 15] lengthy gelding: modest handicapper: stays 1½m: acts on polytrack, best turf form on good going: tried in hood: sometimes wears tongue tie: usually leads. *Tony Carroll* **60**

TIMES UP 9 b.g. Olden Times 121 – Princess Genista 108 (Ile de Bourbon (USA) 133) [2015 116: 14m⁵ 14g⁵ 21.7f⁶ 16s 18m Sep 11] leggy gelding: smart performer at best, twice winner of Doncaster Cup: well below form in 2015: stayed 2½m: acted on soft and good to firm going: often raced towards rear: retired. *Ed Dunlop* **96**

TIME TEST 3 b.c. Dubawi (IRE) 129 – Passage of Time 115 (Dansili 127) [2015 91p: 10m* 10f* 10.4d⁴ 8g* 8g Oct 31] well-made colt: high-class performer: much improved and won handicap at Newbury (by 1¼ lengths from Dissolution) in May, Tercentenary Stakes at Royal Ascot (by 3¼ lengths from Peacock, still pulling when hitting the front over 1f out then quickly going clear) in June and Joel Stakes at Newmarket (by length from Custom Cut, quickening to lead final 1f) in September: never dangerous in International at York and Breeders' Cup Mile at Keeneland (drawn widest): stays 1¼m: acts on firm going, won 2-y-o maiden on good to soft: travels strongly. *Roger Charlton* **125**

Mr K. Abdullah's "Time Test"

TIME WARP 2 ch.c. (Jan 28) Archipenko (USA) 127 – Here To Eternity (USA) 74 **101 p** (Stormy Atlantic (USA)) [2015 p6g⁶ p6g² p6g³ 7.4g⁴ f7s* 7.1m* 7m* 8.2g* Sep 7] €37,000Y: big, strong colt: first foal: dam 7f winner: useful performer: improved and won last 4 starts, namely maiden at Southwell, nursery at Sandown and minor event at Redcar (impressive) in August, and listed race at Craon (by 1½ lengths from Zvalinska, flashing tail final 1f but keeping on well) in September: stays 1m: acts on fibresand and good to firm going: front runner: should continue to progress. *Sir Mark Prescott Bt*

TIMIA 2 b.f. (May 14) Cape Cross (IRE) 129 – Cinerama (IRE) 68 (Machiavellian (USA) **67 p** 123) [2015 p7g⁵ p7g p7m⁵ Dec 16] 42,000Y: useful-looking filly: third foal: half-sister to 6f winner Balliol (by Exceed And Excel) and a winner in Italy by Azamour: dam, 1m winner, half-sister to smart winner up to 2m Namibian: fair form in maidens: will stay 1m: remains with potential. *Ed Dunlop*

TIMONEER (USA) 5 b.g. Elusive Quality (USA) – Gentle Gale (USA) (Storm Cat – (USA)) [2015 8g 7s t8.6f p7f t8.6f⁵ Dec 14] one-time useful winner for Godolphin: off 32 months, well beaten in 5 starts in 2015: stays 1m. *Tim Easterby*

TIM THE TAXI 2 b.g. (Mar 3) Compton Place 125 – Polar Dawn 72 (Polar Falcon (USA) **46** 126) [2015 5d 5.3g⁴ 5.1s⁵ May 19] poor maiden: has been gelded. *Natalie Lloyd-Beavis*

TINCTORIA 5 b.m. Oratorio (IRE) 128 – Blue Indigo (FR) (Pistolet Bleu (IRE) 133) – [2015 t12.2g 11.6m t12.2g Aug 27] maiden: showed nothing in 2015: tried in headgear/ tongue tie. *Adrian Wintle*

TINDARO (FR) 8 gr.g. Kingsalsa (USA) 118 – Star's Mixa (FR) (Linamix (FR) 127) – [2015 14.1m 14g May 23] big gelding: fairly useful handicapper: well below form both starts in 2015: stays 1¾m: acts on firm going: has worn tongue tie: useful chaser. *Paul Webber*

TINDERELLA 2 b.f. (Feb 25) Royal Applause 124 – Flying Finish (FR) (Priolo (USA) **51** 127) [2015 6m p7g 8f Nov 21] 3,200F, €30,000Y: sixth foal: half-sister to several winners, including useful winner up to 7f Common Touch (2-y-o 6f winner, by Compton Place) and useful 1½m-1¾m winner (stayed 2m) Duchess of Gazeley (by Halling): dam, French 2-y-o 7f winner, sister/half-sister to smart performers up to 1½m Flyway and Falcon Flight: modest maiden: left Marco Botti, best effort when seventh at Del Mar (11½ lengths behind Jeremy's Legacy) final start. *Jeff Mullins, USA*

TINGLEO 3 ch.f. Galileo (IRE) 134 – Tingling (USA) 81 (Storm Cat (USA)) [2015 66p: **75** p10g⁵ 12.1g⁵ 10.2m⁴ 11.6g⁴ p13f* 12g p13g Oct 29] rather leggy filly: fairly useful **a82** handicapper: won at Lingfield in July: stays 13f: acts on polytrack and good to firm going: front runner/races prominently. *Roger Varian*

TINGO IN THE TALE (IRE) 6 b.g. Oratorio (IRE) 128 – Sunlit Skies 65 (Selkirk (USA) **63** 129) [2015 70: p13f² p12g Nov 13] compact gelding: modest handicapper: stays 1¾m: acts on polytrack and any turf going: tried in cheekpieces prior to 2015. *David Arbuthnot*

TINKERS KISS (IRE) 3 b.f. Intikhab (USA) 135 – Edmondstown Lass (IRE) 83 **58** (Imperial Ballet (IRE) 110) [2015 62: p5f⁴ Jan 23] modest handicapper: stays 7f: acts on polytrack: in visor sole start in 2015. *Philip McBride*

TIN PAN ALLEY 7 b.g. Singspiel (IRE) 133 – Tazmeen (Darshaan 133) [2015 71: f8g³ **75** f8g p10g⁵ f8d⁵ 10.1d³ 10d² 9.2d³ 9.9m* 9.9m* 9.9m⁴ 9.9m² 9.3d⁶ 9.9m⁴ 10.3m 9g⁶ Sep 25] fair handicapper: won twice at Beverley in June: stays 1¼m: acts on good to firm going: tried in cheekpieces in 2015: usually leads. *David C. Griffiths*

TINSELTOWN 9 b.g. Sadler's Wells (USA) 132 – Peony 108 (Lion Cavern (USA) 117) **59** [2015 76: 10.3d⁶ 12g 12g 12g Jul 22] good-topped gelding: modest handicapper: stays 1¾m: acts on good to firm and heavy going: sometimes wears headgear: usually races prominently. *Brian Rothwell*

TINSILL 4 ch.g. Firebreak 125 – Concentration (IRE) (Mind Games 121) [2015 80: 5d 5m **61** 5s⁶ 5g⁴ 5m 5.5m⁶ 5g⁶ 5m⁶ 5f⁵ 5d 5s⁵ 5d 5m 6m 5m⁶ 5s⁴ 5.1d* p5g⁴ Nov 11] modest handicapper: won at Nottingham in November: best form at 5f: acts on soft and good to firm going: often wears headgear. *Nigel Tinkler*

TIOGA PASS 4 b.f. High Chaparral (IRE) 132 – Seren Devious (Dr Devious (IRE) 127) **100** [2015 100: 12m⁵ 10.2m⁴ 12m⁶ Jul 18] good-topped filly: useful performer: best effort in listed races in 2015 when 4½ lengths fifth to Miss Marjurie at Goodwood on reappearance: stays 1½m: acts on polytrack, good to firm and heavy going: sometimes in headgear. *Paul Cole*

TIPSY STAR 4 b.f. Tobougg (IRE) 125 – Extremely Rare (IRE) 82 (Mark of Esteem (IRE) – 137) [2015 66: p10g³ Jan 7] angular filly: maiden, fair form at best: probably stays 1¼m: acts on good to firm going: often in headgear. *Jonathan Geake*

TIPTREE (IRE) 2 b.f. (Apr 12) Duke of Marmalade (IRE) 132 – Taking Liberties (IRE) **91 p**
57 (Royal Academy (USA) 130) [2015 8.3d 7d* Oct 31] €80,000Y: sister to 10.5f winner
Qatea and closely related/half-sister to several winners, including smart winner up to 1m
Troubadour (2-y-o 6f winner, by Danehill): dam ran once: dropped in trip, improved when
winning 9-runner maiden at Newmarket in October by 1½ lengths from Swiss Range,
flashing tail and just kept up to work: will go on improving. *Luca Cumani*

TIRADIA (FR) 8 b.g. Without Connexion (IRE) 114 – Jimanji (FR) (Kadalko (FR)) [2015 **60**
p13g³ p12m³ Feb 27] modest form in 2 maidens at Lingfield, only outings on Flat: fair
hurdler. *J. R. Jenkins*

TITAN GODDESS 3 b.f. Equiano (FR) 127 – Phoebe Woodstock (IRE) 76 (Grand Lodge **69**
(USA) 125) [2015 55p: p8f t8.6g⁴ 10g⁶ 7.6m 10g^ur p8f² p8f³ p10d⁴ Nov 30] fair maiden:
stays 1¼m: acts on polytrack and tapeta. *Mike Murphy*

TITAN TRIUMPH 11 b.g. Zamindar (USA) 116 – Triple Green 69 (Green Desert (USA) **50**
127) [2015 66: p8m p8f⁴ p8g May 28] well-made handicapper: modest handicapper: stays 1m:
acts on polytrack: tried in hood: wears tongue tie. *Michael Attwater*

TITUS BOLT (IRE) 6 b.g. Titus Livius (FR) 115 – Megan's Bay 82 (Muhtarram (USA) **70**
125) [2015 71: 12.5s² 12.5s⁵ 13d 12.5m⁴ 12.2m⁴ 13.7g⁴ 12.2g² 12.2g* Oct 13] fair
handicapper: won at Musselburgh in October: stays 13f: acts on good to firm and heavy
going: tried in visor prior to 2015. *Jim Goldie*

TITUS SECRET 3 ch.g. Sakhee's Secret 128 – Crimson Fern (IRE) 104 (Titus Livius **–**
(FR) 115) [2015 t8.6g⁵ p7f 9.9m 6g t6g⁶ Aug 6] no form: sometimes in cheekpieces:
sometimes slowly away. *Malcolm Saunders*

TIZ HERSELF (IRE) 2 gr.f. (Mar 5) Dandy Man (IRE) 123 – Pitullie (USA) (Rockport **57 p**
Harbor (USA) 114) [2015 5f⁶ May 11] €4,500F, £17,000Y: sturdy filly: first foal: dam
unraced daughter of useful/untrustworthy 2-y-o 6f winner Rosehearty: 25/1, showed
ability amidst greenness when 5¼ lengths sixth of 13 to Miss Moneypenny in maiden at
Windsor: should do better. *Jonathan Portman*

TIZLOVE REGARDLESS (USA) 4 b.c. Tiznow (USA) 133 – Dianehill (IRE) **86**
(Danehill (USA) 126) [2015 83: t12.2f⁶ t12.2f f8d⁶ t9.5f² t9.5m* p10g p8g⁶ 8.5m² 8.3g²
8g² 8m* 8m 8.5s t8.6g Aug 10] tall colt: fairly useful handicapper: won at Wolverhampton
in April and Newmarket in June: effective at 1m to 11f: acts on polytrack, tapeta, good to
firm and heavy going: wears blinkers nowadays: usually races close up: sent to Saudi
Arabia. *Mark Johnston*

TOAD CORNER 3 b.g. Shirocco (GER) 129 – Didbrook (Alzao (USA) 117) [2015 p12g⁵ **50**
11.8s t12.2m Oct 2] modest maiden: tried in blinkers. *Mary Hambro*

TOARMANDOWITHLOVE (IRE) 7 ch.m. Choisir (AUS) 126 – Deadly Buzz (IRE) **60**
(Darshaan 133) [2015 11.5s⁴ 10m⁴ 10.1d⁵ 11.5s 12.4g⁵ 14.1s Sep 15] fourth foal: half-sister
to 1½m-16.4f winner Bow To No One (by Refuse To Bend): dam unraced: modest maiden:
stays 12.5f: acts on good to firm going. *Susan Corbett*

TOAST OF NEWBURY (IRE) 3 b.g. Captain Rio 122 – Pearl of The Sea (IRE) **72**
(Fusaichi Pegasus (USA) 130) [2015 63: t7.1f² p7m³ p7m⁵ t7.1m⁴ t7.1f³ p8g⁶ f6d* 6m⁴
p6g² p6g² f6d² Jul 27] good-topped gelding: fair handicapper: won at Southwell in
May: left Jamie Osborne after fifth start: stays 6f: acts on all-weather and good to firm
going: tried in cheekpieces in 2015: usually wears tongue tie: consistent. *Heather Dalton*

TOBAGO CAYS 4 b.f. Tobougg (IRE) 125 – Cove Mountain (AUS) 70 (Indian Danehill **–**
(IRE) 124) [2015 –: p8g p12g Aug 17] no form: left John Gallagher after first start.
Mark Rimell

TO BE WILD (IRE) 2 br.c. (Mar 19) Big Bad Bob (IRE) 118 – Fire Up (Motivator 131) **86 p**
[2015 8g⁵ Sep 24] €95,000F, €87,000Y: second foal: dam, lightly raced in France, half-
sister to high-class winner up to 1½m Al Kazeem: 33/1, shaped well when 8½ lengths fifth
of 14 to Mustajeer in maiden at Newmarket on debut, slowly away: will improve.
Hugo Palmer

TOBOGGAN'S FIRE 2 b.f. (Feb 18) Firebreak 125 – Toboggan Lady 75 (Tobougg **75**
(IRE) 125) [2015 7.2s³ 7.5s* 8g 8.3d² 8d Oct 19] leggy filly: third foal: half-sister to 2-y-o
7f winner Toboggan Star (by Lucky Story): dam 1½m-2¼m winner: fair performer: won
maiden at Beverley in July: stays 8.5f: acts on soft going. *Ann Duffield*

TOBOGGAN'S GIFT 3 b.f. Major Cadeaux 121 – Toboggan Lady 75 (Tobougg (IRE) **–**
125) [2015 50: 12.1f 13.1g Jul 20] poor maiden. *Ann Duffield*

TOBOUGGAN RUN 3 b.g. Tobougg (IRE) 125 – Justbetweenfriends (USA) 85 (Diesis **–**
133) [2015 –: 14.1m Apr 18] no form. *Michael Appleby*

TOCORORO (IRE) 3 b.f. Teofilo (IRE) 126 – Firecrest (IRE) 107 (Darshaan 133) [2015 **69**
56p: p11g² 14.1m⁴ t12.2g⁵ Jun 4] fair maiden: stays 11f: acts on polytrack: often starts
slowly: winning hurdler for Gordon Elliott. *Ed Dunlop*

TODD 5 b.g. Gentlewave (IRE) 120 – Voice 79 (Zamindar (USA) 116) [2015 75: p12f⁶ **78**
p15.8g² p16g 16.5m³ 17.2d⁴ p15.8g⁵ p16d* 12v p15.8m² Dec 16] close-coupled gelding:
fair handicapper: won at Kempton in September: stays 17f: acts on polytrack, soft and good
to firm going: tried in headgear. *Anabel K. Murphy*

TODEGICA 3 b.f. Giant's Causeway (USA) 132 – Totally Devoted (USA) 104 (Seeking **87 §**
The Gold (USA)) [2015 77: t9.5m³ 10.3m⁴ a8f² 12f² 9f a8f⁴ Oct 25] fairly useful
performer: left Ralph Beckett, second in 2 allowance races at Delaware: stays 1½m: acts
on polytrack and tapeta: best treated with caution (usually flashes tail). *H. Graham Motion,
USA*

TOE THE LINE (IRE) 6 b.m. Shantou (USA) 125 – Bluebell Line (IRE) 64 (Charnwood **108**
Forest (IRE) 125) [2015 104: 12v³ 14d 14g 12g³ 14g⁴ 14.6m⁴ 16d² 12g³ 15s Oct 25] third
foal: dam 1½m winner: useful performer: placed in listed races at Cork, Roscommon, the
Curragh (neck behind Silwana) and Naas, and fourth of 11 to Gretchen in Park Hill Stakes
at Doncaster sixth start: also ran well in handicaps fifth/final starts, fourth of 19 to Litigant
in Ebor at York and seventh of 23 to Silver Concorde at Leopardstown: stays 2m: acts on
soft and good to firm going: usually races nearer last than first/travels strongly. *John E.
Kiely, Ireland*

TOFFEE APPLE (IRE) 2 b.f. (Apr 23) Zoffany (IRE) 121 – Myrtle Beach (IRE) – **–**
(Kenmare (FR) 125) [2015 p8m p7f⁶ Dec 17] €15,000Y, resold 15,500Y: half-sister to
several winners in Italy, including useful 1m-1¼m winner Dan Grey (by Danehill): dam,
French maiden (second at 1m), half-sister to Oaks d'Italia winner Lady Bentley: well held
in 2 maidens. *Ed Dunlop*

TOGA TIGER (IRE) 8 b.g. Antonius Pius (USA) 123 – Minerwa (GER) (Protektor **82 §**
(GER) 120) [2015 85§: t8.6g* t8.6g 8.9g 8m² p8m Dec 31] clever leggy gelding: fairly
useful handicapper: won at Wolverhampton in January: stays 10.5f: acts on polytrack,
tapeta, firm and good to soft going. quirky sort and not one to rely on. *Kevin Frost*

TOGETHER FOREVER (IRE) 3 b.f. Galileo (IRE) 134 – Green Room (USA) **110**
(Theatrical) [2015 108: 10.4g² 12g 12m⁴ Jul 18] tall, angular filly: smart performer: further
improvement when head second to Star of Seville in Musidora Stakes at York on
reappearance: seventh of 11 in Oaks at Epsom next start (caught in trouble over 1f out),
then shaped much better than distance beaten suggests when 4¼ lengths fourth of 9 to
Covert Love in Irish Oaks at the Curragh, doing too much too soon: stays 1½m: acts on
good to firm and good to soft going. *Aidan O'Brien, Ireland*

TOGETHERWECAN (IRE) 3 b.f. Danehill Dancer (IRE) 117 – Crystal Bull (USA) **53 p**
(Holy Bull (USA) 134) [2015 8.5m⁴ Apr 23] €31,000F, €32,000Y: half-sister to several
winners abroad, including useful Italian winner up to 9f Air Crew (2-y-o 5f-1m winner, by
Pollard's Vision): dam US 9f winner: 17/2, looked in need of experience when fourth of 7
to Goring in maiden at Beverley, racing freely: should do better, *Mark Johnston*

TOHFA (IRE) 3 ch.f. Dutch Art 126 – The Fairies Did It (USA) (Elusive Quality (USA)) **82**
[2015 76: 6s⁵ 6.5m⁴ 7m³ 6g⁵ 6g Sep 24] sturdy filly: fairly useful handicapper: won at
Doncaster in May: stays 7f: acts on good to firm going. *Richard Hannon*

TOLAH 3 ch.f. Mount Nelson 125 – Tropical Barth (IRE) (Peintre Celebre (USA) 137) **50**
[2015 12m³ p12g p12g⁴ p16f Sep 10] 800F, 5,000Y: half-sister to 3 winners in France,
including smart 10.5f winner Cashelgar (by Anabaa) and 7.5f/1m winner Mazayyen (by
American Post): dam French 9.5f winner: modest maiden. *Charlie Fellowes*

TOLEDO 2 b.c. (Mar 21) Exceed And Excel (AUS) 126 – Alovera (IRE) 93 (King's Best **68**
(USA) 132) [2015 6m⁶ p6g⁵ p7g³ Dec 28] good-quartered colt: fair form in maidens at
Windsor and Lingfield (2), off almost 6 months prior to final start. *Richard Hannon*

TOLLY MCGUINESS 4 ch.c. Araafa (IRE) 128 – Golden Flyer (FR) (Machiavellian **49**
(USA) 123) [2015 48: f5s⁵ f5d⁶ p5f⁶ p6m p8fᵇᵘ Mar 4] poor maiden: stayed 6f: acted on
fibresand and tapeta: dead. *Julia Feilden*

TOMBE GIRL 2 b.f. (Jan 18) Royal Applause 124 – Tahfeez (IRE) 61 (Alhaarth (IRE) **53 p**
126) [2015 6g t7.1f⁵ Nov 10] second foal: half-sister to 8.6f winner Sammy's Warrior (by
Myboycharlie): dam, lightly raced, out of useful 6f winner Ghazal, herself sister to
US Grade 3 7f/1m winner Elusive Quality: 100/1, again shaped better than the bare result
when 7½ lengths fifth of 9 to Izmir in maiden at Wolverhampton: has joined Keith
Dalgleish: remains open to improvement. *Ian Semple*

TOMBELAINE (USA) 3 b.c. First Defence (USA) 119 – Kithira 106 (Danehill (USA) **110**
126) [2015 107: 7v* 8g⁵ May 23] good-topped colt: smart performer: won listed race at the
Curragh in May by ½ length from Endless Drama: shaped better than distance beaten
suggests when 4 lengths fifth of 11 to Gleneagles in Irish 2000 Guineas at the Curragh,
hampered 1f out: stays 1m: acts on good to firm and heavy going: usually travels strongly.
D. K. Weld, Ireland

TOM HALL 5 b.g. Pastoral Pursuits 127 – Villarosi (IRE) 77 (Rossini (USA) 118) [2015 **46**
–: p6g³ p6g t6f p6g p8g⁵ 7m 7.1m 11.9d³ 11.9d⁴ 9.9s Oct 15] modest maiden: should prove **a57**
best short of 1½m: acts on polytrack, tapeta and good to soft going: often in headgear in
2015: usually races prominently. *David Menuisier*

TOM HARK (FR) 3 ch.g. Makfi 130 – Raisonable (USA) (El Prado (IRE) 119) [2015 88: **97**
8s⁴ 8.1d 9m 10f² 9.9m 9.9s³ 10.3g⁵ 10s² 9.9g³ 10.2d Oct 14] sturdy gelding: useful
handicapper: best efforts when second at Newbury (neck behind What About Carlo) and
third at Salisbury (4¼ lengths behind Think Ahead) eighth/ninth starts: stays 1¼m: acts on
soft going: front runner/races prominently. *Richard Hannon*

TOMMY DOCC (IRE) 3 b.g. Thewayyouare (USA) 117 – Liturgy (IRE) 83 (Catcher In **102**
The Rye (IRE) 115) [2015 –p: f5g* 7m 8g* 12.5m* 16f² 13m³ 12g Jul 29] sturdy gelding:
useful performer: won maiden at Southwell in March (over 5f) and handicaps at Redcar in
May and Musselburgh in June: improved further when placed in Queen's Vase at Royal
Ascot (½-length second of 13 to Aloft) and Bahrain Trophy at Newmarket (third to
Mr Singh): 25/1, well-held seventh of 9 to Highland Reel in Gordon Stakes at Goodwood
final outing: stays 2m: acts on fibresand and firm going. *Keith Dalgleish*

TOMMYS GEAL 3 b.f. Halling (USA) 133 – Steel Free (IRE) 81 (Danehill Dancer (IRE) **69**
117) [2015 52: p8m⁶ p6g³ p7m p10m⁴ 9.9g** 11.5g⁵ 9.9g⁵ p8g⁵ p10m² p10m³ p10g⁴ Dec
15] compact filly: fair handicapper: won at Brighton in June: stays 1¼m: acts on polytrack.
Michael Madgwick

TOMMY'S SECRET 5 gr.g. Sakhee's Secret 128 – La Gessa 69 (Largesse 112) [2015 **83**
86: p8f³ p8f² 8.3m³ 7f⁴ 8.5m⁴ p8g 8.3g² 8g p8g² p8g⁴ p8f* p8g² p8f⁴ Dec 21] sturdy
gelding: fairly useful handicapper: won at Chelmsford in November: stays 8.5f: acts on
polytrack and good to firm going. *Jane Chapple-Hyam*

TOM SAWYER 7 b.g. Dansili 127 – Cayman Sunset (IRE) 108 (Night Shift (USA)) **85**
[2015 82: t5.1f⁶ f5g⁶ 15.1g 5g 5m* 5m⁵ 5g² 5g Sep 26] strong gelding: fairly useful
handicapper: won at Carlisle in May and Beverley in July: best form at 5f: acts on
polytrack, fibresand, good to firm and good to soft going: wears headgear: usually races
close up. *Julie Camacho*

TONGUE TWISTA 3 b.f. Stimulation (IRE) 121 – Lady-Love 70 (Pursuit of Love 124) **71**
[2015 79: 6m p7g⁵ 8m⁵ Jun 25] leggy filly: fair handicapper: stays 7f: acts on polytrack,
good to firm and good to soft going: tried in blinkers prior to 2015. *Nick Littmoden*

TONI'S A STAR 3 b.f. Avonbridge 123 – Canina 70 (Foxhound (USA) 103) [2015 52: **74**
t5.1g* t5.1f⁴ p5f⁵ t5.1g* 5dʳ t5.1g⁶ 5g* 6m² 5m⁶ 5d⁶ 5.1d² Oct 14] fair handicapper: won
at Wolverhampton in February and April and Haydock (apprentice) in July: effective at
5f/6f: acts on tapeta, good to firm and good to soft going: sometimes in blinkers prior to
2015. *Tony Carroll*

TONKINESE 2 b.c. (Apr 4) Authorized (IRE) 133 – Honky Tonk Sally 86 (Dansili 127) **90**
[2015 6g³ 7g* 7f 7.5s⁶ p7g⁵ Oct 9] 80,000F, 180,000Y: useful-looking colt: fourth foal:
half-brother to useful 2-y-o 5f winner Umneyati (by Iffraaj) and 2-y-o 7f winner Ragtime
Dancer (by Medicean): dam 2-y-o 7f winner: fairly useful performer: won maiden at
Leopardstown (by 3 lengths from Brontide) in June: in first-time cheekpieces, best
subsequent effort when 7¾ lengths fifth of 6 to Hoit It A Bomb in listed race at Dundalk:
stays 7f: front runner/races prominently. *M. Halford, Ireland*

TONTITO (IRE) 2 b.g. (Apr 2) Kodiac 112 – Classical Air (Dubai Destination (USA)) **–**
127) [2015 5g 5m 6g 5g 5m 5d 7g Sep 8] no form: tried in visor. *Nigel Tinkler*

TONTO'S SPIRIT 3 b.g. Authorized (IRE) 133 – Desert Royalty (IRE) 96 (Alhaarth **47**
(IRE) 126) [2015 –: 10g⁵ 14.1m 9.9m 8.3g Jul 22] poor maiden: stays 1¼m: best form on
good going: tried in cheekpieces in 2015. *Michael Dods*

TONY CURTIS 2 b.c. (Mar 23) Rock of Gibraltar (IRE) 133 – Strawberry Lolly 89 **106 p**
(Lomitas 129) [2015 7m* 7f³ 8g* 8d⁶ Oct 24] 16,000F, 48,000Y: fifth foal: closely related
to 1½m-2m winner Strawberry Martini (by Mount Nelson) and half-brother to ungenuine
2-y-o 7f winner (stays 13f) Kolonel Kirkup (by Dr Fong): dam, 8.6f-1¼m winner, half-
sister to smart 1m/9f winner Strawberrydaiquiri: useful performer: won maiden at Epsom
(by length from Daleelak) in July and listed race at Salisbury (by 3¼ lengths from Opal

Tiara) in August: third in Superlative Stakes at Newmarket (1¼ lengths behind Birchwood) in between: softer ground, better than result when sixth of 7 to Marcel in Racing Post Trophy at Doncaster final start (finished tired): likely to stay at least 1¼m: remains with potential. *Richard Hannon*

TOOCOOLFORSCHOOL (IRE) 3 b.g. Showcasing 117 – Spring Surprise 82 (Hector **94** Protector (USA) 124) [2015 112: 7m⁵ 6d 7d Sep 12] workmanlike gelding: smart performer at 2 yrs, well below best in 2015: stays 7f: acts on soft and good to firm going: wears cheekpieces: usually races close up. *K. R. Burke*

TOOFEEG (IRE) 3 ch.g. Approve (IRE) 112 – Zabadani 52 (Zafonic (USA) 130) [2015 **64** 68: f8g⁴ p8f² Jan 30] modest maiden: stays 1m: acts on polytrack and heavy going: wears headgear: often leads: sold 23,000 gns, sent to Italy. *William Haggas*

TOOFI (FR) 4 b.g. Henrythenavigator (USA) 131 – Silver Bark 68 (Royal Applause 124) **112** [2015 107: 6g⁴ 6m² 7g⁶ 6.5m⁷ 6g⁴ Sep 19] sturdy gelding: smart handicapper: good efforts when ¾-length second of 27 to Magical Memory in Stewards' Cup at Goodwood, 1½ lengths second of 11 to Hoof It at Doncaster and ¾-length fourth of 25 to Don't Touch in Ayr Gold Cup at Ayr: stays 7f: acts on good to firm going: visored final start. *Roger Varian*

TOO KAY 3 ch.f. Avonbridge 123 – Too Grand 62 (Zaha (CAN) 106) [2015 p8f p12g⁴ 8.3d **–** p10g Oct 27] first foal: dam winner up to 7f (2-y-o 5f winner): no form. *John Bridger*

TOOLA BOOLA 5 b.m. Tobougg (IRE) 125 – Forsythia 63 (Most Welcome 131) [2015 **–** 8m Jul 6] fourth foal: sister to 2m winner Cowslip: dam maiden (stayed 1½m): 50/1, well held in maiden at Ripon only outing on Flat: poor winning hurdler. *George Moore*

TOO MANY DIAMONDS (IRE) 4 b.g. Diamond Green (FR) 121 – Too Much Color **48** (USA) 63 (Spectrum (IRE) 126) [2015 44: p12m p8g⁵ p8g² p8g⁵ 9.2d 7d p7g 6s⁶ 7.9s a7g⁶ p7g p10.7g Oct 16] poor maiden: stays 1m: acts on polytrack, soft and good to firm going: sometimes wears headgear: in tongue tie in 2015. *Damian Joseph English, Ireland*

TOOMUCH TOSAY (IRE) 2 b.f. (Mar 12) Thousand Words 113 – Doting Amy (IRE) **80** (Mujadil (USA) 119) [2015 5g² 5g² 6g³ 6g⁵ 6g⁶ 6.5g* p7g⁴ 7g² 7m* 6g p7.5g³ 8s 8g p6.5g Nov 30] first foal: dam unraced: fairly useful performer: claimed from J. S. Moore €28,407 after second start: won claimers at Maisons-Laffitte in June and Clairefontaine in July: stays 7f: acts on polytrack: in headgear after first 4 starts. *D. Windrif, France*

TOORMORE (IRE) 4 b.c. Arakan (USA) 123 – Danetime Out (IRE) (Danetime (IRE) **122** 121) [2015 125: 8m² 8f⁴ 7g* 8d⁵ 8g* 7m³ 8g Dec 13] well-made colt: very smart performer: won Lennox Stakes at Goodwood (by ¾ length from Dutch Connection) in July and Topkapi Trophy at Veliefendi (by 2½ lengths from Perfect Warrior) in September: good second in Lockinge Stakes at Newbury (neck behind Night of Thunder) and creditable third in Prix de la Foret at Longchamp (2¾ lengths behind Make Believe): below best in Hong Kong Mile at Sha Tin final start: stays 1m: acts on soft and good to firm going: front runner/races prominently. *Richard Hannon*

TOPALING 4 ch.f. Halling (USA) 133 – Topatori (IRE) 89 (Topanoora 118) [2015 73: **76** t13.9g* t13.9f³ t13.9g² p15.8g t13.9m 14.6d t13.9g⁶ Dec 1] fair handicapper: won at Wolverhampton in January: stays 1¾m: acts on polytrack and tapeta. *Mark H. Tompkins*

TOPAMICHI 5 b.g. Beat Hollow 126 – Topatori (IRE) 89 (Topanoora 118) [2015 83: **83** p10g² p10m p10d* p10g³ p10g⁴ 10d³ 10.2v p10g³ p10f⁵ p12g Dec 2] fairly useful handicapper: won at Chelmsford in March: stays 10.5f: acts on polytrack and heavy going: tried in headgear prior to 2015: often races freely. *Mark H. Tompkins*

Qatar Lennox Stakes, Goodwood—a first success in Godolphin's silks for Toormore (No.6), who beats Dutch Connection (second right in row of horses behind winner) and Safety Check (No.1) in a Group 2 that had its prize money significantly boosted in 2015

TOPARALI 3 b.f. Rail Link 132 – Topatoo 109 (Bahamian Bounty 116) [2015 p8g Dec 2] – 3,000 3-y-o: third foal: half-sister to 1½m winner Toptempo (by Halling): dam 1m-10.4f winner: 66/1, green when well held in maiden at Lingfield, slowly away. *Charlie Wallis*

TOP BEAK (IRE) 2 b.c. (Feb 13) Lawman (FR) 121 – Tree Tops 77 (Grand Lodge (USA) 125) [2015 8.3d* Oct 5] 80,000F, 80,000Y: seventh foal: half-brother to 3 winners, including 1¼m/10.7f winner Snowmane and French/Australian winner up to 15f Martial Law (2-y-o 1m winner) (both useful, by Galileo): dam, maiden (stayed 1¼m), half-sister to very smart US Grade 1 9f winner Tuscan Evening: 25/1, won 11-runner maiden at Windsor by head from Mountain Bell, prominent and rallying to lead again inside final 100 yds: better to come. *Hughie Morrison* **91 p**

TOP BOY 5 b.g. Exceed And Excel (AUS) 126 – Injaaz 99 (Sheikh Albadou 128) [2015 99: p5g³ p5g⁴ 5m t5.1g² 5.1s 5.1g² p5g³ 5m⁴ 5m² 5g³ 5g 5g⁵ 5d³ 5s p6f Oct 15] tall, lengthy gelding: fairly useful handicapper: best at 5f: acts on polytrack, tapeta, good to firm and heavy going: wears headgear. *Derek Shaw* **92**

TOP COP 6 b.g. Acclamation 118 – Speed Cop 104 (Cadeaux Genereux 131) [2015 82: t5.1g⁶ t5.1f⁵ p6m t7.1m⁴ p6f⁵ 6m 6f 5m⁵ 6.1m 5.7m³ 5.1m² 5g² 5.1g³ 5f⁶ 5.7f³ t6m² 5m² t5.1m² 6g⁴ t5.1f⁴ p6m³ t6m³ p5m⁴ Dec 31] big gelding: fair handicapper: stays 7f: acts on polytrack, tapeta, firm and good to soft going: often wears headgear: consistent. *Ronald Harris* **68**

TOP DIKTAT 7 b.g. Diktat 126 – Top Romance (IRE) 105 (Entrepreneur 123) [2015 99, a85: p10g p11g 10g⁴ 8.3v 10.2s* p11g⁶ Dec 9] good-topped gelding: fairly useful handicapper: won at Nottingham (amateur) in November: stays 11f: acts on polytrack, soft and good to firm going. *Gary Moore* **86**

TOP NOTCH TONTO (IRE) 5 ch.g. Thousand Words 113 – Elite Hope (USA) 84 (Moment of Hope (USA)) [2015 119: 8.1d⁴ 8m 7d 8g* 10.4m² 8.9g⁴ 8g² 7g³ 8d 10d³ Oct 31] small gelding: smart performer: won listed race at York in June by 1½ lengths from Gabrial: mainly creditable efforts after, including when second in York Stakes at York (½ length behind Tullius) and Boomerang Stakes at Leopardstown (1¼ lengths behind Custom Cut): stays 10.5f: acts on soft and good to firm going: in cheekpieces last 7 starts. *Brian Ellison* **116**

TOP OFFER 6 b.g. Dansili 127 – Zante 108 (Zafonic (USA) 130) [2015 73, a81: p6g³ p5m³ p5g⁵ p5m⁶ t6g⁵ p6f⁴ 6g p6g⁵ 7m³ 6g⁵ 6s p6g* p7g t5.1f f6g t7.1g⁵ p6m Dec 31] well-made gelding: fair handicapper: won at Kempton in September: left Peter Crate after thirteenth start: stays 1m, effective at shorter: acts on polytrack, tapeta and good to firm going: tried in hood prior to 2015: usually races towards rear: none too consistent. *Patrick Morris* **65 a74**

TOP OF THE ART (IRE) 3 gr.f. Dark Angel (IRE) 113 – Thawrah (IRE) (Green Desert (USA) 127) [2015 6m 6g Jul 25] £130,000Y: sturdy filly: fifth foal: sister to smart 5f and (including at 2 yrs) 6f winner Heeraat and half-sister to 6f/7f winner Dance Every Dance (by Chineur) and useful 2-y-o 5f winner Ambiance (by Camacho): dam unraced half-sister to high-class sprinter 7f Malhub: well held in 2 maidens, blinkered in latter. *Ralph Beckett* –

TOP OF THE BANK 2 b.g. (May 4) Piccolo 121 – America Lontana (FR) (King's Theatre (IRE) 128) [2015 5g² 5d³ 5.4m² 5m² 6g 5.4g⁴ Sep 6] £20,000Y: half-brother to several winners, including useful 5f/6f winner Mayoman (by Namid) and 5.7f winner Libor (by Lend A Hand): dam Italian 5f winner: fairly useful maiden: second in maiden at York and nursery at Haydock: stays 6f: acts on good to firm going: often races prominently: has been gelded. *Kevin Ryan* **85**

TOP OF THE GLAS (IRE) 4 gr.g. Verglas (IRE) 118 – Fury Dance (USA) (Crypto-clearance (USA)) [2015 99: 8m 12g 11.5g³ 10.3g 12m 11.8g⁴ 8g 10g Sep 29] tall gelding: fairly useful handicapper: stays 1½m: acts on good to firm and heavy going: tried in cheekpieces in 2015: often races prominently. *Brian Ellison* **92**

TOP OF THE ROCKS (FR) 2 b.g. (Feb 25) Rock of Gibraltar (IRE) 133 – Runaway Top (Rainbow Quest (USA) 134) [2015 7m⁵ 7.2m⁵ 7.6g⁵ Sep 11] modest form in minor event and maidens: slowly away final outing: has been gelded. *Tom Dascombe* **57**

TOPOLOGY 2 b.g. (Feb 5) Passing Glance 119 – Bold Byzantium (Bold Arrangement 127) [2015 7g 6.5s⁴ Oct 23] 16/1, improved from debut when 2¾ lengths fourth of 9 to Monteverdi in maiden at Newbury. *Joseph Tuite* **75**

TOPOLSKI (IRE) 9 b.g. Peintre Celebre (USA) 137 – Witching Hour (IRE) 88 (Alzao (USA) 117) [2015 –: p16g⁵ May 27] modest handicapper: stays 2m: acts on firm and soft going: tried in cheekpieces/tongue tie. *David Arbuthnot* **58**

TOP

TOP POCKET 3 b.g. Royal Applause 124 – Movie Mogul 64 (Sakhee (USA) 136) [2015 **53**
–: p8f p7f 8f⁵ 10m p8g⁴ Dec 20] workmanlike gelding: modest maiden: stays 1m: acts on
polytrack: often races prominently. *Michael Madgwick*

TOP SET (IRE) 5 ch.g. Tamayuz 126 – Pray (IRE) (Priolo (USA) 127) [2015 70, a76: **56**
p10m⁵ p10f² p13g⁴ p10f⁶ p8m⁴ 8m⁴ 11.9g⁶ Apr 28] good-topped gelding: modest maiden:
stays 13f: acts on polytrack, soft and good to firm going: wears headgear: sometimes
slowly away. *Simon Dow*

TOPSOIL 2 b.c. (Apr 30) Kheleyf (USA) 116 – Edge of Gold 81 (Choisir (AUS) 126) –
[2015 7g 7d 6d Oct 12] well held in maidens: in hood last 2 starts. *Ronald Harris*

TOPTEMPO 6 ch.m. Halling (USA) 133 – Topatoo 109 (Bahamian Bounty 116) [2015 **74**
81: p12f* t12.2g⁴ t12.2f⁶ 10g p12g³ p12f Sep 12] lengthy, angular mare: fair performer:
won seller at Lingfield in January: left Mark H. Tompkins after: stays 1½m: acts on
polytrack, tapeta, soft and good to firm going: tried in blinkers. *Ali Stronge*

TOP TUG (IRE) 4 ch.g. Halling (USA) 133 – Top Romance (IRE) 105 (Entrepreneur **102**
123) [2015 103p: 9m 12m⁶ 9.9g⁵ 12d³ 10s⁴ 11.8s⁴ Oct 26] good-topped gelding: useful
handicapper: third at York (2 lengths behind dead-heaters Libran and Memorial Day) in
August: stays 1½m: acts on polytrack and soft going: well below form in cheekpieces final
start. *Sir Michael Stoute*

TORCH 2 b.g. (Mar 27) Paco Boy (IRE) 129 – Singed (Zamindar (USA) 116) [2015 8.3d **54 p**
Oct 14] 55,000Y: half-brother to 3 winners, including 2-y-o 1m winner On Our Way (by
Oasis Dream), later smart in Hong Kong as Chater Way, and temperamental 1¼m/11f
winner On Her Way (by Medicean): dam French 1m winner: 14/1, shaped as if needed
experience when well held in maiden at Nottingham, slowly away: should do better.
Richard Hannon

TORETTO (IRE) 7 ch.g. Peintre Celebre (USA) 137 – Petite-D-Argent 91 (Noalto 120) **55**
[2015 64: f16d⁶ 17.2f³ 16.2m May 1] modest maiden: stays 17f: acts on tapeta, firm and
good to soft going: tried in headgear. *Bernard Llewellyn*

TORMENT 2 bl.g. (Mar 9) Dark Angel (IRE) 113 – Selkirk Sky 65 (Selkirk (USA) 129) **76**
[2015 6m* 7m³ 6g⁶ 7g Sep 6] useful-looking gelding: fair performer: won maiden at
Windsor in June: stays 7f. *Richard Hannon*

TORNADO BATTLE 5 b.g. War Chant (USA) 126 – Child Bride (USA) (Coronado's **52**
Quest (USA) 130) [2015 p12g p10f p10f p10g p12g⁶ t12.2g p15.8f 11.5d⁶ p12m⁶ 11.5d³ **a41**
10m⁴ 9.9d⁵ 9.9m² 10g⁵ 11.9d 11.9g⁵ 9.9v⁴ 10.1g² p10f t9.5f⁶ p10f Oct 29] sturdy gelding:
modest maiden: stays 1¼m: acts on good to firm going: usually wears headgear/tongue tie.
Phil McEntee

TORNESEL 4 b.g. Teofilo (IRE) 126 – Bezant (IRE) 51 (Zamindar (USA) 116) [2015 69: **67**
8g⁶ 8m 8g³ 10m 8s 9.3g 12.2g Aug 27] good-topped, attractive gelding: fair maiden: best
effort at 7f: acts on good to firm going: usually wears tongue tie. *Brian Rothwell*

TORREMAR (FR) 2 br.g. (Mar 7) Excellent Art 125 – Sabela (IRE) (Sinndar (IRE) 134) **72**
[2015 8d 8s³ 8.3s⁴ Oct 28] fair form in maidens, 4¾ lengths fourth of 8 to Rainbow
Dreamer at Nottingham final start: will stay 1¼m: has been gelded. *Kevin Ryan*

TORRIDONIAN 3 b.f. Kodiac 112 – Scottish Heights (IRE) (Selkirk (USA) 129) [2015 **38**
58: f7g t6g t5.1g⁴ 5g⁵ 5.1m May 30] poor maiden: left James Tate after first start: best
effort at 6f: acts on good to soft going: sometimes in headgear. *John O'Shea*

TOSCANINI (IRE) 3 b.c. Shamardal (USA) 129 – Tuzla (FR) 121 (Panoramic 120) **119**
[2015 107: 5.8d* 6d³ 7f⁵ 6m* 6g² 6g² 5d⁴ 6g⁴ Oct 11] close-coupled colt: smart performer:
won minor events at Navan (by head from Ainippe) in May and Naas (by neck from Letters
of Note) in July: even better form when second in Phoenix Sprint Stakes at the Curragh
(short head behind Mattmu) and Renaissance Stakes at the Curragh (¾ length behind
Moviesta): stays 6f: acts on polytrack, good to firm and good to soft going: in cheekpieces
last 4 starts: front runner/races prominently, often travels strongly. *M. Halford, Ireland*

TOTAL DEMOLITION (IRE) 3 ch.g. Thewayyouare (USA) 117 – Margaux Dancer **60**
(IRE) (Danehill Dancer (IRE) 117) [2015 52: p8f⁵ p7f* p10g* p7m³ p11g⁶ 9d⁵ p8g⁵ Jun
18] neat gelding: modest handicapper: won at Kempton and Lingfield (apprentice) in
February: left Olly Stevens after second start: stays 1¼m: acts on polytrack and good to
soft going. *Pat Phelan*

TOTALIZE 6 b.g. Authorized (IRE) 133 – You Too 74 (Monsun (GER) 124) [2015 100: **103**
16.2g² 16.1m 14d⁶ 14d Sep 26] useful handicapper: second at Haydock (1¾ lengths behind
Seamour) in May: stays 2m: acts on polytrack and any turf going: usually in hood prior to
2015: fairly useful hurdler. *Brian Ellison*

TOTALLY COMMITTED 2 b.c. (Mar 13) Invincible Spirit (IRE) 121 – Zanzibar (IRE) **72 p**
113 (In The Wings 128) [2015 8v 7g 7g Oct 21] 100,000Y: half-brother to several winners,
including smart 9f-1½m winner Spice Route (by King's Best) and smart UAE 7f winner
Zurbriggen (by Raven's Pass): dam 11f/1½m winner, including Oaks d'Italia: fair form:
50/1, best effort when 6¼ lengths seventh of 10 to Mootaharer in maiden at Newmarket
final start, not unduly punished: open to further progress. *Clive Cox*

TOTALLY MAGIC (IRE) 3 b.f. Captain Rio 122 – Hypocrisy 85 (Bertolini (USA) 125) **71**
[2015 7s⁵ 6m⁴ 7.5m⁵ 7m 7d² 7g⁵ 7g* 7s Oct 16] second foal: half-sister to 5f winner
Catwilldo (by One Cool Cat): dam 6f/7f winner: fair performer: won handicap at Catterick
in September: best effort at 7f: acts on good to soft going: in cheekpieces last 4 starts.
Richard Whitaker

TOTAL POWER 2 b.g. (Mar 20) Sleeping Indian 122 – House of Frills 69 (Paris House **72**
123) [2015 5d³ 6d⁶ 5m² 5d* 5m 6.1g³ Aug 2] fair performer: won claimer at Catterick in
July: left Iain Jardine after: will probably stay 7f: acts on good to soft going. *Brian Ellison*

TO THE SKY (IRE) 7 b.g. Saffron Walden (FR) 123 – Tara Tara (IRE) 69 (Fayruz 116) –
[2015 51: 9.9m Jun 30] sturdy gelding: modest handicapper: stays 1¼m: acts on soft and
good to firm going: has worn headgear: fair hurdler/chaser. *Jamie Snowden*

TO THE VICTOR (IRE) 3 b.g. Approve (IRE) 112 – Wonders Gift (Dr Devious (IRE) **50**
127) [2015 –: p8f p7g⁶ 6g⁴ 7d p7g p6g³ 7d 6s p6g⁵ p6m⁴ Nov 14] workmanlike gelding:
modest maiden: stays 7f: acts on polytrack: sometimes in headgear in 2015. *Jim Boyle*

TOTO SKYLLACHY 10 b.g. Kyllachy 129 – Little Tramp (Trempolino (USA) 135) **82**
[2015 88: f8d⁵ f8d* f11g⁴ f8d⁵ f12g³ f8g f8s² f11g* 10.4g 9.9g⁴ 8.5m Jun 10] fairly useful
performer: won claimer at Southwell in January and handicap there in March: stays 1½m:
acts on fibresand and any turf going: tried in cheekpieces. *David O'Meara*

TOTZO (IRE) 2 b.f. (Apr 12) Lilbourne Lad (IRE) 111 – Later (IRE) (Marju (IRE) 127) **51**
[2015 6d⁶ p7g t6f p7g Oct 6] second foal: dam unraced sister to useful performer up to
1¼m Bruges: modest maiden: best effort at 6f. *Paul D'Arcy*

TOUCHED BY LOVE (USA) 2 b.c. (Jan 28) Street Sense (USA) 128 – Love of Dubai **– p**
(USA) 106 (More Than Ready (USA) 120) [2015 7d 7v Nov 3] third foal: half-brother to
a winner in Bahrain by Bernardini: dam 7f (at 2 yrs)/1m (Italian 1000 Guineas) winner:
well held in 2 maidens (11 days apart): should do better in time. *Ismail Mohammed*

TOUCHLINE 3 b.f. Exceed And Excel (AUS) 126 – Trianon 80 (Nayef (USA) 129) [2015 **102**
89: 8f² 8f³ 6.9g³ 7m 5m⁴ 6g p6m Nov 14] useful-looking filly: useful performer: placed
first 3 starts, including third of 17 to Osaila in Sandringham Stakes at Royal Ascot on
second outing: best effort when fourth to Cotai Glory in listed race at Doncaster in September:
stays 1m, may prove most effective at sprint trips: acts on firm going. *Michael Bell*

TOUCH OF COLOR 2 b.f. (Feb 17) Sixties Icon 125 – Shesells Seashells 83 (Tiger Hill **70**
(IRE) 127) [2015 7g⁶ 7.4d⁵ 8.1s³ 7s² 8.3g Oct 19] close-coupled filly: first foal: dam, 1m
winner, half-sister to useful 1½m winner Kassiopeia: fair maiden: should stay 1m: acts on
soft going. *Clive Cox*

TOUCH THE CLOUDS 4 b.g. Sleeping Indian 122 – Aptina (USA) (Aptitude (USA) **57**
128) [2015 79: 5.1s 5.1m 5d p6g 5.1m³ p5f⁶ 5g⁶ 5.1d⁴ f5g⁵ Dec 12] rather leggy gelding:
modest handicapper: stays 6f: acts on all-weather, good to firm and heavy going: has worn
headgear, including last 5 starts: tried in tongue tie: front runner/races prominently.
William Stone

TOUGH CALL (IRE) 3 b.c. Iffraaj 127 – Pivotal's Princess (IRE) 107 (Pivotal 124) **82 p**
[2015 t6g² t6g² Jun 26] 60,000Y, 52,000 2-y-o: fourth foal: half-brother to 3 winners,
including smart 5f/6f winner Robot Boy (by Shamardal) and useful winner up to 7f
Accession (2-y-o 6f winner, by Acclamation): dam 5f winner: fairly useful form when
second in maidens won by Brave Leader and Atletico, both at Wolverhampton in June:
remains open to improvement. *Ismail Mohammed*

TOUJOURS L'AMOUR 3 b.f. Authorized (IRE) 133 – High Heel Sneakers 111 (Dansili **98**
127) [2015 90p: 11.5s* 11.9g May 31] useful form: improved when winning 10-runner
listed Oaks Trial at Lingfield in May by 1¼ lengths from Bellajeu, suited by increase in trip
and well on top at finish: 48/10, only eighth of 9 behind Kataniya in Prix de Royaumont at
Chantilly: should be suited by 1½m: acts on soft going: sold 190,000 gns in December.
William Haggas

TOURNAMENT 4 b.g. Oasis Dream 129 – Concentric 107 (Sadler's Wells (USA) 132) **91**
[2015 97: 8d³ 8m⁵ 7g 8g 8d 7d⁴ p7g⁴ Nov 9] fairly useful handicapper: stays 8.5f: acts on
polytrack, viscoride, good to firm and good to soft going: in tongue tie last 3 starts: often
races in rear: temperament under suspicion. *Seamus Durack*

TOURNY (FR) 2 b.f. (Feb 8) Country Reel (USA) 113 – Maka (FR) (Slickly (FR) 128) **109**
[2015 5g⁴ 5g* 5g² 6g* 6d³ 6d² Sep 21] €32,000Y: second foal: sister to useful French 2-y-o
5f winner Make It Reel: dam French sprint maiden: useful performer: won minor event at
Longchamp in June and Prix de Cabourg at Deauville (by head from Du Pyla) in August:
good 1¼ lengths second to Sasparella in Prix Eclipse at Chantilly final outing: stays 6f: acts
on good to soft going: sold €400,000 in October, sent to USA. *P. Bary, France*

TOURTIERE 7 b.g. Act One 124 – Kindle (Selkirk (USA) 129) [2015 12g* 14.1m² **70**
12.2m* 12.2g³ 12d Sep 15] fair handicapper: won at Ripon (amateur) in June and
Musselburgh in August: stays 1¾m: acts on good to firm going: usually races close up.
Sean Regan

TOWERLANDS PARK (IRE) 2 b.c. (Jan 15) Danehill Dancer (IRE) 117 – Strategy 92 **89 p**
(Machiavellian (USA) 123) [2015 8g 8s⁴ p8g* Dec 9] 120,000Y: sixth foal: brother to
useful US Grade 3 8.5f winner Justaroundmidnight, closely related to 1m-1¼m winner
Havelovewilltravel (by Holy Roman Emperor) and half-brother to useful/temperamental 5f
(including at 2 yrs) winner Boris Grigoriev (by Excellent Art): dam 1¼m/11f winner: fairly
useful form: improved again when winning maiden at Kempton by 2½ lengths from Cape
Banjo, suited by way race developed and leading final 1f: will stay 1¼m: likely to progress
further still. *Michael Bell*

TOWER POWER 4 b.g. Nayef (USA) 129 – Voile (IRE) 102 (Barathea (IRE) 127) [2015 **81**
87: 10.2s 10m² 12m⁴ 10d p10m⁵ Dec 16] strong, good-topped gelding: fairly useful
handicapper: left Ismail Mohammed after fourth start: stays 10.5f: acts on good to firm and
good to soft going: sometimes in cheekpieces/tongue tie. *Phil McEntee*

TOWN ORATOR 3 gr.g. Proclamation (IRE) 130 – Town House 68 (Paris House 123) **–**
[2015 6s t6f t8.6g⁶ Dec 1] no form. *Richard Ford*

TOWN'S HISTORY (USA) 2 ch.c. (Mar 25) Hard Spun (USA) 124 – Smooth Charmer **84 p**
(USA) (Easy Goer (USA)) [2015 t8.6g³ Dec 5] closely related to useful US Grade 3 2-y-o
1m winner Sea Chanter (by War Chant) and half-brother to a winner in Argentina by
Mr Prospector: dam, US 6f/7f winner, half-sister to smart performer up to 1m Mutakddim:
4/6, probably should have won when close third of 11 to Red Verdon in maiden at
Wolverhampton on debut, taking strong hold then keeping on well from poor position: sure
to improve. *Saeed bin Suroor*

TOWNSVILLE 3 b.c. Zamindar (USA) 116 – Rule of Nature 88 (Oasis Dream 129) **82**
[2015 p8f* 8.1g p8g f7f Dec 17] first foal: dam, 2-y-o 6f winner, half-sister to useful
French/US winner up to 12.5f Preferential: fairly useful performer: won maiden at
Kempton (by head from Librisa Breeze) in February: left Amanda Perrett after third start:
best effort at 1m. *Keith Dalgleish*

TOXARIS (IRE) 3 ch.f. Teofilo (IRE) 126 – Right Key (IRE) 108 (Key of Luck (USA) **73**
126) [2015 10m p10g⁶ 9g⁶ 11.5g* p13f 12g Aug 13] 42,000Y: sixth foal: half-sister to
2-y-o 8.4f winner Rightside (by High Chaparral) and useful 2-y-o 1m winner (stayed 2m)
Rising Wind (by Shirocco): dam, winner up to 1¾m (2-y-o 7f winner), sister to useful
performer up to 1¼m Wrong Key: fair performer: won handicap at Lingfield in July: best
effort at 11.5f: acts on polytrack: often races towards rear. *Gary Moore*

TOYMAKER 8 b.g. Starcraft (NZ) 128 – Eurolink Raindance (IRE) 109 (Alzao (USA) **69**
117) [2015 82: p13.3m³ p10f³ t8.6g* p10g³ t8.6g² p10f⁶ t8.6g⁴ t8.6g⁴ 8.5m⁶ p10f⁶ p12m
p8m⁴ Dec 27] strong gelding: fair handicapper: won at Wolverhampton in March: stays
10.5f: acts on polytrack, tapeta and good to firm going: tried in headgear: wears tongue tie:
usually races nearer last than first. *Phil McEntee*

TRADEMARK (IRE) 3 b.c. Galileo (IRE) 134 – Ice Queen (IRE) 118 (Danehill Dancer **–**
(IRE) 117) [2015 11m Apr 18] tall colt: third foal: brother to 1½m winner Exotic and smart
1¼m winner (stays 1½m) Felix Mendelssohn: dam 1¼m-1½m winner, second in Irish
Oaks: 13/2, very green when well held in maiden at Newbury: sent to Czech Republic.
Sir Michael Stoute

TRADER JACK 6 b.g. Trade Fair 124 – Azeema (IRE) 82 (Averti (IRE) 117) [2015 91, **77**
a82: f8d⁶ p5m p6f t8.6f p10f p8f 8d 10.2g* 9g² 11.6g⁵ 8.3g⁴ Aug 3] good-topped gelding: **a62**
fair handicapper: won at Nottingham in May: stays 1¼m: acts on polytrack and any turf
going: tried in headgear/tongue tie: often starts slowly, often races in rear. *David Flood*

TRADE STORM 7 b.h. Trade Fair 124 – Frisson (Slip Anchor 136) [2015 119: 8.9g² 8.9g **112**
Mar 28] strong horse: type to carry condition: smart performer: won Woodbine Mile in
2014: respectable 6½ lengths second to Hunter's Light in Jebel Hatta at Meydan on
reappearance: well-held last of 10 behind Solow in Dubai Turf on same course only
subsequent outing: stays 9f: acts on firm and soft going: sold 65,000 gns in December.
David Simcock

TRAFALGAR ROCK 4 b.g. Mount Nelson 125 – Helter Helter (USA) (Seeking The Gold (USA)) [2015 74: 14g⁵ f12s² p12g² t12.2m² 16d² 13.7m² 15.9g⁵ 13m* p16f⁵ 15.8g* Oct 13] fairly useful handicapper: won at Hamilton in September and Musselburgh in October: stays 2m: acts on good to firm going: consistent. *Mark Johnston* **85**

TRAIL BLAZE (IRE) 6 b.g. Tagula (IRE) 116 – Kingpin Delight (Emarati (USA) 74) [2015 98: 7d 8.3s⁴ 7m⁴ 8.5m 8g 6.9d* 8.3s⁴ 8d⁵ 7d 8g³ 7s² Oct 27] tall gelding: fairly useful handicapper: won at Carlisle in July: stays 8.5f: acts on any turf going: usually wears headgear: usually races close up. *Kevin Ryan* **85**

TRAM EXPRESS (FR) 11 ch.g. Trempolino (USA) 135 – Molly Dance (FR) (Groom Dancer (USA) 128) [2015 –: f16d Jan 2] handicapper, no form in 3 starts since 2013: wears tongue tie. *Shaun Lycett* **–**

TRANQUIL GLEN 3 b.f. Moss Vale (IRE) 126 – Glen Molly (IRE) 97 (Danetime (IRE) 121) [2015 43: p7f⁶ 7m p7g p6f Oct 1] poor maiden: left John Butler after first start: stays 7f: acts on polytrack and tapeta: usually in cheekpieces in 2015. *Dr Jon Scargill* **40**

TRANQUIL TIME 2 b.f. (Mar 14) Poet's Voice 126 – Peaceful Soul (USA) 65 (Dynaformer (USA)) [2015 7.6v³ Aug 13] 30,000Y: first foal: dam, maiden, out of half-sister to US Grade 1 9f winner Include: 3/1, showed a bit when 9 lengths third of 7 to Bell Heather in maiden at Lingfield: capable of better. *James Tate* **59 p**

TRANSFER 10 br.g. Trans Island 119 – Sankaty Light (USA) 55 (Summer Squall (USA)) [2015 –: 14.1m⁴ 14.1g Jun 15] good-topped gelding: handicapper: well held all 3 starts on Flat since 2013: tried in headgear/tongue tie. *Tom Symonds* **–**

TRANSPENNINE STAR 2 ch.g. (Mar 15) Mount Nelson 125 – Brave Mave 83 (Daylami (IRE) 138) [2015 7g 9d Oct 26] 11,000F, 20,000Y: third foal: half-brother to winner up to 12.4f Ryeollian (2-y-o 1m winner, by Haafhd): dam winner up to 1½m (2-y-o 7f winner): well held in 2 maidens: should do better in time. *Michael Dods* **– p**

TRAVIS BICKLE (IRE) 4 b.g. Sky Mesa (USA) 116 – Out of Woods (USA) (Woodman (USA) 126) [2015 70, a60: t12.2f³ t12.2m⁴ 12.1g⁴ Aug 2] good-topped gelding: modest maiden: stays 1½m: acts on polytrack, tapeta, good to firm and heavy going: wears headgear. *John Flint* **56**

TREASURE THE RIDGE (IRE) 6 b.g. Galileo (IRE) 134 – Treasure The Lady (IRE) 95 (Indian Ridge 123) [2015 99, a88: 12m 12m 12s⁵ 16.1m³ 16.4d 16m 14.1s⁴ p14f³ p16f⁴ p16g² p15.8g⁵ Dec 28] sturdy gelding: fairly useful handicapper: stays 2m: acts on polytrack, good to firm and heavy going: often wears headgear. *Andrew Reid* **93**

TREASURY NOTES (IRE) 3 b.c. Lope de Vega (IRE) 125 – Elegant As Well (IRE) (Sadler's Wells (USA) 132) [2015 t8.6g⁴ t7.1g⁶ t8.6g³ t8.6g 8.5d³ 8.3m* 10d³ Oct 19] €28,000Y, 54,000 2-y-o: strong, compact colt: sixth foal: half-brother to 3 winners, including 1½m winner Ebony Boom (by Boreal): dam unraced: fairly useful handicapper: won at Hamilton in September: left Daniel Loughnane after fourth start: stays 1¼m: acts on good to firm and good to soft going: often races towards rear, usually responds generously to pressure. *David O'Meara* **86**

TREATY OF YORK (IRE) 3 b.g. Haatef (USA) 117 – Pretty Woman (IRE) 45 (Night Shift (USA)) [2015 67: p6f⁴ 5m p6g p6g 5g Oct 5] modest maiden: left Henry Candy after second start: stayed 6f: acted on polytrack and tapeta: sometimes in hood: dead. *Paddy Butler* **57**

TRED SOFTLY (IRE) 2 b.g. (Mar 18) Yeats (IRE) 128 – Elayoon (USA) 76 (Danzig (USA)) [2015 7.5m Oct 1] 33/1, last of 10 in maiden at Beverley, slowly away. *John Quinn* **–**

TRENDING (IRE) 6 gr.g. Dark Angel (IRE) 113 – Call Later (USA) (Gone West (USA)) [2015 60: t6g³ p6f p6g³ t5.1f* t5.1g⁴ t6g* t6g⁵ 5.3s⁶ 5.7m⁵ 5.1m 5.3g² 6m 5m p8f⁴ p7g t7.1f Dec 22] plain gelding: fair handicapper: won at Wolverhampton in February and April: stays 1m, effective at shorter: acts on polytrack, tapeta, firm and good to soft going: wears headgear/tongue tie: sometimes slowly away, usually races towards rear: often races freely, temperamental. *Jeremy Gask* **65 §**

TRENDSETTER (IRE) 4 b.g. Mastercraftsman (IRE) 129 – Fashion Trade (Dansili 127) [2015 83: 13.8d² 16.4m³ 13.4g* 14m⁵ 14.1d 12.1d⁴ 13.1g³ Sep 19] fairly useful handicapper: won at Chester in May: stays 1¾m: acts on good to firm and good to soft going: often races prominently, often travels strongly. *John Quinn* **92**

TRES CORONAS (IRE) 8 b.g. Key of Luck (USA) 126 – Almansa (IRE) (Dr Devious (IRE) 127) [2015 112: 8d 10.3s² 10.4g 10.1g Jun 5] leggy gelding: useful handicapper: second at Chester (2¼ lengths behind Collaboration) in May: stays 10.5f: acts on fibresand, good to firm and heavy going: tried in headgear: races towards rear. *David Barron* **105**

TRESPASSED (IRE) 2 b.g. (Apr 2) Thewayyouare (USA) 117 – Trespass (Entrepreneur **74**
123) [2015 t7.1f⁵ p8g⁵ p8f⁴ p8g⁶ Dec 15] €6,500F, €35,000Y: fourth foal: dam, French
maiden (stayed 9.5f), half-sister to useful French 2-y-o 6f/7f winner Inhabitant: fair
maiden: stays 1m. *William Haggas*

TREVE (FR) 5 b.m. Motivator 131 – Trevise (FR) (Anabaa (USA) 130) [2015 129: **129**
10.4g* 11.9m* 11.9s* 11.9m⁴ Oct 4]

The demolition team that arrived with wrecking balls and bulldozers at
Longchamp straight after the Arc meeting, to set about tearing down the old stands
ahead of the track's renovation, did not, after all, find that some of the work had
already been started for them. Another win for Treve in Europe's richest race, in
front of a crowd of more than 58,000, a record for Arc day this century, might have
raised the roof. But there was no historic third victory for the mare who had won
brilliantly as a still-unbeaten three-year-old and then overcome setbacks to become
only the seventh dual winner in the race's history twelve months later. In contrast
to 2014 when Treve's chances of retaining her crown seemed to slip away with
each race, her prospects of a third win in the latest season seemed to improve as
the months wore on. Relatively few outside those closest to Treve had kept faith in
her through an unsuccessful campaign leading up to the 2014 Arc, but there was a
huge amount of public support behind her in the latest season, fuelled partly by a
social media campaign, and she was sent off the first odds-on favourite for the Arc
since Sea The Stars in 2008. If anything summed up the mood on the day, it was the
identical headline on the front page of the Arc day editions of not just *Paris Turf* but
the *Racing Post* as well: Allez Treve.

While Treve's final campaign ultimately ended in disappointment, it was
all too easy to forget that, but for a rethink by connections, she wouldn't have
carried on racing at all as a five-year-old. Speaking the day after Treve had won
her second Arc, Criquette Head-Maarek had ruled out any prospect at all of her
staying in training. 'With the problems she has, no. If she had been sound I would
have said to Sheikh Joaan yesterday, let's go for a third Arc. But not with her
physical problems, it's impossible.' Clearly, Treve must have recovered from her
Arc exertions exceptionally well to have prompted the quick and dramatic u-turn
that resulted, less than a week later, in Al Shaqab's racing manager Harry Herbert
announcing that Treve would, after all, race on, subject of course to her remaining
sound. Fortunately, it turned out that Treve's ailments, which had affected her for
much of her four-year-old season, had been put firmly behind her. Different shoes
corrected problems with her feet, while her back trouble (specifically the condition
known as 'kissing spines') was also a thing of the past.

With her soundness giving her a clear run, Treve's 'bonus' season was geared
firmly around a bid to win the Arc for the third time, something which none of the
previous dual winners of the race had even attempted. Having spent much of the
winter at the Head family's Haras du Quesnay, where she was foaled and raised,
Treve went back into training in early-February and did her first canter of the year on
grass in late-March. Her planned light campaign originally called for her to contest
just two races before the Arc, the Grand Prix de Saint-Cloud at the end of June and
the Prix Vermeille three weeks before her main target. However, with her work going
well, her reappearance was brought forward to the Prix Corrida at Saint-Cloud at the
end of May, with the aim of taking some of the freshness out of her. The Group 2
contest for older fillies and mares, a month before the Grand Prix de Saint-Cloud,
fitted in well and was a particularly apt race for Treve's return. The race is named
after the Marcel Boussac-owned Corrida, the only other filly or mare besides Treve
to have won the Arc twice, her wins coming as a four- and five-year-old in 1936 and
1937. Corrida had been the leading French filly at two and was sent to Newmarket at
three to be trained for the One Thousand Guineas and Oaks but disappointed in both.
She also contested the Arc that season and was beaten a neck and the same by two
other three-year-old fillies, Samos and Peniche who had filled the first two places
in reverse order in the Prix de Diane. Corrida enjoyed a much more lucrative four-
year-old season, having Samos back in fourth when winning her first Arc, and she
was a short-head winner of the race at five on the final start of her career. As well as

Prix Corrida, Saint-Cloud—Treve encounters some trouble in running in a race named after a mare who also won two Arcs, but ultimately gets her fourth season under way with an easy success; the blinkered We Are beats Mayhem (rail) for second

her successes in France, Corrida also won important races in Germany and Belgium and was successful in the Hardwicke Stakes at Royal Ascot during her career, the *Bloodstock Breeders' Review* calculating her earnings of £47,375 to be a record at the time (one now held by Treve) for a mare in Europe.

Treve made a successful return in the Prix Corrida, running out an impressive four-length winner from the previous season's Prix de l'Opera winner We Are. Although the pace was overly-strong, Treve, reported by her trainer not only to have developed physically from four to five but also to have become more relaxed, settled well in mid-division and just had to be pushed clear once a gap came for her. The Corrida had been won three years earlier by Solemia who had gone on to gain a shock win in the Arc later that season. Speaking of upsets, Treve's next race, the Grand Prix de Saint-Cloud has seen more than its share of surprise results over the years. This was another race won by Corrida (it was known as the Prix du President de la Republique in her day), while a more recent Arc winner to have won it is Montjeu. However, since Montjeu's victory in 2000, the only winning favourite had been the previous year's Arc third Sarafina in 2011, after also being successful in the Corrida beforehand. Among the odds-on shots beaten in the interim were no fewer than three who had won the previous season's Arc: Bago in 2005, Hurricane Run who went down by a head at 5/1-on a year later, and Danedream who finished last of four in 2012. Treve also started odds on, in a field of nine. Most of her opponents were some way short of Arc standard, but Treve's two chief rivals Flintshire and Dolniya had finished behind her at Longchamp the previous autumn, when Flintshire had been beaten two lengths into second and Dolniya another couple of lengths or so back in fifth. Flintshire and Dolniya were meeting for the fourth consecutive race in 2015, both having been beaten in a muddling four-runner Coronation Cup last time out. Treve raced more keenly this time and had to work harder to land the odds, but she asserted herself inside the final furlong, getting on top fairly late, to beat Flintshire by a length and a quarter, with Dolniya another two and a half lengths away in third. Flintshire had been the first to go for home in the straight, but Treve always seemed poised to go by him, though she needed a few cracks behind the saddle before finally getting on top.

At the trophy presentation, Treve's trainer thanked the Saint-Cloud crowd for their support, inviting them to come and see Treve at her Chantilly stable. Such openness on the trainer's part was also evident in her backing of 'Follow Treve', an internet and social media campaign by France Galop to publicise Treve's bid to make history. As well as a dedicated website, Treve's followers had their own stand at Longchamp on Arc day. 'I think Follow Treve is a great idea' said Madame Head-Maarek. 'I love racing and I love it is a sport. It brings newcomers to racing and allows you to show them what's involved in preparing an athlete. I've played the game and I always will.' Personally answering fan mail (some of it addressed simply 'Treve, Chantilly') was another commendable example of the trainer 'playing the game', though some would say Criquette Head probably went beyond the call of duty by appearing in a video singing along to the specially written tribute song

'Fly Away Treve'. More comfortable viewing, on the other hand, was to be had from France Galop's impressive publicity clip for the Arc featuring footage of a giant galloping Treve projected on to the facades of buildings as she raced through the night-time streets of Paris before arriving at the Arc de Triomphe.

Before all that, though, there was the Prix Vermeille, which Treve had won in excellent style as a three-year-old (her only success during her short-lived association with her owner's retained rider Frankie Dettori) and in which she had finished only a staying-on fourth a year later. No filly had ever won the Prix Vermeille more than once, and nor had any five-year-old mare been successful, though the race was restricted to three-year-old fillies before 2004 and was not opened to five-year-olds and upwards until 2006 (three- and four-year-olds only in 2004 and 2005). All bar one of Treve's eight rivals were three-year-olds, including the Pretty Polly Stakes winner Diamondsandrubies, the lightly-raced Godolphin filly Beautiful Romance, who had won a listed race at Windsor last time, and the shock Juddmonte International winner Arabian Queen, who was stepping up to a mile and a half for the first time. The pick of the French fillies appeared to be the Aga Khan's Candarliya who had completed a four-timer in the Prix Minerve last time out, while Sea Calisi had finished third in the Yorkshire Oaks. The Al Shaqab second colours were carried by the Andre Fabre-trained Al Naamah. A sister to the Oaks winner Was, she had struggled to live up to her five-million-guinea price tag, including when finishing down the field at Epsom in a bid to emulate her sister.

Conditions at Longchamp on Arc trials day were much softer than for any race Treve had contested since her reappearance in the previous season's Prix Ganay. Whether or not that was a factor, Treve put up a tremendously impressive performance, reminiscent in style of her brilliant Arc win at three. While she had already shown high-class form in her two wins earlier in the year at Saint-Cloud, this was better still. Treve looked to be cantering all over her rivals when making ground in eyecatching style on the downhill 'false straight' before the home turn, Thierry Jarnet having to check her a couple of times to prevent her from hitting the front too soon. Given her head once in line for home, Treve shot clear, the only blemish on her performance being a tendency to hang right, towards the rail. Too far ahead to cause any interference by this stage, she was eased close home as Candarliya and Sea Calisi fought it out for second as they were left behind, Candarliya getting the better of the argument by half a length, with that pair, in turn, six lengths clear of the rest. The judge initially returned Treve's winning margin as four and a half lengths, though that clearly underestimated her superiority and was later corrected to six (because of a 'technical error'), making it the widest margin—though not necessarily the easiest—win of her career (she won her first Arc by an official five lengths, though the distance looked more like four that day). Arabian Queen seemed not to stay in sixth but Treve's overall impressive display, including thrashing the only horse to have beaten Golden Horn, one of her chief Arc rivals, now made Treve an odds-on shot in some books for the Arc.

The ground dried out considerably in the three weeks between the Vermeille and the Arc, something seen as prejudicial to Treve's chances in some quarters, though the Vermeille form was given a timely boost when Candarliya won the Prix de Royallieu twenty-four hours before the big race. In each of her races in the latest season, Treve was supplied with a pacemaker—four different ones to be precise—with the intention of ensuring a strong enough pace to enable her jockey to curb

Grand Prix de Saint-Cloud, Saint-Cloud—a repeat of the 2014 Arc as Treve beats Flintshire (rail), who finishes in front of third-placed Dolniya (noseband) for the first time in 2015; Manatee (rail) is fourth on his first outing at Group 1 level

her free-going tendencies. Treve had had the services of a pacemaker before—the smart Irish mare Belle de Crecy had been bought specifically for the role—but the ploy backfired when she lost her unbeaten record to Cirrus des Aigles in the Prix Ganay on her reappearance at four. On that occasion, Jarnet was ignored in the lead on the pacemaker, while Dettori asked Treve to make ground quickly in the middle of the race to make sure she kept tabs on the eventual winner. There may well have been more to Treve's first defeat than those particular occurrences, of course, but Criquette Head regretted the way things had evolved tactically and Treve went the rest of that season without a pacemaker. There were no plans to supply her with one for the latest Arc, either, in the expectation that the race would be competitive and well-run. However, the prospect of a smaller than usual Arc field, and one lacking Postponed and his own pacemaker who had set such a strong gallop for his stable-companion in the Prix Foy, caused a rethink in the Al Shaqab camp. As it happened, there were seventeen runners in the final field, but the formerly Andre Fabre-trained filly Shahah was drafted in to make the pace for Treve, supplemented at a cost of €120,000. Shahah, who had begun her career with Richard Hannon, had previously been pacemaker for the aforementioned Al Naamah, though had caused an upset on her first start in that role as a two-year-old when holding on in front to win the Prix d'Aumale.

A middle draw in stall eight meant that Thierry Jarnet had more options open to him than in Treve's two previous Arcs. Her eventual position as they made the descent towards the straight was similar to the one from which she had made her run when successful two years earlier from a wide draw, in mid-division on the outside of the field. In contrast, her 2014 win when drawn three had been gained with Jarnet keeping to the inside rail the whole way. The story in the latest Arc might have been different in a more strongly-run race, and on more testing ground, but, as it turned out, Treve ended up poorly placed relative to Golden Horn and the eventual placed horses. The first three home were all close up from a long way out behind Shahah, who had been ideally drawn in stall two to fulfil her role as pacemaker, though she ended up helping Golden Horn's cause much more than Treve's. Jarnet produced Treve, still travelling strongly, wide off the home turn but, in contrast to two years earlier, she was unable to produce the decisive acceleration which had made her such a brilliant winner on that occasion (the relatively steady pace for much of the race meant that those in front of Treve were quickening sharply too, making it harder for her to make up the ground; 'I was going so fast in the last furlong, even a rocket wouldn't have got past me,' said Dettori).

While Golden Horn was quickening away from the Abdullah-owned pair Flintshire and New Bay nearer the rail, Treve, out wider, didn't help Jarnet by again edging to her right, doing no favours to Free Eagle on her inside, which in turn resulted in Dolniya being badly squeezed. Still gaining at the line, Treve failed by just a nose to reel in New Bay for third, beaten just over two lengths by Golden Horn. Treve's connections could probably at least count themselves fortunate that the stewards took no action over the interference which she had caused; miscreants have been demoted for much less under the strict French rules. With the Longchamp stewards' decision not to alter the placings, Treve ended her magnificent career with total prize-money earnings (calculated at exchange rates prevailing at the time of her races) of £5,916,327, the highest by any filly or mare in European history. Coincidentally, the previous holder of that record, Goldikova, also benefited from the leniency of the stewards in her final race, when third in the Breeders' Cup Mile at Churchill Downs in 2011; attempting to win the Mile for the fourth time, Goldikova barged her way out early in the straight and hampered several of her rivals, making herself liable to disqualification under the rules in force in Kentucky at the time, though the stewards decided to take no action. Discretion, it seems, may well have been the better part of valour on both occasions.

Tactically, there's little doubt that the Dettori-ridden Golden Horn received a more inspired ride under the circumstances than Treve, though it might be said that Jarnet could hardly shoulder all the blame for the circumstances in which he found himself, given that he would surely have expected Treve's pacemaker to ensure a stronger pace than the one which resulted. Dettori joined six other jockeys who have ridden four Arc winners, the others including Jarnet himself who had joined that club the year before, Freddie Head, whose final win had come in 1979 on Criquette Head's first Arc winner Three Troikas, and Jacko Doyasbere, who had ridden another of the race's dual winners, Tantieme, in 1950 and 1951. Jarnet found himself having to explain his tactics in the aftermath of Treve's defeat and—perhaps diplomatically—was inclined to blame the firmer ground, saying 'she just didn't quite have the gas.' For her part, Criquette Head-Maarek was reluctant to make excuses. 'I think she had a good race but the only thing is, maybe she could have been a bit closer … maybe the Vermeille was a little tougher than I thought too.' Her brother, on the other hand, was more critical of the tactics employed on Treve which, in his opinion, had been influenced by the intense interest in Treve's bid to

Al Shaqab Racing's "Treve"

make history. 'With the pressure and hype beforehand, I don't think you can analyse the races well, there is something that takes you.' Freddie Head evidently believed Jarnet would have been better served taking the risk of charting a course nearer the rail, tactics which had been so successful the year before. But whether Treve would have enjoyed the same luck round the inside again is another matter. Ryan Moore, who was drawn wide on Found, opted for just such a route, dropping her out from the start and taking her across to the inside rail but, from much further back than Treve, Found met trouble in running in addition to being left with plenty to do, and ultimately passed the post only ninth with running still left in her. For all the ins-and-outs and conjecture afterwards, and the disappointment felt by a Longchamp crowd which wanted only one result, the latest Arc still produced a finishing order that fell into place, with the year's top three-year-old colt chased home by the previous year's runner-up and a stablemate who was the season's leading three-year-old in France.

In any case, now that she has been retired, it will be the two Arcs that Treve won, not the one she lost, for which she will surely be remembered. She was never better than for her first victory in 2013 when achieving a rating of 134, which made her Timeform's Horse of the Year. In the thirty years since Pebbles was awarded that title in 1985, Zarkava, also unbeaten when winning the Arc at the age of three (but then retired to stud immediately afterwards), has been the only other filly honoured with that particular award. Treve's essay in *Racehorses of 2013* acknowledged her winning margin as one of the widest in the history of the Arc, but more importantly noted that her 'performance was right out of the top drawer and has been bettered only by half a dozen fillies and mares aged three or above in the history of the *Racehorses* annual'. Among that half-dozen are just two other Arc winners, Coronation V and Allez France, both rated 135. Allez France, incidentally, also contested the Arc three times, though had never been a potential triple winner after managing to beat only two home on soft ground as a three-year-old. Regarded as needing firm ground for much of her career, Allez France encountered ideal conditions when successful twelve months later, but it was heavy when she still managed to finish third to Sagace as a five-year-old after having only one run beforehand that season.

		Montjeu	Sadler's Wells
	Motivator	(b 1996)	Floripedes
	(b 2002)	Out West	Gone West
Treve (FR)		(br 1994)	Chellingoua
(b.m. 2010)		Anabaa	Danzig
	Trevise (FR)	(b 1992)	Balbonella
	(b 2000)	Trevillari	Riverman
		(b 1987)	Trevilla

Coronation V (well held behind Tantieme when bidding to win the Arc again as a four-year-old) proved infertile for Corrida's owner Marcel Boussac at stud. Corrida herself met an unkind fate, outlined in last year's essay on Treve, but her only surviving produce did win the Prix du Jockey Club. Treve has some much more successful acts to follow among Arc-winning fillies as broodmares. Detroit foaled an Arc winner of her own in Carnegie, Gold River became the great grandam of Goldikova, while Urban Sea, as the dam of Galileo and Arc winner Sea The Stars, has earned even more fame for her stud career than she did for her unheralded Arc win. Zarkava, incidentally, had to wait until the latest season to get off the mark as a broodmare, her fourth foal Zarak being the first of her offspring to reach the track, the two-year-old colt making a successful debut at Deauville a few weeks after the Arc. Zarak is by Dubawi whom Treve is due to visit in 2016, having left Criquette Head-Maarek's stable three weeks after the Arc for Sheikh Joaan's Haras de Bouquetot in Normandy. Although she will be without Treve, Criquette Head will at least have her two-year-old sister Terre in training next season. Billed as one of the star attractions at the Deauville yearling sales in August, the filly bred at the Head family's Haras du Quesnay was led out unsold after the bidding had reached €1,200,000. Although there were parties reportedly interested in buying her privately, those bids evidently fell short of the value placed on her by her breeders and Terre looks set to begin her career, as Treve did, in the all-red colours of the Haras du Quesnay. Treve also failed to find a buyer as a yearling, though in her case the bidding stopped at €22,000! Their three-year-old half-sister Toride (by Fuisse) remains unraced but the year-older Trophee (by Mr Sidney) got off the mark in the States for Christophe Clement during the summer. Successful on turf in a maiden at Belmont and an allowance race at Saratoga, the latter over eleven furlongs, she also finished fourth in a couple of Grade 3 contests in the autumn.

Further details of Treve's illustrious family were given in her essay in *Racehorses of 2013*, and it produced another good mare in the latest season in Odeliz, successful in Group 1 company in both France and Italy. Treve is a quite good-topped mare who took after her sire Motivator in tending to sweat before her races. Her edgy nature was also apparent in a tendency to race keenly, particularly running downhill at Longchamp on the sweeping stretch before the final straight, but, typically held up travelling strongly, she had a particularly potent turn of foot. The first big win of her career came when she won the Prix de Diane in record time on good to firm ground, but, perhaps because she was beaten at odds on under similar conditions on her only outing in Britain in the following year's Prince of Wales's Stakes at Royal Ascot, she was widely portrayed as needing softer going. She certainly looked ill-at-ease at Ascot, not only in the race but also moving to post beforehand, her demeanour, with the benefit of hindsight, signalling the physical problems which ailed her that summer. However, conditions were on the firm side again when she won her second Arc later that year, and also for the Grand Prix de Saint-Cloud in the latest season. She clearly acted on good to firm ground, but, as has been said earlier, her career-best effort came in the 2013 Arc on good to soft and her impressive win in the Vermeille in the latest season came on soft ground. Treve won nine of her thirteen starts and, in fact, earned more than €8m if her prize money earnings are coupled with the bonuses she won as a French-bred. *Mme C. Head-Maarek, France*

TREVISANI (IRE) 3 b.g. Dubawi (IRE) 129 – Geminiani (IRE) 106 (King of Kings (IRE) 125) [2015 10m⁴ 9.9m⁴ 10.1d⁴ p12g* Oct 14] well-made gelding: seventh foal: half-brother to useful 11.5f-1¾m winner Amerigo (by Daylami), stayed 21.7f: dam, 2-y-o 7f winner, closely related to smart 2-y-o 5f/6f winner Damson: fairly useful performer: blinkered first time, won maiden at Kempton in October by 4 lengths from Perche: stays 1½m: acts on polytrack: open to further improvement. *David Lanigan* — **89 p**

TRIASSIC (IRE) 2 b.g. (Jan 24) Vale of York (IRE) 117 – Livadiya (IRE) 111 (Shernazar 131) [2015 6.1m³ 6s² 6d⁵ 6.3d 8.3d² 8.3d⁴ 9d⁶ Oct 31] fair maiden: stays 8.5f: acts on soft going: front runner/races prominently. *Mark Johnston* — **73**

TRIATHLON (USA) 2 b.f. (Mar 20) Hat Trick (JPN) 121 – Relaxed (USA) 94 (Royal Academy (USA) 130) [2015 7m⁵ 8.3g³ Sep 30] fourth foal: half-sister to 2 winners in USA by Empire Maker: dam, 7f and (in USA) 8.5f winner, half-sister to dam of smart performer up to 1½m Slumber: similar form to debut when head third of 9 to Stoney Broke in maiden at Nottingham, leading over 1f out but edged out close home: remains open to improvement. *Sir Michael Stoute* — **73 p**

TRIBESMAN 2 ch.g. (Feb 18) Equiano (FR) 127 – Millsini 55 (Rossini (USA) 118) [2015 5v* 6.1m⁵ 6d p5f⁵ 5.1v⁴ Oct 7] fair performer: won minor event at Musselburgh in April: best effort at 5f: acts on heavy going: in visor final start. *David Brown* — **78**

TRICKY DICKY 2 b.g. (Apr 2) Holy Roman Emperor (IRE) 125 – Tricky Situation 78 (Mark of Esteem (IRE) 137) [2015 6g 6m 7.5g Sep 16] poor maiden. *Olly Williams* — **49**

TRICKY ISSUE (IRE) 3 b.f. Manduro (GER) 135 – Tricky Situation 78 (Mark of Esteem (IRE) 137) [2015 8m⁶ 9.5g⁶ 10m Aug 3] 3,000F: angular filly: first foal: dam, maiden (stayed 1½m), half-sister to useful 1¼m-1¾m winner Trick Or Treat: no form. *Seamus Mullins* — **–**

TRIDENT TESTED 2 gr.g. (Apr 25) Arabian Gleam 122 – Neptune's Girl (IRE) (Verglas (IRE) 118) [2015 p7g 6d 7d⁵ Sep 14] modest maiden: best effort when fifth at Brighton final start. *John Best* — **61**

TRIGGER FINGER 3 ch.g. Double Trigger (IRE) 123 – Galette 94 (Caerleon (USA) 132) [2015 p12m⁵ Apr 8] 14/1, tailed-off last of 5 in maiden at Lingfield. *Jonathan Portman* — **–**

TRIGGER PARK (IRE) 4 ch.g. Tagula (IRE) 116 – Raazi 46 (My Generation 111) [2015 57: t6f⁵ p6f 6.1v³ 7.1s⁵ 8m f7g⁴ t8.6g² f7g³ t8.6f⁴ Dec 21] modest maiden: stays 8.5f: acts on fibresand, tapeta and heavy going. *Ronald Harris* — **56**

TRIKASANA 3 ch.f. Leporello (IRE) 118 – Baileys Honour 61 (Mark of Esteem (IRE) **59**
137) [2015 57: p7g⁵ p6g⁵ p6g⁴ 6g Sep 7] modest maiden: stays 7f: acts on polytrack:
usually races close up. *Clive Cox*

TRIKINGDOM 2 b.g. (Feb 11) Showcasing 117 – Spritzeria 81 (Bigstone (IRE) 126) **65**
[2015 p6g⁴ 6m⁵ 6g⁶ 6.1m⁶ 6v t6f⁴ Sep 19] good-topped gelding: fair maiden: raced only at
6f: acts on polytrack and good to firm going: tried in headgear. *Ed Walker*

TRIMOULET 6 b.g. Teofilo (IRE) 126 – Riberac 110 (Efisio 120) [2015 72: f8g² p10g* **93**
t12.2m* t12.2g⁴ 10.3d p10g³ t12.2g* p13.3f³ t16.5f t12.2f p12g³ p11g* Dec 9] fairly useful
handicapper: won at Chelmsford in January, Wolverhampton in February and August and
Kempton (by length from Royal Warranty) in December: stays 13.5f: acts on polytrack and
tapeta: front runner/races prominently. *Daniel Kubler*

TRINITY STAR (IRE) 4 gr.g. Kheleyf (USA) 116 – Zamiyla (IRE) 86 (Daylami (IRE) **89**
138) [2015 86: 8s³ 8g⁴ 8m* 8m³ 7.9g 8.3m⁴ 8d⁵ 8d 8g 8d* Oct 5] fairly useful handicapper:
won at Pontefract in April and October: stays 1¼m: acts on good to firm and good to soft
going: wears headgear: often races towards rear: has looked quirky. *Michael Dods*

TRIPARTITE (IRE) 2 b.g. (Apr 3) Zebedee 113 – Baltic Belle (IRE) 86 (Redback 116) **65**
[2015 p6g⁶ 5s p6g⁴ Oct 27] fair maiden: best effort when fourth of 10 at Lingfield final
start. *Jeremy Gask*

TRIPLE CHIEF (IRE) 4 b.g. High Chaparral (IRE) 132 – Trebles (IRE) (Kenmare (FR) **–**
125) [2015 82: t9.5m Apr 2] tall, good-topped gelding: maiden, fair form at best: likely to
prove best up to easy 1¼m: acts on polytrack, best turf form on good going: in hood/tongue
tie sole start in 2015. *Chris Down*

TRIPLE CHOCOLATE 5 b.g. Danehill Dancer (IRE) 117 – Enticing (IRE) 116 (Pivotal **92**
124) [2015 94: p6m* p7g 6m 6m p7g⁵ p6g p8g⁶ Dec 7] good-bodied gelding: fairly useful
handicapper: won at Kempton (by ½ length from Light From Mars) in February: stays 7f:
acts on polytrack and good to firm going. *Roger Ingram*

TRIPLE DIP (IRE) 3 ch.f. Three Valleys (USA) 119 – Melpomene 95 (Peintre Celebre **88**
(USA) 137) [2015 72: p12g² 10.2f* 10.2d⁵ 12.5m³ 12.1m⁴ 10.3m³ 10.1m² 12m* 12m⁵
9.9m 12m³ 12d⁴ Aug 26] fairly useful handicapper: won at Bath in April and Doncaster in
July: stays 1½m: acts on firm and good to soft going: sold 8,000 gns, sent to Spain.
Mark Johnston

TRIPLE DREAM 10 ch.g. Vision of Night 115 – Triple Joy 104 (Most Welcome 131) **60**
[2015 72, a89: p5g t5.1f⁵ p6f⁵ p5f⁵ 5.3g 5m³ 5m⁶ 5.3m⁴ 5.1m⁶ 5.1m 5g³ 5g² 5.1g 5d⁶ 5m⁵ **a72**
5.7f² p6g³ 5m³ p6m* p6g² p6m² Dec 16] well-made gelding: modest handicapper on turf,
fair on all-weather: won at Lingfield in November: stays 6f: acts on polytrack, tapeta and
any turf going: has worn headgear/tongue tie: usually leads. *Milton Bradley*

TRIPLE EIGHT (IRE) 7 b.g. Royal Applause 124 – Hidden Charm (IRE) 95 (Big **72**
Shuffle (USA) 122) [2015 77: 12.1m⁶ 11.1s* 11.5d 12.1g Aug 20] rather sparely-made
gelding: fair handicapper: won at Hamilton in July: stays 1¾m: acts on polytrack, good to
firm and heavy going: usually wears headgear. *Philip Kirby*

TRIP TO PARIS (IRE) 4 b.g. Champs Elysees 124 – La Grande Zoa (IRE) 50 **122**
(Fantastic Light (USA) 134) [2015 96: p11g⁴ p12g* 16g* 18.7d* 16.4m² 20f* 16m³
16.4d⁵ 11.9g² 15.9g⁴ 11.9f Nov 29]
    The news that the Gold Cup winner Trip To Paris suffered a tendon injury in
the Japan Cup, on his eleventh start of the season, and is likely to miss the whole of
2016 is a blow to La Grange Stables. He had shown on two starts in Australia (where
he was returned for treatment after Tokyo) that he had all the attributes to become the
latest globe-trotting flagbearer his trainer who has been represented by a number
of tough international performers over the years, from the mares Ouija Board and
Snow Fairy to the ill-fated Red Cadeaux who became the first British-trained horse
to earn £5m in prize money. Like Red Cadeaux, Trip To Paris was sent to contest the
Melbourne Cup in November and started 5/1 second favourite for that race after an
excellent second to Mongolian Khan in the very valuable Caulfield Cup a little over
a fortnight before Flemington. The Caulfield Cup is a mile and a half and Trip To
Paris shaped really well with the Melbourne Cup in mind, staying on strongly, and it
was no surprise to see him make a very bold bid to become the first British-trained
winner of Australia's greatest race. Close up most of the way and ideally placed on
the home turn, Trip To Paris came through to dispute the lead briefly just inside the
final furlong before finishing a good fourth behind 100/1-shot Prince of Penzance,

Betway Chester Cup (Heritage Handicap), Chester—the progressive Trip To Paris (left) defies a 3-lb penalty, beating Irish raider Quick Jack (who landed the Galway Hurdle on his next outing); another Irish challenger Zafayan (noseband) and Gabrial's King complete the frame, the last-named doing best of the five runners owned by Dr Marwan Koukash

two places behind the best-placed European challenger, the Lonsdale Cup winner Max Dynamite, and a place in front of the Goodwood Cup winner Big Orange. The race was marred by the serious injury to Red Cadeaux which is described in the essay on him.

The Lonsdale Cup and the Goodwood Cup were both among the races Trip To Paris had contested in Britain before setting off on his travels and he had to give weight away all round on each occasion because of his Group 1 penalty for winning the Gold Cup at Royal Ascot. The Gold Cup and the St Leger are the only Group 1s run in Britain over a distance of ground, a mile and three quarters or more, while France has only the Prix du Cadran (at potential risk of being downgraded) and the Prix Royal-Oak, and Ireland just the Irish St Leger (the Prix Royal-Oak and the Irish St Leger are both open to horses above the age of three while the St Leger at Doncaster still conforms to the classic tradition by being a race for three-year-olds only). Staying races have always been a valuable part of the variety and spectacle of Flat racing in Britain and it was good to see the Thoroughbred Breeders' Association highlighting the lack of good opportunities for stayers in a report published in April. The programme for staying two-year-olds, for example, is much better in France than it is in Britain, and the downgrading of the Queen's Vase to listed status and the risk to another pattern event for three-year-old stayers, the Bahrain Trophy, were cited as further indicators of a decline that is threatening a vital dimension of British racing. 'British racing is all about diversity. It's the ethos of the TBA to look after the heritage of our racing … and it is important to remember the importance of stayers to National Hunt racing, which in turn contributes to betting turnover,' said the vice-chairman of the Thoroughbred Breeders' Association, Julian Richmond-Watson, unveiling the report.

Breeding stayers for a sales market looking for fast-maturing, speedy horses makes no economic sense—though, as Trip To Paris himself illustrates, chance has a large say in the breeding of racehorses and not all of them conform to their pedigree (he is a thorough stayer from an immediate miling and middle-distance background, and he was acquired at the Newmarket Breeze-Up Sales and won over seven furlongs in the July of his two-year-old season, neither an obvious pointer to his turning into a Gold Cup winner). The TBA advocates the introduction of more restricted two-year-old races for the produce of stallions who have won at a minimum of ten or twelve furlongs, and improvements in the staying programme for three-year-olds—including more three-year-old-only handicaps, some restricted to fillies—to provide more encouragement to breeders and buyers of staying types, who seldom reach their peak anyway until after their three-year-old days. The TBA appealed successfully to the British Horseracing Authority and to racecourses to look at Britain's staying races, a review of which is now being undertaken as part of a wider consideration of the pattern.

The European Pattern Committee has the final say on the status of the top races, but the staying pattern, and having a meaningful 'black type' programme, is an important component of the wider picture, and any further downgrading of such staying events can only accelerate the perceived general decline. There are no fewer than seven Group 1 sprints in Britain for three-year-olds and upwards (though one of them, the Commonwealth Cup, is for three-year-olds only) and there is a very strong case for the stayers to have more than the two Group 1s they have at present. The Goodwood Cup and the Doncaster Cup are the races that have traditionally made up the so-called 'stayers' triple crown' and, with the Goodwood Cup's prize money having been increased markedly with new money made available as part of the rebranding of Glorious Goodwood as the Qatar Goodwood Festival, that race looks the better option to push for Group 1 status. Goodwood is also said to be eyeing the seven-furlong Lennox Stakes and the five-furlong King George Stakes for potential Group 1 upgrades, but Goodwood stages a Group 1 over a mile (the Sussex) and the British calendar is already replete with Group 1 sprints. Although it is close to the Prix Royal-Oak, there is still hope that the Long Distance Cup might soon be promoted from Group 2 to become a fifth Group 1 on British Champions' Day. The sponsors of the Goodwood Festival—who have promised another big rise in its prize money if the Goodwood Cup becomes Group 1—and of British Champions' Day have both shown their ambition, and adding two very richly-endowed staying events to the Group 1 programme at sensible points in the season would certainly help to give the British stayer more prestige. The Long Distance Cup is already run without penalties and the Goodwood Cup should follow the example to make sure it attracts the Gold Cup winner from Royal Ascot on a more regular basis (penalties are hard to justify anyway in a race worth as much as the Goodwood Cup which had a £170,130 first prize in 2015).

Trip To Paris wasn't among the original entries for the Gold Cup but, after being gelded over the winter, he progressed well in handicaps, winning at Lingfield and Ripon in April and then completing his hat-trick in the Chester Cup. Trip To Paris picked up a 3-lb penalty for Chester after winning at Ripon which was just enough to earn him a place in the seventeen-strong line-up. With Trip To Paris forced to delay his challenge as a rival weakened in front of him on the home turn, he did well to peg back the Irish challengers Quick Jack—a horse with a fine record in big handicaps under both codes—and Zafayan. Gabrial's King, runner-up to Trip To Paris at Ripon, repeated that form to finish fourth. With a possible Gold Cup tilt under consideration, Trip To Paris dipped his toe into pattern company in the Henry II Stakes at Sandown where only Vent de Force proved too good, Trip To Paris staying on best of all to take second close home.

Gold Cup, Royal Ascot—Graham Lee gets a clear run up the inside on winner Trip To Paris, but Ryan Moore has to sit and suffer on runner-up Kingfisher (No.9), who finishes well once getting clear; long-time favourite Forgotten Rules (noseband) doesn't find quite so much as seemed likely and has to settle for third, ahead of Simenon (No.6) who makes the frame for the third year in a row

La Grange Partnership's "Trip To Paris"

Supplemented for the Gold Cup at Royal Ascot at a cost of £35,000, Trip To Paris was sent off at 12/1, sixth choice in the twelve-runner field behind the previous season's Long Distance Cup winner Forgotten Rules, the Sagaro Stakes winner Mizzou (who had had Vent de Force—a 10/1-shot in the Gold Cup—back in third) and Ballydoyle's representative Kingfisher, that trio at the head of the market in a strong betting race. The extra half mile on top of the Henry II Stakes trip seemed to suit Trip To Paris and he got home in something of a bunched finish, his jockey Graham Lee (who won the 2004 Grand National on Amberleigh House) keeping to the inside rail in the home straight and enjoying a dream run to lead just inside the final furlong. Staying on strongly, Trip To Paris won by a length and a quarter from Kingfisher, who didn't enjoy the rub of the green, with Ryan Moore having to check his run and switch him inside before getting into the clear all too late. Third place, a neck behind Kingfisher, went to Forgotten Rules who held a short-lived lead before Trip To Paris deprived him of it. Simenon took fourth, finishing in the frame for the third successive year, and Mizzou and Vent de Force came seventh and eleventh respectively. The victory of Trip To Paris revived memories of the Gold Cup forty-one years earlier in which Ed Dunlop's father John was the successful trainer; Ed recalled that the trophy won by Ragstone still takes pride of place on the dining table at the home of his father and mother. 'There are better horses than Trip To Paris running this week but I was brought up to regard the Gold Cup as the highlight of the meeting, this is an incredible day and a hell of a story,' he said. It was the first domestic Group 1 won by the stable since Snow Fairy's Oaks in 2010.

Trip To Paris was the first Gold Cup winner to attempt the Gold Cup/ Goodwood Cup double since Colour Vision in 2013 and, like Colour Vision, the 4-lb Group 1 penalty made his task very difficult. Colour Vision went down by a length and three quarters of a length to the Gold Cup third Saddler's Rock, but Trip

To Paris came even closer to becoming the first to complete the double since Yeats did so in 2008 (for the second time, both when the Group 1 penalty in the Goodwood Cup was 5 lb). Trip To Paris arguably put up an even better performance in the two-mile Goodwood Cup than he had at Royal Ascot, mounting a strong challenge inside the final furlong and going down in a three-way photo only by a neck and a short head to Big Orange and Quest For More, closing all the way to the line and coming out the best horse at the weights. The only other horse before Yeats, incidentally, to achieve the Gold Cup/Goodwood Cup double in the same season, since the Goodwood Cup distance was reduced from two miles five furlongs in the early-'nineties, was Double Trigger in 1995. That was the year that Double Trigger and his year-younger brother Double Eclipse (who received 6 lb more than weight for age) fought out a thrilling finish, with Double Trigger getting home by a neck, the result in doubt right until the end.

Double Trigger went on to complete the stayers' triple crown in the Doncaster Cup, a race that has been the poor relation among the stayers' triple crown races in recent times, both in prize money and prestige and has been usurped by the Long Distance Cup on British Champions' Day as the most significant of the Cup races in the autumn. The Doncaster Cup has also lost ground to the Lonsdale Cup at York's Ebor meeting which is now a Group 2 (Double Eclipse went on to win it after his Goodwood battle with Double Trigger but the Lonsdale had only listed status until becoming a Group 3 in 1997 before being elevated to Group 2 in 2004). Gold Cup winners seldom run in the Lonsdale, though both Colour Vision and Estimate contested it the year after their Royal Ascot triumph. Trip To Paris was the first winner of the Gold Cup to carry the Group 1 penalty in the Lonsdale since 2001 when Royal Rebel managed to finish only seventh of ten. Trip To Paris didn't fare much better, giving a rather flat performance (perhaps entitled to do so after his busy campaign) and coming fifth of eight behind the impressive Max Dynamite. Trip To Paris bounced back to his best, after an eight-week break, to run two fine races in Australia before injuring himself in the Japan Cup, in which he became the only British-trained runner in Japan all year.

Trip To Paris (IRE) (b.g. 2011)	Champs Elysees (b 2003)	Danehill (b 1986)	Danzig
			Razyana
		Hasili (b 1991)	Kahyasi
			Kerali
	La Grande Zoa (IRE) (b 2003)	Fantastic Light (b 1996)	Rahy
			Jood
		Majestic Sister (b 1995)	Last Tycoon
			Royal Sister II

The well-made Trip To Paris went through the sale-ring three times before he saw a racecourse, making 37,000 guineas as a foal and bought back for 35,000 guineas as a yearling, before being returned to Newmarket for the Guineas Breeze-Up Sales at which he was sold for only 20,000 guineas. Trip To Paris is from the first crop of the Juddmonte stallion Champs Elysees who showed more stamina than his brothers Dansili and Cacique, gaining his three Grade 1 wins in North America in the Northern Dancer Stakes, the Hollywood Turf Cup and the Canadian International, all over a mile and a half. La Grande Zoa, the dam of Trip To Paris (her only winner to date, though her colt foal by Invincible Spirit made €135,000 at Goffs November Sale), ran only three times, showing modest form in maidens at up to a mile and a half for Ralph Beckett, and Trip To Paris's grandam Majestic Sister was unraced. Majestic Sister was by Last Tycoon, a top sprinter who also won the Breeders' Cup Mile, and she was a sister to the high-class mile and a quarter performer Ezzoud, winner of the Eclipse and twice successful in the Juddmonte International. Royal Sister II, the great grandam of Trip To Paris, also bred another Group 1 winner in the Sussex and Prix du Moulin winner Distant Relative. There is stamina further back in Trip To Paris's family on the distaff side, Royal Sister II having a half-sister, Ribarbaro, who won at up to two miles and was second in the Chester Cup, while Trip To Paris's great great grandam Ribasha (herself a half-sister to 1948 St Leger winner Black Tarquin) was a half-sister to the dam of Jockey Club Cup winner Blood Royal. Blood Royal's classic-placed sister Arkadina (by Ribasha's sire Ribot and therefore closely related to her) was the dam of the Irish St Leger-winning filly

Dark Lomond. The tough and versatile Trip To Paris is effective at a mile and a half to two and a half miles, and acts on polytrack, firm and good to soft going. He often wore blinkers earlier in his career but wore no headgear as a four-year-old except for being equipped with cheekpieces in the Lonsdale. *Ed Dunlop*

TRIUMPHANT (IRE) 6 b.g. Danehill Dancer (IRE) 117 – Meek Appeal (USA) **95** (Woodman (USA) 126) [2015 107: p15.8g⁴ p15.8m⁵ 13g 18g Oct 10] useful performer, lightly raced on Flat nowadays (winning hurdler): 50/1, shaped better than distance beaten suggests when 10½ lengths nineteenth of 34 to Grumeti in Cesarewitch Handicap at Newmarket final start, going with zest but stamina stretched: stays 2m: acts on polytrack and soft going: often in headgear. *Gary Moore*

TRIXIA (FR) 2 b.f. (Apr 6) Siyouni (FR) 122 – Tianshan (FR) 104 (Lahint (USA)) [2015 **106 p** 7s* 7.7g* 8g* 8s* Oct 21] €85,000Y: third foal: half-sister to French 7.5f winner Calaf (by Elusive City) and French 1m winner Tantris (by Turtle Bowl): dam French 7.5f/1m winner: useful form: unbeaten in 4 starts, namely maiden at Vichy and minor event at Marseilles Borely, both in August, listed race at Lyon Parilly in September and Prix des Reservoirs at Deauville (by 1¼ lengths from Jemayel, leading 1½f out) in October: stays 1m: acts on soft going: joined A. de Royer Dupre: should improve further. *F. Rossi, France*

TRIXIE MALONE 5 b.m. Ishiguru (USA) 114 – Lady-Love 70 (Pursuit of Love 124) **94** [2015 85: 7d⁷ p8g⁵ 8d* 6.9g² 8.3m³ 7s* 7v⁵ Oct 24] fairly useful performer: won claimer at Catterick in April and handicaps at Newcastle in May and Salisbury (by 6 lengths from Wordcraft) in September: stays 8.5f: acts on heavy going: usually leads. *K. R. Burke*

TRODERO 2 b.f. (Mar 30) Mastercraftsman (IRE) 129 – Jules (IRE) 76 (Danehill (USA) **–** 126) [2015 f7g Nov 12] 10,000Y: half-sister to several winners, including smart winner up to 7f Golden Desert (2-y-o 6f winner, by Desert Prince) and useful 1m winner Stosur (by Mount Nelson): dam 7f winner: 33/1, well held in maiden at Southwell. *Dr Jon Scargill*

TROJAN ROCKET (IRE) 7 b.g. Elusive City (USA) 117 – Tagula Bay (IRE) 73 **106** (Tagula (IRE) 116) [2015 98: p6g* p6g⁴ t6m⁶ p6g p6f 6m⁵ f7g Dec 22] workmanlike gelding: useful handicapper: won at Chelmsford in January: stays 7f, usually over shorter: acts on polytrack, tapeta and soft going: wears cheekpieces. *Michael Wigham*

TROOPINGTHECOLOUR 9 b.g. Nayef (USA) 129 – Hyperspectra 91 (Rainbow **86** Quest (USA) 134) [2015 p11f⁵ p11g³ p13.3g⁴ t12.2f² Dec 14] good-topped gelding: fairly useful handicapper: stays 1½m: acts on polytrack, tapeta and heavy going: usually in cheekpieces in 2015: wears tongue tie. *Steve Gollings*

TROPICAL BACHELOR (IRE) 9 b.g. Bachelor Duke (USA) 122 – Tropical Coral **62** (IRE) 82 (Pennekamp (USA) 130) [2015 66: 12f³ 14.1m⁴ 12g² Aug 3] smallish gelding: modest handicapper: stays 14.5f: acts on firm and good to soft going: tried in headgear. *Ruth Carr*

TROPICANA BAY 3 b.f. Oasis Dream 129 – Ballet Ballon (USA) 81 (Rahy (USA) 115) **80** [2015 80: 6d 7m² t7.1g³ 6m³ t7.1m Sep 25] fairly useful maiden: stays 7f: acts on good to firm going: tried in visor in 2015. *Roger Varian*

TROPICS (USA) 7 ch.g. Speightstown (USA) 124 – Taj Aire (USA) (Taj Alriyadh **123** (USA)) [2015 121: 6m* 6f 6f² 6m⁵ Aug 1] strong gelding: very smart performer: won listed race at Windsor in June by ½ length from Lucky Kristale: excellent second in July Cup at Newmarket, caught on line and beaten a nose by Muhaarar: ran well under top-weight (off a mark of 113) when 1½ lengths fifth of 27 to Magical Memory in Stewards' Cup (Handicap) at Goodwood final start, travelling well and leading over 1f out: has won at 7f, best at 6f: acts on polytrack, firm and good to soft going: wears hood. *Dean Ivory*

TROY BOY 5 b.g. Choisir (AUS) 126 – Love Thing 68 (Phountzi (USA) 104) [2015 56: **–** t8.6f 10d⁶ 11.1m Jun 10] modest maiden: out of sorts in 2015: stays 1¼m: acts on polytrack, soft and good to firm going: has worn cheekpieces, including last 3 starts: front runner/ races prominently, usually finds little. *Rebecca Bastiman*

TRUCANINI 5 b.m. Mount Nelson 125 – Jalissa 83 (Mister Baileys 123) [2015 86: 7m* **87** 7g p7g² 7m p7g p7d² Nov 30] strong mare: fairly useful handicapper: won at Newbury in **a94** July: good second at Kempton in September and November: stays 1m: acts on polytrack and firm going: often races towards rear. *Chris Wall*

TRUE COURSE 3 b.f. Dubawi (IRE) 129 – Sugar Free (IRE) 104 (Oasis Dream 129) **63** [2015 57, a72: p6m Jan 24] only modest: best at 5f: acts on tapeta. *Charlie Appleby*

TRUE PLEASURE (IRE) 8 b.m. Choisir (AUS) 126 – Absolute Pleasure 52 (Polar **82** Falcon (USA) 126) [2015 85, a74: p8f f8s⁶ 7d* 8.5m* 8m³ 7s² 8d⁴ 7m² 7.1m⁵ 7.6m⁴ 7.9d⁶ 7.5g⁶ 7.5d⁴ 7v Oct 17] fairly useful handicapper: won at Catterick and Beverley in April:

has won at 9.5f, usually races over shorter: acts on polytrack, soft and good to firm going: usually races towards rear. *James Bethell*

TRUE SOLITAIRE (IRE) 2 b.c. Oasis Dream 129 – Majestic Silver (IRE) (Linamix **104** (FR) 127) [2015 8m² 7d* 8d² 8d² Sep 27] third foal: half-brother to smart 9f/1¼m winner (stays 1½m) Carla Bianca (by Dansili) and useful 7f winner Joailliere (by Dubawi): dam unraced half-sister to 1¼m-1¾m winner (stayed 2m) Profound Beauty and 7f-1¼m winner Rock Critic (both smart): useful form: won maiden at Galway in July: good second after, in Willis Champions Juvenile Stakes at Leopardstown (beaten 1½ lengths by Johannes Vermeer) and Beresford Stakes at the Curragh (beaten short head by Port Douglas): will stay 1¼m. *D. K. Weld, Ireland*

TRUE SPIRIT 5 b.g. Shamardal (USA) 129 – Petonellajill 73 (Petong 126) [2015 62: – t7.1f p7g Dec 10] fair at best, no form in 2015: left Paul d'Arcy after first start: stays 7f: acts on polytrack: tried in headgear: tried in tongue tie. *Heather Dalton*

TRUE STORY 4 b.g. Manduro (GER) 135 – Tanzania (USA) (Darshaan 133) [2015 120: **118** 8.9g* 8.9g² 12g⁴ 12g Mar 28] rangy gelding: smart performer: looked more straightforward when winning listed race at Meydan in January by 3¼ lengths from Mushreq, quickening clear 2f out: in frame next 2 starts, in Al Rashidiya (2 lengths second to Vercingetorix, carrying head awkwardly) and Dubai City of Gold (fourth to Sky Hunter): last of 9 behind Dolniya in Dubai Sheema Classic there final outing: best form at 9f/1¼m: acts on firm and good to soft going: visored/in cheekpieces nowadays. *Saeed bin Suroor*

TRULEE SCRUMPTIOUS 6 b.m. Strategic Prince 114 – Morning Rise (GER) **73** (Acatenango (GER) 127) [2015 73: 10g⁶ 10m² 10.1m⁵ 10m* 10d⁵ 10m⁶ 9.9s⁵ p8f Sep 24] lengthy, angular mare: fair handicapper: won at Newmarket in July: stays 1¼m: acts on soft and good to firm going: wears headgear: front runner/races prominently. *Peter Charalambous*

TRULOVE 2 b.f. (Mar 29) Piccolo 121 – Snow Dancer (IRE) 88 (Desert Style (IRE) 121) – [2015 t5.1f t6f Dec 22] first foal: dam 1m-1½m winner: no form. *John David Riches*

TRUST ME BOY 7 gr.g. Avonbridge 123 – Eastern Lyric 93 (Petong 126) [2015 54: f7g* **63** p8g f7g² f7g³ f7g⁵ f7d⁵ f7s* 7.6s⁴ 7s f8g⁴ f8g Nov 26] compact gelding: modest handicapper: won at Southwell in January and August: stays 7f: acts on fibresand, best turf form on soft/heavy going: has worn visor: often races prominently. *John E. Long*

TRUST THE MAN (IRE) 2 br.c. (May 17) Manduro (GER) 135 – Saree 95 (Barathea **63** (IRE) 127) [2015 7m 7s³ 8g p7g Nov 18] stocky colt: modest maiden: will be suited by 1m: tried in blinkers. *Roger Teal*

TRUTH OR DARE 4 b.g. Invincible Spirit (IRE) 121 – Unreachable Star 81 (Halling **80** (USA) 133) [2015 103: 8d⁶ Sep 4] well-made gelding: useful performer at best, well held only outing in 2015: stays 1½m: acts on good to firm going. *William Muir*

TRYSTER (IRE) 4 b.g. Shamardal (USA) 129 – Min Alhawa (USA) 108 (Riverman **?** (USA) 131) [2015 92: p10g* t9.5g* p10f* p10g* p10f* 10m⁵ p9.2m* Sep 26] **a123**

The days of Mark of Esteem, Halling, Swain, Daylami, Dubai Millennium, Fantastic Light and Sakhee now seem a long time ago for those who have followed Godolphin since its inception. Godolphin's first period of pre-eminence was founded on quality—Saeed bin Suroor operated originally with a string of forty or fifty—but in the last decade it has owed its position among Britain's leading owners to quantity. Godolphin's expanding string in Britain now spreads beyond the in-house operations of Saeed bin Suroor and Charlie Appleby in Newmarket, a situation influenced by a change in policy with the promising stock sourced from other owners, such recruits no longer transferred from their original trainers into the two Newmarket yards. John Gosden, Richard Hannon, Richard Fahey and Roger Varian were among those who continued to train headline horses purchased from their yards by Godolphin, while the 'academy' run by Mark Johnston was also given a higher profile in the latest season (the stable's Coventry Stakes winner Buratino ran in the Godolphin colours and, along with the Sheikh Hamdan bin Mohammed-owned Cheveley Park winner Lumiere, will stay with Johnston).

The sheer weight of winners, rather than the proceeds of big-race wins, ensures Godolphin's place at or near the top of the owners' table these days. Three hundred and seventy individual horses ran for Godolphin in Britain in the latest calendar year, with the royal blue silks carried on no fewer than 1,194 occasions and entering the winner's enclosure on 287 of those occasions, a ratio of wins to runs of nearly one in four. Godolphin had its successes in some of the top races—Night

Coral Easter Classic All-Weather Middle Distance Championships Conditions Stakes, Lingfield—Tryster shows his trademark turn of foot to land the most valuable event on the second All-Weather Championships Finals Day (televised this time); Complicit and Grendisar (cheekpieces)—who were in the frame behind Tryster in the Group 3 Winter Derby the previous month—finish second and third

of Thunder won the Lockinge, Irish-trained Pleascach the Yorkshire Oaks and there were Guineas seconds with Territories and Lucida and a Derby second with Jack Hobbs (who went on to win the Irish Derby)—but Saeed bin Suroor and Charlie Appleby couldn't muster a Group 1 win between them in Britain (or anywhere in Europe for that matter).

Godolphin's tenth British owners' championship must have been a source of satisfaction for its joint-founder Sheikh Mohammed, especially as it was achieved with record first-three prize money of £5,217,268, but the meagre European pattern-race tally of its two private yards over the past couple of years has had to be addressed by the appointment of the Sheikh's bloodstock adviser John Ferguson as Godolphin's chief executive. Ferguson's aim is to continue to restore the stable's reputation, tainted by the steroids scandal of 2013, and to 'ensure that Godolphin continues to represent excellence.' In that regard, Ferguson might consider himself fortunate that he is assuming his new role at a time when Darley's European stallion roster [Darley is being merged with the racing operation] finally has plenty of strength in depth, meaning that Godolphin's trainers should have no shortage of good raw material at their disposal in the coming years. Whether Ferguson can re-establish Godolphin as a real threat on the big stage to its old rival Ballydoyle/Coolmore will be the acid test.

Most of the Godolphin horses at Moulton Paddocks remained at Newmarket over the winter before the latest season, instead of being shipped to Dubai, and, although Charlie Appleby commuted weekly, he had significantly fewer runners at the Dubai Carnival than Saeed bin Suroor (for whom Prince Bishop won the World Cup). Appleby's superb start to the year on the all-weather in Britain looked at the time as if it might spark a revival in Godolphin's fortunes in the big races during the turf season. Moulton Paddocks dominated the all-weather scene through the winter and landed three of the seven finals (each worth at least £150,000) on the richly-endowed Finals Day at Lingfield on Good Friday, with two of the winners, the very smart pair Tryster and Pretend, initially earmarked for Royal Ascot targets, Pretend for the King's Stand and Tryster for the Prince of Wales's Stakes. However, both ran below expectations when switched to turf. All-weather meetings account for roughly a third of the Flat fixtures in Britain and, in a year when the jumps course Wetherby staged its first Flat turf meetings, another northern track Newcastle ripped up its turf course to provide a new venue offering floodlit all-weather racing in 2016.

The All-Weather Championships, which had £1.1m in prize money for Finals Day which attracted a course-record crowd of over 9,000 to Lingfield, shows what can be done.

Tryster's improvement for the switch to synthetic surfaces was dramatic and his dazzling turn of foot made him the undisputed star of the winter all-weather season. Already gelded when making his racecourse debut as a three-year-old, Tryster won a Brighton maiden over a mile and a quarter on the second of three outings on turf that year, when he was not seen out after July. He made his all-weather debut in January in a handicap at Chelmsford—in the first race to be run at the re-opened course formerly known as Great Leighs—but he nearly threw the race away when jinking badly left after hitting the front and just scrambled home. In a change of tactics, he was covered up for as long as possible at Wolverhampton in February before leading in the final hundred yards for a cosy win. Completing his hat-trick in similar style at Kempton in early-March, Tryster stepped out of handicap company to take on a strong field in the coral.co.uk Winter Derby at Lingfield ten days later. In what was by now becoming his trademark style, Tryster quickened sharply to come from second last and hit the front only in the last fifty yards, winning with something to spare from the reliable Big Easy, Grandeur and Complicit.

Tryster started at 2/1-on in the Coral Easter Classic All-Weather Middle Distance Championships, back at Lingfield on Good Friday (early-April, three weeks earlier than the previous year). He completed his five-timer with the kind of performance rarely seen on the all-weather, still six lengths behind the leaders approaching the final furlong before cutting them down with a potent show of finishing speed. Tryster won most impressively by three quarters of a length and a length and a quarter from Complicit and Grendisar, looking a high-class performer in the making. Unfortunately, Tryster finished last of five in the Brigadier Gerard Stakes at Sandown in May on his return to turf and plans for a summer campaign in Britain were shelved (though a possible tilt at the Arlington Million was mentioned). Tryster eventually reappeared at the end of September, maintaining his unbeaten record on synthetic surfaces in a minor event at Chelmsford (leading close home). That outing was said to be part of his preparation for a winter campaign in Dubai.

The well-made Tryster is by the good Darley stallion Shamardal out of the useful mile and a quarter winner Min Alhawa, who was twice placed in listed company for Sheikh Hamdan. Shadwell bred Min Alhawa, a half-sister to Sheikh Hamdan's One Thousand Guineas winner Harayir out of a daughter of the Irish Oaks winner Give Thanks, but she was weeded out at the Keeneland November Sale in 2006 and Tryster, her final foal, was a product of Herbertstown House Stud in Ireland which paid 42,000 dollars for her. Min Alhawa bred a couple of smart middle-distance winners, Ajhar (by Diesis) and Mutasallil (by Gone West), for Sheikh Hamdan before she was sold. Tryster stays a mile and a quarter and acts on polytrack, tapeta and good to firm going. He has been tried in cheekpieces (including on his final start in 2015). He has a fine turn of foot and is best when exaggerated waiting tactics are employed. *Charlie Appleby*

TSARGLAS 4 gr.g. Verglas (IRE) 118 – Russian Empress (IRE) 101 (Trans Island 119) **60**
[2015 59: t7.1f* p7m² p8g t7.1f* 7.2g t7.1f f8g p8g f7m⁵ f8g f11g Dec 29] modest handicapper: won at Wolverhampton in January and March: left Stuart Williams after: stays 1m: acts on polytrack and tapeta: wears headgear: usually in tongue tie. *Colin Teague*

TSEO 3 ch.g. Mount Nelson 125 – Pasithea (IRE) 101 (Celtic Swing 138) [2015 p10m⁶ **61**
p10g³ Dec 9] half-brother to 3 winners, including smart 1m-10.4f winner Educate (by Echo of Light) and 10.4f winner Hippolytus (by Observatory): dam, winner up to 1½m (2-y-o 7.4f winner), half-sister to high-class 6f/7f performer Somnus: better effort when third of 7 in maiden at Lingfield. *David Brown*

TTAINTED LOVE 3 b.f. Mastercraftsman (IRE) 129 – Eve 81 (Rainbow Quest (USA) **81**
134) [2015 10m 10g 10.3m⁶ 10g² p12g t9.5m² 10s⁵ Oct 13] 35,000Y: good-topped filly:
half-sister to several winners, including smart 7f-1½m winner Charm School (by Dubai
Destination) and useful 1m-1¼m winner Dubai Twilight (by Alhaarth): dam 1m winner:
fairly useful maiden: stays 1¼m: acts on tapeta. *Chris Wall*

TUCO (IRE) 3 ch.g. Exceed And Excel (AUS) 126 – Life Rely (USA) (Maria's Mon **97**
(USA) 121) [2015 70p: p7m² p7g² 7m³ 8m* p8g² 9f⁴ Dec 26] useful performer: won
maiden in August: in frame all other starts, in handicap at Lingfield (1¼ lengths
second to Hannington, left Jamie Osborne after) and optional claimer at Santa Anita on last
2 occasions: probably stays 9f: acts on polytrack and good to firm going. *Doug F. O'Neill,
USA*

TUKHOOM (IRE) 2 b.g. (Feb 16) Acclamation 118 – Carioca (IRE) 107 (Rakti 130) **– p**
[2015 8s Sep 18] 100,000Y: second foal: half-brother to smart winner up to 1m Tupi (2-y-o
7f winner, by Tamayuz): dam 1m winner: 20/1, 10½ lengths last of 8 to Stormy Antarctic
in minor event at Newbury, not unduly punished when dropping away 2f out: should do
better. *Marcus Tregoning*

TUKITINYASOK (IRE) 8 b.g. Fath (USA) 116 – Mevlana (IRE) (Red Sunset 120) **57**
[2015 67, a61: t9.5g² t9.5g⁵ 9.9m³ 8.5g 9.9m⁶ 9.9g t9.5f⁵ Oct 27] workmanlike gelding:
modest handicapper: stays 1¼m: acts on polytrack, tapeta, soft and good to firm going:
wears headgear: front runner/races prominently. *Clive Mulhall*

TULIP DRESS 2 ch.f. (Mar 29) Dutch Art 126 – White Dress (IRE) (Pivotal 124) [2015 **57**
5m⁶ 5g⁴ 6m 7d p7g Sep 23] third foal: half-sister to useful 2-y-o 1m winner (stays 1¼m)
Snoano (by Nayef): dam unraced half-sister to smart French winner up to 1¼m Sparkling
Beam: modest maiden: best effort at 5f. *Anthony Carson*

TULLIUS (IRE) 7 ch.g. Le Vie dei Colori 126 – Whipped Queen (USA) (Kingmambo **117**
(USA) 125) [2015 124: 8d* 10d⁴ 8.5g⁴ 10m⁵ 10.4m* 8g⁵ 10d 9.9g⁶ Nov 8] good-topped
gelding: smart performer: won listed race at Doncaster (by ½ length from Glory Awaits) in
March and York Stakes at York (by ½ length from Top Notch Tonto) in July: creditable
seventh of 13 to Fascinating Rock in Champion Stakes at Ascot penultimate start: stays
10.5f: acts on polytrack, good to firm and heavy going: often races towards rear.
Andrew Balding

*Sky Bet York Stakes, York—Tullius (noseband) bounces back to form to beat Top Notch Tonto and
Prince Gibraltar (No.4) and land the third pattern race of his career*

TUMBAGA (USA) 4 b.c. E Dubai (USA) 124 – Brushed Gold (USA) (Touch Gold (USA) 127) [2015 p7g* p8g* a9.9g² Sep 5] first foal: dam, US 1m/8.5f winner (including at 2 yrs), half-sister to smart US Grade 2 8.5f winner Skylighter: left Eoin Harty, USA, much improved and won maiden at Kempton (by 1½ lengths from Tuco) in May and handicap at Chelmsford (by 7 lengths from Bint Dandy) in June: upped in trip, creditable second in Anatolia Trophy at Veliefendi (2 lengths behind Tha'ir) final start: stays 1¼m: acts on polytrack. *Saeed bin Suroor* **111**

TUMBLEWIND 5 ch.m. Captain Rio 122 – African Breeze 79 (Atraf 116) [2015 96: 6v⁵ 6.1g³ 6g³ 6d⁴ Jul 7] fairly useful handicapper: stays 6f: acts on firm and soft going. *Richard Whitaker* **87**

TUNNEL CREEK 3 b.g. Tobougg (IRE) 125 – Free Offer 94 (Generous (IRE) 139) [2015 71p: 7m⁵ 8.3g* 10d⁴ 8.3d 8.3d Oct 5] good-topped gelding: fairly useful performer: won maiden at Windsor in June: stays 1¼m: acts on good to firm and good to soft going. *Henry Candy* **81**

TUOLUMNE MEADOWS 2 b.f. (Jun 5) High Chaparral (IRE) 132 – Seren Devious (Dr Devious (IRE) 127) [2015 p8g³ 8v Oct 24] sister to useful 1½m winner Tioga Pass and half-sister to 3 winners, including smart winner up to 1¼m Circumvent (2-y-o 6f-1m winner, by Tobougg): dam unraced: better effort when third in maiden at Kempton (1½ lengths behind Nessita) in October: will stay at least 1¼m. *Paul Cole* **75**

TUPI (IRE) 3 b.c. Tamayuz 126 – Carioca (IRE) 107 (Rakti 130) [2015 101: 7m² 7f* 7f⁴ 8m* 7g 7d 8g⁴ 7g⁴ Oct 3] strong, useful-looking colt: smart performer: won listed races at Newmarket in May (by ½ length from Latharnach) and July (by 2¾ lengths from Bartel): creditable fourth of 16 to Dutch Connection in Jersey Stakes at Royal Ascot in between: stays 1m: acts on firm going. *Richard Hannon* **114**

TURAATHY (IRE) 2 b.f. (Mar 5) Lilbourne Lad (IRE) 111 – Key Girl (IRE) 48 (Key of Luck (USA) 126) [2015 6m⁶ 7m⁶ 8d Sep 4] £65,000Y: fifth foal: closely related to smart 2-y-o 6f/7f winner Music Theory (by Acclamation): dam maiden half-sister to smart performers Rolo Tomasi (up to 7f in Scandinavia) and Eastern Breeze (up to 1½m): fair maiden: should stay 1m. *Charles Hills* **66**

TURBINE (IRE) 2 b.c. (Mar 22) Cape Cross (IRE) 129 – Chiquita Linda (IRE) (Mujadil (USA) 119) [2015 t7.1f* p7m⁴ Nov 21] €68,000F: half-brother to several winners, including useful winner up to 7f Fiefdom (2-y-o 6f winner, by Singspiel) and 2-y-o 5f winner Puskas (by King's Best): dam Italian winner up to 6f (2-y-o 5.5f winner): won maiden at Wolverhampton in November by 3¼ lengths from Tailwind: well-backed 11/4, still green when 3 lengths fourth of 6 in minor event at Lingfield: remains open to improvement. *Mark Johnston* **92 p**

TURBO CHARGED (IRE) 3 b.g. Jeremy (USA) 122 – House Rebel (IRE) 78 (Spartacus (IRE) 107) [2015 p6f⁶ Nov 6] 25/1, very green when last of 6 in maiden at Chelmsford: unplaced in bumper: dead. *Bill Turner* **–**

TURFDONNA (GER) 3 b.f. Doyen (IRE) 132 – Turfaue (GER) (Big Shuffle (USA) 122) [2015 8.9g* 9.9g⁵ 10.9g³ 10.9g* Aug 2] half-sister to several winners in Germany, including 9f/1¼m winner Turflowe (by Lando) and winner up to 10.5f Turfflamme (2-y-o 7f winner, by Lomitas): dam unraced sister to smart Italian/French performer up to 12.5f Turfrose: smart performer: won minor event at Hoppegarten (by 4 lengths) in April and Preis der Diana at Dusseldorf (further improvement when beating Nightflower ¾ length) in August: stays 11f: raced only on good ground: reportedly suffered minor injury after, then sold privately for stud in Japan. *A. Wohler, Germany* **111**

TURNBURY 4 b.g. Azamour (IRE) 130 – Scottish Heights (IRE) (Selkirk (USA) 129) [2015 72: p10g³ 11.6m p8f⁶ p12m 10m 10g² 10m⁶ 10.1g⁵ p12g* p13f⁵ p12m⁶ p10m* Dec 16] sturdy gelding: fair performer: won claimer at Lingfield in September and seller there in December: left Robert Mills after first start: stays 1½m: acts on polytrack, tapeta and heavy going: sometimes in headgear/tongue tie: front runner. *Laura Mongan* **68**

TURNING THE TABLE (IRE) 2 gr.f. (Apr 16) Mastercraftsman (IRE) 129 – Duchess Dee (IRE) (Bachelor Duke (USA) 122) [2015 8.1v⁴ 7s³ Sep 18] first foal: dam unraced half-sister to smart performer up to 1¾m I'm Supposin: created good impression when winning 5-runner maiden at Chepstow in August by 4 lengths from Rosamaria: only 9¾ lengths third of 5 to Nathra in minor event at Newbury next time, unsuited by drop in trip and still seeming green: remains with potential. *David Simcock* **86 p**

TURNING TIMES (IRE) 3 ro.f. Pivotal 124 – Antiquities 106 (Kaldounevees (FR) 118) [2015 83: p8m³ f8d⁴ Jan 22] fairly useful handicapper: should stay 1¼m: acts on polytrack, raced only on good going on turf: sometimes slowly away, usually races close up. *Charlie Appleby* **80**

TURN ON THE TEARS (USA) 2 ch.f. (Apr 6) Cape Blanco (IRE) 130 – Down The **72**
Well (IRE) 82 (Mujadil (USA) 119) [2015 p6f² t7.1f* Nov 20] $20,000Y: first foal: dam
2-y-o 5f winner: upped in trip, much sharper when winning maiden at Wolverhampton by
1¼ lengths from Theos Lolly, well positioned. *Jamie Osborne*

TURN TIDE 2 ch.c. (Apr 18) Medicean 128 – Quadri (Polish Precedent (USA) 131) [2015 **91**
7g* 7d⁴ 7g² 8g* Aug 31] brother to a winner in Italy, closely related to winner up to 1¼m
Bright Flash (2-y-o 7f winner, by Dutch Art) and half-brother to 2 winners, including 2-y-o
5f winner (stayed 7.5f) Quinine (by Dark Angel): dam unraced half-sister to useful
1m-1¼m winner Fashionable: fairly useful performer: won maiden at Lingfield in June and
nursery at Newcastle (by 1¼ lengths from King's Pavilion) in August: stays 1m.
David Brown

TURPINTINA 2 b.f. (Mar 21) Dick Turpin (IRE) 127 – Cashmere 86 (Barathea (IRE) **–**
127) [2015 5m May 25] £1,000Y: half-sister to 2-y-o 7f winner Stet And Stelio (by
Bertolini): dam, 7f/7.4f winner, half-sister to Irish 1000 Guineas winner Classic Park,
herself dam of Derby runner-up Walk In The Park: 20/1, well held in maiden at Redcar.
Michael Easterby

TURRET ROCKS (IRE) 2 b.f. (Apr 8) Fastnet Rock (AUS) 127 – Beyond Compare **108**
(IRE) 76 (Galileo (IRE) 134) [2015 8m* 7g³ 7g⁴ 8m* 8m² Oct 4] smallish, strong, well-
made filly: fourth foal: half-sister to useful winner up to 11f (including in Australia)
Beyond Thankful (2-y-o 7f winner, by Whipper) and 1¼m winner Vintage Charm (by
Vocalised): dam maiden (stayed 1½m): useful performer: won maiden at Gowran in June
and May Hill Stakes at Doncaster (by ¾ length from Marenko) in September: improved
again when 1¼ lengths second of 8 to Ballydoyle in Prix Marcel Boussac at Longchamp,
sticking to task: will be suited by 1¼m+: acts on good to firm going: in hood first 3 starts:
front runner/races prominently. *J. S. Bolger, Ireland*

TURTLEPLEX 4 b.f. Multiplex 114 – Turtle Bay 64 (Dr Fong (USA) 128) [2015 12g⁶ **–**
Sep 26] third foal: dam maiden (probably stayed 9f): 50/1, well held in maiden at Ripon.
Ann Duffield

TUSCAN GOLD 8 ch.g. Medicean 128 – Louella (USA) (El Gran Senor (USA) 136) **77**
[2015 18s² 21.6g³ 16v* 16d² 17.1g* 18g⁶ 17.1d 18d 18s⁶ Oct 19] well-made gelding: fair
handicapper: won at Ripon in May (awarded race) and Pontefract in June: stays 21.5f: acts
on polytrack, good to firm and heavy going: often starts slowly. *Micky Hammond*

TUTILL 2 ch.f. (Apr 10) Piccolo 121 – Willisa 67 (Polar Falcon (USA) 126) [2015 5m 5.1g **45**
6m 5d³ 6m⁵ t5.1m⁴ 6g t6f⁵ Oct 23] 2,000F, £10,000Y: half-sister to several winners,
including useful 5f and (including at 2 yrs) 6f winner Oil Strike (by Lucky Story) and 6f-
1m winner Polar Annie (2-y-o 7f winner, by Fraam): dam 7f winner: poor maiden: tried in
blinkers: sold 4,000 gns, sent to Italy. *Michael Easterby*

*1stsecuritysolutions.co.uk May Hill Stakes, Doncaster—a second May Hill winner in a row for
Ireland as Turret Rocks relishes the return to a mile and beats Marenko (right) and Opal Tiara (left)*

Mrs J. S. Bolger/John Corcoran's "Turret Rocks"

TUTTI FRUTTI 3 b.f. Teofilo (IRE) 126 – Soft Centre 109 (Zafonic (USA) 130) [2015 **74** 69p: 9.9d³ 11.8m² p12g⁴ Jul 1] fair form in maidens: stays 1½m. *John Gosden*

TUTU NGURU (USA) 2 b.f. (Mar 16) Blame (USA) 129 – Haka Girl (USA) (War Chant **95** (USA) 126) [2015 p6g* 6f 6f* 6g² p6g⁴ 7g⁴ Oct 9] $175,000Y: quite attractive filly: fourth foal: half-sister to winners in USA by Curlin and Mr Greeley: dam, US 1m winner (including at 2 yrs), half-sister to smart US Grade 2 1m/8.5f winner Gotta Have Her: useful performer: won maiden at Lingfield in May and minor event at Doncaster (by neck from Human Nature) in July: creditable efforts after, including when ¾-length second of 20 to Holy Grail in nursery and 2¾ lengths fourth of 12 to First Victory in Oh So Sharp Stakes, both at Newmarket: stays 7f: acts on polytrack and firm going: sometimes slowly away, often travels strongly. *William Haggas*

TWEETHEART 2 ch.f. (Mar 9) Dutch Art 126 – Strictly (USA) (Fusaichi Pegasus (USA) **54** 130) [2015 6g⁶ 6m p6g⁶ Aug 17] 25,000F, 24,000Y: first foal: dam US 1m winner out of US Grade 2 7f winner Dancing: modest form in maidens: blinkered final start. *Marco Botti*

TWEETY PIE (IRE) 4 ch.f. Rock of Gibraltar (IRE) 133 – Princesse Sonia (FR) **74** (Ashkalani (IRE) 128) [2015 76: 5g² 5g⁶ 5m³ 5f⁴ 5m⁴ 6g 7m 5m² 5g³ t6f Oct 17] fair handicapper: stays 5.5f: acts on firm going: tried in blinkers: sometimes slowly away. *Declan Carroll*

TWENTY ONE CHOICE (IRE) 6 ch.g. Choisir (AUS) 126 – Midnight Lace 74 **80** (Tomba 119) [2015 88, a80: 7g 7.1m² 7.6g³ 8.3m 7.4d⁶ 7.4v⁴ p7g* p8f⁴ Oct 10] good-topped gelding: fairly useful handicapper: won at Kempton in September: stays 1m: acts on polytrack and good to firm going: often races towards rear. *Ed de Giles*

1053

TWENTYSVNTHLANCERS 2 b.g. (Mar 13) Hellvelyn 118 – Subtle Move (USA) 60 **73 p**
(Known Fact (USA) 135) [2015 5m⁵ 5s³ 5m² 5m* Sep 8] 800F: sixth foal: half-brother to
a winner in Italy Antonius Pius: dam, maiden (third at 6f), half-sister to smart 6f/7f winner
Demonstrate: fair form: value for extra when winning maiden at Redcar by ½ length from
Bahamian Bird: raced only at 5f: remains open to improvement. *Paul Midgley*

TWICE CERTAIN (IRE) 3 b.f. Lawman (FR) 121 – Leopard Hunt (USA) 89 (Diesis **77**
133) [2015 75p: t9.5m⁶ 10.2s² 10.4d May 30] fair handicapper: stays 1¼m: acts on
polytrack, tapeta and soft going. *Ed Walker*

TWILIGHT ANGEL 7 ch.m. Compton Place 125 – Leaping Flame (USA) (Trempolino **40**
(USA) 135) [2015 53: f5d p6f⁵ p7g Jan 28] poor maiden: stays 5.5f: acts on fibresand,
raced only on good going on turf: in hood in 2015. *Pat Eddery*

TWILIGHT SON 3 b.c. Kyllachy 129 – Twilight Mistress 84 (Bin Ajwaad (IRE) **125**
119) [2015 90p: 6m* 6g* 6d* 6d² Oct 17]

The 2015 season was highly successful for all those involved at Kingston
Warren, the yard of veteran trainer Henry Candy. Kingston Warren's haul of four
pattern races in 2015 was the most for the yard in one season since 2002, when
Kyllachy landed a hat-trick of pattern wins—including the Nunthorpe—and
Airwave won the Cheveley Park Stakes. The yard won just over £900,000 in prize
money in the latest season, surpassing the previous best total—set the year before—
by over £350,000. Three-year-olds Twilight Son (a son of Kyllachy) and Limato
were the yard's two biggest earners in 2015. Limato landed two pattern races from
five starts, and also twice finished second at Group 1 level, but Twilight Son fared
even better, winning on three of his four outings as he progressed rapidly into one
of the top sprinters, making a remarkable debut at pattern level when successful
in the Group 1 Sprint Cup in September. Twilight Son was Candy's second Sprint
Cup winner following Markab in 2010, and he also saddled Twilight Son's half-
brother Music Master to finish third for the same connections in the 2014 renewal.
As mentioned in the entry on Limato, the yard can be confident of having another
good campaign in 2016 with both Twilight Son and Limato set to stay in training.

Whilst the success of Limato in the latest season was hardly a surprise—he
had ended 2014 as Timeform's joint-highest rated juvenile—the rapid strides made
by Twilight Son were a little harder to envisage. Twilight Son had, though, made a
good impression when winning both his races at two, a maiden at Salisbury (where
he beat Desert Force) and a nursery at Thirsk, which earned him the tailpiece 'useful
prospect' at the end of his commentary in *Racehorses of 2014*. Twilight Son started
the latest season with a success in a three-year-old sprint handicap on Two Thousand
Guineas day at Newmarket. Desert Force was again runner-up, beaten comfortably

*888sport Charity Sprint, York—Twilight Son is a clear-cut winner of this competitive three-year-old
handicap, the most valuable event on Macmillan Charity Day, Britain's biggest charity race day;
Grandad's World (check cap) holds on for second after making the running, with
Magical Memory (armlets) and the lighter grey Northgate Lad the others to make the frame*

*Betfred Sprint Cup, Haydock—a second Sprint Cup for trainer Henry Candy
as Twilight Son (centre) maintains his unbeaten record on his first run at pattern level;
outsider Strath Burn (second left) is denied by a short head in second, with Magical Memory
(armlets) third and the 2014 winner G Force (left) fourth*

by two lengths, with a further length and a quarter back to the third, Magical Memory. That proved to be very strong form, Twilight Son doing his own bit to advertise it when following up in the valuable handicap for three-year-old sprinters on the Macmillan Charity Day at York in mid-June. The £100,000 handicap (sponsored by 888Sport in the latest season) is the feature event on Britain's biggest charity race day, which was inaugurated in 1971 and was organised by Timeform for the best part of four decades. Twilight Son looked better than a handicapper as he comfortably shrugged off a 9 lb rise for his win at Newmarket, travelling fluently from the start, and keeping going well after being produced to lead entering the final furlong. He won by a length and a half from Grandad's World, with Magical Memory, who had won at Leicester since Newmarket, finishing third, beaten a further three quarters of a length. The paths of winner and third were to cross again later in the season as both went on to make their mark in pattern company.

Having missed the summer, including an intended engagement at Deauville in late-August, Twilight Son lined up as a 10/1-shot in the Betfred Sprint Cup, now the fourth of five Group 1s in the domestic calendar for the top six-furlong performers aged three and above (though no horse can run in all five, as the Commonwealth Cup is for three-year-olds only and three-year-olds cannot run in the Diamond Jubilee Stakes). Limato had also been set to run in the Sprint Cup but he wasn't among the final declared field, after rain left conditions on the soft side of good. Adaay, who had beaten Limato in the Sandy Lane Stakes over the Sprint Cup course and distance earlier in the season, and Gordon Lord Byron, who hadn't finished out of the first two in the three previous renewals (won in 2013), were sent off joint favourites at 9/2. The 6/1-shot Danzeno and three-year-old Mattmu (7/1), who had been successful in the Phoenix Sprint Stakes at the Curragh and third in the Nunthorpe on his two previous starts, were the others at single-figure odds in what looked a very open renewal. The July Cup winner Muhaarar was a notable absentee but his trainer Charlie Hills still fielded two runners in three-year-olds Strath Burn (33/1) and Magical Memory, the latter sent off at 14/1 after landing two handicaps since his third to Twilight Son at York, notably the Stewards' Cup. The three-year-olds were very well represented with just over half of the fifteen runners, and they dominated the finish, with Twilight Son beating Strath Burn and Magical Memory in a close finish. Travelling strongly in touch, Twilight Son went on over a furlong out but had to dig deep to see off the challenge of Magical Memory well inside the final furlong, having just enough left to hold on by a short head as Strath Burn finished strongly down the outside. Magical Memory came three quarters of a length further back, with the first three pulling nearly three lengths clear of the fourth, the previous year's winner G Force. Twilight Son's unblemished record came to an end on his only subsequent run of the year when he finished two lengths second to champion sprinter Muhaarar in the British Champions Sprint Stakes at Ascot.

Twilight Son beat the rest convincingly, finishing a length and a half ahead of third-placed Danzeno, and he lost little in defeat, the form on a par with that which he achieved at Haydock. Incidentally, Ryan Moore replaced Twilight Son's regular rider Fergus Sweeney at Ascot at the request of Cheveley Park Stud, who bought a majority share in the colt after his success at York ('We have an agreement with him [Ryan Moore] over the years to ride for us when he can,' explained the stud's managing director Chris Richardson).

Twilight Son (b.c. 2012)	Kyllachy (b 1998)	Pivotal (ch 1993)	Polar Falcon, Fearless Revival
		Pretty Poppy (b 1988)	Song, Moonlight Serenade
	Twilight Mistress (b 1998)	Bin Ajwaad (b 1990)	Rainbow Quest, Salidar
		By Candlelight (b 1991)	Roi Danzig, Penny Candle

Bred by his original owner Godfrey Wilson, who retains a part share in the colt, Twilight Son is the third Group 1 winner by his sire Kyllachy following Sole Power and Krypton Factor in Dubai. Twilight Son's dam, the Bin Ajwaad mare Twilight Mistress, was a fairly useful sprint handicapper for David Arbuthnot, winning three races during her four seasons on the track, and she has met with notable success at stud, producing six winners from as many foals to race, Twilight Son being the latest, and the most notable other than him being his two half-brothers by Piccolo (both trained by Henry Candy), the aforementioned Music Master, a very smart Group 3 winner over six furlongs who has finished fourth in the last two renewals of the Diamond Jubilee, and the useful seven-furlong handicapper The

Mr Godfrey Wilson & Cheveley Park Stud's "Twilight Son"

Confessor. Given the propensity for speed in the family and the fact that his dam has only ever been mated with other sprinters, it is hardly surprising that none of Twilight Son's five siblings have won beyond seven furlongs, and he himself looks a sprinter purely and simply (raced only at six furlongs). Twilight Son will presumably join his sire Kyllachy on Cheveley Park's stallion roster once his racing days are over (the stud has a sizeable portfolio of speed-oriented stallions, as explained in the essay on Garswood in last year's *Racehorses*). With just six runs under his belt, there is every chance that the reliable Twilight Son can improve a little further as a four-year-old when he looks set, at this stage, to be a major contender in the top races over six furlongs, starting with the Diamond Jubilee Stakes at Royal Ascot. A well-made colt, the strong-travelling Twilight Son acts on good to firm and good to soft ground. *Henry Candy*

TWIN APPEAL (IRE) 4 b.g. Oratorio (IRE) 128 – Velvet Appeal (IRE) 101 (Petorius 117) [2015 92: 7.2g⁴ 7d* 7g 7m² 7d⁵ 6d f7g³ f7g⁵ Dec 22] useful handicapper: won at Doncaster (by length from George Cinq) in May: stays 7f: acts on fibresand, good to firm and good to soft going: wears blinkers: often races prominently. *David Barron* **97**

TWIN FALLS (IRE) 2 gr.f. (May 7) Zebedee 113 – It Takes Two (IRE) (Alzao (USA) 117) [2015 6m 6m² 6g 7g² p7m² p7g⁵ Dec 18] half-sister to several winners, including smart 5f and (including at 2 yrs) 6f winner Final Exam (by College Chapel) and 1¼m-13f winner Final Opinion (by King's Theatre): dam lightly raced: fairly useful maiden: stays 7f: acts on polytrack and good to firm going. *J. F. Levins, Ireland* **82**

TWINKLE TWINKLE 3 b.f. Exceed And Excel (AUS) 126 – Kalinova (IRE) (Red Ransom (USA)) [2015 –: t7.1f³ 6.9g t7.1g Jul 13] modest maiden: best effort at 7f: acts on tapeta: in hood first 2 starts of 2015. *Julie Camacho* **63**

TWIN POINT 4 br.g. Invincible Spirit (IRE) 121 – Gemini Joan (Montjeu (IRE) 137) [2015 85: t7.1m 7m⁵ 6g 6g⁶ 7m² 10.4m 7g p8m p6g⁵ Dec 16] tall, useful-looking gelding: fair handicapper: left Michael Herrington after eighth start: stays 7f: acts on polytrack and good to firm going: usually wears hood: often races towards rear. *Charlie Fellowes* **78**

TWIN SAILS 2 b.c. (Mar 25) Sir Percy 129 – Atwirl 67 (Pivotal 124) [2015 6.5m* 6m* 7g⁴ 7d⁴ 6.5m³ 6m³ 7g⁶ Oct 10] 25,000Y: angular colt: fifth foal: half-brother to 3 winners, including winner up to 11.5f Amistress (2-y-o 1m winner, by Kalanisi) and 1¼m winner Atwix (by Sakhee): dam 7f winner: useful performer: won maiden at Newbury and minor event at Salisbury first 2 starts, both in June: best effort when fourth of 8 to Galileo Gold in Vintage Stakes at Goodwood third start: stays 7f: acts on good to firm going: in tongue tie final start (out of depth). *Dean Ivory* **103**

TWIN TURBO (IRE) 3 b.g. Dark Angel (IRE) 113 – Scarlet O'Hara (IRE) 100 (Sadler's Wells (USA) 132) [2015 69: p6m² p5g* t5.1m⁶ p5g² 5g³ 5m⁶ Jun 8] lengthy gelding: fair performer: won maiden at Chelmsford in January: best form at 5f: acts on polytrack: in cheekpieces final start: sold 24,000 gns, sent to Macau. *Robert Cowell* **77**

TWISTAWAY (IRE) 3 b.f. Teofilo (IRE) 126 – River Mountain (Reset (AUS) 124) [2015 p8g⁵ Feb 7] 50,000Y: second foal: dam unraced half-sister to useful dam of 1000 Guineas winner Finsceal Beo: 8/1, very green when last of 5 to Zoella in maiden at Lingfield, very slowly away: should do better. *Charles Hills* **– p**

TWISTING HAY 2 b.c. (Jan 17) Cape Cross (IRE) 129 – Blaugrana (IRE) 76 (Exceed And Excel (AUS) 126) [2015 5d² 5m³ 6g⁵ May 17] 140,000F: first foal: dam, 6f winner, out of useful 1¼m-1½m winner Acts of Grace, herself half-sister to very smart sprinter Invincible Spirit: fair form: second of 6 to Gin In The Inn in maiden at Leicester in April: seemed unsuited by track at Ripon final start: should stay 6f: remains with potential. *Mark Johnston* **75 p**

TWITCH (IRE) 3 b.f. Azamour (IRE) 130 – Blinking (Marju (IRE) 127) [2015 66: 9.9d² 10m⁵ 10.2m³ 12m* 12d³ p11g³ 12g² 12m² p13g⁶ 12.4v³ Nov 20] unfurnished filly: useful performer: won maiden at Pontefract in July: good efforts in listed races last 2 starts, at Lingfield (3½ lengths sixth to Urban Castle) and Saint-Cloud (2½ lengths third to Sassella): stays 13f: acts on polytrack, heavy and good to firm going: in cheekpieces last 5 starts: front runner/races prominently. *Hugo Palmer* **96**

TWOBEELUCKY 2 b.g. (Mar 20) Tobougg (IRE) 125 – She's The Lady 64 (Unfuwain (USA) 131) [2015 8.3s² 8.3s² p8g³ Nov 27] third foal: dam, 1½m and bumper winner, half-sister to useful winner up to 11f I'm So Lucky: fairly useful form: 2¼ lengths third of 14 to Red Rannagh in maiden at Dundalk final start, carrying head awkwardly: will be suited by 1¼m+: has been gelded: should continue to progress. *Mark Johnston* **86 p**

TWO FOR TWO (IRE) 7 b.g. Danehill Dancer (IRE) 117 – D'Articleshore (IRE) **106** (Definite Article 121) [2015 108: 8m⁵ 8g⁵ 8m* 8m 8d Aug 20] close-coupled gelding: useful handicapper: won at Ayr (by length from Santefisio) in June: stays 9f: acts on soft and good to firm going: tried in cheekpieces. *David O'Meara*

TWO IN THE PINK (IRE) 5 gr.m. Clodovil (IRE) 116 – Secret Circle (Magic Ring **79** (IRE) 115) [2015 72: p8g* p12f p8g 7m* 7m⁵ 8g² 8f p7g⁶ 7.1g p8g p8g Oct 6] workmanlike **a72** mare: fair handicapper: won at Lingfield in January and Salisbury (amateur) in May: stays 1m: acts on polytrack and good to firm going: tried in headgear/tongue tie prior to 2015. *Ralph Smith*

TWO JABS 5 b.g. Teofilo (IRE) 126 – Red Bravo (USA) (Red Ransom (USA)) [2015 84: **90** t12.2f² 12.1m* 12.3v² 13.4g 12g 12.3g 12g³ 12d⁶ p12g* Nov 18] fairly useful handicapper: won at Mark Brisbourne/off 3 months, improved when also successful at Kempton in November by neck from Precision Five: stays 13.5f: acts on polytrack, tapeta, good to firm and heavy going. *Michael Appleby*

TWO MINDS (FR) 8 ch.g. Choisir (AUS) 126 – Dynamic Dream (USA) 87 (Dynaformer **65** (USA)) [2015 p8f³ p10g⁶ Jun 9] workmanlike gelding: fair handicapper: stays 1¼m: acts on polytrack. *Eugene Stanford*

TWO MOONS 5 b.g. Echo of Light 125 – Forever Loved 86 (Deploy 131) [2015 87: f7d² **87** p8g f7d* f7s⁵ 7d p8g⁵ 8.3s* p8g Nov 9] fairly useful handicapper: won at Southwell in March and Nottingham in October: left Brian Ellison after fifth start: stays 8.5f: acts on fibresand, soft and good to firm going. *Daniel Loughnane*

TWO SHADES OF GREY (IRE) 4 gr.g. Oratorio (IRE) 128 – Elitista (FR) 49 **68 §** (Linamix (FR) 127) [2015 74§: f8g⁴ Jan 8] fair handicapper: stays 1m: acts on fibresand, best turf form on good going or firmer: sometimes in cheekpieces: unreliable: sold 7,500 gns, sent to Italy, where won 5f/6f handicaps at Pisa (2) and Livorno in November/ December. *Richard Fahey*

TWO SMART (IRE) 4 b.f. Cape Cross (IRE) 129 – Smartest (IRE) 76 (Exceed And **61 §** Excel (AUS) 126) [2015 84§: p7f⁶ Feb 21] lengthy, quite good-topped filly: maiden, fairly useful form at best: best effort at 6f: acts on polytrack, good to firm and heavy going: has worn headgear, including usually of late: one to treat with caution. *Daniel Kubler*

TWO SUGARS 7 b.g. Val Royal (FR) 127 – Princess Galadriel 74 (Magic Ring (IRE) **61** 115) [2015 –: 8d³ 8v³ p8f² p8g t8.6f³ Dec 11] modest maiden: stays 13f: acts on polytrack, soft and good to firm going: tried in hood: front runner/races prominently. *Gary Moore*

TWO TURTLE DOVES (IRE) 9 b.m. Night Shift (USA) – Purple Rain (IRE) 46 **60** (Celtic Swing 138) [2015 68, a55: t5.1f⁵ t6g³ p5m t6f⁴ 5.1m⁵ 5.1d⁵ 5m 6m⁴ 5m⁴ 5g⁴ 5.1m⁵ **a51** 5f⁴ 5d³ 5m² 6d* 6g 5s⁴ 5s p5g⁵ p6g Dec 3] leggy mare: modest handicapper: won at Thirsk (amateur) in August: stays 6f: acts on tapeta and any turf going: tried in headgear. *Michael Mullineaux*

TYCHAIOS 5 b.g. Green Desert (USA) 127 – Tychy 102 (Suave Dancer (USA) 136) **71** [2015 77: p7m⁵ p6g⁴ p8f² p8f⁵ 6g³ 7m 7m p7g² p6g* p6f* Oct 22] sturdy gelding: fair handicapper: won at Kempton in October: stays 1m: acts on polytrack, soft and good to firm going: in hood last 3 starts: tried in tongue tie. *Stuart Williams*

TYFOS 10 b.g. Bertolini (USA) 125 – Warminghamsharpish (Nalchik (USA)) [2015 90, **80** a81: 5m 5g⁴ 5f⁵ 5.1m 5m 5m 5.1m² 5m² 5.1s 5.1g Sep 30] lengthy gelding: fairly useful handicapper: stays 7f: acts on polytrack, firm and soft going: tried in cheekpieces: front runner/races prominently. *Brian Baugh*

TY GWR 6 b.g. Echo of Light 125 – House Maiden (IRE) 75 (Rudimentary (USA) 118) – [2015 97: f11s 8m 10.4g 9.8d Jun 2] rather leggy gelding: useful handicapper at best: well held in 2015: stays 1½m: acts on polytrack, tapeta and heavy ground: usually in hood: tried in tongue tie: sometimes slowly away. *Brian Ellison*

TYPHON (USA) 5 b.g. Proud Citizen (USA) 122 – Seven Moons (JPN) (Sunday Silence **59** (USA)) [2015 10sᵖᵘ 12d 12m⁵ 12m⁵ 10g⁶ 10.2m⁵ 15.8sᵖᵘ Oct 6] modest handicapper: stays 10.5f: acts on polytrack and good to firm going: tried in cheekpieces in 2015. *Micky Hammond*

TYRANNICAL 2 br.c. (Apr 5) Dansili 127 – Queen of Mean 79 (Pivotal 124) [2015 7g – 7g p8f Sep 22] down the field in maidens. *Sir Mark Prescott Bt*

TYRELL (IRE) 2 b.g. (Feb 3) Teofilo (IRE) 126 – Sleeveless (USA) 76 (Fusaichi Pegasus **61 p** (USA) 130) [2015 7s 7g 8.3d³ Oct 5] 70,000Y: third foal: dam, maiden (stayed 1m), closely related to Racing Post Trophy runner-up Castle Gandolfo: modest form in maidens, 4¼ lengths third to Gawdawpalin at Windsor final start: will be suited by 1¼m: has been gelded: open to further improvement. *Alan King*

TYRSAL (IRE) 4 b.g. Jeremy (USA) 122 – Blanchelande (IRE) (Subotica (FR) 131) **75**
[2015 77, a71: p7g 8.3s⁵ p8g 7m 6g p6g⁵ 6m⁶ 8.1g⁴ 10m 10g⁵ 10.1g* 10g* 9g⁵ 10.2v 11.6g
p10m* p10g p12g Dec 2] sturdy gelding: fair handicapper: won at Yarmouth (apprentice)
in August, Leicester (apprentice) in September and Kempton in October: stays 1¼m: acts
on polytrack and firm going: tried in headgear: usually races in rear. *Clifford Lines*

<h1 style="text-align:center">U</h1>

UBLA (IRE) 2 ch.g. (Jan 22) Arcano (IRE) 122 – Manuelita Rose (ITY) (Desert Style **59**
(IRE) 121) [2015 7m p7f⁴ Dec 17] €44,000F, 37,000Y: strong gelding: first foal: dam
unraced half-sister to useful 1m-1¼m winner Rose Hip: blinkered, better effort (modest
form) when fourth in maiden at Chelmsford. *Hugo Palmer*

UCHENNA (IRE) 4 b.f. Fastnet Rock (AUS) 127 – Uriah (GER) 109 (Acatenango (GER) **106**
127) [2015 92: t9.5g* 8.5s⁶ 8f* p8.5g⁴ p8.5f* 9d⁴ 10g Oct 18] good-topped
filly: useful performer: won handicap at Wolverhampton in January (left David Simcock
after), optional claimer at Woodbine in May and Grade 3 Ontario Matron Stakes on latter
course (by ¾ length from Strut The Course) in July: respectable fourth to Strut The Course
in Grade 2 Canadian Stakes there next time: behind in E. P. Taylor Stakes on same track
final outing: stays 1¼m: acts on polytrack/tapeta, firm and good to soft going. *Roger L.
Attfield, Canada*

UDODODONTU (IRE) 3 b.g. Lope de Vega (IRE) 125 – Fifer (IRE) (Soviet Star (USA) **99 p**
128) [2015 67p: 8m* 8.1m³ 7g* 8f² Jun 18] useful performer: won maiden at Redcar in
April and handicap at York (by 2¼ lengths from Normandy Barriere) in May: further
improvement when neck second of 28 to War Envoy in Britannia Stakes (Handicap) at
Royal Ascot: stays 1m: acts on firm going: joined Saeed bin Suroor: should continue to
progress. *Richard Guest*

UDONTDODOU 2 b.g. (Feb 9) Fastnet Rock (AUS) 127 – Forever Times 98 (So Factual **82**
(USA) 120) [2015 5.4s 6d³ 6v² Nov 7] 72,000Y, 23,000 2-y-o: sixth foal: closely related to
useful winner up to 7f Sunday Times (2-y-o 6f winner, by Holy Roman Emperor) and half-
brother to useful 6f winner Question Times (by Shamardal) and 1m winner Russian Reward
(by Iffraaj): dam, winner up to 7f (2-y-o 5f winner), half-sister to very smart winner up to
7f Welsh Emperor and smart 5f/6f winner Majestic Times: fairly useful maiden: further
marked improvement when ¾-length second to Sainted at Doncaster (clear of rest).
Richard Guest

UELE RIVER 3 b.f. Refuse To Bend (IRE) 128 – Baddi Heights (FR) (Shirley Heights **92**
130) [2015 73: 10m² 12m⁶ 10m* 10g² 10.1m Sep 16] quite attractive filly: fairly useful
performer: won maiden at Windsor (by 4½ lengths from Burmese) in August: second in
handicap at Newmarket next start: stays 1¼m: acts on good to firm going: front runner/
races prominently, often travels strongly. *Henry Candy*

UGANDA GLORY (USA) 5 br.m. Hat Trick (JPN) 121 – Febrile (USA) (Trempolino **62 §**
(USA) 135) [2015 70§: t12.2g p15.8f² p15.8g⁴ Feb 11] modest handicapper: stays easy
2m: acts on polytrack, tapeta and any turf going: often wears headgear: best treated with
caution. *George Baker*

UJAGAR (IRE) 4 gr.g. Dalakhani (IRE) 133 – No Secrets (USA) (El Corredor (USA) **–**
123) [2015 81: f12s⁶ Mar 17] fairly useful handicapper in 2014, well held only outing in
2015: stays 12.5f: acts on fibresand: wears headgear. *Graeme McPherson*

ULFAH DREAM 2 b.f. (Mar 21) Oasis Dream 129 – Ulfah (USA) 105 (Danzig (USA)) **72 p**
[2015 p6f³ Oct 29] seventh foal: half-sister to 3 winners, including useful 5f/6f winner
Tashqeel (by Medicean) and 8.6f winner Waaleef (by Nayef): dam, winner up to 6.3f
(including at 2 yrs), sister to smart winner up to 7f Haatef: fair form when third in maidens
at Chelmsford, racing too freely latter occasion: remains with potential. *Marco Botti*

ULLSWATER (IRE) 7 b.g. Singspiel (IRE) 133 – Uluwatu (IRE) (Unfuwain (USA) 131) **58**
[2015 f16g³ t12.2f Nov 16] well-made gelding: modest maiden: best effort at 1¼m: acts on
fibresand: winning hurdler. *Philip Kirby*

ULTIMA ORA (IRE) 3 b.f. Thewayyouare (USA) 117 – Prima Volta 80 (Primo Dominie **48**
121) [2015 –: t9.5f 11.7f³ 12.1g 14.1g p13.3m 11.7f t13.9g Jul 13] poor maiden: stays
11.5f: acts on firm going: tried in blinkers. *Mark Johnston*

ULTRA (IRE) 2 ch.c. (Mar 26) Manduro (GER) 135 – Epitome (IRE) 71 (Nashwan **116 p**
(USA) 135) [2015 7g* 8g* 8m* Oct 4]

       The Grand Criterium has been the principal two-year-old race in France for
a century and a half—although its first prize nowadays is almost matched by that for
the Prix Morny—and for most of its history it has successfully done the job for which
it was instituted, that of providing a worthwhile opportunity for high-class two-year-
olds bred to stay. The Grand Criterium's traditional position in the calendar was
the middle of October and its success was one of the inspirations for the Timeform
Gold Cup (now the Racing Post Trophy) which was inaugurated in 1961 and, at that
time, run just a week after the Grand Criterium. Until the advent of the Timeform
Gold Cup, which was by far the most valuable two-year-old race ever staged in
Europe and had the fifth biggest prize for any race in Britain, the most important
event in England for two-year-olds had been the Middle Park Stakes. The Middle
Park was known misleadingly as 'the two-year-old Derby' though its distance of six
furlongs heavily favoured the top sprinting two-year-olds over their staying-bred
counterparts. There were plenty of critics of the Timeform Gold Cup, most of them
objecting to the idea of running a top race for two-year-olds over so long a distance
as a mile and many saying the race was being run too late in the season, increasing
the 'risk' of its being decided on heavy going (something which frequently happened
with the Grand Criterium, though it hadn't stopped that race being won by a string of
horses who went on to become household names in the sport).

       Those critics who objected to the Timeform Gold Cup on the grounds that
a race over a mile for two-year-olds in October would be harmful to the classic
prospects of its participants were quickly put in their place. Like its French
counterpart the Grand Criterium, the Timeform Gold Cup was designed to
provide good staying-bred two-year-olds with a worthwhile prize over a distance
commensurate with their stamina. It was not designed, as Timeform's founder Phil
Bull was at pains to make clear, with the aim of providing a good guide to the
following year's classics. The Timeform Gold Cup was to be valued *as a race* 'not
as something to provide resourceless and thought-lazy journalists with guidance as
to what might win next year's classic races.' As it happened, the first Timeform
Gold Cup field contained the subsequent runner-up in the Two Thousand Guineas,
Romulus, who could fairly be considered the best miler in Europe by the end of his
three-year-old season, and it also had Larkspur and Hethersett, who won the Derby
and the St Leger respectively (the horses that ran in the race went on to win thirteen
races at three, worth the equivalent of more than £1.5m in today's money).

       There were a few early signs in the 'eighties that the Grand Criterium might
be in some danger of losing its lustre and it was moved in 1989 to the Saturday of
Prix de l'Arc weekend in the hope that an earlier date might help. That experiment
lasted for six years before the Grand Criterium was returned to its traditional place
after the 1994 edition attracted just four runners, its smallest field for well over
sixty years. The programme of two-year-old pattern races in France underwent a
major change in 2001 when a new Group 1 event, the Criterium International run
over a mile at Saint-Cloud in November, was created and the Grand Criterium had
its distance reduced to seven furlongs (the changes involved scrapping the historic
seven-furlong Group 1 the Prix de la Salamandre, which had repeatedly upstaged
the Grand Criterium through the 'nineties when it was won by the likes of Zafonic,
Pennekamp and Giant's Causeway). The reduction of the distance of the Grand
Criterium came hand in hand with yet another move in the calendar, back to the
earlier position which had already been tried, this time on to the card on Prix de
l'Arc day itself.

       The tinkering with the Grand Criterium's distance and timing seemed to be
influenced mostly by French trainers worried by the growing plundering of the top
French two-year-old races by foreign challengers. The latest season saw yet another
change, with the Grand Criterium reverting to a mile, its traditional distance (the
Criterium International, which has had a mixed history since its introduction, had
its distance cut to seven furlongs and was run on the same day as the mile and a
quarter Criterium de Saint-Cloud in early-November). Exactly what difference this
series of arbitrary changes has made is anyone's guess. The overall competitiveness

*Qatar Prix Jean-Luc Lagardere (Grand Criterium) sponsored by Al Hazm, Longchamp—
a strong Anglo-Irish contingent but home-trained Ultra comes out on top, beating Cymric (No.4),
Galileo Gold (dark cap) and Johannes Vermeer; the race reverted to its traditional distance of
a mile after being run over seven furlongs since 2001*

of France's top two-year-old races still leaves something to be desired, though this is largely because of the shortage of good French two-year-olds in recent times which must have made the four Group 1s look relatively easy prey sometimes to the major overseas trainers with their strong teams of juveniles.

The latest Grand Criterium—the race has carried the name of the late Jean-Luc Lagardere since 2003—had its first double-figure field since 2002 but there were only three French-trained runners among the eleven starters. The strong Anglo-Irish contingent included representatives from a number of stables that have regularly targeted the Grand Criterium, including that of Aidan O'Brien, who supplied the favourite Johannes Vermeer, winner of the Willis Champions Juvenile at Leopardstown on Irish Champions' Weekend. Up-and-coming Hugo Palmer saddled the second favourite, the Vintage Stakes winner Galileo Gold, his first runner in the race, while two other regulars Jim Bolger and John Gosden were represented respectively by Herald The Dawn, successful in the Futurity Stakes at the Curragh, and Cymric, the last-named making his first appearance in pattern company. The home defence was headed by Ultra, unbeaten after winning a newcomers race at Clairefontaine in July and a minor event over the Grand Criterium course and distance in September.

Godolphin-owned Ultra represented the stable of Andre Fabre, who went on to win the French trainers' championship for a phenomenal twenty-seventh time in the latest season. Fabre had won the Grand Criterium three times before in his long career but he hadn't won the race for twenty years, since landing successive editions in the mid-'nineties with Goldmark (owned by Godolphin's joint-founder Sheikh Mohammed) and Loup Solitaire. Fabre had the first two in both those years, the runner-up spot filled on each occasion by horses owned by the president of France Galop Jean-Luc Lagardere (the sire of that pair, Linamix, who went on to play a big part in establishing the Lagardere bloodstock empire, had come second to the other Fabre-trained winner Jade Robbery in the Grand Criterium a few years earlier).

Ultra was only the eleventh runner in the Grand Criterium saddled by Fabre since Loup Solitaire's victory and only his third in the last eight years, following Lope de Vega, who finished fourth to Siyouni in 2009, and Territories, who was promoted to runner-up in 2014 when Gleneagles was demoted from first for causing interference. Lope de Vega trained on to complete the Poule d'Essai des Poulains/Prix du Jockey Club double and Territories was runner-up to Gleneagles in the Two Thousand Guineas and went on to Group 1 success in the Prix Jean Prat. Some might take that as an encouraging sign for Ultra's prospects as a three-year-old, though the portents might be said to be less encouraging if the subsequent records of Fabre's three previous Grand Criterium winners are examined, none of them managing to win again, Goldmark not seen at all as a three-year-old and both Jade Robbery and Loup Solitaire having their campaigns curtailed severely by injury.

The pace in the latest Grand Criterium was steadier than that in the same afternoon's Prix Marcel Boussac for fillies over the distance and little more than three lengths covered nine of the runners at the finish. Ultra was well positioned throughout, in a rather muddling affair in which it paid to be handy, and he was driven out, after leading with over a furlong to go, to hold off the strong-finishing Cymric (also in the Godolphin royal blue) by a short neck. Cymric was gaining on Ultra all the way to the line after having to race wider than the winner from stall ten (the winner was drawn two). Galileo Gold, a length behind Cymric, and Johannes Vermeer, a further neck away, completed the frame, with Attendu the next French-trained finisher in eighth. Ultra and Galileo Gold weren't seen out again, but Cymric was sent on to Keeneland for the Breeders' Cup Juvenile Turf in which he managed only eighth from a poor draw, while Johannes Vermeer ran twice, finishing runner-up to Marcel in the Racing Post Trophy at Doncaster and winning the Criterium International at Saint-Cloud by a head from British-trained Stormy Antarctic (the Criterium de Saint-Cloud went for export too, won by the Harry Dunlop-trained Robin of Navan, while John Gosden won the summer Group 1 the Prix Morny with Shalaa).

Ultra (IRE)
(ch.c. 2013)

Manduro (GER) (b 2002)
— Monsun (br 1990): Konigsstuhl, Mosella
— Mandellicht (b 1994): Be My Guest, Mandelauge

Epitome (IRE) (b 1999)
— Nashwan (ch 1986): Blushing Groom, Height of Fashion
— Proskona (b 1981): Mr Prospector, Konafa

The good-bodied Ultra is by Manduro, the horse that Andre Fabre once described as the best he had trained (there is more about him in the essay on Vazirabad). Ultra is the tenth foal and the seventh winner out of Epitome who was placed on two of her three starts in maidens at up to a mile and a half as a three-year-old for Luca Cumani and owner-breeder Gerald Leigh. Leigh died before Epitome's racing career was over and, after being part of the bloodstock draft purchased from the Leigh family by Sheikh Mohammed for a reported thirty-five million dollars in 2003, Epitome joined the Darley broodmare band. Her first foal Synopsis (by In The Wings) went on to show useful form at up to an extended twelve furlongs, winning the Prix Minerve for Andre Fabre. Ultra is closely related to Epitome's sixth foal Swedish Sailor (by Monsun, sire of Manduro) who looked a smart prospect when winning his only start at two (beat Noble Mission by five lengths) but finished well held in two races when he returned to action in the autumn of his three-year-old days. Other half-brothers include the useful stayer Exemplary (by Sulamani) and the three-year-old Symbolic Star (by New Approach) who won a seven-furlong Wolverhampton maiden in the latest season. Epitome is a half-sister to several winners including the useful French mile (including at two) winner Calista, and Noesis, the grandam of Act One who won the first Criterium International for Gerald Leigh and went on to win the Prix Lupin and finish second in the Prix du Jockey Club.

Ultra's grandam is the high-class French six- and seven-furlong performer Proskona who is a half-sister to Korveya, the dam of Hector Protector, Bosra Sham and Shanghai, who all won classics in either Britain or France. Hector Protector himself ended his two-year-old season unbeaten with victory in the Grand Criterium. Ultra's family on the distaff side provides a reminder of how long Sheikh Mohammed has been involved in British racing and breeding. Ultra's great grandam Konafa was runner-up in the 1976 One Thousand Guineas but it was her half-sister, Awaasif, a 325,000-dollar yearling purchase, who began Sheikh Mohammed's association with the family. She won the Yorkshire Oaks and finished third in the Arc in the Sheikh's colours and went on to breed Snow Bride who ran in the Sheikh's colours as a two-year-old before winning the Musidora and being awarded the Oaks when carrying the colours of Saeed Maktoum Al Maktoum who also owned Snow Bride's son Lammtarra when he won the Derby, the King George and the Arc. Ultra holds a Derby entry and is bred to stay a mile and a half. He looks the type to progress further as a three-year-old. *A. Fabre, France*

ULYSSES (IRE) 2 ch.c. (Mar 20) Galileo (IRE) 134 – Light Shift (USA) 121 (Kingmambo (USA) 125) [2015 8s⁶ Oct 23] third foal: half-brother to useful 11.6f/1½m winner Dr Yes (by Dansili): dam, won Oaks (also 2-y-o 1m winner), half-sister to high-class 8.5f-10.5f winner Shiva and very smart 1¼m-1½m winner Limnos: 4/1, shaped well when 2½ lengths sixth of 15 to Algometer in maiden at Newbury, considerably handled: sure to progress. *Sir Michael Stoute* — **81 p**

UNCLE BERNIE (IRE) 5 gr.g. Aussie Rules (USA) 123 – Alwiyda (USA) (Trempolino (USA) 135) [2015 81: t16.5g³ p15.8f Apr 3] leggy, close-coupled gelding: fair performer: stays 16.5f: acts on polytrack, tapeta and good to firm going: usually in headgear prior to 2015: sometimes slowly away, usually races in rear. *Sarah Hollinshead* — **78**

UNCLE BRIT 9 b.g. Efisio 120 – Tarneem (USA) 87 (Zilzal (USA) 137) [2015 69: 7s 9.1s³ 7.9v* 8.3s⁴ 8d⁴ 8.5d f7g⁴ f8g³ f8g⁶ f8g Dec 12] modest handicapper: won at Carlisle (apprentice) in June: stays 9.5f: acts on fibresand and heavy going: wears headgear. *Rebecca Menzies* — **63**

UNCLE DERMOT (IRE) 7 b.g. Arakan (USA) 123 – Cappadoce (IRE) (General Monash (USA) 107) [2015 94: 8f 8.5g 7.1m 8.3m 7.5s³ 7.4v² 7d 7s* Oct 26] good-topped gelding: fairly useful handicapper: won at Leicester (amateur) in October: stays 8.5f: acts on good to firm and heavy going: tried in hood: usually leads. *Brendan Powell* — **80**

UNCLE RUFUS (IRE) 4 ch.g. Iffraaj 127 – Astuti (IRE) 84 (Waajib 121) [2015 6.1v⁶ 5.7f⁶ 6d Oct 5] well held in 3 maidens. *Patrick Chamings* — **–**

UNDER APPROVAL 4 b.g. Captain Gerrard (IRE) 113 – Dockside Strike (Docksider (USA) 124) [2015 62: f6s⁵ f5g t5.1g f5g³ f5s⁴ f6g* 6g⁶ 6g⁶ 5g⁴ t6g 5d* 5f 5g⁵ 5m f7s 5s⁵ 5m⁵ 5m⁵ 5s⁵ Oct 6] modest handicapper: won at Southwell in April and Hamilton in June: stays 6f: acts on polytrack, fibresand, soft and good to firm going: usually in headgear. *Karen Tutty* — **58**

UNDER ATTACK (IRE) 2 b.g. (Feb 10) Dubawi (IRE) 129 – Ship's Biscuit 107 (Tiger Hill (IRE) 127) [2015 7m⁴ 7.1m⁶ Jul 22] close-coupled gelding: first foal: dam, 1½m winner who stayed 2m, half-sister to smart 11.6f/1½m winner (stayed 1¾m) Warringah: shaped well on debut when fourth of 12 to Ibn Malik in maiden at Newmarket in June, but failed to build on that in similar event at Sandown: subsequently gelded: will stay 1m: remains capable of better. *Sir Michael Stoute* — **83 p**

UNDERDRESSED 2 b.f. (Apr 2) Elnadim (USA) 128 – Bijan (IRE) 75 (Mukaddamah (USA) 125) [2015 6g³ 6g³ f7g² Nov 12] £10,000Y: half-sister to several winners, including 6f (including at 2 yrs) winner Gung Ho Jack (by Moss Vale) and 5f winner Cliffords Reprieve (by Kheleyf): dam, winner up to 6f (2-y-o 5f winner), half-sister to winner up to 7f Jarn and 5f/6f winner Yomalo, both smart: fair maiden: off 6 months, best effort when neck second to Davey Boy at Southwell. *Keith Dalgleish* — **71**

UNDER REVIEW (IRE) 9 b.g. Danetime (IRE) 121 – Coloma (JPN) (Forty Niner – (USA)) [2015 71: t5.1f Sep 19] good-bodied gelding: poor handicapper: stays 6f: acts on polytrack, fibresand, sand and good to firm going: usually in headgear/tongue tie: sometimes slowly away. *Brian Barr*

UNDER SIEGE (IRE) 3 b.g. Invincible Spirit (IRE) 121 – Interpose (Indian Ridge 123) [2015 6v 6m⁵ 6d* 7v⁴ 6v³ p6f* Oct 10] €52,000Y: closely related to 7f-1¼m winner Go Figure and smart winner up to 1m Rinterval (2-y-o 6f winner) (both by Desert Prince) and half-brother to 11.5f winner Betwixt (by Sinndar): dam unraced: fairly useful performer: won maiden at Hamilton in June (subsequently left Kevin Ryan) and handicap at Chelmsford (apprentice) final start: stays 6f: acts on polytrack and good to soft going: usually races close up. *David Simcock* — **86**

UNDERSTORY (USA) 8 b.g. Forestry (USA) 121 – Sha Tha (USA) 118 (Mr Prospector (USA)) [2015 72: p10g⁵ p10g² p10g⁴ p10g p10g² p10g⁵ p10f⁴ p10m p10d p10g⁶ Dec 30] big, workmanlike gelding: modest handicapper: stays 1½m: acts on polytrack and good to firm going: often in headgear: front runner/races prominently. *Tim McCarthy* — **62**

UNDER THE COVERS 2 b.f. (Apr 30) Stimulation (IRE) 121 – Sakha 109 (Wolfhound (USA) 126) [2015 6d Jul 13] half-sister to several winners, including 1m/9f winner Cantabrico (by Sakhee) and 2-y-o 1m winner Judraan (by Alhaarth): dam 5f/6f winner, including at 2 yrs: 100/1, seventh in maiden at Windsor (5¼ lengths behind Essenaitch) in July: should do better. *Ronald Harris* — **55 p**

UNDERTOW (IRE) 2 b.f. (Feb 8) Arcano (IRE) 122 – Tides 47 (Bahamian Bounty 116) [2015 p6g⁶ t7.1m⁴ Dec 18] half-sister to several winners, including winner up to 6f Hestian and winner up to 7f Invoke (both useful, 2-y-o 5f winners and by Kodiac): dam lightly raced: off 6 months, better effort in maidens when 4½ lengths fourth to Outback Blue at Wolverhampton. *K. R. Burke* — **59**

UNDERWRITTEN 6 b.g. Authorized (IRE) 133 – Grain of Gold 74 (Mr Prospector **72** (USA)) [2015 76: p15.8g 12d 15.8s* 15.8m² 14.6m 16m^pu Jul 1] tall gelding: fair handicapper: won at Catterick in May: left Shaun Harris after third start: stayed 2m: acted on polytrack, tapeta and any turf going: had worn headgear: front runner/raced prominently: dead. *Brian Ellison*

UNDRAFTED (USA) 5 ch.g. Purim (USA) 118 – French Jeannette (USA) (French **126** Deputy (USA) 118) [2015 117: 5.5g³ 5f² 6f* 8f² 5.5g⁵ Oct 31]

The connections of American sprinter Undrafted will have been more than satisfied with the outcome of his gelding's two trips to Britain so far. Fourth in the 2014 July Cup on his first outing outside the States, Undrafted made an even bigger impact in the latest season when he carried off the Diamond Jubilee Stakes at Royal Ascot. Undrafted's win was the high point of another successful Royal Ascot raid by trainer Wesley Ward who is a regular visitor to the meeting. Ward made a big impact with his first batch of Royal Ascot runners in 2009, when Strike The Tiger landed the Windsor Castle Stakes and Jealous Again routed her rivals in the Queen Mary, and since then Ward has fielded runners at Britain's showpiece Flat meeting every year except 2012. After adding another two winners to his Royal Ascot tally in the meantime, courtesy of No Nay Never (2013 Norfolk) and Hootenanny (2014 Windsor Castle), Ward fielded his largest team to date in the latest season, saddling nine runners, and was rewarded with another brace of winners. The impressive Acapulco gave the stable its second success in the Queen Mary on the second day of the meeting, though Ward had little hesitation in nominating Undrafted's success in the Diamond Jubilee as the highlight of his training career—'This is the biggest race I've won. I've won Breeders' Cups and races here in the past, but to come here and be presented with a Group 1 trophy by the Queen was such a fantastic experience.' Undrafted was the first Royal Ascot success outside the two-year-old races for Ward, who also became the first American trainer to saddle a Group 1 winner in Britain. Given his record, Ward will no doubt continue to be a familiar face at Royal Ascot for years to come, and the trainer believes the success of Undrafted in particular will make the big races at the meeting more appealing to other American-trained runners; in addition to Wesley Ward's contingent, the two other North American-trained runners at Royal Ascot were Miss Temple City (fourth in the Coronation Stakes) and Cyclogenesis, who finished down the field in the Commonwealth Cup in which Ward's Hootenanny disappointed after being sent off the 9/4 favourite (the 2014 Kentucky Derby winner California Chrome was due to contest the Prince of Wales's Stakes before being ruled out by a foot abscess and the trainer of American Triple Crown winner American Pharoah, Bob Baffert, has said that he is hoping to have runners in the next season).

Successful twice from three starts as a two-year-old—on his debut at Keeneland and then late in the year (after an absence) at Gulfstream when switched to turf and upped to a mile—Undrafted showed smart form on occasions at three, though he won only one of his seven outings that season, when scoring by a wide margin in an allowance race on his return to turf at Churchill Downs, again over a mile. Undrafted's four-year-old campaign, in which he was dropped in trip and campaigned largely as a sprinter, was more successful. He gained his first win at pattern level in the Grade 3 Jaipur Invitational Stakes over six furlongs at Belmont in June, a race described by his trainer as a '300,000-dollar prep race for the July Cup'. Undrafted started at 25/1 at Newmarket but acquitted himself very creditably in finishing a length and three quarters fourth to Slade Power, seeming suited by a strongly-run race and coming from off the pace. After running below par on his next outing, three months later, when third in a non-graded event at Kentucky Downs, Undrafted ended his four-year-old campaign with another good effort at Grade 1 level, finishing half a length third to Bobby's Kitten in the Breeders' Cup Turf Sprint at Santa Anita, when again staying on well over a strongly-run six furlongs to be beaten a nose for second by stablemate No Nay Never.

With the Diamond Jubilee presumably pencilled in by connections at the start of the latest season, Undrafted was warmed up for Ascot with a brace of encouraging placed efforts in Grade 3 contests over an inadequate five furlongs, finishing third

Diamond Jubilee Stakes, Royal Ascot—a 1, 2 for the strong international contingent as US-trained Undrafted (left) beats Australian raider Brazen Beau (No.3) who races apart from the rest after starting from stall 15; ill-fated Astaire (noseband) and Music Master (stars on cap) fare best of the home-trained runners in third and fourth

in the Shakertown Stakes at Keeneland and then second—beaten three quarters of a length—in the Turf Sprint Stakes at Churchill Downs in early-May. On both occasions Undrafted finished well after being waited with as usual. The return to six furlongs, especially on Ascot's stiff straight course, promised to suit Undrafted much better and, ridden by Frankie Dettori who had also partnered him in the July Cup, he was sent off at 14/1 in a fifteen-runner field for the Diamond Jubilee which had a stronger international flavour than the previous couple of renewals. There were two runners from Australia, the 7/2 joint favourite Brazen Beau, successful in the Group 1 Newmarket Handicap at Flemington on his latest outing, and 10/1-shot Wandjina, who was dropping in trip having landed the Australian Guineas over a mile earlier in the year. There were also five runners from Ireland, including the other joint favourite, the previous year's Jersey Stakes winner Mustajeeb, who had landed the Greenlands Stakes at the Curragh on his reappearance, and Due Diligence from Ballydoyle who was making his second start since returning from a pelvic injury sustained after finishing runner-up to Slade Power in the 2014 Diamond Jubilee. In a truly-run affair, the field raced down the centre of the track, except for Brazen Beau who became rather isolated from the main pack when his jockey Craig Williams elected to keep straight from stall fifteen and race towards the stand rail.

As expected, Undrafted proved very well suited by a strongly-run, stiff six furlongs and, after being waited with on the far side of the pack, he made good progress on the wide outside to head Brazen Beau late on, the latter having travelled strongly all the way and taken it up approaching the final furlong. The pair were separated by half a length, with Brazen Beau a length and three quarters ahead of the third, the ill-fated Astaire, who improved on his sixth in the race the previous year. Music Master finished fourth for the second year running, a place ahead of Mustajeeb, who seemed to lack the basic speed for a top sprint on firmish ground. It was Frankie Dettori's first win in the Diamond Jubilee since it was upgraded to Group 1 (he had landed the equivalent race aboard So Factual in 1995, when it was still run as the Cork And Orrery Stakes). A repeat bid in the July Cup was immediately ruled out by Wesley Ward but a tilt at the Sprint Cup looked on the cards for a while, until it was decided to keep Undrafted on home soil for his two subsequent runs in 2015. He failed to show his best form on either occasion, finishing second in a non-graded event over a mile at Kentucky Downs and managing only fifth when sent off favourite for the Breeders' Cup Turf Sprint at Keeneland where he seemed to find the five and a half furlongs too sharp.

Undrafted (USA) (ch.g. 2010)	Purim (USA) (b or br 2002)	Dynaformer (br 1985)	Roberto
			Andover Way
		Kirsteena (ch 1996)	Lord At War
			Eternal Vow
	French Jeannette (USA) (ch 2000)	French Deputy (ch 1992)	Deputy Minister
			Mitterand
		Fancy Sheba (ch 1993)	Alysheba
			Native Fancy

Purchased for 50,000 dollars at Keeneland as a yearling, Undrafted is part-owned by American football player Wes Welker, whose failure to be selected at the 2004 pre-season NFL draft inspired the name. Undrafted's sire Purim, a son of Dynaformer who has primarily been known for stamina in Europe, won the Shadwell Turf Mile as a five-year-old before being retired at the end of that season, but his time at stud was cut short when he died from colic in 2012. He is also the sire of the very smart American middle-distance turf performer Twilight Eclipse who won the Man o' War Stakes in the latest season. Undrafted is easily the best of the four winners produced by his dam French Jeannette, a minor winner over sprint trips in the States, though, interestingly, Undrafted's year-younger full brother Play Hard To Get has won over as far as a mile and a quarter on turf. Although successful over a mile, Undrafted's very best form has come at six furlongs. Usually held up, he is particularly well suited by a well-run race. Undrafted's four wins on turf have come on firm ground (he also acts on polytrack), though he seemed to handle good to soft well enough in the July Cup (the only time he has encountered softer than good). Although his last ten outings have been on turf, he also has form on dirt and synthetic surfaces. A sturdy gelding, Undrafted wore blinkers on the first four outings of his career. As a gelding, he will presumably be back for more as a six-year-old, with another trip to Royal Ascot likely to be high on the agenda. *Wesley A. Ward, USA*

UNDULATE 4 b.f. Three Valleys (USA) 119 – Singleton 105 (Singspiel (IRE) 133) [2015 72: t7.1g Jan 8] lightly-raced mare: fair winner in 2014, well held only outing in 2015: best effort at 7f. *Peter Niven*   –

UNEX EL GRECO 7 b.g. Holy Roman Emperor (IRE) 125 – Friendlier (Zafonic (USA) 130) [2015 9.9m² 11.9m⁴ p10f p8f Nov 23] good-topped gelding: useful performer at best: left Alan Smith, Bahrain, after second start then off 7 months: stays 1½m: acts on soft and good to firm going. *Martin Smith*   **88**

UNEX MODIGLIANI (IRE) 6 ch.g. Hurricane Run (IRE) 134 – Chronicle (Observatory (USA) 131) [2015 t8.6g t9.5g⁵ p12g² p14g² p13.3m⁶ 14.1v Nov 3] fair maiden: stays 1¾m: acts on polytrack and good to soft going: in tongue tie in 2015, also in cheekpieces final start: sometimes slowly away, often races towards rear. *Derek Shaw*   **65**

UNFORGETTABLE YOU (IRE) 3 br.f. Captain Rio 122 – The Gibson Girl (IRE) (Norwich 118) [2015 –: 6m 8g 5m 7.9g 8g Jul 14] no form in maidens/handicaps: in visor last 2 starts. *Declan Carroll*   –

UNFORGIVING MINUTE 4 b.c. Cape Cross (IRE) 129 – Ada River 102 (Dansili 127) [2015 119p: 7f 8m Aug 8] smart winner of 4 races at Kempton in 2014, well held all 4 starts on turf: stays 1m: acts on polytrack: sold 25,000 gns and joined Barry Brennan. *Clive Cox*   –

UNILIT (IRE) 2 b.f. (Mar 12) Approve (IRE) 112 – Riymaisa (IRE) (Traditionally (USA) 117) [2015 5m² 5m 5.1m⁴ 6g* 6m² 5.1m⁵ 6f³ 6m³ 6g² 6s* 6s³ 6.5m⁶ 6g 6g⁶ 6d³ Oct 24] €10,000Y, resold £20,000Y: smallish filly: fourth foal: half-sister to 2-y-o 6f winner Zacapa (by Majestic Missile): dam, lightly raced, half-sister useful 1¼m winner (stayed 1½m) Riyalma out of smart 1½m winner Riyafa: fairly useful performer: won maiden at Pontefract in June and nursery at Leicester (by neck from Rebel Surge) in August: 20/1, good 2¼ lengths third of 9 to Dhahmaan in listed race at Doncaster final start, well positioned: stays 6f: acts on soft going: sold 78,000 gns. *Mick Channon*   **93**

UNION ROSE 3 b.g. Stimulation (IRE) 121 – Dot Hill (Refuse To Bend (IRE) 128) [2015 96: 5m⁶ 5g² 5.7g 5m 5g 6g 5m⁶ 5s* 5v 5d Oct 24] rangy gelding: useful handicapper: improved to win 20-runner event at York in October by length from Adam's Ale: well held both subsequent starts: best form at 5f: acts on soft going: often wears headgear, not last 3 starts: has been gelded. *Ronald Harris*   **105**

UNISON (IRE) 5 b.g. Jeremy (USA) 122 – Easter Song (USA) (Rubiano (USA)) [2015 85: 10g⁵ 8.1s 8.3m⁴ 10g⁵ 8d⁴ 9s 8.3g⁶ Oct 19] good-topped gelding: fair handicapper: stays 1¼m: acts on soft and good to firm going. *Peter Makin*   **78**

UNNOTICED 3 b.g. Observatory (USA) 131 – Celestial Empire (USA) (Empire Maker (USA) 129) [2015 76: t7.1g⁴ 6.5m⁶ t7.1g⁶ 8m 7.5g² 7.5m³ 7m 8.1g p8f Sep 24] fair handicapper: left Ollie Pears after seventh start: stays 7.5f: acts on tapeta and good to firm going: usually in headgear in 2015. *Denis Quinn*   **78**

UNSUSPECTED GIRL (IRE) 2 b.f. (Feb 14) Rip Van Winkle (IRE) 134 – Sweet Sioux 59 (Halling (USA) 133) [2015 8g p10g⁴ p8g Oct 6] €35,000F: fourth foal: half-sister to useful 1¼m-11.6f winner Running Deer (by Hurricane Run) and 7.4f-1½m winner Heska (by Rock of Gibraltar): dam, maiden (stayed 1¼m), half-sister to smart winner up to 1¾m First Mohican: modest form in maidens, signs of more ability each time: type to do better in handicaps. *David Simcock*   **52 p**

UNTIL MIDNIGHT (IRE) 5 b.g. Moss Vale (IRE) 126 – Emma's Star (ITY) (Darshaan **81**
133) [2015 79: p8g* p8f² 8g 7f p8g p7g⁵ 7g⁴ 7m⁴ t7.1f p7f⁴ p8f Dec 21] fairly useful
handicapper: won at Chelmsford (by neck from Lunar Deity) in January: stays 1m: acts on
polytrack, tapeta and good to firm going: tried in tongue tie: usually races close up.
Eugene Stanford

UPAVON 5 b.g. Avonbridge 123 – Blaina 76 (Compton Place 125) [2015 96: p7f p7g⁵ p6g* **98**
p6f* 6g⁶ p6f p5m⁵ p8f⁶ p6f⁶ p8f⁵ p8g⁵ Dec 7] tall, workmanlike gelding: useful
handicapper: won twice at Chelmsford in April, by ¾ length from Run With Pride on latter
occasion: left David Elsworth after ninth start: stays 1m: acts on polytrack: in hood/tongue
tie last 2 starts: often races towards rear. *Stuart Williams*

UPHOLD 8 b.g. Oasis Dream 129 – Allegro Viva (USA) (Distant View (USA) 126) [2015 **78**
88: p11.9g⁴ 12.4s p11g³ 10m 11m 14.1m⁴ 11.8g 11.9g² 11.9g p12.4g⁶ p11g Sep 5] well-
made gelding: fair handicapper: stays 13f: acts on polytrack, viscoride, good to firm and
heavy going: wears headgear: tried in tongue tie. *Gay Kelleway*

UP IN LIGHTS (IRE) 3 ch.f. Makfi 130 – Spotlight 110 (Dr Fong (USA) 128) [2015 **99 p**
8.3m* p8g⁵ 8g* 8g³ 10.3v Nov 7] 20,000Y: sixth foal: dam winner up to 9f (US Grade 2
winner), also 2-y-o 7f/1m winner: useful performer: won maiden at Nottingham in June
and handicap at Yarmouth (by 1½ lengths from Elusive Guest) in August: seemed unsuited
by heavy ground final outing: will stay 1¼m: acts on good to firm going: usually races
towards rear: remains with potential. *James Fanshawe*

UPPER LAMBOURN (IRE) 7 b.g. Exceed And Excel (AUS) 126 – In The Fashion **46**
(IRE) 88 (In The Wings 128) [2015 50: f5g² p5m⁴ t6g p5g⁵ 5.1g Aug 2] good-bodied
gelding: poor handicapper: stays 6f: acts on fibresand: tried in headgear/often in tongue tie
prior to 2015: usually races prominently. *Christopher Kellett*

UPPISH 3 ch.g. Compton Place 125 – Uplifting 77 (Magic Ring (IRE) 115) [2015 6g 7m **–**
t6g⁶ 7s Oct 6] little impact in maidens/handicap. *Stuart Kittow*

UPSTAGING 3 b.g. Mount Nelson 125 – Corndavon (USA) 95 (Sheikh Albadou 128) **84**
[2015 85: 7m⁵ t8.6g⁴ 8g⁴ 7d⁵ 6g³ 6g³ t6g4² 7g² Jul 25] good-topped gelding: fairly useful
handicapper: stays 6f: acts on polytrack, tapeta, best turf form on good going: sometimes
in blinkers: temperament under suspicion. *Paul Cole*

UPTIGHT (FR) 3 b.g. Zamindar (USA) 116 – Terre d'Espoir (FR) (Oasis Dream 129) **81**
[2015 80p: 5g 5.1g⁴ 5.5g⁶ 5.4m³ 5m³ 6g⁶ p6g Dec 28] sturdy gelding: fairly useful
handicapper: stays 6f: acts on good to firm going: usually races close up. *Kevin Ryan*

UP TO YOU (USA) 2 ch.f. (Feb 6) Giant's Causeway (USA) 132 – Vignette (USA) 93 **72**
(Diesis 133) [2015 p8m³ p8d⁶ Nov 30] sister to 8.5f winner Wing Foot and half-sister to
several winners, including 1m-14.6f (St Leger) winner Lucarno and winner up to 2m
Flying Officer (2-y-o 1m winner) (both very smart and by Dynaformer): dam 2-y-o 6f
winner: promise when third to Danilovna in maiden at Lingfield on debut: below that form
in similar event at Kempton, possibly finding race coming too soon. *John Gosden*

UPWARD TREND (IRE) 3 b.g. Dark Angel (IRE) 113 – Camassina (IRE) 62 (Taufan **56**
(USA) 119) [2015 63: 9.9m 8s⁶ 6.9v³ 7.5g Jul 4] modest maiden: stays 1m: acts on soft
going: in blinkers last 2 starts. *Tim Easterby*

URAMAZIN (IRE) 9 ch.g. Danehill Dancer (IRE) 117 – Uriah (GER) 109 (Acatenango **102**
(GER) 127) [2015 103: p15.8g² p15.8m⁴ p15.8f 14.1m 16gᵖᵘ May 21] tall gelding: useful
performer: second in minor event at Lingfield (4½ lengths behind Anglophile) in January:
pulled up final outing: stays 2m: acts on polytrack, tapeta and good to firm going: wears
headgear: sometimes slowly away, often races in rear. *Philip Hide*

URBAN CASTLE (USA) 4 b.f. Street Cry (IRE) 130 – Cloud Castle 119 (In The Wings **103**
128) [2015 86: t13.9g* t16.5m³ p13.3g⁴ 12g² 12m³ 12m³ 14m⁵ 12g⁴ 12d p13g* Oct 29]
sturdy filly: useful performer: first past post in handicaps at Wolverhampton (by 6 lengths)
in January and Newmarket (demoted to second for causing interference) in May: better
than ever when also won 13-runner listed race at Lingfield final start by length from
California, staying on to lead final 1f: stays 1¾m: acts on polytrack, tapeta and good to firm
going: in headgear last 7 starts: often races towards rear. *James Tate*

URBAN KODE (IRE) 7 b.g. Kodiac 112 – Urbanize (USA) 68 (Chester House (USA) **–**
123) [2015 16s⁶ May 11] handicapper: first run on Flat since 2011 when well held in May:
stays 11.5f: acts on polytrack and good to firm going: usually in headgear: modest hurdler.
Lucinda Russell

URBAN MOON (IRE) 4 b.g. Galileo (IRE) 134 – Velouette (Darshaan 133) [2015 98: **94 §**
12v⁶ 12g⁵ 12m 10.3g 10d³ 10g 10d 10g 18.6f Oct 13] tall, leggy gelding: fairly useful
handicapper: left John Patrick Murtagh after second start: stays 1½m: acts on good to firm
and heavy going: sometimes wears headgear: ungenuine. *Michael Dods*

URBAN SPACE 9 ch.g. Sulamani (IRE) 130 – Rasmalai 71 (Sadler's Wells (USA) 132) **–**
[2015 73: 10.2m 11.6g 10.2s Nov 4] small gelding: handicapper: fair form in 2014, well
held in 2015: stays 1½m: acts on firm and soft going: wears tongue tie. *John Flint*

URIAH HEEP (FR) 6 b.g. Danehill Dancer (IRE) 117 – Canasita 107 (Zafonic (USA) **79**
130) [2015 74: 11.9g³ 14.1g⁶ 13.1g Sep 19] tall gelding: fair handicapper: left Alan King
after second start: stays 13f: acts on polytrack, soft and good to firm going: tried in
cheekpieces: fairly useful hurdler/chaser. *R. Mike Smith*

USE YOUR FILBERT (IRE) 3 b.c. Acclamation 118 – Wishing Chair (USA) (Giant's **83**
Causeway (USA) 132) [2015 83p: 6g³ 7g² 7.1m⁵ 7g⁵ 7g p8f Oct 22] fairly useful handicapper:
stayed 7f: acted on good to firm going: tried in cheekpieces: dead. *Robert Cowell*

U S NAVY SEAL (USA) 3 b.c. War Front (USA) 119 – Questress (USA) (Seeking The **87 p**
Gold (USA)) [2015 –p: 8m³ p10f² t12.2g² f12g^ur p10f* Dec 21] fairly useful performer:
left Aidan O'Brien after reappearance: won maiden at Chelmsford in December: best effort
at 1¼m: acts on polytrack: sometimes slowly away: open to further improvement.
J. R. Jenkins

USTINOV 3 b.g. Exceed And Excel (AUS) 126 – Tamzin (Hernando (FR) 127) [2015 89: **100**
7g 7d 7.1g 6m³ 6g* t7.1m* p7m Oct 21] smallish gelding: useful handicapper: improved
and won at Ayr in September and Wolverhampton (by length from Arlecchino's Leap) in
October: left Brian Meehan after third start: stays 7f: acts on tapeta, best turf form on good
going: races towards rear. *David O'Meara*

U THINK UR FUNNY (IRE) 3 b.f. Zebedee 113 – Northern Tara (IRE) 84 (Fayruz 116) **52**
[2015 48p: 5g² 5g³ 5g t5.1g 5g Jun 20] modest maiden: raced only at 5f: best form on good
going: often wears hood. *Tony Coyle*

<h1 style="text-align:center">V</h1>

VADAMOS (FR) 4 b.c. Monsun (GER) 124 – Celebre Vadala (FR) (Peintre Celebre **117**
(USA) 137) [2015 9.9g* 8g* 10d Oct 17] smart performer: left Francois Rohaut, improved
in 2015, winning minor event at Chantilly in July and Oettingen-Rennen at Baden-Baden
(by 5 lengths from Merry Me) in September: 8/1, well held in Champion Stakes at Ascot
final outing: stays 1½m, best effort at 1m: acts on soft going: usually races close up.
A. Fabre, France

VAGUELY SPANISH 4 b.g. Oratorio (IRE) 128 – Spanish Quest (Rainbow Quest (USA) **63**
134) [2015 67: t12.2g⁶ 8.3m 10.2m⁴ 11.9s⁴ t8.6f² Oct 13] good-topped gelding: modest
handicapper: stays 11f: acts on polytrack, tapeta and good to soft going: often races
towards rear. *Tony Carroll*

VAINGLORY (USA) 11 ch.g. Swain (IRE) 134 – Infinite Spirit (USA) 108 (Maria's Mon **–**
(USA) 121) [2015 83: 10m p11g May 20] smallish gelding: fairly useful handicapper in
2014, well held both starts in 2015: stays 10.5f: acts on polytrack, fibresand, soft and good
to firm going: often races towards rear, often races lazily. *David Simcock*

VALANTINO OYSTER (IRE) 8 b.g. Pearl of Love (IRE) 112 – Mishor 83 (Slip **71**
Anchor 136) [2015 84: 9s 9.9m⁶ 10m⁶ 12d² 12m 12m⁶ 10m* 12m⁴ 10.2m Aug 22] fair
performer: won claimer at Redcar in July: left Tracy Waggott after: stays 12.5f: acts on firm
and soft going: wears headgear: usually leads. *Ali Stronge*

VALBCHEK (IRE) 6 b.g. Acclamation 118 – Spectacular Show (IRE) 79 (Spectrum (IRE) **105**
126) [2015 94, a106: p7g⁶ p7g* 6m 6g³ May 15] strong, sturdy gelding: useful handicapper:
won at Lingfield (by neck from Ishiamber) in April: stays 7f: acts on polytrack, soft and
good to firm going: wears headgear: suspect attitude. *Jane Chapple-Hyam*

VALENTINE BELLE 3 b.f. Monsieur Bond (IRE) 120 – Sheka 68 (Ishiguru (USA) 114) **–**
[2015 –: 6m May 2] no form in maidens. *Paul Midgley*

VALENTINE MIST (IRE) 3 b.f. Vale of York (IRE) 117 – Silvertine (IRE) 84 (Alzao **59**
(USA) 117) [2015 p7g⁶ t7.1m³ f7g⁵ Nov 12] €16,000Y, resold €25,000Y: fourth foal: half-
sister to 2-y-o 6f winner She's Ok (by Xaar): dam, maiden (stayed 7f), half-sister to smart
winner up to 12.3f Mickdaam: modest maiden: best effort when third at Wolverhampton.
Charles Hills

VALENTINE'S GIFT 7 b.g. Presidium 124 – Efipetite 54 (Efisio 120) [2015 61: p12m **47** f11s⁴ t12.2f⁶ p13.3g f14d⁵ Mar 11] poor handicapper: stays 1½m: acts on fibresand, tapeta, good to firm and heavy going: wears headgear. *John Wainwright*

VALE OF IRON (IRE) 3 b.c. Vale of York (IRE) 117 – Lady Van Gogh (Dubai **75** Destination (USA) 127) [2015 64: p8g² p8f³ p8g³ 8g⁴ 9.9g⁵ 8.3d² 8.3m⁴ 7.6g⁵ 8m⁵ p8g² 8.5g² 8.1g p8f⁵ p10f⁵ p10g⁵ p8g⁶ p10g⁴ p12g* Dec 19] tall colt: fair handicapper: won at Lingfield in December: stays 1½m: acts on polytrack, good to firm and good to soft going: tried in cheekpieces in 2015: often races towards rear. *John Best*

VALE OF PARIS (IRE) 3 b.f. Vale of York (IRE) 117 – Paris Glory (USA) (Honour And **79** Glory (USA) 122) [2015 –p: 5g* t5.1g* p5g⁴ 5g* 5d⁴ 5m Sep 11] fair performer: won maiden at Bath and handicap at Wolverhampton in June and handicap at Doncaster in August: best form at 5f: acts on tapeta, best turf form on good going: sometimes slowly away. *Rae Guest*

VALE PARK 3 b.g. Vale of York (IRE) 117 – Sparkle Park 52 (Kyllachy 129) [2015 t7.1f **–** t8.6f p8f t9.5t³ p11g 10.2m May 4] no form: tried in cheekpieces. *David Dennis*

VALIANT FAITH 2 b.f. (Apr 5) Aussie Rules (USA) 123 – Special Destiny (Tobougg **52** (IRE) 125) [2015 5.7f p6g 6g 5f⁴ 5.1m³ p6g Sep 22] smallish filly: modest maiden: stayed 6f: acted on polytrack and good to firm going: dead. *Ronald Harris*

VALID REASON 8 b.g. Observatory (USA) 131 – Real Trust (USA) (Danzig (USA)) **77** [2015 74: p16g³ p16d⁵ p15.8g* p14g² 14m⁵ 16d⁶ May 19] rangy gelding: fair handicapper: won at Lingfield in April: stays 2¼m: acts on polytrack, good to firm and heavy going: usually in headgear/tongue tie: front runner. *Dean Ivory*

VALITOP 2 b.c. (Apr 3) Pivotal 124 – Songerie 115 (Hernando (FR) 127) [2015 7.4d² **89** 8.1g* 8.1g Oct 10] €18,000Y, 33,000 2-y-o: lengthy, rather unfurnished colt: fifth foal: half-brother to 1m winner Tennessee Soul (by Mr Greeley) and useful 1½m-13f winner (stays 15f) Hardstone (by Birdstone): dam, 2-y-o 7f/1m winner who stayed 1½m, sister to smart winner up to 1¾m (stayed 2¼m) Souvenance: fairly useful form: won maiden at Sandown in September by 3 lengths from Absolute Zero: upped in trip, creditable 7¼ lengths eighth of 10 to Glamorous Approach in listed race at Newmarket final start, weakening. *Seamus Durack*

VALKO 2 b.g. (Feb 11) Oasis Dream 129 – Vincennes 109 (King's Best (USA) 132) [2015 **75** 7f⁵ 7m² 6g² p6g* 7g p6f⁵ Oct 15] fair performer: won maiden at Kempton in August: stays 7f: acts on polytrack and good to firm going: in cheekpieces last 3 start: has looked none too keen. *Charlie Appleby*

VALLANCE ROAD 2 b.f. (Apr 10) Kheleyf (USA) 116 – Last Romance (IRE) (Last **73** Tycoon 131) [2015 6g* 6f 7f⁶ 7m⁴ p8f² 7.1m 7g⁶ 6m 7v p8m³ Nov 14] 2,000Y: rather unfurnished filly: closely related to 1m-1¼m winner Rockinger (by Byron) and half-sister to 3 winners, including 5f-1m winner (stayed 11f) Chief Eric (by Slickly) and 1m-1½m winner Napoleon (by Diktat): dam maiden half-sister to winner up to 1¼m Wedding Ring: fair performer: won maiden at Newmarket in May: stays 1m: acts on polytrack: in blinkers final start. *Nick Littmoden*

VALLARTA (IRE) 5 b.g. Footstepsinthesand 120 – Mexican Miss (IRE) 75 (Tagula **88** (IRE) 116) [2015 83: f6g* 6d⁶ 6g² 6m⁴ 6d 6m* 6m 6m³ 6d⁴ 6m 5g³ 6m 6g t5.1f⁴ Oct 9] lengthy gelding: fairly useful handicapper: won at Southwell in March and Ayr in June: has form at 7f, probably best at 6f: acts on fibresand, tapeta and firm going: tried in visor prior to 2015. *Ruth Carr*

VALLEY OF FIRE 3 b.g. Firebreak 125 – Charlie Girl 70 (Puissance 110) [2015 98: 6m **96 p** 6d⁴ Jul 25] useful handicapper: back to form when 2 lengths fourth to Teruntum Star in handicap at Newmarket final outing, running on late having been outpaced: should stay 7f: acts on firm and good to soft going: has been gelded: should do better still. *William Haggas*

VALMINA 8 b.g. Val Royal (FR) 127 – Minnina (IRE) (In The Wings 128) [2015 70, a87: **65** 5m 5.2m 5d 5.4* 5.7s* Aug 26] workmanlike gelding: fair handicapper: won at Ffos Las and Bath in August: stays 7f, races over shorter nowadays: acts on polytrack, firm and soft going: tried in headgear: wears tongue tie: often races towards rear. *Tony Carroll*

VALTASHYRA (IRE) 2 br.f. (Feb 20) Vale of York (IRE) 117 – Tashyra (IRE) 59 (Tagula (IRE) 116) [2015 t5.1f p5f f5g p5m⁶ Nov 21] 3,200 2-y-o: sixth foal: half-sister to 3 winners, including winner up to 7f I'malwaysright (2-y-o 6f winner, by Namid) and 5f winner Simply Black (by Kheleyf): dam maiden sister to useful 6f/7f winner Tagshira: no form. *Ann Stokell*

VANCOUVERITE 5 b.g. Dansili 127 – Villarrica (USA) 84 (Selkirk (USA) 129) [2015 118: 8.9g Feb 12] smart at best: well-held last of 12 in handicap at Meydan on only outing on Flat in 2015: probably stays 1½m: acts on good to firm and good to soft going: blinkered last 3 starts: fairly useful hurdler for John Ferguson. *Charlie Appleby* —

VAN DIEST 3 b.g. Hurricane Run (IRE) 134 – Miracle (Ezzoud (IRE) 126) [2015 8m p10g p12g Jun 4] strong gelding: well held in maidens. *Henry Spiller* —

VAN DYKE 2 b.c. (Apr 15) Excellent Art 125 – Respectfilly (Mark of Esteem (IRE) 137) [2015 p8g2 p8g2 t9.5f2 Dec 14] second foal: dam unraced half-sister to smart winner up to 1¼m Quiz Mistress: fairly useful maiden: runner-up at Kempton (twice) and Wolverhampton : will stay 1¼m. *Hughie Morrison* **82**

VAN ELLIS 6 b.g. Shamardal (USA) 129 – Jalousie (IRE) 108 (Barathea (IRE) 127) [2015 6g 6m4 5f 7fpu Jul 16] big, heavy-topped gelding: fair performer: stays 7f: acts on synthetics, best turf form on good going or firmer: tried in tongue tie in 2015. *Steve Flook* **68**

VAN GERWEN 2 ch.g. (Apr 2) Bahamian Bounty 116 – Disco Ball 75 (Fantastic Light (USA) 134) [2015 5g 5m4 5d5 Sep 17] fair maiden: best efort when fourth at Pontefract: has been gelded. *Les Eyre* **68**

VAN HUYSEN (IRE) 3 br.g. Excellent Art 125 – Tara Too (IRE) 97 (Danetime (IRE) 121) [2015 p7m p8f* 8.3m6 7m p8g2 8m p8g3 p7m3 Dec 31] useful-looking gelding: third foal: half-brother to 1¼m winner (stays 1¾m) Benoordenhout (by Footstepsinthesand): dam winner up to 7f (2-y-o 5f winner): fairly useful performer: won maiden at Lingfield (dead-heated) in January: better form in handicaps subsequently: left Jonathan Portman after seventh start: worth a try at further than 1m: acts on polytrack and good to firm going: usually in hood. *Dominic Ffrench Davis* **82**

VANILLA ROSE (IRE) 3 b.f. Bushranger (IRE) 119 – Vanilla Loan (IRE) 80 (Invincible Spirit (IRE) 121) [2015 6d May 13] €12,000Y: first foal: dam, 6f winner, half-sister to useful 6f-1m winner Film Maker: 33/1, last of 13 in maiden at Newcastle. *Mark Walford* —

VANISHING 3 b.f. Sir Percy 129 – Valoria (Hernando (FR) 127) [2015 72: 10g* 11.6f3 9.9m 12.4g3 12g* 12g4 13.1f2 16.2m2 Oct 1] rather sparely-made filly: fairly useful handicapper: won at Redcar in April and Pontefract in July: stays 2m: acts on firm going: in cheekpieces. *Ed Walker* **83**

VAN MILDERT (IRE) 6 b.m. Observatory (USA) 131 – Vanilla Delight (IRE) 76 (Orpen (USA) 116) [2015 –: f12g Jan 13] no form: tried in cheekpieces: poor winning hurdler. *Dianne Sayer* —

VAN WILDER (IRE) 3 b.g. Rip Van Winkle (IRE) 134 – Zelding (IRE) 108 (Warning 136) [2015 t7.1m3 t6f* t6g* t7.1g4 Jun 2] fair performer: raced only at Wolverhampton, winning maiden in February and minor event in March: best form at 6f: has joined David Loder. *Richard Fahey* **77**

VARIABLE 3 b.f. Sea The Stars (IRE) 140 – Proportional 115 (Beat Hollow 126) [2015 9.5g2 12g* 10m4 12g* Oct 11] second foal: half-sister to winner abroad by Dansili: dam, 2-y-o 7f/1m (Prix Marcel Boussac)winner who should have stayed 1½m, sister to smart winner up to 1m (stayed 1¼m) Vote Often: smart form: won maiden at Cork (by 6½ lengths from Sense of Victory) in May: in first-time hood, much improved when also won 5-runner listed race at the Curragh on final start by 3 lengths from Ebayya, leading over 1f out and driven out: stays 1½m: capable of better still. *D. K. Weld, Ireland* **112 p**

VARSOVIAN 5 ch.g. Refuse To Bend (IRE) 128 – Queen of Poland 109 (Halling (USA) 133) [2015 85: p6g4 p6g* p6f* p6g* p6f4 p6m3 t6m6 Dec 12] lengthy gelding: fairly useful handicapper: won at Lingfield in February and at Chelmsford in March and April: stays 6f: acts on polytrack. *Dean Ivory* **92**

VASTLY (USA) 6 gr.g. Mizzen Mast (USA) 121 – Valentine Band (USA) 104 (Dixieland Band (USA)) [2015 72: 8g 10.2m p8g4 p8f4 t9.5f4 p10d5 p10g6 Dec 15] fair handicapper: stays 1¼m: acts on all-weather: tried in headgear/tongue tie: often races prominently. *Julia Feilden* **69**

VAUNTING (USA) 2 gr.f. (Feb 19) Exchange Rate (USA) 111 – Boasting (USA) (Kris S (USA)) [2015 p7g* Oct 29] lengthy filly: has scope: fifth foal: sister to smart 7f-9f winner Bragging and half-sister to 6f winner Truth To Tell (by Aptitude): dam 1m/9f winner: withdrawn after refusing to enter stalls on intended debut Oct 9: 9/2, shaped well when winning 19-runner maiden at Lingfield comfortably by ½ length from Impressive Day, leading close home: open to significant improvement. *Sir Michael Stoute* **92 p**

VAZIRABAD (FR) 3 b.g. Manduro (GER) 135 – Visorama (IRE) 114 (Linamix **127**
(FR) 127) [2015 10.9s⁶ 14.9g² 14.9s* 13.4g* 14.9g* 14.9m* 15.4d* Oct 25]

He might not have had the speed of Muhaarar or the string of big-race
victories of Golden Horn, but there were few better three-year-olds in Europe by
the end of the year than the top French stayer Vazirabad. Another three-year-old,
Order of St George, was tremendously impressive when thrashing his field by a wide
margin in the Irish St Leger, and Vazirabad himself put up a high-class performance
when also beating older rivals in the Prix Royal-Oak, run at Saint-Cloud in the
latest season. There had been little indication early in his career that Vazirabad
was destined to reach such heights; if anything, he had made an inauspicious start.
Gelded as a two-year-old, it was the following May before he reached the track and
was then beaten on his first two starts, on both occasions fitted with headgear. After
finishing sixth of nine in cheekpieces in a newcomers race at Longchamp, he did
better with his sights lowered when second in a maiden at Dieppe. Blinkered for
that run over fifteen furlongs, the race did at least show that staying was going to be
Vazirabad's game and, with the headgear dispensed with, he didn't look back from
then on, winning his five remaining starts, culminating in that Group 1 success at
the end of October.

After going one better in another maiden over the same distance back at
Dieppe in July, Vazirabad followed up in a minor event at Deauville over a slightly
shorter trip before winning the two big races at Longchamp in the autumn for three-
year-old stayers, the Prix de Lutece and, four weeks afterwards on Arc weekend, the
Qatar Prix Chaudenay. Vazirabad faced six rivals in the Chaudenay, including Big
Blue, Pilansberg and Gaius Caesar who had finished second, fourth and fifth behind
him in the Lutece, while The Twisler, who had upset older rivals in the listed March
Stakes at Goodwood, was the only British challenger. Starting at odds on, Vazirabad
made short work of his field once moving smoothly into the lead two furlongs out
and was five lengths clear before being eased and winning by three from outsider
Tiberian, with Pilansberg, Big Blue and The Twisler the next home. Vazirabad was
the sixth Aga Khan-owned winner of the Chaudenay this century, and all four of his
previous winners who had gone on to the Prix Royal-Oak had finished third, those
being Behkara, Shamdala, Manighar and Shankardeh. Coming three weeks after the
Chaudenay, the Royal-Oak is the logical next step, providing the leading French
three-year-old stayer with the opportunity to take on older rivals, though Jean-Luc
Lagardere's Amilynx in 1999 had been the last to complete the Chaudenay/Royal-
Oak double. Since the successes of Vinnie Roe and Mr Dinos (for Ireland and Britain

*Prix Royal-Oak, Saint-Cloud—a high-class effort from up-and-coming Vazirabad, who becomes
only the second three-year-old winner of this race since 2002; Siljan's Saga pulls clear of the
remainder in second, with Cadran winner Mille Et Mille (second left) third and Cirrus des Aigles
(third right) fourth, the latter having his first try over a staying trip*

respectively) at the beginning of the century, the only other three-year-old winner of the Royal Oak had been the gelding Les Beaufs in 2012 and he had been beaten a neck in the Chaudenay beforehand.

The latest Prix Royal-Oak was the first of Longchamp's Group 1 contests that had to be found a temporary home during the track's two-year redevelopment programme, which was why it was run at Saint-Cloud for the first time. The 2016 Prix de l'Arc weekend will be staged at Chantilly but France's flagship racecourse should be back in action again in time for the 2017 Arc. Other temporary arrangements for Longchamp's big races include the Prix Ganay and the Grand Prix de Paris being run at Saint-Cloud, the Poule d'Essai des Poulains/Pouliches and Prix Saint-Alary at Deauville, and the 'day of trials' at Chantilly. Vazirabad was sent off the 24/10 favourite to beat his twelve rivals in the Royal-Oak, among whom Pilansberg was the only other three-year-old. Considerable interest was added to the field by the presence of Cirrus des Aigles, running at Saint-Cloud in preference to what would otherwise have been his fifth consecutive appearance in the Champion Stakes at Ascot the previous weekend; the nine-year-old had never previously raced at much beyond a mile and a half. With regular partner Christophe Soumillon committed to partnering Vazirabad (on whom he put up a pound overweight, incidentally), the ride on Cirrus des Aigles went to Frankie Dettori instead. Of the proven stayers in the line-up, Mille Et Mille, Kicky Blue and Fun Mac (the last-named the only British runner) had filled the first three places in the Prix du Cadran at Longchamp on Arc day, but it was the pair who had contested the Arc itself, Manatee and Siljan's Saga, who were next in the betting behind Vazirabad. Neither had been the slightest threat to Golden Horn, but the mare Siljan's Saga, winner of the Grand Prix de Deauville in August, had excelled herself at long odds in the Arc for the second year running and hadn't been discredited when fifth in the Royal-Oak the year before. Mille Et Mille had been allowed plenty of rope by his rivals when making all in the Cadran and he led for much of the way, though with a shorter lead, in the Royal-Oak, Cirrus des Aigles one of those kept in touch behind him, while Soumillon dropped Vazirabad out in rear. With the field coming wide into the straight, Vazirabad made his challenge widest of all. Showing something of an ungainly head carriage as he made headway under pressure on the outside of the field, Vazirabad nonetheless responded gamely enough to get on terms with Siljan's Saga, who had taken over from Mille Et Mille in the lead in the straight and had begun to stretch away. Once upsides Siljan's Saga in the final furlong, Vazirabad asserted to win a shade cosily by a length, with a further five lengths back to Mille Et Mille in third, which underlined the fact that Vazirabad had put up a high-class performance. Cirrus des Aigles was beaten seven lengths into fourth, running more like a horse out of form than one who didn't stay.

Vazirabad (FR) (b.g. 2012)	Manduro (GER) (b 2002)	Monsun (br 1990)	Konigsstuhl
			Mosella
		Mandellicht (b 1994)	Be My Guest
			Mandelauge
	Visorama (IRE) (gr 2000)	Linamix (gr 1987)	Mendez
			Lunadix
		Visor (b 1989)	Mr Prospector
			Look

Vazirabad, like the triple Group 1 winner Ervedya, is another top winner resulting from the Aga Khan's acquisition, in 2005, of the bloodstock of Jean-Luc Lagardere following his death. Vazirabad's grandam Visor had been one of the most successful of the Lagardere broodmares before passing into the Aga Khan's ownership, and her daughter Visorama has kept up the good work in the Aga Khan's broodmare band, with Vazirabad her seventh winner from as many foals, all—typically for her owner's studs—by different stallions. Vazirabad is much the best of the septet, though his Dansili half-sister Visoriyna was a useful miler, successful in a listed race at La Teste in 2014 and placed twice in Group 3 company. Visor was by Mr Prospector, a sire whom Jean-Luc Lagardere often made sure featured in the pedigrees of potential broodmares acquired for his own stallion Linamix. Visor was only a six-furlong maiden winner on dirt in the States, but she was well related, being out of a half-sister to the Kentucky Derby and Belmont Stakes winner

Swale. Among her winners at stud, no fewer than seven earned Timeform ratings of 112 or more, including Visorama (by Linamix) who won the Prix de Flore at Saint-Cloud (ridden by Christophe Soumillon) on her final start at three and finished third in the Grand Prix de Saint-Cloud at four. Between them, Linamix and Visor also produced Visionary and Visionnaire, who finished third in the Poule d'Essai des Poulains and Prix de Diane respectively. However, the highest-rated of Visor's offspring was Varenar who caused an upset when beating odds-on Goldikova into third in the 2009 Prix de la Foret. Varenar, by Rock of Gibraltar, had more speed than any of Visor's other foals, though Visor also produced the hot favourite for the 2006 Derby, Visindar. Bred by Jean-Luc Lagardere but by the Aga Khan's Sinndar, he finished fifth in a bid to emulate his sire at Epsom, having won all three of his races beforehand in France, notably the Prix Greffulhe.

The dam's side of Vazirabad's pedigree doesn't wholly account for his abundant stamina, though Linamix sired the aforementioned Amilynx (who went on to win a second Royal Oak at the age of four) and was also responsible for the sire of Siljan's Saga, Sagamix, who won the Prix de l'Arc for Lagardere. Vazirabad's sire Manduro suffered a career-ending injury when winning the Prix Foy on his first start over a mile and a half, having shown himself top class at up to a mile and a quarter, and he was by the proven stamina influence Monsun. Manduro was described at the time of his retirement by his trainer Andre Fabre as the best racehorse he had trained, but he hasn't reached the same heights as a stallion, Vazirabad being responsible for three of the six pattern races won in Europe in the latest season by his progeny (Ultra won the Jean-Luc Lagardere, Ribbons the Blandford Stakes and Fractional the Prix Messidor). Manduro stands at the Haras du Logis in France at €7,000. More big-race success looks sure to come Vazirabad's way if he continues to be campaigned as a stayer, though his trainer intimated after the Prix Royal-Oak that he could be tried back at a mile and a half as a four-year-old. Vazirabad acts on soft and good to firm going and is patiently ridden. He presumably wasn't the most straightforward racehorse in his early days, judging from the fitting of headgear for his first couple of starts, but he has done little wrong since. *A. de Royer Dupre, France*

VECHEKA (IRE) 4 b.g. Lawman (FR) 121 – Lidanski (IRE) 100 (Soviet Star (USA) 128) [2015 74p: 6g⁵ 7g 7s² 7g³ 6m³ 7.5m⁴ 7m⁴ 7.2m 7.9s 7d⁶ 9.3g Sep 15] fair maiden: stays 7f: acts on soft and good to firm going: tried in hood: usually races prominently, often races freely. *Micky Hammond* — **71**

VEENA (FR) 2 b.f. (Feb 19) Elusive City (USA) 117 – Kensita (FR) (Soviet Star (USA) 128) [2015 p7g⁶ p6g* Oct 14] €40,000Y: third foal: dam unraced half-sister to useful 2-y-o 5f/6f winner Keraka out of smart 7f performer (Supreme Stakes winner) Kerita: much improved when winning maiden at Kempton by ¾ length from Catchment, staying on to lead close home and having bit to spare: will prove as effective at 7f as 6f: will go on improving. *David Simcock* — **82 p**

VEERAYA 5 b.g. Rail Link 132 – Follow Flanders 92 (Pursuit of Love 124) [2015 90: p8f 8g 7d² 7m 8f⁴ p8g⁶ p6g² 6m Sep 28] lengthy gelding: fair handicapper: stays 1¼m: acts on polytrack, good to firm and good to soft going: has worn headgear: usually wears tongue tie nowadays. *Julia Feilden* — **74**

VEGAS REBEL (IRE) 3 b.g. Alfred Nobel (IRE) 110 – Van de Cappelle (IRE) (Pivotal 124) [2015 83: 7m 7m² 7g³ 7m 7g⁵ p8m Oct 21] fair handicapper: will prove suited by a return to 7f: acts on polytrack, good to firm and heavy going: usually races towards rear. *Dave Morris* — **76**

VEJOVIS 3 b.g. Fastnet Rock (AUS) 127 – Violet (IRE) 77 (Mukaddamah (USA) 125) [2015 –: t8.6f² p7f* p8f⁶ p7m⁴ p6m³ t7.1m⁴ p6g² p5g³ 5.7f⁶ 6m⁶ Apr 29] fair handicapper: won at Lingfield in January: stays 7f: acts on polytrack and tapeta: has worn headgear, including last 4 starts: sometimes in tongue tie: front runner/races prominently, often races freely: sold 5,000 gns, sent to Denmark. *Stuart Williams* — **67**

VELOCITER (IRE) 3 ch.g. Zebedee 113 – Polly Jones (USA) 48 (Lear Fan (USA) 130) [2015 70: p8f* 10.3d⁴ 8.1m 7m⁴ 7.6g⁶ 7g⁵ 7d 7s⁴ p8f⁶ Oct 22] fair performer: won maiden at Kempton in March: stays 1m: acts on polytrack, soft and good to firm going: temperament under suspicion: sold 8,500 gns, sent to Italy. *Richard Hannon* — **76**

VELVET REVOLUTION 2 ch.c. (May 2) Pivotal 124 – Gino's Spirits 98 (Perugino 73 (USA) 84) [2015 p8f⁵ p8f³ Oct 28] better effort in maidens at Chelmsford when fifth of 14 to Theydon Grey on debut. *Marco Botti*

VENEZIA (IRE) 4 gr.g. Galileo (IRE) 134 – St Roch (IRE) (Danehill (USA) 126) [2015 97 100: p10.7g⁴ 12g 16m⁵ 13g³ 14g⁴ 15g² 13m* 14d⁵ 16g 15s Oct 25] lengthy gelding: useful handicapper: won at Navan (by neck from Hudson's Bay) in September: stays 15f: acts on polytrack, soft and good to firm going: wears cheekpieces nowadays: in tongue tie last 5 starts: often races towards rear. *M. Halford, Ireland*

VENGEUR MASQUE (IRE) 3 b.c. Monsun (GER) 124 – Venetian Beauty (USA) 105 (Lear Fan (USA) 130) [2015 10.9g² 12.4g* 11.9g* 12.4g⁴ 14.6d⁵ Sep 12] fourth foal: half-brother to 3 winners, including useful 1¼m-12.5f winner Vermont (by Muhtathir) and 1¼m winner Virgin Island (by Peintre Celebre): dam unraced half-sister to very smart 1m winner Vetheuil: useful performer: won maiden at Saint-Cloud in May and minor event at Compiegne in June: 2¼ lengths fourth to Loresho in Prix de Reux at Deauville, then far from discredited when 11 lengths fifth of 7 to Simple Verse in St Leger at Doncaster, though never dangerous: probably stays 14.6f: acts on good to soft going: sent to Australia. *M. Delzangles, France*

VENT DE FORCE 4 b.c. Hurricane Run (IRE) 134 – Capriolla 55 (In The Wings 128) 115 [2015 112: 16f² 16.4m* 20f 16.4d⁶ 14d Sep 13] strong colt: smart performer: won Henry II Stakes at Sandown in May by 1¾ lengths from Trip To Paris, making running: also good effort on reappearance when 2 lengths second to Mizzou in Sagaro Stakes at Ascot (waited with, short of room over 1f out): well held all other outings in 2015: stays 16.5f: acts on firm and soft going. *Hughie Morrison*

VENTRILOQUIST 3 ch.g. New Approach (IRE) 132 – Illusion 98 (Anabaa (USA) 130) 79 [2015 82: p7f* Mar 4] useful-looking gelding: fair performer: won maiden at Lingfield in March on only outing in 2015: stays 1m: acts on polytrack: front runner/races prominently: sold £24,000, sent to Hong Kong, where renamed Classier. *Charlie Appleby*

VENTURA CASTLE 3 b.g. Paco Boy (IRE) 129 – Bisaat (USA) (Bahri (USA) 125) 69 [2015 68: p10d³ p10g* 9.8v* May 8] fair performer: in cheekpieces, won sellers at Lingfield in April (subsequently left Richard Hannon) and Ripon in May: stays 1¼m: acts on polytrack, good to firm and heavy going. *David Nicholls*

VENTURA QUEST (USA) 4 b.g. Henrythenavigator (USA) 131 – Ing Ing (FR) 110 88 (Bering 136) [2015 93: p10g⁴ 10.3m⁴ 8.5g⁴ 9.8d* 9g³ Jun 18] well-made gelding: fairly useful handicapper: won at Ripon in June: stays 10.5f: acts on soft and good to firm going: in blinkers last 4 starts: sold 32,000 gns, sent to Saudi Arabia. *Richard Fahey*

VENTURA STORM (IRE) 2 b.c. (Feb 15) Zoffany (IRE) 121 – Sarawati (IRE) 69 104 (Haafhd 129) [2015 7d³ 8g* 8s* 8m Oct 4] €54,000F, €50,000Y, 110,000 2-y-o: useful-looking colt: second foal: half-brother to 1½m winner Bella Varenna (by Lawman): dam lightly-raced half-sister to useful winner up to 1½m Sahool: useful form: won maiden at Newmarket in August and minor event at Salisbury (by 2¼ lengths from Justice Law) in September: not disgraced when never-dangerous 4¾ lengths tenth of 11 to Ultra in Prix Jean-Luc Lagardere at Longchamp final start: stays 1m. *Richard Hannon*

VENTUROUS (IRE) 2 ch.c. (Mar 25) Raven's Pass (USA) 133 – Bold Desire 58 100 (Cadeaux Genereux 131) [2015 7m⁵ 6g* 6m* 6g⁶ Sep 26] 110,000F: well-made colt: fifth foal: half-brother to 3 winners, including smart 2-y-o 5f/6f winner Parliament Square and useful 5f/6f winner Wanting (both by Acclamation): dam ran twice: useful form: won maiden at Newmarket in August and minor event at Doncaster (by ½ length from Madrinho) in September: stiffer task, better than result (8¼ lengths sixth of 7 to Shalaa) in Middle Park Stakes at Newmarket final start, rearing leaving stall but chasing leaders briefly over 1f out: stays 6f. *Charlie Appleby*

VENUS GRACE 4 b.f. Royal Applause 124 – Basque Beauty 96 (Nayef (USA) 129) 69 [2015 83: p8m² p8f p8g⁶ f8g⁵ 10m p8g² 8.3m³ p8f² p8f⁶ f8g⁵ p8g³ p7f³ Dec 17] strong mare: fair maiden: left Dr Jon Scargill after ninth start: stays 8.5f: acts on polytrack and good to firm going: often in cheekpieces in 2015: front runner/races prominently. *Michael Appleby*

VENUS MARINA 4 b.f. Tiger Hill (IRE) 127 – Danvers 63 (Cape Cross (IRE) 129) [2015 78 69, a52: 7m⁶ 7m⁶ 6m⁴ 7g² 7.6s* 7g* 7g⁵ Sep 19] fair handicapper: won at Lingfield and Yarmouth in August: should stay 1m: acts on soft going, probably on good to firm: usually wears hood. *Chris Wall*

VENUTIUS 8 b.g. Doyen (IRE) 132 – Boadicea's Chariot (Commanche Run 133) [2015   **82**
77: 8g 8m² 8.3g² 8.3m* 8.3m⁴ 7.9m* 8.5m* Oct 1] stocky gelding: fairly useful
handicapper: won at Nottingham in July, Carlisle in September and Beverley in October:
stays 8.5f: acts on polytrack, good to firm and good to soft going: front runner/races
prominently. *Ed McMahon*

VERCINGETORIX (SAF) 6 b.h. Silvano (GER) 126 – National Vixen (SAF) (National   **124**
Assembly (CAN)) [2015 124: 8.9g* 8.9g⁶ Mar 7] very smart performer: won Al Rashidiya
at Meydan (by 2 lengths from True Story) in January: reportedly injured sesamoid ligament
in Jebel Hatta on same course next time (had won race in 2014): stayed 1¼m: acted on
good to firm going: standing at Main Chance Farm, South Africa. *M. F. de Kock,
South Africa*

VERERI SENES 3 b.f. Nayef (USA) 129 – Whazzat 105 (Daylami (IRE) 138) [2015 68:   **61**
p10g⁴ 11.9f³ 11.6m⁴ 10m⁴ Jul 17] lengthy filly: modest maiden: seems to stay 1½m: acts
on polytrack and firm going: tried in headgear. temperament under suspicion. *Ed Dunlop*

VERISMO 3 b.g. Hurricane Run (IRE) 134 – Cross Current (Sakhee (USA) 136) [2015   **66**
78p: t12.2g* 10dᵖᵘ Apr 10] fair form: won maiden at Wolverhampton in March; broke
down in handicap at Leicester next time: stays 1½m. *Ed Dunlop*

VERMEULEN 2 b.g. (Feb 19) Fastnet Rock (AUS) 127 – Crystal Maze (Gone West   **–**
(USA)) [2015 7m Oct 3] good-bodied gelding: 40/1, needed race and ran green when well
held in Tattersalls Millions 2-y-o Trophy at Newmarket on debut. *John Gosden*

VERNE CASTLE 2 ch.g. (Mar 21) Sakhee's Secret 128 – Lochangel 119 (Night Shift   **58 p**
(USA)) [2015 p6g 5.1g Sep 30] half-brother to several winners, including useful 6f winner
Strictly Dancing (by Danehill Dancer) and 7f-1¼m winner Star Pupil (by Selkirk): dam,
winner around 5f (including Nunthorpe Stakes and also 6f winner at 2 yrs), half-sister to
lightning fast Lochsong: modest form in maidens at Kempton and Nottingham: has been
gelded: remains open to improvement. *Andrew Balding*

VERSE OF LOVE 6 b.g. Byron 117 – Lovellian (Machiavellian (USA) 123) [2015 94:   **83**
p7f p8m⁴ Feb 28] good-topped gelding: fairly useful handicapper: stayed 1¼m: acted on
all-weather and any turf going: had worn headgear: dead. *David Evans*

VERTUEUX (FR) 10 gr.g. Verglas (IRE) 118 – Shahrazad (FR) (Bering 136) [2015 61:   **–**
14g⁴ 11.9d⁶ Sep 14] poor handicapper: stays 2m: acts on polytrack, firm and soft going:
wears headgear: tried in tongue tie. *Tony Carroll*

VERULAMIUM 3 b.f. Myboycharlie (IRE) 118 – Actionplatinum (IRE) (Act One 124)   **–**
[2015 7g 8.3g 7.1m³ 8m⁶ 8.1g t7.1f Nov 16] smallish filly: first foal: dam unraced: no form.
Nikki Evans

VERUS DELICIA (IRE) 6 b.m. Chineur (FR) 123 – Ribbon Glade (UAE) (Zafonic   **72**
(USA) 130) [2015 83: t6f* p6g² t6g t6g³ p6f⁶ 5.7g 6g³ 6g⁴ 6g⁴ p7g t7.1f⁵ p6f t6f Nov 13]
leggy mare: fair handicapper: won at Wolverhampton in March: stays 6f: acts on polytrack,
tapeta, firm and soft going: wears hood. *Daniel Loughnane*

VERY DASHING 2 br.f. (Apr 3) Dansili 127 – Dash To The Top 116 (Montjeu (IRE) 137)   **82 p**
[2015 7g 8d² Oct 23] fourth foal: closely related to smart 2-y-o 6f winner Dynasty (by
Danehill Dancer) and half-sister to unreliable 2-y-o 7f winner Deep South (by Red
Ransom) and useful 2-y-o 1m winner Seagull Star (by Sea The Stars): dam ungenuine
winner up to 1¼m, also 2-y-o 1m winner: 25/1, much improved from debut when ¾-length
second of 11 to Zest in maiden at Doncaster, keeping on: open to further progress.
Luca Cumani

VERY FIRST BLADE 6 b.g. Needwood Blade 117 – Dispol Verity 60 (Averti (IRE) 117)   **55**
[2015 58: f5d f6s² f5g² f6d* f6g³ f5g⁵ 6.1d 5g² 6m 5g⁴ 7.6g⁶ 5.1m⁴ 5.1s³ 5m 5.1d⁴ 5m⁶ 5g   **a63**
5s⁶ Oct 6] modest handicapper: won at Southwell in February: stays 6f: acts on polytrack,
fibresand, soft and good to firm going: usually wears headgear. *Michael Mullineaux*

VERY GOOD DAY (FR) 8 b.g. Sinndar (IRE) 134 – Picture Princess (Sadler's Wells   **83**
(USA) 132) [2015 86: t16.5g* t16.5m⁵ p12g² t16.5f⁴ Mar 13] strong gelding: fairly useful
handicapper: won at Wolverhampton in January: stays 2¼m: acts on polytrack, tapeta,
good to firm and good to soft going: has worn headgear, including last 4 starts: often races
prominently. *Richard Fahey*

VERY HONEST (IRE) 2 b.f. (Feb 5) Poet's Voice 126 – Cercle d'Amour (USA) (Storm   **– p**
Cat (USA)) [2015 5m⁴ May 26] fourth foal: half-sister to 6f/7f winner Roundelay (by Tiger
Hill) and 11f winner Dorfman (by Halling): dam unraced half-sister to Norfolk Stakes
winner Warm Heart: 15/8 and green, shaped well when 8½ lengths fourth of 10 to Jersey
Breeze in maiden at Leicester on debut, slowly away: sure to progress. *Saeed bin Suroor*

VERY SPECIAL (IRE) 3 ch.f. Lope de Vega (IRE) 125 – Danielli (IRE) 79 (Danehill **106**
(USA) 126) [2015 95p: p8g* p8g² p8g² Nov 18] lengthy filly: useful performer: won minor
event at Kempton (by 2 lengths from Teosroyal) in April: off 7 months, better form when
second in listed races at Lingfield (½ length behind Lamar) and Kempton (1¼ lengths
behind Big Baz): stays 1m: acts on polytrack and good to firm going: wears hood: usually
travels strongly. *Saeed bin Suroor*

VERY TALENTED (IRE) 2 b.c. (Feb 1) Invincible Spirit (IRE) 121 – Crystal House **109 p**
(CHI) (Golden Voyager (USA)) [2015 7m³ 7g² 8m* Sep 10] good sort: seventh foal: half-
brother to winners abroad by Rahy and Smarty Jones: dam, Chilean Derby winner (second
in Chilean 1000 Guineas), sister to Chilean Oaks winner Crystal Clear: useful form: 4/6,
won 8-runner maiden at Doncaster final start easily by 3¾ lengths from Linguistic, travelling
strongly and making all: stays 1m: open to further improvement. *Saeed bin Suroor*

VESNINA 3 b.f. Sea The Stars (IRE) 140 – Safina 100 (Pivotal 124) [2015 91: 7m 7m May —
3] lengthy filly: fairly useful performer in 2014, well below form in 2015: bred to be suited
by 7f+: acts on good to soft going: front runner/races prominently, tends to find little: sold
68,000 gns. *Richard Hannon*

VESTAVIAN (IRE) 2 b.c. (Mar 18) Arcano (IRE) 122 – Vestavia (IRE) (Alhaarth (IRE) **61**
126) [2015 t6g⁴ p6g⁶ 6d t7.1f t6f³ Oct 23] modest maiden: stays 6f: acts on tapeta: tried in
blinkers/tongue tie: sent to Greece. *Brian Meehan*

VEXILLUM (IRE) 6 br.g. (Mar 6) Mujadil (USA) 119 – Common Cause 87 (Polish Patriot **48**
(USA) 128) [2015 –: 8m⁶ 17.2f⁶ Aug 12] sturdy gelding: poor handicapper: stays 17f: acts
on polytrack, good to firm and heavy going: has worn headgear/ tongue tie: winning
hurdler. *Neil Mulholland*

VIBE QUEEN (IRE) 3 b.f. Invincible Spirit (IRE) 121 – Be My Queen (IRE) 104 **93 p**
(Sadler's Wells (USA) 132) [2015 7m⁴ 7v* 7m⁵ 6.9g⁴ Jun 24] good-topped filly: fourth
foal: half-brother to winner up to 1½m Relco Nordic (2-y-o 7f-9f winner, by Raven's Pass):
dam, 1m winner who stayed 1½m, closely related to smart winner up to 6f Imperial
Beauty: useful form: won maiden at Chester (by 5 lengths from Rivers of Babylon) in May:
2 lengths fourth to Excilly in listed race at Carlisle final start, having to wait for gap 2f out:
raced only at 7f: remains with potential. *John Gosden*

VIBRANT CHORDS 2 b.g. (Apr 11) Poet's Voice 126 – Lovely Thought 92 (Dubai **93**
Destination (USA) 127) [2015 6g² 6m* 6d³ p7g² Sep 30] £75,000Y: good-quartered
gelding: third foal: half-brother to smart 5f/5.6f winner High On Life (by Invincible Spirit):
dam, 6f winner (including at 2 yrs), half-sister to very smart/temperamental winner up to
1m Just James and smart winner up to 6f Blue Jack: fairly useful form: won maiden at
Salisbury in August: progressed again when ½-length second to Majdool in nursery at
Kempton final start: stays 7f. *Henry Candy*

VICARAGE GOLD 3 b.f. Kheleyf (USA) 116 – Kyleene 79 (Kyllachy 129) [2015 p7g —
p7f t9.5f⁵ 10.2f May 13] first foal: dam 7f winner: no form. *Shaun Lycett*

VICENNALIA (USA) 2 b.f. (Mar 6) More Than Ready (USA) 120 – Silver Reunion **85**
(USA) (Harlan's Holiday (USA) 124) [2015 7m* p8g⁵ Sep 30] $500,000Y: second foal:
half-sister to a winner in USA by Tapit: dam US Grade 3 8.5f winner out of half-sister to
very smart 6f-1m performer Lucayan Prince: won maiden at Newbury in June by neck
from Heroic Heart: ran no sort of race in minor event at Kempton when next seen 3 months
later: should stay 1m: has joined H-A. Pantall in France. *Charlie Appleby*

VICKY VALENTINE 5 b.m. Rock of Gibraltar (IRE) 133 – Silcasue (Selkirk (USA) **76**
129) [2015 74: 10d* 12g⁶ 12.3f⁵ 13.1s² 13.1g³ 12.4m² 10.4g² 9.8g² Aug 15] fair
handicapper: won at Ayr in May: stays 13.5f: acts on soft and good to firm going: tried in
cheekpieces: usually races prominently, usually travels strongly. *Alistair Whillans*

VICTOIRE DE LYPHAR (IRE) 8 b.g. Bertolini (USA) 125 – Victory Peak (Shirley **83 §**
Heights 130) [2015 98: 7d 7g⁵ 7g³ 7.2s³ 7m 7m 7m² 7f² 7m⁶ 7d 7.5m² 7g² 7g 8g³ Sep 23]
compact gelding: fairly useful handicapper: stays 7f: acts on any turf going: often wears
headgear: often races freely: temperamental. *Ruth Carr*

VICTORIA POLLARD 3 b.f. Sir Percy 129 – Victoria Montoya 104 (High Chaparral **91**
(IRE) 132) [2015 10m* 11.4d 10m 12g³ Aug 4] rather leggy filly: second foal: half-sister
to 1½m winner Cape Victoria (by Mount Nelson): dam, 1¾m winner, half-sister to smart
winner up to 9f Passing Glance: fairly useful performer: won maiden at Newbury in April:
in cheekpieces, good third in handicap at Salisbury final start: stays 1½m. *Andrew Balding*

VICTORIA REGINA (IRE) 4 gr.f. Mastercraftsman (IRE) 129 – For Joy (Singspiel **106**
(IRE) 133) [2015 8g⁴ 8.9g⁴ p8g³ 8.5g 8g* 9.9g Oct 25] useful performer: left David
Simcock/off 4 months, back to form when winning Premio Elena E Sergio Cumani at

Milan in September by neck from Malka: possibly amiss when tailed-off last of 8 behind Odeliz in Premio Lydia Tesio at Rome final outing: stays 9f: acts on good to soft going: has worn tongue tie: sold 130,000 gns in December. *H. F. Devin, France*

VICTORINA 3 ch.f. Kyllachy 129 – Enrapture (USA) 85 (Lear Fan (USA) 130) [2015 –: 8m p10m 8m 7s Oct 6] modest maiden: stays 8.5f: acts on tapeta and good to firm going: tried in blinkers: tends to find little. *Stuart Kittow* — 51

VICTORIOUSLY 3 b.g. Azamour (IRE) 130 – Ambria (GER) (Monsun (GER) 124) [2015 73: 8m 11.6g t9.5g Jun 26] good-topped gelding: maiden: no form in 2015: best effort at 7.5f on firm going: in blinkers last 2 starts: sometimes slowly away. *Brian Meehan* — –

VICTOR'S BEACH (IRE) 5 b.g. Footstepsinthesand 120 – Your Village (IRE) 64 (Be My Guest (USA) 126) [2015 68, a80: p12g⁶ p10.7g⁵ p8g⁶ p8g 7g p10.7g t12.2f Dec 21] modest handicapper: left M. Halford after fourth start: stays 1½m: acts on polytrack, good to firm and good to soft going: often wears headgear: sometimes wears tongue tie: sometimes slowly away. *Mark McNiff, Ireland* — 62

VICTOR'S BET (SPA) 6 b.g. Leadership 124 – Marmaria (SPA) (Limpid 119) [2015 85: 8d 8d p10g Oct 27] fair handicapper: stays 1¼m: acts on dirt, soft and good to firm going: tried in tongue: sometimes slowly away, usually races nearer last than first. *Ralph Smith* — 68

VICTORY BOND 2 b.c. (Jan 20) Medicean 128 – Antebellum (FR) (Anabaa (USA) 130) [2015 8s² Oct 23] fourth foal: half-brother to 9f/9.5f winner Prewar (by Dubai Destination): dam once-raced daughter of half-sister to very smart 1¼m/1½m performer Aquarelliste: 16/1, promising start when ¾-length second of 15 to Algometer in maiden at Newbury, sticking to task under mainly hand riding: sure to progress. *William Haggas* — 85 p

VICTORY CALL (USA) 2 ch.c. (Jan 17) Speightstown (USA) 124 – Batallosa (ARG) (Southern Halo (USA)) [2015 p6g⁵ Nov 11] $200,000Y, 190,476 2-y-o: third foal: half-brother to 1m winner Kimallosa (by Unbridled's Song): dam 2-y-o 5f-7f (including Argentinian Grade 1) winner: 14/1, shaped as if needed experience when 4¼ lengths fifth of 12 to Consulting in maiden at Kempton, nearest finish: will stay 7f: sent to USA: sure to progress. *Olly Stevens* — 63 p

VICTORY MEGASTAR 3 b.c. Medicean 128 – Bourbon Ball (USA) (Peintre Celebre (USA) 137) [2015 83p: 8.3m 10g⁶ Sep 11] fair handicapper: best effort at 7f: acts on polytrack: often races towards rear: sent to Macau. *Clive Cox* — 68

VICTORY STRIKE (IRE) 5 b.g. Kheleyf (USA) 116 – Fairy Festival (IRE) 64 (Montjeu (IRE) 137) [2015 7.4g 7.1s Sep 15] well held in 2 maidens: tongue tied both starts, also in blinkers last time. *Johnny Farrelly* — –

VIED (USA) 4 b.f. Elusive Quality (USA) – Unacloud (USA) (Unaccounted For (USA) 124) [2015 58: t12.2f⁴ p10m⁵ Feb 4] modest maiden: stays 1½m: acts on polytrack, tapeta, best turf form on good to firm going: usually wears headgear: often races prominently. *Ed Vaughan* — 51

VIEWPOINT (IRE) 6 b.g. Exceed And Excel (AUS) 126 – Lady's View (USA) 85 (Distant View (USA) 126) [2015 104: p12g p10f⁶ 10.3d³ 10m 10d 10.2d Oct 14] strong gelding: fairly useful handicapper: stays 1½m: acts on polytrack, good to firm and good to soft going. *Richard Hannon* — 87

VIEW THE MOON 2 b.c. (Feb 26) Eskendereya (USA) 126 – Step Softly 95 (Golan (IRE) 129) [2015 7.2g⁵ 7m p7g 8.3s⁶ 7gᵖᵘ Dec 30] poor maiden: left Mark Johnston after second start, Conrad Allen after fourth: stays 7f: acts on polytrack, soft and good to firm going: tried in blinkers. *Sultan Al Hajri, Qatar* — 39

VIF MONSIEUR (GER) 5 b.h. Doyen (IRE) 132 – Vive Madame (GER) (Big Shuffle (USA) 122) [2015 114: 9.9d 10.4s* 15.4s 13.9g 10.2s* Nov 8] third foal: half-brother to German 1m-1¼m winner Vive Lumiere (by Ransom O'War): dam German 7f/8.5f winner: smart performer: won listed race at Cologne in April and Group 3 Niederrhein-Pokal at Krefeld (for second successive year, beat Nordico by 9 lengths) in November: trained by F. Van Gorp for third/fourth outings then returned to former trainer: stays 1½m: acts on heavy going: usually races prominently. *S. Smrczek, Germany* — 117

VIKING STORM 7 b.g. Hurricane Run (IRE) 134 – Danehill's Dream (IRE) (Danehill (USA) 126) [2015 12f 14.1f³ 14m² Jun 13] fairly useful handicapper: stays 1¾m: acts on polytrack and firm going: tried in hood. *Harry Dunlop* — 90

VIKING WARRIOR (IRE) 8 ch.g. Halling (USA) 133 – Powder Paint 98 (Mark of Esteem (IRE) 137) [2015 61: 8s⁶ Jul 29] leggy gelding: modest handicapper: stays 8.5f: acts on good to firm and heavy going: has worn headgear: not straightforward. *Shaun Harris* — –

VILAZ 4 ch.g. Byron 117 – Flamenco Dancer (Mark of Esteem (IRE) 137) [2015 56: 10m – 10m 8m Jul 21] sturdy gelding: lightly-raced maiden, modest form at best: stays 1¼m: acts on soft and good to firm going: blinkered final start. *Brian Meehan*

VILLA BONITA (USA) 2 b.f. (Feb 15) Elusive Quality (USA) – Villa (USA) (Bernardini **54** (USA) 132) [2015 6m⁶ p7g⁵ Jul 1] $150,000Y: lengthy filly: has scope: first foal: dam lightly-raced half-sister to US Grade 1 8.5f/9f winner Critical Eye: upped in trip, only modest form when fifth of 11 to Hawksmoor in maiden at Kempton, finishing weakly: sold 5,000 gns, sent to France. *John Gosden*

VILLA ROYALE 6 b.m. Val Royal (FR) 127 – Villa Carlotta 110 (Rainbow Quest (USA) **92** 134) [2015 101, a94: 12v p16g f16g³ Dec 18] tall mare: fairly useful handicapper: stays 16.5f: acts on polytrack, fibresand and heavy going: wears headgear: usually races prominently. *Michael Appleby*

VILLORESI (IRE) 6 b.g. Clodovil (IRE) 116 – Villafranca (IRE) (In The Wings 128) **90** [2015 87. 12.3v⁶ 12.3m* 11.5g⁴ Jun 24] angular gelding: fairly useful handicapper: won at Musselburgh in June: stays 13f: acts on polytrack, good to firm and good to soft going: often wears headgear. *John Quinn*

VILMAN (IRE) 3 b.g. Mastercraftsman (IRE) 129 – Velandia (IRE) (Sadler's Wells **87** (USA) 132) [2015 81p: 11.3s² 13m* 13.9g⁶ Dec 5] fairly useful handicapper: won at Navan in June: left M. Halford after second start: stays 13f: acts on good to firm and good to soft going: tried in cheekpieces/tongue tie: front runner/races prominently. *Simon West*

VIMY RIDGE 3 ch.g. American Post 121 – Fairy Shoes 77 (Kyllachy 129) [2015 91: p6g² **96** 5m³ p6m⁵ 5.1m² 5m⁴ 5m⁴ p5g* 6m p6f⁶ 5g⁵ p5m 5m² t6m Dec 18] stocky gelding: useful handicapper: won at Chelmsford in July by ¾ length from Bertie Blu Boy: second at Ascot (neck behind Shipyard) in October: stays 6f: acts on polytrack and good to firm going: in cheekpieces last 7 starts: often races towards rear. *Alan Bailey*

VINAMAR (IRE) 3 b.f. Approve (IRE) 112 – Shalev (GER) (Java Gold (USA)) [2015 52: **47** p6f⁶ 6s p6g³ p6m⁶ Nov 14] poor maiden: stays 6f: acts on polytrack and good to firm going: tried in cheekpieces. *Roger Teal*

VINCENT'S FOREVER 2 b.c. (Jan 30) Pour Moi (IRE) 125 – Glen Rosie (IRE) 102 **90 p** (Mujtahid (USA) 118) [2015 7s* Oct 13] €85,000Y: closely related to 3 winners, including winner up to 1¼m Kings Quay (2-y-o 5f-7f winner) and 9f-10.3f winner (stayed 1¾m) Milne Graden (both useful and by Montjeu) and half-brother to 9.7f-11f winner Fastback (by Singspiel): dam, 2-y-o 5f winner who stayed 1m, half-sister to smart winner up to 1m Hello Soso: 3/1 and in hood, won 10-runner maiden at Leicester on debut by 1¼ lengths from You're Hired, off bridle by halfway but scoring cosily in the end: will be suited by 1m+: will improve. *John Gosden*

VINCENTTI (IRE) 5 b.g. Invincible Spirit (IRE) 121 – Bint Al Balad (IRE) 63 (Ahonoora **83** 122) [2015 88: p6g³ t5.1f³ p5g⁴ p6g t6g² 6.1m² 7.1m⁵ 5.7m² 6g³ 6f 6s* 6s³ 6.1m⁴ 6g 6d⁴ **a75** 6g³ p6m Nov 17] sturdy gelding: fairly useful handicapper: won at Brighton in August: stays 6f: acts on polytrack, soft and good to firm going: wears headgear: tried in tongue tie. *Ronald Harris*

VINCENZO COCCOTTI (USA) 3 gr.g. Speightstown (USA) 124 – Ocean Colors **68** (USA) (Orientate (USA) 127) [2015 t7.1f p8f t7.1f* p7m² p7m² p7f² f8s³ p8g⁶ 8m⁴ 7.1m⁴ 7g⁶ 6v⁴ 6m⁴ Sep 11] good-topped gelding: fair performer: won seller at Wolverhampton in February: left Jamie Osborne after seventh start: stays 1m: acts on all-weather and good to firm going: sometimes in cheekpieces. *Chris Gordon*

VINNIES VIXEN 2 ch.f. (Jan 17) Bahamian Bounty 116 – Feabhas (IRE) 100 (Spectrum – (IRE) 126) [2015 6m 7m Jul 21] 3,800Y: fourth foal: dam winner up to 1¼m, also 2-y-o 7f winner: last of 15 in 2 maidens. *Noel Wilson*

VIOLET DANCER 5 b.g. Bertolini (USA) 125 – Another Secret 87 (Efisio 120) [2015 **67** p12g² Jan 21] workmanlike gelding: lightly-raced maiden, fairly useful form at best: stays 1½m: acts on polytrack: useful hurdler. *Gary Moore*

VIREN'S ARMY (IRE) 2 b.c. (Jan 17) Twirling Candy (USA) 124 – Blue Angel (IRE) **99** 107 (Oratorio (IRE) 128) [2015 6m⁵ 7v* 6.3d⁴ p8m³ 9v* 8.9g³ Nov 8] $35,000Y, resold €115,000Y: first foal: dam, winner up to 1m (2-y-o 7f winner), half-sister to useful winner up to 1m Empowering: useful performer: won maiden at Epsom in August and nursery at Nottingham in October: good third in Premio Guido Berardelli at Rome (¾ length behind Poeta Diletto) final start: likely to stay 1¼m: acts on heavy going: often races prominently. *Richard Hannon*

VIRGINIA CELESTE (IRE) 3 b.f. Galileo (IRE) 134 – Crystal Valkyrie (IRE) 81 **81** (Danehill (USA) 126) [2015 p10g⁵ p12g 12d p12g⁴ 12v² p12g⁶ Nov 13] €295,000Y: sister to useful 1¼m-12.4f winner Granddukeoftuscany, closely related to smart winner up to 2m Above Average (by High Chaparral) and half-sister to several winners, including smart 2-y-o 7f winner Sent From Heaven (by Footstepsinthesand): dam 2-y-o 6f winner who stayed 11f: fairly useful maiden: second in handicap at Epsom (best effort): will prove suited by 1¾m+: acts on heavy going. *Charles Hills*

VIRGO RISING 2 b.f. (Jan 24) Oasis Dream 129 – Rainbow Springs 102 (Selkirk (USA) **65 p** 129) [2015 6g⁴ Jul 17] 200,000Y: sturdy filly: first foal: dam, 9f winner (third in Prix Marcel Boussac), half-sister to smart winner up to 1¼m Sparkling Beam: 3/1, better for run when 2¼ lengths fourth of 7 to Serradura in maiden at Newbury, not quickening immediately but keeping on well final 50 yds and finishing with running left: sent to USA: sure to progress. *Brian Meehan*

VIRILE (IRE) 4 ch.g. Exceed And Excel (AUS) 126 – Winding (USA) (Irish River (FR) **69** 131) [2015 68: p10.7g⁶ 7.1g² 6s 6g 7g 5m⁶ 6m 6g³ 7.9s a6g 6d p8g p7g t5.1f² t5.1f⁸ t6f² **a76** p6m Nov 25] fair handicapper: won at Wolverhampton in October: stays 7f: acts on tapeta and good to firm going: usually wears headgear: tried in tongue tie: often races prominently. *Shane Donohoe, Ireland*

VIRNON 4 b.g. Virtual 122 – Freedom Song 74 (Singspiel (IRE) 133) [2015 12m 11.9d⁶ **75** 12m 16.1m⁴ 14.1s³ 15.8s³ Oct 27] fair maiden: stays 1¾m: acts on soft and good to firm going: fairly useful hurdler. *Alan Swinbank*

VIRTUAL REALITY 3 b.g. Virtual 122 – Regal Riband 79 (Fantastic Light (USA) 134) **70** [2015 66p: p8g³ p8f* t9.5f⁴ 11.6m 8.3s⁴ 9.9m⁴ 8g⁶ 10g t7.1m⁵ 8.3s⁴ t8.6g² 8.3g³ Oct 20] **a80** big gelding: fairly useful performer: won maiden at Kempton in February: good second in handicap at Wolverhampton in September: stays 8.5f: acts on polytrack, tapeta and soft going: usually in headgear nowadays. *Philip McBride*

VIRTUAL SONG 2 b.f. (Mar 27) Virtual 122 – Song of The Desert (Desert Sun 120) **–** [2015 t7.1f t7.1m t9.5f Dec 14] second foal: dam unraced: well held in maidens. *Steph Hollinshead*

VISAGE BLANC 2 b.f. (Apr 30) Champs Elysees 124 – Russian Empress (IRE) 101 **65** (Trans Island 119) [2015 8d 7s⁶ 8v Oct 24] rather leggy filly: third foal: half-sister to 7f/1m winner Tsarglas (by Verglas) and 2-y-o 5f winner Massandra (by Makfi): dam, 6f/7f winner, half-sister to smart winner up to 11.5f Crown of Light: fair maiden: best effort when sixth of 10 to Dutch Destiny at Salisbury second start. *Mick Channon*

VISCOUNT BARFIELD 2 b.c. (Mar 16) Raven's Pass (USA) 133 – Madonna Dell'orto **65** 83 (Montjeu (IRE) 137) [2015 6.5m 7.1f⁵ Jul 3] similar form to debut (some encouragement) when 6¼ lengths fifth of 6 to Miniaturist in maiden at Sandown, not settling fully and weakening over 1f out. *Andrew Balding*

VISERION 3 ch.g. Tamayuz 126 – Frivolity (Pivotal 124) [2015 p8m p8g 7m t8.6f² **72** Dec 14] fair maiden: best effort at 8.5f. *David Simcock*

VITTACHI 8 b.g. Bertolini (USA) 125 – Miss Lorilaw (FR) 104 (Homme de Loi (IRE) **55 §** 120) [2015 56: 11.1s 9.1s 12.5m⁵ 12.5m 12.2g² 12.2m³ 13.7g⁶ 14.1m⁵ 12d⁵ Sep 15] plain gelding: modest handicapper: stays 2m: acts on polytrack, good to firm and heavy going: usually wears headgear: quirky and one to treat with caution. *Alistair Whillans*

VIVACISSIMO (IRE) 8 ch.g. Muhtathir 126 – Valley Orchard (FR) (Zilzal (USA) 137) **64** [2015 12v f11g t16.5m f14g² Dec 12] modest performer: stays 15f: acts on fibresand and good to firm going: sometimes in headgear/tongue tie. *Ivan Furtado*

VIVAT REX (IRE) 4 b.c. Fastnet Rock (AUS) 127 – Strawberry Roan (IRE) 113 (Sadler's **99** Wells (USA) 132) [2015 89: t9.5f p11f p10d⁴ p8f* f8s* p8m 8f⁶ Apr 29] useful handicapper: won at Chelmsford and Southwell (standout effort, by 7 lengths from Toto Skyllachy) 7 days apart in March: stays 1½m: acts on polytrack and fibresand: usually in headgear: sold 32,000 gns in May, sent to France. *Alan Bailey*

VIVA VERGLAS (IRE) 4 gr.g. Verglas (IRE) 118 – Yellow Trumpet 75 (Petong 126) **80** [2015 95§: p6g⁶ f6s² 5v 6s 5.9v² 6m 5s p6g p5f Oct 29] strong gelding: fairly useful handicapper: left David Barron after sixth start: stays 6f: acts on polytrack, good to firm and good to soft going: sometimes wears blinkers: often races in rear. *Daniel Loughnane*

VIVE MA FILLE (GER) 3 b.f. Doyen (IRE) 132 – Vive Madame (GER) (Big Shuffle **94** (USA) 122) [2015 p12f* p12g⁴ 12m² 11.5s 12.3g² 12.5m² 16f⁴ 16m⁵ 14s³ 14.6m Sep 10] €17,000Y: tall filly: fifth foal: sister to smart 1m-1½m winner Vif Monsieur and half-sister to 2 winners, including 1m-1¼m winner Vive Lumiere (by Ransom O'War): dam 7f/8.5f winner: fairly useful performer: won maiden at Lingfield in March: seemingly best effort when 3½ lengths fifth of 11 to Big Orange in Goodwood Cup: creditable third in listed race at Goodwood (4¾ lengths behind The Twisler) next start: stays 2m: acts on polytrack and good to firm going: usually leads. *Mark Johnston*

VIVI'S CHARIS (IRE) 3 ch.f. Rock of Gibraltar (IRE) 133 – Amathusia (Selkirk (USA) 129) [2015 61: t9.5f Jan 5] leggy filly: lightly-raced maiden, modest form at best: looked a difficult ride when well held only outing in 2015. *Stuart Williams* —

VIVO PER LEI (IRE) 3 gr.f. Mastercraftsman (IRE) 129 – Sabancaya 70 (Nayef (USA) 129) [2015 59: p10g t7.1g t8.6g⁵ Jun 2] modest maiden: stays 8.5f: acts on polytrack, tapeta and good to firm going. *Marco Botti* **55**

VIVRE LA REVE 3 b.f. Assertive 121 – Noor El Houdah (IRE) 61 (Fayruz 116) [2015 64: t8.6g⁴ t7.1g t7.1f⁴ t9.5g² Dec 4] fair maiden: stays 9.5f: acts on tapeta. *James Unett* **67**

VIVRE POUR VIVRE (IRE) 2 b.c. (Feb 10) Pour Moi (IRE) 125 – Miss Quality (USA) (Elusive Quality (USA)) [2015 8.1s 8s Oct 23] 75,000F: second foal: half-brother to 2-y-o 1¼m winner Thuit (by Duke of Marmalade): dam, second at 7.5f, half-sister to 9f (minor US stakes) winner Desert Gold: 66/1, showed some ability when 8¾ lengths tenth of 17 to Midterm in maiden at Newbury latter start, weakening over 1f out: remains open to improvement. *Ed Dunlop* **– p**

VIXEN HILL 3 b.f. Acclamation 118 – Heckle 47 (In The Wings 128) [2015 67: 8g⁶ 7g⁴ 7.5g⁴ 10g⁶ 7.1m 7m Jun 18] modest maiden: stays 7.5f: acts on polytrack, tapeta, best turf form on good going: tried in blinkers in 2015. *Tony Coyle* **57**

VIZIER 2 b.g. (Feb 1) Pivotal 124 – Rare Ransom 97 (Oasis Dream 129) [2015 8d 7d t8.6m³ t8.6g² Dec 5] compact gelding: fair maiden: stays 8.5f: tried in cheekpieces. *Roger Varian* **78**

VOCALISE 2 gr.f. (Mar 19) Hellvelyn 118 – Church Hill Queen (Monsieur Bond (IRE) 120) [2015 5m 6g 8g 5g⁶ Sep 16] fourth foal: dam unraced half-sister to useful winner up to 6f Lusciviious: no form. *Charles Smith* —

VODKA CHASER (IRE) 4 b.f. Baltic King 120 – Suffer Her (IRE) (Whipper (USA) 126) [2015 83: 5.1m May 21] close-coupled filly: modest handicapper: best form at 5f: best form on good going or firmer: tried in headgear prior to 2015. *Alison Hutchinson* **64**

VODKA TIME (IRE) 4 b.g. Indian Haven 119 – Cappuccino (IRE) (Mujadil (USA) 119) [2015 77: 6.1m² 6m 6g³ 5s² t6f³ Oct 23] good-topped gelding: modest handicapper: stays 7f: acts on polytrack, tapeta, soft and good to firm going: tried in headgear: often races prominently. *Shaun Harris* **62**

VOICE CONTROL (IRE) 3 gr.g. Dalakhani (IRE) 133 – Scottish Stage (IRE) 112 (Selkirk (USA) 129) [2015 79: 9.9m³ 11.6f 12g³ 11.9v² p12g p13.3f² p16g³ Nov 26] angular gelding: fair maiden: left Sir Michael Stoute after third start: seems to stay 2m: acts on polytrack and good to firm going. *Laura Mongan* **78**

VOICE FROM ABOVE (IRE) 6 b.m. Strategic Prince 114 – Basin Street Blues (IRE) 82 (Dolphin Street (FR) 125) [2015 60: 16m 12s⁴ 13d* 13.1s⁵ 12.1s⁶ 12m⁵ 12.4g³ 12.1g² 12.1m 12v⁴ Oct 17] small mare: modest handicapper: won at Hamilton in June: stays 13f: acts on good to firm and heavy going: tried in headgear prior to 2015. *Patrick Holmes* **62**

VOICE OF A LEADER (IRE) 4 b.g. Danehill Dancer (IRE) 117 – Thewaytosanjose (IRE) 58 (Fasliyev (USA) 120) [2015 –: 10.4g⁴ 10.4m 9.9g 10g 8m 8d 8d t9.5f p10g³ p8g t9.5f Dec 21] lengthy, rather dipped-backed gelding: handicapper: useful form when 2 lengths fourth of 18 to Mahsoob at York on reappearance, but showed little subsequently (left Peter Chapple-Hyam after fourth start): stays 10.5f: acts on polytrack and good to soft going: in hood last 5 starts. *Andi Brown* **105 d**
a72

VOICES OF KINGS 2 b.c. (Apr 18) Poet's Voice 126 – Khubza 86 (Green Desert (USA) 127) [2015 t7.1m Nov 28] 50,000F, 45,000Y: closely related to smart winner up to 8.5f Mujaazef (2-y-o 7f winner, by Dubawi) and half-brother to numerous winners, including winner up to 8.5f Trans Island (2-y-o 6f/7f winner) and 1m winner Welsh Diva (both smart and by Selkirk): dam 7f winner: 33/1, shaped as if needed experience when eighth of 12 in maiden at Wolverhampton: should do better. *William Muir* **– p**

VOLATILE (SWE) 3 b.g. Strategic Prince 114 – Look That Chick (USA) (Souvenir Copy (USA) 113) [2015 100p: a7f⁵ 7g² 7g* a6g* 5.5g³ 7f Jun 17] tall, lengthy gelding: useful performer: won listed race at Meydan (by 1¼ lengths from Mastermind) in February and minor event at Jagersro (by 1¼ lengths from Hall of Fame) in April: third in Prix Texanita at Maisons-Laffitte (beaten 2 heads by Goken) next time: 50/1, turned it in when 9¼ lengths twelfth of 16 to Dutch Connection in Jersey Stakes at Royal Ascot final outing: stays 7f: acts on dirt and good to soft going: wears blinkers: carries head awkwardly: best treated with some caution. *Jessica Long, Sweden* **105**

VOLCANIC JACK (IRE) 7 b.g. Kodiac 112 – Rosaria Panatta (IRE) (Mujtahid (USA) 118) [2015 59: 14.1m⁵ 12g⁵ Jun 18] angular gelding: fair at best, has shown little since 2013: stays 13f: acts on polytrack, firm and good to soft going: front runner/races prominently. *Michael Chapman* –

VOLITION (IRE) 2 gr.f. (Jan 23) Dark Angel (IRE) 113 – Warshah (IRE) (Shamardal (USA) 129) [2015 p6g⁵ Aug 17] 300,000Y: first foal: dam unraced half-sister to smart winner up to 12.3f Mickdaam: 6/1, considerate introduction when 7¼ lengths fifth of 7 to Rosy Morning in maiden at Chelmsford: should do better in time. *Sir Michael Stoute* 55 p

VOLITO 9 ch.g. Bertolini (USA) 125 – Vax Rapide 80 (Sharpo 132) [2015 56, a74: p6m t6g p6f Jan 30] strong gelding: fair at best, no form in 2015: tried in headgear: usually slowly away. *Anabel K. Murphy* –

VOLUNTEER POINT (IRE) 3 b.f. Footstepsinthesand 120 – Piffling (Pivotal 124) [2015 78p: p6f⁴ 8.3m⁵ 8g* 8m 8g² 8m² 8m⁴ 8g 8m 8d³ 8.3g⁴ 8d² 8g* 10.3v⁶ p8f² p8g* p7.5g⁴ Dec 27] rather leggy filly: useful handicapper: won at Haydock in April, Newmarket in October and Chelmsford in December (by head from Mythical Madness) in December: acts on polytrack, best turf form on good going: often races towards rear, usually responds generously to pressure: consistent. *Mick Channon* 104

VON BLUCHER (IRE) 2 ch.c. (Mar 14) Zoffany (IRE) 121 – Tropical Lady (IRE) 117 (Sri Pekan (USA) 117) [2015 7.1m² 7m⁶ 7v² p8g* Oct 27] 55,000F, £95,000Y: strong, lengthy colt: sixth foal: half-brother to 7f winner (stays 9f) Tropical Mist (by Marju): dam 7f-1¼m winner: useful form: much improved when winning maiden at Lingfield final start by 1½ lengths from Ennaadd, pair well clear: best effort at 1m: in tongue tie second/third starts: should progress further. *John Gosden* 106 p

VOSNE ROMANEE 4 ch.g. Arakan (USA) 123 – Vento Del Oreno (FR) 67 (Lando (GER) 128) [2015 72: p10g⁵ t13.9g* p14f⁴ Feb 19] fair handicapper: won at Wolverhampton in February: stays 1¾m: acts on polytrack and tapeta: wears headgear: sometimes slowly away, often races in rear, often travels strongly: fairly useful hurdler. *Dr Richard Newland* 75

VOSTOK 2 ch.g. (Apr 15) Sixties Icon 125 – Cibenze 74 (Owington 123) [2015 5d 6m Jun 15] well held in maiden and a seller. *Mick Channon* –

VOYAGEOFDISCOVERY (USA) 4 b.g. Henrythenavigator (USA) 131 – Look Out Lorie (USA) (Orientate (USA) 127) [2015 91: p8f⁴ p8g² p8g⁴ 8m³ 8.1m p7g p7g⁴ p8g⁴ p7g* Oct 7] compact gelding: fairly useful handicapper: won at Kempton (by 3 lengths from Subversive) in October: stays 8.5f: acts on polytrack and good to firm going: tried in cheekpieces. *Clive Cox* 91

VROOM (IRE) 2 ch.c. (Apr 22) Poet's Voice 126 – Shivaree 88 (Rahy (USA) 115) [2015 6m t6f⁵ p6m⁴ p6g* Dec 15] €8,000F, 45,000Y: useful-looking colt: sixth foal: half-brother to 3 winners, including 5f (including at 2 yrs) winner Geesala (by Barathea) and useful 2-y-o 5f winner Tomintoul Singer (by Johannesburg): dam 2-y-o 6f winner: fairly useful performer: won nursery at Kempton (by 1¾ lengths from Song of Paradise) in December: raced only at 6f: will go on improving. *Charlie Fellowes* 80 p

W

WAABEL 8 b.g. Green Desert (USA) 127 – Najah (IRE) 110 (Nashwan (USA) 135) [2015 62: p6m⁴ p6f f5g⁶ t5.1g⁴ t6m⁶ 6s Oct 15] lengthy, useful-looking gelding: modest handicapper: stays 7f: acts on all-weather, good to firm and heavy going: tried in headgear: wears tongue tie. *Heather Dalton* 53

WAADY (IRE) 3 b.g. Approve (IRE) 112 – Anne Bonney 58 (Jade Robbery (USA) 121) [2015 86p: 5.1d* 5d* 6m⁴ 5m* 5m* 6d Sep 5] rangy gelding: smart performer: much improved after winning handicap at Nottingham in April and won 3 more races, all at Sandown, namely handicap later in April, listed race in June and Sprint Stakes (by ½ length from Wind Fire) in July: off 9 weeks, 20/1, excuses when well held in Sprint Cup at Haydock final start: may prove best at 5f: acts on good to firm and good to soft going: wears hood: usually races towards rear and travels strongly. *John Gosden* 118

WAALEEF 3 ch.c. Nayef (USA) 129 – Ulfah (USA) 105 (Danzig (USA)) [2015 70: t8.6f* p8g³ 8s* 8g⁴ 9.9m⁵ 8m⁴ 8m 10m³ 10d⁵ 8m⁶ Nov 10] fairly useful performer: won handicap at Wolverhampton in January and minor event at Milan in March: left Marco Botti after second start: stays 1m: acts on tapeta: in headgear in 2015: often in tongue tie in 2015: often travels strongly. *G. Marras, Italy* 94

WAANEBE RANGER (IRE) 2 b.f. (Feb 14) Bushranger (IRE) 119 – Jawaaneb (USA) –
87 (Kingmambo (USA) 125) [2015 6g 6d 6g 7s Oct 16] £3,000Y: second foal: half-sister
to a winner in USA by Medaglia d'Oro: dam, 11f winner, out of sister to Prix de l'Arc de
Triomphe winner Sakhee: no form. *Edwin Tuer*

WADI AL HATTAWI (IRE) 5 b.g. Dalakhani (IRE) 133 – Carisolo 71 (Dubai Millennium **121**
140) [2015 109: 12m* 14g^{pu} 13g* 12g^{pu} Sep 25] very smart performer: much improved and
won handicaps at York (by neck from Curbyourenthusiasm) in July and Newmarket (by 3¾
lengths from Intense Tango) in August: pulled up both other starts in 2015, in listed race at
Newmarket final one: stayed 13f: acted on polytrack, good to firm and good to soft going:
wore headgear: dead. *Saeed bin Suroor*

WAFI STAR (IRE) 2 b.g. (Mar 8) Showcasing 117 – Ophelia's Song (Halling (USA) **66**
133) [2015 7.1m^5 p7f^4 Aug 11] good-topped gelding: similar form to debut when 6 lengths
fourth of 10 to Powderhorn in maiden at Lingfield: has been gelded. *Simon Crisford*

WAGSTAFF (IRE) 3 b.g. Rip Van Winkle (IRE) 134 – Ride A Rainbow (Rainbow Quest –
(USA) 134) [2015 12m 10g 12m^5 12m Jun 11] smallish gelding: no form. *Mick Channon*

WAHAAB (IRE) 4 ch.g. Tamayuz 126 – Indian Ink (IRE) 122 (Indian Ridge 123) [2015 **60**
86: p5f 6m p6g^6 p6d p6g Dec 16] well-made gelding: modest handicapper: stays 7f: acts
on firm going: tried in headgear: often races prominently. *Richard Hughes*

WAJEEH (IRE) 3 ch.g. Raven's Pass (USA) 133 – Olympic Medal 66 (Nayef (USA) 129) **77**
[2015 p8m^3 p8f* 10.4d^3 8m Jun 26] angular gelding: fair form: won maiden at Lingfield in
February: third in handicap at Haydock in May: stays 10.5f: sold 24,000 gns in July, sent
to Macau. *Richard Hannon*

WAJEEZ (IRE) 2 ch.c. (Feb 13) Lope de Vega (IRE) 125 – Chanter (Lomitas 129) [2015 **111 p**
8.3s* Nov 4] €48,000Y, resold 190,000Y: fifth foal: half-brother to 3 winners, including
1¼m winners Ladurelli (by Mastercraftsman) and Music Man (by Oratorio): dam unraced
half-sister to King George VI & Queen Elizabeth Stakes winner Belmez: 7/2, created
excellent impression on debut when winning 10-runner maiden at Nottingham impressively
by 7 lengths from Twobeelucky, quickening to lead 2f out and soon clear: will stay 1¼m:
exciting prospect. *John Gosden*

WAKAME (IRE) 2 b.c. (Apr 30) Kodiac 112 – Awwal Mallka (USA) 73 (Kingmambo **64**
(USA) 125) [2015 7.1s^6 p7g^6 p7g t7.1f^5 p8g^3 p7g* Nov 18] modest performer: won
nursery at Kempton in November: stays 1m: acts on polytrack. *Ed de Giles*

WAKEA (USA) 4 b.g. Cape Cross (IRE) 129 – Imiloa (USA) (Kingmambo (USA) 125) **110**
[2015 95p: t13.9m* p13.3g^2 p16f* 16f^4 14g 14m t13.9g^4 p15.8g Dec 28] well-made **a101**
gelding: smart handicapper: won at Wolverhampton in March and Kempton (by 2 lengths
from Buckland) in April: good fourth in Sagaro Stakes at Ascot (5¼ lengths behind Mizzou)
later in April: stays 2m: acts on polytrack, tapeta and firm going: tried in cheekpieces:
usually races prominently, tends to find little. *Jeremy Noseda*

WALAAA (IRE) 2 b.f. (Jan 19) Exceed And Excel (AUS) 126 – Akhmatova 100 (Cape **66**
Cross (IRE) 129) [2015 6d 6g t7.1f^6 p6d* p7g Dec 10] 125,000Y: first foal: dam, 8.3f-1¼m
winner who stayed 1½m, out of close relative to very smart winner up to 1½m Kutub: fair
performer: won nursery at Kempton in November: best effort at 6f: acts on polytrack.
Richard Hannon

WALDNAH 3 ch.f. New Approach (IRE) 132 – Waldmark (GER) 106 (Mark of Esteem **101**
(IRE) 137) [2015 77: p7f* 7.5d 8.9g^3 8g* 8g^4 8.4d^5 Oct 4] useful performer: won maiden
at Kempton in January and listed race at Munich (by ½ length from Rosebay) in July: left
John Gosden after first start, S. J. Stokes after second: stays 9f: acts on polytrack and
tapeta, best turf form on good going: often in hood in 2015. *A. Wohler, Germany*

WALK LIKE A GIANT 4 b.g. Sir Percy 129 – Temple of Thebes (IRE) 92 (Bahri (USA) **77**
125) [2015 75: f8g^5 t9.5g p10g^2 t9.5f* f11g^4 f8d^3 10.3d* 10.1g^5 10g 12s f12g p8g* t9.5f^3
t9.5f^4 Dec 21] fair handicapper: won at Wolverhampton in February, Doncaster (apprentice)
in March and Kempton (apprentice) in December: stays 10.5f: acts on all-weather and good
to soft going: sometimes in cheekpieces, including on last 3 starts: has shown signs of
temperament. *Michael Appleby*

WALK RIGHT BACK (IRE) 4 b.g. Dandy Man (IRE) 123 – Certainlei (IRE) 81 **58**
(Definite Article 121) [2015 67: 5d 5g^4 5m 6g 6g 7.5m 6m Jul 1] modest maiden: stays 7f:
acts on polytrack, best turf form on good going: tried in visor: best treated with caution.
Micky Hammond

WALL OF FIRE (IRE) 2 b.c. (Jan 19) Canford Cliffs (IRE) 133 – Bright Sapphire (IRE) **88**
55 (Galileo (IRE) 134) [2015 6d* 7m^5 Sep 11] 92,000F, 270,000Y: close-coupled colt: first
foal: dam, ran twice, out of Cherry Hinton Stakes winner Jewel In The Sand: won 7-runner

maiden at Ascot in July by ¾ length from Justice Law: similar form when 6½ lengths fifth of 6 to Tashweeq in listed race at Doncaster only other start. *Richard Hannon*

WALL OF LIGHT 2 b.f. (Feb 10) Zamindar (USA) 116 – Veiled Beauty (USA) (Royal **60** Academy (USA) 130) [2015 7g t7.1f⁴ Oct 30] tall, useful-looking filly: half-sister to several winners, including smart 6f and (including at 2 yrs) 7f winner The Cheka (by Xaar) and useful 9f-10.4f winner Wall of Sound (by Singspiel): dam ran twice in France: better effort in maidens when fourth at Wolverhampton (3¾ lengths behind Ice Royal) in October. *Tom Dascombe*

WALLY'S WISDOM 3 b.g. Dutch Art 126 – Faldal 88 (Falbrav (IRE) 133) [2015 75: **69** 8.3m 8.3f p8g p10g³ p10f p12g³ p10f⁴ t13.9f⁵ p12g⁵ p8d Nov 30] stocky gelding: fair maiden: stays 1½m: acts on polytrack and firm going: tried in headgear. *Lee Carter*

WALSINGHAM GRANGE (USA) 2 b.g. (Mar 15) Paddy O'Prado (USA) 121 – Mambo **73** Queen (USA) (Kingmambo (USA) 125) [2015 7f⁴ 7g⁶ 8.5g² 8m 9g Oct 21] strong gelding: fair maiden: stays 8.5f: best form on good going: in cheekpieces final start. *William Haggas*

WALTA (IRE) 4 b.g. Tagula (IRE) 116 – Hi Kationa (IRE) 63 (Second Empire (IRE) 124) **– §** [2015 64§: f8s Jan 20] modest handicapper at best: should prove best at 5f/6f: acts on fibresand: wears blinkers, also tongue tied of late: usually slowly away: held back by attitude and one to be wary of. *Roy Bowring*

WALTZ DARLING (IRE) 7 b.g. Iffraaj 127 – Aljaffliyah (Halling (USA) 133) [2015 70: **60** 16m⁶ 13.8v 14.1v Nov 3] good-topped gelding: handicapper, modest nowadays: stays 2m: acts on good to firm and heavy going: often races towards rear: none too consistent: fairly useful hurdler/chaser. *Keith Reveley*

WALTZING MATILDA (IRE) 4 b.f. Danehill Dancer (IRE) 117 – Simadartha (USA) **108** (Gone West (USA)) [2015 105: 8v 10d³ 12.5g² 10v³ 8g⁴ 10f* 9f Jul 25] useful performer: creditable third in Mooresbridge Stakes at the Curragh (3¾ lengths behind Fascinating Rock) on fourth start: won Grade 2 New York Stakes at Belmont (by ¾ length from Eastern Belle) in June (left T. Stack after): visored, below form when last of 7 in Diana Stakes at Saratoga final outing: stays 12.5f: acts on any turf going: usually in cheekpieces: usually races towards rear. *Thomas Albertrani, USA*

WALZERTAKT (GER) 6 b.h. Montjeu (IRE) 137 – Walzerkoenigin (USA) 116 **118** (Kingmambo (USA) 125) [2015 13.9s⁵ 15.4g³ 15.9g³ 14.9d⁵ 13.9m* 14.9d³ 15.4s* 19.9m⁶ 15.4d⁶ Oct 25] fourth foal: half-brother to 3 winners, including very smart German 10.5f-1½m (including Deutsches Derby) winner Wiener Walzer (by Dynaformer) and smart 1m-1¼m winner Walzertraum (by Rahy): dam German winner up to 1¼m (2-y-o 7f winner): smart performer: campaigned mainly in France in 2015, winning Prix Maurice de Nieuil at Longchamp (by short head from Bathyrhon) in July and Prix Gladiateur on same course (length second to Fly With Me, but later awarded race) in September: also ran creditably in Prix Kergorlay at Deauville (5 lengths third behind Alex My Boy) in between and in Prix Royal-Oak at Saint-Cloud (7½ lengths sixth to Vazirabad) final outing: left Frau M. Rotering after first start: stays 15.4f: acts on soft and good to firm going: in cheekpieces penultimate start. *J-P. Carvalho, Germany*

WANDJINA (AUS) 4 b.c. Snitzel (AUS) 123 – La Bamba (AUS) (Last Tycoon 131) **123** [2015 117: 7g* 8g* 7d² 6f⁶ Jun 20] good sort: brother to Australian 5f winner Rialio, closely related to several winners by Redoute's Choice, including Australian winner up to 1m Lucky Unicorn, and half-brother to 2 winners, including very smart Hong Kong 5f/6f winner Inspiration (by Flying Spur): dam Australian 6f/6.5f winner: very smart performer: won Group 3 C. S. Hayes Stakes at Flemington (by head from Disposition) in February and Australian Guineas at Flemington (by head from Alpine Eagle) in March: good second in All Aged Stakes at Randwick (head behind Dissident) in April: inadequate test when keeping-on sixth of 15 to Undrafted in Diamond Jubilee Stakes at Royal Ascot final start: stayed 1m: acted on soft going: often in blinkers prior to 2015: usually led: standing at Newgate Stud, New South Wales, Australia, fee A$33,000. *Gai Waterhouse, Australia*

WANEEN (IRE) 2 b.g. (Apr 12) Approve (IRE) 112 – Million All Day (IRE) 57 (Daylami **75** (IRE) 138) [2015 6d⁶ 5s 7.6g⁴ 8.3d p7g² 6v³ t7.1f³ Nov 20] fair maiden: stays 7f: acts on polytrack, tapeta and heavy going. *David Evans*

WANNABE FRIENDS 2 ch.c. (Feb 15) Dubawi (IRE) 129 – Wannabe Posh (IRE) 107 **– p** (Grand Lodge (USA) 125) [2015 7g Jul 17] sturdy colt: fifth foal: brother to smart 1m winner Wannabe Yours and half-brother to 1¾m winner Wannabe Your Man (by Halling) and useful 1¼m-1½m winner Wannabe Loved (by Pivotal): dam, 11.6f/1½m winner who stayed 1¾m, half-sister to Cheveley Park Stakes winner/1000 Guineas runner-up Wannabe Grand: 7/1, badly needed experience when eleventh of 12 in maiden at Newbury in July: should do better. *John Gosden*

Britannia Stakes (Heritage Handicap), Royal Ascot—a smart effort under 9-6 from War Envoy, who wears down Udododontu late on; the far-side group provides five of the first six home, the exception being the third Sacrificial (No.16) who fares comfortably best in the other group

WANNABE KOOL (IRE) 2 b.g. (Apr 2) Dandy Man (IRE) 123 – Bobbella (IRE) 75 – (Bob Back (USA) 124) [2015 5g 7m 6m 8g Sep 23] no form. *Brian Ellison*

WANNABE MAGIC 4 b.f. Authorized (IRE) 133 – Wannabe Free 76 (Red Ransom (USA)) [2015 –: 8m 8m⁴ 17.2f p12g Aug 26] poor maiden: best effort at 17f: acts on firm going. *Geoffrey Deacon* **49**

WANNABE YOURS (IRE) 4 b.g. Dubawi (IRE) 129 – Wannabe Posh (IRE) 107 (Grand Lodge (USA) 125) [2015 117: 8g 8f⁵ 8g⁴ 7s⁴ 9.9s² 9g⁵ 10d⁴ Oct 31] strong, useful-looking gelding: smart performer: best effort of 2015 when ¾-length second of 5 to Battalion in listed race at Goodwood in September: stays 1¼m: acts on good to firm and heavy going: often races towards rear: has been gelded. *John Gosden* **112**

WANTING (IRE) 3 b.f. Acclamation 118 – Bold Desire 58 (Cadeaux Genereux 131) [2015 p6g* p6f* t6f² 6m⁴ 5.1v³ 5g* 5m⁵ 6m⁶ 6g Sep 24] 140,000F: fourth foal: sister to smart 2-y-o 5f/6f winner Parliament Square and half-sister to 5f to (at 2 yrs) 7f winner Bunce (by Good Reward): dam, ran twice, sister to useful performer up to 7f Irresistible, herself dam of smart 7f/1m performer Infallible: useful performer: won maiden at Chelmsford in February and handicaps at Kempton in March and Haydock (by 1¼ lengths from Snap Shots) in May: stays 6f: acts on polytrack and good to firm going: often travels strongly. *Charlie Appleby* **99 a93**

WAPPING (USA) 2 b.c. (May 4) Smart Strike (CAN) 121 – Exciting Times (FR) (Jeune Homme (USA) 120) [2015 p7f 7g 8.5m² 10.2g* Oct 18] 90,000Y: half-brother to several winners, including very smart US Grade 1 9.5f winner Gorella (2-y-o 7f winner in France, by Grape Tree Road) and smart French/US winner up to 1m Porto Santo (2-y-o 5f/5.5f winner, by Kingsalsa): dam French maiden: fair form: 4/5, won maiden at Bath in October by 1¾ lengths from Nodachi: stays 1¼m: remains open to improvement. *David Lanigan* **81 p**

WARAPITO 3 b.g. Stimulation (IRE) 121 – Shining Oasis (IRE) 73 (Mujtahid (USA) 118) [2015 –: 9.1g 7g 7m Aug 4] little impact in varied events: in visor last 2 starts. *Richard Guest*

WARBOND 7 ch.g. Monsieur Bond (IRE) 120 – Pick A Nice Name 85 (Polar Falcon (USA) 126) [2015 66: p8g² p8f³ p8f p8m Apr 8] tall gelding: modest handicapper: stays 1m: acts on polytrack, soft and good to firm going: wears headgear. *Michael Madgwick* **54**

WARDAT DUBAI 3 b.f. Mawatheeq (USA) 126 – Efisio's Star (Efisio 120) [2015 80: 7g³ **94** 8.5m* 8s³ t8.6f* Oct 3] fairly useful performer: won maiden at Beverley in June and handicap at Wolverhampton in October, taking well to surface and showing improved form when beating Privileged by short head in latter: stays 8.5f: acts on tapeta, soft and good to firm going: front runner/races prominently. *B. W. Hills*

WARDEN BOND 7 ch.g. Monsieur Bond (IRE) 120 – Warden Rose 61 (Compton Place **63** 125) [2015 61: t8.6f* t8.6g² p8g p8m* p8f t8.6g⁵ t8.6g⁴ t8.6g t8.6f⁴ Dec 21] angular gelding: modest handicapper: won at Wolverhampton in January and Lingfield in April: stays 1¼m: acts on polytrack, tapeta and good to firm going: wears cheekpieces. *William Stone*

WAR DEPARTMENT (IRE) 2 b.g. (Feb 16) Frozen Power (IRE) 108 – On My Kness **92** (FR) (Fasliyev (USA) 120) [2015 6m* 6f 7f 8g p6f⁶ Oct 15] 42,000F, 160,000 2-y-o: fifth foal: half-brother to 2 winners in Italy by Whipper: dam Italian 5f winner: fairly useful form on debut when winning maiden at Leicester in May by 4½ lengths from King's Pavilion: well held subsequently, and gelded after final start (when tried in blinkers): best effort at 6f: acts on good to firm going: has joined Michael Bell. *William Haggas*

WAR ENVOY (USA) 3 b.c. War Front (USA) 119 – La Conseillante (USA) (Elusive **116** Quality (USA)) [2015 110: p7g² 8g⁴ 8g 10.4g 8f* 8m⁴ a8f 8.5f² Dec 20] strong, attractive colt: smart performer: best effort when winning Britannia Stakes (Handicap) at Royal Ascot (by neck from Udododontu) in June: left Aidan O'Brien after seventh start: stays 1m: acts on firm going: tried in blinkers prior to 2015: tried in tongue tie: often races towards rear. *Wesley A. Ward, USA*

WARFARE 6 b.g. Soviet Star (USA) 128 – Fluffy 67 (Efisio 120) [2015 73: f8g* t9.5g² **89** f8d⁶ p8f t9.5g⁴ 7d³ t8.6g² 10d* p11g p10g⁵ 8.5s* 10.4g 10.4d⁶ 10d p8g⁴ t9.5m Dec 30] deep-girthed gelding: type to carry condition: fairly useful handicapper: won at Southwell in January, Ayr in June and Beverley in July: stays 10.5f: acts on all-weather and soft going: tried in headgear. *Tim Fitzgerald*

WAR GIRL (USA) 3 b.f. War Front (USA) 119 – Valarchos Destiny (USA) (Monarchos **–** (USA) 129) [2015 t8.6f t8.6m⁶ 7s⁵ t8.6m Sep 5] $85,000Y: third foal: dam US 8.5f winner: no form. *David Barron*

WAR GLORY (IRE) 2 b.c. (Apr 21) Canford Cliffs (IRE) 133 – Attracted To You (IRE) **86 p** 92 (Hurricane Run (IRE) 134) [2015 t7.1f² Dec 22] first foal: dam 2-y-o 6f winner: 8/1, showed plenty when second in 12-runner maiden at Wolverhampton (1¼ lengths behind Always Welcome) on debut: sure to progress. *Richard Hannon*

WAR IN ROME (IRE) 2 b.g. (Apr 25) Holy Roman Emperor (IRE) 125 – Virginia Rose **–** (IRE) 70 (Galileo (IRE) 134) [2015 7.5g Aug 7] 56/1, tailed-off last of 13 in newcomers race at Deauville in August, only outing. *Jo Hughes*

WAR LORD (IRE) 5 b.g. Aussie Rules (USA) 123 – Carn Lady (IRE) 52 (Woodman **–** (USA) 126) [2015 –: 13.8d⁶ 12.4d Apr 28] fair handicapper in 2013, no form since: stays 1¼m: acts on good to soft going: has worn visor. *George Moore*

WARLU WAY 8 b.g. Sakhee (USA) 136 – Conspiracy 98 (Rudimentary (USA) 118) [2015 **79 §** 84: 8g 10.1d⁴ 11.5m⁴ 11.9m⁶ 10.2m* 10.2m⁵ 9.8m⁵ 10d Jul 7] sturdy gelding: fair handicapper: won at Nottingham (apprentice) in June: stays 1½m: acts on firm and good to soft going: tried in visor/tongue tie: often races prominently: sold 5,500 gns, sent to Germany: unreliable. *Michael Easterby*

WARM ORDER 4 b.f. Assertive 121 – Even Hotter 63 (Desert Style (IRE) 121) [2015 54: **61** t5.1f* t5.1f² 5.1m 5.1m 5.7m 5f² 5m² t5.1g⁵ Aug 27] modest handicapper: won at Wolverhampton in January: stays 5.5f: acts on tapeta and firm going: in headgear last 3 starts: tried in tongue tie. *Tony Carroll*

WARM RECEPTION 3 b.f. Acclamation 118 – Feel (Rainbow Quest (USA) 134) [2015 **65** p7g⁶ t7.1g t9.5g⁵ 8g⁵ Aug 6] third foal: half-sister to Italian 7.5f-11f winner French Alps (by Three Valleys): dam unraced half-sister to smart Italian/French 7f/1m performer Field of Hope: fair maiden: stays 9.5f. *Marco Botti*

WAROFINDEPENDENCE (USA) 3 b.g. War Front (USA) 119 – My Dear Annie **–** (USA) (Smart Strike (CAN) 121) [2015 7.6m⁵ 11.5g p10f Aug 18] lengthy gelding: no form: tried in tongue tie. *Alan Bailey*

WAR PAINT (IRE) 3 br.f. Excellent Art 125 – Stairway To Glory (IRE) 86 (Kalanisi **54** (IRE) 132) [2015 68: p8g 8g⁵ 7m 6m Aug 29] modest maiden: stays 1m: acts on polytrack and good to soft going: tried in headgear. *Ed Walker*

WAR POET 8 b.g. Singspiel (IRE) 133 – Summer Sonnet (Baillamont (USA) 124) [2015 **70 §** 86§: t12.2f 12s⁵ 12m² 13.8m* 8.9g 12m 15.8d Aug 26] good-topped gelding: fair performer: won seller at Catterick in June: stays 1¾m: acts on polytrack, tapeta, soft and good to firm going: tried in headgear/tongue tie: usually races nearer last than first: carries head awkwardly and not one to trust. *Clive Mulhall*

WAR QUEEN (IRE) 2 b.f. (Apr 8) Acclamation 118 – New Deal 76 (Rainbow Quest **89** (USA) 134) [2015 5g⁵ 6s* 6.1m² 6.3d² Sep 13] €67,000Y: sixth foal: sister to 3 winners, including useful winner up to 12.3f Alrasm (2-y-o 6f winner) and winner up to 6f New Pearl (2-y-o 5f winner): dam French 1m winner: fairly useful form: won maiden at Hamilton in July: improved again when ¾-length second of 30 to Glass House in valuable sales event at the Curragh, meeting some trouble 1f out and edging ahead briefly final 100 yds: will stay 7f: sold 100,000 gns in December, sent to USA. *David Brown*

WARRANT OFFICER 5 gr.g. Misu Bond (IRE) 114 – Kilmovee 59 (Inchinor 119) **42** [2015 p12g⁶ 11.9d⁴ Aug 5] poor handicapper: stays 1½m: acts on polytrack and soft going: in cheekpieces last start. *Sheena West*

WARRIOR OF LIGHT (IRE) 4 b.g. High Chaparral (IRE) 132 – Strawberry Fledge **106** (USA) (Kingmambo (USA) 125) [2015 108: 10.3m³ 11.6g² 12f p10m p12g⁴ Dec 19] attractive gelding: useful handicapper: creditable efforts all starts in 2015, 3 lengths fourth of 9 to Barye at Lingfield final one: stays 1½m: acts on polytrack and firm going: tried in cheekpieces: sometimes slowly away, often races towards rear. *David Lanigan*

WAR SINGER (USA) 8 b.g. War Chant (USA) 126 – Sister Marilyn (USA) (Saint **87** Ballado (CAN)) [2015 91: 10d³ 12m p12g Nov 4] fairly useful handicapper: stays 1½m: acts on good to firm and heavy going: usually wears headgear/tongue tie: fairly useful hurdler. *Johnny Farrelly*

WAR STORY (IRE) 2 gr.c. (Apr 25) Myboycharlie (IRE) 118 – America Nova (FR) **85 p** (Verglas (IRE) 118) [2015 p7g² Nov 18] €33,000Y: fourth foal: half-brother to useful 2-y-o 6f/7f winner Sir Patrick Moore (later smart performer renamed Weary up to 1¼m in Australia) and useful French/US winner up to 8.5f Stellar Path (2-y-o 7f/1m winner) (both by Astronomer Royal): dam French 2-y-o 1m winner: 6/1, showed plenty when ½-length second of 9 to Manson in maiden at Kempton, well positioned and keeping on, clear of rest: should progress. *Luca Cumani*

WAR STRIKE (CAN) 3 b.g. Ghostzapper (USA) 137 – Michillinda (CAN) (Candy Ride **86** (ARG) 133) [2015 7d 8f⁵ 7.9g² 7.4g* 8s p8g⁵ Sep 21] $87,000Y: first foal: dam placed up to 1m in Canada: fairly useful performer: won maiden at Ffos Las (by neck from English Style) in July: stays 1m: acts on polytrack, best turf form on good going: front runner/races prominently: sent to UAE. *William Haggas*

WAR WHISPER (IRE) 2 b.c. (Feb 19) Royal Applause 124 – Featherweight (IRE) 89 **85 p** (Fantastic Light (USA) 134) [2015 6g³ 5g* Jun 5] 38,000F, €115,000Y: sturdy colt: second foal: dam, 1¼m winner who stayed 1½m, half-sister to useful 7f winner Carniolan (by Royal Applause): 8/13, value for extra when winning 6-runner maiden at Goodwood in June by 3¼ lengths from Alkhor, quickening clear final 100 yds: will go on improving. *Richard Hannon*

WASEEM FARIS (IRE) 6 b.g. Exceed And Excel (AUS) 126 – Kissing Time 79 **100** (Lugana Beach 116) [2015 86: 6m p5g² 5m³ 5m* 5.3s* 5m³ 5.1d* p5f p5g⁴ p5m² Dec 27] lengthy gelding: useful handicapper: won at Salisbury in June, Brighton in August and Nottingham (by 1¼ lengths from El Viento) in October: left Ken Cunningham-Brown after seventh start, back to form when second at Chelmsford final one: stays 7f: acts on polytrack and any turf going: tried in visor prior to 2015: front runner/races prominently. *Joseph Tuite*

WASHINGTON DC (IRE) 2 b.c. (Mar 10) Zoffany (IRE) 121 – How's She Cuttin' **108 d** (IRE) 99 (Shinko Forest (IRE)) [2015 p5g² 5g* 5g² 5f* 6g² Aug 9] 75,000F, €340,000Y: useful-looking colt: third foal: dam 5f winner: useful performer: won maiden at Tipperary in April and listed Windsor Castle Stakes at Royal Ascot (27 ran, led 1f out and held on by head from Areen) in June: off 8 weeks, further progress when 2 lengths second of 7 to Air Force Blue in Phoenix Stakes at the Curragh: will prove best at sprint distances: often travels strongly: may well do better still. *Aidan O'Brien, Ireland*

WASHINGTON WINKLE 3 b.g. Rip Van Winkle (IRE) 134 – Bluebelle Dancer (IRE) **– p** 70 (Danehill Dancer (IRE) 117) [2015 7g p7g 7s⁵ Oct 6] 62,000F, 70,000Y: third foal: half-brother to a winner in Greece by Cape Cross: dam, maiden (stayed 1m), half-sister to useful 6f winner Catch A Glimpse: well held in maidens: left Shane Donohoe after second start: may well do better in handicaps. *Peter Chapple-Hyam*

WASLAWI (IRE) 2 ch.c. (Feb 23) Halling (USA) 133 – Masaya 101 (Dansili 127) [2015 67 6m⁶ 6.1g² 6g³ 6g Sep 4] fair maiden: best effort second start: raced only at 6f: sold 7,000 gns, sent to Hungary. *Robert Cowell*

WATCHABLE 5 ch.g. Pivotal 124 – Irresistible 98 (Cadeaux Genereux 131) [2015 114: 116 6g² 5m⁵ 6f⁵ 6m⁵ 6m⁴ 6.5g⁴ 6d 5m Oct 4] workmanlike gelding: smart performer: best efforts when second in Abernant Stakes at Newmarket (½ length behind Astaire) and fourth in Prix Maurice de Gheest at Deauville (2 lengths behind Muhaarar) first/sixth starts: stays 7f: acts on soft and good to firm going: wears headgear. *David O'Meara*

WATERCLOCK (IRE) 6 b.g. Notnowcato 128 – Waterfall One 62 (Nashwan (USA) 80 135) [2015 83: 17.1g⁴ 18g⁴ 16.2m² 16.4m 16.2m⁴ Aug 13] rather leggy gelding: fairly useful handicapper: won at Beverley in July: stays 2¼m: acts on good to firm going: wears headgear: fairly useful hurdler. *Jedd O'Keeffe*

WATER DANCER (IRE) 4 ch.g. Ad Valorem (USA) 125 – River Patrol 96 (Rousillon 80 (USA) 133) [2015 t7.1f⁵ t8.6f³ p8f² t9.5f⁴ 10m p8g⁵ p7g⁴ 8.1s p6d* Sep 4] 30,000Y: half-brother to numerous winners, including high-class/temperamental winner up to 9f (stayed 1½m) Norse Dancer (2-y-o 7f winner) and 9.4f winner Romie's Kastett (both by Halling): dam 1¼m winner: fairly useful handicapper: won at Kempton (apprentice) in July and September: stays 7f: acts on polytrack: sometimes in headgear: usually races nearer last than first: sold 6,000 gns, sent to Saudi Arabia. *David Elsworth*

WATERLOO BRIDGE (IRE) 2 b.c. (Mar 12) Zoffany (IRE) 121 – Miss Childrey 106 (IRE) 97 (Dr Fong (USA) 128) [2015 5d⁶ 6d³ 5.8g² 5d* 5f* 7m² a8.5f Oct 31] 350,000Y: compact colt: sixth foal: half-brother to 3 winners, including smart French winner up to 12.5f Forces of Darkness (2-y-o 1m-9.5f winner, by Lawman) and ungenuine 7f winner Independent Girl (by Bachelor Duke): dam 2-y-o 5f/6f winner: useful performer: won maiden at Tipperary and Norfolk Stakes at Royal Ascot (by ½ length from Log Out Island) in June: 4½ lengths second to Gifted Master in valuable sales race at Newmarket and 5 lengths ninth of 14 to Nyquist in Breeders' Cup Juvenile at Keeneland last 2 starts: stays 8.5f: acts on dirt, firm and good to soft going: tried in hood/tongue strap: usually races towards rear, often travels strongly. *Aidan O'Brien, Ireland*

WATERLOO DOCK 10 b.g. Hunting Lion (IRE) 115 – Scenic Air (Hadeer 118) [2015 59 58: p6g² t6g* p6f³ p6g⁵ t6f⁴ t6f t6f t7.1f* t8.6g* 7m⁶ t7.1g 7g⁵ 8.6m t8.6m Sep 14] leggy gelding: modest handicapper: won at Wolverhampton (amateur) in January, March and April: left Emma Baker after eighth start, Brendan Powell after tenth: stays 8.5f: acts on polytrack, tapeta and good to firm going: wears headgear. *Christopher Kellett*

WATERSMEET 4 gr.g. Dansili 127 – Under The Rainbow 107 (Fantastic Light (USA) 112 134) [2015 81: p10f* p12g* p10g* 12f⁴ 12m* 12f⁵ 11.9g² 12m⁴ 14g 12s⁴ Sep 18] good-topped gelding: smart handicapper: won at Chelmsford and Lingfield in March, Chelmsford (by 2¼ lengths from Al Destoor) in April and Newmarket (by 1¾ lengths from Dashing Star) in May: good second of 14 in Old Newton Cup at Haydock (½ length behind Notarised) in July: stays 1½m: acts on polytrack and firm going: front runner/races prominently: quirky sort (sometimes hangs left/flashes tail). *Mark Johnston*

WATER THIEF (USA) 3 b.g. Bellamy Road (USA) 123 – Sometime (IRE) (Royal 75 Academy (USA) 130) [2015 83: p8g⁴ 12f⁴ 10d 8g⁶ p10g Dec 15] fair handicapper: left Mark Johnston after fourth start: stays 8.5f: acts on polytrack and tapeta. *Tim McCarthy*

WATTABOUTSTEVE 4 b.g. Araafa (IRE) 128 – Angel Kate (IRE) 81 (Invincible Spirit 51 (IRE) 121) [2015 –: f7s⁴ f6g³ Dec 29] modest maiden: best effort at 6f: acts on fibresand. *Ralph Smith*

WATT BRODERICK (IRE) 6 ch.g. Hawk Wing (USA) 136 – Kingsridge (IRE) 89 78 (King's Theatre (IRE) 128) [2015 85: t16.5f⁴ t16.5g⁴ t13.9m³ Mar 7] fair handicapper: stays 16.5f: acts on polytrack, tapeta and good to firm going: tried in cheekpieces/tongue tie. *Ian Williams*

WAVELET 3 b.f. Archipenko (USA) 127 – Weather Report (Rainbow Quest (USA) 134) 72 [2015 p12g² p11g³ p13.3f³ p10g* Dec 9] third foal: dam unraced half-sister to smart performer up to 1¾m Flying Cross out of Oaks winner Ramruma: fair performer: won maiden at Lingfield in December: stays 13.5f. *David Simcock*

WAVE REVIEWS 2 b.c. (Feb 8) Fastnet Rock (AUS) 127 – Critical Acclaim 87 (Peintre 95 Celebre (USA) 137) [2015 7g⁵ 7g² Oct 21] lengthy colt: third foal: closely related to useful 1¾m winner (stays 21f) William of Orange (by Duke of Marmalade): dam, 1½m winner, half-sister to smart 1¼m-1½m winner Eagles Peak: progressed from debut when short-head second of 10 to Colour Me Happy in maiden at Newmarket: will be suited by 1m. *William Haggas*

Kilboy Estate Stakes, the Curragh—the highly-tried Wedding Vow breaks her duck in convincing fashion in this Group 2, beating Brooch (rail), Bocca Baciata (right) and Raydara

WAY AHEAD 2 b.c. (Feb 5) Kyllachy 129 – On Her Way 92 (Medicean 128) [2015 7g 7g Sep 7] well held in 2 maidens: in hood first start: sent to Greece. *James Tate* —

WAYSIDE MAGIC 2 b.g. (May 4) Thewayyouare (USA) 117 – Poppy's Rose 85 (Diktat 126) [2015 7m 8d⁶ 7g Sep 23] little impact in maidens. *Michael Dods* —

WAY TO FINISH 9 b.g. Oasis Dream 129 – Suedoise (Kris 135) [2015 8.3d⁵ 10d Sep 17] lightly raced and no worthwhile form. *James Moffatt* —

WAYWARD HOOF 2 b.g. (Apr 8) Equiano (FR) 127 – Mystical Spirit (IRE) 48 (Xaar 132) [2015 6m³ 6m* 7m³ 6d 6g Oct 3] 40,000Y: third foal: half-brother to 2-y-o 7f winner Mystic And Artist (by Excellent Art): dam lightly-raced sister to useful sprinter Mystical Land and half-sister to dam of smart performer up to 9f Forjatt: fairly useful performer: won maiden at Haydock (by ¾ length from Alshalaal) in July: best effort at 6f: acts on good to firm going: tried in visor. *K. R. Burke* **84**

WEALD OF KENT (USA) 3 b.g. Successful Appeal (USA) 118 – Apple of Kent (USA) 118 (Kris S (USA)) [2015 46p: p10g⁵ p10f f12g⁶ f12g* t12.2g⁴ 12g⁶ t13.9f f12g³ f14m f12f Dec 17] fair handicapper: won at Southwell in April: left John Gosden after second start: stays 1¾m: acts on fibresand and tapeta: usually in headgear in 2015: temperament under suspicion. *Michael Appleby* **72**

WEAPON OF CHOICE (IRE) 7 b.g. Iffraaj 127 – Tullawadgeen (IRE) (Sinndar (IRE) 134) [2015 t9.5g Feb 9] lengthy gelding: fair handicapper: stays 10.5f: acts on polytrack, tapeta and any turf going: tried in blinkers/tongue tie: tends to find little. *Dianne Sayer* **74**

WEARDIDITALLGORONG 3 b.f. Fast Company (IRE) 126 – Little Oz (IRE) 71 (Red Ransom (USA)) [2015 49: p8g f8s⁵ 8m 9d* 8.3m 9.9d* p10g⁵ 11.6d p10f Nov 7] sparely-made filly: modest handicapper: won at Lingfield in June and Brighton in August: stays 1¼m: acts on good to soft going: wears headgear. *Des Donovan* **64 a58**

WE ARE (IRE) 4 b.f. Dansili 127 – In Clover 114 (Inchinor 119) [2015 117: 10.4s⁴ 10.4g² 9.9d³ 9.9m³ Oct 4] heavy-topped filly: smart performer: first past post in Prix Saint-Alary and Prix de l'Opera, both at Longchamp, in 2014, but subsequently disqualified from first-named race: placed in 2015 in Prix Corrida at Saint-Cloud (4 lengths second to Treve), Prix Jean Romanet at Deauville (promoted a place after finishing fourth to Odeliz) and Prix de l'Opera at Longchamp (2½ lengths third behind Covert Love, finishing well from hopeless position): stays 10.4f: acts on soft and good to firm going: twice in blinkers. *F. Head, France* **117**

WE ARE NINETY (IRE) 2 b.f. (Feb 8) Thewayyouare (USA) 117 – Brigids Cross (IRE) (Sadler's Wells (USA) 132) [2015 t8.6f* Oct 27] fifth foal: half-sister to 6f winner Lady Brigid (by Holy Roman Emperor): dam unraced sister to Fillies' Mile winner Listen and **76 p**

Moyglare Stud Stakes winner Sequoyah, latter dam of top-class dual 2000 Guineas winner Henrythenavigator: 15/8, overcame greenness when winning 8-runner maiden at Wolverhampton by length from Rasikh on debut, leading 1f out and keeping on well: sure to progress. *Hugo Palmer*

WEATHER FRONT (USA) 2 ch.g. (Jan 19) Stormy Atlantic (USA) – Kiswahili 105   **72**
(Selkirk (USA) 129) [2015 t8.6f⁴ 8m⁴ p8g² Oct 20] tall gelding: nose second to Sahalin in maiden at Lingfield final start, just failing after taking while to knuckle down: stays 1m. *James Tate*

WEDDING VOW (IRE) 3 b.f. Galileo (IRE) 134 – Remember When (IRE) 111   **113**
(Danehill Dancer (IRE) 117) [2015 –p: 10v² 9.5g² 11.5s³ 12f 9d* 9.9m² 9.5d⁵ Aug 15] leggy, angular filly: first foal: dam, maiden (promoted second in Oaks), closely related to Prix de l'Arc de Triomphe winner Dylan Thomas and 1000 Guineas winner Homecoming Queen and half-sister to high-class 2-y-o sprinter Queen's Logic: smart performer: won Kilboy Estate Stakes at the Curragh in July by 2 lengths from Brooch: good efforts last 2 starts, in Nassau Stakes at Goodwood (2¼ lengths second to Legatissimo) and Beverly D Stakes at Arlington (2¾ lengths fifth of 9 to demoted Secret Gesture): should prove effective at 1½m: acts on firm and good to soft going: tried in blinkers: often races towards rear. *Aidan O'Brien, Ireland*

WEDGE (IRE) 2 ro.c. (Apr 28) Zebedee 113 – Jalmira (IRE) 112 (Danehill Dancer (IRE)   **80**
117) [2015 5f.p5m* 5f 6d* 5m⁶ 6m 6g 5.5d Sep 26] €48,000F, 62,000Y: good-topped colt: first foal: dam 1m-9.4f winner: fairly useful performer: won maiden at Chelmsford in June and nursery at Haydock in July: likely to stay 7f: acts on polytrack and good to soft going, probably on good to firm: sold 10,000 gns, sent to Spain. *Richard Hannon*

WEDGEWOOD ESTATES 4 ch.f. Assertive 121 – Heaven 84 (Reel Buddy (USA) 118)   **59**
[2015 65: p6m² t5.1f⁶ p6f t6g⁴ t5.1m⁵ t6m Dec 30] modest handicapper: stays 6f: acts on polytrack, tapeta and firm going. *Tony Carroll*

WEE JEAN 4 b.f. Captain Gerrard (IRE) 113 – Reeli Silli (Dansili 127) [2015 108: 8g 8g   **100**
p8g 8m⁴ 7s 7g 8.1m 8m 7.6m* 7d* 7.6v⁴ 7.6m⁵ 8g 7.2g 7d Sep 26] smallish, workmanlike filly: useful handicapper: won at Chester in July and Newmarket (by 2 lengths from Risen Sun) in July: stays 1m: acts on soft and good to firm going: in visor last 7 starts: front runner/races prominently. *Mick Channon*

WEEKEND OFFENDER (FR) 2 ch.c. (Apr 26) Lope de Vega (IRE) 125 – Huroof   **79**
(IRE) 87 (Pivotal 124) [2015 7g⁶ 7.2g² 7s Oct 10] fair form in maidens at York and Ayr first 2 starts: shaped as if amiss final outing. *Kevin Ryan*

WEET IN NERJA 9 b.g. Captain Rio 122 – Persian Fortune 53 (Forzando 122) [2015 7g   –
Jul 22] good-bodied gelding: poor maiden: usually wears headgear: tried in tongue tie. *Ken Wingrove*

WEETLES 3 b.f. High Chaparral (IRE) 132 – Millestan (IRE) 91 (Invincible Spirit (IRE)   **94 p**
121) [2015 7m 8g⁴ 8.3d* 10d² Oct 30] 36,000Y: close-coupled filly: second foal: half-sister to 6f winner Seraphima (by Fusaichi Pegasus): dam, 1m (at 2 yrs)/8.5f (in USA) winner, half-sister to smart performer (best at 5f/6f) Seeking Magic: fairly useful form: won maiden at Windsor (by 6 lengths from China Girl) in October: improved again when length second to Zamperini in handicap at Newmarket: stays 1¼m: sold 50,000 gns in December: will go on improving. *Clive Cox*

WE HAVE A DREAM 10 b.g. Oasis Dream 129 – Final Shot 91 (Dalsaan 125) [2015 –:   **51**
p6f³ p5g³ p6g Nov 26] good-bodied gelding: modest handicapper: stays 6f: acts on polytrack, good to firm and heavy going: wears headgear/tongue tie. *Heather Dalton*

WEKEYLL 3 b.c. Exceed And Excel (AUS) 126 – Sensible 72 (Almutawakel 126) [2015   **84**
7g⁵ 8.3m* 8.3m a6f⁶ Dec 18] 30,000F, 110,000Y: good-quartered colt: first foal: dam, maiden (stayed 13f), half-sister to smart/temperamental winner up to 1½m Muhannak: fairly useful performer: won maiden at Windsor (by head from Maybe Definitely) in June: left William Haggas after third start: best effort at 8.3f. *D. J. Selvaratnam, UAE*

WELD AL EMARAT 3 b.g. Dubawi (IRE) 129 – Spirit of Dubai (IRE) 103 (Cape Cross   **97**
(IRE) 129) [2015 90p: 8d⁵ 8m² 8d³ 8g Aug 21] useful handicapper: standout effort when second at Ascot (½ length behind Cilento) in May: raced only at 1m: acts on fibresand and good to firm going: sometimes slowly away, often leads: has been gelded. *Kevin Ryan*

WELD AL KHAWANEEJ (IRE) 2 ch.g. (Apr 12) Fast Company (IRE) 126 – Law   **68**
Review (IRE) 63 (Case Law 113) [2015 5g⁶ 5.9g 6d⁶ 6g⁶ 7.2g² t7.1f⁴ p7g t8.6f⁵ Nov 30] fair performer: won nursery at Ayr in September: should stay 1m: acts on tapeta. *Kevin Ryan*

WELD ARAB (IRE) 4 b.g. Shamardal (USA) 129 – Itqaan (USA) 83 (Danzig (USA)) **69** [2015 65: t12.2m p11f* p12f⁴ p10m² 9.9s t8.6g* p8g⁵ p10f p8g⁵ p10m² Dec 27] fair handicapper: won at Kempton in March and Wolverhampton in June: stays 11f: acts on polytrack and tapeta: tried in blinkers: usually races close up. *Michael Blake*

WELEASE BWIAN (IRE) 6 b.g. Kheleyf (USA) 116 – Urbanize (USA) 68 (Chester **77** House (USA) 123) [2015 77: p5g³ p5m p6f⁴ p6f p5f² 6m* 6m⁶ 6v³ 5g⁴ 6g 6m⁶ 5.3d⁴ p6g⁵ p6m⁴ Dec 16] strong gelding: fair handicapper: won at Brighton in April: stays 6f: acts on polytrack, good to firm and good to soft going: tried in headgear/tongue tie: often starts slowly. *Stuart Williams*

WELFORD 2 b.c. (Mar 29) Dubawi (IRE) 129 – Avongrove 108 (Tiger Hill (IRE) 127) **93** [2015 6g⁶ 6s³ 7m² 7.1m* 7m⁶ 7g 7m⁶ Sep 11] rather leggy colt: first foal: dam, French 11f winner, half-sister to smart stayer Veracity: fairly useful performer: won maiden at Musselburgh in June and minor event at Chester (by 1½ lengths from Gerrard's Quest) in July: stays 7f: acts on good to firm going: front runner/races prominently. *Mark Johnston*

WE'LL DEAL AGAIN 8 b.g. Gentleman's Deal (IRE) 114 – Emma Amour 67 (Emarati **78** (USA) 74) [2015 83: t7.1g⁴ 8m⁵ 6s May 9] workmanlike gelding: fair handicapper: stays 7f: acts on polytrack, tapeta, good to firm and heavy going: often in headgear prior to 2015. *Michael Easterby*

WELLIESINTHEWATER (IRE) 5 b.g. Footstepsinthesand 120 – Shadow Ash (IRE) **72** 75 (Ashkalani (IRE) 128) [2015 70: t8.6g 7g* t7.1g⁶ 8.3s⁵ f8m³ p7f² Dec 21] fair handicapper: won at Doncaster in August: stays 8.5f: acts on polytrack, fibresand and soft going: wears visor. *Derek Shaw*

WELL OFF (GER) 3 b.g. Monsun (GER) 124 – Wells Present (GER) 101 (Cadeaux **73** Genereux 131) [2015 8m* p10g⁵ Apr 28] fair form on debut when winning maiden at Redcar in April by head from Spryt: still looked green when disappointing only subsequent start: should stay 1½m: has been gelded. *Saeed bin Suroor*

WELL OWD MON 5 b.g. Vitus 82 – Farina (IRE) 73 (Golan (IRE) 129) [2015 64: **63** t12.2g⁵ t12.2m* t13.9f² t12.2f p12f⁵ 14.1m⁶ 14.6d⁶ t12.2m³ t12.2m⁵ Dec 18] modest handicapper: won at Wolverhampton in February: stays 1¾m: acts on polytrack, tapeta and soft going: wears headgear. *Sarah Hollinshead*

WELL PAINTED (IRE) 6 ch.g. Excellent Art 125 – Aoife (IRE) 83 (Thatching 131) **66** [2015 93: 11.6g* p10g⁶ 10m p12m Nov 19] rangy gelding: fair handicapper: won at Windsor in June: stays 11.5f: acts on polytrack, soft and good to firm going: sometimes in headgear prior to 2015: often wears tongue tie. *Sheena West*

WE'LL SHAKE HANDS (FR) 4 b.g. Excellent Art 125 – Amou Daria (FR) (Kendor **78** (FR) 122) [2015 82: f6s 7d 8g* 8.3s³ 8d⁶ 10.1m* 10.2m⁴ Jul 4] fair handicapper: won at Haydock in April and Newcastle in June: stays 1¼m: acts on soft and good to firm going: in visor last 5 starts: usually races towards rear, often travels strongly. *K. R. Burke*

WELSH GEM 3 b.f. Dylan Thomas (IRE) 132 – Gemini Joan (Montjeu (IRE) 137) [2015 **72** p8f* p8g May 6] 4,000Y: second foal: half-sister to 7f winner Twin Point (by Invincible Spirit): dam unraced half-sister to smart winner up to 1m Tell: fair form when winning 7-runner maiden at Chelmsford in February on debut: well held in handicap there next time. *Mike Murphy*

WELSH INLET (IRE) 7 br.m. Kheleyf (USA) 116 – Ervedya (IRE) (Doyoun 124) [2015 **76** 70, a61: p7g p8f³ p8f² p6f⁶ p8g³ p7m* 7m* 7m³ 6g⁶ 7d 8v* 8s² p8f⁵ 8.3g³ p8m p7m⁴ p7g² **a66** p8g⁴ p8g Dec 30] compact mare: fair handicapper: won at Lingfield (twice) in June and at Brighton in August: stays 8.5f: acts on polytrack, good to firm and heavy going: tried in tongue tie. *John Bridger*

WELSH REBEL 3 ch.g. Cockney Rebel (IRE) 127 – Lasting Image (Zilzal (USA) 137) **51** [2015 –: 10g t8.6g⁶ t9.5g t13.9g⁶ Nov 27] workmanlike gelding: modest maiden: stays 1¾m: acts on tapeta and good to soft going. *Nikki Evans*

WELSH ROSE 2 b.f. (Mar 22) Exceed And Excel (AUS) 126 – Nantyglo 101 (Mark of **78 p** Esteem (IRE) 137) [2015 7m 6g² t6f⁴ Nov 14] 72,000F: useful-looking filly: sixth foal: closely related to 8.6f winner Valley Tiger (by Tiger Hill): dam, winner up to 1m (2-y-o 6f winner), half-sister to useful winner up to 1½m Resplendent Light: fair form: second of 14 to Exist in maiden at Windsor in October, best effort: too free in early stages next time: remains open to improvement. *William Muir*

WENTWORTH FALLS 3 gr.g. Dansili 127 – Strawberry Morn (CAN) (Travelling **86** Victor (CAN)) [2015 105: p5g t5.1f 6m Apr 15] useful-looking gelding: fairly useful performer: stays 6f: acts on polytrack: wears blinkers nowadays: often races in rear. *Charlie Appleby*

WERNOTFAMUSANYMORE (IRE) 2 b.g. (Mar 13) Oasis Dream 129 – Dhanyata (IRE) 109 (Danetime (IRE) 121) [2015 6g⁵ 5.1g⁴ 6d² Oct 26] fair form in maidens at Catterick, Nottingham and Redcar: will prove best at sprint distances. *Kevin Ryan* **76**

WERONAWINNERSHERRY 6 b.m. Needwood Blade 117 – Wizby 59 (Wizard King 122) [2015 7.1m Dec 12] first foal: dam winner up to 1m (2-y-o 5f/6f winner) who stayed 1¼m: 100/1, well held in maiden at Wolverhampton. *Brian McMath* **–**

WESTBOURNE GROVE (USA) 2 b.c. (Mar 25) Munnings (USA) 118 – Catch Me Later (USA) (Posse (USA)) [2015 5m⁶ 5v⁴ t6f³ Oct 16] modest maiden: best effort when third at Wolverhampton. *Robert Cowell* **59**

WEST BRIT (IRE) 7 b.g. High Chaparral (IRE) 132 – Aldburgh (Bluebird (USA) 125) [2015 8.3s* 8.3s May 15] sturdy gelding: fair handicapper: won at Hamilton in May: stays 1¼m: acts on heavy going: tried in tongue tie prior to 2015. *R. Mike Smith* **73**

WEST COAST DREAM 8 b.g. Oasis Dream 129 – Californie (IRE) (Rainbow Quest (USA) 134) [2015 71, a79: t5.1g Jan 19] strong, lengthy gelding: fair handicapper: stayed 7f: acted on polytrack, good to firm and heavy going: had worn headgear: was a front runner/ raced prominently, tended to find little: was none too consistent: dead. *Roy Brotherton* **–**

WEST DRIVE (IRE) 2 ch.c. (Apr 26) Sea The Stars (IRE) 140 – Fair Sailing (IRE) 62 (Docksider (USA) 124) [2015 8.3v 8s⁵ 8.3s² Nov 4] 100,000Y: fourth foal: half-brother to smart winner up to 7f Windfast (2-y-o 6f winner, by Exceed And Excel) and useful 2-y-o 1m winner Montalcino (by Big Bad Bob): dam, maiden (stayed 1¼m), half-sister to high-class 1¼m-1½m winner White Muzzle: fairly useful form: improved again when ¾-length second to Good Trip in maiden at Nottingham final start. *Roger Varian* **83**

WESTERLY 4 b.f. Rail Link 132 – Humility 66 (Polar Falcon (USA) 126) [2015 76: p13g* p13f² t16.5g² 14m 13.3m 12.8m 12.2g³ t12.2m Nov 28] fair handicapper: won at Lingfield in February: left Luke Dace after fourth start: stays 16.5f: acts on polytrack, tapeta, best turf form on good going: usually wears cheekpieces: tried in tongue: often races prominently. *John Mackie* **73**

WESTERN BELLA 4 b.f. High Chaparral (IRE) 132 – Sindarbella (Sinndar (IRE) 134) [2015 67p: 11.8m⁶ 14.1g 12d 12.1m⁶ Sep 10] maiden: fair form in 2014 but well held in 2015: stays 11.5f: acts on soft and good to firm going: sometimes slowly away. *Clive Cox* **–**

WESTERN HYMN 4 b.g. High Chaparral (IRE) 132 – Blue Rhapsody 79 (Cape Cross (IRE) 129) [2015 117: 10d* 10m* 10f³ 10m³ Jul 4] well-made gelding: very smart performer: won Gordon Richards Stakes at Sandown in April by ¾ length from Postponed, leading over 1f out: followed up in Brigadier Gerard Stakes on same course in May, leading close home to beat Arab Spring by head: good third in Prince of Wales's Stakes at Royal Ascot (2¾ lengths behind Free Eagle) and creditable third in Eclipse Stakes at Sandown (8 lengths behind Golden Horn) last 2 starts: stays 1¼m: acts on polytrack and any turf going. *John Gosden* **122**

bet365 Gordon Richards Stakes, Sandown—Western Hymn looks sharper than the pair that chase him home—Postponed and Cannock Chase—in this early-season Group 3 in which four of the five runners are making their reappearance

WESTERN PLAYBOY (IRE) 3 b.g. Kodiac 112 – Dreamalot (Falbrav (IRE) 133) **64 §**
[2015 60, a67: p6g⁴ p7g⁵ 7s⁶ 7m³ p8g³ 8.3m⁴ 7m 8m⁵ 10.2m³ 10.2g⁶ p10g 8g 7d Sep 21]
strong gelding: modest maiden: stays 1¼m: acts on polytrack and good to firm going:
sometimes in headgear/tongue tie in 2015: often races towards rear: best treated with
caution. *Sylvester Kirk*

WESTERN RESERVE (USA) 3 b.g. Indian Charlie (USA) 126 – Visit 116 (Oasis **116**
Dream 129) [2015 p8f³ p8m* 9m² 8f* p9.2m³ p8.5f⁴ Nov 8] lengthy gelding: first living
foal: dam, winner up to 7f (2-y-o 6f winner) who stayed 1¼m, half-sister to Pretty Polly
Stakes winner Promising Lead: smart performer: won maiden at Chelmsford in May and
handicap at Newmarket (by neck from Great Park) in July: good ¾-length third to Tryster
in minor event at Chelmsford in September, having run of race: below-form fourth to Are
You Kidding Me in Grade 2 Autumn Stakes at Woodbine final outing: likely to stay 1¼m:
usually leads: joined William Mott in USA. *Lady Cecil*

WEST LEAKE (IRE) 9 b.g. Acclamation 118 – Kilshanny 70 (Groom Dancer (USA) **68**
128) [2015 66: p7m⁴ p7f⁵ p8f* p7g⁴ p8f* p8f⁴ 8m p7m p8g⁴ p8g⁶ Dec 30] compact,
attractive gelding: fair handicapper: won at Lingfield in March and Kempton in April: stays
1m: acts on polytrack, fibresand and soft going: tried in headgear. *Paul Burgoyne*

WESTMINSTER (IRE) 4 b.g. Exceed And Excel (AUS) 126 – Pivka 90 (Pivotal 124) **93**
[2015 92: f7d* p8g⁵ f7d² f8g⁵ f7d⁴ f8s⁵ Aug 6] well-made gelding: fairly useful
handicapper: won at Southwell in January: stays 7f: acts on fibresand: sometimes in
headgear: sold £6,200. *Michael Appleby*

WEST SUSSEX (IRE) 3 b.g. Teofilo (IRE) 126 – Quixotic (Pivotal 124) [2015 p10g⁴ **60**
10.2m⁴ 8.3g 10.2m⁵ Jul 22] rather leggy gelding: modest maiden: stays 1¼m: tried in
tongue tie. *Paul Cole*

WESTWOOD HOE 4 b.g. Oasis Dream 129 – Disco Volante 105 (Sadler's Wells (USA) **102**
132) [2015 82: 8m² 7g⁴ 8g⁴ 8g 6g 7v* f7g* Dec 12] useful handicapper: won at York
(amateur) in May, Doncaster (by head from Felix Leiter in 22-runner apprentice event) in
November and Southwell (by ½ length from Highland Colori) in December: stays 1m: acts
on polytrack, fibresand, good to firm and heavy going. *Tony Coyle*

WETHER GIRL 3 ch.f. Major Cadeaux 121 – Cyclone Flyer 67 (College Chapel 122) **54**
[2015 6v 6m³ 6s 6m Aug 20] half-sister to 3 winners, including useful winner up to 6f
Autumn Pearl (2-y-o 5f winner, by Orpen): dam, 5f winner, half-sister to very smart
sprinter Bolshoi: modest maiden: raced only at 6f. *Kevin Ryan*

WET SAIL (USA) 3 b.g. Henrythenavigator (USA) 131 – Aljawza (USA) 86 (Riverman **106**
(USA) 131) [2015 104: 6m 6.1g³ 6g 7g⁴ 7s* p8g Nov 18] lengthy, rather unfurnished
gelding: useful performer: won minor event at Salisbury (by ¾ length from Mobsta) in
October: stayed 7f: acted on soft going: dead. *Charlie Fellowes*

WEYBRIDGE LIGHT 10 b.g. Fantastic Light 134 – Nuryana 107 (Nureyev **56**
(USA) 131) [2015 53: f11s³ t12.2f² t12.2f⁴ t12.2g³ 14.1m² 14.1m⁴ 16m* 15.8d² 16.1g³
13.8v⁵ t16.5f⁶ t16.5m f14g⁶ Dec 12] modest handicapper: won at Thirsk (amateur) in
August: stays 2m: acts on polytrack, soft and good to firm going: wears headgear.
David Thompson

WHALEWEIGH STATION 4 b.g. Zamindar (USA) 116 – Looby Loo 71 (Kyllachy **80 §**
129) [2015 93§: p6g p6m p7m² 7d 5m⁵ 6m 7g 6m⁶ 7.1g⁵ p6g p6d 6g 6g³ p6g⁶ f6g Dec 15] **a87 §**
angular gelding: fairly useful handicapper: stays 7f: acts on polytrack, fibresand and good
to firm going: tried in headgear: usually races nearer last than first: temperamental.
J. R. Jenkins

WHARANE (FR) 2 br.g. (Feb 20) Diktat 126 – Nova Lady (USA) (Mr Greeley (USA) **64 p**
122) [2015 7m 7.1g t7.1g⁵ p8g⁵ Dec 15] €8,000Y, €34,000 2-y-o: big gelding: second foal:
dam, Spanish maiden, half-sister to useful US winner around 1m Pearl Turn: modest form
in maidens/nursery: has been gelded: may yet do better. *Ian Williams*

WHAT ABOUT CARLO (FR) 4 b.g. Creachadoir (IRE) 126 – Boccatenera (GER) **109**
(Artan (IRE) 119) [2015 107: p10f 8d⁴ 10.1g 10.4g 10.1g 10m⁴ 12d 10.1v* 10s* 9.9g⁴ 10v
Oct 24] tall gelding: smart performer: back to form to win minor event at Epsom (3 ran, by
3¾ lengths from Fattsota) in August and handicap at Newbury (by neck from Tom Hark) in
September: stays 1¼m: acts on good to firm and heavy going: tried in blinkers: usually
races towards rear. *Eve Johnson Houghton*

WHAT A DANDY (IRE) 4 b.g. Dandy Man (IRE) 123 – Ibtihal (IRE) 75 (Hamas (IRE) **48 +**
125) [2015 64, a76: p8g 9d p8g 7.6d⁵ 7.6s p8g² p8g⁶ p10m p10f² p8g p8f⁶ Dec 21] good- **a74**
topped gelding: fair handicapper: stays 1¼m: acts on polytrack, best turf form on good
going: usually wears headgear: often races prominently. *Jim Boyle*

WHAT A PARTY (IRE) 3 ch.f. Windsor Knot (IRE) 118 – Tarziyma (IRE) (Kalanisi 74 (IRE) 132) [2015 78: p8g p8g p8g 10.2m 8.3m p10f³ t12.2g p10m² Dec 16] fair performer: stays 1¼m: acts on polytrack and good to firm going: often in headgear in 2015: often races towards rear. *Gay Kelleway*

WHAT ASHAM 3 b.g. Pivotal 124 – Coy (IRE) 112 (Danehill (USA) 126) [2015 61: 72 t7.1f⁶ p7m⁵ f8s* f8s* 8.3s t8.6g⁶ a7f⁵ a8.9f Dec 18] fair handicapper: won at Southwell (twice, apprentice event first time) in March; left Ralph Beckett after sixth start: stays 1m: acts on fibresand. *D. Watson, UAE*

WHAT A WHOPPER (IRE) 2 b.f. (Mar 3) Bushranger (IRE) 119 – Chica Whopa (IRE) – 90 (Oasis Dream 129) [2015 p5g Mar 28] 20/1, very green when well held in maiden at Kempton: dead. *David Evans*

WHAT COULD SHE BE (IRE) 3 b.f. Dark Angel (IRE) 113 – Halliwell House 59 81 (Selkirk (USA) 129) [2015 69: f8s² 8g⁵ 7m⁶ 5.9g⁴ 6g 7s² 7v⁴ f8g* f8g³ Dec 15] fairly useful performer: won maiden at Southwell in November: left Bryan Smart after first start: stays 1m: acts on fibresand, best turf form on soft/heavy going: in cheekpieces last 3 starts. *Michael Dods*

WHATDOIWANTTHATFOR (IRE) 2 b.f. (Apr 10) Kodiac 112 – Penicuik 99 (Hernando (FR) 127) [2015 5m² 6d* 5g* 6d³ 5.2s* 6s² 6g⁴ Sep 19] 17,000Y, £50,000 2-y-o: close-coupled filly: fourth foal: dam once-raced half-sister to US Grade 1 9f/1¼m winner White Heart and smart winner up to 1½m Kind Regards: useful performer: won maiden at Leicester and minor event at Windsor in June and listed race at Newbury (by ½ length from Thatsallimsaying) in August: better form when third in Princess Margaret Stakes at Ascot (3½ lengths behind Besharah) in July and second in Dick Poole Fillies' Stakes at Salisbury (4½ lengths behind La Rioja) in September: stays 6f: acts on soft going. *Richard Hannon*

WHAT SAY YOU (IRE) 3 b.f. Galileo (IRE) 134 – Alta Anna (FR) (Anabaa (USA) 130) 90 [2015 89p: 11.4d 8m Aug 8] rangy filly: fairly useful performer: left Rae Guest after first start and returned to former trainer: off 3 months, creditable seventh of 10 to Realtra in listed event at Haydock: bred to stay further than 1m: acts on good to firm going: usually races close up. *K. R. Burke*

WHAT USAIN 3 b.g. Misu Bond (IRE) 114 – Bond Shakira 54 (Daggers Drawn (USA) 71 114) [2015 54: t7.1g* t8.6g* 7.5g t7.1m t8.6f Oct 17] fair handicapper: won at Wolverhampton in January and June: stays 8.5f: acts on tapeta: usually wears headgear: often races prominently. *Geoffrey Oldroyd*

WHEAT SHEAF 3 b.c. Iffraaj 127 – Harvest Queen (IRE) 115 (Spinning World (USA) 91 130) [2015 93P: 8m⁴ 10.2d 8.3m* 8g t8.6f² 10.3d³ Oct 23] good-topped colt: fairly useful performer: won maiden at Windsor in August: better form when placed in handicaps at Wolverhampton and Doncaster last 2 starts: will prove best up to 1¼m: acts on tapeta, good to firm and good to soft going: tried in cheekpieces in 2015: temperament under suspicion: sold 60,000 gns, sent to UAE. *Roger Charlton*

WHERE IT BEGAN (IRE) 2 ch.f. (Mar 15) Strategic Prince 114 – Easy Going (Hamas – (IRE) 125) [2015 t7.1g p7g f6g⁵ f7g t1.1g⁶ Dec 1] €5,500Y: half-sister to several winners, including 6f winner Going French (by Frenchmans Bay) and 2-y-o 5f winner Going Straight (by Princely Heir): dam unraced half-sister to smart sprinter Easycall: no form: sometimes in headgear. *J. S. Moore*

WHERE'S SUE (IRE) 3 br.f. Dark Angel (IRE) 113 – The Hermitage (IRE) 83 (Kheleyf 66 (USA) 116) [2015 –: p6g* 6d p6f 6f⁶ a6f² a6.5f⁵ a6f Oct 21] fair performer: won maiden at Chelmsford in February: left Charles Hills after second start, Brian A. Lynch after fourth: raced only around 6f: acts on polytrack and dirt: often in headgear in 2015. *Shelley Brown, USA*

WHERE'S TIGER 4 b.g. Tiger Hill (IRE) 127 – Where's Broughton 77 (Cadeaux 72 Genereux 131) [2015 73: 10.3d² 10s³ 9g² 9.9g⁶ 11.1s⁶ Aug 1] fair handicapper: left Jedd O'Keeffe after fourth start: stays 10.5f: acts on soft going: usually races prominently: fair hurdler. *Lucinda Russell*

WHERE THE BOYS ARE (IRE) 4 b.f. Dylan Thomas (IRE) 132 – Promise of Love 72 75 (Royal Applause 124) [2015 74: 5g² 5.1d⁴ 5m⁴ 5f 5f Jul 18] lengthy filly: fair handicapper: stays 6f: acts on polytrack, good to firm and good to soft going: usually races close up. *Ed McMahon*

WHILE YOU WAIT (IRE) 6 b.g. Whipper (USA) 126 – Azra (IRE) 102 (Danehill   **57** (USA) 126) [2015 82: p15.8m³ p13f* p15.8f³ 17.2m⁴ p15.8g t12.2g⁶ 14.1g⁶ 12d Aug 15] **a79** strong gelding: fair performer: won claimer at Lingfield in January: left Gary Moore after third start: stays 2m: acts on polytrack and soft going: tried in visor: fair hurdler. *Paul Fitzsimons*

WHINGING WILLIE (IRE) 6 b.g. Cape Cross (IRE) 129 – Pacific Grove 89 (Persian   **84** Bold 123) [2015 86: p11g p10g p12g⁶ p12g* Dec 30] sturdy gelding: fairly useful handicapper: won at Lingfield in December: stays 1½m: acts on polytrack, good to firm and good to soft going: usually in headgear nowadays. *Gary Moore*

WHIPCRACKAWAY (IRE) 6 b.g. Whipper (USA) 126 – Former Drama (USA)   **50** (Dynaformer (USA)) [2015 p10g p10g Jan 16] tall gelding: modest performer: stays 1¼m: acts on polytrack, best turf form on good to soft/soft going: in cheekpieces nowadays. *Peter Hedger*

WHIPLASH WILLIE 7 ch.g. Phoenix Reach (IRE) 124 – Santa Isobel 94 (Nashwan   **–** (USA) 135) [2015 118: 12g⁶ Sep 25] lengthy, angular gelding: smart performer in 2014: well held in listed race at Newmarket only outing in 2015, inadequate test: stays 2½m: acts on polytrack and soft going: often wears headgear. *Andrew Balding*

WHIPPHOUND 7 b.g. Whipper (USA) 126 – Golden Symbol 54 (Wolfhound (USA)   **64** 126) [2015 81, a67: t5.1g⁵ t6g⁴ 6.1d³ p5g 5m t5.1m Oct 2] lengthy gelding: modest handicapper: stays 7f: acts on polytrack, tapeta, soft and good to firm going: tried in cheekpieces: sometimes slowly away. *Mark Brisbourne*

WHIP UP A FRENZY (IRE) 3 b.g. Vale of York (IRE) 117 – Answer Do (Groom   **71** Dancer (USA) 128) [2015 71, a80: p7g 8d² 8g 7m 7m 7g⁵ p6f Dec 17] fair handicapper: left Andrew Oliver after sixth start: stays 1m: acts on polytrack and good to soft going: tried in headgear: usually races close up, tends to find little. *Richard Rowe*

WHISKY MARMALADE (IRE) 3 b.f. Duke of Marmalade (IRE) 132 – Nashatara   **59** (USA) (Nashwan (USA) 135) [2015 59: 10g 14.1g⁵ t12.2g³ 15.8m⁵ Aug 4] modest maiden: left David O'Meara after second start: barely stays 2m: acts on tapeta and good to firm going. *Ben Haslam*

WHISPERED TIMES (USA) 8 b.g. More Than Ready (USA) 120 – Lightning Show   **62** (USA) (Storm Cat (USA)) [2015 69: 7m³ 7g³ 6g⁵ 8g May 26] close-coupled gelding: modest performer: stays 1m: acts on good to firm and good to soft going: wears headgear. *Tracy Waggott*

WHISPERING SOUL (IRE) 2 b.f. (Mar 11) Majestic Missile (IRE) 118 – Belle of The   **53** Blues (IRE) (Blues Traveller (IRE) 119) [2015 6g⁶ 5m⁴ 5m 5d⁶ 6g 5m⁴ Sep 27] €45,000Y: half-sister to several winners, including useful winner up to 1m Talitha Kum (2-y-o 6.3f winner, by Chineur) and 1m-1¼m winner Yojojo (by Windsor Knot): dam ran twice: modest maiden: stays 6f: acts on good to firm going: n headgear last 3 starts: temperament under suspicion. *Ann Duffield*

WHISPERING WOLF 2 b.f. (Mar 3) Amadeus Wolf 122 – Ashover Amber 81 (Green   **45** Desert (USA) 127) [2015 5m⁵ f5d⁴ 5m³ 6m* 6g⁵ 5d 5g⁵ Sep 16] 3,000Y: half-sister to several winners, including winner up to 1m Sir Jasper (2-y-o 7f winner, by Sri Pekan) and 2-y-o 5f/6f winner Fabuleux Cherie (by Noverre): dam 5f/6f winner: poor performer: won seller at Ripon in July: stays 6f: acts on fibresand and good to firm going: tried in cheekpieces. *Ollie Pears*

WHISTLE (IRE) 2 b.f. (Apr 26) Holy Roman Emperor (IRE) 125 – Multaka (USA) 66   **57 p** (Gone West (USA)) [2015 p7g Dec 3] €4,000F: sixth foal: half-sister to 3 winners, including 1m winner Palacefield (by Green Desert) and 9.5f-11½m winner Al Shababiya (by Dubawi): dam, lightly raced, closely related to very smart performer up to 1¼m Bahhare and half-sister to high-class miler Bahri: 14/1, some encouragement when 7¼ lengths seventh of 13 to Kakashan in maiden at Kempton, no extra final 1f after pushed along early in straight: will improve. *Martyn Meade*

WHISTLER MOUNTAIN 3 b.g. Oasis Dream 129 – Canda (USA) 100 (Storm Cat   **69** (USA)) [2015 7d⁵ 8.3d t7.1g 6m 10.2s⁵ t9.5f Oct 20] fair maiden: left Charlie Appleby after fourth start: best effort at 7f: acts on tapeta: tried in cheekpieces: tried in tongue tie: often races prominently. *Mark Gillard*

WHITCHURCH 3 b.g. Mawatheeq (USA) 126 – Silvereine (FR) (Bering 136) [2015 71:   **71** t9.5g* 11.7m⁶ 10m⁴ 10m⁶ 10g⁴ p12g⁶ 12v⁶ 10g 10.2s² 9.9g⁶ 10.2s² t8.6f t9.5f Dec 11] workmanlike gelding: fair performer: won maiden at Wolverhampton in January: left Andrew Balding after tenth start: stays 1½m: acts on polytrack, tapeta, soft and good to firm going: usually in headgear/tongue tie: often races in rear. *Philip Kirby*

WHITE BULLET 2 b.f. (Mar 13) Exceed And Excel (AUS) 126 – Chili Dip (Alhaarth **82** (IRE) 126) [2015 5m³ 6m² 5m² Jul 20] 45,000Y: good-quartered filly: fifth foal: half-sister to 2-y-o 7f/1m winner Zakreet (by Cadeaux Genereux): dam unraced half-sister to grandam of 2000 Guineas/Derby winner Camelot: fairly useful form: placed in listed races at York and Newmarket (neck second of 7 to Katie's Diamond) first 2 starts: 1/8, well below expectations when second in maiden at Beverley final start: has joined Sir Mark Prescott. *Kevin Ryan*

WHITECLIFF PARK (IRE) 2 b.c. (Mar 20) Canford Cliffs (IRE) 133 – Venetian **64** Rhapsody (IRE) (Galileo (IRE) 134) [2015 6g 7.1m 6g 7s p7g⁵ 7g t8.6f⁵ t9.5f³ Dec 11] good-quartered colt: modest maiden: left Richard Hannon after sixth start: will stay 1¼m+: acts on polytrack, tapeta, best turf form on good going: tried in hood. *Brian Ellison*

WHITECREST 7 ch.m. Ishiguru (USA) 114 – Risky Valentine 68 (Risk Me (FR) 127) **85** [2015 80: 5.3g³ 5.7f⁶ 5.3s⁴ 5m* 5.3m* 5g² 5m³ 5f 5m⁶ 5.3g³ 5d³ 5.1v³ 5g 5s⁵ 5sᵘʳ 5.3s⁶ Oct 15] leggy mare: fairly useful handicapper: won at Lingfield and Brighton in June: stays 5.5f: acts on polytrack and any turf going. *John Spearing*

WHITE DOG (IRE) 3 b.g. Le Cadre Noir (IRE) 113 – Little Annie 43 (Compton Place **59** 125) [2015 65: 5m 6.1m 6m⁶ Aug 9] modest maiden: best effort at 7f: acts on polytrack: in headgear in 2015: often races towards rear. *Eugene Stanford*

WHITE ENSIGN (USA) 2 gr.c. (Apr 11) Exchange Rate (USA) 111 – Marianka (USA) **63** (Ascot Knight (CAN) 130) [2015 7.4g⁵ 7m 8.1g 7d Oct 16] compact colt: modest maiden: stays 1m: sold 5,500 gns, sent to Italy. *Richard Hannon*

WHITE FLAG 4 b.f. Sakhee's Secret 128 – Rainbow Spectrum (FR) 57 (Spectrum (IRE) **68** 126) [2015 64: 6g* 6g 6m⁶ 5g² 5f⁶ 6g 6d 5.9g² 6g 6d 7s 6d Oct 26] fair handicapper: won at Thirsk in May: stays 6f: acts on soft and good to firm going: tried in headgear: often races towards rear. *Tim Easterby*

WHITE LAKE 3 b.g. Pivotal 124 – White Palace 80 (Shirley Heights 130) [2015 102p: **106** 8g 8.1m³ 8m⁵ Jul 9] rangy, attractive gelding: useful performer: third in listed race at Sandown (3 lengths behind Consort) in May: not seen to best effect when fifth of 6 in listed race at Newmarket only subsequent start: gelded after: stays 1m: acts on good to firm going: usually races towards rear. *Luca Cumani*

WHITE POPPY (IRE) 2 b.f. (Mar 15) Frozen Power (IRE) 108 – Symbol of Peace **72** (IRE) 85 (Desert Sun 120) [2015 7s⁴ 7g⁴ Oct 21] €42,000Y: lengthy filly: fourth foal: half-sister to 1m winner All Nighter (by Bertolini) and useful 2-y-o 6f/7f winner Treaty of Paris (by Haatef), later successful in Hong Kong: dam 1m-9.5f winner who stayed 1½m: similar form to debut when 5¼ lengths fourth of 11 to Farandine in maiden at Newmarket. *Andrew Balding*

WHITE ROSE RUNNER 4 b.f. Virtual 122 – Entrap (USA) 106 (Phone Trick (USA)) **51** [2015 62: t9.5f t8.6g⁴ t9.5g⁵ 9.9m⁴ 10s⁵ Jul 29] modest maiden: stays 1¼m: acts on tapeta, soft and good to firm going: in visor last 4 starts. *Antony Brittain*

WHITE RUSSIAN 4 ch.f. Sir Percy 129 – Danse Russe (Pivotal 124) [2015 78: p8m³ **79** 7.6d⁵ 7m t7.1g² 8.1g² 8.3d⁵ t7.1m³ t7.1f Oct 13] leggy filly: fair handicapper: stays 1m: acts on tapeta and any turf going: front runner/races prominently: sold 15,000 gns, sent to UAE. *Henry Candy*

WHITE SHAHEEN 2 b.c. (Feb 28) Makfi 130 – Likeable (Dalakhani (IRE) 133) [2015 **76** 7g⁶ 7s² Oct 12] lengthy, useful-looking colt: fair form in maidens at Salisbury, slowly into stride when ¾-length second of 9 to Kismet Hardy: will stay 1m. *William Muir*

WHITE WITCH (USA) 2 b.f. (May 10) Invincible Spirit (IRE) 121 – Ishitaki (ARG) **80 p** (Interprete (ARG)) [2015 6f³ 6m² Jun 26] lengthy filly: second foal: sister to 2-y-o 6f winner Initial: dam useful Argentinian 6f to 7.5f (Grade 1) winner: sweating, improved a little on debut form when 2¾ lengths second of 10 to Lady Macapa in maiden at Newmarket: remains with potential. *Charlie Appleby*

WHITKIRK 2 b.g. (Apr 10) Iffraaj 127 – Bedouin Bride (USA) (Chester House (USA)) **–** 123) [2015 7d 7s 6g 7v Nov 3] tailed off in maidens. *George Moore*

WHITMAN 2 b.c. (May 22) Poet's Voice 126 – Sundrop (JPN) 115 (Sunday Silence **99** (USA)) [2015 6g³ 6m* 6.1m* 6g³ 6g* 6s⁵ Sep 19] sturdy colt: sixth foal: half-brother to 3 winners, including useful 7f winner Volcanic Wind (by Distorted Humor) and French 9f winner Quenching (by Street Cry): dam winner up to 1¼m (2-y-o 7f winner): useful performer: won maiden at Newbury and nursery at Nottingham in July, and listed race at Ripon (by head from Chiringuita) in August: possibly unsuited by soft ground when well held in Mill Reef Stakes at Newbury final start: raced only at 6f: acts on good to firm going: usually races close up. *Mark Johnston*

WHITSTABLE PEARL (IRE) 2 b.f. (Apr 20) Kodiac 112 – Amber's Bluff 80 (Mind Games 121) [2015 6g⁶ 5f³ 6.1s Jul 24] €18,000Y: good-topped filly: half-sister to several winners, including 2-y-o 6f winner Tip Top Gorgeous (by Red Clubs) and 1m winner Red To Amber (by Redback): dam, 6f winner, half-sister to useful sprinter Golden Nun: well held in maidens. *Joseph Tuite* —

WHO DARES WINS (IRE) 3 b.g. Jeremy (USA) 122 – Savignano (Polish Precedent (USA) 131) [2015 73p: t7.1g³ 8.5g⁵ 11g 8.3m⁶ 12m³ t12.2g* 12m* 14f* 14s³ Oct 9] compact gelding: fairly useful performer: won maiden at Wolverhampton in June and handicaps at Salisbury and Sandown in July: creditable third in handicap at York final start: stays 1¾m: acts on tapeta, firm and soft going: in cheekpieces last 5 starts: usually races towards rear: joined Alan King, useful hurdler. *Richard Hannon* 90

WHOLESOME (USA) 2 b.f. (Jan 20) Lemon Drop Kid (USA) 131 – Nite In Rome (CAN) (Harlan's Holiday (USA) 124) [2015 7g⁶ 7g² Sep 26] $75,000Y: good-topped filly: third foal: half-sister to a winner in USA by Broken Vow: dam Canadian 2-y-o 6f winner: much improved from debut when ½-length second of 11 to First Victory in maiden at Newmarket, taking strong hold tracking pace but keeping on: should continue to progress. *K. R. Burke* 88 p

WHOOPIE DO 3 ch.f. Piccolo 121 – Endear (Pivotal 124) [2015 –: 8.3g May 31] no form. *David Bridgwater* —

WHOOPSY DAISY 3 b.f. Champs Elysees 124 – Humility 66 (Polar Falcon (USA) 126) [2015 59p: p7g² p8f⁴ 9.9f³ p10g² p10g 9g⁴ 10.2m⁵ p12f² Sep 12] fair maiden: stays 1½m: acts on polytrack and firm going. *Luke Dace* 77

WHO'S SHIRL 9 b.m. Shinko Forest (IRE) – Shirl 52 (Shirley Heights 130) [2015 82: 7m 8m 8g 7m 7m* 7g⁵ 7m t7.1f t8.6f⁵ t8.6f⁶ Oct 30] workmanlike mare: fair handicapper: won at Doncaster in July: stays 8.5f: acts on polytrack, tapeta, good to firm and good to soft going: usually races towards rear. *Chris Fairhurst* 69

WHO'STHEDADDY 3 br.g. Avonbridge 123 – Lisathedaddy 94 (Darnay 117) [2015 –: 8f² 8g 9.9m* 10g* 10m⁴ p12g⁶ p8g⁵ t9.5m⁵ Dec 18] good-topped gelding: fair handicapper: won at Salisbury and Lingfield in July: stays 1¼m: acts on polytrack and good to firm going: races prominently. *Daniel Kubler* 69

WHOZTHECAT (IRE) 8 b.g. One Cool Cat (USA) 123 – Intaglia (GER) (Lomitas 129) [2015 76: 7g³ 6m 6m⁶ 6g 6.1f 7m 6g⁶ 6.3m 6d 6g* 6m 5g 6s 6m 6.1d 6.1g* 7s² 6g 7v Nov 7] leggy gelding: fairly useful handicapper: won at Thirsk in August and Nottingham in September: good second of 20 at York (apprentice) next start: stays 7f: acts on polytrack, firm and soft going: often wears headgear: front runner/races prominently: moody. *Declan Carroll* 91

WICKEDLY SMART (USA) 3 gr.f. Smart Strike (CAN) 121 – Wickedly Wise (USA) (Tactical Cat (USA) 116) [2015 7m⁵ 8m⁴ p7g² t8.6f* Oct 30] $255,000F, $350,000Y: sixth foal: half-sister to 3 winners in USA, including smart Grade 1 2-y-o 8.5f winner Wickedly Perfect (by Congrats): dam placed all 3 starts (at 6f/7f) in USA: fairly useful performer: won maiden at Wolverhampton in October: stays 8.5f. *Jeremy Noseda* 89

WICKED TARA 5 b.m. Assertive 121 – Tara King 57 (Deploy 131) [2015 21: 8.5g⁵ 8m* 8.5g⁵ 7g⁶ 7g* 8.5d⁶ 9.9d 12d² 11.6g Oct 19] poor handicapper: won at L'Ancresse in May and Les Landes in July: seemingly stays 1½m: acts on good to firm and good to soft going: tried in tongue tie prior to 2015. *Natalie Lloyd-Beavis* 40

WICKED WOO 2 b.f. (Mar 29) Multiplex 114 – Icky Woo (Mark of Esteem (IRE) 137) [2015 5d⁵ 5f⁵ 5.7f 5g³ f5g 6g Aug 7] 8,000Y: fourth foal: sister to winner up to 7f Exzachary (2-y-o 6f winner) and 1½m winner Ickymasho: dam unraced half-sister to useful 6f/7f performer Zilch: modest maiden: stays 6f: best form on good going: often races towards rear. *Jo Hughes* 53

WICKHAMBROOK (IRE) 4 ch.g. Dubawi (IRE) 129 – Beautiful Filly 78 (Oasis Dream 129) [2015 79: t7.1f³ t7.1g² p7g t7.1g⁶ p6g⁵ t6f Oct 9] fairly useful handicapper: stays 8.5f: acts on polytrack, tapeta and heavy going. *Mike Murphy* 80

WICKLOW BRAVE 6 b.g. Beat Hollow 126 – Moraine 71 (Rainbow Quest (USA) 134) [2015 16v* 14v* 21.7f⁴ 14g² 14d³ 16d³ Oct 17] strong, workmanlike gelding: smart performer: won maiden at Gowran (by 2¾ lengths from Jennies Jewel) and minor event at Listowel (by 5½ lengths from Cardinal Palace) in May: further improvement when second in Ebor (Handicap) at York (1½ lengths behind Litigant) and third in Irish St Leger at the Curragh (11¼ lengths behind Order of St George) and in Long Distance Cup at Ascot (2 lengths behind Flying Officer): stays 2m: acts on heavy going: sometimes slowly away, usually travels strongly: very smart hurdler. *W. P. Mullins, Ireland* 115

WIENER VALKYRIE 3 b.f. Shamardal (USA) 129 – Wiener Wald (USA) (Woodman **109**
(USA) 126) [2015 83p: 7g 7f⁶ 7m² 8m³ 8m² 8.1m 8g 8.5f² 9d Nov 21] lengthy filly: useful
performer: second in 2015 in handicap at Lingfield, listed race at Haydock (neck behind
Realtra) and Grade 3 Athenia Stakes at Belmont (excelled herself when beaten ½ length by
Stellar Path): in rear in Grade 3 Cardinal Handicap at Churchill Downs final start: stays
8.5f: acts on good to firm and good to soft going: blinkered last 5 starts: often races towards
rear. *Ed Walker*

WIGGLE 3 ch.f. Dutch Art 126 – Mookhlesa 94 (Marju (IRE) 127) [2015 46: 5g 6g⁴ 6m² **64**
6m* Jul 6] modest handicapper: won at Ripon in July: will prove as effective at 5f as 6f:
acts on good to firm going: tried in blinkers prior to 2015: often races prominently.
Tim Easterby

WILD BLOOM 2 b.f. (Feb 25) Exceed And Excel (AUS) 126 – Wild Gardenia 58 **–**
(Alhaarth (IRE) 126) [2015 p8g Nov 4] third foal: half-sister to 8.6f/9f winner Raheeba (by
Invincible Spirit): dam, maiden (stayed 1½m), half-sister to Irish 2000 Guineas winner
Power and closely related/half-sister to Ribblesdale Stakes winners Thakafaat and Curvy:
40/1, shaped as if needed experience when 8½ lengths ninth of 11 to The Black Princess in
maiden at Kempton. *Ed Vaughan*

WILD CHIEF (GER) 4 b.c. Doyen (IRE) 132 – Wild Angel (IRE) (Acatenango (GER) **118**
127) [2015 115: 8g² 8g⁴ 8d* 8d³ 8s⁵ 8m⁶ Oct 3] third foal: half-brother to German 11f
winner Wild Danger (by Konigstiger): dam German 11f/1½m winner: smart performer:
won Meilen Trophy at Hanover (by 4½ lengths from Felician) in July: creditable efforts
next 2 starts, in Prix Jacques le Marois at Deauville (3 lengths third to Esoterique) and Prix
du Moulin de Longchamp (3 lengths fifth of 6 to Ervedya): showed smart form up to 1½m
at 3 yrs, raced only at 1m in 2015: acts on soft and good to firm going: usually races
prominently. *J. Hirschberger, Germany*

WILD DESERT (FR) 10 b.g. Desert Prince (IRE) 130 – Sallivera (IRE) (Sillery (USA) **65**
122) [2015 66: 14.1m⁵ 14.1m² 13.1m* 14.1g⁴ 17.2f 14.1m 12.1g 13.1m⁴ Sep 28] strong,
angular gelding: fair handicapper: won at Bath in July and Salisbury in August: stays 16.5f:
acts on polytrack, good to firm and good to soft going: tried in headgear: usually leads.
Jennie Candlish

WILDE EXTRAVAGANCE (IRE) 2 ch.g. (Apr 15) Dandy Man (IRE) 123 – **71**
Castanetta (IRE) 90 (Dancing Dissident (USA) 119) [2015 6g⁵ 6g² t6f⁶ Oct 20] fair
maiden: best effort when second of 11 at Pontefract (2¾ lengths behind Yorkee Mo Sabee)
in September. *Julie Camacho*

WILDE INSPIRATION (IRE) 4 ch.g. Dandy Man (IRE) 123 – Wishing Chair (USA) **98**
(Giant's Causeway (USA) 132) [2015 92: 7d² 8g* 7.6g³ 8m 8m 8g⁴ 8g³ 8d⁴ 8.5s³ Oct 9]
workmanlike gelding: useful handicapper: won at Haydock (by 1¼ lengths from Capo
Rosso) in April: good 1½ lengths third of 13 to You're Fired at York final start: stays 8.5f:
acts on heavy going. *Julie Camacho*

WILDES (IRE) 4 b.g. Manduro (GER) 135 – Balloura (USA) 80 (Swain (IRE) 134) [2015 **82**
78: p11f³ 12.3v 12m⁵ p12g⁵ Jul 1] fairly useful handicapper: third at Kempton in February:
stays 1½m: acts on polytrack: sold 26,000 gns, sent to Saudi Arabia. *Ian Williams*

WILD FLOWER (IRE) 3 b.f. Approve (IRE) 112 – Midsummernitedream (GER) 43 **62**
(Thatching 131) [2015 –: 8m 7.5s⁶ p8g⁵ p8g p6f² p7m² p6g⁶ Dec 3] sixth foal: half-sister
to 2-y-o 7.4f winner Stage Flight (by In The Wings) and 7f winner Ceris Star (by Cadeaux
Genereux): dam, German 2-y-o 6.5f winner, half-sister to very smart miler Swallow Flight:
modest maiden: left John Joseph Murphy after fifth start: stays 7f: acts on polytrack:
usually in headgear in 2015: tried in tongue tie. *Jimmy Fox*

WILD HACKED (USA) 2 b.c. (Feb 7) Lemon Drop Kid (USA) 131 – Dance Pass (IRE) **88**
104 (Sadler's Wells (USA) 132) [2015 7d² p7g³ Nov 9] $20,000F, $45,000Y, £22,000
2-y-o: first foal: dam, 1m winner who stayed 1½m, closely related to smart winner up to
1¾m Sense of Purpose: fairly useful form when placed both starts in maidens, 2½ lengths
second to Royal Artillery at Doncaster and ¾-length third to Marylebone at Kempton
(bumped 2f out, finished with running left). *Marco Botti*

WILDOMAR 6 b.g. Kyllachy 129 – Murrieta 57 (Docksider (USA) 124) [2015 69: t13.9f* **70**
p12g t12.2m² Dec 12] tall, rather leggy gelding: fair handicapper: won at Wolverhampton
in March: stays 1¾m: acts on polytrack and tapeta: tried in cheekpieces. *Peter Hiatt*

WILD SIDE (IRE) 2 b.c. (Feb 16) Dark Angel (IRE) 113 – Miss Windley (IRE) 73 **–**
(Oratorio (IRE) 128) [2015 7g 7g⁶ Oct 3] behind in maidens at Brighton and Redcar.
James Tate

WILD STORM 3 b.f. Dubawi (IRE) 129 – The World (Dubai Destination (USA) 127) **97 p**
[2015 83p: 10m* 10g* 12d Oct 30] attractive filly: useful form: won maiden at Windsor in
April and handicap there (by ½ length from Derulo) in October: ran poorly on softer
ground final start: should be suited by 1½m: remains open to improvement. *Saeed
bin Suroor*

WILD TOBACCO 3 br.c. More Than Ready (USA) 120 – Princess Janie (USA) (Elusive **55**
Quality (USA)) [2015 86p: 5m 5.2s 7d t6m⁵ p6f p6f⁶ Nov 19] quite attractive colt: modest
performer: best effort at 5f: acts on good to soft going: tried in headgear in 2015.
Richard Hannon

WILEY POST 2 b.c. (Apr 7) Kyllachy 129 – Orange Pip 89 (Bold Edge 123) [2015 6m 6g **74**
6d 5.1m* 5d⁴ 6g Oct 20] neat colt: fair performer: won nursery at Chepstow in September:
best form at 5f: acts on good to firm and good to soft going: in blinkers last 3 starts.
Richard Hannon

WILFUL MINX (FR) 4 b.f. Le Havre (IRE) 124 – Miskina 67 (Mark of Esteem (IRE) **–**
137) [2015 50: t8.6g⁴ t7.1f Feb 6] lightly-raced maiden, modest form at best. *James Given*

WILLAWAY 2 b.g. (Apr 7) Thewayyouare (USA) 117 – Danjet (IRE) 86 (Danehill Dancer **–**
(IRE) 117) [2015 5m Apr 25] well-grown gelding: 20/1, very green when seventh of 8 in
maiden at Leicester, badly hampered. *David Evans*

WILLBEME 7 b.m. Kyllachy 129 – Befriend (USA) 76 (Allied Forces (USA) 123) [2015 **103**
101: 5m⁵ 5g³ 5m² 6m 6g⁴ 5.1m⁴ 5g 5.6d Sep 12] useful performer: third in handicap at York
(1¼ lengths behind Monsieur Joe) in May and second in minor event at Beverley (½ length
behind Pipers Note) in June: stays 7f: acts on good to firm and good to soft going: front
runner/races prominently. *Neville Bycroft*

WILLEM (FR) 5 b.g. Turtle Bowl (IRE) 121 – Zita Blues (IRE) (Zieten (USA) 118) **–**
[2015 t12.2g Aug 27] maiden: fair form in France for L. Viel, blinkered when well held in
amateur handicap at Wolverhampton only outing in 2015: stays 11.5f: acts on good to soft
going: fairly useful hurdler. *David Pipe*

WILLIAM OF ORANGE 4 b.g. Duke of Marmalade (IRE) 132 – Critical Acclaim 87 **107**
(Peintre Celebre (USA) 137) [2015 95p: 14.1m² 14g³ 16.4m² 12g³ 18ɯ 18g 14.6d³ Oct 23]
strong gelding: useful handicapper: placed 5 times in 2015, 3 lengths third to Magic Circle
at Doncaster final start (found less than looked likely): stays 21f: acts on good to firm and
good to soft going: sold to join Donald McCain 42,000 gns. *Sir Mark Prescott Bt*

WILLIE WAG TAIL (USA) 6 b.g. Theatrical (IRE) 128 – Night Risk (USA) (Wild **91**
Again (USA)) [2015 90: p10m⁶ p14g² Jan 28] tall gelding: fairly useful handicapper:
second at Chelmsford in January: stays 1¾m: acts on polytrack, soft and good to firm
going: tried in headgear: often in tongue tie in 2015: sold 28,000 gns, sent to Saudi Arabia.
Ed Walker

WILL I FINEGOLD 3 b.f. Aqlaam 125 – Angel Song 68 (Dansili 127) [2015 p6m Oct **–**
21] 13,500Y, 43,000 2-y-o: first foal: dam, 6f winner, half-sister to smart sprinter Mood
Music: 7/1 and in blinkers, badly needed experience when well held in maiden at Kempton
on debut. *George Baker*

WILL MAC 4 b.g. Misu Bond (IRE) 114 – Zacinta (USA) (Hawkster (USA)) [2015 7s⁴ 7d **54**
10v³ Nov 3] modest maiden: best effort when third of 5 in claimer at Redcar final outing,
slowly away. *Neville Bycroft*

WILLOW JUBILEE 3 b.f. Champs Elysees 124 – Opera Belle 77 (Dr Fong (USA) 128) **53**
[2015 –: p7f p11g p11g 11.5d⁶ 11.5d⁴ 11.5g⁶ f14s² p16f³ p15.8f p13.3f⁶ p16g Nov 4]
lengthy filly: modest maiden: stays 2m: acts on polytrack and fibresand: usually in
headgear in 2015. *John E. Long*

WILLOW SPRING 3 b.f. Compton Place 125 – Upstream 79 (Prince Sabo 123) [2015 **–**
6m t6g p5g⁶ Aug 17] 8,000Y: rather leggy filly: seventh foal: half-sister to 3 winners,
including 5f winners Ten Down (made all at 2 yrs, by Royal Applause) and Confidential
Creek (by Sakhee's Secret): dam 5f winner: no form. *Conrad Allen*

WILLSHEBETRYING 4 b.f. Act One 124 – Precedence (IRE) 88 (Polish Precedent **–**
(USA) 131) [2015 –: p12m⁵ p12g p16m Feb 18] has shown little in maidens/handicaps on
Flat. *Laura Mongan*

WILLSY 2 b.g. (May 3) Sakhee's Secret 128 – Blakeshall Rose 38 (Tobougg (IRE) 125) **71**
[2015 6g 6m⁴ 6g 5g³ 5.1m³ 6m⁵ 5m³ 7s⁶ 6.1s* 5d 6g Oct 20] rather unfurnished gelding:
fair performer: won nursery at Chepstow in September: stays 6f: acts on soft and good to
firm going. *Mick Channon*

WILLY BRENNAN (IRE) 4 br.g. Bushranger (IRE) 119 – Miss Assertive 88 (Zafonic (USA) 130) [2015 88: t8.6g 8.3d Oct 5] rather leggy gelding: fair handicapper: best effort at 6f: acts on polytrack, fibresand and soft going: tried in tongue tie. *Jo Davis* — **69**

WILLYTHECONQUEROR (IRE) 2 b.g. (Feb 27) Zebedee 113 – Jazzie (FR) (Zilzal (USA) 137) [2015 5d³ 5.7d* 5g 5g Oct 9] 48,000Y: sturdy gelding: closely related to useful winner up to 1m Georgian Bay (2-y-o 7f winner, by Oratorio) and half-brother to several winners, including smart 5f-8.7f winner Bold Thady Quill (by Tale of The Cat): dam French 1m winner: fairly useful form: standout effort when winning minor event at Bath (by length from Shaden) in September: best effort at 5.5f: has been gelded. *William Muir* — **86**

WILSONS RUBY (IRE) 2 b.g. (Mar 31) Lilbourne Lad (IRE) 111 – Atlas Silk (Dansili 127) [2015 5.1g⁶ 5m 5m 5.9m p5f² p6f*] Nov 5] fair performer: won nursery at Chelmsford in November: stays 6f: acts on polytrack. *Brian Ellison* — **72**

WILSPA'S MAGIC (IRE) 2 gr.f. (Apr 28) Zebedee 113 – Triple Zero (IRE) 70 (Raise A Grand (IRE) 114) [2015 5g Jun 13] £20,000 2-y-o: sixth foal: half-sister to winner up to 8.6f Galilee Chapel (2-y-o 7f winner, by Baltic King) and 2-y-o 5f winner Stripped Bear (by Kodiac), later successful abroad: dam 6f-1m winner (including at 2 yrs): 18/1, last of 9 in maiden at Bath, possibly amiss. *Ron Hodges* — **–**

WILY FOX 8 ch.g. Observatory (USA) 131 – Kamkova (USA) 62 (Northern Dancer) [2015 18s p15.8f⁶ Apr 30] modest handicapper: stays 2¼m: acts on polytrack, good to firm and heavy going: wears headgear: fair hurdler. *James Eustace* — **57**

WIMBOLDSLEY 4 ch.g. Milk It Mick 120 – Chrystal Venture (IRE) 71 (Barathea (IRE) 127) [2015 61§: 6g p6g 7g 6.1m 6g t5.1f* t6m⁴ t5.1m t5.1f³ t5.1f³ p6g³ Nov 26] modest handicapper: won at Wolverhampton in September: stays 7f: acts on all-weather and good to firm going: often wears hood: front runner/races prominently. *Scott Dixon* — **58**

WIMPOLE HALL 2 b.c. (Apr 17) Canford Cliffs (IRE) 133 – Sparkling Eyes 80 (Lujain (USA) 119) [2015 6g² 6g³ 7g³ p6f* Oct 15] 40,000F, 65,000Y: fourth foal: half-brother to useful 5f/6f winner Pea Shooter (2-y-o 5.4f winner, by Piccolo) and 6f winner Blurred Vision (by Royal Applause): dam 5f winner (including at 2 yrs): fairly useful performer: won maiden at Chelmsford by 1¾ lengths from Little Swift) in October: should stay 7f: sold 85,000 gns. *William Jarvis* — **85**

WINDFAST (IRE) 4 b.g. Exceed And Excel (AUS) 126 – Fair Sailing (IRE) 62 (Docksider (USA) 124) [2015 107: 7m⁴ 7d 7g³ 7m Oct 3] quite attractive, good-bodied gelding: smart performer: off 12 months, improved form on handicap debut when winning by length from Mister Universe at Newbury in July: subsequently disappointing (eased final start, rider reporting something felt amiss): stays 7f: acts on good to firm and good to soft going. *Brian Meehan* — **115**

WIND FIRE (USA) 4 b.f. Distorted Humor (USA) 117 – A P Dream (USA) (A P Indy (USA) 131) [2015 109: 5m⁶ 5g³ 5f 5m² 5m⁴ 5g 5.2s⁴ 5m⁴ Oct 3] strong filly: smart performer: best efforts when third in Temple Stakes at Haydock (¾ length behind Pearl Secret), second in Sprint Stakes at Sandown (½ length behind Waady) and fourth in World Trophy at Newbury (¼ length behind Steps) on penultimate start: best form at 5f: acts on firm and soft going. *David Brown* — **113**

WINDFORPOWER (IRE) 5 b.g. Red Clubs (IRE) 125 – Dubai Princess (IRE) 105 (Dubai Destination (USA) 127) [2015 72§: 5v* 5g³ 5s² 5g³ 6m² 5g⁶ 5m³ 5.9g⁶ 5.5m* 6g 5g³ 5s⁴ 5m 5d⁴ 5g 5g Sep 23] fair handicapper: won at Musselburgh (apprentice) in April and Wetherby in June: stays 6f: acts on polytrack, good to firm and heavy going: wears headgear: carries head awkwardly. *Tracy Waggott* — **75 §**

WINDHOEK 5 b.g. Cape Cross (IRE) 129 – Kahlua Kiss 103 (Mister Baileys 123) [2015 122: 10.3s⁵ May 7] strong gelding: very smart performer in 2014: probably needed run when 8¾ lengths last of 5 to Maverick Wave in Huxley Stakes at Chester only outing in 2015: subsequently gelded: stays 1¼m: acts on polytrack, tapeta and firm going. *Saeed bin Suroor* — **–**

WIND IN MY SAILS 3 b.c. Footstepsinthesand 120 – Dylanesque 91 (Royal Applause 124) [2015 76p: 8.3m 8g⁵ p7g² 7m² 6.1m 7g* 8g⁶ 8g⁵ 7v Sep 1] fairly useful performer: won maiden at Leicester in July: stays 1m: acts on polytrack and good to firm going. *Ed de Giles* — **83**

WINDMILLS GIRL 2 b.f. (Apr 20) Sir Percy 129 – Cosmic Countess (IRE) 74 (Lahib (USA) 129) [2015 p7d³ p7g 7s Oct 12] half-sister to several winners, including useful 6f winner Dick Bos (by Dutch Art) and 7f/7.6f winner Miss Madame (by Cape Cross): dam 2-y-o 6f winner: well held in maidens. *Jeremy Gask* — **–**

WIN

WINDOW SHOPPING (IRE) 2 b.f. (Feb 4) Lilbourne Lad (IRE) 111 – Stained Glass 41
(Dansili 127) [2015 5.1s p6g³ t5.1m 7g⁴ t8.6g⁴ f8g⁴ f7g Dec 18] €1,200Y: first foal: dam
unraced half-sister to smart winner around 1¼m Mirror Lake: poor maiden: stays 8.5f: acts
on tapeta. *Mark Usher*

WIND PLACE AND SHO 3 br.g. Shirocco (GER) 129 – Coh Sho No 59 (Old Vic 136) 97
[2015 68p: 10s* 11g 14f³ 14g* 14g 14d⁴ 16d² Oct 30] compact gelding: useful performer:
won maiden at Pontefract in April and handicap at Sandown in July: upped in trip,
improved form when ¾-length second to Star Rider in handicap at Newmarket final start:
stays 2m: acts on firm and soft going: front runner/races prominently. *James Eustace*

WINDSHEAR 4 b.g. Hurricane Run (IRE) 134 – Portal 108 (Hernando (FR) 127) [2015 114
118: 12d* 12m⁴ 13.4v⁵ 12m³ 20f 12m³ 13.3d² 11.9g 12m Oct 3] strong, lengthy gelding:
smart performer: won minor event at Doncaster (by ¾ length from Island Remede) in
March: best efforts after when fourth in John Porter Stakes at Newbury (2 lengths behind
Arab Spring), third in Glorious Stakes at Goodwood (3¼ lengths behind Dubday) and
second in Geoffrey Freer Stakes at Newbury (5 lengths behind Agent Murphy) second/
sixth/seventh starts: stays 14.5f: acts on good to firm and heavy going: visored third outing:
has been gelded. *Richard Hannon*

WINDY CITI 4 ch.f. Zamindar (USA) 116 – Windy Britain 106 (Mark of Esteem (IRE) 70
137) [2015 86: 8m⁶ p8g² p8g* p7g p8d⁶ p8g 8.3d⁶ 8d Oct 30] angular filly: fairly useful a92
handicapper: won at Kempton in August: stays 1m: acts on polytrack: often races towards
rear. *Chris Wall*

WINDY MILLER 4 ch.g. Sakhee's Secret 128 – Oatcake 68 (Selkirk (USA) 129) [2015 50
51: p7g⁴ p8f Feb 11] modest maiden: stays 7f: acts on polytrack and tapeta. *Robin Dickin*

WINGED DANCER 2 b.c. (Feb 21) Norse Dancer (IRE) 127 – Winged Diva (IRE) 58 69
(Hawk Wing (USA) 136) [2015 6g 6d 8.3s⁶ p7g⁴ Dec 28] rather unfurnished colt: fair
maiden: stays 8.5f. *Sylvester Kirk*

WINGS OF ESTEEM (IRE) 2 b.f. (Feb 20) Sir Percy 129 – Wings of Fame (IRE) 64 p
(Namid 128) [2015 f8g² Dec 18] €26,000Y: second foal: half-sister to Italian 5f-7f winner
Waylay (by Bushranger): dam unraced half-sister to smart French sprinter Tycoon's Hill:
7/1, some promise when 6 lengths second of 5 to Mayasa in maiden at Southwell: should
progress. *K. R. Burke*

WINK OLIVER 3 b.g. Winker Watson 118 – Nadinska 70 (Doyen (IRE) 132) [2015 66: 72 +
t7.1g* t7.1g³ t7.1g² 7.1m⁵ t7.1g³ 7m⁶ t7.1g 7.5m⁵ 7m⁴ 7m² t7.1m⁵ 7.2g t7.1m⁵ t7.1f³ p7g⁴ a85
p7f* t7.1m² t8.6g³ Nov 27] fairly useful handicapper: won at Wolverhampton in January
and Chelmsford in November: left Kristin Stubbs after thirteenth start: stays 8.5f: acts on
polytrack, tapeta and good to firm going: wears headgear: sometimes slowly away, usually
races nearer last than first, usually travels strongly. *David Dennis*

WINNING HUNTER 3 b.g. Iffraaj 127 – Miss Lacey (IRE) (Diktat 126) [2015 76: p8g 81
6s 7s* Oct 15] fairly useful handicapper: won at Brighton in October: best effort at 7f:
acts on heavy going: sometimes in cheekpieces/tongue tie: sold 2,800 gns, sent to Italy.
Chris Wall

WINN LILY 3 br.f. Captain Gerrard (IRE) 113 – Scisciabubu (IRE) (Danehill (USA) 126) 51
[2015 f5g⁴ f5g³ f6g³ 5g⁴ 5.1g 5g 5f Jul 3] half-sister to several winners in Italy, including
2-y-o 5f/1m winner Susi Applause (by Royal Applause): dam Italian 5f/6f winner, including
at 2 yrs: modest maiden: stays 6f: acts on fibresand: tried in cheekpieces. *Ollie Pears*

WINSLOW (USA) 3 b.g. Distorted Humor (USA) 117 – Justwhistledixie (USA) (Dixie 102
Union (USA) 121) [2015 95: t8.6m⁴ t9.5m⁶ Dec 12] strong, close-coupled gelding: useful
handicapper: better of 2 runs at Wolverhampton in 2015 when good fourth of 10 to Home
Cummins in November: stays 8.5f: acts on tapeta: in tongue tie final outing. *Charlie Appleby*

WINTER HEY LANE (USA) 2 ch.f. (Feb 18) Speightstown (USA) 124 – Clambake 62
(IRE) 64 (Grand Lodge (USA) 125) [2015 6d³ 6g³ p5m⁴ p6g Dec 15] $14,000Y, £50,000
2-y-o: sixth foal: closely related to a winner in USA by Elusive Quality: dam maiden half-
sister to smart performers up to 1½m Art Deco and Somewhat out of sister to 1000 Guineas
winner Sleeptime: modest maiden: stays 6f. *Richard Fahey*

WINTER HOUSE 3 b.g. Cape Cross (IRE) 129 – Villarrica (USA) 84 (Selkirk (USA) 99 p
129) [2015 f8g* Apr 16] sixth foal: brother to smart winner up to 9.5f (UAE Derby/Oaks)
Khawlah (2-y-o 1m winner) and half-brother to 2 winners, including smart French 1¼m
winner Vancouverite (by Dansili): dam, 1¼m/11f winner, half-sister to smart performer up
to 12.5f Masterstroke out of Irish Oaks runner-up Melikah, herself half-sister to Sea The

Stars (by Cape Cross) and Galileo: 11/2, did well under circumstances when winning 12-runner newcomers race at Newmarket by neck from Mustaaqeem, making up a lot of ground to get up close home: sure to progress. *Saeed bin Suroor*

WINTERLUDE (IRE) 5 b.g. Street Cry (IRE) 130 – New Morning (IRE) 115 (Sadler's Wells (USA) 132) [2015 108: 12d Aug 21] smart at best: left Charlie Appleby/off 18 months, no show in handicap at York only outing in 2015: stays 1½m: acts on polytrack, tapeta, best turf form on good going. *Jennie Candlish*

WINTER QUEEN 3 ch.f. Dubawi (IRE) 129 – Straight Lass (IRE) (Machiavellian (USA) 123) [2015 77: t8.6g² p8f⁴ t9.5f⁵ Mar 2] fair handicapper: stays 8.5f: acts on polytrack and tapeta. *Charlie Appleby* **67**

WINTER ROSE (IRE) 2 b.f. (Mar 9) Dark Angel (IRE) 113 – Rose of Battle 80 (Averti (IRE) 117) [2015 6m³ 6g² p7g⁷ 7g⁴ 7s⁴ 7g Oct 10] 50,000Y: compact filly: fifth foal: sister to 6f winner He's My Boy and half-sister to 2-y-o 6f winners Pendle Lady (by Chineur) and Windsor Rose (by Windsor Knot): dam, 2-y-o 5f winner, half-sister to smart 2-y-o 5f/6f winner Orpen Grey: fairly useful performer: won maiden at Kempton (by 3¾ lengths from Peru) in August: stays 7f: acts on polytrack: races prominently. *Richard Hannon* **90**

WINTER SERENADE (ITY) 3 b.f. Fastnet Rock (AUS) 127 – Wickwing 101 (In The Wings 128) [2015 10s⁵ p12g⁴ 11.8m* 11.5m³ Sep 15] sturdy filly: fourth foal: closely related to useful Italian 1¼m/11f winner Delicatezza (by Danehill Dancer) and half-sister to 1¼m winner Speed Boogie (by Oasis Dream): dam Italian 1¼m/11f winner: fairly useful performer: won maiden at Kempton and handicap at Leicester in June: would have benefited from stronger gallop final outing: stays 1½m: sent to Italy: remains with potential. *Marco Botti* **82 p**

WINTERS MOON (IRE) 3 ch.f. New Approach (IRE) 132 – Summertime Legacy 109 (Darshaan 133) [2015 106: 10m³ 10f⁵ 10.1g Jun 26] rather leggy filly: useful at 2 yrs: just fairly useful form in 2015, 9 lengths seventh of 11 to Covert Love in listed race at Newcastle final start: stays 1¼m: acts on firm and soft going: sometimes in headgear. *Saeed bin Suroor* **92**

WINTER SPICE (IRE) 4 gr.g. Verglas (IRE) 118 – Summer Spice (IRE) 88 (Key of Luck (USA) 126) [2015 82: 14.1f p16g² 17.2f⁶ t13.9m⁴ p16g⁶ Dec 9] good-topped gelding: fairly useful handicapper: stays 17f: acts on polytrack, tapeta and firm going: wears blinkers: sometimes slowly away, often races in rear. *Clive Cox* **85**

WINTER THUNDER 4 gr.c. New Approach (IRE) 132 – Summer Sonnet (Baillamont (USA) 124) [2015 119: 12m⁵ May 9] good-topped colt: smart performer in 2014: off 7 months, 7/4, 3¼ lengths fifth of 7 to Agent Murphy in listed race at Ascot only outing in 2015, not seeing race out: stays 1½m: acts on good to firm going: wears hood. *Saeed bin Suroor* **109**

WINTERVAL 3 b.g. Dubawi (IRE) 129 – Festivale (IRE) 107 (Invincible Spirit (IRE) 121) [2015 75: 10m³ 8.3s² 10.4d⁵ 10.2m* Jul 4] fairly useful performer: gelded prior to best effort final start, winning minor event at Nottingham by length from Landwade Lad: stays 1¼m: acts on good and good to firm going. *Luca Cumani* **86**

WINX (AUS) 4 b.f. Street Cry (IRE) 130 – Vegas Showgirl (NZ) (Al Akbar (AUS)) [2015 6g 7s⁵ 7.5g* 9.9g⁵ 11.9s² 8g* 10.9g* 6.5g* 8g* 10.1g* Oct 24] second foal: dam won up to 7f in Australia/New Zealand: high-class form: successful on 3 of her 5 starts in 2014 and 6 out of 10 in 2015: won Group 2 Phar Lap Stakes at Rosehill in March, Group 3 Sunshine Coast Guineas at Sunshine Coast in May, Queensland Oaks at Doomben in May, Group 2 Theo Marks Stakes at Rosehill in September, then Epsom Handicap at Randwick and Cox Plate at Moonee Valley (by 4¾ lengths from Criterion, possibly helped by way race developed), both in October: second in Australian Oaks at Randwick (2½ lengths behind Gust of Wind) in April: stays 11f: best form on good going: likely to progress further. *Chris Waller, Australia* **126 p**

WIOLETTA 2 b.f. (Apr 12) Polish Power (GER) 97 – Wizby 59 (Wizard King 122) [2015 p6g⁵ p6g⁶ Aug 7] 1,800Y: third foal: half-sister to French 2-y-o 6.5f-1m winner Cockney Bob (by Cockney Rebel): dam winner up to 1m (2-y-o 5f/6f winner) who stayed 1¼m: well held in claimer/seller. *J. S. Moore* **–**

WISDEN (IRE) 3 ch.g. Intikhab (USA) 135 – Cayman Sunrise (IRE) 68 (Peintre Celebre (USA) 137) [2015 t8.6g Apr 27] 16/1, very green when well held in maiden at Wolverhampton. *Sir Michael Stoute* **–**

WISETON (IRE) 3 b.g. Majestic Missile (IRE) 118 – Laylati (IRE) 64 (Green Desert (USA) 127) [2015 60: 16f 6d² 5g⁶ 5g 6g⁴ 6m Jun 30] poor maiden: left Garry Moss after fourth start: stays 6f: best form on good going: in headgear in 2015, also in tongue tie last 2 starts: usually leads. *Ivan Furtado* **49**

WISEWIT 3 b.g. Royal Applause 124 – Loveleaves 93 (Polar Falcon (USA) 126) [2015 –: **59**
t6g⁶ t6g⁵ t6g 6d⁶ 8.3d Jul 29] unfurnished gelding: modest maiden: stays 7f: acts on tapeta
and good to firm going: in visor in 2015: sold £600, sent to Germany. *James Toller*

WISHSONG 2 b.f. (Mar 9) Dansili 127 – Princess Janie (USA) (Elusive Quality (USA)) **56**
[2015 6m 5f⁴ p5g⁵ p6f Nov 19] fourth foal: half-sister to 2-y-o 5f winner Wild Tobacco (by
More Than Ready) and a winner in USA by Harlan's Holiday: dam, US 6f winner, half-
sister to Canadian Grade 3 9f/11f winner Raylene: modest maiden: left Richard Hannon
after third start: stays 6f. *David Nicholls*

WISTAR 4 b.c. Dubawi (IRE) 129 – Vallota (Polish Precedent (USA) 131) [2015 79p: 8g⁴ **89**
8m⁵ May 15] fairly useful form: only third outing, still showed signs of inexperience and
better than result when 5¼ lengths fifth of 13 to Musaddas in handicap at Newmarket in
May: raced only at 1m: sold 24,000 gns, sent to Saudi Arabia. *Luca Cumani*

WISTERIA 3 br.f. Winker Watson 118 – Begonia (IRE) 74 (Selkirk (USA) 129) [2015 –: **44**
f6g 7g⁴ 8m 7.5m 7g Aug 6] poor maiden: stays 1m: acts on good to firm and heavy going:
tried in cheekpieces. *David C. Griffiths*

WITH APPROVAL (IRE) 3 b.g. Approve (IRE) 112 – Kelsey Rose 97 (Most Welcome **69**
131) [2015 73: p8f⁴ p8f* p8m³ 8.3m p7f⁴ p8g⁵ 7.1m 8.5g p6g p8m⁴ p7m* p7g Dec 2] **a76**
rather leggy gelding: fair performer: won maiden at Lingfield (dead-heated) in January and
handicap there in October: stays 8.5f: acts on polytrack, good to firm and heavy going:
in cheekpieces last 2 starts: hard to catch right. *Laura Mongan*

WITH A TWIST 4 b.f. Excellent Art 125 – Bint Zamayem (IRE) 95 (Rainbow Quest **– §**
(USA) 134) [2015 –: p7g p8f Jan 21] rather unfurnished filly: no form in maidens/
handicaps, taking little interest final start (in first-time cheekpieces): often in tongue tie:
temperamental: sold £5,000 in February. *Andrew Balding*

WITH CHARM (USA) 3 b.f. Dubawi (IRE) 129 – Secret Charm (IRE) 109 (Green **–**
Desert (USA) 127) [2015 –: t8.6g Mar 24] well held in maidens. *Rod Millman*

WITHERNSEA (IRE) 4 b.g. Dark Angel (IRE) 113 – Charlene Lacy (IRE) 77 (Pips **103**
Pride 117) [2015 100: 6d⁵ 6g² 7g 7m⁵ 7d³ 7s 7g² 8d 7v* Nov 7] good-topped gelding:
useful handicapper: best effort when winning 21-runner event at Doncaster final start by
length from Jamaican Bolt, keeping on to lead final 100 yds: stays 7f: acts on heavy going.
Richard Fahey

WITH HINDSIGHT (IRE) 7 b.g. Ad Valorem (USA) 125 – Lady From Limerick (IRE) **77**
61 (Rainbows For Life (CAN)) [2015 64: p10m⁴ f8s* p8f⁵ f8g 12.1m³ 14.1g² 13.8v*
14.1v² t13.9f* t13.9f* Dec 14] rather leggy gelding: fair handicapper: won at Southwell in
January, Catterick (apprentice) in October, Wolverhampton (amateur) in November and
Wolverhampton in December: left John Spearing after fourth start: stays 1¾m: acts on all-
weather, good to firm and heavy going: front runner/races prominently, often travels
strongly. *Steve Gollings*

WITHOUT DOUBT (IRE) 2 gr.f. (Apr 21) Clodovil (IRE) 116 – Justice System (USA) **53**
57 (Criminal Type (USA)) [2015 6m 7m⁶ p8g⁵ Aug 8] €32,000Y: sister to smart Australian
winner up to 1½m Moriarty (2-y-o 7f/1m winner in Britain) and half-sister to 3 winners,
including 1m winner Leave To Appeal (by Victory Note): dam maiden (stayed 1½m):
modest maiden: best effort at 7f. *Mick Channon*

WITHOUT REGARD (IRE) 7 ch.m. Millkom 124 – Habla Me (IRE) (Fairy King **–**
(USA)) [2015 t8.6g Jan 23] sister to 2 winners, including 2-y-o 6f winner Gipsy Prince,
and half-sister to 2 winners, including 7f/1m winner Neardown Beauty (by Bahhare): dam
Italian 2-y-o 5f winner: 100/1, very green when tailed off in maiden at Wolverhampton.
Mark Walford

WITH PLEASURE 2 b.g. (May 18) Poet's Voice 126 – With Fascination (USA) 111 **77 p**
(Dayjur (USA) 137) [2015 6d⁶ p8f² Nov 6] 14,000Y: half-brother to numerous winners,
including smart winner up to 1¼m With Interest (2-y-o 7f winner, by Selkirk) and useful
French 2-y-o 6f/7f winner Interesting (by Raven's Pass): dam, French 5f to (at 2 yrs) 6.5f
winner, half-sister to very smart US performer up to 1½m With Anticipation: better effort
when second in maiden at Chelmsford (head behind Purple Magic) in November, clear of
rest: will go on improving. *Simon Crisford*

WIZARDESS 2 b.f. (Jan 21) Equiano (FR) 127 – Midnight Fantasy 83 (Oasis Dream 129) **55**
[2015 5m 6g⁶ 5g 6s⁵ Oct 6] 40,000F, 48,000Y: second foal: dam, 6f winner, half-sister to
smart/ungenuine sprinter Out After Dark: modest maiden: best effort at 6f: tried in
cheekpieces: sold 800 gns, sent to Hungary. *Ann Duffield*

WOLF ALBARARI 3 ch.g. Medicean 128 – Pure Song 75 (Singspiel (IRE) 133) [2015 **81**
79p: 11.8m⁵ 12m 10s p11g Sep 30] good-topped gelding: fairly useful handicapper: best
effort at 9.5f: acts on tapeta: wears headgear: sold 16,000 gns, sent to Saudi Arabia.
Marco Botti

WOLF HEART (IRE) 7 b.g. Dalakhani (IRE) 133 – Lisieux Orchid (IRE) 88 (Sadler's **55**
Wells (USA) 132) [2015 54: 8d⁶ 9.1s⁴ 10d³ 10g* Jul 5] modest handicapper: won at Ayr
(dead-heated) in July: stays 1¼m: acts on soft going: often races towards rear. *Lucy Normile*

WOLF OF WINDLESHAM (IRE) 3 ch.g. Mastercraftsman (IRE) 129 – Al Amlah **64**
(USA) (Riverman (USA) 131) [2015 65: p10f p8f 10m 9.2g² p11g³ 12.1m³ Sep 10] lengthy
gelding: modest handicapper: left Charles Hills after second start, Roy Brotherton after
fourth: stays 1½m: acts on polytrack and good to firm going: tried in blinkers: useful
hurdler. *Stuart Edmunds*

WOLOWITZ (IRE) 2 b.g. (May 26) Intense Focus (USA) 117 – Tranquil Sky 91 **90 p**
(Intikhab (USA) 135) [2015 5m⁵ 5m³ f5g* Dec 29] €20,000Y: seventh foal: half-brother to
1¼m winner Diamond Vision (by Diamond Green) and useful 5f/6f winner Discussiontofollow (by Elusive City): dam 2-y-o 6f/7f winner who stayed 1¼m: fairly useful form: off
6 months/gelded, much improved when winning 5-runner maiden at Southwell by 6
lengths from Burmese Whisper, quickening clear final 1f: raced only at 5f: should continue
to progress. *David Barron*

WOMBLE 2 b.c. (Apr 27) Equiano (FR) 127 – Little Caroline (IRE) (Great Commotion –
(USA) 123) [2015 t6m Dec 18] 100/1, last of 9 in maiden at Wolverhampton. *Laura Young*

WONDER LAISH 3 b.c. Halling (USA) 133 – Wonder Why (GER) (Tiger Hill (IRE) **98**
127) [2015 80p: 10g² 11.5d* 12g* 12g Oct 9] lengthy colt: useful performer: won maiden
at Lingfield in May and handicap at Ascot (dead-heated with Duretto) in September: stays
1½m: acts on good to soft going: front runner/races prominently, usually responds
generously to pressure. *William Haggas*

WONDERSTRUCK (IRE) 4 b.f. Sea The Stars (IRE) 140 – Bordighera (USA) 104 **109 p**
(Alysheba (USA)) [2015 102: 11.9d² May 30] strong, good-quartered filly: useful form:
improved when short-head second of 10 to Miss Marjurie in Pinnacle Stakes at Haydock
only outing in 2015, staying on to lead entering final 1f, edged out close home: likely to
stay further than 1½m: acts on soft and good to firm going: often races prominently: open
to further improvement. *William Haggas*

WOODACRE 8 b.g. Pyrus (USA) 106 – Fairy Ring (IRE) 69 (Fairy King (USA)) [2015 **74**
92: 10.4s 10d⁶ Oct 19] strong gelding: fair handicapper: stays 1¼m: acts on good to firm
and good to soft going: tried in cheekpieces. *Richard Whitaker*

WOODBRIDGE 4 ch.g. Exceed And Excel (AUS) 126 – Kristal Bridge 75 (Kris 135) **74**
[2015 77: t7.1f* t7.1g⁵ 7g t7.1g^F Apr 27] workmanlike gelding: fair handicapper: won at
Wolverhampton in March: stays 1m: acts on polytrack, tapeta and good to firm going:
usually races close up. *Richard Fahey*

WOODY BAY 5 b.g. New Approach (IRE) 132 – Dublino (USA) 116 (Lear Fan (USA) **94**
130) [2015 87: 8m⁴ 8s 8d⁵ 7m* 7.9g⁴ 7m² 8m² 8m⁵ 8d⁶ 8d* 7d⁸ 8d³ 8.5s 7s⁶ 7v⁶ Nov 7] tall
gelding: fairly useful handicapper: won at Newcastle in June, and Haydock and Catterick
(by ½ length from Edgar Balthazar) in September: good third at Haydock next start: stays
8.5f: acts on polytrack, soft and good to firm going: tried in blinkers/tongue tie: usually
races prominently. *Mark Walford*

WOOFIE (IRE) 3 b.g. Duke of Marmalade (IRE) 132 – Violet Ballerina (IRE) 85 (Namid **82**
128) [2015 71p: p8m² t7.1f* p8f³ 8.3g* 8m³ 8.3m⁴ 8.1m⁴ 8.1g⁶ p11g⁶ p8g⁶ Dec 9] fairly
useful performer: won maiden at Wolverhampton in January and handicap at Hamilton in
June: left Richard Fahey after fifth start: stays 11f: acts on polytrack, tapeta and good to
firm going: usually in cheekpieces in 2015: front runner/races prominently: quirky.
Laura Mongan

WOOLFALL SOVEREIGN (IRE) 9 b.g. Noverre (USA) 125 – Mandragore (USA) **100**
(Slew O' Gold (USA)) [2015 101: f5s* f5s p6f Feb 21] good-topped gelding: fair on turf,
useful on all-weather: won minor event at Southwell (by head from Dungannon) in
January: well below form both subsequent starts: stayed 8.5f: acted on polytrack, fibresand
and soft going: dead. *George Margarson*

WOOTTON VALE (IRE) 2 b.g. (Apr 24) Wootton Bassett 119 – Shining Vale (USA) –
(Twilight Agenda (USA) 126) [2015 7m 6d 6g Sep 24] useful-looking gelding: well held
in 3 maidens: has been gelded. *Richard Fahey*

WORDCRAFT 3 b.f. Shamardal (USA) 129 – Forensics (AUS) 121 (Flying Spur (AUS)) **103**
[2015 7m* p7g* 7m³ 8m² 7g² 7s² 6g Sep 24] attractive filly: first foal: dam Australian
winner up to 1m, including 5.5f/6f (Golden Slipper Stakes) at 2 yrs: useful performer: won
maiden at Newmarket in May and handicap at Kempton in June: better form when placed
in handicaps at Newmarket next 3 starts: stays 1m: acts on polytrack and good to firm
going: in cheekpieces last 3 starts: usually races towards rear, often travels strongly.
Charlie Appleby

WORDINESS 7 br.g. Dansili 127 – Verbose (USA) 97 (Storm Bird (CAN) 134) [2015 **93**
p13.3g³ p14f⁶ 16m* 14.6m² 14.6m³ 15.9m* 17.2f* 16m* 21g 16m⁵ t13.9m* 18g Oct 10]
smallish gelding: fairly useful handicapper: missed 2014 but returned as good as ever and
won at Newbury in April, Chester in June, Bath and Newbury in July and Wolverhampton
(by length from Soul Searcher) in September: stays 17f: acts on polytrack, tapeta and firm
going: tried in tongue tie prior to 2015. *David Evans*

WORDISMYBOND 6 b.g. Monsieur Bond (IRE) 120 – La Gessa 69 (Largesse 112) **–**
[2015 81: 7.6d 8m 8.3g Oct 19] sturdy gelding: fairly useful handicapper in 2014, no form
in 2015: stays 9f: acts on firm and good to soft going: tried in cheekpieces: front runner/
races prominently. *Peter Makin*

WORDS (IRE) 3 b.f. Dansili 127 – Moonstone 119 (Dalakhani (IRE) 133) [2015 101p: **109 p**
12m* 12m Jul 18] useful form: only second outing when winning 4-runner Munster Oaks
at Cork in June by ¾ length from Carla Bianca, leading final 100 yds: 7/2, run best excused
when 9½ lengths eighth of 9 to Covert Love in Irish Oaks at the Curragh, having hopeless
task from position and not persevered with once held: stays 1½m: in hood last 2 starts:
remains open to further improvement. *Aidan O'Brien, Ireland*

WORKADAY (IRE) 2 ch.g. (Mar 31) Approve (IRE) 112 – Rockyriver Girl (IRE) (Rock **52**
of Gibraltar (IRE) 133) [2015 5m 6g 7g² p6g f8f⁶ Dec 17] modest maiden: left Tim
Easterby after third start: best effort at 6f: usually in headgear: often races prominently.
Garry Moss

WORK (IRE) 2 b.f. (Feb 10) Mastercraftsman (IRE) 129 – Abbeyleix Lady (IRE) **–**
(Montjeu (IRE) 137) [2015 p8g p8g Nov 4] €32,000Y, resold £44,000Y: fourth foal: half-
sister to 5f winner Meebo (by Captain Rio): dam unraced daughter of smart French performer
up to 1½m Premier Amour: well held both starts in Kempton maidens. *David Simcock*

WOR LASS 7 br.m. And Beyond (IRE) 113 – Patience Please 59 (King of Spain 121) **81**
[2015 67: 12.4dᵗ 15.8s⁶ 15s 12.4g⁵ 16.1m⁴ 16m³ 13.1s* 13.1g* 16.1m* 14.4g* 15.8g*
14.4g* Aug 31] fairly useful handicapper: won at Ayr (twice, apprentice event first time)
and Newcastle in July and at Newcastle and Musselburgh in August: career-best effort
when completing 6-timer in 5-runner event at Newcastle later in August by 2 lengths from
Jan Smuts: stays 2m: acts on soft and good to firm going: tried in cheekpieces: usually
travels strongly. *Iain Jardine*

WORLD RECORD (IRE) 5 b.g. Choisir (AUS) 126 – Dancing Debut 83 (Polar Falcon **75**
(USA) 126) [2015 78: p10g⁶ p8g p8g 8m⁵ 8.3g* 7m 8m 8.3g 7g² 7v² 8d⁴ 8v* 8.3g* Oct 20]
lengthy gelding: fair performer: won seller at Leicester in May and handicaps at Brighton
and Windsor in October: stays 8.5f: acts on polytrack, good to firm and heavy going: front
runner/races prominently. *Mick Quinn*

WORLD'S GREATEST (USA) 2 ch.f. (Jan 16) Discreet Cat (USA) 127 – Say You **59**
Will (IRE) (A P Indy (USA) 131) [2015 6m⁶ 6g⁶ t5.1m⁴ Dec 26] useful-looking filly:
second foal: dam, useful US 6.5f-9f winner, out of smart half-sister to Lammtarra: modest
maiden: left Saeed bin Suroor/off 5 months, best effort when fourth of 7 at Wolverhampton
final start. *Stuart Williams*

WORLDS HIS OYSTER 2 b.c. (Jan 23) Pivotal 124 – Regal Salute 91 (Medicean 128) **85**
[2015 6g 6g* p7g Sep 30] £25,000Y, £110,000 2-y-o: first foal: dam, 8.3f winner, out of
sister to Cheveley Park Stakes winner Regal Rose: fairly useful form: won maiden at
Newcastle in September by 3¼ lengths from Spanish City: disappointing in nursery at
Kempton final start: should stay 7f. *John Quinn*

WOTABOND 2 ch.g. (Jan 23) Monsieur Bond (IRE) 120 – Wotatomboy 65 (Captain Rio **39**
122) [2015 6m 5.9g⁶ 6d p6f Nov 19] poor maiden: raced only at 6f. *Richard Whitaker*

WOTABREEZE (IRE) 2 ch.g. (Apr 10) Excellent Art 125 – Sparkling Crystal (IRE) 80 **63**
(Danehill Dancer (IRE) 117) [2015 8s⁶ 7v Nov 3] sixth of 12 to G K Chesterton in October,
better effort in maidens at Redcar: has been gelded. *John Quinn*

WOTALAD 5 b.g. Bertolini (USA) 125 – Cosmic Song 58 (Cosmonaut) [2015 68: t7.1g⁵ **56**
Jan 9] modest handicapper: stays 1m: acts on all-weather and heavy going: usually wears
headgear: front runner. *Richard Whitaker*

WOTNOT (IRE) 3 gr.f. Exceed And Excel (AUS) 126 – Whatami 69 (Daylami (IRE) 138) [2015 p6f² 6m 6m³ 6s⁴ Sep 11] 20,000Y: lengthy filly: second foal: closely related to 2-y-o 5f-7f winner Constantine (by Holy Roman Emperor): dam, maiden (stayed 1½m), half-sister to useful winner up to 1m Whazzis: fair maiden: raced only at 6f: acts on good to firm going. *Henry Candy* **69**

WOWCHA (IRE) 2 b.f. (Mar 21) Zoffany (IRE) 121 – Muravka (IRE) (High Chaparral (IRE) 132) [2015 7.2g⁵ 7v⁴ Oct 17] £150,000Y: second foal: half-sister to smart 2-y-o 6f winner (including Coventry Stakes and Prix Morny) The Wow Signal (by Starspangledbanner): dam unraced: similar form to debut when 3 lengths fourth of 12 to Sunnai in maiden at Catterick, slowly away and badly hampered after 2f: remains open to improvement. *John Quinn* **65 p**

WOWEE 4 b.g. Archipenko (USA) 127 – Katya Kabanova (Sadler's Wells (USA) 132) [2015 71: t8.6f 10m⁶ p8g p10g⁶ 13.1d p8f p10d Nov 30] modest maiden: stays 1¼m: acts on polytrack: sometimes in tongue tie in 2015. *Tony Carroll* **54**

WRAPPED 2 ch.f. (Mar 20) Iffraaj 127 – Muffled (USA) 67 (Mizaaya 104) [2015 7m³ 7g⁴ p8g⁴ Oct 6] 110,000Y: sister to smart winner up to 6f Rafeej (2-y-o 5f winner) and half-sister to several winners, including 2-y-o 5f winner Excello (by Exceed And Excel) and 1m winner Defiant Spirit (by Compton Place): dam 6f winner: fair maiden: didn't progress as seemed likely, racing freely when only fourth to Nessita at Kempton final start. *William Haggas* **77**

WRAP STAR (IRE) 4 b.g. Cape Cross (IRE) 129 – Twinkling (NZ) (Star Way 119) [2015 87: 12m 13g 16.4m³ 15g 16s 16.4s⁶ Oct 10] fairly useful performer: third in handicap at York in July: stays 16.5f: acts on good to firm and good to soft going: often wears headgear, also tried in tongue tie final start: often races towards rear. *Anthony McCann, Ireland* **82**

WREN CASTLE (IRE) 3 b.c. Acclamation 118 – Dixie Eyes Blazing (USA) 56 (Gone West (USA)) [2015 7m p8m May 12] behind in maidens at Newmarket (seventh of 10, not knocked about) and Chelmsford (never on terms): sent to Greece. *Luca Cumani* **–**

WRENINGHAM 10 br.g. Diktat 126 – Slave To The Rythm (IRE) 63 (Hamas (IRE) 125) [2015 60: f5d 5v⁵ p5g Sep 30] angular gelding: poor handicapper: acts on polytrack, fibresand, soft and good to firm going: tried in headgear/tongue tie prior to 2015: usually races prominently. *Pat Eddery* **33**

WRIGHT PATTERSON (IRE) 2 b.g. (Mar 19) Dream Ahead (USA) 133 – Anam Allta (IRE) 117 (Invincible Spirit (IRE) 121) [2015 6d⁶ Oct 26] €65,000Y: first foal: dam, winner up to 7.4f (2-y-o 6f winner), closely related to smart performer up to 2m Opinion and half-sister to very smart performer up to 2m Fox Hunt: 12/1, some encouragement when 6 lengths sixth of 14 to Captain Dion in maiden at Redcar on debut, never nearer: has been gelded: should do better in time. *John Quinn* **48 p**

WROOD (USA) 4 b.f. Invasor (ARG) 133 – Ras Shaikh (USA) 105 (Sheikh Albadou 128) [2015 96: p10m⁵ p10.7g² May 15] fairly useful performer: left James Fanshawe after first start, creditable second in minor event at Dundalk next time: stays 10.5f: acts on polytrack: often races towards rear. *M. Halford, Ireland* **89**

WU ZETIAN 4 b.f. Invincible Spirit (IRE) 121 – China 74 (Royal Academy (USA) 130) [2015 79: p7g 7.5m 8.3m³ 8.3m 8g² 7g⁴ p8f Sep 24] rather sparely-made filly: fair handicapper: stays 8.5f: acts on polytrack, fibresand and good to firm going: in blinkers last 3 starts: front runner/races prominently. *Pam Sly* **71**

WYCHWOOD WARRIOR (IRE) 3 b.c. Lope de Vega (IRE) 125 – Pearlitas Passion (IRE) 53 (High Chaparral (IRE) 132) [2015 82p: 7g⁶ 7g³ p7g* p7g³ 8g² 8.5m Aug 19] useful performer: won minor event at Dundalk in March: third in listed race at Dundalk (1¾ lengths behind Convergence) in April and good second in listed race at Cork (head behind Eshera) in August: stays 1m: acts on polytrack: front runner/races prominently. *M. Halford, Ireland* **103**

WYNFORD (IRE) 2 ch.g. (Apr 28) Dylan Thomas (IRE) 132 – Wishing Chair (USA) (Giant's Causeway (USA) 132) [2015 8g⁶ p8g⁴ p8g⁴ Dec 16] compact gelding: fair maiden: best effort at Newmarket on debut, off over 3 months after: likely to stay beyond 1m: in hood last 2 starts. *Andrew Balding* **78**

X

XCELERATION 2 b.g. (Mar 19) Acclamation 118 – Hijab (King's Best (USA) 132) [2015 6m 6m 6g p7g³ p7g³ 6s Oct 6] rather unfurnished gelding: fair maiden: stays 7f: acts on polytrack: front runner/races prominently: has been gelded. *Ed Vaughan* **68**

XCLUSIVE 5 b.g. Pivotal 124 – Dance A Daydream 67 (Daylami (IRE) 138) [2015 67: 12.1m May 30] fair handicapper in 2014, well held only outing in 2015: stays 1¼m: acts on fibresand, best turf form on good going: tried in cheekpieces: often races prominently. *Ronald Harris*

XINBAMA (IRE) 6 b.h. Baltic King 120 – Persian Empress (IRE) 51 (Persian Bold 123) **96** [2015 95: 11.8g* 12m 12d 12s³ 14.1s p12g⁵ Nov 4] leggy horse: useful handicapper: won at Leicester (by ½ length from English Summer) in July: stays 1½m: acts on polytrack, firm and soft going: has worn tongue tie: sometimes slowly away. *Charles Hills*

X RAISE (IRE) 3 gr.f. Aussie Rules (USA) 123 – Raise (USA) (Seattle Slew (USA)) **60** [2015 65p: 7.1s⁵ 7m 6d 8g⁴ 7.9g 8d⁵ p10f t9.5f² t8.6f⁵ t9.5f t7.1m f7g⁶ f11g Dec 29] rather leggy filly: modest handicapper: stays 9.5f: acts on tapeta and soft going: sometimes in headgear in 2015. *David Brown*

Y

YA BOY SIR (IRE) 8 ch.g. Alhaarth (IRE) 126 – Champs Elysees (USA) (Distant **55** Relative 128) [2015 5m* 5d⁴ 5g 5g⁵ 5g³ 5m⁴ 5m 5m 5g³ 5d* 5m⁶ 5g 5m⁴ 5m 5m⁴ 7.2g Oct 13] modest handicapper: off since 2011, won at Hamilton in June and August: stays 7f, usually over shorter: acts on good to firm and good to soft going: wears headgear: usually races towards rear. *Iain Jardine*

YA HADE YE DELIL 3 br.g. Raven's Pass (USA) 133 – Palatial 101 (Green Desert **82** (USA) 127) [2015 73p: p11g⁴ 10s³ 11.7f* 11g⁶ p12.4g Dec 27] good-topped gelding: fairly useful performer: won maiden at Bath in April: left Richard Hannon 800 gns after fourth start: stays 11.5f: acts on firm going: sometimes slowly away. *Priscilla Peelman, Belgium*

YA HAFED 7 ch.g. Haafhd 129 – Rule Britannia 89 (Night Shift (USA)) [2015 56: 17.2f⁶ **57** Jul 1] modest handicapper: lightly raced on Flat (modest hurdler/poor chaser): stays 2m: acts on polytrack, fibresand, best turf form on good going or firmer: tried in tongue tie. *Sheena West*

YA HALLA (IRE) 3 gr.f. Dark Angel (IRE) 113 – Stormy View (USA) 77 (Cozzene **69** (USA)) [2015 56: t5.1f* t6g p5f p6f⁵ f5d* 5m⁴ 6s 5.1g* 5m³ 5m 5m⁶ Jun 20] fair handicapper: won at Wolverhampton in January, Southwell in March and Nottingham in May: best form at 5f: acts on fibresand and tapeta: wears headgear. *David Evans*

YAIR HILL (IRE) 7 b.g. Selkirk (USA) 129 – Conspiracy 98 (Rudimentary (USA) 118) **68** [2015 74: t6f* t7.1f³ t7.1m⁴ t5.1m² t7.1f⁴ t7.1f 7m⁴ 7g 7m⁶ 5m⁵ 7.6g 7d 5.9d 6d⁵ 6g⁶ 7.9d³ Sep 15] big gelding: fair performer: won claimer at Wolverhampton in January: left Geoffrey Deacon after fourth start, Tony Coyle after eighth: stays 1m: acts on tapeta, firm and soft going: often in headgear: often races towards rear. *Thomas Cuthbert*

YA LATIF (IRE) 3 b.f. Iffraaj 127 – Albahja 111 (Sinndar (IRE) 134) [2015 75: 7m* **81** 8.3m⁴ 7m⁴ 7.1m³ Sep 14] fairly useful handicapper: won at Salisbury in June: stays 7f: acts on tapeta and good to firm going: often travels strongly. *Roger Varian*

YAMLLIK 3 b.g. King's Best (USA) 132 – Anaamil (IRE) 85 (Darshaan 133) [2015 80p: **85** p8f² 9g t8.6g² Jun 4] strong gelding: fairly useful maiden: stays 9f: acts on polytrack: in cheekpieces final start. *Saeed bin Suroor*

YANGTZE 2 b.g. (Mar 23) Dansili 127 – Hi Calypso (IRE) 114 (In The Wings 128) [2015 **73 p** p8g⁴ 8g⁴ Sep 24] fourth foal: half-brother to useful 7f-11.6f winner Evangelist (by Oasis Dream): dam, winner up to 14.6f (Park Hill Stakes, also 2-y-o 7f winner), closely related to 11.6f/1½m winner Mercalta (by Falco) and 10.4f-11.6f winner Rye House (by Dansili), both smart: fair form in maidens at Kempton and Pontefract, still green when fourth of 10 to Percy Street in latter: will prove suited by at least 1¼m: has been gelded: remains open to improvement. *Sir Michael Stoute*

YANKEE MAIL (FR) 3 br.f. American Post 121 – Mercredi (FR) (Groom Dancer (USA) **74** 128) [2015 8g* 8.3m⁴ 10m⁶ 10.3m⁵ 10g⁴ 9.9d⁶ Oct 13] €20,000Y: third foal: half-sister to 10.5f winner Mercalta (by Falco): dam ran twice: fair performer: won maiden at Newcastle in April: stays 10.3f: acts on good to firm going: wore cheekpieces final start. *K. R. Burke*

YARD OF ALE 4 ch.g. Compton Place 125 – Highly Liquid 81 (Entrepreneur 123) [2015 **57** 71: t7.1g p7f⁵ 7g⁶ 8d 10.9g p8f 5g 5s p8g³ f8g⁶ p8g⁴ p8g⁶ Dec 15] modest handicapper: left Kristin Stubbs after fourth start: stays 1m: acts on polytrack, tapeta and soft going: tried in cheekpieces in 2015: usually slowly away, usually races nearer last than first. *Martin Smith*

YARROW (IRE) 3 b.f. Sea The Stars (IRE) 140 – Highland Gift (IRE) 95 (Generous **94** (IRE) 139) [2015 74p: 12m² 11.8m* 16⁰ᵘ 12d Aug 20] lengthy, unfinished filly: fairly useful performer: won maiden at Leicester (by 5 lengths from Stubbins) in May: pulled up next time (reportedly suffered irregular heartbeat), respectable eighth of 16 to Martlet in listed race at York final start: should stay beyond 1½m: acts on good to firm and good to soft going: usually races prominently. *Sir Michael Stoute*

YASIR (USA) 7 b.g. Dynaformer (USA) – Khazayin (USA) 74 (Bahri (USA) 125) [2015 **51 §** 73§: f16g⁴ p13.3g³ f14g³ f14g Mar 31] close-coupled gelding: modest handicapper: stays 16.5f: acts on polytrack, fibresand and heavy going: wears headgear: tried in tongue tie: usually races nearer last than first: unreliable. *Conor Dore*

YASMEEN 3 b.f. Sea The Stars (IRE) 140 – Wissal (USA) (Woodman (USA) 126) [2015 **99** 7m* 8m² 8f 8s⁴ 8m Aug 8] good-topped, attractive filly: closely related to useful 2-y-o 6f-7f winner (stayed 10.4f) Mudaaraah (by Cape Cross) and half-sister to several winners, including smart 7f (including at 2 yrs) winner Muwaary (by Oasis Dream) and useful 6f/7f winner Ethaara (by Green Desert): dam unraced: useful performer: won maiden at Newbury (by 2 lengths from Little Prairie) in April: best effort when ½-length second to Sperry in listed race at York next start: stays 1m: acts on good to firm going: front runner/ races prominently. *John Gosden*

YAT DING YAU (FR) 3 b.f. Air Chief Marshal (IRE) 115 – The Jostler 92 (Dansili 127) **81** [2015 81: p7.5g 8.3s² 8m 8.3m³ 8m⁴ 9.1g⁵ 8.1d 8d⁵ 7.5m Oct 1] plain filly: fairly useful handicapper: may prove best at short of 9f: acts on soft and good to firm going: tried in headgear in 2015. *William Jarvis*

YATTWEE (USA) 2 b.g. (Mar 18) Hard Spun (USA) 124 – Alzerra (UAE) 108 (Pivotal **102 p** 124) [2015 f7m* Dec 8] fourth foal: half-brother to useful 2-y-o 6f-1m winner Majeyda (by Street Cry): dam, 2-y-o 5f/6f winner, half-sister to useful 2-y-o 6f-7f winner Matloob: 11/4, showed useful form and looked good prospect when winning 14-runner maiden at Southwell by 4½ lengths from Always Welcome, leading 2f out: open to improvement. *Saeed bin Suroor*

YAWAIL 4 b.f. Medicean 128 – Al Tamooh (IRE) 84 (Dalakhani (IRE) 133) [2015 65: **59** f11d⁴ f12g 10d⁶ 10m² 10.3m³ 9m⁶ 10.3g⁵ t9.5m Sep 25] modest maiden: stays 11f: acts on fibresand, tapeta and good to firm going: usually wears cheekpieces: sometimes slowly away, usually races nearer last than first. *Brian Rothwell*

YEABUT NOBUT (IRE) 2 b.c. (Mar 29) Tagula (IRE) 116 – Queeny's Princess (IRE) **–** (Daggers Drawn (USA) 114) [2015 7.1s 10.2m Sep 28] well held in maidens at Chepstow and Bath (wore cheekpieces). *J. S. Moore*

YEAGER (USA) 5 b.g. Medaglia d'Oro (USA) 129 – Lucky Flyer (USA) (Fusaichi **96** Pegasus (USA) 130) [2015 101: 8m⁶ 10m² 9m p8g⁵ 8d p8f² Oct 1] good-topped gelding: useful handicapper: second at Redcar (3¾ lengths behind Fire Fighting) and Chelmsford (head behind Second Wave): stays 1¼m: acts on polytrack and firm going: usually in headgear in 2015: tried in tongue tie prior to 2015: sent to USA. *Jeremy Noseda*

YEAH BABY YEAH (IRE) 2 b.f. (Mar 28) Art Connoisseur (IRE) 121 – Royal **92 ?** Interlude (IRE) 67 (King's Theatre (IRE) 128) [2015 p5g³ 5d³ 6d 6.3d Sep 13] €7,000Y: half-sister to several winners, including 2-y-o 6f winner (stays 8.5f) Intermath (by Camacho) and 2m winner Viaduct Joey (by Traditionally): dam maiden sister to 1m-1¼m winner Absolut Taft: fairly useful form at best: standout run when 3 lengths third to Yakaba in listed race at Deauville second start: should stay at least 6f: blinkered final outing. *Gay Kelleway*

YEAH COOL 3 br.g. Kheleyf (USA) 116 – Piverina (IRE) 60 (Pivotal 124) [2015 –: t7.1g⁴ **61** f6s⁵ Feb 3] lightly-raced maiden, modest form: bred to prove best at 7f+: sold 3,000 gns, sent to the Netherlands. *Peter Chapple-Hyam*

YEATS MAGIC (IRE) 3 b.g. Yeats (IRE) 128 – Orinoco (IRE) 53 (Darshaan 133) [2015 **80** 85p: 11g May 15] good-topped gelding: won maiden only start in 2014, eighth of 15 in handicap at Newbury sole outing in 2015: should stay 1¼m+: sold 6,500 gns and joined Ronald Harris. *John Gosden*

YEENAAN (FR) 3 gr.g. Rip Van Winkle (IRE) 134 – Japan (GER) (Key Royal (GER) **91** 110) [2015 93p: p8g² 8.1d 10m 10g⁶ 8.3d⁶ 8.3s Oct 28] well-made gelding: fairly useful handicapper: stays 1¼m: acts on polytrack and heavy going: tried in cheekpieces in 2015: usually races towards rear. *Marco Botti*

YEEOOW (IRE) 6 b.g. Holy Roman Emperor (IRE) 125 – Taraya (IRE) (Doyoun 124) **93**
[2015 100: p6f p6m⁴ p6m p6g⁴ 6g³ 6m* 6.1m 6g 6g p6g² p7m p6f² p6g p6f Dec 17]
sturdy gelding: fairly useful handicapper: won at Pontefract in May: stays 6.5f: acts on
polytrack, firm and good to soft going: usually in headgear in 2015: often races prominently.
K. R. Burke

YENSIR 2 ch.c. (Feb 11) Sir Percy 129 – Yensi 86 (Doyen (IRE) 132) [2015 7v³ 8.1s² 9d⁵ **83**
Oct 11] first foal: dam 1m-9.5f winner: fairly useful form: best effort in maidens when nose
second of 12 to Taskeen at Sandown in September: in hood final start. *Pat Phelan*

YES DADDY (IRE) 7 b.g. Golan (IRE) 129 – Hollygrove Samba (IRE) (Accordion) **81**
[2015 p12g* t16.5f² 14g 14f p16g Aug 19] fairly useful performer: won maiden at
Lingfield in February: stays 16.5f: acts on polytrack, tapeta and firm going: tried in hood:
fair hurdler. *Robert Stephens*

YET AGAIN 3 b.f. Oasis Dream 129 – Quiff 124 (Sadler's Wells (USA) 132) [2015 10m⁵ **85**
10.3m⁴ 12.3m* 12.3g Aug 2] good-topped filly: sixth foal: sister to useful 6f-1m winner
The Great Gabrial and 9.3f/1¼m winner Scallop and half-sister to ½m winner (stays
1¾m) Economy (by Dalakhani): dam 1¼m-1½m (Yorkshire Oaks) winner and second in
St Leger: fairly useful performer: won maiden at Chester in July: best effort at 12.3f: sold
only 3,000 gns in December. *Sir Michael Stoute*

YING YANG (IRE) 3 b.f. Thewayyouare (USA) 117 – Pilda (IRE) (Princely Heir (IRE) **75**
111) [2015 8m 8m⁶ 6m 7.2g* 8s⁵ p8g Sep 25] third foal: dam unraced sister to useful
winner up to 1m Romancero: fair performer: won handicap at Musselburgh in August: best
effort at 7f: often races towards rear: sent to Singapore. *J. J. Feane, Ireland*

YISTY 2 ch.f. (Mar 25) Compton Place 125 – Meditation 88 (Inchinor 119) [2015 5.1g t6g **–**
5.1g t6f p6f Nov 19] fourth foal: dam, winner up to 1¼m (2-y-o 7f winner), half-sister to
1¼m/11f winner Giliberto: no form: sometimes in headgear. *Derek Shaw*

YODELLING (USA) 3 b.f. Medaglia d'Oro (USA) 129 – Echoes In Eternity (IRE) 111 **91**
(Spinning World (USA) 130) [2015 89: a8f⁴ 10.2d⁴ 10.3m⁴ p10g³ Nov 13] fairly useful
handicapper: stays 10.5f: acts on polytrack, dirt and good to soft going. *Charlie Appleby*

YOJOJO (IRE) 6 ch.m. Windsor Knot (IRE) 118 – Belle of The Blues (IRE) (Blues **77**
Traveller (IRE) 119) [2015 94, a86: f8d³ p8f⁴ 9.9g² 8.3d⁶ 11.9m⁶ t8.6g Jul 28] plain mare: **a69**
fair handicapper: stays 1½m: acts on polytrack, firm and soft going: tried in hood prior to
2015. *Gay Kelleway*

YORKEE MO SABEE (IRE) 2 ch.g. (Feb 8) Teofilo (IRE) 126 – Pivotal's Princess **79**
(IRE) 107 (Pivotal 124) [2015 7m 7g 6g* 6d t6f⁵ Oct 31] close-coupled gelding: fair
performer: won maiden at Pontefract in September: best effort at 6f: acts on tapeta: often
races freely. *Mark Johnston*

YORK EXPRESS 3 b.f. Vale of York (IRE) 117 – Star Express 80 (Sadler's Wells (USA) **55**
132) [2015 71: p7g⁵ 7m Jun 18] strong filly: modest maiden: stays 6f: acts on polytrack and
good to soft going: tried in visor. *Ismail Mohammed*

YORK GLORY (USA) 7 gr.h. Five Star Day (USA) 120 – Minicolony (USA) (Pleasant **81**
Colony (USA)) [2015 90: 6g 6d 7g 6m 6m p6g⁴ Aug 26] big, rangy horse: fairly useful
handicapper: stays 7f, usually races at 6f: acts on polytrack, fibresand, good to firm and
good to soft going: wears headgear: tried in tongue tie: sometimes slowly away.
George Peckham

YORKIDDING 3 b.f. Dalakhani (IRE) 133 – Claxon 110 (Caerleon (USA) 132) [2015 75: **97**
10.2s² 12m* 14m* 12.5m⁴ 12f 12m⁶ 13.7m³ 14g 12g⁴ 15.9s² 14s⁶ Oct 9] useful-looking
filly: useful handicapper: won at York and Sandown in May: upped in trip, improved form
when 2¼ lengths second of 5 to Sea of Heaven at Chester in September: stays 2m: acts on
soft and good to firm going. *Mark Johnston*

YORKINDRED SPIRIT 3 b.f. Sea The Stars (IRE) 140 – Paracel (USA) (Gone West **62 +**
(USA)) [2015 72: p12m³ 9.9m 8m 9.2d⁴ 9.9m⁶ 9.9m⁶ 11.5g³ 16.2m* 16g p15.8g² p14g⁶ **a77**
t12.2m* t12.2f² p10f t12.2f⁴ p10g² t12.2f Nov 16] fair handicapper: won at Beverley in
July and Wolverhampton in September: stays 2m, effective at shorter: acts on polytrack,
tapeta and good to firm going: usually wears headgear: often races towards rear.
Mark Johnston

YORK MINSTER (IRE) 2 b.g. (Feb 20) Vale of York (IRE) 117 – Tintern (Diktat 126) **63**
[2015 5.7f⁴ 5m⁵ 5m⁵ 6.1d³ p8g² p8f* 8s⁵ t7.1f⁴ Oct 20] sturdy gelding: fair performer: won **a70**
nursery at Chelmsford in September: will prove suited by a return to 1m: acts on polytrack
and tapeta. *William Muir*

YORKSHIRE DALES (IRE) 3 b.g. Vale of York (IRE) 117 – Rock Exhibition 86 **96** (Rock of Gibraltar (IRE) 133) [2015 67: 8.3s* 8g* 8f Jun 18] useful performer: won maiden at Nottingham in April and handicap at Newmarket (by 1½ lengths from Them And Us) in May: eleventh of 28 to War Envoy in Britannia Stakes (Handicap) at Royal Ascot final start: stays 8.5f: acts on soft going: sent to Hong Kong. *David Elsworth*

YORKSHIRE (IRE) 3 b.g. Tagula (IRE) 116 – Bun Penny (Bertolini (USA) 125) [2015 **62** 56: 5m 7d 6m³ p7m² t7.1m Nov 28] modest maiden: left David O'Meara after fourth start: stayed 6f: acted on good to firm and good to soft going: tried in hood/tongue tie: often travelled strongly: dead. *Ivan Furtado*

YORKSHIREMAN (IRE) 5 b.g. Red Clubs (IRE) 125 – Ossiana (IRE) 72 (Polish **61** Precedent (USA) 131) [2015 59: t16.5g² t16.5m* t16.5g² t16.5g⁵ t16.5f t16.5f⁶ t16.5m⁶ t16.5g Dec 5] neat gelding: modest handicapper: won at Wolverhampton in March: stays 16.5f: acts on tapeta, best turf form on soft/heavy going: sometimes in headgear prior to 2015. *Lynn Siddall*

YORKSTERS PRINCE (IRE) 8 b.g. Beat Hollow 126 – Odalisque (IRE) (Machiavellian **52** (USA) 123) [2015 64: t9.5f⁴ t13.9f⁶ t12.2f Mar 13] lengthy gelding: modest handicapper: stays 1½m: acts on polytrack, tapeta, good to firm and heavy going: wears headgear: tried in tongue tie: front runner, tends to find little. *Marjorie Fife*

YOSEMITE 2 gr.f. (May 3) Makfi 130 – Dansa Queen 89 (Dansili 127) [2015 5.9m² p6g² **85 p** 6d* Oct 11] 6,000Y, €24,000 2-y-o: fifth foal: half-sister to 5f winner Rangooned (by Bahamian Bounty): dam, winner up to 8.3f (2-y-o 7f winner), half-sister to useful winner up to 1¼m Halicardia: fairly useful form: improved/had something in hand when winning maiden at Goodwood final start by neck from Andar, hampered 2f out but staying on to lead final 1f: raced only at 6f: will go on progressing. *Richard Fahey*

YOU BE LUCKY (IRE) 3 b.f. Thewayyouare (USA) 117 – Lovely Dream (IRE) 69 **60** (Elnadim (USA) 128) [2015 64: t7.1g⁵ p7g t7.1f Oct 16] modest maiden: stays 7f: acts on polytrack and tapeta. *Jo Crowley*

YOUCOULDNTMAKEITUP (IRE) 3 b.f. Captain Rio 122 – Miss Donovan 100 **66** (Royal Applause 124) [2015 76: 6d 5g 5g 5d 5m³ 5.1d 5s³ Oct 27] fair handicapper: best form at 5f: acts on soft and good to firm going: wears headgear: also in tongue tie last 4 starts: front runner/races prominently. *Tim Easterby*

YOUM JAMIL (USA) 8 gr.g. Mizzen Mast (USA) 121 – Millie's Choice (IRE) 110 **65** (Taufan (USA) 119) [2015 53: p8f* p8f² p8f⁴ p8f* t8.6f⁶ p8g⁴ 8g Aug 6] rangy gelding: fair handicapper: won at Kempton in January and Lingfield (apprentice) in March: stays 12.5f, effective at shorter: acts on polytrack, good to firm and good to soft going: tried in headgear prior to 2015: in tongue tie: sometimes slowly away, usually races nearer last than first. *Tony Carroll*

YOUNG CHRISTIAN 2 b.g. (Apr 14) Captain Gerrard (IRE) 113 – Shallow Ground **–** (IRE) 97 (Common Grounds 118) [2015 t9.5f Dec 14] 100/1, green and always behind in maiden at Wolverhampton. *Tom Tate*

YOUNG DOTTIE 9 b.m. Desert Sun 120 – Auntie Dot Com 70 (Tagula (IRE) 116) [2015 **71** 68, a78: p10m⁵ p10g⁶ p10m³ p10f⁴ Apr 30] angular mare: fair handicapper: stays 1¼m: acts on polytrack, firm and good to soft going: often races towards rear. *Pat Phelan*

YOUNG JACKIE 7 b.m. Doyen (IRE) 132 – Just Warning (Warning 136) [2015 –: p10m **57** p10m³ t12.2f⁴ p10f⁴ 9.9m⁶ p10m⁴ 12.2g 9.9m* 9.9d² p10m³ p10m⁴ p10g Dec 30] modest handicapper: won at Brighton in June: stays 1¼m: acts on polytrack, good to firm and good to soft going: wears headgear: usually races nearer last than first, usually responds generously to pressure. *George Margarson*

YOUNG JOHN (IRE) 2 b.g. (Apr 20) Acclamation 118 – Carpet Lady (IRE) 70 (Night **85** Shift (USA)) [2015 p5g² 5.1s* 6f 6g⁴ 6s⁵ t5.1f t5.1f Nov 13] €70,000F: brother to 3 winners, including useful 5f (including at 2 yrs) winner Cake and 2-y-o 7f winner Heskin, and half-brother to several winners, including useful 7f-8.3f winner Suited And Booted (by Tagula): dam maiden: fairly useful performer: won maiden at Chester in May: stays 6f: acts on tapeta and soft going: often races nearer rear. *Richard Fahey*

YOUNG TOM 2 b.g. (Mar 11) Sir Percy 129 – Enford Princess 89 (Pivotal 124) [2015 7s **52** 9d⁶ 8.3s⁵ Nov 4] modest form in maidens at Redcar and Nottingham last 2 starts. *Michael Appleby*

YOUNG WINDSOR (IRE) 2 ch.g. (Mar 11) Windsor Knot (IRE) 118 – Invincible **64** Woman (IRE) 87 (Invincible Spirit (IRE) 121) [2015 5.9g⁶ 5m⁶ 6g⁵ 5d⁴ 6d² 5g 6s* t6f⁴ Oct 23] modest performer: won nursery at Catterick in October: stays 6f: acts on soft going: in headgear last 3 starts. *Ann Duffield*

YOU N ME 2 b.f. (Feb 16) Footstepsinthesand 120 – Centenerola (USA) 77 (Century City **64** (IRE) 124) [2015 5.9m⁴ p7g³ 7g⁴ Oct 3] 45,000F, 24,000Y: second foal: half-sister to winner up to 6f Scentpastparadise (by Pastoral Pursuits): dam, 7f winner, half-sister to smart winner up to 10.4f Barefoot Lady out of useful winner up to 1¼m (2-y-o 6f/7f winner) Lady Angharad: modest maiden: should stay at least 7f. *K. R. Burke*

YOUONLYLIVEONCE (IRE) 3 b.g. Lawman (FR) 121 – Caerlonore (IRE) **59** (Traditionally (USA) 117) [2015 57: 8g⁶ 8.3g² 9.9m³ 10.1m⁴ 10.1g³ 12d 9.2d⁶ 8.5g Sep 16] modest maiden: stays 1¼m: acts on good to firm and heavy going: front runner/races prominently. *John Quinn*

YOURARTISONFIRE 5 ch.g. Dutch Art 126 – Queens Jubilee 71 (Cayman Kai (IRE) **98** 114) [2015 97: 8d³ 8.3s* 8g⁵ 8m 8m* 8m 8d 8d Sep 26] sturdy gelding: useful handicapper: won at Nottingham in April and Pontefract (by head from Kiwi Bay) in July: stays 8.5f: acts on good to firm and heavy going: wears visor. *K. R. Burke*

YOU'RE A GOAT 2 b.f. (Mar 25) Notnowcato 128 – Three Wrens (IRE) 99 (Second **56 p** Empire (IRE) 124) [2015 6g p7g p7f⁵ Dec 17] 6,000Y: sixth foal: half-sister to 3 winners, including useful 11f-2m winner (stays 2¼m) Courtesy Call (by Manduro) and 5f/6f winner Gregori (by Invincible Spirit): dam, winner up to 8.2f (including at 2 yrs), half-sister to smart 1m-1¼m winner Thames: signs of ability in maidens: should do better. *Gary Moore*

YOU'RE COOL 3 b.g. Exceed And Excel (AUS) 126 – Ja One (IRE) 74 (Acclamation **81** 118) [2015 68: p6f* t6g* f5s⁵ t5.1g⁵ 6m³ 6.1d⁵ 6d⁶ 5g⁴ 5g⁴ 5g² 5m t6f⁶ t6g⁶ p6f² p5f* t5.1f² t5.1g p5g Dec 10] fairly useful handicapper: won at Kempton in February, Wolverhampton in March and Chelmsford (apprentice) in November: stays 6f: acts on polytrack, tapeta and good to firm going: tried in blinkers. *James Given*

YOU'RE FIRED (IRE) 4 b.g. Firebreak 125 – My Sweet Georgia (IRE) 79 (Royal **111** Applause 124) [2015 96: 8v 8g* 8m² 8f 8m³ 8d 8.5s* 8.3s* 8s Nov 24] angular gelding: smart handicapper: improved again in 2015 and won at Ripon (by 3¼ lengths from Dubai Dynamo) in April, York (by ½ length from Quick Wit) in October and Nottingham (by neck from Storm Rock) in November: also ran well when placed at York in May and July: stays 8.5f: acts on polytrack, soft and good to firm going. *K. R. Burke*

YOU'RE HIRED 2 b.c. (Apr 8) Dalakhani (IRE) 133 – Heaven Sent 116 (Pivotal 124) **81 p** [2015 7s² 8s³ Oct 23] 130,000Y: third foal: half-brother to useful 2-y-o 1m winner Firmament (by Cape Cross): dam, 7f-9f (dual Dahlia Stakes) winner, sister to smart US Grade 1 9f/1¼m winner Megahertz: fairly useful maiden: placed at Leicester (1¼ lengths second to Vincent's Forever) and Newbury (1¼ lengths third to Midterm): will stay beyond 1m: still has scope for improvement. *Amanda Perrett*

YOU'RE MY CRACKER 3 ch.f. Captain Gerrard (IRE) 113 – Dalmunzie (IRE) **84** (Choisir (AUS) 126) [2015 78: 6m² 5.7f² 5.7g² t7.1g² 5.7d³ 6m² t6f⁴ Oct 17] compact filly: fairly useful handicapper: stays 7f: acts on tapeta, firm and good to soft going: sometimes in blinkers: often leads: quirky sort. *Daniel Kubler*

YOUR GIFTED (IRE) 8 b.m. Trans Island 119 – Dame Laura (IRE) 100 (Royal **72** Academy (USA) 130) [2015 58, a70: t5.1g⁵ t5.1f³ t5.1f² t5.1g³ t5.1g⁴ t5.1m 5m⁴ 5m p5g² 5m p5f⁵ t5.1m³ t5.1f* t5.1f³ t5.1f t5.1m Dec 30] fair handicapper: won at Wolverhampton in October: stays 6f: acts on all-weather, good to firm and heavy going: wears headgear. *Lisa Williamson*

YOURHOLIDAYISOVER (IRE) 8 ch.g. Sulamani (IRE) 130 – Whitehaven 116 (Top **59** Ville 129) [2015 52: t12.2m³ t12.2f⁵ t12.2g 12m³ 12.4g² 12.1g⁶ 12.5m⁵ 14.1m 10.1m⁵ **a48** 12.1s³ 12.1m³ 12.1g⁴ 12.4g⁴ Sep 4] modest maiden: stays 1¾m: acts on soft and good to firm going: often in hood in 2015. *Patrick Holmes*

YOURINTHEWILL (USA) 7 ch.g. Aragorn (IRE) 125 – Lenarue (USA) (Gone West **47 §** (USA)) [2015 71§: t9.5f p10m p10f⁵ʰᵘ Feb 2] stocky gelding: poor handicapper: stays 1¼m: acts on polytrack, tapeta and firm going: ungenuine. *Daniel Loughnane*

YOUR LUCKY DAY 3 b.g. Cockney Rebel (IRE) 127 – Fontaine House (Pyramus **59** (USA) 78) [2015 f7g⁴ p8m 7v f6g² Dec 15] modest maiden: best effort at 6f. *Chris Dwyer*

YOUR PAL TAL 5 b.g. Dark Angel (IRE) 113 – Good Health 78 (Magic Ring (IRE) 115) **92** [2015 79: p5g* p6g* p5g* 5.8m 5m⁵ 5m 6.3m² 7g⁵ p5g 6s⁶ 6d 6g Sep 18] fairly useful handicapper: won at Dundalk in January (twice) and February: stays 7f (all wins at 5f/6f): acts on polytrack and good to firm going: tried in headgear prior to 2015. *J. F. Levins, Ireland*

YOURS TRULY (IRE) 3 gr.f. Dark Angel (IRE) 113 – Win Cash (IRE) (Alhaarth (IRE) **72** 126) [2015 8f³ 10m⁵ p12g⁴ t8.6m⁵ p10f* 12d Oct 5] 160,000Y: third foal: sister to 7f (including at 2 yrs) winner Coolnagree and 7f/1m winner Holiday Magic, both useful: dam second over hurdles: fair performer: won handicap at Lingfield in September: stays 1¼m: acts on polytrack, tapeta and firm going: in headgear third to fifth starts: sold 65,000 gns. *Saeed bin Suroor*

YOU WISH 2 b.f. (Feb 16) Poet's Voice 126 – Dignify (IRE) 105 (Rainbow Quest (USA) 134) [2015 6g 6v p7g t7.1g Dec 1] 29,000Y: half-sister to 3 winners, including winner up to 1¼m Personify (2-y-o 6f winner, by Zafonic) and 7f-8.4f winner Declamation (by Shamardal): dam 2-y-o 7f/1m winner: poor maiden: stays 7f. *Gary Moore* **41**

YPRES 6 b.g. Byron 117 – Esligier (IRE) 87 (Sabrehill (USA) 120) [2015 83: 5g⁴ 5m⁴ 6m² 5.5m² 6g³ 5.9m* 5g⁵ 6m³ t6f 6g Sep 26] fair handicapper: won at Carlisle in August: stays 6f: acts on fibresand and good to firm going: sometimes in headgear: quirky sort. *Jason Ward* **77**

YTHAN WATERS 3 b.g. Hellvelyn 118 – Primrose Queen (Lear Fan (USA) 130) [2015 80: 6d⁶ 7.1s⁴ 7.9v³ 8m⁴ 6.9d 7.9m² 7v⁶ 7v t7.1g Dec 5] fair handicapper: stays 1m: acts on tapeta, good to firm and heavy going: in cheekpieces final start. *Bryan Smart* **76**

YUFTEN 4 b.c. Invincible Spirit (IRE) 121 – Majestic Sakeena (IRE) (King's Best (USA) 132) [2015 117: 8m 8g⁶ Jun 13] rather leggy gelding: smart at 3 yrs: just useful form when sixth in listed race at York (blinkered) on second outing in 2015: stays 1m: acts on good to firm and good to soft going: front runner/races prominently. *William Haggas* **98**

YUL FINEGOLD (IRE) 5 b.g. Invincible Spirit (IRE) 121 – Mascara (Mtoto 134) [2015 84: t9.5g² p10g* 10s⁶ p10g⁵ p10g* t12.2g* 12.3v p10m⁵ 11.9d⁵ 10.4f³ p10g⁴ p11g⁶ t9.5g p10g³ 10d³ t8.6g⁶ 10d 10s⁵ p10g⁴ f11g* f12f² f11g⁴ Dec 22] rather leggy gelding: fairly useful performer: left George Baker after reappearance: won handicaps at Chelmsford in March and April and at Wolverhampton later in April, and claimer at Southwell in November: stays 1½m: acts on all-weather and any turf going: tried in headgear: front runner/races prominently: tough. *Conor Dore* **80 a90**

YULONG XIONGBA (IRE) 3 b.g. Kodiac 112 – Moon Legend (USA) 70 (Gulch (USA)) [2015 81: 6g⁶ p7g 7.5d 8d⁶ t9.5f³ t12.2g³ Dec 4] leggy, close-coupled gelding: fair handicapper: left Roger Charlton after second start: will be suited by a return to 1¼m: acts on tapeta and soft going: in hood in 2015: often races prominently. *Julie Camacho* **72**

Z

ZAAKHIR (IRE) 2 b.f. (Feb 21) Raven's Pass (USA) 133 – Zahoo (IRE) 105 (Nayef (USA) 129) [2015 p8d* Nov 30] second foal: half-sister to smart winner up to 7.4f Convergence (by Cape Cross): dam, winner up to 1½m (2-y-o 1m winner), half-sister to very smart 1½m-1¾m winner Tactic and smart 11f winner Yaazy: in hood, 12/1, won 10-runner maiden at Kempton on debut by head from Shaan, staying on to lead final 50 yds: will stay at least 1¼m: sure to improve. *Charles Hills* **86 p**

ZAANEH (IRE) 3 br.f. Aqlaam 125 – Intishaar (IRE) (Dubai Millennium 140) [2015 t8.6f² 7m* t8.6g* 9.9s⁴ 8g Oct 21] sixth foal: half-sister to 3 winners, including 1¼m winner Tabjeel (by Sakhee) and 2-y-o 6f winner Bairam (by Haatef): dam unraced out of useful 2-y-o 6f/7f winner Bint Shadayid: fairly useful performer: won maiden at Wetherby in July and handicap at Wolverhampton in August: stays 8.5f: acts on tapeta and good to firm going: sometimes slowly away, often races prominently. *William Haggas* **89**

ZABDI 2 b.c. (Mar 21) Zebedee 113 – Musical Moonlight (Observatory (USA) 131) [2015 6.5s⁶ p6g³ p6g Dec 3] fair maiden: best effort when third to Mywayistheonlyway at Kempton in November. *Richard Hannon* **72**

ZABEEL STAR (IRE) 3 ch.g. Arcano (IRE) 122 – Deep Winter 94 (Pivotal 124) [2015 –: 8.3m⁵ 8.3m⁵ 8f* 10.3g³ 8.1m³ Aug 22] angular gelding: fairly useful handicapper: won at Haydock in July: stays 10.5f: acts on firm going. *Graeme McPherson* **83**

ZAC BROWN (IRE) 4 b.g. Kodiac 112 – Mildmay (USA) (Elusive Quality (USA)) [2015 71, a98: p5g* f5s⁴ t5.1f p5g⁵ p5g 5m f5g⁶ p6g⁶ Dec 30] useful handicapper: standout effort when successful at Chelmsford (by 3¼ lengths from It Must Be Faith) in January on reappearance: effective at 5f/6f: acts on polytrack and tapeta, best turf form on good going: usually in hood in 2015. *David Barron* **105**

ZAC TRUTH (USA) 3 ch.g. Lookin At Lucky (USA) 127 – Rose of Zollern (IRE) 111 (Seattle Dancer (USA) 119) [2015 65: p10g p9.9g⁵ p10g⁴ p12g⁵ p13g³ p16g Aug 17] fair maiden: stays 1¼m: acts on polytrack: usually in headgear: sent to Singapore. *Gay Kelleway* **69**

ZACYNTHUS (IRE) 7 ch.g. Iffraaj 127 – Ziria (IRE) 109 (Danehill Dancer (IRE) 117) **91** [2015 91: 7d 7.2s* 7m³ 8d 7g 7d 7.2g² 7s 7d Oct 31] fairly useful handicapper: left Shaun Harris, won at Ayr (by 1¼ lengths from Invoke) in July: stays 7f: acts on firm and soft going: tried in headgear/tongue tie. *David O'Meara*

ZAEEM 6 b.g. Echo of Light 125 – Across (ARG) (Roy (USA)) [2015 74: t8.6f³ p8f³ **87** t8.6g* 7m* 8m³ 8m⁶ 7s t8.6f⁶ p7f³ p8m⁵ Dec 27] fairly useful handicapper: left Dean Ivory, won at Wolverhampton, Lingfield and Brighton in June: stays 9f: acts on polytrack, tapeta, firm and good to soft going: wears headgear. *Ivan Furtado*

ZAFAYAN (IRE) 4 b.g. Acclamation 118 – Zafayra (IRE) 101 (Nayef (USA) 129) [2015 **109** 95: 12v* 18.7d³ 15s Oct 25] useful handicapper: won at Leopardstown (by 1¾ lengths from Kabjoy) in April: good 1¼ lengths third of 17 to Trip To Paris in Chester Cup at Chester next start: stays 2¼m: acts on good to firm and heavy going: wears headgear: usually races prominently. *D. K. Weld, Ireland*

ZAFILANI (IRE) 3 b.c. Azamour (IRE) 130 – Zatayra (IRE) 101 (Nayef (USA) 129) **105** [2015 101p: 10v² 9.5g* Apr 26] useful performer: further improvement when winning 3-runner minor event at Gowran in April by ½ length from Royal Navy Ship: second of 3 in Ballysax Stakes at Leopardstown (4½ lengths behind Success Days) on reappearance: likely to stay 1½m: sent to Hong Kong, where renamed Mr Pele. *D. K. Weld, Ireland*

ZAHENDA 3 b.f. Exceed And Excel (AUS) 126 – Impetious 97 (Inchinor 119) [2015 –p: **46** 8.3d 8.3m 8d⁴ 12.1f 8m³ 8g Aug 6] poor maiden: best effort at 1m: acts on firm going: in hood last 2 starts. *Ismail Mohammed*

ZAHRAT NARJIS 2 b.f. (Mar 24) Exceed And Excel (AUS) 126 – Nijoom Dubai 104 **70** (Noverre (USA) 125) [2015 t5.1g⁴ 5m⁵ p6g³ 6m⁶ 7v³ t7.1f Oct 20] leggy filly: third foal: dam, 2-y-o 6f winner who stayed 1m, half-sister to smart winner up to 9f Samitar: fair maiden: best form at 5f: acts on tapeta and good to firm going: often races prominently. *Richard Fahey*

ZAIDIYN (FR) 5 b.g. Zamindar (USA) 116 – Zainta (IRE) 118 (Kahyasi 130) [2015 **86** p14f⁴ Nov 6] strong, good-topped gelding: fairly useful handicapper: stays 1½m: acts on good to firm and heavy going: tried in hood: useful hurdler. *Brian Ellison*

ZAINA RIZEENA 2 ch.f. (Mar 9) Shamardal (USA) 129 – Sweet Lilly 107 (Tobougg **80** (IRE) 125) [2015 7.2d³ 7.5g* 8g⁶ Sep 17] third foal: half-sister to 1m winner Lilly Junior (by Cape Cross) and 2-y-o 7.5f winner Rosy Blush (by Youmzain), both stay 1¼m: dam, winner up to 10.4f (2-y-o 7f-1m winner), half-sister to useful 9.4f-10.4f winner Ofaraby: fairly useful form: won maiden at Beverley in August by 1¼ lengths from Ninetta: still green when last of 6 in minor event at Ayr final start: best effort at 7.5f. *Richard Fahey*

ZAINAT (IRE) 2 b.g. (Apr 18) Masterofthehorse (IRE) 122 – Think Fast (IRE) **69** (Songandaprayer (USA) 118) [2015 7.9m⁵ 8d⁶ 10.2g Oct 18] fair form on first 2 of 3 starts in maidens: ran poorly final outing, subsequently gelded. *K. R. Burke*

ZAIN EAGLE 5 b.h. Dylan Thomas (IRE) 132 – Pearl City (USA) 116 (Carson City **99 §** (USA)) [2015 106: a9.9f a9.9f⁴ a9.9f Dec 3] useful handicapper: left Robert Cowell after first start: stays 11f: acts on polytrack, dirt, good to firm and heavy going: not straightforward (carries head awkwardly), and isn't one to trust. *D. Watson, UAE*

ZAIN EMPEROR (IRE) 2 b.c. (Feb 5) Holy Roman Emperor (IRE) 125 – Love Thirty **73** 93 (Mister Baileys 123) [2015 6d³ 6d 6.5s Oct 23] fair form when third of 10 to Force in maiden at Haydock on debut: disappointing both subsequent starts. *Robert Cowell*

ZAIN TIME 3 b.f. Pivotal 124 – Hypnology (USA) (Gone West (USA)) [2015 5g³ 6g⁵ **55** t5.1f² t5.1f Oct 27] 35,000Y: second foal: half-sister to 1m winner Trust The Wind (by Dansili): dam, unraced, closely related to smart 7f winner Hathal and half-sister to 2 smart winners, out of 1000 Guineas winner Sleepytime: modest maiden: best effort at 5f. *Robert Cowell*

ZAKATAL 9 gr.g. Kalanisi (IRE) 132 – Zankara (FR) (Linamix (FR) 127) [2015 –§: t12.2f **70 §** Dec 22] fair performer: stays 2m: acts on tapeta, heavy and good to firm going: tried in blinkers/tongue tie prior to 2015: temperamental. *Rebecca Menzies*

ZALTY (FR) 5 b.g. Elusive City (USA) 117 – Dubai's Gazal 79 (Fraam 114) [2015 109: **93** 5d⁴ 5m 8g 7g 6d³ 6d Oct 11] strong gelding: fairly useful handicapper: left David Marnane after second start: stays 8.5f, effective at shorter: acts on polytrack, and firm going: sometimes in blinkers: sometimes slowly away, often races in rear. *Ismail Mohammed*

ZAMANI (IRE) 3 ch.f. Teofilo (IRE) 126 – Zam Zoom (IRE) (Dalakhani (IRE) 133) **81** [2015 p10g³ 9.9m* 10m⁴ 12g³ 12.1g Sep 16] lengthy filly: third foal: closely related to useful 1¼m winner Bright Approach (by New Approach) and half-sister to smart winner up to 15.5f Nichols Canyon (2-y-o 9f winner, by Authorized): dam unraced: fairly useful performer: won maiden at Brighton in June: stays 1½m: acts on good to firm going: often races prominently. *James Tate*

ZAMASTAR 4 b.g. Zamindar (USA) 116 – Kissogram 120 (Caerleon (USA) 132) [2015 **67** 7g 6m⁶ 6g² 6s 6d 7s Oct 16] fair maiden: best effort at 6f: sometimes slowly away, often races towards rear. *David Thompson*

ZAMBEASY 4 b.g. Zamindar (USA) 116 – Hanella (IRE) 91 (Galileo (IRE) 134) [2015 **83** 81: p11g⁴ 11.6m 10m³ p12g² 10g* 10m² 10g³ p11g Oct 7] workmanlike gelding: fairly useful handicapper: won at Sandown in July: stays 1½m: acts on polytrack, good to firm and good to soft going: front runner. *Philip Hide*

ZAMOURA 3 b.f. Azamour (IRE) 130 – Move 79 (Observatory (USA) 131) [2015 91p: **100** p10g* 10.3m* 11.4d³ 12f 12d 9.9g² 9.9d Nov 9] useful performer: won maiden at Chelmsford in January and handicap at Doncaster in April: easily best effort when second in listed race at Chantilly (¾ length behind Bilissie) in September: stays 11.4f: acts on polytrack, good to firm and good to soft going. *John Gosden*

ZAMPA MANOS (USA) 4 b.g. Arch (USA) 127 – Doryphar (USA) (Gone West (USA)) **89** [2015 97: p10g² p10g³ p8g⁶ p8g 8.5m⁵ Jul 9] sturdy gelding: fairly useful handicapper: stays 10.5f: acts on polytrack, good to firm and good to soft going: tried in visor: front runner/races prominently: sent to Saudi Arabia. *Andrew Balding*

ZAMPERINI (IRE) 3 ch.g. Fast Company (IRE) 126 – Lucky Date (IRE) 91 (Halling **98** (USA) 133) [2015 67: 8.3g² t8.6g* 10m² 10g² 10v⁴ 10.2g² 10d* Oct 30] good-topped gelding: useful performer: won maiden at Wolverhampton in June and handicap at Newmarket in October, much improved when beating Weetles by length in latter: stays 1¼m: acts on tapeta, good to firm and soft going: visored penultimate start: quirky sort, has high head carriage. *Mike Murphy*

ZAMSINA 3 b.f. Zamindar (USA) 116 – Bolsena (USA) (Red Ransom (USA)) [2015 8f **–** 10s p10f⁴ Sep 22] 4,800Y: sister to useful 1m winner Cactus Rose and half-sister to 11f winner Bloodsuker (by Polish Precedent) and 2-y-o 6f winner Wolf Slayer (by Diktat): dam unraced half-sister to smart US 2-y-o Grade 3 5.5f winner De Niro: signs of ability on last of 3 starts in maidens, when in cheekpieces: also tried in blinkers. *James Toller*

ZAND (IRE) 5 b.g. Zamindar (USA) 116 – Zanara (IRE) 81 (Kahyasi 130) [2015 9.9d³ **101** 11.9g³ 9.9g 10.4m 10s⁵ 11.2f³ p10f 12v Nov 7] lengthy gelding: useful handicapper: third at Wolverhampton (1¼ lengths behind Hamelin) in October: left Frau C. Bocskai in Switzerland after second start: stays 1½m: acts on tapeta, soft and good to firm going. *Mark Johnston*

ZANETTO 5 b.g. Medicean 128 – Play Bouzouki 70 (Halling (USA) 133) [2015 99: 6f³ **100** 6g² 6m 6m⁴ 6m p6f 6g⁵ 6m⁴ 6m Oct 3] rangy, attractive gelding: reportedly has had breathing operation: useful handicapper: third at Newmarket (length behind Eastern Impact) and second at Goodwood (2½ lengths behind Ruwaiyan), both in May: stays 6f: acts on firm going: sometimes in visor, including on last 4 starts. *Andrew Balding*

ZANNDA (IRE) 3 b.f. Azamour (IRE) 130 – Zanoubiya (IRE) 80 (Dalakhani (IRE) 133) **108** [2015 83p: 10v* 10f² 10d² 12g* 10d* Oct 24] useful performer: progressed very well and won maiden at Leopardstown (by ½ length from Wedding Vow) in April, Give Thanks Stakes at Cork (by head from Altesse) in August and listed race at Leopardstown (by head from Torcedor) in October: will prove suited by a return to 1½m: acts on heavy going: in headgear last 4 starts: usually races prominently, usually responds generously to pressure. *D. K. Weld, Ireland*

ZAPLAMATION (IRE) 10 b.g. Acclamation 118 – Zapatista (Rainbow Quest (USA) **–** 134) [2015 10d Jun 8] workmanlike gelding: fair handicapper: off 17 months, well held only start in 2015: stays 2¼m: acts on firm and good going. *John Quinn*

ZAPPED (IRE) 2 gr.c. (Mar 21) Zebedee 113 – Alexander Wonder (IRE) (Redback 116) **62 p** [2015 6d⁴ 6m⁵ 8m Sep 10] €28,000F, 65,000Y: sturdy colt: fourth foal: half-brother to 2-y-o 5f/6f winner Hardy Blue (by Red Clubs): dam unraced half-sister to smart winner up to 6f Triple Aspect: best effort in maidens (fair form) when fourth of 9 to Galesburg at Leicester on debut: should still improve. *Richard Hannon*

ZARAWI (IRE) 4 b.g. Marju (IRE) 127 – Zarwala (IRE) 92 (Polish Precedent (USA) 131) **66** [2015 80: p12m 12g⁵ Jul 16] fair maiden: stays 10.5f: acts on good to firm and heavy going: wears headgear: front runner/races prominently: fair hurdler. *Charlie Longsdon*

ZARI 3 b.f. Azamour (IRE) 130 – Epiphany 81 (Zafonic (USA) 130) [2015 81p: p8g Jul 2] **–** fairly useful winner in 2014: well held on handicap debut only outing in 2015: best effort at 7f. *Roger Varian*

Leopardstown 2000 Guineas Trial, Leopardstown—
the highly-touted Zawraq looks very promising as he easily lands this listed race from
Endless Drama on his reappearance; unfortunately, a crack to his off-fore cannon bone whilst being
prepared for the Derby results in his missing the rest of the season

ZARIA 4 b.f. Tomba 119 – Princess Zara (Reprimand 122) [2015 43: t7.1f⁴ t7.1g⁵ 7d⁵ **62** 8.3m⁵ 7m 8.3g² t8.6g⁶ 7.1m* 8.1g* 8.1d* 8d⁵ 8.3g⁵ 8v⁴ Oct 6] modest handicapper: won at Chepstow in July and August (twice): stays 8.5f: acts on good to firm and good to soft going: in headgear nowadays. *Richard Price*

ZARLIMAN (IRE) 5 ch.g. Zamindar (USA) 116 – Zarlana (IRE) (Darshaan 133) [2015 **59** 70: p8g p10.7m⁶ p10.7g³ p10.7g⁵ p10.7g⁴ t9.5f t8.6f Dec 21] modest maiden: stays 10.5f: acts on polytrack: often in blinkers/tongue tie in 2015: often races prominently. *Denis Hogan, Ireland*

ZAROSA (IRE) 6 b.m. Barathea (IRE) 127 – Shantalla Peak (IRE) 68 (Darshaan 133) **–** [2015 63: 13.8v⁶ 14.1v⁵ Nov 3] modest handicapper: stays 17f: raced only on good going or softer on turf: often races prominently. *John Berry*

ZARWAAN 4 b.g. Dutch Art 126 – Develyn (Pivotal 124) [2015 111: 8d⁶ 7m 7m* 7g⁵ 7d **113** 7g² 7g* Oct 3] smart performer: won handicap at Newcastle (by head from Lulu The Zulu) in June and listed race at Redcar (by ¾ length from So Beloved) in October: stays 1m: acts on firm and soft going: sent to UAE. *Ed Dunlop*

ZAT BE ZAT 8 b.g. Sampower Star 118 – Blakeshall Girl 64 (Piccolo 121) [2015 –: f6d Feb 10] has shown little in maidens/handicap. *Violet M. Jordan*

ZAUFFALY (FR) 2 ch.g. (Feb 25) Zoffany (IRE) 121 – Lady Sadowa (Nayef (USA) 129) **71** [2015 t7.1f t7.1f² p7g² p8f⁵ Dec 21] fair form in maidens, second at Wolverhampton and Chelmsford: should stay 1m. *Ed Dunlop*

ZAWRAQ (IRE) 3 b.c. Shamardal (USA) 129 – Sundus (USA) 80 (Sadler's Wells (USA) **116** 132) [2015 98p: 8v* Apr 12] smart form: won maiden only start at 2 yrs: 11/8, impressive when successful in 7-runner Leopardstown 2000 Guineas Trial at Leopardstown on reappearance, quickening to lead 2f out and beating Endless Drama by 3½ lengths: bred to stay at least 1¼m: second favourite for Derby at Epsom when reported in early-June to have suffered crack in off-fore cannon bone, and missed rest of year. *D. K. Weld, Ireland*

ZAZA ZEST (IRE) 3 ch.f. Approve (IRE) 112 – Happy Talk (IRE) 74 (Hamas (IRE) 125) **76** [2015 71: 8d⁶ 8g³ 7.5m³ 7s* Oct 13] fair performer: won seller at Leicester in October: stays 7.5f: acts on fibresand, soft and good to firm going. *Richard Fahey*

ZEALOUS (IRE) 2 br.g. (Mar 20) Intense Focus (USA) 117 – Velvet Kiss (IRE) (Danehill **83 p** Dancer (IRE) 117) [2015 7.2m 7.9m⁴ 7.2g⁴ 7d* Oct 16] €47,000F, £25,000Y: second foal: half-brother to 10.4f winner Witty Repartee (by Iffraaj): dam 1m winner: fairly useful performer: won nursery at Haydock (by 2½ lengths from Burningfivers) in October: will be suited by 1m+: will go on improving. *Alan Swinbank*

ZEBADIAH (IRE) 2 b.c. (May 9) Zebedee 113 – Kiva (Indian Ridge 123) [2015 6m 7g² **81** 7g* 7g⁶ Aug 29] £35,000F, £140,000Y: smallish colt: half-brother to several winners, including useful 5f (including at 2 yrs) winner Annie Beach (by Redback) and winner up to 6f Cruise Tothelimit (2-y-o 6f winner, by Le Vie dei Colori): dam unraced: fairly useful performer: won maiden at Newbury (by head from Equistar) in July: stays 7f. *Richard Hannon*

ZEBEAD (IRE) 3 gr.c. Zebedee 113 – Sinead (USA) (Irish River (FR) 131) [2015 54: **47** p8m 7.6g p10g³ 11.5g Jul 15] poor maiden: stays 1¼m: acts on polytrack: usually slowly away. *William Jarvis*

ZEBEDEE'S GIRL (IRE) 2 gr.f. (Apr 25) Zebedee 113 – Rafelite 67 (Fraam 114) [2015 **54** 5.1f² 6m⁶ 5g⁶ t6m⁵ Dec 18] €4,000F, €50,000 2-y-o: third foal: half-sister to 2-y-o 5f winner Wolfofwallstreet (by Bushranger): dam maiden half-sister to smart 1¼m-1¾m winner Tartouche: modest maiden: best effort at 5f. *David Evans*

ZEBEDEE'S SON (IRE) 2 gr.g. (Apr 12) Zebedee 113 – Lady Ginevra (IRE) (Touch of **61** The Blues (FR) 125) [2015 6d 6m t6g⁵ p8g⁴ 10.2f² 10.2g p10f Oct 22] rather unfurnished gelding: modest maiden: stays 1¼m: acts on firm and good to soft going: tried in visor: often races lazily. *David Evans*

ZEBELINI (IRE) 3 gr.f. Zebedee 113 – Ma Nikitia (IRE) (Camacho 118) [2015 70: 5g⁶ **60** 5g⁵ 5.1g 5m³ 5m⁶ 5m⁵ t6f Oct 23] modest handicapper: stays 6f: acts on tapeta, soft and good to firm going: in hood last 2 starts: front runner/races prominently. *Ollie Pears*

ZEBELLA 3 b.f. Paco Boy (IRE) 129 – Delittmé (IRE) (Val Royal (FR) 127) [2015 53: 9m 7m p8g Jun 18] sturdy filly: maiden: no form in 2015: tried in cheekpieces. *Rod Millman*

ZEBGREY (IRE) 2 gr.f. (Apr 8) Zebedee 113 – Lear's Crown (USA) 82 (Lear Fan (USA) **72** 130) [2015 5m⁵ 6g³ 5g⁴ 5d³ 6g 5m p6g⁴ p5f⁴ Oct 24] €12,000F, €20,000Y: half-sister to several winners, including winner up to 1m Howya Now Kid (2-y-o 5f/6f winner, by Daggers Drawn) and 2-y-o 6f winner Byronic (by Byron), both useful: dam 1½m winner: fair maiden: best effort at 5f: acts on good to firm going: tried in hood: front runner/races prominently. *Adrian McGuinness, Ireland*

ZEB'S FANTASY (IRE) 2 b.f. (Feb 15) Zebedee 113 – Fantastic Cee (IRE) 71 (Noverre **75** (USA) 125) [2015 7.2m² 5m² 6d³ 7d Sep 11] €17,000 2-y-o: fourth foal: half-sister to 1¼m-11f winner (stays 1½m) Pixie Cut (by Chineur): dam, 7f winner, half-sister to useful 2-y-o 6f winner Yajbill: fair maiden: best effort at 7f. *Ross O'Sullivan, Ireland*

ZEBS LAD (IRE) 3 ro.g. Zebedee 113 – Dubai Princess (IRE) 105 (Dubai Destination **61** (USA) 127) [2015 77, a68: p6m³ p5m* p6f⁴ f5g⁶ t6g 5m 5g⁶ t6g⁵ 5g⁴ 5.1m 5m⁵ 5.3g⁵ 5.1d³ **a71** 5s⁴ 6g 6v² 6s⁵ 15.1f⁴ t6f⁴ t6f* t6g³ t6m⁵ p6m Dec 31] lengthy gelding: fair handicapper: won at Kempton in February and Wolverhampton (apprentice) in November: left Ronald Harris after fourteenth start: stays 6f: acts on polytrack and tapeta: usually wears headgear: tried in tongue tie in 2015: sometimes slowly away. *Nikki Evans*

ZEBSTAR (IRE) 2 b.c. (Apr 15) Zebedee 113 – Zinstar (IRE) (Sinndar (IRE) 134) [2015 **97** 5f* 6g⁶ 6d⁴ 5s³ 5g Oct 9] €3,500Y, resold €16,000Y, £37,000 2-y-o: sturdy colt: sixth foal: half-brother to useful 7f/1m winner (stayed 1¼m) Sinfonico (by Iffraaj) and 5f-7f winner Smokethatthunders (by Elusive City): dam unraced half-sister to smart 7f-1¼m winner (stayed 1½m) Bustan: useful performer: won maiden at Newmarket in May: better form next 3 starts (very stiff tasks first 2), third of 7 in minor event at Longchamp on last occasion: stays 6f. *Gay Kelleway*

ZEB UN NISA 3 b.f. Iffraaj 127 – Tullynally (Dansili 127) [2015 88: 5d² 5m⁴ 5g⁵ 5m p5g **96** Oct 23] angular filly: useful performer: second in handicap at Sandown (2¼ lengths behind Waady) in April: raced mainly at 5f: acts on polytrack, good to firm and good to soft going. *Roger Charlton*

ZED CANDY GIRL 5 ch.m. Sakhee's Secret 128 – Musical Twist (USA) 97 (Woodman **69** (USA) 126) [2015 73: t7.1g⁶ t7.1g* 8.1m⁵ t7.1g³ p8g 7s⁵ t7.1f⁴ t7.1f⁵ t8.6f³ t7.1g³ t7.1f⁴ Dec 22] lengthy mare: fair handicapper: won at Wolverhampton in June: stays 8.5f: acts on polytrack, tapeta and soft going: usually wears cheekpieces: often races in rear. *Daniel Loughnane*

ZEEBEE (IRE) 2 gr.f. (Apr 6) Zebedee 113 – Etta Place 56 (Hawk Wing (USA) 136) **55** [2015 5m 6.1g⁵ p5f⁵ p6g Sep 22] first foal: dam maiden half-sister to useful performer up to 2m Blue Surf: modest maiden: best effort at 5f. *Lady Cecil*

ZEEDA (IRE) 2 b.f. (Mar 4) Zebedee 113 – Beau Petite (Kyllachy 129) [2015 5d⁴ 5m⁵ 5g³ **68** 5m⁵ 5m² 5d³ 5d³ 5m Sep 27] €9,000Y: fourth foal: half-sister to 5f winner Howyadoing-notsobad (by Kodiac): dam once-raced half-sister to smart winner up to 6f Smokin Beau: fair maiden: raced only at 5f: acts on good to firm and good to soft going: usually in tongue tie: usually races close up: sold 4,000 gns, sent to France. *Tim Easterby*

ZEEHAN 2 gr.f. (Feb 11) Aussie Rules (USA) 123 – Cross Current (Sakhee (USA) 136) **58 p** [2015 t7.1m⁵ Dec 18] 9,000Y: third foal: half-sister to 1½m winner Verismo (by Hurricane Run): dam unraced: fair form: 9/2, green when 5 lengths fifth of 11 to Outback Blue in maiden at Wolverhampton on debut, shaping well: will be suited by 1m+: sure to improve. *Clive Cox*

ZEEONEANDONLY (IRE) 2 b.f. (Jan 17) Zebedee 113 – Subtle Shimmer 95 (Danehill **80** Dancer (IRE) 117) [2015 5m 5.2m⁴ 6m² 6m³ 5g⁴ 5.7m* 5m⁶ 6.3d³ 6d* 5.5d 6s⁶ 7v 6v t6g⁶ **a74** f5g³ p6g* p7m⁶ Dec 31] €24,000Y: close-coupled filly: fourth foal: half-sister to 1m winner Schimea (by Footstepsinthesand): dam, 6f/7f winner, sister to useful winner up to 9f Mister Tee: fairly useful performer: won maiden at Bath in July, nursery at Leicester in September and claimer at Lingfield in December: stays 6.5f: acts on polytrack, fibresand, soft and good to firm going: usually in headgear: front runner/races prominently. *David Evans*

ZE KING 6 b.g. Manduro (GER) 135 – Top Flight Queen 82 (Mark of Esteem (IRE) 137) **72 §** [2015 78: p11m⁶ p10f⁵ p10f⁴ t8.6g³ p8g* 8.3m t12.2g⁶ t8.6f Nov 20] unfurnished gelding: fair handicapper: won at Kempton (apprentice) in June: left Chris Wall after sixth start: stays 1½m: acts on polytrack and tapeta: not straightforward. *Donald McCain*

ZENAFIRE 6 b.g. Firebreak 125 – Zen Garden (Alzao (USA) 117) [2015 11.9f 16g 15 9m **72** 12.1m⁵ 11.9d⁷ 11.7g² 14.1v* Nov 3] fair handicapper: won at Redcar in November: stays 2m: acts on good to firm and heavy going: usually wears cheekpieces. *Sarah Hollinshead*

ZEPHYR BREEZE 2 b.g. (Apr 9) Piccolo 121 – Bold Love 47 (Bold Edge 123) [2015 **66** 5v⁴ Apr 3] 50/1, fourth of 6 to Tribesman in minor event at Musselburgh on debut, never a threat. *Noel Wilson*

ZESHOV (IRE) 4 b.g. Acclamation 118 – Fathoming (USA) (Gulch (USA)) [2015 –: 7g⁴ **79** 7m* 7g p7g p8m⁵ Oct 21] angular gelding: fair handicapper: won at Newmarket (awarded race) in July: stays 1m: acts on polytrack and good to firm going: usually wears headgear: usually races towards rear. *Jeremy Noseda*

ZEST (IRE) 2 b.f. (Jan 24) Duke of Marmalade (IRE) 132 – Affinity 76 (Sadler's Wells **86 p** (USA) 132) [2015 8d² 8d* Oct 23] second foal: dam, 1½m winner, half-sister to high-class winner up to 1m Soviet Song: 4/9, progressed from debut when winning 11-runner maiden at Doncaster by ¾ length from Very Dashing, leading on bridle 2f out despite pulling hard: likely to stay 1¼m: open to further improvement. *James Fanshawe*

ZETEAH 5 b.m. Passing Glance 119 – Ajeebah (IRE) (Mujtahid (USA) 118) [2015 52: **57** 9.9s⁵ t8.6g⁴ 8.3g 8g* 8 1d³ t8.6m² 7s Oct 12] good-topped filly: modest handicapper: won at Salisbury in August: stays 8.5f: acts on tapeta and good to soft going: in tongue tie in 2015. *Tony Carroll*

ZHUI FENG (IRE) 2 b.c. (Feb 5) Invincible Spirit (IRE) 121 – Es Que (Inchinor 119) **96** [2015 6m⁶ p6d* 6g* 7m³ Oct 3] 235,000F, 340,000Y: good-bodied colt: fifth foal: half-brother to 3 winners, including very smart winner up to 1½m Dominant (2-y-o 7f winner, by Cacique) and smart winner up to 1m Es Que Love (2-y-o 5f winner, by Clodovil): dam 7.5f winner who stayed 1¼m: useful form: won maiden at Kempton and valuable sales race at Newmarket (by 1¼ lengths from Hillside Dream) in September: creditable 5 lengths third of 14 to Gifted Master in valuable sales race at Newmarket final start: stays 7f. *Amanda Perrett*

ZIFENA 3 b.f. Zamindar (USA) 116 – Luminous Gold 82 (Fantastic Light (USA) 134) **–** [2015 93: 7m Sep 10] fairly useful performer: off a year, out of depth (tailed-off last) in Sceptre Stakes at Doncaster on return: will prove best at sprint trips: acts on firm going: sold 55,000 gns in December, sent to USA. *Jo Davis*

ZIGGERT (IRE) 3 b.g. High Chaparral (IRE) 132 – Billet (IRE) 93 (Danehill (USA) 126) **69** [2015 8m 9.8d⁵ 10m 10.3m⁵ Jun 26] rather unfurnished gelding: fair form at best in maidens/handicap: takes strong hold: has been gelded. *Mick Channon*

ZIGGURAT (IRE) 3 gr.c. Tagula (IRE) 116 – Visual Element (USA) 47 (Distant View **53 p** (USA) 126) [2015 7m Jun 9] £48,000Y: first foal: dam twice-raced half-sister to 1m winner (stayed 1¼m) Enforce and 7f/1m winner Forceful Appeal, both useful: 9/1 and in tongue tie, 8 lengths seventh of 12 to Sirheed in maiden at Salisbury, running green and not unduly punished: entitled to do better. *Hugo Palmer*

ZIGGYS STAR 3 b.g. Compton Place 125 – Ziggy Zaggy (Diktat 126) [2015 t7.1f² t7.1f⁴ **80** t8.6f 8d² 8.3m 10.2m⁶ t7.1f⁶ p7f* Dec 21] 20,000F: sixth foal: half-brother to 7f winner Cheers (by Haafhd) and winner up to 7f Ziggy's Secret (2-y-o 5f winner, by Sakhee's Secret): dam unraced half-sister to very smart winner up to 1½m Imperial Dancer: fairly useful handicapper: in hood, won at Chelmsford in December: stays 1m: acts on polytrack, tapeta and good to soft going: sometimes slowly away. *Michael Appleby*

ZINGIBER 3 ch.g. Manduro (GER) 135 – Titoli di Coda (IRE) (Bertolini (USA) 125) **–** [2015 –: p10g⁴ 9.3g⁴ Jun 15] lengthy, angular gelding: well held in maidens: left Noel Quinlan after first start: tried in hood. *Wilf Storey*

ZINNOBAR 5 gr.m. Ishiguru (USA) 114 – Demolition Jo 89 (Petong 126) [2015 56, a70: **57**
p12m⁴ p13g Jan 21] rather leggy mare: modest handicapper: stays 13f: acts on polytrack,
tapeta, soft and good to firm going: usually wears cheekpieces: front runner/races
prominently: sent to Belgium, where won at 14.2f at Mons in June. *Jonathan Portman*

ZIO GIANNI (USA) 2 b.c. (May 14) Lemon Drop Kid (USA) 131 – August Storm (USA) **74**
(Storm Creek (USA)) [2015 t7.1g⁵ p7g² f7g³ p8g² p7g³ Dec 10] fair maiden: stays 1m: acts
on polytrack and fibresand: sometimes slowly away. *Jamie Osborne*

ZIPEDEEDODAH (IRE) 3 gr.g. Zebedee 113 – Beverley Macca 73 (Piccolo 121) [2015 **77**
74: p6f p5g p5g* f5g Dec 29] compact gelding: fair handicapper: won at Lingfield in
December: best form at 5f: acts on polytrack. *Joseph Tuite*

ZIPPY 2 b.f. (May 11) Hellvelyn 118 – Ziggy Zaggy (Diktat 126) [2015 6s² Oct 26] seventh **65 p**
foal: half-sister to 7f winners Cheers (by Haafhd) and Ziggy's Star (by Compton Place) and
winner up to 7f Ziggy's Secret (2-y-o 5f winner, by Sakhee's Secret): dam unraced half-
sister to very smart winner up to 1½m Imperial Dancer: 4/1, green and shaped with
encouragement when 2½ lengths second of 12 to Flowing Clarets in maiden at Leicester,
staying on and never nearer: capable of better. *Daniel Kubler*

ZIP WIRE (IRE) 6 b.g. Oratorio (IRE) 128 – Jaya (USA) (Ela-Mana-Mou 132) [2015 –: **52**
f12g t13.9f f16g⁴ Dec 29] modest maiden: stays 13f: acts on soft going: sometimes in
cheekpieces in 2015. *Donald McCain*

ZLATAN (IRE) 2 b.g. (Apr 18) Dark Angel (IRE) 113 – Guard Hill (USA) 87 (Rahy **62**
(USA) 115) [2015 6d 7g 6m⁶ 7s³ 7s⁶ p8f 7d Oct 16] sturdy gelding: modest maiden: stays
7f: acts on soft and good to firm going: tried in cheekpieces. *Ed de Giles*

ZMAN AWAL (IRE) 4 ch.f. Dubawi (IRE) 129 – Pivotal Lady (Pivotal 124) [2015 90: **81**
p7m³ Jan 9] good-topped filly: fairly useful handicapper: acts on polytrack and tapeta:
often travels strongly: sold 47,000 gns, sent to Qatar, where won handicap and minor event
at 9f at Doha in April/May. *James Fanshawe*

ZODIAKOS (IRE) 2 b.g. (Feb 9) Kodiac 112 – Zonic 59 (Zafonic (USA) 130) [2015 **91**
7.1m* 8s⁶ p8g² Sep 30] €13,500F, 15,000Y: fifth foal: half-brother to 2-y-o 5f winner
(stayed 1m) Tarita (by Bahamian Bounty) and useful 1m winner Newbury Hall (by Marju):
dam maiden (stayed 7f): fairly useful form: won maiden at Sandown in July by 4½ lengths
from Henry The Explorer: best effort when ¾-length second of 5 to Pure Diamond in minor
event at Kempton final start: stays 1m: has been gelded. *Hugo Palmer*

ZOELLA (USA) 3 b.f. Invincible Spirit (IRE) 121 – Zaeema 93 (Zafonic (USA) 130) **85**
[2015 p8g* 8g⁵ 8.3m Jun 3] sturdy filly: closely related to useful 6f/7f winner Barq (by
Green Desert) and half-sister to several winners, including smart 7f/1m winner Zibelina
(by Dansili) and useful 2-y-o 5.7f/6f winner Floristry (by Fasliyev): dam 2-y-o 7f winner:
fairly useful performer: won maiden at Lingfield in February on debut: best effort when
fifth in handicap at Goodwood next start: raced at 1m: in hood first outing. *Charlie Appleby*

ZOFFANYS PRIDE (IRE) 2 b.c. (Mar 9) Zoffany (IRE) 121 – Lioness 74 (Lion Cavern **80 p**
(USA) 117) [2015 8.3s 8.3s* Oct 28] €10,000Y, €45,000 2-y-o: seventh foal: half-brother
to 3 winners, including useful winner up to 1¼m Mountain Pride (2-y-o 8.3f winner, by
High Chaparral) and 6f-7f winner Wilford Maverick (by Fasliyev): dam maiden half-sister
to smart 7f-11f winner Puppeteer: 7/1, much improved from debut when winning 7-runner
maiden at Nottingham by 4½ lengths from So Celebre, smooth headway and storming clear
1f out: will go on improving. *Andrew Balding*

ZOFFANY'S WAY (IRE) 2 gr.g. (Apr 17) Zoffany (IRE) 121 – Enchanting Way **71**
(Linamix (FR) 127) [2015 6d t8.6f⁵ p7g⁴ p7g p7g Nov 13] fair form in maidens second/third
starts: well held in nursery final outing: stays 8.5f. *James Fanshawe*

ZONDERLAND 2 ch.c. (Feb 21) Dutch Art 126 – Barynya 77 (Pivotal 124) [2015 p7g* **103**
7g⁴ 7v⁵ Oct 24] 70,000Y: third foal: half-brother to useful 1½m winner Osipova (by
Makfi): dam, maiden (stayed 1m), half-sister to useful 7f/1m winner Russian Realm out of
1000 Guineas winner Russian Rhythm: useful form: won 5-runner minor event at Kempton
in September by 5 lengths from Gold Trade: ran creditably both subsequent starts, 1½
lengths fourth of 6 to Sanus Per Aquam in Somerville Tattersall Stakes at Newmarket and
1½ lengths fifth of 9 to Crazy Horse in Horris Hill Stakes at Newbury: raced only at 7f.
Clive Cox

ZOORAWAR 3 b.c. Excellent Art 125 – Sylvan Ride (Fantastic Light (USA) 134) [2015 **67**
10m p10g p12g Jun 4] fair maiden: best effort when seventh of 14 at Kempton on final
start: sent to Morocco. *Charlie Fellowes*

ZOPHILLY (IRE) 2 b.f. (Feb 22) Zoffany (IRE) 121 – Extreme Pleasure (IRE) 72 (High **60**
Chaparral (IRE) 132) [2015 p6g⁶ t6f⁵ p6g Dec 2] 20,000 2-y-o: third foal: dam maiden,
half-sister to 1¼m-2m winner (stayed 2½m) Warm Feeling and winner up to 1¼m (stayed
1½m) Precede, both smart: modest form at best in maidens. *Jeremy Gask*

ZORAIDA (IRE) 2 b.f. (Jan 16) Zebedee 113 – Derval (IRE) (One Cool Cat (USA) 123) **66**
[2015 5m³ 5m⁶ 5m³ 5s⁵ 5m⁵ 5m* 5m³ 5g⁵ p6g⁴ Oct 7] £25,000Y: second foal: dam, of little
account, half-sister to winner up to 1m Sacred Nuts and winner up to 8.5f Them And Us,
both useful: fair performer: won nursery at Musselburgh in July: best at 5f: acts on good to
firm going: sold 4,000 gns, sent to Italy. *Keith Dalgleish*

ZRUDA 4 b.f. Observatory (USA) 131 – Pagan Princess 54 (Mujtahid (USA) 118) [2015 **49**
f8d 8m 7g 8d 10m³ 10g⁵ 12.2g⁶ 10.1g 11.5s 14.1v⁶ Nov 3] sixth foal: half-sister to 9.5f
winner At Wits End (by Orpen): dam maiden half-sister to useful 1½m-1¾m winner
Hambleden: poor maiden: stays 1¼m: acts on good to firm going. *David Thompson*

ZUBAIDAH 3 b.f. Exceed And Excel (AUS) 126 – Bedouin Bride (USA) (Chester House **69**
(USA) 123) [2015 68: p7f 8m⁵ t8.6g⁴ t8.6g³ p8g² 10.2f² 11.7m⁴ 10g 9.9m² 10.2s³ 10s³
p10g⁴ p10m t9.5g⁵ f8g⁶ Dec 18] lengthy filly: fair maiden: left George Baker after eleventh
start: stays 11.5f: acts on polytrack, tapeta, firm and soft going: usually in headgear in
2015: races prominently. *Heather Dalton*

ZUBEIDA 2 b.f. (Apr 9) Authorized (IRE) 133 – Tegwen (USA) 79 (Nijinsky (CAN) 138) **60**
[2015 7.5m 7v⁵ Oct 17] half-sister to several winners, including useful 2-y-o 6f-1m winner
(stayed 1½m) Teggiano (by Mujtahid) and useful 1m-1¼m winner Halawellfin Hala (by
Kris): dam 11f winner who stayed 1¾m: 100/1, improved from debut when 4¾ lengths fifth
of 12 to Sunnua in maiden at Catterick: should prove suited by 1m+. *Ismail Mohammed*

ZUBOON (IRE) 3 b.g. Dansili 127 – Tabassum (IRE) 111 (Nayef (USA) 129) [2015 5d **–**
7.9g⁶ 6s Jul 29] modest form when fifth in maiden at Tours, only outing at 2 yrs: left
J. E. Hammond, last in maidens/handicap in Britain in 2015. *Patrick Holmes*

ZUGZWANG (IRE) 4 b.g. Kodiac 112 – Kris's Bank (Inchinor 119) [2015 90: t7.1m⁵ **95**
p8m⁵ 10.2f* 10m² 8.5g 8m 10.3m³ Jul 18] sturdy gelding: useful handicapper: won at Bath
in April: good second at Newmarket (head behind Amood) in May and creditable third at
Chester (4 lengths behind Racing History) in July: stays 10.5f: acts on polytrack and firm
going: in cheekpieces final start. *Ed de Giles*

ZUHOOR BAYNOONA (IRE) 3 b.f. Elnadim (USA) 128 – Spasha (Shamardal (USA) **94**
129) [2015 96: 5f* 5m⁵ 5m⁵ 6m⁴ 5d Sep 26] quite attractive filly: useful performer: won
listed race at Bath in April by length from Holley Berry at Ascot: stays 6f: acts on firm and good
to soft going: often travels strongly. *Richard Fahey*

ZURIGHA (IRE) 5 b.m. Cape Cross (IRE) 129 – Noyelles (IRE) (Docksider (USA) 124) **107**
[2015 108: 8.9g 8g² 8.9g³ Feb 19] rangy mare: useful performer: creditable efforts at
Meydan in 2015, including when placed behind Cladocera in Cape Verdi (2 lengths
second) and Balanchine (2¾ lengths third): barely stays 9f: acts on polytrack, good to firm
and good to soft going. *Richard Hannon*

ZUZINIA (IRE) 3 b.f. Mujadil (USA) 119 – Sinegronto (IRE) (Kheleyf (USA) 116) [2015 **73**
73: 5.7f⁴ 6m⁴ 6v⁴ 5g⁵ 5f* 6g⁵ 5.3s Oct 15] fair handicapper: won at Bath in September:
stays 6f: acts on any turf going: tried in visor in 2015: often starts slowly/races towards
rear. *Mick Channon*

ZZORO (IRE) 2 b.c. (Apr 8) Manduro (GER) 135 – Krynica (USA) 80 (Danzig (USA)) **87**
[2015 p7g 7m 8g³ t8.6f* Oct 13] 24,000Y: fifth foal: half-brother to 1m winner (stayed
1¼m) Songburst (by Singspiel): dam, 2-y-o 6f winner, half-sister to high-class winner up
to 9f Phoenix Tower out of useful 2-y-o 7f winner Bionic: fairly useful performer: won
maiden at Wolverhampton in October: had left Clive Brittain after previous start: stays
8.5f. *Charles Hills*

1118

SELECTED BIG RACES 2015

Prize money for racing abroad has been converted to £ sterling at the exchange rate current at the time of the race. The figures are correct to the nearest £. The Timeform ratings (TR) recorded by the principals in each race appear on the last line.

MEYDAN Saturday, Mar 28 Turf course: GOOD Dirt course: FAST

1	**Al Quoz Sprint Empowered by IPIC (Gr 1) (3yo+)** £405,405	4f214y (Turf)		
	SOLE POWER *EdwardLynam,Ireland* 8-9-0 RichardHughes (7)	11/2		1
	PENIAPHOBIA (IRE) *A.S.Cruz,HongKong* 4-9-0 (s+t) DouglasWhyte (16)	4/1f	½	2
	GREEN MASK (USA) *WesleyA.Ward,USA* 4-9-0 FrankieDettori (1)	33/1	½	3
	Amber Sky (AUS) *P.F.Yiu,HongKong* 6-9-0 (t) RyanMoore (10)	8/1	1	4
	Bundle of Joy (AUS) *D.J.Hall,HongKong* 6-9-0 JoaoMoreira (2)	8/1	nk	5
	Sir Maximilian (IRE) *IanWilliams,GB* 6-9-0 KierenFallon (6)	22/1	2	6
	Farmah (USA) *FrancoisRohaut,France* 4-8-10 PaulHanagan (5)	16/1	ns	7
	Ahtoug *CharlieAppleby,GB* 7-9-0 (s) WilliamBuick (13)	7/1	nk	8
	Stepper Point *WilliamMuir,GB* 6-9-0 (s) MartinDwyer (9)	20/1	hd	9
	Caspar Netscher *DavidSimcock,GB* 6-9-0 AndrewMullen (11)	20/1	¾	10
	Via Africa (SAF) *M.F.deKock,SouthAfrica* 6-8-10 ChristopheSoumillon (4)	12/1	1¼	11
	Mirza *RaeGuest,GB* 8-9-0 (s) JamesDoyle (8)	33/1	½	12
	Distinctiv Passion (USA) *JeffBonde,USA* 5-9-0 (b+t) EdwinA.Maldonado (14)	20/1	2¾	13
	Caspian Prince (IRE) *TonyCarroll,GB* 6-9-0 (s+h+t) AdamKirby (12)	20/1	1	14
	Hototo *FawziAbdullaNass,Bahrain* 5-9-0 (v) LukeMorris (3)	28/1	2	15
	Lancelot du Lac (ITY) *DeanIvory,GB* 5-9-0 JimCrowley (15)	33/1	16	16
	Mrs S. Power 16ran 57.24secs	123/121/119/115/114/105		
2	**Dubai Golden Shaheen Sponsored by Gulf News (Gr 1) (3yo+)** £810,811	5f212y (Dirt)		
	SECRET CIRCLE (USA) *BobBaffert,USA* 6-9-0 (b) VictorEspinoza (7)	10/3		1
	SUPER JOCKEY (NZ) *A.T.Millard,HongKong* 7-9-0 RyanMoore (12)	20/1	hd	2
	RICH TAPESTRY (IRE) *C.W.Chang,HongKong* 7-9-0 (b+t) OlivierDoleuze (4)	5/1	1¼	3
	El Padrino (NZ) *H.W.Tan,Singapore* 7-9-0 (b+t) OscarChavez (11)	40/1	½	4
	Big Macher (USA) *RichardBaltas,USA* 5-9-0 (b+t) JoelRosario (6)	14/1	¾	5
	Cool Cowboy (USA) *D.Watson,UAE* 4-9-0 PatDobbs (13)	16/1	2¼	6
	Speed Hawk (USA) *RobertCowell,GB* 4-9-0 (s) AndreaAtzeni (2)	22/1	nk	7
	Salutos Amigos (USA) *DavidJacobson,USA* 5-9-0 (b) CornelioH.Velasquez (5)	3/1f	½	8
	United Color (USA) *D.J.Selvaratnam,UAE* 6-9-0 (b+t) OisinMurphy (9)	22/1	nk	9
	Shaishee (USA) *M.AlMuhairi,UAE* 5-9-0 (v) PaulHanagan (10)	22/1	nk	10
	Lucky Nine (IRE) *C.Fownes,HongKong* 8-9-0 (h+b+t) BrettPrebble (8)	7/1	¾	11
	Krypton Factor *FawziAbdullaNass,Bahrain* 7-9-0 (b) KierenFallon (3)	16/1	4	12
	Montiridge (IRE) *B.AlShaibani,SaudiArabia* 5-9-0 JoseLezcano (1)	20/1	7½	13
	Michael E. Pegram, K. Watson & P.Weitman 13ran 1m10.64	122/122/119/117/116/110		
3	**Dubai Turf Sponsored by DP World (Gr 1) (3yo+)** £2,432,432	1m209y (Turf)		
	SOLOW *F.Head,France* 5-9-0 MaximeGuyon (10)	9/4		1
	THE GREY GATSBY (IRE) *KevinRyan,GB* 4-9-0 RyanMoore (6)	6/4f	4¼	2
	MSHAWISH (USA) *ToddA.Pletcher,USA* 5-9-0 FrankieDettori (3)	14/1	¾	3
	Euro Charline *MarcoBotti,GB* 4-8-10 JoaoMoreira (1)	10/1	½	4
	Earnshaw (USA) *S.binGhadayer,UAE* 4-9-0 (b+t) MickaelBarzalona (4)	28/1	sh	5
	Cladocera (GER) *A.deRoyerDupre,France* 4-8-10 ChristopheSoumillon (8)	9/1	½	6
	Umgiyo (AUS) *M.F.deKock,SouthAfrica* 5-9-0 JohnnyGeroudis (2)	33/1	2½	7
	Limario (GER) *D.Watson,UAE* 5-9-0 PatDobbs (5)	50/1	1¾	8
	Farraaj (IRE) *D.J.Selvaratnam,UAE* 6-9-0 OisinMurphy (9)	20/1	3	9
	Trade Storm *DavidSimcock,GB* 7-9-0 AndreaAtzeni (7)	16/1	5	10
	Wertheimer et Frere 10ran 1m47.76	129/121/118/114/118/113		
4	**Dubai Sheema Classic Presented by Longines (Gr 1) (3yo+)** £2,432,432	1m3f216y (Turf)		
	DOLNIYA (FR) *A.deRoyerDupre,France* 4-8-8 ChristopheSoumillon (2)	7/1		1
	FLINTSHIRE *A.Fabre,France* 5-9-0 MaximeGuyon (4)	3/1	2¼	2
	ONE AND ONLY (JPN) *KojiroHashiguchi,Japan* 4-8-13 CristianDemuro (6)	16/1	2	3
	Designs On Rome (IRE) *J.Moore,HongKong* 5-9-0 JoaoMoreira (7)	5/1	½	4
	Sheikhzayedroad *DavidSimcock,GB* 6-9-0 (h) MartinLane (1)	33/1	2	5
	Just The Judge (IRE) *CharlesHills,GB* 5-8-9 AndreaAtzeni (8)	28/1	sh	6
	Main Sequence (USA) *H.GrahamMotion,USA* 6-9-0 (t) RajivMaragh (5)	9/2	ns	7
	Harp Star (JPN) *HiroyoshiMatsuda,Japan* 4-8-8 RyanMoore (9)	11/4f	2¼	8
	True Story *SaeedbinSuroor,GB* 4-8-13 (s) JamesDoyle (3)	25/1	4¼	9
	H.H. Aga Khan 9ran 2m28.21	123/123/121/119/116/111		

5 **Dubai World Cup Sponsored by Emirates Airline (Gr 1) (3yo+)** 1m1f207y (Dirt)
£4,054,054

PRINCE BISHOP (IRE) *SaeedbinSuroor,GB* 8-9-0 (v) WilliamBuick (1) 14/1			1
CALIFORNIA CHROME (USA) *ArtSherman,USA* 4-9-0 (b) VictorEspinoza (9) ... 5/4f	2¾	2
LEA (USA) *WilliamI.Mott,USA* 6-9-0 (t) JoelRosario (5)....................................... 4/1	1¼	3
Candy Boy (USA) *D.Watson,UAE* 4-9-0 (t) PatDobbs (6)................................... 25/1	5¼	4
Hokko Tarumae (JPN) *KatsuichiNishiura,Japan* 6-9-0 HideakiMiyuki (2)............ 8/1	sh	5
African Story *SaeedbinSuroor,GB* 8-9-0 JamesDoyle (3) 8/1	4	6
Long River (USA) *S.binGhadayer,UAE* 5-9-0 (b+t) MickaelBarzalona (7) 66/1	14	7
Side Glance *AndrewBalding,GB* 8-9-0 (b+es) AndreaAtzeni (4)....................... 33/1	8½	8
Epiphaneia (JPN) *KatsuhikoSumii,Japan* 5-9-0 (t) ChristopheSoumillon (8)........ 13/2	7	9

Sheikh Hamdan bin Mohammed Al Maktoum 9ran 2m03.24 126/123/120/114/113/107

NEWMARKET Saturday, May 2 GOOD to FIRM (Rowley Mile Course)

6 **Qipco 2000 Guineas Stakes (Gr 1) (1) (3yo c+f)** £282,841 1m

GLENEAGLES (IRE) *AidanO'Brien,Ireland* 3-9-0 RyanMoore (16).... ... 4/1f			1
TERRITORIES (IRE) *A.Fabre,France* 3-9-0 MickaelBarzalona (19)................ 5/1	2¼	2
IVAWOOD (IRE) *RichardHannon* 3-9-0 RichardHughes (5)............................ 10/1	¾	3
Bossy Guest (IRE) *MickChannon* 3-9-0 CharlesBishop (12)........................... 50/1	½	4
Celestial Path (IRE) *SirMarkPrescottBt* 3-9-0 LukeMorris (1)....................... 14/1	2	5
Home of The Brave (IRE) *HugoPalmer* 3-9-0 (t) JamesDoyle (17) 25/1	1½	6
Dutch Connection *CharlesHills* 3-9-0 WilliamBuick (13)............................... 25/1	¾	7
Mohcet (IRE) *RichardHannon* 3-9-0 FrankieDettori (15)................................ 20/1	sh	8
Ride Like The Wind (IRE) *F.Head,France* 3-9-0 (t) MaximeGuyon (3) 20/1	ns	9
Hail The Hero (IRE) *DavidO'Meara* 3-9-0 (t) DanielTudhope (9)................... 100/1	¾	10
Cappella Sansevero *G.M.Lyons,Ireland* 3-9-0 AndreaAtzeni (10)................. 40/1	½	11
Code Red *WilliamMuir* 3-9-0 MartinDwyer (4) 100/1	1	12
Kool Kompany (IRE) *RichardHannon* 3-9-0 PatDobbs (7)............................ 20/1	½	13
Estidhkaar (IRE) *RichardHannon* 3-9-0 PaulHanagan (6)............................ 6/1	1½	14
Intilaaq (USA) *RogerVarian* 3-9-0 DaneO'Neill (11) 8/1	1	15
Room Key *EveJohnsonHoughton* 3-9-0 JimmyFortune (8) 100/1	1	16
Glenalmond (IRE) *K.R.Burke* 3-9-0 (v) KierenFallon (18)............................ 66/1	6	17
Ol' Man River (IRE) *AidanO'Brien,Ireland* 3-9-0 JosephO'Brien (2).............. 6/1	27	18

Mr M. Tabor, D. Smith & Mrs John Magnier 18ran 1m37.55 125/119/117/116/110/106

CHURCHILL DOWNS Saturday, May 2 Dirt course: FAST

7 **Kentucky Derby Presented by Yum! Brands (Gr 1) (3yo)** £933,421 1¼m (Dirt)

AMERICAN PHAROAH (USA) *BobBaffert,USA* 3-9-0 VictorEspinoza 29/10f			1
FIRING LINE (USA) *SimonCallaghan,USA* 3-9-0 GaryL.Stevens............... 95/10	1	2
DORTMUND (USA) *BobBaffert,USA* 3-9-0 MartinGarcia 43/10	2	3
Frosted (USA) *KiaranP.McLaughlin,USA* 3-9-0 (b) JoelRosario 103/10	nk	4
Danzig Moon (CAN) *MarkE.Casse,Canada* 3-9-0 (b) JulienR.Leparoux 226/10	3¼	5
Materiality (USA) *ToddA.Pletcher,USA* 3-9-0 JavierCastellano 115/10	1¼	6
Keen Ice (USA) *DaleL.Romans,USA* 3-9-0 KentJ.Desormeaux 458/10	1	7
Mubtaahij (IRE) *M.F.deKock,SouthAfrica* 3-9-0 ChristopheSoumillon 144/10	¾	8
Itsaknockout (USA) *ToddA.Pletcher,USA* 3-9-0 LuisSaez 306/10	¾	9
Carpe Diem (USA) *ToddA.Pletcher,USA* 3-9-0 JohnR.Velazquez 77/10	¾	10
Frammento (USA) *NicholasP.Zito,USA* 3-9-0 (b) CoreyS.Nakatani 695/10	1	11
Bolo (USA) *CarlaGaines,USA* 3-9-0 RafaelBejarano 319/10	¾	12
Mr. Z (USA) *D.WayneLukas,USA* 3-9-0 RamonA.Vazquez 366/10	2¾	13
Ocho Ocho Ocho (USA) *JamesCassiday,USA* 3-9-0 ElvisTrujillo 261/10	hd	14
Far Right (USA) *RonaldE.Moquett,USA* 3-9-0 MikeE.Smith..................... 392/10	hd	15
War Story (USA) *ThomasM.Amoss,USA* 3-9-0 JosephTalamo 453/10	3½	16
Tencendur (USA) *GeorgeWeaver,USA* 3-9-0 (b) ManuelFranco 523/10	15¾	17
Upstart (USA) *RichardA.Violettejnr,USA* 3-9-0 JoseL.Ortiz 157/10	25½	18

Zayat Stables LLC 18ran 2m03.02 126/125/122/121/116/115

LONGCHAMP Sunday, May 3 SOFT

8 **Prix Ganay (Gr 1) (4yo+)** £122,443 1¼m97y

CIRRUS DES AIGLES (FR) *MmeC.Barande-Barbe,France* 9-9-2 ChristopheSoumillon 37/10			1
AL KAZEEM *RogerCharlton,GB* 7-9-2 OlivierPeslier 23/10f	1¾	2
FATE (FR) *A.deRoyerDupre,France* 5-8-13 StephanePasquier 55/10	3	3
We Are (FR) *F.Head,France* 4-8-13 ThierryJarnet 53/10	2½	4
Pollyana (IRE) *J.E.Hammond,France* 6-8-13 AntoineHamelin 14/1	1	5
Prince Gibraltar (FR) *Jean-ClaudeRouget,France* 4-9-2 Jean-BernardEyquem 7/1	¾	6
Fractional (FR) *A.Fabre,France* 6-9-2 MaximeGuyon 11/1	20	7

Mr J. C. A. Dupouy 7ran 2m18.07 128/125/116/113/110/113

NEWMARKET Sunday, May 3 FIRM (Rowley Mile Course)

9 Qipco 1000 Guineas Stakes (Gr 1) (1) (3yo f) £232,511 1m

LEGATISSIMO (IRE) *DavidWachman,Ireland* 3-9-0 RyanMoore (13)	13/2		1
LUCIDA (IRE) *J.S.Bolger,Ireland* 3-9-0 KevinManning (11)	9/2f	¾	2
TIGGY WIGGY (IRE) *RichardHannon* 3-9-0 RichardHughes (2)	9/1	4½	3
Malabar *MickChannon* 3-9-0 MartinHarley (7)	11/1	1¼	4
Fadhayyil (IRE) *B.W.Hills* 3-9-0 PaulHanagan (3)	7/1	½	5
Irish Rookie (IRE) *MartynMeade* 3-9-0 FergusSweeney (6)	20/1	1	6
Osaila (IRE) *RichardHannon* 3-9-0 FrankieDettori (9)	15/2	3	7
Queen Nefertiti (IRE) *DavidWachman,Ireland* 3-9-0 W.M.Lordan (12)	25/1	1	8
Terror (IRE) *DavidSimcock* 3-9-0 AndreaAtzeni (10)	25/1	1	9
Local Time *SaeedbinSuroor* 3-9-0 JamesDoyle (4)	16/1	7	10
Redstart *RalphBeckett* 3-9-0 PatDobbs (8)	16/1	10	11
Jellicle Ball (IRE) *JohnGosden* 3-9-0 WilliamBuick (5)	7/1	10	12
Qualify (IRE) *AidanO'Brien,Ireland* 3-9-0 JosephO'Brien (1)	12/1	¾	13

Mr M. Tabor, D. Smith & Mrs John Magnier 13ran 1m34.60 121/119/106/103/101/99

LONGCHAMP Sunday, May 10 GOOD

10 Poule d'Essai des Poulains - Prix Le Parisien (Gr 1) (3yo c) £231,081 7f210y

MAKE BELIEVE *A.Fabre,France* 3-9-2 OlivierPeslier (4)	6/1		1
NEW BAY *A.Fabre,France* 3-9-2 VincentCheminaud (5)	19/1	3	2
MR. OWEN (USA) *FrancoisRohaut,France* 3-9-2 Francois-XavierBertras (12)	11/1	1½	3
Karar *Francis-HenriGraffard,France* 3-9-2 FrankieDettori (13)	9/1	nk	4
Sir Andrew (FR) *F.PerezGonzalez,Spain* 3-9-2 Jose-LuisMartinezTejera (6)	49/1	¾	5
Highland Reel (IRE) *AidanO'Brien,Ireland* 3-9-2 RyanMoore (7)	35/10f	½	6
War Envoy (USA) *AidanO'Brien,Ireland* 3-9-2 ColmO'Donoghue (2)	23/1	sn	7
Muhaarar *CharlesHills,GB* 3-9-2 PaulHanagan (18)	16/1	½	8
Cornwallville (IRE) *Francis-HenriGraffard,France* 3-9-2 OisinMurphy (15)	57/1	¾	9
Hawke (IRE) *MmePiaBrandt,France* 3-9-2 (b) MickaelBarzalona (9)	39/1	sh	10
Flaming Spear (IRE) *KevinRyan,GB* 3-9-2 AndreaAtzeni (10)	66/1	hd	11
The Comissioner (IRE) *X.ThomasDemeaulte,France* 3-9-2 ChristopheSoumillon (17)	19/1	½	12
Tale of Life (JPN) *P.Bary,France* 3-9-2 StephanePasquier (14)	78/10	1¾	13
Maftool (USA) *SaeedbinSuroor,GB* 3-9-2 (s) DaneO'Neill (11)	10/1	hd	14
Borsakov (IRE) *MmePiaBrandt,France* 3-9-2 MaximeGuyon (1)	17/1	½	15
Mind That Boy (IRE) *Y.Durepaire,France* 3-9-2 (s) GregoryBenoist (3)	34/1	hd	16
El Suizo (FR) *H.-A.Pantall,France* 3-9-2 FabriceVeron (5)	21/1	10	17
Smaih (GER) *RichardHannon,GB* 3-9-2 Pierre-CharlesBoudot (8)	34/1	2½	18

Prince A. A. Faisal 18ran 1m36.85 120/112/108/107/106/104

11 Poule d'Essai des Pouliches (Gr 1) (3yo f) £189,066 7f210y

ERVEDYA (FR) *Jean-ClaudeRouget,France* 3-9-0 ChristopheSoumillon (12)	13/10f		1
9 IRISH ROOKIE (IRE) *MartynMeade,GB* 3-9-0 D.F.Sweeney (2)	63/1	¾	2
MEXICAN GOLD (USA) *A.Fabre,France* 3-9-0 VincentCheminaud (9)	43/10	nk	3
Fontanelice (IRE) *MmeC.Head-Maarek,France* 3-9-0 ThierryJarnet (8)	13/1	1¾	4
Qatar Dance (IRE) *G.E.Mikhalides,France* 3-9-0 TonyPiccone (3)	79/1	1	5
Ameenah (FR) *F.Rossi,France* 3-9-0 FranckBlondel (5)	26/1	hd	6
Queen Bee (FR) *E.Lellouche,France* 3-9-0 GregoryBenoist (7)	17/1	½	7
Maimara (FR) *M.Delzangles,France* 3-9-0 AlexBadel (11)	22/1	hd	8
Sainte Amarante (FR) *YvesdeNicolay,France* 3-9-0 Pierre-CharlesBoudot (4)	8/1	1	9
Soft Drink (USA) *A.Fabre,France* 3-9-0 MaximeGuyon (1)	24/1	½	10
Penorka (FR) *B.deMontzey,France* 3-9-0 OlivierPeslier (6)	28/1	hd	11
Bilissic *C.Laffon-Parias,France* 3-9-0 (b) FrankieDettori (6)	20/1	4½	12
Kenouska (FR) *P.Sogorb,France* 3-9-0 AntoineHamelin (10)	63/1	9	13
Royal Razalma (IRE) *JonathanPortman,GB* 3-9-0 AndreaAtzeni (14)	93/1	20	14

H.H. Aga Khan 14ran 1m36.48 114/112/111/107/104/104

YORK Thursday, May 14 GOOD to FIRM

12 Betfred Dante Stakes (Gr 2) (1) (3yo) £90,736 1¼m88y

GOLDEN HORN *JohnGosden* 3-9-0 WilliamBuick (2)	4/1		1
JACK HOBBS *JohnGosden* 3-9-0 FrankieDettori (8)	2/1f	2¾	2
ELM PARK *AndrewBalding* 3-9-0 AndreaAtzeni (4)	7/2	3¼	3
Nafaqa (IRE) *B.W.Hills* 3-9-0 PaulHanagan (3)	14/1	13	4
Lord Ben Stack (IRE) *K.R.Burke* 3-9-0 DanielTudhope (7)	40/1	1¾	5
6 Ol' Man River (IRE) *AidanO'Brien,Ireland* 3-9-0 JosephO'Brien (1)	11/1	¾	6
John F Kennedy (IRE) *AidanO'Brien,Ireland* 3-9-0 RyanMoore (6)	4/1	12	7

Mr A. E. Oppenheimer 7ran 2m08.74 124/118/112/85/82/80

NEWBURY Saturday, May 16   GOOD to FIRM

13   Al Shaqab Lockinge Stakes (Gr 1) (1) (4yo+) £198,485   1m

NIGHT OF THUNDER (IRE) *RichardHannon* 4-9-0 JamesDoyle (3)	11/4jf		1
TOORMORE (IRE) *RichardHannon* 4-9-0 RichardHughes (15)	10/1	nk	2
AROD (IRE) *PeterChapple-Hyam* 4-9-0 AndreaAtzeni (6)	16/1	¾	3
Integral *SirMichaelStoute* 5-8-11 RyanMoore (4)	11/4jf	nk	4
Cable Bay (IRE) *CharlesHills* 4-9-0 JamieSpencer (10)	66/1	½	5
Here Comes When (IRE) *AndrewBalding* 5-9-0 (h) JimCrowley (4)	14/1	1	6
Breton Rock (IRE) *DavidSimcock* 5-9-0 MartinLane (13)	40/1	1½	7
Aljamaaheer (IRE) *RogerVarian* 6-9-0 PaulHanagan (8)	16/1	sh	8
Custom Cut (IRE) *DavidO'Meara* 6-9-0 DanielTudhope (2)	7/1	½	9
Hors de Combat *JamesFanshawe* 4-9-0 FrederikTylicki (7)	25/1	½	10
Cougar Mountain (IRE) *AidanO'Brien,Ireland* 4-9-0 JosephO'Brien (17)	25/1	hd	11
Captain Cat (IRE) *RogerCharlton* 6-9-0 GeorgeBaker (14)	20/1	nk	12
Top Notch Tonto (IRE) *BrianEllison* 5-9-0 SilvestreDeSousa (11)	33/1	¾	13
Master Carpenter (IRE) *RodMillman* 4-9-0 SteveDrowne (16)	100/1	3¼	14
Moohaarib (IRE) *MarcoBotti* 4-9-0 MartinHarley (12)	10/1	4½	15
Yuften *WilliamHaggas* 4-9-0 FrankieDettori (18)	25/1	19	16

Godolphin 16ran 1m38.09   123/122/121/117/119/116

PIMLICO Saturday, May 16   Dirt course: SOFT

14   Xpressbet.com Preakness Stakes (Gr 1) (3yo) £584,416   1m1f110y (Dirt)

7	AMERICAN PHAROAH (USA) *BobBaffert,USA* 3-9-0 VictorEspinoza	9/10f		1
	TALE OF VERVE (USA) *DallasStewart,USA* 3-9-0 JoelRosario	285/10	7	2
	DIVINING ROD (USA) *ArnaudDelacour,USA* 3-9-0 JavierCastellano	126/10	1	3
7	Dortmund (USA) *BobBaffert,USA* 3-9-0 MartinGarcia	45/10	7½	4
7	Mr. Z (USA) *D.WayneLukas,USA* 3-9-0 CoreyS.Nakatani	164/10	1¾	5
7	Danzig Moon (CAN) *MarkE.Casse,Canada* 3-9-0 JulienR.Leparoux	134/10	1	6
7	Firing Line (USA) *SimonCallaghan,USA* 3-9-0 GaryL.Stevens	3/1	26¾	7
	Bodhisattva (USA) *JoseCorrales,USA* 3-9-0 TrevorMcCarthy	299/10	3¼	8

Zayat Stables LLC 8ran 1m58.46   126/115/114/103/100/99

CURRAGH Saturday, May 23   GOOD

15   Tattersalls Irish 2000 Guineas (Gr 1) (3yo c+f) £126,087   1m

6	GLENEAGLES (IRE) *AidanO'Brien* 3-9-0 RyanMoore (2)	2/5f		1
	ENDLESS DRAMA (IRE) *G.M.Lyons* 3-9-0 AndreaAtzeni (8)	9/1	¾	2
6	IVAWOOD (IRE) *RichardHannon,GB* 3-9-0 RichardHughes (9)	11/2	½	3
	Belardo (IRE) *RogerVarian,GB* 3-9-0 (h) JamesDoyle (7)	12/1	½	4
	Tombelaine (USA) *D.K.Weld* 3-9-0 PatSmullen (5)	12/1	2¼	5
	Mohaayed *KevinPrendergast* 3-9-0 C.D.Hayes (3)	66/1	¾	6
	Convergence (IRE) *G.M.Lyons* 3-9-0 C.T.Keane (1)	40/1	½	7
	Smuggler's Cove (IRE) *AidanO'Brien* 3-9-0 (s) SeamieHeffernan (11)	33/1	2¼	8
	Lexington Times (IRE) *RichardHannon,GB* 3-9-0 Francis-MartinBerry (4)	40/1	1	9
	The Warrior (IRE) *AidanO'Brien,GB* 3-9-0 JosephO'Brien (6)	40/1	3	10
	Carbon Dating (IRE) *JohnPatrickShanahan* 3-9-0 DeclanMcDonogh (10)	150/1	nk	11

Mr M. Tabor, Mrs John Magnier & D. Smith 11ran 1m39.30   121/119/118/116/110/108

CURRAGH Sunday, May 24   GOOD

16   Tattersalls Gold Cup (Gr 1) (4yo+) £112,319   1¼m110y

8	AL KAZEEM *RogerCharlton,GB* 7-9-3 JamesDoyle (2)	3/1		1
	FASCINATING ROCK (IRE) *D.K.Weld* 4-9-3 PatSmullen (1)	15/2	nk	2
	POSTPONED (IRE) *LucaCumani,GB* 4-9-3 AdamKirby (6)	3/1	sh	3
3	The Grey Gatsby (IRE) *KevinRyan,GB* 4-9-3 RyanMoore (5)	11/10f	1½	4
	Parish Hall (IRE) *J.S.Bolger* 6-9-3 K.J.Manning (4)	28/1	6	5
	Highly Toxic (IRE) *PatrickJ.Flynn* 4-9-3 Francis-MartinBerry (3)	200/1	5	6

Mr D. J. Deer 6ran 2m13.37   125/125/124/121/109/99

17   Tattersalls Irish 1000 Guineas (Gr 1) (3yo f) £126,087   1m

	PLEASCACH (IRE) *J.S.Bolger* 3-9-0 K.J.Manning (15)	11/2		1
	FOUND (IRE) *AidanO'Brien* 3-9-0 RyanMoore (5)	5/4f	½	2
	DEVONSHIRE (IRE) *W.McCreery* 3-9-0 JamesDoyle (4)	33/1	1½	3
	Jack Naylor *MrsJ.Harrington* 3-9-0 RichardHughes (8)	16/1	ns	4
	Bocca Baciata (IRE) *MrsJ.Harrington* 3-9-0 Francis-MartinBerry (12)	8/1	1	5
	Tamadhor (IRE) *KevinPrendergast* 3-9-0 C.D.Hayes (2)	33/1	¾	6
	Stormfly (IRE) *D.K.Weld* 3-9-0 (b) L.F.Roche (7)	33/1	½	7
9	Malabar *MickChannon,GB* 3-9-0 MartinHarley (9)	14/1	1¾	8
	Joailliere (IRE) *D.K.Weld* 3-9-0 PatSmullen (7)	10/1	nk	9
9	Qualify (IRE) *AidanO'Brien* 3-9-0 SeamieHeffernan (3)	50/1	nk	10
	Raydara (IRE) *M.Halford* 3-9-0 ShaneFoley (17)	16/1	sh	11
	Steip Amach (IRE) *J.S.Bolger* 3-9-0 (s+t) R.P.Whelan (13)	100/1	3¾	12

Plus Ca Change (IRE) *G.M.Lyons,* 3-9-0 C.T.Keane (18)......................................100/1   nk 13
Mainicin (IRE) *J.S.Bolger,* 3-9-0 R.P.Cleary (16)...200/1   2 14
Pastoral Girl *JamesGiven,GB* 3-9-0 TomEaves (6)...100/1   1¼ 15
Russian Punch *JamesGiven,GB* 3-9-0 G.Lee (11)..125/1   1 16
Kissed By Angels (IRE) *AidanO'Brien* 3-9-0 JosephO'Brien (10).....................6/1   1¾ 17
Military Angel (USA) *M.D.O'Callaghan* 3-9-0 EmmetMcNamara (14).............66/1   ½ 18
Mrs J. S. Bolger 18ran 1m39.17   114/113/109/108/106/104

LONGCHAMP Sunday, May 24   GOOD to FIRM

18 **Pour Moi Coolmore Prix Saint-Alary (Gr 1) (3yo f)** £103,514   1m1f207y
  QUEEN'S JEWEL *F.Head,France* 3-9-0 MaximeGuyon 8/10f   1
  WEKEELA (IRE) *Jean-ClaudeRouget,France* 3-9-0 Jean-BernardEyquem 20/1   3 2
  OLORDA (GER) *MichaelFigge,Germany* 3-9-0 (b) CristianDemuro 11/1   6 3
  Princess Charm (IRE) *C.&Y.Lerner,France* 3-9-0 AntoineHamelin ....18/1   sh 4
11 Qatar Dance (IRE) *G.E.Mikhalides,France* 3-9-0 MickaelBarzalona 21/1   4 5
  Olanthia (IRE) *C.Laffon-Parias,France* 3-9-0 OlivierPeslier ....20/1   nk 6
  Varana (FR) *A.deRoyerDupre,France* 3-9-0 ChristopheSoumillon 63/10   15 7
  Viroblanc (FR) *C.Rossi,France* 3-9-0 ThierryThulliez 40/1   7 8
  Raison d'Etre (FR) *FabriceVermeulen,Belgium* 3-9-0 FabriceVeron ....77/1   sh 9
  Wertheimer et Frere 9ran 2m00.87   117/110/101/101/93/93

19 **Prix d'Ispahan (Gr 1) (4yo+)** £103,514   1m1f43y
3 SOLOW *F.Head,France* 5-9-2 MaximeGuyon 6/10f   1
  GAILO CHOP (FR) *A.deWatrigant,France* 4-9-2 JulienAuge 15/1   1½ 2
  SPARKLING BEAM (IRE) *J.E.Pease,France* 5-8-13 ThierryJarnet 30/1   2 3
8 Cirrus des Aigles (FR) *MmeC.Barande-Barbe,France* 9-9-2 ChristopheSoumillon ...28/10   2 4
  Wertheimer et Frere 4ran 1m51.30   123/119/112/110

CHANTILLY Sunday, May 31   GOOD

20 **Prix du Jockey Club (Gr 1) (3yo c)** £607,872   1¼m97y
10 NEW BAY *A.Fabre,France* 3-9-2 VincentCheminaud (13)...............................32/10   1
10 HIGHLAND REEL (IRE) *AidanO'Brien,Ireland* 3-9-2 JosephO'Brien (9).........23/1   1½ 2
  WAR DISPATCH (USA) *Jean-ClaudeRouget,France* 3-9-2 IoritzMendizabal (1) ...75/10   1¾ 3
  Piment Rouge (FR) *C.Scandella,France* 3-9-2 AlexBadel (10) ....17/1   hd 4
  Sumbal (IRE) *Francis-HenriGraffard,France* 3-9-2 AndreaAtzeni (5)..............85/10   1 5
  Mostaneer (IRE) *N.Clement,France* 3-9-2 ThierryThulliez (3) ....21/1   ¾ 6
  Cape Clear Island (IRE) *AidanO'Brien,Ireland* 3-9-2 (b) RyanMoore (7)............11/1   ¾ 7
  Karaktar (IRE) *A.deRoyerDupre,France* 3-9-2 ChristopheSoumillon (12)............ 3/1f   1 8
  Silverwave (FR) *A.Couetil,France* 3-9-2 AdrienFouassier (2)............................45/10   sn 9
  Listan (IRE) *C.Ferland,France* 3-9-2 JulienAuge (14)......................................42/1   1¾ 10
  Kahouanne (FR) *A.&G.Botti,France* 3-9-2 OlivierPeslier (6) ....29/1   ½ 11
  High Dynamite (FR) *A.deWatrigant,France* 3-9-2 CristianDemuro (4) 23/1   1¼ 12
  Campione (FR) *E.Lellouche,France* 3-9-2 (h) AnthonyCrastus (11)..................52/1   12 13
10 War Envoy (USA) *AidanO'Brien,Ireland* 3-9-2 ColmO'Donoghue (8) 53/1   30 14
  Mr K. Abdullah 14ran 2m05.69   121/118/114/114/112/110

EPSOM DOWNS Friday, Jun 5   GOOD

21 **Investec Oaks (Gr 1) (1) (3yo f)** £255,195   1½m10y
17 QUALIFY (IRE) *AidanO'Brien,Ireland* 3-9-0 ColmO'Donoghue (2)...................50/1   1
 9 LEGATISSIMO (IRE) *DavidWachman,Ireland* 3-9-0 RyanMoore (1)................. 5/2f   sh 2
  LADY OF DUBAI *LucaCumani* 3-9-0 AdamKirby (11).....................................7/1   2½ 3
  Diamondsandrubies (IRE) *AidanO'Brien,Ireland* 3-9-0 SeamieHeffernan (5).....14/1   3¼ 4
  Jazzi Top *JohnGosden* 3-9-0 FrankieDettori (10)..16/1   ½ 5
17 Jack Naylor *MrsJ.Harrington,Ireland* 3-9-0 F.M.Berry (9) ....13/2   nk 6
  Together Forever (IRE) *AidanO'Brien,Ireland* 3-9-0 JosephO'Brien (4) 9/1   2¼ 7
  Al Naamah (IRE) *A.Fabre,France* 3-9-0 GregoryBenoist (3).............................11/1   15 8
  Star of Seville *JohnGosden* 3-9-0 WilliamBuick (6)...12/1   15 9
  Crystal Zvezda *SirMichaelStoute* 3-9-0 RichardHughes (8) 7/2   7 10
  Bellajeu *RalphBeckett* 3-9-0 AndreaAtzeni (7) 33/1   1 11
  Mrs C. C. Regalado-Gonzalez 11ran 2m37.41   114/114/110/105/104/103

EPSOM DOWNS Saturday, Jun 6   GOOD to FIRM

22 **Investec Coronation Cup (Gr 1) (1) (4yo+)** £212,663   1½m10y
  PETHER'S MOON (IRE) *RichardHannon* 5-9-0 PatDobbs (5).......................11/1   1
4 DOLNIYA (FR) *A.deRoyerDupre,France* 4-8-11 ChristopheSoumillon (2)......... 8/11f   nk 2
4 FLINTSHIRE *A.Fabre,France* 5-9-0 MaximeGuyon (1) 7/4   1½ 3
4 Sheikhzayedroad *DavidSimcock* 6-9-0 (h) MartinLane (6)...............................12/1   4 4
  Mr John Manley 4ran 2m33.76   121/119/118/111

23   Investec Derby (Gr 1) (1) (3yo c+f) £813,221   1½m10y

12	GOLDEN HORN *JohnGosden* 3-9-0 FrankieDettori (8)..............................13/8f	1
12	JACK HOBBS *JohnGosden* 3-9-0 WilliamBuick (10) 4/1	3½ 2
	STORM THE STARS (USA) *WilliamHaggas* 3-9-0 PatCosgrave (7)..................16/1	4½ 3
	Giovanni Canaletto (IRE) *AidanO'Brien,Ireland* 3-9-0 (s) RyanMoore (9) 6/1	2 4
	Epicuris *MmeC.Head-Maarek,France* 3-9-0 (t) ThierryThulliez (1) 20/1	1¾ 5
	Kilimanjaro (IRE) *AidanO'Brien,Ireland* 3-9-0 (h) JosephO'Brien (6)..............12/1	1¼ 6
	Hans Holbein *AidanO'Brien,Ireland* 3-9-0 (s) SeamieHeffernan (2)..................14/1	1½ 7
15	Carbon Dating (IRE) *JohnPatrickShanahan,Ireland* 3-9-0 R.P.Whelan (4) 150/1	ns 8
	Rogue Runner (GER) *A.Wohler,Germany* 3-9-0 (h) OisinMurphy (11)................50/1	5 9
6	Moheet (IRE) *RichardHannon* 3-9-0 PatDobbs (5)....................................25/1	½ 10
12	Elm Park *AndrewBalding* 3-9-0 AndreaAtzeni (3)......................................9/1	sh 11
	Success Days (IRE) *K.J.Condon,Ireland* 3-9-0 ShaneFoley (12).....................12/1	8 12

Mr A. E. Oppenheimer 12ran 2m32.32   132/124/116/113/110/107

BELMONT PARK Saturday, Jun 6 Dirt course: FAST

24   Belmont Stakes Presented by DraftKings (Gr 1) (3yo) £571,429   1½m (Dirt)

14	AMERICAN PHAROAH (USA) *BobBaffert,USA* 3-9-0 VictorEspinoza 75/100f	1
7	FROSTED (USA) *KiaranP.McLaughlin,USA* 3-9-0 (b) JoelRosario 41/10	5½ 2
7	KEEN ICE (USA) *DaleL.Romans,USA* 3-9-0 KentJ.Desormeaux 172/10	2 3
7	Mubtaahij (IRE) *M.F.deKock,SouthAfrica* 3-9-0 IradOrtiz,Jr 141/10	nk 4
7	Frammento (USA) *NicholasP.Zito,USA* 3-9-0 MikeE.Smith 217/10	7½ 5
	Madefromlucky (USA) *ToddA.Pletcher,USA* 3-9-0 JavierCastellano 146/10	2½ 6
14	Tale of Verve (USA) *DallasStewart,USA* 3-9-0 GaryL.Stevens 199/10	2¾ 7
7	Materiality (USA) *ToddA.Pletcher,USA* 3-9-0 JohnR.Velazquez 54/10	1¾ 8

Zayat Stables LLC 8ran 2m26.65   128/121/119/118/109/106

CHANTILLY Sunday, Jun 14 GOOD

25   Prix de Diane Longines (Gr 1) (3yo) £417,080   1¼m97y

21	STAR OF SEVILLE *JohnGosden,GB* 3-9-0 FrankieDettori 17/1	1
	PHYSIOCRATE (FR) *H.F.Devin,France* 3-9-0 AlexBadel 83/10	1 2
	LITTLE NIGHTINGALE (FR) *M.Delzangles,France* 3-9-0 UmbertoRispoli 13/1	¾ 3
	Desiree Clary (GER) *P.Bary,France* 3-9-0 ChristopheSoumillon 85/10	nk 4
11	Sainte Amarante (FR) *YvesdeNicolay,France* 3-9-0 Pierre-CharlesBoudot 20/1	sn 5
	Sound of Freedom (IRE) *StefanoBotti,Italy* 3-9-0 FabioBranca 28/1	1 6
	Ame Bleue *A.Fabre,France* 3-9-0 MickaelBarzalona 36/1	hd 7
	Nightflower (IRE) *P.Schiergen,Germany* 3-9-0 AndraschStarke 29/1	¾ 8
17	Malabar *MickChannon,GB* 3-9-0 RichardHughes 27/1	sn 9
11	Fontanelice (IRE) *MmeC.Head-Maarek,France* 3-9-0 ThierryJarnet 22/1	nk 10
18	Queen's Jewel (IRE) *F.Head,France* 3-9-0 MaximeGuyon 18/10f	sh 11
	Mojo Risin (IRE) *Jean-ClaudeRouget,France* 3-9-0 GregoryBenoist 48/10	¾ 12
	Absolute Blast (IRE) *F.-X.deChevigny,France* 3-9-0 JulienAuge 124/1	½ 13
	Stay The Night (USA) *Jean-ClaudeRouget,France* 3-9-0 (s) Jean-BernardEyquem ..42/1	1½ 14
	Business Lawyer (IRE) *E.Lellouche,France* 3-9-0 (h) OlivierPeslier 27/1	15 15
	Clarmina (IRE) *C.Laffon-Parias,France* 3-9-0 (b) AurelienLemaitre 54/1	1½ 16
	Moonee Valley (FR) *M.Hofer,Germany* 3-9-0 IoritzMendizabal 75/1	10 17

Lady Bamford 17ran 2m05.69   116/114/112/112/112/109

ROYAL ASCOT Tuesday, Jun 16 FIRM

26   Queen Anne Stakes (Gr 1) (1) (4yo+) £212,663   1m

19	SOLOW *F.Head,France* 5-9-0 MaximeGuyon (4)......................................11/8f	1
	ESOTERIQUE (IRE) *A.Fabre,France* 5-8-11 Pierre-CharlesBoudot (1)..............16/1	1 2
13	COUGAR MOUNTAIN (IRE) *AidanO'Brien,Ireland* 4-9-0 (s) RyanMoore (2)....16/1	nk 3
13	Toormore (IRE) *RichardHannon* 4-9-0 RichardHughes (6)..............................8/1	2 4
13	Night of Thunder (IRE) *RichardHannon* 4-9-0 JamesDoyle (5)........................4/1	1½ 5
	Able Friend (AUS) *J.Moore,HongKong* 6-9-0 (s) JoaoMoreira (7).....................11/4	4 6
	Here Comes When (IRE) *AndrewBalding* 5-9-0 (h) JimCrowley (8)..................33/1	6 7
13	Glory Awaits (IRE) *KevinRyan* 5-9-0 (b) SilvestreDeSousa (3).......................66/1	¾ 8

Wertheimer et Frere 8ran 1m37.97   126/120/123/118/114/103

27   Coventry Stakes (Gr 2) (1) (2yo) £68,052   6f

	BURATINO (IRE) *MarkJohnston* 2-9-1 WilliamBuick (10) 6/1	1
	AIR FORCE BLUE (USA) *AidanO'Brien,Ireland* 2-9-1 RyanMoore (11) 7/2	2 2
	ELTEZAM (IRE) *RichardHannon* 2-9-1 FrankieDettori (4)............................12/1	2 3
	Beaverbrook *MarkJohnston* 2-9-1 JamesDoyle (13)....................................33/1	¾ 4
	Ode To Evening *MarkJohnston* 2-9-1 JamesMcDonald (16)..........................33/1	¾ 5
	Age of Empire *RichardHannon* 2-9-1 RichardHughes (5).............................12/1	2 6
	Round Two (IRE) *J.S.Bolger,Ireland* 2-9-1 KevinManning (12) 9/4f	2¾ 7
	Young John (IRE) *RichardFahey* 2-9-1 TonyHamilton (7)..............................66/1	nk 8
	First Selection (SPA) *SimonCrisford* 2-9-1 SilvestreDeSousa (6)...................20/1	nk 9

Black Beach *J.F.Levins,Ireland* 2-9-1 G.F.Carroll (18) ....25/1 ns 10
Sign of The Kodiac (IRE) *JamesGiven* 2-9-1 TomEaves (17) ....100/1 ¾ 11
Sir Roger Moore (IRE) *CharlesHills* 2-9-1 AndreaAtzeni (1) 25/1 1¼ 12
Maccus (IRE) *BrianMeehan* 2-9-1 JimmyFortune (2) ....25/1 nk 13
Ocean Eleven *JohnRyan* 2-9-1 AdamKirby (15) ....100/1 hd 14
Destroyer *WilliamMuir* 2-9-1 MartinDwyer (8) 100/1 1¼ 15
Qeyaadah (IRE) *EdDunlop* 2-9-1 PaulHanagan (9) 20/1 3¾ 16
War Department (IRE) *WilliamHaggas* 2-9-1 TomQueally (7) 7/1 69 17
Godolphin 17ran 1m13.11 115/108/101/99/96/89

28 King's Stand Stakes (Gr 1) (1) (3yo+) £212,663   5f
GOLDREAM *RobertCowell* 6-9-4 (s) MartinHarley (3) 20/1 1
MEDICEAN MAN *JeremyGask* 9-9-4 (s+t) JoaoMoreira (1) ....50/1 sh 2
MUTHMIR (IRE) *WilliamHaggas* 5-9-4 PaulHanagan (9) ....3/1 nk 3
Pearl Secret *DavidBarron* 6-9-4 AndreaAtzeni (17) ....14/1 ½ 4
1 Sole Power *EdwardLynam,Ireland* 8-9-4 RichardHughes (6) ....5/2f ½ 5
Take Cover *DavidC.Griffiths* 8-9-4 AdamKirby (8) 33/1 2 6
Jack Dexter *JimGoldie* 6-9-4 FergalLynch (12) ....16/1 sh 7
Robot Boy (IRE) *DavidBarron* 5-9-4 GrahamGibbons (7) ....50/1 sh 8
Steps (IRE) *RogerVarian* 7-9-4 (b) JimCrowley (19) ....33/1 nk 9
1 Lancelot du Lac (ITY) *DeanIvory* 5-9-4 RobertWinston (16) ....66/1 nk 10
Rangali *H-A.Pantall,France* 4-9-4 FabriceVeron (18) 25/1 1¼ 11
Spirit Quartz (IRE) *X.Nakkachdji,France* 7-9-4 (s+t) GregoryBenoist (14) ....33/1 nk 12
Shamal Wind (AUS) *RobertSmerdon,Australia* 6-9-1 (t) RyanMoore (4) ....15/2 hd 13
Justice Day (IRE) *DavidElsworth* 4-9-4 (b) JohnEgan (5) ....50/1 ½ 14
Wind Fire (USA) *DavidBrown* 4-9-1 OisinMurphy (15) 20/1 1 15
1 Stepper Point *WilliamMuir* 6-9-4 MartinDwyer (11) ....20/1 nk 16
Hot Streak (IRE) *KevinRyan* 4-9-4 JamieSpencer (10) 18/1 3¾ 17
G Force (IRE) *DavidO'Meara* 4-9-4 PatSmullen (7) 8/1 1¾ 18
Mr J Sargeant & Mrs J Morley 18ran 59.11secs 119/119/118/116/114/105

29 St James's Palace Stakes (Gr 1) (1) (3yo c) £229,854   1m
15 GLENEAGLES (IRE) *AidanO'Brien,Ireland* 3-9-0 RyanMoore (5) 8/15f 1
LATHARNACH (USA) *CharlieAppleby* 3-9-0 WilliamBuick (3) 25/1 2½ 2
CONSORT (IRE) *SirMichaelStoute* 3-9-0 FrankieDettori (6) ....6/1 ½ 3
Aktabantay *HugoPalmer* 3-9-0 (b) JamesDoyle (2) 40/1 2¾ 4
10 Make Believe *A.Fabre,France* 3-9-0 OlivierPeslier (4) 3/1 7 5
Mr M. Tabor, D. Smith & Mrs John Magnier 5ran 1m38.86 125/119/117/110/92

ROYAL ASCOT Wednesday, Jun 17 FIRM

30 Queen Mary Stakes (Gr 2) (1) (2yo f) £56,710   5f
ACAPULCO (USA) *WesleyA.Ward,USA* 2-9-0 (b+t) RyanMoore (20) 5/2f 1
EASTON ANGEL (IRE) *MichaelDods* 2-9-0 PaulMulrennan (1) 13/2 1½ 2
BESHARAH (IRE) *WilliamHaggas* 2-9-0 PatCosgrave (3) 6/1 2½ 3
Kurland (IRE) *MartynMeade* 2-9-0 FergusSweeney (16) 14/1 2½ 4
Kassia (IRE) *MickChannon* 2-9-0 MartinHarley (22) 20/1 2 5
Little Voice (USA) *CharlesHills* 2-9-0 JamieSpencer (6) ....66/1 ¾ 6
Ring of Truth *RichardHannon* 2-9-0 RichardHughes (11) ....25/1 ½ 7
Delizia (IRE) *MarkJohnston* 2-9-0 SilvestreDeSousa (8) 10/1 1 8
Rebel Surge (IRE) *DaveMorris* 2-9-0 LukeMorris (14) ....100/1 nk 9
Rah Rah *MarkJohnston* 2-9-0 WilliamBuick (21) ....8/1 sh 10
Abberley Dancer (IRE) *J.S.Moore* 2-9-0 JohnFahy (12) 100/1 1½ 11
Bruised Orange (USA) *WesleyA.Ward,USA* 2-9-0 (b) FrankieDettori (10) 12/1 1¼ 12
New Road Side *TonyCoyle* 2-9-0 BarryMcHugh (4) ....33/1 ½ 13
Silk Bow *JamesGiven* 2-9-0 TomEaves (5) 33/1 3 14
Pity Cash (IRE) *DavidEvans* 2-9-0 JohnEgan (2) 100/1 1¼ 15
Cry Me A River (IRE) *T.Stack,Ireland* 2-9-0 W.M.Lordan (15) ....9/1 ¾ 16
Secret Tale (IRE) *JamieOsborne* 2-9-0 AdamKirby (23) 50/1 2¼ 17
Just Emma *JosephTuite* 2-9-0 OisinMurphy (19) ....50/1 ½ 18
Rosealee (IRE) *JeremyGask* 2-9-0 FrederikTylicki (13) 66/1 12 19
Shaden (IRE) *LadyCecil* 2-9-0 HayleyTurner (9) 33/1 6 20
Mrs G Smith, Mrs D Tabor, Mrs J Magnier 20ran 1m00.03 114/108/97/87/79/76

31 Prince of Wales's Stakes (Gr 1) (1) (4yo+) £297,728   1¼m
FREE EAGLE (IRE) *D.K.Weld,Ireland* 4-9-0 PatSmullen (4) 5/2f 1
16 THE GREY GATSBY (IRE) *KevinRyan* 4-9-0 (s) JamieSpencer (1) ....9/2 sh 2
WESTERN HYMN *JohnGosden* 4-9-0 FrankieDettori (8) 2¾ 3
The Corsican (IRE) *DavidSimcock* 4-9-0 JimCrowley (6) ....½ 4
Criterion (NZ) *DavidAndrewHayes,Australia* 5-9-0 (b) ChadSchofield (7) ....20/1 ½ 5
Spielberg (JPN) *KazuoFujisawa,Japan* 6-9-0 ChristopheSoumillon (5) ....7/1 nk 6
Cannock Chase (USA) *SirMichaelStoute* 4-9-0 RyanMoore (2) 8/1 1¼ 7

19 Gailo Chop (FR) *A.deWatrigant,France* 4-9-0 (t) JulienAuge (10) ....10/1   hd 8
    Ectot *E.Lellouche,France* 4-9-0 GregoryBenoist (8) 7/1   8   9
    Moyglare Stud Farms Ltd 9ran 2m05.07   128/128/122/121/120/120

ROYAL ASCOT Thursday, Jun 18   FIRM

32 Gold Cup (Gr 1) (1) (4yo+) £229,854   2½m
    TRIP TO PARIS (IRE) *EdDunlop* 4-9-0 GrahamLee (13) 12/1   1
    KINGFISHER (IRE) *AidanO'Brien,Ireland* 4-9-0 (h) RyanMoore (5) 5/1   1¼ 2
    FORGOTTEN RULES (IRE) *D.K.Weld,Ireland* 5-9-2 PatSmullen (10) ....5/2f   nk 3
    Simenon (IRE) *W.P.Mullins,Ireland* 8-9-2 (h) JamesDoyle (9)......................14/1   ½   4
    Bathyrhon (GER) *MmePiaBrandt,France* 5-9-2 MaximeGuyon (4) ....14/1   hd 5
    Scotland (GER) *AndrewBalding* 4-9-0 JimCrowley (14).................................20/1   1¼ 6
    Mizzou (IRE) *LucaCumani* 4-9-0 WilliamBuick (7)..7/2   nk 7
    Forever Now *JohnGosden* 4-9-0 FrankieDettori (1) ....25/1   ½   8
    Havana Beat (IRE) *AndrewBalding* 5-9-2 DavidProbert (3) 25/1   1¼ 9
    Windshear *RichardHannon* 4-9-0 SeanLevey (6)...33/1   37 10
    Vent de Force *HughieMorrison* 4-9-0 RichardHughes (12) ....10/1   nk 11
    Tac de Boistron (FR) *MarcoBotti* 8-9-2 MartinHarley (11) 8/1   99 12
    La Grange Partnership 12ran 4m22.61   120/119/116/116/116/116

ROYAL ASCOT Friday, Jun 19   FIRM

33 Commonwealth Cup (Gr 1) (1) (3yo) £229,854   6f
10 MUHAARAR *CharlesHills* 3-9-3 DaneO'Neill (8)...10/1   1
    LIMATO (IRE) *HenryCandy* 3-9-3 JamesDoyle (12).....................................9/2   3¾ 2
    ANTHEM ALEXANDER (IRE) *EdwardLynam,Ireland* 3-9-0 PatSmullen (9) ......8/1   ¾   3
    Salt Island *CharlesHills* 3-9-3 JamieSpencer (1) ....33/1   sh 4
    Profitable (IRE) *CliveCox* 3-9-3 AdamKirby (18).......................................50/1   ¾   5
6   Home of the Brave (IRE) *HugoPalmer* 3-9-3 (t) JamesMcDonald (2)................18/1   1   6
    Adaay (IRE) *WilliamHaggas* 3-9-3 PaulHanagan (4) ....8/1   hd 7
    Goken (FR) *H.-A.Pantall,France* 3-9-3 OlivierPeslier (4)...........................50/1   1   8
    Tendu *JohnGosden* 3-9-3 FrankieDettori (16)..14/1   1½ 9
6   Kool Kompany (IRE) *RichardHannon* 3-9-3 PatDobbs (10) ....33/1   ¾ 10
    Hootenanny (USA) *WesleyA.Ward,USA* 3-9-3 RyanMoore (14)...................9/4f   1¾ 11
    El Valle (FR) *MlleV.Dissaux,France* 3-9-3 (b) AntoineHamelin (5) ....100/1   ½ 12
    New Providence *HugoPalmer* 3-9-0 TimCrowley (7) ....25/1   ½ 13
    Cyclogenisis (USA) *GeorgeWeaver,USA* 3-9-3 (v+t) JohnK.Velazquez (11)........33/1   1 14
    Ahlan Emarati (IRE) *PeterChapple-Hyam* 3-9-3 SilvestreDeSousa (15) 66/1   10 15
9   Tiggy Wiggy (IRE) *RichardHannon* 3-9-0 RichardHughes (17) 6/1   1 16
17 Pastoral Girl *JamesGiven* 3-9-0 TomEaves (3)..100/1   nk 17
    Jungle Cat (IRE) *CharlieAppleby* 3-9-3 WilliamBuick (13) 33/1   12 18
    Mr Hamdan Al Maktoum 18ran 1m12.05   128/115/109/112/109/106

34 Coronation Stakes (Gr 1) (1) (3yo) £229,854   1m
11 ERVEDYA (FR) *Jean-ClaudeRouget,France* 3-9-0 ChristopheSoumillon (7)........3/1   1
17 FOUND (IRE) *AidanO'Brien,Ireland* 3-9-0 RyanMoore (2).............................13/8f   nk 2
9   LUCIDA (IRE) *J.S.Bolger,Ireland* 3-9-0 KevinManning (9).........................3/1   ½   3
    Miss Temple City (USA) *H.GrahamMotion,USA* 3-9-0 (t) JohnR.Velazquez (3)...50/1   1¼ 4
    Arabian Queen (IRE) *DavidElsworth* 3-9-0 SilvestreDeSousa (5) ....12/1   sh 5
    Sperry (IRE) *JohnGosden* 3-9-0 JamesDoyle (4)...16/1   ½   6
11 Irish Rookie (IRE) *MartynMeade* 3-9-0 FergusSweeney (6) 14/1   2¼ 7
9   Local Time *SaeedbinSuroor* 3-9-0 WilliamBuick (1) 33/1   5   8
    Yasmeen *JohnGosden* 3-9-0 PaulHanagan (1) ....20/1   nk 9
    H.H. Aga Khan 9ran 1m38.46   117/116/115/112/112/111

ROYAL ASCOT Saturday, Jun 20   FIRM

35 Hardwicke Stakes (Gr 2) (1) (4yo+) £113,420   1½m
    SNOW SKY *SirMichaelStoute* 4-9-1 PatSmullen (2) 12/1   1
    EAGLE TOP *JohnGosden* 4-9-1 FrankieDettori (3)......................................2/1   3¾ 2
16 POSTPONED (IRE) *LucaCumani* 4-9-1 AdamKirby (7) ....7/2   ns 3
22 Sheikhzayedroad *DavidSimcock* 6-9-1 (h) MartinLane (4)..........................33/1   3¼ 4
    Hillstar *SirMichaelStoute* 5-9-1 TedDurcan (8) ....16/1   ¾   5
    Telescope (IRE) *SirMichaelStoute* 5-9-1 RyanMoore (6) ....6/4f   sh 6
    Red Cadeaux *EdDunlop* 9-9-1 JamesDoyle (1)...25/1   43 7
    Mr K. Abdullah 7ran 2m31.51   124/117/117/111/109/109

36 Diamond Jubilee Stakes (Gr 1) (1) (4yo+) £297,728   6f
    UNDRAFTED (USA) *WesleyA.Ward,USA* 5-9-3 FrankieDettori (6)...................14/1   1
    BRAZEN BEAU (AUS) *ChrisWaller,Australia* 4-9-3 CraigA.Williams (15) .....7/2jf   ½   2
    ASTAIRE (IRE) *KevinRyan* 4-9-3 JamieSpencer (3).....................................25/1   1¾ 3
    Music Master *HenryCandy* 5-9-3 FergusSweeney (13) 14/1   1¼ 4

Mustajeeb *D.K.Weld,Ireland* 4-9-3 PatSmullen (4) .... 7/2jf ½ 5
Wandjina (AUS) *GaiWaterhouse,Australia* 4-9-3 D.M.Oliver (10) .... 10/1 ½ 6
1 Caspar Netscher *DavidSimcock* 6-9-3 AndrewMullen (2) 25/1 1¼ 7
Gordon Lord Byron (IRE) *T.Hogan,Ireland* 7-9-3 W.M.Lordan (7) .... 20/1 ½ 8
Glass Office *DavidCrowley* 5-9-3 JimCrowley (11) .... 20/1 sh 9
Ansgar (IRE) *SabrinaJ.Harty,Ireland* 7-9-3 (t) JamesDoyle (5) .... 40/1 ½ 10
Moviesta (USA) *EdwardLynam,Ireland* 5-9-3 PaulMulrennan (1) 16/1 1½ 11
28 Pearl Secret *DavidBarron* 6-9-3 AndreaAtzeni (3) 16/1 3¾ 12
Lucky Kristale *GeorgeMargarson* 4-9-0 (b) TomQueally (9) 33/1 1¾ 13
Tropics (USA) *DeanIvory* 7-9-3 (h) RobertWinston (8) 10/1 9 14
Due Diligence (USA) *AidanO'Brien,Ireland* 4-9-3 (t) RyanMoore (12) 5/1 14 15
Wes Welker & Sol Kumin 15ran 1m12.69   126/124/118/114/112/110

CURRAGH Saturday, Jun 27   GOOD to FIRM

37   Dubai Duty Free Irish Derby (Gr 1) (3yo c+f) £517,857   1½m
23 JACK HOBBS *JohnGosden,GB* 3-9-0 WilliamBuick (2) 10/11f 1
23 STORM THE STARS (USA) *WilliamHaggas,GB* 3-9-0 PatCosgrave (7) 10/1 5 2
23 GIOVANNI CANALETTO (IRE) *AidanO'Brien* 3-9-0 (s) JosephO'Brien (8) 8/1 5½ 3
23 Kilimanjaro (IRE) *AidanO'Brien* 3-9-0 (h) SeamieHeffernan (6) .... 20/1 ½ 4
20 Highland Reel (IRE) *AidanO'Brien* 3-9-0 RyanMoore (3) .... 11/4 nk 5
21 Qualify (IRE) *AidanO'Brien* 3-8-11 C.O'Donoghue (4) .... 8/1 hd 6
23 Carbon Dating (IRE) *JohnPatrickShanahan* 3-9-0 R.P.Whelan (1) 150/1 9 7
Radanpour (IRE) *D.K.Weld* 3-9-0 PatSmullen (5) 16/1 13 8
Godolphin & Partners 8ran 2m34.93   127/118/108/107/107/104

CURRAGH Sunday, Jun 28   GOOD to FIRM

38   Sea The Stars Pretty Polly Stakes (Gr 1) (3yo+ f+m) £108,877   1¼m
21 DIAMONDSANDRUBIES (IRE) *AidanO'Brien* 3-8-12 SeamieHeffernan (2) 8/1 1
21 LEGATISSIMO (IRE) *DavidWachman* 3-8-12 RyanMoore (6) .... 6/4f sh 2
RIBBONS *JamesFanshawe,GB* 5-9-10 FrankieDettori (8) .... 8/1 nk 3
Secret Gesture *RalphBeckett,GB* 5-9-10 AndreaAtzeni (4) 8/1 2 4
17 Pleascach (IRE) *J.S.Bolger* 3-8-12 K.J.Manning (3) .... 9/2 ½ 5
Mutatis Mutandis (IRE) *EdWalker,GB* 4-9-10 GeorgeBaker (1) .... 33/1 ns 6
Brooch (USA) *D.K.Weld* 4-9-10 PatSmullen (9) 5/1 1½ 7
8 Pollyana (IRE) *J.E.Hammond,France* 6-9-10 C.T.Keane (5) 50/1 1¾ 8
17 Tamadhor (IRE) *KevinPrendergast* 3-8-12 C.D.Hayes (7) 25/1 1¾ 9
Mrs Richard Henry & Mrs John Magnier 9ran 2m07.38   114/114/115/111/108/110

SAINT-CLOUD Sunday, Jun 28   GOOD to FIRM

39   Grand Prix de Saint-Cloud (Gr 1) (4yo+) £165,623   1m3f205y
TREVE (FR) *MmeC.Head-Maarek,France* 5-8-13 ThierryJarnet 6/10f 1
22 FLINTSHIRE *A.Fabre,France* 5-9-2 VincentCheminaud 7/1 1¼ 2
22 DOLNIYA (FR) *A.deRoyerDupre,France* 4-8-13 ChristopheSoumillon 48/10 2½ 3
Manatee *A.Fabre,France* 4-9-2 MickaelBarzalona .... 19/1 ½ 4
Meleagros (IRE) *A.Couetil,France* 6-9-2 AdrienFouassier 31/1 3 5
Feodora (GER) *A.Fabre,France* 4-8-13 Pierre-CharlesBoudot 50/1 2½ 6
Al Waab *G.E.Mikhalides,France* 5-9-2 SylvainRuis 74/1 10 7
Dauran (FR) *A.deRoyerDupre,France* 4-9-2 (b) FreddyDiFede 80/1 12 8
Altaira *MmeC.Head-Maarek,France* 4-9-2 JeromeClaudic .... 43/1 ds 9
Al Shaqab Racing 9ran 2m27.59   127/128/121/122/115/109

SANDOWN Saturday, Jul 4   GOOD to FIRM

40   Coral-Eclipse (Gr 1) (1) (3yo+) £255,195   1¼m7y
23 GOLDEN HORN *JohnGosden* 3-8-10 FrankieDettori (1) 4/9f 1
31 THE GREY GATSBY (IRE) *KevinRyan* 4-9-7 (s) JamieSpencer (2) 7/2 3½ 2
31 WESTERN HYMN *JohnGosden* 4-9-7 JamesDoyle (3) 10/1 4½ 3
26 Cougar Mountain (IRE) *AidanO'Brien,Ireland* 4-9-7 (b) RyanMoore (4) ...... 10/1 ¾ 4
Tullius (IRE) *AndrewBalding* 7-9-7 OisinMurphy (5) 66/1 1¼ 5
Mr A. E. Oppenheimer 5ran 2m05.77   134/128/119/117/114

NEWMARKET Friday, Jul 10   GOOD to FIRM (July Course)

41   Qipco Falmouth Stakes (Gr 1) (1) (3yo+ f+m) £123,344   1m
AMAZING MARIA (IRE) *DavidO'Meara* 4-9-7 JamesDoyle (4) 17/2 1
3 EURO CHARLINE *MarcoBotti* 4-9-7 AndreaAtzeni (7) 11/1 1 2
AVENIR CERTAIN (FR) *Jean-ClaudeRouget,France* 4-9-7
ChristopheSoumillon (3) .... 7/2 hd 3
Bawina (IRE) *C.Laffon-Parias,France* 4-9-7 MaximeGuyon (1) .... 5/1 ns 4
Fintry (IRE) *A.Fabre,France* 4-9-7 MickaelBarzalona (2) .... 6/1 sh 5
34 Lucida (IRE) *J.S.Bolger,Ireland* 3-8-12 KevinManning (6) .... 2/1f hd 6

34	Arabian Queen (IRE) *DavidElsworth* 3-8-12 SilvestreDeSousa (5)	9/1	2½	7
	Sir Robert Ogden 7ran 1m42.05	118/116/115/115/115/112		

NEWMARKET Saturday, Jul 11 FIRM (July Course)

42 Darley July Cup (Gr 1) (1) (3yo+) £283,550 6f

33	MUHAARAR *CharlesHills* 3-9-0 PaulHanagan (7)	2/1jf		1
36	TROPICS (USA) *DeanIvory* 7-9-6 (h) PatCosgrave (10)	25/1	ns	2
	EASTERN IMPACT (IRE) *RichardFahey* 4-9-6 JackGarritty (11)	50/1	1½	3
28	Sole Power *EdwardLynam,Ireland* 8-9-6 RichardHughes (14)	16/1	nk	4
	Danzeno *MichaelAppleby* 4-9-6 FrankieDettori (4)	12/1	nk	5
33	Anthem Alexander (IRE) *EdwardLynam,Ireland* 3-8-11 PatSmullen (5)	12/1	1	6
36	Brazen Beau (AUS) *ChrisWaller,Australia* 4-9-6 JamesDoyle (15)	2/1jf	nk	7
28	Lancelot du Lac (ITY) *DeanIvory* 5-9-6 HayleyTurner (3)	66/1	¾	8
28	Muthmir (IRE) *WilliamHaggas* 5-9-6 DaneO'Neill (2)	9/1	1½	9
36	Due Diligence (USA) *AidanO'Brien,Ireland* 4-9-6 (t) JosephO'Brien (13)	25/1	1¼	10
36	Astaire (IRE) *KevinRyan* 4-9-6 JamieSpencer (8)	16/1	ns	11
28	G Force (IRE) *DavidO'Meara* 4-9-6 SamJames (9)	25/1	½	12
28	Jack Dexter *JimGoldie* 6-9-6 FergalLynch (6)	25/1	½	13
28	Steps (IRE) *RogerVarian* 7-9-6 (b) JimCrowley (1)	66/1	9	14
	Mr Hamdan Al Maktoum 14ran 1m09.34	121/123/117/116/116/107		

CHANTILLY Sunday, Jul 12 GOOD

43 Prix Jean Prat (Gr 1) (3yo c+f) £162,099 7f210y

6	TERRITORIES (IRE) *A.Fabre,France* 3-9-2 MickaelBarzalona	13/10f		1
6	DUTCH CONNECTION *CharlesHills,GB* 3-9-2 JimCrowley	12/1	½	2
10	SIR ANDREW (FR) *F.PerezGonzalez,Spain* 3-9-2 IoritzMendizabal	33/1	6	3
	Kodi Bear (IRE) *CliveCox,GB* 3-9-2 OisinMurphy	9/1	1¾	4
	Il Segreto (FR) *C.DelcherSanchez,Spain* 3-9-2 Jose-LuisMartinezTejera	26/1	hd	5
10	Mr. Owen (USA) *FrancoisRohaut,France* 3-9-2 ChristopheSoumillon	33/10	2½	6
	Full Mast (USA) *MmeC.Head-Maarek,France* 3-9-2 VincentCheminaud	28/10	8	7
29	Aktabantay *HugoPalmer,GB* 3-9-2 (b) JamesDoyle	41/1	1	8
	Godolphin S.N.C. 8ran 1m36.12	123/122/110/105/105/98		

LONGCHAMP Tuesday, Jul 14 GOOD to FIRM

44 Juddmonte Grand Prix de Paris (Gr 1) (3yo c+f) £244,885 1m3f205y

	ERUPT (IRE) *Francis-HenriGraffard,France* 3-9-2 StephanePasquier	73/10		1
	AMPERE (FR) *A.Fabre,France* 3-9-2 MickaelBarzalona	evsf	2	2
37	STORM THE STARS (USA) *WilliamHaggas,GB* 3-9-2 PatCosgrave	3/1	1¼	3
20	Silverwave (FR) *A.Couetil,France* 3-9-2 AdrienFouassier	13/1	sh	4
	Balios (IRE) *DavidSimcock,GB* 3-9-2 JamieSpencer	35/10	ns	5
	Archangel Raphael (IRE) *AidanO'Brien,Ireland* 3-9-2 (b) JosephO'Brien	17/1	8	6
	Niarchos Family 6ran 2m31.07	120/117/115/115/115/101		

CURRAGH Saturday, Jul 18 GOOD to FIRM

45 Darley Irish Oaks (Gr 1) (3yo f) £165,714 1½m

	COVERT LOVE (IRE) *HugoPalmer,GB* 3-9-0 PatSmullen (8)	7/1		1
21	JACK NAYLOR *MrsJ.Harrington* 3-9-0 Francis-MartinBerry (5)	11/2	1¾	2
	CURVY *DavidWachman* 3-9-0 (s) W.M.Lordan (2)	15/8f	hd	3
21	Together Forever (IRE) *AidanO'Brien* 3-9-0 SeamieHeffernan (7)	7/1	2½	4
	Speedy Boarding *JamesFanshawe,GB* 3-9-0 FrederikTylicki (3)	12/1	1½	5
	Stellar Glow (IRE) *J.S.Bolger* 3-9-0 K.J.Manning (1)	33/1	1¾	6
	Gretchen *JohnGosden,GB* 3-9-0 AndreaAtzeni (4)	14/1	hd	7
	Words (IRE) *AidanO'Brien* 3-9-0 (h) JosephO'Brien (10)	7/2	1¾	8
17	Kissed By Angels (IRE) *AidanO'Brien* 3-9-0 C.O'Donoghue (9)	25/1	41	9
	FOMO Syndicate 9ran 2m30.38	116/113/112/108/105/102		

ASCOT Saturday, Jul 25 GOOD to SOFT

46 King George VI and Queen Elizabeth Stakes (Sponsored by Qipco) (Gr 1) (1) (3yo+) £689,027 1½m

35	POSTPONED (IRE) *LucaCumani* 4-9-7 AndreaAtzeni (9)	6/1		1
35	EAGLE TOP *JohnGosden* 4-9-7 FrankieDettori (3)	5/2f	ns	2
	ROMSDAL *JohnGosden* 4-9-7 WilliamBuick (7)	12/1	3¾	3
	Madame Chiang *DavidSimcock* 4-9-4 JimCrowley (1)	8/1	2	4
	Clever Cookie *PeterNiven* 7-9-7 GrahamLee (10)	4/1	¾	5
35	Snow Sky *SirMichaelStoute* 4-9-7 PatSmullen (5)	3/1	nk	6
	Dylan Mouth (IRE) *StefanoBotti,Italy* 4-9-7 FabioBranca (6)	10/1	8	7
	Sheikh Mohammed Obaid Al Maktoum 7ran 2m31.25	125/125/117/110/111/111		

GOODWOOD Tuesday, Jul 28   GOOD

47   Qatar Lennox Stakes (Gr 2) (1) (3yo+) £170,130   7f

26	TOORMORE (IRE) *RichardHannon* 4-9-3 JamesDoyle (5)	9/4jf		1
43	DUTCH CONNECTION *CharlesHills* 3-8-10 JimCrowley (3)	9/4jf	¾	2
	SAFETY CHECK (IRE) *CharlieAppleby* 4-9-7 WilliamBuick (9)	11/1	hd	3
6	Code Red *WilliamMuir* 3-8-10 MartinDwyer (6)	16/1	¾	4
	Ascription (IRE) *HugoPalmer* 6-9-3 (h+t) GrahamLee (4)	11/2	nk	5
	Aeolus *EdWalker* 4-9-3 GeorgeBaker (8)	16/1	2¼	6
	Tupi (IRE) *RichardHannon* 3-8-10 RichardHughes (1)	6/1	14	7

Godolphin 7ran 1m25.98   118/114/119/111/112/105

GOODWOOD Wednesday, Jul 29   GOOD

48   Qatar Sussex Stakes (Gr 1) (1) (3yo+) £560,200   1m

26	SOLOW *F.Head,France* 5-9-8 MaximeGuyon (5)	2/5f		1
13	AROD (IRE) *PeterChapple-Hyam* 4-9-8 AndreaAtzeni (8)	6/1	½	2
	GABRIAL (IRE) *RichardFahey* 6-9-8 PaulHanagan (2)	50/1	2¼	3
26	Here Comes When (IRE) *AndrewBalding* 5-9-8 (h) JimCrowley (3)	33/1	1	4
40	Cougar Mountain (IRE) *AidanO'Brien,Ireland* 4-9-8 (b) JosephO'Brien (1)	12/1	ns	5
26	Night of Thunder (IRE) *RichardHannon* 4-9-8 JamesDoyle (6)	5/1	1	6
15	Belardo (IRE) *RogerVarian* 3-9-0 (h) WilliamBuick (4)	9/1	sh	7
6	Bossy Guest (IRE) *MickChannon* 3-9-0 CharlesBishop (7)	25/1	1	8

Wertheimer et Frere 8ran 1m39.18   126/125/119/116/116/114

GOODWOOD Thursday, Jul 30   GOOD to FIRM

49   Qatar Richmond Stakes (Gr 2) (1) (2yo) £113,420   6f

	SHALAA (IRE) *JohnGosden* 2-9-3 FrankieDettori (6)	11/8f		1
	TASLEET *WilliamHaggas* 2-9-0 PaulHanagan (7)	7/1	2¾	2
	STEADY PACE *SaeedbinSuroor* 2-9-0 JamesDoyle (1)	4/1	1¼	3
	Adventurous (IRE) *MarkJohnston* 2-9-0 JoeFanning (2)	14/1	1½	4
	Elronaq *CharlesHills* 2-9-0 DaneO'Neill (5)	12/1	½	5
	Riflescope (IRE) *MarkJohnston* 2-9-0 SilvestreDeSousa (9)	11/1	1¾	6
	Log Out Island (IRE) *RichardHannon* 2-9-0 WilliamBuick (4)	6/1	1¼	7
	Barbarous Relic (USA) *K.R.Burke* 2-9-0 JimCrowley (3)	33/1	2¾	8

Al Shaqab Racing 8ran 1m10.82   120/107/102/97/95/89

50   Qatar Goodwood Cup (Gr 2) (1) (3yo+) £170,130   2m

	BIG ORANGE *MichaelBell* 4-9-8 (s) JamieSpencer (1)	6/1		1
	QUEST FOR MORE (IRE) *RogerCharlton* 5-9-8 (b) GeorgeBaker (6)	9/2f	nk	2
32	TRIP TO PARIS (IRE) *EdDunlop* 4-9-12 GrahamLee (11)	5/1	sh	3
	Pallasator *SirMarkPrescottBt* 6-9-8 AndreaAtzeni (9)	11/2	2¾	4
	Vive Ma Fille (GER) *MarkJohnston* 3-8-2 SilvestreDeSousa (8)	14/1	½	5
35	Sheikhzayedroad *DavidSimcock* 6-9-8 (h) MartinLane (12)	16/1	nk	6
	Oriental Fox (GER) *MarkJohnston* 7-9-8 JoeFanning (7)	15/2	2¼	7
32	Simenon (IRE) *W.P.Mullins,Ireland* 8-9-8 (h) FrankieDettori (10)	7/1	5	8
	Aussie Reigns (IRE) *WilliamKnight* 5-9-8 (s) AdamKirby (5)	33/1	2	9
	Eye of The Storm (IRE) *AmandaPerrett* 5-9-8 PatDobbs (4)	10/1	nk	10
	Angel Gabrial (IRE) *RichardFahey* 6-9-8 PaulHanagan (2)	16/1	4½	11

W. J. and T. C. O. Gredley 11ran 3m24.85   115/113/119/109/104/108

GOODWOOD Friday, Jul 31   GOOD to FIRM

51   Qatar King George Stakes (Gr 2) (1) (3yo+) £170,130   5f

42	MUTHMIR (IRE) *WilliamHaggas* 5-9-6 PaulHanagan (3)	3/1f		1
28	TAKE COVER *DavidC.Griffiths* 8-9-2 DavidAllan (9)	20/1	hd	2
	MOVE IN TIME *DavidO'Meara* 7-9-2 JimCrowley (6)	7/1	½	3
	Line of Reason (IRE) *PaulMidgley* 5-9-2 GrahamLee (14)	12/1	1½	4
	Cotai Glory *CharlesHills* 3-8-12 GrahamGibbons (11)	8/1	½	5
	Justineo *RogerVarian* 6-9-2 (b) AndreaAtzeni (2)	12/1	hd	6
28	Justice Day (IRE) *DavidElsworth* 4-9-2 WilliamBuick (8)	33/1	hd	7
	Kingsgate Native (IRE) *RobertCowell* 10-9-2 (h) JamesDoyle (4)	25/1	nk	8
	Katawi *ChrisWall* 4-8-13 (h) TedDurcan (13)	66/1	½	9
	Out Do *DavidO'Meara* 6-9-2 (v) DanielTudhope (15)	8/1	¾	10
1	Caspian Prince (IRE) *DeanIvory* 6-9-2 (h+t) AdamKirby (10)	50/1	½	11
36	Moviesta (USA) *EdwardLynam,Ireland* 5-9-2 (t) PaulMulrennan (1)	5/1	½	12
33	Goken (FR) *H-A.Pantall,France* 3-8-12 OlivierPeslier (5)	12/1	2	13
33	Salt Island *CharlesHills* 3-8-12 JamieSpencer (7)	16/1	1¾	14
	Dikta Del Mar (SPA) *T.Hogan,Ireland* 3-8-9 (t) SilvestreDeSousa (12)	22/1	½	15

Mr Hamdan Al Maktoum 15ran 56.08secs   122/118/115/108/104/105

52   Qatar Nassau Stakes (Gr 1) (1) (3yo+ f+m) £340,260   1m1f192y

38	LEGATISSIMO (IRE) *DavidWachman,Ireland* 3-8-12 W.M.Lordan (8)	2/1		1
	WEDDING VOW (IRE) *AidanO'Brien,Ireland* 3-8-12 ColmO'Donoghue (7)	10/1	2¼	2
41	ARABIAN QUEEN (IRE) *DavidElsworth* 3-8-12 SilvestreDeSousa (5)	25/1	1½	3
3	Cladocera (GER) *A.deRoyerDupre,France* 4-9-7 AntoineHamelin (1)	16/1	¾	4
21	Jazzi Top *JohnGosden* 3-8-12 WilliamBuick (3)	14/1	nk	5
21	Lady of Dubai *LucaCumani* 3-8-12 AndreaAtzeni (1)	5/1	½	6
25	Star of Seville *JohnGosden* 3-8-12 FrankieDettori (4)	6/1	1¾	7
	Bright Approach (IRE) *JohnGosden* 4-9-7 RichardHughes (9)	33/1	2	8
38	Diamondsandrubies (IRE) *AidanO'Brien,Ireland* 3-8-12 SeamieHeffernan (6)	10/3	1	9

Mr M. Tabor, D. Smith & Mrs John Magnier 9ran 2m06.04   118/113/110/110/109/108

53   Prix Rothschild (Gr 1) f+m) (3yo+ f+m) £121,574   7f210y

41	AMAZING MARIA (IRE) *DavidO'Meara,GB* 4-9-2 OlivierPeslier	48/10		1
34	ERVEDYA (FR) *Jean ClaudeRouget,France* 3-8-9 ChristopheSoumillon	evsf	1¼	2
41	BAWINA (IRE) *C.Laffon-Parias,France* 4-9-2 MaximeGuyon	45/10	1¼	3
	Odeliz (IRE) *K.R.Burke,GB* 5-9-2 (s) AdriedeVries	27/1	nk	4
41	Fintry (IRE) *A.Fabre,France* 4-9-2 VincentCheminaud	8/1	sh	5
	Rizeena (IRE) *CliveBrittain,GB* 4-9-2 JamesDoyle	14/1	nk	6
	Usherette (IRE) *A.Fabre,France* 3-8-9 MickaelBarzalona	8/1	¾	7
	Amulet *EveJohnsonHoughton,GB* 5-9-2 (b) TonyPiccone	46/1	2½	8

Sir Robert Ogden 8ran 1m34.72   120/115/112/112/112/111

54   Keeneland Phoenix Stakes (Gr 1) (2yo) £102,113   6f

27	AIR FORCE BLUE (USA) *AidanO'Brien* 2-9-3 JosephO'Brien (4)	9/4		1
	WASHINGTON DC (IRE) *AidanO'Brien* 2-9-3 SeamieHeffernan (5)	10/1	2	2
27	BURATINO (IRE) *MarkJohnston,GB* 2-9-3 WilliamBuick (2)	11/10f	½	3
	Painted Cliffs (IRE) *AidanO'Brien* 2-9-3 (b) C.O'Donoghue (7)	11/2	1½	4
	Rockaway Valley (IRE) *MrsJ.Harrington* 2-9-3 ShaneFoley (1)	9/1	½	5
	Zebstar (IRE) *GayKelleway,GB* 2-9-3 PatSmullen (6)	33/1	½	6
	Sixth Sense (IRE) *MarkJohnston,GB* 2-9-3 JoeFanning (3)	25/1	1½	7

MrsJohnMagnier/MichaelTabor/DerrickSmith 7ran 1m11.88   116/108/107/101/99/97

55   LARC Prix Maurice de Gheest (Gr 1) (3yo+) £140,838   6f102y

42	MUHAARAR *CharlesHills,GB* 3-8-12 PaulHanagan	evsf		1
26	ESOTERIQUE (IRE) *A.Fabre,France* 5-8-9 Pierre-CharlesBoudot	48/10	½	2
36	GORDON LORD BYRON (IRE) *T.Hogan,Ireland* 7-9-2 RichardKingscote	13/1	½	3
	Watchable *DavidO'Meara,GB* 5-9-2 (s) VincentCheminaud	43/1	1	4
	Son Cesio (FR) *H-A.Pantall,France* 4-9-2 FabriceVeron	10/1	sn	5
	Majestic Queen (IRE) *TraceyCollins,Ireland* 8-8-13 JamesDoyle	50/1	sn	6
15	Ivawood (IRE) *RichardHannon,GB* 3-8-12 FrankieDettori	68/10	sn	7
	Coulsty (IRE) *RichardHannon,GB* 4-9-2 SeanLevey	21/1	sh	8
	Gammarth (FR) *H-A.Pantall,France* 7-9-2 (b) MickaelBarzalona	49/1	6	9
25	Fontanelice (IRE) *Mme C.Head-Maarek,France* 3-8-8 CristianDemuro	47/1	hd	10
	Robert Le Diable (FR) *D.Prod'homme,France* 6-9-2 ChristopheSoumillon	10/1	3	11
	Noozhoh Canarias (SPA) *C.Laffon-Parias,France* 4-9-2 OlivierPeslier	29/1	4	12

Mr Hamdan Al Maktoum 12ran 1m15.33   122/118/120/116/116/112

56   Secretariat Stakes (Gr 1) (3yo) £172,452   1¼m

37	HIGHLAND REEL (IRE) *AidanO'Brien,Ireland* 3-8-9 SeamieHeffernan	24/10		1
	CLOSING BELL (USA) *WilliamI.Mott,USA* 3-8-7 JoseLezcano	147/10	5¼	2
	FORCE THE PASS (USA) *AlanE.Goldberg,USA* 3-9-0 JoelRosario	15/10f	hd	3
	Goldstream (ITY) *A.Wohler,Germany* 3-8-11 BrentonAvdulla	56/10	3	4
	Crittenden (USA) *EoinHarty,USA* 3-8-7 WilliamBuick	177/10	1	5
20	War Dispatch (USA) *Jean-ClaudeRouget,France* 3-8-7 IoritzMendizabal	53/10	ns	6
	Granny's Kitten (USA) *MichaelJ.Maker,USA* 3-8-7 IradOrtiz,Jr	91/10	½	7

Mr D. Smith, Mrs J. Magnier, Mr M. Tabor 7ran 2m02.26   123/111/118/110/104/104

57   Beverly D Stakes (Gr 1) (3yo+ f+m) £262,839   1m1f110y
Order as they passed the post: Secret Gesture demoted and placed third for causing interference

38	SECRET GESTURE *RalphBeckett,GB* 5-8-11 JamieSpencer	61/10		1
	WATSDACHANCES (IRE) *ChadC.Brown,USA* 5-8-11 JoeBravo	89/10	1¼	2
	STEPHANIE'S KITTEN (USA) *ChadC.Brown,USA* 6-8-11 IradOrtiz,Jr	37/10	nk	3
41	Euro Charline *MarcoBotti,GB* 4-8-11 JoseLezcano	27/10	¾	4

52 Wedding Vow (IRE) *AidanO'Brien,Ireland* 3-8-5 ColmO'Donoghue ....38/10   ½ 5
Carla Bianca (IRE) *D.K.Weld,Ireland* 4-8-11 PatSmullen 44/10   5¼ 6
Lacy (GER) *W.Hickst,Germany* 4-8-11 EduardoPedroza 346/10   5¼ 7
Maid On A Mission (USA) *PeterR.Walder,USA* 6-8-11 KentJ.Desormeaux .....391/10   pu
Mango Diva *MichaelR.Matz,USA* 5-8-10 FlorentGeroux ....197/10   pu
Qatar Racing Ltd & Newsells Park Stud 9ran 1m57.36   117/114/114/112/113/100

DEAUVILLE Sunday, Aug 16   GOOD to SOFT

58   **Prix du Haras de Fresnay-le-Buffard - Jacques le Marois (Gr 1) (3yo+) £283,674**   7f210y
55 ESOTERIQUE (IRE) *A.Fabre,France* 5-9-1 Pierre-CharlesBoudot 33/10   1
43 TERRITORIES (IRE) *A.Fabre,France* 3-8-13 MickaelBarzalona 13/10f   1½ 2
    WILD CHIEF (GER) *J.Hirschberger,Germany* 4-9-4 AlexanderPietsch 26/1   1½ 3
    Lightning Spear *OllyStevens,GB* 4-9-4 OisinMurphy ....9/1   ns 4
47 Toormore (IRE) *RichardHannon,GB* 4-9-4 JamesDoyle ....9/1   ½ 5
    Karakontie (JPN) *J.E.Pease,France* 4-9-4 StephanePasquier ....53/10   ¾ 6
48 Belardo (IRE) *RogerVarian,GB* 3-8-13 WilliamBuick 28/1   1½ 7
6 Estidhkaar (IRE) *RichardHannon,GB* 3-8-13 PaulHanagan ....12/1   hd 8
    Spoil The Fun (FR) *C.Ferland,France* 6-9-4 JulienAuge 43/1   1¼ 9
Baron Edouard de Rothschild 9ran 1m36.12   123/122/118/118/116/114

YORK Wednesday, Aug 19   GOOD to SOFT

59   **Betway Great Voltigeur Stakes (Gr 2) (1) (3yo) £98,335**   1½m
44 STORM THE STARS (USA) *WilliamHaggas* 3-9-0 PatCosgrave (5)....................3/1   1
    BONDI BEACH (IRE) *AidanO'Brien,Ireland* 3-9-0 (t) JosephO'Brien (1)..........11/4f   ½ 2
37 GIOVANNI CANALETTO (IRE) *AidanO'Brien,Ireland* 3-9-0 (s)
    SeamieHeffernan (4) 13/2   4½ 3
    Tashaar (IRE) *RichardHannon* 3-9-0 FrankieDettori (2) ....4/1   nk 4
    Medrano *DavidBrown* 3-9-0 PhillipMakin (6) 12/1   21 5
44 Balios (IRE) *DavidSimcock* 3-9-3 JamieSpencer (7)...5/1   17 6
    Aloft (IRE) *AidanO'Brien,Ireland* 3-9-0 (b+t) ColmO'Donoghue (3)..................14/1   28 7
Sheikh Juma Dalmook Al Maktoum 7ran 2m30.30   123/122/113/113/72/42

60   **Juddmonte International Stakes (Gr 1) (1) (3yo+) £518,542**   1¼m88y
52 ARABIAN QUEEN (IRE) *DavidElsworth* 3-8-9 SilvestreDeSousa (5)...............50/1   1
40 GOLDEN HORN *JohnGosden* 3-8-12 FrankieDettori (7)....................................4/9f   nk 2
40 THE GREY GATSBY (IRE) *KevinRyan* 4-9-6 (s) JamieSpencer (8) 5/1   3¼ 3
    Time Test *RogerCharlton* 3-8-12 PatSmullen (2)..4/1   1¼ 4
    Dick Doughtywylie *JohnGosden* 7-9-6 (t) RobertHavlin (4)...............................100/1   ½ 5
31 Criterion (NZ) *DavidAndrewHayes,Australia* 5-9-6 (s) WilliamBuick (6)...........22/1   hd 6
48 Cougar Mountain (IRE) *AidanO'Brien,Ireland* 4-9-6 (s+t) JosephO'Brien (1)....50/1   22 7
Mr J. C. Smith 7ran 2m09.92   117/120/112/110/109/108

YORK Thursday, Aug 20   Straight course: GOOD   Round course: GOOD to SOFT

61   **Pinsent Masons Lowther Stakes (Gr 2) (1) (2yo f) £118,893**   6f
30 BESHARAH (IRE) *WilliamHaggas* 2-9-0 PatCosgrave (7) 11/4   1
    LUMIERE *MarkJohnston* 2-9-0 WilliamBuick (2) 9/4f   2¼ 2
30 EASTON ANGEL (IRE) *MichaelDods* 2-9-0 PaulMulrennan (3)............................4/1   2¼ 3
    Lady Clair (IRE) *DavidBarron* 2-9-0 GrahamGibbons (6) 25/1   1 4
    Quiet Reflection *K.R.Burke* 2-9-0 JoeyHaynes (4)...8/1   1½ 5
    Continental Lady *DavidBrown* 2-9-0 OisinMurphy (8) ....20/1   hd 6
    Twin Falls (IRE) *J.F.Levins,Ireland* 2-9-0 G.F.Carroll (9) 50/1   1¼ 7
    Glenrowan Rose (IRE) *KeithDalgleish* 2-9-0 PhillipMakin (5)..........................33/1   1¾ 8
    Ashadihan *KevinRyan* 2-9-0 JamieSpencer (1) 6/1   4½ 9
Sheikh Rashid Dalmook Al Maktoum 9ran 1m11.87   114/105/97/93/87/87

62   **Darley Yorkshire Oaks (Gr 1) (1) (3yo+ f+m) £207,459**   1½m
38 PLEASCACH (IRE) *J.S.Bolger,Ireland* 3-8-11 KevinManning (8)........................8/1   1
45 COVERT LOVE (IRE) *HugoPalmer* 3-8-11 PatSmullen (2).............................15/8f   nk 2
    SEA CALISI (FR) *FrancoisDoumen,France* 3-8-11 MickaelBarzalona (3)...........7/1   nk 3
45 Curvy *DavidWachman,Ireland* 3-8-11 (v) W.M.Lordan (10) ....8/1   hd 4
    Miss Marjurie *DenisCoakley* 5-9-7 PaulHanagan (4)..25/1   ¾ 5
45 Jack Naylor *MrsJ.Harrington,Ireland* 3-8-11 F.M.Berry (9) 7/1   2¼ 6
    Lustrous *RichardHannon* 4-9-7 RichardKingscote (6)......................................50/1   1 7
21 Crystal Zvezda *SirMichaelStoute* 3-8-11 TedDurcan (1).................................14/1   ¾ 8
    Easter (IRE) *AidanO'Brien,Ireland* 3-8-11 (b+t) SeamieHeffernan (5)..............25/1   1¾ 9
52 Lady of Dubai *LucaCumani* 3-8-11 JamesDoyle (11)..8/1   15 10
    Outstanding (IRE) *AidanO'Brien,Ireland* 3-8-11 ColmO'Donoghue (7)............12/1   ½ 11
Godolphin 11ran 2m32.77   116/116/115/115/114/109

63   Coolmore Nunthorpe Stakes (Gr 1) (1) (2yo+) £175,801   5f

	MECCA'S ANGEL (IRE) *MichaelDods* 4-9-10 PaulMulrennan (10) 15/2		1
30	ACAPULCO (USA) *WesleyA.Ward,USA* 2-8-0 (b+t) IradOrtizJr (4) 13/8f	2	2
	MATTMU *TimEasterby* 3-9-11 (s) DavidAllan (5) 12/1	2	3
42	Sole Power *EdwardLynam,Ireland* 8-9-13 FrankieDettori (3) 8/1	½	4
28	Goldream *RobertCowell* 6-9-13 (s) MartinHarley (7) 20/1	hd	5
51	Muthmir (IRE) *WilliamHaggas* 5-9-13 PaulHanagan (12) 13/2	1¼	6
28	Wind Fire (USA) *DavidBrown* 4-9-10 JamieSpencer (11) 33/1	ns	7
36	Pearl Secret *DavidBarron* 6-9-13 OisinMurphy (16) 20/1	1¼	8
51	Move In Time *DavidO'Meara* 7-9-13 DanielTudhope (13) 20/1	2¾	9
33	Profitable (IRE) *CliveCox* 3-9-11 JamesDoyle (2) 20/1	ns	10
51	Cotai Glory *CharlesHills* 3-9-11 GrahamGibbons (8) 25/1	2¼	11
36	Music Master *HenryCandy* 5-9-13 DaneO'Neill (17) 25/1	1¾	12
28	Medicean Man *JeremyGask* 9-9-13 (s+t) PhillipMakin (9) 40/1	¾	13
51	Justineo *RogerVarian* 6-9-13 WilliamBuick (1) 66/1	nk	14
1	Mirza *RaeGuest* 8 9 13 (s) IoritzMendizabal (14) 50/1	½	15
51	Justice Day (IRE) *DavidElsworth* 4-9-13 HayleyTurner (15) 66/1	4½	16
	Canny Kool *BrianEllison* 3-9-11 SilvestreDeSousa (6) 66/1	1	17
51	Line of Reason (IRE) *PaulMidgley* 5-9-13 GrahamLee (18) 50/1	3¾	18
28	Stepper Point *WilliamMuir* 6-9-13 (s) MartinDwyer (20) 40/1	pu	

Mr David T. J. Metcalfe 19ran 57.24secs   129/112/112/110/109/103

64   Irish Thoroughbred Marketing Gimcrack Stakes (Gr 2) (1) (2yo c+g) £124,762   6f

	AJAYA *WilliamHaggas* 2-9-0 GrahamGibbons (9) 7/2		1
	RIBCHESTER (IRE) *RichardFahey* 2-9-0 TonyHamilton (5) 25/1	1¼	2
	RAUCOUS *WilliamHaggas* 2-9-0 PatCosgrave (4) 17/2	2	3
	King of Rooks *RichardHannon* 2-9-0 FrankieDettori (7) 11/2	2½	4
49	Steady Pace *SaeedbinSuroor* 2-9-0 JamesDoyle (1) 4/1	1	5
	Areen (IRE) *KevinRyan* 2-9-0 GrahamLee (6) 12/1	½	6
	Finnegan (IRE) *WesleyA.Ward,USA* 2-9-0 (t) EdgarS.Prado (3) 11/4f	½	7
27	Ode To Evening *MarkJohnston* 2-9-0 WilliamBuick (2) 12/1	15	8

Saleh Al Homaizi & Imad Al Sagar 8ran 1m10.96   117/112/105/96/92/91

65   Breast Cancer Research Debutante Stakes (Gr 2) (2yo f) £48,936   7f

	BALLYDOYLE (IRE) *AidanO'Brien* 2-9-0 JosephO'Brien (1) 11/8f		1
	MINDING (IRE) *AidanO'Brien* 2-9-0 C.O'Donoghue (6) 8/1	2	2
	MOST BEAUTIFUL *DavidWachman* 2-9-0 W.M.Lordan (2) 7/2	nk	3
	Turret Rocks (IRE) *J.S.Bolger* 2-9-0 (h) K.J.Manning (5) 14/1	¾	4
	Alice Springs (IRE) *AidanO'Brien* 2-9-0 SeamieHeffernan (7) 9/2	1	5
	Leafy Shade (IRE) *J.S.Bolger* 2-9-0 R.P.Whelan (3) 25/1	nk	6
	Miss Elizabeth (IRE) *EdwardLynam* 2-9-0 C.D.Hayes (4) 16/1	½	7
	Only Mine (IRE) *JosephG.Murphy* 2-9-0 PatSmullen (8) 11/1	1¼	8

Michael Tabor/Derrick Smith/Mrs Magnier 8ran 1m24.71   113/107/106/103/100/100

66   Darley Prix Morny (Gr 1) (2yo c+f) £141,837   5f212y

49	SHALAA (IRE) *JohnGosden,GB* 2-9-0 FrankieDettori 7/10f		1
	GUTAIFAN (IRE) *RichardHannon,GB* 2-9-0 SeanLevey 4/1	1¾	2
	TOURNY (FR) *P.Bary,France* 2-8-11 GregoryBenoist 43/10	5	3
54	Zebstar *GayKelleway,GB* 2-9-0 Pierre-CharlesBoudot 10/1	2½	4
	Viserano (FR) *D.Prod'homme,France* 2-9-0 MickaelBarzalona 55/10	7	5

Al Shaqab Racing 5ran 1m13.31   123/117/99/94/74

67   Darley Prix Jean Romanet (Gr 1) (4yo+ f+m) £101,312   1m1f207y

Order as they passed the post: Bawina was later disqualified from second
after testing positive for a banned substance

53	ODELIZ (IRE) *K.R.Burke,GB* 5-9-0 (s) AdriedeVries 35/1		1
53	BAWINA (IRE) *C.Laffon-Parias,France* 4-9-0 MaximeGuyon 58/10	nk	2
41	AVENIR CERTAIN (FR) *Jean-ClaudeRouget,France* 4-9-0 GregoryBenoist 4/1	¾	3
8	We Are (IRE) *F.Head,France* 4-9-0 ThierryJarnet 8/1	1½	4
8	Fate (FR) *A.deRoyerDupre,France* 6-9-0 ChristopheSoumillon 7/1	ns	5
38	Ribbons *JamesFanshawe,GB* 5-9-0 FrankieDettori 28/10f	½	6
19	Sparkling Beam (IRE) *J.E.Pease,France* 5-9-0 OlivierPeslier 19/1	1¾	7
39	Feodora (GER) *A.Fabre,France* 4-9-0 Pierre-CharlesBoudot 14/1	1¼	8
46	Madame Chiang *DavidSimcock,GB* 4-9-0 JimCrowley 73/10	½	9
	Persona Grata *EdWalker,GB* 4-9-0 (h) LukeMorris 44/1	4	10

Wunder (GER) *MarkusKlug,Germany* 4-9-0 IoritzMendizabal ....17/1 hd 11
Mrs Barbara M. Keller 11ran 2m14.27 118/117/116/113/113/112

HAYDOCK Saturday, Sep 5 GOOD to SOFT

68 **Betfred Sprint Cup (Gr 1) (1) (3yo+)** £162,191 6f

TWILIGHT SON *HenryCandy* 3-9-1 FergusSweeney (5)....................................10/1 1
STRATH BURN *CharlesHills* 3-9-1 AndreaAtzeni (16).......................................33/1 sh 2
MAGICAL MEMORY (IRE) *CharlesHills* 3-9-1 SilvestreDeSousa (6)...............14/1 ¾ 3
42 G Force (IRE) *DavidO'Meara* 4-9-3 DanielTudhope (12).....................................16/1 2¾ 4
42 Due Diligence (USA) *AidanO'Brien,Ireland* 4-9-3 (t) JosephO'Brien (8)............25/1 1 5
42 Danzeno *MichaelAppleby* 4-9-3 FrankieDettori (2)..6/1 ½ 6
42 Eastern Impact (IRE) *RichardFahey* 4-9-3 JackGarritty (13)................................14/1 1¼ 7
58 Belardo (IRE) *RogerVarian* 3-9-1 (b) JamesDoyle (1)..20/1 ¾ 8
33 Adaay (IRE) *WilliamHaggas* 3-9-1 PaulHanagan (4)...9/2jf 1 9
55 Gordon Lord Byron (IRE) *T.Hogan,Ireland* 7-9-3 W.M.Lordan (3).....................9/2jf ¾ 10
63 Pearl Secret *DavidBarron* 6-9-3 OisinMurphy (11)..20/1 nk 11
55 Watchable *DavidO'Meara* 5-9-3 (s) PhillipMakin (14)..20/1 1 12
Waady (IRE) *JohnGosden* 3-9-1 (h) DaneO'Neill (7)..20/1 ½ 13
63 Mattmu *TimEasterby* 3-9-1 (s) DavidAllan (10)..7/1 3¼ 14
33 Tiggy Wiggy (IRE) *RichardHannon* 3-8-12 SeanLevey (9)..16/1 ns 15
Mr Godfrey Wilson & Cheveley Park Stud 15ran 1m12.86 123/123/120/110/106/104

DONCASTER Saturday, Sep 12 GOOD to SOFT

69 **At The Races Champagne Stakes (Gr 2) (1) (2yo)** £45,533 7f

EMOTIONLESS (IRE) *CharlieAppleby* 2-9-0 WilliamBuick (2)........................8/13f 1
IBN MALIK (IRE) *CharlesHills* 2-9-0 PaulHanagan (3)...7/2 3½ 2
PALAWAN *RichardHannon* 2-9-0 PatDobbs (5)...7/1 7 3
Kentuckyconnection (USA) *BryanSmart* 2-9-0 SilvestreDeSousa (1)..................16/1 2 4
27 Beaverbrook *MarkJohnston* 2-9-0 GrahamLee (6)..14/1 hd 5
Lex Talionis (IRE) *J.F.Levins,Ireland* 2-9-0 DavidNolan ....100/1 ½ 6
Godolphin 6ran 1m27.49 119/109/89/84/83/82

70 **Saint Gobain Weber Park Stakes (Gr 2) (1) (3yo+)** £56,710 7f

33 LIMATO (IRE) *HenryCandy* 3-9-0 AndreaAtzeni (7)..9/2f 1
MARKAZ (IRE) *B.W.Hills* 3-9-0 PaulHanagan (4)...20/1 3¾ 2
13 BRETON ROCK (IRE) *DavidSimcock* 5-9-4 UmbertoRispoli (9)........................10/1 1¼ 3
Naadirr (IRE) *MarcoBotti* 4-9-4 MartinHarley (11)..25/1 nk 4
55 Coulsty (IRE) *RichardHannon* 4-9-4 PatCosgrave (15)...14/1 1¼ 5
13 Cable Bay (IRE) *CharlesHills* 4-9-4 SilvestreDeSousa (14)................................12/1 hd 6
47 Tupi (IRE) *RichardHannon* 3-9-0 PatDobbs (1)...25/1 4½ 7
Lightning Moon (IRE) *EdWalker* 4-9-4 GrahamLee (2)...6/1 nk 8
36 Ansgar (IRE) *SabrinaJ.Harty,Ireland* 7-9-4 (t) RobertWinston (8).........................50/1 8 9
47 Safety Check (IRE) *CharlieAppleby* 4-9-4 WilliamBuick (13)................................7/1 ½ 10
33 Home of The Brave (IRE) *HugoPalmer* 3-9-0 (t) HarryBentley (3)......................11/2 sh 11
Brazos (IRE) *CliveBrittain* 4-9-4 FergalLynch (12)..100/1 sh 12
55 Ivawood (IRE) *RichardHannon* 3-9-0 SeanLevey (10)..8/1 1¾ 13
47 Code Red *WilliamMuir* 3-9-0 MartinDwyer (5)..16/1 7 14
Toocoolforschool (IRE) *K.R.Burke* 3-9-0 (s) GrahamGibbons (6).........................28/1 2 15
Mr Paul G. Jacobs 15ran 1m24.98 126/115/112/111/108/107

71 **Ladbrokes St Leger Stakes (Gr 1) (1) (3yo c+f)** £393,738 1¾m132y

The placings of the first two were reversed on the day after interference between them, but Simple Verse was given the race back on appeal to the BHA

SIMPLE VERSE (IRE) *RalphBeckett* 3-8-12 AndreaAtzeni (1)..............................8/1 1
59 BONDI BEACH (IRE) *AidanO'Brien,Ireland* 3-9-1 (t) ColmO'Donoghue (8)... 2/1jf hd 2
FIELDS OF ATHENRY (IRE) *AidanO'Brien,Ireland* 3-9-1 (h)
SilvestreDeSousa (4)...10/3 1¾ 3
59 Storm The Stars (USA) *WilliamHaggas* 3-9-1 PatCosgrave (3)...........................2/1jf ns 4
Vengeur Masque (IRE) *M.Delzangles,France* 3-9-1 UmbertoRispoli (6)..............16/1 9 5
59 Medrano *DavidBrown* 3-9-1 (h) FergalLynch (5)..25/1 ¾ 6
Proposed *RichardHannon* 3-9-1 PatDobbs (2)..66/1 7 7
QRL/Sheikh Suhaim Al Thani/M Al Kubaisi 7ran 3m07.15 119/122/119/119/105/104

LEOPARDSTOWN Saturday, Sep 12 Enterprise: GOOD to SOFT Remainder: GOOD

72 **KPMG Enterprise Stakes (Gr 3) (3yo+)** £47,445 1½m

16 FASCINATING ROCK (IRE) *D.K.Weld* 4-9-12 PatSmullen (6)..............................2/1 1
PANAMA HAT *AndrewOliver* 4-9-9 (s) C.D.Hayes (2)..5/1 6 2
12 JOHN F KENNEDY (IRE) *AidanO'Brien* 3-9-0 (b+t) JosephO'Brien (3)..............9/2 4¾ 3
Elleval (IRE) *DavidMarnane* 5-9-9 (s) W.M.Lordan (1)..20/1 ½ 4

Answered *J.S.Bolger* 4-9-9 K.J.Manning (4) 15/8f 47 5
Newtown Anner Stud Farm Ltd 5ran 2m38.96 126/113/105/104/

73 **Qipco Irish Champion Stakes (Gr 1) (3yo+)** £465,693 1¼m
60 GOLDEN HORN *JohnGosden,GB* 3-9-0 FrankieDettori (1) 5/4f 1
34 FOUND (IRE) *AidanO'Brien* 3-8-11 SeamieHeffernan (3) 6/1 1 2
31 FREE EAGLE (IRE) *D.K.Weld* 4-9-7 PatSmullen (5) ....10/3 ½ 3
62 Pleascach (IRE) *J.S.Bolger* 3-8-11 K.J.Manning (2)..14/1 2 4
56 Highland Reel (IRE) *AidanO'Brien* 3-9-0 JosephO'Brien (7) ....16/1 nk 5
60 The Grey Gatsby (IRE) *KevinRyan,GB* 4-9-7 (s) JamieSpencer (4) 8/1 1 6
19 Cirrus des Aigles (FR) *MmeC.Barande-Barbe,France* 9-9-7
ChristopheSoumillon (8)..8/1 6 7
Mr A. E. Oppenheimer 7ran 2m05.41 126/121/123/115/118/116

74 **Coolmore Fastnet Rock Matron Stakes (Gr 1) (3yo+ f+m)** £131,387 1m
52 LEGATISSIMO (IRE) *DavidWachman* 3-9-0 W.M.Lordan (4)............................ 7/4f 1
52 CLADOCERA (GER) *A.deRoyerDupre,France* 4-9-5 ChristopheSoumillon (10) 11/1 2¼ 2
AINIPPE (IRE) *G.M.Lyons* 3-9-0 C.T.Keane (3) 16/1 2¼ 3
17 Raydara (IRE) *M.Halford* 3-9-0 ShaneFoley (7)...20/1 ½ 4
57 Euro Charline *MarcoBotti,GB* 4-9-5 FrankieDettori (9) 10/1 2½ 5
17 Steip Amach (IRE) *J.S.Bolger* 3-9-0 K.J.Manning (2)...66/1 2¼ 6
53 Amazing Maria (IRE) *DavidO'Meara,GB* 4-9-5 OlivierPeslier (8).......................15/8 ½ 7
17 Military Angel (USA) *M.D.O'Callaghan* 3-9-0 Francis-MartinBerry (6) 25/1 1 8
38 Brooch (USA) *D.K.Weld* 4-9-5 (b) PatSmullen (1) ....8/1 ½ 9
M. Tabor, Mrs J. Magnier & D. Smith 9ran 1m39.95 121/116/109/108/102/95

CURRAGH Sunday, Sep 13 GOOD to SOFT
75 **Derrinstown Stud Flying Five Stakes (Gr 2) (3yo+)** £87,591 5f
63 SOLE POWER *EdwardLynam* 8-9-7 C.D.Hayes (10) 5/1cf 1
MAAREK *MissEvannaMcCutcheon* 8-9-4 JamieSpencer (3) ....5/1cf hd 2
51 TAKE COVER *DavidC.Griffiths,GB* 8-9-4 DavidAllan (1) 12/1 1 3
Toscanini (IRE) *M.Halford* 3-9-3 (s) JamesDoyle (12)...11/2 nk 4
Great Minds (IRE) *T.Stack* 5-9-4 W.M.Lordan (9)..11/1 ½ 5
68 Pearl Secret *DavidBarron,GB* 6-9-4 OisinMurphy (8)...10/1 nk 6
63 Line of Reason (IRE) *PaulMidgley,GB* 5-9-4 JosephO'Brien (4)..........................10/1 nk 7
Iffraaaj (FR) *RobertCowell,GB* 5-9-1 (h) ShaneFoley (7) 33/1 2½ 8
28 Hot Streak (IRE) *RobertCowell,GB* 4-9-4 (s) C.T.Keane (2)................................16/1 ¾ 9
51 Moviesta (USA) *EdwardLynam* 5-9-4 PaulMulrennan (5)....................................5/1cf 1¾ 10
51 Dikta Del Mar (SPA) *T.Hogan* 3-9-0 (t) B.A.Curtis (6) 66/1 1 11
63 Stepper Point *WilliamMuir,GB* 6-9-4 (s) M.Dwyer (11)..9/1 3¾ 12
Mrs S. Power 12ran 1m01.29 120/117/112/111/109/108

76 **Moyglare Stud Stakes (Gr 1) (2yo f)** £127,007 7f
65 MINDING (IRE) *AidanO'Brien* 2-9-0 SeamieHeffernan (10)..............................15/2 1
65 BALLYDOYLE (IRE) *AidanO'Brien* 2-9-0 JosephO'Brien (7)............................ 5/4f ¾ 2
65 ALICE SPRINGS (IRE) *AidanO'Brien* 2-9-0 (h) M.C.Hussey (8).......................20/1 ½ 3
Tanaza (IRE) *D.K.Weld* 2-9-0 PatSmullen (6)...7/2 2¾ 4
Blue Bayou *BrianMeehan,GB* 2-9-0 JimmyFortune (4) ....6/1 ½ 5
Taisce Naisiunta (IRE) *J.S.Bolger* 2-9-0 R.P.Whelan (5).......................................66/1 ½ 6
Great Page (IRE) *RichardHannon,GB* 2-9-0 SeanLevey (2)......................................18/1 5½ 7
65 Leafy Shade (IRE) *J.S.Bolger* 2-9-0 K.J.Manning (3) ....25/1 ½ 8
Now Or Never (IRE) *M.D.O'Callaghan* 2-9-0 EmmetMcNamara (1) 10/1 1½ 9
Derrick Smith, Mrs J. Magnier & M. Tabor 9ran 1m28.48 114/112/110/102/101/99

77 **Goffs Vincent O'Brien National Stakes (Gr 1) (2yo c+f)** £127,007 7f
54 AIR FORCE BLUE (USA) *AidanO'Brien* 2-9-3 JosephO'Brien (4)..................10/11f 1
HERALD THE DAWN (IRE) *J.S.Bolger* 2-9-3 K.J.Manning (1) 5/2 3 2
BIRCHWOOD (IRE) *RichardFahey,GB* 2-9-3 JamesDoyle (6)............................13/2 1¾ 3
Final Frontier (IRE) *MrsJ.Harrington* 2-9-3 PatSmullen (2)...................................9/1 ½ 4
54 Painted Cliffs (IRE) *AidanO'Brien* 2-9-3 (b) SeamieHeffernan (3).......................14/1 ns 5
MrsJohnMagnier/MichaelTabor/DerrickSmith 5ran 1m29.89 119/110/105/104/104

78 **Palmerstown House Estate Irish St Leger (Gr 1) (3yo+)** £148,175 1¾m
ORDER OF ST GEORGE (IRE) *AidanO'Brien* 3-9-0 JosephO'Brien (9)............ 5/4f 1
AGENT MURPHY *BrianMeehan,GB* 4-9-11 JimmyFortune (10)..........................6/1 11 2
WICKLOW BRAVE *W.P.Mullins* 6-9-11 P.Townend (5)..20/1 nk 3
Second Step (IRE) *LucaCumani,GB* 4-9-11 JamieSpencer (4)..............................13/2 ½ 4
32 Forgotten Rules (IRE) *D.K.Weld* 5-9-11 PatSmullen (8)...9/2 1 5
Gospel Choir *SirMichaelStoute,GB* 6-9-11 K.J.Manning (6)..................................25/1 3¾ 6
Sea Moon *JohnM.Oxx* 7-9-11 DeclanMcDonogh (3)..20/1 7½ 7
32 Kingfisher (IRE) *AidanO'Brien* 4-9-11 (h) SeamieHeffernan (1)..........................20/1 19 8

    32 Vent de Force *HughieMorrison,GB* 4-9-11 GeorgeBaker (11).............................33/1   5½   9
        Good Tradition (IRE) *D.K.Weld* 4-9-11 (v) L.F.Roche (7).....................................100/1   75 10
        Brown Panther *TomDascombe,GB* 7-9-11 RichardKingscote (2) ....13/2   pu
        Michael Tabor/Derrick Smith/Mrs Magnier 11ran 3m03.19   129/112/112/111/109/104

LONGCHAMP Sunday, Sep 13   SOFT

79 Qatar Prix Niel (Gr 2) (3yo c+f) £54,088   1m3f205y
    20 NEW BAY *A.Fabre,France* 3-9-2 VincentCheminaud (3)................................12/10f   1
    44 SILVERWAVE (FR) *A.Couetil,France* 3-9-2 FrankieDettori (7)............................6/1   2½   2
        MIGWAR (FR) *F.Head,France* 3-9-2 OlivierPeslier (1)...............................72/10   1¾   3
    44 Erupt (IRE) *Francis-HenriGraffard,France* 3-9-2 StephanePasquier (2)........21/10   7   4
    12 Ol' Man River (IRE) *AidanO'Brien,Ireland* 3-9-2 ColmO'Donoghue (6).............38/1   5   5
        Ming Dynasty (FR) *M.Delzangles,France* 3-9-2 AndreaAtzeni (5)...................84/10   3   6
        Countermeasure *A.Fabre,France* 3-9-2 Pierre-CharlesBoudot (4)...................236/10   ds   7
        Mr K. Abdullah 7ran 2m35.10   127/123/120/109/101/96

80 Qatar Prix Vermeille (Gr 1) (3yo+ f+m) £145,978   1m3f205y
    39 TREVE (FR) *MmeC.Head-Maarek,France* 5-9-3 ThierryJarnet (8)................... 6/10f   1
        CANDARLIYA (FR) *A.deRoyerDupre,France* 3-8-9 ChristopheSoumillon (1)....49/10   6   2
    62 SEA CALISI (FR) *FrancoisDoumen,France* 3-8-8 MickaelBarzalona (3)...........93/10   ½   3
        Frine (IRE) *C.Laffon-Parias,France* 5-9-3 OlivierPeslier (7).......................216/10   6   4
        Beautiful Romance *SaeedbinSuroor,GB* 3-8-8 WilliamBuick (4) ....173/10   hd   5
    60 Arabian Queen (IRE) *DavidElsworth,GB* 3-8-8 SilvestreDeSousa (6)...........72/10   hd   6
    21 Al Naamah (IRE) *A.Fabre,France* 3-8-8 GregoryBenoist (2)...........................40/1   3   7
    52 Diamondsandrubies (IRE) *AidanO'Brien,Ireland* 3-8-8 ColmO'Donoghue (9)....179/10   1¾   8
        Dihna (FR) *MmeC.Head-Maarek,France* 3-8-8 JeromeClaudic (5) ....97/1   ds   9
        Al Shaqab Racing 9ran 2m34.09   127/120/118/107/107/107

81 Qatar Prix du Moulin de Longchamp (Gr 1) (3yo+ c+f) £187,686   7f210y
    53 ERVEDYA (FR) *Jean-ClaudeRouget,France* 3-8-9 ChristopheSoumillon (6)...... evsf   1
        AKATEA (IRE) *A.deRoyerDupre,France* 3-8-9 ThierryJarnet (10) 122/10   1   2
    58 KARAKONTIE (JPN) *J.E.Pease,France* 4-9-3 StephanePasquier (5).................35/10   1   3
    11 Maimara (FR) *M.Delzangles,France* 3-8-9 GregoryBenoist (8).......................33/10   hd   4
    58 Wild Chief (GER) *J.Hirschberger,Germany* 4-9-3 AlexanderPietsch (9) ....8/1   ¾   5
        Guiliani (IRE) *J-P.Carvalho,Germany* 4-9-3 FilipMinarik (3) ....118/10   hd   6
        H.H. Aga Khan 6ran 1m42.26   119/117/118/114/116/116

82 Qatar Prix Foy (Gr 2) (4yo+) £54,088   1m3f205y
    46 POSTPONED (IRE) *LucaCumani,GB* 4-9-2 AndreaAtzeni (2)...........................26/10   1
        SPIRITJIM (FR) *A.Couetil,France* 5-9-2 FrankieDettori (6)...........................156/10   ¾   2
        BAINO HOPE (FR) *Jean-ClaudeRouget,France* 4-8-13 IoritzMendizabal (1)...32/10   1¼   3
    39 Dolniya (FR) *A.deRoyerDupre,France* 4-8-13 ChristopheSoumillon (3) .... 17/10f   ¾   4
        Free Port Lux *F.Head,France* 4-9-2 MickaelBarzalona (4) 91/10   3½   5
        Roseburg (GER) *LucaCumani,GB* 4-9-2 KevinStott (5) 64/1   4   6
        Kerosin (GER) *J-P.Carvalho,Germany* 4-9-2 FilipMinarik (8) 56/1   8   7
    32 Bathyrhon (GER) *MmePiaBrandt,France* 5-9-2 MaximeGuyon (7) 69/10   5   8
        Sheikh Mohammed Obaid Al Maktoum 8ran 2m32.88   123/122/117/115/113/107

WOODBINE Sunday, Sep 13   GOOD to SOFT

83 Ricoh Woodbine Mile Stakes (Gr 1) (3yo+) £295,647   1m
        MONDIALISTE (IRE) *DavidO'Meara,GB* 5-8-7 FergalLynch (5)....................38/10   1
    5   LEA (USA) *WilliamI.Mott,USA* 6-8-9 JoelRosario (8) .... 23/10f   ½   2
        OBVIOUSLY (IRE) *Philipd'Amato,USA* 7-8-9 JosephTalamo (1).................275/100   1¼   3
        Kaigun (CAN) *MarkE.Casse,Canada* 5-8-7 PatrickHusbands (7).................1235/100   nk   4
        Reporting Star (USA) *,GB* 5-8-9 (b) LuisContreras (9) ....102/10   nk   5
    43 Mr. Owen (USA) *FrancoisRohaut,France* 3-8-0 UmbertoRispoli (6)............885/100   2½   6
        Tower of Texas (CAN) *RogerL.Attfield,Canada* 4-8-9 (b) EuricoRosaDaSilva (4) ...76/10   ½   7
        Turncoat (USA) *L.Silvera,USA* 5-8-5 (b) OmarMoreno (3) 863/10   1¼   8
        Platinum Glory (CAN) *MichaelP.DePaulo,USA* 4-8-6 JesseM.Campbell (2) ...786/10   11¼   9
        Geoff & Sandra Turnbull & Partner 9ran 1m36.66   122/123/119/117/118/108

NEWMARKET Friday, Sep 25   GOOD (Rowley Mile Course)

84 Shadwell Joel Stakes (Gr 2) (1) (3yo+) £56,710   1m
    60 TIME TEST *RogerCharlton* 3-9-0 RyanMoore (2)......................................10/11f   1
    13 CUSTOM CUT (IRE) *DavidO'Meara* 6-9-4 DanielTudhope (4) 15/8   1   2
        DECORATED KNIGHT *RogerVarian* 3-9-0 AndreaAtzeni (3) 7/1   4½   3
    70 Tupi (IRE) *RichardHannon* 3-9-0 PatDobbs (1) 12/1   2   4
        Mr K. Abdullah 4ran 1m35.84   125/122/110/104

1135

85 Connolly's Red Mills Cheveley Park Stakes (Gr 1) (1) (2yo f) £109,876   6f

61	LUMIERE *MarkJohnston* 2-9-0 WilliamBuick (8)..............................10/3		1
	ILLUMINATE (IRE) *RichardHannon* 2-9-0 FrankieDettori (4)....................3/1	½	2
61	BESHARAH (IRE) *WilliamHaggas* 2-9-0 PatCosgrave (7) 9/4f	hd	3
76	Alice Springs (IRE) *AidanO'Brien,Ireland* 2-9-0 RyanMoore (6)................9/2	¾	4
	Bear Cheek (IRE) *G.M.Lyons,Ireland* 2-9-0 AndreaAtzeni (3)....................12/1	3½	5
	Sunflower *AndrewBalding* 2-9-0 DavidProbert (2) 33/1	1½	6
30	Rebel Surge (IRE) *DaveMorris* 2-9-0 WilliamTwiston-Davies (1)..............100/1	1¼	7
	Shadow Hunter (IRE) *PaulD'Arcy* 2-9-0 (h) PhillipMakin (5)....................33/1	½	8

Sheikh Hamdan Bin Mohammed Al Maktoum 8ran 1m11.98   115/113/113/110/98/93

86 Juddmonte Middle Park Stakes (Gr 1) (1) (2yo c) £102,078   6f

66	SHALAA (IRE) *JohnGosden* 2-9-0 FrankieDettori (6) 1/2f		1
54	BURATINO (IRE) *MarkJohnston* 2-9-0 WilliamBuick (1) 13/2	½	2
64	STEADY PACE *SaeedbinSuroor* 2-9-0 HarryBentley (7) 25/1	2	3
64	Ajaya *WilliamHaggas* 2-9-0 GrahamGibbons (4) 6/1	½	4
	Rouleau *CharlieAppleby* 2-9-0 RyanMoore (5)......................................20/1	2¾	5
	Venturous (IRE) *CharlieAppleby* 2-9-0 JamesDoyle (2) 12/1	2½	6
	Madrinho (IRE) *RichardHannon* 2-9-0 PatDobbs (3) 100/1	¾	7

Al Shaqab Racing 7ran 1m11.92   120/118/111/109/100/91

87 Kingdom of Bahrain Sun Chariot Stakes (Gr 1) (1) (3yo+ f+m) £160,915   1m

58	ESOTERIQUE (IRE) *A.Fabre,France* 5-9-3 Pierre-CharlesBoudot (1)..............11/8f		1
13	INTEGRAL *SirMichaelStoute* 5-9-3 RyanMoore (2) 4/1	½	2
34	IRISH ROOKIE (IRE) *MartynMeade* 3-9-0 FergusSweeney (9)......................20/1	1½	3
9	Fadhayyil (IRE) *B.W.Hills* 3-9-0 PaulHanagan (4) 17/2	nk	4
	Realtra (IRE) *RogerVarian* 3-9-0 AndreaAtzeni (5)..................................14/1	½	5
67	Bawina (IRE) *C.Laffon-Parias,France* 4-9-3 MaximeGuyon (3).....................7/1	1¼	6
81	Maimara (FR) *M.Delzangles,France* 3-9-0 FrankieDettori (7)......................12/1	1	7
74	Raydara (IRE) *M.Halford,Ireland* 3-9-0 PatSmullen (8)..............................20/1	½	8
25	Malabar *MickChannon* 3-9-0 (v) SilvestreDeSousa (4) 16/1	1¾	9

Baron Edouard de Rothschild 9ran 1m35.87   120/119/116/115/114/109

88 Total Prix Marcel Boussac - Criterium des Pouliches (Gr 1) (2yo f) £126,044   7f210y

76	BALLYDOYLE (IRE) *AidanO'Brien,Ireland* 2-8-11 (t) RyanMoore (3)............15/10		1
65	TURRET ROCKS (IRE) *J.S.Bolger,Ireland* 2-8-11 KevinManning (5) 127/10	1¼	2
	QEMAH (IRE) *Jean-ClaudeRouget,France* 2-8-11 GregoryBenoist (7)..............13/1	sn	3
	Left Hand *C.Laffon-Parias,France* 2-8-11 MaximeGuyon (2)........................125/10	1	4
	Katie's Diamond (FR) *K.R.Burke,GB* 2-8-11 (h) AndreaAtzeni (4)...................214/10	hd	5
	Aktoria (FR) *C.Laffon-Parias,France* 2-8-11 OlivierPeslier (1)........................41/1	¾	6
	Antonoe (USA) *P.Bary,France* 2-8-11 VincentCheminaud (6)............................evsf	5	7
	Ella Diva (FR) *MmeG.Rarick,France* 2-8-11 MickaelForest (8) 54/1	3	8

Mr M. Tabor, D. Smith & Mrs John Magnier 8ran 1m35.44   111/108/107/104/104/102

89 Qatar Prix Jean-Luc Lagardere (Grand Criterium) Sponsored by Al Hazm (Gr 1) (2yo c+f) £147,051   7f210y

	ULTRA (IRE) *A.Fabre,France* 2-9-0 MickaelBarzalona (2) 55/10		1
	CYMRIC (USA) *JohnGosden,GB* 2-9-0 WilliamBuick (10) 239/10	sn	2
	GALILEO GOLD *HugoPalmer,GB* 2-9-0 FrankieDettori (8)..........................29/10	1	3
	Johannes Vermeer (IRE) *AidanO'Brien,Ireland* 2-9-0 RyanMoore (5).............22/10f	nk	4
27	First Selection (SPA) *SimonCrisford,GB* 2-9-0 Pierre-CharlesBoudot (1).........232/10	hd	5
	Shogun (IRE) *AidanO'Brien,Ireland* 2-9-0 (b) JosephO'Brien (4)..................106/10	sn	6
77	Herald The Dawn (IRE) *J.S.Bolger,Ireland* 2-9-0 KevinManning (6) 6/1	1½	7
	Attendu (FR) *C.Laffon-Parias,France* 2-9-0 MaximeGuyon (11)....................111/10	sh	8
	No Education *JoHughes,GB* 2-9-0 DougieCostello (3)..................................64/1	ns	9
	Ventura Storm (IRE) *RichardHannon,GB* 2-9-0 SeanLevey (9)......................161/10	1½	10
	Rougeoyant (FR) *B.deMontzey,France* 2-9-0 GregoryBenoist (7).....................73/1	1¼	11

Godolphin S.N.C. 11ran 1m37.27   116/116/113/112/112/112

90 Prix de l'Opera Longines (Gr 1) (3yo+ f+m) £168,059   1m1f207y

62	COVERT LOVE *HugoPalmer,GB* 3-8-12 PatSmullen (5).......................36/10		1
52	JAZZI TOP *JohnGosden,GB* 3-8-12 FrankieDettori (2) 54/10	hd	2
67	WE ARE (IRE) *F.Head,France* 4-9-2 ThierryJarnet (12) 51/10	2½	3
18	Wekeela (FR) *Jean-ClaudeRouget,France* 3-8-12 Jean-BernardEyquem (3).......34/1	hd	4
74	Cladocera (GER) *A.deRoyerDupre,France* 4-9-2 ChristopheSoumillon (4).........83/10	sn	5
67	Fate (FR) *A.deRoyerDupre,France* 6-9-2 MickaelBarzalona (1) 196/10	½	6
25	Little Nightingale (FR) *M.Delzangles,France* 3-8-12 UmbertoRispoli (8)............38/1	nk	7

52 Star of Seville *JohnGosden,GB* 3-8-12 WilliamBuick (6)................................ 158/10f hd 8
25 Queen's Jewel *F.Head,France* 3-8-12 MaximeGuyon (11)................................ 35/10f ½ 9
67 Feodora (GER) *A.Fabre,France* 4-9-2 Pierre-CharlesBoudot (13)........................36/1 nk 10
Bourree (GER) *AndreasLowe,Germany* 3-8-12 EddyHardouin (9) ....28/1 ½ 11
80 Diamondsandrubies (IRE) *AidanO'Brien,Ireland* 3-8-12 RyanMoore (7).............18/1 3½ 12
67 Odeliz (IRE) *K.R.Burke,GB* 5-9-2 (s) AdriedeVries (10)..................................184/10 8 13
FOMO Syndicate 13ran 2m04.43 120/120/113/115/113/112

91 Qatar Prix de l'Arc de Triomphe (Gr 1) (3yo+ c+f) £2,100,735 1m3f205y
73 GOLDEN HORN *JohnGosden,GB* 3-8-11 FrankieDettori (14)...........................52/10 1
39 FLINTSHIRE *A.Fabre,France* 5-9-5 MaximeGuyon (11)................................186/10 2 2
79 NEW BAY *A.Fabre,France* 3-8-11 VincentCheminaud (5).................................48/10 nk 3
80 Treve (FR) *MmeC.Head-Maarek,France* 5-9-2 ThierryJarnet (8) .... 9/10f ns 4
79 Erupt (IRE) *Francis-HenriGraffard,France* 3-8-11 StephanePasquier (4)............29/1 1½ 5
73 Free Eagle (IRE) *D.K.Weld,Ireland* 4-9-5 PatSmullen (12) ....168/10 nk 6
8 Prince Gibraltar (FR) *Jean-ClaudeRouget,France* 4-9-5 (b) FabriceVeron (10) ...42/1 sn 7
Siljan's Saga (FR) *J-P.Gauvin,France* 5-9-2 Pierre-CharlesBoudot (7)...............108/1 sn 8
73 Found (IRE) *AidanO'Brien,Ireland* 3-8-8 RyanMoore (15)...................................28/1 ½ 9
79 Silverwave (FR) *A.Couetil,France* 3-8-11 JamesDoyle (17) ....100/1 hd 10
39 Manatee *A.Fabre,France* 4-9-5 MickaelBarzalona (1)..59/1 2 11
82 Spiritjim (FR) *A.Couetil,France* 5-9-5 AndreaAtzeni (18) ....148/1 ¾ 12
82 Dolniya (FR) *A.deRoyerDupre,France* 4-9-2 ChristopheSoumillon (13) 27/1 4 13
80 Frine (IRE) *C.Laffon-Parias,France* 5-9-2 OlivierPeslier (6).................................77/1 ¾ 14
46 Eagle Top *JohnGosden,GB* 4-9-5 WilliamBuick (3) ....46/1 nk 15
Tapestry (IRE) *AidanO'Brien,Ireland* 4-9-2 JosephO'Brien (9) 57/1 15 16
Shahah *MmeC.Head-Maarek,France* 3-8-8 GregoryBenoist (2) 120/1 30 17
Mr A. E. Oppenheimer 17ran 2m27.23 132/128/128/125/125/125

92 Qatar Prix de l'Abbaye de Longchamp (Gr 1) (2yo+) £147,051 4f214y
63 GOLDREAM *RobertCowell,GB* 6-9-11 (s) MartinHarley (5) 9/1 1
28 RANGALI *H-A.Pantall,France* 4-9-11 (b) MickaelBarzalona (11) ....43/1 sn 2
63 MUTHMIR (IRE) *WilliamHaggas,GB* 5-9-11 PaulHanagan (6) 32/10f 1¾ 3
75 Pearl Secret *DavidBarron,GB* 6-9-11 AndreaAtzeni (15) ....50/1 ¾ 4
63 Move In Time *DavidO'Meara,GB* 7-9-11 DanielTudhope (16)...........................74/10 ns 5
63 Mirza *RaeGuest,GB* 8-9-11 (s) IoritzMendizabal (12) ....45/1 hd 6
51 Caspian Prince (IRE) *DeanIvory,GB* 6-9-11 RobertWinston (10)..........................59/1 1¼ 7
42 Steps (IRE) *RogerVarian,GB* 7-9-11 (b) WilliamBuick (3).................................135/10 sn 8
75 Sole Power *EdwardLynam,Ireland* 8-9-11 ChrisHayes (7) ....56/10 sn 9
75 Stepper Point *WilliamMuir,GB* 6-9-11 (b) PatSmullen (1) ....32/1 hd 10
Monsieur Joe (IRE) *PaulMidgley,GB* 8-9-11 JosephO'Brien (9)...........................68/1 1½ 11
75 Take Cover *DavidC.Griffiths,GB* 8-9-11 DavidAllan (8) ....171/10 hd 12
55 Son Cesio (FR) *H-A.Pantall,France* 4-9-11 FabriceVeron (13).............................17/1 sn 13
Humidor (IRE) *GeorgeBaker,GB* 8-9-11 PatCosgrave (4) ....91/1 ½ 14
75 Maarek *MissEvannaMcCutcheon,Ireland* 8-9-11 JamieSpencer (2)..................132/10 ¾ 15
63 Justice Day (IRE) *DavidElsworth,GB* 4-9-11 SilvestreDeSousa (14)....................57/1 1¼ 16
66 Gutaifan (IRE) *RichardHannon,GB* 2-8-7 GregoryBenoist (17)...........................58/10 sn 17
68 Watchable *DavidO'Meara,GB* 5-9-11 (b) VincentCheminaud (18) 35/1 1¼ 18
Mr J Sargeant & Mrs J Morley 18ran 54.79secs 123/122/115/112/112/112

93 Qatar Prix de la Foret (Gr 1) (3yo+) £126,044 6f211y
29 MAKE BELIEVE *A.Fabre,France* 3-9-0 OlivierPeslier (2).................................39/10 1
70 LIMATO (IRE) *HenryCandy,GB* 3-9-0 RyanMoore (9)..................................... 12/10f 1¼ 2
58 TOORMORE (IRE) *RichardHannon,GB* 4-9-2 JamesDoyle (6) 7/1 1½ 3
Amy Eria (IRE) *FrancoisRohaut,France* 4-8-13 GregoryBenoist (4) ....40/1 nk 4
Taniyar (IRE) *A.deRoyerDupre,France* 3-9-0 ChristopheSoumillon (3) ....47/10 hd 5
68 Gordon Lord Byron (IRE) *T.Hogan,Ireland* 7-9-2 W.M.Lordan (10) ....174/10 sn 6
6 Ride Like The Wind (IRE) *F.Head,France* 3-9-0 MickaelBarzalona (12).........204/10 ¾ 7
Suedois (FR) *C.Baillet,France* 4-9-2 AlexBadel (5) 55/1 1¼ 8
La Berma (IRE) *F.Chappet,France* 3-8-10 IoritzMendizabal (7)...........................78/1 sn 9
84 Custom Cut (IRE) *DavidO'Meara,GB* 6-9-2 PatSmullen (8) 269/10 3 10
68 G Force (IRE) *DavidO'Meara,GB* 4-9-2 DanielTudhope (13) 29/1 5 11
11 Penorka (FR) *B.deMontzey,France* 3-8-10 JimmyMartin (11)..............................154/1 ¾ 12
Salateen *KevinRyan,GB* 3-9-0 WilliamBuick (1) 69/1 8 13
Prince A. A. Faisal 13ran 1m17.05 127/123/117/113/117/115

94 Qatar Prix du Cadran (Gr 1) (4yo+) £126,044 2m3f194y
MILLE ET MILLE *C.&Y.Lerner,France* 5-9-2 ThierryThulliez (2)................. 111/10 1
KICKY BLUE (GER) *T.Clout,France* 5-8-13 MickaelBarzalona (3)....................57/1 1½ 2
FUN MAC (GER) *HughieMorrison,GB* 4-9-2 IoritzMendizabal (1)...................49/10 2½ 3
Trip To Rhodos (FR) *P.Tuma,CzechRepublic* 6-9-2 CristianDemuro (6)...........204/10 3 4
82 Bathyrhon (GER) *MmePiaBrandt,France* 5-9-2 MaximeGuyon (8) 31/10 1 5

Walzertakt (GER) *J-P.Carvalho,Germany* 6-9-2 (s) ChristopheSoumillon (4)....31/10 1 6
50 Simenon (IRE) *W.P.Mullins,Ireland* 5-9-2 FrankieDettori (11)..........................124/10 ½ 7
   Iltemas (USA) *FrancoisRohaut,France* 4-8-13 GregoryBenoist (9)....................168/10 1¼ 8
   Achtung (SPA) *J.LopezSanchez,France* 7-9-2 Jose-LuisMartinezTejera (7).........71/1 7 9
   Clondaw Warrior (IRE) *W.P.Mullins,Ireland* 8-9-2 (h) RyanMoore (10)............... 3/1f hd 10
   Nicolas Saltiel 10ran 4m22.61   118/113/115/111/109/108

NEWMARKET Friday, Oct 9 GOOD (Rowley Mile Course)
95 Dubai Fillies' Mile (Gr 1) (1) (2yo f) £302,690   1m
76 MINDING (IRE) *AidanO'Brien,Ireland* 2-9-0 RyanMoore (10) 5/4f 1
   NATHRA (IRE) *JohnGosden* 2-9-0 FrankieDettori (9) 4/1 4½ 2
   HAWKSMOOR (IRE) *HugoPalmer* 2-9-0 PatSmullen (2)........................16/1 2¼ 3
   Coolmore (IRE) *AidanO'Brien,Ireland* 2-9-0 (s) JosephO'Brien (3)..................6/1 hd 4
   Beautiful Morning *LucaCumani* 2-9-0 JamieSpencer (8) 14/1 1½ 5
   Dawn of Hope (IRE) *RogerVarian* 2-9-0 JimCrowley (5) 28/1 6 6
   Promising Run (USA) *SaeedbinSuroor* 2-9-0 WilliamBuick (7) 6/1 1¾ 7
   Marenko *RichardHannon* 2-9-0 SeanLevey (6) ....33/1 nk 8
   Opal Tiara (IRE) *MickChannon* 2-9-0 AndreaAtzeni (4) 100/1 1½ 9
   Dessertoflife (IRE) *MarkJohnston* 2-9-0 JoeFanning (1)..........................100/1 4 10
   Mr D. Smith, Mrs J. Magnier, Mr M. Tabor 10ran 1m37.87   120/107/101/100/96/79

NEWMARKET Saturday, Oct 10 GOOD (Rowley Mile Course)
96 Dubai Dewhurst Stakes (Gr 1) (1) (2yo f) £283,550   7f
77 AIR FORCE BLUE (USA) *AidanO'Brien,Ireland* 2-9-1 RyanMoore (7) 4/6f 1
   MASSAAT (IRE) *B.W.Hills* 2-9-1 PaulHanagan (3)...............................20/1 3¼ 2
   SANUS PER AQUAM (IRE) *J.S.Bolger,Ireland* 2-9-1 KevinManning (6)..........20/1 2¾ 3
   Tashweeq (IRE) *JohnGosden* 2-9-1 DaneO'Neill (1) ....33/1 ns 4
49 Adventurous (IRE) *MarkJohnston* 2-9-1 JamieSpencer (5)........................66/1 1 5
   Twin Sails *DeanIvory* 2-9-1 (t) RobertWinston (4)..............................100/1 ¾ 6
69 Emotionless (IRE) *CharlieAppleby* 2-9-1 WilliamBuick (2)........................7/4 ½ 7
   Mrs John Magnier,Mr M.Tabor & Mr D.Smith 7ran 1m25.34   124/114/106/106/103/101

ASCOT Saturday, Oct 17 GOOD to SOFT
97 Qipco British Champions Long Distance Cup (Gr 2) (1) (3yo+) £195,650   2m
   FLYING OFFICER (USA) *JohnGosden* 5-9-7 (h) FrankieDettori (4)...............6/1 1
46 CLEVER COOKIE *PeterNiven* 7-9-7 GrahamLee (13)............................8/1 1 2
78 WICKLOW BRAVE *W.P.Mullins,Ireland* 6-9-7 RyanMoore (3)....................10/1 1 3
50 Pallasator *SirMarkPrescottBt* 6-9-7 AndreaAtzeni (1)............................8/1 2¾ 4
   Hidden Gold (IRE) *SaeedbinSuroor* 4-9-4 JamesDoyle (5) ....25/1 ¾ 5
   Suegioo (FR) *MarcoBotti* 6-9-7 (s) MartinHarley (9) ....25/1 nk 6
   Amour de Nuit (IRE) *SirMarkPrescottBt* 3-8-11 LukeMorris (8)..................20/1 1¼ 7
78 Forgotten Rules (IRE) *D.K.Weld,Ireland* 5-9-7 PatSmullen (10)...................9/2jf sh 8
   Litigant *JosephTuite* 7-9-7 OisinMurphy (12).....................................7/1 2 9
   Gale Force *JamesFanshawe* 4-9-4 FrederikTylicki (6) ....25/1 sh 10
94 Simenon (IRE) *W.P.Mullins,Ireland* 8-9-7 WilliamBuick (4)........................33/1 1½ 11
78 Agent Murphy *BrianMeehan* 4-9-7 JimmyFortune (11) 9/2jf 1 12
94 Clondaw Warrior (IRE) *W.P.Mullins,Ireland* 8-9-7 (h) VincentCheminaud (1).....20/1 9 13
   Mr George Strawbridge 13ran 3m32.19   118/117/115/111/107/110

98 Qipco British Champions Sprint Stakes (Gr 1) (1) (3yo+) £358,694   6f
55 MUHAARAR *CharlesHills* 3-9-1 PaulHanagan (12) 5/2f 1
68 TWILIGHT SON *HenryCandy* 3-9-1 RyanMoore (20) 4/1 2 2
68 DANZENO *MichaelAppleby* 4-9-2 FrankieDettori (14)........................12/1 1½ 3
   The Tin Man *JamesFanshawe* 3-9-1 TomQueally (6) ....10/1 nk 4
70 Naadirr (IRE) *MarcoBotti* 4-9-2 (s) ChristopheSoumillon (8) 20/1 1¼ 5
68 Adaay (IRE) *WilliamHaggas* 3-9-1 DaneO'Neill (1) ....25/1 nk 6
   Emperor Max (AUS) *S.Gray,Singapore* 6-9-2 (v) CoreyBrown (17)..............33/1 nk 7
47 Aeolus *EdWalker* 4-9-2 GrahamLee (15) ....100/1 nk 8
   Gathering Power (IRE) *EdwardLynam,Ireland* 5-8-13 MickaelBarzalona (19).....66/1 nk 9
   Interception (IRE) *DavidLanigan* 5-8-13 GeorgeBaker (7)......................50/1 hd 10
92 Maarek *MissEvannaMcCutcheon,Ireland* 8-9-2 JamieSpencer (2).................25/1 sh 11
93 Gordon Lord Byron (IRE) *T.Hogan,Ireland* 7-9-2 PatSmullen (18)................16/1 nk 12
70 Lightning Moon (IRE) *EdWalker* 4-9-2 WilliamBuick (9) ....10/1 nk 13
42 Lancelot du Lac (ITY) *DeanIvory* 5-9-2 RobertWinston (10) ....40/1 ½ 14
   Heaven's Guest (IRE) *RichardFahey* 5-9-2 JamesDoyle (16)....................50/1 dh 14
42 Jack Dexter *JimGoldie* 6-9-2 FergalLynch (13) ....33/1 ½ 16
68 Eastern Impact (IRE) *RichardFahey* 4-9-2 JackGarritty (1) ....20/1 nk 17
68 Strath Burn *CharlesHills* 3-9-1 AndreaAtzeni (4) 10/1 5 18
70 Coulsty (IRE) *RichardHannon* 4-9-2 SeanLevey (4)............................66/1 ¾ 19

75 Great Minds (IRE) *T.Stack,Ireland* 5-9-2 W.M.Lordan (11) 66/1 6 20
Mr Hamdan Al Maktoum 20ran 1m13.34 132/125/119/118/114/113

99 Qipco British Champions Fillies' And Mares' Stakes (Gr 1) (1) (3yo+) £327,858 1½m
71 SIMPLE VERSE (IRE) *RalphBeckett* 3-8-12 AndreaAtzeni (12)....5/1 1
JOURNEY *JohnGosden* 3-8-12 (h) FrankieDettori (11)....7/1 ¾ 2
80 BEAUTIFUL ROMANCE *SaeedbinSuroor* 3-8-12 JamesDoyle (1)....20/1 2 3
90 Covert Love (IRE) *HugoPalmer* 3-8-12 PatSmullen (7).... 4/1f nk 4
17 Bocca Baciata (IRE) *MrsJ.Harrington,Ireland* 3-8-12 F.M.Berry (6) ....16/1 ½ 5
80 Arabian Queen (IRE) *DavidElsworth* 3-8-12 SilvestreDeSousa (2) 14/1 1½ 6
80 Sea Calisi (FR) *FrancoisDoumen,France* 3-8-12 MickaelBarzalona (9)....6/1 1½ 7
91 Tapestry (IRE) *AidanO'Brien,Ireland* 4-9-5 RyanMoore (4) 12/1 2¼ 8
45 Speedy Boarding *JamesFanshawe* 3-8-12 FrederikTylicki (5) 25/1 2 9
67 Madame Chiang *DavidSimcock* 4-9-5 JimCrowley (8)....20/1 3¾ 10
80 Candarliya (FR) *A.deRoyerDupre,France* 3-8-12 ChristopheSoumillon (3)....9/2 5 11
Lady Tiana *LucyWadham* 4-9-5 GrahamLee (10)....50/1 4½ 12
QRL/Sheikh Suhaim Al Thani/M Al Kubaisi 12ran 2m32.01 119/118/114/113/112/110

100 Queen Elizabeth II Stakes Sponsored by Qipco (Gr 1) (1) (3yo+) £623,810 1m
48 SOLOW *F.Head,France* 5-9-4 MaximeGuyon (2)....11/10f 1
68 BELARDO (IRE) *RogerVarian* 3-9-1 (h) JamesDoyle (4) ....33/1 ¾ 2
48 GABRIAL (IRE) *RichardFahey* 6-9-4 PaulHanagan (5) 66/1 1½ 3
87 Integral *SirMichaelStoute* 5-9-1 FrankieDettori (9) ....20/1 hd 4
23 Elm Park *AndrewBalding* 3-9-1 AndreaAtzeni (7) ....16/1 nk 5
29 Gleneagles (IRE) *AidanO'Brien,Ireland* 3-9-1 RyanMoore (1) ....9/4 hd 6
58 Territories (IRE) *A.Fabre,France* 3-9-1 MickaelBarzalona (6)....8/1 ½ 7
43 Kodi Bear (IRE) *CliveCox* 3-9-1 GeraldMosse (8) ....7/1 nk 8
13 Top Notch Tonto (IRE) *BrianEllison* 5-9-4 (s) SilvestreDeSousa (3) 50/1 1 9
Wertheimer et Frere 9ran 1m41.92 125/123/119/116/118/118

101 Qipco Champion Stakes (Gr 1) (1) (3yo+) £770,547 1¼m
72 FASCINATING ROCK (IRE) *D.K.Weld,Ireland* 4-9-5 PatSmullen (7)....10/1 1
91 FOUND (IRE) *AidanO'Brien,Ireland* 3-8-11 RyanMoore (8) 9/2 1¼ 2
37 JACK HOBBS *JohnGosden* 3-9-0 WilliamBuick (12) .... evsf ½ 3
Racing History (IRE) *SaeedbinSuroor* 3-9-0 JamesDoyle (1)....16/1 1½ 4
Air Pilot *RalphBeckett* 6-9-5 HarryBentley (10) ....33/1 nk 5
31 The Corsican (IRE) *DavidSimcock* 4-9-5 JamieSpencer (4) 12/1 1 6
40 Tullius (IRE) *AndrewBalding* 7-9-5 JimmyFortune (11)....50/1 1 7
67 Ribbons *JamesFanshawe* 5-9-2 FrankieDettori (6)....14/1 2¾ 8
Palace Prince (GER) *AndreasLowe,Germany* 3-9-0 SilvestreDeSousa (9)....80/1 hd 9
20 Sumbal (IRE) *Francis-HenriGraffard,France* 3-9-0 ChristopheSoumillon (3).....33/1 3¼ 10
Maverick Wave (USA) *JohnGosden* 4-9-5 RobertHavlin (13) 66/1 13 11
58 Lightning Spear *OllyStevens* 4-9-5 OisinMurphy (2)....50/1 8 12
Vadamos (FR) *A.Fabre,France* 4-9-5 VincentCheminaud (5)....8/1 3¾ 13
Newtown Anner Stud Farm 13ran 2m06.31 127/121/123/120/119/117

WOODBINE Sunday, Oct 18 GOOD
102 E. P. Taylor Stakes Presented by HPIbet (Gr 1) (3yo+ f+m) £151,824 1¼m
62 CURVY *DavidWachman,Ireland* 3-8-7 (b) RyanMoore (9).... 245/100f 1
TALMADA (USA) *RogerVarian,GB* 4-8-12 WilliamBuick (12)....1085/100 1½ 2
ROSALIND (USA) *ChadC.Brown,USA* 4-8-12 (b) AlanGarcia (2) ....1455/100 nk 3
Strut The Course (CAN) *BarbaraJ.Minshall,Canada* 5-8-12 LuisContreras (6)...355/100 nk 4
Button Down *JosieCarroll,Canada* 4-8-12 (b) JoelRosario (3) ....915/100 ns 5
Nakuti (IRE) *SylvesterKirk,GB* 4-8-12 AndreaAtzeni (7) ....294/10 ½ 6
17 Devonshire (IRE) *W.McCreery,Ireland* 3-8-7 PatrickHusbands (4) ....124/10 ¾ 7
Yaazy (IRE) *J.E.Hammond,France* 3-8-7 AntoineHamelin (1) ....675/100 ¾ 8
White Rose (USA) *WilliamI.Mott,USA* 5-8-12 ShaunBridgmohan (8)....1555/100 1 9
Eastern Belle *H.GrahamMotion,USA* 4-8-12 JohnR.Velazquez (10).... 110/10 2¼ 10
Uchenna (IRE) *RogerL.Attfield,Canada* 4-8-12 RafaelManuelHernandez (11)...4095/100 ¾ 11
57 Lacy (GER) *W.Hickst,Germany* 4-8-12 MartinLane (5)....470/10 3¾ 12
Mr M Tabor, Mrs J Magnier & Mr D Smith 12ran 2m02.88 113/110/109/109/109/108

103 Pattison Canadian International Stakes (Gr 1) (3yo+) £303,654 1½m
31 CANNOCK CHASE (USA) *SirMichaelStoute,GB* 4-9-0 RyanMoore (2)....11/4f 1
UP WITH THE BIRDS (CAN) *H.GrahamMotion,USA* 5-9-0 (b)
JohnR.Velazquez (5)....1075/100 1½ 2
50 SHEIKHZAYEDROAD *DavidSimcock,GB* 6-9-0 (h) MartinLane (3)....925/100 1 3
83 Kaigun (CAN) *MarkE.Casse,Canada* 5-9-0 PatrickHusbands (10)....1645/100 ½ 4
83 Reporting Star (USA) *PatParente,Canada* 5-9-0 LuisContreras (8)....1545/100 1¾ 5
Triple Threat (FR) *WilliamI.Mott,USA* 5-9-0 JoelRosario (7) ....965/100 nk 6

Danish Dynaformer (CAN) *RogerL.Attfield,Canada* 3-8-7 (b)
EuricoRosaDaSilva (6)..2065/100   ½ 7
Power Ped (USA) *NeilDrysdale,USA* 5-9-0 FlorentGeroux (1).........................230/10   1¼ 8
78 Second Step (IRE) *LucaCumani,GB* 4-9-0 AndreaAtzeni (4)..............................31/10   2 9
Interpol (CAN) *SidC.Attard,Canada* 4-9-0 Emma-JayneWilson (9)...................75/10   ¾ 10
Habibi (NZ) *MarkR.Frostad,Canada* 6-8-11 RobbyAlbarado (11)...............1345/100   3¾ 11
Rabbah Bloodstock LLC Lessee 11ran 2m29.26   119/117/115/114/111/111

DONCASTER Saturday, Oct 24 GOOD to SOFT
104 **Racing Post Trophy (Gr 1) (1) (2yo c+f)** £113,420   1m
MARCEL (IRE) *PeterChapple-Hyam* 2-9-1 AndreaAtzeni (4) 33/1   1
89 JOHANNES VERMEER (IRE) *AidanO'Brien,Ireland* 2-9-1 SeamieHeffernan (1)...7/1   1½ 2
FOUNDATION (IRE) *JohnGosden* 2-9-1 FrankieDettori (6)............................10/11f   2½ 3
Port Douglas (IRE) *AidanO'Brien,Ireland* 2-9-1 (b) EmmetMcNamara (3).........20/1   1½ 4
Deauville (IRE) *AidanO'Brien,Ireland* 2-9-1 (s) JosephO'Brien (5)......................7/2   ¾ 5
Tony Curtis *RichardHannon* 2-9-1 SeanLevey (2)..14/1   5 6
Mengli Khan (IRE) *HugoPalmer* 2-9-1 HarryBentley (7) 8/1   9 7
Mr Paul Hancock 7ran 1m42.19   118/114/107/104/102/88

SAINT-CLOUD Sunday, Oct 25 GOOD to SOFT
105 **Prix Royal-Oak (Gr 1) (3yo+)** £143,878   1m7f90y
VAZIRABAD (FR) *A.deRoyerDupre,France* 3-8-11 ChristopheSoumillon 24/10f   1
91 SILJAN'S SAGA (FR) *J.-P.Gauvin,France* 5-9-1 Pierre-CharlesBoudot 72/10   1 2
94 MILLE ET MILLE *C.&Y.Lerner,France* 5-9-4 ThierryThulliez 9/1   5 3
73 Cirrus des Aigles (FR) *MmeC.Barande-Barbe,France* 9-9-4 FrankieDettori 78/10   1 4
91 Manatee *A.Fabre,France* 4-9-4 MickaelBarzalona ....41/10   nk 5
94 Walzertakt (GER) *J-P.Carvalho,Germany* 6-9-4 FranciscoFrancoDaSilva ....33/1   nk 6
Alex My Boy (IRE) *A.Wohler,Germany* 4-9-4 OlivierPeslier ....57/10   sn 7
94 Fun Mac (GER) *HughieMorrison,GB* 4-9-4 IoritzMendizabal ....47/1   sn 8
Sahrawi (GER) *M.Delzangles,France* 4-9-4 AlexBadel 33/1   2 9
Fly With Me (FR) *E.Libaud,France* 5-9-4 (b) MaximeGuyon ....112/10   sn 10
94 Kicky Bluc (GER) *T.Clout,France* 5-9-1 StephanePasquier 42/1   2½ 11
Zack Hope *N.Caullery,France* 7-9-4 TonyPiccone 132/1   7 12
Pilansberg *D.Smaga,France* 3-8-10 (b) VincentCheminaud 45/1   1½ 13
H.H. Aga Khan 13ran 3m27.61   127/120/117/116/115/115

KEENELAND Friday, Oct 30 GOOD to SOFT
106 **Breeders' Cup Juvenile Turf (Gr 1) (2yo)** £601,307   1m
HIT IT A BOMB (USA) *AidanO'Brien,Ireland* 2-8-10 RyanMoore (14)............72/10   1
AIROFORCE (USA) *MarkE.Casse,Canada* 2-8-10 JulienR.Leparoux (8).......27/10f   nk 2
77 BIRCHWOOD (IRE) *RichardFahey,GB* 2-8-10 JamesDoyle (6)......................185/10   nk 3
Conquest Daddyo (USA) *MarkE.Casse,Canada* 2-8-10 JoeBravo (10)...............133/10   2½ 4
Dressed In Hermes (USA) *JanetArmstrong,USA* 2-8-10 GaryL.Stevens (1)......171/10   1¼ 5
Highland Sky (USA) *BarclayTagg,USA* 2-8-10 (b) CornelioH.Velasquez (5)....178/10   nk 6
Manhattan Dan (USA) *GaryC.Contessa,USA* 2-8-10 RobbyAlbarado (3) 459/10   2¾ 7
89 Cymric (USA) *JohnGosden,GB* 2-8-10 WilliamBuick (13).............................53/10   ns 8
Hollywood Don (USA) *PeterMiller,USA* 2-8-10 JoelRosario (11) ....227/10   ¾ 9
89 Shogun (IRE) *AidanO'Brien,Ireland* 2-8-10 (b) SeamieHeffernan (4)............122/10   nk 10
Ray's The Bar *ChadC.Brown,USA* 2-8-10 JavierCastellano (7) ....82/10   hd 11
Camelot Kitten (USA) *ChadC.Brown,USA* 2-8-10 IradOrtiz,Jr (12) 114/10   5 12
Azar (USA) *ToddA.Pletcher,USA* 2-8-10 JohnR.Velazquez (2) 150/10   1¾ 13
Sky Marshal (USA) *BarbaraJ.Minshall,Canada* 2-8-10 (b) LuisSaez (9)..........310/10   1¾ 14
Mrs E. M. Stockwell 14ran 1m38.86   114/113/113/107/103/103

107 **Breeders' Cup Juvenile Fillies Turf (Gr 1) (2yo f)** £601,307   1m
CATCH A GLIMPSE (USA) *MarkE.Casse,Canada* 2-8-10 FlorentGeroux (3)...64/10   1
85 ALICE SPRINGS (IRE) *AidanO'Brien,Ireland* 2-8-10 RyanMoore (2)........ 29/10f   ¾ 2
NEMORALIA (USA) *JeremyNoseda,GB* 2-8-10 JoelRosario (8) ....141/10   hd 3
Sapphire Kitten (USA) *JoeSharp,USA* 2-8-10 JulienR.Leparoux (6) ....96/10   ½ 4
Time And Motion (USA) *JamesJ.Toner,USA* 2-8-10 MikeE.Smith (14) ....566/10   ½ 5
85 Illuminate (IRE) *RichardHannon,GB* 2-8-10 FrankieDettori (9).....................47/10   ¾ 6
Harmonize (USA) *WilliamI.Mott,USA* 2-8-10 JuniorAlvarado (7)...................45/10   1¼ 7
Mirage (IRE) *SimonCallaghan,USA* 2-8-10 JamieSpencer (12) ....440/10   ½ 8
Pricedtoperfection (USA) *ChadC.Brown,USA* 2-8-10 IradOrtiz,Jr (10) ....251/10   ¾ 9
Last Waltz (IRE) *ChadC.Brown,USA* 2-8-10 JavierCastellano (13) 130/10   6 10
Thrilled (USA) *ToddA.Pletcher,USA* 2-8-10 JohnR.Velazquez (1) ....253/10   nk 11
Gliding By (USA) *WilliamI.Mott,USA* 2-8-10 JoseLezcano (11).....................167/10   2¼ 12
Ruby Notion (USA) *WesleyA.Ward,USA* 2-8-10 RafaelManuelHernandez (4)...287/10   ¾ 13
Andreya's Reward (USA) *MiltonW.Wolfson,USA* 2-8-10 EdgarS.Prado (5)......830/10   1¾ 14
Windways Farm 14ran 1m39.08   111/109/109/108/106/105

KEENELAND Saturday, Oct 31   Dirt course: FAST   Turf course: GOOD

108 Breeders' Cup Filly & Mare Turf (Gr 1) (3yo+ f+m) £718,954   1m1f110y

57	STEPHANIE'S KITTEN (USA) *ChadC.Brown,USA* 6-8-12 IradOrtiz,Jr (9)..... 78/10		1
74	LEGATISSIMO (IRE) *DavidWachman,Ireland* 3-8-8 RyanMoore (2)............... 9/10f	1¼	2
90	QUEEN'S JEWEL *F.Head,France* 3-8-8 MaximeGuyon (5)........................... 132/10	2¼	3
	Sentiero Italia (USA) *KiaranP.McLaughlin,USA* 3-8-8 JoelRosario (1)....... 146/10	nk	4
	Photo Call (IRE) *H.GrahamMotion,USA* 4-8-12 DraydenVanDyke (4) 203/10	hd	5
57	Watsdachances (IRE) *ChadC.Brown,USA* 5-8-12 JoeBravo (6) 496/10	½	6
57	Secret Gesture *RalphBeckett,GB* 5-8-12 FlorentGeroux (10).................... 120/10	2½	7
	Miss France (IRE) *A.Fabre,France* 4-8-12 FrankieDettori (8) 79/10	1½	8
	Dacita (CHI) *ChadC.Brown,USA* 4-8-12 JavierCastellano (7)........................ 51/10	1	9
	Sharla Rae (USA) *DougF.O'Neill,USA* 3-8-8 JoseLezcano (3) 722/10	1½	10
	Kenneth L. & Sarah K. Ramsey 10ran 1m56.22	119/117/113/112/111/110	

109 Breeders' Cup Mile (Gr 1) (3yo+) £718,954   1m

	TEPIN (USA) *MarkE.Casse,Canada* 4-8-11 JulienR.Leparoux (7) 49/10		1
83	MONDIALISTE (IRE) *DavidO'Meara,GB* 5-9-0 DanielTudhope (4).............. 172/10	2¼	2
	GRAND ARCH (USA) *BrianA.Lynch,USA* 6-9-0 LuisSaez (1) 132/10	1½	3
3	Mshawish (USA) *ToddA.Pletcher,USA* 5-9-0 FrankieDettori (10)............... 217/10	½	4
93	Make Believe *A.Fabre,France* 3-8-11 OlivierPeslier (3) 27/10f	nk	5
	Impassable (IRE) *C.Laffon-Parias,France* 3-8-8 MaximeGuyon (5) 154/10	1¼	6
87	Esoterique (IRE) *A.Fabre,France* 5-8-11 Pierre-CharlesBoudot (9)............. 42/10	¾	7
	Tourist (USA) *WilliamI.Mott,USA* 4-9-0 (b) JoseLezcano (6) 128/10	¾	8
83	Obviously (IRE) *PhilipJ.D'Amato,USA* 7-9-0 JosephTalamo (8)................ 175/10	¾	9
84	Time Test *RogerCharlton,GB* 3-8-11 RyanMoore (2) 81/10	hd	10
81	Karakontie (JPN) *J.E.Pease,France* 4-9-0 StephanePasquier (11) 112/10	1¼	11
	Recepta (USA) *JamesJ.Toner,USA* 4-8-11 JohnR.Velazquez (2) 490/10	5	12
	Robert E. Masterson 12ran 1m36.69	125/122/118/117/116/110	

110 Longines Breeders' Cup Turf (Gr 1) (3yo+) £1,078,431   1½m

101	FOUND (IRE) *AidanO'Brien,Ireland* 3-8-7 RyanMoore (9) 64/10		1
91	GOLDEN HORN *JohnGosden,GB* 3-8-9 FrankieDettori (1) 8/10f	½	2
	BIG BLUE KITTEN (USA) *ChadC.Brown,USA* 7-9-0 JoeBravo (7) 58/10	¾	3
	Slumber *ChadC.Brown,USA* 7-9-0 (b) IradOrtiz,Jr (4) 189/10	½	4
	The Pizza Man (USA) *R.Brueggemann,USA* 6-9-0 FlorentGeroux (10)......... 61/10	2½	5
	Da Big Hoss (USA) *MichaelJ.Maker,USA* 4-9-0 JoseL.Ortiz (5) 603/10	2¼	6
	Red Rifle (USA) *ToddA.Pletcher,USA* 5-9-0 JavierCastellano (11) 186/10	nk	7
	Twilight Eclipse (USA) *ThomasAlbertrani,USA* 6-9-0 JoelRosario (6)............ 201/10	2½	8
	Ordak Dan (ARG) *JuanCarlosEtchechoury,Argentina* 7-9-0 JorgeA.Ricardo (12)... 1094/10	3¼	9
	Big John B (USA) *PhilipJ.D'Amato,USA* 6-9-0 RafaelBejarano (3).............. 480/10	6½	10
	Shining Copper (USA) *ChadC.Brown,USA* 5-9-0 LuisSaez (2) 719/10	2¾	11
	Cage Fighter (USA) *JamesL.LawrenceII,USA* 4-9-0 JoshuaNavarro (8)....... 1508/10	1¼	12
	M. Tabor, Mrs J. Magnier & D. Smith 12ran 2m32.06	122/124/120/119/115/112	

111 Breeders' Cup Classic (Gr 1) (3yo+) £1,797,386   1¼m (Dirt)

24	AMERICAN PHAROAH (USA) *BobBaffert,USA* 3-8-10 VictorEspinoza (4) ... 7/10f		1
	EFFINEX (USA) *JamesA.Jerkens,USA* 4-9-0 (b) MikeE.Smith (6)................ 330/10	6½	2
	HONOR CODE (USA) *ClaudeR.McGaugheyIII,USA* 4-9-0 JavierCastellano (8)... 47/10	4½	3
24	Keen Ice (USA) *DaleL.Romans,USA* 3-8-10 IradOrtiz,Jr (2) 97/10	1½	4
	Tonalist (USA) *ChristopheClement,USA* 4-9-0 JohnR.Velazquez (1)............ 60/10	hd	5
	Hard Aces (USA) *JohnW.Sadler,USA* 5-9-0 (b) JosephTalamo (7) 728/10	ns	6
24	Frosted (USA) *KiaranP.McLaughlin,USA* 3-8-10 (b) JoelRosario (3)............. 113/10	hd	7
100	Gleneagles (IRE) *AidanO'Brien,Ireland* 3-8-10 RyanMoore (5) 111/10	12½	8
	Zayat Stables LLC 8ran 2m00.07	138/127/120/119/118/118	

SAINT-CLOUD Sunday, Nov 1   SOFT

112 Criterium International (Gr 1) (2yo c+f) £102,770   6f211y

104	JOHANNES VERMEER (IRE) *AidanO'Brien,Ireland* 2-9-0 RyanMoore 25/10		1
	STORMY ANTARCTIC *EdWalker,GB* 2-9-0 AndreaAtzeni 30/1	hd	2
89	ATTENDU (FR) *C.Laffon-Parias,France* 2-9-0 MaximeGuyon 131/10	1½	3
	Donjuan Triumphant (IRE) *RichardFahey,GB* 2-9-0 AlexBadel 18/10f	1	4
89	No Education *JoHughes,GB* 2-9-0 DanielCostello 67/1	½	5
96	Tashweeq (IRE) *JohnGosden,GB* 2-9-0 PaulHanagan 62/10	sn	6
	Almanzor (FR) *Jean-ClaudeRouget,France* 2-9-0 ChristopheSoumillon 3/1	1¼	7
	Scrutineer (IRE) *MickChannon,GB* 2-9-0 OlivierPeslier 19/1	sn	8
	M Tabor/D Smith/Mrs J Magnier/T Ah Khing 8ran 1m30.15	115/115/111/108/107/106	

113 Criterium de Saint-Cloud (Gr 1) (2yo c+f) £102,770   1m1f207y

	ROBIN OF NAVAN (FR) *HarryDunlop,GB* 2-9-0 TonyPiccone 27/10		1
	CLOTH OF STARS (IRE) *A.Fabre,France* 2-9-0 MickaelBarzalona 26/10	2½	2

1141

NOTTE BIANCA (FR) *S.Kobayashi,France* 2-8-11 AlexBadel 36/1   3   3
Idaho (IRE) *AidanO'Brien,Ireland* 2-9-0 RyanMoore .... 22/10f   hd   4
Millfield (FR) *D.Smaga,France* 2-9-0 GregoryBenoist ....102/10   ½   5
Isfahan (GER) *A.Wohler,Germany* 2-9-0 UmbertoRispoli 9/1   4   6
Ormito (GER) *AndrewBalding,GB* 2-9-0 MaximeGuyon 133/10   3½   7
Indecence Choisie (FR) *C.Ferland,France* 2-8-11 OlivierPeslier ....32/1   sn   8
Ocean Jive *BrianMeehan,GB* 2-9-0 JimCrowley ....88/1   nk   9
Gontchar (FR) *A.M.Shavuyev,CzechRepublic* 2-9-0 IoritzMendizabal 82/1   3 10
Cross, Deal, Foden, Sieff 10ran 2m15.46   114/110/101/104/103/96

FLEMINGTON Tuesday, Nov 3   GOOD

114 **Emirates Melbourne Cup (Handicap) (Gr 1) (3yo+)** £2,565,517   1m7f200y

PRINCE OF PENZANCE (NZ) *DarrenWeir,Australia* 6-8-5 (b+t) MichellePayne ...100/1		1
MAX DYNAMITE (FR) *W.P.Mullins,Ireland* 5-8-9 FrankieDettori 12/1	½	2
60	CRITERION (NZ) *DavidHayes&TomDabernig,Australia* 5-9-1 (b) MichaelWalker ...20/1	¾	3
50	Trip To Paris (IRE) *EdDunlop,GB* 4-8-9 TommyBerry 5/1	¾	4
50	Big Orange *MichaelBell,GB* 4-8-10 (s) JamieSpencer 60/1	½	5
	Gust of Wind (NZ) *J.Sargent,Australia* 4-8-0 (b) ChadSchofield 40/1	nk	6
	Excess Knowledge *GaiWaterhouse,Australia* 5-8-0 KerrinMcEvoy 30/1	½	7
	The Offer (IRE) *GaiWaterhouse,Australia* 6-8-7 DamienOliver 30/1	nk	8
50	Quest For More (IRE) *RogerCharlton,GB* 5-8-6 (b) DamianLane 80/1	½	9
	Our Ivanhowe (GER) *Lee&AnthonyFreedman,Australia* 5-8-11 (b+t) BenMelham 20/1	hd	10
	Who Shot Thebarman (NZ) *ChrisWaller,Australia* 7-8-8 (t) BlakeShinn 20/1	sh	11
	Sertorius (AUS) *JamieEdwards,Australia* 8-8-4 (t) CraigNewitt 100/1	¾	12
	Fame Game (JPN) *YoshitadaMunakata,Japan* 5-9-0 ZacPurton 4/1f	¾	13
	The United States (IRE) *RobertHickmott,Australia* 5-8-4 JoaoMoreira 20/1	hd	14
	Hartnell *JohnO'Shea,Australia* 4-8-10 JamesMcDonald 30/1	hd	15
71	Bondi Beach (IRE) *AidanO'Brien,Ireland* 3-8-4 (t) BrettPrebble 20/1	nk	16
	Hokko Brave (JPN) *YasutoshiMatsunaga,Japan* 7-8-10 CraigA.Williams 40/1	hd	17
	Almoonqith (USA) *DavidHayes&TomDabernig,Australia* 5-8-5 (b) DwayneDunn 16/1	½	18
78	Kingfisher (IRE) *AidanO'Brien,Ireland* 4-8-5 (h+t) ColmO'Donoghue 60/1	sh	19
	Preferment (NZ) *ChrisWaller,Australia* 4-8-5 (s+t) HughBowman 8/1	7	20
	Grand Marshal *ChrisWaller,Australia* 5-8-6 (t) JimCassidy 60/1	¾	21
	Sky Hunter *SaeedbinSuroor,GB* 5-8-7 (h) WilliamBuick 30/1	1¼	22
46	Snow Sky *SirMichaelStoute,GB* 4-9-2 RyanMoore 50/1	2¼	23
35	Red Cadeaux *EdDunlop,GB* 9-8-9 GeraldMosse 25/1		pu

A. McGregor et al 24ran 3m23.15   119/122/127/120/121/113

SHA TIN Sunday, Dec 13   GOOD

115 **Longines Hong Kong Vase (Gr 1) (3yo+)** £803,160   1m3f205y

73	HIGHLAND REEL (IRE) *AidanO'Brien,Ireland* 3-8-9 RyanMoore (9)..............13/4		1
91	FLINTSHIRE *A.Fabre,France* 5-9-0 VincentCheminaud (8).......................	6/4f	1½	2
	DARIYAN (FR) *A.deRoyerDupre,France* 4-9-0 ChristopheSoumillon (6)...........9/1	1½	3
79	Ming Dynasty (FR) *M.Delzangles,France* 3-8-9 UmbertoRispoli (3) 21/1	1¾	4
	Helene Happy Star (IRE) *J.Moore,HongKong* 4-9-0 (h) JoaoMoreira (5)........31/5	1	5
	Dominant (IRE) *J.Moore,HongKong* 7-9-0 (h+t) ZacPurton (2).....................10/1	1½	6
114	Preferment (NZ) *ChrisWaller,Australia* 4-9-0 (s+t) HughBowman (10)...........21/1	½	7
	Khaya (NZ) *J.Size,HongKong* 6-9-0 (es+t) CraigWilliams (7) 78/1	½	8
	Ensuring *J.Size,HongKong* 4-9-0 BrettPrebble (4)................................17/1	sh	9
105	Cirrus des Aigles (FR) *MmeC.Barande-Barbe,France* 9-9-0 OlivierPeslier (12)..51/1	1½	10
103	Cannock Chase (USA) *SirMichaelStoute,GB* 4-9-0 PatSmullen (13).................24/1	½	11
	Harbour Master (USA) *J.Moore,HongKong* 5-9-0 TommyBerry (11).................98/1	3	12
	Helene Super Star (USA) *A.S.Cruz,HongKong* 5-9-0 (s+t) DouglasWhyte (1)......32/1	sh	13

Derrick Smith, Mrs J. Magnier & M. Tabor 13ran 2m28.43   129/126/123/120/118/116

116 **Longines Hong Kong Sprint (Gr 1) (3yo+)** £900,512   5f212y

1	PENIAPHOBIA (IRE) *A.S.Cruz,HongKong* 4-9-0 (s+t) JoaoMoreira (14).........69/20		1
	GOLD-FUN (IRE) *R.Gibson,HongKong* 6-9-0 (v) ChristopheSoumillon (6) 4/5f	½	2
	NOT LISTENIN'TOME (AUS) *J.Moore,HongKong* 5-9-0 (t) HughBowman (2)...63/10	½	3
	Dundonnell (USA) *R.Gibson,HongKong* 5-9-0 (h) DouglasWhyte (1) 46/1	2	4
	Mongolian Saturday (USA) *EnebishGanbat,USA* 5-9-0 FlorentGeroux (4).........30/1	1½	5
	Charles The Great (IRE) *J.Moore,HongKong* 6-9-0 (t) GeraldMosse (7)...........21/1	1	6
	Mikki Isle (JPN) *HidetakaOtonashi,Japan* 4-9-0 (t) SuguruHamanaka (10).........28/1	sh	7
1	Green Mask (USA) *WesleyA.Ward,USA* 4-9-0 (t) JoelRosario (11)..................98/1	½	8
	Straight Girl (JPN) *HideakiFujiwara,Japan* 6-8-10 (t) KeitaTosaki (13) 11/1	nk	9
2	Lucky Nine (IRE) *C.Fownes,HongKong* 8-9-0 (h) BrettPrebble (5)................25/1	sh	10
92	Sole Power *EdwardLynam,Ireland* 8-9-0 ChrisHayes (8) 98/1	nk	11
	Sakura Gospel (JPN) *TomohitoOzeki,Japan* 7-9-0 (h) ZacPurton (12) 59/1	1	12
2	Rich Tapestry (IRE) *C.W.Chang,HongKong* 7-9-0 (b) PatSmullen (3)...............98/1	1¾	13

Huang Kai Wen 13ran 1m08.74   128/126/124/115/109/105

117 Longines Hong Kong Mile (Gr 1) (3yo+) £1,119,556   7f210y

MAURICE (JPN) *NoriyukiHori,Japan* 4-9-0 (t) RyanMoore (11) 63/20		1
GIANT TREASURE (USA) *R.Gibson,HongKong* 4-9-0 (h+b)		
ChristopheSoumillon (1)...17/1	¾	2
26 ABLE FRIEND (AUS) *J.Moore,HongKong* 6-9-0 (s) JoaoMoreira (10) 7/10f	nk	3
109 Esoterique (IRE) *A.Fabre,France* 5-8-10 Pierre-CharlesBoudot (3).....................33/1	1	4
Contentment (AUS) *J.Size,HongKong* 5-9-0 (es) NashRawiller (12)..................69/10	¾	5
Beauty Flame (IRE) *A.S.Cruz,HongKong* 5-9-0 (t) GeraldMosse (5)...................10/1	sh	6
Danon Platina (JPN) *SakaeKunieda,Japan* 3-8-13 MasayoshiEbina (7)...............43/1	sh	7
Rewarding Hero *J.Moore,HongKong* 6-9-0 HughBowman (14) 98/1	½	8
Fiero (JPN) *HideakiFujiwara,Japan* 6-9-0 (h) MircoDemuro (4) 40/1	nk	9
Romantic Touch (AUS) *A.S.Cruz,HongKong* 5-9-0 (t) NeilCallan (8) 45/1	1¼	10
93 Toormore (IRE) *RichardHannon,GB* 4-9-0 JamesDoyle (9)................................98/1	1¾	11
109 Mondialiste (IRE) *DavidO'Meara,GB* 5-9-0 DanielTudhope (13) 98/1	2¼	12
Secret Sham (AUS) *J.Moore,HongKong* 6-9-0 (h) TommyBerry (6) 98/1	2¼	13
Red Dubawi (IRE) *FrauE.Mader,Germany* 7-9-0 AndreasSuborics (2) 98/1	2½	14

K. Yoshida 14ran 1m33.92   126/124/123/116/118/118

118 Longines Hong Kong Cup (Gr 1) (3yo+) £1,216,909   1m1f207y

A SHIN HIKARI (JPN) *MasanoriSakaguchi,Japan* 4-9-0 (h) YutakaTake (12) ...38/1		1
NUOVO RECORD (JPN) *MakotoSaito,Japan* 4-8-10 (h) RyanMoore (3) 84/10	1	2
BLAZING SPEED *A.S.Cruz,HongKong* 6-9-0 (t) NeilCallan (2).............................54/10	1¼	3
4 Designs On Rome (IRE) *J.Moore,HongKong* 5-9-0 JoaoMoreira (6)................. 12/5f	1½	4
Lucia Valentina (NZ) *KrisA.Lees,Australia* 5-8-10 DamienOliver (5).....................41/1	1½	5
Military Attack (IRE) *C.Fownes,HongKong* 7-9-0 (h) ZacPurton (1) 6/1	½	6
Dan Excel (IRE) *J.Moore,HongKong* 7-9-0 (s+t) TommyBerry (8) 98/1	1	7
Beauty Only (IRE) *A.S.Cruz,HongKong* 5-9-0 (t) GeraldMosse (9) 81/10	¾	8
114 Criterion (NZ) *DavidHayes&TomDabernig,Australia* 5-9-0 (b) CraigWilliams (13) ... 11/1	sh	9
Staphanos (JPN) *HideakiFujiwara,Japan* 4-9-0 (h) KeitaTosaki (11) 15/1	1¼	10
Satono Aladdin (JPN) *YasutoshiIkee,Japan* 4-9-0 (t) JamesMcDonald (14)......89/1	sh	11
82 Free Port Lux *F.Head,France* 4-9-0 ThierryJarnet (4) 98/1	½	12
91 Free Eagle (IRE) *D.K.Weld,Ireland* 4-9-0 PatSmullen (9) 41/10	1¾	13

Eishindo Co Ltd 13ran 2m00.60   126/120/121/118/110/113

INDEX TO SELECTED BIG RACES

1143

Straight Girl (JPN) 116
Strath Burn 68², 98
Strut The Course (CAN) 102⁴
Success Days (IRE) 23
Suedois (FR) 93
Suegioo (FR) 97⁶
Sumbal (IRE) 20⁵, 101
Sunflower 85⁶
Super Jockey (NZ) 2²
Tac de Boistron (FR) 32
Taisce Naisiunta (IRE) 76⁶
Take Cover 28⁶, 51², 75³, 92
Tale of Life (JPN) 10
Tale of Verve (USA) 14², 24
Talmada (USA) 102²
Tamadhor (IRE) 17⁶, 38
Tanaza (IRE) 76⁴
Taniyar (IRE) 93⁵
Tapestry (IRE) 91, 99
Tashaar (IRE) 59⁴
Tashweeq (IRE) 96⁴, 112⁶
Tasleet 49²
Telescope (IRE) 35⁶
Tencendur (USA) 7
Tendu 33
Tepin (USA) 109*
Territories (IRE) 6², 43*, 58², 100
Terror (IRE) 9
The Comissioner (IRE) 10
The Corsican (IRE) 31⁴, 101⁶
The Grey Gatsby (IRE) 3², 16⁴, 31³, 40², 60³, 73⁶
The Offer (IRE) 114
The Pizza Man (USA) 110⁵
The Tin Man 98⁴
The United States (IRE) 114
The Warrior (IRE) 15
Thrilled (USA) 107
Tiggy Wiggy (IRE) 9³, 33, 68

Time And Motion (USA) 107⁵
Time Test 60⁴, 84*, 109
Together Forever (IRE) 21, 45⁴
Tombelaine (USA) 15⁵
Tonalist (USA) 111⁵
Tony Curtis 104⁶
Toocoolforschool (IRE) 70
Toormore (IRE) 13², 26⁴, 47*, 58⁵, 93³, 117
Top Notch Tonto (IRE) 13, 100
Toscanini (IRE) 75⁴
Tourist (USA) 109
Tourny (FR) 66³
Tower of Texas (CAN) 83
Trade Storm 3
Treve (FR) 39*, 80*, 91⁴
Triple Threat (FR) 103⁶
Trip To Paris (IRE) 32*, 50³, 114⁴
Trip To Rhodos (FR) 94⁴
Tropics (USA) 36, 42²
True Story 4
Tullius (IRE) 40⁵, 101
Tupi (IRE) 47, 70, 84⁴
Turncoat (USA) 83
Turret Rocks (IRE) 65⁴, 88²
Twilight Eclipse (USA) 110
Twilight Son 68⁴, 98²
Twin Falls (IRE) 61
Twin Sails 96⁶
Uchenna (IRE) 102
Ultra (IRE) 89*
Umgiyo (AUS) 3
Undrafted (USA) 36*
United Color (USA) 2
Upstart (USA) 7
Up With The Birds (CAN) 103²
Usherette (IRE) 53
Vadamos (FR) 101

Varana (FR) 18
Vazirabad (FR) 105*
Vengeur Masque (IRE) 71⁵
Vent de Force 32, 78
Ventura Storm (IRE) 89
Venturous (IRE) 86⁶
Via Africa (SAF) 1
Viroblanc (FR) 18
Viserano (FR) 66⁵
Vive Ma Fille (GER) 50⁵
Waady (IRE) 68
Walzertakt (GER) 94⁶, 105⁶
Wandjina (AUS) 36⁶
War Department (IRE) 27
War Dispatch (USA) 20³, 56⁶
War Envoy (USA) 10, 20
War Story (USA) 7
Washington DC (IRE) 54²
Watchable 55⁴, 68, 92
Watsdachances (IRE) 57*, 108⁶
We Are (IRE) 8⁴, 67⁴, 90³
Wedding Vow (IRE) 52², 57⁵
Wekeela (FR) 18², 90⁴
Western Hymn 31³, 40³
White Rose (USA) 102
Who Shot Thebarman (NZ) 114
Wicklow Brave 78³, 97³
Wild Chief (GER) 58³, 81⁵
Wind Fire (USA) 28, 63
Windshear 32
Words (IRE) 45
Wunder (GER) 67
Yaazy (IRE) 102
Yasmeen 34
Young John (IRE) 27
Yuften 13
Zack Hope 105
Zebstar (IRE) 54⁶, 66⁴

ERRATA & ADDENDA

'Racehorses of 2014'

Green du Ciel   not a maiden, won twice at 1½m in France in 2008

John F Kennedy   p519, 23rd line … was **not** a May foal, foaled in February

Just The Judge   p530, 4 lines from bottom … won the **Irish** One Thousand Guineas

Lamsa   rating 54 **p**

Sagaciously   dam out of sister to Prix de l'Arc de Triomphe winner **Sagamix**

Toormore   7th line … best effort when length **third** to Charm Spirit

THE TIMEFORM 'TOP HORSES ABROAD'

FRANCE   In a year when the Triple Crown was achieved in America for the first time since the 'seventies, in France there was also an attempt at an historic treble that caught the public's imagination. **Treve**'s bid to win a third Prix de l'Arc de Triomphe—none of the six previous dual winners had tried a third time—ultimately failed. But with the physical problems that had dogged her four-year-old season behind her, she had a more successful campaign overall, enjoying an unbeaten build-up in the Prix Corrida, Grand Prix de Saint-Cloud and Prix Vermeille and winning the last-named race for the second time in a style reminiscent of her brilliant first Arc win in 2013. Those wins, along with a sustained publicity campaign from France Galop promoting Treve's bid for her third Arc, ensured she started odds-on (in contrast to twelve months earlier when she had been something of a surprise winner) in October but, unable to quicken into contention from further back than the other principals, she finished only fourth to the Derby winner Golden Horn. A year later than originally scheduled, Treve was retired after the Arc and begins her stud career with a visit to Dubawi in 2016.

The end of the Treve era coincided with the final days of Longchamp racecourse in its current form as work started on major renovation of the course's infrastructure, principally the stands and parade ring, immediately after the latest Arc meeting. Expected to cost in the region of €130m, the work will be financed entirely by France Galop after Arc sponsors Qatar had initially been linked to investing in the project. Longchamp will re-open in September 2017 ahead of the following month's Arc, while in the meantime Chantilly will host the 2016 running and Longchamp's other big races will find temporary homes elsewhere—the French Guineas, for example, will be run over Deauville's straight mile. Treve figured in big races over three seasons, but an even longer career in the top flight, and another intrinsically linked with Longchamp, that looks to be drawing towards an inevitable close is that of the remarkable **Cirrus des Aigles**. The nine-year-old finally seemed on the downgrade for most of the season, but not before another high-class performance to win a third Prix Ganay in May, the first time in his career that he had won on his reappearance. That was his thirteenth win at Longchamp and marked the seventh consecutive season in which he had won a pattern race at the track.

The Arc was one race at Longchamp which Cirrus des Aigles could never contest, and the absurdity of the exclusion of geldings like him from some of the French Group 1 contests was highlighted again when another gelding, **Solow**, developed into the top French miler but was ineligible for races like the Prix Jacques le Marois and Prix du Moulin for the same reason. Having progressed well in France in 2014, Solow flourished as a five-year-old in the latest season, particularly in Britain where he was able to enjoy Group 1 opportunities denied him at home, winning the Queen Anne Stakes, Sussex Stakes and, back at Ascot, the Queen Elizabeth II Stakes. Unbeaten in six starts in 2015, Solow has now lost only one of his last thirteen outings, that defeat coming over fifteen furlongs. That might seem bizarre now that Solow has become established as a high-class miler, but his dam won at that trip. The Prix d'Ispahan at Longchamp in May was one Group 1 open to him on home soil, and with Cirrus des Aigles suffering a broken shoe in that race, Solow was chased home by **Gailo Chop**, another gelding, who won La Coupe de Maisons-Laffitte but had to ply his trade abroad for the most part. Indeed, while there was disappointment for French runners at the Breeders' Cup and Hong Kong International meeting late in the year, Gailo Chop gained an important success in Australia in the Mackinnon Stakes at Flemington.

French-trained horses had better luck abroad earlier in the year in Dubai. Solow burst onto the international stage with an impressive win in the Dubai Turf (formerly the Dubai Duty Free) on World Cup night which also saw a one-two for France in the Dubai Sheema Classic thanks to **Dolniya** and **Flintshire**. The pair had first met in the previous season's Arc and became regular rivals in the latest season. Both were beaten in a muddling Coronation Cup at Epsom but had no excuses when placed behind Treve in the Grand Prix de Saint-Cloud. They contested the Arc again (Flintshire for the third time), with Flintshire runner-up for the second year running under conditions that suit him ideally, while Dolniya couldn't match her fifth place from the year before but was badly hampered in the closing stages, suffering a career-ending injury as a result. Flintshire's only win of the year came when beating inferior rivals in the Sword Dancer Stakes at Saratoga in August; he missed a return trip to the States for the Breeders' Cup but added another to his collection of second places in big races when runner-up in the Hong Kong Vase, a race he had won in 2014. Dolniya's stable-companion **Cladocera** also did well for Alain de Royer Dupre in Dubai, winning the Cape Verdi and Balanchine at the Carnival, and then making the frame in the Duke of Cambridge Stakes, Nassau Stakes and Matron Stakes in Britain and Ireland later in the year.

Other members of the 2014 Arc field to contest the race again were **Prince Gibraltar** and **Siljan's Saga**. Prince Gibraltar finished a good seventh for the second year running having beaten some of Germany's best horses beforehand in the Grosser Preis von Baden. The mare Siljan's Saga was a place behind Prince Gibraltar in the Arc, excelling herself at very long odds as she had done the year before. That was no fluke, however, as she'd previously won the Grand Prix de Deauville (from the 2014 winner **Cocktail Queen**) and finished clear of the rest when a good second in the Prix Royal-Oak after the Arc. The lightly-raced Godolphin colt **Manatee** put up a high-class performance to beat Prince Gibraltar, conceding him weight, in the Grand Prix de Chantilly but didn't quite show the same form subsequently when fourth to Treve at Saint-Cloud and when down the field in the Arc. **Spiritjim**, first past the post in the Grand Prix at both Chantilly and Saint-Cloud in 2014, was towards the rear in the Arc for the second year running (from a poor draw this time) having returned to his best with a close second in the Prix Foy beforehand. Fit from a winter campaign, **Affaire Solitaire** won the first pattern race of the year, the Prix Exbury at Saint-Cloud, at long odds and improved again on his only subsequent start when running Al Kazeem to less than a length in the Prix d'Harcourt at Longchamp.

Solow's absence from the Jacques le Marois left the way clear for the mare **Esoterique**, runner-up to him in the Queen Anne, to peak at Deauville in August for the second year running. The previous season's Prix Rothschild winner was beaten by champion sprinter Muhaarar in the Prix Maurice de Gheest just a week before she landed the Jacques le Marois. Better than ever at the age of five, Esoterique was then supplemented to gain her second Group 1 win of the year in the Sun Chariot Stakes but failed to figure at the Breeders' Cup before a better effort when fourth in the Hong Kong Mile. The 2014 Breeders' Cup Mile winner **Karakontie** made a belated reappearance when sixth in the Jacques le Marois before finishing third in the Prix du Moulin but beat only one home when defending his Breeders' Cup title at Keeneland. His English-born trainer Jonathan Pease retired shortly afterwards at the age of sixty-three with a total of three Breeders' Cup wins to his credit after the earlier successes of Tikkanen in the Turf in 1994 and Mile winner Spinning World three years later. Retirement is seemingly far from the thoughts of Andre Fabre who turned seventy in December and, thanks to the likes of Esoterique and Flintshire among his older horses, became champion trainer for the twenty-seventh time. **Vadamos** was an interesting recruit to the yard and well supported for the Champion Stakes but he finished last at Ascot, having something to find on form despite a five-length win in the Oettingen-Rennen at Baden-Baden beforehand. Smart colt **Elliptique** wasn't among the very best in the Fabre stable but his win in the Grand Prix de Vichy was significant as he was ridden by Amelie Foulon who became the first female jockey to win a pattern race on the Flat in France.

The classic-winning fillies **Miss France** and **Avenir Certain** stayed in training as four-year-olds but neither managed to win a race despite running close to their best. Fabre's One Thousand Guineas winner Miss France made a belated return in the autumn, running her best race when second in the Prix Daniel Wildenstein. Avenir Certain, winner of both French fillies' classics for Jean-Claude Rouget, was dropped back in trip after failing to stay in the 2014 Arc, finishing placed in the Prix Bertrand du Breuil (behind the Fabre-trained **Fintry**) at Chantilly, the Falmouth Stakes and the Prix Jean Romanet. **Bawina** made a good return in the Prix du Muguet at Saint-Cloud when beating **Spoil The Fun** and Esoterique and ran her best race afterwards (though was subsequently disqualified) when beaten a neck by British-trained outsider Odeliz in the Jean Romanet when upped back to a mile and a quarter at Deauville. **We Are** was another smart filly to remain in training at four but without managing to win. She chased home Treve in the Prix

Corrida between fourth places in the Ganay and Jean Romanet (promoted to third) and was left with plenty to do when third to younger rivals in a bid to win the Prix de l'Opera for the second year running.

Catcall's position as France's top sprinter was challenged by younger rival **Rangali**, though neither were at their best for most of the year. Catcall's only win came in a listed event at Fontainebleau in March, while his best effort was reserved for the Prix du Gros-Chene at Chantilly where he finished runner-up for the third year running, losing out only by a short head to British rival Muthmir. 2014 winner Rangali was well held making his reappearance in the same contest but for the second year running was touched off in the Prix de l'Abbaye in which he and stable-companion **Son Cesio** (the Prix de Ris-Orangis winner) were the only French-trained runners. Their trainer Alex Pantall did well with his sprinters and picked up another pattern win when **Gammarth** repeated his 2014 success in the Prix de Seine-et-Oise at Maisons-Laffitte. **Bathyrhon** was the top French stayer in the first part of the year, winning the Prix Vicomtesse Vigier before a creditable fifth in the Gold Cup and then losing out narrowly to the German horse Walzertakt back at Longchamp in the Prix Maurice de Nieuil. **Mille Et Mille** dead-heated for second in the Vicomtesse Vigier, but proved more of a force in the autumn and became the latest good French stayer to graduate from handicaps and/or claimers, making all in the Prix du Cadran where he had a below-form Bathyrhon back in fifth, and then finishing a creditable third in the Prix Royal-Oak.

Besides some leading older horses, Andre Fabre's stable housed three of the leading three-year-old colts who all made their mark in classics. **Make Believe** made all to beat stable-companion **New Bay** in the Poule d'Essai des Poulains where the latter was hampered by a poor draw but went on to prove himself much better suited to middle-distances in any case. Partnered by France's 2014 champion jockey over jumps, Vincent Cheminaud, who switched full-time to riding on the Flat after their victory in the Prix du Jockey Club, New Bay went on to success in the Prix Guillaume d'Ornano and Prix Niel before finishing just behind Flintshire when third in the Arc. While New Bay looks sure to win more good races at four, the lightly-raced Make Believe has been retired to stud having landed a second Group 1 at Longchamp when breaking the track record in the Prix de la Foret. He was then sent off favourite for the Breeders' Cup Mile in which he fared best of the French runners in fifth. Make Believe had been touched off by **Ride Like The Wind** in the Prix Djebel on his reappearance, with the Freddie Head-trained winner going on to contest the Two Thousand Guineas. However, Fabre's **Territories** fared the better of the French pair at Newmarket when second to Gleneagles before running his best races in the summer, winning the Prix Jean Prat at Chantilly and then chasing home stable-companion Esoterique in the Jacques le Marois.

The biggest challenge to New Bay looked like coming from **Erupt** (a son of Dubawi, like New Bay) who was unbeaten in four starts after winning the Grand Prix de Paris in July from New Bay's stable-companion **Ampere**. However, Erupt didn't give his running on soft ground in the Niel but finished much closer to New Bay when fifth in the Arc and went closer still to winning a big prize when sixth in a blanket finish to the Japan Cup. Erupt has the potential to challenge for top honours again at four. Unbeaten in four starts before failing to figure in the Jockey Club and Grand Prix de Paris, **Silverwave** ran well in both the Niel and the Arc, finishing second in the trial before staying on from a hopeless position for tenth in the Arc when poorly drawn. A couple of other colts who developed well to be not far behind the best of their generation over middle-distances later in the season were **Ming Dynasty** and **Migwar** who were first and second in a listed race at Clairefontaine in August and took the same positions in the Prix du Conseil de Paris at Chantilly when clear of some smart older rivals two months later. Migwar fared much the better of the pair in the Niel in between (where Ming Dynasty got worked up), while the latter ended the year with a creditable fourth in the Hong Kong Vase.

The Aga Khan held a strong hand among the leading three-year-olds with the pick of them being **Vazirabad** who proved himself the best stayer of his age with wins in the Prix de Lutece and Prix Chaudenay at Longchamp before putting up a high-class effort to beat some established older rivals in the Prix Royal-Oak which was transferred to Saint-Cloud after Longchamp's closure. Only the second three-year-old since 2002 to win the Royal-Oak, Vazirabad may be aimed at middle-distance prizes in 2016, though has the potential to dominate the staying division in France. **Karaktar** looked like being his owner's Jockey Club horse after a comfortable win in the Prix Noailles, but he finished only eighth when favourite at Chantilly after slipping on the bend and sustaining an injury. Off until the Prix du Prince d'Orange in September, Karaktar made a winning return when beating the Jockey Club fifth **Sumbal** a neck, the pair finishing well clear. Alain de Royer Dupre also had the progressive **Dariyan**, who beat the Jockey Club third **War Dispatch** in the Prix Eugene Adam before a couple of good placed efforts, firstly behind New Bay in the Guillaume d'Ornano at Deauville and then, after a break, in the Hong Kong Vase where he finished third in a race his dam Daryakana had won six years earlier.

The Aga Khan also had a couple of the leading three-year-old fillies, including **Ervedya** who won three Group 1 contests during the year for Jean-Claude Rouget. Runner-up in the Prix Marcel Boussac at two, Ervedya trained on well, with her only defeat at three coming from the older British-trained filly Amazing Maria in the Prix Rothschild. Otherwise, Ervedya racked up wins in the Prix Imprudence, the Poule d'Essai des Pouliches, the Coronation Stakes (where she turned the tables on the Marcel Boussac winner Found) and the Prix du Moulin. The last-named race cut up badly after the ground turned soft (prompting the withdrawal of Esoterique and Territories, among others), leaving Ervedya to beat fellow three-year-old filly **Akatea**. **Candarliya**, trained by Alain de Royer Dupre, was a more typical Aga Khan filly who improved gradually over longer trips. Beaten only by Treve in the Vermeille in a six-race sequence between May and October, Candarliya's biggest wins came in the Prix Minerve at Deauville in the summer and when giving her owner a fourth win and her trainer a fifth in the last seven runnings of the Prix de Royallieu at the Arc meeting. The Fillies & Mares Stakes was probably one race too many when Candarliya ran poorly at Ascot on her final start. **Sea Calisi** also ran below form in the same race at Ascot, but the Prix de Malleret winner had previously run well in Britain when third in the Yorkshire Oaks and then filled the same position behind Treve and Candarliya in the Vermeille.

Impassable would be an interesting rival for Ervedya if their paths cross as four-year-olds as she made into a very smart filly by the autumn, winning four times in all. She was absent during the summer after winning the Prix de Sandringham at Chantilly but came back in the Prix Daniel Wildenstein to account for Miss France and Akatea. That earned her a place in the Breeders' Cup Mile field but she proved no threat when sixth at Keeneland on her first try at the highest level. Another Wertheimer-owned filly to run at the Breeders' Cup was **Queen's Jewel** who was a creditable third in the Filly & Mare Turf. She had looked an exciting prospect when an easy winner of the Prix Saint-Alary (from subsequent Prix Chloe winner **Wekeela**) but disappointed as favourite for the Prix de Diane and wasn't seen to best effect in the Opera. **Physiocrate** fared best of the French fillies in the Diane when runner-up to Star of Seville, who was another big-race winner in France for John Gosden.

There were some important alterations to the autumn programme of French two-year-old races in 2015 as part of wider changes in the European pattern that included the creation of the two-day Future Champions' Festival at Newmarket in October. Most notably, the Prix Jean-Luc Lagardere, formerly run over seven furlongs, reverted to its old 'Grand Criterium' distance of a mile. The penultimate running of the Grand Criterium over a mile in 1999 had attracted just three runners, but there was a field of eleven for the latest running of the Jean-Luc Lagardere which also happened to be the only one of France's five Group 1 two-year-old contests not to go abroad, although winner **Ultra** (trained by Andre Fabre for Godolphin) was one of just three French-trained runners. Unbeaten in three starts, Ultra is bred to stay a mile and a half and looks a good three-year-old prospect. Representing the same connections, the rather headstrong **Cloth of Stars** won the Prix des Chenes from another well-bred colt, the Aga Khan's **Vedevani**, before being placed behind the British-trained Robin of Navan in the Prix des Chenes and Criterium de Saint-Cloud. Fabre's other pattern-winning colt was **Candide** who made it two from two when successful in a four-runner Prix Thomas Bryon. Impassable's half-brother **Attendu** fared the better of just two French-trained colts when third in the Criterium International which was run on the same day as the Criterium de Saint-Cloud for the first time and swapped distances with the Jean-Luc Lagardere to become France's Group 1 seven-furlong contest for two-year-olds. Attendu had finished only eighth in the

Jean-Luc Lagardere (the Criterium International winner Johannes Vermeer was fourth in the same race) after winning the Prix La Rochette from maiden **Lawmaking** beforehand. **Suits You** won both his starts for Eoghan O'Neill, though was exported to Hong Kong after beating subsequent Prix Marcel Boussac winner Ballydoyle in the Chesham Stakes at Royal Ascot. A colt with the potential to figure in pattern company in 2016 is **George Patton**, a brother to War Dispatch, who won both his starts at Deauville during the summer for Jean-Claude Rouget, the second of them a minor event in which he just had to be pushed out to beat Robin of Navan.

    Antonoe was an even-money favourite for the Marcel Boussac after winning her first two starts impressively, including the Prix d'Aumale, but she sustained a pelvic injury when finishing well beaten. **Qemah** had been well beaten by Antonoe on her debut at Deauville but won a minor event at Longchamp in very good style next time and improved again when third in the Marcel Boussac, looking another potentially smart three-year-old filly in the making for Jean-Claude Rouget. Representing the same connections as Attendu (Wertheimer Brothers and Carlos Laffon-Parias), **Sasparella** was the highest-rated French two-year-old filly, winning two of her three starts, including the Prix Eclipse from the Prix de Cabourg winner **Tourny** who had been no match for the British-trained colts Shalaa and Gutaifan in the Prix Morny. **Yakaba** was another speedy Wertheimer-owned filly, who ran poorly in the Prix Robert Papin and Criterium de Maisons-Laffitte, but won her other three starts, notably the Prix d'Arenberg at Longchamp. **Aim To Please** ran her best race when decisively beating colts (including the Cabourg runner-up **Du Pyla**) in the listed Prix Francois Boutin over seven furlongs at Deauville, while **Trixia** kept her unbeaten record on her first start outside the Provinces when winning Deauville's Prix des Reservoirs.

Two-Year-Olds					
116p	Ultra	117	Sumbal	125	Manatee
111	Attendu	117	Taniyar	125	Prince Gibraltar
110p	George Patton	116	Almanaar	123	Dolniya (f)
110	Cloth of Stars	115	Ride Like The Wind	123	Esoterique (f)
110	Sasparella (f)	115	War Dispatch	122	Gailo Chop
109	Aim To Please (f)	115	Wekeela (f)	122	Rangali
109	Tourny (f)	114	Maimara (f)	122	Spiritjim
108p	Suits You	114	Mexican Gold (f)	121	Siljan's Saga (f)
107p	Qemah (f)	114	Physiocrate (f)	119	Catcall
107	Du Pyla	114	Piment Rouge	119	Mille Et Mille
106p	Trixia (f)	114	The Right Man	118	Bathyrhon
106p	Vedevani	114	Toruk	118	Karakontie
106	Lawmaking	113	Baghadur	117	Baino Hope (f)
106	Yakaba (f)	113	Kataniya (f)	117	Bawina (f)
105p	Candide	113	Little Nightingale (f)	117	Fintry (f)
105	Antonoe (f)	113	Mr. Owen	117	Miss France (f)
105	Omar Bradley	113	Yaazy (f)	117	Vadamos
		112	Desiree Clary (f)	117	We Are (f)
Three-Year-Olds		112	La Berma (f)	116	Affaire Solitaire
128	New Bay	112	Sainte Amarante (f)	116	Avenir Certain (f)
127	Make Believe	112	Via Pisa (f)	116	Bello Matteo
127	Vazirabad	112	Vin Chaud	116	Cladocera (f)
125	Erupt	111	De Treville	116	Fate (f)
123	Dariyan	111	Epicuris	116	Free Port Lux
123	Silverwave	111	Meteoric	116	Golden Wood
123	Territories	111	Mostaneer	116	Meleagros
122	Ming Dynasty	111	Night of Light (f)	116	Son Cesio
121	Impassable (f)	111	Sonnerie (f)	116	Spoil The Fun
120	Candarliya (f)	111	Tiberian	115	Amour A Papa (f)
120	Ervedya (f)	110	Extremis	115	Bernay
120	Migwar	110	Finsbury Square	115	Cocktail Queen (f)
118	Karaktar	110	Sarrasin	115	Feodora (f)
118	Queen's Jewel (f)			115	Fly With Me
118	Sea Calisi (f)	**Older Horses**		115	Gammarth
117	Akatea (f)	129	Solow	115	Loresho
117	Ampere	129	Treve (f)	115	Suedois
117	Full Mast	128	Flintshire	114	Fractional
		128d	Cirrus des Aigles	114	Glaring

114	Menardais	112	Best Fouad	111	Peace At Last
114	Smoking Sun	112	Chika Dream	111	Quatorze
114	Spirit Quartz	112	Frine (f)	111	Saint Gregoire
114	Zylpha (f)	112	Meadow Creek	111	Wireless
113	Amy Eria (f)	112	Redbrook	111	Zack Hope
113	Elliptique	112	Robert Le Diable	110	Al Waab
113	Gengis	112	Rosso Corsa	110	Ectot
113	Kalsa (f)	112	Sparkling Beam (f)	110	*Montclair
113	Kicky Blue (f)	111	All At Sea (f)	110	Muharaaj
113	Mayhem (f)	111	Bookrunner	110	*Noozhoh Canarias
113	Narrow Hill	111	*Faufiler (f)	110	Pollyana (f)
113	Norse King	111	Garlingari		
113	Teletext	111	Metropol		

GERMANY   Unlike in recent seasons, there were no high-profile wins for German horses abroad but four-year-old colt **Ito** stamped himself as much the best horse with some clear-cut victories on home turf. Illness forced Ito to miss the Grosser Preis von Baden and he still wasn't at his best when beaten by the placed horses from that race when only fourth in the Preis von Europa at Cologne, but at Munich in November he put up a high-class performance when making all to beat the French-trained Grosser Preis von Baden winner Prince Gibraltar by four lengths. Lightly raced at three when beaten in a handicap on his final start, Ito, a confirmed front-runner, improved rapidly to win his first three starts of the year (by an aggregate of twenty-five lengths), notably the Grosser Preis der Badischen Unternehmer at Baden-Baden, and then found only the Luca Cumani-trained gelding Second Step too strong when beaten three quarters of a length in the Grosser Preis von Berlin. Ito finished tailed off in the Japan Cup on his final start under much firmer conditions than he was used to.

Magic Artist probably emerged with the most credit among Germany's runners abroad. He began the season with two good runs in Italy, winning the Premio Ambrosiano at Milan before being narrowly beaten by the runner-up in that race Cleo Fan in the Premio Presidente della Repubblica at Rome. However, later in the year, having left Wolfgang Figge, Magic Artist joined Andreas Wohler for an Australian campaign in the colours of Protectionist, who had won the Melbourne Cup the year before. Magic Artist twice ran well when beaten only around a length in fourth at Flemington, firstly to the French gelding Gailo Chop when somewhat unlucky in the Mackinnon Stakes over his optimum trip of a mile and a quarter and then in the Emirates Stakes a week later over a mile. Previously successful in the Arlington Million with Silvano, Wohler had a shot at that prize with the Hamburg Trophy winner **Wake Forest** who finished a respectable sixth. On the same Arlington card, Derby Italiano winner Goldstream was fourth in the Secretariat Stakes on his debut for Wohler, while there was German success in the Grade 3 American St Leger when **Lucky Speed** was successful for Peter Schiergen for the first time since winning the 2013 Deutsches Derby.

Back home, the 2014 Grosser Preis von Berlin winner **Sirius** contested all the big mile and a half contests, unable to win one this time but not far away in most of them. After being beaten narrowly in the Hansa-Preis at Hamburg, Sirius went on to finish fourth in a stronger renewal of the Grosser Preis von Berlin than the one he had won in 2014 before finishing third in the Grosser Preis von Baden, second in the Preis von Europa and then a well-held fourth behind Ito at Munich. Ito's stable-companion **Guiliani** was also a Group 1 winner, though successful in a substandard Grosser Dallmayr-Preis (Bayerisches Zuchtrennen), also at Munich, with a below-form Magic Artist in fifth. Former handicapper **Potemkin** denied Guiliani another pattern win when beating him at level weights in the Preis der Deutschen Einheit at Hoppegarten in October. It was the winner's sixth success from seven starts in 2015, a record which would make him an interesting performer in group races again in 2016. For the third year running, **Vif Monsieur** ended his season on a winning note in pattern company and put up a career-best effort when gaining a second consecutive success in the Niederrhein-Pokal at Krefeld with a nine-length beating of **Nordico**. The runner-up had gained his own Group 3 win earlier in the season when beating Guiliani in the Grosser Preis der Wirtschaft at Dortmund.

Preis von Europa, Cologne—
three-year-old filly Nightflower (second left) gets the better of older rivals Sirius (blinkers),
Qatari-trained Dubday (hidden behind winner) and Germany's top horse Ito (left)

Wild Chief headed Germany's older milers, successfully dropping back in trip after being campaigned over middle distances at three. He gained a clear-cut Group 2 success in the Meilen Trophy at Hanover in July and ran well in better company in France subsequently, finishing third in the Prix Jacques le Marois and fifth in the Prix du Moulin. Seven-year-old entire **Red Dubawi** was out of sorts for much of the year (only third in the Meilen Trophy which he had won in 2014) but bounced back to form to win the Premio Vittorio di Capua at Milan in October. **Amaron** was a former winner of that Italian Group 1, and the six-year-old maintained his record of winning at least one pattern race a year when successful in the Fruhjahrsmeile at Dusseldorf for the second year running, from Guiliani, and when beating the same rival a short head in the Badener Meile at Baden-Baden in June. **Pas de Deux** was also a smart winner at a mile when successful in the Grosse Europa Meile at Munich in September, following up another Group 3 success over a mile and a quarter at Baden-Baden in August.

Stayers **Walzertakt** and **Alex My Boy** were both new to their respective stables in 2015 and did well in France. The former was successful in the Prix Maurice de Nieuil and then finished third to the Prix de Barbeville winner Alex My Boy in the Prix Kergorlay at Deauville before being awarded the Prix Gladiateur. Top sprinter was the ex-Irish gelding **Shining Emerald** who won the Silberne Peitsche at Munich in May by seven lengths on soft ground and the Goldene Peitsche (whose Group 2 status was quickly restored in 2015) at Baden-Baden with much less to spare, both times from French opposition. **Donnerschlag** ran below form in both those contests but made all to turn the tables on the previous year's winner **Amarillo** in Hamburg's Flieger-Preis. The other sprinter who deserves a mention is Gamgoom (rated 109) who had a remarkable season which began and ended on the all-weather track at Neuss. He racked up eleven wins during the year for Mario Hofer, notably a listed contest at Milan in September.

Deutsches Derby winner **Nutan** headed the three-year-old crop but didn't get much of a chance to prove himself against older horses, running only once more in a career that spanned just five starts. Nutan provided his trainer Peter Schiergen with a fifth winner of the Deutsches Derby (and his rider Andrasch Starke a seventh, one short of the record) with a five-length victory over **Palace Prince** (a subsequent Group 3 winner at Krefeld but out of his depth in the Champion Stakes), with **Fair Mountain** third, a position he also took behind Ito at Munich. Nutan was injured after finishing third in the Grosser Preis von Berlin and retired to stud. Even less was seen of **Karpino** who looked a promising colt in the spring for Qatar Racing when successful in the Dr Busch-Memorial at Krefeld from **Ajalo** (a good second to Guiliani at Munich later in the year) and the Mehl-Mulhens Rennen which he won by four and a half lengths. Bred to stay further than a mile, Karpino had been talked of as an Epsom Derby possible but was on course for the German version instead when injury ended his season. Karpino is unbeaten in just three starts and would make an interesting four-year-old for Andreas Wohler if returning in 2016.

As well as the top colt, Peter Schiergen had the two best three-year-old fillies, **Nightflower** and **Lovelyn**. A daughter of the Oaks d'Italia winner Night of Magic, Nightflower is closely related to Nutan (their dams are sisters) and represented the same owner-breeders as the Derby winner. She was beaten by **Turfdonna** (not seen out afterwards) in the Preis der Diana after winning the Diana-Trial at Hoppegarten, and was second again in the Grosser Preis von Baden before having a below-par Ito back in fourth when winning the Preis von Europa at Cologne. On her final start, Nightflower didn't get the best of the runs in the Japan Cup but wasn't far off her best form nor beaten very far when eleventh at Tokyo. Stable-companion Lovelyn pulled too hard when favourite for the Preis der Diana but won her other four starts of the year. She gained narrow wins in the Oaks d'Italia and Hansa-Preis (against older rivals) prior to disappointing in the German Oaks and then bounced back in the autumn with a strong staying performance back in Italy to win the Gran Premio del Jockey Club. Retired to stud after injury ruled her out of the Hong Kong Vase, Lovelyn was sadly found dead in her box early in 2016. Two other fillies ran well at Deauville in August where **Holy Moly** met with her first defeat in four starts when second in the Prix de la Nonette and **Bourree** was successful in the Prix de Psyche. Bourree was denied a second French Group 3 later in the year when beaten by the six-year-old mare Si Luna (rated 109) in the Prix de Flore at Saint-Cloud.

There was no stand-out performer among Germany's latest crop of two-year-olds. **Isfahan** (whose three-year-old half-brother **Incantator** was himself a Group 3 winner over a mile and a quarter at Baden-Baden a week later) won the main race for colts, the Preis der Winterfavoriten at Cologne, having dropped back to be last in the straight, but finished only sixth in the Criterium de Saint-Cloud next time. Similar form was shown by the first two in the Herzog von Ratibor Rennen at Krefeld where there was just a nose between **Parthenius** and **El Loco**, the pair pulling clear of the rest. The winner's brother Pastorius won the same race in 2011 before going on to success in the following year's Deutsches Derby. **Noor Al Hawa**, a son of the Sun Chariot Stakes winner Majestic Roi, looked a good prospect when pulling six lengths clear to win a listed race at Dusseldorf in September on just his second start. There was a close finish to the top fillies' race, the Preis der Winterkonigin at Baden-Baden, where less than a length covered the first three home, **Dhaba**, **Serienholde** and **Pagella**, both the placed fillies having finished second on their only previous starts.

Two-Year-Olds					
102p	Dhaba (f)	116	Palace Prince	115	Wake Forest
102p	Parthenius	115	Quasillo	114	Guardini
102	El Loco	114	Ajalo	114	Lucky Lion
102	Isfahan	113	Bourree (f)	114	Lucky Speed
101p	Noor Al Hawa	113	Holy Moly (f)	114	Pas de Deux
100	Pagella (f)	112	Fair Mountain	113	Ajaxana (f)
100	Serienholde (f)	111	Turfdonna (f)	113	Donnerschlag
99	Degas	110	Incantator	113	Potemkin
99	Double Dream (f)	110	Nymeria (f)	112	Kerosin
98	Miss England (f)			112	*Lacy (f)
97	Kosmische (f)	**Older Horses**		112	Nordico
96	Shy Witch (f)	125	Ito	112	Wildpark
95	Fosun (f)	120	Magic Artist	112	Wunder (f)
95	Guizot	118	Sirius	111	Amarillo
95	Millowitsch	118	Walzertakt	111	Daring Match
		118	Wild Chief	111	Ephraim
Three-Year-Olds		117	Alex My Boy	111	Singing
120	Nutan	117	Shining Emerald	111	Victory Song
118	Karpino	117	Vif Monsieur	110	Eric
118	Lovelyn (f)	116	Amaron	110	Felician
118	Nightflower (f)	116	Guiliani	110	Fly First
		116	Red Dubawi	110	Spend The Cash

ITALY With Italian racing's finances seemingly in better shape after some troubled years which led to lengthy delays in the payment of prize money, Italy's big races became more attractive to foreign stables once more in 2015. Eight pattern races went abroad, notably the Oaks d'Italia and three Group 1 contests in the autumn, the Premio Vittorio di Capua, the Gran Premio del Jockey Club and the Premio Lydia Tesio. The last-named

Premio Roma GBI Racing, Rome—Italy's best horse Dylan Mouth (right) is pushed close by younger stable-companion Circus Couture in a race that will be one of just four remaining Group 1 events in Italy from 2016

contest was won by Odeliz who became the first British-trained winner of a pattern race in Italy since Hunter's Light's win in the Premio Roma three years earlier. Italy's big races survived the threat of losing their pattern status during the crisis, but two more Group 1 contests have been downgraded with effect from 2016 after falling short of the required standards, the Premio Presidente della Repubblica and the Gran Premio di Milano, which means that Italy now has no Group 1 races in its calendar until the autumn. Stefano Botti was again overwhelmingly dominant in the trainers' statistics in 2015, with earnings more than four times those of his nearest pursuer, his cousin Endo, and the majority of the horses named below belonged to that one stable.

It wasn't all plain sailing, however, for Stefano Botti who was given a four-month ban late in the year resulting from a doping case which dated back over four years and concerned a listed race won as a two-year-old by the stable's Oaks d'Italia winner Cherry Collect. Another setback for the stable was the complete loss of form in the latest season of four-year-old colt **Priore Philip** who had ended 2014 as Italy's top horse with just two defeats to his name in thirteen starts. Although he made a winning reappearance in a minor event at Rome, his decline was such that he finished tailed off as a 33/1 shot on his final start in the Premio Roma which he had won so impressively twelve months earlier. Stable-companion **Dylan Mouth** won the latest Premio Roma (by a short head from three-year-old stablemate **Circus Couture**) at the end of a season in which he proved better than ever, also winning the Premio Carlo d'Alessio, the Gran Premio di Milano and the Premio Federico Tesio, winning both the last two races at Milan by five lengths. The 2014 Derby Italiano winner, Dylan Mouth was beaten on Italian soil for the first time when going down to the German filly Lovelyn in the Gran Premio del Jockey Club at Milan in October which he had won the year before. For the second year running, Dylan Mouth was much less successful when sent to Ascot (he had run at the Royal meeting as a three-year-old) and finished tailed off in the King George VI and Queen Elizabeth Stakes in July, though he will have more of a chance to prove himself in Britain in future having joined Stefano Botti's cousin Marco at Newmarket. The 2014 Premio Roma runner-up **Cleo Fan** was the champion trainer's other Group 1 winner, making all in a substandard Premio Presidente della Repubblica which sealed that race's fate and was notable for the odds-on defeat of Priore Philip.

Top three-year-old Circus Couture beat older horses in the Premio del Giubileo over nine furlongs at Milan in June and improved further in the autumn, faring best of the home-trained contingent when third in the Premio Vittorio di Capua and then second to older rival **Kaspersky** (trained by Endo Botti) in the Premio Ribot before going so close upped to a mile and a quarter in the Premio Roma. Kaspersky was Italy's best miler, and apart from finishing fourth in the Vittorio di Capua, won his five other starts during the year, notably when making most of the running to beat Circus Couture in the Premio Carlo Vittadini at Milan in May. Apart from the Oaks (another race won by Germany's Lovelyn), the other classics went to Stefano Botti three-year-olds. The previous season's top two-year-old **Hero Look** won the Premio Parioli (2000 Guineas) before being exported to Hong Kong having been first past the post in all five of his races in Italy (demoted in a minor event on his reappearance). **Sound of Freedom** kept her unbeaten record when a four-length winner of the Premio Regina Elena (1000 Guineas) in a faster time than Hero Look had put up on the same day and was runner-up subsequently in the Derby Italiano and the Premio Lydia Tesio before she too joined Marco Botti at the end of the year. Stefano Botti landed the Derby Italiano, Italy's richest race, for the fourth time in the last five runnings with **Goldstream** and saddled both placed horses too, with **Time Chant** taking third behind Sound of Freedom. That was Goldstream's final start in Italy (where he was unbeaten in five races) before joining Andreas Wohler in Germany.

The Botti stable's domination didn't extend to Italy's biggest sprints, however. **Lohit** put up the best performance in this division, though he seemed the only one to handle the conditions when running out a five-length winner of the Premio Omenoni over five furlongs on soft ground at Milan in October. Over six furlongs at Rome there were also smart wins for **Falest** in the Premio Tudini in May (he followed up with a good effort in a listed contest at Milan) and for **Plusquemavie** who beat the Tudini runner-up **Alatan Blaze** a short head in the Premio Carlo e Francesco Aloisi in November.

Biz Heart, a half-brother to one of the stable's Derby Italiano winners Biz The Nurse, became Stefano Botti's third consecutive winner of the Gran Criterium after Priore Philip and Hero Look when beating stable-companion **Basileus** into second. However, the stable's apparent first string **Azzeccagarbugli** ran poorly in Italy's big two-year-old race on soft going but made all on better ground in listed races at Naples (winning by eight lengths), Rome and Pisa. Botti also won the autumn's other two-year-old pattern races, with **Cassina de Pomm** taking the Premio Dormello for fillies at Milan and **Poeta Diletto** and **Voice of Love** making it a stable one-two (separated by a nose) in the Premio Guido Berardelli at Rome. **Saent** had given a five-length beating to Voice of Love in a listed race at Milan but he too ran below form on softer ground in the Gran Criterium. The speedy filly **Fly On The Night**, who subsequently remained in France, won the Prix du Bois for her Italian stable at Chantilly in June.

Two-Year-Olds					
110	Biz Heart	110	Hero Look	114	Cleo Fan
108	Saent	109	Loritania (f)	113	Falest
107	Azzeccagarbugli	109	Ouragan Gris	112	Regarde Moi
104	Basileus	108	Testa O Croce (f)	111	Duca di Mantova
104	*Fly On The Night (f)	108	Time Chant	111	Lodovico Il Moro
104	Zapel	107	Pensierieparole	111	Plusquemavie
102	Aquila Solitaria (f)	107	Right Connection	111	Priore Philip
102	Ottone	107	Zan O'Bowney	110	Sufranel
101	Cassina de Pomm (f)	106	Azari	109	Candiani Street
101	Poeta Diletto	106	Trust You	108	Alatan Blaze
101	Voice of Love	105	Brex Drago	108	Porsenna
100	Lucan Sweet	105	Kyllachy Queen (f)	108	Uniram
		105	Reset In Blue (f)	107	Bertinoro
				107	Harlem Shake
Three-Year-Olds		**Older Horses**		107	Marvi Thunders
120	Circus Couture	121	Dylan Mouth	107	Ottawa
115	*Goldstream	118	Kaspersky	107	Targaryen
113	Sound of Freedom (f)	115	Lohit		

SCANDINAVIA   Unusually, two horses who gained their ratings from sprint handicaps abroad head the Scandinavian ratings. Five-year-old horse **Easy Road** completed a four-timer when successfully conceding weight to some useful rivals in an eighteen-runner contest at Doncaster in October. Runner-up to **Ragazzo** in his first three starts of the year, Easy Road had that rival back in third place in the Polar Cup at Ovrevoll in July (a race Ragazzo had won for the previous two years) and again in the listed Taby Open Sprint in September. A former winner of the Taby Open Sprint, eight-year-old **Beat Baby** was only fourth in the latest renewal and for the second year running ran much his best race all year when making his reappearance in a handicap at the Dubai Carnival; he'd been touched off on turf in 2014 but held on to make all on dirt at Meydan in January. The Carnival is the starting point for the campaigns of a number of Scandinavian performers nowadays, and the other winner there was three-year-old Volatile (rated 105) who was successful in the listed Meydan Classic over seven furlongs. Third in a Group 3 contest at Maisons-Laffitte back in Europe, Volatile was then injured after finishing towards the rear in the Jersey Stakes at Royal Ascot. **Silver Ocean** was the best performer at around a mile, winning the Pramms Memorial at Jagersro in May and a listed contest, also on dirt, at Taby in September, while in between he was beaten a head by Easy Road on turf in the Polar Cup. Meanwhile at Jagersro, dirt sprint specialist **Let'sgoforit** racked up another five wins during the year, including a second successive Zawawi Cup, to take his lifetime record to nineteen successes.

On Scandinavian turf, however, the best performance belonged to the popular Niels Petersen-trained gelding **Bank of Burden** who won a record fourth Stockholm Cup International at Taby at the age of eight from a couple of the season's other pattern winners **Hurricane Red** (Stockholms Stora Pris) and **Eye In The Sky** (Oslo Cup). The latest Stockholm Cup will be the final one run at Taby, with that track set to close in 2016 to be replaced by Stockholm's new track Bro Park which is due to open in June. Also successful in the listed Dansk Jockey Club Cup at Klampenborg for the third year running, Bank of Burden finished runner-up in the Stockholms Stora Pris and third in both the Oslo Cup and Marit Sveaas Minnelop. Bank of Burden also started odds on to win the Scandinavian Open Championship at Klampenborg for a third time but was one of three horses put out of the race in an incident early on. Another eight-year-old, **Berling**, missed the trouble to make all, and ran well afterwards when second to the Oslo Cup runner-up **Fearless Hunter** in the Marit Sveaas Minnelop. Hurricane Red reached the frame for the third year in the Stockholm Cup and ended the season winning a listed race on dirt at Taby. Bank of Burden's stable-companion Eye In The Sky was a new name among the leading older middle-distance performers and has plenty of time on his side as a four-year-old. He won the Norsk Derby and Svensk St Leger in 2014 and stays well as he showed when winning a listed contest over two miles at Hamburg in June prior to the Oslo Cup. Another of Bank of Burden's stable-companions **Energia El Gigante** was found wanting in the bigger races but gave a five-length beating to Hurricane Red in a listed race over a mile and a half at Jagersro in October, though Hurricane Red prevented him repeating his 2014 win in a similar event on dirt at Taby. Three-year-old **Quarterback** was another who began the year at Meydan but he proved suited by longer trips later on, winning the Norsk Derby and showing smart form when second of six in a listed race at Newmarket over a mile and a quarter in October.

Dansk Hesteforsikring Scandinavian Open Championship, Klampenborg—
the grey Berling makes all under Dina Danekilde to win a dramatic renewal of Denmark's Group 3
contest in which favourite Bank of Burden (riderless horse), bidding for a third win in the race,
was one of three casualties in an incident on the first bend

Three-Year-Olds	112	Eye In The Sky	108	Liber
112 Quarterback	112	Hurricane Red	108	Silver Ocean
107 Iceccapada (f)	112	Let'sgoforit	107	Falconet
	111	Fearless Hunter	107	Giftorm
Older Horses	110	Berling	107	Giovanni Boldini
116 Beat Baby	110	Energia El Gigante	107	Over The Ocean
116 Easy Road	110	Ragazzo	107	Saving Kenny
113 Bank of Burden	109	Zen Zansai Zaid		

The following European-trained horses also achieved significant ratings

Three-Year-Olds	112	Cielo Canarias (Spain)	111	Trip To Rhodos
110 Sir Andrew (Spain)	112	Perfect Warrior		(Czech Republic)
		(Turkey)	111	Yildirimbey (Turkey)
Older Horses	111	Arkaitz (Spain)	110	Fly By Me (Turkey)
113 Diego Valor (Spain)	111	Autor (Czech Republic)		

UNITED ARAB EMIRATES   After five editions of the Dubai World Cup run at Meydan on the synthetic tapeta surface, the track's change to dirt resulted, as many had hoped, in attracting some of the best American horses back to the world's richest race after their total absence in 2014 and less frequent participation since the closure of Nad Al Sheba where US-trained dirt performers did much for the race's profile in its early years. According to the betting, therefore, the latest renewal lay between the 2014 Kentucky Derby and Preakness winner California Chrome and the very smart Donn Handicap victor Lea. However, Godolphin's eight-year-old gelding **Prince Bishop** failed to read the script, producing an unlikely last-to-first win after being scrubbed along and detached at the rear. California Chrome and Lea filled the places, but what the World Cup had gained in American participation it predictably lost in competitiveness and strength in depth, the field of nine (down from sixteen in 2014) the smallest for the race at Meydan and attracting a sole European-based horse. That was the Andrew Balding-trained eight-year-old Side Glance (fourth in the two previous renewals) who finished tailed off, beating only the Japan Cup winner Epiphaneia, another who patently failed to handle the dirt. The American raiders didn't go away empty handed on World Cup night, however, with Bob Baffert's 2013 Breeders' Cup Sprint winner Secret Circle taking the Dubai Golden Shaheen under California Chrome's jockey Victor Espinoza. Travelling with enthusiasm towards the head of affairs, Secret Circle took over outright over a furlong out and was always doing enough to hold on by a head and one and a quarter lengths from the Hong Kong-trained pair Super Jockey and Rich Tapestry.

Godolphin had their usual successful Carnival, as they not only had the best dirt performer in Prince Bishop, but also the best turf horse in **Hunter's Light**, he too a son of Dubawi who was no youngster (a seven-year-old) but hit a rich vein of form. After taking a handicap and a listed race, Hunter's Light produced a career best performance on Super Saturday when winning the Jebel Hatta by six and a half lengths from Trade Storm. Injured before World Cup night, Hunter's Light was retired to stand at Darley's Haras du Logis in France. While Prince Bishop and Hunter's Light were trained by Saeed bin Suroor, Godolphin's other trainer Charlie Appleby also tasted Group success at the Carnival, his best performer being **Safety Check**, who recorded a hat-trick of wins. Safety Check started off with a win in handicap company before Group 2 successes in the Al Fahidi Fort and Zabeel Mile, beating Dark Emerald by a length. At his best around seven furlongs to a mile, there was no suitable race for Safety Check on World Cup night, and he was subsequently put away until the summer.

Other notable performances from Godolphin-owned horses came from African Story, Sky Hunter and Ahzeemah. The 2014 World Cup winner **African Story** never really looked at home on the newly-installed dirt surface, though managed to win Round 3 of the Maktoum Challenge by a neck from Prince Bishop in between poor efforts in Round 2 of the Maktoum Challenge (won by **Frankyfourfingers** from Prince Bishop) and the Dubai World Cup.

Back on turf, the very smart **Sky Hunter** won his only start at the Carnival in the Dubai City of Gold when beating Sheikhzayedroad by a length and three quarters. Very smart stayer **Ahzeemah** failed to win but put up two good efforts in defeat, starting with

Godolphin Mile Sponsored by Meydan Sobha, Meydan—
Tamarkuz (striped cap) has to battle to complete a four-timer on Meydan's new dirt track which
replaced tapeta, with British-trained Sloane Avenue (centre) just a short head back in second
ahead of Free Wheeling (star on cap) and Haatheq (second left)

a fine second to stablemate Famous Kid in a handicap (conceding the winner a stone), sharing top weight with **Meandre** who was a close third. Seemingly amiss next time, Ahzeemah returned to form with third in the Dubai Gold Cup behind Brown Panther and Carnival veteran **Star Empire** from the Mike de Kock stable.

Following some disappointing performances from his initial runners on dirt, de Kock was forced to reappraise how his Carnival team would be deployed. 'Unless there are absolutely no other options we won't have another entry on dirt this season. To win on this track you need runners with good gate speed that can jump and lead or sit up second or third. Otherwise you may as well stay at home. The kickback from just behind the front rank is bad, the slower horses get it in the face and sometimes it's so severe that they battle to breathe.'

Ironically, though, it turned out that de Kock had one of the best dirt horses at the Carnival in three-year-old **Mubtaahij**. Off the mark in a maiden at Meydan on New Year's Eve prior to the Carnival, Mubtaahij was beaten only once there (by Godolphin's **Maftool** in the UAE 2000 Guineas) in five starts. Stepping up in trip after that defeat, Mubtaahij inflicted a first defeat on Godolphin's much-hyped Uruguayan import **Sir Fever** in a listed race before running away with the UAE Derby, beating old rival Maftool by eight lengths. So impressive was he there, Mubtaahij was embarked on a US classic campaign, finishing eighth in the Kentucky Derby but running a better race against American Pharoah when fourth in the Belmont Stakes. Mubtaahij wasn't seen again after the Belmont and is to be readied for a 2016 Dubai World Cup campaign.

Stable-companion **Vercingetorix** was again the pick of de Kock's turf performers and looked all set for another successful Carnival when returning with a comfortable victory over Godolphin's **True Story** in the Al Rashidiya. However, he could finish only sixth when bidding to repeat his 2014 win in the Jebel Hatta and was subsequently found to have suffered a career-ending sesamoid injury. A son of the German-trained Arlington Million winner Silvano, Vercingetorix is due to stand at Summerhill Stud in South Africa in 2016.

The Carnival highlight among local trainers was the remarkable improvement of former Godolphin inmate **Tamarkuz**, who was handled expertly by Musabah Al Muhairi having developed an aversion to the stalls following a bad experience earlier in his career. Tamarkuz reeled off four wins in a row, culminating in a gutsy Godolphin Mile win over Sloane Avenue on World Cup night after dominant Group 3 successes in the Firebreak Stakes and Burj Nahaar.

Other local performers worthy of mention are sprinters **Muarrab** and the evergreen veteran **Reynaldothewizard**, who showed his versatility by taking to Meydan's dirt track every bit as well as he had to the tapeta. Winner of the Dubai Golden Shaheen in 2013, Satish Seemar's Reynaldothewizard, even at the age of nine, proved as good as ever when convincingly beating Muarrab by nearly four lengths on his reappearance in a listed race. A win in the Al Shindagha Sprint followed before Reynaldothewizard was forced to miss the Golden Shaheen through injury, although he is fully expected to be back again in 2016. Muarrab returned at least as good as ever late in 2014 after a year's absence, proving particularly effective at Jebel Ali, where the uphill finish seems to bring out the best in him. Beaten just once in nine starts at that track, Muarrab added three more victories to his tally there during 2015, including the listed Jebel Ali Sprint, but also broke new ground when registering a first success at Meydan in a similar event in December.

European-trained horses had the most success on World Cup night, the best performance put up by French gelding Solow in the Dubai Turf (previously the Duty Free) with an impressive beating of The Grey Gatsby. The veteran Irish sprinter Sole Power beat Hong Kong's Peniaphobia in the Al Quoz Sprint (the winner's fifth appearance in the race), while over longer distances, Brown Panther's victory in the Dubai Gold Cup proved to be the last of his career and Dolniya headed a one-two for France in the Dubai Sheema Classic, turning the tables on Arc runner-up Flintshire.

The performances reviewed here are those that took place in the calendar year 2015. Horses which were trained and raced in the UAE but showed significantly better form elsewhere are not included in the list below.

Three-Year-Olds

| 120 | *Mubtaahij |
| 113 | *Maftool |

Older Horses

126	Hunter's Light
126	Prince Bishop
124	*Vercingetorix
123	*Safety Check
123	Tamarkuz
122	*African Story
121	Muarrab
121	*Sky Hunter
120	Ahtoug
120	Ahzeemah
120	*Meandre
120	Reynaldothewizard
119	Frankyfourfingers
118	*Almoonqith
118	Earnshaw
118	Le Bernardin
118	*Mushreq
118	Storm Belt
118	Surfer
118	True Story
117	Free Wheeling
117	Gold City
117	Shaishee
117	*Star Empire
116	Ertijaal
116	Forjatt
116	Haatheq
116	Henry Clay
116	I'm Back
116	Layl
116	Nolohay
116	One Man Band
116	Rafeej
116	Rio Tigre
116	*Umgiyo
115	*Flying The Flag
115	Haafaguinea
115	*Mickdaam
115	Mr Pommeroy
115	Sir Fever
115	*Tha'ir
115	United Color
114	Candy Boy
114	*Fils Anges
114	Kanaf
114	Limario
114	Samurai Sword
114	Silver Galaxy
114	Songcraft
114	Toolain
114§	Interpret
113	Al Saham
113	*Ajeeb
113	Artigiano
113	Encipher
113	*Johann Strauss
113	Master of War
113	Muaanid
113	My Catch
113	*Sanshaawes
113	Sholaan
113	Special Fighter
112	*Anaerobio
112	*Banaadeer
112	Cooptado
112	*Darwin
112	Emirates Flyer
112	Farrier
112	Footbridge
112	*Mujaarib
112	Validus
112	*Zahee
111	*Excellent Result
111	Ghaamer
111	Jutland
111	Mawhub
111	Shamaal Nibras
111§	Iguazu Falls
110	Cool Cowboy
110	Hunting Ground
110	Mashaaref
110	Music Theory
110	Nawwaar
110	Pilote
110	*Rock Cocktail
110§	Busker

NORTH AMERICA   Horse of the Year **American Pharoah** became the first US Triple Crown winner since Affirmed in 1978 and the twelfth in all, and as the first such winner of the Breeders' Cup era (founded in 1984), went on to make history when completing what became known as the 'Grand Slam' when he went on to finish his career in style by taking the Breeders' Cup Classic at Keeneland in October. A tough as well as outstanding racehorse, American Pharoah's feats are chronicled in detail in his essay earlier in this Annual, his rating of 138 the joint highest (along with Cigar) given to a US-trained horse since Timeform started publishing ratings for North American horses in 1993.

One of the best renewals of the Breeders' Cup Classic in recent times was weakened by the withdrawal of top-class mare Beholder, who was found to have a fever and scoped badly the day before the race. That still left a field of eight, however, seven of whom were previous Group/Grade 1 winners. Setting an even pace from the front, American Pharoah cruised clear of **Effinex** (the only runner in the field not to have won a Grade 1 beforehand) and Honor Code, who would have been suited by a stronger gallop. The solidity of the Breeders' Cup Classic form was further validated when Effinex went on to win the Clark Handicap in November, beating **Hoppertunity** by three quarters of a length. The much-improved Effinex remains in training, with further Grade 1 success likely to be forthcoming for this formerly quirky, but now seemingly reformed character.

The leading older horse was the ill-fated **Shared Belief**, who sadly had to be put down after suffering a bout of colic in December. Shared Belief had been sidelined by a hip fracture for the majority of the year after being pulled up in the Charles Town Classic in April. That came after a career-best performance in the Santa Anita Handicap when giving 4 lb and a comfortable beating to **Moreno**. Shared Belief had started his season with an easy win over the previous year's Kentucky Derby winner **California Chrome** in the Grade 2 San Antonio Stakes. In an era when equine stars are sometimes whisked off to stud all too quickly, Shared Belief was a significant loss as, being a gelding, he could otherwise have enjoyed an extended racing career.

Todd Pletcher's top-class **Liam's Map** is one such case. Having made just eight career starts, culminating in a hard-fought victory in the Breeders' Cup Dirt Mile, the grey four-year-old son of Unbridled's Song is set to stand at Lane's End Stud in 2016. As well as his Breeders' Cup win, Liam's Map also took an optional claimer and the Woodward Stakes at Saratoga, travelling powerfully before easing clear of **Coach Inge**. In between those races, Liam's Map had finished second to another horse due to stand at Lane's End in 2016, **Honor Code**. That came in the Whitney Stakes, also at Saratoga, Honor Code getting up in the dying strides to beat Liam's Map by a neck, after the latter, in receipt of 7 lb, had set a strong pace. Honor Code enjoyed something of a renaissance, having had a truncated campaign the year before. He also took the Metropolitan Handicap at Belmont in June, beating Tonalist, the fast pace suiting him ideally there, and had started his year with victory in the Grade 2 Gulfstream Park Handicap, beating Private Zone by half a length, once again coming off the fast pace that was very much needed for the son of A P Indy to be seen to best effect.

Las Vegas Breeders' Cup Dirt Mile, Keeneland—a top-class performance from Liam's Map who retires with six wins from eight starts; Lea (obscured by winner) finishes clear of third-placed Red Vine with the eventual sixth Mr Z (blinkers) also in shot

Travers Stakes, Saratoga—the so-called 'graveyard of champions' claims another victim as American Pharoah (right) suffers a shock defeat, his only one all year, at the hands of Keen Ice after being harried for the lead by eventual third Frosted (blinkers)

Another retiree at the end of 2015 was **Tonalist** (yet another to stand at Lane's End), winner of the 2014 Belmont Stakes. Having proven his stamina in the previous year's campaign, Tonalist showed his versatility by dropping back to a mile with a Grade 3 win at Belmont before that sound effort behind Honor Code in the Metropolitan Handicap. Largely tough and consistent, Tonalist also took the Jockey Club Stakes at Belmont in October for the second time, before bouncing back from a below-par fifth in the Breeders' Cup Classic to take the Cigar Mile at Aqueduct in November.

Four-year-old gelding **Smooth Roller** was an intended runner in the Breeders' Cup Classic until scratched on veterinary advice on the day of the race with a tendon problem. The winner of three of just four starts beforehand, Smooth Roller put up a high-class effort when winning the Awesome Again Stakes at Santa Anita by more than five lengths. The same race, incidentally, saw the final appearance of the previous season's Breeders' Cup Classic winner **Bayern** who was retired after a disappointing campaign.

The aforementioned American Pharoah dominated the three-year-old scene in a season when he not only swept the Triple Crown and Breeders' Cup Classic, but also the Grade 2 Rebel Stakes, the Arkansas Derby, both at Oaklawn in the spring, and a simply stunning performance when taking the Haskell Invitational at Monmouth in August, beating **Keen Ice** by two and a quarter lengths but being value for much more. His one blip came when beaten three quarters of a length by the same rival later that month in the Travers Stakes at Saratoga. The fact that **Frosted** harried American Pharoah for the lead from halfway played very much into Keen Ice's hands as it brought the latter's stamina into play, Keen Ice responding well to take the lead well inside the final furlong.

Consistent as he was (only out of the first four twice in nine starts), the Travers was Keen Ice's only victory in the campaign, his lack of early pace leaving him vulnerable in races not run at an end-to-end gallop. Keen Ice stays in training with a crack at the Dubai World Cup on his early-season agenda. Another of the 2015 classic crop who

Breeders' Cup Mile, Keeneland—much-improved Canadian-trained filly Tepin proves too strong for the European challengers among whom Mondialiste (left) fares much the best in staying on for second ahead of Grand Arch (second right) and Mshawish

has the UAE showpiece as a major target is Frosted, who looked to be going the wrong way in the early part of the year. However, a breathing operation following his second start seemed to correct whatever was ailing him, and he returned to form with a win in the Wood Memorial Stakes at Aqueduct in April before finishing a creditable fourth to American Pharoah in the Kentucky Derby. Solid second places in the Belmont Stakes, the Grade 2 Jim Dandy Stakes and the Travers Stakes followed before Frosted took the Grade 2 Pennsylvania Derby at Parx in September. A subsequent down-the-field finish in the Breeders' Cup Classic is best forgiven.

Two horses that finished ahead of both Frosted and Keen Ice in the Kentucky Derby were **Firing Line** and **Dortmund**. Firing Line had been a wide-margin winner of the Grade 3 Sunland Derby before confirming that form when running the hard-ridden American Pharoah to a length at Churchill Downs. Seemingly set to take high rank among the three-year-olds, Firing Line's season was cut short after a dismal effort in a sloppy-track Preakness Stakes owing to persistent foot problems. He is set to return in 2016, as is the giant Dortmund, who finished third to stable companion American Pharoah in the Kentucky Derby. A fourth in the Preakness followed before Dortmund was given the summer off after bruising his ribs, returning to take a non-graded stakes at Santa Anita (where he had completed an early-season hat-trick in the Santa Anita Derby) in October and then putting up one of his best efforts of the season when taking the Grade 3 Native Diver Stakes at Del Mar in November, beating **Imperative** by four and a half lengths. Given his size and stature, a truncated three-year-old campaign may prove to be a blessing in disguise as Dortmund looks sure to be aimed at all the big middle-distance dirt races in 2016, where he should take high rank.

After finishing her two-year-old season as the leading filly, the unbeaten **Lady Eli** retained that position in her three-year-old season, despite having her year cut short. Chad Brown's turf filly only made the three starts, taking the Grade 3 Appalachian Stakes at Keeneland in April and a non-graded stakes race at Belmont in May, before finishing off with a smooth success in the Belmont Oaks, beating Itsonlyactingdad (rated 112) by two and a half lengths, quickening away to win with plenty in hand despite being forced wide. When diagnosed with laminitis in her front feet shortly after that win, many thought that would be the end of her racing career at the very least—the condition can sometimes even be fatal—but she is described as having made a 'remarkable recovery' and is in training again from Chad Brown's winter Florida base, hopefully ahead of a return to action in 2016.

On the dirt, the three-year-old fillies were a somewhat below-par group, Santa Anita Oaks winner **Stellar Wind** the best of them following her second to the year-older Stopchargingmaria in the Breeders' Cup Distaff. That was Stellar Wind's best effort of a year that saw her win four graded stakes in all, her best winning performance coming in a Grade 3 contest at Del Mar giving weight away all round. At shorter distances, **Cavorting** recorded a hat-trick of wins from June to September, including the Test Stakes at Saratoga. Her form then tailed off a little as she finished her year with fourth place in the Breeders' Cup Filly & Mare Sprint and a third to **Birdatthewire** in the La Brea Stakes at Santa Anita in December. While not one of the very best three-year-old fillies in 2015, the story of Kentucky Oaks winner Lovely Maria (115) is worth documenting as she was partnered in the saddle by Kerwin Clark, giving him his first ever Grade 1 winner in the Ashland Stakes a fortnight before his fifty-sixth birthday, before following up in the fillies' classic at Churchill Downs. That was also a third win in the Kentucky Oaks for the trainer and owner pairing of Larry Jones and Brereton C. Jones.

The year's leading older female **Beholder** stays in training for what will be her fifth year of racing, having taken her form to new heights in 2015 when becoming the first filly or mare to win the Pacific Classic at Del Mar in August from the former Brazilian-trained import (and dual Grade 2 winner) **Catch A Flight**. Beholder was unbeaten in five starts during the year, with her other Grade 1 successes coming in the Clement L. Hirsch Stakes and (for the third year running) Zenyatta Stakes. A fully-fit Beholder would have given American Pharoah plenty to think about in the Breeders' Cup Classic, in receipt of her sex allowance, and it is to be hoped that she will make the line-up in the 2016 renewal.

Del Mar's return to a dirt surface in 2015 seemed to work in Beholder's favour, that track becoming the final major one in the US to switch from synthetics back to dirt. While there is almost unequivocal evidence that synthetic surfaces are safer for thoroughbreds than dirt, it seems the overriding wishes of the leading trainers—so used to preparing and conditioning horses on the more traditional American terrain—have forced the hand of the major racetracks. A few tracks in North America remain with synthetics, the most high-profile being Woodbine in Canada—which is due to switch from polytrack to tapeta in 2016—but by and large, the synthetic era in the US would appear to be well and truly over.

Other performances of note in the older female division came from **Wavell Avenue** and **Stopchargingmaria**, the former improving a great deal to win the Breeders' Cup Filly & Mare Sprint, coming from way off the pace to run down the consistent **La Verdad** in the final furlong. That was a career best effort by some way from Wavell Avenue—and her first at graded stakes level—having previously only been successful in optional claimers and it remains to be seen if she can repeat the form. Stopchargingmaria was another to produce a career best when she took a below-par renewal of the Breeders' Cup Distaff, taking the lead over a furlong out and keeping on well to beat the year-younger Stellar Wind by a neck. That was Stopchargingmaria's first win at Grade 1 level since winning the previous year's Alabama Stakes at Saratoga, taking full advantage of a field that was far from strong.

With dual Horse of the Year Wise Dan failing to make it back to the track in 2015—connections deciding to retire him after another injury derailed an attempt to get him to the Breeders' Cup—the way was left open for a new name to rise to the top of the turf rankings. The one who did so was the four-year-old filly **Tepin** who made remarkable progress for Canadian trainer Mark Casse. Beginning the year with an optional claiming win, Tepin's meteoric rise culminated in her winning the Breeders' Cup Mile, beating the British-trained Woodbine Mile winner Mondialiste by a convincing two and a quarter lengths. In between those successes, Tepin had also won the Just A Game Stakes at Belmont and the First Lady Stakes at Keeneland, as well as the Grade 2 Distaff Turf Mile at Churchill Downs on Kentucky Derby day. The very consistent Tepin seems set to return in 2016, and is very effective on good ground or softer, although she has won on firm ground.

Breeders' Cup Filly & Mare Turf, Keeneland—six-year-old Stephanie's Kitten goes one better than the year before to defeat younger rivals headed by 1000 Guineas winner Legatissimo and French filly Queen's Jewel (left)

Out of luck in the Breeders' Cup Mile, European success came instead in the Breeders' Cup Turf, but it wasn't the result that many envisaged, the filly Found getting the better of Derby and Arc winner Golden Horn, who was possibly feeling the effects of a combination of the dead ground and a long season. That is to take nothing away from Found, who produced the best effort of her career on the day, digging deep in the final furlong to hold on by half a length. Third behind them was the United Nations Stakes and Joe Hirsch Turf Classic winner **Big Blue Kitten**, while fifth was **The Pizza Man**, a reliable, tough and versatile individual who had taken the Arlington Million from Big Blue Kitten earlier in the year. Previously thought of as a staying type (he had won the 2014 American St Leger over an extended thirteen furlongs), The Pizza Man also won races from eight and a half to twelve furlongs during the year, including the Grade 2 Hollywood Turf Cup at Del Mar over the latter trip. He also managed to finish a close second to subsequent Breeders' Cup Mile third **Grand Arch** in the Shadwell Turf Mile at Keeneland, despite finding that an inadequate test.

Beverly D Stakes, Arlington—a controversial finish is about to unfold as Jamie Spencer tracks the pace on first-past-the-post Secret Gesture only to be demoted to third for hampering the Irad Ortiz-ridden Stephanie's Kitten ('R' on cap) but it is the patiently-ridden Watsdachances (pompom on cap) who gets the verdict

Twinspires Breeders' Cup Turf Sprint, Keeneland—
Mongolian Saturday (third left) disputes the lead on the home turn on the way to putting up a
career-best effort from a field that includes 2014 winner Bobby's Kitten (left) who finishes fourth
and Diamond Jubilee Stakes winner Undrafted (black colours on inner) in fifth

Another turf performer of note was **Stephanie's Kitten**, who went one better than the previous year to win the Breeders' Cup Filly & Mare Turf, and was also involved in one of the most controversial incidents of 2015 when finishing second in the Beverly D Stakes on Arlington Million day. The winner of the race on merit was Secret Gesture, who beat Watsdachances (114) by a length and a quarter. However, in so doing, the Jamie Spencer-ridden Secret Gesture drifted into the path of third-past-the-post Stephanie's Kitten, causing her rider Irad Ortiz jr to snatch up in rather dramatic fashion, seemingly costing her the chance of finishing second. Under Illinois rules, the stewards deemed that Secret Gesture's move had been enough to cost Stephanie's Kitten the runner-up spot, and Spencer's mount was subsequently demoted to third behind that rival, handing Watsdachances (who seemed only third best on the day) a most fortuitous win. If anything, the outcome highlights the difference in rules in various jurisdictions, and in particular, the local knowledge of those rules, which Ortiz quite cannily used to his advantage. As well as her Breeders' Cup win, Stephanie's Kitten's other Grade 1 win came in the Flower Bowl Stakes at Belmont. The Breeders' Cup Turf Sprint went to five-year-old gelding **Mongolian Saturday** who put up a career-best effort, while favourite **Undrafted**, winner of the Diamond Jubilee Stakes at Royal Ascot for Wesley Ward earlier in the year, failed to land a blow in fifth.

Back on dirt, the leading sprinter was **Runhappy**, whose successful season was somewhat mired in controversy following his Breeders' Cup Sprint win over Private Zone. Runhappy had started his year in Grade 3 company for trainer Laura Wohlers. He wasn't seen again until July—by that time in the care of little-known trainer Maria Borell—and put that previous effort well behind him with a convincing victory dropped in trip in an optional claimer at Indiana Grand. Following up in a similar race at Ellis Park later that month, Runhappy was then pitched into Grade 1 company, taking the King's Bishop Stakes at Saratoga by four lengths.

Given a break before taking a Grade 3 contest at Parx in October, Runhappy then confirmed himself a high-class and much improved horse with his Breeders' Cup Sprint victory, without doubt the highlight of his young trainer's career to date. However, less than twenty four hours after her finest moment, Borell was shocked to find out she had been sacked as Runhappy's trainer. Owned by furniture magnate Jim 'Mattress Mack' McIngvale, the decision to remove Runhappy from Borell's small Kentucky stable was said to have come after a disagreement between Borell and Runhappy's former trainer, who is also the owner's racing manager as well as sister-in-law.

Twinspires Breeders' Cup Sprint, Keeneland—
three-year-old colt Runhappy (white sleeves, centre) on the way to establishing himself as the
top sprinter on dirt with runner-up Private Zone (stripes) also to the fore

Whatever the rights or wrongs of the situation, the move clearly had little effect on Runhappy as he produced an even better effort when finishing his year back with Laura Wohlers in the Malibu Stakes on Boxing Day. Travelling strongly on the lead under new jockey Gary Stevens, who had taken over from Edgar Prado following Runhappy's trainer change, the three-year-old son of 2010 Kentucky Derby winner Super Saver stormed clear of Marking (114p) to win by three and half a lengths. Despite being blessed with considerable early pace, the tractable Runhappy looks likely to stay a mile, which opens up lots of options for him in 2016, should connections decide to pursue that route. Another point of note in Runhappy's so-far brief but controversial career is that he races without the diuretic furosemide (Lasix). This is one issue that crops up year-in, year-out in US racing—a topic that is dealt with in some detail in the essay on Hit It A Bomb in this Annual.

One horse that is no stranger to trainer changes is Breeders' Cup Sprint runner-up **Private Zone**, who made his final start for Jorge Navarro in that contest. Following that effort, Private Zone was transferred to the care of Brian Lynch, who became the horse's fourth trainer in the space of just over two years. Disappointing on his final start in the Cigar Mile at Aqueduct, Private Zone had previously conceded weight all round when making all in the Forego Stakes at Saratoga over seven furlongs in a season when he also put up solid efforts over a mile. Another sprinter to put up performances of note was Todd Pletcher's **Rock Fall**, who looked set to take high rank before being fatally injured during a morning workout at Keeneland in October. One of the ante-post favourites for the Breeders' Cup Sprint, Rock Fall had shown his class earlier in the year when winning the Alfred G. Vanderbilt Handicap (by a nose from **The Big Beast**) and the Vosburgh Stakes, as well as the Grade 2 True North Stakes.

Somewhat unusually, and by quite a margin, the leading two-year-old was a filly, **Songbird**, whose performance in taking the Breeders' Cup Juvenile Fillies led to her finishing the year with a Timeform rating of 125p, only 1 lb below the mark that American Pharoah achieved when heading the ratings in his juvenile year. Unbeaten in four starts, Jerry Hollendorfer's daughter of Medgalia d'Oro was unchallenged in making all, drawing clear to win by nearly 6 lengths from **Rachel's Valentina**, herself a Grade 1 winner earlier in the year. Songbird's win at the Breeders' Cup was her third at the top level, following on from equally facile successes in the Del Mar Debutante Stakes and the Chandelier Stakes at Santa Anita. Rather disappointingly, connections have stated their intentions to keep Songbird to her own sex, and are unlikely to entertain a shot at the Kentucky Derby.

Other performances of note among the two-year-old fillies came from the aforementioned Rachel's Valentina and **Gomo**. Rachel's Valentina, a beautifully-bred daughter of Bernardini and Rachel Alexandra, won her first two starts at Saratoga, including the Spinaway Stakes. That she proved no match for the high-class Songbird shouldn't be held against her at this stage, but she may need to avoid that filly if she's to gain further success at the top level. Gomo hadn't looked out of the ordinary until really coming into her own around the two turns of the Alciabades Stakes at Keeneland in October, beating **Dothraki Queen** by a convincing two and a quarter lengths. Whether the sloppy conditions or the stiffer test of stamina contributed to her improvement is hard to tell, but her performance on the day was smart.

The two-year-old colts on dirt were a little below the level of previous years, with **Nyquist** and **Mor Spirit** being the best of them. Despite being unbeaten in five starts, Nyquist's performances are best described as workmanlike rather than flashy, his best effort coming in the Breeders' Cup Juvenile when beating **Swipe** by half a length, deserving a bit of extra credit having been wide throughout. That win supplemented previous Grade 1 successes in the Del Mar Futurity and the FrontRunner Stakes at Santa Anita. The more lightly-raced Mor Spirit may have the greater potential of the two, however, his win in the Los Alamitos Futurity hinting at better to come. That win was a step up on Mor Spirit's previous effort when he had finished second to **Airoforce** in the Grade 2 Kentucky Jockey Club Stakes at Churchill Downs. Airoforce himself, switching from turf to dirt that day, is another likely improver in 2016. That same comment can also be applied to **Mohaymen**, unbeaten in three starts for Kiaran McLaughlin. After a winning debut in September, Mohaymen took a pair of Grade 2 contests at Aqueduct, the Nashua Stakes and the Remsen Stakes. An expensive son of elite sire Tapit, Mohaymen is potentially the most exciting prospect amongst 2015's leading juvenile colts.

The best turf performance in North America from a two-year-old colt came courtesy of Aidan O'Brien's Hit It A Bomb, who produced a remarkable effort in taking the Breeders' Cup Juvenile Turf. The half-length margin by which he beat Airoforce doesn't really do justice to his superiority, Hit It A Bomb coming from a long way back and showing a sharp turn of foot to win with plenty in hand. O'Brien was denied a win in the equivalent race for fillies when Alice Springs was beaten three quarters of a length by Tepin's stable-companion **Catch A Glimpse** in the Juvenile Fillies Turf, the winner unbeaten in three starts since switching to that surface. However, Wesley Ward's **Acapulco** produced a better performance at Royal Ascot to win the Queen Mary Stakes before another trail-blazing display, this time against older horses in the Nunthorpe Stakes at York when seeing off all bar Mecca's Angel. Acapulco is likely to return to Royal Ascot as a three-year-old, with the Commonwealth Cup on her agenda.

Two-Year-Olds					
125p	Songbird (f)	111	Street Fancy (f)	119	I'm A Chatterbox (f)
119	Mor Spirit	111	Tap To It (f)	118	Daredevil
119	Nyquist	110p	Off The Tracks (f)	118	Fantastic Style (f)
115p	Mohaymen	110	Annual Report	118	Force The Pass
115	Gomo (f)	110	Riker	118	Om
115	Greenpointcrusader			118	Ready For Rye
115	Rachel's Valentina (f)	**Three-Year-Olds**		118	X Y Jet
115	Toews On Ice	138	American Pharoah	117	Birdatthewire (f)
114p	Airoforce	127	Runhappy	117	Chiropractor
114	Acapulco (f)	125	Firing Line	117	Curalina (f)
114	Nickname (f)	124	Dortmund	117	Embellish The Lace (f)
114	Swipe	124	Frosted	117	Holy Boss
113	Carina Mia (f)	124	Keen Ice	117	March
112	Brody's Cause	124	Lady Eli (f)	117	One Lucky Dane
112	Dothraki Queen (f)	122	Stellar Wind (f)		
111	Catch A Glimpse (f)	121	Carpe Diem	**Older Horses**	
111	Exaggerator	121	Materiality	132	Shared Belief
111	Land Over Sea (f)	120	Cavorting (f)	131	Beholder (f)
111	Mo Tom	120	Texas Red	130	Liam's Map
		120	Upstart	129	Honor Code

128	Tonalist	120	Big Blue Kitten	118	Dame Dorothy (f)
127	Effinex	120	Hard Aces	118	Finnegans Wake
126	California Chrome	120	La Verdad (f)	118	Jack Milton
126	Undrafted	120	Main Sequence	118	Matrooh
125	Private Zone	120	Palace Malice	118	Moreno
125	Rock Fall	120	Protonico	118	Mr Maybe
125	Smooth Roller	120	Red Rifle	118	Mshawish
125	Tepin (f)	120	Ring Weekend	118	Reporting Star
123	Catch A Flight	120	The Pizza Man	118	Shining Copper
123	Lea	120	Wedding Toast (f)	118	Stacked Deck
123	The Big Beast	119	Commissioner	118	Talco
122	Appealing Tale	119	Gabriel Charles	118	V. E. Day
122	Coach Inge	119	Grand Arch	117	Avanzare
122	Constitution	119	Green Mask	117	Bal A Bali
122	Favorite Tale	119	Imperative	117	Big John B
122	Hoppertunity	119	Ironicus	117	Dacita (f)
122	Red Vine	119	Judy The Beauty (f)	117	Got Lucky (f)
122	Salutos Amigos	119	Masochistic	117	Hard Not To Like (f)
122	Secret Circle	119	Noble Bird	117	Kaigun
122	Wavell Avenue (f)	119	Obviously	117	Kobe's Back
122	Wild Dude	119	Palace	117	Midnight Storm
121	Bayern	119	Sheer Drama (f)	117	Seek Again
121	Mongolian Saturday	119	Slumber	117	Stonetastic (f)
121	Race Day	119	Stephanie's Kitten (f)	117	Tourist
121	Stopchargingmaria (f)	119	Twilight Eclipse	117	Tower of Texas
121	Taris (f)	118	Ball Dancing (f)	117	Up With The Birds
121	Untapable (f)	118	Bradester		
121	Wicked Strong	118	Dads Caps		

JAPAN For the first time since 2009 Japan went unrepresented in the Prix de l'Arc de Triomphe. There had been several contenders earlier in the year for the race which has become the most important overseas goal for Japan's top middle-distance performers, but one by one they were ruled out by various setbacks. The previous year's top-class Japan Cup winner Epiphaneia finished last on his dirt debut in the Dubai World Cup on what turned out to be his only start of the year; he was retired to stud after sustaining a tendon injury when being aimed at the Takarazuka Kinen in June. 2013 Arc third **Kizuna**, who missed the 2014 running through injury, returned with a couple of good placed efforts in Group 2 contests early in the year, but after failing to build on those in the Tenno Sho (Spring) his target later in the year was switched from the Arc to the Tenno Sho (Autumn) instead before he too was forced into retirement by a tendon injury. Harp Star, sixth in the 2014 Arc when Japan's top three-year-old filly, was another whose season was cut short after just two runs early on, returning injured when beating only one home after being sent off favourite for the Dubai Sheema Classic. The 2014 Tokyo Yushun (Derby) winner **One And Only** finished third in the Sheema Classic but was ruled out of an Arc challenge after disappointing in the Takarazuka Kinen and was only mid-division in the Japan Cup (seventh for the second year running) and Arima Kinen late in the year.

The latest three-year-old crop also contained some Arc hopefuls, though they too fell by the wayside. **Duramente** was regarded as a potential triple crown winner, as an alternative to the Arc, after completing the Guineas-Derby double of the Satsuki Sho and Tokyo Yushun but he missed the second half of the year after being operated on to have bone chips removed from both forelegs. Winner of the Derby in record time (he beat the record set by his own sire King Kamehameha in 2004), Duramente stays in training so could yet be a future Arc horse. **Real Steel** beat Duramente in a Group 3 contest before finishing runner-up to him in the Satsuki Sho and fourth in the Derby. Injury put paid to Real Steel's Arc hopes as well, though he did make it back in the autumn to be beaten a neck by **Kitasan Black** in the Kikuka Sho (St Leger). The filly **Rouge Buck**, runner-up in the Yushun Himba (Oaks), was the other three-year-old Arc entry, though she was ruled out of a trip to France after having to miss her intended prep run in the Sapporo Kinen in August. Kitasan Black and Rouge Buck contested the Arima Kinen against older horses in December, with the former faring much the better of the pair in third.

Although the Arc challenge came to nothing, there were plenty of other Japanese ventures overseas which yielded some success. In Australia, the 2011 Yasuda Kinen winner **Real Impact** won the George Ryder Stakes at Rosehill before finishing second in the Doncaster Mile at The Championships at Randwick. There were also second places in Australian Group 1 events for **Tosen Stardom** (Ranvet Stakes) and **To The World** (BMW Classic). Less rewarding later in the year was the two-pronged challenge on the Caulfield Cup and Melbourne Cup from **Hokko Brave** and **Fame Game**, though the latter, who had finished second in the Tenno Sho (Spring) (with Hokko Brave back in sixth), shaped promisingly enough when sixth at Caulfield to be sent off favourite at Flemington. The Dubai World Cup meeting proved less successful for Japanese horses than the year before, though One And Only's third place in the Sheema Classic was matched by Golden Barows (rated 109) in the UAE Derby who came out best of three Japanese colts in that contest. Leading dirt performer **Hokko Tarumae** fared better than the year before in the World Cup itself thanks to the change of surface at Meydan, though was still below his best in fifth. Two Japanese horses ran at Royal Ascot, and while Super Moon (rated 106) finished in rear in a messy Wolferton Handicap, the same connections' **Spielberg**, third in the 2014 Japan Cup, was a creditable sixth in the Prince of Wales's Stakes. A much less high-profile runner overseas, but one who made a small piece of history, was the four-year-old filly Esmeraldina who in June became the first JRA horse to win an international stakes race in South Korea, a country with growing ambitions to join the international racing circuit.

However, it was at Sha Tin in December that Japan launched its biggest and most successful foreign raid. A record ten runners from Japan contested the Hong Kong International races, with **A Shin Hikari** and the filly **Nuovo Record** taking the first two places in the Hong Kong Cup and top miler (subsequently also voted Horse of the Year) **Maurice** keeping his unbeaten record for the year in the Hong Kong Mile. A Shin Hikari was Japan's fourth winner of the Hong Kong Cup but the first since Agnes Digital in 2001 as he made all under a superbly-judged ride from Yutaka Take to take his career record to nine wins from eleven starts with much his best effort to date. The Ryan Moore-ridden Nuovo Record, who had beaten Harp Star in the Yushun Himba in 2014, also recorded a career-best. Moore went one better on Maurice who became Japan's third winner of the Hong Kong Mile. They had previously teamed up successfully in the Mile Championship at Kyoto when accounting for the previous year's runner-up **Fiero**, while Maurice, who had changed stables prior to the latest season, also won the Yasuda Kinen at Tokyo in June. Earlier in the year at Sha Tin, **Staphanos** was a good second in the Audemars Piguet Queen Elizabeth II Cup but he wasn't in the same form back there in December. The main hope for Japan in the Hong Kong Sprint was six-year-old mare **Straight Girl** but she ran below form when bidding to better her third place from twelve months earlier. However, at home she gained Group 1 wins in the Victoria Mile and the Sprinters Stakes, stepping

Mile Championship, Kyoto—
Ryan Moore drives out Japan's Horse of the Year Maurice (third left) to remain unbeaten for the year, while the previous season's Guineas winner and Derby runner-up Isla Bonita (striped sleeves) stays on for third behind Fiero (out of picture) who is runner-up for the second year

up on placed efforts in both those races from the year before. **Sakura Gospel**, runner-up in the Sprinters Stakes, and **Mikki Isle**, fourth in the same race and a close third behind the Hong Kong-trained winner Aerovelocity and **Hakusan Moon** in Japan's other Group 1 sprint, the Takamatsunomiya Kinen, were the other Japanese runners in the Hong Kong Sprint. Incidentally, a change in the law will mean that for the first time in 2016 Japanese punters will be able to bet on selected races overseas that have Japanese interest.

Back on home turf, the ranks of Japan's best middle-distance performers may have been a little depleted by the autumn but they were still good enough to hold off four Group 1 winners from abroad in the Japan Cup—it is now ten years since Japan's most international of races went overseas. It was, however, a substandard renewal which resulted in a blanket finish with most of the field covered by around four lengths at the line. Four-year-old filly **Shonan Pandora** (winner of the Shuka Sho in 2014) came out on top on her first start at a mile and a half. After the successes of Vodka, Buena Vista (after being demoted from first twelve months earlier) and dual winner Gentildonna, Shonan Pandora became the fifth female winner of the Japan Cup in the last seven runnings. Ryan Moore had ridden Gentildonna to the second of her Japan Cup wins and he went close again in the latest renewal on the neck runner-up **Last Impact** who was headed close home. Just another neck back in third was favourite **Lovely Day** who enjoyed a tremendous year, winning six group races at ten to twelve furlongs. His first Group 1 success came in the Takarazuka Kinen at Hanshin in June when getting the better of the 2013 Japan Cup runner-up **Denim And Ruby** and Shonan Pandora, while he had Shonan Pandora back in fourth in his other top-level win in the Tenno Sho (Autumn) at Tokyo from Staphanos and **Isla Bonita** who went on to finish third in the Mile Championship.

On his day, **Gold Ship** was still more than a match for the best around at up to two miles, but in his final season, his fourth in the top flight, the six-year-old entire was as unpredictable as ever. He put up one of the best performances all year when conceding weight all round to win the Group 2 Hanshin Daishoten in March for the third year running from Denim And Ruby and Last Impact and made it third time lucky when following up in the Tenno Sho (Spring) from a strong field, with Fame Game, **Curren Mirotic** and Last Impact completing the frame. However, the worst side of Gold Ship's character surfaced when he was sent off at odds on to win the Takarazuka Kinen for the third time. Rearing as the stalls opened, he lost all chance as a result, and he disappointed again, with his usual headgear left off, in both the Japan Cup and Arima Kinen. Others, though, ran good races in defeat in the Japan Cup. Rank outsider **Jungle Cruise** seemed to excel himself in fourth, while fifth was the previous season's St Leger runner-up **Sounds of Earth** who again peaked late in the year, having finished second to Lovely Day in the Group 2 Kyoto Daishoten beforehand. The only Japanese-trained three-year-old in the Japan Cup line-up was leading filly **Mikki Queen** who ran creditably in eighth. She beat Rouge Buck in the Yushun Himba and then landed the autumn leg of the fillies' triple crown, the Shuka Sho at Kyoto. Further down the Japan Cup field, Group 2 winners from earlier in the season **Hit The Target** and **Admire Deus** wouldn't have been far away on their best form. Five-year-old mare **Lachesis** contested the Queen Elizabeth II Cup (which she had won the year before) for fillies and mares instead of the Japan Cup, though she had Shonan Pandora well behind her earlier in the year when putting up one of the best performances by an older filly or mare to win a Group 2 at Hanshin from Kizuna.

The Arima Kinen at the end of December did little to make the pecking order any clearer among the leading middle-distance performers. Shonan Pandora was an absentee, while the placed horses from the Japan Cup, Last Impact and Lovely Day, could finish only twelfth and fifth respectively in a steadily-run race which resulted in another blanket finish. The previous year's Kikuka Sho third **Gold Actor** came out on top to complete a four-timer (after landing a Group 2 contest at Tokyo) by a neck from the strong-finishing Sounds of Earth.

Most of the leading three-year-olds have already been mentioned, but also among the leading fillies were the Oka Sho (1000 Guineas) winner **Let's Go Donki** and **Touching Speech** who had that rival back in fourth when beating Mikki Queen in the Group 2 Rose Stakes at Hanshin in September. Touching Speech was below her best when sixth to Mikki Queen in the Shuka Sho before a better effort when running the older fillies **Marialite** (later fourth in the Arima Kinen) and Nuovo Record close in the Queen Elizabeth II Cup. Among the colts, **Satono Rasen** and **Satono Crown** filled the places in the Tokyo Yushun behind Duramente, while other three-year-olds ran some good races against older horses later in the year. **Ambitious** was fifth in the Tenno Sho (Autumn) at Tokyo (after finishing sixth to A Shin Hikari in a Group 2 there) while **Yamakatsu Ace**, a Group 2 winner against his own age-group earlier in the year, was a close fourth behind smart older rivals in the Group 2 Sapporo Kinen won by **Decipher** in August. The previous season's top two-year-old **Danon Platina** found his best form again late in the year, beating smart older horses in the Group 3 Fuji Stakes at Tokyo before finishing a good seventh behind Maurice as the only three-year-old in the Hong Kong Mile.

The winners of both the JRA Group 1 contests on dirt achieved notable feats. **Copano Rickey** became the first dual winner of the February Stakes at Tokyo, starting a short-priced favourite this time having been a shock winner of the race in 2014. He returned from injury to win the JBC Classic (a local government Group 1) in the autumn, also for the second year. However, in the Champions Cup at Chukyo, Copano Rickey finished only seventh to the six-year-old mare **Sambista** who caused a 65/1 upset in becoming the first of her sex to win either of the JRA Group 1 races on dirt. Three-year-old **Nonkono Yume**, winner of the Japan Dirt Derby, took second in the Champions Cup ahead of the JBC Classic runner-up **Sound True** in third.

Among the two-year-olds, the leading colt and filly respectively were **Leontes** and **Major Emblem** after their Group 1 wins in the Asahi Hai Futurity and the Hanshin Juvenile Fillies. Leontes in particular looks a good prospect after his ready win from the rear at Hanshin on just his second start where the first two finished four lengths clear. He's very well bred, too, being a half-brother to Epiphaneia, and looks another good horse for his sire King Kamehameha. In addition to the likes of Duramente and Lovely Day, King Kamehameha was also responsible for the Futurity runner-up **Air Spinel** whose dam Air Messiah, coincidentally, finished second to Leontes' dam Cesario in the 2005 Yushun Himba. The two Group 1 two-year-old winners were ridden by Mirco Demuro and Christophe Lemaire respectively, the pair having become the first foreign jockeys to be granted permanent licences by the JRA in 2015. Demuro also rode Duramente to his two classic wins, the Italian having already made history in the 2003 Tokyo Yushun when becoming the first foreign jockey to ride the winner of the Japanese Derby on Neo Universe. Demuro and Lemaire finished third and fourth respectively in the jockeys' championship despite both having fewer mounts than the other leading riders.

Two-Year-Olds				Three-Year-Olds	
118p	Leontes	110	Win Fabulous (f)		
116	Air Spinel	109	Battistini	123p	Duramente
116	Major Emblem (f)	109	Dreadnoughtus	121	Ambitious
115	Hartley	108	Black Spinel	120	Kitasan Black
112	Lord Quest	108	Brave Smash	119	Danon Platina
111	Blanc Bonheur (f)	108	Denko Ange (f)	119	Lia Fail
111	Shuji	108	Immortal	119	Nonkono Yume
110	Ball Lightning	108	Respect Earth	119	Real Steel
		108	Smart Odin		

119	Yamakatsu Ace	121	Hakusan Moon	119	Decipher
118	Mikki Queen (f)	121	Jungle Cruise	119	Denim And Ruby (f)
118	Reve Mistral	121	Kizuna	119	Derby Fizz
118	Touching Speech (f)	121	Lachesis (f)	119	Incantation
117	Beruf	121	Mikki Isle	119	Satono Aladdin
117	Let's Go Donki (f)	121	One And Only	119	Toho Jackal
117	Rouge Buck (f)	121	Sakura Gospel	119	Vincennes
117	Satono Crown	121	Sound True	118	Hokko Tarumae
117	Satono Rasen	121	Sounds of Earth	118	Logotype
		121	Wonder Acute	118	Marialite (f)
Older Horses		120	Albert	118	Red Davis
127	A Shin Hikari	120	Fiero	118	Roi Jardin
126	Maurice	120	Hit The Target	118	Tosen Reve
124	Real Impact	120	Hokko Brave	118	Tosen Stardom
123	Copano Rickey	120	Isla Bonita	118	Win Variation
123	Last Impact	120	Mitra	117	Chrysolite
123	Lovely Day	120	Neo Black Dia	117	Clarente
123§	Gold Ship	120	Nuovo Record (f)	117	Danon Legend
122	Fame Game	120	Shonan Pandora (f)	117	Sambista (f)
122	Gold Actor	120	Spielberg	117	Satono Noblesse
122	Staphanos	120	Straight Girl (f)	117	Shonan Bach
122	To The World	120	Suzuka Devious	117	World Ace
121	Admire Deus	119	Best Warrior		
121	Curren Mirotic	119	Danon Shark		

HONG KONG   Having carried all before him at Sha Tin since winning the 2014 Hong Kong Mile, it was with great anticipation that **Able Friend**, later named 2014/15 Horse of the Year in Hong Kong, was sent to Royal Ascot for a clash with another prolific winner, the French gelding Solow, in the Queen Anne Stakes. However, Able Friend ran no sort of race in sixth having become uncharacteristically on edge before entering the stalls. Prior to disappointing at Ascot, Able Friend had again shown top-class form with four easy wins in the Stewards' Cup, the Queen's Silver Jubilee Cup, the Chairman's Trophy (for the second year running) and the Champions Mile. He put up his most impressive display in the last-named contest in which he had finished second twelve months earlier, beating stable-companions **Rewarding Hero** (winner of the Chinese Club Challenge Cup and third in the Stewards' Cup and Chairman's Trophy) and **Dan Excel**. The 2013 Champions Mile winner Dan Excel went on to win his second Singapore Airlines International Cup at Kranji next time, though both that contest and the KrisFlyer International Sprint in which Hong Kong-trained sprinters had a good record were run for the final time in 2015.

Some four months after his failed Ascot raid, Able Friend's return at Sha Tin at the start of the new season came over six furlongs in the Premier Bowl Handicap. Conceding weight all round to some of Hong Kong's best sprinters, Able Friend produced a strong finish to record a win which ranked alongside the pick of his form at his supposed best trip of a mile. While seemingly back to his best, the rest of Able Friend's year didn't go according to plan, however. Defeats in the Jockey Club Mile (third to **Beauty Flame**, who had been runner-up behind Able Friend in his first three wins of the year) and the Hong Kong Mile (third to Japan's Horse of the Year Maurice) followed, the former perhaps excused by a lack of early pace in a race in which Able Friend had to concede weight. The Jockey Club Mile runner-up **Contentment** had returned a much-improved performer in the autumn with handicap wins in the Celebration Cup and Sha Tin Trophy, beating the Hong Kong Classic Mile winner **Beauty Only** in a strong field in the latter. Able Friend may well have had a valid excuse in the Hong Kong Mile too as he was found to have a foot problem on the morning of the race and had to pass the vet three times before being given the green light to line up.

After suffering further lameness, it was announced very early in 2016 that Able Friend would have to miss the rest of the 2015/16 season. Contentment went on to finish a respectable fifth in the Hong Kong Mile, but one who could profit most from Able Friend's absence in the top mile races in 2016 is **Giant Treasure** who took second with a career-best effort in the Hong Kong Mile. A four-year-old who had shown useful form in Britain for Roger Charlton when named Sea Defence, Giant Treasure had finished fifth in the Hong Kong Derby earlier in the year won by **Luger** who finished last in the Champions Mile on his only subsequent start.

The previous season's Horse of the Year **Designs On Rome** was still one of the leading middle-distance performers and followed his 2014 Hong Kong Cup win with successes in the Centenary Vase (giving plenty of weight away in the handicap) and Hong Kong Gold Cup (from **Helene Super Star** and **Blazing Speed**) early in the year. Fourth in the Dubai Sheema Classic next time, Designs On Rome wasn't at his best later in the year, finishing only fourth behind the Japanese pair A Shin Hikari and Nuovo Record, as well as Blazing Speed, when bidding to win the Hong Kong Cup again. The consistent Blazing Speed made up for a luckless run in the Hong Kong Gold Cup when having Designs On Rome back in fourth in an international field for the Audemars Piguet Queen Elizabeth II Cup in April. Sixth in that contest, Helene Super Star narrowly turned the tables on his next start in the Champions & Chater Cup over a mile and a half in which Blazing Speed was a close fourth. **Dominant** and **Helene Happy Star** (the ex-Richard Hannon-trained Barley Mow) filled the places, the latter previously successful over the same trip in the Queen Mother Memorial Cup. In a contest dominated by European visitors and won by Irish three-year-old Highland Reel, Helene Happy Star and Dominant (the 2013 winner) fared best of the locals in the Hong Kong Vase in December when finishing fifth and sixth respectively while Helene Super Star lost his form late in the year and finished last.

Military Attack was Horse of the Year back in 2012/13 but remained among the leading middle-distance performers with some high-class efforts to his name. Returning with fourth place in his hat-trick bid in the Hong Kong Gold Cup, Military Attack went on to finish second to Dan Excel in Singapore (placed for the second year after winning there in 2013) and then ran an excellent race giving around a stone to the first two when third behind Contentment and Beauty Only in the Sha Tin Trophy. The weights were kinder to Military Attack in the Jockey Club Cup next time, when beating Blazing Speed by a head in receipt of 5 lb, but for the fourth year running his year ended in defeat in the Hong Kong Cup, adding a sixth place to the fifth, fourth and second from his previous tries. Yet another Horse of the Year still in action, before being retired at a ceremony in April, was the versatile **Ambitious Dragon**, dual holder of that title (in 2010/11 and 2011/12) and a past winner of the Hong Kong Derby and Hong Kong Mile who was rated 129 at his best. Still capable of some form, he finished fifth to Able Friend in his two appearances in the Stewards' Cup and Queen's Silver Jubilee Cup, Ambitious Dragon's victory in the latter race in 2013 being the last of thirteen wins during his career.

There was a typically strong group of sprinters and the Hong Kong Sprint was won by the previous year's runner-up **Peniaphobia**, whose lightning-fast break compensated for his draw in the widest stall, enabling champion jockey Joao Moreira to cross over to the rail and dictate the pace. Runner-up **Gold-Fun**, who had comprehensively beaten the winner just over three weeks earlier in the Jockey Club Sprint, proved no match on the day, while **Not Listenin'tome** filled third place in both races. After opening his year with a narrow win over **Bundle of Joy** in the Centenary Sprint Cup, Peniaphobia generally struggled to hit the same heights until his Hong Kong Sprint win, one of his better efforts in between coming when runner-up in the Al Quoz Sprint in Dubai on World Cup night. Two more Hong Kong sprinters picked up place money on the same card when **Super Jockey** and **Rich Tapestry** finished second and third in the Dubai Golden Shaheen on dirt.

Longines Hong Kong Sprint, Sha Tin—Peniaphobia makes all to go one better than in 2014; Gold-Fun (spots) stays on to reduce the winner's margin to half a length at the line ahead of Not Listenin'tome and Dundonnell (noseband)

Hong Kong Sprint runner-up Gold-Fun had been campaigned over longer distances prior to 2015, often coming up against Able Friend, but really found his niche as a sprinter, finishing either first or second in five starts over six furlongs, including when beating **Aerovelocity** and **Lucky Nine** in the Chairman's Sprint Trophy in February (Peniaphobia only fourth). His other placed efforts included finishing runner-up to stable-companion **Dundonnell** (later fourth in the Hong Kong Sprint), conceding him weight in the Sprint Cup in April, and when finding old rival Able Friend too strong again when that one dropped down in trip for the Premier Bowl. Aerovelocity, who had beaten Peniaphobia in the 2014 Hong Kong Sprint also had a good year, though his two wins came overseas. After his reappearance behind Gold-Fun, he went on to land the Takamatsunomiya Kinen (becoming the first winner from outside Japan) and the aforementioned KrisFlyer Sprint when having Lucky Nine, winner of the previous two renewals, back in third. Back at Sha Tin, Aerovelocity was found to be lame after finishing last in the Premier Bowl won by Able Friend ruling him out of a defence of his Hong Kong Sprint crown.

Older Horses

130	Able Friend	123	Aerovelocity	119	Charles The Great
128	Peniaphobia	123	Beauty Flame	119	Harbour Master
126	Dan Excel	123	Contentment	119	Rich Tapestry
126	Designs On Rome	122	Helene Super Star	118	California Memory
126	Gold-Fun	122	Lucky Nine	118	Luger
125	Military Attack	122	Super Jockey	118	Redkirk Warrior
124	Blazing Speed	122?	Dundonnell	117	Ambitious Dragon
124	Bundle of Joy	121	Beauty Only	117	Got Fly
124	Giant Treasure	121	Dominant	117	Real Specialist
124	Not Listenin'Tome	121	Helene Happy Star	117	Smart Volatility
		120	Rewarding Hero	117	Thunder Fantasy

AUSTRALIA AND NEW ZEALAND Australia's most prestigious races in the [southern hemisphere] spring, the Melbourne Cup, the Cox Plate and the Caulfield Cup, had all been won by international raiders in 2014, but home pride was restored in the latest season. The large international contingent in the Melbourne Cup, 'the race that stops a nation', mostly took a back seat as media attention was focussed on 100/1-winner **Prince of Penzance** ridden by Michelle Payne, the first female jockey to win a Melbourne Cup. It was by some way the best win of six-year-old Prince of Penzance's career and he became the first winner bred and trained in Australia since Shocking in 2009. Max Dynamite, whose jockey Frankie Dettori was fined and suspended for a month for causing severe interference in the home straight, fared best of the northern hemisphere challengers in second (the pedigree of Prince of Penzance has some familiar names in it from a European view point, as outlined in the essay on Max Dynamite). Third at Flemington was **Criterion** who had built on his excellent campaign the previous year by winning Australia's most valuable weight-for-age race, the A$4m Queen Elizabeth Stakes over a mile and a quarter at Randwick in April. The Queen Elizabeth Stakes is the feature of 'The Championships', Sydney's two-meeting showpiece in the autumn. The

*Emirates Melbourne Cup, Flemington—inside the final furlong and 100/1-shot
Prince of Penzance (light blinkers) takes the lead; Max Dynamite (left) finishes strongly for second
with the other blinkered runner Criterion in third; Trip To Paris (dark colours behind the winner)
completes the frame, while the still-prominent Big Orange (striped sleeves) and
Excess Knowledge (dark colours, light cap) also run well*

resilient and very popular Red Cadeaux, who sadly met with an ultimately fatal accident
in the Melbourne Cup (a race in which he was runner-up three times), finished second in
the Queen Elizabeth and returned to a heartfelt reception as he became the first British-
trained horse to earn more than £5m in prize money. Criterion had won the previous year's
Australian Derby, another of the highlights of 'The Championships', which was won in
2015 by the New Zealand Derby winner **Mongolian Khan** who went on to become a
very good winner of the Caulfield Cup in October (from Red Cadeaux's British-trained
stablemate Trip To Paris). Mongolian Khan looked a strong contender for the Melbourne

*Longines Queen Elizabeth Stakes, Randwick—Criterion lands Australia's most valuable
weight-for-age contest, the feature of 'The Championships' in April; Red Cadeaux (white face)
finishes second to become the first British-trained horse to win over £5m in prize money,
with the consistent Royal Descent (behind winner) also picking up plenty of place money*

BMW Caulfield Cup, Caulfield—Australian Derby winner Mongolian Khan holds off the staying-on British challenger Trip To Paris (right), with the blinkered Our Ivanhowe finishing third; the other British-trained runner Snow Sky (white face) keeps on into fifth

Cup (in which Trip To Paris came fourth) but suffered a bout of colic a week before the race which put an end to his spring campaign. The highlight of the Melbourne Spring Carnival was arguably the emphatic success of the four-year-old filly **Winx** (runner-up in the Australian Oaks at 'The Championships' in April) in the ten-furlong Cox Plate at Moonee Valley where she left runner-up Criterion and third-placed northern hemisphere challenger Highland Reel in her wake, winning in course-record time by four and three quarter lengths, the widest margin of victory in Australia's most prestigious weight-for-age contest since another mare, Sunline, won the 2000 edition by seven. Sunline is one of three mares who have won the Cox Plate twice and Winx looks good enough to emulate her in the next season if she trains on. Winx preceded her Cox Plate win with a clear-cut victory in the Epsom Handicap over a mile at Randwick earlier in October and is the first to achieve the Epsom Handicap/Cox Plate double since Noholme in 1959.

Criterion also raced twice in Hong Kong and twice in Britain during the year, without success. One of his runs in Britain came when he was fifth in the Prince of Wales's Stakes at Royal Ascot where **Brazen Beau** finished a good second in the Diamond Jubilee Stakes (with **Wandjina**, runner-up to Horse of the Year Dissident in the All-Aged Stakes in April, sixth). Brazen Beau had booked his ticket when winning the Newmarket Handicap at Flemington in March comfortably from **Chautauqua**, who went on to win the T J Smith Stakes at 'The Championships' at Randwick and the Manikato Stakes at Moonee Valley in October. Further down the field in the Newmarket Handicap was a below-par **Lankan Rupee** who put up the best performance seen all year on an Australian racecourse for the second year running when dominating his field (Brazen Beau second and previously unbeaten **Deep Field** third) in the Black Caviar Lightning Stakes at Flemington in February. As in 2014, however, Lankan Rupee's form tapered off as his training was interrupted by various minor ailments and injuries. That grand veteran **Buffering**, the last remaining top-level sprinter from the Black Caviar era still in training, returned from nearly a year off the course to win the AJ Moir Stakes at Moonee Valley in October for the third time in his career. He also won the Winterbottom Stakes at Ascot—the eighteenth win of his long career—for the second time when venturing to Western Australia in late-November. It seems that there are plans for Buffering to be seen in Britain in 2016, as there are for the four-year-old **Delectation** who won the Darley Classic over six at Flemington in November. Sprinter-miler **Boban** bypassed the Sydney Autumn Carnival and the Melbourne Spring Carnival but still won two Group 1s, the Doomben 10,000 in May and the Memsie Stakes at Caulfield in August, to take his career record to six Group 1 victories. The mare **Srikandi** landed a seven-furlong Group 1 double in the Stradbroke Handicap at Doomben and the Tattersall's Tiara at the Gold Coast, both in June. The Makybe Diva Stakes over a mile at Flemington in September was won by the 2013 Caulfield Cup winner **Fawkner**, still going strongly at eight years of age. Horse of the Year in 2014/15 **Dissident**, who landed the Memsie/Makybe Diva double in 2014, won twice more at Group 1 level in the autumn—taking the C F Orr Stakes at Caulfield in February and the All Aged Stakes at Randwick in April—before taking up stud duties at Newgate Farm in the spring.

Japanese raiders made their presence felt in some of the big races during the Autumn Carnival—the 2014 Arima Kinen runner-up To The World was second in the BMW and Tosen Stardom second in the Ranvet—but their only winner was Real Impact who followed Irish-trained Gordon Lord Byron as the second successive overseas winner of the George Ryder Stakes at Rosehill in March. Like Gordon Lord Byron, Real Impact went on to contest one of the major races at 'The Championships', in his case the Doncaster Mile in which he finished a very creditable second to **Kermadec** (third in the George Ryder), who gave trainer Chris Waller his third successive Doncaster Mile (the victory of Winx in the Epsom Handicap also gave him a third successive win in that race). Kermadec struck again in the spring too, adding the George Main Stakes at Randwick in September to his Group 1 tally. The Waller stable had a strong team of four-year-olds with Brazen Beau, Winx and Kermadec supported by the likes of the aforementioned Delectation and 2014 Victoria Derby winner **Preferment** (Turnbull Stakes). On the same November day that Delectation won the Darley Classic, Mongolian Khan's New Zealand stable won the Emirates Stakes with the consistent **Turn Me Loose** who has won three of his four starts in Australia and is being aimed at the Sydney Autumn Carnival early in 2016. The Godolphin team had a good year with five Group 1 successes including those by two imported Royal Ascot winners, the Queen's Vase winner **Hartnell** in the mile and a half BMW Stakes at Rosehill in March and the Wolferton Handicap winner **Contributer** who won both the Chipping Norton Stakes at Warwick Farm in February and the Ranvet Stakes at Rosehill in March but wasn't in the same form when returning to action in the spring.

Godolphin also had the year's top three-year-old **Exosphere** who produced a dazzling turn of foot to win the Golden Rose Stakes at Rosehill in September and then destroyed the opposition three weeks later in the Roman Consul Stakes at Randwick, Exosphere's performance in the Roman Consul produced a very high rating for a three-year-old at that

Black Caviar Lightning Stakes, Flemington—five-year-old Lankan Rupee puts up the best performance seen all year on an Australian racecourse, beating the three-year-old Brazen Beau (right) who passes previously unbeaten Deep Field for second late on

Longines Mackinnon Stakes, Flemington—Gailo Chop (right) strikes a blow for Europe at the Melbourne Spring Carnival, winning in a close finish from the blinkered Rising Romance and Godolphin-owned Contributer; German challenger Magic Artist (checked cap) has a nightmare passage on the rail

stage of the season, better than those achieved by Exceed And Excel and Fastnet Rock who won the 2003 and 2004 renewals. Both of those good performers have gone on to be very successful at stud, with Exceed And Excel standing every season in both hemispheres for Darley since being retired in 2004 (fee for his twelfth European season £40,000). The success of Australian stallions in Europe has been a remarkable development and Darley alone will have eight Australian horses on its European roster in 2016, the newcomers in 2016 headed by Brazen Beau. Exosphere tried to emulate Brazen Beau by adding the feature three-year-old sprint in the spring, the Coolmore Stud Stakes at the end of October, but the Flemington track had a bias and Exosphere was one of several fancied runners defeated on the day, managing only fourth behind the pint-sized **Japonisme** who gave Chris Waller his third successive win in the race. Before Exosphere began to dominate in the spring, the best sprinting colt of his generation was **Vancouver** who won the world's richest two-year-old race, the Golden Slipper at Rosehill in March, giving Gai Waterhouse her sixth training success in the event, equalling the record of her father T J Smith. Vancouver was acquired by Coolmore and partners (including the China Horse Club) for a reported A$40m after the Golden Slipper and has joined Aidan O'Brien for a European campaign in 2016. **Xtravagant**, who won the New Zealand 2000 Guineas in November by eight and a half lengths, was set to make his Australian debut after the turn of the year. **Press Statement** won the Caulfield Guineas in October from an awkward, wide draw and looks the sort to go on improving (he is said to be Royal Ascot-bound). Godolphin's former head trainer Peter Snowden completed a Group 1 double with **Pride of Dubai** in the Blue Diamond Stakes at Caulfield in February and the ATC Sires Produce Stakes at Randwick in April. **Stay With Me**, who won the Caulfield 1,000 Guineas in October, was the highest-rated three-year-old filly.

Only a handful of two-year-olds—listed below—had emerged by the end of 2015 who might prove good enough to make their presence felt in the juvenile Group 1 events in the first half of 2016. Away from the track, Australian racing lost one of its greatest figures, 'The Cups King' Bart Cummings, who died aged 87 in August. Still training in partnership with grandson James Cummings at the time of his death, Bart Cummings amassed 266 Group 1 wins in his own name, putting him second only to T J Smith on the all-time list. He won the Melbourne Cup twelve times. Among others mourned were young jockey Tim Bell, one of the leading riders in Queensland who fell to his death from the balcony of his apartment while in Singapore, respected New Zealand trainer Dean Logan who died of cancer at fifty-seven. Two of Australia's best-known senior jockeys, Chris Munce and Jim 'The Pumper' Cassidy, among only seven who have won Australia's 'big four' (Melbourne/Caulfield/Cox/Golden Slipper), both retired from riding. Cassidy is also one of just four Australian-based jockeys who have won more than a hundred Group 1s (George Moore, Roy Higgins and Damien Oliver are the others). The year's major controversy, resulting from the various inquiries into a spate of positive tests for the prohibited substance cobalt, has yet to run its course. A number of trainers have lost their licences, with most of them scheduled to go to appeal in the first part of 2016. Peter Moody, best known as the trainer of Black Caviar, is one of those embroiled in the saga, the outcome of his hearing not expected until after this edition of *Racehorses* has gone to press.

Ratings and text for Australia and New Zealand are supplied courtesy of Gary Crispe (www.racingandsports.com.au) The ages listed below are as at 31st December 2015

Two-Year-Olds

115p	Extreme Choice
115+	Capitalist
109p	Astern
109p	Calliope (f)
107	Concealer (f)
107	Zelady's Night Out (f)
106	Star Turn
105	Dalradian
105	Flying Artie
105	Power Trip
105	Prompt Response (f)
105	Rafha's Choice
105	Souchez
105	Valliano

Three-Year-Olds

127	Exosphere (Aus)
123p	Xtravagant
122	Japonisme
122	Vancouver
120p	Press Statement
119	Tarzino
118p	Pride of Dubai
117	Counterattack
117	Keen Array
117	Stay With Me (f)
116	Headwater
116	Jameka (f)
116	Odyssey Moon
116	Rageese
116	Ready For Victory
116	Sebring Sun
115	English (f)
115	Etymology
115	Furnaces
115	Lizard Island
115	Mahuta

115	Shards
115	Takedown
115?	Zoutenant
114+	Vanbrugh
114	Kinglike
114	King's Troop
114	Mogador
114	Speak Fondly (f)
113	Holler
113	Lake Geneva (f)
113	Perfect Reflection (f)
113	Petits Filous (f)
112	Bassett
112	Bon Aurum
112	Calaverite (f)
112	Dal Cielo
112	Fontiton (f)
112	Haptic
112	Honesta (f)
112	Street Rapper
111	Raphael's Cat
111	Serenade (f)
110	Ambience (f)
110	Demonstrate
110	Le Chef
110	*†Master Zephyr
110	Pasadena Girl (f)
110	Reemah (f)
110	Sacred Eye (f)
110	Tarquin
110	Wicked Intent

Four-Year-Olds

126p	†Winx (f)
126	†Brazen Beau
126	Mongolian Khan
125	Kermadec
125	Turn Me Loose
124	Delectation
124	Hartnell
123	Pornichet
123	Preferment
123	Stratum Star
123	†Wandjina
122	Hallowed Crown
122	Hauraki

121	*†Bow Creek
121	Disposition
121	First Seal (f)
121	Scissor Kick
121	Volkstok'n'Barrell
120	Alpine Eagle
119	It's Somewhat
119	Shooting To Win
119	Sweynesse
118	Bikila
118	Kuro
117	Quick Strike
117	Set Square (f)
117	Werther
116	Eclair Choice
116	Hi World
116	Magicool
116	Tall Ship
115	Amicus (f)
115	Good Project
114	Awesome Rock
114	Gallante
114	Gust of Wind (f)
114	Ruling Dynasty
113	Allergic
113	Amelie's Star (f)
113	Delicacy (f)
113	Fenway (f)
113	Lumosty (f)
113	Najoom (f)
113	Orbec
113	Stolen Dance (f)
113?	Sworn To Silence

Older Horses

130	†Lankan Rupee
127	Chautauqua
127	†Criterion
125	Lucky Hussler
124	Complacent
124	Contributer
124	Dissident
123	Boban
123	Sacred Falls
123	Terravista
122	Buffering

*(f) fillies and mares; *horse trained in the country for only part of the season; † (sections outside Europe and UAE) horse has a commentary in main section.*

INDEX TO PHOTOGRAPHS

PORTRAITS & SNAPSHOTS

RACE PHOTOGRAPHS

Criterium de Saint-Cloud (Saint-Cloud)	*Bertrand*	850
Criterium International (Saint-Cloud)	*Bertrand*	523
Darley Irish Oaks (the Curragh)	*Caroline Norris*	234
Darley July Cup (Newmarket)	*Bill Selwyn*	687
Darley Prix Morny (Deauville)	*Bertrand*	901
Darley Yorkshire Oaks (York)	*Ed Byrne*	781
DBS Premier Yearling Stakes (York)	*Alec Russell*	999
Derrinstown Stud Flying Five Stakes (the Curragh)	*Caroline Norris*	937
DFS Park Hill Stakes (Doncaster)	*Bill Selwyn*	440
Diamond Jubilee Stakes (Royal Ascot)	*John Crofts*	1065
Doom Bar Celebration Mile (Goodwood)	*Ed Byrne*	550
Dubai Challenge Stakes (Newmarket)	*Ed Byrne*	178
Dubai Cornwallis Stakes (Newmarket)	*John Crofts*	818
Dubai Dewhurst Stakes (Newmarket)	*George Selwyn*	48
Dubai Duty Free Irish Derby (the Curragh)	*Peter Mooney*	513
Dubai Duty Free Mill Reef Stakes (Newbury)	*Ed Byrne*	842
Dubai Fillies' Mile (Newmarket)	*Ed Byrne*	655
Dubai Gold Cup Sponsored by Al Tayer Motors (Meydan)	*Bill Selwyn*	169
Dubai Sheema Classic Presented by Longines (Meydan)	*Frank Sorge*	277
Dubai Turf Sponsored by DP World (Meydan)	*Frank Sorge*	938
Dubai World Cup Sponsored by Emirates Airline (Meydan)	*Bill Selwyn*	798
Duchess of Cambridge Stakes (sponsored by Qipco) (Newmarket)	*Ed Byrne*	488
888sport Charity Sprint (York)	*Alec Russell*	1054
E. P. Taylor Stakes Presented by HPIBet (Woodbine)	*Frank Sorge*	243
1stsecuritysolutions.co.uk May Hill Stakes (Doncaster)	*Bill Selwyn*	1052
£500,000 Tattersalls Millions 2YO Trophy (Newmarket)	*Ed Byrne*	397
Fly Aer Lingus From Doncaster Sheffield Flying Childers Stakes (Doncaster)	*Alec Russell*	446
14 Hands Winery Breeders' Cup Juvenile Fillies (Keeneland)	*Frank Sorge*	945
Gigaset International Stakes (Heritage Handicap) (Ascot)	*Ed Byrne*	459
Goffs Vincent O'Brien National Stakes (the Curragh)	*Caroline Norris*	47
Gold Cup (Royal Ascot)	*Caroline Norris*	1043
Grand Prix de Saint-Cloud (Saint-Cloud)	*Bertrand*	1036
Grosser Preis von Berlin (Hoppegarten)	*Frank Sorge*	888
Hardwicke Stakes (Royal Ascot)	*John Crofts*	933
Investec Coronation Cup (Epsom)	*John Crofts*	770
Investec Corporate Banking 'Dash' (Heritage Handicap) (Epsom)	*Ed Byrne*	263
Investec Derby (Epsom)	*Ed Byrne*	414
Investec Derby (Epsom)	*George Selwyn*	415
Investec Oaks (Epsom)	*John Crofts*	812
Irish Stallion Farms European Breeders Fund 'Sovereign Path' Handicap (Leopardstown)	*Caroline Norris*	539
Irish Thoroughbred Marketing Gimcrack Stakes (York)	*Alec Russell*	50
Jersey Stakes (Royal Ascot)	*John Crofts*	292
John Smith's Cup (Heritage Handicap) (York)	*Alec Russell*	631
John Smith's Northumberland Plate (Heritage Handicap) (Newcastle)	*John Grossick*	816
Juddmonte Grand Prix de Paris (Longchamp)	*Bertrand*	318
Juddmonte International Stakes (York)	*John Crofts*	91
Juddmonte Middle Park Stakes (Newmarket)	*Ed Byrne*	902
Juddmonte Royal Lodge Stakes (Newmarket)	*Ed Byrne*	369
Keeneland Phoenix Stakes (the Curragh)	*Caroline Norris*	46
Kentucky Derby presented by Yum! Brands (Churchill Downs)	*ZPhotos*	72
Kilboy Estate Stakes (the Curragh)	*Caroline Norris*	1088
King Edward VII Stakes (Royal Ascot)	*Bill Selwyn*	116
King George VI and Queen Elizabeth Stakes (Sponsored by Qipco) (Ascot)	*John Crofts*	790
Kingdom of Bahrain Sun Chariot Stakes (Newmarket)	*John Crofts*	326
King's Stand Stakes (Royal Ascot)	*Caroline Norris*	429
Ladbrokes St Leger Stakes (Doncaster)	*John Crofts*	919
LARC Prix Maurice de Gheest (Deauville)	*Bertrand*	688
Leopardstown 2000 Guineas Trial (Leopardstown)	*Caroline Norris*	1114

Longines - Grosser Preis von Baden (Baden-Baden)	*Frank Sorge*	801
Longines Breeders' Cup Turf (Keeneland)	*Bill Selwyn*	372
Longines Hong Kong Mile (Sha Tin)	*Frank Sorge*	634
Longines Hong Kong Vase (Sha Tin)	*Frank Sorge*	469
Moyglare "Jewels" Blandford Stakes (the Curragh)	*Caroline Norris*	841
Moyglare Stud Stakes (the Curragh)	*Ed Byrne*	654
Palmerstown House Estate Irish St Leger (the Curragh)	*Ed Byrne*	742
Pastorius - Grosser Preis von Bayern (Munich)	*Frank Sorge*	507
Pattison Canadian International Stakes (Woodbine)	*Michael Burns*	185
Pinsent Masons Lowther Stakes (York)	*John Crofts*	136
Poule d'Essai des Poulains - Prix le Parisien (Longchamp)	*Bertrand*	615
Poule d'Essai des Pouliches (Longchamp)	*Bertrand*	320
Premio Longines Lydia Tesio (Rome)	*Stefano Grasso*	732
Prince of Wales's Stakes (Royal Ascot)	*Frank Sorge*	378
Prix Corrida (Saint-Cloud)	*Bertrand*	1035
Prix de Diane Longines (Chantilly)	*Bertrand*	961
Prix de l'Opera Longines (Longchamp)	*George Selwyn*	235
Prix d'Ispahan (Longchamp)	*Bertrand*	939
Prix du Haras de Fresnay-le-Buffard - Jacques le Marois (Deauville)	*George Selwyn*	325
Prix du Jockey Club (Chantilly)	*Frank Sorge*	713
Prix Ganay (Longchamp)	*Bertrand*	210
Prix Jean Prat (Chantilly)	*George Selwyn*	1005
Prix Rothschild (Deauville)	*Bertrand*	68
Prix Royal-Oak (Longchamp)	*Bertrand*	1071
P. W. McGrath Memorial Ballysax Stakes (Leopardstown)	*Caroline Norris*	979
Qatar King George Stakes (Goodwood)	*John Crofts*	698
Qatar Lennox Stakes (Goodwood)	*Ed Byrne*	1028
Qatar Nassau Stakes (Goodwood)	*Ed Byrne*	572
Qatar Prix de la Foret (Longchamp)	*George Selwyn*	616
Qatar Prix de l'Abbaye de Longchamp (Longchamp)	*George Selwyn*	430
Qatar Prix de l'Arc de Triomphe (Longchamp)	*Bill Selwyn*	422
Qatar Prix du Cadran (Longchamp)	*John Crofts*	652
Qatar Prix du Moulin de Longchamp (Longchamp)	*John Crofts*	322
Qatar Prix Jean-Luc Lagardere (Grand Criterium) Sponsored by Al Hazm (Longchamp)	*John Crofts*	1061
Qatar Prix Vermeille (Longchamp)	*Bertrand*	1037
Qatar Stewards' Cup (Heritage Handicap) (Goodwood)	*Ed Byrne*	609
Qatar Sussex Stakes (Goodwood)	*John Crofts*	941
Qipco 1000 Guineas Stakes (Newmarket)	*John Crofts*	571
Qipco 2000 Guineas Stakes (Newmarket)	*John Crofts*	401
Qipco British Champions Fillies' And Mares' Stakes (Ascot)	*Bill Selwyn*	921
Qipco British Champions Long Distance Cup (Ascot)	*Ed Byrne*	362
Qipco British Champions Sprint Stakes (Ascot)	*John Crofts*	689
Qipco Champion Stakes (Ascot)	*John Crofts*	341
Qipco Falmouth Stakes (Newmarket)	*Ed Byrne*	67
Qipco Irish Champion Stakes (Leopardstown)	*Ed Byrne*	420
Queen Alexandra Stakes (Royal Ascot)	*Bill Selwyn*	745
Queen Anne Stakes (Royal Ascot)	*John Crofts*	940
Queen Elizabeth II Stakes Sponsored by Qipco (Ascot)	*John Crofts*	942
Queen Mary Stakes (Royal Ascot)	*Bill Selwyn*	36
Racing Post Trophy (Doncaster)	*Alec Russell*	624
Ribblesdale Stakes (Royal Ascot)	*Bill Selwyn*	242
Ricoh Woodbine Mile Stakes (Woodbine)	*Michael Burns*	670
Royal Hunt Cup (Heritage Handicap) (Royal Ascot)	*John Crofts*	409
Saint Gobain Weber Park Stakes (Doncaster)	*Alec Russell*	584
Sea The Stars Pretty Polly Stakes (the Curragh)	*Caroline Norris*	268
Secretariat Stakes (Arlington)	*Four Footed Photos*	468
Shadwell Joel Stakes (Newmarket)	*John Crofts*	1022
Shadwell Rockfel Stakes (Newmarket)	*John Crofts*	804
Sky Bet York Stakes (York)	*Alec Russell*	1050
Somerville Tattersall Stakes (Newmarket)	*Ed Byrne*	878

ADDITIONAL PHOTOGRAPHS

The following photos appear in the Introduction:- Trademark flying dismount by Frankie Dettori after the Derby victory of Golden Horn (taken by Bill Selwyn), inset picture of American Pharoah (George Selwyn), Solow wins the Sussex Stakes (Ed Byrne), The Queen and Ryan Moore (Bill Selwyn), Tryster wins the Winter Derby (George Selwyn), Andrea Atzeni and Colm O'Donoghue with the St Leger trophy (George/Bill Selwyn), Peter Dimmock with Peter O'Sullevan (unknown), Pat Eddery (Martin Lynch), Richard Hughes retires, Silvestre de Sousa crowned champion (both Ed Byrne).

Credits for the photographs in 'Top Horses Abroad' are as follows:- Preis von Europa (Frank Sorge), Premio Roma (Stefano Grasso), Scandinavian Open Championship (John Ingles), Godolphin Mile (Bill Selwyn), Breeders' Cup Dirt Mile (Frank Sorge), Travers Stakes (ZPhotos), Breeders' Cup Mile, Breeders' Cup Filly & Mare Turf (both Bill Selwyn), Beverly D Stakes (Four Footed Photos), Breeders' Cup Turf Sprint (Bill Selwyn), Breeders' Cup Sprint, Mile Championship, Japan Cup, Hong Kong Sprint, KrisFlyer International Sprint (all Frank Sorge), Melbourne Cup, Queen Elizabeth Stakes (both Martin King), Caulfield Cup, Lightning Stakes and Longines Mackinnon Stakes (all Bronwen Healy).

BIG RACE WINNERS

The record includes the Timeform Ratings recorded by the winner in the race (not its Timeform Annual Rating), the weight carried (sometimes preceded by age), starting price, trainer, jockey and number of runners. Race conditions and sponsors' names in the race titles are for the 2015 runnings. An asterisk prior to a horse's name denotes that it was awarded the race.

British Classic Races

QIPCO 2000 GUINEAS STAKES (3-y-o colts and fillies) (Newmarket 1m)

Year	Rating	Horse	Trainer	Jockey	Runners
1970	135+	Nijinsky 9-0: 4/7f	M V O'Brien	*L Piggott*	14
1971	141	Brigadier Gerard 9-0: 11/2	W R Hern	*J Mercer*	6
1972	129	High Top 9-0: 85/40f	B van Cutsem	*W Carson*	12
1973	124	Mon Fils 9-0: 50/1	R Hannon	*F Durr*	18
1974	130+	Nonoalco 9-0: 19/2	F Boutin	*Y Saint-Martin*	12
1975	131	Bolkonski 9-0: 33/1	H R A Cecil	*G Dettori*	24
1976	125	Wollow 9-0: 1/1f	H R A Cecil	*G Dettori*	17
1977	125	Nebbiolo 9-0: 20/1	K Prendergast	*G Curran*	18
1978	122	Roland Gardens 9-0: 28/1	D Sasse	*F Durr*	19
1979	130	Tap On Wood 9-0: 20/1	B W Hills	*S Cauthen*	20
1980	130	*Known Fact 9-0: 14/1	A J Tree	*W Carson*	14
1981	125	To-Agori-Mou 9-0: 5/2f	G Harwood	*G Starkey*	19
1982	127	Zino 9-0: 8/1	F Boutin	*F Head*	26
1983	128	Lomond 9-0: 9/1	M V O'Brien	*Pat Eddery*	16
1984	136	El Gran Senor 9-0: 15/8f	M V O'Brien	*Pat Eddery*	9
1985	126	Shadeed 9-0: 4/5f	M R Stoute	*L Piggott*	14
1986	134	Dancing Brave 9-0: 15/8f	G Harwood	*G Starkey*	15
1987	127	Don't Forget Me 9-0: 9/1	R Hannon	*W Carson*	13
1988	124	Doyoun 9-0: 4/5f	M R Stoute	*W R Swinburn*	9
1989	127	Nashwan 9-0: 3/1f	W R Hern	*W Carson*	14
1990	127	Tirol 9-0: 9/1	R Hannon	*M J Kinane*	14
1991	128	Mystiko 9-0: 13/2	C E Brittain	*M Roberts*	14
1992	121	Rodrigo de Triano 9-0: 6/1	P W Chapple-Hyam	*L Piggott*	16
1993	130	Zafonic 9-0: 5/6f	A Fabre	*Pat Eddery*	14
1994	123	Mister Baileys 9-0: 16/1	M Johnston	*J Weaver*	23
1995	130	Pennekamp 9-0: 9/2	A Fabre	*T Jarnet*	11
1996	127	Mark of Esteem 9-0: 8/1	Saeed bin Suroor	*L Dettori*	13
1997	123	Entrepreneur 9-0: 11/2	M R Stoute	*M J Kinane*	16
1998	125	King of Kings 9-0: 7/2	A P O'Brien	*M J Kinane*	18
1999	122	Island Sands 9-0: 10/1	Saeed bin Suroor	*L Dettori*	16
2000	130+	King's Best 9-0: 13/2	Sir Michael Stoute	*K Fallon*	27
2001	122+	Golan 9-0: 11/1	Sir Michael Stoute	*K Fallon*	18
2002	120+	Rock of Gibraltar 9-0: 9/1	A P O'Brien	*J Murtagh*	22
2003	118+	Refuse To Bend 9-0: 9/2	D K Weld	*P J Smullen*	20
2004	129	Haafhd 9-0: 11/2	B W Hills	*R Hills*	14
2005	120	Footstepsinthesand 9-0: 13/2	A P O'Brien	*K Fallon*	19
2006	129+	George Washington 9-0: 6/4f	A P O'Brien	*K Fallon*	14
2007	125+	Cockney Rebel 9-0: 25/1	G A Huffer	*O Peslier*	24
2008	124+	Henrythenavigator 9-0: 11/1	A P O'Brien	*J Murtagh*	15
2009	128+	Sea The Stars 9-0: 8/1	J Oxx	*M J Kinane*	15
2010	124+	Makfi 9-0: 33/1	M Delzangles	*C P Lemaire*	19
2011	135+	Frankel 9-0: 1/2f	Sir Henry Cecil	*Tom Queally*	13
2012	123+	Camelot 9-0: 15/8f	Aidan O'Brien	*Joseph O'Brien*	18
2013	130+	Dawn Approach 9-0: 11/8f	Jim Bolger	*Kevin Manning*	13
2014	126	Night of Thunder 9-0: 40/1	Richard Hannon	*Kieren Fallon*	14
2015	125	Gleneagles 9-0: 4/1f	Aidan O'Brien	*Ryan Moore*	18

QIPCO 1000 GUINEAS STAKES (3-y-o fillies) (Newmarket 1m)

Year	Rating	Horse	Trainer	Jockey	Runners
1970	127	Humble Duty 9-0: 3/1jf	P Walwyn	*L Piggott*	12
1971	121	Altesse Royale 9-0: 25/1	C F N Murless	*Y Saint-Martin*	10
1972	115	Waterloo 9-0: 8/1	J W Watts	*E Hide*	18

1973	116+	Mysterious 9-0: 11/1	C F N Murless	G Lewis	14
1974	118	Highclere 9-0: 12/1	W R Hern	J Mercer	15
1975	121	Nocturnal Spree 9-0: 14/1	H V S Murless	J Roe	16
1976	120	Flying Water 9-0: 2/1f	A Penna	Y Saint-Martin	25
1977	122+	Mrs McArdy 9-0: 16/1	M W Easterby	E Hide	18
1978	119	Enstone Spark 9-0: 35/1	B W Hills	E Johnson	16
1979	113	One In A Million 9-0: 1/1f	H R A Cecil	J Mercer	17
1980	116	Quick As Lightning 9-0: 12/1	J L Dunlop	B Rouse	23
1981	121	Fairy Footsteps 9-0: 6/4f	H R A Cecil	L Piggott	14
1982	125	On The House 9-0: 33/1	H Wragg	J Reid	15
1983	124+	Ma Biche 9-0: 5/2f	Mme C Head	F Head	18
1984	121	Pebbles 9-0: 8/1	C E Brittain	P Robinson	15
1985	119	Oh So Sharp 9-0: 2/1f	H R A Cecil	S Cauthen	17
1986	120	Midway Lady 9-0: 10/1	B Hanbury	R Cochrane	15
1987	123+	Miesque 9-0: 15/8f	F Boutin	F Head	14
1988	121	Ravinella 9-0: 4/5f	Mme C Head	G W Moore	12
1989	117	Musical Bliss 9-0: 7/2	M R Stoute	W R Swinburn	7
1990	122	Salsabil 9-0: 6/4f	J L Dunlop	W Carson	10
1991	120	Shadayid 9-0: 4/6f	J L Dunlop	W Carson	14
1992	117	Hatoof 9-0: 5/1	Mme C Head	W R Swinburn	14
1993	113	Sayyedati 9-0: 4/1	C E Brittain	W R Swinburn	12
1994	115	Las Meninas 9-0: 12/1	T Stack	J Reid	15
1995	119	Harayir 9-0: 5/1	W R Hern	R Hills	14
1996	112+	Bosra Sham 9-0: 10/11f	H R A Cecil	Pat Eddery	13
1997	121	Sleepytime 9-0: 5/1	H R A Cecil	K Fallon	15
1998	126	Cape Verdi 9-0: 10/3jf	Saeed bin Suroor	L Dettori	16
1999	117	Wince 9-0: 4/1f	H R A Cecil	K Fallon	22
2000	117	Lahan 9-0: 14/1	J H M Gosden	R Hills	18
2001	116	Ameerat 9-0: 11/1	M A Jarvis	P Robinson	15
2002	112	Kazzia 9-0: 14/1	Saeed bin Suroor	L Dettori	17
2003	117+	Russian Rhythm 9-0: 12/1	Sir Michael Stoute	K Fallon	19
2004	116	Attraction 9-0: 11/2	M Johnston	K Darley	16
2005	116	Virginia Waters 9-0: 12/1	A P O'Brien	K Fallon	20
2006	115	Speciosa 9-0: 10/1	Mrs P Sly	M Fenton	13
2007	123	Finsceal Beo 9-0: 5/4f	J S Bolger	K J Manning	21
2008	114	Natagora 9-0: 11/4f	P Bary	C P Lemaire	15
2009	117	Ghanaati 9-0: 20/1	B W Hills	R Hills	14
2010	113	*Special Duty 9-0: 9/2f	Mme C Head-Maarek	S Pasquier	17
2011	117	Blue Bunting 9-0: 16/1	Mahmood Al Zarooni	Frankie Dettori	18
2012	120	Homecoming Queen 9-0: 25/1	Aidan O'Brien	Ryan Moore	17
2013	115+	Sky Lantern 9-0: 9/1	Richard Hannon	Richard Hughes	15
2014	112	Miss France 9-0: 7/1	Andre Fabre	Maxime Guyon	17
2015	121	Legatissimo 9-0: 13/2	David Wachman	Ryan Moore	13

INVESTEC OAKS (3-y-o fillies) (Epsom 1½m10y)

1970	120	Lupe 9-0: 100/30f	C F N Murless	A Barclay	16
1971	123	Altesse Royale 9-0: 6/4f	C F N Murless	G Lewis	11
1972	122	Ginevra 9-0: 8/1	R Price	A Murray	17
1973	127	Mysterious 9-0: 13/8f	C F N Murless	G Lewis	10
1974	118	Polygamy 9-0: 3/1f	P Walwyn	Pat Eddery	15
1975	120+	Juiliette Marny 9-0: 12/1	A J Tree	L Piggott	12
1976	123+	Pawneese 9-0: 6/5f	A Penna	Y Saint-Martin	14
1977	119	Dunfermline 9-0: 6/1	W R Hern	W Carson	13
1978	117	Fair Salinia 9-0: 8/1	M R Stoute	G Starkey	15
1979	117+	Scintillate 9-0: 20/1	A J Tree	Pat Eddery	14
1980	127	Bireme 9-0: 9/2	W R Hern	W Carson	11
1981	127	Blue Wind 9-0: 3/1jf	D K Weld	L Piggott	12
1982	124	Time Charter 9-0: 12/1	H Candy	W Newnes	13
1983	130	Sun Princess 9-0: 6/1	W R Hern	W Carson	15
1984	120	Circus Plume 9-0: 4/1	J L Dunlop	L Piggott	15
1985	131	Oh So Sharp 9-0: 6/4f	H R A Cecil	S Cauthen	12
1986	124+	Midway Lady 9-0: 15/8f	B Hanbury	R Cochrane	15
1987	125+	Unite 9-0: 11/1	M R Stoute	W R Swinburn	11
1988	126	Diminuendo 9-0: 7/4f	H R A Cecil	S Cauthen	11
1989	121	*Snow Bride 9-0: 13/2	H R A Cecil	S Cauthen	9
1990	127	Salsabil 9-0: 2/1f	J L Dunlop	W Carson	8
1991	122	Jet Ski Lady 9-0: 50/1	J S Bolger	C Roche	9

1992	128	User Friendly 9-0: 5/1	C E Brittain	*G Duffield*	7
1993	118	Intrepidity 9-0: 5/1	A Fabre	*M Roberts*	14
1994	115	Balanchine 9-0: 6/1	H Ibrahim	*L Dettori*	10
1995	117	Moonshell 9-0: 3/1	Saeed bin Suroor	*L Dettori*	10
1996	122	Lady Carla 9-0: 10/3	H R A Cecil	*Pat Eddery*	11
1997	117+	Reams of Verse 9-0: 5/6f	H R A Cecil	*K Fallon*	12
1998	120	Shahtoush 9-0: 12/1	A P O'Brien	*M J Kinane*	8
1999	123	Ramruma 9-0: 3/1	H R A Cecil	*K Fallon*	10
2000	120	Love Divine 9-0: 9/4f	H R A Cecil	*T Quinn*	16
2001	115	Imagine 9-0: 3/1f	A P O'Brien	*M J Kinane*	14
2002	121	Kazzia 9-0: 10/3f	Saeed bin Suroor	*L Dettori*	14
2003	114	Casual Look 9-0: 10/1	A M Balding	*Martin Dwyer*	15
2004	124	Ouija Board 9-0: 7/2	E A L Dunlop	*K Fallon*	7
2005	117	Eswarah 9-0: 11/4jf	M A Jarvis	*R Hills*	12
2006	123	Alexandrova 9-0: 9/4f	A P O'Brien	*K Fallon*	10
2007	121	Light Shift 9-0: 13/2	H R A Cecil	*T Durcan*	14
2008	123	Look Here 9-0: 33/1	R M Beckett	*S Sanders*	16
2009	122+	Sariska 9-0: 9/4f	M L W Bell	*J P Spencer*	10
2010	115+	Snow Fairy 9-0: 9/1	E A L Dunlop	*R L Moore*	15
2011	117	Dancing Rain 9-0: 20/1	William Haggas	*Johnny Murtagh*	13
2012	115	Was 9-0: 20/1	Aidan O'Brien	*Seamie Heffernan*	12
2013	114+	Talent 9-0: 20/1	Ralph Beckett	*Richard Hughes*	11
2014	117+	Taghrooda 9-0: 5/1	John Gosden	*Paul Hanagan*	17
2015	114	Qualify 9-0: 50/1	Aidan O'Brien	*Colm O'Donoghue*	11

INVESTEC DERBY (3-y-o colts and fillies) (Epsom 1½m10y)

1970	135+	Nijinsky 9-0: 11/8f	M V O'Brien	*L Piggott*	11
1971	130	Mill Reef 9-0: 100/30f	I Balding	*G Lewis*	21
1972	131	Roberto 9-0: 3/1f	M V O'Brien	*L Piggott*	22
1973	125	Morston 9-0: 25/1	A Budgett	*E Hide*	25
1974	125	Snow Knight 9-0: 50/1	P Nelson	*B Taylor*	18
1975	135	Grundy 9-0: 5/1	P Walwyn	*Pat Eddery*	18
1976	128	Empery 9-0: 10/1	M Zilber	*L Piggott*	23
1977	129	The Minstrel 9-0: 5/1	M V O'Brien	*L Piggott*	22
1978	130	Shirley Heights 9-0: 8/1	J L Dunlop	*G Starkey*	25
1979	137	Troy 9-0: 6/1	W R Hern	*W Carson*	23
1980	130	Henbit 9 0: 7/1	W R Hern	*W Carson*	24
1981	140	Shergar 9-0: 10/11f	M R Stoute	*W R Swinburn*	18
1982	133	Golden Fleece 9-0: 3/1f	M V O'Brien	*Pat Eddery*	18
1983	132	Teenoso 9-0: 9/2f	G Wragg	*L Piggott*	21
1984	128	Secreto 9-0: 14/1	D V O'Brien	*C Roche*	17
1985	136	Slip Anchor 9-0: 9/4f	H R A Cecil	*S Cauthen*	14
1986	127	Shahrastani 9-0: 11/2	M R Stoute	*W R Swinburn*	17
1987	134	Reference Point 9-0: 6/4f	H R A Cecil	*S Cauthen*	19
1988	130	Kahyasi 9-0: 11/1	L M Cumani	*R Cochrane*	14
1989	129	Nashwan 9-0: 5/4f	W R Hern	*W Carson*	12
1990	127	Quest For Fame 9-0: 7/1	R Charlton	*Pat Eddery*	18
1991	135	Generous 9-0: 9/1	P F I Cole	*A Munro*	13
1992	127	Dr Devious 9-0: 8/1	P W Chapple-Hyam	*J Reid*	18
1993	126	Commander In Chief 9-0: 15/2	H R A Cecil	*M J Kinane*	15
1994	127	Erhaab 9-0: 7/2f	J L Dunlop	*W Carson*	25
1995	123	Lammtarra 9-0: 14/1	Saeed bin Suroor	*W R Swinburn*	15
1996	125	Shaamit 9-0: 12/1	W J Haggas	*M Hills*	20
1997	125	Benny The Dip 9-0: 11/1	J H M Gosden	*W Ryan*	13
1998	125	High-Rise 9-0: 20/1	L M Cumani	*O Peslier*	15
1999	125	Oath 9-0: 13/2	H R A Cecil	*K Fallon*	16
2000	129	Sinndar 9-0: 7/1	J Oxx	*J Murtagh*	15
2001	132	Galileo 9-0: 11/4jf	A P O'Brien	*M J Kinane*	12
2002	130	High Chaparral 9-0: 7/2	A P O'Brien	*J Murtagh*	12
2003	122+	Kris Kin 9-0: 6/1	Sir Michael Stoute	*K Fallon*	20
2004	125+	North Light 9-0: 7/2jf	Sir Michael Stoute	*K Fallon*	14
2005	131	Motivator 9-0: 3/1f	M L W Bell	*J Murtagh*	13
2006	119+	Sir Percy 9-0: 6/1	M P Tregoning	*Martin Dwyer*	18
2007	132+	Authorized 9-0: 5/4f	P W Chapple-Hyam	*L Dettori*	17
2008	128+	New Approach 9-0: 5/1	J S Bolger	*K J Manning*	16
2009	126+	Sea The Stars 9-0: 11/4	J Oxx	*M J Kinane*	12
2010	133	Workforce 9-0: 6/1	Sir Michael Stoute	*R L Moore*	12

2011	120+	Pour Moi 9-0: 4/1	A Fabre	*Mikael Barzalona*	13
2012	128	Camelot 9-0: 8/13f	Aidan O'Brien	*Joseph O'Brien*	9
2013	120+	Ruler of The World 9 0: 7/1	Aidan O'Brien	*Ryan Moore*	12
2014	127+	Australia 9-0: 11/8f	Aidan O'Brien	*Joseph O'Brien*	16
2015	132	Golden Horn 9-0: 13/8f	John Gosden	*Frankie Dettori*	12

LADBROKES ST LEGER STAKES (3-y-o colts and fillies)
(Doncaster 1¾m132y, Ayr in 1989 and York 1m5f197y in 2006)

1970	127+	Nijinsky 9-0: 2/7f	M V O'Brien	*L Piggott*	9
1971	126	Athens Wood 9-0: 5/2	H T Jones	*L Piggott*	8
1972	124	Boucher 9-0: 3/1	M V O'Brien	*L Piggott*	7
1973	125	Peleid 9-0: 28/1	C W C Elsey	*F Durr*	13
1974	127+	Bustino 9-0: 11/10f	W R Hern	*J Mercer*	10
1975	132	Bruni 9-0: 9/1	R Price	*A Murray*	12
1976	131+	Crow 9-0: 6/1cf	A Penna	*Y Saint-Martin*	15
1977	133	Dunfermline 8-11: 10/1	W R Hern	*W Carson*	13
1978	127	Julio Mariner 9-0: 28/1	C Brittain	*E Hide*	14
1979	126	Son of Love 9-0: 20/1	R Collet	*A Lequeux*	17
1980	128	Light Cavalry 9-0: 3/1	H R A Cecil	*J Mercer*	7
1981	130	Cut Above 9-0: 28/1	W R Hern	*J Mercer*	7
1982	126	Touching Wood 9-0: 7/1	H Thomson Jones	*P Cook*	15
1983	124	Sun Princess 8-11: 11/8f	W R Hern	*W Carson*	10
1984	129	Commanche Run 9-0: 7/4f	L M Cumani	*L Piggott*	11
1985	121	Oh So Sharp 8-11: 8/11f	H R A Cecil	*S Cauthen*	6
1986	128	Moon Madness 9-0: 9/2	J Dunlop	*Pat Eddery*	8
1987	127	Reference Point 9-0: 4/11f	H R A Cecil	*S Cauthen*	7
1988	130	Minster Son 9-0: 15/2	N A Graham	*W Carson*	6
1989	127	Michelozzo 9-0: 6/4f	H R A Cecil	*S Cauthen*	8
1990	130	Snurge 9-0: 7/2	P F I Cole	*T Quinn*	8
1991	125	Toulon 9-0: 5/2f	A Fabre	*Pat Eddery*	10
1992	126	User Friendly 8-11: 7/4f	C E Brittain	*G Duffield*	7
1993	121	Bob's Return 9-0: 3/1f	M H Tompkins	*P Robinson*	9
1994	121	Moonax 9-0: 40/1	B W Hills	*Pat Eddery*	8
1995	120	Classic Cliche 9-0: 10/3f	Saeed bin Suroor	*L Dettori*	10
1996	124	Shantou 9-0: 8/1	J H M Gosden	*L Dettori*	11
1997	124	Silver Patriarch 9-0: 5/4f	J L Dunlop	*Pat Eddery*	10
1998	124	Nedawi 9-0: 5/2f	Saeed bin Suroor	*J Reid*	9
1999	129	Mutafaweq 9-0: 11/2	Saeed bin Suroor	*R Hills*	9
2000	122	Millenary 9-0: 11/4f	J L Dunlop	*T Quinn*	11
2001	126+	Milan 9-0: 13/8f	A P O'Brien	*M J Kinane*	10
2002	125	Bollin Eric 9-0: 7/1	T D Easterby	*K Darley*	8
2003	124	Brian Boru 9-0: 5/4f	A P O'Brien	*J P Spencer*	12
2004	125	Rule of Law 9-0: 3/1jf	Saeed bin Suroor	*K McEvoy*	9
2005	123+	Scorpion 9-0: 10/11f	A P O'Brien	*L Dettori*	6
2006	123+	Sixties Icon 9-0: 11/8f	J Noseda	*L Dettori*	11
2007	120+	Lucarno 9-0: 7/2	J H M Gosden	*J Fortune*	10
2008	127	Conduit 9-0: 8/1	Sir Michael Stoute	*L Dettori*	14
2009	122	Mastery 9-0: 14/1	Saeed bin Suroor	*T E Durcan*	8
2010	123	Arctic Cosmos 9-0: 12/1	J H M Gosden	*W Buick*	10
2011	126	Masked Marvel 9-0: 15/2	John Gosden	*William Buick*	9
2012	123	Encke 9-0: 25/1	Mahmood Al Zarooni	*Mikael Barzalona*	9
2013	120+	Leading Light 9-0: 7/2f	Aidan O'Brien	*Joseph O'Brien*	11
2014	123+	Kingston Hill 9-1: 9/4f	Roger Varian	*Andrea Atzeni*	12
2015	119	Simple Verse 8-12: 8/1	Ralph Beckett	*Andrea Atzeni*	7

King George VI & Prix de l'Arc de Triomphe

KING GEORGE VI AND QUEEN ELIZABETH STAKES (SPONSORED BY QIPCO)
(3-y-o+) (Ascot 1½m; Newbury 1½m5y in 2005)

1970	131+	Nijinsky 3-8-7: 40/85f	M V O'Brien	*L Piggott*	6
1971	139+	Mill Reef 3-8-7: 8/13f	I Balding	*G Lewis*	10
1972	134	Brigadier Gerard 4-9-7: 8/13f	W R Hern	*J Mercer*	9
1973	132	Dahlia 3-8-4: 10/1	M Zilber	*W Pyers*	12
1974	131+	Dahlia 4-9-4: 15/8f	M Zilber	*L Piggott*	10

1975	137	Grundy 3-8-7: 4/5f	P Walwyn	*Pat Eddery*	11
1976	131	Pawneese 3-8-5: 9/4	A Penna	*Y Saint-Martin*	10
1977	135	The Minstrel 3-8-8: 7/4f	M V O'Brien	*L Piggott*	11
1978	133	Ile de Bourbon 3-8-8: 12/1	F J Houghton	*J Reid*	14
1979	133	Troy 3-8-8: 2/5f	W R Hern	*W Carson*	7
1980	129	Ela-Mana-Mou 4-9-7: 11/4	W R Hern	*W Carson*	10
1981	132+	Shergar 3-8-8: 2/5f	M R Stoute	*W R Swinburn*	7
1982	132	Kalaglow 4-9-7: 13/2	G Harwood	*G Starkey*	9
1983	129	Time Charter 4-9-4: 5/1	H Candy	*J Mercer*	9
1984	135	Teenoso 4-9-7: 13/2	G Wragg	*L Piggott*	13
1985	135	Petoski 3-8-8: 12/1	W R Hern	*W Carson*	12
1986	137	Dancing Brave 3-8-8: 6/4	G Harwood	*Pat Eddery*	9
1987	139	Reference Point 3-8-8: 11/10f	H R A Cecil	*S Cauthen*	9
1988	131	Mtoto 5-9-7: 4/1	A Stewart	*M Roberts*	10
1989	131	Nashwan 3-8-8: 2/9f	W R Hern	*W Carson*	7
1990	131	Belmez 3-8-9: 15/2	H R A Cecil	*M J Kinane*	11
1991	138+	Generous 3-8-9: 4/6f	P F I Cole	*A Munro*	9
1992	135	St Jovite 3-8-9: 4/5f	J S Bolger	*S Craine*	8
1993	131	Opera House 5-9-7: 8/1	M R Stoute	*M Roberts*	8
1994	128	King's Theatre 3-8-9: 12/1	H R A Cecil	*M J Kinane*	12
1995	125	Lammtarra 3-8-8: 9/4f	Saeed bin Suroor	*L Dettori*	7
1996	132	Pentire 4-9-7: 10/3	G Wragg	*M Hills*	8
1997	134	Swain 5-9-7: 16/1	Saeed bin Suroor	*J Reid*	8
1998	132	Swain 6-9-7: 11/2	Saeed bin Suroor	*L Dettori*	8
1999	135+	Daylami 5-9-7: 3/1	Saeed bin Suroor	*L Dettori*	8
2000	131+	Montjeu 4-9-7: 1/3f	J E Hammond	*M J Kinane*	7
2001	134	Galileo 3-8-9: 1/2f	A P O'Brien	*M J Kinane*	12
2002	129	Golan 4-9-7: 11/2	Sir Michael Stoute	*K Fallon*	9
2003	133	Alamshar 3-8-9: 13/2	J Oxx	*J Murtagh*	12
2004	132	Doyen 4-9-7: 11/10f	Saeed bin Suroor	*L Dettori*	11
2005	130	Azamour 4-9-7: 5/2f	J Oxx	*M J Kinane*	12
2006	128+	Hurricane Run 4-9-7: 5/6f	A Fabre	*C Soumillon*	6
2007	132	Dylan Thomas 4-9-7: 5/4f	A P O'Brien	*J Murtagh*	7
2008	129	Duke of Marmalade 4-9-7: 4/6f	A P O'Brien	*J Murtagh*	8
2009	130	Conduit 4-9-7: 13/8f	Sir Michael Stoute	*R L Moore*	9
2010	140	Harbinger 4-9-7: 4/1	Sir Michael Stoute	*O Peslier*	6
2011	127	Nathaniel 3-8-9: 11/2	John Gosden	*William Buick*	5
2012	124+	Danedream 4-9-4: 9/1	P Schiergen	*Andrasch Starke*	10
2013	132	Novellist 4-9-7: 13/2	Andreas Wohler	*Johnny Murtagh*	8
2014	127	Taghrooda 3-8-6: 7/2	John Gosden	*Paul Hanagan*	8
2015	125	Postponed 4-9-7: 6/1	Luca Cumani	*Andrea Atzeni*	7

QATAR PRIX DE L'ARC DE TRIOMPHE (3-y-o+ colts and fillies) (Longchamp 1½m)

1970	135	Sassafras 3-8-10: 19/1	F Mathet	*Y Saint-Martin*	15
1971	141	Mill Reef 3-8-10: 7/10f	I A Balding	*G Lewis*	18
1972	133	San San 3-8-7: 185/10	A Penna	*F Head*	19
1973	137	Rheingold 4-9-6: 77/10	B W Hills	*L Piggott*	27
1974	132+	Allez France 4-9-3: 1/2cpf	A Penna	*Y Saint-Martin*	20
1975	133	Star Appeal 5-9-6: 119/1	T Grieper	*G Starkey*	24
1976	132	Ivanjica 4-9-1: 71/10cp	A Head	*F Head*	20
1977	137	Alleged 3-8-11: 39/10f	V O'Brien	*L Piggott*	26
1978	138	Alleged 4-9-4: 14/10f	V O'Brien	*L Piggott*	18
1979	133	Three Troikas 3-8-8: 88/10	Mme C Head	*F Head*	22
1980	131	Detroit 3-8-8: 67/10	O Douieb	*Pat Eddery*	20
1981	132	Gold River 4-9-1: 53/1	A Head	*G W Moore*	24
1982	131	Akiyda 3-8-8: 11/1	F Mathet	*Y Saint-Martin*	17
1983	131	All Along 4-9-1: 173/10	P L Biancone	*W R Swinburn*	26
1984	135	Sagace 4-9-4: 39/10cp	P L Biancone	*Y Saint-Martin*	22
1985	134	*Rainbow Quest 4-9-4: 71/10	J Tree	*Pat Eddery*	15
1986	140	Dancing Brave 3-8-11: 11/10f	G Harwood	*Pat Eddery*	15
1987	135	Trempolino 3-8-11: 20/1	A Fabre	*Pat Eddery*	11
1988	134	Tony Bin 5-9-4: 14/1	L Camici	*J Reid*	24
1989	132	Carroll House 4-9-4: 19/1	M A Jarvis	*M J Kinane*	19
1990	132	Saumarez 3-8-11: 154/10	N Clement	*G Mosse*	21
1991	135	Suave Dancer 3-8-11: 37/10	J E Hammond	*C Asmussen*	14
1992	131	Subotica 4-9-4: 88/10	A Fabre	*T Jarnet*	18
1993	126	Urban Sea 4-9-1: 37/1	J Lesbordes	*E Saint-Martin*	23

1994	129	Carnegie 3-8-11: 3/1cpf	A Fabre	*T Jarnet*	20
1995	134	Lammtarra 3-8-11: 21/10f	Saeed bin Suroor	*L Dettori*	16
1996	136	Helissio 3-8-11: 18/10f	E Lellouche	*O Peslier*	16
1997	137	Peintre Celebre 3-8-11: 22/10f	A Fabre	*O Peslier*	18
1998	129	Sagamix 3-8-11: 5/2jf	A Fabre	*O Peslier*	14
1999	137	Montjeu 3-8-11: 6/4cpf	J E Hammond	*M J Kinane*	14
2000	134	Sinndar 3-8-11: 6/4cp	J Oxx	*J Murtagh*	10
2001	135+	Sakhee 4-9-5: 22/10f	Saeed bin Suroor	*L Dettori*	17
2002	129	Marienbard 5-9-5: 158/10	Saeed bin Suroor	*L Dettori*	16
2003	133	Dalakhani 3-8-11: 14/10cpf	A de Royer Dupre	*C Soumillon*	13
2004	130	Bago 3-8-11: 77/10	J E Pease	*T Gillet*	19
2005	134	Hurricane Run 3-8-11: 19/10cpjf	A Fabre	*K Fallon*	15
2006	132	Rail Link 3-8-11: 236/10	A Fabre	*S Pasquier*	8
2007	127+	Dylan Thomas 4-9-5: 6/1	A P O'Brien	*K Fallon*	12
2008	130+	Zarkava 3-8-8: 1/1f	A de Royer Dupre	*C Soumillon*	16
2009	129+	Sea The Stars 3-8-11: 8/10f	J Oxx	*M J Kinane*	19
2010	133	Workforce 3-8-11: 76/10	Sir Michael Stoute	*R L Moore*	19
2011	132	Danedream 3-8-8: 27/1	P Schiergen	*Andrasch Starke*	16
2012	124	Solemia 4-9-2: 33/1	C Laffon-Parias	*Olivier Peslier*	18
2013	134	Treve 8-8: 48/10	Mme C Head-Maarek	*Thierry Jarnet*	17
2014	129	Treve 4-9-2: 14/1	Mme C Head-Maarek	*Thierry Jarnet*	20
2015	132	Golden Horn 3-8-11: 52/10	John Gosden	*Frankie Dettori*	17

Other Selected Classics

TATTERSALLS IRISH 2000 GUINEAS (3-y-o colts and fillies) (Curragh 1m)

1980	125	Nikoli 9-0: 5/1	P Prendergast	*C Roche*	13
1981	121	Kings Lake 9-0: 5/1	M V O'Brien	*Pat Eddery*	13
1982	128	Dara Monarch 9-0: 20/1	L Browne	*M J Kinane*	14
1983	121	Wassl 9-0: 12/1	J L Dunlop	*A Murray*	10
1984	123	Sadler's Wells 9-0: 10/1	M V O'Brien	*G McGrath*	9
1985	121	Triptych 8-11: 7/1	D V O'Brien	*C Roche*	16
1986	119+	Flash of Steel 9-0: 9/2	D K Weld	*M J Kinane*	6
1987	127	Don't Forget Me 9-0: 6/4jf	R Hannon	*W Carson*	8
1988	121	Prince of Birds 9-0: 9/1	M V O'Brien	*D Gillespie*	14
1989	124+	Shaadi 9-0: 7/2	M R Stoute	*W R Swinburn*	12
1990	116+	Tirol 9-0: 5/4f	R Hannon	*Pat Eddery*	9
1991	122	Fourstars Allstar 9-0: 9/1	L O'Brien	*M Smith*	12
1992	123	Rodrigo de Triano 9-0: 8/11f	P W Chapple-Hyam	*L Piggott*	6
1993	113	Barathea 9-0: 4/7f	L M Cumani	*M Roberts*	11
1994	123	Turtle Island 9-0: 5/4f	P W Chapple-Hyam	*J Reid*	9
1995	121	Spectrum 9-0: 10/3	P W Chapple-Hyam	*J Reid*	10
1996	124	Spinning World 9-0: 7/4f	J E Pease	*C Asmussen*	10
1997	124	Desert King 9-0: 3/1	A P O'Brien	*C Roche*	12
1998	121	Desert Prince 9-0: 8/1	D R Loder	*O Peslier*	7
1999	123	Saffron Walden 9-0: 12/1	A P O'Brien	*O Peslier*	10
2000	118	Bachir 9-0: 4/1	Saeed bin Suroor	*L Dettori*	8
2001	122	Black Minnaloushe 9-0: 20/1	A P O'Brien	*J Murtagh*	12
2002	121+	Rock of Gibraltar 9-0: 4/7f	A P O'Brien	*M J Kinane*	7
2003	117+	Indian Haven 9-0: 8/1	P W D'Arcy	*J F Egan*	16
2004	120+	Bachelor Duke 9-0: 12/1	J A R Toller	*S Sanders*	8
2005	121	Dubawi 9-0: 7/4jf	Saeed bin Suroor	*L Dettori*	8
2006	119+	Araafa 9-0: 12/1	J Noseda	*A Munro*	11
2007	120+	Cockney Rebel 9-0: 6/4f	G A Huffer	*O Peslier*	12
2008	126+	Henrythenavigator 9-0: 5/4	A P O'Brien	*J Murtagh*	5
2009	129	Mastercraftsman 9-0: 6/4f	A P O'Brien	*J Murtagh*	9
2010	123+	Canford Cliffs 9-0: 9/4f	R Hannon	*R Hughes*	13
2011	118+	Roderic O'Connor 9-0: 7/2	Aidan O'Brien	*Joseph O'Brien*	8
2012	117	Power 9-0: 5/1	Aidan O'Brien	*Joseph O'Brien*	10
2013	128	Magician 9-0: 10/3	Aidan O'Brien	*Joseph O'Brien*	10
2014	130+	Kingman 9-0: 4/5f	John Gosden	*James Doyle*	11
2015	121	Gleneagles 9-0: 2/5f	Aidan O'Brien	*Ryan Moore*	11

ETIHAD AIRWAYS IRISH 1000 GUINEAS (3-y-o fillies) (Curragh 1m)

1980	114+	Cairn Rouge 9-0: 5/1	M Cunningham	*A Murray*	18
1981	114	Arctique Royale 9-0: 7/1	K Prendergast	*G Curran*	15
1982	110	Prince's Polly 9-0: 12/1	D K Weld	*W Swinburn*	24
1983	123	L'Attrayante 9-0: 4/1f	O Douieb	*A Badel*	18
1984	114	Katies 9-0: 20/1	M J Ryan	*P Robinson*	23
1985	119	Al Bahathri 9-0: 7/1	H Thomson Jones	*A Murray*	15
1986	113+	Sonic Lady 9-0: 4/1	M R Stoute	*W R Swinburn*	19
1987	103+	Forest Flower 9-0: 4/1	I A Balding	*T Ives*	11
1988	112+	Trusted Partner 9-0: 10/1	D K Weld	*M J Kinane*	16
1989	113	Ensconse 9-0: 13/8f	L M Cumani	*R Cochrane*	13
1990	113	In The Groove 9-0: 5/1	D R C Elsworth	*S Cauthen*	12
1991	114	Kooyonga 9-0: 4/1	M Kauntze	*W J O'Connor*	12
1992	108	Marling 9-0: 4/5f	G Wragg	*W R Swinburn*	9
1993	113	Nicer 9-0: 8/1	B W Hills	*M Hills*	14
1994	115	Mehthaaf 9-0: 5/2	J L Dunlop	*W Carson*	10
1995	121	Ridgewood Pearl 9-0: 9/4	J Oxx	*C Roche*	10
1996	116	Matiya 9-0: 5/1	B Hanbury	*W Carson*	12
1997	115	Classic Park 9-0: 20/1	A P O'Brien	*S Craine*	10
1998	114	Tarascon 9-0: 12/1	T Stack	*J P Spencer*	13
1999	111	Hula Angel 9-0: 16/1	B W Hills	*M Hills*	17
2000	115	Crimplene 9-0: 16/1	C E Brittain	*P Robinson*	13
2001	119	Imagine 9-0: 16/1	A P O'Brien	*J A Heffernan*	16
2002	118	Gossamer 9-0: 4/1f	L M Cumani	*J P Spencer*	15
2003	117	Yesterday 9-0: 11/2	A P O'Brien	*M J Kinane*	8
2004	122+	Attraction 9-0: 2/1f	M Johnston	*K Darley*	15
2005	110	Saoire 9-0: 10/1	Ms F M Crowley	*M J Kinane*	18
2006	113	Nightime 9-0: 12/1	D K Weld	*P J Smullen*	15
2007	110+	Finsceal Beo: 9-0: 9/10f	J S Bolger	*K J Manning*	11
2008	115	Halfway To Heaven 9-0: 13/2	A P O'Brien	*J A Heffernan*	13
2009	115	Again 9-0: 5/2f	D Wachman	*J Murtagh*	16
2010	113	Bethrah 9-0: 16/1	D K Weld	*P J Smullen*	19
2011	117	Misty For Me 9-0: 5/1	Aidan O'Brien	*Seamie Heffernan*	15
2012	116	Samitar 9-0: 12/1	Mick Channon	*Martin Harley*	8
2013	115	Just The Judge 9-0: 2/1f	Charles Hills	*Jamie Spencer*	15
2014	116+	Marvellous 9-0: 10/1	Aiden O'Brien	*Ryan Moore*	11
2015	114	Pleascach 9-0: 11/2	J S Bolger	*K J Manning*	18

DUBAI DUTY FREE IRISH DERBY (3-y-o colts and fillies) (Curragh 1½m)

1980	129	Tyrnavos 9-0: 25/1	B Hobbs	*A Murray*	13
1981	124+	Shergar 9-0: 1/3f	M R Stoute	*L Piggott*	12
1982	128+	Assert 9-0: 4/7f	D V O'Brien	*C Roche*	12
1983	135	Shareef Dancer 9-0: 8/1	M R Stoute	*W R Swinburn*	12
1984	133	El Gran Senor 9-0: 2/7f	M V O'Brien	*Pat Eddery*	8
1985	129	Law Society 9-0: 15/8f	M V O'Brien	*Pat Eddery*	13
1986	135	Shahrastani 9-0: 1/1f	M R Stoute	*W R Swinburn*	11
1987	127	Sir Harry Lewis 9-0: 6/1	B W Hills	*J Reid*	8
1988	119	Kahyasi 9-0: 4/5f	L M Cumani	*R Cochrane*	11
1989	128	Old Vic 9-0: 4/11f	H R A Cecil	*S Cauthen*	8
1990	130	Salsabil 8-11: 11/4	J L Dunlop	*W Carson*	9
1991	139	Generous 9-0: 1/1f	P F I Cole	*A Munro*	6
1992	133	St Jovite 9-0: 7/2	J S Bolger	*C Roche*	11
1993	128	Commander In Chief 9-0: 4/7f	H R A Cecil	*Pat Eddery*	11
1994	131	Balanchine 8-11: 5/1	H Ibrahim	*L Dettori*	9
1995	121	Winged Love 9-0: 5/1	A Fabre	*O Peslier*	13
1996	127	Zagreb 9-0: 20/1	D K Weld	*P Shanahan*	13
1997	124	Desert King 9-0: 11/2	A P O'Brien	*C Roche*	10
1998	124+	Dream Well 9-0: 2/1f	P Bary	*C Asmussen*	10
1999	129+	Montjeu 9-0: 13/8f	J E Hammond	*C Asmussen*	10
2000	132	Sinndar 9-0: 11/10f	J Oxx	*J Murtagh*	8
2001	130+	Galileo 9-0: 4/11f	A P O'Brien	*M J Kinane*	12
2002	127+	High Chaparral 9-0: 1/3f	A P O'Brien	*M J Kinane*	9
2003	130+	Alamshar 9-0: 4/1	J Oxx	*J Murtagh*	9
2004	127	Grey Swallow 9-0: 10/1	D K Weld	*P J Smullen*	10
2005	127+	Hurricane Run 9-0: 4/5f	A Fabre	*K Fallon*	9
2006	127+	Dylan Thomas 9-0: 9/2f	A P O'Brien	*K Fallon*	13
2007	131	Soldier of Fortune 9-0: 5/1	A P O'Brien	*J A Heffernan*	11

2008	122	Frozen Fire 9-0: 16/1	A P O'Brien	*J A Heffernan*	11
2009	130+	Fame And Glory 9-0: 8/11f	A P O'Brien	*J Murtagh*	11
2010	123+	Cape Blanco 9-0: 7/2	A P O'Brien	*J Murtagh*	10
2011	120	Treasure Beach 9-0: 7/2	Aidan O'Brien	*C O'Donoghue*	8
2012	120+	Camelot 9-0: 1/5f	Aidan O'Brien	*Joseph O'Brien*	5
2013	122	Trading Leather 9-0: 6/1	J S Bolger	*Kevin Manning*	9
2014	121+	Australia 9-0: 1/8f	Aidan O'Brien	*Joseph O'Brien*	5
2015	127+	Jack Hobbs 9-0: 10/11f	John Gosden	*William Buick*	8

DARLEY IRISH OAKS (3-y-o fillies) (Curragh 1½m)

1980	127	Shoot A Line 9-0: 6/4f	W R Hern	*W Carson*	8
1981	112+	Blue Wind 9-0: 4/6f	D K Weld	*W Swinburn*	10
1982	119	Swiftfoot 9-0: 4/1	W R Hern	*W Carson*	10
1983	118+	Give Thanks 9-0: 7/4f	J S Bolger	*D Gillespie*	12
1984	118+	Princess Pati 9-0: 9/2	C Collins	*P Shanahan*	11
1985	123	Helen Street 9-0: 3/1	W R Hern	*W Carson*	9
1986	117+	Colorspin 9-0: 6/1	M R Stoute	*Pat Eddery*	8
1987	122+	Unite 9-0: 8/13f	M R Stoute	*W R Swinburn*	8
1988	118	Diminuendo 9-0: 2/9f d-ht	H R A Cecil	*S Cauthen*	
	118	Melodist 9-0: 11/1 d-ht	M R Stoute	*W R Swinburn*	9
1989	124	Alydaress 9-0: 7/4	H R A Cecil	*M J Kinane*	5
1990	116	Knight's Baroness 9-0: 13/8f	P F I Cole	*T Quinn*	10
1991	118	Possessive Dancer 9-0: 8/1	A A Scott	*S Cauthen*	10
1992	115	User Friendly 9-0: 8/11f	C E Brittain	*G Duffield*	9
1993	118	Wemyss Bight 9-0: 9/2	A Fabre	*Pat Eddery*	11
1994	118	Bolas 9-0: 5/2f	B W Hills	*Pat Eddery*	10
1995	121	Pure Grain 9-0: 9/2	M R Stoute	*J Reid*	10
1996	114	Dance Design 9-0: 9/2	D K Weld	*M J Kinane*	6
1997	122	Ebadiyla 9-0: 9/2	J Oxx	*J Murtagh*	11
1998	120	Winona 9-0: 12/1	J Oxx	*J Murtagh*	9
1999	121+	Ramruma 9-0: 4/9	H R A Cecil	*K Fallon*	7
2000	126	Petrushka 9-0: 11/2	Sir Michael Stoute	*J Murtagh*	10
2001	116	Lailani 9-0: 5/1	E A L Dunlop	*L Dettori*	12
2002	120	Margarula 9-0: 33/1	J S Bolger	*K J Manning*	12
2003	117	Vintage Tipple 9-0: 12/1	Patrick Mullins	*L Dettori*	11
2004	117+	Ouija Board 9-0: 4/7f	E A L Dunlop	*K Fallon*	7
2005	124	Shawanda 9-0: 9/2	A de Royer Dupre	*C Soumillon*	13
2006	120+	Alexandrova 9-0: 8/15f	A P O'Brien	*K Fallon*	6
2007	122+	Peeping Fawn 9-0: 3/1	A P O'Brien	*J Murtagh*	12
2008	118+	Moonstone 9-0: 2/1f	A P O'Brien	*J Murtagh*	14
2009	122+	Sariska 9-0: 1/1f	M L W Bell	*J P Spencer*	10
2010	120	Snow Fairy 9-0: 7/2	E A L Dunlop	*R L Moore*	15
2011	118+	Blue Bunting 9-0: 5/2	Mahmood Al Zarooni	*Frankie Dettori*	9
2012	120	Great Heavens 9-0: 5/4f	John Gosden	*William Buick*	7
2013	115+	Chicquita 9-0: 9/2	A de Royer Dupre	*Johnny Murtagh*	7
2014	114	Bracelet 9-0: 10/1	Aidan O'Brien	*C O'Donoghue*	10
2015	116	Covert Love 9-0: 7/1	Hugo Palmer	*Pat Smullen*	9

POULE D'ESSAI DES POULAINS (3-y-o colts) (Longchamp 7f210y)

1990	122	Linamix 9-2: 1/1f	F Boutin	*F Head*	
1991	119	Hector Protector 9-2: 1/10cpf	F Boutin	*F Head*	6
1992	119	Shanghai 9-2: 117/10	F Boutin	*F Head*	9
1993	122	Kingmambo 9-2: 35/10cp	F Boutin	*C Asmussen*	10
1994	120	Green Tune 9-2: 91/10	Mme C Head	*O Doleuze*	7
1995	119	Vettori 9-2: 9/2	Saeed bin Suroor	*L Dettori*	8
1996	118+	Ashkalani 9-2: 4/5f	A de Royer Dupre	*G Mosse*	10
1997	123	Daylami 9-2: 16/10	A de Royer Dupre	*G Mosse*	6
1998	120	Victory Note 9-2: 252/10	P W Chapple-Hyam	*J Reid*	12
1999	127	Sendawar 9-2: 37/10	A de Royer Dupre	*G Mosse*	15
2000	118	Bachir 9-2: 31/10	Saeed bin Suroor	*L Dettori*	7
2001	120	*Vahorimix 9-2: 64/10	A Fabre	*C Soumillon*	12
2002	121	Landseer 9-2: 61/10	A P O'Brien	*M J Kinane*	13
2003	116	Clodovil 9-2: 2/1f	A Fabre	*C Soumillon*	10
2004	119+	American Post 9-2: 4/10f	Mme C Head-Maarek	*R Hughes*	7
2005	120	Shamardal 9-2: 31/10	Saeed bin Suroor	*L Dettori*	15
2006	118	Aussie Rules 9-2: 27/10cp	A P O'Brien	*K Fallon*	11
2007	121	Astronomer Royal 9-2: 34/10cp	A P O'Brien	*C O'Donoghue*	14

2008	122	Falco 9-2: 215/10	C Laffon-Parias	*O Peslier*	19
2009	122	Silver Frost 9-2: 43/10	Y De Nicolay	*C Soumillon*	11
2010	122+	Lope de Vega 9-2: 87/10	A Fabre	*M Guyon*	15
2011	116+	Tin Horse 9-2: 83/10	D Guillemin	*Thierry Jarnet*	14
2012	114	Lucayan 9-2: 33/1	F Rohaut	*Stephane Pasquier*	12
2013	116	Style Vendome 9-2: 9/2	A Clement	*Thierry Thulliez*	18
2014	118	Karakontie 9-2: 11/10f	J E Pease	*Stephane Pasquier*	12
2015	120	Make Believe 9-2: 6/1	Andre Fabre	*Olivier Peslier*	18

POULE D'ESSAI DES POULICHES (3-y-o fillies) (Longchamp 7f210y)

1990	115	Houseproud 9-2: 9/10f	A Fabre	*Pat Eddery*	14
1991	119	Danseuse du Soir 9-2: 4/10cpf	E Lellouche	*D Boeuf*	9
1992	118	Culture Vulture 9-2: 131/10	P F I Cole	*T Quinn*	9
1993	118	Madeleine's Dream 9-2: 49/10cp	F Boutin	*C Asmussen*	8
1994	117	East of The Moon 9-2: 17/10	F Boutin	*C Asmussen*	8
1995	119	Matiara 9-2: 26/10f	Mme C Head	*F Head*	16
1996	112	Ta Rib 9-0: 141/10	E A L Dunlop	*W Carson*	9
1997	112	Always Loyal 9-0: 14/10	Mme C Head	*F Head*	7
1998	118	Zalaiyka 9-0: 6/5f	A de Royer Dupre	*G Mosse*	14
1999	116	Valentine Waltz 9-0: 43/10	J H M Gosden	*R Cochrane*	14
2000	109	Bluemamba 9-0: 184/10	P Bary	*S Guillot*	11
2001	114	Rose Gypsy 9-0: 147/10	A P O'Brien	*M J Kinane*	15
2002	115	Zenda 9-0: 63/10	J H M Gosden	*R Hughes*	17
2003	117	Musical Chimes 9-0: 78/10	A Fabre	*C Soumillon*	12
2004	117	Torrestrella 9-0: 97/10	F Rohaut	*O Peslier*	13
2005	125	Divine Proportions 9-0: 3/10cpf	P Bary	*C P Lemaire*	8
2006	110	*Tie Black 9-0: 87/10	F Rohaut	*J-B Eyquem*	13
2007	117+	Darjina 9-0: 4/1	A de Royer Dupre	*C Soumillon*	13
2008	119+	Zarkava 9-0: 3/10f	A de Royer Dupre	*C Soumillon*	14
2009	118	Elusive Wave 9-0: 54/10	J-C Rouget	*C P Lemaire*	11
2010	113	*Special Duty 9-0: 3/1jf	Mme C Head-Maarek	*S Pasquier*	10
2011	119	Golden Lilac 9-0: 15/10f	Andre Fabre	*Olivier Peslier*	16
2012	118	Beauty Parlour 9-0: 8/13f	E Lellouche	*Christophe Soumillon*	13
2013	120	Flotilla 8-13: 7/1	M Delzangles	*C P Lemaire*	20
2014	119	Avenir Certain 9-0: 74/10	Jean-Claude Rouget	*Gregory Benoist*	16
2015	114+	Ervedya 9-0: 13/10f	Jean-Claude Rouget	*Christophe Soumillon*	14

PRIX DU JOCKEY CLUB (3-y-o colts and fillies) (Chantilly 1¼m110y; 1½m prior to 2005)

1990	126	Sanglamore 9-2: 95/10	R Charlton	*Pat Eddery*	12
1991	126	Suave Dancer 9-2: 6/10f	J E Hammond	*C Asmussen*	7
1992	120	Polytain 9-2: 365/10	A Spanu	*L Dettori*	17
1993	123	Hernando 9-2: 2/1f	F Boutin	*C Asmussen*	11
1994	118	Celtic Arms 9-2: 53/10	P Bary	*G Mosse*	15
1995	122	Celtic Swing 9-2: 1/1f	Lady Herries	*K Darley*	11
1996	117	Ragmar 9-2: 93/10	P Bary	*G Mosse*	15
1997	126	Peintre Celebre 9-2: 31/10	A Fabre	*O Peslier*	14
1998	127	Dream Well 9-2: 78/10	P Bary	*C Asmussen*	13
1999	127	Montjeu 9-2: 7/5cpf	J E Hammond	*C Asmussen*	8
2000	125	Holding Court 9-2: 61/10	M A Jarvis	*P Robinson*	14
2001	118	Anabaa Blue 9-2: 86/10	C Lerner	*C Soumillon*	14
2002	126+	Sulamani 9-2: 199/10	P Bary	*T Thulliez*	15
2003	125+	Dalakhani 9-2: 2/5cpf	A de Royer Dupre	*C Soumillon*	7
2004	118	Blue Canari 9-2: 332/10	P Bary	*T Thulliez*	15
2005	120+	Shamardal 9-2: 68/10	Saeed bin Suroor	*L Dettori*	17
2006	118	Darsi 9-2: 76/10	A de Royer Dupre	*C Soumillon*	15
2007	118+	Lawman 9-2: 72f	J-M Beguigne	*L Dettori*	20
2008	121	Vision d'Etat 9-2: 72/10	E Libaud	*I Mendizabal*	20
2009	124	Le Havre 9-2: 119/10	J-C Rouget	*C P Lemaire*	17
2010	123+	Lope de Vega 9-2: 10/1	A Fabre	*M Guyon*	22
2011	120	Reliable Man 9-2: 79/10	A de Royer Dupre	*Gerald Mosse*	16
2012	118+	Saonois 9-2: 25/1	J-P Gauvin	*Antoine Hamelin*	20
2013	123	Intello 9-2: 15/8f	Andre Fabre	*Olivier Peslier*	19
2014	123	The Grey Gatsby 9-2: 189/10	Kevin Ryan	*Ryan Moore*	16
2015	121+	New Bay 9-2: 32/10	Andre Fabre	*Vincent Cheminaud*	14

PRIX DE DIANE (3-y-o fillies) (Chantilly 1¼m97y)

1990	123	Rafha 9-2: 90/10	H R A Cecil	W Carson	14
1991	119	Caerlina 9-2: 132/10	J de Roualle	E Legrix	13
1992	119	Jolypha 9-2: 36/10	A Fabre	Pat Eddery	12
1993	116	Shemaka 86/10	A de Royer Dupre	G Mosse	14
1994	119	East of The Moon 9-2: 8/10f	F Boutin	C Asmussen	9
1995	118	Carling 9-2: 35/10	Mme Pat Barbe	T Thulliez	12
1996	116	Sil Sila 9-0: 30/1	B Smart	C Asmussen	12
1997	120	Vereva 9-0: 27/10	A de Royer Dupre	G Mosse	12
1998	117	Zainta 9-0: 2/5cpf	A de Royer Dupre	G Mosse	11
1999	117	Daryaba 9-0: 58/10	A de Royer Dupre	G Mosse	14
2000	124	Egyptband 9-0: 57/10	Mme C Head	O Doleuze	14
2001	118	Aquarelliste 9-0: 18/10f	E Lellouche	D Boeuf	12
2002	120	Bright Sky 9-0: 3/1cp	E Lellouche	D Boeuf	15
2003	114	Nebraska Tornado 9-0: 106/10	A Fabre	R Hughes	10
2004	121	Latice 9-0: 9/5f	J-M Beguigne	C Soumillon	17
2005	123+	Divine Proportions 9-0: 4/5f	P Bary	C P Lemaire	10
2006	116	Confidential Lady 9-0: 433/10	Sir Mark Prescott	S Sanders	16
2007	112+	West Wind 9-0: 71/10	H-A Pantall	L Dettori	14
2008	124+	Zarkava 9-0: 2/5cpf	A de Royer Dupre	C Soumillon	13
2009	123	Stacelita 9-0: 13/10f	J-C Rouget	C P Lemaire	12
2010	120	Sarafina 9-0: 1/1f	A de Royer Dupre	C P Lemaire	9
2011	117+	Golden Lilac 9-0: 26/10	Andre Fabre	Maxime Guyon	9
2012	120	Valyra 9-0: 25/1	J-C Rouget	Johnny Murtagh	12
2013	124+	Treve 8-13: 11/1	Mme C Head-Maarek	Thierry Jarnet	11
2014	117	Avenir Certain 9-0: 31/10	Jean-Claude Rouget	Gregory Benoist	12
2015	116	Star of Seville 9-0: 17/1	John Gosden	Frankie Dettori	17

KENTUCKY DERBY PRESENTED BY YUM! BRANDS (Grade 1) (3-y-o)
(Churchill Downs 1¼m Dirt)

1990		Unbridled 9-0: 108/10	C Nafzger	C Perrett	15
1991	123	Strike The Gold 9-0: 48/10	N Zito	C Antley	16
1992	119	Lil E Tee 9-0: 168/10	L Whiting	P Day	18
1993	124	Sea Hero 9-0: 129/10	M Miller	J Bailey	19
1994	123	Go For Gin 9-0: 91/10	N Zito	C McCarron	14
1995	125	Thunder Gulch 9-0: 245/10	D W Lukas	Gary Stevens	19
1996	125	Grindstone 9-0: 59/10	D W Lukas	J Bailey	19
1997	126	Silver Charm 9-0: 4/1	R Baffert	Gary Stevens	13
1998	131	Real Quiet 9-0: 84/10	R Baffert	K Desormeaux	15
1999	124	Charismatic 9-0: 313/10	D W Lukas	C Antley	19
2000	127+	Fusaichi Pegasus 9-0: 23/10f	N Drysdale	K Desormeaux	19
2001	129	Monarchos 9-0: 105/10	J T Ward	J Chavez	17
2002	128	War Emblem 9-0: 205/10	R Baffert	V Espinoza	18
2003	125	Funny Cide 9-0: 128/10	B Tagg	J Santos	16
2004	128	Smarty Jones 9-0: 41/10f	J C Servis	Stewart Elliott	18
2005	123	Giacomo 9-0: 503/10	J A Shirreffs	M E Smith	20
2006	130	Barbaro 9-0: 61/10	M R Matz	E Prado	20
2007	128	Street Sense 9-0: 49/10f	C A Nafzger	C Borel	20
2008	132	Big Brown 9-0: 24/10f	R E Dutrow Jnr	K Desormeaux	20
2009	125	Mine That Bird 9-0: 506/10	B L Woolley Jnr	C Borel	19
2010	121	Super Saver 9-0: 8/1	T A Pletcher	C Borel	20
2011	122+	Animal Kingdom 9-0: 209/10	H Graham Motion	John R Velazquez	19
2012	125	I'll Have Another 9-0: 153/10	Doug O'Neill	M Gutierrez	20
2013	122	Orb 9-0: 54/10	Claude McGaughey III	Joel Rosario	19
2014	123+	California Chrome 9-0: 25/10f	Art Sherman	Victor Espinoza	19
2015	126+	American Pharoah 9-0: 29/10f	Bob Baffert	Victor Espinoza	18

Xpressbet.com PREAKNESS STAKES (Grade 1) (3-y-o) (Pimlico 1m1½f Dirt)

1990		Summer Squall 9-0: 24/10	N Howard	P Day	9
1991	129	Hansel 9-0: 91/10	F Brothers	J Bailey	8
1992	121	Pine Bluff 9-0: 35/10f	T Bohannon	C McCarron	14
1993	121	Prairie Bayou 9-0: 22/10f	T Bohannon	M Smith	12
1994	124	Tabasco Cat 9-0: 36/10	D W Lukas	P Day	10
1995	124	Timber Country 9-0: 19/10f	D W Lukas	P Day	11
1996	125	Louis Quatorze 9-0: 85/10	N Zito	P Day	12
1997	126	Silver Charm 9-0: 31/10	R Baffert	Gary Stevens	10
1998	124+	Real Quiet 9-0: 5/2	R Baffert	K Desormeaux	10

1999	127	Charismatic 9-0: 84/10	D W Lukas	*C Antley*	13
2000	123+	Red Bullet 9-0: 62/10	J Orseno	*J Bailey*	8
2001	126	Point Given 9-0: 23/10f	R Baffert	*Gary Stevens*	11
2002	125	War Emblem 9-0: 28/10f	R Baffert	*V Espinoza*	13
2003	128	Funny Cide 9-0: 19/10f	B Tagg	*J Santos*	10
2004	134	Smarty Jones 9-0: 7/10f	J C Servis	*Stewart Elliott*	10
2005	128	Afleet Alex 9-0: 33/10f	T F Ritchey	*J Rose*	14
2006	125+	Bernardini 9-0: 129/10	T Albertrani	*J Castellano*	9
2007	128	Curlin 9-0: 34/10	S M Asmussen	*R Albarado*	9
2008	125+	Big Brown Jnr 9-0: 2/10f	R E Dutrow Jnr	*K Desormeaux*	12
2009	116+	Rachel Alexandra 8-9: 9/5f	S M Asmussen	*C Borel*	13
2010	121	Lookin At Lucky 9-0: 12/5	R Baffert	*Martin Garcia*	12
2011	124	Shackleford 9-0: 126/10	Dale L Romans	*Jesus Lopez Castanon*	14
2012	129+	I'll Have Another 9-0: 16/5	Doug O'Neill	*M Gutierrez*	11
2013	120	Oxbow 9-0: 154/10	D Wayne Lukas	*Gary Stevens*	9
2014	124+	California Chrome 9-0: 5/10f	Art Sherman	*Victor Espinoza*	10
2015	126+	American Pharoah 9-0: 9/10f	Bob Baffert	*Victor Espinoza*	8

BELMONT STAKES Presented By DraftKings (Grade 1) (3-y-o) (Belmont 1½m Dirt)

1990		Go And Go 9-0: 75/10	D K Weld	*M Kinane*	9
1991	123	Hansel 9-0: 41/10	F Brothers	*J Bailey*	11
1992	123	A P Indy 9-0: 11/10f	N Drysdale	*F Delahoussaye*	11
1993	120	Colonial Affair 9-0: 139/10	S Schulhofer	*Julie Krone*	13
1994	124+	Tabasco Cat 9-0: 34/10	D W Lukas	*P Day*	6
1995	122	Thunder Gulch 9-0: 6/4f	D W Lukas	*Gary Stevens*	11
1996	125	Editor's Note 9-0: 58/10	D W Lukas	*R Douglas*	14
1997	127	Touch Gold 9-0: 265/100cp	D Hofmans	*C McCarron*	7
1998	125+	Victory Gallop 9-0: 9/2	W E Waldon	*Gary Stevens*	11
1999	125	Lemon Drop Kid 9-0: 2975/100	S Schulhofer	*J Santos*	12
2000	122	Commendable 9-0: 188/10	D W Lukas	*P Day*	11
2001	134	Point Given 9-0: 135/100f	R Baffert	*Gary Stevens*	9
2002	125	Sarava 9-0: 7025/100	K G McPeek	*E Prado*	11
2003	129	Empire Maker 9-0: 2/1	R J Frankel	*J Bailey*	6
2004	129	Birdstone 9-0: 36/1	N P Zito	*E Prado*	9
2005	128	Afleet Alex 9-0: 115/100f	T F Ritchey	*J Rose*	11
2006	122	Jazil 9-0: 62/10	K P McLaughlin	*F Jara*	12
2007	125+	Rags To Riches 8-9: 43/10	T A Pletcher	*J Velazquez*	7
2008	120	Da'Tara 9-0: 385/10	N P Zito	*A Garcia*	9
2009	124+	Summer Bird 9-0: 119/10	T Ice	*K Desormeaux*	10
2010	121	Drosselmeyer 9-0: 13/1	W I Mott	*M E Smith*	12
2011	116	Ruler On Ice 9-0: 248/10	Kelly J Breen	*Jose Valdivia jnr*	12
2012	121+	Union Rags 9-0: 11/4	Michael Matz	*J R Velazquez*	11
2013	124	Palace Malice 9-0: 138/10	Todd Pletcher	*M E Smith*	14
2014	119+	Tonalist 9-0: 92/10	Christophe Clement	*Joel Rosario*	11
2015	130+	American Pharoah 9-0: 75/100f	Bob Baffert	*Victor Espinoza*	8

Other Selected Group 1s (3-y-o+)

PRIX GANAY (4-y-o+; geldings excluded prior to 2001) (Longchamp 1¼m97y, 1¼m in 2001)

1990	126	Creator 4-9-2: 3/10cpf	A Fabre	*C Asmussen*	10
1991	122	Kartajana 4-8-13: 39/10	A de Royer-Dupre	*W Mongil*	7
1992	124	Subotica 4-9-2: 74/10	A Fabre	*T Jarnet*	7
1993	125	Vert Amande 5-9-2: 127/10	E Lellouche	*D Boeuf*	8
1994	124	Marildo 7-9-2: 185/10	D Smaga	*G Guignard*	8
1995	125	Pelder 5-9-2: 130/10	P Kelleway	*L Dettori*	10
1996	125	Valanour 4-9-2: 12/10f	A de Royer Dupre	*G Mosse*	10
1997	129	Helissio 4-9-2: 3/5f	E Lellouche	*O Peslier*	8
1998	122	Astarabad 4-9-2: 9/10f	A de Royer Dupre	*G Mosse*	4
1999	122	Dark Moondancer 4-9-2: 43/10	A de Royer Dupre	*G Mosse*	5
2000	124	Indian Danehill 4-9-2: 3/5f	A Fabre	*O Peslier*	4
2001	123	Golden Snake 5-9-2: 10/1	J L Dunlop	*Pat Eddery*	9
2002	115+	Aquarelliste 4-8-13: 7/10f	E Lellouche	*D Boeuf*	7
2003	123	Fair Mix 5-9-2: 41/10	M Rolland	*O Peslier*	9
2004	121	Execute 7-9-2: 219/10	J E Hammond	*T Gillet*	8

2005	121	Bago 4-9-2: 1/2cpf	J E Pease	*T Gillet*	9
2006	124	Corre Caminos 4-9-2: 28/10	M Delzangles	*T Jarnet*	7
2007	127+	Dylan Thomas 4-9-2: 4/10f	A P O'Brien	*C Soumillon*	8
2008	126+	Duke of Marmalade 4-9-2: 38/10	A P O'Brien	*J Murtagh*	6
2009	120+	Vision d'Etat 4-9-2: 14/10f	E Libaud	*I Mendizabal*	8
2010	122	Cutlass Bay 4-9-2: 6/5f	A Fabre	*M Guyon*	9
2011	122+	Planteur 4-9-2: 1/1f	E Lellouche	*Christophe Soumillon*	7
2012	133+	Cirrus des Aigles 6-9-2: 8/13f	Mme C Barande-Barbe	*Olivier Peslier*	6
2013	124	Pastorius 4-9-2: 7/2	Mario Hofer	*Olivier Peslier*	9
2014	129	Cirrus des Aigles 8-9-2: 33/10	Mme C Barande-Barbe	*Christophe Soumillon*	8
2015	128	Cirrus des Aigles 9-9-2: 37/10	Mme C Barande-Barbe	*Christophe Soumillon*	7

INVESTEC CORONATION CUP (4-y-o+) (Epsom 1½m10y)

1990	125	In The Wings 4-9-0: 15/8f	A Fabre	*C Asmussen*	6
1991	123	In The Groove 4-8-11: 7/2	D R C Elsworth	*S Cauthen*	7
1992	126	Saddlers' Hall 4-9-0: 5/4f	M R Stoute	*W R Swinburn*	9
1993	123	Opera House 5-9-0: 9/4jf	M R Stoute	*M Roberts*	8
1994	120	Apple Tree 5-9-0: 12/1	A Fabre	*T Jarnet*	11
1995	122	Sunshack 4-9-0: 10/1	A Fabre	*Pat Eddery*	7
1996	123+	Swain 4-9-0: 11/10f	A Fabre	*L Dettori*	4
1997	127+	Singspiel 5-9-0: 5/4f	M R Stoute	*L Dettori*	5
1998	125	Silver Patriarch 4-9-0: 7/2	J L Dunlop	*Pat Eddery*	7
1999	123	Daylami 5-9-0: 9/2	Saeed bin Suroor	*L Dettori*	7
2000	121+	Daliapour 4-9-0: 11/8f	Sir Michael Stoute	*K Fallon*	4
2001	120	Mutafaweq 5-9-0: 11/2	Saeed bin Suroor	*L Dettori*	6
2002	126	Boreal 4-9-0: 4/1	P Schiergen	*K Fallon*	6
2003	121	Warrsan 5-9-0: 9/2	C E Brittain	*P Robinson*	9
2004	124	Warrsan 6-9-0: 7/1	C E Brittain	*D Holland*	11
2005	125	Yeats 4-9-0: 5/1	A P O'Brien	*K Fallon*	7
2006	126+	Shirocco 5-9-0: 8/11f	A Fabre	*C Soumillon*	6
2007	124	Scorpion 5-9-0: 8/1	A P O'Brien	*M J Kinane*	7
2008	129	Soldier of Fortune 4-9-0: 9/4	A P O'Brien	*J Murtagh*	11
2009	121	Ask 6-9-0: 5/1	Sir Michael Stoute	*R L Moore*	8
2010	130	Fame And Glory 4-9-0: 5/6f	A P O'Brien	*J Murtagh*	9
2011	126+	St Nicholas Abbey 4-9-0: 1/1f	Aidan O'Brien	*Ryan Moore*	5
2012	128	St Nicholas Abbey 5-9-0: 8/11f	Aidan O'Brien	*Joseph O'Brien*	6
2013	128	St Nicholas Abbey 6-9-0: 3/10f	Aidan O'Brien	*Joseph O'Brien*	5
2014	127+	Cirrus des Aigles 8-9-0: 10/11f	Mme C Barande-Barbe	*Christophe Soumillon*	7
2015	121	Pether's Moon 5-9-0: 11/1	Richard Hannon	*Pat Dobbs*	4

QUEEN ANNE STAKES (4-y-o+) (Royal Ascot 1m; York in 2005; Group 2 prior to 2003)

1990	123	Markofdistinction 4-9-5: 7/1	L M Cumani	*L Dettori*	9
1991	119	Sikeston 5-9-8: 9/1	C E Brittain	*M Roberts*	11
1992	118	Lahib 4-9-2: 10/3f	J L Dunlop	*W Carson*	9
1993	116	Allflora 4-9-2: 20/1	C E Brittain	*M J Kinane*	9
1994	123	Barathea 4-9-8: 3/1	L M Cumani	*M J Kinane*	10
1995	116	Nicolotte 4-9-2: 16/1	G Wragg	*M Hills*	7
1996	125	Charnwood Forest 4-9-2: 10/11f	Saeed bin Suroor	*M J Kinane*	9
1997	123	Allied Forces 4-9-5: 10/1	Saeed bin Suroor	*L Dettori*	11
1998	135	Intikhab 4-9-2: 9/4f	Saeed bin Suroor	*L Dettori*	9
1999	125+	Cape Cross 5-9-7: 7/1	Saeed bin Suroor	*Gary Stevens*	8
2000	125	Kalanisi 4-9-2: 11/2	Sir Michael Stoute	*K Fallon*	11
2001	127+	Medicean 4-9-7: 11/2	Sir Michael Stoute	*K Fallon*	10
2002	123	No Excuse Needed 4-9-2: 13/2	Sir Michael Stoute	*J Murtagh*	12
2003	127	Dubai Destination 4-9-0: 9/2	Saeed bin Suroor	*L Dettori*	10
2004	127+	Refuse To Bend 4-9-0: 12/1	Saeed bin Suroor	*L Dettori*	16
2005	127	Valixir 4-9-0: 4/1	A Fabre	*C Soumillon*	10
2006	125	Ad Valorem 4-9-0: 13/2	A P O'Brien	*K Fallon*	7
2007	122	Ramonti 5-9-0: 5/1	Saeed bin Suroor	*L Dettori*	8
2008	125	Haradasun 5-9-0: 5/1	A P O'Brien	*J Murtagh*	11
2009	127	Paco Boy 4-9-0: 10/3	R Hannon	*R Hughes*	9
2010	125+	Goldikova 5-8-11: 11/8f	F Head	*O Peslier*	10
2011	133	Canford Cliffs 4-9-0: 11/8	Richard Hannon	*Richard Hughes*	7
2012	147	Frankel 4-9-0: 1/10f	Sir Henry Cecil	*Tom Queally*	11
2013	125+	Declaration of War 4-9-0: 15/2	Aidan O'Brien	*Joseph O'Brien*	13
2014	126+	Toronado 4-9-0: 4/5f	Richard Hannon	*Richard Hughes*	10
2015	126+	Solow 5-9-0: 11/8f	F Head	*Maxime Guyon*	8

ST JAMES'S PALACE STAKES (3-y-o colts; fillies allowed prior to 1999)

(Royal Ascot 1m; York in 2005)

1990	122	Shavian 9-0: 11/1	H R A Cecil	*S Cauthen*	8
1991	123	Marju 9-0: 7/4f	J Dunlop	*W Carson*	7
1992	121	Brief Truce 9-0: 25/1	D K Weld	*M J Kinane*	8
1993	113+	Kingmambo 9-0: 2/5f	F Boutin	*C Asmussen*	4
1994	123	Grand Lodge 9-0: 6/1	W Jarvis	*M J Kinane*	9
1995	125	Bahri 9-0: 11/4f	J L Dunlop	*W Carson*	9
1996	122+	Bijou d'Inde 9-0: 9/1	M Johnston	*J Weaver*	9
1997	126	Starborough 9-0: 11/2	D R Loder	*L Dettori*	8
1998	122+	Dr Fong 9-0: 4/1	H R A Cecil	*K Fallon*	8
1999	128	Sendawar 9-0: 2/1f	A de Royer Dupre	*G Mosse*	11
2000	120	Giant's Causeway 9-0: 7/2f	A P O'Brien	*M J Kinane*	11
2001	122+	Black Minnaloushe 9-0: 8/1	A P O'Brien	*J Murtagh*	11
2002	129+	Rock of Gibraltar 9-0: 4/5f	A P O'Brien	*M J Kinane*	9
2003	123	Zafeen 9-0: 8/1	M R Channon	*D Holland*	11
2004	121+	Azamour 9-0: 9/2	J Oxx	*M J Kinane*	11
2005	125+	Shamardal 9-0: 7/4f	Saeed bin Suroor	*K McEvoy*	8
2006	125	Araafa 9-0: 2/1f	J Noseda	*A Munro*	11
2007	125	Excellent Art 9-0: 8/1	A P O'Brien	*J P Spencer*	8
2008	127+	Henrythenavagator 9-0: 4/7f	A P O'Brien	*J Murtagh*	8
2009	126	Mastercraftsman 9-0: 5/6f	A P O'Brien	*J Murtagh*	10
2010	122+	Canford Cliffs 9-0: 11/4jf	R Hannon	*R Hughes*	9
2011	123+	Frankel 9-0: 3/10f	Sir Henry Cecil	*Tom Queally*	9
2012	119	Most Improved 9-0: 9/1	Brian Meehan	*Kieren Fallon*	16
2013	126+	Dawn Approach 9-0: 5/4f	J S Bolger	*Kevin Manning*	9
2014	124+	Kingman 9-0: 8/11f	John Gosden	*James Doyle*	7
2015	125	Gleneagles 9-0: 8/15f	Aidan O'Brien	*Ryan Moore*	5

PRINCE OF WALES'S STAKES (4-y-o+; 3-y-o's allowed until 1999)

(Royal Ascot 1¼m; York 1¼m88y in 2005; Group 1 from 2000)

1990	122	Batshoof 4-9-5: 2/1f	B Hanbury	*Pat Eddery*	8
1991	126	Stagecraft 4-9-3: 6/4f	M Stoute	*S Cauthen*	6
1992	119	*Perpendicular 4-9-3: 20/1	H R A Cecil	*W Ryan*	11
1993	116	Placerville 3-8-4: 11/2	H R A Cecil	*Pat Eddery*	11
1994	123	Muhtarram 5-9-7· 6/4f	J H M Gosden	*W Carson*	11
1995	124	Muhtarram 6-9-8: 5/1	J H M Gosden	*W Carson*	6
1996	119	First Island 4-9-3: 9/1	G Wragg	*M Hills*	12
1997	130	Bosra Sham 4-9-5: 4/11f	H R A Cecil	*K Fallon*	6
1998	120	Faithful Son 4-9-3: 11/2	Saeed bin Suroor	*J Reid*	8
1999	124	Lear Spear 4-9-3: 20/1	D R C Elsworth	*M J Kinane*	8
2000	137+	Dubai Millennium 4-9-0: 5/4	Saeed bin Suroor	*J Bailey*	6
2001	134	Fantastic Light 5-9-0: 10/3	Saeed bin Suroor	*L Dettori*	9
2002	129	Grandera 4-9-0: 4/1	Saeed bin Suroor	*L Dettori*	12
2003	128	Nayef 5-9-0: 5/1	M P Tregoning	*R Hills*	10
2004	128+	Rakti 5-9-0: 3/1	M A Jarvis	*P Robinson*	10
2005	128+	Azamour 4-9-0: 11/8f	J Oxx	*M J Kinane*	8
2006	132	Ouija Board 5-8-11: 8/1	E A L Dunlop	*O Peslier*	7
2007	135	Manduro 5-9-0: 15/8f	A Fabre	*S Pasquier*	6
2008	132	Duke of Marmalade 4-9-0: 1/1f	A P O'Brien	*J Murtagh*	12
2009	126+	Vision d'Etat 4-9-0: 4/1	E Libaud	*O Peslier*	8
2010	124+	Byword 4-9-0: 5/2f	A Fabre	*M Guyon*	12
2011	132	Rewilding 4-9-0: 17/2	Mahmood Al Zarooni	*Frankie Dettori*	7
2012	128+	So You Think 6-9-0: 4/5f	Aidan O'Brien	*Joseph O'Brien*	11
2013	127+	Al Kazeem 5-9-0: 11/4	Roger Charlton	*James Doyle*	11
2014	126+	The Fugue 5-8-11: 11/2	John Gosden	*William Buick*	8
2015	128	Free Eagle 4-9-0: 5/2f	D K Weld	*Pat Smullen*	9

GOLD CUP (4-y-o+) (Royal Ascot 2½m; York in 2005)

1990	114	Ashal 4-9-0: 14/1	H Thomson Jones	*R Hills*	11
1991	111	Indian Queen 6-8-13: 25/1	Lord Huntingdon	*W R Swinburn*	12
1992	114	Drum Taps 6-9-2: 7/4f	Lord Huntingdon	*L Dettori*	6
1993	111	Drum Taps 7-9-2: 13/2	Lord Huntingdon	*L Dettori*	10
1994	118	Arcadian Heights 6-9-2: 20/1	G Wragg	*M Hills*	9
1995	114+	Double Trigger 4-9-0: 9/4	M Johnston	*J Weaver*	7
1996	124+	Classic Cliche 4-9-0: 3/1	Saeed bin Suroor	*M J Kinane*	7
1997	121	Celeric 5-9-2: 11/2	D Morley	*Pat Eddery*	13

1998	120+	Kayf Tara 4-9-0: 11/1	Saeed bin Suroor	*L Dettori*	16
1999	126	Enzeli 4-9-0: 20/1	J Oxx	*J Murtagh*	17
2000	117+	Kayf Tara 6-9-2: 11/8f	Saeed bin Suroor	*M J Kinane*	11
2001	123	Royal Rebel 5-9-2: 8/1	M Johnston	*J Murtagh*	12
2002	124	Royal Rebel 6-9-2: 16/1	M Johnston	*J Murtagh*	15
2003	123+	Mr Dinos 4-9-0: 3/1	P F I Cole	*K Fallon*	12
2004	123+	Papineau 4-9-0: 5/1	Saeed bin Suroor	*L Dettori*	13
2005	125+	Westerner 6-9-2: 7/4f	E Lellouche	*O Peslier*	17
2006	122+	Yeats 5-9-2: 7/1	A P O'Brien	*K Fallon*	12
2007	121+	Yeats 6-9-2: 8/13f	A P O'Brien	*M J Kinane*	14
2008	126+	Yeats 7-9-2: 11/8f	A P O'Brien	*J Murtagh*	10
2009	126	Yeats 8-9-2: 6/4f	A P O'Brien	*J Murtagh*	9
2010	124	Rite of Passage 6-9-2: 20/1	D K Weld	*P Smullen*	12
2011	123+	Fame And Glory 5-9-2: 11/8f	Aidan O'Brien	*Jamie Spencer*	15
2012	121	Colour Vision 4-9-0: 6/1	Saeed bin Suroor	*Frankie Dettori*	9
2013	118	Estimate 4-8-11: 7/2f	Sir Michael Stoute	*Ryan Moore*	14
2014	123+	Leading Light 4-9-0: 10/11f	Aidan O'Brien	*Joseph O'Brien*	13
2015	120	Trip To Paris 4-9-0: 12/1	Ed Dunlop	*Graham Lee*	12

CORONATION STAKES (3-y-o fillies) (Royal Ascot 1m; York in 2005)

1990	121	Chimes of Freedom 9-0: 11/2	H R A Cecil	*S Cauthen*	7
1991	123	Kooyonga 9-0: 3/1	M Kauntze	*W J O'Connor*	8
1992	120	Marling 9-0: 8/11f	G Wragg	*W R Swinburn*	7
1993	116	Gold Splash 9-0: 10/3	Mme C Head	*G Mosse*	5
1994	116	Kissing Cousin 9-0: 13/2	H R A Cecil	*M J Kinane*	10
1995	122	Ridgewood Pearl 9-0: 9/2	J Oxx	*J Murtagh*	10
1996	117+	Shake The Yoke 9-0: 1/1f	E Lellouche	*O Peslier*	7
1997	117	Rebecca Sharp 9-0: 25/1	G Wragg	*M Hills*	6
1998	115	Exclusive 9-0: 5/1	Sir Michael Stoute	*W R Swinburn*	9
1999	113	Balisada 9-0: 16/1	G Wragg	*M Roberts*	9
2000	120	Crimplene 9-0: 4/1jf	C E Brittain	*P Robinson*	9
2001	118+	Banks Hill 9-0: 4/1jf	A Fabre	*O Peslier*	13
2002	112+	Sophisticat 9-0: 11/2	A P O'Brien	*M J Kinane*	11
2003	121+	Russian Rhythm 9-0: 4/7f	Sir Michael Stoute	*K Fallon*	9
2004	120+	Attraction 9-0: 6/4f	M Johnston	*K Darley*	11
2005	115	Maids Causeway 9-0: 9/2	B W Hills	*M Hills*	10
2006	119	Nannina 9-0: 6/1jf	J H M Gosden	*J Fortune*	15
2007	122	Indian Ink 9-0: 8/1	R Hannon	*R Hughes*	13
2008	122	Lush Lashes 9-0: 5/1	J S Bolger	*K J Manning*	11
2009	121+	Ghanaati 9-0: 2/1f	B W Hills	*R Hills*	10
2010	120	Lillie Langtry 9-0: 7/2f	A P O'Brien	*J Murtagh*	13
2011	119+	Immortal Verse 9-0: 8/1	R Collet	*Gerald Mosse*	12
2012	121	Fallen For You 9-0: 12/1	John Gosden	*William Buick*	10
2013	120+	Sky Lantern 9-0: 9/2jf	Richard Hannon	*Richard Hughes*	17
2014	112	Rizeena 9-0: 11/2	Clive Brittain	*Ryan Moore*	12
2015	117+	Ervedya 9-0: 3/1	Jean-Claude Rouget	*Christophe Soumillon*	9

CORAL-ECLIPSE (3-y-o+) (Sandown 1¼m7y)

1990	121	Elmaamul 3-8-10: 13/2	W R Hern	*W Carson*	7
1991	126	Environment Friend 3-8-10: 28/1	J R Fanshawe	*G Duffield*	7
1992	125	Kooyonga 4-9-4: 7/2f	M J Kauntze	*W J O'Connor*	12
1993	124	Opera House 5-9-7: 9/2	M R Stoute	*M J Kinane*	8
1994	126	Ezzoud 5-9-7: 5/1	M R Stoute	*W R Swinburn*	8
1995	124	Halling 4-9-7: 7/1	Saeed bin Suroor	*W R Swinburn*	8
1996	130	Halling 5-9-7: 10/3	Saeed bin Suroor	*J Reid*	7
1997	131	Pilsudski 5-9-7: 11/2	M R Stoute	*M J Kinane*	5
1998	125+	Daylami 4-9-7: 6/4f	Saeed bin Suroor	*L Dettori*	7
1999	121+	Compton Admiral 3-8-10: 20/1	G A Butler	*D Holland*	8
2000	130+	Giant's Causeway 3-8-10: 8/1	A P O'Brien	*G Duffield*	8
2001	123+	Medicean 4-9-7: 7/2	Sir Michael Stoute	*K Fallon*	8
2002	125+	Hawk Wing 3-8-10: 8/15f	A P O'Brien	*M J Kinane*	5
2003	126+	Falbrav 5-9-7: 8/1	L M Cumani	*D Holland*	15
2004	128	Refuse To Bend 4-9-7: 15/2	Saeed bin Suroor	*L Dettori*	12
2005	127+	Oratorio 3-8-10: 12/1	A P O'Brien	*K Fallon*	7
2006	124+	David Junior 4-9-7: 9/4	B J Meehan	*J P Spencer*	9
2007	128	Notnowcato 5-9-7: 7/1	Sir Michael Stoute	*R L Moore*	8
2008	124+	Mount Nelson 4-9-7: 7/2	A P O'Brien	*J Murtagh*	8

2009	136+	Sea The Stars 3-8-10: 4/7f	J Oxx	*M J Kinane*	10
2010	122+	Twice Over 5-9-7: 13/8f	H R A Cecil	*T P Queally*	5
2011	131	So You Think 5-9-7: 4/6f	Aidan O'Brien	*Seamie Heffernan*	5
2012	129	Nathaniel 4-9-7: 7/2	John Gosden	*William Buick*	9
2013	128	Al Kazeem 5-9-7: 15/8f	Roger Charlton	*James Doyle*	7
2014	126	Mukhadram 5-9-7: 14/1	William Haggas	*Paul Hanagan*	9
2015	134	Golden Horn 3-8-10: 4/9f	John Gosden	*Frankie Dettori*	5

DARLEY JULY CUP (3-y-o+) (Newmarket 6f)

1990	122	Royal Academy 3-8-13: 7/1	M V O'Brien	*J Reid*	9
1991	128	Polish Patriot 3-8-13: 6/1	G Harwood	*R Cochrane*	8
1992	125	Mr Brooks 5-9-6: 16/1	R Hannon	*L Piggott*	8
1993	125	Hamas 4-9-6: 33/1	P T Walwyn	*W Carson*	12
1994	123	Owington 3-8-13: 3/1	G Wragg	*Paul Eddery*	9
1995	131	Lake Coniston 4-9-6: 13/8f	G Lewis	*Pat Eddery*	9
1996	130	Anabaa 4-9-5: 11/4	Mme C Head	*F Head*	10
1997	125	Compton Place 3-8-13: 50/1	J A R Toller	*S Sanders*	9
1998	128	Elnadim 4-9-5: 3/1f	J L Dunlop	*R Hills*	17
1999	133	Stravinsky 3-8-13: 8/1	A P O'Brien	*M J Kinane*	17
2000	121	Agnes World 5-9-5: 4/1f	Hideyuki Mori	*Y Take*	10
2001	131	Mozart 3-8-13: 4/1f	A P O'Brien	*M J Kinane*	18
2002	121	Continent 5-9-5: 12/1	D Nicholls	*D Holland*	14
2003	128	Oasis Dream 3-8-13: 9/2	J H M Gosden	*R Hughes*	16
2004	120+	Frizzante 5-9-2: 14/1	J R Fanshawe	*J Murtagh*	20
2005	127	Pastoral Pursuits 4-9-5: 22/1	H Morrison	*J F Egan*	19
2006	125+	Les Arcs 6-9-5: 10/1	T J Pitt	*J F Egan*	15
2007	128	Sakhee's Secret 3-8-13: 9/2	H Morrison	*S Drowne*	18
2008	124+	Marchand d'Or 5-9-5: 5/2f	F Head	*D Bonilla*	13
2009	124	Fleeting Spirit 4-9-2: 12/1	J Noseda	*T P Queally*	13
2010	128	Starspangledbanner 4-9-5: 2/1f	A P O'Brien	*J Murtagh*	14
2011	125+	Dream Ahead 3-8-13: 7/1	David Simcock	*Hayley Turner*	16
2012	124	Mayson 4-9-5: 20/1	Richard Fahey	*Paul Hanagan*	12
2013	128	Lethal Force 4-9-5: 9/2	Clive Cox	*Adam Kirby*	11
2014	125	Slade Power 5-9-6: 7/4f	Edward Lynam	*W M Lordan*	13
2015	121	Muhaarar 3-9-0: 2/1jf	Charlie Hills	*Paul Hanagan*	14

JUDDMONTE GRAND PRIX DE PARIS (3-y-o colts and fillies)
(Longchamp 1m3f205y; 1¼m prior to 2005)

1990	131	Saumarez 9-2: 50/10	N Clement	*S Cauthen*	8
1991	121	Subotica 9-2: 27/10	A Fabre	*T Jarnet*	9
1992	120	Homme de Loi 9-2: 37/10	A Fabre	*T Jarnet*	10
1993	117	Fort Wood 9-2: 55/10cp	A Fabre	*S Guillot*	9
1994	118	Millkom 9-2: 34/10cp	J-C Rouget	*J Dubosc*	12
1995	122	Valanour 9-2: 63/10	A de Royer Dupre	*G Mosse*	10
1996	120+	Grape Tree Road 9-2: 10/1	A Fabre	*T Jarnet*	10
1997	119+	Peintre Celebre 9-2: 2/5cpf	A Fabre	*O Peslier*	7
1998	119	Limpid 9-2: 4/1	A Fabre	*O Peslier*	7
1999	119	Slickly 9-2: 9/5f	A Fabre	*T Jarnet*	8
2000	119+	Beat Hollow 9-2: 7/5f	H R A Cecil	*T Quinn*	7
2001	119	Chichicastenango 9-2: no betting	P H Demercastel	*A Junk*	5
2002	117	Khalkevi 9-2: 11/10f	A de Royer Dupre	*C Soumillon*	6
2003	120+	Vespone 9-2: 17/10f	N Clement	*C P Lemaire*	11
2004	118+	Bago 9-2: 1/10cpf	J E Pease	*T Gillet*	4
2005	123+	Scorpion 9-2: 6/4jf	A P O'Brien	*K Fallon*	9
2006	121+	Rail Link 9-2: 1/1f	A Fabre	*C Soumillon*	9
2007	117	Zambezi Sun 9-2: 19/10f	P Bary	*S Pasquier*	7
2008	126	Montmartre 9-2: 5/2f	A de Royer Dupre	*C Soumillon*	13
2009	121	Cavalryman 9-2: 34/10	A Fabre	*M Guyon*	8
2010	123+	Behkabad 9-2: 88/10	J-C Rouget	*G Mosse*	9
2011	122	Meandre 9-2: 55/10	Andre Fabre	*Maxime Guyon*	7
2012	118+	Imperial Monarch 9-2: 6/5f	Aidan O'Brien	*Joseph O'Brien*	9
2013	121+	Flintshire 9-2: 7/10f	Andre Fabre	*Maxime Guyon*	9
2014	120	Gallante 9-2: 62/1	Andre Fabre	*Pierre-Charles Boudot*	11
2015	120	Erupt 9-2: 73/10	Francis-Henri Graffard	*Stephane Pasquier*	6

QATAR SUSSEX STAKES (3-y-o+) (Goodwood 1m)

1990	127	Distant Relative 4-9-7: 4/1	B W Hills	W Carson	7
1991	127	Second Set 3-8-13: 5/1	L M Cumani	L Dettori	8
1992	124	Marling 3-8-10: 11/10f	G Wragg	Pat Eddery	8
1993	126	Bigstone 3-8-13: 14/1	E Lellouche	D Boeuf	10
1994	126	Distant View 3-8-13: 4/1	H R A Cecil	Pat Eddery	9
1995	122	Sayyedati 5-9-4: 11/2	C E Brittain	B Doyle	6
1996	125+	First Island 4-9-7: 5/1	G Wragg	M Hills	10
1997	127	Ali-Royal 4-9-7: 13/2	H R A Cecil	K Fallon	9
1998	124	Among Men 4-9-7: 4/1	Sir Michael Stoute	M J Kinane	10
1999	125	Aljabr 3-8-13: 11/10f	Saeed bin Suroor	L Dettori	8
2000	126+	Giant's Causeway 3-9-0: 3/1jf	A P O'Brien	M J Kinane	10
2001	125	Noverre 3-9-0: 9/2	Saeed bin Suroor	L Dettori	10
2002	124+	Rock of Gibraltar 3-8-13: 8/13f	A P O'Brien	M J Kinane	5
2003	118	Reel Buddy 5-9-7: 20/1	R Hannon	Pat Eddery	9
2004	124	Soviet Song 4-9-4: 3/1	J R Fanshawe	J Murtagh	11
2005	124+	Proclamation 3-8-13: 3/1	J Noseda	M J Kinane	12
2006	126+	Court Masterpiece 6-9-7: 15/2	E A L Dunlop	J Fortune	7
2007	126	Ramonti 5-9-7: 9/2	Saeed bin Suroor	L Dettori	8
2008	128+	Henrythenavigator 3-8-13: 4/11f	A P O'Brien	J Murtagh	6
2009	134	Rip Van Winkle 3-8-13: 6/4f	A P O'Brien	J Murtagh	8
2010	128+	Canford Cliffs 3-8-13: 4/6f	R Hannon	R Hughes	7
2011	139+	Frankel 3-8-13: 8/13f	Sir Henry Cecil	Tom Queally	4
2012	136+	Frankel 4-9-7: 1/20f	Sir Henry Cecil	Tom Queally	4
2013	133	Toronado 3-8-13: 11/4	Richard Hannon	Richard Hughes	7
2014	123+	Kingman 3-9-0: 2/5f	John Gosden	James Doyle	4
2015	126	Solow 5-9-8: 2/5f	F Head	Maxime Guyon	8

QATAR NASSAU STAKES (3-y-o+ fillies and mares)
(Goodwood 1m1f192y; Group 2 prior to 1999)

1990	122	Kartajana 3-8-6: 11/2	M R Stoute	W R Swinburn	6
1991	121	Ruby Tiger 4-9-4: 11/4	P F I Cole	T Quinn	6
1992	119	Ruby Tiger 5-9-1: 2/1	P F I Cole	T Quinn	7
1993	112	Lyphard's Delta 3-8-6: 10/1	H R A Cecil	W Ryan	9
1994	114	Hawajiss 3-8-6: 4/1	M R Stoute	W R Swinburn	9
1995	114	Caramba 3-8-9: 5/2	R Hannon	M Roberts	9
1996	119	Last Second 3-8-6: 7/4f	Sir Mark Prescott	G Duffield	8
1997	119	Ryafan 3-8-9: 9/4f	J H M Gosden	M Hills	7
1998	119	Alborada 3-8-9: 4/1	Sir Mark Prescott	G Duffield	9
1999	114	Zahrat Dubai 3-8-6: 5/1	Saeed bin Suroor	Gary Stevens	8
2000	119+	Crimplene 3-8-6: 7/4f	C E Brittain	P Robinson	7
2001	118+	Lailani 3-8-6: 5/4f	E A L Dunlop	L Dettori	7
2002	119+	Islington 3-8-6: 10/3	Sir Michael Stoute	K Fallon	10
2003	118+	Russian Rhythm 3-8-6: 4/5f	Sir Michael Stoute	K Fallon	8
2004	120	Favourable Terms 4-9-2: 11/2	Sir Michael Stoute	K Fallon	6
2005	122+	Alexander Goldrun 4-9-3: 13/8f	J S Bolger	K J Manning	11
2006	125	Ouija Board 5-9-5: 1/1f	E A L Dunlop	L Dettori	7
2007	120+	Peeping Fawn 3-8-10: 2/1f	A P O'Brien	J Murtagh	8
2008	115	Halfway To Heaven 3-8-10: 5/1	A P O'Brien	J Murtagh	9
2009	122	Midday 3-8-10: 11/2	H R A Cecil	T P Queally	10
2010	123+	Midday 4-9-6: 15/8f	H R A Cecil	T P Queally	7
2011	121+	Midday 5-9-6: 6/4f	Sir Henry Cecil	Tom Queally	6
2012	118+	The Fugue 3-8-11: 11/4	John Gosden	Richard Hughes	8
2013	117	Winsili 3-8-11: 20/1	John Gosden	William Buick	14
2014	118+	Sultanina 4-9-7: 11/2	John Gosden	William Buick	6
2015	118	Legatissimo 3-8-12: 2/1f	David Wachman	W M Lordan	9

PRIX DU HARAS DE FRESNAY-LE-BUFFARD – JACQUES LE MAROIS
(3-y-o+ colts and fillies) (Deauville 7f210y)

1990	125	Priolo 3-8-9: 113/10	F Boutin	A Lequeux	10
1991	124	Hector Protector 3-8-9: 8/10cpf	F Boutin	F Head	10
1992	122	Exit To Nowhere 4-9-4: 23/10cpf	F Boutin	C Asmussen	14
1993	122	Sayyedati 3-8-8: 23/10	C E Brittain	W R Swinburn	8
1994	123	East of The Moon 3-8-8: 9/10f	F Boutin	C Asmussen	9
1995	123	Miss Satamixa 3-8-8: 217/10	A Fabre	S Guillot	9
1996	124	Spinning World 3-8-11: 17/10	J E Pease	C Asmussen	9
1997	130	Spinning World 4-9-4: 29/10	J E Pease	C Asmussen	6

1998	125	Taiki Shuttle 4-9-4: 3/10f	Kazuo Fujisawa	*Y Okabe*	8
1999	124+	Dubai Millennium 3-8-11: 14/10jf	Saeed bin Suroor	*L Dettori*	5
2000	126	Muhtathir 5-9-4: 215/10	Saeed bin Suroor	*L Dettori*	11
2001	118+	*Vahorimix 3-8-13: 33/10	A Fabre	*O Peslier*	9
2002	126	Banks Hill 4-9-1: 17/10f	A Fabre	*O Peslier*	8
2003	124	Six Perfections 3-8-9: 28/10cp	P Bary	*T Thulliez*	12
2004	125	Whipper 3-8-11: 49/10	R Collet	*C Soumillon*	10
2005	129	Dubawi 3-8-11: 42/10	Saeed bin Suroor	*K McEvoy*	6
2006	124	Librettist 4-9-4: 29/10	Saeed bin Suroor	*L Dettori*	10
2007	124+	Manduro 5-9-4: 9/10	A Fabre	*S Pasquier*	6
2008	126	Tamayuz 3-8-11: 5/4f	F Head	*D Bonilla*	8
2009	133	Goldikova 4-9-0: 8/10f	F Head	*O Peslier*	9
2010	130	Makfi 3-8-11: 44/10	M Delzangles	*C Soumillon*	8
2011	126	Immortal Verse 3-8-8: 19/1	R Collet	*Gerald Mosse*	12
2012	128+	Excelebration 4-9-4: 5/2f	Aidan O'Brien	*Christophe Soumillon*	11
2013	129	Moonlight Cloud 5-9-1: 22/10	F Head	*Thierry Jarnet*	13
2014	127+	Kingman 3-8-12: 4/10f	John Gosden	*James Doyle*	5
2015	123	Esoterique 5-9-1: 33/10	Andre Fabre	*Pierre-Charles Boudot*	9

JUDDMONTE INTERNATIONAL STAKES (3-y-o+)
(York 1¼m88y; run at Newmarket 1¼m in 2008)

1990	124	In The Groove 3-8-9: 4/1	D R C Elsworth	*S Cauthen*	9
1991	124	Terimon 5-9-6: 16/1	C E Brittain	*M Roberts*	6
1992	128	Rodrigo de Triano 3-8-12: 8/1	P W Chapple-Hyam	*L Piggott*	12
1993	123	Ezzoud 4-9-6: 28/1	M R Stoute	*W R Swinburn*	11
1994	126	Ezzoud 5-9-6: 4/1	M R Stoute	*W R Swinburn*	8
1995	131	Halling 4-9-6: 9/4f	Saeed bin Suroor	*W R Swinburn*	6
1996	133	Halling 5-9-5: 6/4f	Saeed bin Suroor	*L Dettori*	6
1997	133	Singspiel 5-9-5: 4/1	M R Stoute	*L Dettori*	4
1998	121	One So Wonderful 4-9-2: 6/1	L M Cumani	*Pat Eddery*	8
1999	135	Royal Anthem 4-9-5: 3/1jf	H R A Cecil	*Gary Stevens*	12
2000	131+	Giant's Causeway 3-8-11: 10/11f	A P O'Brien	*M J Kinane*	6
2001	136	Sakhee 4-9-5: 7/4f	Saeed bin Suroor	*L Dettori*	8
2002	127+	Nayef 4-9-5: 6/4f	M P Tregoning	*R Hills*	7
2003	129+	Falbrav 5-9-5: 5/2	L M Cumani	*D Holland*	8
2004	126+	Sulamani 5-9-5: 3/1	Saeed bin Suroor	*L Dettori*	9
2005	127	Electrocutionist 4-9-5: 9/2	V Valiani	*M J Kinane*	7
2006	126	Notnowcato 4-9-5: 8/1	Sir Michael Stoute	*R L Moore*	7
2007	133	Authorized 3-8-11: 6/4f	P W Chapple-Hyam	*L Dettori*	7
2008	127+	Duke of Marmalade 4-9-5: 4/6f	A P O'Brien	*J Murtagh*	9
2009	131+	Sea The Stars 3-8-11: 1/4f	J Oxx	*M J Kinane*	4
2010	129	Rip Van Winkle 4-9-5: 7/4f	A P O'Brien	*J Murtagh*	9
2011	128	Twice Over 6-9-5: 11/2	Sir Henry Cecil	*Ian Mongan*	5
2012	142+	Frankel 4-9-5: 1/10f	Sir Henry Cecil	*Tom Queally*	9
2013	127+	Declaration of War 4-9-5: 7/1	Aidan O'Brien	*Joseph O'Brien*	6
2014	131+	Australia 3-8-12: 8/13f	Aidan O'Brien	*Joseph O'Brien*	6
2015	117	Arabian Queen 3-8-9: 50/1	David Elsworth	*Silvestre de Sousa*	7

COOLMORE NUNTHORPE STAKES (2-y-o+) (York 5f; run at Newmarket in 2008)

1990	131	Dayjur 3-9-3: 8/11f	W R Hern	*W Carson*	6/9
1991	119	Sheikh Albadou 3-9-3: 6/1	A A Scott	*Pat Eddery*	3/9
1992	115	Lyric Fantasy 2-7-8: 8/11f	R Hannon	*M Roberts*	10/11
1993	124	Lochsong 5-9-3: 10/1	I A Balding	*L Dettori*	5/11
1994	112	*Piccolo 3-9-3: 14/1	M R Channon	*J Reid*	4/10
1995	120	So Factual 5-9-6: 9/2	Saeed bin Suroor	*L Dettori*	5/8
1996	124	Pivotal 3-9-7: 10/3	Sir Mark Prescott	*G Duffield*	5/8
1997	118	Coastal Bluff 5-9-9: 6/1 d-ht	T D Barron	*K Darley*	6/15
	118	Ya Malak 6-9-9: 11/1 d-ht	D Nicholls	*Alex Greaves*	4/15
1998	119	Lochangel 4-9-6: 6/1	I A Balding	*L Dettori*	2/17
1999	124	Stravinsky 3-9-7: 1/1f	A P O'Brien	*M J Kinane*	13/16
2000	125+	Nuclear Debate 5-9-9: 5/2f	J E Hammond	*G Mosse*	1/13
2001	126+	Mozart 3-9-7: 4/9f	A P O'Brien	*M J Kinane*	4/10
2002	124+	Kyllachy 4-9-11: 3/1f	H Candy	*J P Spencer*	15/17
2003	129	Oasis Dream 3-9-9: 4/9f	J H M Gosden	*R Hughes*	2/8
2004	118	Bahamian Pirate 9-9-11: 16/1	D Nicholls	*S Sanders*	5/12
2005	119	La Cucaracha 4-9-8: 7/1	B W Hills	*M Hills*	8/16
2006	125+	Reverence 5-9-11: 5/1	E J Alston	*K Darley*	6/14

2007	122	Kingsgate Native 2-8-1: 12/1	J R Best	J Quinn	13/16
2008	125	Borderlescott 6-9-11: 12/1	R Bastiman	P Cosgrave	12/14
2009	123	Borderlescott 7-9-11: 9/1	R Bastiman	N Callan	2/16
2010	125	Sole Power 3-9-9: 100/1	E Lynam	W M Lordan	11/12
2011	122	Margot Did 3-9-6: 20/1	Michael Bell	Hayley Turner	11/15
2012	121+	Ortensia 7-9-8: 7/2jf	Paul Messara	William Buick	8/19
2013	119	Jwala 4-9-8: 40/1	Robert Cowell	Steve Drowne	8/17
2014	123+	Sole Power 7-9-11: 11/4f	Edward Lynam	Richard Hughes	10/13
2015	129	Mecca's Angel 4-9-0: 15/2	Michael Dods	Paul Mulrennan	10/19

QIPCO IRISH CHAMPION STAKES (3-y-o+) (Leopardstown 1¼m)

1990	125	Elmaamul 3-8-11: 2/1f	W R Hern	W Carson	8
1991	136	Suave Dancer 3-8-11: 4/6f	J E Hammond	C Asmussen	7
1992	127	Dr Devious 3-8-11: 7/2	P W Chapple-Hyam	J Reid	8
1993	123	Muhtarram 4-9-4: 7/1	J H M Gosden	W Carson	10
1994	121	Cezanne 5-9-4: 7/2	M R Stoute	M J Kinane	8
1995	126+	Pentire 3-8-11: 9/4f	G Wragg	M Hills	8
1996	122+	Timarida 4-9-1: 3/1	J Oxx	J Murtagh	6
1997	134	Pilsudski 5-9-4: 5/4f	M R Stoute	M J Kinane	7
1998	129	Swain 6-9-4: 6/4	Saeed bin Suroor	L Dettori	8
1999	135+	Daylami 5-9-4: 6/4	Saeed bin Suroor	L Dettori	7
2000	125+	Giant's Causeway 3-8-11: 8/11f	A P O'Brien	M J Kinane	7
2001	134	Fantastic Light 5-9-4: 9/4	Saeed bin Suroor	L Dettori	7
2002	123+	Grandera 4-9-4: 5/2	Saeed bin Suroor	L Dettori	7
2003	128+	High Chaparral 4-9-4: 4/1	A P O'Brien	M J Kinane	7
2004	126+	Azamour 3-8-11: 8/1	J Oxx	M J Kinane	8
2005	128	Oratorio 3-8-11: 7/1	A P O'Brien	K Fallon	10
2006	129	Dylan Thomas 3-9-0: 13/8f	A P O'Brien	K Fallon	5
2007	121+	Dylan Thomas 4-9-7: 8/15f	A P O'Brien	K Fallon	6
2008	124	New Approach 3-9-0: 8/13f	J S Bolger	K J Manning	8
2009	138+	Sea The Stars 3-9-0: 4/6f	J Oxx	M J Kinane	9
2010	130	Cape Blanco 3-9-0: 6/1	A P O'Brien	J A Heffernan	6
2011	131	So You Think 5-9-7: 1/4f	Aidan O'Brien	Seamie Heffernan	6
2012	128	Snow Fairy 5-9-4: 15/8	Ed Dunlop	Frankie Dettori	6
2013	128	The Fugue 4-9-4: 4/1	John Gosden	William Buick	6
2014	128	The Grey Gatsby 3-9-0: 7/1	Kevin Ryan	Ryan Moore	7
2015	126+	Golden Horn 3-9-0: 5/4f	John Gosden	Frankie Dettori	7

QATAR PRIX VERMEILLE (3-y-o+ fillies and mares)

(Longchamp 1m3f205y; 3-y-o & 4-y-o fillies only in 2004 and 2005; 3-y-o fillies only previously)

1990	124	Salsabil 9-2: 4/10f	J L Dunlop	W Carson	9
1991	123	Magic Night 9-2: 30/10	P Demercastel	A Badel	14
1992	119	Jolypha 9-2: 16/10f	A Fabre	Pat Eddery	10
1993	121	Intrepidity 9-2: 25/10	A Fabre	T Jarnet	8
1994	119	Sierra Madre 9-2: 27/10	P Bary	G Mosse	9
1995	119	Carling 9-2: 66/10	Mme Pat Barbe	T Thulliez	10
1996	115	My Emma 9-0: 291/10	R Guest	C Asmussen	10
1997	119	Queen Maud 9-0: 174/10	J de Roualle	O Peslier	9
1998	120	Leggera 9-0: 10/1	J L Dunlop	T Quinn	11
1999	121	Daryaba 9-0: 4/5cpf	A de Royer Dupre	G Mosse	11
2000	120	Volvoreta 9-0: 11/2	C Lerner	M J Kinane	11
2001	122	Aquarelliste 9-0: 8/5f	E Lellouche	D Boeuf	12
2002	121	Pearly Shells 9-0: 19/10f	F Rohaut	C Soumillon	11
2003	117	Mezzo Soprano 9-0: 94/10	Saeed bin Suroor	L Dettori	11
2004	117	Sweet Stream 4-9-2: 308/10	J E Hammond	T Gillet	13
2005	119+	Shawanda 3-8-7: 1/5f	A de Royer Dupre	C Soumillon	6
2006	118+	Mandesha 3-8-7: 26/10	A de Royer Dupre	C Soumillon	11
2007	117	Mrs Lindsay 3-8-9: 183/10	F Rohaut	J Murtagh	10
2008	121+	Zarkava 3-8-8: 1/2f	A de Royer Dupre	C Soumillon	12
2009	117+	*Stacelita 3-8-8: 9/10cpf	J-C Rouget	C P Lemaire	12
2010	118+	Midday 4-9-3: 14/5	H R A Cecil	T P Queally	12
2011	121+	Galikova 3-8-8: 8/10f	F Head	Olivier Peslier	6
2012	122	Shareta 4-9-2: 7/2f	A de Royer Dupre	C P Lemaire	13
2013	127	Treve 3-8-8: 8/10f	Mme C Head-Maarek	Frankie Dettori	10
2014	121	Baltic Baroness 4-9-3: 20/1	Andre Fabre	Maxime Guyon	9
2015	127+	Treve 5-9-3: 12/10f	Mme C Head-Maarek	Thierry Jarnet	9

QATAR PRIX DU MOULIN DE LONGCHAMP (3-y-o+ colts and fillies)
(Longchamp 7f210y)

1990	126	Distant Relative 4-9-2: 26/10	B W Hills	*Pat Eddery*	6
1991	124	Priolo 4-9-2: 33/10	F Boutin	*G Mosse*	12
1992	124	All At Sea 3-8-8: 29/10	H R A Cecil	*Pat Eddery*	10
1993	125	Kingmambo 3-8-11: 27/10cp	F Boutin	*C Asmussen*	11
1994	124	Ski Paradise 4-8-13: 92/10	A Fabre	*Y Take*	7
1995	124	Ridgewood Pearl 3-8-8: 13/10f	J Oxx	*J Murtagh*	8
1996	128	Ashkalani 3-8-11: 8/10f	A de Royer Dupre	*G Mosse*	9
1997	125+	Spinning World 4-9-2: 6/4	J E Pease	*C Asmussen*	9
1998	129	Desert Prince 3-8-11: 41/10	D R Loder	*O Peslier*	7
1999	129	Sendawar 3-8-11: 4/5f	A de Royer Dupre	*G Mosse*	9
2000	122	Indian Lodge 4-9-2: 113/10	Mrs A J Perrett	*C Asmussen*	8
2001	128	Slickly 5-9-2: 43/10	Saeed bin Suroor	*L Dettori*	8
2002	122+	Rock of Gibraltar 3-8-11: 3/5jf	A P O'Brien	*M J Kinane*	7
2003	123	Nebraska Tornado 3-8-8: 146/10	A Fabre	*R Hughes*	14
2004	120	Grey Lilas 3-8-8: 5/1	A Fabre	*E Legrix*	11
2005	128	Starcraft 5-9-2: 122/10	L M Cumani	*C P Lemaire*	9
2006	123	Librettist 4-9-2: 1/1f	Saeed bin Suroor	*L Dettori*	8
2007	128	Darjina 3-8-8: 39/10	A de Royer Dupre	*C Soumillon*	9
2008	123	Goldikova 3-8-8: 7/2	F Head	*O Peslier*	11
2009	125	Aqlaam 4-9-2: 38/10	W J Haggas	*R Hills*	9
2010	122	Fuisse 4-9-2: 99/10	Mme C Head-Maarek	*S Pasquier*	6
2011	126	Excelebration 3-8-12: 22/10f	Marco Botti	*Jamie Spencer*	8
2012	126	Moonlight Cloud 4-8-13: 10/11f	F Head	*Thierry Jarnet*	4
2013	123	Maxios 5-9-2: 3/1	J E Pease	*Stephane Pasquier*	7
2014	126+	Charm Spirit 3-8-12: 61/10	F Head	*Thierry Jarnet*	10
2015	119+	Ervedya 3-8-9: 1/1f	Jean-Claude Rouget	*Christophe Soumillon*	6

QUEEN ELIZABETH II STAKES SPONSORED BY QIPCO (3-y-o+)
(Ascot 1m; Newmarket in 2005)

1990	130	Markofdistinction 4-9-4: 6/1	L M Cumani	*L Dettori*	10
1991	129	Selkirk 3-9-0: 10/1	I A Balding	*R Cochrane*	9
1992	129	Lahib 4-9-4: 8/1	J L Dunlop	*W Carson*	9
1993	126	Bigstone 3-9-0: 10/3	E Lellouche	*Pat Eddery*	9
1994	126	Maroof 4-9-4: 66/1	R W Armstrong	*R Hills*	9
1995	125	Bahri 3-8-11: 5/2	J L Dunlop	*W Carson*	6
1996	137	Mark of Esteem 3-8-11: 10/3	Saeed bin Suroor	*L Dettori*	7
1997	125	Air Express 3-8-11: 9/1	C E Brittain	*O Peslier*	9
1998	130	Desert Prince 3-8-11: 10/3f	D R Loder	*O Peslier*	7
1999	132	Dubai Millennium 3-8-11: 4/9f	Saeed bin Suroor	*L Dettori*	4
2000	131	Observatory 3-8-11: 14/1	J H M Gosden	*K Darley*	12
2001	118	Summoner 4-9-1: 33/1	Saeed bin Suroor	*R Hills*	8
2002	124	Where Or When 3-8-11: 7/1	T G Mills	*K Darley*	5
2003	131+	Falbrav 5-9-1: 6/4f	L M Cumani	*D Holland*	8
2004	129	Rakti 5-9-1: 9/2	M A Jarvis	*P Robinson*	11
2005	123+	Starcraft 5-9-1: 7/2	L M Cumani	*C P Lemaire*	6
2006	132+	George Washington 3-8-13: 13/8f	A P O'Brien	*M J Kinane*	8
2007	126	Ramonti 5-9-3: 5/1	Saeed bin Suroor	*L Dettori*	7
2008	133	Raven's Pass 3-8-13: 3/1	J H M Gosden	*J Fortune*	7
2009	129+	Rip Van Winkle 3-8-13: 8/13f	A P O'Brien	*J Murtagh*	4
2010	126	Poet's Voice 3-8-13: 9/2	Saeed bin Suroor	*L Dettori*	8
2011	143	Frankel 9-0: 4/11f	Sir Henry Cecil	*Tom Queally*	8
2012	133	Excelebration 4-9-3: 10/11f	Aidan O'Brien	*Joseph O'Brien*	8
2013	132	Olympic Glory 3-9-0: 11/2	Richard Hannon	*Richard Hughes*	12
2014	127	Charm Spirit 3-9-1: 5/1	F Head	*Olivier Peslier*	11
2015	125	Solow 5-9-4: 11/10f	F Head	*Maxime Guyon*	9

QIPCO CHAMPION STAKES (3-y-o+) (Ascot 1¼m; Newmarket prior to 2011)

1990	127	In The Groove 3-8-9: 9/2	D R C Elsworth	*S Cauthen*	10
1991	125	Tel Quel 3-8-12: 16/1	A Fabre	*T Jarnet*	12
1992	130	Rodrigo de Triano 3-8-12: 11/8f	P W Chapple-Hyam	*L Piggott*	10
1993	124	Hatoof 4-9-0: 5/2f	Mme C Head	*W R Swinburn*	12
1994	125	Dernier Empereur 4-9-4: 8/1	A Fabre	*S Guillot*	8
1995	126	Spectrum 3-8-8: 5/1	P W Chapple-Hyam	*J Reid*	8
1996	132	Bosra Sham 3-8-8: 9/4	H R A Cecil	*Pat Eddery*	6
1997	125+	Pilsudski 5-9-2: 1/1f	M R Stoute	*M J Kinane*	7

1998	122	Alborada 3-8-8: 6/1	Sir Mark Prescott	G Duffield	10
1999	118+	Alborada 4-8-13: 5/1	Sir Mark Prescott	G Duffield	13
2000	132	Kalanisi 4-9-2: 5/1	Sir Michael Stoute	J Murtagh	15
2001	126+	Nayef 3-8-11: 3/1f	M P Tregoning	R Hills	12
2002	125	Storming Home 4-9-2: 8/1	B W Hills	M Hills	11
2003	126	Rakti 4-9-2: 11/1	M A Jarvis	P Robinson	12
2004	129	Haafhd 3-8-11: 12/1	B W Hills	R Hills	11
2005	127	David Junior 3-8-11: 25/1	B J Meehan	J P Spencer	15
2006	126+	Pride 6-9-0: 7/2	A de Royer Dupre	C P Lemaire	8
2007	126+	Literato 3-8-12: 7/2	J-C Rouget	C P Lemaire	12
2008	132	New Approach 3-8-12: 6/5f	J S Bolger	K J Manning	11
2009	125+	Twice Over 4-9-3: 14/1	H R A Cecil	T P Queally	14
2010	128	Twice Over 5-9-3: 7/2	H R A Cecil	T P Queally	10
2011	133	Cirrus des Aigles 5-9-3: 12/1	Mme C Barande-Barbe	Christophe Soumillon	12
2012	139+	Frankel 4-9-3: 2/11f	Sir Henry Cecil	Tom Queally	6
2013	130+	Farhh 5-9-3: 11/4	Saeed bin Suroor	Silvestre de Sousa	10
2014	128	Noble Mission 5-9-5: 7/1	Lady Cecil	James Doyle	9
2015	127	Fascinating Rock 4-9-5: 10/1	D K Weld	Pat Smullen	13

Other Major Races Abroad

DUBAI SHEEMA CLASSIC – PRESENTED BY LONGINES (Group 1) (3-y-o+)
(Meydan 1½m Turf; Dubai Turf Classic (non-graded) in 1998/9; Group 3 in 2000;
Group 2 in 2001)

1998	119+	Stowaway 4-8-12	Saeed bin Suroor	L Dettori	13
1999	127	Fruits of Love 4-8-12	M Johnston	K Fallon	11
2000	123+	Fantastic Light 4-8-9	Sir Michael Stoute	K Fallon	16
2001	127	Stay Gold 7-8-11: 33/1	Y Ikee	Y Take	16
2002	124+	Nayef 4-8-11: 9/4f	M P Tregoning	R Hills	15
2003	127+	Sulamani 4-8-11: 6/4f	Saeed bin Suroor	L Dettori	16
2004	120	Polish Summer 7-8-11: 10/3jf	A Fabre	Gary Stevens	14
2005	124	Phoenix Reach 5-8-11: 5/1	A M Balding	Martin Dwyer	11
2006	127	Heart's Cry 5-8-11: 11/4	K Hashiguchi	C P Lemaire	14
2007	124	Vengeance of Rain 7-8-11: 9/1	D E Ferraris	A Delpech	14
2008	122	Sun Classique 5-8-7: 15/2	M F De Kock	K Shea	16
2009	123	Eastern Anthem 5-9-0: 14/1	M bin Shafya	A Ajtebi	15
2010	122+	Dar Re Mi 5-8-9: 9/1	J H M Gosden	W Buick	16
2011	125	Rewilding 4-8-13: 2/1f	Mahmood Al Zarooni	Frankie Dettori	14
2012	123+	Cirrus des Aigles 6-9-0: 11/4	Mme C Barande-Barbe	Olivier Peslier	10
2013	121+	St Nicholas Abbey 6-9-0: 11/4	Aidan O'Brien	Joseph O'Brien	11
2014	121+	Gentildonna 5-8-10: 4/1	Sei Ishizaka	Ryan Moore	15
2015	123	Dolniya 4-8-8: 7/1	A de Royer Dupre	Christophe Soumillon	9

DUBAI TURF – SPONSORED BY DP WORLD (Group 1) (Meydan 9f Turf; 9f turf in 2000,
previously 1¼m Dirt) (Group 2 in 2001, Group 3 in 1999/2000, listed in 1998, prestige in 1997)

1996	126	Key of Luck 5-8-12	K P McLaughlin	Gary Stevens	14
1997	119	Tamayaz 5-9-0	Saeed bin Suroor	L Dettori	13
1998	118	Annus Mirabilis 6-9-0	Saeed bin Suroor	Gary Stevens	10
1999	117	Altibr 4-9-0	Saeed bin Suroor	R Hills	9
2000	119	Rhythm Band 4-9-0	Saeed bin Suroor	T E Durcan	11
2001	124	Jim And Tonic 7-9-0: 5/1	F Doumen	G Mosse	15
2002	120	Terre A Terre 5-8-10: 9/1	E Libaud	C Soumillon	16
2003	119+	Ipi Tombe 5-8-10: 1/1f	M de Kock	K Shea	12
2004	118	Paolini 7-9-0: 10/1 d-ht	A Wohler	E Pedroza	11
	118	Right Approach 5-9-0: 12/1 d-ht	M de Kock	W C Marwing	
2005	123	Elvstroem 5-9-0: 8/1	A J Vasil	N Rawiller	14
2006	132	David Junior 4-9-0: 9/2f	B J Meehan	J P Spencer	15
2007	126+	Admire Moon 4-9-0: 11/2jf	H Matsuda	Y Take	16
2008	126	Jay Peg 5-9-0: 50/1	H Brown	A Marcus	16
2009	128	Gladiatorus 4-9-0: 15/1	M bin Shafya	A Ajtebi	16
2010	124	Al Shemali 6-9-0: 40/1	A Al Raihe	R Ffrench	16
2011	124	Presvis 7-9-0: 5/1f	Luca Cumani	Ryan Moore	16
2012	126	Cityscape 6-9-0: 8/1	Roger Charlton	James Doyle	15
2013	121	Sajjhaa 6-8-9: 7/1	Saeed bin Suroor	Silvestre de Sousa	14

| 2014 | 131+ | Just A Way 5-9-0: 3/1f | Naosuke Sugai | *Yuichi Fukunaga* | 13 |
| 2015 | 129 | Solow 5-9-0: 9/4 | F Head | *Maxime Guyon* | 10 |

DUBAI WORLD CUP – SPONSORED BY EMIRATES AIRLINE (Group 1) (4-y-o+)
(Meydan 1¼m Dirt; listed in 1997; Group 1 from 1998; run on tapeta 2010-2014;
run at Nad Al Sheba 1996-2009)

1996	133	Cigar 6-8-12	W Mott	*J Bailey*	11
1997	132	Singspiel 5-9-0	M R Stoute	*J Bailey*	12
1998	132	Silver Charm 4-9-0	R Baffert	*Gary Stevens*	9
1999	126	Almutawakel 4-9-0	Saeed bin Suroor	*R Hills*	8
2000	140	Dubai Millennium 4-9-0	Saeed bin Suroor	*L Dettori*	13
2001	127+	Captain Steve 4-9-0: 7/4jf	R Baffert	*J Bailey*	12
2002	127+	Street Cry 4-9-0: 9/2	Saeed bin Suroor	*J Bailey*	11
2003	131	Moon Ballad 4-9-0: 11/4	Saeed bin Suroor	*L Dettori*	11
2004	130	Pleasantly Perfect 6-9-0: 5/2	R E Mandella	*A Solis*	12
2005	128	Roses In May 5-9-0: 11/8f	D L Romans	*J Velazquez*	12
2006	127	Electrocutionist 5-9-0: 5/4f	Saeed bin Suroor	*L Dettori*	11
2007	132	Invasor 5-9-0: 5/4f	K P McLaughlin	*F Jara*	7
2008	134	Curlin 4-9-0: 4/11f	S M Asmussen	*R Albarado*	12
2009	129	Well Armed 6-9-0: 10/1	E Harty	*A Gryder*	14
2010	125	Gloria de Campeao 7-9-0: 16/1	P Bary	*T Pereira*	14
2011	126	Victoire Pisa 4-9-0: 12/1	K Sumii	*Mirco Demuro*	14
2012	128	Monterosso 5-9-0: 20/1	Mahmood Al Zarooni	*Mikael Barzalona*	13
2013	129	Animal Kingdom 5-9-0: 11/2	H Graham Motion	*Joel Rosario*	12
2014	128	African Story 7-9-0: 12/1	Saeed bin Suroor	*Silvestra de Sousa*	16
2015	126	Prince Bishop 8-9-0: 14/1	Saeed bin Suroor	*William Buick*	9

ARLINGTON MILLION (Grade 1) (3-y-o+) (Arlington 1¼m Turf)

1990	129	Golden Pheasant 4-9-0: 66/10	C Whittingham	*Gary Stevens*	11
1991	124	Tight Spot 4-9-0: 18/10	R McAnally	*L Pincay Jr*	10
1992	125	Dear Doctor 5-9-0: 139/10	J Hammond	*C Asmussen*	12
1993	126	Star of Cozzene 5-9-0: 8/10f	M Hennig	*J Santos*	8
1994	127	Paradise Creek 5-9-0: 18/10f	W Mott	*P Day*	14
1995	124	Awad 5-9-0: 59/10	D Donk	*E Maple*	11
1996	126	Mecke 4-9-0: 155/10	E Tortora	*R Davis*	9
1997	124	Marlin 4-9-0: 29/10f	D Wayne Lukas	*Gary Stevens*	8
1998		No Race (course temporarily closed)			
1999		No Race (course temporarily closed)			
2000	123	Chester House 5-9-0: 38/10	R Frankel	*J Bailey*	7
2001	126	Silvano 5-9-0: 63/10	A Wohler	*A Suborics*	12
2002	123+	Beat Hollow 5-9-0: 7/10f	R J Frankel	*J Bailey*	9
2003	121+	*Sulamani 4-9-0: 28/10	Saeed bin Suroor	*D Flores*	13
2004	121+	*Kicken Kris 4-9-0: 97/10	M R Matz	*K Desormeaux*	13
2005	126	Powerscourt 4-9-0: 52/10	A P O'Brien	*K Fallon*	10
2006	124	The Tin Man 8-9-0: 11/2	R E Mandella	*V Espinoza*	10
2007	121	Jambalaya 5-9-0: 76/10	Catherine Day Phillips	*R Albarado*	7
2008	122	Spirit One 4-9-0: 137/10	P H Demercastel	*I Mendizabal*	7
2009	121	Gio Ponti 4-9-0: 3/2f	C Clement	*R A Dominguez*	8
2010	123	Debussy 4-9-0: 11/1	J H M Gosden	*W Buick*	9
2011	124+	Cape Blanco 4-9-0: 21/10f	Aidan O'Brien	*Jamie Spencer*	10
2012	121+	Little Mike 5-9-0: 39/10	Dale Romans	*R A Dominguez*	11
2013	117	*Real Solution 4-9-0: 84/10	Chad C Brown	*Alan Garcia*	13
2014	120	Hardest Core 4-9-0: 115/10	Edward L Graham	*Eriluis Vaz*	7
2015	120	The Pizza Man 6-9-0: 59/10	R Brueggemann	*Javier Castellano*	13

PATTISON CANADIAN INTERNATIONAL (Grade 1) (3-y-o+) (Woodbine 1½m Turf)

1990	118	French Glory 4-9-0: 18/10	A Fabre	*Pat Eddery*	10
1991	122	Sky Classic 4-9-0: 8/10	J Day	*P Day*	11
1992	122	*Snurge 5-9-0: 50/10	P Cole	*T Quinn*	14
1993	123	Husband 3-8-7: 197/10	J Fellows	*C Asmussen*	11
1994	123	Raintrap 4-9-0: 183/10	A Fabre	*R Davis*	9
1995	121	Lassigny 4-9-0: 77/10	W Mott	*P Day*	15
1996	124	Singspiel 4-9-0: 19/10f	M R Stoute	*Gary Stevens*	7
1997	124	Chief Bearhart 4-9-0: 13/20cpf	M Frostad	*J Santos*	6
1998	129	Royal Anthem 3-8-7: 9/2	H R A Cecil	*Gary Stevens*	8
1999	123	Thornfield 4-9-0: 19/1	P England	*R Dos Ramos*	9
2000	122	Mutafaweq 4-9-0: 4/1	Saeed bin Suroor	*L Dettori*	12

2001	122	Mutamam 6-9-0: 425/100	A C Stewart	*R Hills*	12
2002	123	Ballingarry 3-8-6: 41/10	A P O'Brien	*M J Kinane*	8
2003	120	Phoenix Reach 3-8-7: 54/10	A M Balding	*Martin Dwyer*	10
2004	124+	Sulamani 5-9-0: 85/100f	Saeed bin Suroor	*L Dettori*	10
2005	126	Relaxed Gesture 4-9-0: 112/10	C Clement	*C Nakatani*	10
2006	122	Collier Hill 8-9-0: 108/10	G A Swinbank	*D McKeown*	10
2007	124	Cloudy's Knight 7-9-0: 184/10	F J Kirby	*R Zimmerman*	12
2008	120	Marsh Side 5-9-0: 296/10	N D Drysdale	*J Castellano*	10
2009	124	Champs Elysees 6-9-0: 26/10f	R J Frankel	*G Gomez*	8
2010	121	Joshua Tree 3-8-10: 46/10	A P O'Brien	*C O'Donoghue*	9
2011	124	Sarah Lynx 4-8-11: 225/10	J E Hammond	*Christophe Soumillon*	16
2012	118	Joshua Tree 5-9-0: 87/20	Marco Botti	*Frankie Dettori*	10
2013	118	Joshua Tree 6-9-0: 67/10	Ed Dunlop	*Ryan Moore*	10
2014	119+	Hillstar 4-9-0: 125/100f	Sir Michael Stoute	*Ryan Moore*	9
2015	119	Cannock Chase 4-9-0: 11/4f	Sir Michael Stoute	*Ryan Moore*	11

SPORTINGBET W. S. COX PLATE (Group 1) (3-y-o+) (Moonee Valley 1¼m31y)

1990	130	Better Loosen Up 5-9-4: 2/1f	D A Hayes	*M Clarke*	11
1991	128	Surfers Paradise 4-9-0: 14/1	D J O'Sullivan	*L O'Sullivan*	14
1992	125	Super Impose 8-9-4: 16/1	D L Freedman	*G Hall*	14
1993	121	The Phantom Chance 4-9-0: 4/1	C M Jillings	*R Vance*	9
1994	121	Solvit 6-9-4: 10/1	Ms M J Murdoch	*D Walsh*	14
1995	123	Octagonal 3-7-9: 15/2	J R Hawkes	*R S Dye*	14
1996	127	Saintly 4-9-0: 5/1	J B Cummings	*D Beadman*	8
1997	122	Dane Ripper 4-8-8: 40/1	J B Cummings	*D Oliver*	9
1998	130	Might And Power 5-9-2: 8/11f	J Denham	*J A Cassidy*	11
1999	124+	Sunline 4-8-7: 6/1	T McKee	*G Childs*	11
2000	129	Sunline 5-8-10: 11/8f	T McKee	*G Childs*	13
2001	128	Northerly 6-9-2: 5/2	F Kersley	*D Oliver*	8
2002	129	Northerly 7-9-2: 3/1jf	F Kersley	*P Payne*	9
2003	121	Fields of Omagh 6-9-2: 16/1	T McEvoy	*S R King*	8
2004	116	Savabeel 3-7-9: 14/1	G A Rogerson	*C Munce*	13
2005	125+	Makybe Diva 7-8-10: 1/1f	D L Freedman	*G Boss*	14
2006	123	Fields of Omagh 9-9-2: 18/1	D Hayes	*C Williams*	12
2007	125	El Segundo 6-9-4: 6/1	C Little	*L Nolen*	13
2008	125	Maldivian 6-9-4: 10/1	M Kavanagh	*M Rodd*	12
2009	124	So You Think 3-7-11: 12/1	J B Cummings	*G Boss*	13
2010	131+	So You Think 4-9-1: 1/2f	J B Cummings	*S Arnold*	10
2011	122	Pinker Pinker 4-8-1: 25/1	Greg Eurell	*Craig Williams*	14
2012	128	Ocean Park 4-9-1: 5/1	Gary Hennessy	*Glen Boss*	14
2013	124	Shamus Award 3-7-11: 20/1	Danny O'Brien	*Chad Schofield*	14
2014	124+	Adelaide 3-8-11: 7/1	Aidan O'Brien	*Ryan Moore*	14
2015	126	Winx 4-8-10: 35/10	Chris Waller	*Hugh Bowman*	14

EMIRATES MELBOURNE CUP (HANDICAP) (Group 1) (3-y-o+) (Flemington 1m7f200y)

1990	124	Kingston Rule 5-8-5: 7/1jf	J B Cummings	*D Beadman*	24
1991	122	Let's Elope 4-8-0: 3/1f	J B Cummings	*S R King*	24
1992	123	Subzero 4-8-8: 4/1	D L Freedman	*G Hall*	21
1993	123+	Vintage Crop 6-8-10: 14/1	D K Weld	*M Kinane*	24
1994	123	Jeune 5-8-13: 16/1	D A Hayes	*W Harris*	24
1995	125	Doriemus 5-8-8: 10/1	D L Freedman	*D Oliver*	21
1996	126	Saintly 4-8-10: 8/1	J B Cummings	*D Beadman*	22
1997	126	Might And Power 4-8-12: 7/2f	J Denham	*J Cassidy*	24
1998	118	Jezabeel 5-8-0: 6/1f	B Jenkins	*C Munce*	24
1999	114	Rogan Josh 7-7-12: 5/1	J B Cummings	*J Marshall*	24
2000	114	Brew 6-7-10: 14/1	M Moroney	*K McEvoy*	22
2001	120	Ethereal 4-8-3: 9/1	S Laxon	*S Seamer*	22
2002	117	Media Puzzle 5-8-4: 11/2	D K Weld	*D M Oliver*	23
2003	117	Makybe Diva 4-8-0: 7/1	D Hall	*G Boss*	23
2004	124+	Makybe Diva 5-8-10: 26/10f	D L Freedman	*G Boss*	24
2005	128+	Makybe Diva 6-9-2: 34/10f	D L Freedman	*G Boss*	24
2006	125	Delta Blues 5-8-11: 17/1	K Sumii	*Y Iwata*	23
2007	124	Efficient 4-8-8: 16/1	G A Rogerson	*M Rodd*	21
2008	120	Viewed 5-8-5: 40/1	J B Cummings	*B Shinn*	22
2009	117+	Shocking 4-8-0: 9/1	M Kavanagh	*C Brown*	23
2010	126	Americain 5-8-8: 12/1	A de Royer Dupre	*G Mosse*	23
2011	123	Dunaden 5-8-8: 15/2	M Delzangles	*Christophe P Lemaire*	23

2012	124	Green Moon 5-8-6: 19/1	Robert Hickmott	*Brett Prebble*	24
2013	125	Fiorente 5-8-9: 6/1f	Gai Waterhouse	*Damien Oliver*	24
2014	128+	Protectionist 4-8-13: 7/1	A Wohler	*Ryan Moore*	22
2015	119	Prince of Penzance 6-8-5: 100/1	Darren Weir	*Michelle Payne*	24

BREEDERS' CUP MILE (Grade 1) (3-y-o+) (Various 1m Turf)

1984		Royal Heroine 4-8-11: 17/10cpf	J H M Gosden	*F Toro*	10
1985		Cozzene 5-9-0: 36/10	J H Nerud	*W Guerra*	14
1986	130	Last Tycoon 3-8-11: 359/10	R Collet	*Y Saint-Martin*	14
1987	131	Miesque 3-8-8: 36/10	F Boutin	*F Head*	14
1988	133	Miesque 4-8-11: 2/1cp	F Boutin	*F Head*	12
1989	127	Steinlen 6-9-0: 18/10	D W Lukas	*J Santos*	11
1990	130	Royal Academy 3-8-10: 28/10f	M V O'Brien	*L Piggott*	13
1991	126	Opening Verse 5-9-0: 267/10	R Lundy	*P Valenzuela*	14
1992	127	Lure 3-8-10: 54/10	C McGaughey	*M Smith*	14
1993	129	Lure 4-9-0: 13/10f	C McGaughey	*M Smith*	13
1994	126+	Barathea 4-9-0: 104/10	L M Cumani	*L Dettori*	14
1995	125	Ridgewood Pearl 3-8-7: 255/100f	J Oxx	*J Murtagh*	13
1996	129	Da Hoss 4-9-0: 845/100	M W Dickinson	*Gary Stevens*	14
1997	126+	Spinning World 4-9-0: 21/10f	J E Pease	*C Asmussen*	12
1998	125	Da Hoss 6-9-0: 116/10	M W Dickinson	*J R Velazquez*	14
1999	125	Silic 4-9-0: 72/10	J C Canani	*C Nakatani*	14
2000	122+	War Chant 3-8-11: 7/2jf	N D Drysdale	*Gary Stevens*	14
2001	127	Val Royal 5-9-0: 51/10	J C Canani	*J Valdivia*	12
2002	128	Domedriver 4-9-0: 26/1	P Bary	*T Thulliez*	14
2003	123+	Six Perfections 3-8-7: 53/10	P Bary	*J Bailey*	13
2004	125	Singletary 4-9-0: 165/10	D Chatlos Jnr	*D Flores*	14
2005	124	Artie Schiller 4-9-0: 56/10	J A Jerkens	*G Gomez*	12
2006	126	Miesque's Approval 7-9-0: 243/10	M D Wolfson	*E Castro*	14
2007	126	Kip Deville 4-9-0: 82/10	R E Dutrow Jnr	*C Velasquez*	13
2008	128+	Goldikova 3-8: 18/10f	F Head	*O Peslier*	11
2009	122+	Goldikova 4-8-11: 14/10f	F Head	*O Peslier*	11
2010	129+	Goldikova 5-8-11: 13/10f	F Head	*O Peslier*	11
2011	125	Court Vision 6-9-0: 648/10	Dale L Romans	*Robby Albarado*	13
2012	126+	Wise Dan 5-9-0: 9/4	Charles LoPresti	*J R Velazquez*	9
2013	124+	Wise Dan 6-9-0: 8/10f	Charles LoPresti	*Jose Lezcano*	10
2014	125	Karakontie 3-9-11: 30/1	J E Pease	*Stephane Pasquier*	14
2015	125	Tepin 4-8-11: 49/10	Mark E Casse	*Julien R Leparoux*	12

LONGINES BREEDERS' CUP TURF (Grade 1) (3-y-o+) (Various 1½m)

1984	128	Lashkari 3-8-10: 534/10	A de Royer Dupre	*Y Saint-Martin*	11
1985	126+	Pebbles 4-8-11: 22/10f	C E Brittain	*Pat Eddery*	14
1986	130	Manila 3-8-10: 88/10	L Jolley	*J Santos*	9
1987	133	Theatrical 5-9-0: 18/10cpf	W I Mott	*P Day*	14
1988	124	Great Communicator 5-9-0: 124/10	T D Ackel	*R Sibille*	10
1989	132	Prized 3-8-10: 88/10	N Drysdale	*E Delahoussaye*	14
1990	128	In The Wings 4-9-0: 19/10cpf	A Fabre	*Gary Stevens*	11
1991	125	Miss Alleged 4-8-11: 421/10	P Bary	*E Legrix*	13
1992	127	Fraise 4-9-0: 14/1	W I Mott	*P Valenzuela*	10
1993	126	Kotashaan 5-9-0: 15/10f	R Mandella	*K Desormeaux*	14
1994	130	Tikkanen 3-8-10: 166/10	J E Pease	*M Smith*	14
1995	133	Northern Spur 4-9-0: 395/100	R McAnally	*C McCarron*	13
1996	129	Pilsudski 4-9-0: 137/10	M R Stoute	*W R Swinburn*	14
1997	125	Chief Bearhart 4-9-0: 19/10f	M Frostad	*J Santos*	11
1998	125	Buck's Boy 5-9-0: 36/10	P N Hickey	*S Sellers*	13
1999	135+	Daylami 5-9-0: 16/10f	Saeed bin Suroor	*L Dettori*	14
2000	124+	Kalanisi 4-9-0 46/10	Sir Michael Stoute	*J Murtagh*	13
2001	128	Fantastic Light 5-9-0: 14/10f	Saeed bin Suroor	*L Dettori*	11
2002	127+	High Chaparral 3-8-9: 9/10f	A P O'Brien	*M J Kinane*	8
2003	130	High Chaparral 4-9-0: 49/10 d-ht	A P O'Brien	*M J Kinane*	
	130	Johar 4-9-0: 142/10 d-ht	R E Mandella	*A Solis*	9
2004	126	Better Talk Now 5-9-0: 279/10	H G Motion	*R A Dominguez*	8
2005	128	Shirocco 4-9-0: 88/10	A Fabre	*C Soumillon*	13
2006	124	Red Rocks 3-8-10: 108/10	B J Meehan	*L Dettori*	11
2007	126	English Channel 5-9-0: 3/1	T A Pletcher	*J Velazquez*	8
2008	130	Conduit 3-8-9: 58/10	Sir Michael Stoute	*R L Moore*	11
2009	125	Conduit 4-9-0: 9/10f	Sir Michael Stoute	*R L Moore*	7

2010	125	Dangerous Midge 4-9-0: 85/10	B J Meehan	*L Dettori*	7
2011	127	St Nicholas Abbey 4-9-0: 68/10	Aidan O'Brien	*Joseph O'Brien*	9
2012	126	Little Mike 5-9-0: 25/1	Dale Romans	*R A Dominguez*	12
2013	125+	Magician 3-8-10: 7/1	Aidan O'Brien	*Ryan Moore*	12
2014	124+	Main Sequence 5-9-0: 62/10	H Graham Motion	*John R Velazquez*	12
2015	122	Found 3-8-7: 64/10	Aidan O'Brien	*Ryan Moore*	12

BREEDERS' CUP CLASSIC (Grade 1) (3-y-o+) (Various 1¼m Dirt)

1984		Wild Again 4-9-0: 313/10	V Timphony	*P Day*	8
1985		Proud Truth 3-8-10: 74/10	J M Veitch	*J Velasquez*	8
1986		Skywalker 4-9-0: 101/10	M Whittingham	*L Pincay*	11
1987		Ferdinand 4-9-0: 1/1f	C Whittingham	*W Shoemaker*	12
1988		Alysheba 4-9-0: 15/10	J C van Berg	*C McCarron*	9
1989		Sunday Silence 3-8-10: 2/1	C Whittingham	*C McCarron*	8
1990	128	Unbridled 3-8-9: 66/10cp	C Nafzger	*P Day*	14
1991	128	Black Tie Affair 5-9-0: 4/1	E Poulos	*J Bailey*	11
1992	131	A P Indy 3-8-9: 21/10f	N Drysdale	*E Delahoussaye*	14
1993	128	Arcangues 5-9-0: 1336/10	A Fabre	*J Bailey*	13
1994	127	Concern 3-8-10: 15/2	R Small	*J Bailey*	14
1995	129	Cigar 5-9-0: 7/10f	W Mott	*J Bailey*	11
1996	126	Alphabet Soup 5-9-0: 1985/100	D Hofmans	*C McCarron*	13
1997	131	Skip Away 4-9-0: 18/10f	H Hine	*M Smith*	9
1998	133	Awesome Again 4-9-0: 47/10	P Byrne	*P Day*	10
1999	126	Cat Thief 3-8-10: 196/10	D W Lukas	*P Day*	14
2000	133	Tiznow 3-8-10: 92/10	J M Robbins	*C McCarron*	13
2001	130+	Tiznow 4-9-0: 69/10	J M Robbins	*C McCarron*	13
2002	131	Volponi 4-9-0: 435/10	P G Johnson	*J Santos*	12
2003	126	Pleasantly Perfect 5-9-0: 142/10	R E Mandella	*A Solis*	10
2004	137	Ghostzapper 4-9-0: 25/10jf	R J Frankel	*J Castellano*	9
2005	128	Saint Liam 5-9-0: 24/10f	R E Dutrow jnr	*J Bailey*	13
2006	128+	Invasor 4-9-0: 67/10	K P McLaughlin	*F Jara*	13
2007	131	Curlin 3-8-9: 44/10	S M Asmussen	*R Albarado*	9
2008	131+	Raven's Pass 3-8-9: 135/10	J H M Gosden	*L Dettori*	12
2009	129+	Zenyatta 5-8-11: 28/10f	J A Shirreffs	*M E Smith*	12
2010	129	Blame 4-9-0: 52/10	A M Stall Jnr	*G Gomez*	12
2011	126	Drosselmeyer 4-9-0: 148/10	William I Mott	*Mike E Smith*	12
2012	126	Fort Larned 4-9-0: 9/1	Ian Wilkes	*B Hernandez Jr*	12
2013	128	Mucho Macho Man 5-9-0: 4/1	Kathy Ritvo	*Gary Stevens*	11
2014	127	Bayern 3-8-10: 61/10	Bob Baffert	*Martin Garcia*	14
2015	138	American Pharoah 3-8-10: 7/10f	Bob Baffert	*Victor Espinoza*	8

JAPAN CUP (Group 1) (3-y-o+) (Tokyo 1m3f205y, Nakayama 1m3f in 2002)

1990	125	Better Loosen Up 5-9-0: 52/10	D Hayes	*M Clarke*	15
1991	129	Golden Pheasant 5-9-0: 172/10	C Whittingham	*Gary Stevens*	15
1992	129	Tokai Teio 4-8-13: 90/10	S Matsumoto	*Y Okabe*	14
1993	129	Legacy World 4-8-13: 115/10	H Mori	*H Koyauchi*	16
1994	127	Marvelous Crown 4-9-0: 96/10	M Osawa	*K Minai*	14
1995	128	Lando 5-9-0: 135/10	H Jentzsch	*M Roberts*	14
1996	126	Singspiel 4-9-0: 66/10	M R Stoute	*L Dettori*	15
1997	123	Pilsudski 5-9-0: 36/10	M R Stoute	*M J Kinane*	14
1998	128	El Condor Pasa 3-8-10: 5/1	Y Ninomiya	*M Ebina*	15
1999	125	Special Week 4-9-0: 24/10	T Shirai	*Y Take*	14
2000	128	T M Opera O 4-8-13: 1/2f	I Iwamoto	*R Wada*	16
2001	131	Jungle Pocket 3-8-10: 32/10	S Watanabe	*O Peslier*	15
2002	125	Falbrav 4-9-0: 195/10	L D'Auria	*L Dettori*	16
2003	125	Tap Dance City 6-9-0: 138/10	S Sasaki	*T Sato*	18
2004	125	Zenno Rob Roy 4-9-0: 17/10f	K Fujisawa	*O Peslier*	16
2005	127	Alkaased 5-9-0: 96/10	L M Cumani	*L Dettori*	18
2006	128+	Deep Impact 4-9-0: 3/10f	Y Ikee	*Y Take*	11
2007	127	Admire Moon 4-9-0: 99/10	H Matsuda	*Y Iwata*	18
2008	124	Screen Hero 4-9-0: 40/1	Y Shikato	*M Demuro*	17
2009	123+	Vodka 5-8-10: 26/10f	K Sumii	*C P Lemaire*	18
2010	124+	Rose Kingdom 3-8-10: 78/10	K Hashiguchi	*Y Take*	18
2011	121	Buena Vista 5-8-9: 12/5	Hiroyoshi Matsuda	*Yasunari Iwata*	16
2012	127	Gentildonna 3-8-5: 56/10	Sei Ishizaka	*Yasunari Iwata*	17
2013	116+	Gentildonna 4-8-9: 11/10f	Sei Ishizaka	*Ryan Moore*	17

| 2014 | 132 | Epiphaneia 4-9-0: 79/10 | Katsuhiko Sumii | *Christophe Soumillon* | 18 |
| 2015 | 120 | Shonan Pandora 4-8-10: 82/10 | Tomokazu Takano | *Kenichi Ikezoe* | 18 |

LONGINES HONG KONG VASE (Group 1) (3-y-o+)
(Sha Tin 1m3f205y; first run in 1994; Group 2 1996 to 1999)

1994	121	Red Bishop 6-8-11: 124/10	J E Hammond	*C Asmussen*	4/14
1995	120	Partipral 6-9-0: 5/2f	E Lellouche	*O Peslier*	10/14
1996	124	Luso 4-9-5: 21/10f	C E Brittain	*L Dettori*	6/14
1997	120+	Luso 5-9-5: 9/20f	C E Brittain	*M J Kinane*	12/14
1998	118	Indigenous 5-9-0: 3/1	I Allan	*D J Whyte*	7/14
1999	120	Borgia 5-9-0: 23/1	A Fabre	*O Peslier*	2/11
2000	122	Daliapour 4-9-0: 13/10f	Sir Michael Stoute	*J Murtagh*	9/13
2001	126+	Stay Gold 7-9-0: 105/100f	Y Ikee	*Y Take*	14/14
2002	124	Ange Gabriel 4-9-0: 39/10	E Libaud	*T Jarnet*	4/14
2003	115	Vallee Enchantee 3-8-5: 143/20	E Lellouche	*D Boeuf*	3/14
2004	120	Phoenix Reach 4-9-0: 265/10	A M Balding	*Martin Dwyer*	5/12
2005	119+	Ouija Board 4-8-10: 69/20	E A L Dunlop	*K Fallon*	7/12
2006	121	Collier Hill 8-9-0: 11/1	G A Swinbank	*D McKeown*	10/9
2007	120+	Doctor Dino 5-9-0: 31/4	R Gibson	*O Peslier*	4/13
2008	118+	Doctor Dino 6-9-0-: 13/10f	R Gibson	*O Peslier*	12/13
2009	118+	Daryakana 3-8-6: 57/10	A de Royer Dupre	*G Mosse*	3/13
2010	125	Mastery 4-9-0: 8/1	Saeed bin Suroor	*L Dettori*	2/13
2011	124	Dunaden 5-9-0: 56/10	M Delzangles	*Craig Williams*	3/13
2012	121	Red Cadeaux 6-9-0: 10/1	Ed Dunlop	*Gerald Mosse*	7/12
2013	123	Dominant 5-9-0: 33/1	John Moore	*Zac Purton*	12/12
2014	123+	Flintshire 4-9-0: 11/10f	Andre Fabre	*Maxime Guyon*	4/11
2015	129	Highland Reel 3-8-9: 325/100	Aidan O'Brien	*Ryan Moore*	9/13

LONGINES HONG KONG CUP (Group 1 from 1999) (3-y-o+)
(Sha Tin 1m1f207y; 9f prior to 1999)

1990	115+	Kessem 5-9-0: 8/5f	B Smith	*K Moses*	9/13
1991	118	River Verdon 4-9-0: 8/5f	D Hill	*G Mosse*	13/14
1992		Not run			
1993	119	Romanee Conti 4-8-11: 23/1	L Laxon	*G Childs*	9/10
1993	118	Motivation 5-8-11: 104/10	J Moore	*J Marshall*	8/14
1994	122	State Taj 5-8-11: 203/10	J Riley	*D Oliver*	8/14
1995	119	Fujiyama Kenzan 7-9-0: 40/1	H Mori	*M Ebina*	5/12
1996	120+	First Island 4-9-5: 9/5f	G Wragg	*M Hills*	10/12
1997	116+	Val's Prince 5-9-5: 6/1	J E Picou	*C Asmussen*	2/14
1998	117	Midnight Bet 4-9-0: 42/1	H Nagahama	*H Kawachi*	9/14
1999	124	Jim And Tonic 5-9-0: 7/2	F Doumen	*G Mosse*	7/12
2000	128	Fantastic Light 4-9-0: 19/10f	Saeed bin Suroor	*L Dettori*	10/13
2001	123+	Agnes Digital 4-9-0: 3/1	T Shirai	*H Shii*	12/14
2002	121+	Precision 4-9-0: 65/1	D Oughton	*M J Kinane*	13/12
2003	130+	Falbrav 5-9-0: 7/10f	L M Cumani	*L Dettori*	5/14
2004	121	Alexander Goldrun 3-8-7: 215/10	J S Bolger	*K J Manning*	12/14
2005	126	Vengeance of Rain 4-9-0: 17/20f	D E Ferraris	*A Delpech*	4/10
2006	118	Pride 6-8-10: 51/20	A de Royer Dupre	*C P Lemaire*	9/12
2007	123	Ramonti 5-9-0: 38/10	Saeed bin Suroor	*L Dettori*	4/7
2008	124	Eagle Mountain 4-9-0: 49/10	M F De Kock	*K Shea*	5/14
2009	127	Vision d' Etat 4-9-0: 61/10	E Libaud	*O Peslier*	7/10
2010	119+	Snow Fairy 3-8-7: 7/2f	E A L Dunlop	*R L Moore*	8/13
2011	124	California Memory 5-9-0: 345/100	A S Cruz	*M Chadwick*	1/10
2012	125+	California Memory 6-9-0: 9/4f	A S Cruz	*Matthew Chadwick*	1/11
2013	124	Akeed Mofeed 4-9-0: 7/2	R Gibson	*Douglas Whyte*	1/12
2014	124+	Designs On Rome 4-9-0: 195/100f	J Moore	*Joao Moreira*	3/12
2015	127	A Shin Hikari 4-9-0: 38/1	Masanori Sakaguchi	*Yutaka Take*	12/13

AGE WEIGHT & DISTANCE TABLE
TIMEFORM'S SCALE OF WEIGHT-FOR-AGE FOR THE FLAT: JANUARY-MARCH

Distance	Age	January				February				March			
		1-8	9-16	17-23	24-31	1-8	9-16	17-23	24-29	1-8	9-16	17-23	24-31
5f	4	10-0	10-0	10-0	10-0	10-0	10-0	10-0	10-0	10-0	10-0	10-0	10-0
	3	9-4	9-4	9-4	9-4	9-4	9-4	9-4	9-4	9-6	9-6	9-6	9-6
	2											8-3	8-3
6f	4	9-13	9-13	9-13	9-13	10-0	10-0	10-0	10-0	10-0	10-0	10-0	10-0
	3	9-3	9-3	9-3	9-3	9-3	9-3	9-3	9-3	9-5	9-5	9-5	9-5
	2												
7f	4	9-13	9-13	9-13	9-13	9-13	9-13	9-13	9-13	10-0	10-0	10-0	10-0
	3	9-2	9-2	9-2	9-2	9-2	9-2	9-2	9-2	9-4	9-4	9-4	9-4
	2												
1m	4	9-12	9-12	9-12	9-12	9-12	9-12	9-12	9-12	9-13	9-13	9-13	9-13
	3	9-1	9-1	9-1	9-1	9-1	9-1	9-1	9-1	9-3	9-3	9-3	9-3
	2												
1m1f	4	9-12	9-12	9-12	9-12	9-12	9-12	9-12	9-12	9-13	9-13	9-13	9-13
	3	8-13	8-13	8-13	8-13	9-0	9-0	9-0	9-0	9-2	9-2	9-2	9-2
	2												
1m2f	4	9-11	9-11	9-11	9-11	9-11	9-11	9-11	9-11	9-12	9-12	9-12	9-12
	3	8-11	8-11	8-11	8-11	8-12	8-12	8-12	8-12	9-0	9-0	9-0	9-0
	2												
1m3f	4	9-10	9-10	9-10	9-10	9-10	9-10	9-10	9-10	9-11	9-11	9-11	9-11
	3	8-10	8-10	8-10	8-10	8-11	8-11	8-11	8-11	8-13	8-13	8-13	8-13
1m4f	4	9-10	9-10	9-10	9-10	9-10	9-10	9-10	9-10	9-11	9-11	9-11	9-11
	3	8-9	8-9	8-9	8-9	8-10	8-10	8-10	8-10	8-11	8-11	8-12	8-12
1m5f	4	9-9	9-9	9-9	9-9	9-9	9-9	9-9	9-9	9-10	9-10	9-10	9-10
	3												
1m6f	4	9-8	9-8	9-8	9-8	9-8	9-8	9-8	9-8	9-9	9-9	9-9	9-9
	3												
1m7f	4	9-7	9-7	9-7	9-7	9-8	9-8	9-8	9-8	9-9	9-9	9-9	9-9
	3												
2m	4	9-6	9-6	9-6	9-6	9-7	9-7	9-7	9-7	9-8	9-8	9-8	9-8
	3												
2m1f	4	9-5	9-5	9-5	9-5	9-6	9-6	9-6	9-6	9-7	9-7	9-7	9-7
	3												
2m2f	4	9-5	9-5	9-5	9-5	9-6	9-6	9-6	9-6	9-7	9-7	9-7	9-7
	3												
2m3f	4	9-4	9-4	9-4	9-4	9-5	9-5	9-5	9-5	9-6	9-6	9-6	9-6
	3												
2m4f	4	9-4	9-4	9-4	9-4	9-5	9-5	9-5	9-5	9-6	9-6	9-6	9-6
	3												
2m5f	4	9-4	9-4	9-4	9-4	9-5	9-5	9-5	9-5	9-6	9-6	9-6	9-6
	3												
2m6f	4	9-4	9-4	9-4	9-4	9-5	9-5	9-5	9-5	9-6	9-6	9-6	9-6
	3												

For 5-y-o's and older, use 10-0 in all cases

Note: Race distances in the above table are shown only at 1f intervals. For races over odd distances, the nearest distance shown in the table should be used: thus for races of 1m to 1m 109 yards, use the table weight for 1m; for 1m 110 yards to 1m 219 yards use 9f table.

AGE WEIGHT & DISTANCE TABLE
TIMEFORM'S SCALE OF WEIGHT-FOR-AGE FOR THE FLAT: APRIL-JUNE

Distance	Age	April				May				June			
		1-8	9-16	17-23	24-30	1-8	9-16	17-23	24-31	1-8	9-16	17-23	24-30
5f	4	10-0	10-0	10-0	10-0	10-0	10-0	10-0	10-0	10-0	10-0	10-0	10-0
	3	9-7	9-7	9-7	9-7	9-8	9-8	9-8	9-8	9-9	9-9	9-9	9-9
	2	8-4	8-4	8-5	8-5	8-6	8-6	8-7	8-7	8-8	8-8	8-9	8-9
6f	4	10-0	10-0	10-0	10-0	10-0	10-0	10-0	10-0	10-0	10-0	10-0	10-0
	3	9-6	9-6	9-6	9-6	9-7	9-7	9-7	9-7	9-8	9-8	9-8	9-8
	2					8-3	8-3	8-4	8-4	8-5	8-5	8-6	8-6
7f	4	10-0	10-0	10-0	10-0	10-0	10-0	10-0	10-0	10-0	10-0	10-0	10-0
	3	9-5	9-5	9-5	9-5	9-6	9-6	9-6	9-6	9-7	9-7	9-7	9-7
	2					8-3	8-3	8-4	8-4	8-3	8-3	8-4	8-4
1m	4	10-0	10-0	10-0	10-0	10-0	10-0	10-0	10-0	10-0	10-0	10-0	10-0
	3	9-4	9-4	9-4	9-4	9-5	9-5	9-5	9-5	9-6	9-6	9-6	9-6
	2												
1m1f	4	9-13	9-13	9-13	9-13	10-0	10-0	10-0	10-0	10-0	10-0	10-0	10-0
	3	9-3	9-3	9-3	9-3	9-4	9-4	9-4	9-4	9-5	9-5	9-5	9-5
	2												
1m2f	4	9-13	9-13	9-13	9-13	9-13	9-13	9-13	9-13	10-0	10-0	10-0	10-0
	3	9-1	9-1	9-2	9-2	9-3	9-3	9-4	9-4	9-5	9-5	9-5	9-5
	2												
1m3f	4	9-12	9-12	9-12	9-12	9-12	9-12	9-12	9-12	9-13	9-13	9-13	9-13
	3	9-0	9-0	9-1	9-1	9-2	9-2	9-3	9-3	9-4	9-4	9-4	9-4
1m4f	4	9-12	9-12	9-12	9-12	9-12	9-12	9-12	9-12	9-13	9-13	9-13	9-13
	3	8-13	8-13	9-0	9-0	9-1	9-1	9-2	9-2	9-3	9-3	9-3	9-3
1m5f	4	9-11	9-11	9-11	9-11	9-11	9-11	9-11	9-12	9-12	9-12	9-12	9-12
	3					9-0	9-0	9-1	9-1	9-2	9-2	9-2	9-2
1m6f	4	9-10	9-10	9-10	9-10	9-11	9-11	9-11	9-11	9-12	9-12	9-12	9-12
	3					8-12	8-12	8-13	8-13	9-0	9-0	9-1	9-1
1m7f	4	9-10	9-10	9-10	9-10	9-11	9-11	9-11	9-11	9-12	9-12	9-12	9-12
	3	8-9	8-9	8-10	8-10	8-11	8-11	8-12	8-12	8-13	8-13	9-0	9-0
2m	4	9-9	9-9	9-9	9-9	9-10	9-10	9-10	9-10	9-11	9-11	9-11	9-11
	3									8-11	8-11	8-12	8-12
2m1f	4	9-8	9-8	9-9	9-9	9-9	9-9	9-10	9-10	9-10	9-10	9-10	9-10
	3									8-10	8-10	8-11	8-11
2m2f	4	9-8	9-8	9-9	9-9	9-9	9-9	9-10	9-10	9-10	9-10	9-10	9-10
	3									8-9	8-9	8-10	8-10
2m3f	4	9-7	9-7	9-8	9-8	9-9	9-9	9-9	9-9	9-10	9-10	9-10	9-10
	3									8-8	8-8	8-9	8-9
2m4f	4	9-7	9-7	9-8	9-8	9-9	9-9	9-9	9-9	9-10	9-10	9-10	9-10
	3									8-7	8-7	8-8	8-8
2m5f	4	9-7	9-7	9-8	9-8	9-9	9-9	9-9	9-9	9-10	9-10	9-10	9-10
	3									8-7	8-7	8-8	8-8
2m6f	4	9-7	9-7	9-8	9-8	9-9	9-9	9-9	9-9	9-10	9-10	9-10	9-10
	3									8-7	8-7	8-8	8-8

For 5-y-o's and older, use 10-0 in all cases

Note: Race distances in the above table are shown only at 1f intervals. For races over odd distances, the nearest distance shown in the table should be used: thus for races of 1m to 1m 109 yards, use the table weight for 1m; for 1m 110 yards to 1m 219 yards use the 9f table.

AGE WEIGHT & DISTANCE TABLE
TIMEFORM'S SCALE OF WEIGHT-FOR-AGE FOR THE FLAT: JULY-AUGUST

Distance	Age	July 1-8	July 9-16	July 17-23	July 24-31	August 1-8	August 9-16	August 17-23	August 24-31	September 1-8	September 9-16	September 17-23	September 24-30
5f	4	10-0	10-0	10-0	10-0	10-0	10-0	10-0	10-0	10-0	10-0	10-0	10-0
	3	9-10	9-10	9-10	9-10	9-10	9-10	9-11	9-11	9-11	9-11	9-11	9-11
	2	8-10	8-10	8-10	8-10	8-11	8-11	8-12	8-12	8-13	8-13	9-0	9-0
6f	4	10-0	10-0	10-0	10-0	10-0	10-0	10-0	10-0	10-0	10-0	10-0	10-0
	3	9-9	9-9	9-9	9-9	9-10	9-10	9-10	9-10	9-11	9-11	9-11	9-11
	2	8-7	8-7	8-8	8-8	8-9	8-9	8-10	8-10	8-11	8-11	8-12	8-12
7f	4	10-0	10-0	10-0	10-0	10-0	10-0	10-0	10-0	10-0	10-0	10-0	10-0
	3	9-8	9-8	9-8	9-8	9-9	9-9	9-9	9-9	9-10	9-10	9-10	9-10
	2	8-5	8-5	8-6	8-6	8-7	8-7	8-8	8-8	8-9	8-9	8-10	8-10
1m	4	10-0	10-0	10-0	10-0	10-0	10-0	10-0	10-0	10-0	10-0	10-0	10-0
	3	9-7	9-7	9-7	9-7	9-8	9-8	9-8	9-8	9-9	9-9	9-9	9-9
	2					8-6	8-6	8-7	8-7	8-8	8-8	8-9	8-9
1m1f	4	10-0	10-0	10-0	10-0	10-0	10-0	10-0	10-0	10-0	10-0	10-0	10-0
	3	9-6	9-6	9-6	9-6	9-7	9-7	9-7	9-7	9-8	9-8	9-8	9-8
	2									8-6	8-6	8-7	8-7
1m2f	4	10-0	10-0	10-0	10-0	10-0	10-0	10-0	10-0	10-0	10-0	10-0	10-0
	3	9-6	9-6	9-6	9-6	9-7	9-7	9-7	9-7	9-8	9-8	9-8	9-8
	2											8-5	8-5
1m3f	4	10-0	10-0	10-0	10-0	10-0	10-0	10-0	10-0	10-0	10-0	10-0	10-0
	3	9-5	9-5	9-5	9-5	9-6	9-6	9-6	9-6	9-7	9-7	9-7	9-7
1m4f	4	9-13	9-13	9-13	9-13	10-0	10-0	10-0	10-0	10-0	10-0	10-0	10-0
	3	9-4	9-4	9-4	9-4	9-5	9-5	9-5	9-5	9-6	9-6	9-6	9-6
1m5f	4	9-13	9-13	9-13	9-13	9-13	9-13	9-13	9-13	10-0	10-0	10-0	10-0
	3	9-3	9-3	9-3	9-3	9-4	9-4	9-4	9-4	9-5	9-5	9-5	9-5
1m6f	4	9-13	9-13	9-13	9-13	9-13	9-13	9-13	9-13	9-13	9-13	10-0	10-0
	3	9-2	9-2	9-2	9-2	9-3	9-3	9-3	9-3	9-4	9-4	9-4	9-4
1m7f	4	9-12	9-12	9-13	9-13	9-13	9-13	9-13	9-13	9-13	9-13	9-13	9-13
	3	9-1	9-1	9-1	9-1	9-2	9-2	9-2	9-2	9-3	9-3	9-3	9-3
2m	4	9-12	9-12	9-12	9-12	9-13	9-13	9-13	9-13	9-13	9-13	9-13	9-13
	3	8-13	8-13	9-0	9-0	9-1	9-1	9-1	9-1	9-2	9-2	9-2	9-2
2m1f	4	9-11	9-11	9-12	9-12	9-12	9-12	9-12	9-12	9-12	9-12	9-13	9-13
	3	8-12	8-12	8-13	8-13	9-0	9-0	9-0	9-0	9-1	9-1	9-1	9-1
2m2f	4	9-11	9-11	9-12	9-12	9-12	9-12	9-12	9-12	9-12	9-12	9-13	9-13
	3	8-11	8-11	8-12	8-12	8-13	8-13	9-0	9-0	9-1	9-1	9-1	9-1
2m3f	4	9-10	9-10	9-11	9-11	9-11	9-11	9-12	9-12	9-12	9-12	9-12	9-12
	3	8-10	8-10	8-11	8-11	8-12	8-12	8-13	8-13	9-0	9-0	9-0	9-0
2m4f	4	9-10	9-10	9-11	9-11	9-11	9-11	9-12	9-12	9-12	9-12	9-12	9-12
	3	8-9	8-9	8-10	8-10	8-11	8-11	8-12	8-12	8-13	8-13	8-13	8-13
2m5f	4	9-10	9-10	9-11	9-11	9-11	9-11	9-12	9-12	9-12	9-12	9-12	9-12
	3	8-9	8-9	8-10	8-10	8-11	8-11	8-12	8-12	8-13	8-13	8-13	8-13
2m6f	4	9-10	9-10	9-11	9-11	9-11	9-11	9-12	9-12	9-12	9-12	9-12	9-12
	3	8-9	8-9	8-10	8-10	8-11	8-11	8-12	8-12	8-13	8-13	8-13	8-13

For 5-y-o's and older, use 10-0 in all cases

Note: Race distances in the above table are shown only at 1f intervals. For races over odd distances, the nearest distance shown in the table should be used: thus for races of 1m to 1m 109 yards, use the table weight for 1m; for 1m 110 yards to 1m 219 yards use 9f table.

AGE WEIGHT & DISTANCE TABLE
TIMEFORM'S SCALE OF WEIGHT-FOR-AGE FOR THE FLAT: OCTOBER-DECEMBER

Distance	Age	October				November				December			
		1-8	9-16	17-23	24-31	1-8	9-16	17-23	24-30	1-8	9-16	17-23	24-31
5f	4	10-0	10-0	10-0	10-0	10-0	10-0	10-0	10-0	10-0	10-0	10-0	10-0
	3	9-12	9-12	9-12	9-12	9-13	9-13	9-13	9-13	9-13	9-13	9-13	9-13
	2	9-1	9-1	9-2	9-2	9-2	9-2	9-2	9-2	9-3	9-3	9-3	9-3
6f	4	10-0	10-0	10-0	10-0	10-0	10-0	10-0	10-0	10-0	10-0	10-0	10-0
	3	9-12	9-12	9-12	9-12	9-13	9-13	9-13	9-13	9-13	9-13	9-13	9-13
	2	8-13	8-13	9-0	9-0	9-1	9-1	9-1	9-1	9-2	9-2	9-2	9-2
7f	4	10-0	10-0	10-0	10-0	10-0	10-0	10-0	10-0	10-0	10-0	10-0	10-0
	3	9-11	9-11	9-11	9-11	9-12	9-12	9-12	9-12	9-12	9-12	9-12	9-12
	2	8-11	8-11	8-12	8-12	8-13	8-13	9-0	9-0	9-1	9-1	9-1	9-1
1m	4	10-0	10-0	10-0	10-0	10-0	10-0	10-0	10-0	10-0	10-0	10-0	10-0
	3	9-10	9-10	9-10	9-10	9-11	9-11	9-11	9-11	9-11	9-11	9-11	9-11
	2	8-10	8-10	8-11	8-11	8-12	8-12	8-13	8-13	9-0	9-0	9-0	9-0
1m1f	4	10-0	10-0	10-0	10-0	10-0	10-0	10-0	10-0	10-0	10-0	10-0	10-0
	3	9-9	9-9	9-9	9-9	9-10	9-10	9-10	9-10	9-11	9-11	9-11	9-11
	2	8-8	8-8	8-9	8-9	8-10	8-10	8-11	8-11	8-12	8-12	8-12	8-12
1m2f	4	10-0	10-0	10-0	10-0	10-0	10-0	10-0	10-0	10-0	10-0	10-0	10-0
	3	9-9	9-9	9-9	9-9	9-10	9-10	9-10	9-10	9-11	9-11	9-11	9-11
	2	8-6	8-6	8-7	8-7	8-8	8-8	8-9	8-9	8-10	8-10	8-10	8-10
1m3f	4	10-0	10-0	10-0	10-0	10-0	10-0	10-0	10-0	10-0	10-0	10-0	10-0
	3	9-8	9-8	9-8	9-8	9-9	9-9	9-9	9-9	9-10	9-10	9-10	9-10
1m4f	4	10-0	10-0	10-0	10-0	10-0	10-0	10-0	10-0	10-0	10-0	10-0	10-0
	3	9-7	9-7	9-7	9-7	9-8	9-8	9-8	9-8	9-9	9-9	9-9	9-9
1m5f	4	10-0	10-0	10-0	10-0	10-0	10-0	10-0	10-0	10-0	10-0	10-0	10-0
	3	9-6	9-6	9-6	9-6	9-7	9-7	9-7	9-7	9-8	9-8	9-8	9-8
1m6f	4	10-0	10-0	10-0	10-0	10-0	10-0	10-0	10-0	10-0	10-0	10-0	10-0
	3	9-5	9-5	9-5	9-5	9-6	9-6	9-6	9-6	9-7	9-7	9-7	9-7
1m7f	4	10-0	10-0	10-0	10-0	10-0	10-0	10-0	10-0	10-0	10-0	10-0	10-0
	3	9-4	9-4	9-4	9-4	9-5	9-5	9-5	9-5	9-6	9-6	9-6	9-6
2m	4	9-13	9-13	10-0	10-0	10-0	10-0	10-0	10-0	10-0	10-0	10-0	10-0
	3	9-3	9-3	9-3	9-3	9-4	9-4	9-4	9-4	9-5	9-5	9-5	9-5
2m1f	4	9-13	9-13	9-13	9-13	9-13	9-13	10-0	10-0	10-0	10-0	10-0	10-0
	3	9-2	9-2	9-2	9-2	9-3	9-3	9-3	9-3	9-4	9-4	9-4	9-4
2m2f	4	9-13	9-13	9-13	9-13	9-13	9-13	10-0	10-0	10-0	10-0	10-0	10-0
	3	9-2	9-2	9-2	9-2	9-3	9-3	9-3	9-3	9-4	9-4	9-4	9-4
2m3f	4	9-13	9-13	9-13	9-13	9-13	9-13	9-13	9-13	10-0	10-0	10-0	10-0
	3	9-1	9-1	9-1	9-1	9-2	9-2	9-2	9-2	9-3	9-3	9-3	9-3
2m4f	4	9-13	9-13	9-13	9-13	9-13	9-13	9-13	9-13	10-0	10-0	10-0	10-0
	3	9-0	9-0	9-0	9-0	9-1	9-1	9-2	9-2	9-3	9-3	9-3	9-3
2m5f	4	9-13	9-13	9-13	9-13	9-13	9-13	9-13	9-13	10-0	10-0	10-0	10-0
	3	9-0	9-0	9-0	9-0	9-1	9-1	9-2	9-2	9-3	9-3	9-3	9-3
2m6f	4	9-13	9-13	9-13	9-13	9-13	9-13	9-13	9-13	10-0	10-0	10-0	10-0
	3	9-0	9-0	9-0	9-0	9-1	9-1	9-2	9-2	9-3	9-3	9-3	9-3

For 5-y-o's and older, use 10-0 in all cases

Note: Race distances in the above table are shown only at 1f intervals. For races over odd distances, the nearest distance shown in the table should be used: thus for races of 1m to 1m 109 yards, use the table weight for 1m; for 1m 110 yards to 1m 219 yards use 9f table.